The Routledge Portuguese
Bilingual Dictionary

The Routledge Portuguese Bilingual Dictionary

Portuguese–English and English–Portuguese

Maria F. Allen

Routledge
Taylor & Francis Group

LONDON AND NEW YORK

First edition published 2011 by Routledge
Revised reprint published 2014 by Routledge
2 Park Square, Milton Park, Abingdon, OX14 4RN

and by Routledge
711 Third Avenue, New York, NY 10017

Routledge is an imprint of the Taylor & Francis Group, an informa business

British Library Cataloguing in Publication Data
A catalogue record for this book is available from the British Library

Library of Congress Cataloging in Publication Data
Allen, Maria Fernanda.
   The Routledge Portuguese bilingual dictionary / Maria Allen. – 1st ed.
      p. cm.
   1. Portuguese language–Dictionaries–English. 2. English language–
   Dictionaries–Portuguese. I. Title. II. Title: Portuguese bilingual
   dictionary.
   PC5333.A598 2010
   469.3'21–dc22
         2009037931

ISBN: 978-0-415-43434-8 (hbk)
ISBN: 978-0-415-43433-1 (pbk)
ISBN: 978-0-203-85539-3 (ebk)

Typeset in Minion and Bell Gothic by
Taylor & Francis Books

Contents

Índice

Preface

This compact and up-to-date Portuguese–English and English–Portuguese dictionary is an ideal tool for translators and students alike. It contains approximately 65,000 entries, together with their definitions and examples and many idiomatic expressions in both languages. The dictionary covers the Brazilian variant, where it differs from European Portuguese, as well as some American-English spellings and terms. The reader will also find some popular indigenous words from Portuguese-speaking Africa. In addition, the boxed notes on grammar, false friends and on culture will prove to be of great use to all.

NOTE: European Portuguese is not only spoken in Portugal, Madeira, Azores, but also in five African countries, and in East Timor (as their official language). It is still spoken in Goa and by the Goan, or Goanese, diaspora; in Macao (besides Chinese language) and by large Portuguese communities in Venezuela, USA, South Africa, Australia and other regions. It is the 5th most spoken language in the world.

Key features

♦ Place names and nationalities.
♦ Modern jargon, slang and offensive words.
♦ Formal, informal and colloquial registers
♦ Terminology covering diverse subjects, though not extensively as they would do in a specialized dictionary.
♦ Notes on grammatical points, false friends and general knowledge on the UK, USA, and on all Portuguese speaking countries.
♦ A guide to the new Portuguese orthographic reform, translated into English, and a table of "weights and measures" compliment the book.

It has been written by Maria F. Allen, who for 30 years lectured at the University of Westminster in the School of Languages, in which she developed and co-ordinated "Portuguese Language and Culture" courses. She also taught the prestigious PG/MA Conference Interpreting course from Portuguese into English and other Latin-based languages; the MA Technical and Specialized Translation into English to English graduates; the MA bilingual Translation and the IoL Diploma in Translation.

Dr. Allen was the first teachers' tutor on the first PGCE course for Portuguese teachers at the Thames Polytechnic (now Greenwich University). Apart from courses in Higher Education, the author also initiated some part-time Portuguese courses, leading to A-levels and the Diploma of the Institute of Linguistis examinations, at Chelsea-Kensington and Morley College, London.

She has drawn on her experience and feedback from students, in addition to her continuous professional development, to make this dictionary reliable, user-friendly and up-to-date.

Maria F. Allen is a Fellow of the Chartered Institute of Linguists and a former Member of its Council. As a Member of two Chambers of Commerce, she has also gained experience in business-related matters. She is an author of course books and of articles on language and history.

2nd Dec. 13

Acknowledgements

Mr. Robin Batchelor-Smith for his guidance and help.

Dr. John Flannery – linguist and translator – for his continuous support and belief in my ability.

Mrs. Patricia V Simson – Brazilian linguist and Chartered Interpreter – for her encouragement and praises for the dictionary.

Routledge's editorial and production teams, in particular **Mrs. Roya Tobin**.

I am especially indebted to **Christopher Hook** for coordinating this enormous production task so diligently.

Last but not least, my sincere thanks to **Andrea Hartill, Routledge's Publisher**, without whom this work would not have been possible.

Also to **all my students** who, over the years, have contributed towards my knowledge and whose faith in my teaching and encouragement with my writing, are invaluable.

How to use this dictionary

Entries, known as **headwords** are in bold type, as are derivatives of the headword and examples associated with it. To avoid repetition and to save space, most of those entries having the same stem as the headword are shown with their stems replaced by a swung dash {~}. Parts of speech indicators (*n* for noun, *adj* for adjective, etc.); abbreviations *(BOT, ZOOL, BR, etc.)* and definitions of the word are in italics.

> **aged** *adj (person)* velho,-a, idoso,-a, envelhecido,-a; **2** *(wine, cheese)* envelhecido,-a; **3** *(person)* ~ **three** com três anos de idade; **middle~aged** de meia-idade ♦ *npl* **the** ~ *(the elderly)* os idosos.

When the headword gives rise to **idiomatic expressions**, these are flagged by IDIOM.

Numbers indicate different usages of a headword or entry, whilst semi-colons separate meanings of the same headword. The **diamond** symbol {♦} precedes various grammatical elements and special phrases.

In some cases, the entry is followed by a number in superscript. This indicates that it will be followed or preceded by another entry, which is written the same way but with a different meaning and pronunciation *(homograph)*.

> **devil** *n* Diabo/diabo *m; (evil spirit)* demónio (BR-ô-); **2** *(fam) (person)* diabo; **poor** ~! pobre diabo! **3** *(for emphasis):* **what the** ~ **are you doing?** que diabo estás tu a fazer?; IDIOM *(to be)* **between the** ~ **and the deep blue sea** *(estar)* entre a espada e a parede.
> **Scotch**[1] *adj (Scottish)* escocês *m* escocesa *f.*
> **Scotch**[2] *npr (whisky)* uísque *m.*

Compound nouns-adjectives. A compound noun-adjective or expression has two or three words with one meaning. Look up the first word. Here are some examples:

> **cost-effective** *adj* rentável *m, f;* **far-off** *adj (isolated)* remoto,-a; **out-and-out** *adj* completo,-a, absoluto,-a; **knees-up** *n (fam)* festança *f,* farra *f* **cost, far, out, knees**.

Phrasal verbs. In English grammar a phrasal verb is a phrase that consists of a verb with an adverbial or prepositional particle, which has its own meaning and comes after the main verb. For example: **to take in, take up, take out**, etc. follow the verb "**take**".

Double orthographic entries: entries in the old Portuguese spelling, which are still in current use, but gradually being changed, are found side by side with those in the new spelling. The latter has been introduced in the orthographic reform, guidelines to which are found in the introductory pages of this dictionary. Ex: **anti-séptico,-a/antisséptico,-a** *m,f, adj* antiseptic.

Words which have **c** before **t**, **ç**, etc. (see the guidelines on *Orthographic Changes*) and **p** before **t**, have these letters within parentheses for easy reading.

> Ex: **a(c)ção** *f* action; **se(c)tor** *m* sector; **ó(p)timo,-a** *adj* super, optimum.

Notes on **deceptive meanings, "false friends"** and **grammar** are found in indented and shaded areas.

Cultural information

To understand, speak or translate a language well, it is essential to have an appreciation of its culture. Cultural information is provided in shaded and indented **notes**: that relating to Portugal and other Portuguese-speaking countries *(given in English)* will be found in the Portuguese-English side of the dictionary, while that on the UK and the USA *(given in Portuguese)* is shown in the English-Portuguese part.

Como utilizar este dicionário

Aconselha-se a que o leitor leia com atenção estas explicações

A **entrada**, ou verbete, encontra-se em negrito, assim como sub-entradas e exemplos associados. Para evitar uma repetição da entrada, o símbolo diacrítico {~} substitui o verbete ou a sua radical, nos respetivos exemplos e nas sub-entradas. Ou seja: no verbete **amor**, o sub-verbete ~**zinho** deve ser lido como **amorzinho**.

Os **indicadores gramaticais** – *n, m, f, adj, pron, etc*;- o registo apropriado (*fam, pej, fig, formal*); as **abreviaturas** que destacam as áreas de conhecimento (*AGR, BOT, LITER, etc*) e o contexto em que se usa a palavra, encontram-se em itálico, estando estas últimas três entre parênteses curvos. O mesmo sucede com as abreviaturas *(EP) = Portugal;, (BR) = Brazil; (UK) = United Kingdom; (US) = United States of America.*

> **burro,-a** *m, f (ZOOL)* donkey, ass; ~ **de carga** beast of burden; **2** *(fig)* workhorse; **3** *(fig, pej) (pessoa imbecil)* idiot, ass; **4** *(fig) (pessoa)* ~ **de sorte** lucky devil ♦ *adj (pej) (estúpido)* stupid; **2** *(pej) (teimoso)* obstinate; IDIOM **ele está com os** ~**s** he is in a bad mood; **dar com os** ~**s n'água** *(BR)* to lose out.

Como vimos no exemplo acima, o **losango** {♦} introduz várias categorias gramaticais, enquanto os **números em negrito**, indicam diferentes sentidos da entrada. O 'IDIOM' assinala uma expressão idiomática referente à entrada.

Em alguns casos aparece a mesma entrada, duas vezes, com números sobrescritos. Trata-se de palavras com a mesma grafia, mas com significado diferente e, às vezes, com pronúncia diferente também.

> **sede**[1] {ê} *f* thirst; **sede**[2] {é} *f* seat; **2** headquaters, head office.

Substantivos compostos

O substantivo composto, tal como o título sugere, compõe-se de mais de uma palavra, mas tem um significado próprio. Se o leitor deseja ter a tradução de um substantivo composto, deve procurá-lo na entrada correspondente ao primeiro elemento, mesmo quando os substantivos hifenizados perdem o hífen devido à nova disciplina gráfica:

> **bicho-careta** *(pl: bichos-careta) m (pessoa vulgar)* ordinary person, a nobody; **unhas-de-fome** /unhas de fome *m/f, sg/pl*; skinflint ♦ *adj* stingy; **café-da-manhã/café da manhã** *m (pl: cafés da manhã) (BR)* breakfast.

Grafias duplas

As palavras na grafia anterior à reforma ortográfica, as quais ainda estão em uso*, ou no processo de serem convertidas, precedem as entradas elaboradas na reforma:

> **anti-séptico,-a** /antissético; **pára-quedas**/ paraquedas; **bóia/boia**

*(à data da publicação deste dicionário)

Nas palavras que têm **ct, pt, mn, o, c, p, m**, encontram-se entre parênteses para facilitar. O leitor terá apenas que remover estas na adaptação à nova ortografia.

> **a(c)to; se(c)ção; ta(c)to; ó(p)tica; o(m)nipotente.**

(Veja lista com as novas regras ortográficas)

Notas sobre falsos amigos e gramática encontram-se sombreadas, após a entrada relevante.

Informação cultural

Para entender, falar e traduzir bem uma língua, é essencial ter um bom conhecimento da cultura do país, ou países, onde ela é falada. Sendo este um dicionário e não uma enciclopédia, damos simplesmente, algumas informações gerais, escritas em português, que o leitor encontrará sobre o Reino Unido e os Estados Unidos da América e outras observações, indentadas e sombreadas, na parte inglês-portuguesa do dicionário.

O mesmo se aplica à cultura geral dos países de língua portuguesa, bem como outras observações relevantes, escritas em inglês, que figuram na parte luso-inglesa deste livro.

Notes on Portuguese grammar

Nouns, in general, are either masculine, which end in **o**, or feminine if they end in **a**. There are the exceptions, which may end in **e, m, l, z, ão** are either masculine or feminine, in which case they will be indicated by *m,* or *f:* **o perfume, a gente**; **o capital** (*money*), **a capital** (*city*); **o cão, a mão**, etc. Take note that some nouns, mostly of Greek origin, have **a** as a final vowel, but are masculine: **o poema, o telegrama**, etc. Finally those terminating in **ão** may change to **ã** in the feminine: **irmão, irmã**. The reader should carefully consult the dictionary or a grammar about irregular feminines of "ão" to avoid making mistakes, which could be offensive.

Adjectives agree with the nouns in gender and number.

Plural. As a rule, you add **s** to nouns and adjectives: **meninos bonitos, meninas bonitas**, but when the noun and adjective end in **r, s, z**, you add the termination **es** and remove the circumflex accent from its singular: **francês, franceses; mulher, mulheres; vez, vezes**. Those ending in **al, el, ol, ul**, the **l** changes to **s** and gains an accent on the final vowel, even when the singular has no graphic accent: **amável, amáveis; papel, papéis; espanhol, espanhóis**; (*no accent over* **ul-uis**). **il** has two endings: stressed **il** loses the **l** and gains an **s**: **civil, civis; ardil, ardis**, etc; while those nouns and adjectives ending in unstressed **il**, in other words, have a graphic accent elsewhere, change **il** to **eis** as in the general rule: **fácil, fáceis; viável, viáveis**.

Another exception concerns the plural of nouns and adjectives ending in **ão, são, ção**. The general rule is to change **ão** to **ões, são** to **sões, ção** to **ções**. Ex: **melão, melões; possessão, possessões; coração, corações**. However, there are two other less-common plurals of **ão**:

1 add an **s** to the singular: **mão, mãos; irmão, irmãos; órfão, órfãos**; and a few others.
2 change **ão** to **ães**: **capitão, capitães; alemão, alemães; pão, pães; cão, cães** and a few other cases.

Suggestion to the reader: if you memorize the few examples of number two rule and those of rule number three, you know that all the other plurals of **ão** *will end in* **oes**.

NOTE: in the case of irregular feminines and plurals, these will be shown in parentheses, after their singular entries.

Algumas observações gramaticais sobre o inglês

As principais diferenças gramaticais entre o inglês e o português que um estudante de tradução encara são as seguintes:

Artigo definido – em geral menos usado em inglês do que em português, um problema que se nota frequentemente em traduções e exames.

> **o Senhor Silva** Mr. Silva; **a Carolina** Caroline; **o meu, o seu, etc.** my, your etc. *(o artigo antes dos adjetivos possessivos não é usado no Brasil)*. Em situação indeterminada: o artigo definido em inglês omite-se, mas não em português: **students** os alunos; **dogs bark** os cães ladram.

Adjetivo possessivo – mais usado em inglês do que em português, especialmente quando, em português, nos referimos a roupas e partes do corpo pessoais: **vou lavar as mãos** I am going to wash my hands; **vista o casaco** put on your coat.

Passado simples e composto – o português usa o pretérito simples muito mais do que o inglês ou as outras línguas latinas. Assim, **tenho comido** não significa *I have eaten* – um erro comum – mas *I have been eating* (*past continuous*). Por outro lado, *I have eaten* se traduz por **já comi** (*pretérito simples*).

A voz passiva é muito usada em inglês, pelo que o estudante deve lembrar-se de usar mais a voz ativa em português, quando fala ou traduz. Deve utilizar o impessoal 'se' quando apropriado: **Aqui fala-se chinês** (Chinese is spoken here).

Mais algumas explicações sobre a gramática inglesa

Comparativos e superlativos. A regra geral é acrescentar '**er**' ao adjectivo para formar o comparativo, e '**est**' para formar o superlativo: **great, greater, greatest**. Não é possível escrever estes comparativos e superlativos por extenso no livro, devido à falta de espaço, pelo que damos simplesmente os sufixos entre parênteses. De notar que alguns são irregulares, especialmente os adjectivos que terminam em '**y**'. Neste caso, sera necessário mudar o '**y**' para **i** antes das terminações acima citadas: **dizzy, dizzier, dizziest** = (*-ier, -iest*)

Verbos ingleses: em geral acrescenta-se '**ed**' ou '**d**' à raíz do infinitivo para formar o pretérito e o particípio do passado: **to rule, ruled, ruled** = (*-ed*). Quando eles são irregulares, serão assinalados entre parênteses: verbo **to know** (*knew, known*). Quando a sua regularidade consiste simplesmente em dobrar a consoante – '**ll**', '**tt** or '**rr**' – estas são indicadas entre parênteses: **to regret** (-tt-); **to travel** (-ll-): **they travelled** eles viajaram.

Guide to Orthographic Changes

Portuguese is the official language of eight countries across the world, and during the compilation of this dictionary, the talks about orthographic changes have been going on between Brazil and Portugal. Consultation with the other Portuguese-speaking countries followed. At the time of ratification (2008), there were still four countries who had not signed the agreement on the changes, which have now been resolved (2012). Portugal proposed a ten-year moratorium, from 2008, so that all eight countries may have time to adjust to the new orthography.

Since summer 2012, the Portuguese media started to put the new spelling changes into practice. Otherwise the "old spelling" is being slowly absorbed in all the other Portuguese-speaking countries.

The Routledge Portuguese Bilingual Dictionary will have both versions side by side, where possible.

Advice to examination candidates: until the agreement is better defined and put into practice in all countries, you may write in either the old or the new version, as long as they are consistent with the version you choose. However, consult your university or examination board, depending on which examination you are taking.

The principal changes

Alphabet

The letters **k**, **w**, **y** have been added to the Portuguese alphabet, bringing the number to 26 letters.

A, a *(á)*
B, b *(bê)*
C, c *(cê)*
D, d *(dê)*   J, j *(jota)*
E, e *(é)*   K, k *(capa, cá)*   S, s *(esse)*
F, f *(efe)*   L, l *(ele)*   T, t *(tê)*
G, g *(gê or guê)*   M, m *(eme)*   U, u *(u)*
H, h *(agá)*   N, n *(ene)*   V, v *(v)*
I, I *(i)*   O, o *(ó)*   W, w *(dáblio, dâblio, duplo vê)*
                       P, p *(pê)*   X, x *(xis)*
                       Q, q *(quê)*   Y, y *(ípsilon, i grego)*
                       R, r *(erre)*   Z, z *(zê)*

K, W, Y will also be used in names of people, localities, nationalities, units of currency, sports and other nouns or adjectives derived from foreign languages:

> **Kantismo, Kwanza** (Cuanza), **Frankliano**; **Wagneriano, Washingtoniano, windsurfista**; **yen, yanguiano, yoga, Yorkshire**.

and in abbreviations, symbols, weights and measures:

> **K** = Kelvin, potassium; **Kg** = kilogram; **Km** = kilometre; **W** = watt; West; tungsten; **Yd** = yard; **Gy** = grey, gray.

Silent consonants, such as the **cç**, **cç**, **ct**, **pc**, **pç**, **pt**, **bd**, **bt**, **gd**, **mn**, in which the silent **c**, **p**, **b**, **g**, **m**, are/shall be omitted.

Cc, Cç, Ct

(new spelling is indicated in bold)

direccional – **direcional**; leccionar – **lecionar**; accionar – **acionar**
acção – **ação**; colecção – **coleção**; secção – **seção**
contactar – **contatar**; defectivo – **defetivo**;
infectar – **infetar**; sector – **setor**; olfacto – **olfato**

Pc, Pç, Pt, Mp

decepcionar – **dececionar**; interceptar – **intercetar**; corrupto – **corruto**
concepção – **conceção**; percepção – **perceção**; assumpção – **assunção**; (*NB*: mpç = *nç*)
óptimo – **ótimo**; Egipto – **Egito**; peremptório – **perentório**; (*NB*: mpt = *nt*).

(*NB*: it is expected the agreement will accept both graphic norms, especially when the aforementioned consonants are pronounced. As in **pacto, acepção** in both variants, though "**facto**" in Brazil is simply "**fato**", since its "**c**" is not pronounced).

Ex: **infectar, facto, dactilografia, contactar, defectivo** and others.

Bd, Bt, Gd, Mn, Tm

súbdito – **súdito**; subtil – **sutil**; amígdala – **amídala**; amnistia – **anistia**; indemnizar – **indenizar**
(*NB: as explained in the note above:* **assumpção, peremptório**)

Use of capital and small letters (upper and lower case)

(new spelling is indicated in bold)

Lower case

a) *Months, seasons, days of the week*

Abril – **abril**; Outubro – **outubro**, etc.
Inverno – **inverno**; Verão – **verão**, etc.
Domingo – **domingo**; Quinta-feira – **quinta-feira**, etc.

b) *Cardinal points, except when they refer to countries' names* (as in **África do Sul**)

norte, sul, este, oeste, nordeste, noroeste, sudeste, sueste, és-nordeste, é-sueste, etc.

(However, their abbreviations will be initialled with a capital letter).

c) **fulano, beltrano, sicrano.**

Optional spelling (upper or lower case) in the following cases

a) *Public places, palaces, churches*

Alameda Afonso Henriques – **alameda** Afonso Henriques
Igreja dos Anjos – **igreja** dos Anjos

b) *Academic disciplines*

Línguas – **línguas**; Matemática – **matemática**

c) *Forms of address and holy titles*

Senhor Doutor Silva – **senhor doutor** Silva
Santa Tereza – **santa** Tereza

d) *Book titles except the first element and the proper nouns*

A Praia dos Cães – A **praia dos cães**
O Crime do padre Amaro – O **crime do padre Amaro**

Graphic accents

The diaeresis has finally disappeared from Brazilian Portuguese.

(old) lingüiça; lingüista; agüentar
(new) **linguiça**; **linguista**; **aguentar**.

(NB: *it will remain in words of foreign origin*)

So will the circumflex on **ô** in words ending in **oo** and in those with double **ee** disappeared from both variants.

(old) enjôo; vôo; vôos; abençôo; povôo; lêem; vêem; crêem; dêem
(new) **enjoo**; **voo**; **voos**; **abençoo**; **povoo**; **leem**; **veem**; **creem**; **deem**.

However, the circumflex in **pôde** (*third person singular of the past tense of **poder***) remains unaltered, in order to distinguish it from **pode** (*3rd person singular of the present tense of **poder**). The same applies to **pôr** (*to put*) to differentiate it from **por** (*for, by, through*).
The circumflex accent is also kept in **fôrma** (*mould, block*) to distinguish it from **forma** (*shape, way, manner*).
*Verbs **ter*** – and its "family members": **abster, ater-se, conter, deter, entreter, manter, obter, reter, suster** and **vir, avir, convir, intervir, provir** will keep their graphic accents on their plural forms to differentiate them from their singular forms.

Ex: **ele tem** he has; **eles têm** they have; **você vem** you come/are coming; **vocês vêm** you (plural).

*The acute accent over **í, ú**, when preceded by a diphthong*, will no longer be in use.

feiúra – **feiura**; baiúca – **baiuca**

The same case applies to the tonic **ú** in the verbal forms of the present tense of **arguir** and **redarguir**
There are some exceptions in the verbs ending in **guar, quar, quir**.
Verbs ending in –guar, -quar, -quir present two paradigms

a) they lose the graphic accent on **ú,** though its tonic stress (pitch accent) is maintained

averigue, averigues, averiguem, apazigue, oblique

b) or they keep the tonic and graphic stress on the vowel **i** ou **a**, if they are pronounced.

averíque, averígues, averíguem, delínquam; enxáguo, enxáguas, etc.

Optional use of acute or circumflex accents

a) Verbal forms ending in -*ámos* in the perfect tense of the indicative.

amámos/amamos; (*we loved* or *we love*); **lavámos/lavamos** (*we had a wash* or *we wash*).

(NB: Brazil may continue to use the unaccented past tense, ie, -**amos**, whereas in the Luso-African variant the past tense has always had, and may continue to have, its acute accent).

b) Verbal form: **dêmos/demos** in the present tense of the subjunctive.

Double accentuation (due to different pronunciation)

Final **e** and **o** in acute syllables, especially those from French origin will keep the acute or the circumflex accents, depending on the pronunciation of either variant.

(Luso-African) **bebé cocó puré**
(in Brazil) **bebê cocô purê**

The same will be applicable to words stressed on the third syllable from the end (proparoxytone) com **e** or **o**, followed by **m** or **n**, when the latter are not part of a diphthong:

> (Luso-African) **académico; sénior; anatómico; António; abdómen**
> (in Brazil) **acadêmico; sênior; anatômico; Antônio; abdômen**

Omission of acute accent in grave syllables in the diphthongs ei or oi (in Brazil, thus coming in line with European Portuguese, i.e. Luso-African).

> *(old)* idéia; assembéia; boléia; platéia; asteróide; heróico; jibóia; paranóico.
> *(new)* **ideia; assembleia; boleia; plateia; asteroide; heroico; jiboia; paranoico.**

However, those with acute accents in their final syllables, i.e. **éu, éus, éis, ói, óis** will keep their accents.

> Ex: **véu, véus, troféus, papéis, herói, heróis.**

Homographs, which have respectively open or shut tonic vowels in their grave syllables lose their graphic accents, though their pitch accents will continue to be respected.
It will be a question of deducing the meaning from the context.

> Ex: **pára** (*he/she stops*); **para** (*for, to, so that*) = **para**
> **pêlo** (*animal's hair*); **pelo** (*for the, m*) = **pelo.**
> **pêla** (*vb pelar*) **pela** (*for the, f*) = **pela**
> **pólo** (*pole, polo*) and **pêra** (*pear, goatee beard*) lose their graphic accent.

The use of the hyphen

The hyphen will be kept

a) In compound words which represent one syntactic unit and designate botanic, zoological and other species.

> Ex: **peixe-espada, amor-perfeito, feijão-verde, cobra-capelo, cor-de-laranja, ano-luz, terça-feira, guarda-chuva, mal-me-quer, conta-gotas.**

b) In the prefixes **anti, mini, proto, sobre, super,** when the word in front begins with an **h mudo**.

> Ex: **anti-herói; mini-hotel, proto-história, sobre-humano, super-homem.**

c) Idem if the prefix ends in **r** and the second word begins with an **r**.

> Ex: **super-resistente, inter-relacional, hiper-realista, super-romântico.**

(*NB*: not used in **hipermercado, intermunicipal, superproteção** and similar).

d) With the prefix **sub** when followed by a word beginning with an **r**

> Ex: **sub-região.**

e) With prefixes: **ex-, sota-, soto-, vice-.**

> Ex: **ex-diretor, sota-almirante, soto-capitão, vice-cônsul**

f) With stressed prefixes: **pré-, pró-, pós-, além-, aquém-, ex-, semi-,** if the second element has its own separate function in language.

> Ex: **pré-colonial; pró-romano, pós-graduação, pós-datado, aquém-Minho, além-fronteiras, ex-ministro.**

g) In compound words when the prefix ends in the same vowel as that of the second element.

Ex: **anti-inflamatório, micro-ondas, tele-educação, arqui-inimigo.**

But prefixes **co** and **re** do not follow this rule and are still **coordenar, cooperar, reeditar.**

h) With adverbs **bem, mal,** if the second element begins with a **vowel** or an **h mudo**.

   Ex: **bem-estar, mal-humorado.**

i) With toponyms (place names) and titles preceded by **grão, grã** or those needing definite articles.

   Ex: **Grão-Pará, Grã-Bretanha, Trás-os-Montes, grão-duque.**

j) With prefixes **circum** and **pan** when the next element begins with **m, n,** or **vowel.**

   Ex: **circum-navegação, pan-americano.**

Hyphen will disappear

a) If the prefix ends in a vowel which is different from the vowel of the second element.

   Ex: **antiaéreo, agroindustrial, autoestrada neoexpressionista, infraestrutura, extraescolar, coautor, coocorrência.**

b) In compound words, when the prefix ends in a vowel and the next element starts with an **r** or **s**, in which case the **r** or **s** will be doubled.

   Ex: **antissemita, autorretrato, ultrassom, semissintético, ultrarromântico, antirrugas, minissaia, contrassenso.**

c) When the prefix ends in a vowel and the second element begins with a consonant, other than **r** or **s.**

   Ex: **anteprojeto, autoproteção, microcomputador, coprodução, geopolítica, semicírculo.**

Exception: **vice** = **vice-rei, vice-reitor, vice-almirante, vice-versa** and similar.

d) With the prefixes **hiper, inter, super** and the following element begins with a vowel.

   Ex: **hiperacidez, interestadual, superaquecimento, supereconómico**

e) In compound words when the reason for their composition has been forgotten.

   Ex: **paraquedas, paraquedismo, mandachuva** and those words which were already written without hyphen as in: **girassol, pontapé,** etc.

f) In compound nouns where each of them has a different meaning and grammatical function

   (old) **café-da-manhã, dona-de-casa, mão-de-obra, dia-a-dia**
   (new) **café da manhã, dona de casa, mão de obra, dia a dia**

NB: the following locutions have been respected and remain unaltered:

   água-de-colónia *(BR-ô-)*, **arco-da-velha, cor-de-rosa, deus-dará, mais-que-perfeito, pé-de-meia, queima-roupa.**

Abbreviations/Abreviaturas

abbreviation	*abbr, abr*	abreviatura
adjective	*adj*	adjetivo
administration	*(ADMIN)*	administração
adverb	*adv*	advérbio
aviation, aeronautics	*(AER)*	aviação, aeronáutica
agriculture	*(AGR)*	agricultura
something	*(algo)*	alguma coisa
somebody	*(alguém)*	alguém
anatomy	*(ANAT)*	anatomia
Angola	*(ANG)*	Angola
archaic(dated)	*(arc)*	arcaico
architecture	*(ARCH)*	arquitetura
art	*(ART)*	arte
article	*art*	artigo
astrology	*(ASTROL)*	astrologia
astronomy	*(ASTRON)*	astronomia
Australia	*(AUSTR)*	Austrália
automobile, motoring	*(AUT)*	automobilismo, cars
auxiliary	*aux*	auxiliar
biology	*(BIO), (BIOL)*	biologia
botany	*(BOT)*	botânica
Brazilian	*(BR)*	português do Brasil
slang	*(cal)*	calão
chemistry	*(CHEM)*	química
cinema	*(CIN)*	cinema
colloquial	*(coll), (col)*	coloquial
commerce	*(COMM), (COM)*	comércio
comparative	*comp*	comparativo
computing	*(COMP)*	computação
conjunction	*conj*	conjunção
construction, building	*(CONSTR)*	construção
culinary, cookery	*(CULIN)*	culinária, cozinha
Cape Verde	*(CV)*	Cabo Verde
definite	*def*	definido
ecology	*(ECOL)*	ecologia
economy	*(ECON)*	economia
education	*(EDUC)*	educação
electricity, electronics	*(ELECT)*	electricidade , electrónica
European Portuguese	*(EP)*	português europeu
equivalent (cultural)	*equiv/=*	equivalente cultural
euphemism	*euph, euf*	eufemismo
exclamation, interjection	*exc*	exclamação, interjeição
feminine	*f*	feminino
familiar	*(fam)*	familiar
pharmacy	*(FARM)*	farmácia
railways	*(FERRO)*	ferrovia
figurative sense	*(fig)*	uso figurado
finance	*(FIN)*	finanças
physics	*(FÍS)*	física
physiology	*(FISIOL)*	fisiologia

phonetics	*(fon)*	fonética
photography	*(FOTO)*	fotografia
future	*fut*	futuro
football	*(FUT)*	futebol
geography	*(GEOG)*	geografia
geology	*(GEOL)*	geologia
geometry	*(GEOM)*	geometria
general	*(ger)*	geral
grammar	*(gram)*	gramática
heraldry	*HERALD*	heráldica
history	*(HIST)*	história
idiomatic expressions	*IDIOM*	expressões idiomáticas
imperative	*imp*	imperativo
imperfect	*imperf*	imperfeito
indefinite	*indef*	indefinido
indicative	*indic*	indicativo
invariable	*inv*	invariável
irregular	*irr*	irregular
journalism, press	*(JOURN), (JORN)*	jornalismo, imprensa
law, juridical, legal	*(JUR)*	jurídico, lei, legal
linguistics, language	*(LING), (LÍNG)*	linguística, língua
literature	*(LITER)*	literatura
masculine	*m*	masculino
mathematics	*(MATH), (MAT)*	matemática
mechanics	*(MECH), (MEC)*	mecânica
medicine	*(MED)*	medicina
meteorology	*(METEOR)*	meteorologia
military matters	*(MIL*	military
mineralogy	*(MIN)*	mineralogia
Mozambique	*MOÇ*	Moçambique
music	*(MUS), (MÚS)*	música
noun	*n*	substantivo
nautical, sailing	*(NAUT), (NÁUT)*	náutica
noun (proper noun)	*npr*	nome próprio
numeral	*num*	numeral
oneself	*o.s.*	se
onomatopeia	*onomat*	onomatopeia
pejorative	*(pej)*	pejorativo
pharmacy	*(PHARM)*	farmácia
phonetics	*(phon)*	fonética
photography	*(PHOT)*	fotografia
physics	*(PHYS)*	física
physiology	*(PHYSIOL)*	fisiologia
plural	*pl*	plural
pluperfect	*pluperf*	mais-que-perfeito
past pariciple	*pp*	particípio do passado
politics	*(POL)*	política
prefix	*pref*	prefixo
preposition	*prep*	preposição
present	*pres*	presente
present participle	*pres.p*	particípio presente
pronoun	*pron*	pronome
preterite, past	*pt*	pretérito, passado
psychology, psychiatry	*(PSYC), (PSIC)*	psicologia, psiquiatria
química	*(QUIM)*	química
radio	*(RADIO)*	rádio
railways	*(RAIL)*	ferrovia
regional	*(REG)*	regional
religion	*(REL)*	religião
somebody	*sb*	alguém
Scotland	*(Scot)*	Escócia

singular	*sg*	singular
slang	*(slang)*	calão
somebody	*sb*	alguém
spacial, spatial	*spatial*	espacial
sport	*(SPORT)*	desporto, esporte
something	*sth*	algo
subjunctive	*subj*	subjuntivo,conjuntivo
tauromachy, bullfighting	*(TAUROM)*	tauromaquia
technology, technical term	*(TECH), (TEC)*	técnica, tecnologia
telecommunications, telephone	*(TEL)*	telecomunicações, telefone
theatre	*(THEAT)*	teatro
television	*TV*	televisão
toponym, place name	*(topon)*	nome geográfico
tourism	*(TOUR)*	turismo
typography, printing	*(TYPO)*	tipografia, imprensa
United Kingdom	*(UK)*	Reino Unido
University	*(Univ)*	universidade
United States	*(US)*	EUA
verb	*vb*	verbo
see, Vide	*(Vd)*	vide, veja
veterinary services	*(VET)*	vetrinário, veterinária
intransitive verb	*vi*	verbo intransitivo
reflexive verb	*vr*	verbo reflexivo
transitive verb	*vt*	verbo transitivo
vulgar, offensive	*(vulg)*	ordinário, ofensivo
zoology	*ZOOL*	zoologia
registered trademark	®	marca registada

Portuguese–English

a

A, a *m (letra)* A, a *m*; **de A a Z** from A to Z.
AA *(abr de* **Alcoólicos Anónimos**) Alcoholics Anonymous.
a *art def f (pl:* **as**) the; **a porta/as portas** the door/the doors; **2** *(com nomes próprios)* **a Maria** Mary; **a Menina Alice** (Miss) Alice; **a Senhora Silva** Mrs Silva; **3** *(introduz pronomes)* **as senhoras** you *(pl)* ladies; **que desejam as senhoras?** *(formal)* what would you *(fpl)* like to have?; **4** *(usado em topon.)* **a Inglaterra** England; **5** *(com substantivo abstracto)* **a vida** life; ♦ *prep* to, at, by, on, in, of, towards, from; *(direção, lugar)* **vou a Roma** I am going to Rome; **ela está à janela** *(a+a = * **à**) she is at the window; **ela vai às compras** *(a+as = * **às**) she goes shopping; **2** *(posição)* **à esquerda/à direita** on the left, on the right; **3** *(distância)* **fica a dez minutos daqui** it is ten minutes away *(from here)*; **4** *(tempo, data, frequência)* **de tempos a tempos** from time to time; **a dez de Agosto** on the tenth of August; **dia a dia** day by day; **daqui a duas horas** in two hour's time; **às sextas-feiras cantamos** we sing on Fridays; **5** *(modo)* **a pé** on foot; **a cavalo** on horseback (ride); **ela gritou a plenos pulmões** she shouted out with all her might; **à força** *(a+a = * **à**) by force; **6** *(preço)* **as sardinhas estão a 200 Euros o quilo** sardines are at (cost) 200 Euros a kilo; **7** *(opinião)* **a meu ver** in my opinion; **8** *(aproximado)* **de vinte a vinte e cinco anos** between twenty and twenty five years old; **9** *(indica série)* **de quatro a oito** from four to eight; ♦ *(introduz complemento indirecto)* to; **a alguém** to sb; **vou dar isto a ela** I am going to give this to her; **ele escreveu à mãe** he wrote to his mother; ♦ *(substitui pron dem = * **aquela**, **aquelas***)* the one, that, those; **a de vestido preto** the (that) one in black, in black dress; **as que foram à China** the ones/those/the women who went to China; **a que for mais barata** the one/whichever is the cheapest; ♦ *(introduz pron pess)* **se eu fosse a você** if I were you; **a minha e a dele** mine and his; ♦ *(precede infinitivo)* **ao ver ...** when I saw/on seeing ...; ♦ *(pron pess: her, you (f), it)* **vejo-a** *(BR)* **eu a vejo** I see her/you/it *(f)*; **eu quero vê-la** I want to see her/it; *(ver+a = * **vê-la***)*; **vou comprá-la** I am going to buy it *(comprar+a = * **comprá-la***)* ♦ *(usado na forma perifrástica)*; **está ~ chover** it is raining; **ela aprendeu ~ nadar** she learnt to swim; *(Note: in Brazil, this form is not used; instead:* **está chovendo**, *etc)*; ♦ *(em locuções)* **a partir de** from, starting from.

For other examples using '**a**' plus noun, see the relevant noun. Ex. **a braços com**, see '**braço**'.

à *(= * **a + a***)* to/at the; ♦ **à deriva** *adv* off-course, drifting, floating along; **andar ~** to wander aimlessly.
aba *f (vestuário)* brim; **a ~ do chapéu** the hat's brim; *(de casaca)* tail; **2** *(mobília, envelope)* flap, folding leaf; **3** *(costeleta de vaca)* skirt; **4** *(colina)* foot; **5** *(roof)* eaves.
abacate *m* avocado.
abacaxi *m (BR)* pineapple; *(fam)* tiresome thing; IDIOM **descascar um ~** to get to the root of the problem.
abade, abadessa *m* abbot, *f* abbess.
abadia *f* abbey.
abafadiço,-a *adj* stifling; stuffy.
abafado,-a *adj* stifling; stuffy; **2** *(caso)* hushed up; **3** *(som)* muffled; **4** *(pessoa)* wrapped up; **5** *(vinho)* unfermented.
abafador *m (MÚS)* damper, mute; **2 ~ do bule do chá** tea-cosy; **3** *(de instrumento)* mute.
abafar *vt* to *(sufocar)* suffocate, stifle; **2** *(apagar)* smother *(fogo, chama)*; **2** *(reprimir, conter)* to suppress *(emoções)*; to hold back *(soluço)*; **3** *(ocultar)* to cover, hush up *(rumor, escândalo)*; **4** *(atenuar)* reduce, muffle *(ruído)*; *(MÚS)* damper; **5** *(agazalhar)* to wrap up, keep warm; **6** to cover *(panela)*; **7** *(BR)* *(fazer sucesso)* to steal the show; ♦ **~-se** *vr* to wrap o.s. up.
abafo *m* warm garment; **2** *(fig)* *(carinho)* tender care/gesture/word.
abainhar *(= * **embainhar***)* *vt* to make, sew the hem of a garment.
abaixamento *m (som, altura, nível)* lowering; **2** *(redução)* lowering, reduction, falling of (prices); **3** *(depressão no solo)* hollow; **4** *(emoção)* depression; **5 ~ de temperatura** drop in temperature.
abaixar *(= * **baixar***)* *vt* to lower; to reduce; to bring down; **2** to turn down *(bainha)*; **3** to duck *(a cabeça)*; ♦ **~-se** *vr* to stoop; bend down; **ele abaixou-se para beijar a criança** he stooped down to kiss the child.
abaixo *adv* down, below; **~ o governo!** down with the government!; **encosta ~** downhill; **rio ~** downstream; **mais ~** further down; **~ e acima** up and down; **pela escada ~** down the stairs; **deitar/vir ~** *(árvores, prédios)* to bring/come down; ♦ *prep* **~ de** *(em posição inferior)* below; under.
abaixo-assinado *(pl:* **abaixo-assinados***)* *m* petition, round robin; **2** *(person)* undersigned; **os ~s** the undersigned.
abajur *m* lampshade.
abalada *f* hasty departure, departure; **estamos de ~** we are off.
abalado,-a *adj (inseguro)* shaky *(prédio, amizade, negócio)*; **2** *(doente)* weak, run down, shaky; **a doença deixou-a ~a** the illness left her run down/shaky; **3** *(dente)* loose; **4** *(fig)* *(deprimido)* distressed; **5** *(de susto)* shaken.
abalançar *vt* to hold in equilibrium; **2** make an estimate de *(prejuízos)*; **3** *(impelir)* lead (sb to); ♦ **~-se** *vr* to venture.

abalar vt (fazer tremer) to shake (algo); **2** (fig) to affect, weaken, shake (saúde, espírito, decisões); **3** (fig) (emoção) to move, upset; **4** (ECON) to affect, shake; ♦ vi to rush off, leave.

abalizado,-a adj (lugar) measured out, marked by bounds; confined; **2** (fig) (pessoa) skilled; distinguished; **um médico ~** a renowned doctor; **3** (opinião) expert.

abalizador,-ora m,f (agrimensor) surveyor; **2** m (ferramenta) measuring-rod.

abalizar vt (demarcar) to demarcate, to stake out (land); **2** (questão) survey; ♦ **~-se** vr (fig) to distinguish (oneself) (**em**, in).

abalo m (GEOL) quake; **~ de terra/sísmico** earthquake; **2** (fig) (emoção) shock; upset; jerk.

abanão m (sacudidela) jolt, jerk, shake.

abanar vt to shake; **2** (desaprovação, negação) **~ com a cabeça** to shake one's head; **3** (com o lenço) to wave; **4** (agitar) (animal) to wag (**rabo**, tail); **5** to fan; **~ o lume** to fan the fire; ♦ vr (com leque, jornal) fan oneself; IDIOM **ele veio com as mãos a ~** he came empty-handed (without presents).

abancar vi to sit down; **~ à mesa** to sit at the table; **2** (fig) (permanecer demais) overstay; ♦ **~-se** vr to sit down.

abandalhado,-a adj neglected; **2** (desmazelado) untidy, messy, sloppy.

abandalhar vt to neglect (trabalho, família); ♦ **~-se** vr to disgrace o.s. to let him/herself go.

abandonado,-a adj (terras, navio) abandoned, deserted; **2** (desamparado) neglected, abandoned; **encontraram uma criança ~** a child was found abandoned; **3** (sem trato) neglected (terras, estradas).

abandonar vt (retirar-se) to leave (lugar, barco); **2** (deixar) give up (estudos, projeto); **3** (negligenciar) neglect (animal, propriedade); **4** (desamparar) to abandon, desert; forsake (família, lar); **ele abandonou a mulher** he left/deserted his wife; ♦ **~-se** vr to let o.s. go; **2 ~-se a** (entregar-se a) surrender to.

abandono m desertion; neglect; **andar ao ~** (pessoa sem proteção) to be neglected; out in the cold; **o prédio está ao ~** the building is derelict; **2** (desistência) abandonment; **3** (relaxamento) relaxed (vida, atitude).

abanicar vt to fan (face); ♦ **~-se** vr **~ com um jornal** to fan (oneself) with a newspaper.

abanico m small fan; **2** pl gallantrie; fine, witty words; **3** (pop) **~s** pl bullfighter's moves with his cape.

abano m fan (para fogueira, fogareiro); IDIOM **ter orelhas de ~** to have jug ears.

abarbatar vt (surripiar) to make off with (algo); ♦ **~-se** vr nick, pinch, pilfer (pop).

abarcador,-ora m,f monopolist, racketeer; ♦ adj monopolistic, encompassing.

abarcamento m monopoly.

abarcar vt to include; **2** take on many duties; **3** monopolize; **4** encompass; take in (vista).

abarracamento m (conjunto de barracas) shanty town; **2** (de ciganos) gipsy camp.

abarracar vt to lodge in tents; provide with tents.

abarrotado,-a adj (fam) (sala, transporte) crowded, crammed; (fam) packed; **2** (com comida) stuffed with food; **3 algibeiras ~,-as de dinheiro** pockets full of money.

abarrotar vt to fill up; to crowd, cram; ♦ **~-se** vr to overeat, stuff (oneself) (**de** with).

abastado,-a m,f wealthy person; ♦ adj (rico) wealthy; **3** (provido) (navio, despensa) supplied.

abastança f abundance, surfeit, plenty; **2** wealth; **viver na ~** to live well.

abastardar vt to degrade; to corrupt, to ruin; ♦ **~-se** vr to become corrupt/degenerate.

abastecer vt to supply; **2** to fuel; **3** (AUTO) to fill up; **4** (AER) to refuel; ♦ **~-se** vr: **~-se de** to stock up with.

abastecimento m supply; **2** provisions pl; **3** supplying; **4 ~s** mpl supplies, provisions.

abate m (Vd: abatimento).

abater vt (derrubar) to knock down (algo); **2** to lower; reduce; **3** (animais) slaughter; **4** kill (alguém); **5** (saúde) weaken; **a notícia abateu-o** the news shattered him; ♦ vi (prédio) subside.

abatido,-a adj (moral state) depressed, downcast; **2** (aspeto físico) looking weak, drawn; **3** (gado) slaughtered; **as vacas loucas tiveram de ser abatidas** the mad cows had to be slaughtered; **4** (animal feroz) **o leão foi ~ a tiro** the lion was shot down.

abatimento m weakness; **2** depression, despondency; **3** (animais) slaughtering; **4** (prédios) razing, falling in; **5** (árvores) felling, cutting down; **6** (COM) reduction, rebate; **fazer um ~** give a discount; **7 ~ de terras** shifting of the land; (GEOL, CONSTR) subsidence.

abaulado,-a adj convex; cambered.

abaulamento m curving, arching; **~ das ruas** camber.

abaular-se vr to curve upwards, arch, bulge; ♦ vi to sag, curve.

abcesso m tumour; abscess.

abdicação f abdication.

abdicar vt (**de**) to abdicate, give up; ♦ vi **~ de (algo)** (fig) to forego, go without.

abdómen (pl: **abdómenes**) (BR: -dô-) m abdomen.

abdominal (pl: **-ais**) adj abdominal.

á-bê-cê (abecê) m alphabet, ABC; **2** (fig) rudiments pl; **o ~ da cozinha** the ABC of cooking.

abecedário m alphabet (book).

abegão, abegoa m,f farm hand, overseer; **2** (ZOOL) drone.

abeirar vt to bring near; **2** to approach, go up to (sb, sth); ♦ **~-se** vr: **~-se de** to draw near, to go near to.

abelha f bee; **~-mestra** (pl: **abelhas-mestras**) queen bee.

abelhão m (também: **zângão**) bumblebee.

abelheira f (ninho) bee nest (numa árvore); **2** (BOT) bee-orchid.

abelheiro m bee-eater (bird); **2** bee keeper.

abelhudice f intrusiveness, nosiness; impudence.

abelhudo,-a m,f meddlesome person; ♦ adj (fam) nosy.

abençoadeira *f (BR)* **abençoadeiro** *m* quack doctor, person who cures with charms, prayers.

abençoado,-a *adj* blessed, blissful; *(poet.)* blest; ~ **sejas!** may you be blessed!, bless you!

abençoador,-ora *m,f* the one who blesses; ♦ *adj* blessing.

abençoar, abendiçoar *vt* to bless; **Deus te abençoe!** God bless you!

aberração *f* aberration; **2** error; **3** freak; **uma ~ da natureza** a freak of nature; **4 ~ biológica** *(BIOL)* mutation.

aberrante *adj* hideous, abnormal; incongruous.

abertamente *adv* frankly, openly, freely, candidly.

aberto,-a *(pp irr de abrir) adj* open; **2** clear; **3** exposed; **4** frank; **5** *(floresta)* clearing; **6 nome ~ na madeira** name carved in the wood; **7** *(LITER)* open to interpretation; ♦ *adv* **em ~** incomplete; left open, blank, on-going; IDIOM **estar sempre de pernas ~,-as para fazer** *(col, fam)* to be willing to do anything, to be a doormat; **de boca ~** stunned, gobsmacked *(pop)*.

abertura *f* opening; inauguration; **2** gap, crevice; **3** clearing, glade; **4** *(golfo, ângulo)* width, distance; **5** *(FOTO)* aperture; **6 ~ de falência** declaration of bankruptcy; **7** *(MÚS)* overture; **8** *(POL)* liberalization.

abespinhado,-a *adj* irritated, peevish, huffy.

abespinhar *vr* to irritate, to bother.

abestalhado,-a *adj* dull, stupid; moronic.

abestalhar-se *vr* to become stupid, dull.

abestiar *vt* to make a beast out of sb.

abeto *m (BOT)* fir tree.

abetumado,-a *adj* smeared, covered with bitumen, tar; **2** heavy, soggy *(pão)*.

abieiro *m (BOT)* the abiu, abies *(Pouteria caimito; fruit tree from S. America)*.

abigodado *m* with a moustache, in the shape of a moustache.

abinício, ab initio *adv* from the beginning.

abiotic *adj (MED)* abiotic.

abismado,-a *adj (atónito)* astonished, shocked, dismayed, aghast.

abismal *adj inv (profundo)* deep, bottomless; **2** *(fig) (diferença)* huge, enormous.

abismar *vt (barco)* to sink; **2** *(fig)* to amaze, shock *(alguém)*; ♦ *~-se vr (espantar-se)* to be amazed; **~-se com** be amazed at, appalled (**com** at, by).

abismo *m (precipício)* abyss; depths; **2** *(fig) (situação difícil)* pitfall, depths; **3** *(fig) (grande diferença)* chasm.

abissal *adj inv (GEOL) (cavidade)* abyssal, deep; **2** *(fig) (diferença, distância)* huge, unbridgeable.

abje(c)ção *f* degradation, abjection.

abje(c)to,-a *adj* abject.

abnegação *f* self-denial, renunciation, self-sacrifice.

abnegar *vt* to renounce, abnegate.

abóbada *f (ARQ)* vault; arched roof; **2** *(ASTRON)* dome, ~ **celeste** the roof of heaven (the skies).

abobodado,-a *adj* vaulted, arched.

abóbora *f (BOT)* pumpkin; **2** *(fig) (fam) (mulher gorda)* fatty; roly-poly; **3 ~-carneira** *f* bottlegourd;

4 ~-menina hubbard squash; **5 ~-porqueira** *f* pumpkin (usado para comida dos porcos e na noite do feitiço 'Halloween'); ♦ *exc* **ora ~!** now really!

abolição *f* abolition.

abolir *vt* to abolish, suppress.

abominação *f* abomination.

abominar *vt* loathe, detest.

abominável *adj inv* abominable.

abonação *f* guarantee, warranty, recommendation.

abonado,-a *adj* person with good credit; reliable, **2** *(rico)* well-off person.

abonador,-ora *m,f* guarantor; ♦ *adj* guaranteeing.

abonar *vt* to guarantee, vouch for; **2** *(dinheiro)* to advance; **3** *(conferir)* bestow; ♦ *~-se vr* to boast, flatter oneself.

abono *m* allowance; ~ **de família** child benefit; **2** *(adiantamento)* advance payment; **3** *(garantia)* collateral; **em ~ da verdade** to be absolutely honest, in defence of truth; **falar em ~ de alguém** to speak (well) on sb's behalf; **3** *(fig)* praise.

abordagem *f (contacto)* approach; **2** *(tratamento de tema)* broach, presentation.

abordar *vt (NÁUT)* to come alongside, to accost; **2** to approach *(alguém)*; **3** to broach (subject, conversation).

aborígene *m,f* native, aborigine; ♦ *adj* native, aboriginal.

aborrecer *vt* to annoy; to bore *(alguém)*; ♦ *~-se vr* to get annoyed, bored.

aborrecido,-a *adj* annoying, boring; **ele está ~** *(temporário)* he is bored; **ele é ~** *(característica)* he is boring; **que ~!** how annoying!; how boring!

aborrecimento *m (zanga)* upsetting; **2** *(tédio)* weariness; boredom; **3** *(contratempo)* nuisance; **4** setback; ♦ *exc* **que ~ !** how annoying! how upsetting!

abortar *vi (espontaneamente)* to miscarry, abort; ♦ *vt* to abort; ♦ *vi (plan)* fail, abort.

aborto *m (MED)* abortion; *(interrupção voluntária)* aborto; ~ **espontâneo** miscarriage; ~ **clandestino** back-street abortion; **fazer um ~** to have an abortion.

abotoar *vt* to button (up), to buckle, to fasten; ♦ *~-se com (fig)* to make off with; **eles abotoaram-se com o dinheiro da firma** they made off with the company's money.

abracadabra *m* abracadabra.

abraçar *vt* to hug, to clasp; **2** to include, encompass; **3** embrace *(causa, fé, outra pessoa)*; **abraçámo-nos** we embraced, hugged (each other); **4 ~ uma profissão** to enter a profession; ♦ *vr ~-se a* to cling to; **ela abraçou-se à mãe** she clung to her mother.

abraço *m* embrace, hug; **2 mandar abraços** *(numa carta)* to send one's love.

abrandamento *m* slowing down; **2** softening, mitigating; **3** *(ECON)* slackening; reduction; **4** fall *(em temperatura)*

abrandar *vt* to slow down; ~ **a marcha** to slow down; **2** soften, sooth, attenuate; ♦ *vi* to calm down; **3** case up, ease off.

abrangente *adj inv* broad, ample, wide; **numa perspectiva** ~ in a broad perspective.

abranger *vt (incluir)* to include; **2** *(conter em sua área)* comprise; **3** *(grasp)* to take in; cover; reach, engulf; **a vista abrangia todos os vinhedos** the view took in all the vineyards.

abráquio,-a *adj* born without arms.

abrasado,-a *adj* glowing, ruddy.

abrasador,-ora *adj* **abrasante** *adj inv* burning, scorching; **sob um sol** ~ under a blazing sun.

abrasão *f (GEOL)* erosion; **2** *(MED)* abrasion.

abrasar *vt (queimar)* to burn, overheat, scorch *(os campos)*; **2** *(desbastar)* erode; polish *(superfícies ásperas)*; ♦ *vi* to be on fire.

abrasileirado,-a *adj* Brazilian-like.

abrasileirar-se *vr* to adopt Brazilian customs, traits; speak with Brazilian accent.

abrasivo,-a *adj (produto de limpeza)* abrasive.

abre-boca *m (VET, MED)* a tool to keep the patients and animals' mouths open during surgery, jaw-lever.

abre-cartas *m* letter opener; paper knife.

abre-cu *(Vd:* **pirilampo**).

abre-latas *m* can, tin opener.

abrenúncio! *exc* God forbid!

abreviação *f (de palavra)* abbreviation; **2** *(de resumo)* abridgement; **3** *(diminuição)* curtailment.

abreviado,-a *adj* brief; **2** abridged, condensed.

abreviar *vt (pôr em abreviatura)* to abbreviate; **2** *(tornar breve)* to shorten; **3** *(resumir)* to abridge.

abreviatura *f* abbreviation.

abridor de lata *m (BR)* can, tin opener.

abrigar *vt* to shelter; to protect; ♦ ~**-se** *vr* to take shelter.

abrigo *m (refúgio)* shelter, cover; ~ **subterrâneo** underground shelter; **2 sem** ~ without a roof; **3 os sem** ~ *(pessoas)* the homeless; ♦ *prep* **ao** ~ **de** *(JUR)* under cover of; **ao** ~ **da lei** protected by the law; **2** sheltered from.

Abril, abril *m* April; **primeiro de** ~ *(dia dos enganos)* April's Fool; IDIOM ~ **águas de mil** April's showers.

O 25 de Abril (the 25th of April) refers to the 1974 Revolution in Portugal.

Abrilada (epónimo de: **Abril**) refers to the political rebellion led by D. Miguel against his father and the Constitution, in order to re-establish absolutism (1824).

abrilhantador *m (para a máquina de lavar louça)* rinse product.

abrir *vt* to open, to unlock; **2** to unfasten; **3** to turn on; **4** *(ELECT, TV, RÁDIO)* to switch on; **5** *(vinho)* to uncork; **6** ~ **falência** go bankrupt; **7** ~ **o apetite** whet one's appetite; IDIOM **num** ~ **e fechar de olhos** in the twinkling of an eye.

ab-rogação *f (de lei)* repeal, annulment, abrogation.

ab-rogar *vt (de leis)* to repeal, abrogate, abolish; **2** *(costumes)* discontinue.

abrolhar *vt* to come into bud, to bud, to blossom.

abrolho *m* thorn; **2** *(BOT)* caltrop, kind of thistle; **3** ~**s** *(GEOL)* reefs, under-water pointed rocks; **4** *(fig)* difficulties, troubles.

abrunheiro *m (BOT)* blackthorn tree, damson tree.

abrunho *m (BOT)* damson, (damascus) plum; **2** *(silvestre)* sloe.

abrupto,-a *adj (resposta, movimento)* abrupt, direct, sudden; **2** *(montanha)* steep.

abrutalhado,-a *adj (pessoa)* rough, brutish; **2** *(maneiras)* coarse, rude.

absenteísmo *m (BR)* absenteeism.

absentismo *m (EP)* absenteeism; **2** *(school)* truancy; **3** *(AGR)* absent owner entrusting his estate to a manager.

absentista *adj inv (EP)* absentee; **2** *(comportamento)* withdrawal.

abside, ábside *f (ARQ)* apse, vault.

absolutamente *adv* absolutely; **preciso** ~ **de falar com ele** I really need to talk to him.

absolutismo *m* absolutism.

absolutista *m,f adj inv* absolutist.

absoluto,-a *adj* absolute, unconditional; **2** pure; ♦ *adv (BR)* **em** ~ not at all.

absolver *vt* to absolve, to pardon; **2** *(JUR)* to acquit, set free.

absolvição *f* absolution; **3** *(JUR)* acquittal.

absorção *f* absorption.

absorto,-a *(pp irr de* **absorver**) *adj* absorbed, engrossed **(em** in).

absorvente *adj inv* absorbent; **2** *(fig) (palestra)* fascinating, enthralling; **3** *(fig) (trabalho, família)* demanding.

absorver *vt* to absorb; ♦ ~**-se** *vr:* ~ **em** to concentrate on.

abstémio,-a *(BR: -tê-) m,f* abstainer, teetolar; ♦ *adj* abstemious; **2** teetotal.

abstenção *f (de prazeres)* abstinence; *(de voto)* abstention.

abstencionismo *m (POL)* abstention.

abstencionista *m,f (POL)* abstainer; ♦ *adj inv* abstaining.

abster-se *vr:* ~**-se de** to abstain; refrain from; **2** ~**-se de fazer algo** to refrain from doing sth.

abstinência *f* abstinence; *(de comer)* fasting.

abstra(c)ção *f* abstraction; **2** concentration

abstrair *vt* to abstract; **2** to omit; **3** to separate; ♦ ~**-se** *vr* to become distracted, unaware of anything around.

abstra(c)to *m* abstract; **em** ~ in abstract; ♦ **abstra(c)to,-a** *adj* abstract; **ciência** ~**a** abstract science; **2** *(desatento)* absent-minded; lost in thought.

absurdeza *f* absurdity.

absurdo,-a *m* absurd; absurdity; **é um** ~ it's an absurdity; ♦ *adj* absurd, nonsensical, preposterous, incongruous.

abulia *f* apathy.

abundância *f* abundance; wealth; **viver na** ~ to live in plenty.

abundante *adj* abundant.

abundantemente *adv* abundantly.

abundar *vi* to abound.

aburguesado,-a *adj (pessoa, modos)* bourgeois.

abusar *vi (aproveitar-se)* ~ **de alguém** take advantage *(of sb, sth)*; **ele aproveitou-se da hospitalidade dela** he took advantage of, abused her hospitality; **2** *(sexually)* ~ **alguém** abuse sb, rape sb; **3** *(praticar* *excessos)* ~ **de algo** use too much; ~ **do álcool** to overindulge in drink; ~ **do açúcar** to use too much sugar; **4** *(exceder-se)* to go too far, to overstep the mark.

abusivo,-a *adj (tratamento)* abusive, wrongful; **2** *(trabalho, preço)* excessive.

abuso *m* abuse *(de tabaco, álcool)*; **2** ~ **da inocência** child abuse; **3** *(exagero)* overuse, misuse; **4** ~ **de confiança** breach of trust; **5** *(da lei)* transgression, violation.

abutre *m (ZOOL)* vulture; **2** *(fig)* pessoa cruel; **3** *(usuário)* usurer, vulture.

a.C. *(abr de* **antes de Cristo**) BC.

acabado,-a *adj* finished; **2** complete; **3** accomplished; **4** worn out; **o homem está muito** ~ the man has aged a lot; **é um trabalho bem** ~ it is a well executed work, perfect work.

acabamento *m (de trabalho)* finish, conclusion; **os acabamentos** final/finishing touches.

acabar *vt (terminar)* to finish, conclude; **2** *(pôr fim, encerrar)* to end *(relações, discurso)*; **3** *(chegar ao fim)* come to the end of *(livro)*; *(DESP)* to finish; to end *(filme)*; **4** *(rematar)* to finish off; ♦ *vi (terminar)* to finish, end; **o curso já acabou** the course has finished; **a discussão acabou mal** the discussion ended badly; **2** *(ter tido lugar no momento)* to have just …; **ele acabou de chegar** he has just arrived; **3** *(como consequência)* ~ **em algo** to end up in sth; ~ **em nada** to end up in smoke; **4** *(ter como conclusão)* to end in sth; **a zaragata acabou em desastre** the quarrel ended in disaster; **5** *(arruinar)* ~ **com** to spoil, destroy, finish with; **eles acabaram com as minhas esperanças** they destroyed my hopes; **6** ~ **por** to end (up) by; **ele acabou por fazer o bolo/ acabou fazendo o bolo** he ended up making the cake; ♦ ~**-se** *vr* to be over; to expire; to run out; ♦ *exc* **acabou-se!** that's enough, it's over!

acabrunhado,-a *(deprimido) adj* depressed; downhearted; in low spirits; **2** *(envergonhado)* vexed, embarrassed.

acabrunhador,-ora *adj (situação)* distressing.

acabrunhar *vt (desanimar)* to distress **2** *(envergonhar)* to embarrass, to vex.

acácia *(BOT) f* acacia.

academia *f* academy, college, university; **A~ das Belas Artes** Academy of Fine Arts.

académico,-a *(BR:* -**dê**-*) m,f adj* academic, academician; **2** member of an academy; **3** *(estilo)* conventional.

açafate *m* wicker basket without handles.

açafrão *m (BOT) (planta)* crocus; **2** *(CULIN) (especiaria)* turmeric, saffron.

açaimar *vt* to muzzle, gag; **2** to restrain, repress *(multidão)*.

açaime, açaimo *m* muzzle, gag.

acaju *m (BOT) (planta)* cashew; **castanha de** ~ cashew nut; **2** *(mogno)* mahogany.

acalcanhar *vt (pisar om os calcanhares)* to tread, trample; stamp on/out *(algo)*; **2** *(fig) (oprimir)* to crush *(alguém)*; make someone feel small.

acalcar *vt (Vd:* **calcar**).

acalento *m* lullaby.

acalentar *vt (embalar)* to lull, rock to sleep *(bebé)*; **2** *(alimentar)* to nurture, to cherish *(sonho, desejo)*; ~ **esperanças** to cherish hopes.

acalmar *vt (apaziguar)* to calm down; **2** to soothe, to alleviate; ♦ *vi* to grow calm; ♦ ~**-se** *vr* to calm down.

acalmia *f (bonança)* quiet, lull.

acalorado,-a *adj* hot; **face** *f* ~ hot cheeks; **2** *(conversa, discussão)* heated, excited.

acalorar *vt* to heat; **2** *(fig)* to inflame; ♦ ~**-se** *vr* to liven up; **2** *(fig)* to get heated.

acamado,-a *adj (doente)* bed-ridden; **2** *(em camadas)* in layers, layered; **3** *(seara, erva)* flattened.

açambarcador,-ora *m* monopolist, (of goods); ♦ *adj (alguém)* monopolizing.

açambarcar *vt (mercadorias)* to hoard; **2** to stock up and retain *(para vantagem)*; **3** to monopolize.

acampamento *m* camping; **2** *(MIL)* camp, encampment.

acampar *vi* to camp, set up camp.

acanhado,-a *adj (envergonhado)* shy, bashful; **sinto-me** ~ I don't feel at ease; **2** *(pequeno espaço)* cramped, narrow; **3** *(apertado)* tight, small *(roupa)*.

acanhamento *m* shyness.

acanhar-se *vr:* ~ **de fazer algo** to feel shy about doing sth.

a(c)ção *f (atividade)* action; **2** *(obra, ato)* act, deed, action; **3** *(MIL)* battle; **4** *(JUR)* lawsuit; **uma** ~ **criminal** a criminal action, offense; **5** *(COM, FIN)* share; **6** *(REL)* ~ **de graças** thanksgiving.

acarear *vt (JUR) (testemunhas)* to confront, bring face to face; **2** *(fig)* to attract with affectionate gestures; ~ **algo** to hold sth dear.

acariciante *adj inv (gesto, brisa)* caressing.

acariciar *vt (afagar)* to caress, stroke, fondle; *(animal)* pat, stroke; **2** *(fig) (acalentar)* to cherish, nature *(sonhos, esperanças)*.

acarinhar *vt* to treat someone with love; **ele acarinha-me muito** he is very loving to me; **2** to fondle, stroke.

ácaro *m* mite, acarus.

acarretar *vt* to carry, transport; **2** *(fig) (dar lugar a, causar)* result in, bring about; lead to, cause *(costs, losses)*; **isto acarreta prejuízos** this will cause damages, losses.

acarreto *m (Vd:* **carreto**).

acasalar *vt (animais)* to mate.

acaso *m* chance, accident; **por** ~ by chance; as a matter of fact, actually; **por um** ~ **feliz** by a fluke; **ao** ~ *adv* at random.

acastanhado,-a *adj* brownish; auburn, chestnut.

acatamento *m* respect (for); **2** deference.

acatar *vt* to respect; **2** *(normas, leis)* to obey, observe.

acautelar *vt* to warn; ♦ ~**-se** *vr* to be cautious; to be on guard/watch against; **acautele-se!** watch out!; **acautele-se com os gatunos** beware of thieves.

a(c)cionar *vt (mecanismo)* to set in motion, to activate; to trigger; **2** *(JUR) (processo)* to sue, file a suit.

a(c)cionista *adj inv* shareholder, stockholder.

aceder *vi:* ~ **a** to agree to, accede; ~ **a um desejo** to yield to a wish.

aceitação *f* acceptance, approval.

aceitar *vt* to accept; **2** to acknowledge; **3** agree to.

aceitável *adj inv* acceptable.

aceite (**aceito,-a**) *(pp irr de* **aceitar***) m* acceptance; ♦ *adj* accepted; **2** approved; **as estudantes foram aceitas/aceites** the students were accepted; **o cheque foi aceite/aceito** the cheque was accepted.

aceleração *f* acceleration; **2** *(AUTO)* acceleration, speed; haste.

acelerado,-a *adj* quick, fast; hasty; **o carro ia a uma velocidade ~a** the car was going at a great, high speed.

acelerador *m* accelerator.

acelerador,-ora *adj* accelerating.

acelerar *vt/vi* to accelerate, to speed up; **2** ~ **o passo** to quicken the step, go faster.

acém *f* sirloin *(de vaca)*.

acenar *vi* to wave (com um lenço/mão); **ela acenou com o lenço** she waved good-bye with her handkerchief; **2** *(com a cabeça)* to nod; to beckon; ♦ *vi* *(sinal com os olhos, as mãos, a cabeça)* to make a sign, gesture.

acendedor *m (boiler, cooker)* igniter, ignition, lighter.

acender *vt* to switch on, to light *(forno, cigarro)*; **2** to strike *(fósforo)*; **3** *(fig)* to excite, stimulate.

aceno *m* sign, gesture; **2** wave; **3** nod.

acento *m (FON)* accent; stress; ~ **tónico** (BR: ô) stress; ~ **grave/circunflexo** grave/circumflex accents.

acentuação *f* accentuation; stress.

acentuado,-a *adj* stressed; **2** conspicuous; **3** marked; **tendência** ~ marked tendency, trend.

acentuar *vt (FON)* to put the graphic accent on *(vogal)*; **2** *(sílaba)* to stress the silable; **3** *(enfatizar)* to emphasize, underline; accentuate; ♦ ~-**se** *vr (agravar-se)* get worse *(surdez)*.

ace(p)ção *f* interpretation, sense; ~ **figurada** figurative sense; **na** ~ **da palavra** in the accepted sense of the word.

acepipe *m* tit-bit, delicacy; ~**s** *mpl* hors d'oeuvres.

acerbar *vt (irritar, agravar)* to embitter, to exacerbate, irritate, to acerbate.

acerbo,-a *adj* harsh, bitter, rough.

acerca: ~ **de** *prep* about, on, concerning, as to, as for.

acercar-se *vr:* ~ **de** to approach, draw near to, to go near; ♦ *vt* to go round, to surround.

acérrimo,-a *(superl de:* **acre***) adj* very bitter; **2** *(fig)* staunch, strong, persistent; **ele é um defensor** ~ **do seu país** he is a strong defender of his country.

acertado,-a *adj (correcto)* right, correct; **2** *(fig) (sensato)* sensible, wise.

acertar *vt* to put right; **2** *(relógio)* to set; ~ **o caminho** to find the right way; ♦ *vi* to get it right, be right; **2** to guess right; ~ **no alvo** to hit the target; ~ **com** to hit upon, find out; ~ **em cheio** to hit the nail on the head, bull's eye; ~ **contas** to settle accounts; ♦ *exc* **acertaste!** you got it!

acerto *m* settlement; **2** hit; **3** skill.

acervo *m* heap, pile; **2** *(património)* collection; **3** total assets; **um** ~ **de** a lot of, a load of.

aceso,-a *(irr pp de* **acender***) adj (luz, gás, etc)* on, switched on; **2** *(fogueira, lume)* alight; **3** *(fig) (debate, luta)* heated; **luta** ~ fierce fighting.

acessibilidade *f* accessibility.

acessível *(pl:* -**veis***) adj inv* accessible; approachable; **preço** ~ affordable price.

acesso *m* access, entry; **2** *(MED)* fit, attack; **um** ~ **de cólera** a fit of anger; **3 via de** ~ access road.

acessório *m* accessory, extra; **os** ~**s de casa de banho** bathroom fittings; **2** *(CIN, TEAT, TV)* prop; **3** *(moda)* accessory; ♦ **assessório,-a** *adj (peça)* spare; **2** *(adicional)* accessory, extra.

acetinado,-a *adj (tecido)* silky, satin-like.

acetona *f* nail varnish remover; *(QUÍM)* acetone.

acha *m* log; IDIOM **deitar mais** ~**s na fogueira** to stir things up.

achado *m* find, discovery; **2** bargain; **3** godsend.

achado,-a *adj* found; **perdidos e** ~**s** lost and found; IDIOM **não se dar por** ~ to pretend not to get the meaning, not to understand.

achaque *m (saúde)* ailment.

achar *vt* to find, discover; **2** to think; **acho que sim** I think so; ♦ ~-**se** *vr* to be, to feel, find o.s.; **ele** ~-**se doente** he feels ill, he is ill; **eu achei-me num beco sem saída** I found myself in a blind alley; **2** *(ser de opinião)* **ela acha-se bonita** she thinks she is pretty.

achatado,-a *adj* flattened, squashed; **nariz** ~ flattened nose.

achatar *vt* to squash, flatten.

achegar-se *vr:* ~ **a/de alguém** to approach, come near, close to *(sb)*.

acicate *m* spur; **2** *(fig)* incentive.

acidentado,-a *m,f* injured person; ♦ *adj* rough; **2** *(caminho, região)* uneven, bumpy, hilly; **uma vida** ~**a** a rough life; **3** injured; **4** car in an accident; **5** *(vida, dia)* eventful.

acidental *adj inv* accidental; **2** casual.

acidente *m* accident; **2** misfortune; **3** chance; **4** unevenness, irregularity; **5** *(JUR)* contingency; **6** *(irregularidade)* fault; **7** *(MED) (pop)* fit; **8** *(MÚS)* accidental; **9 por** ~ by accident.

acidente vascular cerebral = AVC *m (MED)* stroke.

acidez *f* acidity.

ácido *m* acid; ♦ **ácido,-a** *adj* acid; **2** sour.

acima *adv* above; up, over; **rio** ~ up river, upstream; **vou lá** ~ I am going upstairs/up there; **mais** ~ higher up; ♦ *prep:* ~ **de** above; beyond; **ele está** ~ **de mim** he is above me; ~ **mencionado** abovementioned, aforementioned; **crianças** ~ **de quatro anos** children over four years of age.

acinte *m* spite, ill-will; provocation; ♦ *adv* **por** ~ out of spice, on purpose.

acintoso,-a *adj* spiteful, malicious.

acinzentado,-a *adj* greyish; **céu** ~ grey/dark sky.

acirrar *vt* to incite; **2** provoke, irritate, exasperate **ele acirrou o animal** he incited/excited the animal; ♦ ~-**se** *vr* to rise against; **2** to get exasperated.

ACL *(abr de* **Academia das Ciências de Lisboa***)* Lisbon Academy of Science.

aclamação *f* acclamation; applause; **grandes aclamações** loud cheers.

aclamar *vt* to acclaim, applaud.

aclaração *f* clarification; **2** clearing (up); **3** brightening.

aclarar *vt* to explain, clarify; ♦ *vi* to clear up; **2** to make it lighter/brighter; ♦ ~-**se** *vr* to become clear.

aclimação, aclimatação *f (BIOL)* acclimatization; **2** *(fig)* adaptation.

aclimatar, aclimatizar *vt (BIOL)* to acclimatize; to adapt.

aclimatizar-se *vr* to become acclimatized; **2** *(fig)* to get used to, to settle down.

acne *f* (MED) acne.

aço *m* steel; **cor de** ~ steel-blue; ~ **inoxidável** stainless steel.

acobardar *vt* to intimidate *(alguém)*; ♦ ~-**se** *vr* to lose courage; to cower, to become fainted-hearted.

acobreado,-a *adj* copper-coloured; **cabelos** ~**s** copper-coloured hair.

acocorar-se *vr* to squat down; crouch.

acode *etc. (pres ind de* **acudir**) *(Vd:* **acudir**): **quem me** ~**?** who will come to my help?

acoimar *vt (lançar coima)* to give a fine to; **2** to blame, reproach; ♦ ~-**se** *vr* to admit to one's guilt, blame oneself.

acoitar *vt* to shelter, give refuge to, harbour (criminal).

açoitar *vt* (= **açoutar**) to whip, lash, flog; **2** *(vento, temporal)* lash.

açoite *m* (= **açoute**) smack on the bottom; **daqui a pouco levas um** ~ you'll get a smack in a moment; **2** *(com chicote)* whip, lash.

acolá *adv* there, over there; **aquela torre** ~ that tower over there; **aqui, ali e** ~ here, there and everywhere.

acolchoado *m* quilt; ♦ **acolchoado,-a** *adj* quilted, padded.

acolchoar *vt* to quilt, to pad, to wad.

acolhedor,-ora *adj* welcoming; hospitable; **2** comfortable; **país** ~ host country.

acolher *vt* to welcome; **2** to shelter; **3** to receive; ♦ ~-**se** *vr* to take shelter/refuge.

acolhida *f* acolhimento *m* reception, welcome; **2** refuge, haven; **ela teve um bom** ~ she was well received; **3 lar de** ~ *m* home for the elderly.

acometedor,-ora *m,f* aggressor, assailant; ♦ *adj* assailing; **2** provoking; **3** bold, enterprising.

acometer *vt (gen)* attack, strike; **a gripe porcina acometeu-o** the swine flu attacked him; **2** *(MIL)* to attack; **3** *(fig) (invadir)* to take over; **4** *(empreender)* to carry out *(algo)*.

acometida *f* sudden attack, assault, onset; **2** undertaking; **3** *(MED)* fit, attack.

acomodação *f (acto de acomodar)* accommodation; adjustment; **2** *(alojamento)* lodgings; **3** *(divisão da casa)* room.

acomodar *vt (alojar)* to accommodate; **2** to make comfortable; ♦ ~-**se** *vr* to make oneself comfortable; **2** settle down; ~-**se a** to conform to, adapt to.

acomodadiço,-a (= **acomodatício, acomodável**) *adj* accommodating, complying with; **2** *(person)* easy-going, adaptable.

acompanhamento *m* attendance; procession; **2** *(MÚS)* accompaniment; **3** *(CULIN)* side dish.

acompanhante *m,f* companion, escort; **2** *(MÚS)* accompanist; ♦ *adj inv* accompanying.

acompanhar *vt* to accompany, go along with; **2** *(MÚS)* to accompany; **3** ~ **a moda** to follow the fashion.

aconchegado,-a *adj* snug, cosy; **2** comfortable; **amigos** ~**s** *(íntimos)* close friends.

aconchegar (= **conchegar**) *vt (na cama)* to tuck in *(alguém)*; **2** to huddle, cuddle; **3** to wrap around *(cachecol, cobertor)*; ♦ ~-**se** *vr* to snuggle down; ~-**se a alguém** to snuggle up to sb.

aconchego (= **conchego**) *m* cosiness, warmth, comfort; **2** *(amparo)* protection.

acondicionamento *m* packing; packaging.

acondicionar *vt (embrulhar)* to wrap; **2** *(embalar)* to package; **3** *(ajeitar, adaptar)* to adapt; ~ **o pessoal à situação económica** to adapt the staff to the economic situation.

aconselhado,-a *adj* prudent, judicious; **mal** ~ ill-advised.

aconselhamento *m* counselling; ~ **legal** legal advice.

aconselhar *vt* to advise; ♦ ~-**se** *vr*: ~-**se com** to consult.

aconselhável *adj inv* advisable.

acontecer *vi* to happen, occur.

acontecimento *m* event; occurrence, happening.

acopolamento *m* coupling; *(FÍS, ELECT, MEC)* coupling.

acoplar *vt* to put together *(elementos)*; **2** *(FIS, ASTRON, MEC, ELECT)* to couple.

açorda *f* traditional Portuguese dish basically made of bread; **2** *(fig)* **um/uma papa** ~ a sluggish, slow-witted person.

acórdão *(pl:* **acórdãos**) *m;* **2** *(JUR)* judgement, sentence.

acordar *vt* to wake (up), awaken; **2** to arouse; ♦ *vi* to agree/accord (with).

acorde *m (MÚS)* chord.

acordeão *(pl:* -**ões**) *m (MÚS)* accordion.

acordo *m* agreement; **de** ~ agreed, O.K.; **estar de** ~ to agree; **chegar a um** ~ to come to an understanding; **de** ~ **com** in agreement with; in accordance with; IDIOM **não dar** ~ **de si** to give no sign of life.

Açores *mpl:* **os** ~ the Azores; **o arquipélago dos** ~ the Azores Islands/Archipelago.

açoriano,-a *m,f adj* Azorean; from the Azores.

acorrentar *vt* to chain *(alguém, algo)*; **acorrentou o boi ao muro** he chained the ox to the wall; **2** to fetter; **3** *(fig)* to enslave, dominate; **4** *(fig)* **ela está acorrentada ao marido** she is chained to her husband; ♦ ~-**se** *vr (submeter-se)* be dominated by.

acorrer *vi* to come to the aid of; **2** ~ **ao lugar do desastre** rush to the place of the accident.

acossar *vt* to pursue, chase (animal); **2** *(atormentar)* to harass, pester.

acostagem *f (NÁUT)* docking, leaning against another vessel.

acostamento *m (NÁUT)* docking; **2** *(BR)* hard shoulder.

acostar *vt* to lean, prop; ♦ *vi (NÁUT)* to bring alongside; **o navio acostou ao cais**, the ship came alongside the quay/port; ♦ *vr*: ~**-se a** *(recostar-se)* to lean back (on, against); **2** to lie down; **3** *(depender de)* **ela acostou-se aos pais** she leant on, became dependent on her parents.

acostumado,-a *adj* used, accustomed; usual, customary; ~ **a fazer a sua vontade** used to having his own way.

acostumar *vt* to accustom; ♦ ~**-se** *vr*: ~**-se a a** to get used to.

açoteia *f* roof terrace; **2** belvedere.

acotovelar *vt* to jostle; **2** to shove (lightly); **3** to nudge; **ele acotovelou-a para chamá-la à atenção** he nudged her to draw her attention.

açougue *m (BR and in some Portuguese regions)* butcher's shop, slaughter-house.

açougueiro *m (proprietário)* butcher.

açoutar *(Vd: açoitar)*.

acovardar-se *(Vd: acobardar-se)*.

acovilhar *vt (meter em covil)* to bring in, put animal in; **2** to shelter.

acre *adj* bitter; sour, sharp; **2** acrimonious, harsh; **3** *(fig)* biting; **4** *(AGR)* acre = a measure of land.

acreditado,-a *adj* qualified; **2** accredited.

acreditar *vt* to believe; **2** to accredit; **3** to guarantee; ♦ *vi*: ~ **em** to believe in; **pode** ~ you can take it from me; ♦ ~**-se** *vr* to consider oneself to be.

acreditável *adj inv* credible, believable.

acrescentamento *m* increase; something added to.

acrescentar *vt* to increase; **2** *(incluir, adicionar)* to add.

acrescer *vt* to increase, add; **acresce um outro facto** there is another fact; **2** to supervene.

acréscimo *m* increase, rise.

acriançado,-a *adj* childlike.

acrílico *m* acrylic.

acrisolar *vt* to refine, purify; to examine, test (metals).

acrobacia *f* acrobatics *pl*; **2** stunt; ~**s aéreas** *fpl* stunt flying.

acrobata *m,f* acrobat.

a(c)ta *f* minutes of meeting; records, record of proceedings; ~**s judaicas** *fpl* Jewish records.

a(c)tivar *vt* to activate.

a(c)tividade *f (gen)* activity; **2** *(energia)* energy; **3** job; **4** *(movimento frântico)* bustle; **em plena** ~ in full swing.

a(c)tivo,-a *adj* active, energetic; **2** lively; **3** *(aroma)* strong; **4 papel** ~ important role; **5** *m (pessoal)* staff; **no seu** ~ on one's staff; **6** *(MIL)* **no a(c)tivo** in the services; **7** *(COM)* *mpl* assets; **ativos e passivos** assets and liabilities *(Vd: ativo)*.

a(c)to *m* act; action, deed; **2** solemn rite.

a(c)tor, a(c)triz *m,f* actor/actress, player; **seguir a carreira de** ~ to go on the stage.

a(c)tuação *f (conduta)* behaviour; **2** *(CIN, TV)* *(desempenho)* performance.

a(c)tual *adj* present, current, today, up-to-date; **a** ~ **situação** the present situation.

A(c)tual is not used in the sense of **'real, true'**, which is **verdadeiro, real**. The same applies to its noun and adverb.

a(c)tualidade *f* current, present day; **a** ~ the present (time); **na** ~ at present, in our days; **a(c)tualidades** *fpl* (current) news; newsreel *sg*.

a(c)tualizar *vt* to update.

a(c)tualmente *adv* at present, nowadays.

a(c)tuar *vi* to act, do; **2** to perform; **3** to put into action.

a(c)tuário *m* actuary; ~ **de seguros** insurance actuary.

açúcar *m* sugar; ~**moído** castor sugar; ~ **mascavado** brown (raw) sugar; ~ **em pó** icing sugar; ~ **pilé** crystal or granulated sugar; **torrão de** ~ a lump of sugar; ~ **em ponto** various stages of burnt sugar: caramel, pearl etc.

açucarado,-a *adj* sugary, sweetened.

açucareiro *m* sugar bowl.

açucena *f (BOT)* white lily.

açude *m (represa)* dam, weir; *(BR)* marginal land of a river for cultivation.

acudir *vi* to come/go to someone's help/aid; **2** assist; **3** *(acorrer)* gather, flock; **acudiram muitos ao sítio para ver o desfile** many people flocked to the place to see the parade; **4** to reply, respond; **5** *(lembrar-se de)* **acudiu-me à memória que já a tinha visto** (it came to mind that) I suddenly remembered I had already seen her; ♦ *exc* **acudam!** help!

acuidade *f* acuity, sharpness; ~ **auditiva** auditive acuity; intensity; **a** ~ **da dor** the intensity of the pain.

açular *vt* to incite; provoke; instigate; ~ **um cão contra alguém** to set a dog on sb.

aculturação *f* acculturation, mixing of cultures.

aculturar *vt* acculturate *(alguém)*; ♦ ~**-se** *vr* to adapt to a new culture/assimilate.

acumulação *f* accumulation.

acumulador *m* accumulator; **2** *(ELECT)* storage battery; ♦ **acumulador,-ora** *adj* accumulative.

acumular *vt* to accumulate; to store; to collect.

acupuntura *f* acupuncture.

acusação *f* accusation, charge; *(JUR)* prosecution, indictment.

acusar *vt* to accuse; to blame; **não me acusa a consciência** my conscience is clear, I am not guilty; ~ **a recepção** *(COM)* *(BR: o recebimento)*(de) to acknowledge receipt (of).

acusado,-a *m,f (JUR)* defendant, offender, the accused; ♦ *adj* accused.

acústica *f* acoustics.

acústico,-a *adj* acoustic.

acutilante *adj inv* cutting, sharp; **2** *(som)* shrill; **um comentário** ~ a cutting/biting remark.

adaga *f* dagger.

adágio *m* adage, proverbial saying; **2** *(MÚS)* adagio.

adamascado,-a *adj* *(sabor, cor)* apricot; **tecido** ~ damask.

adaptabilidade *f* adaptability.

adaptação *f* adaptation.

adaptador *m* *(ELECT)* adaptor; ~ **de rede** *(COMP)* network adaptor.

adaptar *vt* to adapt; to fit; ♦ *vr:* ~-**se a** to adjust to, fit in with.

adega *f* wine cellar.

adejar *vt* to flap; **2** to wave *(lenço, bandeira)*; ♦ *vi* *(esvoaçar)* to flit, flutter.

adelgaçado,-a *adj* thin; **2** narrow; **3** slender; **4** pointed.

adelgaçar *vt* *(tornar delgado)* to make thin *(vara, tábua)*; **2** *(estreitar)* make slim *(cintura)*; **3** *(fazer menos denso)* to dilute.

ademais *adv* besides, moreover.

adendo *m* addendum.

adensamento *m* thickening.

adentro *adv* inside, in; **mata** ~ into the woods; **noite** ~ into the night, through the night.

adepto,-a *m,f* follower; **2** fan, lover of; **3** adherent, partisan.

adequado,-a *adj* adequate; appropriate, suitable.

adequar *vt* to adapt, make suitable.

adereçar *vt* *(enfeitar)* to adorn, decorate; **2** *(ataviar)* to attire, dress up *(alguém)*.

aderecista *m,f* *(TEAT, CIN, TV)* prop *(man woman)*.

adereço *m* adornment; decoration **2** *(da moda)* accessory; ~ **de cama** set of sheets and pillowcases; **adereços** *mpl* **2** *(TEAT)* stage props.

aderência *f* adherence; **2** *(atrito)* adhesion.

aderente *m,f* *(adepto)* supporter, follower; member; **2** *(pagador regular-portagem, etc)* subscriber; ♦ *adj* *(substância)* adherent, sticking.

aderir *vi* to adhere; to stick; **2** *(fig)* to join; **3** *(fig)* to follow, go along with, support; ~ **à causa** to join the cause.

adesão *f* adhesion; **2** *(fig)* support; **3** *(fig)* membership; ~ **à U.E.** accession to, joining the E.U.; **4** *(JUR)* *(fig)* joining.

adesivo,-a *m* sticky tape; sticker; **2** *(MED)* sticking plaster; ♦ *adj* adhesive, sticky.

adestrado,-a *adj* trained, skilled.

adestrar *vt* to train, instruct; to break in *(a horse)*.

adeus *m* goodbye, farewell; **dizer** ~ to say goodbye, bid farewell.

adeuzinho *(pop)* bye-bye!; cheers!

adiamento *m* postponement; **2** delay; **3** adjournment.

adiantado,-a *adj* advanced; **2** *(relógio)* fast; **3** early, **ele chegou** ~ he arrived early; **4** ahead; ~ **nos estudos** ahead in one's studies; **pagar** ~ to pay in advance.

adiantamento *m* advancement, progress; **2** advance payment.

adiantar *vt* to advance; **2** *(antecipar)* to do, say *(algo)* before time; **3** to get on with *(tarefa)*; ♦ *vi* to solve, resolve; **não adianta (nada)** it's no use (at all), it won't solve anything; **5** *(relógio)* be fast; ♦ ~-**se** *vr* *(apressar-se)* to go on ahead; **2**

(antecipar-se) to do, say *(algo)* first; **3** *(avançar)* to make headway.

adiante *adv* in front; **2** forward; **3** onward; **mais** ~ further on; later on; ~! go on!; **passar** ~ to get ahead.

adiar *vt* to postpone, delay; **2** to adjourn.

adição *f* addition; **2** *(MAT)* sum.

adicionar *vt* to add.

adido *m* attaché; **adido,-a cultural** cultural attaché.

adinheirado,-a *adj* with money, wealthy.

aditamento *m* addition.

aditivo,-a *adj* additional; **2** *(QUIM)* *(agente)* addictive.

adivinha *f* puzzle, riddle; **2** guess; **3** *m,f* fortune-teller.

adivinhação *f* fortune-telling; guessing.

adivinhar *vt/vi* to guess; **2** to foretell, to predict; **3** to have a premonition; **você adivinhou!** you guessed it!

adivinho *m* soothsayer, fortune-teller.

adjacente *adj inv* *(contíguo)* adjacent; *(GEOM)* *(ângulos)* adjacente.

adje(c)tivo *m* adjective; ♦ *adj* adjectival.

adjudicação *f* *(concessão)* grant; **2** award; **3** *(JUR)* decision, adjudication; ~ **dos trabalhos** work contract.

adjudicar *vt* to award, grant.

adjunto *m* assistant; **2** **ministro** ~ deputy minister; **3** *(LING)* adjunct; ♦ *adj* assistant; **2** *(gram)* adjunctive.

administração *f* administration; management; **2** Board.

administrador,-ora *m,f* administrator; **2** director; **3** manager.

administrar *vt* to run, manage; **2** to govern.

admiração *f* admiration, wonder; **2** surprise.

admirado,-a *adj;* **estar** ~ to be surprised, amazed; **2** **ser** ~ to be admired.

admirador,-ora *adj:* admirer, lover of.

admirar *vt* to admire, to look at; **estou a** ~ **esta paisagem** I am admiring this landscape; **2** *(respeitar)* to look up to *(sb)* **(por,** for); **eu admiro-o pela sua obra** I admire him for his work; **3** *(surpreendido)* surprised, astonished **(com,** at, by); **não me admira que ele se risse** it doesn't surprise me that he laughed ♦ *exc* **não admira nada!** small wonder!

admirável *adj inv* admirable, amazing, wonderful.

admissão *f* *(aceitação)* admission; **2** *(direito de entrar)* admittance; **3** intake, input; **4** *(TEC)* *(water etc)* inlet; **5** *(of guilt, etc)* acceptance; confession; **exame de** ~ entrance exam; ~ **na Ordem dos Advogados** Bar admission *(UK)*; Bar call *(US)*.

admissível *adj inv* *(permitido)* admissible; **2** *(aceitável)* acceptable.

admitir *vt* to admit; **2** to allow; **3** to confess; **4** acknowledge; **5** to engage *(empregado)*; **admitamos que** let's suppose that; **é de** ~ admittedly; **não te admito que me fales assim** I won't allow you to speak to me in this manner.

admoestação *f* warning; reprimand.

admoestar *vt* *(repreender)* to admonish, reproach, rebuke.

admonitório,-a *adj* *(sermão)* admonishing.

ADN *(abr de* **ácido desoxirribonucleico)** DNA.

adobe *m (terra e barro)* adobe; **2** *(tijolo cozido ao sol)* sun-dried brick.

adoçante *m* sweetener; ♦ *adj* sweetening.

adoçar *vt* to sweeten; **2** *(embate)* to soften; **3** *(apaziguar)* to pacify.

adoção *(Vd:* **ado(p)ção**).

adoçar *vt (açucarar)* sweeten *(chá etc);* **2** *(fig) (suavizar)* alleviate, ease *(life).*

adocicado,-a *adj* sugary, sweetened; **2** *(fam)(voz)* soft.

adocicar *vt* to sweeten slightly.

adoecer *vi* to fall ill, sick; ~ **de/com** to fall ill with.

adoentado,-a *adj* indisposed, sickly, sick; **sentir-se** ~ to feel seedy, under the weather.

adoidado,-a (= **adoudado**) *adj (pessoa)* foolish, rash; touched in the head; senseless.

adolescente *m,f* adolescent, teenager; ♦ *adj inv (moço, moça)* adolescent; **2** *(fig) (governo, democracia)* young.

adopção, adoção *f* adoption.

adoptar, adotar *vt* to adopt; to follow.

adoptivo,-a, adotivo,-a *adj* adopted.

adoração *f* adoration.

adorar *vt* to adore; to worship, venerate.

adorável *adj inv* adorable.

adormecer *vi* to fall asleep; **2** *(ficar dormente)* go numb.

adormecido,-a *adj* asleep, sleeping; **2** *(dormente)* numb; **as pernas estão ~as** the legs have gone numb.

adornar *vt* to adorn, decorate.

adorno *m* adornment.

adoudado *(Vd:* **adoidado**).

adquirente *m,f* acquirer; ♦ *adj inv* acquiring.

adquirido,-a *adj* acquired; **~s** *mpl (JUR)* acquired assets.

adquirir *vt* to acquire; **2** to obtain; **3** purchase; **4** gain; ~ **velocidade** to gain speed.

adrede *adv* on purpose, deliberately; intentionally.

adrenalina *f* adrenaline.

Adriático *npr:* **o** ~ (**mar**) the Adriatic (sea).

adriça *f* halyard.

adro *m* church forecourt, churchyard.

aduana *f* customs (house).

aduaneiro,-a *adj* customs; *m* customs officer; **2** *f* **pauta ~a** customs tariffs *pl.*

adubar *vt* to manure, fertilize.

adubo *m* fertilizer.

adulação *f* flattery.

adulador,-ora *m,f (bajulador)* flatterer; ♦ *adj* flattering.

adular *vt* to flatter; to adulate.

adulteração *f* adulteration, falsification.

adulterado,-a *adj (documento,)* falsified, forged; **2** *(cultura, alimentos)* adulterated; **3** *(costumes)* corrupted; **4** *(verdade, estória)* twisted, garbled.

adulterador,-ora *m,f* adulterator.

adulterar *vt* to adulterate; falsify; corrupt; ♦ *vi* to commit adultery.

adultério *m* adultery.

adúltero,-a *m,f* adulterer, adulteress.

adulto,-a *m,f* adult; ♦ *adj (pessoa)* adult; **2** *(árvore, animal, ideia)* mature.

adunco *adj (nariz)* hooked.

adusto,-a *adj* scorched; parched; burnt.

adventício,-a *adj (extrínsico)* extrinsic; **3** *(BOT) (raíz)* adventitious.

advento *m* advent, arrival; **o A~** *(REL)* Advent.

advérbio *m (gram)* adverb.

adversário,-a *m,f* adversary, opponent, enemy.

adversidade *f* adversity, misfortune.

adverso,-a *adj* adverse, contrary; **sorte adversa** bad luck.

advertência *f* warning; advice; **que isto sirva de ~!** let this be a warning to you!

advertido,-a *adj* prudent; well advised.

advertir *vt* to warn; **2** to advise; **3** to draw attention to.

advogado,-a *m,f* lawyer; advocate; barrister *(UK).*

advogar *vt* to advocate; **2** advocate; **3** *(JUR)* to plead; ♦ *vi* to practise law.

aéreo,-a *adj* air, aerial; **ataque** ~ air raid; **Força Aérea** Air Force; **por via ~a** by air mail; **estar** ~ to be in the clouds.

aerobarco *m (BR)* hovercraft.

aeróbica *f* aerobics *sg.*

aeródromo *m* airfield.

aeromoço,-a *m,f (BR)* steward, air hostess.

aeromodelismo *m (TEC)* model aeroplane making; **2** *(DESP)* model aeroplane flying.

aeronáutica *f* aeronautics, *sg;* **2** *(MIL)* air force.

aeroporto *m* airport.

aerosol *(pl:* **aerosóis**) *m (bomba, sistema)* aerosol.

afã *m* eagerness; **2** great effort, care; **3** toil, ado, hustle-bustle.

afabilidade *f* friendliness, courtesy.

afadigar *vt* to tire (out); ♦ **~-se** *vr* to tire o.s. (out), get tired.

afagar *vt (acariciar)* to caress, fondle *(alguém);* to stroke, to pet *(animal).*

afago *m* caress; endearment; **2** *(agasalho)* wrap.

afamado,-a *adj* renowned, famous, celebrated.

afamar *vt* make famous; ♦ **~-se** *vr* to become famous.

afanado,-a, afanoso,-a *adj* laborious; painstaking.

afanar *vt (fatigar)* to tire, wear out *(alguém);* **2** *(fam) (roubar)* to pilfer; *(carteira)* nick.

afastado,-a *adj* remote; **2** away; **3** secluded; **4** *(perigo)* averted; **5** apart; **muito** ~ far off; ~ **do caminho** off (from) the road; **manter-se** ~ *(pessoa)* to stay clear, away; keep to o.s. **primo** ~ distant cousin.

afastamento *m* distance; **2** separation; **3** *(distanciamento)* withdrawal; **4** pitch; ~ **polar** polar pitch; **3** *(AUTO: rodas)* wheel-gauge.

afastar *vt* to remove, to move away from; **2** to keep off, away; **3** *(AUTO)* to deviate, swerve, turn; ♦ **~-se** *vr* to move, go away; **2** withdraw, to stand back; **~-se do assunto** to keep clear off the subject; **3** *(NÁUT)* to stand off from.

afável *adj* courteous, genial, affable, friendly.

afazer *vt* to accustom; ♦ **~-se** *vr:* **~-se a** to get used to.

afazeres *mpl* work, duties, tasks; **tenho muitos** ~ I have many things to do; **2** ~ **domésticos** household chores.

afe(c)ção *f* *(MED)* *(doença)* ailment; malady; **2** *(PSIC)* affection.

afe(c)tação *f* affectation.

afe(c)tado-a *adj* conceited, affected.

afe(c)tar *vt* *(influenciar, prejudicar)* to affect; have an adverse effect (**em** on); **2** *(simular)* to pretend.

afe(c)tivo,-a *adj* affectionate; **2** *(PSIC)* afective.

afe(c)to *m* affection, fondness; ♦ *adj* ~ **a** related to; **3** in favour of.

afe(c)tuoso,-a *adj* affectionate, tender.

Afeganistão *npr* **o** ~ Afganistan.

afegão *m*, **afegã** *f* (**afegãos** *mpl*, **afegãs** *fpl*) Afghan; ♦ *adj* Afghan.

afeição *f* affection, fondness; **2** devotion.

afeiçoado,-a *m,f* friend, lover; **2** fan, adept (to); ♦ *adj* affectionate; **2** fond of, devoted to; **sou muito ~ à minha casa** I am very devoted, attached to my home; **3** ~ **a algo** to be used to sth.

afeiçoar *vt* to mould, shape, adapt; **2** *(encorajar afeição)* to make another person affectionate; ♦ ~**-se** *vr*: ~**-se a** to take a fancy to, feel inclined towards; **2** to get attached, used to; **3** grow fond of.

afeito,-a *adj*: ~ **a** accustomed to, used to.

aferição *adj* *(medição)* calibration.

aferidor *m* checker; inspector of standards and measures; **2** *(instrumento)* gauge; ~ **de tensão** *(MEC)* strain gauge.

aferir *vt* to gauge, calibrate, check up, inspect; **2** to compare, standardize.

aferrado,-a *adj* obstinate; insistent; *(fig)* attached *(ideia, trabalho)*; **ele é ~ ao trabalho** he is attached/stuck to his work.

aferrar *vt* *(segurar com força)* to grip, grasp; **2** *(NÁUT)* to anchor *(barco)*; ♦ *vi* cast anchor; ♦ ~**-se** *vr*: ~**-se a** to persist in; **2** to cling to, to hold on to.

aferrolhar *vt* *(fechar com ferrolho)* to bolt; **2** *(fig)* *(aprisionar)* to lock up; **3** *(fig)* *(economizar)* to save.

afetação (*Vd:* **afectação**); **afetado** (*Vd:* **afectado**); **afetar** (*Vd:* **afectar**); **afeto** (*Vd:* **afecto**); **afetuoso** (*Vd:* **afectuoso**).

afiado,-a *adj* *(lâmina)* sharp; *(lápis, faca)* sharpened; **3** *(fig)* *(penetrante)* quick, keen; IDIOM **ela tem uma língua muito** ~ she has a sharp tongue.

afiador *m* *(amolador)* knifegrinder.

afia-lápis *m* pencil sharpener.

afiançar *vt* *(JUR)* to stand bail for; to warrant; to guarantee.

afiar *vt* to sharpen; **2** *(lâmina)* to grind.

aficionado,-a *m,f* fan, enthusiast; amateur.

afigurar-se *vt* *(parecer)* to seem, appear; ~**-me que** it seems to me that.

afilhado,-a *m,f* godson, goddaughter; **2** *(de casamento)* man, woman to whom you were best man or witness.

afiliar *vt* to affiliate; to adopt; ♦ ~**-se** *vr*: ~**-se a** to join.

a fim de (*Vd:* **fim**).

afim *m,f* kin, relation, kindred; ♦ *adj inv* (*pl*: **afins**) similar, akin; related, kindred; **almas** ~**s** kindred spirits.

afinação *f* *(MÚS)* tuning, harmony; **2** *(MEC)* tuning up; ~ **do motor** tuning of the engine; ~ **dos travões** adjustment of the brakes; **3** *(metal)* refining.

afinado,-a *adj* *(MÚS: cantor)* in tune; **2** *(MEC)* adjusted; refined; **3** *(fig, fam)* *(ofendido)* offended.

afinador *n* *(técnico)* tuner; ~ **de piano** piano tuner; **2** *(de metais)* refiner.

afinal *adv* at last, finally; **aqui está ela** ~! here she is finally!; ~ **de contas** *adv* after all, when all has been said and done.

afinar *vt* *(MÚS)* to tune; **2** *(MEC)* to tune up; **3** polish (up) refine; ♦ *vi* be in tune, see eye to eye; ♦ ~**-se** *vr* *(fig)* to get irritated.

afinco *m* tenacity, persistence; **trabalhar com** ~ to work doggedly.

afinidade *f* *(semelhança)* affinity.

afirmação *f* affirmation; statement.

afirmar *vt/vi* *(confirmar)* to affirm, assert; **2** to declare, to state.

afirmativo,-a *adj* affirmative.

afivelar *vt* to buckle (up).

afixar *vt* *(fixar)* to fix; **2** *(aviso, cartaz)* put up, affix; **é proibido ~ avisos na parede** it is prohibited to affix *(put up)* notices on the wall.

aflição *f* anxiety; **2** distress; **3** anguish; **4** grief.

afligir *vt* to distress; to worry; ♦ ~**-se** *vr*: ~**-se com** to worry about.

aflito,-a *(pp irr de* **afligir**) *adj* distressed, grieved, anxious, worried.

aflorar *vt* to touch on *(assunto)*; to broach; **2** to touch lightly; **3** to come to the surface.

afluência *f* abundance; **2** flow; **3** crowd, throng; **4** turnout.

afluente *(rio)* attributary; ♦ *adj* copious.

afluir *vi* to flow (**para** into, towards; **de** from); **2** *(pessoas)* to flock to, to congregate, to gather.

afluxo *m* afflux, flow; **2** *(gente)* gathering; **3** in-coming, influx; **4** ~ **do sangue** rush, flow of the blood; **5** *(águas)* flow.

afogadilho *m* hurry, haste; ♦ *adv* **de** ~ in a hurry, hastily.

afogado,-a *adj* drowned; **morrer** ~ to die by drowning; **2** *(motor)* flooded; **3** *(fig)* *(sobrecarregado)* up to one's neck in *(em trabalho, dívida)*; swamped with/in *(perguntas, cartas)*; **4** *(blusa, gola)* highnecked.

afogador *m* *(AUTO)* choke; ♦ *adj* *(colar, gola)* choking.

afogar *vt* *(morrer por imersão em água)* to drown; **2** to extinguish *(fogo)*; **3** *(AUTO)* *(motor, carro)* to flood, stall; **4** to muffle *(voz, passos)*; **5** *(reprimir)* to quell; ~ **a mágoa** to drown one's sorrow; ♦ *vt* to drown o.s.; **2** *(fig)* ~ **em trabalho** to be snowed under with work; ~**-se em pouca água** to get upset easily.

afogo (= **afogamento**) *m* drowning; **2** anguish, worry; **3** *(fig)* haste.

afogueado,-a *adj* *(ferro)* aglow, red-hot; **2** *(rosto)* hot, red, aglow.

afoito,-a (= **afouto**) *adj* bold; **2** intrepid, foolhardy; **2** *(BR)* in a hurry.

afonsino *adj (HIST)* relating to the early Portuguese Kings and King Afonso V; Alphonsine; **2** *(fig) (muito antigo)* old; **nos tempos ~s** in the olden days.

afora *prep* except, save; **2** besides; ♦ *adv* out; **rua ~** down the street; **2** *(além, ao longo)* **Europa ~** throughout Europe.

aforismo *m* aphorism, maxim, saying.

aforístico,-a *adj* sentencious.

aforrador *m* saver.

aforrador,-ora *adj (instituição)* savings.

aforrar *(pôr forro)* to line a garment; **2** economize, save.

aforro *m (de roupa)* lining; **2** savings; **certificado de ~** savings certificate.

afortunado,-a *adj* fortunate, lucky.

afouto *(Vd:* **afoito**).

afrancesado,-a *adj* adopting French ways, French-like.

afrancesar *vt* making sth or sb look French.

África *npr* **a ~** Africa; **~ do Sul** South Africa.

africano,-a *m,f adj* African.

africanista *m,f* expert, scholar in African studies.

afrodisíaco *m* aphrodisiac.

afrodisíaco,-a *adj* aphrodisiac.

afronta *f* insult, outrage.

afrontar *vt (ultrajar)* to insult; to outrage; **2** *(encarar)* to face; **3** *(atacar)* to confront.

afrontamento *m* affront; **2** *(sensação de calor ou indigestão)* flush *(no rosto)*.

aformoseamento *m* embellishment.

aformosear *vt* to embellish; ♦ *~-se vr* to make o.s. beautiful, handsome.

afrouxamento *m* slackening, slowing down; **houve um ~ na economia** there was a slackening in the economy.

afrouxar *vt* to loosen, let go, slacken; **2** *(abrandar)* to slow down; **3** *(moderar)* slacken.

afta *f* mouth ulcer.

aftosa *f (febre que ataca o gado)* mouth and foot disease.

afugentar *vt* to drive off *(pessoa, animal)*, chase away, frighten away.

afundar *vt* to sink; **2** to deepen; **3** to scuttle *(barco)*; **4** *(fig)* to drive *(amigos, família)* into sth; **5** to make things worse **(para alguém** for sb); ♦ *~-se vr* to sink; **2** *(avião)* crash into the sea; **3** *(fig)* arruinar-se.

afunilar *vt* to shape sth like a funnel; **2** to narrow a passage; **3** *(way, pot, trousers)* to taper.

agá *(letra do alfabeto = H) m* H.

agachar-se *vr* to crouch, squat; **2** stoop; **3** to lie low; **4** *(fig)* to cringe, *(humilhar-se)* lower (oneself), bow to *(terms)*.

agarrar *vt* to seize; **2** grab, to catch sb; **ele agarrou-me pela cintura** he grabbed me by my waist; ♦ *~-se vr:* **~-se a** to cling to, hold on to; **agarre-se bem!** hold tight!; IDIOM **~-se com unhas e dentes** to stick to, hold on to obstinately; **~ a ocasião pelos cabelos** to take the bull by the horns, seize the opportunity.

agasalhado,-a *adj* cosy, snug; **2** sheltered.

agasalhar *vt* to shelter; to welcome; **3** *(alguém)* to wrap sb up; ♦ *~-se vr* to wrap o.s. up.

agasalho *m* wrap, warm clothing.

agastar *vt* to irritate, annoy, vex; ♦ *~-se vr: ~-se com* to get angry with.

ágata *f* agate.

agatanhar *vt* to scratch, to claw.

agência *f* agency; office; **2 ~ de correio** *(BR)* post office; **3 ~ de viagens** travel agency.

agenciar *vt* to negotiate for; to obtain.

agenda *f* agenda; **2** diary, notebook; **3** *(ordem de trabalhos)* schedule.

agendar *vt (assunto, reunião)* to schedule; **ficou agendado-a para ...** it was scheduled for ...

agente *m,f* agent; **2 ~ da polícia** policeman; **3** *(COM)* salesperson; **4 ~ de seguros marítimos** shipping underwriter.

ágil *(pl:* **ágeis)** *adj* agile, nimble, active.

agilidade *f* agility.

agilizar *vt* to speed up, activate, hasten *(processo, etc)*.

agiota *m,f* usurer, moneylendert; **2** stockjobber; **3** speculator; **4** *(fig)* miser, stingy.

agir *vi* to act; to behave; **~ bem/mal** to do right/ wrong; **~ com cautela** to play safe.

agitação *f* agitation; **2** disturbance; **3** unrest; **4** *(do mar)* roughness.

agitado,-a *adj* overwrought, disturbed; **2** restless; **mar ~** rough sea; **tempos ~s** stirring times.

agitar *vi* to agitate, disturb; **2** to shake; **3** wag; **o cão** *(BR:* **cachorro)** **agitava o rabo** the dog wagged his tail; **4** to stir; to swing, wave; **ela agitava com o lenço num adeus** she waved good-bye; ♦ *~-se vr* to get upset; **2** get excited.

aglomeração *f* crowd; **2** *(coisas)* pile, stack; **3** built-up area.

aglomerado *m (artefacto)* chipboard; **2** agglomeration; **3** *(CONSTR)* agglomerate; **4 ~ urbano** town dwellings.

aglomerar *vt (coisas)* to heap up, pile up; **2** to swarm; ♦ *~-se vr (pessoas)* to crowd together, swarm.

aglutinação *f* agglutination.

aglutinado,-a *adj (com cola)* glued; **2** agglutinated; **3** *(elementos)* bring together.

agnóstico,-a *adj* agnostic.

agonia *f* agony; anguish; **2** nausea.

agoniado,-a *adj* nauseous; **estar ~** *(estômago)* to be sick.

agoniar-se *vr* to feel sick (nauseous); **agoniou-se com o cheiro do peixe** the fish smell made him feel sick.

agonizante *adj inv* agonizing; **2** dying.

agonizar *vi* to be dying; **2** to suffer agony; **3** *(governo, etc)* in decline, coming to its end.

agora *adv* now, just; **~ mesmo** right now, just now **agora mesmo ouvi as notícias** I have just heard the news; **por ~** for the present; **até ~** so far, up to now; **~ não** not now; ♦ *exc* **ora ~ !/essa ~ !** come now!; really!; **e ~?** now what?; **~ é que eu quero ver!** now I should like to see (that)!; ♦ *conj (mas, todavia)* now, but, however; **subir foi fácil, ~ é que é descer** to go up was easy, but now the problem is to come down.

ágora *f* agora; place of assembly.

Agosto, agosto *m* August.

agourar *vt* to predict, foretell; **2** *(desgraças)* bode.

agouro *m* pressage, prediction, omen; **bom/mau ~** bad sign.

agourento,-a *adj* ominous; **o pio da coruja é ~** the owl's hoot brings bad luck, is a sign of doom.

agraciar *vt (condecorar)* to invest, to honour **(com** with*)*; decorate, reward *(alguém)*; **2** *(honrar com título)* reward with a title; **3** *(conceder mercê)* to pardon.

agraciado,-a *adj* rewarded; **2** honoured.

agradar *vt* to please; ♦ *vi (satisfazer)* **~ a alguém** to please sb; **a comida agradou-lhe** the meal pleased him; **isso não me agrada nada** that doesn't please me at all; ♦ **~-se** *vr*: **~-se de** to like, be pleased with; **~-se do sítio** love the place; **~-se de alguém** be attracted to sb.

agradável *(pl: -eis) adj inv* pleasant, agreeable, nice.

agradecer *vt* to thank, be grateful for; *(dizer obrigado)* to say 'thank you'; **agradeço-lhe** I thank you.

agradecido,-a *adj* grateful, thankful; **mal ~** ungrateful.

agradecimento *m* gratitude; **agradecimentos** *mpl* thanks.

agrado *m* satisfaction; **se for do seu ~** if it is all right with you, if it pleases you; **não foi do meu ~** it was not to my liking; **2** *(BR)* present; **~s** presents.

agrafar *vt* to staple; **agrafador** *m* stapler; **agrafo** *m* staple.

agrário,-a *adj* agrarian; **reforma ~** agrarian reform; **2 exploração ~a** agricultural activity, farming; **3** *(lugar)* rural.

agravamento *m* aggravation; worsening.

agravante *adj inv*: aggravating ♦ **circunstância ~** *f* added difficulty.

agravar *vt* to aggravate, make worse; **2** to offend; ♦ **~-se** *vr (piorar)* to worsen, to get worse; **2** *(JUR)* to lodge an appeal; **3** *(MED)* **a ferida agravou-se** the wound is inflamed, got worse.

agravo *m* offence; injury; **2** *(JUR)* appeal.

agredir *vt (assaltar pessoa)* to attack, cause bodily harm; **2** *(bater)* to hit; **3** *(verbalmente)* to insult.

agregado,-a *m,f* tenant farmer, *(BR)* living-in servant, retainer; **2 ~ familiar** *m* (living-in) family, household; **3** aggregate, sum total; **4** *(MIN, CONSTR)* aggregate; ♦ *adj* attached; with full tenure; **2** *(pessoas)* aggregated, all together.

agregar *vt* to congregate; annex; add; ♦ **~-se** *vr (associar-se a)* join sth.

agressão *f* aggression; **2** attack; assault.

agressividade *f* aggressiveness.

agressivo,-a *adj* aggressive.

agreste *adj inv* rural, rustic, wild, rough; **2** deserted, savage; **paisagem ~** wild scenery *f*.

agrestia *f* roughness.

agrião *m (pl: -ões) (BOT)* watercress.

agrícola *adj inv* agricultural.

agricultor,-ora *m* farmer; landholder; **2** *(arc)* husbandman.

agricultura *f* agriculture, farming.

agridoce *adj inv* bittersweet.

agrilhoar *vt* to chain; **2** shackle; **3** enslave; **4** *(fig)* to restrain, repress *(sentimentos)*.

agrimensão *(also:* **agrimensura***) f* land surveying, survey.

agrimensor,-ora *m,f* land surveyor.

agronomia *f* agronomy.

agrónomo,-a *(BR:* **-grô-***) m* agricultural expert, agronomist.

agro-pecuária *f* farming and cattle-raising; **indústria ~** the farming and cattle-raising industry; mixed farming.

agroquímico,-a *adj* chemicals used in agriculture.

agrupamento *m* gathering, cluster, group; **~ de estrelas** cluster of stars; **2 ~ conjugado** *(ELECT)* ganging.

agrupar *vt* to put into groups; ♦ **~-se** *vr* to gather; to form groups; **eles agruparam-se consoante as idades** they formed groups according to their ages.

agrura *f* roughness; **2** *(fig)* hardship, sorrow.

água *f* water; **~ benta** holly water; **~ calcária** hard water; **~ corrente** running water; **~ das pedras** mineral water; **~ doce** fresh water; **fazer ~** *(NÁUT)* to leak; **~ inquinada** polluted water; **~ potável** drinking water; ♦ **águas** *fpl (do mar)*: **as ~ estão a subir** the tide is rising; **2** *(do parto)* waters; IDIOM **ir por ~ abaixo** to lose everything; **o negócio foi por ~ abaixo** business went down the drain; **deitar ~ na fervura** to pour oil on troubled waters; **fazer crescer ~ na boca** to make one's mouth water; **vem aí uma carga de ~** *(chuva)* a heavy shower is on its way; **pôr ~ na fervura** to cool one's enthusiasm off; **foi um balde de ~ fria** it was a disappointment; **com ~s passadas não mói o moinho** let bygones be bygones; **o casamento ficou em ~s de bacalhau** the wedding was called off; **afogar-se em pouca ~** to get het up about nothing, to get one's knickers in a twist *(fam)*.

aguaceiro *m* sudden shower, downpour; **2** *(zanga ligeira)* light row; **3** *(contratempo)* setback; **4** *(BR) (pé-de-vento)* **~ branco** sudden storm without rain.

água-de-colónia *(BR:* **-lô-***) f* eau-de-cologne.

aguadilha *f* secretion; **2** *(BOT)* sap.

aguado,-a *adj* watery, watered-down; **2** *(cavalo)* foundered; **3** *(fig)* ruined, failed.

água-forte *f (QUÍM)* aqua-fortis, nitric acid.

água-furtada *(pl:* **águas-furtadas***) f (quarto, apartamento no vão do telhado)* garret.

água-marinha *f* aquamarine.

água-oxigenada *f* hydrogen peroxide.

água-pé, aguapé *f* diluted Portuguese wine, new wine.

aguar *vt* to water; to dilute.

aguardar *vt* to wait for, await; **2** to expect; ♦ *vi* to wait; **aguarde um momento se faz favor** please wait a moment.

aguardente *m* Portuguese brandy, firewater; **2 ~ bagaceira** made from husks of grapes; **3** *(BR) (de cana d'açúcar)* cachaça.

aguarela *f* watercolour.

aguarrás *f* turpentine.

água-viva *(pl:* **águas-vivas***) f (alforreca)* jelly fish.

aguçar *vt* to sharpen; **2** *(fig)* excite, sharpen *(curiosidade)*; **3** whet *(apetite)*; **4** *(apurar o ouvido)* to prick up.

agudeza *f (ger)* sharpness; **2** *(som agudo)* shrillness; **3** ~ **de espírito** wit.

agudo,-a *adj (gram)* acute; **acento** ~ acute accent; *(GEOM)* **ângulo** ~ acute angle; **2** pointed; **3** sharp; **4** witty, **5** shrill.

aguentar *vt* to support, to bear; **2** tolerate, stand; **3** put up with; **4** to cope with; **não aguento mais** I can't stand (it) any more; **5** endure; ♦ *vi* support; ♦ ~**-se** *vr* to bear up, pull through; **ele estava nervoso mas lá se aguentou na entrevista** he was nervous but he managed to pull through (do well) in the interview; ~**-se contra a corrente** to stem the tide; IDIOM ~ **e cara alegre** grin and bear it.

aguerrido,-a *adj* warlike, brave; **2** courageous, valiant; **3** *(fig) (pessoa)* bold.

águia *f (ZOOL)* eagle; **2** *(fig)* **olhos de** ~ piercing eyes.

aguilhada *f* goad.

aguilhão *m* spur, goad; spike; sting; stimulus, incentive.

aguilhoar *vt* to goad, stimulate.

agulha *f* needle; **trabalho de** ~ needlework; **enfiar a** ~ to thread the needle; **2** *(NÁUT)* compass; **3** *(FERRO)* points *pl.*

agulheiro *m* needle-case; **2** pin cushion; **3** needle-maker; **4** *(FERRO)* pointsman.

agulheta *f* nozzle.

ah *exc (surpresa)* ah; **ah, foi assim que fizeste!** So, this is the way you did it!; **2** *(compreendendo)* **ah …** I see …; **3** *(apelo)* oh; **oh meu Deus!** Oh my God; **oh que tristeza!** how sad!

ai *exc (dor)* ouch!; **2** ah, oh; **ai de mim!** oh, poor me!; **3** **ai que bom!** oh how nice!; **ai-Jesus!** oh my goodness!; ♦ *m* sigh; groan; *(suspirando)* **ai, se eu fosse rico** if only I were rich; **2** **o ai-Jesus** very dear to sb; **meu neto é o meu ai-jesus** my grandson is the apple of my eye; **3** *(minute)* tick, flash; **ele fez o trabalho num ai** he did the work in a tick; **4** *(advertindo)* **ai, ai, menino, se não te calas, zango-me** now, my boy, if you don't keep quiet, I shall get cross.

aí *adv* there (somewhere); **as luvas estão** ~ (vaguely) the gloves are there (somewhere); **espera** ~! wait!, hang on a minute!; **2** *(ação iminente)* **ela já vem** ~ she is coming; **3** *(conclusão)* there; ~ **o tem** there you have it; **4** *(direção)* **não vá por** ~ don't go that way; **5** *(aprox.)* about; **ela deve ter** ~ **uns trinta anos** she must be around 30 years old; **tens** ~ **três Euros?** have you three Euros by any chance?; ♦ then, at this/that point; ~ **ela se calou,** at this point she kept quiet; **2 para** ~ there; **foste para** ~ **fazer o quê** *(fam)* you went there to do what? why did you go there?; **por** ~ **fora** *(local impreciso)* around, thereabouts, somewhere, there; **3 por** ~ **fora** and so on; **4** *(afora)* all over (place); **ela anda por** ~ she is around; IDIOM ~ **é que está o busílis** there's the rub!, there's the snag/the problem.

aia *f* nursemaid, nanny.

aiatolá *m* ayatollah.

AIDS *f (BR)* AIDS.

ainda *adv* still, yet; **2** even; **3** finally; *(momentos antes)* ~ **agora vi a Ana** I have just seen Ana; **4** ~

mais furthermore; **5** ~ **por cima** to top it all, make things worse; **6** ~ **não** not yet; ♦ *exc* ~ **bem!** just as well! thank goodness! that's good!; ♦ *conj* ~ **que** even if, even though; ~ **assim** even so, nevertheless.

aio *m* valet.

aipo *m* celery.

airado,-a *adj* idle, licentious; **2** *(pop)* **cabeça** ~**a** a head in the air; **3 vida** ~**a** disorderly life; **4** *(BR)* having a chill.

airoso,-a *adj* graceful, elegant; **2** *(vestuário)* light, delicate; **3** *(resposta, desculpa)* proper, gracious.

ajaular *vt* to cage (up).

ajeitar *vt* to fit, adjust; **2** to arrange, fix; ♦ ~**-se** *vr* to adapt; **2** *(fig)* **eu ajeito-me** I'll manage, I can make do with.

ajoelhado,-a *adj* kneeling; **2** *(fig)* humbled.

ajoelhar-se *vr* to kneel (down).

ajuda *f* help; aid; assistance; **sem** ~ unaided; **prestar** ~ **a alguém** to lend sb a hand; **2** grant, subsidy, allowance; ~ **de custo** financial assistance, allowance.

ajudante *m,f* assistant, helper; **2** *(MIL)* adjutant; ~ **de campo** aide-de-camp.

ajudar *vt* to help; **Deus te ajude** God help you.

ajuizado,-a *adj* sensible, wise; **2** discreet.

ajuizar *vt* to judge; **2** to suppose.

ajuramentado,-a (= **juramentado**) *adj* sworn in *(testemunha)*; **tradutor,-ora** ~ officially registered translator.

ajuramentar (= **juramentar**) *vt* swear in *(testemunha)*.

ajuntamento *m (de pessoas)* gathering; crowd, throng.

ajuntar *vt* to join, unite; **2** add; **3** *(dinheiro)* save up; **4** to gather; **5** to muster (an army); **6** *(documentos)* to attach.

ajustado,-a *adj (combinado)* agreed, settled; **2** *(roupa)* tight-fitting.

ajustagem *f (BR) (TEC)* adjustment.

ajustamento *m (EP, BR)* adjustment; **2** settlement, agreement; **3** *(de máquinas)* fitting.

ajustar *vt* to adjust, to adapt; **2** *(acertar)* to settle; ~ **as contas** to settle accounts; *(fig, fam)* *(represália)* ~ **contas com alguém** *(represália)* to settle accounts with sb; to get your own back; **3** *(concordar)* to agree; ~ **um preço** to agree on a price; ♦ ~**-se** *vr* to fit, **o colete ajusta-se bem ao teu corpo** the waistcoat is a good fit; ♦ ~ **a** to conform to, adapt o.s. to.

ajustável *adj inv* adjustable; **2** adaptable.

ajuste *m* agreement; **2** adjustment; **3** *(contrato, acordo)* deal; IDIOM **não estou pelos ajustes** I am not going to put up with it/stand for it.

ala *f* row, file; **2** aisle; **3** wing.

Alá *npr* Allah.

alagação *f* flooding.

alagamento *m* flooding; destruction.

alagar *vt* to inundate, flood; ♦ *vi* to flood.

alalá *m (BR)* newspapers' sensational commentary.

alambazar-se *vr* to cram one's mouth (with food); to eat and drink to the full.

alambicado,-a *adj* having the shape of an alembic; **2** *(fig)* pretentious; with unnatural mannerisms.

alambique *m* alembic; still, vessel/apparatus for distilling, making alcohol.

alameda *f* avenue; grove.

álamo *m* poplar.

alar *vt* line up *(árvores, soldados)*, set in rows/ranks; **2** to be fitted with wings; **3** *(fig) (spirit)* to soar.

alaranjado,-a *adj* orange-coloured; **2** *(cheiro)* orange-scented; **3** *(sabor)* orange-flavoured.

alarde *m* ostentation; **2** boasting; **fazer** ~ **de** to flaunt, show off.

alardear *vt* to show off.

alargamento *m* enlargement, expansion; **o** ~ **da U.E.** the enlargement of the EU; **2** *(largura)* widening, broadening; **3** *(prazo)* extension.

alargar *vt* to extend, enlarge; **2** to widen, broaden *(estrada)*; ~ **o passo** to go faster.

alargado,-a *adj* **num contexto** ~ in a broad context.

alarido *m* uproar; **2** clamour, racket; **3** wailing.

alarma *f* **alarme** *m* alarm, alert; **dar o sinal de** ~ to raise the alarm; **acionar o** ~ to set off the alarm; ~ **de incêndio** fire alarm; ~ **de roubo** burglar alarm; **falso** ~ false alarm.

alarmante *adj* alarming.

alarmar *vt* to alarm; ♦ ~**-se** *vr* to be alarmed.

alarme *(Vd:* **alarma***)*.

alarmista *m,f* alarmist; ♦ *adj* alarming.

Alasca *npr* Alaska.

alarve *m* *(pessoa grosseira)* common lout, boor; ♦ *adj* boorish, charlish; rude; **2** *(que come muito)* glutton; *(col)* greedy pig; **3** *(bronco)* thick.

alastramento *m* spreading.

alastrar *vt* *(propagar, espalhar)* to spread; **as cheias alastraram a outras aldeias** the foods spread to other villages; ♦ ~**-se** *vr* to spread.

alatinado,-a *adj* Latinized.

alaúde *m* lute.

alavanca *f* lever; crowbar; **2** ~ **de mudanças** gear lever; **3** ~ **de pedal** foot-lever.

alazão *m* *(cavalo)* sorrel horse.

Albanês,-esa *m,f adj* Albanian.

Albânia *npr* **a** ~ *f* Albania.

albarda *f* pack-saddle; **2** poorly-made clothing.

alabardar *vt* to put packsaddle **(em** on) *(mula, burro)*; **2** *(fazer trabalho à pressa e mal)* to bungle, scamp; **3** *(CULIN)* to make a type of batter for (fried fish).

albarrā *f* tower of a fort, barbican; **2** *(BOT)* wild onion.

albatroz *m* *(ZOOL)* albatross.

albergar *vt* to provide lodging for; to shelter; to harbour; ♦ ~**-se** *vr* to take lodging; to take shelter.

albergue *m* inn; hospice, shelter; ~ **para jovens** youth hostel.

albino,-a *m,f adj* albino.

albornoz *m* *(tipo de gabão usado pelos árabes)* burnous; **2** wide hooded cape, coat.

albufeira *f* lagoon *(água do mar)*; **2** *(represa artificial)* reservoir.

álbum *m* album; ~ **de fotografias** photo album; ~ **de recortes** scrapbook.

albumina *f* albumin.

alça *f* *(tiras nos ombros)* strap; **as** ~**s do vestido** the dress straps; ~ **da mala** strap; **2** *(NÁUT)* loop; **3** *(MIL) (fusil)* notch of the rear sight; ~ **de mira** sights; ~**s** *fpl* *(suspensórios)* braces.

alcácer *m* fortress; castle.

alcachofra *f (BOT)* artichoke.

alcáçova *f* fortress.

alcaçuz *m* licorice.

alçada *f* jurisdiction; **2** *(cargo)* competence, remit; **3** scope; **4** responsibility; **isso não é da sua** ~ that's nothing to do with you.

alçado *m* *(ARQ)* front elevation; ♦ *adj* lifted; **2 de rabo** ~ *(fam)* in a temper; **3** *(BR) (gado, etc)* run-away.

alcaide *m* *(HIST)* governor of a castle; **2** *(BR) (algo velho, fora da moda)* junk.

alcançar *vt* to reach; **2** to achieve, attain; **3** arrive at; **4** to perceive, understand; **5** to obtain, get; **6** to catch up.

alcance *m* *(acessível)* reach; **preços ao** ~ **das bolsas modestas** affordable prices; **2** power, competence; **3** understanding, grasp; **4** range; **ao** ~ **de** within reach/range of; **ao** ~ **da voz** within earshot; **fora do** ~ **de** *(objecto)* out of reach; *(de entendimento)* out of/beyond sb's grasp.

alcantil *(pl:* **alcantis***) m* slope, crag, precipice.

alcantilado,-a *adj (colina, caminho)* steep; craggy.

alçapão *m* *(abertura no soalho)* trapdoor; **2** *(para pássaros)* bird-trap.

alçar *vt* *(perna)* to lift, lift over; **2** *(voz, braço)* raise *(voz)*; **3** *(carga, viga)* heave; **4** *(flag)* hoist; **5** *(fig) (engrandecer)* exalt, acclaim; ♦ ~**-se** *vr* rise against; to rebel.

alcateia *f* *(de lobos)* pack; **2** *(de ladrões)* gang.

alcatifa *f* carpet.

alcatifado *adj* carpeted *(de parede a parede)*.

alcatrão *m* tar; ~ **de hulha** coal tar.

alcatroado *adj (estrada, caminho)* asphalted.

alcatruz *m* *(duma nora)* bucket on the water-wheel.

álcool *m* alcohol.

alcoólatra *m,f* alcoholic.

alcoólico,-a *adj* alcoholic.

Alcorão *m* Koran; **o** ~ the Koran.

alcova *f* alcove.

alcoviteiro,-a *m,f* gossiper; **2** *(metediço)* busybody; **3** *(proxeneta)* pimp; *(mulher)* go-between *(em relações amorosas)*.

alcunha *f* nickname.

aldeão, aldeã *(mpl:* **aldeãos***) (fpl:* **aldeãs***) m,f* villager, peasant.

aldeia *f* village.

aldraba *(=* **aldrava***) f (trinco da fechadura)* latch; **2** *(batente)* door knocker.

aldravas *fpl (BR)* leggings natives use.

aldrabão, aldrabona *m* liar; **2** cheat *(no trabalho)*; **ela é uma** ~ **no que faz** everything she makes is badly done, is botched.

aldrabar *vt* to tell a fib, to lie; **2** *(inventar)* make up *(stories)*; **3** *(trabalho)* to botch, bungle.

aldrabice *f* lie, deceit; **2** *(vigarice)* swindle; **3** *(fig)* a job badly done, botched.

aleatório,-a *adj* fortuitous, casual, random, uncertain; **2** *(JUR: contrato) (MÚS)* aleatoric; **3** dice-player.

alecrim *m (BOT)* rosemary.

alegação *f* allegation.

alegar *vt* to allege; **2** *(JUR)* to plead; ~ **doença** to feign illness.

alegoria *f* allegory.

alegrar *vt* to cheer (up), gladden; **2** to brighten up; **3** to liven (up); ♦ ~**-se** *vr* to be glad; **2** to get merry; **3** get tipsy.

alegre *adj* cheerful; happy, glad; **2** *(um pouco embriagado)* merry, tipsy; **cores** ~**s** bright colours.

alegrete *m* flower bed in the garden.

alegria *f* joy, happiness.

aleijado,-a *m,f* cripple; ♦ *adj* crippled, disabled.

aleijar *vt* to hurt; to maim; to cripple; ♦ ~**-se** to get hurt *(fisicamente)*.

aleitação *f* **aleitamento** *m* nursing; suckling; ~ **materno** breast feeding.

aleitar *vt* to nurse; to suckle.

aleive *m* slander; treachery.

aleluia *f (REL)* alleluia; **Sábado de A~** Holy Saturday.

além *adv* over there; the other side of; beyond, yonder; **mais** ~ further on; ♦ *prep:* ~ **de** besides; ~ **disso** furthermore; ~**-mar** overseas; ~**-Minho** on the other side of/beyond Minho.

Alemanha *npr:* **a** ~ Germany.

alemão, alemã *m,f adj* German; **os** ~ *mpl* the Germans; *(LÍNG)* **o** ~ German.

alentador,-ora *adj* encouraging.

alentado,-a *adj* encouraged by.

alentar *vt* to encourage; ♦ ~**-se** *vr* to cheer up.

alentejano,-a *m,f adj* from/of Alentejo (Portugal).

alento *m* strength; **2** *(ânimo)* courage, heart; **dar** ~ to encourage; **o desgosto deixou-a sem** ~ **para viver** her grief left her without the heart to live; **ganhar** ~ to recover one's breath.

aleopardado,-a *adj (HERALD) (num escudo, brazão)* rampant lion.

alergia *f* allergy.

alérgico,-a *adj* allergic.

alerta *m* alert, warning; ♦ *adj* alert; **estar** ~ to be vigilant ♦ *adv* on the alert.

alertar *vt* to alert, warn.

aleta *f (ANAT)* nostril; **2** *(pequena fileira)* row.

aletria *f (massa)* vermicelli.

alfa *m (LÍNG)* alpha; **2 de** ~ **a ómega** from alpha to omega; *(ASTRON, FIS, FISIOL)* alpha.

alfabeto *m* alphabet.

alface *f (BOT)* lettuce.

alfacinha *m,f (fam)* Lisbonner, native of Lisbon; **2** *f* small lettuce; ♦ *adj inv (costumes, bairro, etc)* Lisbon.

alfageme *m (arc)* sword cutter; armourer.

alfaia *f* furniture; **2** utensil; **3** ornament; **4** *(AGR)* ~**s agrícolas** agricultural implements/tools.

alfaiataria *f* tailor's shop; tailoring.

alfaiate *m* tailor.

alfândega *f* customs *pl*, customs house.

alfange *m* scimitar.

alfarrábio *m* old book.

alfarrabista *m,f* second-hand book-seller, shop.

alfarroba *f (BOT)* carob.

alfarrobeira *f (BOT)* carob tree.

alfavaca *f (BOT)* aromatic plant akin to basil.

alfazema *f (BOT)* lavender.

alferes *m (MIL)* second-lieutenant; **2** *(NÁUT)* ensign.

alfinete *m* pin; **2** ~**-de-ama** safety pin; **3** ~ **de peito** brooch; IDIOM **isto não vale um** ~ this is not worth a bean.

alfombra *f* carpet; **2** *(relva)* tough turf, lawn.

alforge *m* saddle-bag.

alforra *f* plant rust, mildew.

alforreca *f* jellyfish, medusa.

alga *f* seaweed; **algas** *fpl* algae.

algália *f (MED)* probe, catheter.

algaraviada *f (muits vozes a falar)* hubbub; **2** *(palavreado incompreensível)* gibberish.

algarismo *m* number, digit, figure.

algarvio,-a *m,f adj* from Algarve (Portugal).

algazarra *f* uproar; **2** bawling; racket; **3** hubbub.

álgebra *f* algebra.

algemar *vt* to handcuff; **2** to shackle; **3** *(fig) (obrigar, dominar)* tie down, compel.

algemas *fpl* handcuffs.

algeroz *m* gutter, guttering.

algibeira *f (bolso)* pocket.

algo *adv* somewhat, rather; ♦ *pron indef* something; anything; ~ **de misterioso** something mysterious.

algodão *m* cotton; ~ **hidrófilo** absorbent cotton; ~ **em rama** cotton wool, raw cotton; **2 tecido de** ~ **estampado** printed cotton material.

algodoeiro *m* cotton grower, merchant; ♦ **algodoeiro,-a** *adj* **indústria** ~**a** cotton industry.

algodoal *m* cotton plantation.

algoz *m* hangman, executioner; **2** tyrant, a cruel person.

alguém *pron indef* someone, somebody; *(em interrogativa, negativa)* anyone, anybody; **está** ~ **no quarto?** is there anyone in the room?; **2** *(importante)* **quero ser** ~ I want to be someone.

alguidar *m* large and round earthenware bowl; **2** *(pej)* **políticas de** ~ backyard politics.

algum,-a *(pl: alguns, algumas) adj (indeterminado)* some, any; **fiz** ~**as compras** I did some shopping; ~**a vez** sometime; **em** ~ **lugar** somewhere; **2** *(em negativa, interrogativa)* any; **tens** ~ **dinheiro?** have you any money?; **você foi a** ~ **lado?** did you go anywhere?; ♦ *pron* some, one; ~ **dia** one day/ some day; ~ **vez** sometime; **alguns dizem uma coisa, outros dizem outra** some (people) say one thing and others say another; **na prova dos vinhos, provámos alguns** at the wine-tasting we tried some; **em parte alguma** nowhere; ~**a coisa** something; **coisa** ~**a** nothing; **de modo** ~ in no way, not at all; **ele deve ter feito** ~**a** he must have done something wrong.

algures *adv* somewhere.

alhada *f* dish of, mess of garlic; **2** *(fig)* tangled affair, mess; **meti-me numa** ~ I got in a jam, in a spot of trouble.

alheio,-a *m,f* someone else; stranger; **não se deve rir do** ~ one must not laugh at another person; ♦ *adj (de outra pessoa)* someone else's; **2** *(estranho; pessoa)* stranger, unknown, alien; ~ **a** stranger to; **3** *(desatento)* inattentive, detached; **4** *(ignorante de)* oblivious, unaware; **eu estava** ~ **a essas coisas**

I was oblivious to/I was not aware of such things; **5** *(independente de)* against, alien to; ~ **à minha vontade** against my will; **6 não ~ a** not unconnected with, due to.

alheado,-a *adj* rapt; head in the clouds; detached.

alhear *vt* to alienate, separate; **a paixão alheou-a da realidade** her passion cut her off from reality; ♦ *vr:* ~**-se de** detach (oneself) from.

alho *m* garlic; **um dente de** ~ a clove of garlic; **2 pôr o peixe em vinha d' ~s** to marinate the fish in wine and garlic; IDIOM **misturar ~s com bugalhos** *(conversa)* to go off at a tangent, to confuse two different issues.

alho-porro *(BR:* **alho-poró)** *m (BOT)* leek.

ali *adv (naquele lugar)* there; **ela está** ~ she is there; **2** *(àquele lugar)* there; **ele foi ali** he went there; **3 até** ~ up to there; *(tempo, data)* until/till then; **4** *(aprox.)* **por** ~ round about; **5** *(enfático)* ~ **mesmo**, right there; ~ **dentro** in there; ~ **vem ele!** there he comes!; ♦ **por** ~ *adv (direction)* through there, that way.

aliado,-a *m,f* ally; ♦ *adj* allied.

aliança *f* wedding ring; **2** alliance.

aliar *vt* to ally; ♦ *vr* ~**-se a** to make, form an alliance; **2** to combine with; **a modernidade aliada à tradição** modernity combined with, allied to tradition.

aliás *adv* besides, anyway; **2** actually, as a matter of fact; **3** or rather.

aliás is not to be confused with the English 'alias' in the sense of assumed name.

álibi *m* alibi.

alicate *m* pliers; **2** *(for toenails)* clippers.

alicerce *m* foundation; base.

aliciante *m,f* enticement; ♦ *adj inv* tempting, enticing, delightful.

aliciar *vt* to entice; to lure; **2** *(subornar)* bribe; **3** *(BR)* to get labour unlawfully.

alienação *f* alienation; **2** transfer, sell-off, release *(de bens, propriedade)*; **3** ~ **mental** insanity, psychosis.

alienado-a *m,f* lunatic; ♦ *adj* separated; **2** insane; **3** *(bens)* transferred.

alienar *vt* to transfer *(bens)*; **2** to alienate; keep sb away from; **os problemas domésticos alienaram-no da família** problems at home kept him away from the family; ♦ *vr* ~**-se (de)** to distance oneself from.

aligátor *m (ZOOL)* alligator.

aligeirar *vt* to lighten *(peso)*; **2** *(apressar)* quicken, hasten; **3** *(fig) (aliviar)* to alleviate, assuage.

alimentação *f* food; nourishment; **2** *(abastecimento)* fuel; **3** *(máquina)* feeding; **4** *(ELECT)* supply.

alimentador *m* feeder; ♦ *adj* feeding.

alimentar *adj inv* food; ♦ *vt* to feed; **2** *(esperança)* cherish; **3** *(fig)* encourage, keep up; ♦ *vr* ~**-se de** to feed on.

alimentício,-a *adj* nutritive; **produtos ~s** food products.

alimento *m* food, nourishment; **2** maintenance; ♦ **alimentos** *mpl (JUR)* alimony *sg;* **2** provisions; **3** foodstuffs.

alínea *f* sub-heading; indent, item.

alinhado,-a *adj* elegant; lined up.

alinhamento *m* alignment.

alinhar *vt* to align, line up; ♦ ~**-se** *vr* to form a line.

alinhavar *vt (costura)* to tack, to sew sth loosely; **2** *(fig) (preparar por alto)* to improvise, prepare roughly.

alinho *m* alignment; **2** neatness.

alisar *vt (tornar liso, plano)* to smooth (down) *(cabelo, cama)*; *(terreno)* to even (out); **2** *(madeira)* to plane; **3** *(tirar as rugas de)* to smooth out, to straighten *(papel, tecido)*.

alistamento *m* enlistment.

alistar *vt* to enrol; **2** make a list of sth; **3** *(MIL)* to recruit.

alistar-se *vr* to enlist, join up.

aliviar *vt* to alleviate; **2** to clear up; **3** *(peso mais leve)* to lighten; **4** *(dor)* to relieve, soothe; ♦ ~**-se** *vr* get rid of.

alívio *m* relief, comfort; pause; **que ~!** what a relief!

alma *f* soul, spirit; **ela é a ~ da festa** she is the soul of the party; **ele foi a ~ da revolução** he was the heart and soul of the revolution; **2** *(PSIC)* mind, **o estado de ~** state of mind; **3** *(ânimo)* heart, courage; **4** *(essência)* core, essence; **5** *(carácter)* heart; ~ **danada** evil spirit, bad person; ~ **gémea** kindred spirit, soulmate; **6** *(ghost)* ~ **do outro mundo** spirit; **7** *(generosidade)* **a grandeza de** ~ magnanimity, generosity; **8** *(em arma de fogo)* bore; **9** *(avivar)* **dar** ~ **a algo** to give life to sth, brighten up sth.

almaço *m adj (papel)* foolscap.

almejar *vt* to long for, crave; **2** to covet; **3** to aim, have an aim.

almirantado *m* admiralty.

almirante *m (pessoa)* admiral; ♦ *adj (navio)* flagship.

almoçar *vi* to have lunch.

almoço *m* lunch; **pequeno-~** breakfast.

almocreve *m* mule driver.

almofada *f* cushion; pillow; **2** pad; ~ **de tinta** ink-pad.

almofadão *m* large cushion, pillow.

almofariz *m* mortar.

almôndega *f* meat ball.

alô *exc (TEL) (BR)* hello.

alodial *adj inv (bens)* allodial, unemcumbered (property).

alojamento *m* accommodation; lodgings; **2** *(barco, hotel)* suite; **problema de** ~ housing problem; **3** *(MIL)* quarters.

alojar *vt* to lodge; *(visitas)* to put up; *(MIL)* to billet, quarter.

alojar-se *vr* to stay (**em** at); take lodgings.

alongar *vt (tornar curto)* to lengthen; **2** *(prolongar)* to extend; **3** *(estender)* to stretch out *(braço, perna)*; ♦ ~**-se** *vr* to stretch; **as searas alongavam-se a perder de vista** the cornfields stretched as far as the eye could see; **2** *(levar tempo)* to go on; *(conversa)* ramble on.

alpaca *f (ZOOL)* alpaca; **2** (metal) nickel alloy; **3** *(fam)* **manga de** ~ office-worker.

alpendre *m* shed; **2** porch, veranda.

alpercata (= **alparcata, alpergata**) *f (chinelo)* flip-flop.

alperce *m* apricot.

Alpes *mpl*: **os** ~ the Alps.

alpinismo *m* mountaineering, climbing.

alpinista *m,f* mountaineer, climber.

alpiste *m* canary grass, bird seed.

alquebrar *vt* to weaken; **2** to exhaust; ♦ *vi* (problema dorsal) to stoop, to be bent double; **2** *(NÁUT)* to camber.

alqueire *m* bushel; measure of weight/capacity *(de grão)* varying between 13 and 22 litres; **2** *(de superfície)* area, *(esp. no Brasil)* **1** ~ = 2,42 hectares in São Paulo.

alqueive *m* fallow land.

alquimia *f* alchemy.

alta *(Vd: alto) f (preços, salário)* rise; **2** *(ECON)* upturn; *(FIN) (de cotação)* rise; **estar em** ~ to be rising, on the up; **mercado em** ~ *(ECON)* bull market; **3** *(do hospital, da tropa)* discharge; **ele teve** ~ **do hospital** he was discharged from the hospital; ~ **tensão arterial** high-blood pressure.

alta-costura *f* haute-couture; high fashion.

alta fidelidade *f* hi-fi.

altamente *adv* highly; ♦ *exc (fam) (muito bem)* great! super!

altaneiro,-a *adj [pessoa]* arrogant, haughty; **2** *(ave, plane)* soaring; **3** *(árvore, torre)* towering.

altar *m* altar; **levar alguém ao** ~ to lead, take sb to the altar.

altarmor *m* high altar.

alta-roda *f* high society; upper crust.

alteração *f* change, alteration; **2** falsification; ~ **dos preços** fluctuation of prices.

alterar *vt* to alter; **2** *(JUR)* to amend; **3** to falsify; **4** ~ **o sentido** to twist the meaning; ♦ ~**-se** *vr* to alter; **2** *(exaltar-se)* to get angry, lose one's temper; **3** *(inquietar-se)* to get upset.

altercação *nf* angry dispute, altercation.

altercar *vt* to quarrel, wrangle; **2** to squabble.

alternado-a *adj* alternate; **em dias** ~**s** every other day.

alternância *f* alternation; **2** *(AGR)* crop rotation.

alternar *vt/vi* to alternate; ♦ ~**-se** *vr (revezar-se)* to alternate; to take turns.

alternativa *f* alternative; ♦ **alternativo,-a** *adj* alternative; **2** *(ELECT)* alternating.

alteza *f* height; **2** loftiness; **3** highness; **Vossa A**~ Your Highness.

altifalante *m* loudspeaker.

altíssimo *adj (superl de **alto**)* highest, tallest, loudest; **o A**~ the Almighty.

altista *m (FIN) (especulador, mercado)* bull; ♦ *adj inv (FIN) (mercado)* bullish; upward.

altitude *f* altitude.

altivez *f* haughtiness; loftiness.

altivo,-a *adj* haughty; lofty.

alto *m (cume)* height, top; **o** ~ **do monte/da cabeça** the top of the hill/ of the head; **do** ~ from above; **de** ~ **a baixo** from top to bottom; **2** *(céu, ar)* sky; **lá no** ~ up in the sky; **3** *(elevação)* elevation; *(fig) (saliência)* lump, bump; **tenho um** ~ **no peito** I have a lump on the chest; **4 fazer** ~ to halt; ♦ **altos e baixos** *mpl* ups and downs; ♦ **alto,-a** *adj (pessoa)* tall; **ele está muito** ~ **para a idade** he is very tall for his age; **2** *(som, voz)* **alto,-a; fale mais alto** speak louder; **3** *(object)* high; ~-**falante** *m* loudspeaker; ~-**forno** *m* blast furnace; ~-**relevo** *m* high relief; **mar** ~**o** high seas, open sea; **4** *(GEOG)* upper; **A**~ **Alentejo** upper Alentejo; **5** *(importante)* high; **A**~ **Comissário** High Commissioner; **6** *(perigo)* grave; **7** *(tardio)* **a altas horas da noite** late at night; **8** *(amplo)* broad; ~ **dia** broad daylight; ♦ *adv* loudly, aloud; **fale mais** ~ speak louder; ~ **e bom som** loud and clear; **2 por** ~ roughly; **ler por** ~ to skim through; ♦ *exc* ~ **lá!** halt! stop there!; **mãos ao** ~! hands up!; ~ **lá, não é bem assim!,** come on/stop, it is not quite so!; IDIOM **pôr-se ao** ~ to watch out.

alto-astral *(BR) adj inv (fam)* cool; **estar de** ~ to be cool.

altruísmo *m* altruism.

altruísta *m,f* altruist; ♦ *adj* altruistic.

altura *f* height; **2** time; **3** altitude; **da mesma** ~ of the same height; **na mesma** ~ at the same time; **nessa** ~ then; **ter dois metros de** ~ to be two metres tall; **estar à** ~ **de** to be up to/capable of.

alucinar *vt* to hallucinate.

alucinado,-a *m,f* lunatic, mad person; ♦ *adj (com temperatura, alegria)* delirious.

alucinante *adj inv* hallucinating.

alucinogénio *m* hallucinogen.

alude *m* avalanche.

aludir *vi*: ~ **a** to refer to; allude to; to mention.

alugado *(BR) m* hired hand; ♦ *adj (EP) (carro, ferramenta)* hired; **2** *(casa)* rented; **3** *(BR) (trabalhador)* hired.

alugar *vt (casa, terreno)* to rent, to let, rent out; lease; **2** *(carro, bicicleta)* to hire; ~ **à hora** *(alguém, algo)* to hire out (sb, sth); 'aluga-se' *(quarto, casa)* 'to let'.

aluguel *m (BR) (carro)* rental; *(apartamento)* renting; **2** *(pagamento)* rent.

aluguer *m (EP) (carro, ferramenta)* hire; **2** *(contrato)* rental.

aluição *f* **aluimento** *m (de edifício)* subsidence; *(de terrenos)* landslide.

aluir *vt (derrubar)* demolish, raze, knock down; **2** *(arruinar)* ruin *(reputação)*; ♦ *vi (desmoronar-se)* to fall gradually, to crumble; to collapse, cave in, to subside *(estrutura, terras)*.

alumiar *vt (iluminar)* to light (up); **2** to enlighten; ♦ *vi* to shine *(lanterna)*.

alumínio *m* aluminium.

aluminotérmico,-a *adj (TEC)* aluminothermic.

alunagem *f (BR: alunissagem) (descer na lua)* lunar landing *(astronauta, míssil)*

alunar *(BR: alunissar) vi* to land on the moon.

aluno,-a *m,f* pupil, student; ~ **externo** day pupil; ~ **interno** boarder.

alusão f allusion.

alusivo,-a adj allusive; suggestive.

aluvião f (GEOL) alluvium; flood.

alva f (aurora) daybreak, dawn.

alvará m charter, licence, permit.

alvejante m (BR); ◆ adj inv (de branquear) whitening, bleaching.

alvejar vt to aim at; **2** ~ **a tiro** to shoot, **ele foi alvejado a tiro** he was shot; ◆ vi (BR) whiten, bleach; **2** to gleam white.

alvenaria f masonry.

alvéloa f wagtail.

alvéolo m (cavidade) cavity; (de dentes) socket; **2** (célula do favo das abelhas) cell of the honeycomb; **3** (ANAT) alveolus (pl: alveoli).

alverca f pool, water tank; **2** marsh.

alvíssaras fpl reward; (num anúncio) '**dá-se** ~ **a quem achar o meu gato**' 'reward given to whomsoever finds my cat'.

alvitrar vt to propose, suggest.

alvitre m opinion, view point, suggestion.

alvo,-a m target; **atingir o** ~ to hit the target/bull's eye; **atirar ao** ~ to shoot at a target; **2** (ANAT) (esclerótica) white of the eye; **3** (fig) aim, objective; ◆ adj white, pure.

alvor m (claridade do amanhecer) light; **2** (brancura) whiteness; **3** (fig) (início de algo bom/belo) dawn.

alvorada f dawn; **2** (MIL) reveille; **3** (fig) beginning.

alvorecer vi to dawn; **ao** ~ at daybreak, dawn.

alvoroçar vt to stir up; **2** to excite; ◆ ~-**se** vr to get excited.

alvoroço m commotion, turmoil; **2** enthusiasm; **3** agitation; **4** (pressa) hustle; **5** (motim) riot.

alvura f whiteness; **2** (inocência) purity.

ama f children's nurse, nanny; ~-**de-leite** (pl: **amas-de-leite**) wet nurse; ~-**seca** (pl: **amas-secas**) children's nanny.

amabilidade f kindness; niceness, gentleness.

amabilíssimo (superl de **amável**) adj extremely kind.

amachucar vt to crush, to scrunch up (lata, cartucho); **2** (amarrotar) crease, crumple (roupa, papel); **3** (carro) to dent; **4** (fig) to hurt (sentimentos); **seu orgulho ficou amachucado** his pride was hurt; ◆ vr ~-**se** to crush.

amaciador m (do cabelo, da roupa) conditioner; ◆ adj conditioning.

amaciar vt to soften, make silky; ◆ vi become smooth.

amado,-a m,f beloved, sweetheart, loved one.

amador,-ora m,f amateur, enthusiast, lover; ◆ adj loving.

amadurecer vt/vi to ripen; **2** (fig) to mature.

âmago m (BOT) heart, core, **2** (parte interna) centre; **3** (fig) (essência, cerne) pith, heart; **4** (fig) (íntimo) soul, heart.

amainar vi to abate, soften; **2** to calm down; **3** to subside; **4** (NÁUT) to lower (velas).

amaldiçoar vt to curse (alguém); ◆ vi curse.

amálgama m amalgam.

amalgamar vt to amalgamate; **2** to fuse, blend.

amalucado,-a adj (um pouco louco) nutty.

amamentação f breastfeeding.

amamentar vt to breastfeed.

amaneirado,-a adj affected, conceited, with odd mannerisms.

amanhã m tomorrow; ~ **pode ser nunca** tomorrow may never come; ◆ adv tomorrow; ~ **de manhã** tomorrow morning; ~ **de tarde** tomorrow afternoon; ~ **à noite** tomorrow night; **depois de** ~ the day after tomorrow; **nunca se sabe o dia de** ~ one never knows what the future brings.

amanhar vt to cultivate; to prepare (terra); ~ **a terra** to till the ground; **2** ~ **o peixe** to prepare/clean/scale the fish; ◆ ~-**se** vr (pop) (governar-se) to manage, to do; ~ **bem** (pop) to do well (dinheiro, posição); **amanha-te lá como puderes** see if you can manage.

amanhecer m dawn; **ao** ~ at daybreak; ◆ vi to dawn; **2** to be daybreak.

amanho m (AGR) (cultivo) tillage; **3** (preparação) preparation, arrangement.

amansar vt to tame, to break in (animal); **2** (fig) to calm down (pessoa, ira); ◆ vi to grow calm.

amante m,f lover; f mistress; **2** (apreciador) enthusiast, fan, aficionado,-a; **não sou** ~ **de futebol** I am not a lover of football; ◆ adj inv loving.

amanteigado,-a adj (queijo) creamy, soft, full-fat; (bolacha, biscoito) buttery; **2** (fig) (terno) (pessoa, modo) gentle.

amar vt (ter amor por) to love, gostar muito (de); **2** (fazer amor com) to make love to; ~ **a Deus** to love God; ◆ vi (estar apaixonado) to be in love with; ◆ ~-**se** vr (a si mesmo) to love oneself; **amar-se** (reciprocamente) to love each other.

amarar vt (NÁUT) to set sail, to sail away; **2** (hidroavião) to land on sea.

amarelado,-a adj yellowish; **2** sallow.

amarelecer vt to go/turn yellow.

amarelo,-a m yellow; ◆ adj yellow.

amarfanhar vt (amarrotar) to crinkle; crumble; **2** (fig) (humilhar) to belittle.

amargar vt to make bitter; **2** (fig) to embitter; **ele o amargará** he will suffer for it.

amargo,-a adj bitter.

amargura f bitterness; **2** (fig) sorrow, sadness; **3** (fig) anguish.

amargurado,-a adj embittered; **2** anguished, sad.

amarra f (NÁUT) cable, rope, hawser; **largar as** ~**s** to cast off; **2** (grilhão) shakle; **3** (fig) (amparo) support; **4** (fig, pej) (impedimento) fetter.

amarrar vt to tie (up, together, back, down); **amarra o cabelo** tie back your hair; **ele amarrou o cão à grade** he tied the dog to the railings; **2** (fig) (compromisso, dever) to bind (**a** to); to tie down; ◆ vi (NÁUT) to moor, to anchor; ◆ ~-**se** vr (agarrar-se a algo obstinadamente) stick to (ideia, desejo, person).

amarrotar vt (amachucar) to crumple up, wrinkle (paper, roupa); ◆ vi, vr to crease.

amassadela f (massa) kneading; **2** (amolgadela) dent.

amassar *vt* (*massa*) to knead; **2** (*bolo, mistura*) to mix; **3** (*amachucar*) crush.

ampulheta *f* hour-glass.

amável *adj inv* kind, nice, gentle; **você é muito ~** you are very kind.

amazona *f* Amazon, lady rider; **montar à ~** to ride side saddle.

Amazonas *npr* (*GEO*) (*rio*) the Amazon (river); **2** (*estado*) Amazonas.

Amazónia (*BR*: -zô-) *npr.* **a ~** the Amazon, Amazonas.

amazónico,-a (*PO*), **amazônico,-a** (*BR*) *adj* Amazonian.

> More than half of the area of Amazon (Amazônia) is in Brazil. The Amazon River, which flows to the Atlantic, is the largest in the world, in volume. Amazônia also houses the largest rain forest – 'the world's lung'.

âmbar *m* amber.

ambição *f* ambition.

ambicionar *vt* to aspire to; to crave for.

ambicioso,-a *adj* ambitious.

ambidestro,-a *adj* ambidextrous.

ambiência *f* ambiance, atmosphere; ambient.

ambiental *adj inv* environmental.

ambientador *m* (*air*) freshener.

ambientalista *m,f* environmentalist; conservationist.

ambientar(-se) *vt/vr* to settle; to adapt (o.s.) (**a** to), get used to.

ambiente *m* (*ecologia*) environment; **meio-~** environment; **2** (*fig*) (*social*) atmosphere, ambiance; milieu; scenery; **mudança de ~** change of scenery; ◆ *adj* surrounding; **temperatura ~** room temperature.

ambiguidade *f* ambiguity.

ambíguo,-a *adj* ambiguous.

âmbito *m* ambit, extent, scope, range, field; **no ~ de estudos sociais** in the field of social studies.

ambivalente *adj inv* ambivalent.

ambos,-as *adj* **ambas as irmãs são magras** both sisters are thin; ◆ *pron indef* **preciso de ~** I need both (of them, of you *pl*); **~ os irmãos** both brothers; **de ~ os lados** on both sides.

ambulância *f* ambulance.

ambulante *adj inv* moving; travelling; **vendedor ~** street seller, pedlar; **livraria ~** mobile library.

ambulatório *m* (*MED*) outpatient clinic/department; **2** mobile clinic.

AMC (*abr de* **Acordo Monetário Europeu**) EMA.

ameaça *f* (*intimidativo*) threat; **2** menace (**para** (for)); **3** (*aviso*) warning, scare, notice; **~ de despejo** eviction notice; **~ de bomba** bomb scare; **~ de cancro** risk of cancer; **~ de greve** strike warning.

ameaçador,-ora *adj* threatening.

ameaçar *vt* to threaten; **~ alguém de morte** to threaten sb with death.

amealhar *vt* (*poupar*) to save, economize; **2** (*juntar*) put money in the money-box, in the piggy-bank.

amedrontar *vt* to scare, intimidate; ◆ **~-se** *vr* to be frightened.

amedrontado,-a *adj* scared, terrified of.

ameia *f* (*HIST, ARQ*) battlement.

ameigar *vt* caress, fondle.

amêijoa *f* (*ZOOL, CULIN*) cockle, clam.

ameijoada *f* a kind of cockle stew.

ameixa *f* (*BOT*) plum; **~ passada** prune.

ameixoal *n* (*pomar*) plum grove.

ameixoeira, ameixeira *f* plum tree.

amém *m* amen; **dizer ~ a tudo** to say yes to everything; ◆ *exc* (*REL*) Amen!

amêndoa *f* almond.

amendoeira *f* almond tree.

amendoim *m* peanut.

amenidade *f* amenity; mildness, serenity; affability.

ameninado,-a *adj* boyish, girlish, child-like.

amenizar *vt* to soften; to make pleasant; to ease.

ameno,-a *adj* pleasant; mild, gentle.

América *npr* **a ~** America; **a ~ Central** Central America; **a ~ do Norte/Sul** North/South America; **A~ Latina** *f* Latin America.

americanismo *m* Americanism.

americano,-a *m,f adj* American.

americanizar *vt* to Americanize; ◆ **~-se** *vr* become americanized.

ameríndio,-a *m,f adj* American Indian, Amerindian.

amesquinhar *vt* (*depreciar*) to belittle; to disparage; **2** (*vexar*) to humiliate.

Amesterdã (*BR*) **Amesterdão** (*EP*) *npr* Amsterdam.

amestrar *vt* (*instruir*) to train, coach (*soldados*); **2** (*animal*) to train, to tame.

ametista *f* (*pedra preciosa*) amethyst.

amianto *m* asbestos.

amicíssimo,-a *adj* (*superl de* **amigo**) very, extremely friendly;

amido *m* (*QUÍM*) amylum; **2** (*substância*) starch.

amieiro *m* (*BOT*) alder (*tree*)

amigalhaço,-a *m,f* old pal, old chap, old chum, great friend.

amigável *adj* friendly, amiable; amicable.

amigar-se *vr* (*fam*) to live together (unmarried); (*coll*) to shack up.

amígdala, amídala *f* tonsil; **tirar as ~s** take out the tonsils.

amigdalite *f* tonsillitis.

amigo,-a *m,f* friend; **2** lover, fan; **~ íntimo** close friend; **~ influente** powerful friend; **~ dos animais** animal lover; ◆ *adj* friendly; IDIOM **ele é um ~ às direitas** he is a true friend; **ela tem cara de poucos ~s** she looks unfriendly; **os ~s conhecem-se nas ocasiões** a friend in need is a friend indeed.

amigo-da-onça (*pl*: **amigos-da-onça**) *m,f* false friend, fair weather friend; **2** *mpl* (*LING*) deceptive meanings.

amimado,-a *adj* (*criança*) petted; spoilt.

amimalhar *vt* to spoil (*criança, pessoa*).

amimar *vt* to pet, pamper; to spoil (*criança*).

aminoácido *m* amino acid.

amistoso,-a *adj* friendly, cordial; **2** (*DESP*) (*partida*) friendly.

amiudar *vt/vi* to repeat; to do often; **~ as viagens** to make frequent journeys.

amiúde *adv* often, frequently.

amizade *f* friendship; **2** friendliness; **fazer ~s** to make friends.

amnésia *f* amnesia.

amnésico,-a *m,f adj* amnesic.

amnistia/anistia *f* amnesty.

amo *m* (*arc*) master; **2** (*pres ind, 1ª pessoa de* **amar**) I love.

amodorrado,-a *adj* drowsy; lethargic.

amodorrar-se *vr* to become drowsy.

amoedar *vt* to mint (*ouro, metal*).

amofinar *vt* to vex; **2** to pester, badger; ♦ **~-se** *vr* to fret (over), become upset, distressed, cross.

amolação *f* (*facas, etc*) sharpening, grinding; **2** (*BR*) (*transtorno*) annoyance.

amolador *m* (*faca, tesoura*) grinder, sharpener.

amolar *vt* (*afiar*) to sharpen, grind; **2** (*BR*) to annoy, to pester (*alguém*); ♦ **~-se** *vr* (*BR*) get annoyed.

amoldar *vt* to mould; ♦ *vr* **~-se a** to conform to; **2** to adjust; **3** to get used to.

amolecer *vt* (*tornar mole*) to soften; **2** (*abrandar*) to assuage, mollify; **2** (*fig*) to mellow; ♦ **~-se** *vr* (*comover-se*) to be touched; **2** (*tornar-se brando*) to relent.

amolgadela (= **amolgadura**) *f* dent, indentation.

amolgar *vt* to dent; **2** (corpo) to bruise; ♦ **~-se** *vr* to be dented.

amónia (*BR:* -mô-) *f* **amoníaco** *m* ammonia.

amontoar *vt* to pile up, heap; **2** accumulate; **~ riquezas** to amass a fortune.

amor *m* love; lover; **fazer ~** to make love; **por ~ de** for the sake of; **que ~ !** what a darling!; **não ter ~ à vida** be reckless, foolhardy; **por ~ às crianças** for the children's sake; IDIOM **~ com ~ se paga** love begets love; **não morremos de ~ um pelo outro** there is no love lost between us.

amora *f* mulberry; **~ preta/silvestre** blackberry.

amoral *adj inv* amoral.

amordaçar *vt* (*tapar a boca com mordaça*) to gag.

amoreira *f* (*BOT*) mulberry/blackberry bush.

amorenado,-a *adj* (*pele, tez*) swarthy.

amorfo,-a *adj* amorphous; **2** (*forma*) shapeless; **3** (*caráter*) weak.

amornar *vt* to warm up (*comida, bebida*); ♦ *vi* to get warm/warmer.

amoroso,-a *adj* (*pessoa*) loving, affectionate; **2** loveable; **um caso ~** a love affair; **ela é ~** she is a darling; **3** (*objeto*) lovely.

amor-perfeito (*pl:* **amores-perfeitos**) *m* (*BOT*) pansy, heartsease.

amor-próprio *m* (*auto-estima*) self esteem; **2** (*orgulho*) pride.

amortalhar *vt* to shroud; **2** (*fig*) to enshroud.

amortecedor *m* shock-absorber; **2** muffler (do som).

amortecer *vt* to deaden, lessen, soften; ♦ *vi* to weaken, fade.

amortecido,-a *adj* weak; **2** soft; **3** dim, dull; **4** deadened; **a luz ~ da tardinha** the dim light of the evening.

amortização *f* payment by instalments; paying off (*dívida*), amortization; **2** (*FIN*) (*ações*) redemption of (*título*).

amortizar *vt* to redeem, pay off; **2** to lessen (*choque, queda*).

amostra *f* sample, specimen; example; **2** demonstration; **3** show, display; **uma ~ do feitio dele** a show of his character.

amostragem *f* (*amostra, selecção*) sample, sampling; **2** (*estatística*) selection; **3** show of a home film in preparation.

amotinar *vi* to rebel, to mutiny.

amovível *adj inv* (*nódoa*) removable; **2** (*funcionário*) transferable; **3** (*cargo*) transitório.

amparar *vt* to support, to sustain; to protect, assist; ♦ **~-se** *vr:* **~-se em/contra** (*segurar-se*) to lean on/against; **~-se na lei** to stand on (under the protection of) the law.

amparo *m* (*apoio*) prop, support; **2** protection; **3** aid, assistance; **sem ~** helpless, without any help.

amperagem *f* amperage.

ampère *m* ampere, amp.

ampliação *f* (*aumento, alargamento*) enlargement, extension; **2** (*de ângulo*) widening; **3** (*FOTO*) enlargement; **4** (*de ótica*) magnification.

ampliar *vt* (*de imagem*) to enlarge, magnify; **~ uma fotografia** to enlarge a photo; **2** (*de ângulo*) widen; **3** (*CONSTR*) extend, build an extension; **4** (*negócio*) expand; **5** (*desenvolver – estudos, debate*) broaden; **6** (*fig*) (*história*) to exaggerate.

amplidão *f* (*espaço*) vastness; **2** (*abrangência – de assunto*) extent.

amplificação *f* (*aumento*) enlargement; **2** (*de som*) amplification; **3** (*de ângulo*) widening; **4** (*discurso*) emphasis.

amplificador *m* (*de som*) amplifier.

amplificador,-ora *adj* amplifying; **2** (*ótica*) magnifying.

amplificar *vt* to amplify; **2** widen; **3** to extend.

amplitude *f* (*TEC*) amplitude; spaciousness; extent;

amplo,-a *adj* ample, spacious; **2** numerous; far-reaching.

ampola (= **empola**) *f* blister; vesicle; **2** (*MED*) ampoule, vial.

ampulheta *f* sandglass.

amputar *vt* to amputate.

amuado,-a *adj* sulky, sullen, sulking; **ele está ~** he is sulking.

amuar *vi* to sulk.

amuleto *m* amulet, talisman.

amuo *m* sulkiness.

amurada *f* main rail; wall.

anã *f* female dwarf; (*Vd:* **anão**).

anacronismo *m* anachronism.

anafado,-a *adj* well-fed.

anafar *vt* to fatten (up).

anagrama *m* anagram.

anágua *m* (*tipo de saia*) white petticoat.

anais *mpl* annals.

anal *adj inv* (*ANAT*) (*esfíncter*) anal; **2** (*fístula*) anal.

analfabetismo *m* illiteracy.

analfabeto,-a *m,f* illiterate; ♦ *adj* ignorant.

analgésico *m* (*remédio*) pain killer, analgesic; ♦ **analgésico,-a** *adj* analgesic.

analgia *f* analgesia.

analisar *vt* to analyse.
análise *f (gen)* analysis; **2** *(LÍNG)* parsing; **3** *(MED)* test.
analista *m,f* analyst.
analítico,-a *adj* analytical.
analogia *f* analogy.
análogo,-a *adj* analogous.
ananás *m (EP)* pineapple.
anão, anã *m,f* dwarf.
anarquia *f* anarchy.
anarquista *m,f* anarchist.
anátema *m* anathema.
anatomia *f* anatomy.
anca *f (ANAT) (quadril)* hip; **2** *(fig)* haunch; **3** *(de cavalo)* hindquarters.
ancestral *m* predecessor; **2** ~**ais** *mpl* ancestors; ◆ *adj inv* ancestral; **nossa história** ~ our ancestry.
ancho,-a *adj* broad; **2** conceited.
anchova *f* anchovy.
ancião, anciã *(mpl:* **anciãos, anciães, anciões)** *(fpl:* **anciãs)** *m,f* old man/woman; elder; ◆ *adj* elderly.
ancinho *m (ferramenta de lavoura)* rake.
âncora *f (NÁUT)* anchor; **2** prop, support.
ancoradouro *m* berth; anchorage, pier.
ancorar *vt/vi* to anchor.
andaime, andaimo *m* scaffolding.
andamento *m (prosseguimento)* progress; **2** *(MÚS)* movement, tempo; **3** *(veiculo)* under way, running; **o carro estava em** ~ the car was under way, the car slid into gear; **4** *(ritmo)* pace, pacing; **5** *(modo de andar)* gait *(person, horse)*; **6** *(empreendimento)* development; **7** course; **o** ~ **natural das coisas** the course of nature.
andança *f* walk, pacing; **2** gait, manner of walking; **3** *(fig) (trabalho)* toil; everyday chores; IDIOM **andar sempre nas** ~**s** to be always on the hop.
andante *m,f* walker, transient; ◆ *adj inv* errant, wandering; **o cavaleiro** ~ the wandering knight.
andar *m* flat, apartment, flat, floor, storey; **vivo no 1°** ~ I live on the 1st floor; **ela comprou um** ~ she bought a flat; **é um edifício de quatro** ~**es** it is a four-storey building; **2** *(maneira de caminhar) (pessoa, cavalo)* gait, walk; **3** progress; **com o** ~ **dos tempos** as time goes by; ◆ *vi (movimentar-se em relação à distância e ao tempo)* to go, travel; ~ **de** *(transporte)* travel, go by; ~ **avião/barco/comboio** travel by air/plane/train; ~ **de carro** drive; *(caminhar)* to walk; ~ **a pé** to walk, go on foot; ~ **a cavalo** to ride, go on horseback; **2** *(durante um período)* to be; ~ **triste** to be sad; ~ **grávida** to be pregnant; ~ **a estudar** to be studying; **ando a jardinar** I am gardening *or* I have been gardening; **ele anda à procura do gato** he is looking for the cat *or* he has been looking for the cat; **3** *(funcionar)* **o relógio não anda** the watch/clock isn't working; **os planos andam ou não?** are the plans going forward or not; **4** *(modo de estar/vestir)* **ele anda sempre de calções** he is always in shorts; **5** ~ **com alguém** *(conviver)* go out with sb; **ir andando** to be on one's way; ◆ *exc* **anda!** come on!
andarilho *m,f* fast walker; rambler; **2** *(dated) (lacaio)* footman; **3** **o** ~ **do bebé** baby walker.

andar-modelo *m* apartment on view.
andas *fpl* stilts.
andebol *m (DESP)* handball.
Andes *npr:* **os** ~ the Andes.
andino,-a Andean.
andor *m (veículo em procissão)* litter for carrying images of saints.
andorinha *f (ZOOL)* swallow.
Andorra *npr:* **(o principado de)** ~ (the principality of) Andorra.
andrajos *mpl* rags, tatters.
andrajoso,-a *adj* ragged, tattered.
andrógino,-a *adj* androgynous.
andropausa *f (MED)* male menopause.
anedota *f* anecdote, joke.
anedótico,-a *adj* amusing, funny; **2** *(episódio, evento)* anedoctal.
anel *m (para o dedo)* ring; ~ **de casamento** wedding ring; **2** *(de corrente)* link; **3** *(cabelo)* curl, lock, ringlet.
anelado,-a *adj (cabelo)* curly, in curls.
anelante *adj (ofegante)* panting, breathless; **2** *(fig)* anxious; yearning.
anelar¹ *vt (dar feitio de anel)* to curl *(cabelo)*; ◆ *adj inv (= anular) (forma de anel)* annular; **dedo** ~ ring finger.
anelar² *vi* ~ **por** to pant, gasp for breath; **2** *(desejar)* to yearn, crave **(por** for).
anelo *m* craving, aspiration.
anemia *f* anaemia.
anémico,-a *(BR:* -**nê**-*)* *adj* anaemic.
anémona *f (BOT)* anemone.
anestesiado,-a *adj (paciente)* anaesthetized/ised.
anestesiar *vt (MED)* anaesthetize/tise.
anestésico *m (MED)* anaesthetic; ◆ **anestésico,-a** *adj* anaesthetising.
anestesista *m,f* anaesthetist.
anexação *f (documentos)* attachment; **2** *(de terras)* annexation.
anexar *vt* to annex; **2** *(COMP)* attach; **3** *(CONSTR)* add, build on.
anexo,-a *m* annex; ◆ *adj* enclosed; **2** *(COMP)* attached.
anfetamina *f (FARM)* amphetamine.
anfíbio,-a *adj* amphibious.
anfiteatro *m* amphitheatre *(UK)*; amphitheater *(US)*; **2** *(na universidade)* lecture hall.
anfitrião, anfitriã *m,f* host, hostess.
ânfora *f* amphora.
angariação *f (dinheiro)* fund raising.
angariar *vt* to collect, get; **2** *(dinheiro, fundos)* to raise; **3** ~ **votos** to canvass for; **4** *(recrutar)* enlist; **5** *(fig)* attract, entice *(amizades)*.
angélico,-a *adj* angelic.
angina *f (MED)* ~ **de peito** angina (pectoris); **2** ~**s** *fpl (garganta)* inflammation of the throat, tonsillitis, quinsy.
angioma *m (MED)* angioma, swelling.
anglicanismo *m* Anglicanism.
anglicano,-a *m,f adj (REL)* Anglican; **igreja** ~**a** Anglican Church.
anglicismo *m* Anglicism.
anglófilo,-a *m,f adj* anglophile.

anglófono,-a *m,f* English speaker; ♦ *adj* English-speaking.

anglo-saxónico,-a *adj* Anglo-Saxon.

Angola *npr (República de Angola)* Angola; **em ~** in Angola.

angolano,-a, angolense *m,f adj* Angolan.

> Angola is a republic in SW Africa, on the Atlantic, which includes the enclave of Cabinda. It was discovered by Portuguese navigators in 1482. In 1975, Angola gained its independence from Portugal and is now a member of the CPLP (community of Portuguese-speaking countries). It has one of the fastest-growing economies in Africa. Capital: Luanda.

---

angra *f* bay, cove.

angrense *m,f adj* of/from Angra do Heroísmo (capital of Terceira Island in Azores).

angular *adj* angular; **pedra ~** cornerstone.

ângulo *m* angle; corner.

angústia *f* agony; anguish.

angustiado,-a *adj* anxious; troubled.

angustiar *vt* to cause distress to, worry sb; ♦ **~-se** *vr* upset o.s.; **~-se com algo** to become distressed by sth; **~-se de/por** to be distressed.

angustioso,-a *adj* distressing.

anho *m* lamb.

anil *m (BOT)* indigo plant; *(cor)* indigo.

anilha *f (ger)* ring; **2** *(MEC) (para a torneira)* washer; **3** *(aro)* metal band; **4** identification ring; **5** *(fam)* wedding band.

animação *f* liveliness, bustle, activity; **2** spirit; **ela tem muita ~** she has a lot of spirit; **3** activities; **~ sócio-cultural** socio-cultural acitivities; **4** *(entretimento)* show.

animado,-a *adj* lively; **2** cheerful; **3** *(CIN)* **desenhos ~s** cartoons, animated film.

animador,-ora *m,f* TV presenter; activity leader; ♦ *adj* encouraging; **ele é o ~ da festa** he is the life and soul of the party.

animal *(pl: -ais) m (ZOOL)* animal; **2** *(doméstico)* **~ de estimação** pet; **~ de criação** livestock; **3** *(fig)* brute, animal.

animar *vt (ger)* to liven up; **2** *(encorajar)* **~ alguém a** to encourage sb to; **3** *(fomentar comércio)* to foment; ♦ **~-se** *vr* to become enthusiastic; **2** *(tomar coragem)* to buck up, take heart; **~-se a** to bring o.s. to; to resolve to (do sth); **3** *(alegrar-se)* to cheer up; **4** liven up, brighten up.

ânimo *m* courage; **2** *(temperamento)* spirit; **com bom ~** in good spirits; **recobrar ~** to recover one's spirits; **de ~ leve** *adv* light-hearted; ♦ **ânimo!** *exc* cheer up! courage!

animosidade *f* animosity; bitterness.

animoso,-a *adj* courageous, brave.

aninhar *vt* to nest *(crias)*; *(fig) (aconchegar)* to cuddle up *(alguém, sb)*; ♦ *vi* build a nest; ♦ **~-se** *vr (be in nest)* to nestle; **2** *(fig) (person)* snuggle up, to cuddle up; **ela aninhou-se ao marido** she snuggled up to her husband.

aniquilação *f* annihilation; destruction.

aniquilar *vt* to annihilate; to destroy.

anis *m* aniseed.

anistia *(Vd: amnistia)*.

aniversário *m* anniversary; **~ de casamento** wedding anniversary; **~ natalício** birthday.

anjo *m* angel; **~-da-guarda** guardian angel; **2** *(fig) (pessoa boa)* **ela é um ~** she is an angel.

ano *m* year; **~ bissexto** leap year; **~-bom** *(pl: anos bons)* New Year; **Feliz A~ Novo!** Happy New Year; **~ fiscal** tax year; **~ le(c)tivo** academic year; **o ~ passado** last year; **no próximo ~** next year; **por ~** per annum; **fazer ~s** to have a birthday; **ter vinte ~s** be twenty (years old).

anões *mpl* = **anão.**

anoitecer *vi* to grow dark; *m* nightfall; **ao ~** at nightfall.

ano-luz *(pl: anos-luz) m* light year.

anomalia *f* anomaly.

anómalo,-a *(BR: -nô-) adj* anomalous.

anonimato *m* anonymity.

anónimo,-a *(BR: -nô-) adj* anonymous; **2** *(COM)* **sociedade ~a** limited company; *(US)* stock company.

anoraque *m* anorak.

anorexia *f* anorexia.

anoréxico,-a *adj* anorexic.

anormal *adj inv* abnormal; **2** irregular; **3** unusual, **é uma situação ~** it is an unusual situation.

anotação *f* annotation; *(apontamento)* note.

anotar *vt (apontar)* to note down; **2** to annotate; write down *(comments)*.

ânsia *f* anxiety; **2** longing; **~ de aprender** thirst for knowledge.

ansiar *vi*: **~ por** to yearn for; to long to.

ansiedade *f* anxiety; **2** eagerness.

ansioso,-a *adj* anxious; eager; **estou ~ por te ver** I'm looking forward to seeing you.

anta *f (ARQ)* dolmen; **2** *(ZOOL)* tapir.

antagónico,-a *(BR: -gô-) adj* antagonistic; opposing; **2** *(opiniões, interesses)* conflicting.

antagonismo *m* antagonism; opposition.

antagonista *m,f* antagonist; opponent.

antanho *adv (LITER)* in bygone days; **tempos de ~** in the good old days.

antárctico, antártico *npr o* **A~** *(oceano)* the Antarctic (ocean); ♦ *adj (clima, região, continente)* Antarctic.

Antárctida, Antártida *npr* **a ~** Antarctica.

ante *prep (em frente de)* before; in the presence of, faced with.

antebraço *m* forearm.

antecâmara *f* ante-chamber; **2** waiting-room; **3** *(NÁUT)* cuddy.

antecedência *f* priority; precedence; **com ~** in advance; **com duas semanas de ~** two weeks beforehand.

antecedente *m (precedente)* predecessor; **2** *(LÍNG)* antecedent; *(MAT)* first; ♦ *adj inv (alguém)* previous; *(data, tempo)* prior to; preceding; ♦ **os antecedentes** *mpl* (HIST) *(detalhes do passado)* antecedents, history; *(pessoais)* track record, medical record *sg*; background *sg*; **~ criminais** criminal record *sg*.

anteceder *vt* to precede, go before; **~ a** to precede.

antecessor,-ora *m,f* predecessor; ♦ *adj* preceding.

antecipação *f* anticipation; **2** bringing forward, forestalling; **3** advance payment; **4** expectation, **com dois meses de** ~ two months ahead of time.

antecipadamente *adv* in advance, beforehand.

antecipar *vt* to anticipate, forestall; **2** to bring forward; **3** to expect; ♦ **~-se** *vr* to be early.

antedatar *vt (cheque, etc)* to predate; set an earlier date for.

ante-estreia *f (CIN)* preview.

antemão *adv* **de** ~ beforehand.

antena *f (BIO)* antenna, feeler; **2** *(FÍS)* aerial; ~ **da televisão** television aerial; ~ **parabólica** satelite dish.

antenome *m (BR)* first name; **2** title.

anteontem *adv* the day before yesterday.

anteparar *vt* to put (sth) in front as a shield, protection; **2** to bring *(a horse etc)* to a sudden stop.

anteparo *m (resguardo)* screen; **2** *(fence)* tapume.

antepassado,-a *m* ancestor; **~s** *pl* ancestors, forefathers; ♦ *adj* ancestral.

antepor *vt* to put/set sth before/ahead sth; **2** give preference; **3** *(contrapor)* put against *(proof)*; ♦ **~-se** *vr (antecipar-se)* to forestall; **ele antepôs-se às perguntas** he forestalled the questions; **2** to place o.s. before another.

anteproje(c)to *m* draft, groundwork.

anteproposta *f* preliminary proposal.

anterior *adj* before; previous; former; ~ **a** prior to.

anterioridade *f* priority; precedent.

anteriormente *adv* previously; formerly; **2** before.

antes *adv* before; beforehand; first; **cheguei** ~ I arrived first; **quanto** ~ as soon as possible; **2** (tempo) ~ **havia** in the old days there was/were; **3** rather; **eu** ~ **quero morrer** I would rather die; **4** ~ **pelo contrário** on the contrary; ♦ *prep* ~ **de** before; ~ **do tempo** ahead of time; ~ **de tudo** first of all; ♦ *conj* ~ **que** before; ~ **que seja tarde** before it is too late.

antessala *f* anteroom; *(sala de espera)* waiting room.

antestreia *f (CIN, TEAT)* preview, the day before the première.

antever *vt* to foresee.

antevéspera *f* the day before the eve.

antevisão *f* perception; **2** foresight.

anti *prefix* anti + *adj*.

antiaborto *adj inv* anti-abortion.

antiácido,-a *m adj* antacid.

antiaéreo,-a *adj* anti-aircraft; **abrigo** ~ air-raid shelter.

antibiótico,-a *m* antibiótico; ♦ *adj* antibiotic.

anticiclone *m* anticyclone.

anticlímax *m* anticlimax.

anticoagulante *adj inv* anti-clotting.

anticoncepcional, anticoncecional *(pl: -ais) m, adj* contraceptive.

anticongelante *m* antifreeze.

anticorpo *m (QUIM, ANAT)* antibody.

antidepressivo,-a *adj* antidepressant.

antiderrapante *adj inv* anti-skid.

antídoto *m* antidote.

antigalha *f* antique; **2** junk.

antigamente *adv* formerly; in the old days; years ago.

antigo,-a *adj (velho)* old; **2** *(época)* ancient; **cidade** ~**a** ancient city; **3** *(antecedente)* former *(director, governo)*; **à moda** ~**a** in the old-fashioned way.

antiguidade *f* antiquity, ancient times; seniority; **por ordem de** ~ in order of seniority; **~s** *fpl* antiques, antiquities.

anti-higiénico, antihigiénico,-a *(BR: -ê-) adj* unhygienic, unsanitary.

anti-histamínico, antihistamínico *m* antihistamine.

antihistamínico,-a *adj (medicamento, ação)* anti-allergic.

anti-horário, antihorário *adj* anticlockwise *(sentido, movimento)*.

antilhano,-a, *m,f adj* West Indian *(Caribean)*.

Antilhas *npr:* **as** ~ the West Indies.

antílope *m (ZOOL)* antelope.

antinuclear *adj* anti-nuclear.

antipatia *f* antipathy, dislike.

antipático,-a *adj (pessoa, sítio)* unpleasant; **2** unfriendly; **3** *(pessoa)* nasty.

antipatizar *vi:* ~ **com** to dislike; **antipatizo com ela** I dislike her, I can't stand her.

antipoluente *m* anti-pollution agent; ♦ *adj inv* anti-pollution.

antiquado,-a *adj* antiquated, old-fashioned; **2** out of date; **ele é** ~ he is old-fashioned; *(pop)* he is a square.

antiquário *m* antiquarian.

antiquíssimo,-a *(superl de* **antigo)** *adj* ancient, very old.

anti-racista, antirracista *adj inv* anti-racist.

anti-revolucionário,-a *adj* anti-revolutionary.

anti-roubo/antirroubo *m (dispositivo)* alarme; ♦ *adj inv (produto, acção)* against/protected against theft.

anti-rugas, antirrugas *adj inv (tecido, papel)* crease-free; **2** *(produto de beleza)* anti-wrinkle.

anti-semita, antissemita *m,f* anti-Semite.

anti-semítico,-a, antissemítico,-a *adj* anti-Semitic.

anti-séptico,-a, antissético,-a *m, adj* antiseptic.

anti-sísmico, antissísmico,-a *adj* earthquake-proof.

anti-social, antissocial *adj inv* anti-social.

antitabagismo *m* anti-smoking.

antitabagista *m,f* anti-smoker; ♦ *adj inv* anti-smoking.

antítese *f* antithesis, the direct opposite.

antitoxina *f* antitoxin.

anti-vírus, antivírus *m (BIOL, FARM)* anti-virus; **2** *(COMP)* anti-virus programme.

antojo *m (desejo veemente)* craving; **2** *(capricho)* whim; **3** *(nojo)* disgust.

antolhos *mpl (palas postas nos lados dos animais)* blinkers; **2** *(fig)* fancies, whims.

antologia *f* anthology.

antónimo *m* antonym.

antracite *f (GEOL)* anthracite, stone-coal.

antraz *m (MED, VET) (mosca parasita)* anthrax; **2** *(que afecta os gados)* anthrax, foot and mouth disease.

antro *m* cave, cavern; **2** *(de animal)* lair; **3** *(bandidos)* den.

antropófago,-a *m,f* cannibal.

antropologia *f* anthropology.

antropólogo,-a *m,f* anthropologist.

antropónimo *(BR: -ô-) m* anthroponym.

ANTT (*abr de* **Arquivos Nacionais da Torre do Tombo**) Portuguese National Archives.

Antuérpia *npr* Antwerp.

anual *adj* annual, yearly.

anuário *m* yearbook, directory.

anuência *f* consent.

anuidade *f* annuity; annual payment, annual fee.

anuir *vi*: ~ **a** to agree to; **2** to assent; ~ **com** to comply with.

anulação *f* (*casamento*) annulment; **2** cancellation, invalidation.

anular *m* (*dedo*) ring, finger; ♦ *vt* to annul; **2** (*pena*) to revoke, to rescind; **3** (*invalidar*) to cancel, cancel out, nullify; **4** (*suprimir*) suppress.

anunciante *m* (COM) advertiser.

anunciar *vt* to advertise; to report; to announce; **2** (*rádio, TV*) to broadcast.

anúncio *m* (COM) advertisement; **2** announcement; **3** poster; **4** ~**s classificados** classifieds; **5** ~ **luminoso** neon sign.

ânus *m* (ANAT) anus.

anuviar *vt* to cloud; **2** to darken; ♦ ~-**se** *vr* to cloud over; to grow dark.

anverso *m* obverse.

anzol (*pl*: -**zóis**) *m* fish-hook; **2** (*fig*) bait; **cair no** ~ to swallow the bait, be tricked.

ao (= **a** + **o**) to/at the; in/on; by ~ **acaso** at random; ~ **alcance** within reach; ~ **ar livre** in the open air; **vou ao banco** I am going to the bank; **falar** ~ **telefone** speak on the telephone; ~ **invés** instead of; ~ **passo que** *conj* whereas, while.

aonde *adv* where … to; ~ **vais hoje à noite?** where are you going tonight?; ~ **quer que estejas** wherever you may be.

aorta *f* aorta; **croça da** ~ arch of the aorta.

aos (= **a** + **os**) to/at the; **eles dão esmolas aos mendigos** they give alms (charity) to the beggars.

Ap. (*abr de* **apartamento**) flat, apartment.

apadrinhar *vt* to be a godfather to; **2** (*casamento*) be best man to (*bridegroom*); **3** to protect, support, foster; ~ **um projecto** to foster a project.

apagado,-a *adj* (*fogo, chama*) out, extinguished; **2** (*luz, fogão*) switched off; **3** (*cor*) faded; **4** (*fig*) (*pessoa*) quiet, unobtrusive (*pessoa*); **5** (*expressão*) dull; **ela tem um olhar** ~ she has a lifeless expression in her eyes; **6** (*fig*) (*memória*) erased, wiped out.

apagador *m* (*de quadro preto*) duster; (*de quadro branco*) board eraser; **2** (COMP) eraser; ~ **de memória** bulk eraser; **3** extinguisher.

apagão *m* (*eletricidade*) power cut; **2** ~ **geral** (*país, mundo em hora determinada*) general/global blackout.

apagar *vt* to put out (*fogo, lume, luz*); **2** to switch off, turn out (*luz, fogão*); **3** extinguish (*fogo*); **4** to clean; **5** (*quadro preto/branco*) wipe; **6** to blow out (*vela*); **7** (COMP) to delete; ♦ *vi* (*com borracha, apagador*) rub out, erase; ♦ ~-**se** *vr* (*fogo, lume*) go out, die out; **o fogo apagou-se** the fire went out; **2** (*fig*) (*morrer*) die; **3** (*desvanecer-se*) fade away.

apainelado *m* panelling; ♦ **apainelado,-a** *adj* (*paredes*) panelled, with panels.

apaixonado,-a *adj* passionate; in love with; biased; **ela está** ~**a pelo João** she is mad about John; ♦ ~-**se** (**por**) *vr* to fall in love with.

apalermado,-a *adj* like an idiot; **2** idiotic; **ele é meio-**~ he is a bit of an idiot; **3** (*chocado*) aghast, **fiquei** ~ I was dumbfounded.

apalhaçado,-a *adj* like a clown; clownish.

apaladado,-a *adj* (*comida*) tasty.

apalavrado,-a *adj* (*sob palavra*) agreed upon (*casamento, negócios*).

apalear *vt* to beat (with a stick), to spank.

apalpadela *f* touch; **2** (*fig*) (*em busca*) survey; **andar às** ~**s** to grope about/fumble one's way.

apalpão *m* big pinch.

apalpar *vt* to touch, feel; **2** (*fig, fam*) (*sondar*) probe, search; **3** (MED) examine; ~ **o rabo** pinch sb's bottom; (*fam*) sb's bum; ♦ ~-**se** *vr* examine, feel one's own body.

apanágio *m* (JUR) (*pensão de alimentos a viúvos, etc*) apanage; **2** privilege, attribute.

apanha *f* harvest, ~ **da azeitona** olive harvest; **2** picking; **3** ~ **dos morangos** strawberry picking; **3** rounding up.

apanhar *vt* (*gen*) to catch; ~ **uma constipação** (EP) to catch a cold; **2** to pick up (**do chão**, from the floor); **3** (*fruto*) to gather; **4** (*castigo, experiência*) to get; **5** ~ **sol** to sunbathe.

apanhado,-a (*gatuno,-a*) caught red-handed.

apaniguado,-a *m,f* follower, adept, adherent; **2** favourite, protégé.

apara *f* (*de madeira*) woodchip, shaving; **2** (*de papel*) shred.

aparador *m* sideboard, dresser.

apara-lápis *m* pencil sharpener.

aparar *vt* (*cabelo, papel*) to trim, cut; (*unhas*) clip; **2** (*desbastar madeira*) to pare; **3** (*árvores*) prune, lop; **4** (*lápis, etc*) sharpen; **5** (*ataque*) parry, ward off; **6** to plane off; **7** (*fig*) to tolerate; **8** (*fig*) ~ **algo** to smooth out sth.

aparato *m* (*cerimónia*) pomp, show; **exibir grande** ~ to make a great display; **2** (*conjunto de dispositivos*) apparatus.

aparecer *vi* (*ger*) to appear; **2** to turn up; **as jóias já apareceram** the jewels have been found; ~ **em casa de alguém** to drop in, pop over; **3** (*publicar-se*) be published, come out; IDIOM **quem não aparece se esquece** out of sight out of mind.

aparecimento *m* appearance; **2** (*coisa nova*) novelty; **3** publication; **4** arrival; **5** (*surgimento*) emergence.

aparelhagem *f* equipment, tools, apparatus; **2** (*de som*) sound production apparatus, system; ~ **de alta fidelidade** hi-fi; **3** (*da madeira*) priming; **4** (NÁUT) rigging **5** (*fig*) trappings.

aparelhar *vt* to equip; **2** (CONSTR) prime, plane; **3** to saddle, harness; **4** (NÁUT) to rig; **5** (*fig*) prepare; ♦ ~-**se** *vr* to equip o.s.

aparelho *m* apparatus, equipment, tools; ~ **de escuta** listening apparatus; **2** (*de pesca*) fishing tackle; **3**

(de caça) hunting gear; **4** *(máquina)* machine, kit, appliance; ~ **de barbear** shaving kit; ~ **eletro-doméstico** electrical appliance; **5** ~ **de lavoura** farm implements; **6** ~ **de gesso** plaster cast; **7** *(ANAT)* system; ~ **digestivo** digestive system; ~ **fonador** voice box; **8** *(conjunto)* set; ~ **de rádio/TV** radio/TV set; **9** *(dental)* braces; **10** *(MIL)* trappings.

aparência *f* appearance; aspect; **na** ~ apparently; **manter as** ~**s** to keep up appearances; **sob a** ~ **de** under the guise of.

aparentado,-a *adj (alguém)* related to; **2** resemble; **3 bem** ~ well connected.

aparentar *vt* to look, seem, appear; **ele aparenta ter uns 40 anos** he appears to be around 40 years old ♦ *vr:* ~**-se com** to be, become related to.

aparente *adj* apparent.

aparentemente *adv* apparently.

aparição *f* apparition, ghost.

aparo *m* (pen) nib.

apart. *(abr de* **apartamento)** apartment; flat.

apartado,-a *m (poste restante)* P.O. Box; ♦ *adj (distante)* secluded; distant; **2** *(separado)* parted; away from; **eles estão** ~**s** they are separated/away from each other.

apartamento *m* apartment, flat.

apartar *vt* to separate; to set aside; ♦ ~**-se** *vr* to separate, to be apart; **2** *(animal)* wean; **3** *(separar-se)* ~**-se de** to split, go away from; **4** ~**-se do assunto** to digress, get away from the subject.

aparte *m (em discurso, conversa)* interruption; **2** *(TEAT) (algo dito por um actor, enquanto o outro fala)* aside.

à parte loc adv apart, aside; **pôr uma coisa** ~ to set something apart/aside; IDIOM **amigos, amigos, negócios** ~ don't mix business with pleasure.

aparvalhado *adj* foolish; **2** stupefied; **ficar** ~ to feel like a fool; **ficar** ~ **com a notícia** to be aghast at the news.

apascentar *vt* to take cattle to pasture/to graze.

apatia *f* apathy.

apático,-a *adj* apathetic; indifferent.

apátrida *m,f* stateless person.

apavorado,-a *adj* terror-stricken.

apavorar *vt* to terrify; ♦ ~**-se** *vr* to be afraid, terrified of.

apaziguamento *m* appeasement; pacification.

apaziguar *vt* to appease; to pacify; ♦ ~**-se** *vr* to calm down.

apeadeiro *m (comboio)* stop, halt; **2** small (railway) wayside station.

apear-se *vr* ~ **de** to dismount from; **2** to alight, get off.

apedido *m (BR)* newspaper article, statement or advertisement published at request of, or paid for by, the author.

apedrejar *vt (atirar pedras)* to stone, throw stones.

apeirar *vt* to attach the oxen to the plough.

apegado,-a *adj (afeiçoado)* attached to; **2** adjoining.

apegar-se *vr* to stick (a to), cling (a to); **2** to become devoted to.

apego *m (afeição)* fondness (a, to); **2** attachment; **ter** ~ **às coisas** to be attached to things; **3** *(tarefa)* **com** ~ in earnest.

apelação *f (JUR)* appeal.

apelante *m,f* appellant, petitioner.

apelar *vi:* *(pedir)* to appeal (**a** to) *(compreensão, generosidade)*; **2** *(solicitar)* call for, solicit; **3** *(invocar)* call upon; **4** *(JUR) (recorrer)* appeal; ~ **da sentença** appeal against a sentence; ~ **para o Supremo Tribunal,** to appeal to the High Court; **4** *(BR)* ~ **para** *(ação) (col)* turn nasty.

apelativo *m (LÍNG)* appellative; ♦ *adj (atrativo)* appealing.

apelidar *vt* to name *(pessoa, animal, algo)*; to give a surname to *(alguém)*; **3** *(alcunhar)* to nickname, name; **apelidaram-no de Manel Trouxa** they nicknamed him Manel the Fool; ♦ *vr:* ~**-se de** to go by the name of.

apelido *m* surname; **2** *(alcunha)* nickname.

apelo *m* appeal.

apenas *adv* only; just; ♦ *conj* as soon as; ~ **tinha partido quando** … no sooner had he left when …

apêndice *m* appendix; supplement; **2** *(BOT, ANAT)* appendix; **3** *(ZOOL) (de elefante etc)* appendage.

apendicite *f* appendicitis.

apenso,-a *m* part added to a play; ♦ *adj (documento)* appended, added.

aperaltar(-se) *vr (enfeitar-se)* to dress up.

aperceber *vt (avistar)* distinguish *(vulto)*; ♦ ~**-se** to realize (**de**); **2** *(notar)* notice; **3** to become aware (**de** of).

aperfeiçoamento *m* perfection; **2** improvement; **curso de** ~ training/post-graduation course.

aperfeiçoar *vt* to perfect; **2** to improve; ♦ ~**-se** *vr* to improve o.s.

aperitivo *m* aperitif; appetizer.

aperrar *vt* to cock (a gun).

aperreado,-a *adj (pessoa)* harassed, vexed.

aperrear *vt* to bully, harass; **2** *(açular)* tease, instigate *(cães)*; **3** *(constranger)* constrain, squeeze *(alguém)*.

apertado,-a *adj* tight; **a blusa está-me** ~**a** the blouse is tight on me; **2** narrow; **3** *(em lugar)* squeezed in; **4** *(reduzido: tempo)* short; pressing, urgent; **5** *(sovina)* stingy; **6** *(difícil)* hard; **tempos** ~**s** hard times.

apertão *m* tight squeeze; **2** tightly packed crowd.

apertar *vt* to fasten; ~ **o cinto** to fasten the belt; **2** to squeeze, tighten; **3** ~ **alguém, algo** *(segurar)* clasp, hold sb, sth; **4** shake ~ **a mão a** to shake hands with; **5** *(gatilho)* to pull; **6** *(agarrar com força)* to grip; **7** *(segurança)* step up; **8** *(apressar)* ~ **o passo** to speed up; **9** *(fig) (testemunha)* to put pressure on, insist; **10** *(fig)* ~ **o coração** *(fig) (ter pena)* to wring one's heart; ♦ *vi (roupa, sapatos)* to be tight; to pinch; **os sapatos apertam-me** the shoes are tight on me, they pinch me; **2** *(escassear)* be short; ♦ ~**-se** *vr* to squeeze o.s. into; **2** *(fig) (reduzir gastos)* economize; IDIOM ~ **o cinto** to tighten one's belt; ~ **os cordões à bolsa** to tighten one's purse strings.

aperto *m* pressure; **2** *(shake)* **um ~ de mão** a handshake; **3** *(fig)* trouble, problem; **estou num aperto** I am in a tight spot; **passar um ~** to have a rough time; *(sem dinheiro)* hardship; **4** *(de multidão)* crowd; **evitar ~s** to avoid crowds; **5** *(difícil)* hard, difficult; **vai ser um ~ para acabar esta obra** it's going to be hard, to be a squeeze to finish this work.

apesar *prep*: **~ de** in spite of, despite; **~ disso** nevertheless; ♦ *conj.* **~ de que** despite that, even though; **~ de que não gosto** even though I don't like (it); **~ disso** nevertheless.

apessoado,-a *adj* person with good demeanour; **2** elegant; **homem bem ~** man held in esteem.

apetecer *vt* to feel like, to fancy; **2** *(ter desejos de)* crave for; **apetece-me comer lagosta** I crave for (eating) lobster **2** to fancy; **apetece-me ir ao teatro** I feel like going to the theatre; **3** to be inviting, tempting; **hoje o dia apetece passear** today the day makes one feel like walking, going for a walk.

apetecível *adj* appetizing; **2** tempting; desirable.

apetite *m* appetite; desire; ambition.

apetitoso,-a *adj* appetizing; tempting.

apetrechar *vt* to fit out, equip sb/sth with.

apetrechos *mpl* equipment *sg*; outfit *sg*; utensils; appliances; **~ de pesca** fishing-tackle.

APH *(abr de Academia Portuguesa de História)* Portuguese Academy of History.

ápice *m* summit, top; **2** apex; **num ~** in a trice, in a tick.

apicultura *f* bee-keeping; apiculture.

apiedar-se *vr*: **~ de** to pity; to take pity, compassion on.

apimentado,-a *adj* peppery; *(fig)* spicy.

apimentar *vt* to pepper, spice.

apinhado,-a *adj* crowded, chock-a-block.

apinhar *vt* *(amontoar)* to heap up, pile up *(objetos)*; **2** *(pessoas)* to press together, to crowd; ♦ **~-se** *vr* to crowd, swarm; **a gente apinhou-se para ver …** people swarmed/crowded to see …

apitar *vi* to whistle.

apito *m* whistle.

aplacar *vt* to placate; **2** to assuage; **3** mitigate; **4** subdue; ♦ *vi* to die down; ♦ **~-se** *vr* to calm down, abate.

aplainar *vt* *(nivelar)* to level out, to smooth; **2** *(madeira)* to plane.

aplanar *vt* *(terreno)* to level, flatten; **2** *(amenizar)* to smooth out, iron out *(dificuldades)*.

aplaudir *vt* to applaud, to cheer.

aplauso *m* applause; praise; **2** acclaim *(filme)*; **3** *(fig)* approval.

aplicação *f* application; **~ de uma pomada no joelho** application of an ointment on the knee; **2** *(estudo, trabalho)* effort; **3** *(bordado)* appliqué; **4** *(enfeite)* adornment, applications; **5** *(banco)* investment; **6 ~ da lei** enforcement.

aplicado,-a *adj* hard-working, diligent; **2** *(ligadura, remédio)* applied to sth; **3** *(FIN)* **bem ~** *(dinheiro, investment)* well-spent.

aplicar *vt* *(ger)* to apply sth on another, lay on; **2** *(regras)* enforce, give; **~ uma lei** to enforce a law;

ele aplicou-lhe uma multa he gave her/him a fine; **3** *(ECON) (fundos)* to invest; ♦ *vr*: **~-se a** *(esforçar-se)* to devote o.s. to, apply o.s. to; **ele aplicou-se muito ao trabalho** he worked very hard.

> Not '**apply**' for a job, course, competition, which is 'candidatar-se a', 'inscrever-se em'; 'matricular-se em' (escola, universidade).

aplicativo,-a *adj* adequate, appropriate; **2** *(COMP)* **programa ~** application.

aplicável *adj inv* applicable, relevant.

apneia *f* *(suspensão momentânea da respiração)* apnoea *(UK)*, apnea *(US)*.

Apocalíse *npr* Apocalypse; **2** *(fig)* apocalypse.

apocalíptico,-a *adj* apocalyptic.

apoderar-se *vr*: **~ de** to seize, take possession of, get hold of; **~ de bens** to appropriate.

apodo *m* nickname; **2** taunt, jeer.

apodrecer *vt* to rot; **2** to corrupt; ♦ *vi* to rot, decay.

apodrecimento *m* rottenness, decay; **2** *(fig)* corruption.

apogeu *m* *(ASTRON)* apogee; **2** *(fig) (auge)* summit, height, peak; heyday; **no ~ da sua carreira** at the height of his career.

apoiado,-a *adj* *(que tem apoio, baseado)* based; **história ~ em factos** story based on facts; ♦ *exc* **apoiado!** *(formal)* hear, hear!; well done!

apoiante *m,f adj inv* supporter, backer; who supports, sponsors; **2** backing, sponsoring.

apoiar *vt* to support, encourage; **2** *(fig)* to back up; **3** to second; ♦ *vr*: **~-se em** to lean on, rest on.

apoio *m* prop, support; **2** aid; **3** *(fig)* backing, approval; **4** *(cultural)* sponsorship.

apólice *f* *(documento)* policy, certificate; **~ de seguro** insurance policy; **2** *(acção)* bond, stock.

apolítico,-a *adj* apolitical.

apologia eulogy; **2** *(defesa)* apology.

apontador *m* overseer; **2** *(de jogo)* marker; **3** *(teatro)* prompter.

apontamento *m* note; **2** minute; **3** draft; **tomar ~s** to jot down the minutes, notes.

> Not '**appointment**' in the sense of a '**date**'.

apontar *vt* to aim; **2** to point (out); **3** to note down; **4** to nominate; **5** *(lápis)* to sharpen; **6 ~ para** *(arma)* to aim at; **7** *(com o dedo)* to point at; ♦ *vi* to begin to appear; **2** *(plantas, flores)* to come through, sprout; ♦ *exc* **apontar!** aim!

apoquentação *f* worry, anxiety.

apoquentado,-a *adj*; **estar ~** to be in distress.

apoquentar *vt* to worry; **2** to annoy, pester; ♦ **~-se** *vr* to be worried.

apor *vt* to stick on; **2** attach; **~ os bois ao carro** to attach the oxen to the cart; **3** *(JUR)* inserir, append *(condição)*.

aporrinhar *vt* to pester, annoy.

aportar *vi* *(navio)* to anchor, dock in; arrive, call *(port)*; **o navio aportou em/a Luanda** the ship called at Luanda.

aportuguesar *vt* to be Portuguese-like, to make it appear Portuguese.

após *prep* after.

aposentação (= **aposentadoria, aposentamento**) *f* *(reforma)* retirement; **2** *(vencimentos)* pension.

aposentado,-a *adj* retired; **ficar** ~ to be retired, be pensioned off.

aposentadoria *f* (*Vd:* **aposentação**).

aposentar(-se) *vt/vr* to retire; pension off.

aposento *m* bedroom; **2** lodging; **os** ~**s da rainha** the queen's chambers.

apósito *m (MED)* dressing; ♦ **apósito,-a** *adj* apposite, appropriate.

apossar-se *vr:* ~ **de** to take possession of, seize.

aposta *f (dinheiro)* bet; **2** *(entre pessoas)* wager; **3** *(fig)* aim, faith (**em algo** in sth).

apostar *vt* to bet (**em** on); ~ **que** bet that; **2** *(fig) (confiar)* to trust, believe (**em** in); **3** *(fig)* investir, buy; ♦ ~**-se** *vr (resolver-se)* to decide; be determined; IDIOM ~ **no cavalo errado** to back the wrong horse.

apostate *m,f* renegade.

apóstolo *m* apostle.

apóstrofe *f (retórica)* apostrophe; **2** *(personificação)* invocation.

apóstrofo *m (marca de pontuação)* apostrophe.

apoteose *f* apotheosis.

apoucado,-a *adj* mean, base; **2** scanty.

apoucamento *m* humiliation.

apoucar *vt* to humiliate, belittle; **2** to lessen; ♦ ~**-se** *vr* to lower o.s.

aprazar *vt* to arrange, fix (a time/day); **2** to adjourn; **3** to convoke.

aprazer *vi* to please; **apraz-me fazer isto** I like doing this; **apraz-me saber isso** it pleases me to know that.

aprazível *(pl:* **aprazíveis***) adj* pleasant; **2** delightful; **um clima** ~ a pleasant/mild climate.

apre *exc (col) (irra)* damn!; dammit!

apreçar *vt* to value, to price; **apreçei a máquina na outra loja** I got the machine priced in another shop.

apreciação *f* appreciation; avaliation.

apreciar *vt* to appreciate; **2** value; **3** enjoy, like.

apreciativo,-a *adj* appreciative.

apreciável *adj* appreciable; considerable.

apreço *m* esteem, praise; consideration; **em** ~ under discussion.

apreender *vt (prender, confiscar)* to apprehend, arrest, seize; **2** to understand, grasp *(sentido)*.

apreensão *f* perception, comprehension; **2** *(acto de confiscar)* seizure, arrest; **3** *(preocupação)* apprehension.

apreensivo,-a *adj* apprehensive.

apregoar *vt (proclamar)* announce, proclaim; **2** *(fig)* boast; ♦ *vi (anunciar com pregão) (vendedor da rua)* to cry (one's wares in the street); **'laranjas baratas'** 'oranges going cheap'.

apregoeiro,-a *m,f* street crier; **2** *(arc)* town crier.

aprender *vt* to learn; ~ **de cor** to learn by heart; ~ **a ler** to learn to read; ~ **à sua custa** to learn from one's experience.

aprendiz,-iza *m,f* apprentice; beginner, learner; **aprendizado** *m* apprenticeship; **aprendizagem** *f* training; **2** learning.

apresar *vt (capturar)* to take prisoner, capture.

apresentação *f (mostra, entrega formal)* presentation; ~ **dos seus documentos** presenting his/her/your documents; **2** introduction; **carta de** ~ letter of introduction; **3** *(person)* bearing, appearance.

apresentador,-ora *adj (TV)* presenter; ~ **de um evento** master of ceremonies.

apresentar *vt* to present; show; exhibit; **2** to introduce; **quero apresentar-lhe** ... may I introduce you to ...; **3** *(exprimir, oferecer)* offer *(pêsames, cumprimentos, felicitações)*; **apresento as minhas condolências sinceras** I offer you my sincere condolences; **4** *(submeter ideia, proposta, reclamação)* to present, put forward; ♦ ~**-se** *vr (comparecer)* to appear, turn up; **2** *(parecer)* to seem; **3** ~ **a** *(outros)* to introduce o.s. to (others); **4** *(surgir)* present itself, arise *(oportunidade, negócio)*; **5** *(ter boa aparência)* to look, appear well; **ele apresenta-se sempre bem vestido** he always is, looks well dressed; **6** *(JUR)* to appear; **apresentar-se em juízo** to appear in court.

apresentador,-ora *adj (TV, programa)* presenter.

apressado,-a *adj* hurried, hasty; **estar** ~ to be in a hurry. **apressar** *vt* to hurry, hasten; ♦ ~**-se** *vr* to hurry (up).

apressurar *vt* to urge; **2** to hasten; ♦ ~**-se** *vr* to hurry (up).

aprestar *vt* to equip, fit out; **2** to get ready; ♦ ~**-se** *vr* to get ready.

aprestos *mpl* equipment *sg*, gear *sg*; **2** preparations.

aprisionado,-a *adj* imprisoned.

aprisionamento *m* imprisonment.

aprisionar *vt (apanhar)* to capture; **2** to imprison, arrest *(alguém)*.

aprofundar *vt (tornar fundo)* to deepen; **2** *(investigar, esclarecer)* to get to the bottom of sth, investigate, study in depth; **3** *(aumentar)* increase *(interesse)*; improve *(conhecimento)*; **4** ~ **o olhar em** to look more deeply at, stare at.

aprontar *vt* to get ready, prepare; ♦ ~**-se** *vr:* ~**-se para** to get ready to.

apropriação *f (tirar algo de alguém como seu)* appropriation, takeover; **2** *(tomada)* seizure; **3** *(adequação)* adjustment *(de custos)*; **4** suitability.

apropriado,-a *adj (adequado)* appropriate, suitable, fit; **2** *(tomado)* appropriated, seized.

apropriar *vt (adequar)* to adapt, suit; ♦ ~**-se (de)** *vr* to seize, take possession of; **2** to suit (situation)

aprovação *f* approval.

aprovado,-a *adj* approved; **2 ficar** ~ **num exame** to pass an exam; ♦ *exc* **aprovado!** agreed!; *(formal)* hear, hear!

aprovar *vt* to approve of; **2** to authorize; **3** pass *(aluno no exame)*; ♦ *vi* to approve; **2** *(lei)* pass.

aproveitamento *m* good use, utilization; **2** *(de um aluno)* progress.

aproveitar *vt* to profit by; **2** *(tirar vantagem; servir-se)* to use, make use of, take (good) advantage of; **aproveitou o bónus para comprar o carro** he used his bonus to buy his car; **3 já agora aproveito para comprar** … while I am at it, I am here, I may as well buy …; ♦ *vi* to be of use; ♦ *vr* **~-se de** *(servir-se)* to make use of, avail o.s. of; ♦ *vr* **~-se ao máximo de** to make the most of; **2** *(pej)* to take unfair advantage of; **ela aproveitou-se da minha bondade** she took advantage of my kindness.

aproveitável *adj inv* (recycling) reusable; **2** *(digno de ser aproveitado)* worth using *(ideia)*.

aprovisionamento *m* supply, provision.

aprovisionar *vt* to supply.

aproximação *f* approximation; approach; nearness, closeness.

aproximado,-a *adj* approximate; nearby.

aproximar *vt* to bring near, to bring together; ♦ *vr* **~-se de** to approach, come near; **2** **~ sem ruído** to steal up on sb.

aprumado,-a *adj* (vertical) straight; **2** *(fig)* *(pessoa)* upright, to behave correctly; **3** *(fig) (altivo)* haughty; **4** well groomed, elegant.

aprumo *m* straightness; uprightness; **2** *(compostura)* rectitude; **3** *(altivez)* haughtiness.

aptidão *f* aptitude, ability; **2** knack; **3** **~ para** knack for; **exame de ~** aptitude test; **~ física** physical fitness.

apto,-a *adj* apt; **2** suitable; **3** able, capable; **~ para o trabalho** able to work.

apunhalar *vt* to stab; to knife *(alguém)*; IDIOM **~ alguém pelas costas** stab someone in the back.

apupada *f (no futebol, teatro, políticos)* boo, jeer.

apupar *vt* to boo, jeer; **2** to hoot.

apupo *m (troça)* jeer; *(teatro, futebol)* boo, jeer; hooting; catcall.

apurado,-a *adj* refined; **2** fine, perfect; **comida ~a** food well seasoned; **3** *(escolhido)* selected; **4** *(sentidos)* sharp.

apuramento *m* perfection; **2** *(votos)* counting.

apurar *vt* to purify *(água, sangue)*; **2** refine; **3** to perfect *(estilo)*; **4** to sharpen *(ouvido, vista)*; **5** *(descobrir)* to find out, verify, glean; **6** *(votos)* to count; **7** *(lucros)* to get, gain; **8** *(contas)* to settle, adjust; **9** **~ a verdade** to ascertain the truth.

apuro *m* refinement, elegance; **2** hardship, difficulty; **meter-se em ~s** to get into trouble; **estar em ~s** to be in a fix, cash-strapped, to be hard up.

aquarela *(Vd: aguarela)*.

aquário *m* aquarium; **2** *(ASTRON, ASTROL)* Aquarius.

aquartelar *vt (MIL)* to billet, quarter; ♦ **~-se** *vr (fam)* to install o.s., to settle down.

aquático,-a *adj* aquatic, water; **esqui ~** aquatic ski.

aquecedor,-ora *m* heater; ♦ *adj* warming.

aquecer *vt* to heat, warm; IDIOM **isso não aquece nem arrefece** it is neither here nor there, it's all the same to me; ♦ **~-se** *vr* to grow warm, warm up; **2** *(discussão)* to become heated.

aquecimento *m* heating; **~ central** central heating; warming; **2** *(ECOL)* **~ global** global warming.

aquedar *vt* to calm, quieten.

aqueduto *m* aqueduct.

aquele, aquela, aqueles, aquelas *adj* that; *pl:* those; *(algo, alguém afastado do interlocutor)*; **aquela mulher** that woman *(over there)*; **2** *(determina uma certa pessoa que está ausente da conversa)* that; **~ idiota ainda não compreendeu** that idiot hasn't understood yet; *(pej)* **aqueles malvados** those bastards *(col)*; **3** *(tempo passado)* **aquele dia em que te vi** that day when I saw you; **4** *(ênfase)* that; **aquele comportamento foi indesculpável** that behaviour was inexcusable; ♦ *pron indef* that one, *(pl)* those; *(fam)* **aquela não me engana** I am not taken in by her/that one; **2** *(referência ao que foi dito)* **aquela tem piada!** that really is a joke!; **3** *(irónico)* that really is a joke!; IDIOM **sem mais aquelas** *adv (sem cerimónia)* without so much as a word, as much as by your leave.

àquele, àquela (= a + aquele,-a) *prep* to that, to that one.

aqueloutro,-a (= aquele + outro/a) that other one; **este, esse e ~** this, that and the other.

aquém *adv/prep* here; **2** on this side; **3** beneath; **4** **~ e além** here and there, on all sides; **5** *(abaixo de)* **estar ~ de** to be inferior to; not to come up to; **está ~ das minhas expectativas** it falls short of my expectations; ♦ **de ~-Minho** *adj (of, from)* this side of Minho *(rio)*; **~ de fronteiras** this side of the frontier.

aquentar *vt* to warm, heat; ♦ **~-se** *vr* to get warm.

áqueo,-a *adj* aqueous, watery.

aqui *adv (neste lugar)* here; **~ aqui** come here; **~ dentro** right inside/here; **2** *(neste ponto, nisto)* here, at this point; **~ ele calou-se** at this point he fell silent; **3** *(ênfase)* **~ mesmo** right here; **4** *(pop) (quase)* in a minute; *(avisando)* **estás ~ estás a entornar o vinho** you'll soon spill the wine; **5** *(eis)* **~ tens a verdade** here is the truth; **6** *(espaço, tempo)* now; **até ~ o negócio tem corrido bem** up to now the business has been good; **7 de aqui** (= de + aqui) from here; **de ~ a nada vai chover** *(em breve)* it will rain in a moment; **de ~ para ali** from one place to the other; **anda de ~ para trás** walk backwards; **de ~ para a frente** from now on; from here (on); **8 por ~** *(lugar, direcção)* here, this way, hereabouts; **por ~ e por ali** here and there; **e por ~ me fico** and that's all; **9** *(confidências)* **~ entre nós** … between you and me …; IDIOM **aqui há rato/há caso** *(desconfiança)* I smell a rat (in this).

aquiescência *n* acquiescence, agreement.

aquiescer *vi* **~ a** to accede to; **~ em** to agree to.

aquietar *vt* to calm, quieten; ♦ **~-se** *vr* to calm down.

aquilatar *vt (estimar)* to weigh up *(metais)*; **2** *(sujeitar ouro/prata a análise)* assay.

aquilo *pron* that (thing); **o que é ~?** what is that?; *(refere-se a alguém/algo já mencionado)* **~ é um escândalo!** it is a scandal!; ♦ **àquilo** (= a + aquilo) to that.

aquisição *f* acquisition.

aquoso,-a *adj* aqueous; **2** watery.

ar *m* air; **~ fresco** fresh air; **ao ~ livre** in the open air; **ir tomar ~** to go out for some air; **~ condicionado** air conditioning; **2** *(RADIO, TV)* **no ~** on the air; **3 corrente de ~** draught; **4** *(aparência)* look, appearance, aspect; **5** breeze; **6** *(AUTO)* choke; **7** *(fig) (doença)* **foi um ~ que lhe deu** something made her ill; ♦ **ares** *mpl* air; **mudar de ~** to have a change of air/climate; **2** *(parecença)* **ela dá ~ à mãe** she looks like her mother; **3** *(fig) (emproar-se)* **dar-se ~** to put on airs.

árabe *m,f* Arab; *(LÍNG) m* Arabic.

arabesco *m (estilo de desenho árabe)* arabesque.

Arábia Saudita *npr* a **~** Saudi Arabia.

arábico,-a *m,f* Arabian.

arabista *m,f adj (perito, douto em cultura árabe)* Arabist.

arabizar *vt* ado(p)tar modo/estilo/cultura árabe; ♦ **~-se** *vr* tornar-se semelhante a um árabe.

arado *m (UK)* plough, *(US)* plow.

aragem *f* breeze.

arame *m (fio metálico)* wire; **2 ~ farpado** barbed wire; IDIOM **ir aos ~ s** *(estar furioso)* to hit the ceiling.

aranha *f (ZOOL)* spider; IDIOM **ver-se em palpos de ~** to be in difficulties, in trouble; **andar às ~s** to be at a loss, go around in circles; **ando às ~s à procura do saco** I am going around/I am going mad looking for my bag.

aranhiço *(ZOOL) m* daddy-long-legs.

aranzel *m (arenga)* rigmarole.

arapuca *f (BR) (armadilha)* trap, ambush; **2** *(fig, fam) (estabelecimento)* shady house/company.

arar *vt* to plough *(UK)*, to plow *(US) (terra)*.

arauto *m* herald.

arbitragem *f (JUR) (julgamento)* arbitration; **2** *(DESP) (acto)* adjudication; *(decisão)* decision.

arbitrar *vt* to arbitrate; **2** to referee *(partida)*; **3** *(adjudicar)* **~ algo a alguém** to award sth to sb.

arbitrariedade *f (ação)* arbitrary act.

arbitrário,-a *adj* arbitrary.

arbítrio *m* decision; **ao ~ de** at the discretion of; **livre ~** free will.

árbitro *m (JUR)* arbitrator; **3** *(DESP – ténis)* umpire; **~ de futebol** referee; **2** *(mediador em questão)* mediator, referee.

arborescente *adj inv (árvore)* arborecent, arboreal.

arborescer *vi* to grow into a tree.

arborização *f* tree planting; arborisation.

arborizado,-a *(zona)* woody, wooded; *(rua)* tree-lined.

arborizar *vt* to plant (area) with trees.

arbusto *m* shrub, bush.

arca *f (caixa grande)* chest, trunk; *(para dinheiro)* coffer; **~ do tesouro** treasure chest; **2** *(REL)* ark, **~ de Noé** Noah's Ark; **~ da Aliança** Ark of the Covenant; **3 ~ congeladora** chest freezer; **4 ~ do peito** *(ANAT) (tórax)* chest, thorax.

arcaboiço (= **arcabouço**) *m (estrutura)* framework; **2** *(linhas gerais)* outline; **3** *(ANAT)* torax; **4** *(fig)* capacity.

arcada *f* arcade, arcades; **2** *(arco)* arch; **3** *(ANAT)* arch; **abóboda ~** *adj* arched vault.

arcaico,-a *adj (antigo)* archaic; **2** *(antiquado)* antiquated.

arcaizante *adj inv* archaic.

arcanjo *m* archangel.

arcar *vi (com) (aguentar)* to cope with; **2 ~ com uma responsabilidade** to shoulder the responsibility.

arcebispo *m* archbishop.

arcebispado *m* archbishopric.

archeiro *m (atirador de flechas)* archer; **2** *(MIL)* bowman, archer.

archote *m* torch.

arco *m* arch; **2** *(MIL, MÚS)* bow; **3** *(ELECT, MAT, GEOM)* arc; **4** *(de barril)* hoop; **~-e-flecha** archery, bow and arrow.

arco-da-velha *m (pop)* **história do ~** tall, fantastic story.

arco-íris *m* rainbow.

ar condicionado *m (aparelho)* air conditioner; **2** *(sistema)* air conditioning.

Árctico, Ártico *npr* **o ~** the Arctic; ♦ **árctico, ártico** *adj* arctic.

ardente *adj inv* burning; **2** *(carvão, ferro)* red-hot; **3** *(fig) (fé, paixão)* fervent, ardent; **4 câmara-~** funeral chamber; **em câmara ~** body lying in state.

arder *vi* to burn; **2** sting; **3 ~ em febre** to have a burning fever; **4 ~ em cólera** to boil with rage.

ardil *m* trick, ruse.

ardiloso,-a *adj* cunning; crafty.

ardina *m (vendendo na rua)* newspaper boy, seller.

ardor *m (paixão)* ardour, passion.

ardoroso,-a *adj* ardent.

ardósia *f* slate.

árduo,-a *adj* arduous; **2** *(difícil)* hard, difficult.

are *m (medida de superfície agrária)* are (= 100 metros quadrados) = 119,6 square yards.

área *f (local)* area; **2** *(superfície)* area; **3 ~ de serviço** service point; **4 ~ de conhecimento** field; **5** ground.

areal *m* beach; stretches *pl* of sand; **2** *(lugar)* sandy place.

arear *vt (metais)* to polish; **2** *(panelas)* to scour; **3** *(açúcar)* refinar; **4** to cover with sand.

areeiro *m* sand seller; **2** sand dune.

areia *f* sand; **~ movediça** quicksand; IDIOM **ser muita ~ para a camioneta de alguém** be too hot for sb to handle.

arejado,-a *adj* airy, ventilated; **2** *(fig) (ideias)* open-minded; discussed in the open.

arejar *vt* to air, ventilate *(quarto, roupa)*; **2** *(fig) (tomar ar)* to get some fresh air; **3** *(espairecer)* to have a break (outside).

arena *f* arena; *(espaço central)* ring; *(TAUROM)* arena.

arenito *m* sandstone.

arenga *f (discurso)* harangue; **2** *(palavreado)* rigmarole.

arengar *vt/vi* to argue, harangue.

arenoso,-a *adj (terreno)* sandy.

arenque *m (peixe)* herring.

aréola *f* areola.

aresta *n f (GEOM)* edge; ridge, crest; **2** *(da montanha)* crest, peak; **3** *(esquina)* corner; **4 ~ viva** sharp edge; **5** *(fig) (divergência)* differences; problems.

arfada *f* gasping; **2** *(NÁUT)* pitching.

arfar *vi* to pant, gasp for breath; **2** *(NÁUT)* to pitch.

argamassa *f* mortar.
argamassar *vt* to plaster, apply mortar to.
arganaz *m (ZOOL)* dormouse.
Argélia *npr* **a** ~ Algeria.
argelino,-a *m,f adj* Algerian.
argênteo,-a *adj (de prata)* silver; *(cor de prata)* silvery; like silver; **3** *(voz, som)* silvery, clear.
argentino,-a *m,f adj* Argentinian.
Argentina *npr* **a** ~ Argentina.
argento-vivo *m* quicksilver.
argila *f* white clay, potter's earth; **2** argil.
argiloso,-a *adj* of/from clay; **montanhas ~as** clay/ argillaceous mountains.
argola *f (aro)* ring, hoop; ~ **do guardanapo** napkin ring; **2** ~ **da porta** door-knocker; **3** ~s *fpl* looped earrings.
argolada *f (aldraba)* knock; **2** *(pop)* blunder.
argúcia *f (finura)* subtlety; **2** *(agudeza)* shrewdness, astuteness.
argueiro *m (FÍS)* particle; **2** *(ANAT, BOT)* corpuscle; **3** *(nos olhos)* speck of dust; **4** *(fig) (coisa insignificante)* trifle; IDIOM **de um** ~ **fazer um cavaleiro** to make a mountain out of a molehill.
arguente *m,f (EDUC) (pessoa que examina um candidato sobre a sua tese)* examiner; **2** police who questions suspect; arguer; **3** *(JUR)* plaintiff; ♦ *adj inv* examining, questioning.
arguição *f* argumentation.
arguido,-a *m,f (JUR)* a suspect called in for questioning; being investigated, but not accused.
arguir *vt* to accuse (**de** of); **2** to criticize; **3** *(alegar)* blame (sth); **4** *(JUR)* question; ♦ *vi* to argue; **2** examine.

argumentação *nf* argument; debate.
argumentador,-ora *m,f* arguer; ♦ *adj* argumentative.
argumentista *m,f* screenwriter
argumentar *vt/vi* to argue.
argumento *m* argument (**a favor de/contra**, for, against); **2** *(CIN, TEAT)* script; **3** *(enredo)* plot; **4** *(ópera)* subject.
arguto,-a *adj (sagaz)* shrewd, sharp, quick; **2** *(subtil)* subtle, clever.
ária *f* aria, melody, tune.
ariano,-a *m,f* Aryan; **os** ~ the Aryans.
aridez *f* dryness; dullness.
árido,-a *adj (seco, estéril)* arid, dry; **2** *(fig) (pessoa insensível)* hard; **3** *(fig) (trabalho)* dull.
arisco,-a *adj (pessoa) (esquivo)* dry, snappy; **2** prickly, unfriendly; **3** *(animal)* wild, untameable.
aristocracia *f* aristocracy.
aristocrata *m,f* aristocrat.
aristocrático,-a *adj* aristocratic.
aritmética, arimética *f* arithmetic.
aritmético, arimético,-a *m,f* arithmetician; ♦ *adj* arithmetical, arithmetic.

arlequim *m* harlequin; **2** buffoon; **3** fickle person.
arma *f* arm, weapon; ~ **branca** cold steel weapon; ~ **de fogo** firearm; **a sua inteligência é a sua** ~ her intelligence is her weapon; **2** ~s *fpl* coat of arms; **3 as** ~ **da família** *(brazão)* the family crest; **4** *(MIL)* **pegar em** ~ to take up arms/fight; **seguir as** ~s to join the forces.
armação *f* body, structure; **2** outfitting; **3** *(ato de armar)* setting up; **4** *(de madeira)* framework; **5** *(NÁUT)* rigging; **6** *(pesca)* shipping company; **7** ~ **de óculos** spectacles' frame.
armadilha *f* trap, snare; **cair numa** ~ to fall into a trap.
armadilhado,-a *adj* full of traps, booby-trapped.
armada *f* fleet, navy.
armado,-a *adj* armed; **2** *(CONSTR)* reinforced; **betão** ~ reinforced concrete; **3** *(montado)* outfitted, set up, rigged up; **4** *(fig, fam) (pessoa)* looking, behaving like a; **foi** ~ **em parvo** he went looking like a fool; **5 roubo à mão** ~a armed robbery.
armador *m* shipowner; **2** *(NÁUT)* chandler; trapper.
armadura *f* armour; **2** *(ELECT)* armature; **3** *(CONSTR)* framework, fitting; **4** *(chifres)* antlers, animal's horns.
armamento *m* armament, weapons; **2** *(NÁUT)* equipment.
armar *vt (MIL)* to arm, equip; **2** dress in armour; **3** ~ (alguém) **cavaleiro** to dub sb, to knight sb; **4** *(barracas)* to pitch; **5** *(toldo, circo)* to set up; **6** *(pre-fabricados)* ~ **armários** to assemble cupboards; **7** *(NÁUT)* to fit out, rigg; **8** ~ **uma máquina** to mount an engine; **9** ~ **contendas com** to pick a quarrel with; **10** ~ **uma armadilha** to set a trap; ♦ *vr:* ~-**se de** to arm o.s. with; **2** ~-**se de coragem** to summon up all one's courage; **3** *(fam)* ~-**se em esperto** trying to pass for/to be clever.
armaria *f (MIL)* armoury; **2** heraldry.
armário *m* cupboard; **2** *(de roupa)* wardrobe; **3** *(NÁUT)* ~ **das luzes** lamp locker.
armazém *m* store; **2** warehouse; **3 armazéns frigoríficos** cold storage warehouses; **4** *(MIL)* magazine.
armazenagem *m (= armazenamento) f* storage; **2** ~ **de águas** *m* water deposit.
armazenar *vt* to store; **2** to stock.
armeiro *m* gunsmith.
Arménia *npr f* **a** ~ Armenia.
arménio,-a *adj* Armenian; *(LÍNG) m* Armenian.
arminho *(ZOOL)* stoat; **2** *(pele)* armine.
armistício *m* armistice.
aro *m* ring; **2** *(dos óculos)* frame, rim; **3** *(cinta de metal)* hoop, rim.
aroma *f* aroma, fragrance.
aromático,-a *adj* aromatic, fragrant.
arpão *m* harpoon.
arpoar *vt (pesca)* to harpoon; **2** to grip with a hook; **3** *(fig, fam)* grab (fortune)
arquear *vt* to arch; **2** to camber; ♦ ~-**se** *vr* to bend, arch; **2** to warp.
arqueiro *m* archer.
arquejar *vi* to pant, wheeze.
arquejo *m* panting, gasping.

arqueologia *f* archaeology.
arqueólogo,-a *m,f* archaeologist.
arquétipo *m* archetype.
arquibancada(s) *(fpl)* tiers of seats; benches as in a circus.
arquiduque *m* archduke.
arquitecto,-a, arquiteto,-a *m,f* architect.
arquitectónico,-a, arquitetónico,-a *adj* architectonic.
arquitectura/arquitetura *f* architecture.
arquivar *vt* to file.
arquivo *m* archive; **2** file; **3** ~ **morto** dead file; **4** *(armário)* filing cabinet.
arquivista *m,f* archivist, filing clerk.
arquivo *m*; **2** *(depósito de documentos)* archives; **3** *(móvel)* filing cabinet; **repartição do** ~ record-office.
arrabalde *m* suburbs; **2** ~**s** *mpl* outskirts.
arraia *f* *(peixe)* ray, skate; **2** *(BR)* paper kite; **3** ~-**miúda** *f* *(pej)* ralé, rabble, riff-raff; hoi polloi *pl*; the masses *pl*.
arraial *m* country festival; **2** army camp; **3** camping ground; **4** *(BR)* village; **5 fazer um** ~ to make a fuss.
arraigado,-a *adj* deep-rooted; **2** *(fig)* ingrained.
arraigar *vi* to root; ♦ ~-**se** *vr* to take root; **2** *(fixar-se em)* to settle.
arrais *m* *(NÁUT)* skipper, coxswain.
arrancada *f* pull, jerk, tug; **2** *(motor)* quick start; **3** *(DESP)* final heat.
arrancão *m* jerk, wrench, tug.
arrancar *vt* to pull up/out; **2** to drive away; **3** to take off; **4** to snatch; **5** to extract; **ele arrancou-me dois dentes** he pulled out/extracted two teeth of mine; **6** *(confissão, segredo)* to winkle out; **7** *(fig, fam)* *(fazer sair)* get s.o. to leave/out of; ♦ *vi* *(pegar)* to start up; **o carro não arranca** the car does not start up; **2** *(fig)* start, take off the ground, '**Linha Saúde' arranca hoje** 'Health Line' takes off (is launched) today.
arranco *m* sudden pull, jerk, start; **2** *(arquejo)* **o último** ~ the last gasp; **3** outbreak; **4** ~**s** *pl* convulsions, jerks.
arranha-céu *m* skyscraper.
arranhadura (= **arranhão**) *m f* scratch.
arranhar *vt* to scratch; **2** *(língua)* have a smattering of.
arranjado,-a *adj* tidy; **ela é muito** ~ she is a very tidy person; **2** arranged, done, settled; **já está tudo** ~ all is done/arranged; **o meu cabelo precisa de ser** ~ I need to have my hair done; **3** repaired; **a máquina de costura já está** ~**a** the sewing machine is repaired.
arranjar *vt* to arrange; **2** to tidy (up); **3** to get, to obtain; **vou** ~ **um emprego** I am going to get a job; **4** to repair; ♦ ~-**se** *vr* to get by, to manage; **eu cá me arranjo** I'll manage, I'll get by; **2** to get ready; groom o.s.; **3** ~-**se sem** to do without.
arranjo *m* arrangement; **2** deal; **3** flower arrangement; **4** *(ajuda)* help; **faz-me um grande** ~ it is very useful to me; **5** *(fam)* affaire.
arranjinho *m* *(fam)* *(amor ilícito)* a bit on the side.
arranque *m* sudden start; **motor de** ~ starter motor; **2** *(extração)* pulling up of *(árvores)*; **3** *(DESP)* *(evento)* start.
arras *fpl* surety *sg*; **2** dowry *sg*.

arrasar *vt* to demolish; **2** to raze, level; **3** to ruin; **4** to browbeat; ♦ ~-**se** *vr* to humble o.s.
arrastado,-a *adj* crawling; **2** dragging; **3** *(voz)* drawling.
arrastão *m* tug, jerk; **2** *(pesca)* dragnet; **3** *(fig)* mobbing; **4** *(fig)* *(polícia levando muitos para a prisão)* general arrest.
arrastar *vt* to drag (along); **2** *(temporal)* to sweep (away); **3** *(voz)* to slur, drawl; **4** *(tempo, conversa)* drag on; **5** ~ **a asa** *(fig)* to woo s.o. to pay court to; **6** ~ **os pés** to dance badly; ♦ ~-**se** *vr* to crawl; drag o.s.; **2** *(fig)* to grovel.
arrasto *m* dragging; **2** *(pesca)* **barco de** ~ trawler; **rede de** ~ dragnet.
arrátel *m* old Portuguese unit of weight (459 grammes).
arrazoado *m* *(JUR)* defence.
arrazoar *vt* to argue for (a cause); ♦ *vi* to discuss; **2** to argue.
arre! *exc* *(col)* *(irra)* dammit!; **2** *(incitando burro, cavalo para andar)* giddy-up, giddap.
arrear *vt* to harness.
arrebatado,-a *adj* rash, impetuous; entranced.
arrebatamento *m* impetuosity; ecstasy.
arrebatar *vt* to snatch (away); to carry off; to enrage; ♦ ~-**se** *vr* to be entranced.
arrebentar *vt/vi* to explode; **2** to burst; **3** ~ **a banca** to break the bank *(gambling)* *(Vd: rebentar)*.
arrebitado,-a *adj* **nariz** ~ turned-up nose; **2** pert, snub; **3** cheeky, perky.
arrebitar *vt* to turn up; **2** to curl up; **3** to prick up; **ele arrebitou as orelhas** he pricked up his ears; **4** ~-**se** *vr* to perk up.
arrebol *m* red sky, afterglow.
arre-burrinho *m* *(tipo de balouço para crianças)* seesaw.
arrecadação *f* storehouse, depot; **2** *(em casa)* storeroom.
arrecadar *vt* *(guardar)* put away; to safekeep; **2** *(cobrar)* to collect *(dinheiro, renda)*; **3** *(economizar)* to save.
arredar *vt* *(afastar)* to move away, move back; **2 não** ~ **pé** not to budge, to stand one's ground; ♦ ~-**se** *vr* to withdraw.
arredio,-a *adj* *(animais)* stray; **2** *(pessoa)* reserved, aloof, withdrawn.
arredondado,-a *adj* roundish; *(cara, forma)* rounded.
arredondar *vt* give a round shape to; **2** to round off; ~ **a conta** to make a round sum, to round off an account.
arredores *mpl* suburbs; **2** outskirts.
arrefecer *vt* to cool; ♦ *vi* to cool down; **2** *(emoção)* cool off; **3** to get cold; IDIOM **nem me aquece nem me arrefece** it doesn't matter to me one way or another, I am not bothered.
arregaçar *vt* to roll up *(mangas)*; **2** to turn up *(calças)*.
arregalar *vt*: ~ **os olhos** open the eyes wide; **2** *(fam)* to goggle.
arreganhar *vt* to open; ~ **os dentes** to bare one's teeth, to snarl; ~ **a tacha** to grin.
arreigar *(Vd: arraigar)*.
arreios *mpl* harness *sg*.
arrelia *f* annoyance; trouble; **2** worry.
arreliar *vt* to annoy, irritate; ♦ *vi* to bore; ♦ ~-**se** *vr* get upset; become worried.

arremangar *vt* to roll up *(sleeves)*; **2** *(fig)* to get ready *(para o trabalho ou para uma luta)*.

arrematar *vt (discurso, trabalho)* to conclude; **2** put a finishing touch to; **3** *(adquirir por licitação)* to buy/acquire by auction; *(vender)* to auction off.

arremate *(Vd: remate)*.

arremedar *vt (imitar)* to mimic; **2** imitate.

arremedo *m* mimicry; **2** take-off.

arremessar *vt* to throw, hurl; ♦ ~-**se** *vr* to hurl o.s.

arremesso *m* throw.

arremeter *vi* to lunge; ~ **contra** to attack, assail.

arremetida *f* attack, onslaught.

arrendador,-ora *m,f* landlord, landlady; **2** hirer; **3** leaseholder.

arrendamento *m* renting; lease; rent.

arrendar *vt* to let, rent, lease.

arrendatário,-a *m,f* tenant, leasee.

arrepanhado *adj* tucked up; **2** *(roupa)* rolled up; **3** *(cabelo)* tied back; **4** **pele** ~**a** goose-pimpled skin; **5** *(costura)* puckered.

arrepender-se *vr* to repent; **2** to change one's mind; ~ **de** to regret, be sorry for.

arrependimento *m* repentance; regret.

arrepiado,-a *adj (com frio)* shivering; **2** *(com susto, choque)* horrified; **3** **pele** ~**a** *(com frio, emoção)* goose-flesh, goose-pimpled; **fiquei** ~ **com a notícia da tragédia** my skin went all goose-pimpled when I heard about the tragedy; **4** *(peixe)* **pescada** ~**a** cleaned and hung hake.

arrepiante *adj inv (algo)* horrifying; that makes your hair stand on end; **2** that makes you shiver (com frio/medo).

arrepiar *vt* to horrify; **2** ~ **o cabelo** to pull back (one's) hair; ♦ *vi (estremecer)* to shudder; *(fig)* **é de** ~ **os cabelos** it makes one's hair stand on end; ♦ ~-**se** *vr (pessoa)* to shiver; shudder; **2** to be horrified.

arrepio *m (calafrio)* shiver; **ter sentir** ~**s de frio** to have/feel shivers; **ele causa-me** ~**s** he gives me the creeps; ♦ **ao** ~ *(ao avesso, contrário ao normal)* the wrong way, against the grain.

arrestar *vt (JUR) (bens, propriedade)*, seize, attach assets/property under a court order.

arrestado *adj (JUR) (bens confiscados e congelados por ordem do tribunal)* assets apprehended/seized and confiscated under a court order.

arresto *m* seizure, attachment; **2** confiscation; stoppage; embargo.

arrevesado,-a *adj* obscure; **2** intricate; **3** *(percurso)* tortuous; *(linguagem)* complicada.

arrevesar *vt* to turn inside out/upside down; **2** causing confusion; ♦ ~-**se** *vr (revezar-se)* take it in turns (to do sth).

arria! *exc (NÁUT)* down.

arriar *vt (NÁUT) (velas, roupa)* to lower; **2** (armas) to lay down; **3** *(pneu)* let down; **4** *(mercadoria)* unload; ♦ *vi* to fall down; **2** to sag; **3** *(pneu, bateria)* to go flat; ♦ ~-**se** *vr (fig)* to lose courage, heart, strength; **2** *(fig)* to give up.

arriba *f* high river bank; **2** cliff; ♦ *adv* up, upward(s); **2** onward(s); *exc* ~! *(acima) (pescador, marinheiro)* heave-ho!

arribação *f* arrival in port; **2 ave de** ~ migratory bird.

arribar *vi (NÁUT)* to call at a port, put into harbour; **2** ~ **da rota** go off course; **3** ~ **ao cimo** get to/arrive at the top; **4** *(fig)* to get better, recover; to come around.

arrimar *vt* to support; ♦ *vr:* ~-**se a** to lean against.

arrimo *m* support, prop; ~ **de família** family support.

arriscado,-a *adj* risky; daring.

arriscar *vt* to risk; **2** to endanger, jeopardize; ♦ ~-**se** *vr* to take a risk.

arrivista *m,f* upstart, social climber; **2** opportunist; ♦ *adj inv (alguém)* socially ambitious; **2** opportunistic.

arroba *f (peso)* 32 pounds; **2** *(fig)* **às** ~**s** in great quantities; **3** *(COMP) (arroba)* @ at.

arrochar *vt* to tighten up *(with a stick)*; squeeze tightly.

arrocho *m* short stick; **2** squeeze; **3** *(fig)* hardship.

arrogância *f* arrogance, haughtiness.

arrogante *adj* arrogant, haughty.

arrogar *vt* to arrogate; claim, attribute; ♦ ~-**se** *vr* to take upon o.s.

arrochar *vt* to squeeze, tighten (with a stick); **2** *(fig)* to cause hardship; **3** *(fig)* be severe, exact; **4** *(fig)* to shrink.

arrocho *n* cudgel, tourniquet, short stick; **2** *(fig)* hardship; hard nut to crack; **3** *(fig, fam)* grilling.

arroio *m* stream.

arrojado,-a *adj (sem pensar)* rash, foolhardy; **2** *(ousado)* daring.

arrojar *vt* to hurl; ♦ *vr* ~-**se a** hurl o.s. into; **2** ♦ to dare to.

arrojo *m* audacity; **ter o** ~ *(fam)* to have the nerve/ the cheek.

arrolamento *m (lançamento)* list, inventory; **2** register.

arrolar *vt* to list; **2** *(JUR)* make inventory; **3** *(MIL)* to enlist.

arrolhar *vt* to cork *(bottles etc)*; **2** *(fig) (impedir comunicação)* shut *(boca, ouvidos)*; **3** *(BR)* to round up cattle.

arromba *f* boisterous song accompanied by guitar; ♦ *exc* **de** ~! great!; tremendous!

arrombamento *m* burglary, break-in.

arrombar *vt* to break into, burgle.

arrostar *vt* to confront, face (up to); **2** ~ **o perigo** to brave danger, brave out.

arrotar *vt/vi* to burp, to belch *(fam)*; **2** *(fig)* boast (of); IDIOM ~ **postas de pescada** to show off, blow one's own trumpet.

arrotear *vt* to clear land for cultivation.

arroteia *n (processo)* clearing; **2** *(terra)* cleared.

arroto *m* burp; eructation *(formal)*; belch *(fam)*.

arroubamento *m* ecstasy.

arroubar *vt* to enrapture.

arroubo *m* ecstasy, rapture.

arroxeado *adj* purplish.

arroz *m* rice; ~ **doce** Portuguese rice pudding (traditional at Christmas).

arrozal *m* rice paddy, field.

arruaça *f* street riot.

arruaceiro,-a *m,f adj* hooligan, disorderly person, rowdy.

arruamento *m* planning of the streets; **2** (shopping) mall; row of shops.

arruela *f (TEC)* washer; ~ **de pressão** lock washer.

arrufar *vt* to annoy; **2** *(penas, água)* to ruffle; ♦ *vr* to sulk, become irritated; cheesed off.

arrufo *m (entre namorados)* tiff; sulk.

arrugar *vt* to wrinkle, crease.

arruinar *vt* to ruin, to destroy, to spoil; ♦ *vi* to fall into ruin, go bad; ♦ **~-se** *vr* to be ruined.

arrulhar *vi* to coo.

arrulho *m* cooing.

arrumação *f* arrangement; **2** tidying up.

arrumar *vt (pôr em ordem)* to put in order, to tidy up *(casa, escritório, etc)*; **2** to pack; **ele arrumou as malas e foi-se embora** he packed his bags and went; **3** *(solucionar)* resolver; **4** *(fig, pop) (encontrão, murro)* push, punch sb; **5** *(fig, fam) (casar)* **arrumaram os filhos** they married their children off; ♦ **~-se** *vr* to marry.

arsenal *m (MIL)* arsenal; **2** *(apetrechos)* instruments, tools; **3** ~ **culinário** cooking utensils; **4** *(fig) (quantidade)* stock.

arte *f (ger)* art; **2** *(habilidade)* skill; **com** ~ skilfully; **3** *(astúcia)* cunning; **ela tem uma** ~! she is so cunning!; **4** ~**s e ofícios** arts and crafts; **belas** ~**s** fine arts; **~s e manhas** tricks, artful wiles.

artefacto, artefato *m* article, goods, artefact; ~**s de couro** leather goods.

artelho *m (ANAT)* ankle, ankle-bone.

artemísia *f (BOT)* artemisia.

artéria *f (ANAT)* artery.

arterial *adj (MED)* arterial; **tensão** ~ blood pressure.

arterosclorose *f (MED)* arteriosclorosis.

artesã *f (Vd: artesão)*.

artesanato *m* craftwork, crafts, handicrafts.

artesão,-ã *(mpl: artesãos; fpl artesãs) m,f* artisan, craftsman/woman.

Ártico *npr* **o** ~ the Arctic; **o Oceano Glacial** ~ the Arctic Ocean.

ártico,-a *adj* arctic.

articulação *f* articulation; **2** enunciation; **3** *(ANAT)* joint; **4** *(ligaçã)* connection, link.

articulado *m (JUR)* article(s) of a law; list of facts; ♦ **~-a** *adj* articulated; linked; **cadeira ~a** folding chair.

articular *vt* to articulate; **2** to join together; ♦ **~-se** *vr* to join/fit/work together; **4** to connect, link.

articulista *m,f* newspaper writer, columnist.

artífice *m,f* artisan; craftsperson.

artifício *m (processo)* artifice, ruse, stratagem; **2** *(artemanha)* cover-up, wile, trickery; **3** device; **fogo de** ~ fireworks.

artificioso,-a *adj* skilful; artful.

artigo *m (objeto)* article; ~**s** *mpl* goods; **2** *(JORN)* ~ **de fundo** leading article, editorial; **3** *(gram)* article; ~ **definido** definite article; **4** *(JUR)* clause, provision; **5** *(MIL)* code.

artilharia *f (armamento)* artillery.

artilheiro *m* gunner, artilleryman.

artimanha *f (astúcia)* wile, artifice, cunning; **2** clever stratagem.

artista *m,f* artist.

artístico,-a *adj* artistic.

artrite *f (MED)* arthritis.

artrítico,-a *adj* arthritic.

arvorar *vt* to raise; **2** to hoist *(bandeira)*.

árvore *f* tree; **2** *(TEC)* axle, shaft.

arvoredo *m* woods, grove, trees.

as *pl de:* **a** = the.

às (= **a** + **as**) to/at the; **fui às compras** I went shopping; **ele deu o dinheiro às moças** he gave the money to the girls; ♦ *adv* ~ **escondidas** secretly.

ás *(pl: ases) m (pessoa, carta de jogo)* ace, expert; **ele é um** ~ **no jogo** he is an ace at the game.

asa *f (de pássaro, avião)* wing; **2** *(de louça, cesto)* handle; IDIOM **estar com um grão na** ~ to be tipsy; **dar ~s à imaginação** give free reins to one's imagination.

asa-delta *f* hang-glider.

asbesto *m* asbestos.

ascendência *f (filiação)* ancestry; **2** *(origem)* descent; **3** *(influência)* ascendancy, seniority; **ter** ~ **sobre** have ascendancy over; **4** *(ato de ascender)* rise; ~ **social** social rise.

ascendente *m,f (antepassado)* ancestor, forbear; **2** influence; ♦ *adj inv (ASTROL)* ascendant, ascending; **2** *(curva)* rising, upward.

ascender *vi* to rise, ascend; ~ **a** to amount to.

ascensão *f* ascent; *(fig)* rise; **dia da A~** Ascension Day.

ascensor *m* elevator; lift.

asceta *m,f* ascetic; hermit.

ascético,-a *adj* ascetic, ascetical.

asco *m (aversão)* loathing; **2** *(nojo)* revulsion; **dar** ~ to be revolting; **ter** ~ **a (alguém)** to detest sb; to have aversion to.

áscua *f* ember, incandescent iron; **2** *(fig) (do olhar)* fulmination.

asfalto *m* asphalt.

asfixia *f* suffocation; **2** *(fig)* strangulation.

asfixiante *adj inv (ambiente, calor)* stifling, suffocating; **2** *(regime, attitude)* oppressive, repressive.

asfixiar *vt* to suffocate *(alguém)*; **2** *(fig)* to repress, oppress; ♦ *vi* make breathing difficult; ♦ **~-se** *vr (sufocar-se)* to gasp for air; **2** to be asphyxiated.

Ásia *npr* **a** ~ Asia.

asiático,-a *m,f adj* Asian.

asilar *vt* to give refuge to; ♦ **~-se** *vr* to take refuge.

asilo *m* refuge; **2** support; **3** *(political)* asylum; **4** *(caridade)* Home.

asma *f* asthma.

asneira *f* blunder; nonsense; **2 dizer** ~**s** to talk nonsense; **3** to swear; **3 fazer uma** ~ to make a mistake.

asno *m* donkey; **2** *(fig)* ass, idiot.

aspas *fpl* horns; **2** inverted commas, quotation marks.

aspargo *m* asparagus.

aspecto, aspeto *m* appearance; **2** feature; **3** point of view; **4 ter bom** ~ to look well.

aspereza *f (material)* roughness; **2** *(fig) (voz, castigo)* harshness; **3** *(modos)* abruptness.

aspergir *vt* to sprinkle with holy water.
áspero,-a *adj (caminho)* rough, scabrous; **2** *(vinho, pele, tecido)* rough; **3** *(fig) (maneira, palavras)* harsh; abrupt; crude **4** *(som)* jarring.
aspersão *f* (borrifo) sprinkling.
asperso,-a *(irr pp of:* **aspergir**) *adj* sprinkled.
aspeto *(Vd:* **aspecto**).
aspiração *f* aspiration; strong desire; aim; **2** suction; **3** drawing of breath, inhalation.
aspirador *m*: ~ **de pó** vacuum cleaner; ~ **de ventilação** suction ventilator.
aspirante *m,f* candidate; **2** *(ADMIN)* trainee; **3** *(MIL, NÁUT)* cadet.
aspirar *vt (inspirar)* to breathe in; **2** *(recolher por sucção)* to suck in, to draw by suction; **3** *(LÍNG) (fonética)* to aspirate; ♦ *vi:* ~ **a** *(ter ambição)* to aspire to.
aspirina *f (MED)* aspirin.
asqueroso,-a *adj (casa, lugar)* filthy, disgusting; **2** *(pessoa)* loathsome; **3** *(crime)* vile.
assadeira *f* roasting tin.
assado,-a *adj* roasted; **carne** ~**a** roast meat, roast beef.
assador,-ora *m,f* person who roasts food; **2** *m (utensílio)* roaster; ~ **de castanhas** *(pessoa)* chestnut roaster.
assadura *f (pele)* rash; **2** *(de bebé)* nappy rash *(UK)*, diaper rash *(US)*.
assaltante *m,f* assailant; **2** burglar.
assaltar *vt* to attack, raid; **2** break into; ~ **uma casa** to break into a home.
assalto *m* attack, raid; hold-up; **2** *(DESP: boxe)* round; **3** burglary, break-in.
assanhado,-a *adj* furious, enraged; **2** *(gatos)* provoked, ready to attack; **3** *(BR)* restless, noisy; **4** *(BR, fig)* aroused.
assanhar *vt (provocar)* provoke, tease *(gatos);* **2** *(enfurecer)* enrage *(alguém);* **3** irritate, inflame *(ferida).*
assanhar-se *vr* to get angry; to fly into a rage.
assar *vt (no forno)* to roast; **2** *(no jardim)* to barbecue.
assassinar *vt* to murder; **2** *(POL)* assassinate; **3** *(fig)* destroy; **4** *(não respeitar música, arte)* murder, butcher.
assassinato *m*, **assassínio** *m* murder, assassination.
assassino,-a *m,f* murderer, murderess; **2** assassin.
assaz *adv (bastante)* quite, rather; enough; **3** *(demasiado)* too; **ele ficou** ~ **magoado (para)** he was too hurt (to).
asseado,-a *adj* clean; **2** tidy; neat.
assear *vt* to clean, tidy (up).
assediar *vt* to harass; **2** *(ser importuno)* pester; **3** *(perseguir)* hound; **4** *(sitiar)* to besiege.
assédio *m* harassment; ~ **sexual** sexual harassment; **2** *(cerco, bloqueio)* siege.
assegurar *vt* to secure; **2** to ensure; to assure; ♦ *vr:* ~**-se de** to make sure of.
asseio *m* cleanliness; **2** neatness.
assembléia, assembleia *f* meeting, assembly; **2** *(órgão determinativo)* assembly; ~ **geral** general meeting; **3** **A**~ **da República** Parliament; **4** *(conselho legislativo)* Council.

assemelhar *vt* to liken, compare; ♦ ~**-se** *vr* to be alike; ~**-se a** to resemble, to look like *(alguém).*
assentada, *f (JUR)* court record, sitting; **de uma** ~ in one sitting; all at once.
assentado,-a *adj (firme)* fixed, secure; **2** *(combinado)* agreed, arranged; **3** *(anotado)* entered, written down, recorded.
assentador *m* recorder; **2** scorer; **3** layer; ~ **de tijolos** bricklayer.
assentamento *m* laying of bricks, tiles; **2** *(averbar)* registration; **3** *(nota)* entry, recording; **4** *(acordo)* assent.
assentar *vt* to seat *(alguém, algo);* **2** to place, to set; **ele assentou o banco no relvado** he placed the bench on the lawn; **3** to lay *(tijolos);* **4** *(averbar)* to note/jot down; register; **5** *(poeira)* settle (on, over); **6** *(roupa)* to fit; **esse casaco assenta-te como uma luva,** that coat fits you perfectly/it is a perfect fit; **7** ~ **as tropas** *(MIL)* to set up camp; **8** ~ **uma bofetada** to slap in the face; **9** *(assunto)* be based on; ♦ *vr* to sit down; **2** settle down; **3** ~ **praça** *(MIL)* to enlist.
assente *(pp irr de:* **assentar**).
assentimento *m (aprovação)* assent, consent.
assentir *vi* to agree, concur, assent.
assento *m* chair, bench; **2** seat; **3** *(registo)* book-keeping entry; record; ~ **de nascimento** birth registration; **4** base; **ter** ~ **em** be based on; **5** *(ANAT)* bottom, behind; **6** *(fig) (juízo)* sense; **7** *(JUR)* decision.
assepsia *f (MED)* asepsis.
asséptico,-a, assético,-a *adj* aseptic.
asserção *f*, **assertiva** *f* assertion, affirmation; **2** statement.
assertivo,-a *adj* assertive; **2** positive.
assessor,-ora *m,f* adviser, assessor.
assessoria *f* consultancy; **2** *(órgão)* advisory body.
assestar *vt (visar)* to aim, point.
asseverar *vt (afirmar)* to affirm, assert; **2** *(garantir),* assure.
assiduidade *f* regular attendance; **2** diligence; **com** ~ regularly; **3** diligently.
assíduo,-a *adj* diligent; **2** assiduous.
assim *adv (deste modo)* in this way, thus, so, like this; **sendo** ~ that being the case; **como** ~ **?** how so?; **2** *(portanto)* therefore, so; **3** *(igualmente)* likewise; **tal** ~ *(comparação)* just like; ~ **como** as well as; **mesmo** *(exato)* just so; **assim por diante** and so on; **por** ~ **dizer** so to speak; *(fam)* ~ **e assado** one way or the other; ♦ *conj* **mesmo** ~ /**ainda** ~ even so; ~ **que** as soon as; ♦ *exc* ~ **seja!** let's hope; ~ **é que é!** that's the way!
assim-assim *adv (nem bem nem mal)* so-so; not so bad.
assimétrico,-a *adj* asymmetrical; uneven.
assimilação *f* assimilation.
assimilar *vt (ger)* to assimilate; ♦ *vi* to understand, to take in, to grasp; **2** *(fig)* to absorb; ♦ ~**-se** *vr* to integrate.
assinalado,-a *adj* marked; **2** notable; eminent; **3** *(animais, produtos)* branded.

assinalar *vt* to mark; **2** *(indicar)* indicate; **3** to celebrate *(acontecimento)*; **4** *(observar)* to point out; ♦ ~-se *vr* to distinguish o.s.

assinante *m,f* subscriber.

assinar *vt* *(firmar)* to sign; **2** *ser (assinante)* to subscribe to *(jornal etc)*; **3** *(designar)* assign.

assinatura *f* signature; subscription; season ticket *(opera, theatre)*.

assistência *f* *(presença)* attendance; **2** *(público)* audience; **3** aid, assistance, ~ **médica** medical care; ~ **jurídica** legal aid; ~ **social** social welfare; ~ **técnica** technical support.

assistente *m,f* *(adjunto do professor)* assistant; **2** *(MED)* house physician **3** *(apoio)* helper; ~ **social** social worker; ♦ *adj* attending; **2** assistant.

assistir *vt/vi* to attend, be present at; ~ **a uma reunião** to attend a meeting; **2** *(socorrer)* to assist, help; **3** *(presenciar desastre)* to witness an accident.

assoalhada *f* *(casa/sala com soalho)* room; **quantas ~s tem a casa?** how many rooms has the house?

assoalhado,-a *adj* floored; **uma casa com três ~s** a three-roomed house; **2** *(exposto ao sol)* sunny.

assoalhar *vt* to lay a floor (with planks)

assoar *vt*: ~ **o nariz** to blow one's nose; ♦ ~-se *vr* to blow one's nose.

assoberbar *vt* to belittle; **2** dominate, overwhelm; **3** ~ **alguém** *(com trabalho)* overload sb *(with work)*.

assobiar *vi* to whistle; **o vento assobiava** the wind was whistling; **2** to boo; **os adeptos assobiaram o árbitro** the fans booed the referee; **3** ~ **a** *(chamar)* to whistle at *(o cão, etc)*; *(atrair a atenção das moças, aprovar)* to wolf-whistle.

assobio *m* whistle, whistling; **2** *(a uma mulher bonita)* wolf-whistle; **3** *(apito)* whistle; **4** *(silvo)* hiss.

associação *f* association; **2** society; partnership.

associado,-a *m,f, adj* associate, member; **2** partner.

associar *vt* to associate; ♦ ~-se *vr* *(COM)* to form a partnership; **2** become a member; **3** ~ **a** to associate with; **4** *(juntar-se)* to join.

assolador,-ora *adj* raging; **2** devastating.

assolar *vt* to ravage, destroy; **2** to hit; **o furacão assolou a ilha de Java** the hurricane hit the island of Java.

assomar *vi* to appear; emerge; ~ **à janela** to appear at the window.

assombração *f* dread; *(fantasma)* apparition, ghost.

assombrado,-a *adj* *(pasmado)* astonished; **2** *(lugar com sombra)* shady; **3** *(casa)* haunted.

assombrar *vt* *(assustar)* to frighten, startle; **2** *(pasmar)* astonish; **3** *(fantasma)* haunt; **4** *(tornar escuro)* cover darken *(céu)*; ♦ ~-se *vr* to be amazed; to be clouded over.

assombro *m* astonishment; **2** fright; **3** *(maravilha)* marvel, wonder.

assombroso,-a *adj* astonishing.

assomo *m* *(indício)* first sign, trace, hint; **2** appearance; **3** *(reação súbita)* outburst; **num ~ de cólera** in a fit of anger.

assonância *f* assonance.

assuada *f* gang, mob; **2** hurly-burly; **3** riot; **fazer ~** to cause a row/riot.

assumir *vt* *(encarregar-se de)* to assume, undertake; **2** *(mostrar)* assume, take on *(expressão)*; ♦ *vi* *(pessoa)* *(tomar posse)* to take office; *(algo)* ~ **grandes proporções** (sth) to take on large proportions.

assuntar *(BR)* *vt* to pay attention to; **2** to find out; ♦ *vi* to consider.

assunto *m* *(tema)* subject, matter, topic.

assustadiço,-a *adj* shy, timorous.

assustar *vt* to frighten, scare; **2** *(de súbito)* startle; ♦ ~-se *vr* to be frightened.

asterisco *m* (*) asterisk.

astigmatismo *m* astigmatism.

astral *m* *(humor, ambiente)* mood; ♦ *adj inv* astral, sidereal.

astro *m* star; **2** *(pessoa notável)* star.

astrolábio *m* astrolabe.

astrologia *f* astrology.

astrólogo,-a *m,f* astrologer.

astronauta *m,f* astronaut.

astronave *f* spacecraft.

astronomia *f* astronomy.

astrónomo *(BR:* -trô-*)* *m* astronomer.

astúcia *f* *(esperteza)* sharpness, cleverness, shrewdness; **3** *(ardil)* cunning; trickery, ruse.

astucioso,-a, astuto,-a *adj* *(esperto)* shrewd, sharp, astute; **2** *(manhoso)* crafty, sly; **3** *(resposta)* subtle, clever.

ata *f* *(de reunião)* minutes *pl* *(Vd.* **a(c)ta**); **2** *(BR)* sugar apple.

atabafado,-a *adj* *(atmosfera)* close, stifled; **2** *(som)* muffled; **3** *(CULIN)* covered; **4** *(fig)* *(boato)* covered up.

atabafar *vt* to smother *(fogo)*; **2** *(cobrir com muita roupa)* stifle; **3** hide, cover-up; **4** *(fig)* *(furtar)* to pinch, pilfer.

atabalhoado,-a *adj* *(na fala, gestos)* clumsy; muddled; **2** *(trabalho)* shoddy, slapdash.

atabalhoar *vt* scamp *(trabalho)*; ♦ *(coll)* to bungle.

atacadista *m,f* *(COM)* wholesaler; ♦ *adj* wholesale.

atacado,-a *adj* attacked, under attack; **2** assaulted; **3** *(calçado)* tied, fastened; **4** *(COM)* *(venda)* **por ~** in bulk, wholesale.

atacador *m* *(de sapato)* shoelace; **sapatos de ~es** lace-up shoes; **2** *(variedade de arma de fogo)* ramrod.

atacante *m,f* attacker, assailant; **2** *(DESP)* forward; ♦ *adj inv* attacking; **2** *(palavras)* offensive; **3** *(vírus)* aggressive.

atacar *vt* to attack; **2** assault; **3** hit out; **4** *(fig)* *(tarefa, problema)* to tackle; ♦ *vi* *(vírus)* strike; ♦ *exc* **atacar!** charge!

atado,-a *(pp de* **atar**) *m* *(pessoa sem iniciativa)* wimp; ♦ *adj* *(algo, alguém)* tied, knotted (**a** to); **2** *(BR)* *(fig)* *(desajeitado)* clumsy; **3** *(confuso)* bewildered.

atadura *f* *(ato de atar)* tie, knot; **2** *(ligadura)* bandage.

atafulhado,-a *adj* very full; **2** *(de comida)* stuffed; **3** *(casa, armários)* crammed; **4** *(cabeça)* filled.

atalaia *f (local de vigia)* watchtower, lookout post; **2** *m,f (sentinel)* sentry; **3 de** ~ on the lookout.

atalhar *vt (encurtar)* to intercept, cut short *(caminho, conversa)*; **2** *(interromper)* cut in on another's remark; ♦ *vi* to take a short cut.

atalho *m* short cut; **2** *(fig)* obstacle, hindrance, hurdle; **vencer** ~**s** overcome obstacles.

atamancar *vt (fazer à pressa)* to botch, bangle *(trabalho)*.

atapetar *vt* to carpet.

ataque *m (agressão)* attack, onslaught; ~ **à mão armada** armed attack; **2** *(MIL)* raid; ~ **aéreo** air raid; **3** fit; seizure; stroke; ~ **cardíaco** heart attack; ~ **de tosse** *(de súbito)* coughing fit; ~ **de raiva** *(de fúria)* fit of anger.

atar *vt* to tie (up), fasten; **2** *(fig) (promessa)* bind o.s. to; IDIOM **não** ~ **nem desatar** to waver, be in two minds.

atarantado,-a *adj* confused, embarrassed; **2** half-dazed; **3** stunned.

atarefado,-a *adj* busy; **2** *(apressado)* in a hurry; **3** *(agitado)* flustered.

atarracado,-a *adj (pessoa baixa e forte)* stocky, dumpy, thickset.

atarraxar *vt* to tighten, screw; **ela atarraxou bem o boião** she tightened (the lid) on the jar firmly.

atascadeiro *m* bog; marshy place.

atascar-se *vr* to get stuck in the mud; **2** *(fig)* to be bogged down *(em trabalho, dificuldades)*.

ataúde *m* coffin.

ataviar *vt* to adorn, decorate; ♦ ~**-se** *vr* to get dressed up.

atávico,-a *adj* atavistic.

atavio *m* adornment; **2** attire.

atanazar *(Vd:* **atenazar**).

até *prep* up to, as far as; **2** until, till; **3** ~ **agora** up to now; **4** ~ **certo ponto** to a certain extent; **5** ~ **amanhã** see you tomorrow; **6** ~ **logo** see you later; *(BR)* see you; **7 vou** ~ **Lisboa** I am going to/as far as Lisbon; ♦ *conj* ~ **que** until; ♦ ~ **mesmo** *adv* even, even if; **eu até lhe daria um presente** I would even give (go as far as give) you a present; ♦ *exc* ~ **que enfim!** at last! finally!

atear *vt* to kindle; **2** *(fig)* to incite, inflame; **3** ~ **fogo a** to set light to; **4** ~ **uma questão** to aggravate a quarrel; ♦ ~**-se** *vr* to blaze; **2** to flare up.

ateia *(f de* **ateu**).

ateísmo *m* atheism.

atemorizar *vt (assustar)* to frighten; **2** *(ameaçar)* to intimidate.

atempadamente *adv* in advance; in good time, opportunely.

Atenas *npr* Athens.

atenazar (= **atanazar**) *(apertar com tenaz)* *vt* to grip/hold tightly; **2** *(fig)* to taunt, annoy *(alguém)*.

atenção *f* attention; **falta de** ~ lack of attention; **prestar** ~ to pay attention; **chamar a** ~ **de alguém** to attract sb's attention; **2** *(repreender)* **chamar à** ~ to tell sb off; **3** care; **com** ~ with care; **4** *(correspondência)* **à** ~ **de** for the attention of, c/o; **digno de** ~ noteworthy; ♦ *exc* **atenção!** your

attention, please!; **2** be careful!; ~ **ao degrau!** mind the step!

atencioso,-a *adj* attentive; **2** considerate.

atendedor *m (de chamadas) (EP)* telephone answering machine.

atender *vt* to attend (to); **2** ~ **o telefone** to answer the telephone; **3** ~ **ao balcão** to attend to/help the customer; **4** to pay attention to.

Not: atender uma reunião/entrevista/aula, which is 'assistir' a.

---

atendimento *m* service; **pronto** ~ swift service; **horário de** ~ opening hours.

ateniense *m,f adj inv* Athenian.

atentado *m* attack; **2** attempt on sb's life; **3** ~ **ao pudor** indecent exposure.

atentar *vt* to undertake; ♦ *vi* to make an attempt; **2** ~ **contra** to attempt against; **3** ~ **a/em/para** to pay attention to.

atento,-a *adj* attentive; ~ **ao meu conselho** paying attention to my advice; **2** considerate.

atenuação *f* reduction, lessening.

atenuante *adj inv* extenuating.

atenuar *vt (aliviar)* to attenuate; **2** to soften, relieve; **3** reduce.

aterrador,-ora *adj* terrifying.

aterragem *f (AER)* landing; ~ **de emergência** emergency landing.

aterrar *vt* to terrify; **2** to cover with earth; ♦ *vi (avião)* to land.

aterrissagem *f (BR: AER)* landing.

aterrissar *vi (BR: AER)* to land.

aterro *m* landfill.

aterrorizar *vt* to terrorize.

atestado,-a *m* certificate; confirmation; **2** *(JUR)* testimony; **3** *(fig, fam)* full up; ♦ *adj* certified.

atestador *m (TEC, AUT)* tester; ~ **de baterias** battery tester.

atestar *vt* to certify; **2** *(garantir)* attest, to vouch for; **3** *(encher)* to fill up *(gasolina)*; *(coll) (abarrotar)* cram *(de* with).

ateu *m,* **atéia** *f, adj* atheist.

atiçador *m* poker; **2** instigator.

atiçar *vt (fogo)* to poke; **2** to incite.

atilado,-a *adj* clever; **2** *(ajuizado)* sensible, disciplined.

atilho *m* string, twine around books or a bundle; **2** *(atacador)* lace; **3** *(feixe)* bundle, bale tied with a twine.

atinar *vt* to guess correctly; ♦ *vi* be right; ~ **com** to find, get the hang of; **2** to ponder; **3** to have sense, become sensible.

atingir *vt (alcançar)* to reach; **2** to affect, concern; **3** to attain, achieve *(sonho)*; **4** to understand, grasp; **5** *(alvo)* to hit.

atingível *adj inv* attainable.

atiradiço,-a *adj* flirtatious, cheeky, saucy.

atirador *m* marksman; ~ **de tocaia** sniper.

atirar *vt* to throw; **eu atirei o casaco para cima da cama** I threw the coat *para cima da cama*; **não atires o lixo para o chão** don't throw rubbish onto/on the floor; **2** fling; **ela atirou-lhe os braços à volta**

do pescoço she flung her arms around his neck; **3** to hurl; ~ **insultos** to hurl insults; ♦ *vi* to shoot; ~ **aos pássaros** to shoot at the birds; ♦ ~-**se** *vr (lançar-se)* to throw o.s.; ~ **de pés** to throw o.s. headlong; ~-**se a alguém** *(numa luta)* to hurl o.s. at sb; *(sexualmente)* to make advances, throw o.s. at sb.

atitude *f* attitude; **2** position.

ativar (*Vd*: **a(c)tivar**).

atividade (*Vd*: **a(c)tividade**).

ativo,-a (*Vd*: **a(c)tivo,-a**).

ativo *m* (COM) assets *pl*; **ativa** *f* (MIL): **estar na** ~ to be in active service; **2 da** ~ *(parte do pessoal)* staff; ♦ **ativo-a** *adj (person)* energetic, agile; **2** *(que trabalha)* working.

Atlântico *npr*: **o Oceano** ~ Atantic Ocean.

atlântico,-a *adj* Atlantic.

Atlântida *npr*: **a A~** *(continente lendário)* Atlantis.

atlas *m* atlas; ♦ **Atlas** *npr*: **o** ~ the Atlas Mountains.

atleta *m,f* athlete.

atlético,-a *adj* athlectic.

atletismo *m* athletics *sg*.

atmosfera *f* atmosphere; **2** *(ambiente social)* ambiance, atmosphere.

atmosférico,-a *adj* atmospheric

ato (*Vd*: **acto**).

atoalhado,-a *adj (pano)* towelling; ~**s** *mpl* linen, towels.

atol *m* atoll.

atolar *vi* get stuck in the mud; ♦ *vt* to get muddy; **2** to get bogged down; ♦ ~-**se** *vr (fig)* to get snowed under *(com trabalho)*.

atoleimado,-a *adj (pessoa)* silly, idiotic.

atoleiro *m* mire, quagmire, swamp; **2** *(fig)* base morals.

atómico,-a (*BR*: -tô-) *adj* atomic.

atomizador *m* atomizer, spray.

átomo *m* atom.

atónito,-a (*BR*: -tô-) *adj* astonished; dumbfounded.

átono,-a *adj* (LÍNG) *(vogal, etc)* atonic.

ator (*Vd*: **a(c)tor**).

atordoado,-a *adj* dazed, bewildered.

atordoamento *m* dizziness.

atordoante *adj inv* deafening.

atordoar *vt* to daze, stun.

atormentador,-ora *m,f* tormentor; ♦ *adj* tormenting.

atormentar *vt* to torment; to tease; to plague.

atração (*Vd*: **atra(c)ção**).

atracar *vt/vi (navio)* to come alongside; (NÁUT) to moor.

atra(c)ção *f* attraction; affinity.

atra(c)tivo,-a *m* attraction, affinity; ~**s** *mpl* charms; ♦ *adj* attractive.

atraente *adj inv* attractive.

atraiçoado,-a *adj* betrayed; treacherous.

atraiçoar *vt (ser falso)* to betray.

atrair *vt* to attract; ~ **atenção a si** to catch/to draw attention to o.s.; **2** to entice.

atrapalhação *f* confusion, embarrassment.

atrapalhado,-a *adj* embarrassed; **2** flustered; **3** jumbled, muddled up; **4** clumsy; **5** ~ **com a vida** beset with personal problems.

atrapalhar *vt* to confuse, disconcert; **2** embarrass; **3** hinder; ♦ ~-**se** *vr* to get confused, nervous; to be in a muddle.

atrás *adv (posição)* behind, at the back; **2** *(em classificação)* **estar/ficar** ~ **(de)** to be ranking behind; **3** *(no tempo)* previously, ago, past ♦ *prep*: ~ **de** behind; **2** *(em seguimento)* after; **3** *(em busca de pessoa)* after; **ele anda** ~ **dela** he is after her; *(de objecto, emprego)* to look for; IDIOM *(desconfiado)* **andar de pé** ~ *(desconfiado)* to be suspicious.

atrasado,-a *m* latecomer; ♦ *adj* late, tardy; **2** *(trabalho amontoado)* backlog; **3** *(relógio)* slow; **4** *(pagamento, dívida)* overdue; **5** *(pessoa, aldeia, costumes)* backward; **6** *(edição)* back.

atrasar *vt (fazer demorar)* to delay; **2** *(retardar)* to hold back; **3** *(relógio)* to put back; ♦ *vi (relógio)* to be slow; **2** *(publicação)* to be late; ♦ ~-**se** *vr* to fall behind *(com o trabalho)*; **2** ~-**se para** to be late for.

atraso *m* delay, lateness; **2** backwardness; **em** ~ in arrears; **chegar com** ~ to arrive late; **3** *(fig)* drawback, setback.

atrativo,-a (*Vd*: **atra(c)tivo,-a**).

através *adv* across, through; ♦ *prep*: ~ **de** amongst; **2** by means of, through; ~ **dos séculos** throughout the centuries.

atravessado,-a *adj (de través)* askew; **2** *(cruzado)* crossed; **3** ~ **sobre** lying across; **4** *(fig)* angry, irritated; IDIOM **ter alguém** ~ **na garganta** to bear someone a grudge.

atravessar *vt* to cross *(rua, mar)*; **2** ~ **a correr** to run across; **3** to pass, go through *(túnel); (fig) (dificuldades)* to go through; **4** *(perfurar)* to go through; **5** *(pôr de través)* to place across; *(tábua, etc)* pierce; ♦ ~-**se** *vr* to lie across, to block; to be stuck; **uma espinha atravessou-se na minha garganta** I have a fish bone stuck in my throat; **2** *(fig) (intrometer-se)* to cross *(vida, caminho)*.

atreito,-a *adj* inclined, prone; accustomed (to); **ele é** ~ **a doenças** he is prone to illness.

atrelar *vr*: to put on a leash; **2** to harness; ♦ *vr*: ~-**se a alguém** to stick close to sb.

atrelado,-a *adj* harnessed, behind another vehicle; **2** ~ **a** *(outro veículo)* in tow.

atrever-se *vr*: ~ **a** to dare to; to have courage for; **como se atreve!** how dare you!

atrevido,-a *adj* impudent; bold.

atrevimento *m* boldness; insolence; **que** ~**!** what a cheek! how dare you!

atribuição *f* attribution; award, presentation.

atribuições *fpl* rights, powers.

atribuir *vt* to attribute; **2** to confer.

atribulado,-a *m,f (vida agitada/dura)* troubled, with ups and downs; **2** *(tempos)* hard; **3** *(pessoa)* distressed.

atribular *vt* to trouble, distress; ♦ ~-**se** *vr* to be distressed.

atributo *m* attribute.

átrio *m* church yard; courtyard; atrium; hall.

atrito *nm* friction; **2** (FÍS) attriction; **3** *(fig)* disagreement, conflict.

atriz (*Vd*: **a(c)triz**).

atroador,-a *adj (ruído)* deafening, thunderous.

atroar *vt* to shake *(atmosfera)*; ♦ *vi* to reverberate, thunder.
atrocidade *f* atrocity; **2** *(fig)* outrage.
atrofiado,-a *adj (criança)* underdeveloped, weak; **2** *(órgão, membro, planta)* atrophied.
atrofiar *vt* to cribble; **2** *(definhar)* waste away, wither; ♦ ~**-se** *vr* become weak; *(força, energia)* diminish.
atropelamento *m* accident, running over; **2** ~ **com fuga** hit and run; **3** *(palavras, etc)* stumbling.
atropelar *vt* to knock down, to run over; **3** *(empurrar)* to jostle, to push; **4** *(fig) (baralhar)* to stumble, to muddle up.
atropelo *m* running over, knocking down; **2** *(desrespeito)* abuse; **os** ~**s da lei** the abuses of the law; **3** jostling; scramble; **4 ao** *(confusão)* turmoil.
atroz *adj* merciless; atrocious.
atuação *(Vd* a(c)tuação).
atual *(Vd* a(c)tual).
atualidade *(Vd* a(c)tualidade).
atualizar *(Vd:* a(c)tualizar).
atualmente *(Vd:* a(c)tualmente).
atuar *(Vd:* a(c)tuar).
atuário *(Vd:* a(c)tuário).
atulhar *vt (encher, amontoar)* to fill, to stuff, to cram, clutter up; **a casa estava atulhada de bugigangas** the house was cluttered with knick-knacks.
atum *m* tuna fish.
aturar *vt* to endure, put up with, cope with; **2** *(fig)* to stomach; ♦ *vi* to endure.
aturdido,-a *adj* dazed, stunned; **2** *(fig)* astounded; **ficar** ~ to be stunned.
aturdir *vt* to stun; **2** *(fig)* to bewilder, dazzle.
audácia *f* boldness; audacity, insolence.
audacioso,-a *adj* audacious, intrepid; **2** bold.
audaz *adj* daring; bold; insolent.
audição *(pl:* -**ões**) *f (sentido de ouvir)* hearing; **2** *(resultdo de ouvir)* hearing; ~ **das testemunhas** hearing of witnesses; **3** *(MÚS)* recital, audition.
audiência *f (ger)* audience; **2** *(JUR)* session, hearing; **sala de** ~**s** courtroom; **3** *(RÁDIO – ouvintes)* listeners *pl*; *(TV)* viewers; **4** *(recepção)* audience; **eles tiveram uma** ~ **com o ministro** they had an audience with the minister.
áudio *m* audio.
audiovisual *(pl:* **audiovisuais**) *adj inv* audio-visual.
auditar *vt (FIN)* to audit.
auditivo,-a *adj* auditive, auditory; **problemas** ~**s** hearing problems.
auditor *m* listener; **2** *(FIN)* auditor; **3** *(juíz)* magistrate; ~**ia** *f (serviço)* audit, auditing, audit's department.
auditório *m (assistence)* audience; **2** *(lugar)* auditorium.
audível *(pl:* -**veis**) *adj inv* audible.
auferir *vt* obtain, gain *(juros, lucros)*; **2** ~ **isenção de impostos** enjoy tax exemption.
auge *m (máximo)* pinnacle, zenith; apogee; peak; height, hey-day, **no** ~ **da sua fama** at the height of his fame; **2** despair, **no** ~ **do desespero** in the depth of despair.
augurar *vt* to prophesy, to foretell; **2** wish.
augúrio *m* omen, prophecy.
aula *f* lesson, class; **sala de** ~ class; **2 aulas** *fpl* school, *sg*.

aumentar *vt (ger)* to increase; ♦ *vi* to increase; **2** *(crescer)* to grow.
aumento *m* increase; **2** *(salário)* rise *(UK)*, raise *(US)*; **3** enlargement; **4** *(crescimento)* growth.
aura *f* halo; *(fig)(fama)* aura; **2** breeze.
áureo,-a *adj* golden; **a idade A**~ *(HIST)* Golden Age.
auréola *f* halo; **2** *(ASTRON)* aureola, nimbus.
aurícula *f (ANAT) (do ouvido)* auricle; *(do coração)* atrium, auricle.
aurora *f* dawn; **ao romper da** ~ at daybreak.
auscultação *f (MED)* auscultation; **2** *(sondagem)* survey, opinion poll.
auscultador *m* telephone receiver; **2** *(MED)* stethoscope; **3** *(MÚS)* headphone.
auscultar *vt (MED)* to sound with the stethoscope; **2** *(sondagem)* to sound.
ausência *f* absence; **2** shortage.
ausentar-se *vr* to go/stay away; to be absent.
ausente *m,f* absent person. absentee; ♦ *adj* absent; **estar** ~ to be out/away.
austeridade *f* austerity.
austero,-a *adj* austere.
austral *adj* southern.
Austrália *npr* **a** ~ Australia.
australiano,-a, *m,f adj* Australian.
Áustria *npr* **a** ~ Austria.
austríaco,-a *m,f adj* Austrian.
autarquia *f* autarchy; *(região)* autonomous, regional government.
autenticar *vt* to authenticate, to certify.
autêntico,-a *adj* authentic, genuine, true.
autista *adj inv* autistic.
auto *m* short play, drama; **2** *(JUR)* report, brief; **lavrar um** ~ to make a report; **3** ~**s** *mpl (JUR)* record of proceedings, legal documents; **4** *(prefix)* self, auto.
autobiografia *f* autobiography.
autocarro *m* bus *(EP)*.
autoclismo *m (da sanita)* toilet flush, *(flushing)* cistern.
autocolante *adj inv* sticker; **2** *(envelopes, etc)* self-adhesive.
autoconfiança *f* self-confidence.
autocrata *m,f* autocrat.
autocrático,-a *adj* autocratic.
autocrítica *f* self criticism.
autóctone *adj* indigenous; **2** *m,f* native, aborigine.
auto-de-fé *(pl:* **autos-de-fé**) *m* auto-de fé.
autodefesa *f* self-defence *(UK)*; autodefense *(US)*.
autodeterminação *f* self determination.
autodidacta, autodidata *adj inv* self-taught person.
autodomínio *m* self-control.
autódromo *m* racetrack *(UK)*, racecourse *(US)*.
auto-escola, autoescola *f* driving school.
auto-estima, autoestima *f* self-esteem.
auto-estrada, autoestrada *f* motorway; *(US)* highway.
autografar *vt* to sign, autograph *(livro, etc)*.
autógrafo *m* autograph.
automático,-a *adj* automatic.
automatização *f* automation.
automatizar *vt* to automatize.
autómato,-a *(BR:* -**ô**-) *m* automaton.

automedicar-se *vr* to medicate o.s.

automobilismo *m* motoring; motor car racing.

automobilista *m,f* driver, motorist.

automotora *f* diesel locomotive, rail car.

automóvel (*pl:* **-veis**) *m* motor car; **piloto de ~** racing driver; **~ anfíbio**, amphibious car; **~ de dois lugares** two-seater car.

autonomia *f* autonomy; self government.

autónomo,-a (*BR:* -tô-) *adj* autonomous.

autópsia *f* autopsy; 2 (*fig*) detailed analysis.

autor,-ora *m,f* author; **direitos de ~** author's rights; (*dinheiro*) royalties; 2 inventor; 3 (*de crime*) perpetrator.

auto-retrato, autorretrato *m* self-portrait.

autoria *f* authorship; 2 responsibility.

autoridade *f* authority; 2 **sob a ~ de** under orders of; 3 expert; 4 person in charge; **as ~s** (*indefinidas*) (*ADMIN, POL*) those in charge, the establishment; the powers that be.

autoritário,-a *m,f* authoritarian; ♦ *adj* authoritarian, authoritative.

autorização *f* authorization, permit, permission.

autorizar *vt* to authorize.

auto-satisfação, autossatisfação *f* self-satisfaction.

auto-suficiente, autossuficiente *adj inv* self-sufficient; 2 (*pessoa – confiante*) self-confident.

auto-sugestão, autossugestão *f* auto-suggestion.

autotanque *m* water tanker, fire engine.

autuação *f* fine; 2 (*JUR*) proceedings.

autuar *vt* to fine; to charge; 2 to report (*infractor*).

auxiliar *m* auxiliary, helper; 2 assistant; 3 **~ justice** clerk of the court; auxiliary; 4 aid; ♦ *vt* help.

auxílio *m* aid, help, assistance.

Av (*abr de* **avenida**) avenue, Av.

aval *m* guarantee; 2 backing; 3 (*COM*) surety, warranty.

avalancha, avalanche *f* avalanche; 2 (*fig*) (*grande quantidade súbita*) flood, sudden rush; **uma ~ de cartas** a flood of letters.

avaliação *f* valuation, estimate; assessment, evaluation; **auto~** self-assessment.

avaliar *vt* to estimate; to assess.

avalista *m,f* guarantor, person who gives surety.

avalizar *vt* (*JUR*) vouch for, guarantee; 2 (*fig*) support, back up.

avançada *f* advance; **de uma ~** all at once; **avançado,-a** *m* (*FUT*) forward; **~-centro** *m* centre-forward; ♦ *adj* advanced; ahead; ahead of its time.

avançar *vt,vi* to move forward; advance; put forward; **~ o sinal** to drive through a red light.

avanço *m* advancement; progress; 2 (*TEC*) feed; **~ automático** automatic feed.

avantajado,-a *adj* advantageous, beneficial; 2 (*pessoa forte*) stout.

avarento,-a *m,f* miser; ♦ *adj* greedy; mean, avaricious. **avareza** *f* avarice, greed; meanness.

avaria *f* damage; 2 (*TEC*) breakdown.

avariar *vt* to damage; ♦ *vi* to suffer damage; 2 (*TEC*) to break down.

avaro,-a *m,f* miser; ♦ *adj* greedy; mean.

avassalador,-ora *adj* (*ímpeto, desejo*) overpowering; overwhelming.

AVC *n* (*abr de* **acidente vascular cerebral**) stroke.

ave *f* bird, fowl; **~ de rapina** bird of prey; 2 **~ agourenta** *f* bird of ill omen; **~-do-paraíso** *f* (*BOT, ZOOL*) bird of paradise.

ave-Maria *m* (*oração à Nossa Senhora*) hail Mary!

aveia *f* (*planta, grão*) oats *pl.*; 2 (*farinha*) oatmeal; **papa de ~** porridge.

avelã *f* hazelnut; 2 **cabeça de ~** feather-brained person.

aveludado,-a *adj* silky, velvety; 2 (*voz, olhos*) soft; 3 (*vinho, molho*) smooth.

ave-maria (*pl:* **ave-marias**) *f* prayer to the blessed Virgin; 2 a bead in the rosary; 3 *pl* angelus bell.

avenca *f* (*BOT*) maidenhair, silver fern.

avença *f* agreement; 2 settlement (*entre litigantes*); 3 (*pagamento*) lump sum; 4 **estar de boas ~s** to be on good terms.

avenida *f* avenue, grove.

avental *m* (*vestuário*) apron; (*tipo de bata sem braços*) pinafore.

aventar *vt* to put forward (an idea).

aventura *nf* adventure; exploit.

aventurado,-a *adj* daring; 2 **bem-~** blessed;

aventurar *vt* to risk, venture; ♦ *vr:* **~-se a** to dare to.

aventureiro,-a *m,f* adventurer; ♦ *adj* rash, foolhardy.

averiguação *f* investigation, inquiry.

averiguar *vt* to investigate, ascertain; to verify.

aversão *f* aversion.

avessas: às ~ *adv* upside down, the wrong way round, inside out.

avesso,-a *m* the wrong side, reverse; 2 opposite; ♦ *adj* wrong, opposing; (*do tecido*) reverse; **ao/do ~** inside out.

avestruz *m,f* (*ZOOL*) ostrich.

avezar *vt* to accustom; ♦ *vr:* **~-se a** to get used to; 2 (*pop*) to obtain, possess.

aviação *f* aviation, flying.

aviado,-a *adj* hurried; 2 **receita ~ a** prescription made up (at the pharmacy).

aviador,-ora *m,f* aviator, airman/woman.

aviamentos *mpl* materials, supplies.

avião *m* aeroplane; **~ a jacto** jet plane; **~ de caça** fighter; **~ bombardeiro** bomber.

aviar *vt* (*receita médica*) to make up; 2 to attend to; **~ os fregueses** to attend to the customers; 3 (*executar com rapidez*) to hurry up; **por favor avie-me** please hurry up and see to me/attend to me; ♦ **~-se** *vr* to hurry up; 2 to get ready; **avia-te** hurry up!

aviário *m* aviary.

avícola *adj inv* (*pessoa, indústria*) poultry farmer, farming.

avicultor,-ora *m,f* poultry farmer.

avicultura *n* poultry-raising, poultry-breeding.

avidez *f* greediness; eagerness.

ávido,-a *adj* greedy; 2 eager; **~ de sabedoria** eager/thirsty for knowledge.

aviltamento *m* disgrace, humiliation; abuse.

aviltar *vt* to debase, vilify; degrade; ♦ **~-se** *vr* to demean o.s., to dishonour.

avinagrado,-a *adj* sour, tasting of vinegar, **o vinho está ~** the wine has turned sour.

avir *vt* to reconcile; **2** to adjust; ♦ *vr* ~**-se com** to manage; to get along with.

avisar *vt* to warn; **2** to tell; **3** to notify.

aviso *m (notificação, placa)* notice; **2** *(advertência)* warning; **3** *(informação)* advice, notice; **conforme** ~ as per advice; ♦ *adv* **de** ~ on the alert.

avis rara *f* rare bird.

avistar *vt* to glimpse, to catch sight of; ~ **terra** to come in sight of land; ♦ *vr*: ~**-se com** to have a meeting with.

avivar *vt* to rouse; to intensify, heighten; ~ **o fogo** to stir the fire; ♦ *vi* to revive, recover.

avizinhar-se *vr* to approach, come near.

avo *m* fraction of unity smaller than one-tenth: **cinco treze** ~**s** five-thirteenths.

avô, avó *m,f* grandfather, mother; **avós** *mpl* grandparents; ancestors; IDIOM **do tempo da minha** ~ *adj* old-fashioned.

avoengos *mpl* ancestors, forebears.

avolumar(-se) *vt, vr* to increase, gain in volume, swell, take up space.

à vontade *m* relaxed attitude; ease; *(Vd: vontade)*.

avulso,-a *m* flyer; ♦ *adj* odd, sundry; **2** *(venda)* by weight; **3** *(solto)* loose; **4 papéis** ~**s** sundry papers.

avultado,-a *adj* large, bulky; **uma quantia** ~ a large sum of money; **2** *(negócio, etc)* considerable.

avultar *vt* to enlarge, expand, increase; ♦ *vi* to stand out; **2** exaggerate, emphasize.

axe *exc* **axe!** *(dor repentina)* ouch!

axila *f* armpit.

axioma *m* axiom.

azáfama *f* bustle, frenzied activity, hurly-burly; **a** ~ **de todos os dias** the day-to-day hurly-burly.

azálea *f (BOT)* azalea.

azar *m* bad luck; misfortune; **que** ~! what rotten luck!; IDIOM **ter** ~ **a alguém/algo** to dislike someone/something.

azarado,-a *adj* unlucky; **to be** ~ having the jinx, to be jinxed.

azedar *vt* to sour, curdle; **2** *(fig) (pessoa)* to be/grow bitter; **3** to irritate, exacerbate; ♦ ~**-se** *vr* to turn/go sour.

azedo,-a *adj (produto)* sour; bitter; **2** *(fig) (pessoa)* irritable, bitter.

azedume *m* sourness; bitterness; **2** *(fig)* irritability.

azeite *m* olive oil; IDIOM **estar com os** ~**s** to be in a bad mood; **2** *(BR) (pop)* courtship, going out with sb.

azeitona *f* olive.

azeitoneira *f* dish to put in olives.

azémola *f* beast of burden; **2** *(cavalo velho e cansado)* packhorse; **3** *(fig) (pessoa estúpida)* not very bright.

azenha *f* watermill.

Azerbaijão *npr* **o** ~ Azerbaijan.

azarbaijano,-a *adj* Azerbaijani.

azeteca *m,f* Aztec; **os** ~**s** the Azetecs; ♦ *adj inv* Azetec.

azeviche *m* jet; **2** *(cor negra)* jet black.

azevinho *m (BOT)* holly.

azia *f* heartburn, acid stomach.

aziago,-a *adj (agoirento)* ominous; ill-fated; unlucky; **um dia** ~ an unlucky day.

ázimo *m* **festa dos** ~**s** the Passover; ♦ *m adj (pão sem fermento)* unleavened.

azinhaga *f* country lane; **2** narrow trail.

azinheiro,-a *m,f (BOT) (tipo de carvalho)* holm oak, holly oak, illex.

azo *m* opportunity; **2** pretext; **3 dar** ~ **a** to give full rein to, give occasion to.

azotado,-a *adj (QUÍM)* nitrogenous.

azoto *m* nitrogen, azote.

azougado,-a *adj (pessoa mexida)* restless, lively; **2** *(esperta)* sharp; shrewd; **3** *(BR)* irritable.

azougue *m (QUÍM)* mercury, quick silver; **2** *(fig) (pessoa viva)* live wire, full of life.

azucrinar *vt (BR)* to annoy, pester *(alguém)*.

azul *(pl: azuis) adj m* blue; **2** *(fig)* embarrassed; ~ **celeste** *m* sky blue; ~ **escuro/ferrete** *m* dark blue; ~ **marinho** *m* navy blue; ~ **da Prússia** *(QUÍM) m* dark blue mineral; *(cor)* dark blue; ~ **turquesa** *m* turquoise blue; IDIOM **ver-se** ~ be at one's wits' end.

azulado,-a *adj* bluish.

azulejo *m (ladrilho)* glazed tile.

b

B, b *m (letra)* B, b.

baba *f (saliva)* dribble.

babá *f (BR) (ama-seca)* nursemaid; nanny.

babá-de-moça *(pl: babás-de-moça) m,f (BR) (CULIN)* sweet dish with eggs and coconut; rum baba.

babado *m (folho)* frills, ruffles; **2** *(BR) (fam) (mexerico)* gossip; ♦ **babado,-a** *adj (bebé)* dribbling; *(molhado de baba)* dribbly; **2** *(adulto) (orgulhoso)* doting; **ela é uma mãe** ~ she is a doting mother.

babar *vt* to dribble on *(roupa)*; slaver on ♦ **~-se** *vr (deitar baba)* to dribble, slobber; **o bebé está a ~-se** the baby is dribbling; **2 ~-se por** *(gostar muito de alguém)* to drool over sb; *(estar orgulhoso de alguém)* be proud of *(sb)*.

babeiro *m* baby's bib.

babador *(BR) m* **babete** *(EP) m* baby's, child's bib.

baboso,-a *adj (que se baba)* dribbling; slobbering; **2** drooling, doting; **3** *(orgulhoso)* proud (of/about sb).

baboseira, babosice *f* twaddle; **2** silly compliment.

babugem *f (espuma do mar)* foam, froth; **2** *(baba)* slobber; **3** *(fig) (bagatela)* trifle; **4** *(restos)* left-overs *pl*; **andar à ~** to depend on other people's charity.

babuíno *m (ZOOL)* baboon.

bacalhau *(fish)* cod; **2** ~ **seco** dried cod, codfish. IDIOM **ficar em águas de ~** *(negócio, casamento)* come to nothing; go down the drain.

bacalhoeiro *m (pescador, barco)* cod fisherman, cod fishing boat.

bacalhoada *f* cod stew; **2** a lot of codfish.

bacamarte *m (arma antiga)* blunderbass; **2** *(fig) (livro)* old heavy book.

bacana *(BR) adj inv (col)* great, cool, amazing.

bacanal *m* orgy; **~nais** *pl* festivities in honour of Baco.

bacharel *m,f (UNIV) (alguém)* bachelor, graduate; ~ **em Letras** bachelor in Arts, BA; ~ **em Ciências** graduate in Science, B.Sc.

bacharelar-se *vr* to graduate; to obtain, have a bachelor's degree.

bacharelada *f (conversa pretensiosa)* pretentious talk.

bacharelado, bacharelato *m* bachelor's degree; ~ **internacional** (school-leaving exam) baccalaureate, Baccalauréat; ♦ *adj (alguém)* with a degree, graduate.

bacia *f* basin, bowl; **2** *(GEOG, GEOL, NÁUT)* basin; **3** *(ANAT)* pelvis.

bacilar *adj inv (infecção)* bacillary.

bacilo *m* bacillus; **bacilos** *mpl* bacilli.

bacio *m* chamber pot; **2** *(para criança)* potty.

baço *m (ANAT)* spleen; ♦ **baço,-a** *adj (pele, olhar, vidro) (sem brilho)* dull; **2** *(metal)* tarnished.

bacon *m (tipo inglês)* bacon.

bacorada *f* many piglets, litter; **2** *(fig)* nonsense; **3** *(fig)* obscenity; **dizer ~s** to talk nonsense, to say obscenities.

bacorinho,-a *m* little piglet, suckling pig.

bácoro,-a piglet.

bactéria *f* germ, bacterium; **~s** *fpl* bacteria *pl*.

báculo *m (em cerimónia litúrgica)* staff, crozier.

ba(c)teriologia *f* bacteriology.

ba(c)teriológico,-a *adj* bacteriological.

ba(c)teriogista *m,f* bacteriologist.

badalada *f (relógio)* stroke; **2** *(som do sino)* peal.

badalar *vt/vi (tocar)* to ring; chime; *(sino)* to peal, toll; **2** *(relógio)* strike; **3** *(pop) (falar muito; ser indiscreto)* to talk about; to babble.

badalo *m* clapper; **2** tongue of a bell; **3** *(col)* tongue; IDIOM **dar ao ~** to wag one's tongue, blab.

badalhoco,-a *m,f (fam) (pessoa suja)* slovenly person; *(mulher)* slattern, slut; **2** *(pessoa ordinária)* common person; ♦ *adj* dirty, filthy; **2** *(conversa)* disgusting.

badameco *m (fam) (pessoa de pouca importância)* non-entity; **2** *(rapaz atrevido)* cheeky boy, whippersnapper.

badana *f* scraggy sheep; **2** flap *(de um livro)*.

badanal *m (fam) (azáfama)* hullabaloo, hubbub, racket; **num ~** *adv* in a fluster.

badejo *m (fish)* whiting.

bafejar *vt (sofrar)* to blow on; **2** breathe on; **3** *(destino)* to smile upon/on, to favour.

bafejo *m (sopro)* breath; puff; **2** *(fig) (de sorte)* stroke *(of)*.

bafio *m (mofo)* must, mould; **cheira a ~** it smells musty.

bafo *m (ar quente da respiração)* breath; **limpa o espelho com o teu ~** clean the mirror with your breath; **2** *(cheiro)* smell; **3** *(fig)* protection; **4** *(BR)* **~-de-onça** bad breath.

bafómetro *(BR: -ô-) m* breathalyser.

baforada *f* puff *(de fumo)*; **2** gust *(de ar)*; whiff *(de cheiro)*; **3** *(hálito, mau cheiro)* bad breath, bad smell; **4** *(corrente de ar quente)* warm breeze.

baga *f (fruto)* berry; *(uva)* grape; **2** *(fig) (gota)* drop; bead; ~ **de suor** a bead of sweat.

bagaceira *f* Portuguese brandy.

bagaceiro,-a *(BR)* person who gathers bagasse.

bagaço *m (resíduos de uva, azeitona)* marc; *(de maçã)* pomace; **2** *(aguardente bagaceira)* marc brandy; **3** *(pop) (dinheiro)* dough, lolly; **4** *(BR) (bebida) (feito da cana d'açúcar)* bagasse.

bagageira *f (em carro)* boot (UK), trunk (US); ♦ **bagageiro,-a** *m (carregador)* porter; **2** *(BR) (último cavalo a chegar à meta)* also-ran.

bagagem *(pl: -ens) f* baggage, luggage; **2** *(fig)* knowledge, experience; **3 porta-bagagens** *m (AUTO)* car's boot, trunk.

bagalhoça *f (pop) (dinheiro)* dough.

bagatela *f (coisa insignificante)* bagatelle, trinket; **2** *(fig)* trifle; **3** *(ninharia)* next to nothing; **4** *(bilhar chinês)* bagatelle.

Bagdá *(BR)*, **Bagdade** *(EP) npr* Baghdad.

bago *m (de pequeno fruto)* berry; **2** *(de uva)* grape; **3** *(de romã)* seed; *(de milho)* grain of corn; **4** *(de chumbo)* pellet (shot).

bagulho m *(em pera, romã)* pip; **2** *(uva)* grapeseed; **3** *(col) (dinheiro)* **ter muito ~** to be loaded.

bagunça *(BR) (pop)* f mess; **2** *(barulho, tumulto)* hubbub; clutter; *(BR) (também)* bulldozer.

Bahamas npr **(as ilhas)** ~ the Bahamas.

Bahia npr *(Brasil)* Bahia.

baia[1] f *(barrote que separa os cavalos)* bail, stall; **baias** fpl *(fig) (limites)* restriction; **sem quaisquer** ~s without any impediment.

baia[2] f *(mulher morena) (tez)* dark woman, swarthy woman.

baía f *(GEOG)* bay.

baiano,-a adj of/from Bahia.

baião m Brazilian folk dance.

baila f: **trazer à** ~ to raise the issue; **vir à** ~ *(assunto)* to come up, come to light; IDIOM **andar na** ~ be talked about.

bailado m dance, ballet.

bailar vt *(dançar)* dance.

bailarico m *(baile popular)* village dance; dance party.

bailarino,-a m,f dancer; ballet dancer; f ballerina.

baile m dance; ball; ~ **de máscaras** fancy dress ball; **2** *(fig)* **dar um** ~ **a alguém** to tease sb.

bailio m *(HIST) (comendador)* commander in a religious, military order; **2** *(magistrado)* bailiff.

bainha f *(da espada, do punhal)* sheath, scabbard; **2** *(vestuário)* hem; **descer/subir a** ~ let down/take up the hem.

baio adj *(cor, cavalo)* bay.

baioneta f *(arma)* bayonet; ~ **calada** bayoneted rifle.

bairrista m,f local resident; ♦ adj inv community-based; **2** *(fig)* parochial.

bairro m district, old quarter; **2 o** ~ the neighbourhood; **3** ~-**dormitório** satellite town; ~ **social** m *(UK)* Council housing estate.

baixa f *(diminuição)* decrease; reduction; **2** *(FIN, ECON)* fall, downturn, slump; **3** *(temperatura)* drop, fall; **4** *(depressão de terreno)* hollow; **5 B~** *(centro da cidade)* downtown; **6** *(MIL)* casualties pl, losses pl; **7 dar** ~ **a um caso** *(JUR)* dismiss a case; **8** *(doença)* **ter/estar de** ~ to be on sick-leave; **9 dar** ~ **de algo/alguém num registo** to tick sth/sb off a register.

baixada f *(ELECT)* downlead; **2** *(BR) (depressão de terreno)* lowland; **3** *(descida)* downward, slope.

baixa-mar (= **beixa-mar**) f low tide.

baixar vt to lower *(persiana, bandeira)*; to take down *(bainha do vestido)*; ~ **a cabeça** to bow; to bend one's head; **2** to reduce; **3** *(COMP)* to download; ♦ vi *(descer)* to go/come down, to drop; **a maré baixou** the tide went out; **2** ~ **ao hospital** to go into hospital; **3** *(COMP)* download; ♦ ~-**se** vr *(curvar-se, agachar-se)* to bend down; **2** *(rebaixar-se)* to adopt a humble attitude; to eat humble pie.

baixela f tableware; ~ **de prata** silver tableware.

baixeza f *(ação vil)* meanness, baseness, low-mindedness.

baixinho adv softly, quietly, low; **fale** ~ speak softly/in a low voice; ♦ **baixinho,-a** m,f short; **ele é** ~ he

is quite short; *(móvel)* low; ♦ adv softly, quietly, low; **fale mais** ~ speak (more) softly/in a low voice.

baixio m sandbank; **2** reef; **3** shallow river.

baixista m,f *(MUS)* bass player; ♦ adj inv *(ECON)* *(tendência)* downward; **mercado** ~ *(Bolsa)* bear market; **especulador** ~ *(que joga na baixa)* bear speculator, broker.

baixo m *(NÁUT)* sandbank, shoal; **encalhar num** ~ run aground; **2** *(NÁUT)* lower part of the hull; **3** *(MUS)* bass; ♦ **baixo,-a** adj *(algo)* low; **2** *(alguém)* short; **3** *(depressão)* hollow, shallow; **4** *(temperatura, tensão)* low; **5** *(inclinado para o chão)* lowered *(olhos, cabeça)* **6** *(qualidade)* inferior; **7** *(fig)* *(alguém reles)* common, low; **8** *(região)* lower, **B~ Alentejo** Lower Alentejo; ♦ adv low; low down; **em** ~ below, downstairs; **ela está lá em** ~ she is downstairs, down there; **para** ~ down, downwards, downstairs; **de alto a** ~ from top to bottom; **ele olhou-a de alto a** ~ he looked her up and down; **2** *(fig)* **estar em** ~ *(deprimido)* to be feeling low, to be in the dumps; **3** softly, quietly; **fala mais** ~ speak (more) softly, lower your voice; ♦ prep **por** ~ **de** under, underneath, below.

baixo-relevo m bas-relief.

baixote m *(canino)* basset; ~ **de pelo comprido** Sussex spaniel; ♦ **baixote** m,f adj m undersized, short.

bajulação *(pl: -ões)* f *(pej) (lisonja) (adulação)* adulation, flattery, silly compliment; **2** *(persuação)* cajolery.

bajulador,-ora m,f toady, flatterer, obsequious.

bajular vt *(adular)* to flatter, be a toad; to bow and scrape to *(o patrão etc)*

bala f bullet.

balaço m large ball; **2** cannon shot.

balada f ballad.

balança f scales pl; ~ **comercial** balance of trade; **2** equilibrium; **3** ~ **de estrada** f weighbridge.

Balança *(ASTROL, ASTRON)* Libra.

balançar vt *(baloiçar, oscilar)* to rock, swing; **2** *(compensar)* counteract; **3** *(considerar)* to weigh (up); ♦ vi to shake *(carro, etc)*; ♦ ~-**se** vr to sway; to roll.

balancete m *(COM) (resumo do balanço geral)* summary of the general balance sheet

balanço m *(oscilação)* swinging, rocking; **2** *(de criança)* swing; **3** *(do barco)* rolling; **4** *(solavanco)* jerk; **5** *(TEC)* ~ **térmico** heat balance; **6 os ~s da vida** life's ups and downs; **7** *(COM)* balance, checking of accounts; **8 fazer/dar** ~ to take stock.

It does not mean the results of the balance/accounts (remainder, surplus), which is '**saldo**'.

balão m balloon; **2** aerostat; **3** *(MED)* cylinder *(de oxigéneo)*; **4** *(QUÍM)* flask; **5** ~ **de sondagem/** ~-**sonda** probe, pilot balloon; **6** *(teste de alcoolemia)* breathalyser *(UK)*; breathalizer *(US)*; **7** *(futebol)* high ball; IDIOM **andar de** ~ to be pregnant; **ir no** ~ *(ser enganada)* to be taken for a ride.

balar *(também: balir)* vi *(ovelha)* to bleat.

balastro m ballast.

balaustrada f balustrade.

balbuciante adj inv (criança) babbling; **2** (alguém hesitante) faltering; **3** (gago) stammering.

balbuciar vt/vi to stutter, stammer; **2** (criança) to babble; **3** (hesitar) to falter.

balbúrdia f uproar, bedlam; **2** confusion, disorder.

balcão m shop counter; bar counter; **2** (ARQ) balcony; **3** (empresas, secção) desk; **vá àquele** ~ go to that desk; **4** (TEAT) circle; **primeiro** ~ dress circle; **segundo** ~ upper circle.

Balcãs npl: **os** ~ Balkans.

balcânico,-a m,f adj Balkan.

balda f (col) (desordem) caos, mess; ♦ **à** ~ adv (de qualquer maneira) any (old) how, slapdash.

baldão m (contrariedade) nuisance; **2** (insulto) affront; **3** (onda grande) tidal wave; **4** (azar) stroke of bad luck; **andar aos baldões** to go through a bad time; ♦ **de** ~ adv pell-mell.

baldar vt to frustrate, foil, thwart (plano, esforço).

baldas f, adj inv (pej) (pessoa) slacker.

balde m bucket, pail.

baldeação f transfer (from one container to another); **2** (NÁUT) swabbing of the deck.

baldear vt to decant; **2** to transfer (líquido de um barco para outro); **3** to bail out (líquido).

baldio m wasteland; ♦ adj (terreno) fallow, uncultivated; **terras** ~,-**as** wasteland; **2** (sem dono) common land.

Baleares npr as (ilhas) ~ the Balearic Islands.

baleeira f whaleboat.

baleeiro m (barco, pescador) whaler.

baleia f (ZOOL) whale.

balido m (de ovelha) bleating; bleat.

balir vi (ovelha) to bleat.

balística f ballistics sg.

baliza f (estaca) goalpost; **2** boundary mark; **3** (bóia) buoy; (luminosa) beacon; **4** goal.

balizar vt (DESP) put up goal posts in (campo); **2** demarcate; **3** (cálculo) estimate.

balé, ballet m (dance) ballet.

balneário m spa, bathing resort.

balofo,-a adj (pessoa) flabby, plump; **2** (bolo) fluffy, puffy; **3** (discurso) puffed up; superficial, hollow.

baloiçar, balouçar vt/vi to rock, swing, sway.

baloiço, balouço m (balancé) swing; **andar de** ~ to go on the swing; **2 cadeira de** ~ f rocking chair.

balsa f (BOT) (dorna) briar, thorn-bush; **2** (funil) funnel for wine; **3** (salgadeira) tub; **4** pressed grapes; **5** (BR) raft; **6** (barca) catamaran.

bálsamo m balsam, balm.

Báltico m: **o** (mar) **B**~ the Baltic (sea).

báltico,-a adj relating to the Baltic region; **os países** ~**s** the Baltic countries.

baluarte m rampart, bulwark, stronghold.

balúrdio m (col) (quantia avultada) a packet of (money).

bambo,-a m,f, adj (frouxo) slack, loose (elástico, parafuso); limp, slack (corda); **2** (fig) (instável) wobbly; IDIOM **dançar na corda** ~**a** to walk on a tightrope; **ser bamba em** to be an expert; (BR) (col) to be a shark.

bambear vt (afrouxar) to loosen; to slacken (elastico, corda); ♦ vi (enfraquecer) to become wobbly, weaken (pernas); **2** (fig) (hesitar) to falter.

bâmbi m (veado) deer, fawn.

bambolé (BR: -ê) m hula loop.

bamboleante adj inv swaying (corpo, ancas).

bambolear vt to swing (ancas); ♦ vi to sway; **2** (com passos incertos) totter; wobble.

bambu m (BOT) (cana) bamboo.

banal adj banal, commonplace, ordinary.

banalidade f triviality, banality.

banalizar vt to make/turn common.

banana f (fruto) banana; **2** (col) m coward, spineless (man); **ele é um**~ he has no guts.

bananeira f banana tree.

banca f banking establishment, the Bank; **2** (mesa tosca) table, bench; **3** (jogos) game of chance; **4** tripod; **5** lawyer's office; **6** ~ **de jornais** newspaper stand; **7** ~ **de praça/mercado** market stall; **levar a** ~ **à glória** to sweep the stakes.

bancada f (TEAT) row of seats, tier; (estádio) terraces, bleachers; **2** (assento comprido) bench; **3** (de carpinteiro) workbench; **4** (da cozinha) worktop; **5** (estádio) terraces, bleachers; **6** (parlamento) bench; ~**s de trás** backbenches.

bancar vt (BR) to pretend to be; ♦ vi (jogos) to bank; IDIOM ~ **o difícil** to play hard to get.

bancário,-a m,f bank clerk; ♦ adj bank, banking.

bancarrota f bankruptcy; **ir à** ~ to go bankrupt.

banco m (assento comprido) bench; (pequeno) stool; **2** (mesa de trabalho) workbench; **3** (FIN) bank; **4** ~ **de dados** (COMP) database; **5** (hospital) emergency services; **6** (de igreja) pew; **7** ~ **da frente/de trás** (AUTO) front/back seat; **8** (baixio) ~ **de areia** sandbank; ~ **de coral** coral reef; **9** (peixe) shoal of; **10** ~ **dos réus/das testemunhas** (JUR) witness-stand, dock.

banda f side; **a outra** ~ the other side; (do rio) opposite side; **de todas as** ~**s** from every side; **2** (RÁDIO) band; **3** (MUS) band; **4** (fita) ~ **magnética** magnetic tape; **5** (CIN) track; **6** ~ **larga** (COMP) broadband; **7** ~ **desenhada** cartoon, comic strip; **8** (tipo de cinto) sash; **bandas** fpl (terra de origem, área) **ela é das minhas** ~**s** she is from my area, part of town; ♦ adv **de bóina à** ~ with the cap to one side; **pôr de** ~ to put aside; IDIOM **ficar de cara à** ~ to be taken aback, (col) gobsmacked; **mandar alguém à outra/àquela** ~ to tell sb to get lost; (BR) **sair de** ~ to slip away.

bandada f flock of birds.

bandalheira, bandalhice f undignified behaviour; **2** roguery; **3** shabby trick; **4** person in rags or ridiculous clothing.

bandalho m tramp, ragamuffin; **2** rogue.

bandarilha f (em tourada) bandarilla.

bandear vt to sway from side to side ♦ ~**-se** vr change opinion.

bandeira f flag, banner; ~ **a meia haste** (BR) **a meio-pau** flag at half mast; **2** (taxímetro) flag; **3** weathercock; **4** (de porta) fanlight; IDIOM **ir a** ~**s despregadas** to laugh like mad.

bandeirada f minimum fare on taximeter.

bandeirante m (BR) explorer, pioneer.

Bandeirantes were armed bands, carrying their own flags, who went to explore Brazil's interior in the 17th and 18th century.

bandeirinha *f (DESP)* linesman.
bandeirola *f (CONSTR)* surveyor's pole; **2** *(DESP)* flag; **3** *(obras nas ruas)* traffic flag.
bandeja *f* tray; **receber algo de** ~ to get sth handed to you on a plate.
bandido,-a *m,f* bandit, outlaw.
bando *m* band, group; **2** gang; **3** *(aves)* flock; **4** *(buffalo, etc)* herd; ♦ **em** ~ *adv* all together.
bandó *(BR: -ô) (cabelo)* hairstyle in which the hair is parted in the middle from forehead to nape.
bandoleiro *m (BR)* bandit, highwayman bandoleer.
bandolim *m (MUS)* mandolin.
bandulho *m (pop)* belly; **encher o** ~ stuff the belly.
bangaló *m (casa de campo de um piso)* bungalow.
Bangladesh *npr* o ~ Bangladesh.
Banguecoque *npr* Bangkok.
banha *f (gordura)* fat; *(de porco)* lard.
banhar *vt (objecto)* to bathe (**em** in); **2** *(mergulhar)* to dip (**em** in); **3** *(fig)* to wash; ♦ ~-**se** *vr (no mar, rio)* to bathe (**em** in); go for a swim.
banheira *f* bath (tub).
banheiro *m (BR)* bathroom, toilet; **2** *(pessoa que vigia a praia)* lifeguard.
banhista *m,f* bather.
banho *m* bath; ~ **de imersão** bath; **tomar um** ~ to take a bath; ~ **de chuveiro** shower; ~ **de mar** seabathing, dip; **tomar um** ~ **de mar/piscina** to swim, have a dip; ~ **de assento** hip bath; ~ **de sol** sunbathing; ~ **turco** Turkish bath; **2 fato de** ~ *(BR:* **maiô***)* swimsuit; **calções de** ~ bathing trunks; **3** ~ **de prata/ouro** *(objecto)* dip in silver/gold; **4** ~**s de casamento** marriage banns; **5** *(termas)* spa; **ir a** ~**s** to go to a spa.
banho-maria *(pl:* **banhos-marias***) m (CULIN)* bain-marie, steamer.
banir *vt* to banish.
banjo *m (musical instrument)* banjo.
banqueiro *m* banker; **2** *(jogos)* croupier.
banquete *m* banquet, feast.
banzar *vt* to surprise, astonish; ♦ *vi* to ponder, muse.
banzado,-a *adj* astonished; *(col)* gobsmacked.
banzé *m (fam)* uproar, racket; **2** hullaballoo; **3** *(festa)* romp.
banzo,-a *m (sentimento que afecta africanos)* nostalgia; the blues; low spirits; ♦ *adj* stunned; **2** nostalgic, homesick.
ba(p)tismo *m* baptism, christening.
ba(p)tizar *vt* to baptize, christen; to dilute.
baque *m* thud, thump; **um** ~ **surdo** a dull thud; **2** *(fig) (pressentimento)* feeling, misgiving, hunch.
baquear *vt (cair)* fall, stumble; **2** *(fig) (arruinar-se)* go bankrupt; **3** *(fig) (perder a coragem)* to lose courage; **4** *(fig)* morrer.
bar *m* bar, public house, pub.
baraço *m* twine, cord; IDIOM **estar com o** ~ **na garganta** to be up against the wall.

barafunda *f* bedlam; **2** commotion; **3** clutter.
barafustar *vt (arguir)* to argue, protest; make a fuss; **2** to gesticulate.
baralhar *vt* to shuffle *(cartas)*; **2** *(fig)* to mix up, confuse; ♦ ~-**se** *vr* to get confused.
baralho *m* pack of cards; deck.
barão *m* baron; **2** *(título inglês)* Earl.
barata *f (ZOOL)* cockroach; black beetle; *(Vd: barato).*
baratear *vt* to cut the price of; to undervalue; **2** to bargain down.
barato,-a *adj* cheap, inexpensive; ♦ *adv* cheaply.
barba *f* beard; **fazer a** ~ to have a shave; IDIOM **dar água pela** ~ to be difficult, troublesome; **esta tradução está a dar-me água pela** ~ this translation is causing me a lot of trouble.
barba-azul *m (homem libertino)* bluebeard.
barbado *m* bearded man; **2** *(adulto)* adult; **3** *(AGR)* young vine ready for planting.
barbante *m* string, twine, cord.
barbaridade *f* barbarity, cruelty; **2** *(fig)* nonsense; **3** *(ato)* atrocity; ♦ *exc* **que absurdo!** how absurd!
barbarismo *m* barbarism.
bárbaro,-a *m,f* barbarian; ♦ *adj* cruel, barbaric; **2** rough, crude; **os B**~**s** *(povo)* Barbarians.
barbatana *f (de peixe)* fin; **2** *(de natação)* flipper.
barbear *vt (algo, alguém)* to shave *(sth, sb)*; ♦ ~-**se** *vr* to shave o.s.
barbearia *f* barber's (shop).
barbeiro *f* barber.
barbela *f (peça de ferro)* curb chain; **2** *(ponta farpada)* hook; *(de crochet)* hook; **3** *(barbada)* dewlap; **4** double chin; **5** *(BR) (farpa de anzol)* barb.
barbicha *f* small beard on the chin; goatee.
barbitúrico *m (QUÍM)* barbiturate.
barbo *m (ZOOL) (fish)* barbel.
barbudo *m* fullly-bearded man.
barbuda *f* hairy woman with beard.
barca *f* barge; ferry.
barcaça *f* large barge.
barcarola *f (MÚS) (LITER)* barcarole.
barco *m* boat; ship; ~ **a motor** motorboat; ~ **à vela** sailing boat; ~ **de recreio** pleasure boat; ~ **de remos** rowing boat.
bardo *m (trovador, poeta)* bard, poet; **2** *(sebe)* hedge, fence.
barganha *f* barter; **2** *(trapaça)* swindle; shady deal.
baril *adj inv (EP) (col)* excellent; great; cool.
barítono *m* baritone.
barlavento *m (NÁUT)* windward; **a** ~ to windward.
barómetro *(BR:* **-rô-***) m* barometer.
baronesa *f* baroness.
baronia *f* barony.
barqueiro *m* boatman.
barra *f (metal)* bar, rod; **2** *(madeira)* beam, pole; **3** *(faixa)* strip; **uma** ~ **de azulejos** a strip/frieze of tiles; **4** ~ **de ferro** *(alavanca)* lever, crowbar; **5** *(duma saia)* border, band; **6** *(de sabão, chocolate)* bar; **7 ouro em** ~ gold ingot; **8** *(JUR)* **vir à** ~ to appear before the bar, court of Justice; **9** *(GEOG)*

(entrada de um porto) sandbar, bar; **o navio chegou à** ~ the ship arrived at the bar of the harbour; **10** *(sinal gráfico) (traço)* slash; ~ **de espaços** *(COMP)* space-bar.

barraca *f (ger)* tent; **2** *(em exposição, feira)* stall; **3** *(de madeira)* hut.

barracão *m* marquee; **2** shed.

barraco *m* hut, shack.

barragem *f (represa)* dam; **2** *(MIL) (barreira)* barrage.

barranco *m* ravine, escarpment; **2** gully.

barrar *vt (pôr barras em)* to put bars on (porta, janela); **2** ~ **o caminho** *(não deixar passar)* to bar the way; *(BR) (impedir)* prevent (show, etc) to take place; **3** *(besuntar)* to grease *(lata, fôrma)*; *(cobrir)* cover with *(de manteiga etc.)*.

barreira *f* barrier; fence; ~ **do som** sound barrier.

barrento,-a *adj* muddy; full of clay.

barrete *m* cap, stocking cap; **2** *(clero)* biretta; **3** ~ **turco** tarboosh; ♦ **enfiar um** ~ *(ser logrado)* to be taken in/cheated; **enfiar o** ~ **a alguém** to trick sb; to pull the wool over sb's eyes.

barrica *f* cask, tub; **2** *(pej) (gorda e baixa)* **ela está uma** ~ she is like a tub.

barricada *f* barricade.

barricar *vt* to barricade.

barriga *f (ANAT)* lower abdomen, belly, tummy; **dores de** ~ tummyache; **2** ~ **da perna** calf; **3** bulge, swelling; **4** ~ **grande** potbelly, paunch; IDIOM **ter a** ~ **a dar horas** to be hungry; **ele passa a vida de** ~ **para o ar** he is a layabout, idler; **ter mais olhos do que** ~ to be greedy; **ela chorou na** ~ **da mãe** she was born with a silver spoon in her mouth; **tirar a** ~ **de misérias** to indulge o.s.; **trazer/ter o rei na** ~ to be full of himself, very pleased with himself.

In Portuguese, '**barriga**' is used to mean 'lower abdomen'; not '**estômago**' (stomach).

barrigada *f* bellyful; **2** a large litter *(de animais)*; IDIOM **uma** ~ **de riso** to roar with laughter, to be in stitches; **tive uma** ~ **de riso** I was in stitches.

barrigão *m*, **barrigona** *f* pot-bellied.

barrigudo,-a *adj* with a paunch, big tummy.

barril *m* barrel, casket.

barro *m* clay; **2** mud; **3** terracotta.

barroco,-a *adj* baroque; **2** extravagant.

barrote *m* beam; rafter.

barulhento,-a *adj* noisy, rowdy.

barulho *m* din, noise.

basáltico,-a *adj* basaltic; **basalto** *m* basalt.

basalto *m* basalt.

base *f (ger)* base, foundation, basis; **2** *(fig)* basis, basics; **3** *(motivo)* grounds; **sem** ~ groundless; **4** *(cósmético)* base; **à** ~ **de** based on; ~**s** *fpl (JUR) (cláusulas)* **uma lei de** ~ a statute and common law; IDIOM *(BR)* **tremer nas** ~**s** to shake like a leaf.

basear *vt* to base on; ♦ ~**-se (em)** *vr* to be based on.

básico,-a *adj* basic.

Basileia *npr* Basle.

basófia *f* boasting, bragging.

basquete *m* **basquetebol** *m* basketball.

bastante *adj inv* enough; **2** a lot; **você tem** ~**s vestidos** you have quite a lot of dresses; **3** quite; **é** ~ **bom** it is quite good; ♦ *pron* **ele tem muitas dificuldades; eu também tenho** ~**s** he has many difficulties; I too have plenty.

bastão *m (bordão)* staff; **2** *(vara comprida)* stick; **3** sceptre; **4** (police weapon) truncheon.

bastar *vi* to be enough, be sufficient; ~ **para** to be enough to; ♦ ~**-se** *vr* to be self-sufficient; ♦ *exc* **basta!** (that's) enough!

bastardo,-a *m,f adj* bastard, illegitimate child.

In Portuguese, '**bastardo**' is not a swearword.

bastião *(pl: -ões)* *m* bastion.

bastidor *m* embroidering-frame; **2** ~**es** *mpl (TEAT)* wings; **3** **nos** ~**es** behind the scenes.

basto,-a *adj* thick, dense.

bastonada *f* a blow with a truncheon.

bastonário,-a *m,f* chairperson of an Order/Society/ Chartered Institute; ~ **da Ordem de Advogados** president of the Bar.

bata *f* pinafore; overall; ~ **branca** *(de médico)* white coat.

batalha *f* battle, fight; **2** struggle.

batalhão *m* battalion.

batalhar *vi* to battle; **2** *(esforçar-se por)* struggle, strive *(for)*.

batata *f* potato; ~ **doce** sweet potato; ~**s fritas** chips; ~ **cozidas** boiled potatoes.

batatada *f* a lot of potatoes.

batatinha inglesa *f* crisps *pl*.

bate-chapa *m (operário ou máquina)* panel-beater.

bate-cu *m (fam)* a bump, a thud, a fall on one's bum *(fam)*.

batedeira *f (manual)* beater, whisk; **2** churn; **3** ~ **(elé(c)trica)** (electric) mixer.

batedela *f* light beating.

batedor *m* beater; ~ **de tapetes** carpet beater; **2** *(caça)* beater; **3** scout, forest guard; **4** *(polícia)* escort; **5** ~ **de estrada** military scout, mounted escort; **6** *(DESP) (críquete)* batsman; *(baseball)* batter; **7** ~ **de carteiras** *(BR) (ladrão)* bag snatcher.

batelada *f (carga de um batel)* boatload; **2** *(col) (grande quantidade)* a lot, a load **(de** of).

bátega *f* downpour, sudden shower.

batente *m (ombreira da porta)* doorpost, rabbet; **2** door/window latch, catch; **3** *(meia porta)* half of a door; **4** edge of waves, shoreline; **5** *(col)* job; **no** ~ at work; **5** *(BR)* daily toil; ♦ *adj inv (ondas do mar)* beating.

bate-papo *(BR: fam)* *m* chat.

bater *vt (ger)* beat; **2** *(horas, sino)* strike; **3** thresh, beat out *(trigo)*; **4** *(inspeccionar)* search, go all over; **5** ~ **as asas** *(ave)* flap, flutter the wings; **6** ~ **as botas** *(col) (morrer)* to die, kick the bucket *(col)*; **7** *(CULIN)* ~ **as claras** whisk up the whites of eggs; **8** *(furtar) (BR) (fam)* ~ **carteira** to pickpocket; **9** ~ **os calcanhares** *(col)* to flee, take to one's heels; **10** ~ **os dentes/o queixo de frio**

chatter with cold; **11** ~ **moeda** to mint; **12** ~ **palmas** clap one's hands, applaud; **13** ~ **o pé no chão** to stamp one's foot; **14** ~ **à porta** to knock on/at the door; **15** ~ **em** to strike, hit; **ele bateu na mulher** he struck his wife; **o carro bateu numa parede** the car hit a wall; **16** ~ **com** bang, slam, bump; ~ **com a porta** slam the door; ~ **com a cabeça** bump his head; **17** ~ **contra** collide against/with; ♦ ~**-se** *vr* fight (**por** for); ~ **contra** fight against; IDIOM ~ **com a língua nos dentes** *(segredo)* to let the cat out of the bag; **vieste, mas bateste com o nariz na porta** you came, but I was not in; ~ **sempre na mesma tecla** harp on the same string.

bateria *f* battery; **2** *(MUS)* percussion; **3** ~ **de cozinha** kitchen utensils *pl.*

batida *f* raid; **2** *(AUTO)* collision; **3** *(porta)* knock; **4** *(caça)* rousing; ♦ *adj* beaten; worn, shabby; **2 estrada** ~ a rutty road.

batido *m* beat; **2** slam; **3** knock; **4** ~ **de leite** milk-shake; ♦ *adj* beaten; **2** *(roupa)* worn out; **3** *(estória)* much heard about; **4** (slightly *pej*) *(pessoa)* very experienced, worldwise; (pessoa who has) been around.

batina *f (REL)* cassock; **2** gown.

batismo, batizar *(Vd:* **ba(p)-***)*.

batom *m* lipstick.

batucada *(BR) f* dance percussion group.

batota *f* cheating, **2** *(nas cartas)* double-dealing, trick; **3** gambling house; **4 fazer** ~ to cheat, trick.

batuta *f* baton.

baú *m* old-fashioned trunk, grandmother's trunk.

baunilha *f* vanilla.

bazar *m* bazaar.

bazófia *f* boasting, bragging.

bazuca *f* bazooka.

bê-á-bá *m (abecedário)* alphabet; **2** *(noções básicas)* ABC.

beata *f (ponta de cigarro)* cigarette butt; **2** *(cigarro)* fag.

beatificar *vt* to beatify, bless.

beato,-a *adj* blessed; **2** *(pej)* overpious; *f* old church hen ♦ *(pej)* hypocrite.

bebé *(BR:* **bebê***)* baby; ~ **proveta** *(pl:* **bebés-provetas***)* test-tube baby.

bebedeira *f* drunkenness; **ter uma** ~ to be/get drunk.

bêbedo,-a *m,f adj* drunk.

bebedor,-ora *m,f* drinker; drunkard.

bebedouro, bebedoiro *m* drinking fountain; **2** *(para animais)* drinking trough; **3** *(aves)* bird bath.

beber *vt* to drink; **2** to drink up, *(terra)* soak up; ♦ *vi* to drink.

bebericar *vt/vi (beber pouco a pouco)* to sip; **os passarinhos estão a** ~ the little birds are drinking.

bebida *f* drink.

beca *f* magistrate's gown.

beça *(BR) (fam) adv* **à** ~ plenty, a lot; **eu gosto** ~ **de você** I like you a lot.

beco *m* alley, lane; **2** ~ **sem saída** cul-de-sac; **3** *(fig)* difficult situation.

bedelho *m (de porta)* latch; **2** *(fig) (rapazinho maroto)* little imp; little boy; **meter o** ~ **em** to poke one's nose in *(conversa, na vida das pessoas)*.

beduíno,-a *m,f* Bedouin; **os** ~ *pl* the Bedouin people.

bege *f* beige colour.

begónia *(BR:* -ô-*) m* begonia.

beicinho *m,* little lip; **fazer** ~ to pout, *(criança)* to be near to tears.

beiço *m (fam)* lip; **2** rim, border; **3** *(fig)* **de** ~ **caído** pouting; **fazer** ~ to pout.

beiçudo,-a *adj* thick-lipped.

beija-flor *m* hummingbird.

beijar *vt* to kiss; ♦ ~**-se** (mutually) to kiss (one another).

Beijing *npr* Beijing.

beijinho *m* little kiss, *(fam)* peck.

beijo *m* kiss.

beijoca *f (fam) (grande beijo)* smacker.

beijocar *vt* to kiss often.

beijoqueiro,-a *adj (col)* person who kisses a lot.

beira *f (orla)* edge; **2** *(rio)* bank; border; **à** ~ **de** on the edge of; beside, by; on the verge of.

beiral *m (telhado)* eaves.

Beira *npr* Portuguese province/s; **2** district and city in Mozambique.

beira-mar *f* seaside.

Beirão *m,* **beiroa** *f* of/from Beira (in Portugal)

beirar *vt* to be at the edge of; **2** to skirt.

beirinha *adv:* **à** ~ at/by the very edge.

beisebol *m* baseball.

beladona *f* belladonna.

belas-artes *fpl* fine arts; **Academia das B~-A~** Academy of Fine Arts

beldade *f,* **beleza** *f* beauty; **ela foi uma** ~ **no seu tempo** she was a beauty in her day; **que** ~ **!** how lovely!

belga *m,f adj inv* Belgian.

Bélgica *npl* **a** ~ Belgium.

Belgrado *npr* Belgrade.

beliche *m (navio)* cabin; **2** *(2 camas)* bunk bed *sg.*

bélico,-a *adj* belligerent.

belicoso,-a *adj* bellicose.

beligerante *adj inv* belligerent, quarrelsome.

beliscadura *f* **beliscão** *m* hard pinch.

beliscar *vt* to pinch; nip; **2** *(comer pouco)* to nibble, pick.

belisco *m* pinch; **ele deu um** ~ **no meu rabo** he pinched my bottom.

belo,-a *adj* beautiful, lovely, fine; **um** ~ **cavalo** a fine horse; **que~!** how beautiful!; **2** *(fig)* **uma ~a embrulhada** a pretty mess.

beltrano *m* Mr. So-and-So, the 'what's-his-name'; John Doe *(Vd:* **Fulano, Beltrano e Sicrano***)*.

Belzebu *m (diabo)* Beelzebub, Demon.

bem *m* good; **2 o** ~ **comum** the common good; **o** ~ **público** public welfare; **3** *(pessoa amada)* beloved; **4** *(dádiva)* gift; **a virtude é um** ~ virtue is a gift; ♦ **bens** *mpl (património)* assets; **2** *(produtos)* ~ **de consumo** consumer goods; ~ **imóveis** real estate; ~ **móveis** equipment, liquid assets; **bens mal adquiridos** ill-gotten gains; ♦ *adv (ger)* well; **não me sinto** ~ I am not feeling well; **2** *(enfatizando)*

tu ~ me disseste! you did tell me!, you were right; **3** *(muito)* very; **~ cedo** very early; **4** *(bastante)* really; **~ bom** really good; **5** quite; **não é ~ assim** it's not quite like that; **6** *(aspecto)* good; **as coisas vão ~** things are looking good; **7 nem ~ nem mal** so-so; **8 ~ como** as well as; ♦ *conj* **se ~ que,** even though; ♦ *prep* **a ~ de** for the sake of, for one's good; ♦ *exc* **ora ~!** really! now then!; IDIOM **andar de ~ com** to be on good terms with; **fazer o ~ sem olhar a quem** to do good for its own sake; **a ~ e a torto** by hook or by crook.

bem-amado,-a *adj* beloved, darling.

bem-apessoado,-a *adj (person)* presentable; **2** elegant.

bem-aventurado,-a *adj* fortunate.

bem-criado,-a *adj* well-bred, well-mannered, well brought up.

bem-disposto,-a *adj* in a good mood.

bem-entendido *exc* O.K!; understood!; I got the message!

bem-estar *m* comfort, well-being; **2** *(social)* welfare.

bem-feito,-a *adj* well done, well made; **2** *(de boas formas)* elegant; ♦ *exc* **é ~!** *(irónico)* it serves you right!

bem haja! *exc* God bless (you)!

bem-humorado,-a *adj* good-humoured; **2** in a good mood.

bem-me-quer *(BOT)* daisy (love me, love-me-not) *(Vd: malmequer)*.

bemol *adj inv (MUS)* flat.

bem-parecido *adj* good-looking; pleasant-looking.

bem-posto,-a *adj* well-groomed, elegant.

bem-querer *m* love, friendship; **ele é o meu ~** he is my dearest; ♦ *vt/vi* to love.

bem-querido,-a *m,f* beloved.

bem-vindo,-a *adj* welcome; **bem-vindos, bem-vindas** *pl (a mais que uma pessoa)* welcome.

bem-visto,-a *adj (pessoa)* respected.

bênção *(pl: bênçãos)* blessing.

bendito,-a *adj* blessed.

bendizer *vt* to praise; **2** to bless.

beneficência *f* charity; **beneficente** *adj inv (bondoso)* kind; **2** *(caridoso)* charitable.

beneficiar *vt (favorecer)* to benefit; **2** *(melhorar)* to improve; ♦ **~-se** *vr* to profit.

beneficiário,-a *m,f (herdeiro)* beneficiary.

beneficiente *adj* **obras ~s** charitable, works.

benefício *m* benefit; **2** profit.

benéfico,-a *adj* beneficial; **2** generous; **3** favourable.

benemérito,-a *m,f* distinguished person; ♦ *adj* worthy; distinguished.

beneplácito *m* consent, approval; **~ régio** royal consent.

benevolência *f* benevolence, kindness.

benévolo,-a *adj* benevolent, kind.

benfeitor,-ora *m,f* benefactor, benefactress.

bengala *f* walking stick.

bengaleiro *m* umbrella and hat stand; **2** *(no teatro)* cloakroom.

benignidade *f* kindness.

benigno,-a *adj* kind; pleasant; **2** *(MED)* benign.

benjamim *m (fig)* darling, favourite son; **2** *(BR) (ELECT) (para duas ou mais lâmpadas)* adaptor.

benquerença *f* affection, fondness; well-wishing.

benquisto,-a *adj* well-loved, well-liked.

bens *mpl (Vd: bem)*.

bento,-a *(irr pp of benzer)* blessed; ♦ *adj* holy; **água ~** holy water; **Bento** *npr* Benedict; **Papa ~ XVI** Pope Benedict XVI.

benzedeiro,-a *m,f* witch doctor, sorcerer, sorceress.

benzene *m* benzene.

benzer *vt* to bless; ♦ **~-se** *vr* to make the sign of the Cross.

benzina *f* benzene.

benzol *m (QUÍM)* benzol.

bera *adj inv (fam) (imitação de algo)* poor; **2** *(falso, ruim)* false, deceitful; **esta pessoa é ~** this person is nasty.

berbequim *m (EP)* hand electric drill.

berbere *adj inv (povo, cultura)* Berber; **os Berberes** *mpl* the Berbers.

berbigão *m (marisco)* cockle.

berçário *m* day nursery.

berço *m* cradle; **2** birthplace; **Guimarães é o ~ da Nação** Guimaraens is the cradle of the Nation (Portugal).

This is because the first king of Portugal was born in this town.

beriberi *m (MED)* beriberi.

berimbau *m (MUS)* Jew's harp.

berinjela *f* aubergine, eggplant.

Berlim *npr* Berlin.

berlinda *f (carruagem)* berlin; **2** *(jogo de prendas)* a forfeit; **estar na ~** to pay a forfeit; *(alguém) (alvo de atenção/de crítica)* to be the centre of attention, the butt of jokes.

berlinde *m (jogo de crianças)* marble; **jogar ao ~** play marbles.

berlinense *m,f adj inv* Berliner, from Berlin.

berliques *msg/pl (usado só em):* **~ e berloques** *mpl* tricks, magic; **por artes de ~ e berloques** as by magic, by mysterious means.

berloque *m (objeto insignificante)* trinket; little ornament, charm.

berma *f (beira do caminho)* kerbside, berm(e); **2** *(auto-estrada)* hard shoulder.

Bermudas *npl* **as (ilhas) ~** the Bermudas.

bermudas *f* Bermuda shorts.

bernarda *f (fruit)* variety of pear.

bernardice *f* nonsense, stupidity.

berra *f (cio dos veados)* heat; **2** *(fig)* notoriety; **andar na ~** to be in fashion, to be the topic of conversation.

berrante *adj inv (cor, tom)* flashy, loud; **2** *(algo)* gaudy, showy.

berrar *vi (gritar)* shout, to bellow, yell; **2** *(chorar)* to bawl, wail; **3** *(destoar)* to clash.

berro *m (grito)* yell, bellow, scream; **falar aos ~** to speak too loud; to yell.

besouro *f (ZOOL)* beetle.

besta *f* beast; **~ de carga** beast of burden; **2 ~ fera** wild beast; **3** *(pej)* brute, beast; ♦ *adj (pej)* brutal, stupid, rough; **besta² *f* crossbow.

besta-quadrada *f* quadruped; **2** *(pej)* stupid.

besteira *f (BR)* nonsense, rubbish; **dizer ~s** to talk rubbish.

besteiras *fpl (abertura nas muralhas)* embrasure.

besteiro *m* archer, crossbowman.

bestial *adj* bestial, repulsive; **2** *(col)* **é ~!** it's great! **bestialidade** *f* bestiality, brutality.

besugo *m (peixe)* snapper.

besuntar *vt* to smear, daub, grease; **estás todo besuntado** you are covered in grease; dirty all over.

betão *m* concrete; **~ armado** reinforced concrete.

beterraba *f (BOT)* beetroot.

betoneira *f* concrete mixer.

bétula *f (planta)* birch.

betume *m* bitumen; **2** *(massa artificial para colar vidros)* putty.

bexiga *f (ANAT)* bladder; *(MED)* **~s** *fpl* variola, smallpox; **2 ~s doidas** chickenpox, varicella.

bezerro,-a *m,f* calf, heifer; IDIOM **pensar na morte do ~** to daydream.

BI *(abr* **bilhete de identidade***)* identity card.

bibe *m* pinafore, overall, smoke; **2** *(para crianças)* smoke, bib.

biberão *m* baby's bottle; **vou dar o ~ ao bebé** I am going to give, feed the baby his bottle (of milk).

Bíblia *f* Bible.

bíblico,-a *adj* biblical.

bibliografia *f* bibliography.

biblioteca *f* library.

bibliotecário,-a *m,f* librarian.

bica *f* waterspout, small public spring, spigot; **2** *(EP) (pop)* small black coffee; **3** *(ZOOL)* a kind of catfish; IDIOM **estar à/na ~** to be about to happen/ on the brink of; **correr em ~** to flow, to stream out; **suar em ~** to sweat profusely.

bicada *f* peck; **2** beautifull; **3** *(de um mato)* entrance to/edge of a wood; **4** *(BR)* large spout, guttering; **5 ~s** brushwood.

bicar *vt (dar bicadas)* to peck; **2** *(fig) (comer pouco)* to pick at *(food)*; **3** *(beber pouco)* to sip.

bicarbonato *m* bicabornate; **~ de sódio** baking soda, bicabornate of soda.

bicentenário *m* bicentenary.

bicentenário,-a *adj* bicentennial.

bíceps *m* biceps.

bicha *f* worm; **2** *(fam) (gata, cadela)* cat, bitch; **3** bad tempered woman, nasty; **4** *(EP: col)* queue; **5** *(BR: pej) (homossexual)* queer, poof; **6** *(EP: fam)* *m* pansy.

bicha-de-rabiar *f* firecracker.

bichano,-a *m,f (gato,a) (fam)* puss, pussy-cat.

bicharada *f* animals *pl*.

bicharoco *m* bug, insect, worm.

bicho *m* animal; **2** maggot, bug; **3** *(fam)* pet; **4** *(BR)* energetic person; **~ do mato** *(pessoa)* loner; IDIOM **matar o ~** *(beber)* to wet one's whistle, drink; **algum ~ lhe mordeu** something has upset you/him/her; *(BR)* **virar ~** to turn nasty, get angry.

bicho-careta *m inv (pessoa vulgar)* ordinary person; a nobody.

bicho-carpinteiro *m* woodworm; IDIOM **ter bichos-carpinteiros** to be fidgety.

bicho-da-seda *m* silkworm.

bicho-de-conta *m* woodlouse.

bicho-do-mato *m (fig)* loner, unsociable person.

bicho-de-sete-cabeças *m* puzzle, problem; IDIOM **fazer um ~** to exaggerate, to make a mountain out of a molehill.

bicicleta *f* bicycle, *(col)* bike; **andar de ~** to cycle.

bico *m* beak; **2** point; **3** spout; **4** mouth; **5** *(aparo da caneta)* nib; **6 ~-de-gas** gas jet, gas burner; **7 grão-de-~** chick-pea; **8 ~ do peito** *(ANAT)* nipple; **9 o ~ de pé** the tip of the toe; **10 calar o ~** *(fam)* to shut up; **11 não abrir o ~** *(fam)* to keep mum; **12 abrir o ~** to spill the beans; **13 arranjar uns ~s** *(fam)* to get/do small jobs, errands; **14 em ~s de pés** on tiptoe; IDIOM **jogar com dois ~s** to run with the hare and hunt with the hounds; **melro de ~ amarelo** sly fellow; **meter o ~** to meddle, be nosy; **molhar o ~** drink, wet one's whistle; **levar água no ~** have ulterior motives; **virar o ~ ao prego** to change the subject.

bico-de-obra *m* tricky, difficult job.

bico-de-papagaio *m* hooked, hawk nose; **bicos-de-papagaio** *mpl (MED)* spondylitis.

bicolour *adj inv* two-coloured, bicolour *(UK)*, bicolor *(US)*.

bicorne *m* two-horned animal; ♦ *adj* having two horns; **2 chapéu ~** cocked hat.

bicuda *f (ZOOL)* long-beaked fish; **2** *(galinhola)* woodcock.

bicudo *m (peixe)* a kind of sea bream; ♦ *adj (pau, chapéu)* pointed; **2** *(fig) (difícil)* difficult *(assunto)*; **um caso ~** a tricky case; **3** *(BR)* sulky.

bidé *(BR:* **bidê***)* *m* bidet.

bidente *m* pitchfork.

biela *f* piston rod, connecting rod.

biénio *m* biennium.

biennial *adj* biennial.

bifana *n* Portuguese hot steak sandwich.

bife *m* steak; **~ de porco** pork steak; **~ de vaca** beefsteak; **~ com ovo a cavalo** Portuguese steak with an egg on top; **2** *(alcunha dada a um inglês)* English.

'Bife' is taken from the English word 'beef-steak'. It means any steak and not **beef**, which means 'carne de vaca'.

bifurcação *f (road)* fork.

bifurcar-se *vr* to fork, divide.

bígamo,-a *m,f* bigamist; ♦ *adj* bigamous.

bigode *m* moustache.

bigorna *f* anvil.

bijutaria *f* fancy, costume jewellery.

bilha *f* jug, pitcher; **2** *(de gás)* bottle.

bilhão *m (BR)* billion *(Vd:* **bilião***)*

bilhar *m* billiards *sg;* **taco de ~** cue; **jogar ~** to play billiards.

bilhete *m* ticket; **2** note, card; **3 ~ de ida** single ticket; **~ de ida e volta** return ticket; **~ postal** postcard; **~ de identidade** identity card; **ele recebeu o ~ azul** *(BR)* he was fired.

bilheteira *f (EP)* **bilheteria** *f (BR)* ticket office, booking office, box office.

bilheteiro,-a *m,f* ticket seller.
bilheteria (*Vd:* **bilheteira**).
bilião *num m* billion (= *um milhão de milhões*).
bilingue *adj* bilingual.
bilinguismo *m* bilingualism.
bilionésimo *m* one billionth.
bilro *m* bobbin; **renda de ~s** lace using special bobbins, on a cushion (a tradition of Peniche and its outskirts, Portugal).
bilioso,-a *adj* bilious, liverish, ill-tempered.
bílis *m* bile; **2** (*fig*) bad temper.
bimbo,-a *m,f* (*provinciano*) simpleton, country bumpkin, provincial.
bimensal *adj* twice-monthly.
binário *adj* (*MAT, QUÍM, MUS*) binary; **2** (*COMP*) **dígito ~** binary digit; **3** *m* (*FÍS*) binary fission.
binóculos *m/pl* binoculars *pl*; **2** opera, field glasses *pl*.
biodiversidade *f* biodiversity.
biosfera *f* biosphere.
biofísica *f* biophysics.
bioesfera *f* biosphere.
biografia *f* biography.
biográfico,-a *adj* biographical.
biógrafo,-a *m,f* biographer.
biologia *f* biology.
biológico,-a *adj* biological.
biologista, biólogo,-a *m,f* biologist.
biombo *m* screen, partition.
biópsia *f* biopsy.
bioquímica *f* biochemistry.
biótipo *m* biotype.
bióxido *m* dioxide; **~ de carbono** carbon dioxide.
bipartição *f* bisection.
bipartidarismo *m* two-party system.
bipartidário,-a *adj* partisan.
bíped *m* biped; ♦ *adj inv* (*pessoa, animal*) two-legged.
bipolar *adj inv* (*interruptor, célula*) bipolar; **2** (*MED*) bipolar manic depressive; **3** (*POL*) two-sided.
biqueira *f* (*ponta*) tip; (*de sapato*) toe-cap; **2** (*goteira*) gutter; **3** (*bica*) spout.
biqueiro *m* (*fam*) (*pontapé*) kick (with the toecap); ♦ **biqueiro,-a** *m,f* (*pessoa*) fusspot; ♦ *adj* fussy.
biqueirão (*ZOOL*) *m* anchovy.
biquini *m* bikini.
Birmânia *npr* **a ~** Burma.
birmanês,-a *m,f adj* Burmese; (*LÍNG*) Burmese.
birra *f* wilfulness, obstinacy; **2** aversion; **3 ter ~ com** to dislike, detest; **4** (*criança*) **ter uma ~** to have a tantrum.
birrento,-a *adj* (*pessoa*) sulky; **2** obstinate.
bis *adv* duas vezes; ♦ *exc* encore!
bisar *vt* to repeat, call for an encore.
bisavô, bisavó *m,f* great-grandfather, great-grandmother.
bisbilhotar *vt* pry into, snoop, poke one's nose into; *vi* gossip.
bisbilhoteiro,-a *m,f* meddler, busybody, snoop; ♦ *adj* (*alguém*) nosy.
bisbilhotice *f* gossip; **2** snooping.
bisca *f* (*jogo de cartas*) cribbage; **2** (*fig*) rogue, scoundrel. ♦ *exc* **bisca!** I won!

biscate *m* odd job.
biscateiro *m* odd-job man.
biscoito *m* biscuit (*UK*); cracker (*US*).
bisel *m* bevel; chamfer.
bisnaga *f* tube; **2** (*brinquedo*) water pistol.
bisneto,-a *m,f* grandson, granddaughter.
bisonho,-a *m* (*novato*) novice; green; (*recruta*) raw; ♦ *adj* shy; **2** awkward; inexperienced.
bispado *m* bishopric.
bispo *m* bishop; **2** (*peça de xadrez*) bishop.
Bissau *npr* (*capital de Guiné-Bissau*) Bissau.
bissecção, bisseção *f* bisection.
bisector, bissetor *m* (*GEOM*) bisector.
bissectriz, bissetriz *f* (*GEOM*) bisector, bisecting line.
bissemanal *adj inv* (*duas vezes por semana*) twice weekly (*visita, publicação*).
bissexto,-a *adj:* **ano ~** leap year.
bissexual *adj inv* bisexual; **2** (*flor*) hermaphrodite.
bisturi *m* scalpel.
bit *m* (*COMP*) (*abr do inglês* **binary digit**) bit; (*Vd:* **binário**).
bitola *f* (*medida-padrão*) gauge; **2** measure; **3** standard; IDIOM **medir pela mesma ~** to measure, judge (all) by the same standard.
bivaque *m* (*MIL*) (*acampamento*) bivouac; (*boné de soldado*) bivouac.
bisantino,-a *adj* Byzantine.
bizarria *f* gallantry; **2** elegance; **3** pomp.
bizarro,-a *adj* graceful; **2** elegant; **3** gallant; **4** eccentric; **5** odd, strange.
blablablá *m* (*conversa sem fim*) blather/blether, blah, blah, blah.
blandícia *f* endearment; **2** caress; **3** gentleness; **4** compliment.
blasfemar *vt/vi* to blaspheme; **2** (*palavrão*) swear.
blasfémia (*BR:* -fê-) *f* blasphemy; **2** swearing.
blasfemo,-a *m,f* blasphemer; ♦ *adj* blasphemous.
blaterar *vt* (*camelo*) to bleat.
blenorragia *f* (*MED*) blennorrhagia.
blindado,-a *adj* armoured; **carro ~** armoured car, steel-plated car; (*porta*) reinforced.
blindagem *f* armour, steel plating.
bloco *m* block; **o ~ do leste** the Eastern block; **2** set; **3** (*conjunto de prédios*) block; **4** pad; **~ de notas** writing pad; **5** (*MED*) **~ operatório** operating wing; **6 ~ de carnaval** (*BR*) carnival troupe/revellers; **em ~** *adv* in a block, in a group.
bloqueado,-a *adj* blocked; **2** blockaded; **3 ficar ~** to be speechless.
bloquear *vt* to blockade; **2** to block.
bloqueio *m* (*FIN, MIL*) blockade; **~ económico** economic blockade; **2** (*obstrução*) obstacle; **3** (*tráfico*) jam; **~ do trânsito** traffic jam; **4** (*MED*) blockage, obstruction; **5 ter um ~ mental** to have a mental block; **6** (*ELECT*) cut; **~ da corrente** power cut.
blusa *f* blouse; **~ de lã** cardigan, pullover; **~ de pintor** smock.
blusão *m* jacket; **~ de cabedal** leather jacket.
BM (*abr de* **Banco Mundial**) World Bank.
BN (*abr de* **Biblioteca Nacional**) National Library.
boa¹ *f* (*ZOOL*) boa constrictor.

boa^2 (*feminine de* **bom**) *adj* good; **uma ~ mulher** a good/kind woman; **uma mulher ~** (*fam*) a sexy woman; (*col*) a good lay; **~ fé** *f* good faith, trust; ♦ *exc* **essa é ~!** (*surpresa*) really! you don't mean it! **2** (*piada*) that's a good one; ♦ **às boas** *adv* in a friendly way; **de ~ vontade** willingly; IDIOM **meter-se numa ~** to be in a tight spot; **pregar uma ~ a alguém** to play a trick on sb, to pull sb's leg; (*Vd:* **bom**).

boa-gente *adj inv* good people, trustworthy.

boa-noite! (*pl:* **boas-noites**) *f* good evening!, good night; **dar as ~s** to say good evening.

boa nova *f* white butterfly; **2** good news, good tidings.

boas entradas *fpl* Happy New Year!

boas-festas *fpl* (*Natal, Ano Novo*) Season's greetings.

boas tardes (**boa tarde**) good afternoon.

boas vindas *fpl* welcome; **dar as ~** to welcome.

boato *m* rumour; gossip.

bobagem *f* (*BR*), silliness, nonsense, rubbish; **deixe de bobagens!** stop being silly!

bobina *f* bobbin; **2** coil; **3** spool.

bobinar *vt/vi* to wind, to reel.

bobo,-a *m,f* buffoon, jester; **fazer-se de ~** to act the fool; **2** (*fig*) fool; ♦ *adj* silly, daft.

boca *f* mouth; **2** opening, entrance; **3** slit; **4** (*arma*) muzzle; **5** (*do rio*) mouth; **6** (*mossa*) dent; **7** (*do fogão*) burner, gas jet; **8** ~ **do estômago** pit of the stomach; IDIOM **à ~ pequena** in whispers, in secret; **à ~ da noite** at nightfall; **de ~ aberta** open-mouthed, amazed; **ter o coração ao pé da ~** wear one's heart on one's sleeve; **tiraste as palavras da ~** you took the words out of my mouth; **apanhar alguém com a ~ na botija** catch sb in the act; **de ~** by word of mouth; **de ~ em ~** (*notícias*) going around; gossip **andar nas ~s do mundo** to be gossiped about; (*BR*) **bater ~** to argue.

boca-a-boca *m* (*MED*) mouth-to-mouth resuscitation; (*pop*) kiss of life.

bocadinho *m* (*tempo*) a little while; **2** (*tempo, comida*) a little bit; **espera um ~** wait a little bit.

bocado *m* mouthful, bite; **2** piece, bit; **come um ~** have a bite; **3** (*time*) a while, short while; **esperei um bom ~** I waited quite a while; **vi-o há ~** I saw him a short while ago.

bocal *m* mouth; ~ **do poço**; mouth of a well; **2** (*MUS*) mouthpiece; **3** nozzle.

boçal *adj inv* (*sem cultura*) common, uncouth; boorish; **2** (*ignorante*) simple-minded.

bocejar *vi* to yawn.

bocejo *m* yawn.

boceta *f* (*caixinha*) trinket box; ~ **de rapé** snuff box; ~ **de Pandora** Pandora's Box; **2** (*BR*) fishing tackle; **3** (*BR*) (*vulg*) vulva.

bochecha *f* cheek; **fazer ~s** to blow out one's cheeks.

bochechar *vt* to rinse out (mouth).

bochechudo,-a *adj* chubby-faced.

boda *f* wedding; **~s** *fpl* wedding party, wedding anniversary *sg*; **~s de prata/ouro** silver/golden wedding *sg*.

bode *m* goat; ~ **expiatório** scapegoat.

bodega *f* tavern; **2** (*col*) (*comida*) slop; **3** (*casa*) dump, tip; **4** (*fig, fam*) rubbish.

bofe *m* (*pop*) (*pulmão*) lung; **2** (*fressura animal*) lights *pl*; **3** (*BR*) ugly person; **4 ter maus ~s** to be nasty; **5** ~**s** lungs, lights; IDIOM **deitar os ~ pela boca** to be out of breath; to be fagged out.

bofetada *f* slap (*na cara*).

bofetão *m* hard slap on the face.

bofete *m* (*tabefe*) a light slap.

boi (*pl:* **bois**) *m* ox; oxen; ~ **castrado** bullock; **uma junta de ~s** a team of oxen; IDIOM **ir a passo de ~** to go at snail's pace; **andar o carro adiante dos ~s** to put the cart before the horse.

bóia, boia *f* buoy; ~ **de salvamento** lifebuoy; **2** (*para nadar*) rubber ring, lifebelt; **3** (*para a pesca*) **as ~s das redes de pesca** the floats on fishing nets; **4** ~ **de automobilismo** ballcock; **5** ~ **de sinalização** marker buoy; **6** (*fam*) (*pedaço de pão, etc*) grub; IDIOM **não ligar ~ a** pay no heed to.

boiada *f* herd of cattle.

boião *m* jar, pot.

boiar *vt/vi* (*flutuar*) to float; **2** (*fig*) waver; **3** (*fig*) to hesitate; **4** (*BR*) (*col*) to eat.

boicotar *vt* to boycott.

boicote *m* boycott.

boieiro *m* herdsman.

bóina, boina *f* beret.

boîte *f* nightclub.

bojo *m* (*saliência convexa*) bulge; **2** (*fam*) (*barriga*) paunch, belly; **3** (*de navio*) belly, spread; **4** (*fig, fam*) capacity, ability.

bojudo,-a *adj* (*vaso, lâmpada*) bulbous; **2** (*algo arredondado*) round; **3** (*person*) (*pançudo*) pot-bellied.

bola *f* ball; **2** ~ **de futebol** football; **3** ~ **de sabão** soap bubble; **4 jogar à ~** to play ball/football; **ganhar por duas ~s** to win by two goals; ♦ *exc* **bolas!**, **ora bolas!** bother!, hell; IDIOM **baixar a ~** to keep a low profile; **dar ~ alguém** to play ball/go along with sb; **não regular bem da ~** to have a screw loose.

In Portuguese, the word '**bolas**' is not a vulgar term, since this noun bears no connection to male genitalia.

bolacha *f* biscuit (*UK*); cookie (*US*); ~ **de água e sal** water biscuit, cracker; **2** (*fam*) (*bofetada*) slap.

bolachudo,-a *adj* chubby-cheeked.

bolada *f* stroke of a ball; **2** (*col*) (*dinheiro*) lump sum.

bolandas *fpl* bustle; ♦ *adv* **andar em ~** to rush around, to blunder on.

bolar *vt* (*BR: col*) (*conceber*) to think up, concoct.

bolbo *m* (*da flor*) bulb; **2** (*ANAT*) bulb.

bolboso,-a *adj* (*flor, raiz*) bulbous.

bolchevista *adj inv* Bolshevik.

boléia, boleia *f* driver's seat; **dar uma ~** to give a lift (*BR:* **dar carona**).

boletim *m* bulletin; report; ~ **meteorológico** weather forecast.

bolha *f* (*na pele*) blister; **2** (*glóbulo de ar/água/gás*) bubble.

boliche *m* bowling, skittles *sg.*

Bolívia *npr* Bolivia; **a ~** Bolivia.

boliviano,-a *m,f adj* Bolivian.

bolo *m* (CULIN) cake, pastry; **~ recheado** cake with filling; **~ armado** *(enfeitado)* gateau; **cozer o ~** to bake a cake; **2** *(fig) (massa informe)* mess, wreck; **a cara dele ficou num ~** his face was in a mess; **o carro ficou num ~** the car was a wreck; **3** *(apostas)* stake; **4** *(prémio)* prize.

bolor *m* mould; mildew; mustiness; stale; **a sala cheira a ~** the room smells musty; **o queijo tem ~** the cheese is off.

bolo-rei *m* Portuguese Christmas cake.

bolorento,-a *adj* stale; **2**, mouldy; **3** musty.

bolota *f (BOT)* acorn.

bolsa *f* bag; **2** purse; **3** handbag; **4** *(de estudo)* grant, scholarship; **5** (FIN) **B~** **(de valores)** Stock Exchange; IDIOM **apertar os cordões à ~** to tighten the purse strings.

bolseiro,-a *m,f* treasurer; **2** *(pessoa que recebe a bolsa de estudo)* scholarship holder.

bolsista *m,f (da Bolsa)* speculator, broker.

bolso *m* pocket; **edição/livro de ~** paperback edition/book; IDIOM **encher os ~s** to get rich.

bom (*Vd:* **boa**) *adj* good; **2** *(tempo)* fine; **3** nice, kind; **4** *(MED)* well; **5 ser bom/boa** to be kind, to be good **(em/para** at/for); **ele é um homem ~** he is a kind man; **é um ~ conselho** it is good advice; **meu ~ amigo** my good/dear friend; **6 estar ~** *(saúde)* to be well; **bom-dia** good-morning; ♦ *exc* **bom!** right! good!; **que ~!** how marvellous!; IDIOM **ser bom/boa de contentar** *(pessoa)* to be easy to please; ♦ **bons** *mpl (pessoas honestas):* **os bons** the just, the good people.

bomba *f (MIL)* bomb; **2** *(TEC)* pump; **3 ~ atómica**; **4 ~ de gasolina** petrol station; **5 ~ de incêndio** fire engine, fire hydrant; **6** *(sifão)* siphon; **7 ~ de recalque** pressure pump; **8 dar à ~** to pump; **9** *(BR)* **levar ~** to flunk (exam); IDIOM **a notícia estourou como uma ~** the news burst like a bombshell.

bombástico,-a *adj (estrondoso)* deafening; **2** *(discurso empolado)* bombastic.

bombardear *vt* to bomb, bombard; **2** *(fig)* to bombard.

bombardeio *m* bombing, bombardment.

bombear *vt* to pump; **~ o sangue** to pump up the blood.

bombeiro *m* fireman; **2** *(BR)* plumber; **o corpo de ~s** fire brigade.

bombom *(pl:* **bombons)** *m* chocolate, bonbon, sweet.

bombordo *m (NÁUT)* port.

bom-tom *m* good manners; **ser de ~** to be considered polite, the proper thing to do.

Bona *npr* Bonn.

bonacheirão,-ona *m,f* happy easy-going person, good-humoured person.

bonança *f* fair weather; **2** *(NÁUT)* calm; **3** *(fig)* calm, quiet; **depois da tempestade vem a ~** the lull after a storm.

bondade *f* goodness, kindness; **tenha a ~ de vir amanhã** *(formal)* would you please come tomorrow; be so kind as to come tomorrow *(muito formal).*

bonde *m (BR)* tram, trolley-car.

bondoso,-a *adj (pessoa)* kind-hearted, good.

boné *m* cap.

boneca,-o *f,m* doll; **~ de trapos** rag doll; IDIOM **trabalhar para o ~** to work with no gain; **falar para o ~o** to speak in vain.

bonificação *f (gratificação)* bonus; **2** *(desconto)* reduction; **3** *(melhoramento)* improvement *(em edifício)*; **4** *(banco)* **taxas de ~** preferential rates.

bonifrate *m (fantoche)* puppet; **2** *(fig) (pessoa de fraco carácter)* wimp.

bonina *f (planta, flor)* wild daisy.

bonito *m (peixe)* small tuna, tunny; **2** *(irónico)* **~o!** *exc* fine; ♦ **bonito,-a** *adj* pretty; nice, lovely.

bónus *(BR: -ô-) m* bonus, prize; **2** discount; **3** benefit.

boqueira *f (MED) (feridas no canto da boca)* a form of stomatitis; **2** *(MUS)* mouthpiece; **3** *(mangueira)* nozzle.

boquiaberto,-a *adj* dumbfounded, gaping.

boquilha *f* cigarette holder.

borboleta *f* butterfly.

borboletear *vi* to flutter, flit; **2** *(fig)* to fly about.

borbotão *m* gush, spurt; **sair aos borbotões** to gush out.

borbotar *vt* to pour forth; ♦ *vi* to gush out.

borbulha *f* pimple; **~s** pimples; **2** *(BOT)* shoot; **3** *(fig)* row, quarrel.

borbulhar *vi* to come out in pimples; **2** *(sair em gotas)* drip; **3** *(ferver)* bubble *(líquido)*; **4** *(BOT)* to sprout.

borco *m:* **de ~** upside down; **2** face down.

borda *f (extremidade, orla)* edge, border; **à ~ de** on the edge of; **a ~ da saia é verde** the edge/rim of the skirt is green; **2** *(circular)* brim, rim *(do chapéu, do pires)*; **3** *(do precipício)* brink; **4** *(beira)* side; **~ da estrada** roadside; *(da piscina)* side; **5** *(do rio)* river bank; **pela ~ fora** overboard.

bordado *m* embroidery; ♦ **bordado,-a** *adj* embroidered.

bordão *m* staff; **2** *(MUS)* bass string; **3** support.

bordar *vt* to embroider.

bordejar *vi (NÁUT)* to tack; **2** to stagger.

bordel *(pl:* **éis/eis)** *m* brothel; **2** bawdy house.

Bordéus *npr* Bordeaux.

bordelês,-esa *m,f* Bordelais, of/from Bordéus.

bordo *m* rim; **~ do prato** rim of the plate; **2** *(NÁUT)* side, gunwale; **a ~** on board, aboard; **3 posto a ~** *(COM)* F.O.B. *(free on board).*

boreal *adj inv* north; *(aurora)* boreal.

borga *f (paródia)* a night on the town; **2 andar na ~** *(col)* to go out on the tiles, paint the town red.

borla *f* tassel; **2** pompom; **3 de ~** *(fam) (gratis)* free.

bornal *m* haversack; **2** *(saco para os cavalos)* feedbag, nosebag.

borra *f (de tinta)* blot; **2** *(de vinho)* dregs; **3** *(de café)* grounds *pl*; **4** *(azeite, vinagre)* lees; **5 ~ de chá** tealeaves; **6** *(do casulo que não se fia)* floss; **7** *(fig)* **~ da sociedade** the dregs of society, riff-raff.

borra-botas *m,f (pop)* whippersnapper; good-for-nothing.

borracha *f* rubber; **2** *(para apagar)* eraser.

borracho,-a *m* baby pigeon; **2** *(pop) (embriagado)* drunk(ard); **3** *f (fam)* a pretty girl, a chick; ♦ *adj* drunk.

borradela *f* smudge; blot.

borrador *m* blotter; **2** note book; **3** *(COM)* day book; **4** bad painter, dauber.

borralho *m* embers *pl*; **2** *(fig)* hearth, fireside.

borrão *m* rough draft, sketch; **2** ink stain, blot; **3** **papel mata-~** blotting-paper;

borrar *vt* to blot, smudge; **2** to stain, spoil, ruin (*algo*, sth); **3** *(BR)* to conceal the truth; **4** *(fig)* *(deslustrar)* to taint, stain; **5** *(col)* *(defecar)* to foul, to shit ♦ **~-se** *vr* *(sujar-se com as suas fezes)* to shit o.s.; **~-se de medo** be shit-scared.

borrasca *f* storm; squall.

borrascoso,-a *adj* stormy.

borrego *m* *(cordeiro)* young lamb.

borrifadela *f* *(na roupa)* sprinkle, sprinkling.

borrifador *m* sprinkler.

borrifar *vt* *(salpicar)* sprinkle *(roupa)*; spray *(flores)*; ♦ *vi* drizzle; ♦ **~-se** *vr* *(col)* not care; **estou-me a ~ para o que dizes** I don't give a damn about what you say.

borrifo *m* spray; **2** sprinkle; **3** drizzle.

Bósnia-Herzegovina *npr*: **a ~** Bosnia-Herzegovina.

bósnio,-a *m,f adj* Bosnian.

bosque *m* woods; forest.

bosquejar *vt* to sketch, outline.

bosquejo *m* sketch, outline; **2** *(história)* resumo.

bossa *f (ANAT)* swelling, bump; **2** hump; **3** protuberance; **4** *(NÁUT)* stopper; IDIOM **ter ~ para** to have an aptitude for; **~-nova** *f* Brazilian dance, music.

bosta *f (de animal)* dung; **2** *(fig)* *(cal)* crap.

bostela *f (MED)* blister; pustule.

bota *f* boot; **2** **~s de borracha** wellingtons; **3** **~ de elástico** *(pessoa contra o progresso)* square; **ele é uma ~** he is a square, old fogey; IDIOM **bater as ~s** to kick the bucket.

bota-fora *m (BR) (despedida)* send-off; **2** *(navio)* launching.

botânica *f* botany.

botânico,-a *adj* botanical; botanist *m,f*.

botão *m* button; **2** *(flor)* bud; **~ de rosa** rose bud; **em ~** in bud; **casa do ~** buttonhole; **botões** *mpl*; **~ de punho** cufflinks; IDIOM **falar com os seus ~** to talk to o.s.

botar (= **deitar**, **pôr**) *vt/vi (pôr; vestir, calçar)* to put (in/on); **bota mais açúcar** put more sugar in; **bota esta saia** put on this skirt; **2** *(deitar)* to pour *(líquido, sal)*; **3** *(jorrar, verter)* spurt, spout; **o jarro ~ água** the jug spouts water; **está a ~ sangue** it is spurting blood; **4** *(colocar)* put, place; **5** **~ fora** to throw away; **6** **~ a língua** to stick one's tongue out; *(para outros exemplos, Vd:* **deitar**).

> **Botar** is more commonly used in Brazil and in Portuguese provinces.

bote *m* small boat; **2** dinghy; **3** thrust; **4** **~ de recreio** pleasure boat.

botequim *m* bar, café; **2** local place selling lottery tickets, kiosk.

botica *f* pharmacy, chemist's (shop).

boticário,-a *m,f* pharmacist.

botija *f* (earthenware) jug, bottle; **~ de água quente** hot water bottle; IDIOM **apanhado com a mão na ~** caught red-handed.

botim *m* ankle boot.

boto,-a *adj (lâmina)* blunt; **2** **pé ~** deformed foot, club foot; **3** *(fig)* dull, stupid, thick *(col)*.

botoeira *f* buttonhole.

bouça *f* thicket.

bouquet *(BR:* **buquê)** *m (ramo de flores)* bouquet.

bovino *adj* bovine; **gado ~** cattle.

box e *m* boxing; **combate de ~** boxing match.

boxers *f pl* boxer shorts.

boxeur *m (DESP)* boxer.

BP *(abr de* **Banco de Portugal**) Bank of Portugal.

braça *f (NÁUT)* fathom (6 feet).

braçada *f* armful; **às ~s** by the armful; **2** *(natação)* stroke.

braçadeira *f (para o braço)* arm-band; **2** *(de metal)* clasp; **3** *(cortina)* tie-back; **4** *(argola)* *(para espingarda)* loop; **5** *(para a mangueira)* bracket; **6** *(DESP)* *(correia)* wrist-strap.

braçal *adj inv* manual; **trabalhador ~** manual worker.

bracarense *m,f adj inv* of/from Braga (city in N.W. Portugal)

bracejar *vi* to wave one's arms about, gesticulate.

bracelete *f (pulseira)* bangle, bracelet; **2** *(relógio)* strap.

braço *m* arm; **~ direito** right arm; *(fig)* right-hand man; **2** **~ de mar** inlet; **3** *(de balança)* pointer; **4** *(de toca-discos)* arm; **de ~ dado** arm-in-arm; **braços** arms; **cruzar os ~s** to fold the arms; ♦ **de ~s abertos** with open arms; **a ~s com** struggling with, at grips with; ♦ **de ~ dado** arm-in-arm; **ser levado em ~s** be carried in sb's arms; IDIOM **não dar/dar o ~ a torcer** not give in/give in.

braço-de-ferro *(pl:* **braços-de-ferro**) *m* arm-wrestling; **2** *(fig)* proof of strength; **3** *(fig)* *(de opiniões, princípios, vontade)* clash, conflict of wills.

bradar *vi* to shout, scream; **2** cry out; **3** to proclaim.

Bradesco *(abr de* **Banco Brasileiro de Descontos**) private Brazilian Bank; **saúde B~** Bradesco Health Insurance/Fund.

brado *m* shout, scream.

bragançano,-a *adj* of/from Bragança (capital of Trás-os-Montes, N.E. Portugal).

braguilha *(Vd:* **breguilha**).

braille *m* Braille.

bramido *m* bellow, roar.

bramir *vi* to bellow, roar.

branca *f* white; **2** *(lapso de memória)* slip; **deu-me uma ~** my mind went blank; **3** *(cabelo branco)* white hair; **Branca de Neve** Snow White.

branco,-a *adj (cor)* white; **2** *(espaço)* gap, space; **3** **Livro B~** *(documento do governo)* White Paper; **selo ~** *(selo oficial)* embossed seal ♦ **em ~** *adj, adv (não escrito, não preenchido) (cheque, page etc)* blank; **em ~** in blank; IDIOM **passar a noite em ~** to spend a sleepless night; **~ como a cal** white as a sheet.

brancura *f* whiteness.

brandir *vt* to brandish.

brando,-a *adj (massa, palavras, voz)* soft, gentle; **2** *(CULIN)* medium; **em forno ~** in a medium (temperature) oven; *(lume)* low (flame); **3** *(tempo; febre)* mild; **vento** ~ mild wind.

brandura *f* softness; mildness.

branduras *fpl* caresses.

branqueador *m* whitener; *(pó)* bleaching powder; **2** *(fig)* money laundering.

branqueamento *m* whitening; **2** *(BR)* blanching; **3** *(fig)* ~ **de capitais** money laundering.

branquear *vt (roupa)* to whiten, bleach; **2** *(legumes)* to blanche; **3** *(dinheiro)* to launder; **4** *(metais)* to polish; ♦ *vi (cabelo)* turn white; **2** *(BR) (casa)* whitewash

brasa *f* hot coal, ember; **2 em** ~ red-hot, burning; **3** *(fig, fam)* **ele é uma** ~ he is a dish; IDIOM **estar sobre ~s** to be anxious, be on tenterhooks; **chegar/puxar a** ~ **à sua sardinha** to look after number one; **passar pelas ~s** to have a nap, to slumber.

brasão *m* coat of arms; **2** crest; **3** *(fig)* lema.

braseiro *m* brazier; **2** embers.

Brasil *m* Brazil.

brasileiro,-a *m,f adj* Brazilian; *(LÍNG)* Portuguese.

brasileirismo *m* Brazilianism.

Brasília *npr* Brasilia.

bravata *f* bravado, boasting.

bravatear *vi* to boast, brag.

braveza *f (de pessoa)* fierceness, impetuosity; **2** wildness.

bravio,-a *adj* wild, untamed.

bravo,-a *m,f* brave person; **os ~s daquela guerra** the brave of that war; ♦ *adj* brave; **2** wild, untamed; **3** *(pessoa)* furious; **ela é uma mulher ~a** she is a woman to reckon with; **4** *(mar, etc)* rough, stormy; ♦ *exc* **B~!** Well done!

bravura *f* courage, bravery; **2** fury; **3** prowess.

brazões *(pl de* **brazão***).*

breca *f (MED)* cramp; ♦ *exc* **com a** ~**!** I'll be damned! what about that!; **ser levado,-a da** ~ to be naughty; to be devilish; to be quite a man/a woman.

brecar *vt (BR)* to stop; ♦ *vi* to brake.

brecha *f (abertura)* gap, fissure; opening; crack (na parede); **2** *(ferimento)* wound, cut; **3** *(fig) (lacuna, vaga)* vacancy *(em emprego, cargo)*; **4** *(GEOL)* brechia; **5** *(JUR) (omissão)* loophole; *(prejuízo)* hole; **abrir** ~ to force an opening; *(fig)* suffer damages.

breguilha *f (calças de homem)* fly-front; **2** *(fam)* fly *(US)*; flies *(UK) pl*; **a sua** ~ **está aberta** your fly is open.

brejeirice *f* sauciness; vulgarity.

brejeiro,-a *m,f (brincalhão)* mischief-maker, imp; ♦ *adj* naughty, mischievous, saucy; **2** impish; **3** vulgar.

brejo *m* marsh, swamp, moor.

brenha *f* dense wood, thicket; **2** tangle, maze.

breque *m (carruagem puxada por cavalos)* horse-drawn carriage; **2** *(BR) (travão mecânico)* brake.

Bretanha *npr* Brittany *(França)*.

bretão, bretã *m,f adj (da Bretanha)* Breton; **os bretões** the Bretons.

breu *m* pitch; **escuro como** ~ pitch black.

breve *adj (ger)* short; **2** *(rápido)* fleeting; **3** *(conciso)* brief; ♦ *adv* **em/dentro em** ~ soon, shortly; **até** ~**!**

see you soon!; **ser** ~ to be brief; **seja** ~ make it short; *(REL) (escapulário)* scapular.

brevemente *adv* shortly; briefly; soon.

brevidade *f* brevity, shortness; **2** *(rapidez)* quickly.

breviário *m* breviary; **2** abridgement.

bricabraque *m* junk, bric-a-brac.

bricolage *f (pequeno trabalho)* household repair, do-it-yourself.

briga *f* fight, brawl; **2** *(desavença)* quarrel, row, dispute.

brigada *f (MIL)* brigade; **2** *(agentes de autoridade)* patrol.

brigadeiro *m (MIL)* brigadier.

brigão,-ona *m,f* brawler, trouble-maker; ♦ *adj* quarrelsome.

brigar *vi* to fight; **2** to quarrel; **3** *(destoar)* to clash.

brilhante *m (diamante)* diamond; ♦ *adj* brilliant, bright, shimmering.

brilhar *vi* to shine, glitter, sparkle; IDIOM **nem tudo que brilha é ouro** all is not gold that glitters.

brilho *m (luminosidade)* glow; brightness; **2** *(luz, lustre)* shine; **3** *(fig) (brilhantismo)* splendour, brilliance.

brim *m (tecido forte de algodão)* coarse cloth.

brincadeira *f* fun; **2** joke; **fora de** ~ joking apart; **de/por** ~ for fun; IDIOM **ele não é para ~s** he won't stand for any nonsense; **deixe-se de** ~ stop kidding/mucking about.

brincalhão,-ona *m,f* joker, teaser; ♦ *adj* playful.

brincar *vi (com brinquedos, crianças)* to play; to have fun; **2** *(brincar com)* to joke, tease; **estou a** ~ **contigo** *(BR:* **brincando com você***)* I am joking/pulling your leg; **3** *(jogos):* **vamos** ~ **à cabra-cega** let's play blind man's bluff; **4** ~ **às escondidas** to play hide and seek.

brinco *m (jóia para as orelhas)* earring; ~**s-de-princesa** *mpl (BOT)* fuchsia.

brindar *vt (presentear)* to reward/give a present to; ♦ *vi (fazer uma saudação)* to toast, to make a toast.

brinde *m* toast; **fazer um** ~ to propose, make a toast; **2** *(presente)* free gift, trinket in a Christmas cracker.

brinquedo *m* toy; **loja de ~s** toyshop.

brio *m (honra)* pride; dignity; self-respect; **ter** ~ **na sua casa** to be proud of her home; **2** courage; **3** *(ânimo)* spirit.

brioso,-a *adj* self-respecting; **2** *(orgulhoso)* proud *(de sua casa/seu trabalho)*; **3** *(cavalo)* high-spirited.

brisa *f* breeze, light wind; ~ **marítima** sea breeze.

brita *f* broken stones, macadam; **2** gravel, shingle; ~**deira** *f* pneumatic drill.

britânico,-a *m,f* Briton; *(fam)* Brit; ♦ *adj* British.

broa *f* country/home-made bread with corn flour; **2** traditional Christmas cookie, small cake in the shape of a boat; ~ **castelar** made with honey and almond; ♦ **broas** *fpl (fig)* Christmas box; Christmas bonus.

broca *f* drill; **2** *(eixo da fechadura)* keyhole.

brocar *vt* to drill, bore.

brocade *m* brocade.

brocha *f* tack, small nail; **2** leather strips to tie the oxen to the yoke; IDIOM **estar à** ~ to be in a fix/in some difficulty.

broche *m* (*ornamento*) brooch.
brochura *f* binding; **2** brochure.
brócolos (BR: **brócoli**) *m* (BOT) broccoli *sg*.
broma (*inseto da madeira*) woodworm.
brometo *m* (QUÍM) bromide.
bromo *m* (QUÍM) bromine.
bronca *f* (*barulho, sarilho*) disturbance; commotion; **2** (BR) (*repreeensão*) reprimand; **dar uma ~ a alguém por**; to give a telling-off.
bronco,-a *adj* (*tosco*) rough; **2** (*grosseiro*) (*pessoa*) coarse; common lout; **3** (*fig*) (*pateta*) thick.
brônquio *m* bronchus.
bronquite *f* (MED) bronchite.
bronquite *f* bronquitis.
bronze *m* bronze; **2** suntan.
bronzeado,-a *adj* bronzed; **2** suntanned.
bronzeador *m* sun lotion.
bronzear *vt* to tan; ♦ **~-se** *vr* to get a tan.
broquear *vt* to drill, bore.
broquim *m* (*broca pequena*) small drill.
brotar *vt* to produce; ♦ *vi* to flow; **2** (BOT) to sprout; to spring up.
broto *m* bud; **2** (BR) (*fig*) youngster.
broxa *f* (*pincel largo*) paint brush; **2** (*impotente*) (*vulg*) dickless man.
bruços *mpl* (*natação*) breaststroke ♦ **de** *adv* face down.
bruma *f* mist, haze; **2** uncertainty; **3 nas ~s da história** in the mists of history.
brumoso,-a *adj* misty, hazy.
brunido,-a *adj* polished.
brunir *vt* to polish.
brusco,-a *adj* (*atitude, maneira*) brusque, abrupt; **2** (*palavras*) curt; **3** (*repentino*) sudden.
brutal *adj* brutal; **2** terrible.
brutalidade *f* brutality.
bruto,-a *m,f* (*grosseiro; violento*) brute; ♦ *adj* brutish, coarse, rough; **2** (*diamante*) uncut, rough; **3** (*pedra*) unhewn; **4** (*petróleo*) crude; **5** (*líquido*) gross; **6 em ~** raw, in the rough; ♦ **produto interno ~** (**PIB**) gross domestic product (GDP); **produto nacional** (**PNB**) gross national product (GNP).
bruxa *f* witch; **2** (*fig*) old hag.
bruxaria *f* witchcraft.
Bruxelas *npr* Brussels.
bruxo *m* magician, wizard, sorcerer.
bruxulear *vi* (*tremular*) to flicker (*luz, chama*).
Bucareste *npr* Bucharest.
bucha *f* (*de arma*) wad; **2** (*para parafuso*) plug, Rawlplug®; **3** (*alimento*) morsel; **~ de pão** chunk of bread; **4** (*pessoa gorda*) fatso; **o B~ e o Estica** Laurel and Hardy.
bucho *m* (*do animal*) stomach; **2** (*pop*) (*barriga de pessoa*) belly.
buço *m* down; **2** fuzz over the upper lip.
bucólico,-a *adj* bucolic; (*paisagem, etc*) rustic.
Buda *m* Buddha.
budismo *m* Buddhism.
Budapeste *npr* Budapest.
budista *adj inv* Buddhist.
bueiro *m* (*cano*) drainpipe; **2** (*sarjeta*), gutter; **3** (*respiradouro de fornalha*) cano da chaminé.

bufa *f* (*pop*) fart.
búfalo *m* (ZOOL) buffalo.
bufante *adj inv* (*penteado, saia*) bouffant, fluffy.
bufão *m* jester, buffoon, fool; **2** (TEAT) comedian, comic.
bufar *vi* (*soprar sobre*) to blow; **2** (*ofegar*) pant; **3** (*irritar-se*) huff, puff, fume; **4** (*peidar*) to fart; **5** (*fig*) (*bazofiar*) to boast of, brag.
bufo *m* (*sopro*) puff; **2** (ZOOL) **~ real** eagle owl; **3** (*bobo*) court jester; **4** (*fig, pop*) (*delator*) informer, stool pigeon; undercover agent, mole; ♦ **bufo,-a** *adj* burlesque, comic; **ópera ~** comic opera.
bufete (BR: **bufê**) *m* table d'hôte, buffet (*bar*).
bugalho *m* (BOT) oak-apple; oak gall; gallnut; IDIOM **misturar alhos com ~s** to speak at cross purposes; to speak at a tangent.
buganvília (BOT) bougainvillea.
bugiganga *f* trinket; **~s** *fpl* knick-knacks.
bugio *m* monkey, Brazilian bearded monkey; **2** (*fig*) (*imitador*) ape.
bujão *m* (TEC) cap, plug, stopper; **~ de gas**, gas cylinder, container.
bujarrona *f* (NÁUT) jib.
bula *f* (REL) bull; **B~ Papal** Papal Bull, papal edict; **2** (FARM) printed leaflet for the use of medicines.
bulbo *m* (Vd: **bolbo**).
bule *m* tea/coffee pot.
Bulgária *npr* **a ~** Bulgaria.
búlgaro,-a *m,f adj* Bulgarian.
bulha *f* (*discussão*) row; **2** (*barulho*) din; **andar às ~s** to get into fights.
bulhar *vt* to quarrel.
bulício *m* (*agitação*) bustle, hubbub; flurry.
buliçoso,-a *adj* lively; **2** restless; **3** boisterous.
bulimia *f* bulimia.
bulir *vi* to move, stir; **nenhuma folha bulia** not a leaf stirred; **2 ~ em** to fiddle with sth; **3** (*irritar*) to get/grate on one's nerves.
bum! *exc* (*tiro*) bang!
bumba! *exc* (*zás*) wham!
bumbum *m* continuous noise; **2** (*fala de infante*) água; **3** (BR) (*nádegas*) bottom, bum.
bumerangue *m* boomerang.
bungee-jumping *m* (DESP) bungee-jumping.
bunda *f* (*fam*) (*Angola, BR*) bottom, bum.
buraco *m* hole, orifice; **~ da agulha** eye of the needle; **~ da fechadura** keyhole; **~ de ozono** ozone layer; IDIOM **ter um ~ no estômago** to be hungry.
burburejar *vi* to bubble.
burburinho *m* (*vozes*) buzz, hum; **2** (*fig*) rumour; whisper; **3** (*bulício*) hustle and bustle.
burel *m* (*vestimenta*) coarse woollen cloth; **2** (*hábito*) monk's or nun's habit.
burgau *m* gravel; rubble.
burgo *m* (*castelo e áreas amuralhadas*) borough; town.
burgomestre *m* burgomaster.
burguês,-uesa *adj* middle-class, bourgeois.
burguesia *f* middle class, bourgeoisie.
buril *m* chisel.
burilar *vt* to chisel; to carve.

burla *f (fraude)* fraud, double-dealing; ~**s na portagem** *fpl* fraud in the toll charge; **2** *(zombaria)* jeering.

burlão,-ona *m,f* cheat, swindler.

burlar *vt (ludibriar)* to cheat, to swindle *(alguém)*; to deceive *(alguém)*; **2** *(JUR)* defraud.

burocracia *f* bureaucracy; **2** *(papelada)* red tape.

burocrata *m,f* bureaucrat.

burra *f* she-donkey; **2** *(BR)* mule; **3** *(fig) (moça, mulher)* silly ass, idiot; **4** *(cofre)* safe; **5** *(banco de carpinteiro)* trestle.

burricada *f* a herd of donkeys, asses; **2** *(parvoíce)* nonsense.

burrice *f* stupidity, silliness; **2** *(erro, asneira)* blunder.

burro,-a *m,f* donkey; ass; **2** *(pessoa) (fig, pej)* idiot; **3** ~ **de sorte** lucky devil; ♦ *adj (estúpido)* stupid; *(teimoso)* obstinate; IDIOM **estar com os** ~**s** to be in a bad mood; **ir de cavalo para** ~ to go from bad to worse, go down in the world; **pra** ~ *(BR: col)* a lot.

busca *f (procurar)* search; **em** ~ **de** in search of.

buscar *vt* to look for, search for; **ir** ~ to fetch, go and get; **mandar** ~ to send for.

busílis *m* rub *(arc)*; **aí está o** ~ there is the rub *(arc)*, that's where the problem lies.

bússola *f* compass.

busto *m* (ANAT) bust; **2** *(escultura)* bust.

butano *m, adj* butane; **gás** ~ butane gas.

buxo *m (BOT) (arbusto sempre verde)* box; **2** boxwood; **3 áleas de** ~ box hedges.

buzina *f* horn; **2** hooter; **3** *(BR)* din; ~**da** *f* honk, hoot.

buzinadela *f (toque ligeiro)* toot, hoot.

buzinar *vi* to hoot, sound the horn.

búzio *m* conch; **2** *(ZOOL) (marisco)* dog whelk; **2** *(BR)* **jogar** ~**s** to cast spells, call the spirits.

BV *(abr de* **Bombeiros Voluntários**) Voluntary Fire Brigade.

byte *m (COMP)* byte.

C

C, c *m (letra)* C, c.
Cª *(abr de* **companhia)** Co.
cá *adv* here, over here; **vem ~** come here; **de ~ para lá** to and fro; **~ estou** here I am; **dá ~ a tua mão** give me your hand; **daí para ~** since then; **eu ~ não gosto** I myself don't like it; **já ~ não está quem falou** I take back what I said.
cã *(pl: -ãs) f* white hair.
caaba *f* Kaaba.
caatinga *f (BR) (Vd:* **catinga***)*.
cabaça *f (fruto)* gourd; **2** *(planta)* calabash.
cabaço *m (recipiente)* watering-can; **2** *(fam) (recusa de namoro)* brush-off; **dei-lhe um ~** I gave him the brush-off.
cabal *(pl: -ais) adj inv* perfect; **2** complete; **3** exact.
cabala *f* cabala; **2** *(fig)* conspiracy; intrigue.
cabalar *vi* to plot.
cabana *f* hut, shack.
cabaré *m* night club.
cabaz *m* basket; **2** *(com comida)* hamper.
cabeça *f (ANAT)* head; **abanar a ~** to shake one's head; **fazer sinal com a ~** to nod at; **~ fria** *(fig)* cool-headed, level-headed; **2** tip; head; **parafuso sem ~** headless screw; **~ do alfinete** pin-head; **3** *(inteligência)* mind; brain; brains; **não ter ~ para nada** have no brains, be no good at anything; **passar pela ~** to cross one's mind; **4** *(disposição)* **agora não tenho ~ para isso** I am not in the mood for that now; **5** *(parte coberta pelo cabelo)* scalp, skull; **lavar a ~** to wash one's hair; **6** *(BOT)* head, bulb; **~ de alho** head of garlic; **~ de lança** spear head; ♦ *m,f (fig) (líder)* head, leader; ♦ *adj* **duro de ~** stubborn, pig-headed; ♦ *adv* **à ~ de** at the head of; **da ~ aos pés** from head to toe; **de ~** head first/headlong; **de ~ erguida** *(fig)* with one's head held high; **fazer contas de ~** *(memória)* do sums in one's mind; IDIOM **não estar bem da ~** to be off one's rocker; **perder a ~** *(perder controlo)* to lose one's head.
cabeçada *f (pancada)* head butt; **dar uma ~ na porta** to bang one's head against the door; **2** *(fig) (negócio, amor)* blunder; **dar uma ~** make a mistake; **3** *(FUT)* header.
cabeça-de-alho-chocho *m,f (cabeça no ar)* scatter-brain, featherbrain.
cabeçalha *f (carroça)* front shaft.
cabeçalho *m* headline; **2** caption; letter heading; **3** title page of a book.
cabecear *vt (FUT) (bola)* to head; ♦ *vi (adormecer)* to doze, nod.

cabeceira *f (à mesa)* place of honour; **2** *(cama)* head of a bed; **3** **mesa de ~** bedside table.
cabecilha *m,f* ringleader.
cabeçudo,-a *m,f* person with a large head; ♦ *adj (fig)* obstinate; **2** *(fam)* pig-headed.
cabedal *m* leather; **2** *(musculatura)* body, strength; **3** *(fam) (dinheiro)* money, wealth; **4** *(muitos conhecimentos)* vast knowledge.
cabeleira *f* head of hair; **~ postiça** wig.
cabeleireiro,-a *m,f* hairdresser.
cabelo *m* hair; **~ crespo** frizzy hair; **~ liso** straight hair; **~ louro/loiro** blonde hair; **2** *(fig) (porcelana)* hair-like crack; IDIOM **estar pelos ~s** to be on edge, to do things unwillingly; **é de arrepiar os ~s** to be horrifying, to be hair-raising.
cabeludo,-a *m,f adj* hairy.
caber *vi* to be contained in, to fit in; **os ovos não cabem neste cabaz** the eggs do not fit in this basket; **2** to fall to one's lot/inheritance/responsibility; **cabe a si falar com ele** it is up to you to speak to him; **3** **não cabe aqui fazer comentários** this is not the time or place to comment; IDIOM **ela não cabe em si de contente** she is overjoyed.
cabide *m* rack; **2** peg; **3** coat hanger.
cabidela *f (CULIN)* giblets stew; **arroz de ~** giblet rice; **2** *(fam)* not to have opportunity/acceptance.
cabido¹ *m (assembleia de cónegos)* chapter.
cabido² *(pp d* **caber***) adj* opportune.
cabimento *m (adequação)* sense, reason; **isso não tem ~** that does not make any sense.
cabina, cabine *f* cabin; **2 ~ de piloto** *(AER)* cockpit; **3 ~ telefónica** *(BR: -fô-)* telephone booth.
cabisbaixo,-a *adj* dispirited, crestfallen; **2** downcast.
cabo *m* end; **2** *(utensílio)* handle; **~ da vassoura** broom handle; **3** *(GEOG)* cape; **4** *(ELECT)* cable; **5** *(TV)* cable TV; **6** *(MIL)* corporal; **7 ~ de aço** iron cable; **8** *(NÁUT) (corda)* cable; ♦ **ao ~ de** at the end of; **ao fim e ao ~** after all, at the end of the day; **de ~ a rabo** from one end to the other; from beginning to end; **levar a ~** to carry out; IDIOM **dar ~ de** to destroy, to finish sth/sb off; **ir às do ~** to get furious.
Cabo (= Cidade do Cabo) *npr m f* Capetown.
caboclo,-a *m,f (BR)* mixed white and Indian native; **2** *(agricultor)* peasant.
cabo-de-esquadra *m (argumentos sem fundamentos)* **conversa de ~** *(disparatada)* a lot of poppycock; nonsense.
cabograma *m* cable(gram).
cabouco *m* ditch, trench; **2** *(CONSTR)* foundations.
cabouqueiro *m* ditch digger, navvy.
Cabo Verde *npr* Cape Verde Islands.
cabo-verdiano,-a *m,f adj* Cape-Verdian; **2** *(LÍNG)* Portuguese.

Santiago Island is its capital. Mindelo, in São Vicente Island: a cultural city and important port.

cabra *f (ZOOL)* goat; **2** *(guindaste)* large crane; **3** *(fig) (fam) (mulher de mau génio)* nasty woman; *(pej)* cow, bitch.

cabra-cega *f (jogo)* blind man's buff; **jogar à ~** to play blind man's buff.

cabrão *m (vulg)* bastard; **2** *(pej) m* deceived husband, cuckold; **3** *(cabra) m* billy goat, buck. **cabrona** *f (vulg) (mulher má)* bitch.

cabreiro,-a *m,f* goatherdsman/woman; ♦ *adj* goat's; **queijo ~** goat's cheese.

cabrestante *m* capstan, windlass.

cabresto *m (para cavalos)* halter; **2** *(TAUROM)* lead-ox; **3** *(NÁUT)* bobstay; **4** *(fig) (fam) (sujeição)* halter, restraint.

cabriola *f* leap, skip; *(cambalhota)* somersault; **2** *(fig) (mudança de opinião)* about-face.

cabrito *m* baby goat, kid; **2 ~ montês** *(ZOOL)* mountain goat, ibex.

cabrocha *f (BR)* mulatto girl.

cábula *m,f (aluno que não trabalha)* lazy person; *(que faz gazeta)* truant; ♦ *adj* lazy; slack.

caca *f (fam)* faeces *(US: feces)*, shit; **2** dirt, muck; **3 vai à ~** *(fam) (cal)* get lost!, piss off!

caça *f* hunting, hunt, shooting; **2** *(fig)* chase; **3** quarry, game; **4** *m (AER) (avião)* fighter plane; **5 ~ à baleia** whaling; **6** *(fig)* **à ~ de** in pursuit of.

caçada *f* hunt, hunting trip; **2** *(fig)* chase, pursuit, raid.

caçadeira *f* hunting rifle.

caçador,-ora *m,f* hunter.

caça-minas *m* minesweeper.

caça-níqueis *f* slot machine.

caçar *vt/vi* to hunt, to shoot; **2** *(fig)* to raid, to search, to pursue; **3** to catch; **~ ladrões** to catch thieves.

cacarejar *vi (galinhas)* to cackle, to cluck; **2** *(fig)* to chatter in silly manner, to babble.

cacarejo *m* cackle, clucking; **2** *(fig)* babble.

caçarola *f* saucepan; **2** *(CULIN)* casserole.

caça-submarina *f* underwater fishing.

cacau *m* cocoa; **2** *(BOT)* cacao.

cacetada *f* blow with a truncheon/cudgel/stick.

cacete *m* club; stick; cudgel; **2** *(pão)* French stick; ♦ *adj (BR)* tiresome; **cacetear** *vt* to cudgel.

cachaça *f (BR)* (white) rum; **2** *(BR) (fig)* passion, vocation.

cachaço *m* nape, back of the neck.

cachalote *m* sperm whale, cachalot.

caché *(BR: cachê) m (TV, CIN, TEAT)* fee; **2** *(SPORT)* **os altos ~s** the exorbitant fees.

cachecol *m* woollen neck scarf, football scarf.

Cachemira *npr* **a ~** Kashmir.

cachimbo *m* smoking pipe; **2** *(NÁUT)* funnel.

cachimónia *(BR: -ô-) f (col)* head, noddle; **2** sense; **mete isso na ~** get it into your head.

cacho *m (BOT) (uvas, bananas)* bunch; **2** *(aglomeração)* cluster; **3** *(de cabelo)* ringlets.

cachoeira *f* waterfall.

cachola *f (col) (cabeça)* nut, loaf, noodle; **ele não está bom da ~** he has a screw loose; **2** heads of small fish; IDIOM **ficar com uma grande ~** to suffer a deception.

cachopa *f (fam)* girl, lass.

cachopo *m* lad.

cachorra *f (BR)* she-dog, bitch; **2** *(fig)* slut, strampet.

cachorro,-a *m,f* puppy, pup, cub; **2** *m (ARQ)* corbel, stay, prop; **3** *(BR) (cão)* dog; **4** *(col)* rascal; **5 ~ quente** *m (CULIN)* hot dog; IDIOM *(BR)* **soltar os ~s em cima de** vent one's anger on sb.

cachorrinho,-a *m,f* little puppy.

cacilheiro *m* of/from Cacilhas (on Lisbon's opposite bank); **2** ferry across Tagus.

cacimba *f* drizzle; thick mist.

cacique *m* Indian chief (Americas); **2** *(pej) (mandão)* local political boss.

caco *m* broken piece (of china); **2** *(fam) (pessoa velha ou doente)* wreck; **3** *(fam)* head; **4 ~s** *(CONSTR)* rubble; *(BR)* junk.

caçoar *vt/vi* to mock, tease, make fun of; ♦ *vi* to joke, to jest, to kid.

caçoila, caçoula *f* saucepan, casserole pan.

cacto *m (BOT)* cactus.

caçula *m,f (BR)* youngest child of the family; **2** *(ANGOLA)* the drying or grinding of the corn.

cada *adj inv* each; every; **2 ~ qual** each one; **3 tu dizes ~ uma!** you say such (silly) things!; **4 ~ vez mais** more and more; **5 ela ~ vez está mais linda,** she is more beautiful with each passing day; IDIOM **~ qual tem o seu gosto** each to his own taste; **ganhar o pão-nosso de ~ dia** earn our daily bread.

cadafalso *m* gallows, scaffold.

cadastro *m (prédios)* official register; **2** *(de terrenos)* land registry; **3** *(policial/judicial)* criminal record; **4** census; **5 ~ de pessoa física** tax payer's identity data, records; **6** dossier, record.

cadáver *m* corpse, dead body.

cadavérico,-a *m,f adj* cadaveric, corpse-like.

cadê (= **que é de?**) *adv (BR) (col)* where is …?

cadeado *m* padlock; **2 a ~** under lock and key; **3 fechar a ~** to lock up.

cadeia *f* chain; **2** shackle; **3** prison, jail; **4** *(montanha)* range; **5 ~ alimentar** food chain; **6** (eventos) **uma ~ de acontecimentos** a series of events; **7 ~ de montagem** assembly line; **8 ~ de televisão** TV networks.

cadeira *f* seat, chair; **~ de rodas** wheelchair; **2** seat of authority; **3** *(Univ) (cátedra)* subject, department; **4 ~s** *fpl (ANAT)* hips.

cadeirado *m (igreja, teatro)* stalls, choir-stalls.

cadeirão *m (poltrona)* high-backed chair, large arm chair.

cadela *f (ZOOL)* bitch, she-dog; **2** *(col)* nasty, ungrateful woman; **3** *(pej)* slut.

cadência *f* cadence; **2** rhythm, pace; **3** pause; **marcar a ~** to mark the pause.

cadenciado,-a *m,f adj* rhythmic.

cadente *adj inv (estrela)* fallen, cadent; **2** cadenced, rhythmic.

caderneta *f* notebook; **2** register; **3** passbook; **4** *(BR)* ~ **de motorista** driving licence; **5** ~ **de poupança** savings book, account; **6** ~ **escolar** school register; **7** ~ **predial** property registration booklet.

caderno *m* exercise book; **2** ~ **de encargos** list, contract with rules, terms and conditions **3** ~s **eleitorais** electoral register.

cadete *m* *(MIL)* cadet.

cadilho *m* fringe; **2 cadilhos** *mpl* *(fig)* worries.

cadinho *m* *(TEC)* crucible; **2** ~ **de cultura** melting-pot.

caducar *vi* to lapse, to expire; **seu visto caducou** your visa has expired; **2** to age, to become senile.

caduco,-a *adj* invalid, lapsed, expired; **2** decrepit; **3** obsolete; **4** *(BOT)* deciduous.

cães *(Vd:* **cão***)*.

cafajeste *m,f* *(col)* rogue, yob, thug.

café *m* coffee; ~ **com leite** white coffee; ~ **pingado** coffee with a little milk; ~ **simples** black coffee; *(pop)* bica; **2** *(loja)* café, coffee shop; **3** ~ **da manhã** *(BR)* breakfast.

cafeeiro *m* coffee bush; **indústria cafeeira** *f* coffee industry.

> Vd: 'bica', 'galão', 'meia', = *(EP)* jargon for **café**.

cafeicultor *m* coffee-grower.

cafeína *f* caffeine.

cafeteira *f* coffee pot.

cafezal *m* coffee plantation.

cafezinho *m* *(BR)* small black coffee.

cáfila *f* *(de camelos)* coffle; caravan; **2** *(fig)* rabble, mob.

cafuné *m* caress.

cagaço *m* *(cal)* fright; shock; **apanhar um** ~ to get a fright.

cágado *m* *(ZOOL)* tortoise.

cagalhão *m* *(vulg)* *(fezes)* shit, crap; **2** *(fig, vulg)* **ele é um** ~ he is a piece of shit.

cagança *f* *(prosápia)* crap; **ele é cheio de** ~ he is full of crap.

caganeira *f* *(cal)* *(fezes)* the runs.

caganita *f* goat's, sheep's excrement; **2** *(birds)* droppings *pl*.

caganito *m* *(fam)* small, thin man; **2** slip of a boy.

cagar *vt* *(cal)* *(sujar)* to soil; ♦ *vi* to defecate; *(cal)* to shit; ♦ *vr* to get filthy; **estou todo cagado** *(cal)* I'm covered in muck/shit; IDIOM ~**-se de medo** *(cal)* to have a hell of fright, to be shit scared; **estou-me cagando para o ministro** I don't give a shit about the minister.

cai-cai *m* *(vestido)* strapless dress.

caiador,-ora *m,f* *(de casas)* whitewasher.

caiar *vt* to whitewash.

caiba *(pres subj de* **caber***)* **espero que este presente** ~ **na caixa** I hope this present can go in/fits in the box.

caibo *(pres ind de* **caber***)*.

cãibra *f* *(MED)* cramp.

caibro *m* *(CONSTR)* joist.

caído,-a *m,f adj* fallen; **folhas** ~**as** fallen leaves; **2** dejected; **3** *(fig)* **estar** ~ **por alguém** to have fallen for someone.

caimão *m* alligator, caiman.

caimento *m* fall, falling, slope; **2** *(fig)* *(abatimento)* ruin; **2** despondency.

caipira *m,f* *(BR)* peasant, yokel.

caipirinha *f* *(BR)* cocktail of cachaça, lemon and sugar.

cair *vi* to fall (down); **2** to fall for it; **eu não caio nessa** I won't fall for that one; **3** to drop; **a temperatura caiu** the temperature has dropped; **4** ~ **bem** to suit, go well with; **5** ~ **de cama** to fall sick; **6** ~ **de joelhos** to sink to one's knees; **7** ~ **em exagero** to exaggerate; **8** ~ **em si** to come to one's senses; **9** ~ **no esquecimento** to be forgotten.

cais *m* *(NÁUT)* quay; dock; **2** *(estação de comboios)* platform.

caixa *f* *(gen)* box; **2** *(pagamentos)* cash desk, till; *(empregado,-a)* cashier; **3 livro de** ~ ledger; **4** *(caixote)* box, case; **5** *(estojo)* small box; **6** print; ~ **alta/baixa** *(TIPO)* upper/lower case; **7 C~** *(banco)* national savings bank *(EP)*; ~ **de amortização** *(COM)* sinking fund; ~ **económica** *(BR)* savings bank; **C~ Nacional de Pensões** National Pension Fund; **8** *(cavidade)* ~ **craniana** *(ANAT)* cranium, skull; ~ **do tímpano** *(ANAT)* ear drum; **9** ~ **do correio** letter box; **10** ~ **de fusíveis** *(ELECT)* fuse box; **11** ~ **de mudanças/de velocidades** *(AUTO)* gear box; **12** ~**-forte** safe; strong box; **13** ~ **negra** *(avião)* black box; ♦ **o** ~ **automático** *m* *(EP)*, **o** ~ **eletrónico** *m* *(BR)* cashpoint.

caixa-de-fósforos *f* box of matches, matchbox.

caixão *m* large box, crate; **2** *(esquife)* coffin *(UK)*, casket *(US)*.

caixeira *f* saleswoman.

caixeiro *m* salesman; ~ **viajante** commercial traveller, travelling salesman.

caixilho *m* frame; ~ **da janela** window frame.

caixote *m* packing case, crude box; **2** ~ **do lixo** dustbin.

cajadada *f* a blow with a stick; IDIOM **matar dois coelhos de uma** ~ to kill two birds with one stone.

cajado *m* staff, shepherd's crook.

caju *m* cashew nut.

cajueiro *m* cashew tree.

cal *f* lime; **água de** ~ lime water; **2** calcium oxide; **3 pintar com** ~ to whitewash.

calabouço *m* dungeon, prison.

calado,-a *adj* silent, quiet; **estar** ~ to be, keep quiet; **ser** ~ to be a quiet person; **2** *f* *(NÁUT)* gauge, draft; **3 pela** ~**a** stealthily; **4 pela** ~**a da noite** in the dead of night.

calafate *m* caulker.

calafetagem *f* caulking.

calafrio *m* shiver; **ter** ~s to shiver, to have the shivers.

calamidade *f* calamity, disaster.

calamitoso,-a *adj* disastrous.

calão *m* slang.

calar *vt* to keep quiet about; **2** to silence; *(fam)* **cala a boca!** shut up; ♦ ~**-se** *vr* to keep quiet, silence; **os sinos calaram-se** the bells stopped ringing.

calça *f* trouser.

calçadeira *f* shoe-horn.

calçada *f* cobbled street, paved street; **2** steep street; *(BR)* pavement; **3** *(ART)* the art of paving with stones in a design; IDIOM **isto faz chorar as pedras da ~** this makes one weep, it wrings one's heart.

calçado *m* footwear; **fabrico de ~** footware industry.

calcanhar *m* *(ANAT)* heel; **o ~ de Aquiles** Achiles' heel; IDIOM **não chegar aos ~es de alguém** not be half as good as sb; not be able to hold a candle to sb.

calção *m* shorts *pl*; **~ de banho** swimming trunks *pl*.

calcar *vt* to tread on; **2** to compress, press down; **3** *(fig)* *(humilhar alguém)* to trample on sb; **4** *(fig)* *(sentimentos)* to suppress.

calçar *vt* to put on (gloves/shoes/socks); **2** to wear, **que número calça?** what is your size (of shoe, gloves); **3** *(cavalo)* to shoe; **4** *(rua)* to pave; **5** to put a wedge under *(porta, móvel)*.

calças *fpl* trousers.

calce/calço *m* wedge.

calcetar *vt* *(rua)* to pave; ♦ *vi* to pave artistically with small stones in intricate patterns.

calceteiro *m* man who lays a pavement with small stones in intricate pattern; **mestre ~** *m* the artist in paving.

calcificar *vt* *(GEOL, MED)* to calcify.

cálcio *m* calcium.

calcinhas *fpl* panties.

calço (*Vd: calce*); **calços** *mpl* *(AUTO)* break pads.

calculadora *f* *(máquina)* calculator.

calcular *vt* *(MAT)* to calculate; ♦ *vi* to make calculations; **2** to reckon, to guess; **nem calculas o que me aconteceu** you can't imagine what happened to me.

cálculo *m* calculation; **2** *(MAT)* calculus; **3** *(MED)* stone.

calda *f* syrup; **2** sauce; **3** solution, mixture.

caldear *vt* to weld, to fuse, to turn lime into solution; **2** *(AGR)* to treat with sulphate.

caldeação *f* **caldeamento** *m* welding; **2** mixture.

caldeira *f* boiling pan; **2** *(aquecimento)* boiler; **3** *(do vulcão)* large basin-shaped crater.

caldeirada *f* fish stew.

caldeirão *m* cauldron.

caldeiro *m* bucket.

caldo *m* broth, soup; **o C~ Verde é a sopa típica de Lisboa** Caldo Verde is Lisbon's traditional soup; **2** *(fig)* **temos o ~ entornado** things are looking bad.

caleadela *f* (*=caiadela*) *f* *(parede)* light whitewashing; **2** *(pele)* exfoliation.

calefa(c)ção *f* heating.

caleidoscópio *m* kaleidoscope.

calejado,-a *adj* hardened; **2** *(fig)* experienced; **3** **mãos ~as** horny hands.

calendário *m* calendar.

calendas *fpl* calends; IDIOM **para as ~ gregas** till a day that may never come/never in a month of Sundays.

calha, calhe *f* channel; **2** guttering; **3** rail.

calhamaço *m* *(fam)* a heavy book; a second-hand book.

calhambeque *m* *(fam)* *(carro velho)* bunger.

calhar *vi* to be suitable, fit; **2** to happen; **3 se ~** probably; **4 calha bem** it suits me down to the ground.

calhau *m* stone, pebble.

calhe (*Vd: calha*).

calibragem *f* calibration.

calibrar *vt* *(medir/verificar o calibre)* to calibrate **2** *(dimensão, quality)* to gauge; **3** *(pneu)* to balance.

calibre *m* *(de projécteis e tubos)* calibre, guage; **2** *(volume, tamanho)* capacity, size; **3** *(fig)* *(importância, qualidade)* importance, calibre.

caliça *f* rubble, debris, rubbish.

cálice *m* *(porto, xerez, licor)* glass; **2** *(REL)* chalice.

calicida *m* corn remover.

cálido,-a *adj* warm.

califa *m* caliph.

califato *m* caliphate.

caligrafia *f* calligraphy.

calinada *f* *(erro)* howler, gaffe, blunder

calma *f* *(calor do sol)* heating; **2** *(sosssego)* quiet; **3** *(serenidade)* calm; **conservar/perder a ~** to keep/lose one's temper; ♦ *exc:* **~!** take it easy!

calmante *m* *(MED)* sedative; ♦ *adj inv* soothing, tranquilling.

calmaria *f* *(ondas e vento calmos)* lull, calm.

calmo,-a *adj* calm, tranquil, serene.

calo *m* callus, corn.

caloiro,-a *m,f* (*Vd: calouro,-a*).

calor *m* heat; warmth; **tenho/estou com ~** I am feeling warm; **hoje está ~** today it is hot; **2 ~ humano** human warmth.

caloria *f* calorie.

caloroso,-a *adj* warm; enthusiastic; **2** *(protesto)* fervent.

calota *f* *(AUTO)* hubcap; **2** *(ARQ)* calotte; **3 ~ polar** polar ice cap; **4 ~ craniana** vertex of the skull.

calote *m* *(fam)* *(dívida)* bad debt; swindle; **pregar ~s a alguém** not pay a debt to sb.

calotear *vt* to swindle, fail to pay.

calouro,-a, caloiro,-a *m,f* *(Univ)* *(aluno)* first-year student; fresher; **2** *(fig)* beginner, novice; **3** *(fig)* *(pessoa lorpa)* simpleton; ♦ *adj* *(aluno)* new; **2** *(lorpa)* awkward, simple.

caluda! *exc* shush! hush! quiet; **2** *(pedindo segredo)* not a word!

calúnia *f* slander.

calunioso,-a *adj* slanderous.

calvície *f* baldness.

calvo,-a *m,f* bald patch; ♦ *adj* bald.

cama *f* bed; **~ de solteiro** single bed; **~ de casal** double bed; **estar na ~** to be in bed; **estar de ~** to be sick in bed.

camada *f* layer; **2** coat; **uma ~ de tinta** a coat of paint.

câmara *f* chamber; **música de ~** chamber music; **2** *(CIN, FOTO, TV)* camera; **~ escura** darkroom; **operador,-ora de ~** cameraman; camerawoman; **3 C~ Alta/dos Lordes** House of Lords, Upper Chamber; **C~ Baixa/dos Comuns** House of Commons, Lower Chamber; **4** *(aposento)* bedroom;

~ da rainha queen's chamber; **5** *(conjunto de representantes)* council; **~ de comércio** chamber of commerce, trade council; **6 ~ municipal** Council; Town Hall; **7** *(AUTO)* **~ de ar** *(de pneu)* inner tube; ♦ **em ~ lenta** *adv (CIN)* in slow motion.

câmara-ardente *(pl: câmaras-ardentes) f* funeral chamber, chapel; place where the deceased lies in wake.

camarada *m,f* comrade; companion; **2 ~ de escola** colleague.

camaradagem *f* comradeship.

camarão *m (ZOOL, CULIN)* shrimp; **2 ~ grande** prawn.

camarário,-a *adj* municipal.

camarata *f* dormitory.

camarilha *f* clique; **2** lobby group.

camarim *m (TEAT)* dressing room.

camarote *m (NÁUT)* cabin; **2** *(TEAT)* box.

cambado,-a *adj:* **sapatos ~s** shoes worn at the heels; **2 cambada** *f* a lot of; *(fig)* gang, mob, rabble; **~ de idiotas** bunch of idiots.

cambaio,-a *adj* bow-legged.

cambaleante *adj inv* staggering.

cambalear *vi* to stagger, to reel.

cambalhota *f* somersault.

cambiante *m (cor)* shade; ♦ *adj inv* changing, variable.

cambiar *vt (dinheiro)* to exchange.

câmbio *m* exhange; **taxa de ~** rate of exchange; **2 ~ livre** free trade; **3 ~ negro** black market.

cambista *m,f* money changer; **2** *(BR)* ticket tout.

Camboja *npr* **o ~** Cambodia.

cambojano,-a *m,f adj* Cambodian.

cambota *f (ARQ)* vault; **2** *(MEC)* crankshaft.

camélia *f (BOT)* camellia.

camelo *m (ZOOL)* camel; **2** *(fig)* dunce.

camelô *(BR) m* street pedlar.

câmera *f (Vd:* **câmara***).*

In Brazil both forms of spelling are used for câmera.

camião *(BR:* **caminhão***) m* lorry; truck.

caminhada *f* walk.

caminhante *m,f* walker; **2** wanderer.

caminhão *(BR) m* lorry; truck *(EP =* **camião***).*

caminhar *vi* to walk; to hike.

caminheiro,-a *m,f* walker, hiker; ♦ *adj* walking, on foot.

caminho *m* way; **qual é o melhor ~ para …?** which is the best way to …?; **2** path; **~ apertado** narrow path; **3** *(rumo, rota)* road, route; **4** *(de terra)* track; **5 ~ de ferro** railway; **6 a meio ~** halfway (there); **7 a/em ~** en route; IDIOM **levar ~** to vanish, go astray; **cortar ~** to take a short cut; **ser meio ~ andado,** to be halfway there; **fazer-se/pôr-se a ~** to set out.

camionagem *f* haulage.

camioneta *(BR:* **caminhonete***) f* coach; van.

camionista *m,f* lorry driver.

camisa *f (vestuário de homem)* shirt; **2** *(revestimento)* jacket, liner; **3 ~-de-forças** strait-jacket; **4 ~ de noite/de dormir** nightshirt; **mudar de ~** to

change shirt; *(fig)* to change sides; **5 ~ de onze varas** hairshirt; **6 ~-de-vénus/ ~ de vênus** condom, sheath; IDIOM **meter-se em ~ de onze varas** to be in a jam, to get in trouble.

camisaria *f* shirt makers; shirt shop.

camiseiro,-a *m,f* shirt maker.

camiseta *f (BR)* T-shirt.

camisinha *f* condom, French letter.

camisola *f* sweater; **2** *(BR)* nightdress.

camomila *f (BOT)* camomile.

Camões *npr* Camoens (Portugal's 16th-century bard, famous for his epic: *Os Lusíadas*).

camoniano,-a *adj* related to Camoens; **a grande obra camoniana** the great works of Camoens.

campa *f* gravestone; **2** grave; **3** small bell.

campaínha *f* door/hand bell.

campal *adj inv* rural; **2 batalha ~** pitched battle; **3 missa ~** open-air mass.

campanário *m* bell tower, belfry; **2** *(fig)* parish.

campanha *f* campaign; **2** *(MIL)* field; **3** *(fig)* task.

campânula *f (BOT)* bellflower; campanula; **2** bell-shaped object; bellglass.

campeão, campeã *m,f* champion.

campeonato *m* championship.

campestre *adj inv* rural, rustic.

campina *f* prairie, meadow; **as ~s do Ribatejo** Ribatejo's grassy plains.

campino *m* cowboy, herdsman from Ribatejo (Portuguese province); **2** countryman.

campismo *m* camping; **parque de ~** camp site.

campista *m,f* camper.

campo *m* field; **2** *(rural)* countryside; **gosto do ~** I like the countryside; **3** camp; **~ de concentração** concentration camp; **4** pitch; **~ relvado** green pitch; **5** range; **~ de tiro** shooting range; **6** space; **7** court; **~ de ténis** tennis court; **8 ~ de fundo** *(ART)* background; **9 cm ~ aberto** in the open; **10 trabalho de ~** fieldwork; **11 ele é um perito no ~ da psicologia** he is an expert in the field of psychology; IDIOM **pôr(-se) em ~** to bring, put into action.

camponês,-esa *m,f* countryman/woman; **2** farmer.

campónio,-a *m,f adj (pej)* yokel, country bumpkin.

camuflagem *f* camouflage.

camuflar *vt* to camouflage.

camundongo *(BR) m (ZOOL)* mouse.

camurça *f* chamois; **2** suede; **mala de ~** suede handbag.

cana *f* cane; **~ de açúcar** sugar cane; **2** rod; **3** *(seca)* thatch; **telhado de ~** thatched roof; **4 ~ de pesca** fishing rod; **5 ~ do nariz** nasal bone; **6** *(fig)* **voz de ~ rachada** cracked voice; **7** *(BR) (col)* jail, nick; *(BR)* **ir em ~** to be locked up.

Canadá *npr* Canada; **o ~** Canada.

canadiano,-a *(BR:* **canadense** *inv) adj* Canadian.

canal *m (ger)* channel; **o ~ da Mancha** the English Channel; **~ de irrigação** irrigation channel; **2** *(cavidade)* duct, canal; **~ auditivo** auditory canal; **~ lacrimal** tear duct; **3 ~ de televisão** TV channel; **4 ~s competentes** right/proper channels.

canalha *f (gente)* rabble, mob, riff-raff, gang; ♦ *m,f* scoundrel, swine; shameless person; **2** *(criançada)* kids; ♦ *adj* villainous; **ele tem o ar de** ~ he looks like a villain.

canalização *f* plumbing, piping.

canalizador *m* plumber.

canalizar *vt* to lay pipes, to dig channels; 2 *(fig)* to channel.

canário *m (pássaro)* canary.

canastra *f* large basket, shallow basket which women fishsellers carried on their heads; 2 *(jogo)* canasta.

canavial *(pl: -ais) m* cane field.

canção *f* song; ~ **de embalar** lullaby; **festival da** ~ song contest/festival.

cancela *f (na via férrea)* gate; 2 barred gate; 3 barrier.

cancelamento *m* cancellation.

cancelar *vt* to cancel; to annul.

Câncer[1] *npr m (ASTRON, ASTROL)* Cancer, the crab.

câncer[2] *m (BR) (MED)* cancer; ~ **de mama** breast cancer.

canceriano,-a *adj (ASTROL)* Cancerian.

cancerígeno,-a *adj* carcinogenic; **células** ~**s** cancer cells.

canceroso,-a *adj* cancerous.

cancioneiro *m* song book; traditional book of songs; *(Vd:* **cantiga***).*

cançonetista *m,f* writer of songs, ballads; 2 ballad singer; folk singer.

candeeiro *m* lamp, ~ **de mesa** table lamp.

candeia *f* oil-lamp; 2 candle; **festa das** ~**s** Candlemas; **luz da** ~ candlelight.

candelabro *m* candlestick; 2 chandelier.

candente *adj inv (ardente)* red hot; 2 *(fig)* inflamed.

candidatar-se *vr:* ~ **a um concurso** to be a candidate in a competition; ~ **a um emprego** to apply for a job; *(POL)* to run for election.

candidato,-a *m,f* candidate; 2 applicant.

candidatura *f* candidature, 2 application; **ficha de** ~ enrolment, application form.

candidez, candura *f* innocence, candour, simplicity.

cândido,-a *adj* naïve, innocent; 2 snow-white.

candomblé *m (religião)* Yoruba-Brazilian Cult in Bahia.

candonga *f* black market; 2 pretense of love; 3 flattery; 4 *(BR) (benzinho)* darling, beloved.

caneca *f* mug.

caneco *m* tankard.

canela *f (BOT)* cinnamon; **pau de** ~ cinnamon stick; 2 *(ANAT)* shin; IDIOM *(BR)* **ter** ~ **de cachorro** to be a good walker.

canelada *f* kick on the sheens.

canelado *m* ribbing; ♦ *adj (tricot)* ribbed, 2 *(ARQ) (coluna)* fluted.

caneta *f* pen; 2 ~ **esferográfica** ball-point pen.

cânfora *f* camphor.

canga *f* yoke; 2 *(fig) (domínio)* yoke.

cangaceiro *m (BR)* outlaw; highway-robber.

cangalhas *fpl (para bestas de carga)* wooden pack-saddle; 2 *(fam)* spectacles; 3 **de** ~ topsy-turvy; 4 **cair de** ~ to fall upside down.

cangalho *m* a small yoke; 2 an old good-for-nothing; trash, junk; 3 *(fig)* old person; **ela está um** ~ she has become an old hag.

canguru *m (ZOOL)* kangaroo.

cânhamo *m* hemp; **semente de** ~ *(comida para pássaros)* hemp seed.

canhão *m (MIL)* cannon; 2 **culatra de** ~ breech of a gun; **o troar dos canhões** the roar of guns; 3 the cuff of a coat.

canhestro,-a *adj (pop)* left-handed; 2 inapt, clumsy.

canhoto,-a *m,f* left-handed person; 2 *m (de livro de cheques, recibos)* stub; ♦ *adj* left-handed.

caniçada *adj* trellis, latticework from reeds.

caniço *m* reed, slender cane; 2 fishing rod; 3 *(fam) (perna)* skinny.

canícula *f* height of the summer; 2 heatwave.

canicular *adj inv* hot, sultry.

canil *m* kennel.

canivete *m* penknife, pocket knife; ~ **suíço** army knife; 2 *(fig)* skinny leg.

canja *f* chicken soup; IDIOM **ser** ~ to be a piece of cake; **isso é** ~! that's easy!; *(fam)* easy-peazy!

cano *m* pipe, tube; ~ **entupido** blocked pipe; 2 ~ **de esgoto** drain pipe, sewer; 3 *(da ventilação, do fumo)* shaft; *(gas) (escape)* flue; 4 *(de luva, bota)* **botas de** ~ **alto** high boots; 5 *(arma)* barrel; **espingarda de dois** ~**s** double-barrelled shotgun; 5 *(BR) (negócios)* bad deal, mistake.

canoa *f* canoe.

canoagem *f* canoeing.

canoeiro,-a *m,f* **canoísta** *m,f* canoist.

Cânon *m (LITURG)* Canon.

cânon, cânone *m* rule, precept; 2 church law; 3 *(MAT)* general mathematical order.

canónico,-a *(REL)* canonic(al); **direito** ~ canon law; 2 orderly.

cansaço *m* tiredness, weariness.

cansado,-a *adj* tired, weary.

cansar *vt* to tire; 2 to irritate; 3 to bore; ♦ ~**-se** *vr* to get tired.

cansativo,-a *adj* tiring; tedious.

canseira *f* weariness.

cantar *m* singing, song; **os** ~**res da minha aldeia** the songs of my village; ♦ *vt* to sing; ~ **faz bem** singing is good; 2 *(em cadência)* recitar.

cântaro *m* water jug; 2 pitcher; IDIOM **chover a** ~**s** to rain cats and dogs.

cantarolar *vt* to hum.

canteira *f* quarry.

canteiro *m* stonemason; 2 flower bed; 3 window-box.

cântico *m* hymn, chant, carol, song.

cantiga *f* song, ballad; 2 *(fam) (léria)* smooth talk; **eu não vou na** ~ **dele** I am not taken in by his talk; **isso é uma** ~ that's a tall story!; **ela tem uma grande** ~ she has the gift of the gab; **ele está sempre com a mesma** ~ he is always harping on the same string.

'Cantigas de amigo', 'de amor', 'de escárnio', refer to Portuguese-Galician literature, which was the first Christian literature in the Iberian peninsula. Cantigas were sung by minstrels in the language of the people.

cantil *m* canteen, flask.

cantina *f* canteen.

canto *m* corner; **aos quatro ~s** to the four corners of the earth; **2** chant; **3** song; **4 de ~** edgeways; **5 ~s e recantos** nooks and crannies; **6 pôr para um ~** to disregard, put aside; **7** *(pássaro, cigarra)* chirp; **8** song, singing; **o ~ do rouxinol** the nightingale's song; **9** *(LITER)* Canto; **os C~s de (os) Lusíadas** *(Vd: Lusíadas).*

cantoneira *f* corner shelf; **2** *(reforço)* angle iron.

cantoneiro *m* road mender.

cantor,-ora *m,f* singer.

canudinho *m* straw; **2** *(cabelo)* ringlet.

canudo *m* tube; **2** pipe; **3** *(cabelo)* long ringlet; **4** *(fam)* university diploma.

cânula *f* nozzle.

canzoada *f* pack of dogs.

cão *(pl: -ães)* *m* dog; **2** *(de arma)* hammer; IDIOM **levar uma vida de ~** to lead a dog's life; **preso por ter ~ e preso por não o ter** heads you win, tails you lose; **~ guia** *m* guide dog.

caos *m* chaos; **2** *(desordem)* mess.

caótico,-a *m,f adj* chaotic.

capa *f* cape, cloak; **2 ~ e batina** university attire; **3** *(livro)* cover, wrapper; **4 sob a ~ de** under the cover/guise of; **5 livro de ~ dura** hardback book.

capacete *m* helmet.

capachinho *m* *(cabelo)* hairpiece, toupee.

capacho *m* door mat; **2** *(fig)* toady, servile, doormat.

capacidade *f* capacity; **2** ability; **3** competence.

capado *m* castrated, gelded.

capar *vt* to castrate, to geld; **2** *(plantas)* to prune.

capão *(galo)* capon; *(cavalo)* gelding.

capar *vt* *(animal)* to castrate.

capataz *m* foreman, overseer; supervisor; **2** farm manager.

capaz *adj inv* able, capable; **2** *(bom)* **este trabalho não está ~** this work is no good; **3** *(poder)* **você é ~ de fazer-me este favor?** can you do me this favour?; **4** *(talvez)* **eu sou ~ de ir ao cinema hoje** I may go to the cinema today; **5** *(respeitável)* **ele é uma pessoa ~** he is respectable, well-thought of; **6** *(profissão)* qualified, competent.

capela *f* chapel; **~-mor** chancel.

capelão *(pl: -ães)* *m* *(REL)* chaplain.

capelinha *f* small chapel.

capelo *m* *(capuz dos monges)* hood, cowl; **2** *(de cardeal)* hat; **3** *(CONSTR)* cowl, hood.

capilar *m* *(FIS, ANAT)* capillary; ♦ *adj* capillary; **2** *(loção)* hair lotion.

capilé *m* sweet, cool drink made with sugar, water and spirit.

capim *m* *(BOT)* scrub, undergrowth.

capital *f* *(do país)* capital; **2** *m* *(dinheiro)* capital, funds *pl*; **fuga de ~** flight of capital; **3** *(fig)* of value; **4** essential; **isso é ~** that is most important; **5** *(letra)* capital.

capitalismo *m* capitalism.

capitalista *m,f adj inv* capitalist.

capitanear *vt* to command, to head.

capitania *f* captaincy; **~ do porto** port authority.

capitão *(pl: -ães)* *m* captain; **2** harbour master; **~-tenente** *(pl:* **capitães-tenentes***)* chief petty officer.

capitão-de-mar-e-terra *(pl:* **capitães-de-mar-e-terra***)* captain of a warship.

capitulação *f* capitulation, surrender.

capítulo *m* chapter.

capoeira *f* hen-house, coop; **2** *(BR)* foot-fighting dance.

capota *(BR:* **capô***)* *f* *(AUTO)* bonnet; **2** top.

capotar *vi* to overturn, capsize.

capote *m* cloak; overcoat.

capricho *m* whim, caprice; **2** obstinacy; **3** fad; ♦ *adv* **a ~** properly.

caprichoso,-a *m,f adj* capricious; changeable.

Capricórnio *npr m* *(ASTRON, ASTROL)* Capricorn.

caprino,-a *adj* *(gado)* caprine.

cápsula *f* *(ger)* capsule; **2** *(BOT)* pod, capsule, seed vessel.

captar *vt* *(som)* to pick up; **2** *(águas)* to impound, to dam up; **3** *(fig)* *(compreender)* to catch; **4** *(fig)* *(atenção)* get.

captura *f* *(JUR)* capture, arrest; **2** *(GEOL)* **~ fluvial** river diversion.

capturar *vt* to capture, to arrest; **2** to seize; **3** *(GEOL)* *(water)* to impound.

capuchinho *m* little hood; **a Menina do ~ Vermelho** *(conto infantil)* Little Red Riding Hood; **2** *(frade menor da Ordem de Capucha)* Capuchim monk.

capucho *m* sheaf of rye; **2** hood; Franciscan monk.

capuz *m* *(capelo)* conic hood, cowl.

cáqui *m* *(tecido)* khaki.

cara *f* face; **2** *(BR: col)* chap, guy; **3** *(moeda)* head; **~ ou coroa?** heads or tails?; **4** *(appearance)* **ter boa ~ to look good; este assado tem boa ~** this roast looks good; **ter ~ de mau** he looks nasty; ♦ **dar de ~ com** to bump into *(alguém)*; **ter ~ *(ousadia)*** to dare, have a cheek; **você tem ~ de me dizer isso?** you have the cheek to tell me this!; **virar a ~ a alguém** to turn the face away from sb; ♦ *adv* **à má ~** unwillingly; **2 ~ a ~** face to face; IDIOM **fiquei de ~ à banda/*(BR)* com ~ de tacho** I was dumbfounded, gobsmacked *(fam)*; **ter duas ~s** be two-faced; **ser a ~ chapada de** *(alguém)* to be somebody's spitting image.

carabina *f* rifle.

carabineiro *m* rifleman.

caraça *f* *(máscara)* mask; *(fig)* *(carantonha)* ugly mug.

caraças *exc* *(col)* blimey!

Carachi *npr* Karachi.

caracol *m* *(ZOOL)* snail; **2** *(cabelo)* curl; **3** *(desenho espiral)* **escada em ~** spiral staircase; IDIOM **a passo de ~** at snail's pace.

carácter, caráter *(pl:* **carateres***)* *m* character, nature; **2** *(BIO)* characteristic; **3** printing type.

característico,-a, caraterístico,-a *adj* characteristic; **2** *f* characteristic, feature.

caracterização, caraterização *(pl: -ões)* *f* characterization; **2** *(de actor)* make-up.

caracterizar, caraterizar *vt* to characterize, typify; **2** *(TEAT)* make-up; ♦ **~-se** *vr* be characterized by.

cara-de-pau *(pl:* **caras-de-pau***)* *(BR)* *adj inv* *(fam)* impudent, insolent, shameless.

carago *exc (col)* damn!

caraíba *adj inv* carib, Caribbean.

Caraíbas *npr (as ilhas das)* the Caribbean (Islands).

caramanchão *m* pergola.

caramanchel *m* summer house.

caramba! *exc (fam) (susto, chateação)* blast!, dammit; **2** *(admiração)* gosh!, blimey!

caramelo *m* caramel; **2** sweet.

cara-metade *m,f (esposa/marido)* better half; **esta é a minha ~** this is my better half.

caramujo *m (ZOOL)* periwinkle.

caranguejo *m (ZOOL)* crab; **~ de concha** hermit crab; **2 C~** *(ASTRON, ASTROL)* Cancer, the Crab; IDIOM *(contrário de progresso)* **andar como o ~** go backwards.

carantonha *f (cara feia)* ugly mug; **2** *(aspecto, carranca)* scowl, grimace.

carapaça *f (revestimento duro)* shell, carapace; **~ do cágado** tortoise's shell; **2** *(fig) (proteção)* armour, cover.

carapau *m* jackfish; **~-de-gato** *m* sprat; **2** *(fig)* thin, beanpole; **estar magro como um ~** to be thin as a beanpole.

carapinha *f* frizzy, Afro hair.

carapuça *f* cap, hood; IDIOM **se a ~ serve** if the cap fits; **ele está a enfiar-me a ~** he is pulling the wool over my eyes; **qual ~!** nothing of the kind!; what rubbish!

carapuço *m* hood, cap; **2** filtering bag for making coffee.

caratê *m* karate.

caráter *(Vd: cará(c)ter)*.

caravana *f (que serve the habitação)* caravan *(UK)*, trailer *(US)*; **2** tour group; **3** *(acompanhantes do presidente/rei)* entourage.

caravela *f (NÁUT) (nau portuguesa)* caravel, Portuguese vessel.

carbonato *m (QUÍM)* carbonate; **~ de sódio** sodium carbonate.

carbónico,-a *(BR: -ô-) adj* carbonic.

carbonizar *vt* to carbonize, to char.

carbono *m (QUÍM)* carbon; **sequestro de ~** carbon sequestration.

carburador *m* carburettor *(UK)*, carburetor *(US)*.

carcaça *f (esqueleto de animal)* carcass; **2** *(armação)* frame; *(CONSTR; de um navio)* framework; **3** *(casco velho de navio)* old hull; **4** *(TEC)* **~ do eixo de manivelas** crankcase; **5** loaf of bread; **6** *(col, pej) (pessoa magra, feia e velha)* an old hag.

carcerário,-a *adj* relative to prison; **caução ~a** bail.

cárcere *m* prison, jail.

carcereiro,-a *m* gaoler, warder.

carcomido,-a *adj* worm-eaten; **2** *(fig)* rotten.

carda *f (TEC)* wool card; **2** carding; carding machine.

cardador *m* **cardadeira** *f* carder, **2** wool comber.

cardápio *m* menu; **~ dos vinhos** wine list.

cardar *vt (lã, algodão)* to card, comb; **2** to disentangle; **3** *(fig, pop) (explorar)* to fleece *(pop)*, extort; **4** *(fam)* to scold.

cardeal *(pl: -ais) m (REL)* cardinal; **2** *(ZOOL) (ave)* cardinal; **3** *(BOT)* cardinal flower, lobelia, scarlet

salvia; ♦ *adj inv* cardinal; **2** *(GEOG)* **pontos cardeais** cardinal points.

cardíaco,-a *adj* cardiac; **ataque ~** heart attack.

cardinal *adj inv (MAT)* cardinal; *(número)* cardinal; **2** *(cor)* cardinal red.

cardo *m* thistle.

cardume *m (peixe)* shoal, school; **2** *(fig) (gente)* throng.

careca *m,f (fam)* bald person; **2** *f* baldness; ♦ *adj inv* bald; **2 pêssego ~** nectarine; **3 pneu ~** bald tyre; IDIOM **descobrir a ~ a alguém** to reveal another person's weak points.

carenciado,-a *adj* needy.

carecer *vi* to be in need; **2** to lack.

carência *f* lack, shortage; **2** need; **3** deprivation.

carente *adj inv* wanting; **2** needy, in need of; **3** lacking in.

carestia *f* high prices *pl*; high cost; **a ~ da vida** the high cost of living.

careta *f* grimace; **2** mask; **fazer uma ~** to pull a face.

carga *f* load, loading; **2** cargo; **3** *(ELECT)* charge; **4** lot of; **uma ~ d'água** a lot of rain, downpour; **5** *(fig)* charge, burden; **~ fiscal** the tax burden, contribution; IDIOM **voltar à ~** to insist, to harp on the same string; **ser uma besta de ~** to be a beast of burden; **por que ~ de água…!** why on earth…!

cargo *m* freight; **2** duty, responsibility; **ter alguém a a seu ~** to have to support sb; **3** position, office, **exercer um ~** to hold a position; **4 sem ~** on reserve, free from encumbrances and without reservation.

cargueiro *m* cargo ship; ♦ *adj* cargo.

cariado,-a *adj (MED)* carious, decayed; **dente ~** carious, decayed tooth

caribenho,-a *adj* Caribbean.

caricato *m (TEAT)* satirical actor; burlesque; ♦ *adj* satirical, caricatural; **2** amusing; **3** *(pej) (grotesco)* *(alguém, situação)* ridiculous.

caricatura *f* cartoon; **2** caricature.

caricaturista *m,f* cartoonist.

carícia *f* caress; **fazer uma ~/fazer ~s** to caress sb.

caridade *f* charity; **2** kindness, compassion; **3** *(esmola)* alms *pl*; IDIOM **estender a mão à ~** to beg.

caridoso,-a *adj (pessoa)* charitable.

cárie *f (MED)* caries, tooth decay.

caril *m (CULIN)* curry.

carimbar *vt* to stamp; to postmark; **2** to approve, to rubber-stamp.

carimbo *m* rubber stamp; **2** postmark; **3** official approval; **4** *(fig)* to mark sb.

carinho *m* affection, fondness; **dar ~** to give love/affection; **2** caress; **fazer ~** to caress.

carinhoso,-a *adj* affectionate.

carioca *m,f* native of Rio de Janeiro; **2** *m* weak black coffee; **3 ~ de limão** lemon tea; ♦ *adj inv* relating to Rio de Janeiro.

carisma *m* charism.

carismático,-a *adj* charismatic; **2** *(dom)* gifted.

caritativo,-a *adj* charitable; **2** charity; **OXFAM é uma organização ~a** OXFAM is a charity organization.

cariz *m* nature; countenance; aspect; **2** *(BOT)* caraway, caraway seed.

carmelita *adj inv (REL)* Carmelite.

carmesim *adj* crimson.

carmim *m (corante)* carmine; **2** *(CULIN) (para colorir bolos, etc)* cochineal; **3** *(ZOOL)* cochineal.

carnagem *f* slaughter, carnage.

carnal *adj inv* carnal.

Carnaval *m* carnival; **2** *(fig)* orgy.

carnavalesco,-a *adj* relative to Carnival; Carnival-like.

Carnival, which is celebrated in Portugal during three days, is a legacy left in every Portuguese-speaking country including, of course, Brazil.

carne *f* flesh; **2** meat; **~ de carneiro** mutton; **~ de porco** pork; **~ de vaca** beef; **~ de veado** venison; **~ picada** *(BR:* **moída**) minced meat; **em ~ e osso** in flesh and blood; IDIOM **ser ~ para canhão** to be cannon fodder for.

carneiro *m (ZOOL)* sheep, ram; **2** *(carne)* mutton; **~ castrado** wether; **mãozinhas de ~** sheep's trotters; **3** *(ASTROL)* Aries; IDIOM **olhos de ~ mal morto** *(amoroso)* sheep's eyes.

carniçaria *f* slaughter.

carniceiro,-a *m (magarefe)* butcher ♦ *adj* cruel, feroz.

carnificina *f* slaughter.

carnívoro,-a *adj* carnivorous.

carnudo,-a *adj* plump, fleshy; **2** *(col)* beefy; **lábios ~s** beefy, thick lips.

caro,-a *adj (afectuoso)* dear, darling; **minha cara Maria** my dear/darling Mary; *(formal)* **caro Senhor** Dear Sir; **2** *(preço)* dear, expensive; **sair ~** to cost a lot, pay dearly for; *(fig)* **esta brincadeira vai sair-lhe ~** this joke is going to cost you dearly; ♦ *adv* dear, dearly; IDIOM **o barato sai ~!** the cheapest comes dear; you pay for what you get.

carocha *f* beetle, cockroach; **2** *(cal) (ponte de cigarro)* fag-end.

carochinha *f:* **conto da ~** fairy tale; **2** *(fig)* cock-and-bull story; old wives' tales.

caroço *m (BOT) (de pêssego)* stone; *(de laranja)* pit; *(de algodão)* seed; **2** *(MED) (glândula linfática)* lump; **3** *(fam)* money; **ter muito ~** to have a lot of brass/dough/dosh.

carola *m,f (fam)* overpious person; **2** fan, enthusiast; **3** *(pop) (cabeça)* head nut.

carolice *f* fanaticism.

carona *(BR) f* lift; **viajar de ~** to hitchhike.

carótida, carótide *f (ANAT)* carotid.

carpa *f (peixe)* carp.

carpe diem carpe diem, seize the day.

carpete *f* carpet.

carpideira *f (mulher que antigamente carpia/chorava nos enterros, paga pela família)* hearse-follower; false mourner.

carpintaria *f* carpentry; **2** carpenter's workshop.

carpinteiro *m* carpenter.

carpir *vt/vi* to weep, bewail; to express sorrow; **2** *(BR)* to hoe, weed; **3** *(BR)* to harvest.

carraça *f (ZOOL)* tick, mite, crab louse; **2** *(fam) (pessoa)* pest, nuisance, hanger-on; *(fig)* **ser uma ~** somebody who sticks like a leech.

carrada *f* cart-load; **às ~s** by cartloads; IDIOM **ter ~s de razão** to be absolutely right.

carranca *f* frown, scowl.

carrancudo,-a *adj* surly; **2** sullen; **3** scowling.

carrapato *m (ZOOL)* tick; **2** *(BOT)* **feijão ~** French bean, green bean; **3** *(fam) (homem baixo e gordo)* small and dumpy.

carrapicho *m* hair carelessly tied at the back; *(de cabelo)* a kind of bun.

carrapita *f:* **às ~s** carried on a person's shoulders; pick-a-back.

carrapito *m (Vd:* **carrapicho**).

carrascão *m (vinho)* plonk; rough wine.

carrasco *m* executioner; **2** *(fig)* tyrant.

carraspana *f (col) (bebedeira)* skinful.

carregado,-a *adj (com carga)* loaded; *(pesado)* loaded down, laden with; heavy; **2** *(semblante)* sullen; **3** *(céu)* dark.

carregador *m (bagageiro)* porter; *(transportador)* carrier; **3** *(de arma de fogo)* cartridge clip; **4** *(de pilhas)* battery charger; **5** *(COMP)* loader.

carregamento *m* loading; load, cargo; **2** *(telemóvel) (pôr mais dinheiro)* top up; **~ de 10 euros** 10 curos top-up.

carregar *vt (pôr carga em)* to load; **2** *(transportar/levar)* to carry; **3** *(sobrecarregar)* overload; **4** *(ELECT)* to charge; **5** to press; **~ na campainha** to press the bell hard; **6** *(MIL)* to charge, attack; **7** *(telemóvel)* to top up, charge *(dinheiro)*; ♦ *vi (encher-se)* laden with full of; **2** *(premir)* press; **3** *(calcar)* press down (on); IDIOM **~ a sua cruz** have a cross to bear; **4 ~ o sobrolho** to frown.

carrego *m (carga, peso)* weight, load, burden.

carreira *f (profissão)* career; **2** *(rota habitual)* route; **avião de ~** scheduled plane; **camioneta de ~** regular, scheduled passenger coach; **3** *(fila)* **em ~** in line, row; **4** *(trilha)* track; **5** *(correria)* fast run.

carreira-de-tiro *f* shooting gallery, alley; rifle range.

carreta *f (de duas rodas)* handcart; **2 ~ de peça** gun-carriage; **3 ~ funerária** hearse; IDIOM **deixar passar carros e ~s** to suffer stoically, keep one's chin up.

carrete *m (para linhas, fios)* spool, reel.

carreteiro *m* cart driver.

carretel *m (Vd:* **carrete**) *(cilindro)* reel; **2** *(molinete)* **~ da barquinha** log-reel.

carreto *m (frete)* errand; **2** *(preço de um frete)*

carril *m* steel/iron rail; **2** rut, furrow; **3** track, narrow path.

carrilhão *m* chime; **2** set of bells.

carrinha *f* van, station wagon; **2 ~ da escola** school bus.

carrinho *m* small cart; **2** *(das compras/bagagem)* trolley; **3 ~ de bebé** pram, buggy; **4 ~ de mão** wheelbarrow; **5 ~ de linhas** cotton reel/spool.

carro *m (automóvel)* car; **~ alegórico** *(em desfile)* float; **~ armadilhado** booby-trapped car; **~ blindado** armoured car, armour-clad; **~ de bombeiros** fire engine; **~ de combate** tank; **~ de corrida** racing/

sports car; **2** cart; ~ **de bois** oxen cart; **3** *(RAIL, TEC)* carriage; ~ **elé(c)trico** *m* tram; **4** ~ **fúnebre** hearse; IDIOM **pôr o** ~ **à frente dos bois** put the cart before the horse.

carroça *f* cart, wagon.

carroçaria *f (AUTO)* bodywork; chassis.

carroceiro cart driver; **2** *(pej)* oaf; ♦ *adj* rude, common.

carrocel *m* roundabout, merry-go-round, carousel; **2** ~ **da bagagem** luggage carousel, conveyor belt.

carruagem *f* carriage, coach; **2** *(FERRO)* carriage, car, wagon; **3** ~-**cama** sleeping-car, sleepers.

carta *f* letters; ~ **devolvida** forwarded/returned letter; ~ **extraviada** letter lost in the post; ~ **registada** *(BR:* **registrada***)* registered letter; **2** chart; **C~ do Atlântico** Atlantic Chart; **3** map; **4** diploma; **5** licence; ~ **de condução** driving licence *(BR: Vd:* **carteira***)*; **6** *(jogo)* card; **dar as** ~**s** to deal the cards; IDIOM **pôr as** ~**s na mesa** to lay one's cards on the table, be open/frank.

carta-branca *f* carte blanche.

cartão *m* cardboard; **2** card; ~ **de crédito** credit card; ~ **de visita/da empresa** calling/business card; IDIOM **não passar** ~ to ignore sb or some remark; to give the brush-off.

cartaz *m* poster; **2** bill; **3 ter** ~ to have a good reputation, be famous; **4 cabeça de** ~ *(CIN, TV)* top billing.

carteira *f (escola)* desk; **2** handbag; **3** wallet; **4** ~ **de identidade** *(ID)* identity card; **5** ~ **de chofer** *(BR)* driving licence; **6** *(COM) (no banco)* section, desk; **7** porfolio, list of clients; **temos uma vasta** ~ **de clients** we have a large client portfolio; **8** *(FIN) (de títulos)* portfolio.

carteirista *m,f* pickpocket.

carteiro *m* postman.

cartel *(pl:* **-téis***) m (ECON)* cartel; **2** summons to a dual, provocation; **3** *(fig)* category, class.

cárter *m* crankcase.

cartilagem *f (ANAT)* cartilage.

cartilha *f (livro, texto)* first reader; textbook; **ler a** ~ **a alguém** to give sb a piece of one's mind; a reprimand; **ler pela mesma** ~ to think in the same way; ~ **da coragem** the ABC of courage, the basic principles of courage.

cartográfico,-a *adj* cartographic.

cartógrafo,-a *m,f* cartographer.

cartola *f (chapéu)* top hat; **2** *(pessoa importante)* snob; **3 o** ~ *(BR) (pej) (FUT) (dirigente)* the boss.

cartomância *f* fortune-telling; **2** cartomancy.

cartomante *m,f* fortune-teller.

cartório *m* registry; **2** archive, files; **3** lawyer's office; IDIOM **ter culpas no** ~ morally guilty of some past actions.

cartucheira *f* cartridge belt.

cartucho *m* cartridge; **2** packet; **3** (brown) paper bag.

caruncho *m (ZOOL)* woodworm; **2** dry rot; **3** *(fig)* old age.

carvalho *m (árvore, madeira)* oak.

carvão *m* coal; **2** charcoal; *(frango etc)* **a** ~ barbecued *(chicken)*; ~ **mineral** anthracite; **3** *(lápis-arte)* charcoal; **jazigo de** ~ coalfield.

carvoeiro *m* coal merchant; **navio** ~ collier.

casa *f (habitação)* house, home; **é uma linda** ~ it is a beautiful house/home; ~-**geminada** semi-detached house; **2** *(apartamento)* flat; **é uma** ~ **no segundo andar** it's is a flat on the second floor; **3** *(residência)* abode, dwelling; ~ **com duas assoalhadas** house/flat with two rooms/divisions; **4** *(divisão)* room; ~-**de-banho** bathroom; ~-**de-jantar** dining-room; ~ **de despejo** storeroom, junk room; ~ **das máquinas** engine-room/engine house; ~ **térrea** bungalow, a one-storey house; **5** *(conjunto familiar)* household; **6** *(de descanso/recuperação)* home; ~ **de saúde** nursing home; **7** *(COM)* firm, shop, restaurant; **receita da nossa** ~ our restaurant's recipe; ~ **de câmbio** exchange bureau; **C~ da Moeda** the Mint; ~ **de passe** brothel; ~ **de pasto** cheap restaurant; ~ **de penhores/do prego** pawn-broker's, pawnbroker shop; **8** *(divisão do tabuleiro de xadrez)* square; **9** *(abertura)* ~ **de botão** buttonhole; **10** *(instituição; dinastia)* ~ **da comunidade** community hall; ~ **do povo** community centre; **C~ de Windsor** Windsor dynasty; **11** *(orfanato)* **C~ Pia** school for orphan boys; ♦ **estar na** ~ **dos trinta** to be in one's thirties; **arrumar a** ~ tidy-up the house; *(fig) (POL, COM)* to put one's things in order; **ter saudades de** ~ to be homesick; ♦ *adv* **em** ~ (at) home; **feito em** ~ homemade; **fora de** ~ out, abroad; IDIOM **em sua** ~ **cada qual é rei** an Englishman's home is his castle; **de** ~ **e pucarinho** *(homem e mulher)* living together, co-habiting.

casaca *f (de cerimónia)* morning coat; **2** tails *pl*; **3** *(fig)* **virar a** ~ to be/become a turncoat.

casação *m* big coat, overcoat.

casaco *m* coat; ~ **curto** jacket; ~ **de lã/de malha** cardigan; **fato saia e** ~ suit (coat and skirt).

casa-civil *f* the President's advisory bureau for civil matters *(veja também* **casa***)*.

casado,-a *adj (estado civil)* married.

casadoiro,-a, casadouro,-a *adj* eligible, marriageable; **mulher** ~ woman of marriageable age.

casa-forte *(pl:* **casas-fortes***) f* safe deposit/vault.

casa-grande *(pl:* **casas-grandes***) f* (BR) manor house.

casal *m (par) (de pessoas casadas/juntas)* couple; *(conjunto de alguns animais – macho e fêmea)* pair; **um** ~ **de pombos** a pair of pigeons; **2** *(lugarejo)* hamlet; **3** *(propriedade do campo)* farmhouse.

casamenteiro,-a *m,f* matchmaker; ♦ *adj* matchmaking.

casamento *m* marriage; ~ **por amor** love match; **2** *(cerimónia)* wedding; **3** *(fig) (ligação)* match.

casa-modelo *(pl:* **casas-modelo***) f* house/apartment to view.

casa-torre *f* turret of a castle.

casar *vt* to marry; **2** to give in marriage; **3** *(fig)* ~ **com** match, combine; **o queijo da Serra casa bem com o pão de centeio** the Serra cheese goes well with rye bread; ♦ ~-**se** *vr* to get married; **2** *(fam) (no passivo)* to get spliced; **eles casaram-se ontem** they got spliced yesterday.

casarão *m* large house; **2** *(barracão)* shed.

casario *m* row/group of houses.

casca *f (de árvore)* bark; **2** *(de fruta)* skin, peel; **3** *(de ferida)* scab; **4** *(tartaruga, caracol)* shell; **a ~ do ovo** eggshell; **5** *(de cereais)* husk; **6** *(vagem)* pod; IDIOM **dar a ~** *(agastar-se)* to die; **~ grossa** *f* uncouth person, lout.

casca-de-noz *f (banco frágil)* coracle.

cascalheira *f (riso)* chortle; **2** difficult breathing.

cascalho *m* gravel; **2** *(praia)* shingle; **3** rubble.

cascão *m* crust; grime.

cascata *f* waterfall.

cascavel *m (pequeno guizo dos gatos, etc)* small bell; **2** *(fig)* nasty/hot tempered person; **3** *(ZOOL)* rattlesnake.

casco *m (couro cabeludo)* scalp; **2** *(ossos do crânio)* skull; **3** *(de cavalos/bois)* hoof, hooves *pl*; **4** *(barco)* hull; **5** *(vasilha)* cask, barrel (of wine); **6** *(fam)* drunk; **7** *(fig)* head; *(BR)* empty bottle; IDIOM **C~s de Rolha** the back of beyond.

casebre *m* hovel, shack.

caseiro,-a *adj* home-made; home-loving; **2** homely; ♦ *m,f* farm manager.

caserna *f (MIL)* barracks *pl*.

casino *m* casino.

casmurrice *f* stubbornness.

casmurro,-a *adj* stubborn, pig-headed; **2** sullen; **3** moody.

caso *m (ger)* case; **2** *(JUR)* lawsuit; **3 ~ amoroso** love affair; **4 ~ fortuito** unforeseen circumstances; **5 ~ de vida e morte** a matter of life and death; ♦ *conj* in case, if; **em ~ de** in case (of); **em todo ~** in any case; **fazer pouco ~ de** to make light of; **não fazer ~ de** to ignore; **não faça ~** take no notice; **vir ao ~** to be relevant.

casório *m* marriage; **2** *(fam) (casamento)* splicing.

casote *f (cão)* kennel, doghouse (US).

caspa *f* dandruff.

Cáspio *npr* o **(mar)** ~ the Caspian Sea.

casquilho *m (ELECT) (lâmpada)* base; **2** *(MEC)* coupling; nut to join tubes; **3** *(homem bem vestido)* dandy.

casquinha *f* thin veneer; **2 ~ de madre-pérola** *(botões)* mother-of-pearl veneer; **3** old/silver plated; **4** peel or rind.

cassa *f (tecido)* muslin.

cassação *f (POL)* annulment; *(de documentos)* cancellation.

cassar *vt* annul, *(direitos)* cancel; **2** *(documento, autorização)* cancel, impeach.

cassete *f* cassette, tape; **~ virgem** blank cassette/ tape; **leitor de ~** cassette player.

cassetete *f* truncheon, club.

casta *f* lineage; **2** caste; **3** *(ZOOL)* breed, stock; type, sort; **da mesma ~** of the same kind/race/stock; **toda a ~ de patifes** every kind of scoundrels; **4** *(BOT) (uvas)* species of grapes; **5 sair à ~** *(pai, mãe)* to take after one's parents.

castanheiro *m* chestnut tree.

castanho,-a *adj* brown; **2** *(fruto)* f chestnut; **3 ~ de caju** cashew nut; **4 ~-do-pará** *f* Brazil nut.

castanholas *fpl* castanets.

castelão *m* **castelã** *f* lord, lady of the castle.

castelhano,-a *m,f adj* Castilian.

castelo *m* castle; **~ de areia** sand castle; **2** *(NÁUT)* **~ de proa** quarter deck; **3 ~ de popa** forecastle; **4 claras batidas em ~** egg whites beaten until stiff; IDIOM **fazer ~s no ar** to make castles in the air.

castiçal *m* candlestick.

castiço,-a *adj* pure, genuine; **2** of good stock; **3** *(LÍNG) (estilo)* vernacular.

castidade *f* chastity.

castigar *vt* to punish, to chastise; ♦ **~-se** *vr* to scourge, chastise o.s.

castigo *m* punishment; **2** retribution; **logo por ~** to make things worse; **foi um ~ para apanhar um taxi** it was a nightmare/hell to get a taxi.

casto,-a *adj* chaste, pure.

castor *m (ZOOL)* beaver.

castrado,-a *m,f* eunuch, gelding; ♦ *adj* castrated; **2** *(animal)* neutered, spayed; **3** *(fig)* helpless.

castrar *vt* to castrate.

castro *m* old castle of Roman origin or pre-Roman.

casual *adj inv* accidental; fortuitous.

casualidade *f* chance; accident; **por ~** by chance, accidentally.

casuístico,-a *adj (JUR)* case-by-case, casuistic(al).

casulo *m (de sementes)* boll, seed capsule, pod; **2** *(de larvas)* cocoon.

cataclismo *m (GEOL)* cataclysm; **2** catastrophe.

catacumba *f* catacomb.

catalão, catalã *m,f adj* Catalan; **2** *(LING)* Catalan.

catalizar *vt (CHEM)* to catalyze; **2** *(fig)* to dynamize.

catálise *f* catalysis.

catalogar *vt* to catalogue.

catálogo *m* catalogue; **2 ~ telefônico** *(BR)* telephone directory.

Catalunha *npr* Catalonia; **a ~** Catalonia.

catamarã *f (tipo de jangada)* catamaran; **2** *(BR) (barco de recreio)* yacht.

cataplasma *f (FARM)* poultice.

catapora *f (BR)* chickenpox.

catapulta *f* catapult.

catar *vt* to look for, search for; **2** *(tirar piolhos, carraças)* to delouse.

catarata *f* waterfall; **2** *(MED)* cataract.

catarro *m* catarrh.

catástrofe *f* catastrophe.

cata-vento *m* weathercock.

catecismo *m* catechism, Sunday school.

catedral *f* cathedral.

catedrático,-a *m,f* university professor; **2** Chair of a department, faculty.

catequese *f (ensino religioso)* Sunday school.

categoria *f* category; rank; quality; **de alta ~** first rate.

categórico,-a *adj* categorical.

catinga *f* strong body odour; **2** stench; **3** *(BR) (mato pouco denso)* bush; **4** *(BR) (fig)* **ter ~ de água** to have bad luck; **5** *(BR) m* miser, skinflint.

cativante *adj inv* captivating.

cativar *vt* to capture; **2** to enslave; **3** to captivate; to charm.

cativeiro *m* captivity.

cativo,-a *m,f* captive, slave; **2** prisoner; ♦ *adj (soldado; animal)* captive; **2** *(atraído)* captivated; **3** *(bens)* mortgaged; **4** *(cheque)* held back, retained; **5** *(JUR)* lien.

catolicismo *m* catholicism.

católico,-a *m,f adj* catholic; **2** *(fig)* conventional, traditional; **3** *(fig)* to be/not be in good mood.

catorze *num* fourteen; **estamos a ~ de Agosto** today is fourteenth of August.

catraia *f* small one-man boat; **2** *(EP)* young girl; **3** *(BR) (meretriz)* prostitute.

catraio,-a *m,f (fam)* urchin, kid.

catrapus *(onomat) exc* bang!, crash!, down (he, she, they) went!

caturra *m,f* cantankerous old fogey; ♦ *adj* obstinate, crabby, fault-finding.

caturrice *f* obstinacy.

caução *f (fig)* security, guarantee; **2** *(cuidado)* caution, cautela; **3** *(JUR)* **prestar ~** to stand bail or security *(for)*; **sob ~** on bail; **~ carcerária** bail.

caucho *m* gum tree; rubber.

caucionar *vt* to guarantee, stand surety for; **2** *(JUR)* to stand bail for.

caucionário *m* guarantor.

cauda *f (de animais)* tail; **2** *(de vestido)* train; **3** **piano de ~** grand piano; **4** *(de cometa)* tail; ♦ **na ~ de** *prep* at the end of.

caudal *m* flow; volume of river; torrent.

caudaloso,-a *adj* abundant; torrential.

caudilho *m (POL, MIL)* leader, chief.

caule *m (BOT)* stalk, stem, caulis.

causa *f* cause; **2** motive, reason; **3** *(JUR)* lawsuit, case; **4 em ~** in question; **5 por ~ de** on account of.

causar *vt* to cause, bring about.

cautela *f (cuidado)* caution, care; **tenha ~!** be careful!; **2** lottery ticket; **3 ~ de penhor** pawn ticket.

cauteleiro,-a *m,f* lottery ticket seller.

cauteloso,-a *adj* cautious, wary.

cava *f* pit; **2** *(acto de cavar)* digging; **3** *(da manga de vestuário)* armhole.

cavaca *f* chip of wood.

cavaco *m* firewood; **2** *(fam)* chat; **3** *(fig)* **estar um ~** be a wreck, a dry old stick; **4 não dar ~** not give reply, not pay attention to; **5 dar o ~ por** to be fond of/do anything to get.

cavador,-ora *m,f* digger, ploughman/woman.

cavadora *f* ploughing-machine.

cavala *f (peixe)* mackerel.

cavalaria *f (MIL)* cavalry; **2** horsemanship; **3** chivalry.

cavalariça *f* stable.

cavaleiro *m* rider, horseman; **2** cavalier; **3** knight (de uma Ordem); **~ andante** knight-errant.

cavalete *m* easel; **2** workbench; **3** *(violino)* bridge; **4** *(tortura)* rack; **5 ~ do telhado** ridge of the roof; **6 nariz (de) ~** hook nose; ♦ *adv*: **ao ~** on top of each other.

cavalgada *f* cavalcade.

cavalgadura *f (montada)* mount.

cavalgar *vt* to ride.

cavalheiresco,-a *adj* gentlemanly; chivalrous.

cavalheiro *m* gentleman.

cavalinho *m* pony; **2 ~ de pau** rocking horse.

cavalitas *adv* **às ~ to** piggyback; **andar às ~ de** to be carried on sb's back or shoulders, ride piggyback.

cavalo *m* horse; **~ de raça pura** thoroughbred horse; **2** *(em xadrês)* knight; ♦ *adv* **a ~** on horseback; **2** *(CULIN)* **bife com ovo a ~** a steak with a fried egg on top; **3 andar a ~** to ride; **andar a ~ num burro** ride a donkey; IDIOM **andar de ~ pr'a burro** to go from bad to worse.

cavalo-de-batalha *m* favourite topic; hobby-horse.

cavalo-de-pau *(pl: cavalos-de-pau) m* wheel-spin.

cavalo-marinho *(pl: cavalos-marinhos) m (ZOOL) (do mar)* sea horse; **2** *(ZOOL)* hippopotamus.

cavalo-vapor *m* horsepower.

cavaquear *vi (conversar)* to chat.

cavaqueira *f* chat, prattle.

cavaquinho *m (MÚS)* a small Portuguese guitar, *(tipo de)* ukulele (very popular in Brazil); IDIOM **dar o ~ por** to be very fond of.

cavar *vt (terra)* to dig; **2** *(fig)* **~ a vida** to earn one's living; ♦ *vi* to burrow; **2** *(fig)* to delve; **3** *(fam) (fugir)* scarper; scram; **vai ~!** scram!

cave *f* wine-cellar; **2** *(casa)* basement.

caveira *f* skull.

caverna *f* cavern.

cavername *m (NÁUT)* framework; **2** *(pop)* skeleton.

cavernoso,-a *adj* cavernous; **2** hollow; **3** *(som)* raucous.

cavidade *f* cavity.

cavilha *f* dowel; wooden or metal peg; bolt; **~ de porca** nut bolt.

cavo,-a *adj* hollow; **2** concave.

cavouco *(Vd: cabouco)*.

cavouqueiro *(Vd: cabouqueiro)*.

caxemira *f (tecido de lã fino)* cashmere.

Cazaquistão *npm* **o ~** Kazakistan.

cazaquistanês,-esa *m,f* Kazakistani.

c/c *(abr de conta corrente)* current account.

cear *vt* to have at supper; ♦ *vi* to have supper.

cebola *f* onion.

cebolinha *f* spring onion, small onion *(para conserva)*.

cebolinho *(= cebolo) m (planta, raiz)* chive.

cecear *vi* to lisp.

ceceio *m* lisp.

cedência *f (JUR)* transfer; cession; **~ de quotas** *(numa companhia)* selling of one's shares, partnership; **2** *(da casa)* lending; **3** concession (from both sides), compromise.

ceder *vt* to give up; **2** to hand over; **3** to loan; **4** to loosen; **5** to give way; ♦ *vi* to give in, to yield; to concede.

cedido,-a *adj* given, granted, conceded; **imagens ~as por** *(TV)* photos provided by.

cedilha *f (under the c)* cedilla = ç.

cedinho *adv* very early.

cedo *adv* early; **2** prematurely; **3** soon; **mais ~ ou mais tarde** sooner or later; **4 o mais ~ possível** as soon as possible; **5 bem ~ na vida** at an early age; **6 ~ de manhã** early morning.

cedro *m (BOT)* cedar.

cédula *f* banknote; **2** *(eleitoral)* ballot paper, voter's card; **3 ~ pessoal/~ de nascimento** birth certificate.

cefaleia *f (MED)* migraine.

cefálico,-a *adj (artéria, massa)* cephalic.

cegagem *f (AGR)* removal of eyes from trees.

cegar *vt* to blind; **2** to dazzle; **a luz do outro carro cegou-nos** the light from the other car dazzled us.

cego,-a *m,f* blind man/woman; ♦ *adj* blind; ♦ *adv* blindly; in the dark; by chance; **2** ~ **de ciúmes** blind with jealousy.

cegonha *f (ZOOL)* stork; **2** pillory, post; **3** *(AGR)* ancient water-raising device from a well.

cegueira *f* blindness; **2** *(fig)* ignorance; **3** fanaticism.

ceia *f* evening meal, supper; **a última C~** the Last Supper.

ceifa *f* harvest.

ceifar *vt* to reap, harvest; ~ **vidas** to slaughter.

ceifeiro,-a *m,f* reaper; **~a-mecânica** mowing machine; **~a debulhadora** combine harvester.

Ceilão *npr* **o** ~ Ceylon.

cela *f (de convento, de prisão)* cell.

celebérrimo,-a *(superl de* **célebre)** *adj* very famous.

celebração *f* celebration; **2** commemoration.

celebrante *m,f (REL)* priest; **2** *(pessoa que celebra)* merrymaker, celebrater.

celebrar *vt* to celebrate; **2** to commemorate; **3** *(enaltecer)* to glorify, exult.

célebre *adj inv* famous, well known.

celebridade *f* celebrity.

celebrizar *vt* make sb famous; ♦ ~**-se** *vr* to become famous.

celeiro *m* granary; **2** barn; **o Alentejo é o ~ de Portugal** Alentejo is Portugal's granary.

célere *adj inv (pessoa, animal, acção)* swift, quick.

celeste *adj* celestial, heavenly.

celibatário,-a *m,f* bachelor, spinster; ♦ *adj* unmarried; single.

celibato *m* celibacy.

celofane *m* cellophane.

celsius *adj* Celsius.

celta *m,f* Celt; céltico; ♦ *adj* Celtic.

célula *f (BIO, ELECT)* cell; **2** *(BOT)* cell, nucleous, capsule; **3** *(prisão, convento)* cell; **4** *(fig) (grupo, núcleo)* nucleous; ~ **fotoeléctrica** photoelectric cell.

celular *adj inv* cellular.

celulite *f (nódulos)* cellulite.

celulóide *f* celluloid.

celulose *f* cellulose.

cem *num* hundred; **2** *(último de cem)* hundredth.

cemitério *m* cemetery, graveyard.

cena *f* scene; **2** stage; **em** ~ on the stage; **levar à** ~ to stage; **3** *(fig) (escândalo)* **ela fez uma** ~ **no restaurante** she made a scene in the restaurant.

cénico,-a *adj (arte, espaço, efeitos)* scenic.

cenário *m* scenery; **2** scenario; **3** setting.

cenho *m* scowl, frowning countenance.

cenógrafo,-a *m,f* set designer, scenographer.

cenoura *f (BOT)* carrot.

censo *m* census.

censor *m* censor; critic.

censório,-a *adj* censorial; **mesa ~a** panel of judges.

censura *f* censorship; censure, criticism.

censurar *vt (filme)* to censor; **2** to criticize; **3** reproach (**por**, for).

censurável *adj inv* reprehensible, censorable.

centavo *m* cent, hundredth part of one escudo/ dollar; **não tenho um** ~ I don't have a cent.

centeal *m* rye field; **centeio** *m* rye.

centelha *f* spark; **2** *(fig)* flash.

centelhante *adj inv* sparkling.

centena *f* hundred; **às ~s** in hundreds.

centenário *m* a hundred years; century; centenary; ♦ **centenário,-a** *m,f* centenarian; ♦ *adj (árvore, tradição)* centennial.

centésimo,-a *m,f* hundredth part; ♦ *adj* hundredth.

centiare *m* centiare.

centígrado *m* centigrade.

centímetro *m* centimetre.

cêntimo *m* cent, centime, hundredth part of one euro.

cento *m*: **um** ~ one hundred; **aos ~s** in hundreds; **por** ~ per cent.

Use 'cento' for numbers over 100, e.g. cento e um, etc.

centopeia (*BR:* **-pé-**) *f* centipede.

central *adj inv* central; **2** *f* headquarters, central office; **3** ~ **elé(c)trica** power station; **4** ~ **telefónica** telephone exchange.

centralização *f* centralization.

centralizar *vt* to centralize.

centrar *vt* to centre; **2** *(ponto focal)* to centre on; **3** *(FUT)* centre (bola).

centrifugadora *f* centrifuge; centrifugal machine; **3** *(de sumo)* extractor.

centrifugar *vt* centrifuge; **2** *(roupa lavada)* to spindry.

centrífugo,-a *adj (força)* centrifugal.

centrípeto *aj* centripetal.

centrista *m,f (POL)* centrist, moderator; ♦ *adj inv* moderate, centre.

centro *m* centre; middle; ~ **comercial** shopping centre *(UK)*; shopping mall *(US)*.

centroavante *m* centre forward.

centro-direita *m (POL, DESP)* centre-right.

centro-esquerda *m* centre-left.

centúplo *adj* hundredfold; centuple.

centúria *f* century.

centurião *m (HIST)* centurion.

cepa *f* young grapevine; **2** stump (of any tree); IDIOM **não passar de ~ torta** not make progress/headway.

cepo *m* log; stump.

ce(p)ticismo *m* scepticism.

cé(p)tico,-a *m,f* sceptic ♦ *adj inv* sceptical.

ce(p)tro *m* sceptre.

cera *f* wax, polish.

cerâmica *f* ceramics; **2** *(artefactos)* pottery.

ceramista *m,f* potter, ceramicist.

cerca *f* fence; hedge; **2** enclosed field; **3** enclosure; ♦ *prep*: ~ **de** nearly, about, near by; ♦ *adv* around; near.

cercado *m* enclosure, pen; **2** *(de cavalos)* paddock.

cercadura *f (vedação)* fence, hedge, enclosure; **2** *(decoração)* border *(de saia)*, frieze *(de azulejos: etc)*.

cercanias *fpl* outskirts; **nas** ~ in the neighbourhood *sg*.

cercar *vt* to enclose; **2** to fence in; **3** to surround; **4** *(MIL)* to besiege, lay siege to.

cercear *vt* to cut at the root; **2** to curtail, restrict.

cerco *m* encirclement; **2** enclosure; **3** *(MIL)* siege; **4** **pôr ~ a** lay siege.

cerda *f* bristle.

cerdo *m* boar, hog.

cereal *m* cereal.

cerealífico,-a *adj (cultura, produção)* cereal; **2** *(região)* corn-producing, growing region.

cérebro *m* brain; **2** *(fig)* intelligence, the brains *pl*.

cereja *f* cherry; **doce de ~** cherry jam.

cerejal *m* cherry-orchard.

cerejeira *f* cherry tree; IDIOM **a ~ em cima do bolo** the icing on the cake.

cerimónia *(BR:* -mô-) *f* ceremony; **traje de ~** formal dress; **não faça ~** make yourself at home; ♦ *adv* **sem ~** informally.

cerimonial *m* etiquette; ♦ *adj inv* ceremonial.

cerimonioso,-a *adj* ceremonious; **2** formal.

cério *(QUÍM)* cerium (symbol Ce).

cernar *vt (BOT)* to lay bare the heart of a tree; to cut into the core.

cerne *m (BOT)* heart *(of a tree),* duramen; heartwood; **2** *(fig)* core, heart, nucleous; **3** *(BR)* hardwood log unaffected by water.

cernelha *f* withers. (of a horse, etc); **2** a shock of grain; **3** *(TAUROM)* **pega de ~** catch the bull by the neck.

ceroilas, ceroulas *fpl (roupa)* long johns.

cerração *f* thick fog, mist; **2** *(dificuldade na voz)* thickness, hoarseness.

cerrado *m* enclosure; **2** scrub(-land); ♦ *adj* shut, closed; **2** dense, thick; *(aviso na loja)* **~ amanhã** closed tomorrow.

cerrar *vt* to close, shut; **o banco cerra às cinco** the banks shuts at 5 p.m..

cerro *m* small hill, mound, hillock.

certa *adv* **pela ~** *(BR)* **na ~** certainly, for sure; **2 fica à ~** *(conta)* it will square *(account, sum)* up; IDIOM **levar alguém à ~** *(enganar)* to take sb for a ride, fool sb.

certame *m* fight; **2** contest, competition; **3** discussion; **4** exhibition.

certamente *adv* certainly, of course.

certeiro,-a *adj* well aimed; **2** right, accurate;   steady.

certeza *f* certainty; **com ~** certainly, surely; **ter a ~ de** to be sure of.

certidão *f* certificate; **~ de casamento** marriage certificate.

certificado *m* certificate; **2 ~ de óbito** death certificate; **3** *(FIN)* **~ de aforro** savings certificate.

certificar *vt* to certify; to assure; ♦ **~-se** *vr* (de of) to make sure.

certo,-a *adj* certain, sure; **não estou ~** I am not sure; **ao ~** for certain, exactly; **2** correct, right, exacto; **não está ~** it is not right; **tem horas certas?** what is the right time?; **3** *(positivo)* sure; **estar ~ de** to be sure of; **4** *(verdadeiro)* true, agree; **isso é ~** that is true; I agree; ♦ **o mais ~ é que** likely to, bound to; **por ~** certainly; **até ~ ponto** to some extent; up to a point; **por ~** certainly; ♦ *pron indef* one, a certain person or thing; **~ dia** one day; **a ~a**

altura after a while; **considerar como ~** to take for granted.

cerva *f* hind.

cerveja *f* beer; ale; **~ preta** stout.

cervejaria *f* brewery; **2** beer house, beer pub/bar.

cervical *adj inv (ANAT)* cervical; **2** *(MED)* **traumatismo ~** whiplash injury.

cerviz *f (ANAT) (nuca)* cervix, nape; **2 colo uterino.**

cervo *m* deer, stag.

cerzidura *f* darning.

cerzir *vt* to darn.

cesariana *(MED)* Caesarean section.

césio *m (QUIM)* caesium.

cessação *f* cessation, end, stop.

cessante *adj inv* resigning; ending; **2** *(documento)* ceasing.

cessão *f* transfer, surrender.

cessar *vt* to cease, stop; **2 sem ~** continually; **3 ~ -fogo** cease-fire.

cesta *f* basket; **cestaria** *f* basket work.

cesto *m* small basket; **2** hamper; **3** *(NÁUT)* top; **4 ~ da gávea** crow's nest.

cesura *n (LITER)* cesura; **2** *(MED)* cut, incision.

cesurar *vt (MED)* to make an incision.

cetim *m (tecido)* satin.

ceticismo *m (UK)* scepticism; *(US)* skepticism; **cético,-a** *adj* sceptic(al); skeptic(al).

cetro *(Vd:* **ce(p)tro)**.

céu *m* sky; heaven; **~ carregado** dark, overcast; **2 ~ da boca** roof of the mouth, palate; **3 ~ aberto** in the open, open skies; ♦ *exc* **céus!** good heavens!

ceva *f* fattening; **2** feed; **3** bait.

cevada *f* barley.

cevadal *m* barleyfield.

cevadeira *f* feedbag.

cevado *m* fattened pig.

cevar *vt* to fatten; **2** to feed up; **3** to bait; ♦ **~-se** *vr* to get fat; **2** *(fig)* to get rich.

chá *m* tea; **hora do ~** teatime; **2** *(fig)* **falta-lhes ~** they lack in good manners/in good breeding.

chã *f* plain, plateau.

chacal *m* jackal.

chácara *(BR) f* farm; rural property, estate; **2** country house.

chacina *f* slaughter; **chacinar** *vt* to slaughter.

chacota *f* satirical song; **2** jest, banter; **3** mockery; **ele está na ~** he is making fun.

chacotear *vi* make fun (**de** of), mock.

Chade *npr* **o ~** Chad.

chadiano,-a *m,f adj* from Chad, Chadian.

chafariz *m* public fountain supplying water.

chafurdar *vi (em lama, etc)* to wallow (**em**, in); ♦ *vt (fig) (reputação)* to drag through the mud.

chaga *f (MED)* wound, sore; **as cinco ~s de Cristo** Christ's five wounds; **2** affliction; **3** *(fig) (person)* bore.

chalaça *f* witty remark.

chalado,-a *adj (fam)* crazy, person with a screw loose *(pop)*; **2** boring; **é uma conversa ~a** it is a boring conversation; **ando ~** I am going nuts *(pop)*.

chalé *m* chalet, villa.

chaleira *f* kettle; **2** *(BR)* crawler, toady.

chalota *f (BOT) (da família da cebola)* shallot.

chalupa *f (barco)* sloop.

chama *f* flame; **em ~s** on fire.

chamada *f* call; **2** *(MIL)* roll-call; **3** marginal note; **4** ~ **telefónica** *(BR:* -fô-*)* telephone call.

chamar *vt* to call; **2** to ring, phone; **3** to attract attention; **4 mandar ~** to summon, send for; ♦ *vi* to call (out); ~ **nomes a alguém** to call names to people; ♦ **~-se** *vr* to be called; **chamo-me Maria** my name is Maria.

chamariz *m (caça)* call-bird, decoy; **2** bird call; **3** *(fig)* lure, bait.

chamativo,-a *adj* flashy; **2** *(person)* attractive.

chaminé *f* chimney; **2** *(de barco)* funnel.

champanha *f* **champanhe** *m* champagne.

champô *m* shampoo.

chamuscado,-a *adj* singed, scorched; **imagem ~a** tarnished image.

chamuscar *vt (perna, roupa)* to burn; **2** *(cabelo)*, singe.

chamusco *m* singe, singeing, scald; **2** lightly burn.

chancela *f* seal, official stamp.

chancelaria *f* chancellery, chancery.

chanceler *m* chancellor.

chanfradura *f* bevel.

chanfrar *vt (espelho, pedra)* to bevel; **2** to make grooves; **3** *(fig)* to go nuts; **ele é chanfrado** he is crasy, he is nuts.

chantagem *f* blackmail.

chantagista *m,f* blackmailer.

chão *m* ground; **2** soil; floor; **rés-do-~** ground floor; **3** *(fundo de tecido, pintura)* background.

chapa *f (metal)* plate; *(para grelhar)* hotplate; **2** plaque, **3** metal sheet; **4** *(revestimento de viatura)* chassis; **5 ~ de matrícula** *(AUTO)* number plate; **6** *(pequena peça de metal ou madeira com um número)* disc number; **7** *(da profissão)* badge; **8** *(FOTO)* negative, *(BR)* shot; **tirar uma ~** take an X-ray; **9** *(BR) (camarada)* mate, buddy.

chapelada *f* hatful; **2** *(pop)* greeting with a hat.

chapelaria *f* hatshop; **2** millinery.

chapeleira *f* milliner; **2** hat box.

chapeleiro *m* hatter.

chapéu *m* hat; **~ de coco** bowler hat; **~-de-chuva** umbrella; **~-de-sol** parasol; **de ~** with his/her hat on; **molde de ~** hat block; **pôr o ~ à banda** to cock one's hat over one's ear; IDIOM **ser de se lhe tirar o ~** be worthy of admiration; be top-notch; fantastic.

chapinhar *vi (em água, lama)* to splash.

charada *f* puzzle; riddle.

charco *m* stagnant pond; puddle.

charcutaria, charcuterie *f* delicatessen.

charlatão *m (pl:* -ães*)* **(charlatã** *f)* impostor, charlatan; **2** *(médico, curandeiro)* quack.

charmoso,-a *adj* charming; delightful.

charneca *f* moor, heath; **2** *(BR)* swamp.

charneco *m* blue magpie.

charneira *f (gonzo)* hinge, joint; **2** *(encadernação)* cloth joint; **3** parts of ... gyrating on an axle; **4** *(ANAT)* ginglymus.

charrete *f* small chariot, small carriage pulled by horses.

charro *m (ZOOL) (peixe)* horse mackerel.

charrua *f* plough.

charuto *m* cigar.

chassi *m (AUTO)*, bodywork, chassis.

chata *f* punt, barge *(Vd: chato)*.

chatear *vt* to bore; **2** to annoy, pester sb; ♦ **~-se** *vr* to get bored, upset with; annoyed about/with.

chatice *f (fam)* nuisance; **2** boredom, tedium; **3** worries; **que ~!** what a nuisance!, what a bore!

chato,-a *m,f* bore, nuisance; **2** *(ZOOL) (piolho)* crab-louse; ♦ *adj* flat, level, smooth; **2** *(pop)* tiresome, boring.

chauvinismo *m* chauvinism.

chauvinista *m,f* chauvinist; ♦ *adj inv* chauvinistic.

chavão *m* big key; **2** cake mould; **3** pattern; **4** platitude, hackneyed phrase; **5** important author.

chave *f* key; **2** *(prefixo)* key; **3** *(MÚS)* key; **4** *(solução, razão)* key; **5** ~ **de fendas/de parafusos** screwdriver; **6** ~ **inglesa** (monkey) wrench; **7** ~-**mestra** master key; **8** ~ **de porcas** spanner; **9 fechar à ~** to lock up; IDIOM **fechar a sete ~s** to put under lock and key.

chaveiro *m* key-ring.

chavelho *m (chifre)* horn, antler; **2** *(do caracol)* horns; **3** *(de insecto)* antenna.

chávena *f* cup *(Vd: xícara)*.

chaveta *f* pin, peg; **2** *(sinal gráfico)* bracket.

chazada *f* a lot of tea; **2** *(fam) (coisa sem interesse)* waste of time, rubbish; **3** *(repreensão)* a telling-off.

chazinho *m (fam)* tea; teatime, afternoon tea.

checar *vt (conferir)* to check, go over sth; **2** investigate; **3** *(testar)* check.

checo,-a *m,f adj* Czech; *(língua)* Czech; **a República C~** *npr* Czech Republic.

chefe *m* head, chief; boss; master; ~ **de estação** stationmaster.

chefia *f* leadership.

chefiar *vt* to lead, command.

chegada *f* arrival.

chegado,-a *adj* near; close, intimate **parente ~** a close relative; **recém-~** newly arrived.

chegar *vt* to bring/hold near; **ela chegou a criança ao peito** she held the child close to her bosom; ~ **o copo aos lábios** to bring the glass to the lips; ♦ *vi* to arrive; **eu cheguei atrasado** I arrived late; **2** to reach; **o total quase chegou a um milhão** the total sum nearly reached one million; **3** to be enough; **esta carne não chega para todos** this meat is not enough for all; **4** even, as far as; **chega a parecer mentira** it even sounds like a lie; **ela chegou a bater-lhe** she went as far as beat him; **5** ~ **a** to arrive at; **ele chegou à conclusão** he arrived at the conclusion; ♦ **~-se** *vr* ~ **a** to approach; to be/come close to sb/sth; IDIOM ~ **a brasa à sua sardinha** to think only of one's own interests; ~ **a vias de facto** to get into a fight.

cheia *f (inundação)* flood, flooding; **~s** *fpl* floods.

cheio,-a *adj* full, filled; full up; ~ **de lama** covered in mud; ~ **de si** puffed-up, conceited; ~ **de sorte**

very lucky; **2** *(um pouco gordo)* plump; **3** *(farto)* fed up; ♦ **em ~** *adv* **acertar em ~** to hit the bull' eye.

cheirar *vt* to smell; ♦ *vi:* **~ a** to smell of.

cheiro *m* smell; *(bom)* aroma.

cheiroso,-a *adj* scented.

cheque *m* cheque; **~ cruzado** crossed cheque; **~ em branco** blank cheque; **~ sem cobertura** bounced cheque; **passar um ~** to write a cheque; **uma caderneta de ~s** cheque-book; **~-livro** *m* book token.

cherne *m* *(peixe)* black grouper.

cheta *f* *(fam)* lolly, dough; **estar sem ~** to be hard-up, broke.

chiadeira *f* squeaking (noise).

chiar *vi* *(ratos, carro)* to squeak; **2** *(porta, soalho)* to creak; **3** *(steam)* to sizzle.

chibata *f* *(vara)* cane; stick; birch.

chicharro *m* *(peixe)* horse mackerel.

chichi *m* *(fam)* pee; *(fala de bebé)* wee-wee.

chi-coração *m* *(fam)* bear hug.

chicória *f* chicory.

chicotada *f* whiplash.

chicote *m* whip.

chicotear *vt* to whip, lash.

chifrada *f* horn thrust.

chifrar *(TAUROM)* to gore (the bull).

chifre *m* *(de animal)* horn.

Chiitas *mpl:* **os ~** *(seita muçulmana)* the Shiites, Shias.

Chile *npr* Chile; **o ~** Chile.

chileno,-a *m,f adj* Chilean.

chilique *m* *(fam)* faint; **quando ela viu a conta do gás, deu-lhe um ~** when she saw the gas bill, she freaked out.

chilrear *vi* *(do passarinho)* to chirp, twitter.

chilreio, chilro *m* chirping.

chimpanzé *m* chimpanzee.

China *npr* China; **a ~** China.

chinela *f* mule.

chinelo *m* slipper.

chinês,-esa *m,f adj* Chinese; **a Muralha C~** the Great Wall of China.

chinfrim *m* **chinfrineira** *f* fuss; shindy; hullabaloo; **fazer um ~** to kick up a fuss.

chinó *m* *(cabelo)* hairpiece.

chio *m* *(onomat)* *(som)* creak, squeak.

Chipre *npr* **o ~** Cyprus.

chipriota *m,f* Cypriot.

chique *adj inv* stylish, chic.

chiqueiro *m* pigsty; **2** *(fig)* filth; **3** dump; **4** mess, filthy mess.

chispa *f* *(faísca dos metais)* spark; **2** *(fig)* talent; genius.

chispar *vi* give off sparks; **2** *(fig)* *(ira)* flare up.

chispe *m* pig's trotters *pl*.

chiste *m* joke, quip, ditty; wisecrack.

chita[1] *f* printed cotton, calico; IDIOM *(BR)* **mulher e ~, cada qual é bonita** each to his own taste.

chita[2] *f (BOT)* various kinds of orchids.

chita[3] *(ZOOL)* cheetah.

choca *f* large cowbell.

choça *f* shack, hut.

chocalhar *vt/vi* to rattle; to shake sth; *(fig)* to blab.

chocalho *m* rattle; cow/sheep's bell.

chocar *vt* to hatch, incubate; **2** to shock, offend; ♦ *vi* to collide, crash.

chocho,-a[1] *adj* withered, sapless; **2** *(fig)* dull; **o dia está ~** it is a dull day; **estar/sentir-se ~** *(fam)* to be under the weather.

chocho[2] *m* *(fam)* kiss, smacker *(pop)*.

choco *m* *(ZOOL)* cuttlefish; **2** *(ovo)* addled.

choco,-a *adj* broody; stagnant; **2 galinha ~a** sitting-hen.

chocolate *m* chocolate.

chofer *m* driver.

chofre *m*: **de ~** all of a sudden; **2** full; **o sol batia de ~ na minha cara** the sun fell full on my face.

choldra *f* *(pop)* *(salgalhada)* bedlam; **2** *(ralé)* mob; gang.

chope *m* *(BR)* draught beer.

choque *m* shock; **2** collision; **3** *(MED, ELECT)* shock; impact; **4** *(AUTO)* crash; **5** clash, conflict.

chora *m* *(fam)* **um ~** a moaner, cry-baby; **2** *f* olive-tree flower; **3** *f (Reg) (sopa)* **~ de peixe** fish soup.

choradeira *f* *(fam)* a long cry; weeping.

choramingar *vi* to whine, whimper.

choramingas *m,f,sg,pl* cry baby; whimperer.

chorão[1] *m* **chorona** *f* crybaby; ♦ *adj* snivelling.

chorão[2] *m (BOT)* weeping willow.

chorar *vt/vi* to weep, cry.

choroso,-a *adj* tearful.

choupana *f* shack, hut.

choupo *m* poplar.

chouriço *m* Portuguese garlic sausage; **~ de sangue** black pudding.

chover *vi* to rain; **~ a cântaros/a potes** to rain cats and dogs, pouring down; **2** *(fig)* to rain down, poured in; **choviam insultos** insults rained down; **choviam convites** invitations poured in, kept coming in.

chucha *f* baby's dummy, teat of the bottle.

chuchar *vt* to suck dummy, breast or *(biberão)* bottle; ♦ *vi* to suckle.

chulé *m* foot odour.

chulo,-a *m,f* pimp; ♦ *adj* vulgar, coarse.

chumaço *m* *(vestuário)* padding for the shoulders.

chumbar *vt* to weld, solder; **2** to weight with lead; **3 ~ um dente** to have a tooth filled; ♦ *vt* to shoot *(pássaro)*; ♦ *vi (col) (EP)* to flunk *(exame)*.

chumbo *m* lead; gunshot; **2 cor de ~** leaden; **3 céu de ~** overcast, grey.

chupa-chupa *m* lollipop.

chupar *vt* to suck; **2** *(dinheiro)* to sponge; **3** *(tinta, óleo)* to soak up; IDIOM **ficar a ~ no dedo** to be disappointed.

chupeta *f* *(de bebé) (UK)* dummy; *(US)* pacifier.

churrasco *m* barbecue; **frango no ~** barbecued chicken.

chutar *vt* *(bola)* to kick; **2** *(col)* to throw; to pass on; ♦ *vi* banish.

chuto, chute *m* *(FUT)* kick, shot.

chuva *f* rain; ~ **ácida** acid rain; **~-de-pedra** *f* hailstorm; **~-de-prata** *(BOT)* begonia; IDIOM **quem anda à ~ fica molhada** if you don't take precautions you get pregnant.

chuveiro *m* shower *(apparatus, room)* (Vd: **ducha** for 'shower'/bath).

chuviscar *vi* to drizzle.

chuvisco *m* drizzle.

chuvoso,-a *adj* rainy.

Cia. *(abr de* **companhia***)* Co., company.

ciática *f (MED)* sciatica.

cicatriz *f* scar.

ciciar *vi* to lisp; **2** to whisper; **3** to rustle; **ouviu-se o ~ do vestido de seda** the rustling of her dress could be heard.

ciclismo *m* cycling.

ciclista *m,f* cyclist.

ciclo *m* cycle; **2** *(era)* cycle; **3** *(EDUC)* **o ~ básico, primeiro ~** preparatory/primary school; **4 ~ menstrual** menstrual cycle.

ciclone *m* cyclone, hurricane; twister *(US)*.

ciclónico,-a *adj* cyclonic(al).

ciclovia *f* (road) lane for cyclists.

cidadão *m* **cidadã** *f (pl:* **cidadãos, cidadãs***)* citizen.

cidade *f* town; **2** city.

cidadela *f* citadel.

cidra *f* cider.

cieiro *m (MED)* chap; **ter ~ nos lábios** to have chapped lips; **2** childblains.

ciência *f* science; knowledge.

ciente *adj inv* aware, informed.

científico,-a *adj* scientific.

cientista *m,f* scientist.

cifra *f* cipher; **2** number, figure; **3** sum; **4** code.

cifrão *m* dollar sign, euro sign; **2 cifrões** *pl* money.

cifrar *vt* to write in code; ♦ *vr* amount to; **esta conta cifra-se em** this bill/account amounts to; **2** to come down to; **isto cifra-se em três questões** this comes down to three chief questions.

cigano,-a *m,f* gypsy; *(povo)* Roma; **2** *(pej) (trapaceiro)* cunning, sly (person).

cigarra *f (insecto)* cicada; **2** *(BR)* cricket; **2** *(ELECT)* buzzer.

cigarreira *f* cigarette case.

cigarro *m* cigarette.

cilada *f* ambush; trap; trick.

cilha *f* saddle-girth.

cilício *m* hair-shirt; sackcloth; **2** *(sacrifício)* voluntary sacrifice/penance, torment.

cilindrada *f* cylinder capacity.

cilíndrico,-a *adj* cylindrical.

cilindro *m* cylinder; roller.

cílio *m (pestana)* eyelash; **2** *(BIO, BOT)* cilium.

cima *f* top; **2** summit; **3** crest; **4** apex; ♦ **ao de ~** on the surface; **de ~** from above; **de ~ para baixo** from top to bottom; **ficar de ~** to get the best of it; **em ~ de** on top of, on; **lá em ~** up there; *(andar superior)* upstairs; **para ~** up; **para ~ e para baixo** up and down; **por ~** light, superficial **uma limpeza por ~** a light/quick cleaning; **de ~** over; **ainda por ~** moreover, to top it all; **para ~**

upwards; **para ~ de dez mil** over ten thousand; **para ~ de** on top of; **atirar o casaco para ~ da cama** to throw the coat onto the bed.

címbalo *m (MÚS)* cymbal.

cimeira *f* top, peak, summit; **2** *(BOT)* cyme; **3** *(conferência internacional)* summit meeting, conference.

cimeiro,-a *adj (no alto)* top; **2** highest; uppermost.

cimentar *vt* to cement; **2** *(fig)* to strengthen.

cimento *m* cement; concrete; **~ armado** reinforced concrete.

cimo *m* top; summit; **no ~** at the top.

cinco *num* five, **~ vezes quatro são vinte** five times four come to twenty.

cindir *vt* to split, separate; **2** *(cortar)* cut; **3** *(ar, mar)* cut through.

cineasta *m,f* cinematographer.

cinéfilo,-a *m,f* cinema fan.

cinema *f* cinema, movies *pl*; **~ mudo** silent film.

cinegética *f (arte de caçar)* shooting, hunting.

cinemateca *f* collection of films; place of this collection.

cinematógrafo,-a *m,f* cinematographer.

cinético,-a *adj (FÍS, BIOL)* kinetic.

cingalês,-esa *m,f* native of Sri-Lanka.

cingalês *m (LÍNG)* Sinhalese; ♦ *adj* Singhalese.

cingir *vt* to fasten round one's waist; to encircle; **2** to clasp sb; **3** *(apertar)* to clasp; ♦ **~-se** *vr* to wrap around; **cingiu-se com um manto de veludo** she wrapped herself up in a velvet cloak; **2** *(unir)* **o amor filial que os cingia** the brotherly love that united them.

cínico,-a *m,f (pessoa hipócrita)* cynic; **2** *(FIL)* Cynic; ♦ *adj (filósofo)* cynic; **2** *(pessoa, atitude)* cynical, sarcastic.

cinismo *m (FIL)* cynicism; **2** hypocrisy.

cinquenta *num* fifty; **2** *(página, etc)* fiftieth.

cinquentão,-tona *m,f* person in his/her fifties.

cinquentenário,-a *m* fiftieth anniversary.

cinta *f (faixa)* sash; **2** girdle, roll-on, corset; **3 ~ de jornal** *(tira de papel)* wrapper, postal wrapper; **4 até à ~** up/down to the waist; **pôr a mão na ~** put one's arms akimbo; **agarrar pela ~** to grip someone round by the waist.

cintilar *vi* to sparkle, glitter.

cinto *m* belt; **~ de segurança** safety belt; *(AUTO)* seat-belt.

cintura *f* waist; waistline.

cinza *f* ash, ashes *pl*; ♦ *adj inv (BR)* grey; **quarta-feira de ~s** Ash Wednesday.

cinzeiro *m* ashtray.

cinzel *m* chisel.

cinzelar *vt* to chisel; to carve, engrave.

cinzento *m (cor)* grey, gray; ♦ **cinzento,-a** *m,f adj* grey; **o vestido ~** the grey dress; **o céu está ~** the sky is overcast; **3** ashen; **4** dull.

cio *m* rut; **2** *(peixes)* spawn; **3** *(mamíferos)* heat.

cioso,-a *adj* zealous; **2** possessive, clinging to; **3** *(afectuoso)* protective.

cipó *m (BOT) (planta tropical)* liana, creeper.

cipreste *m* cypress (tree).

cipriota *adj inv* Cypriot.
circo *m* circus.
circuito *m* circuit; **curto** ~ short circuit.
circulação *f* circulation; movement; **2** ~ **de capitais** capital flow; **3 taxa de** ~ road-pricing, congestion charge.
circulante *adj inv* surrounding; **2** circulating, in circulation, itinerant; **3** *(FIN)* **capital** ~ ready/in circulation capital.
circular *f* circular; ♦ *vi* to circulate; **2** to move, flow.
círculo *m* circle, ring; ~ **vicioso** vicious circle.
circum-navegação, circunavegação circumnavigation.
circum-navegar, circunavegar *vt* to circumnavigate.
circuncidar *vt* to circumcise.
circuncisão *f* circumcision.
circunciso,-a *adj* circumcised.
circundante *adj inv* surrounding.
circundar *vt* to surround; **2** to go around; **3** *(com os olhos)* look around.
circunferência *f* circumference.
circunflexo *adj (acentuação)* circumflex; **acento** ~ circumflex accent.
circunscrever *vt* to circumscribe, limit; **2** *(GEOM)* to describe, outline.
circunscrito,-a *adj* circumscribed; **2** restricted.
circunspe(c)ção *f* circumspection.
circunspe(c)to,-a *adj* cautious; **2** serious; **3** circumspect.
circunstância *f* circumstance.
circunstanciado,-a *adj* detailed.
circunstante *m,f* onlooker, bystander; ♦ *adj* surrounding.
circunvagar *vt* to glance over **(algo** sth); **2** *(andar à toa)* to wander about/aimlessly.
circunvalação *f (estrada)* ring road.
circunvizinhança *f* neighbourhood, vicinity; **2** *(arredores)* surroundings.
círio *m (vela grande de cera)* large wax candle.
cirrose *f* cirrhosis.
cirurgia *f* surgery; ~ **plástica** cosmetic surgery.
cirurgião *m,* **cirurgiã** *f* surgeon.
cirúrgico,-a *adj* surgical.
cis *(prefix) (país, fronteira)* this side of.
Cisjordânia *npr* this side of Jordan's frontier, within Jordan.
cisão *f* split, division; **2** *(FIS)* fission; ~ **nuclear** nuclear fission; **3** *(fig)* disagreement.
cisco *m (pó de carvão)* coal-dust.
cisma *m* schism; **2** *f* worry; whim; **3** mania; **4** suspicion; *(BR)* aversion.
cismar *vi* to worry; to dwell on things.
cisne *m* swan.
cisterna *f (depósito de água)* cistern; **2** water tank; **3** *(de águas pluviais)* reservoir.
cisto *m (MED)* cyst.
citação *f* quotation; **2** *(JUR)* summons *sg*; **3** citation.
citar *vt* to quote; **2** *(JUR)* to summon; **3** to cite.
ciúme *m (devido ao amor)* jealousy; **ter** ~**s de** to be jealous of.
ciumento,-a *adj* jealous.
civil *m,f* civilian; ♦ *adj inv* civil; **2** polite.

civilidade *f* civility.
civilização *f* civilization.
civilizar *vt* to civilize.
civismo *m* public spirit; **2** good citizenship.
clã *m* group, clan, gang.
clamar *vt* to clamour for; **2** to cry out; **3** ask for; **4** demand (justice).
clamor *m* outcry, uproar; **2** shout; **3** protest.
clamoroso,-a *adj* noisy; **2** clamorous.
clandestino,-a *adj* clandestine; **mercado** ~ illegal/black market; **2** underground, secret; **3** *(passageiro)* stowaway.
claque *m (fig)* paid applause/audience; **2** group of fans; ~**s de futebol** groups of football fans.
clara *f* white of egg; **2 às** ~**s** in the daylight.
clarabóia *f* skylight.
clarão *m* flash; gleam.
clarear *vi* to dawn; **2** to clear up, brighten up.
clareira *f (no bosque)* glade; clearing.
clareza *f (som, compreensão)* clarity; **2** *(limpidez)* clearness.
claridade *f* brightness, light; **casa com muita** ~ house with much natural light.
clarificação *f (compreensão)* clarification.
clarificador,-ora *adj* purifying.
clarificar *vt* to clarify.
clarim *m* bugle.
clarinete *m (MÚS)* clarinet.
clarinetista *m,f* clarinettist.
claro,-a *adj* clear; bright; **2** light; **3** evident; ♦ *adv* clearly; openly; **em** ~ **passar a noite** ~ to have a sleepless night; **2** *(passar por cim)* skip; **alguns canteiros passar** ~ to skip some flower beds; ♦ *exc* of course! naturally!
classe *f* class; ~ **média/operária** middle/working class.
clássico,-a *adj* classical; **2** *(fig)* classic.
classificação *f* classification.
classificado *adj* classified advert; **2** *(DESP) (competition)* qualified.
classificador *m (arquivo)* file, document.
classificador,-ora *adj (anúncio)* classifying, examining.
classificados *mpl* classified advertisements.
classificar *vt* to classify.
classificativo,-a *adj* classificatory.
claustro *m* cloister; monastic life.
claustrofobia *f* claustrophobia.
claustrófobo,-a *m,f (pessoa)* claustrophobe; ♦ *adj (symptom)* claustrophobic.
cláusula *f* clause.
clausura *f* monastic life; **2** *(seclusão)* seclusion.
clava *f* club, mace.
clave *f (MÚS)* clef; ~ **de sol** treble clef.
clavícula *f* collar bone.
cláxon *m* horn.
clemência *f* mercy.
clemente *adj inv* merciful.
cleptomaníaco,-a *adj* kleptomaniac.
clerical *adj inv (vida, trabalho)* clerical, priestly, ecclesiastical.
clérigo *m* clergyman.

clero *m* clergy.

clicar *vt* (BR) (COMP) to click.

cliché *m* (FOTO) negative; **2** (chavão) cliché, commonplace; **3** (TIPO) (molde) type plate.

cliente *m,f* (de advogado, empresa) client; (loja, restaurante, garage) customer.

clientela *f* clientele; customers *pl.*

clima *m* climate; **2** (fig) (ambiente) environment, atmosphere.

climatérico,-a *adj* climatic.

clínico,-a *m,f* medic, doctor; ~-**geral** general practioner GP; **2** *f* clinic, practice; ♦ *adj* clinical.

clipe *m* clip, paper clip.

clique *m* to form one's own private group; gang; **2** (curto e ligeiro ruído) click; **3** (COMP) (de clicar) click.

clister *m* (MED) enema, clyster.

clitóris *m* (ANAT) clitoris.

clivagem *f* (MIN) cleavage; **2** (separação) split of (minerals).

clonagem (BIOL) cloning; **2** (fig) ~ **de cartões** (falsificar) cloning of credit cards.

clonar *vt* (BIOL) to clone.

clone *m,f* (BIOL) clone.

cloreto *m* (QUÍM) chloride; **2** (para roupa) bleaching powder.

clorídrico,-a *adj* hydrochloric.

clorofórmio *m* chloroform.

clube *m* club; **2** association.

coabitar *vi* to live together as a couple; cohabit.

coação *f* filtering.

coa(c)ção *f* coercion, compulsion, force.

coado,-a *adj* filtered, strained; **2** *f* **luz** ~ dim light; **3** *m* **ferro** ~ pig-iron.

coador *m* strainer, colander.

coadaquirente *m,f* joint purchaser.

coadunar *vt* to join; **2** (ideias, propostas) to combine; **3** get along; ♦ ~-**se** *vr* harmonize, coordinate; **2** ~ **com** to tie in with.

coagir *vt* to coerce, compel.

coagular *vt/vi* (MED, BIOL) to coagulate; to congeal, clot; **2** (milk) curdle; ♦ ~-**se** *vr* to congeal.

coágulo *m* clot.

coalhar *vt/vi* to curd, curdle; ♦ ~-**se** *vr* to curdle.

coar *vt* to strain, filter.

co-autor,-ora, coautor,-ora *m,f* co-author.

coaxar *vi* to croak.

cobaia *f* (ZOOL) guinea pig.

cobarde *m,f* coward; **2** timid; **3** treacherous; ♦ *adj inv* cowardly; shy; treacherous.

coberto,-a (irr pp de **cobrir**) *adj* covered; **2** *f* cover, covering; **3** (NÁUT) deck.

cobertor *m* blanket; **2** cover.

cobertura *f* covering; **2** cover; **cheque sem** ~ bouncing cheque, without cover; **3** coverage (jornais); **4 dar** ~ **a** (em delito) to cover for/give cover to sb; **5** (CONSTR) roof.

cobiça *f* greed; **2** envy; **3** lust.

cobiçar *vt* to covet.

cobiçoso,-a *adj* covetous; greedy; envious.

cobra *f* (ZOOL) snake; **2** serpent; **3** (fig) (pessoa má) a snake in the grass; IDIOM **dizer ~s e lagartos de alguém** to speak ill of sb.

cobra-capelo *f* hooded rattlesnake; **2** ~-**cascavel** *f* rattlesnake; **3** ~-**cuspideira** *f* spitting snake; **4** ~ **do mar** sea serpent.

cobrador,-ora *m* ticket collector; **2** ~ **de impostos** tax collector.

cobrança *f* collection.

cobrar *vt* to collect; **2** to charge; **ele cobrou-me a mais** (dinheiro) he charged me too much; **3** to recover (money).

cobre *m* copper.

cobrir *vt* to cover; **2** to hide, conceal; **3** to protect.

coca *f* (planta) coca; **2** cocaine; **3 à** ~ (fam) (estar à espreita) to be on the look-out.

coça *f* scratching; **2** (sova) thrashing.

coca-bichinhos *m,f sg/pl* fusspot, nitpicker; ♦ *adj* fussy.

cocada *f* coconut sweet.

cocar *vt* (espiar) to spy on.

coçar *vt* to scratch; ♦ ~-**se** *vr* to scratch o.s.

cócaras (Vd: **cócoras**).

cócegas *fpl* tickling; **fazer** ~ to tickle sb; **ter** ~ to be ticklish; **2** (fig) impatience, restlessness; **estar com** ~ (fig) to be impatient, restless, fidgety.

coceira *f* itch, itching.

coche *m* coach, carriage.

cocheira *f* stable; **2** coach house.

cocheiro *m* coachman.

cochichar *vi* to whisper.

cochicho *m* whisper; **2** (ZOOL) skylark; **3** (fig) tiny house; **4** child's toy.

cochilar *vi* to snooze, doze off; **2** to take a nap.

coco *m* coconut; **2 chapéu de** ~ bowler hat; **3** (fig) head, nut; **4** (fig) **comer do** ~ to get a beating; **5** (BR) lots of money.

cocó (BR: -**cô**) *m* (children's language) poo; **fazer** ~ to do, have a poo.

cócoras *fpl*: **de** ~ squatting.

côdea *f* (pão) crust; **2** (queijo) rind.

codificação *f* (COMP) code; **2** (JUR) codification.

codificar *vt* to codify.

código *m* code; **2** (JUR) ~ **civil/comercial** civil law; **3 C** ~ **sobre o rendimento** Corporate Income Tax Code (CIRC); **4 C**~ **de Pessoas Singulares** (CIRS) Individual Tax Code; **5** (de normas) code of practice; **6** ~-**postal**, *m* postal code, postcode.

codorniz *f* (ZOOL) quail.

coeficiente *m* coefficient; **2** factor; **3** ratio.

coeiro *m* (ant.) baby's nappy (UK); diaper (US); (Vd: **fralda**).

coelho *m* rabbit; ~ **bravo** wild rabbit; **2** (CULIN) ~ **à caçadora** Portuguese rabbit stew.

coentro *m* (BOT) coriander.

coerção *f* coercion, compulsion.

coercivo,-a *adj* coercive.

coerência *f* coherence.

coerente *adj inv* coherent.

coesão *f* cohesion.

coeso,-a *adj* (união) coesive, coerente.

coetâneo,-a *adj* contemporary.

coexistência *f* coexistence.

coexistir *vi* to coexist.

coerção *f* coercion; *(JUR)* enforcement, constraint.

coercivo,-a *adj (compulsivo)* compulsive; **2** *(JUR) (medidas)* restraining, constraining.

cofiar *vt* to smooth, *(cabelo, bigode)* to stroke.

cofre *m* safe, strongbox; **2** *(tesouro)* coffer; **os ~s públicos** the public coffers.

cogitar *vt/vi (pensar muito)* to cogitate, think about; **2** *(considerar, reflectir)* to ponder; **~ sobre** think about, deliberate.

cognato,-a *m,f (parente)* blood relation; kindred; **2** *(LÍNG)* cognate.

cognitivo,-a *adj* cognitive.

cognome *m* cognomen; *(algunha)* nickname; **D. (Dom) Heurique por ~ o Navegador** Henry (nicknamed) 'The Navigator'.

cogumelo *m* mushroom; **~ venenoso** toadstool.

coibição *f* restraint, restriction; **2** inhibition.

coibir *vt* to restrain; **~ de** to restrain from; ♦ **~-se** *vr* **(de** to abstain from).

COI *(abr de* **Comité Olímpico Internacional)** IOC.

coice *m* kick; **dar ~s** to kick back; **2** *(de arma)* recoil; **o ~ da espingarda** the kick of the rifle; **3** *(fig, fam) (ingratidão)* ingratitude, no thanks; **dei-lhe uma casa, mas ele pagou-me com um ~** I gave him a house, but he gave me no thanks; **4** *(fig, fam)* bad manners, rude; **ele dá ~s a toda a gente** he is rude to everyone.

coifa *f (touca para o cabelo)* coif; **2** *(de um projéctil)* cap of a projectile.

coima *f (multa)* penalty, fine.

Coimbra *npr* Coimbra; *university city in Portugal.*

coimbrão, coimbrã *m,f adj* from Coimbra; Coimbra; **a história ~** Coimbra's history.

coincidência *f* coincidence.

coincidir *vi* to coincide; to agree.

coisa *f (objecto)* thing; **que ~ é essa?** what kind of thing is that?; **2** matter; problem; **que ~!** what a problem!; **3** *(assunto, negócios)* things; **a ~ vai mal** things are going badly; **4** *(mistério)* **há cada coisa!** strange things happen!; **5** *(motivo)* personal reasons; **cá por ~s, não quero dizer-te** I have my reasons for not telling you; ♦ *adv* **coisa de** *(aproximadamente)* about; **há ~ de meia hora** about half an hour ago; **mais ~ menos ~** more or less, sooner or later; **alguma/qualquer ~** something; **outra ~** something else; IDIOM **dizer ~s e loisas** to say this and that; **~s do arco-da-velha** old wives' tales; incredible things; **não dizer ~ com ~** not make any sense; **aqui há ~** I smell a rat.

coisíssima *f:* **~ nenhuma** *(pop)* nothing at all, not one thing.

coiso *m (pop)* geezer, chap; **aquele ~ deve-me dinheiro pelos livros** that geezer owes me money for the books; **2** thing, thingy; **3** *(fam);* Mr. So-and-So, what's it; **o ~ lá da loja** the what's-the-name who works in the shop.

coitadinho,-a *m,f exc (fam)* poor you!.

coitado *m:* **um ~** a cuckold husband; ♦ **coitado,-a** *adj* poor, wretched; ♦ *exc* **~!** poor dear!; **coitada da mulher!** *(ter pena)* poor woman; **~ de mim!** poor me!

> **Coitado, coitadinho** expresses sympathy in Portuguese and is frequently used; whereas in English, the use of 'poor you, poor girl' is not frequent and is considered to be impolite or too familiar.

coito *m* intercourse, coitus.

cola *f* glue, gum; **2** tail; **3** *(fig)* trail, track.

colaboração *f* collaboration.

colaborar *vi* to collaborate.

colapso *m* collapse.

colar *n* necklace; **2** *(de camisa, casaco)* collar; **3** *(insígnia)* ribbon; ♦ *vt (pôr cola em papel, selo, fragmentos de porcelana/vidro)* to stick, glue (on); **2** *(moldar)* to make cling (to the body) **o suor colou-lhe a roupa ao corpo** the perspiration made her clothes stick to her body; **3** *(fig) (encostar ao ouvido, corpo)* to press; **4** *(vinho)* to purify; ♦ *vi (aderir)* to stick; ♦ **~-se** *vr (pegar-se)* to stick; **2** *(ajustar-se)* to cling; **3** *(encostar-se)* to press against; **4** *(fig, fam) (instalar-se)* to settle down.

colarinho *m* man's shirt collar; **2 ~ postiço** detached collar; **agarrar alguém pelo ~** to grab someone by the collar;

colcha *f* bedspread.

colchão *m* mattress.

colchete *m* clasp, fastening; **2** *(ganho)* hook; **3** square bracket; **4 ~ de gancho** hook and eye; **5 ~ de pressão** press stud.

coldre *m* holster.

cole(c)ção *f* collection.

cole(c)cionar *vt* to collect.

cole(c)ta *f (dinheiro)* collection; **2** taxable income.

cole(c)tar *vt* to tax; **2** to levy.

cole(c)tável *adj inv* taxable.

cole(c)tividade *f* community; **~ recreativa** recreation association.

cole(c)tivo,-a *m,f* group; ♦ *adj* collective; joint.

colega *m,f* colleague.

colegial *m,f* college student.

colégio *m (escola privada, não da universidade)* private school; **2** *(grupo de intelectuais)* college; **3** *(de clérigos)* chapter; **4 ~ de eleitores** electoral college.

cólera *f* anger; rage; *(MED)* cholera.

colérico,-a *m,f (MED)* cholera patient; ♦ *adj* angry; furious.

colete *m* waistcoat; **2** corset; **3 ~-de-forças** straitjacket; **4 ~ de salvação** *(BR:* **salva-vidas)** life jacket; **~ à prova de bala** bulletproof vest.

colheita *f (AGR)* harvest; **2** crop.

colher¹ *vt* to gather, **2** pick; **3** to catch; ♦ *vi* to reap; **quem semeia, colhe** as you sow, so shall you reap.

colher² *f* spoon; **2** *(para servir a sopa)* ladle; **3 ~ de pedreiro** trowel.

colherada *f* spoonful.

colhida *f* goring (by bulls).

colibri *m* hummingbird.

cólica *f (MED)* colic.

colidir *vi*: ~ **com** to collide with, crash into.

coligação *f* coalition.

coligir *vt* to collect; to compile.

colina *f* hill; **2** *(QUÍM)* *f* choline.

colisão *f* collision, crash; **2** *(conflito)* clash; **3** *(desacordo)* disagreement.

coliseu *m* coliseum.

colite *f* colitis.

collants *mpl* tights *(UK)*; pantyhose *(US)*.

colmaça *f* thatched cottage.

colmar *vt* to thatch (a house).

colmatar *vt* to repair, fill, cover; ~ **uma brecha** to fill (up) patch a crack; **2** *(fig) (corrigir erro, lapso)* put right; ~ **um erro** to correct/cover up a mistake.

colmeal *m* apiary.

colmeia *f* beehive; **2** *(fig) (muita gente)* crowd.

colmilho *m (em certos animais)* canine tooth; **2** tusk; **3** fang.

colo *m* neck; area above the breasts; **2** *(regaço)* lap; **no** ~ on one's lap; **ela estava no** ~ **dele** she was on his lap; **4** *(nos braços)* in arms; **levar a criança ao** ~ to carry the child in one's arms.

colocação *f* placing; job, position.

colocar *vt* to place, position; **2** to find a job for; **3** *(COM)* to market.

Colômbia *npr* Colombia; **a** ~ Colombia.

colombiano,-a *m,f adj* Colombian.

Colombo *npr* (= **Cristóvão Colombo**) a Portuguese navigator, originally Genoese *(Vd:* **Madeira***)*.

cólon *m* colon.

colónia *(BR:* -**lô**-*) f (territory)* colony; **2** settlement; ~ **balnear** spa resort; ~ **de férias** summer camp; ~ **de formigas** community of ants; **água-de-C**~ *f (perfume)* eau de Cologne.

colonização *f* colonization.

colonizador-ora *m,f* colonist; ♦ *adj* colonizing; **colonizar** *vt* to colonize.

colono *m* settler.

coloquial *adj inv* colloquial.

colóquio *m* colloquium; seminar; **2** discussion.

coloração *f (de colorir)* dyeing; **2** colouring.

colorau *m* paprika *(em pó)*; **2** ~ **doce** *(não picante)* mild paprika.

colorido *m* colouring, colour; **2** vivacity; brightness; **alimentação do** ~ *f* exciting meals/food; **3 escola** ~**a** colourful school.

colorir *vt* to colour, tint, dye; **2** *(fig)* brighten, highlight; **3** *(fig) (desgosto)* attenuate, disguise; **4** *(mudar de cor)* to turn.

coluna *f* column; pillar; ~ **vertebral** spine.

com *prep* with; **2 sonhar** ~ to dream of; **3 contar** ~ to count on; **gastar** ~ *(coisas)* to spend on; **4 isso é** ~ **ele** that's up to him; **5** ~ **medo** in fear; **6 estar** ~ **fome/sede/pressa/razão** to be hungy/thirsty/in a hurry/right; **7 ela está** ~ **setenta anos** she is seventy years old; **8** ~ **quem você viaja?** whom are you travelling with?; **9** *(intenção)* ~ **vistas a** with a view to; ♦ *exc* ~ **que então**! so!; **co'os diabos!** damn!; ♦ *adv* ~ **certeza** for sure, of course; ~ **vagar** slowly.

coma *m (MED)* coma; **estado de** ~ comatose state.

comadre *f (tratamento entre os pais e a madrinha da criança)* the godmother of your child or vice-versa; **2** *(pej)* gossiper; **3** *(fam, reg) (tratamento entre comparsas)* friend, mate.

comandante *m (MIL)* commander; **2** leader, commandant; **3** *(NÁUT, AER)* captain; **4** *(polícia)* chief officer, *(título)* officer; **5** ~ **dos bombeiros** fire chief.

comandar *vt* to command, give orders, rule; **2** *(dirigir)* to head; **3** *(sobrepor-se, dominar)* to dominate; overlook; command over; **o castelo comanda uma bela paisagem** the castle commands a beautiful view.

comandita *f* commercial partnership that includes one or two sleeping patners; a kind of temporary joint-venture.

comanditário,-a sleeping partner in a 'comandita' arrangement.

comando *m (MIL) (ger)* command; **2** *(MEC)* control; **alavanca de** ~ joystick; **3** *(TV)* ~ **à distância** remote control; **comandos** *mpl (MIL)* commandos.

comarca *f* administrative region; **2** judicial district presided by a judge; **tribunal da** ~ district court.

combate *m* combat, fight; **2** battle; **3** ~ **de boxe** boxing match; **4** ~ **à/contra** fight against fraude.

combatente *m,f* combatant, fighter.

combater *vt* to combat; ♦ *vi* to fight, struggle; ♦ ~**-se** *vr* to fight one another; **2** to compete; **3** to be at war.

combinação *f* combination; **2** arrangement; **3** scheme; **4** *(QUÍM)* compound; **5** *(vestuário)* petticoat.

combinado,-a *adj* combined; **foi um passeio** ~ this trip was already planned/arranged; ~! agreed!; arranged, planned; **pronto, está tudo combinado pr'a amanhã** O.K. that's settled for tomorrow.

combinar *vt (colours)* to combine, match; ~ **com algo** to go with sth; **2** *(plan)* to arrange; agree; fix *(data, encontro)*.

comboio *m (EP)* train; **2** convoy; ~ **aéreo** air convoy.

combustão *f* combustion.

combustível *(pl:* -**íveis***) m* fuel.

começar *vt/vi* to begin, start, commence; ~ **a falar**, *(BR:* ~ **falando***)* to begin to speak; **2** ~ **por** to begin by.

começo *m* beginning, start, commencement.

comédia *f* comedy; **2** play.

comediante *m,f* comedian.

comedido,-a *adj* moderate; discreet.

comedir-se *vr* to control o.s.; **2** to behave modestly.

comemoração *f* commemoration, celebration.

comemorar *vt* to celebrate, commemorate.

comenda *f (benefício)* badge, emblem; **2** insígnia.

comendador *m* commander; knight, **C**~ **da Ordem de D. Henrique** Knight Commander of the Order of Prince Henry.

comensal *m,f* dinner guest.

comentador,-ora *m,f* commentator, critic; **2** broadcaster.

comentar *vt* to comment on/upon; **2** to remark; **3** find fault with.

comentário *m* comment, remark; **2** commentary.

comer *vt* to eat; ~ **à farta/tripa-forra** to eat to one's heart content; ~ **como um abade** to eat like a horse; **2** *(xadrez, damas)* to take, capture; **3** *(corroer)* eat away, corrode; **4** *(fig) (suprimir)* to swallow *(palavras)*; **5** *(fig) (vulg) (sexo)* to bang *(slang, vulg)*; ♦ *vi (alimentar-se)* to eat; **dar de ~ a alguém** to feed sb.

comercial *adj inv* commercial; business.

comercialização *f* comercialization; marketing.

comercializar *vt* to market.

comerciante *m,f* trader; merchant; businessman/woman.

comerciar *vi* to trade; ~ **com** to trade with.

comércio *m* commerce; trade; **2** *(mercado commercial)* **mercado de** ~ business; ~ **de retalho** retail; ~ **por atacado** wholesale.

comes *mpl (fam):* ~ **e bebes** food and drink; **ela gosta de** ~ **e bebes** she is fond of eating and drinking (parties).

comestível *adj inv* edible; **comestíveis** *mpl* foodstuff (s).

cometa *m (ASTRON)* comet.

cometer *vt* to commit; perpetrate *(delito)*; **2** ~ **um erro** to make a mistake; ♦ ~**-se** *vr* to venture.

cometimento *m (infracção)* crime; action; ~ **indigno** vile action; **2** undertaking; *(empreendimento)* enterprise; **3** attack, assault.

comezana, comezaina *f (pop)* a great repast (much food and drink).

comichão *f* itch, itching.

comício *m* political meeting; **2** public rally; ~ **relâmpago** short public rally.

cómico,-a *(BR: cô-) m,f (TEAT,TV)* comedian; *(o que faz rir)* the funny side of; ♦ *adj* comic(al); *(divertido)* funny, amusing.

comida *f* food; **2** meal; **3** ~ **para fora** take-away food; ~ **caseira** home cooking.

comigo *pron* with me; with myself; **a criança está** ~ the child is with me; **esse assunto é** ~ **mesmo** that matter is my own responsibility; **pensei** ~ I thought to myself.

comilão,-lona *m,f (glutão)* glutton; **2** *(pessoa exploradora)* bloodsucker; ♦ *adj* greedy, gluttonous.

cominho *m (BOT) (CULIN) (planta e semente)* cumin; **cominhos** *mpl* cumin.

comiseração *f* commiseration; **2** pity.

comissão *f* commission; **2** committee; ~ **executiva** *(de uma associação)* council, executive committee.

comissário *m* commissioner; **2** *(COM)* agent; **3** ~ **de bordo** cabin steward; **4** ~ **da polícia** chief constable.

comité *(BR: -tê) m* committee.

comitiva *f* retinue, train; *(séquito)* entourage.

como *adv* as; ~ **quiser** as you like; **2** *(de que modo)* how; ~ **assim?** how so? how do you mean?; **a** ~ **estão as uvas?** how much are the grapes (now)?; ~ **disse?** *(o que disse)* sorry? pardon? what?; **3** *(visto que)* seeing that/as, because, since; ~ **ela não come pudim, eu dei-lhe fruta;** seeing that she doesn't eat pudding, I gave her fruit; **4** *(porque, conforme)* because, as, according to; ~ **eu dizia** as I was saying; **5** *(comparativo)* like; **ela é** ~ **a mãe;** she is like her mother; **tão ...** ~ as ... as; **5** and; **tanto ele** ~ **eu** both he and I; *(quanto, quão)* ~ **me magoou a tua resposta!** how your answer hurt me!; **6** *(assim)* such as; like; **tenores** ~ **Plácido** tenores like Plácido; **tal** ~ namely, such as; ♦ *conj* ~ **que** as if; ~ **que por magia** as if by magic; **assim** ~ **assim** in that case; **tal** ~ namely, such as; ~ **não!** but of course! why not!; **seja** ~ **for** be as it may; whatever may be.

comoção *f* commotion; ~ **nervosa** shock.

cómoda *(BR: -ô-) f* chest of drawers.

comodidade *f* comfort; suitability.

comodista *adj (pessoa)* fond of comfort, self-indulgent; *(egoísta)* selfish (person).

cómodo,-a *(BR: cô-) adj* comfortable; **2** convenient; **3** suitable.

comovedor,-ora, comovente *adj inv (cena, gesto, palavras)* moving, poignant.

comover *vt* to move; ♦ ~**-se** *vr* to be moved, overcome with emotion.

comovido,-a *adj* moved, touched.

compa(c)to,-a *adj* compact; **2** thick; **3** solid.

compadecer *vt* to move *(alguém)*; ♦ ~**-se** *vr:* ~ **de** *(ter pena)* take pity on; to sympathize.

compadecido,-a *adj* sympathetic, compassionate.

compadecimento *m* sympathy; pity.

compadre *m* relationship between the godfather and the parents of one's godchild, and vice-versa; **2** *(fam) (amigo)* buddy, pal, mate.

compaixão *m* compassion, pity; mercy.

companheiro,-a *m,f* friend; **2** *(de amor)* partner; **3** *(fam)* buddy, mate; ~ **de trabalho** fellow-worker; ~ **de viagem** fellow traveller.

companhia *f (COM)* company, firm; **2** *(social)* company; **3 fazer** ~ **a alguém** to keep sb company; ♦ **em** ~ **de** accompanied by, along with.

comparação *f* comparison.

comparar *vt* to compare (**a** to; **com** with); ~ **a** to liken to; **comparei o bebé a uma flor** I compared the baby to a flower; **eu comparo uma coisa com a outra** I compare one thing with another; ♦ ~**-se** *vr:* ~ **com** to put o.s. on a level with; to compare o.s. to.

comparativo *m (gram)* comparative; ♦ **comparativo,-a** *adj* comparative.

comparável *adj inv* comparable.

comparecer *vt (tribunal)* to appear (**perante,** before); **2** to show up; **3** to attend.

comparecimento *m* attendance; presence.

comparsa *m,f (TEAT)* extra, stand-in, bit part player; **2** *(cúmplice)* accomplice.

compartilha *f* share, partaking.

compartilhar *vt* to share (**de** in) participate (**de** in); ~ **com alguém** to share with sb.

compartimento *m* compartment; **2** room.

compartir *vt* to share out.

compassado,-a *adj* measured; **2** moderate; **3** regular.

compassar *vt* to measure with compasses; **2** *(MÚS)* time; beat.

compasso *m (NAÚT, MAT)* a pair of compasses; **fora do ~** out of time; **ir a ~** to keep time; **~ binário** binary measure; **a ~** in rhythm.

compatibilidade *f* compatibility.

compatível *adj inv* compatible.

compatriota *m,f* fellow countryman/countrywoman, compatriot.

compelir *vt* to force, compel.

compêndio *m* compendium; textbook.

compenetração *f* conviction.

compenetrar *vt* to convince; ♦ **~-se** *vr* to convince o.s. (**de** of)

compensação *f* compensation; amends; **em ~** on the other hand.

compensar *vt* to make up for, compensate; to offset, counter-balance.

compensatório,-a *adj* compensatory.

competência *f* competence; **2** ability; **3** *(JUR)* legal capacity; **isso não é da minha ~** that is not up to me; not my remit; **4** skill.

competente *adj inv* competent; **2** suitable; **3** proper; **4** lawful.

competição *f* competition; contest.

competidor,-ora *m,f* rival; competitor, contestant.

competir *vi* to compete; to be one's responsibility; **compete-lhe informá-la** it is for you/up to you to inform her.

competitivo,-a *adj* competitive.

compincha *m (fam)* camarada, good friend, good chap/sort; **ele é um velho ~ meu** he is an old colleague of mine.

complacência *f (condescendência)* complacency.

complacente *adj inv* obliging, complacent.

compleição *f (constitution)* build, frame; **2** *(temperamento)* temperament, disposition.

complementar *adj inv* complementary.

complemento *m* complement.

completamente *adv* completely.

completar *vt* to complete, finish; **2** to fill up; **3** *(idade)* to reach; **ao ~ os quarenta, ela decidiu demitir-se do trabalho** on reaching fourty, she decided to leave her job.

completo,-a *m,f* complete, whole; ♦ *adj* full (up) complete; ♦ **por ~** *adv* completely.

complexado,-a *m,f (pessoa)* person with complex; ♦ *adj* hung-up.

complexidade *f* complexity.

complexo,-a *m,f (FIL)* complex; **~ de Édipo** Oedipus complex; **2** *(conjunto de estruturas)* complex, estate; ♦ *adj* complex; complicated.

complicação *f* complication; difficulty.

complicado,-a *adj* complicated.

complicar *vt* to complicate, make difficult; ♦ **~-se** *vr* to become complicated; **2** *(plot)* to thicken.

componente *adj inv* component.

compor *vt (MÚS)* to compose, to write; **2** to comprise; **3** to form; **4** *(TYPO)* to typeset; **5** to arrange; **ela compôs as almofadas** she arranged

the cushions; ♦ **~-se** *vr* to calm down; **2 ~ de** to be made up of, be composed of.

comporta *f* floodgate, canal lock; **2** small door in the wine press.

comportamento *m* behaviour; conduct; **mau ~** misbehaviour; misconduct; **~ do mercado** *(FIN)* market behaviour.

comportar *vt* to put up with, bear; **2** *(permitir)* withstand, take; **3** *(conter)* hold; **o elevador não comporta tanta gente** the lift cannot hold so many people; **4** *(implicar)* imply; ♦ **~-se** *vr* to behave; **~ mal** misbehave, behave badly.

composição *f* composition; arrangement; **2** typesetting.

compositor,-ora *m,f (MÚS, LITER)* composer; **2** *(TIPO)* typesetter.

composto *m (QUÍM)* compound; **2** mixture; ♦ **composto,-a** *adj* composite, compound; **~ de** made up of, consisting of; **2** *(reservado) (pessoa)* reserved, composed; **3** *(bem vestido) (pessoa)* well-turned up, well-dressed.

compostura *f (arranjo)* mending, repair; **2** *(porte, seriedade)* composure.

compota *f* jam; **~ de laranja** orange marmalade.

compra *f* purchase; **fazer ~s** to go shopping.

comprador,-ora *m,f* buyer, purchaser.

comprar *vt* to buy, purchase; IDIOM **~ gato por lebre** to buy a pig in a poke; **~ por tuta e meia** to buy sth for a song.

comprazer *vi* to please; **2** to comply with.

compreender *vt* to understand; **2** to grasp; **3** to comprise, consist of.

compreensão *f* understanding, comprehension.

compreensível *adj inv* understandable, comprehensible.

compreensivo,-a *adj* understanding.

compressa *f (FARM)* compress.

compressão *f* compression.

comprido,-a *adj* long; **ao ~** lengthways.

comprimento *m* length.

comprimido *m,f (FARM)* pill, tablet; ♦ **comprimido,-a** *adj* compressed.

comprimir *vt* to compress; **2** to squeeze; **3** to condense.

comprometedor,-ora *adj* compromising.

comprometer *vt (prejudicar)* to compromise; put at risk *(plan)*; **2** *(por compromisso)* to bind *(pessoas)*; ♦ **~-se** *vr:* **~ a** to undertake, to pledge, to promise to *(alguém)*.

comprometido,-a *adj (namoro)* spoken for, going out with sb; **2** involved; pledged.

comprometido,-a *adj* under obligation, promise; **2** implicated; **3** *(namoro)* engaged.

compromisso *m (JUR)* promise, pledge; **2** obligation; **sem ~** without obligation; **3** *(comprometimento, data)* appointment, engagement, commitment; **tenho um ~ às cinco horas** I have an engagement, appointment at 5 o'clock; **4** agreement; **5** *(encargos)* commitment, debt.

comprovação *f* proof, evidence; **2** *(COM)* receipt, voucher.

comprovar *vt* to prove; **2** to confirm.

comprovativo *m* proof; ♦ **comprovativo,-a** *adj (documento)* of proof.

compulsivo,-a *adj* compulsive.
compulsório,-a *adj* compulsory.
compunção *f* compunction.
computação *f* computation.
computador *m* computer.
computar *vt* to compute; to calculate.
cômputo *m* computation.
comum *m* (*norma*) usual; usual thing; **fora do ~** unusual, out of the ordinary; ♦ a*dj* common; **2** ordinary, usual; **3 ter algo em ~** to have sth in common.
comuna *f* (*governo revolucionário em Paris 1875*) Paris commune; **2** *m,f* (*fam, pej*) (*partidário do comunismo*) red, Commie.
comungar *vi* to take communion; **2** (*fig*) **~ em** to share.
comunhão *f* communion; **2** (*REL*) Holy Communion; **3** (*JUR*) **~ de bens** (*casamento*) joint matrimonial property.
comunicação *f* communication; **2** information; **3** message.
comunicado *m* report; communiqué.
comunicador *m* (*transmissor*) transmitter.
comunicador,-ora *m,f* (*pessoa*) sociable; **2** TV interviewer; ♦ *adj* communicative.
comunicar *vt* to report; **2** to inform; **3** to communicate, broadcast; **4** to tell; **5** to join; **a cozinha comunica com a sala de jantar** the kitchen joins the dining-room; ♦ *vi* to communicate.
comunicativo,-a *adj* communicative; **2** talkative; **3** (*pessoa*) outgoing, sociable.
comunidade *f* community; **a C~ Europeia** European Community; **2 ~ de interesses** interests in common.
comunismo *m* communism.
comunista *adj inv* communist.
comunitário,-a *adj* (*relativo à comunidade*) community; **2** (*propriedade*) communal; **3** (*POL*) comum.
comutador *m* (*ELECT*) switch.
comutação *f* (*JUR*) commutation, reduction.
comutar *vt* (*JUR*) (*sentença*) to commute, reduce; **2** (*trocar*) to exchange; **3** (*ELECT*) (*reverter corrente*) commutate.

> **Comutar** not in the sense of '**commuting**' between places, which is: **fazer o trajecto entre**.

comutável *adj inv* commutable.
concatenar *vt* to link together, to concatenate.
côncavo,-a *m,f* hollow; ♦ *adj* concave; **2** (*cavado*) hollow.
conceber *vt* to conceive; **2** to have the idea, create; ♦ *vi* to become pregnant.
concebível *adj inv* (*imaginável*) conceivable.
conceção, concepção *f* conception; **2** (*noção*) idea; concept; **3** perception; **4** creation.
conceder *vt* (*dar, outorgar*) to grant, give, concede; **2** (*permitir*) to allow, concede; **3** (*admitir*) to admit that.
conceito *m* concept, idea; **2** reputation; **3** opinion.
conceituação *f* conceptualization; **2** (*avaliação*) rating.
conceituado,-a *adj* well thought of, highly regarded.

concelhio *adj* (*relativo a concelho*) municipal.
concelho *m* (*munipício*) council, Town Hall; **2** (*GEO, POL*) municipal authority for the region.
concentração *f* concentration; **2** aglomeration of people.
concentrado *m* (*tomate, garlic*) concentrate, paste; ♦ **concentrado,-a** *adj* concentrated; **2** centralized; **3** immersed; **4** gathered together; **5** (*ódio*) ingrained.
concentrar *vt* to concentrate; **2** to focus; **3** to bring together; **4** (*molho*) thicken; ♦ **~-se** *vr*: **~ em** to concentrate on.
concepção (*Vd: conceção*).
conceptual, concetual *adj inv* concetual.
concernente *adj inv* concerning; related to; about.
concertação *f* agreement; **C~** (*POL*) Social Agreement.
concertado,-a *adj* concerted; **um esforço ~** a concerted effort; **2** planned; **3** sensible; **4** in tune.
concertar *vt* to agree on; **2** to adjust; **3** to plan; ♦ *vi* **~ em** to agree to.
concerto *m* (*MÚS*) concert, concerto; **2** accord; agreement.
concessão *f* concession; permission; grant.
concessionário,-a *m,f* concessionaire.
concha *f* (*ZOOL*) shell; **meter-se na ~** to go into one's shell; **2** (*colher grande para a sopa*) ladle.
conchavar *vt*: **~ em** to fit in; to adjust; **2 ~ com** to conspire with; **conchavo** connivance.
conciliação *f* conciliation; **2** (*entre 2 pessoas*) reconciliation.
conciliador,-ora *m,f* conciliator; ♦ *adj* conciliatory.
conciliar *vt* to conciliate; **2** to reconcile.
conciliatório,-a *adj* conciliatory.
concílio *m* (*REL*) council.
conciso,-a *adj* brief, concise.
concitar *vt* to stir up; **2** rouse to action; **3** to instigate.
concludente *adj inv* conclusive; convincing.
concluir *vt* to end, conclude; **2 ~ um negócio** to close a business deal; ♦ *vi* to deduce.
conclusão *f* end, conclusion; **2** inference; **chegar a uma ~** to come to a decision/conclusion.
conclusivo,-a *adj* conclusive; final.
concluso (*pp de* **concluir**) *adj* (*JUR*) settled, concluded.
concomitante *adj inv* concomitant.
concordância *f* agreement; harmony.
concordar *vi* to agree; to concur; **não concordo!** I disagree!
concórdia *f* harmony; **2** agreement.
concordata *f* bankrupt's certificate; **2** (*REL*) Concordat.
concorrência *f* competition.
concorrente *m,f* competitor.
concorrer *vi* to compete; **2** to run as a candidate; **3 ~ a um lugar** to run as a candidate; to apply for a place, position, contest; **4 ~ para** to contribute to.
concorrido,-a *adj* well-attended.
concretizar *vt* to make real; ♦ **~-se** *vr* to come true; **2** to be realized; **os meus sonhos realizaram-se** my dreams have come true.
concreto *m* (*CONSTR*) concrete; **~ armado** reinforced concrete; ♦ **concreto,-a** *adj* concrete; **2** real; **3** solid; ♦ *adv* **em ~** basically.

concubina *f* concubine.

concupiscência *f* lust.

concurso *m* competition, contest; **2** *(Govt)* public tender; **3** *(multidão)* throng, flow, crowd; **4** concorrence.

concussão *f* concussion; **2** *(JUR)* *(extorsão)* extortion.

condado *m* *(dignidade de um conde)* earldom; **2** *(divisão administrativa da G.B.)* county.

condão *m* talent; **2** *(dom)* gift; magic power; **varinha de ~** magic wand.

conde *m* count, earl.

condecoração *f* decoration; medal.

condecorar *vt* to decorate; to distinguish.

condenação *f* condemnation; **2** *(JUR)* conviction; **3** *(REL)* **~ eterna** damnation.

condenado,-a *adj* condemned; **2** *(JUR)* sentenced; convicted.

condenar *vt* to condemn; **2** *(JUR)* to sentence, to convict.

condensação *f* condensation, thickness.

condescendência *f* acquiescence, compliance, consent.

condescender *vi* to acquiesce, agree, comply, consent.

condessa *f* countess.

condestável *m* constable; *(HIST)* Chief Constable, Supreme Commander of the Army.

O Condestável refers to Nuno Álvares Pereira, the great Portuguese soldier of the 14th century, known for his war tactics and victories, as well as for his kindness towards the vanquished.

condição *f* *(ger)* condition, state; **em boa ~** in good condition/state; **2** rank, status, standing; **~ social** social standing; **com a ~ de que** provided that; **sob ~** on condition; ♦ **condições** *fpl* terms, conditions; **~ costumadas** usual conditions; **~ de seguro** warranty; **~ de venda** terms of sale; **~ de vida** living conditions; **em boas ~ físicas** in good form, fit; **estar em ~ de fazer** to be able to do; **pôr em ~** to put in order; **sob ~** *(COM, JUR)* subject to/under certain conditions.

condicionado,-a *adj* conditioned; **ar ~** air conditioning.

condicional *m* *(modo verbal)* conditional; ♦ *adj inv* conditional; **2** *(JUR)* **liberdade ~** *(JUR)* parole.

condicionamento *m* conditioning.

condigno,-a *adj* worthy, well deserved; **2** fitting, adequate.

condimentar *vt* *(CULIN)* to season; **2** to spice up.

condimento *m* seasoning.

condiscípulo,-a *m,f* class, schoolmate.

condizente *adj inv*: **~ com** in keeping with.

condizer *vi* to match, go well together; **não ~ to** clash.

condoer *vt* to arouse pity, compassion; ♦ **~-se** *vr* to have pity, feel compassion for; **2** to sympathize with.

condoído,-a *adj* *(compaixão)* touched, moved.

condolência(s) *f* *(pl)* condolence, sympathy; **apresentar ~s** to offer condolences.

condomínio *m* *(conjunto de casas)* condominium; **3** *(POL)* condominium.

condução *f* driving; **carta de ~** driving licence *(UK)* driver's license *(US)*; **2** transport; **~ grátis** carriage free; **3** *(FÍS)* conduction; **4** *(direcção)* management, leadership.

conducente *adj inv* conducive (**a** to).

conduta *f* *(procedimento)* conduct, behaviour; **2** *(de pessoas)* conveyance; **3** conduit, duct; **~ de caldeira** flue of boiler; **~ de carvão** coaling shoot, bunker pipe.

conduto *m* *(tubo, cano)* duct, tube, pipe; **2** *(canal)* conduit, channel, canal; **3** *(ANAT)* channel; **4** *(pop)* any food spread on bread.

condutor *m* *(ELECT)* conductor; **2** cable, wire, **~ sem carga** dead wire; **3 ~ de alimentação** feeder; **4** *(de veículos)* driver; ♦ *adj (que dirige)* leading.

conduzir *vt/vi* to drive; **2** *(dirigir)* to guide, manage; **3** *(orquestra)* conduct; ♦ *vi* **~ a** *(levar)* to lead to; **a bebida conduziu-o à morte** drink led him to the grave; ♦ **~-se** *vr* to conduct o.s., behave; **2 ~ mal** to misbehave.

cone *m* *(ger)* cone; **2** *(GEOM, ANAT)* cone; **3** *(gelado)* ice-cream cone; **4 ~ de Seger** *(metal.)* Pyrometric cone; **5 ~ vulcânico** volcanic cone.

cónego *(BR: cô-)* *m* *(REL)* canon.

cone(c)tar *vt* to connect.

cone(c)tor *m* *(ELECT)* connector; ♦ *adj* connective, connecting.

conexão *f* connection.

conexo,-a *adj* linked, joined.

confe(c)ção *f* making, confection; **roupa de ~** ready-made clothes *pl*; ♦ **confe(c)ções** *fpl* manufacturing *sg*; **2** *(vestuário)* clothing, ready-made clothes; **indústria de ~** garment industry.

Not **'confection'** in the sense of cakes, sweets; Vd: **'confeito'**.

confeccionar *vt* to make; to prepare; to manufacture.

confederação *f* confederation; league.

confederado,-a *adj* confederate.

confederar *vt* to unite; ♦ **~-se** *vr* to form an alliance.

confeiçoar *vt* *(MED)* preparar mistura de drogas; **2** *(CULIN)* de ingredientes para bolos.

confeitado,-a *adj* covered in sugar *(or similar)*.

confeitar *vt* to ice *(a cake)*; to preserve with sugar *(fruits)*; to mix medical ingredients.

confeitaria *f* *(arte de pastelaria)* confectionary; **2** *(loja)* cake shop, patisserie; **3** *(de guloseimas)* sweet shop.

confeiteiro,-a *m,f* confectioner.

confeito *m* comfit, sugarplum; **2** sweetmeat; **3** sweets *(UK)*, candies *(US)*.

conferência *f* conference; lecture.

conferencista *m,f* speaker.

conferente *m,f* checker, controller.

conferir *vt* to check; to grant; to confer; ♦ *vi*: **~ com** to confer with; **~ contas** to check accounts.

confessar *vt* to confide; **confesso a ti** I confide in you; **2** to confess; **eu confesso que não gosto disso** I honestly do not like that; **3** *(REL)* to hear confession; ♦ **~-se** *vr* to confess; **~ culpado** *(JUR)* to plead guilty.

confessionário *m* *(REL)* confessional.

confessor m (REL) confessor.

confiado,-a adj (pessoa) confident; **2** ~ **a** entrusted to; **3** (fam) saucy, cheeky, sure of him/herself.

confiança f confidence; **ela está cheia de** ~ she is very confident; **2** trust; **tenho** ~ **em ti** I trust you; **3** familiarity; **você está a tomar muita** ~ you are taking liberties, being very familiar; **4 de** ~ reliable; **5 digno de** ~ trustworthy.

confiante adj inv trusting; **2** confident, self-confident; **3** sure.

confiar vt to entrust; ♦ vi: ~ **em** to trust; **2** to confide in; **3** to rely on, to hope; ♦ **~-se** vr to trust.

confidência f secret; **em** ~ in confidence.

confidencial adj inv confidential.

confidente m,f confidant, confidante.

configuração f configuration; **2** shape, form.

configurar vt to shape, form; **2** to represent; **3** to appear.

confim m barrier, limit.

confins mpl limits; boundaries; **nos** ~ **do mundo** in the remotest corners of the earth.

confinante adj inv bordering upon.

confinar vt to limit; confine; ♦ vi: ~ **com** to border on; ♦ **~-se a** to confine o.s. to.

confirmação f confirmation.

confirmar vt (afirmar algo) to confirm; **2** (REL) (crismar alguém) confirm; ♦ **~-se** vr (algo) be confirmed, justified; **as minhas suspeitas confirmaram-se** my suspicions were confirmed.

confiscação f confiscation, seizure.

confiscar vt to confiscate, seize.

confiscável adj inv liable to forfeiture.

confissão f confession.

conflagração f conflagration, blaze.

conflagrar vt to inflame, set alight.

conflito m conflict; **2** war; **3** fight; **4 entrar em** ~ **com** to clash with; **5** discord; ~ **de gerações** generation gap.

confluente m,f (rio) tributary; ♦ adj inv (ruas, etc) converging; **2** (aspectos) concurrent; **3** (multidão) confluent.

confluir vi to flow together; **2** (rios) meet, converge; **3** (convergir, concentrar-se) converge, merge.

conformação f configuration, shape; **2** resignation.

conformado,-a adj resigned; **ele está** ~ **à sua sorte** he is resigned to his fate.

conformar vt to form, mould; **2** to conform; ♦ **~-se** vr resign o.s. to, agree with, conform; **2** ~ **com** to resign o.s. to.

conforme adj inv like, similar; **2** (JUR) pursuant; **3** in accordance/agreement with; **4** (fig) (alguém) resigned, conform; ♦ prep according to; ♦ adv **isso é** ~ that depends; ♦ conj as, according to, what; ~ **falava, ele olhava em redor** as he spoke, he looked around; ♦ **conformes** mpl (pop) **tudo nos** ~ everything OK.

conformidade f agreement; conformity; **em** ~ **com** in accordance with.

conformista m,f conformist.

confortar vt to comfort, console, sooth; **2** (fig) to cheer sb up.

confortável adj inv comfortable.

conforto m comfort.

confrade m fellow member; **2** (de associação, Ordem) confrère.

confrangedor,-ora adj distressing; **2** grievous; **3** vexing; **4** heart-rending; **5** deplorable.

confranger vt to torment, upset; **2** (espírito) to grieve; **3** (envergonhar alguém) to vex; ♦ **~-se** vr to be distressed; to suffer anguish; **2** to contort, writhe; **seu corpo confrangia-se com a dor** his body contorted/writhed in pain.

confrangido,-a adj distressed, upset.

confrangimento m constraint; distress.

confraria f fraternity; **2** brotherhood.

confraternizar vi to fraternize.

confrontar vt to bring face-to-face; **2** to confront; **3** to compare; ♦ **~-se** vr to face each other.

confundir vt to confuse, mistake; **2** to mix up; **3** to muddle; **4** ~ **com** to mistake for; **confundi o senhor com outra pessoa** I mistook you for another person; **5** to embarrass; **ela ficou confundida quando lhe dei o presente** she was embarrassed when I gave her the present; ♦ **~-se** vr to get mixed up, become confused.

confusão f confusion; **2** mudde; **3** (balbúrdia) chaos, disorder, mess; **4** turmoil, hubbub; ~ **de trânsito** traffic congestion/hubbub; **5** (engano) mistake; ♦ exc **que** ~! what a muddle, mess!

confuso,-a adj (pessoa atrapalhada) confused, muddled; **2** (embaraçado) embarrassed; **3** (misturado) topsy-turvy; **tudo está** ~ everything is topsy-turvy; **4** (algo) (assunto, ideias) obscure, hazy; **5** (equivocado) mistaken.

congelação f freezing; congealing.

congelador m freezer, deep freeze.

congelamento m freezing; **2** (ECON) freeze.

congelar vt to freeze; to congeal; ♦ **~-se** vr to freeze.

congénere (BR: -gê-) adj inv of the same kind, analogous, similar; **2** kindred; **espírito** ~ kindred spirit.

congénito,-a (BR: -gê-) adj congenital.

congestão f congestion; **2** (MED) ~ **nasal** nasal congestion; ~ **cerebral** apoplexy; **2** ~ **de trânsito** traffic congestion.

congestionado,-a adj congested; bloodshot, flushed.

congestionar-se vr to flush, go red.

conglomeração f conglomeration.

conglomerado m (GEOL) conglomerate; **2** (ECON) group; **3** (gente) gathering, crowd.

conglomerar vt to heap together; **2** (TEC) to conglomerate; ♦ vi to form a mass; ♦ **~-se** vr to join together, group together.

cognição f (LING) cognition.

cognitivo,-a m,f (linguagem, processo, função) cognitive.

Congo npr Congo; **o** ~ Congo.

Congo-Quinshasa npr Congo-Kinshasa.

congolês,-esa m,f adj congolese.

congossa f (BOT) periwinkle.

congraçamento m confraternization; harmonization.

congratular vt (alguém) to congratulate; ♦ **~-se** vr to congratulate o.s.

congregação *f (REL)* congregation; gathering.

congregar *vt* to assemble; ♦ ~**-se** *vr* to assemble, gather together.

congressista *m,f* congressman, congresswoman.

congresso *m* congress, convention; **2** (US: parliament) Congress.

conhaque *m* cognac, brandy.

conhecer *vt* to know; to be aware of; **2** to meet for the 1st time; **conheci-o em Paris** I met him in Paris; ♦ ~**-se** *vr* to get to know one another.

conhecedor,-ora *m,f* expert; connoisseur.

conhecido,-a *m,f* acquaintance; **ele é meu ~** he is an acquaintance of mine; ♦ *adj* known; well-known.

conhecimento *m* knowledge; ~**s** *pl* knowledge *sg*; **2** understanding; **3** *(COM)* ~ **de embarque** bill of landing; **4** ~ **de causa** due knowledge; **5** **levar ao** ~ **de alguém** to bring to sb's notice; **6** **ter** ~ **de** to be aware of; **7** **tomar** ~ to take notice.

cónico,-a *adj* cone-shaped, conical; *(GEOM)* *(superfície)* conic.

conífera *f (BOT)* *(arbusto)* conifer.

conífero,-a *adj* coniferous.

conivência *f* connivance; acquiescence.

conivente *adj inv* conniving; **ser ~ em** to connive in.

conje(c)tura *f* *(hipótese)* conjecture, supposition, guess.

conjugação *f* *(união)* linking, union; **2** *(gram)* conjugation; **3** *(de fatores)* combination.

conjugado,-a *adj* *(apartamento)* adjoining; **2** *(GEOM)* linked.

conjugal *adj inv* conjugal; **vida ~** married life.

conjugar *vt* *(gram)* to conjugate *(verbo)*; **2** to link, combine; ♦ ~**-se** *vr* to join together, converge, fit.

cônjuge *m,f* spouse; husband/wife.

conjunção *f* union; meeting; **2** *(gram, ASTRON)* conjunction.

conjuntiva *f* *(membrana)* conjuntive.

conjuntivite *f (MED)* conjunctivitis.

conjuntivo *(gram)* *m* *(modo)* subjunctive; ♦ *adj* *(ANAT)* *(fibras, tecido)* connective.

conjunto *m* whole, collection, combination, set, team; **2** *(MÚS)* group; **3** *(roupa)* outfit; **4** *(habitação)* complex; **5** **em ~ com** together; **6** **tudo em ~** all at the same time; ♦ *adj* joint, adjacent to.

conjuntura *f* conjuncture; **2** situation, combination; **3** opportunity; **4** state of affairs.

conjura, conjuração *f* conspiracy; **2** incantation; **3** exorcism.

conjurado,-a *m,f* conspirator; **2** sworn member of an order or association; **jantar dos ~s** *(de uma associação)* members' dinner.

conjurar *vt* to conspire, plot; **2** to invoke; **3** to swear together; ♦ *vi:* ~ **contra** to plot against.

con(n)osco *pron* with us; **ele vem ~** he is coming with us; **isso é ~** that's up to us; **2** with/to ourselves; about ourselves.

conotação *f* connotation.

conotar *vt* to connote; to imply; **2** ~ **com** *(relacionar)* to consider.

conquanto *conj* although, though.

conquilha *(= cadelinha) (ZOOL)* *(molusco)* coquille.

conquista *f* conquest; **2** achievement, **3** *(fig)* *(amorosa)* conquest.

conquistar *vt* to conquer; **2** *(ganhar)* to win, get; **3** *(alcançar)* to achieve; **4** *(encantar alguém)* to charm, seduce.

consagração *f (REL)* consecration; **2** anointing; **3** acclaim; **4** praise.

consagrado,-a *adj* hallowed; **2** *(lugar)* consecrated; **3** *(bispos)* ordained; **4** ~ **a** dedicated to; **5** established, well-known.

consagrar *vt (REL)* ordain; **2** consecrate; **3** dedicate.

consanguíneo,-a *m,f* blood relation; ♦ *adj* related by blood.

consciência *f* conscience; awareness; conscientiousness; **estar em paz com a ~** to have a clear conscience; **obje(c)tor de ~** conscientious objector; **pôr a mão na ~** to act fairly/with justice; to come clean; **sem ~** inhuman.

consciencialização *f (EP)* awareness *(de* of).

consciencializar *vt (EP)* **alguém de algo** to make sb aware of sth, to raise awareness; ♦ ~**-se** *vr* to become aware **(de** of)

consciencioso,-a *adj* conscientious.

consciente *m (PSIC)* conciousness; ♦ *adj* conscious; aware.

conscientização *f (BR)* awareness *(de* of).

conscientizar *(BR)* *vt (Vd =* **consciencializar**); ♦ ~**-se** to become aware (of sth).

cônscio,-a *adj* aware of.

consecução *f* attainment.

conseguinte *adj:* **por ~** therefore.

conseguir *vt* to get, obtain; **2** to achieve; **3** to be able to, can; **4** ~ **fazer** to manage to do, succeed in doing; **não ~ fazer** to fail to do; **consegues abrir a porta?** can you (manage to) open the door?

conselheiro *m (JUR)* counsellor, counsel; **2** *(JUR)* counsellor at law *(US)*; **3** adviser; **4** ~ **cultural** cultural counsellor; **5** *(município)* councellor.

conselho *m* advice; counsel; board; council; ~ **de ministros** council of ministers, Cabinet; ~ **de família** family council.

consenso *m* consensus; agreement.

consentimento *m* consent, permission.

consentir *vt* to allow, permit; **2** to agree to; IDIOM **quem cala consente** silence gives consent; ♦ *vi:* ~ **em** to agree to.

consequência *f* consequence, result; **por ~** therefore, consequently; **em ~ de** because of; **2** importance.

consequente *adj inv* consequent.

consequentemente *adv* consequently.

consertar *vt* to mend, repair; **2** to rectify.

conserto *m* repair.

conserva *f* *(em lata, boião)* preserve; ~ **de sardinhas** tinned sardines; **2** jam; **3** pickle.

conservação *f* conservation; preservation.

conservado,-a *adj* *(algo)* preserved; **2** well kept; **ele está muito bem ~** he doesn't look his age.

conservador,-ora *m,f* preserver; **2** *(pessoa encarregada dum museu)* curator; **3** *(pessoa oposta a mudança)* conservative; **4** *(POL)* **o partido ~** the conservative party.

conservante *m (alimentos)* preservative.

conservar *vt* to preserve, maintain; **2** to keep, retain; **3** *(sabor)* to conserve; ♦ ~-**se** *vr* to keep (well).

conservativo,-a *adj* conservative; **2** preservative.

Conservatória *f* civil registry.

conservatório *m* conservatoire; **2** drama school.

consideração *f* consideration; **2** esteem; **3** thought; **4** **tomar em** ~ to take into account.

considerado,-a *adj (pessoa)* respected, esteemed; **2** *(algo)* considered, pondered.

considerar *vt/vi* to consider; to think about; **2** to regard; ponder, weigh up; **3** *(alguém)* to esteem, be fond of.

considerável *adj inv* important; **2** large, considerable.

consignação *f (COM)* consignment.

consignar *vt (mercadoria)* to send, dispatch; **2** to ship; **3** *(verbas)* to allocate funds.

consigo¹ *pron pess (com você/o senhor/a senhora)* with/to you; **eu vou** ~ I am coming with you; **é** ~ **mesmo que eu quero falar** it is with you, yourself, I wish to speak; **isso é** ~ that is up to you; **2** *(a pessoa própria) m* with/to him, himself; *f* with/to her, with; **ele não tinha o dinheiro** ~ he didn't have the money on/with him/himself; **ela leva a caixa** ~ she takes the box with her (herself); **gasta mais comigo do que** ~ she spends more on me than on herself; **ele é muito metido** ~ he is very reserved.

consigo² *(pres, ind, 1ª pessoa de* **conseguir***)* **não** ~ **falar com ele** I am not able to speak to him.

consílio *m (assembleia, reunião)* assembly.

consistência *f* consistency; **2** firmness; **3** stability.

consistente *adj inv* solid; **2** thick; **3** consistent; **4** *(duradouro)* stable.

consistir *vi*: ~ **em** to consist of; **2** based on.

consoada *f* Christmas Eve supper.

consoante *f (LÍNG)* consonant; ♦ *adj inv* harmonious; ♦ *prep* according to; *(JUR)* pursuant to; in accordance with; ♦ *conj (como, segundo)* as; **2** *(à medida que)* as.

consola *f (ARQ)* console; **2** *(pequena mesa)* console table; **3** *(COMP, TEC, MÚS)* console; **4** control panel of an electronic system; **5** *(do carro)* dashboard.

consolação *f* consolation.

consolar *vt* to console, comfort; ♦ ~-**se** *vr* to console o.s., to resign o.s. to.

consolo *m* consolation, comfort.

consonância *f* harmony; agreement.

consorciar *vt* to join; ♦ *vi* to unite (**a** with).

consórcio *m* partnership; **2** *(COM)* consortium, association, pool; **3** marriage.

consorte *m,f* partner, companion; **2** spouse; ♦ *adj inv* consort; **príncipe** ~ the Queen's husband, consort.

conspícuo,-a *adj (evidente)* conspicuous; **2** *(ilustre)* distinguished, eminent.

conspiração *f* plot, conspiracy.

conspirador,-ora *m,f* conspirator.

conspirar *vt*: ~ **contra** conspire against; ♦ *vi* to plot.

conspurcar *vt (corromper)* to sully, to corrupt, to stain *(nome, caráter)*; ~ **a alma** to sully one's soul, corrupt one's heart.

constância *f* perseverance; **2** *(barulho)* persistent; **3** *(no amor)* constancy; **4** perseverance.

constante *adj inv* constant persistent; **2** *(amor)* faithful; **3** *(que consta)* pertaining to.

constar *vi* to be known; **2** ~ **de** to consist of; to be written; **isso não consta na minha Bíblia** that is not in my Bible; **3** ~ **que** to be ovious, to be aware that; **não me consta que isso seja a verdade** I am not aware that is the truth; **4 consta que** … it is said that …

constatação *f* fact; **2** verification; **3** proof.

constatar *vt (verificar)* to verify; **2** *(facto)* to report; **3** *(comprovar)* to prove.

constelação *f* constellation; cluster.

constelado,-a *adj* starry.

consternação *f* dismay; distress.

consternado,-a *adj* dismayed.

consternar *vt (alguém)* to upset; ♦ ~-**se** *vr* become upset.

constipação *f (EP) (MED)* cold.

constipado,-a *(EP) adj*: **estar** ~ to have a cold *(BR:* **resfriado,-a***)*.

constipar-se *vr (EP)* to catch a cold.

constitucional *adj inv* constitutional.

constituição *f* constitution; **a C~ Nacional** the National Constitution; **2** *(de um grupo)* formation; **3** bodily strength; **4** *(duma sociedade, firma)* setting up, founding.

constituído,-a *adj* established, set up; **2** *(person)* built; **3** constituted; **4** legally constituted, **Senhor D. não foi** ~ **arguido** Mr D. was not declared under suspicion *(Vd:* **arguido***)*.

constituinte *m,f* voter; **2** *(POL) f* constituent assembly; **3** *(JUR)* client; ♦ *adj inv* representative, constituent.

constituir *vt* to constitute; **2** to establish, set up; ♦ ~-**se** *(como)* to set o.s. up as; **3** to appoint; **4** ~ **família** to get married.

constrangedor,-ora restricting.

constranger *vt* to restrict; to force, compel.

constrangido,-a *adj* uncomfortable.

constrangimento *m* restriction; restraint.

construção *f* building, construction.

construir *vt* to build, construct.

construtivo,-a *adj* constructive.

constructor,-ora *m,f* builder, constructor.

consuetudinário,-a *adj (JUR) (lei, direito)* consuetudinary; **2** *(habitual)* usual, customary.

cônsul *m* consul.

consulado *m* consulate.

consular *adj inv* consular.

consulesa *f* lady consul; **2** consul's wife.

consulta *f* consultation; **horas de** ~ consulting hours; surgery hours; **livro de** ~ reference book.

consultar *vt* to consult; **2** to refer to; **3** to ask sb's opinion or advice; **4** to confer; **5** to have an appointment (with doctor); **6** ~ **o travesseiro** *(pensar numa questão)* to sleep on it.

consultivo,-a *adj* advisory.

consultor,-ora *m,f* adviser, consultant.

consultório *m* surgery, GP's clinic.

consumação *f* consummation; completion; fulfilment.

consumado,-a *adj* perfect; complete; accomplished.

consumar *vt* to consummate; **2** complete; **3** fulfil, carry out.

consumidor,-ora *adj* consumer.

consumir *vt* to consume; **2** to eat away; **3** to use up; ♦ **~-se** *vr* to waste away.

consumo *m* consumption; **artigos de ~** consumer goods.

conta *f* (*ger*) account; **~ à ordem** current account; **~ conjunta** joint account; **~ de terceiros** third party accounts; **~ poupança** savings account; **extracto da ~** bank statement; **2** (*cálculo*) sum, counting; **dar ~s a** to be answerable to; **fazer ~s** to sum up, to do accounts; **prestar ~s** to account for; **isso não é da sua ~** it's none of your business; **3** (*restaurante, etc*) bill; **isso fica por minha ~** (*pagar*) I will pay (the bill); **4** (*de colar, rosário*) bead; **falta uma ~ ao rosário** one bead is missing from the rosary; **5** (*considerar*) **levar em ~** to take into account; **6** (*cuidar*) **tomar ~ de** to look after; **7** (*fingir*) **fazer de ~ que** to pretend that; **8** (*estima*) **tenho-o em grande ~** I have him in high esteem; **9** (*aperceber-se*) **dar-se ~ de** to realize; ♦ *adv* **no fim de ~s** after all, when all is said and done; **trabalhar por ~ própria** work freelance; ♦ *prep* **à ~ de: viver à ~ de** to live off sb; **em ~** (*barato*) reasonably-priced; **por ~ de** on account of; **vezes sem ~** endless times; IDIOM **~s do Porto** (*cada qual paga a sua parte*) to go Dutch; **arredondar a ~** to square up; **por ~, peso e medida** with all the necessary conditions; fair and square; **ajustar ~s com alguém** get one's own back.

contabilidade *f* book-keeping, accountancy; **2** accounts department.

conta(c)to *m* contact; touch; **pôr-se em ~ com** to contact, get in touch with.

contado,-a *adj* counted; **ele está com os dias ~s** his days are numbered; **2** told, related; **3** accounted for; **dinheiro de ~** cash payment.

contador,-ora *m,f* (*COM*) accountant; **2** story-teller; **3** (*aparelho*) (*água, gás, luz*) *m* meter.

contadoria *f* audit department.

contagem *f* counting; **~ regressiva** countdown; **2** score.

contagiar *vt* (*MED*) to infect; **2** to transmit; **3** (*fig*) to corrupt; ♦ **~-se** *vr* to be infected, catch; **4** to affect; **5** (*fig*) to be addicted.

contágio *m* infection.

contagioso,-a *adj* contagious; **2** (*fig*) catching.

conta-gotas *m inv* dropper; **por ~** drop by drop; **a ~** (*fig*) little by little; **o trânsito andava a ~** the traffic was moving at snail's pace.

contaminar *vt* to contaminate; **2** to infect; **3** to corrupt.

contanto que *conj* provided that; **janto contigo ~ tu pagues** I shall dine with you provided you pay.

conta-quilómetros *m* speedometer.

contar *vt* to count; **2** to tell, narrate; **3** to intend; **~ com** to count on, depend on; **4** to expect;

contava com uma coisa e saiu-me outra I was expecting one thing and it turned out to be another.

contemplação *f* contemplation.

contemplar *vt* to contemplate; **2** to gaze at; ♦ *vi* to meditate; ♦ **~-se** *vr* to look at o.s.

contemporâneo,-a *adj* contemporary.

contemporizar *vi* to compromise; **2** to play for time.

contenção *f* contention; **2** quarrel, dispute; **3** restriction, containment; **4** holding back.

contencioso *m* contention; **2** (*JUR*) (*jurisdição*) litigation office; ♦ **~a** *adj* contentious, litigeous.

contenda *f* contention, argument; **2** (*JUR*) litigation; **3** quarrel, dispute.

contentamento *m* happiness; contentment.

contentar *vt* to please; ♦ **~-se** *vr* to be satisfied.

contente *adj inv* happy; **2** content, pleased, satisfied.

contento *m*: **a seu ~** to his satisfaction.

contentor *m* container, recipient; **2** **~ do lixo** large dustbin.

conter *vt* to contain, hold; **2** to restrain, hold back; ♦ **~-se** *vr* to restrain/control o.s.

conterrâneo,-a *adj* person from the same place; **ela é uma amiga ~** she comes from my region/town; **2** compatriot.

contestação *f* challenge; denial.

contestar *vt* to dispute, contest; to challenge.

contestável *adj* questionable; disputable.

conteúdo *m* contents *pl*; **2** (*assunto*) subject; **~ do requerimento** the subject of the petition.

contexto *m* context.

contido,-a *adj* contained; **2** restrained, held back; controlled.

contigo *prep* with (*informal*) you; **janto ~ amanhã** I shall dine with you tomorrow.

contiguidade *f* proximity.

contíguo,-a *adj* next to; neighbouring, adjoining, adjacent.

continência *f* chastity; **2** salute; **fazer ~ a** to salute.

continente *adj inv* chaste; **2** *m* continent; **3** mainland.

contingência *f* eventuality.

contingente *m* quota; (*MIL*) contingent; (*COM*) contingency; ♦ *adj inv* uncertain; conditional.

continuação *f* continuation.

continuar *vt* to continue, carry on; ♦ *vi*: **~ a falar** to keep on talking.

continuidade *f* continuity.

contínuo,-a *m,f* *m* office junior, messenger; **2** (*moça júnior*) girl-Friday; **3** attendant; ♦ *adj* ongoing, continuous; **2** constant.

contista *m,f* short-story writer.

conto *m* tale, story, fable; **~ da carochinha** nursery tale; old wives' tale; (*fam*) fib; **~ de fadas** fairy tale; **~-do-vigário** cock and bull story; confidence trick; **~ policial** detective story, thriller; **2** (*dinheiro*) (*moeda cabo-verdiana*) **um conto** = 1000 escudos; (*BR*) mil reais; **3** (*números*) count; **vezes sem ~** countless times.

contorção *f* contortion; twitch.

contorcer *vt* to twist; ♦ **~-se** *vr* writhe.

contornar *vt* to go round; **2** to skirt.

contorno *m* contour; profile; **2** outline.

contra *m* drawback; **os pros e os ~s** the pros and the cons; **ser do ~** to object in principle; **ter um ~** have a drawback; **2** *(homossexual) (fig)* be of the wrong persuasion; ♦ *prep* against; **2** *(mediante troca de)* in exchange for; **3** counter; ♦ *conj* contrary to; **~ o que eu esperava** contrary to what I was hoping.

contra-almirante *m* rear-admiral.

contra-ataque *m* counterattack.

contrabalançar *vt* to counterbalance; to compensate.

contrabandista *m,f* smuggler.

contrabando *m* smuggling; contraband.

contrabaixo *m* double bass; **2** *(músico)* contrabassist, double bass player.

contrabalançar *vt* counterbalance; ♦ **~-se** *vr* be comparable (**em** in)

contracapa *f (livro)* backcover.

contra(c)ção *f* contraction.

contracenar *vt (TEAT, CIN)* to act (**com**, with).

contrace(p)ção *f* contraception.

contracifra *f* code; key to a cypher.

contradição *f* contradiction.

contraditório *adj* contradictory.

contradizer *vt* to contradict; to refute.

contrafa(c)ção *f* falsification; **2** forgery; **3** counterfeit.

contrafazer *vt* to copy; counterfeit; **2** to falsify; **3** to constrain; **4** to force.

contrafeito,-a *adj* coerced, constrained, against one's will; **fui ~ à reunião** I went to the meeting unwillingly; **2** copied, counterfeited, **sapatos ~s** counterfeited shoes; **3** *(fig)* **um sorriso ~** a forced/false/uneasy smile.

contrafé *f* a true copy of a summons.

contraforte *m* buttress, counterfort; **2** reinforcement.

contraindicação *f (MED)* contraindication.

contrair *vt* to contract; **2** *(doença)* to catch; **3** *(hábito)* to form; **4 ~ amizades** to make friends with; ♦ **~-se** *vr* to shrink.

contralto *m (MÚS)* contralto.

contraluz *f* backlighting.

contramaré *n* ebb tide.

contramão *f* one way, the wrong side of the road; **2** *adv (BR) (fig)* out of the way.

contramestre,-tra *m,f* foreman, supervisor; **2** *(NÁUT)* boatswain.

contrapartida *f* compensation; **2** counterpart; **3** *(COM)* **~ de lançamento** cross-entry; **4 em ~** on the other hand.

contrapeso *m* counterbalance.

contraplacado *m* plywood.

contraponto *m (MÚS)* counterpoint.

contrapor *vt* to oppose; **~ a** to set against; ♦ **~-se** *vr* to be in opposition.

contraposição *f* opposititon, difference, contrast; **em ~** *adv* contrary to; as opposed to; **2** in opposition to, against.

contraproducente *adj inv* counter-productive, self-defeating.

contraprova *f* counter proof; **2** second copy; **3** *(TIPO)* galley proof.

contra-regra, contrarregra *(pl:* **contrarregras)** *m,f (TEAT)* stage manager, prompter.

contra-réplica, contrarréplica *n (resposta)* retort; **2** *(JUR)* rejoinder.

contra-revolução, contrarrevolução *f* counter-revolution.

contrariamente *adv* contrary (to); **~ ao que planeávamos** contrary to what we were planning.

contrariar *vt* to contradict; **2** to thwart; **3** *(JUR) (contraditar)* impugne; ♦ *vi* annoy, be inconvenient.

contrariado,-a *adj:* **fui à festa ~** I went to the party against my will/unwillingly.

contrariedade *f* annoyance, vexation; **2** upsetting; **3** setback, problem; **tive uma ~** I had a setback, problem.

contrário,-a *m,f* adversary; ♦ *adj* contrary; **pelo ~** on the contrary; **2** unfavourable, adverse.

contra-senha, contrassenha *(pl:* **contrassenhas)** password, watchword.

contra-senso, contrassenso *m* nonsense.

contrastar *vt* to differ; ♦ *vi* to contrast.

contraste *m* contrast; opposition; **2 em ~** in contrast.

contratante *adj inv* contracting.

contratador,-ora *m,f (empresa)* contractor, undertaker.

contratar *vt* to contract, to recruit; to engage.

contrato *m* contract; **2** agreement; **~ de arrendamento** letting; **3** lease contract; **~s registados** *(BR:* **registrados)** traded contracts.

contratempo *m (imprevisto)* setback, mishap; **2** problem; **3** *(MÚS)* syncopation.

contratorpedeiro *m (MIL)* destroyer.

contravenção *f* contravention, infringement, transgression.

contraversão *f (versão contrária)* opposite version; **2** *(inversion)* inversão.

contravir *vt/vi* to contravene.

contribuição *f (ajuda)* contribution; **2** donation; **3** *(imposto)* tax; **~ autárquica** council tax.

contribuinte *m,f* contributor; **2** rate-payer, taxpayer; **3 número de ~** tax payer's identification number.

contribuir *vt* to contribute; **~ com/para** contribute to; ♦ *vi* to pay taxes.

contrição *f* contrition, repentance.

contrito,-a *adj* contrite, sorrowful.

controlar *vt* to control; supervise; ♦ **~-se** *vr* to control o.s.

controlo *m* control; **~ remoto** remote control; *(BR)* controle.

controvérsia *f* controversy; debate.

controverso,-a *adj* controversial.

contudo *conj* nevertheless, yet, however.

contumácia *f* obstinacy; **2** *(JUR)* contempt of court.

contumaz *adj inv* obstinate, stubborn; **2** *(JUR: réu)* insubordinate.

contundente *adj inv (ferimento)* contusing, bruising; **2** *(fig) (voz, comentário)* harsh; blunt.

contundir *vt* to wound, bruise, contuse.

conturbação *f* disturbance, unrest, commotion; **2** *(motim)* riot.

conturbado,-a *m,f* troubled; **2** *(espírito)* perturbed.

conturbar *vt* to disturb; **2** to stir up; ◆ **~-se** *vr* to be upset.

contusão *f* bruise.

contuso,-a *adj* bruised.

convalescença *f* convalescence.

convalescer *vi* to convalesce.

convalescente *m,f* convalescent; ◆ *adj inv* convalescent.

convenção *f* convention; agreement.

convencer *vt* to convince; persuade; ◆ **~-se** *vr:* **~ de** to be convinced about.

convencido,-a *m,f* prig, snob; ◆ **estar ~** to be convinced; **2** *(fig, fam) (pretensioso)* smug, conceited; **ser ~** to be full of oneself, to be big-headed.

convencional *adj inv* conventional.

conveniência *f* convenience.

conveniente *adj inv* convenient, suitable; **2** advantageous.

convénio *(BR:* -vên-*)* *m* convention; **2** agreement; **3** pact.

convento *m* convent; **2** monastery.

convergência *f* convergence (**de** of).

convergente *adj inv* convergent.

convergir *vt (direção)* to converge (**para** on); **2** *(mesma tendência)* to aim at (**para**); **3** afluir (**de para**).

conversa *f* conversation; **dois dedos de ~** a brief chat; **~ sem nexo** rambling talk; IDIOM **~ de chacha** hollow talk, hot air; **~ fiada** idle talk; **ir na ~ de (alguém)** to be taken in (by sb); **ter muita ~** *(alguém)* to have the gift of the gab; **as ~s são como as cerejas** one topic falls another.

conversação *(pl:* -ões*)* *f* conversation; **2** *(palestra)* address; **conversações** *fpl (POL)* talk, negotiations.

conversadeira *f* talker, chatterbox; **2** *(cadeira)* double chair (facing each other), lover's bench.

conversador,-ora *m,f* conversationalist, talker; ◆ *adj* talkative, chatty.

conversão *f* conversion.

conversar *vi* to talk, converse; **2 ~ com** to talk to/ with; **3** *(fig)* **vou ~ com o meu travesseiro** *(decidir)* I'll sleep on it.

conversibilidade *f* convertibility.

conversível *adj inv* convertible.

converter *vt* to convert; ◆ **~-se** *vr* to be converted.

convertido,-a *m,f* convert; ◆ *adj* converted.

convés *m (NÁUT)* deck.

convexo,-a *adj* convex.

convicção *f* conviction; **2** certainty.

convicto,-a *adj* convinced; **2** *(JUR)* convicted.

convidado,-a *m,f* guest; ◆ *adj* invited.

convidar *vt* to invite.

convidativo,-a *adj* attractive, inviting.

convincente *adj inv* convincing; **2** persuasive.

convir *vi* to suit, be convenient; **não me convém ir hoje** it doesn't suit me to go today; **2** good, best for; **não convém dizer-lhes isso,** it's not a good idea to tell them that; **3 convém-lhe?** is it all right/O.K. with you?

convite *m* invitation.

convivência *f* living together, familiarity; **ele não é da minha ~** he is not a close friend of mine.

conviver *vi* to live together; to socialize.

convívio *m* sociability; **2** living together; companionship; **o ~ da família** family life; **depois da palestra, haverá festa de ~** after the talk we'll have a get-together.

convocar *vt* to summon, call upon; **2** to convene.

convocatória *f* General Board meeting; notice of a Board meeting.

convosco *pron pl (com vocês, com os senhores)* with you *(pl)*.

convulsão *f (MED)* convulsion; **2** *(fig)* unrest.

convulsionar *vt* to shake; to stir up.

convulso,-a *adj* shaking; **2 tosse ~a** whooping cough.

convulsivo,-a *adj (MED)* convulsive; **2** jerky; **3** *(choro)* convulsive, crying and sobbing.

cooperação *f* co-operation.

cooperar *vi* to co-operate.

cooperativo,-a *m,f (COM)* co-operative; ◆ *adj* cooperative.

coordenação *f* co-ordination.

coordenar *vt* to co-ordinate.

copa *f (árvore)* top; **2** *(chapéu)* crown; **3** pantry; **~s** *fpl*; **4** *(naipe)* hearts; **5 ~ do mundo** *(BR) f* world cup.

copado,-a *adj* leafy, bushy, tufty.

copagem *f* foliage.

cópia *f* copy; **2** *(arte)* reproduction; **3** imitation; **passar uma ~ a limpo** write out neatly; **tirar ~s de** to take copies, duplicate.

copiadora *f (machine)* photocopier.

copiar *vt (transcrever)* to transcribe (text); *(fazer cópia)* to copy; **2** *(imitar)* mimic, imitate *(modos, voz)*; **3** *(col) (escola)* to crib, cheat (**em** in); ◆ *vi (reproduzir)* copy; *(clandestinamente)* copy.

copiosamente *adv* abundantly; **chorar ~** weep profusely.

copioso,-a *adj (comida)* abundant; **2** *(choro)* copious.

copista *m,f* copyist, copier.

copo *m (recipiente)* glass; **~ d'água** *(pl:* **copos d'água***) m* wedding breakfast.

copázio *m* large glass; **2** glassful.

cópula *f* copulation, coitus.

copular *vt* to copulate with; **2** *(acasalar, ligar)* to couple, link; ◆ *vi* to copulate.

coqueiro *m (BOT)* coconut tree.

coqueluche *f (MED)* whooping cough; **2** *(fam) (ídolo)* idol, pet.

coquetel *m (bebida, festa)* cocktail.

coquette *adj* coquetish.

cor[1] [ô] *f* colour; **2 ~-de-rosa** pink; **3** *(da pele)* complexion; **sem ~** pale; IDIOM **~ de burro quando foge** nondescript colour.

cor[2] [ó] *adv (memória)* **de ~** by heart; **aprender de ~** to memorize, commit to memory; IDIOM **saber de ~ e salteado** to know by heart.

coração *m (ANAT)* heart; **2** centro; **o ~ do repolho** the centre/heart of the cabbage; **3** bosom; **4** *(fig)* coragem; **5** feeling; **de bom ~** kindhearted; **6 sem**

~ heartless; ♦ *adv* **de todo o** ~ whole-heartedly; **apertar contra o** ~ to clasp sb against one's bosom; IDIOM **caiu-lhe o** ~ **aos pés** his heart sank; **falar com o** ~ **nas mãos** wear one's heart on the sleeve; **fazer das tripas** ~ to make the best of a bad job; grin and bear.

corado,-a *adj (na face)* ruddy; **2** *(fig) (embaraçado)*, blushed, blushing; **3** *(CULIN)* **o frango está** ~ *(assado)* the chicken has a golden/toasty colour.

coragem *f* courage; nerve.

corajoso,-a *adj* courageous, brave.

coral *(pl:* -ais) *m* coral; **um banco de corais** coral reef; **2** *(MÚS) (grupo de cantores)* choir; ♦ *adj inv (MÚS)* choral; **2** coral.

Corão (o ~) *(=*Alcorão) *m* Koran.

corar *vt* to colour; **2** *(branquear)* to bleach; **3** *(CULIN: tostar)* to brown, toast, turn golden; ♦ *vi* to blush, go red.

corante *m* dye; ♦ *adj inv* colouring.

corça *f (ZOOL)* doe.

corcel *m (ZOOL)* steed, charger.

corço *m (ZOOL)* roebuck.

corcova *f* hump.

corcovar *vt (pessoa)* to be bent, bowed; **2** to arch; ♦ *vi (corpo)* become bent; **2** *(cavalo)* **dar** ~s to buck.

corcovado,-a *m,f* hunchback; ♦ *adj* hunchback(ed).

corcunda *m,f (pessoa)* hunchback; *(corcova)* hump; ♦ *adj* hunchbacked.

corda *f* rope, line, twine; ~ **bamba** slack rope; ~ **de pular** skipping rope; ~ **da roupa** washing line; *(GEOM)* line; **2** *(ANAT)* cord(s); **3** *(MÚS)* string (s); **4** *(de relógio)* spring, **dar** ~ **a** to wind up *(algo)*; **5** **brinquedo de** ~ clockwork toy; IDIOM **dar** ~ **a alguém** *(encorajar conversa)* to allow sb talk on and on; **dançar/andar na** ~ **bamba** to walk the tightrope; **estar com a** ~ **na garganta** to be in a tight spot; **roer a** ~ to go back on word/ promise, let sb down.

cordame *m* rigging.

cordão *m (de seda/algodão)* string; **2** *(têxtil)* twist; **3** cordon, line; **um** ~ **de policiais** a police cordon; **4** *(fio: jóia)* chain; ~ **de ouro** gold chain; **5** *(fileira)* row, chain; ~ **humano** human chain; **6** *(ANAT)* ~ **umbilical** umbilical cord;

cordeiro *m (ZOOL)* lamb.

cordel *(pl:* -éis) *m* string; **2** **literatura de** ~ *(sensacional, banal)* pamphlet/pulp literature; IDIOM **apertar os** ~éis **à bolsa** to economize, to curb spending.

cor-de-laranja *f (cor)* orange; ♦ *adj inv* orange-coloured.

cordelinhos *mpl* strings; IDIOM **mexer os** ~ to pull strings.

cor-de-rosa *m, sg, pl* pink; ♦ *adj inv* rosy; **2** *(fig) (visão romântica)* rosy, rose-coloured/tinted.

cordial *m (bebida)* cordial; ♦ *adj inv* cordial. **cordialidade** *f* warmth, cordiality.

cordilheira *f* ridge, range of mountains.

coreano,-a *adj* Korean; **sul-**~ *(pl:* **sul-coreanos**) South-Korean.

Coreia *npr* **a** ~ Korea.

coreografia *f* choreography.

coreógrafo,-a *m,f* choreographer.

coreto *m (MÚS)* bandstand.

corinto *m (fruta seca)* currant.

corisco *m* flash; **2** *(fig)* bright spark.

corista *m,f* chorister, person who sings in a choir; **2** *f (TEAT)* chorus girl.

corja *f* mob, rabble, gang; **2** band.

córnea *f (ANAT)* cornea.

córneo,-a *adj* relating to horn; **2** *(feitio de)* horn.

cornear *vt (com os chifres)* to gore; **2** *(pop) (trair)* to two-time.

corneta *f* cornet; **2** *(MIL)* bugle; **3** *m* bugler.

corneteiro *m* bugler.

cornetim *m (MÚS)* French horn.

cornija *f (ARQ)* cornice.

corno *m (animal)* horn; **2** *(vulg) (marido)* cuckold; **a mulher pôs-lhe os** ~s his wife made him a cuckold; **3** *(pop) (enganador)* crook, swindler, **você é um** ~! you are a crook *(fig)* a bastard!

Cornualha *npr* **a** ~ *(condado inglês)* Cornwall.

cornudo *adj (animal)* horned; **2** *(fig) (problema, etc)* tricky, difficult; *(cal)* cuckold.

coro *m* chorus; choir.

coroa *f* crown; **as jóias da C~** *(Inglaterra)* the crown jewels; **2** *(de flores)* wreath; **3** *(ARQ) (de cornija)* corona; **4** *(ASTRON)* corona; **C~ Boreal** Corona Borealis; **5** *(careca no topo)* bald patch; **6** *(de uma moeda)* **cara ou** ~ heads or tails; **7** *m,f (BR) (fam) (pessoa velha)* old fogey; **8** *fpl (fam) (moedas)* coppers.

coroação *f* coronation.

coroar *vt* to crown; **2** *(fig)* to reward.

corolário,-a *adj* corollary.

coronário,-a *adj* coronary.

coronel *m (MIL)* colonel.

coronha *f* butt; **à** ~ with the butt (of a rifle).

corpo *m* body; **2** *(MIL)* corps *sg*; ~ **diplomático** diplomatic corps *sg*; **3** ~ **de bombeiros** fire brigade; **4** *(JUR)* ~ **de delito** Corpus delicti; **5** ~ **docente** teaching staff; ♦ *adv* ~ **a** ~ *(luta)* hand to hand; IDIOM **de** ~ **e alma** with heart and soul.

corpulência *f* stoutness.

corpulento,-a *adj* stout; **2** large person; **3** *(animal)* fat.

corpus *(pl:* **corpora**) *m* corpus.

corpúsculo *m* corpuscle.

corre(c)ção *f* correction; **2** marking (school work); **3** ~ **monetária** inflationary adjustment; **4** correctness.

corre(c)to,-a *adj* correct; **2** exact; **3** proper; **4** upright.

corre(c)tor,-ora *m,f (pessoa que corrige)* reviewer, reader; **2** ~ **das provas** proof-reader, copy editor; ~ **tipográfico** proof-reader; **3** *(agente)* broker; *(de imóveis)* estate agent *(UK)*, realtor *(US)*; *(FIN)* ~ **de fundos/de Bolsa** stock broker; ~ **de apostas** bookmaker; *(pop)* bookie; **4** *(de hotel)* tout.

corretora *f (instituição)* agency.

corrediça *f* slide; **de** ~ sliding.

corredor,-ora *m,f* runner; participant in a race; **2** *m (de casa)* corridor; passageway; *(de avião, supermercado)* aisle.

correia *f (tira de couro/borracha)* strap, thong; **2** *(em ventoinha, carro)* belt; *(em carro)* fan belt; **3** dog leash.

correio *m* mail, post; **pôr no** ~ to post; **2** *(estação)* post office *(BR:* **agência dos correios***)*; **3** *(carteiro)* postman, *(US)* mailman; **4** **C~s** Postal service; **5** *(mensageiro)* courier; **6** *(COMP)* ~ **ele(c)trónico** email.

correlacionar *vt* to correlate; **2** to establish a relation between.

corrente *f (do mar)* current; **2** *(de metal)* chain; **3** *(vento)* ~ **de ar** draught; **4** *(ELECT)* current; **5** *(fig) (fluxo)* flow; **6** *(fig) (tendência)* trend; ♦ *adj inv* running; **2** *(actual)* current, present; **3** *(água; prosa)* flowing; **4** *(comum)* usual, common.

correnteza *f (de árvores)* line; **2** *(de casas)* row; **3** *(fig) (andamento)* progresso; **4** *(fig) (no falar)* fluency, ease.

correr *vt* to run, race; **2** *(cortinas)* to draw; **3** to hurry, scurry; **4** *(fama, rumores)* to spread; **5** to pursue; **6** ~ **mundo** to be well travelled; **a cerâmica portuguesa corre mundo** Portuguese ceramic is well known (travels) throughout the world; **7** **porta de** ~ sliding door; **8** ~ **parelhas** to run neck and neck; ♦ *vi* to run; **2** *(rio)* to flow; **3** *(tempo)* to elapse, pass.

correria *f* mad rush; **andar na** ~ to go around in a mad rush.

correspondência *f* correspondence.

correspondente *m,f* correspondent, pen friend; **2** *(JORN)* reporter, correspondent; ♦ *adj inv* corresponding; respective; appropriate.

corresponder *vi:* ~ **a** to correspond to; **2** to be suitable for; **3** to match (up to); **4** to reciprocate; ♦ ~**-se com** *vr* to correspond with.

corretagem *f* brokerage; **2** commission.

corretivo *(Vd:* **correctivo***).*

correto *(Vd:* **correcto***).*

corrida *f (acto)* running, run; rush, dash; **2** *(DESP)* race; **pista de** ~ race-track; **3** *(TAUROM)* bullfight; ♦ **de** ~ *adv* in a rush *(Vd:* **corrido***).*

corridinho *m (MÚS)* Algarve's traditional music and fast dance.

corrido,-a *(pp de* **correr***) adj (expulso)* driven out, sacked; **2** *(tempo)* gone by; **3** *(vexado)* abashed; **4** *(com pressa)* rushed; **5** *(MÚS)* **fado** ~ fast/lively 'fado'; **6** *(TAUROM)* bull that has been fought.

corrigir *vt* to correct, put right; **2** *(trabalho escolar)* to mark; **3** *(repreender)* to reprimand, tell off; **4** *(reparar)* to amend; ♦ ~**-se** *vr* to reform, correct o.s.

corrigível *(pl:* **-veis***) adj inv* corrigible.

corrimão *(pl:* **corrimões/corrimãos***) m* handrail.

corriqueiro,-a *adj (banal)* commonplace; **2** ordinary, trivial; **3** everyday, current; **4** *(BR)* presumptious, affected.

corroboração *f* confirmation, corroboration.

corroborar *vt* to corroborate, confirm; ♦ *vi (dizer que sim)* to agree.

corroer *vt (metal)* to corrode, erode; **2** *(corcomer)* eat away, gnaw; **3** *(fig) (destruir, depravar)* destroy,

undermine, corrupt; ♦ ~**-se** *vr* be consumed; be corrupted.

corroído,-a *adj (metal)* corroded; **2** worn/eaten away.

corromper *vt (deteriorar)* to spoil, damage, polute; **2** *(perverter)* to corrupt; **3** *(adulterar)* to tamper with; **4** *(subornar)* to bribe; ♦ ~**-se** *vr (estragar-se)* to become rotten; deteriorate; **2** *(fig) (pessoa)* to turn to vice.

corrosão *f (QUÍM)* corrosion; **2** *(fig) (uso excessivo)* tear and wear.

corrosivo,-a *adj* corrosive; **2** *(fig) (palavras)* biting.

corrupção *f* corruption; **2** decay, rot.

corrupio *m* children's game; pinwheel; **2** *(fig)* whirl, flurry; **3** hustle and bustle; **andar num** ~ to be always on the go.

corrupto,-a *adj (estragado)* spoiled, rotten; **2** *(cadáver)* decayed; **3** *(fig) (devasso)* depraved; **4** *(LÍNG)* adulterated.

corsa *f (tradicional da Madeira)* cart without wheels pulled by men, a kind of sledge.

corsário *m (NÁUT) (navio)* pirate, corsair; **2** *(homem)* privateer, pirate.

Córsega *npr* **a** ~ Corsica.

córsico,-a *adj* Corsican.

corso *m,f* Corsican; *m (NÁUT)* piracy; **2** *(ZOOL)* school of fish; **3** *(desfile de carros)* parade; **4** *(mar)* surge, billow.

cortadura *f* cut; **2** ditch, gap *(between hills).*

corta-mato *m* cross-country.

cortante *adj inv* cutting; **2** *(fig) (vento frio)* icy; **3** *(som agudo)* shrill, piercing.

cortar *vt (ger)* to cut, chop; *(em fatias)* slice; **2** *(dar golpe)* slash, cut; **3** *(árvore)* cut down; **4** *(tirar parte de)* to cut off; **5** *(impedir)* to cut off; ~ **o gas** to cut the gas off; **6** *(talhar, tirar parte de)* to cut out *(desenho, vestido)*; **7** *(interromper)* to interrupt; ~ **a palavra a alguém** to interrupt/cut sb short; **8** *(em pedaços)* cut up; **9** ~ **com** *(reduzir, acabar com)* cut down on/giveup *(comida, relações)*; **ele acabou com o namoro** he ended his love affair; **10** ~ **os mares** to plough the seas; **11** ~ **o baralho** *(cartas)* cut the deck; **12** *(CIN)* **corta!** cut!; ♦ ~ **-se** *vr* to cut o.s.; IDIOM ~ **o mal à raíz** *(eliminar o mal)* to nip *(sth)* in the bud; ~ **na casaca** to backbite.

corte[1] *[ó] m* cut; cutting; **2** style; **3** ~ **de cabelo** haircut; **4** *(golpe)* gash, incision; **5** *(redução)* cut-back, cut down; ~ **nas despesas** cut-back on expenses; **6** *(de porcos)* pigsty.

corte[2] *[ô]* court; ~ **da rainha** the queen's court; **homem da** ~ courtier; **2** *(DESP)* court; ~ **de ténis** tennis court; **3** *(namoro)* courtship; **fazer a** ~ **a alguém** to flirt with/woe sb; **4** **as C~s** *fpl* the parliament.

cortejo *m* retinue; **2** procession; **3** parade; **4** *(funeral)* cortèje; **5** greetings *pl.*

cortejar *vi (fazer a corte a mulher)* to pay court to; **2** *(adular)* flatter, butter sb up, dance attendance on sb.

cortês *adj inv* polite, courteous.

cortesã *f* courtesan; ♦ *adj f* courtly.
cortesão *m* courtier; ♦ *adj m* courtly.
cortesia *f* courtesy, politeness.
cortex *m (BOT, ANAT)* cortex.
cortiça *f (BOT)* cork; **rolhas de ~** bottle corks.
corticeiro,-a *m,f (tirador da casca)* cork stripper.
cortiço *m* beehive; **2** slum tenement.
cortina *f* curtain; **2 ~ de fumo** smokescreen; **3** *(FOTO)* screen.
cortinado *m* curtain; **~s** *npl* curtains; **2** *(reposteiros)* drapes.
coruja *f (ZOOL) (tipo de mocho)* screech-owl; **2** *(fam)* old witch, hag.
coruscar *vi* to sparkle, glitter; **2** to flash; **3** to send forth.
corvina *f (ZOOL) (peixe do mar)* croaker, jewfish.
corvo *(ZOOL) m* crow, raven; **2** *(BR)* black vulture; **~-marinho** *m* cormorant.
cós *m, sg, pl (tira interior da cintura/do cinto)* waistband; **2** *(base do colarinho)* collar band.
coscuvilheiro,-a *m,f (bisbilhoteiro)* gossiper, tittle-tattler, snooper.
coscuvilhice *f* gossip, tittle-tattle.
coser *vt/vi* to sew, mend stitch; **~ um botão** to sew on a button; **2** to stitch; **3** *(MED)* to sew up, suture.
co-signatário,-a *m,f* cosignatory.
cosmética *f* cosmetics; **2** *(maquilhagem)* make-up.
cosmético,-a *m, adj* cosmetic.
cósmico,-a *adj* cosmic.
cosmografia *f* cosmography.
cosmonauta *m,f* cosmonaut.
cosmopolita *adj* cosmopolitan.
cosmos *m* cosmos.
costa *f* coast, shore; **dar à ~** to wash/run ashore; **2 costas** *(ANAT)* back; **ter dores de ~** tio have a backache; **~s da cadeira** the back of the chair; **~ da mão** *f* back of the hand; **~ curvadas** round-shouldered; **dar as ~s a** to turn one's back on; ♦ *adv* **às ~s** on one's back; **de ~s** from behind; IDIOM **anda mouro na ~** *(suspeitas de namoro)* romance is in the air; **deitar para trás das ~s** to forget an incident/to ignore it; **ver alguém pelas ~s** to wish to see the back of sb; **voltar as ~s a alguém** to turn one's back on sb.
costado *m* back; **2** *(NÁUT)* broadside; IDIOM **ser dos quatro ~s** to be authentic; **os quatro ~s** the four grandparents.
Costa Rica *npr* **a ~** Costa Rica.
costa-riquenho,-a *adj* Costa Rican.
costear *vt* to go round; to round up; ♦ *vi* to follow the coast.
costeiro,-a *adj (região)* coastal.
costela *(ANAT) f* rib; IDIOM **ter uma ~ inglesa** to have English blood/origin; *(BR) (fam)* better-half.
costeleta *f* chop, cutlet; **~ de porco** pork chop.
costumado,-a *adj* usual.
costumar *vt* to accustom; ♦ *vi* to be accustomed to, be in the habit of; **ele costumava dizer** … he used to say …
costume *m* custom, habit; **2 ~s** *pl* customs; **3 de ~** usual(ly).

costumeiro,-a *adj* usual, habitual.
costura *f* sewing, needlework; **modista de alta ~** *f* fashion designer; **2** *(linha de junção)* seam; **sem ~** seamless.
costurar *vt/vi* to sew, stitch; **2** to make clothes.
costureira *f* dressmaker; seamstress.
costureiro *m* tailor, dressmaker; **2** couturier; **3** *(ANAT)* sartorius.
cota[1] *f (FIN)* quota, share; **2** *(membership)* fees, quota; **3** *(GEOM)* measurement, height, distance; **4** *(antiga)* armadura.
cota[2] *m* stub; **2** identification number, marginal note; **3** opposite side of a blade.
cotação *f* quoting; **2** *(preço)* quote; **3** *(avaliação)* rating; **4** *(COM)* value; **5** *(FIN)* list, quotation; *(fig)* prestige, good repute; **~ bancária** bank rate.
cotado,-a *adj* quoted, priced; **2** *(valorizado)* rated; **3** *(na Bolsa)* listed.
cotejar *vt* to compare.
cotejo *m* comparison; collation.
coto *m (ANAT) (braço amputado)* stump; **2** *pl* **~s** knuckles; **3** *(resto da vela)* candle stub; **4** *(ZOOL) (das asas)* part of a bird's wing from which grow the feathers.
cotovelada *f* nudge.
cotovelo *m (ANAT)* elbow; **2** *(rua)* bend; IDIOM **falar pelos ~s** to talk nineteen to the dozen; **dor de ~** to be green with envy.
cotovia *f (ZOOL)* lark.
coube *(pret de caber)*: **os ovos não couberam no cesto** the eggs did not fit in the basket.
couraça *f* breastplate; **2** armourplate.
couraçado *m* battleship.
couro *m* leather; hide; **2 ~ cabeludo** scalp.
coutada *f* game preserve.
coutado,-a *adj* fenced, enclosed.
couto *m* enclosure.
couve *f (BOT) (ger)* cabbage; **~-de-bruxelas** Brussels sprout; **~-flor** cauliflower; **~-galega** kale; **~ lombarda** Savoy cabbage; **~ portuguesa** *f* spring greens, *pl*; **~-roxa** red cabbage.
cova *f (buraco)* pit, hole; **fazer ~s na areia** to dig holes in the sand; **2** cavern; **3** *(sepultura)* grave; **4** hollow, côncavo; **5 ~ da mão** palm; **6 ~ do queixo** dimple; **7** *(toca)* burrow; IDIOM **descer à ~** to be buried; **com o pé pr'a ~** a foot in the grave.
covinha *f (no queixo, face, corpo)* dimple.
covarde (= **cobarde**) *m,f* coward; ♦ *adj inv* cowardly.
coveiro *m* gravedigger.
covil *m* den, lair.
coxa *f (ANAT)* thigh, femur; **2** *(CULIN)* leg.
coxear *vi* to limp, hobble; **2** *(fig)* to wobble.
coxia *f* aisle, gangway.
coxo,-a *m,f* cripple; ♦ *adj* lame; **2** *(passos incertos)* wobbly; **3** *(TIPO) (página)* out of order, shorter/longer than others.
cozedura *f* quick boiling/cooking; **tempo de ~** cooking time; **2** *(das faianças)* firing.
cozer *vt* to cook *(em água e sal: alimentos)*; **~ batatas** boil/cook potatoes; **2** to boil, bring to the boil;

3 *(tratar pelo fogo: azulejos, barro, etc)* to fire; IDIOM ~ **a bebedeira** to sleep it off.

cozido *m (CULIN)*; ~ **à portuguesa** traditional dish of boiled meat, sausages, vegetables; ◆ *adj* boiled, cooked in water; **2** *(barro, vidro, etc)* fired.

cozinha *f* kitchen; **2** cookery; **3** cuisine.

cozinhar *vt/vi* to cook.

cozinheiro,-a *m,f* cook, chef.

CPLP *(abr de* **Comunidade de Países de Língua Portuguesa**) Community of Portuguese-speaking countries (= Angola, Brasil (Brazil), Cabo Verde (Cape Verde Islands), Guiné-Bissau (Guinea-Bissau), Portugal, S. Tomé e Príncipe, Timor Leste (East Timor)).

crachá *m (insígnia)* star; **2** badge.

crânio *m* skull.

crápula *m* libertine; **2** *(malandro)* scoundrel, creep.

craque *m,f* ace, expert; **ele é um ~ no xadrez** he is an ace at chess; **2** *(FUT) m* football star.

crase *f* crasis; **2** temperament, índole.

crasso,-a *adj (espresso)* thick, viscous; **2** *(fig) (grosseiro)* crass.

cratera *f* crater; **2** big hole, opening.

crava *m,f (fam) (pedindo dinheiro, etc)* sponger; cadjer.

cravar *vt* to drive (in), *(pregos)* hammer; **2** *(pedras, jóias)* to set; **3** *(fig)* ~ **os olhos** to stare at sb; **4** *(fig, fam) (dinheiro)* to borrow money, sponge off sb; **5** *(fig)* **cravou-se-me aquela imagem na mente** I retained that image on my mind.

craveira *f* standard measure, price.

craveiro *m (BOT) (planta)* carnation.

cravejar *vt (com cravos)* to nail; **2** *(jóias)* to set stones.

cravelha *f (MÚS)* tuning peg; **2** *(MIL) (obturador dos ouvidos do barulho dos canhões)* plug.

cravinho *m (especiaria)* cloves *pl*; **2** *(flor)* pink; **um ramo de ~s** a bunch of pinks.

cravista *m,f (MÚS)* harpsichordist,

cravo *m (prego)* nail; **2** *(flor)* carnation; **3** *(MÚS)* harpsichord; **4** *(verruga na pele)* wart; **5** *(BR)* clove; **6** *(BR)* blackhead; **7 a Revolução dos C~s** *f (HIST)* Revolution of the Flowers.

Revolução dos Cravos refers to the Portuguese revolution of April 1974, when the soldiers had carnations stuck in their rifle butts, to indicate it was a peaceful revolution.

---

cré *m* chalk, limestone.

creche *f* crèche.

credencial *f* credential.

credenciais *pl* credencials.

credenciamento *m* accreditation.

credenciar *vt (dar credenciais)* to accredit.

credibilidade *f* credibilidade.

credifone *m* phonecard.

creditar *vt* to give credit to; **2** *(contabilizar)* to put on the credit column/list; **3** ~ **alguém with** to credit sb with; ◆ **~-se** *vr* to grant credit; **2** *(fig)* to establish oneself; ~ **como um grande escritor** to establish oneself as a great writer.

crédito *m (ger)* credit; **2** *(FIN)* **a** ~ on credit; **3 digno de** ~ trustworthy; **avaliação de** ~ **de (alguém);** credit rating of (sb); **4** *(reputação)* **ela tinha muito** ~ **na companhia** she was well-thought of in the firm; **5** *(valor no exame)* credit; **6** *(no jogo)* chip.

credível *adj inv (crível)* credible.

credo *m (REL) (fé)* creed; **2** *(oração)* **o C~** Creed; **3** *exc* ~! heavens!; goodness me!

credor,-ora *m,f* creditor; ◆ *adj (merecedor)* worthy, deserving.

credulidade *f* credulity; **2** *(ingenuidade)* gullibility.

crédulo,-a *m,f* innocent; ◆ *adj* credulous; **2** naïve, gullible.

creio *(pres ind de crer)* **eu** ~ **nele** I believe in him/I trust him.

cremação *f* cremation.

cremalheira *f (MEC)* pot-hook and chain; **2** *(régua dentada que engrenha num cilindro)* rack wheel; ~ **e pinhão** rack and pinion; **3** *(trilho dentado)* cog rail.

cremar *vt* to cremate.

crematório *m* crematorium.

creme *adj* cream-coloured; **2** *(CULIN) m* cream, sauce; **3** *(beleza)* ~ **hidratante** moisturizing cream; **4** *(CULIN)* **leite** ~ a kind of custard.

cremoso,-a *adj* creamy.

crença *f* belief, trust; **2** ~**s** beliefs, convictions.

crendice *f* superstition; foolish belief.

crença *f* belief, trust; **2** conviction.

crente *m,f (com fé)* believer; faithful; **2** *(fig) (inocente)* gullible; ◆ *adj* believing.

crepitação *f* crackle, crackling; **2** *(MED)* crepitus.

crepitar *vi (estalar)* crackle; **2** *(MED)* wheeze.

crepuscular *adj inv* crepuscular.

crepúsculo *m* dusk, twilight.

crer *vt/vi* to believe; **2** to think; **3 fazer** ~ to convince; **4** ~ **em** to believe in; ◆ **~-se** *vr* to believe o.s. to be.

crescente *m* crescent; **quarto** ~ *(lua)* first quarter; ◆ *adj inv* growing.

crescer *vi* to grow; **2** to increase; **3** to thrive; **as plantas crescem neste clima** plants grow in this climate; **4** to rise; **o empadão não cresceu** the pie didn't rise.

crescido,-a *adj* grown (up); **2** tall; **o menino está muito** ~ **para a idade** the boy is quite tall for his age; **3** *(unhas, cabelo)* long.

crescimento *m* growth; **2** increase.

crespo,-a *adj (cabelo)* frizzy; **2** rough; **3** *(mar)* choppy, rough.

crestar *vt (pelo tempo)* scorch, burn, singe, sear; **2** *(mel)* collect; ◆ **~-se** *vr (frio, calor)* dry out; **2** *(fig)* to plunder, embezzle.

cretino *m* cretin, imbecile.

cria *f* baby animal, young.

criação *f* creation; **2** *(animais)* raising, breeding; ~ **de gado** livestock; ~ **de suínos** hog-raising; **fazer** ~ to breed animals; **3** *(pessoas)* upbringing; **4 ele é um rapaz da minha** ~ he is a chap from my generation.

criado,-a *m,f* servant, waiter; **2** *f* maid; waitress; ♦ *(pp de* **criar)** *adj* **ele foi muito bem criado** he is well brought up.

criador,-ora *m,f* creator; **2 o C~** the Creator, God; **3** *m* **~ de gado** cattle breeder.

criança *f (ambos os sexos)* child; **as ~s brincam** children are playing **2** *(marota)* brat; ♦ *adj inv* child-like; **a noite ainda é ~** night is still young.

criançada *f* many kids.

criancice *f (acção)* childish.

criar *vt* to create; **2** *(filhos)* to bring up; **3** *(animals)* to raise, breed; **4** to produce; **5** *(plants)* grow; **6 ~ o bebé ao peito** to breastfeed; **7** *(problemas)* to cause; ♦ **~-se** *vr (dar-se bem)* grow well; **2** *(alimentar-se)* to feed.

criativo,-a *adj* creative.

criatura *f* creature; **2 ela é uma ~ antipática** she is a nasty creature; **3 boa ~** good soul.

crime *m* crime.

criminal *adj inv* criminal.

criminalidade *f* criminality, crime.

criminoso,-a *adj* criminal.

crina *f* mane.

crioulo,-a *adj* creole; **2** *(LÍNG)* creole.

cripta *f* crypt vault; **2** *(ANAT)* crypt.

criptografia *f* cryptography.

crisálida *f (ZOOL)* chrysalis.

crisântemo *m (ZOOL)* chrysanthemum.

crise *f* crisis, problem; **2** *(MED)* attack, fit; **3 ~ de choro** a crying fit; **4 ~ de habitação** housing shortage.

crisma *f (REL)* confirmation; **2** chrism, holy oil.

crismar *vt (REL)* to confirm; ♦ **~-se** *vr (REL)* to be confirmed.

crisol *m (pl:* **-óis)** crucible; **2** *(fig) (provação)* hard test, trial; **o ~ da vida** life's trial.

crispar *vt* to contract; **2** *(rosto)* to wrinkle; ♦ **~-se** *vr* to twitch; **2** *(de frio)* to shrink; **3** to be irritated.

crista *f (cume)* crest; **2** *(de galo)* comb.

cristal *m* crystal; **2** *(fig)* **voz de ~** clear voice.

cristaleira *f* glass cabinet, display cupboard.

cristalino,-a *adj* clear; crystal clear; crystalline.

cristalizar *vi* to crystallize.

cristandade *f (qualidade de cristão)* Christianity; **2** Christian community.

cristão *m,* **cristã** *f (pl:* **-tãos/-tãs)** *adj* Christian.

cristianismo *m* Christianity.

cristianizar *vt* to christianize.

Cristo *m* Christ.

critério *m* criterion; criteria *pl*; **2** judgement.

crítica *f* criticism; **2** critique; **3** critics *pl*.

criticar *vt* to criticize, find fault; **2** *(book)* to review, to give a critique.

crítico,-a *adj m,f (de arte)* critic; **2** *(de livro)* reviewer. ♦ *adj inv* critical.

crivar *vt (com balas)* to riddle; **2** (com *punhal/faca)* stab, pierce; **3** *(passar por crivo)* to sift, sieve; **4** *(fig) (com perguntas)* bombard.

crível *adj* credible, believable; **2** *(digno de confiança)* reliable, trustworthy.

crivo *m (peneira)* sieve; **2** *(coador)* colander, strainer; **3** *(do regador)* rose (of the watering-can).

Croácia *npr* **a ~** Croatia.

croata *m,f* Croat; ♦ *adj inv* Croatian.

crocante *adj inv* crunchy.

croché *(BR:* **crochê)** crochet.

crocitar *vi* to caw, croak.

crocito *m (voz de corvo, abutre)* caw, croak.

croco *m (BOT)* crocus.

crocodilo *m (ZOOL)* crocodile; IDIOM **lágrimas de ~** crocodile tears.

cromado *m* chrome; ♦ **cromado,-a** *m,f* chromium-plated, chrome.

cromar *vt* to plate with chromium.

cromático,-a *adj (FÍS, FISIOL, MÚS)* chromatic.

cromato *m (QUÍM)* chromate; **~ de potássio** potassium chromate.

crómio *m* chromium.

cromo chromium; **2** *(imagem impressa a cores)* coloured litograph; **3** *(QUÍM)* chrome.

cromossoma, cromossome *m* chromosome.

cromoterapia *f* colour therapy.

crónica *(BR:* **crô-)** *f* chronicle; **2** newspaper column, report.

crónico,-a *(BR: -ô-) adj* chronic.

cronista *m,f* columnist; **2** chronicler.

cronologia *f* chronology.

cronológico,-a *adj* chronological.

cronómetro *m* stopwatch.

croquete *m* croquette.

croqui *m* sketch.

crosta *f (do pão)* crust; **2** *(GEOL)* crust; **3** *(MED) (de ferida)* scab; **4** *(fig)* shell; **5 a ~ rija** the hard crust.

cru, crua *adj* raw, uncooked; **2** *(grosseiro)* crude, harsh, blunt; **3** *(fig) (ingénuo)* green; **4 pano ~** unbleached cloth; *(seda)* raw; **5** *(luz forte)* naked; ♦ **a ~** *adv* undisguised.

crucial *(pl:* **ais)** *adj inv (forma de cruz)* cross-shaped, cruciform; **2** *(fig) (ponto)* crucial.

crucificação *f* crucification.

crucificante *adj inv (dor)* excruciating.

crucificar *vt* to crucify.

crucifixo *m* crucifix.

crude *m (petróleo)* crude oil.

crudelíssimo,-a *(=* **crueléssimo,-a)** *adj (superl de* **cruel)** very cruel, barbarian.

cruel *adj inv* cruel.

crueldade *f* cruelty.

cruento,-a *adj* bloody, cruel.

crueza *f* crudity, cruelty; **2** rawness; **3** *(estômago)* indigestion.

crupe *m (MED)* croup.

crustáceo *m* crustacean.

cruz *f* cross; **~ gamada** swastika; **C~ Vermelha** Red Cross; **2 braços em ~** crossed arms.

cruzada *f* crusade; **2 raça ~** mixed race.

cruzado,-a *m* crusader; **2** *m* ancient Portuguese coin; former Brazilian currency; ♦ *adj* crossed.

crusador *m (NÁUT)* cruiser.

cruzamento *m (de raças)* cross-breeding; **2** *(estradas)* junction, crossroads.

cruzar *vt* to cross; **~ os braços** to fold one's arms, to do nothing about a situation; **2** *(NÁUT)* to cruise;

(barco) to ply across; **3** *(fogo, bola)* cross; **4** *(acasalar animais, plantas)* cross, mix; **5 cruzes!** *exc* good heavens!, God forbid; ♦ ~**-se** *vr* to cross; **2** ~ **com** to meet/bump into sb; **o nosso olhar cruzou-se** our eyes met.

cruzeiro *m (monumental)* cross; **2** cruise; **3** former Brazilian currency; **4** *(ARQ)* transept.

cruzeta *f (cabide)* coat hanger; hanger.

cu *m (cal)* arse; **olho do** ~ *(cal)* arsehole *(UK: vulg)*; butt *(US)*; **2** *(fam)* bum, bottom, the behind; **3** *(nádegas)* buttocks; IDIOM **cara de** ~ a face like the back of a bus; **o** ~ **de Judas** *(muito, longe)* the back of beyond; **encher o** ~ **a alguém** *(cal)* give lots of money to sb.

cuba *f (vinho)* vat.

Cuba *npr f (GEOG)* Cuba.

cubano,-a *adj* Cuban.

cubata *f* hut.

cúbico,-a *adj* cubic.

cubismo *m* cubism.

cubo *m (ger)*; **2** *(GEOM, MAT)* cube, third power; **3** *(brinquedo)* cubo; **4** *(AUTO)* ~ **de roda** wheel hub.

cubículo *m* cubicle.

cuca *f (fam) (BR)* head; **2** *(mente)* head, intellect; **não andar bem da** ~ not right in the head; **3** *(BR)* sponge cake; IDIOM **encher a** ~ to be drunk; **fundir a** ~ to get muddled up.

cuco *m (ZOOL)* cuckoo.

cuecas *fpl* underpants; **2** knickers.

cueiro *m* nappy *(UK)*, diaper *(US)*.

cuidado *m* care; **aos** ~**s de** in the care of; **2** ~**s** worries; **ter** ~ to be careful; ♦ *exc* ~! watch out!; ~ **com o degrau!** mind the step; ~ **com os carteiristas** be aware of pickpockets.

cuidadoso,-a *adj* careful.

cuidar *vi*: ~ **de** to take care of, look after; **cuide de si próprio** take care of yourself; ♦ ~**-se** *vr* to look after o.s.

cujo,-a/os,-as *pron rel* whose, of which, of whom; **o homem, cujo carro foi roubado ...** the man, whose car was stolen ...

culatra *f (arma)* breech; IDIOM **sair o tiro pela** ~ to backfire.

culinário,-a *f* cookery; ♦ *adj* culinary.

culpa *f* fault, blame; **2** *(JUR)* guilt; **3 ter** ~ **de** to be blame for; be guilty; **4 por** ~ **de** because of; IDIOM **ter** ~**s no cartório** to feel guilty about past sins.

culpabilidade *f* guilt, culpability.

culpado,-a culprit; ♦ *adj* guilty.

culpar *vt* to blame; **2** to accuse; ♦ ~**-se** *vr* to take the blame.

culpável *adj inv* guilty.

cultivar *vt (educar alguém)* to cultivate; **2** *(gosto, espírito, amizade)* develop; **3** *(AGR)* to grow *(cereais, etc)*; **4** *(terra)* till; ♦ ~**-se** *vr* to cultivate one's mind.

cultivável *(pl: -eis) adj inv* arable.

cultivo *m* cultivation, growing; **2** *(letras, arte)* cultivation.

culto *m (ritual)* cult; **2** *(veneração)* worship; ♦ *adj (educado)* cultured; **2** scholarly; **3** *(discurso)* refined.

cultura *f* culture; ~ **geral** general knowdege; **2** refinement; **3** *(AGR)* cultivation; *(da terra)* tillage; **4** *(produto)* culture.

cultural *adj inv (educacional)* cultural.

culturismo *m* body building.

cume *m* top, summit peak; **2** *(fig) (auge, apogeu)* peak, pinnacle.

cumeada *f* succession of peaks, mountain ridge.

cúmplice *m,f* accomplice, accessory; **2** *(fig)* collaborator.

cumplicidade *f* complicity; **acusado de** ~ **no rapto** charged with complicity in the kidnapping; **2** *(fig)* collaboration.

cumprimentar *vt* to greet; to congratulate.

cumprimento *m* fulfilment; **2** abiding (by); **3** compliment; **cumprimentos** *mpl* best regards.

cumprir *vt* to carry out; **2** to fulfil; **3** to honour; **4** to complete; **5** to abide (by); **6** ~ **a sentença** to serve a sentence; **7** ~ **a palavra** to keep one's word; ♦ *vi* to be necessary, be up to; **cumpre-me dizer que** it's up to me/I must tell you that; it is incumbent on me to ...; **fazer** ~ to enforce; ♦ ~**-se** *vr* to be fulfilled.

cúmulo *m* heap, pile; **2** height; **3** accumulation; **4 isto é o** ~! that's the limit!

cunha *f* hatchet; **2** *(calço)* wedge; **3 vértice da** ~ spearhead; **4** *(fam) (empenho)* clout; **5 ter** ~**s** to have connections in high places; **ter/meter uma** ~ to pull strings *pl*; **6** *(fig)* **estar à** ~ *(teatro, restaurante, etc)* to be packed, full.

cunhado,-a *m,f* brother-in-law, sister-in-law.

cunhal *m* angle, outward corner of walls.

cunhar *vt (moeda)* to mint; **2** *(nova palavra, expressão)* to coin.

cunho *m (marca em relevo)* stamp, seal; **2** *(fig) (carácter)* mark; **3** *(TIPO)* coiner's die.

cunilíngua *f* cunnilingus.

cupão *(pl: -ões,-ãos) m* coupon.

cupim *m* termite.

cúpula *f (ARQ)* dome, vault; **2** *(NÁUT)* ~ **de ventilação** cowl; **3** *(BOT)* cup; **4** *(fig)* leader.

cura *f* cure, healing; **2** treatment; **3** *(do queijo)* curing; **4** *m (pároco)* priest, curate.

curador *m (JUR) (de menores)* guardian; **2** *(de bens)* trustee.

curandeiro,-a *m,f (fé)* healer; **2** *(charlatão)* quack.

curar *vt* to cure; **2** to treat, heal; **3** *(secar peixe, queijo)* to cure; **4** *(branquear)* to bleach; ♦ *vi* to heal; **2** to bother; ♦ ~**-se** *vr* to get cured, get well.

curativo *m* treatment; **2** *(emplastro)* dressing; ♦ *adj* medicinal, curative.

curável *adj inv* curable.

Curdistão *npr* **o** ~ Kurdistan.

curdo,-a *adj* Kurd; **2** *(LÍNG)* Kurdish.

curgete *f (BOT)* courgette.

cúria *f* curia; **2 C**~ Papal court.

curinga *m (baralho)* joker; wild card in any game; **2** *(COMP)* wild card.

curiosidade *f* curiosity; curio.

curioso,-a *m,f* an inquisitive person; a curious thing; **2** *(bisbilhoteiro)* snooper, nosy; **3** bystander, onlooker; ♦ *adj* curious; **2** prying, snooping; **3** odd, unusual; **que ~!** how curious!; how remarkable!

curral *m* pen, corral.

currículo *m* curriculum.

curriculum vitae curriculum vitae.

curro *m* *(curral junto à praça de touros)* pen; **2** group of bulls to be fought.

cursar *vt* to follow a course/lectures at university.

curso *m* *(gen)* course; **2** *(EDUC)* **~ de pós-graduação** post-graduation course; **3** *(rumo)* route, distance; **4** *(andamento)* **em ~** in progress; **5** **~ de água** watercourse; **6** *(ASTRON)* path; **o ~ dos planetas** the path of the planets; IDIOM **dar livre ~ a** to let sth take its natural course.

cursor *m* *(peça móvel)* slide-bar; **2** *(COMP)* cursor.

curta-metragem *f* short-length film.

curtido,-a *adj* *(couro)* tanned; **2** *(fig)* *(calejado)* hardened, fed up.

curtidor *m* tanner; **curtimento** *m* tanning.

curtir *vt* *(peles, couro)* to tan; **2** *(azeitonas)* to pickle; **3** *(enrijar)* to toughen up; **4** *(aguentar)* to endure.

curto,-a *adj* *(ger)* short; **a saia está ~a** the skirt is short; **2** brief, concise; **3 ser ~ de vista** be short-sighted; **4** *(FÍS)* *(onda)* short-wave; IDIOM **ser de vistas ~as** to be narrow-minded.

curto-circuito *m* short circuit.

curva *f* *(ger)* curve; **2** *(da rua)* bend; **~ apertada** sharp bend; **3** *(GEOM)* arc; **4 ~s** *(físico de mulher)* curves.

curvar *vt* to bend; curve; **2** *(arquear)* arch; ♦ *vi* *(envergar)* to stoop; ♦ **~-se** *vr* to stoop; bend down; **2** *(inclinar-se)* to bow.

curvatura *f* curvature, contours.

curvo,-a *adj* curved; crooked, bent; **parênteses ~s** round parentheses, brackets.

cuscuz *m* *(BOT, CULIN)* couscous.

cuspir *vi* to spit; **é proibido ~ no chão** spitting (on the floor) is not allowed; **2** *(palavrões, insultos)* to spit out; **3** to throw off; **ele foi cuspido do cavalo** he was thrown off the horse.

custa *f* cost, expenditure; **2 ~s judiciais** *fpl* *(JUR)* court costs; **3 à ~ de** at the expense of.

custar *vt* *(preço)* to cost; **~ caro** to be expensive; **custe o que ~** whatever the cost; **2** *(fig)* *(ameaçar)* **isto vai ~-lhe caro** you/he/she will pay dearly for this; ♦ *vi* to be difficult; **custa-me dizer-lhe** it's hard for me to tell you; **não custa nada provar** it's worth trying; IDIOM **~ os olhos da cara** to cost a fortune.

custear *vt* to bear the cost of.

custeio *m* cost, costs; **2** expenditure; **3** *(estimate)* costing.

custo *m* cost, price; **~ de vida** cost of living; **2** *(despesa)* expenditure; ♦ **a ~ (de)** *prep* with difficulty, **ela sobe as escadas a ~** she climbs the stairs with difficulty; ♦ **a todo o ~** *adv* at all costs.

custo-benefício *m* *(ECON)* *(custo favorável em relação ao lucro)* cost-effective.

custódia *f* custody; **2** protection; **3** detention; **sob ~** in custody; **4** *(REL)* monstrance.

custoso,-a *adj* *(caro)* costly; **2** difficult, hard; **3** painful.

cutâneo,-a *adj* cutaneous.

cutela *f* chopper; **2** carving-knife.

cutelaria *f* cutlery; knife-making.

cuteleiro *m* cutler.

cutelo *m* cleaver.

cutícula *(ANAT, BOT)* cuticle.

cutilada *f* cut, slash with a knife.

cútis *f* skin; **2** complexion.

cutucar *vt* *(BR)* *(pop)* *(tocar com o cotovelo)* to nudge; **2** *(com o dedo)* to poke; **3** *(machucar um pouco)* squeeze sb.

cuzinho *m* *(fam)* little bottom, little bum.

cuva *f* *(peixe)* barbel.

cuvete *f* ice-tray.

czar *m* czar, tsar.

czarina *f* tsarina.

d

D, d *m (letra)* D, d.

da = de + a *(Vd: de)*.

D., Dª *(abr de* **Dom, Dona**)*.

da(c)tilografar *vt* to type.

da(c)tilografia *f* typing.

da(c)tilógrafo,-a typist.

dadaísmo *m* dadaism.

dadaísta *adj* dadaist.

dádiva *f (donativo)* donation; **2** *(oferta, dom)* gift.

dadivoso,-a *adj (BR)* generous.

dado,-a *m,f (pp de:* **dar***); **2** *m (jogos)* die; ~s *mpl* dice; **3** *(COMP)* data, information; **base de ~os** database; ♦ *adj* given, offered; **2** certain, right, **em ~a altura** at a certain point/moment; **3** *(pessoa extrovertida)* friendly; **4** **~ a algo** fond of sth; ♦ **~ que** *conj* given that, seeing that; IDIOM **os ~os estão lançados** the die is cast.

dador,-ora *m,f (doador)* donor; giver; **~ de medula** *(MED)* medulla, bone-marrow donor.

daí (= de + aí) *adv* from there; **sai ~** get out of there; **2** thence, from then on; **3** **~ a um mês** a month later; **4** **~ em diante** from then on; **5** **e ~, ele continuou a viagem** and from there he continued with his voyage; **6** **~ a pouco ele viu** after a while he saw; ♦ **~ que** *conj* consequently; so; **e~, qual é a questão?** and so, what is the problem?

Dalai Lama *npr* Dalai Lama.

dalguém = de + alguém.

algum,-a = de + algum, alguma.

dalgures = de + algures.

dali (= de + ali) *adv (lugar)* from there; **2** **~ a pouco** *(tempo)* after a while; *(distância)* further on.

dália *f (BOT)* dahlia.

dálmata *adj inv (raça de cão)* Dalmatian.

daltónico,-a *(BR: -tô-) adj* colour-blind.

daltonismo *m* colour blindness.

dama *f (mulher nobre/agraciada)* lady, dame; **~ de honor** *(da rainha)* lady-in-waiting; **~ de honor/ de honra** *(num casamento)* maid of honour; bridesmaid; **~ de companhia** lady's companion; **2** *(por cortesia a qualquer mulher)* Senhora; **3** *(baralho/xadrez)* queen; **4 ~s** *fpl (jogo)* draughts.

damasco *m* apricot; **2** *(tecido)* damask.

Damasco *npr* Damascus.

damasqueiro *m* apricot tree.

danação *f (maldição)* damnation; **2** *(ira)* rage, fury.

danado,-a *adj (amaldiçoado)* damned, cursed; **2** *(com raiva)* furious, mad; **cão ~** mad dog; **3** *(menino maroto)* mischievous, naughty; **4** *(pessoa intrépida, enérgica)* **ela é ~a** she is quite a woman; **5 ser ~ para negócios** he is damn good at doing business.

dança *f* dance, ball; **~ de salão** ballroom dance; **~ do ventre** belly dance; **2** *(fig) (agitação)* agitation, bustle; **ando numa ~** *(fam)* I am going around like mad; **3 ~ de São Vito** *(MED) (doença muscular nas crianças)* St Vitus' dance.

dançante *adj inv* dancing, **chá ~** tea-dance.

dançar *vi* to dance; IDIOM **~ na corda bamba** walk the tight rope.

dançarino,-a *m,f (profissional)* dancer; **2** *(amador)* keen dancer; ♦ *adj* dancing.

danificar *vt* to damage; ♦ **~-se** *vr* to get damaged.

daninho,-a *adj* harmful; **ervas ~as** *fpl* weeds.

dano *m (prejuízo)* damage; **2** *(moral)* harm, injury.

dantes *adv (anteriormente)* before, formerly; **2** *(outrora)* in the old days, days gone by.

daquele, daquela = de + aquele/aquela *(Vd: aquele/aquela)*.

daqui (= de + aqui) *adv* from here; from now; **2** **~ a pouco** soon, in a little while; **3** **~ a uma semana** in a week's time; **4** **~ em diante** from now on.

daquilo = de + aquilo *(Vd: aquilo)*.

dar *vt (ger)* to give; **2** *(fornecer)* **~ acomodação a** to give, supply lodgings to; **3** *(causar, fazer)* to give, make; **o vinho dá-me sono** wine makes me sleepy; **4** **~ azar** to bring/give bad luck; **5** *(exprime acção)* **~ cabo de** *(algo, alguém)* to ruin/ destroy sth/sb; **tu dás cabo de mim** you'll be the end of me; **você dá cabo do sofá** *(damage)* you'll ruin the sofa; **6** **~ um grito** to shout, yell; **7** **~ caça a** *(ladrão, etc)* to go after *(thief, etc)*; **8** **~ cartas** to deal the cards; **9** **~ corda ao relógio** to wind the watch/clock up; **10 dar alta a um doente** to discharge a patient; **11** **~ entrada em** *(adoecer)* to be admitted *(to hospital); (em clube, home)* be received; **12** **~ golpes (em alguém)** *(bater)* to strike; **13** **~ mostras de** to show signs of; **14** **~ parte de** *(informar)* to inform/report; **15** **~ um passeio** to go for a stroll/drive/spin; **16** **~ horas** *(relógio)* to strike the hour; **17** **~ de comer/ beber a alguém** to feed sb/give drink to sb; ♦ **~ à costa** *(escombros)* to be washed ashore; **~ à estampa** *(prelo)* to go/give into print; **~ à língua** to wag one's tongue; **~ à luz** to give birth; ♦ **~ em** *(vir a ser)* to become; **ele agora deu em estróina** he has become a bohemian; **~ em nada** *(resultat)* to come to nothing; ♦ **~ com** *(condizer)* to match, go well with; **o chapéu dá com o ves- tido** the hat goes well with the dress; **~ com a porta** *(encontrar)* **não dei com a porta** I didn't find the door *(address); **2** *(encontrar por acaso)* to bump into sb; **3 não dar com** *(cores)* clash; ♦ **~ para** *(direção)* to face/look onto; **a janela dá para o jardim** the window looks onto the garden; **2** *(ser suficiente para)* **esta carne não dá para cinco pessoas** this meat *(portion of)* is not enough for five people; **3** *(jeito)* knack; **ela dá para a costura** she has the knack for sewing; **4** *(ser possível)* **dá para ir esta noite?** are we able to go tonight? ♦ **dar por** *(aperceber-se de)* to notice; **eu dei pelo**

(= **por** + **o**) **ladrão** I noticed, became aware of the thief; **2** *(pagar)* to pay; **quanto deu por esta mesa?** how much did you pay for this table?; ♦ **dar-se** *vr*: **dar-se bem/mal com alguém** to get on (not get on) with sb; **3** *(clima, sítio)* to suit, agree with; **não me dou bem com/em este clima** this climate doesn't agree with me; **2** ~**-se a conhecer** to introduce o.s., make o.s known; **3** ~**-se por vencido** *(ceder)* to give in/up; ♦ *adv* **ao Deus dará** aimlessly; **2 de mãos dadas** hand-in hand; ♦ **tanto se me dá** I don't care one way or another; **quem me dera!** *exc* how I wish! wish it were true!; **isso vem a dar ao mesmo** it all comes to the same; IDIOM ~ **água pela barba** *(tarefa, difícil)* to be difficult; ~ **a mão à palmatória** to give in, agree; **ter a barriga a** ~ **horas** to be hungry; **não** ~ **saída** pretend not to hear; **dar o braço a torcer** *(ceder)* to give in, yield.

dardejar *vt* to fire arrows at; **2** to wound with a dart/arrow; **3** *(fig)* *(olhar, raios)* to flash, sparkle in anger; **4** *(insultos)* to fire.

dardo *m* dart; **2** spear; **3** *(DESP)* javelin.

das = **de** + **as** *(Vd: de)*.

data *f* date; **2 de longa** ~ of long standing; ~ **de validade** sell-by date; **3** *(fam)* *(quantidade)* a lot of.

datação *(pl: -ções) f (processo de datar) f* dating.

data-limite *f* deadline, closing date.

datar *vt (pôr data)* to date; ♦ *vi*: ~ **de** to date from, date back to.

datilo- *(Vd: da(c)tilo-)*.

de (**de** + **o** = **do**; **de** + **a** = **da**; **de** + **os** = **dos**; **de** + **as** = **das**) *prep* of, from; *(posse)* **a casa da Maria** Mary's house; **o carro dele** his car; **2** *(origem)* **sou de Nova Iorque** I am from New York; **uma moça de boas famílias** a girl from good families; **3** *(descrição)* **de pé** standing; **de joelhos** kneeling; **de chapéu na cabeça** with (his) hat on; **de vestido de noite** in an evening dress; **4** *(transporte)* **de carro/barco** by car/boat; **de autocarro** *(BR: ônibus)* on/by bus; **5** *(fam)* **o infeliz do homem** the poor man; **6** *(tempo, situação)* **estar de folga/férias** to be on leave/on holiday; **estar de baixa** to be on sick leave; **7** *(grau de comp.) (do que)* **ela é mais linda do que a irmã** than; she is more beautiful than her sister; **8** *(causa, modo)* **morrer de fome** to die of hunger; **de mansinho** softly; **9** *(obrigação)* **você tem de partir agora** you have to leave now; **10 de quem** *(interrog)* **de quem é esta mala** whose suitcase is this? **11** *(distância)* **perto** ~ near to, nearby; **longe** ~ far from; **falar de** to speak about; ♦ *adv* **de manhã** in the morning; **de dia** by day; **de três em três horas** every three hours; **de dois em dois dias** every other day; **de tempos a tempos** every now and then.

For verbs which require 'de' see the verb in question; e.g. gostar de, lembrar-se de, esquecer-se de, etc.

dê *(pres conj e imperativo de dar)*; **dê-me uma cerveja** give me a beer.

deambular *vi (vaguear)* to wander, stroll (around).

deão, deã *m,f* dean, woman dean.

debaixo *adv* below, underneath; ~ **da prateleira** underneath the shelf; ♦ *prep* ~ **de** under, beneath, below, ~ **da terra** beneath the ground, in the grave; ~ **do braço** under the arm.

debalde *adv* in vain.

debandada *f* stampede, disorderly flight; **2** *(MIL)* rout; **3 em** ~ in confusion.

debandar *vt* to put to flight; ♦ *vi* to disperse.

debate *m* debate; argument.

debater *vt* to debate; to discuss; ♦ ~**-se** *vr* to struggle.

debelar *vt (dominar)* to subdue, defeat; **2** *(doença, problem)* to control, overcome; **3** to make sth disappear, extinguish.

debicar *vt/vi (pássaros)* to peck (at); **2** *(comer pouco)* to nibble (at food) pick at.

débil *(pl: -eis) adj inv* weak, feeble, frail; **2** *(luz, som)* dim, faint; **3** *(vontade)* fainthearted; **4** *(resultados)* poor, weak.

debilidade *f* weakness, frailty, debility; **2** *(PSIC)* ~ **mental** mental debility; **3** *(falta de vigor, poder)* weakness.

debilitar *vt* to weaken; ♦ ~**-se** *vr* to become weak, weaken.

debique *m* nibble; picking (on/at); **2** *(fig)* banter; mockery.

debitar *vt* to debit; to charge.

débito *m* debit.

debochado,-a *adj (pessoa devassa)* lewd, licentious, debauched; **2** *(desleixado)* slovenly, sluttish; **3** *(BR) (trocista)* teaser, joker.

debochar *vt* to corrupt *(alguém)*; to lead astray; **2** *(BR)* to make fun of sb.

deboche *m (libertinagem)* debauchery; **2** *(BR)* mockery, scorn.

debruar *vt (orlar)* to trim, edge, to hem; **2** to adorn; ~ **algo** decorate sth.

debruçar-se *vr* to bend over; ~ **à janela** to lean out of the window.

debrum *m (fita com que se adorna)* binding; border *(de cortina, saia, quadro)*.

debulha *f (de cereais)* threshing.

debulhadora *f* threshing machine.

debulhar *vt* to thresh *(milho, trigo)*; **2** to shell, pod *(ervilhas)*; ♦ ~**-se** *vr*: ~**-se em lágrimas** to burst into tears.

debutante *m,f* debutante; ♦ *adj inv* new.

debutar *vi* to appear for the first time, make one's debut.

década *f* decade.

decadência *f* decadence.

decadente *adj inv* decadent.

decaedro *m* decahedron.

decágono *m* decagon.

decair *vi* to fall, decline; **2** to decay, deteriorate; **3** *(perder o vigor)* to fade, wither.

decalcar *vt (desenho)* to trace; **2** *(fig) (imitar)* to copy.

decalque *m* tracing.

decano *m* deacon, dean; **2** oldest member; senior, elder.

decantar *vt (vinho)* to decant; **2** *(fig)* to purify, cleanse *(alma)*; **3** *(celebrar em verso)* to exalt, sing the praises of.

decapitar *vt* to behead, decapitate.

decassílabo *m* decasyllable; ♦ *adj (verso)* decasyllabic.

decatio *m* decathlon.

decência *f* decency.

decénio *(BR: -cê-) m* a period of ten years; decennium.

decente *adj inv (digno)* decent, respectable; **2** *(trabalho)* proper, suitable; **uma casa** ~ a nice home.

decepado,-a *adj* maimed, amputated.

decepar *vt* to cut off, sever; **2** *(MED) (braço, perna)* to amputate; **3** *(cabeça)* to chop off; **4** *(fig) (interromper)* to cut short *(futuro)*.

dece(p)ção *f* disappointment; **2** deception.

dece(p)cionar *vt* to disappoint, to let down; ♦ ~-se *vr* to be disappointed with.

decerto *adv* certainly, surely, for sure.

decesso *m (morte)* death.

decididamente *adv* decidedly, certainly.

decidido,-a *adj* determined, resolute, decided; **2** *(caso, negócio)* settled, resolved.

decidir *vt* to decide; **2** to resolve; ♦ ~-se *vr*: ~ **a** to make up one's mind to; ~ **por** *(optar)* to opt for, go for.

decifrar *vt* to decipher; **2** to unravel; to work out.

decifrável *adj inv* decipherable; legible.

decimal *adj, m* decimal.

decímetro *m* decimeter.

décimo,-a *num* tenth; ♦ *adj* tenth; **o** ~ **andar** the tenth floor.

decisão *f* decision; **2** resolution; **3** *(qualidade)* decisiveness.

decisivo,-a *adj* decisive; **2** deciding.

declamação *f* recitation; **2** declamation; **3** *(pej)* ranting.

declamar *vt (poema)* to recite; **2** *(pej) (discurso)* to rant.

declaração *f* declaration; statement; **2** ~ **de amor** proposal; **3** ~ **de rendimentos** tax return; **4 de direitos**.

declarar *vt* to declare; **2** to state; ♦ ~-se *vr* to declare o.n.; ~-**se culpado** to plead guilty.

declinação *f (gram)* declension; **2** *(ASTRON)* declination, waning; set; **3** *(declínio)* slope; **4** *(diminuição)* reduction.

declinar *vt* to decline, decay; **2** *(convite, oferta)* to refuse, turn down; ~ **de fazer** to decline to do; **3** *(ASTRON) (diminuir)* to go down, fade; **4** *(inclinado)* to slope; ♦ *vi (fig)* to sink (morally).

declínio *m* decline; **2** *(descida)* going down; **3** *(ASTRON)* setting; **4** *(FÍS) (desvio)* pointing (to).

declive *m* slope, incline.

decolagem *f (BR) (avião)* take-off.

decolar *vt (BR)* to take off. *(EP = Vd: desco-)*

decompor *vt* to analyse, break down; **2** *(MAT)* to decompose; **3** to rot, decay; ♦ ~-se *vr* to decay, decompose; **2** to go rotten.

decomposição *f* decay, rot; **2** *(desintegração)* decomposition; **3** *(division)* breaking down.

decoração *f* decoration; ~ **de interiores** interior decoration; **2** *(TEAT)* stage setting, scenery.

decorador,-ora *m,f (profissional)* decorator.

decorar *vt* to decorate; **2** *(memorizar)* to learn by heart.

decorativo,-a *adj* decorative.

decoro *m* decency; decorum; **com** ~ properly.

decoroso,-a *adj* decent, respectable.

decorrente *adj* resulting from.

decorrer *m*: **no** ~ **do tempo** in the course of, during; **com o** ~ **do tempo** with the passing of time; ♦ *vi (tempo)* to pass, elapse; **2** *(ocorrer)* to take place, happen; ~ **de** to result/stem from.

decotado,-a *adj (vestido)* low-necked.

decotar *vt (vestuário)* to cut a low neckline in.

decote *m* low neckline; décolletage; ~ **redondo** crew neck; ~ **subido** high neck.

decrépito,-a *adj* decrepit, worn out; **2** *(fig) (prédio)* dilapidated; **3** *(fig) (ideias etc., obsoletas)* old-fashioned.

decrepitude *f* decrepitude; **2** *(fig) (decadência)* decline.

decrescente *adj inv* decreasing, diminishing; **por ordem** ~ in descending order.

decrescer *vi* to decrease, diminish.

decréscimo *m (diminuição)* decrease, decline.

decretar *vt* to decree, order; to enact; **2** *(um dever, medida)* establish, to make it a rule, order.

decreto *m* decree, order; ~-**lei** *m* decree, edit, writ; **promulgar um** ~-**lei** to issue a decree, law.

decuplar, decuplicar *vt/vi* to multiply/increase tenfold, ten times over.

décuplo *adj* tenfold, decuple.

decurso *m* course; **no** ~ **de** in the course of, during.

dedada *f* fingerprint; **2** *(marca deixada pelo dedo)* finger stain, mark; **3** *(pitada)* pinch; bit; **uma** ~ **de sal** a pinch of salt.

dedal *m* thimble; **2** thimbleful.

dédalo *m* labyrinth, maze; **2** *(complicação)* mess.

dedeira *f (MÚS)* plectrum; **2** *(para cobrir o dedo no croché)* fingerstall.

dedicação *f* dedication; devotion.

dedicar *vt* to dedicate (**a**, to); to devote (**a**, to); ♦ ~-se *vr*: ~ **a** to devote o.s. to; **2** *(estudos)* to apply o.s. to.

dedicatória *f (mensagem em livro)* signature; dedication; **2** inscription.

dedilhar *vt (MÚS)* to finger, to strum; ~ **a guitarra** to play/strum the guitar.

dedo *m* finger; *(do pé)* toe; ~ **anular** ring finger; ~ **indicador/índice**, index finger; ~ **mínimo** little finger; ~ **polegar** thumb; ~ **médio** middle finger; **ponta dos** ~s fingertips; **nós dos** ~s knuckles; **2** *(fig) (aptidão)* knack, good at; **ela tem dedo para a cozinha** she is good at cooking; IDIOM **estar a dois** ~s **de** be close to; **dar dois** ~s **de conversa** to chat a little; **saber na ponta dos** ~s to know sth well, at one's fingertips; **ter um** ~ **que adivinha** a little bird told me; *(fam)* **ficar a chuchar no** ~ to be left empty-handed, be disappointed; **apontar (alguém) com o** ~ to accuse sb, point the finger at; **meter os** ~s **pelos olhos** (**a alguém**) to impose one's ideas/opinions on sb.

dedução *f* deduction; inference; **2** subtraction.

deduzir *vt* to deduct; ♦ *vi* to deduce, infer.

defecação *f* defecation.

defecar *vt* to defecate.

defecção, defeção *f* defection; desertion; **2** apostasy.

defectivo,-a, defetivo,-a *adj* faulty, defective; **2** *(gram)* defective.

defeito *m* defect, flaw, fault; **pôr ~s em** to find fault with; **com ~** broken, out of order; **ter ~** to be faulty, have a fault.

defeituoso,-a *adj* defective, faulty.

defender *vt* to defend; to protect; ♦ **~-se** *vr*: **~ de** to stand up against; to defend o.s.

defensável *adj inv* defensible.

defensiva *f* defensive; **ficar na ~** to be on the defensive.

defensor,-ora *m,f* defender; **2** *(JUR)* defending counsel, defence *(US)* defense.

deferência *f (respeito)* deference; respect.

deferimento *m* approval; granting.

deferir *vt* to approve; **2** to grant, bestow; ♦ *vi* to concede; **2** to defer.

defesa *f* defence *(UK)*, defense *(US)*; **em legítima ~** in self-defence; **2** protection; **~ do consumidor** consumer's protection; **3** *(JUR)* counsel for the defence, *(US)* defense attorney; **4** *m (FUT)* defence (UK), defense (US); **5** **~s** *fpl* tusks, fangs, horns.

defeso *m (caça, pesca)* close season; **2** *(DESP)* out of season; ♦ *adj (proibido – acesso)* forbidden.

défice *(BR: déficit) m* deficit.

deficiência *f (falta de)* deficiency; **2** *(MED)* **~ física/mental** physical/mental disability.

deficiente *adj inv* deficient, lacking; **2** *(pessoa)* incapacitated; **3** *(MED)* **~ físico/mental** physically/mentally handicapped/disabled.

definhar *vt* to emaciate, weaken; **2** *(secar, plantas)* to wither; ♦ *vi (murchar)* to droop; **2** *(pessoa)* to weaken, waste away.

definição *f* definition.

definido,-a *adj* defined, explained *(programa)* definite; **2** *(gram)* definite.

definir *vt* to define, explain; **2** *(preços, regras)* to determine; ♦ **~-se** *vr* to make out one's mind; **~ sobre** to give one's opinion, position on (against/in favour).

definitivo,-a *adj* defining; **2** *(final)* conclusive, definitive; **3** *(posição)* final.

deflação *f (ECON, GEOL)* deflation.

deflagração *f (incêndio)* deflagration; explosion; **2** *(guerra)* outbreak.

deflagrar *vi (explodir)* to burst, explode; **2** *(espalhar, rebentar)* to break out; **fogos que deflagram** fires that spread/break out.

defloração *f (de mulher)* deflowering.

deformação *f* alteration; **2** distortion.

deformar *vt (corpo)* to deform; **2** *(rosto)* disfigure; **3** *(deturpar)* to distort *(imagem, verdade)*; ♦ **~-se** *vr* to become deformed.

deforme *adj inv* deformed.

deformidade *f* deformity.

defraudação *f* fraud; embezzlement.

defraudar *vt (espoliar)* to defraud, embezzle, to cheat.

defrontar *vt (enfrentar)* to face; **2** *(oponente, concorrente)* to confront; **3** *(problema)* to face up to; ♦ *vi:* **~ com** to come upon; ♦ **~-se com** *vr* to come face to face, to face each other; **2** *(problemas)* to confront.

defronte *adv* opposite, facing, across the road; **2** **~ de** *prep* opposite, facing.

defumado,-a *adj (seco ao fumo)* smoked; **salmão ~** smoked salmon.

defumar *vt (presunto, etc)* to cure-smoke; **2** to fumigate; **3** *(perfumar)* to perfume.

defunto,-a *m,f* dead person; **2** late, former; **a associação ~** the late/former association; ♦ *adj* dead deceased.

degelar *vt* to defrost, thaw; ♦ *vi* to thaw out.

degelo *m* thaw; **2** *(METEOR)* thawing.

degeneração *f* degeneration; **2** corruption.

degenerar *vi* to degenerate *(em into)*; **2** *(deteriorar)* deteriorate; **3** **~ em** *(transformar-se)* to turn into.

degenerativo,-a *adj* degenerative; **doença ~a** degenerative illness.

deglutir *vt/vi* to swallow.

degola, degolação beheading; **2** throat-cutting; **3** *(fig) (BR)* large-scale redundancy; **4** *(DESP) (BR)* sacking.

degolar *vt* to cut sb's throat, to behead.

degradação *f* degradation.

degradar *vt* to degrade, debase; ♦ **~-se** *vr* to demean o.s.

degradado,-a *adj* degraded; **2** *(prédio, área)* rundown.

degrau *m (escada)* step; **2** *(escadote)* rung; **3** *(fig) (para atingir um fim)* means, step up.

degredar *vt* to exile.

degredo *m (pena)* exile.

degustação *f* tasting, sampling.

degustar *vt (vinho, comida)* to taste; to sip (wine).

deificar *vt* to deify.

deitado,-a *(pp de deitar) adj (pessoa)* lying down; in bed; **2** *(object)* set down.

deitar *vt (estender na horizontal)* to lay down; **2** *(dormir)* to put to bed *(alguém)*; **3** to put (in, on), place; **deita a cabeça nesta almofada** put your head on this pillow/cushion; **4** to cast; **5** to pour; **deita mais vinho** pour more wine; **6** **~ sangue** to bleed; **7** **~ abaixo** *(árvore, prédio, pessoa)* to knock down; *(governo)* to overthrow; **8** **~ a** start suddenly, **~ correr** to start running; **9** **~ uma carta no correio** to post a letter; **10** **~ fora** to throw away/out; **11** **~ foguetes** to let off rockets, fireworks; **12** **~ as culpas a (alguém)** to lay the blame on sb; **13** *(NAÚT)* **~ âncora** to drop anchor; **14** **~ para** overlooks (place); **15** **~ a perder** to put in jeopardy; ♦ **~-se** *vr* to lie down; go to bed; **2** *(atacar)* **o lobo deitou-se às galinhas** the wolf attacked the chickens; **3** to throw; **o homem deitou-se à água** the man threw himself into the water.

In Brazil and in some regions of Portugal, the verbs 'jogar' and 'botar' are used in preference to 'deitar'.

deixa *f* hint; **2** *(TEAT)* actor's cue; **3** opportunity, chance; **4** *(legado)* inheritance.

deixar *vt (gen)* to leave (behind); ~ **ficar** *(algo)* leave sth behind; **ele deixou ficar o casaco** he left his coat behind; **2** *(abandonar)* to abandon; *(demitir-se)* resign; **3** *(permitir)* to let, allow; **deixa-o brincar** let him play; ~ **passar** to let go *(alguém)*; to overlook *(algo)*; **4** *(morrer)* **ele deixou dois filhos** he left two children; **5** *(largar, soltar)* **deixa o rapaz** leave the boy alone, let the boy go; **deixe-me em paz!** leave me alone; **6** ~ **cair** to drop, to let fall; ♦ *vi (cessar)* give up, stop; **eu deixei de fumar** I stopped smoking; **2** *(ter de)* must; **não posso** ~ **de lhe falar** I must speak to her/him; **3** *(excluir)* ~ **de lado** to set aside; leave out *(algo)*; ♦ *vr (permanecer)* **ele deixou-se ficar** he stayed; **2** *(separar-se)* **eles deixaram-se** they are separated; they split up; **3** *(abster-se de)* leave off; **deixa-te de vaidades** leave off being vain; **deixa-te de rodeios** stop beating about the bush; ♦ *exc* **deixe-me em paz!** leave me alone!; **deixa estar!** leave it!, let it be!; *(tolerância)* don't worry!; *(ameaça)* just you wait!

deje(c)to *m* defecation; **2** excremento.

dela (= **de** + **ela**) her/hers; **o lápis** ~ her pencil.

delamber-se *vr* to rejoice; to lick.

delambido,-a *m* prig; fop; ♦ *adj (afectado)* saucy, foppish.

delapidar *vt* to dissipate, waste *(fortuna)*.

delatar *vt (denunciar)* to denounce; **2** to inform on; **3** to revel; **4** *(polícia)* to report.

delator,-ora *m,f* informer.

dele (= **de** + **ele**) his; **a mesa** ~ his table.

delegação *f* delegation; ~ **de poderes** transfer of powers.

delegacia *f* delegacy; *(BR)* ~ **de polícia** police station.

delegado,-a *m,f* delegate, representative; deputy; **D~ do Ministério Público** public prosecutor.

delegar *vt* to delegate.

deleitante *adj inv* delightful, delectable.

deleitar *vt* to delight; ♦ **~-se** *vr:* ~ **com** to enjoy, delight in, take pleasure in.

deleite *m* delight.

deleitoso,-a *adj* delightful.

deletério,-a *adj* harmful, noxious; **2** *(companhia, ideias)* bad.

delfim *m (ZOOL)* dolphin; **2** *(peça de xadrez)* bishop; **3** *(HIST)* Dauphin; **4** *(ASTRON)* Delphinus.

delgado,-a *adj* slim, slender; **2** thin; **3** fine; **4** *(ANAT) (intestino)* small (intestine).

deliberação *f* deliberation; decision.

deliberar *vt* to decide, resolve; ♦ *vi* to ponder.

delicadeza *f* courtesy, kindness; **2** delicacy; **3** fragility; **4** *(pele)* softness; **5** *(palavras, atitude)* sweetness.

delicado,-a *adj* delicate; **2** *(modos)* courteous; **3** *(saúde)* frail; **4** sensitive; **5** *(tecido, vidro, objectos)* fine, exquisite; **6** *(pele)* soft, silky.

delícia *f* delight, pleasure; **2** *(CULIN)* a delicacy.

delicioso,-a *adj* delightful, charming; **2** delicious.

delimitação *f* demarcation, limiting the boundaries.

delimitar *vt* to delimit, to bound, demarcate; **2** to mark the limits.

delinear *vt* to outline, sketch; **2** to plan out; **3** to lay out (a course of action).

delinquência *f* delinquency.

delinquente *adj inv* delinquent, criminal.

delirante *adj inv* delirious; overjoyed.

delirar *vi* to be delirious; **2** to go mad, wild.

delírio *m (MED)* delirium; **2** ecstasy; excitement.

delito *m (JUR)* crime; offence; **apanhar alguém em flagrante** ~ to catch red-handed, in the act.

delonga *f* delay; **sem mais** ~**s** without more ado; without further delays.

delta *f* delta.

demagogo *m* demagogue.

demais *adv* moreover, besides; ♦ *pron.dem.* the others, the rest; ♦ **de mais** *adv* too much.

Note: do not confuse 'demais' with 'de mais'.

demanda *f (JUR)* lawsuit; **2** claim; **3** *(JUR)* lawsuit; *(BR: ECON)* demand; **4** search, quest; **em** ~ **de** in search of, in quest of.

Not 'demanda' when you speak of 'demand and supply', which is 'oferta e procura' (EP); except in Brazil = demanda e procura.

demandar *vt (JUR)* to sue; **2** to search for; **3** *(reclamar)* to demand; **ela demandava justiça** she demanded justice; **4** *(BR) (request)* pedir.

demão *f (tinta)* coat, layer; **dar a primeira** ~ to give the first coat (of paint).

demarcação *f* demarcation.

demarcar *vt* to demarcate; to mark out.

demasia *f* excess, surplus; **2** lack of moderation; **3** **em** ~ too much, in excess.

demasiado,-a *adj* excessive, too much; *(pl)* too many; **2** immoderate; ♦ *adv* too much, too; ~ **alto** *(som)* too loud.

demência *f* insanity, madness.

demente *adj inv* crazy, demented.

demissão *f (do empregador)* dismissal; *(do empregado)* resignation; ~ **em bloco** large-scale dismissal; **pedir** ~ to resign.

demissionário,-a *adj* person resigning or being dismissed.

demitir *vt* to dismiss; **2** *(pop)* to sack, to fire sb; ♦ **~-se** *vr* to resign.

Demo *m* devil.

democracia *f* democracy.

democrata *m,f* democrat.

democrático,-a *adj* democratic.

demografia *f* demography.

demográfico,-a *adj* demographic.

demolhar *vt (pôr de molho) (feijão, grão, bacalhau)* to soak.

demolição *f* demolition.

demolir *vt* to demolish, knock down; **2** *(fig)* to destroy.

demoníaco,-a *adj* devilish; satanic.

demónio (*BR*: -mô-) *m* (*criança travessa*) little devil/ monkey; **D~** *npr* Devil, Demon; ◆ *exc* **com os demónios!** Hell!

demonstração *f* demonstration; **2** (*de afecto*) show, display; **3** proof.

demonstrar *vt* to demonstrate; **2** to prove; **3** to show.

demonstrativo,-a *adj* demonstrative.

demora *f* delay; **sem ~** at once, without delay.

demorar *vt* to delay, slow down; ◆ *vi* to stay long; to be late; **~ a chegar** to be a long time coming; **vai ~ muito?** will it take long?; ◆ **~-se** *vr* to stay too long, linger; **não me demoro nada** I shan't be long.

demoroso,-a *adj* tardy; slow.

demover *vt* to dissuade; **2** (*deslocar*) to move.

denegrir *vt* to blacken; **2** to denigrate.

dengoso,-a *adj* languishing; **2** goody-goody; **3** (*maneira*) affected; **4** coy.

dengue *m* affectation, primness; **2** (*MED*) (*febre*) dengue.

denodado,-a *adj* brave, daring.

denominação *f* denomination; **2** name; **3** (*ato*) naming.

denominator *m* (*MAT*) denominator; **~ comum** common denominator.

denotar *vt* (*revelar*) to show, indicate; to denote (*tristeza, miséria*).

densidade *f* density.

densidão *f* denseness.

denso,-a *adj* dense, thick; **2** compact; **3** (*fig*) (*estilo cerrado*) heavy.

dentada *f* bite.

dentado,-a *adj* toothed; **2** serrated; **roda ~** cogged wheel; **3** indented.

dentadura *f* (set of) teeth; **2** dentures *pl.*

dental *adj inv* dental; **fio ~** flossy; **palito ~** tooth pick.

dente *m* tooth; **~ abalado** loose tooth; **~ postiço** false tooth; **~ do siso** wisdom tooth; **chumbar/ obturar um ~** to have a filling, a tooth filled; **arrancar um ~** to have a tooth pulled out; **arreganhar os ~s** (*sorriso falso*) to smile; **2** (*de animal*) fang; tusk; **3** (*de garfo*) prong; **4** (*de alho*) clove; IDIOM **lutar com unhas e ~s** to fight tooth and nail; **dar com a língua nos ~s** to spill the beans; **falar por entre os ~s** to mumble, mutter; **quando as galinhas tiverem ~s** when pigs can fly.

dente-de-cão *m* (*BOT*) (*lillaceae*) bulbous plant from Portugal's hills, a kind of lilly.

dente-de-leão *m* (*BR*) (*BOT*) dandelion.

dentifrício *m* toothpaste.

dentista *m,f* dentist.

dentola *f* (*fam*) large tooth; bucktooth.

dentre (**de** + **entre**) *prep* among, amidst, from among.

dentro *adv* inside; **aí ~** in there; ◆ *prep*: **~ de** inside; within; **~ de dois dias** in/within two days; **2 ~ em breve/em pouco** soon, shortly; **3 de ~ para fora** inside out.

dentuça *f* (*col*) buck-teeth.

dentuço,-a, dentudo,-a *adj* big-toothed, buck-toothed.

denudar *vt* to make bare; to strip.

denúncia *f* denunciation; **2** accusation; **3** (*à polícia*) complaint, report; **4** (*JUR*) indictment; **5** (*contrato*) termination.

denunciar *vt* to denounce, inform against; **2** to reveal; **3** (*em segredo*) to accuse; **4** (*contrato*) to terminate; **5** (*pregão de casamento*) to announce, proclaim wedding banns; ◆ **~-se** *vr* to confess.

deontologia *f* deontology.

deparar *vi* (*encontrar*) to come across; be faced with; ◆ *vr*: **~-se com** to come across/upon, find; **deparou-se-nos a porta aberta** we found/were faced with the door open.

departamento *m* department.

depauperar *vt* (*pessoa, empresa*) to impoverish; **2** to enfeeble,weaken; **3** (*esgotar*) to run out of; ◆ **~-se** *vr* to become weak.

depenado,-a *adj* (*ave*) plucked; **2** (*fam*) broke.

depenar *vt* (*ave*) to pluck; **2** (*fam*) (*extorquir dinheiro*) to fleece sb.

dependência *f* dependence, under the orders (of); **2** dependency; **~ de heroína** drug addiction; **3** (*divisões de casa*) room; (*BR*) annexe.

dependente *m,f* drug-addict; ◆ *adj inv* (*subordinado*) dependent; subject to; **estamos ~s das condições** we are subject to the conditions.

depender *vi*: **~ de** to depend on/upon; be dependent on.

dependurar *vi* to hang sth (on sth); ◆ **~-se** *vr* (*em algo*) to hang from sth.

depilar *vt* to remove hair from.

depilatório *m* hair-remover (cream, wax); ◆ *adj* hair-removing.

deplorar *vt* to deplore; **2** to regret.

deplorável *adj inv* deplorable; **2** regrettable.

depoimento *m* (*JUR*) testimony, evidence, deposition.

depois *adv* afterwards, later; **2** then; **3** next; ◆ *prep* **~ de** after; **2 para ~** afterwards, later; ◆ *conj* besides, what's more; **2 ~ que** after, when; **~ que ele saiu** after (when) he left; ◆ *exc* **e ~?** so what?, and then?

depor *vt* to depose; **2** (*armas*) to hand over, lay down; **3** to dethrone; ◆ *vi* (*JUR*) **~ a favor/contra** to testify (for/against); **2** to deposit; ◆ **~-se** *vr* (*ficar no fundo*) to settle.

deportação *f* deportation.

deportar *vt* to deport.

deposição *f* deposition; **2** dismissal; **3** (*de armas*) laying down; **4** (*JUR*) statement, evidence.

depositar *vt* to deposit; to store; **2** (*voto*) to cast; **3 ~ confiança em** to place one's confidence in; **4** put (sth in sth); ◆ **~-se** *vr* to form a deposit, settle.

depositário,-a *m,f* trustee; **2** (*fig*) confidant, confidante.

depósito *m* deposit; warehouse, depot; **2** (*de lixo*) dump; tank; **~ de bagagens** left-luggage office; **conta ~** savings account.

depravação *f* depravity, corruption.

depravar *vt* to deprave, corrupt; to ruin; ◆ **~-se** *vr* to become depraved.

depreciação *f* depreciation; **2** (*fig*) scorn.

depreciar *vt* to undervalue; to devalue; **2** *(fig)* *(rebaixar)* to belittle, undermine; ♦ ~**-se** *vr* to fall in value; **2** to underestimate.

depredação *f* depredation, plundering.

depredar *vt* to pillage, plunder, loot.

depressa *adv* fast, quickly; **vamos** ~ let's hurry.

depressão *f* depression.

deprimido,-a *adj* depressed, low.

deprimir *vt* to depress; ♦ ~**-se** *vr* to get depressed.

depuração *f* purification.

depurar *vt* *(sangue, água)* to purify; **2** *(petróleo)* to refine; **3** *(fig)* *(sanear)* to purge; ♦ ~**-se** *vr* to become purified, be cleansed.

depurador *m* purifier.

deputado,-a *m,f* deputy; senator, MP (Member of Parliament) *(UK)*; **2** *(US, POL)* Representative.

deque *m* decking *(no jardim, etc)*.

dera *(pluperf de* **dar***)*; *exc* **quem me** ~! how I wish! **quem me** ~ **que fosse assim**! I wish it were so!

derisão *(Vd:* **der(r)isão***)*.

deriva *f* drift; **ir à** ~ to drift; be off-course; **ficar à** ~ to be adrift.

derivação *f* drift; diversion; **2** *(LÍNG)* derivation; **3** *(fig)* origem.

derivada *f* *(MAT)* derivative.

derivado *m* *(LÍNG)* derivative; ~**s** *mpl* *(produto)* by-product(s); **leite e** ~**s** milk and its by-products/dairy products; ♦ **derivado,-a** *adj* derived from.

derivar *vt* to change the course of; **2** *(LÍNG)* ~ **de** to stem from; ♦ *vi* to deviate; go off course/route; **4** *(mudar)* to move, change *(assunto)*.

dermatologia *f* dermatology.

dermatológico,-a *adj* dermatological.

derme *f* *(pele)* skin, dermis, derma.

démico-a *adj* dermal.

dermoprote(c)tor *adj* kind to the skin; **creme** ~ barrier cream, protector.

derradeiro,-a *adj* last, final.

derramamento *m* spilling; shedding.

derramar *vt* *(entornar)* to spill; **2** *(luz)* to shed; **3** *(espalhar)* to spread, strew; ♦ ~**-se** *vr* to pour out; **2** *(lágrimas, sangue)* to flow; ~ **em lágrimas** to weep.

derrame *m* *(de petróleo)* spill; **2** *(MED)* ~ **cerebral** brain haemorrhage; **3** ~ **de líquidos** leakage; **4** *(GEOL)* stream of lava.

derrapagem *f* skidding.

derrapar *vt* to skid, to sideslip.

derreado *adj* *(que não pode endireitar as costas)* bent down, stooped.

derredor *adv prep:* **em** ~ **(de)** around.

derreter *vt* *(liquefazer)* to melt; **2** dissolve; **3** *(consumir)* melt *(velas)*; **4** *(fig)* *(esbanjar)* squander *(dinheiro)*; ♦ ~**-se** *vr* *(gordura, metal)* to melt; *(gelo)* thaw; **2** *(fig)* to feel moved; to dote **(por** on); **ele derreteu-se a ouvi-la** he went all soft listening to her; **ela derrete-se por ele** she dotes on him.

derretimento *m* melting; thawing; **2** *(fig)* tenderness.

der(r)isão *f* derision, mockery, scornful laughter.

derrocada *f* downfall; **2** collapse; **3** destruction, ruin.

derrocar *vt* to overthrow; destroy; demolish.

derrogar *vt* *(JUR)* to annul, revoke, derogate.

derrota *f* defeat; **2** *(NÁUT)* route, course.

derrotar *vt* to defeat; **2** *(jogos)* to beat; **3** *(barco, avião)* to go off course.

derrubar *vt* to knock over, pull down; **2** *(árvores)* to fall; **3** to destroy, ruin; **4** *(poder)* to overthrow.

desabafar *vt* *(destapar)* uncover *(alguém)*; **2** *(fig)* *(livrar-se de ira)* let off steam; ♦ *vi* breathe deeply; **2** to confide *(tristezas)*; open one's heart **(com alguém** to sb); ♦ *exc* **vamos, desabafa!** come on, get it off your chest.

desabafo *m* *(alívio)* relief; **ter um** ~ **com alguém** to cry on sb's shoulder; to open up to sb.

desabalado,-a *adj* excessive; **2** *(espavorido)* **sair/correr** ~ go/run hastily, headlong.

desabamento *m* *(casa)* tumbling down, collapse; **2** *(terras)* landslide.

desabar *vi* to fall, tumble down.

desabitado,-a *adj* unoccupied.

desabituar *vt* ~ **de** *(de fazer algo)* wean sb off *(doing sth)*; ♦ ~**-se** *vr* to lose the habit of.

desabono *m* discredit; ♦ **em** ~ **de** *prep* to the discredit/detriment of *(honra, verdade)*.

desabotoar *vt* to unbutton.

desabrido,-a *adj* *(pessoa)* rude, curt; **2** *(resposta)* sharp; **3** *(tempo)* rough; wild.

desabrigado,-a *adj* unsheltered; **2** unprotected.

desabrochar *vi* *(flores)* to open, bloom, blossom; **2** *(fig)* *(jovem)* to blossom.

desabusado,-a *adj* free from prejudice; **2** unrestrained; bold.

desacatar *vt* to disregard; **2** to desecrate; **3** to scorn.

desacato *m* disrespect; **2** disregard.

desacerbar *vt* to temper; to soften.

desacertar *vt* to miss; **2** to blunder.

desacerto *m* mistake, blunder.

desacordo *m* disagreement; **2** discord.

desacostumado,-a *adj* unaccustomed.

desacreditado,-a *adj* discredited.

desacreditar *vt* to discredit *(alguém)*; ♦ ~**-se** *vr* to lose one's reputation.

desafeto *m* lack of affection.

desafiador,-ora *m,f* challenger; ♦ *adj* challenging; defiant.

desafiar *vt* to challenge; **2** to defy.

desafinado,-a *adj* *(MÚS)* out of tune; **2** out of sorts.

desafinar *vt* to spoil; **2** to put an instrument out of tune; ♦ *vi* to play out of tune.

desafio *m* challenge; **2** *(futebol, etc)* match, game.

desafogado,-a *adj* unencumbered, relieved; **2** *(trânsito)* clear; **3 viver** ~ to live comfortably.

desafogar *vt* *(espírito)* to free; **2** to relieve; **3** *(garganta, trânsito)* to clear; ♦ ~**-se** *vr* to open up to sb; to be at ease; to get out of a crisis.

desafogo *m* relief; **2** *(de trabalho)* break.

desaforado,-a *adj* rude, insolent; **2** *(atrevido)* saucy.

desaforo *m* insolence, insult; IDIOM *(BR)* **não levar** ~ **para casa** not take it lying down.

desafortunado,-a *adj* unfortunate, unlucky.

desagradar *vt* to displease; offend.

desagradável *adj inv* unpleasant.

desagrado *m* displeasure.

desagravar *vt* to make amends for (sth); to make amends to (sb); ♦ **~-se** *vr* to avenge o.s.

desagravo *m* amends *pl*; **2** *(JUR)* compensation, reparation.

desagregação *f* separation; **2** *(dos elementos)* disintegration.

desagregar *vt* to break up, split; **2** to separate; ♦ **~-se** *vr* to break up, split; **2** to separate.

desaguar *vt* to drain; ♦ *vi* *(rio)* to flow (into), to disgorge.

desaire *m* set back; awkwardness; **2** (DESP) rout.

desairoso,-a *adj* awkward, ungainly.

desajeitado,-a *adj* clumsy, awkward.

desajuizado,-a *adj* foolish, unwise, senseless.

desalentado,-a *adj* disheartened.

desalentar *vt* to discourage; to depress.

desalento *m* discouragement.

desalinhado,-a *adj* untidy, disorderly.

desalinho *m* untidiness, carelessness; **em ~** untidy.

desalmado,-a *adj* *(pessoa)* cruel, soulless, inhuman.

desalojar *vt* to dislodge; **2** to remove sth/sb from; to oust; ♦ **~-se** *vr* to move out; **2** to quit.

desamaõ *adv* à **~** out of hand; **3** *(longe)* out of the way.

desamarrar *vt* to untie; ♦ *vi* *(NÁUT)* to cast off.

desamor *m* dislike; antipathy.

desamparado,-a *adj* helpless; abandoned; forsaken.

desamparar *vt* to abandon; forsake.

desamparo *m* lack of help; ♦ *adv* **ao ~** without means of support.

desanda *f* *(pop)* telling-off, reprimand.

desandar *vi* *(mover-se em sentido contrário)* to turn/roll backwards; **2** to unscrew; **3** dar com força *(murro)* **~ uma bofetada** to give sb a slap, blow; **4** *(fig)* *(declínio)* **o mercado está a ~** the market is going to pieces; **5** *(fig)* to change into/turned to; **a festa desandou em zaragata** the party turned into a quarrel; **6 ~ a correr** to break into a run; **7 ~ a chorar** to burst into tears; IDIOM **isto nem anda nem desanda** this thing doesn't go one way or another.

desanimado,-a *adj* disheartened, depressed, dull.

desanimar *vt* to discourage; to depress; ♦ **~-se** *vr* to lose heart.

desânimo *m* despondency, discouragement.

desanuviado,-a *adj* unclouded, clear.

desanuviar *vt* to clear *(céu)*; **2** *(fig)* *(acalmar)* relieve *(mente, espírito)*; ♦ *vi* to become calm, relax; ♦ **~-se** *vr* to clear up; to become tranquil.

desapaixonado,-a *adj* dispassionate.

desaparafusar *vt* to unscrew.

desaparecer *vi* to disappear, vanish.

desaparecido,-a *m,f* missing person; ♦ *adj* lost, missing.

desaparecimento *m* *(sumido)* disappearance; **2** *(morte, fim)* extinction.

desaparelhar *vt* *(retirar os arreios)* to unharness *(cavalo, bois)*; **2** *(desfazer máquina, conjunto)* break up.

desapegado,-a *adj* *(falta de afeição)* indifferent, detached.

desapegar *vt:* **~ alguém de algo** to detach sb from sth; separate; ♦ **~-se** *vr* to detach o.s. from sb/sth.

desapego *m* indifference, detachment.

desapercebido,-a *adj* *(desprovido)* unprepared; **2** devoid of; **3** unequipped.

desapertar *vt* *(sapatos)* to unfasten, unlace; **2** *(gravata)* to untie, undo; **3** *(fig)* *(aliviar)* open up *(coração)*; ♦ **~-se** *vr* *(vestuário)* to loosen; IDIOM **~ os cordões à bolsa** to loosen one's purse strings.

desapiedado,-a *adj* pitiless, ruthless.

desapiedar *vt* to harden sb; ♦ **~-se** *vr* to become hard, harden o.s.

desapontamento *m* disappointment, disillusion.

desapontar *vt* to disappoint.

desapossar *vt* *(alguém de)* to dispossess; **2** *(propriedade)* to take away; ♦ **~-se** *vr* *(renunciar)* to renounce to; **2** to free o.s. from.

desapreço *m* lack of appreciation.

desapropriação *f* seizing of property, dispossession; **2** *(renunciar os bens)* giving up one's assets.

desapropriar *vt* to expropriate; to dispossess *(alguém)*.

desaprovar *vt* to disapprove of; to object to.

desaproveitado,-a *adj* wasted, not used to advantage; **2** *(terra)* undeveloped; **3** *(riqueza)* squandered.

desarborização *f* deforestation.

desarmado,-a *adj* disarmed, unarmed; **2** *(armário)* dismantled.

desarmamento *m* disarmament; **2** *(NÁUT)* unrigging.

desarmar *vt* to disarm; **2** *(desmontar)* to dismantle, take down; **3** *(bomba)* to defuse; **4 ~ uma espingarda** uncock a gun.

desarmonia *f* discord, disagreement; **2** *(MÚS)* disharmony; **3** *(cores)* clash.

desarraigar (= **desarreigar**) *vt* to uproot.

desarranjado,-a *adj* untidy; **2** *(MED)* upset, queasy; **3** *(TEC)* out of order.

desarranjar *vt* to upset, disturb; **2** to mess up.

desarranjo *m* disorder, untidiness, mess; **2** inconvenience; **3** *(avaria)* breakdown; **4** *(pop)* *(aborto)* aborption.

desarreigar *(Vd: desarraigar)*.

desarrolhar *vt* *(garrafa, frasco)* to uncork; **2** *(fig, fam)* *(abir)* to let out.

desarrumado,-a *adj* untidy, messy.

desarrumar *vt* to disarrange, untidy; **2** *(fig)* *(ideias)* to confuse.

desarticulado,-a *adj* *(ossos)* dislocated; **2** *(desfeito)* broken up.

desarticular *vt* to dislocate; **2** to break up, separate; ♦ **~-se** *vr* *(boneca, mecanismo)* to fall to pieces.

desarvorado,-a *adj* *(navio)* dismasted; **2** *(precipitado)* disorientated, very upset.

desarvorar *vt* *(bandeira)* take down, lower; ♦ *vi* *(NÁUT)* to dismast; **2** *(fig)* to break away, bolt.

desassociar *vt* **~ algo/alguém (de)** to dissociate sb/sth from; ♦ **~-se** *vr* to dissociate o.s (from).

desassossego *m* disquiet, uneasiness; **2** restlessness; **3** noise, disturbance; **4** worry.

desastrado,-a *adj* disastrous; **2** awkward, clumsy.

desastre *m* accident; *(de avião)* crash; *(fig)* fracaso.

desastroso,-a *adj* disastrous.

desatar *vt* to unfasten; **2** to undo, untie; ♦ *vi* to start suddenly; ~ **a chorar** to burst into tears; ~ **a rir** to burst out laughing; ~ **a correr** to break into a run; **2** ~ **a língua** to speak freely; IDIOM **isto nem ata nem desata** it doesn't make any progress.

desatarraxar *vt* (*boião, caixa*) unscrew, undo; ♦ ~**-se** *vr* to come undone, loose.

desatenção *f* lack of attention; **2** carelessness.

desatento,-a *adj* inattentive.

desatinado,-a *adj* senseless; (*pessoa*) (*col*) nuts; **2** *adj* crazy.

desatinar *vt* to drive s.o. mad; ♦ *vi* to go mad.

desatino *m* madness, losing one's head; **2** confusion, bewilderment; **em** ~ in confusion.

desatualizado,-a *adj* out of date; **2** (*fora de moda*) old-fashioned; dated.

desavença *f* quarrel; strife, disagreement; **em** ~ at loggerheads.

desavergonhado,-a *m* (*homem*) rogue; ♦ *adj* insolent, impudent, shameless, brazen (faced); **2** (*pop*) cheeky, saucy.

desavir-se *vr* to fall out (**com** with).

desbaratamento *m* defeat; waste.

desbaratar *vt* (*desperdiçar*) to waste, squander; **2** (*derrotar*) defeat, to put to flight (*inimigos*); ♦ ~**-se** *vr* to scatter.

desbarato *m* waste; **2** (*derrota*) defeat; ♦ *adv* **ao** ~ at a low price, cheaply.

desbastar *vt* (*cabelo, arbusto*) to thin (out), to trim; **2** (*alisar*) to smooth; **3** (*fig*) (*gastar*) polish off.

desbastador *m* (*plaina grande*) jack-plane.

desbloquear *vt* to break through a blockade; **2** (*levantar o bloqueio*) to lift the embargo; **3** (*verbas*) to free; **4** (*fig*) to overcome.

desbotar *vt* to discolour; ♦ *vi* to fade; ♦ ~**-se** *vr* to fade.

desbravador,-ora *m,f* (*de mato, terra*) explorer; **2** (*animais*) tamer.

desbravar *vt* to explore; ~ **terras** to clear the land (*de vegetação*), prepare the soil; **2** (*animals*) to tame; (*cavalo*) to break in; **3** (*fig*) (*material, problema*) to study, get to the bottom of.

descabido,-a *adj* (*atitude, perguntas*) improper; **2** (*absurdo*) awkward; **3** (*louvor, crítica*) undeserved.

descair *vt* (*deixar cair*) (*cabeça, braços, ombros*) to lower; ♦ *vi* to go down, drop; **o decote descaía bastante** the décolletage/neckline dropped/went down quite a bit.

descalçar *vt* (*sapatos, luvas*) to take off; ♦ ~**-se** *vr* to take off one's shoes.

descalço,-a *adj* barefoot; **2** (*fig*) unwares; **apanharam-me** ~ I was caught unawares.

descamar *vt* (*peixe*) to scale.

descambar *vt* (*para um lado*) ~ **para** to topple towards, to swerve, slide; **2** to deteriorate into; **3** (*negócio, etc*) to go badly.

descampado *m* open country, desolate land; ♦ *adj* uninhabited.

descansado,-a *adj* rested, calm; **2** slow; **3** **fique** ~ don't worry, rest assured.

descansar *vt/vi* to rest, relax; **2** to lean on/against; **3** (*ficar*) to stand; **4** to calm down; ♦ *exc* (*MIL, DESP*) ~! at ease!

descanso *m* rest, break; **2** easiness; **3** relaxation; **4** peace of mind; **em** ~ at rest; **sem** ~ without a pause.

descapotável *m* (*automóvel*) convertible; ♦ *adj inv* (*viatura*) with folding hood, open.

descarado,-a *adj* cheeky, impudent, saucy, brazen; shameless; ♦ **à** ~**a** *adv* openly.

descaramento *m* cheek, effrontery.

descarga *f* unloading; **2** (*autoclismo*) flush; **3** (*MIL*) volley, gunfire; **4** (*ELECT*) discharge; **5** (*fig*) (*fúria*) give vent to.

descarnado,-a *adj* scrawny, gaunt, skinny.

descarnar *vt* to strip meat off the bones.

descaroçar *vt* (*fruta*) to remove seeds/pits (from), to stone, to core.

descarregadouro *m* unloading place; wharf; **2** (*ELECT*) spark gap.

descarregamento *m* unloading; **2** (*ELEC*) discharge.

descarregar *vt* to unload; **2** to give vent to; **3** to relieve; ~ **a consciência** relieve one's conscience; **4** to fire; **5** (*pancada*) to strike a blow, thump; **6** ~ (*ELECT*) to discharge.

descarrilamento *m* derailment, derailing.

descarrilar *vt* to derail; ♦ *vi* to run off the rails; **2** (*fig*) to go off the rails, stray from the straight and narrow (path).

descartar *vt* to discard; ♦ ~**-se** *vr*: ~ **de** to get rid of.

descartável *adj* disposable.

descasca *f* peeling; **2** (*fig, fam*) a telling off, rebuke.

descascador *m* peeler.

descascar *vt/vi* (*fruta, legume*) to peel; **2** (*ovos*) to shell; **3** to tear a strip off; ♦ ~**-se** *vr* (*casca*) to peel; (*pop*) to undress, strip.

descendência *f* descendants *pl*, offspring *pl*.

descendente *m,f* descendant; ♦ *adj inv* descending, going down.

descender *vi*: ~ **de** to descend/come/derive from; **2** (*descer*) to come/go down; **o riacho descende** the brook goes down.

descentralizar *vt* to decentralize.

descer *vt* to go/come down; **2** ~ **o pano** to bring down the curtain; **3** to lower, take down (*algo*); **4** ~ **a pormenores** to get down to details.

descerrar *vt* to open; **2** (*mistério*) to reveal, disclose.

descida *f* descent; **2** slope; **3** fall, drop.

desclassificar *vt* to disqualify; **2** to discredit.

descoberta *f* (*invenção*) discovery.

descoberto,-a *adj* discovered; **2** bare; exposed; ♦ **a** ~ *adv* openly; **2** (*FIN*) (*sem cobertura*) overdrawn; in the red.

descobridor,-ora *m,f* discoverer; explorer.

descobrimento *m* (*de países*) discovery; **a era dos** ~**s** the age of discoveries/exploration.

descobrir *vt* to discover; **2** uncover; **3** reveal, show; **4** find; **5** discern; ~ **petróleo** strike oil; ♦ ~**-se** *vr* take off one's hat.

descolagem *f* (*EP*) taking off; **2** unsticking.

descolar *vt* to unstick; **2** to detach, remove; **3** (*avião*) to take off.

descolorante *m* whitening, bleach; ♦ *adj inv* bleaching, bleached.

descolorir *vt* to discolour; ♦ *vi* to fade.

descompassado,-a *adj* out of all proportion; **2** out of step with.

descompensado,-a *adj* unrewarded, not compensated for; **2** *(MED) (pessoa, órgão)* deficient.

descompor *vt* to disturb, untidy; **2** to disconcert; **3** *(alguém)* to scold, tell off.

descomposto,-a *adj* improperly dressed; **2** untidy.

descompostura *f* disarray, untidiness; **2** *(reprimenda)* reprimand; **dar uma ~** to give a dressing-down, to reprimand.

descomprimir *vt* to decompress.

descomunal *adj inv* unusual; **2** huge, enormous.

desconcertado,-a *adj* disconcerted; **2** *(avariado)* out of order; **3** in confusion.

desconcertante *adj inv* disconcerting; upsetting.

desconcertar *vt* to confuse, baffle; **2** to fall out; **3** to disagree; ♦ **~-se** *vr* to lose one's composure; **2** to break down.

desconcerto *m* disorder, disarray; **2** disagreement.

desconexo,-a *adj (desunido)* disconnected, unrelated; **2** *(incoerente)* incoherent.

desconfiado,-a *m,f* suspicious person; ♦ *adj* suspicious (of others), distrustful.

desconfiança *f* suspicion, distrust.

desconfiar *vi* to suspect; **eu desconfio que ela saiu** I suspect she has gone out; **~ de** to distrust (sb, sth).

desconforme *adj inv* disagreeing, at variance.

desconforto *m* discomfort; **2** distress; **3** ill at ease.

descongelamento *m* thawing.

descongelar *vt* to defrost; **2** *(fig) (preços)* liberalize; ♦ **~-se** *vr* to melt, thaw.

desconhecer *vt* not to know; **desconheço as razões** I do not know the reasons; ♦ **~-se** *vr* not know o.s.

desconhecido,-a *m,f* stranger; ♦ *adj* unknown.

desconhecimento *m* ignorance.

desconjuntar *vt* to dislocate; ♦ **~-se** *vr (desfazer-se)* to come apart.

desconsolado,-a *adj (triste)* miserable, forlorn.

desconsolar *vt* to sadden, depress; ♦ **~-se** *vr* to despair.

descontar *vt (deduzir)* to deduct; **2** *(preço, verba)* to discount; **3** *(fig) (não levar em conta)* to discount; **4** *(fig)* to ignore.

descontentamento *m* discontent; displeasure.

descontentar *vt* to displease; to go against; to upset.

descontente *adj inv* dissatisfied, discontented, despondent, unhappy, disgruntled.

desconto *m* discount, reduction; **com ~** at a discount; **2** *(fam)* excuse; **tens de lhe dar um ~** you must excuse him.

descontra(c)ção *f* relaxation, unwinding; **~ dos músculos** relaxation/relaxing of the muscles.

descontraído,-a *adj* relaxed, laid-back, easy-going.

descontrair *vt (músculos, tensão)* to relax; ♦ **~-se** *vr* to relax, unwind.

descontrolar-se *vr* to get out of control; **2** to lose one's self-control.

descorar *vt* to discolour; ♦ *vi* to pale, fade.

descortês *adj* discourteous; impolite.

descortesia *f* discourtesy, impoliteness.

descortinar *vt* to find out; **2** to perceive; **3** to unveil; **4** *(avistar)* to make out; **5** to pull back the curtains.

descoser *vt* to unstitch, unpick, undo the sewing; **2** to rip apart; ♦ **~-se** *vr* to come apart at the seams.

descosturar *(BR) (Vd: descoser)*.

descrédito *m* discredit; **2** *(desonra)* dishonour.

descrença *f* disbelief, incredulity.

descrente *m,f* unbeliever, sceptic; ♦ *adj inv* sceptical, unbelieving.

descrer *vi* to disbelieve.

descrever *vt* to describe.

descriminalidade *f* the act of exonerating sb of guilt/crime; of acquiting sb.

descriminar *vt (de crime)* acquit; exonerate, justify.

descrição *f* description.

descritivo,-a *adj* descriptive.

descrito,-a *(pp de* **descrever***)*.

descruzar *vt* to uncross; **ela descruzou as pernas** she uncrossed her legs.

descuidado,-a *adj* careless, negligent; **2** *(desleixado)* unkempt, untidy, slovenly *(trabalho, pessoa)*.

descuidar *vt* to neglect, disregard; ♦ **~-se** *vr* to be careless; **2** to neglect o.s.; **3** *(fig, fam)* to fart, break wind.

descuido *m* carelessness; negligence; **2** *(erro)* oversight, slip; **3** *adv* **por ~** inadvertently.

desculpa *f* pardon, forgiveness; **pedir ~(s)** to apologise; **2** *(justificativa)* excuse; **ela deu uma ~** she gave an excuse.

desculpar *vt (perdoar)* to pardon, to forgive; **2** to excuse; *(para pedir licença ou chamar a atenção)* excuse; *(desculpe-me)* excuse me; *(para pedir perdão)* sorry; *(quando não se ouve bem)* sorry, I beg your pardon; **3** *(argumentação)* to be sorry, to be afraid; **~, mas não concordo** I'm afraid I don't agree/sorry, but I don't agree; ♦ **~-se** *vr* to apologize.

desculpável *adj inv* excusable.

desde *prep* from, since; ♦ *adv* **~ então** since then, ever since; **~ há muito** for a long time (now); **~ já** as from now; right now; **~ quando** since when; ♦ *conj:* **~ que** since, provided that.

desdém *m* scorn, disdain.

desdenhar *vt* to scorn, disdain; **2** ignore.

desdenhoso,-a *adj* disdainful, scornful.

desdentado,-a *adj* toothless.

desdita *f* misfortune, bad luck.

desdizer *vt* to contradict; **2** *(desmentir)* to deny; ♦ **~-se** *vr* to go back on one's word, retract.

desdobramento *m (que se desdobra)* unfolding; **2** *(transporte)* second (bus).

desdobrar *vt (abrir)* to unfold *(papel, tecido)*; **2** *(tropas)* to deploy; **3** *(bandeira)* to unfurl; **4** to divide, separate; ♦ **~-se** *vr (estender-se)* to lay out *(a toalha)*; **2** stretch out *(campos, vista)*; **3** *(empenhar-se)* **(em** algo) *(fig)* to double one's efforts.

desdobrável *m* leaflet; **2** *(transporte)* second *(bus)*; ♦ *adj* additional.

desdouro (= **desdoiro**) *m* (*mácula*) blemish, stain; **2** dishonour, discredit.

desdramatizar *vt* to play down; to soften (*significado*).

desejar *vt* (*querer*) to want, desire; **2** (*desejar*) to wish; **desejo-lhe felicidades** I wish you happiness; **3** to like, want; **que deseja?** what would you like?; ♦ *vi* (*aspirar*) to hope; ~ **ardentemente** to long for.

desejável *adj inv* desirable, attractive; **2** (*estilo*) suitable; **3** (*bom trabalho*) expected.

desejo *m* wish, desire; **2** ~**s** *pl* cravings.

desejoso,-a *adj* eager; **2** ~ **de** wishing for; **3** ~ **de fazer** anxious to do, keen to do.

desemaranhar *vt* to disentangle (*novelo*); **2** to unravel (*mistério, história*).

desembainhar *vt* to unsheathe; to draw (a sword); **2** undo (*bainha*).

desembaraçado,-a *adj* (*nós*) untangled, undone; **2** free, clear; **3** (*pessoa*) agile, quick.

desembaraçar *vt* to disentangle; **2** to free; **3** (*nós*) to undo; ♦ ~**-se de** to get rid of; **2** to do sth well, be quick/efficient.

desembaraço *m* (*agilidade*) speed, gust; **2** promptness; **3** efficiency; **4** ease, self-assurance.

desembarcar *vt* to unload; **2** to put on shore; ♦ *vi* to land, disembark.

desembargador,-ora *m,f* (*JUR*) chief magistrate, high court judge; **2** (*do Tribunal da Relação*) high court judge.

desembargo *m* lifting/raising the embargo, boycott.

desembarque *m* landing, disembarkation.

desembocadura *f* river mouth.

desembocar *vi:* ~ **em** to flow into; (*rua*) to lead into.

desembolsar *vt* to spend, disburse.

desembolso *m* (*gasto*) expenditure.

desembraiar *vt* (*AUTO*) to disengage the clutch.

desembrulhar *vt* to unwrap (*embrulho*).

desembuchar *vt* to feel less full; **2** (*fig, fam*) to confess, blurt/blab out; ♦ *exc* **desembucha!** get it out of your chest! out with it!

desempacotar *vt* to unpack (*pacote*).

desempate *m:* (*jogo*) **partida de** ~ play-off, tie-break.

desempecilhar *vt* to disentangle, remove hindrances.

desempenado,-a *adj* (*madeira, etc*) straight (not warped); **2** (*fig*) (*pessoa*) (*costas, postura*) straight.

desempenar *vt* to straighten; ♦ ~**-se** *vr* to stand up straight.

desempenhar *vt* (*função, dever*) to carry out, fulfil; ~ **um papel** to play a role; **2** to redeem (sth) at a pawn shop; ♦ ~**-se** *vr* to pay off a debt; perform; **ele desempenhou-se da sua promessa** he carried out/fulfilled his promise.

desempenho *m* fulfilment; **2** (*TEAT, CIN*) performance.

desemperrar *vt* (*algo que está perro*) to loosen, to set free.

desempilhar *vt* unstuck (*caixas*).

desempregado,-a *adj* unemployed.

desemprego *m* unemployment.

desencadear *vt* to unleash; **2** (*causar*) to bring about; **3** (*provocar*) to trigger off; ♦ ~**-se** *vr* to break loose; **2** (*tempestade*) to burst, break out.

desencaixar *vt* (*tirar do encaixe*) to force out of joint; **2** to dislodge, gouge out; **3** (*fig*) (*dizer tontices*) to prattle; ♦ ~**-se** *vr* to become dislodged.

desencaminhar *vt* to lead astray; **2** (*enganar*) to mislead; **3** to steal, misappropriate (*fundos*); ♦ ~**-se** *vr* to go astray, stray from (the path); **2** (*corromper-se*) be led astray.

desencantado,-a *adj* disenchanted, disillusioned.

desencantar *vt* to break a spell; **2** to disappoint; **3** (*fig*) to find.

desencanto *m* disillusionment, disappointment.

desencardir *vt* (*roupa/pessoa/casa muito suja*) to clean, remove dirt.

desencarregar *vt* to free from obligation; to exempt; to discharge; ~ **a consciência** to clear one's conscience; ♦ ~**-se** *vr* to discharge o.s., unburden o.s. of sth.

desencontrar *vt* to send in different directions; ♦ ~**-se** *vr* to fail to meet each other; **2** (*opiniões*) to differ, diverge.

desencontro *m* failure to meet; **2** disagreement, divergence.

desenfado *m* amusement; end of boredom.

desenferrujar *vt* (*metal*) to remove rust from; **2** (*fig*) (*a língua*) to polish up, brush up; **preciso de** ~ **o meu francês** I need to brush up my French; **3** to talk; **4** (*pernas*) to stretch.

desenfreado,-a *adj* (*arrebatado*) wild, unbridled; **uma corrida** ~**a** a wild race; **2** (*veículo, cavalo*) out of control.

desenganar *vt* to disillusion; **2** to put sb wise, to open sb's eyes; ♦ ~**-se** *vr* to realize the truth; become disillusioned.

desengano *m* disillusionment.

desengarrafar *vt* to pour from a bottle, to decant; **2** (*fig*) (*trânsito*) to clear.

desengatar *vt* (*livrar do engate*) to unhook, to uncouple; **2** to uncock (*armas*); ♦ ~**-se** *vr* come uncoupled; **2** (*soltar-se*) unharnessed (*do atrelado*); **3** (*acionar*) go off (*arma*); **4** (*fig*) to wiggle.

desengonçado,-a *adj* unhinged; **2** rickety, crooked; **3** (*fig*) (*alguém, movimentos*) clumsy; **4** (*postura*) ungainly.

desenhador,-ora *m,f* artist, sketcher, designer; ♦ *adj* **técnico** ~ draughtsman.

desenhar *vt* to draw; **2** (*TEC*) to design; ♦ ~**-se** *vr* to take shape.

desenhista *m,f* (*TEC*) designer.

desenho *m* drawing; **2** design; **3** (*esboço*) sketch; **4** plan; **5** ~**s animados** cartoons; **6** ~ **gráfico** graphic design.

desenlace *m* outcome; **2** undoing, untangling; **3** (*fig*) ending, end; **um** ~ **infeliz** a tragic ending.

desenrascar *vt* disentangle; **2** (*fig*) help sb out; ♦ ~**-se** *vr* (*col*) to get out of a fix.

desenredar *vt* to disentangle (*novelo, fios*); **2** (*resolver*) to unravel (*mistério, intriga*); ♦ ~**-se** *vr* to extricate o.s.; **2** (*resolver*) to solve, resolve.

desenrolar *vt* to unroll, undo; **2** (*história, factos*) to develop, unfold, take place; ♦ ~**-se** *vr* to unfold; **2**

to uncurl o.s.; **3** *(cobra)* to uncoil itself; **4** *(fig)* *(alongar-se)* to stretch.

desenroscar *vt* to unscrew.

desentender *vt* to misunderstand; ♦ ~**-se** *vr*: ~ **com** to fall out with.

desentendido,-a *adj*: **fazer-se de** ~ to pretend not to understand.

desentendimento *m* misunderstanding.

desenterrar *vt* to exhume, to dig up; **2** to bring to light.

desentoado,-a *adj* discordant; **2** out of tune.

desentranhar *vt* to disembowel; **2** to draw out.

desentupir *vt (canos)* to unblock, unclog; **2** *(trânsito)* to clear; ♦ *vi (fig) (fam) (falar)* **desentupta!** come out with it!; ♦ ~**-se** *vr* to clear, be cleared.

desenvolto,-a *adj* quick; lively; **2** forward; **3** *(linguagem)* quick.

desenvoltura *f* self-confidence; **2** agility; briskness.

desenvolver *vt* to develop; ♦ ~**-se** *vr* to develop; to grow.

desenvolvimento *m* development; growth.

desenxabido,-a *adj (sem gosto) (alimentos)* bland, insipid; **2** *(fig, fam)* dull, boring; **3** *(pessoa) (deslavado)* pale, washed out.

desenxovalhar *vt (limpar)* to clean; **2** *(fig)* to clear one's name.

desenxovalhado,-a *adj (limpo)* clean, spotless.

desequilibrado,-a *adj* unbalanced.

desequilibrar *vt* to throw (sb) off balance.

desequilíbrio *m* lack of balance, loss of equilibrium; **2** *(PSIC)* instability, disturbance.

deserção *f* desertion.

desertar *vt* to desert, abandon; ♦ *vi* to desert.

deserto,-a *m* desert; ♦ *adj* deserted.

desertor,-ora *m,f* deserter.

desesperado,-a *adj* desperate; furious.

desesperança *f* despair; no hope.

desesperar *vt* to drive to despair; ♦ ~**-se** *vr* to despair; to lose hope.

desespero *m* despair, desperation.

desfaçatez *f* impudence; effrontery; *(pop)* cheek.

desfalcar *vt (roubar fundos)* to embezzle, defraud; **2** *(reduzir)* to reduce, lessen.

desfalecer *vt* to weaken, lose heart; ♦ *vi (pessoa)* to collapse, become weak.

desfalque *m (de fundos)* embezzlement, misappropriation.

desfavorável *adj inv* unfavourable.

desfazer *vt* to undo, unmake; **2** *(contrato)* to annul; to break up; **3** ~ **em (alguém, algo)** to belittle sb, undervalue sth; ♦ ~**-se** *vr* to dissolve, crumble, come to nothing; ~ **em pó** to crumble into dust; **2** ~ **em desculpas** to apologize profusely; **3** *(fig)* ~ **em lágrimas** to burst into tears; **4** ~ **em cumprimentos** to be profuse in compliments; **5** ~ **em esforços** to go out of one's way to be of help; **6** ~**-se de** *(algo)* to get rid of, be stripped of sth.

desfechar *vt* to fire *(arma)*; **2** to shoot (arrows); **3** to deal (a blow); **4** to throw; to hurl (an insult); ♦ ~**-se** *vr* to go off.

desfecho *m* ending, outcome.

desfeito,-a *(irr pp de* **desfazer**) *adj* undone; **2** dissolved, crumbled; **3** ended, broken; **4** untidy.

desfeita *f* affront, insult.

desferir *vt* to strike/give *(a blow)*; **2** to shoot; **3** *(raios, sons)* to emit; **4** to throw; **5** ~ **insultos** to hurl insults; **6** ~ **a sua frustração sobre os outros** to take his frustration out on others.

desfiar *vt* unweave; unravel; ~ **o bacalhau** to shred the (salted) cod; **3** *(colar)* to unthread, lose beads; ♦ ~**-se** *vr* to become frayed.

desfigurar *vt (alterar)* to distort; **2** to disfigure *(rosto)*; **3** *(adulterar)* twist *(factos)*.

desfiladeiro *m (passagem estreita)* pass *(entre montanhas)*.

desfilar *vi* to march past, parade past.

desfile *m* parade; (REL) procession.

desflorestar *vt* to deforest.

desflorestação *f* deforestation.

desforra *f* revenge; retaliation; **tirar a** ~ to get even, get one's own back.

desforrar *vt* to get one's revenge; **2** *(forro)* to take out the lining of; ♦ ~**-se** *vr (perdas)* to recoup (losses); **5** *(fig)* to make up for; **desforrei-me a comer** I ate to my hearts' content, I made up for (it) by eating.

desfraldar *vt (navio)* to unfurl; **2** *(bandeira)* to hoist.

desfrutar *vt* to enjoy, to delight in; **daqui desfruta-se uma bela vista** one enjoys lovely views from here; **2** to gain ~ **do conhecimento dele** to gain knowledge from him; **3** *(gozo sexual)* have a good time with; ♦ *vi* ~ **de** to enjoy *(saúde, prestígio)*.

desfrute *m* enjoyment; **2** *(gozo)* fun; IDIOM **dar-se ao** ~ to be a figure of fun/mockery.

desgarrada *f* popular style of song; **cantar/tocar à** ~ to sing/play impromptu to two people (or more) in answer to each other; ♦ **à** ~ *adv (cantiga, guitarra)* in turns.

desgarrado,-a *adj* lost, strayed; **2** *(só)* lonely.

desgarrar-se *vr*: ~ **de** to stray from, lose one's way; **2** to lose sight of sth.

desgastar *vt* to wear away, erode; ♦ ~**-se** *vr* to become worn away/out.

desgaste *m* wear and tear.

desgostar *vt* to displease, upset; **2** *(afligir)* to sadden (alguém); **3** *(incomodar)* to annoy *(alguém)*; ♦ *vi*: ~ **de** to dislike; **não** ~ not to dislike; ♦ ~**-se** *vr*: ~ **de** to get fed up, be displeased (**com** de)

desgosto *m* displeasure; **2** sorrow, grief, sad blow.

desgostoso,-a *adj* grieved; **2** *(triste)* sad; sorrowful.

desgoverno m (má gestão) mismanagement

desgraça *f (azar)* misfortune; **2** *(acontecimento)* calamity; tragedy; **3** *(vergonha)* disgrace; **4** ruin.

desgraçado,-a *m,f* poor soul, poor wretch; ♦ *adj (infeliz)* unfortunate person; **2** *(com azar)* unlucky; **vida** ~**a** miserable life; **3** *(situação)* deplorable, terrible; **4** *(carente)* poor, needy.

desgraçar *vt* to disgrace; dishonour; discredit; **2** to ruin, bring to ruin.

desgrenhado,-a, *adj (cabelo)* dishevelled, tousled; **2** *(descuidado)* unkempt.

desgrudar *vt* to unglue, unstuck sth from sth; **3** *(fig, fam) (afastar)* to drag s.o. away from sb.

desguedelhado,-a *adj (cabelo)* dishevelled; **2** *(alguém)* unkempt.

desidratação *f* dehydration.

desidratar *vt* to dehydrate.

designação *f* designation; **2** appointment; **3** choice.

designar *vt* to designate; **2** to name; **3** appoint.

desígnio *m* purpose, design.

desigual *adj inv (terreno)* uneven, rough; **2** unequal, unmatched; **3** different; **4** irregular.

desigualdade *f* disparity; **2** *(do terreno)* unevenness; **3** *(MAT, FÍS, ASTRON)* inequality; **4** ~ **social** social imbalance/inequality; **5** irregularity, **há algumas ~s nas contas** the accounts have some irregularity.

desiludir *vt* to disillusion; to disappoint; ♦ ~**-se** *vr* to lose one's illusions.

desilusão *f* disillusionment, disenchantment.

desimpedido,-a *adj* free, clear, unencumbered.

desimpedir *vt* to clear; **2** *(fig) (facilitar)* to clear the way for.

desinchar *vt* to deflate; **2** *(MED)* to reduce the swelling of; ♦ ~**-se** *vr* to become less swollen.

desinência *f (gram)* ending.

desinfe(c)ção *f* disinfection.

desinfe(c)tante *adj inv* disinfectant.

desinfe(c)tar *vt* to disinfect.

desinfestar *vt* to kill vermin, pests *(no lugar)*.

desinibido,-a *adj* uninhibited.

desinibir-se to lose one's inhibitions; *(col)* to let one's hair down.

desintegração *f* disintegration, break-up.

desintegrar *vt* to separate; ♦ ~**-se** *vr* to disintegrate, fall to pieces.

desinteressado,-a *adj* disinterested, dispassionate; **2** impartial.

desinteressar-se *vr*: to lose interest (**de** in).

desinteresse *m* lack of interest.

desistência *f* withdrawal.

desistente *m,f* person who gives up; loser; ♦ *adj* desisting.

desistir *vi* to give up, desist.

deslavado,-a *adj (tecido, cor)* faded, washed out; **2** *(pessoa)* pale, colourless; **3** *(pessoa) (sem interesse)* dull, vapid; **4** *(fig) (comida)* insipid, bland.

desleal *adj inv* disloyal.

deslealdade *f* disloyalty.

desleixado,-a *adj* sloven, untidy; **2** unkempt; **3** careless.

desleixo *m* carelessness; **2** slovenliness; **3** mess.

desligado,-a *adj* disconnected; **2** switched off; **3** *(luz)* off.

desligar *vt (TEC)* to disconnect; **2** *(aparelho, máquina)* to turn off; *(RADIO,TV)* to switch/turn off; **3** *(TEL)* to hang up; **não desligue!** *(TEL)* hold the line!; **4** ~ **alguém de** to free sb from.

deslindar *vt (meada, novelo)* to untangle, disentangle; **2** *(apurar, esclarecer)* to unravel, clear up, get to the bottom of it.

deslizar *vt (terra)* to slide; **2** *(no gelo, dança)* to glide; **3** *(AUTO)* to skid; **4** *(conversa)* to turn to; **5** *(do bom caminho)* to make a slip; **6** *(ECON)* to fall.

deslizamento *m* sliding; ~ **de terra** landslide; **2** *(TEC)* slip.

deslize *m (resvalamento)* slide; **2** *(fig) (erro)* mistake, oversight; slip of the tongue.

deslocação *f* move; **2** travelling time; **ele paga os bilhetes e a** ~ he pays for the fares and the travelling time; **3** shifting; **4** *(MED)* dislocation.

deslocado,-a *adj (MED)* dislocated; **2** dislodged; **3** *(fig)* out of place; **os ~s** *mpl* homeless people; displaced people.

deslocamento *(Vd: deslocação) m (GEOG)* movement; **2** *(NAUT, FÍS, MIL)* displacement.

deslocar *vt* to move; **2** to remove; transfer; **3** *(MED) (braço, perna, etc)* to dislocate.

deslumbramento *m* dazzle; fascination.

deslumbrante *adj* dazzling.

deslumbrar *vt (ofuscar)* to dazzle; **2** *(fig) (encantar)* to amaze; to fascinate; ♦ *vi* be dazzling /dazzled; **2** *(alienar-se)* be awe-struck.

desmaiado,-a *adj* unconscious; **2** faint.

desmaiar *vi (perder os sentidos)* to faint, collapse, pass out; *(muito breve, de êxtase)* to swoon.

desmaio *m* faint.

desmamar *vt* to wean.

desmancha-prazeres *m,f (EP)* spoilsport, killjoy.

desmanchar *vt* to undo; **2** *(contrato)* to break; **3** *(noivado)* to break off; ♦ ~**-se** *vr (roupas)* to come undone.

desmancho *m* mess; **a casa está num** ~ the house, place is in a mess; **2** misconduct; **3** *(pop)* abortion.

desmantelar *vt* to demolish; **2** to dismantle, take apart.

desmascarar *vt* to unmask; **2** to expose *(pessoa, mentira)*.

desmatamento *m* deforestation.

desmazelado,-a *m,f* sloven, slob; ♦ *adj* slovenly; unkempt, scruffy; **2** *(casa, etc)* untidy.

desmazelo *m* untidiness, negligence.

desmedido,-a *adj* excessive; **2** inordinate; **3** disproportionate.

desmembramento *m* dismemberment.

desmembrar *vt* to dismember; **2** to separate, divide; ♦ ~**-se** *vr* to break up, be divided.

desmentido *m* denial; contradiction; ♦ *adj* denied, refuted.

desmentir *vt* to contradict; **2** to refute, deny.

desmesurado,-a *adj* immense, enormous.

desmiolado,-a *adj* brainless.

desmontagem *f* disassembling, dismantling; **2** *(fig) (de um texto)* analysis.

desmontar *vt* to take (sth) to pieces, take apart; dismantle; ♦ *vi (do cavalo)* to dismount, get off.

desmontável *adj inv* that can be dismantled, knocked off *(US)*.

desmoralizar *vt* to demoralize; **2** *(corromper)* to pervert, deprave; ♦ ~**-se** *vr* to be demoralized.

desmoronar *vt* to knock down, demolish; ♦ *vi* to collapse; ♦ ~**-se** *vr* to fall down, to crumble; **2** *(fig) (planos, contratos)* to fall through.

desmotivado,-a *adj* discouraged, disheartened, demotivated.

desnacionalização *f* privatization; denationalization.

desnatado,-a *adj* skimmed; **leite** ~ skimmed milk.

desnatar *vt (leite, manteiga)* to skim.

desnecessário,-a *adj* unnecessary.

desnecessariamente *adv* unnecessarily.

desnível *m* drop, uneveness.

desnivelamento *m* unlevelling; ~ **social** social inequality.

desnivelar *vt* to make uneven; **2** to divide, separate levels; ~ **o próximo** to find out about another person's social class; ♦ **~-se** *vr* to become bumpy.

desnorteado,-a *adj* bewildered, confused; **2** crazy; **3** *(direção)* off course; **ando/estou** ~ *(fig, fam)* I am off my rocker.

desnortear *vt* to throw off course; **2** to bewilder; ♦ *vr* to lose one's way; **2** to become confused.

desnudar *vt* to strip, bare; **2** *(fig)* to reveal; ♦ **~-se** *vr* to undress.

desnutrição *f* malnutrition.

desobedecer *vt* to disobey.

desobediência *f* disobedience.

desobrigar *vt* to free from doing, excuse from doing.

desobstruir *vt* to unblock; **2** to clear out/away.

desocupado,-a *adj (casa, lugar)* empty, vacant; **2** *(livre)* free; **3** unemployed.

desocupar *vt* to vacate.

desodorante *m* deodorant.

desolação *f (de um lugar)* desolation; isolation **2** *(fig) (tristeza)* grief, misery.

desolado,-a *adj* desolate; dreary; devastated; **2** *(fig)* distressed, wretched.

desolar *vt (pessoa)* to distress; to sadden.

desolhar *vt (das plantas)* to remove the buds of; **2** to poke sb's eyes out.

desonesto,-a *adj* dishonest; **2** *(alguém devasso)* indecent, despicable.

desonra *f* dishonour; disgrace.

desonrado,-a *adj* dishonoured.

desonrar *vt* to disgrace; **2** to seduce; ♦ **~-se** *vr* to disgrace o.s.

desoras *fpl*: **a** ~ untimely, at a late hour.

desordeiro,-a *m,f* hooligan; ♦ *adj* disorderly.

desordem *f* disorder, confusion; **em** ~ untidy.

desorganizar *vt* to disorganize; ♦ **~-se** *(desordenar-se)* *vr* to get confused.

desorientação *f* bewilderment, confusion.

desorientar *vt* to throw off course; to confuse; ♦ **~-se** *vr* to lose one's way/bearings.

desossar *vt* to bone (a chicken).

desova *f* laying (of eggs); spawn.

desovar *vt* to lay; **2** *(fish)* to spawn.

despachado,-a *adj* determined, resolved; **2** *(ativo)* quick, nimble; **3** efficient; **4** *(pronto)* ready; **já estou** ~ I am ready; I have finished *(tarefa)*.

despachar *vt* to dispatch, send off; **2** to deal with; **3** *(fig)* to kill; ♦ **~-se** *vr* to hurry (up).

despacho *m (mercadoria; carta oficial)* dispatch; **2** *(JUR)* order; **3** speed, promptness.

desparafusar *vt* to unscrew.

despedaçar *vt* to smash, shatter; **2** to tear apart; **3** *(fig) (magoar)* **ela ficou com o coração** ~ her heart was broken.

despedida *f* farewell; **2** dismissal.

despedimento *m (alguém)* dismissal, sacking; ~ **por razão patronal** redundancy.

despedir *vt* to dismiss, sack; **2** to send away; ♦ **~-se** *vr*: ~ **de** to say goodbye to; **2** to give in one's notice.

despegar *vt* to detach, pull apart; ♦ **~-se** *vr (perder afeição)* to go off, lose one's liking for.

despego *m* detachment, indifference.

despeitado,-a *adj* spiteful; resentful.

despeito *m (inveja)* spite; ♦ *adv* **por** ~ out of spite; ♦ *prep* **a** ~ **de** in spite of, despite.

despejar *vt* to pour; **2** to empty; ~ **o lixo** to empty the rubbish (bin); **3** *(duma casa)* to evict.

despejo *m* eviction; garbage; **quarto de** ~ junk room; **2** *(col) (ousadia)* cheek; **ela teve o** ~ **de me chamar sovina** she had the cheek to call me stingy.

despenalizar *vt* to legalize *(algo)*

despender *vt (dinheiro, tempo)* to spend, give; **2** *(fig) (amabilidades, sorrisos)* to give, offer, spread *(around)*.

despenhadeiro *m* cliff, precipice.

despenhar *vt* to hurl down (sth, sb); ♦ **~-se** *vr (avião, carro)* to fall/crash down a precipice.

despensa *f (para a comida)* larder, pantry.

despentear *vt* to dishevel; to tousle *(cabelo)*; **2** to mess up *(penteado)*.

despercebido,-a *adj* unnoticed; **passar** ~ to be/go unnoticed.

desperdiçar *vt* to waste; to squander.

desperdício *m* waste.

despertador *m* alarm clock.

despertar *vt (acordar)* to wake up; **2** *(interesse, sentimentos)* to arouse, excite; **3** to whet, stimulate; **4** *(apetite)* to revive; **5** *(levantar) (suspeita)* to raise; **6** *(fig) (memórias)* to revive; ♦ *vi* to wake up, awake.

desperto,-a *adj* awake.

despesa *f* expense; **uma** ~ **com que eu não contava** an expense I was not expecting.

despido,-a *adj* naked, nude, undressed; **2** *(fig) (desprovido)* ~ **de algo**, lacking sth; stripped (of sth).

despir *vt (roupa)* to take off; to undress; **2** to strip; ♦ **~-se** *vr* to undress.

despistar *vt* to throw off the track, mislead.

despistado,-a *adj* absent-minded.

despistar *vt (fazer perder a pista/atenção)* to put off the track *(alguém)*; *(distrair)* to distract (sb).

despiste *m (AUTO)* skid; **2** *(lapso)* slip, oversight.

despojar *vt (roubar)* to strip; **2** to divest; **3** *(espoliar)* to clean out; ♦ **~-se** *vr* to give up, renounce.

despojo *m* loot, booty; **os** ~**s de guerra** the spoils of war; ~**s mortais** mortal remains.

despoletar *vt (bomba, mina)* to defuse; **2** *(fam) (desencadear)* to spark off.

despolitização *f* depoliticization.

despoluir *vt* control, reduce pollution.

despontar *vt (cortar as pontas)* to cut of the ends of *(ramos, relva)*; **2** ~ **os chifres de** cut the horns of *(gado)*; ♦ *vi* to emerge; **2** *(nascer)* to sprout; **ao** ~ **do dia** at daybreak.

desportista *adj inv* sports person.

desportivo,-a *adj (clube, actividade)* sports; **2** sports-like, sporty; sporting.

desporto *m* sport; **2** pastime; **por** ~ for recreation, as a hobby.

desposado,-a *adj* newly-wed.

desposar *vt* to marry; ♦ ~**-se** *vr* to get married.

déspota *m* despot.

despotismo *m* despotism.

despovoado,-a *m* wilderness; ♦ *adj* uninhabited, deserted.

despovoar *vt* to depopulate.

despregar *vt* to take off, detach; **2** to unfasten sth (from); **3** *(das paredes, etc)* to remove nails; **4** *(do vestido)* to remove pleats; **5** *(fig)* **não** ~ **os olhos de** *(alguém)* not to take one's eyes off sb/sth; ♦ ~**-se** *vr* to get loose; come off/apart.

desprender *vt* to loosen; **2** to unfasten; **3** *(gemido)* to emit; ♦ ~**-se** *vr* to get loose; **2** *(cheiro)* to exude, give off; **3** *(fig)* to remounce; **4** *(fig)* to get detached, indifferent.

desprendido,-a *adj (solto)* loose; **2** *(de emoção, sentimento)* detached.

despreocupado,-a *adj* carefree, unconcerned.

despretensioso,-a *adj* unpretentious, modest.

desprevenido,-a *adj* unprepared, unwary; **2** *(fig)* sem dinheiro.

desprezar *vt* to despise, disdain; **2** to show contempt for; **3** to reject, ignore.

desprezível *adj inv* despicable.

desprezo *m* scorn, contempt; **dar ao** ~ to ignore.

despromovido,-a *adj* demoted.

desproporção *f* disproportion.

desproporcionado,-a, **desproporcional** *adj* disproportionate; **2** unequal.

despropositado,-a *adj* inopportune; irrelevant; preposterous.

despropósito *m* nonsense.

desprovido,-a *adj* deprived (of); lacking in; ~ **de** without; **2** devoid (of).

desqualificar *vt* to disqualify; **2** to consider unfit; **3** to rule out.

desquitar *vt (BR)* to get a legal separation.

desquite *m (BR)* legal separation.

desregrado,-a *adj* disorderly, unruly; immoderate.

desregrar-se *vr* to run riot.

desrespeitar *vt* to disrespect.

desrespeito *m* disrespect.

desrespeitoso,-a *adj* disrespectful.

desse[1] (= de + esse) of/from that *(Vd: esse)*.

desse[2] *(imperf subj de* **dar***):* **se eu** ~ **isso** if I gave that.

dessecar *vt* to dry up; ♦ ~**-se** *vr* to dry up.

destacado,-a *adj (lugar, pessoa)* outstanding.

destacamento *m (MIL)* detachment.

destacar *vt (MIL)* to detach; **2** *(funções)* to assign (to); **3** *(sobressair)* to outline, highlight sth; to make (sth, sb) stand out; ♦ ~**-se** *vr* to stand out; to be outstanding; **entre os melhores candidatos destaca-se João** John is the most outstanding student overall/John stands out among the best.

destapar *vt* to uncover *(tacho, cobertor);* ~ **a panela!** take the lid off the saucepan!

destaque *m* prominence; distinction; **pessoa de** ~ notable person; **em** ~ in evidence, in the limelight; **notícias em** ~ main news, newsflash, news in brief.

deste = de + este *(Vd:* **este***).*

destemido,-a *adj* fearless, intrepid; **2** foolhardy.

destempero *m (falta de tempero)* lacking seasoning; **2** *(disparate)* nonsense; absurdity; **3** *(fig) (fúria)* anger.

desterrar *vt* to exile; **2** *(fig)* to banish.

desterro *m* exile; banishment.

destilação *f* distillation.

destilar *vt* to distil.

destilaria *f* distillery.

destinar *vt* to destine, foretell; **2** *(verbas)* to allocate, put/set aside (for); ♦ ~**-se** *vr:* ~ **a** to be intended for; to decide; **eles destinaram-se a participar** they decided to participate.

destinatário,-a *m,f* addressee; **2** *(TEL)* **chamada a pagar no** ~ reverse call charges; **3** *(LÍNG, LITER)* receiver.

destino *m* destiny, fate; **2** *(fim)* purpose, use; **3** *(direcção)* destination; **4 com** ~ **a** bound for; ♦ *adv* **sem** ~ without destination; **2 andar sem** ~ to walk aimlessly.

destituição *f* dismissal.

destituir *vt* to dismiss; ~ *(alguém)* **de** *(algo)* to deprive sb of sth.

destoante *adj inv* discordant; **2** divergent, different; **3** *(cores)* clashing.

destoar *vi* (MÚS) to be out of tune; **2** to clash **(de** with); **3** to diverge from.

destra *f* right hand; **2 à** ~ **de** on the right of.

destrambelhado,-a *m,f (pessoa-cabeça no ar)* scatterbrain; **2** *(amalucado)* nutter; ♦ *adj (desajeitado)* clumsy, awkward; **2** *(com a cabeça no ar)* crazy, hare-brained.

destrancar *vt* to unbolt, unlock.

destravar *vt (fechadura)* to unlatch; **2** *(AUTO)* to release the brake; **3** to cock a gun; **4** *(fig, fam) (soltar)* ~ **a língua** to wag one's tongue, to loosen; ♦ *vi (fam) (perder o juízo)* to lose one's screw; ♦ ~**-se** *vr* to become loose.

destreza *f* skill; dexterity, adroitness; deftness, cleverness.

destrinçar *vt (episódio, assunto)* to unravel; **2** *(fios)* untangle; **3** to pick to pieces; **4** to describe in detail.

destro,-a *adj* dexterous, deft; **2** agile; **3** *(astuto)* shrewd.

destroçar *vt* to destroy; **2** to smash, break; **3** to ruin, wreck.

destroço *m* destruction.

destroços *mpl (barco)* wreckage *sg*; remains; debris *sg*.

destronar *vt* to depose; **2** to get sb out of his position.

destruição *f* destruction, devastation; **2** extinction.

destruidor,-ora *m,f* destroyer; ♦ *adj* destructive.

destruir *vt* to destroy.

desumanizar *vt* to dehumanize; ♦ ~**-se** *vr* to become dehumanized.

desumano,-a *adj* inhuman; cruel.

desumidificador *m* dehumidifier.

desumidificar *vt* dehumidify.

desunião *f* disunity, falling-out, discord; **2** separation.

desunir *vt*: to separate; **2** *(TEC)* to disconnect; **3** *(fig)* to cause a rift between, break up *(alguém)*; ♦ ~-**se** *vr* separate.

desusado,-a *adj* not used, out of date; **2** *(insólito)* unusual.

desuso *m* disuse; **cair em** ~ to be obsolete.

desvairado,-a *adj* out of one's mind, demented; **2** *(olhar, modo)* mad, insane; **3** *(gente exaltada)* raging, uncontrolled.

desvairar *vt*: ~ **alguém** *(enlouquecer)* to drive (sb) crazy; out of sb's mind.

desvalido,-a *adj* helpless; destitute.

desvalorização *f* devaluation, depreciation.

desvalorizar *vt* *(ECON)* to devalue, depreciate; **2** *(alguém)* to run down sb; **3** to criticize sth; ♦ ~-**se** *vr* to undervalue o.s.; **2** *(ECON)* to lose value, depreciate, go down.

desvanecer *vt* *(dissipar)* to dispel; **2** *(desaparecer)* to fade away; ~ **todas as suspeitas** dispel all suspition; ♦ ~-**se** *vr* to vanish; **2** *(esbater-se)* to wane, fade away.

desvanecido,-a *adj* faded; **2** *(dissipado)* dispelled; **3** *(fig)* puffed up with pride.

desvantagem *f* disadvantage.

desvantajoso,-a *adj* disadvantageous.

desvão *m* *(sótão)* loft; **2** *(recanto)* corner, recess, nook.

desvario *m* madness, folly.

desvelar *vt* to unveil, reveal; ♦ ~-**se** *vr* to be solicitous.

desvelo *m* devotion; zeal, care.

desvendar *vt* to remove the blindfold from; **2** to disclose, unveil, reveal.

desventrar *vt* *(alguém, animal)* to gut.

desventura *f* misfortune; **2** unhappiness.

desventurado,-a *m,f* wretch; ♦ *adj* unfortunate, unlucky; **2** unhappy.

desviar *vt* *(mudar a direção)* to divert, deviate; **2** *(evitar)* to ward off; **3** *(dinheiro)* to embezzle, misappropriate; ~ **fundos da empresa** to embezzle funds from the company; **4** ~ **os olhos** to look away *(conversa)* digress; ♦ ~-**se** *vr* *(fastar-se)* to turn away, step aside; **2** *(carro)* swerve.

desvio *m* diversion; **2** detour, other route; **3** *(da coluna vertebral)* curvature; **4** *(fig)* deviation; **5** *(fundos, dinheiro)* embezzlement, misappropriation.

desvirtuar *vt* to disparage; **2** to misrepresent.

detalhadamente *adv* in detail.

detalhar *vt* to detail.

detalhe *m* *(pormenor)* detail; **entrar em** ~**s** to go into detail.

dete(c)ção *f* detection.

dete(c)tar *vt* to detect, discover.

dete(c)tive *m* detective.

dete(c)tor *m* *(aparelho)* detector; **2** *(ELECT)* indicator, detector.

detenção *f* detention; ~ **domiciliária** house arrest.

detentor,-ora *adj* detainer; **2** holder (**de**, of); ~ **do título** titleholder.

deter *vt* to stop; **2** to arrest, detain; **3** to keep; ♦ ~-**se** *vr* to stop, stay while.

detergente *m* detergent, soap powder.

deterioração *f* deterioration.

deteriorar *vt* to spoil, damage; ♦ ~-**se** *vr* to deteriorate; to worsen.

determinação *f* determination; **2** decision.

determinar *vt* to determine, settle; **2** to decide (on); **3** *(indicar com precisão)* to pinpoint; **4** to lead to; **5** persuade.

detestar *vt* to hate, detest.

detestável *adj inv* horrible, hateful.

detetive *(Vd:* **dete(c)tive)**.

detidamente *adv* minutely, thoroughly.

detido,-a *m,f* *(preso)* detainee; ♦ *adj* detained, held in custody; **2** stopped; **3** retained.

detonação *f* detonation.

detonar *vi* to detonate, go off.

detoxicação *f* detoxication, detoxification.

detrás *adv* behind; ♦ *prep*: ~ **de** behind; **por** ~ (from) behind; **por** ~ **das (minhas) costas** behind (my) back.

detrimento *m*: **em** ~ **de** to the detriment of.

detrito *m* debris *sg*, remains *pl*, dregs *pl*; **2** ~**s nucleares** nuclear waste.

deturpar *vt* to distort, disfigure; **2** to corrupt; **3** to pervert, adulterate.

Deus *m* *(REL)* God; **D**~ **me livre!** God forbid!; **graças a D**~ thank God/thank goodness!; **valha-me Deus!** God help me!; **se D**~ **quiser!** God willing!; **meu D**~**!** good Lord!; **por amor de** ~**!** for God's sake!; **o meu marido, que** ~ **haja ...** my husband, whose soul may rest in peace; IDIOM **o homem põe e** ~ **dispõe** man proposes and God disposes.

deus,-a *m,f* god, goddess.

deus-dará *adv* **ao** ~ at random, haphazardly; aimlessly; **viver ao** ~ to live from hand to mouth, as luck wills.

devagar *adj* slow; ~ **pelo seguro** slow and sure; ♦ *adv* slowly, quietly; IDIOM ~ **se vai ao longe** one step at a time is all it takes (to get you there).

devagarinho *adv* *(pop)* nice and slowly.

devanear *vt* to dream of, muse; ♦ *vi* to daydream; **2** to wander, digress.

devaneio *m* daydream, reverie.

devassa *f* *(JUR)* investigation, official inquiry, inquest; **2** invasion of privacy.

devassidão *f* debauchery, licentiousness.

devasso,-a *m,f* libertine; ♦ *adj* debauched; dissolute; depraved; lewd.

devastar *vt* *(assolar)* to devastate, ruin; **2** *(saquear)* to pillage, sack; **3** *(despovoar)* to drive people out of.

deve *m* *(COM)* debit; ~ **e haver** debit and credit.

devedor,-ora *m,f* debtor; ♦ *adj* owing, in debt.

dever *(pl: -es)* *m* *(obrigação moral)* duty; ~**es de casa** *(EDUC)* homework; ♦ *vt* *(dinheiro favores)* ~ **a** *(alguém)* to owe to sb; **devo-te mil Euros** I owe you one thousand Euros; **tu deves-me uma desculpa** you owe me an apology; **2** *(ter obrigação,* *dúvida)* should; **devias falar com ele** you should speak with him; **que devo fazer?** what should I do?; **3** *(precisar, sugerir)* must; **tens de estudar mais** you must study harder; **você não deve dizer isso** you must not say that; **tu deves estar a troçar** you must be mocking; **4** *(ser possível/ suposto)* ought to, should, may; **ele deve chegar agora** he ought to be arriving now; *(você deve levar um casaco)* **you ought to/should take a coat**; **ela deve ainda vir** he may still come; **5** *(probabilidade)* likely to, probably **deve fazer sol esta tarde** it will probably be sunny this afternoon; ♦ *vi (ter dívidas)* to owe; ♦ *vr* ~**-se a** to be due to, **este sucesso deve-se aos esforços ...** this success is owed to the efforts of ...

deveras *adv* really, indeed.

devesa *f (arvoredo)* shrubbery; **2** *(tapada)* enclosure; small grove.

devidamente *adv* properly, duly, suitably.

devido *m (o que se deve)* debt; **2** *(de direito)* duty; **cumprir o** ~ to do one's duty; ♦ **devido,-a** *adj* proper, owing, due; **2** necessary; ♦ ~ **a** *prep* because of; due to; **em** ~ **tempo** in due course.

devidamente *adv* duly; ~ **preenchida** *(ficha)* duly filled.

devoção *f* devotion.

devolução *f* giving back, return; **2** *(COM)* return; **3** *(JUR)* devolution.

devoluto,-a *adj (vago)* empty, vacant; **fogos** ~**s** vacant houses; **2** *(terrenos)* uncultivated; **3** *(JUR) (propriedade vaga)* repossessed.

devolver *vt* to give back, return; **2** *(COM) (recambiar)* to send back; **3** *(JUR)* to transfer to.

devorar *vt* to devour, eat up; **2** *(comer) (cal)* to gobble; **3** *(fig) (fogo, paixão)* to consume; **4** (quilómetros) to eat up.

devotar *vt* to devote; ♦ ~**-se** *vr* to devote o.s. (**a** to).

devoto,-a *m,f* devotee; ♦ *adj* devout.

dextra *f* right hand.

dextrímano,-a *adj* right-handed.

dez *num m* ten; ♦ *adj inv* tenth; **a** ~ **de Abril/abril, no dia** ~ **de abril** on the tenth of April.

dezanove *num m* nineteen; ♦ *adj inv* **décimo nono** nineteenth.

dezasseis *num m* sixteen; ♦ *adj inv* **décimo sexto** sixteenth.

dezassete *num m* seventeen; ♦ *adj inv* **décimo sétimo** seventeenth; **no século XVII** *(dezassete)* 17th century.

Dezembro, dezembro *m* December.

dezena *f*: **uma** ~ ten; **na casa das** ~**s** in the ten's; **às** ~**s** in tens and tens; **presentes às** ~**s** many presents.

dezenove *(BR) num* nineteen.

dezesseis *(BR) num* sixteen.

dezessete *(BR) num* seventeen.

dezoito *num m* eighteen.

dia *m* day; daylight; ~ **a** ~ daily routine; ~ **folga** day off; **ao romper do** ~ at daybreak; ~ **de anos** birthday; ~ **de Reis** Epiphany, twelveth night; ~ **do juízo final** Doomsday; ~ **útil** weekday, working day; **todo o** ~ all day; **estar/andar em** ~ to be

up to date; **hoje em** ~ nowadays; **dias** *mpl* days, **nos nossos** ~**s** nowadays; ♦ *adv* **todos os dias** everyday, daily; **de** ~ daytime; **de** ~ **para** ~ day by day; **do** ~ **para a noite** overnight; *(fig)* completely; ~ **sim** ~ **não** every other day; **mais** ~ **menos** ~ sooner or later; **um** ~ **por outro** sometimes; **dias e dias** days on end.

diabetes *m* diabetes. **diabético,-a** *adj* diabetic.

Diabo *npr m* the Devil; ♦ **diabo** *m (fam)* **o** ~ **da mulher** the devil of a woman; **2** *(criança)* little devil; ♦ **dos** ~**s** *adv* fiendish, devilish; ♦ *exc* **que** ~! damn!; ~! hell!; **oh,** ~! oh dear!; **por que** ~ ...? why the devil ...?; **aconteceu o** ~ it all happened; ~**s me levem!** I'll be blowed!; ~**s te levem!** go to hell; IDIOM **enquanto o** ~ **esfrega o olho** in the twinkling of an eye; **estar com o** ~ **no corpo** to be restless.

diabólico,-a *adj* diabolical.

diabrete *m (criança travessa)* imp, little devil.

diabrura *f* prank; ~**s** *fpl* mischief *sg.*

diacho *m* deuce, devil.

diácono *m* deacon, dean.

diacrónico,-a *adj* diachronic.

diadema *m* diadem, decorated headband.

diáfono,-a *adj* diaphanous, transparent, translucid.

diafragma *m (ANAT, BOT)* diaphragm.

diagnose *f* diagnosis.

diagnosticar *vt* to diagnose.

diagnóstico *m* diagnosis.

diagonal *adj inv (GEOM)* diagonal; oblique.

diagrama *m* diagram.

dialética, dialé(c)tica *f* dialectics.

dialético, dialé(c)tico *adj* dialectic.

dialeto, diale(c)to *m* dialect.

diálise *f* dialysis.

dialogar *vt (com)* to talk, converse with; **2** to negotiate (with).

diálogo *m* dialogue.

diamante *m* diamond; ~ **bruto** uncut diamond.

diamantífero,-a *adj* diamond-producing.

diâmetro *m* diameter.

diante *prep* ~ **de** in front, in the face of, faced with, before; **não fale assim** ~ **da criança** don't speak like that in front of the child; **daqui em/por** ~ *adv* from now on; **e assim por** ~ and so on; **para** ~ forward.

dianteira *f* lead, vanguard; **tomar a** ~ to get ahead, take the lead; **2** front.

dianteiro *m (DESP)* forward; ♦ **dianteiro,-a** *adj* front; **2** *(carro, etc)* in the lead.

diapasão *f (FÍS)* diapason; **2** *(MÚS)* tuning fork; **3** *(MED)* diaphoretic; **4** *(fig)* range, scope.

diapositivo *m (FOTO)* slide.

diário,-a *m* diary; **2** **D**~ **Oficial** *m* official gazette; **3** *(COM)* ledger; **4** ~ **de bordo** log book; **5** *(jornal)* daily paper; **6** *f (tarifa de hotel)* daily rate; ♦ *adj* daily.

diarréia *f (MED)* diarrhoea; **2** *(fam)* the runs.

diáspora *f* diaspora.

diatribe *f* invective; **2** bitter criticism (against).

dica *f (fam)* hint, clue, lead.

dicção, dição f diction.
dicionário m dictionary; ~ **bilingue** bilingual dictionary.
dicionarista m,f lexicographrer.
dicionarizado,-a adj (palavra, termo, etc) included in, appearing in a dictionary.
dicotomia f dichotomy.
didata m,f teacher.
didática f didactics; teaching.
didático,-a adj instructive, didactic, educational, pedagogic.
diesel m diesel; ♦ adj: **motor a ~** diesel motor.
dieta f diet; **fazer ~** to go on a diet.
dietética f (MED) dietetics.
dietético,-a adj dietetic, dietary.
dietista m,f dietician.
difamação f libel; slander.
difamar vt to slander, libel, to cast aspersions.
diferença f difference.
diferenciar vt to differentiate, distinguish; ♦ ~**-se** vr **to differ.**
diferendo m disagreement.
diferente adj inv different; unusual; **2 ~s** various.
diferentemente adv differently.
diferimento m deferment, postponement.
diferir vi (distinguir) to differ (**de** from); **2** (discordar) differ; ♦ vt to postpone, defer.
difícil adj inv difficult, hard; **2** tricky; **3** (improvável) unlikely; **4 ~ de contentar** hard to please, demanding.
dificilmente adv with difficulty.
dificuldade f difficulty; trouble; **em ~s** in trouble.
dificultar vt to make difficult; to complicate.
difteria f diphtheria.
difundir vt to diffuse, shed out; **2** (propagar) to spread, divulge; **3** (transmitir) to broadcast; ♦ ~**-se** vr (irradiar-se) to be spread, go round; propagate; **a cultura portuguesa difundiu-se pelo mundo** Portuguese culture spread all over the world.
difusão f diffusion; spreading; broadcasting.
diga (pres subj de **dizer**): **quero que lhe ~** I would like you to tell him/her.
digerir vt to digest.
digestão f digestion; **2** (fig) (ofensa) accept, recover from.
digital adj inv: **impressão ~** fingerprint.
dígito m digit.
dignar-se vr: **~ de** to deign to; condescend to; be kind enough to (do, say).
dignidade f dignity; **a ~ humana** human dignity; **2** rank, positon, office; **3** (honestidade) honour; **4** self-respect.
dignificação f dignifying.
dignificar vt (alguém) dignify sb; confer honour on sb.
dignitário m dignitary.
digno,-a adj worthy; dignified; **~ de confiança** trustworthy.
digo (pres indic, 1ª pessoa de **dizer**): **não ~ nada** I am not telling/saying anything.
digressão f digression; **2** excursão, tour.
dilacerante adj inv cutting; **2** (fig) (grito, dor) heartbreaking, piercing.

dilacerar vt to tear to pieces; **2** (ferir) lacerate, gash; **3** (perfurar) pierce; **4** (fig) to tear apart.
dilatação f (FÍS, MED) dilation; **2** (fig) prolongation, spread.
dilatar vt to dilate; **2** (MED) to distend; **3** to expand; **4** to delay.
dilema m dilemma.
diligência f diligence; **2** promptness, speed; **3** inquiry; **4** (carruagem) stagecoach; **5** (JUR) ~ **judicial** judicial proceeding, execution; **fazer todas as ~s** to do one's utmost; **oficial de ~s** bailiff, court clerk.
diligenciar vt to strive for, make every effort.
diligente adj inv hardworking, industrious.
diluente m paint, varnish remover, solvent.
diluir vt to dilute (sth in sth), dissolve; **2** (fig) hide, cover up sth; ♦ ~**-se** vr (fig) (atenuar-se) to grow less; fade (away).
diluviano,-a adj diluvial, torrential.
dilúvio m flood.
dimanante adj inv rising from, emanating; flowing.
dimanar vt to flow, emanate; **2** (origem) to come/spring from.
dimensão f dimension.
dimensões fpl measurements, proportions.
dimensionamento m measurement, size; ~ **da companhia** company's size, number of premises/offices.
dimensionar vt to measure the proportions; calculate the magnitude.
diminuição f reduction.
diminuir vt to reduce, decrease; **2** (MAT) to subtract, take away; ♦ vi to grow less, diminish.
diminuto,-a adj minute, tiny.
Dinamarca npr Denmark; **a ~** Denmark.
dinamarquês,-esa m,f Dane; (LÍNG) m Danish; ♦ adj Danish.
dinâmico,-a adj dynamic.
dinamismo m dynamism; **2** (fig) energy, drive.
dinamitar vt (rochas, etc) to blow up.
dinamite f dynamite.
dinamizar vt to stimulate, dynamize, liven up, give a new life to; ♦ ~**-se** to revitalize.
dínamo m dynamo.
dinastia f dynasty.
dinheiro m money; ~ **de contado** ready money, cash; ~ **miúdo** small change; **sem ~** (fam) broke; ~ **para alfinetes** pin money; **2** (FIN) capital; **a dinheiro** adv cash, for cash; IDIOM ~ **como milho** lots of money.
dinossauro m dinosaur.
dintel m (ARQ) lintel.
diocese f diocese.
diodo m (ELECT) diode.
dióspiro m persimmon.
dioxide m (QUÍM) dioxide.
diploma m (universidade) diploma; **2** (JUR) (texto legislativo) legal charter, decree, statute.
diplomacia f diplomacy; **2** (fig) tact.
diplomata m,f diplomat.
diplomático,-a adj diplomatic; **2** tactful.

dique *m (GEOG)* dam; **2** *(GEO)* dike; **3** *(NÁUT)* dry dock.

dire(c)ção *f* direction; **2** address; **3** *(rumo)* route, way; **4** *(AUTO)* steering; **5** management; **6** *(de partido)* leadership; **7** *(directores)* board of directors; **8** *(gabinete)* manager's/director's office; **9** *(TV, CIN, TEAT)* direction; **10 em ~ a** towards.

dire(c)cionamento *m (COMPUT)* forwarding.

dire-(c)cionar *vt* to channel.

dire(c)ta *f (col)* all-nighter; **fazer uma ~** to stay up all night.

dire(c)tiva *f (MIL, JUR, POL)* directive.

dire(c)tivo,-a *adj (órgão, função)* directive.

dire(c)to,-a *adj (caminho)* direct; **2** *(franco)* direct; **3 comboio ~** through/direct train; **4 transmissão ~ a** *(TV)* live broadcast; **em ~** *(TV)* live; *m (FERRO)* Express.

dire(c)tor,-ora *m,f (COM)* director; **2** *(do banco)* bank manager, manageress; **3** *(do jornal)* editor; **4** *(MÚS)* conductor; **5** *(escola)* headmaster, headmistress; ♦ *adj (MÚS)* directing, guiding.

dire(c)tor-adjunto, dire(c)tora-adjunta *m,f* assistant, deputy director.

dire(c)tor, dire(c)tora-geral *m,f* managing director.

dire(c)triz *f (GEOM)* directrix.

dire(c)trizes *fpl* guidelines.

direita *f* right-hand side; **à ~** on/to/by (your) right, **vire à ~** turn (to your) right.

direito *m* right(s); **2** prerogative; **3** permission; **4** *(JUR)* law; **estudar D~** to read law; **ter ~ a** to have a right to; **dar ~ a** give the right to, entitle; **5 ~s** *mpl (alfândega)* duties; **6** *(de autor)* royalties; **7 ~s autorais** copyright *sg;* ♦ **direito,-a** *adj (pé, margem, etc)* right; **2** *(que não é torto)* straight; **3** upright; **4** *(liso)* levelled; ♦ *adv* **sempre a ~** straight on/ahead; **a torto e a ~** at random, slapdash; **farei isso a torto e a ~** I shall do that by hook or by crook.

dirigente *m,f* leader, director; ♦ leading.

dirigir *vt (filme, actores)* to direct; **2** *(COM)* to manage, run; **3** *(AUTO)* to drive; **4** *(apontar)* to aim; **5** *(guiar)* to lead sb; **6** *(orquestra, coro)* to conduct; **7** *(barco)* to steer; **8** *(avião)* to pilot; ♦ *vt (orientar)* to direct, control; **2** *(estudos)* to supervise; ♦ **~-se** *vr*: **~ a** *(alguém)* speak to, address, approach sb; **2** *(encaminhar-se)* **~ para** go to/ towards, head for.

dirigível *m* airship; ♦ *adj inv* dirigible.

dirimir *vt* to annul; **2** *(obstar)* to impede, hamper; **3** *(resolver)* to solve; **4** to put an end to.

discal *adj inv* relative to a disc; **hérnia ~** slipped disc.

discagem *f* dialling.

discar *vt/vi (TEL)* to dial.

discente *m,f* student; ♦ *adj inv* learning; **corpo ~** student body.

discernimento *m* discernment.

discernir *vt* to distinguish between one and the other; **2** *(perceber)* to recognize.

discernível *(pl: -eis) adj inv* perceptible.

disciplina *f* discipline.

disciplinar *vt* to discipline.

discípulo,-a *m,f* disciple, follower; **2** pupil.

disco *m* disc; **2** *(MÚS)* record; **3** *(DESP)* discus; **4 ~ voador** flying saucer; **5** *(COMP)* disk, **~ compacto** compact disc; **~ flexível** floppy disc; **6** *(fig) (frase/conversa repetida)* **sempre o mesmo ~** always the same old tune; IDIOM **muda o ~ e toca o mesmo** change the tune and play the same; nothing ever changes.

discográfico,-a *adj (rel.* to disco*)* **indústria ~a** disco (discographic) industry.

discotecário,-a *m,f* disc jockey.

discordância *f* discord, disagreement.

discordar *vi* to disagree; to differ.

discórdia *f* discord, strife; **pomo de ~** bone of contention.

discorrer *vi (raciocinar)* to reason; **2** *(compreender)* to work (it) out; **3** *(discursar)* to discourse, talk *(sobre* on*)*; **4** *(apresentar opiniões)* to discuss.

discoteca *f* record-library; discotheque; **2** *(pop)* disco.

discrepância *f* discrepancy; **2** disagreement.

discrepar *vi* to differ (**de** from).

discreto,-a *adj* discreet; **2** *(roupa)* modest, unassuming; **3** *(nódoa, sinal)* little, small.

discrição *f* discretion, good sense; ♦ *adv* **à ~** unlimited, **2 deixo à sua ~** *(decision)* I leave (it) to your discretion.

discriminação *f* discrimination; **2** differentiation; **3** specification.

discriminador,-ora *adj (alguém)* biased, prejudiced.

discriminar *vt (segregar)* to discriminate, isolate; **2** *(especificar)* to specify.

discriminatório,-a *adj (procedimento, medidas)* discriminatory, discriminative; **2** *(lista)* itemized.

discursar *vi* to make a speech; to speak.

discurso *m* speech; **2** *(LÍNG)* discourse.

discussão *f* discussion, debate; **2** argument.

discutido *(pp de discutir) adj* **muito ~** much discussed.

discutir *vt (assunto)* to discuss; ♦ *vi* to argue.

discutível *(pl: -eis) adj inv* open to discussion; **2** arguable.

disfarçar *vt* to disguise; **ele disfarçou um bocejo** he stifled a yawn.

disfarce *m* disguise; **2** mask.

disforme *adj inv* deformed, hideous; **2** colossal.

disfunção *f (MED)* malfunction, dysfunction; **~ erétil** erectile dysfunction

disjunção *f* separation, division, difference; **2** *(GEOL)* split, division; **3** *(LÍNG)* disjunctive.

disjuntor *m (ELECT)* circuit-breaker; **2** *(MAT)* divider.

dislexia *f* dyslexia.

disléxico,-a *adj* dyslexic.

díspar *adj inv* different; **2** disparate.

disparado,-a *adj (tiro, etc)* fired; ♦ *adv (a toda a velocidade)* at full speed; **em ~a** like a shot.

disparo *m* shot; **2** *(estoiro)* bang.

disparar *vt* to shoot, fire; **2** *(lançar pedras)* to hurl; ♦ *vi* to go off; **a arma disparou** the gun went off; **2** *(partir rápido)* to shoot off, bolt; **3 os preços dispararam** prices shot up, soared.

disparatado,-a *adj* silly, absurd.

disparate *m* nonsense, rubbish; **2** blunder; **dizer ~s** to talk nonsense; **fazer um ~** to do a silly thing; to make a blunder.

dispêndio *m* expenditure; **2** *(fig)* loss.

dispendioso,-a *adj* costly.

dispensa *f* exemption; **2** *(de dever, cargo)* dispensation.

dispensário *m* dispensary.

dispensar *vt* to excuse; **2** to do without; **3** to exempt; **ele dispensou a colaboração deles** he did without their collaboration; **4** *(conceder)* to grant.

dispensável *(pl: -eis)* *m* superfluous; ♦ *adj inv* dispensable; **2** *(que pode ser dispensado)* available; **3** unnecessary.

dispepcia *f* dyspepcia.

dispersar *vt* to disperse; **2** to scatter; **3** *(disseminar) (sementes)* to spread; ♦ **~-se** disperse, scatter.

disperso,-a *(pp de* **dispersar***) adj* dispersed; **2** *(nuvens, folhas, casas)* scattered; **3** *(exército)* running in all directions; defeated.

displicência *f* displeasure, annoyance.

displicente *adj inv* unpleasant; indifferent; bored.

disponível *adj inv* available.

dispor *m* disposal; **ao seu ~** at your disposal; ♦ *vt* to arrange; to put in order; ♦ *vi:* **~ de** to have the use of; **não disponho de meios** I don't have the means; **disponha de mim quando quiser** I am at your disposal whenever you like; **2** to have, own; ♦ **~-se** *vr:* **~ a** to be prepared to, be willing to; **ele dispôs-se a falar** he prepared to speak; IDIOM **homem põe e Deus ~** man proposes and God disposes.

disposição *f* arrangement; **2** disposition; **3** intention; **4 à sua ~** at your disposal.

dispositivo *m* gadget, device.

disposto,-a *m* *(JUR)* precept; mandate; regulation, rule; **segundo o ~ na lei** as laid down by the law; ♦ *adj* arranged, ready; **2** disposed, inclined; **3** willing; **4** *(disposição)* **estar bem/mal ~** to be in a good/bad mood; *(saúde)* feel well/be indisposed; **5 sentir-se ~ a fazer** *(algo)* to feel like doing sth.

disputa *f* dispute, argument.

disputar *vt* to dispute; to fight over; **~ uma corrida** to run a race; ♦ *vi* to quarrel, argue; **2** to compete.

disquete *m* *(COMP)* floppy disk.

dissabor *m* *(desgosto)* sorrow, grief; **2** *(contrariedade)* trouble, upsetting; **3** vexation.

disse *(pret de* **dizer***)* **ele ~-me que vinha hoje** he told me he was coming today.

dissecar *vt* to dissect.

disseminação *f* dissemination (**de** of); spreading (**de** of); diffusion (**de** of).

disseminar *vt* to disseminate; to spread.

dissensão *f* dissension, discord.

dissertação *f* *(tese)* dissertation; **2** *(escolar)* essay, composition; **3** lecture.

dissertar *vi:* **~ sobre** *(algo)* to lecture (on sth).

dissidente *adj inv* dissident.

dissimulação *f* pretence; disguise.

dissimular *vt* to hide; to fake; ♦ *vi* to dissemble.

dissipação *f* waste, squandering.

dissipar *vt* to disperse, dispel; to squander, waste; ♦ **~-se** *vr* to vanish.

dissolução *f* dissolving; debauchery.

dissoluto,-a *adj* dissolved; **2** *(JUR) (contracto, acordo)* void, null; **3** *(fig)* dissolute, debauched, licentious.

dissolver *vt* to dissolve, melt; **2** *(dispersar)* to disperse; **3** *(JUR)* to dissolve; **4** *(fig)* to pervert; **5** to evaporate; ♦ **~-se** *vr* to dissolve.

dissuadir *vt* to dissuade; **~ alguém de fazer** to talk sb out of doing, dissuade sb from doing sth.

distância *f* distance; **a grande ~** far away.

distanciar *vt* to distance, set apart; to space out; ♦ **~-se** *vr* to move away.

distante *adj inv* distant, far-off, remote; **2** *(fig) (pessoa) (temperamento)* aloof, reserved.

distar *vi* to be distant (**de** from); **o cemitério ~ a 10 quilómetros da cidade** the cemetery is 10 kilometres distant/away from the city.

distinção *f* difference; **2** distinction; honour.

distinguir *vt* to distinguish, typify; **2** *(separar)* to differentiate, tell s.o./sth apart; **3** *(perceber)* to make out; ♦ **~-se** *vr* to stand out.

distintivo *m* badge; emblem; insignia, honour.

distintivo,-a *adj* distinctive.

distinto,-a *adj* different; distinct; **2** distinguished.

distra(c)ção, distração *f* absent-mindedness; **2** pastime; **3** oversight.

distraído,-a *adj* absent-minded, forgetful; **2** distracted, off one's guard; **3** inattentive; **4** *(entretido)* engrossed (**com** with); *(recreado)*entertained, busy.

distrair *vt* to distract; **2** to amuse; ♦ **~-se** *vr* to amuse/enjoy o.s.; **2** to be distracted; **3** to be engrossed.

distribuição *f* distribution; delivery.

distribuir *vt* to distribute; **2** to share out; **3** to deliver.

distrito *m* district, borough, municipality; **~ eleitoral** constituency.

distúrbio *m* disturbance; **2** *(tumulto)* riot; **3** *(MED, PSIC)* problem; **~ mental** mental disorder.

ditado *m* dictation; **2** *(provérbio)* saying, adage.

ditador,-ora *m,f* dictator.

ditadura *f* dictatorship.

ditame *m* *(ditado pelo íntimo)* dictate; **os ~s da consciência** the dicates of conscience; **2** *(JUR) (regra)* rule; **3** provision.

ditar *vt* to dictate; **2** *(fig)* to impose.

dito *m* saying, adage, proverb; remark; **um ~ chistoso** a witty remark, wisecrack; ♦ **dito,-a** *(pp de* **dizer***) adj* aforementioned, the said (person); ♦ *adv* **~ e feito** no sooner said than done; IDIOM **dar o ~ por não ~** contradict o.s.

ditongo *m* diphthong.

ditoso,-a *adj* happy; lucky; blessed.

diurno,-a *adj* day; **2** daily; **há classes ~as e noturnas** there are day and evening classes.

divagar *vi* to wander; **~ do assunto** to wander off the subject, digress.

divergência *f* divergence; disagreement.

diversão *f* amusement; pastime, entertainment.

diversidade *f* diversity.

diversificar *vt* to diversify; ♦ *vi* to vary.

diverso,-a *adj* different; *(pl)* various; ♦ *pron* ~**s** some, several.

divertido,-a *adj* amusing, funny.

divertimento *m* amusement, entertainment.

divertir *vt* to amuse, entertain; ♦ ~**-se** *vr* to enjoy o.s., have a good time; **diverti-me a valer** I really enjoyed myself, I had a marvellous time.

dívida *f* debt; indebtedness; **contrair** ~**s** to run into debt; ~**s pendentes** outstanding debts.

dividendo *m* (FIN) dividend.

dividir *vt* (ger) to divide; **2** (repartir) to share; **3** (separar) to split; **4** (demarcar) to mark out; ♦ *vi* (MAT) divide; ♦ ~**-se** *vr* to divide, split up.

divindade *f* divinity.

divisa *f* emblem; slogan; (MIL) stripe; **2** ~**s** *fpl* foreign exchange, currency.

divisão *f* division; dissension; **2** (da casa) room.

divisar *vt* (avistar) to see, make out.

divisório,-a *f* partition; ♦ *adj* dividing.

divorciar *vt* to divorce; ♦ ~**-se** *vr* to get divorced.

divórcio *m* divorce.

divulgar *vt* to spread; **2** to publicize, to divulge; **3** (segredo) to disclose; ♦ ~**-se** *vr* to leak out.

divulgação *f* act of spreading, divulging; disclosure.

dizer *m* **o dizer** (modo de expressão) the language; **os dizeres populares** *mpl* people's sayings; ♦ *vt* to say; to tell; ~ **que sim/que não** to say yes/say no; **2 querer** ~ (significar) to mean; **que quer isso dizer?** what does that mean?; **3** (condizer) ~ **bem com** to go well with; **os cortinados dizem bem com as paredes** the curtains go well with/match the walls; ♦ *imp* **digamos** let us say; ♦ *vb impess* **dizem que** it is said/they say that; **diz-se que** it is said that; **diz-se à boca pequena** it is whispered around; ♦ ~**-se** *vr* (afirmar-se) to claim to be; **ela sempre se disse preguiçosa** she has always said she was lazy; ♦ *adv* **por assim dizer** so to speak; ♦ *conj* **a bem dizer** in fact, to tell the truth; **melhor dizendo** or rather.

dízima *f* (antigo imposto) tithe; **2** contribution of one-tenth.

dizimar *vt* (destruir em parte) to decimate; **2** (fig) (dissipar) to squander, waste; ♦ *vi* to devastate.

dl (abr de **decilitro**) decilitre.

do = **de** + **o** (Vd: **de**).

dó *m* pity, compassion; **ter** ~ **de** to have pity on; **2** (MÚS) C, doh; IDIOM **sem** ~ **nem piedade** without pity or mercy.

doação *f* donation, gift; **2** ~ **por morte** bequest; **3** (JUR) legacy.

doador,-ora *m,f* donor; ♦ *adj* donating.

doar *vt* to donate, give.

dobadoira, dobadoura *f* reel.

dobar *vt* to spin (fio); ♦ *vi* to wind up.

dobra *f* (parte que se sobrepõe) fold, flap; **a** ~ **do lençol** the flap/fold of the sheet (turned down); **2** (prega, vestido) pleat; **3** (calças) turn-up (UK), cuffs (US); **4** (envelope, livro) flap; **5** (GEOL) fold, bend.

dobrada *f* (CULIN) tripe.

dobradiça *f* hinge (da janela, porta).

dobradiço,-a *adj* (que se dobra) flexible

dobrar *vt* to double; **2** to fold; **3** (vergar) to bend; **4** (circundar) to turn, go around; **ele dobrou o Cabo das Tormentas** he went around the Cape of Torments; **5** (CIN, TV) (diálogo) to dub; stand in for, be an actor's double; **6** (fazer ceder) to make s.o. give in; ♦ *vi* to double; **2** (sino) to toll; **3** to bend (braço, joelho); ♦ ~**-se** *vr* (curvar-se) to double (up); stoop; **2** (ceder) to give in.

dobro *m* double; (duas vezes mais) twice as much.

doca *f* (NÁUT) dock, quay; ~ **flutuante** floating dock.

doçaria *f* (de doces) confectionery; **2** (loja) confectioner's shop.

doce *m* (CULIN) sweet; **arroz-**~ rice pudding; ♦ *adj inv* sweet.

> Arroz-doce differs slightly from the English rice pudding, in that it is made with with eggs, milk and orange peel. It is traditionally eaten at Christmas.

doce-amargo *adj* bitter-sweet.

docemente *adv* gently, sweetly.

docente *adj inv* teaching; **o corpo** ~ teaching staff.

dócil *adj inv* docile.

docilidade *n* docility.

documentação *f* documentation; papers *pl*.

documento *m* document.

doçura *f* sweetness; **2** (maneira, atitude) gentleness.

doença *f* illness.

doente *m,f* sick person; **2** (paciente) patient; ♦ *adj inv* sick, ill.

doentio,-a *adj* sickly; unhealthy; morbid.

doer *vi* (magoar) to hurt, ache; **2** (fig) (sentir dor) to hurt, grieve; **dói-me tanto ver a miséria** it hurts me to see so much poverty; ♦ ~**-se** *vr* (ressentir-se) to resent, to be offended.

dogma *m* dogma.

dogmático,-a *adj* dogmatic.

doideira *f*, **doidice** *f* madness, foolishness.

doidivanas *m,f sg/pl* crazy person, hair-brained person.

dói-dói *m* (fala de infante) pain, bruise; ♦ *exc* ouch!

doido,-a *m,f* madman, madwoman; ♦ *adj* mad, crazy; ~ **por** mad/crazy about (sb); ~ **varrido** (col) raving mad; **ele ficou** ~ (com fúria) he went mad (with rage).

dois *num* (mpl) two; (f: duas); ~ **a** ~ two by two; ~~**pontos** *m inv* (punctuation) colon; IDIOM ~**pesos e duas medidas** double standards.

dólar *m* dollar.

dolo *m* fraud.

dolorido,-a *adj* painful, sore; **2** (fig) sorrowful.

dom *m* gift, **um** ~ **do céu** it is a gift from Heaven; **2** talent, knack; **o** ~ **da palavra** the gift of the gab; **3 Dom** (= **D.**) (título dado a nobres) = Sir; (endereçando o rei) King; **D. (Dom) Manuel I** King Manuel I; **4** (alto clero) **o cardeal, D. (Dom) José Cerejeira**.

domador,-ora *m,f* tamer.

domar *vt* to tame.

domesticado,-a *adj* domesticated; **2** tame.

domesticar *vt* to tame, housetrain *(animal)*.

doméstico,-a *adj* domestic, household; home; **empregada ~a** home help.

domiciliado,-a *adj (pessoa)* residing in.

domiciliário,-a *adj* domiciliary, home; **2 prisão ~a** house arrest.

domicílio *m* domicile, home, residence, abode; **2** *(JUR)* domicile.

dominação *f* domination.

dominante *adj* dominant; predominant.

dominar *vt* to dominate; to overcome; ♦ *vi* to dominate, prevail; ♦ **~-se** *vr* to control o.s.

Domingo/domingo *m* Sunday; **D~ de Páscoa** Easter Sunday; **D~ de Ramos** Palm Sunday.

domingueiro,-a *adj (relativo a domingo)* Sunday; **no seu traje ~** in his (her, your) Sunday best.

dominicano,-a *adj (REL)* Dominican.

domínio *m* power; domination, control; **~ próprio** self-control; **2** *fig* domain; sphere, ambit, field; **3** *(MAT)* dominium.

dominó *m (traje do carnaval)* domino; **2** *(jogos)* dominoes; IDIOM **fazer ~ para os dois lados** to be two-faced.

dona *f* owner; mistress; **~ de casa** housewife; **2 Dona** *(título dado a mulher casada, professional ou nobre)* **que disse a D. Manuela?** what did (Mrs) Manuela say?; **3** *(princesa)* **D. Mafalda** princess Mafalda; **4** *(rainha)* **Rainha D. Carlota** Queen Charlotte.

donaire *m* elegance, gentility; **2** graceful posture.

donatário,-a *m,f* recipient.

donativo *m* donation.

donde *adv* where from; **~ vem?** where do you come from?

doninha *f (ZOOL)* weasel.

dono *m* owner; **2** *(empregador)* boss; **3** *(pop)* master; **ser ~ do seu nariz/da sua vontade** like to have his own way; be obstinate.

donzela *f (jovem) (HIST)* maiden, maid, damsel; **2** virgin; **a ~ Maria** the maiden Mary; **3** *(aia de nobre)* handmaiden.

dopado,-a *m,f (DESP) (atleta, etc)* drugged; *(cavalo)* doped.

doping *m (DESP)* doping.

dor *f* ache, pain; **~ de cabeça** headache; **2** *(fig) (pesar)* grief, sorrow; **3** *(fig) (dó)* pity; **uma ~ de alma** a poor soul; **4 ~es** *fpl* aches, pangs; **ter ~ de cotovelo** to be green with envy; **ter ~ de corno** *(cal)* be a cuckold.

doravante *adv* from now on, henceforth.

dores *fpl* aches, pains; pangs.

dormente *m,f (FERRO)* railway sleeper; **2** *(do soalho)* beam; ♦ *adj inv* numb, sleeping; **2** *(água)* stagnant.

dormida *f* sleep; **2** *(lugar para uma noite)* lodging; **comida e ~** bed and food.

dorminhoco,-a *m,f* sleepyhead; ♦ *adj* fond of sleep, sleepy.

dormir *vi* to sleep; **~ a sono solto** to sleep soundly; IDIOM **~ como uma pedra** to sleep like a log.

dormitar *vi* to doze.

dormitório *m (coletivo)* dormitory; **2** *(quarto)* bedroom.

dorsal *(pl: -ais) adj inv (ANAT)* dorsal; **coluna ~** spinal column; **2** *(ZOOL) (barbatana)* dorsal.

dorso *m* back.

dos = **de** + **os** *(Vd:* **de**).

dosagem *m* dosage.

dose *f (MED)* dose; **~ excessiva** overdose; **2** *(CULIN)* helping; **3** *(porção)* portion; **4** *(fig)* **ter uma grande ~ de vaidade** to be very vain; **5** *(BR) (fig)* **ser ~ para leão** *(trabalho, tarefa)* be hard, boring.

dossier, dossiê *m* file, dossier.

dotação *f* endowment, allocation.

dotado,-a *adj* gifted; **~ de** endowed with.

dotar *vt* to endow; **2** to give a dowry to.

dote *m* dowry; **2 dotes** *mpl* gifts; **3** accomplishments.

dou *(pres indic, 1ª pessoa de* **dar***):* **eu ~ te um beijo** I give/shall give you a kiss.

dourada *f (peixe)* sea bream, guilthead; **2** *(f de* **dourado***)*.

dourado,-a *adj* golden; **2** gilt, gilded.

dourar *vt (revestir em ouro)* to gild; **2** *(fig) (minimizar: problema etc)* to gloss over.

douto,-a *adj (pessoa)* learned, erudite; **~ em** learned (in), expert on.

doutor,-ora *m,f (título: médico, dentista, veterinário, advogado, pessoa doutorada)* doctor.

doutorado *m* doctorate, Ph.D., person holding a doctorate.

doutoral *adj inv (parecer)* doctoral, doctiorial; **2** *(fig) (pessoa; estilo, Tom)* pompous.

doutorando,-a *m,f* candidate for doctorate.

doutoramento *m (acto)* taking or conferring a Ph.D. degree.

doutrina *f* doctrine.

doze *num* twelve.

Dr/dr, Drª/drª *(abr de* **doutor,-ora***)* Dr.

draga *f (para limpar rio, mar)* dredge; **2** *(barco, pessoa neste trabalho)* dredger; **3** dam barge; **~s** *fpl (NÁUT)* timber, props (to hold up a ship in dry dock); **~-minas** *m (barco para apanhar minas submarinas)* mine sweeper.

dragador *m* dredger.

dragagem *f* dredging.

dragão *m* dragon; **2** *(MIL)* dragoon.

drageia *f (medicamentos)* pill, tablet; **2** *(BR) (gluseima)* sugared almond.

dragona *f (MIL)* epaulette (UK); epaulet (US).

drama *m (TEAT)* play; **2** *(fig) (acontecimento funesto)* tragedy; IDIOM **fazer um ~ (de algo)** to make a drama out of sth.

dramático,-a *adj* dramatic.

dramatizar *vt* to make into play; **2** *(fig) (tornar dramático)* to dramatize, exaggerate.

dramaturgo *m* play-wright, dramatist.

drástico,-a *adj* drastic.

drenagem *f* draining, drainage.

drenar *vt* to drain.

dreno *m (tubo)* drainpipe; **2** *(vala)* drainage ditch.

driblagem *f (DESP)* dribble.

driblar *vt (DESP) (jogador, bola)* to dribble.

drive *f (COMP)* drive.
droga *f* drug; **2** *(fig)* rubbish.
drogado,-a *m,f* drug addict.
drogar *vt* to drug; ♦ ~**-se** *vr* to take drugs; be on drugs.
drogaria *f* drugstore; **2** household, hardware shop.
droguista *m,f* hardware merchant.
dromedário *m (ZOOL)* dromedary.
drope *m inv (rebuçado)* drop.
druida *m* druid.
dto *(abr de* **direito***) (apartamento)* on the right; *(on envelope)* 4º ~ fourth floor on the right.
dualidade *f* duality.
dualismo *m (FIL, REL)* dualism.
duas *(Vd:* **dois***) num* two; ~**-peças** *fpl* two-piece suit; *(de malha)* twinset.
dúbio,-a *adj* dubious; uncertain.
dublado,-a *adj (CIN) (BR)* dubbed.
dublagem *f* dubbing.
dublar *vt* to dub.
Dublin *npr* Dublin.
dublinense *m,f* Dubliner; ♦ *adj inv* of Dublin, Dublin; **associação** ~ Dublin Association.
ducado *m* duchy.
ducentésimo,-a *num* two-hundredth.
dúctil *adj inv* ductile, pliable; **2** *(fig) (dócil)* docile, that can be moulded or trained.
ducha *f (BR)* shower; **duche** *m (EP)* shower; **tomar uma** ~ to take a shower.
dúctil *adj inv (metal)* ductile, flexible, pliable.
ducto *m (ANAT)* duct.
duelo *m* duel; **2** *(fig) (contenda)* duel.
duende *m* goblin, gnome.
dueto *m* duet, duo.
dulcificar *vt (adoçar) (bebida)* to sweeten; **2** *(fig) (suavizar com palavras)* sweeten, soften.
dulcíssimo,-a *(superl de* **doce***)* very sweet.
dum (= **de** + **um**) *m* of/from a.
duma *f* = **de** + **uma**.
duna *f* dune.
duo *m (dueto)* duo.
duodécimo *m* twelfth.
duplex *m (apartamento)* duplex; split-level; ♦ *adj* split-level; **2** *(algo com dois fins)* dual-purpose, **cartão** ~ duplex card.

duplicação *f* doubling, redoubling; **2** second, double.
duplicar *vt* to duplicate; ♦ *vi* to double.
duplicidade *f* duplication; **2** *(fig)* duplicity, double-dealing.
duplo,-a *m,f* double; ♦ *adj* double; **2** *(personalidade)* split.
duque *m (nobre)* duke; **2** *(jogos)* deuce.
duquesa *f* duchess.
durabilidade *f* durability.
duração *f* duration; **de pouca** ~ short-lived.
duradouro,-a, duradoiro,-a *adj* lasting, long-lasting.
durante *prep* during, for.
durão *m* **durona** *f adj (BR)* strict, harsh.
durar *vi* to last; ~ **muito** to last a long time.
durável *adj inv (material, objecto)* durable, lasting.
dureza *f* hardness; **2** *(fig) (severidade)* harshness.
duro,-a *x adj* hard; **água** ~ hard water; **2** harsh; **homem** ~ harsh man; **3** *(resistente)* tough *(material)*; **carne** ~**a** tough meat; **4 pão** ~ stale bread; **5** *(surdo)* ~ **de ouvido** hard of hearing; **ser** ~ **com alguém** to be hard on sb; IDIOM **ser** ~ **de roer** to be a hard nut to crack; hard to take; **dar um** ~ **(para)** *(BR)* do one's utmost, work flat out (for/at sth).
duriense *adj* from Douro province (N. Portugal); relating to Douro.
durmo *(pres ind 1ª pessoa de* **dormir***)*: **eu** ~ **muito bem** I sleep well.
dúvida *f* doubt, uncertainty; **2** indecision; **sem** ~ no doubt; **pôr em** ~ to put in question; **por causa das** ~**s** to be sure.
duvidar *vt* to doubt; **duvido que** I doubt that; ♦ *vi* ~ **de (alguém, algo)** to doubt sb, sth; **2** to be suspicious of/about, suspect; **3** to be uncertain, to hesitate.
duvidoso,-a *adj* doubtful; **2** dubious, suspicious; **3** *(negócio)* uncertain; **4** *(notícia)* unlikely.
duzentos,-as *num* two hundred; ♦ *det* two hundred; ♦ *adj inv* two-hundredth.
dúzia *f* dozen; **meia-**~ half a dozen; ♦ *adv* **à** ~ by the dozen; **às** ~**s** by the dozen; IDIOM ~ **de frade** *(13)*, a baker's dozen.
dzovo *m (MOÇ)* cloth for carrying babies on the back.

e

E, e *m (letra)* E, e.
e *conj* and; **2** ~ **o dinheiro?** what about the money?; **3 E depois?** And then? So? So what?
é *(pres indic de: ser)* he/she/it is, you are.
ébano *m* ebony.
ébrio,-a *m,f* drunkard; ♦ *adj* drunk; ~ **de felicidade** drunk with happiness; **2** ~ **de poder** thirsty for power.
ebulição *f* boiling; **2** fermentation; **3** *(fig)* excitement.
écharpe *f* stole; scarf.
eclesiástico,-a *m* clergyman; ♦ *adj* ecclesiastical, church.
eclipsar *vt* to eclipse; **2** *(fig)* to obfuscate, outshine.
eclipse *m* eclipse; ~ **lunar** lunar eclipse; ~ **solar** eclipse of the sun.
eclodir *vt* to break out; **2** emerge; **3** spring up; bloom.
eclosão *f* emergence; **2** appearance.
eclusa *f (canal)* lock; **2** floodgate.
eco *m* echo; **2 ter** ~ to catch on.
ecoar *vi* to echo, reverberate; **2** repeat.
ecocardiograma *m* echocardiogram, ECG.
ecografia *f* ultrasound scan.
ecologia *f* ecology.
ecológico,-a *adj* ecological.
economia *f* economy; **2** economics *sg pl*; **3** ~**s** *fpl* savings; **4 Caixa** ~**a** savings bank.
económico,-a *(BR: -nô-)* *adj* cheap, economical, thrifty; **2** *(COM)* economic.
economista *m,f* economist.
economizar *vt* to economize, save; **2** *(fortuna)* to amass; ♦ *vi* to be frugal.
ecossistema *m* ecosystem.
ecrã *m (BR:* **ecran***)* screen.
Ecu *(abr de* **Unidade Monetária da União Europeia***)* currency unit.
ecuménico,-a *(BR: -ê-)* *adj* ecumenical; **2** *(GEOG)* worldwide.
eczema *f* eczema.
edema *m* oedema; *(US)* edema.
Éden *m* eden, heaven, paradise.
edição *f* publication, printing, edition; **2** edition, issue; **3** *(TV, CIN) (preparação/revisão de trabalhos para o programa)* editing; preparation; **4** *(TV: notícias)* news broadcast; **5** ~ **a(c)tualizada** *f* revised edition; **6** ~ **pirata** *(CD, DVD)* illegal/pirate copy; **7 a** ~ **em CD** the issuing on CD; **8 de** ~ **oficial** government's publication.
edicto *m* edict, decree, order, proclamation.
edificação *f* construction; **2** *(de monumento)* erection; **3** *(fig)* edification.

edificar to build, erect; **2** *(fig)* edify.
edifício *m* building, edifice, premises; **2** *(fig)* structure; **3** ~ **central** main building; headquarters.
Edimburgo *npr (Escócia)* Edinburgh.
Édipo *m* Oedipus; **2 complexo de** ~ Oedipus complex.
edital *m* genuine copy of an edict, decree, proclamation; **2** ~ **de licitação** tender.
editar *vt* to issue, publish; **2** *(trabalho feito)* to edit, revise, correct, check.
édito *(Vd:* **edicto***)*.
editor,-ora *adj* publishing; **2** *m* publisher; **3** *f* publishers *pl*; **4** ~ **crítico** literary editor; **5 casa** ~**a** publishing firm.
editorial *m* editorial; ♦ *adj inv* publishing.
EDP *(abr de* **Electricidade de Portugal***)* Portuguese Electricity Board.
edredão *(BR: -dom) m (para a cama)* eiderdown.
educação *f* education; **2** upbringing; **3** good manners *pl*; **4** ~ **física** physical training.
educado,-a *adj* educated; wellbred.
educador,-ora *m,f* tutor, educator; ~ **de infância** nursery/kindergarten teacher, carer; ♦ *adj* educating, educational.
educar *vt (criar)* to bring up, raise; **2** to educate, instruct; **3** to train; ♦ ~**-se** *vr* to teach o.s.
educativo,-a *adj* educational.
efe(c)tivamente *adv* really, in fact.
efe(c)tivar *vt* to carry out, realize.
efe(c)tivo,-a *adj* effective; **2** *(trabalho, pessoal)* permanent; ♦ *(MIL) f* military strength.
efe(c)tuar *vt* to carry out, execute.
efeito *m* effect, result; **2** purpose; **3** impression; **4 com** ~ indeed; **5 sem** ~ null and void; **6 fazer** ~ to create an impression; **7 levar a** ~ to carry out; **8** ~**s especiais** *(CIN)* special effects; **para todos os** ~**s** for all intents and purposes.
eféméride *f* daily news items.
efémero,-a *(BR -ê-)* *adj* ephemeral, transitory, short-lived.
efeminado *m* effeminate man; pansy.
efervescente *adj (QUÍM)* effervescent; **2** bubbling, sparkling; **3** *(col)* fizzy; **4** *(fig)* enthusiastic, bubbling.
efes-e-erres *(F's e R's) mpl:* **com todos os** ~ in every little detail; with the smallest details.
efetuar *(Vd:* **efe(c)tuar** and other entries with **efe(c)t-***)*.
effluente *m* affluent; ♦ *adj inv* flowing.
eficácia *f (de pessoa)* efficiency; **2** *(tratamento)* effectiveness.
eficaz *(pl: -es) adj inv (pessoa)* efficient; **2** effective, efficacious.
eficiência *f (eficácia)* efficiency.
eficiente *adj inv* efficient, competent; **2** *(PSIC)* **quociente de** ~ *m* efficiency quota.
efígie *f* effigy, image.
eflorescência *f (BOT, QUÍM)* efflorescence, blooming; **2** *(MED)* rash, skin eruption.
eflúvio *m (fluido)* effluvium, invisible exhalation; **2** emanation; **3** *(poet)* fragrance, aroma.
efluxo *m* efflux.

EFTAR (*abr de* **Estação Fluvial de Tratamento de Resíduos**) Water Treatment Station.

efusão *f* effusion; **2** *(de gás)* spillage; **3** *(fig)* outburst; **4** *(MED)* effusion, shedding; **5** ~ **de sangue** bloodshed; **6 com** ~ effusively.

efusivo,-a *adj* effusive, expressive, enthusiastic; **2** *(GEOL)* extrusive.

Egeu *npr (mar)* **o** ~ Aegean Sea.

égide *f* Aegis; **2** *(fig)* prote(c)ção; **sob a** ~ **de** under the aegis/protection of.

egípcio,-a *adj* Egyptian.

Egi(p)to *m* Egypt, **o** ~ Egypt.

ego *m* ego.

egocêntrico,-a *adj* egocentric person.

egocentrismo *m* egocentrism.

egoísmo *m* selfishness, egoism.

egoísta *m,f* egoist, egotist; ♦ *adj inv* selfish, egotist, self-centred.

egotismo *m* egotism, selfishness.

egrégio,-a *adj* noble, illustrious, distinguished, **nossos ~s avós** our illustrious ancestors.

egresso *m* exit; **2** departure; **3** former monk; **4** *(ASTRON)* the end of an eclipse.

égua *f (ZOOL)* mare.

eguada *(BR)* a herd of mares.

eguariço *m* herdsman of horses, mares, mules; ♦ *adj* of/about mares.

eh! *exc (chamando)* hey!, hey you!

eia! *exc (ânimo)* hey!, courage!, come on!

ei-la, ei-lo, ei-las, ei-los (= **eis** + **a, o, as, os**) here/there she, he, it is; here/there they are; *(Vd:* **eis***);* **você encontrou a chave? sim, ei-la** have you found the key? yes, here it is; **ei-lo finalmente!** here he is at last!

eira *f* threshing floor; IDIOM **nem** ~ **nem beira** to be down and out, in poverty.

eirado *m* roof terrace.

eiró, eirós *f* a kind of eel.

eis *adv* here (it) is, here are, here you have (it); ~ **aqui a prova** here is/you have the proof; **2** ~ **que vimos ao longe** suddenly, we saw in the distance; **3** ~ **senão quando menos esperava** suddenly, when I least expected (it); **4** ~ **então a questão** here, then, is the question; **5** ~ **porque** that is why, here is how/why; **6** ~ **tudo** that is all.

eito *m* sequence of things; ♦ *adv* **a** ~ one after another, non-stop.

eiva *f* flaw; **2** rotten spot in a fruit.

eivar *vt* to contaminate; ♦ ~**-se** *vr* to get infected, **2** *(fruta)* to get rotten; **3** *(vidro)* flawed.

eixo *m* axle; **2** *(MAT)* axis; **3** shaft; **4** basis; ~ **de transmissão** drive shaft; **entrar nos** ~**s** to be on the right track; **pôr nos** ~**s** to set straight.

ejaculação *f* ejaculation; **2** *(fig)* flood.

ejacular *vt* to ejaculate.

eje(c)t *vt* to eject; **2** to spew out; **3** to throw out.

eje(c)tável *adj inv* ejecting.

ela *pron pess (sujeito)* she; *(animal, coisa)* it; ~ **não gosta disso** she doesn't like that; **a chave? aqui está** ~ the key? here it is; **2** *(predicativo)* herself, itself; **nem parece** ~ she doesn't even look herself;

3 *(complemento)* **isto é para** ~ this is for her; **4** *(enfático)* **a** ~ **não dou nada** I don't give anything to her (not to her); ♦ *adv* **dá** ~ **por** ~ it's about the same; **elas** *fpl* they, them, themselves; ~ **já saíram** they have already left; **vou com** ~ I am going with them; ♦ *exc* **quebraste a jarra? agora é que vão ser** ~! you broke the vase? now, there's going to be trouble.

elaboração *f* working out; **2** preparation.

elaborar *vt* to elaborate; **2** to prepare; **3** to set out, draw up.

elanguescer *vt* to go languid, feeble; **2** *(olhos, olhar)* to go/become wistful; ♦ *vi* languish.

elasticidade *f* elasticity; suppleness.

elástico,-a *m* elastic; **2** *(para prender rolo de coisas)* rubber band; **3** *(para o cabelo)* elastic band; ♦ *adj* elastic; **2** *(corpo, membros)* supple, flexible; **3** *(produto)* springy; **4 pastilha** ~**a** chewing gum; **5 bota de** ~ *(fig) (contra o progresso)* old-fashioned person, square, *(pop)* **ele é uma bota de** ~ he is a square.

ele *pron pess (sujeito)* he; it; ~ **é esperto** he is clever; **o melão? aqui está** ~ the melon? here it is; **2** *(predicativo)* himself, itself; **3** *(complemento)* him; it; **ela vai com** ~ she is going with him; **4** *(enfático)* ~ **é que sabe**, he is the one who knows; **5** *(realce)* such, what, ~ **há cada coisa!** what a thing (to happen)!; **6 eles** *mpl* they; them, themselves.

ele(c)tricidade *f* electricity.

ele(c)tricista *m,f* electrician.

elé(c)trico,-a *m* tram, trolley-car; ♦ *adj* electric.

ele(c)trificar *vt* to electrify; **2** *(fig)* to thrill.

ele(c)trizante *adj inv* electrifying.

ele(c)trizar *vt* electrify.

ele(c)tro- *pref* ~**cardiograma** *m* electrocardiogram; ~**cussão** *f* electrocution.

electrocutar *vt* to electrocute.

ele(c)tródio, elé(c)trodo *m* electrode.

ele(c)trodomésticos *mpl* household appliances.

ele(c)trogéneo,-a *adj (aparelho)* producing electricity.

ele(c)trólise *f* electrolysis.

ele(c)trólito *m* electrolyte.

ele(c)trónico,-a *(BR* -ô-*)* *f* electronics *sg*; ♦ *adj* electronic.

elefante,-ta *m,f (ZOOL)* elephant; **2** *(fig)* pessoa grande e pesada; IDIOM ~ **branco** white elephant; **ter memória de** ~ to have an elephant's memory.

elegância *f* elegance.

elegante *adj inv* elegant; **2** fashionable; **3** good figure.

eleger *vt* to elect, to opt for; **2** to choose.

elegia *f* elegy.

elegível *adj inv* eligible.

eleição *f* election; **2** selection.

eleito,-a *(irr pp de* **eleger***)* *adj* elected; **2** chosen.

eleitor,-ora *m,f* voter.

eleitorado *m* electorate.

eleitoral *adj inv* electoral, voting; **campanha** ~ electoral campaign

elementar *adj inv* elementary; **2** basic, fundamental.

elemento *m* element; **2** component; **3** ~**s** *mpl* rudiments.

elenco *m* list; **2** *(actores)* cast.

eletrão *m (FÍS)* electron.

eletri- *(Vd:* **ele(c)tri-**)*;* **eletro-** *(Vd:* **ele(c)tro-**)*.*

elevação *f* elevation; **2** rise; **3** raising; **4** height.

elevado,-a *adj* high; **2** noble; **espírito** ~ noble spirit; **3** *(MÚS)* forte.

elevador *m* lift, elevator; **2** viaduct, overpass.

elevar *vt* to lift up, to rise, to raise; **2** to exalt; ♦ ~**-se** *vr* to rise.

eliminação *f* elimination; **2** defeat.

eliminar *vt* to remove, eliminate; **2** to defeat; **3** *(insectos)* to exterminate.

elite *f* elite; **2 grupo de** ~**s** elitist group.

elitismo *m* elitism.

elitista *adj inv* elitist, adept of elitism.

elixir *m* elixir; **2** néctar; **3** potion, panacea.

elo *m* link; **2** *(da planta)* tendril; **3** bond.

elogiar *vt* to praise.

elogio *m* praise.

eloquência *f* eloquence.

eloquente *adj inv* eloquent; **2** persuasive.

elucidar *vt (explicar)* to explain; to make clear; **2** *(fazer conhecer)* elucidate; enlighten.

em (**em** + **o** = **no; em** + **a** = **na; em** + **essa** = **nessa; em** + **os** = **nos; em** + **as** = **nas**) *prep* in; on; at; *(place)* at, in; **em casa** at home, in the home country; **em Angola** in Angola; **eles estão no jardim** they are in the garden; **2** *(ação, modo)* **em guerra,** at war; **em dire(c)to** *(TV)* *(programa)* live; **em voz baixa** in a low voice; **ele falou em francês** he spoke in French; **a festa já ia em meio** the party was halfway through; **em jejum** (in) fasting; **em pêlo** naked; **ele está na China em negócios** he is in China on business; **3** *(sobre)* on; **o copo caiu no chão** the glass fell on the floor; **ela gasta todo o dinheiro em vestidos** she spends all her money on dresses; **4** *(dentro de)* in, within; **a cópia está na pasta** the copy is in the briefcase; **5** *(tempo)* in, on, at; **vou em Setembro** I am going in September; **na segunda-feira** on Monday; **nessa altura** at that time; **em dois dias** *(dentro de)* in two days time; **6** *(estado, condição)* in; **em bom estado** in good condition/state; **7** *(assunto, matéria)* **ele licenciou-se** ~ **geografia** he graduated in, on geography; **ela é uma perita em culinária** she is an expert on cookery; **8** *(mode of transport)* on; **ela está no autocarro** she is on the bus; **9** *(suplementando certos verbos:* **hesitar, acreditar, crer, pensar, entrar, confiar**) em; **pensei em ti** I thought about you; **hesitei em falar** I hesitated to speak; **muito prazer em conhecê-lo!** I am pleased to meet you!; **10** (*em combina com adjectivo demonstrativo e pronome pessoal objecto*); **eu acredito nela** I believe (in) her; **eu confio neles** I trust them; **ele está naquela loja** he is in that shop; ♦ *(em adv, prep);* ~ **breve** soon; **de quando** ~ **quando** every now and then; **de três** ~ **três horas** every three hours; **em busca de** in search of; **na verdade** in truth, really; ♦ *(em combines with demonstrative adjectives and object pronouns)* **eu acredito nele** I believe him; **eu confio neles** I trust them; **nessa não caio eu** I won't fall for that; **nisto, ele calou-se** at this point, he fell quiet; ~ **baixo** below; ~ **cima** above.

emagrecer *vt* to make thin/slim; ♦ *vi* to grow thin, to slim; ~ **a olhos vistos** to lose weight before one's own eyes.

emagrecimento *m* thinning, slimming; **2** *(pop)* cutting back, thinning out; ~ **do pessoal** the streamlining of staff.

emanar *vi:* ~ **de** to come/emanate from; **um belo aroma emanava do jardim** a lovely aroma came from the garden.

emancipar *vt* to emancipate; ♦ ~**-se** *vr* to come of age.

emaranhar *vt* to tangle; **2** to complicate; ♦ ~**-se** *vr* to get entangled; **2** *(fig)* to get mixed up.

embaçado/embaciado,-a *adj* dull; **2** *(metal)* tarnished; **3** *(vidro, olhos)* misty, cloudy.

embaçar *(Vd:* **embaciar**).

embaciar *vt (vidro, olhos)* to mist up, to cloud; ♦ *vi (metal)* to tarnish.

embainhar *vt* to make a hem, to hem; **2** *(espada)* to sheathe.

embaixada *f* embassy.

embaixador,-ora *m,f* ambassador.

embaixatriz *f* ambassador's wife, ambassadress.

embaixo *adv (BR) (Vd:* **em baixo** *(EP));* ~ **de** underneath; **cá** ~ down here; **lá** ~ downstairs, down there; ♦ *prep* under, below.

embalagem *f* packing, package.

embalar *vt* to pack, wrap up sth; **2** to rock *(berço)*; **3** to lull sb; **4** *(esperanças)* to cherish; **5** *(baloiçar)* swing; **6** *(BR)* to load a gun.

embalo *m* rocking, lulling; **2** *(BR)* impulse, rush; **3** *(drogas)* high; **4** *(fam)* **festa de** ~ swinging party.

embalsamar *vt* to embalm; **2** *(ave)* to stuff.

embaraçar *vt* to hinder, block; **2** to tangle; **3** to embarrass, disconcert; **4** to complicate; ♦ ~**-se** *vr* to become embarrassed.

embaraço *m* hindrance; embarrassment.

embaraçoso,-a *adj* embarrassing.

embaralhar *vt (cartas)* to shuffle; **2** *(confundir)* confuse, to jumble; ♦ ~**-se** *vr* become confused.

embarcação *f* vessel.

embarcadiço,-a *m* sailor, seafarer; ♦ *adj* seafaring.

embarcadouro *m* quay, wharf.

embarcar *vt* to put on board; **2** *(carga)* to load; ♦ *vi* ~ **em** to board, to embark.

embargado,-a *adj (impedido)* blocked; **2** controlled.

embargar *vt (JUR) (apreender)* to seize; **2** *(impedir)* to block.

embargo *m (obstáculo)* embargo, impediment, hampering; **2** *(JUR)* seizure, caviat; **3 sem** ~ **de** *prep* in spite of.

embarque *m* embarkation; **2** *(mercadorias)* shipment.

embasbacado,-a *adj (pasmado)* stunned, dumbfounded, flabbergasted.

embasbacar to astonish, astound.

122

embate *m (choque)* clash; **2** shock; **3** *(resistência)* resistance.

embater em *vi* to collide with, go against *(parede, pessoa)*.

embatucado,-a *adj* flushed with embarassement; **2** dumbfounded.

embatucar *vt* to confound; ♦ *vi* to be lost for words; be nonplussed.

embebedar *vt* to make someone/animal drunk; **já embebedaram o peru?** have you made the turkey drunk?; ♦ **~-se** *vr* to get drunk.

> The practice of making the turkey drunk is to alleviate the pain when he is killed.

embeber *vt (ensopar)* to soak up, absorb; to soak sth in sth; **2** *(cravar)* thrust, plunge *(knife, dagger)*; ♦ **~-se** *vr*: **~ em** to become enraptured in.

embebido,-a *adj* imbibed; **2** *(ensopado)* soaked; **3** *(cravado)* embedded *(no corpo, na madeira)*; **4** *(fig) (absorto)* absorbed *(no trabalho)*; **5** enraptured; **6** *(fig) (impregnado)* riddled (**de** with), full.

embelezamento *m* embellishment, beauty, make-up; **2 cuidados de ~** beauty care; **3 rotina de ~** make-up routine.

embevecer *vt (enlevar)* to fill with joy *(alguém)*; ♦ **~-se** *vr* to be enraptured/ecstatic.

embevecido,-a *adj* enraptured; **2** filled with joy; **3** ecstatic; **4** wrapt up in admiration.

embicar *vi (enlevar)* to stumble, trip over; **2** *(NÁUT)* to enter port, dock; **3** *(fig)* **~ para** to head for; **4** *(BR)* to drink, sip.

embirrante *m,f (pessoa que causa antipatia)* unpleasant person; ♦ *adj inv* annoying; **2** pig-headed; **3** querulous.

embirrar *vi (teimar)* **~ em** to insist on, be obstinate; **2** *(antipatizar)* **~ com** to take a dislike to sb/sth.

embirrento,-a *(Vd: embirrante)*.

emblema *m* emblem; badge.

embocadura *f (rio)* mouth; **2 ~ da ponte** entrance to the bridge; **3** *(MÚS) (bocal)* mouthpiece; **4** *(eixo)* bit.

embolar *vt (pôr bolas)* place padding over *(chifres)*; **2** *(moldar em bolas)* shape into a ball; ♦ *vi (massa)* to rise.

embolia *f* blood clot, embolism.

êmbolo *m (MED) (pistão)* piston; **2** *(coágulo, bolha)* clot, embolus.

embolsar *vt (pôr no bolso)* put sth in one's pocket; to pocket; **2** *(pagar)* to pay out, refund.

embondeiro *m (BOT) (árvore africana)*; **2** *(fibre)* monkey bread, baobab.

embora *adv* away, out; **ir-se/vir-se ~** to go/come away; **mandar alguém ~** to send sb out; send sb away/packing, **mandaram-te ~**; did they throw you out/send you away?; ♦ *conj* though, although, in spite of, albeit; **~ a casa seja pequena, você é bem vinda** though (my) house is small, you are welcome (to stay); ♦ *exc (fam)* **~!** let's go!

emborcar *vt* to turn upside down; **2** *(canoa)* to overturn; **3** *(pop) (beber)* to drain *(garrafa, copos)*.

emboscada *f* ambush; **armar uma ~** to set up an ambush; **cair numa ~** to fall into an ambush.

embotado,-a *adj (lâmina, etc)* blunt; **2** *(fig) (fraco)* numb, weakened.

embotar *vt* to blunt; **2** *(fig)* to deaden, dull.

embraiagem *f, (AUTO)* clutch.

embraiar *vt (AUTO)* to put in gear; ♦ *vi* be put in gear.

embranquecer *vt* to bleach; ♦ *vi* to turn pale; **2** *(cabelo)* to go grey; **3** *(fig) (pessoa)* to go white with fear.

embreagem *(BR) (Vd: embraiagem)*.

embrenhar-se *vr* to conceal o.s. in, to go deep into; **ele embrenhou-se na floresta** he hid, went deep into the forest.

embriagado,-a *adj* intoxicated, drunk.

embriagar *vt* to intoxicate, make drunk sb; ♦ **~-se** *vr* to get drunk.

embriaguez *f* drunkenness; **2** *(fig)* rapture, intoxication.

embrião *m* embryo.

embromar *vt (BR)* to deceive, mislead; **2** to procrastinate; **3** *(promessa não cumprida)* to lead sb up the garden path.

embrulhada *f (trapalhada)* muddle, confusion, mix-up; **2** swindle; **3** *(rixa)* brawl.

embrulhar *vt* to wrap, pack; **2** to put in a bundle; **3** *(enredar)* to muddle (up); **4** *(fig, fam) (enganar)* to cheat, fool; **5** *(negócios)* to screw up; **6** *(estômago)* to upset; ♦ **~-se** *vr* to wrap o.s. up in; **2** get into a tangle, become embroiled; **3** to get involved in a brawl.

embrulho *m* package, parcel; **ir no ~** to be deceived.

embuçar *vt* to disguise.

embuço *m* hood; **2** disguise.

embuste *m* deception; trick.

embusteiro,-a *m,f* liar; cheat, impostor; ♦ *adj* deceitful.

embutido,-a *adj (armário)* built-in, inserted; **2** *(móvel)* in-laid; **uma mesa ~ de madrepérola** a table inlaid with mother-of-pearl.

embutir *vt* to fit/build in *(armário)*; **2** *(jóias, etc)* to inlay, encrust; **3** *(fig) (ideias, etc)* to instill, inculcate.

emenda *f* correction; **2** *(fig)* amendment; **ela não tem ~** she can't be changed/cannot improve; **3** *(JUR)* amendment.

emendar *vt* to correct; **2** to mend; **3** to make amends for; **4** *(JUR)* to amend; ♦ **~-se** *vr* to mend one's ways.

ementa *f (cardápio)* menu; list.

emergência *f* emergence; **2** emergency.

emergente *adj inv* emerging, emergent; **mercados ~s** *(COM, ECON)* emerging markets.

emergir *vi* to emerge, appear; **2** to surface.

emérito,-a *adj (honorário)* emeritus, honorary retired; **professor ~** professor emeritus.

emersão *f* emergence; **2** *(ASTRON)* emersion.

emerso,-a *(pp de: emergir) adj* emerged.

emigração *f* emigration; migration.

emigrado,-a *adj* emigrant.

emigrante *m,f* emigrant.

emigrar *vi* to emigrate.

eminência *f* eminence, salience; **Sua E~ o Cardeal** His Eminence the Cardinal; IDIOM **ser uma ~ parda** to have power behind the scenes.

eminente *adj inv* eminent; **2** *(fig)* distinguished, famous; **3** *(GEOG)* high.

emir *m* emir.

Emirados Árabes Unidos *npr* os ~ the United Arab Emirates.

emissão *f* emission; **2** broadcast; **3** *(FIN)* (moedas, cheques) issuing.

emissor,-ora *m (rádio)* transmitter; *f* broadcasting station; ♦ *adj* issuing.

emitente *m,f (FIN)* issuer; ♦ *adj* issuing.

emitir *vt (documento)* to issue; **2** *(luz, som)* to emit, diffuse; ♦ *vi* to broadcast; to transmit.

emoção *f* emotion; **2** excitement.

emocionado,-a *adj* touched, moved, thrilled.

emocional *adj inv* emotional.

emocionante *adj inv* moving; **foi um gesto ~** it was a touching gesture.

emocionar *vt* to move; **2** to upset; **3** to thrill.

emoldurar *vt* to frame.

emoliente *adj inv* emollient.

emolumento *m* emolument; **2 ~s** *mpl* gain, profit; **3** *(custos legais)* fee.

emotivo,-a *adj* emotional, emotive.

empacotar *vt (presentes, etc)* to pack, wrap up.

empada *f (CULIN)* pie; ~ **de galinha** chicken pie.

empadão *m* large meat or fish-pie.

empadinha *f (BR)* small pies.

empáfia *f* haughtiness, arrogance.

empalar *vt* to impale.

empalhador,-ora *m,f* taxidermist.

empalhamento *m* packing with/in straw; **2** *(animais)* stuffing.

empalhar *vt* to pack up/stuff/fill with straw; ♦ *vi (fam)* to stall, put off; **2** *(BR) (fig)* to feel embarrassed, confused.

empalidecer *vi* to turn pale; **2** to grow dim, weak; **o sol está a ~** the sun is fading.

empanada *f (CULIN)* large pie; **2** *(janela)* cloth covering *(instead of glass)*.

empanado,-a *adj* covered with cloth; **2** *(fig) (honra)* tarnished; **3** *(fig) (espelho)* fogged/steamed up; **4** *(olhar)* dull; **5** *(AUTO) (avaria)* stuck, out of order

empanar *vt* to cover with/wrap in cloth; to bandage; **2** *(fig) (embaciar)* to grow dull *(brilho)*, get fogged up; **3** *(delustrar)* fade *(fama)*; ♦ *vi (fig) (AUTO) (avaria)* to get stuck; break down.

empanturrar *vt* to stuff/cram with food; **2** *(fig)* to fill the mind with ideas hastily; ♦ *vr* to stuff o.s.; **2** *(fig)* be haughty, full of oneself.

empapar *vt (ensopar)* to soak; **2** to turn into a paste; ♦ **~-se** *vr* to get soaked, drenched.

empapuçado,-a *adj (olhos)* puffy; **2** *(rosto)* swollen, bloated; **3** *(cortinas, vestido)* puckered, pleated.

empapuçar *vt (fazer pregas, papos)* pucker; crease.

emparceirar *vt* to join, to match.

emparelhar *vt* to pair off, to put in pairs; **2** to match; ♦ *vi* ~ **com** to be equal to.

empastado,-a *adj (reduzido a pasta)* made into a paste; clotted *(sangue)*.

empatado,-a *adj (bloqueado)* obstructed; **2** *(alguém, trabalho) (retardado)* delayed; **3** *(jogo)* drawn.

empatar *vt (bloquear)* to hold up; **2** *(DESP) (igualar)* to tie, draw **(com** with); to equalize; **3** *(dinheiro)* to tie up, invest; **4** *(perder tempo)* to hinder, delay; take up **(com/em** on); **não me empates** don't waste my time!, don't make me late!; ♦ **~-se** *vr* to be delayed, held up.

empate *m (jogo, votos)* tie, draw; **2** stalemate, deadlock; **3** hindrance, drawback; ♦ *vi (aplicação de fundos)* investment.

empatia *f* empathy.

empecilho *m* obstacle, hindrance; **2** snag; **3** *(pessoa que causa estorvo)* nuisance, burden.

empedernido,-a *adj* stony, hard; **2** *(pessoa)* harsh; **3** *(fig) (coração)* hard-hearted.

empedrado *m* stone paving/pavement; ♦ **empedrado,-a** *adj* stone paved; **2** *(fig)(endurecido)* hardened, tough *(substância)*.

empenado,-a *adj (torto)* warped; **2** *(inclinado)* leaning.

empenar *vt* to warp, bend; **2** to cover with feathers.

empenhado,-a *adj (pessoa, palavra)* pledged; ~ **em**, pledged to; **2** *(coisa no penhor)* pawned; indebted; **3** committed.

empenhamento *m* commitment, promise; **2** devotion.

empenhar *vt* to pawn; **2** *(prometer)* to pledge; **3** *(comprometer)* be at stake *(honra)*; ♦ **~-se** *vr* to commit o.s.; **~-se em fazer** to strive to do.

empenho *m* pawning; **2** commitment; **3** pledge; **4** influence; **ter ~s** to have friends in high places.

emperrado,-a *adj (porta, etc)* stuck, jammed; **2** *(movimentos)* stiff; **3** *(fig)* obstinate.

emperrar *vt (gaveta, etc)* to stick; **2** *(elevador)* to jam; **3** to get stuck **(em,** in); **4** *(teimar)* to be stubborn.

empertigado,-a *adj (direito)* upright, straight; **2 colarinho ~** stiff collar; **3** *(fig) (envaidecido)* **ele anda ~** he walks haughtily, stiffly.

empertigar *vt (costas)* to straighten; ♦ **~-se** *vr* to straighten up; **2** *(fig)* to be puffed up.

empilhadora *f* pallet truck.

empilhamento *m* stacking; heaping up.

empinado,-a *adj* upright, erect; **2** *(cavalo)* rearing up, prancing; **3** *(colina, caminho)* steep; **4** *(fig)* to give oneself airs.

empinar *vt* to raise, uplift; **2** *(peito, nariz)* to thrust out; **3** to tilt *(copo)*; **4** to learn by heart; ♦ **~-se** *vr* *(cavalo)* to rear (up); **2** *(fig, fam)* to become haughty/arrogant.

empírico,-a *m,f* empiric; **2** quake; ♦ *adj* empiric(al).

emplastro *m (MED)* plaster.

empobrecer *vt* to impoverish; ♦ *vi* to become poor.

empobrecimento *m* impoverishment.

empola *f* blister; **2** bubble.

empolado,-a *adj* covered with blisters; **2** *(linguagem)* pompous.

empolgante *adj inv* exciting, gripping.

empolgar vt to excite; **2** to fill with enthusiasm; ♦ vi to get a thrill, be enthusiastic.

empório m market; **2** department store.

empreendedor,-ora m,f entrepreneur; ♦ enterprising.

empreender vt to undertake.

empreendimento m undertaking.

empregabilidade f (capacidade de/para empregos) employability.

empregado,-a m,f employee; worker; ~ **bancário** bank clerk; ~ **de balcão** shop assistant; ~ **doméstico,-a/ de limpeza** cleaner; f maid; mother's help; ♦ adj employed; **2 bem** ~ well done, well spent; **3 ela é mal** ~a **nele** she is wasted on him.

empregador,-ora m,f employer, boss.

empregar vt to employ, engage; **2** to use, ~ **a força** to use force **3** (tempo livre) to spend; **4** (capital) to invest; ♦ ~-**se** vr to get a job.

emprego m job, employment; **2** use; **3** investment.

empreitada f contract work/job; **2** task, burden; **3 de** ~ by contract, by job; **4** (fig) **de** ~ work done quickly and not well; botched job.

empreiteiro m contractor; **2** jobber; **3** ~ **de obras** building foreman.

empresa f firm, company; **2** business; **3** enterprise, **uma** ~ **arriscada** a risky enterprise.

empresarial adj inv business; **sector** ~ business sector; **2** entrepreneurial.

empresário,-a m,f entrepreneur, business person; **2** (TEAT) impresario.

emprestado,-a adj on loan; **2 pedir** ~ to borrow.

emprestar vt to lend.

empréstimo m loan, lending, borrowing.

empunhar vt (faca, espada, pistola) to grasp, seize; **2** (prémio) to raise; **3** to grab, hold up; ~ **o ceptro** to wield the sceptre.

empurrão m push, shove; **ela deu-me um** ~ she pushed me; **aos empurrões** jostling.

empurrar vt to push, shove, jostle.

emudecer vt to silence, to dumfound; ♦ vi to go silent/quiet.

emular vt to emulate, imitate, to compete with.

êmulo,-a m rival, imitator; ♦ adj rivalling, emulating.

emulsão f emulsion.

emulsificar vt to emulsify.

emurchecer vt to wilt, whither; **2** to fade; **3** (pele) to age; **4** (fig) to sadden.

ena! (=ena pai! ena pá!) exc (espanto) wow! gosh! my goodness!; **2** (fam) (UK) great! (US) gee!

enaltecer vt (nome, reputação) to honour, to enhance; **2** (louvar) praise, exalt (alguém).

enamorado,-a adj enchanted; **2** in love, enamoured.

enamorar-se vr: ~ **de** to fall in love with.

encabeçar vt (estar à frente) to head; **2** be at the top of the table/list; **3** (chefiar) lead.

encabritar-se vr to rear up (like a goat); **2** to clamber; **3** to ride sb's back/shoulders; go pick-a-back; **4** (fig) to loose one's temper.

encabulado,-a adj bashful; **2** embarrassed.

encabular(-se) vt,vr to be bashful; **2** (BR) to irritate; **3** to intrigue.

encadeamento m chain; **2** link; **3** sequence.

encadear vt to chain together, attach; **2** to put on handcuffs, chains.

encadernação f bookbinding, binding.

encadernado,-a adj bound; **2** (com capa) hardback.

encadernar vt to bind.

encafuado,-a adj (escondido) hidden; **2** (pessoa) shut away; ~ **no quarto** shut away in the bedroom.

encaixar vt to fit in/on; **2** to insert; **3** to pack; **4** (fig, fam) to grasp the meaning.

encaixe m (cavidade) groove; **2** framing; **3** (junção) joint, fit.

encaixilhar vt (fotos, janelas, portas) to frame.

encaixotar vt to pack into boxes; **2** (fig, fam) to fit, squeeze in.

encalço m pursuit, chase; **ir no** ~ **de** (alguém) to pursue, to go after (alguém); **2 on the trail,** track.

encalhado,-a adj (barco) stranded, aground; **2** (carro) stranded, stuck; **3** (produto) unsold; **4** (assunto) at a standstill.

encalhar vi to get stuck; **2** to stall; **3** (barco) to run aground; **4** (fig) to block, hinder; **5** to bump into sth; **6** (fig) fail.

encamar vt (estar doente de cama) to take to one's bed/confined to bed; **2** (dispor em camadas) to be in/place in layers; ~**a na lista das melhores equipas** to be placed among the best ten teams.

encaminhar vt to direct; **2** to put sb, sth on the right path; ♦ ~-**se** vr: ~ **para/a** to set out for/to.

encanador (BR) m plumber.

encanamento (BR) m plumbing; channelling.

encanar vt (canalizar) to convey, pipe; **2** (pôr entre talas) to put in a splint (perna, braço); **3** (pop) (prender) to arrest, nab, collar; ♦ vi (criar cana) grow stalks.

encandear vt (ofuscar) to dazzle, blind, **as luzes do carro encandearam-no** the car's lights dazzled him; ♦ vr to be dazzled.

encanecido,-a adj (grisalho) grey, grizzled; **2** grey-haired.

encantado,-a adj delighted; **2** enchanted.

encantador,-ora m,f enchanter; **2** (cobra) charmer; ♦ adj delightful, charming.

encantamento, encanto m spell; **2** charm.

encantar vt to bewitch; **2** to charm; **3** to delight.

encapelado,-a adj (mar) rough, choppy.

encapelar vt (mar) to make rough; **2** to confer a doctorate on; ♦ ~-**se** to become rough.

encapetado,-a adj (BR) (criança) michievous.

encapetar-se vr (BR) to get into a tantrum.

encapotado,-a adj cloaked, covered with a cape/ cloak; **2** (fig) concealed, disguised; **3** dissimulated; **4** (céu) overcast.

encapuzado,-a adj hooded; **os ladrões estavam** ~**s** the thieves were hooded.

encapuzar vt to put the hood on (someone); ♦ vr to put on a hood.

encaquestar vt to make believe; ♦ vr (obcecado) be obsessed; (ideia fixa) get sth into one's head.

encaracolado,-a adj curly.

encaracolar *vt/vi* to curl, curled; **2** coiled; ♦ **~-se** *vr* to curl up.

encarapinhado,-a *adj (cabelo)* frizzy; **2** *(bebida congelada)* iced.

encarapinhar *vt (cabelo)* to frizz **2** *(bebida)* to ice.

encarar *vt* to face; **2** to look sb in the eye; **3** *(problema)* to face up to, deal with; ♦ *vi* to come face to face.

encarcerar *vt* to imprison; **2** to incarcerate; **3** *(fig)* ~ **alguém** to shut away sb; **4** *(fig)* to shut o.s. away.

encardido,-a *adj* dirty, filthy; **2** *(roupa)* soiled; **3** *(aspecto)* lousy, filthy.

encardir *vt* to soil, dirt; ♦ *vi* to become dirty.

encarecer *vi* to raise the price of; **2** *(fig)* to exalt, praise; **3** *(fig) (valor)* to exaggerate; ♦ *vi* to go up in price, get dearer.

encargo *m (posto)* charge, office; post; **2** responsibility; **3** *(dever)* duty; **4** assignment; **5** burden; **6** **~s** *mpl* charges, outgoings, expenditure; **7** **~s fiscais** tax burden; **8** *(CONSTR)* **caderno de ~s** specifications; **9 tenho muitos ~s** I have many duties/ responsibilities.

encarnação *f* incarnation; **2** embodiment; **ele é a ~ do diabo** he is the very embodiment of the devil.

encarnado,-a *m (cor)* red; **2** *(ruborizado)* red; **ela ficou ~a de …** she turned red with …

encarnar *vt (REL)* to incarnate, embody.

encarniçado,-a *adj (furioso)* furious, fierce; red in the face.

encaroçar *vi* to come up in lumps; ♦ *vt (comida)* to make lumpy.

encarquilhado,-a *adj (pessoa)* wizened; **2** wrinkled; **3** *(fruta)* shrivelled.

encarquilhar *vt (pele)* to wrinkle; **2** to shrivel.

encarrapitar (= **encarapitar**) *vt (árvore, muro)* to be atop, to perch; ♦ **~-se** *vr* to perch o.s.

encarregado,-a *m,f* person in charge; *(de loja)* supervisor; **2** *(expedição)* leader; *(de obras, fábrica)* *m* foreman; ♦ *adj* **~ de** in charge of.

encarregar *vt* **~ alguém de** to put sb in charge of; ♦ **~-se** *vr:* **~ de fazer** to undertake to do.

encarreirar *vt (guiar)* to lead; **2** to put on the right track; **3** *(negócios)* to run; to have a career (**em**, in).

encarrilhar *vt* to put on the rails; **2** *(fig) (bom caminho)* to put on the right track/path; **3** to get things straight.

encartado,-a *adj* qualified, registered, chartered; **2** *(motorista)* with a driving licence.

encartar *vt* to accredit, certify; **2** *(certificate)* register; **3** to grant a driving licence to.

encastoar *vt (encaixar)* to built in, enchase; *(embutir)* to set *(gems)*; **2** to mount *(canes, sticks)*.

encastrado,-a *adj* inlaid; inserted; **2** *(armário)* built-in.

encavacado,-a *adj (envergonhado)* embarrassed, at a loss for words.

encefálico,-a *adj* encephalic.

encefalite *f* encephalitis.

encenação *f (TEAT)* staging; **2** *(fig)* play-acting.

encenador,-ora *m,f* stage manager; ♦ *adj* stage managing.

encenar *vt (TEAT)* to stage, enact; **2** *(fig)* to play-act; **3** *(na aula)* ~ **uma situação** to do a role-play, re-enact.

enceradora *f (BR:* **enceradeira***) f (machine)* floor polisher.

encerar *vt* to wax; **2** *(com cera)* to polish.

encerramento *m* closing; ~ **por motivo de obras** shut due to building work; **o ~ do ano lectivo** end of academic year.

encerrar *vt* to shut in, lock up; **2** to contain; **3** to hold; **4** to close; **5** *(reunião)* to end; **6** to limit.

encetado,-a *adj* started; **2** *(bolo, queijo)* open, cut.

encetar *vt* to start; **2** *(garrafa, bolo)* to open, first cut; **3** *(subject)* broach.

encharcado,-a *adj (alagado)* flooded; **2** *(ensopado)* soaking wet, soaked through, drenched.

enchente *f* flood, overflow; **2** torrent; **3** abundance; **4** great number of people.

encher *vt* to fill; **2** *(tempo)* to take up; **3** to abound; **4** *(parede)* to cover; ~ **de/com** to fill up with; ♦ **~-se** *vr* to fill up.

enchido *n (CULIN)* sausage, suffing for sausage, etc; **2** *(costura) (chumaço)* padding.

enchova *f* anchovy.

encíclica *f (REL)* encyclical.

enciclopédia *f* encyclopaedia.

encimar *vt* to top, crown.

enclausurar *vt (encerrar num convento)* to cloister; to lock sb up; to shut away; **2** *(encarcerar)* to confine, imprison; **3** *(isolar-se)* to shut o.s. up.

enclave *m* enclave.

enclavinhar *vt (dedos, mãos)* to clasp, entwine.

enclítica *f, adj* enclitic.

encoberto,-a *(irr pp de* **encobrir***) adj (pessoa)* hidden, concealed; **2** *(disfarçado)* disguised, veiled; **3** *(tempo, céu)* overcast, cloudy; **4** *(caso, verdade)* dissimulated.

encobrir *vt* to conceal; **2** to disguise; ♦ **~-se** *vr* to hide; disguise o.s.

encolerizar *vt* to irritate, annoy; ♦ **~-se** *vr* to get angry, get into a rage.

encolher *vt* to shrink; **2** *(ombros)* to shrug; ♦ *vi* to shrink; to grow short, small; ♦ **~-se** *vr* to wince, cringe, cower.

encomenda *f* order; **feito de ~** made to order, custom-made.

encomendar *vt* to order.

encontrão *m* shove, push, jostle.

encontrar *vt* to find, to come across; **2** to meet; ♦ **~-se** *vr* to be/find o.s. (**em** in) **encontro-me em circunstâncias pecuniárias** I am (find myself) in pecuniary circumstances; ~ **à venda** to be on sale.

encontro *m* meeting; **2** *(MIL)* encounter; **3** collision; **4** contest; ~ **marcado** appointment, date; ♦ **ir ao ~ de alguém** to go and meet sb; **ir de ~ a** *(opôr)* to go against, run contrary to; **2** *(colidir)* collide; **ir de ~ contra a parede** to go against/crash into the wall; **3 ir ao ~ das necessidades de** *(COM) (satisfazer)* to meet the needs of.

encorajador,-ora *m,f* promoter; ♦ *adj* encouraging; **2** stimulating.

encorajar *vt* to encourage, promote, incite.

encorpado,-a *adj* stout; **2** well-built; **3** *(vinho)* full-bodied; **4** solid; **5** resistent; **6** *(tecido)* thick, heavy, closely-woven.

encosta *f* slope, hillside; ♦ ~ **abaixo** downhill; ~ **acima** uphill; **pela ~ abaxio** down the slope.

encostadela *f (fam)* taping someone for money or favour; act of importuning; nuisance.

encostado,-a *adj* propped, leaning (on/against); **2** ~ **à parede** flat against the wall; **3** *(junto a)* close to; ~**s um ao outro** next to each other **4** *(fig, fam)* lazy, leaning on others, sponging off others.

encostar *vt* to lean, prop sth on/against; **2** *(cabeça, ombro)* lean; **ele encostou a cabeça ao meu peito** he leaned his head on my chest; **3** ~ **a porta** to leave the door ajar; ♦ ~**-se** *vr* to lean back/against; to lie down *(for a short while)*.

encosto *m* support; prop, stay; **2** back *(of a chair)*.

encovado,-a *adj (faces, olhos)* sunken, hollow; *(tipo de olhos)* deep-set.

encravado,-a *adj (com pregos)* nailed; **2** stuck in, caught; **tenho uma espinha ~a na garganta** I have a (fish) bone stuck in my throat; **3** *(jóias, esmalte)* inlaid, encrusted; **4** *(maquinismo)* clogged, stuck; **5** *(entre lugares/países)* stuck, enclosed; **o Curdistão está ~ nos outros países** Kurdistão is enclosed in by other countries; **6 estar ~** *(fam)* to be in a fix, in debt, embarrassed; **7 unha ~a** in-growth nail.

encravar *vt (jóias, madre-pérola)* to set, inlay, imbed sth in (sth); **2** to fasten with nails; **3** *(mecanismo)* to get stuck/locked/jammed; **4** *(armas)* to spike; **5** *(fig, fam) (enganar)* to trick, deceive; **6** to hinder; ♦ *vr (fam)* to be/put o.s. in a fix; ~ **em dívidas** in debt, to be stuck.

encrenca *f (fam)* trouble, difficulty; **criar ~s** to cause trouble; **meter-se numa ~** to be in a jam/in a fix; **procurar ~s** to look for trouble; **uma ~ dos diabos!** a hell of a mess/trouble!

encrespado,-a *adj (frisado)* frizzy; **2** *(ouriçado)* bristling; **3** *(mar)* choppy; **4** *(fig) (peito, gesto)* puffed up, proud.

encrespar *vt* to curl, crisp; **2** to turn frizzy; ♦ ~**-se** *vr (hair)* to bristle, stand on end; **3** *(sea)* to ripple, get choppy; **4** *(roupa)* to turn rough; ♦ *vi (fig) (pelo de animal)* to get bristled; **2** *(fig)* to get angry, fly into a passion.

encruzilhada *f* crossroads *sg*.

encurtar *vt* to shorten, trim, clip; **2** *(distância)* to shorten, reduce; **3** to summarize, shorten, abridge *(livro, texto)*; **4** to be brief.

endémico,-a *(BR: -ê-) adj* endemic.

endereçamento *m* address; **2** *(COMP)* addressing.

endereçar *vt* to address; **2** to direct to.

endereço *m* address; **2** ~ **electrónico** email address.

endiabrado,-a *m,f* naughty child; ♦ *adj* mischievous, devilish; **2** *(vento, discussão)* infernal, hellish; **3** turbulent.

endinheirado,-a *adj* rich, wealthy, well-off.

endireitar *vt* to straighten; to put right; **2** *(fig)* to straighten out; ♦ ~**-se** *vr* to straighten up.

endívia *f* endire.

endividamento *m* debt.

endividar-se *vr* to run into debt.

endócrino,-a *adj* endocrine.

endógeno,-a *adj* endogenous.

endoidecer *vt* to madden, drive sb mad; ♦ *vi* to go mad.

endomingado,-a *adj* elegant, well-dressed; **ele estava todo ~** he was in his Sunday best.

endoscopia *f* endoscopy.

endossar *vt (COM)* to endorse; **2** *(transferir)* to entrust.

endosso *m* endorsement.

endro *m (BOT)* dill.

endurecer *vt/vi* to harden.

endurecido,-a *adj* hardened; **2** *(fig)* callous; cold-hearted.

enegrecer *vt, vi (dar cor preta)* blacken, darken; **2** *(escurecer)* darken, cloud.

energético,-a *adj* **a política ~a** the energy policy.

energia *f (força)* energy, vitality, drive; **2** *(FÍS)* power, energy; **3** ~ **eléctrica/nuclear/térmica** electric/nuclear/thermic energy; ~ **renovável/eólica** renewable/aeolian *(wind)* energy; **4** ~ **térmicadinâmica** thermodynamic energy.

enérgico,-a *adj (pessoa)* energetic, vigorous; **2** quick.

enervante *adj inv* irritating, annoying.

enervar *vt* to irritate, get on one's nerves; ♦ ~**-se** *vr* to get annoyed; **2** to become nervous.

enésimo *adj (MAT)* nth; **2** *(col) (col)* umpteenth.

enevoado,-a *adj* misty, hazy.

enfadar *vt* to bore; **2** to annoy; ♦ ~**-se** *vr:* ~ **de** to get tired of; ~**-se com** to get fed up with.

enfado *m* annoyance.

enfadonho,-a *adj* tiresome; **2** boring.

enfarinhado,-a *adj (coberto com farinha)* floured, covered with/in flour.

enfarinhar *vt* to sprinkle with flour *(forma)*; to cover with flour *(alguém)*.

enfarruscado,-a *adj (cara, mãos)* blackened with soot; **2** *(roupa, parede)* soiled.

enfarruscar *vt* to blacken; ♦ *vr (sujar-se com carvão)* to get covered with soot.

enfartar *vt* to satiate, fill up.

enfarte *m (obstrução)* clog, blockage; **2** *(MED)* infarct, coronary, heart attack; **3** *(enfartamento)* glutting, stuffing *(com comida)*.

ênfase *f* emphasis, stress.

enfastiado,-a *adj* bored.

enfastiar *vt* to weary; **2** to bore; ♦ ~**-se** *vr:* ~ **de/com** get tired of; get bored with.

enfático,-a *adj* emphatic.

enfatizar *vt* to stress, highlight, emphasize, accentuate.

enfatuado,-a *adj* cocky; conceited.

enfatuar *vt* to flatter *(alguém)*; ♦ ~**-se** *vr* to become/be vain.

enfeitar *vt* to decorate, adorn, embellish; **2** ~ **o touro com bandeirilhas** stick banderillas on the bull; **3** *(fam) (marido atraiçoado)* to betray; ♦ ~**-se** *vr* to dress up.

enfeite *m* decoration, trimming, adornment.

enfeitiçar *vt* to bewitch, cast a spell on.

enfermaria *f* sick room; ward.

enfermeiro,-a *m,f* nurse.

enfermidade *f* illness.

enfermo,-a *m,f* patient; ◆ *adj* ill, sick.

enferrujado,-a *adj* rusty, corroded; **2** *(fig) (língua, memória)* rusty; **3** *(articulações)* stiff; **4** *(ideias)* dated.

enfeudado,-a *adj* feudal; **2** *(fig) (pessoas, economia)* subjected to.

enfezado,-a *adj* undersized, stunted; **2** annoyed, grumpy.

enfezar *vt* to stunt; **2** to make angry *(alguém)*; ◆ **~-se** *vr* become angry.

enfiada *f* string; **2** *(fila)* row, line; **uma ~ de pérolas** a row of pearls; *(BR)* **~ de golos** a string of goals; **3** *(sequência)* series; ◆ *adv* **de ~** at a stretch; one after another.

enfiado,-a *adj* threaded, strung; **2** *(fig)* **estar/parecer ~** to look frightened.

enfiadura *(agulha)* the eye of the needle.

enfiar *vt (agulha)* to thread; **2** to string *(collar)*; **3** *(roupa, sapatos)* to slip on; **4 ~ os filhos na cama** to put the children in bed; **5** *(guardar, pôr)* put, hide sth; **onde é que enfiaste o meu pente?** where did you put my comb?; **6** *(fig)* put in, drive into, head for; ◆ *vi* **~ por/em** take; ◆ **~-se em** *(algo)* *vr* to slip into sth; get into sth, hide o.s. **ela enfiou-se na cama** she got into bed; IDIOM **~ o barrette** *(a alguém)* to pull the wool over sb's eyes.

enfileirar vt to line up, to put in rows; **2** to fall in (into) line.

enfim *adv* finally, at last; **mas ~!** but, anyway!; **até que ~!** finally!, at last! **2** *(resumindo)* in short; to cut a long story short.

enfisema *f* emphysema.

enfolar *vt (papel, tecido)* to crease, pucker; **2** *(fazer fole)* to puff up.

enforcado,-a *adj (pessoa)* hanged; **2** *(fig) (com dívidas)* to be in debt up to his eyes; **3** *(fam) (casamento)* hooked.

enforcamento *m* hanging; **morte por ~** death by hanging.

enforcar *vt* to hang; ◆ **~-se** *vr* to hang o.s.

enfraquecer *vt* to weaken; **2** to lessen, minimize; ◆ *vi* to grow weak; ◆ *vr* to weaken o.s.; to lose power.

enfraquecido,-a *adj* weakened, vulnerable.

enfraquecimento *m* weakening.

enfrascar *vt* to bottle; ◆ **~-se** *vr (pop)* to get drunk.

enfrentar *vt* to face; **2** to confront; **3** to face up to; **4** to defy.

enfronhar *vt* to put the pillow into the pillowcase; **2** *(fig) (instruir)* to teach *(alguém)*; ◆ **~-se** *vr (fig)* be absorbed in *(leitura, trabalho)*.

enfurecer *vt* to infuriate; ◆ **~-se** *vr* to get furious.

engaço *m* stalk of a bunch of grapes; **2** husk of fruits; **3** *(instrumento agrícola)* rake.

engaiolar *vt* to put in a cage; **2** *(fig, fam)* to put sb in jail, to lock up; ◆ **~-se** *vr* to shut o.s. away.

engajado,-a *adj* contracted, employed; **2** *(MIL)* recruited; **3** *(fig)* committed.

engajamento *m* employment, enlistment.

engalfinhar *vt (com dedos, garras)* to grab, dig in; ◆ **~-se** *vr* to grapple (with another); **2** to argue fiercely.

enganado,-a *adj:* **estar ~** to be mistaken; **2 ser ~** to be deceived, cheated, misled; **marido ~** deceived/cockold husband.

enganar *vt* to deceive, cheat; **2** to seduce; ◆ **~-se** *vr* to be wrong/mistaken; fool o.s.; **enganei-me na porta!** wrong door!.

engano *m* mistake, error; **2** deception; **3** trick, ruse, trap.

enganoso *adj* deceitful; **2** *(falso)* misleading.

engarrafamento *m* traffic jam, bottling.

engarrafar *vt* to bottle; **2** *(trânsito)* to cause a bottleneck.

engasgar *vt/vi* to choke; **2** *(fig) (atrapalhar)* to leave sb speechless; **3** *(fig) (no falar, ler)* hesitate, stumble.

engastado,-a *adj (embutido)* inset, mounted.

engastar *vt (embutir)* to set, mount *(jóias)*.

engaste *m* setting, mounting.

engatado,-a *adj* coupled; **2** in gear; **3** *(fig, fam)* hooked.

engatar *vt (atrelar)* to hitch up, couple; **2** *(engrenar)* to put into gear; **3** *(fig, fam) (convencer)* to talk someone into; **4** *(conquistar sexualmente)* to hook.

engatatão *m (col)* lady's man.

engate *m (animais, veículos)* hitching; **2** *(atrelagem)* coupling, connection; **3** *(romance passageiro)* fling, affair.

engatilhar *vt (pistola)* to cock the gun, set the trigger.

engatinhar *vi (baby)* to crawl; **2** *(trepar)* to climb up *(árvore)*; **3** *(fig) (iniciante)* to take first steps.

engelhar *vt/vi* to wrinkle *(pele)*; **2** to shrivel up *(casca)*; **3** to furrow *(solo)*; **4** to crease *(roupa)*; **5** to crumple *(paper)*; ◆ *vi* be shrivelled up.

engendrar *vt* to engender; **2** to invent, create; **3** to beget, produce; **4** to generate, cause.

engenharia *f* engineering.

engenheiro,-a *m,f* engineer.

engenho *m* talent; **2** skill; **3** machine; **4** device; **5** *(BR)* mill.

engenhoca *f (pej)* gadget, contraption; **2** trick, sheme.

engenhoso,-a *adj* clever, ingenious **2** skilful, dexterous; **3** resourceful.

englobar *vt* to include, embody, encompass; **2** to comprise, consist of.

engodar *vt* to lure, entice.

engodo *m* bait; **2** lure, enticement.

engolir *vt* to swallow; **2** *(comer depressa)* gulp down; *(fam)* to gobble down; **3** *(fig)* to bear, accept *(erro derrota)*; **~ a pílula** swallow an insult **4** *(fam)* **~ em seco** to bite one's tongue; **5** *(fig) (fala)* to slur; **6** *(fig) (acreditar)* believe *(mentira)*.

engomar *vt (com goma)* to starch; **2** *(passar a ferro)* to iron, to launder.

engonçar *vt* to hinge, attach with hinges.

engonço *m* hinge; **2 boneco de ~** puppet.

engordar *vt* to fatten; ◆ *vi* to put on weight, get fat.

engordurado,-a *adj (oleoso)* greasy; **2** *(untado)* greased *(forma de bolo)*.

engraçado,-a *m,f (pej)* smarty-pants; ♦ *adj* funny, amusing, witty; **que ~!** how funny!; **2** curious, odd, funny *(episódio)*; **3** *(alguém)* cute, lovely; **4** *(col)* **fazer-se ~ com alguém** *(amoroso)* to get fresh with sb.

engraçar *(com) vt* to take a liking to (sth, sb), fall for (sb).

engradado *m* crate (for packing), **2** enclosed with a grating, railing; **3** shipping crate.

engrandecer *vt* to enlarge, increase; **2** to exalt, glorify; **3** to boost; ♦ *vi* to grow; ♦ **~-se** *vr* to rise; to become great.

engrandecimento *m (crescimento)* enlargement; expansion, spread; growth; **2** *(elevação)* exaltation, celebration; **3** exaggeration *(de factos)*.

engravatado,-a *adj* to be in a tie; **2** dressed up.

engravidar *vt* to get (sb) pregnant; **2** to become pregnant.

engraxador *m* shoe shiner.

engraxador,-ora *adj (col)* flatterer.

engraxar *vt* to polish *(shoes)*; **2** *(col)* to grovel, to suck up to, to be a toad; **3** ~ **as botas a alguém** to butter sb up, to lick sb's boots.

engrenagem *f (AUTO)* gear.

engrenar *vt (AUTO)* to put into gear; **2** to interlock; **3** *(fig) (factos)* to combine; **4** *(BR)* to team up.

engripar *vt* to give one's cold to sb; ♦ **~-se** *vr* to catch the flu.

engrossar *vt/vi (molho, sopa, conspiração)* to thicken; **2** to swell; **3** to increase; *(voz)* deepen; **4** *(fig)* to turn nasty.

enguia *f (ZOOL)* eel.

enguiçar *vi (máquina)* to break down, stall.

enguiço *m* bad luck, evil eye, curse, jinx; **2** *(problema)* snag, hitch.

engulho *m* nausea; **2** *(fig)* temptation, desire.

enho *m* fawn, young deer.

enigma *m* enigma, puzzle, riddle; **2 ~ figurado** picture puzzle; **3** mystery; IDIOM **a chave do ~** the key to the mystery.

enjaular *vt* to cage, cage up.

enjeitado,-a *m,f* foundling, waif.

enjeitar *vt* to reject; to abandon.

enjoado,-a *adj* sick; sea/car/plane-sick; **2** tired of.

enjoar *vt* to make sick, bore sb; ♦ *vi* to be sick.

enjoo *m* sickness.

enlaçar *vt* to tie, bind; **2** to link, join; ♦ **~-se** *vr* to be linked.

enlace *m* link, connexion; **2** marriage, union.

enlameado,-a *adj* muddy.

enlamear *vt* to cover in mud, soil with mud, besmirch; **2** *(fig) (nome, reputação)* to stain.

enlatado,-a *adj* tinned, canned; **2** *(vinhas)* trellised.

enlatar *vt* to can, tin; **2** *(fig) (pessoas)* to squeeze in.

enlear *vt (ligar)* to bind; **2** *(cabelo, fio)* to entangle; **3** to confuse; **4** *(abraçar)* to embrace; **5** *(fig)* to implicate *(alguém)*.

enleio *m* tangle, entanglement, knot; **2** *(fig) (laço)* tie; **3** *(amor)* rapture; **4** *(timidez)* embarrassment.

enlevar *vt* to enrapture; **2** to delight; ♦ **~-se** to be delighted, filled with joy.

enlevo *m* rapture; delight.

enlouquecer *vt* to drive mad *(alguém)*; ♦ *vi* to go mad.

enlutado,-a *adj* in mourning.

enlutar-se *vr* to go into mourning.

enobrecer *vt* to ennoble; ♦ **~-se** *vr* to glorify oneself.

enojado,-a *adj* annoyed, fed up, disgusted, sick.

enojar *vt* to disgust; sicken; ♦ **~-se** *vr* to be annoyed, feel disgust.

enólogo,-a *(= enologista) m,f* oenologist, enologist, expert in wines.

enomania *f* morbid craving for wine.

enômetro *(BR: -ô-) m (TEC) (instrumentro para avaliar o grau alcoólico do vinho)* oenometer: alcoholmeter for testing wines.

enorme *adj* enormous, huge.

enormidade *f* enormity; **2 uma ~ de** a vast quantity of; **3** monstrosity; **4** *(erro)* howler.

enovelar *vt* to wind into a ball; **2** to real; **3** to coil, curl; **4** to be confused; ♦ **~-se** *vr* to curl, roll up.

enquadramento *m* framework, context; **2** framing.

enquadrar *vt* to fit (in); **2** to frame; to make square; **3** *(fig)* to conform.

enquanto *conj (ger)* while, as, when; **bebe o chá ~ eu faço isto** drink your tea while I am doing this; **~ solteiro, ele foi sempre honesto** while (when) he was single/a batchelor he was always honest; **eu for viva sou eu que mando** as long as (while) I am alive, I am the boss; **2 ~ não** until (as long as it is not), **~ não houver solução** until there is a solution; ♦ *adv* **por ~** for the time being, up to now; **~ isso** meanwhile.

enraivecer *vt* to enrage; ♦ **~-se** *vr* to become furious.

enraizado,-a *adj (plantas, hábitos, crença)* deeply-rooted; **2** *(fig)* settled.

enraizar *vi* to take root; **2** *(fig)* to settle.

enrascada *f (fam)* tight spot, trouble, scrape; **estou metido numa ~** *(fam)* I am in a jam, in a fix.

enrascado,-a *adj* **estar ~** to be in trouble; **estou ~ com dívidas** I am in debt up to my eyeballs.

enrascar *vt* to catch sb out; to get sb in trouble ♦ **~-se** *vr* to get in trouble/in a fix.

enredar *vt (emaranhar)* to entangle, to twist; **2** to complicate; **3** to trap; **4** *(fig) (comprometer)* to embroil sb; **5** *(fig) (intrigar)* to plot; ♦ **~-se** *vr* to get entangled.

enredo *m (nó)* entanglement; **2** complication, difficulty; **3** *(ardil, intriga)* trap, intrigue, conspiracy; **4** plot *(of story, film)*; **5** *(mexericos)* plots; **armar ~s** to hatch plots.

enregelado,-a *adj* frozen; freezing; **os meus pés estão ~s** my feet are frozen.

enregelar *vt* to chill; **2** to freeze, turn into ice; ♦ *vi* to become frozen.

enrijecer *(BR: enrijar) vi* to harden, stiffen; **2** to toughen *(carne)*; **3** *(fig)* to fortify, strengthen.

enriquecer *vt* to enrich; ♦ **~-se** *vr* to get rich.

enriquecimento *m (melhoramento)* improvement, enrichment; **2** acquiring of wealth.

enrodilhar *vt (pano, fita)* to twist, roll up *(pano)* *(em forma de caracol)*; **2** *(amarrotar)* to crease *(roupa)*; **3** *(fig)* deceive *(alguém)*; **4** *(envolver)* to involve; ♦ **~-se** *vr* to get entangled.

enrolar *vt (papel)* to roll up; **2** *(fio) (enroscar)* to wind around, reel; **3** *(cabo)* to coil up; **4** *(hair)* to curl; **5** *(enganar)* to deceive, swindle; *(BR)* to complicate; ♦ ~**-se** *vr* to roll up; **2** to wrap o.s. (**em** in), **3** *(fam) (envolver-se)* get involved with *(alguém);* **4** *(cobra)* to coil up.

enroscar *vt* to twist, twine; **2** *(tampa num boião, arame)* to screw in; **3** wind (round); ♦ ~**-se** *vr* roll up *(gato);* to curl up *(cobra).*

enrouquecer *vt* to make hoarse; ♦ *vi* to go hoarse.

enrubescer *vt* to redden; ♦ *vi* to blush, to go red in the face.

enrugamento *m* wrinkling of the skin; **2** *(roupa)* creasing; **3** *(do solo)* roughness; **4** *(GEOL)* corrugation.

enrugar *vt, vi* to wrinkle *(pele);* **2** to crease *(roupa);* ♦ ~**-se** *vr* to wrinckle; **2** to pucker.

ensaboadela *f* a quick wash, lathering; **3** *(fig, fam)* a scolding.

ensaboado,-a *adj* covered with lather.

ensaboar *vt* to soap/lather; **2** *(fig)* ~ **alguém** to reprimand, to get sb het up.

ensaiar *vt* to test, try out, experiment; **2** to practise, train; **3** to rehearse.

ensaio *m* test; ~ **de carga dinâmica** live-load test; **2** attempt; **3** practice; **4** rehearsal; **5** *(LITER)* essay; **6** trial; **balão de** ~ trial balloon; ~**s sucessivos** trial and error; **7** *(DESP) (rugby)* try.

ensaísta *m,f* essayist.

ensanguentar *vt* to stain with blood.

ensarilhar *vt (enrolar) (fio, lã, corda)* to roll up, wind on a reel; **2** *(emaranhar)* to tangle; **3** *(MIL) (armas)* to stack; **4** *(fig) (planos)* mess up; **ele ensarilhou-me a vida** he messed up my life; **5** *(fig, fam)* to make intrigues, gossip.

enseada *f* inlet, cove; **2** bay.

ensebado,-a *adj* greased; **2** greasy, dirty.

ensejo *m* chance, opportunity.

ensimesmar-se *vr* to be lost in thought, day-dream; **2** to meditate, reflect; **3** to muse.

ensinadela *f (fam)* lesson.

ensinar *vt* to teach.

ensino *m* teaching, tuition; **2** education.

ensopado,-a *m* a kind of stew; ♦ *adj* soaked.

ensopar *vt* to soak, drench; **2** *(CULIN)* to soak.

ensurdecedor,-ora *adj* deafening.

ensurdecer *vt* to deafen; ♦ *vi* to go deaf.

entabular *vt* to initiate, open, start; **2** to broach; **3** *(conversa)* to strike up, engage.

entalado,-a *adj* stuck, trapped; **2** *(fig)* to be in a fix.

entalar *vt* to trap; **entalei os dedos na porta** my fingers were trapped in the door; **2** to wedge, jam; **3** to tuck; **entala os lençóis bem** tuck in the sheets well; **4** *(fig)* to put sb in a fix.

entalhar *vt* to carve.

entalhe/entalho *m* groove, notch; **2** *(madeira)* wood carving.

entanto *conj* no ~ however, nevertheless, yet.

então *adv* then; **eu tinha** ~ **os meus 20 anos** I was then about 20 years old; **2** well; well then; ~ **como vai a vida?** well, how is life?; **3** in that case; ~, **já**

não quero ir in that case, I no longer wish to go; **4** so; **ê** ~**?** and so? and then? what of it? **5** ~ **vamos!** come on, let's go!; **6** *(fam)* **com que** ~ **vieste comer?** so, you came just for the food?; **7 vi ontem um filme. E** ~**?** I saw a film yesterday. What was it like?; **8 desde** ~ since then, ever since.

entardecer *m* evening; ♦ to draw on the evening; **2** *(BR)* to get late.

ente *m* being; **2 os meus** ~**s queridos** my loved ones; **3 O E~ Supremo** God.

enteado,-a *m,f* stepson, stepdaughter.

entediar *vt* to bore; ♦ ~**-se** *vr* to get bored.

entendedor,-ora *adj* understanding person; **2** *m* expert; IDIOM **A bom** ~ **meia palavra basta** a word to the wise is enough; you don't have to spell it out.

entender *m* intelligence, knowledge, understanding; **no meu** ~ in my opinion/understanding; ♦ *vt* to understand, to grasp; **2** to think, believe; **3** to mean; **4 dar a** ~ to imply; ♦ ~**-se** *vr* to understand one another; **2** ~ **por** to be meant by; **3** ~ **com** to get along with.

entendido,-a *m,f* expert (**em** in, at); ♦ *adj:* ~ **em** *(conhecedor)* good at, skilled at; ♦ *adv* **bem** ~ naturally, of course; ♦ *exc* **entendido!** I get it!, understood! **2** *(combinado)* agreed!

entendimento *m* understanding; sense; **2** *(acordo)* **chegar a um** ~ to come to an agreement/ compromise.

enternecedor,-ora *adj* moving; **palavras** ~**s**, moving/compassionate words.

enternecer *vt (emoção)* to move, touch; ♦ ~**-se** *vr* to be moved; **enterneci-me pela mágoa dela** I felt moved by her sorrow.

enternecido,-a *adj* tender, moved; **um olhar** ~ a tender look.

enternecimento *m* tenderness; compassion.

enterrar *vt* to bury; **2** to plunge; **3** *(fig)* to cause death to sb; **foi o filho que a enterrou** her son caused her death; **4 enterrei-me em dívidas** I am in debt up to my neck; **5** *(em solidão)* **ela enterrou-se no campo** she buried herself in the countryside; **6 ele enterrou-se na cadeira** he sank down into a chair.

enterro *m* burial; funeral.

entesar *vt* to stiffen; **2** to stretch; **3** to harden; ♦ ~**-se** *vr* to stiffen.

entidade *f* being; entity; ~ **patronal** employer; **2** authority; **as respectivas** ~ the proper authorities/ channels.

entoação *f* intonation.

entoar *vt* to chant.

entontecer *vt* to make dizzy; **2** to daze, stun; ♦ *vi* to become/get dizzy; **2** to go mad, out of one's head.

entontecimento *m* giddiness, dizziness; **2** inebriation.

entornar *vt* to spill; **2** *(garrafa, etc)* to knock over; **3** *(recipiente cheio)* to overflow; **4** *(fig, fam)* to get smashed/drunk.

entorpecente *m* narcotic.

entorpecer *vt* to numb, stupefy; **2** to slow down.

entorpecimento *m* numbness; lethargy.

entorse *f (MED) (distensão anormal dos ligamentos)* sprain, twist; **ter uma ~ no pé** to have sprained/wrenched the foot.

entortar *vt* to bend; **2** *(madeira)* to warp; **3** *(partes do corpo; conversa)* to twist; **4 ~ os olhos** to squint; **5** *(fig, fam)* to insist in his ways, to refuse to listen.

entrada *f* entry; entrance; **2** *(TEC)* inlet; **3** *(COMP)* input; **4** hall; **5** doorway; **6** beginning; **7** ticket; **8** *(CULIN)* starter; **9** down payment; **10** entry; **livro de ~** ledger; *(dicionário)* headword; **11 de ~** at first; ♦ **~s** *fpl* receding hairline; ♦ *adj* **~ em anos** elderly.

entranhado,-a *adj* deep-rooted.

entranhar-se *vr* to penetrate.

entranhas *fpl* bowels, entrails; **2** feelings; **3** *(fig)* heart.

entrar *vi*: **(em)** to go/come in, enter; **2 ~ em consideração** take into account; **3 ~ em contacto** to get in touch; **4 ~ na idade** to get on in age; **5 ~ em vigor** *(lei)* to come into force; **6** *(ingressar)* **~ para um clube** to join a club; **7** *(caber)* to go through; **a mesa não entra** the table doesn't go through; **8 o molhe entra pelo mar dentro** the pier sticks out into the sea; **9 deixar ~** to let in; **10** *(incluir)* **entrar no rol** included in the list/register; **11** *(fam)* to kid sb **estou a ~ contigo** I am kidding you; IDIOM **~ por um ouvido e sair pelo outro** to fall on deaf ears, go in one ear and out the other.

entravar *vt* to obstruct, impede.

entrave *m* restraint, shackle; obstruction, obstacle.

entre *prep* between; **2** *(mais duma pessoa)* among (sth); **você está ~ amigos** you are among friends; **3 por ~** through, between, among; **ele desapareceu por ~ a multidão** he disappeared through the throng; **4 ~ aplausos** amid applause.

entreaberto,-a *adj* half-open, ajar; **2** *(fig) (céu)* clear.

entreabrir *vt* to half open; ♦ **~-se** *vr* to open partly; **2** *(fig) (céu)* **o céu entreabriu-se** the sky has cleared.

entrecho *m (do filme, livro)* plot.

entrechocar *vi* to collide; ♦ **~-se** *vr (fig)* to fight, clash.

entrecortado,-a *adj* intermittent, interrupted.

entrecortar *vt* to intersect; **2** to interrupt; **3** to cross each other.

entrecosto *m* ribs; **2** *(CULIN)* spare ribs.

entrega *f* delivery; **2** handing over, surrender; **3 pagamento contra ~**, cash on delivery (C.O.D.); **4 pronta ~** speedy delivery.

entregar *vt* to hand in/over; **2** to deliver; **3** to give (up/in); ♦ **~-se** *vr* to give o.s. up; to dedicate oneself to.

entregue *(irr pp de* **entregar***) adj inv* **ele foi entregue à polícia** he was handed over to the police; **2** *(absorto)* **~ a pensamentos** engrossed in my thoughts; **3** *(ocupado)* **~ a estudo** busy with studies; **4 ~ ao pai** in his father's care.

entreguismo *m (a exploração de recursos naturais a entidades estrangeiras)* selling out.

entrelaçar *vt* to entwine; interweave; **2** *(cabelo)* to plait; **3** to link; **entrelaçaram seus destinos** their destinies were linked.

entrelinha *f* blank line in between lines; **2 ler nas ~s** to read between the lines.

entremeado,-a *adj* intermingled; **2** layered; **3** *(presunto)* streaky; **4 toucinho ~** *(CULIN)* streaky belly of pork.

entremear *vt* to intermingle.

entremeio *m* break, interval; **2** lace/binding inserted between two parts of material.

entrementes *adv* meanwhile, in the meantime.

entremez *f* intermezzo.

entreolhar-se *vr* to exchange glances.

entrepor *vt* to insert; ♦ **~-se entre** to come between.

entreposto *(pp de* **entrepor***) m* wharehouse, mart; **2** *(COM)* emporium.

entressafra *f* between harvests.

entretanto *m* interim, meantime; ♦ *adv* meanwhile, **no ~** in the meantime; ♦ *conj* nevertheless, however, all the same.

entretela *f* buckram.

entretelar *vt* stiffen *(gola, lapela, punhos)* with buckram.

entretenimento *m* entertainment, distraction, pastime.

entreter *vt* to entertain, amuse; **2** *(amor)* **~ uma moça** to lead a girl on; **3** to cherish (hopes); ♦ **~-se** *vr* to amuse o.s.; occupy o.s.

entretido,-a *adj* occupied; **2** engrossed; **~ a ler** engrossed in reading **3** *(distraído)* entertained.

entrevado,-a *adj* paralysed, crippled.

entrevar *vt* to paralyse, cripple.

entrever *vt* to glimpse, catch a glimpse of; **2** to foresee.

entrevista *f* interview; **marcar uma ~** to make an appointment/book an interview.

entrevistar *vt* to interview; **2** to have an interview.

entrincheiramento *m* entrenchment; **2** *(fig)* evasion.

entrincheirar *vt* to entrench, fortify; ♦ **~-se** *vr* to lock o.s. away.

entristecer *vt* to sadden, grieve; ♦ **~-se** *vr* to feel sad.

entroncamento *m (FERRO)* junction.

entroncar *vt* to join, link; **2** *(corpo, músculos)* to develop; **3** *(árvore)* to thicken.

Entrudo *npr* Carnival; **Terça-feira de ~** Shrove Tuesday, Pancake day; ♦ **entrudo** *m (mascarado)* masked reveller; **2** *(fam) (pessoa malvestida)* fright.

entulho *m* rubble, debris *sg*; **2** *(fam)* junk; **3** various bits; **uma sopa com muito ~** a soup with many bits in it.

entumescimento *m* swelling, tumescence.

entupido *m (cano, nariz)* blocked, plucked up; **2** *(fig) (ficar sem resposta)* speechless.

entupir *vt* to block, clog; **2** *(trânsito)* to congest; **3** *(fig) (ficar embaraçado)* to choke, not reply; ♦ **~-se** *vr* be blocked.

entusiasmado,-a *adj* to be/get excited, enthusiastic; **2** *(acolhimento)* warm; **3** *(BR) (col)* stuck up.

entusiasmar *vt* to fill with enthusiasm; to excite; ♦ **~-se** *vr* to get excited.

entusiasmo *m* enthusiasm; excitement.

entusiasta *m,f* enthusiast; ♦ *adj* enthusiastic.

enumerar *vt* to enumerate, specify, outline, make a list of.

enumerável *adj inv* countless, innumerable.

enunciação *f* enunciation, articulation.

enunciado *m (discurso)* statement; **2** *(exame)* exam paper/sheet.

enunciar *vt* to explain, state; **2** *(teoria)* to define; **3** *(pronúncia)* to enunciate.

enunciativo,-a *adj* enunciative.

envaidecer *vt* to make sb conceited; ♦ **~-se** *vr* to become vain, puffed up with pride.

envaidecido,-a *adj* proud, vain.

envelhecer *vt/vi* to grow old, to age.

envelhecido,-a *adj* old, aged; **ele está ~** he has aged.

envelhecimento *m* ageing.

envelope *m* envelope.

envenenamento *m* poisoning; **~ do sangue** blood poisoning.

envenenar *vt* to poison; **2** *(fig)* to corrupt, to poison.

enveredar *vi*: **~ por um caminho** to follow a road; **2 ~ para** to head for.

envergadura *f (NÁUT)* wingspan, spread of the sails; **2** *(fig)* scope, importance; **missão de grande ~** large-scale mission; *(talento)* **um artista de grande ~** an artist of great talent.

envergar *vt (vestir)* to wear, put on; **2** *(arquear)* to bend; **3** *(cobrir de verga)* to cover sth with wicker; **4** *(velas)* to fasten.

envergonhado,-a *adj* ashamed; **2** shy.

envergonhar *vt* to shame, put to shame; ♦ **~-se** *vr* to be ashamed.

envernizado,-a *adj* varnished; polished; **2** *(sapatos)* patent leather; **3** *(fig) (pessoa)* stuck up.

envernizar *vt* to varnish.

envés *(= invés) m* reverse, wrong side; **ao ~** the other way round, contrary to.

enviado,-a *m,f* envoy, messenger, representative.

enviar *vt* to send.

envidar *vt* to endeavour, endeavour *(US)*; **2** to exert; **3** to raise another player's bet.

envide *f* betting (at poker).

envidraçado,-a *adj (janela)* glazed.

envidraçar *vt* to put glass in the window/door.

enviés *m* slating, bias cutting.

enviesado,-a *adj (obliquamente)* aslant; **2** *(corte de tecido)* on the bias; **3** *(olhos estrábico)* cross-eyed.

envio *m* sending; **2** despatch; **3** remittance; **4** consignment.

enviuvar *vi* to be widowed.

envolto,-a *(irr pp de:* **envolver***)*.

envolver *vt* to envelop; **2** to wrap (up); **3** to cover; **4** to involve; **5** to embrace; ♦ **~-se** *vr* to become involved; wrap o.s. up.

envolvimento *m* involvement; **~ amoroso** liaison, love-affair.

enxabido,-a *adj* insipid, tasteless; **2** *(fig)* uninteresting person.

enxada *f* hoe.

enxadada *f* a blow with the hoe.

enxadrista *m,f (BR)* chess player.

enxaguadela *f* rinse.

enxaguar *vt* to rinse.

enxame *m (abelhas)* swarm.

enxaqueca *f (MED)* migraine.

enxerga *f* straw mattress; **2** poor bed *(no chão)*; **3** pallet.

enxergar *vt* to catch sight of; **2** to make out; **3** to observe, see.

enxertar *vt* to graft; **2** *(fig)* to incorporate.

enxerto *m (BOT)* graft, scion; **2** *(MED)* implant; **3: um ~ de pancada** *(sova)* a hard thrashing.

enxó *m* adze.

enxofre *m* sulphur, brimstone.

enxota-moscas *m* fly swatter.

enxotar *vt (afugentar)* to drive away *(animals)*; to swat *(moscas)*.

enxoval *m* trousseau; **2** *(bebé)* layette.

enxovalhar *vt (manchar)* to stain, soil, dirty; **2** *(amachucar)* crumble, crease; **3** *(fig) (humilhar)* denigrade *(alguém)*; **4** to discredit, stain *(reputação)*; ♦ **~-se** *vr* to get stained, dirty, soiled; **2** to crease; **3** to disgrace o.s., stain one's reputation.

enxugador *m* clothes drier.

enxugar *vt* to dry *(cabelo, mãos, objectos, roupa)*.

enxurrada *f (chuva)* torrent, downpour, deluge; **2** *(fig)* spate, stream.

enxuto,-a *(irr pp de:* **enxugar***) adj* dry, dried out; **a louça já está ~a** the crockery is dry; **2** *(fig) (pessoa magra)* lean.

enzima *f* enzyme.

eólico,-a *adj* aeolian, aeolic; **energia ~a** aeolian/wind energy; **parque ~** aeolic park.

EPAL *(abr de* **Empresa Portuguesa das Águas Livres***)* Portuguese Water Board.

épico,-a *m* epic poet; ♦ *adj* epic.

epicurismo *m* epicureanism.

epicurista *adj inv* epicurean.

epidemia *f* epidemic.

epidémico,-a *(BR: -dê-) adj* epidemic.

epiderme *f (ANAT, BOT)* epidermis.

epidural *adj inv (anestesia)* epidural.

epifania *f (REL)* Epiphany.

epígono *m* epigone, descendant; **2** *(seguidor)* follower; successor.

epígrafe *f* epigraph, inscription; **2** heading, subject, matter in hand.

epigráfico,-a *adj* epigraphic, epigraphical.

epilepsia *f (MED)* epilepsy.

epiléptico,-a *adj* epileptic.

epílogo *m* epilogue.

episcopado *m* episcopate; episcopacy.

episcopal *adj inv* episcopal; **conferência ~** episcopal conference.

episódio *m* episode.

epístola *f (bíblia)* Epistle; **2** *(carta)* letter.

epitáfio *m* epitaph.

epíteto *m* cognomen, epithet; **2** nickname; **3** name, designation; **4** *(fig)* insulto.

epítome *m* epitome.

época *f* time, period; **~ da colheita** harvest time; **naquela ~** at that time; **2** age, epoch; **a ~ vitoriana** the Victorian age; **3** *(FUT)* season.

epónimo *m (LÍNG)* eponym.

epopeia *f* saga, epopee, epic.

equação *f (MAT, FÍS, QUÍM)* equation.

equacionar *vt* to equate, to treat as equal or equivalent.

equador *m (GEOG, METEOR)* equator; **o E~** *m* Ecuador.

equânime *adj inv* fair; unbiased, neutral.

equanimidade *f* equanimity, composure, serenity.

equestre *adj inv* equestrian; **estátua** ~ equestrian statue.

> Not in the sense of 'horseman/woman' which is **equitador**.

equidade *f* equity, fairness; **2** *(JUR) (direito lato)* equal justice.

> **'Equity'** in the financial sense, which is 'património' (BR: **-ô-**), **a(c)ções ordinárias**. Vd: **equity**.

equilibrar *vt* to balance; ♦ **~-se** *vr* to balance.

equilíbrio *m* balance, equilibrium.

equilibrista *m,f* acrobat, tight-rope walker; **2** *(fig)* opportunist, wheeler-dealer.

equimose *f* ecchymosis, bruising.

equino,-a *m (ZOOL) (ouriço)* hedgehog; ♦ *adj inv* equine.

equinócio *m (ASTRON)* equinox.

equipa *f* team.

equipado,-a *adj (casa, fábrica)* equipped, furnished; **2** *(fam)* dressed up.

equipagem *f* crew; equipage.

equipamento *m* equipment, kit, equipage.

equipar *vt* to fit out; to equip.

equiparação *f* equalization, levelling; parity.

equiparar *vt* to compare; ♦ **~-se a** *vr* to equal.

equiparável *adj inv* equal (**a** to); comparável (**a** to).

equipe *f (Vd: equipa) (BR: time)* team.

equitação *f* horse-riding; **2** equitation, horsemanship.

equitador *m* horseman, equestrian.

equitadora *f* horsewoman, equestrian.

equitativo,-a *adj* fair, equitable.

equivalente *m* equivalent; ♦ *adj inv* equivalent.

equivaler *vt:* ~ **a** to be the same as, equal.

equivocado,-a *adj* mistaken, wrong.

equivocar-se *vr* to make a mistake.

equívoco,-a *m* mistake; ♦ *adj* ambiguous.

era[1] *(imperf de: ser)* **ela** ~ **linda** she was beautiful.

era[2] *f* era, age, time, epoch; **E~ Terciária** Terciary Period.

erário *m* exchequer, treasury.

érbio *m (QUIM)* erbium.

erecção/ereção *f (FISIOL)* erection; *(fam) (de pénis)* tesão *(cal)* **2** *(de um sistema)* creation, establishing, institution; **3** *(edificação)* construction, building.

eréctil, erétil *adj inv* erectile.

erecto,-a, ereto,-a *adj* upright, erect; stiff.

eremitão *m* hermit.

eremite *m,f* hermit.

eremitério *m* hermitage.

ergativo *m* ergative.

ergologia, ergometria, ergonomia *f* ergonomics.

erguer *vt* to raise, lift; **2** to build, erect; ♦ **~-se** *vr* to rise, get up; **2** to stand up.

erguido,-a *adj* standing, upright; **2** *(bandeira)* hoisted; **3** rising; **4 andar com a cabeça ~a** to walk with one's head high.

eriçado,-a *adj* bristling; **2** *(cabelo)* on end; **3** spiked; **4** *(fig) (zangado)* with one's hackles up.

eriçar-se *vr* to bristle; **2** *(cabelo)* to stand on end; **3** *(fig) (fazer zangar)* to make one's hackles rise.

erigir *vt* to erect, set up; **2** to edify; **3** to build.

ermida *f* chapel (rural).

ermita, ermitão *(Vd: eremita, eremitão)*.

ermo,-a *m,f* wilderness; **2** *(refúgio de oração)* hermitage; ♦ *adj (isolado)* secluded, remote; **2** *(pessoa)* solitary, reclusive.

erótico,-a *adj* erotic.

erotismo *m* eroticism.

erradicar *vt* to eradicate, eliminate.

errado,-a *adj (equivocado)* wrong, mistaken; **2** inappropriate; **3** *(soma, contas)* incorrect; **dar ~** to go wrong.

errante *adj inv* wandering; **2** straying; **3** *(fig) (espírito)* restless; **4** *(fig)* incerto; **5** *(passos)* unsteady.

errar *vt* to err; **2** to make a mistake, be wrong; **3** *(alvo)* to miss; **4** ~ **o caminho** to lose one's way; ♦ *vi* to wander, roam; **2** to err, be wrong, make a mistake; **3** to sin, trespass.

errata *f* erratum *m*.

errático,-a *adj* erratic; **2** wandering, errant.

erro *m* mistake, error; oversight; ~ **crasso** gross mistake; **salvo ~** unless I am mistaken; **cair no ~** to make the mistake (of); **2** ~ **jurídico** judicial error; *(juízo errado)* misjudgement; **3** ~ **tipográfico** misprint, erratum; IDIOM ~ **de palmatória** unforgiveable mistake, blunder.

erróneo,-a *(BR: -rô-) adj* erroneous, incorrect, wrong, mistaken; **2** false, untrue.

erudição *f* erudition, learning.

erudito,-a *m,f* scholar; ♦ *adj* learned, scholarly.

erupção *f* eruption; **2** *(MED)* eruption; ~ **cutânea** skin rash; **3** *(fig)* outbreak.

eruptivo,-a *m,f* eruptive.

erva *f* grass; **2** *(MED, CULIN)* herb; **3** ~ **daninha** weed, *(fig)* poison; **4** *(BR) (fam)* money.

erva-cidreira *f (BOT)* lemon-scented verbena.

erva-da-fortuna *f* tradescantia.

erva-doce *f* anise.

ervanário *m* herbalist, health shop/store.

ervilha *f (BOT)* pea; **~s congeladas** frozen peas; **~-de-cheiro** *f* sweet pea.

ervilhaca *f (BOT)* tare; **2 semente de ~** *(comida para pássaros)* tare seed.

esbaforido,-a *adj* breathless, panting; **2** puffing and huffing; **3** in a mad rush.

esbanjar *vt* to squander, waste; **2** to dissipate.

esbarrar *vi:* ~ **com** to collide with; ~ **contra** to knock against; ~ **em** to bump into; to come up against.

esbarrigado,-a *adj (fam)* with the belly showing, hanging out; **2** with the trousers hanging down.

esbater *vt (graduar)* to fade, tone down *(cor, tinta)*; **2** *(sombrear)* to shade; **3** *(fig) (atenuar)* mitigate, attenuate; ♦ ~-se *vr* to fade away, die out; fizzle out.

esbatido,-a *adj* faded, dim *(cor, tom)*; **2** *(fig) (memória)* faint, feeble; **3** *(dor)* attenuated.

esbeltez *f*, **esbelteza** *f* slenderness; elegance.

esbelto,-a *adj (pessoa, corpo)* slender, slim, svelte; **2** elegant.

esboçar *vt* to sketch; **2** to outline.

esboço *m* sketch; draft.

esbofetear *vt* to slap sb; ♦ ~-se *vr* to slap oneself.

esbórnia *f* drunken bout; **2** spree.

esboroamento *m* crumbling; **2** *(fig)* falling apart.

esboroar *vt* to crumble to dust.

esborrachado,-a *adj (esmagado)* squeezed, squashed, crushed.

esborrachar *(fig)* to beat up, smash sb; ♦ ~-se *vr* to get crushed.

esbugalhado,-a *adj*: **olhos ~s** open (one's eyes) wide, staring; ♦ ~-se *vr (fig)* to goggle, bulge.

esburacar *vt* to make holes, bore drill; **os ratos esburacaram a parede** the mice made holes in the wall.

esc *(abr de* **escudo**).

escabeche *m (CULIN)* marinade, sauce of spiced vinegar and onion; **2** *(col)* uproar, brawl.

escabroso,-a *adj (encosta)* rugged, craggy; **2** *(caminho)* rough; **3** *(fig) (grosseiro)* crude, indecent, gross.

escacar *vt (rachar)* to split open, to cleave; **2** to open wide *(pernas)*; ♦ ~-se *vr* to sit astride.

escada *f* staircase, stairs *pl*; **2** ~ **de caracol** spiral staircase; **3** ~ **de incêndio** fire escape; **4** ~ **rolante** escalator; **5** *(fig)* stepping stone; ♦ *adv* **em ~** *(cabelo)* in layers.

escadaria *f* large staircase, stairway.

escadote *m* steps, stepladder.

escafandrista *m,f* deep-sea diver.

escafandro *m* diving suit.

escala *f* scale; **2** scaling; **3** *(NÁUT)* port of call; **4** stop; **5 fazer ~ em** to call at; **6 fazer ~** to work in shifts; **7 sem ~** non-stop; **8 em grande ~** in large scale; **9** *(MÚS)* gamut, scale.

escalada *f* act of scaling; climbing; **2** *(MIL)* escalade; **3** *(fig)* rise, mounting.

escalão *m* rank; **2** *(MIL)* **em ~** in echelon.

escalar *vt (montanha)* to climb; **2** *(muro)* to scale; **3** *(DESP) (equipe)* to draw up; **4** *(NÁUT, AER)* to make a stop at.

escaldado,-a *adj* scalded, burnt; **2** *(legumes, etc)* parboiled; **3** *(fig) (enganado)* wary; **já fui ~** I have learnt my lesson; IDIOM **gato ~ da água fria tem medo** once bitten, twice shy.

escaldar *vt* to scald; **2** *(amêndoas, legumes)* to blanch; **3 a areia está a ~** the sand is burning/ scorching; **4** *(com febre)* **a testa dele está a ~** his forehead is burning; ♦ ~-se *vr* to get burnt, scald o.s.

escalfado,-a *adj (ovo)* poached.

escalfar *vt* to scald *(recipiente)*; **2** *(CULIN) (ovos)* to poach.

escalonado,-a *adj* staggered; **2** scheduled.

escalonamento *m* staggering; **2** scheduling; **3** formation in steps; **4** echelon.

escalope *m (CULIN)* scallop; ~ **de porco** porc medallion; ~ **de vitela** veal scallop.

escalpelo *m* scalpel.

escama *f (peixe, réptil)* scale.

escamar *vt* ~ **o peixe** to scale/clean the fish.

escamotar **(escamotear)** *vt* to pinch; **2** to pilfer, filch; **3** *(fig)* to cover up; ♦ *vi* to make sth disappear by sleight of hand.

escancarado,-a *adj* wide open; **deixaste a porta ~a** you left the door wide open; **2** *(pasmado) (boca, sorriso)* wide open.

escâncaras *adv* **às ~** openly, publicly.

escandalizar *vt* to shock, offend, scandalize; ♦ ~-se *vr* to be shocked; be offended.

escândalo *m* scandal; outrage; **fazer um ~** to make a scandal/scene.

escandaloso,-a *adj* shocking, scandalous.

Escandinávia *npr* Scandinavia; **a ~** Scandinavia.

escandinavo,-a *adj* Scandinavian.

escaneador *m (COMP)* scanner.

escanear *vt (BR) (COMP)* to scan.

escangalhar *vt (mecanismo)* to break down; to fall apart; **2** *(partir)* to break to pieces; **3** *(fig) (estragar)* to ruin; **estragaste o meu penteado** you have ruined my hairstyle; ♦ ~-se *vr* to get broken, out of order; **2** *(fig) (desfazer-se)* end *(planos, namoro)*.

escanhoar *vt* to shave perfectly; **2** *(fig) (problema)* to examine in depth; ♦ ~-se *vr* to shave closely.

escaninho *m* pigeonhole, secret drawer, corner.

escanteio *m (BR) (FUT)* corner; **chutar para ~** to kick (the ball) into a corner.

escantilhão *m* standard gauge, compass; ♦ **de ~** *adv* helter-skelter, hastily; **mandar (alguém) de ~** *(fam)* send sb packing.

escanzelado,-a *adj (fam)* scrawny, skinny as a starving dog.

escapada, escapadela *f* temporary escape, slip away/ out; **2** *(leviandade)* escapade; **3** *(vias)* emergency exit (from a tunnel, motorway).

escapamento *m (BR) (Vd:* **escape***)*.

escapar *vi*: ~ **(a/de)** to escape from, get out of, skive; **2 deixar ~** *(segredo)* to slip out, blurt out; **3** ~ **por um triz** to have a narrow escape, escape by the skin of his teeth; **4 ela escapa** she is quite nice; ♦ ~-se *vr* to run away, flee, slip away.

escapatória *f (desculpa)* excuse, subterfuge; **2** *(saída)* way-out, exit.

escapatório,-a *adj* mediocre.

escape *m* leak; **2** *(AUTO)* **tubo de ~** exhaust pipe.

escapulida *f* escapade, runaway.

escapulir-se *vr* to flee, escape *(da prisão)*; **2** *(sair discretamente)* to sneak away, slip away.

escara *f* scab.

escaramuça *f* skirmish.

escaravelho *m (ZOOL)* beetle, scarab.

escarlate *adj inv* scarlet.

escarlatina *f (MED)* scarlet fever.

escarnecer *vt* to scorn, mock, scoff at; sneer (at); make fun of.

escárnio *m* scorn, mockery; **2** taunting; **3** derision.

escarpado,-a *adj* steep.

escarrapachar-se *vt* to straddle, to spread the legs; ♦ *vr* sprawl.

escarrar *vt* to spit (out), expectorate; ♦ *vi* to spit, to hawk up.

escarro *m* phlegm, spit.

escassear *vt* to skimp on; ♦ *vi* to become scarce, short of.

escassez *f* shortage.

escasso,-a *adj* scarce; rare.

escatologia *f* scatology; **2** *(REL)* eschatology.

escavacado,-a *adj* shattered, ruined.

escavação *f* digging, excavation.

escavadeira *f*, **escavadora** *f* *(máquina)* digger.

escavador,-ora *m,f* *(pessoa)* excavator.

escavar *vt* excavate; **2** *(fig)* dig up *(assunto)*.

esclarecer *vt* *(explicar)* clarify; **2** *(elucidar alguém)* shed light upon, enlighten, explain, inform; ♦ *vi* *(céu)* to clear up; ♦ **~-se** *vr* to become clear, to find out; **2** to stand out.

esclarecido,-a *adj* *(pessoa)* enlightned; well informed; **2** *(assunto; problems)* cleared up.

esclarecimento *m* explanation, elucidation, clarification; **2** information; **3** *(anotação)* comment, annotation.

esclavagismo *m* slavery.

esclavagista *adj inv* *(regime, sociedade)* slavery.

esclerose *f* sclerosis; **~ múltipla** multiple sclerosis.

esclerótica *f* sclera, white of the eye.

escoadouro *m* drain, drainpipe.

escoamento *m* drainage, outlet, discharge; **2** *(fig)* flow.

escoar *vt* to drain off; ♦ *vi* to drain away, flow away; ♦ **~-se** *vr* to seep out, trickle, leak.

escocês,-cesa *m,f* Scot, Scotsman/Scotswoman; ♦ *adj* Scottish.

Escócia *npr* Scotland, **a ~** Scotland.

escoicear *vt* to kick sb (like a donkey); ♦ *vi* to give kicks; **2** *(fig)* to offend, kick up a fuss.

escol *m* best; **de ~** of excellence.

escola *f* school; **2 ~ superior** college.

escolar *m,f* pupil, schoolboy/girl; ♦ *adj inv* school.

escolha *f* choice, option, preference.

escolher *vt* to choose, select; **2** prefer.

escolhido,-a *adj* chosen, preferred; IDIOM **ser a dedo ~** to be hand-picked.

escolho *m* reef, rock, cliff; **2** *(fig)* obstacle, pitfall.

escolta *f* escort, guard; **2** *(fig)* entourage.

escoltar *vt* to escort.

escombros *mpl* ruins, debris *sg*; **2** rubble.

esconder *vt* to conceal, disguise; ♦ **~-se** *vr* to hide o.s.

esconderijo *m* hiding place, hideout.

escondidas *f ~* stealthily, on the sly; **jogar às ~** to play hide and seek.

esconjurar *vt* to conjure; **2** to exorcize; **3** to adjure; **4** to curse, swear.

esconjuro *m* swearing, blasphemy; **2** exorcism.

esconso *m* *(recanto)* corner; hideout; **esconso,-a** *adj* secluded; ♦ *adv* **olhar de ~** sidelong glance.

escopo *m* aim, purpose.

escopro *m* chisel.

escora *f* *(CONSTR)* prop, brace; **2** *(ARQ)* flying buttress; **3** *(fig)* support; *(BR)* ambush.

escorbuto *m* scurvy.

escória *f* dross, slag, metal scrap; **2** *(fig, pej)* **a ~ da humanidade** the scum of the earth.

escoriação *f* abrasion; **2** scratch, graze.

escorpião *m* *(ZOOL)* scorpion; **2 E~** *(ASTRON, ASTROL)* Scorpio.

escorraçar *vt* *(com desprezo, violência)* to drive away, banish (person, animal); **2** *(fig)* *(pensamentos tristes)* banish.

escorredor *m* *(para comida)* colander; **2** *(para louça)* draining board.

escorrega *m* *(para crianças)* slide.

escorregadela *f* slip, false step; **2** *(fig)* *(erro)* slip-up.

escorregadiço,-a, escorregadio,-a *adj* slippery.

escorregão *m* *(para crianças)* slide; **2** *(Vd: escorregadela)*.

escorregar *vi* *(deslizar)* to slip; **2** *(resvalar)* to slide; **3** *(FIN)* **o euro voltou a ~** the euro is sliding again; **4** *(fig)* *(erro)* to slip up, blurt out; **5** *(BR)* *(estória)* to exaggerate.

escorreito,-a *adj* *(alguém)* healthy, sound; **2** *(trabalho, texto)* correct, perfect.

escorrer *vt* to drain (off); **2** to pour out; **3** *vi* to drip; **o suor escorria-lhe pelas faces** the sweat dripped down his cheeks.

escorripichar *vt* to empty, drain; **2** to drink up to the last drop.

escorva *f* *(com pólvora)* nipple on a musket; **2** *(dispositivo para foguetes)* cap.

escoteiro *m* scout.

escotilha *f* hatch, hatchway.

escotismo *m* scouting.

escova *f* brush; **~ do cabelo** hairbrush; **~ de dentes** toothbrush; **~ de esfregar** scrubbing brush.

escovar *vt* to brush.

escravatura *f* slave trade; slavery; **2** *(fig)* *(prostituição)* white slave trade.

escravidão *f* slavery; **2** *(fig)* bondage; **levar uma vida de ~** to have a dog's life.

escravizante *adj inv* oppressive.

escravizar *vt* to enslave; to subdue.

escravo,-a *m,f* slave, vassal, serf; ♦ *adj* captive, slavish.

escrevente *m,f* clerk, scribe, copyiest.

escrever *vt/vi* to write **(a, para** = to, **sobre** = on, about); **~ à máquina** to type; IDIOM **Deus escreve direito por linhas tortas** God works in mysterious ways.

escrevinhador,-ora *m,f* hack writer/journalist.

escrevinhar *vt* to scribble.

escriba *m* scribe.

escrita *f* writing; **2** *(caligrafia)* handwriting; **3 fazer a ~** to do the bookkeeping; **4 pôr a ~ em dia** to keep books/things up-to-date.

escrito,-a *m,f* *(irr pp de* **escrever***)* written; **2** *m* piece of writing; **~ à mão** handwritten; **3 dar/pôr por ~** to give/put in writing.

escritor,-ora *m,f* writer, author.

escritório *m* office; **2** *(em casa)* study, workroom.

escritura *f* *(JUR)* deed, writ; **2** *(de compra e venda)* deed; **3** handwriting; **4 Sagradas E~s** Holy Scriptures.

escrituração *f* bookkeeping.

escriturar *vt* to register, enter up.

escriturário,-a *m,f* clerk.

escriva *m* scribe; **2** copyist; **3** *(pej)* scribbler.

escrivaninha *f* writing desk.

escrivão,-vã *(pl:* **escrivães** *m,* **escrivãs** *f) m,f* registrar, recorder; **2** *(JUR)* court's clerk; scribe.

escroque *m* crook, swindler.

escroto *m* scrotum.

escrúpulo *m* scruple, prick of conscience; **sem ~** unscrupulous.

escrupuloso,-a *adj* scrupulous; **2** upright; meticulous.

escrutinar *vt* to scrutinize; count votes.

escrutínio *m* balloting, counting (of votes); **~ secreto** secret ballot; **2** scrutiny.

escudeiro *m* squire; **2** shield-bearer.

escudo *m* shield, escutcheon; **2** coat of arms; **3** Portuguese currency before the Euro; **4 ~ cabo-verdiano** *m* Capeverdian escudo *(dividido em 100 centavos).*

esculhambação *f (col) (BR)* mess, disarray.

esculhambar *(BR, col) vt* to demoralize, ridicule; **2** to mess up; **3** to criticise; **4** to scold.

esculpir *vt/vi* to carve; **2** to scalp; **3** to engrave.

escultor,-a *m,f* sculptor/sculptress.

escultura *f* sculpture.

escuma *f* foam; **2** froth.

escumadeira *f (para líquidos)* skimmer.

escumalha *f* foundry scrap, dross; **2** *(fig, fam)* mob, riff-raff, scum.

escuna *f (NÁUT)* schooner.

escuras *adv:* **às ~** in the dark, blindly; **apalpar às ~** to grope in the dark.

escurecer *vt* to darken, get dark; **ao ~** at dusk.

escuridão *f* darkness, dark; **2** darkening; **3** *(fig)* blindness; **4** ignorance.

escuro,-a *m* darkness, dark; ♦ *adj* dark, **já faz ~** it's getting dark; **azul-~** navy blue; **2** *(céu)* overcast; **3** *(pessoa)* swarthy; **4** *(água)* murky; **5** *(noite)* **estava ~ como breu** it was dark as pitch.

escusa *f* excuse.

escusado,-a *adj* unnecessary; **~ será dizer** … needless to say …

escusar *vt* to excuse; **2** to justify; **3** to dispense with; ♦ *vi* not to need; **escusas de pedir desculpa** you don't have to apologise.

escusar-se *vr* to apologise; ♦ **~-se** *vr* **de fazer** *(algo)* to refuse to do sth.

escuta *f (espiar)* bug; **~ telefónica** telephone tap; **telefone sob ~** bugged telephone; ♦ **à ~** *adv* listening.

escutar *vt* to listen to; ♦ *vi* to listen, hear.

escuteira *f* girl-scout.

escuteiro *m* boy-scout.

esdrúxulo,-a *m,f (GRAM)* proparoxytone; **2** *(verse)* ending in dactyl.

esfacelado,-a *adj* broken up; **2** destroyed; **3** *(em acidente)* mangled; **4** *(MED)* sphacelate.

esfacelar *vt* to destroy.

esfaimado,-a *adj* famished, ravenous.

esfalfado,-a *adj (col):* **estou ~** I'm fagged out.

esfalfar *vt* to wear out, exhaust; ♦ **~-se** *vr* to tire o.s. out.

esfaquear *vt (com uma faca)* to stab sb/sth.

esfarelar *vt* to crumble (into flour); **2** *(fig) (planos)* to crumble; ♦ **~-se** *vr* to crumble.

esfarrapado,-a *adj* ragged, in tatters.

esfarrapar *vt* to tear to pieces; to rip.

esfarripado,-a *adj (cabelo)* sparse, thin; **2** *(pano)* shredded.

esfarripar *vt* tear into pieces; **2** *(desfiar)* to shred; **3** *(hairstyle)* razor cut.

esfera *f (GEOM)* sphere; **2** globe; **3** *(fig)* circle; **4** *(fig)* field, sector; **5** *(fig)* scope, range.

esférico,-a *adj* spherical.

esferográfica *m* ballpoint pen.

esfíncter *m (ANAT, ZOOL)* sphincter.

esfinge *f (MITOL)* sphinx; **2** *(fig)* cold, distant, enigmatic person; **3** *(ZOOL)* hawk-moth.

esfolar *vt (pele)* to flay; **2** *(arranhar)* to graze, scrape *(pele, membros)*; **3** *(sapatos)* to scratch; **4** to strip off the skin *(do coelho)*; **5** *(fig) (cobrar muito)* to rip off, fleece.

esfoliar *vt* to exfoliate *(pele)*.

esfomeado,-a *adj* famished, starving.

esforçar *vt* to force; **2** *(a voz)* to strain; ♦ **~-se** *vr* to exert o.s.; **~ (para)** try hard to, strive to.

esforço *m* effort; **o mínimo ~** as little as possible; **2** endeavour; **3** *(TEC)* stress; **~ axal** longitudinal stress; **4 fazer ~s** to try hard.

esfrangalhar *vt (reduzir a frangalhos)* to reduce to tatters *(algo)*; **2** *(fig)* shatter *(sonhos)*.

esfrega *f* rubbing, rubbing; **2** *(fig)* beating, thrashing.

esfregaço *m (MED)* smear; **2** *(pintura)* scrub.

esfregão *m* scrub cloth, dish rag.

esfregar *vt* to rub; **2** to scrub, scour; **3** *(fig)* to give a hiding; ♦ **~-se (em)** *vr* to rub (against).

esfregona *f* floor mop.

esfriar *vt* to cool, chill; ♦ **~-se** *vr* to grow cold; **2** *(fig)* to cool off.

esfumar *vt* to tone down, soften; **2** to shade; **3** *(perfil, linha)* to blur; **4** to darken with smoke, blacken; **o fogo esfumava as paredes** the fire blackened the walls; ♦ **~-se** *vr* to fade away; **2** to go up in smoke, vanish into thin air.

esfuziante *adj inv* whizzing, whisling; **2** *(fig)* lively; **3** sparkling; effusive.

esgadanhar *vt* to claw; ♦ **~-se** *vr* to scratch o.s.; **2** *(em desespero)* to tear one's hair out.

esgalgado,-a *adj* lean, skinny.

esgalhar *vt (árvore, galhos)* to prune, lop, cut.

esganado,-a *adj* choked; **2** greedy; **3** *(fig)* mean, niggardly.

esganar *vt* to strangle, choke.

esganiçado,-a *adj (voz)* shrill *(voice)*; *(grito)* piercing, shrieking.

esgar *m* grimace.

esgaravatar *vt (terreno)* to rake, scrape; **2** *(fig)* to delve into; **3** *(fig) (gavetas)* to rummage.

esgazeado,-a *adj (olhos, expressão)* staring (eyes); *(fig)* mad *(look)*

esgotado,-a *adj* exhausted, depleted; **2** used up; **3** out of print; **4** sold out; **lotação ~a** all tickets sold.

esgotamento *m* drainage; **2** exhaustion; ~ **nervoso** nervous breakdown.

esgotar *vt (recursos)* to drain; use up; **2** *fazer vender)* sold out; **3** to exhaust *(energia);* ♦ **~-se** *vr* to dry up *(água, memória);* **2** become exhausted; **3** to be sold out.

esgoto *m* drain, sewer; **2 cano de** ~ drainpipe; **3 rede de** ~ sewerage system.

esgrima *f* fencing.

esgrimir *vi* to fence.

esguedelhado,-a *adj* dishevelled.

esguedelhar *vt* to dishevel; ♦ **~-se** *vr* to dishevel o.s.

esgueirar-se *vt* take away *(algo)* artfully; ♦ *vr* to slip away, sneak off.

esguelha *f* slant; **de** ~ *adv* obliquely, side-ways; **2** lopsided; **3** askance.

esguichar *vt* to squirt; ♦ *vi* to squirt out.

esguicho *m* spurt, jet, gush.

esguimista *m,f* fencer, swordsperson.

esguio,-a *adj* lanky; **alto e** ~ tall and slender; **2** narrow; **3** *(pescoço)* long.

Eslovénia *npr:* **a** ~ Slovenia.

esloveno,-a *adj* Slovenian.

esmagar *vt* to crush; **2** to smash, to squeeze; **3** ~ **as batatas** to mash the potatoes; **4** *(com os pés)* to trample; **5** *(fig)* to oppress, overpower; **6** *(fig)* to devastate; **7** *(POL)* ~ **os candidatos** to defeat/ crush the candidates.

esmaltado,-a *adj* enamelled; **2** decorated, studded.

esmalte *m* enamel; **2** nail varnish.

esmerado,-a *adj* careful, neat, fastidious; **2** *(trabalho)* polished, perfect, faultless.

esmeralda *f* emerald.

esmerar-se *vr* to do one's best, to excel o.s.

esmeril *m* emery; **lixa de** ~ emery board.

esmero *m* great care; **2** neatness; **3** accuracy.

esmigalhar *vt* to crumble; **2** *(fig) (reputação)* to destroy, ruin; ♦ **~-se** *vr* to crumble.

esmiuçar *vt* to fragment, crumble; **2** *(assunto)* to examine, explain in detail; **3** *(questão)* to thrash out.

esmo *m* rough estimate; **a** ~ **esmo** *adv* aimlessly; at random; **falar a** ~ to babble.

esmoer *vt* to munch, chew.

esmola *f* alms *pl;* **2** donation, charity; **3 pedir** ~**s** to beg; **4 viver de** ~**s** to live on charity.

esmorecer *vt* to discourage; ♦ *vi* to lose heart/ courage.

esmurrar *vt (dar murros)* to punch, to box.

esnobe *(BR) adj* snob; stuck up.

esnobismo *m* snobbery.

esófago *(BR: -ô-) m* oesofagus *(UK)* esophagus *(US).*

esotérico,-a *adj* esoteric.

espacial *adj* spatial, space; **nave** ~ space-ship.

espaço *m (universo)* space; **2** *(tempo)* period, space, duration; **3** ~ **para duas pessoas** room for two people; **4 a** ~**s** from time to time; **5** *(entre 2 pontos)* distance; **a dois** ~**s** *(TIPO)* with two spaces.

espaçoso,-a *adj* spacious, roomy.

espada *f* sword; **2** ~**s** *fpl (naipe)* spades; **3** *(TAUROM)* matador; **4** *(fam) (pessoa esperta)* ace; IDIOM ~ **de dois gumes** two-edged sword;

entre a ~ **e a parede** between the devil and the deep blue sea.

espadachim *m* swashbuckler.

espadarte *m* swordfish.

espadaúdo,-a *adj* broad-shouldered.

espádua *f* shoulder blade.

espairecer *vt* to amuse, entertain; **2** *(pensamento, espírito)* to clear; ♦ *vi* to relax, pass the time, entertain o.s.

espaldar *m* back; **cadeira de** ~ high backed chair; **2** *(ginásio)* wall bars.

espalha-brasas *m,f* hot head; ♦ *adj (alguém)* rowdy, noisy, impetuous.

espalhafato *m* din, commotion; **2 fazer um** ~ to make a scene.

espalhafatoso,-a *adj (pessoa)* boisterous; **2** *(feito com luxo)* ostentatious; **3** *(fam)* gaudy, loud, showy.

espalhar *vt* to scatter, spread (around); **2** *(luz)* to diffuse, shed; *(aroma)* to give out; ♦ **~-se** *vr* to disperse, disband; **2** spread out.

espalmado,-a *adj* flat.

espalmar *vt* to flatten; **2** to lie flat; **3** *(NÁUT)* to clean and tar.

espampanante *adj inv* splendid, sumptuous; **2** showy, flamboyant.

espanador *m* duster, feather-duster.

espanar *vt* to dust.

espancar *vt* to beat up, spank.

Espanha *npr f* **a** ~ Spain.

espanhol,-ola *adj* Spanish; **2** Spaniard; **3** *(LÍNG) m* Spanish.

espantado,-a *adj* astonished (**com** at); surprised (**com** by).

espantalho *m* scarecrow; **2** *(fig)* fright; **ela parece um** ~ she looks a fright.

espantar *vt* to *(causar assombro)* amaze, astound, marvel; **2** *(surpreender)* to astonish; **3** *(afugentar)* to frighten away, scare off; *(animals)* scatter; drive away *(pessoa, animal);* ♦ **~-se** *vr* to be surprised; **2** *(ficar deslumbrado)* to be awe-stuck, be amazed, be in awe; **3** *(assustar-se) (animals)* to take fright, to be scared.

espanto *m (surpresa)* amazement; **2** *(admiração)* marvel, wonder; **ele é um** ~ he is a marvel/wonder.

espantoso,-a *adj* astounding; **2** *(assombroso)* awesome; **3** marvellous.

esparadrapo *m* (sticking) plaster *(UK);* Band-Aid *(US).*

espargata *f (atletismo)* splits, *pl.*

espargir *vt* to sprinkle; to spray; **2** to spill, shed; **3** *(luz)* to diffuse.

espargo *m (BOT, CULIN)* asparagus.

esparguete (espaguete) *m* spaghetti.

esparramar *vt* to splash; **2** *(líquido)* to scatter; **3** to strew; ♦ **~-se** *vr* disperse, disband.

esparregado *m (CULIN)* pureed spinach.

esparso,-a *(irr pp de espargir) adj* sparce; **2** scattered; **3** *(derramado)* shed *(sangue).*

espartano,-a *adj (vida, atitude)* spartan, frugal, austere; **2 os E~os** *mpl* the Spartans.

espartilho *m* corset, stays, bodice.

espasmo *m* spasm, convulsion.

espasmódico,-a *adj* spasmodic.

espatela *f (MED)* small spatula for depressing the tongue.

espatifar *vt* to tear to pieces; to smah; **2** *(fortuna)* to squander, waste; ♦ ~-**se** to get torn/broken to pieces.

espátula *f* spatula.

espaventar *vt* to frighten.

espavorido,-a *adj* terrified; **2** out of one's mind; **3** terror-stricken.

espavorir *vt* to frighten.

especial *adj inv* special; **2** *(alguém)* special, unusual; **3 em** ~ especially, particularly.

especialidade *f* speciality; **não é da minha** ~ it's not in my line.

especialista *m,f* specialist; expert.

especialização *f* specialization.

especializado,-a *adj* skilled.

especializar-se (em) *vr* to specialize in, be skilled in.

especialmente *adv* specially, expressly.

especiaria *f* spice.

espécie *f (BIO)* species *sg*; **2** sort, kind; **3** ~ **humana** human race; **4 pagamento em** ~ payment in kind; **5 causar** ~ to cause an impression, to perplex; **6 fazer** ~ to raise a doubt; **7 de todas as** ~**s** of all kinds.

especificar *vt* to specify.

específico,-a *adj* specific.

especilho *m (MED)* probe.

espécime *m* specimen, sample.

espe(c)tacular *adj* spectacular.

espe(c)táculo *m* show; **dar** ~ to make a spectacle of o.s.

espe(c)tador,-ora *m,f* onlooker; spectator; member of the audience; **2** ~**es** *mpl* audience *sg*.

espe(c)tral *adj inv* spectrall.

espe(c)tro *m* ghost, phantom; **2** *(FÍS)* spectrum; **3** *(fig) (pessoa muito magra)* skeleton.

especulação *f* speculation, conjecture (**sobre** about).

especulador,-ora *m,f (ECON)* speculator; ~ **na alta/ altista** bull speculator.

especular *vi* to speculate (**sobre** about); *(ECON)* speculate.

especulativo,-a *adj* speculative.

espeleologia *f (DESP)* speleology; **2** *(US)* spelunking.

espelhado,-a *adj* mirrored, refleted.

espelhar *vt* to mirror, reflect; ♦ ~-**se** *vr* to reflect **as estrelas espelhavam-se no mar** the sea mirrored the stars.

espelharia *f* mirror industry.

espelho *m* mirror; **2** *(fig)* model; **3** ~ **retrovisor** *(AUTO)* rearview mirror.

espelunca *f* den; **2** hovel; **3** dump; **4** gambling place.

espera *f* wait, waiting, expectation; **à** ~ **de** waiting for; **à minha** ~ waiting for me; **sala de** ~ waiting-room.

esperança *f* hope; expectation.

esperar *vt/vi* to wait (for), await; **esperando sua resposta** awaiting your reply; **ela espera bebé** she is pregnant; **espero que sim/não** I hope so, not; **fazer alguém esperar** to keep sb waiting; **2** to hope (for); **3** to expect; **4** ~ **em Deus** trust in God.

esperma *f* sperm.

espermatozóide *m* spermatozoon.

espertalhão,-ona *m,f* smart guy/girl; **2** *(col)* slicker; **3** *(fam)* crook; ♦ *adj* alert, sharp; IDIOM **ser um** ~ to be too clever by half.

esperteza *f* cleverness, cunning.

esperto,-a *adj* clever, smart; **2** alert; **estar** ~ to be wide-awake; **3** *(fogo)* bright.

espesso,-a *adj* thick; **2** dense; **3** opaque.

espessura *f* thickness.

espetacu- *(Vd: espe(c)tacu-)*.

espetada *f* skewered meat/fish, kebab.

espetar *vt* to put on a spit; **2** to stick; **3** to prick; **4** *(fig, fam)* to throw; **5** to get stuck.

espetinho *m* skewer.

espeto *m* spit; **2** a sharp-pointed stick; **3** *(fig)* tall and thin person.

espevitado,-a *adj (pavio)* snuffed; **2** *(fogo)* bright; **3** *(fig) (alguém) (esperto, vivo)* clever, sharp, quick, lively; **4** *(fig)* forward, cheeky, pretentious.

espevitar *vt (avivar fogo)* to poke; **2** *(aparar)* snuff; **3** stimulate; ♦ ~-**se** *vr (ser pretencioso)* to show, be stuck up; **2** *(irritar-se)* to fly off the handle.

espia *m,f* **espião,-piã** *m,f* spy.

espiar *vt* to spy on; to watch out for; ♦ *vi* to spy, watch.

espichar *vt (esticar)* to stretch out; **2** to string (fish) together by their gills; **3** to pierce/tap a cask; **4** *(col) (morrer)* to kick the bucket.

espicho *m* spigot; **2** ~ **de um barril** plug; **3 ser um** ~ *(fam)* be skinny, be a stick; **4** *(BR) (fam)* failure.

espiga *f* ear (of corn); **2** spike; **3** hangnail; ♦ *exc* **que grande** ~**!** what a bore!

espigão *m* spike; **2** peak; **3** ridge pole.

espinafre *m (BOT, CULIN)* spinach.

espingarda *f* shotgun, rifle; ~ **de ar comprimido** air rifle.

espinha *f* fishbone; **2** pimple, blackhead; **3** spine; **4** ~ **dorsal** backbone.

espinhar *vt* to prick; nettle; ♦ ~-**se** *vr* to flare up.

espinheiro *m (BOT)* bramble bush.

espinhento,-a *adj* pimply.

espinho *m (BOT)* thorn; spine; prickle; porcupine quill.

espinhoso,-a *adj* prickly, thorny; **2** *(fig)* difficult.

espionagem *f* spying, espionage.

espionar *vt* to spy on; ♦ *vi* to spy, snoop.

espiral *adj inv* spiral; ♦ **em** ~ *adv* in spiral shape.

espírita *m,f* spiritualist.

espiritismo *m* spiritualism, spiritism.

espírito *m* spirit; **2** gost, spectre; **3** mind; **estado de** ~ state of mind; **4** ~**s** spirits *pl*; **E**~ **Santo** *m* Holy Spirit.

espirituoso,-a *adj (pessoa)* lively; **2** witty.

espirrar *vi* to sneeze; **2** to spurt out; **3** *(fig)* to flare up, to burst out.

espirro *m* sneeze.

esplanada *f* esplanade; **2** pavement café; **3** *(beira-mar)* parade.

esplêndido,-a *adj* splendid, marvellous; **2** *(vestuário, aspecto)* stunning.

esplendor *m* splendour, glory.

espojar *vt* to strip sb of sth, to rob; ◆ ~-se *vr* to stretch out on the ground; **2** to wallow; **3** *(animais)* to roll in the dust.

espoleta *f* fuse, cap; **2** detonator.

espoliar *vt* to plunder.

espólio *m (da guerra)* booty, spoils *pl*; **2** *(restos)* left-overs, remains.

esponja *f* sponge; **2** *(beberrão)* sponger; **3** *(fam)* sponge, drunkard.

esponjoso,-a *adj* spongy; **2** porous.

esponsais *mpl* engagement *sg*; **2** betrothal ceremony *sg*.

espontaneidade *f* spontaneity.

espontâneo,-a *adj* spontaneous.

espora *f (gen)* spur; **2** *(do galo)* rooster's spurs; **3** *(ZOOL) (osso de peito das aves)* bird's breastbone.

esporádico,-a *adj* sporadic.

esporão *m* large spur; **2** *(do galo)* cockerel's spur; **3** *(ARQ)* spur, buttress; **4** *(NÁUT)* forepeak.

esporear *vt* to spur on.

esporo *m* spore.

esporte *(BR)* *m* sport.

esportista *m,f* sportsman/woman; ◆ *adj inv* sporting.

esposar *vt* to marry.

esposo,-a *m,f* husband/wife; spouse.

espraiar *vt/vi* to cast/wash ashore; **2** to extend; **3** to spread, stretch; **4** *(olhos)* cast one's eyes over; ◆ ~-se *vr* to sprawl; **2** to expand one's thoughts; **3** *(esquecer tristezas)* to scatter; **4** *(derramar-se)* over flow.

espreguiçadeira *f* long garden chair, deckchair.

espreguiçar *vt (o corpo)* to stretch; ◆ ~-se *vr (depois de dormir)* stretch o.s.

espreita *f* spying, peeping; ◆ à ~ **(de)** *adv* on the lookout (for).

espreitar *vt* to peep; **2** to spy on; **3** to peer; **4** *(esperar)* to watch, ~ **a ocasião** to be on the lookout (for); lurk **o gatuno espreitava por detrás da sebe** the thief lurked from behind the fence.

espremedor *m (de limão, laranja)* squeezer; **2** ~ **eléctrico** juice extractor.

espremer *vt (fruta)* to squeeze; **2** *(borbulha, etc)* to squeeze out; **3** *(roupa)* to wring out; **4** *(fig)* to press, interrogate.

espuma *f* foam, spume; **2** froth; **3** *(sopa)* scum; **4** *(sabão)* lather, sud; **5** *(do champanhe)* bubbles; **6** ~ **para o cabelo** hair mousse.

espumadeira *f* skimmer, skimming spoon.

espumante *m (vinho)* sparkling; ◆ *adj inv* frothy, sparkling.

espumoso,-a *adj* foamy; **2** frothy; **3** sparkling *(vinho)*.

espúrio,-a *adj* spurious; **2** illegitimate, bastard; **3** *(fig)* bogus, false, adulterated.

esq. *(abr de esquerdo)*.

esquadra *f (NÁUT)* fleet; **2** *(MIL)* squadron; **3** police station; IDIOM **conversas de cabo-de-~** arguments without any grounds/reason.

esquadrão *m*, **esquadrilha** *f* flotilla; **2** *(AER)* squadron, formation of two or more flights.

esquadria *f (GEOM)* right angle; right-angle cut; **2** *(de pedreiro)* mitre.

esquadrilhar *vt* to expel from the gang *(alguém)*; **2** to dislocate the hips of *(alguém)*.

esquadrinhar *vt* to scrutinize; **2** to scan.

esquadro *m* set square.

esqualidez *f* squalor.

esquálido,-a *adj* squalid, filthy.

esquartejar *vt (no talho)* to cut up; **2** to quarter.

esquecediço *(pop)* *adj* forgetful.

esquecer *vt/vi* to forget; ◆ ~-se *vr*: ~ **de** to forget.

esquecido,-a *adj* forgotten; **2** *(person)* forgetful.

esquecimento *m* forgetfulness; oblivion; IDIOM **cair no** ~ to be forgotten.

esqueleto *m* skeleton; **2** carcass; **3** framework; **4** *(fig)* outline, rough draft; **5** *(fig) (pessoa muito magra)* bag of bones.

esquema *m* outline; **2** scheme; **3** diagram; **4** plan.

esquemático,-a *adj* schematic; **2** *(pej)* oversimplified.

esquentador *m* water heater (Ascot heater).

esquentar *(BR)* *vt* to heat up; ◆ *vi* to get hot; **2** *(fig)* to get angry.

esquerdino,-a *m,f* left-handed person; **2** left-handed; **3** *(DESP)* left-footed.

esquerdista *m,f (POL)* leftist.

esquerdo,-a *adj* left; **2** à ~a *f* on the left.

esqui *m* ski; skiing; ~ **aquático** water skiing.

esquiar *vi* to ski.

esquilo *m (ZOOL)* squirrel.

esquina *f* (outer) corner; **2** street corner.

esquisitice *f* fussiness; **2** oddity.

esquisito,-a *adj* strange, odd, peculiar; **2** fussy; **sou muito ~ com o peixe** I am very fussy about fish.

esquivar-se *vr*: ~ **de** to escape from, get away from.

esquivo,-a *adj* aloof, standoffish.

esse, essa, esses, essas *adj, pron (sg)* that *(perto da pessoa a quem nos dirigimos)*; *(pl)* those.

essência *f* essence.

essencial *m*: **o** ~ the main thing; ◆ *adj inv* essential.

estabelecer *vt* to establish, set up; ◆ ~-se *vr* to settle, establish o.s.

estabelecimento *m* establishment; business.

estabilidade *f* stability.

estábulo *m* cow-shed; stable.

estaca *f* post, stake.

estaca *f* pole, stake; **2** *(AGR) (rebento)* shoot.

estacada *f* stockade; fencing.

estação *f* station; **2** season; **3** ~ **balneária** seaside resort; **4** ~ **rodoviária** coach station.

estacar *vt* to prop up, support *(com estacas)*; ◆ *vi* to stop short, halt.

estacionamento *m* parking; **2** parking place.

estacionar *vt* to park; ◆ *vi* to park; **2** to remain stationary.

estacionário,-a *adj* stationary; **2** *(COM)* slack.

estada *f*, **estadia** *f* stay, sojourn.

estádio *m* stadium.

estadista *m,f* statesman/woman.

estado *m* state; **2** ~ **civil** marital status; **3 em bom** ~ in good condition; **4 ela anda no seu** ~ **interessante**, she is pregnant; ◆ **em** ~ **de** *prep* in a state of; ~ **de sítio** martial law.

Estado-Maior *(MIL)* *m* General Staff.

estado membro *m* member-state.

estadual *adj inv (BR) (governo, administração)* state.

estafa *f* fatigue; **2** *(fadiga, cansaço)* fatigue, weariness; **que ~!** what a drag! **estafante** *adj inv* tiring; exhausting.

estafar *vt (cansar muito)* to tire out, exhaust; **2** *(esbanjar) (herança, bens)* to squander; ♦ **~-se** *vr* to tire o.s. out.

estafermo *m* scarecrow; **2** *(fam)* nincompoop; **o ~ do rapaz** *(fam)* the nincompoop, the silly boy.

estafeta *m* courier.

estagiário,-a *m,f* probationer; **2** student teacher; **3** junior doctor; **4** student on his/her gap year abroad; working student.

estágio *m* probationary period; **fazer um ~** to be a student teacher/junior doctor; to be on an apprenticeship.

estagnação *f* stagnation.

estagnado,-a *adj* stagnant.

estagnar-se *vr* to stagnate.

estalada *f* slap; **dar uma ~** to slap.

estalado,-a *adj* cracked.

estalagem *f* inn.

estalar *vt* to break; **2** to snap; ♦ *vi* to split, crack; **o espelho estalou** the mirror cracked; **2** to crackle.

estaleiro *m* shipyard.

estalido *m* crack; **2** snap; **3** *(lábios)* smack; **dar ~s com os dedos** to snap one's fingers; **4** *(pinhas na fogueira)* crackle.

estalo *m (estouro) (de chicote)* crack; *(de balão)* pop; *(de dedos)* snap; **dar ~ com os dedos** to snap one's fingers; *(da língua)* click; **2** *(pop) (na cara)* slap; ♦ *adj:* **ser de três ~s** *(comida, etc)* to be splendid, great.

estambre *m* fine wool; wool or silk yarn.

estampa *f* print; **2** picture; **3** stencil; **4** *(children's pictures)* transfer; **5** *(fig)* a beautiful person; **6 dar à ~** publish, press.

estampado,-a *adj (tecido)* printed; **2** *(padrão)* patterned; **3** published.

estampar *vt* to print; **2** to stamp; **3** *(metal)* to engrave; ♦ **~-se** *vr (fig)* to reflect, show; **a sua dor estampava-se na cara dela** her pain was stamped on her face; **2** to fall flat.

estampido *m* bang, crash, loud noise; **2** crack (of a shot).

estampilha *f* stamp; **2** fiscal revenue stamp; **3** *(pop)* slap.

estancar *vt* to stem *(UK)*, staunch/stanch *(US)*; **2** to stop, hold back, block; **3** *(sede)* to quench; ♦ *vi* to run dry; ♦ **~-se** *vr* to halt.

estância *f* ranch; **2 ~ termal** spa resort; **3 ~ balnear** *(BR:* -neária) seaside resort; **4** *(CONSTR)* stockyard; **5** *(LITER)* stanza.

estancieiro *m* rancher, farmer; **2** owner of a timber-yard.

estandardização *f* standardization.

estandardizar *vt* to standardize.

estandarte *m* flag, standard; **2** banner.

estanho *m (metal)* tin.

estanque *adj inv* tight, watertight; **2** *(águas)* stagnant.

estante *f* bookcase; **2** *(MÚS)* stand.

estar *vi* to be *(temporário situação, lugar, estado, acção)*; **~ bem/bom/boa** to be well; **2 está bem!** OK!; **3 ~ bem com** to be on good terms with; **4 ~ com fome/sede/ medo** to be hungry/thirsty/afraid; **5 ~ com pressa** to be in a hurry; **6 ~ de pé** to be standing; **7 ~ de serviço** to be on duty; **8 ~ de boa maré** to be in a good mood; **9 ~ doente** to be ill, sick; **10 ~ em casa** to be in/at home; **11 ~ em dia com** to be up-to-date with; **12 ~ na hora de** to be time to/for; **13 ela está linda** she is looking lovely; **14 eu estou aborrecido** I am bored; **15 está lá?** *(telefone)* hello?; **16 está claro** of course; **17 aí está** there it is! there you have it; **18** to stay; **estamos num hotel** we are in a hotel; **19 ~ para** + *infinitive* to be about to …; **20 ~ por** to be in favour of; **21 ~ por fazer** be yet to be done/made, **a cama está por fazer** the bed is yet to be made; **22** *(aux)* **estou a brincar** *(BR:* **brincando)** I am joking, playing; IDIOM **~ pela hora da morte** to be very expensive, to cost the earth; **~ pelos cabelos/sobre brasas** to be on tenterhooks.

estardalhaço *m (barulho)* clatter; racket, hullabaloo; **2** showing-off; **3** a great stir.

estarola *m,f* harum-scarum, harebrained person; ♦ *adj inv* reckless, wild.

estarrecer *vt* to terrify, scare; ♦ *vi* to be frightened out of one's wits, struck with terror.

estarrecido,-a *adj* terrified.

estatal *adj inv* state; **a imprensa ~** the State press.

estatelar *vt* to knock down, to throw down; **2** *(algo)* to knock over; **3** *(corpo)* to bang (against); ♦ **~-se** *vr* to fall flat.

estático,-a *adj (TEC)* static; **2** motionless.

estatística *f* statistic; statistics *sg.*

estatizar *vt* to nationalize.

estatoscópio *m (METEOR)* statoscope.

estátua *f* statue.

estatual *adj inv* referring to a statue.

estatuária *f (arte)* statuary.

estatueta *f* statuette.

estatura *f* stature; height.

estatuto *m (JUR)* statute, bye-law, rule; **2** *(posição social)* status.

estável *adj inv* stable, firm, steady.

este *m* east; **2** *(vento)* east wind; ♦ *adj inv* eastern.

este, esta, estes, estas *adj (sg)* this; *(pl)* these; ♦ *pron* this one; *(pl)* these.

estear *vt* to prop up.

esteio *m* prop; **2** cane **3** *(fig)* support, protection; **4** *(NÁUT)* stay.

esteira *f* mat; **2 ~ de junco** rush mat; **3** *(NÁUT)* course, wake; **4** track, trail; **5** *(fig)* footsteps; **6** *(BR)* conveyor belt.

esteja *(pres subj de estar):* **espero que ele ~ em casa** I hope he is at home.

estela *f (placas tumulares)* monolith, stele, pilar; **as ~s funerárias** ancient tombs/steles.

estendal *m (para a roupa molhada)* clothesline; *(BR:* Vd: **varal)**.

estender *vt* to stretch out; **2** to extend, expand; **3** to spread out; **4** *(massa)* to roll out; **5** *(roupa)* to hang out; **6** ~ **a mão** to hold out one's hand; **7** to lay out; **8** to hand out; **9** ~ **cabo** *(NÁUT)* to uncoil rope; *(exame)* to fail; ◆ ~**-se** *vr* to stretch; lie down **2** *(ficar deitado)* stretch out.

esteno-dactilógrafo,-a *m,f* shorthand typist.

estenografia *f* shorthand, stenography.

estepe *m* steppe; **2** *(BR)* spare tyre.

esterco *m* manure, dung.

estereo- *pref* stereo.

estereofonico-a *adj* stereophonic; **2** *(col)* stereo.

estereotipar *vt* to stereotype.

estereótipo *m* stereotype.

esteréotipo *m* stereotype; **2** *(fig)* *(lugar comun)* cliché.

estéril *adj inv* sterile, infertile; **2** *(terreno)* barren; **3** *(fig)* futile; **4** *(fig)* *(minas)* burden.

esterilidade *f* sterility, infertility.

esterilizado,-a *adj* *(alimentos)* pasteurized; **2** *(material cirúrgico)* sterilized, disinfected.

esterilizar *vt* to sterilize.

esterlino,-a *m* sterling; ◆ *adj* sterling; **libra** ~**a** pound sterling.

esterno *m* sternum, breastbone.

esteróide *m* steroid.

estética *f* aesthetics *sg*; **2** *(fam)* beauty; **cirurgia** ~ cosmetic surgery.

esteticista *m,f* beautician.

estético,-a *adj* aesthetic *(UK)*, esthetic *(US)*; **2** elegant, tasteful; **3** *(MED)* plastic.

estetoscópio *m* *(MED)* stethoscope.

esteve *(pret de estar)* **ontem** ~ **frio** yesterday, it was cold.

estiagem *f* dry season; **2** aridity.

estiar *vi* to stop raining; **2** to clear up.

estibordo *m* starboard.

estica *f* very thin person; **Bucha e E~** *(famosos cómicos)* Laurel and Hardy.

esticadela *f* *(acto)* stretching; **dar uma** ~to have a stretch.

esticador *m* stretcher, stretching frame; **2** elastic cord; **3** *(para calças)* trouser-press.

esticão *m* pull, jerk, tug; **roubo por** ~ *(mala, carteira)* theft by snatching.

esticar *vt* to stretch, tighten; **2** *(corda)* to strain; **3** to stretch out, ~ **a remada** to stretch out the stroke; **4** ~ **o dinheiro** to make the money go a long way; ◆ ~**-se** *vr* to stretch; IDIOM **esticar o pernil/a canela** *(morrer)* kick the bucket.

estigma *m* mark, scar; **2** *(fig)* stigma.

estigmatizar *vt* to brand; **2** *(fig)* to stigmatize.

estilete *m* stiletto; **2** *(MED)* stylet.

estilhaçar *vt* to splinter; **2** to shatter, smash.

estilhaço *m* fragment, chip, splinter.

estilista *m,f* stylist; **2** dress designer, fashion designer.

estilo *m* style; **2** *(TEC)* stylus.

estima *f* esteem; **2** regard, respect.

estimação *f* *(estima)* esteem, affection; **2** calculation, estimate; **3 animal de** ~ pet animal.

estimar *vt* *(alguém)* to esteem, be fond of; to appreciate, to value; **2** *(preço, value)* to estimate, calculate; **3** *(desejar)* **estimo as suas melhoras** I hope you get better.

estimativa *f* *(calculate)* estimate; **2** appraisal of *(algo)*; ~ **de custo** quote.

estimulante *m* stimulant, tonic; **2** incentive; ◆ *adj inv* stimulating.

estimular *vt* to stimulate; **2** to excite; **3** to encourage.

estímulo *m* stimulus; encouragement, incentive.

Estio, estio *m* summer.

estipêndio *m* stipend, pay; allowance.

estipulação *f* stipulation; condition.

estipular *vt* to stipulate.

estiraçar, estirar *vt* to stretch (out); **2** to lay out; **3** *(corda)* to pull, draw; ◆ ~**-se** *vr* to stretch o.s. out.

estirador *m* drawing board.

estiramento *m* stretching; **2** extension.

estirpe *f* stock, lineage, origin; **2** type, **a** ~ **do vírus** type of virus; **3** *(BOT)* spur.

estive *(pret de estar)*.

estiver *(fut subj de estar)*.

estivesse *(imperf subj de estar)*.

estocada *f* stab, thrust, jab; **2** *(fig)* *(BR)* unpleasant surprise.

estocar *(BR) vt* to stock; *(EP:* **estoquear**).

Estocolmo *npr* Stockholm.

estofa *f* stuff material; woollen fabric; **2** *(fig)* sort, quality; **3** *(maré)* still, without tides.

estofador *m* upholsterer.

estofar *vt* to upholster; **2** to pad, stuff; **3** *(dar volume a tecido)* to stick out, protrude.

estofo *m* padding, stuffing, wadding; **2** *(fig)* moral quality; **sem** ~ without backbone.

estóico,-a *adj* stoic(al); impassive.

estojo *m* small case, box; ~ **de jóias** jewellery box; **2** set; ~ **de unhas** manicure set; **3** kit; ~ **de ferramentas** tool kit.

estola *f* *(do sacerdote)* stole; **2** *(tipo de xaile para senhora)* stole.

estólido,-a *adj* stupid; stolid.

estômago *m* *(ANAT)* stomach; **2** *(fig, fam)* **ter** ~ **para** to tolerate, to have stomach for; IDIOM **ter um buraco no** ~ to feel peckish, hungry; **o meu** ~ **está a dar horas** I am hungry; **dar volta ao** ~ to make one feel sick, be disgusting.

Estónia *npr* **a** ~ Estonia.

estónio *m* *(LÍNG)* Estonian; **estónio,-a** *adj* Estonian.

estonteante *adj inv* stunning, dazzling; **2** perturbing.

estontear *vt* to stun, daze; **2** to bewilder; ◆ *vi* to get giddy, confused.

estopa *f* coconut fiber, flax, tow; IDIOM **não meter prego nem** ~ not lift a finger, take no part in anything.

estopada *f* *(quantidade de)* hurds; **2** *(fig)* nuisance, boring talk; **3** a grind.

estopar *vt* to pad, fill with wadding, etc.

estoque *m* rapier; **2** *m* *(COM)* stock; **em** ~ in stock.

estoquear *vt* to wound with a rapier, thrust; **2** *(BR)* to stock.

estore *m* *(para a janela)* blind.

estória *(BR)* *f* story.

estorninho *m* *(ave)* starling.

estorvar *vt* to hinder, obstruct, make it difficult; **2** *(fig)* to disturb; ~ **alguém de fazer** to prevent sb from doing.

estorvo *m* hindrance, obstacle, difficulty; **2** *(fig)* bother, nuisance.

estourar *vt/vi* to explode, to blow up; **2** to burst; **3** *(pneu)* to blow out; **4** *(fig)* *(fúria)* to blow up; **5** *(fam)* ~ **a banca** to bust the bank; **6** *(dor)* to throb; **7** ~ **os miolos** to blow out (one's or sb's) brains.

estouro *m* explosion, blast, burst, bang; **2** *(de gado)* stampede; **3** *(surpresa)* bombshell; **4** *(BR)* **ser um** ~ *(fam)* to be great, a hit, a sensation.

estouvado,-a *m,f* scatterbrain; daredevil; ♦ *adj* rash, reckless, foolhardy; **2** rattlebrained.

estrábico,-a *adj* *(MED)* cross-eyed, squinting; **2** *(olho)* strabismic.

estrabismo *m* *(MED)* strabismus, squint.

estrada *f* road; ~ **de ferro** railway *(UK)*, railroad *(US)*; **2** ~ **de rodagem** motorway *(UK)*, freeway *(US)*; **3** ~ **de terra** dirt road; **4 código de** ~ Highway Code; **5** ~ **principal** main road *(US)* highway; **6** ~ **de uma só via** one-way road.

Estrada de Santiago *f* *(Via Láctea)* Milky Way.

estrado *m* platform, dais; **2** *(CONSTR)* staging; foot board.

estragão *m* *(BOT)* tarragon.

estraga-prazeres *m,f* *(BR)* (=desmancha-prazeres EP) killjoy, spoilsport.

estragar *vt* to damage; **2** to ruin, wreck; **3** to waste; **4** to deteriorate, *(comida)* to go off; **5** *(fig)* *(amor)* to spoil; **ela estragou o filho** she spoiled her son.

estrago *m* destruction; **2** waste; **3** damage, harm; **os** ~**s da guerra** the ravages of war.

estrambólico,-a, estrambótico,-a *adj* eccentric, weird; **2** unusual, strange.

estrangeirado,-a *adj* foreign-looking; **2** foreign-sounding.

estrangeiro,-a *m,f* foreigner; ♦ *adj* foreign; **no** ~ abroad.

estrangulador,-ora *m,f* strangler; **2** *(TEC)* throttle.

estrangulamento *m* strangling, strangulation; **2** *(asfixia)* suffocation; **3** *(estreitamento)* narrowing *(de rio, passagem)*. **estrangular** *vt* to strangle, choke.

estranhar *vt* to be surprised at, wonder at; **2** to find strange; **3** to feel shy/ill at east; **4** not used to; **estranhei o clima** the climate did not agree with me.

estranho,-a *m,f* stranger; outsider; ♦ *adj* strange, odd, alien.

estratagema *m* *(MIL)* stratagem, manoeuvre; **2** *(fig)* *(manha)* trick, scheme, cunning.

estratega *m,f* *(MIL)* strategist.

estratégia *f* *(MIL)* tactics; **2** strategy.

estratégico,-a *adj* strategic, crucial; **2** cunning, artful.

estrategista *m,f* strategist.

estratego *m* strategist.

estrato *m* *(GEOL)* layer, stratum *(pl:* **strata***)*; **2** *(social)* class.

estratosfera *f* stratosphere.

estreante *m,f* novice, beginner; ♦ *adj inv* *(pessoa)* starting.

estrear *vt* to wear/put on/use/show for the first time; **hoje estreio o meu chapéu** today I am wearing my new hat; **2** to have a première, inaugurate; ♦ *vr* to start, make one's debut.

estrebaria *f* stables, **2** coarse language; **ele só diz** ~**s** he talks like a stable boy.

estrebuchar *vi* *(dor)* to writhe; **2** to toss (about); **3** to shake (in death throes).

estreia *f* première, first appearance, debut; **discurso de** ~ inaugural/maiden speech.

estreitar *vt* to narrow; **2** *(relações)* to strengthen; **3** to hug; **4** *(vestuário)* to tighten; **5** to restrict; ♦ *vi* to narrow; **2** *(roupa)* to shrink; ♦ ~**-se** *vr* to narrow; **2** to deepen; **3** to get stronger.

estreiteza *f* narrowness; **2** closeness; **3** *(fig)* streetness, ~ **de pontos de vista** narrowmindedness.

estreito,-a *m* *(GEOG)* strait; ♦ *adj* narrow; **2** tight; **3** straight; **4** close.

estrela *f* *(ASTRON, CIN)* star; **2** *(TYPO)* asterisk; IDIOM **levantar-se com as** ~**s** to get up at the crack of dawn.

estrela-cadente *f* falling star.

estrelado,-a *adj* *(céu)* starry; **2 ovo** ~ fried egg.

estrela-do-mar *f* starfish.

estrelar *vt* to fill/set/adorn with stars; **2** to fry (eggs); **3** *(BR)* to star (in a film).

estrema *f* end, boundary line.

estremadura *f* border, boundary, confine; **2** E~ western province in Portugal; **3** E~ eastern province in Spain.

estremar *vt* to mark, delimit, bound; **2** to separate; **3** to distinguish.

estreme *m* pure, undiluted.

estremecer *vt/vi* to shake; **2** *(de medo)* to tremble; **3** *(de frio)* to shiver; **4** *(de paixão)* to throb; **5** *(repulsa)* to shudder.

estremecido,-a *m,f* much loved; **o filho** ~ beloved son.

estremecimento *m* shaking, trembling; **2** shiver; **3** deep love.

estremenho,-a *adj* from the Portuguese province of Estremadura.

estremunhado,-a *adj* half asleep, startled from sleep; **2** drowsy.

estrénio,-a *(BR:* -ê-*)* *adj* strenuous.

estrepe *f* thorn, sharp point; **2** *(MIL)* caltrop; **3** *(pl)* broken pieces of glass imbedded in mortar; **4** *(BR: pej)* ugly woman.

estrépito *m* din, racket; **2** *(fig)* fuss.

estrepitoso,-a *adj* noisy, rowdy; **2** *(fig)* sensational.

estria *f* groove, channel, stria; **2** streak, stripe, ~**s de gordura** streaks of fat; **3** ~ **de goma** gum streaks; **4** *(gravidez)* stretch marks; **5** *(MED)* striation, stria; **6** *(GEOL)* stria, striae, striation; *(ARQ)* *(meia-cana)* fluting.

estribar *vt* to put one's (feet) in the stirrups; **2** *(edifício)* to base; **3** to support; ♦ ~-**se** *vr*: ~ **em** to be based on; **2** to lean on.

estribeira *f* stirrup; IDIOM **perder as** ~**s** to lose one's head; to lose control/direction.

estribilho *m (MÚS)* refrain, chorus; **2** catchphrase.

estribo *m* stirrup; **2** footboard, boarding step, *(BR)* platform; **3** running-board; **4** *(CONSTR)* support, prop; **5** *(ANAT)* stapes.

estridente *adj inv (voz, grito)* shrill, piercing; *(barulho)* grating.

estripador,-ora *adj* ripper.

estripar *vt* to rip open, to disembowel.

estrito,-a *adj* strict; **2** restricted.

estrofe *f* stanza; **2** strophe.

estroina *m,f* bohemian; **2** waster; ♦ *adj inv* scatter-brained; **2** extravagant; **3** dissipated, wild; **4** bohemian.

estróncio *m (QUÍM)* strontium.

estrondear *vi* to boom, roar; **2** to rumble, thunder; **3** *(fig)* to cause sensation.

estrondo *m* rumble, din; **2** clap; **3** *(fig)* uproar.

estropiar *vt* to maim, cripple, wound; **2** to wear out *(alguém)*; **3** mutilate; ♦ ~-**se** *vr* to main o.s.

estrugido *m (CULIN)* onions and garlic in olive oil; **2** *(ruído)* din, rumble, roar.

estrumar *vt* to fertilize.

estrume *m* manure.

estrumeira *f* dunghill, heap of manure; **2** *(fig) (lugar sujo)* pigsty.

estrutura *f* structure.

estruturação *f* structure, framework.

estrutural *adj inv* structural.

estruturar *vt* to structure; **2** to build.

estuário *m* estuary.

estucador *m* plasterer.

estucar *vt* to apply plaster, stucco to walls, to plaster.

estuco *m* plaster, stucco.

estudante *m,f* student.

estudantil *adj inv* student.

estudar *vt* to study.

estúdio *m* studio.

estudioso,-a *m,f* student, scholar; ♦ *adj* studious, diligent.

estudo *m* study, survey, research; **em** ~ *(plano etc)* under consideration; **2** ~**s** education, studies; **3** *(MÚS)* études.

estufa *f* greenhouse; **2** *(do fogão)* oven; **3** sterilizer; **4** *(fig)* very hot place.

estufadeira *f* stewpot.

estufado,-a *m (CULIN)* pot-roast; ♦ *adj (carne)* braised; **2** *(aquecido em estufa)* heated.

estugar *vt* to quicken one's step; **2** to spur, urge on; **3** to motivate sb.

Estugarda *npr* Stuttgart.

estulto,-a *adj* foolish, silly.

estupefa(c)ção *f* stupefaction, numbness; **2** amazement, astonishment.

estupefa(c)to,-a *adj* aghast, numb, speechless.

estupefaciente *m* drug, narcotic; ♦ *adj inv* narcotic.

estupendo,-a *adj* wonderful, amazing, fantastic, terrific; ♦ *exc* ~! super!, great!

estupidez *f* stupidity; nonsense.

estúpido,-a *m,f* idiot; **2** *(pessoa inculta)* brute; ♦ *adj* stupid, obtuse, idiotic; *(fam)* thick.

estupor *m* stupor; **2** lethargy; **3** perplexity; **4** *(fam)* *(pessoa feia ou má)* rotter, swine.

estuprar *vt* to rape; **2** to ravish.

estupro *m* rape.

estuque *m (CONSTR)* stucco, plaster; **revestir o muro de** ~ to plaster the outside wall.

estúrdia *f* prank, frolic; **2** spree; **3** high jinks.

esturjão *m (ZOOL) (peixe)* sturgeon.

esturrar *vt* to scorch, parch, burn; ~ **a comida** to burn the food; **2** to become irritated; **3** *(BR)* to growl.

esvaecer-se *vr* to fade away, dissipate; faint *(Vd: esvanecer)*.

esvair-se *vr* to vanish, disappear; **2** *(desfalecer)* to faint, swoon; **3** ~ **em sangue** to lose a lot of blood, to bleed to death.

esvanecer *vt* to vanish, evanesce.

esvaziar *vt* to empty, drain; **2** *(balão)* to deflate; ♦ ~-**se** *vr* to be/become empty; ~ **de sentido** to lose its meaning.

esventrar *vt* to disembowel.

esverdeado,-a *adj* greenish; **azul-**~ greenish blue.

esvoaçante *adj inv* fluttering, flying; **2** *(balão, etc)* floating (in the air).

esvoaçar *vi* to flutter, flit, fly.

etal *m (QUÍM)* ethal, cetyl alcohol.

etanal *adj inv* acetaldehyde.

etano *m* ethane.

etanóico *m* ethanoic acid.

etanol *m (QUÍM)* ethanol, ethyl alcohol.

etapa *f* stage (of journey, progress); **2** *(escala)* stop; **3** phase; **4** *(DESP)* stage; **5** *(MIL)* a day's march, halting place.

ETAR *(abr de* **Estação de Tratamento de Águas Residuais***)* Water Treatment Plant/Station.

etena *f (QUÍM)* ethylene.

éter *m (QUÍM)* ether, **2** ~ **difenilo** phenyl/diphenyl ether.

etéreo,-a *adj (QUÍ)* ethereal.

eternidade *f* eternity.

eterno,-a *adj* eternal.

ético,-a *adj* ethical; **2** *f* ethics *pl.*

etimologia *f* etymology.

Etíope *m,f* Ethiopian; ♦ **etíope** *adj inv* Ethiopian.

Etiópia *npr* Ethiopia; **a** ~ Ethiopia.

etiqueta *f* etiquette, courtesy; **2** label, tag.

etiquetagem *f* labelling.

étnico,-a *adj* ethnic.

etnografia *f* ethnography.

etnográfico,-a *adj* ethnographic.

etnógrafo,-a *m,f* ethnographer.

etnólogo,-a *m,f* ethonolist.

eu *m* the self, the ego; **super-**~ super ego; ♦ *pron (pess, 1ª pessoa)* I; **eu e o meu marido** my husband and I; **agora sou eu a falar** now it is I who speaks/my turn to speak; **2** *(predicativo)* myself, **já não sou eu** I am no longer myself; **3 eu**

mesmo fiz isso *(enfático)* I myself did that; **4** me; **sou eu** it's me; *(de comparação)* me; **ela come mais do que eu** she eats more than me.

EUA *(abr de* **Estados Unidos da América***)* USA.

eucaliptal *m* eucalyptus grove.

eucalipto *m* eucalyptus.

eucalyptol *m* eucalyptus oil.

Eucaristia *f* Holy Communion, Eucharist.

eufemismo *m* euphemism.

eufónico,-a *adj (MÚS)* euphonic, melodious; **2** *(dicção)* euphonious, pleasing.

euforia *f* euphoria.

eufórico,-a *adj* euphoric.

eunuco *m* eunuch; castrated man.

EURATOM *(abr de* **Comunidade Europeia de Energia Atómica***)* EURATOM.

euro *m (moeda)* euro.

eurocrata *m,f* eurocrat; ♦ *adj* eurocratic.

Europa *npr* Europe; **a~** Europe.

europeísta *adj inv* admirer of Europe, pro-Europe.

europeizar-se *vr* to become Europeanized.

europeu, europeia *m,f* European.

eutanásia *f* euthanasia.

Eva *f* Eve.

evacuação *f* evacuation.

evacuar *vt* to evacuate; **2** to leave; **3** *(lugar)* to clear (of people); **4** *(MED, MIL)* to discharge; ♦ *vi* to defecate.

evadido,-a *adj* escaped.

evadir *vt* to evade, ilude; **2** to escape from; **3** *(fam)* to dodge; ♦ **~-se** *vr* to escape.

Evangelho *m* Gospel; **o E~** the Gospel.

evangélico, -a *adj* evangelical.

evangelista *adj inv* evangelist, preacher.

evaporação *f* evaporation.

evaporar *vt* to evaporate; ♦ *vi* to vanish; ♦ **~-se** *vr* to vanish.

evasão *f (fuga)* escape; **2** *(FIN)* **~ fiscal** tax evasion.

evasiva *f,* evasive, excuse; **deixa-te de ~s** stop being evasive; **2** subterfuge; ♦ **evasivo,-a** *adj* evasive.

evento *m* event, happening.

eventual *adj* fortuitous, possible, occasional.

eventualidade *f (casualidade)* possibility, chance, contingency; **nessa ~** in case that should happen.

eventualmente *adv* by chance; potentially.

> Not in the sense of 'ultimate' which is **final, oportunamente**.

evidência *f* evidence, proof; **2** truth; **3** *(relevo)* evidence, highlight.

evidenciar *vt* to prove; **2** to show; **3** to highlight; ♦ **~-se** *vr* to attract attention; **2** to be evident/ obvious; **3** to stand out; **4** to distinguish o.s.

evidente *adj inv* obvious, evident.

evitar *vt* to avoid; **2** to prevent; **3** *(pessoas, problemas)* to shun, dodge; **4** *(murro)* to duck.

evitável *adj inv* avoidable.

evocar *vt* to evoke; **2** to recall.

evolução *f* development; **2** evolution; **3** *(MIL)* manoeuvre; **4** *(FIN)* trend, **a ~ da produção** production trend(s).

evoluir *vi* to evolve, develop; **2** *(MIL)* to manoeuvre; **3** *(FIN)* to perform.

evolutivo,-a *adj* evolutionary.

ex. *(abr de* **exemplo***)*.

exacerbar *vt* to exacerbate, exasperate; **2** to aggravate; ♦ **~-se** *vr* to get worse, become aggravated.

exa(c)tamente *adv* exactly, precisely.

exa(c)tidão *f* accuracy; correctness.

exa(c)to,-a *adj* right, correct, exact.

exagerar *vt/vi* to exaggerate; *(fazer de mais)* to overdo.

exagero *m* exaggeration.

exalar *vt* to exhale; **2** to emit, give off, let out; ♦ **~-se** *vr* to be exhaled; IDIOM **~ o último suspiro** to breathe one's last.

exaltado,-a *m,f* hothead, fanatic; ♦ *adj (irritado)* hot-tempered; angry; *(multidão)* overexcited; **2** *(empolgado)* elated, exalted, carried away; **3** *(fanático)* fanatical.

exaltar *vt (louvar, glorificar)* to praise, extol (sb's qualities); **2** *(entusiasmar)* to excite; **3** to irritate *(alguém)*; ♦ **~-se** *vr (vangloriar-se)* to brag, boast; **2** *(excitar-se)* to get worked up; get carried away; **3** *(enfurecer-se)* to get angry, to fly off the handle.

exame *m* examination, exam; **2** inquiry; **3** scrutiny; **4** review; **fazer um ~** to take an exam; **5** *(de condução)* driving test.

examinador,-ora *m,f* examiner.

examinando,-a *m,f* candidate (for the exam).

examinar *vt* to examine, review; look into.

exangue *adj inv* bloodless; **2** *(fig)* feeble, debilitated.

exarar *vt* to set down in writing; **2** *(actas, opinião)* to register, record; **3** to inscribe, imprint; **4** to engrave.

exasperante *adj inv* exasperating.

exasperar *vt* to exasperate, irritate; ♦ **~-se** *vr* to get exasperated.

exatidão *(Vd:* **exa(c)tidão***)*.

exato,-a *(Vd:* **exa(c)to***)*.

exaurir *vt* to exhaust, drain; **2** *(fig) (energia)* to consume; **3** *(fig)* to dissipate, lose; ♦ **~-se** *vr* to become exhausted; **2** to run dry.

exausto,-a *(irr pp de:* **exaurir***)* exhausted; jaded.

exaustor *m* extractor (fan); ventilator.

exceção *(Vd:* **exce(p)ção***)*.

excecional *(Vd:* **exce(p)cional***)*.

excedentário,-a *m,f* surplus staff; ♦ *adj* extra.

excedente *m* excess; **2** *(COM)* surplus; **3** *(BR)* student on waiting list.

exceder *vt* to exceed; **2** to surpass; **3** to overstep; **4** **~ em peso/brilho** to outweigh/outshine; ♦ **~-se** *vr* to go too far.

excelência *f* excellence; **por ~** par excellence; **V. Exa = Vossa Excelência** Your Excellency; **Sua ~** His/Her Excelency; **V. Exas** *npl* Your Excellencies *m,f pl*.

excelente *adj inv* excellent.

excelentíssimo,-a *(superl de:* **excelente***) adj* most excellent, Madam.

excelso,-a *adj* sublime, eminent.

excentricidade *f* eccentricity.

excêntrico,-a *m,f adj* eccentric.

exce(p)ção *f* exception; **não há regra sem** ~ there is an exception to every rule; **à** ~ **de** except for, save.

exce(p)cional *adj inv* exceptional; **2** special.

exce(p) to *prep* except for, apart from.

exce(p)tuar *vt* to except, exclude; **2** to be let out, excused; ♦ *vi (JUR)* take an exception to; ♦ ~**-se** *vr* make an exception of o.s.

excerto *m* excerpt, **2** *(de uma leitura)* extract.

excessivo,-a *adj* excessive.

excesso *m* excess, ~ **de bagagem** excess luggage; **2** *(COM)* surplus; **3** effort.

exceto *(Vd:* **exce(p)to***).*

excetuar *(Vd:* **exce(p)tuar***).*

excisão *f (MED)* excision.

excisar *vt (MED)* to excise; **2** *(tecido do corpo)* to remove, amputate; **2** to cut/separate.

excitação *f* excitement.

excitado,-a *adj (agitado)* excited; *(sexualmente)* aroused.

excitar *vt* to excite; to arouse; ♦ ~**-se** *vr (entusiasmar-se)* to get excited; **2** *(agitar-se)* to be agitated, get worked out; **não te excites** *(fam)* don't get your knickers in a twist.

exclamação *f* exclamation.

exclamar *vi* to exclaim.

excluir *vt* to exclude; **2** to leave out, shut out.

exclusivo,-a *adj* exclusive; **para uso** ~ **de** for the sole use of.

ex-combatente *m,f* war veteran.

excomungar *vt* to excommunicate.

excreção *(pl:* -**ções***) f (BIOL)* excretion; **2** *(matéria excretada)* excreta.

excremento *m* excrement.

excretar *vt (expelir)* to excrete.

excruciante *adj inv* excruciating.

excursão *f* trip; tour; excursion; **2** *(a pé)* walk, ramble.

excursionar *vi* ~ *(por)* to tour.

excursionista *m,f* tourist; *(por um dia)* day-tripper; **2** *(a pé)* walker.

execrar *vt* to execrate.

execrável *(pl:*-**eis***) adj* execrable.

execução *f* execution; **2** performance; **3** seizure of goods (in default); **4** ~ **hipotecária** *(JUR) f* foreclosure of a mortgage.

executante *m,f* performer; ♦ *adj* executing.

executar *vt* to execute; **2** *(sentence)* to carry out; ~ **um mandado de prisão** to serve a warrant; **3** *(JUR)* to discharge, foreclose; **4** *(MÚS)* to perform; **5** *(peça musical)* execute.

executivo,-a *m,f adj* executive.

executor,-ora *m,f* executor; **2** ~ **testamenteiro** *(JUR)* executor of a will; **3** executioner.

exemplar *adj inv* exemplary; **2** commendable; **3** *m* model, specimen, pattern; **4** copy; ~ **gratuito** free copy.

exemplificação *f* exemplification.

exemplificar *vt* to exemplify.

exemplo *m* example, instance; **por** ~ for example, for instance; **dar o** ~ to set an example; **ser um bom** ~ **de algo** to be a good example of sth; **2**

servir de ~ **a alguém** *(lição)* to serve as a lesson/ warning to sb; **3 a** ~ **de** just like.

exéquias *fpl* funeral rites, exequies.

exequibilidade *f* feasibility.

exequível *adj inv* feasible.

exercer *vt* to exercise; ~ **um direito** exercise a right; ~ **autoridade** exercise/have authority; **2** *(influência)* to exert; **to** ~ **pressão sobre alguém** to exert pressure on sb; **3** *(funções)* to perform, to act; **4** *(profissão)* to practise (medicina, advocacia).

exercício *m (atividade física)* exercise; **2** *(de profissão)* practise, practising; **3** *(MIL)* drill; ♦ *adv* **em** ~ in power, in office; **em** ~ **das suas funções** in the exercise of his functions.

exercitar *vt* exercise; **2** to train.

exército *m* army; **oficial do** ~ army officer.

exibição *f* display; exhibition.

exibir *vt* to show, display; ♦ ~**-se** *vr* to show off, flaunt.

exigência *f* demand; **2** requirement.

exigente *adj inv* demanding; **2** fussy; **3** strict, difficult.

exigir *vt* to demand; **2** to require.

exigível *(pl:* -**veis***) adj inv (condição, requisito)* indispensable; **2** exactable; demandable; ♦ **exigíveis** *mpl (FIN)* liabilities, debts; ~ **a curto prazo** short-term liabilities.

exíguo,-a *adj* small; **2** scanty.

exilado,-a *m,f* exile; ♦ *adj* exiled.

exilar *vt* to exile; **2** to deport; ♦ ~**-se** *vr* to go into exile; **3** *(fig)* to isolate.

exílio *m* exile; **2** deportation.

exímio,-a *adj* eminent, distinguished; **2** excellent; **3** skilled *(JUR)* discharged.

eximir *vt (JUR)* to free, discharge, acquit *(alguém)* **(de** from); **2** *(desobrigar)* ~ **alguém de algo** exempt sb from sth; ♦ ~**-se** *vr* **(de)** to avoid, shun; **2** to get rid (of).

existência *f* existence; **2** being; **3** life; **existências** *fpl (COM)* stock.

existencialismo *m* existentialism.

existir *vi* to exist, to be.

êxito *m* result; **2** success; **3 ter** ~ to succeed, be successful; **4 não ter** ~ to fail; ~ **de bilheteria** box-office hit; ~ **de livraria** bestseller.

Exmo *m* **Exma** *f (abr de* **excelentíssimo,-a***) (regular form of address on an envelope/letter to a man/ woman)* **Exmo Senhor Manuel Pires** Mr. Manuel Pires *ou* M. Pires, Esq; **Exma Senhora D. (dona) Ana Freitas** Mrs Ana Freitas; **Exmo Senhor Dr. A. Silva** Dr. A. Silva; **Exmos Senhores Silva & Pereira** *(empresa)* Messrs Silva Pereira **3** *(em carta) (quando não sabemos o nome da pessoa)* **Exmo/s Senhor/es** Dear Sir/s; **Exma Senhora** Dear Madam.

êxodo *m* exodus.

exonerar *vt (de culpa, encargo)* exonerate, exempt *(from)*; **2** *(despedir)* to dismiss, discharge; ♦ ~**-se** *vr (demitir-se)* to resign (from office).

exorbitante *adj inv* exhorbitant, preposterous; **2** excessive.

exorbitar *vt* to exceed; to go beyond the rules; overstep.

exorcismar *vt* to exorcise.

exorcismo *m* exorcism.

exorcizar *vt* to exorcise.

exortação *f* exhortation; warning.

exortar *vt* to urge on; 2 ~ **alguém a fazer algo** to exhort sb to do sth; to persuade.

exótico,-a *adj* exotic.

expandir *vt* to expand; 2 to unfold; 3 to spread; ♦ ~**-se** *vr* to expand; ~ **com alguém** to be frank with sb.

expansão *f* expansion, spread; 2 effusiveness.

expansivo,-a *adj* outgoing, frank.

expectativa *f* expectation; prospect.

expedição *f* expedition; 2 despatch; 3 shipment.

expediente *m* expedient; 2 day's work; 3 resource; **viver de ~s** to live by one's wits; 4 **ter** ~ to be quick/efficient; 5 *(horário de trabalho)* office hours *pl*.

expedir *vt* to send, despatch; 2 to issue; 3 *(mercadoria)* to ship (goods); 4 to expedite.

expedito,-a *adj* prompt, speedy.

expelir *vt* to expel; 2 to throw out; 3 to eject.

expensas *fpl*: **a** ~ **de** *prep* at the expense of.

experiência *f* experience; 2 experiment, test; 3 **em** ~ on trial; 4 **sem** ~ inexperienced.

experientação *f* experiment.

experiente *m,f* expert ♦ *adj inv* experienced.

experimenta *f*, **experimento** *m* experiment.

experimentado,-a *adj (person)* experienced; 2 *(ideia, pesquisa)* tested, tried.

experimentar *vt (comida)* to taste; 2 *(roupa)* to try on/out; 3 to test, try; 4 to experience; 5 to experiment; 6 *(fig)* to suffer, undergo.

expiar *vt* to atone for.

expiatório,-a *adj* expiatory; 2 **bode** ~ scapegoat.

expirar *vt* to exhale, breathe out; ♦ *vi* to die, pass away; 2 *(caducar)* to end, expire.

explanar *vt* to explain; to elucidate; 2 describe; 3 demonstrate.

explicação *f* explanation; 2 private lesson.

explicar *vt* to explain; 2 to account for; ♦ ~**-se** *vr* to explain oneself.

explícito,-a *adj* explicit, clear.

explodir *vi* to explode, blow up; 2 to burst; 3 *(fig)* *(colérico)* to explode, 4 *(manifestar)* to burst out.

exploração *f* exploration; 2 *(abuso)* exploitation; 3 *(de negócio)* running (a business); 4 *(AGR)* cultivation; 5 *(MIN)* survey.

explorar *vt* to explore; 2 to exploit; 3 to probe; 4 to take unfair advantage **(de alguém** of sb).

explosão *f* explosion, blast; 2 *(fig)* outburst.

explosivo,-a *m* explosive; ♦ *adj* explosive; 2 *(alguém)* hot-headed.

expoente *m,f* exponent, promoter; 2 *(MAT)* exponent; 3 *(figura importante)* great, greatest name.

expor *vt* to expose, reveal; 2 to risk; 3 to explain, report; 4 to display, exhibit; ♦ ~**-se** *vr* to expose o.s.; 2 *(fig)* show off.

exportação *f* export(ing); 2 exports *pl*.

exportador,-ora *m,f* exporter; ♦ *adj* exporting.

exportar *vt* to export.

exposição *f* exhibition; 2 exposition; 3 explanation; 4 statement, account; 5 *(FOTO)* exposure.

expositor,-ora *m,f* exhibitor.

expressão *f* expression.

expressar *vt* to express.

expresso,-a *(pp de* **expressar***) m (comboio)* express; ♦ *adj* definite, clear; 2 expressed, explicit; 3 *(rápido, directo) (correio)* express; 4 *(transporte)* non-stop, direct, express.

exprimir *vt* to express; ♦ ~**-se** *vr* to express o.s.

expropriação *f* expropriation.

expropriar *vt (JUR)* to dispossess, expropriate; 2 to seize, confiscate.

expugnar *vt* to take by storm; 2 to expel (by force of arms).

expulsão *f* expulsion.

expulsar *vt* to expel; 2 to drive out; 3 to throw out.

expulso,-a *(pp de* **expulsar***) adj* expelled.

expurgar *vt* to purge, cleanse.

exsudação *f* exudation, oozing out, transpiration.

exsudar *vt* to exude *(cheiro de suor)* to sweat; *(das árvores)* to sap from the trees.

êxtase *m* ecstasy.

extensão *f (espaço)* expansion; size, vastness; 2 *(area)* expanse; 3 length, duration; 4 *(estrada)* stretch; 5 *(CONSTR) (casa)* adição, extensão; 6 ~**s** *fpl* **do cabelo** hair extensions; 7 *(TEL = ramal); (ELECT)* extension.

extensível *adj inv* extendable.

extenso,-a *adj (area)* wide, vast; long; 2 *(discurso)* lengthy; 3 extended; ♦ **por** ~ *adv (escrita)* in full.

extenuado,-a *adj* worn out.

extenuante *adj inv* exhausting, extenuating.

extenuar *vt* to wear out, exhaust; 2 to weaken.

exterior *m* outside; 2 outward appearance; 3 *(CIN)* **do filme** outdoor shots; 4 **do** ~ from abroad; ♦ *adj* outside, exterior; 2 outward; 3 foreign; 4 non-relevant.

exteriorizar *vt* to exteriorize, show; ♦ ~**-se** *vr* to show/reveal/express oneself.

exterminar *vt* to exterminate, to wipe out; 2 to do away with.

extermínio *m* extermination, wiping out; 2 extinction.

externato *m* day school.

externo,-a *adj* external; 2 outside; 3 **aluno** ~ day pupil; **comércio** ~ foreign trade.

extinção *f* extinction; *(animal, planta, etc)* **em** ~ endangered.

extinguir *vt (fogo)* to put out, extinguish; 2 *(gente, nação)* to exterminate; 3 *(animais)* to wipe out; 4 *(epidemia)* wipe out; ♦ ~**-se** *vr (chama, luz)* to go out; 2 *(BIO)* to become extinct; 3 *(relações)* to end; 4 *(memória)* to fade; 5 *(amor)* die out.

extinguível *adj inv* extinguishable.

extinto,-a *adj* extinguished; 2 dead; 3 extinct; 4 *(partido)* dissolved.

extintor *m (fire)* extinguisher; ♦ **extintor,-ora** *adj (produto, aparelho)* extinguishing.

extirpação *f (MED)* extirpation; 2 eradication.

extirpar *vt (plantas)* to uproot, pull up/out; *(dente)* extrair, pull out; *(MED)* to remove; 2 *(fig) (eliminar)* to eradicate, abolish, wipe out.

extorcionista *m,f* extortioner.

extorquir *vt* to extort; **2** to wring out.

extorsão *f* extorsion; **2** coercion.

extra *m,f (TEAT)* extra; ♦ *adj inv (horas, trabalho)* extra; additional; **2** *(azeite, etc)* finest quality; **3** *(person, etc)* extraordinary.

extra(c)ção *f* extraction; **2** *(MED)* removal; **3** *(sorteio)* draw; **4** *(COMP) (de dados)* retrieval.

extraconjugal *adj inv (relações)* extramarital.

extra(c)to *m (ger)* extract; **2** *(excerto)* excerpt; **3** *(COM)* ~ **do banco** bank statement, printout; **4** *(de uma sinopse, etc)* summary.

extra(c)tor *m,f (pessoa, máquina)* extractor; ~ **de cortiça** *(trabalhador)* cork stripper; ♦ *adj* extracting; extractive.

extradição *f* extradition.

extraditar *vt* to extradite.

extraescolar *adj inv* **actividades** ~**s** after-school activities.

extrair *vt (MED)* to extract, remove, pull out; **3** *(sumo)* to squeeze; **4** *(água do poço)* to draw; **5** *(das minas)* to extract; **6** *(fazer cópia)* to obtain (a copy); **7** *(retirar)* to take, remove; **8** *(extorquir)* to extort.

extramatrimonial *adj inv* extramarital.

extramuros *adv* outside the city; extramural.

extranatural *adj inv* supernatural.

extraordinário,-a *adj* extraordinary; **2** special; **3** additional; **horas** ~**as** overtime *sg*.

extrapolar *vt* to go beyond; **2** *(MAT)* to extrapolate.

extra-sensorial, extrassensorial *adj inv* extrasensory.

extraterrestre *adj inv* extraterrestrial.

extrato *m (Vd: extra(c)to)*; **extrator** *(Vd. extra(c)tor)*.

extra-uterino, extrauterino,-a *adj (gravidez)* ectopic.

extravagância *f* extravagance; **2** eccentricity; **3** excess.

extravagante *adj inv* extravagant; **2** outlandish; **3** prodigal.

extravasamento *m* effusion.

extravasar *vt/vi* to overflow; **2** *(fig)* to overstep; **3** *(fig) (protesto)* to vent, pour one's heart.

extraviado,-a *adj* lost, missing.

extraviar *vt* to mislay; **2** to go astray; **3** *(dinheiros)* to embezzle; ♦ ~**-se** *vr* to get lost; **2** to go astray.

extravio *m (perda)* loss; **2** *(desfalque)* embezzlement; **3** *(fig)* deviation.

extrema direita *f (POL)* extreme-right.

extremado,-a *adj* eminent; **2** extreme.

extrema esquerda *f (POL)* extreme-left.

extremamente *adv* extremely, exceedingly.

extremar to mark out; exalt; ♦ ~**-se** *vr* to distinguish o.s.; ~ **em esforços** to do one's utmost.

extrema-unção *f* last rights, extreme unction.

extremidade *f (ponta)* extremity; end, tip; **de uma** ~ **à outra** from one end to the other; **2** *(limite)* edge, margin; **3** difficult situation.

extremista *adj inv* extremist.

extremo,-a *m,f (limite)* extreme, end, brink; **no** ~ **da miséria** on the brink of poverty; **2** *(máximo)* utmost; **ao** ~ to the utmost; ~ **s** *mpl (exagero)* extremes; ♦ *adj* extreme, far; **o E~ Oriente** Far East; **2** ~ **direito** *m (DESP)* right winger, right wing; ~ **esquerdo** *m (DESP)* left winger, left wing.

extremoso,-a *adj* loving; **2** devoted; **uma mãe** ~**a** a devoted mother.

extrínseco,-a *adj* extrinsic, extraneous; **2** *(valor)* irrelevant, superficial, external.

extroversão *f (MED) (reviramento de um órgão)* extroversion; **2** *(PSIC)* extroversion.

extroverter-se *vr* to become extroverted.

extrovertido,-a *m,f* extrovert; ♦ *adj* sociable, outgoing, friendly.

exu *(BR) m* the devil (voodoo rituals).

exuberância *f* exuberance.

exuberante *adj inv* abundant; **2** exuberant; **3** *(vegetação)* lush; **4** excessive, ostentatious; **5** *(discurso)* flowery; **6** ebullient, enthusiastic.

exultação *f* exultation, jubilation.

exultante *adj inv* jubilant; **2** *(multidão)* excited, thrilled.

exultar *vi* ~ **de** to exalt in.

exumar *vt (corpo)* to exhume; **2** *(fig) (algo de onde estava)* to dig up; **3** *(fig) (tirar do esquecimento)* to dig up.

ex-voto *(pl: ex-votos) m* ex-voto; **2** *(REL) (em cumprimento duma promessa)* offering.

f

F, f *m* (letra) F, f.
fá *m (MÚS)* F, fa.
fã *m,f* fan, admirer.
fábrica *f* factory, mill, plant; ~ **de conservas** cannery; ~ **de papel** paper-mill; ~ **de açúcar** sugar refinery; ~ **de confe(c)ções** textile factory.
fabricação *f* manufacture; production; **2** *(fig)* fabrication.
fabricante *m,f* manufacturer.
fabricar *vt* to manufacture, make; *(fig) (estórias, boatos)* to fabricate.
fabrico *m* manufacture, production; ~ **da casa** our own make/brand.
fábula *f* fable; **2** tale; *(BR)* fortune.
fabuloso,-a *adj* fabulous.
faça *(pres subj de: fazer)* **é preciso que ela ~ tudo hoje** she must do everything today.
faca *f* knife; **2 cabo de** ~ knife handle; **3 fio de** ~ knife's edge; **4 uma ~ de dois gumes** a double-edge sword; IDIOM **ter a ~ e o queijo na mão** hold all the trumps.
facada *f* stab, cut; **2 dar uma ~ numa pessoa** to stab somebody; **3** *(fig)* sting, blow, shock; **4** *(fig) (money)* extortion.
façanha *f* exploit, deed, feat, prowess, achievement.
fa(c)ção *f* faction, party; **2** *(MIL)* exploit.
fa(c)cionário,-a *m,f* party member.
fa(c)cioso,-a *adj* factious.
face *f (rosto)* face; **2** *(bochecha)* cheek; **3** *(superfície)* face, surface *(da terra, água)*; **4** side; **a outra ~ da questão** the other side of the question; **5** *(da moeda)* head; **6 pano de duas ~s** reversible cloth; surface; ♦ *prep* **em ~ de** in view of; ~ **a** ~ face to face; **fazer ~ a** to face up to.
fáceis *(pl: de* **fácil***)*.
faceta *f (facet)* facet; **2** *(characteristic)* feature, aspect, outlook.
facetado,-a *adj* faceted.
fachada *f* facade, front.
facho *m* torch.
facial *adj* facial.
fácil *adj (pl:* **fáceis***) (simples)* easy; **2** *(pessoa dócil)* easygoing; **3** *(pej) (mulher)* easy.
facilidade *f* ease, easiness; **with** ~ easily; **2** *(aptidão)* skill, aptitude; **3** ~**s** *(pl) (condições)* facilities.
facílimo,-a *adj (superl de* **fácil***)* extremely easy.
facilitar *vt* to facilitate, make easy; **2** to provide.
facínora *m,f* criminal, villain; ♦ *adj inv* criminal.
faço *(pres ind, 1ª pessoa de* **fazer***)*: **eu não faço nada** I don't do anything.

fac-símile *m* copy, replica; **2** *(máquina)* fax.
factível *adj inv* feasible.
facto *(EP)* *(***fato***: BR) m* fact, reality; **2** case, event; **3** *(JUR)* fact, evidence; ♦ *adv* **de** ~ in fact, really; **ao** ~ **de** *prep* aware of; **2 um ~ consumado** a fait accompli; IDIOM **chegar a vias de** ~ to come (nearly come) to blows with sb.
fa(c)tor *m* (ECON) factor; **2** agent; **3** element; ~**es de produção** production factors.
fa(c)tura *f* bill, invoice.
fa(c)turação *n (COM)* invoicing.
fa(c)turar *vt* to invoice.
faculdade *f (capacidade)* faculty; **2** *(habilidade, dom)* skill, gift; **3** property, power; **4 F~ de Medicina** faculty of medicine.
facultar *vt* to allow; **2** to grant, facilitate.
facultativo,-a *adj* optional.
fada *f* fairy; **conto de** ~ fairy tale; **2 ter mãos de** ~ to have the ability for handywork *(embroidery, etc)*, wonderful hands; ~**-madrinha** *(pl:* **fadas-madrinhas***) f* fairy godmother.
fadado,-a *adj* fated, destined, doomed; **2 bem** ~ fortunate.
fadar *vt* to destine; to fate.
fadiga *f* fatigue; **2** toil.
fadista *m,f* singer of 'fado'; **2** *(pej)* bohemian, drifter.
fado *m* fate, destiny; **2** *(MÚS)* fado; Portuguese folk song.

Fado is traditionally Portuguese. It originated in Lisbon centuries ago. Another type of fado comes from Coimbra and is sung by its university students.

fagote *m (MÚS)* bassoon.
fagueiro,-a *adj (meigo)* gentle, sweet, caressing; pleasant.
fagulha *f* spark.
faia *f (árvore)* beech.
faial[1] *m* beechwood.
Faial[2] *npr* one of the islands in the Azores.
faina *f* toil, work; **2** task, chore; **a ~ de todos os dias** the daily chores.
faisão *m (ZOOL, CULIN)* pheasant.
faísca *f (fagulha)* spark; **2** *(descarga elétrica)* flash; **3** *(raio)* lightning, thunderbolt; **4** *(eyes)* sparkle.
faiscante *adj inv (de fogo, metal)* sparkling; **2** *(olhos, star)* sparkling, shining, twinkling.
faiscar *vi* to sparkle; to flash; **2** *(cintilar)* to twinkle; **3** *(olhos)* to shine; *(com ódio)* glitter, flash.
faixa *f (para a cintura)* belt, sash, cumberband; **2** *(atadura)* bandage; **3** *(tira de terra)* strip; **a ~ verde** the green belt; **4** *(AUTO) (pista)* lane; **5** *(de pedestres)* pedestrian crossing; **6** *(intervalo, espaço)* interval; ~ **etária** age group; ~ **salarial** salary band; **7** *(mensagens)* banner; **8** *(MÚS) (disk)* track.
faixa-título *(pl:* **faixas-títulos***) f (de disco)* title-track.
fala *f* speech; **2** conversation; **ficar sem** ~ to be speechless.
fala-barato *m,f sg, pl (pop)* loudmouth; chatter; ♦ *adj inv* chattering.

falácia *f* fallacy; **2** *(ardil, engano)* deceit; **3** *(falatório)* prattle, talk.

falacioso,-a *adj* fallacious, erroneous.

falado,-a *adj* talked about; **2** well-known; **3** *(má reputação)* notorious.

falador,-ora *m,f* chatterbox; ♦ *adj* talkative.

falange *f* *(ANAT)* phalanx; **2** *(MIL) (corpo de tropas)* phalanx.

falante *m,f* speaker; ~ **nativo** native speaker; ♦ *adj inv* garrulous, talkative.

falar *m* **o** ~ *(registo de língua)* speech, speaking; **o** ~ **sem cessar é cansante** speaking non-stop is tiresome; **2** idioma, dialecto; **os vários falares de um país** a Country's various modes of speaking; ♦ *vt/vi* to speak; **falo japonês** I speak Japanese; **fale mais alto!** speak louder!; ~ **com** to talk to/ with; **3** *(dialogar)* to talk, discuss; **não quero ~ mais nisso** I don't want to discuss it; **4** *(assunto)* ~ **de/sobre** to talk about; **eles estão a ~ de negócios;** they are talking about business; **5** *(dizer)* say, tell, speak **(de, sobre, em** of, about**); de que falas?** what are you speaking/talking about?; **ela falou-me disso** she told me about that; ~ **a verdade** to tell the truth; **6** *(obrigar alguém a falar)* talk; **ou falas ou eu não te deixo sair** you either talk or I won't let you out; **7** *(criticar, elogiar)* speak: ~ **bem/mal de** to speak well/ill (of); **8** *(significar)* mean; **fala a sério?** do you mean it?; ♦ **falar-se** *vr* to talk, to speak; **eles não se falam há muito tempo** they haven't spoken to each other for ages; **aqui fala-se alemão** German is spoken here; ♦ *adv* **falar por alguém** to speak on behalf of sb; **por** ~ **em** speaking of; by the way; **sem falar de/em** apart from, not to mention; ♦ *exc* **falou!** *(BR)* *(fam)*; IDIOM ~ **por entrte os dentes** to mutter; ~ **com os seus botões** to talk to oneself; **fale sem rodeios!** stop beating about the bush!; ~ **pelos cotovelos** to speak nineteen to the dozen; **ela fala com sete pedras na mão** she speaks in an aggressive manner; **isso vai dar que** ~ this will set people talking/will cause a stir; ~ **de poleiro** to speak with arrogance; **já cá não está quem falou** forget I spoke.

falatório *m* *(vozearia)* chattering, many voices; **2** *(maledicência)* gossip.

falaz *adj* *(raciocínio)* fallacious; **2** *(enganador)* deceptive, misleading; false.

falcão *m* *(ZOOL)* falcon, hawk; **2** *(MIL)* falcon.

falcatrua *f* fraud, trick, swindle.

falecer *vi* to die, pass away; **2** *(escassear)* to fall short of, lack.

falecido,-a *m,f* deceased; ♦ *adj (morto)* dead, late; **o** ~ **Antunes** the late Antunes.

falecimento *m* death; **2** falha; **~s** *pl (necessidades)* needs.

falência *f* *(COM, JUR)* bankruptcy, insolvency; **abrir** ~ to declare o.s. bankrupt; **levar à** ~ to bankrupt; **2** *(fracasso)* failure; collapse; break down.

falésia *f* cliff.

falhanço *m* flop, failure, fiasco.

falha *f* flaw.

falhar *vi* to fail; **2** to miss; **3** to be wrong.

falho,-a *adj* faulty, defective, flawed; ♦ *f* fault; **2** chip; **3** blemish, flaw; **4** *(AUTO)* **falha do motor** engine failure; **5** lapse, omission; **falha de memória** a lapse of memory; ♦ **sem falha** *adv* without fail.

fálico,-a *adj* phallic.

falido,-a *m,f* failure; ♦ *adj (COM)*, bankrupt, ruined.

falir *vi (fracassar)* to fail; **2** *(COM)* to go bankrupt.

falível *(pl: -íveis) adj* fallible.

falo¹ *(pénis)* phallus, penis.

falo² *(pres. ind, 1ª pessoa de falar)* I speak.

falsário,-a *m,f* forger.

falsear *vt* to forge, falsify.

falsidade *f* falsehood; **2** pretence; **3** deceit.

falsificar *vt* to forge, falsify; **2** to adulterate; **3** to misrepresent.

falso,-a *adj* false; **2** deceitful; **3** erroneous; **pisar em** ~ to miss one's step, put a foot wrong.

falta *f (carência)* lack, shortage, scarcity; ~ **de água** shortage of water; ~ **de senso comum** lack of common sense; ~ **de vergonha** shamelessness; **sem** ~ without fail; **2** *(ausência)* absence; ~ **justificada** justified absence; **ter/sentir a** ~ **de (alguém, algo)** to miss sb/sth; to be in need of; **3** *(erro, lapso)* fault; oversight; **ele cometeu uma** ~ he made an error/a mistake; **foi uma** ~ **da minha parte** it was an oversight on my part; **4** *(FUT)* foul.

faltar *vi (não haver)* to be lacking, be wanting; be missing; **falta a carne** the meat is missing; **falta vergonha** there is no shame; **falta sal à sopa** the soup needs salt; **2** *(pessoa)* be absent; ~ **ao trabalho/à escola** to be absent from work/school; **falta-me uma mala** my suitcase is missing; **falta-me dinheiro** I don't have any money/I am short of money; **nada lhe falta** he/she has have everything he/she wants; **3** *(não cumprir, falhar)* to fail; ~ **à palavra** to break one's word; *(desrespeitar)* **ela faltou-me ao respeito** she was rude to me; **4** *(morrer)* to pass away; **ela tinha apenas três anos quando a mãe lhe faltou** she was only three years old when her mother passed away; **5** *(restar por fazer/dizer)* to be left (to be/to do); **faltam vinte para as duas** it is twenty to two; **falta uma hora para chegarmos lá** there is one hour (for us) to arrive there; **ainda falta fazer a cama** the bed is still to be made; **só falta fazer a salada** I/we still have to do the salad/the salad is yet to be done; ♦ *exc* **era (só) o que faltava!** that's all I needed!/that's the last straw!

falto *adj* lacking **(de,** of); short **(de,** of).

fama *f (celebridade)* fame; **2** reputation; **de** ~ by reputation; **de má** ~ of ill-repute, notorious; **3** *(boato)* hearsay.

famélico,-a *adj* starving.

famigerado,-a *adj* well-known, famous; **2** *(pej)* notorious.

família *f* family, household; **abono de** ~ family allowance; ~ **monoparental** one-parent family.

familiar *m,f* relation, relative; ♦ *adj inv* of the family; **2** *(conhecido)* familiar; **3** *(serviços sociais)* **de quantos membros consiste o seu agregado ~** how many family members in your household?

familiaridade *f* familiarity; **2** informality.

faminto,-a *adj* hungry, famished; **2** *(fig)* eager, avid.

famoso,-a *adj* famous.

fanático,-a *m,f* fanatic; addict; ♦ *adj* fanatical; **2 ~ por** crazy about, enthusiastic.

fanatismo *m* fanaticism; extremism.

fancaria *f (loja, comércio)* drapery; *(fig)* **obra de ~** a poorly-done work, bungled.

fandango *m* popular dance in Spain and Portugal; **2** *(fig) (barulho)* revelry, merry-making; **3** noise, brawl.

faneca *f (ZOOL) (peixe)* whiting; **2** *(fam) (pão)* a morsel of bread; **3** an empty nut; **4** *(fig)* thin person.

fanfarrada *f* bragging, boasting; swaggering.

fanfarrão,-ona *m,f* braggard, windbag; **2** bully; ♦ *adj* boastful, bragging.

fanfarronice *f (gabarolice)* boasting, bravado, swaggering.

fanhoso,-a *adj (que fala em tom nasal)* nasal-sounding.

fanico *m (chique)* fit; **ter/dar-lhe um ~** *(pessoa)* to freak out; **2** *(fig) (birra)* to get into a strop; **3** *(prostituição)* **andar ao ~** to be on the game; to be on casual work; **4 ~s** *pl* tiny bits, fragments.

faniquito *m* fainting fit, swoon.

fanqueiro,-a *m,f* draper.

fantasia *f* fantasy, illusion; **2** imagination; **3** fancy, dream; **4** *(de pouco valor)* fancy ornament; **jóias de ~** fancy jewellery.

fantasiar *vt* to imagine, fantasize; ♦ *vi* to daydream.

fantasista *m,f* dreamer; ♦ *adj inv* fanciful.

fantasma *m* ghost; spectre, phantom, apparition.

fantasmagórico,-a *adj* phantasmagorical.

fantástico,-a *adj* fantastic; **2** imaginary; **3** unbelievable; **4** great, sensational; excellent; awesome.

fantochada *f* puppet show; **2** *(fig)* sham.

fantoche *m* puppet.

faqueiro *m* cutlery.

farda *f (MIL, police, etc)* uniform; **2** *(fam, fig) (roupa)* outfit, clothes; **usas sempre a mesma ~** you always use the same clothes.

fardar *vt* to dress in uniform.

fardo *m* bale; **2** bundle; **3** load; **4** *(fig)* burden **a minha vida é um ~** my life is a burden.

farei *(1ª pessoa do futuro de fazer);* **~ o que quiseres** I shall do whatever you wish.

farejar *vt (cheirar)* to smell; sniff (at); **2** *(pressentir)* to sense; ♦ *vi (rasto)* to sniff; to follow the scent.

farejo *n* sniff.

farelo *m (farinha)* bran; **2** *(fig)* trifle.

farfalhada *f (conversa oca)* empty talk, twaddle; **2** *(ruído)* noise; **3** *(fig) (basófia)* bragging.

farfalhar *vi (folhagem ao vento)* to rustle; **2** *(gabar-se)* to boast, brag.

farfalheira *f (rumor)* rustle; **2** *(ruído nos brônquios)* wheezing, chesty cough; **3** *(folhos/adornos no pescoço e peito de senhora)* ruffles.

faringe *f (ANAT)* pharynx.

farinha *f* flour; **~ de primeira** refined four; **~ de mandioca** cassava flour; **2 passar por ~** to coat sth with flour; IDIOM **separar a ~ do farelo** separate the wheat from the chaff.

farinheira *f* a kind of Portuguese sausage used in cooking.

farmacêutico,-a *m,f* chemist, pharmacist; ♦ *adj* pharmaceutical.

farmácia *f* chemist's (shop), pharmacy.

fármaco *m* chemical substance used as medicine.

farmacologia *f* pharmacology.

farnel *(pl: **farnéis**) m* packed lunch.

faro *m (cão)* sense of smell, scent; **2** *(fig) (intuição)* flair, nose, intuition.

farofa *f (CULIN)* Brazilian dish of manioc flour fried in lard or butter.

farófia *f (CULIN)* Portuguese sweet made with milk, sugar and the white of eggs.

farol *(pl: **faróis**) m* lighthouse; **2** *(AUTO)* headlight, head-lamp; **faróis de nevoeiro** *mpl (AUTO)* fog lights.

faroleiro,-a *m,f* lighthouse keeper.

farolete, farolim *m (AUTO)* car light; **~ dianteiro/traseiro** sidelight/rear light.

farpa *f* barb; **2** splinter; **uma ~ no dedo** a splinter in (the) finger; **3** tear.

farpado,-a *adj:* **arame ~** barbed wire.

farpão *m* harpoon.

farra *f* binge; frolic, spree; **andar na ~** to have a night out on the tiles, to paint the town red; **2** *(BR) (fig)* orgy; *(BR) (fam)* jest; **3** *(ZOOL) (peixe)* a kind of salmon.

farrapão *m (maltrapilho)* ragamuffin.

farrapo *m* rag, tatter; **2** shred; **em ~s** in tatters, in rags; **3** *(fig) (pessoa desolada)* shattered.

farripa *f* thin strand of hair; **2** straggly hair.

farrista *m* reveller; ♦ *adj inv (BR)* fun-loving person.

farrusco *adj (com fuligem)* sooty; *(sujo de carvão)* covered in coaldust; **2** *(escuro)* dark; **3** *(pop) (nome dado a gato)* sooty.

farsa *f (TEAT)* farce, satire; **2** *(fig)* farse, sham.

farsante *m,f* joker, buffoon; **2** *(intrujão)* fraud, impostor; ♦ *adj inv* lying; deceitful.

farta *adv:* **~ à** plenty, very much; **comer à ~** to eat plenty/eat to one's heart content; **diverti-me à ~** I enjoyed myself to the full; **ele riu-se à ~** he laughed like mad.

fartar *vt* to satiate, fill up; **2** to tire, sicken; ♦ **~-se** *vr* to gorge o.s.; **~ de** to get fed up with; to have had enough.

fartote *m (fam)* plenty, a lot, lots of; **foi um ~ de riso** it was laughing non-stop.

fartura *f* abundance, plenty; **2 ~s** *fpl (CULIN)* Portuguese sweet fritter.

fascículo *m (publicação)* fascicle; **2** *(plano)* instalment; **3** *(BOT)* fascicle.

fascinação *f* fascination.

fascinante *adj inv* fascinating; alluring; **2** amazing.

fascinar *vt* to fascinate; to charm, spellbind.

fascínio *m* fascination; **2** *(feitiço)* spell, magnetismo; **3** *(atração)* charm.

fascismo *m* fascism.

fascista *adj inv* fascist.

fase *f* phase; **2** stage; **3** *(FÍS)* state; ~ **líquida/sólida**, liquid/solid state.

fasquia *f (ripa)* lath, batten; **2** *(DESP) (para atletas)* bar.

fasquiar *vt* to place/use laths, battens; **2** to saw wood in strips; IDIOM **elevar demasiado a** ~ to demand way too much.

fastidioso,-a, fastiento,-a *adj* boring, wearisome.

> Not 'fastidious' as in 'hard to please'.

fastígio *m* peak, summit, apex; **2** *(fig)* height.

fastio *m* lack of appetite; **2** *(aversão)* disgust; **3** boredom.

fatal *adj* fatal; **2** fateful; **3** inescapable.

fatalidade *f* fate; **2** misfortune; **3** disaster.

fateixa *f (NÁUT)* grapnel.

fatela *adj* kitsch.

fatia *f (pão, fiambre, bolo)* slice; **2** *(CULIN)* ~ **dourada** a type of French toast; **3** *(fig)* share, portion, slice.

fatiar *vt* to cut in slices, to slice *(carne, pão)*.

fatídico,-a *adj* fateful.

fatigante *adj inv* tiring; tiresome.

fatigar *vt* to tire; to bore; ♦ ~-**se** *vr* to get tired.

fato *(Vd: fa(c)to); (BR) m* fact; **2** *(EP) m (roupa)* suit, ensemble; **3** ~ **de banho** swimsuit.

fato-macaco *m* overalls.

fator *(Vd: fa(c)tor).*

fátuo,-a *adj* fatuous, affected; **2** *(conversa)* silly; **3** *(brilho, glória)* fleeting, ephemeral.

fatura *(Vd: fa(c)tura).*

faúlha (fagulha) *f* spark; **2** *(pó fino da faúlha)* dust.

fauna *f* fauna.

fausto *m* pomp, luxury.

faustoso,-a *adj* pompous; **2** extravagant.

fava *f (planta, feijão)* broad bean; **mandar alguém à** ~ to send sb packing/to hell.

favela *f (BR)* slum, shanty town.

favo *m* honeycomb; **2** *(MED)* favus.

favor *m* favour *(UK)*, favor *(US)*; **a** ~ **de** in favour of; **por** ~ please; **faça o** ~ **de** ... would you be so good as to ... kindly ...; **dever** ~**es a alguém** to be obliged to someone, to owe favours.

favorável *adj inv* favourable *(UK)*; favourable *(US)*.

favorecer *vt* to favour.

favorecido,-a *m,f (dotado pelo nascimento) (alguém)* favoured, blessed; **2** *(protegido)* helped, protected; **3** *(melhorado) (alguém)* favoured *(em foto, espelho).*

favoritismo *m* favouritism *(UK)*; favoritism *(US)*, preference, partiality; **2** nepotism.

favorito,-a *adj* favourite.

faxina *f* brushwood, bundle of twigs/faggots; **2** *(MIL) (limpeza)* fatigue (on fatigue duty); **3** limpeza geral, spring-clean.

faxineira *f (BR)* hotel cleaner/porter; **2** cleaner; **3** *(MIL)* soldier on fatigue duty, kitchen duty.

faz-de-conta *m* make-believe; **2** *(BR) (marido enganado)* cuckold.

fazedor,-ora *m,f (criador)* maker; **os** ~**es de História** History-makers.

fazenda *f (grande quinta)* farm, plantation, ranch; **2** estate; **3** assets, property; **4** *(tecido)* ~ **de lã** woollen cloth; **loja de** ~**s** drapers; **5** *(finanças)* treasury; **Ministro da** ~ *m (BR)* Chancellor of the Exchequer.

fazendeiro *m (BR)* plantation-owner; rancher, ranch-owner.

fazer *vt (produzir, formular)* to make; **quantos vestidos faz essa companhia por ano?** how many dresses that company produces/turns out per year?; ~ **barulho** to make noise; **2** ~ **uma pergunta** to ask a question; **3** *(realizar)* ~ **a comida** to cook; ~ **compras** to do/go shopping; ~ **malha** to knit; ~ **as malas** to pack; **4** *(dever, cumprir, praticar)* to do; **faz o que te peço** do as I ask you; ~ **um favor** to do a favour; **eu não faço nada** I don't do anything; **faço ginástica todos os dias** I do exercises every day; **5** *(causar)* **fazer alguém chorar/rir** to make sb cry/laugh; **6** *(anos)* **ela faz anos no domingo e faz cinco anos** her birthday is on Sunday and she will be five years old; **7** *(soma cálculo)* to do; **fazer as contas** to sum up, to total; **8** *(fingir)* ~ **de conta que** to pretend; **9** *(representar)* to play *(de)* **ela fez de prostituta no filme** she played the role of a prostitute in the film; ♦ *vi (causar)* **fazer bem/mal a (alguém/ algo)** to be good/bad for sb/sth; **o tabaco faz mal à saúde** smoking is bad for one's health; **2** *(obrigar, persuadir)* **fazer com que** to make sb do sth, to see to it; **3** *(substituir)* ~ **as vezes de** to substitute; ~ **de** to act as; **4** *(notar)* ~ **caso de** to take notice of, to see to it that; **5** ~ **por** *(esforçar-se)* to make an effort to; ♦ **fazer amor** to make love; ~ **uma queixa** to complain; ~ **uma reclamação** to put in a claim; ~ **beicinho** to pout; **não faz mal** never mind; **tanto me faz** it's all the same (to me); ♦ *v. impess (tempo, duração)* ~ **sol/frio** to be sunny/cold; **faz um ano que** it is a year since; ♦ ~-**se** *vr* to do, become; **faz-se assim** one does it this way; tornar-se; **está a** ~-**se tarde** it is becoming late; ♦ ~-**se de** *(fingir)* to pretend to be, to feign; **ele faz-se de idiota** he pretends to be a fool; **ela faz-se de despercebida** she pretends not to understand; IDIOM ~ **render o peixe** to make sth go a long way; to take unnecessarily long time in doing some work; ~ **ouvidos de mercador** to pretend not to hear; **eu pedi-lhe dinheiro mas ele fez ouvidos de mercador** I asked him for money but (my request) fell on deaf ears/he turned a deaf ear.

fazível *adj inv* feasible; that can be made/done.

faz-tudo *m* jack of all trades, handyman.

fé *f* faith; belief; trust; **de boa/má** ~ in good/bad faith.

fealdade *f* ugliness.

febra *f* strength; **2** lean meat, meat without bones; **3** *(fig)* drive, will, muscle.

febre *f* fever; **2** *(fig)* excitement, thirst for; ~ **dos fenos** hay fever; ~ **palustre** malária.

febril *adj inv* feverish.

fecal *adj inv* faecal *(UK)*; fecal *(US)*.

fechado,-a *adj* shut, closed; **2** *(person)* reserved; **3** **noite** ~a well into the night; IDIOM ~ **a sete chaves** under lock and key.

fechadura *f* lock.

fechar *vt* to close, shut; **2** to finish, conclude *(negócio, contrato)*; **3** *(desligar)* to turn off; **4** ~ **à chave** to lock (up); **com ferrolho** to bolt; ♦ *vi* to close (up), shut; ♦ ~-**se** *vr* to close/shut o.s. off; **2** *(pessoa)* to withdraw; ~ **em copas** to clam up, keep mum (about sth); IDIOM **num abrir e ~ de olhos** in a twinkle of an eye.

fecho *m* *(roupa)* fastener; **2** ~ **éclair** zip fastener; **3** *(de porta)* latch; **4** *(fechadura)* lock; **5** *(ferrolho)* bolt; **6** *(no colar)* clasp; **7** *(fim, encerramento)* closure, closing; **8** *(negócio)* close down.

fécula *f* starch.

fecundar *vt* to fertilize, make fertile.

fecundo,-a *adj* fertile, fruitful; **2** *(fig)* productive; **3** *(fig)* *(artista)* creativo, prolific.

fedelho,-a *m,f (fam)* brat; **seu** ~! you little brat!

feder *vi (mau cheiro)* to stink, reek.

federação *f* federation.

federal *adj inv* federal.

federalismo *m* federalism.

federalista *adj inv* federalist.

federar *vt* to federate; **2** *(grupos)* conferate.

fedor *m* stench.

fedorento,-a *adj (mau odor)* stinking, smelly.

feérico,-a *adj* fairy-like; **2** magical, marvellous; **mundo** ~ make-believe world.

feição *f* form, shape; **2** nature; manner; **3** **à** ~ favourably; **feições** *(rosto) fpl* features.

feijão *m* bean; ~ **carrapato** green bean, runner bean; ~ **encarnado** kidney bean; ~-**frade** black-eye bean; ~ **manteiga** butter bean; IDIOM *(BR) (fig)* **não vale o ~ que come** not worth a bean.

feijoada *f (CULIN)* stew with various beans and pork meat.

Feijoada is a traditional dish from Oporto which was taken to Brazil, where it became its national dish. It is made with beans (the type of beans differs from one country to the other) stewed with pork, trotter, ear, streaky bacon, sausage, 'chouriço', vegetables.

feijoeiro *m (planta)* bean plant, bean stalk.

feio,-a *adj* ugly; **2** grim; **ser** ~ to be ugly; **estar** ~ to look ugly.

feira *f* fair; market; ~ **popular** funfair; **2** *(COM)* trade fair; **3** ~ **da ladra** flea market, car boot sale.

feitiçaria *f* witchcraft, magic.

feiticeiro,-a *m,f* wizard/witch; ♦ *adj* bewitching, enchanting.

feitiço *m* charm, spell.

feitio *m (tailhe)* shape, pattern, cut; **2** *(trabalho)* cutting, making; **de que** ~ **é o teu vestido?** which style is your dress?; **3** *(fig)* nature, manner, **ela tem mau feitio** she has a temper, she is nasty.

feito,-a *(pp irr de* **fazer**) *m (façanha)* act, deed, feat; ♦ *adj* finished, ready, made; ~ **à mão** handmade;

já ~ ready-made; **as malas estão** ~**as** the suitcases are done/ready; **2 homem** ~ grown man; **3** ~ **a** *(acostumado a)* to be used to; **4 isto é** ~ **com cuidado** this is done with much care; **5** *(alguém envolvido)* **ele anda** ~ **com a mulher do vizinho** he is involved (having an affair) with his neighbour's wife; **6 o que é** ~ **da Rita? Não a vejo há muito** what has become of Rita? I haven't seen her for a long time; ♦ *adv* **dito e** ~ no sooner said than done; **desta feita** this time; **de papo** ~ *(alguém)* puffed up; ♦ *exc* **feito!** done!; **é bem feito!** *(irónico)* it serves you right.

feitor,-ora *m,f* maker; **2** *(caseiro)* manager (of a farm); **3** foreman; administrator, steward.

feitoria *f* commercial establishment; **2** administration of land/revenue; **3** *(imposto)* tax.

feitura *f (acto de fazer)* making; doing; **a** ~ **de um jornal** the making of a newspaper.

feixe *m* bundle, bunch; sheaf; ~ **de lenha** fagot; *(TEC)* beam, ~ **de luz** a beam of light; IDIOM **ter os nervos num** ~ to be a bundle of nerves.

fel *m* bile, gall; **2** *(fig)* bitterness.

felação *f* fellatio.

felicidade *f* happiness; **2** good luck; **3** success; ~**s!** *fpl* congratulations!, wishing you much happiness!

felicíssimo,-a *m,f (superl de* **feliz**) *adj* extremely happy, overjoyed.

felicitações *fpl* congratulations, best wishes.

felicitar *vt* to congratulate; ♦ ~-**se** to congratulate o.s.

felino *m* feline.

felino,-a *adj (animal)* feline; **2** *(fig) (pessoa)* treacherous; **olhar** ~ sly look.

feliz *adj inv* happy; **2** fortunate; **3** successful.

felizardo,-a *m,f* very lucky person.

felizmente *adv* fortunately, luckily; **2** happily.

felonia *f* felony.

felpa *f (de tecido)* nap, fleece, fuzz; **2** *(de animal)* down.

felpudo,-a *adj* fuzzy, fleecy; **2** downy; **3** *(fruto)* furry.

feltro *m (recido)* felt.

fêmea *f (BIO, BOT)* female; woman.

feminino,-a *adj* feminine; **sexo** ~ female; **2** *(gram)* feminine.

feminismo *m* feminism.

feminista *adj inv* feminist.

fémur *(BR: -ê-)* femur.

fenda *f* slit, crack; **2** *(GEOL)* fissure.

fender *vt/vi* to split, crack.

fenecer *vi (morrer)* to die; **2** *(extinguir-se)* to die out; **3** *(acabar)* to come to an end, to finish; **4** *(murchar)* to wilt.

fenício,-a *adj* Phoenician.

fénico *m* phenol, carbolic acid.

fénix *f* phoenix.

feno *m (BOT)* hay.

fenomenal *adj inv* phenomenal; **2** amazing.

fenómeno *(BR: -ô-) m* phenomenon.

fera *f* wild animal/beast; **2** *(fig) (colérico)* brute.

féretro *m* coffin, urn.

feriado *m* (bank) holiday.

férias *fpl* holidays *(UK)*, vacation *sg (US)*; ♦ **de** ~ *adv* on holiday.

ferida *f* wound, injury; **2** *(fig)* **tocar na** ~ to re-open a wound, touch/hit a nerve.

ferido,-a *adj* wounded, injured; **2** ~ casualties, injured people.

ferimento *m* injury.

ferir *vt* to injure, wound; **2** *(fig)* to offend, hurt sb.

fermentar *vt* to ferment; **2** *(fig)* to excite; ♦ *vi* to ferment.

fermento *m* yeast; ~ **em pó** baking powder.

fero,-a *adj* fierce; **2** *(fig)* hot-tempered person.

ferocidade *f* fierceness, ferocity; **2** brutality, cruelty.

feroz *adj inv* *(animal, combate, pessoa)* fierce, ferocious; **2** *(acto)* cruel.

ferradela *f* *(mordedela, picada)* bite *(cão, insecto)*.

ferrado,-a *adj* *(cavalo)* shod; **2** *(calçado)* hobnailed; **3** stuck, gripped, nailed; **4** *(fig)* *(sem saída)* done for; **5** ~ **no sono** sound asleep.

ferrador *m* blacksmith.

ferradura *f* horseshoe.

ferragem *f* *(peças)* iron fittings, accessories; **2** ironmongery, ironware; **loja de** ~**s** hardware shop/store; **3** shoeing of the horses.

ferramenta *f* tool; **2** tool kit; **3** *(fig)* *(meio de)* tool, resource; **caixa de** ~**s** tool-box.

ferrão *m* *(de insecto)* sting; **2** *(de aguilhão)* barb, goad.

ferrar *vt* to spike; **2** *(cavalo)* to shoe; **3** *(marcar com ferro)* to brand; **4** *(cravar)* to thrust in (dente, unhas); **5** *(NÁUT)* *(vela)* to furl; ♦ *vi* to anchor; ♦ ~-**se** *vr* ~ **a dormir** to fall asleep; IDIOM ~ **o mono** to cheat; ~ **o galho** to nod off.

ferreiro *m* blacksmith, ironsmith; **2** *(ZOOL)* *(gaivão)* tern; *(peixe)* tree frog; IDIOM **em casa de** ~, **espeto de pau** the cobbler's son always goes barefoot.

ferrenho,-a *adj* iron-like; **2** *(fig)* inflexible, stubborn, uncompromising.

férreo,-a *adj* made of iron; **2** *(fig)* hard, intransigent; **3** ferrous.

ferrete *m* branding iron; **2** *(fig)* *(stigma)* stigma.

ferrinhos *mpl* *(MÚS)* triangle.

ferro *m* iron; **2** ~ **de passar** iron, **passar a roupa a** ~ to iron the clothes; **3** ~ **batido/forjado** wrought iron; ~ **fundido** cast iron; **4** *(NÁUT)* anchor, **levantar/lançar** ~ to raise/drop anchor; **5** ~**s** *mpl* shackles, chains; IDIOM **malhar em** ~ **frio** to knock your head against a brick wall; **ter uma vontade de** ~ to have an iron-will; **ter uma saúde de** ~ have a cast-iron health; **governar com mão de** ~ to rule with an iron rod.

ferroada *f* *(of insect)* sting; **2** *(fig)* *(mordaz)* sarcastic remark.

ferroar *vt* *(picar)* to sting; **2** *(criticar)* to criticize.

ferrolho *m* bolt; **fechar com** ~ to bolt.

ferro-velho *m* *(sucata)* scrapmetal; **2** *(lugar)* scrap-metal yard; **3** junk shop; **4** *(homem ambulante)* rag-and-bone man.

ferrovia *f* railway *(UK)*; railroad *(US)*.

ferrugem *f* rust; **2** *(BOT)* blight; **3** *(fig)* *(velhice)* **já tenho** ~ **nas articulações** my joints are now/have become rusty.

fértil *adj inv* fertile, fruitful, fecund.

fértilidade *f* fertility; fruitfulness.

fértilizante *m* fertilizer; ♦ *adj inv* fertilizing.

fértilizar *vt* to fertilize.

fervedor *m* boiler.

fervente *adj inv* boiling, fervent; **2** *(fig)* *(acalorado)* ardent; **3** *(fig)* eager, zealous.

ferver *vt* to boil; ♦ *vi* to boil, bring to the boil; **2** *(fig)* to seethe, to rage; **3** *(vinho)* *(boiling point)* to bubble; IDIOM ~ **em pouca água** to flare up about nothing.

> The dish 'boiled potatoes, fish, etc.' is translated by 'cozer' not 'ferver' e.g. **vou comer batatas cozidas e creio que elas já estão a ferver** I am going to have boiled potatoes and I think they are already boiling.

fervilhar *vi* to simmer; **2** *(multidão)* to swarm; **3** *(fig)* to overflow.

fervor *m* fervour.

fervoroso,-a *adj* fervent, ardent, passionate.

fervura *f* *(ebulição)* boiling, boiling point; **dar uma leve** ~ bring to a simmer; **2** *(fig)* effervescence, seething; IDIOM **deitar água na** ~ to pour oil on troubled waters.

festa *f* party, feast, festivity, festival; ~ **de anos** birthday party; **dia de** ~ public holiday; ~ **de arromba** great party; hell of a party *(coll)*; **3** *(carícia)* caress; **4** *(reunião)* gathering; **festas** *fpl* caresses; **fazer** ~**s ao gato** to pat the cat; ♦ *exc* Boas F ~**s!** Merry Christmas, Happy New Year; IDIOM **não estar para** ~ to be in a bad mood; **deitar foguetes antes da** ~ to count one's chickens before they are hatched; **fazer a** ~ **e deitar foguetes** to laugh at one's own jokes.

festança *f* *(fam)* big party, banquet; **2** merrymaking; **3** *(fam)* do, blowout, racket.

festão *(ADD)* *m* festoon, garland.

Festas *fpl* (~ **de Natal**; ~ **de Ano Novo**) festive season; ~ **dos Santos Populares** *(EP)*, ~ **Juninas** *(BR)* Popular religious festivities.

> **As festas dos Santos Populares**, known in Brazil as **Festas Juninas**, take place during the month of June: on the 13th we celebrate St Anthony of Lisbon; St John on the 24th and St Peter on the 29th. It is an ancient religious festival, which the Portuguese took to Brazil and other Portuguese-speaking countries. Nowadays, the festival has little of religion, but a lot of merriment: food and drink, bonfires and fireworks, with dancers in colourful costumes parading the streets until the small hours of the morning.

festejar *vt* to celebrate, commemorate.

festejo *m* festivity, celebration, feast.

festim *m* small party/banquet, repast; **2** family gathering; **3** *(diversão)* entertainment.

festinha *f* *(diminuitive; affective term of* **festa***)* little/small party; **2** caress; **fazer** ~ **s à criança** to caress the child; *(ao animal)* to stroke.

festival *n* *(event)* festival; **os** ~ **de música** *mpl* music festivals.

festividade *f* festivity.

festivo,-a *adj* festive.

fetal *adj inv* foetal.

fetiche *m* fetish; **2** *(amuleto)* charm.

fétido,-a *adj* foul; **2** rotten; **3** *(cheiro)* fétido, stinking.

feto *m (MED)* foetus; **2** *(BOT)* fern.

feudal *adj inv* feudal; **~ism** *m* feudalism.

feudo *m* feud.

fêvera *f (carne)* lean meat.

Fevereiro, fevereiro *m* February.

fez[1] *(pret de fazer)* ele ~ os possíveis he did all he could.

fez[2] *m* Turkish cap, tarboosh.

Fez[3] *npr* Moroccan city.

fezes *fpl (de animais)* excrement *sg*; *(de pessoas)* faeces *(US)* feces; *(gíria médica)* stools; **2** *(borras)* dregs, sediment.

fiabilidade *f* reliability, credibility.

fiação *f* spinning; **fábrica de ~** textile mill; **2***(ELECT)* wiring; **fazer a ~** to wire sth.

fiada *f (série)* course; **2** *(fila)* line, row.

fiado,-a *m,f* on credit; **comprar/vender ~** to buy/sell on credit; **aqui não se vende ~** no sale on credit/ we don't sell on tick *(fam)*; **2 ~a** *f* row, line, yarn; **uma ~ de carros** a row/line of cars; **uma ~ de estórias** a string of tales; **conversa ~** *(pop)* a tall story, far-fetched story; ♦ *adj* threaded, spun; **2** trusting.

fiador,-ora *m,f (JUR)* guarantor; **2** *(COM)* backer, sponsor.

fiambre *m* ham.

fiança *f* surety, guarantee; **2** *(JUR)* bail; **prestar ~ por** to stand bail for; **3** trust; **4** guarantee, proof.

fiapo *m* thread; **2** *(cabelo)* thin strand of hair; **3** *(tecido)* rag, shred.

fiar *vt* to spin; **2** to wire; **3** entrust; **4** to sell on credit; ♦ **~-se** *vr*: **~ em** to trust sth, sb.

fiasco *m* fiasco.

fibra *f* fibre; **2** filament; **3** strand; **4** *(fig)* guts.

fibroma *(MED) (tumor)* fibroma, fibrous tumour.

fibromialgia *f* fibromyalgia.

fibrose *f (MED)* fibrosis, fibrositis.

fibroso,-a *adj (tecido)* fibrous.

ficar *vi* remain, be situated, to be; **as chaves ficam aqui** the keys are here; **fico aqui** I shall remain here; **fico à tua espera** I shall remain/be waiting for you; **o banco fica ali** the bank is over there; **2** to stay; remain; **~ fora** to stay out; **~ em casa** to stay at home; **eles vão ~ conosco** they will stay/be staying with us; **~ atrás** to stand behind; **3** *(tornar-se)* to become; **a menina ficou doente** the little girl became ill; **~ escuro** to grow dark; **~ surdo/cego** to go/grow deaf/blind; **~ com** to be, become; **~ com medo** to be afraid; **fiquei contente com as tuas notícias** your news made me happy; **4 ~ com** *(guardar, adquirir)* to be left with, to keep; obter; **fico com a tua mala** I'll keep your bag; **ele ficou com a casa** he acquired the house next door; **5 ~ para** *(ser adiado)* to leave (it) for/until; **fica para trás** to be left behind; to lag behind; to stay for; **não queres ~ para almoço**

don't you want to stay for lunch?; **6 ~ para** *(durar)* to last; **as nossas memórias ficam para sempre** our memories will last forever; **7 ~ bom** *(de doença)* to recover; **8 ~ bem** *(assentar a alguém)* **~ bem** to look good (on sb); **essa cor fica-te bem** that colour becomes you, is good on you; **9** *(condizer)* to go well with; **a saia fica bem com o casaco** the skirt goes well with the coat; **10 ficar por** to stand/to be; *(JUR)* **~ por fiador de** to stand surety for *(alguém)*; to put up bail for; **11** *(ser)* to be; **isso não fica bem assim** that is not right; **12** *(estar, sentir)* to be, to feel; **~ triste/contente** to be sad/happy; **~ atónito** *(de surpresa, choque)* to be flabbergasted; **13** *(insistir)* to stick to; **tu ficas na tua e eu na minha** you have your opinion and I stick to mine; **14** *(do well)* **ele ficou bem no exame** he passed his exam; ♦ **~-se** *vr* to stop short, give up; **2** to restrain o.s.; **3** to end, die; **ele ficou-se no sono** he died in his sleep; **4 ~ por** *(em algum lado)* to settle; **ele ficou-se pelo Brasil** he settled in Brazil; IDIOM **~ de cara à banda** to be gobsmacked; **os planos ficaram em águas de bacalhau** *(frustrado)* the plans went down the drain.

ficção *f* fiction, falsehood; **2** *(livro, filme)* fiction, novel.

ficcionista *m,f* storyteller; fiction writer.

ficha *f (formulário)* form; **preencher a ~** to fill in the form; **2** card; **~ de arquivo** card index; **3** *(de jogo)* chip; **4** *(identificação)* voucher, token; *(com número)* ticket; **5** *(dados pessoais)* dossier, record; **6** *(ELECT)* plug.

fichar *vt* to file, record on index cards; *(BR)* **fazer a ~ de** to put on file; **2** to register.

ficheiro *(BR: fichário) m* filing cabinet; **2** index card, file; **3 ~ de autores** registry; **4** *(jogos)* cashier; **5** *(COMP)* file; folder.

fictício,-a *adj* fictitious.

fidalgo,-a *m,f* nobleman/lady, aristocrat; ♦ *adj* noble, titled; **2** grand, distinguished, dignified; **3** *(fig)* fussy; **mas que ~ que você é!** what a fusspot you are!; IDIOM **~ de quatro costados** full blue blooded nobleperson; **~ de meia tigela** upstart.

fidedigno,-a *adj* trustworthy, reliable; **fonte ~** reliable source.

fidelidade *f* loyalty; **2** exactness.

fiduciário,-a *m,f (JUR)* trustee; ♦ *adj* fiduciary.

fieira *f (fio)* thread; string; **2** *(MIN)* vein.

fiel *adj inv* faithful; **2** accurate; **3** reliable.

fiel *(pl: fiéis) m,f* **os fiéis** *(REL)* the faithful; ♦ *adj inv* faithful.

fielmente *adv* faithfully.

fífia *f (MÚS) (som, nota)* discordant sound; **2** *(fig)* blunder.

figa *f* amulet *(em forma de mão fechada, com o polegar entre os dedos)*; **2 mulher duma ~** a heck of a woman; **3 fazer ~s a** to ward off evil eye *(by putting thumb between two fingers)*; **4 não vale uma ~** it's worth nothing.

fígado *m (ANAT)* liver; **2 de maus ~s** bad-tempered, vindictive.

figo *m (BOT)* fig.

figueira *f* fig tree.

figura *f* figure; **2** shape; **3** *(LING)* ~ **de retórica** figure of speech; **4** *(famoso)* personality; **5** *(GEOM)* symbol; IDIOM **fazer ~s tristes** to cut a sad figure, to make scenes; **fazer ~ de parvo/ idiota** to make a fool of o.s.

figura-chave *(pl: figuras-chave)* *f* key-figure.

figurado,-a *adj (metafórico)* figurative; **em sentido** ~ in a figurative sense.

figurante *m,f (cinema)* extra.

figurão-ona *m (pessoa importante)* big shot, bigwig; **2** *(finório)* toff; IDIOM **fazer um** ~ to cut a fine figure.

figurar *vt* to figure; **2** to represent, symbolize; **3** to look like; ♦ *vi* to depict; **2** to feign; **3** to appear; **4** ~ **em** to act in; **5** ~ **entre/em** to appear on/ among; ♦ **~-se** *vr (imaginar-se)* to imagine o.s.; **não me figura eu ser o campeão** I can't see myself as a champion.

figurativo,-a *adj* figurative; illustrative; pictorial.

figurinista *m,f* clothes designer; **2** *(TEAT, CIN)* costume designer, film set designer.

figurino *m (modelo, manequim)* model; **2** *(molde)* pattern, example model; **3** *(revista)* fashion magazine, pattern book.

FIL *(abr de* **Feira Internacional de Lisboa***)* Lisbon International Fair.

fila *f* row, line; **2** queue; ~ **indiana** single file; **3 cão de** ~ guard dog, mastiff.

filamento *m (FÍS)* filament; **2** fibre; **3** thread.

filantrópico,-a *adj* philanthropic.

filantropo,-a *m,f* philanthropist, benefactor.

filão *m (GEOL)* vein, seam; streak; **2** *(fig)* ~ **de riqueza** source of wealth.

filar *vt* to seize, catch, capture; **2** *(fam)* to cadge, nab; **3** *(BR) (jogo)* to cheat (by peeping).

filarmónica *f* philharmonic.

filarmónico,-a *(BR: -ô-) adj* philharmonic.

filatelia *f* philately.

filatelista *m,f* philatelist, stamp collector.

filé *m* steak; fillet.

fileira *f* file, row, line; ♦ **~s** *fpl (MIL)* ranks.

filete *m (fiozinho)* trickle *(de água, azeite);* **2** *(espiral do parafuso)* thread (of a screw); **3** *(linha fina)* rim, border; **4** *(ANAT)* fibre, filament; **5** *(ARQ)* fillet, moulding; **6** *(TIPO)* rule; **7** *(CULIN)* thin steak; *(de peixe)* filet.

filha *f* daughter.

filharada *f* many children; **2** brood.

filhó *f sg, pl (CULIN)* sweet fritter, *traditionally eaten at Christmas.*

filho,-a *m,f* son/daughter; ~ **único** only son; ~ **pri- mogénito** *m* first-born child; **2** *(ZOOL)* offspring, pup, cub; **3** ~ **de criação** foster son; **4** **~s** *mpl* sons, children; citizens; ~ **ilustres da cidade** the town's illustrious citizens; **5** *(consequência)* resul- tado, product; **6** *(pop)* ~ **da mãe** son of a gun, creep; *(cal)* ~ **da puta** son of a bitch.

filhote *m* young; **2** offspring; **3** pup(py); cub.

filiação *f (pais)* filiation; **2** *(grupo)* affiliation.

filial *f (COM)* branch; ♦ *adj inv (amor)* filial.

Filipinas *fpl:* **as** ~ the Philippines.

filmagem *f* filming; **estar em** ~ to be shooting.

filmar *vt* to film.

filme *m* film, movie; ~ **mudo** silent film; ~ **de longa metragem** full-length film; ~ **de suspense/policial** thriller; **2** *(FOTO) (rolo)* film; **revelar um** ~ to develop a film.

filosofia *f* philosophy.

filósofo,-a *m,f* philosopher.

filtrar *vt* to filter; ♦ **~-se** *vr* to filter; to infiltrate.

filtro *m* filter.

fim *m* end; conclusion; **2** aim, purpose, objective; **ter por** ~ to aim at; **3** *(final)* end, closing, close; **ao ~ da manhã** late in the morning; **ao** ~ **do mês** at the end of the month; **pôr um** ~ **a** to put an end to; **o** ~ **justifica os meios** the end justifies the means; **4** *(ponta)* extremidade; **no** ~ **da rua** at the end of the street; **5** limit; **isto é o** ~ this is the limit; **6;** **~s** *mpl:* **nos fins de Maio** towards the end of May; ♦ *prep* **a** ~ **de** in order to; **sem** ~ endless; ♦ *adv* **por** ~ finally; **no** ~ **de contas** after all; **ao** ~ **e ao cabo** when all is said and done; ♦ *conj* **a** ~ **de que** so that, in order to; IDIOM **ele vive no** ~ **de mundo** he lives in the back of beyond.

fimbria *f (franja)* fringe; **2** *(orla)* hem *(da saia).*

fim-de-semana, fim de semana *m* weekend.

finado,-a *adj* deceased; **dia de ~s** All Souls' Day.

final *m* end; **2** *(última etapa)* end, epilogue, finale; **3** *(MÚS) f* finale; **4** *(DESP) f* final; **chegar à** ~ to get into/reach the finals; **5** *(desfecho)* closing, ending; ♦ *adj inv* final, last, closing; **ponto** ~ final stop; **2** *(derradeiro)* last, ultimate; IDIOM **pôr um ponto** ~ **no assunto** to bring the subject to an end, over and done with.

finalidade *(propósito)* purpose, aim, goal.

finalista *m,f* student in his/her final year; **2** *(DESP)* finalist.

finalizar *vt* to conclude; **2** *(FUT) (goal)* to score.

finalmente *adv* finally, at last.

finanças *fpl* finance *sg;* **Ministro das F~** *(EP)* the Chancellor of the Exchequer.

financeiro,-a *m,f* financier; ♦ *adj (mercado)* financial.

financiamento *m* financing.

financiar *vt* to finance, to fund.

financista *m,f (BR)* financier, banker.

finar-se *vr* to waste away; **2** to die.

finca-pé *m* stubbornness; **fazer** ~ stick to one's guns, put one's foot down.

fincar *vt* to dig into, stick into *(dedos, pés);* in; **2** to fix.

findar *vt/vi* to end, finish.

fineza *f* fineness; **2** kindness, favour; **faça a** ~ **de me dizer** be so kind as to tell me; ~ **de espírito** a fine, shrewd mind.

fingimento *m* pretence.

fingir *vt* to feign; ♦ *vi* to pretend; ♦ **~-se** *vr:* ~ **de** pretend to be.

finito *m* finite; ♦ **finito,-a** *adj* finite.

finlandês,-esa *m,f* Finn; *(LÍNG) m* Finnish; ♦ *adj* Finnish.

Finlândia *npr* Finland; **a** ~ Finland.

fino,-a *adj (requintado)* fine, delicate, elegant; **agora é ~ beber chá na caneca** nowadays it is elegant to drink tea out of a mug; **rosto ~** fine features; **2** slender; thin; **lábios ~s** thin lips; **3** *(lugar)* smart; **4** well-bred, distinguished; **ela é uma senhora muito fina** she is a very distinguished lady; **5** *(voz, dor)* shrill, sharp.

finório,-a *adj (espertalhão)* crafty, sly.

finura *f* fineness; slenderness; **2** *(delicadeza)* finesse; lightness; **3** *(agudeza)* wit.

fio *m (fibra)* thread; **2** string, twine; **3** *(ELECT)* wire; **de dois ~s** two-ply; **4** *(de pesca)* line; **5** *(fig) (gota)* trickle, drop; **deita o azeite ~ a ~** pour the olive oil drop a drop; **6** *(para o pescoço)* chain; **um ~ de ouro** a gold chain; **7 um ~ de contas** a string of beads; **8** *(fig) (gume)* edge, blade; **o ~ da faca** the edge of the knife; **9** *(de feijão)* string; **tirar o ~ aos feijões** to string the green beans; **10** *(líquido)* trickle; **11 um ~ de esperança** a ray of hope; ◆ **a ~** *adj (dias, horas)* on end, without stopping; ◆ **por um ~** *adv* by a thread; **escapei por ~** I escaped by a thread; **estar por um ~** hang by a thread, imminent; **em ~** in a stream; IDIOM **de fio a pavio** *(relato)* from the beginning to the end; **perder o ~ à meada** to lose the thread of conversation.

fio-de-prumo, fio de prumo *m* plumb line.

fiorde *m* fjord, fiord.

firma *f* signature; **2** *(COM)* firm, company.

firmar *vt* to secure; **2** to make firm; **3** to sign; **4** to undersign; **5** to base sth on sth; ◆ **~-se** *vr*: **~ em** to rest on, be based on.

firme *adj inv* firm; **2** stable; **3** solid; **4** steady; **5** *(colour)* fast; **6** resolute, determined; *(fig)* **estou ~ na minha decisão** I won't budge from my decision.

firmeza *f* firmness; stability; steadiness.

fiscal *m,f* supervisor; **2** customs officer; **3** tax inspector; **4 paraíso ~** tax haven.

fiscalizar *vt* to supervise; **2** to inspect, check.

fisco *m (impostos)* tax; **não tem de declarar ao ~** you don't have to declare to the taxman; **fuga ao ~** tax evasion.

fisga *f (para apanhar peixe)* harpoon; **2** *(para apanhar pássaros)* sling, catapult; **3** *(frincha)* crack, chink.

fisgar *vt (peixe, pássaros)* to harpoon, catch; **2** *(fig) (perceber)* to perceive, catch on; **3** *(fig, fam)* **~ a esposa** to catch/hook a wife.

físico,-a *m,f* physicist; **2** *f* physics, *sg*; **3** *m (corpo)* physique, build; ◆ *adj* physical.

fisiologia *f* physiology.

fisiológico,-a *adj* physiological.

fisiologista *adj inv* physiologist.

fisionomia *f* physiognomy.

fisionómico,-a *adj* physiognomic(al).

fisioterapeuta *m,f* physiotherapist.

fisioterapia *f* physiotherapy.

fisioterápico,-a *adj* physiotherapeutical.

fissão *f (FÍS) (ruptura, cisão)* fission.

fissura *f (greta)* crack, split, chink, cleft; **2** *(MED)* fissure; **~ anal** anal fissure.

fístula *f (MED)* fistula; **~ gástrica** gastric fistula; **2** *(flauta pastoril)* flute, reed, pipe; **3** *(BR) (de mau carácter)* bad guy.

fita *f* strip, band; **2** ribbon; **3** tape; **~ métrica** tape measure; **4 ~-cola/colante** Sellotape, sticking tape *(UK)*, *(US)* Scotch tape; **5 ~ elástica** rubber band; **6 ~ virgem** blank tape; **7** scene, **fazer uma ~** to make a scene; **8** *(filme)* film.

fitar *vt* to stare at.

fito,-a *m* aim, intention, target; ◆ *adj* fixed.

fivela *f (de cinto, sapato)* buckle.

fixador *m* fixative; **2** *(para o cabelo)* hair spray; **3** *(FOTO)* **~ de imagem** fixing bath.

fixar *vt* to fix; **2** to stick, fasten; **3** to set; **4** to concentrate on; **~ os olhos em** to stare at; **~ residência** to set up house; ◆ **~-se** *vr* to settle down **(em** in).

fixe *adj inv (pop) (cor, etc)* fixed; **2** *(algo)* nice; **3** *(alguém)* reliable, nice.

fixo,-a *adj* fixed; firm; **2** *(cor)* fast; **3** *(residência)* settled; **4** *(emprego)* stable.

fiz *(pret, 1ª de fazer)* **eu não fiz** I didn't do (it).

fizer *(fut subj de fazer)* **faça o que fizer** whatever you do.

fizesse *(imperf subj de: fazer)* **se você ~ isso** … if you did that …

flácido,-a *adj (músculo)* flabby; **2** *(gesto)* languid, flagging.

flagelar *vt (açoitar)* to flagellate, flog, whip; ◆ **~-se** *vr* to chastise o.s.

flagelo *m* scourge; **2** torment; **estar num ~** be very agitated/worried.

flagrante *adj inv* flagrant; **apanhar em ~** to catch red-handed.

flamejante *adj inv* flaming; blazing; **2** sparkling.

flamejar *vi* to blaze; **2** sparkle.

flamenco *m, adj (bailado)* flamenco.

flamengo *m (LING)* Flemish.

flamengo,-a *adj* Flemish.

flamingo *m (ZOOL)* flamingo.

flâmula *f* small flame; **2** *(NÁUT)* pennant, bunting.

flanar *vi* to stroll; **2 roupa para ~** casual clothes.

flanco *m* flank; **2** side; **3** wing.

flanela *f (tecido)* flannel.

flanquear *vt* attack in the flank; **2** to flank; **3** go alongside.

flash-*back* *(pl: **flash-backs**) m* flash-back.

flatulência *f (MED)* flatulence; **2** *(fig)* presumption.

flatulento,-a *adj* flatulent; **2** *(fig)* presumptious, pretentious.

flauta *f* flute; **~ transversa** transverse flute.

flautear *vt* to flute; **2** *(fam)* to amuse o.s.

flautim *m* piccolo.

flautista *m,f* flute player.

flecha *f* arrow; **2** dart; **arco e ~** bow and arrow; **3** *(ARQ)* spire; ◆ **em ~** *adv (ECON, COM) (aumento, redução)* steeply.

flechada *f (BR)* arrow shot; **2** arrow wound.

fleu(g)ma *f* phlegm; **2** *(fig)* indifference, detachment.

fleu(g)mático,-a *adj* phlegmatical.

flexão *f (músculos)* flexing, flexion; **2 fazer flexões** to do push-ups; **3** *(LÍNG)* inflection.

flexibilidade *f* flexibility.
flexível *adj inv* flexible.
flipar *vt (col)* to flip out; go berserk.
flippers *mpl (jogo electrónico)* pinball.
floco *m (de neve)* snowflake; ~ **de milho** cornflake; ~ **de espuma/sabão** suds; ~ **de nuvens** wisps of clouds.
flor *f* flower; **2** bloom; **3** cream; **em** ~ in bloom; **a fina** ~ the cream, the elite; **à** ~ **de** on the surface of; **4 estar na** ~ **da idade** to be in one's prime; **5** ~ **de estufa** a delicate flower; **6** ~**-de-lis** *(BOT)* fleur-de-lis, lily; *(HERALD)* fleur-de-liz.
flora *f* flora; *(MED)* ~ **intestinal** intestinal floral.
floração *f* blossoming, flowering.
floreado,-a *adj (adorno, enfeite)* flowcry; florid; overwrought.
florear *vt* to embellish.
floreio *m* **florish; floreira** *f* **flower vase.**
Florença *f* Florence.
florescência *f* florescence; **2** *(fig)* brilliance; **3** *(BOT)* blooming, flowering.
florescente *adj inv (planta)* in flower, blooming; **2** *(prosperous)* thriving.
florescer *vt (dar flor)* to blossom, to come into bud; **2** *(fig) (prosperar)* to flourish; to prosper.
floresta *f* forest; ~ **virgem** *f* primeval forest.
florestal *(pl: -ais) adj inv* forest; **guarda** ~ forrester; **incêndio** ~ forest fire.
florestar *vt* to afforest.
florete *m (esgrima)* foil.
floricultor-ora *m,f* flower grower, floriculturist.
florid *adj (em flor)* in bloom; **2** florid.
florir *vt/vi* to flower, blossom; **2** *(fig)* to thrive, develop.
fluência *f* fluency.
fluente *adj inv* fluent.
fluido,-a *m* fluid; ♦ *adj* fluid.
fluir *vi* to flow.
flúor *m (QUÍM)* fluorite.
fluorescente *adj inv* fluorescent; **lâmpada** ~ fluorescent light.
fluoreto *m (QUÍM)* fluorite.
flutuação *f* fluctuation; **2** float, floating.
flutuante *adj inv* floating; **2** *(ao vento)* fluttering; **3** *(FIN) (preço)* fluctuating.
flutuar *vi* to float; **2** to fluctuate; **3** to flutter; **a bandeira flutuava ao vento** the flag fluttered in the wind; **4** *(fig)* to hesitate.
fluvial *adj inv* fluvial; **estação** ~ river port, embankment station/port.
fluxo *m* flow; **2** *(ELECT)* flux; **3** ~**grama** *f* flowchart.
fobia *f* phobia.
fóbico,-a *adj* phobic.
foca *f (ZOOL)* seal; **2** *(pop) (pessoa gorda)* whale; **3** *(pop) (sovina)* skinflint; **4** *(BR) m,f (jornalista)* cub reporter.
focado *adj inv* stressed; **2** in focus.
focagem *f* focus.
focal *adj inv* focal.
focalizar *vt,* **focar** *vt* to focus (on); **2** to concentrate (on).

focinho *m* snout; *(cão)* muzzle; **2** *(col) (face)* mug, **dou-lhe um murro no** ~ I'll punch you on the mug.
foco *m* focus; **2** light, **3** *(projector)* spotlight.
foda *f (vulg)* fuck.
foder *vt/vi (copular)* to fornicate, copulate; *(vulg)* fuck *(alguém)*; **2** *(fig) (lixar, prejudicar)* to fuck *(alguém)*; **3** *(fig) (fazer mau trabalho)* to fuck up, screw up *(plano, negócio)*; ♦ *exc (vulg)* **foda-se!** fuck you!

This word is not used in Portuguese as casually as it is in English.

fofinho,-a *adj* cuddly; **2** *(fam) (pessoa)* plump and cuddly.
fofo,-a *m (tufo de vestuário)* puff, frill; ♦ *adj (cama, almofada, brinquedo)* soft; *(bolo)* spongy; **2** *(fig) (meigo, bonito)* cuddly, cute, lovely.
fofoca *f(BR) (pop)* gossip.
fofoqueiro,-a *m,f* gossip-monger, gossiper; ♦ *adj* gossipy.
fogagem *f (borbulhagem)* pimples, spots, rash.
fogão *m* stove, cooker; **o** ~ **tem 4 bicos** the cooker has four burners.
fogareiro *m* little stove *(made of clay, iron)*; ~ **a petróleo** paraffin burner.
foge *(pres ind 3ª pessoa de* **fugir***)* **ela** ~ **daqui** she runs/is running from here.
fogo *m* fire; **2** *(fig)* ardour; **a** ~ **lento** on a low flame; **abrir** ~ *vt (disparar)* to open fire; **apagar um** ~ to put out the fire; **lançar** ~ **a** to set fire to; **pegar** ~ to catch fire; ♦ ~**s** *mpl* **habitacionais** housing; council housing ♦ ~ **posto** *m* arson; **à prova de** ~ fireproof.
fogo-de-artifício *m* fireworks.
fogo-de-vista *m* fireworks; **2** *(fig)* hot air, show-off.
fogo-fátuo *m* will-o'-the-wisp; **2** *(fig)* flash in the pan.
fogoso,-a *adj* fiery; passionate.
fogueira *f* bonfire; **morrer na** ~ to be burnt at the stake, to die on the pyre; **saltar à** ~ to jump over the bonfire.
foguetão *m (AER)* rocket; **2** *(pirotecnia)* rocket.
foguete *m (pirotecnia, projéctil)* rocket; **2** *(fig, fam)* dynamic person; ♦ *adj inv (pessoa)* lively; **2** *(transporte, visita)* fast, quick; IDIOM **não deites** ~**s antes da festa** don't count your chickens before they're hatched.
foi *(pret 3ª pessoa sg de* **ir, ser***)* **ele** ~ **amável** he was kind; **você** ~ **às compras?** did you go shopping?
foice *f* scythe.
folclore *m* folklore.
folclórico,-a *adj* folkloric.
fole *m* bellows *pl*; **2** *(pop)* stomach.
fôlego *m* breath; **2** *(fig)* courage; **perder o** ~ to lose one's breath.
foleiro,-a *adj (col)* tasteless; tacky.
folga *f* rest, break; **dia de** ~ rest day, day off *(trabalho)*; **estou de** ~ I am off work; **2** fun, frolic.
folgado,-a *adj* easy-going, relaxed; **agora estou mais** ~ I have more time for leisure/to spare now;

2 *(boa vida)* easy, comfortable; **3** *(roupa)* loose, slack; **4** *(BR) (fam)* cheeky.

folgar *vt* to loosen, slacken; ♦ *vi* to rest; **2** to have fun; **3** to be pleased; **folgo muito que esteja melhor!** I am so happy you are better!

folgazão,-ona *m,f* merry-maker, reveller; **2** idler.

folha *f (BOT)* leaf; foliage; **uma ~ de alface** a leaf of lettuce; **2** *(papel)* sheet; page; **~ branca** blank sheet of paper; **~ de pagamento** payroll, payment sheet; **3** *(jornal)* newspaper; **~ de rosto** cover page; **4** *(chapa)* plate, blade; sheet; **~ de alumínio** aluminium foil; **~ de ouro** gold leaf; **~ de estanho** tinfoil; **5** veneer; ♦ *adv* **a ~s tantas** suddenly, at one point; IDIOM **novo em ~** brand new.

folha-de-flandres, folha de flandres *f* tin plate.

folhado *m (CULIN)* puff pastry; **2 folhado,-a** *adj* *(árvores) (muitas folhas)* leafy.

folhagem *f* foliage.

folheado *m* veneer; ♦ *adj (mobília)* veneered, laminated; **2 ~ a ouro** covered with gold leaf; **3 massa ~a** puff pastry.

folhear *vt* to leaf through, to turn the page; **2** *(mobília)* to veneer; **3** to plate; **4** to cover with.

folheta *f* small leaf; **2** tin-plate.

folhetim *m (texto)* serial; **2** *(TV)* soap opera, sit-com.

folhetinista *m,f* writer of serials.

folheto *m* booklet, pamphlet, brochure

folhinha *f* leaflet; newsletter.

folho *m (guarnição de vestido)* frill, ruffle, trimming.

folia *f* revelry, frolic; **2** entertainment; **andar na ~** to lead a life of revelry/fun, paint the town red.

folião,-iona *m,f* reveller; ♦ *adj* revelling, fun-loving.

folículo *m* follicle, cavity; **~ dentário** dental cavity; **~ piloso** hair follicle.

fólio *m* folio.

fome *f* hunger, starvation; **passar ~** go hungry, starve; **ter ~** be hungry; **2** *(míngua)* famine; **3** *(ambição)* greed; **~ de poder** hunger for power; IDIOM **estou a morrer de ~** I am famished, starving; **passar ~ de rabo** to starve.

fomentar *vt* to instigate, promote, foment, encourage.

fomento *m* fomentation; **2** *(estímulo)* encouragement.

fona *m,f* miser, penny-pincher; ♦ *adj inv* stingy, miserly, mean; ♦ *adv* in a hurry, be busy; **andar numa ~** to go around in hurry, on the move.

fonador,-ora *adj* phonic, acoustic; **2** *(aparelho)* speech apparatus.

fonema *m* phoneme.

fonética *f* phonetics.

fonético,-a *adj* phonetic.

fónico,-a *adj* phonic.

fonoaudiólogo,-a *m,f* speech therapist.

fonte *f (nascente)* spring; **2** fountain; **3** *(origem)* source; **4** *(ANAT)* temple; **de ~ limpa/fidedigna** from a reliable source.

for *(fut subj de* ir, ser*)* **se eu ~ ao Brasil** if I go to Brazil.

fora[1] *(pluperf of* ir, ser*)* **ele ~ um grande homem** he had been a great man.

fora[2] *adv (na rua)* out, outside; **2** *(no exterior)* **ele está ~** he is away, out, abroad; **jantei ~** I dined

out; **3 de ~** from the outside; **4 ficar de ~** *(sem participar)* to be left out; **5 deitar a língua de ~** to stick one's tongue out; **6** *(lixo)* out/away; **deitar ~ jogar/botar ~** *(BR and EP Prov)* throw out/away; ♦ *adv* **de dentro para ~** from the inside out; **por ~** on/from outside, on the surface; **por aí ~** and so on; **por esse mundo ~** all over the world; **para ~** out; **ele trabalha para ~** he takes work in; **comida para ~** take-away food; **estar de ~** *(assunto)* to be left out, to be in the dark; ♦ *prep* except for, apart from; **2 ~ de si** furious, beside o.s.; **3 ~ da questão** out of the question; **4 ~ de brincadeiras** no joking; **5 ~ de moda** old-fashioned; **6 ~ do prazo** expired; ♦ *exc* **fora!** out!; *(fam)* piss off!; *(BR)* **dar o ~** *m* gaffe; IDIOM *(BR)* gaffe; **dar um ~** to commit a gaffe; **dar um ~ em alguém** to rebuff sb; **dar o ~** *(partir)* to get out, to skedaddle.

fora da lei *m,f* outlaw; ♦ *adj inv* outside the law, illegal.

fora-de-estrada *adj* off the road.

fora-de-jogo *m, sg/pl (DESP)* *(infracção)* off-side; *adj inv (jogador)* off-side.

foragido,-a *m,f* fugitive; ♦ *adj (refugiado)* refugee.

foral *m (arc) (document in which the king granted privileges and registered/administered the regions)* charter.

forasteiro,-a *adj* stranger; **2** foreigner; **3** traveller.

forca *f* gallows *pl*.

força *f* strength, energy; **~ de expressão** understatement; **2** *(TEC, ELECT, FÍS)* power; **~ de vontade** will-power; **3** *(esforço)* effort; **4** *(pressão)* force, pressure; **5 ~s** *(MIL)* forces, troop; **~s armadas** *fpl* armed forces; ♦ *prep, adv* **à ~** by force; at all costs; **à ~ de** by dint of, by means of; **a toda a ~** full out, full power; **com ~** violently; **por ~ de** of necessity; **pela ~ de** by the force of; ♦ *exc* **força!** *(levando algo pesado)* heave! come on!

forcado *m* pitchfork.

forçado,-a *adj* forced, coerced; **2** false; **3** *(ideia)* far-fetched; **4 trabalho ~** forced labour; **5 riso ~** artificial laughter.

forçar *vt* to force, compel, coerce; **2** *(fechadura)* to break in, break open; ♦ **~-se** *vr:* **~ a** to force o.s. to.

forceps *nsg/pl* forceps.

forçosamente *adv* categorically; **2** definitely.

forçoso,-a *adj* necessary; **2** forceful.

forja *f* forge.

forjar *vt* to forge.

forma[1] [ó] *f* form; *(silhueta)*, shape, figure; **2** manner; **3** *(MED)* fitness; **4 desta ~** in this way; ♦ *adv* **de qualquer ~** anyway; **2 da mesma ~** similarly, likewise; **3 de outra ~** otherwise; **4 de ~ alguma** not at all; ♦ *conj* **de ~ que** so that.

forma[2] [ô] *f (CULIN: molde)* mould; **2 ~ de sapateiro** last; **3 ~ de chapéu** block.

formação *f* formation; **2** training; **3** background; **4** development, growth; **5** education.

formado,-a *m,f* graduate; ♦ *adj* formed; **ser ~ de** to consist of; **ser ~ por** to be a graduate from.

formal *adj inv* formal.
formalidade *f* formality.
formalista *m,f (LITER)* formalist; **2** *(pessoa muito formal)* conventionalist.
formalizar *vt* formalize.
formalmente formally.
formão *m* chisel.
formar *vt* to form; **2** to constitute, make up; **3** to train, educate; ♦ **~-se** *vr* to form; **2** *(EDUC)* to graduate.
formatação *f* formatting.
formatura *f (MIL)* formation; **2** *(EDUC)* graduation.
formidável *adj inv* formidable; **2** *(fam)* tremendous, great, excellent, super.
formiga *f (ZOOL)* ant; **~ branca** termite; **2** *(pessoa trabalhadora)* hard-working person.
formigar *vi* to swarm; **2** to itch.
formigueiro *m* anthill; **2** *(fig)* swarm, *(pessoas)* throng; **3** *(comichão)* itching; **4** *(fig)* impatience; **5** *(fig) (sensação nos membros entorpecidos)* pins and needles (in).
formol *m (QUÍM)* formaldehyde.
formoso,-a *adj* beautiful; superb.
formosura *f* beauty.
fórmula *f* formula; **Fórmula UM** Formula One.
formular *vt* to formulate; **~ votos** to express one's hopes/wishes.
formulário *m (impresso)* form.
fornada *f (quantidade duma vez)* batch, ovenfull **uma ~ de bolos** a batch of cakes; *(fig)* **~ de papéis** a lot of papers.
fornalha *f* furnace, boiler.
fornecer *vt* to supply, provide.
forno *m (CULIN)* oven; **2 ~ de fundição** *(TEC)* furnace; **3 alto ~** blast furnace; **4** *(fig) (quente)* **esta casa é um ~** this house is like an oven.
foro¹ [ó] *m* forum.
foro² [ô] *m (JUR)* Court of Justice; **2** law courts; **3** ground rent; **4 ~s** *mpl* privileges.
forra *f* lining; **2** *(NÁUT) (vela)* tabling, lining; **3 à tripa-~** *(comer, gastar)* to one's heart content; *(BR)* **ir à ~** *(fam)* to get one's own back.
forragem *f* fodder.
forrar *vt* to cover; **2** to line; **3** to paper *(paredes)*.
forró *m* Brazilian pop dance.
forro,-a *m* covering; **2** *(revestimento interno)* lining; ♦ *adj* freed.
forrobodó *m* fun, frolic; **2** clubbing; **3** *(fig)* much noise, hubbub; **4***(BR)* fight.
fortalecer *vt* to strengthen.
fortaleza *f* strength; **2** fortitude; **3** fortress, fort; **ser uma ~** to be as strong as an ox.
forte *m* fort; ♦ *adj inv* strong; **2** hard; **3** *(pessoa)* heavy; **4** rich; **5** loud; ♦ *adv* strongly; **2** loud(ly).
fortificar *vt* to fortify.
fortuito,-a *adj* accidental, fortuitous.
fortuna fortune; **2** luck; **3** wealth; **ter a boa ~ de gozar de saúde** to have the good fortune of enjoying (good) health.
fosco,-a *adj* dull; **2** dim; **3** opaque; *(vidro)* frosted.
fosfato *m* phosphate; **~ de sódio** *(QUÍM)* sodium phosphate.

fosforescência *f* phosphorescence.
fosforescente *adj inv* phosphorescent.
fósforo *m (QUÍM)* phosphorus; **2** match; **caixa de ~s** box of matches; **3** *(prédios) (fig)* small building complexes.
fossa *f* cesspit, cesspool, sewer; **2** *(escavação)* ditch, trench, cova; **3** *(GEOG)* hollow, depression; **4** *(ANAT)* cavity, orifice; **~s nasais** *fpl* nostrils.
Fossa das Marianas *npr (GEOG)* Marianas Trench.
fosse *(imperf subj de* **ir, ser***)* **se eu ~ a ti** if I were you.
fóssil *(pl:* **fósseis***) (GEOL)* *m* fossil; **2** *(fig) (pej) (teoria)* obsolete; **3** *(pej) (pessoa)* old-fashioned, square, fuddy-duddy.
fosso *m (vala)* trench; **2** *(valeta)* ditch; **3** *(em redor do castelo)* moat; **4** *(fig) (abismo)* gulf (**entre** between); *(fig)* gap (**entre** between).
fotão *(EP)*, **fóton** *(BR)* *m (FÍS)* photon.
foto *f* photo.
fotocomposição *f* filmsetting.
fotocópia *f* photocopy.
fotocopiadora *f* photocopier.
fotocopiar *vt* to photocopy.
fotogénico,-a *adj* photogenic.
fotografar *vt* to photograph.
fotografia *f* photography.
fotógrafo,-a *m,f* photographer.
fotólito *m* photolitho.
fotovoltaico *adj* photovoltaic.
foz *f* river mouth.
fração *(Vd:* **fra(c)ção***)*.
fracassar *vi* to fail; go bust; be unsuccessful.
fracasso *m* failure, fiasco, washout.
fra(c)ção *f* fraction.
fraco,-a *m,f* weakling, coward; **2** weakness, weak point; ♦ *adj* weak, **ele é ~** *(carácter)* he is weak; **2 ele está ~** *(saúde)* he is weak, feeble, frail; **3** *(cigarro)* mild; **4** *(sabor, aroma)* delicate; ♦ *adv* weakly.
fractura *f* fracture, break.
frade *m* friar; **2** monk; **~ beneditino** Benedictine monk; **feijão ~** black-eyed bean.
fraga *f* crag, cliff.
fragata *f* frigate.
frágil *(pl:* **frágeis***) adj inv* fragile; breakable.
frágilidade *f* fragility; **2** *(debilidade)* frailty.
frágilizar *vt* to make vulnerable; **2** to weaken.
fragmentar *vt* to fragment.
fragmento *m* fragment.
fragor *m (ruído forte de uma quebra)* bang, crash, blast; **2** *(som forte) (ondas)* crash.
fragrância *f* fragrance; perfume.
fragrante *adj inv* fragrant.
fralda *f* shirt tail; **2** *(de bebé)* nappy *(UK)* diaper *(US)*; **3 ~ descartável** disposable nappy; **4** *(de montanha)* foothill; IDIOM **em ~ de camisa** in (one's) shirt-sleeves.
fraldário *m* baby-changing room *(public)*.
framboesa *f (BOT)* raspberry.
França *npr* France; **a F~** France.
francamente *adv* frankly, honestly.

francês,-cesa *m,f* Frenchman, Frenchwoman; *(LÍNG) m* French; ♦ *adj* French; IDIOM **despedir-se à francesa** to take French leave.

francesismo *m* Gallicism.

frâncio *m (QUÍM)* francium.

franciscano,-a *adj* Franciscan; **ordem** ~ Order of St Francis of Assisi; **frade** ~ Franciscan friar; ♦ *(fig)* **pobreza** ~a *f* extreme poverty.

franco,-a *m (moeda)* franc; ♦ *adj* frank, open-hearted; **2** free; *(loja, porto)* duty-free; **3** ~ **de porte** post paid.

franco-atirador *(pl: franco-atiradores) m* sniper.

francófono,-a *m,f* French speaker; ♦ *adj (país, comunidade)* French-speaking.

Francos *mpl* **os** ~ the Francos.

franga *f* pullet; **2** young and pretty girl; *(fam)* chick.

frangalho *m (farrapo, trapo)* rag, tatter, frazzle; **2** *(pessoa arruinada)* wreck; **ficar feito num** ~ to have one's nerves in a frazzle.

franganita *f (pej)* slip of a girl.

franganito *m (pej) (pessoa)* slip of a lad; wipper-snapper.

frangipana *f (essence)* frangipane.

frango *m (ZOOL)* young chicken; ~ **de aviário** battery hen/chicken; *(CULIN)* chicken; ~ **no churrasco** barbecued chicken.

franja *f (cabelo)* fringe; **ela tem uma** ~ she has a fringe, bangs *(US)*; **2** *(tecido)* **a** ~ **do xaile** the shawl's fringe; **3** edge; **4** margem; IDIOM **tenho os nervos em** ~ my nerves are shattered.

franquear *vt (desimpedir) (via)* to clear; **2** *(isentar)* to exempt from duties; **3** *(pagar transporte)* to pay postage, stamp.

franqueza *f* frankness, honesty; ♦ *adv* **com** ~ frankly; ♦ *exc* **com** ~! really!, what next!

franquia *f* postage; ~ **automática** stamps from an automatic machine; **2** exemption.

franzino,-a *adj* slender, **2** *(pessoa)* frail, puny, slight.

franzir *vt* to pleat, gather; ~ **a saia** *(costura)* to gather the skirt; **2** to wrinkle, crease; **3** ~ **o sobrolho** to frown, to knit the brows.

fraque *m* frock coat.

fraquejar *vi* to weaken.

fraqueza *f* weakness; **2** *(fig) (um pouco de fome)* **estou a sentir** ~ I feel a bit hungry.

fraquinho *m* weakness; **ter um** ~ **por algo** to have a weakness for sth.

frasco *m* flask, phial, small bottle.

frase *f (LÍNG)* phrase, sentence; **2** ~ **feita** set phrase.

fraseado *m* wording; **2** *(MÚS)* phrasing, wording; **3** *(palavreado)* jabbering.

frasear *vt* express in words; phrase; formulate.

fraseologia *f* phraseology; idiomatic phrasing; *(gíria)* jargon.

frásico,-a *adj* phrasal.

frasqueira *f* bootle rack.

fraternal *adj inv* brotherly, fraternal.

fraternidade *f* fraternity, brotherhood.

fraterno,-a *adj* fraternal, brotherly.

fraticida *m,f* fraticide; ♦ *adj* fratricidal.

fratura *(Vd: **fra(c)tura**).*

fraudar *vt* to defraud.

fraude *f* fraud, deception; ~ **fiscal** tax fraud.

fraudulento,-a *adj* fraudulent.

frear *vt (cavalo)* to bridle; **2** to curb, restrain; ♦ *vi (BR) (AUTO)* to brake.

freático,-a *adj (GEOL)* phreatic; **camada** ~**a** aquifer.

freelance *m* freelance.

freguês,-esa *m,f* customer.

freguesia *f* customers *pl*, clientele; **2** *(paróquia)* parish; **3** *(ADMIN) (em grandes cidades) (UK)* borough; *(US)* civil township.

frei *m* friar, monk; **2** *(título)* Brother.

freio *m (cavalo)* bit, bridle; **2** *(BR) (AUTO)* brake; ~ **de mão** *(BR)* hand brake; **3** *(ANAT)* fraenum; **4** *(fig)* restraint, control.

freira *f (REL)* nun.

freixo *m (BOT)* ash tree.

fremente *adj inv* excited, thrilled; **2** flustered; **3** *(mar)* surging, raging.

fremir *vi* to roar; **2** to tremble.

frémito *m* murmur; **2** shudder, shiver; **3** tremor; roaring; thrill; **4** ~ **cardíaco** palpitation (of the heart).

frenesim *m* frenzy.

frenético,-a *adj* frantic, frenzied; **2** restless.

frente *f* front; **2** *(edifício)* front, façade; **rodas da** ~ front wheels; **3** *(MIL, FÍS)* front, ~ **de combate** front line; ♦ *adv/prep* ~ **a** in the face of; **2** ~ **a** ~ face to face, opposite each other; **3** **à** ~/ **na** ~ *(muma fila/marcha)* ahead, in the front, first; **eu estou à** ~ **de você** I am in front of you, I am first; **4** *(principal no cargo)* **ele está à** ~ **da companhia** he is at the head of his company; **5** **de** ~ *(colidir)* head on; **6** ~ **e verso** *(de um livro)* on both sides, front and back; **7** **em** ~ opposite, straight on; **8** **pela** ~ *(frontalmente)* to one's face; **9** **para a** ~ ahead, forward; **ir para a** ~ move on, go forward; **seguir em** ~ go ahead; IDIOM **pôr o carro em** ~ **dos bois** put the cart before the horse; **em** ~ **do nariz (de alguém)** *(fam)* under one's nose.

frequência *f* frequency; **com** ~ frequently, often.

frequentador,-ora *m,f* regular visitor.

frequentar *vt* to frequent, attend regularly.

frequente *adj inv* frequent.

frequentemente *adv* often, frequently.

fresca *f* cool air; fresh breeze; **à** ~ in the open air; **pôr-se à** ~ to be lightly clad.

fresco,-a *adj (ar)* cool; **2** *(food)* fresh; ♦ *adj (tempo)* cool; **2** *(alimentos)* fresh; **3** *(rosto)* fresh; *(BR) (fam) (homossexual)* camp; ♦ *adv* newly; **vestida de** ~ newly dressed up; IDIOM **pôr-se ao** ~ *(fugir)* to take to one's heels.

frescote *adj (tempo)* chilly.

frescura *f* freshness; coolness.

fresta *f* gap, slit, chink.

fretar *vt* to hire, charter.

frete *m* freight, cargo; **2** *(fig, pop) (tarefa)* errand; **3** **fazer um** ~ to do sth you don't want to do; **4** bore; **que** ~! what a bore!

fretenir *vt (cigarra)* to chirr, sing.

freudiano,-a *adj* Freudian.

frialdade *f* coldness; **2** indifference, coolness; **3** frigidity.
friamente *adv* coldly.
friável *adj inv* crumbly, friable.
fricativa *f (LÍNG) (consoante)* fricative.
fricção *f* friction; **2** rubbing; **3** *(MED)* massage.
friccionar *vt (esfregar corpo, etc)* to rub.
frieira *f (MED)* chilblain, kibe.
frieza *f (de frio)* coldness; **2** *(indiferença)* indifference, coldness; **tratar alguém com** ~ to give sb the cold shoulder.
frigideira *f* frying pan.
frígido,-a *adj* cold, frigid.
frigir *vt (fritar)* to fry; **2** *(fig) (irritar)* pester *(alguém)*.
frigorífico,-a *m* refrigerator; *(pop)* fridge; **o congelador do** ~ freezing compartment of the fridge; ♦ *adj* refrigerant; **2 arca** ~**a** freezer; *(armazém)* cold-storage room; **3** *(camião)* refrigerated lorry.
frincha *f* chink, slit, crack; **2** *(BR)* narrow channel.
frio,-a *m* cold; **estou com/tenho** ~ I'm cold; **faz** ~ it's cold; **arrepios de** ~ cold shivers; **2** *(fig)* indifference, coldness; ♦ *adj* cold, chilly; **esta comida está** ~**a** this food is cold; **3** *(pessoa)* insensitive, cold-blooded; ♦ *adv* **a** ~ coldly, in cold blood, cold; **ele anda** ~ **comigo** he is distant with me; **ao** ~ in the cold; IDIOM **um** ~ **de rachar** bitterly cold.
friorento,-a *adj (pessoa)* feeling cold, sensitive to cold weather.
frisa *f (TEAT)* box.
frisado,-a *m* frizz; ♦ *adj* frizzy; curly; **2** *(enfatizado)* stressed, underlined.
frisar *vt* to curl; **2** to stress.
friso *m (ARQ)* frieze; **2** border, row, strip.
fritadeira *f* electric fryer.
fritar *vt* to fry.
frito,-a *adj* fried; **2** *(col)* **estar** ~ to be done for.

A fried egg is '**ovo estrelado**'; not ovo 'frito'.

fritura *f* fried food; frying; fritter.
frivolidade *f* frivolity; futility.
frívolo,-a *adj* frivolous.
froco *m* flake, wisp; ~**s de neve** snow flakes; ~**s de lã** lint.
fronha *f* pillowcase.
frontal *m (ARQ)* frontispiece, façade; **2** *(ANAT)* frontal; ♦ *adj inv (ANAT) (osso, lobo)* frontal; **2** *(fig) (pessoa directa)* blunt, frank; **3** *(choque)* head-on.
frontalidade *f* bluntness.
frontão *m (ARQ)* frontispiece, façade; **2** gable.
fronte *f (ANAT)* forehead, brow.
fronteira *f* frontier, border.
fronteiriço *adj* frontier.
frota *f (NÁUT)* fleet.
frouxidão *f* weakness; **2** *(sem energia)* slackness, lassitude.
frouxo,-a *adj (elástico, economia)* slack; **2** *(roupa, nó)* loose; **3** *(pessoa)* weak; **4** *(fig)* lax, languid, lazy; **5** *(BR) (covarde)* wet, wishy-washy; **6** *(BR) (fig, pop)* impotent.

frufru *m* frill; **2** *(onomat)* froufrou; **o** ~ **da sua saia de tafetá** the froufrou/rustling of her taffeta skirt.
frugal *adj inv* frugal.
frugalidade *f* frugality; **2** *(de hábitos)* simplicity.
fruição *f* fruition.
fruir *vt* enjoy sth, to benefit from; **2** *(JUR)* to have the usufruct.
frúnculo *m (pop) (Vd:* **furúnculo***)*.
frustração *f* frustration.
frustrado,-a *adj* frustrated; failed.
frustrar *vt* to frustrate, hinder; ♦ ~**-se** *vr* to be disappointed.
fruta *f* fruit.
frutaria *f* greengrocer's.
fruteira *f* fruit bowl.
fruticultor,-ora *m,f* fruit-grower. **fruticultura** *f* fruit-farming.
frutífero,-a *adj* fructiferous; fruitful; fruit-bearing.
fruto *m (BOT)* fruit; **2** *(fig)* result, product; **dar** ~ to bear fruit.
fuça *f (fam) (rosto)* ugly mug; snout, nose; **um murro na** ~ *(col)* a punch on the nose.
fúcsia *f (BOT) (brincos de princesa)* fuchsia.
fuga *f* flight, escape; **2** *(de gás, petróleo)* leak, spill, leakage; **3** ~ **ao fisco** tax evasion; **4** ~ **de capitais** flight of capital; **5** *(MÚS)* fugue; **6** *(orifício)* aperture, crack, fissure.
fugaz *adj inv* fleeting.
fugir *vi* to flee, run away, escape; **2** ~ **a** to avoid sth; **3** to slip *(away/out)*; IDIOM **o tempo foge** time flies.
fugitivo,-a *adj* fugitive.
fui *(pret, 1ª pessoa de* **ir, ser***)* ~ **falar com ele** I went to speak to/with him.
fuinha *f (ZOOL)* weasel; **2** *m,f (avarento)* miser.
fulano *m (homem)* chap, guy, bloke *(UK)*, bugger *(US)*; **2** ~ **de tal** Mr. so-and-so; **3** ~**, beltrano e sicrano** Tom, Dick and Harry; **fulana de tal** Jean Doe; *(pej)* **aquela** ~ that woman; that broad *(US)*.
fulcral *adj inv* vital, essencial, basic, key.
fulcro *m* fulcrum.
fulgir *vt/vi* to shine; to glow.
fulgor *m* brilliance, glow, splendour.
fulgor *m (brilho intenso)* glow, brightness, splendour; **2** *(clarão)* blaze; **3** *(mente)* brilliance.
fulgurante *adj inv* resplendent, like lightning.
fulgurar *vt* to shine, sparkle; **2** *(fig) (distinguir-se)* to stand out; irradiate.
fuligem *f* soot, smut.
fulminante *adj inv* devastating; scathing.
fulminar *vt* to strike; **o raio fulminou-a** she was struck by a bolt of lightning.
fumaça *f* smoke; **2** fumes *pl*.
fumador,-ora *m,f* smoker.
fumar *vt* to smoke; ~**ento,-a** smokey.
fumegante *adj inv* steaming; smouldering.
fumegar *vt (emanar fumo)* to smoke; **2** *(vapor)* to steam.
fumigação *f* fumigation, vapour.
fumigar *vt (insectos)* to fumigate; **2** *(defumar) (casa)* to perfume with incense.

fumo *m* smoke; **2** fumes *pl*; **3** *(BR)* tobacco; **4** *(maconha)* dope; **5** *(furioso)* fuming; **6 ter ~s** *mpl* *(fig)* to be haughty; **7 sem ~** to be smokeless; IDIOM **não há ~ sem fogo** there is no smoke without a fire; **desfazer-se como ~** to vanish.

funâmbulo,-a *m,f* *(equilibrista)* acrobat, trapeze artist; **2** *(fig)* *(inconstant)* weathercock, opportunist.

função *f* function; **2** duty, job; **3** role; **4** *(festa)* function; **5 em ~ de** due to; **venho em ~ de** in my capacity as, due to.

funcho *m* *(BOT)* fennel.

funcionalismo *m* practicality.

funcionamento *m* functioning, working; **pôr em ~** to set going, start; **horário de ~** working/opening hours.

funcionar *vi* to function, work, run; **a máquina não funciona** the engine is not going.

funcionário,-a *m,f* official; **2 ~ público** civil servant; **3 ~s** employees, staff.

funda *f* sling; **2** *(MED)* truss, bandage; **3** *(NÁUT)* lashing.

fundação *f* foundation; institution; **fundações** *pl* *(CONSTR)* *(alicerces)* foundations.

fundador,-ora *m,f* founder.

fundamental *adj inv* fundamental, basic.

fundamentalismo *m* fundamentalism.

fundamentar *vt* to substantiate; to base.

fundamento *m* motive; **sem ~** groundless.

fundão *m* whirlpool.

fundar *vi* to establish, found; **2** *(criar)* to start up, launch; ♦ **~-se** *vr* to be based on, founded on.

fundear *vi* to anchor; **2** sink; ♦ *vi* *(NÁUT)* to drop anchor.

fundição *f* foundry, smelting; **2** *(TYPO)* casting.

fundilhos *mpl* *(remendo)* repair on the seat of trousers; seat of trousers.

fundir *vt* *(juntar-se)* to fuse; **2** *(metal, vidro)* to smelt, melt down; **3** *(COM)* to merge, to fuse; **4** *(moeda)* to cast; **5** *(BR)* **~ a cuca** to set one's head spinning; ♦ **~-se** *vr* to melt; **2** to merge; **3** to fuse; **fundiu-se** it's fused.

fundista *m,f* *(JORN)* commentator.

fundo *m* *(parte inferior)* bottom; **o ~ do mar** the bottom of the sea; **2** *(traseira)* back, rear; **o ~ da casa** back of the house; **3** *(profundidade)* depth; **o poço tem pouco ~** the well does not have much depth; **4** *(base; de tecido, papel)* background; **~ da tela** background scenery; **o ~ dos cortinados é amarelo com flores azuis** the background of the curtains is yellow with blue flowers; **5** *(saída no outro lado)* end; **o ~ do túnel** the end of the tunnel; **6** *(íntimo)* heart; **eu gosto dele** I like him from the bottom of my heart; **ela tem bom ~** she is a good-hearted person; **7** *(fundamento, essência)* core, basis, essence; **questões de ~** essential questions; **8** *(ANAT, do olho)* fundus; **9** *(JORN)* **artigo de ~** leading article; **10** *(FIN)* fund, capital; **11** *(FIN)* **~ mútuo** mutual fund; **fundos** *mpl* funds, capital; **a ~s perdidos** no repayment, no returns; **~ de cobertura de risco** hedge funds; ♦ **fundo,-a** *adj* *(buraco)* deep; **2** *(cavado)* *(rosto,*

olheiras) deep; **3** rooted; profound; ♦ *adv* deeply, profoundly; **ele respirou ~** he breathed deeply; **no ~ deep** down, basically.

fúnebre *adj* funeral, funereal; **2** gloomy.

funeral *m* funeral.

funerário,-a *adj* funeral; **casa ~a** undertakers *pl*.

funesto,-a *adj* fatal, disastrous, doomed; **2** *(fig)* gloomy.

fungadela *f* sniff.

fungar *vt/vi* to sniff; **2** *(rapé)* to snuffle.

fungicida *m* fungicide.

fungo *m* fungus.

funicular *m* funicular; **2** *(veículo)* cable-car.

funil *m* funnel.

funileiro *m* tinsmith, panel beater.

furacão *m* hurricane.

furadeira *f* *(MEC)* *(BR)* drill; **~ eléctrica** electric drill.

furado,-a *adj* drilled, pierced; **2** *(pneu)* punctured; **3** *(BR: fam)* unsucceful.

furador *m* *(ferramenta)* awl; *(para bordados)* bodkin; *(de papel)* paper punch.

fura-greves *m,f sg/pl* blackleg, scab.

furão *m* ferret.

furão,-ona *m,f* *(fig)* *(pessoa bibilhoteira)* busybody, nosy; **2** *(pessoa fura-vidas)* go-getter; ♦ *adj* snooping; prying; **2** active, hard-working.

furar *vt* to bore, drill; **2** to penetrate; **3** *(pneu)* to puncture; *(orelha)* pierce; *(alfinete)* prick; **4** *(frustrar)* to fail; **5** *(fila)* jump *(the queue)*; **~ uma greve** to break a strike.

furgão *m* luggage van.

furgoneta *f* van.

fúria *f* fury, rage.

furibundo,-a, furioso,-a *adj* furious.

furna *f* cavern.

furo *m* *(buraco)* hole; **2** *(pneu)* puncture; **3** *(água, petróleo)* bore-hole; **4** *(de reportagem)* scoop.

furor *m* fury, rage; **fazer ~** to be all the rage.

furriel *m,f* *(MIL)* lance-corporal.

furtar *vt/vi* to steal; ♦ **~-se** *vr* **(a)** to avoid, evade.

furtivo,-a *adj* furtive, stealthy.

furto *m* theft.

furúnculo *m* *(MED)* boil.

fusão *f* fusion; **2** *(COM)* union, merger; **~ de empresas** a merger of companies; **3** *(mistura)* blending; **4** melting.

fusco,-a *adj* dark, dusky; **2** gloomy; **3 fusco-fusco** *(BR)* twilight, dusk.

fuselagem *f* *(AER)* fuselage; **furar a ~** to hull.

fúsil *adj inv* *(algo que se pode fundir)* fusible, molten, fused.

fusível *m* *(ELECT)* fuse; **caixa de fusíveis** fuse-box.

fuso *m* *(de tear)* spindle; spool; **2** *(GEOG)* **~ horário** time zone.

fustigação, fustigada *f* flogging; chastisement; *(açoite)* whipping.

fustigar *vt* to beat; **2** to flog, whip; **3** to punish.

futebol *m* football *(UK)*; soccer *(US)*; **~ista** *m* footballer; **~ de salão** indoor football.

fútil *adj inv* futile; trivial.

fútilidade *f* futility.

futricar *(BR)* to rummage; **2** to barter, trade; **3** *(trapacear)* to deal fraudulently; **4** to meddle, gossip.

futurar *vt (predizer)* to foretell, predict.

futurista *m,f (ART)* futurist; ♦ *adj inv* futuristic.

futuro *m* future, hereafter; ~ **próximo** near future; **2** *(GRAM)* future tense; ♦ *adj* future; ~ **incerto** black outlook.

fuxicar *(BR) vt (alinhavar)* to sew loosely, to baste; **2** *(fazer à pressa)* to botch, to bungle; **3** *(mexericar)* to gossip, intrigue, plot.

fuxiqueiro,-a *(BR) adj* gossiper, intriguer.

fuzil *m* rifle; flintlock.

fuzilada *f* a volley of guns, fusillade; firing.

fuzilado,-a *adj* shot down, executed by fire.

fuzilamento *m* fusillade; **pelotão de** ~ firing squad.

fuzilar *vt* to shoot down, to fire; **2** *(fig)* ~ **alguém com os olhos** to look daggers at sb; ♦ *vi (fig) (olhos)* to flash; **2** to sparkle, scintillate.

fuzileiro *m* rifleman; **2** *(MIL)* fusilier; **3** *(naval)* marine; *(US, pop)* leather neck.

g

G, g *m (letra)* G, g.
gabão *m* cloak with hood and cape; ♦ **gabão,-ona** *adj* boastful.
gabar *vt* to praise; **2** to exalt; **3** *(alguém)* to butter up sb; ♦ **~-se** *vr*: **~ de** to boast about, brag; to congratulate o.s.
gabardina *(BR:* **-ne)** *f* raincoat; gabardine.
gabarola *m,f* boaster, braggart.
gabinete *m* government office; **2** *(na universidade)* lecturer's room; **3** *(col)* study; **4** *(escritório)* office; **5** *(ministros)* cabinet.
gabiru *m (fam)* rascal, slydog; **2** *(BR)* clumsy person.
gadanha *f* scythe; **2** *pl (fam) (mãos)* paws, claws.
gadanhar *vt* to reap with a scythe; **2** *(fig)* to grab, claw.
gadanheira *f (AGR)* mowing machine, reaping machine, corn-cutter.
gadelha *f* long and unkempt hair.
gadelhudo,-a *adj* long-haired; **2** hairy; **3** *(desgrenhado)* unkempt (person).
gaditano,-a *adj* of/from Cádiz (Spain).
gado *m* livestock; **2** cattle; **3** herd; **~ bravo** *(fig) (fam)* rabble, riff-raff.
gaélico,-a *adj* Gaelic.
gafa *f (doença de animais)* mange, scabies; **2** *(planta)* mildew; **3** hook, claw; **4** vat with hook for carrying salt.
gafanhoto *m* grasshopper, locust; **praga de ~s** a plague of locusts; **2** *(fam) (enquanto falando)* spittle; **estás a deitar/lançar ~s** you are spitting, throwing spittle.
gafe *f* mistake, error, faux-pas; **cometi uma ~** I made a faux-pas; *(col)* I dropped a brick.
gafeira *f* mange; sheep's pox; **2** disease on olive trees; **3** *(em plantas)* mildew.
gagá *adj inv* gaga, senile.
gago,-a *m,f* stammerer, stutterer; **2** *(fig)* speechless, **fiquei ~ quando o vi** I was speechless when I saw him.
gaguejar *vi* to stammer, stutter.
gaguez *(BR:* **gagueira)** *f* stammer, stutter.
gaiato,-a *m,f* youngster, kid; lad *m,* lass *f,* boy, girl; **2** *m* urchin; ♦ *adj* mischievous (boy, girl); **olhos ~s** naughty eyes; **2** merry; **3** *(atitude)* childlike.
gaio *m (ZOOL)* jay; young sea-gull; **2** *(MÚS)* Portuguese folk dance; **verde-~** light green.
gaiola *f* cage; **2** *(fig) (UK)* gaol; *(US)* jail.
gaita *f (MÚS)* pipe, fife, reed; **2** *(BR)* concertina; **3** *(col)* trash, rubbish; **4** *(col, fam)* nuisance; ♦ *exc* hell!, blast!

gaitada *f (MÚS)* pipes; **2** *(per)* badly played music.
gaita-de-beiços *f* mouth organ, harmonica.
gaita-de-foles bagpipes *pl.*
gaiteira *f (bem vestida)* dressed (up) to the nines.
gaiteiro,-a *m,f* pipe player; ♦ *adj* merry; **2** *m (bem vestido)* dandy.
gaivota *(ave) f* seagull; **2** small paddle boat; **3** *(AGR) (irrigação)* a simple contraption for taking water out of a stream/well, a kind of sweep; **4** *(BR)* simpleton; IDIOM **~s em terra!** *(visita inesperada)* look what the cat has brought in!
gaja *f (pej)* common woman, tart; broad *(US).*
gajo *m (col)* guy, bloke; *(espertalhão)* clever dick, smart alec.
gala *f* full formal dress; **2** gala; **jantar de ~** gala dinner; **3 ~s** *(pl)* accessories.
galã *m* leading actor, idol; **2** *(fig)* heart-throb, charmer.
galaico,-a *adj* referring to Galicia; **2** *(LÍNG, LIT)* Galician; **a Cultura Luso-G~** the Portuguese-Galician Culture.
galante *adj inv* gallant, courteous; **2** romantic; **3** saucy.
galantear *vt* to flatter; **2** to woo; **3** to pay compliments; **4** to chat up.
galanteio *m* flattery; **2** compliment; **3** flirtation.
galão *m (MIL) (oficiais)* gold stripe; **2** galloon, braided ribbon; **3** *(pop) (cerveja)* large glass of beer; **4** white coffee in a glass; **5** *(medida para líquidos)* gallon *(4.546 litres UK; 3.785 liters US);* **6** leap (buck) of a horse; **7** *(NÁUT)* strip of linen used to repair, reinforce the caulking.
galardão *m (distinção, prémio)* award, prize; **2** tribute; **3** *(fig)* reward.
galardoar *vt (dar prémio, homenagear)* to decorate, confer honour; **2** to reward.
galáxia *m* galaxy.
galdéria *f (fig)* tramp, loafer; **2** *(fig)* tart.
galdério,-a *m,f* idler, good-for-nothing; **2** loafer.
galé *f (NÁUT)* galley; **2** printer's galley; **3 ~s** *fpl* forced labour.
gálea *f* helmet.
galeão *m (antiga embarcação)* galleon.
galego,-a *adj* Galician (de Galiza, Norte de Espanha).

O galego is a sister language of Portuguese. Luso-Galician was the first Christian culture in the Iberian Peninsula.

galera *f (NÁUT)* galley; ship; **2** foundry furnace; **3** *(BR)* goods-wagon.
galeria *f* gallery; **2** veranda; **3** *(lojas)* arcade; **4** *(ARQ)* colonnade; **5** *(TEAT = lugares baratos)* gallery; **6** mining shaft/gallery; **7** underground corridor; **8** *(pl)* spectators; **9** *(chuva)* drain; **dirigir-se à ~** play, speak to the public.
Gales *m:* **País de ~** Wales.
galês,-lesa *m,f* Welshman/woman; **2** *(LÍNG) m* Welsh; ♦ *adj* Welsh.
galgar *vt* to leap over; **2** to climb up; **3** to bound, stride rapidly; **4** *(fig) (estatuto, trabalho)* to move up (rapidly).

galgo *m (cão)* greyhound.

galhardia *f* elegance; **2** bravery; **3** gallantry.

galheta *f* cruet; **2** *(fam) (bofetada)* slap.

galheteiro *m* cruet-stand.

galho *m (árvore)* branch; **2** *(de fruto)* bow, sprig; **3** *(de animal)* antler, horn; **4** *(BR) (fam)* hassle, problem; **5 quebrar um/o ~** *(BR)* to patch it up, sort it out.

galhofa *f* fun, banter; prank; **fazer ~** to mock, to make fun of sb; **estar na ~** to be laughing.

galhofeiro,-a *m,f* joker; ♦ *adj* playful; merrymaker.

galicismo *m* Gallicism, French expression or idiom.

gálico,-a *adj* Gallic.

galinha *f (ave)* hen; **2** *(CULIN)* chicken; **3** *(fig) (namoradeira)* easy lay; **4** *(fig, fam) (cobarde)* chicken, yellow; **~choca** broody hen; **pés de ~** *(rugas)* crow's feet; **ter miolos de ~** *(fam)* to be a feather brain; **ela deita-se com as ~s** she goes to bed very early; IDIOM *(arrepiado)* **pele de ~** goose-pimples; **quando as ~s tiverem dentes** when pigs can fly.

galinha-d'angola *(pl:* **galinhas-d'angola)** *(ave) f* guinea-fowl.

galinha-da-índia *(pl:* **galinhas-da-índia)** *f* guinea-foul.

galinheiro *m (pessoa)* chicken farmer, poulterer; **2** *(casa das galinhas)* hen-coop; **3** *(TEAT) (fam) (bilhetes mais baratos)* upper gallery; *(pessoas nesta galeria)* the gods; **4** *(fam)* prison, nick.

galinhola *f (ave)* snipe, woodcock.

Galiza *npr* **a ~** Galicia (Northern Spain).

galo *m (ave)* cock, rooster, male fowl; **Missa do ~** midnight Mass; **2** *(fam) (duma pancada)* lump (on the head).

galocha *f (bota)* rubber boot; wellingtons.

galopar *vi* to gallop; **2** to run fast.

galope *m* gallop, **fazer (algo) a ~** to do sth at a gallop; ♦ *adv* **a ~** full speed.

galvânico,-a *adj (FÍS)* galvanic.

galvanizar *vt* to galvanize; **2** *(fig) (estimular, excitar)* to galvanize ♦ **~-se** *vr* to become galvanized.

gama *f (MÚS)* scale; **2** range, variety; ♦ *adj inv (FÍS)* gamma.

gamado,-a *adj* hooked; **2** *(cruz)* hooked cross; **3** swastika.

gamão *m* backgammon.

Gâmbia *npr* Gambia; **a ~** Gambia.

gambito *m (xadrez)* gambit.

gamela *f* wooden trough; large bowl; IDIOM **comer da mesma ~** to be as thick as thieves.

gâmeta *m (BIOL)* gamete.

gameta *f (nome regional)* lentil; *(Vd:* **lentilha)**.

Gana *npr* Ghana; **a ~** Ghana.

gana *f (desejo)* craving, desire; **2** *(raiva)* ill-will, hate; **ter ~ a alguém** to bear a grudge against sb; **tenho ~s de lhe dar uma sova** I have a good mind to give him a beating.

ganadoria *f* livestock farming.

ganância *f* greed, avarice; **2** *(por meios ilícitos)* illegal profit, usury.

ganancioso,-a *adj* greedy of gain, ambitious.

gancho *m (peça para prender/suspender)* hook; *(tipo de anzol)* fishing hook **2** *(cabelo)* hair-pin; **3** *(das calças)* crotch; ♦ **~s** *(fam) (biscate)* side line job/ earnings, moonlighting; **5** *(boxe)* hook.

ganga *f* denim; **calças de ~** jeans; **2** *(detritos de minerais)* waste, slag.

gânglio *m (ANAT)* ganglion, gland; *pl* ganglia; **~ linfático** lymph gland.

gangorra *f (BR)* seesaw.

gangrena *f (MED)* gangrene; **2** *(fig)* moral decay, rot.

gangue *m* gang.

ganhador,-ora *m,f* winner; ♦ *adj* winning.

ganha-pão *m* living, livelihood; **ele é o ~ da família** he is the family's bread-winner; **2** day-labourer.

ganhar *vt (prémio, etc)* to win; **2** *(salário)* earn; **3** *(lucrar)* gain; **4** *(obter)* get; **~ a vida** to earn a living; ♦ *vi (vencer)* win.

ganho,-a *m,f (irr pp de:* **ganhar)** *m* profit, gain; **2** wage; **bem ~** well-deserved/won.

ganhos *mpl* winnings.

ganir *vi (cão)* to yelp; **2** to whine; **3** to squeal.

ganso,-a *m,f* gander, goose.

garagem *f* garage, car repair workshop, garage.

garagista *m,f* garage owner.

garanhão *m (cavalo)* stud, stallion; **2** *(fig) (homem potente)* stud.

garantia *f* guaranty, surety; **2** assurance; **3** *(fiança)* security; **~ pignoratícia** collateral security.

garantir *vt* to guarantee; **2** to vouch for; **3** to assure; **4** *(dívida, empréstimo)* to secure.

garatujar *vt* to scribble, scrawl; **2** *(desenhar)* to doodle.

garbo *m* elegance; **2** poise, style; **3** gallantry.

garboso,-a *adj* gallant; **2** dashing, debonair, elegant; **3** distinguished.

garça *f (ave)* heron; **~ real** capped, king heron; **~ vermelha** bittern, red heron; **2** *(tecido)* fine gauze.

garção, garçom *m (BR)* waiter.

garço,-a *adj (cor)* bluish-green.

gare *f* railway station; **2** station platform; **3** quay.

garfo *m (de talher)* fork; **2** *(forcado)* hayfork; **3** *(AGR)* scion; **4** *(BR: pente)* metal comb; IDIOM **ser um bom ~** to be a hearty eater, a gourmand.

gargalhada *f* peal/burst of laughter, guffaw; **rir às ~s** to roar with laughter; *(fam)* to be in stitches; **soltar/dar uma ~** to burst out laughing.

gargalo *m (de garrafa)* neck; **2** *(fig) (ANAT)* neck.

garganta *f (ANAT)* throat; **ter dores de ~** to have a sore throat; **2** *(GEOG)* gorge, mountain pass; **3** *(fig) (basófia)* talk, bluff; **ele é só ~** he is all talk; **4** voice; IDIOM **ter algo/alguém atravessado na ~** to have sth/sb stuck in one's gullet, to bear a grudge against s.o.; **estar com a corda na ~** to be in dire straits; **pela garganta abaixo** down the throat.

gargantilha *f (jóias)* choker, necklace.

gargarejar *vi* to gargle.

gargarejo *m* gargling; **2** *(líquido)* gargle; **3** *(hesitação)* voice tremor.

gárgula *f* gargoyle; **2** water spout.
garguleira *f (pássaro)* blue finch.
garimpeiro *m (BR)* gold/diamond prospector, miner; **2** diamond-smuggler.
garoa *f (BR)* drizzle.
garoar *vi* to drizzle.
garotada *f* a group of kids, many children.
garotice *f (ação infantil)* child-like (action); **2** *(partida)* prank.
garoto,-a *m,f* youngster, kid; boy, girl; ~**s da rua** street/slum kids, roguish boys/girls; *m* lad; *f* girl, lass; *(col)* chick; **garoto** *m (pop) (EP)* small white coffee; *(BR)* small beer.
garoupa *f (ZOOL) (peixe)* grouper.
garra *f (de leão, etc)* claw; *(de ave)* talon; **2** long nails, fingers; **3** *(fig) (entusiasmo, energia)* enthusiasm, drive; ~**s** *fpl* clutches.
garrafa *f* bottle; ~ **térmica/-termo** *f* thermos flask; ~ **de gás** gas cylinder/container.
garrafão *m* demijohn.
garrafeira *f* wine cellar; **2** wine cupboard; **3** *(estrutura)* wine-rack; **4** selection of wines.
garraio *m* steer, bullock.
garrano *m (cavalo)* nag.
garrido,-a *adj (vistoso)* smart, dandy; showy; **2** *(cores, estilo)* loud, bright; colourful.
garrote *m* garrotte; **2** *(MED)* tourniquet; **3** *(fig)* anguish.
garrotilho *m (MED)* croup.
garrulice *f* chatter, cackle, prattle.
gárrulo,-a *adj* chattering, cackling; prattling.
garupa *f (de cavalo)* hindquarters, rump; **2** saddle pack; **3** *(de bicicleta)* pillion; **ir na** ~ to ride pillion.
gás *m* gas; ~ **lacrimogéneo** tear gas; **água com** ~ fizzy mineral water; **água mineral sem** ~ still water; ~ **hilariante** laughing gas; **2** *(do intestino)* flatulence, wind.
gasear *vt* to gas.
gaseificado,-a *adj (bebida)* sparkling, fizzy.
gaseificar *vt (QUÍM)* to gasify; **2** *(bebidas)* to carbonate.
gasoduto *m* gas pipeline.
gasogénio *m* gas generator.
gasóleo *m* diesel.
gasolina *f* petrol *(UK);* gas(oline) *(US);* **posto de** ~ petrol station *(UK),* gas station *(US);* **bomba de** ~ petrol pump; ~ **sem chumbo** lead-free petrol.
gasosa *f* fizzy drink; **2** lemonade; **3** soda water *(UK);* soda pop *(US).*
gasoso,-a *adj (bebida)* fizzy; *(água)* sparkling; **água** ~ tonic water.
gáspea *f* vamp; **2** *(fam) (velocidade)* fast; **andar na** ~ walk/move fast.
gastador,-ora *adj* spender.
gastar *vt* to spend; **2** to use up; **3** to wear out; **4** to waste; ~**-se** *vr* to wear out, spend.
gasto *(irr pp de* **gastar***) m (despesa)* expenditure, cost; **2** *(de água, luz)* consumption; ~**s** *mpl* expenses, costs, charges; ~ **imprevistos** incidental expenses ♦ *adj* spent; **2** used up, worn out; **3** *(fig)* worn out, frayed; **frase** ~**a** trite, commonplace.
gástrico *adj (MED)* gastric.

gastrite *(MED) f* gastritis.
gastroenterite *f* gastroenteritis.
gastronomia *f* gastronomy.
gastronómico,-a *(BR: -ô-) adj* gastronomical.
gastrónomo,-a *m,f* gourmet; gastronome.
gata *f* cat, tabby-cat; **2** *(NÁUT)* one-arm anchor; **andar de** ~**s** to crawl on all fours.
Gata Borralheira *f* Cinderella.
gatafunhos *mpl* scribbles, scrawls.
gatanho *m* scratch.
gatilho *m (duma arma de fogo)* trigger.
gatinhar *vi (bebé)* to crawl.
gatinhas *fpl*: **andar de** ~ to go on all fours.
gatinho,-a *m,f* kitten, pussycat.
gato *m* cat, tom-cat; **2** *(erro, lapso)* mistake, oversight; **3** *(grampo)* clamp; **4** ~ **montês** *(ZOOL)* wildcat; IDIOM **comprar** ~ **por lebre** to buy a pig in a poke; **elas dão-se como cão e** ~ they fight like dog and cat; ~ **escaldado da água fria tem medo** once bitten twice shy; **de noite todos os** ~**s são pardos** at night all cats are grey.
gato-bravo *m (ZOOL)* wild cat, lynx.
gato-pingado *m (pop) (sem importância) (pessoa)* pall-bearer; non entity.
gato-sapato *(pl:* **gatos-sapatos***) m* **fazer** ~ **de alguém** to treat sb like a doormat.
gatuno,-a *m,f* thief.
gaúcho,-a *m,f* from Rio Grande do Sul (Brazil).
gaudério,-a *m,f (pop)* scamp; vagrant; loafer.
gáudio *m* pleasure, joy; merrymaking.
gaulês,-esa *m,f* of/from Gaul; Gaulish; **os gauleses** *mpl* the Gauls.
gávea *f (NÁUT)* topsail; **2** top; **cesto da** ~ round top of mast.
gaveta *f* drawer.
gavetão *m* large drawer.
gavião *m* sparrow-hawk.
gavinha *f (BOT)* tendril.
gaza *f,* **gaze** *f* gauze.
gazela *f (ZOOL)* gazelle; **2** *(fig)* young and slender woman, a swan-like girl.
gazeta *f* newspaper, gazette; **fazer** ~ to play truant *(UK);* play hooky *(US).*
gazua *f* skeleton-key, picklock.
geada *f* frost.
gear *vt* to frost.
géiser/geiser *m (GEOL)* geyser.
gel *f (QUÍM)* gel; ~ **de banho** bath gel
geladeira *f (congelador)* freezer; **2** *(compartimento no frigorífico)* icebox; **3** *(BR) (frigorífico)* fridge, refrigerator.
gelado,-a *m* ice-cream; ♦ *adj* frozen.
gelar *vt* to freeze; **2** to chill; **3** *(fig) (paralisado)* to shock; ♦ *vi* to freeze.
gelatina *f (CULIN)* gelatine, jelly; **2** *(QUÍM)* gelatine.
gelatinoso,-a *adj* gelatinous; **2** slimy.
geléia, geleia *f* jelly *(UK);* jello *(US);* **2** jam; ~ **de cenoura** carrot jam.
geleira *f* glacier.
gélido,-a *adj* icy; **2** *(fig)* frozen; **uma expressão** ~**a** a frozen/icy expression.

gelo *m* ice; **2** *(fig)* icy cold; **está uma noite de** ~ it's a chilly night; **quebrar o** ~ to break the ice.

gelosia *f* blind; **2** (latticed) window shutter.

gema *f* (egg) yolk; gem; **2** *(BOT)* shoot; **3** *(pedra preciosa)* gem; **de** ~ genuine, through and through, the real McCoy; **um português de** ~ a Portuguese through and through.

gemada *f* *(ovo com açúcar e/ou conhaque)* egg flip.

gémeo,-a *(BR: gê-) adj* twin; **2 Gémeos** *mpl (ASTROL, ASTRON)* Gemini; the Twins.

gemer *vi* to groan, moan; **2** *(fig) (rodas da carroça)* to creak.

gemido *m* groan, moan.

geminação *f* twinning; **2** *(MIN)* gemmation.

geminado,-a *adj* twin; **casa** ~a semi-detached house.

gene *m* gene.

genealogia *f* genealogy; **2** *(fig)* origin.

genealógico,-a *adj* genealogical.

genealogista *adj inv* genealogist.

genebra *f* gin; **2 G~** *(cidade) f* Geneva.

general *m (MIL)* general; ~ **de Brigada** Brigadier General; ~ **de Divisão** Major General.

> The Portuguese equivalent of the English adjective 'general' is 'geral'.

generalidade *f* generality.

generalização *f* generalization.

generalizar *vi* to generalize; ♦ ~-**se** *vr* to become general, to spread.

generativo,-a *adj* generative.

género *(BR: gê-) m* type, kind; **2** *(ARTE)* genre; **3** *(BIOL)* genus; **4** *(gram)* gender; ~**s** *mpl (artigos)* goods, produce; ~ **alimentícios** foodstuffs; ~ **de primeira necessidade** essentials.

generosidade *f* generosity.

generoso,-a *adj* generous.

génese *f* origin, genesis; beginning.

Génesis *m (REL)* Genesis.

genética *f* genetics *sg.*

gengibre *m (BOT, CULIN)* ginger.

gengiva *f (ANAT)* gum.

gengivite *f (MED)* gingivitis.

genial *adj inv* of genius; **2** brilliant, great; **3** cheerful, genial; **uma ideia** ~ a great idea, a touch of genius.

genica *f (pop)* energy; zest, vigour; pep *(US);* **ter** ~ to have grit; **ela hoje está com a** ~ today she is full of beans.

génio *m* talent; **2** genius; **3** temperament; **de bom/mau** ~ sweet/ill tempered.

genital *adj inv* genital.

genitália *f* genitalia.

genocídio *m* genocide.

genoma *m* genome.

Génova *f (cidade)* Genoa.

genovês, genovesa *m,f* genoese.

genro *(f:* **nora)** *m* son-in-law.

gentalha, gentinha *f* pleb, crowd; *(pej)* riffraff.

gente *f sg* people *pl*, mankind, family; ~ **grande** grown-ups *pl*; **ser** ~ *(importante)* to be somebody; ~ **miúda** small fry; ~ **da mesma laia** birds of a feather; ~**s** *(povos) fpl* people; **direito das** ~ human rights; ♦ **a** ~ *pron* we, one; **a** ~ **gosta de brincar** we like to play; **toda a** ~ everybody; **tanta** ~ so many people.

gentil *adj (suave)* gentle; mild; **2** *(amável)* polite, affable; **o senhor é muito** ~ you are very kind.

gentileza *f* mildness; **2** kindness; **3** *(BR)* **por** ~ **poderia dizer-me ...** would you be so kind as to tell me, have the goodness to tell me ...

gentil-homem *n (fidalgo)* gentleman, nobleman.

gentílico,-a *adj* gentile.

gentio,-a *m,f* gentile; **2** *(pop)* populace; crowd.

gentísico,-a *adj (QUÍM)* **ácido** ~ gentisic acid.

gentisina *f (QUÍM)* gentisine.

genuflexão *f* genuflection.

genuíno,-a *adj* genuine.

geodo *m (GEOL)* geode.

geofísico,-a *m,f* geophysicist; **2** *f* geophysics; ♦ *adj* geophysical.

geófito,-a *adj* geophytic.

geografia *f* geography; ~ **botânica** phytogeography.

geográfico,-a *adj* geographical; **acidente** ~ geographic feature.

geologia *f* geology.

geológico,-a *adj* geological; **geólogo,-a** *m,f* geologist.

geometral *m (perspectiva)* ground plane; ♦ *adj inv (desenho)* geometric.

geometria *f* geometry.

Geórgia *npr* **a** ~ *f* Georgia.

georgiano,-a *adj* Georgian.

geração *f* generation; **de última** ~ *(COMP, TEC)* latest generation.

gerador,-a *m* originator, creator; **2** cause; **3** *(ELECT)* generator; ♦ *adj* procreating, generating; **empresa** ~**a de empregos** job-creating company.

geral *f (TEAT, FUT)* gallery; **2** *m (REL)* General, **o** ~ **dos Jesuítas** the General of the Jesuits; ♦ *adj inv* general; **limpeza** ~ spring cleaning; **dar uma** ~ *(BR)* to clear/clean up; **em** ~ generally.

geralmente *adv* generally, usually.

gerar *vt* to cause; **2** to generate; **3** to procreate, to beget; **4** *(fruta)* to produce; ♦ ~-**se** *vr (negócio)* to grow, develop; **2** to arise.

gerência *f* management.

gerencial *adj inv* management, managerial.

gerenciar *vt, vi* to manage.

gerente *m,f* manager.

gergelim *m (planta, semente)* sesame.

geriatra *m,f* geriatrician.

geriatria *f* geriatrics *(sg).*

geriátrico,-a *adj* geriatrics.

gerigonça *f (fam)* gadget, contraption.

gerir *vt* to manage, to run; to direct *(a business);* to direct.

germânico,-a *adj (natural da Alemanha ou relativo ao alemão);* German; **2** *(LÍNG)* German; Germanic.

germano,-a *adj* German; **os** ~**s** *mpl* the Germans.

germe, gérmen *m* germ; **2** *(fig)* origin.

germicida *m* germicide.

germinar *vi* to germinate, sprout; **2** *(fig)* to develop.

gesso *m* gypsum, plaster, plaster of Paris; **revestimento de ~** plaster cast; **~-cré** gypsum with white limestone.

gesta *f* heroic deed; historical/brave feat; **2** *(façanha)* exploit, feat.

gestação *f* gestation; **em ~** in gestation; in development.

gestante *f* pregnant woman.

gestão *f* management; **2** administration; **curso de G~ de Empresa** Business Management course.

gesticulação *f* gesticulation.

gesticular *vi* to gesticulate, make gestures.

gesto *m* gesture; **fazer ~s** to gesticulate; **ele fez um ~ para eu entrar** he beckoned me to go in.

gestor,-ora *m,f* manager, manageress.

gestual *adj inv* using gestures; **linguagem ~** sign language.

giba *(corcunda)* humpback; *(NÁUT)* flying jib/sail.

gibão *m* gibbon; doublet; a kind of leather jacket worn by shepherds.

gibi *m (BR: col)* small black boy.

giesta *(BOT) f* broom.

gigante,-a *m,f* giant, giantess; ♦ *adj* gigantic, huge.

gigantesco,-a *adj* huge, gigantic, colossal.

gila (= **chila**) *f (a type of pumpkin grown in Portugal, used in cakes and in making jam)* spaghetti gourd.

gilete® *f* razor blade; **2** razor.

gim *m* gin.

ginásio *m* gymnasium, gym; **2** health club; **3** *(BR)* secondary school.

ginasta *m,f* gymnast.

ginástica *f* gymnastics *sg*; **~ rítmica** aerobics; **maças para ~** Indian clubs; **fazer ~** to do (physical) exercise; *(fig, fam) (esforço)* **fazer ~ com (o dinheiro, etc.)** to struggle, outstretch, juggle.

gincana *f* gymkhana.

ginecologia *f* gynaecology.

ginecológico,-a *adj* gynaecological.

ginecologista *adj inv* gynaecologist.

gineta *f (ZOOL)* genet, a kind of civet-cat; **montar à ~** *(à marialva)* short stirrups.

ginete *m (ZOOL)* jennet, small breed of horse; **2** *(pop)* bad temper; **quando lhe dá o ~ ela quebra tudo** when she is in a temper she breaks everything.

gingar *vi (baloiçar o corpo)* to sway; shake *(as ancas)* **2** *(algo) (oscilar)* to wobble.

ginja *f* morello cherry; **2** *(fam)* old man; IDIOM **o dinheiro veio a cair que nem ~s** the money came as a godsend.

ginjeira *f* cherry tree; IDIOM **conhecer alguém de ~** know sb inside out, like the back of one's hand.

ginjinha *f* cherry brandy.

gipsófila *f (BOT)* gypsophila.

gira-discos *m* record-player.

girafa *f (ZOOL)* giraffe.

girar *vt/vi* to turn, rotate; **2** to spin; whirl (round).

girassol *m (BOT)* sunflower.

giratório,-a *adj (porta, prateleira)* revolving; gyratory; **cadeira ~a** *f* swivel chair.

gíria *f* jargon.

girino *m (ZOOL)* tadpole.

giro *m (volta)* turn; **2** *(fam) (passeio)* stroll, drive; **dar um ~** to go for a walk/a stroll/a spin; **3** *(ronda)* beat, circuit; **polícia de ~** police on the beat ♦ **giro,-a** *adj (fam) (pessoa, objecto)* cute; nice; cool; **que coisa tão ~a!** what a lovely thing!; **ela é ~a à farta** she is very gorgeous; **que giro!** how funny!

giz *m* chalk; **~ de alfaiate** French chalk.

glacé *m* icing.

glacial *adj inv* icy.

gladiador *m* gladiator.

gladíolo *m (planta, flor)* gladiolus.

glamoroso,-a *adj* glamorous.

glamour *m* glamour.

glândula *f* gland.

glaucoma *f* glaucoma.

gleba *f (AGR) (for farming)* field, glebe; **2** feudal estate; **3** mineral soil.

glicemia/glicémia *f (MED)* blood sugar.

glicerina *f* glycerine.

glicínia *f (BOT) (planta, flor)* wisteria.

global *adj inv* total, entire, global; **preço ~** overall price.

globalização *f* globalization.

globo *m (mundo)* globe; **2** *(objeto)* glove; **3** *(sphere)* esfera; **4** *(ANAT)* **~ ocular** eyeball.

glóbulo *m (sangue)* blood cell, corpuscle; **~ brancos/ vermelhos** white/red corpuscles.

glória *f* glory; **2** *(honra)* prestige, honour; **jogo da ~** snakes and ladders; IDIOM **levar a banca à ~** to sweep the board, to break the bank.

gloriar-se *vr:* **~ de** to boast of.

glorificar *vt* to glorify.

glorioso,-a *adj* glorious.

glosa *f* footnote; **2** comment, review.

glosar *vt* to comment on, criticize; **2** *(anotar)* to gloss.

glossário *m* glossary.

glote *f (ANAT)* glottis.

GLP *m (abr de Gás Liquefeito de Petróleo)* LPG.

glucose *f (glicose)* glucose.

glutão,-tona *m,f* glutton; ♦ *adj* greedy, gluttonous.

glúten *m (alimento)* gluten.

glutinoso,-a *adj* glutinous.

gnomo *m* gnome.

GNR *(abr de Guarda Nacional Republicana)* Portuguese National Guard.

goela *f* gullet; **2** throat; IDIOM **abrir as ~s** to bawl; **ter muita ~** to be all talk; be a gabbler.

goês ,-esa *m,f adj* of/from Goa.

goiaba *f (fruto)* guava.

goiabada *f* guava jam, jelly.

goiabeira *f* guava-tree.

goiano,-a *m,f* of/from Góias (Brasil).

gol *(pl: goles) m (BR) (DESP)* goal; **2** *(rugby)* try.

gola *f (de camisa, blusa)* collar; **~ alta**, *(BR)* **~ rulê** polo neck.

gole *m* gulp, sip, drop; **de um ~** in a gulp; **um ~ de água** a drop of water.

goleada *f (DESP)* many goals.

goleiro *m* goalkeeper.

golfada *f (líquido)* spurt, gush, jet; **2** vomit; **~ de sangue** spurt, vomit of blood; **3** *(ar)* breath; **4** *(vento)* gust; **às ~s** in spurts, in gushes.

golfar *vt* to throw up; ♦ *vi* to spurt out.
golfe *m (DESP)* golf; **campo de** ~ golf-links, golf course; **taco para jogar** ~ golf-club.
golfinho *m (ZOOL)* dolphin, porpoise; **2** miniature golf.
golfista *adj inv (DESP)* golfer; **2** *(técnica, etc)* golfing.
golfo *m* gulf, bay; **G~ da Biscaia** the Bay of Biscay.
golinho *m* small drop, spot of, *(fig)* thimbleful; **2** tot *(fam)*; **um** ~ **de uísque** a tot of whisky.
golo *m (BR:* **gol)** *(DESP)* goal; **marcar um** ~ to score a goal; **2** drop, gulp, mouthful; **de um só** ~ in one gulp.
golpe *m* blow; **2** cut; **3** punch, hit; ~ **de estado** coup d´état; **de um só** ~ at a stroke; ~ **decisivo** a knockout.
golpear *vt* to slash, hit; **2** to stab; **3** to cut; **4** to strike; **5** to injure; ~ **acertado** to strike home.
goma *f (seiva)* sap, resin; **2** *(para roupa)* starch; **3** *(cola)* glue; **4** *(BR) (pastilha)* chewing-gum; **5** *(BR)* tapioca.
gomo *m (BOT) (broto)* bud; **2** *(de laranja, tangerina)* segment (of orange).
gôndola *f* gondola.
gondoleiro *m* gondolier.
gongo *m (MÚS)* gong.
gonorréia *f* gonorrhoea *(UK)*; gonorrhea *(US)*.
gonzo *m* hinge.
gorar *vt* to frustrate, thwart; ♦ *vi* to fail, go wrong.
goraz *m (ZOOL)* sea bream.
gordo,-a *m,f* fatty; ♦ *adj* fat, stout, plump; **2** bulky.
gorducho,-a *m,f* plump, roly-poly.
gordura *f* fat, fats; **2** grease.
gordurento,-a, gorduroso,-a *adj* fatty; **2** greasy, oily; **tenho as mãos ~as** I have greasy hands.
gorgolejar *vi* to gurgle; **2** to gulp down.
gorgolejo *m* gurgle, gurgling; sound of gurgling.
gorgulho *m (ZOOL)* weevil.
gorila *m (ZOOL)* gorilla; **2** *(fig) (guarda-costas)* bodyguard.
gorjear *vi* to chirp, twitter; **2** to sing, trill.
gorjeio *m* twittering, warbling; **2** *(voz humana)* trill; **3** *(fig)* baby's babble.
gorjeta *f* tip, gratuity.
gorro *m* cap; beret.
gostar *vi (ter prazer)* to like; to enjoy; ~ **de fazer algo** to like doing sth; **2** *(preferir)* ~ **mais de algo do que de** to prefer; **eu gostaria que viesses a minha casa** I would like you to come to my home; **3** *(por curiosidade)* **eu sempre gostaria de saber se ...** I really would like to know if ...; **4** ~ **de alguém** *(sentir amizade)* **eu gosto muito dela** I like her a lot; **ele gosta dela** *(sentir amor)* he loves her; **5** *(comida/bebida = sabor)* **ela gostou do meu assado** she liked my roast; **6** *(aprovar)* **gosto dessa ideia** I like that idea.

In Portuguese, '**gostar de**' is also used to mean 'love'; '**amar**' ('to love') is less common than is 'to love' in the English language, in all senses.

gosto *m* taste; **2** pleasure; **por** ~ for pleasure; **a seu** ~ to one's liking; **de bom/mau** ~ in good/bad taste.

gostoso,-a *adj (comida)* tasty; **2** *(ambiente, cheiro)* pleasant; **3** *(riso)* hearty.
gota *f* drop, droplet; **2** *(de suor)* bead; **3** tear; **4** *(MED)* gout; ♦ *adv* ~ **a** ~ drop by drop; ~**-coral** *f* epilepsy.
goteira *f* gutter; leak.
gotejar *vi* to drip; ♦ *vi* to fall, run down, roll down.
gótico,-a *adj* Gothic.
gotícula *f* droplet.
goto *(Vd:* **glote)** *m (pop)* glottis; IDIOM **dar no/cair no** ~ to please sb; catch/take someone's fancy.
governador,-ora *m,f* governor; ~**-geral** *m,* ~ **ora-geral** *f* Governor-General.
governamentação *f* governability.
governamental *adj inv* governmental.
governanta *f* housekeeper.
governante *m,f* leader, ruler; **2** *adj inv* governing, ruling.
governar *vt* to govern, rule; **2** *(barco)* to steer; **3** *vr* to manage, to make do.
governo *m* government; **2** management, running; **3** *(carro)* control; ~ **da casa** housekeeping.
gozado,-a *m,f adj (BR)* funny; **2** strange.
gozar *vt* to enjoy; **2** *(pop)* to make fun of; ♦ *vi* to enjoy o.s.; ~ **de boa saúde** enjoy good health; ♦ *vr (aproveitar-se de)* ~ **de** to avail o.s. of, rejoice o.s. in.
gozo *(BR:* -ô-*)* *m* pleasure, enjoyment; **2** use, **em pleno** ~ **de** in full use of; **3** fun; **4** *(chacota)* mockery; **ele está no** ~ he is pulling (my) leg, he is (just) kidding.
GPS *m (abr de* **Global Positioning System)** GPS.

'Satellite navigation' is the expression used when this system refers to cars.

grã *adj f (m:* **grão)** *(=grande)* great, grand; ~**-Cruz** Grand Cross; ~**-duquesa** grand-duchesse.
graal *m* grail; **o Santo** ~ the Holy Grail.
Grã-Bretanha *npr* Great Britain; **a** ~ Great Britain.
graça *f* charm; wit; **ela tem muita** ~ she is very funny/cute/witty; **2** joke, prank; **lá está ele com as suas** ~**s** there he is again with his jokes; **3** *(insípido)* **sem** ~ dull, insipid, tasteless; **a sopa não tem** ~ **nenhuma** the soup is tasteless; **3** *(REL)* grace; ♦ *adv* **de** ~ *(gratuito)* free; **eu trabalhei de** ~ I worked for a song; **2** *(devido a)* ~**s a** thanks to, due to; ♦ *excl,* **graças a Deus!** thank God!; **que** ~! how funny!, what a coincidence!
gracejar *vi* to joke, crack jokes.
gracejo *m* joke, jest.
gracinha *f (bebé)* **ser uma** ~ to be a sweetie; **as** ~**s do bebé** *pl* baby's pranks.
graciosidade *f* elegance, grace.
gracioso,-a *adj* charming, elegant; *(moça)* *f* lovely, cute; graceful; **2** witty.
graçola *f* joke in poor taste, coarse joke; **2** wisecrack; **3** *m,f* a coarse joker, jester.
gradação *f* gradação.
gradativo,-a *adj* gradual.

grade f grating; **2** (em grelha) grill; **3** (em vedação) railing; **4** (caixa) crate; **5** (ELECT) grid; **6** (pop) jail; **7** (AGR) harrow; **8** (nas janelas, portas) bars pl.

gradeamento m railing.

gradear vt to rail, put bars up.

grado m (GEOM) grade; **2** (gosto, vontade) liking; **não é do meu** ~ it is not to my liking; ♦ adv: **de bom/mau** ~ willingly/unwillingly; **2 mau** ~ in spite of; ♦ **grado,-a** adj (grande) (cereais) large; **2** (fig) importante.

graduação f graduation; **2** division; **3** rank; **curso de** ~ degree course.

graduado,-a m,f (diplomado) graduate; ♦ adj graduated; **2** graded; **3** (official) commissioned.

gradual adj inv gradual.

gradualmente adv gradually.

graduar vt (curso) to graduate; **2** (dosear) grade, classify; **3** calibrate; ♦ ~-**se** vr to graduate, be a graduate.

gráfica f (empresa) printing company, graphics studio.

gráfico,-a adj graphic; **design** ~ graphic design; ~ **de barras** bar chart.

grã-fino,-a m,f (BR) aristocrat; **2** (fam) snob; socialite; **3** pl the smart set; ♦ adj swanky.

grafite f black lead; **2** graphite; **desenho a** ~ pencil drawing.

grafito m graffito (pl: graffiti); **muros com** ~ outside walls covered with graffiti.

grafonola f gramophone.

grageia f (FARM) coated pill.

grainha f (BOT) pip.

gralha f (ZOOL) magpie (PT), rook, jackdaw; **2** misprint, error; **3** garrulous woman, (fam) parrot.

grama m (FÍS) gramme; **2** f (BR) grass.

gramado m (BR) lawn, turf.

gramar vt (BR) to plant, sow with grass; **2** (EP) (pop) (aguentar) to put up with, to endure; **não a gramo** I can't stand her; (gostar) **eu gramo isto** I like this.

gramática f (disciplina, livro) grammar.

gramático,-a m,f grammarian; ♦ adj grammatical.

gramínea f (BOT) poaceas = grama grass and cereals.

grampa f (NÁUT) cramp iron, clamp; **2** (veículo - por infracção de tráfico) clamp.

grampeador m (BR) stapler.

grampear vt (BR) (papel, tecido) to staple; **2** (BR: TEL) to bug the telephone.

grampo m (de carpinteiro) clamp; **2** (escápula) hook; **3** (BR) (cabelo) slide, hairgrip.

grana (BR) f (pop) money, dough, dosh.

granada f (MIL) grenade; ~ **de mão** hand grenade; **2** (pedra preciosa) garnet.

grande m grandee; ~**s** noblemen; **os** ~**s** (poderosos) the high and the mighty; ♦ adj inv (volume) big, large; **um homem** ~ a large man; **um** ~ **nariz** a big nose; **2** (importância) great; **um** ~ **homem** a great man; **um** ~ **negócio** a great business; **3** grand; **uma** ~ **ocasião** a grand occasion; **4** vast; **uma área grande** a vast area; **5** kind; **um** ~ **coração** a kind heart; **6** (dor) strong; **7** (crescido)

grown up, tall; **o menino está** ~ the boy has grown up/is tall; **8** (somalto) ~ **grito** a loud scream; **9 a G~ Lisboa** Greater Lisbon; **10** (FOTO, CIN) ~ **angular** wide-angle lens; ~ **plano** close-up; **sorte** ~ m stroke of luck; ♦ adv **viver/gastar à** ~ to live/spend lavishly; **em** ~ **escala** on a large scale; ~ **coisa** not much.

grandeza f greatness; vastness; **2** (fig) splendour, grandeur; ~**s** fpl material goods, wealth.

grandiloquência f grandiloquence.

grandiloquente adj inv (orador) grandiloquent.

grandiosidade f magnificence.

grandioso,-a adj magnificent, grand; **2** outstanding, imposing; **3** (alma) noble.

granel m (celeiro) barn, granary; **2** (TIPO) gallery proof; **3** (pop) (confusão) mess, trouble; **4** (COM) **a** ~ in bulk.

granito m granite.

granizo m hail; ~ **miúdo** sleet.

granja f farm; **2** chicken farm.

granjear vt (conseguir) to get, obtain; (fig) to gain, win; ~ **a amizade** to win sb's friendship; ~ **fama** to become famous, to court fame.

grânulo m granule.

grão (pl: **grãos**) m (de areia) grain; **2** (semente) seed; **3** (de café) bean; ~**s** mpl (cereais) cereal; IDIOM (provérbio) ~ **a** ~ **enche a galinha o papo** many a mickle makes a muckle (scot).

grão-de-bico (pl: **grãos-de-bico**) m chick-pea (UK), garbanzo bean (US).

grão-ducado m grand-dukedom.

grão-duque m grand-duke.

grasnar vi (corvo, gralha) to caw; **2** (pato) to quack; **3** (rã) to croak; **4** (fig, fam) (pessoa) to grunt, shout.

grasnido m (do pato) quack; **2** (das gaivotas) cry; **3** (gralha, corvo) caw, croak.

gratidão f gratitude (**por** for).

gratificação f gratuity; **2** tip; **3** (extra) bonus.

gratificante adj inv rewarding, gratifying.

gratificar vt to tip; **2** to reward.

gratinado,-a adj (CULIN) gratiné, au gratin.

grátis adj inv free, for nothing; gratis.

grato,-a adj grateful; **2** (memória, notícia) pleasant, fond; **ficar** ~ **a alguém por** to be grateful to sb for.

gratuito,-a adj free; **2** (opinião, comentário) gratuitous.

grau m (gen) degree; **2** (temperatura, vinhos) degree; **3** university degree; (parentesco) **primo em segundo** ~ twice-removed cousin; **4** stage; **em último** ~ in the final stage; **5** (MÚS) scale; **6** (fig) point.

graúdo,-a m,f grown-up; **os** ~**s** mpl the bigwigs; ♦ adj (feijão, grão) large; **2** (dinheiro) big; **3** (lucros) fat.

gravação f (metal, stone) engraving; **2** (ARQ) inscription; **3** (som, imagem) recording; (de cassettes) tape recording; (de videos) VCR.

gravador,-ora *m* tape recorder; **2** *m,f (profissional)* engraver.

gravar *vt (em metal)* to engrave, cut; **2** *(em madeira)* to sculpture, carve; **3** *(couro)* to emboss; ~ **com água forte** to etch; **4** to stamp; **5** *(fig)* to imprint, etch; ~ **na memória** to commit to/etch on one's memory; **6** to brand; **7** *(TEC)* to record.

gravata *f* tie; ~ **borboleta** bow tie; **alfinete de** ~ tie-pin.

grave *adj inv* serious; **2** grave.

grávida *adj* pregnant.

gravidade *f* gravity.

gravidez *f* pregnancy.

gravilha *f* gravel.

gravitação *f* gravitation; **2** force of gravity.

gravitar *vt* to gravitate; **2** to attract, go round sth; **3** to incline (toward).

gravoso,-a *adj* grievous; **2** vexatious; **3** *(despesas)* onerous; **4** *(COM) (produtos)* overpriced unable to compete in market.

gravura *f* picture, illustration; **2** engraving; ~ **em madeira** wood-cut; ~ **em cobre** copper-plate; **3** *(estampa)* print; ~ **a água forte** etching; ~ **em relevo** relief, embossed engraving; ~ **rupestre** rock engravings.

graxa *f* shoe polish; **2** grease; **3** *(fam) (vinho barato)* plonk; **4** *(col)* flattery; **dar** ~ to butter s.o. up, to lick (their) boots.

graxista *m,f* flatterer; *(pej)* toady; ♦ *adj inv* fawning; flattering.

grazina *adj (pessoa faladora)* chatterbox, prattler; **2** grumbler, moaner.

grazinada *f* hubbub.

Grécia *npr* Greece; **a** ~ Greece.

greco-latino,-a *adj* Graeco-Latin.

greda *f (GEOL)* chalk.

gregário,-a *adj* gregarious.

grego,-a *adj* Greek; **2** *m (LÍNG)* Greek; IDIOM **ver-se** ~ **para** to find it hard to do sth; to be in a bind to do sth; **vi-me** ~ **para encontrar a rua** it was hell to find the street; **isso para mim é** ~ it's all Greek to me; **entre** ~**s e troianos** between the wall and the deep blue sea; **agradar a** ~**s e troianos** to please both sides; **para as calendas** ~**s** for a day that may never come; in a month of Sundays.

gregoriano,-a *adj (calendário)* Gregorian.

grei *f* flock, congregation, society; **2** people, nation; **3** followers.

grelar *vt* to sprout.

grelha *f* grill, roaster; **2** *(grade do fogão/fornalha)* grate, gridiron; **3** *(de lixo, esgoto)* grating; **4** *(de ventilação)* grille, grid; **5** *(ELECT)* grid; **6** *(col) (prisão)* slammer.

grelhado,-a *adj (peixe, carne)* grilled.

grelhar *(CULIN) vt* to grill; ~ **a carvão** charcoal grill.

grelo(s) *m (BOT) (rebento)* shoot, sprout; *(de brócolos)* tendershoot broccoli; *(de nabos)* turnip tops; **2** *m sg (cal)* clitoris; **3** *(distintivo académico)* student's badge.

grémio *(BR:* **grê-***) m* guild; **2** *(associação)* club, association, circle; guild; ~ **literário** literary association.

grená *m, adj (cor)* garnet.

grenha *f (cabelo)* mane, tangled hair; **2** *(bosque)* thicket, dense foliage.

grés *m* sandstone.

greta *f (racha)* crack, fissure; **2** *(fenda)* crevice; **3** *(corte)* chap; ~ **nos lábios** chaps.

gretado,-a *adj (lábio, mão)* cracked, chapped.

gretar *vt (abrir, fender)* to crack *(terra, parede)*; **2** *(cortar)* to chap *(mãos, lábios, pés, pele)*.

greve *f* strike; **fazer** ~ to go on strike; ~ **de fome** hunger strike.

grevista *m,f* striker.

grifa *f* claw, talon; **2** *(ARQ) (base de coluna em forma de garra)* griffe.

grifado,-a *adj* in italics.

grifar *vt* to italicize; **2** *(fig)* to emphasize.

grife *f (BR)* label.

grifo *m* italics; **2** *(cabelo)* curl; **3** *(ZOOL)* vulture; *(animal fabuloso)* griffin (also: griffon).

grilhão *m (corrente forte de metal)* chain; **grilhões** *mpl* chains; *(fig)* fetters.

grilheta *f (argola de ferro)* fetter, shackles; **2** *(fig) (obrigação)* duty.

grilo *m (ZOOL) (inseto)* cricket; **o** ~ **canta** the cricket chirps; **2** *(REL) (pop)* Augustine friar; **3** *(BR, fam) (problema)* worry, hiccup; **4** *(BR) (JUR)* property without legal right; **5** *(BR)* bore; IDIOM **ter memória de** ~ to have a poor memory.

grimaça *f* grimace.

grimpa *f* weathercock, vane; **2** summit, crest, top; **3** *(fig)* haughty bearing; IDIOM **é como a** ~ changeable, fickle; **levantar a** ~ to give o.s. great airs; to get on one's high horse.

grimpar *vi* to climb like a cat, clamber; **2** *(recalcitrar)* to reply back rudely.

grimpo *adj (col)* very cultured person, knowledgeable.

grinalda *f* garland; **2** wreath; **3** tiara; **4** *(ARQ)* cornice, festoon.

gripar[1] *vt (MED)* to catch flu.

gripar[2] *vi (AUTO)* to grip, seize up.

gripe *f* flu, influenza; ~ **das aves** *(BR)*; ~ **aviária** bird flu; ~ **suína/gripe A** swine flu.

grisalho,-a *adj (cabelo)* grey.

grita *f* uproar.

gritante *adj inv* screaming; **2** *(fig)* glaring, gross; **3** *(cor, luz)* bright, vivid; **4** *(fig) (erro)* notorious, blatant.

gritar *vt/vi* to shout, yell.

gritaria *f* shouting, din.

grito *m* shout, scream; **2** cry; call; **dar um** ~ to cry out.

groenlandês,-esa *adj* greenlandic.

Groenlândia, Gronelândia *npr* Greenland; **a** ~ Greenland.

grogue *f (bebida de Cabo Verde) (com aguardente, açúcar, etc)* grog; ♦ *adj inv (pessoa titubeante)* tipsy, groggy.

grosa *f (lima grossa)* rasp, file; **2** *(doze dúzias)* gross.

groselha *f (fruto)* gooseberry; *(sumo)* gooseberry juice.

groselheira *f* gooseberry bush.

grosseiro,-a *m* lout, boor, uncouth; ♦ *adj* coarse, rude; **2** common; **3** indecent; **em linguagem** ~ in strong terms.

grosseria *f* rudeness; **2** churlishness; **3** vulgarity; **dizer/fazer uma** ~ to be vulgar, make a vulgar gesture.

grossista *m,f* wholesaler.

grosso,-a *m* **o** ~ **de um exército** the body of an army; ♦ *adj* bulky, thick; **2** rough; **3** deep; **4** *(BR)* lout; ♦ *adv* in bulk, **por** ~ **e a retalho** wholesale and retail; IDIOM **fazer vista** ~**a** to shut one's eyes to; **ser casca** ~**a** to be thick-skinned; **estar** ~ to be drunk.

grosso modo *adv* roughly.

grossura *f* thickness.

grotesco,-a *adj* grotesque.

grua *f (guindaste)* crane; **2** *(ZOOL)* female crane.

grudar *vt/vi* to glue, stick.

grude *f* glue, paste.

grumete *m* cabin-boy, ordinary seaman.

grumo *m (sólidos)* lump; **2** *(coágulo)* clot, coagulation.

grunhido *m* grunt.

grunhir *vi* to grunt; **2** *(fig)* to growl, groan.

grupo *m* group; ~ **sanguíneo** blood group; **2** *(MED)* group; **3** *(TEC)* unit, set.

gruta *f* grotto, cave; **2** *(covil)* lair, hideaway.

guarda *m,f* policeman, police officer, *(col)* cop; **2** guard, watchman, sentry; ~ **prisional** prison guard, warden; ~ **fiscal** customs officer; ~ **de comporta** lock keeper; *m* **o render da** ~ *(MIL)* the changing of the guard; **estar de** ~ to be on watch; **3** *f (protecção)* care, safe-keeping, **a** ~ **do meu escritório** my office's care/watch; **a G~ Nacional Republicana (GNR)** Republican guard, State Police; ♦ *prep* **à** ~ **de** in the care of; **de** ~ **a** watching, guarding; ♦ *exc* **ó da** ~**!** Police! Help! ~**s** *fpl (duma ponte)* parapets of a bridge; IDIOM **ser da velha** ~ *(fam)* to be of the old school; *(fam)* **esta malta é da nova** ~ this is the new crowd.

guarda-bagagem *(pl: guarda-bagagens) m* baggage room.

guarda-caça *(pl: guarda-caças) m* gamekeeper.

guarda-cancela *m (caminho-de-ferro)* line keeper, flagman at a railway crossing.

guarda-chuva *(pl: guarda-chuvas) m* umbrella, *(pop)* brolly.

guarda-comida *m* larder.

guarda-costas *m,f sg, pl (para defesa)* bodyguard; **o** ~ the bodyguard; **os** ~ the bodyguards; **2** *(NÁUT)* coast-guard boat.

guardador,-ora *m,f* keeper, guardian; ~ **de cabras** goat herdsman; **2** *(BR) (vigia de automóveis)* car watchman.

guardados *mpl (BR)* keepsakes.

guarda-fiscal *m (fronteiras)* customs officer; **2** *(costeiro)* coastguard.

guarda-florestal *m* forester, forest ranger.

guarda-fogo *m* fireguard.

guarda-freio(s) *m* tram driver.

guarda-lamas *mpl (AUTO)* mudguard.

guarda-livros *m,f* bookkeeper.

guarda-loiça, guarda-louça *(pl: guarda-louças) m* china/glass cupboard.

guarda-mor *(pl: guardas-mor) m* commander of the guard; **2** *(UK)* Lord High Steward; **3** *(arc)* chief custodian; **4** *(BR)* Head customs officer.

guardanapo *m* napkin, serviette.

guarda-nocturno, guarda-noturno,-a *(pl: guardas-noturnos) m,f* night watchman.

guardar *vt* to guard; **2** to keep; **3** to watch over; **4** to put away (safekeeping); ~ **(algo) para outro dia** to put off (sth) for another day; ~ **as leis** observe the law; ~ **silêncio** to keep quiet; ♦ ~**-se** *vr* to protect o.s., be on one's own guard.

guarda-redes *m* goalkeeper.

guarda-roupa *(pl: guarda-roupas) m* clothes cupboard, wardrobe.

guarda-sol *m* sunshade, parasol; **2** *(FOTO)* lens hood.

guarda-vento *m* wind screen.

guarda-vestidos *(pl: guarda-vestidos) m* wardrobe.

guardião *(pl: guardiões, guardiães) m* guardian; **2** caretaker; **3** *(comunidade religiosa)* Superior; **4** custodian.

guarida *f* refuge; **dar** ~ to give shelter.

guarita *f* watch-tower; **2** sentry box.

guarnecer *vt (as tropas)* to provide, supply; **2** *(MIL)* to garrison; **3** to decorate, trim; **4** to adorn.

guarnição *f (MIL)* garrison; **2** *(NÁUT)* crew; **3** *(roupa)* trimming; **4** decoration; **5** *(CULIN)* garnish, accompaniment.

Guatemala *npr:* **a G~** Guatemala.

Guatemalteco,-a *m,f adj* Guatemalan.

gude *m (BR)* marbles *pl;* **bola** *f* **de** ~ marble.

gueixa *f* geisha.

guelra *f (de peixe)* gill; IDIOM **ter sangue na** ~ to be full of zest.

guerra *f* war; **2** struggle, battle; ~ **intestina** civil war; ~ **nuclear** nuclear warfare; ~ **santa** holy war; **após** ~ post-war; **conselho de** ~ court martial; **em pé de** ~ on the warpath; **fazer** ~ to wage war.

guerrear *vi* to wage war.

guerreiro,-a *m* warrior, fighter; ♦ *adj (belicoso)* warlike; **2** *(espírito)* fighting.

guerrilha *f* guerrilla warfare.

guerrilheiro,-a *adj* guerrilla.

gueto *m (bairro judeu ou isolado)* ghetto.

guia *m,f (acompanhante de turistas)* guide; **2** *m (manual turístico)* guide, guidebook; *(de instruções)* manual; *(animal ou pessoa que guia outros)* leader; **carneiro de** ~ bellwether; **3** *f (COM)* order, receipt.

Guiana *npr* Guyana; **a G~** Guyana.

guianense *adj* Guyanese, of/from Guyana.

guião *m (REL)* banner; **2** *(MIL)* standard; **3** *(CIN)* script; **4** standard–bearer; **5** *(ZOOL)* a kind of thrush.

guiar *vt* to guide, lead; **2** *(AUTO)* to drive; ♦ ~**-se** *vr:* ~ **por** to go by, guide oneself.

guias sonoras *fpl (estrada)* rumble strips.

guiché *m* ticket window, office, service hatch *(UK);* wicket *(US).*

guicho *adj (Reg)* noisy; **2** clever; **3** *(aprumado)* stiff, upright; **4** blooming of plant.

guidão, guidom *(BR) m (de bicicleta)* handlebars *pl.*

guilherme *m (tipo plaina)* tongue and groove plane; **2** *(nome próprio)* William.

guilhotina *f* guillotine; **2 janela de** ~ sash-window; **3** bookbinder's shear; **4** paper-cutter.

guinada *f (NÁUT)* lurch; **2** swerve; **3** sharp pain.

guinar *vt (carro)* to swerve, veer; **2** *(barco, avião)* to pitch, to yaw.

guinchar *vt (porco, carroça)* to squeal; **2** *(ratos)* squeak; **3** shriek.

guincho *m* squeal, shriek; **2** winch; **3** *(BR)* tow-car.

guindar *vt (com guincho)* to hoist, lift; to winch; **2** *(com guindaste)* to move with crane; **3** *(fig)* to promote; ♦ ~-**se** *vr* to raise oneself; *(fig)* ~ **à alturas** to raise one's expectations.

guindaste *m* hoist, crane.

Guiné-Bissau *npr* Guinea-Bissau; **a G**~ Guinea-Bissau.

guineense *adj inv* Guinean, from Guinea-Bissau.

Guinea-Bissau, a republic in West Africa, was first discovered by the Portuguese in 1446. It became independent in 1974. This beautiful country consists of two parts: the continental and the insular. Its capital is Bissau. Official language: Portuguese. Creole is also spoken.

guinéu *m (dinheiro, moeda de ouro)* English guinea = 21 shillings (old curreny) = £1.05 (actual currency).

guisa *adv:* **à** ~ **de** like, by way of, in the manner/ guise of.

guisado *m* Portuguese stew; **2** *(BR: também* **mince***)*.

guisar *vt* to stew.

guita *f* twine, string; **2** *(pop) (dinheiro)* lolly; **dar** ~ **a alguém** let/make s.o. talk.

guitarra *f* Portuguese guitar; **2** electric guitar.

guitarrista *m,f* guitar player.

A Portuguese guitar differs from its Spanish sister in shape and sound. It has 12 strings and is played – or 'plucked' – with thumb and forefinger. Spanish guitar is known as '**viola**' in Portuguese.

guizo *m (chocalho)* little bell, sleigh bell, cat's bell; **2** child's toy; ~ **de-cascavel** *(pl:* **guizos-de-cascavel***) (BOT) m* rattlebox; **os** ~**s do Carnaval** noisy joviality.

gula *f* gluttony, greed; **2** *(CONSTR)* fillister; **3** *(ARQ)* cyma.

gulodice *f* delicacy; **2** titbit; **3** greediness; **4** *pl* sweets.

guloseima *f* sweet dish; **2** *pl* sweets.

guloso,-a *adj* greedy; **ser** ~ to be fond of sweets, to have a sweet tooth.

gume *m (fio da lâmina)* edge; **2** *(fig) (de inteligência)* sharpness; IDIOM **uma espada de dois** ~**s** a two-edged sword; **estar no** ~ to run a risk.

guri *m (BR)* little boy, kid.

guria *f (BR)* girl; **2** girlfriend.

gurma *f* colt's sickness, during teething.

guru *m* guru.

gusa *m* pig-iron.

guso *m (BR, Angola)* strength, vigour.

gustativo,-a *adj (ANAT) (nervo, papila)* gustative.

gutural *adj inv* guttural.

guturalmente *adv* gutturally.

h

H, h *m (letra: agá)* H, h.
h *(abr de* **hora** hour).
ha *(abr de* **hectare)** *(Vd:* **hectare)**.
hã *exc* what!; what's that?
há *(pres ind 3ª pessoa de* **haver)** there is/there are; ~
muita gente aqui there are many people here; ~
(aqui) **alguém que fale chinês?** is there anyone
who speaks Chinese?; **2** ago; **vi-o ~ muitos anos** I
saw him years ago; **3** for; **estou aqui ~ uma hora**
I have been here for one hour; ~ **que tempos
(que) eu espero** I have been waiting for ages; ♦
~-de *(with the infinitive of another verb means
'will', Vd:* **haver)** **ele ~-de voltar um dia** he will
return one day.

'**Há**', when it means 'there is/there are', is always in the
third person singular in all its tenses.

habeas corpus *m inv* habeas corpus.
hábil *(pl:* **hábeis)** *adj inv* clever, able, skilful, dextrous,
deft; **2** capable; **3** competent.
habilidade *f (aptidão)* skill, ability; *(destreza, jeito)*
deftness, knack, flair; **ela tem ~ para a música**,
she has a knack for music; **2** *(astúcia)* cleverness,
smartness; **3** ~s *pl* skills, talent; **4** acts; ~ **de acrobata**
acrobat acts; **5** *(brincadeiras)* tricks, stunts.
habilidoso,-a *adj* skilful *(UK)*, skillful *(US)*, dextrous,
deft; **2** able, competent; **3** *(esperto)* clever.
habilitação *f* eligibility, qualification; ♦ **habilitações**
fpl (formação documentada) qualifications; **2**
(JUR) documentary evidence, legal formalities.
habilitado,-a *adj (com diploma, certificado)* qualified
(operário), skilful; **2** competent, able.
habilitar *vt (capacitor)* to enable; **2** to prepare; **3**
(direito a) to entitle to; ♦ **~-se** *vr* to become apt; **2**
(JUR) to claim, put oneself forward for; **3** to
equip/prepare o.s. (as, to, for).
habilmente *adv* skilfully; **2** cleverly; **3** efficiently.
habitação *f* dwelling, residence; **2** *(BIO)* habitat.
habitacional *adj inv (relativo a habitação)* housing.
habitante *m,f* inhabitant.
habitar *vt (país)* to live in; to inhabit; **2** *(morar)*
dwell (em in) *(cidade, rua)*. **habitat** *m* habitat.
habitável *adj inv (próprio para habitar)* habitable.
hábito *m (costume)* habit; custom; **conhecer os ~s
de alguém** to know sb's habits; **2** addiction; **o ~
de fumar** smoking habit; **3** *(traje de religiosos)*
habit; IDIOM **o ~ faz o monge** opportunity
makes a thief.
habitual *adj inv* usual, customary.

habitualmente *adv* usually; **2** as usual.
habituar *vt:* ~ **alguém a** to get sb used to, to accustom
sb to ♦ **~-se** *vr:* ~ **a** to get used to.
haematose *f* haematosis *(UK)*, hematosis *(US)*.
Haia *f* The Hague.
Haiti *npr* **o ~** Haiti.
haitiano,-a *adj* Haitian.
haja *(pres subj de* **haver)**; **bem ~!** God bless you!; ~
o que houver whatever there is, whatever happens.
hálito *m* breath; **mau ~** bad breath; **2** *(exalação)* smell.
halo *m* halo; **2** aura; **3** areola; **4** *(ANAT)* areola; **o ~
do mamilo** the areola around the nipple.
halogéneo,-a *(BR: -ê-)* *m* halogen; ♦ *adj (QUÍM)*
halogenous.
haltere *m* dumb-bell, barbell; **~s** *pl (DESP)* weightlifting.
halterofilista *m,f (DESP)* weightlifter; ♦ *adj inv*
weightlifting.
hambúrga, hambúrguer *m* hamburger.
hamster *m,f (ZOOL)* hamster.
hangar *m (aviões)* hangar; **2** large shed.
haraquiri *m (suicídio japonês)* hara-kiri.
hardware *m (COMP)* hardware.
harém *m* harem.
harmonia *f* harmony; **2** peace; **3** agreement; ♦ *adv*
de/em ~ in harmony with, according to.
harmónica *f (MÚS) (de beiços)* mouth organ; **2**
concertina, accordion.
harmónio *m (MÚS)* harmonium.
harmonioso,-a *adj* harmonious; **2** melodious.
harmonizar *vt* to harmonize; **2** conciliate, reconcile;
3 adjust; ♦ **~-se** *vr* go hand in hand, in tune, **as
cores harmonizam-se muito bem** the colours go
well together.
harpa *f* harp.
harpar *vt* to play the harp.
harpista *m,f* harp player.
hasta *f* sale by auction; ~ **pública** public auction.
haste *f* flagpole; **bandeira a meia-haste** flag at half; **2**
(TEC) shaft, rod; **3** *(BOT)* stem, twig; **4** *(chifre)* horn.
hasteamento *m* hoisting.
hastear *vt* to raise, hoist.
haurir *vt (tirar algo do fundo para fora)* to drain;
suck up, absorb; draw off.
havaiano,-a *adj (das ilhas Havaí)* Hawaiian.
havana *m:* **charuto ~** Havana cigar; ♦ *adj inv (BR)
(cor)* light brown, beige.
havanês,-a *(BR) adj* havanese.
havano,-a *adj* from/of Havana.
haver *m (bens)* possessions, assets; **os meus ~es** my
assets; **gente de teres e ~es** people of means; ♦ *vt
(forma impess 3ª pessoa apenas)* there to be; **há**
there is, *(pl)* there are; **há muitos gatos** there are
many cats; **há pouco tempo** recently; **que há?**
what's the matter?; **que há de novo?** what's the
news?; **há que ter paciência** one must have
patience *(Vd:* **há)**; **2** *(fut)* **haverá uma grande luta
amanhã** there will be a big fight tomorrow; **3**
(imperf) **havia tanto barulho!** there was so much
noise!; ♦ *(aux) (quando auxiliar em tempos com-
postos,* **haver** *conjuga-se em todas as pessoas)* to
have; **nós havíamos dito** we had said; **não fui**

tido nem havido, I was not consulted; ♦ **haver +
de** + *infinitive*: will, shall, have to, must; *(intenção)* **hei-de ir ao Brasil** I will go to Brazil; **2**
(obrigação) **havemos-de falar com ele** we must
speak with him; **3** *(probabilidade)* **eles hão-de vir
hoje** they will probably/they should come today;
♦ **~-se** *vr (entender-se, prestar contas)* **ter de ~
com** to have to deal with sb; answer to sb; **2**
(portar-se) to behave, get on; ♦ *exc* **haja saúde!** as
long as there is (good) health!; **bem haja!** bless
you!; ♦ *adv* **haja o que houver** whatever happens; IDIOM **não há duas sem três** it never rains
but pours; **por bem fazer, mal haver** to be paid
back with ingratitude.

haxixe *m* hashish.

hebraico *m (LÍNG)* Hebrew; ♦ *adj (povo, história)*
Hebrew, Hebraic.

hectare *m* hectare = 10.000 sq. metres (= 2.471 acres).

hediondo,-a *adj* vile, revolting; **2** heinous.

hedónico,-a *adj* hedonic.

hedonismo *m* hedonism.

hedonista *adj inv* hedonist.

hegemonia *f* hegemony.

hegemónico,-a *adj* hegemonic.

Hégira *f* Hegira/Hejira.

hei *(pres indic, 1ª pessoa de:* **haver**) *(Vd:* **haver**).

hein! *(tambeín:* **hem**) *exc* what?; **e esta agora, ~?**
and what about this one, eh?

hélice *f* propeller.

helicóptero *m* helicopter.

hélio *m* helium.

heliporto *m* heliport.

Helsínquia *f* Helsinki.

helvético,-a *adj* Swiss, Helvetic.

hem! *(Vd:* **hein**).

hemático,-a *adj (MED)* haematic *(UK)*, hematic *(US)*.

hematite *(MIN)* haematite, red iron ore.

hematócito *m (MED)* haematocyte *(UK)*, blood
corpuscle; hematocyte *(US)*.

hematócrito *m (MED)* haemotocrit *(UK)*, hemotocrit
(US).

hae- in British English, becomes he- in American English.

hematóide *adj inv* haematoid *(UK)*, hematoid *(US)*,
resembling blood.

hematologia *f* haematology *(UK)*, haematology
(US).

hematoma *f (MED)* bruise, haematoma *(UK)*,
hematoma *(US)*.

hemiciclo *m* semi-circle; **2** *(anfiteatro)* semi-circle.

hemisférico,-a *adj* hemispheric.

hemisfério *m (GEOG, FÍS)* hemisphere; **2** *(ANAT)*
~ cerebral cerebral hemisphere.

hemodiálise *f (MED)* dialysis.

hemofília *f (MED)* haemophilia/hemophilia *adj*
haemophilic/hemaphilic.

hemófilo,-a *m,f* haemophiliac/hemophiliac.

hemoglobina *f* haemoglobin/hemoglobin.

hemograma *m* full blood count.

hemopatologia *f* haemopathology/hemopathology.

hemorragia *f (MED)* haemorrhage/hemorrhage;
~ nasal nosebleed.

hemorrágico,-a *adj* haemorrhagic/hemorrhagic.

hemorróidas *fpl (MED)* haemorrhoids/hemorrhoids;
(pop) piles.

hepático,-a *adj* hepatic.

hepatite *f (MED)* hepatitis.

heptagonal *adj inv* heptagonal = having seven
angles.

heptágono *m (GEOM)* heptagon, seven-sided figure.

hera *f (BOT)* ivy.

heráldica *f* heraldry.

heráldico,-a *adj* heraldic.

herança *f (bens herdados)* inheritance; **2** *(bens
deixados a outros)* legacy, bequest; **3** *(o que nos
foi dado de gerações anteriores = cultura)*
heritage; **4** *(qualquer coisa que foi deixada para
gerações futuras)* legacy; **o amor à paz foi a
melhor ~ que nos deixaram** love of peace
was the best legacy they left us; **5** *(transmissão
genética)* heredity; **~ jacente** *(JUR)* hereditas
jacens.

herbáceo,-a *adj* herbaceous, grassy.

herbanário *m* shop/dealer in medicinal herbs; **2**
health shop.

herbicida *m* weed-killer; ♦ *adj inv* weed-killing.

herbívoro,-a *m* herbivore; ♦ *adj (animal)* herbivorous.

herbolário *m* herbalist.

hercúleo,-a *m (ASTRON)* Hercules; ♦ *adj* Herculean;
2 gigantic, strong man, mighty.

herdade *f* large farm; **2** large country estate.

herdar *vt* to inherit (**de** from).

herdeiro,-a *m,f* heir, heiress; **2** beneficiary; **~ fideicomissário,-a** *m (JUR)* trustee heir, fideicommissary.

hereditário,-a *adj (BIOL)* hereditary; **2** *(JUR)*
hereditary.

herege *m,f* heretic.

heresia *f* heresy.

herético,-a *adj* heretical.

hermeticamente *adv* hermetically; **fechado ~**
sealed hermetically.

hermético,-a *adj* airtight.

hérnia *f (MED)* hernia; **~ de disco/discal** slipped disc.

herói *m* hero.

heróico,-a *adj* heroic.

heroína *f* heroine; **2** *(droga)* heroin; **tráfico de ~**
heroin trafficking.

heroismo *m* heroism.

herpes *m (MED)* herpes *sg;* **~ zóster** herpes zoster,
shingles; **~ labial** labial herpes.

hesitação *f* hesitation.

hesitante *m,f (pessoa)* hesitant person; ♦ *adj inv*
hesitant, wavering; **2** *(fig) (caminho, rio)* winding.

hesitar *vi* to hesitate, waver, to be undecided; **ele
hesitou em falar,** he hesitated to speak.

heterodoxo *(REL)* dissenter; **2** *(pessoa)* non-conformist;
♦ *adj* unorthodox, heterodox.

heterogénio,-a *adj (FÍS, QUÍM, MAT)* heterogeneous.

heterógino,-a *m,f (ZOOL)* heterogynous.

heterónimo *m* heteronym; **2** nom de plume; ♦ *adj*
heteronymous.

Fernando Pessoa – a great Portuguese poet, known for his multiple heteronyms. This 20th century genius wrote under his own name, besides several other pen names to which he gave complete biographies and different styles of poetry, including an English heteronym who wrote in English.

heterossexual *adj inv* heterosexual.
hexagonal *adj inv* hexagonal, six-sided.
hexágono *m (GEOM, MIL)* hexagon.
hiato *m (ANAT)* gap, opening; **2** *(LÍNG)* hiatus; **3** *(fig) (intervalo)* gap, interval, lacuna.
hibernar *vt* to hibernate; **2** *(fig)* to stagnate, be at a standstill.
hibérnico,-a *adj* Hibernian, Irish.
hibisco *m (BOT)* hibiscus.
híbrido,-a *adj* hybrid; **2** *(animal)* mongrel, cross-breed; **3** mixed species; **~s recíprocos** *(genetics)* reciprocal hybrids.
hidra *f (MITOL, ASTRON)* Hydra; **2** *(ZOOL)* hydra; **~ d'água** *(ZOOL)* a dogfish, water snake; **3** *(fig) (mal)* evil, plague.
hidratação *f* hydration: **2** *(pele)* moisturizer.
hidratante *m* hydrator; **creme ~** moisturizing cream; ♦ *adj inv (que hidrata) (para a pele)* moisturizing.
hidratar *vt (pele)* to moisturize.
hidrato *m (QUÍM)* hydrate; **~ de cálcio** calcium hydroxide; **~ de terpina** terpinol.
hidráulico,-a *adj* hydraulic; **2** *f* hydraulics; **instalação ~a** waterworks *sg.*
hídrico,-a *adj (QUÍM)* hydric.
hidro *pref* hydro.
hidroavião *(pl: hidroaviões) m* seaplane.
hidroelé(c)trica *f* hydroelectric plant.
hidroelé(c)trico,-a *adj* hydroelectric.
hidrofílico,-a *adj* hydrophilic; **2** hydrophilous.
hidrófilo,-a *adj (algodão)* absorbent.
hidrófito *m (BOT)* hydrophite, aquarian plant.
hidrofobia *f* hydrophobia; **2** *(MED)* rabies *sg.*
hidrofóbico,-a *adj* hydrophobic; **cimento ~** hydrophobic cement.
hidrofrático,-a *adj* water-proof.
hidrogénio *m* hydrogen; **~ pesado** deuterium.
hidrografia *f* hydrography.
hidrográfico,-a *m,f (engenheiro)* hydrographer; ♦ *adj* hydrographic.
hidroplano, hidroplanador *m* hydroplane.
hidrovia *f* waterway.
hidróxido *m (QUÍM)* hydroxide; **~ de alumínio** aluminium tri-hydroxide; **~ de potássio** sodium hydroxide, caustic soda.
hiena *f (ZOOL)* hyena; **2** *(fig) (pessoa interesseira e má)* vulture.
hierarquia *f* hierarchy.
hierárquico,-a *adj* hierarchical.
hieróglifo *m* hieroglyph.
hífen *m* hyphen.
higiene *f* hygiene.
higiénico,-a *adj (MED)* hygienic, sanitary; **papel ~** toilet paper; **penso ~** sanitary towel; **2** *(limpeza)*

cleaning; **ela é uma pessoa muito ~a** she is very fussy about cleaning.
hilariante *adj inv* hilarious, very funny; **gas ~** laughing gas.
hilaridade *f* hilarity, merriment; **2** laughter.
himen *(ANAT) m* hymen.
himénio *m (BOT)* hymenium.
hinário *m* book or collection of hymns.
hino *m* hymn; **~ nacional** national anthem.
hipérbole *f (GEOM)* hyperbola; **2** *(LIT)* hyperbole.
hipertensão *f* high blood pressure.
hípico *adj:* **concurso ~** steeplechase.
hipismo *m* horse racing; **2** horsemanship.
hipnose *f* hypnosis.
hipnótico,-a *m,f* hypnotic.
hipnotismo *m* hypnotism.
hipnotizar *vt* to hypnotize.
hipocondria *f* hypochondria.
hipocondríaco,-a *m,f* hypochondriac.
hipocrisia *f* hypocrisy; deceit.
hipócrita *m,f* hypocrite, two-faced person; ♦ *adj inv* hypocritical, false.
hipodérmico,-a *adj* hypodermic.
hipódromo *m* racecourse, hippodrome.
hipoteca *f* mortgage; **sem ~** free and unencumbered.
hipotecado,-a *adj* mortgaged.
hipotecar *vt* to mortgage.
hipotensão *f (MED)* hypotension, low blood pressure.
hipotermia *f (MED)* hypothermia.
hipótese *f* hypothesis, assumption; **2** possibility; **na ~ de** in the event of; **em nenhuma ~** under no circumstances.
hipotético,-a *adj* hypothetical, uncertain.
hirsuto,-a *adj* hairy, hirsute; **2** shaggy, rugged; **3** *(ZOOL, BOT)* bristly; **4** *(fig) (pessoa, expressão)* harsh, severe.
hirto,-a *adj* stiff, rigid; **2** *(roupa com goma/gelo)* erect, stiff.
hispânico,-a *adj* Hispanic.
histerectomia *f (MED)* hysterectomy.
histéria *f (PSIC)* hysteria.
histérico,-a *adj* hysterical.
história *f* history; **2** *(fábula)* story, tale; **contar uma ~** to tell a story; **reza a ~ (que)** the story goes (that); **3** *(CIN, enredo)* plot, storyline; **4** *(patranha)* fib; **5** *(pretexto)* excuse; **6 ~ em quadradinhos** funnies; **em banda desenhada** comic strip; **7** *(assunto)* **que ~ é essa de te ires embora?** what's this I hear about your leaving?; ♦ *exc* **qual ~!** what nonsense!; **histórias!** *fpl (disparate, invenção)* nonsense, empty talk; **deixa-te de ~s** come off it! stop telling fibs, tales!; IDIOM **~(s) da carochinha** fibs, cock-and-bull story; **~ do arco-da-velha** tall story; **passar à ~** to be old, be forgotten, be obsolete.
historiador,-ora *m,f* historian.
historial *m* various historical facts; **2** record; account.
histórico,-a *adj* historical, historic; **2** traditional, old; **3** true.
historieta *f* anecdote; **2** little tale; **3** *(pej)* novelette.

historiografia *f* historiography.
historiógrafo,-a *m,f* historiographer.
histrião *m* ham actor; *(fig)* buffoon.
histriónico,-a *(BR -ô-) adj* histrionic; theatrical.
HIV *(abr de* **Vírus da Imunodeficiência Humana Adquirida)** HIV.
hodierno,-a *adj* contemporary; present.
hoje *adv* today; **2** now(adays); ~ **em dia** nowadays; ~ **à noite** tonight; ~ **de manhã** this morning; **de** ~ **a um mês** a month from today; **de** ~ **em diante** from now on, henceforth; **mais** ~, **mais amanhã**, sooner or later; **de** ~ **para amanhã** from one day to the next, at any moment; **ainda** ~ this very day.
Holanda *npr* Holland; **a** ~ Holland; the Netherlands
holandês,-desa *m,f* Dutchman/woman; **2** *m (LÍNG)* Dutch; ♦ *adj* Dutch.
holocausto *m* holocaust.
holofote *m* searchlight, holophote; *(foco)* spotlight.
holograma *m (FOTO)* hologram.
hombridade *f* manliness; **2** loftiness; **3** dignity.
homem *m* man; **2** mankind; ~ **de bem** honest/good man; ~ **de confiança** trustworthy; ~ **feito** grown man; ~ **ao mar**, man overboard; ~ **do mar** seaman; ~ **de negócios** businessman; ~ **bem parecido** good-looking man; ~ **bem posto** well-groomed man; ~ **do povo** man in the street; **ser o** ~ **da casa** to wear the trousers; IDIOM ~ **de sete ofícios** jack of all trades; ~ **com H/letra grande** a real man; ~ **do saco** the bogeyman; ~ **prevenido, vale por dois** forewarned is forearmed; **o** ~ **põe e Deus dispõe** man proposes and God disposes.
homem-rã *(pl:* **homens-rãs)** *m* frogman *(pl:* frogmen).
homenageado,-a *adj* honoured; **2** celebrated.
homenagem *f* homage; **2** honour, tribute; **uma de** ~ praise, respect.
homenzarrão *m* big man, tall and stout; **2** *(fig)* big shot.
homeopata *m,f* homeopath; ♦ *adj inv* homeopathic.
homeopatia *f* homeopathy.
homessa *exc* indeed!; you don't say!; certainly not.
homicida *m,f* murderer; ♦ *adj inv* homicidal.
homicídio *m* murder; *(JUR)* homicide; ~ **culposo/ involuntário** manslaughter.
homiziado,-a *m,f* fugitive; ♦ *adj* in hiding.
homiziar *vt* to shelter; **2** to hide.
homófono *m (LÍNG)* homophone; **acento é um** ~ **de assento** 'acento' is a homophone of 'assento'; ♦ *adj* homophonous.
homogeneidade *f* homogeneity.
homogéneo,-a *adj* homogeneous.
homógrafo *m (LÍNG)* homographic.
homologação *f (JUR)* legal approval, ratification; **2** official recognition; **3** confirmation; **4** agreement.
homólogo,-a *m,f* counterpart, colleague; **o Primeiro Ministro francês e seu** ~ **em Portugal,** the French Prime Minister and his counterpart in Portugal; ♦ *adj* homologous, similar, corresponding.
homónimo *m* namesake; **2** *(LÍNG)* homonym; ♦ *adj* homonymous.
homossexual *m* homosexual; *(col)* gay; ♦ *adj inv* homosexual; **2** *(col)* gay.

homossexualidade *f* homosexuality.
hondurenho,-a *adj* Honduran.
honestidade *f* honesty; **2** decency; **3** fidelity.
honesto,-a *adj* honest; **2** frank, outspoken; **um homem** ~ a decent chap.
honorário,-a *adj* honorary.
honorários *mpl* salary, **2** *(de médico, advogado)* fees.
honorífico,-a *adj* honourable.
honra *f* honour *(UK)*, honor *(US)*; **2** virtue; **3** pride; **em** ~ **de** in honour of; **com** ~ **e proveito** with pride; IDIOM **salvar a** ~ **do convento** to save face.
honradez *f* honesty; integrity; honour.
honrado,-a *adj* honest; **2** virtuous; **3** honourable; **uma mulher** ~a a virtuous woman.
honrar *vt* to honour, respect.
honroso,-a *adj* honourable, *(UK)* honorable *(US)*; ~**s** *fpl* honours.
hóquei *m (DESP)* hockey; ~ **em patins** roller-skates hockey; ~ **sobre o gelo** ice-hockey.
hora *f (do dia)* hour; **meia-hora** half an hour; **são quatro horas da manhã** it is four a.m.; **2** *(tempo)* time; **a toda a** ~ all the time; **à última** ~ at the last minute, at the eleventh hour; **a qualquer** ~ at any time; **é** ~ **do almoço** it is lunch hour; **em boa** ~ at the right time, opportunely; **estar na** ~ **de** it is time to; ~ **de dormir** bedtime; **3** *(momento preciso, determinado)* **na** ~ **H** *(agá)* in the nick of time; **ter** ~ **marcada com (alguém)** have an appointment with sb; **4** chance; **a tua** ~ **há-de chegar** you will have your chance; ♦ ~**s** *fpl* **a altas** ~**s (da noite)** in the small hours, early hours; **a que** ~**s** at what time; **chegar a** ~**s**, to be on time; **dar** ~ **s** *(relógio)* to strike the hour; **fazer** ~**s** to pass the time (while waiting); ~**s vagas/de lazer** spare/leisure time; ~**s extraordinárias** *(trabalho)* overtime; ♦ *adv* **mais** ~ **menos** ~ sooner or later; IDIOM **estar pela** ~ **da morte** *(muito caro)* to cost the earth; **ter a barriga a dar** ~**s** to be hungry.
horário *m* timetable; schedule; ~ **de expediente** *m* business hours; ~ **integral** *(trabalho)* full time.
horda *f* horde; **2** *(fig)* mob.
horizontal *f (GEOM)* horizontal; **2** *(fig) (meretriz)* whore; ♦ *adj inv (linha, limite)* horizontal, on the horizon; **2** *(fig)* **pôr-se na** ~ to lie down.
horizontalidade *f* horizontality.
horizonte *m* horizon; ~ **visual** *(ASTRON)* visible horizon; **2** *(fig) (perspectiva)* perspective, horizon.
hormona *f* hormone.
hormonal *adj inv* hormonal.
hormônio *m (BR)* hormone.
horóscopo *m (ASTROL)* horoscope.
horrendo,-a *adj* horrendous, frightful.
horripilante *adj inv* horrifying, hair-raising, hideous.
horripilar *vt* to horrify; ♦ ~**-se** *vr* to be horrified.
horrível *adj inv* awful, horrible; **2** ugly; **3** *(feitio)* dreadful.
horror *m (pavor)* fear, horror; **ter um** ~ **a ratos** I have a horror of mice; **2** *(repulsa, aversão)* horror; **que** ~! how awful!; **3** *(ficar feio)* **depois da operação plástica, ela ficou um** ~ she was/

looked a horror after the cosmetic surgery; **horrores** *pl* terrible things; **ela disse ~ de mim** she said horrible things about me; **2** crimes; **os ~ da Guerra** war crimes; **3** *(pop)* a lot, masses of; **as viagens custaram ~ de dinheiro** the passages cost a fortune, masses of money.

horrorizar *vt (causar medo)* to frighten, terrify; **2** *(causar horror)* to horrify; **3** *(causar repulsa)* disgust *(alguém)*; **os teus hábitos horrorizam-me** your habits disgust me; ♦ **~-se** *vr* be horrified, be terrified; **ela horrorizou-se quando viu a conta do gás** she was horrified when she saw the gas bill.

horroroso,-a *adj* ghastly, appalling; **foi uma cena ~a** it was a ghastly scene **2** dreadful; **3** disgusting; **comida ~** disgusting food; **4** *(tempo)* awful.

horta *f* vegetable garden, kitchen garden; **~ urbana** *f* allotment; vegetable patch.

hortaliças *fpl* green vegetables; **2** *(cal) (genitais masculinos)* male genitals.

hortelã *f* mint; **~ pimenta** peppermint; **~ silvestre** horsemint; **pastilhas de ~** peppermints.

hortelão,-loa *(pl: hortelãos/hortelões) m,f* market-gardener.

horteleiro,-a *m,f (BR)* market-gardener.

hortense *adj inv* of/from Horta *(Azores)*.

hortense, hortênsia *f (BOT)* hydrangea.

hortícola *adj inv* horticultural.

horticultor,-ora *(mpl: -es; fpl: -as) m,f* horticulturist; ♦ *adj inv* horticultural.

hortifrutigranjeiro,-a *adj (BR)* small landholder, grower of fruit, vegetables.

hortigranjeiros *mpl (BR)* farm produce.

horto *m* small vegetable, flower garden; **2** horticultural nursery; **3** patch of land, allotment for growing vegetables.

hospedagem *f* lodging.

hospedar *vt* to put sb up; lodge; give accommodation to; ♦ **~-se** *vr* to stay (at); lodge.

hospedaria *f* inn; **2** hostel, guest house.

hóspede *m,f* guest; **2** lodger; paying guest.

hospedeiro,-a *m,f* inn-keeper; landlord, landlady; **~ de bordo/do ar** air steward, stewardess; ♦ *adj (BOT, BIOL)* host; **2** *(person)* hospitable.

hospício *m* asylum; **2** hospice; **3** nursing home; **4** *(para animais)* home, shelter.

hospital *m* hospital.

hospitalar *adj inv (pessoal, etc)* hospital; **assistência ~** hospital assistance.

hospitalário *m (HIST)* hospitaller.

hospitalários *adj* Knights Hospitallers.

hospitaleiro,-a *adj* hospitable, welcoming.

hospitalidade *f* hospitality.

hospitalizar *vt* to hospitalize (sb).

hoste *f* army, legion, host; **2 ~s** *fpl* rank and file; **3** troops; **enfrentaram as ~s** they faced the enemy.

hóstia *f (REL)* Host; **a Sagrada H~** the Holy Host; **2** *(CULIN, FARM)* wafer.

hostil *adj inv* hostile (**a** to); **2** agressivo,-a.

hostilidade *f* hostility.

hostilizar *vt* to be hostile towards; to antagonize, to make enemies.

hotel *(pl: -éis) m* hotel; *(para automobilistas)* motel *(US)*; **~ de primeira ordem** first class hotel; **gerente do ~** hotel manager.

hotelaria *f* hotel business.

hoteleiro,-a *m,f* hotelier; ♦ *adj* hotel; **rede ~a** hotel chain.

houve *(pt de:* **haver***)*; **~ um erro** an error occurred, there was an error/a mistake.

hui! *exc (dor)* ouch!; *(espanto)* oh!

hulha *f* coal; **~ antracitosa** anthracite, hard coal; **alcatrão de ~** coal tar; **~-branca** *(fpl:* **hulhas-brancas***) f* water power.

hum! *exc (expressando dúvida, impaciência)* hum!; ah, I see! really!

humanidade *f* mankind; **2** humanity.

humanista *adj inv* humanist.

humanitário,-a *adj* humanitarian; **2** humane.

humanizar *vt* to humanize; ♦ *vr* to become more human.

humano,-a *m;* **o ser ~** the human being, mankind; ♦ **humano,-a** *adj* human; **2** *(bom, generoso)* humane; **ela é muito ~a** she is very humane person; **errar é ~!** to err is human!

humedecer *(BR:* **ume-***) vt* to moisten, wet; ♦ *vi* to become humid; ♦ **~-se** *vr* to become moist.

humente *adj inv (Vd:* **húmido***)*.

humidade *f* dampness; **2** humidity.

húmido,-a *adj (terra, relvado)* wet, moist; **2** *(roupa)* damp; **3** *(clima, ar)* humid; **4** *(aquoso)* watery; **5** *(MED) (ferida)* weeping.

humildade *f* humility.

humilde *adj inv* humble; **2** poor; **3** meek.

humilhação *f* humiliation.

humilhado,-a *adj* humiliated; abased; **sentir-se ~** to lose face.

humilhante *adj inv* humiliating.

humilhar *vt* to humiliate; to belittle; to make sb feel small; ♦ **~-se** *vr* to humble o.s.; *(pop)* to eat humble pie.

humílico,-a *adj (superl de* **humilde***)* most humble.

humo *m (Vd:* **humus***)*.

humor *m* mood, temper; **de bom/mau ~** in a good/bad humour; **2** humour *(UK)*, humor *(US)*; **senso de ~** sense of humour; **~ negro** black humour; **3** *(humidade)* dew; ♦ **~es** *npl (ANAT)* bodily fluids; **~ aqueoso/vítreo** aqueous/vitreous humour (in the eye).

humorado,-a *adj:* **mal-humorado** in a bad mood.

humorismo *m* humour.

humorista *adj inv* humorist; **2** humoralist.

humorístico,-a *adj* humorous; witty, funny comical.

humos *m (prato grego/turco feito com grão-de-bico)* houmous, hummus.

humoso,-a *adj* humus, rich in humus.

húmus *m (terra vegetal)* humus, vegetable mould.

húngaro,-a *adj* Hungarian, Magyar.

Hungria *npr* **a ~** Hungary.

Huno, Hunos *m* Hun, Huns; **os ~** *mpl* the Huns.

huri *f (ninfa do Paraíso, na crença islâmica)* houri.

hurra! *exc* hurrah!, hooray!

Hussar, hussardo *m* hussar.

I

I, i *m* (letra) I, i.
ianque *m,f* Yank; ♦ *adj inv* Yankee.
ião *m* (QUÍM, FÍS) ion.
IAPMEI (*abr de* **Instituto de Apoio às Pequenas e Médias Empresas (PME) e Investimento**) the Support Association for SME (Small and Medium Enterprise) and Investment.
iate *m* yacht.
iatismo *m* yachting, sailing.
iatista *m,f* yachtsman, yachtswoman.
ibérico,-a *adj* Iberian.
ibero,-a *m,f* Iberian.
ibi, ibidem, ibid., ib.
içar *vt* (*bandeira, vela*) to hoist, raise.
icebergue *m* iceberg.
ícone *m* icon; **2** (LING) icon; **3** (fig) icon, idol, image.
iconoclasta *m,f* iconoclast; ♦ *adj* iconoclastic.
iconografia *f* iconography.
icterícia *f* jaundice.
ida *f* going, departure; ~ **e volta** round trip; **bilhete de ~ e volta** return ticket; ♦ **~s e vindas** *adv* comings and goings.
idade *f* age; **ter dois anos de ~** to be two (years old); **pessoa de meia ~** middle-aged person; **de menor ~** under age; **a I ~ Média** the Middle Ages; **tenho a mesma ~ que você** I am as old as you; **ele já tem ~ para ter juízo** he is old enough to have some sense; **pessoa da terceira ~** pensioner, senior citizen; ~ **de ouro** the Golden Age/Era; **estar na flor da ~** to be in the prime of life.
ideal (*pl:* **ideais**) *m* ideal, dream; **2** model; ♦ *adj inv* ideal.
idealismo *m* idealism.
idealista *m,f* idealist; ♦ *adj* idealistic.
idealizar *vt* to idealize; **2** to dream; **3** to devise, create; **quem idealizou a EXPO 98?** who created/planned Expo 98?
idear *vt* idealise/idealize; form an ideal.
ideia *f* idea; **2** mind, notion; **mudar de ~** to change one's mind; **não ter ~** to have no idea; **não faço ~ nenhuma** I have no idea/can't imagine; **arrumar as ~s** put one's ideas in order; **tenho uma ~ de que...** I have a notion that...
idem *pron* idem, the same.
idêntico,-a *adj* identical.
identidade *f* identity; **bilhete de ~** identity card.
identificação *f* identification; **placa de ~** identification tag.
identificar *vt* to identify; ♦ **~-se** *vr:* **-se com** to identify o.s. with sb/sth.

ideologia *f* ideology.
ideológico,-a *adj* ideological.
ideólogo,-a *m,f* ideologist.
idílico,-a *adj* idyllic, romantic.
idílio *m* idyll, romance.
idioma *m* language, idiom.
idiomático,-a *adj* idiomatic; **expressões ~as,** idiomatic expressions.
idiota *m,f* idiot, fool; **2** (fam) dunce, blockhead; ~ **chapado-a** drivelling idiot; ♦ *adj* idiotic.
idiotice *f* idiocy; **2** nonsense.
idiotismo *m* idiomatic expression.
ido,-a (*pp de:* **ir**) *adj* departed, gone, left; **ele já tinha ~** he had gone, left; **nos tempos idos** in the bygone days.
idólatra *m,f* idolater, tress; ♦ *adj inv* idolatrous.
idolatrar *vt* to idolize.
idolatria *f* idolatry.
ídolo *m* idol.
idoneidade *f* suitability; competence; ~ **moral** moral probity.
idóneo,-a *adj* suitable, fit; **2** able, capable.
idoso,-a *m,f* old person; **os idosos** the old folks; ♦ *adj* elderly, old.
Iémen *npr* **o ~** Yemen.
iemenita *adj inv* Yemenite.
iene *m* (moeda japonesa) yen.
iglu *m* igloo.
ignaro,-a *adj* ignorant; **2** stupid; **3** (cal) thick.
ignição *f* ignition.
ignóbil *adj inv* ignoble; dishonourable.
ignomínia *f* disgrace, ignominy.
ignominioso,-a *adj* ignominious.
ignorado,-a *adj* unknown; obscure.
ignorância *f* ignorance.
ignorante *m,f* ignorant person; (fam) ignoramus; ♦ *adj inv* ignorant, uneducated.
ignorar *vt* not to know, be unaware of, ignore the fact; **2** (deprezar) to ignore.
ignoto,-a *adj* unknown.
igreja *f* church.
Iguaçu *npr:* **as Cataratas do ~** the Iguaçu Falls.
igual (*pl:* **-ais**) *m,f* equal, match; **coisa ~** the like; ♦ *adj inv* equal; **2** (semelhante) alike even, uniform; **em partes iguais** in equal parts; **ser ~ a** be like; **sem ~** without equal; (MAT) equal (**to** a); **por ~** *adv* equally; IDIOM **cada qual com seu ~** birds of a feather flock together.
igualar *vt* to make equal, equalize, equate (with), match; **2** level; ♦ *vr* **~-se a** be equal to/as good as; be equal.
igualdade *f* equality; **2** evenness, uniformity; **3** (GEOM) equation.
igualha *f* equality of rank, social equality; **gente da mesma ~** of the same ilk; the likes of them.
iguaria *f* (CULIN) delicacy, choice fare; **2** dish.
iídiche, ídiche *m* Yiddish.
ilação *f* inference, deduction.
ilativo,-a *adj* inferential
ilegal *adj inv* illegal, unlawful, illicit.

ilegítimo,-a *adj* illegitimate, illicit; **2** *(filho)* bastardo, illegitimate; **3** *(fig) (infundado)* unacceptable, unfounded.

> The Portuguese word **'bastardo'** is not used in an offensive or in vulgar sense.

ilegível *adj inv* illegible, unreadable; **2** *(documento)* indecipherable.

ileso,-a *adj* unhurt, uninjured; unharmed.

iletrado,-a *adj* illiterate, uneducated.

ilha *f* island.

ilharga *f (ANAT)* hip; **de mãos na ~** with hands on hips, arms akimbo; **2** *(animal)* flank.

ilhéu *m* small island, islet; ♦ *adj* islander.

ilhó, ilhós *(pl: ilhoses) m,f (orifício em roupa, calçado)* eyelet, eyehole, loop, grommet/grummet.

ilhoa *f* islander.

ilhota *f* small island, islet.

ilibar *vt (reconhecer a inocência)* to declare not guilty; **2** to vindicate, justify; ♦ **~-se** *vr* to acquit, justify oneself.

ilição *f (JUR)* fraud.

iliçar *vt* to cheat, deceive, swindle.

ilícito,-a *adj* illicit, illegal, unlawful; **relações ~s** illicit relations.

ilidir *vt (JUR)* to refute, repel; **2** to prove to be false.

ilimitado,-a *adj* unlimited; **2** absolute.

ilimitável *(pl: -veis) adj inv* illimitable.

ilínio *m (QUÍM)* illinium.

ílio *m (ANAT)* hipbone.

ilíquido *adj (COM)* gross, illiquid, without deduction.

il^mo *(abr de* **ilustríssimo)** most illustrious; **2** *(BR)* *(tratamento formal utilizado em cartas/envelopes)* **Il^mo Senhor, Il^ma Senhora** Dear Sir, Madam.

ilógico,-a *adj* illogical; absurd.

iludir *vt* to deceive; **2** to evade; **3** to delude; ♦ **~-se** *vr* to deceive o.s.

iludível *adj inv* deceivable.

iluminação *f* lighting, lights, lights; **2** *(fig)* enlightenment.

iluminado,-a *adj* lit up, alight; **2** enlightened.

iluminar *vt* to light up, illuminate; **2** *(rua com luzes)* to decorate; **3** *(livro com ouro/prata)* to decorate; **4** to enlighten.

iluminismo *m* illuminism.

ilusão *f* illusion; **2** delusion; **3** trick; **~ de óptica** optical illusion.

ilusionista *m,f* illusionist; **2** conjurer; **3** juggler.

ilusório,-a *adj* deceptive; **2** illusive; **3** illusory; **4** unreal.

ilustração *f* illustration; **2** erudition; **3** illustrated magazine; **4** picture, figure, plate.

ilustrado,-a *adj* illustrated; **2** learned; **3** pictorial.

ilustrar *vt* to illustrate; **2** to explain; **3** to clarify, enlighten; ♦ **~-se** *vr* to excel; **2** to educate o.s.

ilustre *adj inv* illustrious, eminent, distinguished.

ilustríssimo,-a *(superl de* **ilustre)** *adj* most illustrious; **~,-a senhor,-a** the honourable gentleman, lady.

ímã¹ *(Vd:* **íman)** *m (BR)* magnet.

ímã² *m (guia religioso)* iman.

imaculado,-a *adj* immaculate, unblemished; **2** undefiled; **3** *(limpo)* spotless; **a I~ Conceição** Immaculate Conception.

imagem *f* image; **2** likeness; **3** picture; **4** *(CIN, Tv, notícias)* picture; **imagens cedidas por** pictures given by.

imaginação *f* imagination.

imaginar *vt* to imagine; **2** to suppose; ♦ *vi* to daydream; ♦ **~-se** *vr* imagine o.s. (to be).

imaginário,-a *adj* imaginary.

imaginativo,-a *adj* imaginative, creative.

imanar *vt (corpo, metal)* to magnetize; ♦ *vi* to be magnetized.

imanente *adj inv* immanent, inherent, intrinsic.

imaterial *adj inv* immaterial, spiritual.

imaturidade *f* immaturity.

imaturo,-a *adj* immature.

imbatível *adj inv* invincible, unbeatable.

imbecil *m,f* imbecile, half-wit; ♦ *adj inv* idiotic, stupid; **2** *(PSIC) (mente)* imbecile.

imbecilidade *f* stupidity.

imberbe *adj inv (jovem)* sem barba, beardless; **2** clean-shaven.

imbricar *vt (dispor, arrange)* to imbricate *(elementos, telhas)*; ♦ **~-se** *vr (dispor-se em estilo de escamas)* overlap.

imbróglio *m* confusion; intricacy.

imbuir *vt* imbue, pervade; **~ de** to imbue with; **~ em,** to soak in; **2** *(fig)* to instil; ♦ **~-se de** *vr* to be imbued with.

imediações *fpl (arredores)* vicinity *sg,* neighbourhood *sg,* near by area.

imediatamente *adv* immediately, right away.

imediato,-a *m,f (NÁUT)* chief officer, first mate; ♦ *adj (rápido)* immediate; **2** *(dia, acontecimento)* next, after; **3** *(lugar)* contiguous, next to; **4** *(MED)* direct; ♦ **de ~** *adv* straight away.

imensidade, imensidão *f* immensity.

imenso,-a *adj* immense, huge.

imerecido,-a *adj* undeserved.

imergir *vt/vi* to immerge, immerse, to plunge (into).

imerso,-a *adj* submerged; **2** immersed.

imidogénio *(BR: -ê-) m (QUÍM)* imidogen; the imido group.

imigração *f* immigration.

imigrante *adj* immigrant.

imigrar *vi* to immigrate.

iminência *f* imminence; **na ~ de** on the verge of.

iminente *adj inv* imminent, about to happen; impending.

imiscuir-se *vr* to meddle **(em** in), interfere; **2** to become involved.

imitação *f* imitation, copy.

imitável *adj inv* that can be imitated.

imitar *vt* to imitate, copy; **2** *(falsificar)* to forge.

imitir *vt* to send, put in; **2** *(JUR)* to vest (on sb).

imobiliário,-a *adj* property, immovable; **2** *(US)* real estate; *f* estate agency.

imolar *vt* to sacrifice; immolate; ♦ **~-se** *vr (fig)* to sacrifice oneself.

imoral *(pl:* **imorais)** *adj inv* immoral.

imortal *(pl:* **imortais)** *adj inv* immortal.

imortalizar *vt* to immortalize.

imóvel *adj inv* motionless, still; **2** immovable; *m* property; **bens imóveis** property.

impaciência *f* impatience.

impacientar-se *vr* to lose one's patience.

impaciente *adj inv* impatient; **2** *(ansioso)* anxious.

impacto *m* impact *(em* on, upon).

impagável *(pl: -eis) adj (pessoa muito cómica)* hilarious; **2** *(inestimável)* priceless; **3** *(dívida, despesa)* unpayable.

impaludismo *m* malaria.

ímpar *(pl: -es) adj (número)* odd; *(lugar, etc)* odd-numbered; **par ou** ~ odd or even; **2** without equal, unique.

imparcial *adj inv* fair, impartial.

imparcialidade *f* impartiality.

impasse *m* one-way street, cul-de-sac, dead end; **2** *(fig)* impasse, deadlock, stalemate.

impassibilidade *f* impassibility.

impassível *(pl: -veis) adj* impassive; **2** expressionless; **3** insensitive.

impávido,-a *adj* fearless, intrepid.

impecável *adj inv* perfect, impeccable.

impedido,-a *m,f (MIL)* batman, orderly; ♦ *adj* hindered, prevented; **2** *(trânsito)* blocked, obstructed; **3** *(linha, telefone)* engaged; **o telefone está** ~ the telephone/line is engaged; **4** *(FUT)* offside.

impedimento *m* obstacle; hindrance; **2** *(JUR)* impediment.

impedir *vt (obstruir)* to obstruct, block; **2** *(coibir)* impede, hinder; ~ **alguém de fazer algo** to prevent sb from doing (sth).

impelir *vt (empurrar para diante)* to drive (on), push forward; **2** *(incentivar)* to impel; **3** *(obrigar)* coerce *(alguém)*.

impene *adj inv* featherless, without plumage.

impenetrável *adj inv* impenetrable; **2** fathomless, unfathomable; **3** *(fig)* reserved, reticent.

impenitente *adj inv* unrepentant.

impensado,-a *adj* thoughtless; **2** unpremediated; **3** unforeseen.

impensável *adj inv* unthinkable.

imperador *m* emperor.

imperar *vi* to reign, rule; **2** *(fig)* to prevail, dominate.

imperativo *m (dever, lei)* imperative, duty; **2** *(gram)* imperative mood; ~**s da moda** dictates of fashion; ♦ *adj* imperative, peremptory.

imperatriz *f* empress.

imperceptível *adj inv* imperceptible; **2** slight.

imperdoável *adj inv* unforgivable, inexcusable.

imperecível *adj inv* imperishable; **2** indestructible.

imperfeição *f* imperfection, flaw.

imperfeito,-a *adj* imperfect; faulty; **2** *(gram) (pt)* imperfect.

imperial *adj inv* imperial; **2** imperious; arrogant; ♦ **uma** ~ *(EP-pop)* glass of draught lager.

imperialismo *m* imperialism.

imperícia *f* incompetence; **2** inexperience.

império *m* empire.

imperioso,-a *adj* domineering; **2** pressing, urgent.

impermeável *m* raincoat; ♦ *adj inv* impervious; waterproof.

impertinência *f* impertinence; **2** irrelevance.

impertinente *adj inv* irrelevant; **2** impertinent; **3** petulance.

imperturbável *adj inv* cool, unmoved; **2** impassive; imperturbable.

impérvio,-a *adj* impervious; **2** *(place)* inaccessible, impassable, impenetrable.

impessoal *adj inv* impersonal.

ímpeto *m* impetus; **2** force; **3** surge, rush; **agir com** ~ to act on impulse.

impetuosidade *f* impetuosity.

impetuoso,-a *adj* headstrong, impetuous; **2** *(águas)* fast-flowing, strong; **3** *(decision)* rash, hasty; **4** *(arrebatado)* enthusiastic, passionate.

impiedade *f (heresia)* impiety, irreverence; **2** *(falta de piedade)* cruelty heartlessness.

impiedoso,-a *adj* merciless; **2** inhuman.

impingir *vt (iludir, enganar)* to palm off *(com mentira, etc)*; **2** to foist/fob a worthless thing on sb; **3** to pass off (one thing for another); **4** *(obrigar alguém a ouvir algo)* **ela impingiu-nos uma longa história** she made us listen to a long, boring story; **5** *(obrigar a ter alguém/algo)* **impingiram-lhe uma tradutora sem qualificações** they made him employ/persuaded him to employ an unqualified translator.

ímpio,-a *m,f* heretic, unbeliever; ♦ *adj* irreligious; **2** inhuman, cruel; **3** pitiless.

implacável *adj inv* implacable; **2** unforgiving; **3** relentless; **4** severe; **5** *(verdade)* grim.

implantar *vt (MED)* to implant; **2** to establish, install; **3** to implement; ♦ *vi (plant)* to take root.

implante *m* implant; **silicone** ~**s** silicone implants.

implementação *f* implementation; **2** execution; **3** development.

implementar *vt* to carry out, execute; **2** *(leis, reformas)* to implement.

implicar *vt* to implicate; **2** to imply; ~ **com** to pick a quarrel with; ♦ ~**-se** *vr* to get involved.

implícito,-a *adj* implicit; implied.

implorar *vt/vi (rogar)* to beg, implore, entreat, plead.

implosão *f* implosion; **2** demolishing of building with explosives.

impoluível *adj inv* unpolluted; that cannot be polluted.

impoluto,-a *adj* spotless, immaculate; **2** pure.

imponderado,-a *adj* thoughtless, heedless, ill-pondered.

imponência *f* splendour, magnificence.

imponente *adj inv* impressive; imposing.

impopular *adj inv* unpopular.

impor *vt* to impose; **2** to command; **3** to demand; ♦ ~**-se** *vr* to impose oneself.

importação *f* importing; **2** imports *pl*.

importador,-ora *m,f* importer; ♦ *adj* importing.

importância *f* importance; **2** sum, amount; **não tem** ~ it doesn't matter, never mind; **sem** ~ not seriously.

importante *m* important (thing); **o** ~ **é** the main/important thing is; ♦ *adj inv* important.

importar *vt (COM)* to import (from abroad); ♦ *vi (ser importante)* to matter; **não importa** it doesn't matter! never mind!; ~ **em** *(atingir valor)* to amount to, add up to; ♦ ~-se *vr (fazer caso)* to mind, care (if); **importa-se que eu fume?** do you mind if I smoke?; **eles não se importam de esperar** they do not mind to wait; **ninguém se importa com a situação** no-one cares about the situation; **não me importo contigo** I am not bothered with you.

importe *m* amount, cost; **o ~ líquido** the net sum, amount.

importunar *vt* to bother, annoy, pester, nag; **2** to disturb.

importuno,-a *adj* annoying; **2** inopportune; **3** impertinent.

impossibilidade *f* impossibility.

impossibilitar *vt* to make impossible; incapacitate; ♦ ~-se *vr* to be unable (**para** to).

impossível *m:* **o ~** the impossible; ♦ *adj inv* impossible; **2** insufferable.

imposto,-a *(pp irr de:* **impor***) m* tax; **~ de rendimento** *(BR:* **de renda***)* income tax; **~ habitacional** Council tax; **~ de circulação** *(zonas proibidas de circular)* congestion charge, road-pricing.

impostor,-ora *m,f* impostor, charlatan.

impostura *f* deception.

impotência *f* impotence.

impotente *adj inv* impotent; **2** powerless.

impraticável *adj inv* impracticable.

imprecação *f (praga)* imprecation, curse.

imprecaução *f (falta de cuidado)* imprudence.

impreciso,-a *adj* vague; **2** inaccurate; **3** imprecise.

impregnar *vt* to impregnate.

imprensa *f* printing; **2** press; **3** printer's.

imprescindível *adj inv* essential, indispensable.

impressão *f (sensação)* impression, feeling; **tenho a ~ que ...** I think that/I have the feeling that ...; **2** printing; **erro de ~** misprint; **3** *(COMP)* imprintout; **~ digital** fingerprint.

impressionante *adj inv* impressive; **2** moving, touching; **3** *(acção má)* shocking.

impressionar *vt* to impress; **2** to move; **3** *(FOTO)* to expose; ♦ ~-se *vr* to be impressed, moved; **isso não me impressiona nada** I am not at all impressed.

impressionismo *m (ART)* impressionism.

impresso,-a *(pp irr de* **imprimir***) m* form; leaflet; ♦ *adj* printed.

impressor,-ora *(pessoa) m,f* printer.

impressora *f (máquina)* printer; **~ laser** laser printer.

impressos *mpl* printed matter *sg.*

impreterível *adj inv* essencial; **2** *(prazo)* final.

imprevidente *adj inv* improvident; **2** *(descuidado)* careless.

imprevisto,-a *adj* unexpected, unforeseen, sudden.

imprimir *vt* to print, to print off *(jornal)*; **2** *(marca)* to stamp; **3** *(inspirar)* to instil; **4** *(COMP)* to print out; ♦ ~-se *vr (gravar-se na memória)* to be stamped/impressed.

improbabilidade *f* improbability, unlikelihood.

ímprobo,-a *adj* dishonest; **2** arduous.

improcedente *adj inv (infundado)* groundless, unjustified.

improdutivo,-a *adj (que não produz)* unproductive, infertile; **2** *(sem lucro)* unprofitable.

improfícuo,-a *adj* useless, futile; **2** unprofitable; **3** fruitless.

impropério *m* insult, affront; **2** vulgarity.

impropriedade *f* unsuitability; **2** incorrectness; **3** impropriety.

impróprio,-a *adj* unsuitable; **2** wrong; **3** *(conduta)* improper, indecorous; **4** *(MAT)* improper.

improvável *adj inv* unlikely.

improvidência *f* rashness; carelessness.

improvidente *adj inv* thriftless; **2** careless.

improvisado,-a *adj* improvised; **2** *(MÚS)* impromptu.

improvisar *vt/vi* to improvise; **2** *(discurso)* to ad-lib.

improviso *m* improvisation; **falar de ~** to speak impromptu/ad hoc.

improvisor,-ora *adj* improviser.

imprudência *f* imprudence; **2** rashness.

imprudente *adj inv* rash; **2** unwise.

impudência *f* impudence; **2** *(fam)* cheek, gall.

impudente *adj inv* shameless, impudent; **3** cheeky, cocky; **4** insolent.

impudico,-a *adj (sem vergonha)* shameless; **2** lewd; **3** immodest; **4** cheeky.

impugnar *vt* to refute, impugn; **2** to oppose, call into question; **3** to veto.

impulsionador,-ora promoter; ♦ *adj* stimulating; **2** driving force.

impulsionar *vt (dar movimento)* to propel; **2** to give impetus to; **3** *(estimular)* to encourage.

impulsivo,-a *adj* impulsive.

impulso *m (impulsão)* impulse, push; impetus; **num ~** on an impulse; **2** *(estímulo)* stimulus, incitement, boost; **3** *(TEL)* unit, period.

impune *adj inv* unpunished. **impunemente** *adv* with impunity.

impunidade *f* impunity.

impureza *f* impurity; **2** dirt, filth; **3** dregs, sediment; **4** *(fig)* unchastity.

impuro,-a *adj* impure; **2** polluted; **3** sordid, lewd.

imputação *f (JUR)* accusation, charge; **~ no crédito** expense deducted from a credit.

imputado,-a *adj (JUR)* **ser ~** to be liable.

imputar *vt* to attribute; **~ algo a alguém** to blame sb for sth.

imputável *adj inv* imputable, imputative; **2** chargeable, liable.

imundícia *f* filth, uncleanness; **2** *(BR)* slum.

imundície *f (Vd:* **imundícia***); 2 (BR)* rabbit hunting.

imundo,-a *adj* filthy, squalid, foul; **2** *(indecente)* immoral, lewd, obscene.

imune *adj inv (BIOL)* immune; **2** exempt; **3** indifferent to.

imunidade *f (BIOL)* immunity; **2** *(JUR, POL)* exemption; **3** privilege.

imunizar *vt* to immunize; **2** *(fig)* to make immune; ♦ ~-se *vr* to become immune.

imuno-deficiência *f* immunedeficiency.

imutável *adj inv* unalterable, unchangeable; **2** immutable.

inabalável *adj inv* unshakeable; **2** firme; **3** *(defesa)* invincible; **4** *(character)* inflexible; **fé ~** deeply-rooted faith.

inábil *adj inv* clumsy; **2** inapt; **3** incompetent; **4** *(atitude)* incorrect; **5** unskilful.

inabilidade *f* incompetence; **2** clumsiness; **3** inability; **4** *(JUR)* incapacity.

inabilitar *vt* to incapacitate; **2** to disqualify (student in an exam).

inacabável *adj inv* interminable, unending.

ina(c)ção *f* inactivity; **2** inertness, inertia; **3** indolence.

inaceitável *adj inv* unacceptable.

inacessível *adj inv* inaccessible.

inacreditável *adj inv* incredible, unbelievable; **2** *(pessoa, obra)* extraordinary; **isso é ~!** that's a tall story!

ina(c)tividade *f* inactivity; inertia; **2** *(reforma)* retirement, redundancy.

ina(c)tivo,-a *adj* inactive, inert; **2** retired; **3** passive.

inadequado,-a *adj* unsuitable, improper; **2** inadequate; **3** *(maneira)* incorrect; **4** *(visita de surpresa)* inconvenient.

inadiável *adj inv* *(algo)* that cannot be put off/ postponed/delayed; **2** urgent, pressing.

inadmissível *adj inv* inadmissible, unacceptable; **2** that cannot be tolerated.

inadquirível *adj inv* unobtainable.

inadvertência *f* oversight, error; **2** carelessness.

inadvertido,-a *adj (sem querer)* unintentional, inadvertent.

inalação *f* breathing in, inhalation.

inalador *m* inhaler; ♦ *adj* inhaling.

inalar *vt* to inhale.

inalcançável *adj inv* unattainable; impossible.

inalterável *adj inv* unchangeable; imperturbable.

inane *adj inv* empty, void; **2** worthless; **3** shallow.

inanição *f* emptiness; **2** *(BIO)* inanition, starvation.

inanimado,-a *adj* lifeless; **2** inanimate; **3** motionless; **4** *(olhar, expressão)* dull, dead.

inaptidão *f* inability, inaptitude.

inapto,-a *m,f* dunce, idiot; ♦ *adj* inapt, unfit; **2** clumsy.

inarticulado,-a *adj (que não tem articulações)* without articulations, joints; *(animal)* jointless; **2** *(no falar)* mal articulado, mal enunciado.

inatingível *adj inv* unreachable, unattainable; **2** *(fig)* inaccessible.

inatividade *f (Vd:* **ina(c)tividade**).

inativo,-a *(Vd:* **ina(c)tivo,-a**).

inato,-a *adj* innate, inborn, inbred; **2** inerente.

inaudito,-a *adj* unheard-of; **2** unprecedented; **3** extraordinary; **4** *(insolência)* shocking.

inauguração *f* inauguration; opening.

inaugurar *vt* to inaugurate; to open.

incalculável *adj inv* incalculable.

incansável *adj inv* tireless, untiring; **2** indefatigable.

incapacidade *f* incapacity; **2** *(inaptidão)* incompetence, inaptitude.

incapacitado,-a *m,f* disabled, handicapped (person); ♦ *adj (inválido)* disabled, handicapped; **2** *(não poder)* unable; **~ de fazer algo** be unable to do sth.

incapacitar *vt* to incapacitate, disable; **2** to deprive s.o. of a right; ♦ **~se** *vr* become unable to.

incapaz *adj:* **~ de fazer** unable to do, incapable of doing; **~ para** unfit for.

inçar *vt* to infest; ♦ *vi* to propagate.

incauto,-a *adj* careless, incautious; **2** unwary; **3** *(ingénuo)* naïve, artless.

incendiar *vt* to set fire to; *(fig)* to inflame; ♦ **~-se** *vr* to catch fire.

incendiáro,-a *m,f* arsonist; ♦ *adj* incendiary; *(fig)* inflammatory.

incêndio *m* fire; **~ premeditado** arson.

incenso *m* incense, frankincense; **2** *(fig)* adulation.

incentivar *vt* to stimulate, encourage.

incentivo *m* incentive, stimulus.

incerteza *f* uncertainty; **2** doubt; **3** indecision.

incerto,-a *adj* uncertain, hesitant; **2** doubtful.

incessante *adj inv* incessant, ceaseless, continuous; **2** continual.

incestar *vi* to commit incest.

incesto *m* incest.

incestuosamente *adv* incestuously.

inchado,-a *adj* swollen; **2** *(fig)* conceited.

inchar *vt* to swell; **2** *(fig) (louvor)* to make sb swell with pride; ♦ *vi* to swell up *(o braço, etc)*; ♦ **~-se** *vr* to swell (up); **2** *(fig)* to become conceited.

incidência *f* incidence; **2** occurrence.

incidente *m* incident.

incidir *vi* to befall, happen; **~ com** to coincide; **~ em** to fall into (error); **~ sobre** *(recair)* to fall on.

incinerar *vt* to burn, incinerate; **3** to cremate.

incisão *f* cut; **2** *(MED)* incision.

incisivo,-a *m (dente)* incisor; ♦ *adj* cutting, sharp; **2** incisive, **um comentário ~** an incisive comment, cutting comment, remark.

incitação *f*, **incitamento** *m* incitement.

incitar *vt* to incite, instigate; **2** to rouse, provoke; to egg on; **3** *(açular)* insite, set on (dog).

incivil *adj inv* rude, ill-mannered, discourteous; **2** boorish.

incivilidade *f* discourtesy; rudeness.

incivilizado,-a uncivilized; **2** barbarian; **3** *(fig)* uncouth.

incivismo *m* want of patriotism or of civility.

inclemência *f* harshness, rigour; **2** inclemency.

inclemente *adj inv* severe, harsh; **2** inclement.

inclinação *f (declive)* inclination; slope; **2** *(atracção)* liking (for); **3** tendency, leaning (towards); **~ da cabeça** nod; *(gesto de saudação ou acordo)*, bow; **4** *(FÍS)* dip; **5** *(NÁUT)* lean, list.

inclinado,-a *adj* inclined, leaning; **2** *(propenso)* inclined towards; **estar pouco ~ a** to loath to (do sth).

inclinar *vt (pender)* to tilt, lean; **2** *(cabeça)* to nod; **3** to bend; *(discussão)* **~ para** to lead round to; ♦ *vi* to slope; ♦ **~-se** *vr* to tilt; **2** to stoop; bend down; **~ a trabalhar** inclined/willing to work; **~ para a ciência** lean towards science.

ínclito,-a *adj* illustrious, renowned.

incluir *vt* to include; **2** to incorporate; **3** to enclose.

inclusão *f* inclusion.

inclusive *adj inv* inclusive; ♦ *prep* including; **2** up to; ♦ *adv* inclusively.

incluso,-a *adj* included; **2** enclosed.

incobrável *adj inv (que não se pode cobrar ou receber)* unrecoverable, uncollectable.

incoerência *f* incoherence.

incoerente *adj inv* incoherent.

incógnito,-a *adj* unknown; ♦ *adv* incognito; **2** unknown; **3** *(MAT)* unknown quantity of factor.

incolor *adj* colourless; **2** *(linguagem)* insipid, bland; **3** uncertain.

incólume *adj inv* safe and sound; **2** unharmed, uninjured; **3** *(pacote, etc)* intact.

incomensurável *adj inv* immense, enormous; **2** measureless; **3** *(MAT)* incommensurable.

incomodar *vt* to bother, trouble; **2** to upset; ♦ *vi* to disturb; ♦ **~-se** *vr* to bother, put o.s. out; **não se incomode!** never mind!, don't trouble yourself.

incómodo,-a *(BR: -ô-) m* nuisance, problem; **2** *(pop)* menstruation; ♦ *adj* inconvenient; **2** uncomfortable; **3** boring.

incomparável *adj inv* incomparable; **2** matchless, without a peer.

incompatibilidade *f* incompatibility.

incompatível *adj inv* incompatible.

incompetência *f* incompetence.

incompetente *adj inv* incompetent.

incompleto,-a *adj* incomplete, unfinished.

incompreensível *adj inv* incomprehensible; **2** unintelligible.

incomum *adj inv* uncommon, unusual.

incomunicável *adj inv* unavailable; **2** incommunicado; **3** *(TEL)* unobtainable; **4** *(preso)* in solitary confinement.

inconcebível *adj inv* inconceivable, unthinkable; **2** incredible.

inconciliável *adj inv* irreconcilable; incompatible.

inconcludente *adj inv* inconclusive.

incondicional *adj inv* unconditional; **2** wholehearted; **3** loyal, staunch; **uma amizade ~ a** staunch friendship.

incôndito,-a *adj (feito sem regra)* disorganized.

inconfesso,-a *adj* secret.

inconfidência *f* disloyalty; **2** indiscretion; **3** *(BR)* *(JUR)* treason.

inconfidente *m (BR)* conspirator; ♦ *adj* disloyal, untrustworthy.

Inconfidente: citizen who took part in the movement against the crown, known as **Inconfidência/Conjuração Mineira**, in Brazil, in the late 18th century.

inconformado,-a *adj* recalcitrant.

inconformismo *m* non-comformity.

inconfundível *adj inv* unmistakable.

incongruente *adj inv* incongruous; inappropriate (to).

inconsciência *f (MED)* unconsciousness, coma; **2** thoughtlessness, irresponsibility.

inconsciente *adj inv* unconscious; **2** unwitting; irresponsible.

inconsequente *adj inv* inconsequent; **2** illogical; **3** *(irrefletido)* hasty.

inconsistente *adj inv* inconsistent; **2** variable; **3** *(líquido)* runny.

inconsolável *adj inv* inconsolable, sad.

inconstância *f* unsteadiness; **2** inconstancy.

inconstante *adj inv* fickle; **2** unstable; **3** changeable.

inconstitucional *adj inv* unconstitutional.

incontável *adj inv (estórias)* that cannot be told; **2** countless, numberless, innumerable.

incontestável *adj inv* undeniable, unquestionable.

incontinência *f* lack of control; **2** *(MED)* incontinence.

incontinente *adj inv* immoderate; **2** *(MED)* incontinent.

incontroverso,-a *adj* indisputable.

inconveniência *f* inconvenience; **2** impoliteness.

inconveniente *m* difficulty, problem; bother; setback; **qual é o ~ ?** what's wrong with it?; ♦ *adj inv* inconvenient; **2** *(inadequado)* unsuitable; **3** *(incivil)* discourteous.

incorporar *vt* to incorporate, include; **2** to add; **3** *(COM)* to incorporate, merge; ♦ **~-se** *vr*: **~ a/em** to join, blend into.

incorre(c)ção *f* inaccuracy.

incorre(c)to,-a *adj (errado)* wrong, incorrect; **2** bad-mannered; **3** *(comportamento)* improper.

incorrer *vi*: **~ em** to incur; **2** to fall (in, into); **incorrer na multa de...** to incur a fine of...

incorreto,-a *(Vd:* **incorre(c)to,-a***)*.

incorrigível *adj inv* incorrigible.

incredulidade *f* incredulity; **2** scepticism.

incrédulo,-a *m,f* unbeliever; ♦ *adj* incredulous; sceptical.

incremento *m* increment, increase, boost; **2** *(COM)* growth, boom.

incriminar *vt* to incriminate.

incrível *adj inv* incredible.

incruento,-a *adj (que não há derrame de sangue)* bloodless; **uma revolução ~a** a bloodless revolution.

incrustar *vt* to encrust; **2** to inlay.

incubadora *f* incubator.

incubar *vt* to incubate; **2** *(ovos)* to hatch.

inculcar *vt* to impress (**em** upon sb); inculcate (**em** on); **2** to instil; **3** *(propor)* to indicate, recommend; ♦ **~-se em** *vr* to ingratiate o.s., to make o.s. be accepted.

inculpar *vt* to blame; **2** to accuse.

inculto,-a *adj (person)* uneducated; **2** *(fam)* uncouth; **3** *(campos)* uncultivated.

incumbência *n (área de responsabilidade)* remit; responsibility, incumbency; **isso não é da minha ~** that is not my responsibility.

incumbir *vt* **~ alguém de** to put sb in charge of; ♦ *vi*: **~ a alguém** to be sb's duty/job; **incumbe ao senhor fazer isso** it's your job to do that; ♦ **~-se** *vr*: **~ de** to undertake, take charge of.

incumprimento *m (faltar ao dever/prometido)* breach, failure to; **~ de contrato** breach of contract, non-compliance; default; **juros de ~** bank charges/interest on overdrafts (non-payments).

incurável *adj inv* incurable.

incúria *f* negligence; **2** carelessness.

incursão *f (MIL)* incursion; **2** foray; **3** inroad; **4** brief passage.

incurso,-a *(pp de* **incorrer***) adj* incurred, liable to.

incutir *vt* to instil, inspire, imbue.

indagação *f* investigation; **2** search; **3** *(JUR)* inquiry.

indagar *vt* to investigate; **2** to ascertain; **3** to research; ♦ *vi*: ~ **de** to inquire about, carry out investigations.

indecente *adj inv* indecent, improper; **2** obscene.

indecisão *f* indecision, hesitation.

indeciso,-a *adj* undecided, hesitant; **2** vague.

indecoroso,-a *adj* indecent, indecorous, improper; **2** scandalous.

indefensável (= **indefensível**) *(pl:* -**veis***)* *adj* defenceless, inexcusable.

indeferido,-a *adj* refused, rejected.

indeferimento *m* refusal.

indeferir *vt* to reject; **2** to turn down; **3** *(JUR)* to deny.

indefeso,-a *adj* undefended; **2** defenceless, helpless.

indefinido,-a *adj* indefinite; **2** vague, undefined; **3** *(gram) (artigo, pronome)* indefinite.

indelével *adj inv* indelible.

indelicadamente *adv* discourteously; tactlessly.

indelicado,-a *adj* discourteous; **2** rude, boorish; **3** tactless.

indemnização, indenização *f* compensation; **2** indemnity.

indemnizar, indenizar *vt* to compensate (for); **2** to reimburse; **3** to pay damages to.

independência *f* independence.

independente *adj inv* independent; **2** self-governing; **3** self-sufficient; **4** *(trabalho)* freelance; **5** *(prédio)* detached.

independentemente *adv* independently; ~ **de** besides, apart from.

indescritível *adj inv* indescribable; **2** *(fig)* extraordinary, fantastic.

indesejável *adj inv* undesirable; **2** unwelcome.

index *(pl:* **índices, indexes***)* *m* index.

indexar *vt* to index; ♦ ~-**se** *vr (ECON)* to be indexed to.

Índia *f* India.

indiano,-a *adj* Indian (from India).

indicação *f (menção)* indication, hint; **2** *(de caminho, etc)* sign; **3** *(termómetro)* reading; **4** sympton; ~ **médica** doctor's advice.

indicador *m* indicator; **2** *(TEC)* gauge, pointer, dial; **3** *(dedo)* index finger; **4** *(AUTO)* indicator.

indicar *vt* to show, indicate; **2** to point to; **3** to register; ~ **o caminho** to show the way.

índice *(pl:* **índices***)* *m* index, table of contents, list; **2** rate **o** ~ **de mortalidade** death rate; **3** *(ANAT)* index.

indício *m* sign; **2** trace; **3** clue, indication; **4** *(JUR)* indicium.

Índico *npr m*: **o** ~ the Indian Ocean; ♦ **índico,-a** *adj (oceano, costa)* Indian.

indiferença *f* indifference; **2** apathy; **3** detachment.

indiferente *adj inv* indifferent (to, towards); **2** apathetic; **isso é-me** ~ it's all the same to me, I couldn't careless.

indígena *adj inv* native, indigenous.

indigência *f* poverty; **2** *(fig)* lack, need.

indigente *m,f* pauper; ♦ *adj inv* needy, poor.

indigerível *adj inv* indigestible; **2** *(fig)* hard to understand, not acceptable.

indigestão *f* indigestion, dyspepsia.

indigesto,-a *adj* undigest, indigested; **2** *(fig) (discurso, etc)* crude, dull, boring.

indigitar *vt* to point out, to indicate.

indignação *f* indignation.

indignado,-a *adj* indignant, furious, angry.

indignar *vt* to anger, exasperate; ♦ -**se (com)** *vr* to get indignant about.

indignidade *f* indignity; **2** outrage.

indigno,-a *adj* unworthy; disgraceful, despicable.

índio,-a *m,f (nativo das Américas)* American Indian, **2** *(pej)* Red Indian; **3** indio *m (QUÍM)* indium.

indire(c)ta *f (col)* insinuation; *(piada)* hint; **mandar uma** ~ to drop a hint.

indire(c)to,-a *adj* indirect; **2** devious, roundabout (manner); **3** *(LÍNG)* **complemento** ~ indirect object; **discurso** ~ indirect/reported speech.

indisciplina *f* lack of discipline.

indisciplinado,-a *m* rebel; ♦ *adj* unruly.

indisciplinar *vt* to cause indiscipline, rebellion; ♦ ~-**se** *vr* to become rebellious.

indiscreto,-a *adj* indiscreet; **2** tactless.

indiscrição *f* indiscretion; **2** tactlessness; **3** blunder, gaffe.

indiscutível *adj inv* indisputable, unquestionable; **2** not open to discussion.

indispensável *(pl:* -**veis***)* essentials *pl*; ♦ *adj inv* essential, vital, necessary.

indisponível *adj* unavailable, busy.

indispor *vt* to disturb, upset; **2** to annoy; ♦ ~-**se** *vr* to get angry; ~ **com um amigo** to fall out with a friend.

indisposição *f* sickness; ~ **gástrica** stomach upset.

indisposto,-a *adj* unwell, poorly.

indistinto,-a *adj* indistinct; **2** vague.

individual *adj* individual, private; **2** single; **lições individuais** lessons on a one-to-one basis.

individualidade *f* individuality.

individualismo *m* individualism.

individualista *adj inv* individualist.

indivíduo *m* person.

indivizível *adj inv (que não se pode dividir)* indivisible.

indizível *adj inv* unspeakable; unutterable; **2** indescribable.

indócil *adj inv* unruly, wayward; **2** *(impaciente)* restless.

indo-europeu,-peia *m,f adj* Indo-European.

índole *f (carácter)* temperament, character, nature; **2** characteristics.

indolência *f* laziness, indolence.

indolor *adj inv* painless.

indomável *adj inv* untameable; indomitable; **2** unmanageable, unruly.

indómito,-a *adj* untamed, wild.

Indonésia *npr* **a** ~ Indonesia.

indonésio,-a *m,f* Indonesian.

indubitável *adj inv* incontestable, beyond doubt, doubtless.

indução *f* induction.

indulgência *f* indulgence, tolerance; **2** *(do juíz)* clemency; **3** *(REL)* indulgence.

indulgente *adj inv* indulgent, clement.

indultar *vt* to pardon, forgive; **2** *(JUR)* to reprieve, reduce sentence.

indulto *m* pardon; reprieve; **2** amnesty; **3** *(REL)* forgiveness, dispensation.

indumentária *f* dress, costume, attire; **2** history of fashion.

indústria *f* industry, business; ~ **caseira** cottage industry; ~ **fabril** manufacturing industry.

industrial *adj inv* industrial, manufacturing.

industrialista *m,f* industrialist.

industrializar(-se) *vt, vr* to industrialize.

indutor *m* *(ELECT)* inductor.

induzir *vt* to induce; ~ **a** to persuade to; ~ **em erro** to lead astray.

inebriante *adj inv* heady, intoxicating.

inebriar *vt* to inebriate, to intoxicate; ♦ **~-se** *vr* to get intoxicated; **2** to be in ecstasy.

inédito,-a *m,f* unpublished work; ♦ *adj* unpublished.

inefável *adj inv* indescribable; unutterable; ineffable.

ineficaz *adj inv* ineffective; ineffectual; **2** *(inútil)* useless; **ineficazmente** *adv* uselessly.

ineficiência *f* inefficiency.

ineficiente *adj inv* inefficient.

inegável *adj inv* undeniable, indisputable.

inépcia *f* ineptitude; **2** incapacity.

inepto,-a *adj* inept, incompetent.

inequívoco,-a *adj* clear, unmistakable, straightforward.

inércia *f* lassitude, lethargy; **2** inactivity, sluggishness; **3** *(FÍS)* inertia.

inerente *adj inv* inherent; inborn, inbred; intrinsic (**a** to).

inerme *adj inv* unarmed; **2** defenceless.

inerte *adj inv* still, motionless; **2** *(FÍS)* inert.

inesgotável *adj inv* inexhaustible; **2** boundless, abundant.

inesperadamente *adv* suddenly, unexpectedly.

inesperado,-a *adj* unexpected, sudden; **2** unforeseen.

inesquecível *adj inv* unforgettable.

inestimável *adj inv* invaluable, priceless.

inevitável *adj inv* inevitable, unavoidable.

inexa(c)tidão *f* inaccuracy, inexactitude.

inexa(c)to,-a *adj* inaccurate; **2** untrue; **3** faulty.

inexcedível *adj inv* unsurpassable.

inexequível *adj inv* impractical, unfeasible.

inexistência *f* absence; **2** lack of.

inexistente *adj inv* non-existent.

inexperiência *f* inexperience.

inexperiente *adj inv* inexperienced.

inexplicável *adj inv* inexplicable.

inexpugnável *adj inv* impregnable; **2** invincible.

infalível *adj inv* infallible, unfailing; **2** inevitable.

infame *adj inv* infamous; **2** vile, shocking, shameful.

infâmia *f* notoriety; **2** disgrace; **3** villainy; **4** shame, dishonour.

infância *f* infancy, childhood.

infanta *f* princess; daughter of Portuguese or Spanish king (not heiress).

infantaria *f* infantry.

infantário *m* nursery school.

infante *m* prince; son of Spanish or Portuguese king (not heir to the throne); **2** *(criança)* child, infant; **Infante D. Henrique** Prince Henry.

infanticídio *m* infanticide.

infantil *(pl: -is)* *adj inv* *(doença)* infantile; **2** *(comportamento, linguagem)* childish, juvenile; **3** childen's; **livros ~is** children's books; **parque ~** children's playground; **trabalho ~** child's labour; **mortalidade ~** infant mortality.

infantilidade *f* childishness.

infarto *(= enfarte, enfarto)* *m* *(MED)* *(mortalidade)* infarct.

infatigável *adj inv* untiring, unflagging, indefatigable; **2** zealous, dedicated.

infausto,-a *adj* unlucky, unfortunate; **2** disastrous.

infe(c)ção *f* infection; contamination.

infe(c)cioso,-a *adj* infectious.

infe(c)tar *vt* to infect, contaminate; ♦ *vi* to be infected.

infelicidade *f* unhappiness; **2** misfortune.

infeliz *m* wretch, poor devil; ♦ *adj inv* unhappy; **2** unfortunate, unlucky.

infelizmente *adv* unfortunately, sadly.

inferior *m* subordinate, underling, inferior; ♦ *adj inv* inferior; **2** lower.

inferioridade *f* inferiority.

inferir *vt* to infer, presume; **2** deduce; **3** imply.

infernal *adj inv* hellish, diabolical; **um barulho ~** terrible noise; **2** *(BR)* *(festa)* wild, great.

inferno *m* hell.

infértil *(pl: inférteis)* *adj inv* infertile, sterile; **2** *(terrenos)* barren.

infertilidade *f* infertility, unfruitfulness.

infestar *vt* to infest; **2** *(invadir)* to overrun; **3** to plague, swarm over.

infetar *(Vd: infe(c)tar)*.

infidelidade *f* infidelity, disloyalty; **2** *(REL)* disbelief.

infiel *(pl: -éis)* *m,f* *(REL)* unbeliever, infidel; ♦ *adj inv* disloyal; **2** unfaithful; **3** *(texto)* inaccurate; **4** *(povo)* heathen.

ínfimo,-a *m* the infinitesimal; ♦ *adj* lowest, smallest, most insignificant.

infindável *(pl: infindáveis)* *adj inv* unending; **2** interminable; **3** endless, infinite.

infinidade *f* infinity; **uma ~ de** countless; **esperei por ti uma ~** I waited for you ages; **2** *(REL)* infinitude.

infinitesimal *adj inv* infinitesimal, tiny (part).

infinitivo,-a *adj* infinitive; **2** countless; **3** *(LÍNG)* infinitive.

infinito *m* the infinite; ♦ **infinito,-a** *adj* countless; **2** boundless; **3** never-ending, eternal.

inflação *f* *(ECON)* inflation.

inflacionário,-a *adj* inflationary.

inflamação *f* *(MED)* inflammation; **2** *(fig)* enthusiasm; **~ das amígdalas** tonsillitis.

inflamado,-a *adj* *(MED)* inflamed; **2** *(oil, etc)* in flames, inflaming; **3** *(fig)* enthusiastic; **4** angry.

inflamar *vt* *(MED)* to inflame, cause swelling; ♦ *vi* to swell up; **2** to set fire to; **3** *(fig)* to excite, arouse; ♦ **~-se** *vr* to catch fire; **2** *(rosto)* to go red; **3** *(fig)* to get excited.

inflar *vt* to inflate, blow up; **2** *(narinas)* to flare (nostrils); **3** to puff up; **4** *(velas de barco)* to fill; ♦ **~-se** *vr* to swell (up).

inflexão *f (flexão)* inflexion, bending; **2** *(voz)* inflection, modulation; **3** *(GEOM, LÍNG)* inflexion, inflection.

inflexível *adj inv* stiff, rigid; **2** *(fig)* unyielding, relentless.

infligir *vt:* ~ **alguma coisa a alguém** to inflict sth upon sb.

influência *f* influence.

influenciar *vt* to influence.

influente *adj inv* influential.

influir *vt* to encourage, cheer up; **2** to inspire; ♦ *vi:* ~ **em** to influence, have an influence on; ♦ ~-**se** *vr* to become enthusiastic.

influxo *m* influx; **2** inflow; **3** high/full tide, inrush; **4** influence, power.

in-fólio *m, adj (TIPO) (formato)* folio *m*.

informação *f* information, report; **2** *(MIL)* intelligence; **3** *(JUR)* inquiry; **4** *(mídia)* news.

informações *fpl* information *sg*, references; **pedir** ~ **sobre** to ask about, enquire, inquire about.

informal *adj inv* informal.

informalmente *adv* informally.

informante *m* informant; **2** *(JUR)* informer.

informar *vt* to inform; ~ **alguém de** to let sb know about; ♦ *vi:* ~ **de** to report on, tell about; ♦ ~-**se de** *vr* to find out about, obtain information.

informática *f (COMP)* information technology, computer science, informatics; ♦ *adj* computer; **estudos de** ~ computer studies.

informativo,-a *adj* informative.

informatização *f* computerization.

informatizar *vt* to computerize; **2** to become computerized.

informe¹ *adj inv* shapeless; **2** *(corpo)* deformed.

informe² *m* report, statement, information; **2** *(MIL)* (of) intelligence.

infortúnio *m* misfortune; adversity.

infra(c)ção *f (de lei)* breach, infringement; ~ **de trânsito** driving offence *(UK)*, driving offense *(US)*; **2** *(DESP)* foul.

infra(c)tor,-ora *m,f* offender, transgressor, infringer.

infra-estrutura *(pl: infra-estruturas) f* substructure; **2** *(ECON)* infrastructure.

infrator,-ora *(Vd: infractor,-ora)*.

infravermelho *(FÍS) m* infra-red; ♦ **infravermelho,-a** *adj* infra-red.

infringir *vt (lei, regras)* to break, violate, contravene; ~ **a lei** to break the law; **2** *(ordem)* to disobey.

infrutífero,-a *adj* fruitless; **2** useless, fruitless, in vain; **a minha visita foi** ~a my visit was in vain.

infundado,-a *adj* groundless, unfounded.

infundir *vt* to infuse, *(chá)* brew; **2** *(derramar)* to pour into; **3** *(fig)* to instil, inculcate, inspire; ♦ ~-**se** *vr* infiltrar-se.

infusa *f* pitcher, earthen pot.

infusão *f* infusion.

ingente *adj inv* huge, enormous.

ingenuidade *f* naivety.

ingénuo,-a *adj* naïve, candid; **2** *(fam)* green; **ela é muito** ~a she is very green; **3** *f (CIN, TEAT)* ingénue.

ingerência *f* interference; **2** meddling.

ingerir *vt* to ingest; **2** to swallow; ♦ ~-**se** *vr* to meddle, interfere; **ele ingere-se nos meus negócios** he interferes in my business.

ingestão *f* ingestion.

Inglaterra *npr* **a** ~ *f* England.

inglês,-esa *m,f* Englishman, Enlishwoman; **2** *m (LÍNG)* English; ♦ *adj* English; ~ **macarrónico** pidgin English; IDIOM **é só para** ~ **ver** it is just for show/to show off.

inglesismo *m (anglicismo)* anglicism.

inglório,-a *adj* inglorious, shameful; **2** *(vida, trabalho)* obscure; **3** *(esforço)* useless, unworthy.

ingovernável *adj inv* unruly; **2** ungovernable, unmanageable.

ingratidão *f* ingratitude, ungratefulness.

ingrato,-a *adj* ungrateful; **2** *(aspecto)* unpleasant; **3** *(fig) (terra)* unproductive.

ingrediente *m* ingredient.

íngreme *adj inv* steep; **uma rua** ~ a steep road.

ingressar *vi:* ~ **em** to enter, go into; **2** to join.

ingresso *m (curso, etc)* entry, admission; **2** *(BR) (bilhete)* entrance ticket.

íngua *f (MED) (inflamação dos glândulos linfáticos)* bubo; **2** *(bubão inguinal)* bubo of the groin.

inhaca *m* Mozambican chief; **2** *(BR)* stink.

inhame *m (BOT)* yam, kind of sweet potato.

inibição *f* inhibition.

inibido,-a *adj* inhibited.

inibir *vt* to inhibit; ~ **de** to prevent from, forbid; ♦ ~-**se** *vr* be embarrassed.

iniciado,-a *m* beginner; **2** initiate; **3** *(REL)* neophyte; ♦ *adj* initiated.

inicial *m* initial; ♦ *adj inv* initial, original.

iniciar *vt* to initiate; **2** to begin, start; ♦ ~-**se** *vr* to begin.

iniciativa *f* initiative.

início *m* beginning; **de/no** ~ at first.

inigualável *adj inv* that cannot be compared, unequal, matchless, peerless; **beleza** ~ unrivalled beauty.

inimicícia *f* enmity; hostility.

inimigo,-a *m,f* enemy, adversary, foe; ♦ *adj* hostile, averse.

inimizade *f* enmity, hatred; **2** animosity.

ininteligível *adj inv* unintelligible.

ininterrupto,-a *adj* uninterrupted.

iniquidade *f* iniquity.

iníquo,-a *adj* iniquitous.

inje(c)ção *f* injection.

inje(c)tado,-a *adj* injected; **2** *(olhos)* bloodshot eyes.

inje(c)tor *m* injector, spray nozzle; ♦ *adj* injecting.

injetar *vt* to inject; **2** to insert.

injunção *f* injunction.

injúria *f* insult; **2** affront, offence; **3** slander; **4** abuse.

injuriar *vt* to insult; **2** to offend; **3** *(sentimentos)* to hurt; **4** to wrong sb; ♦ ~-**se** *vr* to be offended; **2** *(BR)* to get angry with sb.

injurioso,-a *adj (insultuoso)* insulting; **2** injurious; **3** *(calunioso)* slanderous.

injustiça *f* injustice.

injustiçado,-a *adj* unjustly treated, victim of injustice.

injusto,-a *adj* unfair, unjust.
inocência *f* innocence.
inocente *m,f* simpleton; ♦ *adj* innocent; **2** simple, naïve.
inocular *vt* to inoculate; **2** *(fig)* to instill.
inoculável *adj inv (MED)* inoculable.
inócuo,-a *adj* harmless.
inofensivo,-a *adj* harmless, inoffensive.
inolvidável *adj inv* unforgettable.
inoperância *f* inoperativeness, inefficiency.
inoperante *adj inv* inefficient, inoperative.
inopinadamente *adv* unexpectedly.
inopinado,-a, inopinável *adj* unexpected.
inoportuno,-a *adj* inconvenient, inopportune.
inóspito,-a *adj* inhospitable.
inovação *f* innovation; **2** novelty.
inovador,-ora *m,f* innovator, creator; ♦ *adj* innovative.
inovar *vt* to innovate.
inoxidável *adj* rustproof; **aço** ~ stainless steel.
inquebrantável *adj inv (amizade, resolução)* indestructible.
inquebrável *adj inv* unbreakable.
inquérito *m* inquiry, investigation; **2** *(JUR)* inquest; **3** survey; **fazer um** ~ to make a survey.
inquietação *f (desassossego)* inquietude, uneasiness; **2** *(agitação)* restlessness; **3** *(ânsia)* anxiety, worry; **4** tumult.
inquietante *adj inv* disturbing; worrying.
inquietar *vt* to worry, disturb; ♦ ~-**se** *vr* to worry o.s., get restless.
inquieto,-a *adj* anxious, worried; **estar** ~ to be on tenterhooks; **2** *(agitado)* restless; **3** *(animal)* upset.
inquilinato *m* tenancy; **2** *(conjunto de arrendatários)* tenantry.
inquilino,-a *m,f* tenant; **2** *(BIOL)* inquiline.
inquinar *vt (poluir)* polute *(água)*; **2** *(perturbar)* to disrupt *(vida, sossego)*.
inquirição *f* investigation; **2** interrogation; **3** *(JUR)* cross-examination.
inquiridor,-ora *m,f* enquirer.
inquirir *vt (JUR)* to cross-examine; ♦ *vi* to enquire, question.
inquisição *f* inquisition.
inquisidor *m* inquisitor.
insaciado,-a *adj* unsatisfied; **2** insatiate.
insaciável *adj inv* insatiable.
insalubre *adj inv* unhealthy.
insanidade *f* madness, insanity.
insatisfação *f* dissatisfaction.
insatisfeito,-a *adj* dissatisfied; discontented; **2** *(apetite)* not satisfied; **3** *(curiosidade)* insatiate.
inscrever *vt (GEOM)* to inscribe; **2** *(nome, epitáfio)* to carve; **3** *(de um aluno)* to enrol, register; **4** *(perpetuar nome)* to inscribe; ♦ ~-**se** *vr* to enrol; **2** *(para candidatura)* to put oneself forward.
inscrição *f* inscription; **2** enrolment, registration.
inse(c)ticida *m* insecticide.
inse(c)to *m* insect.
insegurança *f* insecurity.
inseguro,-a *adj* insecure.
inseminação *f* insemination.

insensatez *f* folly, madness.
insensato,-a *adj* unwise; **2** foolish.
insensibilidade *f* insensitivity; callousness.
insensível *adj inv (pessoa)* insensitive, unfeeling; indifferent; **2** *(pessoa fria, impiedosa)* cold-hearted; **3** *(dor, parte do corpo)* numb.
inseparável *adj inv* inseparable.
inserção *f (inclusão)* insertion; **2** introduction; ~ **social** *f* social integration.
inserido,-a *(pp com vb ter) adj* inserted; **eu já tinha** ~ I had included.
inserir *vt* to insert (in); **2** to integrate, include; put in; ~ **uma cláusula**, add a clause; ♦ ~-**se** *vr* to be part of, be included.
inserto,-a *(pp irr de: inserir, com vbs ser, estar) adj* inserted, included, added, set in, put in.
inseticida *(Vd: insecticida)*.
inseto *(Vd: insecto)*.
insídia *f* snare, ambush; **2** treachery, treason; **3** plot, stratagem.
insidioso,-a *adj* insidious; **2** crafty, deceitful.
insigne *adj inv* distinguished, eminent, famous.
insígnia *f* insignia; **2** badge; **3** banner; ~ **military colours**; ~**s** *pl* insignia; **as** ~**s da dignidade real**, the Regalia *(UK)*.
insignificante *adj inv* insignificant.
insinuação *f* insinuation, hint.
insinuante *adj* insinuating; ingratiating.
insinuar *vt* to insinuate, imply; ♦ ~-**se** *vr*: ~ **por/entre** to slip into; ~ **na confiança de alguém** to warm one's way into sb's confidence.
insípido,-a *adj* insipid, tasteless; **2** *(pessoa, livro)* dull, tedious.
insistência *f* insistence.
insistente *adj inv* insistent, persistent, stubborn; **2** urgent.
insistir *vi*: ~ **em** to persist in; to insist on; **2** *(fig)* to stress.
in sito in situ.
insociável *adj inv* unsociable; **2** reserved.
insofismável *adj inv* unavoidable; **2** unquestionable, undeniable.
insofrido,-a *adj* impatient, restless, fretful.
insolação *f (METEOR)* insolation; **2** *(MED)* sunstroke.
insolência *f* insolence.
insolente *m,f* insolent person; **ele é um** ~ he is an insolent man; ♦ *adj inv* insolent, rude; bold.
insólito,-a *adj* unusual, uncommon, extraordinary, **o** ~ **caso** the extraordinary case.
insolúvel *adj inv* insoluble.
insolvência *f* insolvency.
insolvent *m,f* insolvent; ♦ *adj inv* insolvent.
insondável *adj inv* unfathomable, impenetrable.
insone *adj inv (pessoa)* insomniac; **2** *(noite)* sleepless.
insónia *(BR: -sô-) f* insomnia.
insonolência *f* sleeplessness.
insonorizado,-a *adj (sala)* sound-proof.
insonorizar *vt* to make (a place) soundproof, insulate.
insonoro,-a *adj* soundless.
insosso,-a *adj (sem sal)* unsalted, tasteless, insipid; **2** *(fig) (pessoa, conversa, etc)* dull, drab, uninteresting, insipid.

inspe(c)ção *f* inspection, survey; **2** check; **3** examination; ~ **médica** medical examination; **4** *(MIL)* inspection board; **5** *(AUTO)* MOT test.

inspe(c)cionar *vt* to inspect, to examine; **2** supervise, survey; **3** check.

inspe(c)tor,-ora *m,f* inspector; controller; surveyor; ~ **da alfândega** Customs Officer; ~-**geral** chief inspector.

inspiração *f* inspiration.

inspirar *vt* to inspire; **2** inhale, breathe in; ♦ ~-**se** *vr* to be inspired; **2** *(fam)* to be exalted.

instabilidade *f* instability.

instalação *f* installation; **2** *(industrial)* plant; ♦ **instalações** *fpl* premises; **2** facilities; **3** fittings; ~ **hidráulica** waterworks *sg*.

instalar *vt* to install (in); **2** to set, put up; ♦ ~-**se** *vr* to install o.s.; **2** to accommodate o.s.; **3** to settle in.

instância *f* urgency; **2** *(solicitação)* plea, entreaty, demand; **3** stages in a lawsuit; jurisdiction; **tribunal de primeira** ~ court of first instance; *(JUR)* ~ **inferior/superior** lower/higher stages; ♦ *adv* **em última** ~ as a last resort; **em primeira** ~ I the first instance/place; **ceder às** ~**s de (alguém)** to give to sb's entreaties.

instantâneo,-a *adj* instant, instantaneous; **2** *m* *(FOTO)* snapshot.

instante *m* instant, moment.

instar *vt* to urge; ~ **com alguém para que faça algo** to urge sb to do sth; ♦ *vi* to be imminent, be about to happen; **2** to be urgent; **3** to insist.

instauração *f* establishment.

instaurar *vt* to establish, set up; **2** to introduce; **3** to institute; **4** *(JUR)* to bring an action against.

instável *adj inv* unstable; **2** *(METEOR) (tempo)* unsettled.

instigação *f* persuasion, encouragement.

instigador,-ora *m,f* instigator, inducer.

instigar *vt* to instigate; **2** to urge, goad on; **3** to provoke; **4** to entice; **ela instigou-o a comprar** she enticed him to buy; **5** *(animal)* to set; **instigou o cão contra o rapaz** he set the dog on the boy.

instinto *m* instinct; **por** ~ instinctively; **to act on** ~ agir por instinct; **2** intuition.

institucionalizar *vt* to institucionalize; ♦ ~-**se** *vr* to become institucionalized; **2** to be an institution; **3** *(pej)* to be officious.

instituição *f* *(organização)* institution; **2** *(POL) (processo)* the setting-up; creation; establishment; **3** *(JUR)* nomination.

instituir *vt* *(criar, fundar)* to institute, found; **2** *(código)* to establish; **3** *(nomear)* to nominate, declare; institute *(herdeiro)*.

instituto *m* institute; ~ **de beleza** beauty clinic, salon; **2** *(arte)* academia.

instrução *f* *(ensino)* instruction; education, learning; **falta de** ~ *(pessoa)* unschooled; **2** *(MIL)* training; **3** *(JUR)* preparation; ~ **de um processo** preparation of a law suit; ♦ **instruções** *(pl)* instructions; *(indicações de uso)* **manual de** ~ handbook; ~ **de manejo** operating instructions.

instruído,-a *adj* educated; **2** informed.

instruir *vt* to instruct; **2** to train; **3** to teach.

instrumento *m* instrument; ~ **de sopro** wind instrument; **2** *(ferramenta)* tool; **3** implement, device; ~ **de medição** gauge device; **ser o** ~ **de** to be instrumental in; **ser o** ~ **de Deus** to be God's medium.

instrutor,-ora *m,f* instructor; private teacher; **2** *(Univ)* tutor, preceptor; **3** *(DESP)* trainer, coach; ♦ *adj* instructing.

ínsua *f* river islet; **2** *(terrenos)* wetlands, land by the river.

insubordinado,-a *adj* unruly, disobedient, rebellious.

insubordinar *vt* to instigate to revolt; ♦ ~-**se** *vr* to rebel, revolt against; rise *(in arms)*; mutiny.

insubsistência *f* lack of support.

insubstituível *(pl: -veis) adj inv* irreplaceable.

insucesso *m* failure; **2** flop.

insuficiência *f* lack, insufficiency; *(MED)* ~ **cardíaca** coronary insufficiency.

insuficiente *adj inv* insufficient.

insuflar *vt* to blow up, inflate; **2** *(fig)* to instil; **3** *(com esperança)* to fill.

insuflável *adj inv* inflatable.

ínsula *f* *(poético)* island.

insular *m,f* islander; ♦ *adj* insular; ♦ *vt* to set apart, isolate; ♦ ~-**se** *vr* cut o.s. off; **2** *(TEC)* to insulate.

insulina *f* insulin.

insultar *vt* to insult, to offend; ♦ ~-**se** to shout insults at each other.

insulto *m* insult, affront.

insumo *m* *(COMP) (data)* input; **2** *(ECON) (fatores de produção)* input goods, supplies entered into a process.

insuperável *adj inv* insurmountable; **2** unsurpassable; **3** unmatched; **4** invincible.

insuportável *adj inv* unbearable.

insurgente *m,f* rebel; ♦ *adj inv* rebellious.

insurgir-se *vr* to rebel, revolt.

insurreição *f* rebellion, insurrection.

insuspeito,-a *adj* unsuspected, beyond suspicion; **2** impartial; **3** *(documento)* reliable.

insustentável *(pl: -veis) adj inv* untenable; **2** unfounded; **3** unbearable; **4** unsustainable.

inta(c)to,-a *adj* intact; **2** *(fig) (puro)* untouched, unspoilt, pure; **3** *(fig) (reputação)* unblemished.

intangível *(pl: -veis) adj inv* intangible.

integérrimo,-a *(superl de* **íntegro***) adj* most upright, most honourable.

íntegra *f* totality; ♦ *adv* **na** ~ word for word, verbatim.

integrado,-a *adj* integrated (in); **2** *(ensino)* comprehensive.

integral *(pl: -ais) f (MAT)* integral; ♦ *adj inv* integral, complete; **pão** ~ wholemeal bread; **arroz** ~ brown rice; **trabalho a tempo** ~ full-time work.

integrar *vt* to unite, combine; **2** to integrate.

integridade *f* integrity.

íntegro,-a *adj* entire; **2** upright, honest; **3** *(fig)* fair, just.

inteiramente *adv* entirely, completely.

inteirar *vt* to complete; ~ **alguém de** to inform sb about/of; ♦ ~-**se** *vr*: ~ **de** to find out about, learn.

inteireza *f* entirety; **2** integrity.
inteiriço,-a *adj* all-in-one; **2** stiff, rigid; **3** *(fig)* inflexible.
inteiro,-a *adj* whole, entire, intact; **2** unharmed; undamaged; **dia ~** all day; **pagar por ~** pay full amount.
intelecto *m* intellect.
intelectual *adj inv* intellectual; **2** *(pej)* **um ~ de meia tigela** a half-baked intellectual.
intelectualidade *f* intellectuality.
inteligência *f* intelligence.
inteligente *adj inv* intelligent, clever.
inteligível *(pl: -veis) adj inv* intelligible, clear, comprehensible.
intempérie *f* bad weather.
intemporalidade *f* timelessness, eternity; **2** spirituality.
intenção *f* intention, intent, purpose; **segundas intenções** ulterior motives; **ter a ~ de** to intend to.
intencionado,-a *adj:* **bem ~** well-meaning; **mal ~** ill-intentioned.
intencional *adj inv* intentional, deliberate.
intendência *f* management, administration.
intensidade *f* intensity.
intensivo,-a *adj* intensive, intensifying.
intenso,-a *adj* intense; **2** deep; **3** vivid; **4** *(MÚS)* volume.
intentar *vt* to try, attempt; *(JUR)* **~ uma a(c)ção contra** *(alguém)* to sue against (sb).
intento *m* aim, purpose, design; **2** *(tentativa)* attempt.
intentona *f* mad plot; **2** wild scheme.
intera(c)tivo,-a *adj* interactive.
interagir *vi* to interact.
intercalar *m,f (de permeio)* insertion; ◆ *adj inv* intercalar(y); ◆ *vt* to insert, intersperce, intercalate; **3** *(TIPO) (folhas)* to interpose; ◆ **~-se** to intermingle; **~ em/entre** to intervene in/between.
intercâmbio *m (divisas)* exchange; **~ cultural** cultural exchange.
interceder *vi* to intercede, mediate; **~ por** to intercede on behalf of; to speak for (sb); **2** to mediate.
intercepção, intercessão *f* interception, intercession; **2** *(sinal de radio)* interference; **3** *(JUR)* pleading.
interceptar, intercetar *vt* to intercept, interrupt; **2** to cut off, stop.
intercostal *(pl: intercostais) adj inv (MED)* intercostal.
interdição *f* prohibition, ban; **2** *(JUR)* interdiction, restraint.
interditado,-a *adj* prohibited, banned; **2** closed; **praia ~a** beach closed/swimming not allowed.
interditar *vt* to forbid, interdict, to ban.
interdito,-a *m (JUR)* interdict, injunction; ◆ *adj* prohibited, banned.
interessado,-a *adj* interested; **2** concerned.
interessante *adj inv* interesting; **mulher ~** attractive woman; **estar no seu estado ~** to be pregnant.
interessar *vt* to interest, be of interest to; ◆ **~-se** *vr* **(em/por)** to take an interest in, be interested in; **2** to be concerned in.
interesse *m* interest; **2** advantage, benefit; **por ~ próprio** out of self-interest; **no ~ de** for the sake of.

interesseiro,-a *m,f* self-interested person; person with ulterior motives; ◆ *adj* selfish; **2** calculating; **3** mercenary.
interestadual *adj inv (JUR)* interstate.
interface *f (COMP, FÍS)* interface.
interferência *f* interference; **2** *(RADIO, TV)* interference.
interferir *vi* to interfere (**em** in).
ínterim *m* interim; **nesse ~** in the meantime.
interino,-a *adj* temporary, interim; **2** acting; **3** provisional.
interior *m (ger)* interior, inside; **2** *(país, região)* centro, heart, hinterland; **no ~** inland, in the country; **navegação ~** inland navigation; **decoração de ~es** interior designing/decoration; ◆ *adj inv* inner, inside, inward; **2** *(íntimo)* innermost; **3** *(COM)* domestic, internal, home, **Ministério do I~** Home Office; **roupa ~** under garments; **~-direito** *m (DESP)* inside right; **~-esquerdo** *m (DESP)* inside left.
interiorização *f* introspection; internalization.
interjeição *f (LÍNG)* interjection.
interligação *f* interconnection; interrelationship.
interligar *vt* to interconnect; ◆ **~-se** *vr (fios)* to meet, be interlocked.
interlocução *f (LÍNG)* interlocution.
interlocutor,-ora *m,f* interlocutor.
intermediário,-a *m,f (medianeiro)* mediator, intermediary, go-between; **2** *(COM) (agente, distribuidor)* middleman; *(GEOL)* intermediate.
intermédio *m* intervention; ◆ *adj* intermediate; ◆ **por ~ de** *adv* by means of, through, via.
interminável *(pl: -veis) adj inv* endless, interminable.
intermissão *f* interval, intermission; **2** pause, break.
intermitente *adj inv* intermittent; **2** spasmodic(al); *(MED)* **febre ~** intermittent fever.
internacional *adj inv* international.
internado,-a *m,f (hospital)* inmate, in-patient; *(no colégio)* boarder; ◆ *adj (admitido) (alguém)* hospitalized; **2** *(recluso)* interned, confined to.
internamento *m (acto de abrigar)* internment; **2** *(admissão a colégio)* admission.
internar *vt (MED)* to admit; **2** *(aluno)* to board; **3** *(POL)* to intern.
internato *m* boarding school, children's home.
interno,-a *m,f (colégio)* boarder; **2** *(médico)* houseman, resident physician *(UK)*, intern *(US)*; ◆ *adj* internal, inside; **2** domestic; *(ECON)* **produto ~ bruto (PIB)** gross domestic product (GDP).
interpelação *f* questioning; **2** *(JUR)* summons.
interpelar *vt* to question, interrogate; **2** to interpellate.
interplanetário,-a *adj* interplanetary.
Interpol *(abr de* **International Criminal Police Organization)** Polícia Internacional, Interpol.
interpolação *f* interpolation; *(inserção)* insertion.
interpolar *vt (narrativa)* to insert; **2** to interpolate.
interpor *vt* to put in, interpose, intervene with; **2** *(JUR)* to lodge, file; **~ recurso** file an appeal; ◆ **~-se entre** *vr* to intervene between; **2** *(contrapôr-se a algo, alguém)* to oppose sb/sth.

interposto,-a *(pp de* **interpor***) m* trading post, emporium, store; ♦ *adj (pessoa)* intermediary; mediator; **2** intervening.

interpretação *f* interpretation; **2** performance.

interpretar *vt* to interpret; **2** *(CIN, TEAT)* to play, perform.

intérprete *m,f (LÍNG)* interpreter; **2** *(CIN, TEAT, TV)* performer, artist.

inter-racial, interracial *adj inv* inter-racial.

interregno *m (período entre dois reinados)* interregnum; **2** interlude; **3** interruption, interval, cessation.

interrogação *f* questioning, interrogation; **ponto de** ~ question mark.

interrogar *vt* to question, interrogate.

interrogatório *m* interrogatory, inquiry; **2** *(JUR)* hearing; ~ **contraditório**, cross-examination; **3** *(várias perguntas)* questionnaire.

interromper *vt* to interrupt; **2** to stop; ♦ ~**-se** *vr* to break off, pause.

interrupção *f (pl:* ~**ões)** interruption, break, pause; **uma leitura sem** ~**ões** a lecture without pauses; **2** *(MED)* ~ **voluntária da gravidez (IVG)** abortion; **3** *(ELECT)* ~ **da corrente eléctrica,** power cut.

interruptor, interrutor *m (ELECT)* light switch.

interse(c)ção *f* intersection.

interse(c)tar *vt/vi* to intersect.

intersideral *adj inv (ASTRON)* interstellar.

intersindical *adj inv:* **acordo** ~ trade union agreement.

intersticial *adj inv (BIOL, MED)* interstitial.

interstício *m (ANAT, REL)* interstice; **2** *(fenda)* crack, chink.

interurbano,-a *adj* interurban; **2** *(transporte)* long distance; **telefonema** ~ long distance, trunk call.

intervalo *m* interval, break, pause; **2** gap; **nos** ~**s** during breaks, in (one's) spare time; **a** ~**s** from time to time.

intervenção *f* intervention, intercession; **2** *(MED)* operation; **3** *(JUR)* mediation.

intervencionista *adj inv* mediator; **2** *(POL)* interventionist.

interveniente *m,f* participant; **2** mediator; **3** *(JUR)* endorser of a bill; guarantor; ♦ *adj inv* intervening, intervenient.

intervir *vi* to intervene; **2** to participate, take part; **3** to be involved in.

intestado,-a *adj* intestate.

intestinal *(pl:* **-ais***) adj inv* intestinal.

intestino *m (ANAT)* intestine; *(pop)* bowels *pl*; ♦ *adj (pop)* bowels; **2** ~ **grosso/delgado** large/small intestine.

intimação *f* notification, summons.

intimar *vt* to announce, inform; **2** to order; **3** *(JUR)* to summon, notify; ~ **alguém a fazer** to order sb to do; **4** *(BR)* to challenge sb to fight; **5** *(BR)* to insult, to offend.

intimidade *f* intimacy; familiarity; **pessoas da minha** ~ people I know well, close friends.

intimidar *vt* to intimidate; **2** to scare, frighten; **3** to buly; ♦ *vi* to be frightening; ♦ ~**-se** *vr* to be intimidated, become disheartened.

íntimo *m (âmago)* heart, innermost, soul, pith; **no** ~ **ele é uma boa pessoa** he's a good person at heart; ♦ **íntimo,-a** *adj (amigo)* intimate; close; **2** *(interior, interno)* inner; **festa** ~**a** family party; **3** *(FÍS, QUÍM) (ligação)* intrinsic.

intitular *vt (dar título)* to title sth; to call sb sth; ♦ ~**-se** *vr* to call o.s. sth.

intocável *adj inv* untouchable; ♦ *adj inv (pessoa)* uncorruptible; **2** *(nome, assunto)* unmentionable.

intolerância *f* intolerance.

intolerável *adj inv* intolerable, unbearable.

intoxicação *f* intoxication; **2** poisoning; ~ **alimentar** food poisoning,

intoxicar *vt* to poison, intoxicate; ♦ ~**-se** to poison o.s.

intraduzível *(pl:* **-veis***) adj inv* untranslatable; **2** *(que não se pode exprimir)* inexpressible.

intragável *adj inv* uneatable, undrinkable; indigestible; *(fam)* disgusting; **2** *(fig) (discurso)* unbearable.

intramuros *adv* intra-mural.

intransigente *adj inv* intransigent; **2** *(fig)* uncompromising; **3** strict, demanding.

intransitável *(pl:* **-veis***) adj inv* impassable.

intransitivo,-a *adj* intransitive; **2** *(gram)* intransitive.

intransmissível *adj inv (bens, títulos)* untransferable, not acceptable; **2** indescribable.

intransponível *(pl:* **-veis***) adj inv (caminho, rio)* impassable; **2** *(problema)* unsurmountable, that cannot be overcome.

intratável *adj inv (MED)* that cannot be treated; **2** *(insociável)* intractable, churlish; **3** anything that is unmanageable.

intra-uterino,-a, intrauterino,-a *(pl:* **intrauterinos, intrauterinas***) m,f (ANAT)* intrauterine.

intravenoso,-a *adj (MED)* intravenous.

intrepidez *f* courage, bravery.

intrépido,-a *adj* daring, intrepid.

intricado,-a *adj* intricate, complicated.

intriga *f* intrigue; **2** plot; ~ **amorosa** love affair; **3** gossip.

intrigante *m,f* trouble-maker, intriguer, schemer; **fazer** ~**s** to make trouble; ♦ *adj (pessoa, história)* intriguing.

intrigar *vt* to intrigue, scheme, plot; ♦ *vi* to be intrigued.

intriguista *m,f* gossip-monger; **2** schemer, plotter, intriguer; ♦ *adj inv* intriguing, scheming.

intrínseco,-a *adj* intrinsic, inherent.

introdução *f* introduction.

introduzir *vt (ideia)* to introduce; **2** *(chave, etc)* to put in, insert; **3** *(apresentar)* to introduce *(alguém)*; **4** *(COMP) (dados)* store (data); ♦ ~**-se** *vr (penetrar)* to get into; **2** *(fumo)* to pervade; **3** to interfere.

intróito *m* beginning, introduction; **2** *(REL)* introit.

intrometer-se *vr* to interfere, meddle.

intrometido,-a *m,f* busybody; ♦ *adj (algo)* inserted; **2** interfering, **3** *(fam)* nosey.

intromissão *f* intromission; **2** meddling, interference (**em** in).

introspe(c)ção *f* introspection, self-analysis.

introspe(c)tivo,-a *adj* introspective.

introversão *f* introversion.

introvertido,-a *m,f* introvert; ♦ *adj* introverted, reserved.

intrujão,-ona *m,f* imposter, deceiver; **2** *(pop)* liar.

intrujar *vt* to trick, swindle, to tell fibs.

intrujice *f* scam, swindle, fib.

intruso,-a *m,f* intruder.

intuição *f* intuition.

intuitivo,-a *adj* intuitive.

intuito *m* intention; **2** aim, purpose; **no ~ de** for the purpose of.

intumescência *f* swelling.

intumescer-se *vr* to swell (up).

intumescido,-a *adj* swollen.

inumação *f* inhumation, burial.

inumano,-a *adj* inhuman.

inumar *vt (sepultar)* to bury, inhume.

inumerável *adj inv*.

inúmero,-a *adj (que não se pode contar)* countless; **2** *(muitos trabalhos)* innumerable.

inundação *f* flood; **2** *(profusão)* flooding.

inundado,-a *adj* flooded; **2** *(fig)* filled.

inundar *vt* to flood; **2** *(fig)* to inundate.

inusitado,-a *adj* unusual, uncommon; never used before.

inútil *m,f (person)* a good-for-nothing; ♦ *adj* useless; worthless; **2** futile; **ser ~** to be of no use, be no good.

inutilidade *f* uselessness, incapacity.

inutilização *f* annulment, invalidation.

inutilizar *vt* to render useless; **2** to thwart; ♦ **~-se** *vr* to become useless.

inutilizável *adj inv* unusable.

inutilmente *adv* uselessly, in vain.

invadir *vt* to invade; **2** to encroach on; overrun; **as ervas daninhas invadiram o jardim** the weeds overran the garden.

invalidar *vt* to invalidate; **2** to render sb incapacitated; **3** to disallow, annul; **4** to discredit.

invalidez *f* invalidity, disablement; **pensão de ~** disablement allowance.

inválido,-a *adj (sem valor)* invalid, void, null; **2** disabled; incapacitated.

invariante *m (FÍS, MAT)* invariant; ♦ *adj inv* unchangeable.

invariável *(pl: -veis) adj inv* invariable; **2** constant.

invasão *f* invasion; **2** raid; **3** *(propagação)* spread.

invasor,-ora *m,f* invader; ♦ *adj* invading.

inveja *f (de coisas materiais)* envy (**de** at, of, towards); **2** *(pop)* the greeneyed monster; **3** *(receio de ser subtituído nas afeições)* jealousy; **estou cheia de ~** I am very envious *or* very jealous; **meter ~ a (alguém)** to make one feel envious; **morder-se/roer-se de ~** to be green with envy.

invejar *vt* to envy; **2** to covet; ♦ *vi* to be envious, **invejo-lhe a boa sorte** I begrudge his good luck.

invejável *(pl: -veis) adj inv* enviable, desirable.

invejoso,-a *adj* envious, jealous.

In Portuguese the line between 'envy' and jealousy is more defined than it is in English, in practice at least. So: **inveja** is caused by resenting other people's success, beauty and material possessions, whereas 'ciúme' (jealousy) is of a sexual nature.

---

invenção *f* invention; **2** *(fig: imaginação)* fabrication; **3** *(fig)* inventiveness.

invencível *adj inv* invincible, unconquerable.

inventar *vt* to invent; **2** *(desculpas)* to make up; **3** *(mentiras, calúnia)* to fabricate; **~ uma história** to make up a story.

inventariar *vt* to make an inventory.

inventário *m* inventory.

inventiva *f* inventiveness.

invento *m* invention.

inventor,-ora *m,f* inventor; ♦ *adj* inventing.

inverdade *f* untruth.

inverídico,-a *adj* untrue, false.

invernação *f (BR)* wintering (of cattle).

invernada *f* hard winter; **2** *(BR)* winter pasture.

invernal *adj inv* wintery.

invernia *f* hard winter.

Inverno, inverno *m* winter; winter weather; **lavra de ~** winter fallow.

invernoso,-a *adj* wintry, wintery.

inverossímil *(pl: -eis) adj inv* unlikely, improbable.

inverossimilhança *f* unlikelihood, improbability.

inversa *f* opposite.

inversão *f (gen)* inversion; **2** *(situação, direção contrária)* reversal, turning round; **~ de marcha** U-turn; **~ da situação** reversal of a situation; **3** *(ANAT)* retroversion; **~ uterina** retroversion of the uterus.

inverso *m* opposite; **ser o ~ de** to be the opposite de; **2** back; **o verso e o ~** front and back; ♦ **inverso,-a** *adj (ordem)* inverse, reverse; **em ordem inversa** in reverse order; **2** *(situação, sentido)* opposite, reversed; **3** *(LÍNG, MAT)* inverse.

invertebrado *m* invertebrate; ♦ **invertebrado,-a** *adj (animal)* invertebrate.

inverter *vt* to invert; **2** to turn upside down; **3** opposite direction; **4** *(ELECT)* to commutate; **5** *(situação, sentido)* to reverse, turn back; **6** *(posições)* to exchange; **7** *(fig) (contrariar)* to turn round backwards; **8** *(BR) (aplicar verbas)* to invest.

invertido,-a *m,f* homosexual; ♦ *adj* invert; *(QUÍM)* invert.

invés *m* wrong side; **ao ~** on the wrong side; **ao ~ de** contrary to.

investida *f* attack; **2** charge, lunge; **uma ~ do touro** a bull's attack, charge; **3** *(tentativa)* attempt; **4** *(verbal)* insinuation.

investidura *f* investiture.

investigação *f* investigation; **2** inquiry, probe; **3** *(pesquisa)* research.

investigador,-ora *m,f* investigator; **2** researcher.

investigar *vt* to investigate; **2** to examine; **3** to inquire into; **4** to research; **5** to carry out a survey.

investimento *m (COM)* investment.

investir *vt (COM)* to invest; *(empossar)* **~ alguém no cargo de presidente** to install sb as chairman; ♦ *vi:* **~ contra** *(arremeter)* to attack, charge against; **~ sobre** fall upon.

inveterado,-a *adj* inveterate; **2** deep-rooted; **3** ingrained.

inviabilizar *vt* to obstruct; **2** to make sth impracticable; ◆ ~-**se** *vr* to become unfeasible.

inviável *adj inv* impracticable.

invicto,-a *adj* unconquered; invincible; **Cidade Invicta** *f (Porto)* the Invincible City.

> **'Cidade Invicta'**: title given to the city of Oporto (Porto), in recognition of its people's indomitable spirit and bravery.

ínvio,-a *adj* pathless, trackless; **2** *(caminho)* impassable.

inviolável *adj inv* inviolable; **2** *(JUR) (deputado, diplomata)* immune.

invisível *adj inv* invisible.

invisual *(pl:* -**ais***) n (pessoa)* blind person; ◆ *adj inv* blind, visually impaired.

in-vitro *m* test tube.

invocar *vt* to invoke, call on.

involução *f (MED, BIOL)* involution; curling inwards; *(ZOOL)* degeneration.

invólucro *m (embrulho)* wrapping; **2** *(BOT) (revestimento)* involucre.

involuntário,-a *adj* involuntary; automatic.

invulgar *adj inv* unusual; **2** exceptional.

invulgarmente *adv* uncommonly, unusually.

invulnerabilidade *f* invulnerability.

invulnerável *ad inv* invulnerable.

iodo *m* iodine.

ioga *f* yoga.

iogurte *m* yoghurt.

ioiô *m (brinquedo)* yo-yo.

íon, iônio (ião) *m (QUÍM, FÍS)* ion.

ionização *f* ionization.

ionizar *vt* to ionize, split into ions.

IPC *(abr de* **Índice de Preços ao Consumidor***)* Consumer Price Index.

ipsis verbis ipse dixit.

ipso facto ipso facto.

ir *vi (deslocar-se)* to go, travel; ~ **a cavalo** to ride (a horse); ~ **a pé** on foot, to walk, to go; **já vou!** I am coming; ~ **de avião** to fly; ~ **de carro/de comboio/de barco** to drive, go by car/go by train/by boat; **vamos!** let us go; come on!; **2** ~ **buscar** to fetch, go and get; ~ **a casa buscar a pasta** *(visita curta)* to go home to get one's briefcase; ~ **para casa** *(por mais tempo)* to go home; **3** ~ **de encontro a** *(embater)* to collide with; **4** ~ **de** *(roupa, cores)* to wear; **o homem ia de chapéu** the man was wearing a hat; **a noiva vai de azul** the bride is wearing blue; *(mascarado)* go as; **ele foi de palhaço** he went as a clown; **5** *(achar-se)* **tudo vai bem** all is/goes well; **então, como vai?** well, how are you?; **como vão os negócios?** how is business?, *(fam)* how goes business?; **6** *(health)* ~ **melhor** to be feeling better; ~ **de mal a pior** to go from bad to worse; **7** *(time duration)* **já lá vão dez anos** ten years have gone by; **8** ~ **com** *(condizer)* to match, go (well) with; **a mala vai com os sapatos** the handbag goes (well) with the shoes; **9** ~ **com** *(acompanhar)*; **vou com eles** I am going with

them; **10 ir a** *(forma progressiva) (prestes a)* about, nearly; **eu ia a sair** I was about to leave/go out; *(seguido de gerúndio)* **eu ia morrendo** I nearly died; **eu ia a falar** I was about to speak; **ele continuou a falar**, *(BR)* **ele continuou falando** he went on speaking; **a noite vai chegando** night is falling; **11** *(sair-se)* go well; **a entrevista foi bem** the interview went well; **12** *(direcção)* **a rua vai até** the street leads to, goes as far as; **o atalho vai ter/dar ao rio** the shot cut leads to the river; ◆ ~-**se** *vr*: **a comida foi-se toda** the food is all gone; ~-**se embora** *(partir)* to go away, go now; **vou-me embora** I am going now; **vai-te embora!** be off with you; ◆ ~ **a pique** *(avião)* to sink, founder; ~ **além de** *(exceder)* to go beyond, overdo; ~ **contra a corrente** to swim against the tide; ~ **com a maioria** to side with the majority, *(fig)* float with the current; ~ **ter com** *(ir encontrar)* to go and meet up with; IDIOM ~ **de vento em popa**, going very well, from strength to strength; ~ **a Roma e não ver o Papa** to go to a place famous for sth and not see it; **o que lá vai, lá vai** let bygones be bygones.

IR *m (abr de* **Imposto de Renda***) (BR)* income tax.

IRA *(abr de* **Exército da República Irlandesa***) Irish Republican Army.*

ira *f* anger, rage, ire; **2** *(REL) (punição)* wrath.

iracundo,-a *adj (furioso)* irascible; **2** irate, furious.

irado,-a *adj* irate, angry.

iraniano,-a *adj* Iranian.

Irão *(BR:* **Irã***) npr* Iran; **o** ~ Iran.

Iraque *npr* Iraq; **o** ~ Iraq.

iraquiano,-a *adj (of, from Iraq)* Iraqui; **2** *(LÍNG)* a variant of Arabic.

irascível *(pl:-* **veis***) adj inv* irritable; **2** irascible, short-tempered.

IRC *(abr de* **Imposto de Rendimento Corporativo***)* corporation tax.

ir-e-vir *(pl:* **ires-e-vires***) m* coming and going.

iridescente *adj inv* iridescent.

iridiano *adj (ANAT, relativo ao olho)* iridian.

irídio *m (QUÍM)* iridium (IR).

íris *m* iris; **2 arco-**~ *m* rainbow; **3** solar spectrum; **4** *(BOT)* iris; **5** *(ANAT) (of the eye)* iris; **6** *(fig)* peace, happiness.

Irlanda *f* Ireland; **a** ~ Ireland.

irlandês,-esa *m,f* Irishman/woman; **2** *(LÍNG) m* Irish; ◆ *adj* Irish.

irmã *f* sister; ~ **colaça** foster sister; **2** *(freira)* Sister; **3** ~**s gémeas** twin sisters.

irmãmente *adv* fraternally, brotherly.

irmanar *vt* to link, unite (as brothers); **2** to match; ◆ ~-**se** *vr* to join (with sb).

irmandade *f* brotherhood, sisterhood, fraternity; **2** *(REL)* friary.

irmão *(pl:* **irmãos***) m* brother; ~ **gémeo** twin brother; ~ **uterino** brother on the mother's side; **meio** ~ stepbrother.

iró *(Vd:* **eiró***).*

ironia *f* irony.

irónico,-a *adj* ironic(al), sarcastic.

irra! *exc* damn!; *(fam)* bloody hell!; **2** *(dor súbita de picada/de corte)* ouch!

irracional *adj inv* irrational, absurd, foolish.

irradiante *adj inv* irradiant; **força** ~ emissivity.

irradiar *vt* to radiate; **2** to spread, diffuse; **3** *(notícias)* to broadcast, transmit; ♦ *vi (fig)* to radiate, shine, brighten up; **2** *(rádio)* to be on the air; ♦ ~**-se** *vr* to spread.

irreal *adj inv* unreal.

irrealizável *(pl: -veis) adj inv* unachievable.

irreconciliável *(pl: -veis) adj inv* irreconcilable.

irreconhecível *(pl: -veis) adj inv* unrecognizable.

irrecuperável *(pl: -veis) adj inv* irrecoverable, irretrievable.

irredimível *(pl: -veis) adj inv* irredeemable.

irredutível *(pl: -veis) adj inv* irreducible; **2** *(MAT) (equação)* irreducible.

irrefle(c)tido,-a *adj* rash, thoughtless.

irreflexão *m* thoughlessness, rashness.

irrefutável *(pl: -veis) adj inv* irrefutable, indisputable.

irregular *adj inv* irregular; **2** *(superfície)* uneven, bumpy; **3** *(tempo, valor)* variable, uncertain, unsettled; **3** erratic.

irremediável *(pl: -veis) adj inv* incurable; **2** hopeless; **3** that cannot be helped, cannot be saved, solved.

irremitente *adj inv* unremitting, unabated.

irreparável *(pl: -veis) adj inv* irreparable, beyond repair.

irreprensível *(pl: -veis) adj inv* irreprehensible; **2** *(maneira, aparência)* impeccable.

irrepremível *(pl: -veis) adj inv (riso, alegria, soluço)* irrepressible.

irrequieto,-a *adj* restless; **2** never still; agitated, fidgety; **3** ill at ease.

irresistível *(pl: -veis) adj inv* irresistible; **2** overwhelming; **3** charming.

irresoluto,-a *adj (problema, questão)* unresolved; **2** *(pessoa hesitante)* undecided, hesitant, irresolute.

irresponsabilidade *f* irresponsibility.

irresponsável *(pl: veis) adj inv* irresponsible; **2** unaccountable, unanswerable.

irreverência *f* irreverence; disrespect.

irreverente *adj inv* irreverent, flippant.

irrevogável *(pl: -veis) adj inv (que não pode ser anulado)* irrevocable.

irrigação *f* irrigation, watering.

irrigador *m* sprinkler, water-can; **2** *(MED)* douche.

irrigar *vt* to irrigate, to water; **2** *(fazer fluir o sangue)* to irrigate.

irrisório,-a *adj* derisive, scornful; **2** ludicrous, laughable; **3** *(fam)* small, petty.

irritação *f* irritation, annoyance; **2** *(MED)* inflammation, itch.

irritante *m,f* irritant; ♦ *adj inv* irritating, annoying.

irritar *vt* to irritate; **2** to annoy, provoke; **3** *(inflamação)* to itch, irritate; ♦ ~**-se** *vr* to get angry; **2** *(algo)* to be itchy, inflamed.

irromper *vt* to break (into, out); ~ **em** *(aplauso, gargalhada, lágrimas)* to burst into; **2** to appear, begin suddenly, rush in.

irrupção *f* irruption; ~ **cutânea** skin irruption; **2** outburst.

IRS *(abr de* **Imposto de Rendimento Social***)* income tax.

isabelino,-a *adj (period, literature)* Elizabethan.

isco,-a *m,f* bait; **2** *f (fig)* lure, bait; ~ **as** *fpl (CULIN)* thin slices of fried liver.

isenção *f* exemption (**de** from); **2** immunity.

isentar *vt* to exempt; **o juiz isentou-a de** the judge cleared her of.

isento,-a *adj* exempt; **2** free; ~ **de impostos** tax-free; **3** *(imparcial)* unbiased.

Islã *(=islame) m (BR) (REL)* Islam.

islâmico,-a *adj* Islamic.

islamita *adj inv* Islamic; **2** *m* Islamist.

Islandês,-esa *m,f* Icelander; **2** *(LÍNG)* icelandic; ♦ *adj* Icelandic.

Islândia *npr* a ~ Iceland.

Islão *(=islame) m (EP) (REL)* Islam; **2** *(conjunto de países islâmicos)* Islam.

isolação *f* isolation.

isolado,-a *adj* isolated; **2** remote; **3** secluded; **4** lonely.

isolamento *m* isolation; **2** *(MED)* isolation ward; **3** *(ELECT)* insulation.

isolante *m (object, material)* insulator; ♦ *adj inv* insulating.

isolar *vt* to isolate; **2** *(ELECT)* to insulate.

isómero,-a *(BR: -ô-) m (QUÍM)* isomeric.

isósceles *adj inv (trapézio)* isosceles.

isótero *adj (FÍS)* isotheral.

isótopo *mpl (FÍS)* isotope; ♦ *adj* isotopic.

isqueiro *m* lighter.

Israel *npr* o ~ Israel.

israelita *m,f* Israeli, Israelite; ♦ *adj inv* Israeli, Israelite; **3** *(LÍNG)* Hebraic.

isso *pron* that, that thing (close to the person you address); ~ **mesmo** exactly; **por** ~ therefore; **é por** ~ that is why; **só** ~**?** is that all?; **apesar disso** nevertheless; **nem por** ~ not really, not that much; ~ **é com** that's up to.

istmo *m* isthmus.

isto *pron* this, this thing; ~ **é** that is, i.e.; **você tem muito a ver com** ~ you have to do much with this; **gosto disto (de+isto)** I like this (one); **nisto (em+isto)** suddenly; ♦ *exc* ~ **é que é vida!** now this is what I call living!

Itália *npr* a ~ Italy.

italianismo *m* italianism.

italianizar *vt* to Italianize sb; ♦ ~**-se** to become Italianized.

italiano,-a *adj* Italian; **2** *(LÍNG)* Italian.

itálico *m* italics *pl.*

item *(pl:* **itens***) m* item; **especificar por** ~ to itemize.

itinerante *adj inv (inspector, juiz, bibiloteca)* itinerant.

itinerário *m* itinerary; **2** route; **3** guide-book.

iva *f (BOT)* yellow bugle.

IVA *(abr de* **Imposto sobre Valor Agregado***)* VAT.

j

J, j *m (letra jota)* J, j.

já *adv* already; ~ **visto** already seen; **2** (imediamente) right now, at once; in a moment; **traz ~ o livro** bring the book at once; **3** just, directly; ~ **vou** I am just coming; **4** *(mesmo dia)* soon; **até ~** see you soon; **5** *(em preguntas) (alguma vez)* ever; ~ **esteve na Escócia?** have you ever been to Scotland?; **6** (eu não) no longer; ~ **não tenho fome** I am no longer hungry; ~ **se vê** it is obvious, of course; ~ **agora** so, since; ~ **agora aproveito para...** since (while) I am here I may as well...?; ♦ **desde ~** *prep* from now on; **para ~** for now; **isto é para ~** this is for now; ♦ ~ **que** *conj* now that, since; **que você quer vir, venha** since you want to come, you may come/come along.

jaburu *m (ZOOL)* variety of stork.

jabuti *m (ZOOL) (BR)* Brazilian tortoise.

jaca¹ *f (BOT)* jack fruit.

jaca² African chief of various tribes.

jacarandá *m (BOT)* jacaranda.

jacaré *m* alligator.

Jacarta *npr* Jakarta.

jacente *m (ponte)* main girder; ~**s** *pl* shallows, reefs; ♦ *adj inv* lying, reclining; **2** *(JUR) (herança)* unclaimed, in abeyance.

jacinto *m (BOT)* hyacinth; **2** *(MIN)* reddish variety of zircon; **3** Jacinto; Jacinta *npr m,f (nome de pessoa)* Hyacinth.

jackpot *m* jackpot.

jacobino,-a *adj* jacobin; **2** *(BR)* xenophobic.

ja(c)tância *f (vaidade)* conceit, arrogance.

ja(c)tar-se *vr:* ~ **de** to boast about, show off.

ja(c)to *m (de água)* jet; **um ~ de luz** a beam,flash of light; **2** *(de areia)* sandblast; **3** *(de ar)* stream; **4** *(golfada, jorro)* gush; **um ~ de sangue** a gush of blood; **avião a ~** jet plane; **motor a ~** jet-propelled, turbo jet; ♦ *adv:* **de ~** at once.

jacúzi *m* jacuzzi.

jade *m (MIN)* jade.

jaez *m (adorno dos cavalos, etc)* harness; **2** *(fig) (laia)* sort; **do mesmo ~** of the same kind/sort.

jaga *f* native chief in Angola; **2** *(BR) (NAÚT)* drain hole in a boat for drainage; **3** stopper to close it.

jaguar *(pl: -es)* *m (ZOOL)* jaguar.

jagunço *m (BR)* hired gunman; thug; **2** hoodlum; **3** *(pej)* bandit.

Jaime *npr (nome de homem)* James.

jaleca *f* **jaleco** *m* short jacket; **2** *(BR)* nickname for Portuguese people.

Jamaica *npr* **a ~** Jamaica.

jamaicano,-a Jamaican.

jamais *adv* never; **2** *(em sentido negativo)* ever; **eu ~ vi uma coisa assim** I have never seen such a thing.

jamanta *f* devilfish, gigantic ray; **2** *(BR) (caminhão)* articulated lorry; **3** *(BR)* unkempt (person).

jan. *(abr de* **janeiro**).

janeiras *fpl* **as ~** traditional songs celebrating the New Year and Epiphany (6th January); **2** New Year's gifts.

Janeiro, janeiro *m* January; **2** ~**s** *pl (pop)* years of age; **quantos janeiros já tem?** how old are you now?

janela *f* window; ~ **corrediça** sliding window; ~ **de guilhotina** sash window; ~ **de sacada** bay window; **peitoral da ~** window-sill; *(fig)* ~**s da alma** eyes; **2** *(COMP)* window.

jangada *f* raft, float.

jangadeiro *m* raft owner.

janota *m* dandy; **ele é um ~** he is a dandy; ♦ *adj inv* **hoje estás muito ~** you're looking very elegant today.

jantar *m* dinner; supper, evening meal; ~ **de cerimónia** formal dinner; **sala de ~** dining-room; ♦ *vt* to have for supper; ♦ *vi* to dine; ~ **fora** to dine out.

jantarada *f* a dinner feast, party; **2** repast.

Japão *npr* Japan; **o ~** Japan.

japonês,-esa *m (LÍNG)* Japanese **2** *adj* Japanese;.

jaque *m (bandeirinha num navio)* jack; **2** *(num navio inglês)* Union Jack.

jaqueta *f* short jacket down to the waist; **2** *m (BR) (fam)* old fogey.

jaquetão *m* double-breasted coat; **2** *(NAÚT)* jacket.

jarda *f* yard (36" = 0,9144 m).

jardim *m* garden; ~ **zoológico** zoo; ~ **infantil/ ~-de-infância** *m* kindergarten, nursery school.

jardinagem *f* gardening.

jardinar *vt* to do gardening, work in the garden.

jardineiro,-a *m,f* gardener; **2** *f* flower, window-box; **3** *f (móvel)* jardinière; **4** *(CULIN)* **guizado à jardineira** meat and vegetables stew.

jardinista *m,f* garden designer; **2** garden lover.

jargão *m* jargon.

jarra *f* vase; **uma linda ~ de flores** a beautiful flower arrangement.

jarrão *m* large decorative vase; **2** *(fig, fam) (senhora sempre sentada nos bailes)* wallflower; **3** *(fig, fam)* inactive person, good-for-nothing.

jarreta *m,f (pessoa que se veste mal)* dowdy person; ♦ *adj inv* old person, old-fashioned; *(fig)* old tramp.

jarrete *m (ANAT)* hollow of a knee; **2** *(cavalo)* hock, hamstring.

jarreteira *f (UK)* garter; **a Ordem da J~** Order of the Garter.

jarro *m* water jug; **2** *(BOT)* arum lily.

jasmim *(pl: -ns)* *m (BOT) (planta, perfume)* jasmine.

jasmineiro *m* jasmine shrub.

jaspe *m (MIN)* jasper; ~ **preto** touchstone.

jato *(Vd:* **jacto**).

jaula f cage; **2** (fig) (prisão) jail, (pop) the nick.

javali m **javalina** f wild boar, wild sow.

javanês,-esa adj from Java, Javanese.

javardo m (ZOOL) wild boar.

jazer vi (estar morto) to lie (at rest, in the grave); **aqui jaz...** here lies...; **2** to rest.

jazida f (GEOL) quarry, mine, deposit bed; **2** (arqueologia) site.

jazigo m tomb, resting place, burial monument, vault; ~ **de família** family vault; **2** (GEOL) ore deposit, mine.

JC (abr de Jesus Cristo) Jesus Christ.

jeira f (antiga unidade de medida) yoke of land (about 25 ares = 2,500 sq meters); **2** a day's work or wages; **3** land ploughed by a team of oxen in one day.

jeitinho (diminutivo de **jeito**) m: **para dar um** ~ to do sth as a special favour; do sth somehow; **2 ter** ~ to have a knack for.

jeito m (modo) way, manner; **isso não tem ~ nenhum** that's not the way to do it; **ele olhou para mim de um certo** ~ he looked at me in a particular way; **2** skill, flair, knack; **ela tem ~ para negócios** she has a flair for business; **3** (ability) special way/touch; **dar um** ~ to do/fix sth somehow, manage to (do); **ele deu um** ~ **e a porta abriu-se** he did something and the door opened; **4** (arrumar) **dar um** ~ **na casa** to give a quick tidy up; **falta de** ~ clumsiness; **5** (torcedura) **dar um** ~ **em** to sprain (ankle, wrist); **6** (favor, ajuda) **dar um** ~ **a** to help; **fazer um** ~ to do a favour; **7 isso dá-me** ~ (conveniente) that suits me fine; **8 ter** ~ **de** (aspeto) air of; **ele tem** ~ **de vigarista** he looks like a crook; ◆ adv **a** ~ at the right time, moment; **de** ~ properly; **de qualquer** ~ in any way; by hook or by crook; **de nenhum** ~! no way!; **com** ~ carefully, tactfully; **estar a** ~ to be close at hand; **pessoa sem** ~ clumsy, person without any flair; ◆ **que** ~ **é esse de você não querer ficar?** what's this (I hear) that you don't wish to stay?; **agora não me dá** ~ now it is not convenient (for me); **só para fazer** ~ **a você** it is just to please you; ◆ **jeitos** mpl (hair) **cabelo com** ~s slightly wavy hair, (to have) a kink in the hair.

jeitoso,-a adj (pessoa) skilful, dexterous; **2** good-looking, gorgeous; **3** (objecto) suitable, nice.

jejuar vi to fast, abstain from.

jejum m fast; **em** ~ on an empty stomach; **estou ainda em** ~ I haven't eaten yet.

Jeová m Jehovah, God.

jerarquia (Vd: **hierarquia**).

jericada f many donkeys; **2** a ride on donkeys; **3** (fig) much stupidity.

jerico m donkey, ass.

jeropiga f unfermented wine.

jesuíta m (REL) Jesuit; ◆ adj inv (pej) crafty, hypocritical.

jesuítico,-a adj (doutrina, arte, vida) Jesuitic(al).

Jesus, Senhor Jesus m Jesus; ◆ exc **Jesus!** Jesus!; **ai Jesus!** oh sweet Jesus!, oh my goodness!

jibóia f (ZOOL) boa constrictor.

jiga f jig, lively dance.

jigajoga f old card game; **2** (coisa improvisada) contraption.

jilaba f Moorish garment.

jipe m (AUTO) jeep.

jiu-jitsu m ju-jitsu, jiu-jitsu.

joalharia (= **joalheria**) f jeweller's shop; **2** jeweller.

joalheiro,-a m,f jeweller.

Joanesburgo npr Johannesburg.

joanete m (no pé) bunion; **2** (NÁUT) topgallant sail.

joaninha f ladybird (UK); ladybug (US); **histórias da** ~ fairy tales; **2** (BR) (também) safety-pin.

joanino,-a adj (relativo a reis de nome João); **dinastia** ~ King John's dynasty; **2** (relativo a S. João) **as festas** ~s Saint John's festivities (on 24th June).

joão-ninguém (pl: **joões-ninguém**) m (fam) (pej) (a) nobody, nonentity, a Joe Bloggs.

joão-pestana m (fam) sleep; **2** (fam: de crianças) Mr. Sandman.

Job (Jó) (figura bíblica) Job; **um pobre de** ~ a poor wretch; **2** very patient person.

joco-sério adj half serious half joking.

jocoso,-a adj jocular, humorous.

joelhada f (DESP) **dar uma** ~ to give sb a knock with the knee.

joelheira f (DESP) knee pad; **2** (armadura) knee-piece; **3** a kneeling-mat for doing some jobs.

joelho m knee; **de** ~s kneeling, on bended knees; **pôr-se de** ~s to kneel down; **até aos** ~s up to the knees, knee-deep.

joelhudo,-a adj having thick knees.

jogada f (jogo, partida) game; **2** (cada vez que se joga cartas) play; move; **3** (dados) throw; **4** shot, stroke.

jogador,-ora m,f player; gambler; ~ **a mais** an odd player; ~ **na alta/na baixa** (ECON) (especulador) bull/bear.

jogar vt to play (games); **2** (arriscar-se) to gamble; **3** (arremessar) to throw, fling (bola, dardo); **4** (BR and Reg) (descartar) ~ **em para dentro** to pour (on); **5** (BR e Prov) (descartar) ~ **fora** to throw away/out; **6** ~ **insultos contra** to hurl insults against; ◆ vi (FÍN) ~ **na Bolsa** to play the stock market; **2** (ter o vício do jogo) to gamble; **3** (agir) help; ~ **a favor dos nossos objectivos** to be on our side, to agree with/be in favour of our objectives; **4** (fam) (bater-se) **os dois jogam à pancada** the two of them are fighting; IDIOM ~ **a última cartada** to sink or swim, play one's last card; ~ **com pau de dois bicos** to double-cross, to hunt with the hounds and run with the hare; ~ **água na fervura** to pour oil on troubled waters; ~ **pela certa** to play safe.

jogata f game, set.

jogatina f habit of gambling.

jogo m play, game; ~ **das escondidas** hide-and-seek game; ~ **de palavras** pun, play on words; ~ **de futebol** football match; ~s **de azar** games of chance; ~s **de salão** indoor games; ~ **de prendas** game of forfeits; ~ **limpo/franco** fair play; **ter um bom** ~ have a good hand; **pôr em** ~ to risk;

gamble; **viciado no** ~ addicted to gambling; **2 um ~ de cama** a set of bed-linen; **3** *(alguém, algo)* **estar em** ~ to be at stake; to be involved.

jogral *m* jester; **2** *(TEAT)* buffoon; **3** *(trovador)* minstrel.

The 'jogral', or 'trovador's literature' – the first Christian culture in the Iberian Peninsula – owes its origin to the religious festivities in **Santiago de Compostela**, in Gallicia (Spain).
Braga (Northern Portugal) was the other religious and cultural centre in medieval times, with a rich minstrel's literature. The language spoken or sung was Luso-Galician.

joguete *m* laughing stock; **2** *(alvo de mofa)* pawn, toy; IDIOM **ser um ~ nas mãos de alguém** to be a tool in sb's hands.

jóia *f* jewel; **2** *(inscrição num clube)* entrance fee; **3** *(fig) (pessoa boa)* wonderful, precious; **ela é uma ~** she is a jewel/a darling.

joio *m (BOT)* darnel; **2** *(AGR) (resíduos dos cereais)* chaff; **separar o trigo do ~** to separate the wheat from the chaff.

jojoba *f* jojoba.

jolda *f* riffraff, gang; **2** revelry, spree; **3** *(REG)* herd, flock of animals.

joldeiro,-a *m,f* reveller; ♦ *adj* revelling, carousing.

jóquei *m* jockey.

Jordânia *npr* **a ~** Jordan.

jordaniano,-a *adj* Jordanian.

jornada *f* day's journey; **2** *(viagem por terra)* journey; **3** *(dated)* a day's work.

jornal *m* newspaper; **2** *(noticiário)* news bulletin; ~ **matutino** morning paper; ~ **vespertino** evening paper; ~ **sensacionalista** yellow press, tabloid; *(relato diário)* ~ **de bordo** log book; **banca de jornais** newsstand.

jornaleco *m* second-rate newspaper; *(pej)* rag.

jornaleiro *m (que trabalha ao dia/à jorna)* labourer; **2** *(pej) (jornalista)* hack; **3** *(ardina)* newspaper boy/seller.

jornalista *m,f* journalist, newspaperman/woman.

jornalístico,-a *adj* journalistic.

jorrar *vi* to flow, pour *(líquido, luz, sangue)*; ♦ *(brotar, correr)* gush, spurt out; *(emanar)*, pour down/in.

jorro *m* jet; **2** *(fig)* stream, *(golfada)* gush, spurt; **3 sol a jorros** blazing sunshine.

jota *m* the letter J; **2** a little bit, iota, jot.

jovem *m,f* young man/woman, youngster; ♦ *adj inv* young.

jovial *adj inv* jovial, cheerful.

jovialidade *f* joviality, good humour.

jovialmente *adv* merrily.

juba *f (de leão)* mane; **2** *(fam) (trunfa)* mane of hair.

jubilação *f* jubilation; **2** *(aposentação)* retirement.

jubilado,-a *adj (aposentado)* retired.

jubilar *vi* to rejoice; **2** to retire, pension off; ♦ ~**-se** *vr* to be delighted; **2** to retire.

jubileu *m* jubilee; ~ **de prata** silver jubilee.

júbilo *m* rejoicing, jubilation, joy, exultation.

judaico,-a *adj* Jewish, Hebrew; **as atas ~as** the Jewish records.

judaísmo *m* Judaism.

Judas *msg* Judas; **2** *(fig)* traitor, false friend; **3** *(BR)* poorly-dressed person; **cu de ~** *(fam) (far)* in the back of beyond.

judeu, judia *m,f* Jew, Jewess; **2** *m (arreliador)* teaser, annoying (person); ♦ *adj* Jewish; ~ **errante** *(fig)* wandering Jew; *(person)* much travelled; **2** *(pej)* stingy; **3** *(fam) (que arrelia)* annoying.

judiar (= **judiciar**) *vt* to torment; tease, annoy sb; **2** to scorn.

judiaria *f (bairro)* jewish quarter, district; **2** *(HIST)* ghetto; **3** *(colectivo judaico)* jews.

judicatura *f (magistratura)* judicature; court; **2** *(cargo)* judge's office.

judicial *adj inv.* **judiciário,-a** *adj* judicial, judiciary; forensic **Polícia ~a (PJ)** Portuguese Criminal Police.

judicioso,-a *adj* judicious, wise, sensible.

judo *(BR: -ô-) m (DESP)* judo.

judoca *adj inv* a person who practises judo.

jugal *adv inv* matrimonial, nuptial; **2** rel. to the zygmatic (cheek) bone; **3** rel. to judo.

jugo *m* yoke; **2** *(fig)* oppression; domination; **sob o ~** under the yoke of.

jugular *adj inv (ANAT)* jugular; **veia ~** the jugular vein.

juiz, juíza *m,f (JUR)* judge, magistrate; ~ **de primeira instância** a judge of a lower court, first instance; ~ **presidente** chief justice, presiding judge; ~ **suplente** *m,f* assistant judge; **2** ~ **de campo** *(DESP)* referee, umpire; ~ **linha** *(DESP)* linesman; ~ **de instrução** coroner.

juízo *m (sentença)* judgement; ~ **Final** Day of Judgement, doomsday; **2** opinion, discernment; **ter confiança no seu ~** to trust his opinion; **3** *(tino)* **ter ~** to be sensible, have good sense; **adquirir ~** to grow wise; **4** *(pop) (mente)* **perder o ~** to lose one's mind; **sem ~** mad, foolish; **em seu perfeito ~** of sound mind; **5** *(JUR)* ~ **arbitral** out-of-court decision; ~ **de menores** juvenile court.

julgamento *m* judgement; trial; hearing; ~ **à revelia** trial by default; **2** *(veredito)* sentence, verdict; **ser submetido a** to stand trial; **3** viewpoint; ♦ *adv* ~ **a portas fechadas/em particular** *(JUR)* in camera trial.

julgar *vt* to judge, to try sb, pass sentence; **2** to think, suppose; **julgas-te muito esperto?** do you think you are very clever?; **3** to criticize; **4** *(avaliar)* to evaluate; ♦ ~**-se** *vr* consider oneself; **julga-se no dever de** he considers it to be his duty to.

Julho, julho *m* July.

juliana *f (CULIN) (sopa de legumes)* julienne.

Juliano *adj* Julian; **calendário ~** Julian calendar.

jumento,-a *m,f* donkey, ass; **2** *(pej) (idiota)* ass; **3** *(BR) (pessoa grosseira)* lout; **4** *(BR) (homem com grande potência sexual)* stud, stallion.

junção *f* junction; joint; **2** joining; **3** merging, fusion; **4** *(FÍS, LING)* conjunction.

juncar *vt* to strew, scatter; **2** to cover all over with flowers/leaves; *(fig)* ~ **a rua de lixo** strew the road with rubble.

junco *m (BOT)* sedge, rush; **2** *(barco)* Chinese junk; **bengala de** ~ rat(t)an, cane.

juncoso,-a *adj* with many rushes.

Junho, junho *m* June.

junino,-a *adj* relating to June; **as festas** ~**s** the June festivities.

júnior *m,f* junior; **2** *(DESP)* junior; ♦ *adj inv (pessoa mais nova)* junior, younger.

junquilho *m (BOT)* jonkil (a kind of narcissus).

junta *f (ANAT, TEC)* joint; **2** *(animais)* pair/team; ~ **de bois** team/yoke of oxen; **3** *(ADMIN)* administrative council; **J~ do Comércio** Board of Trade; ~ **de exportação** Export Commission; *(MED)* Board; ~ **médica/J~ de Saúde** Medical Board; **4** *(GEOL) (fenda)* seam, fault; **5** *(MEC)* coupling, joint; **6** *(MIL, POL)* junta.

juntar *vt* to join, connect; **2** to bring together, unite; **3** *(amealhar)* to save; **4** *(reunir) (pessoas, coisas)* to gather; **5** *(misturar)* to add, mix in; **6** *(coser duas partes)* to join/put together; ♦ ~**-se a** *vr* to get close to sb; **2** to live together (as a couple); IDIOM ~ **os trapinhos** *(fam)* to live as man and wife; ~ **o útil ao agradável** to mix business with pleasure.

junto,-a *(ligado)* joined; **2** *(próximo)* next to; ♦ *adv* near, adjoining; **por** ~ *(ao todo)*, altogether; in all; *(por atacado)* wholesale; **segue** ~ find enclosed, attached; ~**s** together; **viver** ~**s** to live as a couple; ♦ *prep* ~ **a/de** near/next to, close to; ~ **com** together with; **2** *(nesta carta)* here, herewith.

juntura *f* juncture; **2** joint, articulation.

jura *f* oath; **2** *(promessa)* vow; **3** curse; **4** *(BR) (pop)* *(cachaça)* firewater, white rum.

jurado,-a *m,f* juror, member of a jury; **bancada dos** ~**s** jury box; **2** *(de exame)* examination board; **3** *(de avaliação)* ~ **de concurso** competition jury; ♦ *adj* sworn.

juramento *m* oath; **sob** ~ under oath; **fazer** ~ take an oath; **2** *(compromisso)* pledge, vow; promise; ~ **de amor** pledge of love; **prestar** ~ swear allegiance; **fazer** ~ **de bandeira** swear an oath of allegiance to the flag; **3** *(pacto)* ~ **de sangue** blood pact; **4** ~ **falso** forswearing.

jurar *vt* to swear; **ela jurou que era verdade** she swore that it was true; **2** vow; ♦ *vi* to take an oath, be sworn in.

jurássico,-a *adj* jurassic.

júri *m (conjunto de jurados)* jury; ~ **de concurso** jury of the contest; **mandado de intimação a um** ~ juri summons.

jurídico,-a *adj* legal, juridical; forensic; legal.

jurisconsulto *m (JUR)* jurisconsult, jurist; legal expert/consultant.

jurisdição *f* jurisdiction.

jurisprudência *f* jurisprudence; **2** Court decision.

jurista *m,f* jurist, lawyer; *(estudante)* Law student.

juro *m (ECON)* interest; ~ **líquido** net interest; ~**s acumulados** accrued interest; ~**s bonificados** preferential rate of interest; ~**s de mora/moratórios** interest on deferred payment; **taxa de** ~**s** rate of interest.

jus *m (JUR)* right; **fazer** ~ **a** to do justice to; have a right to; to merit.

jusante *adj inv* low tide, ebb-tide; **a** ~ downstream; **2** *(fig)* final phase, end.

justa *f (duelo)* joust, tournament; **2** *(fig)* question to settle, dispute; ♦ *adv* **à** ~ *(quantia, tamanho exato)* exactly right, just enough.

justamente *adv* fairly; **2** precisely; ~ **no meio** in the very middle ♦ *exc* ~! exactly!

justaposição *f* juxtaposition.

justaposto,-a *adj* juxtaposed, side by side.

justeza *f* rightness; fairness; **2** precision; **3** accuracy; **4** legitimacy.

justiça *f* justice; **2** *(equidade)* equity, fairness; **3** righteousness; **4** the law; **oficial da** ~ court's clerk; **com** ~ justly, fairly; **fazer** ~ to see justice done; **fazer** ~ **por suas mãos** take the law into one's hands; **5** *(dar crédito a alguém)* **fazer** ~ **a** to do justice to/to give credit to.

justiceiro,-a *m,f* defender of justice; ♦ *adj* just, righteous; **2** impartial; **3** inflexible.

justificação *f* justification **(para** for); excuse; reason **(para** for).

justificar *vt (JUR) (provar em juízo)* to justify, to prove in a court of Law; **2** *(explicar)* to justify; **3** *(desculpar)* to excuse; ♦ ~**-se** *vr (ser compreensível)* to be understandable; **2** to be excusable; IDIOM **o fim justifica os meios** the end justifies the means.

justificativo,-a *m* justification; ♦ *adj (razão, atitude)* justifiable, justificative; **2** *(documento)* justificatory.

justo,-a *m,f* good person; **os** ~**s** the just; **o sono dos** ~**s** deep sleep; ♦ *adj* just, fair, right, upright, righteous; **2** exact, appropriate; **3** *(roupa, etc)* tight, close-fitting; ♦ **à justa** *adv* just enough; **a** ~ **título** deservedly; ~ **e equitativo** right and proper; IDIOM **paga o** ~ **pelo pagador** some pay for the others.

justura *f* adjustment.

juta *f (BOT)* jute; *(fibra)* jute.

juvenco *f (bezerro) m* calf.

juvenil *(pl:* -**is***) adj inv (caráter)* youthful; **2** *(de jovens) (roupa, moda)* teenage; **3** *(DESP, departamento)* junior.

juventude *f* youth; **2** youthfulness; **3** young people.

k

k, K [ka] *m* [letra- **kapa**] k, K.
K *(símbolo de : **kelvin**) Vd:* **kelvin**.
kafkiano/a *adj* Kafkaesque.
Kalahari *n:* **o deserto de** ~ the Kalahari Desert.
kantismo *m (Kant's* filosphy*)* kantism ♦ **kantista**
  adj Kantian.
karaoke *m* **-1** [atividade] karaoke; **2** [clube noturno]
  karaoke bar.
karaté *(BR: -ê) m* karate.
karateca *m/f* karateca.
kardecismo *m religious doctrine of the Frenchman*
  Allan Kardec.
kart *m* go-cart.
karting *m* karting.
kartódromo *m* go-kart track.
Katmandu *n* Kathmandu; **em** ~ in kathmandu.
kb *(abre de* kilobyte*) m* kilobite, Kb.
Kelvin *n (the basic Si unit of thermodynamic*
  temperature) kelvin.
kepléria *f (BOT) (India palm tree)* kepleria.

ketchup *m* (tomato) ketchup.
Keynesiano/a *adj* Keynesian;
keynesianismo *n* keynesian.
kg *(abre de* quilograma*) m* kg.
Khartum *n* Khartoum; **em** ~ in Khartoun.
Kibutz *m* kibbutz.
Kìev *n* Kiev.
Kilo *m (abr de quilo)* kilo; **kilograma** *m (Vd:*
  quilograma).
kilt *m (Scottish kind of skirt)* kilt.
kimberlito *m (FÍS)* kimberlite.
kimono *m (also: quimono)* kimono.
kit *m* kit.
kitchenette *f* kitchenette.
kitsch *adj inv* kitsch.
kiwi *m* [fruta] kiwi fuit.
kl *m (abr de quilolitro)* kl.
km *(abr de* **kilómetro***) m (also:* **quilómetro***)* kilometer,
  km.
km/h *(abr de quilómetro por hora) m* km/h.
knockout *m (FUT)* knockout
know-how *m* know-how.
KO *m (abr de* **knockout***)*
koeitiano/a *n, adj* from koweit/Kuwait.
Kuala Lumpur *n* Kuala Lumpur; **em** ~ in Kuala
  Lumpur.
kúmel *m (bebida alcoólica com cominho)* kummel.
kunquat *m (also: cunquat) (fruit)* kumquat.
Kuwait/koheit *n Kuwait;* **no** ~ **in Kuwait.**
kw *(abre de quilovátio)* kilowatt *m* kw.
kwanza/cuanza *m (Angola's monetary unit)* kwanza.

L, l *m (letra)* L, l.

L *m (abr de* **Largo***)* Square; **2** Roman numeral: 50.

l *m (abr de* **litro***)* liter.

la *(for rules, please see:* **lo***) (gram) pron pess objecto* her, you *f*, it; **eu quero vê-la** I want to see her; **ele quer amá-la** he wants to love her; **vou fazê-la** I am going to make it; **já puseste a mesa? não, vou pô-la agora** have you laid the table? no, I am going to do it now.

lá *adv* there; ~ **adiante,** over there, further on; *(hora)* **até** ~ until then; *(lugar)* **vou até** ~ I am going (up to) there; ~ **embaixo** down there, downstairs; ~ **em cima** up there, upstairs; ~ **fora** outside, abroad; ~ **mesmo** in that very place; **está** ~? *(TEL)* hello? (are you there?), *(BR)* **alô?**; ~ **vai ela** there she goes; **cá e** ~ here and there; **para** ~ **do** on the other side of; **andar para cá e para** ~ walking back and forth; **toma** ~! take that!; **alto** ~! stop!, wait!; ♦ *(MÚS)* lah.

lã *f* wool; *(pelo)* fleece; ~ **de ovelha** sheepskin; **2** *(tecido)* **fazenda de** ~ woollen material; *(para tricô)* ~ **de dois fios** two-ply wool; **novelo de** ~ ball of wool; **de** ~ woollen, fleece; **3** *(vestuário)* **roupa de** ~ woollies; IDIOM **vir/entrar com pezinhos de** ~ to tiptoe around/approach a subject tactfully.

labareda *f* flame, blaze; **a casa estava em** ~s the house was ablaze; **2** *(fig)* passion, excitement, ardour.

lábia *f (fam)* smooth talk; **ter muita** ~ to be glib; to be cunning; to wheedle; **não vá na** ~ **dele** do not be taken in by his smooth talk; IDIOM **ele tem muita** ~ he has the gift of the gab.

lábio *m (ANAT)* lip; **2** *(genital)* labium; ~ **superior/ inferior** upper/lower lip; ~ **leporino** harelip; **os** ~s **de uma ferida** the lips/edges of a wound; ~ **finos** thin lips; **de sorriso nos** ~s with a smile on the lips.

labioso,-a *adj* crafty, cunning.

labiríntico,-a *adj* winding, sinuous.

labirinto *m* labyrinth, maze; **2** *(fig)* confusion, tangle.

labor *m* hard work, labour, toil.

laboração *f* work, working.

laboral *adj inv* working.

laborar *vt (campos)* to labour, toil, cultivate; ♦ *vi* to work; ~ **em erro** to be in error, be under a misapprehension.

laboratório *m* laboratory.

laborioso,-a *adj (trabalho)* laborious, difficult.

labrador *m (cão)* labrador.

labrego,-a *adj* country bumpkin, lout; **2** *(pej)* churlish, ill-bred, boorish.

labuta *f* constant toil, drudgery; struggle; **a vida é uma** ~ **constante** life is a constant struggle/drudgery.

labutar *vi* to toil, labour; **2** to struggle, strive, endure; scrub; ~ **pela vida** to scrub for a living.

laca *f* lacquer.

laçada *f* loop, slip-knot, bow-knot; **2** one knot in a bow.

lacaio *m* lackey, footman.

laçar *vi* to bind, tie; **2** to fasten with laces; **3** to lasso; **4** to snare.

laçarote *m* beautiful bow, rosette.

laceração *f* laceration, wound; **2** *(MED)* incision.

lacerante *adj inv* lacerating, heart-rending; **grito** ~ heart-rending cry.

lacerar to lacerate, to mangle; **2** to cut into; **3** *(fig)* to afflict, torment, distress; *(fig)* ~ **o coração** to break the heart.

laço *m* knot; **2** bow; **3** bow-tie; **4** trap; **5** noose, lasso; ~s **de sangue** blood ties; **armar um** ~ to set a trap.

lacónico,-a *adj* laconic, terse.

lacraia *f* (**lacrau** *m*) *(ZOOL) (insecto do Amazonas) (espécie de centopeia)* centipede.

lacrainha *f (BR) (insecto)* earwig.

lacrar *vt* to seal (with sealing wax).

lacrau *m* scorpion.

lacre *m* sealing wax.

lacrimal *adj inv (ANAT)* lachrymal; **glândula** ~ lachrymal gland.

lacrimejante *adj inv (voz)* tearful; **2** *(olhos)* full of tears.

lacrimejar *vt (olhos)* to water; **2** *(pessoa)* to cry.

lacrimogéneo,-a *adj* tear-provoking; **gás** ~ tear gas.

lacrimoso,-a *adj* tearful.

lactação *f* suckling, breastfeeding; lactation.

lactante *f* nursing mother; ♦ *adj inv* milk-producing.

lactente *adj inv (criança)* breast-fed, suckling.

lácteo,-a *adj* milky; **Via L~a** Milky Way.

lacticínio *m* dairy product; ~s dairy products; ♦ *adj* made with/from milk.

lacuna *f* gap, blank; space; **2** *(fig)* lack of; **3** *(fig)* omission; **4** *(GEOL)* hiatus; **5** *(MED)* cavity, lesion.

ladainha *f* litany; **2** *(fig)* rambling talk; **sempre a mesma** ~ always the same old talk.

ladear *vt* to flank, border; **2** to walk beside, be alongside; **3** *(contornar)* to surround, skirt; **4** *(fig) (o assunto)* to evade, dodge; ♦ *vi (EQUIT)* to sidestep; ♦ ~-**se** *vr* to surround oneself (**de** with).

ladeira *f* slope, hillside, ramp, hillock; ~ **abaixo** downhill.

ladino,-a *adj (esparto)* smart; **2** lively, **3** *(manhoso)* sharp, cunning.

lado *m* side; **2** *(MIL)* flank; **3** direction, way; **foram por este** ~ they went this way; **ao** ~ **de** beside; **de** ~ sideways; **pôr de** ~ to set aside; **por outro** ~ on the other hand; **de um** ~ **para outro** back and forth; **em/por todo o** ~ everywhere; **de um** ~ **ao outro** from one end to the other; **de** ~ **a** ~ all over; ~s thereabouts; **vou para esses** ~s I am going in that direction; **para os** ~s **de Londres,**

somewhere in/around London; **pôr (algo) de ~** set sth aside.

ladra *f* thief; **Feira da L~** flea market, car-boot market.

ladrão *m* thief, robber; **2** pickpocket; **3** *(casa, carro)* burgler; **4** *(de estrada)* highwayman; **5** *(nas lojas)* shop-lifter; **6** dishonest; **7** *(fam) (rapaz maroto)* little devil; **8** *(fig)* scoundrel; **9** *(MEC) (tubo)* overflow pipe; **10** *(BOT)* sucker (of plants); **cova do ~** hollow in the nape; **cova de ladrões** den of thieves; IDIOM **a ocasião faz o ~** opportunity makes the thief; **andar com pés de ~** to creep about.

ladrar *vi* to bark, bay; *(fig, fam)* **~ à lua** (shout unnecessarily) to bark at the moon; IDIOM **cão que ladra, não morde** a dog's bark is worse than his bite.

ladrido *m (cão)* bark, yap.

ladrilhador,-ora *m,f* tile-layer, tiler.

ladrilhar *vt* to tile, lay tiles/slabs, pave floors.

ladrilheiro,-a *adj* tile-maker, tiler; **cerâmica ~a** tile industry.

ladrilho *m* tile, slab; **~ de vidro** glazed tile.

ladroagem *f* robbery, thievery; **2** thieves; **3** *(acto)* thieving.

ladroeira *f* robbery.

ladrona *f* thief; ♦ *adj* thievish.

lagar *m* fruit press; **2** *(de vinho)* wine press; **3** *(de azeite)* olive press.

lagarta *f (ZOOL)* caterpillar; **2** *(MEC)* caterpillar track of a tractor.

lagartixa *f (ZOOL)* sand-lizard, wall-lizard.

lagarto *m (ZOOL)* lizard; IDIOM **dizer cobras e ~s de (alguém)** to speak ill of sb, to character assassinate.

lago *m (GEOL)* lake; **~ de barragem** reservoir; **2** *(fig) (muita água derramada)* pool.

lagoa *f* pool, pond, lagoon.

lagosta *f (ZOOL)* lobster; **~ comum** *f* crayfish; **~ sapateira** locust lobster.

lagostim *m* small lobster, crayfish.

lágrima *f* tear; drop; **ter a ~ ao canto do olho** to be tearful, about to cry; **2 lágrimas** *fpl* tears; **conter as ~s** to hold back the tears; **as ~s chegaram-lhe aos olhos** tears came to her/his eyes; **derramar ~s** to shed tears; **o saco das ~s** tear duct; **debulhado/ desfeito em ~s** *(pranto)* in tears, weeping; **3** *(fig)* **~s de crocodilo** crocodile tears; **~s da manhã** dew.

laguna *f* lagoon.

laia *f* kind, sort, type; **à ~ de** in the manner of; **os dois são da mesma ~** they are two of a kind.

laico,-a *adj* lay, secular.

lais *m (NÁUT)* yard's end; **~ do navio** squaring *(of the ship)*; **~ de verga** yardarm.

laivar *vt* to sully, taint, stain, blemish.

laivo *m (mancha)* stain; **2** spot, blot; **3** a trickle of blood (from the nose etc); **4** *(desonra)* stain; **5** *(fig)* vestige, mark; **6** vein, streak; **~s** *mpl* smattering of sth, superficial knowledge.

laje *f* paving stone, flagstone.

lajear *vt* to pave (street); to lay slabs down.

lama[1] *f* mud, mire, sludge; **2** *(fig)* disgrace, dishonour; **chafurdar na ~** to wallow in the mud.

lama[2] *m* Lama, Buddhist priest.

lama[3] *m (ZOOL)* llama.

lamaçal *m* quagmire, mud patch, bog.

lamacento,-a *adj* muddy, mud-like.

lambada *f (fam)* slap; **2** *(fig)* telling off, dressing-down; **3** *(BR)* whipping; **4** *(BR)* sip; **5** *(BR)* dance.

lambão,-ona *adj* greedy, gluttonous; having a sweet tooth; **2** sloppy eater.

lambarice *f* greediness; **2 ~s** *fpl* sweetmeats.

lambaz *m* greedy pig; **2** *(NÁUT) (limpar o chão)* mop; ♦ *adj inv* gluttonous.

lambazar *vt* to mop (deck, floor).

lambe-esporas *m (BR)* flatterer, fawner, toady, bootlicker.

lamber *vt* to lick; **~ os beiços** to lick one's lips; **2** *(fig)* lap; **3** *(fig)* swallow up; ♦ **~-se** *vr* to preen oneself, rejoice.

lambida, lambidela *f* lick, licking; **2** flattery; **3** card-game.

lambiscar *vi* to pick at one's food; ♦ *vt* to nibble.

lambisgóia *f* dull, woman; **2** meddler' gossip-monger; affected/conceited woman.

lambreta *f* motor scooter; **andar de ~** to ride a scooter.

lambri *(pl: -s) m (BR)* panelling.

lambril *(pl: -is)*, **lambrim** *m (pl: -ins)* panelling; wainscot.

lambujar *vi* to eat sweet things/tit-bits; to be glutton.

lambuzar *vt (sujar)* to make dirty/greasy/sticky; **2** to smear; ♦ *vr* to get covered with/in, get smeared with/in.

lamecha *adj* overly amorous; **ser ~** to be sentimental.

lamentação *f* lamentations, sorrow; complaint.

lamentar *vt* to mourn *(defunto)*; **2** *(lastimar)* lament; be sorry/sad for, bewail; ♦ **~-se** *vr (queixar-se)* to whinge; to regret; **ele lamenta-se de não se ter casado** he regrets not having married/not to be married.

lamentável *adj inv* regrettable; deplorable.

lamento *m* lament; **2** moan.

lâmina *f (de faca, instrumento cortante)* blade; **2** *(placa de metal)* thin plate; metal plate; **3 ~ de cobre** copper sheet; **4** *(de madeira)* layer/veneer of wood; **5** *(da persiana)* slat; **6** *(de microscópio)* slide; **7** *(MÚS) (palheta)* reed.

laminação *f* lamination; **2** rolling; **~ a frio** cold rolling; **3** *(madeira)* veneering.

laminado,-a *m* laminate; ♦ *adj* laminated; **2** *(revestido de madeira)* veneered; **prata ~a** silver plated.

laminar *vt* to laminate; **2** *(metal)* to cut into strips/plates/sheets; **3** *(a frio)* to cold-roll; **4** *(madeira)* veneer; ♦ *adj inv* laminar.

lâmpada *f* lamp; **~ elé(c)trica** light bulb.

lampadário *m* candelabrum *(pl: **candelabra**)*; chandelier.

lamparina *f* small oil lamp, night lamp; **2** *(fig)* *(bofetada)* slap, box on the ear; **~ de soldar** *(MEC)* blowtorch.

lampejante *adj inv* flashing, twinkling.

lampejar *vt* to twinkle, sparkle, shine, flash.

lampejo *m* sudden flush of light, flare, flash, sparkle; **2** *(fig)* sudden inspiration.

lampião *m* lantern, large lamp; **2** gas lamp.

lampreia *f (ZOOL)* lamprey, catfish; *(CULIN)* ~ **de ovos** a sweet made with eggs and in the shape of a lamprey.

lamúria *f* wailing; lament; complaint; whining.

lamuriante *adj inv* whining; moaning.

lamuriar *vt/vi* to wail, lament; snivel; whine; moan; cry; ♦ ~**-se de** *(algo) vr* to moan about sth, whinge.

lança *f* lance; **2** spear; **3** javelin; **4** pole or shaft of a carriage; **5** boom of a crane; **6** *(FUT) m* striker; **à ponta de** ~ to the utmost; ~ **de guindaste** *(NÁUT)* jib of crane; IDIOM **meter uma** ~ **em África** to set the Thames on fire.

lança-chamas *m sg/pl* flame-thrower.

lançadeira *f* shuttle (of weaving and sewing); ~ **cilíndrica** long shuttle; **2** *(fig)* restless person.

lançador *m (DESP)* thrower; **2** *(leilão)* bidder; **3** *(COM)* promoter; **4** *(DESP) (basebol)* pitcher.

lança-granadas *m sg/pl* grenade launcher.

lançamento *m* throwing; **2** *(COM) (escrituração)* entry; **3** *(leilão)* bidding; **4** *(NÁUT) (evento, livro, satélites)* launching; **5** *(JUR)* summons; **6** *(CONST)* laying (foundations); **7** *(BOT) (broto)* shoot, scion; **8** tax assessment.

lançar *vt* to throw, fling, cast, hurl; **2** *(NÁUT) (ferro)* to drop anchor; **3** *(do navio, evento, satélites)* to launch; **4** *(MED)* to vomit; **5** *(COM)* to enter, register; **6** *(emitir)* to send out, expel; ~ **gafanhotos/ perdigotos** *(saliva, bocados de comida enquanto falando)* to splutter, to spittle; **7 ela lançou a cabeça para trás e cantou** she threw back her head and sang; **8** ~ **um apelo** to make an appeal; **9** ~ **em rosto** to accuse, throw sth at sb's face; **10** ~ **luz sobre** enlighten, explain; **11** ~ **mão** to make use of; IDIOM ~ **(alguém) aos bichos** throw sb to the lions.

lance *m* incident, event; **2** shot, hit; **3** *(leilão)* bid; **4** *(jogo)* bet; **5** *(TEAT) (peça)* launch; **errar o** ~ to miss one's mark; **de um** ~ in one go/moment; ~ **de olhos** fleeting glance; ~ **livre** *(DESP)* free throw.

lanceta *f (MED)* lancet.

lancetar *vt* cortar com lanceta *(tumor)*.

lancha *f (NAUT)* launch; ~ **salva-vidas** lifeboat; ~ **torpedeira** torpedo boat.

lanchar *vt/vi* to have afternoon tea; to take a snack (in the afternoon).

lanche *m* snack; **2** afternoon tea.

lancheira *f* lunch-box.

lancinante *adj inv (dor)* sharp; **2** *(grito)* piercing; **3** *(situação, cena)* heart-rending; **4** *(emoção)* deep, tormenting.

lanço *m (arremesso)* throw; **2** *(conjunto de degraus entre patamares)* flight; **3** *(secção de muro, estrada)* stretch; **4** ~ **de casas** row of houses; **5** *(pesca) (peixe apanhado dume vez)* catch.

languidez *f* languor, listlessness.

lânguido,-a *adj* languid; **2** lazy indolent; **3** *(sem vontade/forças)* listless; **4** *(gesfos; aparência)* voluptuous.

lanho *m (golpe)* slash, gash; **2** *(BR)* strips of meat/ bacon.

lanifício *m* related to wool; woollen fabric/cloth; ~**s** woollen goods; **indústria de** ~ woollen industry.

lanígero,-a *adj* woolly.

lanolina *f* lanolin.

lantejoula *f* sequin; **vestido de** ~**s** sequin-embroidered dress.

lanterna *f* lantern; ~ **de petróleo** paraffin lamp; **2** *(portátil)* torch, flashlight; **3** light-chamber of a limelight; **4** *(ARQ) (telhado de vidro)* roof lantern, kind of skylight; **5** *(pop)* eye, peeper; **6** *(wine bottle or glass)* bottle; **7** *(com dispositivo que esconde a luz)* ~ **furta-fogo** dark lantern.

lanterna-mágica *f (FÍS, CIN)* magic lantern; ~ **de papel** *f* paper lantern.

lanternim *m (ARQ)* fanlight; *(abertura lateral de uma cúpula)* clerestory; **2** *(moinho, azenha)* wheel pivot of a mill.

lanudo,-a *adj* woolly, fleecy; **2** bearing wool.

lanugem *f (pelugem)* down; *(BOT)* fuzz, fluff, pile.

Laos *npr* o ~ Laos.

lapa *f (GEOL) (cavidade)* cave, grotto; **2** *(molusco nos rochedos)* limpet; **3** large overhanging stone, serving as shelter; **4** *(fam) (pessoa chata)* pest; **5** *(BR)* slice, piece.

lapela *f (de um casaco, blusa)* lapel; **ele tem uma rosa na** ~ he has a rose on the lapel.

lapidar *adj inv (gravado em pedra)* engraved; ♦ *vt (talhar, polir)* to cut, polish; **2** *(matar à pedrada)* to stone (to death) *(alguém)*.

lapidaria *f* art of cutting/polishing stones.

lápide *f* tombstone.

lápis *m* pencil; ~**-lazúli** lapis lazuli.

lapiseira *f* propelling pencil; **2** *(caixa)* pencil case.

lapões *mpl* Lapps; **os** ~ the Lapps.

Lapónia *f* a ~ Lapland.

lapónio,-ia *(BR: -ô-) m,f* country bumpkin, boor, yokel; **2** *(fig)* simpleton; ♦ *adj* churlish, uncouth.

lapso *m* lapse; **2** interval; **3** slip (of tongue); **4** *(erro)* oversight, error.

lapuz *m* boor, lout; ♦ *adj inv* uncouth.

laquê *m (BR)* lacquer, hairspray.

lar *m* home; homeland; **no** ~ **da família** in the family bosom; ~ **de terceira idade/de idosos** old people's home.

laracha *f* joke, jest; mockery.

laranja *f* orange; **doce/geleia de** ~ *f* marmalade; **sumo** *(BR: suco)* **de** ~ orange juice.

laranjada *f* orangeade.

laranjal *m* orange grove, orange orchard.

laranjeira *f* orange tree; **flor de** ~ orange blossom.

larapiar *vt* to pilfer.

larápio *m* petty thief.

laré *m* bad/poor dancer; ♦ *adv (fam)* **andar no/ao** ~ to idle, bum around, be always out; **ó** ~ *exc* so there! so what!.

lareira *f* hearth, fireside.

larga *f (acto de largar)* releasing, letting go; **ter consciência ~** to be unscrupulous; **largas** *fpl*; **dar ~ a** to give free rein to, give vent to; **fazer vistas ~s** to ignore, overlook; **viver à ~** live lavishly; **gastar à ~** spend freely; **dar ~s a algo** to give free rein to sth *(imaginação, etc)*; ♦ **larga!** *exc (NÁUT)* cast off!.

largada *f* start; **2** *(partida)* departure, sailing; **3** *(acção)* releasing; **4** *(fam)* joke; ♦ **de ~** *adv* about to leave.

largar *vt (ceder)* to let go of, release; **2** *(desistir)* to give up; **3** *(fam)* to pay up; **4** *(abandonar)* to leave; **5** *(cheiro)* to give off; **6** *(grito, riso)* to let out; ♦ *vi* to leave; **2** *(trabalho)* to finish; **3** *(vela)* to set sail, cast off; **4** to stop (doing); **larga-me** leave me alone; **~ uma bufa** *(fam)* to fart.

largo *m* small square; **2** open sea; **fazer-se ao ~** *(NÁUT)* to sail away, head for the open sea; **3** *(MÚS)* largo movement; ♦ **largo,-a** *adj* broad, wide; **2** *(prolongado)* long; **3** *(roupa folgada)* loose; **4** *(muitos)* several *(centenas, milhares)*; **o vestido custou umas centenas ~as** the dress cost several hundred, *(euph)* a few hundred ♦ *adv* broadly; **ao ~** off the coast; offshore; **a traços ~s** roughly, in broad outline; **a passos ~os** hurriedly.

largueza *f* space, room; **2** *(fig)* generosity, largesse; **3** lavishness.

largura *f* width, breadth, broadness; space, room; **tem dois metros de ~** it is two metres wide.

larica *f (pop)* hunger; **estar com ~** to be peckish.

laringe *f (ANAT)* larynx.

laringite *f (MED)* laryngitis.

larva *f* larva, grub.

lasca *f* splinter; chip (of wood, stone); slice, chunk, fragment; **2** *(em bocados)* flake, sliver; **~s** *(madeira)* shavings.

lascado,-a *adj (louça, madeira)* chipped, cracked, split; **2** *(pedra)* splintered; **3** in pieces, flaked.

lascívia *f* lust, lasciviousness.

lascivo,-a *adj* lewd, lascivious, wanton.

lassidão *f*, **lassitude** *f* lassitude, weariness.

lástima *f* pity, compassion; **2** misfortune; **que lástima!** *exc* what a shame!, what a pity!; **ser digno de ~** to be pitiful.

lastimar *vt* to deplore; to pity; *(BR)* **~ alguém** to wound sb.

lastimar-se *vr* to complain, moan, whinge; to be sorry for o.s.

lastimável *adj inv (merece pena)* pitiful; **2** *(conduta, palavras)* deplorable; lamentable; regrettable.

lastimoso,-a *adj (situação)* pitiful; **2** *(voz)* mournful, complaining, wailing.

lastro *m (NÁUT)* ballast, cargo; **2** broken rock or gravel for bed/covering of road; **3** *(FIN)* gold reserve; **4** *(fam)* appetizer, filler; **5** *(fig)* basis, grounding; **6** *(BR) (cavino de ferro)* switch engine.

lata *f* tin, can, canister; **2** *(de chá)* tea-caddy; **3** tin-plate; **4** *(pej)* old bangle; **5** *(barra de parreira)* crossbar; **6** *(fam) (cara-descaramento)* cheek, nerve; **bairro de ~** shanty town ♦ **que ~!** *exc* what a nerve!, what a cheek!

latada *f (de uvas)* vine trellis; **2** *(de metal)* ironwork; **3** lattice; **4** noise with tins; **5** *(fam)* **dar uma ~** to slap sb.

latão *m* brass; **2** *(grande lata)* bin.

lataria *f (BR)* many tins; **2** *(AUTO)* bodywork.

látego *m* whip; **2** *(fig)* ordeal, scourge; **3** *(fig)* stimulus.

latejante *adj inv (coração)* throbbing, beating; **2** *(arfante)* pulsating.

latejar *vi* to throb, beat; **2** *(cintilar)* to sparkle.

latejo *m* throbbing; gasp.

latente *adj inv* latent, hidden.

lateral *f (FON)* lateral; **as laterais** lateral consonants; **2** *m (DESP)* side, wing, sideline; **3** *(FUT)* outfielder; ♦ *adj inv* side, lateral.

latex *m* latex.

laticínio *m* dairy product.

latido *m* bark(ing), yelp(ing); **~s de consciência** remorse, feel remorse; **~s** *mpl (pop)* empty words.

latifundiário,-a *m,f* big landowner; ♦ *adj* latifundian; large estates' agriculture.

latifúndio *m* large estate, property.

latim *m* Latin; **2** *(fig, fam)* double Dutch; **isso, para mim é ~** it's all double Dutch to me; **3** *(fig, fam)* **~ macarrónico** *(falar com erros)* pidgin talk, kitchen Latin; IDIOM **gastar/perder o seu ~** waste one's breath.

latino,-a *adj* Latin; **o povo ~** the Latin people, race; **2** *(NÁUT)* lateen.

latino-americano,-a *adj* Latin-American.

latir *vi* to bark, yelp; **2** *(fig)* to shout.

latitude *f (GEOL)* latitude; **2** breadth; **3** *(fig)* scope, extent, range, capacity; **4** *(fig)* freedom (of action).

lato,-a *adj* broad, ample, vast; **~ sensu/em sentido ~** in a broad sense.

latoeiro *m* tinker, tin-smith, brass-worker.

latrina *f (pública)* latrine, privy, water-closet, toilet.

latrocínio *m* armed robbery, hold-up, highway robbery.

lauda *f* page of a book; **2** *(REL)* laud, music, song in praise of God.

láudano *m* laudanum; any preparation of opium.

laudativo,-a, **laudatório,-a** *adj* laudatory, praising.

laudável *adj inv* praiseworthy, laudable.

laureado,-a *m,f* honoured, winner; laureate; ♦ *adj* celebrated, laureate.

laurear *vt (homenagem, prémio)* to crown with laurel; **2** to honour, award; **3** to praise.

lauto,-a *adj* sumptuous, opulent; **2** lavish, abundant.

lava *f (GEOL)* lava; **2** *(fig)* torrent; flame, fire.

lavabo *m* washbasin; **2** finger bowl; **3** *(REL)* the priest's ritual washing of hands; **4** *(BR)* bathroom; ♦ **~s** *mpl* lavatory; toilet; **~s públicos** public lavatories, W.C.

lavadeira *f* washerwoman, laundry woman; **2** *(BR)* industrial washing machine for woollen materials.

lavador *m (person who washes: cars, dishes, etc)* washer; ♦ **lavadora** *f (BR)* washing machine.

lavadouro *(= **lavadoiro**) *m* tub, washing tank; public washing place; **2** *(cova junto ao tabuleiro do sal)* salt pan.

lavagante *m* (ZOOL) *(lagosta comum)* spiny lobster.

lavagem *f* washing; **2** *(de roupa)* laundry; **3** *(estômago)* pumping; **4** enema; **5** *(BR)* *(repreensão)* dressing down; **6** *(BR) (DESP)* big victory; **7** *(comida para porcos)* hogwash; ~ **cerebral** *(PSIC)* brainwashing; ~ **de ouvidos** *(MED)* syringing of ears; ~ **de dinheiro** *(fig) (FIN)* money laundering.

lava-louça (= **lava-loiça**) *m* sink.

lavanda *f (BOT)* lavender.

lavandaria (= **lavanderia**) *f* laundry; laundry place.

lavar *vt* to wash; ~ **os dentes** to brush your teeth; **vá ~ as mãos** go and wash your hands; **2** *(fig) (name, honra)* to clear; **3** to cleanse, purify; **4** *(FIN) (dinheiro)* to launder; **máquina de ~ roupa** *f* washing machine; ◆ **~-se** *vr* to have a wash; **lavo-me** I have a wash; **o cão lava-se com a língua** the dog washes himself with his tongue; IDIOM **roupa suja se lava em casa** don't wash your dirty linen in public.

lavatório *m* old-fashioned, mobile wash-basin, washstand, **2** *(BR) (canalizado)* washbasin.

lavoura *f* tilling, ploughing; **2** agriculture, farming; **3** husbandry; **4** *(fig)* work; **casa de ~** farmhouse.

lavra *f* ploughing, tillage; **2** paddy; ~ **de arroz** rice paddy; **3** mining; **4** production; **5** *(obra, trabalho)* of my own; **vinho da minha ~** home-made wine.

lavradio *m* farming, cultivation; ◆ *adj (terreno)* arable, tillable.

lavrado,-a *adj* ploughed *(UK)*, plowed *(US)*; farmed; **2** *(bordado)* embroidered; **3** *(couro)* engraved; **4** *(documento)* drawn up.

lavrador,-ora *m* farmer; **2** landowner; *(BR)* planter.

lavrar *vt (arar)* plough *(UK)*, plow *(US)*; **2** *(lapidar)* carve; **3** *(document)* to draw up; ~ **uma escritura** *(JUR)* draw up a deed.

laxante *m* laxative; ◆ *adj inv* laxative.

laxativo *m adj* laxative.

lazer *m* pleasure; **2** *(ócio, descanso)* leisure.

leal *adj inv* loyal, faithful; **ser ~ a** to be loyal to, keep faith with.

lealdade *f* loyalty; **lealmente** *adv* loyally, faithfully.

lealista *m,f, adj inv (POL)* *(N. Ireland – protestants loyal to UK)* loyalists.

leão *m (ZOOL)* lion; **2** *(ASTROL)* Leo; **~-do-mar** *m* old and experienced sailor.

leão-marinho *(pl: leões-marinhos) m (ZOOL)* sea-lion.

leasing *m (FIN)* leasing.

lebre *f (ZOOL)* hare; **2** *(ASTRON)* constellation Lepus; IDIOM **comprar gato por ~** to buy a pig in a poke.

le(c)cionar *vt* to teach at university; **2** *(disciplina, material)* to lecture in.

le(c)tivo,-a *adj (período, actividade)* academic; **ano ~** academic year.

ledo,-a *adj (poetic) (alegre)* joyful, glad.

legação *f* legation.

legado *m* envoy, legate; **2** legacy, bequest.

legal *adj inv (JUR)* legal, lawful; **2** *(BR: fam)* great, nice, cool.

legalidade *f* legality, lawfulness.

legalizar *vt* to legalize; **2** to authenticate, validate; ◆ *vr* to obtain legal status.

legar *vt* to bequeath, leave (sth to sb); **2** to delegate.

legatário,-a *m,f (JUR)* legatee.

legenda *f (CIN, TV)* subtitle; **2** inscription; **3** caption.

legendar *vt* to subtitle, write captions or subtitles.

legendário,-a *adj* legendary, mythical; **2** relating to captions or subtitle.

legião *f* legion; **2** *(fig)* battalion, many people, crowd.

legislação *f* legislation; ~ **tributária** tax legislation.

legislar *vi* to legislate.

legislativo,-a *adj* legislative.

legitimado,-a *adj (criança)* legitimized.

legitimizar *vt* to legitimize.

legítimo,-a *adj* legitimate; rightful.

legível *adj inv* legible, readable.

légua *f (medida itinerária)* league; ~ **tetrestre** league *(área equiv. a 5 km)*; **2** *(BR: AGR)* 43.57 sq. meters; **3** *(fig)* grande distância; ◆ *adv* **à ~** perfectly, rapidly; **a ~s** miles away/ahead.

legume *m (BOT)* vegetable.

leguminoso,-a *(BOT) adj* leguminous.

lei *f (autoridade)* law; **Decreto-~** decree, law, writ; **2** rule; standard; principle; **a ~ em vigor** the law in force; ~ **de meios** appropriation act; ~ **de talião** retaliation; **fora da ~** *(pessoa)* outlaw; ~ **ordinária** common law; ~ **orgânica** constitutional law, the law of the land; **prata de ~** sterling silver; *(JORN)* ~ **da rolha** censorship; **L~ Seca** *(US)* *(proibindo bebidas alcoólicas)* Dry Law; **sem ~** lawless; **infringir a ~** to break the law; **revogar uma ~** annul/revoke a law.

leia *(pres. subj de: ler)* **não ~ mais** don't read anymore; **é preciso que ele ~ muito** he needs to read a lot.

leigo,-a *m,f* lay person; *m* layman; ◆ *adj (REL)* lay, secular; **2** *(fig)* ignorant.

leilão *m* auction; **vender em ~** to auction off.

leiloar *vt* to auction; ◆ *vi* to cry one's wares.

leiloeiro,-a *m,f* auctionneer.

leira *f (sulco para plantio)* farrow; **2** strip of cultivated land; **3** white grape from Algarve; IDIOM **não ter ~ nem beira** to possess nothing.

leitão *m (ZOOL, CULIN)* suckling pig.

leitaria *f* dairy, dairy shop.

leite *m* milk; ~ **em pó** powdered milk; ~ **desnatado/magro** skimmed milk; ~ **meio-gordo** semi-skimmed milk; ~ **de magnésia** milk of magnesia; **~-creme** *m* custard; *(cosmético)* lotion, ~ **de limpeza** cleansing lotion; **irmão de ~** *(colaço)* brothers through breastfeeding.

leiteiro,-a *m,f* milkman/maid; dairyman/maid.

leito *m (cama)* bed; **2** *(GEOL)* layer, substructure; **3** ~ **do rio** river bed.

leitor,-ora *m,f (pessoa que lê)* reader; **2** *(univ)* foreign language assistant; **3** *(de palestra)* lecturer; **4** *(em algumas universidades)* lector; ~ **de CD's** *(aparelho)* CD player; ~ **de cassetes** tape recorder; ~ **ótico** optical character reader.

leitorado *m* lectureship; *(univ)* foreign language assistants and language lecturers.

leitoso,-a *adj* milky.

leitura *f* reading; **ter muita ~** be well read; **amante da ~** bookworm; ~ **de provas tipográficas**

proof-reading; **2** lecture; **a ~ foi um sucesso** the lecture was a success.

lema *m* *(divisa)* motto; **2** *(publicidade)* slogan.

lembrança *f* recollection, memory; **2** souvenir; **~s** *fpl*: **~s a sua irmã!** regards to your sister!

lembrar *vt* to remind; to recall; to recollect; ♦ **~-se de** *vr* to remember; **eu lembrei-me dela** I remembered her; **ele lembrou-a do vinho** he reminded her about the wine; **fazes-me ~ a minha amiga** you remind me of my friend.

lembrete *m* note; reminder; **2** *(fig)* *(raspanete)* telling-off.

leme *m* rudder; **2** *(NÁUT)* helm; *(fig)* control; **ela está ao ~ da companhia** she is at the head of her company.

lémure *(BR: -ê-)* *m* *(ZOOL)* lemur.

lenço *m* handkerchief; **2** headscarf.

lençol *(pl: lençóis)* *m* sheet; *(extensão de água ou petróleo)* **~ freático/de água** water table; IDIOM **branco como um ~** white as a sheet; **estar em maus lençóis** be in a fix, in deep waters.

lenda *f* legend, tale; **reza a lenda que...** the story goes that...

lendário,-a *adj* legendary.

lêndea *f* *(no cabelo)* nit.

lengalenga *f* rigmarole; balderdash, silly talk; rambling talk; tedious conversation; prolix speech.

lenha *f* firewood.

lenhador *m* woodcutter.

lenho *m* log; timber.

lenitivo,-a *m* *(remédio)* palliative, painkiller; ♦ *adj* soothing, mitigating.

lente *f* lens *sg*; **~s de conta(c)to** *fpl* contact lenses; **2** *m,f* *(univ)* professor; senior lecturer.

lentidão *f* slowness; **~ de caracol** snail's pace.

lentilha *f* *(BOT)* lentil.

lento,-a *adj* slow.

leoa *f* *(ZOOL)* lioness.

leopardo *m* *(ZOOL)* leopard.

lépido,-a *adj* jovial, pleasant; **2** quick, swift, agile, nimble.

leporino,-a *adj* *(relativo à lebre)* leporine; **lábio ~** harelip.

lepra *f* leprosy; **2** *(fig)* plague.

leproso,-a *m,f* leper; **2** *(fig)* moral corruption; **3** *(pej)* filthy beast; ♦ *adj* leprous; **2** *(fig)* *(aspecto)* loathsome; **3** *(cão)* scabby.

leque *m* fan; **como um ~** fan-like; **abóbada de ~** fan vault; **2** range; **um ~ de preços** a range of prices.

ler *vt, vi* to read; **2** to recite; **~ em voz alta** to read aloud, to read out loud; **~ de corrida** to skim through; **3** *(sentimentos)* to understand; **4** *(TYPO)* *(revisão)* to read over; **~ nas entrelinhas** to read between lines.

lerdo,-a *adj* slow, sluggish; **2** heavy-moving; **3** *(idiota)* silly, stupid.

léria *f* *(fam)* poppycock; twaddle; **2** *(fig)* *(treta)* a tall story; **3** *(lábia)* glib talk, the gift of the gab; **4 ~s** crochet stitch.

lero-lero *(pl: lero-leros)* *m* *(BR)* *(pop)* chit-chat.

lés *m*: east; **de ~ a ~** from one end to the other, from east to west, right through; **procurei-o de ~ a ~** I looked for him everywhere.

lesão *f* *(MED)* lesion; injury; **~ corporal** grievous bodily harm; **2** damage; **3** *(JUR)* violation; **4** *(fig)* *(reputação)* damage.

lesa-pátria *f* treason; ♦ *adv* **de ~** against the fatherland.

lesar *vt* to injure, wound; **2** cause damage to, to wrong; **3** *(reputação)* stain; **4** *(JUR)* to violate a person's rights.

lésbica lesbiana *f, adj* lesbian; *(fam)* gay woman; *(col)* dyke, dike.

lésbico *adj* *(amor)* lesbian.

lesionado,-a *adj* *(alguém)* injured, hurt.

lesionar *vt* to injure, hurt *(parte do corpo)*; ♦ *vr* to be injured.

lesivo,-a *adj* *(ofensivo)* damaging, harmful, detrimental.

lesma *f* *(ZOOL)* slug; **2** *(fam)* *(pessoa)* sluggard, slowcoach; ♦ *adj inv* sluggish, lazy.

leso,-a *adj* injured, wounded, hurt; **2** wronged; **3** daft; **crime de ~a majestade** high treason.

leste *m* east; **a ~ de** to the east of; **para ~** eastward; ♦ *adj* easterly; **vento do ~** easterly wind.

letal *adj inv* lethal.

letão *m* *(LÍNG)* Latvian; ♦ **letão,-ã** *adj* Latvian.

letargia *f* lethargy.

letivo,-a *(Vd: lectivo,-a).*

Letónia *npr* **a ~** Latvia.

letra *f* *(do alfabeto)* letter; **2** *(calligraphy)* handwriting; **3** *(de música)* lyrics, *pl*; **4** *(COM, FIN)* letter, bill; **~ maiúscula** capital letter *(COMP)* upper case; **~ minúscula** small letter *(COMP)* lower case; **~ de câmbio** bill of exchange; **~ de imprensa** print; **letras** *fpl* *(curso)* arts, humanities; ♦ *adv* **à ~, ao pé da ~** literally, word for word.

letrado,-a *m,f* man/woman of letters, scholar; ♦ *adj* learned, erudite, well-read.

letreiro *m* lettering, label; **2** notice; **3** *(fig)* poster *(US)* billboard; **~ luminoso** neon sign.

léu *m* *(pop)* *(ócio)* idleness; ♦ **ao ~** *adv* naked, bare; **2** *(BR)* uncovered; **cabeça ao ~** hatless.

leucemia *f* leukaemia *(UK)*, leukemia *(US)*.

leva *f* batch; **2** *(grupo)* bunch, crowd; **3** *(NÁUT)* weighing anchor; **4** *(MIL)* levy; recruitment, call-up.

levada *f* *(para a agricultura)* watercourse; **2** waterfall; *(BR)* slope; ♦ *adv* **de ~** hastily.

levadiça *f* *(ponte)* drawbridge.

levado,-a *adj* taken, carried (away); **2** *(intrujado)* taken for a ride; IDIOM *(criança traquina)* **~ da breca** mischievous, naughty; **mulher ~a da breca** quite a woman, full of the old Nick, the devil of a woman.

leva-e-traz *m,f* gossip-monger; tale-bearer; tittle-tattle.

levantamento *m* lifting, raising; **2** uprising, rebellion; **3** survey; **4** *(retirar dinheiro do banco)* withdrawal; **5** inventory.

levantar *vt* to lift; **levanta a prateleira!** lift (up) the shelf!; **2** to erect; **3** to raise; **~ poeira** raise/provoke dust; **~ o lanço** to raise the bid; **4** to arouse, exalt;

5 (*encurtar vestido*) to take up (*bainha*); ~ **dinheiro** to withdraw money; ~ **voo** (*AER*) to take off; ~ **âncora** to weigh anchor; ♦ **~-se** *vr* to get up, stand up; ~ **contra** to rise up against.

levante *m* (*GEOG*) east; **o** ~ the East, the Orient, the Levant; **2** (*METEOR*) (*suão*) levanter; **3** (*fig*) mutiny, uprising; **4** (*BR*) (*BOT*) horsemint.

levar *vt* to take, bring; **levo-lhe isto amanhã** I am taking/shall take this to you tomorrow (*quando a outra pessoa está presente:* I shall bring this to you tomorrow); (*duração*) **quanto tempo leva isto?** how long will this take?; (*considerar*) ~ **em conta** take into account; (*fig*) (*be cheap*) charge reasonably; **2** to have, lead; **a carta não levava assinatura** the letter didn't have a signature; **ela leva uma vida feliz** she leads a happy life; **3** to take away; **ela levou-me a mala** she took my suitcase away; **4** (*cobrar*) to charge, **quanto me leva você pelo trabalho?** how much will you charge me for the work?; **5** to get; ~ **uma bofetada** to get a slap; ~ **a melhor** get the better of; ~ **um susto** get a fright; **6** (*roupa*) to wear; **ela levava um vestido azul** she was wearing a blue dress; **7** (*conter*) **o elevador leva só cinco pessoas** the lift only takes five people; **8** (*efectuar*) ~ **a cabo** to carry out; **9** (*convencer*) **ele sabe levá-la** he knows how to get around her; **10** ~ **a cabo** to carry out; ♦ *vr* (*partir*) **o barco levou-se de vela** the boat set sail/departed; **~-se pela amizade** be taken in/led by the friendship; IDIOM ~ **a sua avante** to have one's own way in the end; ~ **alguém à certa** to cheat; ~ **a mal/a peito** (*ofender-se*) to take amiss, take to heart; ~ **a bem** to take sth well; **isto leva água no bico** this needs caution; ~ **poucas/uma surra** to get a spanking, take a beating; ~ **couro e cabelo** charge the earth.

leve *adj inv* light; slight; (**ao**) **de** ~ lightly, softly.

levedar to leaven; to ferment (*pão*).

levedura *f* yeast, leaven.

levemente *adv* lightly; **2** slightly; **3** softly; **4** superficially.

leveza *f* lightness; **2** (*com tacto*) delicacy; **3** (*agility*) nimbleness; **4** (*fig*) flippancy.

leviandade *f* frivolity.

leviano,-a *adj* frivolous; fickle.

levitação *f* levitation.

léxia *f* (*LÍNG*) lexis.

léxico *m* (*LÍNG*) lexicon, dictionary; **2** glossary; **3** terminology, jargon.

lexicografia *f* (*LÍNG*) lexicography.

lexicográfico,-a *adj* pertaining to lexicography.

lexicógrafo,-a *m,f* (*LÍNG*) (*dicionarista*) lexicographer.

lexicólogo,-a *m,f* lexicologist.

lezíria *f* (*terra abaixo do nível do rio*) marsh; watery plain.

lha(s) = lhe + a(s) (*gram*) (*Vd:* **lhe**).

lhaneza *f* frankness; **2** candour; **3** simplicity.

lhano,-a *adj* frank; **2** straightforward; **3** amiable.

lhe (*gram*) *pron* to/for him; to/for her; to/for you; **~s** *pl* to/for them; to/for you; **dei-lhe uma prenda** I gave him /her/you a present; **falei-lhe ontem** I spoke to you yesterday; **eu disse-lhes** I told them;

eu fiz-lhe a limpeza toda I did all the cleaning for you; **toquei-lhe no ombro** I touched him/her/you on the shoulder.

lho(s) (= lhe + o(s)) **você deu-me o lápis? sim, dei-lho** did you give me the pencil? yes, I gave it to you; **você deu-me as maçãs? sim, já lhas dei** have you given me/did you give me the apples? yes, I have given them to you.

lia *f* dregs *pl*, sediment; **2** (*imperf de:* **ler**) **ela ~ quando eu entrei** she was reading when I went in.

liamba *f* (*BR*) (*BOT*) hemp; cannabis.

liame *m* tie, bond.

libanês,-nesa *adj* Lebanese.

Líbano *npr* **o** ~ the Lebanon.

libelo *m* (*JUR*) formal indictment, note/bill of indictment; charge sheet; **2** (*BR: também*) satire, lampoon, pamphlet.

> Not **'libel'** in the sense of defamation, which is 'difamação' or 'calúnia'.

libélula *f* dragonfly.

liberação *f* (*COM*) settlement of (a debt); discharge (of certain obligations, restrictions); (*BR*) (*COM*) liquidation. **liberado,-a** *adj* free of obligations; **2** (*BR*) (*JUR*) (*em liberdade condicional*) one who is released on parole or probation.

liberal *m,f* liberal; ♦ *adj inv* generous, liberal; **2** open-minded; **3** (*POL*) Liberal; **4** (*profissão*) free-lance.

liberalidade *f* liberality; **2** generosity.

liberalismo *m* liberalism, tolerance; ~ **económico** free trade.

liberalista *adj inv* liberalist.

liberalizar *vt* (*POL, ECON*) to liberalize, to become accessible.

liberar *vt* to liberate, to free, to release.

liberdade *f* freedom, liberty; ~ **condicional** (*JUR*) probation; ~ **sob palavra de honra** parole; ~ **de expressão** freedom of speech; **tomar a** ~ **de** to take the liberty of; **pôr em** ~ to set free; (*literatura*) ~ **poética** poetic licence; **~s** *fpl* liberties.

Libéria *npr* **a** ~ Liberia.

liberiano,-a *adj* Liberian.

libérrimo,-a (*superl of* **livre**) *adj* very much free, completely free.

libertador *m* liberator; ♦ *adj* liberating; **2** (*palavras*) soothing.

libertar *vt* to free, set free, release; **2** (*desobrigar*) to let off; **3** (*desimpedir*) to free, clear (*o caminho*); **4** (*exprimir*) let out, express; ♦ **~-se** *vr* escape; **2** to gain one's independence; **3** to unbind; **4** to exempt oneself (*de imposto, obrigação*).

libertino,-a *adj* dissolute; loose-living, licentious; **2** *m* libertine, rake; **3** *f* libertine.

liberto,-a (*pp irr de:* **libertar**) (*com vbs* **ser, estar**) freed, liberated.

Líbia *npr* **a** ~ Lybia.

libidinoso,-a *adj* libidinous, lecherous, lustful.

libido *f* libido.

líbio,-a *adj* Lybian.

libra *f (moeda)* pound; ~ **esterlina** pound sterling; **2** *(unidade de peso na G.B = 453,6 gramas)* pound; **3** *(ASTRON)* Libra; **4** *(ASTROL)* Libra.

libré *f* livery; **criados de** ~ servants/employees in livery.

lição *f* lesson; *(fig)* **servir de** ~ **a alguém** to be a lesson to sb; **2** *(repreensão, castigo)* lesson.

licença *f* licence, license *(US)*; **2** permission; **3** *(MIL)* leave; **em** ~ on leave; **com** ~ excuse me; **dá** ~? may I?

licença-maternidade *(pl:* **licenças-maternidades***) f* maternity leave.

licenciado,-a *m,f (univ)* graduate; ♦ *adj* graduated, qualified; **2** *(MIL)* on leave.

licenciar *vt* to grant a licence *(US:* license); to grant a diploma or give a university degree (to sb).

licenciar-se *vr (EDUC)* to graduate, obtain a degree; **2** to obtain a licence/license; **3** to get leave.

licenciatura *f (EDUC)* degree; *(em letras)* BA; *(em ciências)* BsC; **2** *(licenciamento)* licensing.

licencioso,-a *adj (obsceno)* licentious, lewd, lascivious.

liceu *m* secondary/high school.

licitação *f (em leilão)* bid; **vendido a** ~ sale by auction.

licitante *m,f* bidder; ♦ *adj inv* bidding.

licitar *vt* to put up for auction; **2** to bid.

lícito,-a *adj* licit, lawful; **2** fair; **3** permissible.

licor *m* liqueur; **2** *(FARM, QUÍM)* liquor.

licoroso,-a *adj* strong and sweet.

lida *f* toil, work, drudgery; ~ **da casa** housework, chores.

lidar *vi* to toil, to work; **2** to struggle; ~ **touros** to fight bulls; ~ **com** *(tratar/trabalhar com)* to deal/cope with; **vou lidar com ele** I am going to deal with him.

lide *f* bullfight.

líder *(pl:* **líderes***) m (chefe, dirigente)* leader.

liderança *f* leadership.

liderar *vt* to lead, manage, direct; **2** to lead, head *(partido, frente)*; **3** to run *(empreendimento)*.

liga *f* league, association; **2** *(para as meias)* garter; **3** *(QUÍM)* alloy.

ligação *f* joining, binding; **2** coupling, connection; ~ **amorosa** love affair, liaison; **fazer uma** ~ make a telephone call; **caixa de** ~ junction, terminal box; **cano de** ~ service-pipe.

ligado,-a *adj (TEC)* connected; **2** *(lights, radio, etc)* on; **todas as luzes estão ligadas** all lights are on; **3** attached.

ligadura *f* bandage; **2** *(MÚS)* ligature.

ligar *vt* to tie, bind, bandage; **2** to join, connect; **3** to mix, blend; **4** to switch on, turn on; **5** to link; **6** *(motor)* start; ~ **a** to pay attention to; **eu não ligo a essas coisas** I don't pay any attention to such things; ~ **para** to ring up; ♦ ~-**se** *vr* get mixed up (with); **2** *(maritalmente)* to live with; **ela ligou-se a um francês** she lives with a Frenchman.

ligeireza *f* lightness; **2** swiftness; **3** nimbleness.

ligeiro,-a *adj* light; **uma refeição** ~**a** a light meal; **2** slight; **3** quick, fast, swift; **4** *(visita, estada)* short; **5** *(aroma, cheiro)* faint; **6** *(construção)* flimsy; **7** *(pés, dedos)* nimble; **de pés** ~**s** nimble-footed; **8**

(BR) (pessoa) dishonest; ♦ *adv* **à ligeira** quickly, lightly, superficially; **vestir-se à** ~ to dress casually.

lilás *m (BOT)* lilac; **2** *(cor)* lilac; ♦ *adj inv* lilac.

lima *f (BOT) (fruta)* lime; **2** *(árvore)* lime-tree; **3** *(ferramenta)* file; **4** *(para as unhas)* file.

limado,-a *adj* filed, polished; **2** finished.

limão *m (BOT)* lemon.

limar *vt* to file; **2** *(fig) (aperfeiçoar)* to polish; **3** *(fig) (atenuar)* to soothe.

limarense *m,f, adj (pessoa, paisagem, etc)* from Ponte de Lima (a town in the North of Portugal).

limenho,-a *adj (person, produto)* from Lima *(Peru)*.

limeria *f* lime tree.

limiar *m* threshold.

limitação *f* limitation, restriction, limit; **2** drawback.

limitar *vt* to limit, restrict; ♦ *vi* to be confined; ♦ ~-**se** *vr:* ~ **a** to limit o.s. to; refrain from to; ~ **com** to make do with, be bound by.

limite *m* limit; **2** boundary, border; **3** bounds, confine; **4** utmost extent; **passar dos** ~**s** go too far.

limítrofe *adj inv (país, região)* adjacent, adjoining.

limo *m (BOT)* seaweed; slime.

limoeiro *m* lemon tree.

limonada *f* lemonade, lemon soda *(US)*.

limpa-chaminés *m* chimney-sweeper.

limpadela *f (casa, carro)* light, quick cleaning.

limpador *m (MIN)* ~ **de minério** mining van (vanner); **2** *(BR)* (house) cleaner.

limpa neves *m* snow plough.

limpa-para-brisas *m (AUTO)* windscreen wiper.

limpa-pés *m* boot scraper; **2** spatula to clean animal's hooves.

limpa-pratos *m (fig) (lambendo o prato)* glutton.

limpar *vt* to clean; **2** to wipe; ~ **a louça** to dry the dishes; **3** to cleanse, purify; **4** to mop up; **5** *(MIL)* to clean up *(zona)*; **6** *(jardim, etc)* to clear up; **7** *(fam) (roubar)* to clean sb out, to fleece; *(em divórcio)* **a mulher limpou-o** his wife cleaned him out/fleeced him; **8** *(fig) (livrar de)* clear up *(cidade, vândalos)*; **9** *(tirar nódoas)* clear off; ♦ ~-**se** *vr* to have a wash, to clean o.s.; IDIOM ~ **as mãos à parede** to wash one's hands of (the whole affair).

limpeza *f* cleanliness, cleaning; **2** neatness; ~ **grande** *(da casa)* spring-cleaning; ~ **de pele** skin cleansing; ~ **étnica** ethnic cleansing; ~ **de ficheiro** *(COMP)* file clean-up; ~ **da memória** to clear memory; *(razia)* clean out.

límpido,-a *adj* limpid, clear, transparent.

limpo,-a *(irr pp de* **limpar***) adj* clean; **2** *(COM)* net, clear; **3** *(fig)* pure; clean; **passar a** ~ to make a clean copy; **tirar a** ~ to find out the truth, get to the bottom of; **4** *(col) (sem dinheiro)* broke; **5** *(fig) (isento de descontos)* net; **ele ganha oitenta mil euros limpos** he earns eight thousand euros after tax; **céu** ~ clear sky; **consciência** ~**a** clear conscience; IDIOM **pôr (tudo) em pratos** ~**s** to lay the cards on the table.

limusina *f* limousine.

lince *m* lynx; **ter olhos de** ~ to have eyes like a hawk.

linchar *vt* to lynch *(alguém)*.

lindeza *f* beauty.

lindo,-a *adj* beautiful, handsome, lovely; **2** *(fig)* fine, wonderful; **3** *(fam)* **que ~ trabalho!** *(irónico)* what a mess!; **que ~a figura!** *(irónico)* what a sight!

linear *adj inv* linear.

linearidade *f* lineation; simplicity.

linfa *f (FISIOL)* lymph; **2** *(BOT) (seiva)* sap.

linfático,-a *adj (FISIOL)* lymphatic.

linfócito *m* lymphocyte, white cell.

linfoma *m (MED)* lymphoma.

linga *f* sling rope to hoist cargo.

lingote *m* ingot.

língua *f (ANAT)* tongue; **2** *(LÍNG)* language; *(fig)* ~ **afiada** sharp tongue; ~ **materna** mother tongue; ~ **viporina/venenosa** spiteful tongue; IDIOM **dar com a ~ nos dentes** to blab, spill the beans; **estar na ponta da ~** to be on the tip of one's tongue; **não ter papas na ~** not to mince words, be outspoken.

língua-de-gato, língua-de-sogra *f (biscoito)* cat's tongue (or langue-de-chat).

língua-de-trapos *m,f (pessoa que não fala claramente)* mumbler; **2** *(que não guarda segredo)* blabberer.

linguado *m (peixe)* sole; *(BR)* flounder; **2** *(pop) (linguagem ordinária)* swearing; **3** sharp/nasty tongue; **4** *(contacto de línguas)* French kiss.

linguagem *f* language; **2** way of talking; **3** speech; ~ **infantil** baby talk, childish language.

linguajar *m* manner of speaking; **2** *(Reg)* speech; dialect; ♦ *vi* to wag one's tongue; to prattle.

linguarão,-ona (= **linguarudo,-a**) *m,f* chatter-box, blabbermouth; ♦ *adj* talkative, gossipy.

linguareiro,-a *n* gossip-monger.

lingueirão *(BR: -guerão) m (molusco)* razor clam.

lingueta *f* latch; bolt, catch; pawl, lever; languet; ~ **e ranhura** tongue and groove; **2** *(rampa de embarcar)* embarcation ramp; **3** tongue of a shoe; **4** *(BR) (rampa natural sobre o mar/rio)* tongue of land, natural ramp.

linguiça *f* Portuguese thin sausage.

linguista *m,f* linguist.

linguística *f* linguistics *sg*.

linha *f* line; cord; row; ~ **de conduta** code of conduct; ~ **férrea** railway line *(UK)*, railroad *(US)*; **em ~** in line, in a row; ~ **de montagem** assembly line; **sair da ~** to step out of line; **2** *(costura)* thread; **3** *(ELECT)* cable, wire; **4** *(corpo)* figure; **5** *(ANAT)* sinew; **6** *(rosto)* features; ~ **de tiro** firing range; ~**s** lines, outlines; **em ~ gerais** in general terms.

linhaça *f* linseed; **óleo de ~** linseed oil.

linha-dura *(pl: **linhas-duras**) m,f* hardliner; ♦ *adj* hard-line.

linhagem *f* lineage, line; **de alta ~** highborn; **2** *(tecido grosso)* coarse linen fabric.

linhite *m (GEOL)* lignite, brown coal.

linho *m (BOT)* flax; **2** *(tecido)* linen; **minha saia é de ~** my skirt is made of linen; **3** *(encadernação)* binder's cloth.

linhote *m (CONSTR)* joist, beam, girder.

linóleo *m* linoleum; *(fam)* lino.

liofilizar *vt (alimentos)* freeze-dry.

lioz *f (GEOL)* limestone; ♦ *adj (pedra)* limestone.

lipoaspiração *f* liposuction.

liquefazer *vt* to liquefy, dissolve; ♦ *vr* to melt, thaw.

liquefeito,-a *(pp de **liquefazer**) adj* liquefied; *(derretido)* molten.

líquen *m (BOT)* lichen.

liquidação *f* liquidation; **2** *(COM)* settlement (of accounts); repayment, paying off (debts); **3** clearance sale; ~ **total** closing down sale; ~ **da sociedade** *(JUR)* dissolution of the company; ~ **dos bens** sell up of assets; **4** *(fig)* destruction, extermination.

liquidar *vt* to liquidate; to pay, repay; sell off; settle; **2** *(fig)* to destroy, eliminate.

liquidez *f* liquidity.

liquidificador *m* liquidizer.

líquido *m* liquid; ♦ *adj* liquid, fluid; **2** *(COM)* net.

lira *f* lyre; lira.

lírico,-a *adj* lyric(al).

lírio *m (BOT)* iris, lily; ~ **do vale** *(pl: **lírios-do-vale**) m* lily of the valley.

lirismo *m* lyricism; **2** *(fam)* sentimentality.

Lisboa *npr* Lisbon.

lisboeta *m,f* inhabitant from Lisbon, Lisboner; ♦ *adj inv* from Lisbon.

lisbonense *adj inv* rel. to Lisbon, *(clube, tradição)* Lisbon; **clube de futebol ~** Lisbon's Football Club.

liso,-a *adj* smooth, flat; **2** *(tecido, roupa)* plain; **3** *(cabelo)* straight; **4** *(fam) (sem dinheiro)* broke.

lisonja *f (adulação)* flattery; **2** *(mimo)* pampering; **3** *(HERALD) (ornato rombóide)* diamond-shaped.

lisonjeador,-ora *m,f (adulador)* flattererl; ♦ *adj* flattering.

lisonjear *vt (adular)* to flatter; **2** *(agradar a)* to soft-soap *(alguém)*; **3** to honour *(alguém)*; ♦ ~**-se** *vr:* ~ **com** be proud of.

lisonjeiro,-a *adj* flattering.

lista *f* list; agenda; ~ **negra** black list; ~ **telefónica** telephone directory; ~ **de vinhos** wine list; **2** stripe; **às ~s** striped.

listar *vt (COMP)* to list.

listel *m (ARQ)* fillet.

listra *f* stripe.

listrado,-a *adj* striped.

lisura *f* smoothness, softness.

literal *adj inv* literal; exact.

literário,-a *adj* literary.

literato *m* writer.

literatura *f* literature; ~ **comparada** comparative literature; ~ **de cordel** (popular novels) pulp literature; pamphlet literature; ~ **de vanguarda** avant-garde literature.

litigar *vt* to litigate, contend; ♦ *vi* to go to law.

litígio *m (JUR)* lawsuit, litigation; **2** *(fig)* dispute, discussion.

litigioso,-a *adj (JUR)* litigious, contentious.

litografia *f* lithography; **2** *(gravura)* lithograph.

litoral *m (GEOG)* coast; ♦ *adj inv* coastal.

litro *m* litre, *(US)* liter.

Lituânia *npr* **a ~** Lithuania.

lituano,-a *adj* Lithuanian; **2** *m* Lithuanian; **3** *(LÍNG)* Lithuanian.

liturgia *f* liturgy.
litúrgico,-a *adj* liturgical.
Liubliana *npr* **a ~** Ljubljana.
lívido,-a *adj* livid, pale.
livramento *m* release; discharge.
livrança *f* release, liberation; **2** *(COM)* written order for payment.
livrar *vt (libertar, soltar)* to release, to free; **2** *(salvar)* to save; **3** *(preservar)* to redeem, claim; **ela livrou o anel da penhora/da casa de penhor** she redeemed her ring from the pawnbroker; ♦ **~-se de** *vr* libertar-se; **~ de alguém/algo** to free o.s. from sb/sth; **2** *(desembaraçar-se)* to get rid of; **eu livrei-me dos livros** I got rid of the books; **ela livrou-se do namorado** she got rid of/dumped/ ditched *(cal)* her boyfriend; **3** *(salvar-se)* to escape from sth; *(evitar)* to avoid sth; **4** *(casaco, sapato, etc)* take off; **livra-te do casaco!** take off your coat!; **5 ~ duma** *(obrigação)* to get out of an obligation; ♦ *exc* **Deus me livre!** Heaven forbid; **livra!** phew!; **livrei-me a tempo** I got out of it in the nick of time.
livraria *f* bookshop *(UK)*, bookstore *(US)*; **2** *(fam) (many books)* pile of books.
livre *m (DESP)* free kick; ♦ *adj inv* free; **2** unoccupied; **3** clear, open; **4** *(pessoa)* spontaneous; **5** unmarried, unattached; **6** licentious; **ao ar ~** in the open air; **~ de impostos** tax-free; **luta ~** *(DESP)* all-in wrestling; **estar ~ de perigo** to be out of danger; **tradução ~** free translation; ♦ **de ~ vontade** *adv* of (one's) own free will.
livre-arbítrio *m* free will.
livre-câmbio *m* free trade.
livre-docente *m,f* research professor, research fellow.
livreiro,-a *m,f* bookseller.
livresco,-a *adj* pertaining to books, literary; **2** *(pessoa) (fam)* bookish; *(pej)* based on reading but without experience.
livrete *m* note-book, registration book, licence.
livro *m* book; **~ de bolso** pocket-sized book; **~ de bordo** logbook; **~ brochado** paperback; **~ de consulta** reference book; **~ de contabilidade** ledger; **~ de cozinha** cookery book; **~ encadernado** hardback book; **~ de mercadorias** stock book; **~ de ponto** register; **~s cor-de-rosa** love stories; IDIOM **ser um ~ aberto** be an open book.
lixa *f* sandpaper; **~ de unhas** nail file; **2** *(ZOOL) (peixe)* dog-fish.
lixar *vt* to sandpaper; **2** *(cal) (avariar, estragar)* to ruin, brass off, screw up; **ele lixou-me o negócio** he screwed up my business; ♦ **~-se** *vr (cal)* to screw up; **vai lixar-te** go to hell; *(não dar importância)* **estou-me lixando para as tuas gracinhas** I care two hoots for your little jokes; **2** *(fam, pop) (indignar, danar)* to rile; **que se lixe o futebol** damn/screw the football!; **vai-te ~!** *exc (fam)* piss off!
lixeira *f* rubbish dump, garbage dump *(US)*; **2** *(em prédio)* rubbish, garbage chute *(US)*; **3** *(fig, fam)* pigsty.

lixeiro *m* refuse collector, dustbin man.
lixívia *f (QUÍM)* bleach.
lixo *m* rubbish, litter; garbage *(US)*; **~ nuclear** nuclear waste; **o homem do ~** the dustman, refuse collector.
lo *(gram) pron pess* objecto *m* (used after verbal forms ending in **r, s, z**, which are omitted = **him, you** *m*, **it**. This rule is used only in affirmative sentences); **quero vê-lo** I want to see him *(instead of* **quero ver-o***)*; **ela fá-lo** she does/makes it *(instead of* **faz-o***)*; **ela pô-lo** *(instead of* **pôr+o***)*; **2** the pronouns **nos, vos** and *adv* **eis** lose their final *s*; **eu dou-vo-lo** *(instead of* **dou-vos-o***)* I give it to you *(pl) (seldom used except in formal writing)*; **3 ei-lo** (= **eis-o**) here he is; here it is.
ló¹ *m (NÁUT)* windward; luff.
ló² *(CULIN)* **pão-de-~** *(a kind of)* sponge cake.
loba *f* she-wolf; **2** *(AGR)* soil around olive trees (dug up); **3** *(MED) (sobretudo em cavalos)* a kind of tumour; **4** cassock.
lobby *(pl:* **lobbies***) m (POL)* lobby.
lobectomia *(MED)* lobectomy.
lobisomem *m* werewolf.
lobo¹ *m (ZOOL)* wolf; **~ de Alsácia** Alsatian dog; **~ do mar** *(marinheiro)* old sea dog; **~-marinho** *m (BR)* sea-lion; **2** *(têxteis)* carding machine; IDIOM **ser ~ da mesma alcateia** run with the pack; **~ com pele de ovelha** a wolf in sheep's skin.
lobo² *m (ANAT)* lobe.
lobrigar *vt* to glimpse, catch sight of; **2** to discern, make out.
lóbulo *m* ear lobe.
locação *f (arrendamento)* lease, rental contract, renting; **2** *(BR)* installation, premises.
locador,-ora *m,f (JUR)* lessor.
local *m* site, place; ♦ *adj inv* local.
localidade *f* locality; location, area.
localizar *vt* to locate, find; **2** to place; **3** *(precisamente)* to pinpoint; **4** *(fig)* to identify; ♦ *vr* to be situated.
loção *f* lotion; **~ de limpeza** cleansing lotion.
locatário,-a *m,f* lessee; *(inquilino)* tenant.
locativo *m (LÍNG)* locative; ♦ *adj (relativo a aluguer)* renting, leasing.
locomativa *f* locomotive.
locomoção *f* locomotion.
locomotiva *f* railway engine, locomotive.
locomover-se *vr* to move (from place to place); get around.
locução *f* expression; **2** diction; **3** *(gram)* locution.
locutor,-ora *m,f (TV, RÁDIO)* announcer, presenter; **2** *(LÍNG)* speaker.
lodaçal *m* mudhole, bog.
lodacento,-a *adj* muddy, swampy.
lodo *m* mud, slime.
lógico,-a *f* logic; **2** *(raciocínio)* reasoning; ♦ *adj* logical.
logística *f* logistics *(pl)*.
logo *adv* right away, at once; **2** then; later; **3** presently, soon; **4** *(BR)* straightaway, forthwith; **até ~!** cheerio! see you later!; **~ no começo** right at

the start; ~ **ali** right there; **ela foi** ~ **fazer** she went to do it straight away; ~ **depois** soon after; ~ **hoje é que vieste?** you had to come today of all days?; **desde** ~ from that moment on; **para** ~ *(sem demora)* for now; **mais** ~ later on; ♦ *conj* so, consequently, hence; **ele jurou,** ~ **ele fala a verdade** he swore, therefore he is telling the truth; ~ **que** as soon as; ~ **que ele diga-me vier** as soon as he arrives, let me know.

logótipo *m* logo.

lograr *vt* to achieve, to get; ~ **fazer** to manage to do; 2 to enjoy; 3 *(enganar)* to trick, cheat; ♦ *vi* to pay off.

logro *m* enjoyment; 2 swindle; 3 *(confusão)* ruse; 4 *(fiasco)* sham; 5 practical joke.

loiro,-a *adj* (Vd: **louro,-a**).

loja *f (COM)* shop *(UK)*, store *(US)*; ~ **de ferragens** hardware shop, ironmonger's; 2 *(maçónica)* lodge; ~ **do cidadão** *(aconselhamento)* one-stop shop; ~ **dos 300 (trezentos)** *n* poundland *(UK)*, dime store *(US)*; IDIOM **patrão fora, dia santo na** ~ when the cat is away, the mouse goes to play.

lojista *m,f* shopkeeper, tradesman.

lomba *f* ridge; 2 high ground; 3 top.

lombada *f* back; *(animal)* rump; 2 *(livro)* spine.

lombalgia *f* backache.

lombar *adj inv* lumbar.

lombo *m* lower back; 2 *(animal)* loin; ~ **de vaca** *(carne)* sirloin; **costeletas do** ~ loin chops.

lombriga *f (ZOOL)* roundworm.

lona *f (tecido)* canvas; 2 *(cobertura)* tarpaulin; 3 *(AUTO)* ~ **de travão** break lining; IDIOM **estar nas** ~**s** *(sem dinheiro)* to be broke.

Londres *npr* London.

londrino,-a *m,f* Londoner; ♦ *adj* from London; London; **pontes de** ~ London's bridges.

longa-metragem *f (filme)* feature film.

longe *adv* far, distant; far away; **ao** ~ in the distance; **de** ~ from afar; **de** ~ **em** once in a blue moon; IDIOM ~ **dos olhos,** ~ **do coração** out of sight, out of mind; **ir** ~ *(sucesso)* to go far; ♦ *prep*: ~ **de** far from.

longevidade *f* longevity, lifetime; 2 *(FÍS)* lifetime, half-life.

longínquo,-a *adj* distant, remote; **no passado** ~ in the distant past.

longitude *f (GEOG)* longitude.

longo,-a *adj* long; 2 lasting; **ao** ~ **de** *(lugar)* along, alongside; **ao** ~ **dos anos** *(tempo)* over the years.

lontra *f (ZOOL)* otter.

loquaz *adj inv* loquacious, talkative.

lorde *m (titular britânico)* Lord; **Câmara dos L**~**s** House of Lords; IDIOM **viver que nem um** ~ to live like a king.

lorpa *m,f* imbecile, idiot; half-wit; 2 *(grosseiro)* peasant; ♦ *adj inv* foolish, idiotic.

losango *m* diamond; 2 *(GEOM)* lozenge.

lota *f (à chegada dos barcos) (venda por grosso)* fish auction/sale; fish market; **vender/comprar à** ~ sell/buy loose, without weighing.

lotação *f (capacidade) (veículo)* capacity; 2 *(navio)* tonnage; 3 *(vinhos)* blending; 4 *(CIN, TEAT)* full,

crowded; ~ **completa/esgotada** sold out; 5 *(BR)* mini-bus.

lotaria *(BR)* **loteria** *f* lottery; ~ **desportiva** *(BR: esportiva) (futebol)* pools.

lote *m* portion, share; 2 *(em leilão)* lot; 3 *(COM) (ações)* batch, parcel; 4 *(terreno)* plot.

loteamento *m (terreno)* division into plots.

loto *m (jogo)* lotto; 2 *(em clubes, etc)* bingo.

louça (= **loiça**) *f* chinaware, dishware; ~ **de barro** earthenware; 2 *(conjunto)* dishes, crockery; **lavar a** ~ to do the washing up.

louçania *f (garridice)* ostentation; gaudiness; 2 *(beleza)* elegance.

louco,-a *m,f* lunatic, mad person; ♦ *adj* crazy, mad, deranged; ~ **varrido** raving mad; ~ **de** mad with; ~ **por** crazy about.

loucura *f* madness; crazy act; 2 *(paixão)* **ela tem uma** ~ **por ele** she is mad about him.

loureiro *m (BOT)* laurel bush.

louro,-a (= **loiro**) *m (BOT)* laurel; **folha de** ~ *(CULIN)* bay leaf; 2 nickname for parrot; ♦ *adj (cabelo)* blonde; *(person)* blonde, fair.

lousa *f* flagstone; 2 *(túmulo)* gravestone; 3 school children's slate; 4 *(BR)* blackboard; 5 *(GEOM)* slate.

louva-a-deus *m sg/pl (ZOOL)* praying mantis.

louvar *vt* to praise; 2 to exalt; ~ **a Deus** to praise God.

louvável *adj inv* praiseworthy.

louvor *m* praise; 2 glorification.

Ltda *(abr de* **limitada***)* Ltd.

lua *f* moon; **estar na** ~ to have one's head in the clouds; ~**-de-mel** *f* honeymoon.

Luanda *npr* Luanda.

luandense *m,f adj* from Luanda.

luar *m* moonlight.

luarento,-a *adj* moonlit.

lúbrico,-a *adj* slippery; 2 *(lascivo)* lascivious, lewd.

lubrificante *m* lubricant.

lubrificar *vt* to lubricate.

lucarna *f* skylight.

lucas *m,f sg/pl (fam)* fool; **fazer-se** ~ to pretend to be a fool.

lucerna *f (tipo de clarabóia)* roof lantern, lucerne.

lúcia-lima *f (BOT)* lemon-verbena; lippia.

lucidez *f* lucidity, clarity.

lúcido,-a *adj* lucid.

lúcio *m (peixe)* pike.

lucrar *vt* to profit from/by; 2 to enjoy; ♦ *vi* to gain.

lucrativo,-a *adj* lucrative, profitable.

lucro *m* gain; 2 *(COM)* profit.

ludibriar *vt* to dupe, deceive; 2 to mock, deride.

lúdico,-a *adj* amusing, entertaining; **do lado** ~ (on the) amusing side.

lufada *f (rajada de vento)* gust, blast.

lufa-lufa *f* bustle, flurry, hurly-burly; **à** ~ in haste, **fiz o trabalho à** ~ I worked non-stop.

lugar *m* place; 2 room; 3 *(ocupação)* positon, job; 4 *(assento)* seat; 5 *(loja de hortaliças)* greengrocer's; **dar** ~ **a** to give rise to; **dar o** ~ **a** to give the place to sb; **ter** ~ to happen, take place; **pôr-se no** ~ **de alguém** to put o.s. in somebody's shoes; ♦ *prep* em ~ **de** instead of; **em primeiro** ~ in the first place; **em nenhum** ~ nowhere.

lugar-comum *m* common-place, cliché.

lugarejo *m* small village, hamlet.

lúgubre *adj inv* gloomy.

lula *f (ZOOL)* squid; **um cardume de** ~**s** a shoal of squid; ~**s grelhadas** grilled squid.

lumbago *m (MED)* lumbago; **sofrer de** ~ to suffer from lumbago.

lume *m (para cozinhar e aquecer)* fire, flame, hearth; **o** ~ **está fraco** the flame is low/weak; **põe as batatas ao** ~ put the potatoes on; **chega-te aqui ao** ~ come closer to the fire (hearth); **2** light; *(fig)* sparkle; **3** *(cigarro)* light; **você tem** ~**s?** have you got a light?; **vir a** ~ to be published, make known; **dar a** ~ to publish; **4** *(fig)* insight, **ter** ~ **no olho** to be smart.

luminária *f* small lamp, lantern, fairy light; **2** ~**s** *fpl* illuminations.

luminosidade *f* luminosity.

luminoso,-a *adj* luminous, bright, radiant; clear.

lunar *m (sinal na pele)* mole; ♦ *adj inv* lunar.

lunático,-a *m,f* madman, madwoman; ♦ *adj* foolish, lunatic.

luneta *f* eye-glass; **2** type of telescope.

lunetas *fpl* pince-nez.

lupa *f* magnifying glass.

lúpulo *m (BOT)* hop.

lúpus *m (MED)* lupus.

lusco-fusco *m* dusk; nightfall; twilight.

lusíada *adj inv (alma, povo)* Portuguese; **os L**~**s** *mpl* *(LITER)* Lusiads (Camoens' 16th-century epic).

lusitano,-a *adj* Lusitanean, Portuguese; **o cavalo** ~ the Lusitano horse.

luso,-a *adj* Portuguese, Lusitanian.

luso-brasileiro,-a *adj* Luso-Brazilian.

lusófilo,-a *adj* Lusophile.

lusófono,-a *m,f* Portuguese speaker; ♦ *adj* Portuguese-speaking.

lustrar *vt* to polish, clean.

lustre *m* gloss, shine, polish; **2** chandelier; **3** *(fig)* fame; glory, splendour; brilliance.

lustro *m (brilho)* shine, lustre; **2** *(cinco anos)* lustrum, five-year period.

luta *f* fight battle, contest, combat; ~ **livre** wrestling; **2** struggle, effort, toil and moil; **3** conflict, battle, war.

lutador,-ora *m,f* fighter, contender; **2** *(de boxe)* boxer; ♦ *adj* fighting.

lutar *vi* to fight, combat; contend; **2** to wrestle; **3** to struggle (against), strive (for); **4** *(altercar)* to quarrel, dispute; IDIOM ~ **contra a corrente** to stem the tide; ~ **com unhas e dentes** fight tooth and nail; ~ **até ao fim** fight to the bitter end.

luterano,-a *adj* Lutheran.

luto *m* mourning, bereavement; **de** ~ in mourning; **2** *(QUÍM)* *(argamassa)* lute, luting.

lutuoso,-a *adj (aparência)* mournful; **2** *(período)* mourning.

luva *f* glove; **assentar como uma** ~ to fit like a glove; **de** ~**s pretas** with black gloves; **2** ~**s** money under the counter, bribe.

luvaria *f* glover's shop.

luveiro,-a *m,f* glover.

luxação *f* dislocation (of joints); sprain, wrench.

luxar *vt* to dislocate; **2** *(membro)* to sprain, wrench; ♦ *vi* to dress/live in luxury.

Luxemburgo *npr* **o** ~ Luxembourg.

luxemburguês,-a *m,f adj* Luxembourger.

luxo *m* luxury; **de** ~ de luxe; **poder dar-se o** ~ **de** to afford.

luxuoso,-a *adj* luxurious.

luxúria *f (sensualidade)* lust; **2** *(viço das plantas)* lushness.

luxuriante *adj inv (viçoso)* luxuriant, plentiful.

luz *f* light; **a** ~ **do sol** sunlight; **a** ~ **da vela** candle-light; ~ **dos projectores** spotlight; **acender/apagar a** ~ to switch on/off the light; **corte de** ~ power cut; **quebra-**~ lampshade; **2** *(fig)* knowledge; ♦ *prep* **à** ~ **de** in the light of, according to; **vir à** ~ **de** to come to light; ♦ *adv* **à** ~ **do dia** in broad daylight; **à meia-**~ dimly lit; IDIOM **dar à** ~ *(bebé)* to give birth to; **dar à** ~ **uma obra** to publish a work; **uma luz no fundo do túnel** a light at the end of the tunnel.

luzente *adj inv* bright, shining.

luzerna *f (BOT)* alfafa; **2** bright green.

luzes *pl (TEAT)* lights; ~ **da ribalta** floodlights; **filosofia das** ~ *(iluminismo)* enlightenment.

luzidio,-a *adj* shining, glossy.

luzir *vi* to shine, gleam; **2** *(fig)* to be successful.

Lx.a *(abr de* **Lisboa***)* Lisbon.

m

M, m *m (letra)* M, m.

M *(abr de* **Metro***) m* underground; **2** *(abr de* **metro***) m* meter; **3** *(abr de:* **masculino***) m* masculine; **4** M = 1000, in Roman alphabet.

ma (= **me** + **a**) *pron pess* it to me.

má *f adj (Vd:* **mau***)*.

maca *f* stretcher.

maça *f (clava)* mace; **2** *(pilão)* mallet; **3** beetle; **4** *(de bilhar)* cue; **5** club; **6** *(polpa da noz-moscada)* mace.

maçã *f* apple; ~**s do rosto** *(ANAT)* cheekbone; ~**-de-Adão** *(fam)* Adam's apple.

macabro,-a *adj* macabre, gruesome.

macaca *f (jogo)* hopscotch; **2** *(pop)* continuous bad luck.

macacada *f* many monkeys; **2** *(brincadeira)* mischief, tom-foolery; **3** *(BR: fam) (malta)* gang.

macacão *m (BR)* astute, shrewd, sly (man); **2** *(roupa de trabalho)* overalls.

macaco *m* monkey; **2** *(MEC)* jack; **3** *(fam) (muco seco)* snot; **4** *(garatuja)* scribble; **fato** ~ overalls, boiler suit; IDIOM **ser** ~ **de imitação** to be a copycat; ♦ ~**s me mordam!** *exc* I'll be damned!; **mandar pentear** ~**s** to tell sb to get lost.

macacoa *f* ailment, minor sickness.

maçada *f* blow with a club; **2** bore, nuisance; **que** ~! what a nuisance!, what a bore!; **3** inconvenience, **é muita** ~ it's a great inconvenience.

macadame *m* tarmac.

maçador,-ora *adj (aborrecido)* boring; tedious; **2** *(pessoa, tarefa)* tiresome.

macaense *adj inv (de Macau)* of/from Macau, Macanese.

macambúzio,-a *m,f* misery; ♦ *adj (pop) (person)* moody, glum, sullen.

maçaneta *f* knob, *(porta, gaveta)* handle.

maçante *adj inv (BR) (Vd:* **maçador***)*.

mação *m* Freemason.

maçapão *m (CULIN)* marzipan.

macaquear *vt* to imitate, ape; ♦ *vi* to muck around.

macaquice *f* tomfoolery; **2** pulling faces; **fazer** ~**s** to fool around.

macaquinho *m (para bebé)* rompers; IDIOM **meter** ~**s na cabeça de alguém** to put (confusing) ideas in sb's head.

maçar *vt* to bore, annoy, tire sb; bother; **ele está sempre a** ~**-me** he is always bothering me.

maçarico *m* blow torch/lamp; **2** *(ZOOL)* kingfisher; **3** *(lebre)* male-hare; **4** *(fig, fam) (homem inexperiente)* greenhorn.

maçaroca *f (BOT)* head, cob (of corn); **2** *(CULIN)* corn on the cob; **3** *(pop) (dinheiro)* dosh, lolly.

macarrão *m (CULIN)* macaroni; **2** *(BR)* tube to isolate electrical wires.

macarrónico *m (fam)* broken (idiom); **inglês** ~ pidgin English.

Macau *npr* Macao; **o** ~ *m* Macao.

Macedónia *npr* **a** ~ *f* Macedonia.

macedónico,-a *adj* from Macedónia, Macedonian.

macela *f (BOT)* camomile (= chamomile).

macerar *vt (esmagar)* to crush; **2** *(impregnar) (frutos, folhas, couro)* to soften, soak; **3** *(fig)* to torment, mortify, scourge.

machadinha *f* chopper, little axe; **2** butcher's cleaver.

machado *m* axe, hatchet.

machão *m* tough guy, he-man; **2** *(gabão de sua potência sexual)* stud.

machimbombo *m (Angola, Moçambique)* mechanic lift; **2** any rustic heavy vehicle; **3** bus.

machismo *m* male chauvinism, machismo.

macho *m* male; **2** chauvinist; **3** *(prega)* box pleat; **saia de** ~**s** pleated skirt; **4** *(ZOOL)* mule ♦ *adj* male; **2** virile, manly.

machona *f (moça)* tomboy; **2** *(mulher)* butch woman; **3** *(pej) (lésbica)* dyke.

machucar *vt (esmagar)* to crush, crease; **2** *(amarrotar)* crumble, wrinkle; **3** to smash; **4** *(fig) (magoar)* to bruise, injure, **5** *(sentimentos)* to hurt.

macico *m (GEOL) (montanha)* massif; ♦ **maciço,-a** *adj (arvoredo, mata)* thick, dense; **2** *(quantidade)* massive; **3** solid; **4** *(pessoa, robusta)* sturdy.

macieira *f (BOT)* apple tree.

macilento,-a *adj (magro)* gaunt, haggard, very thin; **2** *(pálido)* pale, wan.

macio,-a *adj (pele, tecido)* soft, silky, smooth; **2** *(caminho)* smooth, even; **3** *(palavras, voz)* soft.

maço *m* bundle, packet, pack; **um** ~ **de cigarros** a pack of cigarettes; **2** mallet.

maçonaria *f* masonry; **2** freemasonry.

maconha *f (BR) (BOT)* hemp; **2** *(droga)* cannabis, marijuana; **cigarro de** ~ spliff.

maconhado,-a *adj* high on drugs.

maçónico,-a *adj* masonic.

má-criação *f (rudeza)* rudeness, bad manners *pl*.

macrobiótica *f* macrobiotic diet.

macrobiótico,-a *adj* macrobiotic.

maçudo,-a *adj (cansativo)* dull, tiresome, tedious; **2** *(aborrecido)* dull, tedious; **3** *(forma de maça)* mallet-shaped.

mácula *f* stain, blemish, fault; **2** dishonour; **sem** ~ unblemished, untarnished; **3** *(REL)* sin; **4** *(MED) (na cara)* (red) patch, blotch; **5** *(olhos)* opacity of the cornea.

macumba *f* black magic, voodoo.

Madagáscar (a Ilha de) *npr f* Madagascar.

madagascarense *adj inv* of/from Madagascar.

Madeira *npr* **a (ilha da)** ~ Madeira Island; **vinho da** ~ Madeira wine.

Desertas and Selvagens islets. They were discovered in 1418 by the Portuguese navigators, Tristão V. Teixeira and João G. Zarco. Cristóvão Colombo and his Portuguese wife lived in Porto Santo.

madeira² *f* wood, timber; ~ **contraplacada** plywood; ~ **verde** unseasoned wood; ~ **em branco** unvarnished wood; **de** ~ *adv* wooden; ~ **de lei** hardwood; ♦ ~**s** *fpl* (*MÚS*) woodwind; **2** (*BR*) tree; stick.

madeireira *f* (*empresa*) timber-merchant's, wood-yard.

madeireiro,-a *adj* timber-merchant.

madeirense *adj inv* of/from Madeira, Madeirian.

madeiro *m* log; beam.

madeixa *f* lock of hair, streak of hair; **2** tuft; **3** ~**s** *fpl* (*cabelo*) tresses; (*no cabeleireiro*) highlights.

madorna *f* (*sonolência*) torpor, drowsiness; **2** apathy.

madraço,-a *m,f* (*pessoa*) loafer, idler; lazybones; ♦ *adj* idle, lazy.

madrasta *f* stepmother; **2** (*terra*) harsh, hostile; **3** (*destino*) hard.

madre *f* (*freira*) Mother Superior; **2** nun, sister.

madrepérola *f* mother-of-pearl.

madressilva *f* (*BOT*) honeysuckle.

madrigal *m* (*LITER*) madrigal.

madrileno,-a *m,f adj* of/from Madrid.

madrinha *f* godmother; **2** (*de um casamento*) matron of honour, principal witness.

madrugada *f* morning; dawn, day-break.

madrugador,-ora *m,f* early riser; **2** (*fig*) early bird.

madrugar *vi* to get up very early; **2** (*fig*) to get ahead; **3** to show early tendency for; **madrugava quando** ... dawn was breaking when ...

madurar *vt/vi* to ripen; to mature.

madureza *f* ripeness; maturity.

maduro,-a *adj* ripe; mature.

mãe *f* mother; ~**-coruja** *f* over-protective mum.

maestro, maestrina *m,f* conductor, conductress, maestro; leader of a choral group.

mãezinha *f* mother, mum.

mafarrico *m* devil.

má-fé *f* mallicious intent.

mafioso,-a *m,f* (*pertencente à Mafia*) gangster, mafioso; ♦ *adj* (*pessoa desonesta, má*) crooked.

magano,-a *adj* jovial, roguish; **2** (*mulher*) flirtatious; **3** (*pessoa espirituosa*) wag, witty; **4** (*vigarista*) double-crosser.

magarefe *m* butcher, slaughterer; **2** (*pej*) (*mau cirurgião*) butcher.

magazine *m* (*revista*) magazine; **2** (*BR*) store, boutique.

magérrimo,-a *adj* (*superl de:* **magro**) very thin, thinnest.

magia *f* magic; **fazer** ~ to perform magic; ~ **negra** black magic, voodoo; **2** (*ilusionismo*) conjuring; **truque de** ~ conjuring tricks; ♦ **como que por** ~ *adv* as if by magic.

mágica *f* (*arte, ciência oculta*) sorcery, magic; **fazer** ~ to perform magic; **2** (*fig*) enchantment, magic, fascination; ♦ **mágico,-a** *adj* magical, magic; **varinha** ~**a** magic wand.

magicar *vt* to think hard, ponder; **2** (*estar apreensivo*) to brood (on sth).

mágico,-a *m,f* sorcerer, magician; **2** (*ilusionista*) conjurer.

magistério *m* (*ensino*) teaching; teaching profession; **2** (*instituição de ensino*) teacher training college.

magistrado,-a *m,f* magistrate.

magistral *adj inv* magistral; **2** *f* (*fig*) (*imponente*) magisterial, pompous; **3** (*fig*) masterly.

magistratura *f* magistrature, magistracy.

magnânimo,-a *adj* magnanimous.

magnata *m*, **magnate** *m*, magnate, tycoon.

magnésia *f* (*QUÍM, FAR*) magnesia, **leite de** ~ milk of magnesia.

magnésio *m* (*QUÍM*) magnesium.

magnético,-a *adj* magnetic; **ser um polo** ~ be a magnet.

magnetizar *vt* to magnetize; **2** to attract; **3** to mesmerize.

magnificência *f* magnificence; splendour.

magnífico,-a *adj* splendid, magnificent.

magnitude *f* magnitude.

magno,-a *adj* great; important.

mago *m* magician, conjurer; **2** (*REL*) magus; **os Reis M~s** the Three Kings, the Three Wise Men.

mágoa *f* sorrow, grief.

magoado,-a *adj* **estar/ficar** ~ (**com**) be hurt, offended (by).

magoar *vt* to hurt, injure; **2** to offend.

magote *m* crowd; **a** ~ in a heap.

magreza *f* thinness; **2** (*arte*) slimness; **3** (*fig*) (*infertilidade, falta de*) insufficiency; ~ **da terra** infertility; ~ **de fundos** meagreness of funds; ~ **de ideias** lack of ideas.

magricela *m,f* skinny person; ♦ *adj inv* skinny.

magrinho,-a *adj* thin; **2** (*pej*) skinny.

magro,-a *adj* thin, slim; **2** (*carne*) lean; **3** (*leite*) skimmed; **4** (*rendimento*) poor; IDIOM **o tempo das vacas** ~**as** hard times.

maguala *f* (*MOÇ*) lever for heavy items.

maguimbane *adj* (*MOÇ*) leprous.

magusto *m* St. Martin's feast day, when roasted chestnuts are eaten accompanied by wine.

maia *f* (*BOT*) yellow broom.

Maio/maio *m* May.

maiô *m* (*BR*) swimsuit.

maiombola *f* (*ANG*) magic.

maionese *f* mayonnaise.

maior *m* (*superior*) adult, grown-up; **ser** ~ **e vacinado** grown-up; **2 o/a** ~ the best, greatest; **os** ~**es** the tallest/older (children); **ser o** ~ to be the geeatest; **os nossos** ~**es** our our forbears; ♦ *adj inv* (*comp*) more; ~ **do/do que** bigger, greater larger (than); longer; **quero uma corda** ~ I want a longer rope; ♦ (*superl*) **o, a** ~ (*tamanho*) the biggest; **o** ~ **susto da minha vida** the biggest/the worst nightmare of my life; **2** (*importância*) the greatest, the highest; **ela é a** ~ **cantora do nosso tempo** she is the greatest singer of our time; **3** (*número*) the largest; **a** ~ **parte deles** most of them; **4** (*extensão*) the longest; **o** ~ **rio da**

América the longest river in America; **5** ser ~ **(de idade)** to be of age, adult; ~ **de 18 anos** over 18; **6 em dó** ~ *(MÚS)* in C major; **7** Ursa M~ *(ASTRON)* Great Bear; **8** a ~ **parte de** most of; ♦ **por** ~ **que seja/sejam** however great; **por razões/ motivos de força** ~ for unavoidable reasons.

maioral *m (chefe)* chief, boss, big shot; **2** *(fábrica)* foreman; **3** *(encarregado do gado)* overseer (on a ranch); **4** *(BR) (da turnê)* guide; the biggest, the best, the greatest.

maioria *f* majority; **a** ~ **de** most of.

maioridade *f* adulthood; **atingir a** ~ to come of age.

mais *adv (em comparativos)* more; ~ **de/do que** more than; **ela é** ~ **magra do que eu** she is thinner/ slimmer than me; **2** *(com negativos, interrogativos e pron. indefinidos)* anymore; else; **quem** ~**?** who else?; ~ **alguma pessoa** anybody else?; **ele não anda** ~ he no longer walks; ~ **nada** nothing else; **nunca** ~ never again; **3** *(como superlativo)* **o/a** ~ the most; **o** ~ **rico** the richest (man); **4** *(em locuções)* **a** ~, **de** ~ *(de sobra)* too much/many; **há gente a** ~ there are too many people; **de** ~ **a mais** *(ainda por cima)* moreover; what's more; **ainda** ~ even more; **cada vez** ~ gradually more; ~ **ou menos/ pouco** ~ **ou menos** more or less; **quanto** ~ **melhor** the more the better; **sem** ~ **ou menos** just like that; for no apparent reason; **uma vez** ~ once again, yet again; **5** *(MAT)* plus; **três** ~ **três são seis** three plus three are six; **6** *(ênfase) (tão) que* **moça** ~ **linda!** what a beautiful girl; ♦ *conj* and; **dou-lhe este livro** ~ **a gravura** I give you this book and the picture; **por** ~ **que** however much; **quanto** ~ **não seja/fosse** even if it is/were; IDIOM ~ **vale tarde que nunca**, better late than never.

maisena *f (farinha)* cornflower.

maiúscula *f* capital letter; **escrever em** ~ to write in block letters, *(COMP)* in upper case.

majestade *f* majesty; **S.M.** = **Sua Majestade** His/Her Magesty.

majestoso,-a *adj* majestic.

major *m (MIL)* major; ~ **general** major-general.

mal *m (pl: -es)* evil; **2** *(dano)* harm; **fazer** ~ **a alguém** to harm/hurt sb; **não fiz por** ~ I meant no harm; **3** *(MED) (doença)* illness; **estar** ~ to be seriously ill; **4** *(desgraça)* trouble, misfortune; **falar** ~ **de** to speak ill of; **levar a** ~ to take offence at (sth); **não faz** ~ never mind; ♦ *adv* badly; hardly; **ele** ~ **me falou** he hardly spoke to me; **de** ~ **a pior** from bad to worse; ♦ *conj* ~ **que** as soon as; IDIOM **cortar o** ~ **pela raíz** nip sth in the bud.

mala *f* suitcase; ~**s** *fpl* luggage *sg*; **fazer as** ~**s** to pack; ~ **de senhora** *f (EP)* ladies' handbag.

malabarismo *m (jogo)* juggling; **2** *(fig)* political juggling (balancing act).

malabarista *m,f* juggler.

mal-afortunado,-a *adj* unfortunate, unlucky.

mal-agradecido,-a *adj* ungrateful.

malagueta *f (BOT)* chilli pepper; **pimenta-~** *f* chilli-powder; **2** *(NÁUT)* spoke.

malaio,-a *adj* Malayan.

mal-ajeitado,-a *adj* awkward.

malandragem *f (ociosidade)* idleness; **2** *(patifaria)* villainy, group of rascals.

malandrice *f (criminalidade)* life of crime, of misdeads; **2** *(vagabundice)* vagrancy; **3** *(matreirice)* cunning.

malandro,-a *m,f (patife)* rogue, rascal; **2** *(vadio)* layabout, hooligan; **3** *(ladrão)* double-dealer petty thief; ♦ *adj (ocioso)* idle, vagrant; **2** *(astuto)* sharp.

malaquite *(MIN)* malachite; **2** *(pedra semi-preciosa)* malachite.

malária *f (MED)* malaria.

Malásia *npf* **a** ~ Malaysia.

mal-assombrado,-a *adj (sítio)* eerie, shadowy; **2** *(casa com feitiço)* haunted.

malbaratar *vt (dissipar)* to squander, waste; **2** *(vender barato)* to sell at a loss; **3** *(conselho, tempo)* to make bad use of.

malcheiroso,-a *adj (cheiro)* stinking.

malcriado,-a *adj* ill-mannered, rude.

maldade *f (perversidade)* evil, wickedness; **2** *(criança)* mischief.

maldição *f* curse.

maldisposto,-a *adj (de mau humor)* bad-tempered; **2** *(enjoado)* off-colour, indisposed.

maldito,-a *adj* damned, cursed.

maldizente *m,f* backbiter; gossip-monger; ♦ *adj inv* gossiping.

maldizer *vt (amaldiçoar)* to curse; **2** *(blasfemar)* to swear, blaspheme; **3** *(falar mal de)* to speak ill of sb; to slander.

maldoso,-a *adj (cruel)* wicked; **2** *(mau)* malicious; **3** *(fig)* vicious.

maleabilidade *f (FÍS)* malleability; **2** flexibility, softness; **3** *(fig)* adaptabilty.

maleável *adj inv* malleable, soft.

maledicência *f* slander.

maledicente *m,f* slanderer; ♦ *adj* slanderous, backbiting.

mal-educado,-a *adj* rude, impolite.

maléfico,-a *adj (mau)* evil, wicked; **2** *(nocivo)* harmful, injurious.

maleita *f* ailment, malaise; ~**s** *fpl (pop)* malaria.

mal-empregado,-a *(pl: mal-empregados) adj (desperdiçado)* wasted; **2** *(dinheiro)* badly spent; **3** improper use of; **ele é** ~ **naquela mulher** he is wasted on that woman.

mal-entendido,-a *m* misunderstanding; ♦ *adj* misunderstood.

mal-estar *(pl: mal-estares) m (incómodo)* indisposition; **2** *(inquietação)* uneasiness.

maleta *f (mala)* small suitcase; **2** *(pop) (toureiro)* poor/bad bullfighter.

malevolência *f* malice, spite.

malevolente *adj inv* malicious, spiteful.

malévolo,-a *adj (Vd: malevolente)*.

malfadado,-a *adj* ill-fated, unlucky.

malfeito,-a *adj (má execução)* poorly made; **2** *(disforme)* misshapen; **3** *(fig) (injusto)* wrong, unjust.

malfeitor,-ora *m,f* wrongdoer; **2** criminal.

malga *f (para sopa)* bowl.

malha *f (rede)* mesh; **2** *(ponto)* stitch in knitting; **artigos de** ~ knitwear; **uma camisola de** ~ a sweater; **fazer** ~ to knit; ~ **caída numa meia** ladder/run in a stocking; **3** *(em armadura)* mail of an armour; **4** *(jogo) (chinquilho)* quoits; **5** *(chapa de metal)* quoit; **6** *(NÁUT) (nó)* bowline knot; **7** *(mancha na pele dos animais)* patch; **8** *(fig) (enredo)* web; **9** *(fig) (armadilha)* clutches, snare, net.

malhado,-a *m (HIST)* name given to supporters of the constitutional party during the liberal wars (XIX century); ♦ *adj* spotted, mottled, dappled.

malhão *m* Portuguese folk dance.

malhar *vt (cereais)* to thresh; **2** *(metal)* to beat, strike, hammer; **3** *(manchar)* to discolour, stain; **4** *(fig)* to strive in vain; **5** to repeat, hammer in; ♦ *vi* to hit; **2** *(fig)* to fall into a snare/trap; IDIOM ~ **em ferro frio** flog a dead horse.

malho *m (tipo de martelo)* sledgehammer; **2** *(de calceteiro)* mallet.

mal-humorado,-a *adj* grumpy, sullen, in a bad mood.

malícia *f (maldade)* malice, wickedness; **2** *(astúcia)* slyness, cunning; **3** *(travessura)* mischievousness; **4** *(despeito)* spite; **5** *(ironia)* sarcasm.

malicioso,-a *adj (mau)* malicious, wicked; **2** *(travesso)* mischievous; **3** *(despeitado)* spiteful; **4** *(irónico)* sarcastic.

malignidade *f* malice, spite; **2** *(MED)* malignancy.

maligno,-a *adj* evil, malicious; harmful; **2** *(MED)* malignant.

má-língua *f* slander, backbiting, evil tongue; **2** *m,f (person)* slanderer, backbiter.

malmequer *m (BOT)* marguerite; daisy.

malogrado,-a *adj (falhado)* failed, abortive, frustrated; **2** *(infrutífero)* unsuccessful; **3** *(infortunado)* unlucky.

malograr *vt (estragar)* to spoil, upset; **2** *(frustrar)* to thwart, frustrate; ♦ ~**-se** *vr* to fail.

malogro *m* failure.

malote *m (mala)* small trunk, case; **2** *(mensageiro)* express courier; **3** *(correio)* own mail service.

malparado *adj (negócio)* going badly, in bad hands; **2** *(dinheiro)* at risk.

malpassado,-a *adj* underdone; **2** *(CULIN) (bife)* rare.

malquerença *f* ill will, enmity.

malquisto,-a *adj* disliked; hated.

malta *f* gang, mob; **2** crowd; **3** *(de amigos)* group (of friends).

malte *m (cevada)* malt; **2** *(uísque de qualidade superior)* malt whisky.

maltês,-esa *adj* from Malta; Maltese; **2** *(LÍNG)* Maltese; **3** *(trabalhador)* migrant worker/labourer; **4** *(fig)* vagabond; **5** *(gato)* grey (cat).

maltrapilho,-a *m,f* ragamuffin; ♦ *adj* in rags, ragged, in taters.

maltratar *vt* to ill-treat, mistreat; **2** to ruin, damage; **3** to misuse; **4** *(verbalmente)* to abuse, offend; **5** to mishandle.

maluco,-a *m,f* madman, madwoman; ♦ *adj* mad, crazy, daft.

maluquice *f* madness; **2** silliness, folly.

malva *f (BOT)* rosemallow; ♦ *adj inv (cor)* mauve.

malvadez *f* wickedness.

malvado,-a *adj (pessoa)* wicked, mean; ~ **sejas!** be damned/accursed!; **a ~a da doença!** the accursed influenza!

malversação *(de algo) f (desvio de fundos)* embezzlement; **2** *(desgoverno)* mismanagement.

malversar *vt (desgovernar)* to mismanage; **2** *(desviar fundos)* to embezzle, misappropriate.

Malvinas *npr* as **(ilhas)** ~ the Falklands, the Falkland Islands.

malvisto,-a *adj (person)* ill-regarded; **2** *(desacreditado)* having a bad reputation, distrusted.

mama *f (ANAT)* breast; **cancro da** ~ *(MED)* breast cancer.

mamã *(BR: mamãe) f* mum, mummy.

mamada *f* breastfeed; suckling; feeding; **hora da** ~ feeding time.

mamadeira *f* feeding bottle.

mamão¹ *m (BOT)* papaya.

mamão,-ona² *m,f* child, young animal that sucks a lot; ♦ *adj* suckling; **2** *(fig) (person)* greedy.

mamar *vt* to suck; **2** *(fam)* to drink; **3** *(fig) (apropriar-se)* to pinch sth; **4** *(fig) (ter lucros ilícitos)* to milk dry.

mamário,-a *(adj) (glândula, papila)* mammary.

mamarracho *m (trabalho mal feito)* eyesore; **2** *(autor de obra imperfeita) (col)* bad painter; cowboy.

mamilo *m* nipple.

maminha *f (termo afectivo de mama);* **2** breast nipple of a man; **3** *(BR) (carne)* rump steak.

mamona *f (Vd: mamão).*

mana *f (dated) (termo de afeição)* sister.

manada *f* herd, drove.

manancial *m (nascente)* spring; **2** *(fig)* source.

mancar *vt* to cripple; ♦ *vi* to limp.

mancebo *m* young man, youth.

mancha *f* stain; mark, spot; blotch; **sem** ~ spotless.

manchar *vt* to dirty; **2** to stain; mark; **3** *(fig)* to dishonour.

manchete *f* headline.

manco,-a *adj* crippled, lame; **2** defective, faulty.

mandado *m* order; **2** *(JUR)* writ, injunction; ~ **de prisão/busca** warrant for arrest/search warrant.

mandamento *m* order, command; **2** *(REL)* commandment.

mandante *m,f* instigator.

mandão,-ona *m,f* bossy person; ♦ *adj (fam)* bossy, domineering.

mandar *vt* to order, command; **2** to send, dispatch; ~ **buscar/chamar** to send for; ~ **embora** to send away; ~ **fazer um fato** to have a suit made; ♦ *vi* to be in charge.

mandarim *(pl: -ins) m* Mandarin; **2** *(LÍNG)* mandarin.

mandatar *vt* to commission sb.

mandatário *m* delegate; representative; agent; **2** *(JUR)* attorney-in-fact; proxy.

mandato *m* mandate; order.

mandíbula *f* jaw.

mandinga *f* witchcraft.

mandingas *msg/pl* one of the races from Guinea-Bissau.

mandioca *f* cassava, manioc.

mando *m* command; **a ~ de** by order of; **2** power.
mandona *f (Vd:* **mandão***)*.
mandrião,-ona *m,f* lazybones *sg*, idler; ♦ *adj* lazy.
mandriar *vi* to idle, loaf about.
mandrice *(=* **mândria***) f* lazyness.
manducar *vt/vi* to eat.
maneira *f* way; **2** style, manner; **à ~ de** like; **de ~ a** so as to; **de ~ que** so that; **de ~ alguma/nenhuma** not at all; **de uma ~ ou de outra** somehow or other; **de qualquer ~** whatever, whichever way; **~ s** *fpl* manners.
maneirismo *m (afectação)* affectation, mannerism.
maneiro,-a *adj (veículo)* manageable; **2** *(livro)* easy-reading; **3** *(pessoa hábil)* handy.
manejar *vt (manusear)* to handle; **2** *(administrar)* to manage.
manejável *adj inv* manageable.
manejo *m* handling; **2** use; **3** management.
manequim *(pl:* **-ins***) m,f (pessoa)* model; **2** *(boneco)* dummy.
maneta *adj inv* one-handed, one-armed; IDIOM **mandar alguém para o/pr'ó ~** tell sb to get lost, to piss off *(cal)*.
manga *f (vestuário)* sleeve; **2** *(fruto)* mango; **3** *(filtro)* filter bag; **4** *(AERO)* wind-sock; **5** *(mangueira)* hose *(of a pump)*; **6** cloud-burst; **7** *(AUTO)* part of a car axle; **8** *(tropas)* detachment of troops; **9** *(DESP)* lap; **10 ~-de-alpaca** *m (pej)* civil servant, clerk; IDIOM **em ~s de camisa** in shirt sleeves; **arregaçar as ~s** to set to work, or fight.
manganês, manganésio *m* manganese.
mangar *vi:* **~ com/de** to tease, make fun of, to kid; **2** *(BR) (empatar)* to delay.
mangue *m* mud-flat, swamp; mangrove.
mangueira *f* hose (pipe); **~ de pressão** *(AUTO)* pressure hose; **2** *(árvore)* mango tree.
mangusto *(ZOOL)* mongoose; **2** *(BOT) (árvore, fruto)* mangosteen.
manha *f (astúcia)* guile, cunning, slyness; **2** *(ardil)* trick, craftiness; **3** *(fingimento)* children's ploy; act; **~s** *fpl* habits.
manhã *f* morning; **de ~** in the morning, **amanhã de ~** tomorrow morning; **de ~ cedo** early morning; **hoje de ~** this morning.
manhãzinha *f* early morning.
manhoso,-a *adj (astuto)* crafty, sly; **2** *(esperto)* smart, clever; **3** *(chorão, queixoso)* whining, whingeing.
mania *f (PSIC)* mania; **2** *(obsessão)* obsession, craze, passion; **3** *(capricho)* whim, fad, quirk; **4** *(fixação)* fixed idea; **5** *(hábito)* bad habit; **ela tem a ~ que é muito esperta**, she thinks she is very clever; **~ da grandeza** megalomania.
maníaco,-a *adj* maniac, lunatic, mad.
maniatar *vt* to tie the hands of; to handcuff, manacle; **2** *(fig)* to restrict, constrain.
manicómio *(BR:* **-cô-***) m* asylum, mental hospital.
manicura, manicure *f* manicure; **2** *(pessoa)* manicurist.
manietar *(Vd:* **maniatar***)*.
manifestação *f* demonstration, manifestation; **2** expression; **3** *(sintoma)* sign, show; **4** revelation.
manifestante *adj inv* demonstrator.

manifestar *vt* to show, display; **2** to express, declare; ♦ **~-se** *vr* to show, reveal oneself; express o.s.; **2** to be evident.
manifesto,-a *m* manifesto, public declaration; ♦ *adj* obvious, clear.
manilha *f (grilheta)* shackle, manacle; **2** *(pulseira)* bracelet, bangle; **3** *(cano/tubo de grés)* conduit tube, joint; **4** *(elo de cadeia)* link; **5** *(jogo de cartas)* quadrille; **6** *(nome de algumas cartas)* manille; **7** *(variedade de tabaco)* Manilla/Manila.
maninha *f (diminuitivo de* **mana***)* little sister; **2** raw material for making ropes.
maninho *(diminuitivo de* **mano***) m* brother; **2** *(terreno)* waste, fallow, barren; **~s** *pl:* assets of a deceased without heirs.
manino,-a *adj* very little, tiny.
manipular *vt* to manipulate; **2** *(manusear)* to handle; **3** *(fazer funcionar)* to work, operate; **4** *(medicamentos)* to prepare.
manípulo *m (TEC) (peça mecânica)* lever, arm, handle; **2** *(da porta)* handle, knob; **3** *(punhado)* handful.
manivela *f (TEC)* crank; **~ do eixo** centre crank; **2** handle, winch; **dar à ~** to crank.
manjar *m* food, dish; **2** titbit, choice morsel; **3** *(fig)* feast; **~ branco** blancmange; *(BR)* coconut and milk pudding.
manjedoura *(=* **manjedoira, manjadoura***) f* manger, crib.
manjericão *m (BOT, CULIN)* sweet/wild basil.
manjerico *m (BOT)* sweet basil (house plant grown for its aroma).

Manjerico decorates every window-box during June – the month of the Popular Saints – and is traditionally given to lovers, on St Anthony's Day – 13th June.

manjerona *f (BOT, CULIN)* marjoram.
mano *m (dated) (termo de afeição)* brother.
manobra *f (manejo)* manoeuvre, manoeuvring, handling; **2** *(fig)* trick; **3** *(NÁUT)* steering; **4** *(actividade)* work; **5** *(intriga)* sleaze.
manobrar *vt* to manoeuvre; handle; operate, work; **2** *(barco)* to steer; **3** *(empresa)* to control, run; **4** *(manipular)* to scheme, manipulate; **5** *(MIL)* to manoeuvre.
manquejar *vi* to limp.
mansão *f* mansion; residence.
mansarda *f (aproveitado para habitação)* attic, garret.
mansidão *f* gentleness, meekness.
manso,-a *adj* gentle, soft, quiet, calm; **2** *(domado)* tame.
manta *f* blanket, bed cover; **~ de retalhos** patchwork cover/quilt; **~ de viagem** travelling rug.
manteiga *f (CULIN)* butter; **pão com ~** bread and butter; **2** *(fig)* flattery; **dar ~ a** *(bajular)* to butter sb.
manteigueira *f* butter dish.
manter *vt (preservar)* to maintain; **2** *(prover subsistência a)* to support; **3** *(guardar)* to keep; **~ um segredo** to keep a secret; **4** *(princípios)* to abide

by; **5** *(afirmar)* to affirm; ♦ **~-se** *vr* to support o.s.; **2** *(calmo, alerta, etc)* to remain; **~ firme** to stand firm/one's ground; **~ afastado** to stand aloof; **~ ao corrente** to keep abreast of, to be up to date.

mantilha *f* mantilla.

mantimento *m* *(apoio)* support; **2** *(alimento)* food; **3** *(conservação)* maintaining; **~s** *mpl* provisions, supplies.

manto *m* cloak; robe; **2** *(GEOL, ZOOL)* mantle; **3** *(fig)* mantle, cover.

mantra *f* *(hinduísmo, budismo)* mantra.

manual *m* handbook, manual; ♦ *adj inv* manual.

manuelino,-a *adj* *(estilo, período)* relating to King Manuel I of Portugal, or his time (first decade of the 16th century); **arquitectura ~a** manueline architecture.

manufa(c)tura *f* manufacture; making; **2** craft; **3** *(lugar de fabrico)* factory.

manufa(c)turar to manufacture, make.

manuscrito,-a *m* manuscript; ♦ *adj* handwritten.

manuseamento *m* handling.

manusear *vt* to handle.

manutenção *f* maintenance; **2** *(gerenciamento)* management.

mão *(pl: **mãos**) f* hand, handful; **dar a ~ a** to help; **à ~** by hand, at hand, handy; **à ~ armada** at gunpoint; **aperto de ~** handshake; **feito à ~** handmade; ♦ **mãos** *fpl* hands; **~s ao alto!** hands up!; **~s de arame** butter fingers; **de ~s dadas** hand in hand; **de ~s postas** pleading *(or)* praying; **de ~s a abanar** *(fig)* *(sem prendas)* empty-handed; **~s rotas** spendthrift; ♦ **2 mão** *(de animal)* paw, hoof; **3 ~ de porco** *(no talho)* foot, forefoot; **4** *(da porta, do martelo)* handle; **5** *(de pintura)* coat (of paint); **6** *(jogo de cartas)* hand; **7** *(pequena porção)* small bunch; **~ de papel** quire; **8** *(fig)* control, power; **9** *(estrada)* **fora de ~** out of the way; **10** *(DESP)* leg; IDIOM **uma ~ lava a outra** one turn deserves another; **numa volta de ~** quickly; in the twinkle of an eye; **dar a ~ à palmatória** to accept one is wrong, to give in; **~s à obra!** let's go to work.

mão-cheia *f* handful; **às mãos cheias** by handfuls.

mão-de-obra *f* workmanship, labour; **~ especializada** skilled labour; **2** *(custo do trabalho)* labour costs.

maoísmo *m* Maoism.

maoista *adj inv* Maoist.

Maomé *m* *(o profeta do Islão)* Mahommed.

maometano,-a *adj* Muslim; **2** *(pej)* Mohammedan.

mãos-largas *(BR: **mão-aberta**, **mãos-abertas**) adj* generous.

mãozinha *f* little hand; **2 dar uma ~ a alguém** to give sb a helping hand.

mapa *m* map; chart; graph; **2** *(relação)* list; IDIOM **desaparecer do ~** disappear off the face of the earth.

mapa-múndi, mapa-mundo map of the world.

maple® *m* upholstered arm-chair.

maqueiro,-a *m,f* stretcher-bearer

maqueta, maquete *f* *(esboço de uma escultura)* model; **2** *(TIPO)* layout.

maquiavélico,-a *adj* Machiavellian; **2** *(pérfido)* cruel, sly, cunning, Machiavellian.

maquil(h)agem *f* make-up; making up; **2** *(produtos de beleza)* cosmetics.

maquilhar-se *vr* to put on one's make-up.

máquina *f* machine; **~ de calcular** calculator; **~ de costura** sewing-machine; **~ de escrever** typewriter; **~ de lavar louça** dishwasher; **~ de lavar roupa** washing machine; **~ fotográfica** *(CIN, FOTO)* camera; **~ de filmar** film camera; **~ de projetar** projector; **2** *(TIPO)* press; **~ compositora** typesetter; **~ impressora** printing press; **3** *(FERRO)* *(locomotiva)* engine; *(BR)* car; **4** *(maquinismo)* works, machinery; **5** *(fig)* *(organismo complexo)* workings, mechanism; **a ~ do Governo** the workings of the Government; *(fig)* **ela é uma ~** she is a dynamo; **~s** *fpl* machinery.

maquinação *f* machination, plot.

maquinal *adj inv* mechanical, automatic.

maquinar *vt* to think up, work out; **2** *(conspirar)* to hatch.

maquinaria *f* machinery.

maquinismo *m* mechanism; machinery.

maquinista *m* engine driver.

mar *m* sea; **no ~ alto** on the high seas; **por ~** by sea; **~ picado** choppy sea; **homem ao ~!** man overboard!; **2** *(fig)* great quantity; **~ de gente** a stream of people; **viver num ~ de tristeza** to live drowned in sadness; **num ~ de rosas** in a bed of roses; IDIOM **fazer-se ao ~** to set sail, put out to sea; **nem tanto ao ~ nem tanto à terra** neither one extreme nor the other.

maracujá *m* *(BOT)* passionflower; passion fruit.

marasmo *m* debilitation; wasting away; apathy.

maratona *f* *(corrida)* marathon.

maravilha *f* marvel, wonder; **Alice no País das M~s** Alice in Wonderland; **às mil ~s** wonderfully, like a dream; **2** *(BOT)* marigold.

maravilhar *vt* to amaze; ♦ **~-se de** *vr* to be astonished at, to marvel at.

maravilhoso,-a *adj* marvellous, wonderful.

marca *f* mark; **2** *(COM)* make, brand; stamp; **~ de fábrica** trademark; **3** *(cicatriz)* mark, scar; **4** *(fig)* *(categoria)* calibre.

marcação *f* marking; **2** *(em jogo)* scoring; **3** *(TEAT)* action; *(reserva)* booking.

marcador *m* marker; **~ de livros** book marker; **2** *(DESP)* scoreboard; **3** *(MED, FÍS, BIOL)* tracer.

marçano *m* apprentice.

marcante *adj inv* notable, remarkable; **2** outstanding; distinguishing.

marcar *vt* *(termómetro)* to show; **2** *(DESP)* to score; **3** *(posição)* to define; **4** *(exames, exercícios)* to mark; **~ uma hora** to make an appointment.

marceneiro *m* cabinet-maker, joiner.

marcha *f* march, marching; **2** *(andamento)* course; **3** *(passo)* pace, step; **4** *(AUTO)* gear, **~-atrás** *(BR: ~ à ré)* reverse (gear); **5** *(MIL, MÚS)* march; **6** *(BR)* *(MÚS)* Carnival march; **pôr-se em ~** to set off; **~ festiva** festival, parade; ♦ *adv* **em ~** on the move; **pôr-se em ~** to start off.

marchar *vi* to go; **2** *(caminhar)* to walk; march; **3** *(MIL)* to march.

Marchas fpl: `as Marchas Populares' (Lisbon's colourful and lively song-and-dance parades, which take place at night, during June, in honour of the popular saints: St Anthony on the 13th, St John on the 24th and St Peter on the 29th. These celebrations also take place in other parts of Portugal.

marchetar vt *(trabalhar, embutir em móveis)* to inlay; 2 *(matizar)* to fill with colour.

marcial adj inv martial; **lei ~** martial law.

marciano,-a adj Martian, relating to the planet of Mars.

marco m landmark; 2 monument; 3 *(fig) (fronteira; símbolo)* milestone; 4 *(unidade monetária)* mark; **~ alemão** German mark; 5 *(correio)* **~-do-correio** postbox.

Março, março m March.

maré f tide; **~ alta/baixa** high/low tide; **~ negra** oil slick; 2 *(fig) (ocasião)* opportunity; 3 *(disposição)* mood; **estar de boa/má ~** be in a good/bad mood; **ao sabor da ~** *(fig)* to go with the flow; IDIOM **remar contra a ~** swim against the tide.

marear vt *(barco)* to sail, steer; 2 to make sb seasick; 3 *(oxidar, embaciar)* to tarnish, dim; ♦ vi to be seasick.

marechal *(pl: -ais)* m marshal.

marejar vt to wet, dampen, shed; ♦ vi to flow; ♦ **~-se** vr to be soaked; **~ de lágrimas** to well up with tears.

maremoto m tidal wave.

mareógrafo m tidal gauge.

maresia f sea air, sea breeze; **cheiro a ~** smell of the sea air.

marfim m ivory; **pulseira de ~** ivory bracelet; **o ~ dos dentes** tooth enamel; **cor de ~** ivory-coloured.

margarida f *(BOT)* marigold.

margarina f *(CULIN)* margarine.

margem f *(orla)* edge; **à ~ de** alongside; **viver à ~ de** live on the fringe of; 2 *(de rio)* bank; 3 *(limite)* borderline; 4 *(notas)* margin; **~ de lucro** profit margin; 5 coast; 6 *(fig) (espaço)* room; 7 *(ensejo)* chance.

marginal *(pl: -ais)* adj inv marginal; **avenida ~** coast road; 2 outsider; 3 *(BR)* outlaw; 4 secondary; **notas marginais** marginal notes.

marginalizado,-a adj discriminated against; excluded.

marginalizar vt to discriminate; ostracize.

Maria npr Mary; *(mãe de Jesus)* Mary; **banho-~** *(CULIN)* bain-marie; IDIOM **há mais ~s na terra** you are not the only pebble on the beach.

maria-da-fonte f *(fig)* brawl, disorder, tumult (after the revolutionary movement in Minho, in 1846).

marialva m good horseman; **à ~** following the rules of horsemanship and dressage established by Marquis de Marialva; 2 *(pej)* a dissolute nobleman; young man adopting Marialva's fashion, mannerism; 3 a kind of D. Juan.

maria-maluca f crazy girl/woman (running after men and fun).

maria-rapaz *(pl: marias-rapazes)* f tomboy.

maricas m *(efeminado)* effeminate (man), sissy; 2 *(fig) (medroso)* chicken, yellow (person); 3 *(col) (homossexual)* gay (man).

marido m husband.

marijuana f *(BOT)* marijuana/marihuana, grass, *(col)* pot.

marimbar vi *(MÚS)* to play the marimba; 2 *(jogo)* to win the game of marimba; 3 *(BR) (enganar)* to take sb for a ride; ♦ **~-se** vr *(pop)* **estou-me marimbando para você** I care two hoots about you.

marinada f *(CULIN)* marinade.

marinar vt, vi *(peixe, carne, etc)* to marinade.

marinha f navy; seascape; **Ministério da ~** the Admiralty, Navy Department *(US)*; **arsenal de ~** dock yard; **~ mercante** merchant navy.

marinheiro m seaman, sailor; **~ de primeira viagem** *(fig)* greenhorn; **~ de água doce** fair-weather sailor.

marinho,-a adj sea, marine; **ave ~a** sea bird; **cavalo ~** sea-horse; **biologia ~a** marine biology.

mariola m messenger, courier; 2 scoundrel; 3 *(homem mulherengo)* womanizer, rogue.

marionete f puppet, marionette.

mariposa f *(BOT)* moth; 2 *(jóia em forma de borboleta)* brooch; 3 *(DESP) (natação)* butterfly stroke.

mariquice f effeminate behaviour; pampering; **mas que ~!** what a silly, childish behaviour!

marisco m *(crustáceo)* shellfish.

marítimo,-a adj sea, maritime; **pesca ~a** sea fishing.

marmelada f quince jam *(this is the original marmalade from the Portuguese word: marmelo)*; 2 *(col)* double-dealing; 3 *(pop)* fun; **fazer/estar na ~** *(col)* to snog.

marmeleiro m quince tree.

marmelo m *(fruto)* quince; 2 *(pop) (seio de mulher)* boob.

marmita f *(recipiente)* dixie, soldier's chow pan; 2 *(comida)* packed lunch; 3 *(GEOL)* cylindrical cavity.

mármore m marble.

marmóreo,-a adj marble, marmoreal.

marmorite f marble-cutter.

marmota f *(ZOOL) (animal roedor)* marmot; 2 *(peixe)* young/small hake.

maroto,-a m,f rogue, rascal; 2 *(com afeição)* naughty child; **seu ~/sua ~a!** you naughty boy/girl!; ♦ adj *(olhar, dito de pessoa)* saucy, artful.

marquês,-esa m,f marquis, marchioness.

marquise f *(divisão envidraçada nas traseiras da casa)* small conservatory.

marra f *(maço)* sledge hammer; 2 *(valeta)* ditch alongside the road; **na ~** by force; at any cost.

marrã f a weaned young sow.

marrada f *(cornada)* butt; thrust with the horns; 2 *(cabeçada)* knocking one's head against sth; 3 *(encontrão)* bumping into somebody; **ir aos tombos e às ~s** to go tumbling and bumping.

marrão m *(maço)* heavy sledge hammer; 2 *(col) (aluno)* a student who commits texts to memory without any understanding.

marreco,-a m,f *(corcunda)* hunchback, humpback; 2 *(sagaz)* astute, sharp; 3 *(pato)* duck; 4 f *(bossa)* hump.

marreta f small sledge hammer with long handle; IDIOM **fazer ~** *(BR)* to cheat in a game.

Marrocos npr Morocco.

marrom *adj inv (BR)* brown.

marroquim *m* morocco leather.

marroquinaria *f* morocco leather factory, shop, art; **2** leather goods.

marroquino,-a *adj* from Morocco, Moroccan.

Marselhas *npr* Marseille.

marselhesa *f (hino)* marseillaise.

marta *f (ZOOL)* sable marten; **2** *(pêlo/pelo)* sable, **casaco de** ~ sable coat.

Marte *m (ASTRON, MITOL)* Mars.

martelar *vt* to hammer (on).

martelo *m* hammer.

mártir *m* martyr.

martírio *m* martyrdom; **2** *(fig)* torment.

marujo *m* sailor.

marulhar *vi (mar)* to surge; to crash, pound; **2** to lap; to roar.

marulho *m* surge; **2** tossing; **3** *(fig)* tumult, hubbub.

marxista *adj inv* Marxist.

mas *conj* but; ♦ *pron pess* (= **me** + **as**) them to me.

mascar *vt* to chew.

máscara *f* mask; **sob a** ~ **de** under the guise of.

mascarada *f* masquerade.

mascarado,-a *adj* masked, disguised in a fancy dress.

mascarar *vt* to mask; to disguise.

mascarra *f (mancha de carvão)* soot, smutty mark; ~ **de pó** dust stains; **2** *(fig)* stigma, stain.

mascarrar *vt* to stain; **2** *(maquilhagem)* to smudge; **3** *(fig) (difamar)* to stain, sully; ♦ ~**-se** *vr* to get covered with smuts, get dirty.

mascavado *adj (açúcar não refinado)* **açúcar** ~ brown sugar.

mascote *f (animal)* pet; **2** *(talismã)* lucky charm; **3** *(representante dum grupo/evento)* mascot.

masculinizar *vt* to develop masculine characteristics.

masculino,-a *adj* masculine; **2** *(BIO)* male; **roupa** ~ a men's clothes *pl*; **3** *(gram) (gênero)* masculine.

másculo,-a *adj* mannish, manly.

masmorra *f* dungeon.

masoquista *m,f* masochist.

massa *f (FÍS)* mass; **2** paste; **3** lump; **4** *(CULIN)* dough, mixture; ~ **folhada** puff pastry; **5** *(pop) (dinheiro)* dough, bread, dosh, lolly; **6** *(pop)* stuff; **7** cement; ~ **de vidraceiro** putty; **espectrógrafo de** ~ *(FÍS)* mass spectrograph; **as** ~**s** *fpl* the masses; ♦ *adv* **em** ~ en masse; **produção em** ~ mass; production; IDIOM **estar com a mão na** ~ to be in the middle of doing/dealing with sth; **ser da mesma** ~ be cut from the same cloth.

massacrante *adj inv* annoying.

massacrar *vt* to massacre; torture.

massacre *m* massacre.

massagem *f* massage.

massagista *m,f* masseur, masseuse.

massajar *vt* to massage.

massudo,-a *adj (livro, papéis)* bulky; thick; **2** *(bolo, pão, etc)* heavy.

mastectomia *f (MED)* mastectomy.

mastigar *vt (comer)* to chew; **2** *(pensar no assunto)* to ruminate on, ponder over; **3** *(fig) (falar pouco claro)* mumble.

mastim *m (cão)* mastiff.

mastro *m (NÁUT)* mast; flagpole.

masturbar-se *vr* to masturbate.

mata *f (bosque)* woods, common.

mata-bicho *m* tot of brandy, snifter (taken first thing in the morning).

mata-borrão *m* blotting paper.

matador,-ora *m,f* killer; **2** *m* matador, bullfighter.

matadouro/matadoiro *m* slaughter-house.

matagal *m* bush; **2** thicket, undergrowth.

mata-moscas *m* fly-swat; ~**-mosquito** *m* mosquito spray.

matança *f* massacre; slaughter(ing).

matar *vt (abater)* to kill, murder, slaughter, butcher; **2** *(fig) (sede)* to quench; **3** *(fome)* to satisfy; **4** *(fig) (destruir)* to ruin, destroy; **5** *(fig) (eliminar)* to rule out; ♦ ~**-se** *vr* to kill o.s., to commit suicide; IDIOM ~ **dois coelhos duma cajadada** to kill two birds with one stone.

mata-rato *m* rat poison.

mate *m (BOT)* mate, maté; Paraguay tea; **2** *(jogos)* **xeque** ~ checkmate; **3** *(ponto de meia/tricot)* cast off; ♦ *adj* matt, dull.

matelassé *adj inv* quilted.

matemático,-a *m,f* mathematician; **2** *f* mathematics *sg*, *(pop)* maths *sg*; ♦ *adj* mathematical.

matéria *f* matter; **2** *(TEC)* material; **3** *(EDUC)* subject; **4** *(assunto)* subject; **em** ~ **de** on the subject of.

material *(pl: -ais)* *m* material; **2** *(TEC) (utensílios)* equipment, materials, *pl*; ~ **de escritório** office stationery; ~ **humano** manpower; ♦ *adj* material.

materialismo *m* materialism.

materialista *m,f* materialist; ♦ *adj inv* materialistic.

materialização *f* materialization, concretization.

materializar *vt* to materialize; ♦ ~**-se** *vr* to materialize (itself).

matéria-prima *f* raw material.

maternal *adj inv* maternal; **2** *(fig)* motherly; **escola-**~ *(BR)* playgroup.

maternidade *f (estado)* motherhood, maternity; **2** *(local)* maternity hospital, ward.

materno,-a *adj* motherly, maternal; **língua** ~ mother tongue.

matilha *f (cães)* pack of hounds; **2** *(gente vadia)* rabble, gang.

matinal *adj inv* morning.

matiz *m* shade; **2** *(cores)* blend.

matizar *vt* to tinge, colour; **2** *(cores)* to blend.

mato *m* scrubland, bush; **2 bicho do** ~ *(fig) (solitário)* hermit.

mato-grossense *(pl: **mato-grossenses**)* *m,f* from Mato-Grosso *m* Brazilian State.

matraca *f (brinquedo)* rattle; **2** *(arma)* cudgel, club; **3** *(fig) (barulho)* clatter, racket; **4** *(fig) (chacota)* jeering; **5** *(fig) (falar muito)* be a magpie; **6** *(col) (boca)* gob; **fecha a** ~ *(col)* shut your gob.

matraquear *vi (fazer barulho)* to rattle, clatter; **2** *(repetir)* to repeat; **3** *(falar muito)* to rabbit on; **4** *(chacotear)* to scoff, jeer.

matraquilhos *mpl (jogo de futebol de mesa)* table football.

matreiro,-a *adj* cunning, crafty.

matriarca *f* matriarch.

matricida *m,f* matricide; ♦ *adj inv* matricidal.

matricídio *m* matricide.

matrícula *f (lista)* register; **2** *(inscrição)* enrolment (UK); enrollment (US); **3** *(quantia paga naescola)* fee; **4** *(registo)* registration; **5** (AUTO) number plate (UK), license plate (US).

matricular-se *vr (em curso, exame)* to enrol, register.

matrimónio *(BR: -mô-) m* marriage.

matriz *f (MED)* womb; **2** *(origem)* source, origin; **igreja ~** parish church, mother church; **3** *(imprensa)* mould; **4** *(COM)* head office; **companhia ~** parent-company; **5** *(GEOL)* matrix; ♦ *adj inv* original, founding.

matrona *f* mother of family; **2** *(mulher pesada, idosa)* matron; **3** *(fam) (autoritária, modos masculinos)* butch, virago.

matulagem *f (bando)* bad guys, ruffians; **2** *(vida de vadio)* vagrancy.

matulão,-ona *m (pessoa forte)* large person; strong; **2** *(pej) (vadio)* good-for-nothing; burly.

maturidade *f* maturity.

matutar (em) *vt (pop)* to brood, muse ponder (on).

matutice *f* whim, mania.

matutino,-a *m (jornal)* morning paper; ♦ *adj* morning.

mau, má *m,f (em livro, filme)* **o ~** *m* the baddy *(pop)*; the villain; **os bons e os maus** the good and the wicked; ♦ *adj* bad; evil, wicked; hard; naughty, **ele é ~** he is bad; **ter ~ coração** to be hard-hearted; **~ cheiro** stench; **a vida está má** life is hard; **más línguas** *fpl* evil tongues; **um ~ trabalho** a poor/ bad work; **~ procedimento** misbehaviour; ♦ *adv* **de má vontade** unwillingly; **de ~ humor** ill-tempered, in a bad mood; ♦ *exc* **~! daqui pouco zango-me** oh dear! I am about to get cross; IDIOM **ele está em ~s lençóis** he is in a jam, fix; **passar um ~ bocado** to go through a bad patch/ time; **ter ~s fígados** to be cruel, vindictive; **andar na ~ vida** *(prostituta)* be on the game.

mau-olhado *m* evil eye.

Maurícias *npr:* **as (ilhas) ~** Mauritius.

Maurício *npr (BR)* Mauritius.

Mauritânia *npr* **a ~** Mauritania.

mauritano,-a *adj* Mauritanian.

mausoléu *m* mausoleum.

maus-tratos *mpl* abuse, ill-treatment.

mavioso,-a *adj* affectionate, tender; **2** sweet, melodious.

maxila *f (ANAT)* jawbone.

maxilar *m (ANAT)* jawbone; ♦ *adj inv* maxillary.

máxima *f (axioma)* maxim, saying; **2** *(col)* great! cool!

maximalizar, maximizar *vt* to maximize; **2** *(MAT)* to round up.

máximo *m* maximum, best; **o meu ~** my best; *(fam)* the tops; ♦ *adj* greatest; highest; **~s** *(pl)* (AUTO) beams; **2** peak; **no ~** at most.

maxixe *m (BR) (fruto)* gherkin; **2** *(dança)* 19th-century dance.

mazela *f* sore spot; **2** *(pop) (ailment)* illness, aches and pains; **3** *(fig)* blemish.

MB *(abr de* **megabyte**) *m* MB.

MBA *(abr de* **Master of Business Administration**) (equivalent in Portuguese) mestrado em Gestão de Empresa.

me *pron (directo, indirecto, forma pronominal ou reflexivo)* me; **ainda não ~ vesti** *(negative form)* I haven't (got) dressed yet; **ele deu-~ um beijo**, *(BR)* **ele ~ deu** he gave me a kiss.

meada *f* skein, hank, ball of wool; **2** *(fig)* plot, intrigue; IDIOM **perder o fio à ~** *(estória)* to lose the thread.

meado *m* middle, mid; **em ~s de Maio/maio** in mid-May; ♦ **meado,-a** *adj (dia, mês, ano)* mid.

mealheiro *m* piggy-bank, money box.

meandrar *vt* to meander.

meandro *m* turn, bend, winding; meander; **~s** *mpl* meanderings.

Meca *f* Mecca (Muslim religious city, place of pilgrimage).

meça *(pres subj de* **medir**) **preciso que me ~ a sala** I need you to measure the room (for me).

mecânico,-a *m* mechanic; **2** *f* mechanics *sg*; ♦ *adj* mechanical; **broca ~a** power drill.

mecanismo *m* mechanism.

mecanografia *f* automated indexing.

mecenas *m sg/pl (das artes)* patron, sponsor.

mecha *f (candeia, vela)* wick; **2** *(de explosivo)* fuse; **3** *(cabelo)* tuft, strand; **4** *(cabelo tingido)* streaks, highlights; **5** *(MED)* swab; **6** *(fam)* speed, haste; **7** *(CULIN)* rasher; **8** *(fam)* nuisance; IDIOM **aguentar a ~** put up with things.

mechar *vt* to light a fuse; **2** to fumigate wine casks with sulphurized cloth.

meço *(pres indic de* **medir***)* **eu ~ a mesa** I'll measure/ I measure the table.

meda *f (AGR)* stack, sheaf.

medalha *f* medal.

medalhão *m* medallion.

medalhista *m,f* medallist.

medalhística *f (estudo das medalhas)* study and collection of medals.

média *f (MAT)* mean; **2** average; **em ~** on average.

mediação *f* mediation, intervention; **por ~ de** through; **2** *(JUR, MAT)* mediation.

mediador,-ora *m,f* mediator, go-between.

mediana *f (GEOM)* mediam.

medianeiro,-a *adj* mediator, go-between.

mediano,-a *adj (está no meio)* middle; **2** *(nem grande nem pequeno)* medium, average; **3** *(estatura)* medium.

mediante *prep* by (means of), through; **2** according to, subject to; **~ um acordo** subject to an agreement; **3** thanks to.

mediar *vt* to mediate (for); ♦ *vi* to mediate; **a distância que medeia entre** the distance between.

mediático,-a *adj (notícias, acontecimento)* in the media, in the public eye.

mediatização *f (paz, acordos)* mediation, medicity.

medicação *f* treatment, medication.

medicamento *m (remédios)* medicine, medication.

medição *f (medida)* measurement; **2** *(avaliação do valor)* scale.

medicina *f (ciência)* medicine.

médico,-a *m,f* doctor, medic; ♦ *adj* medical.

medida *f (medição)* measure; measurement; **tomar** ~s to take steps; **encher as** ~s *(col)* to come up to one's expectations; **tirar as** ~s **de** to measure; **feito sob** ~ made to measure; 2 *(ponderação)* prudence; 3 **à** ~ **que** while, as.

medidor *m* meter; ~ **de pressão** pressure gauge; ~ **de terras** *(person)* land surveyor.

medieval *adj inv* medieval.

médio,-a *m (DESP)* halfback; ♦ *adj* middle, mid, midling; **Idade M**~a Middle ages; **M**~ **Oriente** Middle East; **classe** ~a middle class; **dedo** ~ middle finger mean; 2 medium, average; **homem de estatura** ~a a man of medium height.

medíocre *adj inv* mediocre.

mediocridade *f* mediocrity.

medir *vt* to measure; 2 *(ponderar)* to weigh up, consider; 3 *(avaliar)* to judge; ♦ ~-**se** *vr* to compare oneself to another; compete; IDIOM ~ **alguém de alto a baixo** *(com desdém)* look sb up and down; ~ **as distâncias** keep the distances.

meditação *f* meditation.

meditar *vt* to think over; ♦ *vi* to meditate.

mediterrâneo,-a *adj* Mediterranean; *m:* **o M**~ the Mediterranean.

mediterrânico,-a *adj* Mediterranean.

médium *m,f (pessoa vidente)* medium.

medo *m* fear; **com** ~ afraid; **ter** ~ **de** to be afraid of.

medonho,-a *adj* terrible, awful.

medrar *vi (planta)* to thrive, grow, flourish; 2 *(desenvolver)* to develop; 3 *(prosperar)* to prosper.

medrica *m,f (pessoa)* scaredy cat, fraidy cat; ♦ *adj* chicken-hearted, faint-hearted, scaredy.

medricas *sg/pl (Vd:* **medrica**).

medroso,-a *m,f* coward; ♦ *adj (assustado)* scared; 2 *(envergonhado)* timid; 3 *(cobarde)* cowardly.

medronho *m (BOT)* arbustus berry.

medula *f (ANAT)* marrow.

medusa *f (ZOOL)* jellyfish; 2 *(MITOL)* **M**~ Medusa.

megalítico,-a *adj* megalithic.

megalomania *f (PSIC)* megalomania.

megera *f (pej) (mulher)* shrew.

meia *f (vestuário)* stocking, *(curta)* long sock; **um par de** ~**s** a pair of stockings; ~-**calça** *f (pl:* **meias-calças)** tights, collants *(UK)*; pantyhose *(US)*; 2 *(BR) (número seis- no falar)* six; 3 ~-**de-leite** *(col) (café com leite)* white coffee in a large cup; ♦ *adj* half; 2 mid *(Vd:* **meio**); **a** ~ **haste** at half mast; ~-**direita** *f (FUT) (jogador ou posição)* inside-right; ~-**dúzia** *f* half a dozen; ~-**esquadria** *f* half a right angle; *(carpinteiro)* bevel square; ~-**esquerda** *f (FUT)* inside-left; ~-**estação** *f (moda)* mid-season; ~-**final** *f (DESP)* semifinals; ~-**idade** *f* middle age; ~-**lua** *f* half moon; crescent; semi-circle; *(NÁUT)* flat-bottomed boat; ~-**luz** *f* half light, dusk; ~-**noite** *f* midnight; ~-**pensão** *f* half-board; ♦ *adv* **volta e** ~ now and then; 2 *(pop)* **à** ~-**tripa** half full, still hungry; **à** ~ in the gloom; ♦ **meias** *fpl (vestuário)* stockings; 2 halves; ~-**palavras** *fpl* half-truths; **falar por** ~-**palavras**

speak evasively; **ir a** ~ to go halves on; *(comer/beber fora)* to go Dutch.

meia-tigela *f (pessoa sem importância)* common person.

meia-volta *f* half turn; 2 *(MIL)* about face, about-turn.

meia-voz *f* undertone; 2 low voice.

meigo,-a *adj* gentle, sweet; 2 loving, caring.

meiguice *f* tenderness, sweetness, love.

meio *m* **o** ~ **ambiente** the environment; ~ **social** social circle, milieu; 2 way; **um** ~ **de fazer;** a way of doing; **por** ~ **de** through, via, by means of; ~**s** *pl (recursos)* means; **por todos os** ~**s** by all means, in every way; ~**s de comunicação** the media; ♦ **meio,-a** *adj (metade)* half; ~ **quilo** *m* half a kilo; half; **cortar ao/pelo** ~ to cut in half; **a** ~ **de** halfway through; 2 *(DESP) (distância)* middle; **no** ~ **de** *(no centro/interior de)* in the middle/midst (of); ♦ *adv (um tanto)* rather, slightly; ~-**bêbedo** rather drunk, tipsy; ♦ *prep* **a/em** ~ half (done); halfway through; IDIOM **pôr alguém no** ~ **da rua** chuck sb out; **ser** ~ **caminho andado** to be halfway there.

meio-campo *(pl:* **meios-campos)** *m (FUT)* midfield player.

meio-dia *m* midday, noon.

meio-morto,-a *adj* half dead.

meio-sal *adj inv (manteiga)* slightly-salted.

meio-termo *m (posição)* middle; 2 *(fig) (atitude moderada)* compromise; ~**s** *mpl (acção/assunto incompletos)* unresolved, half-done.

meio-tom *(pl:* **meios-tons)** *m (cor)* half tone; 2 *(MÚS)* semitone.

mel *m* honey.

melaço *m* molasses *pl*.

melado *m* molasses, treacle; ♦ **melado,-a** *adj (cor)* honey-coloured; 2 *(textura)* sticky.

melancia *f (fruta)* watermelon.

melancolia *f* sadness, melancholy.

melancólico,-a *adj* sad, melancholy, melancholic.

melão *m (fruta)* melon.

Melbourne *npr* Melbourne.

melena *f* untidy long hair; untidy mop of hair; 2 *(fam)* mane.

melga *f (insecto)* gnat, midge.

melhor *m,f* **o** ~ **de tudo foi** the best of everything was; **levar a** ~ to gain the better of; ♦ *(comp de* **bom/boa)** *adj inv* better, superior; ~ **que nunca** better than ever; **quanto mais** ~ the more the better; **seria** ~ **comermos agora** we had better eat now; **tanto** ~ so much the better; **cada vez** ~ better and better; 2 *(superl de:* **bom, bem)** **o,-a** ~ the best; **é o** ~ **hotel aqui** it's the best hotel (we have) here; **ela é a** ~ **professora que jamais tive** she is the best teacher I ever had; **ela hoje está** ~ *(saúde)* she is better today; **os negócios vão** ~ business is getting better; ♦ *adv* **para** ~ for the better, for better; **casei-me para o** ~ **e para o pior** I got married for better and worse; **pelo** ~ for the best; **fiz pelo** ~ I did it for the best; **à falta de** ~ for want of better (sth); **da** ~ **vontade** with good will, willingly; ♦ *conj* **ou** ~ or rather, that is to say; ♦ exc ~! good!, all the better!; **tanto ~!** so much the better!; IDIOM **ir desta para ~** to die; **fazer/dar o (meu/seu) ~** to give/do one's best.

melhoramento *m* improvement, progress.

melhorar *vt* to improve, make better of; ♦ *vi* to improve, get better.

melhoras *f* improvement; **2** *pl* change, relief, recovery; **tem havido algumas ~** there has been a change for the better; **desejo-lhe as ~!** *(saúde)* I hope you get better soon!

melhoria *f* improvement; betterment; **2** *(CONSTR)* improvements.

meliante *m* scoundrel; tramp; knave.

melífluo,-a *adj (que tem mel)* mellifluous; **2** *(muito doce)* like honey; **3** *(voz)* pleasant, mellifluous, sweet; **4** *(fam) (pessoa lisonjeira)* flattering; *(por interesse)* ingratiating.

melindrar *vt* to offend, hurt; ♦ **~-se** *vr* to take offence, be hurt.

melindre *m* sensitiveness; pique, resentment; **2** *(BOT)* balsam.

melindroso,-a *adj* susceptible, touchy; scrupulous; **2** delicate, tricky; **assunto ~** delicate matter; **3** *(afectado)* foppish.

meloa *f (fruto)* cantaloupe melon.

meloal *m* melon grove; **2** *(conjunto)* many melons.

melodia *f* melody; tune.

melódico,-a *adj* melodic, melodious, harmonious.

melodioso,-a *adj* melodious.

melodrama *m* melodrama.

melodramático,-a *adj* melodramatic.

meloeiro *m* melon plant.

melomania *f* love of music.

melopeia *f (MÚS)* music; **2** *(toada monótona)* boring music, chant

meloso,-a *adj (sabor)* sweet, honeyed; **2** *(textura)* syrupy, sticky; **3** *(música)* corny, sentimental.

melro *m (BOT)* blackbird.

membrane *f* membrane.

membro *m (família, de um clube, organização)* member; **Portugal é ~ da OTAN** Portugal is a member of NATO; **Estados-~s** *(da UE)* Member-States; **2** *(ANAT)* limb; **~ genital** *(ANAT)* penis, male genital; **3** *(LÍNG, MAT)* part.

membrudo,-a *adj* big, with strong limbs; **2** *(fig)* robust.

memorando *m* note; **2** *(COM)* memorandum, memo.

memorável *adj inv* memorable, noticeable, remarkable.

memória *f* memory; **~ fraca** poor memory; **falta de ~** bad memory; **2** *(COMP)* memory; **em ~** *(banco)* in the memory; **~ exclusiva de leitura** *(COMP)* read-only memory ROM; **3** *(recordação)* recollection; **~s** *fpl* memoirs; ♦ **de ~** *adv* by heart; IDIOM **~ de elefante** memory of an elephant; **apagar-se da ~** to forget; **ficar gravado na ~** to be etched on one's mind/memory; **puxar pela ~** try to remember.

memorial *(pl: -ais) m (monumento)* memorial; **2** *(registo)* report, record; **3** *(petição)* memorandum.

memorizar *vt* to commit to memory; memorize.

menção *f* mention, reference; **~ honrosa** honours, distinction; **fazer ~ de** to make a point of.

mencionar *vt* to mention.

mendicância *f* begging.

mendicante *m,f* beggar; ♦ *adj inv* begging; **2** *(REL)* mendicant.

mendicar *vt (pedido, ajuda)* to beg for; ♦ *vi (esmola)* to beg.

mendigo,-a *m,f* beggar.

mendinho *(= mindinho) m* the little finger.

menear *vt* to shake; to swing.

meneio *m* swaying.

menineiro,-a *adj* boyish, girlish; **2** *(aspecto, cara)* very young.

meningite *f (MED)* meningitis.

meninice *f* childhood; **2** *(infantil)* childishness.

menino,-a *m,f* boy/girl, child; youngster; **M~ Jesus** baby Jesus; **menino-prodígio/menina-prodígio** *m,f* whiz-kid; **ó ~s, calem-se!** *(fam)* children keep quiet!; **2** *f (mulher jovem ou solteira)* miss, girl; *(solteirona)* maiden; **~-do-olho** *(ANAT)* pupil (of the eye); IDIOM **ser a ~a dos olhos de (alguém)** to be the apple of sb's eye.

menopausa *f* menopause.

menor *m,f* minor, juvenile; **~ de idade** under age; **em trajes ~es** in underwear; ♦ *adj inv (mais pequeno)* smaller; **2** *(de pouca importância)* minor; **3** *(mínimo)* minimum, least; **4** *(MÚS) (nota)* minor; **5** *(BR)* smaller (than); **o/a ~** the smallest; the youngest; the least, slightest; minimum; **não tenho/faço a ~ ideia** I haven't the slightest idea.

menoridade *f* minority.

menos *m* **o ~** the least, the lesser; **2** *(MAT)* minus; ♦ *adj inv (sg)* less, *(pl)* fewer; least, *(pl)* fewest; ♦ *adv* less; least; **tenho dois Euros a ~** I am short of two Euros; **ao/pelo ~** at least; **mais ou ~** more or less; **sem mais nem ~** just like that, for no reason; **nem mais nem ~** exactly; **~ mal** not too bad; **mais coisa ~ coisa** about, approximately; ♦ *prep* save, except; ♦ *conj* **a ~ que** unless; **por ~ que** even though, however little; **quanto ~ ... melhor** the less... the better.

menosprezar *vt* to underrate; **2** to belittle, scorn.

menosprezo *m* contempt, disdain.

mensageiro,-a *adj* messenger.

mensagem *f* message.

mensal *adj inv* monthly.

mensalidade *f* monthly payment; **2** monthly allowance.

mensalmente *adv* monthly.

menstruação *f* period, menstruation.

menstruar *vi* to menstruate, have a period.

mensurabilidade *f* measurability.

mensurar *vt* to measure.

mensurável *adj inv* measurable.

mental *adj inv* mental.

mentalidade *f* mentality; **2** *(modo de pensar)* mind; **~ retrógrada** reactionary mentality.

mentalização *f* conditioning; **2** making sb aware of (sth).

mente *f* mind; intelecto; **vir à ~** to come to mind; **tenho em ~ fazer isso** *(intenção)* I have in mind to do that; ♦ *adv* **de boa ~** willingly.

mentecapto,-a *m,f* mad person; ♦ *adj* lunatic, mad, insane; **2** *(col, fam)* thick.

mentir *vi* to lie.

mentira *f* lie; lying; **parece ~ que** it seems incredible that; **2** false; **é verdade ou** ~ is it true or false?; **3** *(pequena mentira)* fib; ~ **inocente** white lie *(pop)*.

mentiroso,-a *m,f* liar; ♦ *adj* lying; **2** deceitful, false.

mentol *m* menthol, peppermint.

mentor,-ora *m (orientador)* mentor, guide.

menu *m (ementa)* menu; **2** *(COMP)* menu.

mercado *m* market; **o ~ de fruta** fruit market; **~ de trabalho** labour market; **doméstico/interno** *(COM)* domestic/home market; **M~ Comum** Common Market (EC); **M~ Único** Single Market; **~ negro/paralelo** black market; **~ das pulgas** *(BR)* flea market.

mercador *m* merchant, trader.

mercadoria *f* merchandise, commodity; **~s** *fpl* goods.

mercante *adj inv* merchant; **2** *(navio)* commercial.

mercantil *adj inv* mercantile, commercial.

mercê *f (favor)* favour; reward; **2** *(perdão)* mercy; **à ~ de** at the mercy of; **~ do Senhor X** thanks to Mr X; **3** *(título honorífico)* title; **por ~ régia** by royal decree; **Vossa ~** Your Honor; **4** *(razão)* because of *(arc)*; **~ do seu esforço** because of his efforts.

mercearia *f (loja)* grocer's (shop); **2** *(produto)* grocery, *pl* groceries.

merceeiro *m* grocer.

mercenário,-a *adj* mercenary.

mercúrio *m (QUÍM)* mercury; **2 Mercury** *(ASTRON)* Mercury.

mercurocromo *m (FARM)* mercurochrome.

merda *f (cal)* shit, crap; **2** *(coisa insignificante)* crap; ♦ *exc* ~! Shit!

merdice *f (cal)* filth, crap, shit.

merecedor,-ora *adj* deserving, worthy.

merecer *vt* to deserve, merit; be worth; ♦ *vi* to deserve.

merecido,-a *adj* deserved; **2** *(devido)* just, due; **bem-~** well-deserved.

merecimento *m* desert; merit.

merenda *f (refeição leve)* snack; **2** *(farnel)* picnic; **3** *(lanche)* afternoon tea.

merendar *vi* to have a snack in the afternoon.

merendeiro *m* picnic basket.

merengue *m (CULIN)* meringue; **2** *(MÚS)* merengue.

meretriz *f* harlot, whore, strumpet.

mergulhador,-ora *m,f* diver; **doença de ~** the bends; ♦ *adj* diving.

mergulhão *m* big splash, long dive; **2** *(ZOOL)* grebe.

mergulhar *vt* to dip in, immerse; ♦ *vi* to dive; **2** *(imergir)* to plunge; **3** *(lançar-se)* to throw o.s. (at); **4** *(entranhar)* to penetrate; **ele mergulhou na floresta** he penetrated the forest; IDIOM ~ **em águas turvas** get into deep water.

mergulho *m* dip(-ping), immersion; **2** dive; **3** plunge; **dar um ~** to take a dip; *(da prancha)* to spring.

meridiano *m (GEOG, GEOM)* meridian.

meridiano,-a *adj* meridian.

meridional *adj inv* southern.

meritíssimo *(superl de* **mérito***) m* higly deserving, most worthy; **2** *(forma de se dirigir ao juiz)* Your Honour.

mérito *m* merit; worth, value.

meritório,-a *adj (acção, obra)* worthy of merit.

mero,-a *adj* mere.

mês *m* month; **2** *(salário mensal)* month's pay; **ao ~** *adv* monthly; **de ~ a ~** every month; **de hoje a um ~** in a month's time.

mesa *f* table; **na cabeceira da ~** at the head of the table; **~-de-cabeceira** bedside table; **toalha de ~** table cloth; **pôr/tirar a ~** to lay/clear the table; **~ drobradiça** folding table; **conversa de ~-redonda** round table talk; **2** *(alimentação)* board; **boa ~** good food; **3 M~** *(grupo de pessoas com funções executivas)* Board; **~ eleitoral** polls; **sobre a ~** *(POL, ADMIN) (assuntos)* on the agenda; **4** *(GEOG)* mesa; **5 ~ de raposa** *(NÁUT)* billboard; IDIOM **pôr as cartas na ~** put one's cards on the table.

mesada *f* monthly allowance; pocket money.

mescla *f* mixture.

mesclar *vt* to mix (up); to blend.

meseta *f* plateau, tableland.

mesmo,-a *m* same, all the same; **é sempre o ~** it is always the same thing; **para mim é o ~** it's all the same to me; **2** alike, **eles são todos os ~s** *(pej)* they are all the same; **as coisas ficam na mesma** things never change; **dá no ~/na mesma** it comes to the same; ♦ *adj* same; **temos os ~s hábitos** we have the same habits; ♦ **mesmo,-a o/a** *pron* (who, what) the same; **vi a Antónia ontem e falei com a mesma sobre ...** I saw Antonia yesterday and I spoke to her about ...; **o mesmo rapaz de que te falei** *(citado)* the same young man I told you about; ♦ *adv* **mesmo** *(enfatizar)* just, right, very; really; **este ~ lugar** this very place; **ela era ~ a pessoa que eu queria...** she was the very/just the person I wanted...; **ele está ~ zangado** he is really angry; **nem ~** not even; **até ~ even**; **ao ~ tempo** at the same time; **é assim ~** it's just so; **aqui/hoje/agora** ~ right here/today/now; ♦ *pron dem* **mesmo,-a**, **~os/as** *(próprio)* myself, yourself, him/herself, ourselves, yourselves, themselves; **eu ~ lhe telefonei** I myself rang him up; **eles ~s me disseram** they themselves told me; ♦ *conj* ~ **que** even if, even though; ~ **assim** even so; ♦ **isso ~!** *exc* exactly!, just the thing!.

mesolítico,-a *adj* Mesolithic.

mesquinhez *f (mediocridade)* smallness, insignificance; **2** *(avareza)* stinginess; **3** meanness.

mesquinho,-a *adj (avaro)* mean, *(pop)* meanie; stingy, *(pop)* skinflint; **2** *(tacanho)* narrow-minded, petty person; **3** *(pessoa de estatura fraca)* puny, small.

mesquita *f* mosque.

messe *f (MIL)* mess; **~ dos oficiais** officers' mess; **2** *(AGR)* cornfield; **trabalhar na ~** to work in the harvest.

messiânico,-a *adj (REL) (esperança)* messianic.

messias *m* Messiah.

mestiço,-a *m,f* half-cast, half-breed; ♦ *adj* half-cast, of mixed race; crossbred.

mestrado *m (grau académico)* master's degree.

mestre, mestra *m,f (de escola)* master, mistress; **2** *(CONSTR)* foreman; **~-de-obras** master builder, foreman; **3** *(NÁUT)* boatswain; **4** *(guia espiritual)* spiritual guru; ♦ *adj* master; **chave-~a** master key; **obra ~a** masterpiece; ♦ *adv* **de ~** masterful, masterly; **~-de-cerimónias** master of ceremonies.

mestre de obras *m* foreman, builder, supervisor.

mestria *f* mastery; expertise; **com ~** to perfection.

mesura *f* bow; reverence; **ele está sempre com ~s para com o patrão** he is always kowtowing.

meta *f (marco)* finishing post; finishing line; **2** *(objectivo)* goal; aim; end.

metabólico,-a *adj* metabolic.

metabolismo *m* metabolism.

metade *f* half; middle; **~ de uma laranja** half an orange; **~ do caminho** half way; **a minha cara ~** *(fam) (esposa)* my better half; **2** *(JUR)* moiety; IDIOM **ficar-se pela ~** to leave sth half-done.

metafísica *f* metaphysics.

metafísico,-a *m,f* metaphysician; ♦ *adj* metaphysical.

metáfora *f (LIT)* metaphor.

metafórico,-a *adj* metaphoric.

metal *(pl: metais) m* metal; **~ sonante** hard cash; **~ escovado,-a** brushed, matt metal; **metais** *(MÚS)* brass instruments.

metálico,-a *adj* metallic; metal.

metalinguagem *f* metalanguage.

metalurgia *f* metallurgy.

metalúrgico,-a *adj* metalurgic.

metamorfose *f* metamorphosis.

metamorfosear **(alguém/algo)** *vt* to change sb/sth into; ♦ **~-se (em)** *vr* to change into.

metano *m* methane.

meteórico,-a *adj* meteoric.

meteoro *m* meteor.

meteorológico,-a *adj* **boletim ~** weather forecast.

meter *vt (colocar)* to put (in); **2** *(envolver)* to involve; **3** *(causar)* **ele mete-me raiva** he makes me angry; ♦ **~-se** *vr* to get involved **(em algo** in sth; **com alguém** with sb); **ele meteu-se com a mulher do amigo** he is having an affair with his friend's wife; **~ em** to get into; **meteu-se na cabeça dele** it got into his head; **~ em trabalhos** to get into trouble; **~ na cama** to get into bed; **2** *(esconder-se)* **ela meteu-se no quarto** she shut herself away in the bedroom; **3** *(chatear)* **~ com** to harass someone in street; to pick a quarrel with.

meticuloso,-a *adj* meticulous; overcareful.

metido,-a *(pp de meter) adj (fig)* **ando ~ em maus lençóis/numa enrascada/num sarilho** I am in dire trouble/in a jam/ in a fix; **2** *(caso amoroso)* **andar ~ com** to have an affair with (sb); IDIOM **~ entre a espada e a parede** to be between the sword and the deep blue sea.

metódico,-a *adj* methodical.

método *m* method.

metodologia *f* methodology.

metonímia *f (LIT)* metonymy.

metragem *f (medição em metros)* measurement in metres; **2** *(CIN)* length; **longa ~** feature (film); **curta ~** short (film).

metralha *f* shrapnel; **2** *(chuva de balas)* hail of bullets; **3** *(fig) (quantidade de coisas)* bulk, rubble; **4** *(fig, fam) (falador)* chatterbox; **5** *(CONSTR) (fragmentos de tijolo)* rubble.

metralhadora *f, adj* machine gun.

métrico,-a *adj* metric.

metro *m* metre; **2** underground *(UK)*, subway *(US)*.

metrô *(BR) m* underground *(UK)*, subway *(US)*.

metrópole *f* metropolis; capital.

metropolitano,-a *m* tube, underground *(UK)*, subway *(US)*; ♦ *adj* metropolitan.

meu, minha *adj* my; **a meu ver** in my opinion; **eu estava nos meus vinte anos** I was in my twenties; **eu e os meus** my family and I; **continuo na minha** *(teimosia)* I still think...; **gosto de fazer das minhas** I like to get up to tricks; ♦ *pron* mine; **um amigo ~** a friend of mine; IDIOM **ficar nas ~s tamanquinhas** I stick to my opinion.

mexer *vt (parte do corpo)* to move; **ele não mexe o braço** he can't move the arm; **o cão mexe o rabo de alegria** the dog is wagging his tail out of joy; **2** *(tocar)* to touch; **não mexas no meu cabelo** don't touch my hair; **3** *(agitar)* to stir; **o açúcar está dentro, mexe bem** the sugar is in, stir it well; ♦ *vi* **~ em** to meddle with, mess about, fiddle with; **alguém mexeu nas minhas gavetas** someone has messed about in my drawers; **~ com** to work/deal with (sth); **2** to budge; **empurrei o gato mas ele não mexeu** I pushed the cat but he didn't budge; **3** *(BR) (fig)* **~ com alguém** to tease; ♦ **~-se** *vr* to move, budge; **estou tão cansada que mal me mexo** I am so tired I can hardly move; **2** to get a move on; **mexe-te!** *(fam)*, **mexa-se!** *(não-fam)* get going!, hurry up!; **3** to fidget; **o rapaz está sempre a mexer-se** the boy is always fidgeting; IDIOM **~ os pauzinhos** to pull strings; *(fam)* **pôr-se a ~** to take to his heels, scram.

mexericar *vi* to gossip; make intrigues.

mexerico *m* tittle-tattle; **2** intrigue; **3** gossip.

mexeriqueiro,-a *m,f (pessoa)* gossip, busybody; ♦ *adj* gossiping.

mexicano,-a *adj* Mexican.

México *m* Mexico.

mexida *f (caos)* mess, mayhem; **2** *(trama)* intrigue; **3** *(mudança em posição, emprego)* shuffle, change; *(no governo)* reshuffle.

mexido,-a *adj* mixed up; **2** *(pessoa)* active, energetic; **3 ovos ~s** scrambled eggs.

mexilhão *m* mussel.

mezanino *m (entre dois andares)* mezzanine; **andar ~** mezzanine floor.

mezinha *f (pop) (remédio caseiro)* home-made medication.

miadela *(= miado, miau) f* mew, miaow, miawoing.

miar *vi* to mew.

miasma *m* miasma.

miau *m* miaow.

mica *f (MIN)* mica *(pl: micae)*; **2** *(pequena porção)* morsel; **~ de pão** bread crumb.

micção *f* urination; **~ involuntária** involuntary micturition.

mico *m (ZOOL)* any capuchin monkey.

mico-leão *(pl:* **micos-leão***) m (ZOOL)* golden-lion tamarin.

micose *f* fungal infection, mycosis.

micróbio *m* germ, microbe.

microcomputador *m* microcomputer, PC.

microempresa *f* small business, company, small enterprise.

microfone *m* microphone.

microfonia *f* weak voice; **2** acoustic interference, vibrations in the sound system.

microinformática *f* microcomputing.

microonda *f* microwave; **microondas** *(forno)* microwave oven *sg.*

microscópio *m* microscope.

mictório *m* urinol, male public convenience; ♦ *adj (promover a urina)* diuretic.

mídia *f (órgãos de comunicação social)* media.

migalha *f* crumb; **~s** *fpl* scraps.

migar *vt* to crumble; to crush.

migas *fpl (CULIN)* Portuguese traditional dish made with bread crumbs.

migração *f* migration.

migrar *vi* to migrate.

migratório,-a *adj* migratory; **aves ~as** birds of passage.

mijada *f (fam)* quantity of urine in one go.

mijadela *f (fam)* urine stain; stream of urine.

mijão, mijona *m,f (fam)* child who wets the bed; bed-wetter; **2** *(fig)* coward.

mijar *vt (cal) (urinar)* to piss; to pee; **~ na cama** to wet the bed; ♦ **~-se** *vr* to wet o.s. (with urine).

mijo *m (cal)* pee.

mil *num* thousand; **três ~** three thousand; **~-réis** n old Portuguese and Brazilian currency.

milagre *m* miracle; **por ~** miracously.

milagroso,-a *adj* miraculous.

milanês, milanesa *m,f* Milanese.

Milão *m* Milan.

míldio *m* plant mildew.

milenar *adj inv (que tem um milénio)* millennial.

milenário,-a *adj (tradições, árvore, etc.)* thousand-year-old.

milénio *m* millennium.

milésimo,-a *m,f* thousandth of.

mil-folhas *msg/pl (CULIN)* flaky/puff pastry, mille-feuille.

milha *f* mile (= 1609.3 metres); **~ náutica** nautical/sea mile.

milhafre *m (ZOOL)* kite.

milhagem *f* mileage.

milhão *m (1.000.000)* million (1,000,000).

milhar *m* thousand.

milharal *m* maize field.

milheiro *m* a thousand; **2** *(ZOOL)* finch.

milhentos *mpl (fam) (superior a mil)* thousands; **há ~** thousands of years ago.

milho *m (BOT)* maize *(UK)*; corn *(US)*; **2** *(pop)* dinheiro, lolly; IDIOM **ter dinheiro como ~** to have lots of money.

milícia *f (MIL)* militia; military life; military force; **~s populares** civilian militia.

miligrama *m* miligramme *(UK)*, milligram *(US)*.

milímetro *m* millimetre *(UK)*; millimeter *(US)*.

milionário,-a *adj* millionaire.

milionésimo,-a *m,f (num)* millionth of.

militante *adj* militant.

militar *m* soldier; ♦ *adj inv* military; ♦ *vi (POL)* to be an active member.

mim *pron (complemento indirecto com preposição)* me; **ele gosta de ~** he likes me; **elas jantaram sem ~** they dined without me; **2** *(enfatizando)* **foi a ~ que tu deste a carta** it was to me that you gave the letter; **3** *(opinião)* **para ~, este livro é melhor** in my opinion, this book is better; **4** *(reflexo com preposição)* me, myself; **tenho de tratar de ~** I have to care for myself; **falo de ~ para ~** I am speaking to myself.

mimado,-a *adj* petted; spoilt; pampered.

mimalho *m* spoilt brat: ♦ *adj (criança)* spoiled/spoilt; **2** *(gesto, voz)* loving.

mimar *vt (tratar alguém com carinho)* to pamper; **2** *(fazer todas as vontades a alguém)* to spoil sb; **3** *(expressar por mímica)* to mime, to mimic, to ape; **4** *(fig)* to be a copycat.

mímica *f* sign language; **2** *(TEAT)* mime.

mimo *m (presente)* gift; **2** *(carinho)* tender gesture; **fazer ~s a alguém** caress sb; **3** *(pessoa/coisa linda)* **ela é um ~!** she is a darling!; **estás um ~ nesse vestido** you look a picture in that dress.

mimosa *f (BOT) (árvore, flor)* mimosa.

mimoso,-a *adj* delicate, dainty; **2** tender, loving, sweet; **3** *(pele)* soft; **4** delightful.

mina *f* mine; **~ de diamantes** diamond mine; **2** *(passagem subterrânea)* tunnel; **3 ~ terrestre** land mine; **4** *(fig) (negócio lucrativo)* gold mine; **5** *(grafiti)* lead.

minar *vt (colocar minas)* to mine; **2** *(MIN) (explorar)* to mine, to dig; **3** *(corroer)* corrode; **4** *(fig)* to undermine; **5** *(fig)* exhaust *(paciência)*.

minarete *m* minaret, belvedere.

mindinho *m (Vd:* **mendinho***)*.

mineiro,-a *m* mine; ♦ *adj* mining.

mineração *f* mining, exploration; **2** *(depuração)* purifying (the ores).

mineral *m, adj inv* mineral; **2** *(carvão)* mined.

minério *m* ore; **~ de ferro** iron ore.

míngua *f* shortage, lack of, need; ♦ *prep* **à ~ de** for lack of; ♦ *adv* **à ~** for want of; **morrer à ~** to starve to death.

minguante *m (ASTRON)* wane, decline; **quarto ~** *(ASTRON)* last quarter; ♦ *adj inv* waning.

minguar *vt (importância)* to minimize; **2** to decrease, reduce; ♦ *vi* to wane, dwindle, shrink; become short.

minha *f (Vd:* **meu***)*.

minhoca *f* earthworm; **com ~s na cabeça** *(fig)* with strange/crazy ideas.

minhoto,-a *adj* from Minho, northern province of Portugal.

miniatura *f, adj* miniature.

minifundiário,-a *m,f* small farm owner, smallholder; ♦ *adj (exploração)* on a small scale.

mínima *f (METEOR)* minimum *(temperatura);* **2** *(MÚS)* minim; IDIOM *(BR)* **não dar a ~ para (alguém, algo)** not to have the least concern.

minimalista *m,f* minimalist.

mini-meias, minimeias *fpl* knee-high socks.

minimizar *vt (sofrimento, danos)* to minimize; **2** *(subestimar)* underestimate; **3** *(MAT)* minimize; ♦ **~-se** *vr* to underestimate o.s.

mínimo,-a *m,f* **o ~** *m* the minimum, the least; **é o ~ que posso fazer** it's the least I can do; **no ~** at least; **ao ~** to a minimum; **2** *(dedo mindinho)* little finger; **3** *(car lights)* **os ~s** *mpl (AUT–faróis)* parking lights; ♦ *adj* minimal; **2** *(valor)* lowest, minimum; **preço ~** the lowest price; **3** *(opinião, ideia)* faintest, smallest, least; **4** *(nenhum)* slightest; **não há a ~a chance** there isn't the slightest chance; **não faço a ~a ideia** I don't have the slightest idea; I don't have a clue; **5** *(quantidade)* smallest; **6** *(JUR) (mais brando)* lightest; **~a sentença** lightest sentence; ♦ *prep* **com o ~** with the minimum of.

mínio *m* minium, red lead.

mini-saia, minissaia *f (vestuário)* miniskirt.

ministério *m* ministry; **M~ do Interior** Home Office *(UK);* **M~ das Finanças,** *(BR)* **da Fazenda** Ministry of Finance, H.M. Treasury *(UK);* **M~ dos Negócios Estrangeiros,** *(BR)* **Exteriores** Foreign Office.

ministrar *vt* to administer.

ministro,-a minister; **M~ da Justiça** Justice Minister, Lord Chancellor *(UK);* **M~ das Finanças,** *(BR)* **da Fazenda** Chancellor of the Exchequer *(UK);* Secretary of the State *(US);* **~ sem pasta** minister without portfolio; **M~ dos Negócios Estrangeiros,** *(BR)* **Exteriores** Foreign Secretary; **M~ dos Transportes** Secretary for Transport; **~-adjunto, ~a-adjunta** deputy minister, aide; **2** *(REL)* minister.

minorar *vt* to lessen, reduce, diminish.

minoria *f* minority.

minoritário,-a *adj* in the minority; **línguas ~s** minority languages (least-demanded languages).

minúcia *f* detail.

minucioso,-a *adj* thorough; detailed.

minúsculo,-a *adj* minuscule, minute, tiny; **letra ~a** small letter; **2** *(COMP)* lower case.

minuta *f* rough draft; note, memorandum.

minuto *m* minute; **ponteiro dos ~s** minute-hand; **é só um ~** just a moment; **por ~** per minute.

miolo *m* **~ do pão** inside of the bread; **2** *(fruto)* pulp; core; **3 ~s** *mpl (CULIN)* brains; *(fam) (cérebro)* brains.

mioma *m* myoma.

míope *adj inv* short-sighted.

miopia *f* short-sightedness.

miosótis *m (BOT)* myosotis; *(flor)* forget-me-not.

mira *f (MIL) (arma)* sight, sights; **linha de ~** sight line; **2** aim, purpose; **3** surveyor's pole; **à ~ de** on the lookout; **ter em ~** *(fig)* to have an eye on; to aim/hope for; IDIOM **pôr a ~ muito alta** to set one's sights too high.

mirabolante *adj inv* showy, gaudy; amazing.

miraculoso,-a *m,f (Vd:* **milagroso).**

mirada *f* look, glance.

miradouro, miradoiro *m* viewpoint, belvedere.

miragem *f* mirage; **2** *(fig)* dream, illusion.

miramar *m* sea-view belvedere.

mirante *m* viewpoint, belvedere.

mirar *vt (olhar)* to look at; stare at; **ele mirou-me dos pés à cabeça** he looked me up and down; **2** *(contemplar)* to gaze; **~ os teus olhos** to gaze in your eyes; **3** *(desejar)* to have an eye on (sth); ♦ *vi* to aim at *(animais);* ♦ **~-se** *vr* to look at o.s.; **ele mirava-se ao espelho** he looked at himself in the mirror; **as estrelas miravam-se no mar** the stars were reflected in the water/sea

mirone *m,f* onlooker, bystander, observer.

mirra *f (BOT)* myrrh.

mirrar *vt/vi (flor, árvore, pessoa)* to wither, shrivel; **ela tinha o rosto mirrado** her face was withered, shrivelled; **2** *(terra, fruto)* to dry up, parch; **3** *(tornar magro)* to make thin, waste away.

mirtilo *m (BOT)* blueberry.

misantropia *f* misanthropy.

misantrópico,-a *adj* misanthropic.

misantropo,-a *m,f* misanthrope, misanthropist.

miscelânea *f* miscellany; **2** *(fig)* mixture.

miscigenação *f* miscegenation, interbreeding; **2** *(ZOOL)* cross-breeding.

miserável *(pl: -veis) m,f (azarado)* unfortunate; **2** *(patife)* wretch; **3** *(sovina)* stingy, skinflint; ♦ *adj inv (alguém)* poor, miserable, unfortunate; **2** *(desprezível)* abject, despicable; **3** *(malvado)* wretched; **4** *(sovina)* tight-fisted, mean; **5** *(casa, ambiente)* squalid; **6** *(trivial)* petty, paltry.

miséria *f (pobreza)* poverty; **uma ~** *(de dinheiro)* a pittance; **~ franciscana** *(fig)* extreme poverty; **2** *(avareza)* stinginess.

misericórdia *f* pity, compassion; mercy; **obras de ~** charity work; IDIOM **golpe de ~** coup de grâce.

misericordioso,-a *adj* compassionate.

mísero,-a *adj (pobre)* poor, humble; **uma casa ~a** a humble/poor home; **2** *(estado)* pitiful; **3** *(fig) (escasso)* miserly.

missa *f (REL)* Mass; **~ solene** High Mass; IDIOM **ainda a ~ vai a Santos** much is yet to happen.

missal *m (livro de missa)* missal; **2** *(TYPO)* missal letters.

missanga *f (muitos)* small beads; **2** trinket; **3** *(TYPO)* very small print.

missão *f* mission.

míssil *m* missile; **~ de cruzeiro** cruise missile; **~ de curto/longo alcance** short/long range missile.

missionário *m* missionary.

missiva *f* missive; letter.

mister *m* occupation; *(ofício)* office, profession; **2** purpose; **ser ~ fazer** be necessary to do.

mistério *m* mystery.

misterioso,-a *adj* mysterious, obscure.

misticismo *m* mysticism.

místico,-a *adj* mystic.

mistificar *vt* to mystify; to deceive.

misto,-a *m* mixture; ♦ *adj* mixed; mixed up; **tosta-~a** *f* toasted cheese and ham sandwich.

mistura *f* mixing; mixture; 2 *(QUÍM, FÍS)* compound, blend; 3 *(cimento, etc)* slurry; 4 *(acústico)* mixing; **sem ~** pure.

misturar *vt* to mix, blend; ♦ **~-se com** *vr* to mix in with, mingle with.

mito *m* myth; legend.

mitológico,-a *adj* mythological; legendary.

mitra *f (eclesiástica)* mitre; 2 *(pop) (carapuça)* cap, hat, tifter; 3 *(na inquisição)* paper bag over head.

miudeza *f* precision, detail; ♦ **miudezas** *fpl (víscerars)* giblets; 2 odds and ends, trinkets; **loja de ~** haberdashery *(UK)*, notious shop *(US)*.

miudinho,-a *adj* tiny; **cortar (algo) muito ~** to cut sth very finely; 2 *(pessoa exigente)* fussy; 3 *(mesquinho)* petty.

miúdo,-a *m,f* youngster, kid, boy, girl; **~a muito gira** a cute chick; ♦ *adj (pequeno)* tiny; **despesas ~as** petty expenses; 2 *(magro)* slim; 3 *(em por-menor)* detailed; 4 **arraia ~a** *(pop) (arc)* rabble, the masses.

miúdos *mpl (troco)* small change *sg*; **~s de frango** *(vísceras de aves)* giblets; ♦ **a ~** *adv* often.

mixórdia *f (pop)* confusion, mix-up; 2 *(comida mal feita)* hotchpotch, food thrown together; 3 *(mistura de coisas)* jumble; 4 *(vinho adulterado)* plonk.

mo (= me + o) *pron* it to/for me; **ele deu-te o livro? sim, já mo deu** has he given you the book? yes, he has given it to me.

mó *f* millstone; grindstone.

moagem *f* grinding.

mobilar *vt* to furnish.

mobília *f* furniture.

mobiliário *m* furnishings *pl*.

mobilizar *vt* to mobilize.

moça *f (Vd: moço)*.

moçambicano,-a *adj (from Mozambique)* Mozambican.

Moçambique *npr* Mozambique.

moção *f* motion.

mochila *f* rucksack.

mocho,-a *m (ZOOL)* owl, farm owl; 2 *(banco pequeno)* little stool; ♦ *adj (animal sem chifres)* hornless, without horns; 2 *(pessoa mutilada)* maimed; 3 *(árvore)* branchless.

mocidade *f* youth; young people.

moço,-a *m* young man, lad; **~ de bordo** cabin boy; **~ de cavalariça** groom; **~ de recados** errand-boy, messenger; 2 *(carregador)* porter; 3 *f* girl, young woman; ♦ *adj* young, youthful.

moda *f* fashion; style; 2 *(pop)* rage, craze, fad; **estar na ~** to be in fashion, be all the rage; **fora de ~** out of fashion, old-fashioned; **lançar a ~** to set the fashion; ♦ **~s** *fpl* fashion; 2 *(estilo de música)* Portuguese folk song; 3 *(ESTAT)* mode; ♦ **à ~**, **em ~** *adv* fashionably, in fashion; **à ~ de** like, in the fashion of; **à minha ~** my way, in my fashion; IDIOM **ver em que param as ~s** see how things go, see which way the wind blows.

modalidade *f* mode; 2 *(disciplinas)* module; **o curso tem três ~s** the course has three modules; 3 *(MÚS)* mode.

modelação *f* modelling; 2 *(obra de...)* model, statue.

modelador,-ora *m,f* model-maker, modeller; 2 designer; ♦ *adj* modelling.

modelagem *f* modelling; 2 *(artigo)* moulding *(UK)*; molding *(US)*; 3 *(do corpo)* shape.

modelar *adj (que serve de modelo, exemplar)* model, exemplary; ♦ *vt* to model, make patterns; 2 *(barro, etc)* to mould; 3 *(contornar)* to shape, cling; **a blusa modela os seus seios** the blouse clings to her breasts; ♦ **~-se** *vr* to be modelled on, to adapt oneself to, to model oneself on sb.

modelista *m,f (de aviões, máquinas, etc)* model-maker; 2 *(de vestuário)* designer.

modelo *m* model; **ela foi ~ quando era jovem** she was a model when she was young; **passagem de ~s** fashion show; 2 pattern, style; **não gosto desse ~ de sapato** I don't like this pattern/style of shoes; 3 *(exemplar)* model; **ele é um ~ de bondade** he is a model of kindness; 4 *(norma)* format; 5 *(MAT, FÍS, POL, SOCIAL)* model.

moderado,-a *adj* moderate, tolerant; 2 *(tempo)* mild, moderate; 3 *(trabalho, comida)* tolerable; 4 *(MÚS)* moderate.

moderador,-ora *m,f* moderator, mediator; ♦ *adj* conciliatory.

moderar *vt (regrar)* to moderate; 2 *(restringir)* to control, restrain; 3 *(reduzir)* to reduce; 4 *(afrouxar)* to slow down; ♦ **~-se** *vr* to calm down, slow down.

modernidade *f* modernity.

modernismo *m* modernism, modern; **pensadores do ~** modern thinkers.

modernista *m,f* modernist; ♦ *adj inv* modernistic.

modernização *f* modernization.

modernizar *vt* to modernize; ♦ **~-se** *vr* to keep oneself up to date.

moderno,-a *adj* modern; present-day, up-to-date.

modernoso,-a *adj (BR)* pretending to be modern; 2 *(pessoa)* newfangled, *(pop)*.

modéstia *f* modesty; ~ **falsa** false modesty; ~ **à parte** modesty aside.

modesto,-a *adj* modest; **2** plain; **3** *(negócio)* small; **de origens** ~**s** humble beginnings.

módico,-a *adj* moderate; **preço** ~ low price, reasonable price; affordable; **apartamentos a preço** ~ affordable apartments.

modificação *f* modification, change; **fazer** ~**ões** to carry out modifications/alterations.

modificar *vt* to modify, alter, change (sth).

modificável *(pl: -veis) adj inv* modifiable, changeable.

modilho *m (música)* light song/tune; **2** *(moda)* strict observer of fashion.

modinha *(dim de moda) f*; **2** old folk song/tune; **3** popular Brazilian song (sad and sentimental).

modismo *m* trend, fashion.

modista *f* dressmaker; ~ **de alta costura** haute couture designer.

modo *m* way, manner; **2** *(gram)* mood; ~ **do conjuntivo/subjuntivo** subjunctive mood; **2** *(MÚS)* mode; **3** *(ECON)* method; ♦ *prep* **a** ~ **de** as, so; ♦ *conj* **de** ~ **que** so; (that); **de qualquer** ~ whichever way, anyway; ♦ *adv* **de** ~ **nenhum** in no way; **de algum** ~ somehow; **ao** ~ **de** in the custom of; **a** ~ **de a meu/seu** ~ my/your way; **de certo** ~ in a way; ~**s** *pl* manners; **com bons** ~**s** politely.

modorra *f* drowsiness; lethargy.

moeda *f* coin; money; currency; ~ **sonante** hard cash; **Casa da M~** Mint. IDIOM **pagar na mesma** ~ to give tit for tat.

moela *f* gizzard.

moer *vt* to grind *(café, amêndoa, etc)*; **2** *(carne)* to mince; **3** *(para extrair líquido)* to squeeze/mill, crush *(fruto)*; **4** *(surrar)* to beat (sb); **5** *(cansar)* to tire out; ~ **a paciência/o juízo**, to exhaust one's patience/mind; ♦ *vi* to mull over in one's mind; ♦ ~**-se** *vr* to get tired, fed up; **2** to worry, fret; ~ **uma rosca** to strip a screw; **pedra de** ~ *f* millstone.

mofa *f* mockery, scoffing; **sorriso de** ~ scornful smile.

mofar *vi* to go mouldy/musty; ~ **de** to mock, jeer, scoff at.

mofento,-a *adj* mouldy, musty.

mofino,-a *f* unfortunate person; **sorte** ~**a!** miserable luck!; ♦ *adj* wretched; **2** troublesome; **3** stingy.

mofo *m (BOT)* mould; mustiness.

mogno *m (árvore, madeira)* mahogany.

moído,-a *(pp de moer) adj* ground; **2** *(carne)* minced; **3** *(fruto)* squeezed; **4** *(pessoa)* tired out.

moinho *m* windmill; **2** grinder.

moita *f* thicket; clump, bush; copse, coppice; ♦ ~**!** *exc (segredo)* not a word!

mola *f (TEC)* spring; **2** *(roupa)* peg; **3** *(no vestuário)* press stud; ~**-real** *f* mainspring; ~**-mestra** driving force.

molar *m (dente)* molar.

moldagem *f* modelling; **2** *(CONSTR)* moulding; **3** *(GEOL)* fossile impression.

moldar *vt* to mould, shape; **2** to cast.

Moldávia *npr* **a** ~ Moldavia.

moldavo,-a *adj* Moldavian.

molde *m (modelo)* mould *(UK)*; mold *(US)*; **2** *(de vestido)* pattern; **3** *(escultura)* cast, plaster template, mould, moulding; ~**s** *mpl* way, fashion; ♦ **de** ~ *prep* to the purpose, with the aim of, in such away that.

moldura *f* frame; **2** *(ARQ) (ornatos)* mouldings, panels.

mole *adj* soft; **cama** ~ soft bed; **2** *(pessoa)* lazy, indolent, slow; **3** *(flácido)* flabby; **4** *(feitio)* easy-going, softie.

molécula *f* molecule.

moleiro,-a *m,f* miller.

molengão *m (f: -gona)* slow person; sleepyhead; ♦ *adj* lazy.

molestar *vt (incomodar)* to bother, annoy, trouble; **2** *(magoar)* to offend, hurt; **3** *(estragar)* to cause damage; **4** *(sexualmente)* to molest; ♦ ~**-se** *vr* to be annoyed.

moléstia *f* illness, disease.

molesto,-a *adj (incómodo)* troublesome, annoying; **2** *(perverso)* disturbing; **3** *(doentio)* unpleasant; **4** *(mau)* wicked.

molha *f* soaking.

molhado,-a *adj (húmido)* wet, damp; **2** *(ensopado)* soaked; **3** *(terreno com água)* wetlands.

molhar *vt* to wet; **2** to moisten, dampen; **3** *(líquido)* to dip in; to soak; ♦ ~**-se** *vr* to get wet.

molhe *m* jetty, wharf; **2** *(de maior extensão)* pier.

molheira *f* sauceboat.

molho[¹] [ó] *m* bunch; sheaf.

molho[²] [ô] *(CULIN)* sauce; gravy; dressing; **pôr de** ~ to soak.

moliceiro *m* boat carrying seaweeds (used for manure); **2** *(trabalhador nesta apanha)* boatman.

moliço *m* seaweed.

molusco *m (ZOOL)* mollusc; **2** *(fig, fam) (pessoa mole)* wimp, wet; ~**s** *mpl* the mollusca.

momentâneo,-a *adj* momentary.

momento *m* moment; **a todo o** ~ constantly; **de um** ~ **para o outro** suddenly; **no** ~ **em que** just as; **2** *(TEC)* momentum.

momice *f (esgar)* grimace.

Mónaco *npr* **o** ~ Monaco.

monarca *m,f* monarch; **monarquia** *f* monarchy.

monástico,-a *adj* monastic.

monção *f (METEOR)* monsoon; **2** *(fig)* opportunity.

monco *m (muco nasal)* mucus, snot; **2** *(excrescência sólida)* wattle; IDIOM **andar/ficar de** ~ to be crestfallen.

monda *f (AGR)* weeding, hoeing.

mondar *vt (ervas daninhas)* to weed; **2** *(árvores)* to prune; **3** *(fig)* to weed out.

monegasco,-a *adj* from Monaco, Monegasque.

monetário,-a *adj* monetary; **política** ~**a** monetary policy.

monge *m* monk.

mongol *m,f* Mongol; **o** ~ *(LÍNG)* Mongolian; ♦ *adj (história, cultura)* Mongolian.

Mongólia *(BR: -gô-) npr* **a** ~ Mongolia.

mongolismo *m (MED)* Down's syndrome.

mongolóide *adj inv* person suffering from Down's syndrome, Mongoloid.

monitor,-ora *m,f (EDUC)* instructor, trainer; **2** *m (ger)* monitor; **3** TV screen.

monitorar *vt* to monitor.

monja *f* nun.

mono- *(prefixo em palavras que exprimem uma só unidade)* mono.

mono,-a *m,f* monkey, ape; **2** *(pessoa)* useless; **3** *(pessoa)* ugly; **4** *m (COM)* dead loss; **5** *(fig)* kiss; ♦ *adj* dull, sullen.

monóculo *m* monocle.

monocultura *f* monoculture.

monógamo,-a *adj* monogamous.

monografia *f* monography.

monolítico,-a *adj* monolithic.

monologar *vt (texto, oração)* to recite; **2** to talk to o.s.; **3** *(TEAT)* to give a monologue.

monopólio *m* monopoly.

monopolista *adj inv* monopolist.

monopolizar *vt* to monopolize.

monossílabo,-a *adj* monosyllabic.

monotonia *f* monotony.

monótono,-a *adj* monotonous.

monstro,-a *m* monster; ♦ *adj* monster; **2** *(fig)* fantastic.

monstruoso,-a *adj* monstrous.

monta *f*; **de pouca** ~ trivial, of little account.

montado,-a *m* oak plantation; pasture for pigs; ♦ *adj* mounted, on horseback.

montador,-a *m,f* fitter; ~ **de máquinas** engine-fitter.

montagem *f* assembly, fitting up; **linha de** ~ assembly line; **2** *(ARQ)* erection; **3** *(filme)* editing; **4** *(TEAT)* production.

montanha *f* mountain; **~-russa** *f* rollercoaster.

montanhês,-esa *m,f* highlander; ♦ *adj* (of a) mountain.

montanhista *m,f* mountaineer.

montanhoso,-a *adj* mountainous.

montante *m* total, sum; *(de dinheiro)* amount; **a** ~ upstream; ~ **de vendas** sales figure(s).

montão *m* heap, pile; **em** ~ pell-mell; **aos montões** *mpl* in/by heaps/in piles; *(cartas, presentes)* in shoals.

montar *vt* to mount, *(cavalo)* to get on; to ride; **2** *(mobiliário)* to assemble, put together; **3** *(máquinas)* to fit; **4** *(negócio)* to set up; ♦ ~ **a/em** *vi* to get on, mount; **2** *(CIN)* to edit; **3** *(TEAT)* to produce.

montaria *f* hunting; mount; side-saddle.

monte *m (terreno)* hill; **2** *(pilha de coisas)* heap, pile; **3** *(prov)* a cluster of houses; **4** *(pessoas)* crowd; ♦ **aos** ~**s** *adv* in/by heaps.

montenegrino,-a *adj* from Montenegro.

montepio *m* trust fund.

montês,-esa *adj* mountainous; **cabra** ~ mountain goat.

montevideano,-a *adj* from Montevideo.

montículo *m (pequeno amontoado)* mound; **2** *(pequeno monte)* hillock.

montívago,-a *adj* roving in the mountains.

montra *f* shop window.

monturo *m (lixeira)* dump, tip; **2** *(monte de lixo)* heap of rubbish.

monumental *adj inv* monumental; **2** *(fig)* magnificent, splendid.

monumento *m* monument.

moquear *vt* to dry meat.

moquenquice *f (careta)* grimaces; **2** *(lábia)* wheedling, fawning.

morabeza *f (Cape Verde) (amabilidade)* kindness.

morada *f* address; **2** dwelling; **3** domicile.

moradia *f* detached house, villa.

morador,-ora *m,f* resident.

moral *f* ethics *pl*, morality; **2** *m (ânimo)* morale; **o** ~ **dos soldados estava em baixo** the soldiers' morale was low; ♦ *adj inv* moral.

moralidade *f* morality.

moralismo *m* moralism.

moralista *adj inv* moralist.

moralizar *vi* to moralize.

moralmente *adv* morally.

morango *m* strawberry.

morangueiro *m* strawberry plant.

morar *vi* to live, reside.

moratória *f (JUR)* moratorium.

moratória,-o *adj (JUR)* delaying, moratory.

mórbido,-a *adj* morbid; sickly.

morcego *m (BIO)* bat.

morcela *f* black pudding.

mordaça *f (açaime)* muzzle; **2** *(fig) (para tapar a boca a alguém)* gag.

mordaz *adj inv (incisivo)* biting, mordant; **2** caustic *(comentário)*.

mordedura *f* bite, teethmark.

morder *vt (trincar)* to bite; to bite into; ~ **a língua** to bite one's tongue; **2** *(corroer)* to corrode; ♦ **~-se** *vr*: ~ **de inveja** to be green with envy.

mordomo *m* butler.

moreno,-a *adj* olive-skinned; **ele é** ~ he is dark-skinned; **ela está ~a** she is bronzed/sun-tanned; **2** *f* brunette.

morfina *f* morphine.

morgadio *m (sistema de)* right of primogeniture *(male line)*; **2** assets; **3** estate; ♦ *adj (solar)* manor *(house)*.

morgado *m* heir to an entailed estate; **2** such an estate.

morganático,-a *adj (casamento)* morganatic.

morgue *f* morgue.

moribundo,-a *adj* moribund, dying.

morigerado,-a *adj* upright.

mormacento,-a *adj* sultry.

mormente *adv* chiefly, especially.

mórmon *(pl: mormones) adj inv* Mormon.

morna *f* Cape Verde's traditional song.

morno,-a *adj* lukewarm, tepid.

moroso,-a *adj* slow, sluggish.

morrer *vi* to die; ~ **afogado** to drown; **ela morreu atropelada** she was run over by a car and died; **2** *(fig)* ~ **de fome, de sede, de amores, de saudade** to die of hunger/thirst/love/of longing; ~ **por** to be mad about; ~ **de rir** to die laughing; **2** *(AUTO)* to stall.

morro *m* hill; **2** *(BR: favela)* slum.

mortadela *f* a kind of salami.

mortal *adj inv* mortal; deadly.

mortalha *f* shroud; **2** cigarette rolling paper.

mortalidade *f* mortality; death rate.

mortandade *f* slaughter; **2** loss of life.

morte *f (falecimento)* death; **às portas da ~** at death's door; **2** *(fim)* end; **3** *(desgraça)* ruin; **4** deathly; **silêncio de ~** deathly silence; IDIOM **tão certo como a ~** as sure as death; **pensar na ~ da bezerra** to daydream; **estar pela hora da ~** to be very expensive; **tu serás a minha ~** you will be the end of me.

morteiro *m (MIL)* mortar; **2** *(pirotecnia)* banger.

mortiço,-a *adj (luz, chama)* dying, fading; **2** *(olhos, olhar)* dull, lifeless, dim; **3** *(festa)* boring.

mortífero,-a *adj* deadly, lethal.

mortificar *vt* to torture; **2** to annoy, torment.

morto,-a *(pp irr de matar/morrer) m,f* dead man/woman; **2** *(cadáver)* body, corpse; **velar o ~** keep vigil over the body; **3 ponto ~** *(AUTO)* neutral; ♦ *adj (falecido)* dead, deceased; **estar ~** to be dead; **dado como ~** presumed dead; **ser ~** to be killed; **ele foi ~ na guerra** he was killed in action (war); **bebé nascido ~** stillborn baby; **2** *(exausto)* exhausted; **3** dying, **estar ~ de fome** dying of hunger; **~ de cansaço** dogtired; **4** *(ansioso)* eager, longing for; **estou ~ por sair daqui** I am dying to leave this place; **5** *(olhar, expressão)* dull, deadpan; **natureza ~a** *(ARTE)* still life; **6** *(NÁUT) (águas)* stagnant; IDIOM **não ter onde cair ~** to have nothing; **estar mais ~ do que vivo** be more dead than alive.

mortuário *adj* mortuary, funerary.

mos (= me + os) *pron pess* them to/for me; **ele deu-mos** he gave them to me.

mosaico *m* mosaic.

mosca *f (ZOOL)* fly; **2** *(sinal postiço preto)* dot, patch; ♦ *adv* **às ~s** *(sala, teatro)* empty; IDIOM **(estar a) apanhar ~s** to have one's mouth open; **estar com a ~** be fidgety; **não faria mal a uma ~** would not hurt a fly; **não se ouvia uma ~** not a sound could be heard; **andar picada da ~** to be furious/mad; **acertar na ~** *(BR)* to hit the target/jackpot; **comer ~** *(BR)* be cheated; not understand; **~-morta** *f* slowcoach; **papa-~s** *m,f (pej)* fool, gullible person.

moscada *adj* **noz-~** nutmeg.

moscardo *(ZOOL)* horsefly.

moscatel *m (BOT)* Muscat; ♦ *adj* muscat, muscadine; **vinho ~** Muscatel wine.

moscovita *adj inv* from Moscovo, Moscavite.

Moscovo *npr* Moscow.

mosquete *m (MIL) (arma antiga)* musket; **2** *(cavalo pequeno e corredor)* small racehorse.

mosqueteiro *m* musqueteer.

mosquiteiro *m* mosquito net.

mosquito *m* mosquito.

mossa *f (amolgadela)* dent; **2** *(cavidade)* hole, cavity, notch; **3** *(falha)* nick; **fazer ~** *(fig) (impression)* to affect.

mostarda *f* mustard.

mosteiro *m* monastery; convent.

mosto *m* must; **2** *(suco, sementes, tubérculos)* juice; **~ de aloés/azebres** aloe-vera juice; *(BR) (enxame)* swarm of bees.

mostra *f* display, show, exhibition; **2** sign, indication, appearance; **3** sample, example; **dar ~s de** to show signs of.

mostrador *m (relógio)* face, dial.

mostrar *vt* to show; to display; to prove; ♦ **~-se** *vr (parecer)* to appear, seem; **2** *(exibir-se)* to show off; **~ os dentes** to snarl.

mostrengo *m* monster; **2** *(pej) (pessoa feia, bruta)* monster; **3** *(pej) (indolente)* layabout.

mostruário *m* display case, showcase; **2** samples catalogue.

mote *m* motto; **2** theme.

motejar *vt* to taunt, mock; ♦ **~ de** *vi* to jeer at, make fun of.

motejo *m* mockery, derision; **2** joke.

motim *m* riot, rebellion; mutiny.

motivar *vt* to cause, bring about; **2** to motivate.

motivo *m* cause, reason; **2** motive; **3** *(MÚS)* motif.

moto *f* motorbike; ♦ *adv* **de ~ próprio** of one's own free will.

moto *f*, **motocicleta** *f*, **motociclo** *m* motorbike; (motor-)scooter.

motociclista *m,f* motor-cyclist.

motoniveladora *f* bulldozer.

motoqueiro,-a *m,f* biker, motorcyclist.

motor *m* motor, engine, source of energy; **~ de arranque** *(AUTO)* starter (motor); **~ de explosão** internal combustion engine; **~ de popa** *(NÁUT)* outboard motor; **2** *(fig)* instigator; ♦ *adj* driving.

motorista *m,f* driver.

motorizado,-a *f* motorbike; ♦ *adj* motorized.

motosserra *f* chainsaw.

motricidade *f* driving force; **2** *(FISIOL)* movement.

motriz *adj inv* motive; **força ~** motive/driving power; **roda ~** traction wheel.

motu proprio of one's own free will.

mouco,-a *adj* deaf, hard of hearing; IDIOM **fazer orelhas ~as** to turn a deaf ear.

mouraria *f* Moorish quarter.

mourisco,-a *adj (arte, cultura)* Moorish; **2** *(ARQ) (arco)* horseshoe.

mouro,-a *m,f* Moor; **2** native of Mauritania.

movediço,-a *adj* easily moved; unsteady; **areia ~a** quicksand.

móveis *mpl (peças de)* furniture *sg*; **bens ~** personal property.

móvel *m* piece of furniture; ♦ *adj inv* movable.

mover *vt* to move, to set in motion; **2** *(partes do corpo)* to move, swing; **3** *(JUR)* **~ um processo** to sue; ♦ **~-se** *vr* to move; **2** *(emoção)* to be moved.

movido,-a *adj (impelido)* driven; **~ a pilhas** battery-operated; **2** *(fig) (emoção)* **~ a** moved (to); **~ por** driven by.

movimentado,-a *adj (vida, ruas)* busy.

movimentar *vt (deslocar)* to move; **~ uma conta** to operate an account; **2** *(dinamizar)* to liven up; **3** to form a movement.

movimento *m* movement; **2** *(TEC)* motion; **3** activity, bustle.

movível *adj inv* movable.

moxama *f* all kinds of smoked fish.

moxinifada *f* *(salsada)* mixture, miscellany, medley; **2** *(FARM) (de ingredientes)* mixture.

muar *m,f* *(ZOOL)* mule; ♦ *adj inv* *(animal)* stubborn, mulish.

mucano *m* *(ANG) (culpa)* guilt; **2** *(JUR)* sentence.

muco *m* mucus.

mucosa *f* *(ANAT)* mucous membrane.

muçulmano,-a *m,f adj* Muslim.

muda *f* change; **~ de cavalos** change of horses; **~ de voz** *(rapaz)* voice breaking; **2** *(BOT)* seedling; ♦ *adj (Vd:* **mudo***)*.

mudança *f* change; move; **2** *(AUTO)* gear.

mudar *vt* to change; **~ de roupa/de assunto/de emprego** to change clothes/subject/job; **2** *(de casa, de escritório)* move, transfer; ♦ *vi (modificar)* to change ♦ **~-se (de)** *vr (casa, lugar)* to move; **2** *(modificar-se)* to change.

mudez *f* dumbness, muteness; **2** silence.

mudo,-a *m,f* dumb person, mute; ♦ *adj* dumb; **2** silent; **3** *(fig) (incapaz de falar)* speechless; **~ de susto**, dumb with fright; **~ de surpresa** dumb-struck, dumbfounded; **4** *(TEL)* dead; **5** *(CIN, filme)* silent; **6** *(FON) (consoante)* silent.

muge/mugem *m* *(ZOOL) (peixe)* grey mullet.

mugido *m* *(voz de vaca)* moo; **2** *(de touro)* bellow.

mugir *vt* to moo; IDIOM **sem tugir nem ~** without a whimper.

muito,-a *m* great deal; ♦ *adj* a lot of; *(sg)* much, *(pl)* many; **muitas vezes** often; ♦ **muito** *adv* a lot; very; much; too much; *(de tempo)* long; **há ~ tempo** a long time ago; **em ~** a great deal; **~ melhor** a lot/much/far better; *(frequente)* **você vem aqui ~?** do you come here often?; ♦ *conj* **por ~ que** however much; **~ embora** although; ♦ *pron* a lot; much; many; **mais que ~** more than enough; IDIOM **falar ~ sem dizer nada** to talk a lot of hot air; **ter ~ de seu** be rich.

mula *f* *(ZOOL)* mule; **2** *(fig) (teimoso)* stubborn person.

mulato,-a *m,f adj* mulatto.

muleta *f* crutch; **2** *(fig)* support.

mulher *f* woman; **~-a-dias** cleaning lady; **~-feita** *f* grown woman; **foi ~ aos 11 anos** her periods started when she was 11 years old; **2** *(esposa)* wife; **3** *(amante)* lady-love; **~ da má vida** prostitute; **~-objecto** sex object; **~ de mau porte** tart; **4** *(vivendo juntos)* companheira, parceira.

mulheraça *f* *(mulher)* tall, stout and attractive.

mulherengo *m* womanizer; ladies' man; ♦ *adj* womanizing.

mulherio *m* a lot of women.

mulo *m* *(ZOOL) (macho)* mule.

multa *f* fine; **levar uma ~** to get fined.

multar *vt* to fine.

multicolor *adj inv* multicoloured *(UK)*; multicolor *(US)*.

multidão *f* crowd; **uma ~ de** lots of.

multifacetado,-a *adj* multifaceted.

multilateral *adj inv* multilateral.

multiplicação *f* *(MAT)* multiplication; **2** *(aumento)* increase, growth.

multiplicador *m* multiplier.

multiplicar *vt* *(MAT)* to multiply; ♦ **~-se** *vr* to propagate; **2** more and more; **ele multiplica-se em atenções** he has become more and more considerate.

multíplice *adj inv* complex, multiple; **2** *(dados)* manifold.

múltiplo,-a *m* multiple; ♦ *adj* multiple.

multiprocessamento *m* *(COMP)* multiprocessing.

multiusos *adj inv* multi-purpose; **pavilhão ~** multi-purpose pavillion.

mulungo *m* *(MOÇ)* white man; **2** *(form of address)* Senhor.

múmia *f* *(cadáver humano)* mummy.

mumificar *vt* to mummify.

mundano,-a *adj* worldly; mundane.

mundial *m* world championship; **o ~ de futebol** the World Cup; ♦ *adj inv* worldwide.

mundo *m* world; **todo o ~** everybody; **um ~ de** lots of, a great many; **Terceiro M~** *(dated)* Third World; **os confins do ~** the ends of the earth; ♦ *adv* **enquanto o ~ for ~** as long as the world goes on; IDIOM **correr ~** to travel the world; **nas bocas do ~** be the subject of gossip; **o ~ às avessas** topsy-turvy world; **ele prometeu-lhe ~s e fundos** he promised her the earth and the moon.

mungir *vt* *(extrair)* to milk *(vaca, cabra)*.

munição *f* ammunition; shot; **2** *(MIL)* munitions *pl*, supplies *pl*.

municipal *adj inv* municipal; of local council; **imposto ~** council tax.

municipalidade *f* municipality; city council.

municipality *f* municipality, local authority.

munícipe *f* *(cidadão)* citizen; **2** *(citadino)* townsman/woman, *(pl)* townsfolk.

município *m* municipality; **2** *(divisão administrativa)* borough; **3** *(câmara)* city/borough council.

munificência *f* generosity, munificence.

Munique *npr* Munich.

munir *vt*: **~ de** to provide with, supply with; ♦ **~-se de (algo)** *vr* to equip o.s. with sth; to arm o.s. with.

mural *m* *(arte)* mural.

muralha *f* rampart; **2** *(paredão)* wall; **3** wall; **a Grande M~ da China** the Great Wall of China.

murchar *vt* *(BOT)* to wither, *(folhas, flores)* to droop; **2** *(fig) (sentiment)* to fade, wane, diminish; ♦ *vi (BOT)* to wither, wilt.

murcho,-a *adj* withered; wilted, droopy; **2** *(fig)* faded; **um ar ~** *(pessoa)* downcast/droopy look; **flores ~as** dead flowers; **3** *(coisa)* soft, droopy, inert.

murmuração *f* muttering.

murmurar *vi* to murmur; **2** *(ao ouvido)* to whisper; **3** to mutter.

murmurejar *m* *(de seda, folhas)* rustling; ♦ *vi* to murmur.

murmurinho *m* *(vozes)* murmuring; **2** *(boato)* rumour, gossip.

murmúrio *m* murmur, hum, whisper, undertone; **2** *(de água)* swishing; *(do lago)* rippling; **3** *(seda, folhas)* rustling.

muro *m* (outside) wall, garden wall; **o M~ das Lamentações** the Wailing Wall.

murro *m* punch, sock; **dar ~s** to punch sb.

murta *f (BOT)* myrtle.

musa *f* muse.

musculado,-a *adj* vigorous, sturdy.

músculo *m* muscle.

musculoso,-a *adj* muscular.

museológico,-a *m,f* museologist; ♦ *adj* museological.

museu *m* museum; IDIOM **ser uma peça de ~** to be old-fashioned.

musgo *m* moss.

musgoso,-a *adj* mossy.

música *f* music; **2** *(fig) (treta, lamúria)* fuss, noise, talk.

musicado,-a *adj* set to music, musical arrangement.

musical *m, adj inv* musical.

músico,-a *m,f* musician; ♦ *adj* musical.

musicólogo,-a *m,f* musicologist.

musse *f (para o cabelo)* mousse; **2** *(CULIN)* mousse.

musselina *f (pano)* muslim (cloth).

mutação *f* change, alteration; **2** *(BIO)* mutation.

mutante *adj inv (BIO)* mutant.

mutável *adj inv* variable, changeable, inconstant.

mutilado,-a *adj* maimed, disabled.

mutilar *vt* to mutilate, maim; **2** *(estátua)* to destroy in part.

mutismo *m* muteness; **2** dumbness.

mutualidade *f* reciprocity, mutuality; **vantagens da ~** mutual advantages.

mutualismo *m (sistema social de previdência)* mutualism; **2** *(BIOL, SOCIAL)* mutualism, interdependence.

mutuamente *adv* mutually, reciprocally.

mutuante lender; ♦ *adj inv* lending.

mutuário,-a *m,f (JUR)* borrower.

mútuo,-a *m (JUR, FIN) (contrato)* loan, exchange.

n

N, n *m (letra)* N, n.
na (= em + a) in the, on the, at the; **ela está ~ praia** she is on the beach.
nababo *m (antigo título indiano dos altos dignatários da corte do império Mogul)* Nabob; **2** *(presentemente na Índia e Paquistão)* big landowners; tycoon, nabob.
nabal *m* turnip field; **2** many turnips.
nabiça *f (BOT) (CULIN)* tender foliage of turnip-plant; turnip-top.
nabo *m (BOT)* turnip; **2** *(BR) (vulg)* penis, dick; IDIOM **ser (um) ~** to be a halfwit; **tirar ~s da púcara (de alguém)** to try to get/winkle information out of (sb); to be nosy *(fam)*; **comprar ~s em saco** to buy a pig in a poke.
nação *f* nation, country; **Nações Unidas** *fpl* United Nations.
nácar *m* mother-of-pearl; **2** *(cor, brilho semelhante)* pearly, rosy.
nacional *adj inv* national.
nacionalidade *f* nationality.
nacionalismo *m* nationalism, patriotismo.
nacionalista *m,f* nationalist; ♦ *adj inv* nationalistic, nationalist.
nacionalização *f* nationalization.
nacionalizar *vt* to nationalize.
naco *m (pedaço)* piece, slice, chunk; **um ~ de pão** a chunk of bread.
nada *m* **o ~** nothingness, the void; **2** *(ninharia)* **um ~** a trifle; **3** *(pej) (pessoa)* non-entity, nobody; ♦ *pron indef* nothing; **não dizer ~** to say nothing, not to say anything; **~ mau** not bad; **~ de novo** nothing new; **~ de sustos** let's not be frightened; **de ~** *(resposta a obrigado)* not at all!, it's O.K.!; **2** little, slight; **foi uma coisa de ~** it was (just) a little thing; ♦ *adv* **em ~** not at all, in no way; **antes de mais ~** first of all; **daqui a ~** in a minute; **por tudo e por ~** for the slightest thing; **~ mais, ~ menos** *(exatamente)* no less than; IDIOM **não faltava mais ~!** that's all we need; **não dar por ~** not to notice a thing; **a polícia não deu por ~** the police didn't notice anything; **não presta para ~** it's good for nothing.

In Portuguese you use double negatives in verbal forms: **não tenho nada**.

nadador,-ora *m,f* swimmer; **~-salvador** lifeguard; ♦ *adj* swimming.
nadar *vi* to swim; **sabe ~?** can you swim?; **~ em dinheiro** *(fig)* to be rolling in money.

nádegas *(ANAT)* buttock; **2** *(ZOOL)* haunch; **~s** *fpl* buttocks.
nadinha *f (dim. de nada)* m *(fam)* a bit, a little; **nem mais um ~** not even a little bit; **2 daqui a um ~** *(momento)* in a little while.
nado² *m (de nadar)* swim, swimming; **~ de peito** breaststroke; **~ de costas** backstroke; ♦ **a ~** *adv* swimming; **atravessar a ~** to swim across.
nado,-a¹ *adj (nascido, nato)* born; **~ e criado em Maputo** born and brought up in Maputo.
nado,-a morto,-a *m, adj* stillborn.
nafta *f (QUÍM)* naphtha.
naftalina *f* naphthalene; **bolas de ~** moth balls.
naipe *m (cartas)* suit; order.
nalgum,-a (= em + algum) *(Vd: algum,-a)*.
namoradeiro,-a *m,f* flirt; ♦ *adj* flirtatious.
namorado,-a *m,f* boyfriend, girlfriend, living-in partner; sweetheart.
namorar *vt* to be going out with (sb); to date (sb); *(arc) (cortejar)* to court (sb); **2** *(fig) (cobiçar)* to covert (sth); to have one's eye on (sth); ♦ *vi* to have a boyfriend/girlfriend; ♦ **~-se** *vr* **eles namoram-se há muito tempo** they have been going out (together) for ages.
namoricar (=**namosricar**) *vt* to flirt with.
namorico *m* a passing courtship, flirt.
namoro *m* courtship; relationship; **~ de criança** calf love.
nana *f (bebé)* lullaby to put to sleep.
nanismo *m (MED)* dwarfism; **2** *(anomalia de crescimento)* stunted growth; **~ dentário** microdontism.
nanocéfalo,-a *adj (MED)* microcephalic; microcephalus.
Nanquim *npr* Nanking/Nanjing; **2 nanquim** *m (cor, tecido)* nankeen; **3** *(tinta da China)* Indian ink.
não *m (refusal)* no; **ele deu-me um ~** he gave me a refusal; ♦ *adv* not; no; **~ sei** I don't know; **~ muito** not much; **~ só... mas também** not only but also; **agora ~** not now; **~ é?** isn't it?; **ela fala francês, ~ fala?** she speaks French, doesn't she?; **~ faz mal** never mind, it doesn't matter; **~ raro** often; **pelo sim, pelo ~** just in case; **dia sim, dia ~** every other day; **dizer que ~** to deny; **2** to refuse; **~ tem de quê** *(resposta formal a 'obrigado')* not at all, you are welcome; ♦ *conj* **a ~ ser que** unless; ♦ *exc* **como ~?** why not?, how so?; **pois ~!** why not!, of course!
não- *pref* non-; **~-agressão** non-aggression.
não-alinhado,-a *adj* non-aligned.
não-conformista *adj inv* non-conformist.
não-cumprimento *m (JUR)* nonfeasance, non-compliance.
não-me-esqueças *m (BOT)* forget-me-not, myosotis.
não-me-toques *m,f* a touch-me-not person, a haughty/aloof person.
não-pagamento *m (JUR)* non-payment.
não-sei-quê *m (inexplicável)* a vague something; **eu senti um ~** I felt something/I felt I don't know what; **2** *(BR)* firewater.
não-ser *m (FIL)* non-being.
napa *f (pele de carneiro macia)* nappa; nappa leather.

naperão *m* crochet table mat.
napoleónico,-a *adj (relativo a Napoleão)* Napoleonic.
Nápoles *npr* Naples.
napolitano,-a *adj* Neapolitan.
naquele, naquela (= **em** + **aquele/aquela**) in/on that.
naquilo (= **em** + **aquilo**) in/on that.
narceja *f (ave pernalta)* snipe.
narcisismo *m* narcissism.
narcisista *m,f* narcissist; ♦ *adj inv* narcissistic.
narciso *m (BOT)* narcissus.
narciso-amarelo *m (BOT)* daffodil.
narcótico,-a *adj* narcotic.
narcotráfico *m* drug traffic.
nardo *m (BOT) (erva aromática)* spikenard, nard.
narigão *m (pej)* large bulbous nose.
narigudo,-a *adj (fam)* big-nosed.
narigueta *f (pej)* big nose, conk(UK), schnozzle (US).
narina *f (ANAT)* nostril.
nariz *m (ANAT)* nose; IDIOM **meter o ~ em** to poke one's nose into; **torcer o ~ para** to turn one's nose up at; **dar com o ~ na porta** to go to sb's house and the person is not in; **ser dono do seu ~** to be of one mind, obstinate; **não ver um palmo à frente do ~** *(col)* to be thick, stupid.
narração *f* narration, story; **2** *(relato)* account.
narrador,-ora *m,f* narrator, storyteller.
narrar *vt* to narrate, recount.
narrativo,-a *f* narrative, story; ♦ *adj* narrative.
narval *m (ZOOL)* narwhal, the Arctic dolphin with tusk/long tooth.
nas (= **em** + **as**) in the *(Vd:* **em***)*.
nasal *adj inv* nasal.
nasalado,-a *adj (vogal, voz)* nasalized.
nasalização *f* nasalization.
nascença *f* birth; **de ~** from birth; **2** *(origin)* beginning; **3** *(pop) (tumor)* growth.
nascente *f (fonte)* spring; **2** *(GEOL)* source; **3** *m* East; ♦ *adj inv (planta, organização)* sprouting, budding.
nascer *m* **o ~ do dia** daybreak; **o ~ do sol** sunrise; ♦ *vi* to be born; **2** *(planta)* to sprout; **3** *(sol)* to rise; *(dia)* to dawn; **4** *(ter origem em)* to come into being; **5** *(cabelo)* to grow; **6** *(dente)* to come through.
nascido,-a *(pp de* **nascer***) adj* born.
nascimento *m* birth; **2** *(fig)* origin; descent.
nascituro,-a *adj (ser)* unborn.
nastro *m*: **fita de ~** *(fita estreita de algodão)* tape.
nata *f (CULIN)* cream; the fat part/skin of the milk; **2** *(fig)* the pick of the bunch; **pastéis de ~** Portuguese cream tarts.
natação *f* swimming.
natal *m* Christmas; **Feliz N~** Merry Christmas; ♦ *(pl:* **-tais***) adj* natal; native; **cidade ~** home town; **terra ~** birthplace.
natalício *m* birthday; ♦ *adj* **aniversário ~** birthday.
natalidade *f* **taxa/índice** *f* **de ~** birth rate.
natimorto,-a *m,f (BR) (bebé)* stillborn baby.
natividade *f* nativity.
nativo,-a *m,f* native; ♦ *adj* native; **2** innate, inborn.
nato,-a *adj* born; **2** *(congénuo)* **um cantor ~** a born singer.

natural *m,f* natural (de); **ele é ~ do Porto** he is from Oporto; **os ~ais de Setúbal** the people from Setubal; ♦ *adj inv* natural; **2** *(gesto, riso)* spontaneous, natural; **água ~** spring water; **3** *(seda)* pure; **4** *(filho,-a)* natural; **é ~ que ele venha** he is likely to/is bound to come; **ao ~** *adv (bebida)* without ice, at room temperature.
naturalidade *f* naturalness, lack of affectation; **2** *(origem)* origin.
naturalismo *m* naturalism.
naturalista *m,f* naturalist.
naturalização *f* naturalization.
naturalizar-se *vr* to become naturalized.
naturalmente *adv (certamente)* naturally, of course.
natureza *f* nature; **2** kind, type; **~ morta** still life; **por ~** by nature.
nau *f* vessel, ship.
naufragar *vi* to be shipwrecked; **2** *(fig)* to fail.
naufrágio *m* shipwreck; **2** *(fig)* failure.
náufrago,-a *m,f* castaway, ship-wrecked survivor.
náusea *f* nausea; **sentir ~s** *(agoniado)* to feel sick.
nauseabundo,-a, nauseante *adj (cheiro)* nauseating, sickening; **2** *(aspecto)* disgusting.
náutico,-a *f* seamanship; ♦ *adj* nautical.
naval *adj inv (NÁUT)* naval; **construção ~** shipbuilding.
navalha *f* knife; **2** *(de barba)* razor; **3** pocket knife; **~ de ponta e mola** flick knife.
navalhada *f* stabbing, knifing; **ele deu-lhe uma ~** he stabbed him with a knife, a blade.
nave *f (ARQ)* nave, aisle; **2** ship; **~ espacial** spaceship.
navegabilidade *f* seaworthiness; navigability.
navegação *f* navigation, sailing; voyage; **~ aérea** air traffic; **~ costeira** coastal shipping; **agência de ~** shipping agency.
navegador *m* navigator; **2** *(COMP)* surfer.
navegante *m,f* marine, sailor, navigator.
navegar *vt* to pilot, navigate; ♦ *vi* to sail, fly; **~ na internet** *(COMP)* to surf the Net; IDIOM **~ nas mesmas águas** to be of the same mind.
navegável *adj inv* navigable.
navio *m* ship; **~ à vela** sailing boat; **~ de carga** freighter, cargo ship; **~-cisterna** tanker; **~-escola** training ship; **~ de guerra** warship; **~ de pesca** fishing vessel/boat; **~ petroleiro** oil tanker; **~ porta-aviões** aircraft-carrier; IDIOM **ficar a ver ~s** to be left high and dry.
nazi, (EP) **nazista** (BR) *m,f adj inv* Nazi.
neblina *f* fog, mist; haze.
nebuloso,-a *adj* foggy, misty; cloudy; **2** *(fig)* vague; **3** *f (ASTRO)* nebula.
necessariamente *adv (sem falta)* must; necessarily; **2** *(provavelmente)* be bound to.
necessário *m* **o ~** necessary; **fiz o ~** I did what was necessary; ♦ **necessário,-a** *adj* necessary, needful; **é ~ que estudes muito** you must study hard.
necessidade *f* need, necessity; **2** poverty, privation; **ter ~ de** to have need of.
necessitado,-a *adj* needy, poor.
necessitar *vt* to need, require; ♦ *vi* to be in need of.
necrologia *f* obituary column.
necrológio *m* obituary.

necromância *f* necromancy.

necrópole *f (ARC)* necropolis; **2** *(arc)* cemetery.

necrotério *m* mortuary, morgue.

néctar *m* nectar.

nectarine *f (fruit)* nectarine.

nédio,-a *adj (animais)* plump and sleek; well-fed.

neerlandês,-esa *m,f adj (pessoa, lingua)* Dutch.

Neerlândia *npr* a ~ the Netherlands *pl*.

nefando,-a *adj (perverso) (crime, act)* abominable, heinous, nefarious; **2** *(malvado)* wicked.

nefasto,-a *adj (nocivo)* harmful; **2** *(agourento)* ominous; tragic; **consequências** ~**as** tragic consequences.

negaça *f* lure, bait, decoy.

negacear *vt* to entice; to decoy.

negação *f* negation; refusal, denial.

negar *vt* to refuse; to deny; ♦ *vi* to say no, refuse; ♦ ~**-se** *vr* to refuse (**a** to).

negativa *f* refusal; **2** *(gram)* negative.

negativo *m (TEC, FOTO)* negative; ♦ **negativo,-a** *adj* negative.

negável *adj inv* deniable.

negligência *f* negligence, carelessness.

negligenciar *vt* to neglect.

negligente *adj inv* negligent, careless.

negociação *f* negotiation; transaction.

negociador,-ora *m,f* negotiator; ♦ *adj* negotiating.

negociante *m,f* businessman/woman; merchant.

negociar *vt/vi* to negotiate; transact; deal; ♦ *vi* to deal in, do business with.

negociável *adj inv* negotiable.

negócio *m (COM)* business; **2** deal, transaction; **3** *(fam) (questão, problema)* matter, business; *(BR) (fam)* thing; **homem/mulher de** ~**s** businessman/woman; **fechar o** ~ to close the deal.

negócios *mpl* affaires; ~ **de compadres** family affaires; ~ **escuros** underhand/shady deals; **Ministério dos N~ Estrangeiros** Foreign Office; **em** ~**s** on business; IDIOM **um** ~ **da China** a profitable deal, a bargain; **amigos amigos,** ~**s à parte** don't mix business with pleasure.

negra *f (mulher, raça)* black woman; **2 nódoa** ~ bruise.

negrito *m (TYPO)* bold type, boldface.

negro,-a *m,f (pessoa, cor)* black person; ♦ *adj* black, dark; **mercado** ~ black market; **2** *(fig) (sombrio)* gloomy; **um futuro** ~ a gloomy future.

negróide *adj inv (raça)* Negroid.

negrume *m* darkness, blackness; **2** *(trevas)* darkness; **3** *(tristeza)* sadness, gloom.

negrura *f* blackness.

nela, nele (= **em + ela, em + ele**) *(Vd: em)*: **eu confio nele** I trust (in) him.

nem *conj* **nem... nem** neither... nor, either... or, not... either; **não vi esse filme** ~ **quero vê-lo** I didn't see that film nor do I want to see it; ~ **ele** ~ **a irmã dele são simpáticos** neither he nor his sister are nice; **sem nome** ~ **fortuna** without name or fortune; **2** *(negação enfática)* not even; ~ **quero saber** I don't even want to know; ~ **sempre** not always; ~ **um só** not a single one; ~ **que** not even if; **que** ~ like; **ela dançou que**

~ **uma bailarina** she dances like a dancer; ♦ *adv* ~ **sequer** not even; **ela** ~ **sequer olhou para mim** she didn't even give me a glance; ~ **por isso** not really, not specially; **sem mais** ~ **menos** just like that, without as much as by your leave; ♦ *exc* ~ **imaginas!** you have no idea! you can't (even) imagine!; ~ **pio!** not a word!; IDIOM ~ **oito,** ~ **oitenta/** ~ **tanto ao mar,** ~ **tanto à terra** neither one extreme nor the other.

nené *(BR: -ê)* *m* baby.

nenhum,-a *adj* no, not any; **não tens** ~ **dinheiro?** don't you have any money?; ♦ *pron* none, not one; **ele não está em** ~ **lado (em lado** ~**)** he is nowhere; ~ **a das cinco irmãs é bonita** none of the five sisters is pretty; ♦ *adv* **de modo** ~ in any way; not at all.

nenhures *adv (em nenhum lugar)* nowhere.

nénia *(BR: -ê-)* *m* elegy, lament for the dead; dirge.

nenúfar *m* water lily.

neoclássico,-a *adj* neoclassic, neoclassical.

neófito,-a neophyte, convert.

neogótico *m (ART)* Neo Gothic; ♦ **neogótico,-a** *adj* Neo Gothic.

Neolítico *m* Neolithic Age.

neolítico,-a *adj* Neolithic.

neologismo *m* neologism.

néon *m (QUÍM)* neon; **2** *(luzes)* neon lights.

neoplasia *f (MED)* neoplasm.

neoplásico,-a *adj (tumor, célula)* neoplástico.

neozelandês,-desa *m,f adj* New Zealander.

Nepal *npr* **o** ~ Nepal.

nepalês,-esa *m,f* Nepalese.

nepotismo *m* nepotism.

Neptune, Netúnio *npr (ASTRON)* Neptune.

neptúnio, netúnio *m (EWÍM)* neptunium.

nervo *m (ANAT)* nerve; ~ **ciático**; sciatic nerve; **2** *(fig)* energy, strength; **3** *(tendão, na carne)* gristle, sinew; **4** *(fig) (força principal, motor)* hub, driving force; IDIOM **estar uma pilha de** ~**s** to be a bag of nerves.

nervosismo *m* nervousness; irritability.

nervoso,-a *adj* nervous; **esgotamento** ~ nervous breakdown.

néscio,-a *adj* ignorant; foolish; **2** *(falta de educação)* ignoramus, *(fam)*.

nesga *f* scrap of cloth; **2** little bit; **3** *(fenda)* crack.

nêspera *f (fruto)* loquat.

nespereira *f (BOT)* loquat tree.

nessa(s) (= **em + essa(s)**) *f, fpl* in that (those); IDIOM **não caio nessa** I won't fall for that.

nesse(s) (= **em + esse(s)**) *m, mpl* in that (those); **não mexo nesses assuntos** I don't touch such matters.

nesta(s) (= **em + esta(s)**) *f, fpl* in this (these); **meti-me nesta brincadeira** I am involved/stuck in this mess.

neste(s) (= **em + este(s)**) *m, mpl* in this (these); **nasci nestes campos** I was born in these fields.

neto,-a *m,f* grandson, daughter.

netos *mpl* grandchildren.

neuralgia *f (MED)* neuralgia.

neurastenia *f (PSIC)* neurasthenia; **2** *(fam)* depression, irritability.

neurasténico,-a *adj* neurasthenic; **2** *(fam)* irritable person.

neurocirurgião, neurociurgiã *m,f* neurosurgeon.

neurose *f* neurosis.

neuroléptico,-a *adj (FARM) (produto)* neuroleptic.

neurónio *m* neuron; nerve cell.

neurose *f* neurosis; **2** anxiety.

neurótico,-a *adj* neurotic.

neutral *adj inv* impartial, neutral.

neutralidade *f* neutrality.

neutralizar *vt* to neutralize; to counteract.

neutrão *(BR: nêutron) m* neutron.

neutro,-a *m (gram)* neuter; ♦ *adj* neutral.

nevada *f* **nevão** *m* snowfall; **2** *(acumulada)* snowdrift.

nevar *vi* to snow.

nevasca *f* snowstorm; blizzard.

neve *f* snow; **branco de ~** snowwhite; **Branca-de-~** *f (estória da)* Snowhite.

neviscar *vi* to snow lightly.

névoa *f* fog, mist.

nevoeiro *m* thick fog; **um dia de ~** a foggy day.

nevrálgico,-a *adj* neuralgic.

nexo *m* connection, link; **sem ~** disconnected, incoherent.

nhoque *m (CULIN)* gnocchi.

Niágara *m* Niagara; **as cataratas do ~** the Niagara Falls.

Nicarágua *npr* **a ~** Nicaragua.

nicaraguense *adj* Nicaraguan.

nicho *m (vão na parede)* niche; recess; **2** *(recanto)* corner, nook; **novos vinhos procuram um ~ no mercado** *(COM)* new wines are looking for a niche in the market.

Nicósia *npr* Nicosea.

nicotina *f* nicotine.

nidificar *vi* to nest, to make a nest.

Nigéria *npr* **a ~** Nigeria.

nigeriano,-a *adj* Nigerian.

nimbado,-a *adj (céu, astro)* wrapped, swathed; **2** *(fig) (pessoa)* with a halo; with an aura.

nimbo *m (METEOR)* nimbus; **2** *(fig)* halo; rain cloud.

nímio,-a *adj* excessive.

ninar *vt (BR) (bebé)* to lull to sleep.

ninfa *f* nymph; **2** *(ANAT)* nympha; **3** *(ZOOL)* damselfly.

ninfomania *f* nymphomania.

ninguém *pron* nobody, no one; **não vi ~** I saw no one, I didn't see anybody; **~ mais** nobody else.

ninhada *f (conjunto de aves nascidas)* brood; **2** *(cachorros, gatos, coelhos)* litter; **3** *(fam) (filharada)* brood.

ninharia *f (coisa insignificante)* trifle; triviality.

ninho *m* nest; **2** *(de lobos)* lair; **3** *(de víboras)* pit; **4** *(fam)* home; **~ de ladrões** den of thieves; *(fig)* **~ de ratos** tangle, mess; **o cabelo dela é um ~** her hair is a tangled mess; IDIOM **fazer o ~ atrás da orelha** to pull the wool over sb's eyes.

nipónico,-a *adj* Nipponese, Japanese.

níquel *m* nickel.

niquelar *vt (TEC)* to nickel-plate.

niquento,-a *m,f (pessoa difícil de satisfazer)* fusspot; **2** *(que critica)* nit-picker; ♦ *adj* fussy; **2** *(que se ocupa de ninharias)* petty; **3** *(rabugento)* peevish.

niquice *f* impertinence; fuss; **2** *(bagatela, insignificância)* trifle.

nirvana *m inv* nirvana.

nissei *(BR) m,f* child of Japanese parents born in Brazil.

nisso (= **em** + **isso**) in/on that; **já te meteste ~?** have you got involved in that?

nisto (= **em** + **isto**) in/on this; **~, ele apareceu** suddenly, he appeared.

nitidez *f* clarity; brightness; sharp.

nítido,-a *adj* bright; clear.

nitrato *m* nitrate.

nitrogénio *(BR: -gê-) m* nitrogen.

nível *m (ger)* level; **~ de bolha** spirit level; **curvas de ~** *(GEOG)* contour lines; **~ de vida** *(ECON)* standard of living; **2** *(LÍNG)* register; **3** *(categoria)* class; ♦ *prep* **ao ~ de** up to the level of.

nivelação *f* **nivelamento** *m* levelling.

nivelar *vt (aplainar) (terreno)* to level out; **2** *(medir)* to measure with a spirit level; **3** *(aplanar, reconciliar)* to even out, level out; ♦ **~-se** *vr* to put o.s. on the same level; **~-se com/a** *(alguém)* to measure up to sb.

no (= **em** + **o**) in/on the; **estou no jardim** I am in the garden.

nó *m* knot; **~ corredio** slipknot; **2** *(pomo-de-adão)* Adam's apple; **~s dos dedos** knuckles; **~ rodoviário/ferroviário** road/rail junction; **3** *(fig) (dificuldade)* crux; **4** *(fig, fam) (casamento)* knot; **5** *(NÁUT)* knot; **6** *(ASTRON, GEOM, FÍS)* node; IDIOM **ter um ~ na garganta** have a lump in the throat; **não dar ponto sem ~** do nothing without an ulterior motive.

nobiliário *m* book of the peerage; ♦ **nobiliário,-a** *adj* nobiliary.

nobilíssimo,-a *(superl de nobre) adj* very noble.

nobilitar *vt* to ennoble; ♦ **~-se** *vr* to keep dignity.

nobre *m adj* noble.

nobreza *f* nobility.

noção *f* notion; **~ vaga** inkling.

nocivo,-a *adj* harmful.

noctâmbulo,-a, notâmbulo,-a *m,f* sleepwalker.

noctívago,-a, notívago,-a *m,f (pessoa)* night owl; **2** *(animal)* nocturnal.

nocturno,-a, noturno,-a *adj* nocturnal, nightly.

nódoa *f* spot; stain; **~ negra** bruise; **2** *(reputação, nome)* stain, taint.

nódolo *m (ANAT)* nodule; **2** *(BOT) (nas raízes das plantas)* nodus; **3** *(MED)* lump, node, nodul.

nodoso,-a *adj (que tem nós)* knotty; knotted.

nogueira *f* walnut tree; walnut.

noitada *f* whole night; **2** night out.

noite *f* night; **à/de ~** at night; **~ adentro** into the night; **~ passada** last night; **esta ~** tonight; **ontem à ~** last night; **~ em branco** sleepless night; **~ descansada** a good night's sleep; **camisa/(BR) camisola de ~** nightdress; **~ de Natal** Christmas eve; **da ~ para o dia** from one day to the next; ♦ *exc* **boa ~!** good evening! good night!; ♦ *adv* **de ~** at night; **alta ~** late at night, in the small hours of the morning; IDIOM **passar a ~ em claro** to have a sleepless night, up all night; **na/pela calada da** ~ in the dead of the night.

noitinha *f:* **à** ~ in the evening, at dusk.

noivado *m* engagement.

noivo,-a *m,f* fiancé, fiancée; **2** bridegroom, bride.

noivos *mpl* engaged couple; **2** newlyweds.

nojento,-a *m,f* disgusting person; ♦ *adj* filthy, despicable.

nojo *m* nausea; **2** loathing; disgust; **3** *(luto)* mourning.

no-la (= **nos** + **a**) **no-lo** (= **nos** + **o**) it to us; **no-las** (= **nos** + **as**), **no-los** (= **nos** + **os**) them to us; **eles já vos deram o dinheiro? eles dão-no-lo amanhã** have they given the money to you *(pl)*? they will give it to us tomorrow.

nómada *(BR:* -ô-*) m,f* nomad; ♦ *adj* nomadic; **2** *(fig)* wandering.

nome *m* name; fame; **2** *(LÍNG)* noun; ~ **de ba(p)-tismo** Christian name, first name; **em** ~ **de** in the name of; on behalf of; ~ **de guerra** assumed name; **chamar** ~**s a alguém** *(palavras feias, alcunhas)* to call someone names/nicknames; ~ **de guerra** assumed name.

nomeação *f* nomination; appointment.

nomeada *f* fame.

nomeadamente *adv* namely.

nomeado,-a *adj* appointed.

nomear *vt* to nominate; to appoint; to name.

nomenclatura *f* nomenclature.

nona *f (fruit)* custard apple.

nonagenário,-a *adj* nonagenarian.

nonagésimo,-a *adj* ninetieth.

non-alcoólico,-a *m,f* teetotaller; ♦ *adj (bebida, etc)* soft drink, non-alcoholic.

nongentésimo,-a *adj* nine hundredth.

nónio *m (MAT, FÍS)* vernier.

nono,-a *num, adj* ninth; **um** ~ *(fraction)* one ninth.

nora[1] *f* daughter-in-law.

nora[2] *f (AGR) (poço)* water wheel (pulled by a donkey or cow).

nordeste *m (GEOG)* northeast; **o N**~ North-east region of Brazil.

nordestino,-a *(BR) m,f* northeasterner; ♦ *adj (from Nordeste)* northeastern.

nórdico,-a *adj* Nordic; ♦ **os N**~**s** *npr mpl* the Nordic race, the Nordic people.

norma *f* standard, norm; rule; **como** ~ as a rule.

normal *adj inv* normal; natural, usual.

normalidade *f* normality.

normalizar-se *vr* to return to normal; get into a routine.

normalmente *adv* normally, habitually, usually.

normativo *m* law, rule.

normativo,-a *adj* standard.

noroeste *m (GEOG)* northwest; ♦ *adj inv* north-west.

norte *m* north; **2** *(fig)* bearing, direction; **ao** ~ **de** to the north of; ♦ *adj inv* northern, north.

norte-americano,-a *adj* North American.

nortenho,-a *adj* north-country person, from the North (of Portugal).

Noruega *npr* **a** ~ Norway.

norueguês,-esa *adj* Norwegian.

nos *prep* **em** + **os** in/on/at the; ♦ *pron pess objecto* us, to/from us, ourselves; **ele fez-nos o jantar** he made dinner for us *(BR:* **nos fez o jantar***).*

nós *pron pess objecto* we; **a/para** ~ to/for us; **venha a nós o vosso reino** *(REL)* thy kingdom come.

nosso,-a *m,f* **N**~**a Senhora** *f* Our Lady; **os** ~**s** *mpl* our family; ♦ *adj* our; ♦ *pron* ours; **um amigo** ~ a friend of ours; ♦ **nossa!** *(BR)* goodness!

nostalgia *f* nostalgia.

nota *f* note; **um bloco de** ~ pad book; **2** *(resultado de exame)* mark; **3** *(FIN) (dinheiro)* bill, bank-note; ~**s contrafeitas,** counterfeit notes; *(anotar)* **tomar** ~ take note, note down; ~ **de rodapé** footnote; ~ **promissória** promissory note IOU; **4** **digno de** ~ noteworthy; **5** *(MÚS)* note; **6** *(importancia)* **pessoas de** ~ people of repute.

notabilidade *f* notability; remarkable person.

notabilizar *vt* to make famous; ♦ ~**-se (em/por)** *vr* to become famous (for).

notar *vt* to notice, note; **é preciso** ~ **que** it must be noted that; **fazer** ~ to call attention to; ♦ ~**-se** *vr* to be obvious.

notarial *adj inv* notarial.

notário,-a *m,f* notary; **2** *(repartição de registos, declarações)* notary, Commissioner for Oaths.

notável *adj inv* notable, remarkable.

notícia *f* (the) news; ~**s** *fpl* news *sg;* **2** *(texto informativo)* news item; **tive uma má** ~ I had bad news, **pedir** ~**s de** to enquire about s.o./sth; **ter** ~**s de** to hear from.

noticiar *vt* to announce, report, communicate, publish.

noticiário *m (jornal)* news section, (the) news; **2** *(RÁDIO, TV)* bulletin; *(CIN)* newsreel; ~ **de última hora** latest news, newsflash.

noticioso,-a *adj (referente a notícias)* news.

notificação *f* notification; **2** *(JUR)* instruction.

notificar *vt* ~ **algo a alguém** to notify sb of/about sth; **2** *(JUR)* instruct.

notívago,-a *(Vd:* **noctívago***).*

notoriedade *f* notoriety; publicity; **2** fame.

Not in the sense of bad notoriety, which is: **má fama**.

notório,-a *adj (pessoa)* well-known; **2** evident, blatant; **é público e** ~ **que...** it's public knowledge and clear that.

Not 'notorious' in the sense of bad reputation, which is **conhecido; de má fama**.

noturno,-a *(Vd:* **no(c)turno,-a***).*

noutro,-a (= **em** + **outro,-a**).

nova *(f de* **novo***, Vd:* **novo***) f* news item; ~**s** *fpl* news *sg;* **que** ~**s trazes?** (what's the news) what news do you bring?; **boas** ~**s!** good news!*;* IDIOM **nem** ~**s nem mandatórias** no news at all; **fazer-se de** ~**s** to feign ignorance.

Nova Escócia *npr* **a** ~ Nova Scotia.

Nova Gales *npr* **a** ~ New South Wales.

Nova Guiné *npr* **a** ~ New Guinea.

novaguinense *adj inv* of/from New Guinea, New Guinean.

nova-iorquino,-a *adj* of/from New York.

Nova Jérsia *npr* a ~ New Jersey.

novamente *adv* again, once again.

Nova Orleães *npr* New Orleans.

novato,-a *m,f* beginner, novice; **2** *(pessoa inexperiente)* greenhorn; ♦ *adj* inexperienced, raw.

Nova Zelândia *npr* a ~ New Zealand.

nova-zelandês,-esa *adj* new Zealander.

nove *num* nine; ♦ *adj* ninth; **dia ~ de Maio** ninth of May; ~ **vezes mais** ninefold; *(jogo)* ~ **de copas** nine of hearts; ♦ **a ~** *adv* quickly; IDIOM **cheia de ~ horas** dressed up to the nines; *(BR)* **cheio de ~ horas** full of airs; fussy.

novecentos,-as *num* nine hundred.

novela *f* short novel, novella; **2** soap opera.

novelesco,-a *adj* soppy.

novelista *m,f adj inv* novelist; script writer; romance writer.

novelo *m* ball of yarn/wool.

Novembro, novembro *m* November.

novena *f (REL)* novena.

noventa *num* ninety.

noviciado *m (REL)* novitiate.

noviço *m (REL)* novice.

novidade *f* novelty; **a mini-saia é a última ~**; **2** news; **sem ~** without incident; **há alguma ~?** is something wrong?; ~**s** *fpl* news *sg*; **que ~s me trazes?** what news do you bring me?

novilho,-a *m,f* young bull, heifer.

novinho,-a *adj (pessoa)* very young; **2** *(objecto)* new; ~ **em** *(BR: de)* **folha** brand new.

novo,-a *m,f* the new; **os ~s** *mpl* the young; ♦ *adj* new; young; **Ano N~** New Year; **o que há de ~?** what's new?; ♦ *adv* **de ~** again.

novo-rico, nova-rica *m,f* nouveau-riche; ♦ *adj* upstart.

novo-riquismo *m* flashiness.

noz *f* nut; walnut; ~ **moscada** nutmeg.

nú, nua *m,f* nude; ♦ *adj* naked, bare; stripped; ~ **em pelo** stark naked; **a verdade ~a e crua** the bare/naked truth; **a realidade ~a e crua** the stark reality; ♦ **a nú** *adv* bare; **ficar a ~** to be laid bare.

nuança, nuance *f* nuance.

núbil *adj inv (pessoa)* marriageable, nubile.

nublado,-a *adj* cloudy, overcast.

nublar *vt* to darken; ♦ ~**-se** *vr* to cloud over.

nuca *f* nape.

nuclear *adj inv* nuclear.

núcleo *m (ASTRON, FÍS, BIO)* nucleus *sg*; **2** centre; **3** *(BOT) (de fruta)* stone; *(miolo)* kernel.

nudez,-a *f* nakedness, nudity.

nudismo *m* nudism.

nudista *m,f* nudist.

nulidade *f* nullity, invalidity; **2** insignificance; **3** *(inaptidão)* uselessness; **4** *(pessoa inapta)* numbskull; **5** nonentity.

nulo,-a *adj* null, void; **2** *(pessoa)* inept, useless, stupid; **3** *(resultado)* nil.

num (= **em** + **um**) **num dia lindo** on a lovely day; ~ **abrir e fechar d'olhos** in a twinkle of an eye.

numa (= **em** + **uma**); **numas** (= **em** + **umas**); **numa casa portuguesa** in a Portuguese home.

numeração *f* numbering, numbers *pl*.

numerador *m* numerator; number machine; ♦ *adj* numbering.

numeral *m* numeral.

numerar *vt* to number; **2** to enumerate, count.

numerário *m* cash; money; **pagar em ~** to pay cash.

numérico,-a *adj* numerical.

número *m* number; **2** *(revista, jornal)* issue; ~ **par/ímpar** even/odd number; **3** *(LIT)* metre; ~ **primo** *(MAT)* prime number; ♦ *adv* **sem ~** countless; IDIOM **estar a fazer ~** stand around.

numeroso,-a *adj* numerous.

numismata *m,f* numinatist.

nunca *adv* never; ~ **mais** never again; **como ~** as never before; **quase ~** hardly ever; **mais do que ~** more than ever; ~ **digas...** don't ever say...; ~ **mais pára/para de chover** when will it ever stop raining?

nuns (= **em** + **uns**) in, on some.

nupcial *adj inv* nuptial; **a marcha ~** the wedding march.

núpcias *fpl* nuptials, wedding *sg*; **segundas ~** second marriage; **ela casou em segundas ~** she remarried.

Nuremberga *npr f* Nuremberg.

nutrição *f* nutrition, feeding.

nutricionismo *m* dietetics.

nutricionista *m,f* dietician; ♦ *adj inv* dietetic, dietary.

nutrido,-a *adj* well-nourished.

nutriente *m (alimento)* food; ♦ *adj inv* nourishing.

nutrimento *m* nourishment.

nutrir *vt* to nourish, feed; **2** to nurture; **3** to encourage.

nutritivo,-a *adj* nourishing, nutritive.

nuvem *f* cloud; **céu carregado/coberto de ~s** overcast/dark sky, cloudy; **2** *(insectos)* swarm; **3** *(fig) (de gente)* throng; **4** haze, mist; **5** sadness, shadow; **uma ~ passou pelos olhos dela** a shadow/sadness came over her eyes; ~ **de fumo** cloud of smoke; **uma ~ de setas** *(fig)* a shower of arrows; **uma ~ de setas**; **nuvens** *fpl* clouds (of); **sem ~** cloudless; ~**s de neblina** streaks of mist; **nuvens de neblina** IDIOM **cair das ~s** be astounded; **ir às ~s** to see red, hit the roof; **estar nas ~s** to daydream; **elevar às ~s** to praise to the skies.

O

O, o (letra) *m* O, o.

o (*pl*: **os**) (*f*: **a, as**; *Vd*: **a, as**) the; *art def m* **o homem/os homens** the man/men; **2** *(com substantivo abstracto)* **o amor** love; **os cães ladram** dogs bark; **3** *(com nomes próprios)* **o Carlos** Charles; **o Senhor Silva** Mr Silva; **o Japão** Japan; **o Tâmisa** *(rio)* the Thames; **os Estados Unidos da América** United States of América; **4** *(before senhor/senhores = the formal 'you')* **o senhor onde vai?** where are you going?; **vi os senhores ontem no parque** I saw you yesterday in the park; **5** *(em datas, períodos)* the; **o 4 de Março,** the forth of March; **o pós-guerra** the post-war (times); *(em títulos)* **D. Afonso, o Conquistador** King Afonso, the Conqueror; ♦ *prep* to, at, in, on, towards, from, by; *(lugar, destinação)* **ele está no** *(em + o = no)* **escritório** he is in the office; **vamos ao** *(a + o = ao)* **Brasil** we are going to Brazil; **esquiámos nos Pirenéus** we skied on the Pyrenees; ♦ *(pron pess, 2 ª, 3ª pessoa sg/pl)* him/you/it/them; **vi-o** I saw him/it/you (sg); **quero amá-lo** I want to love him; *(omite-se o r, s, z, finais das formas verbais, antes do pron: o, os, a, as, na afirmativa somente)*; **você pode fazer o vestido? sim, posso fazê-lo** *(fazer+o)* can you make the dress? yes, I can make it; **2** *(fut)* **vê-lo-ei esta noite** I shall see him tonight; **3** *(na terceira do plural, acrescenta-se n ao o, os)* **os meninos comem os morangos? sim comem-nos** are the children eating the strawberries? yes, they are; **4** *(na negativa)* **eu não os quero** I don't want them; ♦ *pron dem (equiv: aquele, aqueles)* **o, os (que)** the one(s) (that, those), what; **o do carro preto** the one in the black car; **o que mais quero** what I want most; **os que foram para o Quebeque** (the ones/those) who went to Quebec; **o que for mais barato** whichever is cheaper; **o que what; **o que diz você?** what do you say?; **o que é?** what is it?; ♦ *(com adj)* the; **prefiro os maiores** I prefer the largest ones; **2** *(antes do adj e pron)* **o meu e o dele** mine and his; **3** *(com adj possessivo)* **o meu, os seus, etc** my, your, etc; **o meu carro** my car; **os seus filhos** your children; **o nosso jardim** our garden.

ó *exc* oh!, hey!; **ó Maria!** Maria!; **ó minha mãe!** oh, mummy!; **ó da casa!** *(fam)* is anyone at home?; **ó rapazes!** hey, boys!; **ó da guarda!** police!

oásis *m* oasis.

oba *(BR) (exc) (de alegria)* great!, whoopee!, wow!; **2** *(cumprimento)* hi!

obcecação *f* obsession; *(teimosia)* stubborness, persistence *(em erro)*.

obcecado,-a *m,f* maniac; ♦ *adj* obsessed, obsessive; *(ofuscado)* blind, dazzled; **estar ~ (por/com)** to be obsessed by/with.

obcecar *vt* to obsess *(alguém)*; **2** *(ficar uns momentos sem ver)* blind, dazzle; **os faróis do carro obcecaram-me** the car's headlights blinded me; **3** obsess *(alguém)*.

obedecer *vt* to obey; ♦ *vi* to be obedient.

obediência *f* obedience.

obediente *adj inv* obedient.

obelisco *m* obelisk.

obesidade *f* obesity; **~ mórbida** morbid obesity.

obeso,-a *adj* obese.

óbice *m* obstacle, hindrance.

óbito *m* death, demise; **certidão de ~** death certificate.

obituário,-a *m* obituary; ♦ *adj* obituary; relating to a death.

obje(c)ção, objeção *f* objection; **2** obstacle; **fazer ~ a** to make an objection.

objectar, objetar a *vt* *(contestar)* to object, reply; ♦ *vi* object to.

objectiva, objetiva *f* *(FOTO)* lens; **~ normal** standard lens; **~ grande-angular** wide-angle lens; **~ olho-de-peixe** fish-eye lens.

objectivação, objetivação *f* execution, completion; **2** realization.

objectivar, objetivar *vt* *(visar a)* to aspire, aim, target *(algo)*.

objectividade, objetividade *f* objectivity; **2** impartiality.

objectividade, objetividade *f* objectivity.

objectivo *m* objective; aim; purpose; ♦ **obje(c)tivo,-a** *adj* objective, impartial; ♦ *adv* **sem ~** aimlessly.

obje(c)to, objeto *m* *(coisa)* object, thing; **este ~ é pesado** this thing is heavy; **2** *(FIL)* object; **~ de paixão** the object of passion; **3** *(material)* matter; **4** *(conteúdo)* subject; **o ~ deste reunião é** the subject of this meeting is; **5** *(gram)* **~ pessoal** personal object.

objector, objetor,-ora *m,f* objector, opposer.

oblação *(pl*: **ões)** *f* *(REL)* oblation, offering, sacrifice; **2** *(pl)* offerings, donations.

oblíqua *f* *(GEOM)* oblique line.

obliquar *vt* to diverge from a course; ♦ *vi* *(MIL)* to advance obliquely.

obliquidade *f* obliquity, slant; **2** indirectness, ambiguity; **3** *(desvio)* diverging; **4** *(fig) (maldade)* perversity.

oblíquo,-a *adj* *(ângulo)* oblique; **2** *(diagonal)* slanting; **3** *(rua, caminho),* sloping, sinuous; **rua ~a à estrada principal** street leading off the main road; **4** *(MIL) (marcha)* sideways; **5 um olhar ~** a sidelong glance; **6** *(resposta)* ambiguous; **7** *(fig) (pessoa) (ardiloso)* cunning, devious.

obliteração *f* obliteration.

obliterador *m* *(para selos)* franking machine; *(para bilhetes)* punch machine; ♦ **obliterador,-ora** *adj* *(processo)* obliterating, effacing; *(MED) (coágulo)* obstructing.

obliterar *vt (apagar)* to obliterate, erase, efface; **2** *(tapar)* to block, obstruct.

oblongo,-a *adj* oblong, elongated.

obnóxio,-a *adj* obnoxious; **2** *(servil)* subservient; contemptible; **3** *(funesto)* doleful.

oboé *m* oboe.

oboísta *m,f* oboe player.

óbolo *m (esmola)* alms *(pl)*.

obra *f* work, job; **2** building, construction; **em ~s** under repair; **3** ~ **dramática** play, drama; ~ **literária** literary work; ~ **prima** masterpiece, opus; **4** ~**s públicas** *(CONSTR)* public works, road works; **5** *(ação)* deed.

obrar *vt (trabalhar)* to work, make; **2** *(fabricar)* produce, build, manufacture; **3** *(causar)* to cause, bring about; ♦ *vi* to act, work, take effect; **2** to defecate; *(gíria médica)* pass motions.

obreiro,-a *m,f* worker, labourer; ♦ *adj* working.

obrigação *f (dever)* obligation, duty; **2** *(COM)* bond, note, liability; ~ **de taxa variável** floating rate note; ~ **de alta rentabilidade** high yield bond.

obrigacionista *m,f* bondholder; ♦ *adj inv* related to bonds; **mercado** ~ bond market, debenture bond market.

obrigado,-a *adj* obliged, grateful; **2** compelled to; **3** *(por lei)* obliged, bound; ♦ *exc* ~! thank you!, thanks!, *(fam)* cheers!; **muito** ~ thank you very much; much obliged, many thanks.

obrigar a *vt* to force, compel (a to); ~ **sb a fazer algo** to compel sb to do sth; **2** *(requerer, exigir)* require, demand; **3** to bind *(contrato, promessa)*; **4** *(sentir-se grato)* **sinto-me obrigado a você** I feel obliged to you/ I am in your debt; ♦ ~**-se** *vr* *(responsabilitar-se)* to assume responsibility **por** for.

obrigatório,-a *adj* obligatory; compulsory; mandatory.

obscenidade *f* obscenity.

obsceno,-a *adj* obscene, indecent.

obscurantismo *m* obscurantism, opposition to reform/progress.

obscurantista *m,f* obscurant; ♦ *adj inv* obscurantist.

obscurecer *vt (sala)* darken; **2** *(factos)* to hide; **3** *(significado)* disguise, make vague; **4** *(entristecer)* overshadow; ♦ ~**-se** *vr* to become dark; become obscure; **2** *(fig)* become dim, fade.

obscuridade *f* darkness; **2** *(falta de clareza, anonimato)* obscurity; **3** *(fig) (esquecimento)* **ela depressa caiu na** ~ she was soon forgotten.

obscuro,-a *adj (escuro)* dark, sombre; **2** *(fig) (ideia, compreensão)* unclear, confused; **3** *(vulto, objecto)* indistinct, hazy; **4** *(fig) (personagem)* obscure, unknown; **5** *(matéria, data, história)* little known, vague; concealed.

obsequiador,-ora *m,f* kind person; ♦ *adj* obliging, helpful.

obsequiar *vt* to do a favour to; **2** to give presents to; **3** to treat sb kindly.

obséquio *m* favour *(UK)*; favor *(US)*; **faça o** ~ **de me dizer** kindly tell me; ♦ **por** ~ *adv* please; as a favour.

obsequioso,-a *adj* obliging, helpful; kind.

Not 'obsequious' in the sense of subservient.

observação *(pl:- ões) f* observation; **2** remark, comment.

observador,-ora *m,f (que observa)* observer; **2** *(cumpridor)* respecter (**de** of); ♦ *adj inv* observant, watchful.

observância *f* observance; compliance; obedience; ~ **do jejum** observance of a fast.

observante *m,f* onlooker, spectator; ♦ *adj* observant.

observar *vt* to observe; **2** to look at, watch; **3** *(notar)* notice; **4** make a comment, remark; **5** *(respeitar)* respect, obey; **ela observa sempre as regras** she always observes/respects the rules; **6** *(considerar)* take into account.

observatório *m* observatory.

observável *adj inv (eclipse)* observable; **2** *(grandeza)* significant.

obsessão *(pl:-ões) f* obsession.

obsessivo,-a *adj* obsessive.

obsessor,-ora *adj* obsessive.

obsidiana *f (MIN)* obsidian.

obsidiar *vt* to besiege, harass *(alguém)*; **2** *(fig)* to spy on someone.

obsoleto,-a *adj* obsolete, antiquated, out of use.

obstáculo *m* obstacle, hindrance, difficulty; **3** *(barreira)* barrier; **corrida de ~s** obstacle race; **4 prova de** ~ hurdle race.

obstante *adj inv* obstructive, hindering; ♦ **não** ~ *conj* nevertheless, however; ♦ *prep* in spite of, notwithstanding.

obstar *vt, vi* to hinder, impede, prevent; **2** *(contrariar)* to oppose, withstand.

obstetra *m,f (MED)* obstetrician.

obstetrícia *f sg* obstetrics.

obstétrico,-a *adj* obstetric(al), pertaining to midwifery.

obstinação *(pl: ões) f* obstinacy.

obstinado,-a *adj* obstinate, stubborn; **2** determined.

obstinar-se *vr* to be obstinate; ~**-se em** to persist in, insist on.

obstipação *f (MED)* obstipation, severe constipation.

obstrução *(pl: -ões) f* obstruction; **2** *(MED)* blockage; **3** *(fig) (bloqueio)* opposition; **fazer** ~ **a** to oppose.

obstruente *adj inv* obstructive.

obstruir *vt (bloquear)* to obstruct, block (up); **2** *(progresso)* impede, hinder.

obstrutivo,-a *adj* obstructive.

obstrutor,-a *m,f* obstructor; ♦ *adj* obstructive; hindering.

obtemperar *vt* to temper, respond mildly to; **2** to acquiesce, agree, give in.

obtenção *f* acquisition; **2** attainment, achievement.

obtenível *(pl: -eis) adj inv* obtainable.

obter *vt* to obtain, get *(informação, dinheiro)*; **2** to win *(prémio, aposta)*; **3** *(objetivo, sucesso)* to attain, achieve.

obturação *(pl: -ões) f (MED) (dente)* filling; **2** *(MED) (bloqueio)* obstruction; sealing, obturation; ~ **das trompas** sealing of the Fallopian tubes.

obturador *m* stopper; **2** *(foto)* shutter; **3** *(usado nas armas)* obturator; ♦ *adj inv (ANAT) (artéria, etc.)* obturating.

obturar *vt (cavidade)* to fill; **2** *(impedir)* to obstruct, stop, plug, close.

obtuseângulo *m, adj (GEOM)* obtuse-angled, obtuse-angular.

obtuso,-a *adj (arredondado)* blunt, rounded, not sharp; **2** *(GEOM) (ângulo)* obtuse; **3** *(fig, fam) (alguém estúpido)* stupid, slow; thick *(col)*.

obus *m (MIL) (peça)* howitzer; **2** *(projéctil)* howitzer shell.

obviamente *adv* obviously.

óbvio *m* o ~ the obvious; **dizer o** ~ to state the obvious; ◆ **óbvio,-a** *adj* obvious, clear.

obviar *vt* to obviate, alleviate, remedy; **2** to prevent; ◆ *vi (dificuldade)* to counteract, oppose.

obvir *vi (JUR)* to accrue, pass to, fall to.

oca *f* large hut in some S. American Indian settlements; **2** *f (BOT)* S. American wood-sorrel; *(Vd:* **oco***)*.

ocapi *m (ZOOL)* okapi.

ocarina *f* wind instrument.

ocarinista *m,f* ocarina player.

ocasião *f* opportunity, chance; **2** occasion, time; **3** event; **as grandes ocasiões** the great events; **4 de** ~ fleeting, ocasional; **5** *(BR)* **preço de** ~ bargain price, bargain; IDIOM **a ocasião faz o ladrão** opportunity makes the thief.

ocasionador,-ora *m,f* causer; ◆ *adj* causing.

ocasional *adj inv (fortuito)* chance, casual *(olhar)*; **2** *(esporádico)* occasional, unexpected.

ocasionalmente *adv* occasionally.

ocasionar *vt* to cause, bring about; **2** *(proporcionar)* enable; afford *(algo a alguém)* sb sth.

ocaso *m* sunset; **2** the west; **3** *(fig)* decline.

occipício, occipúcio *m (ANAT)* occiput, back of the head.

occipital *adj inv* occipital; **osso** ~ occipital bone.

oceanário *m* oceanarium.

Oceânia *npr (GEOG)* Oceania; **a** ~ Oceania.

oceânico,-a *adj* oceanic; **crosta** ~ oceanic crust.

oceano *m* ocean; **o O~ Glacial Antártico** *npr* the Antarctic Ocean; **o O~ Glacial Ártico** *npr* the Arctic Ocean; **o O~ Atlântico** *npr* Atlantic Ocean; **o O~ Índico** *npr* Indian Ocean; **o O~ Pacífico** Pacific Ocean; **2** *(fig) (imensidão)* great quantity.

oceanografia *f* oceanography.

oceanográfico oceanographic(al).

oceanógrafo *m* oceanographer.

oceanologia oceanology.

oceanólogo oceanologist.

ocelado,-a *adj (ZOOL)* ocellated.

ocelo *m* ocellus; **2** eyespot *(pavão, borboleta)*.

ocelote *m (ZOOL)* ocelot.

ocidental *m,f* westerner; ◆ *adj inv* western.

ocidentalizar *vt* to westernize; ◆ ~-**se** *vr* to become westernised.

ocidente *m* west, occident; **o O~** *npr m* the West.

ócio *m (inacção)* idleness, indolence; **2** inactivity; **3** *(descanso)* leisure.

ociosidade *f* idleness, laziness; **2** indolence.

ocioso,-a *m,f* idler; ◆ *adj* idle, lazy, indolent; **horas** ~**as** time of leisure, hours to idle away.

oclocracia *f* ochlocracy, mob rule.

oclocrático,-a *adj* ochlochratic(al).

oclusão *f (fechamento)* occlusion; **2** *(MED)* obstruction.

oclusiva *f (FON)* occlusive consonant; ◆ **oclusivo,-a** *adj* occlusive.

ocluso,-a *adj* occluded, obstructed; **2** closed, shut.

oco,-a *adj (da árvore)* hollow, **2** *(fig) (palavras)* hollow, trivial, futile; **3** *(pej)* **cabeça** ~ brainless, empty head.

ocorrência *f* occurrence, event, happening, incident; ~ **policial** police matter.

ocorrente *adj inv* occurring.

ocorrer *vi* to happen, occur; **2** *(vir à memória)* to come/spring to mind.

ocra, ocre *f (MIN)* ochre; **2** *(cor)* yellow ochre.

ocráceo,-a *adj* ochreous, pertaining to ochre, ochre's colour.

ócrea *f (BOT)* ochrea.

ocreado,-a *adj* oc(h)reate.

octaedro *m (GEOM)* octahendro.

octeto *m (MÚS)* octet.

octingentésimo,-a *adj* eight hundredth.

octogenário *m* octogenarian.

octogésimo,-a *adj* eightieth.

octogonal *adj inv* octagonal.

octógono *m* octagon.

octossilábico,-a *adj* octosyllabic.

ocular *adj inv* ocular; **testemunha** ~ eye-witness.

oculista *m,f* optician.

óculo *m* spyglass; **óculos** *m pl* glasses, spectacles; ~ **de sol**, ~ **escuros** sunglasses, *(fam)* shades; ~ **de natação/de proteção** goggles.

ocultação *f (efeito de esconder)* concealing; **2** holding back; **3** *(ASTRON)* eclipse.

ocultar *vt* to hide, conceal.

ocultismo *m* occultism.

ocultista *m,f* occultist.

oculto *m* occult; ◆ *adj* hidden, concealed; **2** *(sobrenatural)* occult, unknown; **3** secret; **às ocultas** *adv* in secret, stealthily.

ocupação *f* occupation; ~ **selvagem** illegal occupation, squatting.

ocupacional *adj inv* occupational.

ocupado,-a *adj (lugar, tempo)* busy, occupied, filled, engaged; **o telefone está ocupado** the telephone is engaged.

ocupante *m,f (de casa)* occupier; **2** tenant; **3** *(ilegal)* squatter.

ocupar *vt* to occupy; **2** to take possession of; ◆ ~-**se de/com/em** *vr* to concern o.s./deal with; look after; ~ **a** be busy at.

odalisca *f* odalisque/odalisk, female slave.

ode *f* ode.

odiar *vt* to hate, detest.

Odiar is not as casually used as is 'hate' in English. Ex: 'I hate cabbage'. In Portuguese you would say, 'detesto couves' or 'não gosto de couves'.

odiento,-a *adj* odious; offensive; repugnant.

ódio *m* hate, hatred.

odioso *m* the worst/most difficult part (**de algo** of sth).

odioso,-a *adj* odious, hateful, nasty.
odisseia *f* odyssey.
odontologia *f (MED)* odontology; dentistry.
odontológico,-a *adj* odontological; pertaining to teeth or odontology.
odontologista *m,f* odontologist; dentist.
odor *m* smell, fragrance.
odorante *adj inv* fragrant, sweet-smelling.
odorífico,-a *adj* odoriferous.
odre *m* wineskin.
oés-noroeste *m* west-north-west.
oés-sudoeste *m* west-south-west.
oeste *m* west; **vento de ~** westerly wind; **dirigir-se para ~** to head (towards) west; **em direcção ao ~** westwards; **2 Oeste** *npr (Ocidente):* **o O~** the West; ♦ *adj inv* west; *(part, fronteira)* westerly, western.
ofegante *adj inv* breathless, panting, wheezing.
ofegar *vi* to pant, puff; **2** to gasp.
ofender *vt* to offend, insult, hurt; **2** to wound, injure; ♦ **~-se** *vr* to take offence, resent.
ofensa *f* offence, insult; **2** *(JUR)* abuse, offense; **3** *(REL) (pecado)* sin; **sem ~** no offense.
ofensiva *f (MIL)* offensive, attack.
ofensivo,-a *adj* offensive; **2** *(maneira)* aggressive.
oferecer *vt* to offer; **~ resistência** to offer resistance; **2** give; **o rapaz ofereceu-nos uma bebida** the young man gave us a drink; **3** to suggest, propose; ♦ **~-se** *vr* **~ para fazer (algo)** to offer o.s. to do (sth); **2** to volunteer; **3** *(sexualmente)* to give o.s. (a to).
oferecimento *m* offer.
oferenda *f (REL)* offering.
oferta *f* offer; gift; **2** *(ECON) (quantia proposta num leilão, etc)* bid; **3** *(ECON) (no mercado)* supply; **~ e procura** *(EP)* supply and demand; *(BR:* **oferta e demanda***);* **~ pública de aquisição** tender offer.
ofertar *vt* to offer, give, bestow; **2** to make an offering.
ofertório *m (REL)* offertory.
off-line *adv (COMP)* off-line.
off-set *m* offset printing.
oficial *m (funcionário)* official; **2** *(MIL)* officer; **~ do estado-maior** general staff officer, field officer; **~-às-ordens** military aide, ADC; **3** *(JUR)* clerk; **~ de diligências** clerk of the court, bailiff; **4 ~ da polícia** *(pl:* **oficiais da polícia***)* officer (of the law, of police); ♦ *adj inv* official; **tradutor,-ora ~** registered translator.
oficializar *vt* to officialize.
oficiar *vt* to officiate; **2** *(REL)* serve at Mass, officiate.
oficina *f* workshop; **~ mecânica** garage, auto-repairs; **~ de reparações** repair shop.
ofício *m (ocupação manual)* job, art, craft; **~ liberal** freelance job; **2** profession, trade; **3** *(REL)* service, office; **Santo O~** Holy Office; **4** *(documento formal do governo)* minute; **ofício nº ...** minute nº; ♦ **ofícios** *pl* intervention, help; **bons ~s** good/kind help; **fazer os bons ~s** to pacify, conciliate (in a row); IDIOM **os ossos do ~** occupational hazards; **homem dos sete ~s** Jack of all trades.

oficioso,-a *adj* informal, un-official, semi-official; **em cará(c)ter ~** unofficially.
ofídico,-a *m* ophidian; ♦ *adj (ZOOL)* ophidian, pertaining to snakes.
oftálmico,-a *adj (MED)* ophthalmic, pertaining to the eye.
oftalmologia *f* ophthalmology.
ofuscação *f (perda por momentos da visão)* momentary loss of vision; **2** *(fig)* **~ da mente** mental disturbance; **3** *(fig)* dimness; loss *(fama, prestígio)*.
ofuscante *adj inv (luz, brilho)* dazzling, blinding; **2** *(fig) (beleza)* dazzling.
ofuscar *vt (encobrir)* to obfuscate, hide, obscure, darken; **2** *(fig)* to lessen; darken; overshadow *(fama)*; **3** *(fig) (cegar)* to cloud, bewilder *(juízo)*; **4** to confuse; ♦ *vi (a vista)* to dazzle, **as luzes ofuscaram-me** the lights dazzled, blinded me.
ogiva *f (ARQ)* ogive, vault, arch; **2** *(MIL)* ogive, warhead; **~ nuclear** nuclear warhead.
ogre, ogro *m* ogre.
oh! *exc* oh!, ah!; **~ que bom!** marvellous!, how wonderful!, **~, se fosse verdade!** ah, if only it were true!
oi *(BR) exc (fam)* hi!; hello! **2** *(chamando)* hey, eh; **~, você aí!** hey, you there!
oiço, oiro, oiropel, oiriço, oiteiro *(Vd:* **ouço, ouro, ouropel, ouriço, outeiro***).*
oídio *m (BOT) (fungos)* oidium; **2** *(parasitas afetando estes)*, blight.
oitante *m* octant.
oitão *m (Vd:* **oitão***).*
oitava *f (MÚS)* octave; **2** *(LITER) f* octave; octet; **~-rima** *f* stanza of eight lines of verse.
oitavado,-a *adj (coluna)* eight-sided; octagonal.
oitavar *vt* to divide into eight equal pieces.
oitavino *m* small flute in C.
oitavo,-a *m* eighth; ♦ *adj* eighth.
oitenta *m (núm)* eighty; **na década dos ~s** in the eighties; ♦ *adj inv* eighty; **~ vezes** *adj* eightyfold; **~ e um** *m (núm)* eighty-one; ♦ *adj inv* eighy-first; IDIOM **nem oito nem ~** not so much, nor so little; **é oito ou ~** it's all or nothing.
oitentão,-ona *m,f (fam)* octogenerian.
oito *m (núm)* eight.
oitocentista *adj inv* pertaining to the 18th century.
oitocentos, oitocentas *num, adj* eight hundred; **~ e um/uma** eight hundred and one.
ojeriza *(BR)* grudge.
olá *exc* hello!
olaia *f (BOT)* judas-tree.
olaré *exc (fam) (alegria ou surpresa)* well, well!; cheers!, good!, oh yes!
olaria *f* pottery factory; **2** brickyard; **forno de ~** kiln.
olarila *exc (Vd:* **olaré***).*
olé *exc (fam) (chamamento, saudação)* high!, hello!; **2** *(concordando)* O.K., right; **3** *(de satisfação)* well done!
oleáceas *f pl (BOT)* oleaceae.
oleáceo,-a *adj* oleaceous; pertaining to the family Oleaceae *(oliveira, jasmim, lilás)*.

oleado,-a *m* oil cloth, tarpaulin; ♦ *adj* oily, greasy.

oleagíneo,-a *adj* pertaining to the olive tree.

oleaginoso,-a *adj* oleaginous; oily, greasy; **2** *(fig)* smooth, obsequious.

oleandro *m (BOT)* oleander.

olear *vt* to oil, lubricate.

olearia *f* oil factory, oil mill.

oleato *m (QUÍM)* oleate, salt of oleic acid.

oleiro *m* potter; **2** brickmaker.

óleo *m* oil; ~ **alimentar** cooking oil; ~ **bronzeador/ de bronzear** sun-tan oil; ~ **de combustível** engine oil; ~ **de fígado de bacalhau** cod liver oil; **pintura a** ~ oil painting; ~ **de rícino** castor oil; ~ **voláto** essential oil.

oleoduto *m (petróleo)* pipeline, oil-duct; **montagem de um** ~ the laying of a pipeline.

oleoso,-a *adj* oily; greasy.

olfacto, olfato *m* scent, smell; **2** sense of smell.

olga *f (leira)* vegetable allotment.

olha *f (CULIN)* thick soup; ~-**podrida** *f* type of stew with meat sausage, chick-peas, etc.

olhada *f* glance, look.

olhadela *f* peep, quick glance.

olhar *m* look, glance; ~ **apagado** dull/lifeless look; ~ **de espanto** statled look; ~ **fixo** stare; ~ **meigo**, loving look; gaze; ~ **de ódio** a look of hatred; ♦ *vt (ger)* to look (at); ~ **mas não ver** *(alguém)* to look through sb, looking but not seeing; **2** *(ver)* to see; view; **3** *(contemplar)* to gaze (out); **ela olhava o mar com um ar saudoso** she gazed out to sea nostalgically; **4** *(julgar, considerar)* to look on; **5** *(prestar atenção)* to mind; **olhe bem o que o médico lhe disse** mind what the doctor said (to you); **6** *(avaliar)* to look, to eye *(alguém)*; **ele olhou-a com desconfiança** he eyed her with suspicion; **ela olhou-me dos pés à cabeça** she eyed me from top to toe; **7** *(cuidar de)* to keep an eye on; ♦ *vi* fitar, stare; **2** *(voltado para)* to face, look out on; **o meu quarto olha para o rio** my bedroom looks on to the river; ♦ ~ **a** *(reparar, ter em conta)* to notice; **eu não olho a essas coisas** I don't notice such things; ~ **de alto** *(alguém)* to look down one's nose (at sb); ~ **à volta** to look round; ~ **de esguelha/de revés/de soslaio** *(alguém)* to look sideways/askance; to sneer, leer (at sb); ~ **para** to look at; ~ **para o ar** to daydream; ~ **para baixo/cima** to look up/down; ~ **para fora** to look out; ~ **por** *(cuidar de alguém/ algo)* to take care of; to keep an eye on; ~ **por cima do ombro** to look over one's shoulder; ♦ *exc* **olhe!** *(chamada de atenção)* hey! look!; **2 olhe lá** *(admoestar)* look here!; ♦ ~-**se** *vr* to look at one another; **2** *(mirar-se)* ~ **ao espelho** to look at o.s. in the mirror; ♦ *exc* **olhe!** look!, hey!; **olhe lá!** look here!; **olha quem fala!** look who is talking!; IDIOM **a cavalo dado não se olha ao dente** don't look a gift horse in the mouth.

olheiras *f pl* dark rings/circles under the eyes.

olheiro *m* foreman, supervisor; **2** observer, informer; **3** fountain, jet of water.

olhete *m* eyelet, small opening.

olho *m* eye; **2** *(furo)* eye; ~ **da agulha** eye of the needle; *(de alguns vegetais)* heart; ~ **de couve/ alface** the heart of a cabbage/lettuce; **3** *(TIPO)* typeface; **4** *(buraco)* ~**mágico** *(da porta)* peephole; **5** *(vulg) (ânus)* hole; **o** ~ **do cu** *(vulg)* asshole *(col)*; **no** ~ **da rua** *(col)* out in the street; **6 não pregar** ~ to not sleep a wink; **7 piscar o** ~ to wink ♦ **a** ~ *adv (CULIN)* by the rule of thumb; **a** ~ **nu** with the naked eye; ♦ ~ **alerta!** watch out!, keep your eyes open.

olho-de-boi *m (ARQ, TEC, NÁUT)* bull's eye, skylight, small circular window; **2** *(BOT)* ox-eye daisy.

olho-de-gato *(pl: olhos-de-gato)* *m (MIN)* cat's eyes; *(sinalização nocturna)* reflector; Catseye®.

olho-de-perdiz *m (calo)* corn; **2** *(tecido de lã pintalgado)* dog-tooth check.

olho-de-tigre *m (MIN)* tiger's eye.

olhos *mpl* eyes; ~ **azuis** blue eyes; ~ **s inchados** swollen eyes; **cravar os** ~ **em alguém** to stare fixedly at sb; ~ **de água** spring of water; **piscar os** ~ to blink; **revirar os** ~**s** turn up one's eyes; ♦ *adv* **a** ~**s vistos** before one's very eyes, visibly; IDIOM **num abrir e fechar de** ~**s** in a flash, in the twinkling of an eye; **ver com bons** ~**s** to approve of; ~**s rasos de água** eyes full of tears; **ela é a menina dos meus** ~**s** she is the apple of my eye; ~**s de carneiro mal morto** *(amoroso)* languid or wistful look, sheep's eyes; **saltar aos** ~**s de** to be obvious/clear to; **deitar,-atirar poeira aos** ~ **de (alguém)** *(enganar)* to throw dust in sb's eyes.

olhudo,-a *adj* big-eyed, goggle-eyed.

olibano *m* frankincense.

oligarquia *f* oligarchy.

Olimpíada *f (Hist)* Olympiad: **as O~s** the Olympics.

olímpico,-a *adj* olimpic.

oliva *f (LITER) (oliveira)* olive tree.

oliváceo,-a *adj* olivaceous, olive-green.

olival, olivedo *m* olive grove.

oliveira *f* olive tree.

olivicultura *f* olive growing.

olmo *m* elm.

olvidar *vt (LITER)* to forget.

Omã *npr* Oman.

ombrear *vt* go/be shoulder to shoulder; **2** *(igualar-se)* match; rival with.

ombreira *f (ARQ)* doorpost; **2** *(vestuário)* shoulder pad.

ombro *m (ANAT)* shoulder; ~ **a** ~ shoulder to shoulder; **encolher os** ~**s** to shrug one's shoulders.

OMC *f (abr de* **Organização Mundial do Comércio***)* WTO.

ómega *m* omega.

omeleta, omelete *f* omelette *(UK)*; omelet *(US)*.

omissão *f* omission; **2** *(JUR)* nonfeasance, withholding; **salvo erro ou** ~ errors and omissions excepted; ~ **fiscal** *f (COM)* tax loophole.

omisso,-a *adj (descuidado)* neglectful, remiss; **2** *(faltando)* omitted, left out.

omitir *vt* to omit, leave out; withhold *(informação)*.

omnipotência, onipotência *f* omnipotence.

Omnipotente, Onipotente o ~ the Almighty; ♦ *adj inv* omnipotent.

omnipresente, onipresente *adj inv* omnipresent.

omnívoro,-a, onívero,-a *adj* omnivorous.

omoplata *f* shoulder blade.

OMS *f (abr de* **Organização Mundial da Saúde)** WHO.

ónagra *f (BOT)* evening primrose.

ónagro *m (ZOOL)* onager, wild ass; **2** *(MIL)* type of machine for catapulting rocks.

onanismo *m* onanism; **2** coitus interruptus; **3** masturbation.

onanizar-se *vr* to masturbate.

onça *f (ZOOL)* ounce, jaguar; **~-parda** *f* puma; **~-preta** *f* panther; **2** *(unidade de peso britânica)* ounce (1 ounce = 28,35 gramas); *(em Portugal antiga unidade)* equiv to: 29, 691 gramas; IDIOM **amigo da ~** false friend; **amigos da ~** *(palavras)* deceptive meanings, false friends.

oncologia *f (MED)* oncology.

oncológico,-a *adj* oncological; pertaining to tumours.

oncologista *m,f* oncologist.

oncotomia *f* oncotomy.

onda *f* wave; **~ sonora/luminosa** sound/light wave; **2** *(RADIO)* **~ curta/média/longa** short/medium/long wave; **3 ~ de calor** heat wave; **4 ~ de frio** cold snap; **5 ir na ~** to be taken in; **6 fazer ~s** to provoke argument.

onde *adv* where; **~ fica a loja?** where is the shop?; **para ~ ?** where to?; ♦ *pron rel* **não sei ~ ela está** I don't know where she is; **por ~** through which; **2 por ~?** which way?; **3 ~ quer que estejas** wherever you may be.

ondeado,-a *(Vd:* **ondulado**).

ondeante *(Vd:* **ondulante**).

ondear *vi (Vd:* **ondular**).

ondulação *f (das ondas)* undulation; **2** *(de uma superfície)* unevenness.

ondulado,-a *adj (do cabelo)* wavy; **2** *(chapa de metal)* corrugated.

ondulante *adj inv* undulating; **as searas ~s** undulating cornfields; **2** *(bandeira)* fluttering, waving; **3** *(saia)* flowing; **4** *(lago, águas)* rippling.

ondular *vt* (hair) to wave, curl; ♦ *vi (bandeira)* flutter.

onerar *vt* to charge; **2** to burden, weigh down.

oneroso,-a *adj* onerous, burdensome.

onfalite *f (MED)* omphalitis, inflammation of the umbilicus.

onglete *m* engraving tool.

ônibus *(BR) m sg/pl* omnibus, bus; **2** coach; **ponto de ~** *(BR)* bus stop.

onipotência *(Vd:* **o(m)nipotência**).

onipotente *(Vd:* **o(m)nipotente**).

onipresente *(Vd:* **o(m)nipresente**).

onírico,-a *adj (delírio)* oneiric.

onívoro,-a *(Vd:* **o(m)nívoro,-a**).

ónix *(BR:* **ônix**) *m (MIN)* onyx.

on-line *(COMP)* on-line.

onomástica *f (LÍNG)* onomastics.

onomástico,-a *adj (LÍNG) (classificação, ciência)* onomastic.

onomatopéia, onomatopeia *f (LÍNG)* onomatopoeia; **miau é uma ~** miaow is an onomatopoeia.

ontem *adj* yesterday; *adv* **~ à noite** last night; **~ à tarde** yesterday afternoon; **~ de manhã** yesterday morning.

ontologia *f* ontology.

ontológico,-a *adj* ontologic(al).

ónus *(BR:* **ônus**) *m* onus, burden, responsibility; **~ da prova** *(JUR)* onus probandi, burden of proof.

onze *num* eleven; ♦ *adj* **no dia ~** on the eleventh; IDIOM **meter-se em camisa de ~ varas** get into a mess/trouble.

onzeneiro *m* money lender.

o-ó *(linguagem de criança)* beddy-byes; **fazer ~** to go to sleep, to go beddy-byes.

opa (**= ova**) *f (capa sem mangas)* sleveless surplice *(dos frades)*; ♦ *exc (BR) (fam) (de admiração)* wow!

opacidade *f* opaqueness; thickness.

opaco,-a *adj* opaque; dark.

opala *f (MIN)* opal; **2** fine muslin-like material.

opalino,-a *adj (MIN)* opaline; opalescent.

opção *f* option, choice; **2** first claim, right; **3** *(COM)* **~ de a(c)ção** share option.

OPEP *f (abr de* **Organização dos Países Exportadores do Petróleo)** OPEC.

ópera *f* opera; **~-bufa/cómica** comic opera.

operação *f* operation; **2** *(COM)* transaction; **~ de cobertura de risco** hedge.

operacional *adj inv* operational.

operador,-ora *m,f* operator; **2** surgeon; **3** projectionist; **4** cameraman/woman.

operar *vt* to produce, bring about; **2** *(MED)* to operate on; ♦ *vi* to act, function; ♦ **~-se** *vr* to take place; **2** *(MED)* to have an operation.

operária *f (bee, ant)* worker.

operariado *m* the workers, proletariat.

operário,-a *m,f* worker; **~ de uma fábrica** factory worker; ♦ *adj* working.

operativo,-a *adj* working; **operatório,-a** *adj* operative; **cuidados pós-~** after surgery care; post-operational.

opereta *f* operetta.

opiáceo,-a *adj* opiate, soporific; **2** *(FARM) (medicamento)* containing opium.

opinar *vt* to give an opinion, to judge; ♦ *vi* to express an opinion.

opinião *f* opinion, view, belief.

opinioso,-a *adj* opinionated, conceited.

ópio *m* opium.

opiomania *f* opium addiction.

oponente *m,f* opponent, adversary; ♦ *adj inv* opposing.

opor *vt* to oppose; **2** to put up, offer; ♦ **~-se** *vr* to object; **2** to resist.

oportunidade *f* opportunity.

oportunismo *m* opportunism.

oportunista *m,f* opportunist, social climber; ♦ *adj inv* opportunistic.

oportuno,-a *adj* opportune, right; **2** convenient, suitable.

oposição *f* opposition; **em ~ a** in opposition to, against; *(POL)* **o Ministro da Saúde da ~** *(UK)* the Shadow Health Minister; ♦ *adj inv* opposition, opposer; **2** *(candidato)* competitor.

oposicionista *m,f* person in opposition.

opositor,-ora *m,f* opponent.

oposto,-a *adj* opposite; facing; **2** contrary.

opressão *f* oppression.

opressivo,-a *adj* oppressive.

opressor,-ora *m,f* oppressor.

oprimido,-a *m,f*: **os ~s** the oppressed; ♦ *adj* oppressed, persecuted.

oprimir *vt* to oppress; **2** *(fig) (angustiar)* to weigh on *(pessoa, consciência)*; **3** *(fig)* repress.

opróbrio *m* ignominy; **2** shame, disgrace.

optar *vt,vi* to choose, select; **2** to make a choice; **~ por** to opt for.

optativo,-a *adj* optative.

óptica *f sg* optics; **2** *(fig)* point of view.

óptico,-a *m,f* optician; ♦ *adj* optic(al), pertaining to sight; **nervo ~** optic nerve.

o(p)timismo *m,f* optimism.

o(p)timista *m,f* optimist.

o(p)timizar *vt* to optimize.

ó(p)timo *m* optimum; **ó(p)timo,-a** *adj* excellent, splendid; ♦ *(exc)* ~! great!, super!

optometria *f (ciência de testar a visão)* optometry.

opugnar *vt* to oppugn, disputar; lutar contra; **2** *(fig)* to attack (sb) in writing.

opulência *f* opulence, riches, wealth; *(fig)* abundance.

opulento,-a *adj* opulent, wealthy, affluent; **2** rich, profuse, luxurious.

opúsculo *m* opuscule.

ora *adv* now; **de ~ em diante** from now on; **por ~** for the time being; ♦ **~ conj** now; well; **~ aqui, ~ ali** sometimes here, sometimes there; **~ sim, ~ não** now you say yes, then you say no ♦ *exc* **~!** well now!; **~, ~!** oh, come on!; **~ essa!** the very idea!, *(em resposta a um 'obrigado')* not at all!, *(reposta a alguém pedindo licença)* by all means!; **~ bem!** now then!; **~ viva!** hello there! **~ bolas!** damn! blast!

oração *f (rel)* sermon, prayer; **~ fúnebre** funeral oration/elegy; **lugar de ~** place of worship; **roda de ~** prayer wheel; **2** oration, discourse; **3** *(LÍNG)* sentence.

oráculo *m* oracle.

orador,-ora *m,f* speaker; **2** preacher.

oral *adj inv* oral, pertaining to the mouth.

orangotango *m (ZOOL)* orang-utan.

orar *vi (REL)* to pray, plead; **orai por nós** *(ora pro nobis)* pray for us.

oratória *f* oratory; **2** rhetoric.

oratório *m (MÚS)* oratorio; **2** *(REL)* oratory, small shrine or chapel; ♦ **oratório,-a** *adj* oratorical; **2** rhetorical.

orbe *m* orb, circle; **2** sphere; **3** *(fig)* the world.

orbícola *adj inv* everywhere; **2** *(fig)* cosmopolitan; **orbicular** *adj inv* round, circular.

órbita *f* orbit; **2** *(fig)* range; **~ de olho** eye socket; **orbitar** *vt* to orbit.

orca *f (ZOOL)* killer whale.

orçamentação *f (COM)* budgeting.

orçamento *m* budget, estimate; **2 ~ aproximado** rough estimate.

orçar *vt* to estimate, calculate, give a quotation; ♦ *vi* to prepare a budget.

ordeiro,-a *adj* law-abiding; orderly.

ordem *f (encomenda)* order; **2** command, order; **3 ~ de prisão** warrant of arrest; **eviction ~** ordem de despejo; **4** *(disposição)* tidiness, neatness; **pôr em ~** to tidy up; **5 ~ do dia** agenda; **6** rate, order; **de primeira ~** first-rate; **7** *(renque, fileira)* row; **8** *(sociedade profissional ou honorífica)* order, associação; **O~ dos Advogados** Bar Association; **Ordem da Jarreteira** *npr f* Order of the Garter; **9** *(confraria)* religious order; **O~ de São Francisco** the Order of St Francis; ♦ *adv* **à ~** on sb's orders; **até nova ~** until further notice; **com ~** orderly; **fora de ~** out of order, untidy; **por ~** in sequence; ♦ *prep* **à ~ de** at the orders of; **conta à ~** current account; **em ~** ready; **por ~ de** by order; ♦ *conj* **em ~ a que** so that; in such a way that; ♦ *exc*; **às suas ordens** at your service; IDIOM **andar às ordens de** *(alguém)* to be at sb's beck and call; **meter na ~** *(alguém)* to make sb behave.

ordenação *f (REL)* ordination; **2** arrangement, classification; **Ordenações** *fpl* decree, statute law.

ordenado,-a *m,f* salary, wages *pl*; ♦ *adj* in order, organized; **2** orderly; **3** carried out; **4** *(REL)* ordained.

ordenança *m (MIL, ADMIN)* orderly, messenger boy; **2** *f (regulamento)* ordinança, regulation.

ordenar *vt* to order, command; **2** to arrange, put in order; ♦ *vi* to give orders; ♦ **~-se** *vr (REL)* to be ordained.

ordenha *f* milking; **~ manual** milking by hand; **ordenhar** *vt/vi (vaca, cabra)* to milk.

ordinal *adj inv* ordinal.

ordinarice *f (fam)* vulgarity.

ordinário,-a *adj (habitual)* common; **2** *(qualidade)* mediocre; **3** *(pej) (grosseiro)* coarse, vulgar; ♦ *adv* **de ~o** usually.

Do not confuse **'ordinário'** with the English word **ordinary** which in Portuguese is **'vulgar'**.

---

orégano, orégão *m (BOT)* oregano, wild marjoram.

orelha *f (ANAT)* ear; **2** *(de um livro)* flap of a book jacket; **3** *(martelo)* claw of hammer; ♦ *adv* **até às ~** put to the ears in; **até às ~ com a papelada** I am snowed under with paper work; IDIOM **fazer ~s moucas** to turn a deaf ear; **estar com a pulga atrás da ~** to smell a rat, be suspicious; **de ~s murchas** crestfallen; **ser de trás da ~** *(comida)* excellent.

orelhão *m (fam)* big ears **2 levar um ~** to get a scolding; **3** *(MED) (fam)* mumps; **4** *(BR) m* glass public telephone box.

orelhudo,-a *adj* big-eared; **2** *(fig)* idiotic; **3** *(fig)* stubborn.

órfã *f (Vd: órfão)*.

orfanato *m* orphanage.

órfão *(pl: órfãos) m* **órfã** *(pl: órfãs) f* orphan.

orfeão *m (MÚS)* choir, choral society.

organdi *m* organdie, organdy; fine muslin.

orgânico,-a *adj* organic.
organismo *m* organism; **2** body, organization.
organista *m,f* organist.
organização *f* organization.
organizacional *adj inv* organizational.
organizado,-a *adj* organized; **2** orderly, methodical.
organizar *vt* to organize.
organza *f (tecido de seda transparente)* organza.
órgão *(pl: órgãos) m (MÚS)* organ; **2** *(BIO, ANAT)* organ; **3** *(organismo)* body; **os ~s de comunicação social** the media.
orgasmo *m* orgasm.
orgia *f* orgy; **2** *(fig) (excesso, desordem, profusão)* riot, profusion.
orgíaco,-a *adj* orgiastic; licentious; riotous.
orgulhar-se *vr* ~ **de** to be proud of, pride o.s. of.
orgulho *m* pride; **2** arrogance.
orgulhoso,-a *adj* proud; haughty.
oricterope *m (ZOOL)* aardvark.
orientação *f* direction; **2** position; **3** tendency; **4** *(EDUC)* training, guidance.
orientador,-ora *m,f* tutor; **2** *(conselheiro)* adviser; **3** *(guide)* guia.
oriental *adj inv* eastern.
orientalismo *m* orientalism.
orientalista *m,f* orientalist, scholar in oriental studies.
orientar *vt* to orientate; **2** to direct, guide; ♦ **~-se** *vr* to get one's bearings.
oriente *m*: **O~** *npr* the East; **Extremo O~** *npr* Far East; **O~ Médio/Próximo** *npr* Middle/Near East.
orifício *m* hole, opening.
origem *f* origin; **2** lineage, descent; **lugar de ~** birthplace.
originador,-ora *m,f* originator, creator; ♦ *adj* originating.
original *m,f* **um/uma ~** an eccentric, an original person; ♦ *adj inv* original; **2** *(fig)* strange, odd.
originalidade *f* originality.
originar *vt* to originate, cause, bring about; ♦ **~-se** *vr* to arise.
originário,-a *adj (proveniente de)* native of.
oriundo,-a *adj* arising from; coming from; **2** native of.
Orixà *m*, **Orixalá** *m (Afro-Brazilian)* divinities.
orizicultura *f* rice growing.
orla *f* edge, border; **2** *(de vestuário)* hem; **3** *(tira)* strip; **4** *(de árvores)* a row of trees by the side of avenue, road.
ornamentar *vt* to decorate, adorn, garnish.
ornamento *m* ornament, decoration.
ornar *vt* to adorn, decorate.
ornato *m* adornment, decoration, embellishment.
ornitologia *f* ornithology.
ornitologista *m,f* ornithologist.
ornitorrinco *m (ZOOL)* duck-billed platypus.
orquestra *f* orchestra; **~ de câmara/filarmónica/ sinfónica** chamber/philharmonic/symphony orchestra.
orquestrar *vt (ger)* to orchestrate.
orquidário *m* orchid house.
orquídea *f (BOT)* orchid; any plant of the family Orchidaceae.

orquidófilo *m* grower of orchids.
orto *m (ASTRON)* rising of a star or planet.
ortodontia *f (dental)* orthodontia, orthodontics.
ortodóntico,-a *adj* orthodontic.
ortodontista *m,f* orthodontist.
ortodoxia *f* orthodoxy.
ortodoxo,-a *adj* orthodox.
ortoépia *f (LÍNG)* orthoepy, pronunciation.
ortogonal *(GEOM) adj inv* orthogonal.
ortografia *f* orthography, spelling.
ortográfico,-a *adj* orthographic.
ortopedia *f (MED)* orthopaedics.
ortopédico,-a *adj* orthopaedic.
ortopedista *m,f* orthopaedist.
orvalhar *vt* to sprinkle with dew; **começa a ~** the dew begins to fall.
orvalho *m* dew; **gotas de ~** dewdrops.
os *mpl (Vd:* **o***)*; **os sem-abrigo** *(pessoas)* the homeless.
oscilação *f* oscillation; **2** fluctuation; **3** hesitation.
oscilar *vi* to oscillate, sway, swing; **2** to hesitate.
ósculo *m* kiss.
osga *f (ZOOL)* house lizard.
Oslo *npr* Oslo.
osmose *f (FÍS)* osmosis.
ósseo,-a *adj* bony.
ossificação *f* ossification.
osso *m* bone; **2** difficulty; IDIOM **um ~ difícil/duro de roer** a hard nut to crack; **~s do ofício** occupational hazards; **ser pele e ~** to be nothing but skin and bones.
ossuário *m* ossuary; charnel-house.
ossudo,-a *adj* bony, big-boned.
ostaga *f (NÁUT)* halyard, rope for hoisting a sail.
ostensivo,-a *adj* ostensible, apparent.
ostentação *f* ostentation; **2** display, show.
ostentar *vt* to exhibit; **2** to show off, flaunt.
ostentoso,-a *adj* ostentatious, showy.
osteopata *m,f (MED)* osteopath.
osteopatia *f* osteopathy.
osteoporose *f (MED)* osteoporosis.
ostra *f (ZOOL)* oyster.
ostráceo *adj* oyster-like.
ostracismo *m* ostracism.
ostreira *f* oyster-bed.
OTAN *f (abr de* **Organização do Tratado do Atlântico Norte***)* NATO.
otário,-a *m,* sucker; ♦ *adj* credulous, gullible.
otimismo *(Vd:* **o(p)timismo***)*.
otimista *(Vd:* **o(p)timista***)*.
ótimo,-a *(Vd:* **ó(p)timo,-a***)*.
otite *f (MED)* otitis, inflammation of the ear.
otologia *f* otology.
otologista *m,f* otologist.
otomano *m*: **o Império O~** the Ottoman Empire.
otorrinolaringologia *f (MED) (ouvido, nariz e garganta)* otorhinolaryngology.
otosclerose *f (MED)* otosclerosis.
ou *conj* or; **~ este ~ aquele** either this one or that one; **~ seja** in other words; i.e.
ouça *(também:* **oiça***) (pres subj de:* **ouvir***)* **espero que vocês me ~ bem** I hope you can hear me

well; **que Deus ~ as minhas preces** may God listen to my prayers.

ouço *(também:* **oiço)** *(pres indic, I^a pessoa de* **ouvir)**
eu não ~ nada I don't hear anything.

oura *f* dizziness; **2** vertigo.

ourar *vi* to feel dizzy; ♦ *vt* to decorate with gold.

ourela *f* edge, border.

ouriço (= **oiriço)** *m (ZOOL)* hedgehog; **~-cacheiro**
m hedgehog; **~-do-mar** *(pl:* **ouriços-do-mar)** *m*
sea urchin.

ourives *mpl* goldsmith, jeweller.

ourivesaria *f* goldsmith's art; **2** *(loja)* jeweller's.

ouro (= **oiro)** *m* gold; **2** *(cartas)* **naipe de ~** suit of
diamonds; **3 ~ de lei** hallmarked; **4 de ~** golden;
5 ~ em folha gold leaf.

ouropel (= **oiropel)** *m* tinsel; **2** bauble.

ousadia *f (audácia)* daring, bravery, courage.

ousado,-a *adj* daring, audacious.

ousar *vt/vi* to dare.

outeiro (= **oiteiro)** *m* hill, hillock.

outonal *adj inv* autumnal.

Outono, outono *m* autumn, *(US)* fall.

outorga *f* grant, concession, bestowal.

outorgante *m,f (JUR)* grantor; ♦ *adj* granting.

outorgar *vt (conceder)* to grant; **2** to execute, to
draw up; **3** *(conferir)* to bestow.

outrem *pron indef sg* somebody else; *pl* other
people.

outro,-a *adj sg (pessoa, objecto)* other, another; **os
outros rapazes** the other boys; ♦ *pron indef ~
(pessoa)* somebody else; **um outro, uma outra**
other (one); **~s** *pl* others; **um ou outro** one or the
other; **um ao outro** each another; **uns aos outros**
one another; **nem um, nem ~** neither one nor
the other; **alguns ~s** a few others; **2** *(objecto)* **~a
coisa** something else; **~ qualquer** any other; **de ~
modo/de ~a maneira** otherwise; **~ tanto** the
same again; as much more; **no ~ dia** the other day.

outrora *adv* formerly, a long time ago, in times past;
**a língua portuguesa foi ~ a língua franca do
mundo** Portuguese was once/in times gone by
the world's lingua franca.

outrossim *adv* also, likewise, moreover.

Outubro, outubro *m* October.

ouvido *m (ANAT)* ear; *(audição)* hearing; **ter bom ~
para a música** have a good ear for music; **de ~** by
ear; **dar ~ s a** to listen to, lend one's ear to; **dizer
ao ~ de** to whisper in one's ear; **dor de ~s** earache; IDIOM **entrar por um ~e sair pelo outro**
go in one ear and out the other; **fazer ~ de mercador** turn a deaf ear; **ter os ~ cheios** to be fed
with listening to stories.

ouvidor *m* listener, hearer; **2** magistrate.

ouvinte *m,f (ger)* listener.

ouvir *vt* to hear, listen to; **2** pay attention to; **3 ouvi
dizer que** I heard that/I heard it said; **4 ~ falar**

de algoal/guém, to hear of/about sth/sb; IDIOM
tu vais ~ you are going to have a telling off.

ova *f* ova; spawn; **2** *pl* fish roe; ♦ **uma ~!** *exc*
fiddlesticks!, stuff and nonsense!, no way!

ovação *f* ovation, acclaim.

ovacionar *vt* to acclaim.

oval *f (GEOM)* oval.

ovalado *adj* oval, egg-shaped.

ovante *adj inv* triumphant; joyous.

ovário *m (ANAT)* ovary.

ovas *fpl (de peixe)* roe.

ovelha *f* sheep, ewe; **~ desgarrada** stray sheep; **2
rebanho de ~s** a flock of sheep/ewes; **3 ~ negra/
tinhosa** *(fig)* black sheep; **4** *(REL)* the flock;
IDIOM **cada ~ com sua parelha** birds of the
same feather flock together.

ovino,-a *adj* ovine; **gado ~** sheep; **2** sheep-like;
criação ~a sheep breeding.

OVNI *m (abr de* **Objeto Voador Não-Identificado)**
UFO (Unidentified Flying Object); **ovnilogia** *f*
ufology.

ovo *m* egg; **~s cozidos/duros** hard-boiled eggs; **2 ~s
escalfados** *(BR:* **pochê)** poached eggs; **3 ~s estrelados** fried eggs; **4 ~s mexidos** scrambled eggs; **5
~s quentes** soft-boiled eggs; **~ de Páscoa** Easter
egg; IDIOM **ser o ~ de Colombo** be easy when
you know how; **não contes com o ~ no cu da
galinha** *(fam)* don't count your chickens before
they are hatched.

ovóide *adj inv (que tem forma de ovo)* egg-shaped,
oval, ovoid.

ovulação *f* ovulation.

ovular *vt* to ovulate.

óvulo *m* ovum.

oxalá *(excl)* God willing!, let's hope so!; **~ ele venha**
hopefully/I hope he comes; **~ fosse assim!** if only
it were so!.

oxiacetilénico,-a *adj (gás)* oxyacetylene.

oxidação *f* oxidation; **2** rusting.

oxidante *m* oxidant, oxidizer/oxidiser; ♦ *adj* oxidizing.

oxidar *vi* oxidize/oxidise; ♦ **~-se** to cause
oxidization, be rusty.

óxido *m (QUÍM)* oxide; **~ de ferro** iron oxide; **~ de
carbono** carbon monoxide.

oxigenação *f* oxigenation.

oxigenado,-a *adj (QUÍM)* oxygenated; **água ~a**
hydrogen peroxide.

oxigenar *vt (QUÍM)* to oxygenate; **2** to bleach *(cabelo)*.

oxigénio *m (QUÍM)* oxygen; *(MED)* **balão de ~**
oxigen tent.

oxítono *m (gram)* oxytone, a word which has an
acute accent on the last syllable.

oxiúro *m (ZOOL)* oxyuris, pinworm.

ozonar *vt (impregnar de ozono)* encher de ozono.

ozonizar *vt (tratar com ozono)* ozonize.

ozono *(EP)* **ozônio** *(BR);* **camada de ~** ozone layer.

p

P, p *m (letra)* P, p.

p. ex. *(abr de* **por exemplo***)* e.g. (for example).

P.e. *(abr de* **Padre***) (REL)* Father.

p.f.v. *(abr de* **por favor volte***)* PTO *(please turn over)*.

pá *f* shovel; spade; *(hélice, ventilador)* blade; ~ **da praia** spade; *(MEC)* ~ **giratória** rotor vane; ~ **mecânica** power shovel; **2** *(perna das reses)* shoulder; **3** *(BR) (quantidade)* a lot; **4** *m (fam)* pal, mate, man; **ó ~!** hey, you!, **ó ~ dá-me cinco paus!** come on, man; give me five quids! *(UK)*, bucks! *(US)*.

PAC *(abr de* **Política Agrícola Comum***)* Common Agricultural Policy.

pacatez *f* quietness.

pacato,-a *adj* quiet, peaceful; **um homem ~** a quiet man.

pachola *m,f (fam) (indolente)* lazybones, slowcoach; **2** *(bonacheirão)* wag; ♦ *adj inv* lazy; **2** *(com bom feitio)* easygoing; good-natured; **3** waggish; **4** *(BR) (pessoa pedante)* conceited.

pachorra *f (fam)* slowness, sluggishness.

pachorrento,-a *adj* patient, easygoing, lumbering.

paciência *f* patience; endurance; **ter ~** to be patient; IDIOM **abusar da ~ de (alguém)** try someone's patience; **perder a ~** to lose one's patience; **tenha ~!** be patient!; *(a um mendigo, quando não se dá dinheiro)* may God help you!

paciente *m,f (doente)* patient; ♦ *adj inv* patient; **ser ~ com alguém** to be patient with sb.

pacificação *f* pacification.

pacificador,-ora peacemaker; ♦ *adj* pacifying, soothing, appeasing.

pacificar *vt* to pacify, appease; calm (down); ♦ **~-se** *vr* to become calm.

Pacífico *npr:* **o (Oceano) ~** the Pacific Ocean.

pacífico,-a *adj* peace-loving; peaceful, tranquil; pacific.

pacifismo *m* pacifism.

pacifista *m,f* pacifist.

paço *m* palace; **2** *(fig)* court; **3** **paços** *mpl* **do concelho** *(ADMIN)* Town Hall.

pacote *m* packet; **um ~ de açúcar** packet of sugar; **2** *(embrulho)* parcel, package; **3** *(embalagem)* packet, carton; **~ de leite** milk carton; **4** *(ECON)* package; **5** *(turismo)* **~ de viagem** package holiday; **6** pack, number; **um ~ de propostas** a pack, a number of proposals; IDIOM *(BR) (pop)* **ir no ~** to be taken in.

pacotilha *f* trash; cheap junk; **de ~** second-rate.

pacóvio,-a *(pej) m,f* simpleton, dunce; ♦ *adj* foolish, silly.

pacto *m (acordo)* pact, agreement; **~ de não-agressão** non-aggression pact.

pactuante *adj inv (países, membros)* members of a pact.

pactuar *vt* to agree on; ♦ *vi* **~ com alguém** to be in an agreement/in league with sb; **2** *(ceder)* go along with sth.

padaria *f* bakery, baker's (shop).

padecer *vt* to suffer, undergo (**de** from); **2** *(aguentar)* to put up with, endure; ♦ *vi* **~ de algo** suffer from sth.

padecimento *m* suffering; pain.

padeira *f* baker's wife, female baker.

padeiro *m* baker.

padiola *f (maca)* stretcher; **2** handbarrow.

padrão *(pl:- ões) m* standard; **~ de vida** standard of living; **2** *(desenho, tecido)* pattern, outline; **3** stone monument.

padrasto *m* stepfather.

padre *m* priest; **o Santo ~** *m (Papa)* the Holy Father; **2** **~-nosso** *m (Pater Noster)* our Father; the Lord's Prayer.

padrinho *m (REL) (de baptismo)* godfather; **2** *(de casamento)* best man, witness; **3** *(duelo)* second; **4** *(fig)* sponsor; **padrinhos** *mpl (padrinho e madrinha)* godparents.

padroado *m (privilégios)* patronage; grace and favour.

padroeiro,-a *m,f* patron/patroness; **2** patron saint; **Santo António é o ~ de Lisboa** St. Anthony is Lisbon's Patron Saint.

padronização *f* standardization.

padronizar *vt* to standardize.

paelha *f (CULIN)* paella.

pães *mpl (Vd:* **pão***)*.

pagã *(pl:* **pagãs***) f adj* pagan.

paga *f* payment, pay; wages; **2** *(fig) (vingança)* payback, revenge; **3** *(reward)* recompensa *f*; ♦ *adv* **em ~ de** in return (for), as payment.

pagador,-ora *m,f* payer; **2** pay clerk, pay master; ♦ *adj* paying.

pagamento *m* payment; **~ a contado/a dinheiro** cash payment; **~ a prestações** payment in instalments, hire-purchase; **dia de ~** pay-day; **folha de ~** payroll.

pagão *(pl:* **-ãos***) m adj adj* pagan.

pagar *vt (satisfazer)* to pay *(dívida)*; **2** *(reembolsar)* to pay back, repay; **3** **~ por algo** pay (for sth); **~ caro** to pay dearly; **~ a pronto/**(BR) **à vista** to pay on the spot; **4** *(retribuir)* to return *(amabilidade, visita, elogio)* pay off; ♦ *vi (liquidar)* repay; pay off; **2** *(expiar)* pay for; IDIOM **paga o justo pelo pecador** to pay for someone else's mistakes; **~ na mesma moeda** an eye; give for an eye; give tit for tat.

pagável *adj inv* payable.

página *f* page; **~ de rosto** facing page; **2 a ~s tantas** *adv* suddenly.

paginação *f* pagination.

paginar *vt* to paginate *(livro, etc)*; to number pages; **2** *(TYPO)* do the lay-out.

pago,-a (*irr pp de* **pagar**) *adj* paid; **2** (*dívida*) paid, settled; **3** (*fig*) even; **estamos** ~**s** we are even; **4** (*recompensado*) rewarded.

pagode *m* (*templo*) pagoda; templo; **2** (*pop*) (*gente*) crowd; **3** (*fig*) (*farra*) fun, high jinks *pl*; **andar no** ~ to go on the spree, paint the town red (*pop*); **4** (*BR*) (*zombaria*) joke, trick.

págs (*abr de* **páginas**) *fpl* pp.

pai *m* father; ~ **adotivo** adoptive father; ~ **de criação** foster father; ~**s** *mpl* parents; IDIOM **tal** ~, **tal filho** like father, like son.

pai-de-santo *m* (*BR*) witch-doctor.

Pai-Natal *m* Santa Claus, Father Christmas.

painel (*pl*: -**éis**) *m* (*ger*) panel; **2** picture; **3** (*porta, janela*) frame; **4** (*expositor*) board, panel; **5** (*AER, AUTO*) ~ **de instrumentos** dashboard; **6** (*NÁUT*) ~ **da popa** counter; **7** (*fig*) (*reunião*) panel.

Pai-nosso *m* (*REL*) (*oração*) Our Father; the Lord's prayer; IDIOM **ensinar o** ~ **ao vigário** to teach one's grandmother how to suck eggs.

paio *m* a kind of large smoked sausage.

paiol *m* (*NÁUT*) arsenal, storeroom; **2** barn; **3** (*MIL*) ~ **de pólvora** powder magazine, keg; **4** ~ **de carvão** coal bunker.

pairar *vi* (*estar no ar, sobranceiro*) to hover (**em/ sobre** in/over, about); **a águia pairava sobre os telhados** the eagle hovered about the roofs; **2** (*NÁUT*) to lie to; **3** (*iminente*) loom, hang over; **a ameaça paira sobre nós** the threat hangs over us; **4** (*fig*) (*estar irresoluto*) to hesitate, waver; **5** (*permear*) **o mau cheiro pairava** the bad smell lingered on.

país *m* country; land; ~ **encantado** fairyland; ~ **natal** native land, homeland.

paisagem *f* scenery, landscape.

paisagista *m,f* landscape painter; (*arquitecto*) landscape architect.

paisagístico,-a *adj* (*panorama, impacto, vista*) relating to landscape.

paisana *m* civilian; **à** ~ *adv* (*traje civil*) in plain clothes, in mufti; (*MIL*) (*col*) civvy (*pl*: civvies).

paisano,-a *m,f* civilian; **2** fellow; ♦ *adj* civilian.

País de Gales *npr* Wales; **o** ~ Wales.

Países Baixos *npr* **os** ~ the Netherlands.

paixão *f* passion; **2** (*REL*) **Semana da P**~ holy week; **Sexta-feira da P**~ Good Friday.

paixoneta *f* crush, puppy love.

pajem *m* (*moço*) page.

pala *f* (*de boné*) peak; **2** (*para proteger os olhos*) eye shade; **3** (*de sapato*) tongue; **4** cloth with which the priest covers the chalice; **palas** *fpl* (*para burro, cavalo*) blinkers; ♦ *prep* **à** ~ **de** *prep* at the expense of; **to live à** ~**de alguém** to live at sb's expenses; (*a pretexto de*) out of; **à** ~ **de interesse** out of interest.

palacete *m* mansion, small palace.

palaciano,-a *adj* palatial, courtly.

palácio *m* palace; (*JUR*) ~ **da Justiça** Law courts.

paladar *m* taste, flavour; **isto está sem** ~ this has no taste, this is tasteless. **2** (*ANAT*) palate.

paladino *m* paladin, champion, knight-errant; **2** (*fig*) (*defensor de uma causa*) defender.

palafita *f* (*ARQ*) pile; (*habitação*) casa built on piles; **2** lake-dwelling.

palanque *m* stand.

palatal *m* palatal; ♦ *adj inv* palatal.

palavra *f* word; **2** (*expressão verbal*) speech; **3** promise, **dou-lhe a minha** ~ I give you my word; **4** floor; **ter a** ~ have the floor; **5** right to speak; **cortar a** ~ to interrupt, cut sb short; **cumprir a** ~ to honour one's word; **dirigir a** ~ to address; **faltar à** ~ to break one's word; **pedir a** ~ **alguém** (*num debate*) to ask permission to speak; **ter o dom da** ~ to have the gift of the gab; ~**s cruzadas** *fpl* cross-word (puzzle); ♦ *exc* ~ really!; ~ **de honra!** honestly!; ♦ *adj* **sem** ~ untrustworthy, unreliable; ♦ *adv* ~ **por** ~ word for word; **em poucas** ~**s** briefly; IDIOM **não estar com meias** ~**s** not to mince words.

palavra-chave (*pl*: **palavras-chave**) *f* keyword; **2** (*identificação*) password.

palavrão *m* (*palavra obscena*) swearword; **2** (*difícil de pronunciar*) mouthful; **3** jargon; ~ **técnico** technical jargon.

palavreado *m* chatter, gable, palaver; **2** (*lábia*) gab, smooth talk; **3** a lot of words/talk; **4** bad language, sharp tongue.

palavrinha *f* (*fam*) little word; **quero ter uma** ~ **com você** I want to have a word with you.

palco *m* (*TEAT*) stage; **2** (*cenário*) scene; **3** ~ **de reuniões** venue for the meetings.

paleio *m* prattle, idle talk; **estar no** ~, (*BR*: **estar no bate-papo**) to be chatting; nattering with (sb).

paleolítico,-a *adj* Palaeolithic.

paleontologia *f* paleontology.

paleontólogo,-a *m,f* palaeontologist.

palerma *m,f* fool; ♦ *adj* silly, foolish; **2** (*col*) daft.

palermice *f* foolishness; stupidity.

Palestina *npr* **a** ~ Palestine.

palestino,-a, palestiano,-a *adj* Palestinian; from Palestina.

palestra *f* lecture; talk.

palestrante *adj* (*em conferências*) speaker.

paleta *f* (*de pintor*) palette; **2** (*pincel de dourar*) brush used in gilding.

paletó *m* overcoat; **2** (*BR*) jacket, coat; **3** (*BR*) (*pop*) **abotoar o** ~ morrer.

palha *f* straw, chaff; **2** (*feno*) hay; **fardos de** ~ bundles of hay/straw; **3** (*fig*) (*ninharias*) trifle; **4** (*na escrita*) waffle, rubbish; IDIOM **por dá cá aquela** ~ for no obvious reason; **ela não mexe uma** ~ (**em nada**) she doesn't lift a finger (to do) anything.

palhaçada *f* clowns; **2** (*acto, dito de palhaço*) antics, tricks; **3** (*brincar como palhaço*) clowning, buffoonery.

palhaço *m* clown; **fazer de** ~ to play the fool.

palha-de-aço *f* steel wool.

palheiro *m* hay loft, haystack; **2** (*casa pobre*) straw hut; **uma agulha em** ~ a needle in a haystack.

palheta *f* (*ART*) palette; **2** (*de modular*) pallet; **3** (*de persiana*) slat; **4** (*calçado*) tongue; **5** (*MÚS*) (*lâmina de madeira ou metal*) reed; (*de marfim, osso*) plectrum; **instrumento de** ~ reed instrument.

palhete *m (vinho)* light red (wine); ♦ *adj inv* straw-coloured.

palhinha *(tubo de plástico para beber líquidos)* straw; **2** *(para cadeira)* **assentos de** ~ straw, split cane seats.

palhoça, palhota *f (cabana coberta de colmo)* thatched hut; **capa de** ~ straw cape *(de Trás-os-Montes)*

paliar *vt (disfarçar)* to disguise, gloss over; **2** *(fig)* to mitigate, alleviate, palliate; ♦ *vi* make excuses.

paliativo,-a *m* palliative ♦ *adj* palliative;.

paliçada *f* palisade, (cane) enclosure, fence; **2** *(MIL)* stockade.

palidez *f (cor)* paleness; **2** *(de pessoa)* pallor.

pálido,-a *adj* pale, pallid, *(rosto)* white.

pálio *m (LITURG)* pallium.

palitar *vi* ~ **os dentes** to pick one's teeth.

paliteiro *m* tooth-pick, cocktail-stick holder.

palito *m* small stick; **2** ~ **dental** toothpick; **3** *(de cocktail)* cocktail stick.

palma *f (BOT) (de palmeira)* palm; **2** *(ANAT) (da mão)* palm; **3** ~**s** applause; **bater** ~**s** to clap; **4** *(fig)* laurels; IDIOM **levar a** ~ **a alguém** to carry off the palm, surpass sb; **trazer alguém nas** ~**s da mão** to treat sb with care/tact; **conhecer** *(pessoa/ lugar)* **como a** ~ **da mão** to know (sb, sth) like the back of one's hand, to know inside out.

palmada *f* slap, smack; **dar/levar umas** ~**s** to smack, be smacked.

palmar *m* palm grove; ♦ *adj inv (palma da mão)* relative to the palm; **2 erro** ~ *(grande erro)* a howler; ♦ *vt (pop) (futar)* to nick.

palmatória *f* ferule; **dar a mão à** ~ to give in, acknowledge one's mistake, defeat; **erro de** ~ a howler.

palmeira *f (BOT)* palm tree.

palmilha *f (sapato)* insole, inner sole; **2** *(parte da meia)* sole of sock/stocking.

palmilhar *vt (sapato)* to tread; **2** *(distância a pé)* to trudge; ~ **quilómetros** to walk for miles.

palminhas *fpl*: **dar** ~ *(criança)* to clap; **2 andar (com alguém) nas** ~ to pamper s.o., take great care of (sb).

palminho *m*; **ter um** ~ **de cara** be a pretty face.

palmo *m (mão)* handspan; **2** *(fig)* short distance; **3** *(fig) (grande)* huge; **ele tem um nariz de** ~ **e meio** he has a huge nose; ♦ *adv* ~**a** ~ inch by inch; **a** ~**s** in leaps and bounds; IDIOM **não ver um** ~ **adiante do nariz,** not able to see beyond (the end of) one's nose; **ficar de nariz de** ~ **e meio** be disappointed; **ter língua de** ~ **e meio** have a sharp tongue.

PALOP *(abr de* **Países Africanos de Língua Oficial Portuguesa)** Portuguese-speaking African countries.

palpável *(pl:* -**veis***) adj* palpable, tangible; **2** *(fig)* obvious, evident.

pálpebra *f (ANAT)* eyelid.

palpitação *f* beating, throbbing; **palpitações** *fpl* palpitations.

palpitante *adj* throbbing; **2** *(fig)* thrilling, quivering.

palpitar *vt (coração)* to beat, to pulsate; **2** *(pressentir)* forecast, have a feeling; ♦ *vi (coração agitado)* throb, palpitate.

palpite *m* palpitation; **2** *(fig) (intuição)* hunch, inkling; **3** *(fam)* opinião; **dê-me o seu** ~ give me your opinion.

palpiteiro,-a *m,f* opiniated person; ♦ *adj* opiniated.

palpo *m (ZOOL)* palpus, feeler; ~**s-de-aranha** *mpl* spider's palpi; IDIOM **estar em** ~**s de aranha** to be in a tricky situation/in a jam.

palrar *vi* to chatter as a parrot; **2** *(falar sem sentido)* to babble; **3** *(falar sem cessar)* prattle, jabber; *(col)* rabbit on.

palude *m* marsh, swamp.

paludismo *m (MED)* malaria.

palustre *adj* marshy; marsh-dwelling.

pampa *f* pampa; *(GEOG)* pampas; **as** ~**s argentinas** *fpl* Argentinian pampas.

pâmpano *m (BOT)* vine tendril/shoot; **2** *(fish)* type of pompano.

Panamá *npr* **o** ~ Panama.

panamenho,-a *(BR) adj;* **(EP) panamense** *adj inv* from Panama; Panamanian.

pan-americano,-a *adj* pan-American.

panar *vt (CULIN)* cover sth *(carne, peixe, etc)* with breadcrumbs.

panasca *m (pop)* sissy, pansy.

pança *f (fam)* belly, paunch.

panca *f (col) (mania)* crank; **ele tem uma** ~ sb has a screw loose.

pancada *f* blow, hit; **2** *(porta)* knock; **3** *(relógio)* stroke; **4 dar uma** ~ **com a cabeça** to bang one's head; **dar** ~ **em alguém** to hit sb; **levar (uma)** ~ to get hit.

pancadaria *f (muitas pancadas)* thrashing; **2** *(desordem)* brawl *(with blows).*

pâncreas *f sg/pl (ANAT)* pancreas.

pançudo,-a *adj* fat tummy, potbellied.

pandarecos *mpl (fam) (cacos)* broken pieces, fragments; **em** ~ in pieces, shattered

pândega *f* merrymaking, high jinks; **uma noite de** ~ a night on the tiles.

pândego,-a *m,f (alguém brincalhão)* wag, reveller; ♦ *adj* fun-loving; **2** waggish, flippant.

pandeireta *f (MÚS)* tambourine.

pandeiro *m (MÚS)* timbrel.

pandemia *f* pandemic.

pandemónio *(BR:* -ô-*) m* pandemonium

pane *f (AUTO)* breakdown.

panela *f* pot; saucepan; ~ **de pressão** pressure cooker; **2** *(fig)* death-rattle; IDIOM **muita gente a mexer na** ~ too many cooks spoil the broth.

paneleiro *m* potter; tinker; **2** *(pej) (homosexual)* gay.

panfleto *m* pamphlet.

pânico *m* panic; **em** ~ panic-stricken.

panificação *f* bread-making, baking industry.

panificar *vt* to make bread.

pano *m* cloth; **2** *(fig)* skin blemish; **3** *(TEAT)* curtain; ~ **de boca** safety, stage curtain; ~ **de cozinha** dishcloth; ~ **cru** unbleached cotton; ~ **de pó** duster;' **4** ~ **de fundo** backdrop; **5** *(mesa de jogo)* baize; **6** *(NÁUT)* sail; **7** *(ARQ)* front/face; **8** *(fig)* **por baixo do** ~ **debaixo do** ~ on the sly; **9** ~**s quentes** half measures; ♦ *adv* **a todo o** ~ under

250

full sail, at full speed; IDIOM **talhar/cortar o fato conforme o ~** to cut one's coat according to one's cloth.

panorama *m* panorama, scene, view; **2** *(fig)* survey.

panqueca *f* pancake.

pantanal *m* swamp, marshland.

pântano *m* marsh, swamp.

pantanoso,-a *adj* marshy, swampy.

panteão *m* pantheon.

panteísta *m,f* pantheist; ◆ *adj* pantheistic.

pantera *f* panther.

pantomima *f* pantomime.

pantufa *f* winter slipper.

pão *(pl:* **pães)** *m* bread; **um ~** a loaf; **~ de forma** sliced loaf; **~ caseiro** home-made bread; **~ com manteiga** bread and butter; **~ integral** whomeal bread; **miolo de ~** crumb; **~ ralado** breadcrumbs; **~ ázimo** unlevelled bread; **~-de-ló** *(pl:* **pães-de-ló)** *m* sponge cake; **2** *(fig) (sustento)* **ganhar o ~ de cada dia** to earn a livelihood; IDIOM **nem só do ~ vive o homem** man does not live on bread alone, all work and no play makes Jack a dull boy; **ser ~ ~, queijo, queijo** *(ser directo)* be blunt, to call a spade a spade.

pão-duro *(pl:* **pães-duro)** *(BR) m m,f* miser; ◆ *adj inv* miserly, stingy.

pão-ralado *m* breadcrumbs.

pãozinho *(pl:* **pãezinhos)** *m* (bread) roll.

papá *m* dad; daddy.

papa *f (comida para bebés)* mush, pap, baby food; **2** *(substância mole)* mash, pulp; **3** P~ *m* Pope; IDIOM **não ter ~s na língua** to be outspoken, not to beat about the bush; **ir a Roma e não ver o P~** to miss the main attraction in a place/point.

papa-açorda *m,f (pessoa)* slowcoach, dawdler, slow-witted person.

papada *f (fam)* double chin.

papado *m* papal throne; **2** *(reino, tempo do reino)* papacy.

papa-formigas *m sg/pl (ZOOL)* anteater.

papagaio *m* parrot; **2** *(de papel)* kite.

papaguear *vt (repetir)* to repeat like a parrot; ◆ *vi* to chatter away.

papai *(BR) m* dad, daddy; **P~ Noel** Santa Claus, Father Christmas.

papaia *f (BOT)* papaya.

papaieira *f* papaya tree.

papa-jantares *m,f sg, pl, (fam)* sponger, scrounger.

papal *adj inv* papal; **2 as bulas papais** papal edicts.

papalvo *m (pej)* simpleton; ◆ *adj* simple; **2** *(ingénuo)* naïve, gullible.

papa-moscas *m,f (pej)* simpleton, ninny; gaper; **2** *(ZOOL)* fly-catcher.

papanicolau *(MED) (fig) (esfregaço)* cancer smear.

papão *m* bogeyman.

papar *vt (child's talk), (fam) (comer)* eat (up); **2** *(fig) (ganhar prémios)* gobble up; ◆ *vi* to eat; **vamos, papa tudo** come on, eat up.

paparicar *vt* to pamper.

paparicos *mpl* pampering *sg*.

papeira *f (MED)* mumps.

papel *(pl:* **-éis)** *m* paper; **~ de alumínio** tinfoil; **~ de embrulho** wrapping paper; **~ higiénico** toilet paper; **~ ofício** headed paper; **~ pardo** brown paper; **~ químico** carbon paper; **~ de rascunho** scrap paper; **~ de seda** tissue paper; **2** role; **fazer o ~ de** to play the part of; **fazer o ~ de** *(fig)* to play the fool; IDIOM **confiar ao ~** put in writing.

papelada *f* pile of papers; **2** red tape.

papelão *m* cardboard; **2** papier-maché; **3** *(CIN, TEAT) (fig) (figura de ridículo)* fiasco.

papelaria *f* stationer's (shop).

papelzinho *m* scrap of paper.

papo *m (de ave)* crop; **2** *(de pessoa)* double chin; **3** *(fig)* **de ~ para o ar** to be idle, to sit on one's hands; **4** *(BR) (fam)* chat; **bater ~** to chat, to have a natter.

papoila (= **papoula**) *f (BOT)* poppy.

papo-seco *m* Portuguese bread roll; **2** *(fam)* dandy; **3** *(rapaz bonito, galante)* heartthrob.

papudo,-a *adj* double-chinned

paquete *m (NÁUT) (grande navio de passageiros)* liner, steamship.

paquiderme *m* pachyderme; **2** *(pop) (pessoa corpulenta)* elefante.

paquistanês,-esa *adj* Pakistani; *(LÍNG)* Urdu.

Paquistão *npr* o ~ Pakistan.

par *(pl:* **-es)** *m (dupla)* pair; couple; **um ~ de candieiros** a pair of lamps; **um ~ de namorados** a couple of lovers; **um ~ de ovos** a couple of eggs; **2** *(em dança)* partner; **3** P~ *(UK) (antigo membro da câmara alta)* Peer; **a Câmara dos Pares** The Chamber/House of Peers/Lords; ◆ *adj inv (MAT) (número)* even; alike; symmetrical; ◆ *adv* **a ~** in twos, abreast; **aos pares** in pairs; **de ~ em ~** wide open; **sem ~** without equal/peerless; ◆ **estar a ~ de** to be aware of (situation, subject; to be well informed about sth).

para *prep (direcção, objectivo)* for, to, at (towards); **as flores são ~ ti** the flowers are for you; **olhei ~ ele** I looked at him; **ela foi ~ cima/baixo** she went upstairs/downstairs; **2** *(destino, estágio longo)* **vou para o Brasil trabalhar** I am going to work in Brazil; **vou ~ casa** I am going home; **3** *(motivo, fim)* (in order to) to; **vim a tua casa ~ te consolar** I came to your home to (in order to) comfort you; **~ quê?** what for?; **4** *(orientação)* **o quarto dá ~ a rua**, the room overlooks the street; **~ onde?** where to?; **5** *(horas)* **faltam vinte ~ as cinco** it's twenty to five; *(hora marcada)* **tenho uma consulta ~ as oito** I have a doctor's appointment for eight o'clock; **6** *(tempo futuro)* **~ a semana** next week; **7** *(comparação, opinião)* for; **o casaco está grande demais ~ você** the coat is too big for you; **~ mim está tudo bem** for me/as far as I am concerned everything is all right; **8** *(iminência)* **estou para sair** I am about to go out; **9** *(capacidade)* **ele é a pessoa própria ~ este trabalho** he is the right person for this job; **10** *(quantidade)* **~ cima de** in excess of, on top of; **~ com** *(attitude)* towards; **ele é bom para com todos** he is kind to (towards) everyone; ◆ *adv* **~ além**

251

de beyond, over, furthermore; ~ **sempre** for good, for ever; ♦ *adv* ~ **sempre** for ever; ♦ *conj* ~ **que** so that, in order that, so as to.

parabéns *mpl* congratulations; happy birthday *sg*; **dar** ~ **a** to congratulate; to wish happy birthday to.

parábola *f (LITER)* parable; **2** *(GEOM)* parabola.

parabólica *f (GEOM) adj* parabola; **2** *(TV)* satellite dish.

pára-brisas, para-brisas *m sg pl* windscreen; **2** *(US)* windshield.

pára-choques, para-choques *m sg pl (AUTO)* bumper; shock absorber; **2** *(FERRO)* buffer.

parada *f* parade; **2** stake (gambling); **3** halt; **4** *(BR)* stop; ~ **do ônibus** bus-stop.

paradeiro *m (lugar onde se pára)* stopover; **2** *(endereço, lugar onde se encontra)* whereabouts, address.

paradigma *m* paradigm; example.

paradigmático,-a *adj* paradigmatic.

paradisíaco,-a *adj* paradisiac; paradise-like; idyllic; heavenly.

parado *adj (alguém)* still, motionless; **2** *(máquina, etc)* stopped; **3 expressão** ~**a** expressionless, dull; **4** *(sem progresso)* standstill.

paradoxal *adj inv* paradoxical, contradictory.

paradoxo *m* paradox.

parafernália *f* paraphernalia; **2** equipment; **3** *(cenário)* props.

parafina *f (QUÍM)* paraffin.

paráfrase *f* paraphrase.

parafrasear *vt* to paraphrase.

parafuso *m* screw; **chave de** ~**s** screw-driver; IDIOM **ter um** ~ **a menos** to have a screw loose.

paragem *f* stop; ~ **do autocarro** *(EP)* bus stop; **2** *(MED)* ~ **cardíaca** cardiac arrest; **paragens** *fpl* places, spot, parts; **estive nestas** ~ **ontem** I was in this area yesterday.

parágrafo *m* paragraph.

Paraguai *npr* Paraguay; **o** ~ Paraguay.

paraguaio,-a *adj* Paraguayan.

paraíso *m (lugar lindo)* paradise; **2 P**~ *(REL)* Paradise, Garden of Eden; **3** ~ **fiscal** tax haven.

pára-lamas, para-lamas *m (AUTO)* mudguard.

paralela *(GEOM)* parallel; **2** ~**s** *(DESP)* parallel bars.

paralelepípedo *m* paving stone; **2** *(GEOM)* parallelepiped.

paralelo,-a *f* parallel line; ♦ *adj (GEOM)* parallel; **2** equivalent.

paralisar *vt* to paralyse; **2** to bring to a standstill; ♦ ~**-se** *vr* to become paralysed; **2** *(fig)* to come to a standstill.

paralisia *f* paralysis.

paralítico,-a *adj* paralytic.

paramédico,-a *adj* paramedic.

paramento *m (LITURG)* vestment; **2** ornament; ♦ ~**s** *mpl* vestments; **2** hangings; **3** *(enfeites)* trimmings.

parametrizar *vt* to follow parameters; to place *(subject, problem)* within the parameters.

parâmetro *m* parameter.

paramilitar *adj* paramilitary.

parangona *f (TYPO)* large print; ~**s** *fpl* headlines.

paranóia, paranoia *f* paranoia.

paranóico,-a, paranoico,-a *adj* paranoid, paranoiac.

paraolimpíadas *fpl (DESP)* Paralympics, Parallel Olimpics.

parapeito *m* parapet; **2** *(muro de protecção)* wall; ~ **da janela** windowsill; ~ **da chaminé** mantelpiece.

paraplégico,-a *m,f adj* paraplegic.

pára-quedas, para-quedas *m inv (AER)* parachute; **lançar-se de** ~ to bail out; **2** *(pop) (sutiã)* bras.

paraquedista *m,f* parachutist; ♦ *m (MIL)* paratrooper.

parar *vi* to stop; to stay; ♦ *vt* to stop; **fazer** ~ to stop; ~ **na cadeia** to end up in jail; ~ **de fazer** to stop doing.

pára-raios, para-raios *m inv* lightning conductor, rod.

parasita *m,f* parasite; **2** *(fig) (pessoa)* parasite; ♦ *adj inv* parasitic.

pára-vento, para-vento *m* windscreen; windbreaker.

parceiro,-a *m,f (em jogo, dança, vida conjugal)* partner; **2** *(POL) (entidades representativas)* representatives; **3** *(em crime)* accomplice, partner; **4** associate.

Not in a commercial sense, which is '**sócio**'.

parcela *f* piece, bit, part; **2** *(de terra)* plot; **3** *(cada número duma adição)* number.

parcelamento *n (de pagamento)* pay in instalments; **2** *(de terras)* distribution.

parcelar *vt* pay in instalments.

parceria *f* partnership; **2** *(AGR, ECON, JUR)* cooperative, association; **em** ~ in partnership; **de** ~ **com** in conjunction with.

parcial *adj inv* partial; **2** biased; **3** *(tempo)* part, **trabalho a tempo** ~ part-time job.

parcialidade *f* partiality, bias, unfairness; **2** *(favoritismo)* preference.

parcimónia *(BR: -ô-)* parsimony, frugality; **2** moderation.

parcimonioso,-a *adj* scanty; thrifty, parsimonious.

parco,-a *adj (que poupa)* economical; **2** *(moderado)* sparing; **3** *(meios escassos)* meagre, scanty; **4** *(comida)* frugal.

parcómetro *m* parking-meter.

pardacento,-a *adj* brownish, greyish; **as águas** ~**as do rio** the murky waters of the river; **2 céu** ~ dark, grey sky.

pardal *m (ZOOL)* sparrow; **2** *(fig, fam)* wise-guy.

pardieiro *m* ruin; **casa em** ~ ruins of (a house), dilapidated (area); **2** *(casebre)* squalid dwelling, hovel.

pardo,-a *adj (cor) (acinzentado)* grey, greyish; **2** *(cinza acastanhado)* dun; **3** *(céu nublado)* cloudy, overcast, dull; **4** *(papel)* brown; **5** *(fig) (pessoa)* shadowy; IDIOM **à noite todos os gatos são** ~**s** at night, every cat is grey.

parecença *f* similarity, likeness.

parecer *m* opinion; **no meu** ~ in my opinion; **2** *(pessoa)* **de bom** ~ good-looking; ♦ *vi* to look, seem; **ele parece cansado** he looks tired; **2** to look like, seem; **parece que vai chover** it looks like raining (it is going to rain); **ele parece diferente** he seems different; ♦ **~-se** *vr* to look alike, resemble each other; **~ com o pai** to take after one's father; ♦ *adv* **ao que parece** apparently; **parece-me que** it seems to me that; **que lhe parece?** *(pedindo a opinião)* what do you think? (of idea etc).

parecido,-a *adj* alike, similar; **~ com** like; **ele é ~ com o pai** he looks like/takes after his father.

paredão *m* high, thick wall; **2** steep river bank, breakwater; **3** *(avenida pedonal à beira-mar)* promenade.

parede *f (CONSTR)* wall; **2** *(ANAT)* walls; ♦ **viver ~s com** *prep* next door to, sharing (an apartment); IDIOM **entre a espada e a ~** between the devil and the deep blue sea; **ir à ~** *(irritar-se)* to hit the ceiling; **pôr os pés à ~** *(insistir no seu parecer)* dig in one's heels.

parelha *f (junta)* team; **uma ~ de bois** a team of oxen; **2** *(fig, fam)* pair; **uma ~ de idiotas** a pair, couple of idiots.

parental *adj inv* parental.

parente *m*, **parenta** *f* relative, relation, kin; **~s afastados** distant relatives; **~s próximos** next of kin.

It does not mean '**parents**' i.e. **father, mother**.

parentela *f* family relations, family line; **2** *(pej)* sect, cult.

parentesco *m* relationship; **2** *(fig)* similarity, connection.

parêntese *m* parenthesis, brackets; **~ curvo/recto** round/square brackets; **abrir/fechar ~s** to open/close brackets.

páreo *m (corrida a cavalo entre dois competidores)* horse-race; **estar fora do ~** to be out of the race.

pargo *m (peixe)* porgy, a kind of large snapper.

pária *(pessoa)* pariah; **2** *(pessoa marginalizada)* outcast; ♦ *adj inv (grupo, população)* low cast, outcast.

paridade *f* equality; **2** *(ECON) (câmbios)* parity; *(ECON: ajuste gradual da paridade) (col)* crawling peg; **3** *(FÍS, MAT)* parity; **~ ímpar** odd parity.

parir *vt (fam)* to give birth to; ♦ *vi (animals)* to bring forth young, to lamb, whelp.

parisiense *m,f* Parisien, Parisienne; ♦ *adj inv (monumento, vida, etc)* from Paris.

parka *f* headed jacket, parka.

parlamentar *m,f* member of Parliament, deputy; ♦ *adj inv* parliamentary.

parlamento *m* Parliament.

parmesão *adj (queijo)* parmesan.

pároco *m* parish priest.

paródia *f* parody, burlesque; **2** *(humor)* joke; **3** *(gozo)* fun; **ontem foi uma grande ~** last night it was a lot of fun.

parodiar *vt* to copy, parody; **2** *(gozar)* take off; ♦ *vi* mimic, take-off.

parolice *f (rusticidade)* coarseness; **2** *(tagarelice)* chatter.

parolo,-a *m,f (pej)* country bumpkin, boor, lout.

parónimo *(LÍNG) m* paronym; ♦ *adj* paronymous.

paróquia *f (REL)* parish.

paroquiano,-a *m,f* parishioner; ♦ *adj* parochial.

paroxismo *m (MED)* paroxysm; fit, attack; **~ s** *mpl* death throes.

parque *m* park; **2** *(reserve)* park; **~ nacional** national park; **3** *(coutada)* game reserve; **4 ~ de estacionamento** car-park; **5 ~ industrial** industrial estate.

parqueamento *m* car park; parking; *(residentes)* resident's park area.

parquet *(CONSTR) (soalho)* parquet.

parquete *(Vd:* **parquet**).

parquímetro *m* parking meter.

parra *f* vine leaf.

parreira *f* trellised vine; **2** *(armação)* trellis.

parte *f* part, fraction; **2** *(quinhão)* share; **3** *(papel de actor)* role, part; **4** *(JUR, ECON)* party; **ambas as partes** both parties; **5** *(lado)* **~ interna** inside/lower; **chamar à ~** to call sb aside; ♦ **a maior ~ de** most of; **da ~ de** from, on behalf of; **dar ~ de** inform about; **dar ~ de fraco** show weakness; **de ~ a ~** mutually; **~ aside**; **pôr de ~** to set aside; **fazer ~ de** to belong; to participate; **em grande ~** to a great extent; **em ~** partly; **5** *(lugar)* **em ~ alguma** nowhere; **por toda (a) ~** everywhere; **6 partes** *fpl* parts; **vejamos isto por ~s** let us look at this methodically (one by one); **por exclusão de ~s** by the process of elimination; **~s íntimas** *(ANAT)* private parts; IDIOM **mandar (alguém) à outra ~** tell sb to get lost.

parteira *f* midwife.

partição *f* sharing (out); **2** *(COMP)* partition; **3** *(of a country/room)* division, separation.

participação *f* participation, partaking; **2** announcement, notification, notice; **3** *(ECON)* **~ nos lucros** profit-sharing; **4** *(à polícia)* complaint.

participante *m,f* participant.

participar *vt* to inform; **2** announce; **3** notify, report; ♦ *vi* to participate, take part in; **2** to share in; **3 ~ de** *(denunciar)* complain about.

particípio *m (LÍNG)* participle.

partícula *f (gen)* particle.

particular *m* particular; **2 ~ es** *mpl* details; ♦ *adj inv (modos, estilo, sabor, questão)* particular; **2** *(quarto, caminho, carro)* private; **3** *(atenção, simpatia)* special; **em ~** *(privativo)* in private; *(especialmente)* in particular, especially.

particularizar *vt* to specify; to give details of; ♦ **~-se** *vr* to distinguish o.s.; to stand out.

particularmente *adv* privately; particularly, especially.

partida *f* departure, leaving time, start; **ponto de ~** starting time; **2** *(DESP)* game, match; **uma ~ de futebol** a football match; **3** *(fam) (brincadeira)* joke; **pregar uma ~ a** to play a joke on; **4 fazer uma ~ a (alguém)** to let someone down; **à ~** *adv* at first; **fazer ~s** to play tricks.

partidário,-a *m,f (POL) (membro/simpatizante de um partido)* member, supporter of a party; **2** *(seguidor)* follower; *(de uma causa)* partisan; ♦ *adj* party; follower.

partido *m* (POL) party; (UK) P~ **Conservador** Conservative Party; P~ **Trabalhista** Labour Party; 2 (apoio, defesa) side; **ela tomou o ~ do marido** she took her husband's side; 3 (parceiro de boa posição social) catch, match; **um bom ~** a good catch; 4 advantage; **tirar ~ de** to profit from, take advantage of, make the most of; ♦ **partido,-a** *adj* broken; 2 (partilhado) divided (up), cut; **pão ~ em fatias** bread cut into slices.

partilha *f* division; **fazer ~** to divide up a inheritance.

partilhar *vt* to share (**com** with); 2 (distribuir) to share out; ♦ *vi* (compartilhar) **~ de algo** to share in sth.

partir *vt* to break; 2 to divide, split; ♦ *vi* to set off, set out; to leave, go away; 2 **~ de** to start/arise from ♦ **~-se** *vr* to break; ♦ *adv* **a ~ de** (starting) from, as from; **a ~ de amanhã** starting from tomorrow.

partitivo *m* (gram) partitive.

partitura *f* (MÚS) partiture.

parto *m* (MED) birth; **dores de ~** labour pains; **~ pélvico** breech delivery.

parturiente *f* (mulher, fêmea) in childbirth/in labour.

parturir *vt/vi* to give birth to.

parvalhice (=parvoíce) *f* silliness, imbecility.

parvo,-a *m,f* fool idiot; **armado em ~** acting like/ pretending to be a fool; ♦ *adj* silly, idiotic, foolish; 2 (fig) **fiquei ~ com o que vi** I was dumbstruck with what I saw.

parvónia *f* (pej) (lugar distante) countryside; 2 middle of nowhere; the back of beyond.

Páscoa *f* Easter; Passover; **Domingo de ~** Easter Sunday.

Pascoela *f* (REL) Low Sunday.

pasmaceira *f* (fam, pej) apathy; 2 star-gazing; 3 (tédio) bore; **a vida no campo é uma ~** life in the country is a bore.

pasmado,-a *adj* astonished, dumbfounded; 2 (com ar distante, alheio) rapt in thought; 3 (pessoa apalermada) stupid-looking.

pasmar *vt* (deslumbrar) to amaze; (surpreender) astonish; (com boca aberta) to gape; ♦ **~-se** (com) *vr* to be amazed at, be astonished at.

pasmo *m* (estupefação) amazement; 2 stupefaction; 3 dullness; IDIOM **morrer de ~** to die of boredom/ be bored stiff.

paspalhão,-ona *m,f* idiot; ♦ *adj* (ar, gesto) idiotic, foolish.

paspalho *m* scarecrow; 2 simpleton; numskull, dunce.

pasquim *m* satirical pamphlet; lampoon satire; 2 (fig) (jornaleco) rag.

passa *f* raisin; 2 (pop) (mulher seca e enrugada) dried up old stick; IDIOM **passar as ~s do Algarve** go through hell.

passada *f* step, pace, footsteps; **~ grande** stride; **ele ouviu ~s** he heard footsteps; 2 footprint; 3 **dar uma ~ por** to pop in, drop by; 4 **numa ~** (de uma vez) in a jiffy; IDIOM **perder as ~s** fail to obtain results from one's efforts.

passadeira *f* (carpete de corredor) runner; **~ para peões** zebra crossing; (estrado sobre a areia) walkway; 2 (BR) (engomadeira) ironing-woman; 3 (alpondras) *pl* stepping-stones.

passadiço,-a *m* (NÁUT) footbridge; 2 passageway, gallery; 3 narrow alley; ♦ *adj* (moda, ideias) passing.

passado *m* past; 2 (LÍNG) (tempo) past (tense); ♦ **passado,-a** *adj* past, last; **o ano ~** last year; 2 old-fashioned; 3 (fruto) bad; 4 (peixe) off; 5 (CULIN) (bife) **bem ~** well done steak; **mal ~** rare; 6 (banzado) stupefied (person); **um tempo bem ~** an enjoyable time.

passador *m* (utensílio da cozinha) strainer; colander.

passador,-ora *m,f* (de contrabando) trafficker, smuggler, receiver and passer.

passageiro,-a *m* passenger; 2 *adj* passing, fleeting.

passagem *f* (viagem, preço de) passage; fare; (bilhete) ticket; **~ de ida e volta** return ticket; (US) round trip ticket; 2 (caminho) passage; way; **~ de nível** (FERRO) level crossing; **~ subterrânea** subway; **~ de peões** pedestrian crossing; 3 (tempo) passage; **com a ~ dos anos** as the years went by; 4 (excerto) passage, section 5 (de modelos) fashion show; ♦ **de ~** *adv* in passing, briefly; **diga-se, de ~, que não achei grande coisa** actually, I didn't think much of (it); **de ~ por** *prep* passing through.

passajar *vt* to darn; **hoje em dia, já não se passaja as peúgas** nowadays, one no longer darns the socks.

passamento *m* (falecimento) passing, demise; 2 (efeito de passar) pushing; **~ de droga** drug pushing.

passante *m* passer-by; ♦ *adj inv* (que ultrapassa) passing, **~ de** over; 2 **~ de** (prep) exceeding.

passaporte *m* passport.

passar *vt* (movimentar-se) to pass, to go; 2 (atravessar) **~ por** to cross; to go through; 3 (ultrapassar) overtake (carro); to go beyond, exceed; **ela já passa dos cinquenta anos** she is well over fifty; **~ à frente** to get ahead; 4 (sofrer, aguentar) endure; **~ por** (coar) to sieve; (líquido) to strain; 5 (tarefa da escola) to set; 6 (tempo) to spend; 7 (expedir) send; 8 **~ a ferro** to iron; 9 **~ a** to go onto; **passo a responder** I'll go onto replying/I am now going to reply; (change the subject) **~ a** to go onto another (topic); **passemos ao assunto em questão** let's go onto the matter in question; 10 (aprovar) pass; 11 enact, pass; (JUR) **~ uma lei** to enact a law; (sentença) to pronounce; ♦ *vi* (ger) to pass; (ficar aprovado no exame) to pass the exam; 2 to go; to go past; (mudar de assunto) **~ a** to go onto another subject; (tempo) to go by; **~ em/por** go in/through; **~ pela cabeça** to cross one's mind; **~ fome** to go hungry; (tempo) to go by; (sofrer) **~ por privações** to go through hardship/ endure; **~ de moda** to go out of fashion; 3 (fingir) **~ por** to pass o.s. off as; **~ por esperto** to pretend to be clever; 4 (estar) to be; **~ bem/mal** to be well/ not well; (ser mais tarde que) to be past; **já passa da meia-noite** it is past midnight; 5 (quick visit)

passar por casa de to drop by; **6** ~ **a ser** to become; **7** *(ser apenas)* **não** ~ **de** to be but, be just; **não passa duma brincadeira** it is just a joke; ~ **sem** to do without; ♦ **~-se** *vr* to go on, happen; **o que se passa?** what is happening?; **2** ~ **para** *(mudar de posição)* to go over to; **ele passou-se para o Benfica** he went over to Benfica.

passarada *f* many birds, flock of bids.

passarela *f* gangway; **2** *(BR) (para pedestre)* footbridge; **3** *(estrado elevado) (para manequim)* catwalk.

passarinho *m* little bird.

pássaro *m* bird; **2** *(homem astuto)* crafty fellow; IDIOM **mais vale um** ~ **na mão do que dois a voar** a bird in the hand is worth two in the bush.

passatempo *m* pastime; **2** hobby; **como** ~ for fun.

passável *adj inv* passable; **2** *(aceitável)* passable, so-so, all right; bearable, tolerable.

passe *m* *(licença)* pass; ~ **social** travel card.

passear *vt* to take *(pessoa, animal)* for a walk; **2** *(exibir)* to show off; ♦ *vi (a pé)* to go for a walk/stroll; ~ **a cavalo** to go for a ride; ~ **de carro** go for a drive/ spin; IDIOM **mandar alguém** ~ to send sb packing.

passeata *f (fam)* stroll *(de carro)* spin, drive; **2** *(BR)* demonstration, march.

passeio *m* walk, stroll, outing, drive, ride; **2** *(excursão)* trip; **3** *(lado da rua)* pavement; *(US)* sidewalk.

passe-vite *n (utensílio da cozinha)* potato, vegetable masher.

passivo,-a *adj* passive; ♦ *m (COM)* liabilities *pl*; **activos e ~s** assets and liabilities.

passo *m* step; footstep; **ouvir ~s** to hear footsteps; **2** stride, pace; **não consigo acompanhar teu** ~ I can't keep up with your pace; **apertar o** ~ to hurry up; **acertar o** ~ keep in step; **ceder o** ~ to give way; **dar um** ~ to take a step; **3 dar um mau** ~ to go astray; **4** *(ruído de passos)* footsteps; **5** *(pegada)* footprint; **~s na neve** footprints in the snow; **6** *(modo de andar)* gait; **7** ~ **em falso** the wrong move *(fig)* slip-up; **8** *(MIL)* **marcar** ~ to mark time; **9** *(REL)* station; **os ~s da paixão de Cristo** the stations of the cross; ♦ *adv* **a cada** ~ constantly, at every turn; **2** *(distância)* **fica a dois ~s** it is very near; **3 a** ~ **de caracol** at snail's pace; ♦ *conj* **ao** ~ **que** whereas, while.

pasta *f* paste, slurry; **pasta de dentes/dentrífica** toothpaste; **2** briefcase; **3** folder; **4** portfolio, **ministro sem** ~ minister without portfolio; **5** *(CULIN)* paté; **6** ~ **de papel** paper pulp.

pastagem *f* pasture.

pastar *vt* to graze on; ♦ *vi* to graze.

pastel *m (CULIN)* savoury fritter, turnover, tart; pastry; ~ **de bacalhau** Portuguese cod croquette; ~ **de massa tenra** meat turnover; ~ **de nata** Portuguese custard tart; **2** pastel drawing; **3** *(fig, fam) (pessoa indolente)* wimp; ♦ *adj inv (cor)* pastel.

pastelada *f (arte)* stroke of the brush; **2** a lot of cakes and fritters.

pastelão,-ona *m,f (fig)* lazy-bones; **2** *m (CULIN)* big pie.

pastelaria *f* patisserie.

pasteleiro,-a *m,f* pastry cook.

pasteurizado,-a *adj* sterilized (milk, etc.) by Pasteur's method).

pastiche *m* pastiche; imitation.

pastilha *f (MED)* tablet, pill; *(para a tosse, garganta)* pastille, lozenge; **2** *(COMP)* chip; **3** ~ **elástica** chewing gum.

pasto *m* grass; **2** pasture; **casa de** ~ eating-house, diner.

pastora *m,f* shepherd/shepherdess; ♦ *m (REL)* clergyman, pastor.

pastoral *m (LIT)* pastoral; ♦ *adj (campestre)* rustic.

pastorela *f (MÚS)* pastoral, pastoral poem.

pastorícia *f* herding; grazing.

pastoril *adj* pastoral, bucolic, rural.

pata *f* animal's foot, paw; ~ **dianteira/traseira** forefoot/hindfoot. **2** *(female)* duck; **3** ~ **de âncora** fluke/palm of the anchor; **4** *(fig, fam)* **meter a** ~ **(na poça)** to put one's foot in it.

pataca *f (BR and old Port.)* silver coin; **2** unit of currency in Macau.

pata-choca *(fig) (pej) (mulher gorda)* rolly-polly.

pataco *m* ancient Portuguese coin; **isso não vale um** ~ that isn't worth twopence.

patada *f* kick, blow.

patamar *m (da escada)* landing; **2** *(fig)* level.

patamar, patamarim *m (embarcação indiana)* coastal boat in India.

patavina *f (fam)* nothing; **não compreendi** ~ I didn't understand a word; it was all Greek, double Dutch to me.

patego,-a *m,f (pessoa do campo)* peasant, country-bumpkin; **2** *(fig) (fam)* simpleton.

patente *f (COM)* patent; **2** *(MIL)* commission; **altas ~s** high-ranking officers; ♦ *adj* obvious, evident.

patentear *vt* to show, reveal; **2** *(COM)* to patent; **3** *(franquear)* open, exibit; ♦ **~-se** *vr* to be shown, evident; show off.

paternal *adj inv* paternal; fatherly.

paternidade *f* paternity.

paterno,-a *adj* paternal; **casa ~a** family home.

pateta *m,f* idiot; ♦ *adj* stupid, daft.

patetice *f* silliness; **foi uma** ~ it was a silly thing.

patético,-a *adj* pathetic, tragic; **2** moving.

patíbulo *m* gallows.

patifaria *f (velhacaria)* villainy, wickedness.

patife *m (velhaco, enganador)* scoundrel, crook; **2** *(descarado)* rouge, rascal; ♦ *adj* villainous.

patilha *f (MEC, ELECT)* ~ **de segurança** safety/security catch; **2** *(do selim)* cantle; **~s** *pl (barba)* sideburns, side whiskers.

patim *m* skate; ~ **de rodas** roller skate.

patinagem *f* skating; skating rink.

patinar *vi* to skate; *(AUTO) (derrapar)* to skid.

patinhar *vi* to dabble; **2** to splash about, slosh; **3** ~ **pelas lezírias** to trudge through the marshes.

patinho *m* duckling; **o** ~ **feio** the ugly duckling; **2 ser um** ~ to be a sucker, naïve; IDIOM **ele caiu que nem um** ~ he fell for the bait.

pátio *m* patio, backyard; courtyard; **2** *(MIL)* parade ground; ~ **de recreio** playground.

pato *m* duck; drake; **2** ~ **bravo** mallard, wild duck; **3** *(fam) (lorpa)* sucker; **cair como um** ~ to swallow the bait, fall for it, be easily taken in.

patogenético,-a, **patogénico,-a** *(MED)* *adj* *(organismo, germe, acção)* pathogenic.

patologia *f (MED)* pathology.

patológico,-a *adj* pathological.

patologista *m,f* pathologist.

patranha *f (com fantasia, exagero)* tale, tall story; **2** *(mentira)* fib.

patrão *(f: -oa) (mpl: -ões; fpl: -oas) m (chefe, empregador)* boss, employer; **2** *(pessoa importante)* bigwig; **3** *(dono)* proprietário, owner; **4** *(da taberna)* landlord; **5** *(NÁUT)* skipper; **6** *(pop) (tratamento de afeição)* guv'nor, guv, gaffer; **7** *(marido, mulher)* boss; **pergunta à patroa** ask the wife/the boss.

pátria *f* native land, homeland.

patriarca *m (REL)* Patriarch; Bishop; **2** *(chefe de família)* patriarch.

patriarcal *(pl: -ais) adj inv* patriarchal.

patrício,-a *m,f* compatriot.

património *(BR: -mô-) m* patrimony; **2** *(JUR, ECON)* assets; **3** *(herança)* inheritance; **4** *(histórico)* heritage; ~ **cultural** cultural heritage.

patriota *m,f* patriot.

patriótico,-a *adj* patriotic.

patriotismo *m* patriotism.

patroa *f* female boss; **2** *(fam)* boss's wife; **3** wife, lady of the house; **4** landlady.

patrocinador,-ora *m,f* sponsor, patron.

patrocinar *vt* to sponsor; to support.

patrocínio *m* sponsorship, backing; **2** *(JUR)* patronage.

patronal *adj inv* sponsoring, supporting; **2 entidade** ~ employer.

patronato *m* the body of employers; management; **2** patronage.

patrono *m* patron saint; **2** *(JUR) (defensor)* lawyer.

patrulha *f* patrol.

patrulhar *vt/vi* to patrol.

patuscada *f (manjar)* eating spree; **2** *(ao ar livre)* garden party; *(churrascada)* barbecue party.

pau *m* wood; stick, beam; **de** ~ wooden; ~ **de vassoura** broomstick; **2** ~ **de canela/baunilha** a cinnamon/vanilla pod; **3** ~ **de bandeira** flagpole; **a meio** ~ at half-mast; **4** ~s *mpl (naipe)* clubs; **5** *(fam) (dinheiro)* quid, buck; **empresta-me 100 paus** lend me 100 bucks; IDIOM **cara de** ~ poker-faced; **jogar com um** ~ **de dois bicos** to hunt with the hounds and run with the hare; **pôr-se a** ~ to look out; **ser** ~ **para toda a obra** willing to do any work; be a Jack-of-all-trades.

pau-brasil *m (BOT)* Brazil wood.

This tree acquired its name due to its flaming colour (brasa). Thus the country that had been named Vera Cruz and then Santa Cruz, became Brazil.

pau-de-cabeleira *m (col)* chaperon; **servir de** ~ *(col)* to play gooseberry.

paul *m* marsh, swamp.

paulada *f* blow (with a stick).

paulatinamente *adv* gradually.

paulatino,-a *adj* slow, gradual.

paulista *m,f* from São Paulo State (Brazil).

paulistano,-a from the city of São Paulo; ♦ *adj inv (economia, indústria, etc)* of São Paulo.

pau-mandado *m* cat's-paw, servile person.

paupérrimo,-a *adj* poverty-stricken.

pau-preto *m (BOT)* ebony tree.

pau-rosa *m (BOT)* rosewood.

pausa *f* pause; **2** break; rest.

pausado,-a *adj* slow; leisurely; **2** *(cadenciado)* rhythmic; **3** *(palavras)* measured.

pauta *f* (guide)line; **2** *(MÚS)* staff; **3** list; **4** ruled paper; **5** ~ **de alfândega** customs tariff; **6 sem** ~ plain.

pautado,-a *adj* ruled, with lines; **2** *(mercadorias)* on a list; **3** *(fig) (seguindo regras)* **redacção** ~**a** draft according to rules.

pavão *m* peacock.

pavilhão *m* pavilion, ~ **de desportos** sport pavilion; **2** *(feira)* stand, stall; **3** annex, lodge; **4** *(abrigo)* tent; **5** ~ **de isolamento** isolation ward; **6** *(bandeira)* flag; **7** *(cortina do sacrário)* tabernacle curtain; **8** *(ANAT)* auricle.

pavimento *m (revestimento de ruas, pistas)* pavement; *(do solo)* paving, road surface; **2** *(chão)* flooring.

pavio *m* wick (of a candle); ♦ *adv (fam) (história)* **de fio a** ~ from beginning to end; **ela contou o filme de fio a** ~ she told the story of the film from beginning to end.

pavoa *f (ZOOL)* peahen.

pavonear *vt* to show off; ♦ *vi (pej)* to strut; ♦ ~**-se** *vr* to show off; to dress up.

pavor *m* dread, terror; **ter** ~ **de** to have a horror of; **2** *(fig)* **esta mulher é um** ~ this woman is awful.

pavoroso,-a *adj* dreadful, terrible, horrible, frightful.

paz *f* peace; **fazer as** ~**es** to make up, be friends again; **deixa-me em** ~ leave me alone/in peace; **ele/ela jaz em** ~ he/she lies in peace.

pazada *f (quantidade de uma pá)* spadefull; a blow with a spade or similar tool.

PB *(abr de Peso Bruto)* gross weight.

pé *m (ANAT)* foot; **a** ~ walking/on foot; ~ **chato** flat foot; **a planta do** ~ the sole of the foot; **2** *(de alguns objectos)* stem; ~ **do copo** stem of the glass; **3** *(de animal)* hoof, paw, foot; **4** *(de mobília)* foot, leg; **o** ~ **da mesa** the table's foot; **5** *(CULIN)* ~ **de porco** pig's trotter; **6** *(BOT)* stem, foot, cutting (of a plant); **7** *(fundo)* bottom, depth; **8** *(base)* pedestal, base; **9** *(do vinho)* dregs: **este vinho tem** ~ this wine has dregs; **10** *(fig)* **ter** ~ be within one's depth; **11** *(medida inglesa)* foot; **12** *(NÁUT)* foot; **13** *(fig)* pretexto, excuse; **14** *(estado)* **em que** ~ **estão os negócios?** how is business now (on what footing/stage)?; ♦ *adj* **a/de** ~ standing, on foot; **2 pôr-se de** ~ to stand up; **3 de** ~ **atrás** suspicious, on one's guard; **4 de** ~ **descalço** barefoot; ♦ *adv* **em** ~ **de guerra** on a warlike footing; **2 em** ~ **de igualdade** on equal terms; **3 ao** ~ **da letra** literally; **4 de** ~ **para a mão**

quickly, roughly, **isto não se faz de ~ para a mão**
this is not done just like that/quickly; **5 ~ ante ~**
on tiptoe; **6 com o ~ às costas** easily; **7 dos ~s à
cabeça** from head to toe; ♦ *prep* **ao ~ de** near,
close, compared with; IDIOM **não arredar ~** not
to budge; **acordar com o ~ direito/esquerdo**
wake up in a good/bad mood; **não chegar aos ~s
de (alguém)** not to be as good as (sb else), not
hold a candle to (sb else); **entrar/começar com o
~ direito** to enter/start on the right foot; **ficar
com os cabelos em ~** hair standing on end;
lamber os ~s de boot-licking; **meter os ~s pela
cabeça** to get confused, to go haywire; **sem ~s
nem cabeça** without head or tail, without any
sense.

peanha *f* small pedestal, block; **2** *(de tear)* treadle,
foot pedal.

peão *m* pedestrian; **2** *(nos estádios)* standing spectator; **3** *(HIST)* foot soldier; **3** *(xadrês)* pawn; **4**
(BR) farm labourer.

peça[1] *pres. subj de:* **pedir**.

peça[2] *f* piece, portion, bit; item; **2** *(AUTO)* part ~
sobressalente spare part; **3** *(habitação)* room; **4**
(TEAT) play; **5** *(serviço)* **pago por ~** piecework; **6**
~ de roupa garment; **7** *(de mobília)* móvel; **8**
(fam) trick; **pregar uma ~a alguém** to play a
trick on someone; **9** *(fam) (mau caracter)* **ser
uma boa ~** to be nasty.

pecado *m* sin.

pecador,-ora *m,f* sinner, wrongdoer.

pecaminoso,-a *adj* sinful,

pecar *vi* to sin; to do wrong; **~ por excesso de zelo**
to be overzealous.

pecha *f* bad habit; IDIOM **pôr ~ em tudo** find fault
with everything.

pechincha *f* bargain.

pechinchar *vi* to bargain, haggle.

peço *(vb pres indic, 1ª pessoa de* **pedir***)*.

peçonha *f* poison; **2** *(fig)* malice.

peçonhento,-a *adj (cobra)* poisonous, venomous; **2**
(epidemia) deadly; **3** *(pop)* repugnante.

pé-coxinho *m (jogo de crianças)* hop-scotch; ♦ *adv*
andar ao ~ to limp.

pecuária *f* cattle-raising, cattle-breeding, livestock;
♦ *adj (indústria, produtos)* cattle; **agro-~** farming
and livestock.

peculiar *adj* special, peculiar; particular.

pecúlio *m* savings *pl*; wealth.

pecuniário,-a *adj* pecuniary.

pé-d'água *(pl:* **pés-d'água***) m* downpour, heavy rain.

pedaço *m* piece, chunk, bite; **um ~ de pão** a chunk
of bread; **2** *(fig) (tempo)* long time; **esperar um ~**
to wait a long time; **3** *(área)* **um ~ de terra** a
piece of land; *(fig, fam) (mulher bem feita)* to be a
bit of all right *(col)*; ♦ *adv* **a ~s** here and there;
aos ~s in pieces; **em ~s** into pieces *(fig)* shattered;
IDIOM **ser um ~ de asno** be an ass; **ser um ~ de
homem** *(pop) (bem feito)* to be a hunk; **ser um ~
de mulher** *(pop) (bem feito)* to be a bit of alright;
ser um ~ de mau caminho *(BR) (fig) (person)* to
be bad news.

pedágio *m* bridge toll.

pedagogia *f* pedagogy.

pedagógico,-a, *adj* pedagogic.

pedagogo,-a *m,f* pedagogue.

pedal *m* pedal.

pedalar *vt* to pedal; ♦ *vi* to pedal; to cycle.

pedante *adj* pedantic, priggish, pretensious; ♦ *m,f*
pedant, prig.

pedantice *f;* **pedantismo** *m* pedantry, pretensiousness,
ostentation, vanity.

pé-de-atleta *m* athlete's foot.

pé-de-boi *(pl:* **pés-de-boi***) m* old-fashioned man, old
fogy; plodder.

pé-de-cabra *(pl:* **pés-de-cabra***) m (alavanca)* crowbar;
2 *(fam)* devil.

pé-de-galinha *(pl:* **pés-de-galinha***) m (rugas)* crow's
foot/feet.

pé-de-galo *(pl:* **pés-de-galo***) m (BOT) (lúpulo)* hop.

pé-de-meia *(pl:* **pés-de-meia***) m (economias)* nest
egg, savings.

pederasta *m,f* pederast *(UK)*, paederast *(US)*.

pederastia *f* pederasty.

pederneira *f* flint.

pé-descalço *m (pessoa)* down and out, pauper; **viagens de ~ com** *(com pouco dinheiro)* trips on a
shoestring.

pedestal *m* pedestal.

pedestre *m,f* pedestrian; ♦ *adj* foot; **soldado ~** foot
soldier.

pé-de-vento *m (vento forte)* gust of wind, squall; **2**
(fam) **fazer/armar um ~** make a fuss.

pediatra *m,f* paediatrician *(UK)*; pediatrician *(US)*.

pediatria *f* paediatrics *sg (UK)*; pediatrics *sg (US)*.

pedicuro,-a *m,f* pedicure; chiropodist; *(US)* podiatrist.

pedido *m* request, application, petition, appeal; **~ de
casamento** proposal (of marriage); **~ de demissão**
resignation; **~ de divórcio** divorce petition; **~ de
informação** inquiry; **~ de emprego** job application;
2 *(COM) (encomenda)* order.

pedinchão *m,* **pedinchona** *f* scrounger; ♦ *adj*
always asking for things; **2** *(voz)* whining, pleading.

pedinchar *vt (esmola, favores)* to beg for; ♦ *vi* to
beg.

pedinchice *f* begging.

pedinte *m,f (em todos os sentidos)* beggar; ♦ *adj*
begging; **2** *(sentido: súplica) (mãos, olhos)*
entreating.

pedir *vt* to ask for; **2** *(encomendar)* to order; **3** to
demand; **4** to apply (for) **~ auxílio** to ask for
help; **~ alguma coisa a alguém** to ask sb for sth;
~ informações to enquire; ♦ *vi* to ask; **~ por** to
plead for; **~ a alguém que faça** to ask sb to do; **~
esmola** to beg; **~ desculpa** to apologize; **~
emprestado** to borrow.

pé-direito *m* right foot; **2** *(desejando boa sorte)*
'**entre com o ~!**' *(casa, emprego)* I wish you good
luck; **3** *(ARQ)* height of a ceiling.

peditório *m (de dinheiro)* collection; **2** *(caridade)*
appeal; **3** *(de pedinte)* begging.

pedofilia *m* paedophilia *(UK)*; pedophilia *(US)*.

pedófilo *m* paedophile *(UK)*, pedophile *(US)*.

pedonal *adj inv (zona, area)* pedestrian; **acesso ~** access to pedestrians only; **ponte ~** footbridge.

pedra *f* stone; *(qualquer variedade de rocha)* stone; **2** *(variedade calcária)* limestone; **3 ~ de amolar** grindstone; *(peça abrasiva)* flint; **4 ~ angular** corner-stone; **5 ~ preciosa/fina** precious stone/gem; **6 pedra de gelo/açúcar** ice/sugar-cube; **7 ~ de sabão** bar of soap; **as ~s do sal** salt grins; **8 ~ de toque** touchstone; **9** *(granizo)* hail; **10 as ~s** *fpl* grains of salt; **pés frios como ~s** cold-stone feet; IDIOM **dormir como uma ~** to sleep like a log; **falar com quatro ~s na mão** jump down sb's throat; **fazer chorar as ~s da calçada** to inspire pity; **pés frios como ~s** stone-cold feet.

pedrada *f* stone throwing; **andar à ~** to throw stones *(a alguém/a algo, at sb, at sth)*; **2** *(fig)* to accuse, cast aspersions; ♦ *vt (matar)* to stone.

pedra-pomes *(pl: pedras-pomes)* *f* pumice stone.

pedra-sabão *(pl: pedras-sabão)* *f* soapstone.

pedregal *m* stony ground.

pedregoso,-a *adj* stony, rocky.

pedregulho *m* boulder.

pedreira *f* quarry.

pedreiro *m* bricklayer.

pedreiro-livre *m (mação)* freemason.

pedrês *adj inv (ave com plumagem branca e preta)* **galinha-~** speckled hen; **2** *(fig) (mosaico)* black and white.

pega[1] *f (tourada) (agarrar o touro pelos chifres)* grapple; **2** *(pequeno pano para segurar utensílios quentes)* holder; **3** *(fig) (briga)* quarrel.

pega[2] *f (ZOOL)* magpie; **2** *(NÁUT) (peça de mastreação)* relating to masts; cap.

pegada *f* footprint; **2** track, trace.

pegadiço,-a *adj* sticky; **2** *(MED)* infectious, catching.

pegado,-a *adj* stuck; together; **a casa ~** the house next door.

pegajoso,-a *adj* sticky; tacky; **2** *(fig) (pessoa maçadora)* clinging.

pegar *vt* to take hold of; **2 ~ em** to pick (up); **ela pegou na menina** she picked the little girl up; **3** *(BR) (transporte)* to catch, take; **~ o ônibus** to catch the bus; **4** *(BR) (ir buscar)* fetch, pick up *(alguém)*; **5** *(transmitir)* set, transmit; **~ fogo a** to set fire to; **ela pegou-me uma gripe** she gave me the flu; ♦ *vi* to stick; to take, to catch; **a polícia pegou o ladrão a roubar** police caught the thief stealing; **2** *(AUTO)* to start; **o carro não pega** the car won't start; **o lume não pega** the fire does not light; **a carne pegou ao tacho** the meat stuck to the pan, start off, catch on *(pop)*; **a música inglesa pegou** English music has caught on, it's catchy; **~ com** to be next door to; ♦ **~-se** *vr* to stick; **2** to come to blows.

peia *f* hindrance.

peidar *vt (fam)* to fart; **peido** *m (fam)* fart.

peitar *vt (enfrentar)* to face; **2** *(subornar)* to bribe.

peitilho *m* shirt front.

peito *m (ANAT)* chest; breast; **~ do pé** instep; **~ do frango** chicken breast; **de braço ao ~** with the arm in a sling; **tomar a ~** to take to heart; **dar o ~**

ao bébé to breast-feed a baby; **ela chorou no ~ dele** she cried on his chest; *(fig) (ânimo)* courage, guts *(col)*.

peitoril *m* windowsill.

peitudo,-a *adj* big-chested; with big bosom; **2** *(valente)* plucky.

peixaria *f* fishmonger's.

peixe *m* fish; **~-agulha** swordfish; **~-espada** *m* scabbard fish; **Peixes** *(ASTROL)* Pisces; IDIOM **estar como ~ na água** to be in one's own element; **falar/pregar aos ~s** to speak to the wall.

peixeiro,-a *m,f* fishmonger/fishwife.

pejar *vt* to fill up, cover; **os livros pejavam as paredes** the books covered the walls; **2** *(estorvar)* encumber, hinder; **3** *(coração, memória)* to fill ♦ *vi* to become pregnant; ♦ **~-se** *vr* be embarrassed.

pejo *m* shyness; **ter ~** be embarrassed, to be bashful.

pejorativo,-a *adj* pejorative.

pela (= **por + a**) **pelas** (= **por + as**) **pelo** (= **por + o**) **pelos** (= **por + os**) *prep* by/through the/for the; **~ porta** through the door; **~ minha parte** I for one; **~ força** by force; ♦ **~ calada** on the sly; **~ calada da noite** in the quiet of the night; **~ madrugada** at dawn; *(approx)* **~s seis horas** about six o'clock; **ele fugiu ~ traseiras** he ran out through the back (door); (Vd: **pelo, pelos**).

péla *f (descortiçamento)* bark, stripping, peeling; **a ~ dos sobreiros** the stripping of the cork-trees.

pelada *(MED)* alopecia, baldness; **2** *(floresta)* clearing.

pelado,-a *adj* skinned; shorn; peeled; bald; naked; **2** *(BR) (fam)* broke.

pelagem *f (de animais)* fur, fleece, coat.

pélago *m (oceano)* high seas *pl*, ocean; **2** *(mar profundo)* depths *pl*; **3** *(fig)* abyss.

pelar *vt (tirar a pele)* to skin; **2** *(fruta, legumes)* to peel; **3** *(por efeito do calor)* peel; **4** *(tirar o pelo)* lose fur *(animal)*; **as queimaduras pelaram o gato** the cat lost its fur due to the burns; **4** *(fig)* to fleece; ♦ **~-se** *vr*: to strip/undress; **2 ~ por** *(gostar muito)* to be crazy about, adore.

pele *f* skin; **2** leather, hide, pelt; **3** fur *(coat)*; **~ de ovelha** sheepskin; **4** *(fruta, queijo)* peel, rind; **5** *(tez)* complexion; **6** *(flácida)* loose skin; IDIOM **cortar na ~ de alguém** to backbite; **estar na tua/sua ~** to be in your shoes.

pele-de-galinha *f* goose flesh, goose pimples.

peleiro *m* furrier.

peleja *f* fight; battle; row.

pelejar *vi* to fight; to quarrel; **~ pela paz** to struggle for peace.

pelica *f* kid (leather).

pelicano *m (ZOOL)* pelican.

película *f (CIN, FOTO)* film; **2** *(de pele)* membrane; **3** *(camada fina)* layer.

pelintra *m,f (pessoa)* penniless but 'slick' dresser; ♦ *adj* poor but pretentious; **2** shabby; **3** *(fig)* stingy.

pelo (= **por + o**); **pelos** (= **por + os**) *prep* by/through /for the; **~ correio** by post; ♦ **~ sim, ~ não** just in case; **~ rio/caminho** along the river/the road; **~ que me diz** according to what you tell me; **~ que sei** as far as I know; **~ menos** at least;

~ **contrário** on the contrary; ~ **vistos** apparently, evidently; IDIOM estar ~ **cabelos** to be push for time in a rush, in a panic (*Vd:* **pela, pelas**).

pêlo, pelo *m* hair; fur; **em** ~ stark naked; **montar em** ~ to ride bareback.

pelota *f (bolinha)* pellet; ♦ **estar em** ~ to be stark naked.

pelotão *m* platoon, squad.

pelourinho *m* pillory.

peluche *m* plush; **2** *(brinquedo)* soft toy; **urso de** ~ teddy bear.

pelúcia *f* plush.

peludo,-a *adj* hairy, shaggy.

pélvico,-a *adj* pelvic.

pélvis *f (ANAT)* pelvis.

pena *f* feather; **2** pen; **3** writing; **ele vive da** ~ he is a writer; **4** *(JUR)* sentence, punishment; ~ **de morte** death sentence; **sob** ~ **de** on pain of; **5** *(NÁUT)* ~ **de vela** peak of a sail; **6 as** ~**s de amor** the pangs of love; ♦ **ter** ~ to have regrets; **ter** ~ **de** feel pity/ be sorry for; **tenho muita** ~ I am so sorry/so sad; **valer a** ~ to be worth while; ♦ *exc* **que** ~! what a pity, what a shame!

penacho *m (de plumas)* plume.

penado,-a *adj* grieved; **alma** ~**a** tormented soul.

penal *adj* penal; **código** *m* ~ penal code.

penalidade *f* penalty; punishment; **impor uma** ~ **a** to penalize.

pênalti *m (futebol)* penalty.

penar *vt* to grieve; **2** make amends for; ♦ *vi* to suffer, to be afflicted.

penca *f (folha grossa)* pulpy leaf; **2** *(pop)* long nose; **3** *(BR) (grande quantidade)* bunch; ♦ *adv* **em** ~ in heaps.

pendência *f (contenda)* dispute, quarrel.

pendente *m (joia)* pendant ♦ *adj inv* hanging; **2** pending; **3** sloping; **4 dívida** ~ outstanding debt.

pender *vt* to hang; ♦ *vi* to hang; **2** sag, droop; ~ **de** to hang from; ~ **para** to lean/inclined towards; to tend to; ~ **a** to be inclined to.

pendor *m (vertente)* inclination; slope; **2** *(obliquidade)* slant; **3** *(fig) (tendência)* flair; **ter** ~ **para a arte** to have a flair for art.

pêndulo *m* pendulum.

pendura *m,f* hanger-on; **2 andar na** ~ to be a hanger-on, relying on others to pay.

pendurado,-a *adj* hanging; ~ **da árvore** hanging from the tree.

pendurar *vi:* ~ **de** to hang from.

penedo *m* rock, boulder; *(fig)* obstacle.

peneira *f* sieve; *(máquina)* sifting machine; **2** *(fig) (chuva miúda)* drizzle; **3 peneiras** *fpl (fig) (ilusão, vaidade)* vanity, snobbery; **ter** ~**s** *(fazer-se importante)* give o.s. airs and graces; to be conceited/ snobbish.

peneirar *vt* to sift, sieve; **2** select; ♦ *vi* to drizzle.

peneirento,-a *m,f (pej)* prig, snob, show-off, stuck up person; ♦ *adj (pej)* conceited.

penetra *m,f* gatecrasher.

penetração *f* penetration, entering; **2** *(compreensão)* insight, sharpness.

penetrante *adj (mente)* searching, sharp; **2** *(dor, som)* penetrating; **3** *(gaze)* piercing.

penetrar *vt* to get into, penetrate; **2** go deep; **3** pervade; **o cheiro penetrava a sala** the smell pervaded the room; **4** infiltrate/filter; ♦ *vi* enter; **2** go/get through; **3** break into.

penetrável *adj* permeable, pervious, penetrable.

penha *f* crag, cliff.

penhasco *m* cliff, ravine.

penhor *m* pledge; **2** pawn; **casa de** ~**es** pawnshop; **dar em** ~ to pawn; **3** *(JUR)* guarantee; **4** *(prova)* proof.

penhora *f (JUR)* seizure, confiscation.

penhorado,-a *adj:* **sentir-se/estar** ~ **a alguém** to be indebted to sb.

penhorar *vt* to pledge; **2** pawn, *(fam)* hock; **3** *(JUR)* confiscate; **4** *(fig)* to put under an obligation.

penhorista *m,f* pawnbroker; money-lender; ♦ *adj (actividade)* pawn.

penichense, penicheiro,-a *adj* from the town of Peniche, Portugal; **amigos de Peniche** *mpl* fair-weather friends.

penicilina *f* penicillin.

penico *m (fam) (vaso urinário)* chamber pot.

península *f (GEOG)* peninsula.

peninsular *adj* peninsular; *(referente à Península Ibérica)* **Guerra P~** the Peninsular War (in Portugal and Spain, 1807–1814).

pénis (*BR:* **pê-**) *m (ANAT)* penis.

penitência *f* penitence; **2** *(REL) (expiação)* penance, contriction; **3** *(fam) (maçada)* bore, punishment, sacrifice.

penitenciária *f* prison, penitentiary.

penitente *m,f* penitent, repentant sinner; ♦ *adj* repentant, contrite.

penoso,-a *adj (que causa mágoa)* painful; **2** *(trabalho)* hard; **3** *(assunto)* distressing; **4** *(tratamento)* harsh.

pensado,-a *adj* deliberate, intentional.

pensador,-ora *m,f* thinker.

pensamento *m* thought; **2** thinking; ~ **negativo** negative thinking; **3** mind.

pensante *m,f* thinker; ♦ *adj inv* thoughtful; **2** *(reflectido) (gente)* intelectual.

pensão *f* boarding house; board; ~ **completa** full board; **2** ~ **de velhice/de reforma** (*BR:* **de aposentadoria**) old age, retirement pension.

pensar *m* idea, opinion; **no meu** ~ the way I see it; **2** *(fam) (juízo)* sense; ♦ *vi* to think; **2** imagine; **3** ~ **em** to think of/about; **4** ~ **fazer** intend to do; **5** ~ **sobre** to ponder over; **pensando bem** on second thoughts; ~ **alto** to think out loud; IDIOM ~ **na morte da bezerra** daydreaming; **dar que** ~ it makes one think; ♦ *exc* **nem** ~ **nisso!** don't even think it!, it doesn't bear thinking about it!

pensativo,-a *adj* thoughtful, pensive.

pênsil *adj (suspenso)* hanging.

pensionista *m,f* pensioner; **2** *(hospedado em)* boarder.

penso *m (MED)* dressing; **pôr um** ~ **na perna** to put, apply a dressing on the leg; **2** *(adesivo anti-séptico)* sticking plaster; **3** *(menstruação)* sanitary

towel; **4** *(comida para animais)* food ration; ♦
penso,-a *adj (pendido)* hanging.

penta *(elemento que exprime cinco)* ~**campeão** *m*
five-times champion; ~**cordo** *m (MÚS)* pentachord.

pentagonal *adj inv* pentagonal.

pentágono *m (GEOM)* pentagon.

pente *m (do cabelo)* comb; **2** *(de pistola)* cartridge.

penteadela *f* hasty combing, brushing through the
hair.

penteado *m* hairdo; ♦ **penteado,-a** *adj* combed,
groomed.

pentear *vt (cabelo, bigode)* to comb, style; **2** *(cão,
gato)* brush; **3** *(cavalo)* groom; ♦ ~**-se** *vr* to comb
one's hair; IDIOM **vai ~ macacos!** get lost!

Pentecostes *m (REL) (festa judaica)* Passover; **2** *(festa
cristã)* Pentecost; **Domingo de ~** Whit-Sunday.

pente-fino *m* fine-tooth comb; **passar (algo) a ~** to
go through (sth) with a fine-tooth comb.

penugem *f* down; fluff.

penúltimo,-a *adj* last but one, penultimate.

penumbra *f* twilight, dusk; **2** *(arte)* shading; **3**
(luz fraca) half-light, dim light; **4** darkness; **5**
(obscuridade) shadows.

penúria *f* poverty, destitution; **2** lack of sth.

peónia *f (BOT)* peony.

pepino *m (BOT)* cucumber; IDIOM **de pequenino
se torce o ~** spare the rod and spoil the child.

pepita *f (de ouro)* nugget.

pequenada *f (muitas crianças)* little ones, children; **2**
(filhos) kids.

pequenez *f* smallness; **2** infancy; **3** *(fig)* meanness;
with a small mind.

pequenino,-a *m,f* little one; *adj (tamanho pequeno)*
(objecto) tiny, wee, small.

pequeno,-a *m* boy, *f* girl; **faço bordados desde ~a** I
have been embroidering since I was a little girl; **2**
(COM) **as ~s e médias empresas (PME)** small
and medium enterprises (SME); ♦ *adj* small, little;
2 slight; **3** *(mesquinho)* mean, petty; small-
minded; IDIOM **à boca ~a** in a whisper; **dizer à
boca ~** to spread rumours, gossip.

pequeno-almoço *m* breakfast *(in Brazil = café da
manhã)*.

pequeno-burguês, pequeno burguesa *m,f* petit-
bourgeois; middle class.

pequerrucho,-a *(termo de afeição)* baby, little baby,
meu ~ my little one.

pequinês *m (cão)* Pekinese.

pêra, pera *f (BOT)* pear; **2** *(pequena barba no
queixo)* goatee beard.

peralta *m* dandy, fop; **2** *(BR) (ocioso)* idler; **3** mischief-
maker; ♦ *adj inv (BR) (criança)* mischievous.

perambular *vi* to walk about, wander, roam.

perante *prep* before, facing, in the presence of; ~ **a
lei** in the eyes of the law; **2** *(fig)* in the face of.

pé-rapado *(BR) (pej)* pauper.

perca (= **perda**) *f (peixe)* perch.

percalço *m* difficulty, setback, drawback, hitch, snag,
pitfall.

perceber *vt (pelos sensos)* to perceive, sense; **2**
(compreender) to understand, realise; **3** *(distinguir)*

make out; **4** *(notar)* be aware of, to notice; **5 dar a
~** to make sb understand.

percentagem *f* percentage.

percepção *f (dos sentidos)* perception.

perceptível *adj* perceptible, noticeable; audible.

percevejo *m (ZOOL)* bug; bedbug; **2** *(prego)* drawing
pin, tack.

percorrer *vt* to travel (across/over); **2** to go through,
search through; **percorri as lojas todas e não
encontrei** I went to every shop and couldn't find;
3 *(distância)* cover; **4** *(examinar)* go over, to run
over sb with one's eyes.

percurso *m* distance (covered); **2** route; **3** journey;
fazer o ~ entre to travel between.

percussão *f (MÚS)* percussion; **percutir** *vt* to
strike.

perda *f* loss; **2** damage; **3** waste; **4 ~ de direitos**
forfeiture; **5 ~s e danos** losses and damages; **6**
(peixe) perch.

perdão *m* pardon, forgiveness; ♦ *exc* ~! sorry!; **peço
~** I beg your pardon; I apologize.

perdedor,-ora *m,f* loser.

perder *vt* to lose; **2** *(desperdiçar)* to waste; **estás a ~
tempo** you are wasting time; **3** to miss; **perdi o
comboio** I missed the train; **4 a ~ de vista** as far
as the eye can/could see; ♦ *vi* to lose; ~ **as estribeiras** to lose one's bearing; ♦ ~**-se** *vr* to be/get
lost; **2** *(fig)* to be ruined; **perdeu-se** it got lost/it
disappeared.

perdição *f (fraqueza)* weakness; **fumar é a minha ~**
smoking is my weakness; **2** perdition, ruin; **Amor
de ~** *(romance/filme português)* ill-fated love.

perdido,-a *adj* lost; **2** depraved; **3** done for; **4 ~ (de
amor) por** desperately in love with; **eu estava ~
de riso** I was in stitches; **5** *(olhar desorientado)*
vague, lost; **perdidos** *mpl* lost; ~ **e achados** lost
and found.

perdigão *m (ZOOL)* male partridge.

perdigoto *m* young partridge; **2** *(pop) (salpico de
saliva)* splatter of spittle; **lançar ~s** to spittle.

perdigueiro *m (cão)* pointer, setter.

perdiz *f (ZOOL)* female partridge; *(BR)* tinamou.

perdoar *vt* to forgive; pardon; to excuse; to spare; **a
morte não perdoa a ninguém** death does not
spare anyone.

perdulário,-a *m,f* wasteful, big spender, spend-thrift;
2 generous person; ♦ *adj* wasteful; **2** generous.

perdurar *vi* to last a long time; **2** to still exist; **a
minha memória dele perdura** my memory of
him lives on.

perdurável *adj inv* long-lasting; durable.

pereba *f (BR) (ferida)* sore; **2** *(em animais)* mange;
skin eruption.

perebento,-a *adj* covered in sores; mangy.

perecedoiro,-a, perecedouro,-a, perecedor,-ora
adj liable to perish; perishable, mortal.

perecer *vi* to perish; to die; to come to nothing.

perecível *adj inv* perishable.

peregrinação *f* long tour, journey, travels *pl*; **2**
(REL) pilgrimage.

peregrinar *vi* to travel; *(REL)* to go on a pilgrimage.

peregrino,-a *m,f* pilgrim; *(viajante)* wanderer; ♦ *adj* travelling; **2** *(fig) (teoria)* uncommon, strange; **3** *(ZOOL) (falcon)* peregrine falcon.

pereira *f* pear tree.

peremptório,-a, perentório,-a *adj* final, decisive.

perene *adj* everlasting; *(BOT)* perennial.

perfazer *vt* to come to, amount to; **2** *(tarefa)* to carry out.

perfe(c)cionismo *m* perfectionism.

perfe(c)cionista *adj inv* perfectionist.

perfeição *f* perfection.

perfeitamente *adv* perfectly; ♦ *exc* ~! of course!

perfeito,-a *adj* perfect; **2** *(gram) (tempo)* perfect (tense).

perfídia *f* treachery.

pérfido,-a *adj* treacherous.

perfil *m* profile; **2** *(fig) (retrato)* silhouette, outline; **3** *(ARQ)* (cross-)section, sectional drawing; **4** *(MIL)* alignment.

perfilar *vt* to line up; to straighten up; ♦ ~-**se** *vr* to stand to attention.

perfumado,-a *adj* scented.

perfumar *vt* to perfume; ♦ ~-**se** *vr* to put perfume on, spray scent on.

perfume *m* perfume; scent.

perfurador,-ora *m* borer, drill; punch; ♦ *f* punch machine.

perfurar *vt* to drill a hole in; to punch (a hole in).

perfurante *adj* piercing.

pergaminho *m* parchment; **2** diploma.

pergunta *f* question; query; **fazer uma** ~ **a alguém** to ask sb a question.

perguntar *vt* to ask; to question; ♦ *vi* ~ **por alguém** to ask after sb; **pergunta-se** … the question is …

perícia *f* expertise; **2** mastery; skill.

pericial *adj inv* expert; **testamunha** ~ expert witness.

periclitante *adj inv* unstable; uncertain; **2** risky; **3** *(em perigo)* in danger.

periferia *f* periphery; outskirts *pl.* **periférico,-a** *m* peripheral; ♦ *adj* peripheral; **estrada periférica** ring road.

perífrase *f* circumlocution.

perifrástico,-a *adj (gram)* periphrastic.

perigo *m* danger; **correr** ~ to be in danger.

perigosidade *f* danger.

perigoso,-a *adj* dangerous; risky.

perímetro *m* perimeter.

periodicidade *f* frequency, periodicity.

periódico,-a *adj* periodic; occasional; recurrent; ♦ *m* magazine, periodical.

período *m* period; season; ~ **lectivo** academic term/time.

peripécia *f* episode, interesting incident; **2** adventure.

periquito (=**budgie**) *m (ave)* budgerigar.

periscópio *m* periscope.

peritagem *f* expert inspection.

perito,-a *m,f* expert, specialist; ♦ *adj* skilled, experienced; ~ **em matéria de** expert in.

peritonite *f (MED)* peritonitis.

perjurar *vt* renounce; betray *(princípios)*; ♦ *vi* to commit perjury, perjure.

perjúrio *m (falso testemunto)* perjury.

perjuro,-a *m,f (pessoa ue jura falso)* perjurer; ♦ *adj* perjurious.

permanecer *vi* to stay; to remain, keep; ~ **parado** to keep still.

permanência *f* stay; permanence; continuance.

permanente *f (cabelo)* perm, permanent wave; **fazer uma** ~ have a perm; ♦ *adj inv* constant, continuous; **2** permanent; **3** *(cor)* fast, permanent; **caneta de tinta** ~ fountain pen.

permeável *adj* permeable.

permeio *adv*: **de** ~ in between, among.

permissão *f* permission, consent.

permissivo,-a *adj* permissive.

permitir *vt* to allow, permit; to grant; ~ **a alguém fazer** to let sb do, allow sb to do; ♦ ~-**se** *vr* to let/allow o.s. to do.

permuta *f* change; **2** *(troca)* exchange, swap, barter; **3** *(ideias)* exchange (**de** of).

permutação *f (MAT)* permutation; exchange.

permutar *vt* to exchange; *(col)* to swap; ♦ *vi* to change.

perna *f (ANAT)* leg; **barriga da** ~ calf of the leg; *(dos móveis)* leg; IDIOM **passar a** ~ **a alguém** to trip someone up; ~**s para que te quero** to take to one's heels; **de** ~**s abertas** *(cal)* obliging, ever willing; **de** ~**s para o ar** upside down.

pernada *f* long stride; **2** *(from a horse)* kick; **3** *(BOT)* large branch; **4** *(pequeno curso do rio)* stretch, tributary.

pernalta *adj (alguém)* long-legged; long-legged bird, wader; ♦ *adj inv (ave)* wading.

perneta *m,f (fam, pej)* one-legged person

pernicioso,-a *adj* harmful; bad; *(MED)* malignant.

pernil *m* thin leg; **2** *(CULIN)* leg, haunch; IDIOM **estender o** ~ *(morrer)* to kick the bucket.

pernoitar *vi* to stay overnight.

pernóstico,-a *adj* pretentious, person using 'posh' words without knowing their meaning.

pêro *m* sweet apple (Golden Delicious, Starker type); IDIOM **são como um** ~ as fit as a fiddle.

Pêro differs from the 'cox' or 'Granny Smith' types, which translate 'maçã'. It is a cross between apple and pear and it is sweeter than 'maçã'; more like the English 'starker' apples.

pérola *f* pearl.

perónio *m (ANAT)* fibula.

perpassar *vt* run/go through *(com a mão, dedos)*; ♦ *vi (passar junto)* to pass by; go through; **ela perpassou um mau bocado** she went through a difficult time; **2** pass over, lightly touch; **um sorriso perpassou-lhe pelos lábios** a smile passed over his lips.

perpendicular *adj inv (GEOM)* perpendicular; **ser** ~ **a** to be at right angles to.

perpetração *f (JUR)* perpetration.

perpetrar *vt* to perpetrate, commit.

perpetuar *vt* to perpetuate; ♦ ~-**se** *vr* to last.

perpetuidade *f* eternity.

perpétuo,-a *adj* perpetual, eternal; forever; **prisão perpétua** life imprisonment.

perplexidade *f* confusion, bewilderment.

perplexo,-a *adj* bewildered, puzzled; uncertain.

perrice *f* stubbornness, obstinacy.

perro,-a *(que resiste) (porta, etc)* stiff; **a janela está ~a** the window is stiff/stuck; **2** *(ideias, pessoa)* obstinate.

persa *adj* Persian; **2** *(LÍNG)* Persian.

perscrutar *vt* to scrutinize, examine; **2** *(alma)* to look into.

perseguição *f* pursuit; **2** *(REL, POL)* persecution.

perseguidor,-ora *m,f* pursuer; **2** *(REL, POL)* persecutor.

perseguir *vt* to pursue, to chase; **2** *(REL)* to persecute; **3** to harass, pester, torment.

perseverança *f* persistence; perseverance.

perseverante *adj inv* persistent.

perseverar *vi* to persevere; **~ em** persevere in; **~ em erro** keep on doing sth wrong.

persiana *f* venetian blind; **subir/baixar a ~** to pull up/let down the blind; **2** *(portinha exterior)* shutter.

persignar-se *vr (REL)* to cross o.s., to make the sign of the cross.

persistência *f* persistence; persistency.

persistente *adj inv* persistent.

persistir *vi* **~ em** to persist; **2** *(teimar)* insistir.

personagem *m,f* famous person, celebrity; **2** character.

personalidade *f* personality.

perspectiva *f* perspective; **2** view; **3** *(fig)* point of view; **4** *(melhoria)* prospect, outlook, possibility; ♦ *adv* **em ~** *(futuro)* in prospect; **2** *(três dimensões)* in perspective; ♦ **perspectivas** *fpl (horizontes)* horizon.

perspicácia *f* insight, perceptiveness.

perspicaz *adj* observant, perspicacious; **2** *(fig)* shrewd.

persuadir *vt* to persuade; convince; **~ alguém a fazer** to persuade sb to do; ♦ **~-se** *vr* to make up one's mind.

persuasão *f* persuasion; conviction.

persuasivo,-a *adj* persuasive.

pertencente *adj inv* belonging; **~ a** pertaining to.

pertencer *vi* belong (**a** to); **2** *(dizer respeito a)* to concern.

pertences *mpl* belongings, possessions; **2** *(escritório, fábrica)* equipment; **3** *(JUR)* goods and chattels.

pertinácia *f* obstinacy.

pertinaz *adj* persistent; obstinate.

pertinente *adj* relevant, pertinent; appropriate.

perto,-a *adj inv* nearby; ♦ *adv* near; **~ da casa** close to the house; **conhecer de ~** to know very well; **de ~** closely; **~ de 50 escudos** about 50 escudos; **seguir de ~** to follow close on the heels of; **ao ~** close to; **por ~** nearby; *(quase)* nearly.

perturbação *f* distress, upset; **2** *(MED)* trouble; **3** *(POL)* disturbance.

perturbado,-a *adj* upset; disturbed, perturbed; *(METEOR) (tempo)* turbulent.

perturbado,-ora *m,f* disturber, trouble-maker; ♦ *adj (facto, ruído)* disturbing.

perturbante *adj inv* disturbing.

perturbar *vt* to perturb; **2** disturb; **3** to upset, trouble; ♦ *vi (atordoar)* to pester; ♦ **~-se** *vr* be worried; be embarrassed.

Peru *npr* Peru; **o ~** Peru.

peru *m (ave)* turkey; **perua** *f (fêmea)* hen turkey; **2** *(BR) (pej) (mulher atraente)* hussy; **3** *(US)* station wagon.

peruano,-a *adj* Peruvian.

peruca *f* wig.

perversão *f* perversion.

perversidade *f* perversity.

perverso,-a *m,f* pervert; *adj* perverse; wicked, wayward.

perverter *vt* to corrupt, pervert.

pervertido,-a *m,f* pervert; ♦ *adj* perverted.

pesadão,-ona *adj* very heavy, weighty; **2** slow-moving; **3** *(fig) (discurso)* tedious.

pesadelo *m* nightmare.

pesado,-a *adj* heavy; **2** hard; **3** dull, boring; **um discurso ~** a boring speech; **4** *(atmosfera)* close, sultry; **5** *(ambiente)* tense; **6** *(andar, ar)* slow, clumsy; **7** *(anedota)* coarse; **8** *(comida)* stodgy; **9** *(MÚS)* heavy metal.

pesadume *m (ressentimento)* bitterness, grudge; **2** *(pesar)* sorrow.

pesagem *f* weighing; *(equitação)* weighing-in.

pêsames *mpl* condolences, sympathy *sg*; **dou-lhe os meus sinceros ~** (I offer you) my condolences, my sympathy.

pesar *m* sorrow, sadness; remorse; ♦ *vt* to weigh; **2** *(fig) (considerar)* to weigh up; ♦ *vi (ser pesado)* to weigh, to carry weight; **2** *(ser encargo)* be a burden; **3** *(fig) (ter sono) (olhos)* grow heavy; **4** *(recair)* **~ sobre** to fall upon.

pesaroso,-a *adj* sorrowful, sad; **2** regretful, sorry.

pesca *f* fishing; catch; **ir à ~** to go fishing; **2** *(fig)* **andar à ~** to look for (sth).

pescada *f (peixe)* hake; **arrotar postas de ~** to blow one's own trumpet.

pescado *m (nome colectivo)* peixe; **2** *(apanha)* catch.

pescador,-ora *m,f* fisherman/woman; **~ à linha** angler.

pescar *vt* to catch, to fish; **2** *(pérolas, tesouro)* fish for; **3** *(retirar da água)* to fish out; ♦ *vi (pop)* to understand.

pescaria *f* fishing trip; **~ de corrico** troll fishing; **~ de sondar** deep-sea fishing.

pescoço *m* neck; throat, nape; scruff; *(fig)* **~-de-cisne** long neck, swan's neck; **2** *(da garrafa)* neck; ♦ **até ao ~** *adv (very involved)* up to his neck; *(cheio)* be fed-up.

peso *m* weight; **~ bruto/líquido** gross/net weight; **argumento de ~** weighty argument; **2** *(fig)* burden; **3** influence; **pessoa de ~ no ministério** influential person in the ministry; **4** *(fig)* force; **em ~** in full force, en masse, heavily; **a ~ de ouro** very expensive; IDIOM **tirar o ~ de cima de (alguém)** to take a weight off (sb); **valer o seu ~ em ouro** to be worth one's/its gold.

peso-morto *m* dead-weight.

peso-pesado *m* heavy weight.

peso-pluma *m* feather-weight.

pespegar *vt* dar; ~ **um beijo/uma bofetada** give a
kiss/a slap; **2** *(colocar)* to leave (behind); **ela
pespegou o garoto na casa da mãe** she left her
kid at her mother's; **3** *(fig) (ficar sem ser convidado)* to stick to; **ele pespegou-se na minha
casa sem ser convidado** he stuck to/stayed on
uninvited.

pespontar *vt* backstitch, stitch.

pesponto *m* backstitch.

pesqueiro,-a *adj* fishing.

pesquisa *f* inquiry, investigation; research; ~ **de
mercado** market research, survey.

pesquisador,-ora *m,f* researcher.

pêssego *m* *(fruta)* peach.

pessegueiro *m* peach tree.

pessimista *m,f* pessimist; ♦ *adj* pessimistic.

péssimo,-a *(superl de* **mau)** *adj* very bad, awful.

pessoa *f* person; ~**s** *fpl* people; ♦ *adv* **em ~** personally;
personified; **ela é a bondade em ~** she is kindness
in person; ♦ *pron inv* **uma ~** one; **no que toca à
minha ~** as for me, as far as I am concerned; **na
~ de** on behalf of …

pessoal *m* personnel *pl*; **2** staff *pl*; **3** *(col)* people,
folk; ♦ *adj inv* personal, individual; **2** *(conversa)*
private.

pessoano,-a *adj (texto, estilo, obra) (relativo a Fernando
Pessoa)* Pessoa's, by Pessoa.

pestana *f (ANAT)* eyelash; **2** *(MÚS)* nut; **3** *(NÁUT)*
fluke.

pestanejar *vi* to blink; **2** flutter eyelashes.flirt.

peste *f (epidemia)* epidemic, plague; ~**-negra** *(HIST)*
black death; **2** *(fig)* pest, nuisance, scourge; **3** *(fig)*
(mau cheiro) stink, stench.

pesticide *m* pesticide.

pestífero,-a *adj* noxious; poisonous.

pestilência *f* plague; **2** pestilence; **3** *(fedor)* stench.

peta *f* lie; *(col)* fib.

pétala *f* petal.

petardo *m (MIL)* petard; **2** *(fogo de artifício)* small
bomb, cracker; **3** *(FUT)* powerful kick.

petéquias *fpl (MED)* petechiae, *pl.*

petição *f* petition; **2** *(JUR)* plea, petiton.

peticionário,-a *m,f* petitioner; *(JUR)* plaintiff; **em ~
de miséria** in a sorrowful state.

petinga *f* small fish/sardine; **2** *(na pesca)* bait.

petiscar *vt* to nibble at peck at; ♦ *vi* to have a snack.

petisco *m* savoury, titbit; **2** delicacy.

petiz *m* (small) boy.

petrechos *(=* **apetrechos)** *mpl* equipment *sg*; **2**
(MIL) stores, equipment; **3** utensils.

pétreo,-a *adj* petrous, stony; **2** *(fig)* hard-hearted.

petrificado,-a *adj* petrified; **2** fossilized.

petrificar *vt* to petrify; **2** to harden; **3** to stupefy; ♦
~**-se** *vr* to be petrified.

petroleiro,-a *m (navio)* oil tanker.

petróleo *m (mineral)* oil, petroleum; ~ **bruto** crude
oil; **poço de ~** *m*, **jazida de ~** *f* oil well.

petrolífero,-a *adj*: **indústria ~a** oil industry.

petulância *f* impertinence, arrogance; **2** *(fam)* cheek.

petulante *adj* arrogant; impudent, insolent; cheeky.

petúnia *(BOT)* petunia.

peúga *f* sock.

peugada *f* footprint; **2** vestige; **na ~ de** on the
trail of.

pevide *f (BOT)* seed; *(da laranja, limão, melão)* pip.

pez *m* resin; **2** *(alcatrão)* tar, pitch.

pezinho *m* little foot; **2** *(BOT)* cutting; **dê-me um ~
da sua planta** give me a cutting from your plant;
~ **s** *mpl* little feet; IDIOM **andar com ~s de lã**
walk on tiptoe; IDIOM **vir com ~s de lã** to
pussyfoot.

pia *f (para animais)* trough; **2** *(para despejar restos
líquidos de comida) (EP)* a kind of lavatory; **3**
(EP, BR) baptismal font; **4** *(BR)* sink, basin.

piaçá, piaçaba *m* toilet brush; **2** fibres from a Brazilian
piassaba palm (used for making brooms).

piada *f (pio)* trill, chirp; **2** joke, quip, gag, wisecrack;
3 *(provocação)* jibe, gibe; **estás a dar-me ~s?** are
you getting at me/taking a jibe at me?; ♦ **que ~!**
exc how funny!; **ela tem ~** she is funny, cute; **5**
satire, skit; **a peça era/dava ~ ao ministro ao
governo** the play was a skit on the minister/was
getting at the government; ~**s porcas** dirty jokes.

pianista *m,f* pianist.

piano *m* piano.

pião *m (brinquedo)* top.

piar *vi (voz dos pássaros)* to cheep, chirp; *(mocho,
coruja)* to hoot.

PIB *(abr de* **Produto Interno Bruto)** Gross
Domestic Product, GDP.

pica *m (fam)* public transport inspector; **2** *m* hoe; **3**
(entalhe no pinheiro) incision; **4** *(dose injectada
de droga)* shot.

picada *f* prick; **2** *(de insecto)* sting, bite; **3** *(bicada)*
peck; **4** ~**s de traça** moth holes; **5** *(dor aguda)*
sharp pain, stab; **6** ~ **de sarcasmo** a touch of
sarcasm; **dar a ~ ao solo** to hoe the ground; **a
vaca andava ~ da mosca** *(fig) (furioso)* the cow
had gone raving mad.

picadeiro *m (MIL)* riding-school; **2** *(estância de madeiras)*
woodyard; **3** *(BR)* (circus) ring.

picadinho *m (CULIN)* mince.

picado,-a *adj* pricked; **2** stung; **3** bitten; **4** pecked; **5**
(fig) angry, easily offended, touchy; **6** *(cebola, alho)*
chopped; **7** *(mar)* choppy; **8** *(CULIN)* minced; **9**
(avião a pique) nosedive; **10** *(touro)* pricked.

picante *adj* hot, spicy; **2** stinging; biting; **3** risqué,
saucy.

pica-pau *m* woodpecker.

picar *vt* to prick; to sting; to bite; to peck; to goad;
to mince; to shred; to chop up; ♦ *vi* to take the
bait; to sting; ♦ ~**-se** *vr* to be offended/cross; to
prick oneself.

picardia *f* trickery; **2** *(acção)* knavish.

picaresco,-a *adj* comic, farcical.

picareta *f* pickaxe.

pícaro,-a *m,f* crook; **2** *(LITER)* hero of a picaresque
novel; *adj* crafty, cunning, clever, sly.

piçarra *f* shale.
picles *mpl* pickles.
pico *m* peak; **2** thorn; **3** a bit; **duas e ~s** just after two o'clock.
picolé *(BR) m* iced lolly.
picotar *vt* to perforate; **2** *(bordado)* picot-embroidery.
pictórico,-a *adj* pictorial.
piedade *f* piety; **2** pity; **ter ~ de** to have pity on; **piedoso,-a** *adj (REL)* pious; merciful.
piegas *m,f* softy; cry-baby; ♦ *adj inv* sentimental; *(fam)* soppy.
pieguice *f* sentimentality, soppiness.
pieira *f (fam) (respiração)* wheezy breathing.
piela *f (fam)* booze; **estar com uma ~** to be tight, be smashed.
pifar *vt* (col) to snatch; pinch, pilfer; **2** *(BR) (beber demasiado)* drink too much; **3** to be a flop, go wrong, fall through.
pífaro *m (instrumento de sopro)* pipe; *(pessoa que o toca)* piper.
pigarrear *vi* to hawk; **2** clear one's throat.
pigarro *m (fam)* phlegm; **2** *(fig)* a frog/tickle (in one's throat).
pigmento *m* pigment, pigmentation.
pigmeu, pigméia *adj* pigmy.
pijama *m* pyjamas *pl*.
pila *f (vulg) (pénis)* willy *(UK)*; dick *(US)*.
pilantra *m (BR) (dishonest person)* rogue.
pilão *(pl: -ões) m* pestle; **2** *(pop) (pelintra)* rogue, devil; ♦ *adj (pop) (alguém)* poor devil.
pilar *m* pillar; **2** column; ♦ *vt* to crush with pestle; **2** *(cereal)* remove husk.
pilha *f* battery; **2** pile, heap; **3** *(de pratos)* stack; **4** *(de nervos)* a bag of nerves; IDIOM **meter ~ de raiva** be annoying, infuriating.
pilhagem *f* pillage, plunder, booty.
pilhar *vt* to plunder, pillage; **2** to rob, steal; **~ carteiras** pinch wallets.
pilhéria *f* jest, joke, quip.
pilim *m (fam) (dinheiro)* dosh.
pilinha *f (linguagem de criança) (pénis)* little willy.
pilotagem *f* flying; **escola de ~** flying school.
pilotar *vt* to fly; to steer.
pilotis *mpl (ARQ)* stilts.
piloto *m (modelo)* pilot; **2** *(avião, barco)* pilot; **cabine de ~** *(de avião)* cockpit; **3** *(DESP) (de corrida)* (racing) driver; **4** *(bico de gás)* pilot light.
pílula *f* pill.
pimenta *f* pepper; **grão de ~** peppercorn; **~-do-reino** *(BR)* black pepper.
pimentão *m* green/red pepper.
pimenteira *f* pepper plant.
pimenteiro *m* pepper-mill, pepper shaker.
pimpão,-ona *m,f* show-off, boaster, braggart; ♦ *adj* smart, haughty, neat.
pimpolho *m (de vinha)* young shoot; **2** lovely baby, healthy youngster.
pinacoteca *f* art gallery, pinacotheca.
pináculo *m* pinnacle, summit.
pinça *f* tweezers *pl*; **2** tongs *pl*; **3** *(MED)* forceps *pl*.
píncaro *m* summit, peak; **2** *(apogéu)* height.

pincel *m (vertical)* brush; **2** paintbrush; **~ de barba** shaving brush.
pincelada *f (brush)* stroke.
pincho *m* hop; jump.
pindérico,-a *m,f, adj (pej)* shabby person; shabby.
pinga *f* drop; **~s de chuva** raindrops; **ir tomar umas ~s** to go boozing; **mais uma ~?** a little more wine?
pingado,-a *adj (com pingos)* **~** splashed *(de* with); **2** wet, dripping; **3 café ~** *(pop)* coffee with a little milk.
pingar *vi* to drip; **2** *(sujar)* get a spot/drip (on sth) **ele pingou a camisa com o molho** he got a spot of gravy on his shirt; **3 ~ do nariz** drop from the nose, snivel; **o teu nariz está a ~** your nose is running/runny; ♦ *vi* to start to rain.
pingente *m* pendant; earring.
pingo *m* drop; **~s de sangue/de chuva** drops of blood/raindrops; **2 um ~ de** a tiny bit; **3** *(sinal ortográfico)* dot; **aos ~s** drop by drop.
pingue-pongue *m* ping-pong, table tennis.
pinguim *m* penguin.
pinha *f (BOT)* pine cone; **2** *(pop)* head; **não regular bem da ~** not be right in the head; ♦ **à ~** *adv* in a heap, packed.
pinhal *m* pine grove.
pinhão *m* pine kernel.
pinheiro *m* pine (tree).
pinho *m* pine.
pino *m* **a ~** upright; **fazer o ~** to stand on one's head; **o sol está a ~** the sun is at its height.
pinote *m (de cavalo)* caper; curvet.
pinta *f* spot, dot; **saia preta com ~s** black polka-dot skirt; **2** *(fig)* appearance; **ter boa ~** to look good; **3** *(na pele)* mole.
pintainho,-a *m,f* little chick.
pintar *vt* to paint; **2** to describe; **3 ~ o cabelo** to dye the hair; ♦ **~-se** *vr* to put on one's make-up; ♦ *vi* to paint; **2** change colour **o milho já pinta** the corn is changing colour; IDIOM **~ o sete** to paint the town red.
pintarroxo *m* robin; **2** linnet.
pintassilgo *m (ave)* finch.
pinto,-a *m,f* chick.
pintor,-ora *m,f* painter.
pintura *f* painting, picture; **~ a óleo** oil painting; **~ rupestre** cave painting; **2** make-up.
pio,-a *m,f* pious; charitable; ♦ *adj* cheep, chirp; *(da coruja, do mocho)* hoot.
piolho *m* louse.
pioneiro,-a *m* pioneer; ♦ *adj* pioneering.
pior *m*: **o ~ de tudo** worst of all; ♦ *adj adv* worse; the worst; **piora** *f* worsening, deterioration.
piorar *vt* to make worse, worsen, aggravate; ♦ *vi* to get worse.
piorio *m (fam) (gente)* the lowest of the low; scum.
piorreia *f (MED)* pyorrhoea.
pipa *f (recipiente)* barrel, cask; **2** *(medida de capacidade)* hogshead; **3** *(fam) (pessoa gorda)* tub; **4** *(BR) (de papel)* kite.
piparote *m* flick, flip; **2** *(fig) (falha, insucesso)* fall, flop; **3** *(fig, fam) (ignorar alguém)* brush-off.

pipi *m (fala de infante – nome para pássaro)* birdie.

pipilar *m* chirp; **o ~ do passarinho** the little bird's chirp; ♦ *vt* to chirp, twitter, chirrup.

pipo *m* small barrel, keg; **2** nozzle; **3** *(fam) (grávida)* **andar de ~** to be pregnant.

pipoca *f* popcorn.

pique *m (lança)* pike; **2** piquancy; **3** spite, grudge; **4** **a ~** vertically, steeply; **cair a ~** *(plane)* nosedive; **a ~ de** on the verge of; **ir a ~***(navio)* to sink.

piquenique *m* picnic; **fazer (um) ~** to have a picnic.

piquete *m (MIL)* squad; **2** *(de greve)* picket.

pira *f (fogueira sagrada)* pyre; **2** *(pop)* **dar o ~** *(escapar)* to scarper, scram, make off; abscond.

pirâmide *f* pyramid.

piranha *f (ZOOL)* piranha.

pirar *(fam) vi (BR)* scarper; **2** enlouquecer, go mad; ♦ **~-se** *vr (EP) (fam)* to slip away, disappear; **pira-te!** get lost!

pirata *m* pirate, buccaneer; **2** *(de avião, navio)* hijacker; **3** *(fam)* rogue; **4** *(BR)* ladies'man; ♦ *adj (rádio, cópia)* pirate.

pirataria *f* piracy; **~ aérea** hijacking of planes; **2** *(fig, fam)* **viver como um ~** to live like a villain, rascal.

piratear *vt (pilhar)* to plunder; **2** *(COMP)* to hack; **3** plagiarize.

Pireneus *npr* **os P~** *mpl* the Pyrenees.

pires *m inv* saucer.

pirilampo *m* glow-worm.

piropo *m* a compliment made to women; **2** *(MIN)* garnet.

pirotecnia *f* pyrotechnics *sg*, art of making fireworks.

pirraça *f (provocação)* spite, spiteful joke; **fazer ~ a alguém** *(irritar, provocar)* tease, spite sb.

pirralho *m (criança)* little boy; **2** *(BR)* small man.

pirueta *f* pirouette.

pirulito *m* fizzy drink (in a special bottle); **2** *(fam) (pénis de criança)* little willy.

pisada *f* footstep; **2** footprint.

pisadela *f* trampling; **dar/levar uma ~** to tread on/ be trodden.

pisa-papéis *(pl: pisas-papéis) m* paper–weight.

pisar *vt* to walk (on); **2** tread (on) **~ o pé de (alguém)** tread on sb's foot; **3** *(esmagar alimentos)* press, crush; pound; **~ as nozes** pound/crush the nuts; **4** *(espezinhar)* walk all over, trample on (sb); ♦ *vi* to walk; to put one's foot down.

piscadela *f* blink; **2** wink; **3** *(para atrair atenção)* signal.

pisca-pisca *(pl: pisca-piscas) f (AUT)* indicator, blinker; **2** person with an eye tic.

piscar *vt* to blink; **2** **~ o olho** to wink; **3** *(estrelas, luz ao longe)* twinkle; **num ~ de olhos** in a twinkle of an eye.

piscatório,-a *adj* fishing; **uma zona ~a** a fishing area/zone.

piscina *f* swimming pool; **2** fish pond.

piso *m* floor, storey; **o prédio tem quatro ~s** the building has four floors; **2** *(chão)* surface; **3** tread; **4** *(GEOL)* layer.

pisotear *vt (BR) (pisar)* to trample (on); **2** *(fig) (humilhar)* to trample over.

pista *f* track, trail; **~ de hipismo** race-track; **2** *(dica, vestígio)* clue, trace; **3** *(AER)* runway; **4** *(circo, estádio)* ring; **5** *(de estrada)* lane; **a avenida tem 4 ~s** the avenue has 4 lanes; **6** *(dance)* floor.

pistácio *m (BOT)* pistachio.

pistão *m* piston; **2** *(MÚS)* valve.

pistola *f* pistol, revolver, gun; **2** *(aparelho de pintura)* spray gun.

pistoleiro *m* gunman; **2** *(BR)* overseer of a ranch.

pita *f (BOT) (fibras das folhas do piterd)* agare's leaves or fibres; **2** *(pop) (palinha nova)* spring chicken.

pitada *f (um pouco)* pinch; **uma ~ de sal** a pinch of salt; **2** bad smell; IDIOM **não perder ~ (de algo)** not miss a clue.

pitanga *f (BOT) (BR)* Brazil cherry.

pitão *m (ZOOL)* python; **2** tip of the bull's horn; **3** cork-tree's trunk (cut down).

pitar *vt/vi* to smoke.

piteira *f* cigarette-holder.

piteria *f (BOT)* agave, aloe (tree).

pitéu *m* titbit, delicacy.

pitoresco,-a *adj* picturesque.

pitosga *adj inv* short-sighted.

pituitária *adj (ANAT)* pituitary.

pivete *m* nasty smell; **2** *(fam)* naughty, mischievous child.

PJ *(abr de* **Polícia Judiciária***)* CID.

PL *(abr de* **peso líquido***)* net weight.

placa *f (chapa)* plate, *(AUTO)* number plate, *(US)* license plate; **2** metal sheet; **3** *(inscrição)* plaque; **~ de sinalização** road sign; **4** *(MED) (nos dentes)* plaque, *(na pele)* rash, spot, scab; **5** *(CONSTR)* block, slab; **6** *(FÍS, GEOG, FOTO)* plate.

placagem *f (DESP)* tackling.

placa-mãe *f (COMP)* motherboard.

placar *vt (acalmar)* to calm down; **2** *(DESP)* to tackle.

placebo *m* placebo.

placenta *f (MED, BOT)* placenta.

placidez *f* peacefulness, serenity.

plácido,-a *adj* calm; placid.

plagiar *vt (imitar, apresentar como seu)* to plagiarize.

plágio *m* plagiarism.

plaina *f (de carpinteiro)* plane.

planador *m* glider.

planáltico,-a *adj* referring to plateau, upland.

planalto *m* tableland, upland plateau.

planar *vi (voar sem motor)* to glide; **2** *(pássaros)* hover; **3** *(fig) (viver num plano elevado)* to rank.

planeamento *(BR:* **planejamento***) m* planning, design, plan.

planear *(BR:* **planejar***) vt* to plan; **2** to design.

planejamento *vt (BR) (Vd:* **planeamento***)*.

planejar *vt (BR) (Vd:* **planear***)*.

planeta *m* planet.

planetário,-a *adj* planetary.

plangente *adj (canto, voz)* plaintive, mournful.

planície *f (GEOG)* plain.

planificar *vt* to plan out; **2** to make a plan for; **3** *(traçar)* to design, make a plan of; **4** *(GEOM, MAT)* outline.

planilha *f (formulário)* table; **2** *(COMP)* spreadsheet.

planisfério *m* planisphere.

plano,-a *m* plan, outline; **2** *(MAT, GEOM)* plane; **3 em primeiro/em último** ~ in the foreground/background; **4** ~ **inclinado** *(ARQ)* slope; **5** *(fig)* slippery slope; **6***(CIN, TEAT)* shot; **7 grande** ~ close-up; ♦ *adj* flat, level, plane; **2** smooth.

planta *f (BOT)* plant; **2** *(ARQ)* drawing, plan, blueprint; **3** ~ **do pé** sole of the foot; **4** ~ **da cidade** street map, street atlas; **5 isto não tem** ~ **nenhuma** this doesn't look good/nice at all; **ela não tem** ~ **nenhuma** she is quite plain.

plantação *f* planting; planted land.

plantão *(MIL)* on duty; **médico de** ~ doctor on duty; **ficar de** ~ stand around waiting.

plantar *vt* to plant; **2** to sow; **3** *(estaca, bandeira)* put up; **4** to set up, install.

plantel *m (DESP) (jogadores, etc. selecionados)* the best team; **2** *(gado)* breeding herd.

plantio *m* plantation; crops.

planura *f* plain.

plaqueta *f* small board; **2** *(sangue)* platelet; ~ **sanguínea/ trombócita** (thrombocyte) blood platelet.

plasma *m (ANAT)* plasma.

plasmar *vt (em barro, gesso)* to mould, shape.

plástico,-a *m* plastic; **comida de** ~ *f* fast food; **2** *f* modelling; ♦ *adj* plastic.

plastificar *vt* to laminate, cover sth with plastic.

plataforma *f* platform; **2** *(FÍS)* ~ **giratória** turntable; **3** ~ **de teste** test bed; **4** *(de petróleo)* oil rig; **5** *(de lançamento)* launching pad; **6** *(GEOG)* shelf; **7** *(proposta de conciliação)* **encontrar uma** ~ find a middle ground; **8** position.

plátano *m* plane tree.

plateia *f* stalls *pl (UK)*; orchestra *(US)*; **fundo da** ~ pit; **2** *(público)* audience.

platina *f* platinum.

platinado,-a *adj* platinum; **loura** ~**da** platinum blonde; ♦ *mpl* **platinados** *(MEC)* contact points.

Platão *m* Plato.

platónico,-a *adj* platonic.

platonismo *m* Platonism.

plausibilidade *f* plausibility.

plausível *adj inv* credible, plausible.

plebe *f* common people, populace; **2** *(pej)* riff-raff, rabble.

plebeu,-éia *m,f* pleb; ♦ *adj* plebeian, commoner.

plebiscite *m* referendum, plebiscite.

plectro *m (MÚS)* plectrum.

plêiade *f (ASTRON)* Pleiades; **2** pleiad; **uma** ~ **de cientistas** a pleiad of scientists.

pleitear *vt (JUR)* to plead for; **2** to sue for; **3** contest, compete.

pleito *m* lawsuit, case; **2** *(fig)* dispute.

plenamente *adv* fully, absolutely.

plenário,-a *adj* plenary.

plenitude *f* peak, prime, plenitude; fullness.

pleno,-a *adj* full, complete; **em** ~ **dia** in broad daylight; **em** ~ **mar** on the high sea; **em** ~ **inverno** in mid-winter; **ele gritou a** ~**s pulmões** he shouted with all his might.

plenopotenciário,-a *adj* plenipotentiary; with full powers.

pleonasmo *m* pleonasm; redundancy.

plica *f (TIPO)* accent.

plinto *m* plinth; **2** *(DESP)* plinth, springboard.

plissado,-a *adj (vestuário)* pleated.

plissar *vt* to pleat, tuck.

pluma *f* feather; plume; **chapéu com** ~**s** hat with feathers; **2** *(para escrever)* quill (dated).

plumagem *f* plumage.

plural *(pl: -ais)* *m* plural.

pluralidade *f* majority; **2** variety, diversity.

pluralismo *m (FIL, POL)* pluralism.

pluridisciplinar *adj inv* many-sided, covering various subjects.

Plutão *(ASTRON)* Pluto.

plutocrata *m,f* plutocrat; ♦ *adj* plutocratic.

plutónio *(BR: -tô-)* *m* plutonium.

pluvial *adj* pluvial, rain; **as florestas pluviais** the rain forests.

pluviosidade *f* rainfall.

pluvioso,-a *adj* rainy.

PNB *(abr de **Produto Nacional Bruto**)* Gross National Product, GNP.

pneu *m* tyre, *(US)* tire.

pneumático,-a *m* tyre, *(US)* tire; ♦ *adj* pneumatic.

pneumonia *f* pneumonia.

pó *m* powder; dust; **limpar o** ~ to dust; **pano do** ~ duster; **2** ~**-de-arroz** face powder; **açúcar em** ~ icing sugar; **canela em** ~ ground cinnamon; **leite em** ~ powdered milk; **3** *(cocaine)* snow; **reduzir a** ~ to destroy sth, to disintegrate.

pobre *m,f* poor person; **os** ~**s** the poor; ♦ *adj* poor; ~ **de espírito** poor in spirit.

pobreza *f* poverty.

pobrezinho,-a *m,f* beggar; *(pessoa/animal digno de compaixão)* poor thing, poor wretch; ♦ *adj* poor.

poça[1] *f* puddle, pool; ~ **de sangue** pool of blood; IDIOM **meter o pé/a pata na** ~ *(cometer um erro)* to put one's foot in it; to blow it.

poça[2] *exc (cal)* blimey!

poção *f* potion, draught.

pocilga *f (casa de suínos)* pigsty; **2** *(lugar imundo)* pigsty, hovel, *(fam)* dump.

poço *m (ger)* well; ~ **de petróleo** oil-well; **2** *(do rio)* eddy, whirlpool; **3** *(da mina)* (mine) shaft, pit; **4** *(que se aprofunda para obter água)* bore hole; **5** ~ **de ar** *(AERO)* air-pocket; **6** *(TEAT) (da orquestra)* orchestra-pit; **7** *(fig)* abysm, chasm; IDIOM **ser um** ~ **de ciência** a learned person; **ser um** ~ **sem fundo** a person who keeps secrets.

poda *f* pruning.

podadeira *f* pruning knife.

podado,-ora *m,f* pruner.

podão *m* pruning-hook; **2** *(fig, fam) (pessoa desajeitada)* ham-fisted person.

podar *vt/vi* to prune.

podengo,-a *m,f (cão de caça)* setter, pointer; **2** *(qualquer cão)* dog.

poder *m* power; authority; **plenos** ~**es** full powers; ~ **aquisitivo** purchasing power; ♦ *vt* to be able to, be capable of, can; to be allowed to, may; **pode ser que** it may be that; **não posso ir** I can't go;

pode não ser verdade it may not be true; **ele não pode com a despesa** he can't afford the expense; **não posso com ela** I cannot cope with her; **querer é** ~ where there's a will there's a way.

poderio *m (dominio)* might; *(poder)* power; authority.

poderoso,-a *adj* mighty, powerful.

pódio *m (muro circundante da arena)* podium; **2** *(DESP) (lugar/estrado de honra)* podium.

podre *adj* rotten, putrid; **2** *(fig)* rotten, corrupt.

podridão *f* decay, rottenness, putrification; **2** *(fig)* corruption.

põe, pões *(pres. ind. = pôr, 2nd, 3rd person sg).*

poeira *f* thick dust; ~ **radioactiva** fallout.

poeirento,-a *adj* dusty.

poejo *m (BOT) (planta aromática, usada na culinária)* pennyroyal.

poema *m* poem.

poente *m (ASTRON, GEOG)* west; **2** *(sol)* sunset; ♦ *adj inv (sol)* setting; **2** *(ocidental)* western.

poesia *f* poetry; *(composição em verso)* poem.

poeta *m* poet.

poético,-a *adj* poetic.

poetisa *f* poetess.

pois *adv* well (then); so; yes; ~ **bem/~então** well then; ~ **é** that's right, so it is, indeed; ~ **naturalmente/claro!** *exc* but, naturally! of course! ~ **não!** of course!; **ah pois?** really?; ♦ *conj* as, because, therefore; **pois que** since.

'**Pois**' has a wide variety of meanings, often depending on intonation. Very common to let the chatter-box at the other end of the line think you are still listening: **pois** ... **pois** ... Ah **pois:**.. yes ... oh yes ... yes ... really!

---

poisar *vt* to put, place, rest; **ela pousou as mãos na mesa** she put her hands down on the table; **a borboleta poisou na flor** the butterfly rested on the flower; **avião poisou** the plane touched down; ♦ *vi* settle, land, alight, rest, stop, pause.

poise *f (FÍS) (unidade de viscosidade dos líquidos, CGS)* poise.

poisio *m (AGR) (descanso à terra)* fallow.

pojadoiro, pojadouro *m* topside of the beef (leg).

pojante *adj (NÁUT)* strong; swift, fast.

polaco,-a *(BR:* **polonês, polonesa***) m,f (pessoa)* Pole; ♦ *m (LING)* Polish; ♦ *adj* Polish.

polar *adj* polar; **Estrela P~** North Star.

polaridade *f* polarity.

polarizar *vt* to polarize.

poldra *f (BOT) (rebento duma árvore)* shoot.

poldro,-a *m,f (ZOOL)* colt/filly.

polé *m (roldana)* pulley; **2** *(instrumento de tortura)* strappado; **3** *(no riacho)* stepping stone.

polegada *f (medida britânica, antes do metro ser adaptado)* inch.

polegar *m* thumb.

poleiro *m* perch.

polémica *(BR:* -lê-*) f* controversy, dispute.

polémico,-a *adj* polemic, controversial.

pólen *m* pollen.

polichinelo *(TEAT)* punch (and judy show); **2** (artista de saltibanco etc) travelling entertainer; **3** *(fam)* fool, buffoon.

polícia *f* police, police force; ♦ *m,f* policeman/woman; **agente de** ~ police constable; ~ **marítima** coastguard; ~ **rodoviária** traffic police; **esquadra da** ~ police station.

policial *adj* police; **novela/romance** ~ detective story.

policiamento *m* ~ **das ruas** street policing, police on the beat.

policiar *vt* to police, patrol, supervise.

polidez *f* good manners *pl*, politeness.

polido,-a *adj (metal, cera)* polished, shiny; **2** *(maneiras)* well-bred, polite.

poliéster *m* polyester.

poliestireno *m* polystyrene.

poligamia *f* polygamy.

polígamo,-a *m,f* polygamist; ♦ *adj* polygamous.

poliglota *adj* polyglot.

polimento *m* polishing; **2** refinement, polish.

polínico policlinico,-a *adj (BOT) (ue contem pdén)* polliniferous (=poleniferrous).

polinizar *vt/vi* to pollinate.

pólipo *m (MED) m* polyp.

polir *vt (metal, vidro, mobília)* to polish; **2** *(discurso, texto)* polish up; ♦ ~-**se** *vr (fig)* polish up one's manners.

polissílabo *adj* polysyllabic.

politécnica *f* polytechnic.

politicagem *(Vd: politiquice).*

político,-a *m,f* politician; **2** *(fig) (pessoa conciliadora)* diplomat; ♦ *f* politics *sg*; **2** policy; ♦ *adj* political; crafty.

politiqueiro,-a *m,f (pej)* wheeler-dealer; ♦ *adj* politicking.

politiquice *f* political dabbling, politicking; **2** *(discussão vã);* empty political talk.

politização *f* politicization.

politizar *vt* politicise, make sb politically aware; ♦ *vr* become politically aware.

pólo *m (GEOG/ELECT)* pole; **P~ Sul** South Pole; **2** *(fig) (elemento)* side; **3** *(DESP)* polo; ~ **aquático** water polo.

polonês,-esa *(BR)* ♦ *m,f* Pole; ♦ *m; (LÍNG)* Polish; ♦ *adj* Polish *m,f.*

Polónia *npr* a ~ Poland.

polpa *f (dos vegetais)* pulp; **2** *(massa de consistência fraca)* pap; **3** ~ **de cellulose** paper pulp.

polpudo,-a *adj (fruto, vegetal)* pulpy; **2** *(lábio carnudo)* fleshy; **3** *(negócio, etc)* profitable; **4** *(de vulto)* sizeable.

poltrão,-ona *m,f* coward, timid; ♦ *adj* cowardly.

poltrona *f* high-backed chair with arms, armchair.

poluente *m* pollutant; ♦ *adj inv* pollutant.

poluição *f* pollution.

poluir *vt* to pollute; **2** *(fig) (honra, nome)* sully.

polvilhar *vt* to sprinkle, powder, dust; **polvilhe a forma com açúcar** dust the cake tin with sugar; ♦ *vr* sprinkle o.s.

polvo *m* octopus.

pólvora *f* gunpowder.

polvorosa f fuss, commotion; **em ~** adv *(muito desarrumado)* in a mess, in confusion.

pomada f pomade, ointment, cream; **2** *(para sapatos)* shoe polish; **3** *(pop)* good wine; **4** *(BR)* vanity.

pomar m orchard.

pomba f dove; **ter coração de ~** to have a kind heart.

pombal m dovecote.

pombo m pigeon; **~ bravo** wild-pigeon.

pomo m *(BOT)* pome; **~ de discórdia** bone of contention; **~-de-Adão** m Adam's apple.

pompa f pomp, ceremony; **~ e circunstância** pomp and circumstance.

pomposo,-a adj ostentatious, pompous.

ponche f *(bebida com rum e fruta)* punch.

poncho m poncho, cape; IDIOM *(BR)* **passar por baixo do ~** to smuggle in.

ponderação f consideration, meditation.

ponderado,-a adj prudent, well-considered.

ponderar vt to consider, weigh up; ♦ vi to meditate, muse.

ponha *(pres. subj de* **pôr**).

ponho *(pres. indic. de* **pôr**, *first person).*

ponta f point, tip; **2** end; **3** bit; **~ de cigarro** cigarette end; **na ~ da língua** on the tip of one's tongue; **na (s) ~(s) do(s) pé(s)** on tiptoe; **4** *(DESP)* **~ esquerda** outside-left, left-winger; **5 uma ~ de febre** a touch of fever; **6 ~ de lança** centre-forward; **7** apex; ♦ adv **de ~ a ~** from one end to the other; IDIOM **esta farto,-a até à ~ dos cabelos** I am fed up to the back of my teeth; **hora de ~** rush hour.

pontada f *(dor aguda e passageira)* sharp pain, twinge; *(de lado)* stitch.

pontão m *(small bridge)* pier; **~ em T** pier in T *(shape)*; **2** pontoon bridge; **3** *(prop)* escora.

pontapé m kick; **dar ~ em** to kick; **~ de saída** kick-off.

pontaria f aim; **fazer ~** to take aim; **errar a ~** to miss one's aim.

ponte f bridge; **~ aérea** air shuttle, airlift; **~ levadiça** drawbridge; **~ pênsil** suspension bridge; **~ pedonal** footbridge; **2** *(NÁUT)* bridge; **3** *(fig)* *(circuito de contacto)* link.

ponteado,-a m stipple; ♦ adj stippled, dotted.

pontear vt to dot, stipple; **2** to sew, stitch.

ponteiro,-a m *(vara para apontar o quadro)* pointer; **2** *(relógio)* hand; **3** needle; **4** *(MÚS)* plectrum; **5** *(DESP)* striker.

pontiagudo,-a adj sharp, pointed.

pontificado m pontificate.

pontífice m pontiff, Pope.

pontilhado m dot … dot … dotted; ♦ adj dotted, pitted, spotted; **linha ~a** dotted line.

pontilhar vt to dot, stipple.

pontinha f tip, point; **2** end; **uma ~ de ciúme** a touch of jealousy.

ponto m point; dot; *(pontuação)* **~ final** full stop; **~ de exclamação/interrogação** exclamation mark; **2** *(costura, bordado)* stitch; **~ da cruz** cross-stitch; **3** aim, object; **4** *(TEAT)* prompter; **5** spot, place; **6** examination paper; **7** *(CULIN)* **açúcar em ~** sugar at point of caramelization; **8** mark, score; **marcar**

~s to keep score; *(GEOG)* **pontos cardeais** cardinal points; **9 ~ negro** *(poro sujo)* black head; **10 ~ morto** *(AUTO)* neutral; **11 ~ de partida** starting point; **12 ~ de táxi** *(BR)* taxi stand; **~ de vista** *(opinion)* viewpoint; ♦ adv **em ~** sharp, on the dot; **ele chegou à uma hora ~** he arrived at one o'clock sharp; **até certo ~** to a certain extent; **em que ~ está o trabalho** at what stage is the work? **estar a/no ~ de** be about to; ♦ **aí é que bate o ~!** exc that's just the point!; IDIOM **não dar ~ sem nó** have an ulterior motive, to look after number one; **pôr os ~s nos ii** to dot the ii's; **dar um ~ na boca** clam up, to shut one's mouth.

pontoar vt *(coser)* *(a pontos largos)* to tack, baste; **2** to mark with points.

ponto-e-vírgula *(pantuação)* semicolon.

pontuação f punctuation; **2** *(atribuição, lista de pontos)* marksheet, scoring list.

pontual adj punctual.

pontualidade f punctuality.

pontuar vt to punctuate.

popa f *(tecido)* stern, poop; **à ~** astern, aft; **o negócio vai de vento em ~** business is going from strength to strength; **a venda vai de vento em ~** selling like hot cakes.

popelina f *(tecido)* poplin.

populaça f *(gonte)* mob, rabble.

população f population.

popular adj popular; of the people; common, current.

popularidade f popularity.

popularizar vt to popularize, make popular; ♦ **~-se** vr to become popular.

póquer *(BR: pô-)* m poker (cards).

pôr m **o ~ do sol** sunset; ♦ vt *(colocar)* to put; to place; **ele pôs os pratos na mesa** he put the plates on the table; **2 ~ a mesa** to set/lay the table; **3 ~ a carta no correio** post the letter; **4** *(vestuário)* put on, **ponha o chapéu** put on your hat; **5 ~ a culpa em alguém** to blame sb; **6 ~ de lado** set aside; **7 ~ defeito em algo, alguém** find fault with sb, sth; **8** *(dúvidas, questão)* to raise; **9** *(TEAT, CIN)* **~ em cena** to stage a play; **10 ~ fora (alguém)** put (sb) out; **11** *(ovos)* to lay; **12** *(deitar algo em algo)* pour in/into, put in, **não ponha açúcar no meu café** don't put any sugar in my coffee; **~ o azeite na garrafa** pour the olive-oil into the bottle; ♦ vr **~-se de pé** to stand up; **~ zangado** to become angry; **~ a** to begin to; **~ a caminho** to set off; IDIOM **~ tudo em pratos limpos** to clear a matter up; to clarify; **pôr-se a pau** to be wary.

por **(por + o = pelo; por + a = pela; por + os = pelos; por + as = pelas)** prep *(duração do tempo, frequência)* for; **estive na África ~ 4 meses** I was in Africa for 4 months; **falo com ela duas vezes ~ semana** I speak to her twice a week; **vi-a pela primeira vez** I saw her for the first time; **~ hoje é tudo** that's all for today; **2** on behalf of, for the sake of, in exchange for; **faço isso ~ ela** I do that for her; **~ Deus** for Heaven's sake; **troco o chapéu verde pelo preto** I change (exchange) the green hat for the black one; **3** through, by; **viemos**

pelo parque, we came through the park; **perdi o avião ~ cinco minutos** I missed the plane by five minutes; **4** *(na voz passiva)* by; **isso foi dito por mim** that was said by me; **5** *(data aproximada)* about; **pelas três horas** about three o'clock; **6** around, by, over, all over; **vou viajar pelo Natal pela China** I am going to travel all over China around Christmas; **7** *(maneira de)* **ele levou-a pelo braço** he took her by the arm; **8** per; **o telefonema custa 2 euros ~ minuto** the phone call costs 2 euros per minute; **9** *(direcção)* **vá ~ ali** go (through) way; **10** along, by; **passeámos ao longo do mar** we walked along the shore; **11** *(razão)* because, due to; **não trabalhei ~ estar doente** I didn't go to work, because I was sick; **12** *(ainda não feito)* **isso ficou ~ fazer** that is yet to be done; **13** *(enfático)* **por mim, não me importo** (as for me) I don't mind, that's fine by me; **14** *(completa o significado de vários verbos, adjectivos, substantivos)* **apaixonar-se ~** be in love with; **~ fora** outside, outwardly; **~ dentro** inside, inwardly; **~ atacado** wholesale; **~ fim** finally, at last; **escrito** in writing; **louco ~** mad about; **~ mês** monthly; **~ dia** daily; **~ alto,** superficially; **~ miúdo,** in detail; **~ um lado** on the other hand; **~ assim dizer** so to speak; **~ isso** therefore; **~ que razão;** for which reason; **~ mais rico que ele seja** however rich he may be.
porão *m* *(NÁUT)* hold.
porcalhão, porcalhona *m,f* *(animal, pessoa)* pig; **2** *(fam)(depravado)* swine, scumbag; ♦ *adj* dirty, filthy, messy, obscene, nasty; IDIOM **dormir como um ~** to sleep like a log.
porcaria *f* filth; **2** *(fig)* mess; **3** *(fig)* rubbish.
porção *f* portion, piece; **uma ~ de** a lot of.
porcelana *f* porcelain, bone china.
porco,-a *m* *(ZOOL)* pig, hog; ♦ *f* sow; *(CULIN)* pork; **2** *(MEC)* nut; **3** *(pessoa suja)* pig; ♦ *adj* *(casa etc. imunda)* filthy.
porco-espinho *m* porcupine.
porco-montês *m* wild boar.
porém *conj* yet, but, nevertheless.
porfia *f* discussion, talk; **2** dispute, wrangle; **3** stubbornness, obstinacy; **à ~** *adv* *(em desafio no canto)* in competition; **cantar ~** to sing in turns.
porfiado,-a *adj* disputed; **2** stubborn; persistent.
porfiar *vt* **~ em** to insist, persist in.
pormenor *m* detail; **entrar em ~s** to go into detail.
  pormenorizar *vt* to detail; ♦ *vi* tell in detail.
pornografia *f* pornography.
pornográfico,-a *adj* pornographic.
poro *m* *(BIOL)* pore.
poroso,-a *adj* porous.
porquanto *conj* since, seeing that, even more so.
porque *conj* because, why, since; **eis ~** that's why; why; ♦ **~ não?** *adv* why not?
porquê *m* **o ~** *(motivo)* the reason (for); the wherefore; **não entendo o ~** I don't understand the reason; ♦ *adv* why, what for?; **ela não disse ~** she didn't say why; **~ que ele foi?** why did he (have to) go?

Not to be confused with: **por que =** why, for which reason; **por que você fez isso?** why did you do that?

porquinho,-a *m,f* little pig, piglet; **~-da-índia** *(ZOOL)* *m* *(cobaia)* guinea-pig.
porra *f* cudgel; **2** *(cal)* damned thing; **3** *(cal)* penis; **4** *(BR)* sperm, spunk; ♦ *exc* *(cal)* *(ira)* ~ shit!, bullocks!, hell!
porrada *f* *(cal)* beating, thrashing, blow, hell of a beating; **ele dá ~ à mulher** he spanks his wife; **2** *(pop)* *(quantidade)* a lot, loads of; **gastei uma ~ de dinheiro** I spent a lot of money; ♦ **de ~** *adv* *(fam)* suddenly.
porre *(BR)* *m* *(pop)* *(bebedeira)* booze; **ficar de ~** to be plastered; **2** *(copo de aguardente)* a glass of spirits; a skinful *(pop)*; **ser um ~** to be a drag.
porreiro,-a *adj* *(pop)* nice, great, likeable; **ele é ~** he is nice/cute/O.K.; ♦ *exc* great!
porrete *m* *(pop)* cudgel, truncheon, club.
porro *m* club, cudgel; **2** *(BOT)* **alho-~** leek.
porta *f* door, doorway; entrance; gate; **~ corrediça** sliding door; **~ giratória** revolving door; **a ~ das traseiras** *(BR: dos fundos)* back door; **a ~s fechadas** behind closed doors, **à ~ fechada** in private; **2** *(fig)* *(possibilidade)* opportunity; **3** *(COMP)* **~ serial,** serial port; IDIOM **bater à ~** to knock on the door; **bater com a ~** slam the door; **dar com a ~ na cara de (alguém)** slam the door on sb's face; **bater com o nariz na ~** to find the door closed to one; **fora de ~s** on the outskirts; **por ~s travessas** by indirect or illicitous means, by a side door; **surdo como uma ~** deaf as a post.
porta-aviões *m inv* aircraft carrier.
porta-bagagens *m inv* *(AUTO)* boot *(UK)*, trunk *(US)*; parcel rack.
porta-bandeira *(pl:* **porta-bandeiras***)* *m,f* standard-carrier; *(MIL)* standard-bearer.
porta-chaves *m inv* key-holder.
portador,-ora *m,f* bearer; **ao ~** *(COM)* payable to bearer; **2** *(of title, document)* holder; **3** *(MED)* carrier, *(BR)* porter.
portagem *f* toll.
portal *m* main door/gate, doorway; **2** *(COMP)* portal, site.
portaló *m* *(NÁUT)* gangway.
porta-luvas *m inv* *(AUTO)* glove compartment.
porta-malas *(BR)* *m inv* *(AUTO)* boot *(UK)*, trunk *(US)*.
porta-moedas *m* purse.
portanto *conj* so, therefore.
portão *m* gate.
portar *vt* to carry; ♦ **~-se** *vr* to behave.
portaria *f* principal entrance of a convent, portal; convent's entrance hall; **2** *(do porteiro)* doorkeeper's office/desk/lodge, reception desk; **3** *(JUR)* edict, decree, administrative rule/ruling.
portátil *adj* portable.
porta-voz *m,f* spokesman/woman.
porte *m* transport; **2** freight charge, carriage; **3** *(NÁUT)* tonnage, capacity; **4** *(postura)* bearing, **ela tem um ~ de senhora** she has a bearing of

lady; **5** ~ **pago** post paid; **6** *(fig) (tamanho)* scale; **de grande** ~ great stature, important.

porteiro,-a *m,f* caretaker, doorman *(UK)*; janitor *(US)*.

portento *m* wonder, marvel.

portentoso,-a *adj* amazing, marvellous.

pórtico *m (ARQ)* portico.

portinhola *f* (small) door, trap-door; **2** *(NÁUT)* porthole; **3** *(BR) (braguilha)* fly, flies; **sua** ~ **está aberta** your fly is open.

porto *m* port, harbour; **2** *(vinho)* port; **3** ~ **de escala** port of call; **4 o P~** *(capital do Norte de Portugal)* Oporto.

portuense *adj inv* from Oporto.

Portugal *npr* Portugal.

português,-esa *m (LÍNG)* Portuguese; ♦ *adj* Portuguese.

portunhol *m (col, fam) (português incorrecto)* a mixture of Portuguese and Spanish.

porventura *adv* by chance, maybe, probably; **se** ~ **você vir** if, by any chance, you see/come across.

porvir *m* future.

pôs *(pret de:* **pôr***)* **onde** ~ **você a minha mala?** where did you/have you put my suitcase?

pós- *(prefixo, prep)* post.

posar *vi (FOTO, servir de modelo)* to pose.

poscénio *m (TEAT)* backstage.

pós-datado,-a *adj* post-dated.

pós-datar *vt* to postdate.

pose *f (postura)* pose; **2** affectation; **3** *(FOTO)* exposure.

pós-esrito *m* postscript.

posfácio *m* notes *(no fim do livro)*, postface.

pós-graduação *f (grau universitário)* post-graduation.

pós-guerra *m* post-war.

posição *m* position, place; **~-chave** *f* key-position; **2** standing, status, rank; **3** *(opinião)* opinion, standpoint.

posicionar *vt* to position, put in position.

positivamente *adv* positively.

positivo,-a *adj* positive.

pospor *vt* to put after, add later; **2** *(adiar)* postpone; **3** *(amesquinhar) (questão)* belittle, scorn; **4** *(preterir)* put … before.

possa *(pres subj de* **poder***)*.

possante *adj* powerful, strong.

posse *f* possession, ownership; **2** tenure; **tomar** ~ to take office; **tomar** ~ **de** to take possession of; **tomada dos membros do governo** *(POL)* **investidure** of the Cabinet; **~s** *fpl* possessions, means; ♦ *prep* **na** ~ **de** in possesion of.

possessão *f* possession, ownership.

possessivo,-a *adj* possessive.

possesso,-a *adj* possessed, crazed.

possibilidade *f* possibility; chance; **~s** *fpl* means.

possibilitar *vt* to make possible, permit.

possível *adj* possible, likely; **fazer o melhor** ~ to do one's best.

posso *(pres indic de* **poder***)*.

possuidor,-ora *m,f* owner, possessor.

possuir *vt* to own, possess; **2** to enjoy; **3** to hold.

posta *f (cortes paralelos) (peixe, carne)* slice, piece, cutlet; **2** rewarding job; **arrotar** **~s de pescada** boast, show-off.

postal *m* postcard, card; ♦ *adj inv* postal, post.

postar *vt* post (**alguém**, sb); **2** *(BR)* to post (letters); **3** *vr (posicionar-se)* to post o.s.; **4** *(pôr-se de vigia)* take up post.

posta-restante *f* post-office box *(número)*; P.O. box number.

poste *m (pau vertical)* post; **2** *(TEC)* pole, post; **3** *(ARQ)* pillar; **4** *(para condenados)* stake; **5** *(DESP)* goal post.

postergar *vt (deixar para trás)* to postpone; **2** offend, break rules; **3** show contempt for.

posteridade *f* posterity.

posterior *m (pop)* posterior, bottom, bum *(pop)*; ♦ *adj* later, after; **2** *(parte, acesso)* rear, back.

posteriormente *adv* later, afterwards, subsequently.

postiço,-a *adj* false, artificial; **cabeleira** ~ wig, hairpiece; **dentes** **~s** false teeth.

postigo *m* little window/door; **2** window shutter; **3** *(repartição pública)* guichet, window; **4** *(NÁUT)* porthole cover.

posto,-a *(irr pp de* **pôr***) m* position; job; ~ **de gasolina** service/petrol station; ~ **de polícia** police station ♦ *adj* put, placed ♦ **a postos** *adv* at the ready, be prepared ♦ *conj* ~ **que** although, since, given that.

postulado *m* postulate, assumption.

postular *vt* to request, ask (for), plea, beg (for); **2** propose, put forward.

póstumo,-a *adj* posthumous.

postura *f* posture, position; **2** attitude.

potassa *f* potash.

potássio *m* potassium.

potável *adj* drinkable; **água** ~ drinking water.

pote *m* jug, pitcher; small clay pot, jar; ♦ **a/aos ~s** *adv* plenty; **chover a ~s** to rain cats and dogs.

potência *f (gen)* power, strength, force, energy; **2** *(MEC)* horsepower; **3** *(sexual)* potency; **~s** *pl* powers.

potencial *m* potential; ♦ *adj* potential.

potencialidade *f* possibility.

potenciar *vt (valor, potencial)* to raise, reinforce increase.

potentate m potentate.

potente *adj* powerful, potent.

potro,-a *m,f* colt/filly; foal.

pouca-vergonha *f (pop)* shameful/disgraceful behaviour; shameless.

pouco,-a *adj (sg)* little; *(pl)* few; **há** ~ **tempo** a short time ago; **~as vezes** rarely; ♦ *pron* not much, little; **muito** ~ very little, **muitos ~s** *(pl)* few; ♦ *m* **um** ~ *(pequena quantidade)* little piece, a little bit; *(pouco tempo)* a bit, a while; ♦ *adv* ~ **a** ~ gradually, bit by bit; **por** ~ almost; **por** ~ **eu não te encontrava** I very nearly missed you; **aos ~s** gradually; **daqui a ~/dentro em** ~ shortly, in a while; **fazer** ~ **de** *(zombar)* to make fun of; **dizer/ouvir ~as e boas** to say/hear some home truths; **poucochinho** little; **um** ~ very little.

poupado,-a *adj* economical, thrifty.

poupar *vt* to save, to economize on; **2** to spare; **poupa-me os detalhes** spare me the details.

pousada *f* inn, resting place.

pousar *vt* to place, set down; to put down, rest; ♦ *vi* to rest; *(pássaro)* to perch.

povo *m* people; **2** race.

póvoa, povoação *f* village, settlement, hamlet; **2** population.

povoado,-a *m* village, settlement; ♦ *adj* populated colonized.

povoar *vt* to people, populate; **2** to stock.

pra, pr'a (= para) **pr'à** (= para a); *(fam)* **vamos pr'à frente** let's go, let's get a move on.

praça *f* square; **2** *(mercado)* market; **3** ~ **de táxis** taxi rank; **4** *(COM)* city, trading centre; **representante da nossa** ~ our city's representative; **5** *(hasta pública)* public auction; **6** ~ **de touros** bull ring; **7** ~ **forte** stronghold, fort; **8** *(MIL)* *(soldado)* private (soldier); **fazer** ~ to enlist in the army; **fazer** ~ **de** divulge, make a show of.

praceta *f* small square.

pradaria *f* prairie.

prado *m* meadow, grassland; **2** *(BR)* racecourse.

praga *f* pest, plague; ~ **de gafanhotos** a plague of grasshoppers; **2** curse; **3** calamity.

Praga *npr* Prague.

pragana *f* a beard of corn.

pragmático,-a *adj* pragmatic.

praguejar *vt/vi (infestar)* to infest; **2** *(amaldiçoar)* to curse; direct invectives against.

praia *f* beach, shore, seashore.

praiense *adj inv* from Praia (Cape Verde's capital); **2** from Praia da Vitória (in the Azores).

prancha *f* plank; **2** *(NÁUT)* gangplank.

prantear *vt* to mourn; ♦ *vi* weep.

pranto *m* weeping, sobbing; **ela rompeu num** ~ she burst into tears; **2** wailing.

prata *f* silver.

prateado,-a *adj* silver-plated; silvery; **cabelo** ~ salt and pepper hair, silver hair.

prateleira *f* shelf.

praticante *m,f* apprentice; **2** practionner; ♦ *adj inv* practising.

praticar *vt* to practise, perform; **2** commit, perpetrate.

praticável *adj* practical, feasible.

prático,-a *m,f* expert; ♦ *m (NÁUT)* pilot; ♦ *f* practice; **2** experience, know-how; **3** habit; **em** ~ in practice; ♦ *adj* practicable.

prato *m (louça)* plate, dish; **2** *(comida)* dish, course; **almoço de; 3** ~**s** a three-course lunch; ~**s** *mpl (MÚS)* cymbals.

praxe *f* custom, usage; **2** etiquette; praxis; **3 é da** ~ it's a must, it's the done thing.

praxis *f sg/pl* praxis.

prazenteio *m* compliment, gallantry, flattery, pleasantry.

prazenteiro,-a *adj* cheerful, pleasant.

prazer *m* pleasure; **muito** ~ **em conhecê-lo** pleased to meet you; ♦ *vi* to please; **praza a Deus que** if it pleases God that; **praz-me ver** it pleases me to see.

NOTE: prazer is only used in the 3rd person singular in all tenses.

prazo *m* term, period; **2** expiry date, deadline; **a curto/longo** ~ short-/long-term; ~ **final** deadline; **pôr dinheiro a** ~ money in a savings account; **pagar a** ~ to pay in instalments/installments, on credit.

pré *(MIL)* soldier's daily wage in the old days.

pre, pré *prefix* = pre.

preamar *f (BR)* high tide, high water.

preâmbulo *m* preface, introduction, preamble; ~**s** *pl* rigmarole *sg.*

pré-aviso *(pl: pré-avisos) m* (advance) notice.

preçário *m* price-list.

precário,-a *adj* precarious, insecure.

precatado,-a *adj* cautious.

precatar *vt* to warn, put on the alert; ♦ ~**-se** *vr* to take precautions, be careful, be prepared

precatória *f (JUR)* rogatory letter.

precatório,-a *adj* precative, precatory; supplicatory.

precaução *f* precaution.

precaver-se *vr:* ~ **de, contra** *(algo)* to be on one's guard, be forewarned; take precautions.

precavido,-a *adj* cautious.

prece *f* prayer; **2** supplication.

precedência *f* precedence; **2** seniority; **3** priority.

precedente *m* precedent; ♦ *adj inv* previous.

preceder *vt* to precede.

preceito *m* precept, rule; **fazer algo a** ~ to do sth perfectly, as it should be done.

preceituar *vt* to decree, prescribe.

preceituário *m (conjunto de regras)* etiquette, book on etiquette.

prece(p)tor,-ora *m,f* tutor, teacher.

precificação *f* pricing policy.

precificar *vt* to price.

preciosidade *f* gem; treasure.

preciosismo *m* preciosity.

precioso,-a *adj* precious, valuable; **2** *(fino)* refined, fine.

precipício *m* precipice; **2** *(fig)* abyss.

precipitação *f* haste; rashness; **2** *(QUÍM, FÍS)* precipitation.

precipitado,-a *m,f* impetuous person ♦ *adj* hasty; rash.

precipitar *vt* to fling, hurl down, throw; ♦ ~**-se** *vr* to rush, to make a rash decision; **2** do/say sth in advance/before time; **3** throw o.s. into; plunge headlong; **4** *(QUÍM)* precipitate.

precisão *f* precision, exactness; **2** need, necessity.

precisar *vt* to need; **2** specify, state in detail; **sem** ~ unnecessarily; ♦ *vi* ~ **de** to need; **não precisa dizer** you don't have to say; **precisam-se enfermeiras** nurses required.

preciso,-a *adj* precise, exact; **2** necessary, imperative; **é preciso** it's necessary.

preclaro,-a *adj* famous, illustrious; **2** *(cara, figura)* beautiful.

preço *m* price, cost, tariff; ~ **de custo** cost price; ~ **por atacado/a retalho** wholesale/retail price; *(BR,*

Port province) ~ **a varejo** retail price; ~ **de ocasião** bargain price; ~ **líquido** net price; **a todo/ qualquer** ~ at any price/cost.

precoce *adj* precocious; **2** early; **3** *(idade)* premature.

precocidade *f* precociousness.

preconcebido,-a *adj* preconceived.

preconceito *m* prejudice, bias.

preconizar *vt* to extol, praise; **2** to proclaim; **3** recommend; **4** *(prever)* foretell.

precursor,-ora *m,f (o que antecede)* predecessor; **2** precursor, forerunner; harbinger; **os ~es da doença cardíaca** the harbingers of heart disease; ♦ *adj* early, preceding; innovative.

predador,-ora *m,f* predator.

pré-datado,-a *adj (cheque, etc)* predated.

predatório,-a *adj* predatory.

predecessor *m* predecessor.

predestinação *f* predestination, fate.

predestinado,-a *adj* predestined, destined for; *(REL)* chosen (by God).

predeterminado,-a *adj* predetermined.

predeterminante *adj inv (factor, etc)* predeterminate.

predial *adj inv* property, real-estate; **crédito** ~ mortgage loan.

predicado *m* quality, attribute; **2** *(gram)* predicate.

predição *f* prediction, forecast.

predile(c)ção *f* preference, predilection.

predile(c)to,-a *adj* favourite.

prédio *m* building; ~ **de apartamentos** block of flats.

predispor *vt* to predispose; ♦ *vi* ~ **a** predispose to; ♦ *vr* ~**-se a fazer** be predisposed to do.

predisposto,-a *adj* predisposed; **2** *(doença)* prone.

predizer *vt* to predict, forecast.

predominância *f* predominance, prevalence.

predominar *vi* to predominate, prevail.

predomínio *m* predominance, supremacy.

preeminência *f* pre-eminence, superiority.

preeminente *adj* pre-eminent, superior.

preencher *vt (completar)* to fill in/out, complete, **preencha o formulário** fill in the form; ~ **o tempo** spend the time; **2** *(vaga)* fill; **3** *(satisfazer)* to fulfil, meet.

pré-estreia *f* preview.

pré-fabricado,-a *adj* prefabricated.

prefácio *m* preface.

prefeito *(BR) m* mayor.

prefeitura *(BR) f* town hall.

preferência *f* preference; **de** ~ preferably.

preferir *vt* to prefer.

preferível *adj* preferable.

prefixo *m (LING)* prefix.

prega *f (vestuário)* pleat, fold.

pregação *f* sermon.

pregadeira *f (alfinete de peito)* brooch; **2** ~ **de alfinetes** *f* pin cushion

pregador *m* preacher; ♦ *adj* preaching.

pregão *m* proclamation, patter; **2** (street) cry; **pregões** *mpl* marriage banns.

pregar¹ [pré-] *vt/vi* to preach; to proclaim.

pregar² [pre-] *vt* to nail, hammer in; **2** to pin, fasten; ~ **uma partida** *(BR:* **peça)** to play a trick; **3** ~ **os**

olhos em to fix one's eyes on; ~ **um susto a** to give a fright to; ~ **uma peta** tell a lie/fib; **não** ~ **olho** not to sleep a wink.

prego *m* nail; **2** *(pop)* pawnbroker; **pôr algo no** ~ to pawn sth; **3** *(CULIN) (coll)* Portuguese hot steak sandwich; IDIOM **nadar como um** ~ sink like a stone; **não meter** ~ **nem estopa** do nothing about (it); *(BR)* **dar o** ~ to collapse.

pregoeiro *m* town crier; **2** auctioneer.

preguear *vt* to pleat, fold.

preguiça *f* laziness; sloth.

preguiçoso,-a *adj* lazy.

preia-mar *(pl:* **preia-mares)** *f* high tide, high water.

preito *m* homage, tribute; **render** ~ **a** to pay homage to.

prejudicar *vt (negócio, colheita, reputação, saúde)* to damage, hurt, impair; **2** *(transtornar)* cause inconvenience, detract from; ♦ ~**-se** *vr* to suffer loss(es), damage.

prejudicial *adj inv* harmful, detrimental; **este tempo frio é** ~ **à saúde** this cold weather is harmful to one's health.

prejuízo *m (dano)* damage; **a geada causou** ~ **às colheitas** the frost damaged the crops; **2** *(financeiro)* loss; **3** *(JUR)* prejudice; **4 em** ~ **de** in detriment to.

prelação *f* preference, prelation.

prelada *f* abbess.

prelado *m* prelate.

prele(c)ção *f* public lecture, talk.

preliminar *f* preliminary; ♦ *adj* preliminary.

prélio *m* battle; **2** *(DESP)* competition.

prelo *(TIPO)* press; **livro no** ~ book in print, being printed.

prelúdio *m* prelude, beginning; **2** *(MÚS)* overture.

prematuro,-a *adj* premature.

premeditação *f* premeditation, forethought.

premeditado,-a *adj* premeditated.

premeditar *vt* to premeditate; scheme beforehand.

premente *adj inv* pressing, urgent.

premiado,-a *adj* prize-winning.

premiar *vt* to award a prize to; to reward.

prémio *m* prize; premium.

premir *vt (carregar campainha, tecla, gatilho)* press; click; **2** *(comprimir – dedos)* to squeeze; **prima a campainha** press the bell.

premissa *f (FIL)* premise.

premonição *f* premonition, pressentiment; **2** aviso por instincto.

premonitório *adj* forewarning, premonitory.

prenda *f* present, gift; **2** *(fig) (dote)* skill, gift; **3** *(BR) (em jogo)* forfeit; **prendado,-a** *adj* skilled.

prendedor *m* fastener; ~ **de roupa** clothes peg; ~ **de papéis** paper clip.

prender *vt (amarrar)* to fasten, hitch, tie, fix; **ela não prendeu o cortinado bem** she did't fix the curtain properly; **2** *(capturar)* to arrest, capture, seize; **3** *(reter)* confine, lock in; **prendemos o cão na garagem** we locked the dog up in the garage; **4** hinder, impede; **5** *(atrair)* attract, captivate; **6** *(vincular)* hold, bind; ♦ *vi* hold; ~ **a atenção** hold one's attention; ♦ ~**-se** *vr* to get caught; **2** stick;

3 to hold back; **4** be related to; **isto prende-se a outro assunto** this relates to another subject; **5** (*afeiçoar-se*) **prendi-me ao gato** I got attached to the cat; **os olhos prenderam-se** the eyes locked.

prenha *adj f* grávida.

prenhe *adj inv* **mente ~ de projectos** a mind full of ideas; **2** (*fig*) (*embebido*) impregnated.

prenome *m* forename, (*BR*) surname.

prensa *f* (*aparelho de compressão*) **~ de vinho** wine press; **2** (*TIPO*) **printing press**; **~ hidráulica** hydraulic press; **~ rotativa** rotative press; **~ de encadernador** screw press.

prensar *vt* to press (*uvas, azeitonas*); **2** to compress.

prenunciar *vt* to predict, foretell, forewarn.

prenúncio *m* sign, harbinger, omen, forewarning.

pré-nupcial *m* pre-nuptial.

preocupação *f* worry, concern.

preocupante *adj inv* worrying, disturbing.

preocupar *vt* to worry; ♦ **~-se** *vr* **~ com** to worry about (sth, s.o.), be concerned about.

preparação *f* preparation; preparations.

preparado,-a *adj* prepared; **2** (*pronto*) ready; **3** (*arranjado*) groomed.

preparar-se *vr* **~ para** to prepare to/for.

preparativos *mpl* preparations, arrangements.

preparatório,-a *adj* (*preliminar*) preparatory.

preparo *m* preparation; **2** (*da papelada*) drawing up (of the papers).

preponderância *f* preponderance, predominance.

preponderante *adj inv* important, predominant; **2** considerable.

preposição *f* proposal; **2** (*LÍNG*) preposition.

prepotência *f* abuse of power; **2** being overbearing; **3** oppression, tyranny.

prepotente *adj inv* predominant; **sectores ~s** predominant sectors; **2** authoritarian, despotic.

prepúcio (*ANAT*) prepuce.

prerrogativa *f* prerogative, privilege.

presa *f* (*acto de apresar*) seizure; **2** (*na guerra*) spoils, pl; **3** (*preia*) prey; **4** (*dente canino*) canine, fang, tusk; **5** (*garra de ave*) talon; **6** (*açude*) pool; **7** (*BR*) vítima.

presbita *adj inv* long-sighted.

presbiteriano,-a *adj inv* (*REL*) Presbyterian.

presbitério *m* presbytery.

presbitia *f*, **presbitismo** *m* long-sightedness.

presciência *f* foreknowledge, foresight.

presciente *adj* far-sighted, prescient.

prescindir *vi*: **~ de algo** to do without sth; **2** (*abstrair*) to disregard sth.

prescindível *adj* dispensable.

prescrever *vt* to prescribe; ♦ *vi* (*data, documento*) to expire; to fall into disuse; **2** (*JUR*) to lapse.

prescrição *f* order, rule; **2** (*MED*) prescription; **3** (*JUR*) lapse.

presença *f* (*ger*) presence; **ter boa ~** have good appearance; **2** figura; **livro de ~s** register; ♦ *adv* **à ~** here; **à ~ de** before; **em ~ de** in presence of, faced with; **comunicação em ~** face to face communication.

presencial *adj inv* (*depoimento, etc.*) witnessed.

presenciar *vt* to witness, be present at.

presente *m* (*tempo*) **o ~** the present; **2** (*pessoa que comparece*) present; **3** (*fig*) (*prenda*) present, gift.

presentear *vt* give presents to, to present with.

presentemente *adv* presently.

presépio *m* Nativity scene, crib.

preservação *f* preservation.

preservar *vt* to preserve, protect.

preservativo *m* preservative; sheath, condom.

presidência *f* presidency; chairmanship; **assumir a ~** to take the chair.

presidente *m* president; chairman; **2** Lord Mayor.

presidiário *m* convict, prisoner.

presídio *m* military prison; fortress.

presidir *vt* to preside over; **2 ~ à** (*obra*) supervise.

presilha *f* strap with buttonhole; **2** loops; **pôr o cortinado nas ~s** put the curtain through the loops; **3** (*fivela*) buckle.

preso,-a *m,f* prisoner; ♦ *adj* (*na prisão*) imprisoned; **2** detained, under arrest; **3** (*atado, fixado*) tied, held, fixed; **~ por um fio** held/tied/hanging by a thread; **4** (*fig*) (*no tráfico*) stuck; **5** (*fig*) (*ligado*) **estar ~ a detalhes** to be bogged down in detail; **6** (*fig*) **língua ~a** tongue tied; **com a voz ~** a catch in one's voice; **7** (*fig*) (*casado*) spoken for; IDIOM **estar ~ a sete chaves** to be under lock and key; **ser ~ por ter cão e ~ por não o ter** can't win either way.

pressa *f* hurry, speed; **2** (*afã*) rush; **não tem ~** there is no rush; ♦ **à ~** *adv* quickly; **ele respondeu à ~** he replied hastily; **a toda a ~** at full speed; **sem ~** unhurriedly; **estou com ~** I am in a hurry.

pressagiar *vt* to foretell, presage.

presságio *m* omen, sign.

pressão *f* pressure; **~ sanguínea** blood pressure.

pressentimento *m* premonition, presentiment.

pressentir *vt* to foresee; **2** to sense, have a premonition of; **3** to suspect.

pressionar *vt* (*apertar, comprimir*) to press; **2** (*coagir*) **~ alguém a fazer** to pressurize sb to do, put pressure on.

pressupor *vt*, to presume, assume; **2** presuppose; **3** imply.

pressuposto *m* belief, assumption; **2** (*JUR*) pre-supposition ♦ *adj* expected; **2** presupposed; **3** implied; ♦ *pp of* **pressupor.**

pressurizado,-a *adj* pressurized, under pressure.

pressuroso,-a *adj* hurried, in a hurry; keen, eager.

prestação *f* (*ger*) instalment; **a prestações** on hire purchase; **2 ~ de serviços** (*trabalho*) services rendered; **3** (*FUT*) (*desempenho*) performance.

prestamista *m,f* moneylender.

prestar *vt* to give, render; **2** to provide; **3** be of use, good for; **isto não presta nada** this is of no use; **4 ~ atenção** pay attention; **5** (*JUR*) **~ juramento** take an oath; **6** (*MIL*) (*continência*) to salute; ♦ **~-se** *vr* **~ a** to be suitable for; **2** to offer, make o.s. available; **ela prestou-se a fazer a limpeza** she offered to do the cleaning.

prestativo,-a *adj* (*attitude*) obliging.

prestável *adj* helpful.

prestes *adj inv* **~ a** ready to, about to; **estou ~ a sair** I am ready to go/about to go out.

presteza *f* promptness, agility.

prestidigitação *f* sleight of hand, conjuring, magic tricks.

prestidigitador *m* conjurer, magician.

prestígio *m* prestige, reputation.

prestigioso,-a *adj* prestigious, eminent.

préstimo *m* use, usefulness; **sem** ~ useless, worthless; ~**s** *mpl* favours, services.

presumido,-a *adj* vain, self-important.

presumir *vt* to presume, suppose; **2** to assume.

presunção *f* presumption; conceit, self-importance.

presunçoso,-a *adj* vain, self-important.

pretendente *m,f* claimant; candidate, applicant; suitor.

pretender *vt* to want to; **2** to intend; **3** to hope to get.

pretensão *f* claim; pretention; **2** *(intenção)* aim, aspirations; **pretensões** *fpl* pretentiousness.

pretensioso,-a *adj* pretentious.

preterir *vt* to ignore, disregard.

pretérito *m* past, bygone; ♦ *m (gram)* preterite.

pretérito,-a *adj* past, last.

pretexto *m* pretext, excuse; **sob o** ~ **de** under the pretext of.

pretidão *f* blackness, darkness.

preto,-a *m (raça negra) (pej)* black; **2** *(cor)* black; ~ **de azeviche** jet black; **estar de** ~ *(luto)* be in mourning; ♦ *adj* black; **2** *(fig)* dark; sombre; **3** **quadro-**~ blackboard; **4** *(fig) (sujo)* black; **tens a cara** ~**a** your face is black; **pôr o preto no branco** to put down in writing; **as coisas estão** ~**as** things are (looking) bad.

pretor *m* praetor.

prevalecente *adj* prevailing.

prevalecer *vi* to prevail, predominate; ~ **sobre** to outweigh; ♦ ~**-se** *vr* to take advantage **(de** of).

prevalência *f* predominance.

prevaricador,-ora *m,f* transgressor.

prevaricar *vi* to fail in one's duty; to misbehave.

prevenção *f* prevention; warning; caution; ~ **rodoviária** road safety; **a** ~ **é melhor do que a cura** forewarned is forearmed.

prevenido,-a *adj* cautious, wary; forewarned, prepared.

prevenir *vt* to prevent; to warn; to anticipate; to prepare; ♦ ~**-se** *vr* to take precautions; **2** to equip o.s.

preventivo,-a *adj* preventive.

prever *vt* to foresee, anticipate; **2** *(profetizar)* predict.

previamente *adj* previously.

previdência *f* foresight; precaution; ~ **social** social welfare/security; **Caixa de P**~ **de saúde** health fund.

previdente *adj inv (que prevê)* provident; **2** *(cauteloso)* cautious.

prévio,-a *adj* previous, prior; preliminary.

previsão *f* foresight; forecast; ~ **meteorológica** weather forecast.

previsível *adj* foreseeable.

previsto,-a *adj* foreseen.

prezado,-a *adj* prized; esteemed; respected; well-known **2** *(em cartas)* **P**~ **Senhor,** Dear Sir.

prezar *vt* to cherish; **2** to respect; ♦ ~**-se** *vr* have self-respect; **2** pride o.s.; **prezo-me de ser honesta** I pride myself of being honest.

primado *m* primacy; **2** *(fig)* superiority; **3** *(fig)* pre-eminence.

primar *vi* to excel, stand out.

primário,-a *adj* primary, elementar; **2** *(tinta de base)* primer; **3** *(ECON)* **sector** ~ agricultural sector.

primate *m (ZOOL)* primate.

Primavera/primavera *f* spring.

primavera *f (BOT)* primrose; *(fig)* youth.

primaveril *adj* vernal, spring; youthful.

primaz *m (REL)* primate; ♦ *adj inv (principal)* prime, principal.

primazia *f* period as Primate; **2** superiority, primacy; **3** preference.

primeira *f (Vd: primeiro)*; **à** ~ at first; **2 de** ~ *(qualidade)* best; **produto de** ~ first-class product; *(carne)* **de** ~ prime.

primeira-dama *f* first lady.

primeira-mão *f (DESP)* first round; **2 em** ~ new, **carro em** ~ new car, in first-hand.

primeiro,-a *num* first; **2** *m,f (o melhor)* the first one, the best, top of; ♦ *adj* first, foremost; prime; ~**s socorros** first-aid.

primeiro,-a-ministro,-a *m,f* prime-minister.

primeiro-de-abril *m* first of April; **2** *(pop)* April's fool.

primeiro-sargento *m (MIL)* serjeant-major.

primitivo,-a *adj* primitive; original.

primo,-a *m,f* cousin; ~ **direito,** first cousin; ~ **co-irmão** *(BR)* first cousin; ~**-s afastados** distant cousins; ♦ *adj* prime.

primogénito,-a *adj* first-born.

primor *m* excellence, perfection; **a mesa é um** ~ the table is perfect; **2** *(beleza)* beauty; **o bebé é um** ~ the baby is a beauty, adorable; ♦ *adv (esmero)* **com** ~ perfectly, thoroughly.

primordial *(pl: -ais) adj inv* primordial, primitive; **2** fundamental, important; **3** *(razão, questão)* main, principal.

primórdio *m* exordium; **nos** ~**s** *mpl (princípio)* origin(s), beginnings.

primoroso,-a *adj* excellent, exquisite.

princesa *f* princess.

principado *m* principality.

principal *m* head, chief, principal; **2 o** ~ the main thing; ♦ principal, main.

príncipe *m* prince.

principiante *m,f* beginner; ♦ *adj* inceptive, inexperienced.

principiar *vt* to begin.

princípio *m* beginning, start; **no** ~ in the beginning; **2** origin; **3** *(norma)* principle, rule; **4** assume; **parti do** ~ **de que** I assumed that; ♦ ~**s** *mpl* rudiments; **2** *(morais)* principles; **em** ~ *adv* on principle.

prior *m (REL)* parish priest; prior.

priorado *f (REL)* priorate.

prioridade *f* priority; **ter** ~ **sobre (alguém)** to have priority over sb.

prioritário,-a *adj (assunto, etc)* of priority.

priorizar *vt* prioritize.

prisão *f* imprisonment; **2** *(cadeia)* prison, jail; **3** *(acção)* arrest; **ordem de** ~ warrant for arrest; **sob**

~ under arrest; ~ **domiciliária** house arrest; ~ **perpétua** life imprisonment; ~ **preventiva** preventive custody; ~ **de ventre** constipation.

prisional *adj inv (edifício, guarda, etc.)* prison.

prisioneiro,-a *m,f* prisoner, captive.

prisma *m (GEOM, MIN)* prism; **2** *(fig) (perspectiva)* angle, perspective, point of view; **sob esse** ~ from that perspective.

privação *f (falta de)* deprivation, loss; ~ **de audição** loss of hearing; **2 sintomas de** ~ **de tabaco** tobacco withdrawal symptoms; **3** ~ **de direitos** denial of rights.

privacidade *f* privacy.

privações *fpl (penúria)* hardship *sg*.

privado,-a *adj* private; **2** deprived.

privar *vt* to deprive; ♦ *vi*: **privar com** to be on intimate terms with; ♦ **~-se** *vr*: **privar-se de** to dispense with; to refrain from, to go without.

privativo,-a *adj* private.

privatizar *vt* to privatize.

privilegiado,-a *adj* privileged; **2** distinguished; **3** excepcional.

privilegiar *vt* to favour *(UK)*; to favor *(US)*.

privilégio *m* privilege.

pro = *para o*.

pró *m* pro; **os** ~**s e os contras** the pros and cons; **nem** ~ **nem contra** neither for nor against; ♦ *adj* for/in favour of.

proa *f (NÁUT)* prow; **2** *(frente)* front; **ir à** ~ to go in front; **3** *(fig) (presunção)* conceit, pride.

probabilidade *f* probability, likelihood; **segundo todas as** ~**s** in all probability; **2** *(fig) (COM)* prospects; off-chance.

probidade *f* honesty, uprightness.

problema *m* problem.

problemática *f (muitas questões)* theme; **2** *(conteúdo dessas)* problem.

problemático,-a *adj* problematic(al); **2** tricky; **3** uncertain.

probo,-a *adj (pessoa)* honest, upright.

procedência *f (origem)* source, origin; **2** *(lugar donde se provém)* place of departure; **3** *(correio)* **remeter à** ~ return to sender.

procedente *adj inv (vindo de)* coming from; **2** *(assunto)* arising from; derived from.

proceder *vt (vir)* ~ **de** originate, come from; **2** *(comportar-se)* behave; **3** *(levar a efeito)* carry on, proceed; **4** *(JUR)* ~ **a** take legal action; ~ **ao tribunal** to take (sb) to court; ~ **contra (alguém)** to sue sb.

procedimento *m* conduct, behaviour; **2** procedure, method; **3** *(JUR)* proceedings, *pl*.

procela *f* storm, tempest; **2** *(fig)* troubles, problems.

proceloso,-a *adj* stormy.

processador *m (COMP)* processor; ~ **de texto** word processor.

processamento *m* processing.

processar *vt (JUR)* to sue, prosecute; **2** to check, verify; **3** *(COMP)* to process.

processo *m (método)* process; **2** *(regra)* procedure; **3** *(JUR)* lawsuit, legal proceedings; **4** *(documentação)* evidence.

procissão *f* procession.

proclamação *f* proclamation.

proclamar *vt* to proclaim.

procrastinar *vt* to put off, procrastinate.

procriação *f* procreation.

procriar *vt (gerar)* to engender; ♦ *vi* to multiply.

procura *f* search; **à** ~ **de** in search of; **2** *(ECON)* demand; **a oferta e a** ~ demand and supply; **(algo) com** ~ selling well.

procuração *f (JUR)* power of attorney; **2** *(documento)* proxy.

procurador,-ora *(JUR)* attorney; ~ **Geral da República** Attorney General.

procurar *vt* to look for, seek; **procuro o meu livro** I am looking for my book; **2** *(tentar obter)* **ele procura casa** he is looking for a house; **3** try to, attempt; **procuro dizer** I am trying to say; ♦ *vi* ~ **por** *(perguntar)* to ask about, enquire about; IDIOM ~ **agulha em palheiro** to look for a needle in a haystack.

prodigalidade *f* prodigality, abundance, generosity.

prodigalizar *vt (dissipar)* squander, **2** *(dar em excesso)* overdo.

prodígio *m (pessoa)* prodigy; **2** *(maravilha)* feat.

prodigioso,-a *adj* prodigious; **2** wonderful.

pródigo,-a *adj* prodigal; **2** *(perdulário)* wasteful; **3** *(generoso)* lavis; **filho** ~ the prodigal son.

produção *f* production; **2** *(volume)* output; ~ **em massa/em série** mass production;

produtividade *f* productivity.

produtivo,-a *adj (fértil)* productive; **2** *(lucrativo)* profitable.

produto *m* product; **2** production; **3** *(AGR)* produce; ~**s alimentícios** foodstuffs; **4** *(fig)* consequência; **5** proceeds *pl*; ~ **interno bruto** (PIB) gross domestic product (GDP).

produtor,-ora *m,f* producer; *f (empresa)* production company; ♦ *adj* producing.

produzir *vt* to produce, make; **o brinquedo produziu muito barulho** the toy made much noise; **2** *(causar)* bring about, provoke; **você deve produzir provas** you must present proof; ♦ **~-se** to happen; *(BR)* to dress up.

proeminência *f* prominence; **2** protuberance.

proeminente *adj inv* proeminent.

proeza *f* exploit, feat.

profanação *f* sacrilege, profanation; **2** *(fam) (irreverência)* lack of respect.

profanar *vt (santidade, templo)* to profane, desecrate, violate; **2** *(arte)* debase, treat with irreverence.

profano,-a *m,f (leigo)* lay person; **2** layman; ♦ *adj* profane.

profecia *f* prophecy.

proferir *vt (discurso)* give; **2** *(dizer)* utter, say; **3** *(JUR) (decretar)* pronounce.

professar *vt (propagar)* to profess, affirm one's beliefs; **2** *(exercer profissão)* to practise; ♦ *vi (REL)* to take holy orders.

professo,-a *adj (REL)* professed, avowed; **2** *(fig) (perito)* skilled, expert.

professor,-ora *m,f* teacher; ~ **universitário** university lecturer, ~ **catedrático/titular** university professor.

professorado *m (magistério)* professorship; **2** *(conjunto de professors)* teaching profession.

profeta,-tisa *m,f* prophet.

profético,-a *adj* prophetic(al).

profetizar *vt/vi* to foretell, predict.

proficiência *f* proficiency, competence.

proficiente *m,f* proficient, competent.

profícuo,-a *adj* useful, advantageous.

profissão *f* profession, job; ~ **liberal** freelance profession.

profissional *adj inv* professional.

profissionalismo *m* professionalism.

pró-forma *m* formality, pro forma.

profundamente *adv* deeply.

profundas *fpl* depths, hell.

profundidade, profundeza *f* depth; **tem 2 metros de ~** it is two metres deep; **nas profundezas** in the depths.

profundo,-a *adj* deep; **2** *(fig) (intenso)* profound.

profusão *f* profusion.

profuso,-a *adj* profuse.

progénie *(BR: -ê-) f (descendência)* progeny, offspring; **2** *(ascendência)* lineage, ancestry.

progenitor,-ora *m,f* progenitor; **progenitores** *mpl* parents; **2** *(antepassado)* ancestors.

progénito,-a *m,f* descendant.

prognóstico *m (predição)* prognostic; **2** *(MED)* prognosis.

programa *m* programme *(UK)*, program *(US)*; **2** *(COMP)* program.

programação *f* program(m)ing.

programador,-ora *m,f* program(me) planner;*(COMP)* programmer; ~ **visual** graphic designer.

programar *vt* to program(me); **2** *(planear, (BR) planejar)* to plan, schedule.

progredir *vi (aumentar)* make progress, do well; **2** *(MED) (agravar-se)* get worse.

progressão *f* progression; advance.

progressista *adj inv* progressive.

progressivo,-a *adj* progressive.

progresso *m* progress, advance; **fazer ~s em** to make progress in (sth).

proibição *f* prohibition.

proibido,-a *adj* forbidden, banned; **é ~ fumar** smoking is not allowed.

proibir *vt* to forbid, prohibit; **2** *(interdizer)* to ban.

proibitiro,-a *adj* prohibitive, interdictory.

proje(c)ção *f* projection, planning; **tempo de ~** running time; **2** protuberance, bulge, overhang; **3** *(fig)* prominence.

proje(c)tar *vt (ger)* to project; **2** *(planear)* to plan, devise; **3** *(arremessar)* to cast, hurl; **4** *(ARQ)* to design; ♦ **~-se** *(sombra, filme)* be cast, be projected; **2** *(atirar-se)* throw o.s.; **3** *(tornar-se famoso)* achieve fame, project o.s.

projé(c)til *(pl: -teis) m* projectile.

proje(c)to *m (ger)* project, plan; **2** *(empreendimento)* projecto; **3** *(ARQ)* plan, blueprint; **4** *(esboço do texto)* draft; ~ **de lei** bill.

proje(c)tor *m* projector; searchlight.

prol *m* advantage, profit, benefit; **em ~ de** *adv* on behalf of, for the benefit of.

prolapso *m (MED)* prolapse.

prole *f (filhos)* offspring, children; **2** *(geração)* progeny, descendants.

proletariado *m* proletariat, working class.

proletário,-a *m,f* proletarian.

proliferação *f* proliferation.

proliferar *vi* to proliferate, reproduce.

prolífico,-a *adj* prolific, fertile, productive.

prolixo *adj (verboso)* lengthy, long-winded, tedious, prolix.

prólogo *m* prologue.

prolongação *f* extension.

prolongado,-a *adj* prolonged.

prolongamento *m* extension.

prolongar *vt* to extend, lengthen; to prolong; ♦ **~-se** *vr* to extend.

promessa *f* promise.

prometer *(ger)* to promise; ~ **não fazer isso** to promise not to do that; **2** *(ter potencial)* be promising.

prometido *m (a coisa)* promised; **o ~ é devido** a promise is binding; **2** *m,f* fiancé; ♦ **prometido,-a** *adj* promised.

promiscuidade *f* promiscuity; **2** *(desordem)* confusion, mess.

promíscuo,-a *adj* promiscuous; **2** disorderly.

promissão *f* promise; **terra da ~** Promised Land.

promissor,-ora *adj* promising.

promissória *f* promissory note.

promoção *f* promotion; **2** *(COM)* publicity (campaign).

promocional *adj* promotional.

promontório *m* headland, promontory.

promotor,-ora *m,f* promoter; supporter; patron; ~ **de justiça** prosecutor; ♦ *adj* promoting.

promovedor,-ora *m,f* promoter.

promover *vt (ger)* to promote; **2** *(encontros)* organize; **3** *(JUR)* move *(processo)*; ♦ **~-se** *vr* to promote o.s.

promulgação *f* promulgation; ~ **um decreto** promulgation of a decree.

promulgar *vt* to promulgate; to publish.

prono *adj* prone, bending forward; *(fig)* prone to, inclined to.

pronome *m (gram)* pronoun; ~ **pessoal** personal pronoun.

prontidão *f* readiness; promptness, speed.

prontificar-se *vr* ~ **para fazer** to volunteer for.

pronto,-a *adj* ready, prepared; **2** quick; **3** willing; **estou ~ para tudo** I am prepared for anything; ♦ **pronto** *adv* promptly, readily; **a ~** *(imediato)* prompt, ready; **a ~ pagamento** (COM), ~ **pagamento** prompt payment ♦ *exc*; ~ **right!** that's it!; **vim para a Madeira e ~ fiquei** I came to Madeira and that was that, I stayed.

pronto-a-vestir *m (roupa)* ready-made, off the peg *(pop)*.

pronto-socorro *m* first aid; **2** *(hospital)* emergencies, first-aid post; **3** *(AUTO) (reboque)* breakdown truck, service.

prontuário *m* handbook; record.

pronúncia *f* pronunciation; **2** *(JUR)* indictment.
pronunciado,-a *adj (JUR)* indicted; **2** prominent.
pronunciamento *m* proclamation, pronouncement.
pronunciar *vt* to pronounce; to make, deliver; *(JUR)* to indict; ~ **mal** to mispronounce; ♦ ~**-se** *vr* to express one's opinion.
propagação *f* propagation.
propaganda *f (POL)*. propaganda; *(COM)* advertising.
propagandista *m,f* propagandist.
propagar *vt* to propagate, spread.
propalar *vt* to divulge.
propender *vi* ~ **para/a** to lean towards.
propensão *f* inclination, tendency.
propenso,-a *adj* inclined; **ser** ~ **a** to be inclined to, have a tendency to.
propiciar *vt/vi (favorecer)* to favour *(UK);* favor *(US);* to provide, allow sb sth.
propício,-a *adj (favorável)* ~ **a algo** favo(u)rable, propitious for sth; **2** *(oportuno)* opportune, propitious.
propina *f (dinheiro para inscrição)* fee; **as** ~ **escolares** school fees; *(BR) (gratificação)* tip; **2** bribe.
propor *vt* to propose; **2** *(JUR) (acção)* to move; ♦ *vr* ~**-se a fazer** to aim to do; **2** to offer to do.
proporção *f* proportion; **à** ~ **de** at the rate of; **à** ~ **que,** as; **2** *(MAT)* proportion.
proporcionado,-a *adj* proportionate, harmonious.
proporcional *adj inv* proportional.
proporcionar *vt* to provide, give; **2** to adjust, adapt sth to sth; ♦ ~**-se** *vr* to present itself *(the moment, etc).*
proporções *fpl (tamanho)* dimensions.
proposição *f (proposta)* proposition, proposal.
propositado,-a *adj* intentional.
proposital *(pl: -ais) adj inv* intentional.
propósito *m* purpose, aim; ♦ *adv* **a** ~ by the way; suitably; **a** ~ **de** with regard to; **de** ~ on purpose; **fora de** ~ irrelevant.
proposta *f* proposal, proposition; **fazer uma** ~ to make a proposal; **2** *(oferecimento)* offer.
proposto,-a *(pp de* **propor)** *adj* proposed.
propriamente *adv* exactly, really, aptly; **ele não é** ~ **meu marido** he is not really my husband; **2** ~ **dito** strictly speaking, per se; **3** *(adequadamente)* suitably, properly; **ela chegou** ~ **vestida** she arrived suitably/properly dressed.
propriedade *f* property; ~ **alodial** freehold; ~ **imobiliária** real estate; **2** ~ **horizontal** property shared by two or more rightful owners; **3** *(característica)* attribute, quality; **4** ownership; **5** **com** ~ correctly, with propriety; **portar-se com** ~ to behave correctly; ~**s químicas** chemical properties.
proprietário,-a *m* owner, proprietor; **2** *(de imóvel de alugar)* landlord; ♦ *f* owner; **2** landlady.
próprio,-a *adj* own, of one's own; **com os meus** ~**s olhos** with my own eyes; **por si** ~ of one's own accord; **2** proper; **não é** ~ it's not proper; **3** self; **eu** ~ I myself; **ele** ~ he himself; **eu** ~ **disse** I myself said; **4 o** ~ **homem** the very man; ♦ *adv* **por mão** ~**a** by hand; **no momento** ~ at the right

moment; **é o Senhor Luz** ~**?** **sou o** ~ is that Mr Luz? it is I.
propulsão *f* propulsion; ~ **a ja(c)to** jet propulsion.
propulsar *vt* encourage.
propulsor,-ora *m* propeller ♦ *adj* propelling.
prorrogação *f* extension; **2** *(COM)* deferment; **3** *(JUR)* adjournment; **4** *(FUT)* extra time **prorrogar** *vt* to defer, adjourn.
prorromper *vi* ~ **(de)** to burst (out of); ~ **em** to burst into.
prosa *f (LITER)* prose; **2** *(fig, fam) (manha)* lip, gab; **3** *(conversa)* chat, chit-chat; **4** braggard; ♦ *adj* boastful, puffed up.
prosaico,-a *adj* prosaic; **2** *(fig) (vulgar)* commonplace, dull.
prosápia *f* lineage; **2** *(fig)* vanity, boasting.
proscénio *m* proscenium.
proscrever *vt* to prohibit; **2** *(desterrar, afastar)* to exile, proscribe, banish; **3** *(abolir)* to do away with.
proscrição *f* proscription; **2** prohibition, ban; exile.
proscrito,-a *m* exile; ♦ *adj* banished, exiled; **2** forbidden.
prosélito,-a *m,f* proselyte, convert; **2** *(fig) (partidário)* advocate, follower.
prosódia *f (LÍNG)* prosody.
prosopopéia *f (LITER)* prosopopoeia, personification; **2** *(fig, pej) (discurso)* diatribe.
prospe(c)ção *f (GEOM)* prospecting; ~ **de petróleo** oil exploration; **2** *(ECON)* survey; ~ **de mercado** market survey.
prospe(c)tivo,-a *adj* prospective.
prospe(c)to *m* prospects, outlook; **2** *(folheto)* leaflet; *(de cursos)* prospectus.
prospe(c)tor,-ora *(GEOL) (que faz sondagem)* prospector; **2** *(pessoa que faz pesquisa)* researcher.
prosperar *vi (enriquecer)* to prosper; **2** *(progredir)* thrive.
prosperidade *f* prosperity; **2** success.
próspero,-a *adj* prosperous; **2** thriving; successful.
prossecução *f* continuation.
prosseguidor,-ora *m,f* pursuer, follower.
prosseguimento *m* continuation.
prosseguir *vt* to continue, carry on with; to follow; ♦ *vi* to continue, go on.
prostate *f (ANAT)* prostate gland.
prostático,-a *adj* prostate.
prosternar *(Vd:* **prostrar).**
prostíbulo *m* brothel.
prostituição *f* prostitution.
prostituir *vt* to prostitute; **2** debase; ♦ ~**-se** *vr* to debase/lower o.s.; become a prostitute.
prostituta *f* prostitute.
prostituto *m* male prostitute.
prostração *f* prostration; **2** *(fig) (abatimento)* exhaustion; dejection.
prostrado,-a *adj* prostrate.
prostrar *vt* to knock down, throw down; **2** to tire out; ♦ ~**-se** *vr (em reverência)* to prostrate o.s.; **2** humble o.s.
protagonista *m,f* protagonist.
prote(c)ção *f* protection; support, backing.

prote(c)cionismo *m* protectionism.

prote(c)torado *m* protectorate.

prote(c)tor,-ora *m,f* protector; ♦ *adj* protective, protecting.

proteger *vt* to protect.

protegido,-a *m,f* ward, protégé(e); ♦ *adj* protected; **2** *(coberto)* shielded, protected.

proteína *f (QUÍM)* protein.

protelação *f* delay.

protelar *vt* to postpone, put off.

prótese *f (LÍNG, (MED)* prothesis.

protestante *adj inv* Protestant.

protestantismo *m* Protestantism.

protestar *vt* to protest; **2** to declare, affirm; **3** *(zangar-se)* to kick up a row; ♦ *vi* ~ **contra** protest (against); ~ **por** claim.

protesto *m* protest; **2** objection.

protetor *(Vd:* **protector***)*.

protocolar *adj inv (questão, caracter)* of protocol, formal; **sector** ~ registry; ♦ *vt* to register.

protocolo *m (ger)* protocole; etiquette, formality; **2** *(acordo)* agreement.

protótipo *m* prototype; **2** *(exemplo)* epitome, **ser o** ~ **de** *(algo)* to be the prototype of (sth).

protuberância *f (ANAT)* protuberance, bulge; **2** saliência, projection; **3** *(ASTRON)* prominence.

protuberante *adj inv* protuberant, bulging; **2** projecting.

prova *f* proof; **2** *(EDUC)* mock examination, test; **3** *(DESP)* contest; **4** *(comida, bebida)* taste, **uma** ~ **de vinhos** wine tasting; **5** *(vestuário)* fitting **o vestido precisa de duas** ~**s** the dress needs two fittings; **6** *(FOTO)* proof; **7** *(tribulações)* trial **as** ~**s da vida** life's trials; **8** *(TIPO)* proofs; **9** *(JUR)* evidence, proof; ~ **indiciária** circumstancial evidence; ♦ *prep* **à** ~ **de água/de bala/fogo** waterproof/ bullet-proof/fireproof.

provação *f* proof; **2** *(dificuldade)* hardship.

provador *m (em loja)* fitting room; ~**es** *(pl)* changing rooms; **2** *(de vinho)* taster; ♦ *adj* tasting.

provar *vt (ger)* to prove; **2** *(comida)* to taste, try; **3** *(experimentar roupa, calçado)* to try on; **4** *(testar)* to test.

provável *adj* probable, likely.

provavelmente *adv* probably.

provedor,-ora *m,f* provider; **2** *(COM)* supplier, purveyor; **3** *(chefe de instituição caritativa)* director, Head; **4** **P~** *(de justiça)* *(independente e non-jurídico)* *(UK)* Omsbudsman.

proveito *m* advantage, profit, **tirar** ~ **de** take advantage of, profit by; **2** *(utilidade)* benefit, gain, use; ♦ *exc (antes da refeição)* **bom** ~**!** enjoy it!

proveitoso,-a *adj* useful, advantageous, worthwhile.

proveniência *f* source, origin.

proveniente *adj* ~ **de** coming from, originating from.

provento *m* profit; **2 proventos** *mpl* proceeds.

prover *vt (vaga, posto)* fill; **2** *(promover)* to promote sb; **3** *(JUR)* defer; **4** supply, provide; ♦ *vi (atender a)* provide.

proverbial *adj inv* proverb.

provérbio *m* proverb.

proveta *f* test tube; **bebé de** ~ test-tube baby.

providência *(REL)* God; **2** providence **P~ Divina** Divine Providence; **3** *fpl (acção, medida)* measures; **tomar** ~**s** take measures/steps; to be in charge of (a situation); ♦ *adj m (do Estado)* Welfare State.

providencial *adj inv* provential; **2** cautious, wise; **3** *(fig)* opportune, lucky.

providenciar *vt* to provide; **2 tomar** ~**s contra para algo** take precautions/measures against/for sth; **3** to see to sth, to arrange; ♦ *vi* to make arrangements, make provision; ~ **para que** to see to it that.

providente *adj* provident; prudent, careful.

provido,-a *adj* provided with; **2** *(dotado)* gifted with; ~ **de** supplied with; **despensa bem** ~**a** well stocked larder **3** *(pessoa)* cautious, prudent, far-seeing.

provimento *m* stocking up; **2 dar** ~ *(JUR)* to grant a petition.

província *f* province.

provincianismo *m* provincialism.

provinciano,-a *adj* provincial; **2** *(pej)* country bumpkin.

provindo,-a *(pp de: provir) adj*; ~ **de** coming from.

provir *vt* to come/originate from; derive from.

provisão *f* provision, supply; **provisões** *fpl* provisions; supplies.

provisório,-a *adj* provisional, temporary.

provocação *f* provocation; **2** *(sensual)* attraction.

provocador,-ora *m,f* provoker, instigator; **2** cause; ♦ *adj* provocative.

provocante *adj inv (sensual)* provocative; **2** *(questão)* provocative, provoking.

provocar *vt* to provoke; **2** to cause; **3** to tempt, attract; **4** to instigate.

provocativo,-a *adj* provocative.

proxeneta *m* pimp; *f (mulher)* madame.

proximidade *f* proximity, nearness; **2** *(semelhança)* similarity; **3** *(afinidade)* closeness; **4** ~**s** *fpl arredores)* neighbourhood, vicinity, *sg*, surroundings.

próximo,-a *m* fellow man, neighbour; **amar o** ~ love thy neighbour; ♦ *adj* near, close (de to); **fica** ~ **daqui** it is near here; **2** *(seguinte)* next, **no** ~ **mês** next month; **futuro** ~ near future; **até a** ~ see you soon; **fica para a** ~ **vez** leave it for another time.

'**Próximo'** = **next**, always refers to future dates, events, etc., and not to the past, as in English, e.g. 'the next day I went'.

prudência *f (REL)* prudence; **2** wisdom, common sense; **3** *(cuidado)* care; **com** ~ carefully, with caution.

prudente *adj inv (sensato)* sensible, prudent, wise; **2** *(cuidadoso)* careful, cautious.

prumo *m (CONSTR) (fio de* ~*)* plumb-line; **2** *(NÁUT)* lead, prow, sounding-lead; ♦ *adv* **a** ~ vertically, overhead, up and down.

prurido *m (MED)* pruritis; *(comichão)* itch; **2** *(fig) (desejo)* yearning, urge.

pseudónimo *(BR:* -**dô**-*) m* pseudonym.

psicanálise *f* psychoanalysis.

psicanalítico,-a *adj* psychoanalytic(al).

psicodélico,-a *adj (estado, música, drogas, visões, cores, luzes)* psychedelic.

psicofármaco *m (MED)* psycopharmacologic; ♦ *adj (medicamento)* psychotropic, psychopharmacologic.

psicolinguista *m,f* psycholinguist.

psicolinguística *f* psycholinguistics.

psicologia *f* psychology.

psicológico,-a *adj* psychological.

psicólogo,-a *m,f* psychologist.

psicopata *m,f* psychopath.

psicose *f* psychosis.

psicotécnico *m* response test; ♦ **psicotécnico,-a** *adj* response.

psicoterapeuta *m,f* psychotherapist.

psiquiatra *m,f* psychiatrist.

psiquiatria *f* psychiatry.

psiquiátrico,-a *adj* psychiatric.

psíquico,-a *adj* psychic.

psoríase *(MED) f* psoriasis.

PSP *(abr de* **Polícia de Segurança Pública***)* Police Force, Metropolitan Police.

PT *(abr de* **Portugal TELECOM***)* Portuguese Telecommunications.

pua *f (tipo de broca para abrir furos na madeira)* bit, prong, auger; **2** *(ponta aguçada)* sharp point; **3** *(haste da espora)* spur; **4** *(BR) (col) (bebedeira)* drunkenness.

puã *f (ZOOL)* kind of small crab.

puberdade *f* puberty.

púbere *m,f* puberty; ♦ *adj inv* pubescent.

pubescent *adj inv* pubescent.

púbico,-a *adj (ANAT)* pubic.

púbis *m,f (ANAT)* pubis.

publicação *f* publication.

publicar *vt* to publish; **2** to broadcast; **3** to announce *(decisão, regras)*; **4** to make well known.

publicidade *f* publicity; *(COM)* advertising; *(TV)* commercials.

publicitário,-a *adj* publicity; *(COM)* advertising.

público,-a *m* **o ~** the public; **2** *(plateia)* audience; ♦ *adj* public; **biblioteca ~a** public library; ♦ *adv* **em ~** in public.

púcara *f (recipiente de barro para cozinhar)* pot, **frango na ~** chicken in the pot; **2** *(para beber vinho)* mug.

púcaro *m (recipiente com asa, para beber café, leite)* mug; *(quantidade nele)* mugfull.

pude + *endings (p perf. de* **poder***)* I could; I was able to.

pudendo,-a, *adj* **pudente** *adj inv* bashful, shy, prudish, modest; ashamed.

pudera! *exc* no wonder!, small wonder!

pudibundo,-a *adj (recatado)* bashful, shy, private; **2** modest; **3** *(pej)* prudish.

pudico,-a *adj (pessoa com pudor)* shy, bashful, modest.

pudim *m (CULIN)* pudding.

pudor *m* modesty, shyness; **ter ~** I am shy/ashamed, embarrassed; **2** *(decoro)* decency; *(JUR)* **atentado ao ~** indecent assault.

puerícia *f (idade)* youth, childhood; **2** *(conjunto de indivíduos nesse período)* children, young people.

puericultura *f* child care.

pueril *adj* puerile, silly, inane.

puerilidade *f* childishness, foolishness.

pufe *m (uma grande almofada como assento)* pouffe.

pugilato *m (DESP)* boxing, fighting.

pugilismo *m* boxing.

pugilista *m* boxer.

pugna *f* fight, struggle.

pugnar *vi* to fight; **2 ~ pelo,-a** to fight for, to stand up for.

pugnaz *adj* pugnacious.

puído,-a *adj (desgastado)* frayed, worn.

puir *vt* to fray, wear out.

pujança *f* strength, vigour, great energy; **2** exuberance, vigorous growth; **estar na ~ da vida** to be in the prime of life.

pujante *adj inv (corpo)* vigorous, robust; **2** *(obra, exército)* powerful, great; **3** *(floresta)* exuberant, luxuriant, dense.

pula-pula *(pl:* **pula-pulas***) m (BR) (para crianças pular) (cama elástica)* bouncy castle; **2** *(ave)* golden-crowned warbler.

pular *vt* to jump, leap; **~ de alegria** jump for joy; **2** *(dar pulos)* jump about, hop, skip; **~ à corda** to skip rope; **3** *(fig)* **~ de galho** switch sides; **4** *(fig) (omitir linha, trecho)* to skip; **você saltou duas linhas** you jumped two lines; **5** to grow.

pulga *f* flee; IDIOM **estar em ~s** to be anxious; **estar com a ~ atrás da orelha** to be suspicious.

pulgão *m* greenfly; any plant louse, aphid.

pulguento,-a *adj (casa, animal, roupa)* flee-ridden.

pulha *m (fam)* rogue, creep, cad; ♦ *adj inv (pessoa)* lying, rotten; **2** lazy; **3** common, vile, despicable.

pulmão *m (ANAT)* lung; **2** *(zona verde)* lung, **Monsanto é o ~ de Lisboa**; Monsanto is Lisbon's lung; ♦ *adv* **gritar a plenos pulmões** shout at the top of one's voice.

pulmonar *adj inv* pulmonary, lung.

pulo *m* jump, leap; **2 dar um ~ até** to pay a flying visit to, pop (over); **3** *(palpitar)* to skip a beat; **coração aos ~s** (one's) heart thumping; **4 de um ~** in one bound; **5 num ~** in a tick, in a flash; **6 aos ~s** by leaps and bounds.

pulôver *m (roupa)* pullover.

púlpito *m* pulpit.

pulsação *f* pulsation, beating; **2** *(MED)* pulse; **pulsar** *vi* to pulsate, throb, beat.

pulseira *f (jóia)* bracelet; *(para o tornozelo)* anklet; **2** *(preso)* **~s electrónicas**, electronic wristbands; *(BR)* handcuffs.

pulso *m (ANAT)* wrist; **2** *(MED)* pulse; **tomar o ~ de alguém** to take sb's pulse; **3** *(fig) (vigour)* autoridade, energia; **homem de ~** energetic man, with authority; **com ~** forceful; **4 ~ de ferro** iron will; ♦ *adv* **a ~** by one's own steam/will-power; **à força de ~** with physical force, *(trabalho)* with hard work; **a todo o ~** at all speed.

pulular *vi* to swarm, spring up.

pulverizador *m* spray, spray gun.

pulverizar *vt* to pulverize; **2** *(AGR)* to spray; **3** *(pedra, vidro)* grind, shatter.

pum!, pumba! *exc (queda, pancada)* bang!, boom!; **2** *(acção rápida)* **whoosh!** ... **e pumba!** ... and that was that.

puma *f (ZOOL)* puma, wildcat.

punção *m* punch; **gravar a ~** to engrave with a punch; **2** *(instrumento)* stylus, awl; **3** *(TIPO)* stamp; ♦ *f (MED)* puncture.

pundonor *m* dignity, self-respect.

pungente *adj inv (cheiro, gosto)* sharp, pungent; **2** *(fig) (de dor/mágoa; grito, olhar)* painful, moving; sharp, piercing.

punha (+ *endings) (imperf de pôr)* **eu ~ a mesa** I was setting/laying the table.

punhada *f (pancada com o punho)* a blow with fist.

punhado; *m* **um ~ de** a handful of.

punhal *m* dagger; **2** *(fig) (o que magoa)* knife.

punhalada *f* a stab (from dagger/knife); **espetou-lhe (o punhal) no peito** he stabbed him in the chest; **2** *(fig) (ofensa moral)* moral blow; **3** *(fig) (injúria maliciosa)* stab in the back.

punho *m* fist; **de ~ cerrado/fechado** with a clenched fist; **2** cuff; **camisa sem ~s** shirt without cuffs; **botões de ~** cuff links; **3** *(cabo de alguns utensílios)* handle; **4** *(NÁUT)* clew; **5~ de remo** grip/grasp of an oar; ♦ **em punho** in hand; **com a espada em ~** the drawn sword; IDIOM **de seu próprio ~** in his/her/your own handwriting; **verdades como ~s** home truths; **ter ~s de renda,** have refined/gracious manners, to be particular about manners.

punição *f* punishment; **2** *(fig) (penoso)* the cross, suffering.

punir *vt* to punish; chastise; inflict penalty/punishment.

punitivo,-a *adj* punitive; **medidas ~as** punitive measures.

punível *adj inv* punishable.

pupila *(ANAT) (do olho)* pupil.

pupilo,-a *m,f* pupil, student; **2** *(a cargo do tutor)* ward.

puré *(BR: purê) m* purée; **~ de batatas** mashed potatoes.

pureza *f* purity; **2** clarity

purga *f (MED) (purgativo)* purge; **2** *(eliminação)* cleansing, purification.

purgante *adj inv* purgative.

purgar *vt* to purge, cleanse, purify.

purgativo,-a *adj* purgative.

purgatório *m (REL)* Purgatory; **2** *(fig) (vida difícil, sofrimento)* purgatory.

purificação *f* purification, cleansing.

purificador *m* purifying.

purificar *vt* to purify; **2** to refine.

purista *m,f* purist.

puritanismo *m* puritanism.

puritano,-a *m,f* puritan; ♦ *adj* puritanical; puritan.

puro,-a *adj* pure; **2** clear; **3** clean; **4** genuine; **5** complete, absolute; **6** chaste.

púrpura *f* purple.

purpúreo,-a *adj* crimson, purple.

purulento,-a *adj* festering, suppurating.

pus *m (MED)* pus; ♦ *(pret = pôr- 1st person sg);* **eu ~ a chave na mesa** I put (have put) the key on (top of) the table.

pusilânime *adj* fainthearted; shy; cowardly.

puta *f (vulg) (mulher má)* bitch, cow; **2** whore; **3 a ~ de vida;** bloody life; **aquele filho da ~** that so and so, bastard.

putativo,-a *adj* putative.

puto *m (pop) (miúdo)* kid; ♦ *adj (esperto)* brilhante, hell of a kid.

putrefa(c)ção *f* rotting, putrefaction.

putrefazer *vt* putrify; ♦ **~-se** *vr* to rot.

pútrido,-a *adj* putrid, rotten.

puxa *(BR) exc* gosh!, goodness!

puxadela *f* a little pull, jerk, tug.

puxado,-a *adj(corda)* taut, stretched; **2** *(fam) (preço)* expensive; **3** well-dressed; **4** *(BR) (exame)* difficult.

puxador *m* handle, knob; *(BR) (fumador de maconha)* person addicted to marijuana.

puxão *m* tug, jerk, pull; **2** *(col)* **um ~ de mulher** quite a woman, a lot of woman.

puxar *vt* to pull; **puxa a porta** pull the door; **~ as orelhas a alguém** to box sb's ears; **2** *(tirar)* take out; **3** *(arrancar)* to pull out, jerk; **4** *(arrastar)* tug; **5** pull up; **puxa a saia para cima** pull up the skirt; **6** *(tosse)* to provoke; **7 ~ assunto** bring up the subject; **8 ~ conversa** to strike up a conversation; **9 ~ briga** to pick a fight; **10 ~ a alguém** to take after sb; **11 ~ para algo,** to incline towards sth; **12 ~ espada** to draw the sword; IDIOM **~ a brasa para a sua sardinha** to draw water to one's mill; **palavra puxa palavra** one word leads to another; **~ pelos cordelinhos** to pull strings; **~ pelos cordões à bolsa** to pay; **~ pela cabeça/cachimónia** think hard; *(BR)* **puxar-saco** flatter, butter sb up.

puxa-saco *(BR) m* flatterer, creep, crawler, toady.

puxo *m (cabelo)* hair bun.

q

Q, q *m (letra)* Q, q; **2** *(abr de* **quintal***)* one hundred kilos.

Qatar *npr* Qatar; **o ~** Qatar.

quacre *m (REL)* Quaker.

quadra *f* square enclosure, quadrangle; **2** *(ténis)* tennis court; **3** *(LITER)* quatrain, four-line stanza; **4** *(fig)* period, season, age; **a ~ natalícia** Christmas season; **a melhor ~ da minha vida** the best period of my life; **5** *(em jogos)* four; **6** flag of a flagship; **7** *(muralha)* stretch of wall; **8** *(BR) (4 ruas em quadrado)* block; **9** lineal measure of 132 metres.

quadradinhos *mpl (banda desenhada)* cartoon squares; **história aos** *(BR:* **em***)* **quadradinhos** *f* comic strip.

quadrado,-a *m (polígono, objecto)* square; **2** *(MAT, MIL, GEOG)* square; ♦ *adj* square, squared, quadrate; **2** *(vela)* square; **3** checked; **tecido aos ~s** checked cloth; **4** *(fig, pej) (bronco)* thick; **5** *(fig) (pessoa baixa e atarrecada)* squatty; IDIOM **ver o sol aos ~s** be in prison.

quadragésimo,-a *m,f* fortieth; *f* space of forty days.

quadrangular *adj inv (GEOM) (aspecto, figura)* quadrangular.

quadrângulo *m (GEOM)* quadrangle.

quadrante *m (GEOM, ASTRON, FÍS)* quadrant.

quadrar *vt* to square; ♦ *vi* **~ a** to suit; fit in, agree with.

quadrícula *f* small square.

quadriculado,-a *adj (paper)* squared; **2** *(shirt, fabric)* checked.

quadril *m (ANAT)* hip, haunch; *(BR)* rump.

quadrilátero *m* quadrilateral; four-sided figure.

quadrilha *f (de ladrões)* gang; **2** *(dança)* quadrille.

quadrimestral *adj inv (período)* four-monthly.

quadringentésimo,-a *m,f* the four-hundredth; ♦ *adj* four-hundreth.

quadro *m (pintura)* picture, painting; **2** **~-preto/branco** black/white board; **~ de avisos** notice board, bulletin; **3** *(tabela, gráfico)* chart, table; **4** *(TEC) (painel)* panel; **5** *(ADMIN)* staff; **6** *(fig) (TV, CIN)* scene; **7** *(situação)* picture; **8** **~ de reserva** *(MIL)* reserve list.

quadrúpede *m (ZOOL)* quadruped.

quádruplo,-a *adj* quadruple; foursome.

qual *(pl:* **quais***) adj pron interrog* which, what; **~ chapéu prefere?** which hat do you prefer?; **qual é o seu nome?** what is your name?; **qual deles deseja?** which one do you want?; ♦ *(exclamativas)* nonsense, nothing of the sort; **ele ganhou um** prémio? **qual coisa!** he, winning a prize? nonsense!; **qual nada!, qual o quê!** no such thing!; ♦ *pron rel* whom, that which; **os livros sobre os quais te falei** the books that I spoke to you about; **João tem quatro casas, uma das quais em Angola** John has 4 houses, one of which (is) in Angola; **2** *(especificando o sujeito)* **encontrei a Maria no armazém, a qual me disse** I met Maria in the store, who told me; ♦ *pron indef* each one; **cada qual tem o seu gosto** each (one) to his own taste; ♦ *conj* like, as; **seja ~ for** whatever it may be; **~ seja** such as; **tal ~** just like.

qualidade *f (ger)* quality; **azeite de ~** good quality olive-oil; **baixa ~** low grade, ilk; **2** *(representação)* capacity; **na minha ~ de testemunha** in my capacity as a witness.

qualificação *f* qualification.

qualificado,-a *adj* qualified; classified; graded; **~ como** regarded as; **non-~** unqualified.

qualificar *vt* to qualify; **2** **~ de/como** to classify as, regard as; ♦ **~-se** *vr* to qualify, become qualified.

qualificativo,-a *m* label; **2** *(LÍNG)* qualifier; ♦ *adj* qualifying.

qualitativo,-a *adj* qualitative.

qualquer *(pl:* **quaisquer***) adj* any; **~ pessoa** anybody **~ pessoa serve** anybody will do; **~ dia** one of these days; **2** *(em frases negativas)* **uma mulher sem qualquer talento** a woman without any skills; **3** *(pej) (pessoa, objecto vulgar)* any old (thing) any; **não é uma casa ~, é um palácio** it is not any house (just a house) it is a palace; ♦ *pron indef* any, anyone, all, every; anyone; **um lápis ~** any pencil (you like), any odd pencil; **ele vai a quaisquer países** he goes to all countries/every country; **4** *(pej) (pessoa comun)* someone or other; *(depois do sujeito)* **ele é uma pessoa ~** he is a nobody; **5** *(maneira)* **de ~ jeito/forma/maneira** in any way; **6** *(cada um)* any of; **~ dos dois** either; **~ de nós** one of us, any of us; **~ outro** any other; **~ dia** any day; **~ dia que lhe seja conveniente** whichever day is convenient to you; **7** *(ao dizer adeus)* **adeus e até ~ dia!** until we meet again!, be seeing you!

quando *adv* when; ♦ *conj* when; *(ao passo que)* while; if, even if; while; **de vez em ~ / de ~ em ~** every now and then; **~ menos** at least; **~ muito** at most; **mesmo ~** even when; **~ mais não seja,** if only, at least; **~ quer que** whenever.

quanta *mpl (FÍS)* quanta (*Vd:* **quantum***)*.

quantia *f* sum, amount.

quântico,-a *adj (relativo à teoria dos quanta)* quantum; **teoria ~a dos campos** quantum field theory.

quantidade *f* quantity, number; **2** amount; **grande ~ de arroz** a large amount of rice.

quantificador *m* quantifier.

quantificar *vt* quantify *(custos, diferenças)*.

quantitativo,-a *adj* quantitative.

quanto,-a *m* **o ~** how much; **nem sei o ~ ele me contou** I don't even know how much he told me; ♦ *adj (interrogativo)* how; **~ custa?** how much does (it) cost?; ♦ **quantos,-as** how many; ~ **as camas tem o quarto** how many beds has the room?; ♦ *adj indef* some, as many; **tantos alunos** ~**s os professores** as many students as teachers; ♦ *adv* ~ **tempo?** how long?; ♦ *pron rel (intensidade)* **tudo** ~ everything that, as much as; **fiz tudo** ~ **me disse** I did everything you told me (to do); **gosto de tudo** ~ **é lindo** I like all that is beautiful; ♦ *(exclamativo)* **quantas mães choraram!** how many mothers wept!; **um tanto ou** ~ somewhat, a little; **tantos** ~**s** as many as; ~ **antes** as soon as possible; ~ **mais cedo melhor** the sooner the better; ~ **mais come, mais ele engorda** the more he eats the fatter he gets; ~ **mais não seja** at least, if only; **não compro vestidos,** ~ **mais um carro** I don't buy dresses, let alone a car; ♦ *prep* ~ **a** with regard to, as to/for; ~ **a mim** as for me, as far as I am concerned; ♦ **quantas** *pron pl (fam)* **a** ~ **at** what stage.

quantum *msg* quantum.

quantum satis (q.s.) (o bastante) enough, as much as is sufficient.

quão *adv* how; ~ **belos estes versos são!** how beautiful these verses are!; ♦ *conj* **tão ...** ~ as, both ... and; **ela é tão linda** ~ **generosa** she is as beautiful as she is generous.

quarenta *num* forty; ♦ *adj inv (século, página, dia)* fourtieth.

quarentão,-ona *m,f* man in his/woman in her forties; ♦ *adj inv* fourty-year-old.

quarentena *f* quarantine.

Quaresma, quaresma *f* Lent.

quarta-de-final *(pl: quartas-de-final) f (DESP)* quarter final.

quarta-feira *(pl: quartas-feiras) f* Wednesday; **Q~ de Cinzas** Ash Wednesday.

quarteirão *m (de prédios)* block; **2** quarter (of a hundred); **um** ~ **de sardinhas** *(arc)* 25 sardines.

quartel *m (MIL)* barracks *sg*; quarter; ~ **general** *(pl: quartéis-generais)* headquarters; **2** quarter-century; **o último** ~ **do ano** the final quarter of the year; **3** *(NÁUT, HERALD)* quarter; *(NÁUT)* ~ **das escotilhas** hatches.

quarteto *m (MÚS)* quartet.

quartilho *m* pint.

quarto *num* fourth; **moramos no** ~ **andar** we live on the fourth floor; **D. João IV** King John the fourth; ♦ *m* quarter, ¼; **2** *(horas)* **são duas menos um** ~ it is a quarter to two; **3** *(parte de rés)* quarters; haunch; **4** *(divisão)* room; ~ **de banho** bathroom; ~ **de dormir** bedroom; ~ **de casal** double bedroom; ~ **de solteiro** single room; **5** *(MIL) (plantão)* watch; **6** *(ASTRON) (da lua)* ~ **crescente/minguante** first/last quarter; *(fig)* **passar um mau** ~ **de hora** to go through a bad time; ♦ **quarta** *f* quarter; **2** *(medida)* quart; **3** *(MÚS)* perfect fourth.

quartos-de-final *mpl (DESP)* quarter-finals.

quartzo *m* quartz.

quase *adv* almost, nearly; **a sopa está** ~ **a ferver** the soup is almost boiling; **eu** ~ **não falei com ele,** I

hardly spoke to him; **ela** ~ **perdeu o avião** she very nearly missed the plane; ~ **nada** almost nothing; ~ **nunca** hardly ever.

quaternário,-a *m: Q~ (GEOL) (período)* Quaternary; ♦ **quaternário, -a** *adj* quaternary.

quatorze *num (BR)* fourteen.

quatrilião *num* quadrillion.

quatro *num* four; ~**centos,-as** *num* four hundred.

que *adj inv (interrogativa)* what?, which?; ~ **camisa?** which shirt?; ~ **é que você tem?** what do you have? what is the matter with you?; ~ **é de** where? *(BR:* **cadê***) (col)* **que é da tua mãe** where is your mother?; **o** ~ **?** what?; **o** ~ **se passa?** what is going on?; ♦ *pron rel* who, which, that; whom, that; **foi ela** ~ **me avisou** it was she who warned me; **aqui está o livro** ~ **me pediste** here is the book (that) you asked me for; **o pincel com** ~ **pinto é reles** the brush with which I paint is rotten (poor quality); **o** ~ what, (the thing that); **o** ~ **ele quer é dinheiro** what he wants is money; ♦ *adv (exclamativa)* ~ **sorte!** what luck!; ~ **horror!** how awful!; ~ **pena!** what a shame, what a pity!; **2** *(enfático)* **há meses** ~ **não o vejo** I haven't seen him for months; **nisso é** ~ **não acredito** that is what I don't believe; ♦ *prep* have to; **tenho** ~ **fazer isto** I have to do this; **2** *(excepto)* all: **não quero mais** ~ **dormir** all I want is to sleep; **nada** ~ **fazer** nothing to do; ~ **nem** like; **ela parece** ~ **nem um anjo** she looks like an angel; ♦ *adv* **ao** ~ as far as; **ao** ~ **parece** as far as (I) can see; apparently; **2** ~ **tal?** how about it?; ♦ *conj* that; **de modo** ~ so that; **2 que, do que** than; **3** *(subst:* porque*)* and, **vai indo** ~ **eu já vou** you go and I'll follow soon; **4** *(usado no subjuntivo)* **espero** ~ **ele venha** I hope he comes; **eu quis** ~ **ele fosse** I wanted him to go; **ele** ~ **faça** he should do it.

quê *m* something; complication; **a questão tem os seus** ~**s** the question has its drawbacks; **2 um não sei** ~ something I can't define; vague feeling; **3** *(resposta cortês a obrigado)* **não tem/há de** ~ you are welcome; **sem** ~ **nem para** ~ just like that; without rhyme or reason; ♦ *(pron. inter.)* **para** ~**?** what for?; **com** ~ with what?; **o** ~ what?

quebra *f* break, rupture; **2** *(COM) (perda)* loss; **3** *(FIN)* drop, fall; **uma** ~ **no euro/nas vendas** a fall in the euro/a drop in the sales; **4** *(declive)* slope.

quebra-cabeças *m sg/pl (jogo)* puzzle, jigsaw; brainteaser; **2** *(dificuldade)* problem; **3** *(jogo de palavras)* crosswords.

quebrada *f (encosta)* slope, hillside; **2** *(caused by rains)* slide; **3** *(desabamento das terras)* landslide.

quebradiço,-a *adj* fragile, breakable.

quebrado,-a *adj (louça, etc)* broken; **2** *(fig) (cansado)* worn out; **3** *(fig) (sem dinheiro)* broke; **4** *(fig) (desanimado)* down-hearted; **5** *(BR) (falido)* bankrupt.

quebradura *f (fenda)* rupture; **2** crevice; **3** *(fam) (hernia)* hernia.

quebra-galho *(pl: quebra-galhos) m (BR)* makeshift, stopgap; contrivance; **2** *(fig) (pessoa)* Mr. Fixit.

quebra-gelo *msg (NAUT)* ice-breaker.

quebra-luz *m (abajur)* lampshade.

quebra-mar *m* breakwater, mole.

quebra-nozes *m* nutcrackers *pl.*

quebrantar *vt* to break; **2** to weaken, wear out; **3** *(demolir)* raze; **4** *(domar paixões)* quell; ♦ ~-**se** *vr* to grow weak.

quebranto *m* weakness; **2** *(cansaço)* lassitude; **3** *(desânimo)* depression; **4** *(pop) (mau olhado)* blight, evil eye.

quebrar *vt* to break; ~ **algo ao meio** to split sth in half; **2** *(enfraquecer)* to weaken; **3** break off; **ele quebrou com os amigos** he broke off with his friends; ♦ *vi (BR) (falir)* to go bankrupt; ♦ ~-**se** *vr (desfazer)* to break; shatter, get broken; **o copo quebrou-se** the glass got broken; IDIOM **parece que ele não quebra um prato** butter wouldn't melt in his mouth.

queca *f (vulg)* sexual act, shag.

queda *f* fall; drop; decline; downfall; inclination; ~-**d'água** *f* waterfall.

quedar *vi* to be still/quiet; ♦ ~-**se** *vr* stand, remain still; **quedei-me a contemplar o mar** I stood still gazing at the sea.

quedo,-a *adj* quiet, motionless; ~**e mudo** silent and still.

queijada *f* Portuguese little cheesecake, tart; ~**s de Sintra** little cheesecakes (a tradition from Sintra); **2** a lot of cheese.

queijadinha *(BR) f (doçaria)* coconut-ice.

queijaria *f* cheese making.

queijo *m* cheese; ~ **da Serra**, Serra cheese from Portugal; ~ **flamengo** Dutch cheese; *(BR)* ~-**prato** Edam cheese; ~ **ralado** grated cheese; IDIOM **ter o ~ e a faca na mão** to have the power to do sth, have the ball at one's feet; **eu sou pão, pão, ~, ~** *(ser franco)* I call a spade, a spade.

queima *f* burning; **2** cremation; **3** *(AGR)* nip caused by frost; **4** ~ **das fitas** *(universidade) ritual no fim do ano/do curso* the burning of the ribbons; **5** *(BR) (COM)* clearance, sale.

'**Queima das fitas**' refers to the traditional students' festivities, particularly at Coimbra University, which take place at the end of every academic year. During this event, the finalists burn their ribbons in public, to celebrate the end of their courses and the obtention of their degrees. The ribbons and sashes are of many colours to represent each College of the university.

queimado,-a *adj (comida, mão)* burnt, burning; **açúcar** ~ caramelized sugar; **2** ~ **do sol** *(bronzeado)* sunburnt, tanned; **3** *(flora)* scorched, burnt down; **4** *(fig) (alguém)* discredited.

queimadura *f* light/superficial burn.

queimar *vt (ger)* to burn; **2** *(plantas)* scorch; **o sol queimou a urze** the sun scorched the heather; **2** *(líquido fervente)* to scald; **3** *(pele)* to tan; **4** *(pôr fogo)* to set fire to; **5** *(murchar)* to wither, nip; **6** *(fig) destroy,* ruin; **7** *(fig) (fortuna, vida)* blow, waste; ♦ *vi* to burn; be burning hot; ♦ ~-**se** *vr* to burn o.s.; to burn down; *(BR)* to get angry.

queima-roupa, à ~ *adv* point-blank.

queira *(pres subj de* **querer**); **quer** ~ **quer não** ~ **tenho de ir** whether I like it or not I have to go.

queiró *f (BOT)* heather.

queirosiano,-a *adj* of/from Queirós; (*Eça de Queirós Portuguese writer of* the Realism (1845–1900).

queixa *f* complaint; **2** moan; **3** grievance; **4** *(JUR)* formal accusation; **ter razão de** ~ to have cause for complaint.

queixada *f (ANAT)* jawbone.

queixar-se *vr* complain (**de** about sth, sb); **2** *(lamentar-se)* to moan; **3** *(JUR)* make an accusation.

queixo *m* chin; jaw; IDIOM **de** ~ **caído** amazed, open-mouthed; **dar aos** ~**s** to eat; **levar nos** ~**s** to get a punch in the jaw.

queixoso,-a *m (JUR)* plaintiff; ♦ *adj* complaining, doleful; **2** *(ofendido)* aggrieved.

queixume *m* lament, wail; **2** groan.

quelha *f (viela)* alley; narrow lane.

quem *pron rel* who, whom, that; **foi ela** ~ **mo disse** it was she who told it to me; **2** *(in a question)* who? whom?; ~ **é?** who is it?; who is there?; ~ **vem lá?** *(MIL)* who goes there?; **3** *(posse)* **de** ~ whose, of which, of/about whom; **de** ~ **é esta mala** whose suitcase is it?; **a mulher, de** ~ **te falei** the woman I spoke to you about (of/about whom); **4** *pron indef* those who, whoever; **quem come muito, engorda** those who eat a lot get fat; **5** whomsoever, whoever; **dou este bolo a** ~ **quiser** I give this cake to whoever/whomsoever wants it; **seja** ~ **for** whoever he may be; ♦ *exc* ~ **me dera!** how I wish!; ~ **me dera ir a ...!** I wish I could go!/would that I could/if only I could go; ~ **tal diria!** who would have thought!; ~ **sabe!** who knows; IDIOM ~ **quer vai,** ~ **não quer, manda** if you want a good job done, do it yourself.

Quénia *npr* **o** ~ Kenya.

queniano,-a *adj* Kenyan.

quente *adj* hot; **2** *(caloroso)* ardent, sensual; **3** *(fig) (temperamento)* fiery; **4** ardent; **5** *(temperatura)* warm; IDIOM **ficar com a batata** ~ to be left holding the baby.

quentura *f* heat, warmth.

quepe, quepi *m (mil)* kepi.

queque *m (tipo de bolo)* muffin.

quer *conj* either, or; ~ **chova** ~ **faça sol** whether it rains or shines; ~ **queiras,** ~ **não** whether you like it or not; **2** both, both of; ~ **um** ~ **outro** both of them/either; **onde** ~ **que** wherever; **quem** ~ **que** whoever; **quem que seja, diz-lhe que não estou** whoever it is, say that I am not in.

querela *f* dispute; quarrel; **2** *(JUR)* accusation; **3** *(LITER)* plaint.

querelado *m (JUR)* defendant, accused.

querelante *m,f (JUR)* plaintiff.

querelar *vt (JUR)* to prosecute, sue; ♦ *vi:* ~ **contra/ de** to lodge a complaint against.

querença *f (amizade)* liking, affection; **2** wish, desire; **3** *(teimosia)* conviction.

querer *m* will, wanting; ~ **é poder** where there is a will, there's a way; ♦ *vt* to want, wish; **2** ~**a**

(alguém) to be fond of; **3** ~ **bem a** to love; **4** ~ **mal a** to hate; **5** ~ **dizer** to mean; **6 queria** wanted, would like; **eu queria um chá** I would like (to have) a tea; ♦ ~-**se** *(recíproco)* **querem-se muito** they love each other; ♦ *adv* **sem** ~ unintentionally; **por** ~ on purpose; **2 queira, queiram** *pres subj* (used when expressing wish, doubt, hope, etc, and in forms of courtesy); **queira dizer-me** would you kindly tell me; **queira sentar-se** please be seated; **Deus queira!** God willing!; **Deus queira que não chova** I hope it will not rain.

querido,-a *(pp de querer) m* darling; **bem-~** beloved; **2** *(fam)* cute; ♦ *adj* dear; loved.

quermesse *f (pavilhão de vendas; vendas de beneficiência)* bazaar.

querosene *m (QUÍM)* paraffin oil, kerosene.

querubim *m (anjo)* cherubim; **2** *(ART)* cherub; **3** *(fig) (criança adorável)* cherub.

quesito *m* query, question; **2** an issue for which a response/an opinion is required; **3** requisite.

questão *(pl: -ões) f (pergunta)* question; **responder à** ~ answer the question; **2** *(assunto, tema)* question, subject, matter; **uma** ~ **de dignidade** a matter/ question of dignity; **discutir uma** ~ to debate an issue; **fazer** ~ **de** to insist on, make a point of; **3** *(disputa)* **há umas questões na família** there are some disputes in the family; **4** *(JUR)* case; **5** *(coisa, algo, aprox.)* about; **isso aconteceu há** ~ **de dois meses** that happened about/some two months ago.

questionamento *m* questioning.

questionar *vi* to argue, wrangle; ♦ *vt* to question, call into question.

questionário *m* questionnaire.

questionável *(pl: -eis) adj inv* questionable.

questiúncula *f (discussão)* triviality, debate of minor importance.

questões *f (pl de questão)*.

quezilar *vt* to upset, annoy *(alguém)*; ♦ *vi* pick a quarrel with, tease.

quezilento,-a *adj (que provoca brigas)* quarrelsome, rowdy; **2** *(pessoa impaciente)* grumpy.

quezília *f (briga)* quarrel; **2** *(antipatia)*, strong dislike, aversion.

quiabo *m* ochra.

quiasmo *m (LITER)* chiasmus.

quiçá *exc (LITER)* who knows!; **2** perhaps, may be.

quíchua *(indígena do Brazil) adj* Quechuan.

quietinho,-a *adj (crianças)* nice and quiet, still as a mouse.

quieto,-a *adj* still; **estar** ~ to be/keep still; **2** calm, quiet.

quietude *f* calm, tranquillity.

quilate *m* carat; **2** *(fig)* excellence, calibre *(UK)*, calibre *(US)*.

quilha *f (NÁUT)* keel; ~ **corrediça** centreboard; **2** *(ZOOL)* carina.

quilo *m* kilo; **compro a** ~ I buy by the kilo; ~**grama** *m* kilogram(me); ~-**padrão** kilogram(me) prototype.

quilometragem *f* distance in kilometres, mileage.

quilómetro *(BR: -ô-) m* kilometre.

quilovate *m (BR)* kilowatt.

quilovátio *m (BR)* kilowatt; ~-**hora** *m (ELECT)* kilowatt-hour.

quimera *f* chimera.

quimérico,-a *adj* imaginary, fanciful.

químico,-a *m,f* chemist; ♦ *f* chemistry; ♦ *adj* chemical; **papel** ~ *m* carbon paper.

quimioterapia *f (MED)* chemotherapy.

quimono *m* kimono.

quina[1] *f (canto)* corner, edge; *(ângulo)* sharp edge; **2** *(esquina)*, corner of the street; **3** *(de cartas, dominó)* five; *(jogo do loto) (linha horizontal de cinco números)* row of five numbers, bingo; **4** *(escudo, brasão)* shield, **as ~s da bandeira portuguesa** the shields of the Portuguese flag; **5 de** ~ edgeways, edgewise *(US)*.

quina[2] *(QUÍM)* quinine; *(BOT) (casca de planta)* chinchona bark.

quinar *vi (jogo do loto)* win at lotto; ♦ *exc* ~! bingo!, jackpot!; ♦ *vt* **prepare medicinal drink with quinquina.**

quingentésimo,-a *adj* five-hundredth.

quinhão *m (parte)* share, portion.

quinhentista *adj inv (período, estilo, literatura)* (of the) sixteenth century.

quinhentos,-as *num* five hundred.

quinina *f (QUÍM)* quinine; sulphate.

quinquagenário,-a *m,f* quinquagenerian, in his/her fifties; ♦ *adj* fiftieth.

quinquenal *adj inv* quinquennial, a five-year period.

quinquénio,-a *(BR: -ê-)* quinquennium.

quinquilharias *fpl* odds and ends; knick-knacks; **2** *(cheap jewellery)* trinkets, baubles.

quinta *f* farm; rural estate/property; country house with land; manor house; **2** fifth; **3** *(MÚS)* fifth; **4** *(abr de* **quinta-feira)** **telefono-te na** ~ I shall ring you up on Thursday; IDIOM **estou nas minhas sete** ~ I am as pleased as Punch, I am in my seventh heaven.

quinta-essência *f* quintessence; epitome.

‛**Feira**‛ in terça-feira, quarta-feira, quinta-feira and sexta-feira, is often omitted in speech and informal writing.

quinta-feira *f* Thursday; **às** ~/**às quintas nunca estou em casa** I am never home on Thursdays.

Quinta-feira Santa *f* Maundy Thursday.

quintal *(pl: -ais) m (de casa)* backyard; kitchen-garden.

quintarola *f (pej)* small farm.

quinté *m (SRP)* an area for festivities.

quinteiro *m (feitor)* manager of a farm.

quinteto *m (MÚS)* quintet.

quintilha *f* a five-verse stanza.

quinto,-a *adj* fifth; **2** *(fracção)* one fifth, 1/5; *(papa, rei)* fifth; **D. Jorge V** King George V (the fifth); *(Vd:* **quinta)**.

quintuplicar *vt* multiply by five.

quíntuplo *m* quintuple, fivefold; ♦ **quíntuplo,-a** *adj* quintuple, fivefold.

quinze *num* fifteen; *(horas)* **são duas e** ~ a quarter past two; **2 passar** ~ **dias na praia** to spend two weeks on the beach.

quinzena *f* fortnight; two weeks.

quinzenal *adj* twice monthly, fortnightly.

quinzenalmente *adv* fortnightly.

quinzo *m (ANG)* mercado.

quiosque *m* kiosk, band stand; ~ **dos jornais** news stand; **2** food, drink stand.

quiproquó *m* quid pro quo, mistake, mix-up.

quiqueriqui *m (canto do frango)* cock-a-doodle-doo; **2** *(pessoa insignificante)* a nobody; *(coisa insignificante)* trifle.

quiromancia *f* palmistry.

quiromante *m,f* palmist, fortune teller.

quis *(pret de* **querer**).

quiser *(fut subj de* **querer**).

quisesse *(imp subj de* **querer**).

quisto *m (MED)* cyst.

quitação *f (dívida)* discharge; **2** *(pagamento total)* settlement; **3** *(recibo)* receipt.

quitanda *f* small grocer's shop/stall; **2** (BR) greengrocer.

quitandeiro,-a *m* grocer; (BR) greengrocer; *f* market seller, street seller of sweets.

quitar *vt (pagar)* to pay off, to settle; **2** *(desobrigar)* release sb from sth; **3** *(saldar dívida)* discharge;

♦ ~-**se** *vr (livrar-se de)* to get rid of; **2** *(desquitar-se)* to get divorced.

quite *adj (livre de algo)* free; **2** *(contas, dívidas)* squared up; **estamos** ~**s** we are even.

quitenho,-a *adj* from Quito.

quitina *(QUÍM)* chitin.

Quito *npr* Quito.

quitute *f (iguaria)* (BR) titbit *(UK)*, tidbit *(US)*; tasty dish.

quivi *m (BOT)* kiwi.

quixotesco *adj* quixotic, romantic.

quociente *m* quotient; ~ **de inteligência** (Q.I.) intelligence quotient (I.Q.)

quórum *m (assembleia)* quorum.

quota *f (quinhão)* quota; ♦ *(parte do capital)* share, portion; **2** fee, subscription.

quota-parte *f* share.

quotidiano *m* daily life; ♦ **quotidiano,-a** *adj* daily, everyday.

quotização *f (cotização)* distribution of quotas; establishment of fees, subscriptions.

quotizar *vt* to distribute shares.

q.v. *(abr de* **quod vide** (=**queira ver**)) see.

r

R, r *m (letra)* R, r.

R *(abr de* **Rua***)* street.

rã *f* frog.

rabada *f* fish tail; **2** *(trança)* pigtail, plait of hair; **3** *(pop)* rump; bum; **4** *(BR) (fig)* tail end.

rabanada *f (pancada com o rabo)* whack, blow with the tail; **2** *(CULIN)* French toast; **3** ~ **de vento** gust/blast (of wind).

rabanete *m (BOT)* radish.

rábano *m (BOT)* black radish; ~ **picante** horseradish.

rabeca *f (MÚS)* fiddle; **2** *(NÁUT)* small sail.

rabecão *m (MÚS)* fiddler; **2** *(BR) (carro funerário)* hearse.

rabejador *m (TAUROM)* bull catcher, person who grabs the bull's tail.

rabelo *m* Douro's traditional boat.

rabi *m (REL)* rabbi.

rabiça *(AGR)* plough-handle, plough tail.

rabicho *m (trança)* pigtail; **2** *(da sela)* crupper (of the harness).

rabino *m (REL)* rabbi.

rabino,-a *adj (criança)* naughty, mischievous.

rabiscar *vt* to scribble, scrawl; ♦ *vi (fazer rabiscos)* to doodle; to scribble.

rabisco *m* scribble, doodle; *pl* scribbles.

rabo *m (cauda)* tail; ~ **de cavalo** horsetail; **2** *(cabelo)* ponytail; **3** *(cabo)* handle; **4** ~ **de boi** *(CULIN)* ox-tail; **5** *(fam)* bottom, buttocks; IDIOM **passar fome de** ~ be as hungry as a wolf; **meter o** ~ **entre as pernas** to put one's tail between one's legs; **levar fogo no** ~ to run like blazes; **com o** ~ **do olho** out of the corner of one's eye; **aqui é que a porca torce o** ~ that's the snag; **de cabo a** ~ from head to tail, from end to end.

rabo-de-palha *m (fam)* blot, blemish on sb's reputation.

rabo-de-raposa *m (BOT)* foxtail grass.

rabuge, rabugem, rabugeira *f* ill temper, grouchiness, peevishness; **2** *(VET)* mange.

rabugento,-a *adj* grumpy, crabby; **2** peevish, sullen.

rabugice *f* churlishness, petulance; **2** fretfulness.

rabujar *vi* to grumble; **2** *(de criança)* whine.

rábula *f (TEAT)* small part; **2** *(cena)* sketch.

raça *f* race; **2** *(ZOOL)* breed, strain, stock; **cavalo de** ~ thoroughbred horse; **cão de** ~ pedigree dog; **3** *(étnia)* race; **4** *(boas qualidades)* character, breeding, refinement; **de boa** ~ highbred, well-bred; **5** *(fam)* **ter** ~ to have courage.

ração *f (porção de comida)* ration, portion, helping; **2** *(alimento para animais)* fodder, feed.

racha *f (em parede, rocha, terra)* split, crack, fissure, crevice; **2** *(em madeira)* splinter, chip, crack; **3** *(fam) (corte)* cut; **4** *(em vestuário)* slit; IDIOM **sair o pau à** ~ be a chip off the old block; like father, like son.

rachador *m* woodcutter.

rachadura *f* crack.

rachar *vt* to split, cleave; **2** *(lenha)* chop (wood); **3** divide lengthwise, slit; **4** *(fam)* crack (open); **ele rachou a cabeça dele** he cracked his skull; ♦ *vi* split, crack; IDIOM **um frio de** ~ bitterly cold; **ou vai ou racha** it's sink or swim.

racial *adj inv* racial.

rácio *m (estatística)* ratio.

raciocinar *vi* to reason.

raciocínio *m* reasoning.

racional *adj* rational.

racionalizar *vt* to rationalize.

racionamento *m* rationing.

racionar *vt* to ration out; to ration.

racismo *m* racialism, racism.

racista *adj inv* racist.

radar *m* radar.

radiação *f* radiation.

radiador *m* radiator; ~ **eléctrico** electric radiator.

radiante *adj inv* radiant; overjoyed.

radicado,-a *adj (algo)* deeply-rooted; **2** *(alguém)* settled (**em** in), based (**em** in).

radical *m* radical; **2** *(LÍNG)* root; ♦ *adj inv* radical; **2** *(MAT, QUÍM)* ~ **livre** free radical; **3** *(DESP)* extreme.

radicalismo *m* radicalism.

radicalizar *vt* to favour radicalism; ♦ ~**-se** *vr* to become radical, take radical attitudes.

radicar *vt* radicate; ♦ *vi* arise from; ♦ ~**-se** *vr* to take root; to settle (down); **ele radicou-se na França** he settled in France.

rádio *m (aparelho)* radio; **ligar o** ~ turn on the radio; **2** *(QUÍM)* radium; **3** *(ANAT)* radius.

radioa(c)tivo,-a *adj* radioactive.

radiodifusão *f* radio broadcast(ing).

radiodifusora *f* radio station.

radioemissora *f* radio broadcasting station.

radiografar *vt* to X-ray.

radiografia *f* X-ray.

radiograma *m* cablegram.

radiojornal *m* radio news.

radiologia *f* radiology.

radiologista *m,f* radiologist.

radiopatrulha *f (serviço)* radio patrol; **2** *(veículo)* patrol car.

radioso,-a *adj* radiant; **2** *(luminoso)* shining, brilliant, glowing; **3** *(fig) (alegre)* radiant, ecstatic, overjoyed.

radioterapia *f (MED)* radiotherapy.

rafeiro *m (cão)* mongrel.

ráfia *f* raffia.

raia *f (linha)* line, stripe; **2** *(limite)* boundary; frontier; **chegar às** ~**s** to reach the limit; **3** marker; ~ **de tiro** firing range; **4** *(peixe)* ray, skate; **5** *(pop)* blunder, silly mistake; **dar** ~ to make silly mistakes.

raiado,-a *adj (tecido, asa)* striped; **2** *(piscina)* divided in lanes; **3 céu** ~ streaky sky; **4** *(cano, arma)* rifling.

raiano,-a *m,f* person from a border place; ♦ *adj (terra, gente, etc)* being/living in a border area.

raiar *vi* to shine, to dawn; to appear; **o sol raiava** the sun was shining/breaking through; **2** border on; ♦ *vr* be streaked.

raínha *f* Queen; **2** *(jogo de cartas)* queen of clubs.

rainha-cláudia *(BOT)* greengage.

rainha-mãe *(pl: **rainhas-mães**) f* Queen Mother; ~ **viúva** Queen Dowager.

raio *m* ray; beam; **2** *(de roda)* spoke (of a wheel); **3** *(METEOR)* flash of lightning; **4** *(MIL)* range; **5** *(GEOM)* radius; **~s X (XIS)** X-rays; **6** *(fam)* blasted, bloody, damned; **o ~ da mulher que faltou outra vez!** the damned woman didn't turn up yet again; **que ~ de cantiga é essa?** what kind of bloody tale is that?; ♦ *(cal)* exc **raios o partam!** damn him!

raiva *f* *(MED, VET)* rabies *sg*; **2** *(fig) (ira)* rage; ~ **surda** blind rage; **3** *(fig) (ódio)* aversion, hatred; **4** *(dentinhos do bebé)* teething; ♦ **ter ~ a** to hate; **meter ~** to irritate; **tu metes-me ~** you infuriate me.

raivoso,-a *adj (alguém)* furious, raging; **2** *(cão)* rabid, mad.

raiz *f* *(ger)* root; *(MAT)* ~ **quadrada** square root; **2** *(origem)* source; **3 bens de ~** real estate; **4** *(fig)* root; IDIOM **farto,-a até à ~ dos cabelos** fed up to the back of one's teeth; **criar raízes** to put down roots; **cortar o mal pela ~** to root it out, to eradicate the problem, to nip in the bud *(problema)*.

rajá *m* rajah.

rajada *f* *(de vento)* gust; **2** *(de tiros)* volley, barrage of shots; **3 uma ~ de insultos** a barrage of insults.

ralado,-a *adj* **pão ~** breadcrumbs *pl*; **queijo ~** grated cheese; **2** *(fig)* worried.

ralador *m* grater.

ralar *vt* to grate; **2** to crumble; **3** *(fig) (irritar alguém)* to annoy; ~ **a paciência** try sb's patience; ♦ **~-se** *vr* be worried.

ralé *f* the common people, riff-raff.

ralear *vt/vi* to thin out, to make thin; **2** grow sparse.

ralhar *vi* to scold; ~ **com alguém** to tell sb off.

rali *m* rally.

ralo *m* grater; **2** *(de farinha)* sieve; **3** *(de regador)* rose; **4** *(para líquidos)* colander, strainer; **5** *(da banheira, pia)* drain; **6** *(da porta)* peephole; **7** *(ZOOL)* mole-cricket; ♦ **ralo,-a** *adj (cabelo)* thin; **2** *(vegetação)* sparse.

RAM *(abr de: **Random Access Memory**) f* RAM.

rama *f* branches *pl*, foliage; **2** *(TIPO)* printer's chase; **em ~** raw; **algodão em ~** raw cotton; **pela ~** superficially.

ramada *f* branches *pl*, foliage; **2** *(abrigo para o gado)* lean-to.

Ramadão *(BR: **Ramadã**) m (REL)* Ramadan, Ramadham.

ramagem *f* branches *pl*, foliage.

ramal *m* *(FERRO)* branch line; **2** *(estrada)* branch road; **3** *(de mina)* transverse gallery; **4** *(BR) (de telefone)* extension.

ramalhete *m* bouquet, posy.

ramalhudo,-a *adj (planta)* leafy; **2** *(bigode)* thick; **3** *(tecido)* flowery.

rambóia *f* *(pândega)* fast living, revel; IDIOM **andar na ~** paint the town red.

rameira *f* *(pej)* whore, prostitute; **2** *(BOT)* large pine branch.

ramela *(Vd: **remela**).*

ramerrão *m* *(rotina)* rotina; grind.

ramificar-se *vr* to branch out.

ramo *m* *(de flores)* bunch, bouquet; **2** *(COM)* branch; **3** *(área de actividade)* line; **Domingo de Ramos** Palm Sunday.

rampa *f* ramp; **2** slope; ~ **de lançamento** launching pad; ~ **de embarque** gangway; **3** *(TEAT)* stage.

rampante *adj inv (HERALD) (leão, touro)* rampant; **2** *(ARQ)* arch; **arco ~** rampant arch.

> '**Rampante**' is not 'rampant' in the sense of 'unbridled', which is **desenfreado**, or in the sense of 'luxuriant' which is **viçoso**.

rançar *vi* to go rancid.

rancheiro *m* *(que prepara o rancho)* cook; **2** *(fazendeiro)* farmer.

rancho *m* group; **2** *(MÚS)* band; **3** *(MIL)* mess; **4** *(BR)* hut; small farm.

ranço *m* *(sabor)* rancidity; **a manteiga sabe a ~** the butter tastes/is rancid; **2** *(cheiro)* rank smell.

rancor *m* bitterness; hatred.

rancoroso,-a *adj* bitter, resentful; **2** *(ódio)* hateful.

rançoso,-a *adj* rancid; musty.

ranger *vi* *(ruído de porta)* to creak; ♦ *vt*: ~ **os dentes** to grind one's teeth.

rangido *m* creak.

ranho *m* *(muco nasal)* mucus; **2** *(fam)* snot.

ranhoso,-a *f* *(ZOOL)* cuttle-fish; **2** *(mulher desmazelada)* shabby woman, down-at-heel; ♦ *adj (fam)* snotty; **2** *(nariz)* runny; **3** *(criança)* snivelling; **4** *(fig, pej) (reles)* common.

ranhura *f* *(entalhe)* groove, rabbet; **2** *(para moeda)* slot; **3** incision; **4** *(TIPO)* notch; ~ **de um disco** track of a record.

ranicultor,-ora *m,f* frog breeder.

ranúnculo *m* *(BOT)* buttercup.

rapace *adj* rapacious; plundering; ♦ *f* bird of prey.

rapacidade *f* rapacity, rapaciousness.

rapadeira *f* scraper, knife for scraping.

rapagão *m* *(col)* big lad.

rapagona *f* *(girl)* big lass.

rapapé *m* bowing and scraping; flattery.

rapar *vt* *(parede etc)* to scrape, rub out; **2** *(cabelo)* to shave off; **3** *(cenoura, etc)* grate; **4** *(fam)* to pinch, nick; IDIOM ~ **frio e fome** to go cold and hungry; ~ **frio** get bitterly cold.

rapariga *f* girl, moça, lass; **2** *(BR)* prostitute.

raparigaça *f* *(moça robusta)* strapping girl.

raparigada *f* group/bevy of girls.

rapaz *m* boy, young man, lad; **2** *(fam) (homem)* old friend/fellow/chap.

rapaziada *f* *(grupo de)* lads, gang of boys.

rapazote *m* lad; young man.

rapé *m* snuff.

rapel *m* (*DESP*) abseil (*UK*), rappel (*US*).

rapidez *f* speed, rapidity.

rápido,-a *m* (*comboio*) express; ♦ *adj* quick, fast; ♦ *adv* fast, quickly.

rapina *f* (*pilhagem*) robbery; **2 ave de ~** bird of prey.

raposa *f* (*ZOOL*) vixen, female fox; **2** *m,f* (*fig*) (*pessoa manhosa*) sly old fox/person; **3** (*falhar no exame*) be ploughed.

rapsódia *f* rhapsody.

raptar *vt* to kidnap; **2 ~ um avião** hijack; **~ um carro** carjack.

rapto *m* kidnapping.

raptor,-ora *m* kidnapper.

raqueta, raquete *f* (*de ténis, badminton*) racquet; **2** (*tennis de mesa*) bat.

raquítico,-a *m* (*MED*) person suffering from rickets; ♦ *adj* (*MED*) rachitic; **2** (*pop*) puny, feeble.

raquitismo *m* rickets *sg*.

raramente *adv* rarely, seldom.

rarear *vt/vi* to make/become scarce; **2** (*cabelos*) to thin; **3** (*população*) to thin out.

rarefeito,-a *adj* rarefied; **2** dispersed.

raridade *f* rarity.

raro,-a *adj* rare; extraordinary; thin; ♦ *adv* rarely, seldom.

rasante *adj* low-flying.

rasar *vt* (*medir*) measure (cereals); **2** (*nivelar*) to level, flatten; **3** (*roçar*) to skim; **4** (*vinho*) fill to the brim; ♦ *vr* fill up.

rasca *f* (*pesca*) trawl-net, dragnet; small fishing boat; **~ das lagostas** lobster basket; **2** (*pop*) share in the profits; ♦ *adj inv* (*pop*) cheap, tawdry; IDIOM **ver-se à ~** (*col*) to get into a jam, be in trouble; **ter ~ na assadura** share the spoils.

rascunhar *vt* to draft, make a rough copy of.

rascunho *m* rough copy, draft.

rasgado,-a *adj* (*roupa*) torn, ripped; **2** (*papel*) torn up; **3** (*panorama*) wide, sweeping; **4** (*olhos, boca*) wide; **5** (*fig*) (*elogio, gesto*) hearty, generous; **elogios ~** generous praises; **6** (*fig*) (*sorriso*) wide, open, frank.

rasgão *m* tear, rip.

rasgar *vt* to tear (up), rip; **2** (*furar*) make an opening; **3** (*cavar*) dig; **4** (*ferir*) wound, cut open; **5 ~ os mares** to plough through the seas; **6** separate, cleave through (*nuvens, trevas*); **7** (*rua*) widen; ♦ **~-se** *vr* to tear.

rasgo *m* tear, rip; **2** (*arranhão*) graze, scratch; **3** (*CONSTR*) groove; **4** (*de imaginação*) flight; **5** (*fig*) (*ato nobre*) feat; (*ímpeto*) burst; **6** (*MEC*) **~ de chaveta** key way.

raso,-a *adj* (*sapato, terreno*) flat; **2** (*pouco fundo*) shallow; **3** (*liso*) even, level, full; **olhos ~s de lágrimas** eyes full of tears; **4** (*rente*) close-cropped (*cabelo, relva*); **5** (*MIL*) (*campo*) flatland; **6** (*prédios destruídos*) flattened; **soldado ~** private.

raspa *f* (*lasca*) wood shavings, chips *pl*; **2** (*de laranja, limão*) (grated) peel, zest; **3** (*de comida*) scrapings *pl*.

raspadeira *f* scraper; **2** (*CONSTR*) chisel.

raspadela *f* scrape.

raspadinha *f* (*jogo*) scratch card.

raspagem *f* scrape; **2** shaving; **3** (*MED*) curettage.

raspanete *m* (*fam*) scolding, telling off.

raspão *m* scratch, graze; **de ~** *adv* graze.

raspar *vt* (*alisar*) to scrape, scratch; **o carro raspou o muro** the car scraped the wall; **2** (*tirar a pele*) scrape, peel; **3** (*ralar*) grate; **4** (*ferir*) (*de raspão*) graze; **5** (*madeira, bigode*) shave (off); **6** (*tinta*) to rub out; **7 ~ uma palavra** to scratch, erase a word; ♦ **~-se** *vr* to bolt, sneak off, take to one's heels, scram.

rasteira *f* (*BOT*) low-growing creeper; **2** trip; **passar uma ~ a alguém** to trip sb up.

rasteiro,-a *adj* (*animal*) crawling, creeping; **2** (*planta*) creeping; **3 cão ~** short-legged dog; **4** (*voo*) low; **5** (*fig*) (*pessoa, modos*) common.

rastejante *adj inv* (*planta*) creeping; **2** (*animal*) crawling.

rastejar *vi* (*animal, planta*) to crawl, to creep; **2** (*pessoa*) crawl, (*fig*) grovel; **3** (*seguir o rasto*) trace, track.

rastejo *m* trace, track, tracing, tracking; **2** pursuit, search.

rastilho *m* (*de pólvora*) fuse; **2** (*pista*) trail of gunpowder.

rasto *m* (*pegada*) track; **2** (*vestígio, pista*) trail, trace; **3** (*de sapato*) footprint; **4 no ~ das caravelas** in the wake of the caravels; **andar de ~s** to crawl, go on all fours; **de ~s** crawling/grovelling; **estar de/a ~** (*fig*) to be ruined; **preço de ~s** very low price; **levar de ~s** to drag along; **pôr alguém de ~s** slander someone; **no ~** (**de** of) on the scent/trail.

rastreio *m* (*MED*) screening; **2** (*exame citológico*) (*rasto*) cancer smear; **3** (*TEC*) track, tracking.

rasura *f* erasure; crossing out; **sem ~** (*cheque, carta*) without erasure, clean; **2** (*de ervas medicinais*) scraping, grating.

rasurar *vt/vi* to erase, rub out; **2** grate.

ratar *vt* to gnaw like a rat; **2** (*fig*) (*col*) **~ na casaca de alguém** to run sb down, to backbite.

ratazana *f*, big rat; **2** *m,f* (*pessoa ridícula*) odd person, clown; **3** (*pessoa manhosa*) sly person; **4** (*BR*) (*larápio*) thief.

ratear *vt* to share out, distribute fairly.

rateio *m* sharing; distribution; allotment.

rateiro,-a *adj* (*cão, gato*) rat-catcher, ratter; ♦ *adj* rat-catching.

raticida *f* rat poison, raticide.

ratificação *f* ratification.

ratificar *vt* to confirm, ratify.

rato,-a *m,f* (*ZOOL*) mouse; **2 ~ de biblioteca** bookworm; **3** (*COMP*) mouse; ♦ *adj* (*fig*) crafty; IDIOM **calado como um ~** quiet as a mouse.

ratoeira *f* rat trap, mouse trap; **2** (*fig*) (*armadilha*) trap, snare.

ratoneiro *m* pilferer, petty thief.

ravina *f* ravine, gorge.

razão *f* reason; **2** (common) sense; **3** reasoning, argument; **ter/não ter ~** to be right/be wrong; **dar ~ a** to side with; **4** (*MAT*) ratio, quotient; **5** (*FIN*) account; ♦ *m (COM)* ledger; ♦ *adv* à ~ **de** at the rate of; **em ~ de** on account of.

razia *f (invasão)* plunder, raid, foray; **2** destruction; **3** *(mau resultado)* disaster.

razoar *vi* to reason.

razoável *adj* reasonable; **2** fair.

razoavelmente *adv* reasonably.

r/c *(Vd. rés do chão).*

RDP *(abr de* **Radiodifusão Portuguesa***)* Portuguese Broadcasting Service.

ré *f (JUR)* defendant, accused; **2** *(MÚS)* re, D; **3** *(NÁUT)* stern; **à ~!** astern!; **dar marcha à ~** *(BR) (AUTO)* reverse, back up.

reabastecer *vt (avião, navio)* to refuel; **2** *(despensa)* to restock.

reabastecimento *m* refuelling; restocking.

reabertura *f* reopening.

reabilitação *f* rehabilitation; reform; **2** *(de crédito)* recovery.

reabilitar *vt* rehabilitate; **2** *(JUR)* rehabilitate, reform; **2** restore the reputation of; ♦ ~-**se** *vr (regenerar-se)* to be rehabilitated.

reabrir *vt* to reopen.

rea(c)ção *f* reaction; **2** *(FÍS)* reaction; ~ **em cadeia** chain reaction **3** response.

rea(c)cionário,-a *adj* reactionary.

reacender *vt (fogo, luz)* relight; **2** *(paixão, ânimo)* to rekindle; **3** *(polémica)* to stir up.

rea(c)tivar to reactivate.

rea(c)tivo,-a *adj* reactive.

rea(c)tor *m* reactor; ♦ **rea(c)tor,-ora** *adj* reacting.

reagente *m (QUIM)* reagent; ♦ *adj inv* reactive, reacting; **papel ~** test paper.

reagir *vi* to react (to), respond; **2** ~ **a/contra** to resist to, oppose, fight; **3** *(recuperar-se)* to rally.

real *(pl:* **reais***) adj inv* royal, regal; **Sua Alteza R~, S.A.R.** His Royal Highness, H.R.H.; **2** *(verdadeiro)* true, genuine; **3** *(moeda do Brasil) (antiga moeda portuguesa)* real *(pl:* **réis***).*

realçar *vt* to accentuate, emphasize; *(fig)* to highlight.

realce *m* emphasis; **2** distinction; **dar ~ a** to enhance.

realejo *m (MÚS)* barrel organ; **tocador de ~** organ grinder.

realeza *f* royalty; **2** *(fig)* magnificence, grandeur.

realidade *f* reality; **na ~** actually; IDIOM **chamar** (**alguém**) **à ~** bring down to earth.

realimentação *f (ELECT)* feedback.

realização *f* fulfilment, achievement; **2** execution, carrying out; **3** *(JUR)* consummation; **4** *(FIN)* turnover; **5** *(CIN)* direction.

realizador,-ora *m,f* accomplisher, executor; **2** *(CIN)* director.

realizar *vt* to achieve; **2** to carry out; **3** *(converter em dinheiro)* to realize (capital); **4** *(filme)* to direct; ♦ ~-**se** *vr* to take place; **2** *(sonho, desejo)* to come true; **3** to achieve one's goal, feel fulfilled.

Not in the sense of 'understanding', which is **perceber.**

realizável *adj inv* achievable; **2** feasible; **3** *(FIN) (obrigações)* marketable.

realmente *adv* really, actually, indeed.

realojar *vt* rehouse *(alguém)*; ♦ ~-**se** to move, settle elsewhere.

reanimar *vt* to revive; **2** to encourage; ♦ ~-**se** *vr* to cheer up.

reaparecer *vi* to reappear.

reatar *vt* to resume, take up again; **2** to retie.

reativar *(Vd:* **rea(c)tivar***).*

reativo,-a *(Vd:* **rea(c)-tivo,-a***).*

reato *m (JUR)* reatus; **2** *(REL)* obligation of atonement after absolution.

reator *(Vd:* **rea(c)tor***).*

reaver *vt* to recover, get back.

rebaixa *f (de altura, de preço)* reduction, lowering.

rebaixar *vt* to lower; **2** ~ **o preço de** undersell; **3** *(fig)* to belittle; ♦ *vi* to drop; ♦ ~-**se** *vr* to lose self-respect.

rebaixe *m* lowering; **2** wainscot.

rebaixo *m* stair recess; **2** *(sob o telhado)* loft; **3** *(inclinação)* slope.

rebanho *m (de carneiros, cabras)* flock; **2** *(de gado)* herd; **3** *(REL) (fiéis)* flock.

rebarbativo,-a *adj* double-chinned; **2** *(pessoa)* surly; uncouth, gruff; **3** *(tom)* aggressive; **4** *(discurso)* boring, tiresome.

rebate *m* alarm; ~ **falso** false alarm; **2** *(COM)* discount; **3** incursion.

rebater *vt (socos)* to counter; **2** to strike again *(ferro)*; **3** to refute; **4** *(COM)* to discount *(cheque)*; **4** *(refrear)* to control; **5** *(bola)* to kick back.

rebelar *vt* to cause to revolt; ♦ *vr* to rebel, rise against.

rebelde *m,f* rebel; ♦ *adj inv* rebellious; **2** unruly, wild.

rebeldia *f* rebellion; **2** *(tendência)* rebelliousness; **3** stubbornness; **4** defiance.

rebelião *f* rebellion.

rebentar *vi (ger)* to break; **2** *(guerra)* to break out; **3** *(líquido)* to gush out; **4** to burst, explode; **os canos rebentaram** the pipes burst; ~ **de/em** burst with/into; **5** ~ **com a fortuna** go bankrupt; **6** *(roupa)* to split; **7** *(borbulhas)* burst, break.

rebento *m (BOT)* shoot; **2** *(fig)* off-spring.

rebite *m (TEC)* rivet.

reboar *vi* to resound, echo.

rebocador *m* tug (boat); **2** plasterer.

rebocar *vt (CONSTR)* to plaster; **2** *(carro, barco)* to tow; *(levar carro por infração)* to tow away.

reboco *m (CONSTR)* plaster.

rebolar *vt (corpo, ancas)* to swing; ♦ *vi* to roll, tumble; ♦ ~-**se** *vr* to roll over; swagger; **2** *(BR) (fig) (fam)* to work hard.

rebolo *m* grindstone; **2** *(pop)* cylinder.

reboludo,-a *adj* roundish, plump.

reboque *m* tow; **taxa de ~** towage; **2 carro-~** trailer; ~-**guincho** tow-truck; **3 a ~** on tow.

rebordo *m* rim, edge; **2** *(espelho, vidro)* bevelling.

rebote *m* carpenter's plane.

rebuçado *m* sweet *(UK)*; candy *(US)*.

rebuliço *m* commotion, hubbub, bustle.

rebuscado,-a *adj (fig)* searched for, sought after; **2** *(estilo)* refined; **3** *(pej)* recherché; pretentious; **4** *(discurso elaborado)* flowery.

rebuscar *vt* to search carefully for; rummage; ~ **as gavetas** rummage the drawers; ~ **a casa** ransack the house; **2** *(fig)* to refine, over-elaborate.

recado *m* message; **mandar** ~ to send word; **menino de** ~**s** errand boy.

recaída *f (MED)* relapse; **2** *(ECON)* slump; setback; **3** *(fig) (reincidência)* recurrence.

recalcado,-a *(terra, rua)* beaten down; pressed down; well-trodden; **2** *(fig) (sentimentos)* repressed; **3** *(assunto)* reiterated.

recalcar *vt (comprimir)* to tread down/upon; **2** *(reprimir)* repress; **3** *(PSIC)* inhibit; **4** repeat.

recalcitrante *adj* recalcitrant.

recambiar *vt (restituir)* to send sth back; **2** send sb back, **3** *(fam) (mandar alguém embora)* send sb packing.

recanto *m* corner, nook; **2** hiding place.

recapitulação *f* recapitulation, recap, revision, review.

recapitular *vt* to sum up, recapitulate; repeat, revise.

recarga *f (substituto duma embalagem)* recharge; **2** *(segunda investida)* second charge/attack.

recatado,-a *adj (pudico)* modest; **2** reserved.

recato *m (pudor)* modesty; **2** restraint, circumspection.

recauchutado,-a *adj*: **pneu/pneumático** ~ *(AUTO)* retread, remould.

recear *vt* to fear; ♦ *vi* to be afraid; **receio que chova hoje** I fear/am afraid it may rain today.

recebedor,-ora *m,f* receiver.

receber *vt (ger)* to receive; **2** *(abrigar)* to take in; **3** *(entreter)* to entertain, welcome, have guests.

recebimento *m* receipt; **acusar o** ~ to acknowledge receipt of; **2** reception, receiving; **3** acceptance.

receio *m* fear; **ela tem** ~ **de sair à noite** she is afraid to go out at night, **sem** ~ no fear; **2** *(apreensão)* worry, concern.

receita *f* income; **2** *(FIN)* revenue; ~ **do Estado** public revenue **3** *(MED)* prescription; **4** *(CULIN)* recipe.

receitar *vt* to prescribe.

receituário *m (FARM)* pharmacopoeia; **2** prescription-pad/book.

recém *adv* recently, newly; ~-**casado,-a** *adj* newly-wed.

recender *vi*: ~ **um aroma** to exhale or emit an odour.

recenseamento *m* census.

recensear *vt* to take a census of.

recente *adj inv* recent; **2** new, fresh, latest; **as notícias** ~**s** latest news.

recentemente *adv* recently, lately, of late.

receoso,-a *adj (com susto/medo)* frightened, afraid; **2** *(apreensivo)* fearful **(de** of) worried; *(COM)* cautious, uneasy.

rece(p)ção *f (recibo)* reception, receipt; **acusar a** ~ **de** to acknowledge receipt of; **2** *(entrada de hotel, etc)* reception; **3** *(festa, acolhimento)* reception.

rece(p)cionista *m,f* receptionist, desk clerk.

rece(p)tação *f (JUR)* receipt of stolen goods.

rece(p)táculo *m* receptacle, container, vessel, pot.

rece(p)tador,-ora *m,f (JUR)* receiver, receptor; ♦ *adj* of receiving.

rece(p)tar *vt* to receive *(dinheiro, espólio)*.

rece(p)tivo,-a *adj* receptive **(a** to); open-minded; welcoming.

receptor *m (TEC, RADIO)* receiver.

recessão *f (ECON)* recession.

recesso *m (lugar afastado)* retreat, place of retirement; **2** *(vão)* recess, alcove, niche; *(o mais intime)* depths; ♦ **recesso,-a** *adj* hidden away.

Note that 'school recess' is **hora de recreio**.

recheado *m (comida)* stuffing, filling; **2** *(algo cheio de penas, etc)* stuffing; ♦ **recheado,-a** *adj* stuffed, filled; ~ **com** filled with; **2** *(mobiliado)* furnished; **3** *(fig) (enriquecer)* **carteira** ~**a** well stuffed wallet = rich.

recheio *m* stuffing *(do peru)*; filling *(do bolo)*; **2** *(da almofada)* stuffing; **3** *(da casa)* contents *pl*.

rechem-chegado,-a *m,f* newcomer, newly-arrived.

rechem-falecido,-a *adj* recently deceased.

rechem-nascido,-a *adj* newborn (child).

rechonchudo,-a *adj* chubby, plump; **um bebé** ~ a chubby baby.

recibo *m* receipt.

reciclagem *f (de material)* recycling; **2** *(de pessoal)* retraining.

recidiva *f* recurrence.

recife *m* reef.

Recife city in Brazil.

recinto *m* enclosure; area.

recipiente *m* recipient, receiver; **2** *(vasilha)* container, receptacle, recipient; **3** *(FÍS)* receiver.

recíproca *f* reciprocal.

reciprocar *vt* to reciprocate, give and take; **eu reciproco os seus desejos** I wish you the same.

recíproco,-a *adj* reciprocal.

récita *f* performance.

recitação *f* recitation.

recital *m* recital.

recitar *vt* to recite.

reclamação *f* complaint; **2** protest; **3** *(JUR)* claim.

reclamante *m,f* claimant.

reclamar *vt (reivindicar)* to demand, claim; ♦ *vi*: **reclamar contra** to complain about; **2** *(exigir)* ~ **por** to demand.

reclame *m*, **reclamo** *m* advertisement, ad, advert; **2** *(cartaz)* poster, billboard; ~ **luminoso** neon display; **3** *(JUR)* claim.

reclinar *vt (cabeça, corpo, braço)* to recline, lean back, to rest **(em, sobre** on, against); **2** to incline, bow, ~ **a cabeça** incline one's head; ♦ ~-**se** *vr (recostar-se)* to lean back.

reclusão *f* seclusion; **2** confinement, prison; **3** *(doença infectuosa)* quarantine, isolation; **4** *(afastamento social)* solitude.

recluso,-a *m,f* recluse, hermit; **2** prisoner; ♦ *adj* reclusive; **2** *(preso)* shut up, confined.

recobrar *vt* to recover; ♦ ~-**se** *vr* ~ **de algo** to recover from sth.

recolha *f (colheita)* gathering, picking; **2** *(abrigo)* sheltering; **3** ~ **do lixo** rubbish collection; **4** *(pesquisa)* collecting.

recolher *vt* to collect *(água, mel, dados)*; **2** to bring in *(algo)*; **3** *(colher)* to gather together; **4** *(abrigar)* to give shelter to; **5** *(angariar)* collect; **6** *(retrair)* to withdraw, draw in; ♦ *vi* to return ~ **a casa** to get back home; ♦ **~-se** *vr* to go home; **2** to go to bed, retire to *(cama, quarto)*; **3** shelter; **recolhi-me da chuva** took shelter from the rain; **4** *(meditar)* meditate.

recolhido,-a *adj (lugar)* secluded; **2** *(retraído)* withdrawn; **3** absorbed; **4** *(dentro de casa)* housebound; **5** collected.

recolhimento *m* retirement; **2** meditation.

recomeçar *vt* to begin/start again; ♦ *vi* recommence, return; **o vento recomeçou** the wind has returned.

recomendação *f* recommendation; **carta de ~** testimonial; **2** advice; **3** warning; **recomendações** *fpl* regards.

recomendar *vt* to recomend, advise; **recomende-me à sua tia** give my best regards to your aunt; **2** remind, urge.

recomendável *adj* recommendable, advisable.

recompensa *f* reward, recompense; **2** award.

recompensar *vt* to reward; **2** to compensate for; **3** to thank for.

recompor *vt (reorganizar)* to reorganize; **2** to restore, rearrange; ♦ **~-se** *vr (a compustura)* to recover oneself.

recomposição *f* rearrangement, reorganization; **2** reshuffle, **a ~ do governo** the government's reshuffle.

recôncavo *m (enseada)* bay, cove; **2** *(concavidade)* deep recess, hollow; **3** ~ **baiano** *(GEOG)* large and fertile area on the coast of Bahia (Brazil); *(fig) (HIST)* **os dias do ~ baiano** the golden days of Bahia.

reconciliar *vt* to reconcile; ♦ **~-se** *vr* to be reconciled.

recondicionado,-a *adj* reconditioned.

recondicionar *vt* to recondition.

recôndito,-a *m* nook, corner; **2** *(fig) (íntimo)* secret place, depths; ♦ *adj* concealed; **2** obscure; **3** *(íntimo)* innermost.

recondução *f* forwarding; **a ~ de um pacote** the forwarding of a parcel.

reconduzir *vt* to lead sb back to.

reconfortante *adj inv* comforting, soothing; relaxing.

reconfortar *vt* to comfort; ♦ **~-se** *vr* to be invigorated.

reconhecer *vt (ger)* to recognize; **2** *(admitir)* acknowledge, accept; **3** be grateful for; **4** *(MIL)* to reconnoitre; **5** witness *(assinatura)*.

reconhecido,-a *adj* grateful; **2** *(assinatura)* authenticated; **3** recognized, accepted, acknowledged.

reconhecimento *m* recognition; **2** gratitude; **3** *(MIL) (exploração)* reconnaissance.

reconquista *f* reconquest.

reconquistar *vt (território)* to reconquer; **2** *(confiança)* to regain.

reconsiderar *vt/vi* to reconsider.

reconstituinte *m (FARM)* tonic.

reconstituir *vt (grupo)* to reconstitute; **2** *(doente)* to revive, invigorate; **3** to reconstruct.

reconstrução *f* reconstruction, rebuilding.

reconstruir *vt* to rebuild, reconstruct; **2** to restore.

recontro *m (MIL)* clash, fight.

reconversão *f* reconversion; back to its original state.

reconverter *vt* convert; **2** *(região)* develop; **3** *(prédio)* modernize.

recordação *f (memória)* memory; **2** *(objecto)* souvenir, memento; **recordar** *vt* to remember; **2** *(fazer lembrar)* remind *(algo, alguém)*; **recordei-lhe o nosso encontro** I reminded him of our meeting; **ele recorda-me o meu filho** he reminds me of my son; ♦ **~-se** *vr* (**de**) to remember; **não me recordo de você** I don't remember you.

recorde *m* record; **em tempo ~** in record time; **bater um ~** to break a record.

recorrente *m,f (JUR)* appellant; ♦ *adj inv (que se repete)* recurring

recorrer *vi*: ~ **a** *(pedir ajuda)* ask for help to, turn to sb; **2** to resort to; **3** *(JUR)* appeal; ~ **da sentença** appeal against a sentence.

recortado,-a *adj (papel)* cut; **2** *(sinuoso)* outlined, contoured *(cumes, litoral)*.

recortar *vt* to cut out; scallop; **2** *(fazer destacar)* outline *(figura)*.

recorte *m* cutting out; cutting, clipping; **álbum de ~** scrapbook.

recostar *vt* to recline; **2** *(a cabeça, o corpo)* rest *(em, sobre)* on; ♦ **~-se** *vr* to lean back *(em)*; lean on.

recreação *f* fun, recreation; **por sua alta ~** just for fun.

recreativo,-a *adj* recreational; leisure; amusement.

recreio *m* recreation; **2** fun; **3** *(pátio da escola)* playground; **hora de ~** break; playtime; **viagem de ~** pleasure-trip.

recriação *f* re-creation; **2** *(peça)* new production; **3** *(filme)* remake.

recriar *vt (história)* to re-create.

recriminação *f* recrimination, reproach.

recriminador,-ora *adj* reproachful.

recriminar *vt* to reproach, reprove.

recrudescência *f* recrudescence, becoming worse.

recrudescer *vi (sintomas, epidemia, situação)* grow worse, intensify.

recrudescimento *m* recrudescence, new outbreak; **2** *(disease, crime)* increase.

recruta *m,f* recruit.

recrutamento *m (MIL)* recruitment; **2** *(contrato, angariação)* recuitment.

recrutar *vt* to recruit.

recta *f (GEOM) (linha direita)* straight (line); **2** **estrada ~** straight road; **3** *(DESP)* lap; **4 à ~** just right/exactly.

re(c)tidão *f* rectitude; **2** straightness.

re(c)tificação *f* adjustment.

re(c)tificador *m* rectifier.

re(c)tificar *vt* to rectify.

re(c)to,-a *m (ANAT)* rectum; ♦ *adj (GEOM)* straight; **traçar uma ~** to draw a straight line;

ângulo ~ right angle; **2** *(pessoa)* upright, just; **juiz** ~ upright judge; **3** *(fig)* **caminho** ~ the right path.

récua *f (bestas de carga)* pack, train (of animals); drove (of packhorses); **2** *(carga)* load; **3** band, group; **4** *(pej)* gang.

recuar *vt/vi* to move back; **2** put back, move sth further back; **3** *(carro)* to back; **4** *(retirar-se)* retreat; **5** *(desistir)* go back on *(promessa)*; **6** ~ **ao tempo de** to recall the days of.

recuo *m* stepping backwards; **2** *(MIL)* retreat; *(de canhão)* recoil; kick.

recuperação *f* recovery; **2** recuperation.

recuperar *vt* to recover; **2** to make up for; **3** to rehabilitate; ♦ ~**-se** *vr* **(de)** to recuperate from.

recurso *m* o ~ **a algo**, having recourse/resorting to sth to; **2** *(uso)* recourse; **em último** ~ as a last resort; **3** *(JUR) (reclamação)* appeal; **4** ~**s** *mpl (dinheiro)* means, resources; **ela tem** ~**s** she can afford; **sem** ~**s** without funds.

recusa *f* refusal; **2** denial; **3** rejection.

recusar *vt* to refuse; **2** *(negar)* to deny; **3** to reject; ♦ ~**-se** *vr*: ~ **a** to refuse to.

reda(c)ção *f* composition, essay; editing; editorial staff; editorial office.

reda(c)tor,-ora *m,f* journalist; editor; ~**-chefe** *m,f* editor in chief.

redarguir *vi* to retort, reply sharply.

redator,-ora *(Vd: reda(c)tor,-ora)*.

rede *f (ger)* net; **2** *(de vedação)* wire netting; **3** *(cabelo)* hairnet; **4** *(leito)* hammock; **5** *(cilada)* trap; *(TEC)* network, grid.

rédea *f* rein; **dar** ~ **larga a** to give free rein to.

redemoinho *(Vd: remoinho)*.

redenção *f* redemption; **2** ~ **de um título** redemption of a bond.

Redentor *(REL)* Redeemer, Saviour; ♦ *adj* redeeming.

redigir *vt*, to compose, draft; **2** *vi* write.

redil *m (curral)* pen, fold, sheepfold; **2** *(fig) (REL)* congregation, flock.

redimir *vt (REL) (salvar)* redeem; **2** *(expiar)* to atone for; **3** to set free *(prisioneiros)*; **4** *(resgatar) (penhor, etc)* redeem from; ♦ ~**-se** *vr* **(de)** *(faltas)* make up for, compensate; *(do castigo)* to escape (punishment).

redobrar *vt* to fold again; **2** to redouble; ♦ *vi* to increase; **2** to ring out; **os sinos redobravam** the bells were ringing.

redoma *f* glass case/cover; glass dome; IDIOM **viver numa** ~ to be over-protected, be wrapped up in cotton wool.

redondel *m (TAUROM)* bull ring, arena; **2** *(rotunda)* roundabout.

redondeza *f* roundness; **2** *(area)* vicinity; **nas** ~**s** in the outskirts.

redondo,-a *adj* round, cylindrical, circular; **rosto** ~ round face; IDIOM **um não** ~ a blunt 'no'; **cair redondo** to fall down flat.

redor *m*: **ao/em** ~ **(de)** around, round about.

redução *f (ger)* reduction; **2** *(COM)* abatement, rebate; **3** conversion.

redundância *f* redundancy; excess; verbosity; tautology.

redundante *adj inv* superfluous; **2** *(palavroso)* wordy; **3** *(pleonástico)* redundant, tautological.

redundar *vt* overflow, abound; **2** ~ **em** to result in, end in, tend to.

reduto *m (MIL)* stronghold, fort, bulwark; **2** *(fig) (abrigo)* refuge, shelter.

reduzido,-a *adj* reduced; **2** limited; **3** small.

reduzir *vt (ger)* to reduce; **2** to convert; **3** to abridge; **4** to shorten; ~ **ao silêncio (alguém)** to silence; **5** *(fig)* ~ **à expressão mais simples** to simplify; ♦ ~**-se** *vr* to be reduced (**a** to).

reembolsar *vt* to reimburse; **2** to refund; **3** pay back.

reembolsável *adj inv* repayable, refundable, reimbursable.

reembolso *m* refund, repayment; **2** *(seguros)* compensation; **3** **contra-**~ cash on delivery, C.O.D.

reencarnação *f* reincarnation.

reentrância *f (ângulo para dentro)* concavity, cavity; *(para estátua)* recess.

reentrante *m (GEOM) (curva, ângulo)* concave.

refazer *vt* to redo, do again; **2** to rebuild, build up; **3** to restore; ♦ ~**-se** *vr* **(de)** *(MED)* to recover from *(doença, susto)*.

refego *m (na pele)* fold, wrinkle; **2** *(num vestido)* pleat, tuck.

refeição *(pl: -ões) f* meal; ~ **rápida** fast food.

refeitório *m* dining hall, refectory.

refém *m* hostage.

referência *f* reference; **com** ~ **a** with reference to, about.

referendar *(BR) vt* to countersign, endorse.

referendum *m (POL)* referendum.

referente *adj*: ~ **a** concerning, regarding.

referido,-a *adj* aforesaid, aforementioned.

referir *vt* to relate, tell; ♦ ~**-se a** *vr* to refer to; **2** *(aludir)* to allude to.

refestelar-se *vr* to stretch out; *(em cadeira, sofá)* lean back comfortably; to sprawl.

refilão,-lona *m,f* grumbler, recalcitrant.

refilar *vi (ripostar)* to retort, answer back; **2** to protest *(resmungar)*.

refinado,-a *adj* refined.

refinamento *m* refinement.

refinar *vt* to refine; **2** *(fig)* to perfect, polish.

refinaria *f* refinery.

refle(c)tido,-a *adj* reflected; **2** thoughtful.

refle(c)tir *vt (luz)* to reflect; **2** *(sobre, em)* to think about; **3** *(som)* to echo; ~ **em** to consider, think about; ♦ ~**-se** *vr* to be reflected.

refle(c)tor,-ora *m* reflector; ♦ *adj* reflecting.

reflexão *f* reflection; thought, contemplation; remark, comment.

reflexivo,-a *adj* reflexive.

reflexo *m (ger)* reflection; **2** *(MED)* reflex; ♦ **reflexo,-a** *adj (luz)* reflected; **2** *(movimento)* reflex; **3** *(gram) (verbo, pronoune)* reflexive.

reflorestamento *m* reforestation.

reflorestar *vt* to reforest.

refluxo *m* ebb.

refogado *m* sautéed (onions) (as a basis for Portuguese stew); **2** *(com cebola, tomate sautée)* gravy.

refogar *vt* to sauté.

reforçado,-a *adj* strengthened; strong; *(ARQ)* reinforced.

reforçar *vt* to reinforce, strength; **2** *(ânimo)* invigorate; ♦ *vi* to grow stronger; **2** to emphasize.

reforço *m* reinforcement, strengthening; **2** *(aumento)* increase; **3** support, help.

reforma *f (ger)* reform; ~ **agrária** agrarian reform; **2** *(EP)* retirement; **pensão de** ~ retirement pension; **3** *(CONSTR)* repair, renovation; **4** *(REL)* Reformation.

reformado,-a *adj* retired *(not in Brazil)*; **2** reformed; **3** rebuilt, improved.

reformar *vt* to rebuild, alter, renovate; ♦ ~**-se** *vr* to retire; **2** *(corrigir-se)* to reform, mend one's ways.

reformatório *m (para delinquentes)* reform school, reformatory.

refra(c)tário,-a *m,f (MIL) (que foge do serviço militar)* deserter; ♦ *adj (TEC)* resistant, refractory, **tijolo** ~ refractory brick, fire-brick; **2** *(fig) (pessoa)* unruly, rebellious.

refrão *m (estribilho)* refrain; chorus; **2** *(provérbio)* saying, adage.

refratário,-a *(Vd:* **refra(c)tário,-a**).

refrear *vt (reprimir)* to restrain, suppress; **2** *(cavalo)* rein in; **3** *(cólera)* cool down, control; ♦ ~**-se** *vr* to restrain o.s.

refrega *f* fight.

refrescante *adj* refreshing.

refrescar *vt* to cool, chill (**algo** sth); **2** to refresh; ♦ *vi (tempo)* to cool down; ♦ ~**-se** *vr* to be refreshed, refresh o.s.

refresco *m* cool drink, soft drink, refreshment.

refrigeração *f (de comida)* refrigeration; **2** *(de ambiente)* air-conditioning.

refrigerador *m* refrigerator, *(fam)* fridge; ♦ **refrigerador,-ora** *adj* refrigerating.

refrigerante *m* cool drink, soft drink.

refrigerar *vt* to chill, freeze; **2** *(ambiente)* to cool, cool down, freshen.

refrigério *m (consolo devido a frescura)* refreshment; **2** *(consolação)* comfort.

refugiado,-a *adj* refugee.

refugiar-se *vr* (**em**) *(abrigar-se em)* to take refuge/ cover/shelter in; **2** *(fig)* to seek solace.

refúgio *m (abrigo)* shelter, hideaway; **2** *(DESP) (de montanha)* mountain cabin; **3** *(apoio, amparo)* refuge.

refugo *m* waste, rubbish *(UK)*, garbage *(US)*; ~ **de metal** metal scrap; **negócio de** ~ scrap; business.

refulgência *f* brilliance.

refulgente *adj inv* shining.

refulgir *vi* to shine; **2** *(fig) (destacar-se)* to stand out.

refundir *vt (metal)* to recast; **2** *(texto)* reformulate; ♦ ~**-se** *vr* to melt.

refutação *f* refutation; denial.

refutar *vt* to refute.

refutável *adj* refutable.

rega *f* watering; irrigation.

regabofe *m (fam)* noisy party, revelry.

regaço *m* lap; **o menino sentou-se no** ~ **da vovó**; the little boy sat on his grandma's lap; **2** *(fig) (seio)* bosom.

regadia *f,* **regadio** m watering, irrigation; ♦ *adj* watered; **campo de** ~ irrigated field.

regador *m* watering can.

regalado,-a *adj* delighted; **2** comfortable; **levar uma vida** ~**a** to live in the lap of luxury; ♦ *adv* comfortably.

regalar *vt* to delight; **2** to regale; **3** to feel pleasure; ♦ ~**-se** *vr* to treat/gratify o.s.; ~**-se a comer** to eat/feast lavishly.

regalia *f* privilege, prerogative; **2** *pl* special allowances, perks; ~ **fiscais** tax allowances.

regalo *m* pleasure, treat; **2** *(agasalho das mãos)* muff.

regar *vt* to water, irrigate; **2** *(fig)* to wash down, drink; **3** *(CULIN) (peixe, carne)* baste, pour over *(com vinho, etc)*.

regata *f* regatta.

regatear *vt (baratear)* to haggle over, bargain for; ♦ *vi* to haggle.

regateio *m* haggling, bargaining.

regateiro,-a *m,f* street-seller, standholder; **2** *(que discute preços)* wrangler, haggler; **3** *(pessoa que alterca)* quarrelsome; *(fig) (pop) (pessoa grosseira)* fishwife.

regato *m* brook, stream.

regelado,-a *adj* frozen; ~ **até aos ossos** chilled to the bone.

regelar *vt* to freeze.

regência *f* regency; **2** *(LING)* government; **3** *(MÚS)* conducting.

regeneração *f* regeneration.

regenerar *vt* to regenerate; **2** to reform.

regente *m (POL)* regent; **o príncipe** ~ the Prince Regent; **2** *(MÚS)* conductor; **3** *(de escola, curso)* director, leader.

reger *vt* to govern, rule; **2** *(MÚS)* to conduct; **3** *(EDUC)* ~ **a cadeira de Recursos Humanos** to hold the Chair of Human Resources; ♦ ~**-se** be ruled/run (**por** on); **a associação rege-se pela democracia** the association is run on democracy.

região *f (ADMIN)* region; **a Madeira é uma** ~ **autónoma** Madeira is an autonomous region.

regicida *m,f (criminal)* regicida.

regicídio *m (assassínio do rei)* regicide.

regime *m (ger)* system; **2** *(dieta)* diet; **fazer** ~ to go on a diet; **3** *(POL, JUR)* regime.

regimento *m (MIL)* regiment; **2** *(normas)* regulations *pl*, rules *pl*.

régio,-a *adj* royal; **2** regal; **carta** ~**a** royal charter.

regional *adj* regional.

regist(r)ador,-ora *m,f* registrar, recorder; **caixa registadora** cash register; ♦ *adj* registering.

registar *(BR:* -**trar**) *vt* to register, record.

registo *(BR:* -**tro**) *m (ger)* registration; enrolment; **2** *(ger, LÍNG)* register; *(livro de)* register; **3** *(MÚS)* range, *(voz)* register; ~ **civil** registry office; **4** ~ **de tropas** muster-roll; **5** log; **6** *(JUR)* recording.

rego *m (pequena vala)* channel, duct; **2** *(para água)* (irrigation) ditch, trench; **3** *(de arado)* furrow, rut; **4** *(de roda)* cart-track; **5** *(do cabelo)* parting; **6** *(ANAT) (entre os seios)* ~ **do peito** cleavage; **7** *(fam) (entre as nádegas)* bum crack *(col)*.

regozijar *vt* to gladden, cheer up; ♦ ~**-se** *vr* **(com algo/por)** to be delighted at/with, rejoice at.

regozijo *m* joy.

regra *f (norma)* rule; **em** ~, **por via de** ~ as a rule, usually; **2 estar em** ~ to be in order; **3 estabelecer a** ~ to lay down the rule; **4 sair da** ~ step out of line; **5** ~**s** *fpl (MED)* menstruation; **6** *(MAT)* **as quatro** ~**s** the four rules.

regrado,-a *adj* methodical, moderate.

regrante *adj inv* ruling.

regrar-se *vt* to regulate; ♦ *vr* ~ **por** to be guided by sth.

regressão *f* regression; **2** *(MED)* relapse.

regressar *vi* to come/go back, return **(de/a** from/to); **regresso** *m* return.

régua *f* ruler; ~ **de cálculo** slide rule.

régua-tê (réguas-tê) *f (ARQ)* T-square.

regueira *f* drainage ditch.

regulador,-ora *m (medicamento)* regulator; ♦ *adj* regulating.

regulamentação *f* regulation; **2** *pl* rules, regulations *pl*. **regulamentar** *adj inv* standardizing; ♦ *vt* to regulate.

regulamento *m* rules *pl;* statute; **2** *(JUR)* (administrativa) by-law.

regular *adj* regular; **2** average, medium; **3** normal, usual; ♦ *vt (ger)* to regulate; **2** adjust; **3** to verify, check; ♦ *vi* to function; **não** ~ **bem da cabeça** not be right in the head; **2** *(conter gastos)* moderate; ♦ ~**-se** *vr:* ~ **por** abide by.

regularidade *f* regularity.

regularizar *vt (normalizar)* to legalize, to regularize; ♦ ~**-se** *vr* return to normal.

regularmente *adv* regularly.

régulo *m* tribal chief, chieftain.

regurgitar *vt/vi* regurgitate.

rei *(pl:* **reis)** king; **bolo-~** *(CULIN)* Christmas cake; **os três Reis Magos** the Magi, the Three Kings (Epiphany); IDIOM **sem** ~ **nem roque** haphazardly; **trazer o** ~ **na barriga** to be stuck up, proud.

reimprimir *vt* to reprint.

reinado *m* reign.

reinante *m,f* ruler; ♦ *adj inv* ruling; **2** prevailing; **a paz** ~ the prevailing peace; **3** *(arte, moda)* popular.

reinar *vi (governar)* to reign; **2** *(fig) (predominate)* to prevail; **3** *(fig, fam) (troçar)* to kid, to have/makefun.

reincarnação *f* reincarnation.

reincidência *f* relapse; **2** recurrence; **3** repetition.

reincidir *vi* to recur; ~ **em algo** to do sth again; **2** *(JUR)* relapse.

reino *m* kingdom, reign, realm.

Reino Unido *npr* **o** ~ the United Kingdom.

> Note that 'Reino Unido' refers to England, Wales, Scotland and Northern Ireland.

reintegrar *vt* to reinstate; **2** to restore; **3** to readmit.

Reiquiavique *npr* Reykjavik.

réis *mpl of* **real** old Portuguese currency.

reiterar *vt/vi* to reiterate, repeat.

reitor,-ora *m f (de escola)* principal; **2** *(faculdade)* rector; *(universidade)* vice-chancellor, university's rector.

reitoria *f (universidade)* central office; **2** *(do pároco)* vicarage, rectory.

reivindicar *vt* to claim.

rejeição *f* rejection.

rejeitar *vt* to reject; **2** to refuse.

rejubilar-se *vr* to rejoice.

rejuvenescer *vt* to rejuvenate; ♦ *vr* ~**-se** *vr* to be rejuvenated.

relação *f (analogia)* relation; **2** connection, relationship; **3** *(MAT)* ratio; **4** *(rol)* list; **5** *(JUR)* **Tribunal da R~** court of appeal; ♦ **com/em** ~ **a** *adv* regarding, with reference to; ♦ **relações** *fpl* relations; ~ **públicas** public relations; **estar de boas relações (com)** be on good terms (with); **cortar** ~**s com** break off with sb; **relações sexuais** sexual intercourse.

relacionar *vt* to make a list of; **2** to connect; **3** *(comparar)* ~ **algo com algo**; ♦ ~**-se** *vr* **(com alguém)** to be connected with sb, to be acquainted with; **2** to be related to, have to do with sth.

relâmpago *m (METEOR)* lightning; **2** flash of lightning; **3** *(rapidamente)* **passar como um** ~ to flash past.

relampejar *vi* to flash; **relampejava** the lightning flashed; **2** *(cintilar)* shine, glitter, sparkle.

relançamento *m* relaunching; **2** *(livro)* re-editing; **3** put back in play.

relançar *vt* to throw again *(bola, projéctil)*; **2** to relaunch; start again *(profissão)* ~ **o olhar** to throw a glance at.

relance *m* glance; **ver de** ~ to glance at; **num** ~ in a flash.

relapso,-a *(JUR)* second-time offender; ♦ *adj (criminoso)* hardened; **2** *(REL)* impenitent; **3** *(não cumpridor de deveres)* slack, negligent.

relatar *vt* to give an account of.

relatividade *f* relativity.

relativo,-a *adj* relative; ~ **a algo** relative (to sth); **2** regarding; *(gram) (pronome)* relative.

relato *m* account, report; **2** description.

relator,-ora *m,f (pessoa que relata)* commentator; *(JUR)* relator.

relatório *m* report.

relaxação *f* relaxation; **2** slovenliness.

relaxado,-a *adj* relaxed; **2** slack; **3** slovenly, sloppy.

relaxamento *m (descanso)* relaxation; **2** *(desleixo)* slovenliness.

relaxar *vt (descontrair)* to relax; **2** *(enfraquecer, atenuar)* relax; ♦ *vi (afrouxar)* to slacken, become loose; **2** to weaken; ♦ ~**-se** *vr* to relax; **2** become lax; **3** loose; slacken.

relaxe *m* relaxation; **2** negligence.

relegar *vt* to relegate.

relembrar *vt* to recall, bring to memory.

relento **ao** ~ *prep* open air; **dormir ao** ~ to sleep rough/in the open.

reles *adj inv (produto)* poor quality; **2** *(pessoa)* common, vulgar; **3** *(conversa, trabalho, salário)* lousy *(fam)*.

relevância *f* relevance.

relevante *adj inv* outstanding; **2** pertinent.

relevar *vt (pôr em relevo)* to project, emphasize; **2** *(atenuar)* to relieve; **3** *(perdoar)* to pardon; ♦ *vi* stem/come from.

relevo *m (GEOG)* relief; **2** *(arte)* relief; **3** *(fig)* prominence, importance; **pôr em** ~ emphasize; **com** ~ with focus on.

relha *f* ploughshare, blade of plough.

relicário *m* reliquary, **2** shrine.

religião *f* religion.

religiosidade *f* piety; **com** ~ religiously.

religioso,-a *m,f* monk/nun ♦ *adj* religious.

relinchar *vi (cavalo)* to neigh.

relincho *m* neigh; neighing.

relíquia *f* relic; ~ **de família** family heirloom.

relógio *m* clock; ~ **de pé** grandfather clock; ~ **de pulso, algibeira** watch; ~ **despertador** alarm clock.

relojoeiro *m* watchmaker.

relutância *f* reluctance.

reluzente *adj* brilliant, shining.

reluzir *vi* to gleam, shine.

relva *f (para o jardim)* grass; lawn.

relvado *m* lawn, turf.

REM *(abr de* **Rapid Eye Movement***) m* REM.

remanescente *m (sobejo)* rest, remaining; **2** *(JUR)* residue; **3** surplus; leftovers *pl*; ♦ *adj inv* leftover, residual.

remanso *m* stillness, quiet; **2** *(retiro)* peace and quiet, seclusion; *(BR)* backwater.

remar *vt/vi* to row; ~ **ao longo** to row with long strokes; **perícia de** ~ oarmanship. IDIOM ~ **contra a maré** to row/swim against the tide.

rematado,-a *adj* completed, complete.

rematar *vt* to finish off; ~ **a bainha** to finish off the hem; **2** *(concluir)* conclude.

remate *m* end, conclusion; **2** *(acabamento)* finishing touch; **3** *(de piada)* punchline; **4** *(ARQ)* top, finial; **5** *(FUT)* strike.

remediado,-a *adj* comfortably off.

remediar *vt* to put right, repair; **2** *(aliviar)* alleviate; **3** *(socorrer)* help; ♦ ~-se to make do with sth; **a carne não chega, mas vou ~-me com os ovos,** I don't have enough meat, but I'll make do with some eggs; IDIOM **mais vale prevenir que** ~ forewarned is forearmed.

remédio *m* medicine medication; **2** remedy; **3** help; **4** *(JUR)* recourse; **5** *(fig)* solution; **não tem** ~ it can't be helped; **não havia outro** ~ **mas aceitar** there was no other way but to accept; **que** ~! what else can one do?

remela *(também:* **ramela***) f (olhos)* sticky secretion, rheum.

remelento,-a, remeloso,-a *adj (olhos)* bleary-eyed, rheumy.

remendar *vt (roupa, pneu, etc)* to mend; to patch; repair; **2** *(erros)* rectify, correct.

remendo *m (de pano, borracha)* patch; **2** *(de couro)* repair; **3** *(fig) (solução)* temporary solution; **4** excuse.

remessa *f (COM)* shipment, dispatch; **2** remittance; **3** consignment, stock.

remetente *m,f* sender; **2** *(COM)* shipper.

remeter *vt* to send, dispatch; **2** to remit *(dinheiro)*; **3** to hand over; **4** forward *(carta, etc)*; ♦ ~-**se** *vr* ~ **a** to refer to.

remexer *vt* to move; **2** *(revolver)* to stir (up); **3** *(papéis)* to shuffle; ♦ *vi* ~ **em** rummage through; **2** fidget; ♦ *vr* to roll.

reminiscência *f* reminiscence, memory.

remir *vt (ger)* to redeem; **2** *(livrar)* to free; **3** *(compensar)* to make up for; ♦ ~-**se** *vr* to redeem o.s.

remissão *f* remission; **2** forgiveness; **3** payment; **4** *(MED)* abatement; **5** *(em texto)* cross-reference.

remisso,-a *adj* remiss, careless.

remível *adj* redeemable.

remo *m* oar; **2** *(DESP)* rowing.

remoção *f* removal.

remoçar *vt* rejuvenate *(alguém)*; ♦ *vi* to be rejuvenated, look younger.

remodelação *f* renovation, renewing.

remodelar *vt* to modify, renew, upgrade; **2** *(reorganizar)* reshuffle.

remoer *vt* grind again; **2** *(mastigar bem)* chew; **3** *(animais)* to ruminate; **4** *(fig)* turn sth over in the mind; ♦ *vr* to fret.

remoinho *m* whirl; **2** *(de fumo, cigarro)* eddy; **3** *(água)* whirlpool; **4** *(de vento)* whirlwind.

remontar *vt* to re-assemble; **2** *(TEAT)* to restage; ♦ *vi (no tempo)* ~ **a** date back to; **2** *(em cavalo)* to remount; **3** to soar.

remoque *m* gibe, taunt, scoff.

remoquear *vt* to taunt.

remorso *m* remorse.

remoto,-a *adj* remote, far off.

remover *vt (ger)* to remove; **2** *(transferir)* to transfer.

remuneração *f* remuneration; **2** *(pagamento)* payment.

remunerador,-ora *adj* remunerative, rewarding.

remunerar *vt* to remunerate; **2** pay; **3** to reward.

remunerável *adj inv (trabalho, material)* remunerable.

rena *f* reindeer.

renal *adj inv* renal, kidney.

renascença *f* rebirth; **2** *(fig)* revival; **3** **a R** ~ the Renaissance.

Renascentista *m,f (escritor, artista)* Renaissance figure; ♦ *adj inv (pensamento, arte)* **a Arte** ~ the Renaisance Art.

renascer *vi* to be reborn; **2** *(fig)* to be revived.

renascimento *(Vd:* **renascença***).*

renda *f* rent; **a** ~ **da casa** the rent of the house, apparatus; **2** *(tecido)* lace; needlework, crochet; **3** *(de imóveis)* income; ~ **proveniente de capital** unearned income; ~ **bruta/líquida** gross/net income; **4** ~ **vitalícia** life annuity/pension; **5** ~**s**

públicas public revenue; **6 imposto de** ~ (BR) income tax.

rendado,-a m lacework; ♦ adj lace, lacy.

rendeiro,-a m,f (fabricante de renda) lacemaker; **2** (de terrenos) tenant.

render vt (dar rendimento) (produto, lucro) to produce, yield; **a cortiça rende milhões de euros** the cork yields millions of euros; **2** (substituir) to relieve (guarda); **3** (prestar) to render, pay (homenagem); ♦ vi (ser produtivo) be productive; (trabalho, tempo) **hoje, o meu dia não rendeu nada** today the day has not been productive; **2** (durar = comida) to last, go a long way; **a carne rende mais do que o peixe** meat goes further than fish; **3** (fig) **fazer** ~ **o peixe** (fam) (trabalho pago à hora) to work slowly; **4** (estalar) rent, give way; **5** (entregar armas) surrender; ♦ **~-se** vr (capitular) to bow to; **2** to give in; surrender.

rendibilidade (Vd: rentabilidade).

rendibilizar (Vd: rentabilizar).

rendição f surrender, capitulation; **2** (substituição) changing.

rendido,-a adj subdued; ~ **a algo** overcome by sth.

rendimento m (montante de salário, lucros, benefícios) income; (do Estado, empresa) revenue; **declarar os** ~**s** to declare one's income; **2** (de produção) yield; output; (produtividade) productivity; **3** (de juro) interest; **4** (motor) performance; **5** (aproveitamento, sucesso) success.

rendível (Vd: rentável).

rendoso,-a adj profitable; productive.

renegado,-a m,f adj renegade; (fam) turncoat.

renegar vt to renounce; **2** to disclaim; **3** repudiate, deny; **4** betray (ideal); ♦ vi (descrer) renege.

> Not 'renege' in the sense of going back on one's promise, which is **faltar à palavra**.

renhido,-a adj (debate, jogo) heated, intense; **2** (fam) fierce, hard-fought; (fam) bloody.

renhir vt to contest; ♦ vi to wrangle, contend.

renina f (quimosina) rennin.

rénio, rênio m (QUÍM) rhenium.

renitência f obstinacy.

renitente adj inv obstinate; recalcitrant, renitent.

renome m fame, renown; **de** ~ renowned.

renovação f renewal; **2** (ARQ) renovation.

renovador,-ora m,f renovator; ♦ adj reform; renewing, renovating.

renovar vt to renew; **2** to renovate; ♦ vi to be renewed; **2** to be revamped.

renovável adj inv renewable; **energias renováveis** renewable energies; **2** (substituível) replaceable.

renovo m sprout, shoot.

rentabilidade f profitability.

rentabilizar vt to make a profit; **2** (informação) make the most of.

rentável adj inv rentable, profitable.

rente adj (cabelo) close-cropped; **2** ~ **a** (junto a) next to, nearby; ♦ adv close to; ~ **ao passeio** close to the pavement.

renúncia f renouncement.

renunciar vt ~ **a algo** (recusar) renounce; **2** give up (direitos).

reorganizar vt to reorganize.

reparação f (concerto) mending, repair; **2** (emenda) correction; **3** compensation, reparation; **4** (REL) redemption.

reparar vt to repair; **2** to restore; **3** to compensate for, make amends for; ♦ ~ **em** vi (notar) to notice, look at; **não repare no que ela diz** pay no attention to what she says; **eu reparei que ele não tinha gravata** I noticed he was not wearing a tie; **repare naquela mulher** look at that woman.

reparo m (concerto) repair; **2** (crítica) criticism; **3** observation, comment.

repartição f distribution; **2** (partilha) sharing; allocation (de fundos etc); **3** (ADMIN) government office, department; **R~ das Finanças** Finance Department, Treasury; ~ **do registo civil** registrar's office.

repartir vt (distribuir) to distribute; **2** (dividir em) divide (up); **3** (partilhar) to share out; ♦ **~-se** vr divide; **2** to spread.

repassar vt to go over sth again; **2** (revisar) revise; **3** iron again (roupa); **4** (tecido) soak; **5** (cheio) be full; seeped in.

repasto m banquet, repast.

repatriação f repatriation.

repatriar vt to repatriate; ♦ **~-se** vr to go back home.

repelão m push, shove; **de** ~ brusquely, with a jerk; **ela passou por mim de** ~ she passed by me brusquely.

repelente m adj repellent.

repelir vt to drive away; **2** (afastar) repel, stave (off); **3** (expulsar) expel; **4** (repudiar) to reject.

repente m suddenness; **2** (ímpeto) flash: ♦ adv **de** ~ suddenly; **num** ~ on an impulse.

repentino,-a adj sudden.

repercussão f repercussion.

repercutir vt/vi (som) to echo, reverberate; **2** (luz) to reflect; **3** (fig) (notícia) divulge, spread; ♦ **~-se** vr (em) to affect, to have repercussions (on); **2** (grito, som) to be heard/felt.

repertório m list; **2** (conjunto) collection; **3** (MÚS) repertoire.

repetente m,f student who repeats a year or an examination; ♦ adj inv repeating.

repetição f repetition.

repetido,-a adj repeated; ~ **s vezes** repeatedly, again and again.

repetir vt to repeat; ♦ **~-se** vr to be repeated.

repicar vt/vi (sino) to ring, chime, peal; **os sinos repicavam** the (church) bells were ringing; **2** (carne, veg) to mince; to chop again ♦ vi to ring (out).

repimpado,-a adj (fam) comfortably settled (in armchair, etc), lounging; **2** well-fed.

repique m peal, chiming; **2** (da campainha) ring.

repisar vt to repeat, stress; **2** (uvas, cereais) to tread, crash; **3** (fam) (repetir o mesmo assunto) harp on, nag; ♦ vi rub in.

repleto,-a *adj* full, packed; **a casa está ~a de antiguidades** the house is full of antiques.

réplica *f* replica; **2** *(resposta)* reply, retort; **3** *(JUR)* replication; **4** *(TEAT)* repartee.

replicar *vt* to answer *(back)*, reply to.

repolhado,-a *(vegetal, como o repolho)* hearty, leafy.

repolho *m (BOT)* green cabbage.

repor *vt (colocar)* to put back, replace; **2** *(devolver)* to pay back; ♦ **~-se** *vr* to recover o.s.

reportagem *f* reporting; report; reporters *pl*.

reportar *vt* to take back; ♦ **~-se** *vr*: **a** to refer to.

repórter *m,f* reporter.

reposição *f* replacement, restitution; **em ~** *(filme)* showing again.

reposteiro *m* heavy curtain; **~ s** heavy drapes.

repousar *vi* to rest.

repouso *m* rest.

repreender *vt* to reprimand; **2** *(fam)* to tell off.

repreensão *f* rebuke, reprimand.

repreensível *adj* reprehensible.

represa *f* dam; **2** *(água acumulada nessa)* pool.

represália *f* reprisal, retaliation.

representação *f* representation; petition; performance.

representante *m* representative.

representar *vt* to represent; to play a part/role; **~ um anjo** to play the part of an angel; ♦ *vi (JUR)* to make a complaint.

representativo,-a *adj* representative.

repressão *f* repression.

repressivo,-a *adj* repressive.

reprimir *vt* to repress.

réprobo,-a *adj* reprobate; *(pessoa)* depraved.

reprodução *f* reproduction.

reproduzir *vt* to reproduce; to repeat; ♦ **~-se** *vr* to breed, multiply; to be repeated.

reprovação *f* disapproval; **2** failure.

reprovado,-a *adj* failed (in exam).

reprovar *vt* to disapprove of; **2** to fail.

réptil *m adj inv (ZOOL)* reptile.

repto *m* challenge, provocation.

república *f* republic; **Assembleia da R~** Parliament; **2** *(fig, fam) (desordem)* mess, free-for-all; **3** students' hostel.

republicano,-a *adj* republican.

repudiar *vt (rejeitar)* to repudiate, reject; **2** to disown; **3** *(acusações)* deny, refute.

repúdio *m* rejection, repudiation.

repugnância *f (ger)* repugnance.

repugnante *adj inv (nojento)* disgusting, repulsive.

repugnar *vt* to be repugnant to; ♦ *vi* to be repulsive; **2 ~ a alguém** to disgust sb.

repulsa *f* rejection; **2** repulsion, aversion, repugnance, disgust.

repulsivo,-a *adj* repulsive.

reputação *f* reputation.

reputado,-a *adj* renowned.

reputar *vt (considerar)* to consider *(algo, alguém)*; ♦ **~-se** *vr* to consider o.s.

repuxado,-a *adj (apertado)* tight; **2** *(esticado)* stretched; *(cabelo)* pulled back; **3** *(fig) (esmerado) (alguém)* refined.

repuxar *vt (colar, gola)* to pull on; **2** *(cabelo)* pull back; **3** *(vestido, corda)* to pull tight, stretch; **4** *(costura)* to pucker.

repuxo *m (fonte)* water spout; **2** *(jorro de água)* spurt, jet.

requebrado *m (que tem requebros: nos gestos, corpo)* swaying; *(na voz)* warble, trill.

requebrar *vt* to wiggle, sway; swing *(hips)*; ♦ **~-se** *vr (saracotear-se)* to move the hips, dance; **2** *(voz)* to trill, warble.

requeijão *m* fresh cottage cheese, curd cheese.

requentado,-a *adj* reheated; **2** *(fig) (quando se finge ser novo – ideia, etc)* rehashed, hashed-over.

requerente *m,f (JUR)* petitioner, plaintiff.

requerer *vt (solicitar)* to apply for; **2** *(pedir)* to request, require; **3** *(exigir)* to demand; **4** *(JUR)* to petition for; ♦ *vi (JUR)* to make a petition.

requerimento *m* application; **2** request; **3** petition.

réquiem *m* requiem.

requintado,-a *adj* refined, elegant.

requinte *m* refinement, finesse; **2** *(excesso)* height, acme *(de perfeição, estupidez)*.

requisição *f (pl: -ões)* requisition; **livro de ~ções** order book; **2** claim; **3** *(JUR)* court order; **4** *(MIL)* requisition *(de material, homens)*

requisitado,-a *adj* requested; **2** *(muito procurado)* in demand.

requisitar *vt* to make a request for; **2** to order **(algo,** *sth)*; **3** *(JUR, MIL)* to requisition.

requisito *m* requirement, requisite.

requisitório *m* requisitory; **2** *(JUR)* indictment; report.

rês *f* head of cattle; **reses** *fpl* cattle, livestock *sg ou pl*.

rescaldo *m (cinzas)* cinders; **2** *(fig)* aftermath.

rescindir *vt (JUR) (contracto)* to rescind; to revoke, annul.

rescisão *f (JUR)* rescission.

rés-do-chão *m* ground floor *(UK)*; first floor *(US)*.

resenha *f (descrição)* report, review; **2** summary, minute description.

resenhar *vt* to review; **2** to list/report in detail.

reserva *f (ger)* reserve; **2** extra supply, stock, store; **de ~** in store; **3** *(recursos disponíveis)* reserves; **~ de dinheiro** savings; **4 ~ de água** reservoir; **5** *(MIL) reserve;* **6** *(fig) (marcação)* reservation; **7** *(fig)* inhibition, reserve; **8** *(fig) (dúvidas)* reservation, doubts; **9** reticence, discretion; **com ~** guardedly, cautious; **sem ~** unconditionally.

reservado,-a *adj (bilhetes, espaço)* reserved, booked; *(lugar especial)* restricted **(a** to); **2** *(posto de parte)* set aside *(dinheiro);* **3** *(atitude da pessoa)* reserved; unsociable.

reservar *vt (guardar)* to reserve; **2** to book, reserve; **3** *(poupar)* save; **4** to hold in store; **5** *(opinião, decisão)* hold back; ♦ **~-se** *vr (preservar-se)* to save o.s.; keep o.s.

reservatório *m (de água)* reservoir; **2** *(depósito)* tank.

reservista *adj inv (MIL)* reservist.

resfolegar *vi (respirar)* to pant, to gasp for breath; **2** *(fig) (expelir)* puff, wheeze; **3** *(pop)* to snort.

resfriado,-a *m* cool, chill; **apanhei um ~ à noite** I caught a chill last night; **2** (*BR*) common cold; ♦ *adj* chilled; **2** (*fig*) (*desapontado*) disillusioned, in the dumps.

resfriar *vt* to cool, chill; ♦ **~-se** *vr* to catch (a) cold, catch a chill.

resgatar *vt* (*ger*) to rescue; **2** (*liberar*) to ramson; **3** (*pagar*) to pay off, pay back (*dívida*); **4** redeem (*título*).

resgate *m* ransom; **2** (*FIN*) (*ajuda*) bailout; **3** (*JUR*) remittance; **4** redemption (*de hipoteca, títulos*); (*REL*) (*de pecados*) redemption.

resguardar *vt* (*proteger*) to protect, shelter (**de** from); **resguarda o cão da chuva** protect the dog from the rain; ♦ **~-se** *vr*: **~ de** to guard against; to protect o.s.

resguardo *m* protection; **2** (*cuidado, defesa*) care, safeguard; **3** (*debaixo do lençol*) undersheet, mattress cover; **4** (*para cobrir livros*) cover, jacket.

residência *f* (*morada*) residence, home, abode; **2** (*casa*) house.

residencial *m* (*para dormidas*) boarding house, residential hotel; ♦ *adj inv* (*zona*) residential.

residente *adj* resident; ♦ *adj* residing.

residir *vi* to live, reside.

residual *adj inv* residual; **2** (*fig*) secondary.

resíduo *m* residue.

resignação *f* resignation (**a com** to).

resignado,-a *adj* (*conformado*) resigned.

resignar-se *vr* **~ com** to resign o.s.

resina *f* resin.

resistência *f* (*geral*) resistance (**a** *to*); **2** (*moral*) endurance, stamina; **3** (*MIL*) resistance; **linha de ~**.line of defense; **4** (*ELECT*) resistor.

resistente *adj inv* (*ger*) resistant; **2** (*produto*) hardwearing, strong; **~ a traças** mothproof; **~ a fogo** flame resistant, fire-proof; **3** (*planta*) hardy; **4** (*pessoa*) strong, healthy; **5** (*que se opõe*) resistant to.

resistir *vi*: **~a** to resist to, stand up to; **2** (*durar*) to last, defy; **~ à velhice** to defy old age; (*roupa*) **~ ao uso** wear well.

resma *f* ream.

resmungão,-gona *m,f* grumbler, grouch; ♦ *adj* grumpy, crotchety, cantankerous.

resmungar *vt/vi* to grumble, mutter.

resmunguice *f* whining, whinging; **~ de criança** whining; **2** grumbles, moaning; **tanta ~!** so much moaning!

resolução *f* (*ger*) resolution; **2** decision, resolve; **3** solution.

resoluto,-a *adj* resolute, determined.

resolver *vt* (*solucionar*) to solve; **2** (*decidir*) decide, resolve; **3** to settle; **ele resolveu a disputa** he settled the dispute; **4** (*JUR*) annul; ♦ **~-se** *vr*: **~ a** to make up one's mind to; **2** (*tumor*) disappear; **3** be reduced to.

resolvido,-a *adj* solved, resolved; (*pessoa*) determined; **2** (*combinado*) settled, closed; **um caso ~** a settled case;

respaldo *m* (*de cadeira, assento*) back; **2** (*de montanha*) slope.

respe(c)tivamente *adv* respectively.

respe(c)tivo,-a *adj* respective.

respeitar *vt* to respect, honour.

respeitável *adj* respected; **2** respectable; **3** (*algo*) considerable, sizeable.

respeito *m* (*deferência*) **~ a /por** respect; **a ~ de/com ~ a** (*sobre*) as to, as regards, about; **dizer respeito a** to concern; **faltar ao ~ a** to be rude to; **respeitos** *mpl* regards; ♦ *adv* **com o devido ~** with due respect.

respeitoso,-a *adj* respectful, polite, reverent.

respingar *vt/vi* to splash, spatter (*alguém, algo*); **2** (*responder de forma agressiva*) answer back.

respingo *m* splash.

respiração *f* breathing; **2** (*fôlego*) breath; **3** (*MED*) respiration.

respirador *m* respirator.

respiradouro *m* vent.

respirar *vt/vi* to breathe; **2** (*descansar*) to have a respite; **3** (*fig*) (*sentir alívio*) breathe freely; **4** (*fig*) (*fruir*) enjoy.

respiratório,-a *adj* respiratory.

respiro *m* (*respiração*) breath; **2** (*fig*) rest; **3** (*abertura*) vent.

resplandecente *adj* resplendent.

resplandecer *vi* to gleam, shine (out).

resplendor *m* brilliance; (*fig*) splendour; glory.

respondão,-ona *adj* insolent, snappy.

responder *vt/vi* to answer; **~ por** to be responsible for, answer for.

responsabilidade *f* responsibility, duty; **assumir a ~** to take on the responsibility **2** (*COM*) **sociedade de ~ limitada** limited liability company; **3** (*ECON, JUR*) liability; **4 ficar à ~ de** be left in someone's charge.

responsabilizar *vt* **~ alguém** to hold sb responsible, blame sb; ♦ **~-se** *vr*: **~ por** to take responsibility for, take charge of.

responsável *m,f* person in charge; **2** (*culpado*) person responsible; ♦ *adj inv* **~ por** responsible for; liable for; **2** (*consciente*) sensible, reliable.

resposta *f* answer, reply; **2** (*reacção*) response; **3** (*de mau modo*) retort; **4** (*JUR*) appeal; **5** (*MED*) reaction.

resquício *m* (*vestígio*) trace, fragment; **2** (*pequeno fragmento*) residue; **3** (*frincha*) crack, gap.

ressaca *f* (*do mar*) undertow, surf; **2** (*fluxo e refluxo*) ebb and flow; **3** (*fig*) (*de bebida*) hangover; **4** (*fig*) after-effects.

ressaibo *m* unpleasant taste; **2** (*fig*) (*indício*) trace, sign; **3** resentment.

ressaltar *vt* to emphasize, underline; ♦ *vi* to stand out.

ressalva *f* note, precaution; **2** (*MIL*) (*certidão de isenção*) exemption certificate; **3** correction; **4** (*documento de salvaguarda*) safe conduct, safeguard; **5** exception; ♦ **sem ~** *adv* freely, without restrictions.

ressarcimento *m* compensation, reparation.

ressarcir *vt* to compensate (for); **~ alguém de** to compensate sb for.

ressecar vt (roupa, terra) dry up, overdry; **2** (MED) to resect; ♦ vi become dry, dry out.

ressentido,-a adj hurt, resentful.

ressentimento m resentment.

ressentir-se vr: ~ **de** (sentir mágoa) to resent, be hurt by; **2** (sofrer) to suffer from, feel the effects of.

ressequido,-a adj parched; dried up, overdried.

ressoar vi to resound, to echo.

ressonância f (acústicos) resonance; **2** echo; **3** (MED, FÍS, MÚS) resonance; ~ **magnética, RM** magnetic resonance, MR; **caixa de** ~ soundbox.

ressonar vt to snore.

ressurgimento m resurgence; **2** revival.

ressurgir vi to reappear; **2** (revitalizar-se) to revive.

ressurreição f resurrection.

ressuscitar vt to revive, resuscitate.

restabelecer vt to re-establish **2** restore; ♦ ~**-se** vr to recover, recuperate.

restabelecido,-a adj (saúde) recovered.

restante m (resto) rest, remainder; **ela vai comigo, o** ~ **fica aqui** she is coming with me, the rest (of you) can stay here; ♦ adj remaining.

restar vi (sobrar) to be left over; **não lhe resta nada** he has nothing left; **2** (faltar) **resta-me comprar o casaco** I still have the coat to buy; **3** (subsistir) to remain; **resta dizer que ...** it remains to say/be said.

restauração f repair, restoration; **2** (saúde) recovery; **3** re-establishment (de um pacto); **4** R~ **da monarquia** Restoration of the monarchy.

restaurante m restaurant.

restaurar vt (reparar) to restore; **2** to recover; **3** (renovar) to renew; **4** re-establish (tradição).

réstia f (de luz) ray, beam; **uma** ~ **de esperança** a ray of hope; **2** (de cebolas) string (of onions).

restituição f restitution, return; repayment.

restituir vt (devolver) to return, give back; **2** (compensar) to repay; **3** (restaurar) to restore.

restituível adj inv restitutory; restorable; returnable.

resto m rest, remainder; **o** ~ **do dia passei-o ao sol** I spent the rest of the day in the sun; **o** ~, **não interessa** otherwise, it is of no interest; **2** ~**s** mpl remains; **os** ~**s mortais** the mortal remains; **3** (de comida) scraps, leftovers; **dei os** ~**s ao cão** I gave the scraps to the dog; **4** (fig) (um pouco) vestige; **5** (MAT) left over; ♦ adv **de resto** besides, in any case.

restolho m (o que fica na terra depois da ceifa) stubble; **2** (BR) (de pouco valor) leftovers, pl; residue.

restrição f restriction.

restringir vt to restrict; to reduce.

restritivo,-a adj restrictive.

restrito,-a adj restricted; reduced.

resultado m result, score; **dar** ~ to succeed.

resultante f outcome, result; **2** (FÍS, GEOM) resultant: ♦ adj inv resulting.

resultar vi ~ **de** (ter origem) to result (from); **disto resulta que**; from this, it follows that; **2** ~ **em** end in; **o concurso resultou numa desordem** the contest ended in disorder; **3** to turn out to be.

resumido,-a adj abbreviated, abridged; **2** concise; **3** ~ **a** reduced to; **o contracto ficou** ~ **a nada** the contract was reduced to nothing.

resumir vt to abbreviate; **2** to sum up; **3** to reduce; ♦ ~**-se** vr: ~ **a** to consist in/of; be summed up.

resumo m summary, résumé, précis, brief; ♦ **em** ~ adv in short, briefly.

resvaladiço,-a adj (caminho, encosta) slippery.

resvalamento m sliding.

resvalar vt (deslizar) to slip, roll, skid; **o carro resvalou colina abaixo** the car skidded downhill; **2** to slide, glide.

resvés adv even with, close; **2** just right, exactly; **3** near enough.

reta,-o (Vd: **recta, recto**).

retábulo m altar-piece.

retaguarda f (MIL) rearguard; **2** back, rear.

retalhar vt (em pedaços) to cut up; **2** divide up; **3** (papel, tecido) cut out; **4** (golpear) to slash; **5** (dilacerar) hurt, break.

retalho m remnant, piece; **colcha de retalhos** patchwork quilt; **2 vender/comprar a** ~ to sell/buy at retail.

retaliação f retaliation.

retaliar vt to retaliate, retort.

retardado,-a m,f (PSIC) mentally retarded; ♦ adj delayed, prorogued.

retardar vt to hold up, slow down; **2** to postpone.

retardatário,-a m,f latecomer; ♦ adj (pessoa) late, tardy.

retardo m (retardamento) (BR) (PSIC) retardedness.

retenção f (MED) (de líquidos) retention; **2** detention.

reter vt to retain; **2** hold up, detain; ♦ ~**-se** vr to restrain o.s.

retesado,-a adj taut; **2** (alguém) stiff.

retesar vt to tighten; **2** to tense, to stretch; ~ **a vela** to flatten the sail.

reticência f reticence, reserve; **2** ~**s** fpl (sinal gráfico) (3 pontinhos) ellipsis.

reticente adj reticent.

reticulado m mesh, network; ♦ adj netlike.

retidão (Vd: **re(c)tidão**).

retifi- (Vd: **rectify**).

retina (ANAT) retina.

retinir vt (tinir) to clink, ring, jingle, clang; **2** (ressoar) to resound.

retinite f (MED) retinitis, inflammation of the retina.

retintim (pl: -tins) m jingling, clanging; **2** the sound of brass instruments.

retinto,-a adj (tingido de novo) re-dyed; **2** (cor muito escura) pitch, inky.

retirada f withdrawal, retreat; **bater em** ~ to beat a retreat.

retirado,-a adj (pessoa) retiring; **2** (lugar) isolated, remote.

retirar vt (dinheiro, etc) to withdraw; **2** (tirar) to remove; **3** (retrair) take back; ♦ vi to withdraw (ajuda); ♦ vr to retire.

retiro m (isolamento) retreat; **2** (lugar) hideaway, haunt; **3** (casa de fados) traditional fado restaurant; **4** (BR) ranch.

reto,-a (*Vd:* **re(c)to,-a**).

retocar *vt (pintura, etc)* to touch up; **2** *(texto)* to tidy up, to perfect.

retomar *vt (tomar de novo)* to take up again, resume, return to *(posição)*; **2** *(reaver)* to take back, regain.

retoque *m* finishing touch.

retorcer *vt (torcer de novo)* to twist; **2** *(roupa)* wring out over and over; ♦ **~-se** *vr* wriggle, writhe; **2** *(mover os lábios)* twist; *(os olhos)* roll (the eyes) upwards; **3** *(fig) (usar evasivas)* to dodge, try everything.

retorcido,-a *adj* twisted, winding; **2** *(espiralado)* coiled; **3** **bigode** ~ twisted, turned up; **4** *(fig) (discurso, escrita)* elaborate; **5** *(fig) (alguém, mente)* warped, twisted.

retórica *f* rhetoric; **figura de** ~ figure of speech; **poder de** ~ persuasive power.

retornado,-a *m,f* a person who returns to his/her country of origin from the ex-colonies; expatriate.

retornar *vt* to return, regress; **2** *(retomar)* come/go back (a to).

retorno *m* return; **2** retrogression; **3** *(COM)* barter, exchange.

retorquir *vt* to retort; *vi* reply, answer back.

retra(c)ção *f* contraction; **2** shrinkage; *(da gengiva)* receding.

retra(c)tar *vt* to retract, recant.

retráctil (*pl:* **-eis**) *adj inv* retractable.

retraído,-a *adj* retracted; **2** *(fig)* reserved, timid;

retraimento *m* withdrawal; contraction; *(fig)* timidity, shyness.

retrair *vt* pull in, draw in; **o caracol retrai o corpo** the snail pulls in its body; ♦ **~-se** *vr* to withdraw; go back (on); shrink.

retranca *f* crupper; **2** *(NÁUT)* boom; **3** *(frugalidade)* thrift, pinch *(fam)*; **à/na** ~ *adv (na poupança)* with a brake on spending, tightening the purse's strings.

retransmissor *m (TELECOM)* transmitter.

retratar, retra(c)tar *(fazer retrato)* depict, paint; **2** *(descrever)* portray.

retratista *m,f* portrait painter.

retrato *m* portrait, picture; **2** *(FOTO)* photo(graph); **3** description; IDIOM **ser o** ~ **de alguém** be the spitting image of sb.

retrato-robô *m* photo-fit, robot-picture.

retrete *f* toilet; *(pop)* the loo *(UK)*; the john *(US)*; **~s públicas** public toilets, WCs

retribuição *f* retribution, retaliation; **2** reward, recompense; **3** remuneration; ♦ **~-se** *vr* to portray o.s.

retribuir *vt* to reward, recompense; **2** to remunerate; **3** reciprocate; **4** to return, pay back *(elogios, desejos, visita)*.

retro *pref* back.

retroceder *vi (recuar)* to step back, fall back; **2** *(desistir)* ~ **em** to withdraw (from); **3** *(decair)* to decline, to regress.

retrocesso *m* setback; **2** step backwards; **3** recurrence; **4** *(COMP) (na tecla)* backspace; **5** *(ECOM)* slowdown.

retrógrado,-a *m,f* retrograde; backward; ♦ *adj* retrograde.

retroproje(c)tor *m* overhead projector.

retrós (*pl:* **-ses**) *m (costura)* twisted sewing silk thread; **2** *(BR) (cilindro de plástico, para enrolar o fio)* bobbin.

retrosaria *f (loja/departamento de artigos para costura)* haberdashery *(UK)*, notions *(US)*.

retrospectiva *f* retrospective; **2** *(recapitulação)* hindsight, recollection.

retrospectivo,-a *adj* retrospective.

retrospecto *m* retrospect; **em** ~ in retrospect.

retroversão *f* retroversion; **2** translation back into the source language.

retrovisor (*pl:* **-es**) *m* rear-view mirror.

retrucar (*Vd:* **retorquir**).

retumbante *adj inv (som)* loud, resounding; **2** *(fig) (fama, êxito)* resounding.

retumbar *vi* to resound, echo; **2** rumble.

réu *m* **ré** *f* defendant, accused.

reumático,-a *m,f* rheumatism sufferer; ♦ *adj* rheumatic.

reumatismo *m* rheumatism.

reumatologia *f* rheumatology.

reunião *f* meeting; **vou assistir à** ~ I am going to attend the meeting; **2** ~ **de cúpula** *(BR)* summit; **3** reunion: party.

reunir *vt* to bring/join together; **2** *(juntar)* to gather; **3** unite; ♦ **~-se** *vr (aliar-se)* to be combined; **2** to meet, gather.

Rev.º *(abr de* **Reverendo***)* Reverend, Rev.

revalidar *vt* to renew, revalidate.

revanche *f* **revanchismo** *m (desforra)* revenge, spite, vengeance; **2** *(FUT)* return match.

revelação *f* revelation; **2** *(FOTO)* development.

revelar *vt* to reveal, show; **2** *(FOTO)* develop; ♦ **~-se** *vr* to turn out to be.

revelia *f* defiance, default; **à** ~ *(JUR)* by default; **2** **à** ~ *adv (ao acaso)* to luck; **3** **à** ~ **de** *prep* in defiance of.

revenda *f* resale, wholesale; **desconto para** ~ trade discount.

revendedeira *f* wholesaler; **~s** *(do carros)* dealer.

revendedor *m,f* middleman, wholesaler.

revender *vt* to resell.

rever *vt* to see again; **2** to scrutinize; **3** to check, revise.

reverberar *vt (luz, calor)* reverberate, reflect; ♦ *vi (brilhar)* shine brightly.

Not in the sense of sound. Vd: **retumbar**.

---

reverdecer *vt/vi* to turn green again.

reverência *f* reverence, respect; **2** bow, curtsey.

reverenciar *vt* to revere, venerate; **2** to obey.

reverendo,-a *m* priest, clergyman; ♦ *adj* venerable.

reverente *adj* reverent, respectful.

reversão *f* reversion.

reversível *adj* reversible.

reverso *m* reverse; **o** ~ **da medalha** *(fig)* the other side of the coin.

reverter *vi (retroceder)* ~ **a** return to, revert; **2** ~ **a favor de alguém** to revert to sb: ~ **em favor de** in sb's favour.

revés *m (inverso)* reverse, inside out; **2** *(contrariedade)* setback, mishap, vicissitude; ♦ **ao** ~ *adv* back to front; **ao** ~ **de** contrary to, against; **de** ~ *(olhar)* sideways, askance; **2** *(tiro)* slanting.

revestimento *m* covering, wrapping; **2** lining, coating; cladding; **3** *(MEC)* lagging; **4** *(CONSTR)* ~ **a argamassa** buttering.

revestir *vt* to put on, to don *(traje de gala)*; **2** to cover, coat; ~ **de azulejos a parede** to cover the wall with tiles; ♦ ~**-se** *vr*: ~ **de** *(munir-se)* to summon up *(coragem, etc)*; **2** ~ **de autoridade** assume authority, give o.s. airs.

revezar *vt* to relieve, substitute *(alguém)*, alternate; ♦ ~**-se** *vr* to take turns, rotate, relieve one another.

revigorar *vt* to refresh, reinvigorate *(alguém)*; ♦ ~**-se** *vr* become stronger.

revirado,-a *adj (casa, etc)* untidy, upside down.

revirar *vt* to turn over/upside down; turn inside out *(bolso, camisa)*; **2** *(remexer)* turn out *(gavetas, etc)*; **3** *(os olhos)* to roll *(one's eyes)*; to rotate; ♦ *vr (dar voltas na cama)* twist and turn.

reviravolta *f (mudança radical)* turnabout; **2** *(giro em torno de si)* spin, pirouette; **3** sudden turn.

revisão *f (do trabalho)* revision; ~ **de provas** proofreading; **2** *(de máquinas)* overhaul; **3** *(carro)* service; **4** *(JUR)* re-evaluation.

revisar *vt* to revise; **2** to check.

revisor,-ora *(pl: -res) m,f* ticket inspector; **2** *(TIPO)* proofreader; ♦ *adj* checking.

revisor oficial de contas (R.O.C.) *(FIN, COM)* officially registered accountant; chartered accountant.

revista *f (JUR)* review; **2** *(MIL)* inspection, review; **3** magazine, *(académico)* journal; **4** *(TEAT)* revue; **5** *(busca)* search; **passar** ~ **a uma casa** to inspect the house; **passar em** ~ *(tropas)* to review.

revistar *vt* to search, check through.

revoada *f* taking flight *(again)*; **uma** ~ **de andorinhas** a flock of swallows in flight; **2** *(de folhas)* whirl.

revocar *vt (fazer lembrar)* to recall; **2** *(restituir)* to give back.

revogação *f* repeal.

revogar *vt (JUR)* to revoke, repeal; **2** *(cancelar)* to cancel.

revolta *f* revolt, revolution.

revoltar *vt* to disgust; ♦ ~**-se** *vr* to rebel, revolt.

revolto,-a *(irr pp de* **revolver***) adj* turbulent; troubled; **2** *(pessoa, casa, etc)* untidy; **3** *(mar, etc)* rough; **4** *(terra)* dug up; **5** *(multidão)* rebellious.

revolução *f* revolution.

revolucionar *vt* to revolutionize.

revolucionário,-a *adj* revolutionary.

revolver *vt (examinar)* to go over; **2** rummage through; **3** *(olhos)* roll; **4** *(terra)* turn over; ♦ *vi* to revolve; **2** to roll over.

revólver *m* revolver, gun.

rezar *vt* to pray; **2** *(missa)* to say, celebrate *(mass)*; ♦ *vi* to pray; **2** *(ler, dizer)* to say (read); **o livro reza que** the book says that.

ria *f (GEOG)* estuary, canal.

riacho *m* stream, brook.

riba *f* high riverbank; ♦ *adv (pop)* **à** ~ on the banks of; **de** ~ from up,/from North; ♦ *prep* **para** ~ **de** *(pop) (para cima de)* **para** ~ **do Tejo** beyond the Tagus, north of the Tagus.

ribalta *f (luzes)* footlights *pl*; **2** *(espectáculo)* theatre, stage; **3** *(fig) (cena)* limelight.

ribanceira *f* steep river bank; **2** steep slope, cliff.

ribeira *f* riverside; **2** stream.

ribeirão *m (BR)* stream.

ribeirinho,-a *adj* riverside.

ribeiro *m* brook, stream; *(US)* creek.

ribombar *vi (trovão)* to rumble; **2** *(canhão)* boom; **3** *(eco)* to resound.

ricaço,-a *m,f* very rich person.

rícino *m (BOT)* castor-oil plant; **óleo de** ~ castor oil.

rico,-a *m,f* rich person; ♦ *adj* rich, wealthy; **2** fertile; **3** sumptuous; **uma** ~**a mulher** *(fig)* a beautiful/sexy woman; **uma mulher** ~**a** a rich woman; **um** ~ **homem** a nice man; **um homem** ~ a rich man.

> Note the position of the adjective.

ricochete *m* ricochet; **fazer** ~ to rebound.

ridente *adj inv (alguém)* laughing, smiling; **2** *(expressão)* cheerful; **3** *(fig)* promising; **futuro** ~ promising/rosy future.

ridicularizar, ridiculizar *vt* to ridicule, make fun of, to mock, jeer at.

ridículo,-a *adj* ridiculous, laughable.

rifa *f (do sorteio)* raffle, raffle ticket.

rifão *m* proverb, saying.

rifar *vt* to raffle; **2** *(pop) (descartar)* to dump.

rigidez *f* rigidity, stiffness; **2** *(MED)* rigor mortis; **3** *(fig) (austeridade)* strictness, inflexibility, severity.

rígido,-a *adj (teso)* rigid, stiff; **2** *(material)* hard; **3** *(fig)* strict, severe, inflexible, harsh.

rigor *m* rigidity; harshness, severity; **2** precision; **a** ~ strictly speaking; **de** ~ essential, obligatory; **no** ~ **do inverno** in the depths of winter; **no** ~ **do verão** in the height of summer; **traje de** ~ formal dress; **criado a** ~ brought up strictly.

rigorosamente *adv* strictly; **2** precisely, exactly.

rigoroso,-a *adj* strict, harsh; **2** *(pessoa)* demanding; **3** precise, exact.

rijo,-a *adj (material)* tough, hard; **2** *(fruta verde)* unripe; **3** *(carne)* tough; **4** *(fig) (pessoa)* sturdy, strong; **um homem** ~ **apesar dos seus oitenta anos** he is still robust despite being eighty years old; **5** *(intense)*, heavy; **chuva** ~**a** heavy rain.

rim *(pl:* **rins***) m (ANAT)* kidney; **rins** *mpl (pop)* small of the back *sg*.

rima *f* rhyme; **2** verse, poem.

rimar *vt* to put into verse; ♦ *vi* to rhyme; **2** *(fig)* ~ **com** to agree with, tally with.

rímel *(pl: -eis) m* mascara.

rinçagem *f (BR)* rinse.

rinçar *vt* to rinse.

rinchar, rincho (*Vd:* **relinchar, relincho**).

ringue *m* (*DESP*) ring; **2** (*argola de borracha para jogar*) ring.

rinite *f* (*MED*) rhinitis.

rinoceronte *m* (*ZOOL*) rhinoceros.

rinque *m* (*DESP*) rink; ~ **de patinagem** roller-skating rink.

rio *m* river.

Rio de Janeiro *npr* o ~ Rio de Janeiro.

ripa *f* lath, batten, strip of wood.

ripar *vt* to lath (*paredes*); **2** cut wood in strips; **3** to strip fruit from its tree; **4** (*couve, alface*) rip out leaves; **5** to clear soil; **6** (*riçar o cabelo*) to backcomb.

ripostar *vt* to retort; to answer back; **2** to retaliate.

riquexó *m* rickshaw.

riqueza *f* wealth, riches *pl*; **2** (*luxo*) richness; **3** abundance; **4** fertility.

rir *vi*, **rir-se** *vr* to laugh; ~ **de** to laugh at.

risada *f* laughter; guffaw.

risca *f* (*traço*) line; **2** stripe; **blusa às ~** blouse with stripes; **3** (*cabelo*) parting; ♦ **à ~** *adv* to the letter, strictly.

riscar *vt* to score, mark; **2** (*fazer riscas na parede etc*) scratch; **3** to draw/trace lines on; **4** (*apagar*) cross out; **5** (*fósforo*) strike (*match*); **6** (*excluir alguém*) strikeout/off; ~ **alguém da lista** strike sb off the list.

risco *m* (*perigo*) risk, danger; **correr o ~** to run the risk; **2** (*traço*) scratch; **3** (*hair*) parting; **4** line; **5** (*esboço*) sketch.

risível *adj* laughable, ridiculous.

riso *m* laughter; **2** (*estrondoso*) guffaw, horse-laugh; **3** ~ **amarelo** wan smile; **morrer de riso** to split one's sides; **morri de** ~ I was in stitches.

risonho,-a *adj* laughing, smiling; **2** cheerful, happy.

risota *f* laughter; **2** giggle; **3** (*de escárneo*) sneer; **foi uma ~ pegada** it was laughter all the way.

rispidez *f* harshness.

ríspido,-a *adj* sharp, curt; **2** harsh.

riste *m*: **em ~** pointing; pointed; **orelhas em ~** pointed ears.

rítmico,-a *adj* rhythmic(al).

ritmo *m* rhythm.

rito *m* rite; cult.

ritual *m adj* ritual.

rival *m,f adj inv* rival.

rivalidade *f* rivalry.

rivalizar *vt* to rival; ♦ *vi*: ~ **com** to compete with, vie with.

rixa *f* quarrel, fight.

robalo *m* (*peixe*) sea bass.

robô/robot *m* robot.

robótica *f* automation, robotics, *sg.*

robustecer *vt* to strengthen; ♦ ~**-se** *vr* to become stronger.

robustez *f*, **robusteza** *f* robustness, vigour.

robusto,-a *adj* strong, robust.

R.O.C. (*abr de* **Revisor Oficial de Contas**) (*Vd:* **revisor**).

roça *f* plantation; **2** clearing of underwood; **3** (*BR*) (*campo*) country.

roçado *m* clearing of brush; **2** (*clareira*) clearing.

roçar *vt* (*terreno*) to clear; **2** to graze; ♦ *vi*: ~ **em/por** (*tocar de leve*) to graze, brush/rub against (sb).

roceiro (*BR*) *m* peasant, yokel; **2** farm-hand.

rocha *f* rock, ~ **calcária** limestone.

rochedo *m* crag, steep rock, reef; **2** (*ANAT*) petrous bone.

rochoso,-a *adj* rocky.

rococo *m* (*ARTE*) rococo style: ♦ *adj* over-elaborate, pretentious.

rocola *f* (*BOT*) (*enura*) (wild) rocket.

roda *f* (*ger*) wheel; ~~**-dentada** cog (wheel); **2** (*círculo*) circle; ~ **de amigos** a circle of friends; **3 alta ~** high society; **4** (*de saia*) hoop; **saia com muita ~** full skirt; **5** (*fig*) lottery; **6 à ~ de** *prep* round, around; **7 cabeça à ~** head in a spin.

rodada *f* rotation; **2** (*de bebidas de um grupo*) round; **a próxima ~ pago eu** the next round is on me; **3** wheeltrack; **4** round-table meeting.

rodagem *f* (*MEC*) (*de máquinas*) set of wheels; **2 em ~** (*AUTO*) running-in; (*CIN*) filming; **3** (*em estrada*) **faixa de ~** (*em autoestrada*) lane.

rodapé *m* (*de página*) foot; **nota de ~** footnote; **2** (*parede*) skirting-board; **3** (*de cama*) valance.

rodar *m* moving, passing; ♦ *vt* to turn (*algo*); **2** (*distância*) cover; **3** (*CIN*) film, shoot; ♦ *vi* turn around; spin; roll down.

roda-viva *f* bustle, commotion; hustle and bustle; **andar numa ~** to rush to and fro.

rodear *vt* to go round; **2** encircle, surround.

rodeio *m* circumlocution; **2** (*evasiva*) subterfuge; **3** (*de gado*) round-up; IDIOM **deixe-se de ~s** stop beating about the bush; **fale sem ~s** speak frankly.

rodela *f* round slice; **uma ~ de chouriço** a slice of chourizo.

rodilha *f* rag; **2** (*para limpar*) dishcloth; **3** rolled cloth to put on the head for carrying heavy loads = cloth pad.

rodízio *m* (*para pés de mesa*) castor, caster; **2** (*em restaurante*) buffet service going round the tables.

rodo *m* (*AGR*) rake; **a ~s** *adv* in abundance, plenty.

rodopiar *vi* to whirl around, swirl.

rodopio spin; IDIOM **andar num ~** run/bustle around, be in a spin.

rodos (*Vd:* **rodo**).

rodovalho *m* (*peixe*) turbot.

rodovia *f* motorway (*UK*), highway (*US*).

rodoviário,-a bus transport, bus station; ♦ *f adj* relating to roads.

roedor,-ora *m* rodent; ♦ *adj* gnawing.

roer *vt* to gnaw, nibble; **2** ~ **as unhas** to bite the nails; **3** (*corroer*) erode; **4** (*fig*) (*inquietar*) gnaw at, weigh on (*mente, consciência*); ♦ *vr* ~~**-se de inveja** be green with envy; IDIOM **osso duro de ~** a hard nut to crack; ~ **a corda a (alguém)** (*negócio, promessa*) to let sb down.

rogado (*pp de vi* **rogar**) **fazer-se ~** to play hard to get.

rogar *vt/vi* to implore, entreat, beg; **2** (*orar*) pray; **3** ~ **pragas** to curse.

rogatório,-a *adj* pleading; **2** (*discurso em que se roga*) appealing; **3** (*JUR*) (*pedido a tribunal estrangeiro*) **carta ~a** rogatory letter.

rogo *m* plea, request; **a ~ de** at the request of; **4** prayer; **Deus oiça meus ~s** may God hear my prayers.

rogo *m (súplica)* plea, appeal; **2** request; **3** *(oração)* prayer; **assinar a ~** sign on behalf of an illiterate.

rojo: de ~ *adv* **levar algo, alguém de** ~drag sth/sb along (the ground); **andar de ~s** to crawl along the ground.

rol *m (lista)* list; **~ da equipagem** *(NÁUT)* muster-roll.

rola *f* (turtle)-dove.

rolamento *m* rolling *(of a ship)*; **2** *(MEC)* ball bearing.

rolante *adj inv* moving; **escada ~** escalator; **passadeira ~** *(no supermercado, airport)* travelator.

rolar *vt (virar cabeça)* to turn; **2 ~ um cigarro** roll a fag; **3** *(cair)* roll, fall; **4** rock; **5** to cut a tree trunk into logs; ♦ *vi (rola)* to coo.

roldana *f* pulley.

roldão *m* rashness, haste; **de ~** hastily, clumsily, pell-mell; **levar de ~ (algo)** to snatch sth.

roleta *f* roulette; **2 ~ russa** Russian roulette.

rolha *f (para garrafas)* cork, stopper; **tirar a ~** to uncork (a bottle); **2** *(fig)* gag; **meter uma ~ na boca (de alguém)** to shut sb up, gag sb; **lei da ~** censorship; IDIOM **cascos de ~ rolhar** *vt* to cork; the back of beyond.

rolhar *vt* to cork.

roliço,-a *adj* plump, chubby; **2** cylindrical.

rolo *m (para pintar paredes; nivelar solo)* roller; **2** *(para estender massa)* rolling pin; **3** *(papel, arame)* roll; *(FOTO)* roll of film; **4** *(TIPO)* cylinder roll; **5** *(para o cabelo)* rollers.

Roma *npr* Rome; IDIOM **ir a ~ e não ver o Papa** to go to a place famous for sth and fail to see it; **~ e Pavia não se fizeram num dia** Rome was not built in one day.

romã *f* pomegranate.

romagem *f* pilgrimage.

romance *m (LITER) (em prosa)* novel; **2** *(caso amoroso)* romance, romantic story; **~ policial** detective story, thriller; **3** *(LÍNG)* romance.

romanceado,-a *adj* exaggerated, fanciful.

romancear *vi* fantasize.

romancista *m,f* novelist.

românico,-a *adj (língua)* Romance; **românica(s)** *(línguas latinas* Romance languages; **2** *(ARQ)* Romanesque.

romano,-a *m,f adj* Roman.

romântico,-a *adj* romantic.

romantismo *m* romanticism.

romaria *f (peregrinação)* pilgrimage; **2** folk festival; **3** a throng of people going to the same event; crowd.

romãzeira *f* (BOT) pomegranate tree.

rombo *m (furo)* large hole; **2** *(MAT)* rhombus; **3** *(fig) (desfalque)* embezzlement; **4** *(fig)* deficit; ♦ *adj (ponta, faca)* blunt.

romeiro,-a *m,f* pilgrim.

Roménia *npr* **a ~** Romania.

romeno,-a *m,f adj* Romanian; ♦ *m (LÍNG)* **R~** Romanian.

rompante *m* outburst; impulse; **2** rashness; ♦ *adj* arrogant; **2** hasty; **de ~** *adv* busting in.

romper *m* **ao ~ do dia** at daybreak; ♦ *vt/vi* to tear, puncture *(pneu)*; **2** to break off; **3** *(sulcar os mares)* cut through (the waves); **~ o silêncio** break the silence; **~ pela multidão** push through the crowd; ♦ *vr* to get broken/torn; broken off.

rompimento *m* hole, rupture; **2** *(de cano, barragem)* bursting; **3** *(de relações, negócios)* break, breaking-off.

roncar *vi (no sono)* to snore; **2** *(grunhir)* grunt.

ronco *m* snore; *(MED)* rale; **2** grunt; **3** *(ruído)* rumble.

ronda *f* patrol, beat; **fazer a ~** to go the rounds; **2** *(fig) (conversações)* talks, round-table talks; **3** *(DESP)* round.

rondar *vt* to patrol; **2** *(espreitar)* to prowl, go round; **3** *(cifrar)* around/about; **o salário dele ronda uns vinte milhões** his salary is about 60 million; ♦ *vi* to prowl about, lurk.

ronha *f (VET)* mange, scabies; **2** *(pop)* wile, artfulness; **estás doente a sério ou estás na ~** are you really sick or are you pretending?

ronqueira *f* wheeze.

ronrom *m (do gato)* purring.

ronronar *vi* to purr.

roque *m (no xadrês)* rook; **2** *(MÚS) (dança)* rock (and roll); IDIOM **sem rei nem ~** at sixes and sevens, any-which-way.

ror *m (muitos)* heaps, loads, a lot of, a pile; **um ~ de caixotes** a pile of boxes.

rosa *f (BOT)* rose; **~ de lobo** peony; **~-moscada** musk rose; ♦ *adj inv* rose-coloured, pink; **2** *(ARQ)* rose window; **3 ~ dos ventos** *f (NÁUT)* compass card/points; wind-rose; **4** *(fig) pl* happiness, joys *pl*; **mar de ~s** a sea of roses.

rosácea *f (ARQ)* rose-window, rosace.

rosáceas *fpl (BOT)* rosaceae.

rosado,-a *adj* rosy, pink; **2** *(vinho)* rosé.

rosário *m (REL)* rosary.

rosbife *m* roast beef.

rosca *f (de saca-rolhas, etc)* spiral; **2** *(da cobra)* coil; **3** *(MEC)* thread; **~ do parafuso** screw-thread; **4** ring-shaped loaf *(of bread)*; **5** *(tampa de frasco, etc)* screw cap; **6** *(pop) (embriaguês)* skinful.

roscar *vt* to screw in.

roseira *f* rosebush.

roséola *f* rash.

roseta *f (roda dentada)* rowel; **2** *(na lapela)* rosette.

rosmaninho *m* rosemary.

rosnar *vi (pessoa)* to mutter, mumble; grumble; **2** *(animal)* to growl, snarl.

rossio *m* large square.

rosto *m (ANAT)* face; **2 página de ~** title page; **3** *(do edifício)* frontispiece; IDIOM **lançar em ~** *(acusar)* to throw accusations/insults in one's face.

rota *f* route, course; **2** *(fig) (caminho)* track, way; **3 em/de ~ batida** in full speed, without stopping.

rotação *f* rotation.

rotativo,-a *adj* rotative, alternate.

roteiro *m* itinerary; **2** *(de viagem)* guide-book, road map; **3** *(NÁUT)* log-book; **4** *(fig)* norm, rule; **5** *(BR) (CIN)* script.

rotina *f* routine.

rotineiro,-a *adj* routine.

roto,-a (*irr pp de* **romper**) *adj* ruptured; torn; in rags, with holes; IDIOM **ser mãos ~as** be open-handed.

rótula *f* (*ANAT*) kneecap, patella.

rotular *adj inv* rotatory; ♦ *vt* to label; 2 (*fig*) (*qualificar*) classify, label (*alguém*).

rótulo *m* label, tag.

rotunda *f* (*círculo de ruas*) roundabout; 2 (*ARQ*) rotunda.

rotundo,-a *adj* (*redondo*) round; 2 (*gordo*) plump, rotund.

roubalheira *f* (*muitos furtos*) robbery, thieving; 2 (*fig*) (*preço exagerado*) daylight robbery; outright robbery.

roubar *vt* (*furtar, plagiar*) to steal; 2 (*casa, banco, etc*) rob; ~ **um beijo** to steal a kiss.

roubo *m* theft, robbery; stolen goods.

rouco,-a *adj* hoarse.

roufenho,-a *adj* (*voz fanhosa*) nasal-sounding.

rouge *f* (*cosmético*) blusher.

roupa *f* clothes *pl*, clothing; ~ **de baixo** underwear; ~ **de cama** bedclothes *pl*, bed linen; ~ **domingueira** Sunday best (*clothes*); ~ **usada** secondhand clothing; **à queima-~** point-blank; IDIOM **chegar a ~ ao pêlo a** (**alguém**) give sb a hiding; ~ **suja se lava em casa** don't wash your dirty linen in public.

roupagem *f* clothing, apparel; 2 (*fig*) appearance.

roupão *m* dressing gown; (*de banho*) bathrobe.

roupeiro *m* clothes cupboard; ♦ **roupeiro,-a** *m,f* closet assistant, person in charge of locker room (*em clube*).

roupeta *f* (*batina*) cassock; 2 (*pej*) (*padreca*) jesuit.

rouquidão *f* hoarseness.

rouxinol (*pl: - óis*) *m* (*ZOOL*) nightingale.

roxo,-a *adj* (*cor*) purple, violet.

RP (*abr de* **relações públicas**) *fpl* public relations, PR.

RTP (*abr de* **Radiotelevisão Portuguesa**) Portuguese TV Station.

rua *f* street; ~ **de sentido único** one-way street; ♦ *exc* (*fam*) ~! get out!, clear off; **pôr no olho da ~** (*fam*) kick sb out.

rubéola *f* (*MED*) rubella, German measles.

rubescência *f* reddening, flush, rubescence.

rubi *m* ruby.

rubor *m* blush, flush; 2 (*fig*) shyness, bashfulness.

ruborizar *vt* go red, redden; 2 embarrass (*alguém*); ♦ *vr* to blush.

rubrica *f* (*assinatura*) rubric; (*assunto*) rubric, item; ~ **de capítulo** heading of a chapter; 2 instructions to actors; 3 (*assinatura*) initials *pl*.

rubricar *vt* to initial, countersign.

rubro,-a *adj* bright red, glowing; 2 (*rosto*) ruddy; 3 ~ **branco** white heat; 4 **ao ~** red hot.

ruço,-a *adj* (*cor*) dun; 2 (*tecido*) worn; 3 sandy hair; 4 (*grisalho*) grey-haired; 5 (*BR*) (*fig*) tricky; 6 (*BR*) *m* dense fog.

rude *adj inv* (*algo*) rough, crude, rustic; 2 (*grosseiro*) (*alguém*) uncouth, boorish; 3 (*tempo, trabalho*) harsh, hard.

rudeza *f* roughness, crudity.

rudimentar *adj inv* rudimentary, primitive, elementary.

rudimento *m* rudiment; ~**s** *mpl* rudiments; (*fig*) principles.

ruela *f* lane, alleyway.

rufar *vt* (*tambor*) to beat, play; 2 (*vestido, saia*) ruffle, pleat; ♦ *vi* to drum.

rufião (*pl:* **rufiões/rufiães**) *m* ruffian, hooligan; 2 (*que vive à custa de prostitutas*) pimp.

ruflar *vt* (*agitar as asas*) to flutter, flit; **o pombo ruflava as asas** the pigeon fluttered its wings; 2 (*tafetá*) to rustle.

ruga *f* (*na pele*) wrinkle; 2 (*na roupa*) crease.

rúgbi *m* rugby.

ruge-ruge *m* rustling sound (*da seda*); 2 child's bell; 3 rumour, gossip.

rugido *m* (*de leão*) roar; 2 (*grito semelhante*) roar; ~ **do mar,** the roaring of the sea.

rugir *vi* to roar; 2 bellow; 3 to thunder.

rugoso,-a *adj* (*pele*) wrinkled; 2 (*roupa, papel*) creased, crampled; 3 (*terreno*) rough, uneven, rugged.

ruído *m* noise, din.

ruidoso,-a *adj* noisy.

ruim *adj inv* bad,wicked, evil (*person*); 2 (*BR*) useless, faulty.

ruína *f* (*degradação*) ruin; 2 (*colapso*) downfall, destruction; 3 (*falência*) ruin.

ruínas *fpl* ruins, remains.

ruindade *f* wickedness; 2 poor quality.

ruir *vi* to collapse; 2 (*fig*) (*desintegrar-se*) crumble away, fall apart; 3 (*fig*) go into ruin.

ruivo,-a *m,f* redhead; 2 (*ZOOL*) (*ave*) redwing, thrush; 3 (*peixe*) gurnard; ♦ *adj* (*alguém*) redhead, auburn.

rum *m* rum.

rumar *vi* (*NÁUT*) to steer course (*barco*) 2 ~ **para** head for.

ruminante *m* (*ZOOL*) ruminant.

ruminar *vt/vi* to ruminate, chew the cud; 2 (*fig*) to ponder, brood over.

rumo *m* (*do compasso*) rhumb; 2 (*direcção*) course, route; 3 *prep* ~ **a** bound for, toward; **sem** ~ *adj* adrift, aimless; 4 ~ **de vida** way of life.

rumor *m* (*de vozes*) hum, buzz; 2 (*do rio*) murmur; 3 (*boato*) rumour (*UK*); rumor (*US*).

rumorejante *adj inv* murmuring; whispering.

rumorejar *vi* to murmur, to whisper.

rupestre *adj inv* (*planta*) rupestrian, growing on rocks.

rupia *f* (*unidade monetária*) rupee.

ruptura *f* hole, rupture; 2 ~ **no cano** burst pipe; 3 (*MED*) rupture, hernia; 4 (*fig*) break, break off (*relações*); 5 breach.

rural *adj inv* rural, rustic.

rusga *f* (*pequena briga*) brawl; 2 (*batida policial*) search, raid; **fazer uma** ~ to make a search.

Rússia *npr* Russia; **a** ~ Russia.

russo,-a *m,f adj* Russian; (*LÍNG*) Russian.

rústico,-a *adj* rustic; 2 unsophisticated, simple.

ruténio/roténio *m* (*QUÍM*) ruthenian.

rutilante *adj inv* (*cor*) bright, shining; 2 (*luz*) shining, bright.

rutilar *vt* to shine, to glitter.

rutura (*Vd:* **ruptura**).

S

S, s *m (letra)* S, s.

S. (*abr de* **Sul**) South; **2** (*abr de* **Santo/Santa/São**) Saint.

sã *f* (*Vd:* **são**).

S.A. (*abr de* **Sociedade Anónima**) *f* limited company, Ltd.

Saara *npr* o (**deserto do**) ~ Sahara Desert.

saariano,-a *adj* Saharian.

sábado *m* Saturday; **aos** ~**s** on Saturdays; **no** ~ on Saturday; **no** ~ **passado** last Saturday; **no próximo** ~ next Saturday; **todos os** ~**s** every Saturday; **S~ de Aleluia** Easter Saturday.

sabão *m* soap; ~ **em pó** washing powder; **2** (*fig*) (*pop*) (*reprimenda*) **passar um** ~ **a** (**alguém**) to tell sb off.

sabático,-a *adj* sabbatical; **licença** ~ sabbatical leave.

sabedor,-ora *m, f* (*person*) informed; **2** with knowledge.

sabedoria *f* (*bom senso*) wisdom, common sense; **2** knowledge.

saber *m* knowledge; common sense; learning; **a** ~ *adv* namely; ♦ *vt* to know; to know how to, can ~ **de cor e salteado** to know off by heart; **ele sabe nadar?** can he swim?; **sabe-se lá!/sei lá!** (*fam*) who knows! you can never tell!; **que eu saiba, não** not that I know of; **2** (*indagar*) find out; **3** (*ter notícia*) hear, learn; **soube que ele tinha partido** I learnt he had left; ♦ *vi* to taste; **sabe bem** it tastes good; ~ **a** to taste of; **2** ~ **de** (*interessar-se por*) to ask after sb; **quero** ~ **da Ana** I want to ask about Ana.

sabiá (*ZOOL*) *m* mockingbird.

sabichão,-ona *m,f* (*fam*) know-all, smart alec.

sabido,-a *m,f* shrewd, cunning person; ♦ *adj* (*aprendido*) learned; **2** (*conhecedor*) knowledge-able; **3** (*conhecimento geral*) **como é** ~ as is know; ♦ (*person*) astute; cunning, sly; IDIOM **é certo e** ~ everyone knows it; it is a well-known fact.

sábio,-a *m,f* scholar, learned person, sage; ♦ *adj* learned, wise.

sabões (*pl de* **sabão**).

sabonete *m* toilet soap.

sabor *m* taste, flavour; wit; ♦ *prep* **ao** ~ **de** at the mercy of.

saborear *vt* to relish, savour.

saboroso,-a *adj* tasty, delicious.

sabotador,-ora *m* saboteur.

sabotagem *f* sabotage.

sabotar *vt* to sabotage.

sabrina *f* (*calçado*) pump.

sabugo *m* (*ANAT*) root of a nail; **2** pith of an elder tree.

sabugueiro *m* elder tree; **baga de** ~ *f* elderberry.

sabujar *vt* to flatter, cringe.

sabujo,-a *m,f* cringer; fawner.

saburrento,-a *adj* (*crosta branco-amarelada na língua em doença*) furry; **2** (*animal, tecido*) furry.

saca *f* sack, large bag.

sacada *f* (*ARQ*) balcony; **janela de** ~ French window; **2** (*saco cheio*) sackful.

sacado,-a *m,f* (*COM*) drawee.

sacador,-ora *m,f* (*COM*) drawer (*de cheque*).

sacana *m, adj* (*cal*) (*canalha*) swine, bastard; **2** (*esperto*) sharp, foxy; **3** (*BR*) (*libertino*) randy; **4** (*brincalhão*) raffish, mischievous.

sacanagem *f* (*EP*) **sacanice** *f* (*BR*) dirty trick; **2** (*libidinagem*) screwing; **3** rascals.

sacão *m* (*puxão violento*) jerk, jolt; **2** (*do cavalo para sacudir o cavaleiro*) buck.

sacar *vt* (*arma, etc*) to take out, pull out; **2** (*tirar à força*) snatch; **3** (*no banco*) withdraw (*quantia*); ~ (**contra/sobre**) draw (against/from); **4** get, obtain (*dados*); **5** (*DESP*) serve; **6** (*fam*) (*compreender*) get, catch.

sacarina *f* saccharin.

saca-rolhas *m sg/pl* corkscrew(s).

sacerdócio *m* priesthood.

sacerdote *m* priest.

sachar *vt* to hoe, weed; **2** (*escavar*) dig over, rake, grub up.

sachê *f* (*BR*) sachet.

sacho *m* weeding-hoe.

saciante *adj inv* satisfying; **saciar** *vt* to satiate; **2** to quench (*sede*); ♦ ~**-se** *vr* to be contented; **2** (*fartar-se*) to be satisfied to the full.

saco *m* sack, bag; ~ **de água quente** hot-water bottle; ~ **de dormir** sleeping bag; **2** (*cavidade de organismo*) sac; **3** (*BR*) (*vulg*) (*testículos*) balls; **encher o** ~ **de** (*alguém*) (*BR: col*) to annoy, get one's goat (*col*); IDIOM **meter a viola no** ~ shut up; **cair em** ~ **roto** to fall on stony ground; **despejar o** ~ get it off one's chest, to spit it out (*col*).

sacola *f* (*school*) satchel; **2** (*bornal de pedinte*) bag, bundle; **3** (*alforge*) saddlebag.

sacramento *m* (*REL*) sacrament.

sacrário *m* (*REL*) tabernacle.

sacrificar *vt* to sacrifice.

sacrifício *m* sacrifice; **2** (*prejudicar*) damage; ♦ ~**-se** *vr* endure, suffer; **2** (*sujeitar-se*) give in to.

sacrilégio *m* sacrilege.

sacrílego,-a *adj* sacrilegious.

sacristão *m* sacristan, sexton.

sacristia *f* (*REL*) sacristy; vestry.

sacro *m* (*ANAT*) sacrum; ♦ **sacro,-a** *adj* sacred; **2** (*ANAT*) sacral.

sacudidela *f* shake, jolt.

sacudido,-a *adj* (*pano do pó, tapete*) shaken; **2** (*pessoa*) quick, energetic.

sacudir *vt* to shake; **ela sacudiu o pano de pó** she shook the duster; **2** dust/brush off (*pó, poeira*);

3 *(abanar)* shake *(cabeça)*; 4 *(agitar)* **o cão agitava a cauda** the dog wagged his tail; 5 *(mar)*
rocked *(barco)*; ~ **levemente** joggle, jolt.

sádico,-a *m,f* sadist.

sadina, sadino *adj* relating to the Portuguese river
Sado, or the city of Setúbal.

sadio,-a *adj* healthy; wholesome.

sadismo *m* sadism.

safa ! *exc* phew! good heavens!

safado,-a *m (pop)* rogue; ♦ *adj (gasto)* worn out *(roupa)*;
2 faded *(desenho)*; 3 *(pop) (pessoa)* shameless.

safanão *m (puxão)* tug.

safar *vt* to pull off *(camisa)*; 2 *(NÁUT)* clear; 3 erase;
♦ ~-se *vr* escape, duck; *(barco)* heave off.

safari *m* safari.

safio *m (ZOOL)* conger eel.

safira *f* sapphire.

safo *adj (col) (de perigo)* clear; 2 *(livre)* free.

safra *f* harvest; **ano de** ~ good production year; 2
(pesca) fishing season; 3 *(bigorna)* smith's anvil; 4
hustle and bustle.

sagacidade *f* sagacity; 2 discernment; 3 shrewdness.

sagaz *adj inv* sagacious, intelligent; 2 shrewd, wise;
astute.

Sagitário *npr m (ASTRON, ASTROL)* Sagittarius.

sagração *f (REL) (bispo)* ordination, consecration.

sagrado,-a *m* holy; ♦ *adj* sacred, hallowed, sanctified.

sagrar *vt* to consecrate; 2 hallow, sanctify; 3 venerate,
respect; **a História sagra os nomes de ...** History
venerates the names of ...; ♦ *vr* ~-se win the title
(of); **Rosa Mota sagrou-se campeã mundial na
maratona** Rosa Mota became the world champion
in the marathon.

Sagres® *npr* well-known Portuguese beer; 2
(GEOG, HIST) place in Western Algarve.

It is believed the Sagres School for aspiring navigators
was founded in this place, from where the first caravels
would have departed in their conquest of the seas and of
the unknown world in the 14th century. Henry the Navigator
died nearby.

sagu *m (BOT)* sago palm; 2 *(CULIN) (tipo de farinha)*
sago.

saguão *m (pátio estreito)* inner yard/court; 2
(entrada) porch, lobby.

saia *f* skirt; ~ **escocesa** kilt; 2 ~s *(fam)* women;
andar atrás de ~s run after skirts; ~-**calça** *(pl:
saias-calça)* culottes.

saibro *m* gravel.

saída *f* exit, way out; 2 *(partida)* departure; 3 outing,
going out; 4 *(demissão)* resignation; 5 outlet; 6
(venda) sale, ready market; 7 **ter boas** ~s give
witty answers; IDIOM **beco sem** ~ blind alley;
deadlock.

saiote *m (saia debaixo de saia)* slip.

sair *vi* to go/come out; 2 to leave, depart; 3 *(parecer-se
a)* ~ **a** *(alguém)* take after (sb); ~ **bem** *(resultar)*
to turn out well; ~ **do emprego** to leave the job; ~
do *(avião, etc)* get off; ~ **do carro** get out; ~ **por**
(custar) to come to; ~ **caro** be expensive, cost

dearly; ♦ ~-se *vr*: ~-se **bem/mal** be successful/
unsuccessful; 2 *(dizer)* ~-se **com** to come out with.

sal *(pl: sais) m* salt; **uma pitada de** ~ a pinch of salt;
sem ~ *(manteiga)* unsalted; *(gosto)* bland; ~
amargo Epsom salts; 2 **sais de cheiro** smelling
salts.

sala *f* room; *(de visitas)* lounge, drawing room; ~ **de
jantar** dining room; ~ **de espera** waiting room; ~
de estar living room; ~ **de operações** operating
theatre; 2 *(EDUC: aula)* classroom; 3 *(NÁUT)*
deck saloon; ~ **de audiências** courtroom.

salabórdia *f* tastelessness; insipid talk.

salada *f (CULIN)* salad; 2 *(fig)* confusion, mix-up;
temperar a ~ season/dress the salad; 3 ~ **russa**
Russian salad; *(fig)* medley.

saladeira *f* salad-bowl.

salafrário *m (pop)* scoundrel, rascal.

salamaleque *m* salaam, Muslim greeting; 2 ~s *(fig)*
(mesura) exaggerated bow; bowing and scraping.

salamandra *f (ZOOL)* salamander; 2 *(mitolofia)*
Salamandra; 3 *(para aquecimento da casa)* wood-
burning stove.

salame *m* salami.

salão *m* large room, hall, salon, saloon; ~ **de vendas**
showroom; **jogos de** ~ indoor games; ~ **de bilhar**
billiards saloon.

salarial *adj inv (política, aumento)* relating to salary.

salário *m* wages *pl*, salary; ~ **líquido** net salary.

saldar *vt (contas)* to settle *(accounts)*; *(dívidas)* pay
off, liquidate; ~ **agravos antigos** settle old scores.

saldo *m* balance; 2 *(excedente)* surplus; 3 ~ **negativo**
debit balance, overdraft; 4 sale; 5 *(fig) (resultado)*
outcome.

saleiro *m* salt cellar; 2 *(moedor)* salt-mill.

saleta *f* small living-room.

salgadeira *f* salt-vat, tank for preserving meat.

salgadinho(s) *mpl (CULIN)* snacks; hors d'oeuvres.

salgado,-a *adj* salty, salted; 2 *(fig) (piada)* saucy,
risqué; 3 *(fig)* steep.

salgar *vt* to salt.

sal-gema *m* rock salt.

salgueiro *m* willow; ~ **chorão** weeping willow.

saliência *f* prominence, projection.

salientar *vt* to point out, stress, emphasize; 2
(ressaltar) highlight; ♦ *vr* stand out.

saliente *adj inv* jutting out, prominent, salient; 2 *(fig)*
(notável) outstanding, remarkable; 3 conspicuous.

salina *f (terreno)* salt-pan.

salino,-a *adj* saline.

salitre *m (QUÍM)* saltpetre, nitre.

salitroso,-a *adj (terra, água)* saliferous.

saliva *f* saliva; 2 *(baba)* slobber, dribble; 3 *(de cuspir)*
spittle.

salmão *m* salmon.

salmo *m (REL)* psalm.

salmonella *f (MED, VET)* salmonella.

salmonete *m (peixe)* red mullet.

salmoura *f* brine.

salobro,-a *adj* salty, brackish; 2 *(mar)* briny.

saloio,-a *m,f* from the outskirts north of Lisbon; 2
(pop, pej) country bumpkin, yokel *(UK)*; hillbilly

(US); (pej) (pessoa crédula) gullible, fool; **tu és uma ~a** you are an idiot; ♦ *adj:* **queijo/pão ~** home-made cheese/bread from that region; **esperteza ~a** low cunning, cheap, trick.

salpicado,-a *adj (peixe, carne)* sprinkled with salt; **2** *(roupa, parede)* splashed, spattered; **3** *(animal com pequenas malhas no pêlo)* speckled; **4** *(permeado)* dotted; **5** **~ com açúcar** dusted with sugar.

salpicar *vt* to sprinkle with salt; **2** *(deitar salpicos)* splash, spatter.

salpico *m (pingo sujo)* spot, speck; **2** *(um pouco de sal)* pinch of salt.

salsa *f (BOT)* parsley; **2** *(MÚS)* salsa.

salsada *f* mess; **2** muddle.

salseira *f* sauce boat.

salsicha *f* Portuguese sausage, a kind of chipolata.

salsichão *m* large garlic sausage.

salsicharia *f* sausages department, butcher-shop.

saltada *f* big leap; **2** *(assalto)* assault, attack; **3** **dar uma ~ (a casa de alguém)** to drop in, pay a sudden visit.

saltar *vt* to jump (over), leap (over); **2** *(passar)* skip, **você saltou duas páginas** you skipped/missed two pages; ♦ *vi (pular)* **~ (de/sobre)** jump (from, on), alight; **2 ~ da cama** jump out of bed; **3 ~ de contente** jump for joy; **4 ~ à corda** skip the rope; **5** come off; **o botão saltou do casaco** the button came off the coat; **6 ~ para trás** to start/spring back; **7 ~ por cima** jump over; **8 ~ à vista/aos olhos** to be obvious, strike the eye.

salteado *adj (alternado)* alternate; **saber de cor e ~** to know (sth) off by heart.

salteador,-ora *m,f* highwayman/woman, mugger.

saltimbanco *m* travelling acrobat.

saltitante *adj inv* hopping.

saltitar *vt* hop; **~ de um pé para o outro** hop from one foot to the other; **2** *(divagar)* **~ de um assunto/duma coisa para outro,-a** jump from one subject/thing to the other, digress.

salto *m* jump, leap; **2 ~ de anjo** swan dive; **3** vault; **~ à vara** pole vault; **4 ~ em altura** high jump; **5 aos ~s** leaping; **6 ~ de vento** *(NÁUT)* shift of wind; **7** *(sapato)* heel, **~s altos/baixos** high/low heels; **8 dar um ~** to jump, leap, *(fig) (jovem)* grow fast; **9 ~-mortal** *(pl:* **~s mortais)** *m* back-flip jump(s); IDIOM **dar um ~ à loja** to pop into the shop.

salubre *adj* healthy, salubrious.

salutar *adj* salutary, beneficial, wholesome; **conselhos ~es** sound advice.

salva *f (BOT)* salvia, sage; **2** *(tabuleiro)* salver, tray; **3** *(MIL)* salvo, salute; **~ de artilharia** salvo of guns; **4** *(de palmas)* round (of applause).

salvação *f (REL)* salvation; **2** *(remédio, solução)* remedy; **não há ~ possível** there is no remedy; **3** *(salvamento):* **barco de** *(EP)* **~** lifeboat; **bóia de** *(EP)* **~** lifebuoy; **colete de ~** *(EP)* lifejacket.

salvador,-ora *m,f (person)* saviour; **S~** *npr (REL)* Saviour; **2** *(na praia)* **nadador-~** *n (EP)* lifeguard; ♦ *adj (exército,etc)* liberating.

salvadorenho,-a *n, adj* from Salvador, Salvadorean.

salvados *mpl (de acidentes)* salvage.

salvaguarda *f* protection, safeguard; ♦ *vt* to safeguard.

salvamento *m* rescue.

salvar *vt* to save, rescue; **2** to salvage; ♦ *vr* to escape; ♦ *vp* save o.s.

salva-vidas, salvavidas *adj inv (BR)* lifebuoy; lifeguard; **barco ~** *(BR)* lifeboat; *(person) (BR)* lifeguard; *(jaqueta) (BR)* life jacket; **estação ~** *(EP, BR)* safeguard post/centre.

salve! *exc (fam)* cheers!; **~-rainha** *f* Hail Mary.

sálvia *f (BOT) (Vd:* **salva).**

salvo,-a *adj* safe; ♦ *adv* **a salvo** in safety; **pôr-se a salvo** to run to safety; **são e ~** safe and sound; ♦ *prep* save, except, unless; **todos ~ ele** all except him.

salvo-conduto *(pl:* **salvos-condutos)** *m* safe-conduct.

samaritano,-a *m,f* Samaritan; **2** *(fig, pej)* do-gooder.

samarra *f* Portuguese heavy, rough woollen coat with a cape over it *(tipo usado por Sherlock Holmes)*; **2** sheepskin garment.

samba *f* samba.

sambar *vi* to dance the samba.

sambista *adj* samba dancer, composer of samba.

samovar *m* samovar.

samurai *m* samurai.

sanar *vt (curar)* to cure, heal *(alguém, doença)*; **2** to remedy; to solve *(problem)*.

sanatório *m* sanatorium.

sanável *adj* curable; remediable.

sanção *f* sanction.

sancionar *vt* to sanction; **2** to authorize; **3 ~ contra** sanction against.

sandália *f* sandal.

sândalo *m* sandalwood.

sande *(Vd:* **sanduíche).**

sandeu *m* fool; numbskull.

sandia *f* foolish woman; **2** *(BOT)* water-melon; ♦ *adj* foolish, idiotic.

sandice *f* folly, nonsense.

sanduíche *f* sandwich.

saneamento *m (limpeza básica)* sanitation; **2** cleansing; **3 ~ dos bairros de lata** clearance of shanty towns; **4** *(POL) (fig)* purging.

sanear *vt* to clean up, cleanse; **2 ~ terrenos** drain the marshes; **3** purge *(políticos, regime)*.

sanefa *f (para cortinados)* pelmet; **2** *(em soalhos)* cross beams.

sangra *f (extracção da seiva)* tapping.

sangradura *f* bleeding, blood-letting; **2** *(golpe nos pinheiros, etc)* tapping.

sangrar *vt/vi* to bleed; **2** *(para tirar líquido da árvore)* tap; **3** *(fig) (enfraquecer)* drain; **4** *(fig)* grieve.

sangrento,-a *adj (batalha)* bloody; **2** bloodstained; bleeding; **3** *(bife, rosbife meio-cru)* rare.

sangue *m* blood; **2 tirar ~** to take blood; **3** *(raça)* **puro ~** thoroughbred; **4 exame de ~** blood test; **5 ~-frio** cold-blood, sangfroid; **6 a ~ frio** *adv* in cold blood; IDIOM **ter ~ na guelra** to have guts; **chorar lágrimas de ~** to cry bitter tears.

sanguessuga *f* leech, blood-sucker.

sanguinário,-a *adj* blood-thirsty, cruel.

sanguíneo,-a *adj* blood; **vaso ~** blood vessel; **2** sanguine; **3** *(cor no rosto)* ruddy.

sanha *f* rage, fury.

sanidade *f* health; 2 *(mental)* sanity.

sanita *(BR:* **vaso sanitário** *m)* *f* lavatory bowl, toilet.

sanitário,-a *adj* sanitary.

sânscrito *m (LÍNG)* Sanskrit.

santidade *f* holiness, sanctity; 2 *(o Papa)* **Sua S~** His Holiness.

santificar *vt* to sanctify, canonize; 2 make holy.

Santíssimo *m* Blessed Sacrament; ♦ **santíssimo,-a** *adj* holy; **~a Trindade** Holy Trinity.

santo,-a *m,f* saint; ♦ *adj* holy, sacred; **S~a Sé** Holy See; **Terra S~a** Holy Land; **Santo António (S.to)** Saint Anthony (St); **Santa Tereza** St. Thereza; **dia ~** holy day; **dia de todos os Santos** All Saints' Day; **todo o ~ dia** the whole day long; **sexta-feira ~a** Good Friday; **uma ~ mulher** a good woman; *(soul)* saintly; IDIOM **~s da casa não fazem milagres** no-one is a prophet in his own country.

santo-e-senha *m* password, motto.

santola *f (ZOOL, CULIN)* spider crab.

santuário *m* shrine, sanctuary.

sanzala *(Vd:* **senzala)**.

são, sã *adj* healthy; **ela é uma moça sã;** she is a healthy girl; 2 *(da mente)* sane; 3 sound **são e salvo** safe and sound.

São *m* Saint; **~ Jorge** Saint George; **~ Pedro** Saint Peter.

São Tomé e Príncipe *npr* São Tomé and Principe.

são-tomense *m,f* native from São Tomé; ♦ *adj* of/ from São Tomé.

> The Portuguese-speaking Republic of São Tomé and Príncipe is situated off West Africa, in the Gulf of Guinea. The archipelago consists of the islands of St Tomé, Príncipe and other small islands, and was discovered by Portuguese navigators between 1469 and 1471. Capital: St António. The country became independent in July 1975.

sapa *f (pá)* shovel; spade; **trabalho de ~** underhand work.

sapador *m (MIL)* sapper; 2 *(bombeiro)* fireman.

sapal *m (terreno alagadiço)* marshland.

sapataria *f* shoe shop.

sapateado *m* tap-dancing.

sapateira *(ZOOL, CULIN) (marisco)* large crab; 2 shoemaker's wife; 3 shoe-cupboard.

sapateiro *m* shoemaker, cobbler.

sapatilha *f (DESP)* sneaker; 2 gym shoe; ballet shoe; pump.

sapato *m* shoe; **~s rasos** flat shoes; **~ de camurça/ verniz** suede/patent leather shoe.

sapiência *f* wisdom, learning, erudition.

sapiente *adj inv* wise, erudite; 2 *(conhecedor)* knowledgeable.

sapo *m (ZOOL)* toad.

saque *m (COM)* draft, bill; 2 *(DESP)* serve; 3 plunder, pillage.

saquear *vt* to pillage, plunder; 2 *(de casa)* ransack.

saqueta *f* sachet; **~ de chá** tea bag.

SAR *(abr de* **Sua Alteza Real)** His/Her Royal Highness, H.R.H.

sarabulhento,-a *adj (louça, vidro)* rough, uneven; 2 *(fig) (cara, corpo)* scabby.

saracotear *vi* to shake one's hips.

saraiva *f* hail.

saraivada *f* hailstorm; 2 *(fig) (grande quantidade)* barrage.

saraivar *vi (cair saraiva)* to hail; ♦ *vt* to pelt.

sarampo *m* measles *sg ou pl.*

sarapatel *m* haggis; 2 *(fig)* confusion; pell-mell.

sarapintado,-a *adj* spotted, speckled; dotted.

sarar *vt* to cure, heal; ♦ *vi* to recover, be cured.

sarau *m* soirée, social evening.

sarça *f (BOT)* bramble (bush).

sarcasmo *m* sarcasm.

sarcástico,-a *adj* sarcastic.

sarcófago *m* sarcophagus.

sarda *f (na pele)* freckle; 2 *(peixe)* horse-mackerel.

sardanisca *(ZOOL)* wall lizard.

sardão *(ZOOL)* green lizard; 2 *(BOT)* holm-oak.

Sardenha *npr* Sardinia.

sardenho,-a, sardo,-a *m,f* from Sardinia; *adj* relating to Sardinia.

sardento,-a *adj* freckled.

sardinha *f* sardine; **conserva de ~s** tinned sardines, IDIOM **como ~s em lata** *(muita gente num sítio)* packed in like sardines; **chegar/puxar a brasa à sua ~** bring grist to one's mill.

sardinheira *(BOT)* geranium.

sardónico,-a *(BR:* -dô-) *adj* sardonic, sarcastic.

sargaço *m (BOT)* sargasso, seaweed; **mar de ~** Sargasso Sea.

sargento *m* sergeant; **~-mor/primeiro ~** sergeant-major.

sargo *m (peixe)* sea bream.

sarilho *m* winch, reel, winding frame; 2 *(rodopio do corpo)* gyration, turn; *(no trapézio, na barra)* somersault; 3 *(pop) (confusão)* hullabaloo; **fazer um ~** raise a fuss; 4 *(pop) (problema)* trouble, difficulty; **meter-se em ~s** get into trouble, get into a jam; 5 *(pop) (roda-viva)* mad rush; *(fig)* **andar num ~** to run around in circles; **armar ~s** to cause trouble, to make intrigues; ♦ **que ~!** what a mess! what a nuisance!

sarja *f (tecido)* serge.

sarjeta *f* gutter.

SA(RL) *(abr de* **Sociedade Anónima de (Responsabilidade Limitada)** PLC.

sarna *f (doença em animal)* scabies *sg*; 2 *(pessoa importuna)* pest; nuisance.

sarnento,-a *(cão, cobaia doente)* mangy; 2 *(fig)* scruffy.

sarrabulho *m* clotted pig's blood; 2 *(CULIN)* a dish made of pork, liver, blood; 3 *(pop)* uproar, hubbub; 4 *(pop)* mess.

sarro *m (dentes)* tartar; 2 *(língua)* fur *(on the tongue).*

Satã, Satanás *npr m* Satan, the Devil.

satânico,-a *adj* satanic(al).

satélite *m (astro)* satellite; 2 *(país)* satellite state; ♦ *adj inv (nação, cidade)* satellite; 3 *(fig)* follower, hanger-on.

sátira *f* satire.

satírico,-a satirical.

satisfação *(pl: -ões) f* satisfaction; **2** amends, explanation, **não preciso de lhe dar satisfações** I don't have to give him any explanation/explain my acts.

satisfatório,-a *adj* satisfactory.

satisfazer *vt* to satisfy; **2** ~ **a fome** appease hunger; **3** ~ **os regulamentos** comply with regulations; **4** *(convencer)* **essa história não me satisfaz** that story does not convince me; **5** *(contentar)* to please; ♦ *vi* be satisfactory; **2** *(ECON)* to meet, fulfil ~ **a procura** meet demand; ♦ ~**-se** be content, satisfied.

satisfeito,-a *adj* pleased, glad; **2** *(comida)* satisfied, full; **3** *(pedido)* granted.

saturado,-a *adj* saturated; **2** *(farto)* fed up.

saturar *vt* to saturate (**de**, of).

saudação *f* greeting; **2** homage.

saudade *f* longing, yearning; home-sickness, nostalgia; **ter/sentir** ~**s de (algo, alguém)** to long for, to miss (sb, sth); **tenho** ~**s de Lisboa** I miss Lisbon; **deixar** ~**s** to be greatly missed; **morrer de** ~**s de (alguém)** to be pining for sb; **dá** ~**s ao Paulo** give Paul my regards/love; *(terminando uma carta amiga)* **Saudades** Love.

saudar *vt* to greet, salute; **2** to welcome.

saudável *adj* healthy, wholesome.

saúde *f* health; toast; **beber à** ~**de** to drink to, toast to sb's health; **casa de** ~ private hospital; **vender** to be bursting with health; ♦ *exc (brindar)* **à** ~! cheers!, **à sua** ~ to your health!

saudosismo *m* nostalgia.

saudoso,-a *adj* nostalgic; **2** homesick; **3** dearly missed; **4** heartfelt.

sauna *f* sauna.

savana *f* savanah.

saxão, saxã *m,f adj* Saxon.

saxofone *m (MÚS)* saxophone.

saxofonista *m,f* saxophone player.

sazão *f (época)* season, time.

sazonado,-a *adj* ripe, mature; **2** seasonal.

sazonalidade *f* seasonal variation.

se *conj* if, whether *(quando se trata de factos ou em dúvida)*; **não sei se ela vem** I don't know whether she is coming; **se ela engorda é porque come muito** if she is fat it's because she eats so much; **se por acaso eu não ouvir o despertador, acorda-me** if (by any chance) I don't hear the alarm, wake me up; **2** *(sujeito a condição, desejo, possibilidade, etc. e usado no futuro e imperfeito do conjuntivo)* if, when, whenever; **irei ao Japão se eu tiver dinheiro** I shall go to Japan if I have money; **se for possível** if it is possible; **se eu tivesse bebido menos, não me teria embriagado** if I had drunk less, I would not have got drunk; **3** *(em interrog. indirecta)* what if; **e se falássemos com ele?** what if we were to speak with him?; **e se ele não pagar?** and what if he does not pay?; **3** ~ **bem que** although, even though; **se bem que eu goste dele, não quero casar-me** although I like him, I do not want to get married; ♦ *pron pessoal reflexo*

himself, herself, itself, oneself, yourself, yourselves, themselves (NOTE: in English you don't always write "himself" etc); **a menina veste-se** the little girl dresses herself; **vocês já se levantaram?** have you got up/are you up?; **2** *(complemento recíproco)* each other; **eles amam-se** they love each other; ♦ *pron indef* one; **nunca se pode dizer** one can never tell; **diz-se que** ... it is said that/one says; **aqui fala-se inglês** English is spoken here.

sé *f* cathedral; **Santa S**~ Holy See.

SE *(abr de* **Sudeste***)* SE (South East)

seabórgio *m (QUÍM)* seaborgium.

seara *f* wheat/corn field; **2** tilled field; **as** ~**a do Alentejo** Alentejo's cornfields.

seareiro,-a *m,f* sower of cornfields; ♦ *adj (escritor, militante)* relating to the Seara Nova literary movement.

sebácio,-a *adj* sebaceous.

Sebastianismo *m* Sebastianism *(belief in the return of King Sebastian, who disappeared in the tragic battle of Alcacer-Kibir, 1578).*

Sebastianista *adj inv* Sebastianist; **2** *(fig)* retrograde.

sebe *f* fence; ~ **viva** hedge; **saltar a** ~ jump over the fence.

sebenta *f (caderno de apontamentos)* rough book for notes *(in the old days, it was passed down from student to student).*

sebento,-a *adj* greasy; **2** dirty, filthy.

sebo *m* fat, suet, tallow; **2** *(secreção das glândulas)* sebum; **3** *(pej) (gordo)* fat, flab; **4** *(BR)* second-hand bookshop.

seboso,-a *(BR) adj* greasy, oily; **2** dirty; *(fam, pej) (pessoa)* conceited.

seca *f (falta de chuva)* drought; **2** *(secagem)* drying; **3** *(fig, pop)* nuisance; **que grande** ~! what a bore!; ♦ *adj Vd:* **seco**.

secador *m* dryer; *(de cabelo)* hair dryer; *(de roupa)* tumble dryer; ♦ **secador,-ora** *adj* drying.

secagem *f* drying.

seção *(BR)* seção *(Vd:* **se(c)ção***)*.

secar *vt (gen)* to dry; **2** to parch; **o sol secou a vegetação** the sun parched the vegetation; **3** dry, cure *(peixe, peles)*; ♦ *vi (evaporar)* to dry up/out *(lago, fonte)*; **2** *(tornar murcho)* to wither *(plantas)*; ♦ *vr* ~**-se** become dry.

se(c)ção *f* section.

sec(c)ionar *vt* to section; divide into sections.

secessão *f* secession.

seco,-a *adj (ger)* dry, dried; **2** *(terra)* arid; **3** *(fig, fam) (pessoa magra)* thin, skinny; **4** *(fig) (tom, modos)* curt, brusque, cold; **5** *(pão)* stale; **6** *(fig) (pancada)* dull; **7** *(BR)* eager, dying for; **pôr em** ~ to run aground; ♦ ~**s** *mpl* dry provisions (cereals, etc); **soldada a** ~ wages without board; ♦ **a** ~ *adv* **limpeza a** ~ dry-cleaning; **engolir em** ~ suffer in silence.

secreção *f* secretion.

secretaria *f* general office; **2 S**~ **de Estado** Secretary of State.

secretariado *m* secretariat; *(lugar)* administrative office.

secretário,-a *m,f* secretary; ♦ *f (mesa)* desk; 2 *(BR)* ~ **eletrônica** answering machine.

secreto,-a *adj* secret; 2 hidden; ♦ **os serviços secretos** the Secret Services.

sectário,-a *m,f* follower, sectarian; ♦ *adj* sectarian.

sectarismo *m* sectarianism.

se(c)tor *m* sector; ~ **empresarial** business sector; ~ **primário** agricultural sector; ~**secundário** industrial sector; ~ **terciário** tertiary/services sector.

secular *adj* secular, lay, worldly; 2 centenary; **comemoração** ~ commemorative centenary; 3 *(muito antigo)* age-old.

século *m* century; ~ **XXI** the twenty-first century; 2 *(época)* age, time; 3 *(fig)* for ages; **há** ~**s que não te vejo** I haven't seen you for ages.

secundar *vt* to support, back up; 2 reinforce.

secundário,-a *adj* secondary; 2 *(actor)* supporting; 3 *(estrada)* B road.

secura *f* dryness; 2 *(falta de chuva)* drought; 3 *(fam) (vontade de beber)* thirst; 4 *(fig) (frieza de tom/ modos)* coldness.

seda *f (tecido)* silk; **papel de** ~ tissue paper; **bicho da** ~ silkworm.

sedativo,-a *adj* sedative.

sede¹ [é] *f* headquarters, head office; 2 *(do governo)* seat; 3 *(REL)* diocese; 4 *(lugar, centro)* site.

sede² [ê] *f* thirst; **ter** ~ to be thirsty; **matar a** ~ to quench one's thirst; 2 *(fig) (desejo)* craving/thirst (for); IDIOM **ter** ~ **a alguém** feel like hitting sb.

sedentário,-a *adj* sedentary.

sedento,-a *adj* thirsty; 2 *(fig)* eager, avid.

sediar *vt (instalar)* set up, to base; 2 *(ter sede)* be the venue for; **Brasil sediou a cimeira sobre o Meio Ambiente** Brazil hosted the conference on Environment.

sedição *f* sedition.

sedicioso,-a *adj* seditious.

sedimentar *adj inv (GEOL)* sedimentary; ♦ *vi* form sediment; 2 consolidate.

sedimento *m* sediment, *(vinho)* dregs *pl.*

sedoso,-a *adj* silky.

sedução *f* seduction; 2 allure, charm.

sedutor,-ora *adj* seductive; 2 alluring, tempting; ♦ *m,f* seducer.

seduzido,-a *adj* seduced; 2 attracted to; **senti-me** ~**a por aquela voz** I felt attracted to/taken by that voice.

seduzir *vt (desonrar)* to seduce; 2 to fascinate, attract, entice; 3 *(desencaminhar)* to lead astray.

sega *f*, **segada** *f* harvest-time; 2 mowing, reaping time.

segadeira *f (foice grande)* scythe; 2 mowing machine, harvester.

segador *m* harvester, reaper; ~ **mecânica** reaping machine.

segar *vt* to harvest, reap; 2 *(fig)* mow down.

segmentação *f* segmentation.

segmentar *vt* to divide; 2 *(fraccionar)* split up *(grupo, equipa)*; ♦ ~**-se** *vr* break into pieces.

segmento *m* segment, section, piece.

segredar *vt* to whisper.

segredo *m* secret; 2 secrecy; discretion; **em** ~ in private, in confidence; 3 mystery.

segregação *f* segregation.

segregar *vt* to segregate, separate.

seguido,-a *adj* following; 2 *(consecutivo)* consecutive, one after another; **dois dias** ~**s** two days running; **comi dois bolos** ~ I ate two pastries one after another; ♦ *adv* **de/em seguida** straight away, directly; **em** ~**a** afterwards, next.

seguidor,-ora *m,f (partidário)* follower; 2 pursuer; ♦ *adj* following, in pursuit.

seguimento *m* continuation; **dar** ~ **a algo** proceed with sth; **em** ~ **de** after.

seguinte *m,f* the following; 2 *(citando)* as follows, **a história é a** ~ the story is as follows; ♦ *adj inv* next, following; **na manhã** ~ **fui ao mercado** the following morning I went to the market; **na paragem** ~ next stop.

seguir *vt (ger)* to follow; 2 to come after, 3 *(perseguir)* chase, pursue; 4 *(continuar)* carry on; ♦ *vi* proceed, go (on); 2 *(ser enviado)* **a carta já seguiu** the letter has gone; ♦ *vr* ~**-se** *(vir depois)* follow, come after; **seguiram-se dias exilirantes** there followed exciting days; ♦ *adv* **logo a** ~ straight away; **a** ~ *(na fila)* after; **estou a** ~ I am next, it is my turn; **segue-se que** it follows that; **que se segue?** what next?

segunda *f* second; 2 *(MÚS)* second; 3 *(abre de segunda-feira)* Monday; **ele vem na** ~ he is coming on Monday; **ele vem às** ~**s** he comes (every) on Mondays; 4 *(AUTO)* second; **conduzir em** ~ to drive in second gear; ♦ *adj (qualidade infertior)* second; **de** ~ **classe** second class/rate; ~~-**mão** *f (compras)* second-hand; **em** *(BR: de)* ~ **mão** in second-hand; ~ **intenções** ulterior motives.

segundo,-a *m,f* second; 2 *(de tempo)* **só um** ~ just a second; ♦ *adj* second; **João Paulo II** Pope John Paul II (the second); 2 *(FUT)* ~ **tempo** second half; 3 *(double)* **conversa com** ~ **sentido** a talk with a double meaning; ♦ *prep* according to; ♦ *conj* as; ~ **disse** as he said, from what he said; ♦ *adv* secondly, **em** ~ **lugar** in second place.

segurado,-a *m,f* person insured; *(UK)* **o/a** ~ the assured.

segurador,-ora *m,f (agente)* insurance broker; 2 *f* insurance company.

seguramente *adv* surely, certainly; 2 safely; **a jovem conduz** ~ the young girl drives safely; 3 firmly.

segurança *f* safety; **alfinete de** ~ *m* safety pin; **cinto de** ~ *m* safety belt; **normas de** ~ *fpl* safety standards *(MEC)* **válvula de** ~ *f* safety valve; 2 *(protecção)* security; *m* security man; **S~ Social** *f* Social Security; 3 *(certeza, confiança)* certainty, assurance; **com** ~ assuredly.

segurar *vt (pegar)* to hold; 2 *(firmar)* secure, fix; 3 *(suster)* hold up; 4 *(manter)* keep; 5 *(fig)* guarantee, ensure; 6 *(COM)* ~ **algo/alguém contra** to insure sth/sb against; ♦ *vr (aguentar-se)* hold on; 2 *(manter-se)* stand; 3 control o.s.

seguro,-a *m (COM)* insurance; ~ **de vida** life insurance; **apólice de** ~ *f* insurance policy; **fazer** ~ take out an insurance; ♦ *adj* safe; 2 secure; 3 sure; 4

firm; **5** *(de confiança)* trustworthy, reliable; **6** *(tempo)* settled; **7** *(pouco seguro)* unsteady; IDIOM **o ~ morreu de velho** prevention is better than cure.

sei *(pres indic saber)* I know.

seio *m (ANAT)* breast, bosom; **o bico do ~** the nipple; **2** *(fig) (intimidade)* heart; **no ~ de** in the heart of, in the bosom of; **3** *(profundeza)* depths, centre; **no ~ da terra** in the depths of the earth; **4 o ~ de Deus** Paradise.

seira *f (cesto para figos)* esparto basket (made from esparto grass); **2** bag or basket made of esparto for straining the olives; (kind of) colander.

seis *num* six; **sessenta e ~** sixty-six; **o menino fez ~ anos no domingo** the little boy was six years old last Sunday.

seiscentista *adj inv (moda, arte, escritor)* seventeenth century.

seiscentos *num* six hundred.

seita *f* sect; **2** *(partido)* faction; **3** *(pej) (bando)* gang.

seiva *f (BOT)* sap; **2** *(fig) (energia)* vigour, vitality.

seixal *m* area of pebbles.

seixo *m* pebble.

seja *etc (pres subj de ser)*: **espero que ele ~ bom** I hope he is good; *conj* **~ como for** be that as it may; **ou ~** that is, i.e.; **quem for** whoever may be; **~ onde for** wherever it may be; **~ assim!** *exc* so be it!

sela *f* saddle.

selado,-a *adj* sealed, stamped; **papel ~** (papel com o selo oficial) legally/officially stamped paper; **2** *(cavalo)* saddled.

selar *vt (ger)* to seal; **~ uma bela amizade** seal a beautiful friendship; **2** *(pôr selo)* stamp; **3** close; **4** *(cavalo)* saddle.

sele(c)ção *f* selection, choice; **2** collection *(de discos, etc)*; **3** *(FUT)* team.

selec(c)ionado *m* member of the team; ♦ *adj* chosen, picked, selected.

selec(c)ionador *m* selector, chooser.

selec(c)ionar *vt* to select, choose.

sele(c)tivo,-a *adj* selective.

sele(c)to,-a *f* anthology; ♦ *adj* select, choice.

selim *m* small saddle, side saddle.

selo *m* stamp; **~ fiscal** revenue stamp; **2** seal, **~ branco** embossed seal.

selva *f* jungle, forest.

selvagem *adj (pessoa, paisagem)* wild; **2** *(feroz)* savage, fierce; **3** *(ermo)* desolate.

selvajaria *f* savagery; cruelty.

sem *prep* without; **passar ~ algo** to go without; **sem que** *conj (followed by subjunctive)* without.

sem-abrigo *m,f sg, pl* homeless; **os ~** the homeless.

semáforo *m (AUTO)* traffic lights *pl*; **2** *(FERRO)* signal.

semana *f* week; **~ sim, ~ não** every other week; **a ~ que vem** next week; **a ~passada** last week; **há uma semana** a week ago; *(REL)* **~ Santa** Holy week; ♦ *adv* **à ~** by the week; **para a ~** next week.

semanada *(dinheiro)* weekly pocket money.

semanal *adj* weekly.

semanário *m* weekly (publication).

semblante *m (rosto)* face, countenance; **2** *(fig) (aspecto)* appearance, look.

sem-cerimónia *f* informality; **2** abruptness, offhandedness.

sêmea *f* wheat bran.

semeador,-ora *m,f* sower; **2** *(máquina)* seed-drill, sowing machine; ♦ *adj* sowing; **2** *(fig)* spreader, carrier *(de virus, etc)*.

semeadura *f* sowing, seeding.

semear *vt (plantar)* to sow; **2** *(fig) (disseminar)* spread; **3** scatter seed; **4** *(fig) (fomentar)* lead to, start *(terror, confusão)* lead to, start; **~ a cizânia/ ~ a discórdia** to sow discord; IDIOM **estar à mão de ~** *(muito perto)* handy, within reach.

semelhança *f* similarity, resemblance; ♦ **à ~ de** *prep* like; ♦ **à ~ do que** *conj* as.

semelhante *m* fellow creature, neighbour; ♦ *adj* similar, resembling; ♦ *pron dem (tal)* any such.

sémen *(BR: -ê-) m* semen, sperm.

semente *f* seed.

sementeira *f* sowing; **2** *(o que está semeado)* crop; **3** **tempo das ~s** sowing-time.

semestral *adj* half-yearly.

semestre *m (EDUC)* semester.

sem-fim *m* endless number, etc; endless space, immensity.

semiaberto,-a *adj (portas, janela)* half-open, ajar.

semicírculo *m* semicircle.

semiconsciente *adj* semiconscious.

semifinal *f (DESP)* semifinal.

semifinalista *m,f* semi-finalist.

semi-frio *m* soft ice-cream.

semifusa *f (MÚS)* semiquaver.

seminário *m (EDUC) (conferência)* seminar; **2** *(REL)* seminary.

seminarista *m,f* seminarian, seminarist.

seminu,-a *adj (alguém com pouca roupa)* half-naked.

semiótica *f* semiology; semiotics.

semítico,-a *m,f* Semite; ♦ *adj inv* semitic.

semitismo *m* semitism.

sem-número *m* countless, a great number of.

sêmola *f* semolina.

semovente *adj* self-moving, self-propelled; **bens ~s** *mpl* livestock *sg, pl*.

sem-par *adj* unique, unequalled, without its peer.

sempiterno,-a *adj* everlasting, eternal.

sempre *adv* always, ever, forever; **amo-te para ~** I love you forever; **como ~** as always; **a história de ~** the same old story; **2** really; **você ~ gostou do filme?** did you really like the film?; **3** still, yet, after all, finally; **você ~ vai?** are you still going?; **~ compraste o carro?** did you buy the car in the end?; **4 ~ quero ver isso!** I really want to see that!; I should like to see that!; ♦ *conj* **~ que** whenever; ♦ *adv* **até ~** forever, ever more; **desde ~** since always; **quase ~** nearly always; **para todo o ~** for ever and ever; **até ~ !** so long!

sem-razão *f* wrong, injustice.

sem-valor *adj* worthless.

sem-vergonha *m,f* shameless person.

311

senado *m* senate.

senador,-ora *m,f* senator.

senão *m* flaw, hitch, hiccup *(fig)*; ◆ *conj* otherwise, if not; **não mintas ~ eu digo ao pai** do not tell lies, otherwise I'll tell daddy; **2** nothing but; **ele não bebe ~ água** he drinks nothing but water; **3** suddenly, then; **~ quando** when suddenly; **4 ~ que/ também** but also, but rather; ◆ *prep* except, save.

senda *f* path; **~ da virtude** path of virtue.

Senegal *npr* **o ~** Senegal.

senegalês,-esa *m,f adj* Senegalese.

senha *f* password; **2** *(comprovativo)* receipt, voucher; **3** *(lugar na fila – banco, etc)* ticket.

senhor *m* man, gentleman; **2** *(feudal)* lord; *(proprietário)* owner; **~ de muitas terras** owner/lord of many lands; **3** Mr, Sir; **o S~ Ministro** Minister, Sir, you; **S~ (Sr) Silva** Mr. (Mister) Silva; *(numa carta formal)* **Excelentíssimo (Ex.mo) ~/ (BR) Ilustríssimo (Il.mo) S~** Dear Sir; *(carta comercial)* **Caro ~** Dear Sir; **5 Nosso S~** Our Lord; **6** *(pron pess) (tratamento respeitoso ou para um desconhecido)* you; **o ~ já encomendou?** have you ordered?; **7** *(enfático)* **sim ~**, yes, Sir; IDIOM **ser ~ de si** be one's own master; **ser ~ do seu nariz** opinionated, wilful, to know one's own mind.

senhora *f* lady; **2** wife; **3** Mrs., madam; **Excelentíssima (Ex.ma) S~a** Dear Madam; **a ~a** you; **Nossa Senhora** *npr f* Our Lady.

senhoria *f* landlady; **Vossa S~** *m,f* Your Honour.

senhorial *adj* seigneurial; **2** *(casa)* manor.

senhoril *adj* lordly; **2** ladylike.

senhorinha *f* (very formal) young unmarried woman.

senhorio *m* *(de terras)* seigneur, Lord; **2** *(de casa)* landlord.

senhorita *f* *(BR) (very formal)* miss; young lady; **2** *(pron. pess)* you.

senil *adj inv* senile.

senilidade *f* senility.

sensaboria *f* insipidity, dullness.

sensação *f* sensation, feeling; **causar ~** to cause a sensation.

sensacional *adj* sensational.

sensatamente *adv* wisely.

sensatez *f* good sense.

sensato,-a *adj* sensible, level-headed, wise.

sensibilidade *f* sensitivity; **2** *(susceptibilidade)* feelings.

sensibilização *f* *(acto de comover)* moving; **2** *(de consciência)* awareness; **3** *(MED)* sensitiveness; **4** *(FOTO)* sensitization.

sensibilizar *vt (comover)* to touch, move, affect; **seu gesto sensibilizou-me muito** your gesture touched me very much; ◆ **~-se** *vr* to be moved; **2** be sensitive to to; be aware of; be moved.

sensitivo,-a *adj (ger)* sensitive; **ser ~ a** be sensitive to.

sensível *adj* sensitive; touchy; **2** perceptible.

sensivelmente *adv* perceptibly, markedly; ◆ *adj inv* nearly.

Do not confuse '**sensível**' with the English word '**sensible**' which means '**sensato**'.

senso *m* sense; **~ comum** common sense; **~ de humor** sense of humour; **o ~ moral** moral judgement.

sensorial *(pl:* -ais*) adj inv* sensory.

sensual *(pl:* -ais*) adj inv* sensual, sensuous/

sensualidade *f* sensuality; **2** lust.

sentar *vt* to sit down *(alguém)*; ◆ *vi* to sit; **~-se** *vr* to sit down, take a seat; **queira ~** please be seated; **2** settle down.

sentença *f (JUR)* sentence; penalty; **~ absolutória** acquittal; **cumprir uma ~** to serve one's sentence/ time; **dar uma ~** to pass sentence.

sentenciar *vt* to pass judgement on; **2** *(condenar)* to sentence **(to a)**.

sentido,-a *m* sense; **em certo ~** in a sense; **não faz ~ nenhum** it doesn't make any sense; **2** meaning; **~ duplo** double meaning; **no ~ figurado,** in the figurative sense; **sem ~** meaningless; **3** direction, **~ único** one-way; **~ anti-horário** anticlockwise; **4 ~s** senses, **perder/recobrar os ~s** lose/recover consciousness; ◆ *adj (magoado)* offended, hurt; **estou muito ~ com ela** I am very upset with her; ◆ **~ no ~ de** *prep* with the purpose of; ◆ *exc (MIL):* **~!**; attention!; **tome ~!** be careful!

sentimental *adj* sentimental.

sentimentalismo *m* sentimentalism.

sentimento *m* sentiment; **~s** *mpl* feelings; **2** *(pêsames)* **meus sentimentos!** condolences!

sentina *f (MIL)* latrine; **2** *(NÁUT)* bilge; **3** *(fig) (lugar sujo)* pits; **este lugar é a ~ da aldeia** this place is the pits of the village!

sentinela *f* sentry, guard; **estar de ~** to be on guard duty; **render ~** to relieve the guard.

sentir *vt (ger)* to feel; **~ a falta de** to miss (sb, sth); **2** *(por meio de sentidos)* perceive, sense; **3** *(lamentar)* to regret, feel sorry; **sinto muito que ele tenha falecido** I am so sorry he passed away; ◆ *vi* feel; **2** to grieve, suffer; ◆ **~-se** *vr* to feel; **como se sente hoje?** how are you feeling today?; **2** to imagine o. s. to be, feel like; **3** *(melindrar-se)* be offended/ hurt; **4** be affected.

senzala *(também* **sanzala***) f* Angolan village; *(BR)* slave quarters in Brazil.

separação *f* separation; **2** partition.

separado,-a *adj* separate, separated; **em ~** separately, apart.

separar *vt* to separate; **2** to divide; **3** *(reservar)* to set aside; ◆ **~-se** *vr* to separate; **2 ~ em** *(rio, caminho)* to divide into.

separata *f (TIPO)* offprint.

separatismo *m* separatism.

separatista *m,f* separatist.

sépia *f (ZOOL)* sepia; **2** *(tinta escura que este molusco segrega)* sepia; **retrato pintado a ~** a sepia portrait.

septicemia *f (MED)* septicaemia, blood poisoning.

séptico,-a *adj* septic.

septuagésimo,-a *num* seventieth.

sepulcral *adj inv* sepulchral.

sepulcro *m* tomb, sepulchre; **o Santo S~** the Holy Sepulchre; **2** *(lugar desolado)* grave.

sepultar *vt (ger)* to bury; **2** *(fig)* to hide *(enclausurar)* enclose sb in.

sepultura *f* grave, tomb.

sequaz *m* follower, adherent.

sequela *f (sequência)* sequel; 2 *(consequências)* after-effects; 3 *(MED)* sequela.

sequência *f* sequence, succession.

sequer *adv* at least, even; **nem ~** not even; **ela não trazia ~ um guarda-chuva** she didn't even bring an umbrella.

sequestrador,-ora *m,f* sequestrator; kidnapper; abductor; 2 *(avião, barco)* hijacker.

sequestrar *vt (JUR)* to seize, confiscate; 2 kidnap *(alguém)*; 3 *(avião, barco)* hijack.

sequestro *m* seizure, sequestration; 2 *(rapto)* abduction, kidnapping; 3 *(MED)* sequestrum.

sequioso,-a *adj (alguém)* thirsty; 2 *(solo)* dry; 3 *(fig)* eager, **~ de aprender** eager to learn; 4 *(fig) (cobiçoso)* greedy.

séquito *m* retinue, suite.

ser *m* being, **o ~ humano** human being; ♦ *vi* to be *(característica inerente)* **ele é alto** he is tall; 2 *(para designar o que faz, mesmo que temporário)* **eu sou médica** I am a (medical) doctor; **nós somos turistas e eles são estudantes** we are tourists and they are students; 3 *(origem ou posse)* **~ de** to be/come from, to belong to; **ele é do Brasil** he is from Brazil; **esta mala é daquele senhor** this suitcase is that man's; **que é da Maria?** where is Mary?; 4 *(dizer as horas)* **são cinco horas** it is five o'clock; **é uma hora** it is one o'clock; 5 *(descrever)* **Lisboa é linda** Lisbon is beautiful; **era uma tarde verão** it was a summer afternoon; **ele foi o maior poeta** he was the greatest poet; 6 *(em frases impessoais)* **isto é impossível** this is impossible; **foi preciso chamar a ambulância** it was necessary (we had to) call the ambulance; 7 *(na voz passiva)* **o pão foi comprado por mim** the bread was bought by me; 8 **ser para** to be for, **esta água não é para beber** this water is not for drinking; 9 **pode ~** may be; **era uma vez ...** once upon a time; **será que ... ?** I wonder if ...; ♦ *adv* **é sim,** yes, it is; **não é?** isn't it?; **pois é** so it is; **a não ser** except for; ♦ *conj* **a não ~ que** unless; **ou seja** or rather; **isto é** that is to say; **seja ... seja ...** whether ... or ...; **sendo assim** that being the case, thus.

serafim *m (REL)* seraphim; 2 *(pessoa de beleza angélica)* cherub.

serão *m* night work, overtime; **fazer ~** to work overtime; 2 *(reunião familiar, depois do jantar)* evening.

serapilheira *f* sackcloth, jute sackcloth.

sereia *f* mermaid; 2 *(alarme)* alarm siren; *(do navio)* siren; **ouvia-se a ~ do navio** one heard the ship's siren/foghorn/the ship's siren was heard.

serenar *vt* to calm (down); ♦ *vi* to calm down; ♦ **~-se** *vr* to grow calm.

serenata *f* serenade.

serenidade *f* calmness, tranquillity.

sereno,-a *m* damp dew; evening mist; ♦ *adj* calm; fine, clear; **noite serena** still evening.

seriado,-a *m* serial; ♦ *adj* in a series, serialised.

seriar *vt* to arrange in series.

série *f* series *sg*, row; sequence, succession; **uma ~ de acontecimentos** a succession/train of events; **uma ~ de mentiras** a web of lies; 2 *(coisas análogas)* categories; 3 *(conjunto)* set; 4 **~ limitada** limited edition; 5 *(BR) (EDUC)* year; 6 *(QUÍM, ELECT, MAT, FÍS)* series; ♦ **~ em** *adv* serial; **produção em ~** mass production.

seriedade *f* seriousness; 2 *(circunspecção)* sobriety; 3 honesty, integrity.

seringa *f* syringe.

seringal *m* rubber plantation.

seringalista *m* rubber plantation owner.

seringueira *f* rubber tree.

seringueiro *m* rubber tapper.

sério,-a *adj* serious; 2 honest; ♦ *adv* really; seriously; **a ~?** really?; **falo a ~** I mean it; **levar algo a ~** to take to heart.

sermão *m* sermon; *(fig)* lecture; **pregar um ~** to give a lecture, *(fig)* a reprimand.

serôdio,-a *adj (tardio)* late *(fruta, etc)*; 2 *(carta, resposta, etc)* belated, tardy.

seronegativo,-a *m,f* person who is HIV negative.

seropositivo,-a *m,f* person who is HIV positive.

serpeante *adj* wriggling; *(fig)* winding, meandering.

serpear *vi* to wriggle; 2 *(fig)* to wind, meander.

serpente *f (ZOOL)* snake, serpent; **encantador de ~s** snake-charmer.

serpentear *(Vd: serpear)*.

serpentina *f (TEC) (conduto)* coil; 2 *(fita de papel)* streamer; 3 *(MÚS)* French horn; 4 *(MIN)* serpentine; 5 *(BOT)* dragon-wort

serra *f* mountain range; 2 *(ferramenta)* saw; **~ de cadeia** chain-saw; IDIOM **ir à ~** to hit the ceiling, fly into a rage.

serração *f* sawmill.

serrado,-a *adj (madeira)* sawn; *(folha)* serrated.

serradura *f* sawdust.

serragem *f* sawing.

serralharia *f (oficina)* smithy's; **serralheiro** *m* locksmith, blacksmith.

serrania *f* mountain range.

serrano,-a *m,f* highlander; ♦ *adj* highland.

serrar *vt* to saw, cut.

serraria *f* sawmill.

serrote *m* hand-saw; *(para metal)* hacksaw.

sertã *f* frying-pan.

sertanejo,-a *m,f (do Sertão)* inhabitant of Sertão; ♦ *adj* relating to Sertão (Brazil).

sertão *m (interior do país)* backwoods, bush country.

servente *m,f* assistant; 2 **~ de pedreiro** bricklayer's labourer; 2 *(BR)* caretaker *(UK)*; janitor *(US)*.

serventia *f* service, utility; 2 use; 3 entrance.

Sérvia *npr* **a ~** Serbia.

serviçal *m,f* servant; 2 wage earner; ♦ *adj* helpful, obliging.

serviço *m* service; 2 job; 3 *(conjunto louça, etc)* set; **um ~ de chá** a tea-set; 4 **~ de estrangeiros** immigration department; 5 **~ a(c)tivo** *(MIL)* active duty; 6 **~ doméstico** housework; 7 **~ militar** military service; **porta de ~** tradesmen entrance;

serviços públicos public utilities; **prestar** ~ to be of help; **estar de** ~ to be on duty.

servidão *f (escravidão)* servitude, serfdom.

servido,-a *adj* served; **2** worn; ~ **de** supplied with, provided with; **é servido,-a?** would you care to join us (for lunch/dinner)?

servidor,-ora *m,f* servant; **2** employee; **3** ~ **do Estado** civil servant; **4** *(COMP)* server.

servil *adj inv (subserviente)* servile (**a** to), obsequious; **2** cringing.

sérvio,-a *m,f* Serb; *(LÍNG)* Serbian.

servir *vt/vi* to serve; **2** to be of use; **esta panela serve para a sopa** this pan is good for (making) soup; **isto não serve para nada** this is good for nothing; ♦ ~**-se** *vr* to serve o.s.; **sirva-se** *(de comida/ bebida)* help yourself (to); **2** ~**-se de** to use, make use of; **3** to fit; **este vestido não me serve** this dress doesn't fit me.

servo,-a *m,f* serf; servant.

sésamo *m (BOT)* sesame; IDIOM **abre-te** ~! open (thee) sesame!

sesmaria *f* wasteland; **a Lei das** ~**s** *(HIST)* 14th-century law which divided and allotted land (the first agrarian 'reform').

sessão *f* session; **2** meeting; **3** showing; **bilhetes para a primeira** ~ tickets for the first performance.

sessenta *num* sixty; ♦ *adj inv* sixtieth.

sesta *f* siesta, nap.

seta *f* arrow, dart.

sete *num* seven; ♦ *adj inv* seventh; IDIOM **estou nas minhas** ~ **quintas** I am as pleased as Punch/I am in my seventh heaven; **bicho de** ~ **cabeças** tricky problem; **homem dos** ~ **ofícios**; handyman, fixer.

setecentista *adj inv (arte, moda, etc)* relating to the 17th century.

setecentos *num* seven hundred.

setembrismo *m political movement in September 1822, which defended the Constitution.*

Setembro, setembro *m* September; **em meados de** ~ mid-September; **no dia 1 de** ~ on the first of September.

setenta *num* seventy; ~ **e quatro** seventy-four; ♦ *adj inv* seventieth.

setentrional *adj* northern.

sétimo,-a *adj* seventh.

setor *m (BR)* sector (*Vd:* **sector**).

seu, sua *adj (dele)* his; *(dela)* her; *(neuter)* its; *(deles, delas)* their; *(de você/vocês)* your; ♦ *pron* his; hers; theirs; yours; **seu parvo!** *(fam, pop)* you, idiot! **seu António** *(BR e províncias portuguesas) (fam)* Mr António, hey António!

seus *(pl de seu)* ~ **livros** his/her/your/their books.

severidade *f* severity, harshness; *(para com os filhos)* strictness.

severo,-a *adj* severe, harsh, strict.

sevícia *f* ill treatment.

sevícias *fpl* inhumanity, cruelty.

sexismo *m* sexism.

sexista *adj inv* sexist.

sexo *m* sex; **o bebé é do** ~ **feminino** the baby is a girl/female sex

sexta-feira *f* Friday; **S**~ **Santa** Good Friday; **eu vou na sexta** I am going on Friday.

sexto,-a *adj* sixth.

sexual *adj* sexual. **sexualidade** *f* sexuality.

sezão *f (MED) (intermitente)* fever from malaria; **2** *(ímpeto)* force, vigour.

s.f.f. *(abr de se faz favor)* if you please.

si *pron* oneself; himself; herself; itself; yourself; *(de você)* you; yourselves; themselves; **falava de si para si** he was speaking to himself; **este dinheiro é para si** this money is for you; **eles falavam entre si** they were speaking among themselves.

siamês,-mesa *adj* Siamese.

Sibéria *npr* **a** ~ Siberia.

siberiano,-a *adj* Siberian.

sibilante *adj inv (consonant)* sibilant; **2** *f (pronúncia)* hissing; **3** *(vento)* whistling.

sibilar *m* **o** ~ **do vento** the whistling of the wind; **o** ~ **da serpente** the snake's hissing; ♦ *vi (silvar) (vento)* to hiss; whistle; **2** *(seta, bala)*, whiz (past); **uma flecha passou sibilando** an arrow whizzed past **sibilo** *m* hiss, whistling sound.

sicário *m* hired assassin.

Sicília *npr* **a** ~ Sicily.

siciliano,-a *m,f* Sicilian.

sicrano *m* Mr So-and-so; **aquele** ~ that chap/bloke.

siderurgia *f* iron and steel industry.

siderúrgico,-a *adj* iron and steel; **fábrica** *(BR:* **usina)** ~**a** steel works; ♦ *f* steel works, *sg*.

sidra *f* cider.

sifão *m* syphon.

sífilis *f sg pl* syphilis.

siflítico,-a *adj* syphilitic.

siga *(etc vb: pres subj de* **seguir)** ~ **este caminho** follow this road; **é preciso que eles sigam os meus conselhos** they should follow my advice.

sigilo *m* secret; secrecy; **guardar** ~ **sobre** to keep secret.

sigiloso,-a *adj* secret.

sigla *f (abreviatura)* acronym; *(sinal)* initial.

signa *f* ensign, flag, standard.

signatário *m* signatory, undersigned; ♦ *adj (país, companhia)* signatory.

significação *f* significance.

significado *m* meaning; **significar** *vt* to mean, signify.

significativo,-a *adj* significant.

signo *m* sign; **2** *(ASTROL)* sign; **Touro é um** ~ **do Zodíaco** Taurus is a sign of the Zodiac; **3** *(expoente)* banner.

signo-saimão *(pl:* **signos-saimões)** *m* talisman, amulet, charm.

sigo *(pres indic, 1ª pess sg de* **seguir)**.

sílaba *f* syllable.

silenciador *m (AUTO, MIL)* silencer.

silenciar *vt (calar)* to silence; **2** *(omitir)* omit, conceal; **3** *(abafar boatos)* to hush up; ♦ *vi* to keep quiet, remain silent; **2** kill; **3 guardar** ~ **sobre** keep quiet about; **romper/quebrar o** ~ to break the silence.

silêncio *m* silence, quiet; **2** *(MÚS)* pause; **em** ~ in silence; **quebrar/romper o** ~ to break the silence.

silencioso,-a quiet, noiseless; *(sem falar)* speechless.

silhueta *f* silhouette, outline.

silício *m* silicon.

silo *m* silo.

silva *f* bramble bush; **amora de** ~ blackberry.

silvar *vi* *(ger)* to hiss; **2** *(vento)* to whistle; **3** *(bala, seta)* whizz; **silvestre** *adj* *(flora)* wild.

silvicultura *f* forestry.

sim *adv* yes; **acho/creio que** ~ I think so; **isso** ~! that's it!; **dia** ~, **dia não** every other day; **pelo** ~, **pelo não** just in case; **claro que** ~ of course; *(enfatizando)* **vou sim** yes, I am coming/going; ♦ *m* consent; **dar o** ~ to consent.

simbiose *f* symbiosis; **simbiótico,-a** *adj* symbiotic.

simbólico,-a *adj* symbolic.

simbolismo *m* symbolism.

simbolizar *vt* to symbolize, represent.

símbolo *m* symbol, sign.

simetria *f* symmetry.

simétrico,-a *adj* symmetrical.

similar *adj* similar.

similaridade *f* similarity.

simpatia *f* *(por algo alguém)* liking sb; **2** affection; **3** affinity, fellow feeling; **por** ~ out of kindness.

> Not in the sense of 'condolences' which is `**pêsames**'.

simpático,-a *adj* *(amável, agradável)* nice, pleasant, friendly; **2** kind; **3** attractive; **4** *(ANAT)* sympathetic; **sistema do grande** ~ parasympathetic system.

> Not sympathetic in the sense of 'compassionate', which is `**condoído**'.

simpatizante *m,f* *(causa)* sympathizer; **2** adherent.

simpatizar *vt* (**com alguém**) to take an instinctive liking to sb; **2** ~ **com uma causa** to sympathize with a cause; **3** *(aderir)* agree to.

> In the sense of feeling sad/sorry for sb, it is `**condoer-se**', `**ter pena**'.

simples *m,f* *(pessoa cândida)* simpleton; ♦ *adj inv* *(ger)* simple, plain; **2** mere, unique, single; **um bilhete** ~ a single ticket; **3** *(ingénuo)* naïve; **4** *(puro)* **café** ~ black coffee; **iogurte** ~ natural yoghurt; **uísque** ~ neat whisky; **5** *(pessoa modesta)* unaffected, modest.

simplesmente *adv* simply.

simplicidade *f* simplicity; **2** naiveté; **3** plainness; **4** artlessness; **5** simple-mindedness.

simplicíssimo,-a *(superl de* **simples***)* extremely simple.

simplificação *f* simplification.

simplificar *vt* to simplify.

simplista *adj inv* simplistic.

simplório,-a *m,f* simpleton; ♦ *adj* innocent, gullible.

simpósio *m* symposium.

simulação *f* simulation; **2** *(fingimento)* pretence; **3** *(imitação)* fake.

simulacro *(ger)* simulation; **2** *(imitação)* bad copy, imitation.

simulado,-a *adj* simulated; **2** *(fingido)* false; **3** *(sorriso, espanto)* feigned; **4** *(negócio)* fake, sham.

simular *vt* simulate; **2** to feign; **3** to imitate.

simultaneamente *adj* simultaneously.

simultâneo,-a *adj* *(factos, eventos)* simultaneous; *(interpetação)* simultaneous.

sina *f* fate, destiny; **ler a** ~ to read one's fortune.

sinagoga *f* synagogue.

sinal *(pl:* **sinais***)* *m* sign, signal; **2** *(mancha no rosto/corpo)* mole, birthmark, beauty spot; **3** *(marca)* mark; ~ **de pontuação** punctuation mark; **4** *(prova)* proof; **5** *(prenúncio)* sign, omen; **6** *(COM)* **dar de** ~ to give as a deposit; **7** ~ **rodoviário** road sign; **8** ~ **de impedido** *(telefone)* engaged tone; **9** **fazer** ~ *(num gesto)* to signal; **10 fazer o** ~ **da Cruz** to cross o.s. make the sign of the Cross; ♦ **por** ~ *adv* actually, as it happens.

sinaleiro *m* traffic policeman; **2** *(FERRO)* signalman.

sinalização *f* signalling; **2** *(na estrada)* road sign; **3** *(AUTO)* traffic signs *pl*; **4** *(FERRO)* railway signal.

sinalizar *vi* *(a outra pessoa)* to signal; ♦ *vt* *(estrada)* road sign.

sinceramente *adv* sincerely.

sinceridade *f* sincerity.

sincero,-a *adj* sincere, frank.

síncope *f* *(MED)* syncope, faint, fainting fit.

sincronia *f* synchrony. **sincronizar** *vt* to synchronize.

sindical *(pl:* **-ais***)* *adj inv* union, trade union.

sindicalista *m,f* trade unionist.

sindicância *f* (**de/sobre**) inquiry (into), investigation.

sindicato *m* trade union; syndicate.

síndico,-a *m* *(de prédio)* residents' representative; **2** trade union leader; **3** investigator; **4** *(BR)* *(de falência)*; receiver.

síndroma *f* *(MED)* syndrome; **2** *(indicadores de estado/situação)* syndrome; ~ **de abstinência** withdrawal symptoms, *pl*.

sineiro *m* bell-ringer; bell-maker.

sineiro,-a *adj* rel. to bell; **a torre** ~**a** the bell tower.

sinergia *f* synergy, *(pl: synergies)*; **2** combined action.

sineta *f* small bell, hand bell.

sinete *m* seal, signet; **anel de** ~ signet ring.

sinfonia *f* symphony.

sinfónico,-a *(BR:* **-ô***)* *adj* symphonic.

Singapura *npr* Singapore.

singeleza *f* simplicity; **2** *(pureza, sinceridade)* innocence, openness.

singelo,-a *adj* simple; **2** *(alma, coração)* pure, innocent; **3** *(pessoa)* sincere; **uma flor** ~**a** a simple (and pure) flower.

singrar *vt* *(navegar)* to sail; **2** *(fig)* *(progredir)* to do well.

singular *m* *(LÍNG)* singular; ♦ *adj* singular, exceptional, unique; **2** *(estranho)* odd, peculiar, unusual.

singularidade *f* strangeness, peculiarity.

singularizar *vt* to single out; **2** list; ♦ ~**se** *vr* to stand out, distinguish o.s.

sinistra *f* the left hand.

sinistrado,-a *m* injured person, casualty; ♦ *adj* *(alguém)* injured; **2** *(algo)* damaged.

sinistro *m* disaster, accident; **2** damage; ♦ **sinistro,-a** *adj* sinister; *(ambiente, lugar)* dark, gloomy.

sino *m* bell; **os ~s da igreja repicavam** the church bells were ringing.

sinónimo,-a *(BR: -nô-) m* synonym; ♦ *adj* synonymous.

sinopse *f* synopsis.

sinta *(pres subj de* **sentir)** **espero que ele se ~ melhor** I hope he feels better.

sintá(c)tico,-a *adj* syntactic(al).

sintaxe *f* syntax.

síntese *f* synthesis, summary, précis; **em ~** in short.

sintético,-a *adj* synthetic, concise; **2** *(produzido artificialmente)* synthetic.

sintetizar *vt* to synthesize; **2** to summarize.

sinto *(pres indic, 1ª pess de* **sentir)** **~ saudades de Lisboa** I miss Lisbon.

sintoma *m (MED)* symptom; **2** *(fig)* sign.

sintomático,-a *(MED) adj* symptomatic, indicative of; **2** *(fig)* significant.

sintonia *f (ELECT)* tuning; **2** *(fig)* harmony.

sintonizador *m (aparelho)* tuner; ♦ *adj* tuning.

sintonizar *vt (RADIO, TV)* to tune (in), synchronize; ♦ *vi (ELECT)* **~ com** to tune into; **3** *(fig)* get on with, harmonise with.

sinuosidade *f (do caminho)* winding, twisting, bend.

sinuoso,-a *adj (que descreve curvas)* sinuous, winding; **2** *(fig) (complicado)* devious; **3** *(fig) (astucioso)* shrewd, sharp.

sinusite *f (MED)* sinusitis.

sionismo *m* Zionism.

sionista *adj inv* Zionist.

sirene *f (da ambulância, polícia)* siren.

siri *m (ZOOL) (BR)* type of crab.

Síria *npr* **a ~** Syria.

sirigaita *(também:* **serigaita)** *f (ZOOL)* wren; **2** *(fam) (menina espevitada)* clever Miss; **3** *(mulher alegre)* lively, frolicsome girl.

sírio,-a *adj* Syrian.

siroco *m (vento quente e seco)* sirocco.

sirvo *(pres indic de* **servir)**.

sisa *f (JUR)* property transfer tax.

sisal *(BOT) m* agave; **2** *(fibra)* sisal.

sísmico,-a *adj* seismic.

sismo *m* earthquake.

sismógrafo *m* seismograph.

siso *m* good sense, wisdom; **dente do ~** wisdom tooth.

sistema *m (ger)* system; **2** *(modo)* method, way; **3** *(fig) (regime estabelecido)* establishment; ♦ **por ~** *adv* as a rule.

sistemática *f (estudo de sistemas)* systematics.

sistemático,-a *adj* systematic, methodical.

sistémico,-a *adj* systemic.

sístole *f* systole.

sisudo,-a *m,f (pessoa que fala ou ri pouco)* dour/sour person; ♦ *adj* serious, taciturn; **2** *(prudente)* wise, circumspect.

sitiante *adj inv* settler.

sitiar *vt (cercar)* to besiege, lay siege to; **2** *(rodear quinta)* surround; **3** *(assediar)* to harass.

sítio *m* place, location; **2** *(MIL)* siege; **estado de ~** state of siege, martial law.

situação *f (ger)* situation; **2** location, position; **3** placing; **4** *(estado)* state; **5** *(estado social)* status.

situacionista *adj inv* supporter of the "establishment" member of the governing party.

situar *vt* to place; **2** to situate, locate; **3** *(calcular algo)* estimate sth; ♦ **~-se** *vr (colocar-se) (pessoa)* place o.s.; **2** be placed/situated; **3** be considered, **este edifício situa-se entre os mais famosos** this building is considered (to be) among the most famous; **4** *(passar-se num determinado tempo)* take place; **5** *(em questão)* to take a position.

skate *m* skate; **andar de ~** to skate; **prancha de ~** skateboard.

skinhead *m,f* skinhead.

slogan *m* slogan.

smoking *m* dinner jacket.

snifar *vt (cd)* to sniff *(droga, coca)*.

snobe *m,f* snob; ♦ *adj inv* snobbish.

snobismo *m* snobbery; *(comentário snobe)* snobbish comment/remark.

só *adj inv* alone, by o.s., by itself; **estou ~** I am alone; **a s~s** alone; **conversa a ~s** chat between two people; **2** *(único)* single, only; **3** *(solitário)* solitary, lonely; **um ~** only one; ♦ *adv* only, just; **por si ~** by itself; *(tudo)* **é ~ isso?** is that all?; ♦ *conj* **não ~ … mas também…** not only … but also; **~ que** except that; ♦ *exc* **~ visto!** you would have to see it!

soalheiro,-a *adj* sunny, **uma casa ~a** a sunny house; ♦ *f* heat of the sun; ♦ *m* sunny spot.

soalho *m* (wooden) floor.

soar *vi* to sound, go off, ring; **o alarme soou** the alarm went off; **2** *(horas)* to strike; **3** echo; **4 ~ a** to sound like, seem like; **5** *(chegar)* come; **soou o momento de** the moment has come to; **soou-me aos ouvidos** it has come to my ears.

sob *prep (debaixo)* under; **~ a mesa** under the table; **2** *(mediante)* under, on; **~ pena de** on pain of; **~ minha palavra** on my word; **~ juramento** on oath; **~ emenda** subject to correction; **~ ameaça** under threat.

sobejar *vi (sobrar)* to be left over; **sobrou muita comida** a lot of food was left over; **2** *(abundar)* more than enough, abound; **ainda sobeja tempo** there is still plenty of time.

sobejo *m (vestígio)* trace; **um ~ de honra** a trace of honour (left); **~s** *mpl* remains, left-overs; ♦ *adj* surplus; **2** plenty of; **de ~** *adv* plenty.

sobem *(pres indic de* **subir)** **~ as escadas** they are going up the stairs; **elas, eles vocês sobem as escadas** they, you (pl) go up the stairs.

soberania *f* sovereignty.

soberano,-a *m,f (monarca)* sovereign; ♦ *adj* sovereign; **2** *(fig)* supreme.

soberba *f* arrogance, pride; **2** *(sobranceiro)* important.

soberbo,-a *adj* haughty, arrogant; **2** magnificent, splendid, superb; **um ~ cavalo** a splendid horse; **um jantar ~** a superb dinner; **3** *(pop) (avarento)* stingy.

sobra *f* surplus, remnant; **de ~** spare, extra; in abundance; **ficar de ~** to be left over; **~s** *fpl* leftovers, remains.

sobraçar *vt* to hold under one's arm.

sobrado *m* floor.

sobral *m* plantation of cork oaks, cork oak grove.

sobrancear *vt* to tower above.

sobranceiro,-a *adj (que está acima)* ~a above; **2** over-looking, prominent; **3** *(fig)* lofty.

sobrancelha *f* eybrow; **franzir as** ~s to frown.

sobrar *vi* to be left over; **sobra-me uma libra** I have £1 left; **não me sobrou tempo para** I had no time (left) to/for.

sobre *prep* on; **2** *(por cima de)* over; **as lindas pontes (por)** ~ **o Tâmisa** the beautiful bridges over the Thames; **3** *(em cima de)* on top of; **4** *(a respeito de)* about, concerning; **5** *(acima de)* above; **6** besides; **7** around; **ele chegou** ~ **a noite** he arrived at night/around night-time; **8** one after another; **cerveja** ~ **cerveja** one beer after another; **tomar** ~ **si** take upon him/herself; IDIOM **pôr uma pedra** ~ **o assunto** close the subject.

sobrealimentar *vt* to overfeed.

sobreaquecimento *m* overheating; ~ **global** global warming.

sobreaviso *m*: **estar/ficar de** ~ to be on the alert, on one's guard.

sobrecapa *f (de livro)* dust jacket.

sobrecarga *f* excess load, overloading.

sobrecarregar *vt* to overload; **2** *(pessoa)* to overburden; **3** *(fig)* overdo.

sobrecasaca *f* morning coat.

sobrecenho *m* frown, scowl.

sobrecéu *m* canopy.

sobredotado,-a *adj (pessoa)* gifted.

sobre-humano,-a *adj* superhuman, extraordinary.

sobreiro *m (BOT)* cork tree.

sobrelevar *vt* to tower above, rise above; **2** to raise; **3** to overcome; ♦ *vi* to stand out; ♦ ~-**se** *vr* to stand out.

sobreloja *f (piso)* mezzanine.

sobrelotado,-a *adj* full, overloaded.

sobremaneira *adv* really; **2** exceedingly, very, extremely; **3** extraordinarily.

sobremesa *f* dessert.

sobrenatural *adj* supernatural.

sobrenome *m* second name; **2** *(apelido)* surname, family name.

sobrepeliz *f* surplice.

sobrepor *vt* to put on top, overlap, overlay; **2** *(acrescentar)* to add; **3** *(antepor)* to put sth first, value more; ♦ ~-**se a** *vr*: to take over; **o seu desejo sobrepunha-se a tudo mais** her/his desire took over everything else; *(fig)* to overcome.

sobreposição *f* overlapping.

sobreposto,-a *(pp irr de: pôr) adj* overlapped; **2** ~ **a** superimposed, placed on top of.

sobrepujar *vt* to rise above; **2** to excel, surpass *(algo)*, exceed; **3** *(superar)* to overcome; ♦ *vi* stand out.

sobrescrito *m* envelope; address.

sobressair *vi (estar saliente)* to stand out; **esta cor sobressai do tom da parede** this colour stands out against the wall.

sobressalente *adj inv* spare; **um pneu** ~ a spare tyre.

sobressaltar *vt (assustar)* to startle, to frighten, make people jump; **2** *(inquietar)* to upset/worry; ♦ ~-**se** *vr* to be startled.

sobressalto *m* shock; scare; **de** ~ *adv* suddenly.

sobretaxa *f* surcharge.

sobretudo *m* overcoat; ♦ *adv* mainly, especially, above all.

sobrevalorizar *vt (mérito, qualidades)* over-estimate.

sobrevento *m* squall, a gust of wind; **2** sudden/unexpected event; **3** trouble.

sobrevir *vi* to occur, arise (after a previous event); **2** ~ **a** to follow (on); **sobreveio-lhe a morte** death overtook him.

sobrevivência *f* survival.

sobrevivente *m,f* survivor; ♦ *adj* surviving.

sobreviver *vi* to survive.

sobrevoar *vi* to fly over.

sobriedade *f* sobriety, soberness; **2** moderation, simplicity; **3** *(fig) (reserva)*, restraint.

sobrinha *f* niece.

sobrinho *m* nephew.

sóbrio,-a *adj (não embriagado)* sober; **2** *(nos seus hábitos)* moderate; **3** *(reservado)* controlled, restrained.

sobrolho *m* eyebrow; **2** ~ **carregado** scowl; **3** *(área superior do olho)* brow; **carregar/franzir o** ~ to scowl/frown.

soca *f (tamanco de madeira)* clog; **2** *(BOT)* rootstalk; **3** *(pop) (dinheiro)* dosh; **4** *(BR)* second production of sugar.

socalco *m* cultivated mountain terrace, ledge on the slope of a mountain; **os** ~s **do Minho e da Madeira cobertos de vinhas** Minho's and Madeira's mountain terraces covered in vines.

socapa *f* stealth; ♦ **à** ~ *adv* furtively, on the sly, sneakily; **entrar/sair à** ~ sneak in/sneak out; **rir à** ~ to laugh up one's sleeve.

socar *vt* to punch; **2** *(esmagar)* to crush; **3** *(amassar)* to knead.

socavar *vt* to excavate, dig out a mine.

social *(pl: -ais) adj inv* social; **assistência** ~ social welfare; **colunas** ~**ais** *(jornal)* social columns; *(COM)* **capital** ~ capital (stock); **2** sociable, friendly.

social-democrata *m,f* social-democrat; ♦ *adj inv* social-democratic.

socialismo *m* socialism.

socialista *adj* socialist.

socializar *vi* to socialize.

sociável *adj* sociable.

sociedade *f* society; **alta-**~ high society; **2** association; **3** *(ECON)* company; ~ **anónima** joint-stock/limited company; ~ **em comandita** limited partnership; ~ **de responsabilidade limitada** limited (liability) company; **4** partnership.

sócio,-a *m (membro)* member; ~ **benemérito** *(a mais alta distinção de um membro de uma associação)* Fellow; ~ **honorário** honorary member; **2** *(COM)* partner, associate; ~ **comanditário** *(COM)* silent/sleeping partner.

sócio-económico,-a *(pl: sócio-económicos,-as) adj* social-economic.

sociologia *f* sociology.

sociológico,-a *adj* sociological.

sociólogo,-a *m,f* sociologist.

soco *m* blow, punch, cuff; **dar um ~ (a alguém,** *(BR)* **em alguém)** to punch sb; **2** *(pop) (prejuízo)* blow; **3** *(ARQ)* socle; *(peanha)* small pedestal.

soçobrar *vt* to sink, wreck, turn upside down; **2** put at risk, jeopardize *(algo)*; ♦ *vi (naufragar)* to sink, capsize, founder; **2** fall, in danger of falling; come to ruin; **3** to lose courage; **não ~** to be buoyant.

soco-inglês *m* boxing.

socorrer *vt* to help, assist, relieve; **2** to rescue; ♦ **~-se** *vr*: **~ de** to resort to, have recourse to, turn to for help.

socorro *m* help, assistance; **ir em ~ de** to come to the aid of; **primeiros ~s** first aid *sg*; **posto de ~** first-aid centre; *(hospital)* casualty department; **2** *(reforço de tropas)* reinforcements; ♦ *exc* **socorro!** help!

soda *f (QUÍM)* soda; **~ cáustica** caustic soda; **2** *(água gaseificada)* soda water.

sódio *m* sodium chloride.

sodomia *f* sodomy.

sodomita *m* sodomite.

sodomizar *vt* to sodomize.

soerguer *vt (levantar um pouco)* to raise, lift *(cabeça)*; ♦ **~-se** *vr* to raise oneself; **2** *(pôr-se num nível acima)* rise above.

sofá *m* sofa, settee; **~-cama** *m* sofa-bed.

Sófia *npr* Sofia.

sofisma *m* sophism; **2** *(fig)* false statement; **3** *(BR) (col)* trick, deception.

sofismar *vt* to alter (facts), tell half-truths; ♦ *vi* mislead.

sofisticado,-a *adj* sophisticated.

sôfrego,-a *adj* greedy; **2** impatient (for); **3** *(ávido)* eager.

sofreguidão *f* greed; **2** eagerness; **3** impatience.

sofrer *vt* to suffer; **2** *(aguentar)* bear, put up with; **3 ~ prejuízos** incur loss *sg*; ♦ *vi (padecer)* to suffer; **~ de** suffer from.

sofrido,-a *adj* endured; **2** long-suffering; **sofrimento** *m* suffering; endurance.

sofrível *(pl: -eis) adj* bearable.

sogro,-a *m,f* father-in-law, mother-in-law.

sois *(2nd pers pres de ser) (arc, REL)* you are.

sóis *(Vd: sol).*

soja *f (planta)* **2** *(alimento, feijão)* soya bean.

sol *(pl: sóis) m* sun; **o nascer/o pôr do ~** sunrise/ sunset; **ao/no ~** in the sun; **faz ~** it is sunny; **tomar banho de ~** to sunbathe; **2** *(a luz do sol)* sunshine, sunlight; **3** *(MÚS)* G, Soh; ♦ **de ~ a ~** from dawn to dusk.

sola *f (do sapato)* sole; **2** *(ANAT)* **~ do pé** sole of the foot.

solapar *vt (minar)* to dig into; **2** *(fig)* to undermine; **3** *(arruinar)* destroy.

solar *m* manor house; ♦ *adj inv* solar; **energia ~** solar energy.

solarengo *adj* manorial.

solário *m* solarium.

solavanco *m* jolt, bump; **andar aos ~s** to jog along.

solda *f (material metálico fuzível)* solder; **2** *(soldadura)* welding; **3** *(antigo pagamento anual a empregados de lavoura)* wages; **4** *(fig) (aderência)* adherence, link.

soldadesca *f (pej)* soldiers, soldiery, troops.

soldado *m* soldier; **~ raso** private soldier; *(fig)* **~ de chumbo** *(de brinquedo)* tin soldier, toy soldier.

soldador *m* welder.

soldar *vt* to solder, weld; ♦ *vr* to unite, join, link.

soldo *m (MIL)* soldier's pay; wages.

soleira *f* doorstep, threshold; **2** *(EQUIT) (parte do estribo)* tread of the stirrup; **3** *(GEOL)* plateau.

solene *adj inv* solemn, formal.

solenidade *f* solemnity.

solenizar *vt* to solemnize.

soletrar *vt* to spell out; **2** read out slowly.

solfejo *m (MÚS)* sol-fa, solfeggio.

solha *f (fish)* plaice.

solicitação *f* request; **solicitações** *fpl* inducement *sg*, appeal *sg*.

solicitador,-ora *m,f* solicitor.

solicitante *m,f* petitioner; ♦ *adj* petioning.

solicitar *vt* to ask for; **2** *(emprego, etc)* to apply for; **3** *(amizade, atenção)* to seek; **4** *(cortejar)* go after, chase.

solícito,-a *adj* diligent; **2** helpful.

solicitude *f* great care; **2** concern, thoughtfulness; **3** *(empenho)* commitment.

solidão *f* solitude, isolation; **2** loneliness; **3** *(fig)* wilderness, desert.

solidariedade *f* solidarity.

solidário,-a *adj* sympathetic; **2** jointly responsible; *(na dor)* united.

solidarizar-se *vr* **~ com** to sympathize with.

solidez *f* solidity; **2** stability; **3** strength.

sólido,-a *adj* solid; **2** *(firme)* strong; **3** *(argumento)* sound.

solilóquio *m* soliloquy.

solista *m,f* soloist.

solitário,-a *m,f* recluse; *m* hermit; **2** *(jarra estreita)* vase for one flower; **3** *(anel de um diamante)* solitaire (ring); **4** *f (ténia)* tapeworm; **5** *(cela)* solitary (confinement); ♦ *adj* lonely, solitary.

solo *m* ground, soil, land; **2** *(MÚS)* solo.

sol-pôr *m* sunset; **ao ~** *adv* at sunset.

solstício *m (ASTRON)* solstice.

soltar *m (libertar)* set free, release, let go; **2** *(desatar)* to loosen, untie, unfasten; **3** *(afrouxar)* to slacken; **4** *(emitir)* to let/burst out; **eles soltaram gargalhadas** they burst out laughing; **ele soltou insultos** he let out insults; ♦ **~-se** *vr* to *(desprender-se)* come loose/off; **2** to escape, free o.s.; **3** *(bandeira, velas)* unfurl; **~ a língua** to loosen one's tongue.

solteiro,-a *m* bachelor; ♦ *f* single woman, spinster; ♦ *adj* unmarried, single; **solteirona** *f* old maid, spinster.

solto,-a *(irr pp de soltar) adj* loose; **2** free; **3** *(roupa larga)* baggy, loose; **4 verso ~** blank verse; **5 intestino ~** loose bowels; **à ~a** *adv* freely, loosely, on the loose; **IDIOM dormir a sono ~** to sleep like a log.

soltura *f* looseness; **2** release, discharge.

soluçante *adj inv* (*que soluça*) with hiccups; **2** (*choro*) sobbing; **3** (*relato, motor, etc*) with stops and starts, hiccupping.

solução *f* resolução solution; **2** (*FARM, FÍS*) solution; **3** (*obrigação de pagar*) pay-off.

soluçar *vi* (*choro*) to sob, weep; **2** (*MED*) to hiccup.

solucionar *vt* to solve.

soluço *m* sob; **2** (*MED*) hiccup, hiccough; **3** (*ruído intermitente*) hiccup.

solúvel *adj* soluble.

solvência *f* solvency.

solvente *adj* solvent.

solver *vt* to solve; to pay.

som *m* sound; (*MÚS*) tone; **2** (*BR*: aparelho) hi-fi, stereo; (*BR*) music; ♦ **ao ~ de** (*MÚS*) *prep* to the tune/accompaniment of; (*falar*) **alto e bom ~** *adv* to speak out; IDIOM **sem tom nem ~** without rhyme or reason; **dançar ao ~ dos caprichos de** (**alguém**) dance to sb's tune.

soma[1] (*MED*) *m* (*corpo*) the body.

soma[2] *m* tribal chief (*Angola*).

soma[3] *f* sum, total.

somar *vt* to add (up); **2** (*totalizar*) to add up to, amount to; ♦ *vi* to add up.

somático *adj* somatic, physical; **células ~as** body cells.

somatório m total sum; **2** (*totalidade*) total.

sombra *f* (*projeção, silhueta*) shadow; **2** (*lesão, mancha*) shadow; **ele tem uma ~ no pulmão** he has a shadow on the lung; (*cosmético*) eye shadow; (*estar mudado para pior*) **ela é uma ~ do que era** she is a shadow of what she used to be; **3** (*vestígio*) trace; **não vejo ~ dele** I don't see any trace of him; **4** (*fig*) ghost; bodyguard; **5** (*área*) shade; **à ~** in the shade; **à ~ de** in the shade of; (*fig*) under the protection of; **nem por ~s!** not a chance, don't even dream of it!; **sem ~ de dúvida** without a shadow of a doubt; IDIOM **fazer ~ a alguém** to outshine sb, put sb in the shade.

sombreado,-a *adj* shady; (*ARTE*) shading.

sombrear *vt* to shade.

sombrinha *f* lady's umbrella.

sombrio,-a *adj* (*lugar*) shady, dark; **2** (*pessoa*) gloomy.

some (*pres indic, 3ª pessoa sg, pl de* sumir) **as coisas somem-se** things vanish; **some-te!** get lost!

somenos *adj* inferior, poor; **de ~ importância** unimportant.

somente *adv* only, merely.

somítico,-a *adj* stingy, mean.

somos (*pres indic, 1ª pessoa pl, de* ser).

sonambulismo *m* sleepwalking.

sonâmbulo,-a *m,f* sleepwalker; ♦ *adj* sleepwalking.

sonante *adj inf* sounding, ringing, clinking; **2** (*voz, tom*) noisy, loud; **3 metal ~** (*dinheiro*) hard cash.

sonata *f* sonata.

sonda *f* (*examinar terreno, água*) plummet, plumb-line, sounding-line; **2** (*MED, FÍS*) probe; **3** (*MED*) (*de alimentação*) drip; **4** (*GEOL*) bore; **5** (*TEC*) (*de petróleo*) drill; **~ a diamante** diamond drill; **6** (*NÁUT*) sounding lead; **7 ~ espacial** space probe.

sondagem *f* (*terreno, mar*) sounding, exploration; **2** (*petróleo*) drilling; boring; **3** survey; **~ pública** opinion poll.

sondar *vt* (*NÁUT*) to sound; **2** (*perfurar com sonda*) probe, drill; **3** (*investigar*) to sound out (*terreno, rochas*); **4** (*METEOR*) take soundings, probe; **5** (*estatísticas*) survey; take a survey of; **6** (*fig*) (*investigar*) sound out, fathom.

soneca *f* short nap; have a snooze; (*fam*) forty winks.

sonegação *f* (*ocultação*) concealment, withholding; **~ de impostos** tax evasion.

sonegador,-ora *m,f* (*de impostos*) tax dodger; ♦ *adj* (*impostos*) fraudulent.

sonegar *vt* (*omitir*) to conceal, withhold; **2** dodge (*impostos, declaração*); ♦ *vr* fail/refuse to carry out an order/duty.

soneto *m* sonnet.

sonhador,-ora *m,f* dreamer; ♦ *adj* dreamy, dreaming.

sonhar *vi* to dream; **~ com** to dream about; **2** (*desejar*) dream, **~ em fazer algo** to dream of doing sth; **~ acordado** to daydream; **nem ~!** don't even dream it!

sonho *m* dream; **tu és o meu ~** you are my dream; **2** (*CULIN*) kind of doughnut.

sono *m* sleep; **estar com ~/ter ~** to be sleepy; **pegar no ~** to fall asleep.

sonolência *f* drowsiness.

sonolento,-a *adj* sleepy, drowsy.

sonoridade *f* (*timbre*) sound quality; **2** resonance.

sonorizar *vt* set up the sound for; **2** (*filme*) make the soundtrack for.

sonoro,-a *adj* sonorous; resonant, resounding; **vias ~as** (*auto-estrada*) rumble strips; **2** (*FÍS*) (*onda*) sound; **banda ~a** soundtrack; **3** (*FON*) voiced.

sonso,-a *adj* sly, artful, pretending to be innocent.

sopa *f* (*CULIN*) soup; **2** (*fig*) **estar uma ~** to be soaked; **3** *excl* **ou sim ou ~!** take or leave it!; IDIOM **andar às ~s** living off/sponging off someone.

sopapo *m* (*bofetada*) slap, cuff; ♦ **de ~** *adv* without thinking; IDIOM **dar um ~ na carteira** to nick from a wallet; **dar um ~ em alguém** to slap sb.

sopé *m* (*GEOG*) (*da montanha*) foot, bottom.

sopeira *f* tureen for soup; **2** (*pop*) (*arc*) kitchen maid, domestic employee.

sopesar *vt* to weigh in one's hand; to calculate the weight by hand.

sopitar *vt* to make sb sleepy; **2** to calm (down), appease.

soporífero,-a *adj* soporiferous.

soprano *adj* soprano; **meio ~** mezzo-soprano.

soprar *vt* (*com sopro*) to blow; **2** (*apagar*) to blow out; **3** blow up (*saco, balão*); **4 ~a** (**alguém**) to whisper (*sth to sb*); ♦ *vi* (*vento*) blow.

sopro *m* blow, puff; **2** (*de aragem*) gust, breeze; **3** (*ânimo*) breath; **4** (*MED*) **~ no coração** heart murmur; **5 instrumento de ~** wind instrument.

soquete *m* ankle sock.

sordidez *f* (*sujidade*) filth, squalor; **2** (*torpeza*) sordidness, baseness.

sórdido,-a *adj* squalid; **2** *(torpe)* sordid, vile.
sorna *f* *(moleza)* laziness, sluggishness; **2** *(pessoa)* lazybones; ◆ *adj* idle, slow.
soro *m* *(MED)* serum; **2** *(de leite)* whey.
soropositivo *adj* soropositive.
sóror *f* *(REL)* sister.
sorrateiro,-a *adj* sly, sneaky, stealthy.
sorridente *adj* smiling.
sorrir *vi* to smile; ~ **para** to smile (at); *(sorte)* to smile on.
sorriso *m* smile; ~ **amarelo** forced smile, wry smile.
sorte *f* *(ventura)* luck, chance; **ter** ~ to be lucky; **a** ~ **grande** the lottery, the jackpot; **pouca** ~ hard luck; **a** ~ **é caprichosa** Lady Luck is capricious; **2** *(destino)* fate, destiny, lot(s); **abandonada à** ~ left to her fate; **tirar à sorte** to draw lots; **à** ~ at random; **desta** ~ so, thus; **de** ~ **que** so that; **por** ~ *(acaso)* by chance, luckily.
sortear *vt* to draw lots for; **2** to raffle; **3** *(sortir)* mix *(bolos, etc)*; **4** *(MIL)* to draft.
sorteio *m* draw; **2** *(rifa)* raffle; **3** *(MIL)* draft; **4** selecção; **o** ~ **de três prémios** selection of three prizes (in the draw).
sortido,-a *m* assortment, variety; ◆ *adj* *(fornecido)* supplied, stocked; **2** *(variado)* varied, assorted.
sortilégio *m* *(feitiço)* sorcery, spell; **2** *(encanto)* charm, fascination; **3** *(truque)* trick, divination by drawing lots.
sortimento *m* assortment, stock.
sortir *vt* to supply, stock; **2** to vary, mix.
sorumbático,-a *m,f* uncommunicative person; ◆ *adj* gloomy, sullen, glum.
sorvedouro *m* *(redemoinho)* whirlpool; **2** *(abismo)* chasm; **3** *(fig)* ~ **de dinheiro** a drain on resources; **4** soaking up.
sorver *vt* *(beber, engolir)* to sip, gulp; **2** *(comer ruidosamente)* to slurp; **3** *(tragar)* swallow (up); **4** *(aspirar fundo)* breathe in; **5** *(cheirar aroma)* to sniff; **6** *(absorver)* absorb, soak (up/in); **7** *(chupar)* suck; ◆ *vi* *(aspirar)* to suck.
sorvete *m* ice cream.
sorvo *m* *(gole)* sip, gulp; **2** sucking, slurping.
sósia *m,f* double; **2** *(fam)* spitting image.
soslaio *adv* **de** ~ sideways, obliquely, askew; **olhar algo de** ~ to look out of the corner of one's eye.
sossegado,-a *adj* peaceful, calm, quiet.
sossegar *vt* to calm *(down)*, quieten; **2** *(espírito)* soothe; ◆ *vi* to rest.
sossego *m* peacefulness, calm, peace (and quiet).
sotaina *f* cassock.
sótão *m* attic, loft.
sotaque *m* accent.
sotavento *m* *(NÁUT)* lee; **a** ~ to leeward; **2** *(região)* eastern part, east.
soterrar *vt* to bury.
soturno,-a *adj* sad, gloomy; **2** *(assustador)* frightening.
sou *(pres ind, 1ª pessoa de ser)* ~ **médico** I am a doctor (medicine).
soube *etc* *(pret de: saber)* ~ **pela Rita que tu ias casar** I learnt from Rita you were getting married.
soutien (= **sutiã**) *m* bra(ssiere).

sova *f* beating, thrashing; **2** *(fig)* *(ralhar)* scolding; **3** *(BR)* *(de fruta, sementes)* crushing; *(de massa)* kneading.
sovaco *m* armpit.
sovar *vt* *(bater em)* to beat, to thrash; **2** to tread.
sovela *f* awl; **2** *(ZOOL)* avocet.
sovina *m,f* miser, skinflint; ◆ *adj* miserly.
sovinice *f* stinginess; **2** meanness, pettiness, stinginess.
sozinho,-a *adj* (all) alone, by oneself; **2** *(solitária)* lonely; **3** *(único)* by itself.
sprintar *vt* to sprint.
Sr. *(abr de senhor)* Mr.; **Sr.ª** *(abr de senhora)* Mrs.
Srs. *(abr de senhores; senhores e senhoras)*
Sr.ta *(BR)* *(abr de senhorita)* Miss.
sua *(Vd. seu)*.
suado,-a *adj* *(de suor)* sweaty; **mãos ~as** sweaty hands; **2** *(fig)* *(fam)* *(obtido com esforço)* hard-earned.
suão *m* hot south wind; ◆ *adj* south.
suar *vi* *(transpirar)* to sweat, perspire; **2** *(fig)* *(esforçar-se)* strive for, sweat; *(adquirir com esforço)* with the sweat of one's brow; IDIOM **suar às estopinhas** sweat like a pig.
suas *(fpl de sua)* *(Vd: seu, sua)*.
suave *adj* soft, gentle; **voz** ~ soft voice; *(brisa, carícia)* gentle; **2** *(temperatura)* mild; **3** *(cabelo, pele, vinho)* smooth; **4** *(trabalho, castigo)* light; **5** *(cor, aroma)* delicate.
suavidade *f* softness, delicacy; **2** gentleness; **3** *(brandura)* mildness.
suavizar *vt* to soften, tone down; **2** *(mitigar)* lessen; **3** *(amaciar-pele)* smooth; ◆ *vr* *(amenizar)* to lessen; **2** *(luz)* fade.
subalimentado,-a *adj* undernourished.
subalterno,-a *m* *(MIL)* subaltern; ◆ *adj* subordinate.
subalugar, subarrendar *vt* to sublet.
subchefe *m,f* assistant director; **2** *(da polícia)* assistant chief of police.
subconsciência *f* subconscious.
subconsciente *m* the subconscious; ◆ *adj inv* subconscious.
subdesenvolvido,-a *adj* underdeveloped.
subdesenvolvimento *m* underdevelopment.
sú(b)dito *m* *(de um governo, país)* subject; **um** ~ **de Sua Majestade** Her Majesty's subject.
subemprego *m* *(ECON)* under-employment
subentender *vt* to assume, infer, imply.
subido,-a *f* ascent, climb; **2** *(encosta)* slope; **3** *(aumento)* rise; **houve uma** ~ **de preços** there was a rise in prices; **4** *(das saias)* shortening.
subir *vt/vi* to go up; ~ **as escadas** go up the stairs; **2** *(colina, árvore)* climb (up); **3** to rise; **subir a** to mount, get on to; **4** *(elevador)* go up; **5** *(socialmente)* go up in the world; **6** ~ **à cabeça** *(fig)* *(vinho)* go to one's head; **7** *(ECON, COM)* **os preços sobem em flecha** prices are rising steeply.
súbito,-a *adj* sudden; **de** ~ suddenly.
subjacente *adj* subjacent, underlying.
subje(c)tivo,-a *adj* subjective.
subjugar *vt* *(dominate)* to subjugate; **2** *(moralmente)* subdue; **3** *(derrotar)* to overpower.
subjuntivo *m* *(gram)* subjunctive.
sublevação *f* (up)rising, revolt.

sublevar *vt* to stir up in revolt; ◆ ~-**se** (**contra algo/ alguém**) *vr* to revolt, rebel (against sth/sb).

sublime *adj* sublime, noble.

sublinhar *vt (linha, palavras)* to underline; **2** *(enfatizar)* to emphasize, stress.

sublocatário,-a *m,f (inquilino que arrenda/aluga quarto, apartamento)* sub-tenant, lodger.

submarino,-a *m* submarine; ◆ *adj* underwater.

submergir *vt* to submerge; **2** *(afundar)* sink; **3** *(engolfar)* swallow up; **4** *(esconder-se)* be plunged.

submersão *f* submersion.

submerso,-a *adj* submersed, flooded; **2** *(fig)* ~ **em** absorbed, engrossed (in).

submeter *vt* to subdue; **2** to submit *(pessoa, proposta)* ◆ ~-**se** *vr*: ~ **a** to submit to, give in; **2** to undergo.

submissão *f* submission, obedience; **2** *(MIL)* surrender.

submisso,-a *adj* submissive, docile.

submundo *m* underground world.

subnutrição *f* malnutrition.

subordinado,-a *adj* subordinate, dependent.

subordinar *vt* to subordinate.

subordinável *adj inv (autoridade, funcionário, posição)* that can be subordinated, controlled.

subornar *vt* to bribe.

suborno *m* bribery.

subproduto *m* secondary product.

sub-reptício,-a *adj* surreptitious, furtive.

subscrever *vt (assinar)* to sign; **2** *(aprovar)* to subscribe to; agree with, give support to; ◆ ~-**se** *vr* to sign one's name.

subscrição *f* subscription; **2** *(assinatura)* signature.

subscrito,-a *(pp de* **subscrever***) adj* undersigned.

subscritor,-ora *m,f* subscriber; ◆ *adj (alguém)* subscribing.

subsecretário,-a *m,f (do governo)* under-secretary, ~ **adjunto** deputy under-secretary.

subsequente *adj* subsequent, following.

subserviência *f* subservience.

subserviente *adj inv* subservient, servile, obsequious; **2** *(que lisonja)* cringing, fawning.

subsidiar *vt* to subsidize; **2** back, support.

subsidiário,-a *f (COM)* subsidiary (company); ◆ *adj* subsidiary.

subsídio *m (estatal)* subsidy, aid; ~ **de desemprego** unemployment benefit/allowance; **receber** ~ **de desemprego** be on the dole; **2** grant; ~ **a fundo perdido** non-returnable grant; **subsídios** *mpl (dados, contribuições)* information *sg*.

subsistência *f (sobrevivência)* subsistence; **2** *(sustento)* livelihood.

subsistir *vi* to survive, subsist.

subsolo *m (GEOL)* subsoil; **2** *(de um prédio) (garagem, casa de arrecadação)* basement, underground.

substância *f* substance; **2** *(ANAT)* matter; ~ **cinzenta** grey matter (the brain); ◆ **em** ~ *adv* in general, basically.

substancial *adj inv* substantial.

substantivo,-a *m ((GRAM)* noun; ~ **próprio** proper noun; ◆ *adj (relativo a substância)* substantive.

substituir *vt (fazer as vezes de alguém) (temporário)* to substitute, stand in for (sb); *(tomar o lugar de*

outro permanentemente) replace; **2** *(trocar/mudar máquina, etc.)* change; **3** ~ **a sentinela** change the guard.

substituível *adj inv* replaceable.

substituto,-a *adj* substitute.

substrato *m (GEOL)* substratum; **2** *(LÍNG)* roots; **3** *(substância)* foundation, essence.

subterfúgio *m* subterfuge, evasion; **2** trick.

subterrâneo,-a *adj* subterranean, underground; **passagem** ~**a** subway.

su(b)til *adj inv* subtle; **2** fine, delicate.

su(b)tileza *f* subtlety; **2** fineness, delicacy.

subtilmente *adv* subtly.

subtítulo *m* subtitle.

subtra(c)ção *f (MAT)* subtraction; **2** *(furto)* theft.

subtrair *vt* to subtract, deduct; **2** to steal, embezzle; ◆ ~-**se** *vr (fam)* get rid of.

suburbano,-a *adj* suburban.

subúrbio *m* suburb.

subvenção *f* subsidy, grant.

subvencionar *vt* to subsidize.

subversivo,-a *adj, m,f* subversive.

subverter *vt* to subvert.

sucata *f* scrap metal; **2** *(local)* scrapyard, junkyard.

sucateiro,-a *m,f* scrap metal merchant.

sucção *f* suction.

sucedâneo,-a *m* substitute; ◆ *adj* substitute.

suceder *vi* to happen, occur; **2** ~ **a** to befall; **3** ~ **a alguém** to succeed sb, take the place of; **4** *(vir a seguir)* follow; ◆ ~-**se** *vr (repetir-se)* **os anos sucedem-se** year follows year; year after year.

sucedido,-a *m* occurrence, what happened; **isto foi o** ~ this is what happened; ◆ *adj*: **bem** ~ successful.

sucessão *f* succession.

sucessivo,-a *adj* successive, succession.

sucesso *m* success; **não ter** ~ to fail; **2** *(filme)* hit.

sucessor,-ora *m,f* successor.

súcia *f* gang, band.

sucinto,-a *adj* concise, succinct.

suco *m (BR)* juice.

suculento,-a *adj* succulent, juicy.

sucumbir *vi (ceder)* to succumb, yield; **2** *(morrer, esmorecer)* to die, perish, fade; **3** *(acabar)* close down *(empresa)*.

sucursal *f (COM) (de empresa)* branch; **2** *(de jornal, etc)* subsidiary.

sudanês,-nesa *m,f adj* Sudanese.

Sudão *npr* Sudan; **o** ~ Sudan.

sudário *m (lençol em que se enrola o cadáver)* shroud.

sudeste *m* the South East; ◆ *adj* south-east.

súdito *(BR) (Vd:* **sú(b)dito***)*.

sudoeste *m* the South West; ◆ *adj* south-west.

Suécia *npr f* Sweden; **a** ~ Sweden.

sueco,-a *m (LÍNG)* Swedish; ◆ *m,f* Swede; ◆ *adj* Swedish.

sueste *m* the South East; ◆ *adj* south-east.

suéter *m,f* sweater.

suficiência *f* sufficiency; **2** *(capacidade)* competence, aptitude.

suficiente *adj* sufficient, enough.

sufixo *m (gram)* suffix.

sufocante *adj inv* suffocating; **2** *(calor, ar)* sweltering, stifling.

sufocar *vt/vi (asfixiar)* to suffocate, choke; **2** *(matar por asfixia)* smother; **3** *(abafar-voz, passos)* muffle; **4** *(reprimir – choro, riso)* restrain, hold back.

sufrágio *m* suffrage, vote.

sugar *vt* to suck; **2** *(fig)* to extort.

sugerir *vt* to suggest, insinuate.

sugestão *f* suggestion; **2** hint.

sugestionável *adj inv* suggestible, easily influenced.

sugestivo,-a *adj* suggestive.

Suíça *npr f* Switzerland; **a ~** Switzerland.

suíças *fpl (na cara)* sideburns.

suicida *m,f* suicidal person; **2** suicide.

suicidar-se *vr* to commit suicide.

suicídio *m* suicide.

suíço,-a *adj* Swiss.

sui generis *adj inv* unique, sui generis.

suincultor,-a *m,f* pig breeder.

suíno,-a *m* (ZOOL) pig, swine; ♦ *adj* pig-like, porcine.

sujar *vt* to soil, dirty; **2** *(macular)* sully, disgrace; ♦ **~-se** *vr* to get dirty; **2** *(por actos indignos)* debase/lower o.s.

sujeição *f* subjection; **2** subordination; **3** *(fig)* submission.

sujeira *f* dirt, dirtiness, filth, mess; **2** *(fam)* common behaviour; *(fig)* **foi uma ~** it was a scandal/shameful scene.

sujeitar *vt (subordinar)* to subdue; **2** *(submeter)* to subject, submit; ♦ **~-se** *vr (submeter-se)* to submit, given in, yield (to).

sujeito *m (pessoa)* fellow, gentleman; **não conheço aquele ~** I don't know that gentleman; **2** *(gram)* subject; **3** *(LITER) (assunto)* subject.

sujeito,-a *adj* subjected (to); liable to.

sujidade *f* dirtiness; filth, muck.

sujo,-a *adj* dirty, filthy.

sul *m* the south; ♦ *adj inv* south, southern.

sulcar *vt (o mar)* to plough; **~ os mares** to plough the seas; **2** *(fazer sulcos na terra)* plough; **3** *(cavar)* furrow.

sulco *m (rego na terra)* furrow; **2** *(no rosto)* wrinkle; **3** *(rasto do navio pelo mar)* wake.

sulfato *m* sulphate.

sulfúrico,-a *adj* sulphuric.

sultana *f (raínha)* Sultana; **2** *(variedade de uva/passas)* sultana.

suma *f* summary; **em ~** in short.

sumamente *adv* extremely.

sumariar *vt* sum up; summarize; abridge.

sumário *m* summary; abstract; **2** *(índice)* index; ♦ **sumário,-a** *adj* brief, concise.

sumaúma *f (fibra, árovre)* kapok; **prefiro almofadas de ~** I prefer pillows (filled) with kapok.

sumiço *m (pop)* disappearance; **dar ~ a** a spirit away, to do away with, lose sth; **levar ~** to disappear.

sumidade *f* highest point; **2** *(fig) (pessoa)* very important.

sumido,-a *adj* vanished; **2** *(apagado)* faint, indistinct; **3** *(olhos)* sunken; **4** *(voz)* low.

sumidouro *m* drain; **os ~s da rua estão entupidos** the drains in the street are clogged up.

sumir *vt* make disappear; **2** *(desembaraçar-se de algo)* get rid of; **3** *(perder)* lose; ♦ *vi* disappear, run away, make off with; **some daqui** get out of here!; ♦ **~-se** *vr* disappear, vanish; **2** *(extinguir-se)* fade, die.

sumo *m (fruto)* juice; ♦ **sumo,-a** *adj* supreme, maximum; **~ sacerdote** high priest; **S~ Pontífice** Pope; **assunto de ~a importância** matter of great importance.

sumptuoso,-a, suntuoso,-a *adj* sumptuous.

súmula *f* epitome; summing up.

sunga (BR) *f* swimming trunks; jock-strap, athletic support.

suor *m* sweat, perspiration; **2** *(fig)* **fiz este jardim com o meu próprio ~** I made this garden by the sweat of my brow.

superaquecer *vi, vt* to overheat.

superaquecimento *m* overheating.

superar *vt (vencer)* to overcome; **ela superou a sua perda** she overcame her loss; **2** *(ultrapassar)* to exceed, surpass.

superável *adj inv (problema, desgosto)* that can be overcome; superable; **2** surpassable.

superávit *m* (COM) surplus.

superestrutura *f* superstructure.

superficial *adj* superficial.

superfície *f* surface; area.

supérfluo,-a *adj* superfluous, unnecessary.

super-homem *(pl: super-homens)* *m* superman; supermen.

superintendência *f* management.

superintendente *m* superintendent, supervisor, overseer.

superior *m,f* superior; **2** (REL) superior; **Superiora** *f* Mother Superior; ♦ *adj inv (mais alto)* superior, higher, upper; **2 ~ a** better/greater /higher than, superior to; **3** (ANAT) *(lábio, membros)* upper; **4 ensino ~** higher education.

superioridade *f* superiority.

superlativo,-a *m (gram)* superlative; ♦ *adj* superlative.

superlotado,-a *adj (transport, teatro)* overcrowded, packed; **2** *(bilhetes para teatro etc)* sold out.

supermercado *m* supermarket.

superpotência *f* superpower.

superpovoado,-a *adj* over-populated.

superprodução *f* over-production.

supersensível *(pl: -veis)* *adj inv* hypersensitive.

supersónico,-a (BR: -sô-) *adj* supersonic.

superstição *f* superstition.

supersticioso,-a *adj* superstitious.

supervisão *f* supervision.

supervisionar *vt* to supervise.

supervisor,-ora *m,f* supervisor.

superavit *m* (FIN) surplus in revenue.

supetão *adv* **de ~** all of a sudden.

suplantar *vt (vencer)* to supplant, beat, supersede; **2** *(dominar)* override.

suplementar *adj inv* additional, extra; (GEOG) supplementary; ♦ *vt (fornecer)* to provide; **2** reinforce; **3** to supplement.

suplemento *m (provisão)* supply; **2** supplement; **3** ~ **policial** police reinforcement; **4** *(jornal,revista)* supplement.

suplente *m,f* substitute; ♦ *adj inv (alguém, pneu, peça)* extra, spare.

súplica *f* supplication, plea.

suplicante *m* supplicant; **2** *(JUR)* plaintiff; suitor; ♦ *adj inv* pleading.

suplicar *vt* beg for; *vi* to plead.

suplício *m* torture.

supor *vt* to suppose, think, presume; **suponhamos que** let us suppose (that).

suportar *vt* to hold up, support *(alguém, algo)*; **2** to bear, tolerate; **não suporto este calor** I can't bear this heat.

suportável *adj inv* bearable, tolerable; **2** reasonably good.

suporte *m* support, prop, stand; **2** *(material básico antes de aplicar a tinta)* primer.

suposição *f (conjectura)* supposition, assumption.

supositório *m* suppository.

supostamente *adv* supposedly.

suposto,-a *m* assumption; ♦ *(pp de* **supor***) adj* supposed; **2** *(falso) (alguém)* so-called.

supracitado,-a *adj* aforementioned, above.

supra-sumo *(pl:* **supra-sumos***) m* highest, top, cream, acme, ideal.

supremacia *f* supremacy.

supremo *m* Supreme; **o S~ Tribunal** Supreme Court; ♦ **supremo,-a** *adj* supreme, highest; **2** utmost.

supressão *f* suppression; omission.

suprimento *m (fornecimento)* supply; **2** *(suplemento)* subsidy, supplement; **3** loan; **4** aid, assistance.

suprimir *vt (omitir)* to suppress; **2** *(cortar)* to cut back; **3** eliminate; **4** *(abolir)* abolish.

suprir *vt (provir)* to supply, provide; **2** *(atenuar)* to make up for; **3** *(substituir)* take the place of; ♦ *vi* to make do with.

supurante *adj inv (abcesso)* suppurative.

supurar *vt, vi (fazer criar pus)* to fester, suppurate.

surdez *f* deafness.

surdina *f (MÚS)* mute; **em** ~ stealthily, on the quiet.

surdo,-a *m,f (que não ouve)* deaf person; hearing-impaired; ♦ *adj* deaf; **2** *(passos, som)* muffled, dull); ~-**mudo,-a** *adj* deaf and dumb.

surgir *vi* to emerge, appear; **2** *(sobrevir)* to arise; **surgiu uma questão** a question arose; **3** *(ideia)* come up with.

surpreendente *adj inv* surprising, amazing.

surpreender *vt* to surprise, amaze; **2** to take sb unawares.

surpresa *f* surprise; **de** ~ by surprise.

surpreso,-a *(pp de* **surpreender***) adj* surprised.

surra *f* beating, thrashing; **dar uma** ~ **em alguém** to give sb a hiding.

surrado,-a *adj* beaten (up); **2** *(muito usado)* worn out.

surrar *vt* to beat; to thrash.

surriba *f (AGR)* deep trenching *(para melhorar qualidade)*; excavation.

surripiar *vt (pop)* to take on the sly; to filch.

surtida *f (MIL)* sortie, sally.

surtir *vt* to produce, bring about; **2** ~ **efeito** to turn out well.

surto *m (irrupção)* burst, outburst; **2** *(doença)* outbreak; **3** impulse, upsurge; **4** *(ECON)* boom; **5** ~ **de frio** cold spell.

susce(p)tível *ad jinv* susceptible.

suscitar *vt* to excite, stir up, provoke, cause; **2** ~ **dúvidas** to raise doubts; **3** *(despertar)* awake in, inspire, revive; ~ **interesse** to awaken interest.

suspeição *(pl: -ões) f* suspicion; **2** lack of trust.

suspeita *f* suspicion; **levantar/afastar** ~**s** to raise/avert suspicions; **lançar** ~**s** to cast suspicion on.

suspeitar *vt/vi (desconfiar de alguém)* to suspect, distrust; **2** *(crer)* suspect, think; **suspeito que ele venha tarde** I suspect he may come late.

suspeito,-a *m,f (pessoa)* suspect; ♦ *adj (que causa suspeita)* suspicious; **2** suspected.

suspeitoso,-a *adj (desconfiado)* suspicious; **2** *(em questão, dúvida)* questionable.

suspender *vt (ger)* to suspend; **2** *(levantar)* hold/lift up; **3** *(adiar)* postpone; **4** ~ **a sessão** adjourn the meeting; **5** to stop.

suspensão *f (ger)* suspension; **2** interruption; **3** postponement; **4** temporary dismissal; **5** *(AUTO)* **roda de** ~ wheel suspension; **6** *(de pagamento)* stoppage.

suspense *f* suspense; **filme de** ~ thriller.

suspenso,-a *(pp de:* **suspender***) adj* suspended, hanging; **2** *(encomenda)* cancelled; **3** *(JUR) (sentença)* suspended.

suspensórios *mpl (das calças)* braces *(UK)*; suspenders *(US)*.

suspirar *vi* to sigh; ~ **de alívio** to sigh with relief; **2** ~ **por algo** to long for sth.

suspiro *m* sigh; **2** *(CULIN)* meringue.

sussurrar *vt/vi* to whisper; **2** to murmur.

sussurro *m* whisper; **2** *(rumorejo)* buzz; **3** *(boato)* rumour.

sustância *(também* **substância***) f (vigor)* strength; **2** *(comida)* nourishment.

sustar *vt/vi* to stop, halt *(processo)*.

sustentáculo *m (apoio)* prop; **2** *(pessoa)* supporter, mainstay.

sustentar *vt* to sustain; **2** to hold up, support; **3** to maintain; **4** bear, undergo; **5** nourish, feed.

sustentável *adj inv* sustainable.

sustento *m* food, sustenance; maintenance.

suster *vt* to support, hold up, sustain; **2** to restrain, hold back.

susto *m (soressalto)* fright, shock; *(de medo)* scare, fear; *(alguém que se aproxima de surpresa)* **que** ~! you startled me!; **2** *(de medo)* what a fright! **apanhar um** ~ *(de choque)* to get a fright.

sutiã *m* bra.

sútil *(Vd:* **su(b)til***;* **su(b)tileza***;* **su(b)tilmente***)*.

sutura *f (MED)* suture.

suturar *vt* to suture, stitch.

t

T, t *m (letra)* T, t.

ta (= **te** + **a**) *pron* it *(f)* to you; **deste-me a maçã? sim, dei-ta** did you give me the apple? yes, I gave it to you.

tabacaria *f (owner, loja)* tobacconist's (shop).

tabaco *m* tobacco.

tabagismo, tabaquismo *m (abuso do tabaco)* smoking; 2 *(MED)* nicotine addition; *(intoxicação)* nicotine poisoning.

tabefe *m (soro de leite)* whey; 2 *(CULIN)* a kind of custard; 3 *(fam) (bofetada)* slap.

tabela *f* table, chart; *(preço)* list; *(horário)* schedule; 2 *(pauta oficial)* official rates; 3 billiards board; 4 *(DESP)* backboard; ♦ **à ~** on time/schedule; at the standard/fixed price; **por ~** indirectly.

tabelado,-a *adj (produto)* controlled; 2 *(preços)* price-controlled; 3 *(items, dados)* listed.

tabelar *vt (algo)* to set/fix the price of; 2 to list.

tabelião,-iã *m,f (notário)* notary public.

taberna *f* public house; 2 *(fam)* pub *(UK)*; tavern, bar *(US)*.

tabernáculo *m (santuário do Templo de Jerusalém)* Tabernacle; 2 *(mesa de trabalho do ourives)* goldsmith's bench.

taberneiro,-a *m,f* publican; pub or bar owner, keeper.

tabique *m* partition, dividing wall; 2 *(vedação)* fence; 3 *(ANAT, BOT)* septum.

tablado *m (palco)* stage; 2 *(palanque, estrado)* raised platform, stage, dais; 3 boxing ring.

tablete *f* bar; **~ de chocolate** bar of chocolate; 2 *(medicamento)* tablet.

tabu *m adj* taboo.

tábua *f* plank, board; **~ de passar roupa** ironing-board; *(de cortar legumes, carne)* chopping-board; 2 *(outro material liso e fino)* plate; 3 **~ de mesa** table flap/leaf; 4 *(lista)* list, index; 5 *(MAT)* table; **~s** *pl (TEAT)* boards; IDIOM **~ de salvação** last resort.

tabuada *f (MAT)* tables.

tabulador *m* tab key, spacebar.

tabuleiro *m (de levar comida)* tray; 2 *(peça semelhante)* tray; 3 *(para o forno)* baking tray; 4 *(de jogos)* board; 5 *(via de uma ponte)* **superior/ inferior ~** upper/lower carriageway of a bridge; **a Ponte 25 de Abril tem um ~ inferior para os comboios** the 25th April Bridge has a lower carriageway for trains; 6 *(divisão de salina)* salt pan; 7 *(piso)* stair landing.

tabuleta *f* sign, signboard, board; *(para pequenos anúncios, notas)* notice board; 2 *(placa)* name plate, board.

TAC *f (abr de* **tomografia axial computadorizada***) (MED)* CAT scan.

taça *f (copo)* glass; **~ de champanhe** glass of champagne; 2 *(troféu)* cup; **~ mundial** world cup; *(BR)* **copa mundial**.

tacada *f (DESP)* stroke, strike; **de uma só ~** *(fig)* in one go, at a stroke; 2 *(bilhar) (pancada de taco)* a shot with a cue.

tacanho,-a *m,f (pessoa estúpida)* narrow-minded person; ♦ *adj (de baixa estatura)* squat; 2 *(fig)* mean, niggardly.

tacão *m (no sapato)* heel.

tacha *f (prego cabeça achatada)* tack; 2 *(em cadeira)* stud; 3 *(fam) (cara)* face, look; 4 *(fig) (mácula)* blemish; IDIOM **arreganhar a ~** grin like a Cheshire cat.

tachada *f (tacho cheio)* a panful (of food).

tachar *vt* to find fault with; **~ de** to brand sb/sth as sth.

tachinha *f* drawing pin *(UK)*; thumbtack *(US)*.

tacho *m* saucepan; **sirvo-me de um ~ para o guisado** I use a saucepan for the stew.

tácito,-a *adj* tacit, implied.

taciturno,-a *adj* taciturn, reserved.

taco *m (DESP) (de bilhar)* cue; *(de golfe)* club; *(de hóquei)* stick; *(de pólo)* mallet; 2 *(pedaço de madeira)* wedge; 3 *(bucha de artilharia)* wad; 4 *(de soalho)* parquet block; 5 **taco a ~** *adv* tit-for-tat.

tactear, tatear *vt/vi* to grope (for, after); 2 *(apalpar)* feel; 3 sound out.

táctico, tático,-a *f* tactics *pl*; strategy; ♦ *adj* tactical.

táctil, tátil *adj* tactile; tangible.

tacto/tato *m* touch; tact.

tafetá *m (tecido)* taffeta.

tagarela *m,f* chatter-box; ♦ *adj* talkative.

tagarelar *vi* to chatter, prattle, gossip.

tagarelice *f* chat, prattle, gossip.

tágide *f* a nymph of the river Tagus.

tailandês,-esa *adj* Thai; 2 *(LÍNG)* Thai.

Tailândia *npr* **a ~** Thailand.

tainha *(ZOOL) f* grey mullet.

taipa *f* lathe-and-plaster wall; **parede de ~** mud wall, mud wall; **casa de ~** loam hut, mud hut.

tal *(pl:* **tais***) adj* such; **a surpresa foi ~ que** the surprise was such that ...; **tais coisas não me interessam** I am not interested in such things; 2 **~ e coisa** this and that; 3 **um ~ Sr. X** a certain Mr. X; **a ~ senhora** the aforementioned lady; 4 **que ~ ?** what do you think? how are things?; **que ~ uma cerveja?** how about a beer?; 5 *(semelhança)* **~ pai, ~ filho** like father, like son; ♦ *adv* so, as; **~ como** just as; **~ qual** just like, just as it is; ♦ *pron* such a thing.

tala *f (MED)* splint.

talante *m* will, choice; **a seu belo ~** at his sweet will.

talão *m (duplicado de recibo)* receipt; 2 *(parte do livro de cheques, etc)* counterfoil, stub; 3 stump of a vine *(left after pruning)*; 4 *(calcanhar ou coisa que o cobre)* heel.

talco *m* talc; **pó de ~** talcum powder.

talento *m (aptidão)* talent; ability.

talentoso,-a *adj* talented.

talha *f (de barro)* large earthen pitcher, vessel; **2** *(madeira)* carving; **3** cut; **4** *(metal)* hand engraving; **5** *(NÁUT) (aparelho, corda)* tiller rope; **6** *(MED)* **operação da** ~ *(cirurgia para tirar pedras da vesícula)* lithotomy.

talhada *f (fatia) (de melão, melancia, queijo)* slice; ♦ **às ~s** *adv* in slices.

talhado,-a *adj* cut in slices; **2** *(roupa)* cut; **3** *(esculpido)* carved; **4** *(pessoa elegante)* svelte, shaped; **5** *(alguém)* made for.

talhão *m (porção de terreno para cultura)* alotment; patch; **2** *(para construção de prédio)* small plot of land.

talhar *vt (ger)* to cut; **2** slice, cut up; **3** carve, sculpt; **4** *(vestido)* cut out; ♦ *vi (leite)* to curdle; **2** make *(alguém)* for.

talhe *m (de roupa)* cut; **2** *(feições)* features; **3** *(desenho, aparência)* shape.

talher *m* item of cutlery; **2** place setting; **~es** *mpl* cutlery *sg*.

talho *m (corte)* cut, cutting; **2** slicing; **3** butcher's (shop).

Talho is not used in Brazil. Vd: **açougue**.

talião *m* talion, retaliation; **a lei de** ~ the law of retaliation, an eye for an eye.

talidomida *f (FARM)* thalidomide.

talismã *m* talisman; **2** *(objecto)* lucky charm.

Talmude *npr m* Talmud.

talo *m (BOT)* stalk, stem *(de couve)*; **2** *(ARQ)* shaft.

taluda *f (pop) (o maior prémio da lotaria)* jackpot.

talude *m (rampa, declive)* talus, slope, incline.

taludo,-a *adj (adulto – corpulento)* stout, stocky; **2** *(fig)* important, big; **3** *(criança)* grown up; **4** *(couve, etc)* stalky.

talvez *adv* perhaps, maybe; ~ **haja alguém que** perhaps there is someone who.

tamanco *m* clog; **tamancada** *f* blow with a clog.

tamanduá *m (BR) (ZOOL) (urso-formigueiro)* anteater.

tamanhão *adj (pop)* very big/large.

tamanho,-a *m (volume)* size; **2** *(medida)* size, number; **qual é o seu** ~ what size are you?; **3 em** ~ **natural** life-size; ♦ *adj (tão grande) (área, acidente, queda)* so big, such a great; **nunca vi** ~ **multidão** I have never seen such a crowd; **tenho uma dor de cabeça** ~a I have a huge headache; **carro** ~**-família** family size car.

tâmara *f (BOT) (fruto)* date.

também *adv* also, too, as well; **ele fala** ~ **chinês** *(além das outras línguas)* he also speaks Chinese; **ela** ~ **trabalha muito** she too works a lot; **eu falo francês e ele** ~ I speak French and so does he; **2** ~ **não** *(negativo)* neither, nor; **eu não bebi nada e o meu marido** ~ **não** I didn't drink anything nor did my husband; **3** besides, apart from that; **e** ~, **ela é mentirosa** and besides, she is a liar.

tambor *m (MÚS)* drum; **2** *(vasilha)* drum, ~ **de óleo** oil drum; **3** *(cilindro das máquinas)* drum; **4** cylinder; **5** *(TIPO)* ~ **de provas** proof press; *(ANAT)* eardrum.

tamborete *m (banco)* stool; **~s** *(NÁUT)* reinforcement planks.

tamboril *m (ZOOL)* monk fish, frog-fish; **2** *(MÚS)* small drum.

tamborilar *vt (imitar o som do tambor com os dedos ou semelhante)* to drum.

tamborim *m (MÚS)* tambourine.

Tamisa *(BR: Tâ-) npr* **o** ~ river Thames.

tampa *f (de panela, caixa)* lid, cover; **2** *(caneta, garrafa)* top, cap; **3** *(laje)* gravestone; **4** *(fig, fam) (recusa a um convite)* brush-off.

tampão *m (ger)* cover; **2** *(na banheira)* stopper, plug; **3** *(do carro)* hubcap; **4** *(MED)* compress; **5** *(penso vaginal)* tampon; **6** earplugs.

tanga *f (pano à volta das ancas)* loincloth; **2** *(BR)* scanty bikini, G-string; **3 estar de** ~ *(col) (em penúria)* to be broke.

Tanganica *npr* **a** ~ Tanganyika; **o Lago T**~ Lake Tanganyika.

tangente *adj* tangent, touching.

tanger *vt (MÚS)* to play; **2** *(sinos)* to ring; **3** *(guitarra)* to pluck; ♦ **no que tange a** with regard to.

Tânger *npl* Tangier

tangerine *(BOT)* tangerine.

tangerineira *f (BOT)* tangerine tree.

tangível *(pl: -veis) adj inv (real)* tangible; **2** attainable.

tango *m (dança)* tango.

tanoaria *f* cooper's shop; **tanoeiro** *m (conserta barris)* cooper.

tanque *m (MIL)* tank; **2** *(de lavar roupa)* wash-tub; **3** *(para líquidos)* vat, tank.

tântalo *m (QUIM)* tantalum.

tanto,-a *m* **um** ~ **de** some, a certain amount; ♦ *adj (sg)* so much; as much; **~s** *(pl)* so many; as many; **vinte e tantos** twenty-odd, twenty something; **tantas casas** so many houses; ~ **como/ quanto** as much as; ♦ *adv* so much; ~ **melhor/ pior** so much the better/too bad; ~ **se me dá** it's all the same to me; ~ ... **quanto** as much ... as; **ela tem** ~ **dinheiro como ele** she has as much money as he; ~ **eu como meu marido** both my husband and I; **nem** ~ not that much, not quite so; **um** ~ **ou quanto** somewhat; **se** ~ if that; **às tantas** *(fam)* very late *(in the hour)* **ele chegou às tantas da manhã** he arrived in the early hours of the morning; **2** *(a certa altura)* after a while, suddenly; **às tantas, já não sei o que estou a fazer** after a while I no longer know what I am doing; **a páginas tantas** suddenly, at a certain point/ time; ♦ *pron:* **ele deu-me muito, mas eu eu não queria** ~ he gave me a lot, but I didn't want so much; **nunca os problemas foram tantos** there never were so many problems; ~ **quanto sei** as far as I know; ♦ *conj* ~ **que** so much so that.

Tanzânia *npr* **a** ~ Tanzania.

tão *adv* so; ~ **rico como/quanto** as rich as; ~ **cedo quanto possível** as soon as possible.

tão-pouco *conj (nem)* nor; ~ **o mencionei** nor did I mention it.

tão-só, tão-somente *adv* only, simply, but.

tapa *f (bofetada)* slap; **levar uma ~ de (alguém)** to be slapped by sb.

tapada *n* game park; enclosed park.

tapado,-a *adj (coberto)* covered (up); **2** *(nariz)* blocked; **3** *(fam) (estúpido)* thick.

tapa-misérias *m, sg, pl* coat put on to hide a poor dress/suit.

tapar *vt* to cover sth with lid, blanket; **2** *(garrafa de vinho)* to cork, put the cork back in.

tapeação *f (BR) (engano, logro)* hoax, con.

tapeçaria *f* tapestry, wall hanging.

tapeceiro,-a *m,f (fabricante, vendedor)* carpet manufacturer/ seller.

tapete *m* carpet, rug.

tapioca *f (fécula de mandioca)* tapioca.

tapume *m* fencing, boarding; **2** hedge; **3** *(divisória)* partition.

taquigrafia *f* shorthand *(UK)*; stenography *(US)*.

taquímetro *m* speedometer.

tara *f (peso de recipiente)* tare; deduction allowed for the weight of wrapping, boxes; **2** *(peso de veículo sem carga)* tare; *(fig)* mania, obsession; derangement.

tarado,-a *m,f (fam) (desequilibrado)* nutcase; loony, maniac; **~ sexual** sex-maniac.

taralhouco,-a *adj (pessoa) (senil)* gaga.

taramela *f* mill clapper, wooden bolt; **2** *(fig, fam) (muita conversa)* claptrap; **dar à ~** to babble on.

tarântula *f (ZOOL)* tarantula.

tardança *f* delay, slowness.

tardar *vi* to delay, be slow; **2** to be late; **sem mais ~** without delay; **ele tardou a vir** he was long in coming; he took his time to come; ♦ *vt* to delay.

tarde *f* afternoon; evening; **hoje à ~** this afternoon; ♦ *adv* late; **mais ~** later, afterwards; **muito ~** too late.

tardeza *f* tardiness.

tardiamente *adv* late, too late.

tardinha *f* evening, late afternoon.

tardio,-a *adj* late, belated.

tareco,-a *m,f (criança que não está quieta)* restless, fidget; **2** *(gato)* pussy cat; **3 tarecos** *mpl (objectos)* knick-knacks, bits and pieces; old (personal) things; **eu pego nos meus ~ e vou-me embora** I'll take my things and leave.

tarefa *f* task; **2** *(trabalho com pagamento)* job.

tareia *f* beating, hiding, spanking.

tarifa *f* tariff; **2** fare.

tarifário *m* price list, price chart; ♦ *adj (preço tributo coberto pela)* by tariff.

tarimba *f (MIL) (cama)* bunk; plank-bed **2** *(fig)* army life; **3** *(fig)* hardships.

tarimbar *vi (fam)* to serve in the army.

tarja *f (orla)* border, edging, outline; **2** *(contorno em papel, desenho)* outline, edging; **3** *(papel de luto)* black border.

tarraxa *f (peça roscada)* rosca; screw; **2** *(em espiral)* thread of a screw; **3** screw cutter; IDIOM **apertar a ~** put the screws on.

tartamudear *vi/vt (gaguejar, falar com hesitação)* stammer, stutter.

tartamudo,-a *m,f* stammerer, stutterer.

tártaro *m* tartar.

tartaruga *f (ZOOL) (grande)* turtle; **2** *(pequena)* tortoise; **o fecho da mala é de ~** the handbag's clasp is of tortoiseshell.

tas (= **te** + **as**) them to you; **onde estão as chaves? Eu dei-tas ontem** where are the keys? I gave them to you yesterday.

tasca *f* cheap eating place.

tatear (*Vd:* **ta(c)tear**).

tático,-a (*Vd:* **tá(c)tico,-a**).

tátil (*Vd:* **tá(c)til**).

tato (*Vd:* **ta(c)to**).

tatu *m (ZOOL)* armadillo.

tatuagem *f (desenho)* tattoo; **2** *(técnica)* tattooing.

tatuar *vt* to tattoo.

tauromaquia *f* bullfighting.

tauromáquico *adj (espectáculo, arte)* bullfighting.

tautologia *f* tautology.

tavão *m (ZOOL)* horsefly.

taxa *f* rate; **~ de câmbio** exchange rate; **~ fixa** flat rate; **~ de juros** interest rate; **~ de mortalidade** death rate; **2** charge, dues; **~ de circulação urbana** *(UK)* congestion charge; **~ de doca** *(NÁUT)* dock dues; **3** *(imposto)* tax.

taxar *vt* to fix the price of; **2** to tax; **3** *(fig) (classificar, censurar)* classify, accuse *(alguém)*; ♦ *vr (ter-se em conta de)* to call o.s., consider o.s. to be.

taxativo,-a *adj* taxing; **2** restricting.

táxi *m* taxi, cab.

taxímetro *m* taxi meter.

taxista *m,f* taxi driver, cab driver.

tcheco *(LÍNG)* Czech; ♦ **tcheco,-a** *adj* Czech.

tchecoslovaco,-a *m,f* Czechoslovak; ♦ *adj* Czechoslovakian.

Tchecoslováquia *npr (antiga)* **a ~** Czechoslovakia.

te *pron* you, yourself, to you; **já ~ dei uma resposta** I have already given you an answer.

tear *m (têxtil)* loom; **~ manual** hand-loom.

teatral *adj* theatrical; **2** *(fig)* showy, artificial.

teatro *m* theatre *(UK)*, theater *(US)*; **2** plays *pl*, dramatic works *pl*; **3 ~ de variedades** variety show; **4** *(MED)* **~ de operações** surgery theatre; **5** *(fig) (desfecho)* **um golpe de ~** dramatic gesture; **6** *(fig)* **fazer ~** *(exagerar)* to dramatize; make scenes.

tecelagem *f* weaving.

tecelão,-lã *m,f* weaver.

tecer *vt* to weave *(linho, algodão, fazenda)*; to spin; **2** *(fig) (engendrar)* **~ intrigas sobre/contra (alguém)** to devise/contrive (plots); **3** *(fig) (fazer)* **~ elogios a (alguém)** to praise sb.

tecido *m (têxtil)* cloth, material; **2 o ~ social** the social fabric; **3** *(BIOL)* tissue; ♦ *(pp de tecer) adj* woven, spun; plotted.

tecla *f* key; **~ de tabulação** tab key; IDIOM **bater na mesma ~** harping on the same subject.

teclado *m* keyboard.

técnico,-a *m,f* technician; *(pop)* engineer; **2** *(especialista)* expert; ♦ *f* technique; ♦ *adj* technical.

tecnocrata *m,f* technocrat; ♦ *adj* technocratic.

tecnologia *f* technology.

tecnológico,-a *adj* technological.

tecto, teto *m* ceiling; **2** *(telhado)* roof; **partilhar o mesmo** ~ to live under the same roof; **2** ~ **solar** *(AUTO)* sunroof; **3 sem** ~ homeless; **os sem** ~ the homeless; **4** *(limite)* ceiling; ~ **salarial** maximum salary increase.

tectónico,-a, tetónico,-a *adj (camada, lago)* tectonic.

tédio *m* tedium, boredom; IDIOM **morrer de** ~ to die of boredom.

tedioso,-a *adj* tedious; boring.

Teerão *(BR:* **Teerã)** *npr* Teheran.

teia *f (ZOOL)* web; ~ **de aranha** spider's web, cobweb; **2** intrigue, plot; **3** *(organização)* network.

teimar *vi:* ~ **em** to insist on; to persist in.

teimosia *f* obstinacy, stubbornness; **2** perseverance.

teimoso,-a *adj* obstinate, stubborn; **2** *(fig) (pessoa)* pig-headed; **3** *(pertinaz)* tenacious; **4** *(vento, dor)* persistent.

teipe *f* tape.

teixo *m (BOT)* yew.

Tejo *npr (rio)* Tagus.

tela *f* (de pintura) canvas; **2** *(CIN, COMP, TV)* screen; **3** *(pesca)* nets; **4** *(BR) (de arame)* wire netting.

tele *pref* tele; **~comando** *m* remote control; **~comunicação** *f* telecommunications *pl.*

teleférico *m* cable car.

telefonar *vt/vi* to telephone, phone; to call, ring up.

telefone *m* phone, telephone.

telefonema *m* phone call.

telefónico,-a *adj* telephone.

telefonista *m,f* telephone operator.

telegrafar *vt/vi* to telegraph, wire.

telegrama *m* telegram, cable.

teleguiado,-a *adj* remote-controlled; **2 míssil** ~ guided missile.

telejornal *(pl:* **-ais)** *m* television/TV news *sg.*

telémetro *m* telemeter, rangefinder.

telemóvel *m* cellular phone, mobile *(pop).*

telenovela *f* TV soap opera.

teleobje(c)tiva *f* telephoto lens.

telepático,-a *adj* telepathic.

telescópico,-a *adj* telescopic.

telescópio *m* telescope.

telespe(c)tador,-ora *m,f* viewer; ♦ *adj* viewing

teletexto *m* teletext.

teletipo *m* teletype.

televisão *f* television; ~ **a cores** colour television.

televisivo,-a *adj* television.

televisor *m* television (set), TV (set).

telex *m* telex; **enviar um** ~ to send a telex.

telha *f* roof tile; **2** ~ **de vidro** glass tile; **3** *(fam) (cabeça)* head; **deu-me na** ~ **para fazer isto** it got into my head to do this; **4** *(fam) (mania, mau humor)* mood, strange mood; **estar com a** ~ to be in a bad mood.

telhado *m* roof; IDIOM **quem tem ~s de vidro, não deve andar à pedrada** people who live in glass houses, should not throw stones.

telha-vã *f (telhado sobre ripas)* unlined tiled roof.

telheiro *m (abrigo)* lean-to; **2** *(fabricante)* roof tile maker.

telhudo,-a *adj (fam) (alguém)* crazy.

telintar *vt (som de telim)* clink *(copos, etc);* jingle *(moedas, sinos, campainha);* tinkle *(chocalho).*

tema *m (ger)* theme; **2** *(de palestra)* subject.

temático,-a *adj* thematic; **2** *f* thematics *sg.*

temente *adj inv* fearing.

temer *vt* to fear, be afraid of; ~ **a Deus** to fear God; **temo que ele faça um erro** I fear he may commit an error.

temerário,-a *adj (corajoso)* brave, fearless; **2** *(destemido)* reckless, foolhardy.

temeridade *f (valentia)* courage, boldness; **2** *(imprudence)* rashness, foolhardiness, foolhardy act.

temeroso,-a *adj* dreadful; **2** fearful, afraid.

temível *adj* fearsome, terrible.

temor *m* fear, dread.

têmpera *f (ger)* tempera; **2** *(de metais)* tempering, temper; **3** *(fig) (força física)* mettle; **4** *(fig) (honestidade)* integrity.

temperado,-a *adj (clima)* temperate, mild; **2** *(ferro)* hardened; **3** *(CULIN)* seasoned; *(marinado)* marinated.

temperamental *m,f* temperamental person; ♦ *adj inv* temperamental.

temperamento *m* temperament, nature.

temperar *vt (metal)* to temper, harden; **2** *(CULIN)* to season; to marinate.

temperatura *f (FÍS, METEOR)* temperature; **2** *(MED)* temperature; **tirar a** ~ **a (alguém)** take somebody's temperature.

tempero *m (CULIN)* seasoning, condiment; *(líquido)* dressing; **2** *(tempera)* temper; **3** *(fig)* remedy, lenitive.

tempestade *f* storm, tempest; **2** *(fig)* tumult, agitation; IDIOM **fazer uma** ~ **em copo d'água** to make a storm in a tea cup.

tempestuoso,-a *adj* stormy; **2** *(fig) (carácter)* tempestuous.

templo *m* temple; church.

tempo *m (ger)* time; **a** ~ on time; **ao mesmo** ~ at the same time; **com o andar dos ~s** as time goes on; **dá** ~ there is/we have plenty of time; **de ~s em ~s** from time to time; **a seu** ~ in due course; **há muito** ~ a long time ago; ~ **livre** spare time; **nos velhos ~s** in the old days; **quanto** ~ **leva?** how long does it take?; **2** *(METEOR)* weather; **bom/mau** ~ good/bad weather; **previsão do** ~ weather forecast; **3** *(gram)* tense; **4** *(MÚS)* time, rhyme; *(velocidade)* timing; IDIOM **matar o** ~ to pass the time; **no** ~ **das vacas gordas** in good times; **perder** ~ to dilly-dally, to waste time.

têmpora *f (ANAT)* temple.

temporada *f (período de tempo)* season, spell; **2** *(espaço de tempo)*, time.

temporal *m (METEOR)* storm, gale; **2** *(ANAT)* temple; ♦ *adj inv* temporal; **2** temporary.

temporão,-rã *m,f adj (antes do tempo esperado)* premature, early.

temporário,-a *adj* temporary, provisional.

tenacidade *f* tenacity.

tenaz *f (ferramenta)* tongs *pl*; **2** *(do caranguejo)* pincers; ♦ *adj (pessoa)* tenacious.

tença *f (pensão para pagamento de serviços)* annuity, endowment, pension; **às ~s de** *adv* on a hand-outs.

tencionar *vt/vi* to intend, plan; **tenciono ir a Angola** I intend to go to Angola.

tenda *f (barraca)* tent; **2** *(barraca de feira)* stall; **3** *(pequena loja na província)* local shop.

tendão *m (ANAT)* tendon.

tendência *f (propensão)* tendency; **~ a fazer** tendency to do; **2** *(vocação)* inclination; **3** *(de moda)* trend.

tendencioso,-a *adj* tendentious, partial, biased.

tender *vt (estender massa)* roll out (the pastry); ♦ *vi (inclinar-se)* **~ a/para** to tend to, have a tendency to; **2** *(vocação)* have a flair for; **3** *(encaminhar-se)* on the way to; **ela tende para a miséria** she is on the way to poverty.

tenebroso,-a *adj (noite)* dark; **2** *(ambiente)* gloomy; **3** *(figura, mar)* terrifying; **4** *(caminho)* tortuous, winding.

tenente *m* lieutenant; **~-coronel** *m* lieutenant-colonel.

tenha *(pres subj de* **ter***)* **espero que ele ~ sorte** I hope he is lucky.

tenho *(pres indic, 1ª pessoa de* **ter***)*.

ténia *(BR:* **tê-***) f* tapeworm.

ténis *(BR:* **tê-***) m* tennis; **~ de mesa** table tennis; *(sapatos)* trainers *(UK)*; sneakers *(US)*.

tenista *m,f* tennis player.

tenro,-a *adj (fácil de mastigar)* tender; **2** *(que é viçoso)* young, tender; **de ~a idade** of tender age.

tensão *f (estado de esticado)* tension, tightness; **2** *(pressão)* pressure, strain; **3** *(PSIC)* stress; **4** *(ELECT)* voltage; **5** *(MED)* pressure; **~ arterial** blood pressure.

tenso,-a *adj (esticado)* taut, tight, stiff; **2** *(pessoa, ambiente)* tense, strained.

tenta *f (MED)* probe; **2** mock fight between young men and newly branded young bulls.

tentação *f* temptation.

tentáculo *m* tentacle.

tentador,-ora *m,f* tempter, temptress; ♦ *adj* tempting, seductive.

tentar *vt/vi (intentar)* to try, attempt; **2** *(seduzir)* to tempt, entice.

tentativa *f* try, attempt; **fazer uma ~** to make an attempt; *(JUR)* attempt; **~ de roubo** attempted robbery.

tentear *vt (sondar com tenta)* to probe, examine; **2** to grope, feel one's way.

tentilhão *m (ZOOL)* chaffinch.

tento *m (tino)* common sense; **2** *(cuidado)* attention, care; **3** *(casino)* chip; **4** *(DESP)* point, goal.

ténue *(BR:* **tê-***) adj inv (argumento)* tenuous, weak; **2** *(luz, som)* faint; **3** *(camada)* thin, fine, flimsy, slight.

teologia *f* theology.

teológico,-a *adj* theological.

teólogo *m* theologian.

teor *m (modo)* tenor, meaning, drift, wording; **2** *(conteúdo)* contents; **3** *(QUÍM) (proporção)* content, grade.

teorema *m* theorema.

teoria *f* theory.

teoricamente *adv* theoretically.

teórico,-a *adj* theoretical.

tépido,-a *adj* tepid, lukewarm.

ter *m (estado de posse material)* **a cultura do ~ dos nossos dias** today's obsession with having/with possession; **2** *mpl (com bens)* **gente de teres e haveres** rich people; ♦ *vt (ger)* to have; **~ fome/ rio/razão** to be hungry/cold/right; *(idade)* **ela tem vinte anos** she is twenty years old; *(tamanho)* **tem dois metros de altura** it is two metres high; *(saúde, disposição)* **que é que tem?** what's the matter with you? what have you?; **tenha cuidado!** be careful!; **tenha a bondade/fineza/gentileza de** be so kind as to; **2** *(possuir)* to have, hold; **eles têm uma casa linda** they have a beautiful house; **ele tem um mestrado** he holds a master's degree; **3 ~ mão** *(controlar)* to restrain; **4** *(conter)* contain; **o balde tem muita água** the bucket contains a lot of water; **5 ~ a ver com** to concern, have to do with; **não tenho nada a ver com isso** I have nothing to do with it; **6 ir ~ a** to lead to; **7 ir ~ com** to (go and) meet; ♦ *v aux* **~de/que** have to, must; **tenho de terminar isto** I have to finish this; ♦ **~-se** *vr* consider o.s.; **ela tem-se como esperta** she considers herself clever; **2** *(aguentar-se)* hold on; **ter-se em pé** to stand; IDIOM **ter o coração ao pé da boca** to wear one's heart on one's sleeve.

terapeuta *m,f* therapist.

terapeuta *m,f* therapist;

terapêutico,-a *f* therapeutics; ♦ *adj* therapeutic(al).

terapia *f* therapy.

terça *f (parte de herança)* third; **~-feira** *f* Tuesday; **~-feira gorda** Shrove Tuesday; **2** *(abr de* **~-feira***)* **vou na ~** I am going on Tuesday; **3** *(LITURG)* terce, tierce; ♦ *adj f (fracção)* third (part).

terça *f (MED) (febre)* tertian; ♦ *adj* tertian, that occurs every three days.

Terceira *npr (Ilha nos Açores)* Terceira (Island)

terceiro,-a *num* third; **2** *f (AUTO)* **em ~a** in third (gear); **3 ~s** *mpl (pessoas)* others, third parties; ♦ *adj* third; **a ~a idade** pension age, senior citizen.

tercenário,-a *m,f* person who receives a third part of an inheritance.

terceto *m (LIT)* tercet; **2** *(MÚS)* trio.

terciário,-a *adj (cor; ordem) (EDUC)* tertiary; **educação ~** further eduction; **2** *(ECON)* **sector ~** services sector; **3** *(GEOL)* Tertiary.

terciarização *f* policy of adopting the tertiary trends in the market outsourcing.

terço *m* third (part); **2** rosary.

terçol, terçolho *m (pop)* sty.

tergiversar *vi* to prevaricate, evade the issue; **2** hesitate.

termal *adj inv* thermal.

termas *fpl (estabelecimento)* spa *sg*, hot springs.

térmico,-a *adj* thermal; **2** *(prato que conserva calor)* hot *(plate)*.

terminação *f (ger)* end, termination; **2** *(gram)* ending; **3** *(ANAT)* endings.

terminal *m (ELECT)* terminal; **2** *(de transporte)* terminal, terminus; ♦ *adj inv* last, terminal; *(MED) (doença)* terminal.

terminante *adj inv* categorical; **2** *(decisivo)* final.

terminantemente *adv* absolutely, categorically, expressly.

terminar *vt/vi* to finish, end; ♦ *aux* ~ **de fazer** (**algo**) to finish doing sth.

término *m* end, terminus.

terminologia *f* terminology.

terminológico,-a *adj* terminological.

térmita *f* termite.

termo *m* end, termination; **pôr** ~ **a** to put an end to; **2** *(limite)* limit, boundary; **3** *(prazo)* period, term **a curto/longo** ~ in the short/long term; **meio** ~ compromise; **4** *(LÍNG)* term, expression; **5** *(garrafa)* thermos (flask); ♦ **termos** *mpl* terms; **em** ~ **gerais** in general terms; **em** ~ **de** in terms of; **2** *(maneiras, postura)* manners; **3 fora de** ~ longe.

termómetro *(BR:* -mô-*) m* thermometer.

termóstato *m* thermostat.

terno *m (conjunto de três)* trio, threesome; **2** *(cartas de jogo)* three; **3** *(queda)* tumble; **4** *(BR) (traje)* suit; ♦ **terno,-a** *adj (carinhoso)* tender, loving.

ternura *f* tenderness, gentleness.

terra *f* T~ *(planeta)* Earth, World; **2** *(solo)* earth, soil; **3** *(terreno)* ground, land; ~ **firme** dry land; **4** *(pátria)* homeland; ~ **natal** birthplace; ♦ *adv* **por** ~ *(ao chão)* down; ♦ T~ **fria** *f (GEOG)* = Trás-os-Montes *(N.E. Portugal)*; ~ **a** ~ *(pessoa)* down to earth; ~ **de ninguém** no man's land; ~ **à vista!** *(NÁUT)* land ahoy!

terraço *m (veranda)* terrace; **2** *(telhado plano)* roof terrace; **3** *(socalco na montanha)* terrace.

terracota *f* terracotta.

terramoto, terremoto *m* earthquake.

Terra Nova *npr* **a** ~ Newfoundland.

terraplenagem *f* levelling of the ground.

terráqueo,-a *m,f* earthling.

terreiro *m* public square; **2** *(adro)* yard; **3** threshing floor; **4** *(BR)* area for camdomblé festivities.

terreno *m* ground, soil; **2** plot of land; **3** *(para construção)* site; **4** *(GEO)* terrain; soil; **5** *(MIL)* ground; **6** *(de pesquisa)* field; ~ **baldio** wasteland; IDIOM **ganhar/perder** ~ to gain/lose ground; **sondar o** ~ sound out the ground.

térreo,-a *m,f* **casa** ~**a** *(só com um nível)* bungalow, cottage; ♦ *adj* ground (level), low; **andar** ~ *(BR)* ground floor, *(US)* first floor; **2** *(chão sem soalho)* of beaten earth.

terrestre *adj inv* terrestrial; **2** *(transporte)* by land; **3** *(prazeres, seres)* earthly; **4** *(mundano)* worldly.

terrificante, terrífico,-a *adj* dreadful, frightful, terrifying.

terrina *f* tureen.

territorial *adj inv.* **território** *m* territory; district, region.

terrível *adj inv* terrible, horrible.

terror *m (medo)* terror, dread.

terrorismo *m* terrorism.

terrorista *m,f* terrorist.

tertúlia *f* gathering (of friends), family reunion.

tesão *m* stiffness; **2** *(fig)* vigour, impetuosity; **3** *(desejo sexual)* randiness; **estar com uma** ~ be horny, have a hard-on.

tese *f (argumento)* thesis; dissertation; ~ **de doutoramento** doctoral thesis; **em** ~ *adv* in theory.

teso,-a *adj (hirto)* stiff, upright; **2** *(esticado)* taut; **3** strong; **4** *(fig)* inflexible, rigid; **5** *(fam)* **estar** ~ *(sem dinheiro)* to be broke; be skint.

tesoura (= **tesoira**) *f* scissors *pl*; **uma** ~ a pair of scissors; ~ **de unhas** nail scissors; **2** *(MEC)* shears; **3** ~ **de podar** secateurs; **4** *(fig)* sharp criticism; *(falar mal duma pessoa)* backbiting.

tesoureiro,-a *m,f (do banco, associação)* treasurer; **2** *(de empresa)* financial director; **3** *(de escola, navio)* bursar.

tesouro *m* treasure; **2** *(COM)* treasury, exchequer.

testa *f* brow, forehead; **à** ~ **de** at the head of; **franzir a** ~ to frown; ~**-de-ferro** *(pl:* **testas-de-ferro***) f* figurehead.

testamentário,-a *m,f* beneficiary; ♦ *adj* of a will.

testamento *m* will, testament; **Velho/Novo T~** Old/New Testament.

testar *vt* to test, try out; **2** to examine.

teste *m* test; ~ **surpresa** pop quiz.

testemunha *f* witness; ~ **ocular** eye-witness; **2** *(num duelo)* second.

testemunhar *vi* to testify, be witness ♦ *vt* (**sobre**) to give evidence of/about; **2** *(gratidão, suporto)* express.

testemunho *m* evidence, testimony; **falso** ~ slander; **dar** ~ to give evidence; **2 prova, como** ~ **do meu amor** as proof/token of my love.

testículo *m (ANAT)* testicle.

testudo,-a *adj* with high forehead; **2** *(fig)* stubborn, headstrong.

teta *f (de mamal)* udder, teat; *(de gata)* nipple; *(de mulher) (seio) (fam)* breast, teat; **2** *(fig, fam) (manancial, fonte)* source.

tétano *m (MED)* tetanus.

tetina *f (teta do biberão)* teat.

teto *(Vd:* **tecto***)*.

tetracampião,-piã *m,f* four times champion.

tetraedro *(GEOM)* tetrahedron.

tetraplégico,-a *adj (MED)* quadriplegic.

tétrico,-a *adj (pensamento, visão)* gloomy, dismal; gruesome; frightening.

tétum *m (língua)* Tetum.

teu, tua *(2ᵃ pessoa sg) adj* your; **a tua filha é linda** your daughter is beautiful; ♦ *pron* yours.

teve *(pret, 2ᵃ, 3ᵃ pessoas de* **ter***)* **ela teve um acidente** she had/has suffered an accident.

têxtil *(pl:* **têxteis***) m* textile.

texto *m* text; **2** *(TV, CIN)* lines; **3** *(JUR)* wording.

textual *adj* textual; **2** *(análise)* discourse; **3** *(fig)* exa(c)to.

textura *f* texture.

texugo *m (ZOOL)* badger.

tez *f (pele)* complexion.

ti *pron pess (2ᵃ pessoa sg =* **tu***) (depois de preposição)* you; **gosto de** ~ I like you; **isto é para** ~ this is for you.

tia *f* aunt; ~**-avó** great-aunt.

tiara *m (para a cabeça)* tiara; ~ **de diamantes** diamond tiara; **2** *(REL) (mitra)* tiara.

tibetano,-a *(LÍNG)* Tibetan; **2** *adj* Tibetan.

Tibete *npr* o ~ Tibet.

tíbia *f (ANAT)* tibia, shinbone; **2** *(pop) (perna, canela)* shin.

tíbio,-a *adj* tepid, lukewarm; **2** *(fig)* unenthusiastic.

tica *f (pop) (ponta de cigarro)* butt of cigarette, fag; **2** *(em Moçambique) (ZOOL)* hyena.

tição *m (lenha)* firebrand, piece of burnt wood; **2** *(fig)* sun-tanned person, person covered in soot.

tido,-a *(pp de ter) adj (considerado)* ~ **como** considered; **ele é** ~ **como perito** he is considered an expert.

tifo *m* tiphus.

tifóide *adj* typhoid *(fever)*.

tigela *f* bowl; **2** *(BR) (litro)* litre; **3** *(pop) (pej)* **de meia-~** mediocre; petty; **gente de meia-~** common people, uncouth people.

tigelada *f* bowl-full.

tigre *m (ZOOL)* tiger.

tigresa *f* tigress.

tijolo *m (CONSTR)* brick; ~ **refra(c)tário** fire-proof brick, refractory brick.

til *m (acentuação)* tilde: *sã, põe, vão, mãe*.

tília *f (BOT)* linden, lime-tree; **chá de** ~ lime tea.

tilintar *(Vd:* **telintar***)*.

timão *m (NÁUT)* helm, tiller.

timbrado,-a *adj (papel)* headed (paper).

timbre *m (insígnia)* crest, emblem; **2** *(em papel)* stamp; *(MÚS) (de voz, instrumento)* timbre, tone; **3** *(fig) (hábito, estilo)* class.

timidez *f* shyness, timidity.

tímido,-a *adj* shy, timid.

timoneiro *m (NÁUT)* helmsman, coxswain; **2** *(fig)* leader, guide.

Timor (= **Timor Leste**) *npr* East Timor.

> **Timor Leste** is a beautiful country situated in the archipelago of Sunda, in South-East Asia. It was discovered by the Portuguese in 1512. In 1974, it was given independence from Portugal, but was immediately invaded by Indonesia. Its independence was finally recognized in 2002. Languages: Portuguese and Tetun (língua franca). Capital: Dili.

timorato,-a *m,f (medroso)* timid; **2** *(cauteloso)* over-cautious.

tímpano *m (ANAT)* ear-drum, tympanum, tympanic membrane; **2** *(MÚS)* kettle drum, timbal; **3** *(ARQ)* tympanum.

timpanoplastia *f (MED) (cirurgia)* ear-drum surgery.

tina *f (vasilha de aduelas)* wooden tub; **2** *(para uso industrial)* vat, vessel; **3** *(para lavar o ouro)* sluice-box; **4** bath tub.

tingido *(pp de tingir)* dyed.

tingir *vt (alterar a cor)* to dye; **2** *(fig) (colorir)* to tinge *(rosto, céu)*; ♦ *vr* tinge.

tinha *etc (imperf de ter)* **eu** ~ **sono** I was sleepy; ♦ *f (MED)* scurf; **2** tinea (ringworm).

tinhoso,-a *adj (com tinha) (cão, cobaia)* mangy.

tinido *m (som)* ring; tinkle; **2** *(sinos)* jingle; **3** *(zumbido)* buzzing.

tinir *vi (campainha)* ring; **2** *(sinos, moedas, chaves)* to jingle; **3** *(ferrinhos, chocalhos, copos)* tinkle.

tinite *f (MED) (zumbido nos ouvidos)* tinnitus.

tino *m (senso, juízo)* discernment, common sense, judgement; **perder o** ~ to lose one's senses; **2** *(intuição)* feel, knack.

tinta *f (para paredes, arte)* paint; ~ **de água** matt paint; ~ **de esmalte** oil paint; **2** *(para escrever)* ink; **3** *(para o cabelo, roupa)* dye; **4** *(ZOOL, CULIN) (das lulas)* ink; **5** ~-**da-china** Indian ink; IDIOM **estar-se nas** ~**s (para)** not care a damn (to, for).

tinteiro *m* inkwell.

tintim *m* ~ **por** ~ *(história)* in full detail.

tinto,-a *(irr pp de tingir, com vb ser/estar) adj* dyed, stained; **2** red; **vinho** ~ red wine.

tintura *f* dying; **2** *(solução)* dye; **3** *(FARM)* tincture, ~ **de iodo** tincture of iodine; **4** *(fig) (rudimentar)* smattering.

tinturaria *f* dyer's; **2** dry-cleaners.

tintureiro,-a *m,f* dry-cleaner; **2** *(que tinge)* dyer.

tio *m* uncle; ~-**avô** *m* great-uncle.

típico,-a *adj* typical, characteristic.

tipificar *vt* to typify.

tipo *m (espécie)* type, kind; **2** *(TIPO)* type; *(letra)* font; **3** *(fam)* guy, bloke; **4** *(woman) (pej)* floozy.

tipografia *f* printing, typography; printing, printer's office.

tipógrafo *m* printer.

tique *m (espasmo)* spasm; **2** *(MED)* twitch; ~ **nervoso** nervous tic; **3** *(som)* tick.

tiquetaque *(pl: tique-taques) m* tick-tack; **2** *(do relógio)* tick-tock; **3** *(palpitação do coração)* pit-a-pat.

tiquete *m (BR)* voucher, ticket.

tira *f* strip *(de pano, papel)*; **fazer em** ~**s** to tear to pieces, into strips; ~ **de banda desenhada** comic strip; **2** *m (BR: col) (agente de polícia)* cop.

tira-agrafos *m* staple-remover.

tiracolo *m* shoulder belt; **a** ~ slung from the shoulder, over the shoulder, cross-wise.

tirada *f (caminho longo)* stretch; **2** *(dito)* tirade.

tira-dentes *m,f (pop)* dentist; **T~** place in Brazil.

tiragem *f (de revista, jornal)* circulation; **2** collection (of post).

tira-linhas *m sg/pl* drawing pen, stylo.

tirania *f* tyranny.

tiranizar *vt* tyrannize/tirannise.

tirano,-a *m,f* tyrant; ♦ *adj* tyrannical.

tira-nódoas *m sg pl* stain remover.

tirante *m* trace, strap; **2** *(correia)* harness; **3** *(MEC)* connecting rod; **4** *(viga)* tie beam; ♦ *adj inv:* **uma cor** ~ **a azul** a bluish colour; ♦ *prep* except for.

tirar *vt (ger)* to take; ~ **um curso/diploma/uma fotografia** to take a course, a diploma, a photo; **2** *(remover)* to remove, take away; **ela tirou-me a escova** she took away my brush; **3** *(despir)* take off *(roupa, chapéu)*; **4** *(sacar, puxar)* to take out, withdraw, pull out *(dinheiro, arma)*; **5** *(extrair)* extract; **6** *(eliminar)* remove, take off; **este produto tira nódoas** this product removes/takes off stains; **a cirurgia plástica tirou-te dez anos** the cosmetic surgery took ten years off you; **7** take out from; **tira os garfos da caixa** take the forks out of the box; **8 tirei-o da escola** I took him out of the school; **9** *(transcrever)* write/take (down); **10** *(ganhar)* **ela tira uns trinta mil euros por mês** she earns about thirty thousand euros per month; **11** ~ **donde tirou essa história?** where did you get that story from?; **12** ~ **informações** to enquire; **13** deduct, subtract; **14** ~ **à sorte** to draw lot; ♦ *vi (semelhante)* **ele tira ao pai** he looks like his father; ♦ *vr (sair de)* get out (of, from); **2** *(livrar-se)* get rid of; ♦ **sem ~ nem pôr** *adv* precisely.

tiritar *vi* to shiver.

tiro *m* shot; **2** shooting, firing; team; ~ **ao alvo** target practice; **sair o ~ pela culatra** *(fig)* to backfire; *(AUSTRAL)* to boomerang.

tirocínio *m* apprenticeship, training.

tiroide *adj (ANAT)* thyroid; **glândula** ~ thyroid gland.

tiroteio *m (troca de tiros)* shooting; shootout; volley of shots; **2** *(fig)* bombardment.

tísico,-a *f* consumption; ♦ *adj* consumptive.

tisnar *vt* to smudge; **2** to blacken, to brown *(pão, etc)*; become sunburnt.

titâneo *m* titanium.

títere *m (fantoche)* puppet.

titubear *vt (gaguejar)* stutter; **2** hesitate; **3** *(cambalear)* to totter, stagger; **sem ~** without faltering.

titular *m,f* titled noble person **2** *(do ministério)* incumbent, minister; **3** *(possuidor)* holder; ♦ *adj inv (efe(c)tivo) (juiz)* incumbent; *(professor)* tenured; ♦ *vt* to title.

título *m* title; **2** *(em jornal)* headline; **3** *(COM) (papel de crédito)* bond, certificate; **4** ~ **de propriedade** title deed; **a título de** *prep* by way of, as, on the pretext of; **a justo ~** with reason.

tive *(pret, 1ª pessoa de* **ter)** ~ **boas notícias** I have had/received good news.

to (= **te** + **o**) it to you; **já me deste o dinheiro? sim, dei-to** have you given me the money? yes, I have given it to you.

toa *f (NÁUT)* tow-rope; **2 à** ~ *adv* at random; carelessly; **andar à** ~ to walk aimlessly.

toada *f (MÚS)* tune, melody; **2** *(ruído, som)* noise, sound (of); **3** *(boato)* rumour.

toalete *f (traje)* outfit; **2 fazer a** ~ to groom o.s., wash and get dressed; **3** *(BR) m (banheiro, casa de banho)* toilet.

toalha *f (de banho/do rosto/da praia/das mãos)* bath/face/beach/hand towel; **2** ~ **de mesa** tablecloth.

toalheiro *m* towel rail.

toalhete *m (higiene)* tissue; **2** *(pequena toalha)* ~ **do rosto** face flannel; ~ **de bidé** bidet towel.

toar *vi* to sound, resound; **2** to thunder; **os trovões toavam** the thunder resounded.

toca *f (covil)* burrow, hole, warren; **2** *(de animal selvagem)* den, lair; **3** *(de ladrões)* hiding place, hide-out.

toca-discos *(BR) m inv* record-player.

tocado,-a *adj (que recebeu um toque)* bumped, bruised; **2** *(fig) (meio embriagado)* tipsy; **3** *(BR)* touched (in the head).

toca-fitas *msg/pl (BR)* cassette-player, tape-recorder.

tocaia *f (BR)* ambush, snare; **de** ~ *adv* in hiding; on the look-out.

tocaio *m (homónimo)* namesake.

tocante *adj inv (de emoção)* moving, touching; **2 no** ~ **a** *prep* regarding, concerning.

tocar *vt* to touch; **2** *(sensibilizar)* move, touch; **o seu gesto tocou-me** his gesture touched/moved me; **3** *(MÚS)* to play; **4** *(campainha, sino)* to ring; **pelo que me toca** as far as I am concerned; ♦ *vi* to *(telefone)* ring; ~ **em algo** to touch upon sth; **2** ~ **em alguém** *(apalpar)* to touch; **3** *(na ferida)* to hurt one's feelings; **4** *(fazer escala em)* to stop off in.

tocha *f* large candle; **2** *(archote)* torch.

toco *m* tree stump; **2** *(resto de algo)* stub; **3** *(de um membro decepado)* stump; **4** *(de cigarro)* butt (-end).

todavia *conj* yet, however, nevertheless; ♦ *adv* notwithstanding.

todo,-a *m* whole; **como um** ~ as a whole; **todos** *mpl* everybody *sg*; ♦ *m*: **o T~-poderoso** the Almighty; ♦ *adj* all; **o país todo, todos nós** all of us; **2** every; ~**a a gente,** *(BR)* ~**o o mundo** everyone, everybody; **em toda a parte** everywhere; **3** ~ **todo o dia** all day; ~**s os dias** every day; **a** ~**a velocidade** at great speed; ♦ *adv* whole; **ao** ~ in all; **de** ~ completely.

Todo-poderoso,-a *adj* almighty, all-powerful.

todo-o-terreno *m* land rover.

toga *f* toga; **2** *(de professores, advogados)* gown.

toiro *(Vd: touro)*.

tojo *m (BOT)* gorse, furze.

tola[1] *f (pop)* head; **com a** ~ **descoberta** bareheaded.

tola[2] *f (Vd: tolo)*.

toldo *m* awning, sun blind, wind-breaker.

toleima *f* foolishness; silliness.

tolerância *f* broadmindedness, tolerance; toleration, forbearance.

tolerante *adj* broadminded, understanding.

tolerar *vt* to tolerate, allow; to put up with, bear.

tolerável *adj* tolerable, bearable; passable.

tolher *vt* to impede, prevent; **2** *(movimento)* hinder; **3** *(entorpecer)* numb *(dedos, membros)*; ~ **a voz** silence the voice.

tolice *f* stupidity, idiocy; **2** *(dito de tolo)* nonsense; **3** *(vaidade)* conceit.

tolo,-a *m,f (pessoa)* idiot, nitwit; **2** *(cândido)* sucker, dope; ♦ *adj* silly, idiotic; **2** vain, conceited; **3** *(doido)* crazy.

tom *m (som, voz)* tone, intonation; **2** *(cor)* shade.

toma *f (acto de ingerir)* dose, dosage; **2** *(pop) (manguito)* rude gesture (com os braços); ♦ *exc* **toma!** *(aprovando castigo)* it serves you right!, I told you so!

tomada *f* capture, conquest; **2** *(acto de tomar)* taking (up); **3** ~ **de consciência** awareness; **4** *(ELECT)* plug, *(na parede)* socket; **5** ~ **de posse** investiture; **6** *(CIN, TV)* take; **7** ~ **de preços** tender.

tomado,-a *adj (por boca)* taken; **2** seized; overtaken; ~ **de pânico** panic-striken.

tomar *vt (ger)* to take; **2** to capture, seize; **3** *(tomar posição, oferta)* take up; **4** *(beber)* to have; ♦ ~**-se** *vr*: ~ **de** to be overcome with.

tomara *exc* how I wish!, wish it were so!, let us hope so!, ~ **que ele venha** let us hope he comes (soon); ~ **que ele fosse rico** how I wish he were rich!; ~ **que não chova** I hope it doesn't rain.

tomate *m* *(BOT)* *(fruto, planta)* tomato; **um quilo de** ~ a kilo of tomatoes; **2** ~**s** *pl* *(vulg)* *(testículos)* balls *(cal)*.

tomateiro *m* tomato plant.

tombada *f* watershed.

tombadilho *m* *(NÁUT)* poop deck, quarter deck.

tombar *vi* *(cair)* ~ **em/de/para** to fall (down, over), tumble down; **algo tombou do céu** something fell from the sky; **2** go down; **o sol tombava** the sun was going down; **3** *(inclinar)* to lean, tilt; ◆ *vt* *(derrubar)* to knock down, knock over, topple over; **2** *(inventariar)* to list; IDIOM **cheira que tomba!** what a stench!

tombo *m* *(queda)* fall, tumble; **2** *(jogos)* throw; **3** archives *pl*, records *pl;* **Torre do T~** The Portuguese National Archives for Historical Documents; IDIOM **andar aos** ~**s** to stumble along.

tômbola *f* bingo, lotto, tombola.

tomilho *m* *(BOT)* thyme.

tomo *m* *(part)* tome; **2** volume; **3** *(fig)* importance, value.

tomografia *f* *(MED)* *(exame radiológico)* ~ **axial computarizada, TAC** computerized axial tomography, CAT (scan).

tona *f* *(água)* surface; **à** ~ afloat; **vir à** ~ to come to the surface; **2** *(fig)* to come to light, bring up *(assunto)*.

tonalidade *f* *(MÚS)* key, tonality; **2** shade, colouring.

tonel *m* *(recipiente)* tun, largecask, hogshead; **2** *(fig, fam)* *(beberrão)* boozer, guzzler.

tonelada *f* *(medida)* ton, tonne; **2** *(tonel cheio)* tun.

> **Tonelada Americana** = short ton = 2000 lbs; ~ **inglesa** long ton = 2,240 lbs; ~ **métrica** = metric ton = 1000 kilos, 2,204.6 lbs.

tonelagem *f* *(capacidade)* tonnage; ~ **de arqueação** gauge tonnage.

tónico,-a *(BR:* tô-*)* *f* *(água)* tonic; ◆ *adj* tonic; **2** **nota** ~**a** *(assunto principal)* keynote; **3** **acento** ~ stress, pitch, tonic accent.

tonificante *adj* invigorating.

tonificante *adj inv* invigorating.

tonificar *vt* to invigorate, to tone.

toninha *f* porpoise.

tonitruante *adj inv* *(canhões, voz ronca)* thundering.

tono *m* air, melody, song; **2** *(TEC)* tone.

tons *mpl* *(Vd:* tom*)*.

tonsure *f* tonsure.

tonta *f* *adj* *(Vd:* tonto*)*; **2** head; *(pop)* crazy; **mulher** ~ crazy woman; **3** *(BR)* **à** ~, **às tontas** *(atarantadamente)* in a fluster.

tonteira *f* *(tolice)* nonsense; **2** *(vertigem)* dizziness, dizzy spell.

tontice *f* stupidity, silly idea.

tonto,-a *adj* dizzy; **2** lightheaded; **3** *(fam)* silly, crazy.

tontura *f* *(vertigem)* giddiness; **ter uma** ~ to have a dizzy spell.

tónus *m* *(FISIOL)* tonus; ~ **muscular** muscular tone, muscular contraction.

top *m* *(roupa)* top; *(tabela de vendas)* charts.

topa-a-tudo *m* *(pop)* Jack-of-all-trades, a know-all.

topada *f* a trip, tripping, a stumble, stumbling; **dar uma** ~ to stub one's toe.

topar *vt* *(encontrar)* to find, come across, spot *(algo/ alguém,* sth/sb*)*; **2** *(pop)* *(perceber)* to get, to understand, to figure out; ◆ *vi* ~ **(com)** to meet up (with); **2** ~ **em** to trip/stumble over; **3** *(fam)* *(gostar)* fancy, agree to; **você topa um sorvete?** do you fancy an ice cream?; ◆ ~**-se** *vr* catch sight of; ~ **em cheio** *(chocar-se)* bump into.

topázio *m* *(pedra preciosa)* topaz.

tópico,-a *m* topic, subject; ◆ *adj* topical; *(MED)* a topical remedy.

topo[1] *m* *(cimo, cume)* top, peak, crest; ~ **da mesa** table top; **2** extremity.

topo[2] *(choque)* bump; **2 de** ~ *adv* suddenly.

topografia *f* topography.

topográfico,-a *adj* topographical.

topónimo *(BR:* -ô-*)* *m* *(LÍNG)* toponym, place name.

toque *m* *(contacto)* touch, tap; **dei-lhe um** ~ **no ombro** I touched/tapped her/him on the shoulder; **2** *(som)* *(campainha)* ringing, sound; *(dos sinos)*, peal; ~ **de clarim** bugle call; **o** ~ **da sereia** the wail of the siren; **3** *(telefonema)* ring, buzz; **dá-me um** ~ **para o escritório** give me a buzz at the office; **4** touch; **um** ~ **de génio** a touch of genius; **5 pedra de** ~ touchstone.

Tóquio *npr* Tokyo.

torácico,-a *adj* thoracic; **caixa** ~**a** thoracic cage.

toranja *f* *(fruto)* grapefruit; *(árvore)* grapefruit tree.

tórax *m* *(ANAT)* thorax.

torção *m* twist, twisting, wringing; **2** *(MED)* torsion of an artery; *(do pé, braço)* spraining; **3** *(MEC)* *(metal torcido)* torque.

torcedura *f* *(rodar em si)* twist; **corda sem nós nem** ~**s** rope without knots or twists; **2** *(torcer algo molhado)* wringing; **3** *(braço, pé)* sprain, wrench.

torcer *vt* to twist, to turn; **2** ~ **um pano molhado** to wring a wet cloth; **3** to sprain, twist ~ **o pulso** to sprain the wrist; **4** ~ **o nariz** to turn one's nose up at; **5** *(conversa)* to distort, misconstrue; ◆ *vi* *(apoiar)* to on the side of, support; **2** *(voltar-se)* turn round; ◆ ~**-se** *vr* to squirm, writhe; **ela torcia-se com dores** she writhed with pain; **2** *(fig)* *(render-se)* to give in to, enjoy; **ele torceu-se à tentação** he gave in to the temptation.

torcicolo *m* *(MED)* stiff neck.

torcida *f* *(pavio)* wick; **2** *(BR)* supporting; *(BR)* *(claque)* fans, supporters.

torcido,-a *adj* *(algo que se torceu)* twisted; **2** *(caminho, rio)* winding, tortuous; **3** *(alguém de mau cará(c)ter)* twisted.

tordo *m* *(ZOOL)* thrush.

torga *f* *(BOT)* heather.

tormenta *f* storm, tempest; **2** *(fig)* agitation, trouble; **3** *(angústia)* torment, anguish.

tormento *m* torment, suffering; **2** *(suplício)* torture; **3** *(fig)* agony, anguish, suffering; **passar por ~s** to go through hell.

tormentoso,-a *adj* stormy, tempestuous; **2** *(difícil)* hard.

tornado *m* *(METEOR)* tornado, hurricane.

tornar *vi* to return, go back; **tornei à minha terra** I returned to my land; **2 ~ a fazer algo** to do sth again; **ele tornou a ler o jornal** he read the paper again; ♦ *vt* to render, make; ♦ **~-se** *vr (vir a ser)* to become.

tornas *fpl* compensation; part of the inheritance.

tornassol *m* *(QUÍM)* litmus.

torneado,-a *adj (arredondado)* rounded, turned; **2** *(fig)* **corpo bem ~** shapely body.

tornear *vt* to turn, turn on a lathe; **2** *(rodear)* by-pass, go around; **3** *(madeira)* shape; ♦ *vi* work with a lathe.

torneio *m (torneamento)* rounding, turning; **2** *(competição de desporto)* tournament, match; **3** *(de cavaleiros)* joust.

torneira *f* tap *(UK)*; faucet *(US)*; **a ~ do lava-louças está a pingar** the sink's tap is dripping.

torniquete *m (MED)* tourniquet.

torno *m (máquina para tornear = madeira, metal)* lathe; **2 ~ de mão** vice *(UK)*, vise *(US)*; **3** *(clavilha)* wooden peg; **4** *(tubo com rolha para pipas)* spigot; **5** *(em olearia)* potter's wheel; **em ~ (de)** *adv/prep* around, about.

tornozelo *m (ANAT)* ankle; **torcer o ~** twist/sprain the ankle.

toro *m (de árvore)* stump, trunk; **2** *(árvore, cortada e limpa)* log; **3** *(corpo humano)* trunk, torso; **4** *(ARQ)* torus.

torpe *adj inv (obsceno)*, disgusting, disgraceful; **2** *(vil)* foul, vile; **3** dishonest, shameful; **4** *(que perdeu vigor)* lethargic.

torpedeiro *m (MIL)* torpedo boat; sailor who fires torpedos.

torpedo *m* torpedo.

torpeza *f (baixeza)* vileness; **2** disgrace; **3** obscenity.

torpor *m* torpor, numbness; **2** *(indiferença)* apathy, inertia, indifference.

torrada *f* toast.

torradeira *f* toaster.

torrão *m (terra endurecida)* soil; **2** *(arável)* land; **3** *(país)* **~ natal** native land; **4** lump; **~ de açúcar** lump of sugar.

torrar *vt (pão)* to toast; **2** *(amêndoas, etc)* to roast; **3** *(vegetação)* to parch; ♦ *vi (queimar)* burn, be burning hot.

torre *f* tower; **2** *(igreja)* steeple, bellfry; **3 ~ de menagem** keep; **4** *(xadrez)* castle, rook; **5** *(em submarino)* conning tower; **6** *(AERO)* turret; **7** *(ELECT)* pylon; **8** (TV, RADIO) mast; **9 ~ de vigia** watchtower; **~ de escritórios** office tower.

torrefa(c)ção *f (de café, etc)* roasting; **2** *(estabelecimento)* coffee-roasting house.

torrencial *adj inv* torrential.

torrente *f* torrent.

torresmo *m (CULIN)* crackling (of roast pork), pork scratchings, *pl.*

tórrido,-a *adj* torrid.

torso *(ANAT)* trunk; **de ~ nu** bare to the waist.

torta *f* pie, tart; **2** *(contorção da videira)* bending arch; **3** *(bebedeira)* skinful; **4** *(contra(c)ções do útero após parto)* afterbirth pains *(Vd: **torto**)*.

torto,-a *adj* twisted, crooked, not straight, bent; **2** *(olhos)* squinting; **3** *(argumento)* wrong; **4** *(pessoa má, vingativa)* wicked; ♦ *adv* rudely; **a ~ e a direito** recklessly, every which way; IDIOM **não passar da cepa ~a** make no progress.

tortuoso,-a *adj* winding; **2** *(fig) (mente)* tortuous; **3** *(fig) (carácter)* devious.

tortura *f* torture; **2** *(fig)* anguish, agony.

torturante *adj inv (espera)* agonizing; **2** *(dor)* excruciating.

torturar *vt* to torture; **2** *(fig)* to torment.

torvação *f* perturbation, agitation; **2** *(cólera)* anger.

torvelinho *m* whirlwind, whirl; **2** whirl, swirl; **andar num ~** to be in a whirl, be always on the go.

torvo,-a *adj* angry; **2** *(expressão)* grim; **3** *(ambiente)* gloomy, dark.

tos (= **te** + **os**) them to you; **já me deste os papéis? ainda não ~ dei** have you given me the papers? I have not given them (to you) yet; **dei-tos ontem** I gave them to you yesterday.

tosa[1] *f (tosquia)* shearing; **2** *(pêlo)* trimming, clipping.

tosa[2] *(fam) (tareia)* hiding; **2** *(fig, fam) (censura)* lashing, scolding.

tosão *m (pêlo do carneiro)* fur, fleece; **2** net to catch trout.

tosar *vt* to shear; **2** to crop.

tosco,-a *ad (em bruto, primitivo)* rough, unpolished; **2** (grosseiro) coarse, crude.

tosquia *f* sheep-shearing.

tosquiador,-ora sheep-shearer.

tosquiar *vt (carneiro)* to shear; *(aparar pêlo)* to clip.

tosse *f* cough; **~ convulsa ou comprida** whooping cough; **~ seca** dry cough.

tossir *vi* to cough; *(expelir)* to cough up.

tosta *f* toast; **~ mista** toasted cheese and ham sandwich.

tostado,-a *adj (pão, etc)* toasted; **2** *(pessoa)* tanned.

tostão *m (antiga moeda portuguesa)* penny, farthing, money, cash; **não tenho um ~** I haven't got a penny/a cent/any cash; IDIOM **não valer um ~** not be worth a tinker's cuss.

tostar *vt* to toast; ♦ **~-se** *vr* to get tanned, get sunburnt.

totabola *m (jogo)* (football) pools.

total *m* total; **no ~** in total; ♦ *adj inv* total, complete.

totalidade *f* totality, entirety.

totalitário,-a *adj* totalitarian.

totalizador *m (aparelho relativo aos jogos de apostas)* totalizator, tote.

totalmente *adv* totally, utterly.

totem *m* totem pole.

totoloto *m* lottery, draw.

touca *f* child's/woman's bonnet; **2** nun's coif.

toucador *m (mobília)* dressing table; **2** *(touca ou rede para segurar o cabelo)* hair net.

toucinho *m* salted pork fat, pork belly; **~ entremeado** streaky bacon.

toucinho do céu *m* (*CULIN*) cake made with almonds and eggs.

toupeira *f* (*ZOOL*) mole; **2** (*fig*) numbskull, ignoramus, dimwit.

tourada *f* bullfight; **2** drove of bulls; **3** (*fig*) brawl, riot, tumult.

tourear *vi* to fight (bulls).

toureio *m* bullfighting.

toureiro *m* bullfighter.

tournée *f* tour; ~ **de pé descalço** (*sem dinheiro*) tour on a shoestring.

touro *m* (*também* **toiro**) (*ZOOL*) bull; **corrida de ~s** bullfight; **2** **T~** (*ASTROL*) Taurus; **praça de ~s** bullfight amphitheatre; **arena da praça de ~s** bullring; IDIOM **pegar o ~ pelos cornos** take the bull by the horns.

tóxico,-a *adj* poisonous, toxic.

toxicodependência *f* drug addiction.

tóxicodependente/toxicómano,-a *m,f* drug addict.

toxicomania *f* drug addiction.

toxina *f* toxin.

trabalhado,-a *adj* (*lavrado*) (*prata, ouro, madeira*) elaborate; (*iron*) wrought; **2** (*estilo, discurso*) prepared carefully.

trabalhador,-ora *m,f* labourer, worker; employee; ♦ *adj* hard-working; **a classe ~** working class.

trabalhão *m* (*fam*) a lot of work.

trabalhar *vi* to work, labour; **2** to function; ♦ *vt* to work, operate; **2** ~ **a terra** to till the ground; IDIOM ~ **de borla/de graça** to work for nothing; ~ **de sol a sol** work all day long; ~ **p'ró** (= **para o**) **boneco** work for nothing; ~ **sem proveito** work in vain.

trabalhista *adj* (*POL*) labour member; **Partido T~** Labour Party.

trabalho *m* work, labour; **2** occupation, job, task; ~ **braçal** manual work; (*ECON*) **força de ~** work force; (*JUR*) **~s forçados** hard labour; IDIOM **morto de ~** dead beat; **carga de ~s** a lot of work; **dar ~** (*algo*) be hard work.

trabalhoso,-a *adj* laborious, arduous.

traça *f* (*ZOOL*) (*de roupa*) moth; **2** (*de livro*) bookworm; **3** (*de traçar*) sketch, outline; **4** (*CONSTR, ELECT*), blueprint.

traçado *m* sketch, plan.

tracção (*Vd*: **tracção**).

traçar *vt* to draw, sketch; **2** (*planear*) to draw up; **3** (*pôr linhas em cheque*) cross; **4** (*demarcar*) map out; **5** (*cruzar pernas*) to cross (legs).

tracção, tração *f* traction, pull.

tracinho *m* (*hífen*) hyphen.

traço *m* line; **2** (*sinal de pontuação*), dash; **3** ~ **de união** hyphen; **4** trace, vestige; **5** (*característica*) feature, trait, characteristics; **6** (*fig*) (*pedaço*) piece; **um ~ de carne de vaca** a piece/slice of beef; **7** (*pop*) (*mulher atraente*) a stunner, a dish; ♦ **a ~s largos** in broad lines, roughly; **de um ~** in one go.

tractor, trator *m* tractor.

tradição *f* tradition.

tradicional *adj* traditional.

tradução *f* translation; ~ **consecutiva/simultânea** consecutive/simultaneous translation.

tradutor,-ora *m,f* translator; ~ **juramentado,-a** accredited/registered translator.

traduzir *vt* to translate; **2** (*expressar*) express; **3** (*manifestar, significar*) to reveal, to mean; ♦ ~-**se** *vr* (*manifestar-se*) be expressed.

traduzível *adj inv* translatable.

tráfego *m* trade, commerce; **2** (*fluxo de veículos circulantes*) traffic; **3** ~ **aéreo** air traffic; **4** toil, work.

traficante *m,f* trafficker, dealer; **os ~s de drogas** drug dealers.

traficar *vt/vi* to trade, deal; **2** (*tráfico ilícito*) traffic in.

tráfico *m* to trade, deal; **2** (*negócio fraudulento*) trafficking; ~ **de armas** arms trafficking; ~ **de influência** backscratching (*fam*).

trafulha *m,f* (*fam*) (*pessoa que engana/mente*) cheat, crook, trickster, knave.

traga (*pres ind de* **tragar**); **2** (*pres subj de:* **trazer**) **eu quero que ele me ~ água** I want him to bring me water.

tragar *vt* (*engolir*) to swallow; **ele traga com dificuldade** he is swallowing with difficulty; (*comer*) swallow down; **2 o mar tragou tudo** the sea swallowed everything up; **3** (*fig, fam*) (*aguentar*) to tolerate, stand (*alguém, algo*); **4** (*acreditar*) swallow; ♦ *vi* (*aspirar fumo*) breathe in, inhale.

tragédia *f* tragedy.

trágico,-a *adj* tragic; **2** over-dramatic.

tragicomédia *f* tragicomedy.

trago *m* mouthful, gulp; **2** (*dose*) shot; **bebi de um ~** I drank in one gulp/go; ♦ (*pres ind, 1ª pessoa de* **tragar**).

traguei, tragou (*pt de* **tragar**).

traição *f* (*POL*) treason, treachery; **2** (*deslealdade*) betrayal, disloyalty; **3** (*infidelidade*) infidelity.

traiçoeiro,-a *adj* (*acção*) treacherous; **2** (*pessoa*) disloyal.

traidor,-ora *m,f* traitor, traitress; ♦ *adj* (*acção*) treacherous; **2** (*pessoa*) (*infiel*) unfaithful, disloyal; **3** (*mar*) treacherous.

traineira *f* (*NÁUT*) (*pesca*) trawler, fishing boat.

trair *vt* to betray, be disloyal to; **ela traiu o marido** she was unfaithful to her husband.

trajar *vt* to wear; ♦ ~-**se** *vr*: ~ **de branco** to be dressed in white.

traje (*também* **trajo**) *m* dress, clothes *pl*, attire; **em ~ domingueiro** in one's Sunday best; ~ **de fantasia** fancy dress; ~ **de noite** evening gown, dress suit; ~ **de passeio** informal dress; **a rigor** formal dress; **em ~s menores** in underclothes.

trajecto, trajeto *m* course, path.

trajectória, trajetória *f* trajectory, path, course.

tralha *f* fishing net; **2** (*fam*) junk, stuff (*col*).

trama *f* (*fios que cruzam a urdidura*) woof, weft, the threads that cross the web; **2** (*tecido*) texture, woven material; **3** secret scheme, plot, intrigue; **4** (*ANAT*) lung tissue.

tramar *vt* to weave; **2** (*fazer planos secretos*) to scheme, plot; **3** (*pop*) get into trouble; **4** (*prejudicar*) to spoil; **ele tramou os meus planos** he spoiled my plans; ♦ ~-**se** *vr* to get oneself in trouble; IDIOM **estar/ficar tramado** to be in a jam; **tramado com (alguém)** to be fed up with sb.

trambelho *m (juízo)* common sense.

trambolhão *m* tumble, fall; **levar um** ~ be knocked down; have a setback; **andar aos trambolhões** to stumble along.

trambolho *m (empecilho)* encumbrance; **2** *(pessoa que é um encargo)* burden; **3** log attached to animals' legs.

trâmite *m* path; **2** course; ♦ ~**s** *mpl* formalities, standard procedure *sg*; **2** *(JUR)* legal channels.

tramoia *f (pop)* swindle, trick; **2** plot, intrigue.

tramontana *f* Pole Star; north wind; **2** *(rumo)* way; **perder a** ~ to lose one's bearings.

trampa *f (caca)* shit, dung; crap.

trampear *vt/vi* to deceive, to cheat.

trampolim *m* trampoline; ~ **para mergulhar** diving board; **2** *(fig) (uma via para progredir)* springboard.

trampolina *f* trickery, fraud, cunning.

trampolineiro *m (intrujão)* cheat, trickster.

trampolinice *f* trick, lie, deceit.

tranca *f (da porta)* bolt, bar; **2** *(de carro)* lock.

trança *f (cabelo)* plait; **2** *(fita, fios entrelaçados)* braid.

trançar *vt (cabelo)* to plait; **2** *(palha)* weave; **3** *(fios)* braid.

trancar *vt* to bar, bolt, lock up; **2** *(impedir, cancelar)* to put a stop to, cancel *(documento)*; ♦ ~-**se** *(fechar-se)* lock o.s. in; IDIOM ~ *(algo, alguém)* **a sete chaves** to lock sb/sth under lock and key.

tranco *m (andar do cavalo)* trot; **2** *(solavanco)* jolt; **3** *(esbarrão)* bump, shove; **aos** ~**s** in jolts; ♦ **aos** ~**s e barrancos** *adv* with difficulty.

tranquilidade *f* quietness; peacefulness; calm.

tranquilizar *vt* to calm, quieten; ~ **alguém** to reassure, assure sb.

tranquilo,-a *adj* tranquil; **2** quiet; **3** calm; **4** peaceful.

transacção, transação *f (COM)* transaction, deal.

transacto, transato,-a *adj (ano, semana, mês)* past, previous, ult(imate), last.

transamazónico,-a *(BR: -ô-)* trans-Amazónia.

transatlântico,-a *m* liner; ♦ *adj* transatlantic.

transbordante *adj inv (rio, etc)* overflowing; **2** *(fig) (de alegria)* overjoyed, bursting with.

transbordar *vi* to overflow, to spill over; ~ **de felicidade** be overjoyed.

transbordo *m* overflow; **2** *(NÁUT)* transfer.

transcendente *adj* transcendent.

transcender *vt* to transcend, exceed.

transcorrer *vi (decorrer)* to elapse, go by.

transcrever *vt* to transcribe; **2** *(copiar)* copy.

transcrição *f* transcription.

transe *m* ordeal, plight; **2** *(aflição)* anguish, distress; **3** *(hipnose)* trance; ♦ *adv* **a todo** ~ at all costs.

transeunte *m,f* passer-by, pedestrian.

transferidor *m* protractor.

transferir *vt* to transfer; **2** *(adiar)* postpone.

transfiguração *f* transformation; **2** *(REL)* transfiguration.

transfigurar *vt* to transform, turn (into); ♦ ~-**se** *vr (REL)* be transfigured.

transformação *(pl: -ões)* *f* transformation.

transformador *m (ELECT)* transformer; **2** processor; **indústria** ~**a** processing industry.

transformar *vt* to transform, change, alter; **2** *(modificação)* conversion; **3** *(DESP)* conversion (into a goal).

trânsfuga *m (MIL) (desertor)* deserter; renegade; **2** *(POL) (pessoa que muda de partido, seita)* turncoat.

transfusão *f* transfusion.

transgredir *vt* to transgress, infringe.

transgressão *f* transgression, infringement.

transgressor,-ora *m,f* transgressor, lawbreaker.

transição *f* transition, change.

transido,-a *adj (de frio)* numb, benumbed *(with cold)*; **2** *(de medo, susto)* shaking *(with fear, fright)*.

transigência *f* compliance, agreement; **2** acquiescence.

transigente *adj inv* compliant, willing to compromise.

transigir *vi (ceder)* compromise, make concessions; ~ **com alguém** to meet sb half-way; **2** give in, yield.

transistor/transístor *m (ELECT)* transistor; **2** *(RÁDIO)* portable, transistor radio.

transitar *vt (percorrer)* to go through; ♦ *vi*: ~ **por** *(pessoa, veículo, mercadoria)* to move about/ through, circulate.

transitável *adj inv* passable, practicable.

transitivo,-a *adj (gram) (verbo)* transitive; **2** *(transitório)* passing.

trânsito *m* transit, passage; **passageiros em** ~ transit passengers; **2** traffic, flow; ~ **interdito/impedido** no entry.

transitório,-a *adj* transitory, passing.

transladar *(Vd:* **trasladar***)*.

translúcido,-a *adj (que deixa passar a luz)* translucent; **2** diaphanous; **3** *(fig)* clear; *(pessoa)* enlightened, clear.

transmissão *f (RÁDIO, TV)* transmission, broadcast; **2** *(mensagem, etc)* sending; **3** *(JUR, MEC, MED)* transmission; **4** *(bens, cargo)* transfer; **5** *(de poderes)*, transference; **6** ~ **de pensamentos** mind-reading.

transmissões *fpl* communications.

transmissor *m* transmitter.

transmitir *vt (RÁDIO, TV)* to broadcast, transmit; **2** to transfer; **3** *(por contágio)* infect; **4** *(mensagem)* give, send.

transmontano *(Vd:* **trasmontano***)*; ♦ *adj* **of/from Trás-os-Montes**.

transparecer *vi (aparecer)* ~ **através de** to come/ show through; **2** be visible through/in.

transparência *f* transparency; **2** *(em projector)* slide.

transparente *adj* transparent; **2** *(roupa)* see-through; **3** *(fig) (óbvio)* clear, obvious.

transpiração *f* sweating, perspiration.

transpirar *vi (suar)* to perspire, sweat; **2** *(revelar-se)* become known, transpire.

transplantar *vt* to transplant, plant out; **2** *(MED)* transplant, graft *(órgão)*.

transplante *m* transplant.

transpor *vt (ger)* to transpose; **2** *(passar além)* to cross over; **3** leap/ go over *(muro, etc)*; **4** ~

um obstáculo overcome a difficulty; **5** *(mudar de/ lugar)* change the position; *(MÚS) (de tom)* change the key; ♦ **~-se** *vr* to vanish; **2** *(TIPO)* transpose.

transportadora *f* haulage company.

transportar *vt (levar)* to transport, carry; **2** *(MÚS)* transpose; **3** *(fig) (arrebatar)* enrapture, transport; ♦ **~-se** *vr (de lugar)* to move; *(fig) (remontar mentalmente)* cast one's mind back to.

transporte *m* transport, conveyance; **2** *(COM)* haulage; **3** amount carried forward; **4** rapture, delight.

transtornado,-a *adj* disturbed, confused; **estou ~** I don't know whether I am coming or going; **2** *(planos, etc)* upset, unsuccessful.

transtornar *vt* to upset; **2** disrupt; ♦ *vr* get upset.

transtorno *m (acção)* inconvenience; **causar ~** (a alguém) to cause inconvenience (to sb); **2** *(contrariedade)* upsetting, disturbance; **desculpe o ~** sorry to disturb you.

transversal *f* transversal; ♦ *adj inv (GEOM)* transversal; **2** *(rua)* side; **3** *(FÍS) (ondas)* transverse; **4** *(secção, corte)* cross.

transviado,-a *adj (pessoa)* wayward, erring; **2** *(carta)* gone astray; **3** *(carneiro)* stray.

transviar *vt (desencaminhar)* to lead astray; to deviate; **2** *(fig)* to corrupt; ♦ **~-se** *vr* to go astray.

trapaça *f* cheating; *(fraude)* swindle, fraud, scam.

trapaceiro,-a *m,f* swindler, cheat, con-man; ♦ *adj (person)* dishonest.

trapalhada *f* confusion, mix-up; **2** disorder; **que ~!** what a mess!

trapalhão,-lhona *m,f* bungler, blunderer; ♦ *adj* clumsy.

trapézio *m* trapeze; **2** *(GEOM)* trapezium.

trapezista *m,f* trapeze artist.

trapo *m* rag, old cloth; **manta de ~s** patchwork bedcover; **2** *pl (fig)* clothes; IDIOM **dizer ~s e farrapos (de)** to back-bite.

traqueia *f* windpipe.

traquinas *m,f sg, pl imp,* naughty (boy/girl); ♦ *adj inv* mischievous, troublesome.

trarei *(fut, 1ª pessoa de* **trazer)** **~ o dinheiro quando puder** I shall bring the money when I can.

trás *prep adv* behind; **de ~ para a frente** from back to front; **para ~** backwards; **por ~ de** behind; **dar para ~** *(algo)* back out; **ficar para ~** *(ultrapassado, atrasado)* to fall behind.

traseira *f (carro)* back, rear; **as ~s** *(casa)* the back (of house).

traseiro *m (ANAT) (col)* bottom, behind, backside; ♦ **traseiro,-a** *adj* back, rear.

trasladação *f (transferir) (algo/alguém de um lado para outro)* transfer; **2** *(JUR),* transfer; **3** *(adiar)* defer, postpone; **4** *(dum documento)* transcription.

trasladar *vt* to remove; **2** transfer; **3** to transcribe; **4** deferment, postponement.

trasmontano,-a *m,f* a native of Trás-os-Montes (province in northeast Portugal); ♦ *adj* pertaining to Trás-os-Montes.

traste *m* piece of junk, trash; **2** old piece of furniture; **~s** chattels; **3** *(fig)* rogue, a bad lot; **4** *(mulher sem moral)* hussy.

tratado *m* treaty, pact; **2** *(obra)* treatise; ♦ **tratado,-a** *adj* treated; **fui muito bem ~** I was very well treated, looked after.

tratamento *m (MED)* treatment; **2** *(forma de tratamento)* form of address (sb).

tratante *m* crook, rogue.

tratar *vt (MED)* to treat; **2** to look after; **3 ~ com** *(COM) (resolver)* to deal with; **4 ~ de** *(encarregar-se de)* to discuss, attend to; to manage; **5 ~ por** *(forma de se dirigir)* to address; **ele trata-me por Senhora** he addresses me by Mrs.; **trate da sua vida** mind your own business; **de que se trata?** what's it about?; **trata-se de** it is a question of, it is about.

tratável *adj inv (doença)* treatable; **2** *(pessoa)* approachable.

trato *m* treatment; **2** handling; **3** *(acordo)* agreement; **sem ~** uncouth; **ser de mau/ruim ~** to be hard to deal with; **a criança sofreu maus ~s** the child suffered ill-treatment; IDIOM **dar ~s à imaginação** *(col)* **à bola** to give rein to one's imagination, to cudgel one's brains.

trator *(Vd:* **tractor)**.

trauma *m (PSIC)* trauma; **2** *(MED)* injury.

traumatismo *m* traumatism.

trautear *vt/vi (cantarolar)* to hum, sing to oneself; **2** *(pop) (importunar)* to annoy, pester; **3** *(pop) (intrujar)* deceive sb.

travado,-a *adj (preso, seguro)* locked, secured; **2** restrained; **3** *(carro)* with break on; **4 língua ~a** tongue-tied.

trava-línguas *m* tongue-twister.

travão *m* brake.

travar *vt* to apply the brakes; **2** *(roda)* to lock; **3** *(obstruir)* to block; **4** *(impedir)* stop, prevent; **5** engage in, start/strike up *(conversa, etc)*; **~ amizade com** to make friends with; **6** *(combater)* fight; ♦ *vi* to brake.

trave *f (CONSTR) (de madeira/metal)* beam, crossbeam; **2** *(DESP)* crossbar.

travejamento *m* timberwork; framework.

través *m* slant, incline; **de ~** *adv* on the slant, obliquely; crosswise; **olhar de ~** to give a sidelong glance.

travessa[1] [é] *f* platter, long serving dish; **2** *(para segurar/enfeitar o cabelo)* sidecomb; **3** *(FERRO)* sleeper; **4** *(rua)* alleyway, lane; **5** *(CONSTR)* crossbeam; IDIOM **por portase ~s** by stealth, by devious means.

travessa[2] [ê] *adj (Vd:* **travesso)**.

travessão *m (balança)* beam; **2** *(tipo de gancho para o cabelo)* slide; **3** *(sinal gráfico)* dash.

travesseiro *m (almofada longa da cama)* bolster; IDIOM **consultar o ~** to sleep on it, think it over.

travessia *f* journey, crossing.

travesso,-a *adj (maroto)* mischievous, naughty.

travessura *f (de criança)* mischief; **2** *(brincadeira)* prank, trick.

travesti *m* travestite; **2** *(artista)* drag artist.

travo, travor *m (gosto)* acrid taste, tang, unpleasant after-taste; **2** *(impressão)* unpleasant impression.

trazer *vt (ger)* to bring; **2** *(causar)* to bring about, cause; **3** ~ **à baila** bring a (subject) up for discussion/to air sth; **4** ~ **à memória** to bring to mind; **5** have, hold, contain; **o avião trazia poucas pessoas** the plane had few people; **o jarro trazia sangria** the jug held sangria; **6** *(usar roupa)* wear; **elas traziam vestidos azuis** they wore/were wearing blue dresses; **ela trouxe-me muita sorte** she brought me much luck; IDIOM ~ **o coração aos pulos** to be excited; ~ **o rei na barriga** to be conceited, full of o.s.

trecho *m (MÚS, LITER)* passage; **2** *(de um lugar)* stretch.

treçolho (= **terçol**) *m (MED) (no olho)* sty, stye.

trégua *f (MIL)* truce; **2** respite, rest.

treinador,-ora *m,f* trainer; **2** *(FUT)*, coach.

treinar *vt* to coach; ~ **cães** train dogs; ♦ ~**-se** *vr* to train, to exercise.

treino *m* training.

trejeito *(gesto, expressão)* sign, gesture, twist; **2** *(cómico)* funny/wry face; **3** ~ **de dor** grimace with pain.

trela *f* lead, leash; **o cão não tem** ~ the dog is without a leash; **2** *(pop) (conversa)* chat; **dar** ~ **a** give rope to; to lead on.

trem *m* carriage, coach; **2** *(BR)* train; *(BR)* ~ **de carga** freight train; *(BR)* ~ **correio** mail train; **3** *(conjunto)* set; ~ **de cozinha** kitchen utensils; **4** *(AERO)* gear, ~ **de aterragem** landing gear; **trens** *mpl (pop)* gear *sg*, belongings *pl*.

trema *m (sinal m gráfico)* diaeresis *(agora ultrapassado em ambas as variantes de português)*.

tremedal *m (terreno alagadiço)* bog, quagmire.

tremelica *m,f* coward, milksop; ♦ *adj inv* cowardly, faint-hearted.

tremelicar *vi (de susto/frio)* to tremble, shiver.

tremelique(s) *m sg/pl* quivering, trembling; **com** ~ in fear and quivering.

tremeluzir *vi* to flicker, twinkle, glimmer, shine; **as luzes do carro tremeluziam** the car lights were flickering.

tremendo,-a *adj* tremendous, enormous; **2** horrible, awful; **ventania** ~**a** huge gale.

tremente *adj inv (luz)* flickering, tremulous.

tremer *vt (medo, frio)* to shake, tremble *(de, with)*; ♦ *vi (tiritar)* shiver; **2** *(voz)* quaver; **3** *(com horror)* shudder; **4** *(vela, chama)* flicker; IDIOM ~ **como varas verdes** to shake like a leaf.

tremoçal *m* lupin field.

tremoço *m (BOT) (semente)* lupin seed; **2** *(planta)* lupin; ~ **amarelo** yellow lupin.

tremor *m (pessoa, mãos, pernas, voz)* trembling, shaking; **2** tremor; ~ **de terra** earth tremor, earthquake.

tremular *vi (bandeira)* to flutter; **2** *(luz)* flicker.

trémulo,-a *adj* trembling; *(voz passo)* shaky, faltering; **2** *(fig)* timid.

trenó *m* sledge, sleigh *(UK)*; sled *(US)*.

trepadeira *f (BOT)* creeper, climbing plant.

trepar *vt (escalar)* to climb; ♦ *vt/vi* to rise in the world; ~ **com** *(BR) (fam)* sleep one's way to the top; **2** *(fig)* to be cheeky; **3** *(BR)* to speak ill of sb, gossip.

trepidação *f* trepidation, shaking.

trepidante *adj inv* shaking; **2** restless.

trepidar *vi* to tremble, shake; **2** to hesitate.

três *num* three.

tresandar *vt* to make one walk back; **2** to upset, disturb; ♦ *vi* go backwards; **2** *(exalar mau cheiro)* stink, reek.

tresloucado,-a *adj* crazy, deranged; **olhar** ~ crazy look.

tresloucar *vi* to go mad.

tresmalhar *vt/vi (perder as malhas)* to drop the loops in knitwear; **2** to let escape; **3** to scatter, disperse; ♦ *vi (animal)* to stray.

Três-Marias *fpl (ASTRON)* Orion's Belt; **2** *(BOT, pop)* bougainvillea.

trespassar *vt* to go through, pierce, penetrate; **o punhal trespassou o corpo dele** the dagger went through his body; **2** *(fig) (violar)* to overstep; **3** *(COM)* to transfer *(loja, quinta, negócio)*.

trespasse *m* transfer, handover *(negócio)*; lease.

treta *f (esgrima)* feint; **2** *(labia)* tale; **não venhas cá com essa** ~ don't come with such tales; **3** fib; ~**s** *fpl* nonsense; fibs.

trevas *fpl (escuridão)* darkness *sg*; **2** *(fig)* ignorance, obscurity.

trevo *m (BOT)* clover.

treze *num* thirteen; ♦ *adj inv (dia, página, etc)* thirteen, thirteenth; **dia** ~ **de Julho** thirteenth July; **século treze (XIII)** thirteenth century.

trezentos,-as *num* three hundred; ♦ *adj* three hundred, three hundredth.

triagem *f (seleção)* sorting; screening.

triatlo *m (DESP)* triathlon.

triangular *adj* triangular.

triângulo *m* triangle.

tribo *f* tribe, clan.

tribulação *f* tribulation, affliction.

tribuna *f* platform, dais, tribune; **2** *(de orador)* rostrum; **3** *(REL)* pulpit; **4** ~ **da imprensa** press gallery.

tribunal *m (JUR)* court; **T~ de apelação** Court of Appeal; **T~ de Contas** Government's Audit Office (Dept. of the Exchequer); **T~ de Justiça** Law Court; **T~ de Primeira Instância** Country Court; **T~ de Pequenos Delitos** Police Court, County Court; **T~ da Relação** High Court of Justice; **Supremo T~ de Justiça** Supreme Court of Judicature *(UK)*, High Court of Justice; **ministro do Supremo T~** Lord Chief of Justice *(UK)*; Attorney General *(US)*; **T~ Criminal Central** Central Criminal Court.

tribuno *m* tribune.

tributação *f* taxation.

tributar *vt* to tax; **2** to pay tax on.

tributário,-a *m,f* taxpayer; **2** *m (rio)* tributary.

tributável *adj inv* taxable.

tributo *m (imposto)* tax; **2** *(o que um Estado paga a outro)* tribute; **3** *(fig)* (onus) duty.

triciclo *m* tricycle.

tricot *(BR: tricô) m* knitting.

tricotar *(fazer malha) vt/vi* to knit.

tridimensional *adj inv* three-dimensional.

trienial *adj inv* triennial.

triénio *m* three-year period.

trigésimo,-a *num, m,f* thirtieth.

trigo *m* wheat.

trigueiro,-a *adj* dark, swarthy.

trilar *vt,vi* to warble, trill, quaver.

trilha *f (caminho)* path, track; **2** *(rasto)* trail; **3** *(COMP)* track; **4** *(CIN)* soundtrack; **5** *(exemplo)* follow.

trilhado,-a *adj* trodden; beaten, **caminho** ~ beaten track; **2** *(cereais)* thrashed, ground.

trilhar *vt (caminho)* to tread; **2** *(cereais)* thrash.

trilho *m (FERRO)* rail; **2** *(AGR) (utensílio para cereais)* harrow; **3** *(para fazer queijo)* churn-staff; **4** ~ **de roda** tread of a wheel; **5** *(fig) (norma)* rail, **sair do** ~ go off the rails.

trimestral *adj inv* quarterly.

trimestre *m* term; quarter (of a year); **pagamento** ~ quarterly payment.

trinado *m (canto dos passarinhos)* warble, chirp, trill; **2** *(MÚS)* trill.

trinar *vt* to trill, warble.

trinca-espinhas *m,f* tall and thin; **2** *(pernas)* spindleshanks.

trincar *vt (comer)* to chew; *(nozes, bones)* crunch; **2** *(morder)* to bite.

trincha *f* thick paintbrush; **2** *(ferramenta)* adze.

trinchar *vt (CULIN)* to carve, cut up *(carne)*.

trincheira *f (MIL)* trench; **2** *(TAUROM)* barrier; **3** *(BR) (baluarte)* stronghold.

trincheira *f* trench.

trinco *m (ferrolho)* latch.

trindade *f (REL)* Trinity; **Santíssima T~** the Holy Trinity; **2** *(fig) (tríade)* trio, threesome; **3** ~**s** *fpl* angelus *sg*.

trineto,-a *m,f* great-great-grandson/daughter.

trinómio *(BR: -ô-) m (MAT)* trinomial.

trinta *num* thirty.

trintão,-ona *m,f* man/woman in (their) thirties.

trio *m* trio; **2** ~ **elé(c)trico** music float.

tripa *f (de animal)* gut, intestines; ~**s** *fpl* bowels, guts; *(CULIN)* tripe *sg*; **tripas à moda do Porto** a kind of stew of tripe and beans; IDIOM **à ~-forra** for nothing; **comer à ~-forra** to gorge o.s.; **fazer das** ~**s coração** to make do with/do one's best out of a poor situation.

tripar *vt (descontrolar-se)* to freak out.

tripé *m* tripod; **2** three-legged stool; **3** *(para panela de três pés)* trivet; **4** *(BR)* threesome.

tripeiro,-a *m,f (pop)* nickname given to a citizen from Oporto.

tripla *f (ELECT) (ficha)* three-pin plug.

triplicado *adj* triplicate, threefold.

triplicar *vt* to triplicate, treble.

tríplice *adj inv* triple.

triplo,-a triple, threefold.

tríptico *m (ARTE) (quadro de três panos)* triptych; **2** *(obra em três partes)* trio, trilogy.

tripulação *f* crew.

tripulante *m* crew member.

tripular *vt (dirigir)* to man, *(barco)* to crew; **2** supply crew.

triques *m (janota)* dandy; ♦ *adj inv* smart; **todo** ~ **à beirinha** all togged up, dressed to the nines.

trisavô,-ó *m,f* great-great-grandfather/grandmother.

trismo *m (MED)* lockjaw.

triste *adj inv (pessoa)* sad, unhappy; miserable, wretched; **2** *(algo)* depressing.

tristeza *f* sadness; **2** sorrow.

triturado,-a *adj* crushed, ground.

triturador *m (de papel)* paper shredder; **2** *(legumes, carne)* food processor; **3** *(de lixo)* waste disposal unit; **4** *(de minério)* ore grinder; **5** ~ **de escória** *(MEC)* slag breaker.

triturar *vt (reduzir a fragmentos)* to grind; **2** *(minério)* stamp; **3** *(fig) (magoar)* to hurt; **3** *(fig) (argumento) to* crush.

triunfal *adj inv* triumphal.

triunfante *adj inv* triumphant.

triunfar *vi* to triumph, win.

triunfo *m* triumph, success.

trivial *adj inv* common(place), ordinary; **2** trivial, trifling.

trivialidade *f* triviality, banality, pettiness.

triz *m:* **por um** ~ by a hair's breath; **escapar por um** ~ to have a narrow escape, to escape by the skin of one's teeth.

troca *f* exchange, swap; **em** ~ **de** in exchange for; **2** *(ECON)* barter, ~ **de bens** barter of goods; ~ **de palavras** quarrel, exchange of words; IDIOM ~ **e baldrocas** shady business.

troça *f* ridicule, mockery; **fazer** ~ **de** to make fun of.

trocadilho *m* pun, play on words.

trocado,-a *m* exhanged, changed; **tem dinheiro** ~ **?** have you any change?

trocar *vt* to exchange, swap; **2** to change.

troçar *vt* to ridicule, make fun of.

trocista *m,f* joker, wag, tease; ♦ *adj* playful, teasing, mocking.

troco *m (dinheiro)* small change; **2** retort, rejoinder; **a** ~ **de** in exchange for.

troço *m* broken piece; **2** rough stick; **3** *(duma couve)* stalk; **4** *(de estrada, rio)* stretch; ~ **de via-férrea** branch line.

troço *m (BR)* thing, thingamajig; **2** *(pessoa influente)* big shot; **3** **ter um** ~ *(sentir-se mal)* to have an ache/pang.

troféu *m* trophy.

Tróia *npr (city)* Troy.

troiano *adj* trojan; **2** *(fig)* **entre gregos e** ~**s** between opposing parties; between the devil and the deep blue sea.

troika *f* troika.

trolha *m (pedreiro)* building worker/workman.

tromba *f (de animal)* trunk; snout; **2** *(pop)* cara; **estar de** ~**s** *(fam)* to look sullen; with a long face, **ela está de** ~**s comigo,** she is cross with me.

trombada *f* blow with a, elephant's trunk; **2** *(fig)* violent hit/blow; **3** *(colisão)* crash.

tromba d'água *f* downpour.

trombeta *f* trumpet, bugle.

trombone *m* trombone.

trombose *f (MED)* thrombosis.

trombudo,-a *adj (fam)* sulky, sullen.

trompa *f (MÚS)* horn; **2** *(ANAT)* tube; ~ **de Falópio** Fallopian tube.

trompete *m* trumpet.

trompetista *m,f* trumpeter.

tronchar *vt* to cut close, crop; **2** to chop off, mutilate.

troncho,-a *m* stump; ♦ *adj (mutilado)* ~ **de um braço** one-armed.

tronco *m (de árvore)* trunk; **2** *(ANAT)* torso, trunk; **3** *(de família)* lineage; *(fig)* stock.

troncudo,-a *adj* stocky.

trono *m* throne.

tropa *f (MIL)* army, troops; **ir para a** ~ to join the army; **fazer a** ~ do military service; **2** *(bando)* gang, troop; **3** ~ **de choque** *(polícia)* riot squad.

tropeçar *vi* to stumble; ~ **em algo** trip over sth; **2** *(fig) (errar)* to blunder; **3** ~ **em dificuldades** to come up against difficulties.

tropeço *m* obstacle, hindrance, setback; **pedra de** ~ stumbling block.

trôpego,-a *adj* shaky, unsteady, wobbly; **2** *(fig, fam)* *(pessoa desajeitada)* clumsy, awkward.

tropel *m (multidão desordenada)* mob, throng; **2** tramping of feet; **3** clatter of hooves; **4** *(fig)* confusion, hubbub; **entrar de** ~ to come bursting in.

tropelia *f* tumult, confusion, disorder.

tropical *adj* tropical.

trópico *m* tropic.

trotar *vi* to trot.

trote *m* trot; ~ **largo** canter; ~ **travado** jerky trot; **andar a** ~ trotting, *(fig)* in haste, on the go.

trouxa *f* bundle of clothes; **2** *(col)* sucker, idiot.

trouxe *(pret de trazer)* **ele** ~**-me flores** he brought/ has brought me flowers.

trova *f* ballad, folksong.

trovador *m* troubador, minstrel.

trovão *m* thunder, clap of thunder; **2 voz de** ~ thundering voice.

trovejar *vi* to thunder.

trovoada *f* thunderstorm.

truão *m* clown, buffoon.

trucidar *vt (matar com crueldade)* to slaughter, massacre; **2** to butcher *(povo, exército)*; **3** mutilate *(alguém)*; **4** *(fig)* crush *(alguém)*.

truculento,-a *adj (alguém)* truculent, fierce.

trufa *f (BOT)* truffle.

truncar *vt (separar do corpo)* to chop/cut off, to mutilate; **2** *(texto, discurso)* shorten, cut out, omit; **3** *(GEOM)* intercept.

trunfo *m* trump card, trumps; IDIOM **ter os** ~**s na mão** to have the ball at one's foot.

truque *m (ardil)* trick, gimmick, ploy, bluff; **ele usou um** ~ **para entrar** he bluffed his way in; **todos os** ~**s** every trick.

truta *f* trout.

tu *pron (familiar)* you; **tu deste-me dinheiro a mais** you gave me too much money; **tu não digas isso** don't say that; **ser tu cá tu lá** to be familiar, be on familiar terms; **você pode tratar-me por *tu*** you can address me by 'tu'.

tua *(Vd: teu).*

tuba *f (MÚS) (instrumento de sopro)* tuba, bass horn; **2** *(fig)* epic style.

tubagem *f (canalização)* pipes; **2** *(MED)* tubing, system of tubes.

tubarão *m (ZOOL)* shark; **2** *(fig) (pessoa que aufere grandes vencimentos de muitos cargos)* shark.

tubérculo *m (MED) (excrescência/tumor)* tubercle; **2** *(BOT)* tuber.

tuberculose *f* tuberculosis; TB.

tuberculoso,-a *m,f* TB sufferer; ♦ *adj (MED)* tubercular; **2** *(BOT)* tuberous.

tubo *m* tube, pipe; ~ **de escape** exhaust pipe; **2** *(QUÍM)* tube, ~ **de ensaio** test tube; **3** *(embalagem)* tube.

tucano *m* toucan.

tudo *pron* all, anything, everything; **há um pouco de** ~ there is a little of everything; ~ **quanto faço** all that I do; **é tudo?** is that all?; ~ **o que fizer** whatever you do; ♦ *adv* **acima de** ~ above all; **antes de** ~ first of all; **apesar de** ~ despite everything; **em** ~ in every way; ~ **contado** all in all; ~ **ou nada** all or nothing; **como** ~ as anything.

tufão *m* typhoon, hurricane.

tufar *vt* blow about *(saia, pano)*; ♦ *vi (inflar)* fluff up; **2** *(dilatar)* swell, puff.

tufo *m (conjunto de pelos, penas, vegetação)* tuft.

tugúrio *m* hut, shack; shelter.

tule *m (tecido)* tulle.

tulha *f* olive-bin; **2** granary.

túlio *m (QUÍM)* thulium.

tulipa *f (BOT)* tulip.

tumba *f* coffin; **2** tomb; **3** *(infeliz ao jogo)* unlucky devil; ♦ *exc (onomat)* crash! bang!

tumefação *(pl: -ões) f* swealing.

tumor *m (MED)* tumour (UK), tumor (US); ~ **cerebral** brain tumour.

tumular *adj* of tomb; **pedra** ~ tombstone.

túmulo *m* tomb, vault, sepulchre.

tumulto *m* tumult, uproar.

tumultuar *vt* to rouse, incite.

tumultuoso,-a *adj* tumultuous; stormy.

tuna *f* university's or regional musical group.

tunda *f* thrashing, beating; **2** *(fig) (descompostura)* dressing-down.

túnel *m* tunnel.

tungsténio *(QUÍM) (volfrâmio)* tungsten.

túnica *f* tunic.

Tunísia *npr* Tunisia; **a** ~ Tunisia.

tunisino,-a *adj* Tunisian.

turba *f* crowd, throng.

turbante *m* turban.

turbar *vt* to darken, cloud; **2** upset, disturb; ♦ ~**-se** *vr* to be troubled/upset; **os olhos turbaram-se** the eyes clouded over.

turbilhão *m* whirlwind; whirlpool.

turbina *f* turbine.

turbo *m (MEC)* turbo.

turbulência *f* turbulence.

turbulento,-a *adj* turbulent, stormy.

turco,-a *m,f (pessoa)* Turk; **2** *(língua)* Turkish ♦ *adj* Turkish; **pano** ~ *m (tecido felpudo)* towelling *(cloth)*.

turfa *f* turf.

túrgido,-a *adj* swollen, bloated.

turismo *m* tourism; tourist industry.

turista *m,f* tourist.

turístico,-a *adj* tourist.

turma *f (escola)* class; **2** *(de amigos)* group, gang; **3** *(de trabalhadores)* shift.

turné *f* tour.

turno *m* shift, shift work; period of work; **por** ~s alternately, by turns, in turn.

turquês *f* pincers *pl,* pliers.

turquesa *f (pedra, cor)* turquoise.

Turquia *npr* Turkey; **a** ~ Turkey.

turra *f* argument; **2** head butt; **andar às** ~s to be at loggerheads; **3 turra!** *(com crianças)* knocking foreheads.

tuturdona *m,f* bisavô, bisavó; ~s *mpl* great-grand parents, ancestors.

turvar *vt (vista)* to cloud; **2** *(céu)* to darken; ♦ *vr* ~-se *(vista, vinho)* to become cloudy; **3** *(pessoa)* to be concerned, disturbed.

turvo,-a *adj* clouded, muddy.

tuta e meia *f (col)* a bit, trifle; bargain; **comprar algo por** ~ to buy sth for a song, very cheaply.

tutano *m (ANAT)* marrow.

tutela *f (JUR)* protection; guardianship; **estar sob a** ~ **de (alguém)** to be under somebody's guardianship; **estar sob a** ~ **judicial** *(criança)* to be a ward of the court.

tutelar *adj* protecting, guardian; **anjo** ~ guardian angel; **2** *(JUR)* tutelary; ♦ *vt* to watch over, protect.

tuto *f* ballerina's skirt; **2** *(BR)* Brazilian dish; **3** *(BR) (fam)* dinheiro, cash.

tutor,-ora *m,f (JUR)* guardian; **2** *(EDUC)* tutor.

TV *(abr de televisão)* television.

TVI *(abr de* **Televisão Independente***)* = ITV.

tweed *m (tecido de lã grossa, feito na Escócia)* tweed.

txapo-txapo *adv (MOÇ) (depressa)* quick, hurry up.

u

U, u *m (letra)* U, u.
úbere *m* udder; ♦ *adj* fertile.
ubérrimo,-a *adj (superl)* very fertile.
ubiquidade *f* ubiquity.
ubíquo,-a *adj* ubiquitous.
Ucrânia *npr* a ~ Ukraine.
ucraniano,-a *(LÍNG)* Ukrainian; ♦ *adj* Ukrainian.
UE *(abr de* **União Europeia)** *npr* European Union, EU.
UEFA *(abr de* **União Europeia de Futebol)** Union of European Football Associations.
ufa *exc (exprimindo alívio, cansaço)* phew!
ufanar *vt* to make (sb) proud, to flatter; ♦ ~-**se** *vr* to boast; ~ **de** to pride o.s. (on).
ufanismo *m* vainglory; **2** national pride.
ufano,-a *adj* proud; vain; **estar** ~ to be puffed up.
Uganda *npr* a ~ Uganda; **ugandês,-esa** *mf, adj* Ugandan.
ui *exc (dor)* ouch! **2** *(surpresa)* oh! hey!; **3** *(desagrado)* pooh!
uísque *m* whisky, *(US)* whiskey.
uivada *f* howl.
uivante *adj inv* howling.
uivar *vi (cão, lobo, vento)* to howl; **2** *(fig) (vociferar)* to bawl.
uivo *m* howl.
úlcera *f* ulcer; **2** ~ **de estômago** gastric ulcer; **3** *(ferida aberta)* sore.
ulcerar *vi* to ulcerate; **2** *(afligir)* lacerate.
ulceroso,-a *adj* ulcerous.
uliginoso,-a *adj (pantanoso)* swampy; humid.
ulmeiro *(=olmeiro)* *m (BOT)* elm tree.
ulterior *adj inv (posterior)* subsequent; further; future; following; later.
ulteriormente *adv* later on, subsequently.

> Not in the sense of 'hidden motive/idea' which is **oculto**, **interesseiro**, **preconcebido**.

última *f (col) (novidade)* news, latest *(Vd: último)*; **já ouviste a** ~ have you heard the latest (news) yet?; **dizer as** ~**s a alguém** to insult sb; **estar nas** ~**s** *(moribundo)* to be on one's last legs; **2** *(pobreza)* to be down and out; ♦ *adv* **à** ~ **hora** at the last minute; **em** ~ **análise** finally, as a last resort.
ultimação *f* conclusion, finishing.
ultimamente *adv* recently, lately; **ele não tem trabalhado** ~ he hasn't worked lately.
ultimar *vt* to finish, complete; **2** *(fechar)* bring to a close/an end/a conclusion; ♦ *vi* to come to an end.
ultimato *m* ultimatum.

último,-a *adj (sequência)* last; **2** *(recente)* latest; **o** ~ **escândalo** the latest scandal; **3** *(finalizado)* final; **esta é a minha** ~ **oferta** this is my final offer; **os** ~ **remates** the final touches; **4** *(segundo pessoa mencionada)* latter; **5** *(piso)* top; **o** ~ **andar** top floor; **6** *(fig)* extreme; ♦ *adv* **em** ~ **caso** as a last resort; **por** ~ finally; of late.
ultra *m,f (pessoa muito conservadora)* stick-in-the mud; **2** ~ *prefix* ultra-.
ultrajado,-a *adj* affronted, offended.
ultrajante *adj inv (atitude)* insulting, outrageous.
ultrajar *vt* to insult, offend, outrage.
ultraje *m* insult, outrage.
ultraleve *m (AER)* microlight; ♦ *adj* ultralight.
ultramar *m* o ~ overseas.
ultramarino,-a *adj* overseas; ultramarine.
ultramoderno,-a *adj (algém)* ultramodern; **2** *(modelo, linhas)* state-of-the-art.
ultrapassado,-a *adj (prazo, data)* out-of-date; **2** *(desatualizado)* old-fashioned; **3** *(que ficou para trás)* overtaken.
ultrapassagem *f (UK)* overtaking; *(US)* passing.
ultrapassar *vt (transpor)* to cross, go beyond; **2** exceed; **o negócio ultrapassou as minhas expectativas** the deal exceeded my expectations; **3** *(superar)* to surpass; **4** overcome; ~ **as dificuldades** overcome the difficulties; **5** *(AUTO)* to overtake.
ultra-rápido,-a *adj (serviço, acção)* ultra-fast.
ultrassom *m* ultrasound.
ultrassónico,-a *adj* ultrasonic; *(MED)* ultrasound.
ultrassonografia *f* ultrasound scanning.
ultravioleta *m (FÍS)* ultraviolet; ♦ *adj (raios, radiação)* ultraviolet.
ululante *adj inv* howling; *(BR)* screaming *(fig)* *(facto, verdade)* obvious, glaring, blatant.
ulular *vi* to howl, wail.
um *m* **uma** *f art indef* a, an; **um ovo** an egg; **uma moça** a girl; *(indeterminado)* someone; **vi uma pessoa** I saw someone; **uns** *mpl*, **umas** *fpl* some; **uns homens** men; **umas mulheres** (some) women; **2** *(algum, alguns)* **escolhi uns sapatos que me agradaram** I chose (some) shoes that I liked; **3** *(certo)* a, some; **conheci um Senhor Lopes** I met a Mr. Lopes; ♦ *adj (aprox)* **havia uns quatro** there were about four; **2** *(data indefinida)* **um dia hei-de voltar** I shall return one day; **o artigo fala-nos de um Obama muito diferente** the article gives us a very different picture of Obama; **3** *(este, aquela)* a; **tem aqui um bolo** here it is a cake; ♦ *num* one; **um e** ~ **são dois** one plus one are two; **2** *(quantidade)* **um kilo** one kilo; **uma tonelada** a ton/tonne; **3** *(enfâse)* **está um calor!** it is so hot!; *(mau dia)* **hoje é** ~ **daqueles dias** today is one of those days; ♦ *pron indef* one; **dê-me mais um** give me another (one more); **um deles** one of them; ♦ *adv* ~ **e outro** both; ~ **a um, por** ~ one by one; ~ **ao outro** one another; **uns aos outros** each other; **um deles** one of them; **todos à uma** they all; **todos à uma concordaram** they all agreed; **ele sentou-se sem mais uma palavra** he sat down

without a word; ♦ *exc* **uma figa**!; *(fam)* **uma gaita**!; damn!; **isto é uma pouca-vergonha!** this is a disgrace!

umbamba *(BOT)* bramble palm.

umbanda *f* Afro-Brazilian cult.

umbigo *m (ANAT)* navel, belly button; IDIOM **olhar para o ~** *(fig) (absorto em si mesmo)* navel-gazing.

umbilical *adj inv (ANAT)* umbilical.

umbral *m (de porta)* doorway; **2** *(limiar)* threshold; **3** *(CONSTR)* door jamb/post.

umbroso,-a *adj (que dá sombra, à sombra)* shady.

umedecer *vt (BR)* to dampen; ♦ *vr* **~-se** to mist over; become moist; *(EP:* **humedecer**).

umedecido,-a *adj (BR)* moist; damp; *(EP:* **humedecido**).

umidade *f (de clima)* humidity; **2** *(na casa)* damp; *(EP:* **humidade**).

úmido,-a *adj (BR)* damp; *(EP:* **húmido**).

unânime *adj inv* unanimous.

unanimidade *f* unanimity.

unção *f (REL)* unction; anointing; **2** *(suavidade no falar)* excessive or affected suavity.

undécimo,-a *m adj* eleventh.

ungir *vt* to rub with ointment; **2** *(REL)* to anoint.

unguento *m* ointment.

unha *f* nail; **~ encravada** ingrowing nail; **roer as ~s** to bite one's nails; **2** *(de animais) (garra)* claw; **~s do gato/do caranguejo** cat's/crab's claws; *(ave de rapina)* talon; **3** *(do pé)* toe-nail; *(sheep's, horses)* hooves; **4 ~s da âncora** *(NÁUT)* flukes; **5** *(poder, domínio)* mão; **cair nas ~s de alguém** to fall into sb's hands; ♦ *exc* **à unha!** *(na tourada ou a comer)* with bare hands!; IDIOM **lutar com unhas e dentes** to fight tooth and nail; **escapar por uma ~ negra** to escape by the skin of one's teeth/a hair's breadth; **ser ~ e carne com** to be hand in glove with (sb); **ferrar a ~** to exploit, sell very dear.

unhada *f* (nail) scratch.

unhas-de-fome, unhas de fome *m,f* skinflint; ♦ *adj inv sg, pl* stingy, miserly.

unheiro *m* sore nail, hangnail.

união *f* union, uniting, joining; **2** unity; **3** marriage; **4** *(TEC) (junção)* joint, bond, *(canos)* coupling; **5** *(CONSTR)~* **de fita** tape joint; **6** *(ligação)* connexion, link; **7 traço de ~** hyphen; IDIOM **a ~ faz a força** united we stand, divided we fall.

unicamente *adv* only, solely, exclusively.

único,-a *adj* only; **o ~ sobrevivente** the only survivor; **2** unique; **ele é uma pessoa ~a** he is unique; single; one and only, exceptional; **mão única** *(BR) (AUTO: tráfego)* one-way.

unicórnio *m (MITOL)* unicorn.

unidade *f (medidas) (ECON, FIN, MIL)* unit; **~ fabril** factory, unit; **~ hoteleira** hotel facility; **2** *(COMP)* **~ de visualização** screen; **~ de disco** disc drive; **3** *(união)* unity.

unidimensional *adj inv* one-dimensional.

unido,-a *adj* joined, linked; **2** *(fig) (pessoas)* united; **manter-se unidos** to stick together.

unificar *vt* to unite; **2** unify, bring together; ♦ **~-se** *vr* to merge; **as companhias unificaram-se** the companies merged.

uniforme *m* uniform; ♦ *adj inv* uniform; **2** alike, similar; **3** even.

uniformidade *f* uniformity.

uniformizado,-a *adj* uniformed.

uniformizar *vt* to standardize; **2** to put on uniform; ♦ **~-se** *vr* to put on one's uniform; **2** to become standardized.

unilateral *adj* unilateral.

unionista *m,f* unionist; ♦ *adj* unionistic.

unir *vt* to join together; **2** to unite; **3** to mix; to tie together; **4** combine; **~ o útil ao agradável** to mix business with pleasure; ♦ **~-se** *vr* to join together; **2** to be united; **3** *(conciliar-se)* to be reconciled; **4** to join in matrimony.

unissexo *adj inv* unisex.

uníssono *m*: **em ~** in unison.

unitário *adj* unitary; **preço ~** price per unit.

universal *adj inv* universal; general; worldwide.

universalidade *f* universality.

universidade *f* university.

universitário,-a *m,f (docente)* lecturer; *(estudante)* university student; ♦ *adj* university.

universo *m* universe.

uno,-a *adj (indivisível)* one; single.

uns *(pl de* **um***)*.

untar *vt* to rub; to grease, oil; **2** *(MED)* to rub with ointment.

unto *m (gordura de porco)* fat, lard.

untuoso,-a *adj (oleoso)* greasy, oily; **2** *(fig) (voz)* unctuous.

untura *f (REL)* anointing; ointment.

upa! *ex (subindo, levantando)* up; **vamos, ~!** up we go!; **2** *(alguém caindo)* oops!; **3** *(levantar criança)* upsy-daisy.

Urais *npr* **os ~** *mpl* the Urals.

urânio *m* uranium.

Urano *m (ASTRON)* Uranus.

urbanidade *f* urbanity; **2** *(cortesia)* civility, courtesy, politeness.

urbanismo *m* town planning.

urbanização *f* urbanization.

urbanizado,-a *(zona, área)* urbanized, built up.

urbanizar *vt* to urbanize.

urbano,-a *adj* urban; *(comportamento)* polite.

urbe *f* city, town.

urdidura *f (tecelagem, conjunto de fios)* warping; **2** *(fig) (intriga)* intrigue, plot, machination.

urdir *vt (dispor em tela)* to warp; **2** *(tecer)* to weave; **3** *(fig) (maquinar)* to plot, to hatch *(intrigas)*.

Urdu *m (língua oficial do Paquistão)* Urdu.

urgência *f* urgency; speed, haste; **com toda ~** as quickly as possible.

urgente *adj* urgent; **entrega ~** special delivery.

urgir *vt* **~ alguém (para, a)** to urge sb to do sth; ♦ *vi* to be pressing; to necessitate; **o tempo urge** time presses on.

úrico,-a *adj (ácido)* uric.

urina *f* urine.

urinar *vi* to urinate, pass water; **2 ~ sangue** to pass blood; **3 ~ na cama** to wet the bed; ♦ **~-se** *vr* wet o.s..

urinário,-a *adj* urinary.

urinol (*pl*: **-óis**) *m (sanitárias públicas)* public lavatory, urinal; **2** *(recipiente para doentes na cama)* bedpan; **3** *(BR)* chamber pot, *(para crianças)* potty.

urna *f* urn; **2** *(caixão)* coffin *(UK)*, casket *(US)*; **2 ~ eleitoral** ballot box; **3 ~ electrónica** computerized vote; **ir às ~s** to go to the polls.

urologia *f (MED)* urology.

urológico,-a *adj (exame, etc)* urologic(al).

urologista *m,f* urologist; **2** *adj inv* urologic.

urrar *vt/vi (bramir)* scream, roar, bawl, bellow; **2** *(de dor)* scream, groan; **3** *(animal)* roar.

urro *m (of person)* yell, roar; **2** *(animal)* roar.

Ursa Maior *npr (ASTRON)* Great Bear; Ursa Major.

Ursa Menor *npr (ASTRON)* Little Bear; Ursa Minor.

ursinho *m (para criança)* teddy-bear.

ursino,-a *adj* relating to bear.

urso,-a *m* bear; **~ branco,-a** *m,f* polar bear; IDIOM **fazer figura de ~** to cut a poor figure.

urso-formigueiro, ursa-formigueira *n (ZOOL)* anteater.

urso-pardo, ursa-parda *f* grisly bear.

urticária *f (MED)* nettle rash, urticaria.

urtiga *f* nettle.

urubu *m (BR)* black vulture.

Uruguai *npr* **o ~** *m* Uruguay.

uruguaio,-a *adj* Uruguayan.

urze *m* heather.

usado,-a *m,f (algo)* used item; **loja de usados** second-hand shop; ♦ *adj (utilizado/em uso)* used; **2** *(gasto, fora de moda)* worn, worn out; **3 ~ a** accustomed to, used to.

usar *vt (utilizar)* to use; **pode ~ o meu martelo** you may use my hammer; **2** *(roupa, cabelo, penteado)* to wear; **ela usa o cabelo ao alto** she wears her hair pulled up; **3** *(ter o hábito de fazer algo)* be in the habit of doing sth; **eu uso passar as férias no Porto** I usually spend my holidays in Oporto; **4** *(pej) (aproveitar-se de)* use; exploit *(pessoa, bondade, inocência)*; **ela aproveitou-se dele para arranjar emprego** she used him to get a job; ♦ **~-se** *vr (gastar)* wear out, get worn; **2** *(servir-se de)* make use of; make the best of; **3** *(impessoal)* **agora usa-se a saia comprida** the long skirt is now in fashion; **hoje em dia usam-se muitos estrangeirismos** nowadays one uses many foreign words.

usável *adj* wearable.

usbequistanês,-esa *m,f* Uzbek.

Usbequistão *npr* Uzbekistan.

username *m (COMP) (nome de uso pessoal)* username.

usina *f (BR) (lugar fabril)* factory, plant, works; **~ de aço** steelworks; **2** *(AGR)* **~ de açúcar** sugar mill; **~ elétrica/hidrelétrica** power plant.

usineiro,-a *m,f* sugar mill owner; ♦ *adj (BR)* plant, factory.

uso *m* use; **objectos de ~ pessoal** personal belongings; **2** practice, exercise; **o ~ é enviar uma resposta** it is usual to send a reply; **3** fashion; **em ~** in fashion; **fora de ~** out of fashion; **4** *(tradição)* usage, custom; **segundo o ~** according to custom; **fazer ~ de** make use of; IDIOM **o ~ faz o mestre,** practice makes perfect.

usocapião *m (JUR) (arc)* udal *(dated in UK)*.

usofrutuário,-a *m,f adj* beneficiary, usofructuary.

usual *adj* usual; common.

usualmente *adv* usually, normally.

usuário *m,f (BR)* user; ♦ *adj* useful.

usufruir *vt* to enjoy the benefits of; **2 ~ de** *(desfrutar) (da beleza, do saber, da companhia/amizade de alguém)* enjoy.

usufruto *m* usufruct, enjoyment; **2** *(JUR)* usufruct.

usura *f (juro exagerado)* usury; **2** *(pop) (avareza)* avarice, greed.

usurário,-a *m (agiota)* usurer; **2** *(pej) (pessoa)* avaricious, miserly; **3** *(acção)* usurious.

usurpador,-ora *m,f* usurper; ♦ *adj* usurping.

usurpar *vt* to usurp; arrogate; appropriate unlawfully; ♦ *vi* to encroach upon.

úteis (*pl de*: **útil**).

utensílio *m* utensil, instrument, tool, implement; **~s** *pl* kitchen gear, kitchenware.

utente *m,f adj inv (de lugares ou serviços públicos)* user.

uterino,-a *adj* uterine.

útero *m (ANAT)* womb, uterus; **o colo do ~** the neck of the womb.

uteroscopia *f (MED) (exame ao útero)* uteroscopy.

útil (*pl*: **úteis**) *adj* useful; **2** helpful; **3 dias úteis** weekdays, working days;

utilidade *f* utility, usefulness; **2** advantage.

utilitário,-a *adj (ideal)* utilitarian; **2** *(viatura)* utility; **3** *(BR) m* utility vehicle.

utilizador,-ora *m,f* user.

utilizar *vt* to use, utilize; ♦ **-se** *vr*: **~ de** to make use of, utilize.

utilizável *adj inv* usable; practicable.

Utopia *npr* Utopia; **2** *(fig)* dream.

utópico,-a *adj* Utopian; **2** utopian.

utopista *m,f (pessoa)* utopian; **2** *(pej)* dreamer.

uva *f* grape; **um bago de ~** a grape; **cacho de ~s** bunch of grapes; **semente de ~** grape pip; **2** *(uva seca)* **~-passa** raisin; **ao preço da ~ mijona** *(col)* very cheap, dirt cheap.

úvula *f (ANAT)* uvula.

uxuricida, uxoricídio uxuricide.

V

V, v *m (letra)* V, v.

vá *etc. (pres subj de* ir*)* **espero que você** ~ I hope you go; *(command form)* ~ **ali** go there.

vã *f (Vd:* **vão***).*

vaca *f (ZOOL)* cow; **carne de** ~ beef; **mugir as** ~**s to** milk the cows; **2** *(pej) (moral duvidoso)* strumpet; *(ingrata, má)* bitch; IDIOM **no tempo das** ~**s gordas/das** ~**s magras** in the good (old) days/in lean times.

vaca-fria, voltar à ~ to harp on the same string, to be on one's hobby-horse.

vacância, vacatura *f* vacancy; **2** *(JUR)* avoidance.

vacante *adj inv* vacant.

vacaria *f* cowshed.

vacilação *f* hesitation; **2** *(balanço)* swaying.

vacilante *adj inv* hesitant; **2** *(oscilação)* vacillating, swaying; **3** *(pouco seguro)* unsteady, wobbly; **4** *(luz, chama)* flickering.

vacilar *vi* to hesitate; **2** vacillate, sway; **3** *(cambalear)* to totter.

vacina *f (MED)* vaccine.

vacinar *vt* to vaccinate; ♦ ~**-se (contra)** to be vaccinated (against).

vacuidade *f* emptiness, hollowness.

vacum *adj (relativo a gado)* bovine.

vácuo *m (FÍS)* vacuum; **2** *(espaço vazio)* gap; void; space; **3** *(fig) (sentimento)* void, hollow, emptiness.

vadeação *f (acto de superar obstáculos)* wading (through).

vadear *vt* to wade through.

vadiagem *f* vagrancy.

vadiar *vi (vaguear)* to wander, roam, to idle about; **2** *(vida de ocioso)* lounge around.

vadio,-a *m (ocioso)* vagabond, vagrant, tramp; ♦ *adj* lazy, idle; **2** *(conversa)* wandering.

vaga *f (do mar)* wave; **maré** ~ low tide; **horas** ~**s** spare time; **2** *(haver vaga)* vacancy, availability.

vagabundagem *f* vagrancy; **2** *(vadiagem)* roaming, loafing.

vagabundar *vi* to wander, roam about.

vagabundo,-a *m,f* tramp, rover, bum; **2** *(quem passeia)* wanderer; ♦ *adj* idle, vagrant; wandering.

vagalhão *m (mar)* breaker, roller.

vaga-lume *m* firefly.

vagão *m* carriage; wagon; ~ **de carga** freight-car; ~**-cama** *(pl:* **vagões-cama***) m* sleeping car; ~**-cisterna** tank-car.

vagar *m* leisure, spare time; **não ter** ~ **para** to have no (free) time to; **fazer algo com** ~ to do sth at leisure; ♦ *vi* to wander about, ramble; **2** *(lugar)* to be vacant; **3** to drift about.

vagaroso,-a *adj* slow, sluggish; **2** *(pessoa)* easy-going.

vagem *f* green bean; **2** *(fava, ervilha, etc)* pod.

vagido *m* wail, whimper.

vagina *f (ANAT)* vagina.

vago,-a *adj (indefinido)* vague; **2** *(lugar)* vacant, free, empty; **3** *(indistinto)* faint; **um** ~ **cheiro** a faint smell; **4** *(pessoa)* vague, confused.

vaguear *vi* to wander, roam; **2** to ramble; ~ **pelas ruas** to wander through the streets.

vai *(pres indic and imp de:* ir*)* ~ **ali** *(imp)* go there; **quando** ~ **você?** when are you going?

vaia *f* booing.

vaiar *vt/vi (apupar)* to boo, hiss.

vaidade *f* vanity; **2** futility.

vaidoso,-a *adj* vain, conceited.

vai-não-vai, vai não vai *adv (quase)* almost, on the point of, about to; **estive** ~ **para ir** I very nearly went.

vaivém *m (de pessoas)* coming and going, to-and-fro; **2** *(AER)* shuttle; ~ **espacial** *(nave)* space shuttle; **3** *(porta, pêndulo)* swing; **vaivéns** *mpl* **os** ~ comings and goings; **os** ~**s da vida** *(fig)* life's ups and downs.

vala *f* ditch, trench; **2** *(sepultura)* ~ **comum** common grave.

valada *f* long ditch.

valado *m (elevação que rodeia terra)* stockade, hedge; **2** *(vala)* ditch.

valado,-a *adj (quinta cercada)* fenced in.

valdevinhos *mpl* rogue, rascal; *(fam)* rotter.

vale *m (GEOG)* valley, vale; **2** voucher **3** *(de correio)* ~ **postal** postal order; **4 correr montes e** ~**s** over hill and dale.

valência *f* validity; **2** *(QUÍM, BIOL)* valence.

valentão,-tona *m,f* bully; *(col)* show-off.

valente *adj* brave, courageous, intrepid, bold; **2** *(alguém forte)* tough, strong.

valentia *f* courage, bravery, boldness; **2** *(façanha)* valour, prowess, feat.

valer *vt,vi (ger)* to be worth; **isto vale uma fortuna** this is worth a fortune; **vale a pena** to be worthwhile; **2** *(digno de crédito)* **a palavra dele vale tudo** his word is worth everything; **3** *(ser equivalente a)* be worth; **uma libra quantos ecus vale?** how many ecus is worth one pound?; **4** *(ser válido)* to be valid; *(em jogos)* to be fair; **assim não vale** that is not fair; **5** *(vigorar)* be in force; **este visto já não vale** this visa is no loger valid; **6** *(significar)* to mean, signify; **vale dizer** in other words; it is worth saying; **7** *(ser útil)* be useful/of help **quando eu precisei de dinheiro foi ela que me valeu** she came to my help when I needed money; ♦ ~**-se** *vr* ~ **de** to use, make use of; **eu vali-me do martelo** I used the hammer; ♦ *exc* **valha-me Deus!** may God help me!; ♦ **tanto vale** it's all the same, it makes no difference; **não vale a pena** it isn't worth it; ~ **por** *(equivaler a)* be worth to; **ela é velha, mas vale por duas jovens** she is old, but she is worth two young women; **valer a** ~ *(BR:* **para** ~*)* very much, for real, really;

ela canta a ~ she sings very well/ she really sings well; **eu gosto dele a ~** I really like him; IDIOM **não ~ um caracol** it's not worth a nickel/a penny/a bean; **mais vale um pássaro na mão do que dois a voar** a bird in hand is worth two in the bush.

'Valer' is a regular verb except for the first person sg of pres. indicative and the pres. subjunctive – all persons – as seen above.

valeta *f* gutter, drain; 2 channel; ~ **empedrada** paved gutter.

valete *m* jack (at cards), knave.

valha (*pres subj de* **valer**) **espero que ele ~ a nossa confiança** I hope he is worth/he merits our trust.

valho (*1ª pessoa pres indicativo, de* **valer**) **eu não ~ nada** I am not worth anything, I am nobody.

valia *f* value; 2 worth; 3 merit; **de ~** valuable; **de pouca ~** of little value/worth.

validade *f* validity; **prazo de ~** expiry date.

validar *vt* to validate.

validez *f* validity.

válido,-a *adj* valid.

valioso,-a *adj* valuable.

valor *m* value, worth; 2 courage; 3 price; 4 importance; **dar ~ a** to value; **sem ~** worthless; **no ~ de** to the value of; **obje(c)tos de ~** valuables.

valores *mpl* (*dum exame*) marks; 2 (*princípios*) values; 3 (*COM*) securities; ~ **imóveis** *npl* real estate; ~ **móreis** chattels.

valorização *f* increased value, rise in value.

valorizar *vt* (*pessoa, trabalho*) to value, appreciate; 2 (*moeda*) to raise the value of; ♦ ~**-se** *vr* to go up in value; 2 value oneself.

valoroso,-a *adj* brave, courageous, valiant; 2 (*importante*) valuable; **obra ~a** valuable work.

valsa *f* (*MÚS*) waltz.

valsar *vi* to waltz.

válvula *f* valve; ~ **de escape** escape, exhaust valve; (*fig*) (*tensão*) escape valve; 2 ~ **de segurança** safety valve.

vampe *f* vamp.

vampiro *m* vampire.

vandalismo *m* vandalism.

vândalo,-a *m* Vandal; 2 (*fig*) vandal, hooligan; ♦ *adj* destructive.

vangloriar-se *vr* to boast (**de** of about).

vanguarda *f* (*MIL*) vanguard; 2 (*DESP*) forefront, front, advanced line, forward; 3 (*frente*) front line; 4 (*arte*) avant-garde.

vantagem *f* advantage; **tirar ~** to make use, to take advantage of; 2 (*lucro*) profit, benefit; 3 (*fig*) privilege, perk.

vantajoso,-a *adj* advantageous; 2 profitable; 3 beneficial.

vão, vã *m* void; opening; (*vazio*) empty space; **no ~ da janela** in the window recess/alcove; ~ **das escadas** space under the stairs; ♦ *adj* futile, useless; ♦ *adv* **em ~** in vain.

vapor *m* steam, vapour; **peixe cozido no ~** steamed fish; 2 (*barco*) steamer; **panela a ~** steamer;

barco a ~ steamboat; ♦ **a todo o ~** *adv* full steam ahead.

vaporização *f* evaporation; 2 (*FÍS*) vaporation.

vaporizador *m* atomizer, sprayer; ♦ *adj* spraying, atomizing.

vaporoso,-a *adj* steamy, misty; 2 exhaling vapours; 3 (*vestido*) light, transparent; 4 (*figura*) diaphanous, dainty.

vaqueiro,-a *m,f* cowboy, cow-girl, cowhand.

vara *f* stick; 2 rod, cane, staff; 3 (*de porcos*) herd (of swine); 4 (*JUR*) jurisdiction; 5 (*DESP*) **salto à ~** pole vault; **à ~ larga** *adv* freely, footloose and fancy-free; **tecido de ~** rough woollen material; IDIOM **tremer como ~s verdes** to shake like a leaf; **meter-se em camisa de onze ~s** (*situação difícil*) to be in a tight spot.

varado *m adj* (*NÁUT*) stranded, run aground; 2 ~ **de** (*trespassado*) riddled (*com*), pierced; 3 (*fig*) (*atónito*) stunned; 4 spanked with a rod; 5 one of the ecclesiastic divisions in India.

varal *m* shaft (of a cart/carriage); 2 pole; 3 ~ **do arado** plough beam; 4 (*BR*) (*estendal*) clothes line.

varanda *f* verandah; balcony.

varandim *m* (*pequena varanda*) balcony.

varão *m* man, male; 2 (*de ferro*) rod, rail; **o ~ para as cortinas** curtain rod, rail; ♦ *adj* **filho ~** (*descendente, herdeiro*) male.

varapau *m* stick, staff, pole; 2 (*BR*) (*pessoa alta e magra*) beanpole.

varar *vt* to pierce, shoot through; 2 (*atravessar rio*) to cross; ♦ *vi* (*NÁUT*) to beach, run aground.

vareja *f* (*ZOOL*) (*mosca*) bluebottle, blowfly; 2 the knocking-down of fruit from trees.

varejar *vt* (*sacudir com vara*) to beat-shake with a stick (*ávores*); knock down (*fruta.*)

varejista (*BR*) *m,f* retailer.

varejo *m* (*BR and Port. regions*) (*COM*) retail trade.

vareta *f* (*pequena vara*) ramrod, rod; ~ **do guarda-chuva** umbrella's rib/stretcher; 2 (*haste de compasso*) leg.

variação *f* variation, alteration, change.

variado,-a *adj* varied, assorted.

variante *n* (*LING*) variant.

variar *vt/vi* to vary; 2 to change; 3 to diversify; **é só para ~** it's only for a change.

variável *adj* variable, changeable.

varicela *f* chicken pox.

varicose *f* (*MED*) varicose; 2 (*tumor causado por estas veias*) varicocele.

variedade *f* variety, diversity; ~**s** *fpl* variety show *sg*.

variegado,-a *adj* (*BOT*) (*folhas*) motley, variegated; **planta ~** variegated plant; 2 multicoloured; 3 (*gente*) mixed.

varim *m* long narrow boat.

varina *f* fishwife.

Lisbon's traditional 'varina' has now disappeared from the streets, but she was one of the most colourful sights in this city until the 1960s. She is now legally established in municipal markets.

varinha *f* wand; ~ **de condão** magic wand; **2** pointer.

vário,-a *adj* varied, diverse; ~**s** *pl* various, several; **por** ~**as razões** for several reasons; **2** *(COM)* sundry; **3** *(cor)* varied, colourful; ♦ *pron indef (alguns)* some, a few, several; **há** ~ **s dias** several days ago.

varíola *f* smallpox.

variz *f (MED)* varix; **varizes** *(MED) fpl* varices, varicose veins.

varonil *adj* manly, virile, masculine.

varrão *m (ZOOL)* boar, pig not castrated.

varredela, varridela *f* a quick light sweep.

varredor,-ora *m,f* road sweeper; ~ **de rua** road sweeper.

varrer *vt* to sweep; to sweep out/up; **máquina de** ~ carpet sweeper.

varrido,-a *adj* swept; *(fig)* raving; **doido varrido/ doida varrida** completely mad.

Varsóvia *npr* Warsaw.

várzea *f* meadow, field, lea; **2** *(arrozal)* rice-paddy.

vasa *f* slime, mire; **2** *(fig)* riff-raff, rabble, mob.

vasculhar *vt* to sweep and dust; **2** *(revistar)* rummage through, search; **3** *(fig) (pesquisar)* to search, examine.

vasculho *m (vassoura de cabo comprido)* broom; **2** *(lixo)* rubbish, garbage.

vasectomia *f* vasectomy.

vaselina *f* vaseline, petroleum jelly.

vasilha *f* vessel, container.

vaso *m (decorativo)* pot, vase; *(para plantas)* flowerpot; **2** *(REL)* chalice; **3** ~ **capilar** capillary (vein); **4** *(NÁUT)* vessel; ~ **de guerra** warship; **5** ~ **sanitário** *(sanita)* lavatory pan; **6** *(MED)* ~ **sanguíneo** blood vessel.

vasoconstrição *f (MED)* vascular constriction.

vassalagem *f* servitude; submission.

vassalo,-a *m,f* vassal, subject of; ♦ *adj* servile, submissive.

vassoura *f (longa)* broom; *(curta)* brush; **a pá e a** ~ brush and pan.

vastidão *f* vastness, immensity.

vasto,-a *adj* vast, huge.

Vaticano *npr* **o** ~ Vatican.

vaticinar *vt/vi* to foretell, predict.

vaticínio *m* prophecy, prediction.

vau *m* ford; **atravessar o rio a** ~ to cross a river on foot; to ford a river; **2** ~**s** *(NÁUT)* beams.

vaza *f (no jogo)* trick.

vazadoiro, vazadouro *m (despejo)* dump, dumping ground, tip.

vazamento *m (derrame)* leak, spill, leakage *(de água, gás)*; ~ **de petróleo** oil spill, slick; **2** *(descarga)* discharge *(da barragem)*; **3** *(acto de vazar)* emptying; **o** ~ **do lixo para o depósito** the emptying of the rubbish to the depot.

vazante *f (maré)* ebb tide.

vazão *f* flow; **2** *(consumo)* outlet, drainage; **dar** ~ **a** to give vent to; **3** *(COM)* **dar** ~ to clear.

vazar *vt (despejar)* to empty; to pour out; ♦ *vi* to run out; to leak; **2** *(desaguar)* to flow into; **3** *(maré)* to go out; **4** *(trespassar)* **a bala vazou-lhe o olho** the

bullet gouged out his eye; **5** *(fig) (information)* to leak out.

vazia *f (pop)(quadril)* haunch; **2** *(carne desta area)* rump; **bife da** ~ rumpsteak.

vazio *m* vacuum, emptiness, void; ♦ **vazio,-a** *adj* empty; **2** *(fig)* **cabeça** ~ empty-headed, frivolous.

veado *m (ZOOL) (macho)* deer, buck, stag; *(fêmea do veado)* hind *(também:* **corça***)*; **2 carne de** ~ venison; **3** *(pop) (marido traído)* cuckold; **4** *(BR) (pej) (pederasta passivo)* poof, pansy.

vedação *f* barrier, fence, enclosure.

vedado,-a *adj* forbidden; enclosed.

vedar *vt* to ban, prohibit; **2** to stop the flow of; to stop up.

vedeta *f (CIN)* star; **2** *(NÁUT)* speedboat.

vedor,-ora *m,f* inspector, fiscal; **2** *(especializado em descobrir nascente de água)* water diviner.

veemência *f* vehemence; passion; vigour.

veemente *adj* vehement; intense.

vegetação *f* vegetation.

vegetal *m* vegetable; ♦ *adj inv* vegetable, plant.

vegetar *vi (plant)* to grow; **2** *(fig)* to vegetate.

vegetariano,-a *adj,* vegetarian.

vegetativo,-a *adj (fig)* vegetative.

veia *f (ANAT, BOT)* vein; **2** *(filão de minério)* seam; **3** *(fig, fam) (jeito)* vein, streak; **ter** ~ **para** to have a flair for; IDIOM **ferve-lhe o sangue nas veias** she is hot-headed/hot-tempered.

veicular *adj inv (LÍNG)* vehicular; ♦ *vt* to send out, to convey; **2** *(divulgar)* to spread.

veículo *m* vehicle; ~ **articulado** articulated lorry; **2** *(fig) (de informação)* means sg.

veio¹ *m (GEOL)* vein, thread, seam; **2** *(de madeira)* grain, vein; **3** *(em rochas)* fissure; **4** *(MEC)* shaft, ~ **motor** crank shaft; **5** *(fig) (ponto principal)* heart *(of the matter)*; ♦ **veio** *(pret de* **vir***, 2*ª*/3*ª *pessoa, sg)* **a que horas você** ~**?** (at) what time did you come?

veio² *(pret de* **vir***, 3*ª *pessoa, sg)* **ela** ~ **falar comigo** she came to speak to me; **quando** ~ **você?** when did you come?

veja *(pres subj de* **ver***)* **é bom que eles** ~ **isso** it is good that (they should) see (to) that; **2** *(command form)* ~ **o que eu fiz** see what I have done.

vela *f (de cera)* candle; **2** *(AUTO)* sparking plug; **3** *(NÁUT)* sail; **fazer-se à/de** ~ to set sail; **4** ~ **mestra** mainsail; **5** *(velar defunto)* vigil, wake; IDIOM **ir-se à** ~ *(algo sem sucesso)* to go down the drain.

velame *m (NÁUT) (conjunto)* sails, pl.

velar *f, adj (LÍNG)* velar; ♦ *vt (cobrir)* to hide, conceal; **2** *(som, vista)* to blur, dim; **3** *(tornar sombrio)* cloud over, overshadow; **4** *(doente)* to watch over; to keep vigil for; **5** *(defunto)* to keep vigil, have a wake for; ♦ *vi* to stay up; **2** *(cuidar)* to keep watch; ♦ ~-**se** *vr (cobrir-se com véu)* to veil o.s., to cover o.s.; **2** *(olhos)* cloud over.

veleidade *f* whim, fancy, caprice; fickleness.

veleiro *m* sailing boat; ♦ *adj* sailing.

velejador,-ora *m,f (DESP) (pop)* person who mans a sailing boat.

velejar *vi* to sail, go sailing.

veleta *f* weather vane, weather cock.

velhacaria *f* dishonesty.

velhaco,-a *m,f (desonesto)* crook, knave, scoundrel; ♦ *adj (pessoa falsa)* two-faced, villainous, *(fig)* a snake in the grass; **2** crafty, shifty; **3** *(desonesto)* crooked, untrustworthy.

velha-guarda *f (fig)* old guard; old school.

velharia *f* old stuff, junk; **~s** old-fashioned objects, antiques.

velhice *f* old age.

velhinho,-a *adj* very old person.

velho,-a *m,f* old man/old woman; **os ~s** the old folk; ♦ *adj* old; **nos ~s tempos** in the old/olden days.

velhote,-a *m,f (fam)* old person; **2** *(com afeição)* old dear; ♦ *adj* old, elderly.

velocidade *f* speed, velocity; **2** *(FÍS) (da luz)* speed of light; **3** *(AUTO)* gear; **em alta ~** at high speed.

velocímetro *m* speedometer.

velocípede *m* velocipede, bicycle.

velocíssimo *(superl de* **veloz***) adj* very rapid, fast; high speed.

velocista *m,f* sprinter.

velódromo *m* cycle track.

velório *m (acto de velar um defunto)* wake.

veloz *adj* fast, swift, quick.

velozmente *adv* speedy, quickly.

veludo *m* velvet; **~ cotelê** corduroy.

venal *adj inv (que se pode vende/comprar)* saleable, purchaseable; **2** *(subornável)* corrupt, corruptible, venal; **3 valor ~** selling price.

vencedor,-ora *m,f* winner, victor; ♦ *adj* winning, victorious.

vencer *vt (ger)* to win; **2** *(superar)* to overcome, master; **3** defeat; **4** *(exceder)*, outdo sb in sth; ♦ *vi (ganhar)* to win; to win through; **2** *(prazo)* to run out, expire; **3** *(dívida, letras, juros)* to be due, to mature.

vencimento *m* triumph; **2** *(salário)* salary, income; **3** *(COM)* (termo de prazo) expiry/due date; maturity; **4 dar ~ a** (algo) to cope with (sth); **não dou ~ a tanto trabalho** I can't manage/cope with so much work; **5 folha de ~s** payroll.

venda *f* sale, selling; **à ~** on sale, for sale; **2** *(pequena loja rural)* local general store; **3** *(nos olhos)* blindfold.

vendar *vt (os olhos de alguém)* to blindfold.

vendaval *m* gale; **2** *(fig)* tumult; *(livro, filme)* **O Monte** (*BR:* **O morro**) **dos Vendavais** Wuthering Heights.

vendável *adj* marketable.

vendedor *m* seller.

vender *vt* to sell; **~ por atacado/a retalho** to sell wholesale/retail; (*BR:* **= varejo**); **2 ~ fiado,-a a prestações** to sell on credit/in instalments.

vendido,-a *(pp de* **vender***) adj* sold.

vendilhão *m* pedlar.

veneno *m* poison; **2** *(fig)* venom.

venenoso,-a *adj* poisonous; **3** *(fig)* venomous.

veneração *f* reverence.

venerar *vt* to revere; *(REL)* to worship.

venéreo,-a *adj* venereal.

veneta *f* fancy, whim; **dar na ~** to take a fancy to.

Veneza *npr* Venice.

veneziana *f (porta, janela) m* louvred *(UK)*, louvered *(US)*.

veneziano,-a *adj* Venetian.

Venezuela *npr* **a ~** Venezuela.

venezuelano,-a *adj* Venezuelan.

venha *etc (pres subj de:* **vir***)* **duvido que ele ~ a** I doubt if (that) he will come; **~ cá** come here.

vénia *(BR:* **vê-***) f* curtsy, bow; **fazer uma ~** to curtsy.

venial *adj inv (pecado)* venial; **2** *(desculpável)* forgiveable.

venta *f (pop) (narina)* nostril; *(cara)* face; **2 ~s** *fpl (pop)* nose, mug *sg;* IDIOM **estar de ~s** be in a bad mood, with a long face; **dar nas ~s** punch sb's nose.

ventania *f* gale, strong winds, windstorm.

ventar *vi (soprar)* to blow; **2** be favourable; **se a sorte ~** if a fair wind blows.

ventilação *f* ventilation.

ventilador *m* ventilator; **2** *(ELECT)* fan.

ventilar *vt* to ventilate, to air; **2** *(fig)* to discuss.

vento *m* wind; *(filme)* "**E tudo o ~ levou**" 'Gone with the Wind'.

ventoinha *f* fan; **2** *(AUTO)* fan; **3** *(grimpa)* weathercock.

ventoso,-a *adj* windy.

ventre *m (ANAT) (barriga)* belly, paunch; **2** *(útero)* womb; **3 prisão de ~** constipation.

ventríloquo,-a *m* ventriloquist.

ventura *f* luck; **2** happiness; **desejo-lhe as melhores ~s** I wish you the best of luck; **3** fate; **4** chance; **à ~** at random, haphazardly; **ir à ~** to try one's fortune/luck.

Vénus *(BR:* **-ê-***) f* Venus.

ver *m* opinion; **a meu ~** in my opinion; ♦ *vt* to see; **2** to look at; **3** watch; **vejo a TV à noite** I watch the TV in the evening; **4 não poder ~ algo/ alguém** not able to bear/stand sb sth; **ter a ~ com**, to have to do with; **este assunto tem a/que ~ com** this subject has to do with; **eu não tenho nada a ~ com isso** it's nothing to do with me, none of my business; **5 é de ~** it's worth seeing; **6** *(ter dúvidas)* **estar para ~** we shall see; ♦ **~-se** *vr* to see one another; **2** to meet one another; **vimo-nos uma vez por semana** we meet once a week; **3** look at o.s.; **ele vê-se ao espelho** he is looking at himself in the mirror; **4** find o.s. **ela viu-se em apuros** she found herself in a jam/in trouble; **5 ~-se com** to settle accounts with; ♦ *conj* **bem se vê que** it's obvious that; **já se vê** of course, it is obvious; ♦ *exc* **veja lá!** be careful!; **veja lá se não cai** mind you don't fall; **2** just imagine!; **3 eu logo vi!** I knew it!; **4 vejamos!** let us see!

veracidade *f* truthfulness, veracity.

veraneante *m,f* summer holidaymaker *(UK)*; summer vacationer *(US)*.

veranear *vi* to spend the summer.

veraneio *m* summer holidays *pl (UK)*, summer vacations *(US)*; **estância de ~** summer resort.

Verão, verão *m* summer; **estação de ~** summer season.

veraz *adj inv* truthful, true.

verba *f* funds, funding, budget; **a ~ para a Educação** Education budget/funding; **~s desviadas** funds gone astray/diverted; **2** *(JUR)* clause, article; **3** note.

verbal *adj inv* verbal, spoken, oral.

verbalizar *vt* put into words, verbalize.

verberar *vt* to whip, flagellate; **2** *(censurar)* disapprove of *(alguém);* reproach *(attitude).*

verbete *m (dicionário)* entry.

verbo *m (LÍNG)* verb; **2** *(eloquência)* eloquence; **3** *(REL)* **o V~** *m* the Word.

verborreia, verbosidade *f* verbosity.

verbose,-a *adj* wordy, verbose; prolixe.

verdade *f* truth, fact, reality; **dizer a ~** to tell the truth; **faltar à ~** to be economical with truth; **2** *(JUR)* **a ~ e só a ~** the truth, the whole truth and nothing but the truth; ♦ *adv* **em ~** in truth; **na ~** in fact, indeed; **de ~** really; **eu dancei de ~** I really danced; **~?** really?; ♦ *exc* **é ~!** **quando vens cá?** by the way, when are you coming here?; ♦ *conj* **a ~ é que** the truth is/the fact is that; IDIOM **a ~ crua e nua** the naked truth, the plain facts; **dizer umas ~s** to speak plainly; **ser a ~ personificada** to be the truth personified; **as ~s amargas** the bitter truth.

verdadeiramente *adv* in fact, truly; really, indeed.

verdadeiro,-a *adj* true, real; **2** *(leal)* loyal; reliable **um amigo ~** a staunch friend; **na ~a acepção da palavra** in the real sense of the word.

verde *m (cor)* green; ♦ *adj inv (fruta)* green, unripe; **2** *(madeira)* not seasoned; **3** *(fig) (pessoa)* immature; **4** *(POL)* **os V~s** the Green Party; environmentalists; **5** *(POL)* **o Livro V~** *(documento do governo)* the Green Paper; IDIOM **dar luz ~** to give the go-ahead.

verdejante *adj inv (campos, etc)* green, verdant.

verdejar *vi (campos, etc)* to turn/go green.

verdelhão, verdilhão *m* green linnet.

verdor *m (do que é verde)* verdure, greenness; **2** *(imaturidade)* inexperiência.

verdugo *m* executioner; **2** *(fig) (pessoa má)* beast, monster.

verdura *f (BOT)* greenery, vegetation; **2** *(cor verde)* greenness; **3** **~s** *fpl (hortaliça)* greens, green vegetables.

vereação *f (organismo)* town council.

vereador,-ora *m,f* councillor, alderman.

vereda *f* narrow path.

veredi(c)to *m (JUR)* verdict.

verga *f (pau delgado, flexível)* stick, twig; **2** *(vime)* wicker; **artigos de ~** wickerwork; **3** *(NÁUT) (para o mastro)* pole; **4** *(viga)* rod.

vergadiço,-a *adj* flexible.

vergão *m (pau)* pole; **2** *(marca na pele)* weal.

vergar *vt* to bend; **2** *(fig)* to submit, to humble; ♦ *vi* to bend; **2** to stoop; **3** *(ceder)* give in, bow; **4** *(com o peso)* sag.

vergastada *f* whiplash, caning.

vergastar *vt* to whip, to beat with a cane; **2** *(fig) (criticar)* censure, reprove.

vergel *m* orchard, kitchen garden, allotment *(para cultivar verduras).*

vergonha *f* shame; **que falta de ~!** how disgraceful!; **ela não tem ~** she is shameless, brazen; **2** embarrassment; **eu sinto ~ de falar com ele** I feel embarrassed to speak to him; **3** timidity, shyness; **ela tem ~ de usar vestidos decotados** she is too shy to wear low-necked dresses; **4** *(desonra, ultraje)* shame, outrage; **sofrer uma ~** to be outraged; **5** **com ~** in shame.

vergonhoso,-a *adj* shameful; **2** *(indecoroso)* indecent; **3** *(indigno)* disgraceful.

vergôntea *f (BOT) (rebento de planta)* shoot; **2** *(ramo, haste)* twig; **3** *(fig) (filho)* offspring.

verídico,-a *adj* true, truthful; *(testemunho)* veridical.

verificação *f* checking; verification.

verificar *vt* to check, to verify; **2** confirm; ♦ **~-se** *vr* to happen; to come true.

verme *m (ZOOL)* worm, grub; **2** *(pessoa desprezível)* worm.

vermelhão *m (cor)* vermilion; **2** *(QUÍM)* cinnabar.

vermelhidão *f* redness, vermilion.

vermelho,-a *m,f (cor)* red; **2** *(corar)* red, blush, ruddiness; **ela pôs-se ~a** she blushed, she turned/went red; **olhos ~s de chorar** eyes red with crying; **3** *(QUÍM)* cinnabar; ♦ *adj* red.

vermicida *m* vermicide.

vermute *m* vermouth.

vernáculo,-a *m* vernacular; ♦ *adj (língua)* vernacular; **2** *(gastronomia)* traditional.

verniz *m* varnish, polish; **2** patent leather; **mala de ~** patent leather handbag; **3** *(fig) (aparência)* veneer.

verosímil *(BR: -ssí-) adj inv (história, desculpa)* believable; *(crível)* credible; **2 é pouco ~** hard to believe; it is unlikely.

verosimilhança *(BR: -ssi-) f* verisimilitude; **2** *(probabilidade)* credibility; **3** likelihood.

verrina *f* violent accusation *(em discurso público);* harsh criticism.

verruga *f (MED)* wart.

verruma *f (MEC)* gimlet, bit, drill, borer.

versado,-a *adj:* **~ em** good at, versed, specialised.

versão *f* version.

versar *vt (pesquisar)* to study, research *(autor, obra);* ♦ *vi (tratar de)* to deal **(sobre** with); **2** *(dizer respeito)* to be about, to concern.

versátil *adj* versatile.

versatilidade *f* versatility.

versejar *vi* to write in verse, versify, rhyme.

versículo *m (REL)* versicle, verse; **2** *(de artigo)* paragraph.

verso *m* verse; line of poetry; **2** *(da página, moeda)* other side, reverse; **vide ~** see over(leaf).

vértebra *f* vertebra.

vertebrado,-a *adj* vertebrate.

vertente *f (encosta)* slope.

verter *vt (vazar)* to pour out, to tip; **2** *(entornar)* to spill; **3** *(traduzir)* **(para)** to translate (into); **4** *(lágrimas)* to shed; ♦ *vi* to leak; **a torneira verte** the tap leaks; **2** *(brotar)* **3 ~ de** *(jorrar)* to spring /gush from *(fonte);* **4** *(gota a gota)* to seep **(de** from, through) *(do teto).*

vertical *f (GEOM)* vertical line; *(GEOG)* longitude; ♦ *adj inv* vertical; **2** *(posição)* upright, standing.

vértice *m (GEOM)* vertex *(pl:* **vertices**); **2** *(cimo, cume)* summit, peak, top.

vertigem *f* dizziness; *(MED)* vertigo; **ter** ~ feel dizzy, giddy.

vertiginoso,-a *adj* vertiginous; **queda** ~**a** headlong fall; *(COM)* sharp fall; **2** *(sensação, medo de alturas)* dizziness, guiddiness.

vesgo,-a *adj* cross-eyed.

vesícula *f* sac; ~ **biliar** gall-bladder.

vespa *f (BOT)* wasp; **2** *(fig) (pessoa intratável)* acrimonious person.

vespão *m (ZOOL)* hornet.

vésper *m* evening star, Venus.

véspera *f* the day before; ~ **de Natal** Christmas Eve; ~ **de Ano Novo** New Year's Eve; ~**s** *fpl (REL)* vespers; **estar nas** ~**s de** to be about to.

vespertino,-a *adj* evening; **jornal** ~ the evening paper.

veste *f* garment; **2** *(REL)* vestment, robe.

vestiário *m (num teatro)* cloakroom; **2** *(loja, ginásio)* changing room.

vestibular *m (BR)* senior grade, entrance examination to get into university; ♦ *adj inv (função)* vestibular.

vestíbulo *m* hall(-way), vestibule; **2** foyer.

vestido,-a *m* dress; ~ **de baile** long dress; ~ **de noite** evening dress; ♦ *adj* dressed; **vestida** *f* **de preto** dressed in black.

vestidura *f (REL)* robe, vestment; **2** religious, formal occasion; **3** garments, clothing.

vestígio *m (pegada)* trail, footprint; *(do carro)*, mark, track; **2** *(indício)* sign, trace; **3** ~**s** *(ARQ)* remains.

vestimenta *f (Vd:* **vestidura**).

vestir *vt* to dress, clothe, to put on, to wear; to make clothes for; ♦ ~**-se** *vr* to dress; to get dressed; to dress up.

vestuário *m (roupas)* clothing, attire, apparel; **2** *(TEAT)* costumes *pl*, wardrobe.

vetar *vt (opor proposta, lei, etc)* to veto.

veterano,-a *adj* veteran.

veterinário,-a *m,f* vet, veterinary surgeon; ♦ *adj* veterinary.

veto *m* veto.

vetor (**vector**) *m (MAT)* vector.

vetusto,-a *adj* ancient, very old; time-honoured.

véu *m* veil; ~ **de freira** wimple; **tomar o** ~ *(freira)* take the vows/veil; **2** *(algo oculto, pretexto)* **sob um** ~ **de mistério** under a veil of mystery; **3** silk cloth covering holy host; **4** *(ANAT)* ~ **palatino** soft palate.

vexame *m (vergonha)* shame, scandal; **foi um** ~**!** it was a scandal!; **2** humiliation.

vexar *vt (envergonhar)* to embarrass; **2** to put to shame; humiliate; ♦ ~**-se** *vr* to be ashamed/embarrassed.

vexatório,-a *adj* humiliating.

V. Exª *(abr de* **Vossa Excelência**) (in formal address) Sir, Madam, your Excellency; **Exªs** Your Excellencies.

vez *f* time; **uma** ~ once; **era uma** ~ once upon time. **alguma** ~ ever; **já alguma** ~ **viu?** have you ever seen?; **algumas** ~**es** a few times; **às** ~**es** sometimes,

at times; **cada** ~ **mais** more and more, gradually; **cada** ~ **que** every time that; **de** ~ **em quando** from time to time; **desta** ~ this time; **em** ~ **de** instead of; **mais uma** ~ again, once more; **raras** ~**es** seldom; **uma** ~ **ou outra** once in a while; **de** ~ for good, forever; **2** turn, **é a** ~ **dele** it's his turn, **fazer as** ~**es de** to stand in for; to replace; **3** *(MAT)* times; **dois** ~**es dois são quatro** two times two are four; ♦ *conj* **uma** ~ **que** since, as.

via *f (caminho)* path, lane, route, way; ~ **da esquerda** left-hand lane; ~ **férrea** railway; **por** ~ **aérea/marítima/terrestre** by air/sea/overland; ~ **pública** public way; ~ **rápida** *(autoestrada)* fast lane; **2** *(ANAT)* duct; **3** *(de drenagem)* channel, duct; **4** *(ASTRON)* way; **5** ~**s** *fpl* roads; channels; ~**s legais** legal channels; **vias sonoras** *(nas ruas)* rumble strips; ♦ *prep (modo, meio de)* **por** ~ **de** through, by means of; **por via de regra** as a general rule; **por** ~ **das dúvidas** just in case; **em** ~**s de** about to; in the course of; IDIOM **chegar a vias de facto** *(pancada)* to come to blows.

viabilidade *f* viability, feasibility.

viação *f* transport; bus/coach company; **acidentes de** ~ road accidents.

viaduto *m* viaduct, flyover; *(para peões)* footbridge; *(subterranean)* tunnel.

viagem *f* journey, trip, travel; ~ **de ida e volta** return trip, round trip; ~ **de barco** voyage; ~ **de núpcias** honeymoon trip; ~ **inaugural** *(barco)* maiden voyage.

viajante *m* traveller; **caixeiro** ~ *(COM)* commercial traveller; ♦ *adj inv* travelling.

viajar *vi* to travel *(para* to; *por* by, across through).

viajata *f* short holiday trip.

Via Láctea *npr f (ASTRON)* Milky Way.

viandante *m,f (viajante)* walker, pilgrim; **2** *(transeunte)* pedestrian.

viário,-a *adj* road, *(regulamentos, etc)* related to traffic, streets.

via-sacra *f (REL)* stations of the Cross; Via Dolorosa; *(fig) (percurso difícil; a vida)* calvário *m*.

viatura *f* vehicle; ~**s usadas** second-hand vehicles.

viável *adj inv* feasible, viable.

víbora *f (ZOOL)* viper; **2** *(fig)* hot-tempered person.

vibração *f* vibration; **2** *(tremor na voz etc)* quivering.

vibrador,-ora *m* vibrator; **2** vibrating.

vibrante *adj inv* vibrant, resonant; **2** *(fig) (discurso)* vibrant, thrilling.

vibrar *vt* to vibrate; **2** *(fazer soar sinos, tambor)* to play; **3** *(brandir)* brandish, strike; ♦ *vi* to vibrate; **os sinos vibravam** the bells tolled; **2** *(tremer)* shake; **3** *(soa)* to echo; **4** *(entusiasmar-se)* be thrilled.

vibrião *m (MED)* vibrio.

vicejante *adj inv (pomar, campos)* lush, exhuberant.

vicejar *vi (vegetar, estar viçoso)* to flourish.

vicentino,-a *adj (confraria, ordem)* St. Vincent de Paul's Order; **2** *(obra, era)* relativo a Gil Vicente.

Gil Vicente was the best-known playwright and poet of his time, 14th/15th c. Founder of the theatre in Portugal.

vice-presidente *m* vice-president.
vice-rei *m* viceroy.
vice-reitor,-ora *m,f* vice-rector, pro-rector, deputy head.
vice-versa *adv* vice-versa.
viciado,-a *m,f (dependente)* addict; 2 *(fig) (apreciador)* avid; **um ~ no cinema** cinema-goer; ◆ *adj* addicted (to); **~ em drogas** drug addict; 2 *(ar, ambiente)* foul, polluted; 3 *(produto)* vitiated, adulterated.
viciante *adj inv* addictive.
viciar *vt* to make addicted to; 2 to falsify; 3 to spoil; 4 to corrupt; ◆ **~-se** *vr* to become addicted to.
vício *m (mania)* vice; 2 *(erro)* failing; 3 bad habit; 4 *(dependência)* addiction.
vicioso,-a *adj* defective; 2 *(comportamento)* licentious, depraved; 3 *(pessoa, vida)* corrupt; 4 *(círculo)* vicious.
vicissitude *f* vicissitude; **as ~s** *fpl* **da vida** the ups and downs of life.
viço *m (da vegetação)* vigour, greenness; 2 freshness; 3 *(fig)* force, vigour; **o ~ da mocidade** the vigour of the youth.
viçoso,-a *adj* luxuriant, verdant; 2 *(fig)* exuberant; 3 *(da pele)* glowing.
vida *f* life; lifetime; living; 2 *(existência)* **esperança de ~** life expectancy; **ela trabalhou toda a ~** she worked all her life; **com ~** alive; **em (sua) ~** in one's lifetime; 3 *(subsistência)* living; **custo de ~** cost of living; **ganhar a ~** to earn one's living; **mulher da ~** prostitute; 4 *(modo de viver)* **padrão de ~** the standard of living; 5 *(morte)* life beyond; 6 *(FÍS)* **meia-~** *(desintegração de detritos)* half-life, lifetime; 7 *(fig) (vitalidade)* vitality; **ela tem muita ~** she is very energetic, lively; ◆ *prep, adv;* **para toda a ~** forever; **sem ~** dull, lifeless, dead; **andar à boa ~** to idle around; *exc* **que ~ esta!** what a life!; **meta-se na sua ~!** mind your own business!; IDIOM; **~ airada** easy life; **~ de cão** a dog's life; **fazer a ~ negra a (alguém)** to make somebody's life a hell; **meter-se na ~ (de alguém)** to poke one's nose into other people's life; **meta-se na sua ~** mind my own business.
vide[1] *f* twig of a creeping /twisting vine.
vide[2] *vt* see; **~verso** see overleaf.
videira *f (BOT)* grapevine, vine.
vidente *m,f* clairvoyant, visionary, seer.
vídeo *m* video.
vídeodisco *m* videodisc.
vídeoteca *f (colecção)* video collection/library; 2 *(loja)* video-shop.
vídeoteipe *f (fita)* videotape; ◆ *adj (processo)* videotaping.
vidoeiro *m (BOT)* birch.
vidraça *f* window pane.
vidraceiro *m* glazier.
vidrado,-a *adj* glazed; **cerâmica ~a** glazed pottery.
vidrão *m (recipiente)* bottle-bank.
vidraria *f* glass factory; glassware; glassmaking.
vidreiro *m* glassmaker, glass-blower; **indústria** *f* **~a** glass industry.
vidro *m* glass; **~ fosco** frosted glass; **~ fumado/fumê** smoked glass; **serviço de ~** glassware.

viela *f* alley, lane.
Viena *npr* Vienna.
vienense *adj inv* Viennese.
vier *(fut subj de* vir) **se ele ~ amanhá** if he comes tomorrow; **quando você ~** when (whenever) you come.
viés *m* slant; 2 bias strip; ◆ **de ~** *adv* sideways, diagonally.
viesse *(imperf subj de* vir) **esperei que ele ~** I was hoping/I hoped he would/might come.
vieste *(pret de* vir, 2ª *pessoa, sg)* **tu ~ muito tarde** you came very late.
Vietnã *npr (BR)* **o ~** Vietnam.
Vietname *npr (EP)* **o ~** Vietnam.
vietnamita *(LÍNG)* vietnamese; 2 *adj inv* Vietnamese.
viga *f (madeira)* beam; 2 *(concreto)* girder; **~ de aço** steel girder; **~ mestra** *f* main beam.
vigamento *m* rafters *mpl*.
vigarice *f* swindle.
vigário *m* vicar; 2 *(pop)* parish priest; IDIOM **cair no conto do ~** to be taken for a ride, taken in by a confidence trickster; **ensinar o pai-nosso ao ~** to teach your grandmother how to suck eggs.
vigarista *m,f* swindler, confidence trickster.
vigarizar *vt* to swindle, to cheat (sb).
vigência *f* validity.
vigente *adj inv (lei, contracto)* in force, valid, current.
vigésimo,-a *num* twentieth.
vigia *f* watching, surveillance; 2 *(orifício da porta)* peephole; 3 *(NÁUT)* porthole; 4 **de ~** on watch; ◆ *m* night watchman.
vigiar *vt* to watch, keep an eye on; to keep watch over; ◆ *vi* to be on the lookout.
vigilância *f* vigilance, surveillance; 2 *(school)* supervision.
vigilante *m* vigilant; 2 watchman; 3 sentinel; 4 *(at exams)* invigilator; ◆ *adj* watchful, alert; 2 vigilant; 3 attentive; 4 sleepless.
vigília *f (estar junto de um doente/defunto)* vigil; 2 *(MIL)* watch; 3 *(insónia)* sleeplessness; 4 **~ pascal** Easter eve.
vigor *m* energy, vigour; 2 **falar com ~** speak vehemently; 3 **em ~** in force; 4 **entrar/pôr em ~** to take/put into effect.
vigorar *vi* to be in force.
vigoroso,-a *adj* vigorous, robust, strong; **aperto de mão ~** strong handshake.
vil *(pl:* vis) *adj inv* vile, low (person).
vila *f* town; 2 *(moradia)* villa.
vilã *(Vd:* vilão).

Vila-Francada rebellion against the Constitutional regime, which took place in Vila-Franca de Xira, Portugal, in 1823.

vila-diogo *f;* **dar às de ~** *(fugir)* to take to one's heels.
vilania *f* villainy.
vilão,-ã *m,f (termo antigo)* townsman; 2 villain, rogue; **mulher vilã** wicked woman.
vilarejo *m* hamlet, small village.

vileza *f* mean trick.

vilipendiar *vt* to vilify *(nome, memória)*; ♦ ~-se to disgrace o.s.

vim *(pret de:* **vir**, 1ª *pessoa, sg)* **eu** ~ **vê-lo** I came to see you/him.

vime *m (ramo de viveiro)* wicker; **2** *(planta)* willow, osier.

'**Vime**' and '**verga**' have the same translation of 'wicker'. However, 'vime' is soft, chiefly used in the fabric of some baskets and table mats, while 'verga' is generally used for making furniture or tough baskets.

---

vinagre *m* vinegar.

vinagreira *f* vinegar plant; **2** vinegar bottle/cruet.

vinagrete *m* vinaigrette.

vincar *vt (fazer vinco) (roupa, papel)* to crease *(calças)*; **2** *(rosto)* to wrinkle; **3** *(sulco)* to furrow.

vinco *m* crease; **2** wrinkle; **3** furrow.

vinculado *adj* joined; **2** linked; **3** tied; **4** bound.

vincular *vt* to tie; **2** *(ligar)* join; **3** *(comprometer)* link; **4** *(por obrigação)* to bind; ♦ ~-se *vr* to embrace; **2** entail.

vinculativo,-a *adj (promessa, contracto)* binding.

vínculo *m (amizade)* bond; **2** *(entre países)* tie; **3** link, connection.

vinda *f* arrival, coming from; **dar as boas** ~**s** to welcome.

vindicar *vt* to vindicate; **2** to claim; **3** to demand.

vindima *f* grape harvest.

vindimar *vt (fig)* to harvest; ♦ *vi* to gather grapes.

vindo *(pp irr de* **vir**) **eu já tinha** ~ **aqui** I had already come/been here; ♦ **vindos,-as** *adj pl* **vocês são bem** ~ you are welcome.

The past participle of **vir = vindo** is invariable when conjugated with **ter and haver**, but with the verbs **ser**, **estar**, it varies in gender and number.

---

vindouro,-a *adj (ano)* coming; **2** *(geração)* future; ♦ ~**s** *mpl* future generations.

vingador,-ora *m,f* avenger; ♦ *adj* avenging.

vingança *f* vengeance, revenge.

vingar *vt* to avenge; ♦ *vi* to be successful; to thrive; ♦ ~-se de *vr* to take revenge on sb; **2** *(de um insulto)* avenge.

vingativo,-a *adj* vindictive, revengeful.

vinha¹ *(imperf de* **vir**) **eu** ~ **a caminho, quando encontrei a Maria** I was on my way when I met Mary.

vinha² *f* vine, vineyard.

vinha d'alhos *f (CULIN) (peixe, carne)* marinade of wine and garlic.

vinhateiro,-a *m,f adj* vine-grower; vine-growing; **uma região vinhateira** a vine-growing region.

vinhedo *m* vineyard, many vines.

vinheta *f (em medicamento, receita)* stamp; **2** *(desenho marca)* vignette.

vinheto *m (vinho ordinário)* plonk.

vinho *m* wine; ~ **espumante** sparkling wine; ~ **tinto** red wine; ~ **do Porto** port wine; ~ **a martelo** plonk.

vinícola *adj inv* wine-growing; **2** *(produção)* wine.

vinicultor,-ora *m,f* wine-grower.

vinicultura *f* viniculture.

vinil *m* vinyl.

vinte *num* twenty; ♦ *adj inv (dia, página)* twentieth; **no dia** ~ on the twentieth; **século XX** twentieth century; ~ **e um** *num* twenty one; ♦ *adj inv (folha, século)* twenty-first; IDIOM **acertar no** ~ to hit the nail on the head.

vintém *m (moeda antiga)* farthing; **2** *(pop)* **sem** ~ penniless, broke; **3 três vinténs** *mpl (pop) (arc)* virginity.

vintena *f* twenty, a score.

viola¹ *f (MÚS) (instrumento de cordas)* Spanish guitar; IDIOM **meter a** ~ **no saco** to shut up.

viola² *(BOT) f* viola, small violet.

violação *f (de pessoa)* violation, rape; **2** ~ **da lei** infringement, lawbreaking; **3** *(de casa)* housebreaking.

violador *m* rapist; ♦ **violador,-ora** *adj (transgressor)* breaker; **2** *(profanador)* profaner.

violão *m (MÚS) (de seis cordas)* large guitar, French guitar.

violar *vt (pacto, direitos, lei)* violate, infringe, break; **2** *(usar violência)* violentar; **3** *(estupro)* to rape *(pessoa)*; **4** *(casa)* to break in; **5** *(terra alheia para caçar)* to poach *(on another's reserves)*; **6** *(segredo)* breach; **7** *(lugar sagrado)* desecrate; **8** *(correspondência)* to open, interfere.

violência *f (acto)* violence; **2** *(força)* force, strength.

violentar *vt* to use violence against; **2** to force; **3** rape; **4** *(factos, história)* to distort, alter.

violento,-a *adj* violent, heavy; **2** impetuous; **3** intense; **4** *(dor)* sharp; **5** *(vida, desporto)* rough.

violeta *f (BOT)* violet; **2** *(cor)* violet.

violinista *m,f* violinist.

violino *m* violin.

violoncelista *m,f* cellist.

violoncelo *m* cello.

VIP *(abr de* **Very Important Person**) VIP.

viperino,-a *adj* viper-like; **2** *(venenoso)* venomous, viperish.

vir *vi (chegar)* arrive; **o avião veio às oito horas** the plane came/arrived at eight o'clock; **2** *(ger)* come; **você veio tarde** you came late; **vem/venha cá** come here; *(futuro)* **o mês que vem** next month; **3** *(estar)* to be; **a tradução vinha errada** the translation was wrong; **4** to go; **quem vem lá?** who goes there?; ♦ ~ **abaixo** to collapse; desmoronar(-se); *(prédio)*; ~ **a saber** *(descobrir)* to find out, come to know; ~ **a ser** *(tornar-se)* become, to be; **que vem a ser isto?** what's this about?; **tornar a** ~ *(voltar)* to come back; ~ **a si** *(recuperar sentidos)* to come round; **mandar** ~ *(encomendar)* to send for; ~ **de** *(provir)* to come from; **donde veio esta coisa?** where did this thing come/spring from?; ~ **em auxílio de** to come to the help of; IDIOM ~ **ao mundo** nascer; ~ **à baila** *(assunto, questão)* to come up in conversation; **não** ~ **ao caso** to be irrevelant; ~ **à cabeça** to spring to mind; ~ **de carrinho** to waste one's time; **lá vens**

tu com as tuas gracinhas there you go again with your jokes.

vira¹ *f* welt (of a shoe).

vira² *m* popular dance in the north of Portugal.

viração *f* sea-breeze.

vira-casaca, vira-casacas *m,f sg pl* turncoat.

virada *f* turning.

viragem *f* turning, change; **2** *(AUTO)* turning, swerve; **3** *(FOTO)* toning.

vira-lata *m* *(col)* mutt.

virar *vt* to turn; *(contornar)* turn, go around ~ **a esquina** turn the corner; **2** ~ **de cabeça para baixo** to turn upside down; **3** ~ **as costas** to turn one's back; **4** *(veículo)* to veer, change direction; **5** *(pôr do avesso)* turn inside out; **6** ~ **o disco/o bife** to turn over the record, the steak; **7** ~ **a dobra do lençol** turn down the sheet; ♦ *vi* *(alterar-se)* to change; **2** *(mudar de direção; dar voltas)* to turn; ~ **para** to face, turn towards; **3** ~ **de bruços** to turn on one's tummy; ~ **do avesso** to turn inside out; ♦ **~-se** *vr* to turn; to turn round; **2** *(AUTO)* capsize; **3** *(revoltar-se)* rebel, turn **(contra**, against, on); IDIOM **vira o disco e toca o mesmo** change the record and play the same/it's always the same old thing.

viravolta *f* *(volta inteira)* turning, spin; **2** somersault; **3** *(fig)* *(mudança)* reversal, setback, turnabout.

virgem *f* virgem; **a V~ Maria** the Virgin Mary; **2** *(ASTROL)* Virgo; ♦ *adj* pure; **mel** ~ pure honey; **2** *(pessoa)* virgin; **3** *(floresta, etc)* unused, virgin; **4** *(cassete, discos, etc)* blank.

virginal *adj inv* virginal.

virgindade *f* virginity.

vírgula *f* *(pontuação)* comma; **2** *(MAT)* *(decimal)* *(entre números)* point.

viril *(pl:* **viris)** *adj* virile.

virilha *f* *(ANAT)* groin.

virilidade *f* virility.

virose *f* viral infection.

virtual *adj inv* *(mercado, sucesso, etc)* virtual; *(FÍS, COMP)* virtual.

virtualmente *adj* virtually.

virtude *f* *(qualidade moral)* virtue, merit; **2** *(castidade)* chastity.

virtudes *fpl* virtues *pl.*

virtuoso,-a *m,f* *(músico de grande talento)* virtuoso; ♦ *adj* *(pessoa que tem virtudes)* virtuous.

virulência *f* virulence.

virulento,-a *adj* virulent.

vírus *m* virus.

vis *(pl de* **vil).**

visado,-a *adj* *(cheque, passaporte)* valid, stamped.

visão *f* vision, sight; **2** *(MED)* eyesight; **3** *(ponto de vista)* view; **4** *(alucinação, percepção do futuro)* vision, intuition.

visar *vt* *(apontar arma, ter por fim)* to aim at, target; **2** *(DESP)* *(ter como alvo)* shoot at; **3** *(vistos)* to stamp; ♦ *vi* to aim.

víscera *f* viscus.

vísceras *fpl* vicera, bowels.

visco *m* mistletoe; **2** *(fig)* bait, bird-lime.

visconde *m* viscount.

viscondessa *f* viscountess.

viscoso,-a *adj* *(planta)* sticky, viscous; **2** slimy; **3** *(fig)* *(person)* nuisance.

viseense *adj inv* from Viseu, relating to Viseu (town in northeast Portugal).

viseira *f* visor.

visibilidade *f* visibility.

Visigodos *mpl* **os** ~ the Visigoths.

visionário,-a *adj* visionary.

visita *f* visit, call; **2** *(pessoa)* visitor; **fazer uma** ~ **a alguém** to visit sb; ~ **de cerimónia** formal. official visit; **3** ~ **de médico** flying visit; **4** *(fam)* *(mênstruo)* menstruation; ♦ *adv* **de** ~ visiting; **estar/vir só de** ~ just passing by/visiting.

visitante *m,f* visitor.

visitar *vt* to visit, call on sb; **2** *(inspeccionar)* to inspect; ♦ **~-se** *(recíproco)* to visit one another.

visível *adj* visible, clear; **2** obvious, clear.

visivelmente *adv* visibly, clearly.

vislumbrar *vt* *(entrever)* to glimpse, catch a glimpse of, see; **2** *(conjecturar)* think up.

vislumbre *m* *(luz)* glimmer, flicker; **2** *(fig)* *(vestígio, sinal)* glimmer; **3** *(olhar rápido)* glimpse.

vista *(pp irr de:* **ver)** *f* view, sight; **que bela ~!** what a lovely view!; **2** *(MED)* eyesight; ~ **curta** short-sightedness; **ter** ~ **para o mar** to look on to the sea; ♦ *adj* seen; ♦ *adv* **à** ~ in sight; **pagamento à** ~ cash payment; **até à ~!** so long!; **pôr à** ~ to display, to show; **desenho à** ~ drawing from a model; **conhecer de** ~ to know (sb) by sight; **dar na(s)** ~ **(s)** to be striking; to attract attention; **ter em** ~ to have in mind; IDIOM **dar uma** ~ **de olhos em** to give a quick glance (at, through); **fazer** ~ **grossa** *(pop)* turn a blind eye to; **fogo de** ~ *(pop)* a flash in the pan; **a perder de** ~ as far as the eye can see; **longe da ~, longe do coração** out of sight, out of mind.

visto *m* visa; **2** *(garantia, validade)* stamp; *(sinal)* tick; **pôr um** ~ **em (algo)** *(como prova que foi visto)* to tick (sth); ♦ *(pp irr de:* **ver)**; ♦ *adj* seen, known; **chapéu muito** ~ very popular hat; **2** *(conhecido)* ver common; ♦ *adv* **a olhos ~s** visibly, rapidly; **pelos ~s** apparently, by the look of it; **está** ~ **que** it is obvious that; ♦ ~ **que** *conj* seeing that, since.

vistoria *f* inspection; **2** *(JUR)* survey; **3** *(busca)* search.

vistoriar *vt* to inspect; **2** survey; **3** *(NÁUT)* overhaul.

vistoso,-a *adj* *(person)* *(ger)* eye-catching; nice; handsome *(man).*

visual *m* *(aparência)* appearance; **ela mudou de** ~ she changed her appearance, she has a new look; ♦ *adj inv* visual.

vital *adj* vital; essential.

vitalício,-a *adj* for life.

vitalidade *f* vitality.

vitalizar to vitalize.

vitamina *f* vitamin.

vitaminado,-a with vitamins.

vitela *f* *(ZOOL)* calf; **2** *(CULIN)* veal; **escalopes de** ~ veal fillets.

vítima *f* victim; **fazer-se de** ~ to play the victim.

vitimar *vt (matar)* to claim the life of; **2** *(danificar)* to destroy.

vitivinicultura *f (AGR)* vitiviniculture, vine–growing and wine production.

vitória *f* victory, win.

vitorioso,-a *adj* winning, victorious.

vitral *m (arte) (painel decorativo, técnica)* stained glass (window).

vítreo,-a *adj* glassy, vitreous; **2** *(fig)* transparent, crystal clear.

vitrificar *vt* vitrify, to turn into glass.

vitrina, vitrine *f* glass case, display cabinet; show-window.

vitrola *f* gramophone; **2** ~ **automática** jukebox; **3** *(fig, fam)* gossip.

vituperar *vt* to insult, abuse, revile.

vitupério *m* vituperation, insult, abuse.

viuvez *f* widowhood.

viúvo,-a *m,f* widower widow; ♦ *adj* widowed.

viva *exc* ~! hurray!; **2** ~! hello!; **ora** ~! well, hello!; **3** ~ **o rei!** long live the king!

vivacidade *f* vivacity, liveliness; **2** spirit; **3** brilliance.

vivalma *f* living soul; **nem** ~ not a living soul.

vivaz *adj inv (espécie)* long-lived; **2** *(planta)* perennial; **3** *(fig)* lively.

viveiro *m (de plantas)* nursery; **2** *(de pássaros)* aviary; **3** *(de peixe)* fish pond.

vivenda *f* detached house; villa.

viver *vt* to live, be alive; **ela ainda vive/está viva?** is she still alive?; ~ **bem** to live comfortably; **2 ela vive do seu trabalho** she lives by/off her work; ~ **dos seus rendimentos** to live on one's income; **3** *(residir)* **eu vivo em Londres** I live in London; **4** ~ **fora** to live out; **5** *(experiência)* to live through; **ele viveu a guerra civil** he lived through the civil war; **viver à custa de (alguém)** *(col)* to sponge off sb; ~ **para** to live for; ~ **juntos** *(cohabit)* to live together; IDIOM ~ **da pena** to live by/off writing; ~ **à larga** to live in great style; ~ **a trabalhar/trabalhando** do nothing but work; ~ **à tripa-forra** to live in ease and plenty; ~ **e deixar** ~ to live and let live.

víveres *mpl* provisions.

vivido,-a *adj (pessoa)* **muito** ~ very experienced, been around.

vívido,-a *adj (ger)* vivid; **2** *(animado)* vivacious.

vivificar *vt* to vitalize, give life to, revive.

vivissecção *f* vivisection.

vivo *m:* **os** ~**s** the living; ♦ **vivo,-a** *adj* alive, living; **2** strong; **3** *(cor)* bright; **4** *(alegre)* lively; ♦ *adv (TV, RADIO)* **ao** ~ live; **de** ~**a voz** by word of mouth.

vizinhança *f* neighbourhood.

vizinho,-a *m,f* neighbour; ♦ *adj* neighbouring; nearby.

voador,-ora *adj* flying; **2** swift; **disco** ~ flying saucer; **objecto** ~ **não identificado** unidentified flying object, UFO.

voar *vi* to fly; to blow up, explode; **fazer** ~ **(pelos ares)** to blow up; ~ **pelos ares** explode; ~ **alto** *(fig)* to aim high.

vocabulário *m* vocabulary.

vocábulo *m* word; term.

vocação *f* vocation; **2** *(orientação)* calling, vocation.

vocacional *adj inv* vocational.

vocal *adj* vocal.

vocálico,-a *adj* vocal.

vocalista *m,f* vocalist.

você *(pron pess, sg) (informal, but not familiar)* you; ~ **está acordado?** are you awake?; **vou com** ~ I am coming with you.

vocês *(pron pess, pl) (informal)* you; ~ **estão cansados** you are tired; **ele lembra-se de** ~ he remembers you *pl*.

vociferar *vt/vi (bramar)* to shout, roar out, bluster; **2** *(clamar)* to bawl, clamour, vociferate; ~ **contra** rant against.

vodka *(BR:* **vodca**) *f* vodka.

vodu *m* voodoo.

voejo *m* fluttering, flapping.

voga *f (moda)* fashion, vogue; **estar em** ~ to be fashionable; **2** *(fig)* popularity; **3** *(NÁUT) (cadência)* rowing; **4** *(impulsão com os remos)* stroke; **à** ~ **surda** with muffled; **5** *(pessoa)* oarsman, strokeoar.

vogal *f (LÍNG)* vowel; ♦ *m,f* voting member; committee officer/member.

vogar *vi* to row, sail; **2** to float, drift; **3** to be popular, be in vogue.

voile *m (tecido)* voile; **cortina de** ~ net curtain.

volante *m (AUTO)* steering wheel; **2** *(motorista, piloto)* driver; **3** *(MEC)* ~ **de máquina** flywheel; **4** *(peça que se atira num jogo)* shuttlecock; **5** *(esse jogo)* badminton game; **6** *(BR) (impresso para apostas)* betting slip.

volátil *adj* volatile.

voleibol *m* volleyball.

voleio *m* volley.

volfrâmio *m* tungsten, wolfram.

volição *f (FIL, PSI)* volition; wish, will.

volt *m (FÍS)* volt.

volta *f* turn; **dar** ~ **à chave** to turn the key; **2** return; **bilhete de ida e** ~ return ticket *(UK)*, round trip ticket *(US)*; **estar de** ~ to be back; **3** string; **uma** ~ **de pérolas** a string of pearls; **à/na** ~ on the way back; **dar** ~ **a um argumento** twist an argument around; **dar** ~ **ao juízo** to go crazy; **dar** ~**s à casa/às gavetas** *(rebuscar)* to go through the house/the drawers; **dar** ~**s na cama** twist and turn in bed; **dar uma** ~ **à casa** *(limpeza ligeira)* give the house a clean; **dar uma** ~ *(a pé)* go for a walk/stroll, *(de carro)* spin/drive; *(curta viagem)* trip; **numa** ~ **de mão** in a jiff/jiffy; **4** bend, curve; **5** *(DESP)* lap, circuit; **6** *(MIL)* **dar meia-volta** to about turn *(UK)*, about-face *(US)*; ♦ *prep* **por** ~ **de** about, around; **à** ~ **de** round; **à/na** ~ **de** on the way back; **na** ~ **do correio** by return post; **às** ~**s com**, busy with, struggling with; ♦ ~ **e meia** *adv* from time to time; ~ **e reviravoltas** twists and turns, windings and turnings.

voltado,-a *adj (de frente, para)* facing; ~ **para a parede** facing the wall; **2** *(concentrado)* focussed, turned to.

voltagem *f* voltage.

voltaico,-a *adj (FÍS)* voltaic.

voltar *vt* to turn (**a, para** to, towards); ~ **para trás** to turn/go back; ♦ *vi* to return (**a, para,** to; **de,** from), go/come back; **2** ~ **para casa** to go home; **3** ~ **com a palavra atrás** to go back on one's word; **4** ~ **a si** *(reanimar)* to come to, come round; **5** *(fazer outra vez)* ~ **a** + *verbo* to do ... again; **ele voltou a ler** he read again; ♦ **~-se** *vr* to turn (**contra** against); **2** SAT (**para** towards); **3** ~-**se na cama,** toss and turn, turn over; **4 ela voltou-se para ele** she turned to him.

voltear *vt (contornar)* go round; **2** *(fazer girar)* to turn, revolve; **3** *(esvoaçar)* flutter, swirl, whirl; **4** spin round.

voltímetro *m (ELECT)* voltmeter.

volubilidade *f* fickleness.

volume *m* volume; **2** *(quantidade)* bulk; **3** *(embrulho)* package.

volumoso,-a *adj* bulky, big.

voluntário,-a *m,f* volunteer ♦ *adj* voluntary.

voluntarioso,-a *adj* headstrong, stubborn.

volúpia *f* pleasure, sensuality; **2** desire.

voluptuoso,-a *adj* voluptuous.

volúvel *adj inv* fickle, changeable, inconstant.

volver *vt/vi* to turn; ♦ *vi* ~ **a** to go/come back, return.

vomitar *vt/vi (MED)* to vomit; to bring up, throw up *(vómito)*; *(fig)* to pour out.

vómito *m* vomiting; vomit; **ter ~s** to retch, feel sick.

vontade *f* will; wish, craving; **má ~** ill will; **fale à ~** speak freely, be frank; **esteja à ~** make yourself at home, be at ease; **ter ~ de ...** to feel like/fancy ...; **não tenho ~ de comer** I don't feel like eating; **estou-lhe com uma ~!** *(ódio)* I feel like killing (him, her); **fazer todas as ~s a** *(mimar)* to please/spoil sb, satisfy sb's whims; ~ **de ferro** a strong-will; ♦ **de má ~** unwillingly; **contra ~** against own's will; **ela comia com ~** she ate heartily; **pouco à ~** be uncomfortable.

voo *m* flight; **levantar ~** to take off.

voragem *f* abyss, gulf; **2** whirlpool.

voraz *adj* voracious, greedy.

vórtice *m* whirlpool, whirlwind.

vos *(pron pess objecto) pl* you, to you *pl*; **dou-vos o meu livro** I give my book to you; **já ~ disse** I have already told you.

vós *pron pess, sujeito, segunda pessoa sg/pl (arc)* you; thou *(arch)*; ~ **sois meu/meus convidado/s** you/ thou are my guest/s. *(Note: vós is almost obsolete, except in old poetry and in church services, particularly in Portugal's northern regions);* **vós** (**na função de complimento indirecto**) you; **a** ~ (**a vocês**) **é que compete falar** it is you *(pl)* who should speak; **2** *(enfático)* **ele disse-vos isso, a vós**

he said that to you *(pl)* (inference: and to nobody else); **3** *(complemento preposicionado)* **a** ~, **para** ~ to/for you; **por** ~ by you; **estes presentes são para** ~ *(para vocês)* these presents are for you *(pl)*; **eu acredito em** ~ I believe (in) you.

vosso,-a *adj* your; ♦ *pron:* (**o**) ~ yours; **a vossa casa** your house *(sujeito no pl; objecto no sg)*; **vossos/as** *pl,* **as vossas casas** *(ambos sujeito e objecto no pl)* your houses; **os vossos trabalhos** your jobs/works.

votação *f* vote, ballot; voting; **votante** *m,f* voter.

votar *vt* to vote for; to devote; to make a vow of; ♦ *vi* to vote; ♦ **~-se** *vr:* ~ **a** to dedicate o.s. to; ~-**se ao silêncio** keep silent.

voto *m* vote; **assembleias de** ~ polling stations; **2** *(REL)* vow; **votos** *mpl (desejos)* wishes; ~ **de felicidade** wish you happiness; **com os melhores** ~ **para as festas** with the best wishes for the season; **fazer ~s (para, por)** to wish (for).

vou *(pres indic de:* **ir,** *1ª pessoa)* (**eu**) ~ **dormir** I am going to sleep; ~ **ao mercado** I am going to the market.

vovô *m* grandad.

vovó *f* grandma.

voz *f* voice; rumour; ~ **alta/baixa** loud/low voice; ~ **arrastada** a drawl; ~ **de cana rachada** rasping voice; ~ **aguda** high-pitched, shrilling voice; **dar** ~ **de prisão** announce an arrest; **ter** ~ **a(c)tiva em** be an authority, have a say in; *(gram)* ~ **a(c)tiva/ passiva** active/passive voice; **2** *(boato)* **ser** ~ **por aí** be rumoured around ♦ *adv* **em** ~ **alta** aloud; **a meia** ~ in a whisper; **de viva** ~ orally.

vozearia *f* shouting, bawling; clamour; hullabaloo.

vozeirão *m* strong voice, loud voice.

v.s.f.f. (= **volte se faz favor**) p.t.o. (please turn overleaf).

vulcânico,-a *adj* volcanic; **2** *(fig)* violent, impetuous.

vulcão *m* volcano.

vulgar *adj (comum)* common, ordinary, usual; commonplace.

vulgaridade *f (banalidade)* triviality; platitude **2** commonness; **3** *(pej) (dito maneira)* rudeness.

vulgarizar *vt* to popularize; **2** *(tornar reles)* to vulgarize; ♦ **~-se** *vr* become commonplace; **2** *(reles)* become common/coarse.

vulgarmente *adv* generally.

vulgo *m (povo)* common folk; ♦ *adv* vulgus, commonly known as.

vulnerabilidade *f* vulnerability.

vulnerável *adj inv* vulnerable.

vulto *m (figura, sombra)* figure, form; **2** *(fig) (importância)* stature; **de** ~ important, famous; **tomar** ~ take shape.

vultuoso,-a *adj (volumoso)* bulky; **2** *(soma de dinheiro)* great, large; **3** *(transa(c)ção)* weighty; **4** important.

vulva *f (ANAT)* vulva.

W

W, w *m (letra dubloV)* W, w

W *(abr de watt Internacional) m* International watt.

W *(QUÍM) (símbolo para volfrâmio) m* wolfram, tungsten; **2** *m (GEOG) (símbolo para Oeste).* West.

wagnerianismo *m (teorias musicais e música do compositor alemão Wagner)* Wagnerianism

wagneriano,-a *m,f adj (adepto, etc de Wagner)* Wagnerian.

walkie talkie *(pl: walkie-talkies) m* walkie-talkie.

Walkman® *m* walkman.

WAN *(abr de Wide Area Network) f* WAN.

Washington *n* Washington; **em** ~ in Washington.

Washingtoniano,-a *m,f adj* Washingtonian.

watt *m* watt.

watt-hora *m (unidade de energia)* watt-hour, Wh.

wattímetro *m* wattmeter.

WC *(abr de water-closet) (retrete)* WC.

WEB *(world wide web) m (COMP)* web.

webmail *(pl: webmails) m (COMP)* webmail.

webmaster *(pl: webmasters) m (COMP)* webmaster.

wellingtoniano,-a *m,f adj* Wellingtonian.

western *m (de films americanos)* western.

Wh *(abr de watt-hora)*

whist *m (jogo parecido com a bisca)* whist.

windsurfe *m* windsurf.

windsurfista *m,f* windsurfer.

won *m (unidade monetária da Coreia do Norte e do Sul)* won.

workshop *m* workshop.

wurtzitem *(MIN) (sulfureto de zinco)* wurtzite.

WWW *(abr de World Wide Web) f* WWW.

X

X, x *m (letra: xis)* X, x.

xá *m* shah; **o antigo ~ da Pérsia** the former Shah of Persia.

xácara *f* ballad, romance.

xadrez *m (jogo)* chess; chessboard; **2** *(tecido)* checked cloth; **3** *(fam) (prisão)* jail, clink *(col)*; ◆ *adj inv* checked.

xadrezista *m,f* chess player.

xaile, xale *m* shawl.

xampu *(BR: champô) m* shampoo.

xará *(BR) m* namesake.

xaropada *f* cough syrup; **2** *(col)* boring talk.

xarope *m* syrup.

xaveco *m* small, old and ordinary boat; **2** *(BR) (objecto sem valor)* a piece of junk.

xelim *m (velha moeda britânica, 1/20 de uma libra esterlina)* shilling.

xelindró *m (col)* jail.

xenofobia *f* xenophobia.

xenófobo,-a *m,f* xenophobe; ◆ *adj* xenophobic.

xeque *m (chefe de tribo árabe)* sheik; **2** *(jogo)* chess; **~-mate** *m* checkmate.

xereta *adj inv (fam)* busybody, snoop.

xeretar *vi (BR)* to poke one's nose in, to snoop.

xerez *m (vinho)* sherry; **2** *(cidade espanhola)* Xerez.

xerife *m* sheriff.

xerocópia *f* photocopy.

Xérox *m (cópia)* photocopier.

xeta *f (BR: fam)* blown kiss.

xi *m (fala de criança) (Vd: chi).*

xícara *f* cup.

xicarada *f* cupful.

xiita *adj (seguidor da seita muçulmana)* shiita.

xilofone *m* xylophone.

xingar *vt/vi (BR)* to swear at; **2 ~ alguém de algo** to call sb sth, call names to sb, insult; **3** to bother sb.

xis *m (letra)* x.

xixi *m (fala de criança) (urinar)* wee-wee; **fazer ~** to do a wee-wee, *(fam: entre adultos)* to pee.

xisto *m (pedra, rocha)* schist.

xistoso,-a *adj (terreno, montanha)* schistaceous; **2** *(cor)* slate-grey.

xó! *exc (onomat) (para fazer parar as mulas, os bois)* whoa!

xô! *exc (onomat) (para mandar as galinhas embora)* shooing away the chickens; shoo!

xodó *m (BR)* flirting; sweetheart.

y

Y,y *(ípsilon, i-grego) m* Y,y twenty-fifth letter in the new Portuguese alphabet; **2 Y** *(QUÍM) (símbolo de ítrio)* yttrium *(y. oxide)*.

yaca *f (BOT) (AUSTRAL)* yacca, grass tree.

yanguiano,-a *adj (FÍS) (relativo ao físico chinês Chen Ning Yang or ao seu trabalho)* of Yang.

Yangtze *m (o rio mais longo da China)* Yangtze.

Yankee *m,f, adj* ianque.

Yd *(símbolo de: **yard**)*.

yeatsiano *adj (relativo ao poeta irlandês William Butler Yeats ou à sua obra)*; of Yeats.

yen *m (unidade monetária do Japão)* yen.

yersiniano,-a *adj (relativo ao médico francês Alexandre Yersin ou à sua obra)*; of Yersin.

yeti *m* ieti.

yoga *m*=ioga.

yorkshiriano,-a *m,f adj (do condado ao norte da Inglaterra)* from Yorkshire.

younguiano,-a *adj (relativo ao poeta inglês, Edward Young ou à sua obra)* of Young.

yuan *m (unidade monetária da China)* yuan.

yuppie *m inv (jovem executivo bem sucedido)* yuppie.

Z

Z, z *m (letra)* Z, z.

zabumba *m (bombo)* brass drum.

zaga *f (BOT)* a kind of palm tree; **2** *(MIL)* rear, rearguard; **3** *(BR) f (FUT)* fullback position.

zagueiro *m (FUT)* fullback.

zagaia *f (arma de arremesso)* assegai.

zagalote *(para espingardas) m* small bullet.

Zaire *npr* o ~ Zaire.

zairense *adj inv* native of Zaire; relative to Zaire.

Zâmbia *npt* a ~ Zambia.

zambiano,-a *adj* native of Zâmbia; relative to Zâmbia.

zanga *f* anger, rage; **2** quarrel.

zangado,-a *adj* angry; annoyed; **estamos ~s** we are not on speaking terms.

zangão *(pl: zangões) m (insecto)* drone.

zangar *vt* to annoy, irritate; ♦ **~-se** *vr* to get annoyed; ~ **com** to get cross/angry with; ~ **a sério** had a falling out.

zaragata *f* uproar, turmoil; squabble.

zaragateiro,-a *m,f* rioter; bustler; ♦ *adj* rowdy.

zarolho,-a *adj* blind in one eye; **2** *(estrábico)* cross-eyed.

zarpar *vt* to weigh anchor, set sail; **2** *(afastar-se à pressa)* scarper, run away.

zás *exc (onomat) (batida)* wham, whack; **a cozinheira deu-lhes com a frigideira na cabeça, ~!** the cook whacked them with the frying-pan, wham!

Zé *m,f (diminutivo e alcunha de* **José, Maria José**).

zebra *f* zebra; *(fig)* silly ass; collapse, surprise result.

zebu *(ZOOL)* zebu.

zelador *m (doméstico)* caretaker; **2** superviser, inspector.

zelar *vt* to look after; to watch over.

zelandês,-a *(também:* **neo-zelandês,-esa**) *adj* New-Zealander.

zelo *m* devotion, zeal.

zeloso,-a *adj* zealous; **2** hardworking.

zé-ninguém *m:* **um ~** a nobody, a non-entity.

zénite *(BR: zê-) m (ASTROL)* zenith; **2** *(fig) (auge)* high/culminating point.

zé-pereira *m* player of a big drum at rural festivities; busker.

zé-povinho *m* the man in the street; Joe Bloggs; **2** *(povo)* common people, the masses *pl;* **o ~ estava nas ruas a celebrar** the people were celebrating in the streets.

zero *m* zero, naught; **abaixo/acima** ~ below/above zero; **2** none; nothing; **3** *(DESP)* nil; **a ~** *adv* zero;

IDIOM **ser um ~ à esquerda**, a nobody; **eu sou um ~ em ciência** I know nothing about science; **começar do ~** start from scratch.

zeugma *f (LÍNG)* zeugma.

ziguezague *m* zigzag; IDIOM **andar aos ~s** to stagger.

ziguezaguear *vi* to zigzag.

zimbabuano,-a, zimbabuense *adj* native of Zimbabwe; relative to Zimbabwe.

Zimbabué *npr* o ~ Zimbabwe.

zimbório *m (ARQ)* dome.

zimbro *m (BOT)* common juniper.

zinco *m (QUÍM)* zinc; **folha de** ~ corrugated iron; ~ **refundido** galvanized zinc.

zincogravura *f (TIPO)* zincograph.

zipar *vt (BR) (COMP)* to zip.

zíper *(pl: -es) m (fecho éclair, EP)* zip, *(UK)* zipper *(US)*.

zircon *(mineral)* zircon.

zircónio *(BR: -ô-)* zirconium.

zoada *(também:* **zoeira***) f* hum, buzz, whiz(zing).

zoar *vi (zumbir)* to buzz; **2** *(vento)* haul; **3** *(BR, also = barulho)* make a din.

zodíaco *m* zodiac.

zombado,-a *adj* mocking.

zombar *vi:* ~ **de alguém** to make fun of sb; to sneer at sth.

zombaria *f* mockery; **2** ridicule.

zombeteiro,-a *m,f* joker; ♦ *adj* joking; **um comentário** ~ a comment in jest.

zona *f* zone, area, district; **a ~ franca** free trade zone; ~ **urbana** urban area; ~ **eleitoral** electoral district; ~ **periférica** outskirts; **2 a ~ verde** *(ambiente)* the green belt; **3** *(GEOG)* zone; **4** *(MED)* herpes, shingles.

zoneamento *m* zoning.

zonzo,-a *adj (BR)* dizzy, confused, bewildered.

zoo *(BR):* **zôo***) m* zoo.

zoófilo,-a zoophile.

zoologia *f* zoology.

zoológico,-a *adj* zoological; **jardim** ~ *m* zoo.

zoólogo,-a *m* zoologist.

zootecnia *f* animal breeding.

zootécnico,-a *m,f* animal breeder.

zorra *m,f* low, four-wheel cart to carry forest materials, dray; **2** *(fig)(vagaroso)* slow, slowcoach; **3** *(ZOOL)* old, cunning fox; **4** *(para crustáceos)* trawl-net; **5** *(BR) (fam)* mess.

zorro *m (ZOOL)* fox cub; **2** *(EP)* illegitimate child; **3** *(pessoa falsa, astuta)* fox; **4** *(BR)* lazybones; **5** old servant.

zum *m* zoom.

zumbido *m (de insecto)* buzz(ing); **2** *(de vozes, motor)* hum; **o ~ das abelhas** the buzzing of the bees; **3** *(no ouvido)* ringing.

zumbir *vi* to buzz; **2** to hum; **um mosquito zumbia à minha volta** a mosquito buzzed around me; **3 o vento zumbia** the wind was whistling.

zunido *m* whistling; whir(ring), buzz.

zunir *vi (vento)* to whistle; **2** *(passar rapidamente)* to whiz past, fly by; **3** *(serpente)* to hiss.

zunzum *m* buzz(ing); rumour; **há um ~ por aí que o ministro vai demitir-se** it is rumoured that the minister is going to resign.

zurrapa *f* rough wine; *(pop)* plonk.

zurrar *vi (voz do burro)* to bray, to heehaw; **2** *(fig) (fam) (dizer tolices)* to bray, talk nonsense.

zurraria *f* many asses braying.

zurre! *exc* scram!, off with you!

zurro *m* braying, heehaw; **2** rattle (with this sound).

zurzir *vt (açoitar)* whip, flog, lash; **2** *(fig) (repreender)* to lampoon, scold.

English–Portuguese

a

A, a *n (letter)* A, a *m;* **2** *(MUS: note)* lá *m;* **3** *(school: the highest mark)* A; **the A to Z** *(map)* roteiro *m* da cidade, carta *f* da cidade; **to get from A to B** ir de um lado para o outro; andar de cabo a rabo.

a, an *art* um, uma; **a beautiful day** um lindo dia; **an intelligent woman** uma mulher inteligente; **I want a beer** eu quero uma cerveja; **a Mr. Allen** um certo Senhor Allen; ♦ *prep (prices, ratio, time)* por, à, a, cada; **£10 an hour** dez libras por/à hora; **many a time** muitas vezes; **twice a week** duas vezes por semana.

"a" usa-se antes de palavras começadas por consoantes *(a boy),* "h" pronunciado *(a host),* por "y" *(a yankee),* e do som "iu" *(a unicorn);* an emprega-se antes de palavras que começam por vogal *(an article),* ou "h" mudo *(an hour).*

aback *adv* para trás; **to be taken ~** *(by sth)* ficar surpreendido,-a; colhido,-a de surpresa.

abacus *(pl:* **abacuses** or **-ci**) *n* ábaco *m.*

abandon *n* abandono *m* despreocupação *f;* **with ~** *(relaxed)* sem inibição, despreocupadamente *m;* **2** desamparo *m;* ♦ *vt (leave)* abandonar, deixar; **2** *(idea, plan)* desistir de, renunciar a; **to ~ o.s. to** entregar-se ao abandono, abandonar-se a.

abase *vt (humble)* **to ~ oneself** rebaixar-se; **2** reduzir, baixar *(esteem, in rank).*

abashed *adj* envergonhado-a, embaraçado,-a.

abate *vt/vi (to become less)* abater, abrandar, amainar; **the storm has abated** a tempestade abrandou; **2** *(reduce)* diminuir, reduzir; **3** *(lower)* baixar; **4** *(JUR) (annul)* anular *(writ).*

abatement *n (decrease, termination)* alívio *m,* diminuição *f.*

abattoir *n* matadouro *m.*

abbess *n* abadessa, madre *f* superiora.

abbey *n* abadia *f,* mosteiro *m;* convento *m.*

abbot *n* abade *m.*

abbreviate *vt* abreviar, resumir.

abbreviation *n* abreviatura *f.*

ABC *n (alphabet)* ABC *m,* abecedário *m;* **2** *(fig) (rudiments)* **the ~ of** o ABC de, o bê-á-bá de.

abdicate *vt,vi* abdicar, renunciar a *(throne);* **to ~ a right** abdicar a um direito; **2** *(responsability)* demitir-se de.

abdication *n* abdicação *f;* renúncia *f.*

abdomen *n* abdómen *(BR:* -dô-*) m.*

abdominal *adj* abdominal.

abduct *vt* raptar; arrebatar.

abduction *n* rapto *m,* sequestro *m.*

abductor *n (kidnapper)* raptor,-ora.

aberrant *adj (person, behaviour)* aberrante; *(result)* anormal.

aberration *n* aberração *f;* anomalia *f.*

abet (-tt-) *vt* incitar; **2** *(in crime)* encorajar a.

abeyance *n (formal):* **in ~** em desuso,-a; **2** *(JUR)* suspenso temporariamente; em estado jacente.

abhor (-rr-) *vt* detestar, abominar.

abhorrent *adj* detestável, repugnante, abominável.

abide *(pt, pp* **abode** *or* **abided)** *vt* aguentar, suportar; **I can't ~ sth** não posso suportar (algo); **to ~ by** *vt* cumprir.

abiding *adj* constante, permanente.

ability *n* capacidade f **(to** de, para); **to the best of my ~** o melhor que posso; **2** talento *m;* **3** *(skills)* habilidades *fpl,* competências *fpl;* **4** *(school)* aptidões *fpl.*

abject *adj* miserável, abjecto,-a; **~ poverty** miséria *f.*

ablaze *adj* em chamas, a arder.

able *adj (capable)* capaz; **to be ~ to** ser capaz de; poder, conseguir; **2** *(skilled)* talentoso,-a, competente; **3** *(MIL)* apto,-a; **~ in body and mind** são de corpo e espírito; **~-bodied** *adj* são *m,* sã *f;* robusto,-a; **~ seaman** *n (ordinary seaman)* marujo.

ably *adv* habilmente, com competência.

abnormal *adj* anormal.

abnormality *n* anormalidade *f.*

aboard *adv* a bordo; ♦ *prep* a bordo de; **to go ~** embarcar.

abode *(pt, pp of* **abide**) *n (home)* residência *f,* domicílio *m;* **of no fixed ~** sem domicílio *m* certo, fixo.

abolish *vt* abolir; revogar.

abolition *n* abolição *f,* extinção *f.*

abominable *adj* abominável, detestável; **~ snowman** *n* o abominável homem das neves.

aborigine *n* aborígene *m,f.*

abort *vt* abortar, fazer abortar *(foetus);* **2** *(plan)* abortar, fracassar.

abortion *n* aborto *m;* **to have an ~** fazer um aborto.

abortive *adj* abortado,-a, **2** *(raid)* fracassado,-a.

abound *vi* abundar **(with** *em);* estar cheio,-a/repleto,-a.

about *prep* **(on)** acerca de, sobre, a respeito de; **2** *(around)* em redor de, cerca de, mais ou menos; **she was ~ twelve years old** ela tinha cerca de doze anos; **it's ~ right** está mais ou menos bem; **3** *(imminent)* quase, prestes; **he is ~ to leave** ele está prestes a partir; **I was ~ to say** eu ia a dizer; **4** *(thereabouts)* por, por aí; **there is a prowler ~** anda por aí um gatuno ♦ *exc* **~ time too!** já não era sem tempo! **what/how ~ it?** que tal ...?; **what ~ a beer?** Que tal uma cerveja?; **what is it ~** de que se trata? **what ~ you?** e você? e tu *(fam)?;* **there isn't much of that ~** não há muito disso agora; **he is up and ~** *(from sleep)* ele já está acordado; *(from sick bed)* ele já está bom; ♦ **to jump ~** saltitar; **to wander ~** vaguear, deambular, andar por aí fora; IDIOM **don't beat ~ the bush** deixe-se de rodeios.

about-face *(US),* **about-turn** *(UK)* *exc (MIL)* meia volta; **2** reviravolta *f,* mundança radical.

above *adv* em/por cima; acima; ♦ *prep* sobre, acima de, por cima de; **mentioned ~** acima mencionado, supracitado; ♦ ~ **all** *adv* sobretudo, acima de tudo; ~ **board** *adj* legítimo,-a, honesto,-a, limpo,-a.

abracadabra *exc* abracadabra!

abrasion *n* desgaste *m*; **2** *(skin)* esfoladura, esfoldela *f*.

abrasive *adj* abrasivo,-a; **2** *(manner)* cáustico,-a; ~ **paper** lixa *f*.

abreast *adv* lado a lado; **to keep ~ of** estar a par de.

abridge *vt* resumir, abreviar, encurtar, reduzir; **~d** *adj* resumido,-a.

abridgement *n* resumo *m*.

abroad *adv* lá fora; **to be ~** estar no estrangeiro; estar fora; **to go ~** ir ao estrangeiro.

abrogate *vt* *(JUR)* *(repeal)* revogar, abrogar.

abrupt *adj* *(person, tone)* brusco,-a inesperado,-a; áspero,-a.

abruptly *adv* bruscamente.

ABS *n* *(abbr for:* **anti-lock breaking system**) ABS *m*.

abscess *n* abscesso *m*.

abscond *vi* fugir, esconder-se, evadir-se; **to ~ with sth** sumir com algo.

abseil *n* (SPORT) rapel *m*; ♦ *vt* fazer rapel.

abseiling *n* *(UK: SPORT)* descida *f* em rappel.

absence *n* ausência *f*; falta *f*.

absent *adj* ausente *m,f* *(from de)*; **to be ~** ausentar-se.

absentee *n* absentista *m,f*; ausente *m,f*.

absenteeism *n* absentismo *m*; *(BR)* absenteismo *m*.

absent-minded *adj* distraído,-a; desatento,-a.

absent-mindedness *n* distra(c)ção *f*.

absinth(e) *n* *(drink)* absinto *m*.

absolute *adj* absoluto,-a; **2** verdadeiro; **an ~ idiot** um verdadeiro idiota; **the ~ truth** a pura verdade; **3** *(PHYS)* *(scale)* máximo,-a.

absolutely *adv* absolutamente, sem dúvida.

absolution *n* absolvição *f*.

absolve *vt* *(acquit)* absolver *(from, de)*; **2** *(from sin)* perdoar; **3** *(from responsibility)* desobrigar.

absorb *vt* *(liquid, energy)* absorver; **2** *(be engrossed)* estar absorto, concentrar-se (**in**, a); **3** *(sound)* amortecer.

absorbent *adj* absorvente.

absorbing *adj* *(story)* empolgante, cativante.

absorption *n* absorção *f*; ~ **factor** *n* *(PHYS)* fator de absorção; **2** *(engrossed)* concentração *f*; **3** *(of impact)* amortecimento *m*.

abstain *vi* *(REL)* abster-se (**from** de); privar-se de.

abstemious *adj* *(person)* abstémio,-a, sóbrio,-a.

abstention *n* abstenção *f*, desistência *f*.

abstentionism *n* abstencionismo *m*.

abstinence *n* abstinência *f*, sobriedade *f*.

abstract *n:* **the ~** o abstrato; **in ~** em teoria, em sinopse; **2** *(JUR)* ~ **of title** *(property law)* extrato/certidão de registo de móveis ♦ *adj* abstrato,-a ♦ *vt* resumir *(from de)*.

abstruse *adj* confuso,-a, obscuro,-a.

absurd *adj* absurdo,-a; ridículo,-a; disparate *m*.

absurdity *n* absurdo *m*, disparate *m*.

abundance *n* abundância *f*.

abundant *adj* abundante.

abundantly *adv* suficientemente; ~ **clear** suficientemente claro; **2** *(in large quantity)* em abundância.

abuse *n* insultos *mpl*, injúrias *fpl*; ♦ *vt* *(maltreat)* maltratar; **2** insultar; **3** *(misuse)* abusar de.

abusive *adj* ofensivo,-a, grosseiro,-a (**to** para com); **2** *(improper)* abusivo,-a.

abut (-tt-) *vt* ser contíguo,-a, confinar (**on/onto** a); ♦ *vi* **to ~ against sth** apoiar-se a algo.

abysmal *adj* abismal; profundo,-a; ~ **ignorance** ignorância total.

abyss *n* abismo *m*.

Abyssinia *npr* Abissínia; **in ~** na Abissínia.

Abyssinian *npr adj* abissínio,-a.

AC *(abbr for:* **alternating current**) CA *(abbr. for:* **corrente alternada**).

a/c *(abbr for* **account/current account**) c.c. *f*.

acacia *n* acácia *f*

academia *n* o mundo académico.

academic *adj* académico (*BR:* -dê-), universitário; *(debate, question)* teórico; **that's just ~** isso é só em teoria; ~ **year** *n* ano *m* le(c)tivo.

academy *n* academia *f*; instituto *m*, colégio *m*; **military ~** academia militar; **2** *(learned society)* academia.

accede *vi* *(agree)* **to ~ to sth** consentir (em), aceder a (algo); **2** *(monarch)* ~ **to the throne** subir ao trono.

accelerate *vt/vi* apressar, acelerar; **2** *(of inflation, growth)* disparar.

acceleration *n* *(of car)* aceleração *f*; **2** *(growth)* disparada *f*.

accelerator *n* (AUT, CHEM, PHYS) acelerador *m*.

accent *n* *(in speaking)* sotaque *m*; **2** *(graphic)* acento *m*; **acute ~** acento agudo.

accentuate *vt* *(put the stress on)* acentuar; **2** *(emphasize)* sublinhar, destacar.

accept *vt* *(gen)* aceitar; **2** aprovar; **3** *(admit)* admitir, reconhecer *(own fault)*; **4** *(person- into a group)* acolher; **5** *(agree to do)* assentir.

acceptable *adj* aceitável, admissível.

acceptance *n* aceitação *f*; aprovação *f*.

accepted *pp, adj* aceite, aceito,-a; **she was ~** ela foi aceite/aceita.

access *n* acesso, entrada; **to have ~ to** ter acesso para/a.

accessible *adj* acessível.

accession *n* *(power)* ascensão *f*; **2** *(entry)* ingresso *m*.

accessory *n* acessório; **2** *(JUR)* ~ **to a crime** cúmplice num crime; **accessories** *npl* acessórios *mpl*.

accessorize/ise *vt* completar com acessórios.

accident *n* acidente *m*, desastre *m*, casualidade *f*; **~s will happen** tudo pode acontecer; **by ~** sem querer, por acaso; **traffic ~** acidente de viação.

accidental *adj* acidental.

accidentally *adv* *(inadvertently)* sem querer, **2** *(meet)* casualmente, por acaso; **~-prone** *adj* *(person)* com tendência para/propenso,-a (**to** a) acidentes.

acclaim *n* aclamação *f*, aplausos *mpl*; ♦ *vt* aclamar, aplaudir.

acclamation *n* acalamação *f*.

acclimatize, acclimatise (UK), **acclimate** (US) *vt*: **to become ~d** aclimatar-se a, habituar-se a.

accolade *n* *(praise, special honour)* honra *f*, galardão *m*; **2** cerimónia de conferir o grau de uma Ordem.

accommodate *vt* *(provide room for)* acomodar, alojar; **2** adaptar-se a *(change)*; **3** *(oblige)* conciliar, comprazer a.

accommodating *adj (person, obliging)* prestável *m,f* (**to** para, com); pronto,-a a ajudar.

accommodation *(UK)*, **accommodations** *(US) n (lodging)* alojamento *m*, acomodação *f*, lugar *m*; **2** *(gen)* adaptação; **3** **~s** *npl (work premises)* instalações *fpl*.

accompaniment *n (MUS)* acompanhamento.

accompany *(pt, pp* -**ied)** *vt* acompanhar; **he accompanied me** ele acompanhou-me; *(MUS) (with instrument)* **to ~ sb on sth** acompanhar alguém em algo.

accomplice *n* cúmplice *m,f*.

accomplish *vt (attain)* alcançar; **2** realizar, levar a cabo; **3** *(manage)* conseguir.

accomplished *adj* talentoso,-a; prendado,-a; **2** *(task)* acabado,-a, completo,-a; perfeito; **an ~ fact** facto *(BR:* fato*)* consumado.

accomplishment *n* acabamento, conclusão com sucesso; realização *f*; **~s** *(skills)* habilidades *fpl; (social graces)* dotes *mpl*.

accord acordo; ♦ *vt* conceder; ♦ *vi* concordar; **of his own ~** por sua iniciativa; por sua livre vontade; ♦ **in accordance with** de acordo com.

according to *prep* segundo; conforme.

accordingly *adv* por conseguinte, consequentemente.

accordion *n (MUS)* acordeão *m*.

accost *vt* dirigir-se a, aproximar-se de; **2** meter conversa com (alguém); abordar *(subject)*.

account *n (COMM)* conta *f*; **current ~** *(EP)* conta à ordem; *(BR)* conta corrente; **deposit ~** conta a prazo; **savings ~** conta poupança; **to settle an ~** liquidar uma conta; **2** *(bill)* fa(c)tura *f*; **3** *(description)* relato *m*; **she gave me a detailed ~** ela deu-me um relato detalhado; **4** importância *f*, valor *m*; **to be of no ~** não ter importância; **on no ~** de modo algum; **5 on ~ of** *(because of)* por causa de, devido a; ♦ **to take sth into ~** levar algo em consideração, ter algo em conta; **to ~ for** *(explain)* justificar, explicar; **2** *(represent)* representar *(proportion)*; ♦ **accounts** *npl (department)* contabilidade *f sg*; **by all ~** *adv* segundo dizem.

accountability *n (gen)* responsabilidade *f*.

accountable *adj inv* responsável; **to be held ~ for sth** ser responsabilizado,-a por algo.

accountancy *n* contabilidade *f*.

accountant *n* contabilista *m,f* contador,-ora; revisor oficial de contas, ROC; **chartered ~** *(UK)* perito,-a contabilista registado,-a; membro da associação, da ordem de contabilistas.

accumulate *vt* acumular, amontoar; ♦ *vi* acumular-se.

accumulation *n* acumulação *f*.

accuracy *n* exatidão *f*, precisão *f*.

accurate *adj* exa(c)to,-a; corre(c)to,-a; preciso,-a.

accusation *n* acusação *f*.

accuse *vt* acusar; culpar.

accused *n* culpado,-a.

accustom *vt* acostumar.

accustomed *adj* acostumado,-a (**to** a).

ace *n (playing card)* ás *m*; **~ of** *(hearts, clubs, diamonds, spades)* ás de (copas, paus, oiros, espadas); **2**

(expert) ás; **he is an ~ at tennis** ele é um ás no ténis; **3** *(fig)* trunfo.

acerbic *adj* acerbo,-a.

acerbity *n* sabor amargor; **2** *(attitude, voice)* aspereza *f*, azedume *m*

acetate *n* acetato *m*.

acetone *n (nail varnish remover)* acetone *f*.

ache *n* dor *f*; ♦ *vi* doer; **I am aching all over** todo o corpo me dói.

achieve *vt* alcançar; **2** realizar; **3** obter.

achievement *n* realização *f*; sucesso *m*; façanha *f*.

Achilles' heel *n* calcanhar *m* de Aquiles.

acid *n (CHEM)* ácido *m*; **2** *(coll) (drug)* LSD, ácido; ♦ *adj* ácido,-a; **~ rain** chuva *f* ácida; **2** *(fig) (remark, voice)* áspero,-a; **3** *(bitter)* amargo,-a.

acidic *adj (CHEM)* acidífero,-a.

acidity *n* acidez *f*; **2** *(fig) (manner)* aspereza *f*.

acknowledge *vt* reconhecer; **~ sb as sth** reconhecer alguém como algo; **2** acusar a recepção *(BR:* o recebimento*)* de *(letter, message)*; **3** admitir, aceitar; **I ~ defeat** eu aceito a derrota, dou-me por vencido.

acknowledgement *n* reconhecimento, notificação *f* de recebimento.

acme *n:* **the ~ of** o auge de.

acne *n* acne *f*.

acorn *n (BOT)* bolota *f*.

acoustic *adj* acústico,-a; **~s** *npl (of room)* acústica *fsg*.

acquaint *vt* tornar conhecido; informar; **to ~ sb with sth** avisar alguém de alguma coisa; pôr alguém ao corrente de alguma coisa; ♦ *vr* **to ~ o.s. with sth** familiarizar-se com algo; **to be ~ed with** conhecer; saber.

acquaintance *n* conhecimento *m*; conhecido,-a; **an ~ of mine** um conhecido meu, uma pessoa do meu conhecimento.

acquiesce *vi:* **to ~ in** aquiescer em, concordar com.

acquiescence *n* aquiescência *f*.

acquire *vt (gen)* adquirir; **2** *(details)* obter; **~d taste** gosto adquirido/adotado.

acquisition *n (of property)* aquisição *f*; **2** *(of documents)* obtenção.

acquisitive *adj* ávido,-a; *(pej)* consumista *m,f*.

acquit (-**tt**-) *vt (JUR)* absolver; **to ~ o.s. well** desempenhar-se bem.

acquittal *n (JUR)* absolvição *f*.

acre *n* acre *m* (= 40.47 ares = 4046,9 m²) terreno *m* de cultura.

acreage *n* area medida em acres.

acrimonious *adj* mordaz; acrimonioso.

acrimony *n* azedume *m*.

acrobat *n* acrobata *m,f*.

acrobatics *npl* acrobacia *fsg*.

across *prep* no outro lado de; através de; **~ from** em frente de; ♦ *adv* transversalmente; **2** de um lado ao outro; **3 the lake is thirty metres ~** o lago tem trinta metros de largura; **to swim ~** atravessar a nado; **to run ~ the street** atravessou a rua a correr, *(BR:* correndo*)*; **4 to look ~ at sb** olhar em direção a; **5** *(in crosswords)* cruzado,-a.

act *n* a(c)to; **2** *(in music hall etc)* número *m*; **3** *(law)* lei *f*; ♦ *vi* funcionar; **2** agir; **3** *(take steps)* tomar medidas; **4** *(THEAT)* representar; **to ~ a part** desempenhar um papel; **5** *(pretend)* fingir; ◆ *vt* representar; **to ~ as a fool** fazer-se de bobo; **to ~ on/upon** agir conforme conselho; ◆ **to ~ out** *vt (feeling)* expressar; **2** representar; ◆ **to ~ up** *vi (fam) (machine)* emperrar; *(person)* comportar-se mal; IDIOM **act of God** *n* catástrofe *f* natural.

acting *n (in play, filme)* atuação *f*; **to love ~** gostar de atuar; ◆ *adj (interim)* interino,-a; **~ director** director interino.

action *n* a(c)ção *f*; **2** *(MIL)* batalha *f*, combate *m*; **3** *(JUR)* processo *m*; ação *f* judicial; **to bring an ~ against** *(JUR)* intentar uma ação contra; **take ~** agir proceder; **it's time for ~** é a altura de agir; **forward and backward ~** movimento de vaivém; **out of ~** *(machine)* desativado,-a, avariado,-a.

activate *vt* a(c)tivar.

active *adj* a(c)tivo,-a enérgico,-a; em a(c)tividade; **2** *(JUR) (law)* em vigor; **be on ~ service** estar no a(c)tivo.

actively *adv* a(c)tivamente.

activist *n* a(c)tivista *m,f*.

activity *n* a(c)tividade *f*.

actor *n* a(c)tor *m*.

actress *n* a(c)triz *f*.

actual *adj* real, existente; exato,-a; **the ~ name for that is …** o nome disso propriamente dito é …

actuality *n* realidade *f*; **in ~** na realidade.

actually *adv* realmente, de facto; *(BR)* fato; **in ~ fact** na verdade, de facto.

> Não confundir com as palavras portuguesas: **actual**, **actualidade**, **actualmente**, as quais têm significados diferentes em inglês.

actuary *(pl: -ies)* *n (FIN)* atuário *m*.

actuate *vt* a(c)cionar (machine, alarme); **2** *(motivate)* estimular, motivar.

acuity *n (sharpness in vision, thought)* acuidade *f*.

acumen *n* perspicácia *f*; **business ~** tino *m* para os negócios.

acupuncture *n* acupuntura *f*.

acute *adj (sharp, intelligent)* perspicaz; engenhoso,-a; **~ eyesight** vista *f* apurada; **2** *(severe, intense)* agudo,-a, fino,-a; **~ pain** dor aguda; **3** *(MED) ~ treatment** cuidados *mpl* intensivos; **4 ~ crisis** situação *f* grave; **5 ~ pleasure** prazer *m* intenso; **6** *(LING) ~ accent* acento *m* agudo; **7** *(MATH) (angle)* agudo,-a.

acutely *adv* intensamente; extremamente.

acuteness n agudeza *f*; perspicácia *f*.

ad *n (abbr for* **advertisement**) anúncio.

AD *adv (abbr for* **Anno Domini**) d.C.

adage *n* adágio *m*.

Adam *npr* Adão; **~'s apple** *n* maçã-de-Adão *f*; *(BR)* pomo-de-Adão *m*.

adamant *adj (determined)* inflexível.

adapt *vt* adaptar; acomodar; ◆ *vi* adaptar-se (**to** a).

adaptable *adj* ajustável; adaptável.

adaptation *n* adaptação *f*, ajuste *m*; ◆ *adj* adaptado,-a, próprio,-a.

adapter *n (ELECT)* adaptador *m*.

add *vt* juntar, acrescentar; **you have to ~ more water to the soup** você tem de juntar/acrescentar água à sopa; **to ~ in (sth)** incluir (algo); **to ~ to (sth)** acentuar *(irritation)*; **2** acrescentar a *(trouble, work)*; **~ together/up** *(MATH) (total)* somar, adicionar; ◆ **to ~ up** *vi (make sense)* fazer sentido; **2** acumular; IDIOM **to ~ insult to injury** fazer o mal e a caramunha; ainda por cima.

added *adj* suplementar; **~ to which …** a que se junta…

addendum *(pl: -da)* *(additional section/entry)* adendo *m*.

adder *n (ZOOL)* víbora *f*.

addict *n (drug user)* toxicómano; dependente *m,f*; **2** *(health, filmes)* fanático,-a; *(coffee, tea)* viciado,-a *(no café/chá)*.

addicted *adj*: **to be (become) ~ to** ser viciado,-a; ser dependente (**to** de).

addiction *n (to alcohol, drugs)* dependência *f*; *(to music, sweets)* paixão *f*; *(smoking)* vício.

adding machine *n* máquina de somar.

Addis Ababa *npr* Adis Abeba; **in ~** em Adis Abeba.

addition *n* adição *f*; soma; **in ~** além disso; **in ~ to** além de.

additional *adj* adicional.

additionally *adv* adicionalmente; **2** *(moreover)* além do mais.

additive *n* aditivo *m*; **food ~** aditivo alimentar; ◆ *adj (drugs, etc)* que cria dependência; habituação *f*.

addled *adj (confused)* confuso,-a.

address *n (residence)* ende-reços, morada, direção *f*; **~ book** *n* agenda *f* de endereços, livrinho *m* de moradas; **2** *(speech)* discurso; ◆ *vt* endereçar; dirigir-se a, dirigir a palavra a.

addressee *n* destinatário,-a.

adenoidal *adj (voice)* nasalado, fanhoso.

adenoids *npl* adenóides *fpl*.

adept *n* especialista *m,f* (**at/in** em); ◆ *adj* hábil.

adequacy *n* adequação *f*; suficiência *f*.

adequate *adj (competent)* adequado,-a; **2** suficiente.

adhere *vi*: **to ~ to sth** aderir a *(algo)*; **2** *(fig)* manter-se fiel a; apegar-se a; *(fig)* perfilhar.

adherence *n*: **~ to sth** *(surface)* aderência *f* a; *(party, belief)* adesão *f* a *(algo)*; **2** *(rules, decision)* respeito *m*, observância *f*.

adherent *n (of party)* membro, partidário,-a; **2** *(of doctrine)* aderente.

adhesion *n (sticking/attaching to)* aderência *f*; *(joining)* adesão a *(party, ideology)*.

adhesive *n* adesivo *m*, cola *f*; ◆ *adj (sticky)* adesivo,-a, pegajoso,-a; **self-~** autocolante *m*; **~ tape** *n* fita *f* adesiva, fita-cola *f*.

ad hoc *adj* ad hoc; improvisado,-a.

adjacent *adj*: **~ to** adjacente a, contíguo a.

adjectival *adj* adjectival, adjetival.

adjective *n (gram)* adje(c)tivo *m*.

adjoin *vt* unir.

adjoining *adj* adjacente, contíguo,-a; *(next door)* vizinho,-a; **~ house** a casa vizinha; ◆ *prep* ao lado (de).

adjourn *vt (postpone, defer)* adiar (**for** para); ◆ *vi (temporary close/stop)* suspender; **2** *(of a court)* encerrar a sessão; **3** *(fam) (to move to another place)* ir para; **let us ~ to the drawing-room** vamos para a sala.

adjudge *vt (usually in the passive)* declarar; **he was ~ed the champion** ele foi declarado o campião; **2** *(JUR)* julgar, sentenciar; declarar *(decree).*

adjudicate *vt/vi* adjudicar; **~ a claim** arbitrar uma pretensão; escolher (**between** entre).

adjudication *n (of contest)* julgamento; **2** *(JUR)* decisão *f* judicial; **under ~** sob apreciação.

adjudicator *n* juiz *m*, árbitro.

adjust *vt* ajustar *(amount)*; **2** *(TECH)* arranjar; regular *(machine)*; ♦ *vi* adaptar-se (**to** a).

adjustable *adj* ajustável.

adjustment *n (TECH) (of machine, fitment)* re(c)tificação *f*; **2** adaptação *f*; ajuste.

adjutant *n (MIL)* adjunto *m.*

ad-lib *n (abbr for **ad libitum**)* improvisação *f*; ♦ *adj* improvisado,-a; ♦ *vt/vi* improvisar.

administer *vt* dirigir; gerir; **2** *(medicine, justice, punishment)* aplicar.

administration *n* administração *f*; *(JUR) (of an estate)* administração judicial; **~ of an oath** *(in court)* prestação *f* de juramento. **administrative** *adj* administrativo,-a.

administrator *n* administrador,-ora; *(of hospital)* director,-ora, administrator,-ora.

admirable *adj* admirável.

admiral *n (NAUT)* almirante *m*; **Rear A~** *n* contra-almirante; **red ~** *(butterfly)* vanessa.

admiralty *n* Ministério *m* da Marinha, Almirantado; **First Lord of the ~** *(UK)* Ministro da Marinha.

admiration *n* admiração *f.*

admire *vt* admirar alguém, algo (**for** por); **2** apreciar **I ~ the peaceful countryside** eu aprecio muito a tranquilidade do campo.

admired *adj*: **to be ~** ser admirado,-a.

admirer *n* admirador,-ora; **2** *(suitor)* pretendente; **3** *(enthusiast)* fã *m,f.*

admission *n (entry)* entrada; admissão *f*; **to gain ~ to** ser admitido em; **2** confissão *f*; **~ of guilt** admissão de culpa; **3** *(school, univ)* matrícula, inscrição *f.*

admit (-tt-) *vt* admitir; **to ~ defeat** *(fig)* dar-se por vencido,-a; **to be ~ted into hospital** ser hospitalizado,-a; **2** *(allow)* permitir; **3** reconhecer, aceitar; **I ~ I was wrong** reconheço que estava enganado; **4 to ~ to** confessar.

admittance *n* entrada; '**no ~**' 'proibida a entrada'.

admittedly *adv* evidentemente, reconhecidamente.

admonish *vt* repreender; avisar.

admonishment *n (reprimand)* repreensão f; **2** advertência.

admonitory *adj (comment)* reprovador; de censura.

ad nauseam *adv (discuss, repeat)* exaustivamente, até nunca mais acabar, até enjoar.

ado *n*: **without (any) more ~** sem mais cerimónias *(BR: -mô-)*; **much ~ about nothing** muito barulho por nada.

adolescence *n* adolescência.

adolescent *n adj* adolescente *m,f.*

adopt *vt (a child)* ado(p)tar, perfilhar; *(attitude, idea, etc)* adotar, escolher; **to ~ some measures** adotar medidas.

adopted *adj* ado(p)tivo.

adoption *n* ado(p)ção *f.*

adorable *adj* adorável.

adore *vt* adorar; **I ~ him** eu adoro-o, *(BR)* eu o adoro.

adorn *vt* adornar, enfeitar *(with, com)*; **~ment** *n* adorno, enfeite *m.*

adrenalin *n* adrenalina *f.*

adrenals *npl (MED)* (glândulas) suprarenais.

Adriatic *npr*: **the ~ (Sea)** o (Mar) Adriático.

adrift *adv* à deriva; **to come ~** desprender-se.

adroit *adj* destro,-a, hábil *m,f.*

adroitness *n* habilidade *f*, destreza *f.*

adspeak *n* linguagem *f* publicitária.

adulation *n* adulação *f.*

adulator *n, adj* adulador,-ora; bajulador,-ora.

adult *n* adulto; ♦ *adj* adulto,-a; *(film, DVD = porn)* para adultos; **~ literacy classes** curso *m* aulas *fpl* de alfabetização.

adulterate *vt* adulterar.

adulterer *n* adúltero.

adulteress *n* adúltera.

adultery *n* adultério *m.*

advance *n (MIL)* avanço *m*, avançada *f* (**on** sobre); **~ guard** *n (MIL)* vanguarda; **2** *(of money)* adiantamento, empréstimo; **3** progresso *m*, passo *m* em frente; **4** *(prior)* **~ warning** aviso *m* prévio; ♦ **in ~** *adv* antecipadamente; de antemão, adiantadamente; **three months in ~** três meses de antecedência; **in ~ of** antes de; ♦ **advances** *npl (sexual overtures)* provocação *f*; assédio *m*; **he made some ~ to her** ele tentou captá-la, assediá-la; **2** *(business)* propostas *fpl*; ♦ *vt (ger)* avançar; **2** desenvolver, promover; **3** adiantar, emprestar; ♦ *vi (move forward)* avançar (**on** sobre, **towards** em direção a); **2** *(fazer progresso)* progredir.

advanced *adj* avançado,-a; **2** *(EDUC)* adiantado,-a; **3 ~ in years** entrado,-a em anos; **~ notice** *n* pré-aviso *m.*

advancement *n* avanço, progresso *m*; **2** *(of person in career)* promoção *f*; *(social rung)* ascenção *f.*

advantage *n* vantagem *f*; **2** *(tennis)* a favor de; **to take ~ of** *(positive use)* aproveitar-se de; *(negative use)* abusar de; tirar proveito de.

advantageous *adj* vantajoso,-a; favorável.

advent *n* vinda, chegada; **A~** *(REL)* Advento.

adventure *n* aventura; *(film, book)* de aventuras; **~ playground** *n* área de jogos e de lazer para crianças.

adventurer *n* aventureiro *m*; aventureira *f*; *(also: pej)* namoradeira.

adventurous *adj* venturoso,-a; **2** *(daring)* audaz, temerário,-a; **3** *(with ideas)*, ousado,-a, inovador,-ora.

adverb *n (gram)* advérbio *m.*

adversary *n* adversário,-a.

adverse *adj* adverso, contrário (**to** a).

adversity *n* adversidade *f*; desgraça.

advert *n (abbr for **advertisement**)* anúncio *m.*

advertise *vi* anunciar, fazer propaganda; **2** *(in newspaper etc)* publicar um anúncio; ♦ *vt* anunciar.

advertisement n anúncio; (in small ads) anúncio classificado.

advertiser n anunciante m,f.

advertising n publicidade f, anúncios mpl.

advice n conselhos mpl; **a piece/word of** ~ conselho; aviso; **to take legal** ~ consultar um advogado; **2** (COMM) parecer m, opinião f.

advisable adj aconselhável, conveniente.

advise vt aconselhar; informar; **you are well ~d to study harder** é/seria melhor você estudar muito mais.

adviser n (official capacity) conselheiro; consultor m.

advisory adj consultivo,-a.

advocate n advogado,-a; ♦ vt defender; advogar.

aegis n **under the** ~ **of** sob a égide de.

aeolian adj (wind) eólico,-a, eóleo,-a.

aerial n antena; ♦ adj aéreo,-a.

aerobics n aeróbica f ginástica.

aerodrome n aeródromo m.

aerodynamic adj aerodinâmico,-a.

aerodynamics npl (science) aerodinâmica f.

aeronautics n aeronáutica sg.

aeroplane n avião m.

aerosol n aerossol m.

aesthetic (UK) **esthetic** (US) adj estético.

aesthetics estética sg.

afar adv: **from** ~ de longe, à distância.

affable adj afável, simpático,-a.

affaire n negócio m; **2** (ceremony) acontecimento m; **3** romance m; **love** ~ aventura f amorosa, namoro m; **he is having an** ~ **with a married woman** (pej) ele anda metido com uma mulher casada; **4** (subject, manner) assunto m; **state of** ~s estado m de coisas.

affect vt afe(c)tar, tocar, comover.

affectation n afe(c)tação f; fingimento m.

affected adj afe(c)tado,-a.

affection n afe(c)to; afeição f.

affectionate adj (loving) meigo,-a carinhoso,-a afe(c)tuoso,-a.

affectionately adv afe(c)tuosamente.

affidavit m declaração escrita sob juramento; depoimento m.

affiliate n (company) filial f, sucursal f; **2** (person) filiado,-a, consórcio,-a; ♦ vt/vi filiar; perfilhar; **2** (combine) filiar-se (**with sth** a algo).

affiliation n afiliação f.

affinity n afinidade f.

affirm vt/vi (assert) afirmar; **2** (assure) garantir, assegurar; **3** (JUR) ratificar, homologar.

affirmation n afirmação f (**of sth** de algo); declaração f; homologação.

affirmative adj afirmativo,-a.

affix vt afixar, colar (stamp); **do not** ~ **notices on this wall** proibido afixar avisos na parede.

afflict vt afligir; **to be** ~**ed with** sofrer de.

affliction n (illness) doença f; **2** (anxiety) ânsia f, angústia f.

> Não confundir com a palavra portuguesa 'aflição' a qual significa, em geral: **distress; anxiety.**

affluence n riqueza, opulência.

affluent adj rico,-a, opulento,-a.

afford vt fornecer, dar; **can we** ~ **it?** temos dinheiro para comprar isso?; **we can't** ~ **wasting time** não podemos perder tempo.

affordable adj (price) razoável; (propriety, product) a preço acessível.

afforestation n florestação f; (BR) florestamento m.

affray n (UK) desordem f, tumulto m; rixa f, briga f.

affront n afronta f, ofensa f (insult), insulto m.

affronted adj insultado,-a ofendido,-a.

Afghan npr adj afegão m, afegã f.

Afghanistan npr Afganistão m; **in** ~ no Afganistão.

afield adv longe; **further** ~ mais longe; **to go far** ~ afastar-se para muito longe.

aflame adj, adv em fogo; **to be** ~ (cheeks) estar em brasa; **to be** ~ **with desire** arder em desejo.

afloat adv (floating) à tona de água, a boiar; **2** (in circulation) **there is a story** ~ anda por aí uma história; **to keep (o.s.)** ~ (without debts) manter-se sem dívidas; (FIN) **keep the economy** ~ manter a economia equilibrada.

afoot adv a pé; **there's something** ~ algo está a pé/acontecendo; **a rumour is** ~ corre um boato; **to set (sth)** ~ pôr (algo) em movimento.

aforesaid adj supracitado,-a, referido,-a.

afraid adj (creature, fright) receoso, assustado; **to be** ~ **of/to** ter medo de, recear; **2** (apology) **I am** ~ **I can't go** lamento não poder ir.

afresh adv de novo, outra vez.

Africa npr África f.

African npr adj africano,-a.

Afrikaner n, adj africânder.

Afro-American n adj afro-americano,-a.

aft adv (NAUT) à ré; à popa.

after prep depois de; atrás de; após; **day** ~ **day** dia após dia; **the day** ~ **tomorrow** depois de amanhã; **2** (wooing) atrás de; **he is** ~ **you** ele anda atrás de ti; **3** (in pursuit of) **the police are** ~ **him** a polícia anda á procura dele; **4** (repeated action/time) após; **month** ~ **month** mês após mês; **5** (in spite of) ~ **all** apesar de tudo; afinal; afinal de contas; ~ **all we did!** depois de tudo que fizemos!; ~ **all, it was a lie** afinal, era uma mentira; **6** segundo, conforme; ~ **the fashion of...** conforme a moda de; **7** (similarity) **she takes** ~ **her grandmother** ela parece-se com a avó; **what are you** ~? o que pretende você?; **she looks** ~ **the house** ela toma conta da casa; **to enquire** ~ **sb** perguntar por alguém (saúde); ♦ adv depois, mais tarde, em seguida, posteriormente; **soon** ~ pouco depois; (following) **the month** ~ o mês seguinte; ♦ conj depois que, de; **2** (once) since; ♦ ~ **you!** (you go first) faz favor!, passe primeiro!

afterbirth n (MED, ANAT) placenta f; secundinas fpl.

aftercare n (MED) acompanhamento m médico, assistência f pós-operatória f.

after-effect (MED) sequela f; (fig) repercussão f; ~**-effects** npl efeitos secundário mpl, consequências fpl.

afterlife n (US) vida depois da morte.

aftermath n rescaldo m; consequências fpl.

afternoon n tarde f; **in the** ~ à tarde; **yesterday** ~ ontem à tarde; **late** ~ à tardinha; ~ **tea** n chá das cinco, lanche m; **good** ~! boa tarde!

afterpains *npl* (US) dores uterinas.

afters *npl* (UK) sobremesa; **what have we for ~?** *(fam)* o que temos para a sobremesa?

after-sales service *n* serviço pós-venda.

aftershave *n* (lotion) pós-barba; aftershave.

aftersun lotion *n* loção hidratante após-sol.

aftertaste *n* ressaibo, mau sabor.

afterthought *n* reflexão *f.*

afterwards *adv* depois, mais tarde; **immediately ~** logo depois.

again *adv* outra vez, de novo; **to do sth ~** voltar a fazer algo; **~ and ~** repetidas vezes; **now and ~** de vez em quando.

against *prep* contra, em oposição a; **2 as ~** em vez de; comparado,-a com; **3** em, sobre; **4** *(close to)* junto de/a; **~ the wall** encostado à parede; **~ a red background** sobre um fundo vermelho; **to run ~ sb** encontrar alguém por acaso.

agape *adj adv* de boca aberta, boquiaberto,-a, estupefato,-a; **with eyes ~** de olhos arregalados.

age *n* (of person, animal) idade *f;* **to be under ~** ser menor de idade; **to come of ~** atingir a maioridade; **I am twice your ~** tenho o dobro da sua idade; **you don't look your ~** você não aparenta a sua idade; **~ group** *n* faixa *f* etária; **to be in the same ~ group** ter a mesma idade; **~ limit** *n* idade *f* mínima; **2** *(wine, cheese)* tempo *m;* **this cheese improves with ~** este queijo melhora com a idade; **3** *(period, era)* era *f,* época *f,* período *m;* **the Edwardian ~** a época Eduardiana (de: Eduardo VII da Grã-Bretanha); ♦ **ages** *mpl* tempos, séculos, idade; **the Middle A~** *npl* a Idade das Trevas; **I haven't seen you for ~** há tempos que não te vejo; **through the ~** através dos séculos; **~ and ~** muito tempo; **in past ~** *n* tempos *mpl* idos; **to last for ~** durar séculos; ♦ *vt/vi* envelhecer.

aged *adj* velho-a, envelhecido,-a; *(wine, cheese)* envelhecido; **middle-~ man** *n* homem *m* de meia-idade; **~ three** com três anos de idade; **the ~** *n* (elderly) os idosos.

ageing *n* envelhecimento; ♦ *adj (person)* envelhecido,-a, idoso,-a; **~ population** população *f* idosa.

ageism, agism *n* idadismo *m;* discriminação *f* etária.

ageless *adj* eterno,-a; sempre jovem; intemporal.

agency *n* agência; **2** *(government)* órgão *m;* **3 through/by the ~ of** por meio de.

agenda *n* ordem *f* do dia; *(fig)* (list of priorities) programa *m,* lista de assuntos.

agent *n* agente *m,f;* representante *m,f;* **secret ~** *(spy)* agente secreto; **3** *(chemical substance)* reagente *m,* agente *m.*

age-old *adj (very old)* antigo,-a; secular, ancestral.

age range *(also: ~ **bracket**);* **children in the 11–16 ~** as crianças na casa dos 11–16 anos.

agglomerate *vt/vi* aglomerar.

agglomeration *n* aglomeração *f.*

aggravate *vt* agravar; irritar.

aggravation *n* irritação *f.*

aggregate *n* conjunto *m;* agregado *m.*

aggression *n* agressão *f.*

aggressive *adj* agressivo,-a.

aggressor *n* agressor,-ora *m,f.*

aggrieved *adj* ofendido,-a; *(hurt, upset)* magoado,-a.

aggro *n* (UK: coll) violência; *(in a gang)* arruaça *f.*

aghast *adj* horrorizado,-a, espantado,-a **(at** por).

agile *adj* ágil.

agility *n* agilidade *f.*

aging *(Vd:* **ageing***).*

agitate *vt* agitar; perturbar.

agitation *n* agitação *f.*

agitator *n* agitador,-ora.

aglow *adj, adv* radiante; resplendecente **(with,** com).

AGM *n* (abbr for **annual general meeting**) *(UK)* assembleia *f* geral annual.

agnostic *n, adj* agnóstico,-a.

ago *adv:* **one month ~** há um mês; **not long ~** há pouco tempo; **how long ~?** há quanto tempo?

agog *adj (eager)* ansioso,-a; impaciente; **2** com curiosidade; **to be all ~** arder de impaciência.

agonizar *vi* agonizar; **to ~ over/about sth** *vt* atormentar-se *(com algo).*

agonizing *adj* agudo,-a; angustiante.

agony *n* agonia *f;* dor *f;* **2** *(sorrow)* angústia *f;* **to be in ~** sofrer dores terríveis.

agoraphobia *n* (PSYCH, MED) agorafobia *f.*

agoraphobic *adj* agorafóbico,-a.

agree *vt* combinar, ajustar; ♦ *vi* combinar; **to ~ (with)** concordar (com), estar de acordo (com); **to ~ to do** aceitar fazer; **to ~ to** consentir em; **to ~ that** admitir; **the climate does not ~ with me** não me dou bem com o clima.

agreeable *adj* agradável; simpático,-a; disposto,-a.

agreed *adj* combinado; **as ~d** como combinado.

agreement *n* acordo *m;* *(COMM)* contra(c)to *m;* **in ~** de acordo.

agricultural *adj* agrícola.

agriculture *n* agricultura *f.*

agronomist *n* agrónomo,-a.

aground *adv:* **to run ~** *(NAUT)* encalhar.

ah *exc* ah! *(expressing pain, disappointment, pleasure);* **~ well!** ah bem!

aha *exc (triumph at finding sth)* ah-ah!

ahead *adj adv (in advance)* adiantado,-a, adiante, à frente; **to get ~** ir à frente; **2 ~ of** *(more advanced)* à frente de; adiantado,-a; **he is ~ of his studies** ele está adiantado nos seus estudos; **3** *(in time)* antes, próximo,-a, futuro,-a; **in the months ~** nos meses futuros; antes de; **4** *(in directions)* **right/straight ~** mesmo em frente; **to be/go ~** *(in competition)* passar à frente dos outros, ultrapassar; **to go ~ with (sth)** prosseguir (com algo); ir avante (com algo); **to look ~** olhar para o futuro.

ahoy! *exc (NAUT)* **~ there!** *(calling)* ó do barco! **land/ship ~** terra/barco à vista!

aid *n* ajuda, auxílio; **first ~** pronto-socorro *m;* ♦ *vt* ajudar, auxiliar; **in ~ of** em benefício de; **to ~ and abet** *(JUR)* ser cúmplice de.

aide *n* assistente *m,f;* **~-de-camp** *n (pl: aides-de-camp)* *(MIL)* ajudante-de-campo.

aider *n* ajudante *m,f;* auxiliar *m,f.*

aiding and abetting *(JUR)* cumplicidade *f* num crime; instigação *f* a um crime.

AIDS/Aids n Sida f; (BR) Aids.

ail vt/vi afligir, doer; **what ~s you?** que te dói?, que se passa contigo?

ailing (fig): **to be ~** (business) andar mal, fraco,-a; (person) indisposto,-a; sentir-se mal.

ailment n doença, achaque m.

aim n (in firing) mira f, pontaria f, alvo m; **to take ~ at** apontar (para) fazer pontaria; **miss one's ~** falhar o alvo; **2** (objective) objetivo, fim; meta; ♦ vt visar algo, apontar (**at**, a; **for**, para); (stone) atirar (**at**, a); **2** (intention) aspirar (**at**, **for**, a); **~ to do** pretender fazer; **3 to ~ at one's efforts at** envidar os seus esforços para; ♦ vi **to ~ high** almejar.

aimless adj sem propósito, destino.

aimlessly adv ao acaso; (person) sem rumo, ao Deus-dará.

air n ar m; **in the open ~** ao ar livre; **by ~** de avião; **~ freshener** n purificador de ar; **~ hostess** n hospedeira; (BR) aeromoça; **hot ~** n (coll) conversa f; **2 to be on the ~** (RADIO, TV programme) estar no ar; **3** (appearance) aparência f, aspecto m; **to clear the ~** (be rid of tension) desanuviar a atmosfera; (coll): pôr tudo em pratos limpos; **vanish into thin ~** desaparecer de repente; **plans are in the ~** os planos estão a ser decididos; **to walk on ~** sentir-se elevado/exultante; ♦ adj aéreo,-a; ♦ vt (ventilate) arejar; **2** (express) exprimir, export (view, grievance); (broadcast) difundir, anunciar.

airborne adj (por avião) aerotransportado; **2** (bird, seed) trazido pelo vento.

air carrier n porta-aviões m inv.

air conditioning n ar m condicionado.

aircraft/plane n avião m.

air cushion almofada f pneumática.

airdrop (delivery) entrega de mercadoria por paraquedas.

Air Force n Força Aérea, Aviação f.

airgun n espingarda de pressão/de ar; (BR) pistola de ar comprimido.

airily adv (light-hearted) despreocupadamente.

airing n (of linen) secagem f; **2** (ventilation) arejamento m; **~ cupboard** n armário que contém a caldeira e onde se areja a roupa depois de engomada.

airless adj (weather, room) abafado,-a.

airlift n ponte aérea; ♦ vt **to ~ sb** evacuar (alguém) através da ponte aérea.

airline n linha aérea.

airmail n: **by ~** or avião, via aérea.

airpocket poço de ar.

airport n aeroporto.

air pressure n pressão f atmosférica.

air pump n bomba f de ar.

air raid n ataque m aéreo.

airs npl: **to give o.s. ~/put on ~** (pej) dar-se ares mpl de pessoa importante.

air-shaft respiradoiro, respiradouro.

airsick adj enjoado,-a; **to be ~** enjoar-se.

airstrip n pista f de aterragem.

airtight adj hermético.

air-traffic control n controlo m de tráfego aéreo.

air tube n câmara f de ar.

airwaves npl ondas fpl de rádio.

airways n rota/companhia aérea; **2 the ~** (ANAT) vias fpl respiratórias.

airy adj (place) arejado,-a, ventilado,-a; **2** (person) indiferente, aéreo,-a; **3** (not heavy) ligeiro,-a.

aisle n (of church) nave f; (of theatre) corredor m; coxia.

ajar adj entreaberto,-a.

a.k.a. (abbr for also known as) também conhecido como.

akimbo adv **with arms ~** de mãos na ilharga/na cinta.

akin adj (similar) **~ to** parecido,-a com, semelhante a.

alabaster n alabastro m.

alacrity n alacridade f; entusiasmo m.

alarm n alarme m; **~ clock** n despertador m; **2** inquietação f; ♦ vt alarmar, inquietar.

alarming adj alarmante.

alas adv infelizmente; ♦ exc (commiserating) ai de mim!; (re: another person) coitado!

Albania npr Albânia; **in ~** na Albânia.

Albanian n adj albanês,-esa; (LING) albanês.

albatross n (ZOOL) albatroz m.

albeit conj embora, não obstante.

albino n adj albino,-a.

Albion npr (arc) nome poético da Inglaterra.

album n álbum m; LP m.

alcohol n álcool m; **the ~ content** o teor de álcool.

alcoholic n adj alcoólico; alcoólatra m,f.

alcoholism n alcoolismo m.

alcove n alcova f, recanto m na parede.

alder m amieiro m.

alderman (pl: -men) vereador da câmara municipal.

ale n cerveja f.

alert n alerta m, alarme m; **to be on the ~** estar de sobreaviso/alerta; ♦ adj atento,-a; esperto,-a; ♦ vt alerter.

A-level (abbr for advanced level) (UK: school) nível, exame do 12º de escolaridade.

alfalfa n (BOT, CULIN) luzerna f; alfalfa f.

alfresco adj, adv ao ar livre.

algebra n álgebra f.

Algeria npr Algéria; **in ~** na Argélia.

Algerian npr adj argelino,-a.

algorithm n algoritmo m.

alias n outro nome, pseudónimo (BR: -dô-); nome suposto; ♦ adv também chamado.

alias não traduz os outros significados da palavra portuguesa 'aliás'.

alibi n (JUR) álibi m; (fam) (excuse) desculpa f (EP); escusa (BR).

alien n estrangeiro,-a; **2** (from space) extraterrestre m,f; **3** (stranger) estranho,-a; ♦ adj estranho,-a, alheio,-a (**to** a).

alienate vt alienar.

alienation n alienação f.

alight adj (light, stove) aceso; **2** (house, forest) em chamas; ♦ vi (get off bus, train) appear, descer (**from** de); **2** (bird) pousar (**on** em, sobre).

align vt alinhar (**with** com).

alignment *n (car wheels, etc)* alinhamento *m*.

alike *adj* semelhante, parecido,-a; **to be** ~ ser parecido; ♦ *adv* igualmente, do mesmo modo; **they look** ~ eles são parecidos.

alimony *n (JUR)* pensão *f* alimentar, sustento *m*.

alive *adj (living)* vivo,-a; com vida; **to stay** ~ sobreviver; ~ **and kicking** bem vivo; **2** *(lively person)* animado,-a, alegre.

alkali *n* álcali *m*.

alkaline *adj* alcalino,-a.

all *adj* todo; *(pl)* todos,-as; ♦ *pron* tudo; *(pl)* todos; ♦ *adv* todo, completamente; ~ **alone** completamente só; **not at** ~ de modo algum; **nothing at** ~ absolutamente nada; ~ **along** sempre; ~ **the time** todo o tempo; **after** ~ afinal de contas; ~ **of them** todos eles; **not as hard as** ~ **that** não tão difícil como isso; **in** ~ **comes to £20** *(total)* ao todo vem a dar vinte libras; **2** *(resuming)* **in** ~ **it was a great success** ao todo foi um grande sucesso; ~ **in** *(price)* tudo incluído; **on** ~ **fours** de gatas; **the best of** ~ o melhor de todos; ~ **the same** mesmo assim; **it's** ~ **the same to me** tanto se me dá; **and** ~ **that** e tudo isso, et cetera; ♦ *adv* **for** ~ **that** apesar disso; ~ **but** *(nothing but)* quase, todosmenos; **2** *(with negative)* **do you mind if I smoke? not at** ~ importa-se que eu fume? de modo algum; ~ **right** *adv* bem; está bem!; **she was** ~ **smiles** ela estava toda sorridente; **is that** ~? é tudo?

All-Fools' Day *(1st April)* Dia das Petas.

Allah *npr (in Islam: God)* Alá.

allay *vt* dissipar *(fears, doubts)*; acalmar; aliviar, suavizar.

all clear *m (MIL)* sinal de fim de alerta; **2** *(fig) (the go-ahead)* dar luz verde a alguém.

allegation *n (JUR)* alegação *f* (**against** contra).

allege *vt* alegar; **she is** ~**ed to be in prison** diz-se que ele está na prisão.

allegiance *n* lealdade *f* (**to** a)*; (JUR)* vassalagem *f*.

allegoric *adj* alegórico,-a.

allegory *n* alegoria.

allergic *adj* alérgico,-a (**to** a).

allergy *n* alergia.

alleviate *vt* aliviar.

alley, alleyway *n* viela *f*, beco *m*.

alliance *n (POL, MIL)* aliança.

allied *adj* aliado,-a; aparentado,-a.

alligator *n (ZOOL)* aligátor *m*, jacaré *m*.

all-important *adj* crucial.

all-in *adj* tudo incluído; **2** exausto,-a; ~**-all** ao todo; ~ **wrestling** *n* luta *f* livre.

alliteration *n* aliteração *f*.

all-night *adj* aberto toda a noite; que dura toda a noite.

allocate *vt* distribuir; **2** designar.

allocation *n* atribuição *f*; distribuição *f*; **2** *(of time)* alocação *f*.

allot *(-tt-) vt (resources, assets)* distribuir, repartir; **2** *(time)* dedicar.

allotment *n* distribuição *f*, partilha; **2** *(em leilão)* lote *m*; **3** *(urban vegetable plot)* loteamento *m*, horta *f* urbana.

all-out *adj (effort)* máximo; ♦ *adv* com todas suas forças; **2** *(speed)* a toda a velocidade.

allow *vt* permitir, deixar; **2** dar, conceder; **3** admitir; **to** ~ **that** reconhecer que; **to** ~ **sb to do** permitir a alguém fazer; **to** ~ **for** *vt* levar em conta.

allowance *n* concessão; **2** *(grant)* subsídio *m*; **family** ~ abono *m* de família; **3** *(FIN) (tax exemption)* isenção *f*; **4** *(pocket money) (per month)* mesada *f*.

alloy *n (metals)* liga *f*; ♦ *vt* ligar (**with**, com).

all right *adj (film, book, food)* assim, assim; **2 to be** ~ estar bem; **it's** ~ *adv* não há problema; de acordo, tudo bem.

all-round *(UK)*, **all round** *(US) adj* completo,-a; geral; **2** *(worker, athlete)* versátil.

all-rounder *n (person)* pessoa com jeito para tudo; ♦ *adj* polivalente.

All Saints' Day *npr* Dia de todos os Santos.

All Soul's Day *npr* Dia de Finados.

all-star *adj* de estrelas; **an** ~ **cast** um elenco cheio de estrelas.

all-terrain *adj (vehicle)* todo-o-terreno.

all-time *adj (record)* absoluto,-a, insuperável.

allude *vi* (**to** a) aludir.

alluring *adj* tentador,-ora, sedutor,-ora.

allusion *n* alusão *f*.

ally *n* aliado,-a; ♦ *vr*: **to** ~ **o.s. with** aliar-se com.

Almighty *n*: **the A~** *(God)* o Todo Poderoso; ♦ *adj* o(m)nipotente; **2** *(acontecimento)* formidável, tremendo-a; ♦ *exc* **God** ~! meu Deus!

almond *n* amêndoa; ~ **tree** *n* amendoeira *f*.

almost *adv* quase.

alms *npl* esmolas *fpl*, esmola *sg*.

aloft *adv* em cima, no alto; *(NAUT)* no alto do mastro.

alone *adj* só, sozinho; **all** ~ completamente só; ♦ *adv* só, somente; **leave me** ~ deixe-me em paz; **leave it** ~ não toque nisso; **let** ~ … sem falar em …; **too tired to eat, let** ~ **to talk** demasiado cansado para comer, quanto mais falar.

along *prep* por, ao longo de; ~ **the road** pela estrada fora; ♦ *adv*: **is he coming** ~ **with us?** ele vem co(n)nosco?; **I don't get** ~ **with them** não me dou com eles; ♦ ~ **with** junto com, em companhia de; ~**side** *prep* ao lado de; ♦ *adv (NAUT)* encostado.

aloof *adj (reserved)* afastado,-a reservado,-a; ♦ *adv*: **to stand** ~ afastar-se; isolar-se; **to remain** ~ **to sb/sth** ficar indiferente a alguém/a algo.

aloud *adv* em voz alta.

alpaca *n* alpaca

alphabet *n* alfabeto.

alphabetical *adj* alfabético,-a.

alpine *adj* alpino,-a, alpestre.

Alps *npr*: **the** ~ os Alpes.

already *adv* já.

alright *adv* = **all right**.

Alsace *npr* Alsácia; **in** ~ na Alsácia.

Alsatian *npr, adj* alsaciano,-a; **2** *(dog)* pastor alemão.

also *adv* também; **not only but** ~ não só como também.

altar *n* altar *m*.

alter *vt* alterar, modificar; ♦ *vi* alterar-se, modificar-se.

alteration *n* alteração *f*, modificação *f*.

altercation *n* altercação *f.*

alternate *adj* alternado,-a; **on ~ days** em dias alternados; ♦ *vi* alternar-se.

alternately *adv* alternadamente.

alternating *adj* alternado,-a.

alternative *n* alternativa *f;* ♦ *adj* alternativo,-a.

alternatively *adv:* **~ one could** ... por outro lado se podia ...

alternator *n* (*AUT*) alternador *m.*

although *conj* embora; se bem que, ainda que; **~ I want to go on, I can't anymore** embora eu queira continuar, já não posso mais.

altitude *n* altitude *f.*

alto *n* (*singer, voice*) contralto *f;* alto.

altogether *adv* totalmente, de todo; no total, ao todo; **he was in his ~** (*naked*) ele estava em (pêlo) pelo.

altruism *n* altruísmo *m.*

altruist *n* altruísta *m,f.*

altruistic *adj* altruísta *m,f.*

aluminium *n* alumínio.

always *adv* sempre; **I ~ remember you** eu sempre me lembro de ti.

am (*Vd:* **be**) **I ~ happy** eu sou/estou muito feliz.

a.m. *adv* (*abbr for* **ante meridiem**) da manhã; **it is 4 ~** são 4 da manhã.

amalgamate *vi* amalgamar-se; unir-se; ♦ *vt* amalgamar, unir.

amalgamation *n* (*COMM*) amalgamação *f,* união *f.*

amass *vt* acumular, amontoar; **to ~ a fortune** acumular uma fortuna.

amateur *n* amador,-ora.

amaze *vt* surpreender, espantar; **2** (*stun*) abismar; aturdir.

amazed *adj* admirado,-a; (*stronger*), atónito,-a, estupefa(c)to,-a; **I am ~ that** admira-me que.

amazement *n* surpresa *f,* admiração *f,* espanto *m;* **to everyone's ~** para espanto geral.

amazing *adj* espantoso,-a, exce(p)cional; **2** (*price, cost*) exorbitante; (*reaction, surprise*) incrível, surpreendente.

Amazon *npr* (*GEOG*) (*river*) o Amazonas *m;* (*forest, land*): **in the ~** na Amazónia (*BR:* -ô-); **the rainforest ~** a floresta amazónica (*BR:* -ô-); **2** (*woman, legend*) amazona.

Amazonian *adj* amazónico,-a, (*BR*) amazônico,-a.

ambassador *n* embaixador,-ora; **~-at-large** *m* (US) embaixador *m* itinerante; **ambassador's wife** embaixatriz.

amber *n* âmbar *m;* **at ~** (*AUT*) em amarelo.

ambidextrous *adj* ambidestro.

ambience *n* ambiente *m,* ambiência *f;* **in a pleasant ~** num ambiente muito agradável.

ambiguity *n* ambiguidade *f;* duplo sentido.

ambiguous *adj* ambíguo,-a.

ambit *n* âmbito *m.*

ambition *n* ambição *f.*

ambitious *adj* ambicioso,-a; grandioso,-a.

ambivalence *n* ambivalência.

ambivalent *adj* ambivalente.

amble *vi:* (**along**) andar devagar, caminhar, passear; **2** (*cavalo*) andar a furta-passo.

ambulance *n* ambulância *f.*

ambush *n* emboscada; ♦ *vt* emboscar; **2** (*fig*) atacar de surpresa.

ameliorate *vt/vi* melhorar.

amen *exc* (*prayer*) amém! assim seja!; IDIOM **~ to that!** (*approval*) apoiado!; **I say ~ to that!** ainda bem!, de acordo!

amenable *adj* (*obliging*) amável; acessível; **~ a sth;** receptivo,-a a algo.

amend *vt* (*JUR*) alterar; emendar (*law*); **2** (*correct*) corrigir; **3** modificar (*contract*); ♦ *vi* emendar-se.

amendement *n* emenda *f;* alteração *f;* corre(c)ção *f.*

amends *npl:* **to make ~s** (**for,** por) compensar, inde(m)nizar; **2** (*reedem s.o.*) redimir-se.

amenity *n* (*pl:* **-ies**) (*facilities*) serviços *f;* **2** (*premises*) comodidades *fpl;* **3** atrativos *mpl;* vantagens *fpl.*

America *npr* América; **in ~** na América; **the United States of ~,** USA os Estados Unidos *mpl* da América, EUA.

American *n adj* americano,-a; (*LING*) inglês americano; **A~ Indian** *npr* índio *m* da América, ameríndio,-a.

americanism *n* americanismo *m.*

amethyst *n* ametista *f*

amiable *adj* (*person*) amável, simpático,-a (**to, towards sb** para com alguém).

amiably *adv* amavelmente.

amicable *adj* (*friendly*) amigável, afável *m,f.*

amicably *adv* amigavelmente, cordialmente.

amid(st) *prep* entre, no/pelo meio de.

amino acid *n* aminoácido *m.*

amiss *adj* (*wrong*) errado,-a, impróprio,-a; ♦ *adv* fora do lugar, mal; **to take sth ~** levar algo a mal, ficar ofendido.

ammeter *n* amperímetro *m.*

ammo *n* (*coll*) munições *fpl.*

ammonia *n* amoníaco *m.*

ammunition *n* (*MIL*) munição *f;* munições *fpl,* armas *fpl;* **~ dump** *n* paiol *m;* **~-pouch** *n* (*for cartridges*) cartucheira; **2** (*fig*) (*argument*) argumento *m,* arma *f* verbal.

amnesia *n* amnésia.

amnesty (*pl:* **-ies**) *n* a(m)nistia *f;* **A~ International** *n* Amnestia *f* Internacional.

amoeba *n* amiba *f,* ameba *f.*

amok *adv* freneticamente, desenfreadamente; **to run ~** (*animal, people*) correr em frenesi; **2** perder a cabeça; **3** (*prices*) disparar; **4 to run ~ with one's thoughts** dar largas à imaginação *f*/a pensamentos *mpl* desenfreados.

among(st) *prep* entre (vários), no meio de; **~ many others** entre muitos outros; **~ themselves** entre eles.

amoral *adj* amoral.

amorous *adj* amoroso,-a; apaixonado,-a; enamorado,-a.

amorphous *adj* amorfo,-a.

amortize *vt* amortizar.

amount *n* (*quatity*) quantidade *f;* **2** (*dinheiro*) quantia *f,* importância *f,* montante *m;* ♦ *vi:* **to ~ to sth** (*add up*) perfazer, chegar a; **2** (*cost*) atingir; **3** (*to be worth*) equivaler a, ter importância; **it doesn't ~ to much** (*quantity*) não é muito.

amp *n* ampere; **2** (*coll*) amplificador *m.*

amperage n (ELECT) intensidade f de corrente.
amp(ere) n ampere m.
amphibian n anfíbio,-a.
amphibious adj anfíbio,-a.
amphitheatre n anfiteatro.
ample adj amplo,-a extenso,-a; abundante; suficiente;
~ **room** bastante espaço.
amplifier n amplificador m.
amplification n (of sound) amplificação f; (of idea, subject) ampliação f.
amplify vt amplificar, aumentar; 2 (explain) explicar.
amply adv amplamente; consideravelmente.
ampoule (UK), **ampule** (US) n ampola f.
amputate vt amputar, cortar.
amputation n amputação f.
Amsterdam npr Amsterdão; (BR) Amsterdã.
amuck (Vd: **amok**).
amuse vt (cause laughter) divertir; 2 (entertain) entreter; 3 (not be pleased) agradar; **their comments didn't ~ us** os comentários deles não nos agradaram; **I'm not ~d** não acho piada nenhuma; ♦ vr (have fun) divertir-se; 2 entertain o.s. by doing sth) entreter-se (a fazer algo).
amusement n diversão f, divertimento m; entretenimento, (hobby) passatempo m.
an indef. art (Vd: **a**).
anachronism m anacronismo m.
anachronistic adj anacrónico,-a.
anaconda n (ZOOL) anaconda f.
anaemia (UK), **anemia** (US) n anemia.
anaemic (UK), **anemic** (US) adj anémico (BR: -nê-); 2 (fig) insípido.
anaesthesia (UK), **anesthesia** (US) n anestésico.
anaesthetic (UK), **anesthetic** (US) n anestésico.
anaesthetist (UK), **anesthetist** (US) n anestesista m,f.
anaesthetize (UK), **anesthetize** (US) vt anestesiar.
anagram n anagrama m.
anal adj (ANAT) anal.
analgesic n adj analgésico.
analogous adj análogo (to, with a).
analogy n analogia f.
analyse (UK) **analize** (US) vt analisar.
analysis (pl: -ses) n análise f.
analyst n analista m,f.
analytic(al) adj analítico,-a.
anarchist n anarquista m,f.
anarchistic adj anarquista m,f.
anarchy n anarquia f.
anathema n (REL) anátema; 2 (fig) aversão f.
anatomy n (BIOL, MED) anatomia f; 2 (fig) (of subject) análise f detalhada.
ancestor n antepassado,-a; avoengo,-a; 2 (of vehicle, machine) antecessor,-ora.
ancestry n ascendência, linhagem f; 2 antepassados mpl.
anchor n âncora; **to weigh** ~ levantar âncora/ferro; 2 (fig) (person) esteio m, apoio m; ♦ vi (NAUT) ancorar, fundear; ♦ vt (fig) segurar, amarrar; 2 (RADIO, TV) (present) apresentar.
anchorage n (NAUT) ancoradouro m; 2 (means of securing) ancoragem f.

anchovy (pl: -vies) n enchova, anchova f.
ancient n (person) ancião,-anciã m,f; velho,-a; ♦ adj antigo,-a; ~ **castle** castelo m antigo; **in ~ times** antigamente.
ancillary adj (department, etc) serviço m auxiliar; 2 (person) auxiliar m,f, subordinado,-a.
and conj e; (as well as) e; **bread ~ butter** pão com manteiga; **my husband ~ I** eu e o meu marido; (in numbers) e; **one hundred ~ eighty two** cento e oitenta e dois; **now ~ then** de quando em quando; **richer ~ richer** cada vez mais rico; **go ~ get me a spoon** vá buscar-me uma colher; ~ **so on/and so forth** adv e assim por diante; ~ **all that** e tudo isso;
Andes npr pl: **the** ~ os Andes.
androgynous adj andrógino,-a.
android n andróide m,f.
anedoctal adj (event, memoirs) anedótico,-a; ~ **evidence** n fontes não confirmadas.
anecdote n anedota f, história f jocosa/trocista.
anemone n (BOT) anémona (BR: -nê-) f.
anew adv de novo, outra vez.
angel n anjo m; **guardian** ~ anjo-da-guarda; 2 (fig) (generous, lovely) **she is an** ~ ela é um anjo; ~**-like** como um anjo; ~**fish/~shark** n anjo-do-mar m.
angelic adj angélico,-a.
anger n cólera, zanga; ♦ vt irritar, zangar.
angina n (MED) angina; quinsy; ~ **pectoris** (affecting heart's muscles) angina f de peito, angina pectoris.
angle n (MATH) ângulo m; perspe(c)tiva f; ponto de vista; **from their** ~ do ponto de vista deles; ♦ **camera** ~ ângulo de visão; 2 (corner) esquina f, canto m; ♦ vt (tilt) orientar (light, focus); inclinar (algo); ♦ vi pescar (à linha); 2 (try to obtain) tramar, tentar obter (work, compliments).
angler n pescador m à linha; (BR) pescador de vara.
Anglia npr antigo reino anglo-saxão; 2 província f inglesa.
Anglican npr adj anglicano,-a.
angling n pesca à linha; (BR) pesca com vara.
Anglo- pref anglo-; ~**-Portuguese** adj anglo-português.

Aliança anglo-portuguesa – a mais velha no mundo – data de 1373.

Anglo-Saxon npr anglo-saxão m; **the** ~**s** npr pl os anglo-saxões mpl.
Angola npr Angola f.
Angolan npr adj angolano,-a; (official language) português.
angrily adv com zanga, furiosamente.
angry adj zangado,-a; **to be ~ with sb/at sth** estar zangado com alguém/algo; **to get ~** zangar-se.
angst n ânsia f; angústia f; existencial.
anguish n angústia f; 2 (sorrow, suffering) dor f, sofrimento m.
anguished adj angustiado,-a; aflito,-a.
angular adj (PHYS) (distance) angular; 2 (face) anguloso,-a; 3 (building) cheio de ângulos.
animal n animal m; bicho m; ♦ adj animal; 2 (person) (pej) animal, bruto,-a, desumano,-a.

animate *vt* animar; encorajar.
animated *adj* animado; ~ **cartoon/film** *n* desenhos *mpl* animados.
animation *n* animação *f*; entusiasmo *m*; 2 *(show)* entertainment.
animosity *n* animosidade *f*.
aniseed *n* erva-doce *f*, semente *f* de anis *f*.
ankh *n* cruz ansada.
ankle *n (ANAT)* tornozelo *m*.
anklet *n (decoration)* argola para o tornozelo.
annals *n* anais *mpl*.
annex, annexe *n* anexo; ♦ *vt* anexar; ajuntar.
annihilate *vt* aniquilar.
anniversary *n (of wedding etc.)* aniversário *m*; **today is my wedding** ~ hoje é o meu aniversário de casamento.
annotate *vt* anotar, comentar.
annotations *npl* anotações *fpl*.
announce *vt* anunciar.
announcement *n (public)* anúncio *f*; 2 notícia *f*; 3 *(of death, birth)* participação *f*.
announcer *n (RADIO, TV)* locutor,-ora; apresentador, -ora.
annoy *vt* aborrecer, irritar; *(noise)* incomodar; **don't get ~ed!** não se irrite.
annoyance *n* aborrecimento; irritação *f*.
annoying *adj* aborrecido,-a; importuno,-a; irritante.
annual *n (plant)* planta *f* sazonal; 2 *(book)* anuário *m*; ♦ *adj* anual; ~ **general meeting, AGM** reunião *f* geral anual; convocatória *f* anual.
annually *adv* anualmente, cada ano.
annuity *n (FIN)* anuidade *f*; 2 renda *f* annual; **lifetime** ~ renda *f* vitalícia; 3 *(annual payment of credit card etc.)* pagamento annual.
annul (**-led, -ling**) *vt* anular, cancelar; *(JUR)* revogar.
annulment *n* anulação *f*; revogação *f*.
annum *n:* **per** ~ por ano.
Annunciation *n (REL):* **the** ~ a Anunciação *f*.
anode *n (TECH)* ânodo *m*.
anoint *vt (REL)* ungir (**with** de/com).
anomaly *n* anomalia *f*.
anon *adv (LITER)* em breve; sem demora; 2 *(abb for* **anonymous**).
anonymity *n* anonimato *f*.
anonymous *adj* anónimo,-a *(BR:* -nô-).
anorak *n* anorak *m*, anoraque *m*.
anorexia *n (MED)* anorexia *f*.
another *adj (additional)* outro; um outro; ~ **drink?** mais um copo?; ♦ *pron* outro; *(also:* **one**) **to fight one** ~ brigar um com o outro; **they kissed one** ~ eles beijaram-se.
answer *n* resposta; **give me your** ~ dê-me a sua resposta; **in** ~ **to sth** em resposta a (algo); 2 *(solution)* solução *f*; **the** ~ **to your problem is** ... a solução para o seu problema é ...; ♦ *vi (respond)* responder; 2 atender *(telephone, door);* **to** ~ **to sb** *(give account)* prestar/dar razões/responder perante alguém; 3 responsabilizar-se por alguém; **to** ~ **back** *(retort)* retorquir; 4 *(insolently)* refilar, respingar, responder torto; grimpar *(cal);* ♦ *vt* responder; 2 ~ **the door!** veja quem é/quem bate

à porta!; *(JUR)* **to** ~ **a charge** responder a uma acusação; 3 **to** ~ **to a/the name** dar por um/pelo nome; **to** ~ **to** *vt (meet)* corresponder a *(description)*.
answerable *adj (accountable):* ~ **to sb for sth** responsável perante alguém por algo; **you are** ~ **to me** tu tens de me dar/prestar contas.
answering-machine *n (TEL)* atendedor *m*; caixa *f* do correio; *(BR)* secretária eletrônica *f*.
ant *n* formiga *f*.
antacid *adj* antiácido,-a.
antagonist *n* antagonista *m,f*; adversário,-a.
antagonistic *adj* antagónico *(BR:* -gô-), hostil; oposto,-a contrário,-a.
antagonize *vt* contrariar, hostilizar.
Antarctic *npr:* **the** ~ o Antártico.
Antarctica *npr* Antártica *f*.
anteater *n (ZOOL)* papa-formigas *m*; *(BR)* tamanduá *m*.
antecedent *n (precedent)* antecedente *m*; 2 *(ancestor)* antepassado,-a; ♦ *adj* anterior (**to** a).
antelope *n* antílope *m*.
ante meridien (= **a.m.**) ante meridiem; **it is 8 o'clock** ~ são oito horas da manhã.
antenatal *adj* pré-natal; ~ **clinic** clínica *f* pré-natal.
antenna *(pl:* **-e**) *n* antena *f*.
anteroom *n* antessala; antecâmara.
anthem *n:* **national** ~ hino *m* nacional.
anthill *n* formigueiro *m*.
anthology *n* antologia.
anthracite *n (type of coal)* antracite.
anthrax *n (disease)* antraz; carbúnculo.
anthropologist *n* antropologista *m,f*; antropólogo,-a.
anthropology *n* antropologia.
anti- *pref* anti-, contra; ~-**aircraft** *adj* anti-aéreo.
antibiotic *n, adj* antibiótico,-a.
antibody *n (BIOL)* anticorpo *m*.
anticipate *vt (expect)* prever, contar com, esperar; 2 *(preemp)* antecipar-se a; 3 *(await)* aguardar; ~**ed** previsto.
anticipation *n* antecipação *f*; expectativa *f*; **in** ~ antecipadamente.
anticlimax *n* desapontamento; anticlímax *m*.
anticlockwise *adv* em sentido antihorário.
antics *npl (comical)* palhaçadas *fpl*; 2 *(of child)* travessuras *fpl*; gracinhas *fpl*; 3 *(pej) (of politician, etc)* chalaças, trapaças *fpl*.
anticyclone *n* anticiclone *m*.
antidepressant *n adj* antidepressivo,-a.
antidote *n* antídoto *m*, remédio *m*.
antiestablishment *n adj* contestatário,-a.
antifreeze *n* antigelante *m*.
antiglare *n (screen)* anti-reflexo/antirreflexo.
Antigua and Barbuda *npr* Antígua e Barbuda.
antihistamine *n* antihistamínico *m*.
antipathetic *adj (uncongenial)* contrário (**to** a) hóstil (**to, towards sb** a/para com alguém); **be** ~ **to sb/sth** *(strong aversion)* detestar alguém/ algo.
antipathy *(pl:* **-ies**) *n (dislike for sb/sth)* antipatia *f*; antagonismo *m*.
antiperspirant *n, adj* desodorizante *m*.
antipodes *npl* antípodas.

antiquated *adj* (*idea*) antiquado,-a; (*term, machine*) obsoleto.

antique *n* antiguidade *f*, antigualha; ♦ *adj* antigo,-a; ~ **dealer** *n* antiquário; ~ **shop** *n* loja de antiguidades/ de velharias *fpl*.

antiquities *npl* (*ancient objects, statues*) antiguidades.

antiquity *n* (*ancient times*) antiguidade *f*; **2** (*relic*) relíquia *f*.

antiracism *n* antirracismo *m*.

anti-riot *n* anti-motim *m*.

anti-Semitic *adj* anti-semita/antissemita *m,f*.

antiseptic *n adj* anti-séptico, antisséptico,-a.

anti-smoking *n* antitabaco; **2** ~**addition/consumption** *n* antitabagismo.

antisocial *adj* anti-social/antissocial *m,f*.

anti-theft *n* (*device*) anti-roubo/antirroubo *m*; ~ **camera** câmara *f* de vigilância; ~ **steering lock** bloqueador *m* da direção.

antithesis (*pl: -theses*) *n* antítese *f*.

anti-virus *adj* antivírus.

antlers *npl* (*on stag*) chifres *mpl* de veado; armação *f*, haste *f* de veado.

antonym *n* antónimo *m*.

Antwerp *npr* Antuérpia; **in** ~ em Antuérpia.

anus *n* (*ANAT*) ânus *m*.

anvil *n* bigorna *f*.

anxiety *n* (*worry, apprehension*) inquietação *f*, aflição *f*; ansiedade *f*; **2** (*eagerness*) ânsia *f*, anseio *m*.

anxious *adj* (*worried*) inquieto,-a, aflito,-a (**about sb/sth** com algo, alguém); **2 to be** ~ **to do sth** (*eager*) desejoso,-a; ansioso,-a (por fazer algo); **I am** ~ **to leave** estou ansioso de me ir embora.

anxiously *adv* ansiosamente.

any *adj* (*in interrogative and conditional sentences – some*) algum,-a; alguns, algumas; **have you** ~ **change?** você tem algum dinheiro?; **2 if you have** ~ **shame …** se tens alguma vergonha …; **3** (*no matter which*) qualquer, todo, tudo; ~ **will do** qualquer (um) serve; ~ **day that suits you** qualquer dia que lhe convenha; **I am ready to do** ~ **work you need** estou pronto a fazer todo o trabalho que quiser; **4** (*negative sense*) nenhum,-a; qualquer; **I haven't** ~ **money** não tenho dinheiro; **I don't have** ~ **interest** não tenho qualquer (nenhum) interesse; ♦ *adv* **at** ~ **moment** a qualquer momento; **in** ~ **case** em todo caso; **at** ~ **rate** de qualquer modo; (*at all*) de maneira nenhuma; **2** (*with comparatives*) ~ **more,** ~ **longer** não mais; **I don't like him** ~ **more** não gosto mais dele; **it won't take** ~ **longer** não irá demorar mais; **are you feeling** ~ **better?** você sente-se melhor?; ♦ *pron* (*in negative and interrogative sentences*) algum; nada; **I haven't** ~ não tenho nenhum; **can** ~ **of you speak English?** algum de vocês sabe falar inglês?

anybody, anyone *pron* qualquer; (*in interrogative sentences*) alguém; **would** ~ **like wine?** alguém quer vinho?; ~ **else?** mais alguém?; **2** (*negative sentences*) **I don't see** ~ não vejo ninguém.

anyhow *adv, conj* de qualquer maneira; seja como for; sem cuidado; **2** (*work, action*) à toa.

anyone (= ~-**body**).

anything *pron* algo, qualquer coisa; ~ **you wish** qualquer coisa que queiras; **2** (*in negative sentences*) nada; ~ **but that** tudo menos isso; ~ **will do** qualquer coisa serve; ~ **you want** (tudo) o que quiser.

anytime *adv* a qualquer momento/hora; ~ **you want to come …** a qualquer hora que queira vir.

anyway *adv* de qualquer modo; **2** aliás; **I didn't go to the cinema;** ~ **I have seen the film** não fui ao cinema; aliás já vi o filme.

anywhere *adv* em qualquer parte; algures; **2** (*negative sense*) em parte nenhuma; nenhures; ~ **else** em qualquer outra parte.

aorta *n* (*MED*) aorta *f*.

apace *adv* (*LITER*) rapidamente.

apart *adv* (*distance in time/space*) afastado,-a, (em) separado; **ten miles** ~ separados por dez milhas; **to set** ~ pôr de lado, reservar; **I can't tell them** ~ não consigo distingui-los (um do outro); ~ **from** *prep* além de; ~ **from being far …** além de ser longe …; **2** (*aside, exceto*) à parte; **I spoke with him** ~ falei com ele à parte; **joking** ~ fora de brincadeira; a sério.

apartheid *n* apartheid *m*.

apartment *n* apartamento *m*; ~ **building** *n* prédio *m* de apartamentos, indiferente *m,f*.

apathetic *adj* (*by nature*) amorfo,-a; (*from depression*) apático,-a, indiferente, indeferença *f*.

apathy *n* apatia *f*.

ape *n* macaco *m*; **2** (*fig*) imitador,-ora; ♦ *vt* macaquear, imitar.

aperitif *n* aperitivo *m*.

aperture *n* orifício *m*; **2** (*PHOT*) abertura *f*.

apex (*pl: apices*) *n* ápice *m*; (*fig*) cume *m*.

aphrodisiac *n adj* afrodisíaco.

apiary *n* (*pl: -ies*) colmeal *m*, apiário *m*.

apiculture *n* apicultura *f*.

apiece *adv* cada um, por cabeça.

aplenty *adv* em quantidade.

aplomb *n* auto-domínio *m*; firmeza *f*.

apocalypse *n* (*Bible*) **the A~** o Apocalipse *m*.

apocalyptic *adj* apocalíptico,-a.

apogee *n* apogeu *m*.

apologetic *adj* apologético,-a, cheio de desculpas.

apologetically *adv* apologeticamente.

apologize, apologise *vi* pedir desculpa; **to** ~ **for** desculpar-se de.

apology *n* desculpa, apologia; **to demand an** ~ exigir satisfações.

apoplectic *adj* (*MED*) apoplético,-a; **2** (*fig*) (*furious*) furioso,-a.

apoplexy *n* (*MED*) apoplexia *f*.

apostle *n* apóstolo *m*.

apostrophe *n* apóstrofo *m*.

apothecary *n* boticário,-a.

appal (*UK*) (*-ll-*), **apall** (*US*) *vt* horrorizar.

appalled *adj* horrorizado,-a; chocado,-a.

appalling *adj* pavoroso,-a; horrível; espantoso,-a.

apparatus (*pl: inv or -ses*) *n* (*equipment*) aparelho *m*; (*in gym*) aparelhos *mpl* (de ginástica); (*in lab*) instrumentos.

apparent *adj* aparente; claro,-a.

apparently *adv* aparentemente, pelo(s) visto(s).

apparition *n* aparição *f*; fantasma *m*.

appeal *n* (*JUR*) apelação *f*; recurso *m*, apelo; **2** (*call*) apelo *m*; ~ **for understanding** apelo à compreensão; **3** (*REL*) súplica; **4** (*attraction*) atra(c)ção *f*, encanto *m*; ◆ *vt/vi*: **to** ~ **for** (*call*) apelar a; (*request*) solicitar; ◆ **to** ~ **to** suplicar a; **2** atrair, agradar; ◆ (*JUR*) **to** ~ **against a sentence** recorrer de uma sentença; **to** ~ **to sb for mercy** pedir misericórdia a alguém; IDIOM **it doesn't** ~ **to me** não me atrai.

appealing *adj* atraente *m,f*; apelativo,-a.

appear *vi* (*gen*) aparecer; **2** (*to seem*) parecer; **it would** ~ **that** parece que; **3** (*book, article*) **to** ~ **in print** ser publicado; **4** (*THEAT, TV*) aparecer em cena; **5 to** ~ **before** (*JUR*) comparecer perante o juiz.

appearance *n* (*look*) aparência *f*; aspecto *m*; **2** (*arrival*) chegada *f*; **3** (*apparition*) aparição *f*; (*be visible/found*) aparecimento *m*; **4** (*JUR*) comparência *f* (**in**, **before** em, perante); ◆ **appearances** *fpl* (*external show*) aparências; ~ **are deceptive** as aparências iludem; **to all** ~ ao que parece ...; **to keep up** ~ manter as aparências.

appease *vt* apaziguar, acalmar.

appeasement *n* apaziguamento *m*.

appellant *n* (*JUR*) apelante, recorrente *m,f*.

append *vt* (*formal*) ~ **sth to sth** anexar (**to**, a); juntar algo a algo.

appended *adj* anexado,-a.

appendage *n* anexo *m*; **2** (*addition to an animal's trunk*) acrescentamento *m*; **3** (*fig*) apêndice *m*; acessório *m*.

appendant *adj* apenso,-a, ligado,-a (**to** a); **2** (*JUR*) (*property law*) direito subordinado a.

appendicitis *n* (*MED*) apendicite *f*.

appendix (*pl*: **-dices**, **-dixes**) *n* apêndice *m*; **to have one's** ~ **removed** ter/sofrer a remoção do apêndice.

appertain *vt* (*formal*) pertencer (**to**, a); **2** dizer respeito (**to**, a).

appetite *n* apetite *m*; **2** (*fig*) (*desire*) desejo *m*.

appetizer *n* (*CULIN*) (*food, drink*) aperitivo *m*; **2** (*fig*) (*starter*) entrada *f*.

appetizing *adj* apetitoso,-a.

applaud *vt/vi* (*clap*) aplaudir; **2** (*approve of*) aprovar, louvar, elogiar.

applause *n* aplausos *mpl*; ovação *f*.

apple *n* (*fruit*) maçã *f*; ~**-tart** (*CULIN*) torta *f* de maçã; **the (Big) A~** *npr* Nova Iorque; ~ **of discord** pomo *m* de discórdia; **Granny Smith** ~ *npr* maçã reineta *f*; IDIOM **she is the** ~ **of my eye** ela é a menina dos meus olhos, o meu ai-jesus.

apple-tree *n* macieira *f*.

appliance *n* (*TECH*) aparelho *m*; **home** ~**s** ele(c)trodomésticos *mpl*.

applicable *adj* aplicável; **2** apropriado,-a, adequado,-a; **3** (*regulation, law*) em vigor; **if** ~se assim for.

applicant *n* (*courses, job*) candidato,-a; (*to competition*), concorrente *m,f*; **2** (*JUR*) (*to a claim, benefit, etc*) requerente *m,f*; **3** (*for shares*) subscritor.

application *n* (*claim, request*) requerimento *m*; **2** (*courses, exams*) matrícula *f* inscrição *f*; **3** (*job,*

competition) candidatura *f*; ~ **form** *n* formulário *m* de candidatura; ficha de inscrição *f*; **4** (*for a loan*) pedido de empréstimo; **5** ~ **to study** aplicação *f*; ~ **of sth on sth** aplicação de algo em algo; **6** (*implementation of law, fine*) aplicação; **7** (*use*) utilização *f*; **8** (*layer*) camada *f*.

applied *adj* (*LING, science*) aplicado,-a.

appliqué *n* (*sewing*) aplicação *f*.

apply *vt* (*rule, fine*) aplicar; **2** (*ointment, paint*) aplicar (**to** em); **3** (*use*) utlizar; exercer (*force, pressure*) (**to** em); **to** ~ **one's mind to sth** concentrar-se em algo; concentrar-se; ◆ *vi*: **to** ~ **to** apresentar-se a; **2** ser aplicável a; **3** dizer respeito, referir-se a; **it doesn't** ~ **to you** não se refere a você; **to** ~ **for** (*course, job*) candidatar-se a, matricular-se a; **to** ~ **the brakes** travar, (*BR*) frear; **to** ~ **o.s. to** (*work, study*) aplicar-se a, dedicar-se a.

appoint *vt* nomear; marcar.

appointment *n* encontro *m*, entrevista *f*, marcação *f*; compromisso *m*; nomeação *f*; cargo *m*.

apportion *vt* repartir, fazer partilhas.

appraisal *n* avaliação *f*, apreciação *f*.

appreciable *adj* apreciável, notável.

appreciably *adv* (*noticeably*) visivelmente, sensivelmente.

appreciate *vt* (*esteem*) estimar; **2** (*appreciate*) valorizar, apreciar; **3** (*understand*) compreender, perceber; **4** (*grateful for*) agradecer, reconhecer; **I** ~ **your kindness** agradeço a sua amabilidade; ◆ *vi* (*COMM*) valorizar-se.

appreciation *n* apreciação *f*, estima *f*.

appreciative *adj* (*grateful*) agradecido,-a, reconhecido,-a; elogioso,-a.

apprehend *vt* (*arrest*) apreender; prender, deter.

apprehension *n* (*anxiety*) apreensão *f*; **2** (*fear*) receio.

apprehensive *adj* (*anxious*) apreensivo,-a, receoso,-a; **2** (*worried*) preocupado,-a (**about** acerca de).

apprentice *n* aprendiz *m,f*; estagiário,-a.

apprenticeship *n* aprendizagem *f*; (*BR*) aprendizado.

approach *n* aproximação *f*; **2** (*access to route, etc*) acesso; **3** (*problem, subject*) abordagem *f*; **4** (*proposal*) proposta; **a new** ~ uma nova atitude; ◆ *vi* (*draw near*) aproximar-se de; ◆ *vt* aproximar-se (de); **to** ~ **sb** dirigir-se a alguém; **2** (*make overture*) sondar alguém; fazer diligências junto de alguém; **3** (*getting near*) aproximar-se, estar perto de; **she is approaching middle age** ela está perto da meia idade; **4** (*deal with*) abordar (*topic, problem*); **to** ~ **a problem** aflorar, abordar um problema.

approachable *adj* tratável; acessível.

approaching *adj* (*event*) iminente; próximo,-a.

approbation *n* (*JUR*) (*formal*) aprovação *f*.

appropriate *adj* apropriado,-a, adequado,-a, próprio,-a; **2** (*authority*) competente; ◆ *vt* apropriar-se de; **to** ~ **sth for** (*allocate*) destinar algo para.

appropriation *n* (*stealing*) apropriação *f*; **2** allocation; **3** (*JUR*) (*removal*) apropriação *f*.

approval *n* aprovação *f*; **2** (*official agreement*) sanção, homologação *f*; **3** (*COMM*) **on** ~ sob condição; **to nod** ~ acenar aprovativamente.

approve *vt* aprovar.

approximate *adj* aproximado,-a; ~ **to** próximo de; ♦ *vt* aproximar-se de; **2** ~ **to** *(similar to)* assemelhar-se a algo.

approximately *adv* aproximadamente; *(about)* perto de, cerca de.

approximation *n* *(calculation; guess, figure)* (**of** de) aproximação *f*.

apothecary *n* boticário,-a.

apricot *n* *(fruit)* damasco *m*, alperce *m*; *(BR)* abricó; ~ **tree** *n* damasqueiro *m*.

April *npr* abril *m*; ~ **Fool's Day** *npr* dia um de abril, Dia *m* dos Enganos, das Petas; ~ **showers** *npl* abril chuvoso.

apron *n* *(garment)* avental *m*; **2** *(AER)* área de estacionamento, pista *f* frente a um hangar; placa *f* de manobra; **3** *(conveyor)* passadeira, esteira *f* rolante; IDIOM **tied to sb's** ~ **strings** agarrado,-a às saias da mãe.

apropos *adj* *(comment)* oportuno,-a; ♦ *adv* a propósito (**of** de).

apse *n* ábside *f*.

apt *adj* apto,-a; adequado,-a; apropriado,-a; ~ **to do** estar sujeito,-a, apto,-a a fazer.

apt *(abbr for* **apartamento**).

aptitude *n* aptidão *f* (**for sth** para algo); talento *m*.

aptly *adv* com aptidão, habilidade.

aqua-fortis *n* água-forte *f*.

aqualung *n* aparelho respiratório autónomo; escafandro *m*.

aquamarine *n* *(gem)* água-marinha *f*; **2** *(colour)* verdemar, azul marinho; ♦ *adj (colour)* verde-azulado,-a.

aquarium *n* aquário *m*.

Aquarius *npr* *(sign)* Aquário *m*; **2** *(person)* aquariano,-a.

aquatic *adj* *(plants, etc)* aquático,-a.

aquatics *npl* *(SPORT)* desportos *mpl* náuticos.

aqueduct *n* aqueduto *m*.

aqueous *adj* aquoso,-a; ~ **humour** *n* *(PHYS)* *(watery fluid in the eyeball)* humor *m* aquoso.

aquiescence *n* aquiescência *f*.

aquiline *adj* *(nose, features)* aquilino,-a.

Arab *npr* *(person)* árabe *m,f*.

arabesque *n* *(ART)* arabesco *m*.

Arabia *npr* Arábia *f*; **Saudi** ~ *npr* Arábia Saudita; **in Saudi** ~ na Arábia Saudita.

Arabian *adj* *(desert, etc)* árabe, da Arábia; **the** ~ **Nights** *(book)* as Mil e Uma Noites.

Arabic *npr* *(LING)* árabe; ♦ *adj* arábico.

Arabist *n* *(scholar in Arabic culture/language)* Arabista *m,f*.

arable *adj* cultivável.

Aran sweater *n* *(garment)* camisola *f* irlandesa (das Ilhas Aran).

arbitrary *adj* arbitrário,-a.

arbitrate *vi* arbitrar.

arbitration *n* arbitragem *f*. **arbitrator** *n* árbitro *m*.

arc *n* *(curved line)* arco.

arcade *n* *(arches)* arcos *mpl*; *(shopping)* galeria *f* de lojas.

arch *n* arco *m*; abóbada *f*; ♦ *vt* arquear, curvar; ♦ *vi (rainbow)* fazer um arco.

archaeologist *n* arqueólogo,-a.

archaeology *n* arqueologia *f*.

archaic *adj* arcaico,-a.

archbishop *n* arcebispo *m*.

archduchesse *n* arquiduquesa *f*.

archduke *n* arquiduque *m*.

arched *adj* abobodado,-a; **2** *(eyebrows)* arqueado,-a.

archenemy *n* arqui-inimigo,-a.

archer *n* arqueiro,-a; **the A~** *(ASTROL, ASTRON)* Sagitário.

archery *n* tiro *m* ao arco.

archetype *n* arquétipo *m*.

archipelago *n* arquipélago *m*.

architect *n* arquite(c)to,-a.

architectural *adj* arquitectónico,-a *(BR:* -tô-*)*.

architecture *n* arquite(c)tura *f*.

archive *m* *(often plural)* arquivo *m*, arquivos *mpl*; ~ **file** *n* *(COMP)* arquivo armazenador.

archway *n* arco *m*.

Arctic *adj* ár(c)tico; *(fig)* glacial; ♦ *npr*: **the** ~ o Ár(c)-tico; ~ **Circle** *n* *(GEOG)* círculo *m* polar *m* ártico.

ardent *adj* ardente, apaixonado,-a; *(fervent)* fervoroso,-a.

ardour *(UK)*, **ardor** *(US)* *n* ardor *m*; fervor *m*.

arduous *adj* *(task)* árduo,-a; difícil.

are *(pres. ind.* = **to be**)

aren't = **are not** *(pre. ind.* = **to be**).

area *n* área; superfície *f*, extensão *f*; zona, região *f*.

arena *n* arena *f*; picadeiro *m*; pista *f*.

Argentina *npr* Argentina; **in** ~ na Argentina.

Argentinian *npr adj* argentino,-a.

arguable *adj* discutível.

arguably *adv* discutivelmente.

argue *vi* argumentar, arguir; **2** *(quarrel)* discutir; **to** ~ **that** sustentar, demonstrar que.

argument *n* argumento *m*; **2** debate *m*; **3** *(quarrel)* disputa *f*, discussão *f*.

argumentative *adj* argumentativo,-a; questionador, -ora.

argy-bargy *n* *(argie-bargie)* *(coll)* discussão *f* acalorada; *(BR)* bate-boca.

aria *n* *(MUS)* ária *f*.

arid *adj* árido,-a.

Aries *npr* *(ASTRON, ASTROL)* Áries *m*; *(sign)* Carneiro *m*.

arise *(pt* **arose**, *pp* **arisen**) *vi* levantar-se, erguer-se; **2** surgir; **to** ~ **from** resultar de.

aristocracy *n* aristocracia *f*.

aristocrat *n* aristocrata *m,f*.

arithmetic *n* aritmética *f*.

ark *n*: **Noah's A~** arca de Noé.

arm *n* *(ANAT)* braço; ~ **in** ~ de braço dado; **child in one's** ~**s** criança *f* ao/de colo; **to fold one's** ~**s** cruzar os braços; **in/within** ~**'s reach** à mão, ao alcance da mão; **2** *(COMM)* filial *f*, ramo *m*; **3** *(TECH)* *(of record player, anchor, sea)* braço; ♦ **arms** *npl* armas *fpl*; **2** *(HERALD)* brasão *m*; **3** ~**s race** corrida ao armamento, *(BR)* corrida armamentista; **to take up** ~**s** pegar em armas; *(fig)* revoltar-se; ♦ *vt* armar; **to** ~ **o.s.** armar-se (com); IDIOM **keep sb at** ~**'s length** manter alguém à distância; **a list as long as my** ~ uma lista muito longa; **to cost an** ~ **and a leg** custar os olhos da cara; ~**chair** n poltrona f; **2** (upholstered) maple m.

armada n (fleet of boats, ships) armada f.

armadillo n (ZOOL) tatu m.

armament n (ZOOL) (usually pl) (weapons) armamento m.

armband n (faixa) f; **black** ~ braçadeira de luto.

armed adj armado; ~ **car** n carro blindado; ~ **robbery** n assalto à mão armada.

Armenia npr Arménia; **in** ~ na Arménia.

Armenian npr adj arménio,-a; (LING) arménio m.

armful n braçada f.

armhole n (of garments) cava f.

armistice n armistício; **A**~ **Day** Dia do Armistício, 11 de novembro.

armor (US) (Vd: **armour**).

armorial adj armorial.

armour (UK) **armor** (US) n armadura.

armoury n arsenal m.

armpit n (ANAT) axila, sovaco.

army n exército.

arnica n arnica f.

aroma n aroma.

aromatic adj aromático.

arose (pt of **arise**).

around adv em volta, ao redor; **2** (near) perto; ♦ prep em redor de, em volta de; **2** (approx.) cerca de; **it's** ~ **5 o'clock** são cerca das cinco horas; **3** (in vicinity) **he is** ~ ele anda por aí; **4** (the opposite) **to do the wrong way** ~ fazer o contrário; **to put on the blouse the other way** ~ vestir a blusa ao contrário/do avesso; **5** (in circulation) **there are still honest people** ~ ainda há pessoas honestas; **6** (fig) (experienced) **he has been** ~ ele é um homem vivido.

arousal n (of feelings) despertar m.

arouse vt (from sleep) despertar, acordar (alguém); **2** despertar, estimular (interest); **3** provocar, excitar, causar (anger, passion, envy).

arrange vt/vi (tidy up) arranjar, arrumar; **2** organizar; **3** fazer preparativos; **4** combinar (appointment, etc) **to** ~ **sth with sb** combinar algo com alguém); **5** **to** ~ **for** providenciar, dar instruções para; **6** (flowers) arranjar; **7** (MUS) fazer um arranjo (musical).

arrangement n arranjo m; **2** (agreement) acordo m; (BR) combinação; **3** (of furniture etc) disposição f; **4** (of meetings, agenda) organização; ♦ **arrangements** npl planos mpl; **2** medidas fpl; **3** providências mpl; **to make** ~ **for** tomar providências para.

array n (of objects) gama f, série f; **2** (of troops) formação f; **3** (of attire) vestuário m, traje m; **4** (COMP) matriz f (BR) array; **5** (MATH) sequência de números, símbolos; ♦ vt (objects, troops) disport; **2** (JUR) constituir (juri); **3** **to be** ~**ed in sth** (dressed) trajar algo/estar vestido com algo; ♦ vr (adorn o.s.) enfeitar-se com algo.

arrears npl atrasos mpl; **to be in** ~ **with one's rent** estar/andar atrasado,-a com a renda (BR: aluguel).

arrest n detenção f, prisão f; **under** ~ (person) sob detenção; preso,-a; ♦ vt prender, deter; **2** (sb's attention) chamar, prender; (stop) deter.

arresting adj (striking) interessante, cativante, impressionante.

arrival n chegada; **new** ~ n recém-chegado,-a; (fig) (baby) recém-nascido,-a.

arrive vi chegar; **to** ~ **at a conclusion** chegar a uma conclusão; **2** (baby) nascer.

arrogance n arrogância.

arrogant adj arrogante.

arrogantly adv presunçosamente.

arrow n flecha, seta; **2** (sign) seta; **to mark with an** ~ marcar/assinalar com uma seta; ~**head** n ponta de flecha.

arrow root n (BOT) araruta f.

arse (UK), **ass** (US) n (vulgar) cu m (cal); (Angolan, BR) bunda f; traseiro m; **get off your** ~ (slang) fora daqui, põe-te a andar; **move your** ~ ! (slang) mexe-te!; ~**hole** n (vulg) cara de cu

arsenal n arsenal m.

arsenic n arsénico (BR: -sê-).

arson n incêndio premeditado, fogo posto.

arsonist n incendiário,-a, pirómano m.

art n (creativity) arte f; **2** (skill) habilidade f, jeito m; técnica f; ~ **gallery** n museu m de belas-artes; galeria de arte; ~ **college** n escola/academia de belas-artes; ♦ **arts** (culture) npl artes fpl; ~ **and crafts** mpl artes e ofícios; **2** (univ subject) Letras fpl; **BA** (bachelor of Arts) licenciado,-a em Letras; ~ **deco** arte f deco.

artefact n artefato m.

arterial adj (ANAT) arterial; **2** (of road) de grande circulação f.

artery n (MED) artéria; **2** (road) estrada principal; (RAIL) linha f principal.

artful adj (crafty) astucioso,-a; **2** (skilful) engenhoso,-a; **3** (sharp, sly) espertalhão,-lhona finório,-a.

artfully adv (arranged skilfully) engenhosamente; **2** (in speaking) artificiosamente.

arthritic adj artrítico,-a.

arthritis n artrite f.

arthrosis n artrose f.

artic (UK: fam) (Vd: **articulated lorry**).

artichoke n alcachofra f; **Jerusalem** ~ topinambo m.

article n (gram) artigo m; **2** (object) artigo m, obje(c)to m; **luxury** ~**s** artigos mpl de luxo; **3** (JOURN) artigo m (**about on** sobre); **leading** ~ editorial m; **4** (JUR) (provision) cláusula f, artigo; **under A**~ **no. 24/99** ao abrigo da cláusula (BR) sob a cláusula 24/99; **articles of association** npl (of a registered company) constituição f, estatutos mpl de uma companhia.

articled adj: ~ **clerk** (UK) estagiário,-a contratado,-a.

articulate adj (eloquent) articulado; (speech) claro; ♦ vt articular; ~**d lorry** n camião m (BR: caminhão) articulado.

articulation n (enunciation) articulação f; **2** (in words) expressão f.

artifice n artifício m; estratégia f engenhosa.

artificial adj artificial; **2** postiço,-a, falso,-a; ~ **respiration** n respiração f artificial.

artillery n (guns) artilharia f.

artisan n (craftsperson) artesão m, artesã f.

artist n artista m,f; **2** (MUS) intérprete m,f; **hair** ~ cabeleireiro,-a artístico,-a.

artista *n (entertainer)* artista *m,f.*

artistic *adj* artístico,-a.

artistry *n* arte *f,* maestria.

artless *adj* natural, simples, despretensioso,-a; ~ **reply** resposta *f* desajeitada.

as *conj (in the way/manner that)* como; ~ **usual** como de costume; 2 *(since, given that)* já que, visto que; **I solved the problem ~ you were not here** eu resolvi o problema já que não estavas aqui; 3 *(according to, what)* conforme, segundo; **I did ~ you said** fiz conforme me disse; 4 *(while, when)* quando; enquanto; à medida que; ~ **we went along ...** à medida que caminhávamos ...; **he arrived just ~ I was leaving** ele chegou quando eu saía; 5 *(introducing statement)* ~ **you know** como você sabe; 6 *(although)* embora, ainda que; 7 *(time)* **as soon as** logo, assim que; 8 *(provided that)* **as long as** desde que, contanto que; ♦ *prep (in the role of)* ~ **your friend, I tell you ...** como amigo, eu digo-lhe ...; 2 *(as for, as regards, as to)* quanto a; ~ **for me** quanto a mim; 3 *(as if/though)* **as it were** como se fosse; 4 ~ **if to say** como que a dizer; 5 *(existing matters)* ~ **the situation is, I cannot ...** tal como a situação está, eu não posso ...; 6 *(date from)* ~ **from March ...** a partir de Março; ~ **soon ~ possible** tão cedo quanto possível; ♦ *adv (in comparisons)* **rich ~** tão rico como/quanto; **twice ~ big** duas vezes maior que; ~ **much/~ many** tanto/s ... como/quanto/s; ~ **much ~ I want** por muito que eu queira; ~ **many ~ 250 boxes** pelo menos 250 caixotes; **the same ~** o mesmo que; **I thought ~ much** foi isso que/foi o que pensei; 2 ~ **it were** por assim dizer; 3 *(up to now)* ~ **nothing has arrived** nada chegou até agora; 4 ~ **well (that)** ainda bem (que); 5 **just ~ well!** *exc* ainda bem!; ~ **well** ~ também; *conj* assim como.

asap (a.s.a.p.) *(abbr for* **as soon as possible***)* tão cedo quanto possível.

asbestos *nsg* asbesto *m,* amianto *m.*

ascend *vt (stairs, steep road)* subir; 2 **to ~ to the throne** ascender ao trono; ♦ *vi* elevar-se, subir.

ascendancy *n* ascendência *f;* 2 domínio *m (sobre* alguém).

ascendant *n (ASTROL)* ascendente *m.*

ascension *n* ascenção *f;* **the A~** *(REL)* a Ascenção *f.*

ascent *n (of smoke, cycle, ramp)* subida; 2 *(of ballon, soul)* elevação *f; (in mountaineering)* escalada; ascensão *f.*

ascertain *vt* averiguar, verificar, apurar; **to ~ the truth** para apurar a verdade.

ascetic *adj* ascético,-a.

ascribe *vt:* **to ~ sth to** atribuir algo a.

asexual *adj* assexuado,-a.

ash *n* cinza *f;* freixo *m;* **as pale as ~es** branco como a cal; **burnt to ~es** reduzido,-a a cinzas; **A~ Wednesday** Quarta-feira de Cinzas; 2 *(tree)* freixo *m;* **~-coloured** *adj* acinzentado,-a.

ashamed *adj* envergonhado,-a; **to be ~ of** ter vergonha de.

ashen *adj (turned pale)* pálido,-a; 2 *(grey)* cinzento,-a.

ashore *adv (on land)* em terra; **to go ~** desembarcar; **sb/sth washed ~** levado,-a pela maré.

ashtray *n* cinzeiro *m.*

Asia *npr* Ásia; **in ~** na Ásia; ~ **Minor** *npr* Ásia Menor *f.*

Asian, Asiatic *npr adj* asiático,-a.

aside *n (remark)* aparte *m;* observação *f;* ♦ *adv (to one side, in private)* à parte; **to speak to sb ~** falar com alguém à parte; **to brush sth ~** ignorar algo; 2 *(apart from)* com excessão de; 3 *(to one side)* de lado, de parte; **to set ~** pôr de lado.

ask *vt* perguntar; **to ~ sb a question** fazer uma pergunta a alguém; 2 exigir; 3 *(invite)* convidar; **to ~ for** *(request)* pedir *(por);* **to ~ for payment** exigir o pagamento; **to ~ after sb** perguntar por alguém; **~ after sb's health** perguntar pela saúde de alguém; **to ~ sb to do sth** pedir a alguém para fazer algo; **to ~ sb out to lunch** convidar alguém para almoçar.

askance *adv:* **to look at sb ~** olhar para alguém de soslaio; 2 *(with mistrust)* olhar com desconfiança.

askew *adv (not straight)* torto, de esguelha; **to hang a picture ~** pendurar um quadro às três pancadas.

asking *n:* **for the ~** por pouco, sem esforço; sem ser caro; ~ **price** *n* preço *m* marcado.

asleep *adj* adormecido,-a, dormindo,-a; **to fall ~** adormecer.

asp *n (ZOOL) (venomous snake)* áspide *f;* 2 *(short for* **aspen***).*

asparagus *n (BOT, CULIN)* aspargo, espargo *m.*

aspect *n* aspecto, aparência; 2 orientação *f;* **to have a northern ~** estar virado para o norte.

aspen *n (BOT)* álamo *m;* faia *f* preta.

aspersions *npl:* **to cast ~ on sb** difamar, caluniar alguém.

asphalt *n* asfalto *m; (road)* estrada asfaltada.

asphyxiate *vt* asfixiar, sufocar; ♦ *vi* asfixiar-se, sufocar-se.

asphyxiation *n* asfixia, sufocação *f.*

aspic *n* aspic; gelatina para carnes frias, etc; *(BR)* geleia *f* (de carnes, peixes).

aspidrista *n (BOT)* aspidistra *f.*

aspirant *n* aspirante *m,f.*

aspirate *n (LING: sound)* som *m* aspirado; ♦ *vt* aspirar.

aspiration *n* aspiração *f;* 2 *(fig)* ambição *f.*

aspire *vi* aspirar **(to, after** a); ambicionar **(to, after** a); **he aspired to the position of director** ele ambicionava a posição de director, ambicionava a carreira de director.

aspirin *n (PHARM)* aspirina *f.*

aspiring *adj* aspirante; **these ~ politicians** estes aspirantes a políticos.

ass *n (donkey)* jumento,-a, burro,-a *m;* 2 *(coll)* estúpido,-a; **to make an ~ of o.s.** fazer-se ridículo, fazer papel de idiota.

assail *vt (attack)* atacar; 2 *(fig) (beset)* acometer (alguém); **to be ~ed by questions** ser crivado,-a de perguntas.

assailant *n* assaltante *m,f;* aggressor,-ora.

assassin *n* assassino.

assassinate *vt* assassinar.

assassination *n* assassinato *m,* assassínio *m.*

assault n (MIL) ataque m; 2 (physical) agressão f; ~ and battery (JUR) agressão seguida de lesões; **indecent** ~ atentado m ao pudor; **verbal** ~ insultos mpl; **to make an** ~ **on a record** (SPORT) tentar bater o recorde; ~ **course** (MIL) pista f de ataque; ♦ vt assaltar, atacar; 2 (physically) agredir (person); 3 (sexually) violar, violentar.

assemble vt (gather) reunir; 2 (TECH) (parts, furniture) montar; ♦ vi reunir-se.

assembly n (meeting) reunião f; 2 (POL, ADMIN) assembleia; **National A~** Assembleia Nacional; 3 (of church) congregação f; 4 (MIL: signal) toque m de reunir; 5 (TECH) montagem f; ~ **line** n linha f de montagem.

assent n assentimento m; consentimento m; aprovação f; **with one** ~ por unanimidade; ♦ vi consentir, assentir, aquiescer.

assert vt afirmar; fazer valer; **to** ~ **one's own rights** defender os seus direitos.

assertion n afirmação f.

assertive n assertivo,-a.

assess vt avaliar (ability, work, students); 2 julgar (candidate); 3 (calculate) estimar (loss, damage); 4 (tax) tributar; (BR) taxar.

assessment n avaliação f; apreciação f (of de); (tax) tributação f; **self-~** (school, univ) auto-avaliação f.

assessor n (JUR) assessor,-ora; 2 (FIN) analista m,f; inspe(c)tor,-ora; (TAX) avaliador,-ora do fisco.

asset n (of value) bem m, a(c)tivo; 2 (quality, person) vantagem f; **she is a great** ~ **to the school** ela é uma grande vantagem para a escola; ♦ **assets** npl (COMM) (o) a(c)tivo sg, fundos mpl; ~ **and liabilities** a(c)tivo e passivo.

assiduous adj assíduo,-a.

assign vt (attribute) atribuir (responsibility); 2 (allocate) conceder (funds); (delegate) designar (task, role) (**to sb** algo a alguém); 3 (appoint) nomear; 4 (JUR) (transfer) ceder, transmitir (rights).

assignation n encontro m (**with sb** com alguém).

assignment n designação f; (task) tarefa f; missão f; (diplomatic/military post) cargo, posto m; 2 (JUR) transmissão f (of rights).

assimilate vt assimilar (**to** a); ♦ vi assimilar-se (**to** a).

assimilation n assimilação (of ideas); absorção f (of people).

assist vt ajudar, auxiliar.

assistance n ajuda, auxílio; subsídio.

assistant n assistente m,f auxiliar m,f; **shop** ~ caixeiro,-a, empregado,-a de balcão; (BR) balconista m,f; ~ **manager** gerente m,f adjunto,-a.

assizes npl sessões de tribunal criminal e civil que se reunia quatro vezes por ano, no principal tribunal de cada condado. Este sistema terminou em 1971.

associate n colega m,f; 2 (in crime) cúmplice m,f; 3 (in business, association) sócio,-a; (academic body) membro; ♦ adj pp (member, idea) associado,-a; ♦ vt associar (**with** a); ♦ vi: **to** ~ **with sb** associar-se a alguém; ♦ vr: ~ **o.s. with sth** associar-se a algo.

associated pp adj (person, idea) associado,-a, sócio,-a; **the discussion and its** ~ **complications** a discussão e as complicações daí decorrentes.

association n (club, association) associação f; 2 (COMM) sociedade f; 3 (relationship between people, business) relações fpl; (sexual) ligação f íntima (**with** com); **to have ~s with sth** recordar/lembrar/evocar algo.

assonance n assonância f.

assort vt classificar; dispor; sortir.

assorted adj sortido,-a variado-a, vários mpl; 2 (people) heterogéneo,-a.

assortment n sortido m, diversidade f.

assuage vt (soften) suavizar (pain, fury); 2 acalmar; (mitigate), mitigar, aliviar, atenuar.

assume vt (presume) supor, presumir; ~**d innocent** presumivelmente inocente; 2 (take on) assumir; ado(p)tar; **under an ~d name** sob um nome suposto.

assuming conj; ~ **that** ... supondo que ...

assumption n suposição f, hipótese f; 2 (of power) tomada f; 3 assunção f; **the A~** (REL) a Assunção.

assurance n garantia f, segurança f; 2 promessa f; 3 (being sure of) certeza; 4 (FIN) (insurance) seguro m; 5 (confidence) segurança f.

assure vt assegurar, garantir; (be certain of) estar seguro de.

assured n: **the** ~ (insured) o segurado; ♦ adj segurado,-a; 2 (confident) seguro,-a (attitude, voice); **self** ~ (person) autoconfiante m,f.

asterisk n asterisco m.

astern adv (NAUT) à popa; à ré.

asteroid n asteróide m.

asthma n (MED) asma.

asthmatic n adj asmático,-a.

astigmatism n astigmatismo m.

astir adj adv (awake and up) a pé; 2 em movimento; ativo,-a.

astonish vt surpreender; 2 (to shock) pasmar, espantar; 3 causar admiração.

astonished adj surpreendido,-a; pasmado,-a; atónito,-a.

astonishing adj surpreendente, espantoso, 2 (price, fact) incrível.

astonishment n espanto m; **to my** ~ para minha surpresa.

astound vt (amaze) aturdir; espantar, assombrar, estarrecer.

astounded adj espantado,-a.

astounding adj assombroso,-a, espantoso,-a.

astray adj (mail, item) extraviado, perdido; ♦ adv: **to go** ~ perder-se; **to lead sb** ~ desencaminhar alguém.

astride adj adv (ride, sit) escarrapachado,-a, escarranchado,-a; 2 (stand) de pernas afastadas; ♦ prep (seated) a cavalo, montado sobre.

astringent n adstringente m; ♦ adj (MED; cosmetic) adstringente; 2 (criticism, tone) severo,-a, duro,-a.

astrologer n astrólogo,-a.

astrology n astrologia f.

astronaut n astronauta m,f.

astronomer n astrónomo,-a (BR: -trô-).

astronomical adj astronómico,-a (BR: -nô-); (fig) enorme.

astronomy n astronomia f.

astrophysicist *n* *(ASTRON, PHYS)* astrofísico,-a.
Astroturf® *npr* *(SPORT)* gazão *m* artificial.
astute *adj* astuto,-a, esperto,-a.
astuteness *n* astúcia *f*.
asylum *n* asilo *m*, refúgio *m*; **political** ~ asilo *m* político; *(for the mentally ill)* *(dated, pej)* manicómio *(BR: -cô-)* *m*.
asymmetric(al) *adj* assimétrico,-a.
at *prep* em, a; ~ **the door** à porta; ~ **Easter** na Páscoa; ~ **first** em primeiro lugar; ~ **home** em casa; ~ **my aunt's house** na casa da minha tia; ~ **night** à noite; **nothing** ~ **all** absolutamente nada; ~ **6 o'clock** às seis horas; ~ **once** já, imediatamente; ~ **a stroke** de um golpe; ~ **that time** naquela altura; ~ **the top** no cimo; ~ **the same time** ao mesmo tempo; ~ **times** às vezes; **two** ~ **a time** de dois em dois; **to be** ~ **large** andar à solta; **to be good** ~ **sth** ser bom em algo; **to be angry** ~ **sth** estar zangado por causa de algo/ ~ **sb** com alguém; IDIOM **I don't know what he is getting** ~ *(insinuation)* não percebo a que ele quer chegar; não sei o que ele quer dizer com isso.
atavistic *adj* atávico,-a.
ate *(pt of* **eat***)*.
atheist *n* ateu, ateia *(BR:* atéia*)*.
Athenian *npr adj* ateniense *m,f*.
Athens *npr* Atenas *f*.
athlete *n* atleta *m,f*.
athletic *adj* atlético,-a.
athletics *n* atletismo *msg*.
Atlantic *npr*: **the** ~ o Atlântico; ~ **(Ocean)** o (Oceano) Atlântico.
Atlantis *npr* *(legendary continent)* Atlântida *f*.
atlas *n* atlas *m*; **road** ~ atlas rodoviário; **A~ Mountains** *npr* Montes *mpl* Atlas.
atmosphere *n* atmosfera; **2** *(fig)* *(ambiance)* ambiente *m*.
atmospheric *adj* atmosférico,-a; **2** *(captivating)* envolvente.
atom *n* átomo.
atomic *adj* atómico,-a *(BR: -tô-)*; ~ **bomb** *n* bomba atómica.
atomizer *n* atomizador *m*, pulverizador *m*.
atone *vi*: **to** ~ **for** expiar *(sin, crime)*; reparar *(error)*.
atrocious *adj* atroz; *(fig)* horrível, detestável.
atrocity *n* atrocidade *f*.
attach *vt* *(document)* juntar, anexar; **2** *(blame)* atribuir; **3** *(fasten)* prender **(sth to sth** algo a algo); **4** *(COMP)* anexar.
attaché *n* adido,-a; ~ **case** *n* pasta/maleta executiva.
attached *adj* junto, anexo; **to be** ~ **to sth** estar ligado a; ~ **to sb** *(feeling)* ter afeição por alguém/ algo/ser apegado a alguém/algo.
attachment *n* *(device)* acessório *m*, dispositivo *m*; **2** *(fondness)* ~ **(to)** afeição *f* (por); **3** *(COMP)* anexo *m*; **4** *(MIL)* destacamento *m*; **5** *(fastening)* fixação *f*; ~ **of earnings** *(JUR UK)* retenção *f* sobre o salário.
attack *n* assalto, ataque *m*; *(on sb's life)* atentado, *m*; agressão *f*; **heart** ~ *(MED)* ataque *m* cardíaco; **nervous** ~ uma crise *f* de nervos; ♦ *vt* *(gen)* atacar, assaltar; **2** agredir *(victim)*; **3** *(fig)* atacar *(task, book)*; *(job)* empreender.

attacker *n* agressor,-ora, assaltante *m,f*.
attain *vt*: **to** ~ **(to)** alcançar, atingir; **2** realizar *(ambição)*.
attainable *adj* acessível; realizável.
attainment *n* *(of goal)* realização *f*; **2** *(qualification, skill)* qualificação *f*; dotes *mpl*, talento *msg*.
attempt *n* tentativa *f*; ~ **on sb's life** atentado contra a vida de alguém; ♦ *vt* *(try)* tentar, intentar; ~**ed murder** assassínio *m* frustrado, tentativa *f* de assassinato.
attend *vt* *(be present at)* assistir a; **2** *(go regularly to)* frequentar; ♦ *(patients)* tratar **(to** de); **2** *(telephone, customer)* atender a; ♦ *vi* **to** ~ **to** *(work)* ocupar-se de; **2** prestar atenção a; **3** comparecer.
attendance *n* comparecimento; presence; **to be in** ~ **to sb** cuidar de alguém; acompanhar alguém.
attendant *n* empregado,-a; assistente; acompanhante; **2 flight** ~ hospedeira *(BR)* aeromoça *f*; comissário,-a de bordo; **3** *(for royalty)* membro *m* dum séquito; ♦ *adj* associado,-a; relacionado,-a; **2** *(symptom)* concomitante.
attention *n* atenção *f*; **medical** ~ assistência *f* médica; **for the** ~ **of** *(ADMIN)* *(in correspondence)* atenção de; ao cuidado de; **to draw** ~ chamar a atenção para; **2** atrair; **to pay** ~ prestar atenção; ♦ *exc* *(MIL)* sentido!
attentive *adj* atento,-a; cortês.
attest *vi*: **to** ~ **to** *(affirm)* atestar; *(prove)* provar, dar testemunho de.
attic *n* sótão *m*; *(with dormer windows)* água-furtada *f*.
attire *n* *(clothes)* traje *m*; vestuário *m*.
attired *pp adj* vestido,-a, trajado,-a; **the lady president was elegantly** ~ a presidenta estava elegantemente vestida.
attitude *n* atitude *f*; disposição *f*.
attorney *n* *(US)* *(lawyer)* advogado,-a; procurador, -ora; **A~ General** *npr* procurador-geral.
attract *vt* atrair; **2** suscitar *(interest)*; **to be** ~**ed to** ter uma atração por; ser atraído,-a **(to**, a).
attraction *n* *(entertainment)* atra(c)ção *f*; diversão *f*; **2** *(allure)* atra(c)ção *f*; **3** *(feature)* atra(c)tivo,-a.
attractive *adj* *(looks)* atraente; **2** *(idea, offer)* atrativo,-a.
attractively *adv* de modo atraente.
attribute *n* *(quality)* atributo, apanágio; ♦ *vt*: **to** ~ **sth to sb** atribuir algo a alguém; *(blame)*, imputar algo a alguém.
attrition *n* *(MIL, GEOL)* atrito *m*; **2** desgaste *m*.
attuned *adj* *(accustomed to)* acostumado a; adaptado a; familiarizado com algo; **2** *(tuned in)* sintonizado,-a.
atypical *adj* atípico,-a.
aubergine *n* *(BOT, CULIN)* berinjela *f*.
auburn *adj* castanho-avermelhado,-a.
auction *n* leilão *m*; **fish** ~ lota *f*; ♦ *vt* leiloar; ~ **off** *vt* leiloar.
auctioneer *n* leiloeiro,-a; **fish** ~ contador *m*.
audacious *adj* audaz, atrevido,-a; **2** *(cheeky)* descarado,-a, impudente.
audacity *n* audácia *f*; atrevimento *m*; **2** descaramento *m*.
audible *adj* audível.

audience *n* auditório *m*; **2** *(concert, show)* público *m*; **3** *(radio listeners)* ouvintes *mpl*; **4** *(formal meeting)* audiência *f*.

audio-visual *adj* audiovisual.

audit *n* peritagem *f* (às contas); auditoria *f*; **Government's A~ Office** *(UK)* *(equiv)* Tribunal *m* de Contas *(EP)* (de notar que sistemas nestés países diferem e que a tradução é uma equivalência); ♦ *vt* fiscalizar, examinar contas, audit.

audition *n* audição *f*; **to go for an ~** ter um audição; **2** *(for a part in a play/film)* fazer um teste para.

auditive *adj* auditivo; **~ device** *(hearing aid)* aparelho auditivo.

auditor *n* auditor,-ora perito,-a contabilista; **official ~** revisor,-ora oficial de contas (ROC).

auditorium *(pl: -ria)* *n* auditório *m*.

au fait *adj*: **to be ~ with sth** estar a par de algo.

augment *vt* aumentar; ♦ *vi* aumentar-se.

augur *n* vidente *m,f*; ♦ *vt/vi* agoirar; **it ~ s well** é de bom augúrio.

augury *n* agoiro, presságio *m*, augúrio *m*.

August *n* Agosto, agosto *m*; ♦ **august** *adj* augusto,-a, majestoso,-a.

augustinian *adj* *(relating to Saint Augustin or to his doctrine)* augustiniano.

auk *n* *(ZOOL)* alca *f*, penguim *m*.

Auld Lang Syne *npr* canção tradicional escocesa cantada na noite do ano-novo. Escrita pelo poeta Robert Burns em 1789.

aunt *n* tia.

auntie, aunty *(dim of* **aunt)** tiazinha, titi *(fam)*.

au pair *n* (estudante empregada como doméstica a tempo parcial e residente) au pair.

aura *n* *(of person)* aura *f*; **2** emanação *f*; **3** *(place)* ambiente *m*.

aural *adj* auditivo,-a; auricular *m,f*.

aurora *n* aurora *f*; **~ australis/borealis** aurora austral/boreal.

auspices *npl*: **under the ~ of** sob os auspícios de.

auspicious *adj* prometedor,-ora, auspicioso,-a.

Aussie *npr adj* *(fam)* australiano,-a.

austere *adj* *(person)* austero,-a; **2** *(manner)* severo,-a.

austerity *n* austeridade *f*.

Australasia *npr* Australásia *f*.

Australia *npr* Austrália; **in ~** na Austrália.

Australian *npr adj* australiano,-a; *(LING)* inglês.

Austria *npr* Áustria; **in ~** na Áustria.

Austrian *npr adj* austríaco,-a.

authentic *adj* autêntico,-a.

authenticate *vt* autenticar.

authenticity *n* autenticidade *f*.

author *n* autor,-ora.

authorship *n* autoria *f*.

authoritarian *adj* autoritário,-a.

authoritative *adj* *(voice, manner)* autoritário,-a; **2** *(source)* bem informado,-a.

authority *(pl: -ies)* *n* *(gen)* autoridade *f*; **2** *(expert)* **he is an ~ in Art** ele é uma autoridade em Arte; **3** *(permission)* autorização *f*; **to have it on good ~** saber de fonte *f* segura; **4 the ~ies** *(people in power)* as autoridades *fpl*.

authorize, authorise *vt*: **to ~ sb to do sth** autorizar alguém a fazer algo.

autism *n* autismo *m*.

autistic *adj* autista.

auto *n* *(coll)* carro, automóvel *m*.

autobiographical *adj* autobiográfico,-a.

autobiography *n* autobiografia *f*.

autocracy *n* autocracia *f*.

autocrat *n* autocrata *m,f*.

autocratic *adj* autocrático,-a.

Autocue® *npr* *(UK)* teleponto *m*; teleprompter *m*.

autograph *n* autógrafo *m*; ♦ *vt* autografar.

automate *vt* automatizar.

automatic *n* *(gun)* pistola *f* automática; ♦ *adj* automático,-a.

automation *n* *(of process, factory)* automatização *f*. **industrial ~** robótica *f*.

automaton *(pl: -mata)* *n* *(robot)* autómato *m,f*; *(BR)* robô *m*.

automobile *(US)* *n* carro, automóvel *m*.

autonomous *adj* autónomo,-a (BR: -tô-); independente.

autonomy *n* autonomia *f*.

autopsy *n* *(MED)* autópsia *f*.

autumn *n* Outono/outono *m*; **in ~** no outono; **an ~ morning** uma manhã outonal.

auxiliary *n adj* auxiliar *m,f*; ajudante *m,f*.

avail *n* vantagem *f*, utilidade *f*; **to no ~** em vão, inutilmente; ♦ *vt*: **to ~ o.s. of** aproveitar/valer-se de.

availability *n* disponibilidade *f*.

available *adj* disponível; utilizável; **'venison ~'** 'carne de veado à venda'.

avalanche *n* avalanche *f*, alude *m*.

avant-garde *adj* de vanguarda.

avarice *n* avareza *f*.

avaricious *adj* avarento,-a avaro-a.

avdp *(abbr for* **avoirdupois)**.

Ave *(abbr for* **Avenue)**.

avenge *vt* vingar; **to ~ oneself** vingar-se; **~ing angel** *n* anjo *m* exterminador.

avenue *n* avenida *f*; caminho *m*; **to explore every ~** explorar todas as vias.

aver **(-rr)** *vt* *(formal)* asseverar, assegurar.

average *n* média *f*, termo médio; **on ~** em média; ♦ *adj* médio,-a; comum; ♦ *vt* calcular a média de; **to ~ out** *vt* fazer a média (de algo); ♦ *vi*: **to ~ out at** resultar como média, fazer em média, ser por regra geral.

averse *adj* avesso,-a adverso,-a; **to be ~ to sth/to doing** ser avesso a algo/a fazer algo.

aversion *n* aversão *f*, repugnância *f*; **her pet ~** o que ela mais detesta.

avert *vt* *(avoid)* prevenir, evitar; **to ~ danger** evitar o perigo **2** *(turn away)* desviar *(gaze)*.

aviary *n* aviário *m* viveiro de aves.

aviation *n* aviação *f*.

avid *adj* ávido **(for** de).

avidity *n* avidez *f* **(for** por).

avidly *adv* avidamente; *(support)*, com fervor.

avocado *n*: **~ pear** abacate *m*.

avoid *vt* evitar, escapar.

avoidable *adj* evitável.

avoidance *n* evitamento *m*, prevenção *f*; **tax** ~ fuga ao fisco.

avoirdupois *n* sistema de pesos usado no comércio e baseado na libra-peso; **2** *(fig)* **the** ~ **of a book** o valor dum livro segundo o seu peso (em vez de conteúdo).

avow *vt* declarar, afirmar; **2** *(admit)* admitir, confessar.

avowed *adj* declarado,-a, manifesto,-a.

await *vt* esperar, aguardar; **I** ~ **your answer** aguardo a sua resposta.

awake *adj* acordado,-a, desperto,-a; ♦ *(pt* **awoke,** *pp* **awoken** *or* **awaked)** *vt/vi* despertar, acordar; **to be** ~ **to sth** ter consciência de algo; estar ciente de algo.

awaken *vt/vi* despertar, acordar *(feelings, memories).*

awakening *n (of emotion, interest)* despertar *m.*

award *n* prémio *(BR:* prê-); condecoração *f*; distinção *f* honorífica; **2** *(JUR)* decisão de um árbitro; **3** *(civil court)* compensation; ♦ *vt (grant, prize)* atribuir (**to**, a); **2** conceder; **3** galardoar; **4** *(JUR)* adjudicar.

award-winner *n* galardoado,-a; premiado,-a.

aware *adj* consciente (**of** de); informado,-a; a par de; **to become** ~ **of** reparar em, dar-se conta, conscializar-se; **to make sb** ~ conscencializar, sensibilizar alguém.

awareness *n* consciência de; sensibilização *f*; conscializalização *f*; *(BR)* conscientização *f.*

awash *adj* inundado,-a; **2** *(ship, person)* levado pelas ondas; ♦ *adv (afloat)* à tona da água.

away *adv* fora; **far** ~ muito longe; **thirty kilometres** ~ a trinta quilómetros de distância; **three hours** ~ **by car** a três horas de carro; **the trip was two weeks** ~ faltavam duas semanas para a viagem; ~ **from** longe de; **right** ~ imediatamente; **he's** ~ **for a week** está ausente por uma semana; ♦ **to take** ~ *vt* levar; **to go** ~ *vi* ir-se embora; **to work/pedal** ~ trabalhar/pedalar sem parar; **to**

fade ~ desvanecer-se; ♦ ~ **match** *n (SPORT)* jogo fora de casa.

awe *n* temor *m* respeitoso; reverência *f.*

awe-inspiring, **awesome** *adj* imponente; impressionante, temível; *(US) (coll)* fenominal.

awestruck *adj* pasmado,-a; temente.

awful *adj* terrível, horrível.

awfully *adv* muito; ~ **kind** muito generoso,-a.

awhile *adv* por algum tempo, um pouco, por um momento.

awkward *adj (clumsy)* desajeitado,-a; **2** *(inconvenient)* incómodo,-a *(BR:* -cô-); difícil; *(embarrassing)* embaraçoso,-a.

awning *n (over the shop)* toldo *m.*

awoke *(pt of* **awake**).

awoken *(pp of* **awake**).

awry *adj (picture)* oblíquo, torto; ♦ *adv:* **to be** ~ estar de viés/de esguelha/de través; **to go** ~ dar para o torto; sair mal, falhar.

axe *n* machado; *fig* **the** ~ **falls on ...** a desgraça abate-se sobre ...; ♦ *vt* cortar; **2** *(projects)* abandonar; **3** *(jobs, costs)* reduzir; **to** ~ **sb** despedir alguém; IDIOM **to have an** ~ **to grind** não dar ponto sem nó; ter um interesse pessoal.

axiom *n* axioma *m.*

axis *(pl:* **axes**) *n (abstract)* eixo.

axle *n* eixo *m (de roda).*

ay(e) *adv (UK) (POL) (yes)* sim; **the** ~**s** *npl (in voting)* os votos a favor; ~, ~ **Sir** *(NAUT)* Sim, Senhor.

Azerbaijan *npr* Azerbaijão.

Azerbaijani *n (língua)* azerbaijano, azerbaijanês; ♦ *n, adj (person)* azerbaijanês,-esa.

azimuth *n* azimute *m.*

Azorean *npr adj* açoriano,-a.

Azores *npr* Açores.

Aztec *npr adj* asteca *m,f.*

azure *n adj (colour)* azul-celeste *m.*

b

B, b *n (letter)* B, b *m*; **2** *(MUS)* si *m*.
b. *(abbr for* **born**); *(Vd:* **born**).
BA *(abbr for* **Bachelor of Arts)** Licenciado, Bacharel *m* em Letras, Ciências Humanas/Sociais.
baa *n (goat, sheep)* balido; ◆ *vt* balir.
babble *n (of babies)* balbucio; ◆ *vi (baby)* balbuciar; **2** falar de mais, palrar; **to ~ out a secret** deixar escapar um segredo.
babe *n* bebé *m inv*; **a ~ in arms** *(fam)* menina ingénua; **2** *(US) (coll) (attrative woman)* boneca *f*; garota *f*; **3** *(term of affection)* querida, amorzinho.
babel *n* babel *f*; algazarra, confusão *f*.
baboon *n* babuíno.
baby *n* criança, bebé *(BR:* -bê) *m,f*; *(BR)* nené *m*; **~ pram/buggy** *(UK)*, **~ carriage** *n (US)* carrinho de bebé; **~ food** comida para/de bebé *f*; **~hood** *n* infância, meninice; **~ish** *adj (pej)* infantil, criança; **~-sit** *vi* tomar conta de crianças; **~-sitter** *n* pessoa que toma conta de crianças; IDIOM **to throw the ~ out with the bath water** deitar tudo a perder.
baccalaureate *n (US) (univ) (diploma)* bacharelato *m*; **2** *(school)* **European International B~** exame final do ensino secundário europeu internacional.
bachelor *n* solteiro, celibatário; **old/confirmed ~** solteirão *m*; *(EDUC)* bacharel *m*; **2** *(EDUC)* **B~ of Arts, BA** *n* licenciado,-a, formado,-a em Letras; **B~ of Science (BsC)** *n* licenciado,-a em Ciências.
back *n (gen)* costas *fpl*; **the ~ of the hand** as costas da mão; **the ~ of a chair** as costas de uma cadeira, encosto *m*; **with one's ~ to the wall** encostado,-a à parede; *(fig) (in trouble)* entre a espada e a parede; **be (flat) on one's ~** *(ill)* estar de cama; **to turn one's ~ on sb/sth** virar as costas a alguém/a algo; **2** *(of animal, in gen.)* dorso *m*; *(of meat)* lombo; *(of horse)* garupa *f*; **the ~ of a horse** a garupa do cavalo; **3** *(rear of sth)* traseiras *fpl (BR)* fundos *mpl*; **the ~ of the house** as traseiras da casa; **4** *(SPORT)* defesa *m*, *(BR)* zagueiro *m*; **5** *(reverse, wrong side)* reverso *m*; *(of book)* contracapa *f*; *(of page, cheque)* verso *m*; *(of medal, coin)* reverso *m*; *(of book)* contracapa *f*; *(of fabric, clothes)* avesso *m*; **the ~ of a carpet** o avesso de uma carpete; ◆ *adj (at the rear)* traseiro,-a, de trás, atrás; **the ~ door** a porta de trás; *(of page)* último,-a; *(magazines)* números antigos/anteriores; **2** *(road)* secundário,-a; **3** *(behind time)* **~ orders** ordens *fpl* pendentes; **~ payments** pagamentos *mpl* atrasados; retroativos *mpl*; **~ rent** renda *f*, *(BR* aluguel *m)* em atraso; ◆ *adv* para

trás; **push ~** empurra para trás; **2** *(ago, last)* atrás; passado; **two days ~** dois dias atrás; **~ in March** em março passado; **3** *(be behind)* atrás de; **~ and forth** ir e vir, de um lado para o outro; **~ to front** *(the wrong way)* ao contrário, de trás para a frente; **~ to ~** costas com costas; ◆ **to answer ~** replicar, retorquir; **to be ~** *(person, fashion)* estar de volta; **I'll be ~ later** volto mais tarde; **to call ~** chamar de novo, telefonar; **to give sth ~** devolver; **to pay ~** *(debt)* pagar; *(compliment)* retribuir; *(revenge)* vingar-se de (alguém); ◆ *vt* **to ~** *(reverse)* recuar, fazer marcha a trás, *(BR: de ré)*; **2** *(support)* apoiar; *(with money)* financiar; **3** *(a cheque)* endossar; **4** *(to bet on: horse, deal)* apostar em; ◆ *vi* retornar; ◆ **~ away** afastar-se; **~ down** desistir; **~ off** afastar-se, recuar; **~ on to** *(facing)* dar para as traseiras, ter as traseiras viradas para; **~ out** *(of) (promise)* faltar ao prometido, voltar com a palavra atrás; **~ up** apoiar; **2** *(COMP)* fazer cópia de segurança: IDIOM **the ~ of beyond** *(far removed place)* em Cascos de Rolha; no cu de judas *(cal)*; **be at the ~ of sth** estar na origem de algo; **break one's ~** *(work)* trabalhar duro, de mais; **get sb's ~ up** irritar alguém; **get one's ~** *(on sb)* *(take revenge)* vingar-se (de alguém); **to put one's ~ into sth** *(work with gusto)* deitar mãos à obra.
backache *n* dor *f* de costas/nas costas.
back bacon *n* bacon, presunto *m* magro.
backbench *n (UK) (parlamento)* assento *m*/bancada *f* de trás dos deputadossem cargo.
backbencher *n (UK) (parlamento)* deputado sem pasta, no governo ou na oposição.
backbite *(pt* **bit**, *pp* **bitten** *or* **bit)** *vi* dizer/falar mal de *(alguém) (pelas costas)*; ratar na casaca *(fam)*.
backbiting *n* maledicência.
backbone *n* coluna *f* vertebral; **2** *(of fish)* espinha *f* dorsal; **3** *(main support)* pilar *m*; **to be the ~ of** ser o pilar de; **4** *(fig) (courage)* tutano *m*.
backbreaking *adj (exhausting)* estafante, de arrasar.
backburner *n (postpone work)* **to put sth on the ~** *(fig)* deixar algo em segundo plano, para mais tarde.
backcloth *n (THEAT)* pano de fundo.
backcomb *(tease the hair)* ripar o cabelo.
backdate *vt* antedatar; **~ed to March** estar datado com efeito retroactivo a Março.
backdrop *n (THEAT)* pano *m*/cortina *f* de fundo.
backer *n (POL)* partidário,-a, apoiante *m,f*; promotor,-ora; financiador,-ora; **2** *(FIN)* avalista *m,f*.
backfire *vi (fail: plans)* ter o efeito oposto, *(fig, fam)* sair o tiro pela culatra; **2** *(car)* produzir explosões no escape; *(BR)*engasgar.
backgammon *n* gamão *m*.
background *n (HIST)* origem *f*; antecedentes *mpl*; **2** *(picture, scene)* fundo; **3 ~ music** de fundo; **4** *(education)* formação *f*; **5** *(unobtrusive)* **to be in the ~** ficar em segundo plano; estar nos bastidores; *f*; **6 ~ radiation** *n* nível *m* baixo de radiação.
backhand *n (TENNIS)* revés *m*; **2** *(writing)* escrita *f* inclinada para a esquerda.

backhanded *adj* *(blow)* com as costas da mão; **2** *(fig)* ambíguo.

backhander *n* *(fam)* suborno *m*.

backing *n* *(fig)* *(FIN)* apoio *m*, endosso *m*; **2** *(MUS)* acompanhamento *m*; **3** *(reverse side)* revestimento *m* interior.

backissue *(Vd:* **backnumber***)*.

backlash *n* *(adverse reaction)* rea(c)ção violenta, revolta *f*.

backlog *n* *(work)* acúmulo *m* (de trabalho); trabalho em atraso.

backnumber *n* número anterior; **2** (algo) for-a de moda.

backpack mochila *f*.

backpassage *n* *(ANAT)* recto.

backpay *n* pagamento atrasado.

backroom *n* quarto dos fundos.

backside *n* *(ANAT)* *(fam)* traseiro *m*.

backslide ter uma recaída.

backslider *n* recaída *f*, reincidente *m*.

backspace *n* recla *f* de retorno.

backstage *adv* nos bastidores.

backstairs *npl* escada de serviço *f*.

backstitch *n* *(sewing)* ponto atrás.

backstreet *n* ruela *f*; **~-abortion** *n* aborto clandestino.

backstroke *n* *(swimming)* nado *m* de costas.

backtrack *vt* retroceder; **2** mudar de ideias.

backup *n* *(police)* reforços *mpl*; **2** apoio *m*; **3** *(COMP)* cópia de segurança; ♦ *adj* de reserva.

backward *adj* *(move, step)* para trás; **2** *(person, country)* atrasado, retardado; **3** retrógrado,-a; **4 ~ roll** cambalhota *f*; **5** *(read a list)* às avessas; de trás para frente; **6 ~ fall** *n* queda de costas.

backward-looking *adj* retrógrado,-a.

backward(s) *adv* para trás; **to know sth ~** saber *(algo)* de salteado.

backwash *n* *(situation)* repercussão *f*.

backwater *n* *(fof dam)* água represada; **2** lugar isolado; *(pej)* buraco *m*.

backwoods *n* *(remote place)* confins *mpl*.

backyard *n* quintal, pátio *m* traseiro,-a.

bacon *n* *(prosciutto type)* presunto; **2** *(English bacon)* bacon; **a rasher of ~** uma fatia de presunto; IDIOM **to bring home the ~** ser o ganha-pão da família.

bacteria *npl* bactérias *fpl*.

bacterium *n* bactéria *f*.

bad *n* **the good and the ~** o bom e o mau; ♦ *adj* *(comp:* **worse***; superl:* **worst***)* mau, má, ruím; *(language)* grosseiro,-a; **2** *(serious)* grave, sério,-a; **3** *(spoilt, rotten)* estragado,-a; **to go ~** estragar-se; **to have/get a ~ name** ter/ganhar má reputação; **to be in a ~ mood** estar zangado,-a; *adv* mal; **to go from ~ to worse** ir de mal a pior; **it will look ~** isso parece mal; **I feel ~ *(sick)*** sinto-me mal; **I feel ~ about** *(guilty)* sinto-me mal por/sentir-se culpado,-a; **it's too ~!** é pena!; **it's ~ enough** já é mau; **it's ~ to do** é errado fazer; ♦ **~ boy/girl!** *(naughty)* maroto,-a; mauzinho,-a; IDIOM **in a ~ way** *(in trouble)* em maus lençóis; **2** *(seriously ill)* estar muito mal.

bad blood *n* *(anger)* ódio, hostilidade; **there is ~ between them** eles estão de relações cortadas *fpl*.

bad cheque *(US:* **check***)* *n* cheque *m* sem cobertura, *(BR)* sem fundo.

bad debt *n* dívida *f* perdida.

baddie, baddy *(pl:* **-ies***)* *n* *(person in a film)* vilão *m*, vilã *f* **2** *(pop)* o mau da fita.

bade *(pret* of **to bid***)*.

bad feeling *n* *(resentment)* resentimento, rancor *m*.

badge *n* emblema *m*; crachá *m*.

badger *n* texugo *m*.

badly *(comp* **worse***; superl* **worst***)* *adv* mal; **she thinks ~ of me** ele pensa mal de mim; **2** *(poorly)* mal; **she is ~** ela está muito mal; **3** *(seriously)* gravemente; **~ wounded** gravemente ferido; **to be ~ in need of** *(very much)* precisar muito; **he needs it ~** isso faz-lhe grande falta; **to be ~-off** *(for money)* estar pobre; *(col)* estar nas lonas; **4** ser carente, necessitado; **5** *(in need of sth)* ter falta de algo *(roupa, espaço)*.

bad-mannered *adj* malcriado,-a, mal-educado,-a.

badminton *n* badminton *m*.

badness *n* maldade *f*.

bad-tempered *adj* *(irritable)* mal-humorado; **to be ~** *(by nature)* ter mau feitio, ter génio.

baffle *vt* *(puzzle)* confundir, desconcertar.

baffled *adj* confuse, perplexo, estupefa(c)to.

baffling *adj* desconcertante.

bag *n* saco *m*, saca *f*; **~ of potatoes** saca *f* de batatas; **school ~** sacola; *(baggage)* mala; *(hunting = quantity of)* caça; **~ of bones** *(coll)* *(person)* very thin person; **an old ~** *(mulher)* *(pej)* velha e feia *f*; **in the ~** *(fam)* *(about to succeed)* no papo; **bags of** *(coll: lots of time, money)* montes *mpl* de; ♦ *(-gg-)* *vt* *(coll: save, get, achieve)* guardar, reservar, apanhar; **she ~ged a lot of fruit** ela apanhou muita fruta; *(catch, steal)* levar; **the thief ~ged all my silver** o ladrão levou toda a minha prata; IDIOM **bags and baggage** com armas e bagagem.

bagful *(pl:* **bagsful***)* *n* saco cheio.

baggage *n* *(luggage)* bagagem; **2 cultural ~** *(knowledge, experience)* conhecimento *m*, bagagem *f* cultural *f*; **3** *(MIL)* *(army's portable equipment)* equipamento *m* portátil; **~ room** *n* *(US)* guarda-volumes *m*.

baggy (ier, iest) *adj* largo, amplo; hanging loose.

bagpipes *npl* gaita de foles.

bagsnatcher *n* batedor,-ora de carteiras.

Bahamas *npr* Baamas *fpl*; *(BR)* Bahamas.

Bahgdad *npr* Bagdade; *(BR)* Bagdá.

Bahrain, Bahrein *npr* Barein; ♦ **Bahreini** *n, adj* bareini.

bail *n* *(JUR)* fiança *f*; ♦ *vt* **to release sb on ~** libertar alguém sob fiança/caução; **2** *(NAUT)* *(also:* **bale***)* baldear (do barco); **~ out** *vt* libertar sob fiança; **2** *(from a predicament)* desenrascar(-se) *(coll)*; **3** *vi* *(emergency)* saltar de paraquedas.

bailout *n* ajuda *f* financeira, resgate *m*.

bailiff *n* *(in court)* oficial *m,f* de justiça; oficial *m,f* de diligências; **2** *(steward of a landowner)* feitor; **3** *(in charge of repossessions)* administrador,-ora; magistrado,-a local.

bailout n ajuda f financeira.
bain-marie n (CULIN) banho-maria m.
bait n (food to entice fish, etc) isca; (fig) **to take/rise to/swallow the** ~ morder a isca; (fig) (enticement) engodo; ♦ vt (to put food on) iscar (hook, trap); 2 (entice) engodar; 3 (tease) apoquentar.
baize n (kind of felt, usually green) baeta; repes.
bake vt (CULIN) cozer, assar no forno; ~**d potato** batata f assada com casca (no forno); 2 (kiln) cozer; 3 (sun) secar (ao sol); (dry, harden) endurecer; 4 (of weather) fazer um calor terrível.
baker n padeiro, pasteleiro.
bakery n padaria; pastelaria.
baking n (process) cozedura; fornada; ♦ adj (weather) escaldante ~ **powder** n fermento em pó; ~ **tin** n fôrma f; ~ **tray** n assadeira.
balance n (equilibrium) equilíbrio; **to catch sb off** ~ (fig) apanhar alguém desprevenido; **to hang in** ~ (fig) estar em jogo; ♦ **on** ~ adv feitas as contas, de um modo geral; 2 (COMM) (of bank account) saldo m; (remainder of debt, sum) resto m, restante f; ~ **of payments/of trade** n balança f de pagamentos/comercial; ♦ ~ **sheet** balancete m sumário geral; ♦ vt fazer o balanço; 2 (compare, compensate for) contrabalançar; (AUT) calibrar (wheels); (weigh up) medir, pesar; ♦ vi (maintain equilibrium) equilibrar-se.
balancing act n número m de equilibrista, malabarista m,f.
balcony n varanda; 2 (closed) marquise f; 3 (THEAT) segundo balcão m.
bald adj (head, person) calvo,-a; (fam) careca m,f; 2 (AUT) (tyre) liso, careca; ~ **eagle** n águia f americana (símbolo dos E.U.A.).
balderdash n (coll) disparate m, tolice f; ♦ exc tretas! cantigas!
balding adj começo de calvície; **he is** ~ ele está a ficar calvo,-a.
baldness n calvície f.
bale n (AGR) fardo m; pacote m; ♦ vt **to** ~ **cotton/hay** enfardar, empacotar; ~ **out** (Vd: bail out).
baleful adj (harmful, vindictive) maléfico; 2 funesto; 3 (dejected) tristonho.
balk, baulk n impedimento; ♦ vt (thwart) frustrar; ♦ vi mostrar-se relutante; 2 (recoil) recuar (**at/from sth** perante algo).
Balkan adj balcânico,-a.
Balkans (= The Balkans) npl os Balcãs.
ball n (gen) bola; (of iron, lead) pelota; (of wool) novelo m (BR) bola f de lã; 2 esferas; ~ **bearing** n (MEC) rolamento m de esferas; ~ **cock** (MEC) válvula f de depósito de água; 3 (dance) baile; **the** ~ **of the foot** (ANAT) parte redonda da sola do pé; IDIOM **to keep the** ~ **rolling** (progress of a plan) manter a bola em jogo; **to be on the** ~ manter-se informado; **the** ~ **is in your court** é a tua/sua vez de agir; **to have a** ~ divertir-se.
ballad n balada.
ball-and-socket joint n (also: ball joint) (MEC) articulação esférica f; junta articulada f.
ballast n lastro.

ballerina n bailarina.
ballet n ballet, balé m, bailado m; ~ **dancer** n bailarino,-a.
ball game n (fig) (situation) **it's a whole new** ~ é outra história.
ballistic missile n míssil m balístico.
ballistics n balística f.
balloon n balão m; bola de soprar.
balloonist n balonista m inv.
ballot n votação f secreta; boletim m de voto; ~ **box** n urna; ~ **paper** n cartão de eleitor, (BR) cédula eleitoral.
ballouist n aeronauta m,f.
ballpark n estádio de basebol; 2 nível.
ballpoint pen n (pen) (caneta) esferográfica.
ballroom n salão m de baile; ~ **dancing** n dança f de salão.
balls npl (slang) (testicles) tomates mpl, (BR) saco m; (fig) (guts): **to have** ~ (slang) ter colhões (vulg).
balls-up n (US: ball-up) (slang) confusão; ♦ vt semear a confusão.
balm n bálsamo n.
balmy (-ier, -iest) adj (of weather) ameno, suave.
baloney n (fam) (rubbish) asneira f; 2 (US) mortadela f.
Baltic npr **the** ~ (**Sea**) o (Mar) Báltico.
balustrade n balaustrada f.
bamboo n bambu m; ~ **curtain** cortina de bambu.
ban n proibição f, interdição f; ♦ (pt, pp -**ned**) vt banir, proibir, interditar; excluir.
banal adj (trite, common) banal, vulgar.
banality n banalidade f.
banana n banana; ~ **republic** n (pej) república f das bananas; ~ **skin** casca f de banana.
band n (musical group) banda; 2 (gang) bando m, quadrilha f; 3 (long strip) correia; (of land, of colour) faixa; 4 (of waistband) cinta f, faixa f; 5 (for hair) fita f; 6 (for arm) braçadeira f; 7 (wedding ring) aliança f; ~ **master** n (MUS) mestre/conductor m de banda; **to** ~ **together** vi juntar-se a, associar-se a.
bandage n ligadura, (BR) atadura; ♦ vt ligar (**contra against**) enfaixar.
bandanna n lenço m de pescoço de cabeça.
bandit n bandido; **one-armed** ~ caça-moedas, (BR) caça-níqueis.
bandstand n coreto m.
bandwagon n (US) vagão que leva a banda; IDIOM **to jump on the** ~ (fig) seguir a corrente, juntar-se aos que triunfam.
bandy vt (exchange words) trocar (insultos); ~-**legged** adj de pernas arqueadas, cambaio, cambeta; ♦ vi discutir.
bang n (crack of a plate, etc) estalo; 2 (loud noise) estrondo; 3 (blow) pancada; ~ **goes my job** posso dizer adeus ao meu emprego; ♦ adv ~ **on time** à hora certa; **with a** ~ (successfully); **the party went with a** ~ a festa foi um estouro; ♦ vt (hit, bump,knock hard) ~ **one's head on** bater com a cabeça em; (slam: door, window) bater com/fechar com violência; ♦ vi **to** ~ **into** (bump) bater em, chocar com; ♦ exc **bang!** bum; IDIOM ~ **one's head against a brick wall** tentar realizar o impossível.

banger *n (UK) (fam) (old car)* calhambeque *m*, carroça *f*; **2** *(firework)* petardo *m*; **3** *(CULIN) (pop)* salsicha *f*.

Bangladesh *m npr* Bangladesh; **in** ~ no Bangladesh.

bangle *n* bracelete *m*, pulseira *f*.

banish *vt (gen)* desterrar, exilar; banir; **2** *(dismiss)* afugentar.

banister(s) *n(pl) (of the staircase)* corrimão *m*.

banjo *(pl: -es or -s) n* banjo *m*.

bank *n (FIN)* banco, *m*; ~ **account** *n* conta bancária; ~ **charges** *n* encargos *mpl* bancários; ~ **clerk** *n* empregado,-a bancário,-a; ~ **draft** *n* ordem *f* bancária ~**er** *n* banqueiro; ~ **holiday** *n* feriado nacional; **banking** *n* transações *fpl* bancárias; banca; ~ **manager** *n* gerente de banco; ~**note** *n* nota *f*, cédula *f*; ~ **rate** *n* taxa *f* referencial de juros; ~**roll** *n* fundos *mpl*; ~ **statement** *n* extra(c)to bancário *m*; **2** *(of river, lake)* borda, margem *f*; **3** *(slope)* rampa, ladeira; **sand** ~ banco de areia; **4** *(MED)* **sperm** ~ banco de espermas *m*; ◆ *vi (AER)* inclinar lateralmente; **2** *(border)* ladear; **3** *(FIN)* depositar num banco; **to** ~ **with** ter conta em; ◆ **to** ~ **on** *vt (rely on)* contar com; **to** ~ **up** *(mud, snow)* amontoar.

bankrupt *n adj* falido,-a; *(person)* insolvente, arruinado,-a; **to go** ~ falir; ◆ **to** ~ **a company** levar uma empresa à falência.

bankruptcy *n* falência; bancarrota.

banner *n* bandeira; estandarte *m*; **2** *(in protest or festival)* bandeirola *f*.

banns *npl (of wedding)* banhos *mpl*; **to publish the** ~ proclamar os banhos.

banquet *n* banquete *m*.

bantam *n*: **cock**~ garnisé *m*.

banter *n* brincadeira, gracejo; ◆ *vi* gracejar, estar na brincadeira.

baptism *n* ba(p)tismo.

baptize *vt* ba(p)tizar.

bar *n (of chocolate, soap, in gym, etc)* barra *f*; ~ **chart** *n* gráfico *m* de barras. ~ **code** *n* código de barras. **2** *(MUS)* compasso; **3** *(on gate, window)* tranca; **4** *(prison)* grades; *(fig)* obstáculo; impedimento; **5** *(of drinks)* bar *m*; *(counter)* balcão *m*; **6** *(limit)* **age** ~ limite *m* de idade; **7** *(JUR) (in courthouse)* barra *f*; **the Bar** a advocacia, o corpo de advogados; **to read for the B~** estudar Direito; ◆ *prep* exce(p)to; **at the** ~ em tribunal; **behind** ~**s** na prisão; ◆ *(-rr-) vt* obstruir; trancar; *(prevent)* excluir; barrar; **he barred my way** ele barrou-me o caminho.

barb *n (on hook, arrow tip)* barbela *f*; farpa *f*.

barbarian *n* bárbaro.

barbaric *adj* bárbaro.

barbarous *adj* bárbaro, desumano.

barbecue *n (CULIN, party)* churrasco *m*; *(grill)* churrasqueira; ◆ *vt* assar (na churrasqueira).

barbed *adj (with hook)* com farpas; **2** *(comment)* áspero, cáustico, mordaz; ~ **wire** *n* arame *m* farpado.

barbel *n (river fish)* barbo.

barber *n* barbeiro; ~**'s shop** barbearia.

barbiturate *n* barbitúrico.

bard *n (great poet)* bardo; **Shakespeare is England's** ~ Shakespeare é o bardo da língua inglesa.

bare *adj (naked)* despido, nu; ~**foot(ed)** descalço; **2** *(field)* descoberto; **3** *(empty)* vazio; **4** *(basic)* mínimo,-a; **the** ~ **necessities** as necessidades básicas *fpl*; ◆ *vt (uncover)* destapar, descobrir; **to** ~ **one's teeth** arreganhar os dentes; ◆ ~**back** *adv* em pêlo; sem arreios.

barefaced *adj (without make-up)* deslavado; **2** *(cheeky)* descarado.

barely *adv* mal, quase não; **he** ~ **speaks** ele quase não fala.

bareness *n* nudez.

bargain *n* deal, negócio; **2** *(very cheap)* pechincha; ◆ *vi* negociar; **2** *(haggle)* regatear; **to** ~ **for** *vt* contar com, esperar; **to get a** ~ comprar muito barato; **into the** ~ ainda por cima; **we got more than we bargained for** conseguimos mais do que esperávamos; IDIOM **a** ~ **is a** ~ o combinado é combinado.

bargain hunter *n* pechincheiro.

bargaining *n* regateio *m*, *(BR)* barganha.

barge *n* barcaça; barca; ◆ **to** ~ **in** *vi* entrar sem permissão; **2 to** ~ **into sb/sth** esbarrar com, deparar-se com (alguém/algo); ◆ *vt* ~ **in (on sb/sth)** interromper; **2** *(shove)* empurrar; ~ **one's way through** abrir caminho aos encontrões.

bargee *n* barqueiro.

bargepole *n*: IDIOM **I wouldn't touch him/it with a** ~ não o quero nem de graça.

baritone *n* barítono.

bark *n* casca (de árvore); **2** *(dog's)* latido; ◆ *vi* ladrar, latir; ◆ *vt (order)* ~ **out (at sb/sth)** ladrar, gritar; IDIOM **his** ~ **is worse than his bite** cão que ladra não morde.

barking *n* ladrar *m*; ◆ *adj* que ladra; **the dog is** ~ o cão está a ladrar, *(BR)* ladrando; **the man is** ~ **mad (furious)** o homem está/anda louco.

barley *n* cevada *f*.

barmaid *n* empregada (de bar), *(BR)* garçonete *f*.

barman *n* empregado (de bar), *(BR)* garçom *m*.

barmy *adj (coll) (UK)* maluco,-a, chalado,-a, *(BR)* pirado, encucado,-a.

barn *n (granary)* celeiro; **2** *(for cattle)* estábulo; **3** *(for horses)* estrebaria *f*; ~ **owl** *n (ZOOL)* coruja *f*.

barnacle *n (cirripedia)* lapa *f*, *(BR)* craca *f*; **2** *(ZOOL) (bird)* bernaca; **goose** ~ *(fig) (person, thing difficult to be rid of)*; sarna *f*.

barometer *n (MET)* barómetro *(BR*: -rô-*)*.

baron *n* barão *m*; **oil/press** ~ *(tycoon)* magnata *m,f* do petróleo/da imprensa.

baroness *n* baronesa *f*;

barony *n* baronia; baronato.

baroque *n adj* barroco *m*.

barracks *npl* quartel *m*, caserna *f*.

barracuda *f (fish)* barracuda.

barrage *n (MIL)* bombardeio *m*; **2** *(dam)* barragem *f* represa *f*; **3** *(continuous questions, words)* bombardeio.

barrel *n (barrel)* barril *m*, barrica; **2** *(of gun)* cano (de arma); ~~**organ** *n* realejo.

barren *adj* estéril, árido, improdutivo, inútil.

barricade *n* barricada; ◆ *vt* barricar.

barrier n (wall) barreira; **2** (fig) obstáculo; ~ **cream** n (UK) loção f protectora; (**ticket**) ~ n (RAIL) cancela; **to put up a** ~ (PSYC) fechar-se, ser reservado, introvertido,-a.

barring prep (except for, unless) exce(p)to; salvo; a menos que; ~ **rain** a menos que chova.

barrister n (UK) advogado,-a.

barrow n (for garden, building) carrinho de mão.

bartender n (US) empregado (de bar), (BR) garçom m, barman m.

barter n permuta, barganha, troca; ♦ vt: **to** ~ **sth for sth** (exchange) trocar algo por algo; (haggle) negociar por troca.

base n (gen) base f; **2** (MIL) base, centro de operações; **3** (of mountain) sopé m; **4** (of edifice) alicerce m; **5** base f; fundamento m ♦ adj ignóbil, vil, baixo,-a; (language) grosseiro,-a; **2** (quality) inferior, falso,-a; ♦ vi fundamentar (**on**, em), basear (**on**, em); ♦ **to be off** ~ (US) estar muito errado; **touch** ~ contatar.

baseball n basebol m, (BR) beisebol m.

based adj pp (person, company) sediado,-a, estabelecido,-a (**at**, em); **2** (plan, theory) baseado,-a (**on**, **upon**, em).

baseless adj infundado,-a.

basement n cave f; (BR) porão; **2** (ARCH) (foundations) envazamento m.

baseness n baixeza f, vileza f.

base rate n (FIN) taxa f de referência.

bash (pl: -es) n (punch, blow) murro m, sova f; **2** (dent) amolgadela f; **3** (party) farra; ♦ vt (coll) **to have a** ~ **at sth** tentar (fazer) algo; **2 to** ~ **on/ against** (hit, knock) bater com (a cabeça) em/ contra; **3** (strike) sovar, dar uma surra a/em; **4** ~ **the door down** arrombar a porta; **5** ~ **into** (collide with sb/sth) embater em, esbarrar com; **6** criticar, (BR) xingar.

bashful adj tímido, envergonhado.

bashfully adv timidamente.

bashing n (coll) sova, surra, tareia; **2** (fig) (criticism) crítica f sistemática.

basic adj básico,-a; elementar; simples inv.

basically adv fundamentalmente, basicamente.

basics npl bases fpl.

basil n (BOT, CULIN) manjericão m.

basin n (vessel) bacia; (non-plumbed) alguidar m; **2** (GEOG) bacia; doca; **wash**~ lavatório m, bacia f, (BR) pia f.

basis (pl: -ses) n base f.

bask vi (relax) refastelar-se; **to** ~ **in the sun** apanhar sol, (BR) pegar sol; **2** ~ **in his love** (enjoy) gozar do seu amor.

basket n cesto m, cesta f; cabaz, alcofa; canastra; ~ **ball** n basquete (bol) m; ~**work** n obra de verga; trabalho de vime.

Basle npr Basiléia f.

Basque adj basco,-a.

bas-relief n baixo-relevo m.

bass n (fish) perca; **2** (MUS) baixo; **3** (sound/voice) grave m; **double** ~ (MUS) contrabaixo.

bassoon n (MUS) fagote m.

bassoonist n fagotista m,f.

bastard n adj (pej) (person) canalha, filho da mãe, pulha; **2** (illegitimate child) bastardo,-a, ilegítimo,-a.

baste vt (CULIN) regar com molho; **2** (sewing) (loose stitches) alinhavar; **3** (thrash) espancar.

bastion n baluarte m.

bat n (ZOOL) morcego; **2** (SPORT: baseball) bastão m; (table tennis) raquete f; (cricket) pá m; ♦ adj **off one's own** ~ de sua livre vontade; ♦ adv **at full** ~ (slang) (speed, rate) a toda a velocidade; ♦ (-ted, -ting) vt/vi bater com força; IDIOM **blind as a** ~ ser míope; **he didn't** ~ **an eyelid** ele nem pestanejou.

batch n (of cakes, bread) fornada; **2** (of work) porção f; **3** (papers, letters) monte m; **4** (of books, orders) remessa, lote; ~ **file** n (COMP) arquivo em lote.

bated adj: **with** ~ **breath** contendo a respiração, com a respiração suspensa (de ansiedade).

bath n banho; **2** (tub) banheira; ~**s** (swimming) piscina f; **3** (public) balneários mpl; (in spa) termas f; **to have a** ~ tomar um banho (in the tub or sea); ~**mat** n tapete m de banho (BR) de banheiro; ~**robe** n roupão m; ~**room** n casa/quarto de banho, (BR) banheiro; ~ **towel** n toalha de banho; ♦ vt **to** ~ **sb** dar banho a (alguém).

bathe vi banhar-se; ♦ vt banhar, lavar (**sth, sb** algo, alguém); (swim) nadar.

bather n banhista m,f.

bathing n banho; **to go** ~ ir dar um mergulho; ~ **cap** n touca de banho; ~ **costume** n fato de banho, (BR) roupa de banho, maiô m; ~ **trunks** npl calções mpl de banho.

bathhouse n (public) balneário m.

batman (pl: -men) n (UK) (MIL) (officer's servant) (o) ordenança, impedido m.

baton n (MUS) batuta; bastão; **2** (de polícia) bastão, cassetete m; **3** (baseball, cricket) (estafeta) testemunho m.

batsman n (SPORT) batedor m.

battalion n (MIL) batalhão m.

batten n (CONSTR) (door, floor) travessa; (roofing) sarrafo m, ripa f; **2** (piece of wood) tábua f; **3** (NAUT) (in sail) fasquia; **4** (THEAT) (for lights) gambiarra; ♦ vt reforçar com ripas, travessas; (NAUT) correr as escotilhas; IDIOM ~ **down the hatches** preparar-se para o pior.

batter n (CULIN) massa; ♦ vt/vi (child, wife) bater em, espancar; **2** (door, wall) arrombar, derrubar.

battered adj amassado,-a; **2** (item) muito usado, estragado, (car, etc) amolgado; **3** (subjected to violence) **a** ~ **child** criança espancada; **4** (subjected to criticism) amarfanhado,-a.

battering-ram n (MIL) aríete m.

battery n (for car) bateria; (ELECT) pilha; **2** (group of things) série f; **a** ~ **of questions** um bombardeio de perguntas; **3** (MIL, MUS) bateria; **4** (JUR) agressão, espancamento; ~ **charger** n carregador m de bateria; ~ **farming** n criação de aves; ~ **hen** n frango m de aviário/(BR) de granja.

battle n batalha; **2** (fig) luta; **to be half the** ~ ser meio caminho andado; ♦ vi lutar.

battlefield n campo de batalha.

battlements *npl* ameias *fpl.*

battleship *n* couraçado.

bauble *n* bijutaria; **2** *(trinket)* bugiganga; ninharia; **3** bola, enfeite *m* de Natal.

bawdy *n* obscenidade *f*; ♦ **(-ier, -iest)** *adj* indecente; immoral, obceno,-a.

bawl *vi (shout)* gritar; **2** *(weep)* berrar; **to ~ out sb for** *vt* repreender, censurar alguém por.

bay *n (GEOG)* baía; **to hold/keep at ~** *(fig)* manter à distância; **2** *(BOT)* **~ leaf** folha *f* de louro; **~ tree** loureiro *m*; **3 residents' ~** *(individual car parking)* parcamento *m*; **4** *(horse)* cavalo *m* baio; **5 ~ window** janela *f* saliente/de sacada; ♦ *vi (dog, wolf)* latir; IDIOM **to bring someone to ~** *(impossible retreat)* encostar alguém à parede.

Bay of Biscay *npr* **the ~** o Golfo da Biscaia.

bayonet *n* baioneta.

bazaar *n* bazar *m.*

bazooka *n (MIL)* bazuca *f*; lança-foguetes *m inv.*

b&b, B&B *n (abbr for* **bed and breakfast)** *(UK)* cama e pequeno-almoço, *(BR)* cama e café da manhã.

BBC *npr (abbr for* **British Broadcasting Corporation)** BBC.

BC *(abbr for* **before Christ)** antes de Cristo, a.C.

be *(pres:* **am, are, is**; *pt* **was, were**; *pres p* **being**; *pp* **been)** *aux vi* ser; *(inherent state, characteristic)* **I am tall** sou alto; **she is boring** ela é aborrecida; **he is fat** ele é gordo; **who is it?** quem é?; **2** *(profession, vocation, civil status)* **are you the manager?** você/o senhor é o gerente?; **we are tourists** somos turistas; **3** *(stating a fact/opinion)* **it is impossible** é impossível; **the climate is good** o clima é bom; **this is beautiful, isn't it?** isto é lindo, não é?; **4** *(price, cost)* **how much is it?** quanto é?; **5** *(time)* **que horas são?** what time is it?; *(in passive voice)* **the book was given by me** o livro foi dado por mim; **be cheated/misled** ser enganado,-a; ♦ *exc* **so be it!** (OK) assim seja!; ♦ *(temporary condition/action/place)* estar; **I am tired** estou cansado; **você está aborrecido?** are you bored?; **how are you?** como está?; **the weather is bad** o tempo está mau; **she is (looking) fat** ela está gorda; **we have been here for two hours** estamos aqui há duas horas; **I was being polite** estava a ser, *(BR)* sendo cortês; **she was sick** ela estava doente; **2** *(in progressive tense)* **it is raining** está a chover, *(BR)* está chovendo; **3** *(to be hungry, thirsty, cold, etc)* estar com/ter; **I am hungry** estou com/tenho fome; *(age)* **I am twelve years old** tenho doze anos; **4** *(compound tenses)* **where have you been?** onde tem estado; *(BR)* onde você estava?; **5** *(about to, almost)* **I was about to go out** eu estava prestes a sair; **be mistaken** estar enganado,-a.

Notar as diferenças entre os significados nos exemplos da verbete acima: `aborrecido,-a', `enganado,-a', `gordo,-a'.

beach *n* praia; ♦ *vt (fish, sth)* dar à costa; *(boat, whale)* encalhar.

beacon *n (lighthouse)* farol *m*; **2** *(radio beacon)* radiofarol; **3** *(buoy)* bóia *f* de sinalização; **4** *(of aviation)* baliza *f*; **5** sinal *m* luminoso; **6** *(warning fire, invasion)* fogaréu; **7** *(guide, inspiration)* guia *m*; ♦ *vt* guiar, avisar por meio de luz.

bead *n (in necklace, rosary)* conta; pérola; *(small-glass beads)* missanga *f* **2** *(drop of sweat)* gota (de suor); ♦ *vi:* **to draw a ~ on** *vi* fazer pontaria.

beady **(-dier, -iest)** *adj (eyes)* pequenos e brilhantes; **~-eyed** *adj (person)* com olhos penetrantes; IDIOM **I have my ~ eye on you** tenho-te debaixo de olho.

beak *n (of bird, mouth of some animals)* bico *m*; **2** *(de pessoa)* nariz aquilino; **3** *(coll)* magistrado; professor/reitor.

beaker *n* taça *f* com bico; **2** *(CHEM) (recipient)* proveta *f.*

be-all and end-all *n (fam) (end, justification)* o mais que tudo; a razão de ser; **2** *(providing help)* **the ~ of this group** a razão de ser do grupo; **3** *(humour) (person who needs no improvement)* o sabichão.

beam *n (ARCH)* viga *f*, trave *f*; **2** *(of light)* raio *m*, feixe *m*; ♦ *vi* irradiar; **3** *(sign)* emitir.

beaming *adj* radiante.

bean *n* feijão *m*; **full of ~s** muito animado; **to spill the ~s** revelar um segredo; **broad ~** vagem *f*; fava; **coffee ~** grão *m* de café; **runner ~** feijão *m* verde.

bear *n* urso,-a; *(FIN) (especulador, market)* baixista *m,f*; ♦ *(pt* **bore**, *pp* **borne)** *vt (carry)* levar, carregar; **2** *(sustain, tolerate)* suportar, aguentar; **I can't ~ that woman** não suporto, aguento aquela mulher; **3** *(suffer)* sofrer; **4** *(pay)* pagar; **he bore the expense** ele pagou a despesa; **5** *(give birth to)* dar à luz, parir; **she bore a son** ela deu à luz um filho; **6** *(feel, have)* **she bears him a grudge** ela tem-lhe rancor; ♦ *vi* virar; **to ~ right/left** virar à direita/à esquerda; **2 ~ to/on sb** *(influence, pressure)* exercer influência/pressão sobre alguém; **~ down on sb/sth** cair sobre, abater-se sobre algo,-alguém; **to ~ in mind** lembrar-se de, tomar em conta; **~ off** desviar-se, fazer-se ao largo; **~ out** confirmar; **~ up** resistir, conservar a coragem; **~ upon** referir-se a; **~ with** tolerar; **~ witness** prestar testemunho.

bearable *adj* suportável; tolerável.

beard *n* barba.

bearded *adj* barbado, com barba; **beardless** *adj* imberbe.

bearer *n (of good/bad news)* portador,-ora; **2** *(of new title)* detentor,-ora; **3** *(of stretcher)* carregador,-ora.

bearing *n (posture, manner)* porte *m*, comportamento *m*; **2** *(relevance)* relação *f* com; **it has no ~ on this matter** isso não tem nada a ver com este assunto; **~s** *npl* orientação *fsg*, rumo *m*; **to get one's ~s** *(direction)* tentar orientar-se; **to lose one's ~s** perder o rumo.

bearish *adj (ECON) (market)* em baixa.

beast *n* besta, animal *m*; **2** *(coll)* bruto, selvagem *m.*

beastly *adj* repugnante *m,f*; horrível *m,f*; bruto,-a.

beat *n (gen)* batida; **2** *(MUS)* ritmo, compasso; **3** *(of policeman)* ronda *f*; **4** *(of heart, pulse)* batimento *m*, pulsar *m* do coração; **5** *(of the drums)* rufar *m* *(do tambor)*; **6** *(flap of birds's wings)* bater *m*; **dead ~** *(exhausted)* morto,-a de fadiga; ♦ *(pt* **beat***, pp* **beaten***) vt (hit)* bater em; **2** *(defeat)* vencer, derrotar; **your question beats me** não compreendo a tua pergunta, declaro-me vencido; **3** *(arrive before)* chegar antes, vencer; **you ~ me to it** você venceu-me; **4** *(drums)* tocar, rufar; **5** *(MUS) (rhythm)* marcar; ♦ **to ~ sb black and blue** *(coll)* espancar, dar uma tareia em alguém; **to ~ a retreat** *(gen) (MIL)* bater em retirada; **~ it!** *(fam)* põe-te a mexer!; *(CULIN) (mixture, eggs)* bater; ♦ *vi (heart)* bater; **2** *(strike) (rain, sea)* bater (**against** contra); **to ~ about the bush** *(fig)* falar com rodeios; **to ~ down** *(rain, hail)* cair fortemente; *(sun)* bater de chapa (**on** sobre); *(force to lower prices) vt* fazer baixar os preços; **~ out sth** *(metal)* martelar; *(flames)* abafar (as chamas); **to ~ one's brain out** *(fig)* queimar os neurónios; **to ~ the truth out of sb** arrancar a verdade a alguém; ♦ *vt* repelir; **to ~ up** *vt (col)* dar uma sova em.

beaten *adj* vencido, derrotado; **2** *(metal)* forjado,-a, martelado,-a; **3** *(path)* batido,-a; **~ track** rota batida.

beater *(electric) n* batedeira; **2** *(de tapete)* batedor *m*; **3** *(of person)* aggressor,-ora.

beatify *vt (REL)* beatificar.

beating *n (gen)* batida; **2** sova, surra; **get a ~** apanhar uma tareia; **take a ~** *(coll) (rough treatment)* ser maltratado,-a; **3** *(heart)* pulsação *f*; **4** *(SPORT)* derrota.

beat-up *adj (coll)* a cair aos pedaços, desconjuntado,-a.

beautician *n* esteticista *m,f*.

beautiful *adj* belo,-a, lindo,-a, formoso,-a; **a ~ horse** um belo cavalo; **a ~ woman** uma mulher bela; maravilhoso,-a, excelente *m,f*; *(weather)* magnífico.

beautily *adv* maravilhosamente, lindamente.

beautify *vt* embelezar.

beauty *n* beleza, formosura; beldade *f*; **2** *(advantage)* **the ~ of it is that ...** a vantagem disto é que ...; **~ contest** concurso de beleza; **~ salon** *n* salão *m* de beleza; **~ sleep** primeiro sono; **~ spot** *n (on the skin)* sinal *m* (de beleza); **3** *(place)* recanto; IDIOM **~ is in the eye of the beholder** quem o ama, bonito lhe parece.

beaver *n (ZOOL)* castor *m*.

bebop *n (fam)* dançar ao som de música pop.

becalmed *adj* imóvel *m,f*, parado, devido a calmaria.

became *(pt of* **become**).

because *conj* porque; ♦ **~ of** *prep* por causa de.

béchamel sauce *n* molho branco *m*

beck *n* aceno, gesto, sinal *m*; **to be at the ~ and call of** estar sempre às ordens de/à disposição de alguém.

beckon *vt:* **~ to** *(make a sign to)* chamar com sinais/gestos, acenar para; **he ~ed her to approach** ele fez sinal para que ela se aproximasse.

become *(irr: like* **come***) vt* favorecer, ficar bem, ser próprio; *(clothes)* **it ~s you!** fica-lhe bem!; **2** ficar, acontecer; **what has ~ of her?** o que foi feito dela?; ♦ *vi (+ noun)* fazer-se, tornar-se; vir a ser; *(+ adj)* tornar-se, ficar; **to ~ fat** engordar.

becoming *adj* decoroso; **2** *(clothes)* elegante; **3** *(appropriate)* adequado,-a.

BEd *(abbr for* **Bachelor of Education***)* Licenciado,-a em Ciências da Educação.

bed *n* cama *f*; **2** *(layer)* camada *f*, base *f*; *(CULIN)* **on a ~ of watercress** sobre uma camada de agriões; **3** *(GEOL)* leito *m*; **~rock** *(layer)* leito de rocha; **4** *(of river)* leito, *m*; **5** *(poetic, regal) (cama)* leito; **6** *(of sea)* fundo; **a ~ of roses** *(fig) (easy)* um mar de rosas; **7** *(in the garden)* canteiro; ♦ **to go to ~** ir deitar-se; **to be in ~** estar/ficar na cama/deitado,-a; **to make the ~** fazer a cama; ♦ **~ and full board** *n* quarto *m* e pensão *f* completa; **~-bath** *(also:* **blanket bath***) (for patient)* lavagem *f* na cama; **~bug** *n* percevejo *m*; **~-chamber** *(the queen's)* quarto *m* de dormir; **~chamber pot** *n (jerry)* bacio *m*; penico *m (fam)*; *(child's potty)* bacio; **~ clothes** *npl*/**~-clothing** *sg* roupa *f* de cama; **~ linen** *n (sheets, pillowcases)* roupa de cama; **~ room** quarto *m* de dormir; **single/double ~** cama de solteiro/de casal; **~-settee** *n* sofa-cama *m*; **~side** *n* cabeceira *f*; **at sb's ~** à cabeceira de alguém; **to have a ~ manner** ser carinhoso,-a para com os doentes; **~ table** *n* mesinha *f* de cabeceira; **~ sitter** *n (bedroom and sitting room)* conjugado *m*, bed-siter *m*; **~ sore** *n* escara *f*; **~spread** *n* colcha *f*; **~stead** *n* aro *f* da cama; **~time** *n* hora *f* de dormir; **~-wetting** *n (MED)* enurese, incontinência urinária; *(of children)* chichi *m* na cama; ♦ *(-ded, -ding) vt* **to ~ out plants** plantar num canteiro; IDIOM **to get out of ~ on the wrong side** acordar de mau humor; **you have made your ~, now you must lie on it** quem boa cama fizer, nela se deitará.

bed and breakfast (= B and B) *n (EP)* cama e pequeno almoço; *(BR)* cama e café da manhã.

bedazzle *vt* deslumbrar alguém; ofuscar; impressionar alguém com seu brilho, beleza.

bedding *n* colchão *m*, roupa *f* de cama; *(for animals) (straw, etc)* cama *f*.

bedeck *vt* enfeitar, decorar; **the town was ~ed with bedspreads** a cidade estava decorada com colchas.

bedevil *(UK: -led, -ling; US: -ed, -ing) vt* **~ sb** atormentar, arreliar alguém; **2** fazer diabruras.

bedfellow *n* companheiro, *(fig)* **they make odd ~s** eles formam uma dupla estranha.

bedlam *n* confusão *f*, caos *m*.

bedouin *n* beduíno,-a.

bedpan *n (for sick people)* arrastadeira *(para doentes)*.

bedraggled *adj (person, clothes)* enlameado,-a, sujo,-a; *(hair)* emaranhado; *(sloven)* descuidado.

bedridden *adj (sick)* acamado,-a, de cama.

bee *n* abelha; **queen-~** abelha-mestra/-rainha; **~hive** *n* colmeia; **~keeper** *n* apicultor,-ora; **~line** *n:* **to make a ~line for sth** ir dire(c)to a algo; IDIOM **to have a ~ in one's bonnet** ter macaquinhos no sótão; ter ideia fixa.

beech *n (BOT)* faia *f*.

beef *n* carne *f* de vaca; **roast ~** rosbife *m*; **~steak** *n* bife *m (de vaca)*; ♦ **to ~ about sth** *vi (complain)* reclamar; **~ up** *vt (strength)* reforçar.

Beefeater *npr* guarda da Torre de Londres de traje antigo.

beefy *adj (person, lips)* robusto,-a, carnudo,-a.

Beelzebub *n* Belzebu.

been *(pp of* **be**).

beep *n (som)* bipe.

beeper *n (device)* bíper; ♦ *vi* bipar.

beer *n* cerveja *f*.

beeswax *n* cera *f* de abelha.

beet *(sugar beedt)* acelga *f*; **2** *(US)* beterraba.

beetle *n (ZOOL)* escaravelho, besouro.

beetroot *n (BOT)* beterraba.

befall *(pt* **fell**, *pp* **fallen)** *vt/vi* suceder, acontecer.

befit *(-ted, -ting)* *vt* convir a, ser próprio de; **as it befits a young lady** como é próprio de uma menina.

befitting *adj (formal)* adequado, maneira apropriada.

before *prep (of time)* antes de, anterior a; **the day ~ yesterday** anteontem; **2** *(in front of)* diante de, em frente de; **don't shout ~ the children** não grites diante das crianças; **the taxi stopped ~ the door** o táxi parou em frente da porta; **3** *(facing the law, the truth, God)* perante; **I am innocent ~ God** estou inocente perante Deus; **to appear ~ the Court** comparecer perante o tribunal; ♦ *adj* anterior; **the week ~** a semana anterior; ♦ *conj* antes que/de; **~ he comes** antes que ele venha; ♦ *adv (time)* antes, anteriormente; **I was thin ~** eu antes era magra; **2** *(in front of, ahead)* diante, adiante; **you go ~ me (ahead)** vai adiante; **long ~** já; **have you seen this picture ~** já viu este quadro?

beforehand *adv (earlier, ahead of time)* antes, antecipadamente, de antemão; **I bought the tickets ~** comprei os bilhetes de antemão.

befriend *vt* fazer amizade com; ser amigo de; **2** *(support)* favorecer.

beg *(-ged, -ging)* *vt/vi (money, food)* pedir **(from, a)**; **~ alms** pedir esmolas, mendigar; **2** *(favour, forgiveness)* **I ~ you to do this for me** peço-lhe o favor de me fazer isto; **I ~ your pardon** desculpe! como disse?; **3** *(entreat, plead)* rogar, suplicar, implorar; **I ~ you not to tell my husband** rogo-lhe que não diga nada ao meu marido.

began *(pt of* **begin**).

beget *vt (begot, begotten)* gerar.

beggar *n* mendigo,-a, pedinte *m,f*; **~s can't be choosers** *(coll)* a cavalo dado não se olha o dente.

beggarly *adj (very poor)* miserável; **2** *(salary)* irrisório,-a.

begging *n* pedido *m*, súplica *f*; **he is ~** ele pede esmolas.

begin *(pt* **began**, *pp* **begun**, *cont* **-ning)** *vt/vi (star)* começar, principiar; **to ~ to do sth** começar/principiar a fazer algo; **he began by telling us** ele começou por dizer-nos; **2** *(initiate)* iniciar; **3 to ~ with** *adv* para começar, em primeiro lugar.

beginner *n* principiante, iniciante *m,f*; aprendiz *m,f*.

beginning *n* princípio, começo, início; **in the ~** no início, ao princípio; **from ~ to end** do princípio ao fim.

beginnings *fpl (origins)* origens.

begonia *n (BOT)* begónia *f*.

begrudge *vt (envy)*: **to ~ sb sth** invejar algo de alguém; **2** *(to do/give sth unwillingly)* dar, fazer algo de má vontade.

beguile *vt (entice sb)* iludir, enganar; **2** *(charm)*, seduzir, encantar.

beguiling *adj* encantador.

begun *(pp of* **begin**).

behalf *n*: **on ~ of** em nome de; **on my ~** no meu interesse.

behave *vi* portar-se, comportar-se; **2** *(machine, etc)* funcionar; ♦ *vr* **to ~ o.s.** portar-se (bem); **~ yourself!** porte-se bem.

behaviour *(UK)* **behavior** *(US) n* comportamento *m*, conduta *f*.

behavioural *(UK)* **behavioral** *(US) adj* comportamental; **~ contagion** propagação de um tipo de comportamento; **~ science** *n* aplicação de métodos científicos.

behead *vt* decapitar.

beheld *(pt, pp of* **behold**).

behind *prep* atrás de; ♦ *adv* atrás, detrás, para trás; ♦ *n* traseiro; **~ one's back** pela calada; por trás das costas; **~ the scenes** nos bastidores; **~ time** atrasado; **~ the times** antiquado.

behindhand *adj* com atraso; **2** *(debt)* dívida em atraso.

behold *(irr: like* **hold**) *vt* contemplar; observar.

beholder *n* observador,-ora; espetador,-ora.

beholden *adj (formal) (indebted-moral obligation)* em dívida (para com alguém).

beige *adj* bege.

being *n* existência *f*; ser *m*; **to come into ~** nascer, aparecer.

Beijing *npr* Beijing.

Belarus *npr* Bielorrússia *f*.

belated *adj* atrasado, tardio; **~ greetings** os meus desejos (de felicidade) tardios.

belately *adv* demasiado tarde, tardiamente.

belch *vi* arrotar; ♦ *vt*: **to ~ out** vomitar; expelir.

beleaguer *vt (MIL) (city)* cercar, sitiar; **2** *(harass)* assediar.

belfry *(pl:* **-ries**) *n* campanário.

Belgian *npr adj* belga *m,f*.

Belgium *npr* Bélgica *f*; **in ~** na Belgica.

Belgrade *npr* Belgrado.

belie *(cont:* **belying**) *vt* desmentir, contradizer.

belief *n* opinião *f*; **my ~ is that he is out of town** a minha opinião é que ele está fora; **2** fé *f*; **3** crença, convicção *f*; **beyond ~** inacreditável.

believable *adj* crível, acreditável.

believe *vt/vi* crer em, acreditar em; **1 ~ so!** acho que sim!; **I ~ her** *(truth)* eu acredito nela; **I ~ in God** *(faith/trust)* creio em Deus.

believer *n* crente *m,f* fiel *m,f*; **2** *(POL)* partidário,-a.

belittle *vt* amesquinhar, depreciar.

bell *n (of the church)* sino; **2** *(of the door, cycle)* campainha; **3** *(cat, toy)* guizo; **4** *(cow, goat)* chocalho; **5** *(sound) (church, clock)* badalada; **it rings a ~** isso traz à memória; **~boy** *n* moço de recados; mensageiro (de hotel).

belligerent *adj (POL)* beligerante; **2** *(person, attitude)* agressivo,-a.

bellow *n (of bull)* mugido; **2** *(fig) (angry person)* berro, grito; ♦ *vi (bull)*, mugir; bramar; ♦ *vt (order)* gritar; berrar.

bellows *npl nsg* fole *m*.

bell-push *n* campainha.

bell-ringer *n* sineiro.

belly *n (lower abdomen)* barriga *f*, ventre *m*; ~-ache dor *f* de barriga; **a ~ from laughing** uma barrigada de riso; ~ **button** *n inv* umbigo *m*; ~ **dancing** *n* dança *f* do ventre; ~ful **(of)** *(coll)* *n* cheio de; **to have a ~** fartar-se de algo.

belong *vi*: pertencer **(to** a); *(of club, association)* ser sócio de.

belongings *npl* bens *mpl*, pertences *mpl*.

beloved *n adj* querido,-a, bem-amado,-a.

below *prep (under)* por baixo de; **2** *(numbers; text; inferior in rank)* abaixo de; ~ **zero** abaixo de zero; **3** *(unworthy)* indigno de; ♦ *adv* de baixo, abaixo; **see** ~ ver abaixo.

belt *n (clothing)* cinto; **safety ~** *(AUT)* cinto de segurança; **2** *(of land, sea)* faixa; **3** zona; **green ~** zona verde; **4** *(TECH)* correia, cinta; **seat~** cinto *m* de segurança; ~**way** *n (US)* via circular; **5** *(SPORT) (judo)* cinturão *m*; ♦ *vt (coll) (punch)* surrar, dar um soco; ♦ *vi* ~ **along/down the street** *(very fast) (person, car)* descer/ir a correr pela rua fora; **to ~ off** (person) ir a toda a pressa; **to ~ out** berrar; cantar a plenos pulmões; **to ~ up** *(coll)* calar a boca/o bico *(fam)*; IDIOM **to tighten the** ~ *(economizar)* apertar o cinto; **have sth (years, etc.) under one's ~** *(experience)* ter algo de experiência.

belvedere *n* miradouro, mirante *m*.

bemoan *vt (to grieve over)* lamentar; ~ **one's fate** lamentar a sua sina, seu destino.

bemuse *vt* estar confuso, perplexo.

bemused *adj (lost in thought)* alheio,-a; **2** *(bewildered)* estupidificado,-a.

bench *n (seat)* assento *m*, banco *m*; **2** *(British parliament)* assento; **3 the B~** *(JUR)* tribunal *m*; magistratura *f*; **4** *(workshop)* banco.

benchmark *n (standard)* ponto *m* de referência; **2** *(COMP)* padrão *m* de desempenho; *(FIN)* indicador de referência.

bend *n* curva *f*, ângulo *m*, curva *f*; ♦ *(pt, pp* **bent)** *vt* dobrar; curvar; dobrar; ♦ *vi* dobrar-se, inclinar-se; **to ~ down** dobrar-se; ~ **to** curvar-se para; **to ~ over** inclinar-se; IDIOM **to go around the ~** *(fig)* andar maluco,-a, andar às voltas.

beneath *prep/adv* sob, debaixo de; por baixo (de); ~ **the table** sob a mesa; ~ **the window** debaixo da janela; **2** abaixo de; **she married ~ her** ela casou-se com uma pessoa de categoria social inferior; **3** indigno; **it is ~ you to do that** não é digno de você fazer isso.

benediction *n* bênção; bênção do Santíssimo.

benefactor *n* benfeitor,-ora; **2** benemérito,-a.

beneficent *adj* caritativo, beneficente.

beneficial *adj* proveitoso, benéfico.

beneficiary *n* beneficiário,-a.

benefit *n* benefício, proveito; lucro; subsídio; ♦ *vt* beneficiar, aproveitar; ♦ *vi*: **he'll ~ from it** ele se beneficiará disso.

benevolence *n* benevolência.

benevolent *adj* benévolo, benevolente.

benign *adj* benigno, afável *m,f*.

benignancy *n* bondade *f*.

bent *(pt, pp of* **bend)** *n* inclinação *f* para algo; **to have a ~ for sth** *(aptitude)* ter queda para; ♦ *adj* torto; **2** *(fig)* corrupto; **3** *(person, body)* curvado; **to be ~ on doing sth** estar determinado a fazer algo.

benumbed *adj* entorpecido,-a.

benzene *n* benzeno *m*; benzina *f*.

bequeath *vt (money, property)* legar, deixar em testamento; **2** *(fig) (idea, tradition)* passar, transferir.

bequest *n* legado, herança.

berate *vt*: ~ **sb** *(scold)* repreender alguém (severamente), ralhar com alguém.

bereave *(pt, pp* **bereft)** *vt* privar **(of** de); desolar.

bereaved *n*: **the ~** *(persons)* os enlutados *mpl*.

bereavement *n* luto *m*.

bereft *adj* privado de.

beret *n* boina *f*.

bergamot *n (BOT)* bergamota *f*.

beriberi *n* beriberi *f*.

berk *n (UK) (fam)* palhaço,-a.

Berlin *npr* Berlim.

Berlinner berlinês-esa.

berm *n (US)* berma *f*.

Bermuda *npr* as Bermudas *fpl*; ~ **shorts** *n* bermudas.

Bern *npr* Berna.

berry *n (fruit)* baga *f*; **2** *(dried kernel)* grito *m*; **3** *(egg of lobster and similar)* ova *f*.

berserk *adj* desvairado,-a, furioso,-a; **to go ~** perder as estribeiras, ficar furioso,-a.

berth *n (NAUT, RAIL)* cama; beliche *m*; **2** *(in harbour)* ancoradouro; ♦ *vi (NAUT)* ancorar.

beseech *(pt, pp* **besought)** *vt* suplicar, implorar; **I ~ you not to do that** imploro-lhe que não faça isso.

beset *(pt, pp* **beset**; *p.pres.* **-ting)** *adj* assediado,-a, preocupado,-a **(by, with sth,** com, de algo); ~ **with problems** estar cheio,-a de problemas.

beside *prep* junto de, ao lado de, ao pé de; **to be ~ o. s.** *(with anger)* fora de si; *(with happiness)* estar louco de alegria; **that's ~ the point/question** isso está fora de questão; isso não vem ao caso.

besides *adv* além disso; ♦ *prep* além de; exceto.

besiege *vt* sitiar, cercar; **2** *(fig)* assediar.

besieged *n* sitiante.

besmirch *vt* manchar, sujar.

besotted *adj (in love)* obcecado,-a (~ **with sb**, por alguém); apaixonado,-a como um louco.

besought *(pt, pp of* **beseech**).

bespatter *vt (formal)* salpicar.

bespectacled *adj* com óculos.

bespoke *adj (UK)* feito por encomenda, feito à medida.

best *(superl of* **well)** *adj* o melhor; ♦ *adv* (o) melhor; **the ~ part of** a maior parte de; **at ~** quando muito; **to get the ~ of sb** vencer, levar a melhor;

make the ~ **of** tirar o maior partido possível de; **make the** ~ **of one's time** aproveitar o tempo (ao máximo); **to the** ~ **of my knowledge** que eu saiba; **I'll do my** ~ farei os possíveis, farei o meu melhor; ~ **man** *n* padrinho de casamento; **in one's Sunday** ~ no seu fato (*BR:* terno) domingueiro.

bestial *adj* brutal *m,f*; bárbaro.

bestow *vt:* **to** ~ **sth on sb** conferir, dar; **2** conceder, outorgar algo a alguém.

bestowal *n* outorga *f*; concessão *f*.

bestseller, best selling *n* o mais vendido, de grande êxito; **2** (*book*) sucesso de vendagem/de livraria *m*, best-seller *m*.

bet *n* aposta *f*; (*forecast*) aposta; ♦ (*pt, pp* **bet** *or* **betted**) *vt/vi* apostar (**on** em), jogar; **to** ~ **one's boots on** (*coll*) estar certo de; **your best** ~ **is to…** melhor é você…; **I** ~ **he won't come** aposto que ele não vem.

beta *n* (*US*) beta; ~ **blocker** *n* bloqueador-beta.

bête-noir *n* (*besta negra*) pessoa a quem se tem aversão.

Bethlehem *n* Belém.

betray *vt* trair, atraiçoar; denunciar.

betrayal *n* traição *f*.

betrothed *adj* (*dated*) (*engaged*) prometido,-a (**to sb**, a alguém).

better *n* **the** ~ **of the two** o,-a melhor dos dois/das duas; **one's** ~ **half** (*coll*) (*wife*) cara-metade; **our** ~**s** os nossos superiores *npl*; **so much the** ~/**all the** ~ tanto melhor; **to get the** ~ **of** levar vantagem sobre, levar a melhor; ♦ *adj* (*comp of* **good**) **this material is** ~ **than the other one** este tecido é ~ do que o outro; **to get** ~ melhorar (*MED*) recuperar; **things are getting** ~ as coisas vão melhor; **the sooner, the** ~ quanto mais cedo, melhor; ~ **off** em melhor situação (*financeira*); ♦ *adv* (*comp of* **well**) **I had** ~ **do this now** é melhor eu fazer isto agora; **he thought** ~ **of it** pensou melhor sobre o (assunto); **to do** ~ (*career*) ser mais bem-sucedido; ~ **and** ~ cada vez melhor; ♦ *vt* melhorar.

betterment *n* melhoria *f*; melhoramento *m*.

betting *n* jogo *m*, aposta *f*; ~ **shop** *n* agência de apostas.

between *prep* no meio de, entre; ~ **you and me** cá entre nós, aqui entre nós; ♦ *adv* no meio.

bevelled (*UK*), **beveled** (*US*) *adj* (*mirror, glass*) chanfrado,-a; biselado-a.

beverage *n* (*non-alcoholic*) bebida *f*.

bevy *n* grupo (**of**, de); **2** (*birds*) bando *m*; **a** ~ **of beautiful girls** um grupo de beldades.

beware *vi* precaver-se (**of** de), ter cuidado (**de** com); ♦ *exc* cuidado!

bewildered *adj* perturbado, perplexo.

bewildering *adj* desconcertante *m,f*.

bewitch *vt* enfeitiçar; encantar.

bewitching *adj* feiticeiro, encantador, sedutor.

beyond *prep* além de; acima de, fora de; superior a; ~ **doubt** fora de dúvida; ~ **repair** irreparável; ~ **reach** fora do alcance; ♦ *adv* além, mais longe; **at the back of** ~ (*coll*) em cascos de rolha; no fim do mundo, no cu de Judas (*vulg*).

bezel *n* bezel *m*; chanfradura *f*.

Bhutan *npr* Butão; **Bhutanese** *npr*, *adj* butanês,-esa.

biannual *adj* semestral.

bias *n* (*prejudice*) preconceito *m*; **2** propensão, *f* tendência *f*, parcialidade *f*; (*in favour of*) a favor de; **3** (*sewing*) em viés *m*; **to cut on the** ~ cortar em viés; **4** ~ **binding**/~**tape** (*for hems, etc*) fita *m* mastro em viés; ♦ **bias, biased** *adj* (*slanting*) inclinado; **2** (*opinion*) propenso a, tendencioso; **3** (*prejudiced*) preconceituoso; **in favour of**/**against sb, sth** a favor de, contra algo, alguém; **4 to be** ~ (*opinion, taste, person*) ser parcial; **5** (*text, statistics*) sem objectividade.

bib *n* babeiro, babete *m*; **2** (*of apron*) peitilho de avental; (*BR*) babador.

Bible *npr* Bíblia.

biblical *adj* bíblico.

bibliography *n* bibliografia.

bibliophile *n* bibliófilo.

bicabornate *n* (~ **of soda**) bicabornato de soda *m*.

bicentenary, bicentennial *n* bicentenário *m* (**of** de).

biceps *npl* biceps.

bicker *vi* (*argue, row*) discutir, altercar, brigar (por coisas simples).

bickering *n* discussão *f*; conflito *m*; ♦ *adj* conflituoso,-a.

biculturalism *n* biculturalismo *m*.

bicycle *n* bicicleta; **andar de** ~ to ride a bicycle.

bicyclist *n* ciclista *m,f*; ~ **path** *n* ciclovia *f*.

bid *n* (*at auction*) lance *m*; oferta *f*; **2** (*COMM*) (*for*/ *of contracts*) proposta *f* para/de; **to invite** ~**s** abrir concurso; **3** (*attempt*) tentativa; ♦ (**bade** *or* **bid**, *pp* **bidden** *or* **bid**) *vt* (*company, auction, Bridge*) fazer uma oferta (**for** para); **2** (*COMM, FIN*) licitar; ♦ *vt* **to** ~ **sb to do** (*request*) pedir alguém para, ordenar; **the judge bade her to keep silent** o juiz pediu-lhe que se calasse; **2 to** ~ **farewell** despedir-se.

De notar que quando o verbo 'to bid' significa **licitar**, o seu pretérito e particípio do passado são invariáveis (**bid**).

---

bidder *n* (*COMM*) licitador *m*; **the highest** ~ quem oferece mais.

bidding *n* lance *m*; **2** (*COMM*) licitação *f*; **3** ordem *f*.

bide *vt:* **to** ~ **one's time** esperar o momento adequado; dar tempo ao tempo.

bidet *n* bidé *m*.

bid-up *vb, adv* aumentar o preço no mercado de algo através de lances artificiais.

biennial *adj* (*every two years*) bienal.

bier *n* féretro, padiola *m*.

bifocals *npl* bifocais *mpl*.

big (*comp* **-ger** *superl* **-est**) *adj* (*ger*) grande; **2** importante; **3** (*older*) mais velho, o mais velho; ~ **with child** (*pregnant*) grávida; **in a** ~ **way** em grande estilo; **Big Apple** (**the**) *npr* Nova Iorque; **Big Bang theory** (**the**) a teoria do Big Bang; **Big Ben** (**the**) (*clock*) Big Ben (em Londres); ~ **deal!** *exc* (*scorn*) que grande coisa!; ~ **dipper** *m* montanha *f* russa; ~ **fish** pessoa muito importante; ~ **game** (*fig, fam*) o objeto de um grande empreendimento; ~ **game hunting** *n* caçada a animais de grande porte; ~ **hand** *n* (*on clock*) ponteiro *m* grande, dos minutos; **2** *(fam)* *(applause)* salva de palmas; ~ **screen** *(CIN)* *n* cinema *m*, o grande ecrã; ~ **shot** *m* *(fam)* figurão; pessoa influente; **(the)** ~ **time** *n* *(fam)* o auge, sucesso; ~ **top** *n* *(tent)* tenda *f* de circo; ~**wig** *n* *(coll)* o manda-chuva; *m* *(fam)* IDIOM **to grow too ~ for one's boots** tornar-se presunçoso,-a; **a ~ fish in a small pond** o,-a mais importante/mais influente num pequeno grupo de pessoas.

bigamist *adj* bigamista *m,f*.

bigamy *n* bigamia *f*.

bighead *n* *(pej)* fanfarrão,-rona.

bigheaded *adj* *(pej)* presunçoso,-a.

big-hearted *adj* generoso,-a; com bom coração.

bigmouth *n* *(indiscreet or boastful person)* indiscreto,-a, pessoa que tem uma grande língua *(BR)* língua solta; ~ **name** *n* *(famous person)* grande figura.

bigot *n* *(person)* fanático, intolerante *m,f*.

bigoted *adj* fanático, intolerante.

bigotry *n* fanatismo, intolerância.

bike *n* bicicleta.

bikini *n* biquíni *m*.

bilateral *adj* bilateral.

bile *n* bílis *f*.

bilingual *adj* bilíngue.

bill *n* *(sum for what you owe)* conta; *(invoice)* factura; ~ **of exchange** *n* letra *f* de câmbio; **2** *(POL)* projeto de lei; **to pass/reject a** ~ aprovar/rejeitar um projecto de lei; **3** *(US)* *(banknote)* nota *f*; **4** *(ZOOL)* *(beak)* bico; **5** *(printed notice/poster)* cartaz *m*; **stick no ~s** é proibido afixar cartazes; **to fit/fill the** ~ *(coll)* preencher os requisitos; ~**board** *n* quadro *m* de anúncios; ~ **of lading** *n* *(NAUT)* conhecimento de carga; **to be given a clean** ~ **of health** *(MED)* obter um atestado de boa saúde; ♦ *vt* *(COMM)* faturar, enviar a conta; **to be** ~**ed as** ser anunciado como; **the play is** ~**ed for next month** a peça está anunciada para o próximo mês.

billabong *n* *(Austral)* ribeiro *m*.

billboard *n* *(US)* painel *m* publicitário.

billet *n* *(MIL)* aboletamento, aquartelamento; **2** *(job)* emprego.

billhook *n* *(tesoura)* podadeira *f*.

billiard/s *npl* bilhar *m*; ~ **ball** *n* bola *f* de bilhar; ~ **cue** *n* taco *m* de bilhar.

billion *num* bilião; *(BR)* bilhão.

Atualmente, na Grã-Bretanha e em muito outros países, inclusivamente Brasil, um bilião equivale a um milhar de milhões (nove zeros = 10^9). Antes, escrevia-se com 12 zeros (10^{12}) e equivalia a um milhão de milhões. Esta última é a norma em Portugal e em muitos outros países.

---

billionnaire *n* bilionário,-a, multimilionário,-a.

Bill of Rights *n:* as 10 primeiras emendas da Constituição dos E.U.A.

Estas emendas garantem os direitos fundamentais de um cidadão, tais como, liberdade de expressão, de crença e de reunião. Baseou-se no estatuto britânico de 1689.

---

bill of sale *n* contrato de venda ou de trespasse de uma propriedade, ou de garantia contra empréstimo.

billow *n* *(mar)* vaga; **2** *(of smoke, steam)* nuvem; ♦ *vi* *(sea)* encapelar-se; **2** *(clouds, smoke)* redemoinhar; ~ **out** *vt* *(sail)* enfunar-se; *(skirt)* levantar-se, subir, enfunar.

billowy *adj* encapelado, cheio de redemoinhos.

billy goat *n* bode *m*.

bimbo *n* *(fam)* *(girl)* bonita mas cabeça oca; *(BR)* burra *f* gostosa.

bin *n* *(gen)* caixa; **2** *(for rubbish)* caixote/recipiente *m* do lixo; **3** *(for bread)* caixa/lata *f* do pão.

binary *adj* binário; *(COMP)* ~ **digit** *n* dígito binário; *(FIS)* ~ **fusion** *n* fissão *f* binária.

bind *(pt, pp* **bound)** *vt* *(tie up, fasten)* atar, amarrar; **bound hand and foot** de mãos e pés atados; **2** *(band/bandage around)* pôr atadura/ligadura em; **3** *(in bookbinding)* encadernar *(in* em); **4** *(law, duty)* obrigar; **duty bound** sujeito ao dever; **5** ~ **together** *(people)* unir; **6** ~ **o.s. to** comprometer-se a; **6** *(CULIN)* ligar, juntar; ♦ *vi* (cohere) *(BIOL, CHEM)* ligar-se *(to* a); **2** ~ **on sth** prender(-se); *(LAW)* ~ **sb over** *vt* obrigar alguém legalmente **(to** a).

binder *n* capa *f* de argolas; **2** *(person)* encadernador,-ora.

binding *n* cinta; ~ **tape** *(ELECT)* fita *f* isoladora; ♦ *adj* obrigatório, sujeitante.

binge *n* *(coll)* *(of drinking)* bebedeira *f*; **2** *(of eating)* patuscada, farra *f*; **to go on a** ~ fazer uma farra ♦ **to** ~ *vi* comer entre refeições.

bingo *n* bingo *m*.

binoculars *npl* binóculos *mpl*.

bio- *pref:* bio-; ~**chemistry** *n* bioquímica; ~**degradable** *adj* biodegradável; ~ **diversity** *n* biodiversidade *f*; ~ **washing powder** sabão *m* em pó com enzimas.

biological *adj* biológico,-a.

biology *n* biologia.

biopic *n* filme biográfico *m*.

biopsy *(pl:* -**ies)** *n* biópsia *f*.

biosphere *n* bioesfera *f*.

bipartite *adj* bipartido,-a.

birch *n* *(tree)* bétula; **2** *(for punishment)* vara de vidoeiro; ♦ *vt* vergastar.

bird *n* *(ZOOL)* ave *f*, pássaro; ~ **of prey** *n* ave *f* de rapina; **2** ~**cage** *n* gaiola *f*; **3** *(coll)* rapariga, moça; **4 early** ~ *n* madrugador,-ora; **5 little** ~ *n* passarinho *m*; IDIOM **a** ~ **in the hand is worth two in the bush** mais vale um pássaro na mão que dois a voar.

birdie *n* *(infant's talk)* passarinho.

birdseed *n* alpista.

bird's-eye view *n* vista aérea; **2** vista *f* panorâmica.

biretta *n* barrete *m* de clérigo.

birth *n* nascimento *m*; **2** *(MED)* parto *m*; **to give** ~ **to** dar à luz, parturar; *(animals)* parir; **at** ~ à nascença; **by** ~ por nascimento; **from/since** ~ de nascença/ao nascer; **of low** ~ de origem *f* humilde; ~ **certificate** *n* certidão *m* de nascimento; ~ **control** *n* controlo *m* de natalidade.

birthday *n* dia *m* de anos; aniversário; **Happy B~!** Parabéns!

birthmark *n* sinal *m* de nascença.

birthplace *n* lugar *m* de nascimento.

birthrate *n* taxa de natalidade.

birthright *n* direito *m* inato; *(HIST)* direito de primogenitura; IDIOM **to be in one's ~-suit** andar nu/ao léu como Adão e Eva.

Biscay *npr*: **the Bay of ~** o Golfo de Biscaia.

biscuit *n* bolacha *f*, biscoito *m*.

bisect *vt* cortar ao meio; dividir em duas partes.

bisexual *adj* bissexual *m,f*.

bishop *n* bispo *m*.

bishopric *n* bispado *m*, diocese *m*.

bison *n (ZOOL) (buffalo)* bison, bisonte *m*.

bissextile *adj (year)* bissexto.

bistro *n* bar *m*, café *m*.

bit *(pt of* **bite***) n* pedaço, bocadinho *m*; **2** *(in music, history, film)* passagem, bocado; **I like that ~ where he sings** gosto daquele bocado em que ele canta; **3** *(of horse)* freio; **4** *(COMP)* bit; **5** *(of drill)* broca *f*; **~s and pieces** bugigangas *fpl*; **a ~ of** um pouco de; **a ~ more** um pouco mais; **a ~ tired** um pouco cansado; **~ by ~** pouco a pouco; **it won't do a ~ of good** isso não vai servir para nada; **to do one's ~** fazer a sua parte.

bitch *n (female dog)* cadela, cachorra *f*; **2** *(offensive slang) (spiteful woman)* cabra, vaca *(cal)*; **3** *(slang) (difficult problem)* um osso duro de roer; ♦ *vi (complain)* resmungar; **2 to ~ about sb** *(maliciously)* falar mal de alguém.

bite *n* dentada, mordedura; *(of insect)* picada, picadela; *(of dog)* mordidela, *(BR)* mordida; **my husband gave me a love ~** o meu marido deu-me uma dentada; **2** *(coll) (sth to eat)* qualquer coisa *f* de comer; **let us have a ~** vamos comer qq coisa; **3** *(of wind, cold)* golpe *m*; **4** *(sharp flavour, UK)* picante; **mustard ~s the tongue** a mustarda é picante; **5** *(to cut into)* cortar; **the bra is biting into my back** o sutiã está a cortar as minhas costas; **6** *(policy, unemployment,* etc*)* fazer-se sentir; ♦ *(pt* **bit** *pp* **bitten***) vt* morder; **the dog bit me** o cão mordeu-me; **2** *(insect, snake)* picar; **3** *(nails)* roer (as unhas); ♦ **to ~ back** *vt/vi* conter; conter-se, evitar responder; **2 to ~ into** *(cut into)* cortar; *(fig)* to affect; *(policy, unemployment)* fazer-se sentir; **to ~ through** *(wind, acid)* trespassar; IDIOM **to ~ off more than one can chew** meter-se em cavalarias altas; **once bitten twice shy** gato de rabo escaldado, da água fria tem medo.

biting *adj* cortante; **~ cold** um frio *m* cortante; **2** *(remark, wit)* mordaz; *(wind)* penetrante.

bitten *(pp of* **bite***)*.

bitter *n (beer)* cerveja *f* amarga; ♦ *adj (sour)* amargo; **~sweet** *adj* agridoce; **2** *(resentful) (person)* amargoa; **3** *(acrimonious)* violento, feroz, pungente; **they are ~ enemies** eles são inimigos fidagais; **till the ~ end** até ao fim, até à morte; **4** cortante; **~ cold** um frio cortante, um frio de rachar.

bitterly *adv* amargamente.

bitterness *n* amargor *m*; amargura *f*.

bizarre *adj* esquisito,-a, estranho,-a.

blab *(pt, pp* **bleb***) vi (gossip)* dar à língua; **2** *(revelar segredos)*, dar com a língua nos dentes; despejar o

saco *(coll)*; *(BR)* fazer fofoca; ♦ *vt (talk idly)* tagarelar; *(BR)* estar no bate-papo; **to ~ out** revelar, chocalhar.

black *n (dark)* negro; **2** *(colour)* preto; **3** *(race, person)* negro,-a; *(pej)* preto,-a; **to wear ~** vestir/andar de luto; **~-and-blue** *(bruised)* roxo,-a; **~ art/magic** magia *f* negra; **~ ball** *(veto)* votar contra, veto; **~ beetle** escaravelho *m*; **~ belt** *(martial arts)* faixa-preta *m,f*; **~berry** *(BOT)* amora preta/silvestre; **~bird** *(ZOOL)* melro; **~board** quadro preto/-negro, lousa; **~ box** *(recorder)* caixa preta *f*; **~ comedy** tragicomédia *f*; **~ currant** *(BOT)* groselha *f* negra; **~ death** *n* peste *f* negra *f*; **~ economy** *n* economia *f* paralela; **~ eye** olho *m* pisado; **give sb a ~ eye** dar um murro nos olhos de (alguém); **~ future** *n (gloomy)* futuro incerto/sombrio; **~ head** *n (impure pores)* pontos *mpl* negros; **in ~** *(pictures)* a preto e branco; **to be in ~** *(solvent)* em crédito, sem dívidas; **in ~ and white** *(writing)* a preto e branco, por escrito; **~ leg** *n* fura-greve; **~list** *n* lista *f* negra; **~ look** *n (glance)* olhar fulminante; **~mail** *n* chantagem *f*; ♦ *vt* fazer chantagem; **~mailer** chantagista *m,f*; **~ mark** *n* informação/mancha *f* negativa; **~ market** mercado *m* negro; **~ness** *n (darkness)* escuridão *f*, negrume, *m*; **~ pudding** *n* chouriço *m* de sangue; **~ sheep** *n (fig)* ovelha *f* ronhosa/negra; **~smith** *n* ferreiro *m*; **~ tie** *n* fato de cerimónia, *(BR)* terno *m* de gala; **~ widow** *(ZOOL = spider)* viúva *f* negra; ♦ *adj (hair, clothes, car)* preto; **2** *(night, cloud)* escuro; **~ing** *n (polish)* graxa; **~ish** escuro; ♦ *vt (darken, dirt)* enegrecer; **2** *(polish shoes)* engraxar, *(BR)* lustrar; **3** *(ECON)* boicotar; ♦ *vi* desmaiar; perder os sentidos; ♦ **to ~ out** *vi* perder os sentidos; *(news)* to stop broadcasting.

Black Country *n região central da Inglaterra, muito industrializada em outros tempos.*

blacken *vt (darken)* enegrecer; **2** *(fig) (reputation, name)* denegrir; **3** *(sky)* escurecer.

Black Forest *npr* Floresta *f* Negra.

blackout *n (general power cut)* apagão *m*; **2** perda temporária dos sentidos; **3** blackout; **news ~** blackout informativo.

blackspot *m (dangerous place on road etc.)* lugar *m* fatídico; ponto *m* negro (or cego); **2** *(situation)* situação *f* problemática; **3** (BOT) *(disease of roses)* doença *f* das rosas.

bladder *n (ANAT)* bexiga.

blade *n* folha *f*; lâmina *f*; **a ~ of grass** uma folha de relva.

blame *n* culpa; **to be to ~** ter a culpa; **~less** *adj* inocente; **~worthy** *adj* culpável; ♦ *vt*: **to ~ sb for sth** culpar alguém por algo.

blanch *vt/vi (person: turn pale)* empalidecer; **2** *(almonds, laundry etc)* branquear.

blanching *n (roupa)* branqueamento.

bland *adj* suave; leve; brando.

blank *n* lacuna *f*, espaço *m* em branco; **2** *(MIL)* cartucho, sem bala; **3** *(empty look)* ar vazio, ar ausente, sem expressão; **my mind went ~** deu-me uma branca ♦ *adj (unmarked)* em branco; **~ cheque** *(UK)*, **check** *(US)* cheque em branco; **2**

(unused cassette) virgem; ♦ *vt* **to ~ sth out from memory** apagar algo da memória; IDIOM **to draw a ~** tirar leite da pedra, não chegar a nenhum lado.

blanket *n* cobertor *m*, manta; **2** *(of smoke)* nuvem; **3** *(of fog)* cortina *f*, manto *m*; **4** *(of flowers)* tapete *m*; ♦ *vt* cobrir, tapar.

blanket bath *n (for bedridden people)* lavagem na cama (para doentes).

blankly *adv* sem expressão, com uma expressão *f* vaga; com um ar pasmado.

blare *vi (car)* buzinar; **2** *(very loud)* soar; **~ out** *vi* soar muito alto, ressoar.

blasé *adj* indiferente.

blasphemy *n* blasfémia (*BR*: -fê-).

blast *n (gust)* rajada; pé-de-vento *m*; **2** *(of trumpet)* toque *m*, sopro *m*; **3** *(of bomb)* explosão *f*; **4** *(noise of whistle)* assobio; **5** *(car horn)* buzinadela *(BR)* buzinada *f*; **at full ~** *(music) adv* com o volume no máximo; *(car speed)* a toda a velocidade *f*; **~ furnace** *n* altoforno; **~-off** *(space)* lançamento *m*; ♦ *vt* fazer voar; **2** bombardear; **3** *(open hole tunnel)* dinamitar; **4** *(rocket)* deslocar, *(BR)* decolar; ♦ **blast!** *exc (UK)* co'os diabos!

blasted *adj* destruído; queimado.

blatant *adj (shameless, direct)* descarado; direto, frontal.

blaze *n (fire)* incêndio; **2** *(flames)* chamas *fpl*; **3** *(burst: of light)* clarão, brilho; **4** *(of colour)* esplendor de cores; **5** *(of anger)* acesso de fúria; **6** *(fig)* explosão *f*; ♦ *vi* arder; *(news)* difundir; **2** *(with colour)* resplandecer; ♦ *vt*: **to ~ a trail** *(fig)* abrir (um) caminho.

blazer *n* casaco desportivo, blazer *m*.

blazing *adj (pres p) (house, car)* em chamas; **2** *(row)* violento; **3** *(coll)* furioso; *(sun)* ardente.

bleach *n*: **household ~** lixívia; *(BR)* água sanitária, alvejante *m*; ♦ *vt* branquear.

bleached *adj* oxigenado,-a; alvejante.

bleaching *n* branqueamento *m*; **~ powder** cloreto, pó *m* de branquear.

bleak *n (fish)* mugem *m*; ♦ *adj (place)* desolado, escuro, desanimador; **2** *(dismal future)* sombrio; **3** *(tempo, dia)* frio e triste.

bleap *n* apito; *(signal)* bip-bip; ♦ *vt/vi* apitar, chamar alguém (através do sinal sonoro).

bleaper *n* bipe *m*; bíper *m*.

blear *adj* turvo; ♦ *vt* turvar.

bleary-eyed *adj* remelento, de olhos cansados, com olho-de-peixe-morto.

bleat *n (of sheep)* balido; ♦ *vi (sheep, goat)* balir; **to ~ out** *(person: gossip)* contar a toda a gente, revelar, chocalhar.

bleed *(pt, pp bled) vt/vi* sangrar; **2** *(fig) (money)* extorquir; **3** *(TECH)* purgar; **to ~ to death** esvair-se em sangue.

bleeding *n (MED)* hemorragia; ♦ *adj (pres p)* ensanguentado,-a; que sangra; **~ heart** coração *m* despedaçado.

blemish *n* mancha, mácula; **2** defeito; ♦ *vt* manchar; **2** desfigurar; **3** *(reputation)* desonrar, manchar.

blench *vi (shy away)* desviar-se, recuar por timidez ou medo.

blend *n* mistura; ♦ *vt* misturar; ♦ *vi* **~ in** *(colours)* combinar-se, harmonizar; **2** *(smells)*, misturar-se; **~ in (sth)** incorporar; **~ into** *(person)* confundir-se (com).

blender *n* batedeira *f*, liquidificador *m*.

blending *(CULIN)* mistura.

bless *(pt, pp blessed or blest) vt* abençoar; **God ~ you!** Deus te abençoe!; *(after sneezing)* santinho,-a!; **to be blessed with sth** ser abençoado,-a (com algo), usufruir (de algo); **~ o.s.** *vr* benzer-se, fazer o sinal da cruz.

blessed *n* **the ~** *mpl (REL)* os bem-aventurados; ♦ *adj (place, name)* sagrado, santo; bendito; **the B~ Virgin** Santíssima Virgem; **2** *(good)* benéfico.

blessing *n* bênção *f*; **2** *(fig)* benefício; IDIOM **a ~ in disguise** *(misfortune)* há males que vêm por bem.

blether *vi* disparatar, dizer disparates.

blew *(pt of blow)* **his hat ~ off** *(in the wind)* o chapéu dele voou; o vento levou-lhe o chapéu.

blight *n (plants)* míldio; **2** *(fig) (curse)* praga, chaga, desgraça *f*; ♦ *vt* arruinar *(plants)*, queimar.

blimey *exc (coll)* meu Deus!, caramba!, *(BR)* nossa!

blind *n* cego,-a; invisual; **the ~** os cegos, os invisuais *mpl*; **2** *(blunt: razor)* cego *m*; ♦ *adj* cego,-a; **2** *(corner, etc)* sem visibilidade; **to go ~** ficar cego; **to be ~ to sth** estar cego a *(algo)*; **3** *(with anger)* cego-a de fúria; ♦ *adv (not looking)* às cegas; **2** sem visibilidade ♦ *vt* cegar; **2** *(cover eyes)* vendar *(os olhos)*; **3** *(sun)* ofuscar; ♦ **~ alley** beco sem saída; **~ corner** *n* curva sem visibilidade; **~ date** *n* encontro *m* com um desconhecido; **~fold** *n* venda *f*; **~folded** *adv* de olhos vendados; **~ man's buff** *(child's game)* cabra-cega; **~ spot** *n* ponto *m* cego/oculto; IDIOM **to turn a ~ eye to sth** fazer vista grossa a *(algo)*.

blind *n (for window)* persiana *f*; estore *m*.

blinder *n (UK-sport)* grande golo, grande partida.

blinding *adj (luz)* ofuscante; **2** *(coll)* fantástico,-a.

blindly *adv* às cegas; cegamente; sem refletir.

blindness *n* cegueira *f*.

blink *vi (of eye)* piscar; **2 without a ~** sem pestanejar; **on a ~** *(coll) (machine)* enguiçado,-a, com problemas; ♦ *vi (eyes)* piscar; **2** *(lights)* cintilar; *(do carro)* piscar; ♦ *vt (person)* pestanejar, piscar.

blinkered *adj (fig) (view, attitude)* limitado, de vistas curtas; *(BR)* bitolado,-a.

blinkers *npl (AUT) (emergency)* luzes *fpl* intermitentes; faróis *mpl* pisca-pisca; **2** *(for horse)* antolhos *mpl*.

blinking *n (of an eye)* piscar *m* de olhos; ♦ *adj (coll)* **this ~ …** este danado/maldito…; **~ idiot** grande idiota *m,f*.

bliss *n* felicidade *f*; bem-aventurança; **2** *(fig)* êxtase *m*; **~ful** *adj* feliz.

blister *n* bolha, empola; ♦ *vt* empolar-se, formar bolhas.

blistering *n (of skin)* formação *f* de borbulhas/bolhas; ♦ *adj (sun)* tórrido; **2** *(heat)* sufocante; **3** *(comment, criticism)* causticante; **4** *(tongue)* afiada; **5 ~ speed** velocidade alucinante.

blithe *adj* alegre *m,f*; feliz *m,f* despreocupado,-a.

blithering *adj (col)*: **this ~ idiot** esta besta quadrada.

blitz *n* bombardeamento *m* aéreo, bombardeio *m*; *(HIST)* **the Blitz** o Blitz; **to have a ~ on sth** dar uma geral em algo.

blizzard *n* tempestade *m* de neve, nevasca.

bloated *adj (swollen)* inchado,-a; **2** *(having eaten too much)* empanturrado,-a; **3** *(fig) (puffed up)* empolado.

blob *n (drop)* gota *f*, pingo *m*; **2** *(of colour)* mancha *f*; **3** *(stain of ink)*, borrão *m*.

block *n (gen)* bloco; **2** *(of buildings)* quarteirão *m*, quadra *f*; **3** *(obstruction)* obstáculo, entrave; **~ and tackle** moitões para grandes pesos *mpl*; **~ letters** letras *fpl* maiúsculas; ♦ *vt* obstruir; **2** *(FIN, SPORT, streets)* bloquear; **3** *(impede)* impedir; **to ~ in** esboçar, traçar; **~ off** *(seal off)* barrar, obstruir; **~ out** tapar *(view)*; **~ up** entupir.

blockade *n* bloqueio *m*.

blockage *n (arteries)* obstrução *f*; **2** bloqueio.

blockbuster *n (coll) (book, film)* estouro; de grande sucesso.

blockhead *n (fam)* imbecile; *(BR)* cabeça dura

blocking *n (drains)* entupimento *m* obstrução *f*.

blog *n (blogger, weblog)* jornal *m* escrito para online, blogue *m*.

blogger *n* jornalista para online, blogo.

blogsphere *n* (o mundo do blog) bloguesfera *f*.

bloke *n (UK: slang)* tipo *(fam)*; gajo *(coll)*; *(BR)* cara *m (fam)*.

blond(e) *n adj* louro,-a.

blood *n* sangue *m*; **~ bank** banco *m* de sangue; **~ donor** *n* dador,-ora de sangue; **~ group** *n* grupo sanguíneo; **2 blue ~** *(lineage)* sangue azul; ♦ **in cold ~** a sangue frio; **to make one's ~ boil** fazer alguém furioso/danado.

blood bath *n* banho *m* de sangue.

blood-curdling *adj* arrepiante; de fazer gelar o sangue.

bloodhound *n* sabujo.

bloodless *adj (person)* exangue, esvaído,-a; **2** pálido,-a.

blood poisoning *n (MED)* septicemia *f*.

blood pressure *n* tensão *f* arterial, *(BR)* pressão *f* sanguínea.

bloodshed *n* derramamento *m* de sangue.

blood-shot *adj (eyes)* injetados de sangue.

bloodstream *n* corrente *f* sanguínea.

bloodsucker *n* sanguessuga *m,f*.

blood transfusion *n* transfusão *f* de sangue.

bloody (-ier, -iest) *adj adj* sangrento,-a; **2** *(stained)* manchado de sangue; **3** *(coll) (in anger)* raio, maldito,-a; **that ~ man** esse maldito; **the ~ car...** o raio do carro; **not ~ likely!** nem pensar!; **~-minded** *adj (coll)* antipático,-a; obstinado,-a.

bloom *n* flor *f*, *(fig)* florescimento, viço; **in ~** em botão/em flor; **in the ~ of youth** na flor da idade; ♦ *vi* florescer.

blooming *adj* viçoso, em flor.

blossom *n* flor *f*; ♦ *vi* florir; *(fig)* desabrochar-se.

blot *n* borrão *m*; ♦ *vt* secar; manchar; **to ~ out** *vt* apagar, ocultar.

blotch *n* mancha *f*.

blotchy *adj* cheio de manchas.

blotting paper *n* mata-borrão *m*.

blotto *n (coll: dead drunk)* grosso, bêbedo (sem consciência).

blouse *n (garment)* blusa *f*.

blow *n* golpe *m*, pancada *f*; **a ~ to the back of the head** uma pancada na cabeça; *(with fist)* murro *m*, soco *m*; **we nearly came to ~s** quase chegámos a vias de facto; *(fig) (shock)* **it was a ~ to my pride** foi um golpe para o meu orgulho; **2** *(setback)* revés *m*; ♦ *(pt* **blew**, *pp* **blown)** *vi (wind)* ventanejar, soprar; **2** *(by mouth)* soprar; **3** *(sound) (horn, car)* soar; **4** *(lightbulb)* fundir; **5** *(fuse, gasket)* queimar; **6** *(leave quickly)* raspar-se *(fam)*; ♦ *vt* soprar; **2** *(horn, trumpet)* soar, tocar; **3** *(safe, etc)* dinamitar; **4 ~ the nose** assoar o nariz; **one's nose** assoar-se; **5 to ~ the whistle** apitar; **to ~ the whistle on (sb)** denunciar alguém; **6 to ~ money** esbanjar; **7 to ~ one's chances** perder/desperdiçar oportunidades; **to ~ one's trumpet** *(coll)* gabar-se; ♦ **to ~ away** voar longe; **2** *(shoot sb)* matar alguém; **to ~ down** derrubar; **~ off** levar (in the wind); **to ~ out** *vi (candle)* apagar; **2** *(tyre)* estourar; ♦ **~ over** *vi (incident, argument)* passar, ser esquecido; **2** *(storm)* cessar; **3** *(plant)* cair (por causa do vento); ♦ **~ up** *vi (bomb)* explodir; **2** *(row, trouble)* rebentar; **3 ~ sth up** *(inflate)* encher *(tyre, balloon)*; **4** *(enlarge)* ampliar (foto); **5** exagerar; **6** *(fig)* perder a paciência, irritar-se; ♦ **~ by ~** *adj* detalhadamente.

blow-dry *n (hairstyle)* brushing *m*.

blowed *adj* **I'll be ~** *exc* macacos me mordam! *(BR)* nossa!

blowfly *n* mosca *f* varejeira.

blowjob *m (vulg) (fellatio)* mamada *f*, broche *m (vulg)*.

blowlamp, blowtorch *n* maçarico *m*.

blown *(pp:* **blow***)*.

blowout *n (tyre)* furo; estouro *m*; **2** *(oil, gas escape)* fuga; **3** *(ELECT)* curto-circuito *m,f*; *(mining)* jorro *m*.

blowpipe *(UK)*, **blowgun** *(US)* *n* zarabatana *f*.

blowy *adj* ventoso,-a.

blowzy *adj*: **~ woman** mulher *f* desleixada.

blub *(pt, pp:* **blubbed***)* *vi* chorar muito alto.

blubber *n* óleo de baleia; ♦ *vi* chorar descontroladamente; *(fig, pej)* chorar como um cabrito desmamado.

blubbering *adj* chorão *m*/chorona *f*, choroso,-a; **~ session** *f* pranto *m* descontrolado.

blue *n (colour)* azul *m*; **~ (colour) suits you** o azul fica-te bem; **to win a ~** ganhar o prémio desportivo das universidades de Oxford (azul-escuro) e Cambridge (azul-claro); **~ baby** *(MED)* bebé *m* cianótico; **~ bell** *(BOT)* campânula *f*, campainha *f* azul; **~bottle** *(ZOOL) (mosca)* varejeira *f* azul; **~ chip** *(FIN)* ação *f* segura, de primeira; **~ chip investment** investimento seguro; **~ moon** *m* da lua cheia; **once in a ~ moon** uma vez na vida; **~-print** anteprojeto; *(CONSTR)* planta; **~ tit** *(ZOOL)* melharuco *m* azul; **out of the ~** inesperadamente; **the ~s** *npl (MUS)* o blues; *(sad)* depressão moral; **to have the ~s** ter a neura; sentir-se deprimido,-a; ♦ *adj* blue; **~-black** azul-azeviche, azul-ferrete; ~ **collar worker** operário *m*, trabalhador *m* manual; **~-eyed** de olhos azuis; ~ **film/joke** filme/anedota picante *or* pornográfico,-a.

bluff *n (deception)* logro; **2** *(false claim)* basófia; **3** *(cliff)* penhasco; **4** *(bank)* escarpa; ♦ *vi* enganar, mentir, iludir, blefar; **2 to ~ sb into doing sth** convencer alguém a fazer algo; **3 to call sb's ~** desmascarar alguém; confrontar com sua decepção; **4** *(tease or pretend to tease)* **I was bluffing** estava a brincar com você.

bluish *adj* azulado,-a.

blunder *n* asneira *f*, disparate *m*, erro *m* crasso, gaffe; ♦ *vi* cometer um erro; **2** *(move clumsily)* tropeçar, ir de encontro a (**sth**, algo); ~ **around** andar às cegas.

blunt *adj (blade, knife)* embotado, cego; sem corte; **2** *(person)* direto, indelicado; franco; **in a ~ manner** *(discurso)* de um modo *m* frontal; ♦ *vt* embotar.

bluntly *adv* francamente; bruscamente.

bluntness *n* franqueza; frontalidade *f*; aspereza.

blur *n* borrão *m*, mancha *f*; **2** névoa *f*, imagem *f* enevoada; **3** *(memory)* lembrança *f* vaga, confusa; ♦ *(pt, pp* **-red,** *cont.* **-ring)** *vt* nublar, *(vision)* embaçar; ♦ *vi* toldar-se, tornar-se indistinto; **2** obscurecer; **3** *(smudge)* fazer borrões.

blurt *vt:* **to ~ out** deixar escapar, dizer impensadamente; *(confess, get it out of your chest)* desembuchar *(fam)*.

blush *n* rubor *m*; vermelhidão *f*; ♦ *vi* corar, ruborizar-se; ♦ *vt* envergonhar-se.

blusher *n* rouge *f*.

bluster *n (noise)* estrondo; **2** *(angry talk)* discussão *f*; **3** *(boasting)* basófia; ♦ *vi (angrily)* vociferar, barafustar, esbravejar; **2** *(boasfully)* fanfarronar; **3** *(wind)* soprar em rajadas.

blustering *n (boasting)* basófia; **2** *(rage)* fúria, ímpetus *mpl*; **a ~ wind** uma grande ventania; ♦ *adj (angry)* aos berros.

blustery *adj (weather)* tempestuoso,-a.

boa *(ZOOL) n* jiboia *f*; ~ **constrictor** *n* boa *f*.

boar *(ZOOL) (wild)* javali *m*.

board *n* tábua; **2** *(school)* quadro *(preto/branco)*; **3** *(of games)* tabuleiro *m*; **4** *(ADMIN)* conselho *m*; ~ **of directors** conselho administrativo; **5** ~ **of inquiry** comissão *f* de inquérito; **6** B~ **of Education** Ministério da Educação; **7** *(accommodation)* ~ **and lodging/full** ~ pensão *f* completa; **8 ironing** ~ tábua de engomar, de passar a ferro; **9 notice** ~ placa *f*, quadro *m* de avisos, notícias; ♦ **on** ~ *adv* a bordo; **across the** ~ em geral, a todos os níveis; ♦ *vt (embark)* embarcar; **2** hospedar; **to take sth on** ~ *(fig)* tomar algo em consideração; **to ~ over/up** (sth) fechar algo com tábuas, entaipar; IDIOM **to go by the** ~ *(fig) (lost)* ir por água abaixo; **these days courtesy goes by the** ~ hoje em dia a cortesia vai por água abaixo; **to sweep the** ~ ganhar tudo.

boarder *n* hóspede *m,f; (student)* interno.

boarding *n* embarque *m*; **2** *(MIL)* abordagem; **3** hospedagem *f*; ~ **pass** *n* cartão *m* de embarque; ~ **school** *n* colégio *m* interno.

boast *n* jactância, basófia *f*; ♦ *vi* gabar-se; ♦ *vt* ostentar; *(be proud)* orgulhar-se de; **the library ~s a large collection** a biblioteca orgulha-se da sua grande coleção.

boastful *adj* gabarola *m*, fanfarrão,-ona *m,f*.

boasting *n* fanfarronice *f*.

boat *n* barco, navio *m*; *(rowing)* bote *m*; *(sailing)* veleiro *m*; **by** ~ de barco; **life-~** barco sava-vidas; **in the same** ~ *(fig)* nas mesmas circunstâncias; **ferry-~** barco fluvial; **~er** *n (hat)* chapéu *m* de palha, palhinhas; **~ing** *n (SPORT)* remo; **~man** *n* barqueiro; **~swain** *n* contramestre *m*; IDIOM **to rock the** ~ fazer ondas *(fam)*, complicar.

bob *n* mesura *f*; **2** *(haircut)* corte *m* de cabelo para mulher; **3** *(coll: former UK money, shilling)* xelim *m*; ♦ *vi:* **to ~ up and down** *(person, boat)* balouçar-se; mexer-se para cima e para baixo; **to ~ up** flutuar; ressurgir; **to ~ one's head** *(greeting)* inclinar a cabeça.

bobbin *n (spool)* bobina, carretel *m*; **2** *(for lace-making)* bilro *m*.

bobble *n* pompom *m*.

bobby *n (UK) (coll)* polícia *m,f*.

bobcat *n (ZOOL)* lince *m*.

bobsled, bobsleigh *n* trenó.

bode *vi (LITER)* **to ~ well/ill (for sb, sth)** ser bom/mau presságio para (algo,-alguém).

bodge *vt (UK) (coll)* remendar mal; fazer trabalho mal feito/atabalhoado.

bodice *n (of dress)* corpete *m*.

bodily *adj* físico, corporal; ♦ *adv (carry, lift)* em peso.

body *n (person, animal)* corpo; **2** *(dead)* cadáver *m*; **3** *(of car)* carroçaria; **4** *(of plane)* fuselagem; **5** *(organization)* entidade; **6** *(large volume of water)* extensão *f*; **7** *(of wine)* corpo; **8** *(of persons, opinions)* conjunto *m*; **9** *(of hair)* volume; **in a ~** todos juntos; **~guard** *n* guarda-costas *m,f inv*; ~ **odour** *(US:* **odor)** *n* odor *m* corporal; ~ **search** *n* revista *f* corporal; ~ **shop** *n* academia *f* de ginástica; **~-stocking** *n* macaquinho *m* colante *(for gymnastics)*; IDIOM **over my dead** ~ só por cima do meu cadáver.

body-building *n* musculação *f*; ♦ *adj (exercise)* muscular.

boffin *(UK) (coll)* perito, entendido *m*.

bog *n* pântano, atoleiro; **2** *(UK: slang) (toilet)* retrete *f*; *(BR)* privada *f*; ♦ *vt:* **to get ~ged down in sth** atolar-se em algo.

bogey (man) *n* papão *m*.

boggle *vi* ficar atónito,-a ou confuso,-a; **the mind ~s!** é de ficar pasmo! isso ultapassa a imaginação!

boggy (-ier, -iest) *adj* lamacento.

bogie *n (RAIL)* truque.

bogus *adj* falso; **2** fingido, farsante.

bohemian *adj* boémio *(BR:* boê-).

boil *n (MED)* furúnculo; **to come to the** ~ começar a ferver; ♦ **~ing point** *n* ponto de ebulição; ♦ *vt* cozer; cozinhar; ♦ *vi* ferver; **to ~ down to** *(fig)* reduzir-se a; **to ~ dry** evaporar(-se).

boiler *n* caldeira; ~ **suit** *n* fato-macaco *(BR)* macacão *m*.

boisterous *adj* barulhento; **2** *(child)* turbulento; **3** *(crowd, sea)* agitado,-a.

boisterously *adv* de modo barulhento.

bold *m (TYPO)* negrido *m;* **in** ~ em negrido; ♦ *adj* valente, audaz; **2** *(cheeky)* atrevido; **3** *(pej)* descarado; **4** *(design, colour)* forte; **he is as ~ as brass** ele tem muita lata.

boldness *n* arrojo *m,* coragem *f;* audácia *f,* descaramento *m.*

Bolivia *npr* Bolívia; **in** ~ na Bolívia.

Bolivian *npr adj* boliviano,-a.

boll *n* casulo.

bollard *n (AUT) (on the road)* meco *m;* **2** *(for the boat)* posto *m* de amarração.

bollocks *npr (UK) (vulg) (testicles)* tomates *(coll);* *(BR)* saco *(coll);* ♦ *exc* **bollocks!** *(coll) (nonsense)* tretas *fpl* merda!, *(BR)* saco! ♦ *exc* caramba!

bolshy *adj (coll) (child)* rebelde; **2** *(adulto)* chato, incómodo.

bolster *n* travesseiro *m;* ♦ *vt* **to ~ up** encorajar, apoiar, promover.

bolt *n* trinco, ferrolho; **2** *(with nut)* parafuso, cavilha; **a ~ of lightening** relâmpago; **3 to make a ~ for it** pôr-se ao fresco *(fam)* sitting; ~ **upright** direito como um fuso, hirto; ♦ *vt* trancar; **2** aparafusar; ~ **down** *(food)* devorar; ♦ *vi (horse) (flee)* disparar; **2** *(raposa)* fugir; IDIOM **a ~ out of the blue** *(news, etc)* (cair) como uma bomba.

bolt-hole *n* esconderijo, refúgio.

bomb *n* bomba; ~**shell** *n* granada *f* de artilharia; *(fig)* bomba *f;* ♦ *vt* bombardear.

bombard *vt* bombardear; *(fig)* assediar.

bombardment *n* bombardeamento; ~ **disposal** *n* desa(c)tivação *f* de explosivos.

bombastic *adj* bombástico; pomposo.

bomber *n (AER)* bombardeiro.

bona fide *adj* sincero, autêntico; ♦ *adv* de boa-fé.

bond *n* título; **2** *(ECON)* obrigação *f;* ~ **market** mercado *m* obrigacionista; **3** vínculo, laço *m;* ~-**holder** *n* obrigacionista *m,f.*

bondage *n* escravidão *f.*

bone *n* osso; *(of fish)* espinha; ♦ *vt (fish)* tirar as espinhas de; *(of meat)* desossar; **to feel in one's ~s** pressentir; ♦ ~-**dry** *adj* completamente seco; ~**idle** *adj* mandrião,-ona; preguiçoso,-a; ♦ ~-**setter** *n (quake)* curandeiro; ~ **of contention** *n* causa da contenda.

bonfire *n* fogueira (ao ar livre, em festas).

bonnet *n* capota *(BR:* capô *m)* de automóvel.

bonus *n* bónus *m (BR:* bô-), prémio *(BR:* prê-) *m.*

bony *adj (arm, face, tissue)* ossudo; **2** *(meat)* cheio de ossos; **3** *(fish)* cheio de espinhas.

boo *n* vaia *f;* ♦ *vt (jeer)* apupar, vaiar; ♦ *exc* **boo!** *(to frighten sb)* bu!

boob *n (mistake)* asneira *(EP);* bobagem *(BR);* **2** *(breast) (fam)* seio *m;* ~ **tube** *(kind of bra without straps)* tomara-que-caia *m inv;* **boobs** *(fam) (teats)* tetas *fpl.*

booby *n* palerma *m,f;* ~ **prize** *n* prémio *(BR:* prê-) de consolação; ~ **trap** *(prank)* armadilha; **2** *(bomb)* bomba camuflada ♦ **to ~-trap** ♦ *vt* colocar explosivos em (carro, casa).

book *n* livro; caderno; ~**s** *(COMM)* as contas; ♦ *vt* reservar; contratar; IDIOM **to be in sb's good ~s** estar nas boas graças de alguém.

bookcase *n* estante *f* para livros.

booking office *n (RAIL, THEAT)* bilheteira, *(BR)* bilheteria.

book-keeping *n* escrituração *f,* contabilidade *f.*

booklet *n* livrinho, brochura.

bookmaker *n* agente *m,f* de apostas.

bookseller *n* livreiro,-a.

bookshop *n* livraria.

bookstall *n* banca de livros.

boom *n* barulho, estrondo; **2** aumento rápido; **3** *(ECON)* fase *f* de prosperidade; **baby** ~ *n* aumento súbito do índice de natalidade.

boomerang *n (AUSTRAL)* bumerangue *m;* ♦ *vi (~ed)* voltar para trás; **the plan ~ed** o plano retrocedeu; o tiro saiu pela culatra.

boon *n* benefício; conforto.

boor *adj* grosseiro.

boost *n* estímulo; ♦ *vt* estimular, levantar, aumentar.

booster *n (MED)* revacinação *f.*

boot *n* bota *f;* **2** *(AUT)* porta-bagagem *m, (BR)* porta-malas; **to give the** ~ despedir; ♦ *adv* ainda por cima, também; ♦ *vt (kick)* dar um pontapé no rabo, na bunda, no cu *(slang);* **to ~ out** *(expel)* expulsar; pôr alguém na rua/no olho da rua *(slang);* ♦ ~ **up** *vi (COMP)* inicializar, arrancar; IDIOM **to lick sb's** ~ lamber as botas, engraxar os sapatos a alguém; **too big for his/her** ~ ter pretensões.

bootee *n (for baby's feet) (knitted)* botinha *f* de lã; **2** *(of leather)* botina *f, (BR)* butim *m.*

booth *n (at fair, market)* barraca *f,* tenda *f;* **telephone** ~ cabina *f* telefónica *(BR:* -fô-); **2** ~ **voting** cabina de votação; *(BR)* cabine *f* eleitoral.

bootleg *adj (alcohol)* de contrabando; **2** *(recording)* gravação *f* pirata.

bootstrap *n (shoe lace)* atacador; *(COMP)* programa *f* de inicialização.

booty *n* despojos *mpl;* pilhagem *f;* espólio *m.*

booze *n (coll) (drink)* pinga *f;* bebida *f;* ♦ *vi* embebedar-se.

boozer *n (coll)* bêbedo,-a; *(BR)* bebum; **2** *(UK)* bar, pub.

booze-up *n* farra *f* de copos.

boozy *(-ier, -iest) adj (fam) (drunken)* bêbedo,-a; ~ **party** uma festa de borrachões; **2** *(euph) (meal)* bem regado,-a.

bop[1] *n (fam) (blow)* golpe *m;* *(punch)* murro *m;* ♦ *(-pp-) vt* esmurrar.

bop[2] *(MUS)* tipo de jazz.

bo-peep *n (children's game)* **to play** ~ jogar às escondidas.

border *n* borda, margem *f,* limite *m,* fronteira, beira, orla; ~**line** *n (fig)* fronteira; **2** *(jardim)* canteiro; ♦ *adj* fronteiriço; ♦ **to ~ on** *vt* confinar com; *(fig)* chegar às raias de.

bore *(pt of* bear*) n (tedious person, task)* maçador, -ora, chato,-a; *(coll)* chato; **2** *(arma)* calibre *m;* **3** perfuração *f;* ~**hole** furo (de sondagem); **what a ~!** que maçada, *(coll)* que chatice!; ♦ *vt* furar, perfurar; aborrecer, maçar, chatear *(coll).*

bored *adj (person) (que se aborrece)* aborrecido,-a; **to be/get** ~ *(temp.)* estar aborrecido, aborrecer-se.

boredom tédio *m*, chatice *f*.

boring *n* (*drilling*) (*rock, wood*) perfuração *f*; ♦ *adj* aborrecido,-a, maçador,-ora; chato,-a (*coll*); **to be ~** (*characteristic*) ser aborrecido; **it is a ~ job** é um trabalho, emprego chato.

born (*pp of* **bear**) *adj* nascido, nato; **to be ~** nascer; **I was ~ in 1951** nasci em 1951; **~-again** *adj* renascido; (*fig*) convertido; **first-~** *adj* primogénito (*BR*: -gê-); **newly-~** *adj* recém-nascido; **high-~** de alta linhagem *f*.

borne (*Vd:* **bear**).

borough *n* município; bairro; distrito.

borrow *vt*: **to ~ sth** (**from sb**) pedir algo emprestado a alguém.

borrower *n* o que pede emprestado; tomador,-ora de empréstimo.

borrowing *n* empréstimo *m*.

borstal *n* reformatório (para menores); casa *f* de correção; reinserção *f* social; (*BR*) instituto *m* correcional para jovens.

Bosnia-Herzegovina *npr* Bósnia-Herzegovina.

bosom *n* (*chest*) peito *m*; **2** (*breast*) seio; **3** (*fig*) coração, seio; **~ friend** *n* amigo,-a íntimo,-a; **in the ~ of** no seio de.

Bosphorous *npr* **the ~** o Bósforo.

boss *n* (*stud*) saliência, relevo; **2** (*on wheel*) cubo; **3** (*person in charge*) chefe *m,f*; patrão *m*, patroa *f*; manda-chuva *m inv* (*fam*); ♦ *adj* (*slang*) excelente; **a ~ hand at carpentry** excelente na carpintaria; ♦ *vt* mandar; **to ~ about/around** (*coll*) mandar em alguém, dar ordens a outrem.

bossy (**-ier, -iest**) *adj* mandão,-dona; (*BR*) manda-chuva *m,f*.

bosun *n* (*boatswain*) contramestre *m*.

botanist *n* botânico.

botany *n* botânica.

botch *n* trapalhada *f*; ♦ *vt*: **to ~ up** estropiar, atamancar, fazer uma trapalhada de algo; (*BR*) fazer nas coxas.

both *adj pron* ambos, os dois; **~ of us went** ambos fomos; ♦ *adv*: **~ she and I** tanto ela como eu.

bother *n* (*inconvenience*) incómodo (*BR*: -cô-) *m*; maçada *f*; chatice *f* (*fam*); **it's no ~** não é incómodo nenhum; não tem problema; **what a ~!** que maçada!, que chatice! (*fam*); ♦ *vt* (*worry*) preocupar; **2** (*upset*) aborrecer; **3** (*be inconvenient*) incomodar; **this pain ~s me** esta dor incomoda-me; **does the smoke ~ you?** o fumo incomoda-te?; **3** (*pester*) chatear; ♦ *vi*: **to ~ o.s.** preocupar-se; **to ~ to do** dar-se ao trabalho de fazer algo; **I can't be ~ed to do that** não estou disposto a fazer isso; **to ~ about** preocupar-se com.

bothersome *adj* incomodativo,-a; **2** (*worrying*) preocupante *m,f*; **3** (*fam*) chato,-a.

Botswana *npr* Botsuana *f*.

bottle *n* garrafa *f*; **2** (*smaller*) frasco *m*; **3** (*baby's*) biberão *m*, (*BR*) mamadeira *f*; **4** (*fig*) (*alcohol*) **to be on the ~** gostar da pinga; **5** (*for preserve, jam*) boião *m*; ♦ *vt* (*wine, etc*) engarrafar; **2 to ~ up** *vt* (*anger, grief*) reprimir, refrear; **to hit the ~** meter-se na bebida; ♦ **~ bank** *n* vidrão; **~-fed** *adj* alimentado,-a a biberão; **~neck** (*of bottle*) *n* gargalo

m; **2** (*traffic jam*) engarrafamento; **~-opener** *n* saca-rolhas *m inv*; (*BR*) abridor *m* de garrafas.

bottled *adj* engarrafado.

bottom *n* (*of sea, pile, bottle*) fundo; **2** (*of hill*) sopé *m*; **3** (*of page; far end*) fim *m*, final *m*; **4** (*ANAT*) traseiro, (*coll*) rabo *m*, bunda *f*; **5** (*of ship*) casco *m*; **6** (*root, cause*) **at the ~** por trás de, ao fundo; ♦ *adj* inferior, de/em baixo; último; **~ line** *n* (*fig*) no fundo; **the ~ is that …** a questão toda é que…; **~ shelf** a última prateleira, a prateleira *f* de baixo; **~ drawer** *n* enxoval *m*; **from top to ~** de alto a baixo; ♦ **to ~ out** *vi* (*fam*) to reach the lowest point; ♦ **~s up!** (*in one gulp*) (*cheers*) à saúde!

bottomless *adj* sem fundo; **2** infinito; (*fig*) insondável.

botulism *m* (*kind of food poisoning*) botulismo.

bough *n* (*of tree*) galho *m* (de árvore).

bought (*pt, pp of* **buy**).

boulder *n* pedregulho *m*, matacão *m*.

bounce *n* salto *m*; **2** (*fig*) energia, vigor; **on the ~** *adv* em movimento; no ar; ♦ *vi* saltar, pular; **2** (*cheque*) ser devolvido, não ter cobertura; ♦ *vt* fazer saltar; **to ~ back** *vi* (*after an illness, setback*) restabelecer-se, recuperar.

bouncer *n* (*coll*) (*at the club, hotel*) gorila *m*.

bouncing *adj* robusto; **~ baby** um bebé robusto.

bouncy (**-ier, -iest**) exuberante; **2** (*springy*) (*ball*) que ressalta, saltitante; (*bed, trampoline*) que tem molejo; elástico.

bound (*pt, pp of* **bind**) *n* pulo *m*, salto *m*; **2 ~s** *npl* limites *mpl*; ♦ *adj*: **~ by** limitado por, (*obliged*) obrigado (**by** por); **to be ~ to do sth** fazer algo de certeza; **I am ~ to say …** devo dizer que; **2** (*book*) encadernado; **3 ~ for** (*heading for*) em direção a; (*plane*) com destino a; **4 ~ to** (*connected*) ligado a algo; **5** (*confined to*) retido; **out of ~s** entrada proibida, fora dos limites; **~ up with** dependente de.

boundary *n* (*GEOG*) limite *m*, fronteira *f*.

boundless *adj* ilimitado, sem fim; **2 ~ energy** energia *f* sem limites, energia incrível.

bountiful *adj* (*ample*) abundante.

bounty *n* generosidade; **2** (*reward*) recompensa.

bouquet *n* (*of flowers*) ramalhete *m*, ramo *m*; **2** (*of wine*) aroma *m*.

bourgeois *n* *adj* burguês,-esa, bourgeoisie *m*, burguesia *f*.

bout *n* ataque *m*; surto *m*; **2** (*of cough*) acesso de tosse; **drinking ~** bebedeira *f*; **3** (*boxing*) combate *m*; **4** (*outbreak*) crise *f*.

bow¹ *n* (*curtsy*) vénia (*BR*: vê-); **2** (*of boat*) proa; ♦ *vt/vi* curvar-se; (*head forward*) inclinar a cabeça, cumprimentar; **to ~ down to/before** ceder ante/perante, submeter-se a, render-se a.

bow² *n* laço *m*; (*small*) lacinho; **2** (*MUS, SPORT*) arco *m*; ♦ *vi* manejar o arco.

bowed (*pt, pp of* **bow**) *adj* (*head*) descaída; **2** (*back*) curvada.

bowels *npl* intestinos *mpl*; (*fam*) tripas *fpl*; **2** (*fig*) (*inner depths*) entranhas; **in the ~ of earth** nas entranhas da terra; **~ cancer** cancro intestinal.

bowl n (small) tigela, **a ~ of soup** uma tigela de sopa; **2** (larger) taça grande; **3** (for salad) saladeira f; **sugar ~** açucareiro m; **3 lavatory ~** sanita f; **4** (SPORT) bola de madeira; **5** (of pipe) fornilho m; ♦ vi (cricket) lançar a bola; **~s** n jogo de bowling; (BR) jogo de boliche ♦ **~ over** vt (knock over) derrubar; **2** (fam) (astound) surpreender, aturdir; **I was ~ed over with the news** fiquei atónito,-a com a notícia.

bowlegged adj de pernas arqueadas, (BR) cambota.

bowler n (cricket) lançador m (da bola); **2 ~ hat** chapéu m coco.

bowling n bowling m, (BR) boliche m; **~ alley** n pista de bowling; (BR: boliche); **~ green** n campo, cancha de bocha, de bowling, (BR) gramado para boliche; **~s** n (SPORT) jogo m de bocha.

bow out (resign) despedir-se; (withdraw graciously) afastar-se.

bow tie n gravata-borboleta f; laço m.

box n caixa, caixote m; **2** (for jewels) estojo; **3** (THEA) camarote m; **4 the ~** (fam) a television; **5** (BOT) buxo m; **~ junction** (UK) cruzamento de ruas com faixas amarelas, no qual um veículo não pode avançar a não ser que o caminho esteja livre; **~ number** n caixa f postal, apartado; **~ office** n bilheteira, (BR) bilheteria; **~room** n quarto pequeno de arrumação; ♦ vt encaixotar; ♦ vi (SPORT) socar, jogar o boxe, (BR) boxear.

boxer n pugilista m, jogador m de boxe, (BR) boxeador m; **2** (dog) boxer m; **~ shorts** n cuecas mpl (de homem).

boxing n (SPORT) boxe m, pugilismo; **B~ Day** npr Dia de Santo Estêvão (26 de Dezembro festejado na Inglaterra); **~ gloves** npl luvas fpl de boxe; **~ ring** n ringue m de boxe.

boy n menino; (kid) garoto; (older) moço, rapaz m.

boycott n boicote m (**against, of** a, de); ♦ vt boicotar.

boyfriend n namorado, amigo, companheiro.

boyish adj (figure, face) de menino; jovem; **2** (manner, grin) juvenil.

boy scout n escuteiro.

bra n (under garment) soutien m, sutiã m.

brace n (CONSTR) (bean, prop) reforço, braçadeira; **2** (on teeth) aparelho m dentário; **3** (MED) (broken limb) tala f; **4** (tool) arco m de pua; **5** (pair) par, parelha f; **a ~ of partridges** um par de perdizes fpl; **6** (graphic symbol) chaveta f; ♦ vt (CONSTR) reforçar; ♦ vr (fig) precaver-se, preparar-se (**for** para); **~ yourself for what is going to happen** prepare-se para o que vai acontecer; ♦ vi (invigorate) fortalecer, tonificar; **braces** n (for trousers) suspensórios fpl.

bracelet n pulseira, bracelete m.

bracing adj tonificante; revigorante m,f; **the morning breeze is ~** a brisa da manhã é revigorante.

bracken n (BOT) feto, (BR) samambaia.

bracket n (TECH) (for shelf) suporte m; mão francesa f; **2** (group) classe f, faixa f; **3** escalão m; **his income is in the lower ~** o salário dele está no escalão mais baixo; **4** (characters) parêntesis; **round/square ~s** parênteses curvos/retos; ♦ vt

(enclose in brackets) meter entre parênteses; **2** (group) **to ~ sb/sth** (**together**) **with sb/sth** agrupar, equiparar algo, alguém a algo, alguém.

brackish adj (água) salobra.

bradawl n bradal m.

brag n (boast) fanfarronice f; **2** jogo m de cartas semelhante ao póquer; ♦ (**-ged, -ging**) vi (boast) gabar-se (**about** de).

braggart, bragger n gabarola m fanfarrão m, fanfarron f.

bragging adj boastful; **he is ~** ele está se gabando.

braid n (trimming) galão m; **2** (of hair) trança; ♦ vt entrançar; **2** (curtain, etc) ornar de galão.

Braille npr braile m.

brain n cérebro; **2** (mind) cabeça; **3** (intelligent person) génio; **~child** n invenção f; **~ death** morte f cerebral; **~ drain** fuga f de cérebros (para outro país); **~less** adj desmiolado, idiota m,f; **to ~wash** vt (fig) fazer lavagem f cerebral a; **~wave** n inspiração f, ideia (BR: idéia) luminosa; ♦ **brains** npl inteligência, sabedoria, (coll) miolos mpl; **he has no ~** ele não tem miolos; **2** (CULIN) **sheeps' ~** miolos de carneiro; IDIOM **to beat one's ~ out** dar voltas ao miolo/juízo/à cabeça.

brainy adj inteligente m,f; muito esperto.

braise vt (CULIN) estufar.

brake n travão m, (BR) freio, breque m; ♦ vt/vi travar, (BR) frear; **~ block** calço m de travão; **~drum** n tambor m de freio; **~ fluid** n óleo de freio; **~ lining** revestimento m do travão; **~man** n guarda-freio m braking n travagem f.

bramble n (BOT) (plant) silva f, sarça; **~-berry** amora-silvestre f; **~ bush** sarçal m.

brambling m (ZOOL) tentilhão m.

bramley adj (BOT): **~ apple** (English cooking apple) maçã reineta f.

bran n (CULIN) farelo.

branch n (of tree) ramo m, galho m; **2** (of pipe, railway, road) ramificação f, secção f, ramal m; **3** (COMM) sucursal f, filial f; **4** (of bank) agência f; ♦ vi: **to ~ off** (road, railway) bifurcar-se, ramificar-se; **to ~ off from** separar-se de; **~ out** (person, company) diversificar-se; **~ line** n linha f secundária; (BR) ramal m secundário.

brand n (COMM) marca f; **~ name** n marca f registada, (BR: registrada); **2** tipo, género m; **3** (mark on animals) marca de ferro em brasa; ♦ vt ferrar (animal); **2** (fig) (stigmatize, denounce) rotular, estigmatizar, denunciar alguém; **3** **~ed** (engraved in one's mind) gravado,-a na mente.

brandish vt brandir (sword).

brand-new adj novo em folha, completamente novo.

brandy n conhaque m.

brash adj descarado,-a, atrevido,-a, petulante m,f; **2** (loud) (colour, style) berrante; **3** (rash) irrefle(c)tido,-a.

brass n latão m; bronze m; **2** (MUS) os metais; **~ band** n banda de música, fanfarra f: (BR) charanga f; **~ rubbing** n técnica de decalque; gravura em latão; **~ tacks** npl (fam): **to get down to ~**

tacks ir direto ao assunto; ♦ **brasses** *npl* ornamentos *m,f* em latão.

brassière *n (undergarment)* sutiã *m*, soutien.

brassy *adj (US)* acobreado; **2** *(som) (de metais)* metálico; *(loud)* estridente; **3** *(showy)* espalhafatoso.

brat *n (coll) (pej) (child)* pirralho, fedelho; *(BR) (pej)* capeta *m*.

bravado *n* bravata.

brave *n* guerreiro índio, bravo; ♦ *adj* valente, corajoso; ♦ *vt* desafiar; enfrentar; **to ~ out** *(danger)* enfrentar.

bravely *adv* corajosament.

bravery *n* coragem *f*, bravura.

brawl *n* briga, rixa *f*; ♦ *vi* brigar, andar à pancada.

brawler *n* zaragateiro,-a, *(BR)* brigão *m*, brigona, *f*; **2** barulho, alarido ♦ *adj* barulhento,-a.

brawn *n (muscle)* músculo *m*;, força *f* muscular; **2** *(CULIN) (from pig's head)* paté *m* de carne.

brawny (-ier, -iest) *adj* musculoso,-a, musculado.

bray *n (of donkey)* zurro; **2** *(of person)* cacarejo *m*; ♦ *vi* zurrar; **2** *(person's laugh)* cacarejar uma gargalhada *f*.

brazen *adj* descarado; imodesto; ♦ *vt*: **to ~ it out** portar-se descaradamente, enfrentar alguém.

brazier *n* braseiro *m*.

Brazil *npr* Brasil *m*; **in ~** no Brasil.

Brazilian *npr adj* brasileiro,-a; **~-like** *n (mannerism, etc)* brasileirismo.

Brazil nut *n* castanha-do-pará.

breach *vt n* brecha *f*, rotura *f*; **2** *(of contract, rights)* quebra *f*; **3** *(LAW) (infringement)* **a ~ of the law** uma transgressão/infração *f* da lei; **4 ~ of peace** perturbação *f* de ordem pública; **5** *(of relations)* de rompimento *m*; **6 ~ of trust** abuso de confiança; **7** *(of professional secret)* violação *f*; **8** *(breaking of the sea on shores)* o quebrar das ondas; ♦ *vt* abrir uma brecha; **2** desrespeitar, infringir; **3** *(whale)* saltar, livrar-se das ondas.

bread *n (CULIN)* pão *m (pl:* **pães)**; **~ and butter** *n* pão com manteiga; **two loaves of ~** dois pães; **~ bin** caixa *f* caixote *m* do pão; **a slice of ~** uma fatia de pão; **~ crust** côdea *f* do pão; **~-crumbs** *npl* pão ralado *sg*; migalhas *fpl*; **escalopes coated in ~** escalopes panados; **~-line** limiar *m* da pobreza; **stale ~** pão duro; **2** *(fig) (livelihood)* o ganha-pão *m*; **to earn one's (daily) ~** ganhar o pão de cada dia; **3** *(coll: money)* massa; ♦ *adj* básico, essencial; ♦ *vt (CULIN) (cutlet in bread)* panar; **~ cutlet** costeletas panadas.

breadth *n* largura; *(mind)* abertura; *(fig)* amplitude *f*.

breadwinner *n* ganha-pão *m*, sustento da família, *(BR)* arrimo de família.

break[1] *n (crack)* racha, fenda *(china, wall)*; **2** *(gap)* brecha, abertura; **3** *(circular rupture)* ruptura; *(hole)* rombo; **4** *(in relations)* rompimento; **5** *(day, clouds)* romper; **at the ~ of day** ao romper do dia, ao alvorecer; **6** *(bones, etc)* fratura *f*; **7** *(pause in conversation, work)* pausa *f*; **8** *(intermission)* intervalo; **a ~ in transmission** uma interrupção na transmissão; **9** *(from prison)* fuga; **10** *(weather)* mudança *f*; **11 Christmas ~** as férias do Natal; **12** *(coll) (opportunity)* oportunidade, chance; **13**

golpe, corte; **a lucky ~** um golpe de sorte; **I need a ~** preciso de um descanso; **without a ~** sem parar; **give me a ~!** deixa-me em paz!; **give it a ~** deixa isso!

break[2] *(pt* **broke**, *pp* **broken)** *vt* quebrar, partir, fracture; **2** *(tear, rupture)* romper; **3** *(of promise, etc)* faltar a; **4** *(silence)* romper; **5** *(secret, news)*, revelar; **6** *(soften fall)* amortecer; **7** interromper; **8** violar, transgredir; ♦ *vi (smash)* quebrar-se, partir-se; fraturar-se; **2** *(scandal)* rebentar; **3** *(weaken) (moral)* esmorecer; ♦ **to ~ away** *vt (escape)* escapar, livrar-se à força de (algo), afastar-se; **2** *(relationship)* **(from sb)** romper (com alguém); ♦ **to ~ the bank** *(finances)* arruinar; **to ~ down** *vt (analyse)* analisar, separar *(items, elements)*; **2** *(demolish)* destruir, derrubar; **3** *(not function – machines, car)* avariar-se; **4** *(weep)* desatar a chorar, romper em choro/lágrimas; ♦ *vi* desarranjar-se; **2** *(TECH)* enguiçar; **3** *(MED)* sofrer um colapso; **4** *(negotiations)* fracassar; **5** *(AUT)* avariar-se; **to ~ even** *vi* sair sem ganhar nem perder; **to ~ free/loose** *vi* escapar-se, libertar-se; **to ~ ground (for)** preparar o terreno (para); **to ~ in** *vt (horse etc)* domar; *(car)* fazer a rodagem de; ♦ *vi* forçar uma entrada; **2** *(conversation, etc)* interromper; **~ sb in** acostumar alguém ao trabalho; **to ~ into** *vt* arrombar; forçar *(cofre, fechadura)*; **3** *(encroach)* ocupar; **4** *(to begin to do)* começar a, desatar a (+ *verb)*; **she broke into singing** desatou a cantar; **5** *(COMM) (pessoa)* penetrar em *(market, show)*; **to ~ off** *vt (snap off)* cortar, partir-se; ♦ *vi* interromper-se; **~ sth off** *(become detached)* quebrar-se; *(engagement)* romper, terminar; **to ~ off doing** parar de fazer, cessar; **to ~ open** *vt* abrir com esforço, forçar; ♦ **to ~ out** *vi (start suddenly)* rebentar,explodir, estalar; **to ~ out in spots** aparecer coberto de manchas; **to ~ out in a cold sweat** começar a suar frio; ♦ **to ~ through** *vt, vi (to force the waythrough)* romper, abrir caminho por; **2** avançar; ♦ **to ~ up** *vi* (alliance, relationship) romper-se; ♦ *vt (ice in small pieces)* partir; **2** *(car, wreck)* desmontar; **3** *(membership)* desmembrar (-se), dissociar-se; **4** *(crowd)* dispersar-se; **to ~ up with sb** acabar com/romper com alguém; ♦ *vi* **to ~ waters** *(pregnancy)*; **her waters have broken** as águas dela já romperam; **to ~ wind** *(fart)* bufar.

breakable *adj* quebradiço, frágil.

breakage *n* quebra.

breakaway *adj inv* dissidente.

breakdown *n (AUT) (machine)* avaria; **2** *(in communications)* interrupção *f*; **3** *(of negociations)* ruptura *f*; **4** *(of relations)* rompimento *m*; **5** *(of plan)* falhanço; **6** *(of analysis)* em detalhe, detalhamento *m*; **7** *(MED =* **nervous ~)** esgotamento nervoso *m*, depressão *f*, colapso *m*; **8 ~ crane** grua *f*, guindaste *m* de manutenção; **9** *(truck, van)* de pronto-socorro; **~ even** *n (accounts, price)* ponto *m* de equilíbrio; **~ fast** *n* pequeno-almoço *m*; *(BR)* café *m* da manhã.

breaker *n (wave)* onda *f* grande; **2** *(person)* domador *(of animals)*; **3** *(machine)* quebra-pedras; **4** *(ELECT) (short for:* **circuit ~)** interruptor *m* do circuito.

breakfast *n* pequeno-almoço *m*, *(BR)* café *m* da manhã.

break-in *n* arrombamento *m*.

breaking and entering *n (JUR)* invasão *f* de domicílio; transgressão *f*.

breaking point *n* limite *m*, ponto *m* de ruptura; **2** *(fig)* colapso.

breakneck *adj:* **at a ~ speed** a uma velocidade excessiva, vertiginosa.

breakthrough *n* avanço *m*.

breakup *n (of system)* dissociação *f*; **2** *(of relationship)* rompimento *m*; **~ value** *(COMM) n* valor *m* de liquidação.

breakwater *n (mole)* quebramar *m*, molhe *m*, paredão *m*.

bream *n (fish)* sargo *m*; **sea-~** dourada *f*.

breast *n (ANAT) (chest)* peito; *(woman's)* seio, mama; **~ cancer** *n* cancro da mama; **~ pocket** *n* bolso *m*, algibeira *f* do peito; **large ~s** grandes seios *mpl*; **~-stroke** *n (swimming)* nado de bruços, *(BR)* nado de peito; ♦ *vt* enfrentar; **to ~ feed** *(pt, pp fed) vt* amamentar; IDIOM **To make a clean ~ of it** confessar, ficar com a consciência mais tranquila.

breath *n* fôlego *m*, hálito *m*, respiração *f*; **a ~ of life** um sopro de vida; **a ~ of fresh air** uma lufada de ar fresco; *(mouth odour)* hálito *m*; **to hold one's ~** reter, suster a respiração; **out of ~** ofegante, sem fôlego; **to say sth under one's ~** *(mutter)* falar entre dentes; **take a ~** fazer uma pausa; **to take sb's ~ away** ser surpreendente; **waste one's ~** falar em vão; falar para a parede; **don't waste your ~** não gaste o seu latim, a sua saliva; **with bated ~** *adv* ansiosamente.

breathalyser *(US: -zer) n* bafómetro *m*, alcoolímica *f*.

breathe *vt/vi* respirar; **to ~ in** respirar, inspirar; *(inhale)* inalar; **to ~ freely** respirar com alívio; **to ~ one's last** morrer, dar o último suspiro; **to ~ out** exalar; IDIOM **to ~ down sb's neck** *(watch sb closely)* vigiar alguém; ter alguém debaixo do olho *(fam)*; *(be close behind)* estar sempre em cima de alguém *(fam)*.

breather *n (short break)* momento de descanso, pausa.

breathless *adj* ofegante, sem fôlego; **2** *(out of panic)* espavorido,-a.

breathtaking *adj (beautiful)* lindo,-a; incrível.

breath test *n (UK)* teste *m* de alcoolémia.

bred *(pt, pp of* **breed**).

breech *n (of gun)* culatra *f*; **~ delivery** *n (MED)* parto *m* pélvico; ♦ **breeches** *npl (gen)* calções; calções antigos; **2** *(riding)* calças *fpl* de montar.

breed *n* raça, casta *f*; ♦ *(pt, pp* **bred**) *vt* criar, gerar; ♦ *vi* reproduzir-se, procriar-se.

breeder *n (of animals)* criador,-ora.

breeding *n* educação *f*; **2** *(of animals, plants)* criação *f*, reprodução *f*; **~-ground** *n (fig) (ideas)* fonte *f*.

breeze *n* brisa, aragem *f*.

breezeblock *n* tijolo *m* leve.

breezy *(-ier, -iest) adj* ventoso,-a; **2** *(person)* jovial.

Breton *npr* bretão *m*, bretã *f*; *(LING)* bretão.

brevity *n* brevidade *f*.

brew *vt (beer)* fermentar, **2** *(tea)* preparar; ♦ *vi (infuse)* preparar-se; **2** *(fig) (crisis, trouble)* armar-se; **3** *(storm)* formar-se; **4** *(quarrel) (coll)* tramar-se; **5** *(plot)* maquinar-se; **a storm is ~ing** vem aí uma tempestade.

brewer *n* cervejeiro, fabricante *m,f* de cerveja.

brewery *n* cervejaria *f*, fábrica *f* de cerveja.

bribe *n* suborno; ♦ *vt* subornar.

bribery *n* suborno.

brick *n* tijolo; **fire-proof ~** tijolo refratário **~layer** *n* assentador *m* de tijolos; pedreiro; **~work** *n* alvenaria *f*; **~yard** fábrica *f* de tijolos; **2** *(toy)* cubo; **to ~ in/up** *vt* tapar com tijolos; IDIOM **to drop a ~** meter o pé na argola.

bridal *adj* nupcial.

bride *n* noiva.

bridegroom *n* noivo.

bridesmaid *n* dama *f* de honor, *(BR)* dama de honra.

bridge *n* ponte *f*; *(NAUT)* ponte de comando; **~ head** cabeça-de-ponte **2** *(link)* ligação *f*; **3** cavalete *m* (de violino); **4** osso *m* (do nariz); **5** *(cards)* bridge *m*; ♦ *vt* construir uma ponte; **2** estabelecer ligação; **to ~ the gap** efetuar uma aproximação; *(between opponents)* harmonizar; **~ a gap** preencher uma lacuna em *(knowledge)*, um vazio em *(in conversation)*.

bridle *n* cabeçada *f*, freio *m*; ♦ *vt* enfrear; aparelhar; **2** *(fig)* refrear, conter; **~path** *n* pista/vereda *f* para cavaleiros.

brief *n (JUR)* causa *f*; **2** *(statement)* declaração *f*; **3** *(gen)* instruções; ♦ *adj* breve, curto,-a; **be ~!** seja breve!; ♦ *vt* informar; dar instruções a (on, sobre); **fully ~ed** completamente informado,-a; **in ~** em resumo.

briefcase *n* pasta *f*.

briefing *n* instruções *fpl*.

briefly em resumo; **2** laconicamente.

briefs *npl* cuecas *fpl*, *(BR)* calcinha *fsg*.

Brig *(abbr for:* **brigadier**) Brigº.

brigade *n (MIL)* brigade; **2 the anti-~ smoke** a brigada anti-tabaco.

brigadier *n* general *m* de brigada, brigadeiro *m*.

bright *adj (full of light)* claro,-a; **2** *(star, eyes)* brilhante; **3** *(colour)* vivo,-a; **he went ~ red** ele ficou todo vermelho; **4** *(lively)* alegre, animado,-a; **5** *(clever)* esperto,-a, inteligente.

brighten *vt* alegrar; ♦ *vi (sky)* clarear; **to ~ up** animar-se, alegrar-se; *(situation)* melhorar; *(light)* intensificar-se; **~ lights** *npl* centro de diversão da cidade.

brightly *adj (dressed)* de cores vivas; *adv* intensamente, animadamente.

brightness *n* brilho *m*; **2** claridade *f*; **3** vivacidade.

brill *n (ZOOL)* espécie de rodovalho *m*.

brilliance *n* brilho, claridade *f*.

brilliant *adj* brilhante; admirável; inteligente.

Brillo pad® *n* esfregão (de aço com sabão) esfregão Bravo.

brim *n (cup, etc)* bordo; **2** *(hat)* aba; **~ful** *adj* cheio até transbordar; **eyes ~ming with tears** olhos rasos de lágrimas; ♦ **~ over** *vt* transbordar (**with**, de).

brine *n (CULIN)* salmoura.

bring *(pt, pp.* **brought) (to the addressee)** trazer; 2 atrair; **the talk brought many people** a palestra atraíu muita gente; 3 *(JUR)* **to ~ charges against sb** acusar alguém em tribunal; 4 **to ~ nearer** aproximar; ♦ **to ~ oneself to do** *vr* decidir-se a *(fazer)*; ter a coragem de fazer; 2 **you brought it on yourself** a culpa é tua/sua; ♦ **to ~ about** *vt* causar, efetuar, conseguir fazer; **to ~ alongside** *vt (NAUT)* atracar; **to ~ back** *vt* trazer de volta, devolver; **to ~ sth down** *(cause to fall)* derrubar; deitar abaixo; 2 fazer baixar *(plane)*; 3 *(reduce)* reduzir; baixar *(price)*; 4 *(fig) (THEAT)* **to ~ down the house** causar grande aplauso; **to ~ forth** gerar; originar; **to ~ forward** antecipar, adiantar; 2 *(accounts)* transportar; **to ~ in** *(introduce)* apresentar, introduzir; 2 *(yield)* render, recolher; 3 *(JUR) (verdict)* pronunciar; **to ~ off** *(difficult task)* ter êxito *(em)*, sair-se bem; levar a cabo; **to ~ on** causar, provocar; **to ~ out** *vt (COMM) (new product)* apresentar, lançar; 2 publicar; 3 *(stand out, reveal)* ressaltar, salientar; **to ~ sb round** *(also:* **around)** *(regain senses)* fazer alguém recuperar os sentidos; reanimar; 2 convencer *(to, a)*; **to ~to an end** acabar com *(algo)*; **to ~ to mind** *(recall)* recordar; **to ~ together** reunir; **to ~ up** *(mention)* abordar, falar de; 2 vomitar; 3 educar, criar; ♦ **well/badly brought up** bem/mal criado,-a; IDIOM **bring and buy sale** *(UK)* venda *f* para a caridade.

brink *n (edge)* borda; beira; **on the ~ of** à beira de; prestes a; **on the very ~ of** mesmo à beirinha.

brisk *adj* vigoroso; 2 rápido; 3 a(c)tivo; **a ~ walk** um passeio vigoroso; **a ~ gust of wind** uma forte rajada de vento.

brisket *n* carne *f* de peito de vaca.

bristle *n (on brush, face, plant)* pelo; 2 *(on pig)* cerda; ♦ *vi (stand up)* eriçar-se; 2 **to ~ with** estar cheio de; ♦ *vi (hair)* eriçar-se; 2 indignar-se **(at,** com).

bristly *adj (hair, beard, fibres)* hirsuto, cabeludo; coberto de pelos; 2 *(fig)* irritadiço; áspero.

Brit *(abbr for* **Briton)** *(fam)* pessoa britânica, inglês,-esa.

Britain *npr* =**Great Britain** a Grã-Bretanha.

British/Britannic *adj* britânico,-a; inglês, -a; **the B~** *(people)* os ingleses; **the ~** *npr pl* os britânicos, os ingleses; **the ~ Isles** *npr pl* as Ilhas Britânicas; **the ~ Council** *n* o Conselho Británico *(in Portugal)* o Instituto Británico.

Briton *npr (fam)* pessoa británica; **we, Britons …** nós, os britânicos …

brittle *adj* quebradiço, frágil; 2 *(person, instance)* susce (p) tível, melindroso.

broach *vt* abordar *(subject)*; 2 *(coll)* trazer à baila.

B road *n* estrada *f* secundária.

broad *adj* amplo, largo, extenso; **~ lands** terras *fpl* extensas; 2 **~ shoulders** ombros *mpl* largos; 3 *(accent)* carregado; 4 *(smile)* aberto; **to drop ~ hints about sth** fazer alusões evidentes a algo, dar piadas a algo; **in ~ daylight** em pleno dia; IDIOM **it's as ~ as it's long** vai dar no mesmo.

broadband *n (TV, COMP)* banda *f* larga.

broad bean *n (BOT)* fava *f.*

broadcast *n* transmissão *f*; ♦ *(pt, pp* **-cast)** *vt (RADIO, TV)* transmitir.

broadcaster *n* locutor,-ora de rádio.

broadcasting *n* radiodifusão *f*, transmissão *f*; **~-time** *n* tempo de emissão *f.*

broaden *vt* alargar; ♦ *vi* alargar-se; **~ out** ampliar-se.

broadening *n* alargamento *m*, extensão *f.*

broadly *adv* em geral; **~-speaking** em termos gerais; 2 *(smile)* abertamente.

broadminded *adj* tolerante, liberal.

broadsheet *n* jornal *m* (de tamanho grande).

broadside *n (NAUT)* costado *m*; 2 *(criticism)* ataque *m* severo; **on ~** de través, de lado.

> **Broadsheet,** na Grã-Bretanha, e **Broadside,** nos Estados Unidos da América, são jornais de formato grande e de maior prestígio e reputação.

brocade *n* brocade *m.*

broccoli *n* brócolos *mpl.*

brochure *n* folheto, brochure; prospeto.

brogue *n (accent)* sotaque *m* forte; **Irish, Scottish ~** sotaque irlandês, escocês.

broil *n (quarrel)* disputa; ♦ *vt* assar na grelha, tostar.

broiler *n (UK, US) (young tender chicken)* frango para grelhar, assar na grelhar; *(BR)* galeto; 2 *(fig) (sun, day)* escaldante.

broiling *adj (sun)* abrasador, escaldante.

broke *(pt of* **break)** *adj (coll) (insolvent)* sem vintém; teso,-a, *(BR)* duro,-a.

broken *(pp of* **break)** *adj (in pieces)* quebrado, partido, fraturado; 2 *(interrupted)* interrompido, quebrado; 3 *(not working)* estragado, avariado; 4 *(coastline)* recortado; 5 *(contrato, casamento)* desfeito; 6 **a ~ man** um homem abatido; **in ~ English** num inglês incorreto, macarrónico; **~-down** *(car, machine)* avariado; 2 *(in ruins)* estragado, *(BR)* duro,-a; **~-hearted** *(pessoa)* com o coração despedaçado.

broker *n* corretor,-ora; *(foreign exchange)* cambista *m,f.*

brokerage *f (FIN)* corretagem *f.*

brolly *n (umbrella) (fam)* guarda-chuva *m*; 2 *(coll)* chuço.

bromide *n (PHARM)* brometo *m.*

bromine *n* bromo *m*, bromine *f.*

bronchial *adj (infection)* dos brônquios; **~ tubes** brônquios *mpl.*

bronchitis *n (MED)* bronquite *f.*

bronze *n* bronze *m*; ♦ *vt/vi* bronzear(-se).

bronzed *adj* bronzeado,-a; acobreado,-a.

brooch *n* broche *m*; pregadeira *f*; alfinete *m.*

brood *n (of animals)* ninhada; 2 *(fam)* filhos *mpl*; prole *f*; ♦ *vi (birds, poultry)* chocar; 2 *(ponder)* cismar, matutar; **~ about, over** *(fig)* ruminar.

brooding *adj (person)* pensativo,-a cismático,-a **(on, over, upon,** sobre); sorumbático,-a.

broody *adj (-ier, -iest)* deprimido, cismático; 2 *(of bird)* **a ~ hen** uma galinha choca; 3 *(woman)* **to feel ~** desejar ficar gávida/ter um filho.

brook *n* arroio, ribeiro; ♦ *vt* tolerar; permitir.

broom *n* vassoura; **2** *(BOT)* giesta *f*; ~**stick** *n* cabo *f* de vassoura.

Bros *(abbr for* **Brothers***)*.

broth *n (soup)* caldo; IDIOM **too many cooks spoil the** ~ muitos a mexer a panela entornam o caldo.

brothel *n* bordel *m*.

brother *n* irmão *m*; ~**-in-law** *n (pl:* **brothers-in-law***)* cunhado.

brotherhood *n (REL)* irmandade; ~ **of men** fraternidade.

brotherly *adj* fraterno,a.

brought *(pt, pp* of **bring***)*.

brow *(eyebrow)* sobrancelha *f*; **2** *(forehead)* testa *f*; **to knit one's** ~ franzir a testa, carregar o sobrolho; **3** *(of hill)* cimo, cume *m*.

browbeat *vt* intimidar; **to** ~ **sb into doing** forçar alguém a fazer algo; **to** ~ **sb into silence** silenciar.

brown *n (colour)* castanho, cor *f* castanha; ♦ *adj (in colour)* castanho, *(BR)* marrom; **2** *(tanned)* bronzeado, moreno; ~ **bread** pão *m* integral; ~ **paper** *n* papel *m* pardo; ~ **rice** *n* arroz *m* integral; ~ **sugar** *n* açúcar *m* mascavo; ♦ *vt* tostar; **2** bronzear; **3** *(CULIN)* dourar.

brownie *n (junior guide)* menina-escoteira.

brownish *adj* acastanhado,-a.

browse *vt/vi (in shop)* dar uma vista de olhos *(por)*; *(fam)* dar uma olhada; **2 to** ~ **through a book** folhear um livro; **3** *(COMP)* **to** ~ **the Web** navegar na Web; ♦ *vi (graze deer, sheep)* pastar *(on)*; alimentar-se de.

browser *n (COMP)* navegador *m*.

bruise *n* equimose *f*, contusão *f*, nódoa *f* negra; **2** *(on fruit)* mancha *f*, pisadura *f*, toque *m*; ♦ *vt* magoar, contundir; **2** *(feelings)* magoar; **to** ~ **fruit** estragar, pisar.

bruised *adj* magoado, aleijado; ~**eyes** olhos pisados.

brunch *n (late breakfast and early lunch)* pequeno-almoço tardio em vez de almoço.

brunette *n (woman)* morena, trigueira.

brunt *n* a pior parte de; **to bear the** ~ ser o mais afetado,-a.

brush *n (hair, clothes, teeth)* escova; **2** *(painting)* pincel *m*, brocha *f*; **3** *(small for sweeping up)* vassoura; **4** *(BOT)* mato rasteiro, matagal; **5** *(confrontation)* escaramuça; ♦ *vt (clean)* escovar; **to** ~ **sth with** pincelar; ~ **against/past sb/sth** roçar; ~ **aside** afastar (do pensamento), pôr de parte; ~ **off** limpar; **2** repelir; **3** não fazer caso de; ~ **up** *vt* rever; retocar; relembrar.

brushing *n* escovadela; ~ **stroke** *n* pincelada.

brush-off *n*: **to give the** ~ **sb** despedir alguém; não ligar importância a alguém, fingir que não vê a pessoa.

brushy *adj* áspero; ~ **wood** *n* mato, matagal *m*.

brusque *adj* brusco, áspero.

brusquely *adv* bruscamente.

Brussels *npr* Bruxelas; ~ **sprout** *n* couve-de-bruxelas *f*.

brutal *adj* brutal.

brutality *n* brutalidade *f*.

brute *n* bruto; animal *m*; ♦ *adj* cruel *m,f*.

BSc *(abbr for* **Bachelor of Science***)* bacharel, licenciado,-a em Ciências.

bubble *n* bolha *f*, empola *f*; **2** *(FIN, COMM)* preço *m* inflacionado; **soap-~** bola de sabão; ♦ *vi (form bubbles)* borbulhar; *(boiling liquid)* ferver; ~ **over/~with** transbordar (de); ~ **bath** *n* banho *m* de espuma; ~ **gum** *n* pastilha elástica, *(BR)* chiclete *m*.

bubbling *(sound) (brook)* murmúrio *m*; **2** efervescente.

bubbly *adj (wine)* espumante; **2** *(fig)* alegre.

buccaneer *n* pirata *m*.

buck *n (animal)* macho; **2** cavalo de volteio; **3** *(US) (coll) (dollar)* dólar *m*; *(coll)* massa *f*; ♦ *vt (horse)* derrubar; *(oppose)* ir contra; ♦ *vi (horse)* corcovear; **to pass the** ~ fazer o jogo do empurra; passar a responsabilidade para; ♦ **to** ~ **up** *vi* animar-se; **2** apressar-se.

bucket *n* balde *m (of a water-wheel)* alcatruz *m*; **to kick the** ~ *(coll) (die)* esticar o pernil *(BR:* as canelas*)*; ~ **down** *vt (rain)* chover a cântaros.

bucketful *n* balde cheio; ♦ **by the** ~ *(a lot)* às carradas.

buckle *n* fivela; ♦ *vt* afivelar; **2** *(legs)* ceder, dobrar; ~ **down** *(work harder)* empenhar-se (em), pôr mãos à obra.

buckshot *m* chumbo *m* de espingarda; ~**skin** *n* pele *f* de cervo.

buckteeth *n* dentes *mpl* salientes.

buckwheat *n* trigo mouro, mourisco.

bucolic *adj* bucólico,-a.

bud *n* broto, rebento; botão *m*; ♦ *(pt* -**ded***)* *vi* brotar, desabrochar; *(fig)* florescer; **to nip in the** ~ cortar o mal pela raiz.

Buddha *npr* Buda.

Buddhism *npr* budismo.

Buddhist *npr* budista *m,f*.

budding *adj* em botão, nascente; **2** promissor,-ora, principiante *m,f*.

buddy *n (US)* camarada *m*, companheiro; pá.

budge *vt* mover; **2** *(fig)* fazer ceder; **she won't** ~ **an inch** ela não vai ceder/mudar de opinião; ♦ *vi* mexer-se.

budgerigar *n* periquito.

budget *n* orçamento *m*; **the B~** *(UK)* o Orçamento Nacional; **2** *(amount included in the budget for)* verba; **the** ~ **given to the Health sector is shameful** a verba destinada ao setor da Saúde é vergonhoso; ♦ *vt* estimar; ♦ *vi* calcular.

budgeted *pp, adj (amount)* orçamentado; ~ **for sth** incluído no orçamento.

budgetary *adj* orçamentário,-a.

budgie *n* = **budgerigar**.

buff *n (colour)* cor *f* de camurça; **2** *(leather)* pele *f* de búfalo; **3** *(expert)* perito,-a; ♦ *adj* aficionado,-a, doido,-a (por); ♦ **in the** ~ *(coll)* em pêlo; nu(a); ♦ *vt (polish)* polir *(nails, metal)*, engraxar *(shoes)*; puxar o lustro *(on waxed furniture)*.

buffalo *(pl:* -**s** *or* -**es***)* *n* búfalo *m*; *(US)* bisonte *m*.

buffer *n (RAIL) (car)* pára-choques *m sg pl*, amortecedor *m*; **2** *(fig) (protection)* tampão *m*; ~ **state** *n* estado tampão *m*; **3** *(COMP)* buffer *m*; **4** *(any cloth, pad used to give shine)* esponja *f*, pano *m* que dá lustro *(nails, furniture)*; **old** ~ *(person)* antiquado,-a.

buffet *n* bar *m*; cafeteria *f*; bufete *m*, *(BR)* bufê *m*; 2 *(slap)* bofetada *f*; ~ **car** carruagem-restaurante, vagão-restaurante *m*; ♦ *vt (slap)* esbofetear; 2 *(wind, sea)* fustigar.

buffoon *n* bobo *m*; 2 palhaço,-a; 3 *(fam)* idiota.

bug *n* inseto *m*; **bed** ~ percevejo; 2 *(germ)* micróbio, vírus; 3 *(COMP) (fault)* erro; **the millennium** ~ o erro do milénio; 4 *(hidden microphone)* escuta *f* telefónica, *(BR)* grampo *m*; 5 *(coll) (craze)* mania *f*; *(US)* fanático,-a; **a samba** ~ um fanático do samba; ♦ *(pt, pp* -ged*) vt (coll) (bother)* chatear *(fam)*; ♦ *vi* pôr sob escuta; grampear (telefone).

bugaboo *m* papão; ~**bear** bicho-papão, pesadelo.

bugger *n (vulg)* sodomita *m*; 2 cabrão *m (vulg)*; 3 *(slang)* gajo, tipo; 4 *(coll)* chato,-a; ♦ *vt (vulg)* enrarar; *(vulg)* **stop bugging me** *(slaug)* não me chateies!; ♦ **bugger**! *exc (slang) (UK)* porra!, merda!; *(coll)* ~ **off** *exc (vulg) (get lost)* vai á merda! *(vulg)*.

buggy *(pl:* -ies*) n (pushchair)* carrinho *m* de bebé *(BR:* -ê*)*.

bugle *n* trompa, corneta.

build *n (physique)* talhe *m*, estatura; ♦ *(pt, pp* **built**) *vt* construir, edificar; ~ **in/into** embutir em, encaixar; ~ **on** ampliar; 2 *(fig) (relationship)* basear-se em, contar com; ♦ ~ **up** acumular; 2 *(of levels)* desenvolver; 3 *(urban)* urbanizar; 4 *(MED)* fortalecer.

builder *n* construtor *m*.

building *n* construção *f*; *(structure)* edifício, prédio; ~ **company** construtora; ~ **society** *n* agência *f* predial; financiadora, sociedade de crédito para a habitação; ~ **site** *n* terreno de construção.

build-up *n (of zone)* urbanização *f*; 2 *(of traffic)* intensificação *f*; 3 *(of objects, people)* acumulação *f*; 4 *(of levels)* desenvolvimento *m*.

built *(pt, pp* of **build**) *adj*: **he is well** ~ ele é bem constituído.

built-in *(closet)* embutido; 2 *(clause)* incorporado.

bulb *n (BOT)* bulbo; 2 *(ELEC)* lâmpada.

bulbous *adj* bulboso,-a.

Bulgaria *npr* Bulgária; **in** ~ na Bulgária.

Bulgarian *npr adj* búlgaro,-a.

bulge *n* bojo *m*, saliência *f*; ♦ *vi* inchar-se; fazer bojo.

bulging *adj (stomach)* inchado,-a, saliente *m,f*; 2 *(eyes)* desorbitado; 3 *(wallet)* a aborrotar.

bulimia *n (MED)* bulimia *f* nervosa.

bulk *n (of person)* massa, corpulência *f*; 2 *(letters, etc)* volume *m*; 3 parte *f* principal, grosso; 4 *(CULIN)* fibra *f*; **in** ~ *(COMM)* a granel, por atacado; **the** ~ **of** a maior parte de.

bulkhead *n (division)* tabique *m*; 2 *(NAUT)* antepara.

bulky *adj* volumoso; *(person)* corpulento,-a; *(BR)* troncudo,-a.

bull *n (of cattle)* touro; 2 *(of elephant, whale, etc)* macho *m*; 3 *(ASTROL)* Touro; 4 ~ **speculator** *(FIN)* especulador altista; 5 *(coll: nonsense)* disparate *m*; 6 *(darts)* o centro, o alvo; 7 **papal** ~ *n* bula *f* papal *f*; ♦ *adj (FIN) (market)* na alta; ~ **headed** *adj* teimoso,-a; ~**ring** *n* arena; IDIOM **to take the** ~ **by the horns** afrontar o perigo.

bulldog *(breed of dog)* buldogue, cão *m* de fila; ~ **clip** *n* clipe *m* gigante.

bulldoze *vt (knock down)* derrubar; aplainar; 2 *(fig)* **to** ~ **one's way** forçar a passsagem.

bulldozer *n* escavadora *m*.

bullet *n* bala; ~**proof** *adj* à prova de balas; 2 *(irrefutable)* irrefutável; ~ **wound** *n* ferida de bala.

bulletin *n* boletim *m*; 2 comunicado oficial; 3 noticiário; ~ **board** *n (US)* quadro de anúncios.

bullfight *n* tourada.

bullfighter *n* toureiro.

bullfighting *n* os touros *mpl*; tauromaquia.

bullfinch *(pl:* -es*) n (bird)* pisco *m*.

bullion *n* ouro/prata em barras.

bullish *adj (FIN):* ~ **market** mercado em alta; 2 o(p)timista.

bullock *n* boi castrado.

bullring *n* arena de touros.

bullrush *(pl:* -es*) n* junco *m*.

bull's-eye *n (target)* centro do alvo, mosca (do alvo).

bullshit *n (slang) (nonsense)* tretas *fpl*, asneiras *fpl*; ♦ aldrabar; vir com tretas para cima (de alguém).

bully *n (who annoys/teases)* arreliador,-ora; 2 valentão *m*, valentona *f*; ♦ *vt* intimidar; 2 tiranizar; 3 arreliar.

bulwark *n* baluarte *m* (**against** contra); 2 prote(c)ção *f*; ♦ **bulwarks** *npl (NAUT)* amurada *f*.

bum *n (coll) (buttocks)* traseiro, *(BR, Angola)* bunda; 2 *(vagrant, lay-about)* vagabundo, vadio; ♦ *vi:* **to** ~ **about/around** mandriar, vadiar.

bumble *vi (mumble)* resmungar; 2 deambular, andar aos tropeções.

bumblebee *n (ZOOL)* abelhão *m*, zângão.

bumbler *n* pessoa atarantada.

bumbling *adj (clumsy)* desajeitado.

bumf, bumph *n (coll) (documento)* papelada *f*.

bump *n* choque *m*, embate *m*; 2 *(jolt)* sacudida; *(vehicle)* solavanco; 3 *(on the head)* bossa *f*, galo *m*; *(lump on the leg, etc)* inchaço; 4 *(elevation on the road)* elevação; 5 *(sound of fall)* baque *m*; ♦ *exc* pum!; ♦ *vt* bater contra, dar encontrão em; ♦ *vi* dar sacudidas; **to** ~ **into sth** *vt* chocar com/contra, colidir com algo; ~ **into sb** *(meet by chance)* dar com, esbarrar com alguém; ~ **off** *(coll)* liquidar alguém, matar; ~ **up** *(tax, prices)* aumentar; IDIOM **to come down to earth with a** ~ cair das nuvens com um trambolhão.

bumper *n (AUT)* pára-choques *m inv*; ♦ *adj (crop, harvest)* abundante.

bumpkin *(also:* **country** ~*) n (coll) (pej)* labrego *m*.

bumpy *adj (road)* cheio,-a de altos e baixos; acidentado,-a.

bun *n (CULIN)* pão *m* de leite, *(BR)* pão *m* doce; **hot cross** ~ pão doce com passas pela Páscoa; 2 *(hair)* rolo, chignon *m*. ♦ **to have a** ~ **in the oven** *(coll)* estar grávida.

bunch *n (of flowers)* ramo *m*; *(of carrots, watercress, keys)*; molho; *(of grapes, bananas)* cacho *m*; *(of people)* grupo *m*; **a** ~ **of idiots** uma cambada *f* de idiotas; **the best of the** ~ a flor do rancho; ♦ *vt* agrupar, fazer molhos/ramos de.

bundle *n* embrulho, pacote *m*; *(of twigs)* feixe, fardo *m*; *(of papers)* maço *m*; *(of clothes)* trouxa *f*; ♦ *vt:*

to ~ up embrulhar, atar; **to ~ sth/sb into** enfiar algo alguém à pressa em; **to ~ off** despachar alguém; **to ~ up** empacotar, atar; *(of clothes)* fazer uma trouxa; **be in a ~ of nerves** estar numa pilha de nervos.

bung *n* tampão *m*, tampo *m*; **2** *(of barrel)* batoque *m*; *(of bottle)* tapulho *m*, rolha *f*; ♦ *vt* abatocar; **to ~ into** *(coll)* pôr em, *(BR)* botar em; **to ~ up** *vt/vi (block; drain, nose)* fechar; entupir; **2** *(nose)* congestionar.

bungalow *n* bangalô *m*; casa *f* térrea; chalé *m*.

bungee-jump *n (SPORT) n* jumpee jump *m*.

bungee-jumping *n* bungee jumping *m*.

bungle *vt* estropear; fracassar; fazer malfeito.

bungled *adj* frustrado, gorado.

bungler *n (person)* trapalhão *m*, trapalhona *f*.

bunion *n (of foot)* joanete *m*.

bunk *n* tolice *f*; disparate *m*; **2** *(MIL) (kind of bed)* tarimba; **~ beds** *npl* beliche *msg*.

bunker *n* carvoeira; **2** *(MIL)* abrigo, casamata; **3** *(in golf)* obstáculo, bunker *m*.

bunny *n* (= **~ rabbit**) coelhinho; *(from Playboy club) (girl)* coelhinha.

Bunsen burner *n (stove, cooker)* bico *m* de Bunsen.

bunting *n* bandeirinhas enfiadas em fio para enfeitar ruas ou barcos em dias de festa.

buoy *n* bóia; **life ~** *n* bóia salva-vidas; ♦ **to ~ up** *vt* fazer boiar; *(fig)* sustentar, animar.

buoyancy *n* capacidade *f* de flutuaçâor; **2** otimismo.

buoyant *adj* flutuante; **2** *(person)* alegre; **3** *(COMM)* otimista *m,f*; dinâmico,-a.

burble *n (of stream, voices)* burburinho *m*; **2** *(rambling talk)* aranzel *m*; ♦ *vt* gorgolejar; **2** falar excitadamente.

burden *n (load)* carga, fardo; *(fig) (responsibility)* peso, *f* fardo; **2 the ~ of truth** *(LAW)* o ónus da prova; **3** *(refrain)* refrão; ♦ *vt* carregar; **2 to ~ sb with sth** sobrecarregar alguém com algo; **3** *(fig) (bother)* incomodar alguém; **~some** *adj* pesado; opressivo; *(fig)* incómodo *(BR: -ô-)*.

bureau *n (writing desk) (dated)* escrivaninha *f*, *(UK)* secretária *f*; *(US)* cómoda *f*; **2** *(agency)* escritório, agência; **3** *(government)* departamento governamental.

bureaucracy *n* burocracia.

bureaucrat *n* burocrata *m,f*.

burgeon *n* botão, rebento de árvore; ♦ *vt (give buds)* deitar rebentos; ♦ *vi (grow rapidly)* fluorescer; multiplicar-se.

burger *n (CULIN) (short for hamburger)* hambúrguer.

burglar *n* ladrão *m*, ladra *f*; **~ alarm** *n* alarme *m* antirroubo.

burglary *n (house, car)* roubo por arrombamento.

burgle *vt (break-in)* arrombar; ♦ *vt/vi* assaltar.

burial *n* enterro; **~ ground** *n* cemitério; **~-service** *n* enterro; **~ solemnities** *n* exéquias *fpl*.

burlesque *n* paródia; ♦ *adj* burlesco.

burly *adj (person)* robusto, forte, corpulento.

Burma *npr* Birmânia *f*.

Burmese *npr, adj* burmês,-esa.

burn *n* queimadura; ♦ *(pt, pp* **burned** or **burnt***) vt* queimar; incendiar; ♦ *vi* queimar-se; **2** *(be on*

fire) incendiar-se; **3** *(CULIN)* queimar; *(stick to pan)* pegar no fundo; **4** *(feelings)* arder; **~ with desire for** arder de desejo de/por; **5** *(to smart)* **this ointment ~** esta pomada arde; **6 the fire ~s in the hearth** o fogo arde na lareira; **7 the sand is ~ing** a areia está a escaldar; ♦ **to ~ to ashes** reduzir a cinzas; **~ down** *vt (house, forest)* incendiar-se, destruir pelo fogo; **2** *(fire)* extinguir-se; ♦ **to ~ in** gravar a fogo; **~ off** *(evaporate)* evaporar-se; ♦ **~ out** *(candle, fire)* extinguir-se; **2** *(pessoa)* desgastar-se, ficar exausto,-a; *(MED) (device)* queimar-se; *(fig)* ficar inoperativo; IDIOM **to ~ the candle at both ends** *(exhaust one's energy)* esgotar-se.

burner *n (on cooker)* bico de gás, queimador.

burning *adj* ardente; intenso; **a ~ sensation** uma sensação viva; **a ~ question** uma questão *f* escaldante; **the sand is ~** a areia está a escaldar; **there's a smell of ~** cheira a queimado.

burnish *vt/vi* polir, dar lustro.

burnous *n* albornoz *m*.

burnt *(pt, pp of* **burn***) adj* queimado; **everything has ~** ficou tudo queimado.

burntout *n* falha dum mecanismo; desgaste *m*; *(business)* colapso *m*; *(person's energy)* esgotamento *m*.

burp *n (coll)* arroto; ♦ *vi* arrotar.

burrow *n* toca, lura; ♦ *vt* fazer uma toca, cavar.

bursar *n* tesoureiro; bolseiro, *(BR)* bolsista *m,f*.

bursary *n* bolsa *f* de estudos.

burst *n* estouro *m*; explosão *f*; rebentamento *m*; **a ~ of colour** uma explosão de cores ♦ *(pt, pp* **burst***) vi* rebentar, estourar/estoirar; explodir; **the pipes ~ open** os canos rebentaram; **to ~ in** começar subitamente; **to ~ in on sth** interromper bruscamente; **to ~ into** irromper; **to ~ into flames** irromper em chamas; **to ~ into laughter/tears** desatar a rir/a chorar, desfazer-se em lágrimas; **to ~ out shouting** exclamar; desatar a; *(leave)* sair de repente **(of**; de); ♦ **the door ~ open** a porta abriu-se de repente.

bursting *adj* repleto,-a; **to be ~ at the seams** estar completamente cheio,-a.

bury *vt* enterrar, sepultar.

bus *n* autocarro, *(BR)* ônibus *m*; *(Angola, Mozambique)* machimbombo; **by ~** de autocarro; de ônibus.

bush *n (plant)* arbusto; **2** mato *m*, mata *f*, matagal *m*; **to beat about the ~** falar com rodeios.

bushel *n (unit of capacity)* alqueire *m*; *(fam)* large amount; **hide one's light under a ~** não mostrar (nossas) qualidades, aptidões.

Bushmills® *npr* cerveja *f* irlandesa muito conhecida.

bushy *adj* espesso, denso.

busily *adv* atarefadamente.

business *n* negócio *m*; comércio, negócios *mpl*; **2** *(firm)* empresa, casa; **3** profissão *f*; **4** *(subject)* assunto; **~ is ~!** contas são contas!, *(BR)* negócios são negócios; **it's my ~ to …** encarrego-me de …; **it's none of my ~** eu não tenho nada a ver com isto; **mind your own ~** *(fam)* não te metas onde não és chamado; **that's my ~** isso é cá comigo; **he means**

~ ele fala a sério; ~ **card** *n* cartão *m* de visita; ~ **class** *n* classe *f* executiva; ~ **like** *adj* eficiente, profissional; ~**man**/~**woman** *n* homem/mulher de negócios, empresário,-a, comerciante *m,f*.

busker *n* (*street musician/singer*) artista *m,f* da rua.

bus-stop *n* paragem *f* de autocarro, (*BR*) ponto de ônibus.

bust *n* (*sculpture*) busto *m*; **2** (*woman's*) peito, seio *m*; **3** festa de comes e bebes; **4** (*US*) fracasso *m*; **5** (*police-raid*) rusga *f*; **6** (*relationship*) discussão e rompimento; ♦ *adj* (*coll*) rompido, estragado; ♦ *vt* (*pt, pp* **bust** or ~**ed**) estragar; dar cabo de; **2** (*US*) **to ~ sb** prender alguém; **3** (*coll*) falir.

bustle *n* (*frenetic activity*) azáfama *f*; movimento *m*; ♦ *vi* andar atarefado.

bustling *adj* movimentado,-a.

bust-up *n* (*brawl*) discussão *f*, luta; **2** rompimento *m*. ♦ **to bust up** *vt* (*relationship*) romper, acabar.

busy *adj* ocupado, atarefado; **2** (*lively place*) animado, movimentado; **3** (*TEL*) interrompido, (*BR*) ocupado; ♦ *vr*: **to ~ o.s. with** entreter-se a/com; ~**body** *n* bisbilhoteiro,-a, metediço,-a (*fam*); ~ **lane** *n* corredor *m* para transportes públicos.

but *conj* mas, porém; ♦ *prep* exce(p)to, menos, senão, a não ser; **everything ~ that** tudo menos isso; **all ~ finished** tudo menos acabado/quase tudo acabado; ~ **for** sem, se não fosse; **nothing ~** só; **the last ~ one** o,-a penúltimo,-a.

butane *n* butano *m*.

butch *n* (*coll*) (*of woman*) machona, (*BR*) sapatão; **2** (*of man*) *n* machão, latagão (*fam*); ♦ *adj* (*slang*) (*of woman – manner etc*) viril.

butcher *n* homem *m* do talho, talhante; (*BR*) açougueiro *m*; carniceiro; **2** (*fig*) (*killer*) carniceiro; ~**'s** (**shop**) *n* talho, açougue *m*; ♦ *vt* abater (*animal*), chacinar; (*fig*) (*kill people*), massacrar.

butchery *n* slaughter; **2** (*of people*) massacre *m*, carnificina *f*.

butler *n* mordomo *m*.

butt *n* (*thick end*) extremidade; **2** (*of barrel*) tonel *m*; **3** (*of rifle*) coronha *f*; **4** (*of cigarette*) (*fam*) ponta, beata, prisca, (*BR*) bagana *f*, toco *m*; **5** (*fam: US*) (*bottom*) rabo (*fam*), cu *m* (*vulg*); (*BR, Africa*) bunda *f*; **6** (*target*) alvo, barreira atrás do alvo; (*of ridicule*) **to be the ~ of jokes** ser o bobo da festa, (*of attention*) estar na berlinda; ♦ *vt* (*person*) dar cabeçadas contra; (*goat etc*) marrar, dar marradas; **2** (*CONSTR, NAUT*) (*joint*) unir a topo, pelos topos; **to ~ in** interromper, intrometer-se; ~ **out!** (*fam*) fora! não te metas!

butter *n* manteiga; **bread and** ~ pão com manteiga; ♦ *vt* (*grease sth*) untar com manteiga; **to ~ sb up** (*fig*) bajular; dar graxa a alguém (*fam*); ♦ ~ **bean** *n* feijão-manteiga *m*; ~**cup** *n* (*BOT*) botão-de-ouro *m*; ranúnculo; ~ **dish** *n* manteigueira *f*; ~**fingers** *n* (*person*) desajeitado,-a; ♦ *adj* amanteigado,-a; IDIOM (**it looks as if**) ~ **wouldn't melt in her mouth** parece que não faz mal a uma mosca.

butterfly *n* borboleta; ~ **stroke** (*swimming*) *n* mariposa *f*.

buttermilk *n* soro do leite *m*.

butternut *n* (*BOT*) (*pumpkin, squash*) tipos de abóbora *f*.

butterscotch *n* (*sweet made with butter*) caramelo duro *m*.

buttery *n* (*for wines*) despensa ♦ *adj* amanteigado,-a.

buttocks *npl* nádegas *fpl*.

button *n* (*on coat, bell, machine*) botão *m*; (*US: tip of chin*) a ponta *f* do queixo; (*US: badge*) crachá; **on the ~** (*coll*) em cheio; ~**ed-up** *adj* (*fam*) retraído; ~**hole** *n* casa de botão; flor *f* na lapela; ♦ *vt* **to ~ up** (*garment*) abotoar; **2** (*fam*) (*conclude business*) concluir o negócio com sucesso; **to undo the ~** desabotoar.

buttress *n* contraforte *m*; (*fig*) apoio, esteio.

buxom *adj* (*esp. of woman*) saudável e gorducha; **2** arredondada, rechonchuda (*with large breasts*) de seios grandes.

buy *n* compra; ♦ (*pt, pp* **bought**) *vt* comprar **to ~ sb sth** comprar algo para alguém; **to ~ sth from sb** comprar algo a alguém; **to ~ sb off** subornar alguém; **to ~ up** açambarcar.

buyer *n* comprador,-ora; gerente *m,f* de compras.

buying *n* achat *m*; ~ **power** poder *m* de compra.

buyout *n* compra maioritária de acções.

buzz *n* (*of insect*) zumbido *m*; **2** (*conversation*) burburinho *m*, rumor *m*, boato *m*; **3** (*coll*) (*phone call*) telefonadela *f*; **give me a ~** (*coll*) telefona, apita (*fam*); ♦ *vi* (*inseto*) zumbir; **2** chamar alguém pelo intercomunicador; (*fig*) **her head ~ed with ideas** a cabeça dela fervilhava de ideias; ~ **off!** põe-te a mexer! pira-te! (*fam*); (*BR*) dê o fora!

buzzard *n* (*UK*) (*hawk*) gavião *m*; (*US: vulture*) abutre *m*, urubu *m*.

buzzer *n* sirene *f*; **2** (*bell*) campainha; **3** botão *m* do intercomunicador.

buzzing *n* zumbido; **2** (*coll*) *adj* (*town*) animado,-a.

buzzword *n* palavra *f* da moda.

by *prep* (*expressing cause, agent*) por; **this made ~ him** isto foi feito por ele; **to begin ~ cleaning** começar por limpar; **2** (*by means of*) **to pay ~ cheque** pagar por cheque; (*similarity*) **I recognized him ~ his nose** reconheci-o pelo nariz (*NOTE: por + o = pelo*); (*transport*) de; ~ **car, boat/air** de carro/de barco/de avião; **3** (*means, method*) por, a, de; ~ **means of** por meio de; ~ **kilo or ~ the dozen?** ao quilo ou à dúzia? (*NOTE: a + o = ao, a + a = à*); ~ **force** à força; **leave ~ the back door** saia pela porta traseira; **4** (*according to*) em, por; ~ **my watch it is one o'clock** no meu relógio é uma hora; ~ **law** por lei; **it is O.K. ~ me** por mim tudo bem; (*approx. time*) ~ **two o'clock** pelas duas horas; (*before*) ~ **tomorrow it will be ready** amanhã já estará pronto; (*in measurements, division*) por; **fifty divided ~ five,** cinquenta dividido por cinco; **four multiplied ~ four** quatro vezes quatro são dezasseis; (*rate*) à, por; ~ **the hour** à/por hora; (*by degrees*) a; **little ~ little** pouco a pouco; **one ~ one** um a um; (*origins, profession*) de; ~ **birth** de nascimento; ~ **profession** de profissão; (*near, beside*) de perto de, ao pé de, junto a; **a car went ~ my house** um carro passou por/pela minha casa; ~ **the window** junto/ao pé da janela; *(as a result of)* ~ **chance** por acaso; ~ **mistake** por engano; *(with reflexive pronouns)* ~ **o.s.** sozinho,-a, por si só; ♦ *adv* **close by** perto daqui/dali; **drop ~ my home** passa por minha casa; (*Vd:* **pass, go, drive**); ~ **and large** em geral; ~ **the ~/~ the way** a propósito.

bye(-bye) *exc* adeus, até logo, tchau! *(fam).*

by-election *n (UK, US) (POL)* eleição suplementar para preencher um lugar vago (por morte ou outra razão) na Câmara Baixa.

by(e)-law *n* lei *f* municipal; estatuto; regulamento.

bygone *adj (days, years, event)* passado, antigo; IDIOM **let ~s be ~s** o que lá vai, lá vai; *(BR)* o que passou, passou.

by-line *n (newspaper)* nome do jornalista no início de um artigo.

bypass *n (AUT)* via secundária, desvio; *(MED) (surgery)* ponta *f* de safena; ♦ *vt (AUT)* contornar; **2** *(fig)* evitar.

by-product *n* subproduto; **2** produto derivado; **3** *(fig)* efeito secundário.

bystander *n* espe(c)tador,-ora; observador,-ora; curioso,-a, presente *m,f.*

byte *n (COMP)* byte *m.*

byway *n* desvio; *(fig)* periferia; ~**s** recantos.

byword *n (symbol, synonym, proverbial);* **to be a ~ for sth** ser conhecido por; ser um exemplo de algo.

C

C, c *n (letter)* C, c *f*; **2** *(abbr for* **carat**); **3** *(abbr for* **circa**) **c. 1920** por volta de 1920; **4** *(abbr for* century); **5** *(US abbr for* **cent**); **6** *(MUS: note)* dó *m*; **C major/minor** dó maior/menor; **7** *(school grade)* **C-mark/note** 12 em 20 valores; **8** *(abbr for* **Celsius, Centigrade**).

CA *(abbr for* **chartered accountant**); **2** *(abbr for* **Consumers Association**).

cab *n* táxi *m*; **2** *(of truck)* cabine *f* do motorista; ~ **driver** *n* taxista *m,f*, motorista *m,f* de praça; ~ **rank** *n* praça *f* de táxis.

CAB *(abbr for* **Citizens' Advice Bureau**) Centro britânico (gratuito) de Aconselhamento legal e Informação ao cidadão.

cabala *n* cabala *f*.

cabaret *n* cabaré *m*.

cabbage *n* couve *f*, repolho; **2** *(coll) (brain-damaged person)* pessoa em estado vegetativo; ◆ *vt (coll) (pilfer)* roubar.

cabby *n* taxista *m,f*, motorista *m,f* de praça.

cabin *n* cabana, **2** *(NAUT)* camarote *m*, cabine *f*; ~ **boy** *(NAUT)* grumete *m*; ~ **crew** tripulação *f*; ~ **cruiser** *n* *(NAUT)* navio a motor com um ou mais camarotes.

cabinet *n* *(POL)* conselho de ministros, gabinete *m*; **a ~ reshuffle** uma remodelação *f* de ministros; **2** armário; **display** ~ armário com vitrina; **~-maker** *n* marceneiro.

cable *n* *(rope)* cabo *m*; **2** *(ELECT)* fio *m* (eléctrico); **high voltage** ~ cabo de alta tensão; ~ **car** teleférico *m*; ~ **railway** funicular *m*; ~ **television** *n* televisão por/a cabo; **3** *(telegram)* telegrama *m*, cabograma *m*; ◆ *vt (telegraph)* enviar um telegrama.

caboodle *n* *(coll)* bando *m*; *(fam)* **the whole ~ (kit and)** a tralha toda.

cabotage *n* *(NAUT)* cabotagem *f*, navegação *f* costeira.

cabriolet *n* cabriolé *m*.

cachalot *n* *(ZOOL)* cachalote *m*.

cache *n* esconderijo; ~ **memory** *n* *(COMP)* memória cache *f*; ◆ *vt* esconder; ◆ *vt* armazenar em cache.

cachet *n* cunho *m*, prestígio *m*; **2** distinguished mark.

cachinnate *vi* dar gargalhadas.

cackle *n* *(of chicken)* cacarejo *m*; **2** *(fig) (chat)* tagarelice *f*; falatório *m*; *(BR)* bate-papo *m*; ◆ *vi (hen)* cacarejar; **2** *(person)* tagarelar.

cacky *adj (coll)* sujo,-a, vil, sem valor ou gosto.

cacodemon *n* espírito *m* mau, demónio, *m*.

cacoepy *n* cacoépia *f*.

cacoethes *n* mania *f*, vício *m*.

cacophony *n* balbúrdia *f*; cacofonia *f*.

cactus *(pl: -ti) n (BOT)* cacto *m*.

cad *n (coll: vulgar fellow)* brutamontes *m sg/pl*.

CAD *n (abbr for* **computer-aided design**) CAD *m*.

cadaverine *n (CHEM)* cadaverina *f*.

cadaverous *adj* cadavérico,-a.

caddie *n (golf)* caddie *m*, carregador *m* de tacos de golfe; cadie.

caddy *n* lata *f* para chá.

cadence *n* ritmo *m*, cadência *f*; **2** *(intonation)* entoação *f*.

cadet *n (MIL)* cadete *m*.

cadge *vt* cravar, *(BR)* filar.

cadger *n* crava *m,f*; *(BR)* filante *m,f*.

cadmium *n* cádmio *m*.

caesarean (section) *n (MED)* cesariana *f*.

caesium *(UK)*, **cesium** *(US) n* césio *m*.

caesura *n (LITER)* cesura *f*, pausa métrica *f*.

C.A.F. *(abbr for* **cost and freight**) custo e frete.

café *n* café *m*.

cafeteria *n* café *m*, cantina *f*.

caffein(e) *n* cafeína *f*.

cage *n* gaiola, jaula *f*; ◆ *vt* engaiolar, enjaular; IDIOM **to rattle someone's ~** *(coll)* transtornar ou enfurecer alguém.

cagey (-ier, -iest) *adj (coll)* apreensivo,-a, cauteloso,-a; **2** reservado,-a.

cahoots *npl*: **to be in ~** estar em conluio *(fam)* (**with** com).

cairn *n* monte *m* de pedras sobre um túmulo ou no cume duma montanha.

Cairo *npr* Cairo.

caisson *n* ensecadeira *f*.

cajole *vt* lisonjear; **to ~ sb into doing sth** aliciar; convencer alguém, por meio de lisonja, a fazer algo.

cake *n* bolo, queque *m*; **2** *(soap)* barra; **~d with** empastado de; IDIOM **one cannot have one's ~ and eat it** ter um no papo e outro no saco; **that's a piece of ~** *(coll: very easy)* isso é canja; **to sell like hot ~s** vender-se rapidamente.

CAL *(abbr for* **computer-aided learning**) ensino *m* assistido por computador.

calaboose *n (US: coll)* choça *f*, prisão *f*, calabouço *m*.

calamari *n (CULIN)* lulas cortadas às rodelas, panadas e fritas.

calamine lotion *n* loção *f* de calamina.

calamitous *adj* calamitoso,-a, desastroso,-a.

calamity *n* calamidade *f*.

calash *n* caleche *f*.

calcareous *adj (CHEM)* calcário,-a.

calcification *n (MED)* calcificação *f*.

calcium *n (CHEM)* calico *m*.

calculate *vt* calcular.

calculating *adj* astucioso,-a; *(sharp)* esperto,-a; **2** calculista.

calculation *n* cálculo *m*.

calculator *n* calculadora *f*.

calculus *n (MATH)* cálculo; **2** *(MED)* cálculo *m*.

Calcutta (Kolkata) *npr* Calcutá, Kolcata.

calendar *n* calendário *m*; **2** ~ **month/year** mês/ano *m* civil.

calender *n (machine for paper/cloth)* calandra *m*.

calendula *n (BOT) (marigold)* calêndula *f.*

calf (*pl:* **calves**) *n (baby animal – of cow)* bezerro,-a; *(of elephant, whale, etc)* filhote *m,f; (gen)* cria *m,f;* **2** *(skin)* calfe; **3** *(ANAT)* barriga *f* da perna; ~ **love** *n* namorico de adolescentes.

calibrate *vt* calibrar.

calibre *n* calibre *m.*

caliche *n (GEOL)* caliche *f,* depósito calcário.

calico *n* tecido fino de algodão; morim *m.*

California *npr* Califórnia.

Californian *npr adj* californiano,-a.

calix (*pl:* **calices**) *n (chalice)* cálice *m;* cup.

call *n (cry – of person)* grito *m; (of bird)* canto *m;* **2** *(TEL)* telefonema *m,* chamada *f* telefónica; **to make a** ~ telefonar; **3** *(calling)* chamada *f;* ~**box** *n* cabine *f* telefónica (BR: -fô-); (BR) orelhão *m;* **final** ~ última chamada; **4** *(appeal, demand)* apelo *m,* pedido *m;* **a** ~ **for help** apelo para ajudar; **5** *(allure)* **the** ~ **of the wild** o apelo, a atração da natureza agreste; **6** *(brief visit)* visita; **to pay a** ~ **to** fazer uma visita a; **the doctor made two** ~**s to our home** o médico veio duas vezes; **6** *(need)* necessidade *f;* **there is no** ~ **for that** não há necessidade disso; ~ **of nature** *(euph)* necessidade urgente de ir à casa de banho; **7** *(COMM) (demand)* **there isn't much** ~ **for this product** não há muita procura para este produto; **8** *(JUR) (summons)* chamada *f;* **9** *(REL)* apelo *m;* vocação *f;* **10** *(FIN) (of redeemable bonds)* pedido *m* de reembolso; **11** *(demand on one's time)* **to have many** ~**s on one's time** ser muito concorrido,-a; ♦ **at/on** ~ *prep* à disposição, a postos; ♦ *vt/vi* chamar, telefonar; **to** ~ **back** voltar a chamar; **to** ~ **for** *vt* pedir, ir buscar; **to** ~ **in** *vi* visitar; **to** ~ **in question** duvidar; **to** ~ **off** *vt* cancelar; fazer parar; **to** ~ **on** *vt* visitor; apelar a (alguém), recorrer a; ♦ **to** ~ **out** *vi* gritar; **2** *(summon)* chamar; **3** convocar *(union members, witnesses);* ♦ **to** ~ **round** visitor, passar por *(sb's home);* ♦ **to** ~ **up** *vt* chamar *(on phone);* **2** *(MIL) (summon for military service)* mobilizar; chamar às fileiras; **3** *(evoke)* recordar *(the past);* invocar *(spirits).*

caller *n (visitor)* visita *m,f;* **2** pessoa que faz o telefonema.

call girl *n prostitute;* (BR) garota *f* de programa.

calligraphy *n* caligrafia.

calling *n* vocação *f;* **2** profissão *f;* ~ **card** *n* (US) cartão *m* de visita.

callipers (UK), **calipers** (US) *n (MATH)* calibrador *m,* compasso *m.*

callisthenics *n* calistenia *f,* ginástica *f* rítmica.

callous *adj* insensível *m,f,* duro,-a.

callousness *n* insensibilidade *f.*

call-up *n* mobilização *f.*

callow *adj* imaturo,-a, inexperiente *m,f.*

callus (*pl:* -**es**) *m* calo *m.*

calm *n* calma *f,* tranquilidade *f;* ♦ *adj* calmo,-a, sereno,-a; ♦ *vt* acalmar, tranquilizar; ♦ **to** ~ **down** *vi* acalmar-se, tranquilizar-se.

calmative *adj (of a remedy or an agent)* calmante.

calmly *adv* tranquilamente, com calma.

calmness *n (of person)* calma *f.*

Calor gas® gás *m* butano.

calorie *n* caloria *f.*

calorific *adj* calorífico,-a.

calumny *n* calúnia *f.*

Calvary *n (REL)* Calvário *m; (fig),* calvário *m.*

calve *vi (cows)* parir.

calves (*pl* **of calf**).

calvities *n (baldness)* calvície *f.*

CAM *n (abbr for* **computer-aided manufacturing***)* produção *f* assistida por computador; **2** *(abbr for* **content addressable memory***)* memória *f* de conteúdo endereçável.

camaraderie *n* camaradagem *f.*

camber *n (NAUT)* abaulamento, arqueamento *m; (AER)* curvatura *f* da asa *(of beam, girder)* curvatura.

cambist *n (foreign exchange) (agent)* cambista *m,f.*

Cambodia *npr* Camboja *m;* **in** ~ na Camboja.

Cambodian *npr adj* cambojano,-a.

Cambridge *npl* Cantabrígia.

camcorder *n* câmara *f* de vídeo, filmadora *f.*

came *(pt of* **come***).*

camel *n* camelo *m;* ~**eer** *n* cameleiro *m;* ~ **hair** *n* pêlo *m* de camelo.

camellia *n (BOT)* camellia *f.*

cameo *n* camafeu *f;* **2** breve atuação de famoso ator.

camera *n* máquina fotográfica, *(CIN, TV)* câmara; **2 in** ~ em câmara, em privado; ~ **phone** telemóvel com máquina fotográfica; ~**man** *n* operador *m* de câmara, cameraman *m.*

Cameroon *npr* Camarões; **in** ~ nos Camarões.

camisole *n (lady's vest)* camisola *f* do interior.

camomile *n (BOT)* camomila *f;* ~ **tea** *n* chá *m* de camomila.

camouflage *n* camuflagem *f;* ♦ *vt* camuflar.

camp[1] *n* campo *m,* acampamento *m;* **holiday** ~ colónia de férias; ♦ *vi* **to** ~ **out** acampar.

camp[2] *adj (exaggerated) (person)* cabotino; *(manner)* efeminado, amaneirado, teatral.

campaign *n (MIL, POL)* campanha *f;* ♦ *vi* fazer campanha.

camper *n (person)* campista *m,f; (also:* ~ **van***)* roulette *f,* caravana *f.*

camping *n* campismo, camping *m;* **to go** ~ fazer campismo, camping.

camporee *n* reunião de escuteiros.

campsite *n* parque *m* de campismo; (BR) área *f* de camping.

campus *n* campus *m* universitário.

camshaft *n* eixo *m* de cames.

can[1] (*pt, pp* **could**) *aux (have the right to, be allowed to)* poder; **you cannot park here** não pode estacionar aqui; ~ **I have a drink?** posso beber alguma coisa?; ♦ *vi (able to, be skilled, fit);* **as soon as I** ~ **I shall write to you** assim que eu possa/puder *(pres/fut subj)* escrevo-te; **the patient cannot leave the hospital** *(be discharged)* o paciente não pode ter alta do hospital; **2** *(polite request)* ~ **you do me this favour?** pode/é capaz de fazer-me este favor?; **3** *(be capable of)* **he can't do this job** ele não é capaz de fazer este trabalho;

4 *(manage to)* conseguir; **I can't open this door; it is stuck** não consigo abrir esta porta; está perra; **5** *(know how to)* **I ~ swim** sei nadar; **6** *(in condit. clauses)* **you could have rung me up** podias ter-me telefonado; **if I could I would have done it** se eu pudesse o teria feito (= tê-lo-ia feito); **7** *(expressing possibility, doubt)* poder; **she could be sick** ela pode estar doente; **how ~ that be?** como pode ser isso?; **8** *(occasionally)* **they ~ be/get nasty** eles às vezes são antipáticos.

can² *n* lata *f*; **~ of sardines** lata *f* de sardinhas; **beer ~** uma lata de cerveja; **oil~** *n* oleadeira *f*; ◆ **(-ned)** *vt* enlatar, conservar em latas; **canned food** conservas *fpl*; ◆ *(arranged, agreed) (fam)* **in the ~: the business contract is in the ~** o contra(c)to do negócio está quase feito; IDIOM **to carry the ~** *(coll)* levar/ficar com as culpas; **~ of worms** *(coll)* problema complicado.

Canada *npr* Canadá *m*; **in ~** no Canadá.

Canadian *npr adj* canadiano,-a; *(BR)* canadense *m,f*.

canal *n* canal *m*.

canalization *n* canalização *f*.

canalize *vt* canalizar.

canard *n* mentira *f*, rumor *m* falso.

canary *n* *(bird)* canário *m*; **C~ Islands** *npl* (Ilhas) Canárias *fpl*.

cancel *vt* cancelar, anular; *(cross out)*, riscar.

cancellation *n* cancelamento *m*; **2** anulação *f*.

cancer *n* cancro *m*, *(BR)* câncer *m*; **~ smear** exame *m* citológico, esfregaço *m* ao útero; *(pop)* papanicolau; **2 C~** *(ASTROL)* Caranguejo *m*, Câncer *m*.

Cancerian *n, adj* Canceriano,-a

cancerophobia *n* cancerofobia *f*.

candid *adj* franco,-a, cândido,-a.

candidate *n* candidato,-a.

candidature *n* candidatura *f*.

candidly *adv* ingenuamente; sinceramente.

candle *n* vela *f*; **~ holder**, **~stick** castiçal *m*; **~light** *n* luz *f* da vela; IDIOM **not hold a ~ to sb** *(coll)* não chegar aos pés de (alguém).

can-do *adj* pró-a(c)tivo, expedito; **a ~ attitude** uma postura pró-a(c)tiva.

candour *n* franqueza *f*, candura *f*.

candy *n* açúcar *m* cristalizado; **2** *(US) (confectionery)* doce *m*, confeito, rebuçado *m*; **~ floss** *n* algodão *m* doce.

cane *n* *(bamboo)* cana *f*; **sugar ~** cana *f* d'açúcar; **2** *(stick)* vara *f*; **3** *(walking stick)* bengala *f*; **4** *(police)* bastão *m,f*; **5** *(for making furniture)* palhinha *f*; ◆ *vt* *(with cane)* bater, espancar.

canine *adj* canino,-a.

canister *n* caixa *f*, lata *f*.

cannabis *n* *(BOT)* cânhamo *m*, maconha *f*.

canned *adj* em lata, enlatado; *(coll)* bêbedo,-a.

cannery *n* fábrica de conservas.

cannibal *n* canibal *m,f*.

cannibalism *n* canibalismo.

cannibalistic *adj* canibalesco.

cannon *(pl: cannon or -s)* *n* canhão *m*; **~ball** *n* bala (de canhão); **2 ~ fodder** *n* carne *f* para canhão.

cannot = **can not**.

canny *adj* astuto, esperto.

canoe *n* canoa *f*; **2** *(SPORT)* **to go ~ing** *vt* remar uma canoa.

canoeist *n* canoeiro.

canon *n* cónego *(BR: cô-)*; cânone *m*; **~ law** *n* direito canónico *(BR: -nô-)*; **~ hour** *n* hora canónica *(BR: -nô-)*.

canonize *vt* canonizar.

canoodle *vi* *(slang) (kiss, pet)* fazer marmelada *(cal)*.

can opener *n* abre-latas *m inv*, *(BR)* abridor *m* de latas.

canopy *n* dossel *m*; **2** *(ARCH)* baldaquino; **3 ~ of heavens** abóbada celeste.

can't = **can not** = **cannot**.

cant *(slant)* inclinação *f* de um ponto vertical ou horizontal; chanfradura *f*.

Cantab *(abbr for Cantabrigiensis)* Cambridge.

cantankerous *adj* embirrento,-a, conflituoso,-a, rabugento,-a.

canteen *n* cantina *f*, cantil *m*; **2** jogo *f* de talheres.

canter *n* meio galope *m*; ◆ *vt* ir a meio galope.

cantle *n* pedaço *m*, porção *f*.

canton *n* cantão *m*; ◆ *vt* *(MIL)* aquartelar.

cantonment *n* *(MIL)* aquartelamento *m*.

cantor *n* chantre *m*, director de coro.

canvas *n* lona; **2** *(painting)* tela; **3** *(NAUT)* velas *fpl*; **under ~** em barracas.

canvass *vt/vi* *(POL)* pedir votos (de); **to ~ from door to door** fazer a praça.

canyon *n* *(MIL)* canhão *m*; **2** *(GEOG)* garganta *f*, desfiladeiro *m*.

cap *n* *(for head) (of wool)* gorro, barrete *m*; *(of canvas, felt)* bone *m*; **2** *(for bottle, jar)* tampa *f*, cápsula *f*; **3** *(emblematic cap) (POL, SPORT)* **to wear the ~ of** (**team, party**) representar o partido, a equipa; **4** *(MED)* diafragma *m*; **5** *(of tooth)* esmalte de um dente; ◆ **(-ned)** *vt* rematar; **2** superar; **3** *(SPORT)* sele(c)cionar *(for the national team)* para a equipa nacional; **4** *(usually in passive)* cobrir; IDIOM **to ~ it all** ainda por cima, para culminar; **if the ~ fits** a carapuça é para quem a enfia.

CAP *n* *(abbr for Common Agricultural Policy)* *(in the EU)* Política Comum de Agricultura.

capability *n* capacidade, aptidão *f*.

capacious *adj* amplo,-a, espaçoso,-a.

capacitance *n* *(ELECT)* capacidade *f* eléctrica.

capacitor *n* *(ELECT)* condensador *m*.

capacity *n* capacidade *f*; **2** posição *f*; **3 filled to ~** com a lotação *f* esgotada.

cap-à-pieds *adv* *(dressed, armed)* dos pés à cabeça.

cape *n* *(garment)* capa *f*; **2** *(GEOG)* cabo *m*, promontório *m*.

Cape of Good Hope *npr* *(GEOG)* Cabo da Boa Esperança *m*.

caper *n* *(CULIN)* alcaparra; **2** *(playful leap)* cabriola *f*; **3** *(escapade, frolic)* travessura *f*; **cop ~** comédia *f* policial; ◆ *vi* cabriolar, dar pulos.

Cape Town *npr* Cidade do Cabo *f*.

Cape Verde *npr* Cape Verde *(Islands)*.

capillary *n adj* capilar *m*.

capital *n* *(city)* capital *f*; **2 ~ letter** *n* letra *f* maiúscula; **3** *(FIN, ECON)* capital *m*; **~ gains tax** *n* imposto *m* sobre os lucros; ~ **levy** *n (ECON)* imposto de capitais; **4** *(JUR)* ~ **charge** *n* acusação passível de pena de morte; ~ **sentence** *n* pena de morte.

capitalism *n (ECON, POL)* capitalismo *m*.

capitalist *n* capitalista *m,f*.

capitalization *n (market value)* capitalização *f*.

capitulate *vi* capitular, render-se.

capitulation *n* capitulação *f*, rendição *f*.

capon *n (ZOOL, CULIN) (castrated cock)* capão *m*.

capricious *adj* caprichoso,-a.

Capricorn *npr (ASTROL)* Capricórnio *m*, bode *m*.

capsicum *n* pimentão *m*.

capsize *vt/vi* virar-se, voltar-se; **2** soçobrar; capotar.

capstan *n (machine)* cabrestante *m*.

capsule *n* cápsula *f*.

captain *n* capitão *m*; ♦ *vt* liderar, ser o capitão de.

caption *n* título *m*; **2** legenda *f*.

captivate *vt* cativar, fascinar (**sb** alguém).

captive *n adj* cativo,-a.

captivity *n* cativeiro *m*.

captor *n* captor,-ora.

capture *n* captura *f*, tomada *f*; **2** *(person, animal)* presa *f*; ♦ *vt* prender, aprisionar, tomar; **2** captar; **3 to ~ the market** *(COMM)* apoderar-se do mercado.

car *n* carro, automóvel *m*; **2** *(RAIL)* vagão *m*, carruagem *f*; **sleeping/dining** ~ *n* carruagem-cama, restaurante, *(BR)* carro-leito, restaurante; *(also:* **street/tram~**) *n* carro-eléctrico, *(BR)* bonde.

carafe *n* garrafa de mesa.

caramel *n* caramelo *m*.

caramelize/ise *vt* caramelizar.

carat *n* quilate *m*.

caravan *n (vehicle)* caravana; *(on camels in the desert)* caravana *f*; **to go ~ning** *vi* viajar em caravana/roulotte.

caraway *n (plant)* alcaravia *f*, cariz *m*; ~ **seed** *n* semente *f* de alcaravia.

carbohydrate *n (CHEM)* hidrato de carbono, carboidrato.

carbon *n (CHEM)* carbono, carbónio; **2** papel *m* químico; ~ **copy** *n* cópia de papel químico; ~ **dioxide** *n* dióxido de carbono; ~ **footprint** *n* pegada ecológica; ~ **paper** *n* papel *m* químico, *(BR)* papel carbono.

carbonated *adj* gaseificado,-a; **2** carbonatado,-a.

carbonic *adj* carbónico (*BR*: -bô-).

car-boot sale *n (market of used articles brought by owners in their cars)* feira da ladra (in Portugal).

carbuncle *n (MED) (infection of boils)* antraz *m*; **2** *(gemstone)* carbúnculo *m*.

carburettor *n (MEC)* carburador *m*.

carcass *n (animal)* carcaça *f*; **2** *(of boat)* casco *m*; **3** armação.

carcinogenic *adj (MED)* substancia *f* cancerígena.

carcinoma *n (MED)* carcinoma.

card *n (gen)* cartão *m*; **credit~** cartão de crédito; **business/visiting** ~ cartão de visita; **2 ~board** cartolina; **3 post~** postal *m*; **4** *(playing card)* carta *f* de jogar; **pack of ~s** baralho *m*; **5** *(fibres of wool)* carda *f*; IDIOM **to hold all the ~s** ter todos os trunfos; **to lay the ~s on the table** pôr as cartas na mesa.

cardamon *n (BOT)* cardamomo *m*.

cardiac *adj* cardíaco,-a; ~ **arrest** *n* paragem cardíaca.

cardigan *n* casaco de lã/de malha; *(BR)* cardigã.

cardinal *n (REL)* cardeal; **2** *(MATH) (number)* número *m* cardinal; ♦ *adj* primordial.

card index *n* ficheiro, *(BR)* fichário.

carding *n (of wool)* cardação *f*.

cardiograph *n* cardiógrafo *m*.

cardiology *n (MED)* cardiologia *f*.

cardiovascular *adj (MED)* cardiovascular *m,f*.

cardsharp *n (person)* trapaceiro,-a, batoteiro,-a.

care *n (looking after)* cuidado *m*; **he takes ~ of his niece** ele toma conta da sobrinha; **to be taken ~ of** ser entregue aos cuidados duma instituição social; **take ~ with that!** toma cuidado com isso!; **2** *(of concern)* preocupação *f*; **3 in sb's** ~ a cargo de alguém; ~ **of/in** ~ **of** ao/s cuidado/s de; **social** ~ assistência *f* social; ~ **attendant** *(social welfare)* professional que vai a casa dos doentes cuidar deles; prestador de cuidados; ♦ *vi* **to** ~ **about** preocupar-se com; *(mind)* importar-se com; **I don't** ~ não me importo; **he couldn't** ~ **less about doing this work** ele está-se nas tintas para fazer este trabalho; **2** *(of love)* **I** ~ **for you** eu gosto muito de ti; **I didn't know you ~d** eu não sabia que eu era importante para ti; **3** *(formal)* **would you** ~ **to tell me if ...** queira dizer-me se/importa-se de me dizer se ...; **4** *(groom o.s., look after o.s.)* cuidar-se.

career *n* carreira *f*, profissão *f*; ♦ *vi:* **to** ~ **along** correr a toda a velocidade; **to** ~ **off the road** descarrilar; **to** ~ **out of control** entusiasmar-se, descontrolar-se.

careerist *n (pej)* carreirista *m,f*.

careers adviser *n* orientador,-ora vocacional.

carefree *adj* despreocupado; irresponsável *m,f*.

careful *adj* cuidadoso,-a, cauteloso,-a (**with**, com); **2** *(wise)* prudente; **be ~!** tenha cuidado; seja prudente!

carefully *adv* com cuidado, cuidadosamente.

careless *adj* descuidado,-a, desatento,-a.

carelessly *adv* sem cuidado, sem preocupação.

carelessness *n* descuido, falta de atenção.

careline *n* linha *f* de apoio ao cliente.

carer *n* prestador,-ora de cuidados; **2** *(relative)* pessoa que cuida de um familiar doente ou incapacitado.

caress *n* carícia *f*; ♦ *vt* acariciar.

caretaker *n (JUR)* curador,-ora *(of child assets)*; **2** zelador,-ora; **3** *(school)* porteiro; ~ **government** *n* governo provisório.

car-ferry *n* barco de transporte de carros, *(BR)* balsa para carros.

cargo *n (pl:* **-oes**) carregamento, carga; **2** frete *m*.

Caribbean *npr:* **the** ~ **(Sea)** Mar *m* das Antilhas, Mar das Caraíbas.

caricature *n* caricature *f*; ♦ *vt* caricaturar.

caries *n (MED)* cárie *f*.

caring *adj (person)* carinhoso,-a, afe(c)tuoso,-a.

carnage *n* carnificina *f*.

carnal *adj* carnal, sensual; **2** *(JUR)* **to have** ~ **knowledge (of)** ter relações sexuais (com).

carnation *n (BOT)* cravo *m*.

carnet n (document) caderneta f; **2** (tax) (for goods) guia f de trânsito.

carnival n carnaval m.

carnivorous adj carnívoro,-a.

carob n (BOT) alfarroba f; ~ **tree** m alfarrobeira f.

carol n (Christmas) cântico de Natal.

carotene n (CHEM) carotene m.

carotid n (ANAT, MED) carótida f.

carousal n farra f.

carouse vi andar na farra.

carousel n (US) (at fair) carrossel; **2** (airport) tapete m rolante; **3** (for slides) carreto.

carp n (fish) carpa f; ♦ vi to ~ **at** praguejar (**about**, **against** sobre, contra) queixar-se de.

car park n parque m de estacionamento.

carpenter n carpinteiro,-a.

carpentry n carpintaria f.

carpet n (loose) tapete m, carpete f; (all over the floor) alcatifa f; ~ **slippers** npl pantufas fpl; ~ **sweeper** n máquina f de varrer carpete; ♦ vt atapetar, alcatifar (room).

carpool vi (also: **car share**) utilizar o sistema de boleia organizada (among parents, friends).

carport n abrigo para automóveis, tipo de telheiro.

carpus (pl: -pi) n (ANAT, TECH) (wrist) carpo m.

carriage n carruagem f; coche m; **2** (RAIL) vagão m; **3** transporte m; porte m; ♦ ~ **clock** n relógio m de viagem; ~ **free** franco de porte; ~ **paid** porte pago; ~**way** n faixa (de rodagem), (BR) pista; **dual** ~**way** com duas faixas de rodagem, (BR) pista dupla.

carrier n carregador,-ora, transportador,-ora; **2** empresa de transportes; **3** mensageiro,-a; ♦ **aircraft**-~ n porta-aviões m; ~ **bag** n saco das compras, (BR) sacola; ~ **pigeon** n pombo-correio.

carrillon n (MUS) carrilhão m.

carrot n cenoura f; **2** (fig) incentivo m.

carry (-ied) vt (transport) levar; transportar; **2** (message, disease) transmitir; **3** (be equipped with) dispôr de; **4** (motion) aprovar; **5** (involve) implicar; **6** (bear, support) suportar (bridge, weight, traffic); **7** (POL) (win) vencer, levar a melhor; **8** (be pregnant) estar grávida; **I am carrying his child** estou grávida dele; **9** (stock, supplies) abastecer, vender; ♦ vi (sound) proje(c)tar-se; ser audível; ♦ vr to ~ **o.s.** mover-se; **2** comportar-se; **he carries himself well** ele comporta-se muito bem; ♦ **to ~ away** levar; **to get ~ entusiasmar-se**; deixar-se levar; ♦ **to ~ off** (sth) vt (succeed) levar a melhor; arrebatar (prize); ♦ **to ~ on** vi continuar, prosseguir; (fam) disparatar; **to ~ on with sb** vt (coll) andar metido com alguém; ♦ **to ~ out** vt concluir, levar a cabo; ♦ **to ~** (sth) **over** (FIN) transferir (algo); ♦ **to ~ through** vt levar a efeito; **2** (humour) animar (person).

carrycot m (for baby) alcofa f; Moisés m inv.

carry-on m (UK) alvoroço m.

carshare (Vd: carpool).

carsick adj (travel by car) enjoado,-a.

cart n carroça, carreta; **2** (US) carrinho (de supermercado) ♦ vt transportar (em carroça); IDIOM **to put the ~ before the horse** pôr o carro à frente dos bois; **to ~ sb off** (coll) levar alguém à força.

carte blanche n carta f branca.

cartel n (ECON) cartel m; **2** (POL) aliança f política.

cartilage n (ANAT) cartilagem f.

cartogram n cartograma m.

cartographer n cartógrafo.

carton n caixa (de papelão); **2** pote m.

cartoon n (JOURN) caricatura, cartum m; **2** bonecos mpl animados, (BR) desenho animado; banda f desenhada.

cartoonist n caricaturista m,f; desenhador,-ora, (BR) cartunista m,f; (EP) cartonista m,f.

cartridge n (for shotgun) cartucho m; **2** (for pen) recarga f; **3** (COMP) cartucho m; **4** (for camera) rolo m de filme.

cart-track n caminho m de carroças.

cartwheel n roda f de carroça; **2** (gymnastics) roda f; **to do a ~** fazer a roda.

carve vt (meat) trinchar; **2** (wood, stone) cinzelar, esculpir; (metal) gravar; **3 to ~ up** dividir, repartir.

carvery n restaurante com serviço de bufete.

carving n escultura, obra de talha, de entalhe; **2** ~ **knife** n trinchante m, faca de trinchar.

cascade n cascata, queda d'água f; **2** (fig) cachoeira; ♦ vi cair em cascata.

case[1] n caixa f; (for jewels, spectacles,) estojo; (crate) caixote m; **brief**~ pasta (de executivo); **suit**~ mala f; **2 show**~ vitrina f; **3** (LING) caso m; **4** (COMP) **upper ~** letra maiúscula; **lower ~** letra f minúscula; **5** (MED) caso m; (patient) doente m,f; ♦ vt (recognition) fazer o reconhecimento de (área, local).

case[2] n (JUR) (suit) processo m judicial; (inquiry) causa f; **case-by-case** caso-a-caso; **criminal ~** processo-crime; **the ~ for the Crown** (UK), **the ~ for the State** (US) acusação f para o Ministério m Público; ~ **for the defense** para a defesa; **make a good ~** ter bons argumentos; argumentos mpl convincentes; **a ~ in point** um caso m típico; **to state the ~** expor os factos; ♦ **in ~** (of) adv em caso (de); **in any ~** adv em todo caso; ♦ conj caso; **in ~ I go out …** caso eu vá sair …; **just in ~** conj se por acaso; ♦ adv por via das dúvidas, por precaução; **in no ~** em caso algum.

case history n (MED) os antecedentes; (BR) o histórico m; prontuário m.

case law m (UK) (based on previous cases) lei f caso a caso.

casement n caixilho; ~ **window** n janela f de batente.

case work n (analysis of background etc) trabalho social.

cash n (= hard ~) dinheiro de contado (BR: em espécie); **2** (immediately) dinheiro m à vista; ~ **in hand** dinheiro na mão; **to pay (in) ~** pagar em dinheiro, pagar em numerário; ♦ vt cobrar, descontar (cheque); **to ~ in** (in exchange for money) vt resgatar (bond, insurance, etc); **2 ~ in on sth** (fig) tirar proveito de algo; ~ **on delivery, COD** reembolsar contra entrega (of goods); ~~**and-carry** n sistema de 'pague-e-leve' armazém grossista m; ~**book** n livro-caixa m; ~ **desk** n caixa; ~

dispenser *n* caixa *f* automática; ~ **point** *m* caixa *f* multibanco; ~ **register** *n* caixa-registradora.

cashew *n* caju *m*; ~ **nut** castanha de caju.

cashier *n* caixa *m,f*; encarregado da caixa.

cashmere *n* caxemira, cachemira.

casing *n* cobertura *f*; *(of boiler etc)* revestimento *m*.

casino *n* cas(s)ino *m*.

cask *n* barril *m*, casco *m*, pipa *f*.

casket *n* cofre *m*, guarda-jóias *m*; **2** *(US: coffin)* caixão *m*.

cassava *n* *(BOT)* mandioca *f*.

casserole *n* *(pan)* caçarola *f*; **2** *(CULIN)* estufado *m*.

cassette *n* cassete *m*; **2** ~ **player** *n* gravador *m*.

cassock *n* *(priest's clothes)* sotaina *f*, batina *f*.

cast *n* *(CIN, TV)* *(actors)* elenco *m*; **2** *(MED)* *(plaster)* gesso *m*; **3** *(art)* molde *m*, forma *f*; **4** *(snake skin)* muda *f*; ♦ *(pt, pp* **cast***)* *vt* *(throw)* lançar, atirar *(stone, dice)*; *(light, shadow)* proje(c)tar; *(direct)* dirigir *(torch, glance)*; **to ~ one's glance over one's shoulders** olhar por cima dos ombros; **to ~ one's mind over sth** relembrar-se de algo; **to ~ light on sth** esclarecer algo; **2** *(discard)* mudar, perder *(snake skin)*; **3** fundir *(metal)* **4** *(THEAT)* distribuir papéis; **to ~ one's vote** *(POL)* votar; ♦ *vi* *(fishing)* lançar a linha; lançar; **to ~ about/around** *(for sth)* vasculhar *(memory); (search)* procurar; **she ~ about for an idea** ela tentou procurar uma ideia para ...; ♦ *vt* **to ~ aside** rejeitar; ♦ **to ~ away** *vt*: **be ~ away** estar naufragado,-a; ♦ **to ~ back** *(one's memory)* relembrar-se do passado; ♦ **to ~ down** *vt* baixar *(eyes)*; **2** *(make sad)* *vt* desalentar, deixar deprimido,-a; **be ~ down** *vi* sentir-se deprimido,-a; ♦ **to ~ loose** soltar; **to ~ off** *(stitches)* *vt* *(in knitting)* rematar as malhas; **2** *(discard sth)* livrar-se de *(algo)*; **3** *(NAUT)* largar *(cabo, bóia)*; soltar as amarras; **4** *(printing)* calcular o número de espaços requerido *(em um livro)*; ♦ **to ~ on** *(in knitting)* montar as malhas; **to ~ out** *(sb, sth* alguém, algo*)* expelir, expulsar, descartar.

castanets *npl* castanholas *fpl*.

castaway *adj* náufrago,-a.

caste *n* casta *f*.

caster *n* *(shaker)* polvilhador *m*; ~ **sugar** *n* açúcar *m* pilé, açúcar branco refinado; **2** rodízio *m*.

castigate *vt* repreender, castigar *(for doing sth* por ter feito algo*)*.

Castilian *npr adj* castelhano,-a.

casting *n* *(throwing)* lançamento *m* *(of stone, etc)*; ~ **vote** *n* voto *m* decisivo, voto de desempate.

cast iron/steel *n* ferro,-aço *m* fundido; **2** *(fig)* *adj* firme, incontestável *m,f*.

castle *n* castelo; **2** *(chess)* torre *f*; IDIOM **to build ~s in the air** fazer castelos no ar.

castle nut *n* *(MECH)* porca *f* castelada.

cast-off *adj* discarded, abandoned; ♦ **cast-offs** *n* roupa *f* posta de lado; **to wear sb's ~** usar as roupas velhas de alguém; **society's ~** *(fig)* *npl* os marginalizados da sociedade.

castor *n* *(ZOOL)* *(bearer)* castor *m*; **2** *(also:* **caster***)* *(for chairs etc)* rodízio; ~ **oil** *n* óleo *m* de rícino.

castrate *vt* castrar; **2** *(fig)* censurar.

casual *adj* *(encounter)* fortuito,-a; **2** *(clothes, relaxed)* informal; descontraído,-a; **3** *(attitude)* despreocupado,-a; **4** *(relationship)* passageiro,-a, acidental *m,f*; **to the ~ eye it would seem that** um observador superficial diria que.

casually *adv* casualmente, sem refletir; *(dress, attitude)* informalmente.

casuals *npl* *(clothes)* roupa *f* desportiva.

casualty *(pl:* -ies*)* *n* *(dead/injured person)* vítima *m,f* *(de acidente)*; **2** *(MIL)* baixa; ~ **department** *(in hospital)* urgência(s); ♦ **casualties** *npl* *(MIL)* baixas *fpl*.

casuist *n* *(REL)* casuísta *m,f*.

casuistic *adj* *(case-by-case)* casuístico,-a.

casuistry *n* *(philosophy)* casuística *f*.

cat *n* gato; **2** felino; **~-and-dog life** contínua discórdia; IDIOM **he is a bag of ~s today** *(Ireland)* ele hoje está com a telha; **to let the ~ out of the bag** revelar um segredo *(por acidente)*; **to rain ~s and dog's** chover a cântaros, a potes.

CAT *(abbr for* **Computer Aided Training***)* ensino assistido por computador.

cataclysm *n* cataclismo *m*.

catafalque *n* *(funeral)* essa.

Catalan *npr adj* catalão *m*, catalã *f*.

catalogue *n* catálogo; ♦ *vt* catalogar.

Catalonia *npr* Catalunha *f*.

catalyst *n* catalisador *m*.

cataplexy *n* *(MED)* cataplexia *f*.

catapult *n* catapulta *f*.

cataract *n* *(waterfall)* *(also: MED)* catarata *f*.

catarrh *n* catarro *m*.

catastrophe *n* catástrofe *f*.

catastrophic *adj* catastrófico,-a.

catcall *n* vaia *f*.

catch *n* captura *f*; **2** *(trick)* armadilha *f*, manha *f*; **3** *(fishing)* pesca, apanha de peixe; **4** *(door's fastener)* trinco *m*; **5** *(of ball, etc)* pegada *f*; **he is a good ~** *(fig) (marriage)* ele é um bom partido; ♦ *(pt, pp: caught)* *vt* *(transport, sickness)* *(EP)* apanhar; *(BR)* pegar; **I didn't ~ the bus** *(EP)* não apanhei o autocarro; *(BR)* não peguei o onibus; **2** *(arrest)* deter, agarrar; ~ **thief!** agarra ladrão!; **3** *(discover, surprise in the act)* *(EP)* surpreender, apanhar; *(BR)* flagrar; **the police caught him red-handed** *(EP)* a polícia apanhou-o em flagrante; *(BR)* a polícia o flagrou; **4** *(attention, interest)* despertar; **5** *(animal)* capturar; **6** *(coll)* *(perceive)* entender; **do you ~ my meaning** entendes o que eu quero dizer?; ♦ *vi* *(be stuck)* prender-se; **my shoe was caught in the lift** o meu sapato ficou preso no elevador; **2** *(start fire)* pegar fogo; atear-se; ♦ **to ~ on** perceber, entender; **2** *(music, fashion, idea)* tornar-se popular; pegar rapidamente; **to ~ on sleep** tentar recuperar o sono; **to ~ sight of sb/sth** conseguir avistar alguém/algo; **to ~ sb out** apanhar alguém de surpresa; **2** *(trick)* enganar; *(BR)* embromar; **3** *(SPORT)* eliminar *(batsman)*; **to ~ up** alcançar; **2** *(fig) (work)* pôr em dia *(with, com)*; **3 to ~ up**

with sb *(chat, friendship)* recuperar terreno; **caught up in** *(traffic, scandal)* metido em; **to ~ up on/with the news** pôr-se ao corrente das notícias, estar atualizado; IDIOM **it's a catch-22 situation** preso por ter cão e preso por não ter.

catching *adj (MED and gen)* contagioso,-a.

catchment *n* reservatório *m* de água; **~ area** *n (MED)* zona *f* de contágio.

catchphrase *n* cliché *m*, frase feita *f*.

catchword *n* slogan; **2** *(THEAT)* deixa *f*.

catchy (-ier, -iest) *adj (tune)* atraente, fácil de lembrar.

catechism *n (REL)* catecismo *m*.

categoric(al) *adj* categórico,-a, terminante *m,f*.

categorize *vt* classificar.

category *n* categoria, classe *f*.

cater *vi*: **to ~ for** fornecer; abastecer; atender a.

caterer *n* fornecedor *m*, abastecedor *m*.

catering *n* serviço de bufete.

caterpillar *n (insect)* lagarta *f*; *(TECH)* **~ track** *n* esteira (de lagarta); **C~** *n* tra(e)tor *m* de lagarta.

catfight *n (coll)* briga entre mulheres.

catflap *n* portinhola *f* para gatos.

catharsis *(pl:* **catharses)** *n (PSYCH)* catarse *f*; **2** *(MED)* purgação *f*.

cathedral *n* catedral *f*.

Catherine wheel *n (UK)* roda *f* de fogo de artifício.

cathode *n (PHYS)* cátodo *m*.

catholic *adj* católico,-a; **C~** *npr adj (REL)* católico,-a.

cathouse *n (US) (coll)* bordel *m*.

catkin *n (BOT)* amentilho *m*.

catlike *adj* felino,-a.

cat litter *n* areia *f* no tabuleiro para gatos urinar.

catnap *n* sesta *f*; **to have a ~** dormitar.

CAT scan *n (MED)* tomografia axial computatorizada (TAC).

catseye® *n (UK: on roads etc) (providing light)* olho-de-gato *m*.

cat's eye *n (MIN) (gem)* olho-de-gato, cimofana *f*.

cattle *n (function as plural)* gado *m*; **~-raising** *n* pecuária *f*; **~ grid** *(UK)*, **~ guard** *(US)* *n* grelha *f* (de barras no chão do caminho para impedir o gado de atravessar).

catty *adj* malicioso,-a, rancoroso,-a; **a ~ remark** um comentário *m* malicioso.

catwalk *n* passarela *f*.

Caucasian *npr adj* caucásio,-a.

Caucasus *npr*: **the ~** o Cáucaso.

caucus *n (US) (meeting)* reunião *f* de chefes dum partido político; **2** *(of same interest)* ala *f*; grupo *m*.

caught *(pt, pp of* **catch)**.

cauliflower *n (BOT)* couve-flor *f*; **~ cheese** *n* couve-flor gratinada.

caulk *vi* calafetar, vedar.

cause *n (gen and JUR)* causa *f*, motivo *m*, razão *f*; **2 to make common ~ with** aliar-se a; ♦ *vt* causar; provocar; **to ~ sth to be done** fazer com que algo seja feito.

causeway *n* caminho *m* pavimentado; **2** travessa *f* por sobre água ou pântano.

caustic *n (CHEM)* cáustico; ♦ *adj* cáustico; **2** *(fig)* mordaz; **~ soda** *n* soda *f* cáustica.

cauterize *vt* cauterizar.

caution *n* cautela *f*, prudência *f*; **2** *(warning)* aviso *m*; advertência *f*; ♦ *vt* advertir *(against, a respeito de)*.

cautious *adj* cauteloso, prudente, precavido.

cautiously *adv* com cautela.

cautiousness *n* cautela, prudência.

cavalier *(dated) n* cavaleiro *m*.

cavalry *n* cavalaria *f*.

cave *n* caverna, gruta; **~man** *n* troglodita *m,f*, homem, mulher das cavernas; ♦ *vi* **to ~ in** dar de si; ceder.

cavern *n* caverna *f*.

cavernous *adj* imenso,-a.

caviar(e) *n* caviar *m*.

cavil *vi* querelar, carpir (**at, about** sobre).

caving *n (sport)* espeleologia; **2** desabamento.

cavity *n* buraco, cavidade *f*; **2** *(teeth)* cárie *f*.

cavort *vi (also:* **~ around, about)** fazer cabriolices, brincar; **2** andar na pândega; divertir-se.

caw *n* grasnido; ♦ *vi* grasnar.

cayenne *n* colorau *m* picante.

CBI *npr (abbr for* **Confederation of British Industry)**.

CBT *n (abbr for* **Cognitive Behavioural Therapy)** Terapia *f* de Comportamento Cognitivo.

CBW *n (abbr for* **Chemical** *or* **Biological Weapon)**.

cc *(abbr for* **cubic centimetres**; **carbon copy)**.

CD *n (abbr for* **compact disc)**; **2 ~ player** *n* leitor de CDs; **3 ~-RW** *n* CD regravável; **4 ~ writer** *n* gravador de CDs.

cease *n*: **without ~** sem cessar; ♦ *vt/vi* cessar; **~fire** *n* cessar-fogo *m*.

ceaseless *adj* contínuo, incessante.

ceaselessly *adv* sem parar, sem cessar.

cedar *n (BOT)* cedro *m*.

cede *vt/vi (JUR)* ceder, transferir *(rights, land)* (**to** a, para); **2** admitir.

cedilla *n* cedilha *f*.

ceilidh *n* festa tradicional realizada na Escócia e Irlanda, na qual as pessoas cantam e dançam ao som de música e canções folclóricas.

ceiling *n* te(c)to; **2** *(fig)* limite *m*, te(c)to *m* máximo.

celebrate *vt* celebrar; ♦ *vi* divertir-se.

celebrated *adj (person, event)* célebre.

celebration *n* festa; celebração *f*, comemoração *f*.

celebrity *(coll:* **celeb)** *n* celebridade *f*.

celeriac *n (BOT)* aipo nabo *m*.

celerity *n* presteza, rapidez *f*.

celery *n (BOT)* aipo *m*.

celestial *adj* celeste *m,f*; celestial *m,f*.

celibacy *n* celibato *m*.

celibate *adj* celibatário.

cell *n (prison, convent)* cela; **2** *(BIOL)* célula; **3** *(ELECT)* pilha; **4** *(of honey)* alvéolo *m*; **5** *(US)* telemóvel *m*.

cellar *n* cave *f*; **2** *(for wine)* adega, garrafeira *f*; **3** *(BR) (basement)* porão *m*.

cellist *n (MUS)* violoncelista *m,f*.

cello *n (instrument)* violoncello *m*.

cellophane® *n* celofane *m*.

cellphone *n* telemóvel *m*, *(BR)* celular *m*.

cellular *adj* celular *m,f*.

cellulite *n* celulite *f*.

cellulose *n* celulose *f*.

Celsius *adj* = **centigrade**.

Celt *npr adj* celta *m,f.*

celtic *adj* celta.

cement *n* cimento *m* *(with cement)* argamassa *f;*
~ **mixer** *n* betoneira *f;* ♦ *vt* cimentar; **2** *(fig)*
fortalecer, cimentar *(alliance, friendship).*

cemetery *n* cemitério *m.*

cenotaph *n* cenotáfio *m.*

censor *n (of film, book)* censor,-ora; ♦ *vt* censurar
(cut) cortar.

censorship *n* censura.

censure *n* reprimenda *f;* ♦ *vt* censurar, criticar.

census *n* censo, recenseamento *m.*

cent *n (US: coin)* centavo *m,* cêntimo *m.*

centaur *n* centauro *m.*

centenarian *n adj* centenário,-a.

centenary *n* centenário *m.*

centennial *adj* centenário,-a, secular *m,f.*

center *(US) (Vd:* **centre**).

centi- *pref* centi-; **~grade** *adj* centígrado; ♦ **~litre,**
~liter *n* centilitro; **~metre, ~meter** *n* centímetro *m.*

centipede *n (ZOOL)* centopeia *f.*

central *adj* central; **C~ African** *adj* centro-africano,-a;
C~ African Republic *npr* a República Centro-
Africana; **C~ America** *npr* América *f* Central; **C~**
American *adj* centro-americano; ~ **government**
n governo *m* central; ~ **heating** *n* aquecimento *m*
central; ~ **locking** *n (AUT)* sistema *f* de fecho
centralizado; ~ **nervous system** *n* sistema *m*
nervoso central.

centrally *adv* no centro *m;* **a ~-planned economy**
uma economia *f* de planificação centralizada.

centralize *vt* centralizar.

centre *(UK),* **center** *(US) n* centro; ~ **of attention**
centro das atenções; **the ~** o centro *m;* **2** *(seat)*
sede *f;* **the ~ of power** a sede do poder; **~back** *n*
(SPORT) centromédio; **~fold** *n (newspaper)*
póster *m* central; ~ **forward** *n (SPORT)* centro-
avançado, *(BR)* centroavante *m,* centro; ~ **half** *n*
(SPORT) centromédio; **~piece** *n* centro *m* de
mesa; ~ **stage** *n (THEAT)* centro *m* do palco; **2**
(fig) prime position; ♦ *vt* centralizar; ~ **around/**
on *vt* **2** concentrar-se sobre.

centred *adj* centrado,-a.

centrifuge *n* centrifugadora; ♦ *vt* centrifugar.

centripetal *adj* centrípeto,-a.

centurion *n* centurião *m.*

century *(pl:* **-ies**) *n* século *m,* centúria *f;* **18th ~**
século dezoito; **centuries-old** muito antigo; **2**
(SPORT) (cricket) **to score a ~** marcar cem
pontos.

CEO *n (abbr for* **chief executive officer**) executivo,-a
chefe.

ceramic *adj* cerâmico,-a; de cerâmica; **~s** *npl*
(objects) cerâmica; faiança *f;* ~ **hob** *n (cooker)*
placa *f* de vitrocerâmica.

cereal *n* cereal *m.*

cerebellum *n (pl:* **cerebella**) cerebelo *m.*

cerebral *adj* cerebral *m,f;* ~ **palsy** *(MED)* paralisia *f*
cerebral.

ceremonious *adj (person, event)* formal, cheio,-a de
cerimónia.

ceremony *n* cerimónia *(BR:* -mô-) *f;* ritual *m;* **2**
(protocol) etiqueta; **don't stand on ~** deixe-se de
cerimónias.

cert. *(abbr for* **certificate**) certificado *m.*

certain *adj* certo,-a; **to be ~ of** *(sure)* ter a certeza de;
2 *(sure)* confiante *m,f* **(about,** de/em); **a ~ girl I**
know uma certa moça que eu conheço; **to a ~**
extent até certo ponto; **to make sure of** certificar-
se de, verificar; ♦ *pron* alguns; **certain of the**
members may doubt alguns dos sócios duvidam;
♦ *adv* **for ~** definitivamente.

certainly *adv* certamente, com certeza; **he is ~ a**
nice guy ele é certamente (sem dúvida) um bom
rapaz; **~ not!** de modo algum!

certainty *n* certeza *f,* segurança *f.*

CertEd *(abbr for* **Certificate in Education**) diploma
universitário em Educação.

certifiable *adj (insane)* demente *m,f.*

certificate *n (gen)* certificado *m;* **2** *(MED)* atestado
m; ~ **of birth** cédula *f,* certidão *f;* ~ **of death**
certidão *f* de óbitos.

certification *n* certificação *f.*

certified *adj (person)* habilitado,-a; **2** *(document)*
autenticado,-a; ~ **public accountant** *(US)* perito-
contador,-ora.

certify *vt* certificar, atestar **(that** que).

cervical *adj* cervical; ~ **cancer** cancro do útero. *(Vd:*
cancer).

cervix *n (pl:* **-es,** cervices) colo do útero.

cessation *n* cessação *f,* interrupção *f.*

cesspit *n* fossa; **2** pilha de estrume *f.*

CET *(abbr for* **Central European Time**).

cf. *(abbr for* **compare**).

Chad *npr* Chade; **in ~** no Chade.

chafe *vt (rub)* roçar; ♦ *vi (skin – sore)* esfolar; **2** *(fig)*
(be annoyed) irritar-se.

chaff *n (AGR) (husk)* palhiço *m* casca/palha de
cereais; *(fodder)* forragem *f;* ♦ *vt* zombar, brincar;
IDIOM **to separate the wheat from the ~**
separar o trigo do joio.

chaffinch *n* tentilhão *m.*

chagrin *n* mortificação *f,* descontentamento *m.*

chain *n* corrente *f,* cadeia *f;* ~ **reaction** *n* rea(c)ção *f*
em cadeia; ~ **saw** *n* motosserra *f;* **~-smoke** *vi* fumar
um cigarro atrás do outro; **~store** *n* grande
armazém *m;* ♦ *vt (=* **to ~ up**) encadear.

chair *n* cadeira *f;* **arm-~** *n* cadeira de braços; **deck-~**
espreguiçadeira *f;* **high-back ~** *n* cadeira de
espaldar, poltrona *f;* **swivel ~** *n* cadeira giratória;
wheel ~ *n* cadeira de rodas; **2** *(Univ)* cátedra; **3**
C~ person presidente,-a *(of association, etc);*
(Univ) chefe de Departamento, reitor da Faculdade; ♦ **to take the ~** *vt* presidir; **to take a ~**
sentar-se.

chairlift *n* cadeirinha *f* de teleférico.

chairmanship *n* presidência *f.*

chalet *n (mountain)* chalé *m.*

chalice *n* cálice *m.*

chalk *n (GEOL)* greda *f;* **2** *(for writing)* giz *m;* **3**
~board *n (US) (school)* quadro; ♦ **to ~ out** *vt*
delinear, descrever em linhas gerais; **to ~ up** *vt*

(attain) obter; IDIOM **as different as** ~ **and cheese** tão diferentes como a água e o vinho.

challenge *n* desafio *m; (motivating)* repto *m;* ♦ *vt* **to** ~ **sb for sth** desafiar alguém para algo; **2** questionar, contestar; **3** *(test)* pôr à prova *(skill, etc); (JUR)* recusar *(jury, witness).*

challenger *n (SPORT)* competidor,-ora.

challenging *adj* desafiante; *(tone)* de desafio.

chamber *n (gen)* câmara *f;* **C~ of Commerce** Câmara do Comércio; **Council** ~ o gabinete do Conselho; sala de reuniões; ~ **music** música de câmara; **Upper/Lower** ~ *(UK) (parliament)* Câmara Alta./Baixa; **2** *(cavity)* cavidade *f;* **3** *(formal)* aposento *m;* **chambers** *npl* **the Queen's ~s** os aposentos da Raínha; **2** *(JUR)* gabinete de magistrado/do juíz; **I want to see you in my ~s** quero vê-lo em privado *(or)* /no meu cartório; **in** ~**s** *(JUR) (in camera)* à porta fechada.

chamberlain *n (UK)* camareiro *(BR:* camarista*) m* da corte; **Lord** ~ **of the Household** camareiro-mor *(BR:* camarista-mor*)* da corte.

chambermaid *n (hotel)* camareira *f;* criada de quarto.

chamber pot *n* bacio *m; (fam)* penico *m.*

chameleon *n (ZOOL)* camaleão *m.*

chamois *n* camurça *f.*

champ *n (coll)* campeão,-eã; ♦ *vt/vi (coll)* roer, mastigar com ruído.

champagne *n* champanhe *m.*

champion *n* campeão,-eã.

championship *n* campeonato.

chance *n* sorte *f,* oportunidade *f;* acaso *m;* possibilidade *f;* risco *m;* **to take a** ~ **on sth/on doing sth** arriscar-se (em algo/a fazer algo); ♦ *adj* fortuito, casual; ♦ *vt* arriscar; **to** ~ **it** aventurar-se, arriscar-se; **to** ~ **one's arm** arriscar, tentar; ♦ *adv* **by** ~ por acaso.

chancel *n* coro *m,* capela-mor *f.*

chancellor *n* chanceler *m;* **C~ of the Exchequer** *npr* Ministro das Finanças/*(BR)* da Fazenda.

chancy (-ier, -iest) *adj (fam)* arriscado.

chandelier *n* lustre *m.*

chandler *n* comerciante *m,f* distribuidor *m.*

change *n (small cash)* troco *m;* **have you any** ~? você tem (algum) troco?; **2** *(alteration)* mudança *f* de *(of attitude, plan, weather, job, ideas);* ~ **of heart** mudança de opinião; *(of clothes)* muda de roupa; ~ **of life** *n* menopausa; **3** modificação *f;* **I have made some** ~**s to the dress** fiz algumas modificações ao vestido; **4** transformação *f;* ♦ *(alter)* mudar; alterar; **she has** ~**ed a lot** ela mudou muito; **2** *(exchange)* **I want to** ~ **the blue hat for the black one** quero trocar o chapéu azul pelo preto; **3** transformar; **the house is completely** ~**d** a casa está completamente transformada; **4** *(currency)* cambiar, trocar **(for/into,** para); ♦ *vi* trocar-se, mudar-se; **2** transformar-se; **the princess** ~**ed into a beggar** a princesa transformou-se numa mendiga; **to get** ~**ed** *(clothes)* mudar de roupa; **to** ~ **hands** *(business, shop)* mudar de dono; **to** ~ **one's mind** mudar de ideias; **to** ~ *(transport – bus, train)* mudar de; *(underground – connection)* fazer correspondência; **you must** ~ **the underground**

at Victoria Station deve fazer correspondência do metro em Vitória; ♦ **to** ~ **for the better** melhorar; **for a** ~ para variar; **it makes no** ~ não faz diferença.

changeable *adj* variável, instável.

changeful *adj* inconstante.

changeless *adj* imutável.

changeling *n* criança trocada por outra supostamente pelas fadas.

changeover *n* mudança *f;* **2** *(policy; leaders)* remodelação *f;* **3** *(of guards)* rendição *f.*

changing *adj* variável; ~-**room** *n* vestiátio *m;* **2** *(in shop)* gabinete *m* de provas.

channel *n* canal *m;* **2** *(groove)* ranhura; estria; **3** *(TV, RADIO)* canal; **4** *(ARCH) (fluted)* canelura; *(fig)* meio, via; **the (English) C~** o Canal da Mancha; **the C~ Islands** Ilhas Anglo-Normandas; **the C~ Tunnel** o Túnel da Mancha; ♦ *vt* canalizar.

chant *n* cântico *m;* ♦ *vt* cantar; **2** *(fig)* entoar.

chaos *n* caos *m,* tumulto *m;* desordem *f;* confusão *f;* balbúrdia *f.*

chaotic *adj* caótico,-a.

chap *n (UK) (lips)* cieiro *m;* **2** *(man) (coll)* tipo, fulano, rapaz; *(BR)* cara; **an old** ~ um velho amigo; um velho cara; ♦ **(-pp-)** *vt/vi* fender, rachar, gretar (-se); **my lips are** ~**ped** os meus lábios têm cieiro/ estão gretados.

chap. *(abbr for* **chapter)** cap. (capítulo).

chapbook *n* livro *m* de histórias populares.

chapel *n* capela *f;* ~ **of rest** *n* câmara *f* ardente.

chaperon(e) *n* acompanhante *f;* **2** *(for young lovers)* chaperona; *(coll)* pau de cabeleira.

chapiter *n (ARCH)* capitel.

chaplain *n* capelão *m.*

chapter *n* capítulo *m.*

char *vt* tostar, queimar, chamuscar.

character *n (moral nature)* charácter; **2** estilo *m,* personalidade *f;* **3** *(of film)* personagem *m,f;* **4** *(fam) (unusual person)* tipo, ponto *m;* **5** *(printing – letter, symbol)* carácter *m (pl:* caracteres *mpl).*

characteristic *n* caraterística *f;* ♦ *adj* caraterístico,-a.

characterize, characterise *vt* caraterizar.

charade *n* charada *f.*

charcoal *n* carvão *m* (de lenha).

charge *n (ELECT, MIL)* carga; **2** *(JUR)* acusação *f;* **3** *(burden)* encargo *m;* **to be in** ~ **of** estar encarregado de; **to take** ~ **of** encarregar-se de; **4** *(cost)* preço custo; **free of** ~ gratuito,-a, grátis; **5** incumbência *f,* responsabilidade *f;* **she is in my** ~ ela é a minha responsabilidade, estou encarregado,-a dela; **the employees in (under) my** ~ os empregados a meu cargo; ♦ *vt (JUR: with)* acusar de; **2** *(MIL)* atacar; **3** *(ELECT)* carregar; **4** *(FIN, COMM)* levar, cobrar; **how much do you** ~? quanto leva, quanto cobra?; ~ **it to my account** ponha (algo) na minha conta; **5** *(JUR)* inculpar, acusar; **to** ~ **sb to do** encarregar alguém de fazer; ♦ *vi (MIL) (rush at enemy, etc)* cair sobre, investor; **2** *(to run)* precipitar-se **(into** para dentro de; **out of** para fora de); **3** *(demand payment)* cobrar.

chargeable *adj (costs)* debitável *m,f* **(to sb/sth** de alguém/algo); **2** *(offence)* imputável *m,f.*

chargé d'affaires n adido,-a comercial.

charger n (ELECT) carregador (of batteries); **2** (soldier's horse) cavalo m de batalha.

charges npl: **bank** ~ taxas bancárias; (fee) encargos mpl; **free of** ~ grátis; (TEL) **to reverse the** ~ telefonar a cobrar.

chargrilled adj (CULIN) grelhado,-a na brasa.

chariot n coche m.

charisma n carisma m.

charismatic adj carismático,-a.

charitable adj caritativo,-a.

charity n caridade; **2** compaixão; **3** esmolas; ~ **shop** loja f/de beneficência f/de reinserção social.

charlady n (dated) mulher a dias f, mulher de limpezas, (BR) faxineira.

charlatan n charlatão m, charlatã f, impostor,-ora.

charlotte n (CULIN) (dessert) charlota.

charm n charme m; encanto m; **2** feitiço m; **3** amuleto m; ~ **bracelet** n pulseira com berloques; ♦ vt encantar, enfeitiçar.

charmer n encanto m; **she is a real** ~ ela é um encanto; **2 snake** ~ encantador de serpents.

charming adj encantador,-ora, charmoso,-a; adorável.

charred adj carbonizado,-a.

chart n quadro m; gráfico m; mapa m; **2** (NAUT) carta de roteiro m maritime; **charts** npl (sales) tabelas fpl; (CD's etc) top; ♦ vt fazer; **2** (plan) delinear, traçar.

chartbuster n (coll) (MUS) êxito m.

charter n (POL, JUR) decreto m, **2** (NAUT) carta f de roteiro marítimo; **3** (govt authorization – for business) alvará m; **4** (doc. from the sovereign or State specifying rights of a region or borough) foral m, carta régia; **5** (transport) fretamento m; **6** (POL) (of organization) constituição f; ♦ vt (hire) fretar, alugar; ~**ed flight** n voo m fretado.

chartered n membro de uma instituição com alvará, a qual concede o Diploma de 'chartered'– peritagem – a especialistas nos seus campos, após terem prestado exames de especialização e de terem satisfeito os critérios do seu Conselho: – engenheiro, linguista, etc; ~ **accountant** n perito contabilista, (BR) perito contador; ~ **surveyor** agrimensor perito; (of real estate) perito,-a de imobiliária.

Chartism npr (HIST) movimento, no século XIX, para uma reforma parlamentar e social.

chartist n (ECON) analista m técnico (Stock Exchange).

chartography n cartografia f.

chary (-ier, -iest) adj (wary, cautious) cauteloso,-a, prudente; **2** (finicky) muito esquisito, picuinhas; **3** relutante m,f; **to be ~ of** hesitar em.

chase n perseguição f (of person); caça f (of animal); ♦ vt perseguir; **2** caçar, dar caça a; **to ~ after sb/ sth** correr atrás de (alguém/algo); **to ~ away** vt afugentar; **to ~ up** pressionar (**about**, a respeito de).

chaser n perseguidor,-ora; **2** (plane) caça m

chasm n abismo m.

chassis n chassi m.

chaste adj casto,-a.

chasten vt (dated) punir; disciplinar.

chastise vt (formal) castigar; **2** (verbally) repreender.

chastisement n castigo m; **2** repreensão f.

chastity n castidade f.

chat n cavaqueira f; conversa f (BR) bate-papo m; ~ **line** n linha f de conversação; ~ **show** n (TV) programa m de entrevistas, debates; ♦ vi (= **to have a** ~) conversar, tagarelar cavaquear; **2 to ~ sb up** (pop) tentar conquistar (alguém); atirar-se a alguém (fam); (to obtain sth) dar manteiga a alguém (fam).

chatter n (of people) tagarelice f; (of birds) chilreio m; ♦ vi (person) falar; (birds) chilrear; **2** (teeth) bater os dentes (with cold); ~**box** n tagarela m,f, falador,-ora.

chatty adj (style) familiar; **2** (person) tagarela m,f, loquaz.

chauffeur n condutor m,f, (BR) chofer m, motorista m,f.

chauvinismo m chauvinismo.

chav (UK) (coll) (derogatory) n jovem da classe operária, cujos gostos são caros mas ordinários.

cheap adj barato,-a; **to buy/sell on the** ~ comprar/ vender ao desbarato, por uma ninharia; ~ **rate** n (TEL) tarifa f económica; **2** (vulgar) de mau gosto; **3** (pej: shoddy) de fraca qualidade; **4** (success, woman) (easy) fácil; **5** (despicable) mesquinho,-a, miserável m,f; ♦ adv barato.

cheapen vt desvalorizar (life, etc); **2** (degrade) rebaixar; (price) embaretecer; ♦ vr **to ~ o.s.** rebaixar-se.

cheaply adv a/por baixo preço.

cheapness n baixo preço m; **2** (vulgarity) mau gosto m; **3** (mean deed) baixeza f.

cheat n (person) vigarista m,f; (at cards) batoteiro,-a, (BR) trapaceiro,-a; **2** (dishonest action) vigarice f, fraude f; ♦ vi fazer batota, (BR) fazer trapaça; **2 to ~ on** (relationship) trair; ♦ vt defraudar, enganar, (BR) embromar; **to fell ~ed** sentir-se enganado,-a.

cheating n vigarice f; (BR) trapaça; (at cards, exam) batotice (fam); (BR) blefe m, cola f.

check n controlo m, (BR) controle (**on** sobre); **in** ~ sob controlo; inspe(c)ção f; **2** (medical) exame m; **3** (pattern – in cloth/paper) xadrez; **4** (in chess) xadrez m; ~**list** n lista f de verificação; ~**out** n caixa f; ~**point** n (ponto) de controlo m; ~**up** (MED) exame m geral; **2** (of machine) revisão f, inspe(c)ção f; ♦ vt (restrain) controlar, conter; **2** (facts) verificar; **3** (halt) impedir, deter; ♦ **to ~ in** vi (hotel) regist(r)ar-se; **2** (in airport) fazer o check-in; **3** (luggage) vt despachar; ♦ **to ~ on sth** examinar; **to ~ out** vi (of hotel) pagar a conta e sair; ♦ **to ~ up** vi informar-se; **to ~ up on sth** verificar algo, procurar se há algo; **to ~ up on sb** investigar alguém, informar-se sobre alguém.

checked adj (paper, etc) quadriculado,-a.

checker n (COMM) (employee) controlador.

checkers n (US) jogo m de damas.

checking account (US) n conta f corrente.

cheek n bochecha, f, face f; **to dance ~ to** ~ dançar face a face; **2** (impudence) atrevimento m, descaramento m, lata f (fam); **what a ~!** que lata!

cheekbone n maçã f do rosto, osso m malar.

cheeky *adj* insolente *m,f* descarado,-a.

cheep *n* (*of birds*) pio *m*, chilreio *m*; ♦ *vt* piar, chilrear, chiar.

cheer *n* (*shout*) vivas; ♦ *vt* dar vivas; **2** (*gladden*) *vt* animar; ♦ *vi* aplaudir, gritar com entusiasmo, aclamar; ♦ *vt* **to ~ up** animar; ♦ *vi* animar-se, alegrar-se.

cheerful *adj* alegre *m,f* jovial *m,f*.

cheerfully *adv* alegremente; **2** (*willingly*) de boa vontade.

cheerfulness *n* alegria *f*.

cheering *n* animação *f*, vivas *fpl*; ♦ *adj* (*words*) reconfortante *m,f*; **everybody was ~** toda a gente estava a aplaudir; (*BR*) todo mundo estava aplaudindo.

cheerio *exc* até logo!, adeus!

cheerleader *n* chefe *m* de claque.

cheerless *adj* triste *m,f*, sombrio,-a.

cheers *npl* aplausos *mpl*; ♦ **cheers!** *exc* (*to toast sb*) saúde!; **2** (*coll*) (*thanks*) obrigado,-a.

cheese *n* queijo; **~board** *n* travessa de queijos; **~cake** *n* torta *f* de queijo; **~cloth** gaze *f*; ♦ *vt* (*coll*) parar.

cheesed off (*coll*) chateado,-a; **I am really ~** estou mesmo chateado.

cheesy (-ier, -iest) *adj* (*tasting, smell*) de queijo; (*grin*) foleiro; **2** (*broad grin*) rasgado,-a; **3** (*bad taste*) banal, foleiro,-a.

cheetah *n* (*ZOOL*) chita *f*.

chef *n* cozinheiro-chefe *m*.

chemical *n adj* químico; **~ warfare** guerra química.

chemist *n* farmacêutico,-a; **~'s (shop)** *n* farmácia; **2** (*scientist*) químico,-a.

chemistry *n* química.

chemotherapy *n* (*MED*) quimioterapia *f*.

cheque *n* cheque *m*; **blank ~** cheque em branco; **bounced ~** cheque sem cobertura; **crossed ~** cheque cruzado.

chequebook *n* livro (*BR*: talão *m*) de cheques.

chequered *adj* (*fig*) variado,-a, acidentado,-a; **a ~ career** carreira *f* com altos e baixos; **2** (*patterned*) axadrezado,-a; **~ flag** *n* bandeirinha preta e branca que se mostra no fim das corridas de automóvel.

cherish *vt* querer muito a (**sb** alguém); **2** cuidar de (**sth** algo); **3** (*hope, ambition*) acalentar.

cherry *n* cereja *f*; **2** (*vulg*) (*virginity*) cabaço *m*; **3 ~ jam** compota/doce de cereja; **to ~-pick** *vt* (*choose the best to one's advantage*) escolher o melhor para sua vantagem.

cherry tree *m* cerejeira *f*; **~ orchard** *n* pomar *m* de cerejeiras.

cherub *n* querubim *m*; (*angel*) anjinho,-a.

chervil *n* (*BOT*) cerefolho, cerefílio *m*.

chess *n* xadrez *m*; **~board** *n* tabuleiro (de xadrez); **~man** *n* peça, pedra (de xadrez).

chest *n* (*ANAT*) peito; **2** (*box*) caixa *f*, cofre *m*; **3 ~ of drawers** *n* cómoda; **4 to get (sth) off one's ~** desabafar.

chesty *adj* grande peito; **2** do peito.

chestnut *n* (BOT) castanha *f*; **~ (tree)** *n* castanheiro *m*.

chew *vt* (*food*) mastigar; **2** (*tobacco*) mascar; ♦ **~ed up** *adj* (*coll*) preocupado; ♦ **~ out** *vt* (*US*) (*coll*)

repreender; **~ over sth** ponderar, (*fig*) ruminar sobre algo; **~ up** roer.

chewing gum *n* chiclete *m*, pastilha elástica.

chic *adj* elegante *m,f*, chique *m,f*.

chick *n* pinto, pintainho; **2** (*fam*) moça *f*, garota; **what a lovely ~** que linda garota!

chicken *n* galinha; frango; **2** (*fam*) cobarde *m,f*; **3 ~pox** *n* varicela *f*, (*BR*) catapora *f*.

chickpea *n* (*BOT*) grão-de-bico *m*.

chicory *n* (*BOT*) chicória *f*; escarola *f*.

chief *n* (*gen*) chefe *m,f*; (*boss*) patrão,-oa; ♦ *adj* principal; **~ executive officer** (**CEO**) *n* director,-ora geral executivo,-a.

chiefly *adv* principalmente.

chieftain *n* chefe *m,f*, líder *m,f*.

chiffon *n* (*material*) chiffon *m*.

chilblain *n* (*MED*) frieira *f*.

child (*pl:* **-ren**) *n* criança *f*; (*offspring*) filho,-a; **~ abuse** *n* abuse de menores; **~-bearing** *n* maternidade *f*; **~ benefit** *n* abono *m* de família; **~birth** *n* parto *m*; **~hood** *n* infância *f*, meninice *f*; **~ish** *adj* infantil, pueril; **~like** *adj* acriançado,-a; ingénuo,-a; **~minder** *n* cuidadora de crianças (*BR*) babá *f*; **~ prodigy** *n* criança *f* prodígio; **~proof** *n* (*lock*) seguro *m* à prova de criança; **that is ~'s play** (*fam*) isso é canja.

children (*pl of* **child**).

Chile *npr* Chile; **in ~** no Chile.

Chilean *npr adj* chileno,-a.

chill *n* frio *m*; **2** (*MED*) resfriamento; *m*, resfriado; *m*; **to catch a ~** apanhar um resfriamento; ♦ *vt* esfriar; arrefecer; **2** (*CULIN*) semicongelar; ♦ **he is ~** (*coll*) ele é porreiro; **to ~ out** *vt* relaxar.

chilli *n* (*BOT*) malagueta *f*; **~ powder** *n* colorau picante; piri-piri *m*.

chilling *adj* (*frightening*) arrepiante; **2** (*very cold*) gelado,-a.

chilly *adj* (*of weather*) frio; **2** (*remark*) (*person, attitude*) pouco cordial *m,f*; frio,-a; **3** gélido,-a.

chime *n* (*of clock, church bell, doorbell*) (*sound*) repique *m*, som *m*; ♦ *vi* repicar, soar; **to ~ in with sth** estar em concordância com algo.

chimerical *adj* imaginário,-a, quimérico,-a.

chimney *n* chaminé *f*; **~pot** *n* cano *m* de chaminé; **~ sweep** *n* limpa-chaminés *m,f*.

chimpanzee *n* chimpanzé *m*.

chin *n* queixo *m*; **2 ~ up!** não desanimes!; IDIOM **to take it on the ~** enfrentar as adversidades.

china *n* porcelana *f*, louça fina *f*.

China *npr* China; **the People's Republic of ~** a República Popular da China; **in ~** na China.

china clay *n* caulim *m*.

China Sea *npr:* **the ~** o Mar da China.

Chinatown *npr* bairro chinês em Londres.

chinchila *n* chinchilla *f*.

chine *n* coluna *f*, espinha *f*.

Chinese *npr adj* chinês,-esa; **the ~** os chineses; (*LING*) *n* chinês *m*.

chink *n* (*narrow opening*) greta, abertura, fresta *f*; **2** (*sound of glasses*) tinido *m*; ♦ *vi* tilintar.

chintz *n* tecido *m* de algodão estampado, chita *f*.

chinwag *n* cavaqueira *f*; (BR) bate-papo; **to have a ~ with** dar dois dedos de conversa com.

chip *n* (CULIN) batata *f* frita; **2** (*fragment – of glass, stone*) lasca *f*, (*of wood*) aparas; **3** (*flaw*) defeito *m*, lasca (*in cup, etc*); **4** (*game*) ficha; **5** (COMP) chip; **6** (SPORT) tacada *f*; **7** ~(**s**) batata *f* em forma de dedo, frita; **fish and ~s** peixe e batata frita; ♦ *vt* lascar; ♦ **to ~ in** *vi* interromper; **2** (*with money*) compartilhar as despesas; ♦ *vt* **to ~ off** lascar; ♦ IDIOM **a ~ off the old block** tal pai, tal filho; **when the ~s are down** em tempos difíceis, quando chega a hora da verdade; **to have a ~ on one's shoulder** ter um complexo de inferioridade.

chipboard *n* (*wood*) aglomerado *m*.

chipmunk *n* (ZOOL) tâmia *m*.

chippings *npl* (*fine fragments*) aparas *fpl*; cavacos *mpl*; (*for garden, etc*) cascalho *m*.

chiropodist *n* pedicuro; quiropodista *m,f*.

chiropractor *n* chiroprá(c)tico,-a.

chirp *n* chilreio, gorjeio *m*; ♦ *vt/vi* chilrear, gorjear, cantar.

chirpy (**-ier, -iest**) *adj* alegre *m,f*, vivo,-a.

chisel *n* (*of wood*) formão *m*, escopro *m*; (*of stone*) cinzel *m*; ♦ (**-led**) *vt* esculpir, talhar com cinzel; cinzelar; **finely-~led features** (*fig*) *npl* traços *mpl* bem chinzelados.

chit *n* talão *m*, vale *m*.

chitchat *n* cavaqueira, tagarelice *f*, (BR) bate-papo *m*.

chivalrous *adj* cavalheiresco.

chivalry *n* (*system*) cavalaria *f*; **2** (*courtesy*) cavalheirismo *m*.

chives *npl* (BOT) cebolinhos *sg*.

chlorinate *vt* desinfectar com cloro.

chlorine *n* (CHEM) cloro *m*.

chloroform *n* (CHEM) clorofórmio *m*.

chloroplast *n* (BIO) cloroleucito *m*.

choc-ice *n* (UK) sorvete, gelado *m* coberto de chocolate.

chock *n* calço *m* (para roda de veículo).

chock-a-block (*full*) *adj* abarrotado,-a, apinhado,-a, à cunha (*fam*).

chocolate *n* chocolate *m*.

choice *n* (*variety*) sele(c)ção *f*; opção *f*, escolha; preferência; ♦ *adj* de qualidade sele(c)to, escolhido.

choir *n* coro; ~**boy** *n* menino de coro.

choke *n* (AUT) ar *m*; **2** obturador *m* de arranque; (BR) afogador *m*; ♦ *vt* (*smoke, heat, plastic bag*) sufocar, asfixiar; (*person*) estrangular; **2** (*block*) obstruir, entupir; ♦ *vi* engasgar-se (*on food*).

choker *n* colar *m* curto, gargantilha *f*; ~ **coil** *n* (ELECT) bobina *f* de indução.

cholera *n* cólera *f*.

cholesterol *n* colesterol *m*.

chomp = **champ**.

choose (*pt* **chose**, *pp* **chosen**) *vt* escolher (**between** entre); **2** optar; **to ~ to do sth** optar por fazer algo; ♦ *vi* **to ~ from sth** sele(c)cionar; **well chosen** bem escolhido,-a.

choosy (**-ier, -iest**) *adj* exigente *m,f*; difícil de contentar; picuinhas (*fam*).

chop *n* (*meat*) costeleta; **lamb ~** costeleta *f* de carneiro; **2** (*blow*) golpe *m*, corte *m*; **to get the ~** (UK)

(*coll*) ser despedido,-a; **3** (*in table tennis*) golpe *m* de esquerda; ~**s** *npl* (*thick lips*) beiços *mpl*; ♦ *vt* cortar; talhar; **2** (*wood*) rachar; **3** (CULIN = **to ~ up**) cortar em pedaços; **4** picar (*onion, meat*); **5** (*funding*) cortar; **6** (*fig*) reduzir (*expense deficit*); **to ~ and change** (*person*) ser inconstante *m,f*; **to ~ (sth) down** abater, derrubar; **to ~ off** (*discard*) cortar (*hand, branch, end of sth*).

chopper *n* (*axe*) machado *m*; (*for kitchen*) cutelo *m*; **2** (*coll*) (*helicopter*) heli *m* (*col*); ~**s** *npl* (*col*) dentes *mpl*.

choppy (**-ier, -iest**) *adj* (*sea*) picado, agitado.

chopsticks *npl* pauzinhos *mpl* (para comida oriental).

choral *adj* de coral; ~ **society** *n* grupo *m* coral.

chord *n* (MUS) acorde *m*.

chore *n* tarefa *f*; trabalho *m* de rotina.

choreographer *n* coreógrafo,-a.

chorister *n* corista *m,f* membro de um coro.

chortle *n* gargalhada *f*; cacarejo *m*; ♦ *vi* rir alto.

chorus *n* coro; **2** estribilho *m*.

chose (*pt of* **choose**).

chosen (*pp of* **choose**).

chowder *n* (CULIN) sopa ou caldeirada de peixe.

Christ *npr* Cristo *m*; **the ~ Child** *npr* o Menino Jesus.

christen *vt* (REL, NAUT) ba(p)tizar; (*give name to*) dar o nome a.

Christendom *npr* cristandade *f*.

Christening *n* ba(p)tismo *m*.

Christian *npr adj* cristão,-tã; ~ **name** *n* primeiro nome, nome de ba(p)tismo.

christianity *n* cristianismo.

Christmas *npr* Natal *m*; **Merry ~!** Feliz Natal!; **2** ~ **carol** *n* canção *f* do Natal; (REL) cântico *m* do Natal; ~ **Eve** *n* véspera do Natal; ~ **Eve dinner** consoada *f*; ~ **season** *n* estação *f* natalícia; ~ **stocking** *n* meias de Natal de cada pessoa, penduradas na lareira (para presentes).

chrome, chromium *n* (CHEM) cromo *m*.

chromosome *n* (BIOL) cromossomo *m*.

chronic *adj* crónico,-a (BR: crô-).

chronicle *n* crónica *f* (BR: crô-).

chronological *adj* cronológico,-a.

chrysalis (*pl*: **-lises**) *n* (*insect*) crisálida *f*.

chrysanthemum *n* (BOT) crisântemo *m*.

chubby *adj* roliço,-a, rechonchudo,-a; (*cuddly*) fofo,-a; **2** ~ **cheeks** bochechas; **he has ~ cheeks** ele é bochechudo.

chuck *vt* lançar, deitar; **to ~ out** *vt* rejeitar, deitar, fora, (BR and prov) jogar fora; **she ~ed out her boyfriend** ela abandonou o namorado; **3** (US) (*coll*) vomitar.

chuckle *n* (*suppressed laughter*) riso *m* discreto; risadinha *f*; ♦ *vi* rir baixinho; ~ **to o.s.** rir à socapa.

chuffed *adj* (UK) (*fam*) ~ **with sth/with doing sth** muito satisfeito com algo/por fazer algo; **I am ~!** estou contentíssimo,-a!

chug *n* ruído; ♦ *vi* (*machine*) andar fazendo ruído da descarga.

chum *n* camarada *m*, amigo.

chummy *adj* amigável.

chump *n (coll)* idiota *m,f;* **2** *(wood)* cepo; ~ **chop** *n* costeleta de lombo de carneiro.

chunk *n (of bread)* pedaço *m, (of cheese)* naco *m;* **2** *(large amount)* grande parte.

chunky (-ier, -iest) *adj* pesado; **2** *(sweater)* grosso,-a.

church *n* igreja; **to go to** ~ ir à igreja; ~**goer** *n* fiel *m,f* devoto,-a; ~**man** *n* clérigo *m,* eclesiástico *m.*

Church of England *npr:* **the** ~ a Igreja Anglicana.

Church of Scotland *npr:* **the** ~ a Igreja presbiteriana da Escócia.

churchyard *n* adro *m* da igreja.

churlish *adj* grosseiro,-a, rude *m,f.*

churn *n (for making butter)* batedeira *f;* **2** *(for milk)* lata *f,* vasilha *f;* ♦ *vt* bater, agitar.

chute *n* plano *m* inclinado, rampa *f;* **2** *(rubbish)* conduta *f* de lixo *(BR)* calha *f.*

chutney *n (CULIN)* condimento picante.

CIA *npr (abbr for* **Central Intelligence Agency**) *(US)* Agência Central de Informações.

cicerone *(pl:* -**nes** *or* -**ni**) *n* guia *m,f* turístico.

CID *npr (abbr for* **Criminal Investigation Department**) *(UK)* Brigada de Investigação Criminal.

cider *n* sidra *f.*

cigar *n* charuto *m.*

cigarette *n* cigarro; **2** ~ **butt/end** *n* ponta de cigarro; beata *(fam);* ~ **case** *n* cigarreira *f;* ~ **holder** *n* boquilha, *(BR)* piteira; ~ **lighter** *n* isqueiro *m;* ~ **paper** *n* mortalha *f.*

C-in-C *npr (abbr for* **Commander-in-Chief**) comandante supremo; *(BR)* Comandante-em-chefe *m.*

cinch *n (coll) (easy task)* fácil *m,f;* **the exam was a** ~ o exame foi canja *(fam).*

Cinderella *npr* gata *f* borralheira.

cinders *npl* cinzas *fpl,* escória.

cine camera *n* câmara cinematográfica.

cine-film *n* filme *m* cinematográfico.

cinema *n* cinema *m.*

cinematic *adj* cinematográfico,-a.

cinephile *n adj* cinéfilo.

cinnamon *n (BOT)* canela *f.*

cipher *n* cifra *f.*

circa *adv (date)* aproximadamente.

circle *n* círculo *m;* **2** *(in cinema)* balcão *m;* ♦ *vi* dar voltas; ♦ *vt* rodear, cercar; dar a volta; **to come full** ~ terminar.

circuit *n* circuito; **2***(track)* pista; **3** *(SPORT) (lap)* volta; ~-**breaker** *n (ELECT)* disjuntor *m;* ~ **training** *(gym)* circuitos cardiovasculares.

circuitous *adj* tortuoso, indire(c)to.

circular *n* circular *f;* ♦ *adj* circular *m,f;* ~ **saw** *n* serra *f* circular.

circulate *vi* circular; ♦ *vt* pôr em circulação, espalhar.

circulation *n* circulação *f; (of newspaper)* tiragem *f.*

circumcise *vt* circuncidar.

circumcision *n* circuncisão *f.*

circumference *n* circunferência *f.*

circumflex *n (graphic accent)* acento *m* circunflexo.

circumnagivate *vt* circum-navegar, circunavegar.

circumscribe *vt* limitar, demarcar, circunscrever.

circumspect *adj* circunspe(c)to, prudente.

circumstances *npl* circunstâncias *fpl;* **under the** ~ nestas circunstâncias; **due to** ~ **beyond our control** por motivos alheios à nossa vontade; **2** *(financial condition)* situação *f* económica.

circumstantial *adj* circunstancial; ~ **evidence** *n* prova *f* circunstancial; **2** acidental.

circus *n* circo; **2** *(road – roundabout)* praça *f* circular.

cirrhosis *n (MED)* cirrose *f.*

cissy *(also:* **sissy**) *(pl:* -**ies**) *(UK) (fam) (man)* maricas *m inv.*

cistern *n* tanque *m,* reservatório; **2** *(in toilet)* autoclismo.

citadel *n* cidadela *f.*

citation *n* citação; **2** *(JUR)* citação; judicial; **3** condecoração **(for** por).

cite *vt* citar.

citizen *n (POL)* cidadão,-dã; habitante *m,f;* **C~'s Advice Bureau** *(CAB) npr (UK)* Centro de Apoio e Aconselhamento legal ao Cidadão = Loja *f* do Cidadão *(Portugal).*

citizen's arrest *n* detenção *f* feita por um cidadão.

citizenship *n* cidadania *f.*

citric *adj* cítrico; ~ **acid** *n (CHEM)* ácido *m* cítrico.

citrus fruit *n* citrinos *mpl,* cítricos *mpl.*

city *n* cidade *f;* **2 the C~** centro financeiro de Londres; **3** ~ **hall** *n* câmara municipal (de Londres); *(BR)* prefeitura *f.*

civic *adj* cívico,-a, municipal *m,f;* ~ **centre** *n* casa *f* do povo.

civil *adj* civil *m,f;* delicado,-a, cortês *m,f;* educado,-a; ~ **engineer** *n* engenheiro,-a civil; ~ **servant** funcionário,-a público,-a; ~ **rights** *npl* direitos *mpl* civis.

civilian *n, adj* civil, paisano,-a; **in** ~ **clothes** vestido à paisana.

civilise *(US),* **civilize** *(UK) vt* civilizar.

civilization *n* civilização *f.*

civilized *adj* civilizado,-a.

Civil List *n* verba anual designada pelo parlamento britânico para a manutenção da Família Real.

civvies *n (coll)* traje *m* civil, à paisana.

clad *adj (dressed);* ~ **in sth** vestido,-a de algo.

cladding *n (building, boiler)* revestimento *m.*

claim *n* reclamar; **2** *(insurance)* pedido de indenização; **3** *(for expenses)* pedido de reembolso; **4** *(demand)* reivindicação *f;* **5** *(JUR)* direito *m,* pretensão *f;* **6** *(assertion)* afirmação, alegação *f;* ♦ *vt* exigir, reclamar; **2** *(rights to)* reivindicar; **3** *(assert – innocence, truth)* afirmar, alegar, asseverar **(to,** que); dizer **(to,** que); **4** reivindicar; **to** ~ **responsibility for** reivindicar a responsabilidade por; **to** ~ **(on,** a) **the insurance** participar ao seguro; **to** ~ **back expenses** pedir um reembolso das despesas.

claimant *n* reclamante; **2** *(ADMIN, JUR)* requerente; **3** *(throne)* pretender.

clairvoyant *n* clarividente *m,f.*

clam *n (seafood)* berbigão *m; (BR)* sururu *m;* ♦ **to** ~ **up** *vi* fechar-se em copas, não dizer mais nada.

clamber *n (up)* escalada *f; (down)* descida *f;* ♦ *vi* **to** ~ **up/down** trepar/descer com dificuldade.

clammy (~**ier**, ~**iest**) *adj (weather)* húmido,-a; **2** *(hands)* pegajoso,-a.

clamour *(UK)*, **clamor** *(US)* n *(noise)* clamor m; ♦ vi *(demand) (shout-crowd)* bradar, chamar a atenção, protestar (**about/over sth** por/devido a); **2** *(demand)* reclamar (**sth** algo).

clamp n grampo, gancho de ferro; **2** *(car-wrong parking)* bloqueador de rodas; **3** *(secured to bench)* torno m; ♦ vt segurar; apertar; **2** *(TECH)* prender com grampos; **3** *(parking: immobilize a car)* bloquear; **to ~ down on** suprimir, impôr restrições; conter, controlar.

clampdown n (**on sth**) medidas fpl de repressão, restrição f sobre algo.

clan n clã m.

clanish adj dedicado ao clã; **2 to be ~** ter espírito limitado.

clandestine adj clandestino,-a.

clang n *(onomat)* retintim m *(of coins, keys)*; som m metálico; clangor m; ♦ vi retinir.

clanger n *(coll)* grande erro m; erro m de palma-tória *(fam)*.

clap n *(with hand)* palmada f (**on**, em); **2** *(applause)* aplauso m; **3** *(noise – thunder)* ribombar m do trovão; ♦ (-**ped**) vi aplaudir; ♦ vt bater palmas; **to ~ one's hand over** *(mouth, ears)* tapar; **to ~ one's eyes on sb** fixar os olhos em; **to ~ hold of sb** agarrar alguém de repente.

clapped-out adj *(machine)* estragada, a cair aos pedaços.

clapperboard n indicador m de cenas, claquete f.

clapping n aplausos mpl.

claptrap n *(coll)* discurso bombástico m; parlapatice f *(fam)*; ♦ adj *(empty talk)* vazio,-a, oco,-a.

claret n clarete m, vinho m palhete.

clarification n esclarecimento m.

clarify vt esclarecer, aclarar, clarificar.

clarinet n clarinete m, clarineta f.

clarity n claridade f.

clash n colisão f; *(fig)* conflito; choque m; *(disagree-ment)* divergência; ♦ vi colidir, chocar (**against** contra); **2** estar em conflito, discordância; **3** *(colours)* não combinar, destoar, chocar; **to ~ with sth** *(dates)* coincidir com algo.

clasp n *(fastener)* fecho m; *(of necklace) (buckle)* fivela; ♦ vt afivelar; **2** apertar; **to ~ sb in one's arms** abraçar, apertar nos braços; *(against one's breast)* apertar (alguém contra o peito).

class n *(gen)* classe f; **2** *(EDUC)* aula, turma f **3** *(style)* estilo m, classe; ♦ adj de classe; ♦ vt classificar.

classic n obra f clássica; ♦ adj clássico,-a.

classical adj clássico,-a.

classicism n *(ART, LITER)* classicismo.

classification n classificação f.

classified adj classificado; secreto.

classify vt classificar.

classmate n colega m,f de aula.

classroom n sala de aula.

classy n *(coll)* elegante m,f.

clatter n *(noise)* tinido m, estrépito m; **2** *(of dishes)* bater m de pratos; **3** *(of horses)* ruído de cascos; ♦ vi fazer barulho; repicar.

clause n cláusula; **2** *(LING)* oração f.

claustrophobia n claustrofobia f.

clavichord n clavicórdio m.

clavicle n *(ANAT)* clavícula f.

claw n *(wild animal)* garra f; **2** *(bird)* presa, garra; **3** *(cat, dog)* unha; **4** *(crab, lobster)* pinça; **5** *(TECH)* unha; ♦ vt **to ~ at** arranhar; **to ~ back** *(UK)* recuperar; **to ~ one's way up** subir a pulso; **to ~ one's ~s into sb** deitar as garras a alguém.

clay n argila; f gesso m; **red ~** *(terracotta)* barro m; **~ pigeon shooting** n tiro m ao prato.

clean adj limpo,-a; **2** nítido,-a; **3** *(paper)* em branco; **to come ~** confessar; ♦ adv completamente; ♦ vt limpar; ♦ **to ~ out** limpar a fundo; **2** *(coll) (rob)* depenar (**sb**, alguém).

clean-cut adj limpo,-a; nítido,-a; **2** *(features)* regulares.

cleaner n *(in house)* mulher a dias; *(in office)* empregado,-a de limpeza *(BR)* faxineiro,-a.

cleaning n *(gen)* limpeza f.

cleanliness n limpeza.

cleanse vt limpar *(skin, etc)*; **2** lavar *(wound)*; **3** purificar *(blood; soul)*.

cleanser n *(make-up)* limpador m; demaquilador m, creme m de limpeza.

clean-shaven adj de cara raspada, de barba feita.

cleansing n purificação f; **ethnic ~** limpeza f étnica.

clear n: **in the ~** fora de perigo; *(free from suspicion)* acima de suspeita; ♦ adj claro,-a; **~ head** mente f lúcida; **2** óbvio,-a; **3** *(free)* livre m,f; **4** transpa-rente; *(water)* límpido,-a; **5** *(conscience)* tran-quilo,-a; ♦ adv, exc *(out of the way)*; **stand ~!** afaste-se!; **~ off!** *(fam)* desaparece!; **2** *(free of)* a salvo de; ♦ vt *(pipe)* desentupir; *(throat)* limpar; **2** *(of obstacles)* desimpedir; **3** *(JUR)* absolver, livrar de culpa; **4** *(debt)* liquidar, saldar; ♦ vi dissipar-se *(fog, etc)*; **2** *(sky)* clarear; **3** *(skin)* tornar-se clara; **4** *(headache)* passar; ♦ **to be ~ about** vt ter a certeza de; **to ~ away** *(objects)* arrumar; **2** *(after a meal)* levantar a mesa; **to ~ out** *(discard)* deitar fora, *(BR)* jogar fora; **2** ir-se embora; **to ~ up** *(tidy)* arrumar; **3** *(solve)* resolver; *(problem)*; esclarecer *(confusion)*; **4** *(mist)* dissipar-se.

clearance n despejo m; **2** *(permission)* autorização f; **3 customs ~** despacho m alfandegário; **4** *(of trees)* derrube m; *(of woods)* desbravamento; **5** *(of land mines)* remoção f; **6** *(free space)* vão m livre; ♦ **~ order** n ordem f de despejo; **~ sale** n liquidação f.

clear-cut adj bem definido,-a, nítido,-a.

clearheaded adj lúcido,-a.

clearing n clareira; **~ bank** n câmara de compensação.

clearly adv claramente.

clearout n *(coll)* limpeza f geral, arrumação f.

clear-sighted adj *(person)* perspicaz m,f.

clearway n *(UK) (AUT)* via f espressa.

cleavage n *(between breasts)* rego m do peito; *(in the dress)* decote m.

cleave *(pt clove or cleaved; pp cleft or cleaved)* vt *(split)* rachar, fender; **2** separar, dividir; ♦ vi *(be attached to)* aderir a, ser fiel a.

cleaver n machadinha, cutelo *(de talho, de açougue)*; **2** *(BOT)* amor-de-hortelão.

clef *n* (MUS) clave *f.*

cleft *n* fissura; fenda; **2** cova no queixo; **3** ~ **palate** fenda palatina.

clemency *n* clemência *f.*

clemente *adj* ...

clementine *n* (fruit) clementina *f.*

clench *vt* apertar, (teeth, fists) cerrar; ~ **the fists** cerrar os punhos.

clergy *n* clero *m.*

clergyman *n* clérigo, pastor *m.*

clerical *adj* clerical *m,f;* **2** de escritório.

clerk (US) *n* caixeiro,-a; empregado,-a.

clever *adj* inteligente *m,f;* **2** (sharp) esperto,-a; **3** (skilful) hábil *m,f;* **4** (ingenious) engenhoso,-a; **5** (pej) (sly) manhoso,-a.

clever-clogs, clever Dick *n* (coll) chico-esperto; espertalhão *m,* espertalhona *f.*

cleverness *n* esperteza *f;* **2** (skill) habilidade; **3** (pej) manha *f.*

cliché *n* cliché *m,* frase *f* feita.

click *vt* (tongue) dar estalido com; **2** (COMP) clicar; **3 to ~ the heels together** bater com os calcanhares.

client *n* cliente *m,f.*

clientele *n* clientela.

cliff *n* penhasco *m;* ~**hanger** *n* (film, story) suspense *f.*

climate *n* clima *m;* **2** (fig) ambiente *m.*

climax *n* clímax *m,* ponto culminante.

climb *n* subida *f;* ♦ *vi* subir, trepar; ♦ *vt* subir; trepar; escalar; ♦ **to ~ down** *vi* recuar, ceder.

climber *n* alpinista *m,f,* (plant) trepadeira.

climbing *n* alpinismo *m.*

clinch *vt:* **to ~ a deal** fechar/concluir um negócio; **2** (POL) firmar um acordo; **3 the lovers were ~ed** os namorados estavam abraçados.

cling (pt, pp **clung**) *vi:* **to ~ to** pegar-se a, aderir a; **2** (of clothes) agarrar-se a (sb, sth), ajustar-se a, colar-se a.

clingfilm *n* película aderente.

clinic *n* clínica *f.*

clinical *adj* clínico,-a.

clink *n* tinido *m;* ♦ *vi* tinir.

clip *n* (for hair) gancho *m;* **2** (= **paper** ~) mola, clipe *m;* **3** (ELECT: for wire) grampo *m;* ♦ *vt* cortar; aparar; (clamp) grampear; prender; IDIOM **to ~ sb's wings** cortar as asas a alguém, frustrar–lhe os planos.

clippers *npl* (gardening) podadeira *sg;* **2** (hair, nails) tesoura *f sg;* corta-unhas *m.*

clipping *n* recorte *m.*

clique *n* (fig) camarilha *f;* grupo *m* exclusivista.

clitoris *n* (ANAT) clítoris *m.*

cloak *n* capa, manto; **2** (disguise) disfarce *m;* ♦ *vt* (fig) encobrir.

cloak and dagger *adj* (story) misterioso,-a, secreto,-a.

cloakroom *n* (in theatre, hotel, etc) (for coats) vestiário *m;* **2** (in house) (euph for toilet) casa de banho; (BR) banheiro *m.*

clobber *n* (personal things) tralha *f;* ♦ *vt* (coll) espancar; **2** (fig) vencer; **3** criticar severamente.

clock *n* relógio; **2** (in taxi) taxímetro.

clockwise *adv* em sentido horário.

clockwork *n* mecanismo de corda; **like** ~ com regularidade, como um relógio; ♦ *adj* de corda.

clog *n* tamanco *m;* ♦ *vt* entupir, bloquear; ♦ *vi* entupir-se.

cloister *n* claustro *m.*

clone *n* (BIO) clone *m;* ♦ *vt* clonar.

clonk *n* (noise) baque *m.*

close *n* (end) fim *m,* conclusão *f,* desfecho *m;* (short street) pequena rua, beco sem saída; ♦ *adj* próximo,-a, reservado,-a; **2** (print, weave) denso,-a, compacto,-a; **3** (friend) íntimo,-a; **4** (connection) estreito,-a; **5** (examination) detalhado,-a, minucioso,-a; **6** (weather) abafado,-a; (atmosphere) sufocante; (room) mal arejado; ♦ *adv* perto, próximo; ♦ *vt* (shut) fechar, encerrar; **2** acabar; ♦ *vi* fechar; concluir, terminar; **to ~ down** *vi* fechar-se definitivamente.

close-cropped *adj* (grass, hair) rente *m,f.*

closed *adj* fechado,-a; ~-**circuit television** *n* televisão em curto-circuito.

closedown *n* (TV) fim *m* de emissão; **2** (of shop, etc) fechamento.

close-fisted *adj* (person) (with money) forreta *m inv.*

close-fitting *adj* (garment) justo,-a.

close-lipped *adj* (person) calado,-a, reservado,-a.

closely *adv* fielmente; de perto.

close-off *vt* interditar.

closet *n* armário *m,* guarda-roupa *m;* **2** (short for water closet) lavabo *m.*

close-up *n* (PHOT) grande plano.

closing *n* encerramento *m.*

closure *n* encerramento, fechamento *m;* **2** fim *m.*

clot *n* (= **blood** ~) coágulo; (in milk) coalho; **2** (coll) imbecil *m,f;* ♦ *vi* coagular-se, coalhar-se.

cloth *n* tecido, fazenda; (rag) pano, trapo; **table**~ *n* toalha de mesa.

clothe *vt* vestir; **2** (fig) revestir.

clothes *npl* roupa *sg,* vestuário; **to take one's** ~ **off** despir-se, tirar a roupa; ~ **brush** *n* escova *f* de roupa; ~ **horse** *n* (for drying clothes) estendedor *m* de roupa; **2** (fig) pessoa que se preocupa só com o andar na moda; ~**line** *n* estendal, (BR) varal *m;* ~ **peg** (UK), ~ **pin** (US) *n* mola *f* de roupa; (BR) prendedor *m* de roupa.

clothing *n* = **clothes.**

clotted cream *n* creme de nata muito espessa (tradicional da Cornualha).

cloud *n* nuvem *f;* **to be in the** ~**s** andar nas nuvens; **to be on** ~ **nine** estar no sétimo céu.

cloudberry *n* framboesa-amarela.

cloudburst *n* aguaceiro.

cloudless *adj* (sky) limpo, claro.

cloudy *adj* nublado; (liquid) turvo.

clout *vt* (blow) dar uma bofetada em.

clove *n* cravo(-da-Índia); **2** ~ **of garlic** dente *m* de alho.

clover *n* (BOT trevo *m.*

clown *n* palhaço *m;* ♦ *vi* (= **to** ~ **about/around**) fazer palhaçadas.

cloying *adj* enfadonho,-a; enjoativo,-a.

club n clube m, (dancing) discoteca f; **2** (weapon) clava f, cacete m (da polícia); **2** (golf) taco m; **clubs** npl (cards) paus mpl; ♦ (**-bb**) vt bater com (sth algo); ♦ vi **to go ~bing** correr as discotecas, os clubes; ~ **together** (UK) fazer uma vaquinha; IDIOM **join the ~!** junte-se a nós!, temos a mesma experiência!

clubcar n (US) vagão-restaurante m.

clubfoot n pé m torto/chato; **to have a ~** ser aleijadao,-a.

clubhouse n sede do clube.

cluck vi cacarejar.

clue n sinal m; indício; pista f; **I haven't a ~** não faço ideia (BR: idéia).

clued-up adj sagaz, bem informado.

clueless adj (coll) alheio,-a, ignorante m,f.

clump n (group) (of trees) arvoredo m, (of bushes) moita f; **2** (of grass) tufo m; ♦ vt **to ~ together** plantar em grupos; ♦ vi mover-se pesadamente.

clumsy adj desajeitado, sem graça; **2** (object) tosco,-a.

clung (pt, pp of **cling**).

cluster n grupo; algomerado; **2** (BOT) cacho, ramo; ♦ vi agrupar-se, apinhar-se; **2 ~ bomb** n bomba f de fragmentação.

clutch (pl: **-es**) n garra f; (fig) (power) **in the ~es of** nas garras de, nas mãos de; **2** (AUT) embraiagem f, (BR) embreagem f; **3** vt empunhar, pegar em; **she ~ed her bag** ela agarrava o saco.

clutter n desordem f, tralha por todo o lado, (BR) bagunça; ♦ vt abarrotar, encher desordenadamente;

Co. (abbr for **county**; **company**).

c/o (abbr for **care of**) a/c, ao cuidado de.

coach n camioneta, (BR) ônibus; **2** carruagem f, coche m; (of train) vagão m; ~ **class** n (US) classe f turística; ~ **station** n estação f rodoviária; **3** (SPORT) treinador m; instru(c)tor m; ♦ vt (SPORT) treinar; preparar, ensinar.

coaching n (SPORT) treino m, treinamento m.

coagulate vi (milk, blood) coagular-se.

coal n carvão m; hulha; **~face** n veio m de carvão; **~field** n jazida f de carvão; **~man**, **~-merchant** n carvoeiro; **~mine** n mina de carvão; ~ **miner** n mineiro de carvão.

coalition n (POL) coligação f, (BR) coalizão f.

coarse adj grosso, áspero; **2** grosseiro, ordinário.

coast n costa, litoral m; ♦ vi (AUT) ir em ponto morto.

coastal adj costeiro.

coaster n embarcação f costeira, barco de cabotagem; ♦ (US) (abbr for **roller-~**) montanha-russa; porta-copo m.

coastguard n guarda costeira.

coastline n litoral m; IDIOM **the ~ is clear** (coll) o perigo já passou.

coat n casaco, (BR) paletó m; sobretudo; **2** (of animal) pêlo, lã f; **3** (of paint) demão f, camada; ♦ vt cobrir, revestir; ~ **of arms** n brasão m; ~ **hanger** n cabide m.

coating n (of protection; dust) camada f; **2** (covering) revestimento m; **3** (edible) cobertura f.

coax vt persuadir com meiguice.

cob n espiga (de milho).

cobbler n sapateiro-remendão m.

cobblers (coll) npl porcarias, tretas; **that's a load of ~** isso são tretas.

cobbles, **cobblestones** npl pedras fpl arredondadas.

cobra n (snake, cobra) cobra f.

cobweb n teia f de aranha.

cocaine n cocaína f.

cock n galo m; (male bird) macho; **2** (gun) cão; **3** (vulg) pénis (BR: pê-), (BR) pinto (cal); ♦ vt engatilhar; ♦ vt/vi levantar, emproar-se, pôr o chapéu à banda; **~-and-bull story** n história f da carochinha, do arco da velha.

cock-a-doodle-doo (onomat) (cock's crowing) cocorocó.

cockatoo n cacatua.

cockerel n frango, galo pequeno.

cockeyed adj (fam) vesgo,-a; **2** (askew) torto; **3** (fig) absurd.

cockfight n rinha f, luta f de galos.

cockle n (mollusc) amêijoa f.

cockney n pessoa que nasceu no leste de Londres, em geral, da classe trabalhadora; (accent) cockney.

cockpit n (AER) cabina f.

cockroach n (insect) barata f.

cockscomb n crista f (do galo).

cocktail n (EP) cocktail m; (BR) coquetel m; ~ **cabinet** n móvel-bar m; **Molotov ~** (EP, BR) (explosivos) cocktail molotov.

cockup n (UK) (slang) (shoddy work) cagada f.

cocky adj convencido,-a, presunçoso,-a.

cocoa n cacau m; (drink) chocolate.

coconut n coco m.

cocoon n casulo m.

cod n bacalhau m.

COD (abbr for **cash on delivery**) entrega à cobrança.

code n código; cifra; ~ **name** n pseudónimo m; ~ **of practice** n código m de conduta.

codec n (ELECT) codec m.

codeine n codeína f.

codify vt codificar.

codswallop n (UK) (fam) asneira f, treat f.

coeducational adj (school) misto,-a.

coefficient n (MATH) coeficiente m.

coerce vt forçar, obrigar.

coercion n coerção f.

coexistence n coexistência.

coffee n café m; (in a glass) galão m (pop); ~ **bean** n grão m de café; **black ~** (small cup, much sugar) bica f (EP) (pop), café simples; ~ **grounds** npl borras fpl de café; ~ **pot** n cafeteira; ~ **set** serviço de café; ~ **table** n mesinha de centro or de lado; **white ~** (with milk) garoto m (pop).

coffer n cofre m; **~s** npl fundos mpl disponíveis.

coffin n caixão m; ♦ vt meter em caixão.

cog n dente m; **~wheel** n roda dentada; ♦ vt fazer batota.

cogent adj persuasivo,-a; convincente.

cogitate vt cogitar (**about/on** em); meditar (**about/on** em)

cognate n, adj cognado,-a.

cognition n cognição f.

cognizant adj consciente m,f; conhecedor,-ora.

coherent adj coerente m,f.

coil n rolo m; corda f enrolada; **2** (ELECT) bobina; **3** (contraceptive) espiral f, DIU m; ♦ vi enrolar-se, espiralar-se.

coin n moeda; ~-**box** n caixa de moedas, mealheiro; ♦ vt cunhar, criar; **new coined word** neologismo m; IDIOM **to pay sb back in their own** ~ pagar na mesma moeda.

coinage n (making coins) cunhagem f; **2** (word, phrase) invenção f.

coincide vi coincidir; **2** (agree) estar de acordo.

coincidence n coincidência f.

coitus n coito m.

coke n (coal) coque m; **2** (drink) coca-cola f.

colander n (kitchen utensil) coador m, passador m.

cold n adj frio; **it's** ~ está frio; **to be** (feeling) ~ ter frio, estar com frio; **it is getting** ~ está a arrefecer; **2** (person) (~-blooded) frio,-a, insensível; cruel; **a** ~ **welcome** um acolhimento frio; **in** ~ **blood** a sangue frio; ♦ n (MED) **to catch a** ~ (EP) apanhar uma constipação; (BR) pegar um resfriado; ♦ **to** ~-**shoulder sb** vt tratar alguém com frieza; **to throw** ~ **water on sth** desanimar; ♦ ~ **sore** n (MED) herpes m labial; ~ **store** n câmara f frigorífica; ~ **sweat** n suores mpl frios; ~ **turkey** n (slang) (drug addition) desmame m. IDIOM **to be out** ~ estar inconsciente m,f sem sentidos; **to have** ~ **feet** (before doing sth) não ter coragem de fazer algo); **to go** ~ **on sth** abster-se de algo.

coldly adv friamente; **to turn sb down** ~ rejeitar completamente.

coleslaw n (CULIN) salada de repolho cru.

colic n cólica f.

coliseum n coliseu m.

collaborate vi colaborar.

collaboration n colaboração f.

collage n colagem f.

collapse n (MED) colapso m, queda f; **2** ruína f; ♦ vi cair, tombar; **2** (MED) desmaiar.

collapsible adj dobrável, desmontável m,f.

collar n (of coat, shirt) colarinho m, gola f; **2** (ornamental) colar m; **3** (dog) coleira f.

collarbone n clavícula f.

collate vt cotejar, confrontar, comparar.

collateral n garantia; ♦ adj colateral.

colleague n colega m,f.

collect n (REL) cole(c)ta f; ♦ vt (gather) reunir, juntar; **2** (information) recolher; **3** (rent) cobrar; **4** (donations) pedir, colher; **5** (material) colher; **6** (as hobby) cole(c)cionar; ♦ vi (gather) (people) reunir-se; **2** (objects) acumular-se.

collectable adj (potential antique) colecionável m,f.

collection n cole(c)ção f; (anthology) coletânea f; **Summer** ~ (fashion) cole(c)ção do verão; **2** (of people) reunião f, grupo m; **3** (of donations) angariação f; **4** (Post) (from letterbox) tiragem f.

collective adj cole(c)tivo,-a; ~ **bargaining** npl negociações entre o patronato e o sindicato; ~ **ownership** n propriedade f conjunta.

collector n cole(c)cionador,-ora; ~'s **item** n peça f de cole(c)ção; **2** (of taxes etc) cobrador m.

college n colégio; **2** (faculty) faculdade f.

collide vi chocar, colidir, embater em.

collie n cão m pastor.

colliery n mina f de carvão e instalações.

collision n choque m, colisão f; **head-on** ~ colisão f frontal.

colloquial adj familiar, colloquial.

colloquialism n coloquialismo m.

collude vi conspirar; **to** ~ **with sb** entrar em conluio com alguém.

collusion n trama m, conspiração f.

Colombia npr Colômbia f; **C~ian** adj colombano,-a

colon n (punctuation) dois pontos; **2** (ANAT) cólon m.

colonel n (MIL) coronel m.

colonial adj colonial m,f.

colonize vt colonizar.

colonnade n colunada f.

colony n colónia f.

colorant n corante m.

colossal adj colossal m,f.

colour (UK), **color** (US) n cor f; ~-**blind** adj daltónico; ~**ed** adj a cores; colorido; ~ **film** n película a cores; filme m colorido; ~ **scheme** n combinação f de cores; ~ **television** n televisão f a cores; ♦ vt colorir; pintar; (dye) tingir; ♦ vi (blush) corar.

colourful, colorful adj colorido,-a; **2** (lively) animado,-a.

colouring, coloring n colorido m; **2** (skin) tez; **3** (in food) corante m.

colourless, colorless adj incolor, sem cor, **2** pálido,-a.

colours npl bandeira que indica nacionalidade; **to show one's** ~ mostrar seu íntimo.

colt n potro m.

column n coluna.

columnist n colunista m,f, cronista m,f.

coma n coma m.

comb n (for hair) pente m; **2** (side ~ for hair) travessa; **3** (of cock) crista f; **4** (textile) carda f; **5 honey** ~ favo (de mel); ♦ vt (hair) pentear; **2** (area) vasculhar; **3** (textile) cardar; IDIOM **to go over (a place) with a fine-toothed** ~ (search) passar (casa, sítio) a pente fino.

combat n combate m; ♦ vt combater.

combination n combinação f; ~ **lock** n fechadura f de código.

combine[1] n (COMM) consórcio m; ♦ vt combinar (qualities); **2** reunir (activities, colours); **3** (CULIN) misturar; ♦ vi combinar-se (colours, events); **2** associar-se (people).

combine[2] n (coll) (harvester) n ceifeira, ceifadeira, colheitas.

combustible n adj combustível m,f.

combustion n combustão f.

come n esperma f; ♦ (pt **came**, pp **come**) vi vir; chegar; **I'm coming!** vou já!; **you are free to** ~ **and go** tens a liberdade de ires e vires; **to** ~ **about** vi suceder, acontecer; **to** ~ **across** vt deparar-se com; encontrar; **to** ~ **after** perseguir (alguém); **to** ~ **back** vi voltar; **to** ~ **before the court** (JUR) comparecer perante o juíz; ♦ **to** ~ **by sth** vt (acquire) obter, adquirir (sth); **2** (travel) vir de; ♦

to ~ clean confessar; ♦ **to ~ down** vi descer; **2** acalmar-se; **3** *(building)* desabar; desmoronar-se; ♦ **to ~ for** vir buscar; **I ~ my parcel** vim buscar o meu embrulho; ♦ **to ~ forward** vi apresentar-se; **to ~ from** *(origin)* vir de; ♦ **to ~ in** vi entrar; chegar; **2** *(fashion)* entrar na moda; **to ~ in for** vt merecer; **to ~ into** vt *(money)* herdar; ♦ **to ~ near** aproximar-se; ♦ **to ~ off** vi desprender-se, soltar-se; **2** *(have success)* realizar-se; ♦ **to ~ on** vi avançar, fazer progressos; **come on!** vamos!; **~ let's go!** vamos, despacha-te! ♦ **to ~ out** revelar-se; **2** *(stain)* sair; **to ~ out for or against** declarar-se por/contra; ♦ **to ~ to** vi *(recover senses)* voltar a si; **the total ~s to** o total vem a dar; ♦ **to ~ through** trespassar, atravessar; ♦ **to ~ up** vi subir; aparecer; surgir; **to ~ up with** vt encontrar, ter *(idea, solution)*; **to ~ upon sth** encontrar, achar.

comeback n regresso m; **2** *(THEAT)* reaparição f.
comedian n comediante m,f; cómico m.
comedienne n cómica f.
comedown n revés m, desilusão f.
comedy n comédia f.
comely adj atraente m,f.
comet n cometa m.
comfort n comodidade f; conforto; bem-estar m; **2** consolo; **3** *(relief)* alívio; ♦ vt confortar, aliviar.
comfortable adj confortável, cómodo (BR: cô-).
comic n humorístico,-a, (BR) gibi m; adj (= ~**al**) cómico,-a (BR: cô-); ♦ **~ strip** n história em quadrinhos; banda desenhada.
coming n vinda, chegada, advento; ♦ adj que vem, vindouro; **2** ~**(s) and going(s)** n(pl) *(activity)* vaivém m, azáfama f; **3 to have it ~** merecer.
comma n *(punctuation)* vírgula f.
command n ordem f, mandado m; *(MIL)* comando m; domínio m; ♦ vt mandar; ordenar; dispor de; merecer.
commandeer vt *(MIL)* requisitar.
commander n *(MIL)* comandante m,f, chefe m,f.
commando n comando m.
commemorate vt comemorar.
commemoration n comemoração f.
commemorative adj comemorativo,-a.
commence vt/vi começar, iniciar.
commend vt elogiar, louvar; recomendar; encomendar.
commendable adj louvável.
commendation n elogio, louvor m, recomendação f.
commensurate adj proporcionado, igual a.
comment n comentário m; ♦ vi fazer comentários, comentar.
commentary n comentário.
commentator n comentador,-ora; (BR) comentarista m,f.
commerce n comércio m.
commercial n *(TV)* anúncio m, publicidade f ~ **break** n intervalo m publicitário; **~ traveller** n caixeiro-viajante m; ♦ adj commercial m,f.
commercialize vt comercializar.
commie n adj *(fam, pej)* comuna f.
commiserate vi: **to ~ with** comiserar-se de, condoer-se de.

commission n comissão f; incumbência; **2** vt *(MIL)* dar patente oficial; comissionar, **3** *(work of art)* encarregar; encomendar; **out of ~** fora do serviço a(c)tivo.
commissionaire n porteiro; rececionista m,f.
commissioner n comissário; *(police)* chefe m, delegado,-a.
commit vt cometer; **2** *(to sb's care)* entregar; **3 to ~ o.s. (to do)** comprometer-se (a fazer); **to ~ suicide** suicidar-se; **to ~ to memory** memorizar.
commitment n compromisso m, empenhamento m.
committed adj *(devoted)* devoto,-a **(to** a), empenhado **(to** em); **to be ~ to do sth** consagrar-se a fazer; **2 ~ to sb** comprometido com alguém.
committee n comité *(BR)* comitê m; **2** *(to investigate)* comissão f.
commodity n mercadoria f, produto, m.
common n *(UK)* *(public land)* mata f; ♦ adj *(gen)* comum, frequente; **2** *(ordinary)* banal, vulgar; **3** *(UK)* *(pej)* *(behaviour)* ordinário,-a; **4** *(everyday)* banal, trivial; ♦ **in ~ with** em comum com; **it's ~ knowledge;** é do conhecimento geral; **~ law** n lei f consuetudinária; **C~ Market** npr Mercado Comum; **~ room** n *(school)* n sala de convívio; **~ sense** n bom senso.
commoner n plebeu,-eia.
commonly adv geralmente.
commonplace n lugar-comum.
Commons n *(UK)* **the House of ~** a Câmara dos Comuns, Deputados.
Commonwealth npr **the (British) ~** a Comunidade f Britânica.
commotion n tumulto m, agitação f.
communal adj comunal m,f.
commune n comuna; ♦ vi: **to ~ with** conviver com.
communicate vt comunicar; ♦ vi: **to ~ (with)** comunicar-se com.
communication n comunicação f; **~ cord** n sinal, cordão m de alarme.
communion n *(REL)* (= **Holy C~**) comunhão f; *(gen)* comunhão f.
communiqué n comunicado m.
communism n comunismo.
communist n adj comunista m,f.
community n comunidade f; **2** *(large group)* multidão f; **3** *(locals)* vizinhança; **~ centre** n centro social; **~ service** serviço m comunitário.
commute vi viajar diariamente; ♦ vt *(JUR)* comutar *(sentence)*; **2** *(FIN)* converter; ♦ vi **to ~ between** *(two places)* fazer o traje(c)to regularmente entre ... e ...
commuter n viajante m,f habitual.
compact n *(for face powder)* caixinha f, estojo m; **2** *(US)* *(AUT)* *(car)* de médio porte; ♦ adj *(compressed)* compa(c)to,-a; ♦ vt comprimir, acalcar; *(BR)* compactar.
companion n companheiro,-a; **~ animal** n animal m de estimação.
companionship n companhia, companheirismo.
company n companhia; **2** *(COMM)* sociedade f, companhia; **joint-stock ~** sociedade anónima;

limited ~ companhia limitada; **to keep sb** ~ fazer companhia a alguém; **to part** ~ separar-se de.

comparable *adj* comparável *m,f.*

comparative *adj* comparativo,-a.

compare *vt* comparar; cotejar; ♦ *vi:* **to** ~ **with** comparar-se com.

comparison *n* comparação *f;* **in** ~ **with** em comparação com, comparado com.

compartment *n* compartimento *m.*

compass *n* bússola; **2 compasses** *npl* compasso *sg.*

compassion *n* compaixão *f.*

compassionate *adj* compassivo,-a.

compatible *adj* compatível *m,f.*

compatriot *n* compatriota *m,f.*

compel *vt* obrigar.

compelling *adj (fig)* convincente *m,f.*

compendium *n* compêndio *m.*

compensate *vt* compensar; ♦ *vi:* ~ **for** compensar; recompensar.

compensation *n* compensação; *(for loss)* inde(m)-nização.

compere *n* apresentador,-ora; ♦ *vt* apresentar *(show, programme).*

compete *vi* competir, concorrer; fazer competição (com).

competence *n* competência, capacidade *f.*

competent *adj* competente *m,f,* capaz *m,f.*

competition *n* concurso *m;* **2** *(ECON)* concorrência *f;* competição *f;* **to put up for** ~ pôr a concurso.

competitive *adj (ECON)* competitivo,-a; competidor de rivalidade; ~ **exclusion** *n* exclusão *f* competitiva.

competitor *n (rival)* competidor,-ora; **2** concorrente *m,f.*

compilation *n* compilação *f,* cole(c)ção *f.*

compile *vt* compilar, coligir.

complacency *n* satisfação *f* consigo mesmo, complacência *f.*

complacent *adj* demasiado confiante en si mesmo.

complain *vi* queixar-se; reclamar.

complaint *n* reclamação *f,* queixa; **2** *(JUR)* querela *f;* **3** *(MED)* queixa, doença *f.*

complement *n* complemento; **2** *(ship's crew)* tripu-lação *f.*

complementary *adj* complementar *m,f.*

complete *adj* inteiro, completo; acabado; ♦ *vt* completar; acabar; preencher.

completely *adv* completamente.

completion *n* conclusão *f,* término; realização *f.*

complex *n adj* complexo *m.*

complexion *n (of face)* cor *f,* tez *f;* **2** *(fig)* aspe(c)to *m.*

complexity *n* complexidade *f.*

compliance *n* submissão *f;* conformidade *f;* **in** ~ **with** de acordo com; **2** obediência; *(rules)* acatamento (**with** de).

compliant *adj* obediente *m,f;* **2** *(COMP)* compatível.

complicate *vt* complicar.

complicated *adj* complicado.

complication *n* complicação *f.*

complicity *n:* ~ **in sth** cumplicidade *f* em algo.

compliment *n* cumprimento; **2** *(praise)* galanteio, elogio *m;* **to pay sb a** ~ elogiar, cortejar alguém;

to return the ~ retribuir o elogio; **compliments** *npl (regards)* cumprimentos *mpl.*

complimentary *adj* lisonjeiro,-a; *(free)* gratuito,-a; **2** ~ **ticket** entrada grátis; ~ **copy** *n* oferta *f.*

comply *vi* obedecer; **2 to** ~ **with** aquiescer, cumprir com; agir de acordo com.

component *n (TECH)* peça, componente *m,f.*

compose *vt* compor; **to be** ~**d of** compor-se de; **to** ~ **o.s.** *vr* tranquilizar-se.

composed *adj* calmo.

composer *n* compositor,-ora.

composite *n adj* composto.

composition *n* composição *f.*

compositor *n (printing)* compositor.

compost *n* adubo; ~ **bin** *n* compostor *m.*

composure *n* serenidade *f,* calma, compostura *f.*

compound *n (CHEM, LING)* composto; recinto; ♦ *adj* composto; complicado; ~ **fracture** fra(c)tura exposta.

comprehend *vt* compreender; **2** abranger.

comprehension *n* compreensão *f.*

comprehensive *adj* extensor,-ora; abrangente *m,f;* **2** *(insurance)* contra todo risco, global; ~ **school** *n* escola (secundária) polivalente.

compress *n (MED)* compressa; *vt* comprimir.

compression *n* compressão *f.*

comprise *vt:* **be** ~**d of** compreender, constar de, consistir de.

compromise *n* acordo; meio-termo; **to reach a** ~ chegar a um acordo; ♦ *vi (undermine reputation, etc)* comprometer, expor a perigo; ♦ *vt* transigir, chegar a um acordo, comprometer-se.

compulsion *n (strong desire)* compulsão *f; (force)* coação *f.*

compulsive *adj (gambler, liar)* inveterado,-a; **2** *(compelling)* envolvente *m,f;* fascinante; **3** *(PSYCH)* compulsório,-a.

compulsory *adj* obrigatório,-a; **2** *(retirement)* coercivo,-a, imposto,-a, coercivo,-a; ~ **purchase** *n* expropriação *f.*

compunction *n* remorsos *mpl.*

computer *n* computador; ~ **programmer** *n* progra-mador,-ora; ~ **programming** *n* programação *f;* ~ **science** *n* ciência de computadores *(BR:* da computação); ~ **hacking** *n* pirataria.

computerize *vt* computerizar, informatizar.

computing *n* informática *f.*

comrade *n* camarada *m,f;* ~**ship** *n* camaradagem *f.*

con *(abbr for* **convict)** *n (coll)* presidiário,-a; ♦ (**-nn-**) *vt* enganar, defraudar; ~**man/woman** *n* vigarista *m,f.*

concave *adj* côncavo,-a.

concavity *n* concavidade *f.*

conceal *vt* ocultar, dissimular.

concede *vt* conceder, admitir; ♦ *vi* ceder, conceder.

conceit *n* presunção *f.*

conceited *adj* presunçoso,-a.

conceivable *adj* concebível, imaginável *m,f.*

conceive *vt/vi (baby, plan, idea)* conceber; **2** *(under-stand)* compreender; **I cannot** ~ **such an audacity** não posso compreender tal arrojo.

concentrate *vi* concentrar-se; **2** concentrar.

concentration *n* concentração *f*; ~ **camp** *n* campo de concentração.

concentre, concenter *vt/vi* concentrar; **2** convergir (**in** para).

concentric *adj* concêntrico,-a.

concept *n* conceito *m*.

conception *n* *(idea)* conceito, ideia, *(BR)* idéia; **2** *(BIOL)* concepção *f*.

concern *n* *(matter)* assunto; **2** *(COMM)* empresa; **3** *(anxiety)* preocupação *f*; ◆ *vt* dizer respeito a; **to be concerned** (**about**) interessar-se (por); preocupar-se (com).

concerning *prep* sobre, a respeito de, acerca de.

concert *n* concerto; ~ **hall** *n* sala de concertos; ~ **master** *(US)* *n* primeiro violino de uma orquestra.

concertina *n* concertina, sanfona *f*.

concerto *n* concerto *m*.

concession *n* concessão *f*; **2 tax** ~ incentivo *m* fiscal; **3** *(transport)* *(discount)* redução *f*, tarifa *f* reduzida.

concessionaire *n* concessionário,-a.

concessionary *adj* *(rate, fare)* reduzido,-a, com desconto.

concierge *n* porteiro,-a, encarregado,-a.

conciliate *vt* conciliar.

conciliation *n* conciliação *f*.

conciliatory *adj* conciliador.

concise *adj* conciso,-a.

conclave *n* *(REL)* conclave; **2** reunião secreta.

conclude *vt* *(finish)* acabar, concluir; **2** *(treaty etc)* firmar; *(agreement)* chegar a; **3** *(decide)* chegar à conclusão de.

conclusion *n* conclusão *f*; **to jump to** ~ tirar conclusões precipitadas; **a foregone** ~ uma conclusão previsível.

conclusive *adj* conclusivo,-a, decisivo,-a.

concoct *vt* *(CULIN)* confecionar, preparar; **2** *(story, plot)* inventar; tramar; engendrar.

concordance *n* aceitação *f*, harmonia; **2** *(LING)* concordância *f*.

concourse *n* *(crowd)* afluência; **2** confluência *f*, conjunção *f* *(of events)*; hall *(in hotel, airport, etc)*.

concrete *n* concreto, betão *m*; ◆ *adj* concreto,-a, palpável *m,f*.

concur *vi* estar de acordo, concordar.

concurrent *adj* simultâneo,-a.

concurrently *adv* simultaneamente; *(with)* em concordância.

concussion *n* concussão *f* cerebral, choque *m*.

condemn *vt* condenar.

condemnation *n* *(gen)* condenação *f*; **2** censura *f*.

condensation *n* condensação *f*; **2** resumo *m*.

condense *vi* condensar-se; ◆ *vt* condensar; resumir; **2** ~**d milk** *n* leite *m* condensado.

condescend *vi* *(be patronizing)*: **to** ~ **to sb** condescender em alguém; **to** ~ **to** (**do sth**) dignar-se a (fazer algo); ser condescendente para com alguém.

condescending *adj* condescendente.

condescension *n* condescendência.

condiment *n* tempero *m*.

condition *n* condição *f*; **on** ~ **that** na/com a condição de; **on no** ~ de maneira nenhuma alguma; ◆ *vt* condicionar; **2** *(skin, hair)* tratar de.

conditional *adj* condicional; **2** dependente (**upon**, de).

conditioner *n* *(hair, clothes)* amaciador *m*; **2** *(skin)* hidratante *m*.

condole *vi*: **to** ~ **with** dar pêsames a alguém.

condolences *npl* pêsames *mpl*, condolências *fpl*; 'sincere ~!' 'meus sinceros pêsames!'

condom *n* *(MED)* preservativo *m*; camisinha *f* *(fam)*.

condominium *n* condomínio *m*.

condone *vt* perdoar, conceder perdão.

condor *n* *(ZOOL)* condor *m*.

conducive *adj*: ~ **to** conducente para/a.

conduct *n* *(behaviour)* conduta, comportamento; ◆ *vt* *(lead)* conduzir; **2** *(manage)* orientar, dirigir; ◆ *vi* *(MUS)* reger; **to** ~ **o.s.** *vr* comportar-se.

conductor *n* *(MUS)* regente *m,f*, maestro *m*, maestrina *f*; **2** *(on bus)* cobrador *m*; **3** *(RAIL)* revisor *m*; **4** *(ELEC)* condutor *m*.

cone *n* cone *m*; *(for ice-cream)* cone, *(BR)* casquinha; ◆ *vt* ~ **off** *(on road)* colocar cones de sinatização.

confectioner *n* pasteleiro; confeiteiro; ~**'s** (**shop**) *n* pastelaria; confeitaria.

confectionery *n* *(cakes)* bolos *mpl*; *(sweets)* doces *mpl*.

confederation *n* confederação *f*.

confer *vt*: **to** ~ **on/upon** *(rights, honour)* outorgar a alguém; ◆ *vi* conferenciar.

conference *n* conferência *f*; congresso *m*; **in** ~ em reunião.

confess *vt* confessar, admitir; ◆ *vi* confessar-se.

confession *n* confissão *f*.

confessional *n* confessionário; ◆ *adj* confessional.

confessor *n* confessor *m*.

confetti *n* confete *m*, confetti *m* *(for wedding)*; **2** papelinhos *mpl*, serpentinas *fpl* usados no Carnaval.

confidant *n* confidente *m*.

confidante *n* confidente *f*.

confide *vi* confidenciar (**to** a); **2 to** ~ **in** *(trust)* confiar em.

confidence *n* confiança; **2** confidência; ~ **trick** *n* conto do vigário; ~ **trickster** *n* escroque, vigarista.

confident *adj* *(sure of o.s.)* confiante *m,f*, convicto,-a.

confidential *adj* confidencial; *(secretary)* de confiança.

configure *vt* *(also COMP)* configurar.

confine *vt* limitar; encarcerar.

confined *adj* reduzido, retido.

confinement *n* prisão *f*; reclusão *f*; *(MED)* parto; ~**s** *npl* confins *mpl*.

confirm *vt* confirmar.

confirmation *n* confirmação *f*.

confirmed *adj* inveterado,-a; **a** ~ **drunkard** um bêbedo inveterado,-a.

confiscate *vt* confiscar.

confiscation *n* confiscação *f*, confisco *m*.

conflict *n* conflito *m*; ◆ *vi* opor-se, chocar.

conflicting *adj* oposto,-a, contraditório,-a.

conform *vi* conformar-se; **to** ~ **to** ajustar-se a, acomodar-se a.

conformist *n* conformista *m,f*.

confound *vt* frustrar; lançar em confusão.

confounded *adj* confuso,-a; **2** *(coll)* maldito,-a.

confront *vt* confrontar-se com; deparar-se com; defrontar-se com.

confrontation n confrontação f.

confuse vt desconcertar; confundir.

confused adj confuso; perplexo.

confusing adj confuso.

confusion n confusão f.

confute vt refutar.

congeal vi congelar-se; coagular-se.

congener n congénere.

congenial adj simpático,-a, agradável m,f.

congenital adj congénito (BR: -gê-).

conger eel n enguia f marinha.

congested adj (MED) congestionado,-a; **2** (of road) congestionado,-a; (passage) obstruído,-a; **3** (town, area) superpovoado,-a.

congestion n (MED) congestão f; **2** (of road) congestionamento m; **traffic** ~ engarrafamento m de trânsito; ~ **charge** n (UK) taxa de circulação em certas áreas da cidade.

conglomerate n (COMM) conglomerado m.

conglomeration n conglomeração f, aglomeração f.

Congo npr Congo; **in** ~ no Congo; (river) o Congo.

Congolese npr adj congolês,-esa.

congratulate vt felicitar; dar os parabéns a (alguém).

congratulations npl parabéns mpl.

congregate vi reunir-se, congressagar-se.

congregation n (REL) (in church) assembleia dos fiéis mpl; (of cardinals) congregação f.

congress n congresso; **Congress** npr (US) Congresso m.

congressional adj (POL) parlamentar m,f.

congressman/woman n (US) congressista.

conical adj cónico (BR: cô-).

conifer n conífera.

coniferous adj conífero.

conjecture n conjetura f, hipótese f; ♦ vt supor, conjeturar, presumir.

conjugal adj conjugal m,f.

conjugate vt conjugar; ♦ vi (LING) conjugar-se.

conjunction n (gen) (LING) conjunção f; **2** (of events) associação f; **in** ~ **with** conjuntamente com, em conjunto com.

conjunctivitis n (MED) conjuntivite f.

conjure vt adjurar; **to** ~ (**up**) vt (by magic) fazer aparecer; praticar magia; (BR) fazer macumba; ♦ vi fazer truques de prestidigitação.

conjurer n prestidigitador,-ora; ilusionista m,f.

conjuring trick n truque de ilusionismo; mágica f.

conk n (coll) (nose) nariz m; penca (fam); ♦ **to** ~ **out** vi (fam) (person) (breakdown) estar em frangalhos; **2** (break down) (car) entrar em pane, avariar-se.

conker m (coll) castanha-da-india.

connect vt juntar, unir; **2** (ELECT) ligar; **3** (fig) relacionar, unir; ♦ vt/vi: **would you** ~ **me to Mr ...?** ligava-me ao Sr ...?

connected adj: **well** ~ de boa família; bem relacionado.

connection n ligação f, união f; **2** (ELECT, RAIL) conexão f; **3** (TEL) comunicação f; (fig) relação f.

connive vi: **to** ~ **at** ser conivente em.

connoisseur n conhecedor,-ora, apreciador,-ora.

connotation n conotação f.

connubial adj conjugal.

conquer vt conquistar; vencer; dominar.

conqueror n conquistador m.

conquest n conquista f.

cons npl (Vd: **pro**).

conscience n consciência f; ~**-stricken** adj arrependido, com remorsos.

conscientious adj conscencioso,-a, escrupuloso,-a; **2** (objection) de consciência.

conscious n: **the** ~ (PSYC) o consciente; ♦ adj consciente; **to be** ~ **of** (aware) ser consciente de; (MED) consciente m,f.

consciousness n consciência; noção f.

conscript n recruta m,f.

conscription n serviço m military obrigatório.

consecrate vt consagrar.

consecration n (REL) consagração f.

consecution n sucessão; sequência lógica.

consecutive adj consecutivo,-a seguido,-a.

consecutively adv consecutivamente.

consensus n consenso m.

consent n consentimento m; ♦ vi: **to** ~ **to** consentir em.

consequence n consequência f.

consequently adv por conseguinte, consequentemente.

conservation n conservação f, preservação; **2** (of nature) prote(c)ção; ~ **area** n zona f (oficialmente) protegida.

conservationist adj (person) ecologista m,f.

conservative adj conservador; **2** (cautious) moderado; ♦ **the C~ party** npr o Partido Conservador.

conservatoire n (MUS) conservatório m.

conservatory n (MUS) conservatório; **2** marquise f; sala envridraçada em anexo, sala-lanterna f; **3** (greenhouse) estufa.

conserve vt conservar, preservar.

consider vt (gen) considerar; **2** (take into account) levar/ter em consideração; **3** (study) examinar.

considerable adj considerável; significativo.

considerate adj atencioso,-a, delicado,-a.

consideration n consideração f; **2** (reward) remuneração f; **3** reflexão f; **to be under** ~ estar em estudo; **for a** ~ (fee) mediante pagamento; **money is no** ~ não se faz questão de dinheiro.

considering prep em vista de; tendo em vista que.

consign vt consignar.

consignment n consignação f.

consist vi: **to** ~ **of** consistir em, ser formado de.

consistency n (of text, etc) coerência f; **3** (thickness) consistência f.

consistent adj consistente; (logical) coerente m,f; unifome.

consolation n consolação f, consolo m.

console[1] vt consolar (**with sth** com algo).

console[2] n (peça f ornamental) consola; **2** (video cabinet) armário m.

consolidate vt consolidar.

consommé n (CULIN) caldo.

consonant n (letter) consoante f; ♦ adj conforme; em harmonia (**with** com).

consort n: **prince** ~ príncipe consorte; ♦ vi: **to** ~ **with** acompanhar com.

consortium *n* consórcio.

conspicuous *adj* visível *m,f*; conspícuo,-a; **to be ~** dar nas vistas.

conspiracy *n* conspiração *f*, trama *m*.

conspire *vi* conspirar.

constable *n* polícia *m,f*; **chief ~** chefe *m* de polícia.

constabulary *n* polícia (distrital), força *f* policial.

constancy *n* constância *f*; **2** fidelidade.

constant *adj* contínuo,-a, constante *m,f*; **2** *(loyal)* leal, fiel.

constellation *n* (ASTRON) constelação *f*.

consternation *n* consternação *f*.

constipation *n* prisão de ventre.

constituency *n* (POL) círculo, distrito eleitoral.

constituent *n* (POL) eleitor,-ora; **2** *(part)* constituinte *m,f*, componente *m,f*.

constitute *vt* constituir.

constitution *n* constituição *f*.

constitutional *adj* constitucional.

constrain *vt* *(person)* coagir; **to ~ sb to do sth** forçar alguém a fazer algo.

constrained *adj* constrangido,-a, compelido,-a.

constraint *n* força, coa(c)ção; **2** restrição *f*; **3** *(shyness)* acanhamento *m*.

constrict *vt* *(part of body)* apertar, comprimir; **2** *(person)* restringir.

construct *vt* construir.

construction *n* construção *f*.

constructive *adj* construtivo,-a.

constructivism *n* (ART, PSYC) construtivismo *m*.

construe *vt* interpretar.

consul *n* cônsul *m,f*.

consulate *n* consulado.

consult *vt/vi* consultar.

consultant *n* (MED) médico,-a especialista; **2** consultor,-ora; **3** assessor,-ora.

consultation *n* consulta.

consulting room *n* consultório *m*.

consume *vt* comer; beber; consumir, gastar.

consumer *n* consumidor,-ora; **~ goods** *npl* bens *mpl* de consumo.

consumerism *n* consumismo *m*.

consuming *adj* profundo,-a; que consome; **a ~ ambition** uma profunda ambição *f*.

consummate *vt* consumar *(marriage)*.

consumption *n* consumo *m*.

cont *(abbr for* **continue**).

contact *n* conta(c)to *m*; **2** *(coll)* *(friends in high places who recommends)* pistolão *m*; ♦ *vt* entrar, pôr-se em contacto com; **he has good ~s** tem boas relações; **~ lenses** *npl* lentes *fpl* de conta(c)to.

contagious *adj* contagioso,-a.

contain *vt* conter; **2** *(feelings)* reprimir **to ~ o.s.** conter-se.

contained *adj* *(unemotional)* contido,-a.

container *n* recipiente *m*; **2** (COMM) contentor *m*; cofre *m* de carga.

containment *n* contenção *f*.

contaminate *vt* contaminar.

contamination *n* contaminação *f*.

cont'd *(abbr for* **continued**).

contemplate *vt* contemplar; contar com; pretender, pensar.

contemplation *n* contemplação *f*.

contemporaneous *adj* contemporâneo.

contemporary *n adj* contemporâneo.

contempt *n* desprezo, desdém *m*; **to have ~ for sb/ sth** desprezar, desdenhar.

contemptible *adj* desprezível.

contemptous *adj* desdenhoso,-a.

contend *vt* afirmar; argumentar; ♦ *vi* lutar; contender.

contender *n* *(in fight)* oponente *m,f*; **2** (POL) candidato,-a.

content *n* *(of copper, etc)* teor; **2** *(basket, speech)* conteúdo *m*; **3** *(satisfaction)* contentamento *m*; **to your heart ~'s** quanto te/lhe apetecer; ♦ *adj* contente; satisfeito; ♦ *vt* contentar, satisfazer.

contented *adj* contente *m,f*, satisfeito,-a.

contention *n* contenda; argumento.

contentious *adj* conflituoso,-a, contencioso,-a.

contentment *n* contentamento *m*.

contents *npl* conteúdo *sg m*.

contest *n* *(fight, competition)* concurso *m*; (SPORT) certame *m* desportivo; **2** (JUR) contestação *f*; *(fight)* luta *f* (**between** entre); ♦ *vt* disputar; **2** (JUR) contestar *(will)*; **3** concorrer; **4** (POL) ser candidato a.

contestant *n* competidor,-ora, oponente.

context *n* contexto.

contextual *adj* contextual.

contiguous *adj* *(proximity)* contíguo,-a, adjacente *m,f* (**to/with**, a).

continent *n* continente *m*; ♦ *adj* continente.

continental *adj* continental.

contingency *n* contingência.

contingent *n* contingente *m*.

continual *adj* contínuo.

continually *adv* constantemente.

continuation *n* prolongamento *m*; continuação *f*.

continue *vi* prosseguir, continuar; ♦ *vt* seguir, **2** persistir em.

continuity *n* continuidade *f*.

continuous *adj* contínuo; **~ assessment** *n* avaliação *f* contínua.

contort *vt* retorcer, contorcer.

contortion *n* contorção *f*.

contortionist *n* contorcionista *m,f*.

contour *n* contorno *m*; **~ line** curva de nível.

contraband *n* contrabando *m*.

contrabass *n* (MUS) *(instrument)* contrabaixo.

contraception *n* contracepção *f*.

contraceptive *n adj* contrace(p)tivo, anticonce(p)-cional; **~ pill** *n* pílula *f* contrace(p)tiva.

contract *n* contra(c)to *m*; ♦ *vi*: **to ~ to do sth** (COMM) comprometer-se por contrato a fazer algo; *(become smaller)* contrair-se, encolher-se; ♦ *vt* contrair; **to ~ out** *vi* contratar.

contraction *n* contra(c)ção *f*.

contractor *n* contratante *m,f*.

contradict *vt* *(deny)* desmentir; *(be contrary to)* contradizer.

contradiction *n* contradição *f* (**between** entre).

contraflow n (UK) (AUT) circulação f em sentido alternado numa estrada (em reparação).

contraindication n (MED) contraindicação.

contralto n (MUS) contralto.

contraption n (device) (fam, pej) engenhoca f, gerigonça f.

contrariwise adv (on the other hand) por outro lado.

contrary n adj oposto,-a, contrário,-a; **on the** ~ pelo contrário; ~ **to my expectations** ao contrário das minhas expectativas.

contrast n contraste m; ♦ vt contrastar, comparar.

contrasting adj oposto,-a.

contravene vt opor-se a; 2 (JUR) infringir, transgredir.

contravention n (JUR) infracção, transgressão; (of rules) violação f.

contribute vt contribuir; ♦ vi: **to** ~ **to** (gen) contribuir para; (newspaper) escrever para.

contribution n (money) contribuição f; 2 (to debate) intervenção f; 3 (to newspaper) colaboração f.

contributor n (to newspaper) colaborador,-ora.

contrite adj arrependido,-a.

contrition n (REL) contrição f; arrependimento m.

contrivance n (contraption) dispositivo m; 2 (ploy) artimanha f.

contrive vt (invent) idealizar; 2 (carry out) efe(c)tuar; 3 (plot) tramar; ♦ vi: **to** ~ **to** conseguir.

contrived adj forçado,-a; simulado,-a; artificial.

control n (command) controlo m (BR) controle; 2 autoridade f; **to lose** ~ **of sth** perder o controlo; **to lose one's** ~ perder o auto-domínio; **to take** ~ **of plane** tomar os comandos; ♦ vt (gen) controlar; 2 (traffic etc) dirigir; 3 (machinery) regular; 4 (temper) dominar; ~ **panel** n painel m de comando; ~ **room** n sala de comando; ~ **tower** n (AER) torre f de controle.

controversial adj discutível m,f, controverso,-a, polémico,-a.

controversy n controvérsia f.

contumacious adj irreverente, obstinado.

contusion n (MED) equimose f.

convalesce vi convalescer.

convalescence n convalescença.

convalescent adj, n convalescente m,f.

convector n (heater) convetor m; (BR) aquecedor m de convecção.

convene vt convocar; ♦ vi reunir-se.

convenience n (comfort) comodidade f; 2 (advantage) vantagem f; 3 conveniência; **at your** ~ (when it suits you) quando lhe for conveniente; quando lhe der jeito (fam); 4 **at your earliest** ~ (formal) assim que possível; 5 **public** ~s lavabos mpl, (BR) banheiro público.

convenient adj cómodo,-a; 2 (useful) útil; 3 (place) acessível; 4 (time) oportuno, conveniente.

convent n convento; ~ **school** n colégio de freiras.

convention n convenção f; 2 (meeting) assembleia f; 3 congresso.

conventional adj convencional m,f.

converge vi convergir.

conversant adj: **to be** ~ **with** estar familiarizado com.

conversation n conversação f, conversa; **to hold a** ~ manter uma conversa.

conversational adj familiar; (talkative) loquaz.

converse n inverso m, contrário m; 2 (MATH) proposição f recíproca; ♦ vi conversar.

conversely adv inversamente.

conversion n conversão f; ~ **table** n tabela de conversão.

convert n (REL, etc) convertido,-a; ♦ vt converter; transformar.

convertible n (car) convertível, conversível; descapotável m,f; (bed) dobrável m,f.

convex adj convexo,-a.

convey vt levar, transportar; 2 (thanks) comunicar; 3 (idea) exprimir.

conveyance n transporte; 2 (JUR) cedência f.

conveyor belt n (in factory) correia f transportadora; (in airport) (for luggage) tapete m rolante; (of goods, luggage) transportador.

convict n (person) presidiário,-a; ♦ vt condenar; (sentence) declarar culpado.

conviction n condenação f; 2 (belief) fé f, convicção f.

convince vt convencer.

convincing adj convincente m,f.

convivial adj aprazível, jovial m,f.

convocation n assembleia f, convocação f.

convoy n escolta f.

convulse vt convulsionar; 2 fazer morrer de rir.

convulsion n convulsão f; ataque m; acesso m.

coo vi (dove) arrulhar.

cooing n arrulho m.

cook n cozinheiro,-a; ♦ vt/vi cozinhar; cozer.

cooker n fogão m.

cookery n arte f culinária; ~ **book** n livro de receitas.

cookie n (US) bolacha, biscoito.

cooking n cozinha f, culinária f.

cookout n (US) churrascada.

cook-up vt (story) engendrar, inventar, fabricar.

cool adj fresco; tépido; 2 frio; 3 calmo; ~ **box** n caixa f frigorífica; 2 (relaxed) descontraído,-a; ♦ vt esfriar; **to** ~ **off** vi acalmar(-se); ~ **it!** (coll) tem calma!; 4 (coll) (elegant) **you look** ~! estás o máximo!

coolant n refrigerante, fluido de refrigeração.

cooling adj refrescante.

coolness n frescura; frieza; indiferença.

coop n (chicken's ~) galinheiro, capoeira; ♦ vt: **to** ~ **up** (fig) confinar.

co-op n (abbr for **Co-operative (Society)**).

cooper n tanoeiro.

co-operate n cooperativa f; ♦ vi cooperar, colaborar.

co-operation n cooperação f; colaboração f.

co-operative adj cooperativo.

co-opt vt cooptar.

co-ordinate vt coordenar.

co-ordination n coordenação f.

cop n (coll) polícia m.

cope vi: **to** ~ **with** lidar com; estar à altura de; aguentar (work, tension, person).

Copenhagen npr Copenhaga; (BR) Copenhague.

copilot n co-piloto.

copious *adj* copioso, abundante *m,f.*

cop-out *n (excuse)* desculpa *f*; escapatória *f*; ♦ **to cop out** *vt* escapar-se a/de responsabilidades.

copper *n* cobre *m*; **2** *(coll) (UK)* polícia *m*; **3** ~**s** *npl* moedas *fpl*, tostões *mpl*; **4** *(hair)* acobreado.

coppice, copse *n* bosquete *m*; matagal *m*, souto *m.*

coprocessor *n (COMP)* co-processador.

copulate *vi* copular.

copulation *n* cópula, união *f* sexual.

copy *n* cópia; exemplar *m*; **2** originais *mpl*; ♦ *vt* copiar.

copycat *n (fam)* macaco de imitação; *(crime)* idêntico.

copyeditor *m* revisor,-ora de provas.

copyist *n* copista *(of old texts)*; **2** falsificador,-ora.

copyright *n* direitos *mpl* de autor; direitos *mpl* autorais.

copytypist *n* digitador,-ora.

copywriter *n* redator,-ora de material publicitário.

coquet (-tt-) *vi* gracejar; comportar-se de forma sedutora, flirtear.

coral *n* coral *m*; ~ **reef** *n* recife *m* de coral.

cord *n* corda; **2** *(ELECT)* cordão *m*, cabo.

cordless *adj (electrical device)* sem fios.

cordial *n* cordial *m*; ♦ *adj* cordial.

cordon *n* cordão *m*; ♦ *vt* **to** ~ **off** isolar.

cords *n* calças de bombazina.

corduroy *n* bombazina, *(BR)* veludo cotelê.

core *n* centro, núcleo; *(of fruit)* caroço; ♦ *vt* descaroçar.

coriander *n* coentro *m.*

cork *m (product)* cortiça; **2** *(for bottle)* rolha *f.* ~**-tree** sobreiro *m.*

corkage *n* taxa cobrada nos reastaurantes por servirem bebidas trazidas pelos clientes.

corked *adj (vinho)* com sabor a rolha.

corking *adj (coll)* excelente *m,f.*

corkscrew *n* sacarolhas *m inv.*

cormorant *n (ZOOL)* cormorão *m*, corvo marinho.

corn *n* trigo; *(US)* milho; grão *m*; cereal *m*; **2** *(on feet)* calo *m*; **3** ~ **on the cob** *(CULIN)* espiga de milho.

cornea *n (ANAT)* córnea *f.*

corned beef *n (CULIN)* carne *f* de boi enlatada.

corner *n* ângulo; esquina; canto; curva; **2** *(football)* canto, corner *m*; ♦ *vt* açambarcar; *(COMM)* monopolizar; ♦ *vi* dobrar a esquina; **to cut** ~**s** trabalhar à pressa.

cornerstone *n* pedra *f* angular.

cornet *n (MUS)* cornetim *m.*

cornfield *n (of wheat, maize)* seara; *(of maize: also)* malharal *m.*

cornflour *n* farinha *f* maisena.

cornice *n (ARCH)* cornija *f.*

Cornish *adj* relativo a Cornualha.

cornstarch *n* amido *m* de milho.

Cornwall *npr* Cornualha.

corny *adj (coll)* velho, gasto; **2** caloso; **3** a ~ **joke** uma anedota já com barbas; **4** *(story)* lamechas *fpl.*

corollary *n* corolário *m.*

coronary *n (MED) (thrombosis) (coll)* enfarte *m* do miocárdio.

coronation *n* coroação *f.*

coroner *n* magistrado que investiga mortes suspeitas.

coronet *n* coroa aberta, diadema.

corpora *(Vd: corpus).*

corporal *n (MIL)* cabo *m*; ♦ *adj* corpóreo,-a.

corporate *adj* corporativo,-a; cole(c)tivo,-a.

corporation *n (of town)* junta; **2** *(COMM)* corporação *f*; ~ **tax** *n* imposto *m* sobre rendimento de corporações.

corporeal *adj* corpóreo,-a.

corps *(pl: corps)* *n (MIL)* unidade *f*; corpo *m* (diplomático etc).

corpse *n* cadáver *m.*

corpulent *adj* corpulento, encorpado.

corpus *(pl: corpora)* *n* corpus *m.*

corpuscle *n (blood)* glóbulo *m*; **red** ~**s** glóbulos vermelhos.

corral *n* curral *m*, cerca; ♦ *vt* encurralar.

corrasion *n (GEOL) (erosion)* corrasão *f.*

correct *adj* justo, exa(c)to; corre(c)to; ♦ *vt* corrigir.

correction *n* corre(c)ção *f*, re(c)tificação *f*; emenda.

corrective *adj* correctivo.

correlate *vt* correlacionar.

correspond *vi* corresponder-se (com); corresponder; equivaler.

correspondence *n* correspondência; ~ **course** *n* curso por correspondência.

correspondent *n* correspondente *m,f.*

corresponding *adj* correspondente.

corridor *n* corredor *m*, passagem *f.*

corrigible *adj* remediável *m,f.*

corroborate *vt* corroborar.

corrode *vt* corroer; ♦ *vi* corroer-se.

corrosion *n (GEOL) (erosion)* corrosão *f.*

corrosive *adj* corrosivo.

corrugated *adj* ondulado,-a; ~ **iron** chapa ondulada/ enrugada.

corrupt *adj* corrompido,-a; **2** *(dishonest)* corrupto,-a; **3** pervertido,-a; ♦ *vt* corromper; *(bribe)* subornar.

corruption *n* corrupção *f.*

corsage *n* raminho *m* de flores que se leva no vestido ou na lapela do casaco.

corset *n* espartilho *m.*

Corsica *npr* Córsega; **in** ~ na Córsega.

Corsican *npr, adj* corso,-a.

cortege *n* séquito, cortejo.

cortex *n (ANAT)* córtex *m.*

cortisone *n* cortisona.

coruscate *vi* reluzir, cintilar.

corysa *n (MED)* rinite *f.*

cos *n (lettuce)* alface-repolho *f.*

cosh *n (pl: -es) (bludgeon)* moca *f*; ♦ *vt* bater/agredir com uma moca.

cosiness *n* conforto; aconchego *m.*

cosmetic *n* cosmético *m*, produto *m* de beleza; ♦ *adj* cosmético,-a; ~ **surgery** cirurgia *f* estética.

cosmetician *n* este(c)ticista.

cosmic *adj* cósmico,-a.

cosmology *n* cosmologia *f.*

cosmonaut *n* cosmonauta *m,f.*

cosmopolitan *adj* cosmopolita *m,f.*

cosmos *n* cosmos *m*, universo *m.*

cosset *vt* acarinhar, afagar, mimar.

cost *n* custo *m*, despesa *f*; **2** preço *m*; **at a ~ of** ao preço de; **~ price** preço de custo; ◆ **~s** *(JUR)* npl custas *fpl*; **at all ~s** a todo o custo; ◆ **~-effective** *adj* rentável *m,f*; ◆ *(pt, pp* cost) *vi* custar, valer; ◆ *vt* custar; avaliar; **to ~ a lot of money** *(coll)* sair caro.

costing *n (estimate)* estimativa dos custos; custeamento *m*.

co-star *n* co-estrela *m,f*.

Costa Rican *npr adj* costarriquenho,-a.

costly *adj* caro,-a, dispendioso,-a.

costume *n* traje *m*, trajo *m*; **~ jewellery** *n* bijutaria *f*; **swimming ~** *(EP)* fato de banho *m*, *(BR)* maiô *m*; **~ ball** baile de máscaras.

cosy *(UK)*, **cozy** *(US) adj* cómodo,-a *(BR:* cô-); confortável; aconchegante; **tea-~** *n* abafador do chá.

cot *n* cama *f* (de criança), berço *m*; **~ death** n *(MED)* morte *f* súbita de recém-nascido

coterie *n (group)* tertúlia.

cottage *n* casa *f* de campo; **2** *(rustic)* cabana *f*; **3 ~ cheese** *n* espécie de queijo-fresco; **~ industry** *n* indústria *f* caseira (de artesanato); **~ pie** *n* empadão *m* de carne picada e puré *m* de batata.

cotton *n* algodão *m*; **2** *(thread)* fio *m*, linha *f*; **to ~ on (to)** *vi (begin to understand)* perceber; **~ candy** *n* algodão *m* doce; **~-mill** fábrica *f* de fiação *m*; **~ wool** *n* algodão em rama.

couch *n* sofá *m*.

cough *n* tosse *f*; **~ drop** *n* pastilha para a tosse; **~ syrup** *n* charope *m* para a tosse; ◆ *vi* tossir; **to ~ up** *vt* expelir.

could *(pt of* can).

couldn't = **could not**.

council *n* conselho *m*; assembleia *(BR:* -bléia) *f*; **city/town ~** câmara municipal; **~ estate** *n* (conjunto residencial subvencionado pelo governo) fogos *mpl* habitacionais; bairro *m* social; **~ house** *n* casa *f* de habitação social; **~ tax** *n (UK)* imposto camarário de habitação.

councillor *n* vereador,-ora.

Council of Europe *npr* Conselho *m* da Europa.

counsel *n (advice)* conselho; *(JUR)* advogado,-a; **~ for the defence** advogado de defesa; **~ for the prosecution** advogado,-a de acusação; ◆ *vt* aconselhar; ◆ *vr* **to take ~** aconselhar-se.

counselling *(UK)*, **counseling** *(US) n* terapia *f*; *(practical advice)* orientação *f* psicológica.

counsellor *(UK)*, **counselor** *(US) n (adviser)* conselheiro,-a, advogado,-a; **2** orientador,-ora.

count *n* conta *f*; **2** contagem *f*; cálculo *m*; **I have lost ~ of** já perdi conta de; **on both ~s** em ambos os pontos; **3** *(JUR)* acusação; **4** *(title)* conde; ◆ *vt* contar; incluir; ◆ *vi* contar; ◆ **to ~ against** *vt* pesar contra; **~ in** *vt* incluir; **~ on** *vt (rely)* contar com; ◆ **~ out** *vt* excluir; **2** contar um a um; IDIOM **that doesn't ~!** isso não vale!

countdown *n* contagem *f* decrescente.

countenance *n (face)* semblante *m*; expressão *f*; **2** compostura *f*; **to keep one's ~** manter a compostura; ◆ *vt* tolerar, permitir.

counter *n* balcão, guiché; **2** contador; **3** *(game)* ficha; ◆ *vt* contrariar.

counteract *vt* neutralizar.

counterattack *n* contra-ataque *m*.

counterbalance *n* contrapeso *m*; ◆ *vt* contrabalançar.

counter-espionage *n* contra-espionagem *f*.

counterfeit *n* falsificação *f*, contrafação *f*; ◆ *adj* falso, falsificado; ◆ *vt* falsificar.

counterfoil *n (of cheque, receipt)* talão *m*; *(BR)* canhoto *m*.

countermand *n* contraordem *f*; ◆ *vt* revogar.

counterpart *n* hómologo *f*; **the Prime Minister and his Brazilian ~** o Primeiro Ministro e seu homólogo.

counterproductive *adj* contraproducente *m,f*.

counter-revolution *n* contrarrevolução *f*.

countersign *n (MIL)* contrassenha *f*, rubrica *f*; ◆ *vt (document)* ratificar.

countess *n* condessa *f*.

countless *adj* inumerável *m,f*.

country *n* país *m*; *(nation)* pátria *f*; **2** *(countryside)* campo *m*; **3** região *f*, terra; **~ club** *n* clube *m* de campo; **~ dancing** *n* dança regional; **~ house** *n* casa de campo.

county *n* condado *m*; **~ council** *n* conselho *m* regional.

coup *(pl:* -s) *n* golpe *m*; **~ d'état/de grâce** golpe de estado/de graça.

coupé *n* cupé *m*.

couple *n* par *m*; **a ~ of eggs** um par de ovos; **a ~ of lovers** um par namorados; **2** casal; **a married ~** um casal; **a ~ of pigeon** um casal de pombos; ◆ *vt (join)* unir, juntar; **3** *(connect)* ligar; **3** engatar, atrelar; **4** associar; **5** *(animals)* acasalar.

couplet *n (stanza)* dístico *m*.

coupling *n (RAIL)* engate *m*.

coupon *n* cupão *m*, *(BR)* cupom *m*; **pools ~** cupão da lotaria.

courage *n* valentia *f*, coragem *f*; **to pluck up ~** encher-se de coragem.

courageous *adj* corajoso,-a, valente.

courgette *n (BOT)* curjete *f*.

courier *n* correio; **2** mensageiro; **3** guia *m,f*, agente *m,f* de turismo.

course *n* direção *f*; caminho *m*; rumo *m*; **2** *(plane)* rota *f*; **3** *(study)* curso *m*; **4** *(golf)* campo *m*; **5** *(CULIN)* prato; ◆ *adv* **of ~** claro, naturalmente; **in due ~** oportunamente; na devida altura; **(sth) has run its ~** já deu o que tinha a dar.

court *n (royal)* corte *f*; **2** *(JUR)* tribunal *m*, Palácio de Justiça; **3** sessão *f* de tribunal; **4** *(tennis)* campo de ténis, *(BR)* quadra de tênis; **5** *(palace)* palácio; ◆ *vt* atrair; solicitar; **2** *(dated)* namorar; ◆ **the banks are ~ing disaster** os bancos estão à beira dum desastre; **to take to ~** levar ao tribunal.

courteous *adj* cortês *m,f*.

courtesan *n* cortesã *f*.

courtesy *n* cortesia *f*; **by ~ of** por gentileza de; graças à generosidade de *(sponsor)*.

courtier *n* cortesão *m*, cortesã *f*.

court-martial *(pl:* -s-martial) *n* conselho de guerra; ◆ *vt* submeter a conselho de guerra.

courtroom *n* sala de tribunal.

courtship *n* galanteio, namoro.

courtyard *n* pátio.

couscous *n* (*CULIN*) cuscuz *m*.

cousin *n* primo,-a; **first ~** primo em primeiro grau; **far-removed ~s** primos afastados.

cove *n* angra, enseada.

coven *n* reunião de bruxas.

covenant *n* convénio (*BR*: -vê-); ajuste, pacto; **2** (*UK*) promessa escrita; **Ark of the C~** Arca da Aliança.

Coventry *npr cidade inglesa*; **to send sb to ~** ignorar alguém; mandar a pessoa à fava.

cover *n* (*gen*) cobertura, coberta *f*; **2** (*cladding*) revestimento *m*, forro *m*; **3** (*protection*) abrigo; **4** (*lid*) tampa; **bed~** colcha *f*; **under ~** abrigado; **under ~ of** ao abrigo de; (*fig*) sob a capa de; ♦ *vt* cobrir (*cushion, table*); tapar (*saucepan, child*); **2** (*clad*) revestir; **3** percorrer (*ground*); **4** (*take in*) abranger (*view, etc*); abrigar.

coverage *n* (*of news*) cobertura *f*.

covering *n* cobertura, invólucro; **~ letter** *n* carta *f* explicativa em anexo.

covert *adj* secreto,-a, oculto,-a; **2** (*glance*) furtivo; **3** (*payment*) clandestino,-a.

cover-up *n* encobrimento *m*; ♦ *vt* encobrir, esconder.

covet *vt* cobiçar.

cow *n* vaca *f*; **2** (*female of elephant, seal, etc*) **3** (*pej*) (*nasty woman*) vaca; ♦ *vt* intimidar; IDIOM **till the ~s come home** até as galinhas terem dentes.

coward *n* cobarde *m,f*, covarde *m,f*.

cowardice *n* covardia.

cowardly *adj* cobarde, covarde.

cowboy *n* vaqueiro, campino; **2** (*unscrupulous in business/work*) trapaceiro.

cower *vi* encolher-se (de medo).

cowl *n* capuz *m* de frade.

co-worker *n* colega, sócio.

cowpat *n* bosta *f*.

cowshed *n* estábulo *m*.

coxswain *n* timoneiro,-a.

coy *adj* acanhado,-a, recatado,-a, (*often pej*) sonso,-a.

coyote *n* coiote *m*.

cozy (*US*) (*Vd*: **cosy**).

cp. (*abbr for* **compare**).

CPD *n* (*abbr for* **Continuing Professional Development**) (*EDUC*) desenvolvimento *m* continuo profissional.

CPR (*abbr for* **cardiopulmonary resuscitation**) ressuscitação cardiopulmonar.

crab *n* caranguejo; **2 ~ apple** *n* maçã *f* ácida.

crabbed *adj* (*coll*) irritável.

crack *n* (*fine line in cup, ground, wall*) fenda *f*; (*wall ceiling*), racha *f*, rachadura *f*; (*GEOL*) fissure *f*; (*small opening*) fresta *f*; (*in door*) frincha *f*; **2** (*noise*) estalido *m*; **3** (*of whip*) estalo; **4** (*joke*) piada; **5** (*cocaine*) crack *m*; **6** (*attempt*) **to have a ~ at sth** tentar fazer algo; ♦ *adj* de elite, de primeira; (*~ shot*) de campeão; ♦ *vt* (*mirror, cup*) rachar, quebrar, (*egg, nut*) partir; **2** (*paint, varnish, twig*) estalar; **3** (*safe*) arrombar (cofre); **4**

(*of whip, joint*) estalar; **to ~ the whip** (*fig*) (*assert one's authority*) agitar o chicote; **5** (*fig*) (*joke*) contar (uma piada); **6** (*solve-problem*) resolver; **7** (*code*) decifrar; ♦ *vi* achar-se; (*skin, lips*) gretar-se; ♦ **to ~ down** (**on sb, sth**) *vi* tomar medidas *fpl* severas, linha *f* dura (contra alguém/algo); **to ~ sth open** *vt* abrir algo forçosamente; **~ up** sofrer um colapso nervoso; **2** (*US*) (*laugh*) ter um ataque de riso.

crack-brained *adj* disparatado,-a, doido,-a.

crackdown *n* medida *f* severa (**on** contra); **~ on crime** medidas *fpl* anti-crime/anticrime.

cracker *n* (*biscuit*) biscoito *m*; **2** (*for Christmas*) tubo de cartolina decorado, contendo um brinde e um estalinho; **2** (*person, show*) espantoso,-a; **she is a ~** ela é fantástica; **fire-~** petardo; **~s** *adj* (*coll*) doido,-a.

crackerjack *adj* (*coll*) excelente, fantástico,-a; **2** (*UK*) *children's TV programme*.

cracking *adj* (*fam*): **to get ~** (*work*) pôr mãos à obra; (*walk*) andar a passos largos.

crackle *vi* (*fire*) crepitar; (*sounds of burning*) dar estalinhos.

crackling *n* (*sound of*) crepitação *f*; estalidos *mpl*; **2** (*RADIO*) interferência; **3** (*skin of roasted pork*) estaladiça de porco assado.

cradle *n* berço; ♦ *vt* embalar (*baby*) (*in one's arms*).

craft *n* (*skill*) arte *f*; ofício; **2** (*cunning*) astúcia; **3** (*boat*) barco.

craftsman *n* artífice *m*, artesão *m*.

craftsmanship *n* artesanato *m*; **2** habilidade *f*.

crafty *adj* astuto,-a; (*sly*) manhoso,-a.

crag *n* penhasco.

craggy *adj* escarpado.

cram *vt* encher, abarrotar; **2** preparar para exames.

crammed *adj* abarrotado.

cramp *n* (*MED*) cãibra; **2** (*TECH*) grampo *m*; ♦ *vt* (*limit*) restringir; **2** (*annoy*) estorvar.

cramped *adj* apertado, confinado.

crampon *n* grampo, gato *m* de ferro.

cranberry *n* (*BOT*) arando.

crane *n* (*CONSTR*) guindaste *m*, grua *f*; **2** (*bird*) grou *m*; ♦ *vt* esticar (*the neck*).

craniology *n* craniologia *f*.

crank *n* (*TECH*) manivela; **2** (*person*) excêntrico,-a; **~case** *n* (*MEC*) carter; **~shaft** *n* veio motor, eixo de manivelas; (*MEC*) cambota *f*.

cranky *adj* excêntrico; (*bad-tempered*) irritadiço,-a.

cranny *n* (*Vd*: **nook**).

crap *n* (*slang*) (*excrement*) merda *f* (*cal*); **2** (*nonsense*) tretas; **you're full of ~** só dizes tretas.

crape *n* (*fabric*) crepe; **2** (*mourning – arm band*) fumo.

crappy (-ier, -iest) *adj* (*person*) (*slang*) de péssima qualidade.

crash *n* (*noise*) estrondo; **2** (*of cars, planes etc*) acidente *m*, colisão *f*; **3** (*COMM*) falência, quebra; ♦ *vt* cair; (*plane*) espatifar; ♦ *vi* (*plane*) despenhar-se; (*cars*) chocar, bater; **~ course** *n* curso intensivo; **~ helmet** *n* capacete *m* prote(c)tor; **~ landing** *n* aterragem *f*; (*BR*) aterrissagem *f* forçada.

crass adj (person) abjecto,-a, grosseiro,-a.
crate n caixote m; cesta f; **2** (of beer) grade, (BR) engradado.
crater n cratera f.
cravat n (for man) lenço de pescoço.
crave vt: **to ~ for** ansiar por; desejar, ter desejos
craving n (food) desejo incontrolável m,f; ânsia f.
crawl n rastejo; (swimming) crawl m; ♦ vi arrastar-se; rastejar; **2** (child) gatinhar, (BR) engatinhar; **3** (vehicle) andar a passo de caracol, (BR) tartaruga.
crayfish npl inv lagostim m.
crayon n lápis m; de pastel, crayon m.
craze n mania f; moda f.
crazy adj louco, maluco, doido; disparatado.
creak n rangido m; ♦ vi chiar, ranger.
cream n (of milk) nata; creme m; **2** (fig) a fina flor; ♦ adj (colour) creme; **to ~ off** vt selecionar.
creamy adj cremoso.
crease n ruga; vinco; **2** vt vincar (with iron); (face) enrugar; (clothes) amarrotar; ♦ vi enrugar-se; amarrotar-se.
create vt criar; produzir.
creation n criação f.
creative adj criativo,-a; ~ **tension** n tensão f criativa.
creator n criador,-ora.
creature n animal m, bicho m; criatura f.
crèche, creche n creche f.
credentials npl credenciais fpl.
credibility n credibilidade f.
credible adj crível m,f.
credit n confiança, crédito; **2** mérito, honra; **3** (COMM, FIN) crédito m; ~ **card** n (bank's) cartão m de crédito; ♦ vt creditar; **2** (merit) reconhecer.
creditable adj respeitável; **2** louvável.
credit broker n intermediário,-a, financeiro,-a.
credit crunch n crise f de crédito severa.
credit note n (COMM) nota f promissória; (FIN) letra f de câmbio.
creditor n (FIN, COMM) credor m.
credit rating n classificação f do crédito (of a private person or business).
credits npl (CIN) fichas técnicas fpl.
credit squeeze n (ECON, FIN) restrições fpl de crédito.
creditworthy adj merecedor,-ora de crédito.
credo n credo m.
credulity n credulidade f.
creed n credo; crença; **2** (POL) doutrina.
creek n ria, enseada; (US) arroio.
creep n (coll) verme m, estafermo m; **2** (coll) lambe-botas m inv; ♦ (pt, pp **crept**) vi (move slowly), arrastar-se; (furtively) andar furtivamente; **2** trepar; **3** (grovel) rastejar (**before sb** diante de alguém); **4** vr arrepiar-se; **it gives me the ~s** horroriza-me, dá-me arrepios; **to ~ in/into** surgir, avançar, penetrar gradualmente; **to ~ up on** aproximar-se furtivamente.
creeper n (plant) trepadeira.
creeping adj gradual.
creepy adj horripilante.
creepy crawley n (coll) (insect) bicho m (rastejante).
cremate vt cremar.

cremation n cremação f.
crematorium (pl: -ria) n crematório.
creole n adj crioulo,-a.
creosote n creosote f.
crepe n (fabric rubber) crepe m; ~ **paper** n papel m crepe; (BR) papel crepom m; ~ **bandage** n atadura de crepe; **2** (CULIN) crepe m.
crepe-soled shoes npl (UK) sapatos mpl com sola emborrachada.
crepitate vi (sound) crepitar; estalejar.
crept (pt, pp of **creep**).
crepuscular adj crepusculino.
crescent n (moon) quarto-crescente; **2** (shape) crescente f; **3 C~** npr (Islam) Crescente.
cress n (BOT) agrião m.
crest n (on bird's head, of wave) crista; (of mountain) cimo, topo, cume; **2** (coat of arms) brasão m.
crestfallen adj desanimado,-a.
Crete npr Creta.
cretin n cretino, imbecil.
crevasse n (ice, glacier) fenda f, fissura f.
crevice n (in rock) fenda f, greta f.
crew n tripulação f; bando, quadrilha; (MIL) guarnição f; ~ **cut** n corte m à escovinha; ~**man** n tripulante; ~**-neck** n gola f arredondada.
crib n (Nativity) presépio; **2** (US) berço; ♦ (-bb-) vt (coll) copiar algo de alguém, plagiar.
crick n (neck) torcicolo; ♦ vt dar mau jeito.
cricket n grilo; **2** (game) críquete m, cricket m.
crime n crime m; delito.
criminal n criminoso,-a; ♦ adj criminal; (JUR) penal; **the C~ Investigation Department (CID)** Departamento de Investigação Criminal.
crimp vt (hair) frisar; (fabric) plissar.
crimson adj inv carmesim.
cringe vi (grovel) portar-se servilmente; **2** (out of fear/ timidity) encolher-se, recuar **3** ficar embaraçado.
crinkle n (in skin) ruga f; (clothes) prega f; ♦ vt enrugar, engelhar; (clothes) amarrotar.
crinkly adj enrugado, amarrotado,-a.
cripple n coxo, aleijado; ♦ vt aleijar, inutilizar.
crisis (pl: -ses) n crise f.
crisp adj (greens) fresco; **2** (bread, biscuit) torrado, estaladiço; **3** (hair) crespo; **4** (manner) decidido, seco,-a.
crispness n aspereza f.
crisps npl batatinha frita, inglesa.
criss-cross adj cruzamento de linhas, com linhas cruzadas.
criterion (pl: -ria) n critério, critérios.
critic n crítico,-a.
critical adj crítico; grave.
critically adv gravemente.
criticism n crítica.
criticize vt criticar.
croak n grasnido m; ♦ vi coaxar; crocitar.
Croat npr croata m,f.
Croatia npr Croácia.
Croatian npr adj (LING) croata.
crochet n croché m.
crock n vaso de barro; **2** (coll) caco m velho.

crockery n (dishes, etc) louça; faiança f.
crocodile n (ZOOL) crocodile m.
crocus n (BOT) açafrão-da-primavera m.
croft n pequena quinta, (BR) pequena chácara.
crofter n arrendatário,-a/dono,-a de pequena quinta.
crone n velha encarquilhada; (fig) bruxa f.
crony n camarada m,f, compincha m,f; **my old** ~ a minha velha companheira.
crook n vigarista m,f; **2** (of shepherd) cajado; **3** (of arm) curva; ♦ vt dobrar, curvar.
crooked adj torto; tortuoso; (fig) desonesto.
croon vi sussurrar, cantar baixinho.
crop n colheita; safra; ♦ vt cortar, ceifar; **to ~ up** vi aparecer, surgir; (topic) vir à baila.
cropper n (fam): **to come a** ~ levar um tombo; cair desastradamente; **2** (fig) falhar.
crop spraying n pulverização f.
croquet n croquet m.
croquette n (CULIN) croquete m.
cross n cruz f; **2** (fig) (torment) cruz; **3** (breed) cruzamento m; **4** (boxing) cruzado; ♦ adj zangado,-a (**with** com); ♦ vt (street, sea) atravessar; **2** (legs, arms, cheque) cruzar; ♦ vi benzer-se, fazer o sinal da cruz; **2** (meet) cruzar-se; **to ~ one's mind** passar pela cabeça; **to ~ out** riscar; **to ~ over** passar para, atravessar.
crossbar n tranca, viga; **2** (SPORT) barra transversal.
crossbreed n raça cruzada.
cross-country n (race) corrida f de corta-mato.
cross-dressing n travestismo.
cross-examination n interrogatório; instância.
cross-examine vt interrogar, instar.
cross-eyed adj estrábico, vesgo.
crossfire n fogo m cruzado.
crossing n faixa f de segurança; **2** (sea journey) travessia f; (road) cruzamento m; (RAIL) passagem f de nível; **pedestrian** ~ passadeira para peões, (BR) passagem para pedestres.
cross-legged adv de pernas fpl cruzadas.
crossly adv com irritação f.
cross purposes npl obje(c)tivos contrários; **to be at** ~ divergir; não entender-se.
cross-reference n referência remissiva.
crossroads npl cruzamento m, encruzilhada f.
cross-section n corte m transversal; **2** (of population) grupo representativo.
crosswind n vento costal.
crosswise adv em diagonal.
crossword (puzzle) palavras mpl cruzadas.
crotch n (area, trousers) entrepernas; (BR) (trousers) grampo m.
crotchet n (MUS) semínima.
crotchety adj extravagante.
crouch vi agachar-se; estar de cócoras.
croup n (MED) difteria.
croupier n (game) banqueiro, crupiê m,f.
crow n (bird) corvo m; **2** (of cock) canto, cocorocó m; ♦ vi (cock) cantar; ~**'s feet** n (lines around the eyes) pés-de-galinha mpl.
crowbar n alavanca, pé-de-cabra m.

crowd n multidão f; chusma, populaça, (SPORT) público; tropel m, turba; ♦ vt amontoar; encher; ♦ vi reunir-se; amontoar-se.
crowded adj apinhado, concorrido, repleto.
crown n coroa; **C~** npr Monarquia f; ~ **jewels** npl jóias fpl da Coroa; ~ **prince** n príncipe m herdeiro; **2** (of head) topo, alta; **3** (of hat) copa; **4** (of hill) cume m; **5** (artificial tooth) coroa; ♦ vt coroar.
crowning n coroação f; ♦ adj culminante m,f.
crozier n (of bishop) croça f.
crucial adj decisivo,-a.
crucible n (TECH) cadinho, crisol m.
crucifix n crucifixo.
crucifixion n crucificação f.
crucify vt crucificar.
crud n (sticky substance) resíduo; matéria pegajosa.
cruddy adj (coll) repugnante, sujo.
crude adj cru, bruto; **2** tosco; rude; **3** ~ **(oil)** n petróleo, crude m.
cruel adj cruel.
cruelty n crueldade f.
cruet n galheta f, galheteiro m.
cruise n cruzeiro, viagem f de recreio (por mar); ~ **missile** míssil de cruzeiro; ♦ vi fazer um cruzeiro.
cruiser n cruzador m.
crumb n migalha f, farelo; **wipe the** ~ **off the table** limpa as migalhas da mesa.
crumble vt esmigalhar; ♦ vi desintegrar-se; desmoronar-se; **to ~ into dust** desfazer-se em pó.
crumbly adj quebradiço.
crummy adj pobre, inferior, barato.
crumpet n (CULIN) bolo leve; **she is a piece of** ~! (fam, offensive) ela é um pedaço de mulher!, gostosa; (BR) gostosona.
crumple vt enrugar; amarrotar.
crunch n (under feet) rangido m; (eating) mastigação f; ♦ vt (food etc) trincar, mastigar; **2** (underfoot) fazer ranger.
crunchy adj crocante; ruidoso,-a; **2** (gravel) estaladiço,-a.
cruor n (MED) cruor m, coágulo.
crusade n cruzada f.
cruse n vasilha de barro.
crush n aperto; aglomeração f; ♦ vt esmagar; **2** amachucar; **3** enrugar; **4** (fruit) espremer; comprimir; **to ~ grapes** pisar uvas; **to have a ~ on** ter uma paixoneta por.
crushing adj esmagador,-ora.
crust n côdea; (MED) crosta.
crutch n muleta f.
crux n ponto m crucial; âmago, cerne m.
cry n grito; choro; **street vendor's** ~ pregão m; ♦ vi chorar; **2** spregoar; ~ **for help** pedir ajuda; ~ **out** gritar.
cryonics nsg criogenização f.
crypt n cripta f.
cryptic adj enigmático, secreto, oculto.
cryptography n criptografia.
crystal n cristal m; ~ **ball** n bola de cristal; ~**-clear** adj cristalino,-a; **2** (meaning) claro,-a.
crystalize vt cristalizar; ♦ vi cristalizar-se.

C-section *n (US) (MED)* cesariana *f.*

cub *n* filhote *m.*

Cuba *npr* Cuba; **in ~** em Cuba.

Cuban *npr adj* cubano,-a.

cubbyhole *n* esconderijo *m.*

cube *n* cubo; ♦ *vt (MATH)* elevar ao cubo; **~ root** *n* raiz *f* cúbica.

cubic *adj* cúbico.

cubicle *n* cubículo *m.*

cubism *n* cubismo *m.*

cuckoo *n* cuco *m;* **~ clock** *n* relógio de cuco.

cucumber *n* pepino *m.*

cuddle *n* abraço *m;* ♦ *vt* abraçar; embalar; ♦ *vi* abraçar-se.

cuddly *adj* mimoso,-a, fofinho,-a.

cudgel *n* cacete; ♦ *vt* desancar, espancar.

cue *n (billiards, snooker)* taco *m;* **2** *(hint)* dica *f,* sinal *m;* **3** *(THEAT)* deixa; **on ~** no momento certo.

cuff *n (of sleeve)* punho *m;* **2** *(blow on face)* bofetada *f,* tapa *f;* **off the ~** *(fam) adv* improvisado; ♦ *vt* bater, dar uma bofetada.

cufflinks *npl* botões-de-punho *mpl, (BR)* abotoaduras *fpl.*

cuirass *n* couraça.

cuisine *n (CULIN)* cozinha *f.*

cul-de-sac *n* beco sem saída.

culinary *adj* culinário,-a.

cull *vt* reduzir *(size of herd,* flora); **2** *(small animals)* matar seletivamente; **3** *(people, society)* sanar.

culminate *vi* culminar; **to ~ in** terminar em.

culmination *n* culminação *f,* auge *m.*

culpability *n* culpabilidade *f.*

culpable *adj* culpável *m,f.*

culprit *n* culpado,-a, acusado,-a.

cult *n* culto *m.*

cultivate *vt* cultivar.

cultivated *adj (field, garden)* cultivado; **2** *(fig) (cultured)* culto.

cultivation *n* cultivo; *(fig)* cultura.

cultural *adj* cultural.

culture *n* cultura.

cultured *adj* culto.

culvert *n* bueiro.

cumber *n* obstrução *f;* ♦ *vt* obstruir.

cumbersome *adj* pesado,-a, incómodo,-a *(BR:* cô-).

cumbrance *n* estorvo *m,* incómodo *m.*

cumin *n* cuminho *m.*

cumulative *adj* cumulativo,-a.

cumulus *n (cloud)* cúmulo *m.*

cunning *n* astúcia; manha, esperteza; ♦ *adj* astuto; IDIOM **as ~ as a fox** manhoso como uma raposa.

cup *n (EP)* chávena *f; (BR, Reg)* xícara; **2** *(of prize)* taça *f; (BR)* copa *f;* **3** *(of bras)* copa; ♦ *(-pp-) vt* dispor (as mãos) em forma de concha; ♦ **it's not my ~ of tea** isso não é do meu agrado; **~ tie** jogo *m* eliminatório.

cupboard *n* armário; guarda-louça.

cupcake *n (CULIN)* queques decorados.

Cupid *npr* Cupido *m.*

cupola *n (ARCH) (domed roof)* cúpula *f.*

cur *n* cão *m* vadio, rafeiro *m;* **2** *(fig)* vira-latas *m inv;* patife *m,f.*

curable *adj* curável *m,f.*

curate *n* coadjutor *m.*

curator *n* curador,-ora; *(museum)* conservador,-ora.

curb *n* freio, controlo *m;* **2** borda de passeio, *(BR)* meio-fio; ♦ *vi* refrear, controlar.

curbside *n (US) (road)* berma *f.*

curd cheese *n (UK)* requeijão *m.*

curdle *vi (cheese, milk)* coalhar; **2** *(blood)* coagular.

cure *n* tratamento, cura; ♦ *vt* curar.

cure-all *n* panaceia *f.*

curfew *n* hora de recolher obrigatório.

curia *n (REL)* cúria *m.*

curio *n* antiguidade *f.*

curiosity *n* curiosidade *f.*

curious *adj* curioso,-a.

curl *n (of hair)* anel *m;* caracol *m;* **2** espiral *m;* ♦ *vt (hair)* encaracolar-(se); **to ~ one's lip** fazer beicinho; **to ~ up** enroscar-se; enrolar-se; **3** *(edges)* dobrar.

curler *n (for hair)* rolo de cabelo; *(BR)* bobe *m.*

curling tongs *npl* ferros *mpl* de frisar.

curly *adj (hair)* encaracolado.

curmudgeon *n* pessoa carrancuda, trombudo.

currant *n* passa de corinto; groselha.

currency *n* moeda, dinheiro; divisa *f;* valor *m* cambial.

current *n* corrente *f;* ♦ *adj* corrente, atual; em curso; **2** *(law)* vigente; **~ account** *n (EP)* conta à ordem; *(BR)* conta corrente; **~ affairs** *npl* a(c)tualidades *fpl.*

currently *adv* a(c)tualmente.

curriculum *(pl:* **-s** *or* **-la)** *n* programa *m* de estudos; **~ vitae** *n* curriculum *m* vitae.

curry *n* caril *m;* **~ powder** *n* caril em pó; curry *m;* **2** *vt (horse)* escovar; **to ~ sb's favour** captar, obter as boas graças de alguém.

curse *n* maldição *f;* **2** *(swearword)* palavrão *m,* asneira *f;* ♦ *vi* praguejar, blasfemar; ♦ *vt* maldizer, amaldiçoar.

cursed *adj* maldito,-a, detestável *m,f.*

cursive *n adj (TYPO)* cursivo.

cursor *n (COMP)* cursor *m.*

cursory *adj* rápido,-a, superficial *m,f.*

curt *adj* seco, brusco.

curtail *vt (visit etc)* abreviar, encurtar; *(expenses etc)* reduzir.

curtain *n* cortina; **2** *(THEAT)* pano; **behind the ~** nos bastidores *mpl;* **~ call** *n (THEAT)* chamada dos actores ao palco; **~ raiser** *n* preâmbulo *m,* prelúdio *m;* **~ ring** *n* argola; ♦ **to ~ off** separar com cortina.

curts(e)y *n* mesura, reverência; ♦ *vi* fazer reverência *f.*

curvature *n* curvature *f.*

curve *n* curva; ♦ *vt* encurvar, torcer; ♦ *vi* encurvar-se, torcer-se; **2** *(road)* curvar, fazer (uma) curva.

curvy *adj (person)* cheio,-a de curvas.

cushion *n* almofada *f;* **2** *(bilhar)* tabela; ♦ *vt (seat)* almofadar; **2** *(shock)* amortecer.

cushy *adj (work, living)* fácil; **~ job** *(coll)* um bom tacho.

cusp *n (ASTROL)* cúspide *f;* **2** ponta alongada.

cuss *n* maldição *f;* praga *f;* IDIOM **not give a tinker's ~** estar-se nas tintas.

custodian *n* guarda *m,f; (in museum)* conservador, -ora; *(traditions; children)* guardião,-iã.

custody *n* custódia *f,* guarda *f;* **to take into** ~ deter, prender.

custom *n* costume *m,* hábito *m;* **2** *(JUR)* norma *f;* **3** *(COMM)* clientele, freguesia.

customary *adj* costumeiro, habitual; **it is** ~ ... é costume ...

customer *n* cliente *m,f,* freguês,-esa *m,f.*

customise *(UK)* **customize** *(US) vr* personalizr.

custom-made *adj (US)* feito sob/por medida.

customs *npl* alfândega *sg;* ~ **duties** *npl* direitos *mpl* *(BR:* impostos *mpl)* alfandegários; ~ **officer** *n* empregado *m,f* de alfândega; **Customs and Excise** *m* Departmento britânico responsável por arrecadar os impostos sobre compras e vendes de bens importado.

cut *n (gen)* corte *m;* golpe *m; (in salary etc)* redução *f; (of meat)* peça, corte; **power** ~ corte de energia; ♦ *(pt, pp* **cut**) *vt* cortar; *(price)* baixar; *(record)* gravar; *(reduce)* reduzir; *(hurt)* ferir; ♦ *vi* cortar; *(intersect)* interceptar-se; **2 to** ~ **a tooth** sair, nascer um dente; ♦ **to** ~ **across** *(short cut)* cortar caminho por (atalho); ♦ ~ **back** *(trees)* podar, reduzir; ~ **back on** *(sth)* reduzir; ♦ **to** ~ **down** *vt (tree)* derrubar; reduzir; **to** ~ **in on sb** interromper alguém, cortar em frente (de alguém); ♦ **to** ~ **off** *vt (gen)* cortar; **2** *(take from)* deserdar; **3** *(troops)* cercar; ♦ **to** ~ **out** *vt (shape)* recortar; **2** *(delete)* suprimir; exclude; **to** ~ **through** *vi* abrir caminho; ♦ *exc* ~ **out!** para com isso!

cut-and-dried *adj* rotineiro,-a, definicivo,-a.

cut-and-paste *vt (COMP)* cortar e colar.

cutaneous *adj* cutâneo,-a.

cutback *n* corte *m,* redução *f* em.

cute *adj* bonito, engraçado,-a, jeitoso,-a.

cut glass *n* vidro *m* lapidado.

cutie *n (coll) (child, woman)* coisa/coisinha fofa.

cuticle *n* cutícula.

cuting *n (JOURN)* recorte *m; (RAIL)* corte em; ~ **room** *n (CIN)* sala *f* de edição; ♦ *adj* cortante; *(remark)* mordaz.

cutlass *n* alfange *m.*

cutlery *n* talheres *mpl.*

cutlet *n (meat)* costeleta *f.*

cutoff *n (limit)* limite.

cutout *n (on machine)* disjuntor; figura para recortar.

cut-price *(UK),* **cut-rate** *(US) adj* a preço reduzido.

cutter *n* cortador *m.*

cut-throat *n* assassino; ♦ *adj* impiedoso, feroz.

cuttlefish *n* choco *m.*

CV *(abbr for* **Curriculum Vitae**).

cyan *n, adj (colour)* ciano,-a.

cwt *(abbr for* **hundredweight**).

cyanide *n (CHEM)* cianeto *m.*

cyber- *pref (COMP)* ciber-.

cybercafé *n (COMP)* cibercafé *m.*

cyberculture *n (COMP)* cibercultura *f.*

cybernetics *n (COMP)* cibernética *f.*

cyberspace *n (COMP)* ciberespaço *m.*

cyclamen *n (colour)* cíclame *m.*

cycle *n* ciclo *m;* **2** *(bicycle)* bicicleta; ♦ *vi* andar de bicicleta.

cyclic(al) *adj* cíclico,-a.

cycling *n* ciclismo; ~ **helmet** *n* capacete *m* de ciclismo.

cyclist *n* ciclista *m,f.*

cyclone *n* ciclone *m.*

cyclorama *n* ciclorama *m.*

cygnet *n* cisne *m* novo.

cylinder *n* cilindro; tubo; ~ **capacity** *n* capacidade *f* cilíndrica; ~ **head** *n* culatra *f,* cabeça *f* de cilindro.

cymbals *n (MUS)* címbalos *mpl; (fam)* pratos *mpl.*

Cymru *npr* nome dado ao País de Gales pelos seus habitantes (nome em galês).

cynic *n* cínico,-a.

cynical *adj* cínico.

cynicism *n* cinismo, ce(p)ticismo *m.*

cynophobia *n* cinofobia.

cypress *n (BOT)* cipreste *m.*

Cypriot *n adj* cipriota *m,f.*

Cyprus *npr* Chipre; **in** ~ no Chipre.

cyst *n* cisto.

cystic fibrosis *n (MED)* fibrose quística *f.*

cystitis *n* cistite *f.*

cytology *n (MED)* citologia *f.*

czar = **tsar** *n* czar *m.*

czarina = **tsarina** *n* czarina.

Czech *npr adj* checo,-a.

Czechoslovakia *npr (the former)* Checoslováquia, *(BR)* Tchecoslováquia.

Czech Republic *npr* República Checa.

d

D, d *n (letter)* D, d.

D *n (MUS)* ré; **D sharp** ré sustenido; **2** *(school marks)* medíocre.

D. *(US) (POL) (abbr for Democrat, Democratic)* democrata *m,f;* democrático,-a.

D/A *adj (abbr for Digital to Analogue)* D/A.

DA *(abbr for District Attorney) (US) (EP)* Procurador da República, *(BR)* Promotor/Procurador público.

dab *n* pincelada; **2** gota, pequena quantidade *f;* ♦ *(pt, pp dabbed) vt* tocar ligeiramente; pintar de leve.

dabble *vt (splash, dip)* salpicar, molhar *(hands);* ♦ *vi:* **to ~ in** interessar-se por.

dab hand *n (UK) (fam)* **to be a ~ at sth** ser um craque em algo.

dab on *vt* aplicar um pouco de *(algo)* em; aplicar ligeiramente

dactyl *n* dáctilo *m;* dedo *m.*

dactylogram *n* impressão *f* digital, dactilograma *m.*

dactylology *n (EDUC)* dactilologia, quirologia *f.*

dad, daddy *n* papá *m,* paizinho, *(BR)* papai *m;* **daddy-longlegs** *n (insect)* pernilongo.

Dada *n* dada; dadaísmo.

dado *(pl: dadoes) (ARCH)* dado *m;* corpo *m* de pedestal, lambrim *m.*

daffodil *n (BOT)* narciso-dos-prados *m.*

daft *adj* estúpido,-a, idiota *m,f, (BR)* bobo; **to be ~ about** ser louco por.

dagger *n* punhal *m,* adaga *f;* **to look ~s at sb** lançar olhares fulminantes a alguém.

dago *n (pej) (person of Portuguese or Spanish origin in the USA)* luso-americano, hispano-americano.

dahlia *n (BOT)* dália *f.*

Dahomey *npr (GEOG)* Daomé; **in ~** no Daomé.

daily *n (newspaper)* diário *m;* **2** *(cleaner)* mulher *f* a dias, *(BR)* diarista; ♦ *adj* diário,-a, **2** quotidiano,-a, *(BR)* cotidiano,-a; **on a ~ basis** ser pago ao dia; ao dia/por dia; ♦ *adv* diariamente, cada dia, todos os dias: **twice ~** duas vezes por dia.

daintily *adv* delicadamente, graciosamente; **to eat ~** comer com delicadeza.

dainty *adj* delicado,-a; gracioso,-a; ♦ guloseima *f.*

dairy *n (shop)* leitaria *f, (BR)* leiteria *f;* **2** *(farm) n* vacaria *f;* ♦ *adj (industry)* indústria *f* de la(c)ticínios; **~ farming** criação *f* de vacas leiteiras, *(BR)* fazenda de gado leiteiro; **~ produce** *n* produtos *mpl* lá(c)teos, la(c)ticínios.

dais *n* estrado *m,* tablado *m.*

daisy *n (BOT)* pequeno malmequer *m,* margarida *f;* IDIOM **fresh as a ~** fresco como uma alface; **pushing up the daisies** (estar) morto e enterrado.

daisy wheel *n (COMP, TYPO)* margarida *f* de impressão; **~ printer** *n* impressora *f* de margarida.

Dakar *npr (GEOG)* Dacar; **in ~** em Dacar.

Dalai Lama *npr:* **the ~** o Dalai Lama.

dale *n* vale *m;* **the Dales** (= **Yorkshire Dales**) os Vales de Yorkshire; **2** *(horse)* uma raça de cavalos de Yorkshire.

dally *vt* perder tempo; **2 to ~ with** agir frivolamente *(com).*

dalmatian *n (ZOOL)* dálmata *m.*

daltonian *adj (MED)* daltónico *(BR:* -tô-).

daltonism *n (MED)* daltonismo *m.*

dam *n (across river)* represa, barragem *f,* dique, açude *m;* ♦ *(pt, pp -med) vt* represar; **2** construir barragem em *(river);* **to ~ up** *(block up)* obstruir, bloquear.

damage *n* dano, estrago *m;* **2** avaria *f;* **3** *(JUR)* prejuízo; **~s** *npl (JUR)* inde(m)nização *f* por perdas e danos; **~s to property** *npl* danos materiais; ♦ *vt* prejudicar, danificar.

damaging *adj* **(to)** prejudicial *m,f.*

Damascus *npr* Damasco.

dame *n (US) (coll)* tipa, gaja; **Dame** *n (UK)* título honorífico concedido a uma mulher por serviços prestados ao país.

dammit! (= **damn it**) *exc* bolas!; raios!

damn *n* praga, maldição *f;* **2** *(coll) (not caring)* **I don't give a ~** tanto me faz; estou-me nas tintas **(to do para fazer)** (para alguém algo) *(fam);* ♦ *exc* **~ you!** maldito sejas, raios te partam *(fam);* **2 ~ your job!** que se lixe o teu emprego! **3** *(coll)* raios!, bolas!, *(BR)* droga!; ♦ *adj* **~ the boy** o maldito do rapaz; ♦ *adv* raio, diabo; **~ the man** o raio do homem; **2 ~ near** quase, prestes a; **I ~ near told him to go** eu quase lhe disse para ir-se embora; ♦ *vt (REL)* condenar, censurar; **2** *(curse)* amaldiçoar, maldizer; **3 ~ sb for sth** culpar alguém por algo.

damnable *adj (coll)* condenável, horrível *m,f.*

damnation *n* danação *f,* maldição *f.*

damned *n:* **the ~** *(REL)* os condenados; ♦ *adj (REL)* condenado,-a; **2** *(accursed)* maldito,-a; *(Vd:* **damn**); **I'll be ~ if ...** diabos me levem, raios me partam se ...; **I'll be ~!** *(expressing surprise)* essa agora!; **I'll be ~ if I know!** sei lá!, como se eu soubesse!, diabos me levem se eu ...; ♦ *adv (intensifier)* muito *(really);* **she is ~ beautiful** ela é linda a valer.

damnedest *n (fam) (utmost):* **do your ~** faz todos os possíveis.

damning *adj* grave *m,f;* prejudicial; **~ evidence** prova grave/incriminatória.

damp *n* (h)umidade *f;* **~ course** *(also:* **~-proof course)** *n* impermeabilização *f;* ♦ *adj* (h)úmido; molhado; ♦ *vt* (= **-en**) molhar levemente, *(BR, prov)* jogar água fria em; **2** (h)umedecer; **3** *(fig) (emotion)* esfriar.

damp down *vt (fire)* abafar; extinguir; **2** *(sound)* amortecer; **3** *(enthusiasm)* desanimar; reduzir.

dampen *vt* molhar levemente; **2** *(joy, emotion) (fig)* esfriar; *(BR, Reg)* jogar água fria em; **3** (h)umedecer.

dampness *n* (h)umidade *f.*

damsel *n (LIT)* donzela, menina; ~ **in distress** uma donzela em perigo.

damson *n (fruit)* abrunho *m*; ~ **tree** *n* abrunheiro *m*.

dance *n* dança *f*; baile *m*; ~ **floor** pista de dança; ~ **hall** salão *m* de baile; ♦ *vt* bailar, dançar; **to ~ about** saltitar.

dancer *n* dançarino,-a; bailarino,-a.

dancing *n* dança *f*, baile *m*.

dandelion *n (BOT)* dente-de-leão *m*.

dandle *vt (up and down)* mover, balouçar uma criança nos joelhos; **2** *(in one's arms)* embalar.

dandruff *n* caspa *f*.

dandy *(pl:* -**ies**) *n (man who likes to dress well)* janota *m*; ♦ *adj (coll: US)* excelente, ótimo; *(BR)* bacana.

Dane *npr* dinamarquês,-esa.

danger *n* perigo; risco; **to be in ~ of** correr o risco de; **there is a ~ of** … há o risco de …; **out of ~** fora de perigo; **in ~** em perigo; ~ **list** *(MED)* na lista dos pacientes graves *(hospital list)*; **on the ~ list** *(MED) (patient)* num estado crítico, grave; ~ **money** prémio *m* de risco *m*; ~ **zone** zona de perigo.

dangerous *adj* perigoso,-a.

dangerously *adv* perigosamente.

dangle *vt/vi (keys, rope, etc)* suspender; **2** *(swing legs, feet)* baloiçar; balançar; **3** *(enticing)* **he ~d the ruby before his eyes** ele baloiçava/oscilava o rubi diante de seus olhos.

Danish *npr adj* dinamarquês,-esa; *(LING)* dinamarquês *m*; **2** ~ **pastry** *n* doce *m* (de massa com frutas).

dank *adj* frio e (h)úmido.

Danube *npr (GEOG)* (o rio) Danúbio.

dapper *adj* garboso,-a, brioso,-a.

dappled *adj (animal)* malhado,-a; ~-**grey** *(US:* **gray**) *n (horse)* cavalo cinzento-malhado; **2** *(shade)* cinzento malhado.

Dardanelles *npr pl (GEOG)* **the ~** o estreito *m* de Dardanelos.

dare *n* audácia, ousadia *f*; **2** *(have the cheek)* atrevimento *(fam)*; ♦ *vt:* **to ~ sb to do sth** desafiar alguém a fazer algo; ♦ *vi:* **to ~ (to) do sth** atrever-se a/ousar fazer algo; **I ~ say** acho provável que; **how ~ you!** como se atreve!

daredevil *n* intrépido,-a, audacioso,-a, arrojado,-a.

daren't = **dare not**.

daring *adj* arrojado,-a, ousado,-a; *(cheeky)* atrevido,-a *(fam)*.

dark *n* escuridão *f*; **to get ~ anoitecer**, escurecer *m*; **D~ Ages** *npr pl* a Idade Média *fsg*, a idade *f* das trevas; *(fig)* **the ~ forces** *npl (evil)* as forças do mal; **in the ~** às escuras, na escuridão; **at ~** ao anoitecer; **to be left in the ~** *(about sth) (fig)* ser deixado,-a ignorante (sobre algo); **to be in the ~** estar no escuro, desconhecer; ♦ *adj* escuro,-a; ~ **blue** azul-escuro *m*; **2** *(complexion)* moreno,-a; **3** *(sad)* triste, sombrio,-a; **4** *(fig)* secreto,-a; **keep it ~!** guarda segredo!; **5** sinistro,-a, negro,-a; ~ **chocolate** *n* chocolate *m* amargo; ~ **glasses** *npl* óculos *mpl* escuros; ~ **room** *n (PHOT)* câmara *f* escura; IDIOM **to look on the ~ side** ver só o lado negro das coisas, ser pessimista *m,f*.

darken *vt* escurecer; **2** *(make dark)* obscurecer *(sky, sun)*; ♦ *vi* escurecer-se, anuviar-se; *(face, expression)* toldar-se.

darkened *(pt, pp of* **darken**) *adj (house, street, countenance)* sombrio,-a.

dark horse *n (enigmatic person)* enigma *m*, mistério *m*; **you are a ~** você é um mistério; **2** *(US) (POL)* candidato surpresa.

darkly *adv* de forma sombria.

darkness *n* escuridão *f*, trevas *fpl*; **plunged in the ~** mergulhado nas trevas.

dark-skinned *adj* moreno,-a.

darling *n adj* querido,-a.

darn¹ *(exc)* damn; **this ~ car won't start** este maldito carro não pega.

darn² *vt* remendar *(patches)*; cerzir passajar *(socks)*; ~**ing needle** *n* agulha *f* de cerzir.

darnel *n (BOT)* joio *m*.

dart *n* dardo *m*; **2** movimento rápido; **3** *(in sewing)* costura *f* afunilada; ♦ *vt* lançar, arremessar; ♦ *vi* precipitar-se; sair precipitadamente; ~**board** *n* alvo.

darts *n* jogo *m* de dardos.

dash *n (punctuation mark) (long)* travessão *m*; *(short)* hífen *m*, traço *m*; **2** *(rush)* correria; **3** *(bit)* pequena quantidade, pitada *f*; ♦ *vt (hurl)* arremessar; **2** *(fig) (hopes)* frustrar, desfazer; ♦ *vi* ir depressa, precipitar-se; **to ~ off** *vi (a letter)* escrever rapidamente, rabiscar; **2** *(go out)* sair a correr.

dashboard *n* painel *m* de instrumentos.

dashing *adj (handsome young man)* elegante, atraente, jeitoso, catita; *(lively)* vivaz.

data *npl (COMP)* dados *mpl*; *n* informação *f*; ~**bank** *n* banco m de dados; ~**base** *n* base *f* de dados; ~ **capture** *n* entrada de dados; ~ **management** *n (COMP)* gerenciamento *m* de dados; ~ **processing** *n* processamento de dados, informática; ~ **transmission** *n* transmissão de dados.

date¹ *n (BOT)* tâmara *f*; *(tree)* tamareira *f*.

date² *n (in time)* data *f*; ~ **of birth** *(d.o.b.)* *n* data *f* de nascimento; ~**book** *n (US)* agenda *f*; **closing ~** data de encerramento; ~**line** *n* meridiano ou linha *f* de data; **out of ~** *(edition, coursebook)* desa(c)tualizado; **up-to-~** moderno, a(c)tualizado; **to bring up to ~** *(correspondence)* pôr em dia; *(method)* modernizar; ~ **rape** *n* estupro após um encontro social; ~ **stamp** carimbo *m* datador; **2** *(with friend)* encontro *m*; **she is my ~** ela é a minha namorada; ♦ *adv* **at a later ~** mais tarde; ♦ *vt* datar; **2** *(to go out with sb)* sair com alguém, namorar; ♦ *vi (originate)* **to ~ from** datar de; **to ~ back to** remontar a; **the cathedral ~s back to the 15th century** a catedral remonta ao século XV.

dated *adj (old, ancient)* antiquado,-a; **2** *(style)* fora de moda; ultrapassado,-a.

dateless *adj* sem data; imemorável *m,f*.

dateline *n (newspaper)* cabeçalho *(do artigo)*.

dating *n* datação *f*; ~ **agency** *n* agência de contatos.

dating agency *n* clube *m* de encontros.

dative *n adj (gram)* dativo,-a.

daub *n (coll)* borrada, mancha *f;* ♦ *vt* borrar, manchar (algo); **to ~ paint on a wall** esborratar uma parede; pintar sem cuidado.

daughter *n* filha; **~-in-law** *n* nora.

daunt *vt* intimidar; **2** desanimar, desalentar.

daunting *adj (prospect)* desanimador,-ora; *(work)* assustador,-ora; **2** *(person)* intimidante *m,f.*

dauntless *adj* destemido,-a, intrépido,-a.

dawdle *vi (waste time)* perder tempo; andar devagar.

dawn *n* madrugada *f,* alvorada *f,* amanhecer *m;* ♦ *vi* amanhecer; **2** *(fig)* despertar; **~ (up) on** aperceber-se de; **it ~ed on me that** … comecei a perceber que …; ♦ **at ~** ao amanhecer; **~ chorus** *n* canto dos pássaros na alvorada; **from ~ to dusk** de manhã à noite; **at the crack of ~** ao romper da manhã.

day *n* dia *m;* **2** *(working)* dia útil; **the ~ before** véspera; **the ~ before yesterday** anteontem; **the following ~** o dia seguinte; **the ~ after tomorrow** (o dia) depois de amanhã; **all/whole ~** todo o dia, todo o santo dia *(fam);* **by ~** de dia; **~ in ~ out** dia após dia; **every other ~** dia sim dia não; **every ~** todos os dias; **the ~ to ~** *(routine)* o dia-a-dia; **these ~s/nowadays** hoje em dia; **in three ~'s time** daqui a três dias; **the good old ~s** os bons velhos tempos; **the ~s gone by** outrora, antigamente; **wiser by the ~** cada vez mais sensato; **to be on a ~'s release** ter dispensa de um dia; **open ~** dia de visitas, casa aberta; **~ return (ticket)** *n* bilhete de ida e volta; **~ shift** *n* turno *m* diurno; **~ student** *n* estudante *m,f* externo; **~time** *n* dia; **in the ~ time** durante o dia; **~-tripper** excursionista *m,f;* IDIOM **to make a ~ of it** aproveitar o dia; **to call it a ~** dar por terminado (o dia de trabalho).

daybreak *n, vt* amanhecer.

daydream *n* devaneio *m.*

daydreamer *adj* sonhador,-ora.

daylight *n* luz *f* do dia; **in broad ~** à luz do dia, em pleno dia; **~ saving time, DST** *n* hora *f* de verão.

day-to-day *adj* diário, quotidiano.

daze *n*: **in a ~** aturdido,-a; ♦ *vt* aturdir.

dazzle *vt* deslumbrar; **I was ~d by her beauty** fiquei deslumbrado com a beleza dela; **2** *(lights)* encadear.

dazzling *adj* deslumbrante *m,f.*

DBE *npr (abbr for* **Dame Commander of the Order of the British Empire)** (agraciada com a distinção de:) Comendadora da Ordem do Império Britânico.

DBS *(abbr for* **direct broadcasting direct by satellite)** transmissão *f* dire(c)ta via satélite.

DC *(abbr for* **direct current)** *(ELECT)* corrente contínua ou galvânica; CC.

DD *(abbr for* **Doctor of Divinity)** título universitário.

dd. *(abbr for* **delivered)** entregue.

D-day *n* dia *m* D.

DDE *(abbr for* **Dynamic Data Exchange)** *(COMP)* intercâmbio dinâmico de dados; **2** *(abbr for* **Direct Data Entry)** entrada dire(c)ta de dados.

deacon *n* diácono *m;* **2** *(lay assistant)* acólito *m.*

deaconess *n* diaconisa *f.*

deactivate *vt* desativar.

dead *n* morto,-a; falecido,-a, defunto; **the ~** *npl* os mortos *mpl;* ♦ *adj* morto,-a; **2** *(telephone)* cortado; **3** *(ELECT)* desligado, sem corrente; **4** *(insensitive)* dormente; ♦ **~ duck** *n (coll)* fracasso *m;* **~ drunk** a cair de bêbedo; **~ easy** *(coll)* bastante fácil; **~ letter** *n (fig) (law)* letra *f* morta; **~line** *n* prazo final; **~lock** *n* impasse *m;* **~locked** *adj* paralisado,-a; **~ season** *n (turism)* baixa estação *f;* **~stock** *n* apetrechos/equipamento da quinta; **~ tired** morto de cansaço; estafado,-a; **~ weight** *n* peso *m* morto; **2** *(US) (unproductive staff)* pessoal a mais; **~ wood** *n (fig) (fam)* estorvo *m;* ♦ *adv* completamente; ♦ **to stop ~** estacar.

deadbeat *n (US) (coll) (lazy)* mandrião *m,* mandriona *f.*

deaden *vt (blow, sound)* amortecer; **2** *(pain, sorrow)* aliviar, abrandar.

dead end *n (street)* beco sem saída; **2** *(fig)* impasse *m;* **dead-end job** *n* emprego *m* sem perspectivas.

deadhead *n (fig) (stupid)* cabeça *f* oca; ♦ *vt* tirar as folhas secas (das plantas).

dead heat *n (SPORT)* empate *m.*

dead loss *n (COMM)* perda *f* sem indemnização; **2** *(coll) (useless person)* traste *m,f;* **to be a ~** ser um zero à esquerda; **3** *(thing)* não prestar para nada.

deadly (-ier, -iest) *adj* mortal, fatal; **2** *(weapon)* mortífero; **3** preciso,-a, exato,-a; ♦ *adv (extremely)* terrivelmente.

deadly nightshade *n* beladona *f.*

deadpan *adj (person, face)* sem expressão.

dead ringer *n* sósia **(of sb** de alguém).

Dead Sea *npr (GEOG)* **the ~** o Mar Morto.

deaf *adj* surdo; **~-mute** *n* surdo-mudo; **stone-~** *adj* surdo como uma porta *(fam).*

deafen *vt* ensurdecer.

deafening *adj* ensurdecedor,-ora

deafness *n* surdez *f.*

deal *n* acordo; **2** *(COMM)* transa(c)ção *f,* negócio *m;* **3** *(cards)* mão *f,* distribuição *f;* ♦ *(pt, pp* **dealt)** *vt (cards)* dar; **to strike a ~ with sb** fechar um negócio com alguém; **it's a ~** *(coll)* negócio *m* fechado; **a great ~ (of)** bastante, muito; **to ~ in** negociar; **to ~ with** *vt (people)* tratar com/de, ocupar-se de; *(COMM)* negociar com.

dealer *n* negociante *m,f;* *(for cars)* concessionário,-a; **2** *(for products)* revendedor,-ora; **scrap ~** *n* ferro-velho, sucateiro,-a.

dealings *npl* negócios *mpl,* relações *fpl,* transacções *fpl.*

dean *n (REL)* decano *m;* **2** *(UK, EDUC)* reitor,-ora de faculdade *m,f; (US)* orientador,-ora de estudos.

dear *n (affectionate)* querido,-a; **my ~** meu querido, minha querida; ♦ *adj (~er, ~est)* caro,-a; *(form of address on formal/business letters)* **D~ Sir/Madam** Caro Senhor/Cara Senhora; *(very formal)* Exmo (excelentíssimo) Senhor/Exma Senhora; **2** *(costly)* **it is very ~** isso é muito caro; ♦ *adv* **that mistake has cost me ~** esse erro saiu-me caro; ♦ *exc* **~ me!** oh meu Deus!

dearly *adv* caro,-a; **2** *(lovingly)* carinhosamente.

dearth *n* escassez *f,* carência *f.*

death *n* morte *f*; *(ADMIN) n* óbito; ~**bed** *n* leito de morte; **to be at ~'s door** estar à beira da morte; ~ **certificate** *n* certidão *f* de óbito; ~ **duties** *npl (JUR)* imposto de transmissão *f causa mortis*; ~ **knell** *n (of church bell)* dobre a finados; **2** *(fig)* prenúncio de morte ou desastre; *f*; ~ **penalty** *n* pena de morte; ~ **rate** *n* (índice *m* de) mortalidade *f*; ~ **row** *n (US)* corredor *m* da morte; ~ **sentence** *n* sentença de morte; ~ **squad** *n* esquadrão *m* da morte; ~-**toll** *n* número de mortos *(em acidentes)*; ~-**trap** *n* perigo; **this street is a** ~-**trap** esta rua é perigosíssima; ~-**watch** *n (vigil)* velório m.

deathly *adj* mortal; **2** *(ghostly)* pálido,-a; **3** *(silence)* profundo,-a, sepulcral *m,f*; ♦ *adv* mortalmente.

deb *n (abbr for* **debutante***)* debutante *f*.

debacle *n* fracasso *m*.

debar *vt* excluir, privar de; **to ~ sb from doing sth** proibir alguém de fazer algo.

debase *vt* degradar, desvalorizar, agravar.

debatable *adj* discutível *m,f*.

debate *n* debate *m*; ♦ *vt* debater, discutir; ♦ *vi*: **to ~ whether** perguntar-se se..., perguntar a si mesmo se...

debauchery *n* libertinagem *f*, deboche *m*.

debenture *n (bond)* obrigação do Tesouro; *(BR)* debênture; ~ **market** mercado *f* obrigacionista.

debilitate *vt* debilitar.

debilitating *adj* debilitante *m,f*.

debit *n* débito; ~ **balance** *n* saldo devedor; **direct ~** dèbito *m* dire(c)to; ~ **note** *n* nota de débito; ♦ *vt*: **to ~ a sum** debitar uma quantia.

debrief *vt* interrogar; **2** fazer o relatório oral (de uma missão); **3** recolher o testemunho *m* de.

debriefing *n* interrogatório *m*.

debris *n* escombros *mpl*; **2** *(rubbish)* lixo *m*.

debt *n* dívida; **to be in ~** ter dívidas; **bad ~** dívida incobrável; ~ **collector** *n* cobrador,-ora de dívidas; **national ~** *n* dívida pública.

debtor *n* devedor,-ora.

debug (**gg**) *vt* remover as escutas de; **2** *(COMP) (program)* depurar.

debunk *vt (myths, ideas)* desvendar, desmascarar.

début *n* estreia *f*.

Dec. *(abbr for* **December***)* dez.

decade *n* década *f*.

decadence *n* decadência *f*.

decadent *adj* decadente *m,f*.

decaf *n (fam)* café *m* descafeinado.

decaffeinated *adj* descafeinado.

decagon *n* decágono *m*.

decahedron *n* decaedro *m*.

decal *n (US)* adesivo *m* decalque *m*.

decalcify *vt* descalcificar.

decamp *vi (coll)* safar-se, esquivar-se; escapulir-se.

decant *vt (wine)* decantar.

decanter *n* garrafa ornamental.

decarbonize *vt (AUT)* descarbonizar.

decay *n* decadência *f*; ruína *f*; **2** *(fig)* deterioração *f*; podridão *f*; **tooth ~** cárie *f*; ♦ *vi* apodrecer-se; deteriorar-se; **2** *(fig)* decair.

decease *n* morte *f*, falecimento, óbito *m*; ♦ *vi* falecer, morrer.

deceased *n* defunto,-a, falecido,-a.

deceit *n* engano *m*; fraude *f*.

deceitful *adj* enganador,-ora, *(BR)* enganoso,-a; fraudulento,-a.

deceive *vt* enganar, iludir.

decelerate *vt* moderar a marcha de, desacelerar.

December *npr* dezembro *m*.

decency *n (respectability)* decência *f*; **2** boas maneiras *fpl*; **3** *(morality)* noção *f* da moral.

decent *adj* decente *m,f*; **sorry, but I am not ~** desculpe, mas não estou vestido,-a devidamente; **he is a ~ chap** ele é um rapaz, homem honesto, bem educado.

decently *adv* decentemente.

decentralization *n* descentralização *f*.

decentralize *vt* descentralizar.

deception *n* engano, decepção *f*, fraude *f*.

deceptive *adj (appearance)* enganador,-ora.

decibel *n (sound)* decibel.

decide *vt (person)* decide; ♦ *vi* decidir-se; **to ~ on sth** decidir-se por algo; **to ~ on/against doing** decidir fazer/não fazer.

decided *adj* decidido,-a; nítido,-a, definido,-a.

decidedly *adv* decididamente.

deciding *adj* decisivo,-a.

deciduous *adj (BOT)* decíduo,-a; caduco,-a; efémero,-a *(BR: -fê-)*.

decimal *n (MATH)* fra(c)ção *f* decimal; **2** *adj* decimal; ~ **point** *n* vírgula de decimais.

decimalize *(UK) vt* decimalizar.

decimate *vt* dizimar.

decimetre *n (measurement)* decímetro *m*.

decipher *vt (writing)* decifrar.

decision *n (gen)* decisão *f*, **to take a ~** tomar uma decisão; **2** determinação *f*; ~-**making** tomada *f* de decisão.

decisive *adj* decisivo,-a; categórico,-a.

deck *n (NAUT)* convés *m*; **2** *(on bus, plane)* andar *m*; **3** *(of cards)* baralho *m*; **3 to go up on ~** subir ao convés; ♦ *vt* enfeitar, ornamentar; **to ~ out** enfeitar-se.

deckchair *n* cadeira de lona, espreguiçadeira.

deckhand *n* taifeiro,-a.

decking *n* soalho *m* no terraço *ou* jardim.

declaim *vt* declamar, discursar.

declamation *n* declamação *f*.

declamatory *adj (US)* declamatório, enfático.

declaration *n* declaração *f*.

declare *vt/vi* declarar; **to ~ for/against sb/sth** pronunciar-se a favor/contra de alguém/algo.

declassify *vt* tornar público.

decline *n* declínio *m*; **2** *(ECON)* diminuição *f*, baixa, decréscimo *m*; ♦ *vt* recusar, declinar; ♦ *vi* decair; diminuir; baixar; ~ **in living standards** quebra *f* nos padrões de vida; **to ~ to do sth** recusar-se a fazer algo.

declutch *vi* desengatar, desembrear, *(BR)* debrear.

decode *vt* decifrar, descodificar.

decoder *n* descodificador *m*.

decolonization (*also*: **-isation**) *n* descolonização *f*.
decompensation *n* (*MED*) de(s)compensação *f*.
decompose *vi* decompor-se.
decomposition *n* decomposição *f*; **2** (*PHYS*) desintegração *f*.
decompress *vt* descomprimir; ♦ *vt* (*COMP*) descompactar.
decompression *n* descompressão *f*; ~ **chamber** *n* câmara de descompressão.
decongestant *n* (*MED*) descongestionante *m*.
deconstruct *vt* (*LING*) desconstruir.
deconstruction *n* (*LING*) desconstrução *f*.
decontaminate *vt* descontaminar.
decontrol *vt* (*prices, etc*) liberar, liberalizar.
décor *n* decoração *f*; (*THEAT*) cenário *m*.
decorate *vt* ornamentar, decorar; **2** (*the room*) pintar; decorar com papel de parede.
decoration *n* (*on garment*) adorno, enfeite *m*; **2** ~ **work** (*by painter*) trabalhos de decoração *f*; **3** (*MIL*) condecoração *f*.
decorative *adj* decorativo,-a.
decorator *n* pintor,-ora; **interior** ~ *n* decorador,-ora de interiores.
decorum *n* decoro *m*.
decoy *n* engodo, chamariz *m*; ♦ *vt* atrair, apanhar.
decrease *n* diminuição *f*, redução *f*; ♦ *vt* diminuir, reduzir; **to be on the** ~ estar a diminuir; ♦ *vi* reduzir-se.
decreasing *adj* decrescente.
decree *n* (*JUR*) decreto *m*, ordem; *f*; **2** (*judgement*) sentença; deliberação *f*; ♦ *vt* decretar; ~ **nisi** *n* (*JUR*) (*in divorce*) ordem *f* provisória de divórcio; ~ **absolute** *n* sentença *f* final de divórcio.
decrepit *adj* decrépito,-a; (*building*) a cair aos pedaços.
decrepitude *n* (*US*) decrepitude *f*, velhice *f*.
decriminalize (*also*: **-ise**) *vt* liberalizar (*the category of the crime*).
decry (*pt*, *pp* **-ied**) *vt* denegrir, decriminalizar; **2** depreciar; censurar.
dedicate *vt* dedicar; consagrar.
dedicated *adj* dedicado,-a.
dedication *n* dedicação *f*; **2** (*in a book*) dedicatória *f*; **3** (*on radio*) mensagem *f*.
deduce *vt*: ~ **sth from sth** deduzir (algo de algo).
deduct *vt* deduzir; **2** descontar.
deductible *adj* dedutível *m,f*.
deduction *n* (*conclusion*) dedução; **2** (*FIN*, *ECON*) (*on wages*) retenção *f*; **3** (*on price, bill*) desconto, abatimento *m*; **4** (*MATH*) subtra(c)ção *f*.
deed *n* feito *m*, façanha *f*; **2** (*JUR*) escritura, título; **3** (*JUR*) ~ **poll** *n* alteração *f* de nome; ~ **of covenant** *n* escritura *f* de transferência; **title** ~ *n* (*JUR*) título *m* de propriedade.
deem *vt* julgar, supor, crer; **to** ~ **highly** ter em grande consideração; **to** ~ **it wise to do** julgar prudente fazer.
deep *adj* profundo,-a; ~ **grief** desgosto profundo; **2** fundo,-a; ~ **bowl** tigela funda; ~ **fat fryer** *n* (*for chips, etc*) frigideira *f* por imersão; ~ **freeze** *n* congelador *m*; ~ **mourning** *m* luto *m* pesado; ~-**rooted** *adj* enraizado, profundo; ~-**sea fishing** *n*

pesca *f* de alto-mar; ~-**seated** *adj* (*beliefs*) arraigado; ~-**set** *adj* (*eyes*) fundo, encovado; **he took a** ~ **breath** ele respirou fundo; **3** (*voice, sound*) baixo,-a, grave *m,f*; ~ **voice** voz grave; **4** (*carpet, snow*) espesso,-a; **I had my feet** ~ **in mud** eu tinha os pés enterrados na lama; **5** (*colour*) escuro,-a, intenso,-a; ~ **green eyes** olhos dum verde intenso; **6** (*absorbed*) ~ **in thought/book** absorto,-a em; ♦ *adv* fundo, profundidade; **to be 3 metres** ~ ter 3 metros de profundidade; **to be** ~ **in debt** estar endividado até ao pescoço; **he had his hands** ~ **in his pockets** ele tinha as mãos enfiadas nos bolsos; (*long way in*) ~ **in the city** no coração da cidade; IDIOM **to be in** ~ **water** (*trouble*) estar em maus lençóis.
deepen *vt/vi* aprofundar(-se), aumentar; intensificar.
deep end *n* tanque *m* grande; IDIOM **to jump in at the** ~ pegar o touro pelos cornos (*fam*).
deepening *adj* (*problem*) cada vez mais grave.
deeply *adv* profundamente, sinceramente; **to go** ~ **into sth** analisar algo; estudar em profundidade.
deepness *n* profundidade *f*.
deer *n* (*ZOOL*) veado *m*, cervo *m*; ~ **skin** *n* camurça, pele *f* de cervo; ~ **stalker** *n* caçador de veados; **2** (*hat*) chapéu de abas.
deface *vt* desfigurar, deformar.
defamation *n* difamação *f*, calúnia.
defamatory *adj* difamatório, difamante.
defame *vt* difamar, caluniar.
default *vi* não pagar; **2** (*SPORT*) não comparecer; (*JUR*) inadimplemento; **by** ~ (*JUR*) à revelia; (*SPORT*) por ausência; ~ **value** *n* (*COMP*) valor *m* de default; ~ **option** *n* (*COMP*) opção *f* de default.
defaulter *n* devedor,-ora; **2** incumpridor,-ora.
defeat *n* derrota *f*; ♦ *vt* derrotar, vencer; **2** (*efforts*) frustrar.
defeatism *n* derrotismo.
defeatist *n adj* derrotista *m,f*.
defecate *vi* defecar.
defecation *n* defecação *f*.
defect *n* defeito, falha; ♦ *vi* (*MIL*) deserter (**from**, de).
defective *adj* defeituoso,-a.
defector *n* trânsfuga *m,f*, dissidente *m,f*; (*POL*) asilado *m* político; **physical/mental** ~ defeito físico/ mental.
defence *n* defesa *f*; **in** ~ **of** em defesa de; **the Ministry of D**~ Ministério da Defesa; **self-**~ *n* legítima defesa, auto-defesa.
defenceless *adj* indefeso.
defend *vt/vr* defender(-se), proteger(-se); (*JUR*) contestar.
defendant *n* (*JUR*) acusado,-a; réu/ré *m,f*.
defender *n* defensor,-ora.
defending champion *n* (*SPORT*) a(c)tual campeão,-peã.
defending counsel *n* (*JUR*) advogado(a) de defesa.
defensive *adj* defensivo,-a; **on the** ~ na defensiva.
defer *vt* adiar; ♦ *vi* submeter-se (**to** a).
deference *n* deferência, respeito, consideração *f*; **in** ~ **of** em deferência a.

deferential *adj* deferente *m,f.*
deferment, deferral *n* adiamento *m.*
deferred *adj* diferido,-a.
defiance *n* desafio *m;* provocação *f;* desobediência *f;* **in** ~ **of** sem respeito por; indiferente a.
defiant *adj* provocador,-ora; desafiador,-ora.
defiantly *adv* desafiadoramente.
defibrillation *n* desfibrilador *m.*
deficiency *n* deficiência *f;* falta *f;* imperfeição *f.*
deficient *adj* deficiente; incompleto; imperfeito; ~ **in** falto de, carente de.
deficit *n* (ECON) deficit *m,* défice *m;* **trade** ~ *n* deficit *m* na balança comercial; **2** falta (**in**, **de**).
defile¹ *n* (gorge) desfildeiro *m;* soldados em fila indiana.
defile² *vt* (holy place) profanar; **2** (purity) macular; **3** (reputation) manchar.
defilement *n* profanação *f;* maculação *f.*
define *vt* definir; determinar.
definite *adj* definitivo; claro, categórico; **he was** ~ **about it** ele foi categórico; ~ **article** *n* (gram) artigo definido.
definitely *adv* claramente, sem dúvida.
definition *n* definição *f;* (PHOT) nitidez *f.*
definitive *adj* definitivo,-a, conclusivo,-a.
deflate *vt* (baloon, tyre) esvaziar; (fig) (person) diminuir; **2** (ECON) deflacionar.
deflation *n* (ECON) deflação *f.*
deflationary *adj* (ECON) deflacionário,-a.
deflect *vt/vi* desviar(-se).
deflection *n* desvio *m.*
deflower *vt* (LIT) (virgin) desflorar.
defog *vt* (US) (AUT) desembaciar, (BR) desembaçar.
defogger *n* (US) (AUT) desembaciador *m,* (BR) desembaçador *m.*
deforest *vt* (clear forest of vegetation) desflorestar, desbravar.
deforestation *n* desflorestação *f,* desflorestamento *m,* desarborização *f.*
deform *vt* deformar; distorcer.
deformed *adj* deformado; desfigurado.
deformity *n* deformidade *f.*
deformation *n* deformação *f;* **2** (MED) *n* malformação *f.*
defraud *vt* defraudar (**sb of sth** alguém de algo); enganar.
defray *vt* (costs, expenses) pagar; custear.
defrock *vt* despadrar.
defrost *vt* descongelar.
defroster *n* (US) desembaciador *m* de pára-brisa(s), de parabrisas.
deft *adj* destro,-a, hábil *m,f;* (in movement) ágil *m,f.*
defunct *adj* (no longer operative) extinto,-a (company); **2** (person) morto,-a, defunto,-a, falecido,-a.
defuse *vt* (bomb) desa(c)tivar, tirar a espoleta de; **2** (situation) desagravar, atenuar.
defy *vt* opor-se a; desafiar; desobedecer.
degenerate *adj* degenerado,-a; ◆ *vi* degenerar, deteriorar, degradar(-se).
degeneration *n* degeneração *f.*
degenerative *adj* (MED) degenerativo,-a.

degradation *n* degradação *f.*
degrade *vt* degradar.
degrading *adj* degradante *m,f.*
degree *n* grau *m;* **five** ~**s below zero** cinco graus abaixo zero; **2** (EDUC) diploma *m,* título académico; ~ **in economics** formatura/licenciatura em economia; **by** ~**s** gradualmente, pouco a pouco; **to a certain** ~ até certo ponto; **third-** ~ **burns** *npl* queimaduras *fpl* de terceiro grau.
dehumanization (also: -**isation**) *n* desumanização *f.*
dehumanize (also: -**ise**) *vt/vr* desumanizar.
dehumidifier *n* desumidificador *m.*
dehydrate *vt* desidratar; ◆ *vi* desidratar-se.
dehydrated *adj* desidratado,-a.
dehydration *n* (MED) desidratação *f.*
de-ice *vt* descongelar.
de-icer *n* (AUT, etc) substância *f* descongelante; **2** dispositivo para remover o gelo.
deign *vi:* **to** ~ **to do** dignar-se a fazer.
deity *n* divindade *f,* deidade *f.*
dejected *adj* abatido, desanimado, deprimido; triste.
dejection *n* desânimo *m.*
delay *n* demora *f,* atraso *m;* ◆ *vt* demorar, atrasar; ◆ *vi* retardar-se, atrasar(-se); **to be** ~**ed** estar atrasado; **without** ~ sem demora, sem atraso.
delayed-action *adj* de a(c)ção retardada.
delectable *adj* delicioso,-a, aprazível *m,f;* ~ **places** locais *mpl* aprazíveis.
delegate *n* delegado,-a; ◆ *vt* delegar; **to** ~ **sth to sb/ sb to do sth** delegar algo a alguém/alguém para fazer algo.
delegation *n* delegação *f.*
delete *vt* eliminar, riscar; **2** (COMP) apagar, (BR) deletar.
deletion *n* exclusão *f.*
Delhi *npr* Delhi.
deliberate *adj* intencional; pausado, lento; **a** ~ **lie** uma mentira premeditada; ◆ *vi* deliberar.
deliberately *adv* de propósito; deliberadamente, lentamente.
deliberation *n* deliberação *f.*
delicacy *n* (tact) delicadeza *f;* **2** (food) iguaria *f.*
delicate *adj* (instrument) delicado,-a; **2** (china) frágil *m,f;* **3** (features) fino,-a; **4** ~ **health** saúde *f* débil, fraca; **5** ~ **taste** gosto *m* apurado; **6** (flavour, colour) suave; **7** (subject) sensível; **8** (touch) ligeiro,-a.
delicately *adv* delicadamente.
delicatessen *n* charcutaria *f.*
delicious *adj* delicioso,-a, saboroso,-a.
delight *n* prazer *m,* deleite *m;* **2** encanto, delícia; ◆ *vt* encantar, deleitar; **to take** ~ **in** deliciar-se com; ter prazer em.
delighted *adj* deleitado, deliciado; **to be** ~ **to do sth** ter muito prazer em fazer algo; **I'd be** ~ eu adoraria.
delightful *adj* encantador,-ora, delicioso,-a, aprazível *m,f.*
delimit *vt* delimitar.
delineate *vt* delinear; (fig) definir.
delinquency *n* delinquência *f;* **juvenile** ~ delinquência juvenil.

delinquent *n adj* delinquente *m,f.*

delirious *adj* delirante; **to be** ~ delirar.

delirium *n* delírio *m.*

deliver *vt* distribuir; **2** *(hand in)* entregar; **3** libertar; proferir *(sermon)*; **4** *(blow)* dar, desfechar; **to** ~ **the goods** *(fig)* dar conta do recado.

deliverance *n* libertação *f.*

delivered *adj* entregue; *(MED)* **to be** ~ **of** dar à luz.

delivery *n* entrega *f*; distribuição *f*; *(goods)* remessa *f*; **to take** ~ **of** receber; **2** *(MED)* *(birth)* parto; **3** *(liberation)* libertação *f*; **4** *(SPORT)* *(of ball)* arremesso *m*; ~ **note** *n* nota *f* de entrega; guia *f* de remessa; ~ **van** *(US:* ~ **truck)** camioneta de entrega; **recorded** ~ **letter** *(UK)* carta registada, *(BR)* registrada.

delta *n* delta *m.*

delude *vt* enganar, iludir.

deluge *n* dilúvio *m*; inundação *f*; ♦ *vt* inundar.

delusion *n* ilusão *f*, erro *m*; IDIOM **to have** ~**s of grandeur** ter mania de grandeza.

de luxe *adj (edition)* de luxo; **2** *(accomodation)* luxuoso,-a.

delve *vi:* **to** ~ **into** investigar, sondar, pesquisar.

Dem. *(abbr for* **Democrat, Democratic)** *(US)* Democrata; Democrático.

demagogic *adj* demagógico,-a.

demagogue *n* demagogo,-a.

demand *n* exigência *f*; **2** *(request)*, pedido *m*; **3** *(claim)* reclamação *f*; **4** *(ECON)* procura; **to be in** ~ *(popular)* ser muito, popular; ser muito concorrido,-a; ter muita procura; **today I am much in** ~ hoje estou a ser muito concorrido; **on** ~ a pedido; **supply and** ~ *n* oferta e procura *f*, *(BR)* oferta e demanda *f*; ♦ *vt* pedir; *(forcefully)* exigir, reclamar; **I** ~ **to know** procuro saber; *(forcefully)* exijo saber.

demanding *adj (person)* exigente; **2** *(work)* absorvente *m,f*, extenuante *m,f.*

demarcate *vt* demarcar, delimitar.

demarcated *adj* demarcado,-a.

demarcation *n* demarcação *f.*

dematerialize *(also:* -**ise)** *vi* desmaterializar-se.

demean *vt:* **to** ~ **o.s.** rebaixar-se.

demeaning *adj* humilhante *m,f*, vexatório *m.*

demeanour *(UK)* **demeanor** *(US)* *n (behaviour)* conduta *f*; *(bearing)* comportamento *m.*

demented *adj* demente *m,f*, doido,-a; **become** ~ enlouquecer, endoidecer.

dementia *n (MED)* demência *f.*

demerara sugar *n* açúcar *m* mascavo.

demigod *n* semideus *m.*

demijohn *n* garrafão *m.*

demilitarize *(UK)*, **demilitarise** *(US)* *vt (MIL)* desmilitarizar; ~**ed zone** *n* zona desmilitarizada.

demise *n (euph for death)* morte *f*, falecimento *m*; **2** *(fig)* *(of hopes, plans)* fim *m*; **3** *(JUR)* *(property law)* transferência of lease; *(on owner's death)* transferência de propriedade (por herança).

demisemiquaver *n (UK)* *(MUS)* fusa *f.*

demist *vt* desembaciar, *(BR)* desembaçar.

demister *n (AUT)* desembaciador *m*, *(BR)* desembaçador *m* de pára-brisa/parabrisa.

demobilize *(also:* -**ise)** *vt* desmobilizar.

democracy *n (POL)* democracia *f.*

democrat *n* democrata *m,f*; **Social D~** *npr* social-democrata *m,f.*

democratic *adj* democrático,-a.

democratize *(also:* -**ise)** *vt* democratizar.

démodé *adj* fora da moda; ultrapassado,-a.

demographic *adj* demográfico,-a.

demolish *vt* demolir, derrubar; **2** *(argument)* refutar, contestar.

demolition *n* demolição *f*, destruição *f*; **2** *(of argument)* refutação *f*, contestação *f.*

demon *n (evil)* demónio; **2** *(fig)* *(skilful)* fantástico; **he is a** ~ **at tennis** ele é um/a craque de ténis.

demonic *adj (US)* demoníaco.

demonstrate *vt* demonstrar; ♦ *vi* manifestar-se; **to** ~ **(for** *or* **against)** manifestar-se a favor/contra.

demonstration *n (POL)* manifestação *f*, protesto *m*; **2** prova, demonstração *f.*

demonstrative *adj (person showing affection)* demonstrativo,-a; *(enthusiasm)*, efusivo,-a; **2** *(gram)* ~ **pronoun** *n* pronome *m* demonstrativo.

demonstrator *n (POL)* manifestante *m,f.*

demoralize *vt* desmoralizar.

demote *vt* despromover; fazer baixar de categoria, *(BR)* rebaixar de posto.

demotion *n* despromoção *f*, *(BR)* rebaixamento.

demur *n* obje(c)ção, refutação; **without** ~ sem obje(c)-ção; ♦ **(-rr-)** *vi* opor-se, obstar.

demure *adj* recatado,-a, reservado,-a.

demystification *n* desmistificação *f.*

demystify *vt* desmistificar.

den *n (fox, mole)* toca *f*; *(lion's)* cova *f*, antro *m*; *(fig: of thieves)* covil *m*; **2** *(small room-secluded)* esconderijo *m*; recanto *m.*

denationalization *n (ECON)* privatização (de empresas).

denationalize *vt (ECON)* privatizar.

denial *n* refutação *f*; negação *f*; desmentido; **self-~** abnegação *f*; **in** ~ *(PSYCH)* em negação.

denigrate *vt* denegrir.

denigration *n* difamação *f.*

denim *n (material)* ganga; ~**s** *npl* calças *fpl* de ganga, jeans *mpl.*

denizen *n* habitante *m,f*; *(UK)* pessoa permanente-mente resideute no estrangeino.

Denmark *npr* Dinamarca; **in** ~ na Dinamarca.

denomination *n (FIN)* valor *m*; **2** *(REL)* denomi-nação *f*; seita *f.*

denominator *n* denominador *m.*

denote *vt* indicar, designar, significar.

denouement *n* desenlace *m*; desfecho *m.*

denounce *vt* denunciar; acusar.

dense *adj* denso,-a; *(fam, pej)* estúpido, bronco,-a *(fam).*

densely *adv* densamente; ~ **populated** com grande densidade populacional.

density *n* densidade *f*; **double** ~ **floppy** *(COMP)* disquete de densidade dupla.

dent *n* amolgadura, mossa; ♦ *vt* (= **to make a** ~ **in)** amolgar, dentar.

dental *n (LING)* dental; ♦ *adj* dental *m,f;* dentário,-a; ~ **clinic/surgery** *n* consultório *m* dentário; **2** *(treatment, surgery)* cirurgia *f* dentária; ~ **floss** *n* fio dentário; ~ **surgeon** *n* odontologista *m,f;* cirurgião,-ã dentista.

dentifrice *n* dentífrico *m,* *(BR)* dentifrício *m.*

dentist *n* dentista *m,f.*

dentistry *n* odontologia.

dentition *n (MED)* dentição *f.*

dentures *npl* dentadura *sg.*

denude *vt* desnudar(-se).

denunciation *n* denúncia *f.*

deny *vt* negar; desmentir; **he denies saying it** ele nega ter dito isso.

deodorant *n* desodorizante *m,* *(BR)* desodorante *m.*

deoxyribonucleic acid (DNA) *n (MED)* ácido deso-xirribonucléico.

depart *vi* ir-se, partir; **to** ~ **from** *(fig: differ from)* afastar-se de, divergir de.

departed *adj* falecido.

department *n* departamento *m;* **2** *(COMM)* se(c)ção *f;* **3** *(POL)* ministério, repartição *f;* ~ **of State** *n (US)* Ministério *m* dos Negócios Estrangeiros, *(BR)* Ministério das Relações Exteriores; ~ **store** *n* grande armazém *m,* *(BR)* loja de departamentos.

departmental *adj* departamental *m,f;* ~ **manager** *n* chefe *m,f* de serviço.

departure *n* partida *f,* ida *f;* saída *f;* ~ **gate** porta de embarque; ~ **lounge** *n* sala *f* de embarque; **~s board** horário *m* de partidas; **a new** ~ nova orientação; **place of** ~ ponto de partida.

depend *vi:* **to** ~ **on** depender de; **2** *(rely on)* contar com.

dependable *adj (person)* de confiança, seguro.

dependant *(also:* **dependent)** *n* dependente *m,f;* **2** *(addicted)* dependente; **to be** ~ **(on)** ser dependente (de).

dependence *n* dependência.

depict *vt* pintar; representar.

depilate *vt* depilar.

depilatory *n* depilatório; ~ **cream** *adj* creme *m* depilatório.

deplete *vt* reduzir, esgotar *(resources).*

depleted *adj* gasto,-a, esgotado,-a, empobrecido,-a.

depletion *n* redução *f.*

deplorable *adj* deplorável, lamentável *m,f.*

deplore *vt* deplorar, lamentar.

deploy *vt* dispor, distribuir.

deployment *n* disposição *f,* distribuição *f.*

depopulate *vt* despovoar.

depopulation *n* despovoamento *m.*

deport *vt* deportar.

deportation *n* deportação *f.*

deportee *adj* deportado.

deportment *n* comportamento *m;* postura *f.*

depose *vt* depor *(king, president).*

deposit *n (part of payment)* depósito *m,* sinal *m,* entrada *f;* **2** *(CHEM)* sedimento *m;* **3** *(of ore, oil)* jazida *f* ♦ *vt* depositar; ~ **account** *n* conta a prazo.

depositor *n* depositante *m,f.*

deposition *n (of king, President)* deposição *f;* **2** *(JUR) (statement)* depoimento *m.*

depot *n (storehouse)* armazém *m;* **2** *(for buses)* garagem *f;* **3** *(train)* estação *f* de caminho-de-ferro *(BR:* de trem).

deprave *vt* depravar, perverter.

depraved *adj* depravado,-a, pervertido,-a.

depravity *n* depravação *f,* perversão *f.*

deprecate *vt* desaprovar, reprovar.

deprecating *adj* desaprovador,-ora.

depreciate *vt/vi* depreciar(-se), desvalorizar, denegrir.

depreciation *n* depreciação *f.*

depress *vt* deprimir.

depressed *adj* deprimido,-a; **to be** ~ estar depri-mido,-a.

depressing *adj* triste *m,f,* deprimente *m,f.*

depression *n* depressão *f.*

deprivation *n* privação *f;* perda *f.*

deprive *vt:* **to** ~ **sb of** privar alguém de.

deprived *adj* pobre *m,f,* destituído,-a, carente *m,f.*

depth *n* profundidade *f;* abismo *m;* **2** *(of knowledge)* vastidão *f;* **in** ~ a fundo, em detalhe; **out of one's** ~ perder o pé; fora do alcance; **in the** ~ **of despair** profundamente desesperado,-a; **~s** *npl* profundezas *fpl.*

deputation *n* delegação *f.*

depute *vt* encarregar, incumbir.

deputize *vi:* **to** ~ **for sb** substituir alguém.

deputy *n* substituto,-a, suplente *m,f;* *(POL)* depu-tado,-a; representante *m,f;* ♦ *adj* substituto, adjunto, vice; ~ **chairman**, vice-presidente *m,f;* ~ **head** dire(c)tor,-ora adjunto,-a.

derail *vt* descarrilar; **to be ~ed** descarrilar-se.

derailment *n* descarrilamento *m.*

deranged *adj* louco,-a, transtornado,-a.

deregulate *vt* liberar, liberalizar.

deregulation *n* liberação *f,* liberalização *f.*

derelict *adj (building, area)* abandonado,-a.

derision *n* zombaria *f,* troça *f,* irrisão *f.*

derisive *(also:* **derisory)** *adj (laughable)* irrisório,-a; **2** *(scornful)* zombeteiro,-a, desdenhoso,-a.

derivation *n* derivação *f.*

derivative *n* derivado; *(MATH)* derivada; ♦ *adj* derivado; **2** *(ART)* pouco original.

derive *vt* derivar, provir; ♦ *vi:* **to** ~ **from** derivar de.

dermatitis *n (MED)* dermatite *f.*

dermatologist *n* dermatologista *m,f.*

derogatory *adj* pejorativo,-a, depreciativo,-a.

derrick *n* guindaste *m,* torre *f* de perfuração.

derv *n* gasóleo *m.*

dervish *n (Muslim ascetic)* dervixe, dervis; **~-like** *adj (frenzied dance etc)* como um dervixe, dervis.

DES *n (abbr for* **Department of Education and Science)** Ministério da Educação e das Ciências.

desalination *n* dessalinização *f.*

descaler *n (UK)* destartarizante *m.*

descant *n* descante *m,* melodia *f;* *(in music)* con-traponto *m;* ♦ *vi* comentar, discursar; **to** ~ **on upon the beauty of** cantar as belezas de.

descend *vt/vi (go down)* descer *(slope, stairs);* **2** **to** ~ **from** *(get off)* descer de; *(through affiliation)* **to** ~ **from** descender de; **3** *(suddenly arrive, fall upon)* invadir, cair sobre; **her relatives ~ed upon**

her os parentes dela invadiram-na; **night** ~**ed upon us** a noite caiu sobre nós; **4** *(sink in morals)* rebaixar-se.

descendant *n* descendente *m,f* (**of sb** de alguém).

descending *adj:* **in** ~ **order** em ordem decrescente.

descent *n* descida *f;* declive *m,* ladeira *f;* **2** descendência *f;* **by** ~ por filiação *f;* **3** invasão *f;* **collateral/lineal** ~ *n* descendência *f* em linha colateral/recta.

descrambler *n (TV)* descodificador *m.*

describe *vt* descrever.

description *n* descrição *f;* classe *f,* espécie *f;* **of every** ~ de toda a espécie, de todo o tipo.

descriptive *adj* descritivo.

desecrate *vt* profanar.

desecration *n* profanação.

desegregate *vt* desagregar.

desert *n (GEOG)* deserto *m;* *(fig)* deserto; ♦ *vt* abandonar; ♦ *vi (MIL)* desertar.

deserted *adj* abandonado,-a; *(place)* deserto,-a.

deserter *n* desertor *m.*

desertification *n* desertificação *f.*

desertion *n (MIL)* deserção *f;* **2** *(JUR)* abandono *m* do lar, do domicílio *m* conjugal.

deserve *vt* merecer.

deservedly *adv* merecidamente.

deserving *adj* merecedor,-ora; *(worthy)* digno,-a de *(respect, etc); (cause)* louvável *m,f* meritório,-a.

desiccated *adj* desidratado,-a, resseguido,-a; **2** *(AGR)* árido, seco,-a; **3** ~ **coconut** coco ralado.

design *n* desenho *m; (sketch),* esboço; **2** plano, modelo; **3** proje(c)to; **4** propósito, intenção *f;* ♦ *vt* desenhar; proje(c)tar.

designate *vt (appoint sb)* apontar; nomear; **2 to** ~ **sb to do** designar alguém para fazer; **3 to** ~ **sth for sth** destinar algo para algo; considerar; **this place was** ~**d as ...** este lugar foi considerado como ...

designation *n* nomeação *f;* designação *f;* **2** classificação.

designer *n (ART)* artista *m,f* gráfico,-a; *(TECH)* desenhador,-ora, *(BR)* desenhista *m,f;* proje(c)tista *m,f;* **fashion** ~ estilista *m,f.*

desirable *adj* desejável *m,f;* apetecível *m,f;* atraente *m,f.*

desire *n* desejo, anseio *m;* ♦ *vt* desejar, querer; IDIOM **to leave a lot to be** ~**d** deixar muito a desejar.

desirous *adj* desejoso,-a, ansioso,-a.

desist *vt* desistir (**from** de).

desk *n (writing table)* secretária; *(bureau)* escrivaninha; *(in school)* carteira; recepção *f; (in bank)* carteira *f; (in shop)* balcão *m;* ~ **clerk** *n* recepcionista *m,f;* **information** ~ *n* balcão *m* de informações; ~**top computer** *n* computador de secretária.

desolate *adj* deserto,-a; desolado,-a; ♦ *vt* despovoar; **2** lançar na desolação.

desolation *n* desolação *f.*

despair *n* desespero, aflição *f;* ♦ *vi:* **to** ~ **of** desesperar-se com; **to be in** ~ estar desesperado.

despairing *adj* desesperante *m,f.*

despatch *n, vt* = **dispatch**.

desperate *adj* desesperado; **to be** ~ **for sth** estar louco por algo.

desperately *adv* desesperadamente; terrivelmente.

desperation *n* desespero *m,* exasperação *f;* **in** ~ desesperado,-a.

despicable *adj* desprezível *m,f,* vil *m,f.*

despise *vt* desprezar; menosprezar.

despite *prep* apesar de, a despeito de.

despoil *vt* espoliar, despojar; saquear.

despoiler *n* espoliador, saqueador.

despoilment *n* espoliação *f,* despojamento *m.*

despondent *adj* abatido,-a, desanimado,-a.

despot *n* déspota *m,f,* tirano,-a.

despotic *adj* despótico, tirânico.

despotism *n* despotismo *m.*

dessert *n* sobremesa; ~ **spoon** *n* colher *f* de sobremesa.

destabilize/ise *vt* desestabilizar, desequilibrar.

destination *n (ultimate end of journey/purpose)* destino *m.*

destine *vt* destinar.

destined *adj* destinado; **to** ~ **to do sth** estar destinado a fazer algo.

destiny *n (fate)* destino *m;* sina *f;* fado *m,* sorte *f.*

destitute *adj* indigente *m,f,* necessitado,-a; ~ **of** desprovido de.

destroy *vt* destruir; acabar com.

destroyer *n* destruidor; *(NAUT)* contratorpedeiro.

destruction *n* destruição *f;* devastação *f; (fig)* ruína *f.*

destructive *adj* destrutivo,-a, destruidor,-ora.

desultory *adj* desconexo,-a; desordenado,-a; esporádico,-a.

Det. *(abbr for* **Detective**) dete(c)tive.

detach *vt* separar; desprender (**from** de); **to** ~ **oneself from** distanciar-se de; **2** *(MIL)* destacar.

detachable *adj (coupon)* destacável *m,f;* **2** *(TECH)* desmontável; **3** *(collar, lining)* separável *m,f.*

detached *adj (opinion)* imparcial, obje(c)tivo,-a; **2** *(object)* destacado,-a, separado,-a; **3** *(house)* isolada, independente; **4** *(person) (emotionally)* desinteressado,-a, desprendido,-a; distanciado,-a; **5** *(MED)* ~ **retina** retina *f* descolada.

detachment *n* separação *f;* **2** *(MIL)* destacamento; *(fig)* obje(c)tividade *f,* imparcialidade *f.*

detail *n* detalhe *m;* pormenor *m;* ♦ *vt* detalhar; *(MIL)* destacar; **in** ~ pormenorizado, em detalhe; **to go into** ~**s** entrar em detalhes.

detailed *adj* detalhado,-a.

detain *vt (police)* deter; prender; **he** ~**ed me for an hour** ele deteve-me por uma hora; **2** reter, demorar.

detainee *n (arrested person)* detido,-a.

detect *vt* descobrir; identificar; detectar.

detection *n* descoberta *f;* identificação *f;* **crime** ~ investigação *f* de crimes.

detective *n* dete(c)tive *m,f;* ~ **story** *n* romance *m* ou história policial.

detector *n* dete(c)tor *m;* **lie** ~ dete(c)tor de mentiras; **mine** ~ dete(c)tor de minas.

detention *n* detenção *f,* prisão *f;* ~ **centre** *n* casa *f* de correcção; **be given a** ~ *(school)* ficar de castigo na escola.

deter (-**rr**-) *vt (dissuade)* desencorajar; dissuadir; (**from** de); **2** impedir (**from** de).

detergent n detergente m.
deteriorate vt deteriorar.
deterioration n deterioração f.
determinant n adj determinante, firme m,f; **2** (MATH) n determinante m.
determination n determinação f; firmeza; resolução f; (JUR) decisão f.
determine vt determinar; definir; **2** (dispute) resolver.
determined adj (person) resoluto,-a, decidido,-a; ~ **to do sth** decidido a fazer algo.
determiner n (gram) determinante m.
deterrence n dissuasão f, coibição f.
deterrent n dissuasivo m.
detest vt detestar, odiar.
detestable adj detestável m,f.
dethrone vt destronar.
detonate vi explodir, rebentar; ♦ vt detonar.
detonation n detonação f, explosão f.
detonator n detonador m.
detour n desvio m.
detox n (fam) desintoxicação f.
detoxification n desintoxicação f.
detoxify vt desintoxicar.
detract vi: **to** ~ **from** tirar o prazer de; depreciar; **2** (reputation) caluniar.
detractor n detra(c)tor,-ora, difamador,-ora.
detriment n: **to the** ~ **of** em detrimento de.
detrimental adj prejudicial (**to** a).
detritus n (waste) detrito, resíduo, resto m.
deuce n (tennis) empate m; (in cards) dois; **like the** ~ muito rápido; **what the** ~! mas que raio!; **where the** ~ **is my coat?** mas por onde se meteu o casaco?
devaluation n desvalorização f.
devalue vt (ECON, FIN) desvalorizar.
devastate vt devastar (land, place); **2** (fig) aniquilar (person); **he was** ~**ed by the news** as notícias deixaram-no arrasado.
devastated adj devastado; desolado.
devastating adj devastador,-ora; assolador,-ora.
devastation n devastação f.
develop vt desenvolver; **2** (PHOT) revelar; **3** (disease) contrair; **4** (engine trouble) começar a ter; ♦ vi desenvolver-se; progredir; aparecer.
developer n (PHOT) revelador; **property** ~ n empresário,-a de imóveis.
developing country país m em (vias de) desenvolvimento.
development n desenvolvimento m; progresso m; **2** (of land) urbanização f; ~ **area** n zona a ser urbanizada; **housing** ~ n zona residencial.
deviate vi desviar-se (**from**, de); **2** divergir (**from**, de).
deviation n desvio m; **sexual** ~ perversão f sexual.
device n (scheme) estratagema m, plano; **2** (apparatus) dispositivo m, aparelho m; **3** (method) artifício m; IDIOM **leave sb to their own** ~**s** deixar alguém por sua conta/alguém fazer o que quer; (child) deixar a criança entreter-se.
devil n diabo m, demónio m, (BR: -mô-); **2** (person) **poor** ~! pobre diabo!; **3** (for emphasis) **what the** ~ **are you doing?** que diabo estás tu a fazer?;

IDIOM **between the** ~ **and the deep blue sea** estar entre a espada e a parede; **speak of the** ~ fala-se no diabo e aparece-lhe o rabo.
devilish adj diabólico,-a.
devil-may-care adj despreocupado,-a, descuidado,-a.
devilment n coisa diabólica; **2** diabrura f.
devil's advocate n advogado,-a do diabo.
devious adj (person) astuto,-a, maldoso,-a; (foxy) matreiro,-a; **2** (winding road) tortuoso,-a.
devise n (JUR) legado m; ♦ vt inventar (product); conceber (plan).
devitalize vt desvitalizar.
devoid adj desprovido,-a (**of** de).
devolution n (JUR) (giving back) devolução f (**to** a) (original owner); **2** (transfer) transferência f (of rights; **3** (POL) descentralização f.
devolve vt delegar (**to** em); ♦ vi **to** ~ **on/upon sb** (be the responsability of) incumbir a; **2** (JUR) transferir (**to** para).
devote vt dedicar, devotar; **to** ~ **yourself to sb/sth** dedicar-se a alguém ou algo.
devoted adj (loyal) leal, fiel; dedicado; **the book is** ~ **to economics** o livro trata de economia.
devotee n adepto,-a, entusiasta m,f; **2** (REL) devoto,-a.
devotion n dedicação f; (REL) devoção f.
devour vt devorar.
devout adj (REL) devoto,-a.
dew n orvalho m; **night** ~ relento m.
dewy adj orvalhado,-a; **a** ~ **morning** uma manhã orvalhada.
dewy-eyed adj comovido,-a; **2** inocente, ingénuo,-a.
dexterity n destreza, agilidade f, habilidade f.
dext(e)rous adj destro,-a, ágil, hábil m,f.
dextrin(e) n (CHEM) dextrina f.
dextrose n (CHEM) dextrose, glicose f.
DfEE (abbr for **Department for Education and Employment**) Ministério da Educação e do Emprego.
diabase n diábase f.
diabetes n diabetes fpl.
diabetic n adj diabético,-a.
diabolic, diabolical adj diabólico; **2** (fig) horrível m,f.
diacritic n adj (LING) diacrítico; **2** distinto,-a.
diadem n (for the head) diadema m, coroa f.
diaeresis (UK), **dieresis** (US) diérese f.
diagnose vt diagnosticar.
diagnosis (pl: **-ses**) n, **diagnostic** adj (MED) diagnóstico m.
diagonal n adj diagonal m,f.
diagram n diagrama m, esquema m.
dial n (clock, watch) mostrador m, **2** (on phone) disco; ♦ (**-led**) vt (TEL: number) marcar, (BR) discar.
dialect n diale(c)to m.
dialectic n dialé(c)tica, lógica; ♦ adj dialé(c)tico.
dialling n (TEL) maração f; (BR) discagem f; ~ **code** n (TEL) indicativo m; (BR) código m; ~ **tone** n sinal m para marcar o número.
dialogue n diálogo, conversa; ~ **box** n (COMP) caixa de diálogo.

dialysis *(pl: -lyses)* *n (CHEM)* diálise *f*.

diamanté *n (artificial jewel)* paste; ♦ *adj (decorated fabric, trim etc)* de vidrilhos, lantejoulas.

diameter *n* diâmetro *m*.

diametrically *adv*: ~ **opposed (to)** diametralmente oposto (a).

diamond *n (stone)* diamante *m*; ~ **ring** anel *m* de diamante(s); *(BR)* brilhante(s); **2** *(shape)* losango; ~ **Jubilee** *n* 60^0 aniversário dum acontecimento; ~ **wedding** *n* bodas *fpl* de diamante.

diamonds *npl (cards)* ouros *mpl*.

diaper *n (US) (baby's nappy)* fralda.

diaphanous *adj* diáfano,-a, transparente *m,f*.

diaphragm *n (ANAT)* diafragma *m*.

diarist *n* autor,-ora de um diário (íntimo); **2** *(journalist)* que escreve crónicas *m,f*.

diarrhoea *n* diarréia *f*.

diary *(pl: -ries)* *n* diário *m* íntimo; **2** *(for appointments)* agenda; **to keep a** ~ ter um diário.

diaspora *n* diáspora *f*, dispersão *f*.

diatonic *adj (MUS)* diatónico.

diatribe *n* diatribe *f*, crítica *f* severa.

dice *n inv (game)* dados *mpl*; ♦ *vt (CULIN)* cortar em cubos; IDIOM **no** ~! nada feito!; **to** ~ **with death** *vi* brincar com o fogo.

dicey *adj* arriscado, perigoso; **it's a bit** ~ é um pouco arriscado.

dichotomy *n* dicotomia *f*.

dick *n (coll)* pénis *(BR*: pê-); **2** *(coll)* dete(c)tive, **private** ~ dete(c)tive privado; **3 D~** *(nickname for Richard)* Ricardo; **clever** ~ *n (a know-all)* sabichão *m*, sabichona *f*.

dickens *n (euph for devil)*: **what the** ~**?** mas porque diabo?; co'os diabos!

Dickensian *adj* relativo a Dickens ou à sua obra

(Charles Dickens, famoso escritor do século XIX).

dicky, dickey *adj (false shirt front)* peitilho; **2** *(coll) (in poor health, shaky)* abalado,-a; ~ **heart** coração *m* fraco.

dicky-bird *n (child's talk)* passarinho *m*; IDIOM **not say a** ~ não dizer nada de jeito.

dicotyledon *n (BOT)* dicotiledónia *(BR*: -dô-).

dictate *n* ordem *f*; ~**s** *npl* ditames *mpl*; **the** ~**s of one's conscience** os ditames da consciência; ♦ *vt* ditar; dar ordens *fpl*.

dictating machine *n* máquina de ditar.

dictation *n* ditado *m*.

dictator *n* ditador *m*, déspota *m,f*.

dictatorial *adj* ditatorial *m,f*.

dictatorship *n* ditadura *f*.

diction *n* dicção *f*; **2** estilo *m* (de expressão), elocução *f*.

dictionary *n* dicionário *m*.

dictum *(pl: -a, -ums)* *n* dito popular; máxima; **2** declaração, afirmação formal.

did *(pt of* **do***)*.

didact *n* dida(c)ta *m,f*.

didactic *adj* didá(c)tico, instrutivo.

didactics *nsg* didá(c)tica *fsg*.

diddle *vt (usually in passive) (coll)* burlar; **to** ~ **sb out of sth** extorquir algo a alguém; **2** *(COMP)* manipular dados ilegalmente.

didn't = **did not**.

dido *(pl: -oes)* *n* travessura *f*, truque *m*.

die[1] *n (of games)* dado *m*; **the** ~ **is cast** a sorte está lançada; **2** *(for casting)* molde *m*.

die[2] *(pt, pp* **died**, *pres.p: dying) vi* morrer, falecer; **to** ~ **of/from** morrer de; **to** ~ **a pauper** morrer na miséria; **2** *(plant)* murchar; ~ **away** *vi (light, flame)* extinguir-se lentamente; **to** ~ **down** *vi* apagar-se; abrandar; *(noise)* cessar; **to** ~ **out** *vi (become extinct)* desaparecer, *(light)* apagar-se; IDIOM **the** ~ **is cast** a sorte está lançada.

diehard *n (POL)* rea(c)cionário,-a; **2** *(conservative person)* conservador,-ora extremista; **3** *(stubborn)* obstinado,-a, irredutível *m,f*.

dieresis *n (LING)* diérese *f*.

diesel *n* gasóleo; ~ **engine** *n* motor *m* diesel; ~ **(oil)** *n* óleo diesel.

diesis *n (MUS)* diese *f*, sustenido, meio tom.

diet *n* dieta *f*; regime *m*; ♦ *vi* (= **to be on a** ~) estar de dieta, fazer regime.

dietary *adj* dietético,-a.

dietetic *adj* dietético,-a; ~ **advice** conselho dietético; **2** ~**s** *nsg* dietética *f*.

dietician, dietitian *n* dietista *m,f*, nutricionista *m,f*.

differ *vi* ser diferente de, diferenciar-se de; **2** discordar.

difference *n* diferença; **2** desacordo, divergência; **time** ~ *n* fuso *m* horário; IDIOM **it makes no** ~ **to me** não me faz diferença, para mim dá no mesmo.

different *adj* diferente, desigual.

differently *adv* diferentemente.

differential *n adj (AUT, MATH)* diferencial; **2 wage/price** desnível *m* salarial, de preços.

differentiate *vt* distinguir, diferenciar; ♦ *vi* diferenciar-se; **to** ~ **between** distinguir entre.

differently *adv* de outro modo, de forma diferente.

difficult *adj* difícil *m,f*, árduo,-a.

difficulty *n* dificuldade *f*.

diffidence *n* timidez *f*; acanhamento *m*, insegurança.

diffident *adj* tímido, acanhado.

diffidently *adv* timidamente.

diffract *vt (PHYS)* difra(c)tar.

diffraction difra(c)ção.

diffuse *adj* difuso,-a, prolixo,-a; ♦ *vt* difundir.

diffusion *n* difusão *f*, propagação *f*.

dig *n (coll) (unkind jibe)* piada *f*, alfinetada *f (BR)* indireta; **2** *(poke with elbow)* cotovelada *f*; **3** ~**s** *npl (coll) (UK)* quarto *m* mobilado; alojamento simples; **4** *(ARCHEOL)* escavações *fpl*; ♦ *(pt, pp* **dug**, *pres p* **digging**) *vt* cavar *(ground, gravel)*; **2** *(ARCHEOL)* escavar; **to** ~ **in** *(MIL)* cavar trincheira; **3** *(to eat)* encetar *(cake, etc)*, comer; **4 to** ~ **in one's heels** ser firme/obstinado,-a; *(coll)* bater o pé; **to** ~ **in the ribs** chamar a atenção de (alguém); **to** ~ **into sth** cravar; **she dug her nails into the palm of her hand** ela cravou as unhas na palma da mão dela; ♦ **to** ~ **out** *vt* escavar *(car, etc)*; **2** extirpar *(root, weed)*, desenterrar; ♦ **to** ~ **up** *vt* desenterrar; arrancar; *(discover)* pôr a nu, revelar *(details, information)*.

digest *n* sumário *m,* resumo *m;* publicação *f;* **2** *(CHEM)* decompor; *(JUR)* digesto, compilação *f* de decisões jurídicas; ♦ *vt* digerir *(food);* assimilar *(information).*

digestible *adj* digerível *m,f.*

digestion *n* digestão *f.*

digestive *adj* digestivo,-a; ~ **biscuits** bolachas *fpl* digestivas; **2** ~ **tract** aparelho *m* digestivo.

digger *n* cavador *m,* escavador *m;* **2** máquina escavadora.

digit *n (ANAT)* dedo *m;* **2** *(MATH)* dígito *m,* algarismo *m.*

digital *adj* digital *m,f;* ~ **camera** *n* câmara *f (BR:* -me-) digital.

digitize *(also:* -**ise**) *vt (COMP)* digitalizar.

dignified *adj (person)* grave *m,f,* sério,-a; **2** *(posture)* nobre *m,f.*

dignify *vt* dignificar, exaltar.

dignitary *n* dignitário,-a.

dignity *n* dignidade *f.*

digraph *n (LING)* dígrafo, digrama *m.*

digress *vi* divagar, digressar; **to** ~ **from** afastar-se de.

digression *n* digressão *f,* divagação *f.*

digs *npl (coll)* quarto *m* mobilado, alojamento *m* simples.

dihedral *n adj (MATH)* diedro *m.*

dike = **dyke**.

diktat *n (imposed by ruler/nation)* declaração *f* dogmática, imposição *f.*

dilapidate *vt* delapidar, destruir, arruinar.

dilapidated *adj* degradado,-a, arruinado,-a, estragado,-a; **the building is** ~ o prédio está em mau estado.

dilapidation *n* degradação *f,* ruína *f;* **2** *(property law)* negligência.

dilatation *n* dilatação *f.*

dilate *vt* dilatar; ♦ *vi* dilatar-se.

dilation *n* dilatação *f.*

dilatory *adj* dilatório,-a; **2** *(slow)* vagaroso,-a.

dildo *n* vibrador *m.*

dilemma *n* dilema *m.*

dilettante *n (pej)* amador,-ora.

diligence *n* diligência *f,* zelo *m,* cuidado *m.*

diligent *adj* diligente, cuidadoso,-a, estudioso,-a.

dill *n* endro, funcho *m.*

dilly-dally *vt (to waste time)* perder tempo; **2** ser indeciso,-a

diluent *n, adj* diluente *m.*

dilute *adj* diluído,-a; ♦ *vt* diluir.

dilution *n* diluição *f.*

dim *adj (sight, sound)* fraco,-a; **2** *(not clear)* turvo,-a; indistinto,-a; **3** *(memory)* vago,-a; **4** *(dark)* sombrio,-a; **5** *(coll)* estúpido,-a; ♦ *vt* diminuir, baixar; *(US: AUT)* baixar os faróis; IDIOM **to take a** ~ **view of sth** desaprovar algo.

dime *n (US)* moeda de dez cêntimos de dólar; ~ **novel** *n* romance *m* em folhetim; ~ **store** *(US) n (equiv)* loja dos 300 *m;* IDIOM **they are a** ~ **a dozen** *(coll)* encontram-se por aí aos pontapés.

dimension *n* dimensão *f,* medida *f,* tamanho *m.*

diminish *vt/vi* diminuir(-se).

diminished *adj (profits, level)* reduzido,-a; **2** *(support, praise)* diminuído,-a; **3** *(person)* menos prezada; ~ **responsibility** *n (JUR)* responsabilidade *f* atenuada; incapacidade *f* penal por doença mental.

diminishing returns *npl* rendimentos *mpl* decrescentes.

diminutive *n (LING)* diminutivo *m;* ♦ *adj* diminuto,-a.

dimity *n (strong cotton fabric)* fustão *m.*

dimly *adv* fracamente; indistintamente.

dimmer *n (ELECT)* redutor *m* de tenção; ~**s** *npl (US: AUT)* faróis *mpl* baixos; **2** *(parking lights)* pisca-alerta *m;* ~ **switch** *n* regulador (da luz ambiente) dimmer.

dimple *n (on chin, cheek, child's knee)* covinha *f.*

dimwit *n* palerma *m,f.*

dim-witted *adj* obtuso,-a, imbecil *m,f.*

din *n (of machines)* barulho *m,* barulheira *f; (of people)* chinfrim *m;* ♦ *vt* fazer barulho; **to** ~ **sth into sb** *(coll)* meter algo na cabeça de alguém.

dine *vi* jantar; ~ **in** jantar em casa; ~ **out** jantar fora.

diner *n* cliente *m,f* (de restaurante); comensal *m,f; (RAIL)* vagão-restaurante *m;* **3** *(US: by the roadside)* snack-bar *m.*

ding *vt (repeatedly) (door bell)* tocar, tilintar; **2** *(church bell)* tocar, repicar.

ding-dong *n (UK) (row)* zaragata *f;* ♦ *adv (onomat) (sound of bell)* tlim-tlão; *(of church bells)* tão-balalão.

dinghy *n (NAUT)* caiaque *m,* bote *m;* **rubber** ~ *(inflatable)* barco, bote *m* de borracha.

dingle *n* pequeno vale *m* arborizado.

dingo *(pl:* -**es**) *n (wild dog of Australia)* dingo *m.*

dingy (-ier, -iest) *adj (dirty, drab)* sujo,-a *(street);* **2** *(colour)* de cor baça, desbotado,-a; descolorido,-a *(building).*

dining: ~ **car** *n* carruagem *(BR:* carro)-restaurante *f;* ~ **room** *n* sala *f* de jantar; ~ **table** *n* mesa *f* de jantar.

dinner *n* jantar *m;* **gala** ~ banquete *m;* ~ **jacket** *n* smoking *m;* ~ **time** *n* hora de jantar; ~ **set** *n* serviço *m* de jantar.

dinosaur *n (ZOOL)* dinossauro *m.*

dint *n (dated)* mossa *f;* **2 by** ~ **of** à força de, por meio de, a poder de.

diocese *n* diocese *f.*

diode *n (ELECT)* díodo *m.*

dioxide *n (CHEM)* dióxido *m;* **carbon** ~ *n* dióxido *m* de carbono.

Dip. *(UK) (abbr for* **Diploma**).

dip *n (slope)* inclinação *f;* **2** *(in sea)* mergulho; **3** *(CULIN)* molho para salgados; ♦ *vt (in water)* mergulhar; **2** *(ladle etc)* meter; **3** *(AUTO) (lights)* baixar, pôr os médios; ♦ *vi* mergulhar-se; **to** ~ **into his wallet** ver se tem dinheiro, procurar algo; ~ **into his money** tirar o dinheiro.

diphtheria *n (MED)* difteria *f.*

diphthong *n (LING)* ditongo *m.*

diploma *n* diploma *m.*

diplomacy *n* diplomacia *f.*

diplomat *n* diplomata *m,f.*

diplomatic *adj* diplomático; **to break off** ~ **relations (with)** romper relações diplomáticas (com); ~ **bag** mala diplomática; ~ **immunity** imunidade *f* diplomática.

dipper n (ladle) concha, colherão m; **2** (ZOOL) mergulhão m; **3** (coll) (pickpocket) carteirista m,f; **the Big D~** n Ursa Major; **the Little** ~ Ursa Menor.

dippy adj (person) excêntrico,-a.

dipsomania n (MED) dipsomania f.

dipsomaniac n adj dipsomaníaco,-a.

dipstick n (AUT) vareta f medidora do nível do óleo.

dipswitch n (AUT) interruptor m da luz alta e média.

dire adj terrível, extremo,-a; de mau agouro; ~ **need** necessidade urgente; **to be in** ~ **straits** estar em apuros.

direct adj (gen) dire(c)to,-a; franco,-a; ~ **access** (COMP) acesso dire(c)to; **2** ~ **object/speech** (gram) obje(c)to m, discurso dire(c)to; ♦ vt dirigir; indicar.

direction n dire(c)cão f; **2** indicação f; **3** (letter) endereço m; **4** administração f, gerência f; ~**s** npl ordens fpl, instruções fpl; ~**s for use** modo de emprego, modo de usar.

directive n (ADMIN, POL) dire(c)tiva f; ♦ adj (tending to instruct) dire(c)tivo,-a, dire(c)cional m,f.

directly adv (in straight line) dire(c)tamente; **2** (at once) imediatamente.

directness n (person) franqueza f.

director n dire(c)tor,-ora; ~ **general**, **DG** dire(c)tor,-ora geral; **D~ of Public Prosecutions** Procurador,-ora Geral da República; **funeral** ~ agente m,f funerário; **managing** ~ dire(c)tor,-ora, gerente m,f.

directorate n (board of directors) dire(c)toria f.

directory n (TEL) lista (telefónica), (BR) catálogo; **2** (COMM) anuário comercial; **3** (COMP) dire(c)tório; ~ **enquiries** npl serviço m informativo; informações fpl.

direct rule n governo m central.

dirge n canto m fúnebre; **2** canção f solene/fúnebre.

dirigible n (MIL) avião m, balão m ou arma de guerra dirigível; ♦ adj dirigível m,f, manobrável m,f.

dirt n sujidade f, (BR) sujeira f; **2** (pej) (gossip) mexeriquice f; ~**-cheap** adj baratíssimo; **that was** ~**-cheap** isso foi uma pechincha; IDIOM **to treat sb like** ~ espezinhar alguém.

dirtiness n sujidade f, porcaria f (fam); **2** grosseria, obscenidade.

dirt-track n (road) estrada f de terra batida; **2** (SPORT) pista f de corridas para motociclos.

dirty adj (gen) sujo,-a; **2** (person) porco,-a; **3** (obscene) indecente; ~ **cheat** adj (person) desonesto,-a, sem escrúpulos; **to play** ~ jogar, agir duma maneira desonesta; ~ **joke** n anedota f obscena; ~ **look** n olhar m furioso, desdenhoso; ~ **trick** n (despicable action) patifaria, sujeira f; ~ **weekend** n fim-de-semana m com amante; ~ **white** branco sujo; ~ **word** n palavrão m; ~ **work** n a(c)tividade f desagradável ou ilícita; ♦ vt sujar; (stain) manchar; IDIOM **do not wash your** ~ **linen in public** (reveal secrets/gossip) a roupa suja lava-se em casa; **to do the** ~ **on sb** atraiçoar alguém, fazer uma patifaria a alguém.

disability n incapacidade f; **2** (JUR) inabilidade f, incompetência f; **3** (MED) invalidez f, incapacidade física; ~ **allowance** n pensão f por invalidez.

disable vt inabilitar, incapacitar; **2** (tank, gun) inutilizar; **3** (JUR) desqualificar, invalidar; **4** (COMP) desa(c)tivar.

disabled adj incapacitado,-a, deficiente m,f, aleijado,-a; **the** ~ npl os deficientes mpl; os incapacitados mpl.

disablement n incapacidade f, invalidez f.

disabuse vt desenganar, desiludir.

disadjustment n desafinação f; desarranjo m.

disadvantage n desvantagem f; inconveniente m.

disadvantaged adj (person) menos favorecido,-a; em desvantagem.

disadvantageous adj desvantajoso,-a.

disaffected adj descontente; **2** dissidente.

disaffirm vt desmentir, negar; **2** (JUR) anular, revogar.

disagree vi discordar; **to** ~ (**with**) não concordar (com).

disagreeable adj desagradável m,f.

disagreement n desacordo m; briga f, desavença f, discórdia f.

disallow vt desaprovar, não admitir; **2** (goal) anular; **3** (JUR) vetar, proibir.

disappear vi desaparecer; **to be fast** ~**ing** estar em vias de extinção.

disappearance n desaparecimento m; **2** (of animals, plants, civilization) extinção f.

disappoint vt desapontar; desiludir; frustrar.

disappointed adj decepcionado,-a, desapontado,-a.

disappointing adj frustrante, decepcionante.

disappointment n dece(p)ção f; desilusão f.

disapprobation n (moral, social) desaprovação f, censura f, reprovação f.

disapproval n desaprovação f.

disapprove vi: **to** ~ **of** desaprovar; reprovar.

disapproving adj (look, remark) desaprovador,-ora.

disarm vt desarmar.

disarmament n desarmamento; deposição f de armas; **nuclear** ~ n desarmamento nuclear.

disarming adj (smile) encantador,-ora.

disarray n desordem f; **in** ~ (clothes, appearance) em desalinho; **to throw into** ~ (troops) desbaratar, dissipar; **2** (government) deixar em agitação ♦ adj (office, business) desorganizado,-a, caótico,-a; **2** (thoughts) confuso,-a ♦ vt desordenar, desalinhar.

disassemble vt (furniture) desmontar; **2** separar, desunir.

disassociate vt: **to** ~ **from sb** desligar-se de alguém.

disaster n desastre m; **2** (natural) catástrofe f, calamidade f.

disastrous adj desastroso,-a.

disavow vt negar, desmentir; desautorizar.

disavowal n negação f, desmentido m.

disband vt dispersar; ♦ vi debandar.

disbandment n dispersão f, debandada f.

disbar vt expulsar membro da ordem dos advogados.

disbelief n incredulidade f; **in** ~ adj incrédulo,-a.

disbelieve vt desacreditar, descrer.

disbeliever n descrente m,f.

disc (also: **disk**) n disco; **2** (BOT) receptáculo; **3** ~ **brake** n (AUT) travão m de discos (BR: freio a disco); **4** (COMP) compact disc = **CD**; ~ **drive**

unidade *f* de disco; **floppy** ~ *n* disquete *m*; **hard** ~ *n* disco rígido.

discard *vt* desfazer-se de; *(fig)* descartar.

discern *vt* perceber; discernir.

discerning *adj* perspicaz *m,f*, sagaz *m,f*; com discernimento.

discharge *n* *(ELEC)* descarga *f*; **2** *(dismissal)* demissão *f*; **3** *(of duty)* desempenho *m*; **4** *(of debt)* pagamento, resgate *m*; **5** *(JUR)* absolvição *f*; **6** *(MED)* secreção *f*; **to ~ one's gun** descarregar a arma, disparar; ♦ *vt* *(duties)* cumprir; **2** saldar, liquidar *(debt)*; **3** *(patient)* dar alta a *(from hospital)*; **4** *(soldier)* ter baixa, licença do (exército); **5** *(JUR)* anular; **6** *(of oath, promise)* desobrigar; **7** *(conscience)* aliviar.

disciple *n* discípulo,-a; **2** *n* apóstolo.

disciplinary *adj* disciplinar; **to take ~ action against sb** mover uma a(c)ção disciplinar contra alguém.

discipline *n* disciplina; **self-~** autodisciplina; ♦ *vt* disciplinar, punir.

disclaim *vt* negar; recusar; **2** *(JUR)* renunciar (a um direito).

disclaimer *n* desmentido; **to issue a ~** publicar um desmentido; **2** *n* *(JUR)* renúncia a um direito legal.

disclose *vt* revelar; divulgar.

disclosure *n* revelação *f*; divulgação *f*.

disco *n* *(abbr for **discotheque**)* discoteca.

discography *n* discografia *f*.

discolour *vt* descorar, desbotar, descolorar.

discolouration *n* descoloração *f*, desbotamento *m*.

discomfit *vt* *(usually in the passive)* desconcertar, embaraçar.

discomfort *n* desconforto; inquietação *f*; mal-estar *m*.

disconcert *vt* desconcertar.

disconcerting *adj* desconcertante *m,f*.

disconnect *vt* separar, desunir; **2** *(ELECT, etc)* desligar.

disconnected *adj* desligado; **2** *(speech)* desconexo, incoerente.

disconsolate *adj* *(depressed)* desconsolado,-a, inconsolável *m,f*.

discontent *n* descontentamento.

discontent *adj* descontente.

discontinue *vt* interromper; suspender; **2 ~d line** *(COMM)* fora de linha.

discontinuous *adj* descontínuo,-a, interrompido,-a.

discord *n* discórdia *f*; **2** *(MUS)* dissonância.

discordance *n* discordância *f*; **2** *(MUS)* dissonância *f*.

discordant *adj* dissonante *m,f*.

discotheque = **disco**.

discount *n* desconto, abatimento *m*; ♦ *vt* descontar, abater, reduzir; **~ for cash** desconto por pronto pagamento; **~ rate** taxa de desconto.

discourage *vt* *(dishearten)* desanimar; desencorajar; dissuadir; **~ sb from doing sth** desencorajar alguém de fazer algo.

discouragement *n* desânimo, desalento.

discouraging *adj* desanimador,-ora.

discourse *n* *(LITER)* discurso *m*; **2** *(talk, lecture)* palestra; dissertação *f*; ♦ *vi* discursar (**on** em sobre).

discourteous *adj* descortês *m,f*, indelicado,-a.

discourtesy *n* descortesia *f*, grosseria *f*.

discover *vt* descobrir; **2** *(missing person)* encontrar.

discover *n* descobridor,-ora; investigador,-ora.

discovery *n* descoberta *f*; descobrimento *m*; **a voyage of ~** uma viagem de exploração; **2** *(object)* achado,-a.

discredit *n* descrédito *m*; **2** vergonha *f*; ♦ *vt* desacreditar; questionar, desabonar.

discreditable *adj* desabonador,-ora; **2** indigno,-a.

discreet *adj* discreto,-a; circunspe(c)to,-a.

discreetly *adv* discretamente.

discreetness *n* discrição *f*; prudência.

discrepancy *n* diferença *f*; discrepância *f*; disparidade *f*.

discrete *adj* distinto,-a, separado,-a; **2** *(MAT)* discreto,-a.

discretion *n* discrição *f*; prudência, circunspecção *f*; **use your ~!** aja, faça segundo o seu critério!

discretionary *n* discricionário,-a, arbitrário,-a.

discriminate *vt/vi* discriminar, distinguir, diferenciar; **to ~ between** *vi* fazer distinção entre; **to ~ against** *vi* discriminar contra.

discriminating *adj* criterioso,-a; **2** *(differences)* distintivo,-a.

discrimination *n* discernimento *m*; discriminação *f*; **racial/sexual ~** discriminação racial/sexual.

discursive *adj* discursivo,-a; digressivo,-a.

discus *n* disco; **2 the ~** *(SPORT)* lançamento do disco, *(BR)* arremesso do disco.

discuss *vt* discutir; debater; tratar de.

discussion *n* discussão *f*; debate *m*.

disdain *n* desdém *m*; desprezo *m*; ♦ *vt* desdenhar; desprezar.

disdainful *adj* desdenhoso,-a.

disease *n* doença *f*, enfermidade *f*.

diseased *adj* doente *m,f*, **2** doentio,-a.

disembark *vt/vi* desembarcar.

disembarkation *n* desembarque *m*.

disembody *vt* desencarnar, desincorporar.

disembowel *vt* desentranhar, estripar.

disenchanted *adj*: **~ with sth** desencantado,-a, desiludido,-a

disenchantment *n* desencanto, desilusão *f*.

disenfranchise *vt* privar do direito ao voto; **2** *(COMM)* retirar a concessão de.

disengage *vt* *(gen)* soltar; desprender; **2** *(AUT, TECH)* desengatar *(gear, machines)*; **to ~ the clutch** desembraiar. *(BR)* desembrear.

disengagement *n* desimpedimento; **2** desprendimento, desligamento *m*.

disentangle *vt* desenredar; *(wool, wires)* desemaranhar; **2** *(get out of a problem)* desenrascar-se.

disenthrall *vt* *(US)* livrar, libertar.

disequilibrium *n* *(ECON)* desequilíbrio.

disestablishment *n* laicização *f*; separação da Igreja e do Estado.

disfavour *(UK)*, **disfavor** *(US)* *n* desaprovação *f*; **2** *vt* desagradar a (alguém), desaprovar; **to fall into ~** cair em desgraça.

disfigure *vt* desfigurar, deformar.

disfigurement *n* desfiguração *f*.

disgorge vt (MED) desobstruir; **2** despejar, escoar (crowd, liquid); **3** expelir.

disgrace n ignomínia f; vergonha f, desonra; ♦ vt desonrar; envergonhar.

disgraceful adj vergonhoso,-a.

disgruntled adj descontente m,f, mal-humorado,-a.

disguise n disfarce m; ♦ vt disfarçar; **to ~ o.s. (as)** disfarçar-se (de); **in ~** disfarçado,-a.

disgust n repugnância f, aversão f; ♦ vt repugnar a (alguém), enojar.

disgusting adj repugnante m,f, nojento,-a.

dish n (CULIN) (recipient) travessa f; **butter ~** n manteigueira f; (CULIN) (food) prato m; **cod is Portugal's national ~** o bacalhau é o prato nacional de Portugal; **to do/wash the ~es** lavar os pratos or a louça; **2 TV ~** (also: **satellite**) antena f parabólica; **3** (fam) (attractive person) **she is a ~** ela é um traço m; ♦ vt **to ~ out/up** servir (food); **2** (fam) distribuir algo casualmente; **cards were ~ed out by the businessmen** os empresários distribuíram os seus cartões de visita; **2 to ~ sth up** vt apresentar, preparar algo dum modo atraente.

disharmony n desarmonia f; discórdia f.

dishcloth n pano da louça.

disheartened adj desanimado,-a.

disheartening adj desanimador,-ora, desencorajante m,f.

dishes npl pratos mpl; louça fsg; **to wash the ~** lavar a louça.

dishevel vt desgrenhar, despentear.

disheveled adj despenteado,-a, desgrenhado,-a.

dishonest adj desonesto, desleal.

dishonesty n desonestidade f; deslealdade f.

dishonour n desonra f; ♦ vt desonrar.

dishonourable adj desonroso,-a, vergonhoso,-a.

dishtowel n pano m de louça.

dishwasher n máquina f de lavar louça.

dishy (-ier, -iest) adj (good-looking) atraente m,f; **he is ~** ele é um puxão m de homem uma brasa.

disillusion n desilusão f, dece(p)ção f; ♦ vt desiludir, desenganar.

disincentive n falta f de incentivo, desmotivação f.

disinclined adj: **~ to do sth** pouco disposto,-a a fazer algo.

disinfect vt desinfe(c)tar.

disinfectant n adj desinfe(c)tante m.

disinfection n desinfecção f.

disinflation n (ECON) deflação f.

disingenuous adj falso,-a, dissimulado,-a, fingido,-a.

disinherit vt (JUR) deserdar.

disintegrate vi desagregar-se, desintegrar-se.

disinterested adj desinteressado, indiferente, imparcial.

disjoin vi desunir(-se), desligar(-se).

disjointed adj desconjuntado,-a; **2** (programme) desconexo,-a; (speech) incoerente m,f.

disjunct adj desunido,-a, separado,-a, desconexo,-a.

disjunction n disjunção f; desunião f, **3** (GEOL) (of rock) divisão f.

disjunctive n (gram) conjunção f disjuntiva; **2** adj disjuntivo.

disk n (COMP) disco m; (Vd: **disc**).

disk drive n unidade f de disco.

dislike n antipatia, aversão f; ♦ vt antipatizar com, não gostar de; **he ~s the idea** ele não gosta da ideia (BR: idéia); **to take a ~ to sb** antipatizar com alguém.

dislocate vt (MED) deslocar; **he has ~d his foot** ele deslocou o pé; **2** (disrupt) perturbar (system).

dislocation n (MED) (hip) luxação f.

dislodge vt deslocar, desalojar (**from** de).

dislodgement n desalojamento.

disloyal adj desleal m,f (**to** para com); infiel m,f.

disloyalty n deslealdade f, infidelidade f.

dismal adj (bleak) sombrio,-a, lúgubre m,f; **2** (coll) lamentável, deprimente m,f.

dismantle vt desmontar, desmantelar.

dismay n consternação f; ♦ vt consternar; **much to my ~** para minha consternação.

dismember vt (corpse) desmembrar, **2** desagregar.

dismemberment n desmembramento, desagregação f.

dismiss vt (job, position) demitir, despedir (**sb from** alguém de); **2** (idea) rejeitar; **3** (possibility) excluir; **4** (JUR) (case, session) encerrar, terminar; **5** (claim, appeal) rejeitar, indeferir; **6** (bad thoughts) pôr de parte, banir; **7** (comment) menosprezar; **8** mandar embora.

dismissal n despedimento (of employee); demissão f (of boss); **2** (MIL) baixa; demissão f; **3** (JUR) (case) encerramento m; **unfair/wrongful ~** demissão f infundada, sem justa causa.

dismount vi desmontar, apear; **2** (bicycle) descer.

disobedience n desobediência; **civil ~** resistência f passiva.

disobedient adj desobediente m,f.

disobey vt desobedecer.

disorder n desordem f; **in ~** em desordem, desordenado,-a; **2** (rioting) desordens fpl; **civil ~** motins mpl; **3** (MED) indisposição f; doença; **bowel ~** problema intestinal.

disorderly adj (untidy-room) desarrumado,-a; **2** (person) desordenado,-a; **3** (unruly – crowd) agitado,-a; **4** (JUR) **~ conduct** n perturbação f da ordem pública.

disorganized (also: **-ised**) adj desorganizado,-a.

disorientated, disoriented adj desorientado,-a; **2** (confused) desnorteado,-a.

disown vt renegar, repudiar, enjeitar (child).

disparage vt menosprezar, depreciar, denegrir.

disparaging adj depreciativo,-a; **to be ~ about sb** troçar de alguém.

disparite adj desigual, díspar.

disparity n disparidade f, desigualdade f.

dispassionate adj imparcial m,f, calmo,-a, impassível m,f.

dispassionately adv imparcial, calmamente.

dispatch n (stock) remessa f; **2** (sending) expedição f; **3** (report, JOURN) comunicação f, comunicado m; **4** (speed) prontidão f; (MIL) parte f; **~ rider** n emissário,-a; (MIL) estafeta m,f; ♦ vt send, expedir; **2** (euph) (kill) despachar (fam).

dispel (also: **-led**) vt dissipar.

dispensable adj dispensável, prescindível m,f.

dispensary *n (in hospital)* dispensário *m; (shop)*, farmácia *f*.

dispensation *n (REL, MIL)* dispensa; **2** licença.

dispense *vt (JUR)* administrar, aplicar; **2** *(MED)* preparar (e vender) medicamentos; **3** aviar *(prescription at the pharmacy)*; **to ~ with** *vt* prescindir de; dispensar.

dispenser *n (machine)* distribuitor *m* automático; **cash ~** *(bank) n* caixa *f* automática; **soft drink ~** máquina *f* de refrigerantes; **3** *(for liquids)* doseador *m*.

dispensing chemist *n* farmacêutico,-a.

dispensing optician *n* oculista *m,f*.

disperse *vt* dispersar, espalhar; ♦ *vi* dispersar-se.

dispirited *adj* desanimado,-a, desalentado,-a.

displace *vt* deslocar.

displaced person *n (POL)* destituído,-a; exilado,-a.

displacement *n* deslocamento *m*.

display *n* exposição *f*, mostra; **2** *(MIL)* parada; manifestação *f*; **3** *(pej)* ostentação *f*; **4** *(COMP)* apresentação *f* visual; **5** *(show)* espe(c)táculo; ♦ *vt* expor, mostrar; manifestar; ostentar; **on ~** à mostra, em exibição; **~ advertising** *n* anúncios *mpl*; **~ cabinet** armário com vitrina; *(COMP) n* **~ screen** tela de vídeo.

displease *vt* ofender; desagradar; desgostar; **~d with** descontente com.

displeasure *n* desagrado *m*.

disposable *adj* disponível *m,f*; **2** descartável *m,f*; **~ nappy** *(UK)*, **diaper** *(US) n* fralda descartável.

disposal *n* disposição *f*, arranjo *m*; **2** *(COMM) (property)* venda, trepasse *m*; **3** *(of rubbish)* remoção *f*; **4** (of *waste*) destruição *f*; **at your ~** à sua disposição; **waste ~ unit** *n* triturador *m* de lixo.

dispose *vt*: **to ~ of** *(time, money)* dispor de; **2** *(unwanted goods)* desfazer-se de; **3** *(throw away)* atirar *(BR:* jogar) fora; **4** *(COMM)* vender, transferir (propriedade).

disposed *adj*: **~ to help** disposto a ajudar; **to be ~ to violence** ser propenso à violência; **well-~ to(wards)** *adj* favorável a.

disposition *n* disposição *f*; **2** *(temperament)* índole *f*.

dispossess *vt (JUR)* **to ~ sb (of)** despojar alguém de; **2** *(land)* desapossar de; **3** *(house)* expropriar alguém de.

dispossessed *adj* despojado,-a; **2** *(family, property)* expropriado,-a.

disproportion *n* desproporção *f*, disparidade *f*.

disproportionate *adj* desproporcionado,-a.

disprove *vt* refutar.

disputable *adj* discutível *m,f*, contestável *m,f*.

dispute *n* disputa *f*; discussão *f*; (= **industrial ~**) contenda, disputa; ♦ *vt* discutir; questionar.

disqualification *n* *(SPORT)* desqualificação *f*, desclassificação *f*; **2** *(JUR)* inabilitação *f*, incapacidade *f*.

disqualify *vt* desqualificar; **to ~ sb from doing sth** desqualificar alguém para fazer algo; **2** *(AUT, JUR) (from driving)* ser proibido de (conduzir).

disquiet *n* inquietação *f*, perturbação *f*.

disregard *n* negligência *f*, desleixo *m*; **~ (for)** desconsideração *f (por)*; ♦ *vt* desconsiderar; não fazer caso de.

disrepair *n* mau estado; ruína; **to fall into ~** ficar arruinado,-a, estar estragado,-a.

disreputable *adj* de má fama; vergonhoso,-a.

disrepute *n* descrédito, má reputação *f*.

disrespect *n* desrespeito.

disrespectful *adj* desrespeitoso.

disrobe *vi (formal)* despir(-se).

disrupt *vt* desfazer; transtornar; interromper.

disruption *n* *(inconvenience)* transtorno *m*; **2** *(ELECT)*, interrupção *f*; **3** *(upheaval)* perturbação *f*, perturbações *fpl*.

disruptive *adj (person)* perturbador,-ora; *(ELECT)* **~ discharge** descarga *f* disruptiva.

dissatisfaction *n* descontentamento *m*, desagrado *m*.

dissatisfactory *adj* insatisfatório,-a.

dissatisfied *adj* descontente *m,f*; insatisfeito,-a.

dissect *vt (MED, ANAT, BIOL)* dissecar; **2** decompor *(molecule);* **3** analisar *(book theory)*.

dissection *n* dissecação *f*.

dissemble *vt* dissimular, disfarçar.

dissembler *n* dissimulador, fingido.

disseminate *vt (spread)* divulgar *(information)*; espalhar, propagar *(seed)*.

dissemination *n* disseminação *f*, propagação *f*; **2** divulgação *f*; **3** *(MED)* alastramento *m* de *(virus, infection)*.

dissent *n (POL, SPORT)* contestação; **2** desacordo, divergência; ♦ *vi (JUR)* contestar; **2** divergir.

dissenting *adj (gen)* dissidente; contestatário,-a; *(REL)* inconformista *m,f*.

dissenter *n adj (REL, POL)* dissidente *m,f*, separatista *m,f*.

dissertate *vi* dissertar, prele(c)cionar.

dissertation *n* dissertação *f*, tese *f*.

disservice *n* prejuízo *m*; **to do sb a ~** prejudicar alguém.

dissident *n* dissidente *m,f*.

dissimilar *adj* dissimilar *m,f*, diferente *m,f* (de); dessemelhante *m,f*.

dissimilarity *n* diferença, dissemelhança.

dissimilitude *n* dissimilhança *f*.

dissimulate *vt/vi* dissimular, fingir, disfarçar.

dissipate *vt/vi* dispersar; dissipar(-se), desperdiçar.

dissipated *adj* disperso,-a; dissoluto,-a.

dissociate *vt (CHEM)* dissociar, separar, desagregar, decompor.

dissoluble *adj* dissolúvel *m,f*.

dissolute *adj* dissoluto,-a; **~ man** libertino,-a.

dissolution *n (CHEM, JUR)* dissolução *f*.

dissolve *vt* dissolver; ♦ *vi* dissolver-se; **to ~ in(to) tears** desfazer-se em lágrimas; **2** *(JUR)* anular, rescindir.

dissonance *n* discordância *f*; **2** *(MUS)* dissonância *f*; **3** *(PSYCH)* **cognitive ~** dissonância cognitiva.

dissuade *vt*: **to ~ sb (from)** dissuadir alguém (de).

distaff *n* roca *f* de fiar; fuso *m*; **2** *(fig)* women's work; **~ side** lado, ramo materno da família.

distal *adj* (ANAT) distal *m,f*.

distance *n* distância; **in the ~** ao longe; **it's within walking ~** pode-se ir a pé; **keep your ~ (from sb/ sth)** manter-se à distância (de alguém/algo); ♦ *adj* **long-~** *(travel)* de longa distância; *(phone)* interurbano.

distant *adj (far)* distante *m,f*; afastado,-a; **2** *(person)* reservado,-a, distante *m,f*.

distaste *n* desagrado *m*; aversão *f*.

distasteful *adj* desagradável *m,f*.

distemper *n* tinta plástica; **2** *(VET) (dog's disease)* cinomose *f*.

distend *vt* distender, alongar, dilatar.

distended *adj* inchado, dilatado.

distention *n (MED)* distensão *f*, dilatação *f*.

distil *vt* destilar.

distillation *n* destilação *f*.

distillery *(pl: -ies) n* destilaria *f*.

distinct *adj* distinto,-a; claro,-a; nítido,-a; **as ~ from** diferente de.

distinctive *adj* distintivo.

distinction *n* diferença *f*; *(excellence)* distinção *f* (**between** entre); **to draw a ~ between** fazer distinção entre; **a writer of ~** um escritor de destaque.

distinctive *adj* care(c)terístico,-a (de).

distinctly *adv* claramente.

distinguish *vt* distinguir, diferenciar; ♦ *vi:* **to ~ between** distinguir entre; **to ~ o.s** distinguir-se.

distinguished *adj (person)* eminente *m,f*, notável *m,f*; **~-looking** com um ar distinto.

distort *vt* alterar; deturpar; distorcer.

distortion *n* deturpação *f (of truth)*; **2** *(ELECT, PHOT)* distorção *f*, deformação *f* visual ou auditiva.

distract *vt (person – attention)* distrair; desviar.

distracted *adj* distraído,-a; preocupado,-a.

distraction *n* distra(c)ção *f*; IDIOM **to drive sb to ~** fazer alguém louco; **be driven to ~** perder a cabeça.

distraught *adj* perturbado,-a, transtornado,-a.

distress *n* angústia *f*, aflição; **2** *(physical)* dor *f*; perigo; **in ~** em perigo; ♦ *vt* afligir; doer.

distressing *adj* aflitivo,-a, angustioso,-a; **~ signal** *n (AER, NAUT)* sinal *m* de perigo, pedido *m* de socorro.

distribute *vt* distribuir; repartir.

distribution *n* distribuição *f*; *(profits)* partilha; **2** *n (COMM)* **~ cost** custo de distribuição.

distributor *n (AUT)* distribuidor *m*; **2** *(COMM)* distribuidor,-ora.

district *n (gen)* distrito *m*; **2** *(ADMIN)* bairro *m*, comarca *f*; **~ attorney** *n (US)* procurador *m*, *(BR)* promotor *m* público; **~ council** *n* câmara municipal, *(BR)* município; **~ Court** *n (US)* Tribunal *m* de primeira instância; **~ nurse** *n (UK)* enfermeira visitadora; domiciliária (do distrito).

distrust *n* desconfiança, suspeita; ♦ *vt* desconfiar de, suspeitar de.

disturb *vt (interrupt)* perturbar; incomodar; **sorry to ~ you** desculpe incomodá-lo!; **2** *(upset, inconvenience)* inquietar, transtornar; **3** *(disarrange)* desarrumar; ♦ *vr* **to ~ o.s.** *(inconvenience)* incomodar-se.

disturbance *n (agitation)* perturbação *f*; **2** *(upheaval)* tumulto *m*; *(riots)* distúrbios; **to cause a ~** *(JUR)* perturbar a ordem pública.

disturbed *adj (PSYCH)* perturbado,-a, desnorteado,-a; **mentally ~** com perturbações *fpl* mentais; **2** *(sleep, night)* agitado,-a; **3** *(concern)* inquieto,-a.

disturbing *adj* perturbador,-ora; *(worrying)* inquietante *m,f*.

disuse *n:* **to fall into ~** cair em desuso.

disused *adj* desusado, abandonado.

disyllabic *adj (LING)* dissilábico.

ditch *n (AGR)* fosso *m*; rego *m*, vala *f*; ♦ *vt (coll) (get rid of)* desfazer-se de *(clothes, car)*; **she had to ~ the car** ela teve de abandonar, desfazer-se de, *(BR)* descartar o carro; **2** *(unwanted visitor)* desembaraçar-se de; **3** *(employee)*; despedir; **4** *(girlfriend, boyfriend)* livrar-se de, desembaraçar-se; **5** *(AER) (plane)* aterrar de emergência na água; **6** *(US) (evade)* escapar *(police)*.

ditchwater: IDIOM **as dull as ~** chato,-a, insípido,-a.

dither *vt (hesitate, be nervous)* hesitar, ser indeciso; **2** *(speech)* titubear.

ditto *adv* idem, o mesmo; **~ marks** *npl* aspas *fpl*.

ditty *n* cantiga, música ligeira, modinha.

diuretic *n adj (MED)* diurético.

diva *n* diva, cantora (de ópera) notável.

divan *n* divã *m*.

dive *n (from board)* salto; mergulho; *(plane, bird)* voo *m* picado; **2** *(coll) (bar, pub)* taberna, espelunca, bodega; **3** *(sudden fall)* queda *f* súbita; **4** *(coll) (SPORT)* **to take a ~** ir ao tapete; ♦ *vi* mergulhar; fazer mergulho; **2** *(plane)* descer a pique; **3** *(person)* atirar-se para.

dive-bomb *vt* bombardear em voo picado.

diver *n* mergulhador,-ora; **deep-sea ~** *n* escafandrista *m,f*; **2** *n (ZOOL)* mergulhão *m*.

diverge *vi* divergir.

divergence *n* divergência *f*, discordância *f*.

diverse *adj* diferente *m,f*.

diversify *vt/vi* diversificar, variar.

diversion *n (traffic, money)* desvio *m*; **2** *(distraction, MIL)* diversão *f*.

divert *vt (turn aside)* desviar; *(attention)* distrair.

divest *vt (idea)* banir; *(person)* despojar, privar de; **to ~ sb of sth** privar alguém de algo; **2** *(JUR)* desapossar, privar.

divide *vt (MATH)* dividir; separar; repartir; **~ out (between/among)** distribuir, repartir (entre); ♦ *vi* dividir-se; *(road)* bifurcar-se.

divided *adj* dividido,-a; **~ highway** *n (US)* pista-dupla; **~ skirt** *n* saia-calça *f*.

dividend *n (FIN)* dividendo; **to pay ~s** trazer benefícios *mpl*, vantagens *fpl*.

divider *n (space)* divisória *f*; **2** *(voltage potential) (ELECT)* divisor de tensão; **3** *(dossier)* separador *m*; **4 ~s** *npl* compasso de ponta seca.

divine *adj* divino,-a, sagrado,-a; ♦ *vt* adivinhar; predizer; *(water)* descobrir.

diving *n (SPORT)* salto *m*; *(underwater)* mergulho; **~ board** *n* prancha de saltos; trampolim *m*; **~ suit** *n* escafandro.

divinity *n* divindade *f*; *(EDUC)* teologia.

divisible *adj (MATH)* divisível *m,f* (por).

division *n (MATH, MIL, BIO)* divisão *f*; **2** *(sharing out)* repartição *f*, distribuição *f*; **3** *(disagreement)* desavença *f*; **4** *(POL)* votação *f*.

divisive *adj* que semeia discórdia, causa divisão *f*.

divorce *n* divórcio; ◆ *vt* divorciar-se de; **she ~d him** ela divorciou-se dele; **to file for/sue for ~** *(JUR)* intentar uma a(c)ção de divórcio; **to grant a ~** *(JUR)* decretar o divórcio; **to be ~d from sth** *(fig)* dissociar-se de, desligar-se de *(idea, reality)*.

divorcé *n* divorciado.

divorced *adj* divorciado,-a.

divorcée *n* divorciada.

divot montículo *m* de relva

divulge *vt* divulgar, revelar.

dixie *n (MIL)* caldeirão de metal para cozinhar.

Dixie *(also: **Dixieland**) n* estados *mpl* do sul dos EUA.

Dixieland *n* tipo de jazz oriundo de Nova Orleães.

DIY *(abbrev for **do-it-yourself**)* faça-você-mesmo.

dizziness *n* vertigem *f*, tontura *f*.

dizzy *adj (person)* tonto,-a; *(height)* vertiginoso; **to have ~ spells** ter vertigens; **to feel ~** sentir-se tonto, sentir-se atordoado,-a.

DJ *n (abbr for **disc jockey**)*.

DJIA *n (abbr for **Dow Jones Industrial Average**) (US) (ECON)* índice *m* da bolsa de valores de Nova Iorque.

Djibouti *npr* Djibuti.

Djiboutian *npr adj* djibutiano,-a.

dl *n (abbr for **decilitre**)* decilitro.

DLitt *(abbr for **Doctor of Letters**)* doutor,-ora em letras, doutorado,-a em letras.

DLL *n (abbr for **Dynamic-Link Library**) (COMP)* Biblioteca de Ligação Dinâmica.

DM *(abbr for **Deutschmark**)* marco *m* alemão *(before the Euro)*.

DNA *n (abbr for **deoxyribonucleic acid**)* ADN *m* ácido m desoxirribonucleico.

D notice *(UK) n* aviso *m* do governo aos órgãos de comunicação social para não divulgarem informações sensíveis.

do *n (UK)* festa *f*; **2 do's and don'ts** *(pop)* coisas que se devem ou não fazer; ◆ *(3rd pers, sg: **does**, pt: **did**, pp: **done**, pres.p: **doing**) vt aux (gen)* fazer; **2** *(be busy with)* **to ~ the ironing** passar a ferro; **to ~ the garden** tratar do jardim; *(grooming o.s)* **go and ~ your hair** vai pentear-te; **I have already done my teeth** já lavei os dentes; **to ~ the dishes** lavar a louça; **2** *(emphatic)* **I ~ like this colour** eu realmente gosto desta cor; **3** *(in negatives)* **I don't like** não gosto; **she doesn't (does not) care about it** ela não se interessa por isso; **4** *(in questions)* **do you want to go out?** você quer sair?; **you said yes, didn't you?** tu disseste que sim, não disseste?; **do you agree? yes I do** você concorda? sim; **no, I don't** não, não concordo; **I don't either** eu também não; **how did you do it?** como é que você fez isso? *(fam)*; **how do you manage**

to do it? como consegue fazer isso?; *(finish with doing sth)* **have you done with crying?** já acabaste com o choro?; **5** *(formal talk) (on introduction)* **how do you do!** *(pleased to meet you)* muito prazer; **do sit down!** queira sentar-se!; **6** *(in comparisons)* **she sings better than I do** ela canta melhor do que eu; **7** *(be enough)* **that will do!** basta! chega!; ◆ *vt (perform)* fazer; **she always does that** ela sempre faz isso; **she has done it again** ela voltou a fazer isso; *(noticing change)* **what have you done to your face?** que fizeste à tua cara?; **it's done!** *(completed)* está feito!; **well done!** apoiado! **nothing doing!** *(no way)* nem pensar!; *(course subjects)* estudar; **I am doing geography** estudo geografia; **I am doing a course** estou a fazer/fazendo um curso; ◆ *vi (behave)* **do as you are told** faz o que/como te dizem; **2** *(purpose)* servir; **that cloth will ~** esse pano serve; **3** *(business)* prosperar; **4 ~ well/wrong** *(get on/ not get on)* sair-se bem/mal; **5** *(THEAT) (a play)* representar; ◆ **to ~ away with** exterminar, ver-se livre de *(sth algo)*; descartar; **to ~ in** *(coll)* matar; **to ~ over** *vt* repetir; ◆ **to ~ up** *vt (laces)* atar; **2** *(zip)* fechar; **3** *(dress, coat)* abotoar; ◆ **to ~ well** *(progress, prosper)* prosperar, ter êxito; *(health)* **they are doing well** eles estão bem; **~ without** prescindir de; passar sem; **I can ~ without it** eu cá me arranjo.

DOA *(abbr for **dead on arrival**)* já era cadáver.

doable *adj* exequível *m,f*, viável *m,f*.

d.o.b. *n (abbr for **date of birth**)* data *f* do nascimento.

dobbin *n* cavalo *m* manso, *(BR)* matungo *m*.

doc *n (abbr for **doctor**) (coll)* médico,-a.

docile *adj* dócil *m,f*, manso,-a, submisso,-a.

docility *n* docilidade *f*, mansidão *f*.

dock *n (in harbour)* doca *f*, ancoradouro, cais *m*; **2** *(JUR; in court))* banco (dos réus); **3** *(BOT)* azeda *f*; ◆ *vi (ship)* chegar; atracar; **come into ~** *(ship)* entrar no cais; *(go into the shipyard)* entrar no estaleiro; **2** *(passengers)* chegar; ◆ *vt (in a game)* descontar *(point or money)*; *(in wages)* reduzir; **2** *(cut dog's, sheep's tail)* cortar, fazer a cauda do animal mais curta; pequena; **3** *(connect two computers)* acoplar; *(two spacecrafts)* acoplar duas naves espaciais enquanto orbitando.

docker *n* trabalhador *m* portuário, estivador *m*.

docket *n (consignment) (delivery)* guia *f*; **2** resumo *m*, extra(c)to *m*; **3** *(JUR)* lista das sentenças, sumário oficial dos casos/processos.

docking *n (NAUT)* amarração *f*; entrada em doca; **2** *(spacecraft)* acoplagem *f*.

dockland *n* zona *f* portuária.

dockyard *n* estaleiro *m*.

doctor *n* médico,-a; **2** *(PhD)* doutor,-ora; ◆ *vt (fig)* tratar; *(VET)* castar *(dog, cat)*; **2** falsificar *(accounts)*; adulterar *(food, wine)*; **~'s clinic** *n (US)* consultório.

doctorate *n* doutoramento *m*, doutorado *m*.

doctrinaire *n* visionário,-a, escolástico,-a, teorista *m,f*, ideólogo,-a; ◆ *adj* doutrinário,-a, teórico,-a, dogmático,-a.

doctrine *n* doutrina *f*.

docudrama *n* dramatização *f*.

document *n* documento *m*; ♦ *vt* documentar.

documentary *n* documentário *m*; ♦ *adj (evidence)* documental *m,f*.

documentation *n* documentação *f*.

DOD *npr (abbr for* **Department of Defense)** *(US)* Departamento/Ministério da Defesa dos EUA.

dodder *vi* cambalear, titubear; **2** *(BOT)* cuscuta *f*.

doddering *adj (person)* cambaleante *m*; **2** *(senile)* senil, gagá *(fam)*; *(legs)* trôpegas.

doddle *n (UK) (coll) (easy work)* **it's a ~!** é canja!

dodecagon *n (MATH)* dodecágono.

dodecahedron *n (MATH)* dodecaedro.

Dodecanese (Islands) *npr pl* (Ilhas *fpl* do) Dodecaneso.

dodge *n (idea)* evasiva; *(fig)* trapaça *f*; ♦ *vt* esquivar-se, evitar; **2** *(tax)* sonegar; ♦ *vi*: **to ~ out of the way** safar-se.

Dodgems® *npl (bumper car)* carros *mpl* de choque.

dodger *n* trapaceiro,-a, desonesto,-a.

dodgy *adj* arriscado,-a; desonesto,-a; **it sounds ~ to me** parece-me duvidoso/desonesto.

dodo *n (ZOOL) (extinct animal)* dodó, droute *m*.

doe *n (ZOOL) (of deer)* corça; *(female of rat, kangaroo, ferret)*; *(female rabbit)* coelha.

DOE *(abbr for* **Department of Environment)** Ministério do Ambiente.

doer *n (active, energetic) (person, horse)* enérgico,-a; *(of good deeds)* **a ~ of good** uma boa pessoa.

does *(3rd pess sg* of **do)**.

doesn't = **does not** *(Vd:* **do)**.

doff *vt* despir; **2** tirar o chapéu *(saudação)*.

dog *n* cão *m*, *(puppy)* cachorro,-a, *(female dog) (BR) (any size dog)* cachorro,-a; cadela *f*; ~ **breeder** *n* criador,-ora de cães; ~'**s club** associação *f* canina; ~ **collar** *n* coleira; *(fig)* gola de padre; ~-**eared** *adj (book)* com os cantos dobrados *or* gastos; ~-**end** *n (cigarette)* prisca *f*; ~**fish** *(ZOOL)* pequeno tubarão *m*, cação *m*; **guard** ~ cão de guarda; **guide** ~ cão guia; ~**house** canil *m* **to be in the ~house** *(fig) (person)* cair em desagrado; **hot** ~ *(CULIN)* cachorro-quente *m*; ~-**leg** *n (AUT) (sharp turn)* viragem *f* brusca; ~ **show** *n* exposição *f* canina; **D~ Star** *npr (ASTROL)* Sírio *m*; ~-**tired** *adj* estafado,-a; **2** *(fam) (person)* **you lucky ~!** seu felizardo!; **3** *(CONSTR) (gen)* gancho *m*; ♦ *(-gg-) vt* seguir os passos de; perseguir; **to be ~ged by bad luck** ser perseguido pela má sorte; IDIOM **it's a ~'s life** é uma vida de cão *(also:* uma vida burro); **you don't have a ~'s chance** você não tem a mínima hipótese; *f* **barking dogs seldom bite** cão que ladra, não morder.

dogfight *n* luta *f* de cães; **2** *(between people)* zaragata *f*, *(BR)* brigalhada *f*.

dogged *adj* tenaz *m,f*; persistente *m,f*.

doggerel *n* verso *m* de pé quebrado, versalhada *f*.

doggie *(also:* **doggy)** *n* cãozinho *m*, *(female)* cadelinha; *(child's talk)* béu-béu; ~ **bag** *n* saco *m* para levar restos de comida.

dogma *n* dogma *m*.

dogmatic *adj* dogmático.

dogmatics *n (EDUC)* dogmática.

dogmatism *n* dogmatismo.

dogmatist *n* dogmatista.

do-gooder *n* pessoa com boas intenções mas que interfere; uma bom/um boa samaritano,-a; **2** *(pej) (person)* um bonzinho, uma boazinha.

dogsbody *n (UK) (coll) (person)* o a faz-tudo.

doh *n (MUS)* dó *m*.

doily *n* naperão *m* de papel *(to put under cakes)*.

doing *n*: **it's all your ~!** é tudo a tua/sua culpa!; ♦ ~**s** *npl* acontecimentos *mpl*; a(c)tividades *fpl*.

do-it-yourself (DIY) *n* faça-você-mesmo; **2** bricolagem *f*.

doldrums *npl*: **to be in the ~** estar abatido; **2** *(ECON)* estar parado/estagnado.

dole *n (UK)* subsídio de desemprego, fundo de desemprego; ~ **queue** *n* fila *f* de espera (na agência de desemprego); **to be on the ~** estar desempregado; ♦ *vt* **to ~ out** *(food, money)* repartir, distribuir.

doleful *adj* triste *m,f*, lúgubre *m,f*.

doll *n* boneca, **2** *(coll)* mulher bonita; ~ **house** *n* casa de bonecas; **rag** ~ *n* boneca de trapos; ♦ *vt* **to ~ o. s. up** ataviar-se *(BR:* embonecar-se)*.

dollar *n* dólar *m*; ~ **sign** *n ($)* cifrão *m*.

dolled-up *adj (coll)* embonecado,-a.

dollop *n* colherada *(of* de); *(fig)* dose *f* (*of* de).

dolly *n (fam)* boneca, bonequinha *f (child's language)*; **2** *(CIN, TV) n* plataforma móvel para câmara cinematográfica.

dolman *n (MIL)* hussardo; **2** casaco feminino com mangas soltas; manto.

dolmen *n (MIN) (white mineral)* dolomite *m*.

dolomite *n (MIN) (white mineral)* dolomite *m*.

Dolomites *npr pl*: **the ~ Peaks** *(part of the Alps)* os Pináculos *mpl* das Dolomitas; os Dolomitas *mpl*.

dolomitic *adj* dolomítico,-a.

dolmen *n* dólmen *m*.

dolphin *n (ZOOL)* golfinho *m*.

dolt *n* tolo, parvo, estúpido, pateta *m,f*.

doltish *adj* estúpido, lerdo.

domain *n* território, propriedade *f*; **2** *(sphere)* domínio *m*; ~ **name** *n (COMP)* nome *m* de domínio.

dome *n (ARCH)* cúpula *f*; abóbada *f*, zimbório *m*; **2** *(GEOG)* cume *m* arredondado (dum monte).

Dome of the Rock *npr (Mosque in Jerusalém)* a Cúpula do Rochedo.

Domesday Book *n (HIST)* registro das propriedades rurais inglesas e dos seus proprietários (1086).

domestic *adj (home, house-work related, market)* doméstico,-a, interno,-a; *(flight)* doméstico,-a; ~ **appliance** *n* ele(c)trodoméstico *m*; ~ **help** *n* empregado,-a doméstica; ~ **problems** *npl* problemas *mpl* de família/conjugais; **2 gross ~ product (GDP)** *n (ECON)* produto interno bruto (PIB).

domestically *adv (POL, gen)* internamente.

domesticity *n* domesticidade *f*, vida caseira.

domicile *n* domicílio; habitação *f*, residência *f*.

dominance *n (control)* domínio *m*, dominância *f*; **2** influência *f*; **3** *(importance)*, predomínio *m*.

dominant *n (MUS)* dominate *f*; ♦ *adj* dominante, predominante *m,f*.

dominate *vt* dominar, controlar.

domination *n* domínio *m*; inação *f*.

domineering *adj (person, character)* dominador, -ora, mandão *m*, mandona *f*.

Dominica *npr* Dominica.

dominical *adj* dominical; relativo ao domingo; *(REL)* relativo ao Senhor.

Dominican *adj (from Dominica)* dominicano,-a; **2** referente a São Domingues (pregador castelhano); **3** ~ **Republic** *npr* República; Dominicana; **in the** ~ na República Dominicana.

dominion *n* domínio *m*; autoridade *f* (**over** sobre); **2** *(territorial possessions)* domínios *mpl*; *(former British colonies)* império *m*.

domino *(pl:* **-es***) n* peça de dominó; ~ **effect** *n* efeito dominó; **-es** *npl (game)* dominó *msg*.

don *n (UK)* professor,-ora universitário,-a; ♦ (**-ned**) *vt* trajar, vestir.

donate *vt* doar.

donation *n* doação *f*, donativo.

donator *n* doador,-ora, dador,-ora.

done *(pp of* **do***) adj* feito, acabado, concluído,-a; **well** ~ *(approving)* apoiado!; **2** *(it serves you right)* bem feito!, *(CULIN)* cozido ou assado no ponto; ♦ *exc* feito!, combinado! aceite, aceito,-a!; *(Vd:* **do***).*

donée *n (JUR)* donatário,-a.

donkey *n (ZOOL)* burro, asno, jumento; **2** *(fig)* idiota *m,f*, estúpido; ~**-work** *n (coll)* labuta; **to do the** ~**'s work** fazer o pior trabalho.

donor *n* doador,-ora; **blood** ~ *n* doador,-ora, dador,-ora de sangue.

don't = **do not**.

doodle *n* rabisco *m*, gatafunho *m*; ♦ *vt* rabiscar, garatujar.

doom *n* (má) sorte *f*, perdição *f*; morte *f*, fado *m*; ♦ *vt* condenar *(person, object)*, fadar.

doomed *adj (business, mission)* condenado,-a; **to be** ~ **to failure** estar destinado/fadado ao fracasso.

Doomsday (Domesday) *n* dia do Juízo Final, fim do mundo.

doomwatch *n (ECOL)* previsão de catástrofe; **2** vigilância do meio-ambiente

door *n* porta *f*; entrada *f*; **back** ~ *n* porta das traseiras, *(BR)* porta dos fundos; ~**bell** *n* campainha *f* da porta; **front** ~ porta da rua/da frente; ~ **handle** *n* puxador *m*, maçaneta *f*; ~ **knocker** *n* batente, aldraba *f*; ~**keeper** *n* porteiro,-a; ~**mat** *n* capacho *m*; *(fig)* **I am not your** ~ não sou o teu capacho; ~**post** *n* ombreira *f* da porta; ~**step** *n* degrau *m* da porta; **trap** ~ alçapão; **two-~ car** *adj (AUT)* carro de duas portas; ~**way** *n* limiar da porta, entrada *f*; ♦ **next** ~ *adv* aqui ao lado, na casa ao lado; ♦ *adj* vizinho,-a; ~**-to-~** de porta a porta; **behind closed** ~**s** à porta fechada; '**mind the doors, please**' atenção às portas (automáticas); **to slam the** ~ **in sb's face** bater com a porta no nariz de alguém; **to show sb the** ~ pôr alguém na rua; IDIOM **as one** ~ **closes another one opens** quando se fecha uma porta abre-se uma janela.

dope *n (coll)* imbecil *m,f*; **2** droga *f*, narcótico *m*, *(BR)* maconha; **3** estimulante *m,f*; *(medicine) (to*

induce sleep) sonífero *m*; *(coll)* informação confidencial, dica *f*; ♦ *vt* drogar; dopar.

dopey (-ier, -iest) *adj* grogue *m,f*; **2** *(silly)* tonto,-a.

dormancy *n* letargia *f*, sonolência *f*; **2** *(BIOL)* dormência *f*.

dormant *adj* ina(c)tivo,-a; latente *m,f*.

dormer *n (in the building's roof)* água-furtada *f*, trapeira *f*; ~ **window** *n* janela *f* de água-furtada.

dormitory *n* dormitório *m*.

dormouse *(pl:* **-mice***) n (ZOOL)* arganaz *f*; rato (de campo).

dory *n (US) (NAUT)* barco de pesca (com remos).

DOS *n (abbr for* **Disc Operating System***) (COMP)* DOS *m* (sistema operacional de disco).

dosage *n (MED)* dose *f*, dosagem *f*, posologia *f*.

dose *n (MED)* dose *f*; ♦ *vt (MED)* **to** ~ **o.s.** medicar-se; dosear, dosificar.

dosh *n (slang) (money)* massa *f*.

doss-house *n* pensão *f* barata, casa de dormidas, *(BR)* cômodos; albergue *m*.

dossier *n* dossiê *m*; pasta *f*.

dot *n* ponto *m*; **2** *(on material)* mancha *f*; **3** ~,~,~ *(ellipsis)* reticências *fpl*; ♦ (**-tt-**) *vt (CULIN) (sprinkle)* salpicar; ~**ted with** salpicado de; **2** *(scattered over/along)* espalhar; **3** *(in writing)* pôr os pontos no i, j; ♦ *adv* **on the** ~ em ponto.

dotage *n*: **to be in one's** ~ estar na segunda infância.

dotcom *adj* ponto.com.

dote *vt*: **to** ~ **on** adorar; ter um fraco por, idolatrar.

doting *adj (person)* que adora *(children, spouse)*; baboso,-a, babão *m*, babona *f*; **a** ~ **father** um pai baboso.

dot-matrix printer *n (COMP)* impressora *f* matricial ou de agulhas.

dotted *adj (fashion – on fabric)* com pintas *fpl*, às pintas, com pintinhas *fpl*; ~ **line** *adj (paper)* pontilhado,-a; '**tear along the** ~ **line**' cortar pelo ponti-lhado.

dotty *adj (coll)* pateta *m,f*.

double *n (two of the same)* dobro *m*; **to be paid** ~ **time** ser pago o dobro; **2** *(look-alike person)* sósia; **3** *(ator)* duplo *m*; *(BR)* dublê; **to throw a** ~ *(games)* dobrar; **4** *(twice)* duas vezes; **she earns** ~ **the amount I earn** ela ganha duas vezes mais do que eu; ♦ **doubles** *npl (tennis)* pares *mpl*; *(BR)* dupla *f*; ♦ *adj (portion)* duplo,-a; **a** ~ **whisky** um uísque duplo; ~ **glazing** *n (windows)* vidro duplo; **2** ~ **figures** números de dois algarismos; **to go into** ~ **figures** *(inflation)* passar a fasquia do 10%; **Mellor is spelt (spelled) with a ~ 'l'** Mellor escreve-se com dois ll's; ♦ *adv* dobro, ao meio, em dois; **to cost** ~ custard o dobro; **to bend** ~ dobrar ao meio; **at/on the** ~ a/em passo acelerado; rápido; imediatamente ♦ *vt* duplicar; **2** *(prices, sales)* dobrar; **3** *(betting) (UK)* **to** ~ **the stakes** dobrar a aposta; ♦ **to** ~ **as** *(dual purpose)* servir de/como; também funcionar como; **to** ~ **back** voltar para trás; **to** ~ **for sb** *(CIN, THEAT)* for sb dobrar alguém; **2** *(work, dancing)* fazer as vezes de; **to** ~ **over** *(fold)* dobrar ao meio; **to** ~ **up** *vi (bend)* dobrar-se, curvar-se em dois; IDIOM **to**

~ **up with laughter** morrer de riso; ~ **standard** ter dois pesos e duas medidas; ◆ ~**-barrelled** *(UK)*, ~**-barreled** *(US) adj (rifle)* de dois canos; **2** *(person' surname)* apelido composto, 'Bottomworth-Smith'; ~ **bass** *n* contrabaixo *m*; ~**-breasted** *(jacket)* de trespasse; *(BR)* trespassado; ~**-check** *vt* tornar a verficar; ~ **chin** *n (fam)* papada *f*; *(on animals)* dewlap; ~**-chinned** *adj* com duplo queixo; ~**-cross** *vt* enganar; **2** atraiçoar; ~**-dealer** *n (person) (coll)* *(person)* pessoa de duas caras; enganador,-ora; ~**-dealing** *n* jogo *m* duplo; ~**-decker** *n* autocarro *m (BR)*: onibus *m* de dois andares; *adj (beds)* de duas camas; ~**-dutch** *n* **to talk** ~ falar chinês; ~**-edged** *adj (blade)* de dois gumes; ~ **entendre** *n (sentence, remark)* duplo sentido; ~**-jointed** *adj (person)* com articulações flexíveis; ~**-park** *vt* estacionar em segund fila; ~**-quick** *adj* **in** ~ **time** num ápice; **2** *adv* rapidamente; ~ **room** *n* quarto *m* de casal; ~**-sided** *adj (COMP)* dupla face; ~ **talk** *n (gibberish)* algaraviada *f*; ~**-tongued** *adj* hipócrita *m,f*.

doubloon *n (old Spanish gold coin)* dobrão.
doubly *adv* duplamente.
doubt *n* dúvida *f*; desconfiança *f*; ◆ *adj* indubitável *m,f*; ◆ *adv* sem dúvida alguma; ◆ *vt* duvidar; desconfiar de; **I** ~ **that** duvido que; **there is no** ~ **that** não há dúvida que.
doubtful *adj* duvidoso,-a, incerto,-a; **to be** ~ **about** ter dúvidas quanto a.
doubtless *adj* indubitável *m,f*, sem dúvida; ◆ *adv* indubitavelmente, certamente.
dough *n* massa; **2** *(coll) (dinheiro)* massa *(cal)*, *(BR)* grana *(cal)*; ~**nut** *n* bola de Berlim, *(BR)* sonho.
dour *adj* severo,-a, austero,-a.
douse (dowse) *vt* encharcar; **2** *(flames)* apagar.
dove *(US: pt of* **dive***)* *n (ZOOL)* pomba; ~**cote** *n* pombal; ~**tail** *vi (furniture)* encaixar-se.
dowager *n* viúva que herda o título ou os bens do marido; **2** senhora idosa da alta sociedade.
dowdiness *n* desalinho *m*, desmazelo *m*, desleixo *m*.
dowdy *adj* desleixado; fora de moda; pouco elegante.
down *n (fluff)* lanugem *f*; *(feathers)* penugem *f*; ◆ *adv* abaixo; para baixo; por terra; **I am coming** ~ já vou para baixo; **I am coming** ~ **with the flu** estou a ficar engripado,-a; **to come** ~ **on a person** censurar, ralhar com; **to come** ~ **to business** trabalhar, falar a sério; ◆ *prep* em baixo, abaixo; ~ **there**; ◆ *adv* lá em baixo; ~ **the river** pelo rio abaixo; **put my name** ~ **(for)** inscreva-me (para); ~ **to the last detail** até o último detalhe, em grande pormenor; ◆ *vt (gulp down)* beber depressa; **2** *(food)* devorar; ◆ **to back** ~ *vi* desistir; **to go** ~ descer; **the business has gone** ~ o negócio está em declínio, fracasso; **the wind is gone** ~ o vento abateu, amainou; **grade** ~ *vt* rebaixar; ~**hearted** *adj* desanimado; ~**-market** *adj* barato,-a, de qualidade *f* inferior; ~ **payment** *n* depósito *m*, sinal *m*, entrada *f*; ~ **play** *vt* minimizar; ~**pour** *n* aguaceiro *m*; ◆ *exc* **with the tyranny!** abaixo a tirania!
down-and-out *n* vagabundo,-a; ◆ *adj* sem futuro.

down-at-heel *adj (shabby) (person)* desmazelado,-a.
downbeat *adj* desanimado,-a.
downcast *adj* deprimido,-a cabisbaixo,-a.
downer *n (coll)* calmante.
downfall *n* queda, ruína.
downhill *n (skier)* descida *f*; ◆ *adj*: **to go** ~ *(skier)* ir morro abaixo; descer a encosta; ◆ *adv (downwards)* para baixo; *(fig)* estar em declínio, ir de mal a pior.

download *vt (COMP)* descarregar, *(BR)* baixar.
downmarket *adj* de má qualidade.
downright *adj (person)* franco,-a; **2** ~ **lie** perfeita mentira; **3** *(denial)* categórico,-a; **4** completo,-a; ~ **rude** grande malcriado,-a.
Downs *npr pl*: **the** ~ colinas *fpl* ao sul da Inglaterra.
downsize *vt (workforce)* reduzir.
Down's syndrome *n* síndrome *m* de Down, trissonia.
downstairs *adj* do andar de baixo; ◆ lá em baixo; **to go** ~ descer (as escadas).
downstream *n adv* juzante *f*; rio abaixo.
down-to-earth *adj* prá(c)tico, realista *m,f*.
downtown *adv (US)* do/no centro da cidade; baixa *f*.
downtrodden *adj* pisado,-a, oprimido,-a.
downturn *n (ECON)* queda *f*, declínio *m*; viragem *f* para pior.
down under *adv* da/na Austrália.
downwards *adj inv* descendente; ◆ **downwards** *adv* para baixo; ~ **tendencies** tendências negativas.
downwind *adv* a favor do vento.
downy *adj* com penugem *f*; macio,-a; felpudo,-a; *(pillow)* fofo,-a.
dowry *n* dote *m*; **Catarina de Bragança brought an enviable** ~ **to Britain's crown** Catarina de Bragança trouxe um dote invejável para a coroa britânica; **2** dom *m*, talento *m*.
doz. *(abbr for* **dozen***)*.
doze *n* soneca, *(BR)* cochilo; ◆ *vi* dormitar, *(BR)* cochilar.
dozen *n* dúzia; ~**s of times** milhares de vezes.
dozing (~ off) *adj*: **I was** ~ estava a cair no sono,-a dormitar.
dozy *adj* sonolento,-a, adormecido,-a.
dr *(abbr for* **doctor***)*; **2** *(street) (abbr for* **drive***)*.
drab *adj* monótono,-a, desinteressante *m,f*.
draft *n (first copy)* rascunho *m*; **2** *(POL)* proje(c)to de lei; **3** *(COMM)* saque *m*, letra; *(US: call-up)* recrutamento; ◆ *vt (plan)* redigir; esboçar; *(conscript)* recrutar; ~ **up** *(document)* redigido,-a, elaborado,-a.
draftee *n (MIL)* recruta *m*.
drag *n (coll)* estorvo *m*, obstáculo *m*, maçada *f (fam)*; **2** *(of cigarette)* fumaça *f (BR)* tragada *f*; **3** *(AER, NAUT)* resistência *f*; **in** ~ em travesti; ◆ *vt* arrastar; **2** *(river)* dragar; **to** ~ **away (from)** desgrudar (de); ◆ *vi* rastejar; **to** ~ **on** *vi* arrastar-se; prolongar-se.

dragnet *n* rede *f* de arrasto; **2** diligência *f* policial.

dragon *n* (ZOOL) dragão *m*; **2** *(fam)* pessoa intratável, megera *f*.

dragonfly *n* (ZOOL) libélula *f*.

dragoon *n* (MIL) dragão (soldado de cavalaria); ♦ *vt* acossar, perseguir com tropas; **to ~ sb into doing sth** forçar alguém a fazer algo.

drain *n* dreno *m*; sarjeta *f*; cano *m* (de esgoto); *(in street)* bueiro; escoamento; **2** *(loss)* perda *f*; **3** *(on resources)* sorvedouro *m*; ♦ *vt* esvaziar; escoar; drenar; ♦ *vi (strength, resources)* esgotar-se; **2** desaparecer; **the colour ~ed from her face** o rosto dela ficou sem pinta de sangue; IDIOM **down the ~** *(wasted, lost)* por água abaixo; **the wedding went down the ~** o casamento foi por água abaixo.

drainage *n* *(act)* drenagem *f*, escoamento *m*; **2** *(MED, AGR)* dreno *m*; *(sewage)* esgoto *m*.

drain away *vt* desaparecer.

drainer *n* escoador do lava-louças.

draining *n* escoamento *m*, esvaziamento *m*; ♦ **~ board** *n* escorredor da loiça/louça.

drainpipe *n* cano *m* de esgoto; **2** caleira *f*.

drake *n* (ZOOL) pato *m*, marreco *m*; **2** inse(c)to usado como isca (pesca).

dram *n* trago *m*.

drama *n* *(art)* teatro *m*; *(play)* drama *m*.

dramatic *adj* dramático,-a.

dramatically *adv* dramaticamente.

dramatist *n* dramaturgo,-a.

dramatize *vt/vi* dramatizar.

drank *(pt of* **drink***)*.

drape *vt* ornar; drapejar; **2 ~ over sth with sth** *(fig)* cobrir algo com algo; **~d** envolto,-a (**in**, **em**); **be ~ed over** *(fig) (casually)*; **she was ~ed over the sofa** ela estava reclinada sobre o sofa; ♦ **~s** *npl* (US) *(heavy curtains)* reposteiros *mpl*.

draper *n* negociante *m* de tecidos, fanqueiro,-a.

drastic *adj* severo,-a; drástico,-a; enérgico,-a.

drastically *adv* drasticamente.

draught (UK) **draft** (US) *n* *(air current)* corrente *f* de ar; **2** *(gulp: drink)* trago *m*; **on ~** *(beer)* da pipa, do barril; *(over counter)* (EP) imperial *f* *(col)*; (BR) chope *m*; **3** (NAUT) calado; **~ horse** cavalo *m* de tra(c)ção; **~s** (UK) *n* jogo de damas *fpl*; **~board** *n* tabuleiro de damas.

draughtsman *n* desenhista *m,f*, proje(c)tista *m,f*; **~ship** *n* *(art)* desenho industrial, *(technique)* habilidade *f* de desenhista.

draughty (UK), **drafty** (US) com correntes *fpl* de ar.

draw *n* (SPORT) empate *m*; *(lottery)* sorteio; atra(c)ção *f*; ♦ *(pt* **drew***, pp* **drawn***) vt* puxar, tirar; retirar; *(attract)* atrair; *(picture)* desenhar; *(money)* tirar, receber; **to ~ a check** emitir um cheque; **to ~ a curse** lançar um maldição; **to ~ apart** afastar-se; **to ~ a weapon** sacar uma arma; **to ~ blood** tirar sangue; **to ~ one's last breath** expirar; ♦ *vi* (SPORT) empatar; **to ~ back** *vi* fazer retroceder ou recuar; **to ~ in** *vi* chegar; encostar; **to ~ near** *vi* aproximar-se; **to ~ out** *vi* esticar, alargar; **to ~ up** *vi* parar(-se); ♦ *vt (document)* redigir.

drawback *n* inconveniente *m*, desvantagem *f*.

drawbridge *n* ponte *f* levadiça.

drawee *n* (COMM) sacado.

drawer *n* gaveta; **2** *n* (COMM) sacador; emitente (de cheque); **~s** ceroilas, (BR) ceroulas; ♦ **drawers** *npl* *(legged undergarment)* ceroulas, ceroilas *fpl*.

drawing *n* desenho; **~ board** *n* prancheta; **~ desk** *n* estirador *m*, mesa de desenho; **~ pin** *n* percevejo, (BR) tachinha; **~ room** *n* sala de visitas.

drawl *n* fala arrastada; ♦ *vi* falar arrastadamente.

drawn *(pp of* **draw***) adj (appearance)* abatido,-a, deprimido,-a; **2** *(curtain, blind)* fechado,-a, corrido,-a; **~-out** *adj* esticado,-a.

drawstring *n* cordão *m*.

dray *(also:* **drey***) n (type of cart)* zorra *f*; carreta *f*.

dread *n* medo, temor *m*; ♦ *vt* temer, recear, ter medo de.

dreaded *adj* temido,-a.

dreadful *adj* terrível.

dreadlocks *npl (hair style)* rastas *fpl*.

dream *n* sonho *m*; ♦ *(pt, pp* **dreamed** *or* **dreamt***) vt/vi* sonhar; **sweet ~s!** sonha com os anjos; **~ up** *vt* inventar.

dreamer *n* sonhador,-ora.

dreamy *adj* sonhador, distraído; sentimental.

dreary *adj* monótono,-a, maçador,-ora.

dredge *vt* dragar; **~ up** *vt (with dredger)* tirar do fundo, dragar; **2** *(fig)* trazer à tona, descobrir.

dredger *n* (NAUT) draga; (= **sugar ~**) polvilhador *m*.

dregs *npl* fezes *fpl*; **2** *(of coffee, wine)* borras *fpl*; *(of tea)* folhas *fpl*; **3** escória, resíduo; **4** *(of society)* ralé *f*.

drench *vt* encharcar, ensopar; **to get ~ed** molhar-se, encharcar-se.

dress *n* vestido; roupa; **~ circle** *n* primeiro balcão; balcão *m* nobre; **~ designer** *n* estilista *m,f*; **evening ~** *n (man's)* traje *m* de cerimónia (BR: -mô-), *(woman's)* vestido de noite; **~maker** *n* costureira, modista; **~making** *n* (arte *f* da) costura; **~ rehearsal** *n* ensaio geral; ♦ *vt* vestir; **2** *(wound)* fazer curativo; **3** (CULIN) preparar, temperar; **4** (MIL) alinhar (soldados); **5** *(hair)* arranjar, pentear; **6** *(shop window)* adornar, enfeitar; ♦ *vi* vestir-se; **to ~ down** *vt* repreender; **to ~ up** *vi* vestir-se com elegância, a rigor; fantasiar-se.

dresser *n* *(piece of furniture)* aparador *m*; **2** (US) cómoda (BR: cô-).

dressing *n* (MED) penso; curativo; (CULIN) molho; **~ gown** *n* roupão *m*; **~ room** *n* (THEAT) camarim *m*; (SPORT) vestiário; **~ table** *n* toucador *m*; (BR) penteadeira.

dressy *adj (coll)* chique, elegante no trajar.

drew *(pt of* **draw***)*.

drib *n*: **in ~s and drabs** *(small quantity)* às pinguinhas, aos poucos.

dribble *n* *(of liquid)* fio, fiozinho; *(drop)* gota; pequena quantidade; finta; **2** *(saliva)* baba *f*; **3** (SPORT) dribble; ♦ *vi* gotejar, pingar; **2** babar-se; **3** (SPORT) driblar.

dried *(pt, pp of* **dry***) adj* seco,-a; *(milk)* em pó.

drift *n* movimento; **a ~ back to** um movimento, retorno *m* progressivo a *(method)*; **2** *(trend)* tendência *f*; **3** *(of events)* curso; **4** *(of current)* corrente *f*, correnteza *f*; **5** *(of plane, ship)* deriva *f*; **6** *(of projectile)* desvio *m*; **7** *(GEOL)* deposits, sediments *mpl*; **~-sand** *n* areia movediça; **~wood** *n* madeira flutuante, afasta-se de algo; **8** *(meaning)* **to catch the ~ of** *(conversation, argument)* compreender o sentido de; **I don't catch/follow your ~** não compreendo, percebo onde você quer chegar; ♦ *vi (pile up)* amontoar-se, acumular-se *(of snow, leaves)*; **2** *(plane, balloon)* voar à deriva; **3** *(be carried by wind and tide)* ser arrastado pelo vento ou corrente *(boat)*; andar à deriva; **to ~ along** *(aimlessly)* vaguear, andar sem destino; **to ~ away from sth** afastar-se gradualmente de algo; **to ~-apart** *(lovers)* separar-se, afastar-se aos poucos; **to ~ in** *vt* entrar por acaso; **to ~ off** *vt* adormecer.

drifter *n* nómada *m,f*, *(BR)* nômade; **2** *(fig)* vagabundo,-a; **3** *(boat)* traineira *f*.

drill *n* furador *m*; *(dentist)* broca; *(MIL)* exercícios *mpl* militares; ♦ *vt* furar, brocar; *(MIL)* exercitar; ♦ *vi* perfurar.

drilling *n* *(for oil)* perfuração *f*; **~ rig** *n* torre *f* de perfuração.

drink *n* bebida; **to have a ~** tomar uma bebida; ♦ *(pt* **drank** *pp* **drunk)** *vt/vi* beber; **to ~ to sb/sth** brindar a alguém/algo; **to ~ in** *vt* embeber-se em; **to ~ up** *vt* beber todo/tudo.

drinkable *adj (water)* potável; **2** *(wine, etc)* bebível.

drinker *n* bebedor,-ora.

drinking *n* alcoolismo; **~ fountain** *n* bebedoiro, *(BR:* -dou-); **~ water** *n* água potável.

drip *n* goteira; gota, pingo; **2** soro *m*; *(device)* conta-gotas *m*; **3** *(insipid person)* deslavado,-a; *(fam)* mosca-morta; ♦ *vi* gotejar, pingar; **2** *(plant)* regar a conta-gotas.

drip-dry *adj* de lavar e vestir.

drip-feed *n* *(MED)* alimentação *f* intravenosa de soro/sangue, etc.

dripping *n* gordura; **2** gotejamento *m*; **~ wet** *adj* encharcado,-a.

drive *n* passeio (de carro); viagem *f*; **2** *(short street)* rua; caminho *m* privado; *(~way)* entrada; energia, vigor *m*; **3** *(PSYCH)* impulso; **4** *(SPORT)* tiro *m*, golpe *m*; ♦ *(pt* **drove,** *pp* **driven)** *vt* conduzir; guiar, *(BR)* dirigir; fazer trabalhar; impelir; cravar; empurrar; ♦ *vi (AUT)* andar de carro; conduzir; **left-/right-hand ~** dire(c)ção *f* à esquerda/direita.

drivel *n* disparate *m*; ♦ *(-ll-)* dizer asneiras; **2** *(slaver)* babar-se.

driven *(pp of* **drive) power ~** elétrico,-a.

driver *n* motorista *m,f*; chofer *m*; *(RAIL)* maquinista *m,f*; **2** *(MEC)* propulsor, roda motriz; **co-~** *n (in race)* co-piloto; *(in lorry)* segundo motorista; **~'s license** *n (US)* carta de condução, *(BR)* carteira de motorista; **lorry ~** *n* camionista *m,f*, *(BR)* caminhoneiro.

driving *n* automobilismo *m*; condução *f*, *(BR)* direção *f*; **~ belt** *n* correia *f* de transmissão; **~ force** *n* força *f* motriz; **~ instructor** *n* instrutor,-ora de condução, *(BR:* de auto-escola); **~ lesson** *n* lição *f* de condução, *(BR)* aula de direção; **~ licence**

n (UK) carta de condução, *(BR)* carteira de motorista; **~ mirror** *n* (espelho) retrovisor *m*; **~ school** *n* escola de condução, *(BR)* auto-escola *f*; **~ test** *n* exame *m* de condução *(BR:* de motorista); ♦ *adj* intenso, energético; *(force)* impulsionador,-ora; **~ rain** chuva torrencial.

drizzle *n* chuvisco *m*; ♦ *vi* chuviscar.

drizzly *adj* chuvoso.

droll *adj* engraçado,-a, cómico,-a *(BR:* cô-).

drollery *n* brincadeira *f*, graça *f*.

dromedary *n* *(ZOOL)* dromedário *m*.

drone *n* zumbido, zunido; *(ZOOL)* zangão *m*; ♦ *vi* zumbir, zunir; **~ on** *vi* falar monotonamente.

drool *vt* babar(-se); **to ~ over sth** adorar algo.

droop *n* inclinação *f*; *(sagging)* frouxidão *f*; ♦ *vi (hang downwards limply)* pender; *(head)* inclinar-se, baixar; *(fig) (spirits)* desanimar-se; *(flowers)* murchar; *(eyelids)* cair, tombar; *(mustache)* descair; **the corners of her mouth ~ed** os cantos da boca dela descaíram.

drop *n* *(of liquid, rain, blood)*, gota *f*; **a ~ in the ocean** uma gota no oceano; **2** *(of wine, tea)* pinga *f*, gole *m*; **another ~ (of wine)?** mais uma pinga?; **3** *(MED)* gota *f*; **~ by ~** gota a gota; **4** *(in prices, demand)* baixa *f*, queda *f*; *(in salary)* redução *f*; **5** *(slope)* escarpa, declive *m*; (= **parachute ~)** salto *m*; **there is a ~ of about 30 m from the top to the bottom** há um altura de 30 m de cima para baixo; **6** *(sweet)* rebuçado *m*; *(for cough, etc)* pastilha *f* (para a tosse); **7** *(delivery of supplies) (from plane)* lançamento *m*; *(from lorry)* entrega *f*; ♦ *(-pp-)* *vt (person-accidentally)* deixar cair; *(door, window, shoulders)* descair; **the door ~ped by a few centimeters** a porta descaíu uns centímetros; *(fall-by itelf)* cair; **the vase ~ped to the floor** a jarra caiu ao chão; *(from aircraft)* largar; **2** *(lower)* baixar *(price, temperature, hem)*; descair **3 to ~ a hint** fazer alusão a; *(with malice)* dar piada a **(sb** alguém); ♦ **to ~ sb sth** *(at a place) (also:* **~ off)** deixar (ficar); **I'll ~ you at the station** deixo-te na estação; ♦ *vi (fall, descend)* cair; descer; **the curtain ~ped** *(THEAT)* o pano desceu; **the plane ~ped to an altitude of** o avião desceu até à altitude de; **2** *(lower)* baixar *(price)* diminuir *(interest, speed, noise)*; **3** *(let fall) (in amazement)* **his mouth ~ped** ele ficou de boca aberta/boquiaberto; **4** *(stop doing)* parar, deixar de; **~ the subject!** deixa lá o assunto!; **~ that!** *(doing that)* para com isso!; **to ~ back/behind** *(walking, in progress)* ficar para trás, atrasar-se; **to ~ by/in** passar pela casa de **(sb** alguém); **~ in any time** venha cá à casa quando quiser; **to ~ off** *vi (fall asleep)* adormecer; **to ~ sb/sth off at** deixar (ficar) alguém/algo *f*; **to ~ out** *vi (fall out)* cair **(of** de); **2** *(withdraw)* desistir, retirar-se **(of from** de) *(project, competition)*; *(from studies)* abandonar os estudos; *(from society)* marginalizar-se; **to ~ round sth** *(to sb's house/office)* devolver, entregar algo; ♦ IDIOM **to have a ~ too much** estar embriagado,-a; estar com um grão na asa; **to ~ a brick/clanger** meter o pé na argola, meter a pata na poça.

drop leaf *n* (*flap of table*) aba (de mesa).

droplet *n* gotinha, gotícula.

dropout *n* marginal *m,f*; **2** (*from school, univ*) desistente *m.f.*

dropper *n* conta-gotas *m inv.*

droppings *npl* (*excrement*) (*of sheep, goat, rabbit, birds*) caganitas *fpl.*

drops *npl* gotas *fpl.*

drop-shot *n* (*tennis*) deixada *f.*

drop-shutter *n* (PHOT, TV, CIN) obturador *m* de guilhotina.

dross *n* (TECH) (*waste-of molten material*) refugo *m*; **2** (*of mine*) ganga; **3** (*fig*) (*rubbish*) escória *f*, lixo *m.*

drought *n* seca *f*, estiagem *f.*

drove (*pt of* **drive**) *n* rebanho, manada; (*of people*) multidão *f.*

drown *vt* (*kill*) afogar; ~ **out** *vt* (*sound*) abafar; ♦ *vi* afogar-se, morrer afogado,-a.

drowning *n* afogamento *m.*

drowse *vi* dormitar.

drowsiness *n* sonolência *f*, torpor *m.*

drowsy *adj* sonolento,-a; **to be** ~ ter sono.

drudge *n* (*fig*) (*person doing heavy menial tasks*) burro *m* de carga; ♦ *vi* matar-se a trabalhar.

drudgery *n* trabalho *m* monótono e árduo.

drug *n* (MED) medicamento *m*, droga *f*; **2** (*narcotic*) droga *f*, estupefaciente *m*; ~ **addict** *n* toxicómano (BR:-có-), drogado,-a; ~**gist** *n* (US) farmacêutico,-a; ~ **peddler** *n* traficante *m,f* de drogas; ~**store** *n* (US) drogaria (*for household/cleaning goods*); ♦ (-**gg**-) *vt* drogar; **to be on** ~**s** (*addict to*) estar viciado em drogas, drogar-se; (SPORT) dopar-se; (MED) estar sob medicação.

drugged (*pp of* **drug**) *adj* drogado,-a; (*state*) entorpecido,-a.

druid *n* (REL) druida *m inv.*

drum *n* tambor *m*, bombo *m*; ~ **brake** *n* freio *m* de tambor; **2** (*for oil*) barril *m*; **3** (ANAT) (*ear*) tímpano; **4** (ARCH) coluna; ~**s** *npl* bateria *sg*; ♦ *vt* tocar tambor; tamborilar; **3** ~ **up** *vt* (*support*) angariar.

drumbeat *n* rufo *m* (*de tambores*).

drummer *n* baterista *m,f*; tocador *m* de tambor.

drumstick *n* (MUS) baqueta *f*; (*of chicken*) perna *f.*

drunk (*pp of* **drink**) *n* bêbedo,-a (*also:* bêbado); (*tipsy*) ébrio,-a; ♦ *adj* embriagado,-a, bêbedo,-a; **to get sb** ~ embriagar alguém; **to get o.s** ~ embriagar-se.

drunkard *n* beberrão *m*, borrachão *m*, beberrona *f*, borrachona *f.*

drunken *adj* bêbedo,-a; **2** (*state*) *n* embriaguez *f.*

dry (-ier, -iest) *adj* seco,-a; **we had the driest April in 30 years** tivemos o abril mais seco em 30 anos; **2** (*climate*) árido,-a; **as** ~ **as a bone** muito duro; **on** ~ **land** em terra firme; ♦ ~-**cleaner** *n* tintureiro,-a; ~ **cleaner's** *n* lavandaria (a seco); ~-**cleaning** *n* limpeza *f* a seco; ~ **dock** *n* doca *f* seca (BR) dique *m* seco; ~**er** *n* (*for hair*) secador *m*; ~ **ice** *n* neve *f* carbónica; ~ **land** *n* terra *f* firme; ~**ly** *adv* secamente; ~**ness** *n* secura *f*; **2** (*of soil*) aridez *f*; ~ **rot**

n putrefa(c)ção *f* fungosa, apodrecimento *m* da madeira (de casa); ~ **run** *n* (*practice*) ensaio *m*; ~ **ski slope** *n* rampa *f* de esqui artificial; ♦ *vt* secar, enxugar; (*tears*) limpar; ♦ *vi* secar-se; **to** ~ **off** (*person*) secar-se; ♦ **to** ~ **out** (*river, etc*) secar completamente; **2** (*wiping crockery*) limpar a louça; **3** (*funds, supplies*) (*also:* ~ **up**) esgotar-se; ♦ **to** ~ **up** *vi* (*dishes*) secar; **2** (*speaker*) calarse; **to** ~-**clean** *vt* lavar a seco.

DST (*abbr for* **daylight saving time**) (US) horário de verão nos E.U.A.

DTP *n* (*abbr for* **desktop publishing**) DTP.

dual *n* (LING) dual; ♦ *adj* dual, duplo; ~ **carriage way** *n* faixa/pista *f* dupla; ~-**control** duplo comando; ~-**purpose** *adj* com duas funções.

dualism *n* dualismo *m.*

Dubai *npr* Dubai.

dubbed *adj* (CIN) dobrado, (BR) dublado; **2** (*nicknamed*) alcunhado; **to be** ~ **Knight** ser armado cavaleiro.

dubbing *n* (CIN) dobragem *f*, (BR) dublagem *f*; **2** (*sound mixing*) mistura *f.*

dubious *adj* duvidoso,-a, suspeito,-a; (*person undecided*) dúbio,-a, indeciso,-a.

dubiously *adv* duvidosamente; **2** (*look at*) com um ar inseguro.

Dublin *npr* Dublin; **in** ~ em Dublin.

Dubliner *npr adj* dublinense *m,f.*

duchess *n* duquesa *f.*

duck *n* (ZOOL) pato,-a; ~**bill** *n* (ZOOL) ornitorrinco; ♦ **to** ~ baixar(-se), desviar(-se); **to** ~ **one's head** baixar a cabeça; **2** (*push under water*) meter debaixo de água; mergulhar; **3** (*fig*) (*try to avoid*) esquivar-se de (*blow*); **4** evitar (*issue*); ♦ (*move down quickly*) abaixar-se; curvar-se; **to** ~ **out** (**of sth/of doing sth**) safar-se de (algo, de fazer algo); IDIOM **he took to it like a** ~ **to water** ele estva como um peixe na água.

duckling *n* patinho,-a; **the ugly** ~ *n* o patinho feio.

duct *n* (*pipe*) tubo *m*; **2** (*air, water*) conduto *m*, canal *m*; **3** (ANAT) ducto *m.*

dud *n* (*coin, cheque*) falso,-a; (*not functioning*) falhado,-a (*shell, bullet*); **it's a** ~ não presta; ♦ *adj*: ~ **cheque** cheque *m* sem cobertura.

dude *adj* (US, Canada) (*coll*) (*man*) tipo *m* (BR) cara *m*; **2** (*dandy*) janota *m.*

dudgeon *n* ressentimento *m*, indignação *f*; **in high** ~ bastante irritado,-a.

due (US) *n* (*debt*) dívida *f*; **2** (*praise, recognition*) crédito, justica *f*; **one must give her** ~ é preciso fazer-lhe justiça; **dues** *npl* direitos, *npl*; **customs** ~ direitos alfandegários, aduaneiros; **3** (*for membership*) cotização *f*; ♦ *adj* (*payable*) **to be/fall** ~ vencer-se; ~ **date** (data *f* de) vencimento; **on** ~ **date** em … data; **2** devido,-a; esperado,-a; **she is** ~ **to arrive tonight** … espera-se que ela chegue esta noite; **3** oportuno; **in** ~ **course** na devida altura, no devido tempo; ♦ *adv* dire(c)tamente, na dire(c)ção exata; oportunamente ~ **north** exa(c)tamente ao norte; ~ **to** devido a; **the train is** ~ **at 5 o'clock** o comboio (BR: trem) deve chegar às 5 horas.

duel *n* duelo *m*; **2** *(fig)* duelo *(of words)*.

duet *n (MUS)* dueto, duo.

duff *adj (UK) (fam)* inútil *m,f*; **2** *(fake)* falso,-a, simulado,-a.

duffle bag *(also:* **duffel)** *n (type of)* mochila *f*; saco *m* de marinheiro; ~ **(duffel) coat** *n* canadiana *m*, casaco *m* com capuz.

dug *(pt, pp of* **dig)**.

dugout *n* canoa *f*, piroga *f*; **2** *(MIL)* abrigo escavado e coberto; **3** *(SPORT) (BR)* fosso.

duke *n* duque *m*.

dull *adj (dark)* sombrio,-a; **a** ~ **day** um dia sombrio, nublado; **2** *(boring)* enfadonho,-a; **3** insípido,-a *(food, person)* **4** *(listless-person)* sem energia, animação; **5** *(slow to understand)* obtuso,-a; **6** *(thud, sound)* surdo,-a; **7** *(colour)* opaco,-a; **8** *(expression-listless)* apagado,-a, mortiço,-a; ♦ *vt* aliviar, entorpecer.

dullness *n* monotonia *f*; obtusidade *f*.

duly *adv* devidamente; como era de esperar.

dumb *adj* mudo,-a; **2** *(pej)* estúpido, pateta; **to be struck** ~ emudecer; ~**bell** *n (SPORT)* haltere *m*; ~**founded/struck** *adj* pasmado,-a; ~ **waiter** *n* elevador para a comida *(da cozinha)*.

dumbo *(pl:* -**s**) *n* estúpido,-a.

dummy *(pl:* -**ies)** *n (model of human figure)* manequim *m*; **2** *(ventriloquist)* boneco,-a; **3** *(UK)* chupeta *f*, chucha *f (for baby)* (US = **pacifier**); **4** *(coll) (idiot)* papalvo *m*; ♦ *adj (document)* falso,-a; **2** *(furniture, etc)* de imitação *f*; **3** *(bomb)* de exercício *m*; ~ **run** *n* ensaio *m; (MIL)* ataque *m* simulado.

dump *n (rubbish heap)* montão *m* de lixo; *(place)* despejadouro *m*, descarga *f* pública; **rubbish** ~ *(UK)* **garbage** ~ *(US)* lixeira *f*; **2** *(MIL)* depósito *m* de armas; **3** *(coll, pej)* chiqueiro *m*; **the house was a** ~ *(filthy)* a casa era um chiqueiro, uma pocilga; barraca *f*; ♦ *vt (throw away)* depositar, descarregar; **2** *(get rid of)* desfazer-se de, livrar-se de; **she** ~**ed her boyfriend** ela livrou-se do namorado; **3** *(COMM)* exportar ou importar a baixo preço; inundar o mercado com; ♦ **dumps** *npl:* **to be (down) in the** ~ estar deprimido,-a, estar neura/na neura *(BR)* estar na fossa.

dumper *n (person, thing)* que deprime, *(fig)* um balde *m* de água fria; ~ **truck** *n* camião, *(BR)* caminhão, basculante *m*.

dumping *n* despejo de lixo; **2** *(ECON)* exportação *f* de bens a preço inferior ao do mercado doméstico; '**no** ~' 'proibido deitar lixo'; *(BR and prov)* jogar lixo; ~ **ground** *n* depósito *m*.

dumpling *n (CULIN)* bolinho de farinha e ovo que acompanha o rosbife (= *Yorkshire pudding*).

dumpy *adj* atarracado,-a, gorducho,-a.

dunce *n (slow at learning)* estúpido,-a, burro,-a *(coll)*; ignorante *m,f*.

dunderhead *n* estúpido, imbecil *m,f*.

dune *n* duna *f*.

dung *n (for manure)* estrume *m*, esterco *m*.

dungarees *npl* fato-macaco, *(BR)* macacão *msg*.

dungeon *n* calabouço *m; (in the castle)* masmorra *f*.

dunk *vt* molhar o pão, bolo (no café/leite).

Dunkirk *npr* Dunquerque.

duo *n (THEAT) (double act)* dupla; *(MUS)* duo, dueto.

duodenal *adj: (MED)* **ulcer** ~ úlcera *f* duodenal.

dupe *n* otário,-a, trouxa *m,f (fam);* ♦ *vt* enganar, ludibriar.

duplex *n (US)* casa *n* geminada; ~ **apartment** dúplex *m*.

duplicate *n* duplicado,-a; *(key, CD, painting)* cópia *f*; **in** ~ em duplicado; ♦ *vt* duplicar; ♦ *vi (BIOL)* reproduzir-se.

duplicator *n* duplicador *m*.

duplicity *n (trait)* duplicidade *f*.

durability *n* durabilidade *f*, solidez *f*.

durable, durables *npl* bens *mpl* douradouros; ♦ *adj* durável *m,f*; **2** *(metal, plastic)* resistente *m,f*; **3** *(equipment)* sólido,-a, duradouro,-a.

duration *n* duração *f*.

duress *n (JUR)* coação *f*, coerção *f*; **under** ~ sob coação.

during *prep* durante.

dusk *n* crepúsculo *m*, anoitecer *m*.

dusky (-ier, -iest) *adj* escuro,-a; *(sky)* sombrio,-a; *(complexion)* moreno,-a.

dust *n* pó *m, (thicker dust)* poeira *f*; ~**bin** *n* caixote *(BR*: lata) de lixo; ~ **bowl** *n* área, zona *f* de desertificação; ~ **cover** (= ~ **jacket**); ~**er** *n* espanador *m; (cloth)*, pano de pó; ~**ing** *n (cleaning)* limpeza *f* do pó; **2** *(layer)* camada *f*; ~ **jacket** *n (on book)* sobrecapa *f*; ~**man** *n* homem do lixo, almeida *(BR)* lixeiro; ~ **mite** *n* ácaro *m*; ~**pan** *n* pá *f* de lixo; ~ **sheet** *n (for floor, furniture)* capa *f*, lençol *m* prote(c)tor; ~**storm** *n* tempestade *f* de poeira; ♦ *vt* limpar o pó de; **2** *(CULIN)* polvilhar *(cake, etc)* **(with** de); **to** ~ **sth off** *(brush off)* escovar, espanejar; limpar *(crumbs off the table)*; IDIOM **when the** ~ **settles** quando as coisas estiverem mais calmas.

dusty *adj* poeirento,-a; *(covered in dust)* empoeirado,-a.

Dutch *npr, adj* holandês,-esa; **the** ~ os holandeses *mpl*; *(LING)* holandês *m*; ~ **auction** *n* leilão no qual o preço do artigo vai baixando até haver um comprador; ~ **cap** *n* diafragma *m*; ~ **courage** *n* coragem *f* produzida pela embriaguês; ♦ *adv* **go** ~ *(invitation to eat out)* cada um paga a sua parte; fazer contas à moda do Porto *(fam)*.

dutiable *adj* tributável; *(by customs)* sujeito a impostos alfandegários.

dutiful *adj* zeloso,-a; conscencioso,-a; obediente *m,f*.

duty *(pl:* **duties)** *n* dever *m*; **to do one's** ~ cumprir o seu dever; **2** obrigação *f*; **it is your** ~ **to pay your debt** é a tua obrigação pagares a dívida; **3** *(tax)* imposto *m*; **on** ~ de serviço; de plantão, de guarda; **off** ~ de folga; ~**bound** *adj (obliged)* obrigado,-a *(a fazer algo)*; ~-**free** *adj* isento de taxas aduaneiras; ~ **officer** *n (MIL, police)* oficial *m* em serviço; ♦ **duties** *npl* funções *mpl*; **2 customs** ~ direitos *mpl* aduaneiros/alfandegários.

duvet *n* edredão *m*, acolchoado *m;* ~ **cover** *n* fronha *f* do edredão.

dwarf *(pl:* **dwarves)** *n* anão, anã; ♦ *vt* diminuir-se, ananicar.

dwell *(pt, pp* **dwelt)** *vi* morar; **to** ~ **on** *vt* divagar sobre, repisar.

dweller *n* morador,-ora, habitante *m,f*.

dwelling *n* residência, habitação *f*.

dwelt (*pt, pp of* **dwell**).

dwindle *vi* minguar, diminuir.

dwindling *adj* decrescente *m,f*, minguante *m,f*.

dye *n* (*product*) tinta *f*; **hair** ~ tinta para o cabelo; **fast/ permanent** ~ cor *f* fixa, tinto *m* fixo; **2** (*substance*) corante *m*; ♦ (*pt, pp* -**ed**; *cont*: **dyeing**) *vt* tingir.

dyed *adj* tingido,-a; **to have sth** ~ mandar tingir.

dyed-in-the-wool *adj* pessoa de fortes convicções.

dyer *n* (*person*) tintureiro,-a; ~**s shop** (= **dry- cleaners** *UK*) tinturaria *f*.

dyestuffs *npl* corantes *mpl*.

dying¹ to be ~ **for a drink** estar a morrer de sede; **to be** ~ **to** (**do sth**) estar morto,-a por (fazer algo).

dying² (*cont of* **die**) *adj* (*about to die*) moribundo,-a; (*condition*) agonizante; final; **his** ~ **words** as suas palavras derradeiras; **2 she is** ~ **to go to China** ela está ansiosa, a morrer por ir à China.

dyke *n* dique *m*, represa *f*.

dynamic *adj* dinâmico,-a, enérgico,-a; ~**s** *npl* (*PHYS*) dinâmica *sg*.

dynamism *n* dinamismo *m*.

dynamite *n* dinamite *f*; ♦ *vt* dinamitar.

dynamo *n* dínamo *m*.

dynasty *n* dinastia *f*.

dysentery *n* (*MED*) disenteria *f*.

dysfunction *n* (*MED*) disfunção *f*.

dyslexia *n* (*MED*) dislexia *f*.

dysmenorrhea *n* (*MED*) dismenorreia *f*, cólica *f* menstrual.

dyspepsia *n* (*MED*) dispepsia *f*.

dyspeptic *adj* dispéptico,-a.

e

E, e *n (letter)* E, e; **2** *(MUS)* mi *m*; **3** *(abbr of* East*)*; **4** *(exam classification)* mau; **5** *(COMP) (prefix)* e-.

each *adj (every)* cada *inv*; ♦ *pron (every one)* cada um, cada qual; **2** ~ **other** *(reciprocal)* um ao outro.

eager *adj (keen)* ávido,-a, desejoso,-a **(to, for** por); **she is** ~ **to learn** ela está ávida por aprender; *(anticipation)* ansioso,-a, impaciente *m,f*; **we are** ~ **to see our house** estamos desejosos/ansiosos por ver a nossa casa; **to be** ~ **to do sth** ansiar por fazer algo; **to be** ~ **to please sb** procurar agradar a (alguém).

eagerly *adv* ansiosamente; animadamente.

eagerness *n* ânsia *f* **(to,** de); entusiasmo *m* **(for,** por).

eagle *n (ZOOL)* águia *f*.

eagle-eyed *adj (sharp-eyed person)* com olhos de lince.

eaglet *n (young eagle)* águia *f* nova, aguieta *f*.

ear *n (ANAT – external)* orelha *f*; *(inner)* ouvido *m*; **2** *(hearing, perception)* **to have good** ~ **(for)** ter bom ouvido para á música; **to play music by** ~ tocar de ouvido; ~ **trumpet** *n* corneta *f* acústica; ~**wax** *n* cerúmen *m* dos ouvidos; **3** *(BOT) (of corn, wheat)* espiga *f*; IDIOM **to be all** ~**s** ser todo ouvidos; **to keep one's** ~**s to the ground** estar consciente do que se passa à volta, prestar atenção à opinião pública; **to be up to one's** ~**s (in debt/ in work)** estar enterrado em dívidas, enterrado até ao pescoço com trabalho; **in at one** ~ **and out of the other** entrar por um ouvido e sair por outro; **to turn a deaf** ~ fazer ouvidos de mercador.

earache *n* dor *f* de ouvidos.

eardrum *n* tímpano *m*.

earl *n* conde *m*.

earldom *n* condado *m*.

earlier *adj* anterior; mais cedo; **I prefer an** ~ **date to the one you mentioned** prefiro uma data anterior à que (àquela que) sugeriu; ♦ *adv* antes; **the plane will arrive** ~ **than expected** o avião vai chegar antes do esperado; **the** ~ **the better** quanto mais cedo melhor.

earliest *adj (first)* primeiro,-a; o mais cedo; **at your** ~ **convenience** o mais cedo que puder; **in the** ~ **days of science** nos primórdios da ciência.

earlobe *n* lóbulo *m* da orelha.

early (-ier, -iest) *adj adv* cedo; **to have an** ~ **dinner** jantar cedo; ~ **in life** enquanto novo,-a; **2** *(death, delivery of baby)* prematuro,-a; **3** *(BOT) (fruit, vegetable)* temporão *m*, temporã *f*; **4** *(first)* primeiro,-a; *(era, man)* primitivo,-a; ~ **bird** *n (person)* madrugador,-ora; **5** *(start of)* princípio, começo *m*; **6** antecipado,-a; **in the** ~ **part of the XX century** nos princípios do século XX; ~ **closing** *n (shops)* meio-feriado; ~ **retirement** *n (EP)* reforma *f* antecipada, *(BR)* aposentadoria *f* antecipada; ~ **warning** *n* aviso *m* prévio, com antecedência; ~ **opening** abertura *f* antecipada; ♦ *adv* a tempo; com antecedência; ~ **in the morning** de manhã cedo; **2** *(very)* de manhãzinha; ~ **on** desde o princípio; ~ **on I realized that ...** desde o princípio que eu vi logo que ...; **3** *(before)* antes de; **sorry to arrive** ~ peço desculpa por ter chegado antes da hora; **as** ~ **as I can remember** desde que me lembro; **at an** ~ **date** *(future)* (dentro) em breve; **arrange an** ~ **date** marcar uma data para breve; **to retire** ~ reformar-se, aposentar-se cedo; IDIOM **the** ~ **bird gets the worm** Deus ajuda a quem cedo madruga.

earmark *vt* reserva (para); destinar (para); assinalar.

earmuffs *npl* tapa-orelhas *m inv*.

earn *vt* ganhar; **to** ~ **one's living** ganhar a vida, o pão de cada dia; **2** *(deserve)* merecer *(respect, praise, reward)*; **3** *(COMM)* obter, gerar; ~**ed income** *n* rendimento *m* do trabalho.

earner *n (person)* assalariado,-a; **2** *(COMM)* fonte *f* de recursos.

earnest *n (seriousness)* **to be in** ~ não estar a brincar; ♦ *adj* sério,-a; sincero,-a; *(desire, plea)* profundo,-a, ardente *m,f*; **in** ~ *adv* a sério.

earnestly *adv (talk)* seriamente; **2** *(wish)* sinceramente, do coração.

earnings *npl (of person)* salário *msg*, ordenado *msg*; *(of business)* rendimentos *mpl*; ~**-related** *n adj (pension, benefits)* proporcional aos rendimentos.

earphones *npl* auscultadores *mpl*, *(BR)* phones *mpl* de ouvido.

earpiece *n* audiofone *m*.

earplugs *npl* prote(c)tores *mpl* de ouvido.

earring *(for the ear)* brinco *m*.

earshot *n*: **within/out of** ~ ao alcance/fora do ouvido/da voz.

earsplitting *adj (noise)* ensurdecedor,-ora, *(voice, shout)* estridente *m,f*.

earth *n* terra *f*, solo *m*; *(ELECT–wire)* fio terra *m*; ♦ *exc* **how/what on** ~!/? como que diabo!, como é que ... ?; **where on** ~...? onde por que diabos...?; ♦ *vt (ELECT)* ligar, *(BR)* conectar à terra; **down to** ~ prá(c)-tico,-a; IDIOM **to cost the** ~ custar uma fortuna.

earthenware *n* louça de barro.

earthling *n* habitante da terra.

earthly *adv (terrestrial)* terrestre *m,f*; **2** *(coll)* **there is no** ~ **reason** não há razão nenhuma.

earthquake *n* terramoto; *(BR)* terremoto.

earth-shattering *adj* espantoso,-a.

earthward(s) *adv* em dire(c)ção à terra.

earthwork *n* excavação *f*; fortificação, trincheira *f*.

earthworm *n (ZOOL)* minhoca *f inv*.

earthy (-ier, -iest) *adj (person)* sensual *m,f*; **2** *(smell, taste)* a terra *f*; **3** *(joke)* grosseiro,-a.

earwig *n (insect)* fura-orelhas *m inv*; lacraia *f*; ♦ (-**gg**-) *vt (fam) (eavesdrop)* estar à escuta à porta; **2** *(dated)* insinuar algo.

ease *n* facilidade *f*; alívio *m*; tranquilidade *f*; ♦ *vt* facilitar; soltar; afrouxar; aliviar; **to ~ sth in/out** meter/tirar algo com cuidado; **at ~!** *(MIL)* descansar!; **to be at ~** estar à vontade; ♦ **to ~ off** *vi* diminuir; ♦ **to ~ up** *vi (rain, storm)* acalmar; *(person)*, acalmar-se, moderar-se; **2** *(relax)* descontrair-se; **~ up on sb** ser menos severo,-a.

easel *n* cavalete *m*.

east *n* leste *m*, este *m*; ♦ *adj* do leste; ♦ *adv* de leste; **the E~** o Oriente; **E~ End** *n* a zona leste de Londres; **E~ Europe** *n* Europa do Leste; **the Middle E~** o Oriente Médio; **the Far E~** o Extremo Oriente; IDIOM **too far ~ is west** os extremos tocam-se.

eastbound *adj* em dire(c)ção ao leste.

Easter *n* Páscoa *f*; **~ egg** *n* ovo de Páscoa; **Happy ~!** Páscoa Feliz!; **~ Island** *n* Ilha *f* da Páscoa.

easterly *adj* para o leste; do leste; **~ wind** vento *m* do leste.

eastern *adj* do leste, oriental; *(person)* oriental *m,f*; **Portugal is on Spain's ~ side** Portugal fica a leste da Espanha; **the E~ bloc** *n (POL, HIST) (the former)* o (antigo) bloco *m* oriental (da Europa).

East Timor *npr* Timor-Leste.

East Timorese *adj* timorense *m,f*.

eastward(s) *adv (direction)* rumo a leste, para leste.

easy (-ier, -iest) *adj (work, question)* fácil; simples; *(pace)* lento, tranquilo; **2** *(smile, attitude)* descontraído,-a; **to feel ~ (about sth)** não se preocupar com/estar à vontade com; **3** *(having no preference)* **'white or red wine?' 'I am ~'** 'branco ou tinto?' 'tanto se me dá'; **4** *(coll) (promiscuous person)* fácil *(fam)*; ♦ *adv*: **to take it/things ~** levar as coisas com calma; ir devagar; ♦ *(MIL)* **'stand ~!'** 'descansar!'; IDIOM **to be ~ on the eye** *(pretty/handsome)* ser agradável *m,f* à vista; **easier said than done** mais fácil dizer que fazer.

easy-care *adj (UK) (clothes)* que não precisa de ser passado (a ferro).

easy chair *n* poltrona.

easy-going *adj (person) (good natured)* bona-cheirão,-rona; *(BR)* bonachão,-chona; **2** *(relaxed)* descontraído,-a, relaxado,-a.

easy-peasy *adj (pop)* fácil; **this is ~!** isso é canja!

eat *(pt:* **ate**, *pp:* **eaten**) *vt* comer *(food)*; **to ~ very much** ser um bom garfo; **to ~ through the whole meal** devorar a refeição; **to ~ humble pie** humilhar-se; **to ~ one's words** *(coll)* engolir as palavras, desdizer-se; ♦ **to ~ away at/into** *(gnaw) vt* roer *(wood)*; corroer *(metal)*; **2** *(with worry)* consumir; **to ~ out** *vt* comer fora; **to ~ up** comer tudo; **3** consumir; **4** *(car)* devorar *(miles)*.

eatable *n (eatables)* produtos, pratos de comida; ♦ *adj (edible)* comestível *m,f*; próprio,-a para comer.

eaten *(pp of* **eat***)*: **have you ~?** já comeu?; **I have never ~ such a good dish** nunca comi um prato tão bom; **to be ~ up with** estar cheio de *(curiosity, desire)*; ser consumido por *(remorse)*.

eater *n* comedor,-ora; **she is a big ~** ela é comilona; **I am a fussy ~** eu sou muito esquisita na comida; **to be a good ~** ser um bom garfo.

eating *n* comer, alimentação *f*; **~ disorder** *n* distúrbio *m* alimentar; ♦ *(pres p of* **eat***)* comendo, a comer; **I am not ~ well** não estou a comer, *(BR)* comendo bem.

eau de Cologne *n* (água de) Colónia *(BR:* -lô-*)*.

eaves *npl (of roof)* beiral *msg*.

eavesdrop *vi* escutar (secretamente) à porta; bisbilhotar: **~ on sb** bisbilhotar alguém.

ebb *n* maré *f*; **~ tide** *n* baixa-mar, maré *f* vazante; **the ~ and the flow of life** *(fig)* os altos e baixos da vida; **to be at a low ~** sentir-se deprimido, estar cabisbaixo,-a; ♦ *vt (tide)* baixar, vazar; **2** declinar.

ebony *n (wood)* ébano *m*.

ebullient *adj* exuberante *m,f*; excitado,-a; entusiasmado,-a.

EC *(abbr of* **European Community***); (the former)* Comunidade *f* Europeia *f*, CE; **2** **(European Commision)** Comissão *f* Europeia.

e-cash *n (COMP)* dinheiro *m* electrónico *(BR:* -ô-*)*.

eccentric *n adj* excêntrico.

eccentricity *n* excentricidade *f*.

ecclesiastical *adj* eclesiástico,-a.

echelon *n (formal) (level in organization)* escalão *m*.

echinacea *n* equinácea *f*.

echo *(pl:* -**es***) n* eco *m*; ♦ *vt* ecoar, repetir; **2** *(opinion)* repercurtir; ♦ *vi* ressoar, repetir.

echoing *adj* sonoro,-a.

ECHR *(abbr for* **European Convention on Human Rights***)* CEDH (Convenção Europeia dos Direitos da Humanidade).

eclipse *n* eclipse *m*; **~ total/partial** eclipse total/parcial; **2** *(fig)* declínio *m*; ♦ *vt* eclipsar; **2** *(overshadow)* eclipsar, ofuscar.

eco- *pref (combining form)* eco-.

eco-friendly *adj* amigo,-a do ambiente.

ecological *adj* ecológico,-a.

ecologically ecologicamente.

ecologist *n* ecologista *m,f*.

ecology *n* ecologia *f*.

e-commerce *n* comércio ele(c)trónico *(BR:* -ô-*)*.

economic *adj* económico,-a *(BR:* -ô-*)*; **2** *(profitable)* rentável *m,f*.

economical *adj* económico,-a *(BR:* -ô-*)*; **2** *(person)* poupado,-a; **to be ~ with the truth** dizer meias-verdades.

economics *n* economia *f*.

economist *n* economista *m,f*.

economize *vi* economizar **(on** em)*(gas, etc)* poupar.

economy *n* economia *f*; **to make economies** fazer economias; **~-class** *n (AER)* classe *f* turística; **~ size** *n* embalagem *f* económica.

ecosystem *n* ecossistema *m*.

ecstasy *(pl:* -**ies***) n* êxtase *m*; enlevo *m*; **2** *(drug)* ecstasy *m*.

ecstatic *adj* extasiado,-a; **to be ~ about** extasiar-se com/perante *(idea, landscape)*.

ectopic pregnancy *n (MED)* gravidez *f* extra-uterina.

Ecu *n (abbr of* **European currency unit***)* écu; **hard ~** écu forte e estável.

Ecuador *npl* Equador; **E~ian** *n, adj* equatoriano,-a.

ecumenical *adj* ecuménico,-a (BR: -ê-).

eczema *n* eczema *m.*

eddy *(pl:* **eddies***) n* turbilhão *m;* redemoinho *m;* **eddies** *(of smoke)* fumo *m* em espiral; ♦ *(pt, pp* **eddied***) vi* redemoinhar *(tide, wind); (smoke)* rodopiar.

Eden *n* Éden *m,* paraíso *m* terrestre.

edge *n (of blade)* fio *m;* gume *m;* **2** *(table)* bordo *m;* **3** *(lake)* margem *f;* **4** *(of skirt, avenue, woods)* borda, orla *f;* **5** *(outer limit)* borda *f,* perífero *m;* **to be on the ~ of sth** estar à beira de algo; **to be on ~** *(fig)* estar nervoso,-a, inquieto,-a; **6** *(in voice)* rispidez *f;* ♦ *vi (move)* avançar de lado; **he ~s his way through the crowd** ele abre caminho através da multidão; **2** *(decorate garments)* debroar; orlar *(avenue);* **to ~ away from** afastar-se pouco a pouco de.

edged *adj* cortante *m,f,* afiado,-a; orlado,-a *(por* algo); **a two-~ sword** uma espada de dois gumes.

edgeless *adj* sem fio, embotado,-a *(blunt)* cego,-a.

edgeways *adv* de lado; **he couldn't get a word in ~** ele não conseguiu abrir bico; não conseguiu meter a colherada na conversa.

edging *n (gen)* borda *f; (in sewing)* fímbria *f.*

edgy (-ier, -iest) *adj* nervoso,-a, impaciente *m,f.*

edible *adj* comestível *m,f.*

edict *n (HIST)* edito *m; (POL, JUR)* decreto *m.*

edifice *n* edifício *m.*

edify *vt* edificar.

edifying *adj* edificante *m,f.*

edit *vt (gen)* editar; **2** *(correct)* revisar *(book),* modificar com cortes; preparar para publicação; **3** *(TV, CIN)* realizar a montagem; **4** *(COMP)* editar (data); **to ~ out** *vt (word, sentence)* cortar.

edition *n (JOURN)* edição *f.*

editor *n (gen)* editor,-a; *(of newspaper)* reda(c)tor,-a; dire(c)tor,-a de revista, jornal; chefe *m,f* de redacção; **2** *(copy editor)* revisor,-a chefe *(book).*

editorial *n adj* editorial.

educate *vt* educar; instruir.

educated *adj* educado,-a, culto,-a.

education *n* educação *f;* ensino *m,* instrução *f;* formação *f;* **primary/secondary ~** ensino primário/ secundário; *(method)* ensino pedagógico.

educational *adj* educacional; educativo,-a **~ system** sistema *m* educativo.

educationalist *n* educacionista *m,f.*

educator *n (person)* educador,-ora; especialista *m,f* em educação.

Edwardian *adj* da época do Rei Eduardo VII, eduardiano,-a.

EEC *n (abbr of* **European Economic Community***) (former)* Comunidade *f* Económica *(BR:* -nô-) Europeia.

eel *n* enguia *f.*

eerie *adj* estranho,-a; misterioso,-a, medonho,-a; **there was an ~ silence** o silêncio era inquietante.

efface *vt* apagar.

effect *n (result)* efeito *m;* **to come into ~** *(JUR, ADMIN)* entrar em vigor; **to take ~** *(pills, price increase)* fazer efeito; **to use sth to good ~** utilizar algo com sucesso; **2** *(impression)* efeito *m;* **words to this ~** palavras nesse sentido; **personal ~s** *npl* bens *mpl,* pertences; **in ~** na realidade; ♦ *vt* efe(c)tuar; levar a cabo.

effective *adj* eficaz *m,f,* **2** *(impressive)* impressionante; **the speech was ~** o discurso foi impressionante; **3** *(regulation)* efe(c)tivo,-a, em vigor; **2 to become ~** entrar em vigor.

effectiveness *n* eficácia *f.*

effeminate *adj* efeminado,-a.

effervescent *adj* efervescente *m,f.*

efficiency *n* eficiência *f;* rendimento *m.*

efficient *adj* eficiente, competente.

effigy *n* efígie *f.*

effluent *n* efluente *n.*

effort *n* esforço *m;* **to make an ~ to** esforçar-se por.

effortless *adj* sem esforço, com desenvoltura *f.*

effrontery *n* descaramento *m,* atrevimento *m.*

effusive *adj* efusivo,-a.

eft *n (ZOOL)* lagartixa *f.*

EFTA *(abbr of* **European Free Trade Association***)* Associação *f* Europeia do Comércio Livre.

e.g. *adv (abbr of* **exempli gratia***)* por exemplo.

egalitarian *n, adj* igualitário,-a.

egalitarianism *n* igualitarismo *m.*

egg *n* ovo *m;* **~-nog** *n* gemada; **~plant** *n (US)* berinjela; **~shell** *n* casca de ovo; **fried ~** ovo estrelado; **hard-boiled ~** ovo cozido; **poached ~** ovo escalfado; **soft-boiled ~** ovo quente; **scrambled ~s** ovos mexidos; ♦ **to ~ on** *vt* incitar, animar a.

ego *n* ego.

egocentric *adj* egocêntrico,-a.

egoism *n* egoísmo.

egoist *n* egoísta *m,f.*

egotist *n* egotista *m,f.*

egregious *adj* muito mau, ruim; flagrante; **2** *(arc)* eminente.

Amigo falso: embora 'egregious' no sentido de 'distinguished', 'eminent' seja agora arcaico em inglês, o adjectivo 'egrégio' em português continua a ter os significados de 'ilustre', 'eminente' no registo formal. Não tem outro significado.

Egypt *n* Egi(p)to; **in ~** no Egipto.

Egyptian *n adj* egípcio,-a.

eiderdown *n* edredão *m,* edredon *m.*

eigenfunction *n* (MATH, PHYS) função *f* própria.

eight *num* oito.

eighteen *num* dezoito.

eighteenth *n* décimo oitavo *m;* **~ century** século XVIII; **2** *(MATH) (fraction)* dezoito avos *mpl;* ♦ *adj* décimo oitavo; ♦ *adv:* **to finish ~** acabar em décimo oitavo lugar/em décima posição.

eighth *n adj* oitavo,-a; **~ note** *n (US) (MUS)* colcheia *f.*

eightieth *n adj* octogésimo,-a; **it is his ~ birthday** é o seu octogésimo aniversário; *(MATH) (fraction)* oitenta avos *mpl.*

eighty *(pl:* -**ties***) num* oitenta; **she is in her 80s (eighties)** ela está na casa dos oitenta; **~-one** oitenta e um,-a; **my grandmother is 81 today** minha avó faz hoje oitenta e um anos.

Eire *n* República *f* da Irlanda; Eire *m*.

either *det* cada; qualquer; ambos, um ou outro; **on ~ side** de cada lado, de ambos os lados; ♦ *pron:* ~ **(of them)** ambos, cada um, qualquer um (deles); **I don't like** ~ não gosto nem de um nem do outro; ♦ *adv* tão-pouco, tampouco, também não; **no, I don't** ~ eu tão-pouco, eu também não; ♦ *conj:* **either ... or** ou ... ou; **either yes or no** ou sim, ou não.

ejaculate *vt* ejacular.

eject *vt* expulsar, expelir; despejar.

ejector seat *n* assento eje(c)tor.

eke *vt:* **to ~ out** *(by saving)* fazer durar *(money, supplies)* **(by** à força de**)**; **to ~ out a living** manter-se a custo; suprir as deficiências de.

elaborate *adj* complicado,-a; elaborado,-a, detalhado,-a; ♦ *vt* elaborar; ♦ *vi* explicar minuciosamente.

elapse *vi (time)* decorrer.

elastic *n adj* elástico; **~band** *n* tira de borracha, elástico.

elasticity *n* elasticidade *f*.

elate *adj* orgulhoso,-a; entusiasmado,-a; exultante *m,f*; ♦ *vt* elevar, extasiar, exaltar.

elation *n* exaltação *f*.

elbow *n* cotovelo *m*.

elder *n (older person)* o mais velho; ancião *m*, anciã *f*; **2** *(of church)* presbítero *m*; **~ statesman/ stateswoman** *n* estadista *m,f* experiente.

elder (tree) *n (BOT)* sabugueiro *m*; **~berry** *n (BOT)* baga *f* do sabugueiro, sabugo *m*.

elderly *n:* **the ~** as pessoas de idade; os idosos; ♦ *adj* idoso, de idade madura.

eldest *n adj (oldest)* o mais velho.

elect *adj (party, president)* eleito,-a; ♦ *vt* eleger; **2** *(choose)* escolher, optar; **to be ~ed** optar por ser.

election *n* eleição *f*; **Council ~s** *npl* as eleições *fpl* autárquicas; **~ campaign** *n* campanha *f* eleitoral.

electioneering *n (pej)* propaganda *f* eleitoral; eleitoralismo *m*.

Na Grã-Bretanha, as eleições realizam-se de 5 em 5 anos, podendo o primeiro-ministro convocar eleições em qualquer altura. Nos E.U.A. o presidente não pode ser eleito mais que duas vezes consecutivas, sendo cada mandato de 4 anos.

elective *n (school, univ)* disciplina *f* optional.

elector *n* eleitor,-ora.

electoral *adj* eleitoral; **the ~ register/roll** *n* o registo *(BR)* registro *m* eleitoral.

electorate *n* eleitorado *m*.

electric *n (fam) (car, train)* elétrico *m*; ♦ *adj* elétrico,-a; **~ blanket** *n* cobertor *m* elé(c)trico; **~ cable** *n* cabo elé(c)trico; **~ chair** *n* cadeira elé(c)trica; **~ drill** *n* perfurador *m* elé(c)trico; *(BR)* furadeira *f* elétrica; **~ eel** *n* gimnoto *m*; enguia *f* elé(c)trica; **~ eye** *n* célula *f* fotoelé(c)trica; **~ fence** *n* cerca *f* elé(c)trica; **~ iron** *n* ferro elé(c)trico (de engomar).

electrical *adj* elétrico,-a; **~ appliances** *npl* eletrodomésticos; **~ engineer** *n* engenheiro,-a eletrotécnico,-a.

electrically *adv* ele(c)tricamente.

electrician *n* ele(c)tricista *m,f*.

electricity *n* ele(c)tricidade *f*.

electrify *(-***ied***) vt* ele(c)trificar; **2** *(fig) (excite)* ele(c)trizar.

electrifying *adj (fig)(exciting)* ele(c)trizante *m,f*.

electro- *pref* ele(c)tro-.

electrocute *vt* ele(c)trocutar.

electrode *n* elé(c)trodo.

electrolysis *n (CHEM)* electrólise; *(cosmetics)* depilação *f* elé(c)trica.

electromagnetic *adj* ele(c)tromagnético.

electron *n* electrão *m*, *(BR)* elétron *m*.

electronic *adj* electrónico,-a, *(BR)* eletrônico,-a; **~ data processing** *n* processamento *m* ele(c)trónico de dados; **~ organizer** *n* agenda *f* ele(c)trónica; **~s** *npl (TECH)* electrónica, *(BR)* electrônica *f*; **2** *(equipment)* componentes *mpl* ele(c)trónicos.

elegance *n* elegância *f*.

elegant *adj* elegante *m,f*.

elegantly *adv* elegantemente.

elegy *(pl:* -**ies***) n* elegia *f*.

element *n* elemento *m*; **2** rudimentos *mpl*; **3** *(of nature)* forças *fpl* da natureza.

elementary *adj* elementar; rudimentar; *(school, education)* primário.

elephant *n (ZOOL)* elefante *m*; **~ bull** macho *m* elefante; **~ cow** fêmea *f* elefante; **white ~** *(fig) (useless and expensive thing)* elefante branco.

elephantine *adj (person)* elefantino,-a; **2** *(task)* gigantesco,-a.

elevate *vt (promote)* elevar *(person, quality)*, ascender **(to** a**)**; **2** *(raise)* levantar.

elevated *adj (formal) (rank, voice, sentiment)* elevado,-a; *(person)* digno,-a; **~ railroad** *n (US)* ferrovia *f* elevada.

elevation *n* elevação *f*; **2** *(in status)* ascensão *f*; **3** *(ARCH)* proje(c)ção *f* frontal, lateral, fachada *f* frontal; **4** *(height)* altura *f*.

elevator *n (US)* elevador *m*, ascensor *m*.

eleven *num* onze.

eleven plus *n* exame *m* de entrada no 6° ano de escolaridade.

elevenses *n* refeição ligeira no meio da manhã; **2** *n (SPORT) (of football, cricket team)* o onze.

eleventh *n adj* décimo-primeiro; undécimo,-a; **2** *(fraction)* onze avos *mpl*; **at the ~ hour** à última hora.

elf *(pl:* **elves***) n* elfo, duende *m*.

elicit *vt* obter *(opinion)* (**from** de); provocar *(reaction)*; extrair *(information)* (**from** de).

eligibility *n (suitability)* elegibilidade *f*.

eligible *adj* elegível *m,f*, apto,-a (**for**, para); **to be ~ for sth** ter qualificações/habilitações para algo; **to be ~** *(benefit, allowance)* ser qualificado,-a, ter as condições requeridas; **2 an ~ man/woman** *(for marriage)* ser um bom partido.

eliminate *vt* eliminar; suprimir; excluir.

elimination *n* eliminação *f*, exclusão *f*.

elite *n* elite *f*.

elitism *n (pej)* elitismo *m*.

elitist *n adj (pej)* elitista *m,f*.

elixir *n (magic drink)* elixir *m*; **2** *(fig) (magic cure)* poção *f* mágica.

Elizabethan *adj (HIST)* isabelino,-a.

elk *n* alce *m*.

ellipse *n (GEOM) (shape)* elipse *f*.

ellipsis *(pl:* -**pses**) *(LING) (word, verb omitted in text)* elipse *f*; **2** *(in punctuation)* reticências *fpl*.

elliptical *adj* elíptico,-a.

elm *n (wood)* olmo *m*; ~ **tree** *n* ulmeiro *m*.

elocution *n* elocução *f*.

elongated *adj* alongado,-a.

elope *vi* fugir (de casa) com namorado,-a.

elopement *n* fuga do lar paterno.

eloquence *n* eloquência *f*.

eloquent *adj* eloquente *m,f*.

else *adv* outro, mais; **everywhere** ~ por todo lado (menos aqui); **something** ~ outra coisa; **somewhere** ~ em outro lugar, algures; **nobody** ~ **came** ninguém mais veio; **there was little** ~ **to do** não havia outra coisa a fazer; **what** ~ **can we say?** que mais podemos dizer?; **who** ~**?** quem mais?; ~**where** *adv (be)* em outro lugar; *(go)* para outro lugar; **where** ~ **shall I look for it?** em que mais lugares devo procurar isso?; ♦ **or** ~ *conj* senão, ou então; **shut up or** ~ **...** cala-te senão ...

elucidate *vt* esclarecer, elucidar.

elude *vt* fugir à *(police)*; **2** escapar *(observation)*; **3** *(obligation)* evitar; **4** *(baffle)* confundir.

elusive *adj* esquivo,-a; evasivo,-a.

elver *n* enguia *f* nova.

elves *(pl of* **elf**).

emaciated *adj (person, features)* emaciado,-a, macilento,-a.

emanate *vi* emanar, provir, desprender-se de.

emancipate *vt* emancipar.

emancipated *adj* emancipado,-a.

emancipation *n* emancipação *f*, libertação *f*.

emasculate *vt* enfraquecer; emascular, efeminar *(man)*.

embalm *vt* embalsamar.

embankment *n* aterro *m*; **2** dique *m*, represa *f*; cais; **3** *(along the river)* margem.

Em Londres, ao longo do rio Tamisa, as margens têm os seus nomes conforme os distritos: **Victoria** ~, **Albert** ~, **Chelsea** ~, **Putney** ~, entre muitas outras.

embargo *(pl:* -**es**) *n* embargo (**on** sobre; **against** contra); **2** *(fig) (ban)* proibição *f* (**on sth** de algo).

embark *vt/vi* embarcar; **to** ~ **on** *(fig)* empreender, começar.

embarkation *n* embarque *m*.

embarrass *vt* embaraçar (alguém); **to be/feel** ~**ed** estar, sentir-se embaraçado,-a envergonhado,-a; **to be** ~**ed by** ser embaraçado por.

embarrassed *adj (self-conscious)* envergonhado,-a, embaraçado,-a; **to be financially** ~ estar com problemas financeiros.

embarrassing *adj (question, situation)* embaraçoso-a, incómodo-a.

embarrassment *n* embaraço; dificuldades *fpl*.

embassy *n* embaixada *f*.

embed (-**dd**-) *vt (in wall)* encastrado,-a; *(in soil, cement)* enterrado,-a em; firmado,-a em; **2** *(in wood)* cravar *(a nail)*; **3** *(fig) (ingrained)* enraizado,-a; **4** *(fig) (in mind)* gravar.

embellish *vt* embelezar; *(fig)* adornar.

ember *n* brasa *f*; borralho *m*; **2** *(fig) (remains of past)* **the** ~**s of his love** as cinzas do seu amor.

embers *npl* brasa *sg*, borralho *sg*, cinzas *fpl*.

embezzle *vt* desfalcar, desviar *(funds)*.

embezzlement *n* desvio (de fundos).

embitter *vt* amargar; *(fig)* azedar, irritar.

embittered *adj* amargurado,-a.

emblem *n* emblema *m*.

embodiment *n* personificação *f*.

embody *vt* incorporar; incluir.

embolden *vt* encorajar.

embolism *n* embolia *f*.

embolus *n (MED)* êmbolo *m*.

embossed *adj* realçado; gravado em relevo; ~ **with** ornado com relevos de; ~ **seal** *n* selo *m* branco.

embrace *n* abraço; ♦ *vt* abraçar, dar um abraço em; abarcar, abranger; ado(p)tar; ♦ *vi* abraçar-se.

embrocation *n* linimento *m*.

embroider *vt (sewing)* bordar; **2** *(pej)* fantasiar, acrescentar; ♦ *vi* bordar.

embroidery *n* bordado *m*.

embroil *vt:* **to be/get** ~**ed in sth** envolver-se, meter-se em algo.

embryo *n (BIOL)* embrião *m*.

embryonic *adj (fig) (emergent)* embrionário,-a.

emcee *n (abbr of* **master of ceremonies**) *(US)* mestre *m* de cerimónias.

emend *vt* emendar, corrigir.

emerald *n (gem)* esmeralda *f*; **2** *(colour)* verde-esmeralda.

emerge *vi* emergir, sair, aparecer; surgir.

emergence *n* aparecimento *m*.

emergency *n* emergência; crise *f*; necessidade *f* urgente; **in an** ~ em caso de urgência; **in times of** ~ em tempos de crise; **state of** ~ estado de emergência; ~ **brake** *n (AUT)* freio *m* de mão; ~ **exit** *n* saída de emergência; ~ **landing** *n* aterragem *f* de emergência *(BR:* aterrissagem *f* forçada); ~ **medical services** *npl* serviços médicos urgentes; ~ **meeting** *n* reunião *f* extraordinária; **to rise to the** ~ portar-se à altura da situação; ~ **ward** *n* sala *f* de urgências.

emergent *adj* emergente *m,f*; **2** *(industry)* novo,-a.

emerging *pres p, adj (market)* em desenvolvimento; ~ **markets** novos mercados.

emery *n* esmeril *m*; ~**board** *n* lima/lixa *f* de unhas; ~ **paper** *n* lixa *f*, papel *m* de esmeril.

emetic *n adj* emético *m*; que provoca vómitos.

emigrant *n* emigrante *m,f*.

emigrate *vi* emigrar.

emigration *n* emigração *f*

eminence *n* eminência; **E**~ or, **Eminency** (cardeal) Eminência..

eminent *adj (person, position)* eminente *m,f,* notável *m,f.*

eminently *adv* eminentemente.

emir *n* (título muçulmano) emir *m.*

emirate *n* emirado *m.*

emissary *n* emissário,-a (**to** junto a).

emission *n* emissão *f* (**from** de).

emit (-tt-) *vt (discharge)* emitir *(radiation, signal, light, sound)*; *(to utter)* **she emitted a shrill scream** ela emitiu um grito estridente; **2** emanar *(gas, smell)*; **3** lançar, cuspir *(lava).*

emollient *n* emoliente *m.*

emolument *n (payment, fee)* honorários *mpl (of doctor, lawyer)*; **2** *(salary, bonus)* remuneração *f.*

emotion *n* emoção *f.*

emotional *adj* sentimental; comovente.

emotionally *adv* com emoção.

emotive *adj* emotivo,-a.

emperor *n* imperador *m.*

emphasis *(pl: -ses)* *n* ênfase *f.*

emphasize *vt* enfatizar; dar, pôr ênfase; acentuar; salientar.

emphatic *adj* enérgico; enfático.

emphatically *adv* com ênfase.

empire *n* império *m.*

empirical *adj* empírico,-a.

emplacement *n (position)* plataforma para canhão.

employ *vt* empregar *(person, capital).*

employability *n (capable of being employed)* empregabilidade *f.*

employable *adj (person)* empregável *m,f.*

employee *(UK)* **employe** *(US)* *n* empregador,-ora; **body of** ~**s** *n* patronato *m.*

employer *n* empregador,-a patrão,-roa *m,f*; entidade *f* patronal.

employment *n* emprego; trabalho; ~ **agency** *n* agência de empregos; ~ **exchange** *n* bolsa de trabalho.

emporium *(pl: -s or -ria)* *n* empório *m.*

empower *vt* dar poderes a; **to** ~ **sb to do sth** autorizar alguém a fazer algo; *(fig)* capacitar; **to be** ~**ed** ter plenos poderes.

empress *n* imperatriz *f.*

empties *npl (UK) (fam) (bottles)* tara *f,* garrafas *npl* vazias.

emptiness *n* vazio, vácuo; vacuidade *f*; solidão *f*; *(fig)* nulidade *f.*

empty (-ier, -iest) *adj* vazio,-a; deserto,-a; desocupado,-a; inútil *m,f*, vão *m,* vã *m,f*; ~-**handed** *adj* de mãos vazias; ~-**headed** *adj* de cabeça oca; ♦ *vt* esvaziar; evacuar; ♦ *vi* esvaziar-se; ficar desocupado; ficar deserto.

EMS *(abbr of* **European Monetary system)** SME; **2** *(abbr of* **emergency medical services).**

emu *n (ZOOL)* emu *f.*

EMU *n (abbr of* **Economic and Monetary Union)** UME *f.*

emulate *vt* emular; imitar; *(COMP)* copiar, emular.

emulsion *n (PHOT)* emulsão *f*; **2** *(paint)* tinta *f* plástica.

enable *vt* capacitar; proporcionar; **to** ~ **sb to do sth** permitir que alguém faça algo.

enact *vt (JUR)* decretar, aprovar; *(bring into effect)* promulgar; **as by law** ~**ed** nos termos da lei; **2** *(THEAT)* representar, desempenhar um papel.

enactment *n (JUR)* promulgação *f*; **2** *(THEAT)* representação *f.*

enamel *n* esmalte *m.*

enamoured *(UK),* **enamored** *(US)* *adj*: **to be** ~ **of** estar apaixonado,-a por/enamorado,-a por (alguém); estar encantado,-a.

encampment *n (gen)* acampamento *m.*

encapsulate *vt*: **to** ~ **sth in** resumir algo em.

encase *vt* revestir (de); meter (em).

encased *adj*: ~ **in** coberto,-a de; encaixado,-a em; *(MED) (plaster)* estar metido,-a em.

encash *n (UK) (cheque)* descontar.

encephalic *adj* encefálico,-a.

enchant *vt* encantar.

enchanted *adj (charmed)* encantado,-a.

enchanting *adj* encantador,-a.

encircle *vt (troops)* cercar; *(fence)* circundar, rodear; **2** cingir *(waist).*

encl. *(abbr for* **enclosed)** anexo *m,* junto *m,* incluso *m.*

enclave *n* enclave *f.*

enclose *vt (surround)* cercar; anexar *(in letter etc)*; incluir; **please find** ~**d** anexamos; junto enviamos; segue anexo.

enclosure *n (closed-in) (for animals)* cercado *m; (for people)* recinto *m*; **2** *(fence)* cerca *f*; **3** *(in letter)* anexo *m.*

encompass *vt (include)* abranger, abarcar, incluir *(land, view, ideas).*

encore *n* bis *m*; repetição *f*; **to do an** ~ bisar; **the play had two** ~**s** a peça bisou duas vezes; ♦ ~! *exc* bis! outra!

encounter *n* encontro *m*; ♦ *vt* encontrar; *(problem, danger)*, deparar-se com; enfrentar.

encourage *vt* encorajar; animar; incitar, estimular.

encouragement *n* encorajamento *m*; estímulo *m*; fomento *m.*

encroach *vi*: **to** ~ **on/upon** *(vegetation; land)* invadir, trespassar; **2** ocupar, apossar-se de (algo); **3** *(rights)* abusar de; **4** *(enemy)*, usurpar a; **5** *(privacy)* invadir.

encrusted *adj*: ~ **with** incrustado de.

encrypt *vt* encrptar; **encryption** *n* encriptação *f.*

encumber *vt* sobrecarregar *(person, family)*; **2** estorvar, obstruir *(street, person)*; **to be** ~**ed with** estar carregado, sobrecarregado com.

encumbrance *n* estorvo *m.*

encyclop(a)edia *n* enciclopédia *f.*

encyclical *n* encíclica *f.*

end *n* fim *m,* final *m*; cabo *m*; **at the** ~ **of two hours** ao cabo de duas horas; **at the** ~ **of the month** no fim do mês; **at the** ~ **of the day** *(fig) (after all)* afinal de contas, ao fim e ao cabo; **2** *(at the bottom)* **at the** ~ **of the street** ao fundo/no fim da rua **to bring to an** ~/**to put an** ~ **to** acabar com, pôr fim a; **in the** ~ ao fim, por fim, finalmente; **for hours on** ~ durante horas seguidas, sem fim; **to no** ~ em vão; **to get to the** ~ **of** chegar ao fim de; **3** *(limit)* **there is no ~ to his knowledge** o conhecimento dele não tem limites; **4** *(of story, talks)* conclusão *f*; **5** *(extremity) (fam)* ponta *f*, extremo *m* *(of nose, etc)*; **from one ~ to the other** dum extremo ao outro; *(of scale)* extremidade *f*; **6** *(aim)* finalidade, obje(c)tivo, fim; **7** *(side of two ends)* lado *m*; **8** *(SPORT)* lado; **9** **~s** *npl (of meat, etc)* restos *mpl*; **odds and ~s** coisas *fpl* miúdas; ♦ *vt/vi* acabar, terminar, pôr fim a; **2** *(marriage, relations)* romper; **to ~ in** acabar em; **to ~up (in)** ir parar em; **to ~ up being/doing** acabar por ser/ fazer; IDIOM **to stand on ~** *(hair)* arrepiar-se; **there is no ~ to it** isto é um nunca acabar; **and that's the ~ of that!** acabou-se!; **a means to an ~** um meio para alcançar um fim; **the ~ doesn't justify the means to** os fins não justificam os meios; **I am at the ~ of my tether** não aguento mais; **he is at his wit's ~** ele está atarantado; não sabe o que fazer.

endanger *vt* *(health, life)* pôr em perigo; **2** *(environment)* ameaçar; **3** *(position)* comprometer; **~ed species** espécie *f* em vias de extinção.

endear *vr*: **to ~ o.s. to sb** conquistar a afeição de alguém, cativar alguém.

endearing *adj* cativante *m,f*, atraente *m,f*, afe(c)-tuoso,-a.

endearment *n* carinho *m*, meiguice *f*; *(smile)* sedutor; *(discurso)* tocante.

endeavour *(UK)*, **endevor** *(US)* *n* *(effort)* esforço *m*; tentativa *f*; empenho *m*; **to make every ~ to** fazer todos os possíveis/esforços para; ♦ *vi*: **to ~ to do** esforçar-se em fazer; tentar fazer.

endemic *n* endemia *f*; ♦ *adj* endémico,-a **(in to** em).

ending *n* fim *m*, conclusão *f*; *(outcome)* desfecho *m*, desenlace *m*; **2** *(LING)* terminação *f*.

endive *n* *(BOT)* endívia *f*, chicória *f*.

endless *adj* interminável, infinito, sem fim.

endlessly *adv* interminavelmente.

endorse *vt* *(approve)* endossar; aprovar; **2** assinar nas costas do cheque; garantir pagamento; **3** *(to record offenses) (UK)* **to have one's driving licence ~d** receber pontos, ter cadastro na carta de condução.

endorsement *n* *(of cheque)* endosso *m*; aprovação *f*, sanção; **2** descrição *f* das infra(c)ções na carta de condução.

endorser *n* endossante *m,f*.

endow *vt* *(with money)* doar; dotar; **2** fundar, financiar *(operating theatre, etc)*; **to be ~ed with** *(gifted)* ser dotado de; **well-~ed** *(physically) (large)* grande.

endowment *n* dote *m*; *(for charity)*, doação; dotação *(of money)*; **2** *(fig)* talento *m*, dom *m*; **~ insurance/ assurance** *n* *(in a mortgage)* seguro *m* dotal.

> Tipo de seguro de vida que paga a hipoteca ao designatário no caso de morte do titular da apólice.

endurance *n* resistência; **~ test** *n* prova *f* de resistência.

endure *vt* sofrer; *(to bear)* aguentar, suportar; resistir; ♦ *vi* perdurar.

enduring *adj* paciente *m,f*; durável *m,f*, resistente *m,f*.

enema *n* *(MED)* clister *m*.

enemy *n adj* inimigo,-a; **the ~** o inimigo *m*.

energetic *adj* *(lively)*; enérgico,-a; *(exercise)* vigoroso,-a; **~s** *n* *(PHYS)* energética *f*.

energy *(pl: -ies)* *n* *(vitality)* energia *f*; **2** *(power)* energia; **~-saving** *n* *(device)* poupança *f* de energia; **renewable ~** energias *fpl* renováveis.

enervating *adj* enervante *m,f*, desgastante *m,f*.

enfold *vt* *(LITER)* *(engulf)* envolver; **2** *(embrace)* abraçar.

enforce *vt* obrigar; *(JUR)* fazer cumprir.

enforceable *adj* aplicável *m,f*.

enforced *adj* obrigatório.

enforcement *n* coa(c)ção *f*; cumprimento *m*.

engage *vt* travar *(conversation)* **(with sb** com alguém); **2** *(TECH)* engrenar; **3** *(employ)* contratar; **to ~ in** dedicar-se a algo, ocupar-se com, envolver-se em.

engaged *adj* ocupado,-a em algo; **2 ~ to sb** estar noivo/noiva; **to get ~** ficar noivo; **he is ~ in research** dedica-se à pesquisa; **~ tone** *n* *(TEL)* sinal *m* de interrompido/ocupado.

engagement *n* encontro *m*; **2** *(commitment)* compromisso; **3** noivado *m*; **~ ring** *n* anel *m* de noivado.

engaging *adj* atraente *m,f*; cativante *m,f*; simpático,-a.

engender *vt* *(beget)* engendrar; **2** *(generate, produce)* gerar, produzir.

engine *n* *(AUT)* motor *m*; máquina *f*; *(RAIL)* locomotiva; **~ driver** *n* maquinista *m,f*; **~ room** *n* casa *f* das máquinas.

engineer *n* *(university qualified)* engenheiro,-a; **civil ~** engenheiro,-a civil; **2** técnico,-a; *(US: RAIL)* maquinista *m*; **borough ~** pessoal de limpeza da câmara; ♦ *vt* *(construct)* construir; **2** *(contrive)* tramar, urdir *(plot)*.

engineering *n* engenharia *f*; **light/heavy ~** indústria leve/pesada.

England *n* Inglaterra; **in ~** na Inglaterra.

English *n adj* inglês, esa; **the ~** *npl* os ingleses *mpl*; ♦ *n* *(LING)* inglês *m*.

English Channel *n:* **the ~** o Canal da Mancha.

English Heritage *n* organização financiada em parte pelo governo, que olha pelos monumentos e edifícios históricos.

Englishman, Englishwoman *n* inglês *m*, inglesa *f*.

engorge *vt* *(MED) (blood)* congestionar-(se); **2** *(eat)* devorar.

engrave *vt* *(metal, glass)* gravar **(on** em, **with** com); **2** *(fig) (on one's memory)* gravar **(on** em); **~r** *n* gravador *m*.

engraving *n* gravura, gravação *f*.

engross *vt* *(absorve)* absorver **(in** em); **to be ~ed in** estar absorto em; **2** copiar/passar a limpo *(manuscript)* em letra legível.

engrossing *adj* *(book, film)* absorvente *m,f*, cativante *m,f*.

engulf *vt* *(waves)* tragar; *(fire)* devorar, engolir *(fire)*; **2** *(silence, fog)* envolver; **3** *(overwhelm)* **to be ~ed by debts** estar imerso em dívidas; **4 to be ~ed by fear** ser apoderado de medo.

enhance *vt* melhorar; **2** realçar; **3** *(COMP)* optimizar, otimizar.

enhancement *n* realce *m;* **2** melhoria *f,* aumento *m.*

enigma *n* enigma *m.*

enigmatic *adj* enigmático,-a.

enjoy *vt* *(gen)* gostar de; desfrutar de *(view, beauty, climate); (food)* comer com gosto; *(ART, MUS)* apreciar; **2** gozar *(health, life, position);* **to ~ o.s.** *vr (have a good time)* divertir-se.

enjoyable *adj* agradável; divertido.

enjoyment *n* prazer *m;* gozo *m,* satisfação *f.*

enlace *vt* enlaçar, abraçar.

enlarge *vt* aumentar; estender, alargar; **2** *(PHOT)* ampliar; ♦ *vi:* **to ~ on** desenvolver, estender-se sobre.

enlargement *n* engrandecimento *m;* **2** *(dimension)* expansão *f;* alargamento *m;* **Europe's ~** o alargamento da Europa; **3** *(PHOT)* ampliação *f;* **4** *(MED)* *(of eye)* dilatação *f; (of tumour)* hipertrofia *f.*

enlighten *vt* esclarecer, informar, instruir.

enlightened *adj* culto,-a; bem informado,-a; compreensivo,-a; "**the ~ despot**" *(Marquês de Pombal)* 'o déspota esclarecido'.

enlightening *adj* elucidativo,-a.

enlightenment *n* esclarecimento *m;* **the E~** *(HIST)* Iluminismo *m;* **the age of ~** o século das Luzes.

enlist *vt* *(MIL)* recrutar; **2** *(support)* **to ~ sb's help** assegurar–se da ajuda de alguém; ♦ *vi* alistar-se.

enlistment *n* recrutamento, alistamento *m.*

enliven *vt* animar *(conversation).*

enmesh *vt* *(passive use)* emaranhar, enredar; **to become ~ed in** envolver-se em; *(bird in a net)* emaranhado,-a.

enmity *n* inimizade *f.*

ennoble *vt* *(dignify)* enobrecer; **2** *(raise to noble rank)* nobilitar.

enormity *n* enormidade *f.*

enormous *adj* enorme, grande.

enough *adj, pron* bastante, suficiente; **~ time/things** bastante tempo/bastantes coisas; **he is old ~ to know** ele já tem idade para saber; **to have ~ (of sb/sth)** *(fed up with)* estar farto,-a de (alguém, de algo); **that's ~!** já chega!, basta!; **~ for today** por hoje chega; ♦ *adv:* **large ~** suficientemente grande; **sure ~** sem dúvida; **curiously ~ ...** por estranho que pareça ...

en passant *adv* de passagem; a propósito.

enquire *vt* *(to ask a question)* perguntar; informar-se (**about** de/sobre); **to ~ (after sb's health)** perguntar por alguém (pela saúde de alguém); *(Vd: inquire).*

enquiry *(pl: -ies)* *n* pedido *m* de informações; **to make enquiries** colher informações *(Vd: inquiry).*

enrage *vt* enfurecer, enraivecer.

enraged *adj* furioso,-a.

enrapture *vt* encantar; **to be ~d** estar, ficar extasiado,-a.

enrich *vt* enriquecer.

enrol *vt* inscrever; *(EDUC)* matricular; ♦ *vi* inscrever-se, matricular-se.

enrolment *(UK),* **enrollment** *(US)* *n* inscrição *f;* matrícula *f* (**in, for, at** em); *(MIL)* recrutamento *m.*

en route *adv* no caminho; **~ to** a caminho de.

ensemble *n* conjunto *m.*

enshroud *vt* *(hide with, cover)* cobrir; esconder, ocultar.

ensign *n* bandeira *f;* **2** símbolo *m,* emblema *f;* **3** *(MIL: lowest rank officer)* alferes *msg;* *(US: NAUT)* guarda-marinha *m.*

enslave *vt* escravizar.

ensnare *vt* apanhar *(animal or sb)* numa armadilha; **2** enganar, iludir.

ensue *vi* seguir-se; resultar (**from** de); acontecer.

ensuing *adj* subsequente *m,f.*

ensure *vt* assegurar, garantir; **to ~ (that)** assegurar (-se) que.

ENT *(MED)* *(abbr of* **ear, nose and throat**) otorrino.

entail *vt* *(involve)* implicar, envolver.

entangle *vt* enredar, emaranhar.

entanglement *n* emaranhado.

entente *n* entendimento *m;* acordo *m.*

enter *vt* entrar em *(room);* **2** *(join)* ficar, fazer-se sócio de; **3** *(MIL)* alistar-se em; **4 to ~ in** *(register)* inscrever-se em *(course, competition);* **5** *(record)* anotar, apontar *(book, ledger);* ♦ *vi* entrar; **to ~ for** *vt* apresentar-se para; ♦ **to ~ into** *vt* entrar em *(conversação, negociação);* **2** tomar parte em; ♦ **to ~ (up) on** *vt* entrar para; **to ~ upon** *vt* *(start)* encetar.

enteritis *n* *(MED)* enterite *f.*

enterprise *n* empresa *f;* iniciativa *f;* **free ~** livre iniciativa; **private ~** iniciativa privada.

enterprising *adj* *(person)* empreendedor,-ora; dinâmico,-a; **2** *(plan)* audacioso,-a.

entertain *vt/vi* *(amuse)* divertir, entreter; **2** receber (em casa), acolher *(guest);* **3** *(idea)* considerar.

entertainer *n* artista animador,-ora.

entertaining *adj* divertido,-a.

entertainment *n* diversão *f;* espe(c)táculo *m;* festa *f,* entretenimento *m.*

enthral *vt* encantar, enfeitiçar; cativar.

enthralled *adj* encantado,-a, enfeitiçado,-a.

enthuse *vi:* **to ~ about sth** entusiasmar-se com.

enthusiasm *n* entusiasmo *m.*

enthusiast *n* entusiasta *m,f.*

enthusiastic *adj* entusiástico,-a; **to be ~ (about)** entusiasmar-se (por).

entice *vt* atrair, aliciar, engodar.

enticing *adj* sedutor,-ora, tentador,-ora.

entire *adj* inteiro,-a, completo,-a; total *m,f,* todo,-a.

entirely *adv* totalmente.

entirety *n:* **it its ~** na sua totalidade, no seu conjunto.

entitle *vt* autorizar, dar direito a; **to ~ sb to sth** dar a alguém direito a algo.

entitled *adj* *(book)* intitulado; **to be ~ to do** ter direito de fazer.

entitlement *n* direito *m* (**to** a).

entity *n* entidade *f.*

entomology *n* entomologia *f.*

entourage *n* séquito *m,* comitiva *f.*

entrails *npl* entranhas *fpl.*

entrance *n* *(way-in, act of entering)* entrada *f; (hall)* vestíbulo *m;* **2** *(entry)* acesso *a;* **to gain ~ to** ser admitido,-a em; **~ examination** *n (school)* exame *m* de admissão; *(civil/diplomatic services)* concurso *m* de admissão; **3** ~ **fee** *n* matrícula *f*, propina *(BR)* preço do ingresso; *(to club)* jóia *f (BR)* taxa de admissão.

entrancing *adj* encantador,-ora; fascinante *m,f*.

entrant *n* participante *m,f*; novato,-a.

entrap (-pp-) *vt* apanhar numa armadilha, atrair (para o perigo).

entrapment *n* armadilha *f (for person)*.

entreat *vt* rogar, suplicar.

entreaty *n* rogo *m*, súplica *f*.

entrée *n (CULIN)* entrada *f*.

entrenched *adj (MIL)* entrincheirado,-a; **2** *(idea, opinion)* fixo,-a, inabalável *m,f*; *(tradition)* enraizado,-a.

entrepreneur *n* empresário,-a.

entrust *vt*: **to** ~ **sth to sb** confiar algo a alguém.

entry *n (gen)* entrada *f*; **2** *(admission)* acesso *m* **(to** a); **3** *(in register)* assento, regist(r)o *m*; **4** *(in diary)* nota *f*, anotação *f*; **5** *(in dictionary)* entrada; **6** *(COMM) (in ledger)* lançamento *m*; **7** *(in competition; to school)* inscrição *f*; *(competition – person)* concorrente; ~ **form** *n* ficha *f*, formulário *f* de inscrição; ~ **phone** *n* porteiro ele(c)trónico; **7** *(COMP)* entrada *f* de dados; **8** *(road)* '**no** ~' 'sentido proibido'.

entwine *vt/vi* enroscar(-se); entrelaçar(-se) **their hands were** ~**d** as mãos deles estavam entrelaçadas; **the snake** ~**d around the tree** a cobra enroscou-se em redor da árvore.

E number *n (COMM) (UK)* número (depois do prefixo E) de aditivo alimentar (substância química no alimento).

enumerate *vt* enumerar.

enunciate *vt (pronounce clearly)* pronunciar; **2** *(express clearly)* enunciar.

envelop *vt* envolver; **she** ~**ed the child in a blanket** ela envolveu a criança num cobertor.

envelope *n* envelope *m*.

enviable *adj* invejável *m,f*.

envious *adj* invejoso,-a; de inveja.

Os significados de **envy** e de **jealousy** não são tão distintos como em português, podendo-se usar um ou outro, com o mesmo sentido.

environment *n (gen)* ambiente *m*; **the** ~ o meio ambiente *m*; **friendly** ~ ambiente *m* amigável.

environmental *adj* ambiental, do meio ambiente; ~ **group** grupo *m* ecologista.

environmentalist *n* prote(c)tor,-ora do ambiente; ambientalista *m,f*.

environmentally *adv*: ~ **safe** que não prejudica o meio ambiente; ~ **friendly** amigo do ambiente; ~ **aware** sensível aos problemas ambientais; *(person)* consciente dos problemas ambientais.

Environmental Protection Agency *n (US)* **the** ~ a Secretaria Especial do Meio Ambiente.

environs *npl* subúrbios, arredores *mpl*.

envisage, envision *vt (foresee)* prever, imaginar.

envoy *n* emissário,-a, enviado,-a.

envy *n* inveja; ♦ *vt* ter inveja de; **to** ~ **sb sth** invejar alguém por algo, cobiçar algo de alguém.

enzyme *n* enzima *f*.

e.o. *(abbr for* **ex officio***)*.

EOC *(abbr for* **Equal Opportunities Commission***)* Comissão para a Igualdade.

eon *(US) (Vd:* **aeon***)*.

epaulet(t)e *n* (adorno militar) dragona *f*.

ephemeral *adj* efémero *(BR:* -ê-*)*.

epic *n* epopéia; ♦ *adj* épico,-a.

epicentre *n* epicentre *m*.

epidemic *n* epidemia *f*.

epidermis *n (ANAT)* epiderme *f*.

epidural *n adj (MED) (anaesthetic)* epidural *m*.

epigram *n* epigrama *m*.

epilepsy *n* epilepsia.

epileptic *n adj* epiléptico,-a.

epilogue *(UK)*, **epilog** *(US)* epílogo *m*.

epiphany *(pl:* -ies*)* *n* epifânia; **E**~ *(REL)* Epifânia *(6th Jan)*, dia dos Reis.

episode *n* episódio *m*.

epistle *n* epístola *f*.

epitaph *n* epitáfio *m*.

epitome *n* epítome *m*.

epitomize *vt (embody)* epitomar, personificar, encarnar.

epoch *n* época *f*.

eponym *n (LING)* epónimo *m*.

eponymous *adj* eponímico.

equable *adj (person)* plácido,-a, equilibrado,-a; *(climate)* uniforme *m,f*, temperado,-a.

equal *n* igual *m* **to have no** ~ não haver um igual; **she has no** ~ não há nenhuma como ela; ♦ *adj* igual *m,f*; equitativo,-a, equivalente *m,f*; **to be** ~ **to sth** ser igual a algo; **on** ~ **terms** em igualdade de condições; **of** ~ **rank** da mesma patente, categoria; **all men are** ~ **in the sight of God** somos todos iguais perante Deus; ♦ *(UK pt, pp* -led, *US pt, pp* -ed*)* *vt* **to be** ~ *(MATH)* ser igual a; **2** *(SPORT)* igualar *(time, record)*; **3** igualar-se a.

equality *n* igualdade *f*.

equalize *vt/vi* igualar; *(SPORT)* empatar.

equalizer *n* empate *m*.

equally *adv* igualmente; por igual.

equanimity *n* equanimidade *f*, serenidade *f*; re(c)tidão *f*.

equate *vt*: **to** ~ **sth with** equiparar algo com.

equation *n (MATH)* equação *f*.

equator *n*: equador *m*.

equatorial *adj* equatorial.

equerry *(pl:* -ies*)* *n* funcionário *m* da Casa Real britânica.

equestrian *n* equestre *m,f*, equitação *f*; ♦ *adj* equestre *m,f*.

equilibrium *n* equilíbrio *m*.

equine *adj (species)* cavalar *m,f*; *(disease)* equino,-a.

equinox *n* equinócio *m*.

equip (-ped) *vt* equipar *(for* para*)*; prover, **(sb with sth)** munir alguém com algo; **to be well** ~**ed** estar bem preparado,-a, equipado,-a.

equipment *n* equipamento *m*; aprestos *mpl*, apetrechos *mpl*.

equitable *adj* equitativo,-a.

equities *npl (FIN)* a(c)ções *fpl* ordinárias.

equity *n (fairness)* equidade, justeza *f; (JUR)* justiça; **E~** *n (Actors' Equity Association) (UK)* sindicato *m* dos a(c)tores.

equivalent *n* equivalente *m;* ♦ *adj* equivalente *m,f;* **to be ~ to** ser equivalente a.

equivocal *adj (remark)* equívoco,-a; ambíguo,-a.

equivocate *vi* equivocar.

era *n* era *f,* época *f.*

eradiate *vi* irradiar.

eradicate *vt* erradicar, extirpar.

erase *vt* apagar, raspar.

eraser *n* borracha (de apagar).

erect *adj (standing)* erguido,-a, vertical *m,f; (straight)* ere(c)to,-a; direito,-a; **2** *(stiff)* hirto,-a; **3** *(penis)* em ere(c)ção; **4** *(head)* levantada; ♦ *vt* erigir *(statue);* **2** levantar *(head, arm);* **3** montar *(tent);* **4** instalar *(board, screen).*

erection *n (of building, statue)* construção *f;* **2** *(tent)* montagem *f;* **3** *(PHYSIOL) (of penis)* ere(c)ção *f;* **to have an ~** *(coll)* ter uma tesão.

ergonomics *n* ergonomia *f.*

ERM *n (abbr for* **Exchange Rate Mechanism**) MTC *m.*

ermine *n (animal, fur)* arminho *m.*

erode *vt (GEOL)* causar erosão; corroer.

erogenous zone *n* zona *f* erógena.

erosion *n* erosão *f;* desgaste *m.*

erotic *adj* erótico,-a.

eroticism *n* erotismo *m.*

err *vi* errar, equivocar-se, enganar-se; **2** *(REL)* pecar.

errand *n* recado, missão *f; ~* **boy** *n* mensageiro; moço de recados; *~* **of mercy** missão *f* de caridade; **to run ~s** fazer recados; fazer pequenos serviços.

errant *adj* errante *m,f;* **knight** *~* cavaleiro *m* andante.

erratic *adj* errático,-a; irregular *m,f.*

erroneous *adj* erróneo,-a *(BR: -ô-),* falso,-a.

error *n (mistake)* erro *m;* **to commit an ~** cometer um erro; *~* **of judgement** erro de julgamento; **in ~** por erro; **to see one's ~s** reconhecer nossos erros.

ersatz *n adj (substitute)* artificial, sucedâneo,-a.

Erse *n (Irish Gaelic)* erse *(língua gaélica).*

erst, erstwhile *adj* antigo,-a, anterior *m,f; ~* **friends** *npl* velhos amigos *mpl;* ♦ *adv (dated) (long ago)* outrora, antigamente.

erudite *n* erudito,-a, douto,-a.

erudition *n* erudição *f.*

erupt *vi* entrar em erupção; **2** *(MED)* causar erupção; **3** *(fig)* explodir.

eruption *n* erupção *f; (fig)* explosão *f.*

escalate *vi (spread)* alastrar-se, intensificar-se; **2** *(inflation)* subir em flecha.

escalation *n (of violence)* escalada *f* (**of** de); **2** intensificação *f;* **3** *(of costs, prices)* aumento *m.*

escalator *n* escada *f* rolante.

escapade *n (adventure, fun)* travessura *f;* escapadela *f,* escapada *f.*

escape *n* fuga *f;* escapatória *f;* **to have a narrow ~** escapar por um triz; **2** *(accident)* fuga *f (of gas);* ♦ *vi* escapar, evadir-se; **2** *(avoid)* fugir a *(work,*

responsibility); ♦ *vt* evitar, fugir de; **to ~ from** escapulir de; livrar-se de; **2** *(elude name, fact)* escapar a; não lembrar; **his name ~s me now** não me lembro agora do nome dele.

escape clause *n (in a contract)* cláusula *f* de exce(p)ção (que permite revogar).

escapee *n* evadido,-a.

escape route *n (from fire)* saída *f* de emergência; **2** *(from prison)* rota *f* de fuga/evasão.

escape valve *n (TECH and fig)* válvula *f* de escape.

escapism *n* fuga à realidade, escapismo *m.*

escapologist *n* ilusionista *m,f.*

escarpment *n* escarpa *f.*

eschew *vt* evitar; **2** abster-se (de).

escort *n* acompanhante *m,f;* **2** *(MIL)* escolta; **3** acompanhamento, séquito; ♦ *vt* acompanhar; **2** *(MIL)* escolta.

escutcheon *n* brasão *m;* **2 ~ plate** *(door lock)* escudete *m.*

Eskimo *n* esquimó *m,f.*

esophagus *(US) (Vd:* **oesophagus***).*

esoteric *adj* esotérico,-a.

ESP *(abbr for* **extrasensory perception**) percepção *f* extrasensorial.

espadrille *n* alpargata *f.*

especially *adv* especialmente; sobretudo; em particular.

Esperanto *n* esperanto *m.*

espionage *n* espionagem *f.*

esplanade *n* avenida *f,* beira-mar *m;* esplanada *f.*

espouse *vt* casar com, desposar; **2** *(cause)* abraçar.

Esq. *(abbr for* **Esquire***) (title of respect used in correspondences, instead of 'Mr.');* **S. Scott Esq.** Exmo Senhor S. Scott.

esquire *n (dated)* escudeiro.

essay *n (school)* reda(c)ção *f,* composição *f* (**on** sobre); **2** *(Univ) (LITER)* ensaio *m* (**on** sobre), tratado *m* literário.

essayist *n* ensaísta *m,f.*

essence *n* essência *f;* **in ~** em essência.

essential *adj* indispensável *m,f;* essencial *m,f.*

essentially *adv* essencialmente, basicamente; **2** *(really)* sobretudo.

essentials *npl (basic necessities)* o essencial *m;* **2** *(important elements)* elementos *mpl* essenciais, fundamentos *mpl.*

establish *vt (set up)* estabelecer; criar; fundar; **to ~ that** demonstrar, provar.

established *adj (person, business)* com boa reputação; fixo,-a.

establishment *n* estabelecimento *m;* **2** instituição *f;* **the E~** a classe dirigente.

estate *n (manor house with lands)* solar *m,* quinta *f (BR)* fazenda *f;* **2** *(inheritance)* herança *f* bens *mpl; ~* **agent** *n* agente *m,f* imobiliário; *~* **car** *n (UK)* furgão *m;* **housing ~** fogos *mpl* habitacionais; urbanização *f;* **industrial ~** zona industrial.

esteem *n* estima, consideração; apreço *m;* **to hold sb in high ~** ter grande consideração/estima; por alguém; ♦ *vt* estimar.

estimate *n (assessment of size,etc)* avaliação *f,* estimativa *f;* **2** *(calculation)* cálculo; **3** *(COMM)* orçamento; ♦ *vt* avaliar, calcular; ♦ calcular, estimar; ♦ *vi* (COMM) fazer um orçamento de algo.

estimated *pp adj* aproximado,-a; ~ **time of arrival** (ETA) hora *f* prevista de chegada.

estimation *n* opinião *f*; **2** cálculo *m*; **3** estimativa *f*; **4** (esteem) consideração *f*.

Estonia *npr* Estónia (BR: -ô-); **in** ~ na Estónia.

Estonian *n adj* estoniano,-a.

estrange *vt* (usually in passive) alienar, afastar.

estranged *pp adj* (husband, wife) separado,-a de; (son, daughter) alienado,-a (o filho, a filha, etc) com quem não fala.

estrangement indiferença *f*, afastamento *m*.

estrogen (US) (Vd: **oestrogen**).

estuary *n* estuário *m*.

ETA (abbr for **estimated time of arrival**) (Vd: **estimated**).

et cetera *adv* e assim por diante; etc.

etch *vt* (engrave) gravar a água forte; **2** (fig) **our farewell is ~ed on my memory** o nosso adeus está gravado na minha memória.

etching *n* gravura, estampa a água-forte *f*; (arte de) gravar a água-forte.

ETD (abbr for **estimated time of departure**) (Vd: **estimated**).

eternal *adj* eterno,-a.

eternally *adv* eternamente.

eternity (pl: -ies) *n* eternidade *f*.

ethanol *n* (QUÍM) etanol *m*.

ether *n* éter *m*.

ethereal *adj* etéreo,-a.

ethic *n* ética *f*.

ethical *adj* ético,-a; honrado,-a.

ethics *n* ética *f*; **2** moral *f*; **medical** ~ ética médica.

Ethiopia *npr* Etiópia; **in** ~ na Etiópia.

Ethiopian *n adj inv* etíope.

ethnic *adj* étnico,-a; ~ **cleansing** saneamento *m* étnico, limpeza *f* étnica.

ethnologic *adj* etnológico,-a.

ethos *n* característica, cultura *f* dum povo, duma comunidade; sistema *m* de valores.

etiquette *n* etiqueta *f*.

Eton (GEOG) cidade inglesa famosa pelo seu colégio; **Eton College**, colégio privado, para rapazes – 'jovens cavalheiros'; fundado em 1411.

Eton crop *n* corte de cabelo à rapaz para mulheres.

etymology *n* etimologia *f*.

EU (abbr for **European Union**) a União Europeia, UE.

eucalyptus *n* (BOT) eucalipto *m*.

Eucharist *n* (REL) Eucaristia *f*.

eulogize/ise *vt* louvar, elogiar.

eulogy (pl: -ies) *n* grande elogio *m*; **2** discurso laudatório *ou* fúnebre; **3** panegírico *m*.

eunuch *n* eunuco *m*.

euphemism *n* eufemismo *m*.

euphoria *n* euforia *f*.

euphoric *adj* eufórico,-a.

Euphrates *n* (river) Eufrates *m*.

Eurasian *n adj* euroasiático,-a.

eureka *exc* heureca!, eureka!

Eurocrat *n* (pej) eurocrata *m,f*.

Eurocurrency (pl: -ies) *n* divisa *f* europeia, euro-divisa.

Euro MP *n* deputado,-a ao parlamento europeu.

Europe *npr* Europa; **in** ~ na Europa.

European *n, adj* europeu *m*, europeia *f*.

European Commission *npr*: **the** ~ a Comissão *f* Europeia.

European Council *n* Conselho *m* Europeu.

European Court of Justice *npr*: **the** ~ o Tribunal Europeu de Justiça.

European currency unit, ECU *n* Unidade *f* de moeda europeia, ECU, ecu *m*.

Europeanism *n* europeísmo *m*.

Europeanization *n* europeização *f*.

European Monetary System *n*: **the** ~ o Sistema Monetário Europeu.

European standard *n* normas *fpl* europeias.

European Union *n*: **the** ~ a União *f* Europeia.

Eurosceptic *adj* eurocético,-a.

Eurostar *n* comboio rápido entre a Inglaterra (Southampton) e França (Paris) pelo Canal da Mancha, Eurostar.

euthanasia *n* eutanásia *f*.

evacuate *vt* evacuar (**from**, de; **to**, para); **2** (defecate) evacuar.

evacuation *n* evacuação *f*.

evade *vt* (question) evadir, evitar; **2** fugir a; **to** ~ **the police** fugir à polícia.

evaluate *vt* avaliar; determinar o valor de; **2** avaliar (situation).

evaluation *n* avaliação *f*.

evangelist *n* evangelista *m,f*; evangelizador,-ora.

evaporate *vi* evaporar-se; ♦ *vt* evaporar; ~**d milk** *n* leite *m* evaporado.

evaporation *n* evaporação *f*.

evasion *n* (responsibility) evasão *f*; fuga *f*; **tax** ~ fraude *f* fiscal; fuga ao fisco; **3** (fig) (lie) evasiva.

evasive *adj* evasivo,-a.

Eve *n* (woman) Eva *f*.

eve *n* véspera *f*; (the day before) **on the** ~ **of** na véspera de; **Christmas** ~ *n* véspera do Natal.

even *adj* (flat, smooth) plano,-a; liso,-a; uniforme *m,f*; **2** (number) número par *m*; **3** equilibrado,-a; (SPORT) igual *m,f*; ~**minded** calmo,-a, equilibrado,-a; ♦ *adv* (emphasis) até, mesmo, ainda; ~ **more** ainda mais; ~ **so** mesmo assim; **not** ~ nem mesmo, nem sequer; ~ **if** ainda que; ♦ *conj* ~ **as** (while) enquanto; ~ **if** mesmo que, se; ~ **though** ainda que; ♦ **to be** ~ quite; **we are** ~ estamos quites; **to get** ~ **with sb** vingar-se de alguém; **to make** ~ igualar, saldar; ♦ **to** ~ **out** *vt/vi* nivelar; **2** distribuir equalitariamente; **to** ~ **up** compensar, equilibrar.

even-handed *adj* (impartial) justo,-a, imparcial *m,f*.

evening *n* tardinha *f*, fim *m* de tarde; anoitecer *m*, entardecer; noite *f*; **good** ~! boa noite!; **tomorrow** ~ amanhã à noite; **2** (entertaining) serão *m*; **a musical** ~ (**soirée**) um serão *m* musical; ~ **class** *n* aula no(c)turna; ~ **dress** *n* trajo de cerimónia; traje a rigor; (for woman) vestido de noite; (for man) smoking.

evenly *adv* igualmente; **2** (speak, do) calmamente; **3** (distribute) uniformemente.

event *n* acontecimento *m*; **2 social** ~ evento *m* social; **3** *(SPORT)* prova; **field** ~ prova *f* de atletismo; **at all** ~**s/in any** ~ em todo caso, aconteça o que acontecer; **in the** ~ **of** no caso de.

even-tempered *adj* calmo,-a, plácido,-a.

eventful *adj* notável, momorável *m,f*; **2** cheio,-a de acontecimentos/de incidentes; **3** agitado,-a.

eventide *n (poetic)* o anoitecer *m*.

eventing *n (UK) (dressage)* competição *f* de corridas e saltos de cavalos; **2** concurso de torneios.

eventual *adj* final; definitivo.

eventuality *n* eventualidade *f*.

eventually *adv* finalmente; por fim, oportunamente, em dado momento.

ever *adv* já, alguma vez; nunca, jamais; alguma vez; **better than** ~ melhor que nunca; **the best** ~ o melhor que já se viu; ~ **again** nunca mais; **hardly** ~ quase nunca; ~ **more** cada vez mais; **have you** ~ **seen it?** já alguma vez viu/viste isto?; **2** *(emphatic)* **she is** ~ **so pretty!** ela é tão linda!; **I shan't speak to you,** ~/~ **again** jamais te falarei; ~ **such a fight!** tamanha luta!; **for** ~ **and** ~ para sempre; ~ **the same smile** sempre o mesmo sorriso; ~ **since** *adv* desde então; ♦ *conj* depois que.

Everest *npr:* **the Mount** ~ o Monte Everest.

Everglades *npr:* **the** ~ região pantanosa da Flórida E.U.A., os Everglades.

evergreen *n (BOT)* sempre-verde.

everlasting *adj* eterno,-a, perpétuo,-a.

every *adj* cada; todos; ~ **day** todos os dias; *(BR)* todo dia; ~ **other week** semana sim, semana não; ~ **now and then** de vez em quando; ~ **two** de 2 em 2 dias; ~**body** *pron* todos *mpl*, toda a gente, todo o mundo; ~**day** *adj* diário; corrente; comum; vulgar; rotineiro; quotidiano; ~ **one** cada um, todos *mpl*; ~**thing** *pron* tudo; ~**thing else** todo o resto; **I help in** ~ **way I can** eu ajudarei em tudo quanto eu puder; ~**where** *adv* em/por toda parte; ~**where else** em qualquer outro lugar; ~ **which way** em todos os sentidos; IDIOM **she is** ~ **inch a lady** ela é uma senhora até à raiz dos cabelos; ~ **man for himself** cada um por si.

evict *vt* expulsar; desalojar.

evictee *n* inquilino com ordem de despejo.

eviction *n (from house)* despejo *m*; ~ **order** *n (JUR)* ordem *f* de despejo.

evidence *n (JUR) (forensic data)* prova(s) *f (pl)*; **2** *(testimony)* testemunho *m*, *(deposition)* depoimento; **to give** ~ testemunhar, prestar declarações; **circumstantial** ~ prova *f* indire(c)ta; **external** ~ provas extrínsecas; **to turn King's/Queen's state** ~ *(for the prosecution)* depor contra os próprios cúmplices; **2** *(sinal, trace)* evidência *f*; **to be in** ~ estar em evidência.

evident *adj* evidente *m,f* patente *m,f*.

evidently *adv* naturalmente, evidentemente.

evil *n* mal *m*, maldade *f*; **there is good and** ~ **in all of us** há de bom e de mal em todos nós; **she is pure** ~ ela é a maldade personificada; ♦ *adj* mau *m*, má *f*; funesto,-a; horrível *m,f*; ~ **doer** *n* malfeitor,-ora; ~ **eye** mau olhado; ~ **fate**

(misfortune) desgraça *f*, pouca sorte *f*; ~ **gossip** *n* maledicência *f*; **king's** ~ *(dated) (MED)* escrófulas *fpl*; ~**-minded** malvado,-a; ~ **tongue** *n (coll)* má língua; **to have an** ~ **tongue** ser maldizente *m,f*; **the E~ One** o demónio, diabo; ♦ *adv* mal.

evince *vt* evidenciar.

evocation *n* evocação *f*.

evocative *adj* evocativo,-a, sugestivo,-a.

evoke *vt* evocar.

evolution *n* evolução *f*, desenvolvimento *m*.

evolve *vt* desenvolver, evoluir; ♦ *vi* desenvolver-se.

ewe *n* ovelha *f*

ewer *n (pitcher)* jarro *m* para a água.

ex- (former) *prefix* ex- (eis); **my ex-husband** o meu ex (eis), o meu ex marido;

exacerbate *vt* exacerbar.

exact *adj* exa(c)to,-a; ♦ *vt;* **to** ~ **sth (from)** exigir algo (de).

exacting *adj* exigente *m,f* difícil *m,f*.

exactitude *n* exa(c)tidão *f*.

exactly *adv* exa(c)tamente; no ponto.

exaggerate *vt/vi* exagerar.

exaggeration *n* exagero *m*.

exalt *vt (glorify)* exaltar.

exalted *adj* sublime; **2** *(position, rank)* elevado,-a.

exam *n (abbr for examination)* exame *m*, prova *f*; **to take/sit an** ~ fazer um exame; **to pass/fail an** ~ passar/reprovar *(col* = chumbar*)* num exame; ~ **paper** *(test, exam)* enunciado *m*.

examination *n* exame *m*; **mock** ~ prova *f*, teste *m*; **2** *(of accounts)* verificação *f*; **3** inquérito *m*; ♦ **under** ~ sob investigação *f*; **2** *(JUR) (police; in court)* interrogatório *m*.

examine *vt (gen)* examinar; inspe(c)cionar; **2** *(JUR)* interrogar.

examiner *n* examinador,-ora; **external/internal** ~ examinador,-a externo,-a/interno,-a.

example *n* exemplo; exemplar *m*; **for** ~ por exemplo.

exasperate *vt* exasperar, irritar.

exasperating *adj* irritante *m,f*.

excavate *vt (dig)* escavar.

excavation *n* escavação *f*.

excavator *n (ARCHEOL) (person)* escavador *m*; **2** *(machine)* escavadora *f (BR)* escavadeira.

exceed *vt* exceder; ser superior a; **2** *(over limit)* ultrapassar *(speed, expectations)*.

exceedingly *adv* extremamente, muitíssimo.

excel *vt* exceder **(in** em); ~ **o.s.** exceder-se; ♦ *vi* sobressair, distinguir-se.

excellence *n* excelência *f*.

Excellency *n:* **His/Her** ~ Sua Excelência; **Your** ~ Vossa Excelência *m,f*.

excellent *adj* excelente *m,f*.

except *prep (=* ~ **for, -ing)** exce(p)to; salvo, menos; ♦ *vt* exce(p)tuar, excluir; ~ **if/when** exce(p)to se/ quando; ~ **that** salvo que.

excepting à exce(p)ção de; **present company** ~**ed** à exce(p)ção dos presentes.

exce(p)tion *n* exce(p)ção *f*; **to take** ~ **to** ressentir-se de, melindrar-se com; IDIOM **the** ~ **proves the rule** a exce(p)ção faz a regra.

exceptional *adj* excepcional *m,f.*

excerpt *n* extra(c)to, excerto; ♦ *vt* sele(c)cionar, extrair.

excess *n* excesso; **2** *(COMM)* excedente *m*; ~ **baggage** *n* excesso de bagagem.

excessive *adj* excessivo,-a.

exchange *n* *(swap)* troca *f*; **in** ~ **for sth** em troca de algo; **2** ~ **of words/discussion** troca de palavras, discussão *f*, altercação *f*; **3** *(FIN)* câmbio *m*; ~ **broker** *n* corretor,-ora *m,f* de câmbios; ~ **of posts** *n* permuta *f* ~ **rate** *m* taxa de câmbio *f*; **stock** ~ bolsa *f* (de valores); **4 telephone** ~ central *f* telefónica *(BR:* -fô-); **5** *(EDUC) (visit)* intercâmbio (cultural); ♦ *vt* trocar, permutar.

exchequer *n* *(UK)* **the E~** *(ADMIN)* o Tesouro *m* Público, Ministério das Finanças; *(BR)* Ministério da Fazenda; **the Chancellor of the E** ~ o Ministro das Finanças *(BR:* da Fazenda).

excise¹ *n* imposto *m* de consumo; ~ **duties** *(~ tax)* imposto *m* indire(c)to (**on** sobre).

excise² *vt* excisar, amputar.

excitable *adv* excitável *m,f.*

excite *vt* *(person)* excitar; entusiasmar; **2** *(interest, suspicion)* despertar; **to get ~d** entusiasmar-se; *(temper, nerves)* agitar-se.

excitement *n* excitação *f*; agitação *f*; entusiasmo *m.*

exciting *adj* estimulante; emocionante *m,f*; **how ~!** fantástico! que estupendo!

exclaim *vi* exclamar.

exclamation *n* exclamação *f*; *m* ~ **mark** *n* ponto ~ de exclamação.

exclude *vt* excluir; exce(p)tuar.

exclusion *n* exclusão *f*; ~ **zone** *n* zona *f* interdita.

exclusive *adj* exclusivo,-a; **2** *(club, district)* privativo,-a, fechado,-a; ~ **of tax** sem incluir os impostos.

exclusively *adv* exclusivamente, unicamente.

excommunicate *vt* excomungar.

excommunication *n* excomunhão *f.*

excrement *n* excremento *m*, fezes, *fpl.*

excrete *vi* excretar.

excruciating *adj* torturante *m,f*; atroz *m,f*; *(pain)* insuportável *m,f.*

excursion *n* excursão *f*, turné *f.*

excursionist *n* *(day-tripper)* excursionista *m,f.*

excusable *adj* perdoável, desculpável *m,f.*

excuse *n* desculpa, escusa; pretexto; ♦ *vt* desculpar, perdoar; **to** ~ **sb from doing sth** dispensar alguém de fazer algo; **to** ~ **o.s.** *vr* pedir licença (para se ausentar) desculpar-se; ~ **me!** *(apology)* desculpe!, perdão; **2** *(right of way, reaching across sb)* com licença.

ex-directory *n* *(UK) (person's number not on the telephone directory)* interdito a estranhos.

execrable *adj* abominável *m,f.*

executable *adj* executável *m,f.*

execute *vt* realizar, cumprir; **to** ~ **orders** cumprir as ordens; **2** *(task)* levar a cabo; **3** *(JUR)* executar *(criminal);* ~ **a will** legalizar um testamento.

execution *n* realização *f*; execução *f.*

executioner *n* verdugo, carrasco.

executive *n* *adj* *(COMM, POL)* executivo,-a.

executor *n* executor *m*; **2** *(JUR)* testamenteiro,-a.

exemplar *n* exemplar *m*; modelo *m.*

exemplary *adj* exemplar *m,f.*

exemplify *vt* exemplificar.

exempt *adj*: ~ **from** isento de; ♦ *vt*: **to** ~ **sb from** dispensar, isentar alguém de.

exemption *n* isenção *f*; dispensa; imunidade *f.*

exequies *(sg:* -**quy**) *npl* *(funeral rites)* exéquias *fpl.*

exercise *n* exercício; ~ **book** *n* caderno; ♦ *vt* exercer; **2** valer-se de *(rights)*; **3** *(dog)* levar para passear; ♦ *vi* fazer exercício.

exert *vt* exercer *(influence, pressure)* (**on sb** sobre alguém); **to** ~ **o.s.** esforçar-se, empenhar-se; **2** trabalhar demasiado.

exertion *m* esforço *m.*

exfoliant *n* cosmético *m* abrasivo, exfoliante *m.*

exfoliate *vi* *(wash skin with granular cosmetic)* exfoliar; **2** *(of bark, leaves)* esfoliar.

ex gratia *n* *(UK)* ~ **payment** gratificação *f.*

exhaust *n* escape *m*, exaustor *m*; escapamento *m* (de gás); ♦ *vt* esgotar.

exhaustion *n* exaustão *f*; **nervous** ~ esgotamento *m* nervoso.

exhaustive *adj* exaustivo,-a.

exhibit *n* *(ART)* obra exposta; **2** *(JUR)* objecto exposto; ♦ *vt* manifestar; demonstrar, acusar; apresentar; expor.

exhibition *n* exposição *f*; **to make an** ~ **of o.s.** fazer figura de tolo.

exhibitionist *n* exibicionista *m,f.*

exhilarating *adj* estimulante *m,f*, divertido,-a, tónico,-a *(BR:* tô-).

exhort *vt* exortar.

exhume *vt* exumar, desenterrar.

exigence *n* exigência *f*, imposição *f.*

exigent *adj* exigente *m,f*; urgente *m,f.*

exile *n* exílio; exílado; ♦ *vt* desterrar, exilar; ~**d** *n* exilado,-a.

exist *vi* existir; viver.

existence *n* existência *f.*

existentialist *adj* existencialista *m,f.*

existing *adj* existente *m,f*, atual *m,f.*

exit *n* saída *f*; ~ **poll** *n* *(UK) (POL)* pesquisa *f* de boca de urna.

exodus *n* êxodo *m.*

ex officio *adj* ex ofício; ♦ *adv* em ex ofício.

exonerate *vt*: **to** ~ **sb from** *(culpa)* exonerar alguém de; **2** *(obrigação)* desonerar (**from** de).

exorbitant *adj* exorbitante *m,f.*

exorcism *n* exorcismo *m.*

exorcize *vt* exorcizar; esconjurar.

exotic *adj* exótico,-a.

expand *vt* aumentar *(influence)*; *(size, activity)* expandir, alargar; **2** *(COMM)* desenvolver; ♦ *vi* expandir-se; dilatar-se; ~ **on/upon** *(subject)* entrar em detalhes, ampliar.

expanse *n* extensão *f*; vastidão *f.*

expansion *n* *(gen)* expansão *f*; **2** desenvolvimento; **3** ampliação *f*; **4** *(PHYS)* dilatação *f.*

expansionism *n* expansionismo *m*

expansive *adj* *(friendly, talkative)* expansivo,-a, pessoa muito dada; **2** capaz de expandir-se.

expatriate *n* expatriado,-a; ♦ *vt* expatriar; exilar.

expect *vt* esperar; contar com; supor; ♦ *vi*: **to be ~ing a baby** *(pregnant)* estar à espera de bebé *(BR*: nené).

expectancy *n*: **life ~** esperança de vida.

expectant *adj (person, crowd)* ansioso,-a **~ mother** *n* gestante, grávida.

expectantly *adv* ansiosamente.

expectation *n* esperança *f* expectativa *f;* **she improved beyond my ~s** ela melhorou além das minhas expectativas.

expectorant *n* expectorante *m*.

expedience, expediency *n* conveniência *f*, oportunidade *f*.

expedient *n* expediente *m*, recurso; **to resort to ~s** recorrer a expedientes; ♦ *adj* conveniente, oportuno.

expedite *vt* expedir; acelerar.

expedition *n* expedição *f*.

expel *vt* expelir; **2** *(school)* expulsar.

expend *vt* gastar, despender; consumir.

expendable *adj* prescindível.

expenditure *n* gasto, despesa; consumo; **the national ~** os gastos públicos, a despesa pública.

expense *n* gasto *m;* despesa *f;* custo *m;* **~s** *npl (COMM)* gastos *mpl;* **at the ~ of** à custa de; **~ account** *n* relatório de despesas.

expensive *adj* caro,-a, dispendioso,-a.

experience *n* experiência *f;* ♦ *vt (try)* experimentar; *(suffer)* sofrer.

experienced *adj* experimentado,-a, experiente *m,f*.

experiment *n* experiência; **2** *(science)* experimento *m;* prova; ensaio; **as an ~** a título de experiência; ♦ *vi* fazer experiências; **2** *(science)* fazer experimentos; experimentar, ensaiar.

experimental *adj* experimental *m,f*.

expert *n* perito,-a, especialista *m,f;* ♦ *adj* perito,-a, conhecedor,-ora.

expertise *n* perícia *f*, habilidade *f*.

expire *vi (become out of date)* caducar; terminar; **2** *(run out)* vencer *(payment);* **3** *(respiration)* expirar; **4** *(LITER)* falecer.

expiry *n* caducidade *f;* vencimento *m;* **~ date** prazo de validade.

explain *vt* explicar; **to ~ sth to sb** explicar algo a alguém; **2** *(clarify)* esclarecer; expor; **3** *(justificar)* justify.

explanation *n* explicação *f*.

explanatory *adj* explicativo,-a.

expletive *n* imprecação *f*.

explicit *adj* explícito,-a.

explode *vt (set off)* detonar, fazer explodir; **2** *(fig) (disprove)* desacreditar, derrubar; ♦ *vi* estourar, explodir; **2** *(fig)* rebentar *(with* de) **to ~ with laughter** rebentar de riso.

exploit *n* façanha *f*, proeza *f;* feifo *m;* ♦ *vt* explorar; **2** *(fig) (person's goodness)* abusar de, aproveitar-se de.

exploitation *n (mine,workers)* exploração *f*.

exploration *n (of theory, study)* exploração *f* ; **oil ~** prospe(c)ção petrolífera.

exploratory *adj (fig)* exploratório,-a, de pesquisa.

explore *vt* explorar; *(fig)* examinar, pesquisar.

explorer *n* explorador,-ora.

explosion *n* explosão *f*.

explosive *n adj* explosive,-a; **~ device** *n* dispositivo *m* explosivo.

exponent *n* expoente *m,f; (supporter)* defensor,-ora.

exponential *adj* exponencial *m,f*.

export *n* exportação *f;* ♦ de exportação; ♦ *vt* exportar.

exportation *n* exportação *f*.

exporter *n* exportador,-ora.

exposé *n (public)* revelações *fpl* comprometedoras; **2** *(study)* exposição *f*.

expose *vt* expor; revelar; **2 to ~ o.s.** desnudar-se, exibir-se; **3** mostrar *(ignorance);* **4** *(unmask)* desmascarar-se; **5** denunciar *(injustice, person).*

exposed *adj* exposto,-a; **2** *(area)* desabrigado,-a; **3** *(found out)* descoberto,-a.

exposure *n* revelação *f;* **2** descoberta, desmascaramento *m;* **3** *(PHOT)* exposição *f;* fotografia *f;* **northern ~** voltado para o norte; **to die from ~** morrer de *(cold, heat);* **~ meter** *n* fotómetro *(BR:* -tô-) *m*.

expound *vt* expor, explicar; ♦ *vi* dissertar **(on** sobre).

express *n (train)* rápido *m;* expresso *m;* ♦ *adj* expresso,-a, explícito,-a; urgente *m,f;* ♦ *adv* correio expresso/azul; ♦ *vt* exprimir; espremer.

expression *n* expressão *f*.

expressionism *n* expressionismo *m*.

expressive *adj* expressivo,-a.

expressly *adv* expressamente.

expressway *n* auto-estrada/autoestrada, via rápida.

expropriation *n (of house, lands)* expropriação *f*.

expulsion *n* expulsão *f*.

expurgate *vt* limpar, purificar, expurgar.

exquisite *adj* belo,-a; delicado,-a; bizarro,-a; **2** *(taste, manner)* requintado,-a; **3** *(object)* raro,-a.

exquisitely *adv* de maneira primorosa; **~ dressed** elegantemente vestido,-a.

ex-serviceman *n* ex-combatente *m*.

extant *(US) adj* existente *m,f*.

extemporize *vt/vi* improvisar.

extend *vt* prolongar; dilatar; **2** *(space)* ampliar; **3** *(condolences)* oferecer; **4** *(hand)* estender; **5** *(credit)* conceder.

extension *n (CONSTR)* extensão *f;* alargamento *m;* anexo *(UK);* **2** *(TEL) (number)* extensão *f, (BR)* ramal; **3** *(deadline)* prolongamento *m*, adiamento *m; (JUR)* prorrogação *f;* **4** *(growth)* expansão *f*.

extensive *adj* extenso,-a; vasto,-a, amplo,-a; **2** *(loss)* considerável *m,f;* **3** *(PHYS)* extensivo,-a.

extensively *adv (amount)* extensivamente; *(in range)* consideravelmente.

extent *n* extensão *f;* alcance *m;* **to some ~** até certo ponto; **to the ~ of** ... a ponto de ...; **to such an ~ that** ... a tal ponto que ...; **to what ~?** até que ponto?

extenuate *vt* atenuar.

extenuating *adj* atenuante; **~ circumstances** *n* circunstâncias *fpl* atenuantes.

exterior *n* exterior *m, aspe(c)to *m;* ♦ *adj* exterior, externo,-a.

exterminate *n* extermínio *m*; ♦ *vt* exterminar; eliminar.
extermination exterminação *f*.
external *adj* externo,-a, exterior *m*; **2** E~ **Affaires** Negócios Estrangeiros.
externally *adv* por fora.
extinct *adj* extinto,-a.
extinction *n* extinção *f*; **on the verge of** ~ em vias de extinção.
extinguish *vt* (*smoke, fire*) extinguir, apagar.
extinguisher *n* extintor *m* (de incêndio).
extol *vt* louvar; exaltar (*person, virtues*).
extort *vt* (*confession*) arrancar à força; **2** extorquir.
extortion *n* extorsão *f*.
extortionate *adj* (*price*) excessivo,-a, exorbitante *m,f*.
extra *n* extra *m*; **2** (*CIN*) figurante *m,f*, **3** (*newspaper*) edição *f* especial; ♦ *adj* adicional; de mais, extra; extraordinário; ~ **charge** suplemento *m*; **the wine is** ~ o vinho é à parte; ♦ *adv* adicionalmente.
extra ... *pref* extra ... .
extract *n* (*excerpt*) trecho *m*, excerto (**from** de); **2** (*CULIN*) extrato (**from**, de); concentrado; ♦ *vt* tirar (*tooth*); extrair (*coal*); **2 to** ~ **sth from sb** (*obtain illicitly*) extorquir, tirar (*algo de alguém*); arrancar (*from sb, a alguém*).
extraction *n* (*from mines*) extração *f*, **2** (*origin*) origem *f*; **of English** ~ de origem inglesa.
extractor *n* (*gen*) extra(c)tor *m*; ~ (**fan**) *n* exaustor (na cozinha, etc); ventoínha de extra(c)ção *f* de ar (*in the window*).
extracurricular *adj* extracurricular.
extradite *vt:* **to** ~ **sb** (**from/to**) extraditar alguém (de/para).
extradition *n* extradição *f*.
extramarital *adj* extraconjugal *m,f*.
extramural *adj* extra-muros, externo,-a; (*course, student*) de extensão *f* universitária.
extraneous *adj* (*of external origin*) secundário,-a; irrelevante *m,f*; **2** ~ **to** alheio,-a (a), extrínseco,-a.
extraordinary *adj* (*esquisite*) extraordinário,-a; exce(p)cional *m,f*; **2** (*odd*) esquisito,-a.
extrapolate *vt* extrapolar (**from** de)
extraterrestrial *n adj* extraterrestre *m,f*.
extra-time *n* (*SPORT*) prolongamento *m*.
extravagance *n* (*excess*) extravagância *f*.
extravagant *adj* (*excessive*) extravagante *m,f*.
extreme *n* extremo *m*; **in the** ~ ao maximo; ♦ *adj* extremo,-a; excessivo,-a, exce(p)ional; **2** (*POL*) radical; **extreme unction** (*REL*) Extrema-Unção *f*; ~ **sports** desportos radicais.
extremely *adv* extremamente.
extremist *n adj* extremista *m,f*.
extremities *pl* (*ANAT*) extremidades *fpl*.

extremity *n* extremidade *f*; **2** ponta *f*; **3** apuro *m*, necessidade *f*.
extricate *vt* (*from difficult situation*) livrar, desembaraçar (**from** de); **2** (*from tangle, trap*) livrar, soltar (*bird, etc*); ♦ **to** ~ **o.s.** *vr* libertar-se de, livrar-se de.
extrovert *n* extrovertido,-a.
exuberant *adj* eufórico,-a; exuberante *m,f*.
exude *vt/vi* (*ooze*) ressumar (*liquid*); exsudar (*sap*), exalar (*smell*); **2** (*fig*) (*be full of*) irradiar, exalar (*charm*).
exult *vi* regozijar-se; alegrar-se (**at**, **in** com).
eye *n* (*ANAT and general*) olho *m*; ~**ball** *n* globo ocular; ~**bath** *n* recipiente *m* para lavar os olhos; ~**brow** *n* sobrancelha; ~-**catching** *adj* de chamar a atenção; ~ **contact** *n* troca *f* de olhares; ~**drops** *npl* gotas *fpl* para os olhos; ~**glasses** *npl* óculos *mpl*. ~**lash** *n* cílio *m*; pestana *f*; **to flutter one's** ~**lashes** fazer olhinhos a alguém; ~**let** *n* ilhó *f sg*; ~**lid** *n* pálpebra; ~-**opener** *n* revelação *f*, grande surpresa *f*; ~ **patch** *n* pala *f*; ~**shadow** (*cosmetic*) sombra *f*; ~**sight** *n* vista *f*, visão *f*; ~**sore** *n* monstruosidade *f*; ~**tooth** *n* (*pl:* ~**teeth**) (*dente*) canino *m* superior; **to give one's** ~**teeth for sth** dar tudo por algo/para fazer algo; ~**wash** *n* (*fig*) (*nonsense*) disparates *mpl*; ~**witness** *n* (*JUR*) testemunha *f* ocular; ♦ **to have one's** ~ **on sth** (*desire*) querer, ter algo sob o olho; (*aim*) ter algo em vista; **to have an** ~ **for sth** (*ability to recognize sth*) ter olho para algo; **to keep an** ~ **on sb/sth** vigiar, ficar de olho em (alguém/algo); **as far as the** ~ **can see** a perder de vista; ♦ **eyes** *npl* olhos *mpl*; **in my** ~ a meu ver; **with large brown** ~**s** de olhos grandes castanhos; **to cry one's** ~**s out** chorar até não poder mais; **to keep one's** ~**s peeled** manter-se atento,-a; **to make sheep's** ~**s at sb** (*to look amorously*) fazer, ter olhos de carneiro mal morto; **to run one's** ~**s over sth** percorrer algo com os olhos; **to shut one's** ~**s to sth** (*fig*) recusar-se a ver (*truth, etc*); **in the** ~**s of the law** perante a lei; **2** (*of needle*) buraco *m*; **3 hook and** ~ colchete e ilhó *or* aselha *f*; **4** (*on potato*) olho *m*; ♦ *adj* (*of disease, problem*) ocular; (*medication*) para os olhos; ~**ed** *adj* **a blue-eyed kitten** uma gatinha de olhos azuis; ♦ *vt* olhar, observar; **to** ~ **up** *vt* encarar (*problem, etc*); (*ogle sb, sth*) comer com os olhos (alguém, algo); IDIOM **to turn a blind eye to sth** fazer vista grossa (**to** a); **there is more to this than meets the** ~ isto é mais complicado do que parece; **I am up to my** ~**balls in work** (*coll*) estou cheio,-a de trabalho.
eyeful *n* olhar *m* demorado; **2** (*coll*) pessoa atra(c)tiva; **to get an** ~ **of sb, sth** regalar-se a olhar (alguém, algo).
eyrie, aerie *n* ninho de ave de rapina.

f

F, f *n (letter)* F, f, *m*; **2 F** *n (MUS) (key)* fá *m.*
F *(abbr for* **Fahrenheit***).*
FA *n (abbr for* **Football Association***)* Federação
britânica de Futebol.
fable *n* fábula *f*, conto *m.*
fabric *n* tecido, pano; **2** *(fig) (building, society)*
estrutura; **social** ~ tecido social/da sociedade.
fabricate *vt* fabricar; construir; **2** forjar; inventar
(stories); **to ~ a document** forjar um documento.
fabrication *n (manufacture)* construção *f*; **2** invenção
f; **3** *(lie)* mentira *f*, maquinação *f.*
fabulous *adj* fabuloso,-a.
fabulously *adv* fabulosamente.
façade *n (ARCH)* fachada *f*; **2** *(fig)* countenance.
face *n (ANAT)* cara *f*, rosto *m*, face *f*; **2** *(of clock)*
mostrador *m*; **3** *(surface)* face *f*; **4** *(building)*
façade; **5** *(of coin)* cara *f*; **6** *(appearance)* cara *f*,
aspeto *m;* **to keep a straight** ~ mostrar uma cara
séria, controlar o riso; **7** *(expressão)* **to pull/make
a ~ at sb** fazer uma careta/fazer caretas a alguém;
to fall flat on one's ~ cair de cara no chão; **to
have the ~ to (do sth)** *(coll)* ter o descaramento
de (fazer algo); **to lose** ~ *(fig) (dignity, reputation)*
ficar malvisto; ♦ *adj* ~-**to**-~ cara a cara; ♦ *adv* **in
the ~ of** em vista de; na presença de (alguém); **in
the ~ of (death, danger)** perante, diante (a
morte, o perigo); **it was staring me in the ~**
(algo) saltava aos meus olhos; **on the ~ of it** a
julgar pelas aparências, à primeira vista; ~ **down**
(person) de bruços; *(object)* virado para baixo; ~
up virado para cima; de costas; ♦ *vt* encarar;
about-~ dar meia-volta; *(MIL)* fazer meia-volta;
♦ **to ~ up to** *(situation)* enfrentar; **2** assumir; **3**
(look on to) dar para *(algo);* **4** *(enemy, problem)*
confrontar; ♦ *vi* ~ **backwards/forward** estar de
costas/de frente para; ~ **towards sth** estar voltado,-a para algo; IDIOM **to fly in the ~ of sth**
desobedecer abertamente; **to ~ the music** arcar,
arrostar com as consequências; **to put a bold ~
on it** fazer das tripas coração; fazer o melhor
duma má situação; **to save one's** ~ salvar a honra
do convento.
faced *adj* com face; virado para; **bold-~** descarado,
atrevido; **ill-~** mal encarado; **two-~** hipócrita *m,f*,
pessoa com duas caras; ~ **with** perante, diante,
face a.
faceless *adj (fig)* anónimo,-a.
facelift *n (cosmetic surgery)* lifting *m*, operação *f*
plástica; **2** *(fig) (of house)* renovação *f.*
facemask facepack *n* máscara *f* facial.

facepowder *n (make up)* pó *m* de arroz.
face-saving *adj* para salvar/manter as aparências.
facet *n* faceta *f*; **2** aspe(c)to *m.*
facetious *adj (remark)* jocoso,-a, brincalhão,-lhona.
face-value *n (ECON)* valor *m* nominal, **2 to take
sth at** ~ *(fig)* tomar algo ao pé da letra; **to take sb
at** ~ julgar alguém pelas aparências.
facial *n* limpeza *f* de pele; ♦ *adj* facial.
facile *adj (pej) (superficial)* trivial, fácil.
facilitate *vt (make easy)* facilitar; **2** *(growth, etc)*
favorecer.
facility *n (ability)* facilidade *f* (**for** para); **2** *(feature)*
recurso *m*, função *f.*
facilities *npl (building)* instalações; **2** *(amenities)*
serviços *mpl*; **3** *(equipment)* equipamento *m;* ~
for the disabled instalações para deficientes físicos;
4 vantagens *fpl.*
facing *n (sewing)* debrum; *(of jacket)* forro; **2**
(CONSTR) revestimento *m*; ♦ *adj* em frente,
defronte; ♦ *prep* em face de, virado para.
facsimile *n* fac-símile *m*; **2** *(sculpture)* reprodução;
~ **machine** *n* aparelho *m* de fax.
fact *n* fa(c)to; **to know sth for a** ~ ter a certeza de algo;
♦ *adv conj* **in** ~ na verdade; **as a matter of** ~ aliás,
de facto; **a matter-of-~ person** pessoa positivista,
prática.
fact-finding *adj (tour, etc)* obtenção *f* de investigação.
faction *n* facção *f*; **2** *(discord)* dissensão.
factional *adj* faccionário, faccional.
factious *adj (argument)* faccioso,-a.
fact of life *n* facto *m* consumado; ~**s of life** *(sex)* of
fa(c)tos da vida; **2** as realidades da vida.
factor *n* fa(c)tor *m*, causa (**in** de); **2** *(COMM)*
(person, goods) agente, fator; **at** ~ **cost** a custo de
fa(c)tores; **3 protection** ~ *(of sun lotion)* índice *m*
de proteção; **4** *(níveis)* coeficientes.
factor in/into *vr* tomar em linha de conta.
factorage *n* comissão paga a um factor.
factoring *n* (comprar dívidas a um desconto com
vistas a fazer lucro) factoring.
factorise, factorize *vt* factorizar, decompor em
factores.
factory *n* fábrica *f*; *(BR)* usina *f*; ~ **farming** *n* criação *f*
intensiva; ~ **ship** *n* navio-fábrica *m.*
factotum *n* faz-tudo.
factsheet *n* ficha *f* de informação.
factual *adj* real, fa(c)tual, concreto,-a.
facula *n (ASTRON)* fácula.
facultative *adj* facultativo,-a.
faculty *n* faculdade *f*, aptidão *f*; **2** *(teaching staff)* corpo
m docente; **mental** ~**ties** faculdades *fpl* mentais.
fad *n* mania *f*; **2** capricho *m*; **3** voga *f.*
faddish, faddy *adj (UK) (person)* difícil, caprichoso,-a
(**about** acerca de); *(fig)* chato,-a.
fade *vi (colour)* desbotar; **2** *(sound)* diminuir; **3** *(hope,
memory)* desvanecer; ♦ *vi (light, lettering)* apagar-
se; **2** *(flowers, smile)* murchar; **3** *(person) (grow
weak)* definhar; **to ~ into the crowd** desaparecer;
~ **away** *(person)* definhar-se; *(sound)* apagar-se; ~
in aumentar gradualmente *(sound);* ~ **out** *(fizzle
out)* desaparecer gradualmente.

faded *adj (colour)* desbotado,-a; **2** *(wall paper)* amarelecido,-a; **3** *(picture)* esbatido,-a.

faecal *adj* fecal.

faeces *(UK)*, **feces** *(US)* *npl* fezes *fpl*.

faecula *n* fécula *f*.

faff *vi:* ~ **about/around** *(fam: UK) (fuss)* preocupar-se com qualquer coisa; **don't** ~ **about!** deixe-se dessas coisas!

fag *n (coll) (cigarette)* cigarro; beata; ~ **end** *n* ponta de cigarro, pirisca, *(BR)* bagana *f*; *(abbr for* **faggot**).

fagged out *adj (coll) (exausto)* estafado,-a.

faggot *(UK)*, **fagot** *(US)* *n (CULIN) (meat ball)* almôndega *f*; **2** *(firewood)* feixe *m*; **3** *(bundle of anything)* molho *m*; **4** *(US) (homosexual or effeminate) (pej) (EP)* maricas, paneleiro; *(BR)* bicha.

Fahrenheit *n* Fahrenheit; **40 degrees** ~ 40 graus Fahrenheit.

fail *n (exam)* reprovação *f*; chumbo *m (fam)*; **without** ~ sem falta; ♦ *vt (exam)* não passar, ser reprovado, *(coll: EP)* chumbar; **2** *(not succeed in)* **to** ~ **to do sth** não conseguir fazer algo; **3** *(neglect)* **to** ~ **to do sth** deixar de fazer algo; **she** ~**ed to keep her word** ela faltou à palavra dada; **4** *(let down)* faltar aos compromissos para com *(employer, lender)*; **words** ~ **me!** faltam-me as palavras; **if all else** ~**s** em último recurso; ♦ *vi (exam, candidate)* reprovar; **2** *(attempt, plan)* fracassar, falhar; **3** *(weaken)* enfraquecer; **4** *(not function)* falhar *(engine, etc)*; *(food supply)* faltar.

failing *n* defeito; fraqueza; ♦ *prep* na/à falta de; ~ **that** se isso não resultar.

fail-safe *adj (device, system)* com sistema de segurança integrado.

failure *n (lack of success)* fracasso *m*; insucesso *m*; ~ **to honour a contract** inadimplemento, incumprimento *m* de um contra(c)to; **2** *(MEC) (malfunction)* falha *f*, avaria; **3** *(MED) (kidney, etc)* insuficiência renal; *(MED)* **heart** ~ ataque *m* cardíaco.

faint *n* desmaio, desfalecimento *m*; ♦ *adj (weak)* fraco,-a; **2** vago,-a; **a** ~ **feeling** uma vaga sensação; **3** *(voice, sound)* indistinto; ♦ *vi* desmaiar; **to feel** ~ sentir-se desfalecer; ♦ ~**-hearted** *adj* cobarde; medroso,-a; **the** ~**est idea** a mínima ideia.

faintly *adv* levemente, vagamente.

faintness *n (feeling weak)* fraqueza *f*; mal-estar *m*; **2** *(dimness of image)* imprecisão *f*; **3** *(of memory)* debilidade *f*.

fair *n (trade)* feira *f*; **2** *(UK: funfair)* parque *m* de diversões; *(of entertainment)* feira *f*; **3** *(for charity)* quermesse; ♦ *adj (person, ruling, action)* justo,-a; **it's not** ~! não é justo; **to be** ~ para ser honesto; **to be** ~ **game** ser alvo, presa fácil **(for sb** para alguém); **to play** ~ fazer jogo limpo; **2** *(hair colour)* louro,-a; **3** *(complexion)* claro,-a; **4** *(weather)* ameno; *(good enough)* razoável *m,f*; **that's a** ~ **answer** é uma resposta razoável; **5** *(sizeable)* considerável; ~ **amount** bastante; ♦ *exc* ~ **enough!** *(UK)* de acordo!, tudo bem!; ♦ **with her own** ~ **hands** com as suas belas mãos;

IDIOM ~ **weather friend** amigo de Peniche, amigo só para as ocasiões; ~ **weather sailor** marinheiro de água doce.

fair and square com justeza e honestidade.

fairish *adj* razoável; **2** *(hair colour)* aloirado,-a.

fairly *adv* bastante; **2** com justiça; honestamente.

fair-minded *adj* imparcial; justo,-a.

fairness *n* justiça, equidade; **2** *(of judgement)* imparcialidade.

fair play *n* jogo lícito, honesto; **to have a sense of** ~ ter o senso de justeza e respeito pelas regras (do jogo).

fair-sized *adj* de bom tamanho.

fair-spoken *adj (person)* cortês, suave.

fair trade *n* acordos de reciprocidade nas transa(c)ções internacionais comerciais.

fairway *n (of river, harbour)* parte *f* navegável; **2** *(of golf)* parte plana entre os buracos.

fairy *(pl:* -**ies**) *n* fada *f*; **2** *(pej) (male homosexual)* maricas *m*; ~ **godmother** fada madrinha *f*; ~**land** país *m* encantado; ~ **lights** *npl* luzes, *(BR)* lâmpadas *fpl* decorativas; ~**like** *adj* feérico,-a; ~ **tale** *n* conto *m* de fadas.

fait accompli *n* fa(c)to *m* consumado.

faith *n (trust)* fé *f*, confiança *f*; **in good** ~ em boa fé; **2** *(REL)* religião *f*, fé, crença *f*.

faithful *n (REL)* **the** ~ os fiéis *mpl*; ♦ *adj* fiel; leal.

faithfully *adv* fielmente; **yours** ~ *(at the end of a formal letter)* atenciosamente.

faith healer *n* curandeiro,-a.

faithless *n (husband, etc)* infiel; ♦ *adj (employee, etc)* desleal.

fake *n* falsificação *f*; **2** *(person)* impostor,-ora, falsário,-a; ♦ *adj* falso,-a; *(fur, etc)* de imitação; *(flowers)* artificial *m,f*; ♦ *vt (counterfeit)* falsificar, forjar; **2** *(pretend: emotion, illness)* fingir.

faker *n* falsificador,-ora; fingidor,-ora.

fakir *n* faquir.

falcon *n (ZOOL)* falcão *m*.

falconer *n* falcoeiro,-a.

falconry *n* falcoaria *f*.

Falkland Islands *npr pl* **the** ~ as Ilhas *fpl* (das) Malvinas.

fall *n* queda; **2** decadência; **3** *(prices)* baixa; **4** *(slope)* inclinação *f*; **5** *(US)* Outono; ♦ *(pt* **fell**, *pp* **fallen**) *vi (gen)* cair; **he fell from the roof** ele caiu do telhado; **2** *(let fall)* deixar-se cair; **she fell into a chair** ela deixou-se cair numa cadeira; **3** *(night, silence)* descer; **4 to** ~ **on** cair **(on** sobre**)**; **5** *(day, data)* calhar; **her birthday** ~**s on a Friday** os anos dela calham a uma sexta-feira; **6** *(temperature, prices, production)* baixar; cair; **7** *(speed, quality)* diminuir; **8** *(government, enemy)* cair, ser derrubado; **9** *(MIL, DESP)* ser derrotado, perder; ♦ ~ **about** *vi (UK) (fam):* **to** ~ **laughing** cair de riso, torcer-se a rir; ♦ **to** ~ **apart** *(also:* ~ **to pieces)** *vi (book furniture)* cair aos pedaços; **2** *(house)* desmoronar-se, ruir; **3** *(clothes, shoes)* desfazer-se; ♦ **to** ~ **asleep** *vi* adormecer; ~ **sick** adoecer; ~ **in love with** apaixonar-se por; ♦ **to** ~ **back** *vi (lag behind)* recuar; **2** *(troops, police)* bater em retirada; ♦ **to ~ back on** *(resort to)* *vt* recorrer a; **to ~ backwards** *vi* cair de costas; ♦ **to ~ behind** *(fail to keep up)* ficar para trás; *(with payments)* atrasar-se com; **2** *(performance)* perder terreno; ♦ **to ~ down** cair; **2** *(businesss, project)* fracassar, ir por água abaixo; **~ the stairs** cair pelas escadas abaixo; ♦ *vi (building)* desabar; cair por terra; **2 to ~ due (on)** *(date) vi* vencer *(payment, bond)* (em); **3 to ~ for** *vt (be deceived by)* deixar-se enganar por; ♦ **to ~ in with** *vt* concordar; **2** *(in love with)* apaixonar-se por; *(BR)* ficar caído,-a por; ♦ **to ~ in** *vi (roof)* desabar; **2** *(MIL)* enfileirar-se, formar fileiras, *(BR)* entrar em forma; ♦ **to ~ into the habit** *vi* habituar-se a; ♦ **to ~ off** *vi* cair; **2** *(detach itself/oneself)* desprender-se; **3** *(diminish)* diminuir; ♦ **to ~ on** *vt (attack)* cair, lançar-se sobre, atacar; **2** *(eyes/gaze)* dirigir-se para; fitar; ♦ **to ~ out** *vi (drop out)* cair; **2** *(quarrel with sb)* ficar de mal com alguém; brigar; **3** *(soldiers, police)* dispersar; ♦ **to ~ over sth** *vt* tropeçar em; **2 ~ all over sb** desdobrar-se em amabilidades; ♦ **to ~ short** *vi (be short of)* ser insuficiente; **to ~ through** *vi (fail)* falhar, fracassar; **to ~ to** *vt (duty, responsibility)* caber a; **it fell to me to check accounts** coube a mim verificar as contas.

fallacious *adj* enganador,-ora ilusório,-a.

fallacy *n (error)* erro; **2** engano *m*; **3** *(misconception)* falácia *f*.

fallen (*pp of* **fall**): **the ~** *n* os mortos *mpl* no campo de batalha; ♦ *adj (leaf)* caído,-a; **the ~ leaves** as folhas caídas; **2** *(dated) (woman)* mulher perdida.

fallible *adj* falível.

falling *adj (going down)* em declínio; **~ star** estrela *f* cadente.

Fallopian tube *n (ANAT)* trompa *f* de Falópio.

fallout *n* partículas *fpl* radioa(c)tivas; **2** *(fam)* consequências *fpl* secundárias.

fallow *adj (land)* inculto,-a; de/em pousio; **2** *(state of mind)* inativo,-a; **3** *(interval)* de pausa; ♦ **to ~** *vr* deixar *(land)* sem sementes.

fallow deer *n* gamo *m*.

falls *npl* cataratas *fpl*, quedas d'água *fpl*.

false *adj* falso,-a; **2** *(of hair, teeth)* postiço,-a, artificial; **3** *(person)* desleal, traidor,-ora; **~hood** *n* mentira; **2** falsidade *f*; **~ note** *n* fifia *f (fam);* **2** *(in film music)* som dissonante, com falsidade; **~ start** *n* tentativa *f* frustrada; **~ teeth** *npl* dentadura *f* postiça.

falsely *adv* falsamente, com falsidade.

falsification *n* falsificação *f*.

falsifier *n* falsificador,-ora.

falsify *vt* falsificar; enganar.

falsity *n* falsidade *f*.

falter *vi* vacilar; **2** hesitar.

faltering *adj (steps, voice)* vacilante, hesitante; *(voice)* balbuciante.

fame *n* fama *f*.

famed *adj* famoso,-a, célebre.

familiar *adj* familiar; **2** conhecido,-a; **on ~ ground** num lugar conhecido; **3 be on ~ terms with sb** ser tu cá tu lá (com alguém); **4 ~ friend** amigo

íntimo; **5** *(pej) (overly familiar)* pessoa que toma liberdades; **6 to be ~ with** *(conversant)* estar familiarizado com.

familiarity *n* familiaridade *f*; **2** *(impropriety)* liberdades; **3** *(with place, rules)* conhecimento *m* de algo.

familiarize, familiarise *vr*: **to ~ o.s. with** familiarizar-se com.

family *n* família *f*; **2 ~ business** *n* negócio *m* de família; **3 ~ doctor** *n* médico,-a de família; **4 F~ Division** *(High Court)* Tribunal de Família; **5** *(parents and children)* família *f* imediata; **6 ~ planning** *n* planeamento, *(BR)* planejamento *m* familiar; **7 single-parent** *(ADMIN, SOCIOL)* família *f* mononuclear; **to be in the ~ way** *(pregnant)* estar grávida.

famine *n* fome *f*; **~ relief** *n* luta *f* contra a fome.

famished *adj (pop)* faminto,-a, esfomeado,-a, famélico,-a.

famous *adj* famoso,-a, célebre, famigerado,-a.

famously *adv* maravilhosamente.

fan *n (hand ~)* leque *m; (for fire)*, abano; **2** *(ELECT)* ventilador *m*; ventoinha *f*; **~-belt** *n* correia *f* da ventoinha, corrente *f* do ventilador; **3** *(person)* fã *m,f*; aficionado,-a; ♦ *vt* abanar; atiçar (fogueira, fogo); **to ~ out** *vi* espalhar-se.

fanatic *n* fanático,-a.

fanatical *adj* fanático.

fanatically *adv* fanaticamente.

fanaticism *n* fanatismo.

fanciable *adj* atraente; **2** imaginário,-a.

fanciful *adj* fantástico,-a; **2** *(elaborate)* extravagante; **3** *(odd)* estapafúrdio,-a.

fancifully *adv* de uma maneira fantasista; extravagante.

fancy *n (whim)* capricho *m*; **2** *(liking)* inclinação *f*; gosto; **to take a ~ to sb** gostar de, simpatizar com alguém; **3** fantasia *f*; ♦ *adj* ornamental; luxuoso,-a; decorativo,-a; ♦ *vt* desejar, querer, apetecera; gostar de; **I ~ a custard tart** apetece-me um pastel *m* de nata; imaginar; crer; **she fancies him** ela gosta dele; ♦ *exc* **~ that!** imagine, imaginem!

fancy dress *n* vestido *m* de fantasia/de máscara; **in ~** mascarado,-a.

fancy-free *adj* descontraído,-a; com o coração livre; **footloose and ~** livre como um passarinho.

fancy man *n* namorado,-a; **2** *(coll)* chulo,-a.

fancy woman *n* namorada *f*; **2** *(coll)* amante.

fandango *n (Spanish and Portuguese folk dance)* fandango *m*.

fanfare *n* fanfarra *f*; **2** *(speech, display)* com ostentação.

fang *n* presa; dente *m* canino.

fanfaronade *n* fanfarrada.

fanlight *n (UK) (janela, porta)* bandeira *f*; *(US)* clarabóia *f*.

fanny *(pl:* **-nies)** *n (vulg) (female genitals)* cona *f (vulg)*, rata *(vulg); (US) (coll) (backside)* cu *m (coll)*, rabo *m (fam)*.

fantasize, fantasise *vt* fantasiar (**about** sobre).

fantastic *adj* fantástico,-a; estranho,-a; ilusório,-a.

fantastically *adv* fantasticamente.

fantasy *n* fantasia *f*.

far *(comp* **farther, further,** *superl* **farthest, furthest)** *adj* (= **~away**) *(place)* longe, distante; remoto,-a;

2 *(extreme)* extremo,-a; *(POL)* **the ~ left** a extrema esquerda; **3** *(memory, time)* longínquo,-a; **4** *(not present)* ausente; **5** *(level)* bastante, muito; **~ better (than)** muito melhor (que); **to be ~ above average** estar bastante acima da média; ♦ *adv (distance)* longe; **by ~ de** longe; **how ~ is the beach?** a que distância estamos da praia; **2** *(distance, degree, extent)* **how ~?** até onde, até que ponto?; **3** *(exceed)* **it has gone too ~** já passa dos limites; **4** *(time)* **so ~** até agora; **as ~ as I know** que eu saiba, tanto quanto sei; **as ~ as I am concerned** no que me diz respeito, quanto a mim; **so ~ so good** até aqui tudo bem; **5** *(everywhere)* **~ and wide** por toda a parte; **6** *(level, state)* **~ from that** longe disso; **~ be it from me to say such a thing!** nem me passa pela cabeça dizer uma coisa dessas!; **~ gone** em estado avançado *(of deterioration)*.

faraway *adj (fig) (LITER)* longínquo,-a; distante; **2** *(person)* alheado,-a; **with a ~ look** com um olhar distante.

farce *n* farsa *f*.

farcical *adj* farsante, ridículo,-a.

fare *n* preço do bilhete *m*, tarifa *f*; **2** *(person)* passageiro,-a; **3** *(food)* comida *f*; ♦ *vi* **to ~ well/badly** passar bem/mal; **2** *(do well/badly; manage)* sair-se bem/mal; **how did you ~ in the exam** como é que você se saiu do exame?

Far East *npr* Extremo Oriente *m*.

farewell *n* despedida *f*; adeus *m*; **~ party** festa da despedida; ♦ *exc* **farewell!** adeus!

far-fetched *adj* forçado,-a, rebuscado,-a; pouco plausível; **2** *(história)* exagerado,-a.

far-flung *adj (remote)* longínquo,-a; **2** *(widely distributed) (towns, places)* afastados uns dos outros.

farinose *adj* farinhoso,-a, farináceo,-a.

farm *n* quinta, herdade *f*; *(BR)* fazenda; ♦ *vt* cultivar; **2** dirigir uma quinta; ♦ **to ~ out (sth)** *vt (land)* arrendar; **2** *(work)* contratar, delegar em; **chicken ~** aviário *m*.

farmed *(pt, pp of farm) adj (fish)* peixe criado no viveiro.

farmer *n (EP)* lavrador,-ora; *(BR)* fazendeiro,-a, *(EP, BR)* agricultor,-ora.

farmhand *n* trabalhador *m* agrícola, rural, *(BR)* peão *m*.

farmhouse *n* casa *f* da quinta; granja; casa rústica.

farming *n (activity)* agricultura *f*; **2** *(of land)* exploração; **pig/poultry ~** *n* criação *f* de porcos/ de aves de capoeira.

farmland *n* terra de cultivo.

farmstead *n* granja *f*.

farmworker *n (Vd:* **farmhand***)*.

farmyard *n* terreiro *m* da quinta; curral *m*.

far-off *adj* remoto,-a, distante; **2** *(time, memory)* longínquo.

far-out *adj (bizarre)* estranho,-a; *(idea)* de vanguarda; **2** excelent; ♦ *exc (of wonder, admiration)* fantástico!; porreiro!

far-reaching *adj (effect, implication)* de longo, grande alcance; **2** *(chances)* considerável, abrangente; **~ consequences** *npl* consequências *fpl* graves.

farrier *n* ferrador *m*.

farrow *n* ninhada *f* de porcos; *vi* (porca) parir.

far-sighted *adj (person)* prudente; **2** previdente, perspicaz; **3** *(US) (long-sighted)* hipermetrope.

fart *n (vulg)* peido; bufa *(coll)*; ♦ *vi* peidar-se, dar um peido; dar uma bufa.

farther *adv* mais distante, mais afastado; **~ away** mais para lá; ♦ *(comp of far) adj* mais longe; **~most** *adj (distance, time)* o mais distante; remoto.

farthest *(superl of far) (place)* a mais remota; **2** *(time)* **at the ~** o mais tardar.

farthing *n (old English money)* a quarta parte de um péni (dinheiro); IDIOM **I don't have a ~** não tenho um tostão.

Far West *npr (US)* faroeste.

fascia *n (ARCH)* friso *m*; **2** *(over shop)* faixa *f*; **3** *(de edifício)* fachada; **4** *(dashboard) (UK)* painel *m* de instrumentos.

fascicle *n* fascículo *m*.

fascinate *vt* fascinar.

fascination *n* fascinação *f*.

fascinating *adj* fascinante, encantador,-ora.

fascism *n* fascismo *m*.

fascist *n adj* fascista *m,f*.

fashion *n* moda; **2** *(way, manner)* maneira; **after a ~** de certo modo, até certo ponto; **after the ~ of** à maneira de, à moda de; **in ~** na moda; **in the Greek ~** à grega; **to come into ~** tornar-se moda; **~ designer** *n* estilista *m,f*; **out of ~** fora da moda; **~ show** *n* passagem *f* de modelos, *(BR)* desfile *m* de modas; ♦ *vt (mould)* moldar.

fashionable *adj* na moda elegante, em voga.

fashionably *adv* à moda; elegantemente.

fashioning *n* acto de talhar, moldar; **2** fabrico *m*.

fast *n* jejum; **to break ~** quebrar o jejum; ♦ *adj (quick)* rápido; **2** *(colour, hold)* firme, que não desbota; **3** *(dye)* permanente; **4 the clock is ~** o relógio está adiantado; **5 to lead a ~ life** levar uma vida de prazer; **6** *(pej) (woman)* fácil, de vida fácil; **7** *(PHOT)* de alta sensibilidade; ♦ *adv* rapidamente, depressa; **2** firmemente; **~ asleep** profundamente adormecido; ♦ *vi* jejuar; IDIOM **to pull a ~ one on sb** enrolar, enganar alguém.

fast breeder reactor *n* rea(c)tor super-regenerador.

fasten *vt (seat belt)* apertar, **2** *(ribbon)* atar; **3** *(with buttons)* abotoar; **4** *(door, window)* fechar, trancar; **5** *(attach)* fixar *(notice, poster)*; **6** *(a brooch)* prender; **7** *(fig) (fix)* **~ one's eyes on sb** cravar os olhos em, olhar alguém fixamente; ♦ *vi* amarrar, fixar-se; **to ~ on sb/sth** agarrar-se a alguém/a algo; **2** concentrar-se (em); **to ~ down** *(carpet etc)* prender, fixar; **to ~ up** fechar, apertar; **~ your boots!** aperta as botas!

fastener *n (clasp: necklace, bag)* fecho *m*; **2** *(clothes)* fecho *m; (zip)* fecho de correr/fecho éclair *m*; **snap ~** mola *f* de pressão; **paper ~** agrafo *m*.

fastening *n* fechadura; **2** *(window)* trinco *m*.

faster *n* jejuador; ♦ *adj adv* mais rápido.

fast food *n* comida *f* pronta; fast food.

fast-forward *n (audio)* avanço *m* rápido; ♦ *vi* avançar rapidamente.

fast-growing *adj* em pleno desenvolvimento; em crescimento rápido.

fastidious *adj* meticuloso,-a; minucioso,-a, miudinho,-a (**about** acerca de).

Fastidious não significa '**fastidioso**' em português.

fastidiousness *n* meticulosidade *f*.

fast lane *(AUT)* via *f* rápida.

fat *n* gordura *f*; **2** *(for cooking)* banha *f*; ♦ *adj* gordo,-a; gorducho,-a; **to get ~** engordar; **2** *(food)* com muita gordura; **3** *(volume)* espesso,-a; grosso,-a; pesado,-a; **4** *(money, profit)* avultado,-a; **a ~ sum of money** uma soma avultada de dinheiro; IDIOM **to have a ~ chance** ter poucas probabilidades; **to live off the ~ of the land** viver à grande (e à francesa).

fatal *adj* fatal; **2** mortal; **3** funesto.

fatalism *n* fatalismo.

fatalistic *adj* fatalista *m,f*.

fatality *n* fatalidade *f*; **2** *(accident)* vítima *m,f* mortal.

fatally *adv* fatalmente; **~ injured** mortalmente ferido.

fate *n* fado *m*, sina *f*, destino *m*, sorte *f*.

fated *adj* fadado,-a; predestinado,-a; marcado,-a pelo destino.

fateful *adj* fatídico,-a.

fat-free *adj* *(food)* magro,-a; sem gordura.

fathead *n* estúpido,-a.

father *n* pai *m*; **~hood** *n* paternidade *f*; **~-in-law** *n* sogro; **2** F~ **Christmas** *npr* Pai Natal; *(BR)* Papai Noel; **3** **the Land of our Fathers** a terra dos nossos antepassados; ♦ *vt* **to ~ a child** conceber.

fatherly *adj* paternal, como um pai.

fathom *n* *(NAUT)* braça *f* (medida de profundidade = 1,83 metros); ♦ *vt* *(NAUT)* sondar; **to ~ sth out** deslindar, desvendar; **to ~ sb out** compreender alguém; **I don't ~ you** não te compreendo.

fathomless *adj* insondável.

fatidic(al) *adj* fatídico,-a; profético,-a.

fatigue *n* fadiga *f*, cansaço *m*, **2** *(MIL)* *(work)* serviço de faxina; **to be on ~** estar de faxina; ♦ *vt* cansar; fatigar.

fatigues *n* farda *f* de serviço.

fatness *n* *(of person, animal)* gordura *f*, corpulência *f*; **2** *(soil)* fertilidade do solo.

fatso *(pl: -es)* *n* *(coll)* *(pej)* bucha, *m,f*.

fatten *vt* engordar, fazer engordar; *(animal)* fazer engordar, cevar; *(land)* enriquecer.

fattener, fattening *n* (o) que faz engordar.

fattish *adj* um tanto gordo; *(fam)* rechonchudo,-a.

fatty *(pl: -ies)* *n* gorducho,-a; bucha *m,f*; ♦ *(-ier, -iest)* *adj* *(substance)* gorduroso,-a; oleoso,-a; adiposo,-a.

fatuous *adj* estúpido,-a.

fatwa *n* mandado *m* religioso islâmico,-a.

faucet *n* *(US)* torneira *f*.

fault *n* defeito *m*, imperfeição *f*; **2** *(error)* falta *f*, erro *m*; **3** culpa *f*; **it's my ~** é a minha culpa; **4** *(GEOL)* falha; **to find ~ with** criticar, implicar com; **to be at ~** estar errado/culpado.

faultage *n* *(GEOL)* deslocação de estratos.

fault-finding *n* tendência para criticar.

faultily *adv* incorrectamente; imperfeitamente.

faultless *adj* impecável; irrepreensível.

faulty *adj* imperfeito,-a; defeituoso,-a.

fauna *n* fauna *f*.

faux pas *n* passo em falso; gafe *f*; **2** *(slip, oversight)* deslize *m*, lapso *m*.

faveolate *adj* *(style of dress)* com favos, com alvéolos.

faveolus *n* alvéolo *m*, favo *m*.

favour *(UK)*, **favor** *(US)* *n* favor *m*; **2** apoio; **3** aprovação *f*; ♦ *vt* favorecer, aprovar; auxiliar; **to ask a ~ of** pedir um favor a; **to do sb a ~** fazer um favor a alguém; **to find ~ with** cair nas boas graças de; **to be in ~ of** estar/ser a favor de.

favourable *adj* favorável.

favourably *adv* favoravelmente.

favoured *adj* favorecido,-a; **well-~** bem-parecido,-a.

favouring *adj* favorável, que favorece.

favourite *n adj* favorito-a.

favouritism *n* favoritismo.

fawn *n* *(ZOOL)* cervo *m* novo; cervato *m*; **in ~** *(of deer)* grávida; ♦ *adj* (= **~-coloured** *(UK)*, **~-colored** *(US)*) castanho-claro, fulvo; ♦ *vt* parir cria; **2** *(adulate)* bajular.

fawner *n* *(flatter)* adulador,-ora, bajulador,-ora.

fax *(pl: faxes)* *n* fax; **~ machine** *n* máquina de fax; **to send by ~** enviar por fax; **to send ~ to** enviar um fax para.

fay *n* *(LITER)* fada *f*.

faze *vt* desconcertar (alguém), preocupar (alguém).

FBI *npr* *(US: abbr for* **Federal Bureau of Investigation**) Polícia *f* Judiciária do Estado.

fear *n* medo *m*, temor *m*; ♦ *vt* ter medo de, temer; **for ~ of** com medo de.

feared *adj* temido,-a.

fearful *adj* medonho,-a; **2** *(person)* medroso,-a; **3** *(UK-coll)* terrível.

fearless *adj* corajoso,-a; destemido,-a; audaz.

fearsome *adj* temível; **2** assustador,-ora.

feasibility *n* viabilidade, possibilidade *f*.

feasible *adj* possível; viável.

feast *n* banquete, festim *m*; **big ~** *(lots of food)* *(pop)* comezaina/comezana *f*, **2** *(fig)* *(for eyes, senses)* festa, regalo; **3** *(REL:* = **~ day)** festa, festividade *f*; ♦ **to ~ on/off sth** *vt/vi* *(food)* banquetear-se, regalar-se a comer; **2 to ~ one's eyes on sth** *(fig)* deleitar-se a ver algo; regalar-se com algo.

feasting *n* acto de festejar.

feat *n* façanha *f*, proeza *f*, feito *m*.

feather *n* pena *f*, pluma *f*; **~ bed** *n* cama *f*/colchão *m* de penas; **~-brained** *adj* despistado,-a; **a ~ person** um,-a cabeça de vento; **~ duster** *n* espanador *m*; **~weight** *n* *(boxing)* peso-pena *m*; IDIOM **that's a ~ in his cap** isso é mais um penacho com que ele fica; **birds of a ~** da mesma laia; **birds of a ~ flock together** diz-me com quem andas, dir-te-ei quem és; **to ~ one's nest** encher os bolsos.

feature *n* característica *f*; **2** *(landscape)* aspe(c)to *m*; **3** *(ANAT)* feição *f*, traço *m*; **4** *(of machine)* recurso *m*, programa *m*; **5** *(JOURN)* artigo *m* de fundo (**on** sobre), reportagem *f* especial; **6** *(TV)* programa *f* especial; **7** *(CIN)* *(main actor)* atra(c)ção *f* principal; ~ **film** *n* filme *m* de longa metragem; **~s** *npl (ANAT)* feições *fpl*; ♦ *vt* apresentar; ♦ *vi (appear, figure)* figurar em (algo).

featureless *adj* sem traços caraterísticos.

February *npr* Fevereiro, fevereiro *m*.

fecal *adj* fecal.

feces, faeces fezes *fpl*.

feckless *adj (helpless)* incapaz; **2** *(feeble)* fraco,-a; **3** inepto,-a, irresponsável; **3** tíbio,-a, inepto,-a, irresponsável.

fecula *n* fécula.

feculent *adj* fétido,-a; sujo,-a; com sedimento.

fecund *adj* fecundo,-a.

fecundity *n* fecundidade *f*.

fed *(pt, pp of* **feed**).

federal *adj* federal.

federation *n* federação *f*.

fed-up *adj (coll)* farto,-a **(with** de) **to be ~ with sb/ sth** estar farto,-a de (alguém/algo)

fee *n* taxa; **school ~s** propinas *fpl*; *(BR)* taxa *f* de matrícula; **2** *(doctor, lawyer)* honorários *mpl*; **3** *(arrangement)* comissão *f*; **4** *(club, association)* jóia, quota *f*.

feeble *adj* fraco,-a, débil; **~-minded** *adj* imbecil.

feed *n* comida *f*, alimento *m*, sustento *m*; **2** *(animal)* ração *f*; **2** *(TECH)* alimentação *f*; ♦ *(pt, pp* **fed**) *vt* alimentar, comer; **2 to ~ one's family** sustentar a família; **to breast-~** amamentar; *(BR)* dar a mamada; **bottle ~** dar o biberão *m*, *(BR)* a mamadeira *f*; **3** *(put, insert)* inserir algo em algo, meter em, introduzir em; **4** *(TECH)* alimentar; **to ~ on** *vi* alimentar-se de; **to ~ the forwards** dar jogo aos avançados; **5 to ~ up** engordar, comer bem.

feedback *n (from people)* reacção *f*, opinião; **2** *(EDUC) (from tests, exams)* comentários *mpl*; **3** *(experiment)* repercussão *f*; **4** *(TECH) (audio)* reacção *f* parasita; **5** *(COMP)* feedback.

feedbelt correia *f* de alimentação *f*.

feeder *n* pessoa que dá alimento; **2** *(bottle)* biberão; **3** *(bib)* babete *m*; **4** *(road)* nó *m* de ligação; **5** *(printer)* alimentador *m* de papel.

feeding *n* alimentação *f*; **2** *(bottle)* biberão *m (BR)* mamadeira *f*; **3** *(SPORT)* fazer um passe de *(ball)*; **~-time** *(for animals)* hora de comer; *(for children)* *(pop)* hora de papar.

feedstuff *n* comida para animais.

feed-valve válvula de alimentação.

feel *n* sensação *f*; ta(c)to *m*; **get the ~ of** habituar-se a; ♦ *(pt, pp* **felt**) *vt* tocar, apalpar; sentir; crer; acreditar; **it ~s soft** é macio; **to ~ about/around** apalpar, ta(c)-tear; **to ~ for** compadecer-se de, lamentar; **to ~ blue** sentir-se triste; **to ~ cheap/ small** sentir-se envergonhado,-a, atrapalhado,-a; **to ~ hungry/cold** ter fome/frio, estar com fome/ frio; **to ~ like** ter vontade de; **to ~ up to** sentir-se à altura de (fazer algo).

feeler *n (of insects)* antena *f*; **to put out ~s** *(fig)* sondar opiniões; **2** *(fig)* apalpar o terreno.

feelgood *adj (pej)* falsamente tranquilizador,-ora; **to play on the ~ factor** tentar dar uma impressão (ilusória) de bem-estar.

feeling *n* sensação *f*; pressentimento *m*; opinião *f*; sentimento *m*; **no hard ~s** sem ressentimento.

feet *(pl of* **foot**).

feign *vt* fingir, simular.

feigned *adj* simulado,-a, fingido,-a.

feigning *n* simulação *f*.

feint *n (SPORT, MIL)* finta; simulação; ♦ *vi* simular; fintar.

feinter *n (SPORT)* jogador que faz uma finta.

feisty (-ier, -iest) *adj (fam)* vivo,-a, autoconfiante; determinado,-a; *(US, CANADA)* irritável.

felicitate *vt* felicitar.

felicitous *adj* apropriado,-a; adequado,-a.

felicity *n* felicidade, alegria *f*.

feline *n adj* felino,-a.

fell¹ *(pt of* **fall**).

fell² pele *f* de animal com pelo.

fell³ *n* serras, colinas rochosas (no norte da Inglaterra); ♦ *adj (arc)* terrível; **the ~ necessity** a dura necessidade; ♦ *vt* lançar por terra; derrubar; **to ~ a tree** derrubar uma árvore.

fella, feller¹ *(variant of* **fellow**) *n* indivíduo, *(coll)* tipo, gajo *m*.

fellatio, fellation *n* felação *f*.

feller² pessoa que derruba árvores, rachador (de lenha).

fellmonger *n* peleiro, peliqueiro.

fellow *n* indivíduo, man; *(older person)* sujeito; *(younger man)* rapaz; **he is a nice ~** ele é um rapaz/homem/sujeito bom; **2** *(fam)* tipo, camarada, *(BR)* cara *m*; **3 ~ citizen** *n* concidadão,-dã; **4 ~ countryman** *n* compatriota; **5 ~ men** *npl* semelhantes *mpl*; **our ~** nossos semelhantes, nossos irmãos; **6 ~ students** colegas *m,fpl* de curso; **7 ~ traveller** *n* companheiro,-a de viagem; **8 Fellow** *m,f (Univ)* (professor) membro *m* do corpo docente; a mas alta distinção profissional de uma Ordem/Associação; **F~ of the Royal Australasian College of Surgeons, FRACS** Fellow-membro da Associação Australasiana de Cirurgiões; **F~ of the Chartered Institute of Linguists** Fellow-membro da Ordem de Linguistas; *(from prestigious learned academy/ society)* Membro de academia ou sociedade literária ou científica; **F~ of the British Society** Membro da Academia Britânica; **9 ~ researcher** bolseiro.

De notar que no mundo britânico o **'Fellow'** de uma ordem ou sociedade está acima de membro das mesmas ordens ou sociedades; como este distintivo não está traduzido em português, o equivalente é 'Membro' ou deixá-lo em inglês.

fellowship *n* amizade *f*, camaradagem *f*; **2** *(EDUC: grant)* bolsa *f* de estudo; **3** *(association)* sociedade, associação *f*.

felon *n* criminoso,-a.

felony *n (JUR)* delito *m* grave.

felt *(pt, pp of* **feel**); *n* feltro; **~ hat** chapéu *m* de feltro; **2 ~-tip pen** *n* caneta de feltro, *(BR)* hidrocor *m*.

female *n* mulher *f*; **2** *(ZOOL)* fêmea; ♦ *adj* feminino,-a; **~ circumcision** *n (MED; traditions)* excisão *f*.

feminine *adj* feminino,-a.

femininity *n* feminilidade.

feminism *n* feminismo.

feminist *n* feminista.

femur *n* fémur.

fen *n* pântano, charco; **~land** terra pantanosa; **2** **~-man** habitante dos Fens; **3** **the Fens** *(flat low-lying area with marshes)* lezíria *f (in Portugal)*.

fence *n* sebe *f*; cerca *f*, cercado *m*; **2** *(in show jumping)* barreira *f* obstáculo *m*; **3** *(coll) (receiver of stolen goods)* rece(p)tador; ♦ *vt* cercar, vedar, construir um sebe; ♦ *vi (SPORT) (fight with sword)* esgrimir; **2** *(fig) (evade)* esquivar-se a perguntas directas argumentos **(with** a), dar respostas evasivas; **3** *(receive stolen goods)* rece(p)tar mercadoria roubada; **to ~ in/off** *vt (cattle)* encurralar; **2** *(land)* separar com cerca, cercar; **3** confinar; **he ~d in his livestock** ele encurralou o gado; **to ~ off an attack** defender-se, evitar; IDIOM **to sit on the ~** não tomar partido.

fenceless *adj (without fence)* sem vedação; **2** sem defesa.

fencer *n* esgrimista *m,f*.

fencing *n (SPORT)* esgrima *f*; **2** *(fences)* cerca *f*, cercado *m*; **3** *(material)* material para fazer cercas.

fend *vi*: **to ~ for o.s.** *(provide for)* arranjar-se sozinho; *(fam)* desenrascar-se; ♦ *vt*: **to ~ off sb/sth** desviar-se de *(attacker, blow)*; **2** *(evade)* esquivar-se **(with** a) *(questions)*.

fender *n (round fireplace)* guarda-fogo *m*; **2** *(US) (AUT)* párachoque *m*; **3** *(buoy or similar on side of boat)* prote(c)ção *f*, parachoque *m*.

fennel *n* funcho *m*, erva-doce *f*.

fent *n* retalho *m*, pedaço de tecido *m*; **2** fenda *f*.

fenugreek *n (BOT)* fenacho.

ferment *n* fermento; **2** *(fig)* agitação *f*; ♦ *vt* fermentar.

fermentation *n* fermentação *f*.

fern *n* feto *m*, *(BR)* samambaia.

Fernando de Noronha *npr (GEOG) (in the Atlantic)* **the Island of ~** a Ilha de Fernando de Noronha.

Fernando Pó *npr (GEOG)* **the Island of ~** Ilha ohe Fernando Pó (assim chamado até 1973) agora: Bioko.

fernery *n* fetal, terreno onde crescem fetos.

ferocious *adj* feroz.

ferocity *n* ferocidade *f*.

ferreous *adj (CHEM)* ferroso,-a.

ferret *n (ZOOL)* furão *m*; **2** *(fig)* furão *m inv*; **3** fita de seda ou algodão; ♦ *vt*: **to ~ sb/sth out** *(drive from hiding) (animal)* desentocar, desenterrar; **2** *(person)* seguir a pista de *(thief, etc)*; investigar; **3** descobrir *(object, bargain)*.

ferreter *n* caçador que utiliza o furão.

ferric *adj* férrico,-a.

ferro-alloy *n* liga *f* de ferro.

ferrous *adj (CHEM)* ferroso,-a.

ferry *n* barco (de travessia); **~boat** balsa; **Lisbon ~boat** cacilheiro *m*; ♦ *vt* transportar em barco.

fertile *adj* fértil; **2** *(BIOL)* fecundo,-a.

fertility *n* fertilidade *f*; fecundidade *f*; **~ drug** *n* medicamento *m* para/contra a esterilidade/infertilidade *f*.

fertilization *n* fertilização *f*; **2** *(insemination)* fecundidade *f*.

fertilize *vt (land)* fertilizar; **2** *(of human, plant, egg)* fecundar; **3** *(AGR)* adubar.

fertilizer *n* adubo *m*, fertilizante *m*.

ferule (= **ferrule**) *n (small, ring)* aro, virola.

fervent *adj (believer)* fervoroso,-a; **2** *(passion, hope)* ardente *m,f*, apaixonado,-a, vivo,-a.

fervently *adv* ardentemente.

fervour *(UK)*, **fervor** *(US)* *n* fervor, ardor.

fester *vi (wound)* inflamar, supurar, ulcerar; **2** *(fig) (become bitter)* inflamar, ulcerar; **resentment ~ed his imagination** o resentimento *m* inflamou a sua imaginação.

festering *adj* ulceroso,-a.

festival *n (REL)* festa *f*; **2** *(ART, MUS)* festival *m*.

festive *adj* festivo,-a, alegre; **the ~ season** a época do Natal.

festivities *npl* festas *fpl*, festividades *fpl*.

festoon *n* festão *m*; ♦ *vt* ornar **(with** com) festão.

fetal *adj (Vd: foetal)*.

fetch *vt (go and get)* ir buscar, trazer; **I am going to ~ the children from school** vou buscar as crianças à escola; **2** *(sell, cost for a price)* render; **that picture ~ed a fortune** aquele quadro rendeu uma fortuna; IDIOM **to ~ and carry for sb** ser moço de recados de alguém.

fetching *adj (attractive)* atraente *m,f*; *(child)* encantador,-ora; **this dress is very ~ on you** este vestido fica-te lindamente.

fête, fete *n (church)* quermesse *f*; **2 charity ~** festa *f* de caridade, beneficiência; ♦ *vt* festejar *(em honra de alguém)*; **a much-feted (fêted) author** um autor muito festejado/celebrado.

fetid *(UK)* **foetid** *(US)* *adj* fétido,-a.

fetish *n* fetiche *m* **(about,** por); **2** *(object)* feitiço *m*; **to have a ~ about sth** estar obcecado por algo.

fetishism *n* fetichismo *m*.

fetlock *n (horse's leg joint)* boleto *m*; **2** *(tuft of hair on this part)* topete *m*.

fetter *(usually plural -s)* *npl (chains around ankles)* grilhões *mpl*, grilhetas *fpl*; **2** *(restraint)* **in ~s** a ferro; **3** *(fig)* obstáculo *m*, restrição *f*; ♦ *vt* agrilhoar, acorrentar, refrear.

fettered *adj* agrilhoado,-a, acorrentado,-a.

fettle *n (mood)* disposição *f*; **in fine/good ~** com boa disposição, com boa saúde, em excelente forma.

fettler *n (UK)* operário,-a que trata das vias férreas.

fetus, foetus *(pl: -tuses)* feto *m*.

feud *n* feudo *m*; **2** disputa *f*, contenda *f*, querela **(with** com, **between** entre).

feudal *adj* feudal *m,f*.

feudalism *n* feudalismo *m*.

feudalist *n* feudalista *m*.

feuding *adj (families)* em conflito.

fever *n* febre *f*; temperatura *f*; **2** *(fig) (craze)* febre; **bout of ~** acesso de febre; **3** *(fig) (frenzy)* frenesi.

feverish *adj* febril; **2** *(with dreams)* delirante; **3** *(frenzied)* frenético;

fever pitch *n* ponto *m* máximo/intenso; **our excitement reached ~** a nossa excitação estava no auge, no máximo.

few *adj* poucos; alguns; **the ~** a minoria; **a ~** *adj* uns poucos; ♦ *pron* alguns; **the thinking ~** a minoria pensante; **in the next ~ days** nos próximos dias;

quite a ~ vários, bastante; **I know a** ~ conheço alguns; ♦ *pron* poucos; IDIOM **I have had quite a** ~ **(drinks) too many** já bebi demais.

fewer (*comp of few*) *adj pron* menos; **no** ~ **than** não menos do que; **the** ~ **the better** quanto menos, melhor.

fewest (*sup of few*) *adj* o menos (possível).

fez (*pl*: -**zes**) *n* fez, barrete árabe.

fiancé *n* (*engaged*) noivo.

fiancée *n* noiva.

fiasco *n* fiasco *m*.

fiat *n* sanção *f* oficial; **2** autorização *f*; **3** ordem *f* arbitrária.

fib *n* (*little lie*) (*coll*) peta *f*; patranha *f* (EP); potoca, lorota (BR); ♦ (-**bb**-) *vt/vi* (*coll*) mentir mentir; contar petas (EP); contar lorotas (BR).

fibber *n* (*coll*) mentiroso,-a; **2** (*joker*) gracejador,-ora; **he is a** ~ ele mente por brincadeira; ele está a brincar.

fibre (UK) **fiber** (US) *n* fibra *f*; ~-**glass** *n* fibra *f* de vidro; ~ **optics** *n* fibra *f* óptica.

fibreless *adj* sem fibra; **2** (*fig*) sem energia.

fibroid *n* (*MED, ANAT*) fibroma; ♦ *adj* fibroide.

fibromyalgia *n* fibromyalgia *f*.

fibrosis *adj* fibroso.

fibrous *adj* fibroso,-a.

fibula *n* perónio *m*; fíbula *f*.

fickle *adj* inconstante, volúvel.

fickleness *n* inconstância *f*.

fiction *n* ficção *f*; obras de ficção; romances.

fictional *adj* de ficção.

fictioneer *n* romancista barato.

fictitious *adj* fictício,-a; falso-a; **a** ~ **address** um endereço falso.

fictionist *n* ficcionista.

fid *n* (*NAUT*) cavirão *m*; cunha *f* do mastaréu.

fiddle *n* (*MUS*) violino *m*; **2** (*coll*) rabeca *f*; **3** (*dishonest plan*) fraude *f*, intrujice *f*, trapaça; **tax** ~ fraud *m* fiscal; ♦ *vt* defraudar; falsificar (*figures*); **2 to** ~ **with** *vt* brincar com; **3** (*to adjust*) ajustar, mexer em (*device, knobs*); **4** (*accounts*) **to** ~ **with the figures** fazer uma trapaça com as contas/os números; IDIOM **to be as fit as a** ~ estar são como um pero, de ótima saúde; **to play second** ~ to sb desempenhar uma posição subalterna, secundária; **to** ~ **about** passar o tempo sem fazer nada; **to** ~ **about with** estar sempre a mexer em algo.

fiddledeedee *exc* ora adeus!, não acredito!, que disparate!

fiddle-faddle *n* bagatelas, patetices; ♦ *exc* histórias!; tolice; ♦ *vi* perder tempo com frívolidades.

fiddler *n* músico de rabeca; violinista de música folclórica; **2** pessoa que perde tempo ou mexe em tudo; **3** trapaceiro,-a.

fiddlesticks *exc* (*fam*) cantigas!, disparates!

fidelity *n* fidelidade *f*; exactidão *f*.

fidget *vi* estar irrequieto, mexer-se!; **to be in a** ~ não sossegar; **to have the** ~**s** estar enervado, estar excitado.

fidgety *adj* inquieto, nervoso, desassossegado.

fiduciary *adj* (*JUR*) (*having the nature of a trust*) fiduciário,-a; ~ **issue** *n* emissão *f* de notas de banco sem o apoio de de ouro.

fie *exc* fora!; que vergonha!; ~ **upon you** devia mais era ter vergonha!

field *n* (*gen*) (*GEOG*) campo *m*; **2** (*fig*) (*knowledge, profession*) esfera, especialidade *f*, âmbito *m*; **3** (*SPORT*) (*ground*) *n* campo; **to lead the** ~ tomar a dianteira; ~ **glasses** *npl* binóculo *m sg*; ~ **hospital** hospital *m* de campanha; ~ **marshal** *n* marechal-de-campo *m*; ~ **mouse** *n* (*ZOOL*) arganaz; ~ **of vision** *n* campo visual; ~ **work** *n* trabalho *m* científico de campo *m*; ♦ *vi* **to hold the** ~ aguentar-se, manter-se

field day *n* (*Univ, school*) saída, visita (para estudo); **2** (*MIL*) dia *m* de manobras; IDIOM **to have a** ~ ter um dia em cheio.

fielder *n* (*SPORT*) jogador de críquete cuja função é apanhar a bola jogada pelo batedor.

field-grey *adj* cinzento, pardo; **2** *n* soldado alemão.

fiend *n* demónio (BR:-mô-) *m*; **opium-**~ opiómano.

fiendish *adj* diabólico; **2** pessoa viciada em.

fiendishly *adv* diabolicamente.

fiendlike *adj* diabólico,-a, satânico,-a.

fierce *adj* feroz; violento,-a; intenso,-a.

fiercely *adv* furiosamente, ferozmente.

fierceness *n* ferocidade *f*, fúria *f*; brutalidade *f*.

fiery *adj* ardente, impetuoso,-a; **2** apaixonado,-a; arrebatado,-a.

fife *n* pífaro; ♦ *vt/vi* tocar pífaro.

fifer *n* tocador de pífaro.

fifteen *num* quinze.

fifteenth décimo quinto; **today is the** ~ hoje é dia quinze.

fifth *n* adj quinto,-a; **he was in** ~ **place** ele ficou em quinto lugar.

fifthly *adv* em quinto lugar.

fiftieth *adj* quinquagésimo.

fifty *num* cinquenta; **to go fifty-fifty** ir a meias; **to go** ~-~ **with** repartir igualmente.

fig[1] *n* (*BOT*) figo *m*; **dried** ~**s** figos *mpl* secos; ~-**garden/-orchard** figueiral; IDIOM **I don't care a** ~ **for it** não quero saber disso para nada.

fig[2] (*abbr for* figure); (*abbr for* figurative).

fight *n* briga, luta *f*; **2** (*MIL*) combate *m*; **hand to hand** ~ luta corpo a corpo; ♦ (*pt, pp* **fought**) *vt* lutar, combater; ♦ *vi* brigar, lutar; **2** (*to argue*) discutir sobre; **3** (*fig*) (*overcome*) superar; ~ **off** libertar-se de; (*troops*) vencer; (*attack*) repelir.

fighter *n* combatente; **2** (*fig*) lutador,-ora; **3** (*plane*) caça.

fighting *n* luta *f*; batalha *f*; **close** ~ luta corpo a corpo; ♦ *adj* batalhador,-ora.

figment *n*: **a** ~ **of the imagination** um produto da imaginação.

fig tree (*BOT*) figueira *f*.

figurant *n* (*CIN, THEAT*) figurante *m,f*.

figuration *n* figuração; **2** embelezamento *m*.

figurative *adj* (*meaning*) figurado,-a; **2** (*representation*) figurativo,-a.

figuratively *adv* em sentido figurado, metaforicamente.

figure *n* (*ART, MATH*) figura *f*, desenho *m*; ~ **skating** *n* patinagem *f*, (BR) patinação artística; ~ **of fun** pessoa ridícula; ~ **of speech** figura de retórica; **to cut a fine** ~ fazer boa figura; **2** (*number, digit*) algarismo, número, cifra; **a four-~ amount** uma quantia com quatro algarismos; **3** *(shape of body)* talhe *m*, forma, linha *f*; **she has a lovely ~** ela tem uma bela linha; ♦ *vt* imaginar; ♦ *vi* figurar; **to ~ on** contar com; **to ~ out** *vt* compreender; **to ~ it out** calcular; ♦ *exc* **that ~!** isso expl.

figured *adj* com desenhos, com figuras; florido.

figurehead *n (on ship)* carranca de proa, figura de proa; **2** *(fig)* chefe *m* nominal, testa-de-ferro *(fam)*.

figurine *n (US)* estatueta *f*.

figuring *n* cálculo *m*.

Fiji *npr* Fiji; **in ~** em Fiji.

Fijian *adj* fijiano,-a.

filament *n* filamento *m*.

filature *n* fábrica de fiação de seda.

filbert *n* avelã *f*; **~ tree** *n* avelaneira *f*.

filch *vt (pilfer)* surripiar; *(coll)* fanar, pifar.

filcher *n* larápio *m*, ladrão *m*, ladra *f*.

filching *n* furto, gatunice.

file *n (for nails,wood, metals)* lima *f*, lixa *f*; **2** *(of documents)* ficheiro *m* **(on** sobre**)**; dossier *m*, arquivo *m* **(on** sobre**)**; *(folder)* pasta *f*; **3** *(COMP)* ficheiro *m*; **4** *(row)* fila *f*, coluna *f*; **in single ~** em fila indiana ♦ *vt (nails etc)* lixar; **2** *(documents)* arquivar; **3** *(JUR) (claim)* apresentar, dar entrada em; ♦ *vt* lixar; arquivar; **2** *(documents)* arpuivar; **3** *(JUR) (claim)* apresentar, dar entrada em; **to ~ away** arquivar; **to ~ in/out** *vi* entrar/sair em fila; **to ~ past** *vt* desfilar em frente de/ante.

filing *n* classificação *f*, arquivamento *m*; **~ cabinet** *n* fichário, arquivo *m*; **~ clerk** *n* arquivista *m,f*.

filemot *n* cor de folha seca, amarelo acastanhado.

filer *n* limador; **2** ficheiro, classificador.

filet *n* filé *m*.

filial *adj* filial; sucursal.

filiation *n* filiação; **2** *(JUR)* investigação de paternidade.

filibeg *n* saiote *m* escocês.

filibuster *n* flibusteiro; obstrucionista *m,f*; **2** obstrução *f* à a(c)tividade parlamentar; ♦ *vi (POL)* fazer discursos obstrucionistas.

filigree *n* filigrana *f*.

filings *n* limalha *f*.

Filipino *npr adj* filipino,-a.

fill *n:* **to eat one's ~** *(of food)* fartar-se de comer; *(fig)* **I've had my ~ of it** já estou farto,-a disso; ♦ *vt (room, container)* encher **(with** com**)**; **to ~ in** *vt (form)* preencher; **2** *(hole)* tapar; **3** *(inform)* pôr ao corrente **(sb** alguém**)**; **4** *(substitute)* substituir **(for sb** alguém**)**; ♦ *vi (AUT)* abastecer; **to ~ a tooth** obturar um dente; **to ~ a vacancy** prencher uma vaga.

filler *n (CONSTR) (for cracks)* massa para tapar buracos/rachas; betume *m*, enchimento; *(for windows)* massa *f* de vidraceiro,-a.

fillet *n* filete *m*; lombo, *(BR)* filé *m*; **2** *(ARCH)* filete; ♦ *vt* ornar com filete.

fill-in *n (person)* substituto,-a.

filling *n (CULIN)* recheio; **2** *(for tooth)* obturação *f*; chumbo; **~ station** *n* bomba *(BR:* posto*)* de gasolina; ♦ *adj* que satisfaz, que sacia *(alimento)*.

fillip *n* estímulo; **2** piparote *m*; ♦ *vt* dar um piparote *m*.

filly *n* potra *f*.

film *n (CIN)* filme, *m*; **2** *(layer)* película *f*; **3** *(PHOT)* película *f*; ♦ *vt/vi* rodar, filmar; **~ fan** *n* apaixonado,-a do cinema; **~ director** *n* realizador,-ora; **~goer** *n* cinéfilo,-a; **~ industry** *n* indústria *f* cinematográfica; **~ maker** *n* cineasta *m,f*; **~ing** *n* filmagem *f*; **~set** *n (CIN)* cenário *m*; **~ star** *n* astro, estrela de cinema; **short/long ~** curta, longa metragem; **the films** *pl* o cinema, a cinematografia; **to shoot a ~** *vt* rodar um filme; **~ studio** estúdio de cinema.

filmy *adj (dress)* transparente *m,f*, diáfano,-a; **2** *(cloudy) (glass, lens)* embaciado,-a.

filter *n* filtro; **2 ~ tip** *n* piteira; ♦ *adj* com filtro; ♦ *vt* filtrar; **2 to ~ out** tornar-se conhecido.

filtered *adj* filtrado,-a.

filtering *n* filtragem.

filth *m* sujidade *f*, *(BR)* sujeira; porcaria, imundície *f*.

filthiness *n* imundície, porcaria; obscenidade *f*.

filthy *adj* sujo; **2** *(language)* indecente, obsceno, imoral; **~ rich** podre de rico.

fin *n (of fish)* barbatana *f*.

final *adj* final *f*; ♦ *adj* final *m,f*, último,-a, derradeiro,-a; **2** definitivo,-a; ♦ **~ adjustment** afinação final; **~ clause** *n (LING)* oração *f* final; **~ stage** *n* fase *f* final.

finale *n (MUS, THEAT)* final *m*.

finalist *n (SPORT)* finalista *m,f*.

finalize *vt* concluir, completar.

finally *adv* finalmente, por fim; definitivamente.

finals *npl (EDUC) (exams)* exames finais; *(SPORT)* as finais.

finance *n* finança, fundos *mpl*; ♦ *vt* financiar.

financial *adj* financeiro,-a; económico,-a *(BR:*-nô-*)*.

financially *adv* financeiramente.

financier *n* financista *m,f*; financeiro, *(BR)* investidor,-ora.

find *n* achado *m*, descoberta *f*; ♦ *(pt, pp* **found***) vt* encontrar, achar; **2** descobrir; notar; *(JUR)* **to ~ sb guilty** declarar alguém culpado,-a; **to ~ against** decidir contra; **to ~ fault with** censurar alguém; **to ~ one's feet** ganhar confiança; **to ~ out** *vt* verificar; descobrir; IDIOM **all found** *(included)* = **£100 a week all found** 100 libras por semana e cama e mesa; **seek and you will ~** quem procura, sempre alcança.

finder *n* aquele que encontra algo.

findings *n* descobrimento, descoberta; **2** *(JUR) npl* veredito *sg*, decisão *fsg* do júri; **3** *(of report)* recomendações *fpl*.

fine *n (JUR)* multa *f*; coima *f* ♦ *adj* fino; bom/boa; **2** *(small, thin)* delgado; bonito; **~ arts** *npl* belasartes *fpl*; **~-looking** elegante, atraente; **~-spoken** bem-falante; **~ work** trabalho de precisão; *(weather)* **to be ~** fazer bom tempo; ♦ *adv* bem; ♦ *vt (JUR)* multar; IDIOM **~ feathers make ~ birds** o hábito faz o monge.

fine herbes *npl (CULIN)* ervas *fpl* aromáticas.

finely *adv* admiravelmente; com delicadeza *f*.

fineness *n* finura *f*; **2** *(precious metals)* quilate *m*.

finery *n* traje *m* chique; **2** afinação *(de metais)*.

finesse *n* subtileza *f*; artemanha; delicadeza.

fine-tooth comb *n:* **to go over sth with a ~** passar algo a pente fino.

finger *n (ANAT)* dedo *m*; **2** *(small quantity in a glass)* dedo; **~ alphabet** *n* alfabeto dos surdos-mudos; **~board** *n (MUS)* braço (de instrumento de cordas); **~ed** *adj* digitado,-a; **~mark** *n* dedada; **~nail** *n* unha; **~print** *n* impressão *f* digital; **~ stall** *n (finger cover)* dedeira; **~tip** *n* ponta do dedo; **little/index ~** dedo mínimo/indicador; **middle ~** dedo médio; **ring ~** dedo anelar; ♦ *vt (touch)* manusear; mexer; **2** *(MUS)* dedilhar. IDIOM **to have a ~ in every pie** ser pau para toda a obra; **not to lift a ~** não mexer uma palha em (nada); **to lay a ~ on (sb)** pôr mãos em; bater em (alguém); **to point the ~ at sb** apontar para alguém; acusar alguém; **to be all ~s and thumbs** *(clumsy)* ser desajeitado,-a; **to be at one's ~tips** ter algo à mão.

fingering *n (MUS)* dedilhado.

finial *n (ARCH)* florão *m*.

finicky *adj (person)* esquisito,-a, meticuloso,-a, miudinho,-a (**about** acerca de); *(task)* minucioso,-a.

finis *n* fim (página de livro).

finish *n* fim *m*; remate *m*; **2** aperfeiçoamento; **3 ~ surface** superfície *f* polida; ♦ *vt/vi* terminar, concluir; **to ~ off** *vt* acabar; liquidar; **to ~ up** acabar por fazer; **to ~ with sb** romper com *(boyfriend, etc)*; separar-se.

finished *adj* acabado,-a; **she ~ third** ela acabou em terceiro lugar.

finishing *n* acabamento; **the ~ blow** golpe *m* de misericórdia; **~ coat** *(paint)* última demão de tinta; **~ line** *n* linha de chegada, meta; **~ touch** *n* toque *m* final, acabamento *m*, aperfeiçoamento *m*.

finite *adj* finito,-a, limitado,-a.

Finland *npr* Finlândia; **in ~** na Finlândia.

Finn *npr* finlandês,-esa.

finned *adj* com barbatanas.

finner *n* baleia anã *f*.

Finnish *npr adj* finlandês,-esa; *(LING)* *n* finlandês *m*.

fiord *n* fiorde *m*.

fir *n* abeto *m*; **~-cone** *n* pinha; **~ tree** *n* abeto *m*.

fire *n* fogo *m*; **on ~** em chamas; **2** *(blaze)* incêndio *m*; **3** *(essence of fire)* *(for cooking, warmth)* lume; **4** *(for warmth in the open)* fogueira *f*; **5 bon~** fogueira; **to jump over the ~** *(for fun)* saltar à fogueira; **6** *(fire in the hearth)* lareira *f*; **to catch ~** pegar fogo; **to come under ~** *(MIL)* ser atacado; *(fig) (criticized)* ser censurado, criticado; **to extinguish ~** apagar, extinguir; **7** *(enthusiasm)* ardor; ♦ **~ alarm** *n* alarme *m* de incêndio; **~arm** *n* arma de fogo; **~ball** *n* bola *f* de fogo; *(fig)* pessoa dinâmica; **~basket** *n* braseira *f*; **~ bomb** *n* bomba *f* incendiária; **~break** *n* corta-fogo; **~brick** *n* tijolo *m* refratário; **~ brigade** *n* (corpo de) bombeiros *mpl*; **~ cracker** *n* rojão *m*; **~ drill** *n* simulação *f* de incêndio; **~-eater** *n (performer)* engolidor,-ora de fogo; **~ engine** *n* carro de bombeiro; **~ escape** *n* escada de incêndio; **~ extinguisher** *n* extintor *m* de incêndio; **~-fly** *(pl: -ies)* *n (nocturnal beetle)* pirilampo *m*; **~grate** grelha; **~ guard** guarda fogo; **~ hazard** *n*

risco de incêndio; **~ kiln** *n* fornalha *f*; **~ lighter** *n* acendalha; *(for cigarette)* isqueiro *m*; **~man** *n* bombeiro; **~place** *n* lareira *f*, fogão *m* de sala; **~-raiser** *n (person who causes fire on purpose)* incendiário,-a; **~side** *n:* **to sit by the ~** sentar-se junto à lareira; **~proof** *adj* à prova de fogo; **~station** *n* quartel *m* dos bombeiros; **~-tongs** *n* tenazes *fpl*; **~trap** *n* prédio sujeito a risco de incêndio; **~-water** *n* aguardente *f*; **~wood** *n* lenha; ♦ *vt (shoot)* disparar; **2** *(set fire to)* incendiar; **3** *(coll) (dismiss)* despedir *(alguém)*; **4** *(fig)* **to ~ questions at** bombardear alguém com perguntas; **5 to ~ sb's imagination** inflamar a imaginação de alguém, entusiasmar; ♦ *vi* incendiar-se; **to ~ at** atirar em; **to ~ away** *(question)* disparar; **to ~ up** *(ignite)* acender; **2** irritar-se; IDIOM **there is no smoke without ~** não há fumo sem fogo.

fireworks *npl* fogo *m* de artifício; **2** *(fig) (of temper)* explosão *f*.

firing *n (MIL)* tiroteio *m*, tiros *mpl*; **~ line** *n* linha *f* de fogo; **~ squad** *n* pelotão *m* de fuzilamento.

firkin *n* pequeno barril; **2** medida de capacidade para nove galões.

firm *adj* firma, empresa; ♦ *adj* firme; resoluto; ♦ *vt* firmar.

firmament *n* firmamento *m*.

firmly *adv* firmemente.

firmness *n* firmeza.

firn *n* camada de neve endurecida, nevada *f*.

first *n* primeiro,-a; **the ~ of May** o primeiro de Maio; **2** *(AUT) (gear)* primeira *f*; ♦ *adj* primeiro,-a; ♦ *adv* primeiro; em primeiro lugar; **at ~** a princípio; **~-aid** *n* pronto-socorro; **~born** *n* primogénito,-a *(BR:-gê-)*; **~ cousin** *n* primo,-a direito,-a; **~ degree murder** homicídio premeditado; **~ floor** *n* primeiro andar *m*; **~-hand** *adj* em/de primeira mão; **F~ Lady** *n* Primeira-dama; **~ name** nome de ba(p)tismo; **~ of all** antes de tudo, antes de mais nada; **~-rate** *adj* de primeira categoria; **~ things ~** vamos ao mais importante, sem demora.

first-class *n adj adv* (de/em) primeira classe; *(gen)* excelente; **2** *(Post)* correio *m* azul; **3** *(Univ = degree)* com louvor.

firstly *adv* primeiramente, em primeiro lugar.

firth *n* braço *m* de mar, estuário *m*.

fiscal *adj* fiscal *m,f*; **2 ~ year** *(FIN)* ano *m* fiscal.

fish *n, pl inv* peixe *m*; ♦ *vt/vi* pescar *m*; **2** *(fig) (testing)* procurar saber; **to ~ around** *(in the bag, drawer)* remexer; **to ~ out sth from** tirar algo de algo; **~bone** *n* espinha *f* de peixe; **~-breeding** *n* piscicultura; **~bowl** *(small)* aquário *m*; **~cake** *n (CULIN)* bolinho/pastel/croquete *m* de peixe; **~-fig** *n* arpão *m*; **~ hook** *n* anzol *m*.

fisherman *n* pescador *m*.

fishery *n* pescaria *f*.

fishing *n* pesca *f*; **~ boat** *n* barco de pesca; **deep-sea ~** *n* pesca no mar alto; **to go ~** ir à pesca; **~ line/rod** *n* linha; vara *f* de pesca; **~ tackle** *n* apetrecho (de pesca).

fishmonger *n* peixeiro,-a; **~s** *n (shop)* peixaria *f*.

fishnet *n adj (tights, stockings)* de rede.

fishpond *n* viveiro *m* de peixes.

fish-spear *n* arpão *m*.

fishwife *n (seller)* peixeira *f*; **2** *(fig)* mulher regateira.

fishy *adj (smell, taste)* a peixe; **2** *(fig)* suspeito,-a, esquisito,-a.

fission *n (PHYS)* cisão *f*, divisão *f*; **nuclear** ~ fisão *f* nuclear; desintegração *f* nuclear; ~ **products** *npl* produtos *mpl* de fisão; **2** *(BIOL)* fissiparidade *f*.

fissure *n* fenda *f*, fissura *f*, greta *f*.

fist *n* punho; **2** ~ **law** lei do mais forte.

fistful n punhado *m*.

fistical *adj* pugilístico,-a.

fistula *n* fístula; **2** respiradouro (de baleia).

fit *n (MED)* ataque *m*; **to have a** ~ *(of nerves, anger, laughter)* ter um ataque *f*; **a coughing** ~ um acesso *m* de tosse; ♦ *adj (MED, SPORT)* em (boa) forma; adequado,-a; apto,-a; **not** ~ **for** impróprio para; não estar em condição de; ♦ **(-tt-)** *vt* ficar bem a, assentar a; **2** *(clothes)* experimentar, provar; **3** ajustar; **the coat is a good** ~ **(on me)** o casaco fica-me bem; **to** ~ **sth with sth** equipar algo com algo; **to have sth ~ted** instalar algo; ♦ *vi (correct size)* servir; **the suit doesn't** ~ **me** o fato não me serve; **'one size ~s all'** 'tamanho único'; ♦ *(give space or time for)* **to** ~ **in** encaixar-se em; caber em; **the blanket doesn't** ~ **in that suitcase** o cobertor não cabe nessa mala; **the key doesn't** ~ **in the keyhole** a chave não encaixa na fechadura; **to** ~ **in with sth** *(accommodate)* enquadrar-se **(with** com); **it doesn't** ~ **with my plans** isso não se enquadra nos meus planos; **2** *(not get on with people, job)* integrar-se, misturar-se (outros); **he does not** ~ **in with (other people)** ele ná se dá bem com os outros; está fora do seu lugar; ♦ **to** ~ **out sth** (= **to** ~ **up)** *vt* equipar, prover, fornecer; **to** ~ **together** *vt* unir-se; **2** *(make sense)* fazer sentido; IDIOM **as** ~ **as a fiddle** são como um pêro; **fits and starts** *(machine, transport)* aos solavancos.

fitch *n* pêlo *m* de furão.

fitful *adj* espasmódico,-a; agitado,-a; intermitente *m,f*.

fitfully *adv (sleep, rain)* intermitentemente; **2** *(AUT)* aos arrancos; de uma maneira incerta.

fitment *n* móvel *m*; peça *f* de mobília.

fitness *n (MED)* saúde *f*, boa condição física; **2** aptidão *f*.

fitted *adj* adequado **(for** para); **2** *(tailored)* ajustado,-a; na medida; **3** *(built-in)* embutido,-a *(cupboard)*; *(kitchen)* integrado,-a; ~ **carpet** alcatifa; **room with** ~ **carpet** quarto alcatifado; ~ **sheet** n lençol de baixo com elástico.

fitter *n (of furniture)* montador *m*; **2** *(of equipment, electricals, etc)* mecânico, técnico.

fitting *adj* próprio,-a, apropriado,-a; **it isn't** ~ **to speak like that** não é próprio que fales assim; **2** *(of clothes)* n prova; **when is the second** ~**?** quando é a segunda prova?; ~**-room** sala de provas, *(BR)* provador; ~**s** *npl (taps, etc)* instalações *fpl*, acessórios *mpl*.

five *num* cinco; **2** *(GEOM)* ~ **angled** pentagonal; **3** **fiver** *n (UK: coll)* nota de cinco libras.

fivefold *adj adv* quíntuplo; ao quíntuplo.

fives *n (UK) (coll)* jogo de bola, semelhante ao squash, mas em que a bola é batida com mão ou taco.

fivesome *n* partida de golfe com cinco jogadores.

five-star *adj (hotel)* de cinco estrelas.

fix *n* inje(c)ção *f* (de droga); **2 to be in a** ~ estar em apuro(s); **3 to** ~ **a date** marcar uma data; ♦ *vt* fixar, colocar; **2** *(repair, put together)* arranjar; consertar; **to** ~ **on, to** ~ **upon** resolver, decidir, escolher.

fixation *n (PSYC)* fixação *f*; obsessão *f*.

fixative *n (for hair)* fixador *m*.

fixed *adj* fixado,-a; fixo,-a; firme; ~ **bar** barra fixa; ~ **beam** viga encastrada; ~ **idea** ideia *f* obstinada, fixa, mania *f*; ~ **assets** *npl (ECON)* a(c)tivos *mpl*.

fixedly *adj* fixamente.

fixer *n (PHOT)* fixador *m*; **2** *(fig) (schemer)* intriguista, maquinador,-ora.

fixing *n* acção de fixar (algo).

fixity *n* fixidez *f*, firmeza *f*, imutabilidade *f*.

fixture *(CONSTR)* instalação *f*; **2** móvel, acessório fixo (em lugar); ~**s and fittings** *npl* equipamento que faz parte duma casa (e que tem de ficar quando a casa é vendida); **2** *(UK: property law)* lei sobre propriedade imobiliária; **3** *(SPORT)* desafio, encontro *m*; **4** figura *f* constante.

fizz *n (of drink)* efervescência *f*; **2** *(sound)* chiado *m*; ♦ *vi* efervescer; ♦ *vi* fazer espuma (champanhe); *(firework)* crepitar.

fizzle out *vi (romance, campaign)* acabar mal, desaparecer; *(firework)* extinguir-se.

fizzy *adj* gasoso,-a; gaseificado,-a; efervescente *m,f*.

fjord *n* = **fiord**.

flab *n* flacidez *f*.

flabbergast *vt* espantar, confundir; **I am** ~**ed** estou pasmado,-a.

flabbiness *n* flacidez *f*, moleza *f*, frouxidão *f*.

flabby *adj (skin, muscle)* frouxo,-a, flácido,-a; **2** *(fig) (person)* mole.

flaccid *adj* flácido,-a.

flag *n* bandeira *f*; **2** *(as a signal) (RAIL, etc)* bandeirola *f*; ♦ **(-gg-)** *vi* acabar-se, descair; *(person)* desanimar; **to** ~ **sth down** *(taxi, etc)* fazer sinais a alguém/algo para parar; **the fly and hoist of a** ~ o comprimento e a largura duma bandeira; **to hoist the** ~ içar a bandeira; **to keep the** ~ **flying** *(fig)* não se deixar dominar; **to strike the** ~ arriar a bandeira; ~ **at half-mast high** bandeira a meia-haste.

Flag Day *n* dia da bandeira nos E.U.A. (14 de junho).

flagellant *adj* flagelante.

flagellation *n* flagelação *f*.

flageolet *n* flautim *m*; **2** *(BOT) (bean)* feijão *m*.

flagon *n* garrafão *m*; garrafa *f* bojuda para o vinho.

flagpole *n* mastro de bandeira.

flagrancy *n* flagrância *f*.

flagrant *adj* flagrante.

flagship *n* navio *m* almirante.

flagstaff *n* mastro *m* de bandeira.

flagstone *n* laje *f*.

flag-waving *n (fig)* patriotismo *m* exagerado.

flail *n* malho *m*; ♦ *vt (AGR)* malhar; **to** ~ **about** *vt* agitar *(arms, legs)*; ♦ *vi (person)* debater-se.

flair *n* aptidão *f*, jeito *m* especial; talento *m*.

flake n (of paint) lasca f; **2** (of snow) floco m; ♦ vt escamar (fish); ♦ vi (also: ~ **off**) (paint) descamar-se; (skin) esfoliar-se.

flak jacket (UK) ~ **vest** (US) n colete m; anti-balas.

flaky adj em flocos, em lascas; **2** (skin) descascado,-a, a descascar (due to sunburn); ~ **pastry** n massa f folhada.

flam n (falsehood, sham) falsidade f, peta f; **2** rufo do tambor.

flambeau n archote m.

flamboyant adj espalhafatoso,-a, espampanante; extravagante.

flame n chama; labareda f; **in ~s** em chamas; **to burst in ~s** irromper em chamas; **to go up in ~s** inflamar-se; **2** (fig) paixão; **an old ~** paixão antiga; **to fan the ~s** atiçar o fogo; **~proof** adj à prova de chama; **~-retardant** adj resistente m,f ao fogo; **~-thrower** n lança-chamas m inv; (fig) atiçar as paixões; **3** (coll) email insultuoso ou zangado; **4 ~ colour(ed)** cor de fogo; ♦ vi (be on fire) arder, estar queimado; **2** (fire) flamejar; **3** (cheek) ruborizar-se; **4** (passion) inflamar-se; **5** (send email) enviar abusos por correio ele(c)trónico.

flaming n envio de emails insultuosos; ♦ adj (fire-coloured) de cor-de-fogo; **2** (sending flames) chamejante, em chamas; **3** (row) violento,-a; **4** (UK) (in frustration) maldito,-a; ♦ exc ~ **work!** maldito trabalho!

flamingo n (ZOOL) flamingo m.

flammable adj inflamável.

flan n pudim; tarte f; (BR) torta.

Flanders npr Flandres; **folha de flandres** n tin-plate; (BR) tin can.

flange n (on beam) rebordo m; ♦ vt colocar um rebordo ou saliência.

flank n flanco m; lado m; ♦ vt ladear, flanquear; proteger flanqueando; acompanhar lado a lado.

flannel n (material) flanela; (for cleaning) pano de rosto, banho; ~s npl calças fpl de flanela.

flap n aba (of hat, envelope, table); **2** dobra (of sheet, etc); **3** (of wings) o bater das asas; ♦ (-pp-) vt bater; ♦ vi ondular; ~-**up seat** assento dobradiço; ~-**table** mesa com abas; **in a ~** agitado; **to ~ away the flies** enxotar as moscas; **to get in a ~** enervar-se, agitar-se.

flapdoodle n (coll) disparate, tolice.

flapjack n biscoito de farinha de aveia e mel (com frutas secas).

flapped adj com abas.

flapper n pato bravo muito novo; perdiz nova; **2** (coll) mão.

flapping adj que se agita, batente.

flare n fogacho, chama; **2** (MIL) sinal m luminoso; ♦ vt **to ~ about** brilhar, cintilar aqui e ali; **to ~ up** vi chamejar; **2** (fig) encolerizar-se; irromper.

flared adj (skirt) evasé; (trousers) calças à boca de sino.

flash n (of lightning) relâmpago m; (of light, torch) clarão; **2** (sudden idea, inspiration) lampejo; **3** (= news ~) notícias fpl de última hora; **4** (PHOT) flash m; **in a ~** num instante, de repente; **he ~ed by/past me** ele passou por mim como um raio; ♦ vt

(lights, torch) acender; ♦ vi (stars, teeth) brilhar; relampejar; **2** (angry eyes) faiscar; **3** (jewels) cintilar; **to ~ on and off** (AUT) piscar; IDIOM **a ~ in the pan** (sudden but brief success) sol de pouca dura; (BR) fogo de palha; **it ~ed into my mind ...** ocorreu-me de repente ao espírito, à mente ...

flashback n flashback m; **2** recordação f.

flashbulb n lâmpada de flash.

flasher n (AUT) pisca-pisca m; **2** (coll) (man – indecent exposure) exibicionista.

flashgun n disparador m de flash.

flashing n (CONSTR) material m isolante prateado (for roof, etc); **2** adj intermitente m,f; ~-**light** luz de farol; (US: torch) lanterna f de bolso; ~ **of lightning** relâmpago m.

flashing point n (explosive row) moment m crítico; **the conflict reached** ~ o conflito atingiu o momento crítico; **2** (CHEM) ponto m de inflamação.

flashy adj (pej) (party, car) espalhafatoso,-a; **2** (colour) gritante, berrante m,f.

flask n frasco m; (also: **vacuum** ~) garrafa térmica.

flat n andar m, apartamento m; **2** (MUS: note) bemol m; **3** (AUT) pneu m furado, (BR) pneu m murcho; **4** (of hand) palma; ♦ adj (level) plano,-a, **2** (smooth floor, road) liso,-a; **3** (of shoes, feet) raso,-a; **a ~ spoonful of** uma colher rasa; **4** (MUS) abaixo do tom; (instrument) desafinado,-a; **5** (drink - no longer fizzy) choca; ~ **beer** cerveja f choca; **6** (COMM, FIN) estacionário,-a; **7** (ELECT) descarregado,-a; **to feel ~** (in the dumps) (coll) sentir-se chocho, deprimido, em baixo; ♦ adv em posição f horizontal; **at a ~ rate** a preços mpl invariáveis; ~-**chested** adj de seios mpl pequenos; ~ **out** adv a todo o vapor ~ **race/racing** n (SPORT) corrida f de cavalos sem obstáculos; ~ **rate** preço de tabela; taxa f fixa; ~ **refusal** adj recusa f formal; ~ **tyre** n pneu m vazio; ~-**footed** adj (MED) de pés mpl chatos; **2** (exactly) **in five minutes** ~ exa(c)tamente em cinco minutos; **3 to fall** ~ (coll) (joke) ser um falhanço.

flatly adv categoricamente; **2** de modo liso.

flatmate colega que partilha o apartamento.

flatness n insipidez, monotonia; **2** ausência de relevo, planura.

flat-pack adj (furniture, etc. wrapped) para montar.

flatstone n pedra tumular.

flatten vt (= ~ **out**) aplanar; ♦ vi alisar-se, nivelar-se; **2** (demolish) derrubar; **3** (coll) esmagar.

flatter n adulator,-ora, bujulador,-ora; ♦ vt adular, lisonjear, gabar.

flattering adj lisonjeiro,-a.

flattery n bajulação f.

flatulence n flatulência f.

flatulent adj flatulento,-a; **2** presunçoso,-a.

flaunt vt ostentar, pavonear.

flaunter n exibicionista m,f, vaidoso,-a.

flaunting n ostentação f, exibição f.

flautist n flautista m,f.

flavour n sabor m, gosto; ♦ vt condimentar, temperar, aromatizar; ~**ed with** temperado com.

flavouring n condimento m.

flavourless *adj* sem sabor, insípido,-a.
flavoursome *adj* saboroso,-a.
flaw *n* defeito.
flawed *adj* com defeito; cheio,-a de defeitos.
flawless *adj* impecável.
flax *n* linho.
flaxen *adj* de cor de linho, feito de linho.
flay *vt* esfolar, tirar a pele; **2** criticar sem dó nem piedade, deitar abaixo alguém.
flea *n* pulga *f*; ~-**bite** ferradela, picada de pulga; ~-**market** mercado de velharias; ~**pit** *n* (*EP*) (*CIN*) espelunca *f*; (*BR*) pulgueiro *m*.
fleck *n* (*speckle*) pequena nódoa *f*, salpico *m*.
flecky *adj* às manchas, às pintas, pintalgado,-a, salpicado,-a.
fled (*pt, pp of* **flee**).
fledge *vt* cobrir de penas ou penugem, emplumar.
fledg(e)ling *n* passarinho que começou a voar; **2** pessoa inexperiente.
flee (*pt, pp* **fled**) *vt* fugir (de), abandonar; ♦ *vi* desaparecer, fugir.
fleece *n* velo; **2** (*wool*) lã *f*; ♦ *vt* tosquiar; extorquir; **2** (*coll*) pelar, depenar.
fleecy (-ier, -iest) *adj* em flocos, com aspecto de lã, lanoso.
fleeing *adj* em fuga.
fleet *n* frota; (*of ships*) esquadra.
fleeting *adj* fugaz, passageiro, rápido.
fleetingly *adv* transitoriamente.
Fleet Street *npr* rua no centro de Londres.

Fleet Street esta rua situada na City era o antigo centro de jornalismo e de jornalistas. Continua a ser designada como tal, apesar da imprensa inglesa ter-se mudado para outros lugares.

Flemish *npr adj* (*person*) flamengo,-a; (*LING*) flamengo *m*.
flench (*also:* **flense, flinch**) *vt* esquartejar (baleia); esfolar (foca).
flesh *n* carne *f*; (*of fruit*) polpa; **2 of ~ and blood** de carne e osso; **ones's own ~ and blood** pessoas de família mais chegada; **3 to put on ~** engordar; **4** ~-**wound** ferimento *m* sperficial.
fleshly *adj* (*fat*) carnudo,-a.
fleur-de-lis *n* flor-de-lis.
flew (*pt of* **fly**).
flews *n* beiços grossos e pendentes de certos cães.
flex *n* (*ELECT*) fio *m*, cabo *m*; ♦ *vt* (*muscles*) dobrar, flexionar.
flexability *n* flexibilidade *f*.
flexible *adj* flexível.
flexi disc *n* (*AUDIO*) disco *m* flexível.
flexion *n* (*of muscles*) flexão *f*.
flexitime *adj* horário *m* flexível.
flibbertigibbet *n* pessoa frívola, pateta *m,f* cabeça no ar.
flick *n* pancada *f* leve; **2** (*with finger*) piparote *m*; **3** (*with whip*) chicotada; ♦ *vt* dar pancada leve em; **to ~ through** (*book*) folhear; **2** (*throw in the air – coin*) lançar ao ar; **3** (*switch on/off*) ligar, acender/apagar (*light, TV*); **4** (*press*) premir (*bell, button*).

flicker *n* movimento oscilante; **2** (*light of candle*) luz *f* bruxuleante, tremulação *f*; **3** (*of hope*) centelha; ♦ *vi* (*candle*) bruxulear, tremeluzir; **2** (*shadow*) tremer.
flickering *n* vacilação *f*, tremulação *f*; ♦ *adj* tremente, tremeluzente, vacilante.
flick knife (*UK*) canivete *m* de ponta e mola.
flier *n* (*pilot*) aviador *m*; **2** (*also:* **flyer**) (*advertising leaflet*) folheto *m* publicitário (*Vd:* flyer).
flight *n* voo *m*; **2** (*escape*) fuga *f*; ~ **of capital** (*ECON*) fuga *f* de capitais; **3** (= ~ **of steps**) lance *m*; **4** bando (de pássaros); **to take ~** fugir, pôr-se em fuga; **to put to ~** pôr em fuga; ~ **attendant** *n* comissário,-a de bordo, hospedeira *f* de bordo; ~ **crew** *n* tripulação *f* de voo; ~ **deck** *n* (*of aircraft*) cabine *f* de pilotagem, de comando; ~ **path** trajectória de voo; ~ **recorder** *n* (*black box*) caixa negra *f*.
flighty (-ier, -iest) *adj* volúvel, inconstante.
flimflam *n* disparate, tolice.
flimsy (-ier, -iest) *adj* (*clothes, fabric*) fino,-a, ligeiro,-a; **2** (*argument, excuse*) fraco,-a, (*BR*) furado,-a.
flinch *vi* (*shy away*) vacilar, hesitar (*from duty*); **to ~ from** (**doing sth**) esquivar-se a (fazer algo); **2 to ~ at** estremecer perante (*shock, sudden pain cold*); **3** (*reaction*) retroceder de súbito.
flinders *n* fragmentos *mpl*, estilhaços *mpl*.
fling *n* (*coll*) (*spree*) estroinice, bora *f*; **2** (*casual sexual affair*) aventura *f*, caso *m*; **3** (*for any theory, ideology*) simpatia *f* passageira (**with** por); **4** (*coll*) (*attempt at doing sth*) experiência *f*; **5** dança *f* escocesa; ♦ (*pt, pp* **flung**) *vt* lançar, arremessar; **to ~ o.s. at** (**another person's mercy/feet**) lançar-se (à mercê de, aos pés de); **2** (*throw*) atirar (*ball, stone*) (**onto, into** para); **to ~ sb** (**to the ground**) atirar alguém por terra; **to ~ one's arms around sb's neck** abraçar, pôr os braços à volta do pescoço de alguém; **to ~ the door open** abrir de repente, abir de par em par.
flint *n* (*rock*) sílex *f*; **2** (*in lighter*) pedra *f* do isqueiro.
flip *n* piparote *m*; **2** (*AER, SPORT*) cambalhota *f*; ♦ *vt* (-**pp**-) dar a volta em; **2** (*toss*) lançar, atirar ao ar (**sth** algo); (*coin*) tirar cara ou coroa; virar (*pancake, egg*); **3** mover dum lado para o outro rapidamente; ♦ *vi* (*coll*) (*get angry*) zangar-se; **to ~ on, ~ off** (*switch*) ligar, desligar; **at the ~ of a switch** ao toque dum interruptor; **to ~ through** sth *vt* folhear, dar uma vista d'olhos por (*book, magazine*).
flip chart *n* (*used in meeting for writing*) quadro *m* de folhas soltas de papel.
flip-flop *n* (*slipper type*) chinelo *m* de praia.
flippancy *n* desembaraço, desenvoltura; **2** irreverência, falta de respeito.
flippant *adj* (*not serious*) petulante, desenvolto,-a; (*lacking respect*) irreverente.
flippantly *adv* irreverentemente; de maneira inconsiderada.
flipper *n* barbatana *f*; **2** (*fam*) mão *f*.
flipperty-flopperty *n* solto,-a, pendente.

flipping *adj adv (slang) (for emphasis)* tremendo, horrível; **what a ~ nuisance!** que raio de chatice!

flip side *n (of record)* lado B.

flirt *n* namorador,-deira *(EP)*; paquerador,-ora *(BR)*; ♦ *vi* namoriscar *(BR)* flirtar.

flirtation *n* namoro, namorico, *(BR)* flerte *m*; **2** interesse *m* passageiro em algo.

flirtatious *adj (smile, wink)* sedutor; **2** galanteador,-ora, flerte.

flit (-tt-) *vi (bird)* esvoaçar, voar; **2** *(person)* passar rapidamente; **to ~ from one thing to the other** passar/saltar duma coisa à outra.

flitch *n (a steak cut from certain fish)* posta; *(cut from the side of a tree)* talhada, lascada.

flix *n* pêlo de castor.

float *n* bóia *f*; **2** *(in procession)* carro alegórico; **3** *(money)* caixa; *(FIN) (in till)* fundo *m* de maneio; ♦ *vi* flutuar; boiar; **2** *(money)* circular; ♦ *vt* fazer flutuar; **2** *(company)* lançar, emitir.

floatable *adj* flutuável.

floater *n* flutuador,-ora; banhista que bóia; **2** pessoa de moralidade pouco sólida; **3** pequena mancha escura que aparece às vezes nos olhos.

floating *adj* flutuante; **2** variável; *(not attached)* solto,-a; ~ **voter** *n (POL)* eleitor *m* indeciso, eleitora *f* indecisa.

flock *n (of sheep, goats)* rebanho *m*; **2** *(of birds)* bando *m*; ~ **of birds** bando de passarinhos; **3** *(of people)* multidão *f*; ♦ *vi* afluir, congregar-se.

floe *n* massa *f* de gelo flutuante.

flog (-gg-) *vt* açoitar; chicotear; **2** *(coll)* empenhar, pôr no prego.

flogging *n* castigo *m*, punição *f*; açoite *m*.

flood *n* cheia, inundação *f*; torrente *f*; ♦ *vt* inundar; transbordar, jorrar; **in a ~ of tears** numa torrente de lagrimas; **~-gate** *n* comporta, dique *m*; **~ing** *n* inundação *f*; **~light** *n* holofote *m*; proje(c)tores *mpl*.

floor *n* chão *m*; pavimento; *(wooden)* soalho; **2** *(storey)* andar *m*, piso *m*; **3** *(of sea)* fundo; **4** pista de dança; **first ~** primeiro andar; **ground ~** *(US: **first ~**)* rés-do-chão, *(BR)* andar térreo; ~ **lamp** *n* candeeiro *m* de pé; ~ **manager** *n (COMM) (of large stores)* gerente *m,f* de se(c)ção; **2** *(TV)* dire(c)tor de estúdio; ~ **polish** *n* cera *f* (para o chão); ~ **polisher** *n* enceradora *f*; ~ **show** *n* espe(c)táculo *m (in cabaret, bar)*; ~ **walker** *n (in shops)* supervisor,-ora de se(c)ção; ♦ *vt* confundir, pasmar; **to take the ~** *(speech)* tomar a palavra.

floorboard *n* tábua *f* de soalho (BR: de assoalho).

flooring *n* pavimentação *f*; a(c)to de pavimentar, de assoalhar.

floozy *(pl: -ies)* *n (pej)* mulher leviana; *(fig) (pej)* puta *(cal)*.

flop *n* fracasso, fiasco, baque *m*; ♦ *vi* fracassar.

floppy *adj* frouxo,-a, mole *m,f*; **2** *(ears)* pendente *m,f* caído,-a; **~-eared rabbit** coelho de orelha pendente; ~ **hat** *n* chapéu de abas caídas; **3** *(clothes loose on body)* largo,-a.

floppy disk *n* disquete *f*.

flora *n (BOT)* flora.

floral *adj* floral.

Florence *npr* Florença; **in ~** em Florença.

florescence *n* florescência *f*.

floret *n* cada uma das flores que compõem um florão, florinha.

florid *adj* florido,-a; **2** *(ruddy)* corado,-a.

Florida *npr* Flórida; **in ~** na Flórida.

florist *n* florista *m,f*; **~'s (shop)** *n* florista, floricultura.

floss *n (of fine silky fibres)* fios de casulo ou de plantas; **2** *(for embroidery)* fio *m* seda; **3 dental ~** *(for cleaning teeth)* fio *m* dental.

flotation *(also: floatation)* *n (ECON)* flutuação *f*.

flotilla *n* flotilha *f*.

flotsam *n* destroços, restos de naufrágio; **2** viveiro *m* de ostras.

flounce *n (frill)* folho *m*; ♦ *vi* agitar-se com impaciência; **to ~ down** sentar-se com violência; **to ~ out of a room** retirar-se, de modo brusco, dum aposento.

flounder *n (fish)* solha *f*; ♦ *vi (be in difficulty)* debater-se **(in** em); *(on snow, mud)* andar com dificuldade; **2** *(in speech)* atrapalhar-se; **the project ~ed because of lack of funds** o proje(c)to atrapalhou-se devido à falta de capital.

flour *n* farinha; **2 ~-mill** moinho; **~-milling** fábrica de moagem; ♦ *vt* moer.

flourish *n (gesture)* gesto *m* teatral; floreado; ♦ *vi* florescer.

flourishing *adj* próspero,-a; **2** florescente *m,f*.

floury *adj* afarinhado, farinhento.

flout *vt* zombar, desrespeitar *(conventions, etc)*.

flouting *n* zombaria, chacota.

flow *n (of water, tide)* fluxo *m*; **2** *(of blood, transit)*, circulação *f*; **3** *(fig) (of time)* curso *m*; decurso *m*; ♦ *vi (traffic, speech, ideas)* fluir; **2** circular; **3** *(liquid, electricity)* correr; **4** *(hair)* correr, ondular, **her hair ~ed down her back** o cabelo dela corria solto pelas costas abaixo; **5** *(tide)* subir; **to ~ from** correr; **to ~ in/back** afluir/refluir; **to ~ into** *(river)* desaguar em; **in her long ~ing dress** no seu longo e elegante vestido; **in full ~** discursar fluente e entusiasticamente.

flow chart gráfico de operações; *(COMP)* organograma *m*, fluxograma m.

flower *n* flor *f*; ♦ *vi* florescer, florir; **in ~** em flor; **in the ~ of one's age** na flor *f* da idade; ~ **arrangement** *n* composição de flores; ~ **bed** *n* canteiro; **~-bud** *n* botão de flor; **~pot** *n* vaso *m*.

flowered *adj* florido,-a; com padrão/desenho de flores.

flowering *n (BOT)* floração *f*; **early/late ~** floração precoce/tardia; ♦ *adj* em flor.

flowery *adj* florido,-a; **2** *(dress)* às flores; **3** *(scent)* floral; **4** *(language, speech) (pej)* floreado,-a, com floreados.

flowing *n* inundação; ♦ *adj* corrente; **2** *(language, style)* fluente; **3** *(hair/dress)* solto,-a.

flown *(pp of fly)*.

flu *n (fam)* gripe *f*; **bird ~** gripe das aves, *(BR)* gripe aviária; **swine ~** gripe *f* suína, gripe A.

fluctuate *vi* flutuar.

fluctuating *adj* flutuante, variável.

fluctuation *n* flutuação *f*.

flue n tubo *(for smoke, steam from cooker)*; **2** *(of chimney) (stack)* cano m (de chaminé).

fluency n fluência, facilidade em falar.

fluent *adj* fluente; **he's ~ in Portuguese** ele fala português fluentemente.

fluently *adv* fluentemente.

fluff n *(down)* felpa *f*, penugem *f*.

fluffy (-ier, -iest) *adj* macio,-a; fofo,-a; felpudo,-a.

fluid *adj*, n fluido m; líquido m.

fluke n *(coll) (chance)* sorte, acaso feliz, obra do acaso; **to win by a ~** ganhar por um acaso; **by a ~** por uma questão de sorte.

flume n calha *f*; ravina com torrente.

flummery *(pl: -ies)* n *(nonsense)* disparate m, conversa tola.

flummox *vt (fam)* desconcertar, confundir, desorientar.

flump *vt* mover-se pesadamente, deixar cair ruidosamente; ♦ *exc* ~! *(in a fall)* pumba!

flung *(pt, pp of fling)*.

flunk *(mostly US) vt (fail exam)* chumbar *(EP, fam)*; levar pau *(BR, fam)*; ser reprovado,-a; **2** *(teacher)* reprovar *(class, student)*.

flunkey, flunky *adj (person)* servil, bajuladolor,-ora; **2** *(pej) (manservant in attire)* lacaio m.

fluoresce *vi* brilhar, entrar em fluorescência.

fluorescence n fluorescência.

fluorescent *adj* fluorescente.

fluoride n fluoreto m.

fluorine n *(CHEM)* fluor m.

flurry *(pl: -ies)* n *(shower, wind)* lufada *f*, **2** *(bustle)* agitação *f*; ~ **of activity** n azáfama *f*; **to be in a ~** andar numa lufa-lufa; **3** *(FIN)* ligero aumento dos preços das acções.

flush n *(blush)* rubor m; **2** *(in the sky)* clarão m vermelho; **3** *(surge of anger)* acesso de; **4** *(in toilet)* descarga *f* (do autoclismo); **5** *(full of)* **to be ~ with money** nadar em dinheiro; ♦ *adj (level)* ~ **with sth** nivelado,-a; ♦ *vt* lavar com água; inundar; **to ~ the toilet** puxar, descarregar o autoclismo *(EP)*; dara descarga na privata *(BR)*; ♦ *vi* ruborizar-se; **to ~ out** *(the dirt from pipes)* lavar o cano com ja(c)to de água; **to ~ out/from** *(person, animal)* fazer sair **(from** de) *(hiding place)*.

flushed *adj (red face)* ruborizado, corado; ~ **with happiness** radiante.

flushing n *(face)* rubor m; **2** limpeza (por jacto de água).

fluster n agitação *f*, excitação *f*.

flustered *adj* atrapalhado,-a.

flute n flauta.

flutist n flautista.

flutter n agitação *f*; **2** *(of eyelashes)* pestanejo m; **3** *(of wings)* bater m de asas; **4** *(of heart)* pulso m, palpitação *f*; **5** *(fam) (bet)* aposta *f*; ♦ *vt* bater *(as asas)* ruflar; esvoaçar; **2** *(eyelashes)* pestanejar; ♦ *vi (of wings, insects)* agitar; **the butterfly ~ed in the sun** a borboleta esvoaçava ao sol; **2** *(heart)* palpitar *(with excitement, etc)*; *(pulse)* bater fracamente; **3** *(flag, ribbons)* flutuar; **to be in a ~** estar todo agitado,-a, andar num rodopio; **to make a ~** causar sensação.

fluttering n agitação, excitação *f*; ruflar m (de asas).

fluvial *adj* fluvial.

flux n fluxo m, enchente *f*, torrente *f*; **2 in a state of ~** mudando continuamente.

fly *(pl: flies) (insect)* mosca *f*; **2** *(opening in trousers)* braguilha *f*; *(BR)* breguilha; **your ~ is undone** a sua braguilha está aberta; **~-past** n *(AER) (UK)* desfile m aéreo; **~-sheet** n *(on tent)* te(c)to duplo; ~ **spray** n bomba *f* insecticida; **~-weight** *(boxing)* peso mínimo, peso-mosca; **~wheel** n *(TECH)* volante m; **flies** *fpl (THEAT)* bambolinas *fpl*; ♦ *(pt flew, pp flown) vt* fazer voar; **2** *(transport by air)* transportar (de avião); **3** *(cover distance)* percorrer; **4** *(display flag)* hastear; ♦ *vi (gen)* voar; **2** *(go by air)* ir de avião; **3** *(pilot)* pilotar; **4** *(move fast)* voar; **time flies** o tempo voa; ♦ **to ~ a flag** arborar, hastear uma bandeira; **to ~ at sb** atacar subitamente; lançar-se sobre alguém; **to ~ across/over** *(place)* sobrevoar; **to ~ away** ir-se embora; **to ~ into a rage/temper** enfurecer-se; perder a paciência.

flyaway *adj (hair)* solto,-a; *(dress, hair)* ao vento.

fly-by-night *adj (person)* irresponsável *m,f*; **2** duvidoso,-a.

fly catcher m *(ZOOL)* papa-moscas m; **2** *(product)* mata-moscas m.

flyer *(Vd: fly)*.

flying n aviação *f*; voo m; ♦ *adj*: ~ **visit** *(fig)* visita *f* de médico; **2** *(exam, interview)* **with ~ colours** com êxito; ~ **officer** n *(UK)* tenente-voador; **~over** n *(UK)* viaduto m; **2** *(US)* desfile m aéreo; ~ **saucer** n disco voador; ~ **squad** n *(UK)* radiopatrulha *f*; ~ **start** n *(SPORT)* excelente partida.

FM n *(abbr for Field Marshal)* Marechal m; **2** *(abbr for frequency modulation) (RADIO)* FM.

foal n potro m; **to be in ~** estar prenhe.

foam n *(sea, bath, drink)* espuma; **2** *(on horse) (froth)* suor; *(dog, etc, from mouth)* baba; ♦ *vi (at the mouth)* espumar; deitar baba; ~ **rubber** n espuma de borracha.

foaming n espuma; ♦ *adj* cheio de espuma; **the dog is ~ at the mouth** o cão está a deitar baba, saliva; *(fig)* raivoso.

foamy (-ier, -iest) *adj (with bubbles)* coberto,-a de espuma; espumoso,-a; espumante.

fob n *(pocket in waistcoat)* pequena algibeira *f*; *(for pocket watch)* corrente *f*; berloque m; ♦ *(-bb-) vt* enganar; **to ~ sth off on sb** impingir algo a alguém; **to ~ sb off with excuses** dar desculpas a alguém *(BR)* escusas; desembaraçar-se de alguém com uma desculpa, escusa.

fob watch n relógio m de algibeira, de corrente.

focal *adj* focal; ~ **point** n ponto m central; **2** *(report, etc)* foco m.

focalize *vt* focar.

focus *(pl: -es)* n foco m; ♦ *vt* focar, *(BR)* enfocar; ♦ *vt* realçar; **to get the right ~** regular a focagem, **to ~ on** focar, focalizar; **in/out of ~** focado/desfocado.

focussed *adj (mentally)* concentrado,-a, determinado,-a; *(image)* focado,-a.

fodder n *(animal feed)* forragem *f*.

foe *n* inimigo,-a, adversário,-a, antagonista *m,f.*

foetal *adj* fetal.

foetus *n (MED)* feto *m.*

fog *n* nevoeiro *m; (mist)* neblina *f.*

fogey: old ~ *n (pej) (old-fashioned)* bota *f* de elástico.

foggy (-ier, -iest) *adj* cerrado de nevoeiro; **it's ~!** está enevoado; **2** *(fig) (notion)* confuso,-a indistinto,-a; **I haven't the foggiest idea** não tenho a mínima ideia.

fog-horn *n (NAUT)* sirene *f* (de nevoeiro).

foglights *npl* faróis *mpl* de nevoeiro.

foible *n* ponto fraco, lado fraco; pequena excentricidade.

foil *n* folha *f* metálica; **2** (= **kitchen ~**) folha, papel *m* de alumínio; **3** *(fencing)* florete *m;* ♦ *vt* desorientar, despistar.

foist *vt* impingir, enganar.

fold *n (crease)* vinco *m*, prega *f*, dobra *f; (on face, body)* ruga *f;* **2** *(AGR)* redil *m*, curral *m;* ♦ *vt* dobrar *(sheet, paper);* **to ~ one's arms** cruzar os braços; **to ~ s.o. in one's arms** abraçar, estreitar; ♦ *vi (collapse) (also: ~ up)* abrir falência; *(project)* fracassar; ♦ **~ away** dobrar e arrumar *(clothes);* **2** fechar *(chair);* ♦ **~ in** *(CULIN)* meter, deitar; **~ in the eggs** deite os ovos sem mexer.

folder *n (for papers)* dossier *m*, pasta; **2** *(brochure)* folheto *m.*

folding *adj (table, etc)* dobrável, flexível *m,f.*

foliage *n* folhagem *f.*

foliate *adj (ARCH) (design with leaves)* folheado,-a; **2** *(in layers)*, laminado,-a; ♦ *vt/vi* estanhar espelhos; laminar.

foliated *adj* laminado, em lâminas/lascas.

folic acid *n (CHEM)* ácido *m* fólico.

folio *n (book)* folio *m.*

folk *npl* gente *f*, povo; **~s** *npl* família *sg*, parentes *mpl;* **my ~s are coming to dinner** meus pais vêm jantar; ♦ *adj* popular, folclórico; **country ~** *npl* gente *f* das aldeias; **~ song** *n* canção *f* popular folclórica.

folklore *n* folclore *m.*

follicle *n* folículo *m.*

follow *vt* seguir; **you should ~ this road** você deve seguir este caminho; **2** *(understand)* compreender; **are you ~ing?** compreende-me?; **3** *(persue)* perseguir; **the police ~ed the thief** a polícia perseguiu o ladrão; ♦ *vi (come after)* seguir-se; **as ~s** como se segue; **2** *(result, as a consequence of)* resultar de; **she ~ed suit** ela fez o mesmo; **3 to ~ through** *vt* completar, levar a cabo *(task, project);* ♦ **to ~ up on** *vt* responder a *(advertisement);* **2** *(pursue, investigate)* seguir, investigar *(lead, story);* **3** dar continuidade a *(discussion, meeting).*

follower *n (of an artist, philosopher)* discípulo,-a; *(POL)* partidário,-a; *(of tradition, football)* adepto,-a.

following *n* seguinte *m;* **you need the ~** você precisa do seguinte; **2** séquito *m*, adeptos *mpl.*

follow-on *n* seguimento *m.*

follow-up *m (of film, story)* continuação (**of** de); *(MED) (after treatment)* acompanhamento *m;* **~ (with)** *(after an accident)* assistência *f* social.

folly *n* loucura; tolice *m*; extravagância *f.*

foment *vt* fomentar, promover, favorecer.

fomentation *n* fomentação, estímulo, apoio.

fond *adj (affectionate)* carinhoso,-a; **to be ~ of** gostar de.

fondant *n* doce que se derrete rapidamente na boca.

fondle *vt* acariciar.

fondling *n* carícia *f*, afago *m*, carinho *m;* ♦ *adj* carinhoso,-a.

fondness *n (liking)* gosto *m;* afeição *f;* **2** *(love)* ternura *f;* **3** *(inclination)* tendência *f.*

font *n* pia ba(p)tismal; **2** *(COMP)* fonte *f.*

food *n* comida *f;* **~ mixer** *n* batedeira; **~ poisoning** *n* intoxicação alimentar; **~stuffs** *npl* géneros *mpl* alimentícios; IDIOM **~ for thought** é caso pra pensar/dá que pensar.

fool *n* tolo,-a, bobo,-a; **April Fool's Day** *(first of April)* dia da mentira; **2** *(CULIN)* puré *m* de frutas com creme; ♦ *vt* enganar; ♦ *vi (gen: ~ around)* brincar; perder tempo; **to make a ~ of o. s.** fazer fraca figura; fazer papel de bobo; **2** *(affair)* andar metido com.

foolhardy *adj* temerário,-a; irrefletido,-a; imprudente.

foolish *adj (unwise)* imprudente; idiota; bobo,-a; **what a ~ thing!** que coisa tão estúpida!; **2** *(laughable)* ridículo,-a.

foolishly *adv* estupidamente, idioticamente.

foolishness *n* disparate *m*, tolice *f*, loucura *f*, patetice *f.*

foolproof *adj* infalível.

foolscap *m* (UK) *(size of paper)* papel *m* de ofício.

foot *(pl: feet) n (ANAT)* pé *m;* **2** (medida inglesa) pé (= 304 mm); **3** *(of dog, rabbit, cat)* pata *f;* ♦ **at the ~ of a mountain** no sopé da montanha; **on ~** a pé; **from head to ~** da cabeça aos pés; **to have/get cold feet** perder a coragem no último momento; **to put one's ~ down** ser firme, não ceder; **to help sb to her/his feet** ajudar alguém a levantar-se; **to be on one's feet again** estar restabelecido,-a; **to put one's ~ in it** *(fig)* cometer um lapso/uma gaffe; **to loose one's ~** desequilibrar-se; ♦ *exc* **my ~!** *(of disbelief)* ora adeus!, uma fava!; ♦ **~lights** *npl (THEAT)* ribalta *sg;* **~ling** *adj (fam) (person)* parvo,-a; *(thing)* trivial; mesquinho,-a; **~-loose** livre, sem compromissos; **~-soldier** *n (MIL)* soldado de infantaria; **~sore** *adj* com os pés doloridos; **~step** *n* passo; **~stall** *n* pedestal; **~stool** *n* banquinho para os pés; **~way** *n* caminho para peões; **~wear/gear** *n* calçado *m;* ♦ *vt (fam)* **to ~ the bill (for sth)** pagar a conta por algo; **2** *(AUT)* acelerar; IDIOM **one ~ in the grave** *(very old/dying)* com o pé na cova.

footage *n (of film)* metragem *f;* **2** *(measure)* comprimento *m* (em pés).

foot-and-mouth disease *n* febre *f* aftosa.

football *n* bola de futebol; *(game)* futebol *m;* **~ ground** *n* campo *m* de futebol; **~ match** *n* desafio *m*/partida *f* de futebol; **~ pools** *npl* (UK) totobola *f.*

footballer *n* futebolista *m.*

footbrake *n* travão *m* (BR: freio) de pé.

footbridge *n* passadiço, ponte para peões.

footer *n (COMP)* rodapé *m.*

footfault *n (tennis)* falta.

foothills *npl* contraforte *msg.*

foothold n apoio para o pé.

footing n pé m; base f; (fig) posição f; **to lose one's ~** escorregar; **to put sth on a legal ~** legalizar algo; **on an equal ~ with sb** em pé de igualdade com alguém.

footman n lacaio m.

footnote n nota de rodapé, ao pé duma página.

footpath n senda, vereda, caminho.

footprint n pegada f.

footsie: to play ~ brincar com o pé de alguém debaixo da mesa.

Footsie n (UK) (FIN) = **Financial Times Stock Exchange 100 index** = FTSE (Vd: **FTSE**).

footstep n passo m.

foozle n jogada que saiu mal (golfe); **2** trabalho malfeito.

fop n (man) (obsessed with fashion) janota m.

for prep (intention, purpose, reason) para; **these flowers are ~ you** estas flores são para si; **what for?** para quê?; (scheduled time) **I have an appointment with the doctor ~ 10 o'clock** tenho hora marcada com o médico para as dez horas; (opinion) **this coat is too big ~ her** este casaco é grande demais para ela; (expressing destination) (to) para; **I am going to Portugal ~ work** vou para Portugal trabalhar; **2** (on account of, for the sake of) por; **he fought ~ his country** ele lutou pelo seu país; **I shall speak ~ you** eu falarei por si; **as far as I am concerned, all is well, ~ me everything is O.K** por mim, está tudo bem; **3** (expressing time) por, durante; **he is going out ~ a few minutes** ele vai sair por uns minutos; **I saw him ~ the first time;** vi-o pela primeira vez; **4** (expressing price) por; **I bought the hat ~ £30** comprei o chapéu por 30 libras; **s** (apologising) **I am sorry ~ breaking your vase** peço desculpa por ter quebrado o jarrão; ♦ conj pois, porque; ♦ **as ~ me** quanto a mim; **~ as much as** porquanto; **~ all I know** tanto quanto sei; **~ certain** de certeza; **~ good ~ ever** para sempre; **~ or against?** a favor ou contra?; **once and ~ all** de uma vez por todas; "**~ sale**" "vende se"; **~ short** em suma; para abreviar; **~ the present** por agora; **~ the time being** por enquanto; IDIOM **I bought it ~ a song** comprei-o por uma pechincha.

forage n forragem f.

foray n incursão f.

forbade (pt of **forbid**).

forbear n antepassado,-a; ♦ vt/vi abster-se, reprimir-se; **to bear and ~** tolerar.

forbearance n paciência f; indulgência f.

forbears npl antepassados mpl.

forbid (pt **forbade**, pp **forbidden**) vt proibir.

forbidding adj lúgubre; severo,-a; ameaçador,-ora.

force n força f; ♦ vt forçar; **to ~ o.s. to** forçar-se a; **the F~s** npl Forças Armadas; **in ~** em vigor.

forced adj forçado,-a; **~ to do sth** obrigado a fazer algo.

force-feed vt alimentar à força.

forceful adj (power) forte m,f; **2** (words) contundente; **3** enérgico,-a; **a ~ argument** um argumento convincente.

forcefully adv energicamente.

forcemeat n (CULIN) recheio m de carne.

forceps npl fórceps m inv.

forcible adj eficaz; **2** (using force) feito,-a à força, contra vontade; **3** (argument) enégico, convincente.

forcibly adv à força.

ford n vau m; ♦ vt vadear.

fore n the front part; **2** (NAUT) proa ♦ adj dianteiro,-a; anterior; **~-tooth** dente da frente; **to bring to the ~** (subject) pôr em evidência, destacar-se, chamar a atenção.

forearm n antebraço; ♦ vt precaver, prevenir.

foreboding n presságio, mau pressentimento.

forecast n prognóstico; **weather ~** previsão f do tempo; ♦ (irr: like **cast**) vt prognosticar; prever.

forecaster n (MET) meteorologista m,f; **2** (ECON) analista m,f.

forecastle n (NAUT) castelo m de proa.

foreclose vt (FIN, JUR) executar uma hipoteca; ♦ **to ~ on sb** vi privar alguém do direito de resgatar uma hipoteca; **2** (shut out) excluir; **3** impedir excluir (possibility).

foreclosure n execução de uma hipoteca; **2** privação do direito de resgatar uma hipoteca.

forecourt n (COMM) área f de estacionamento.

foredoom vt pressagiar, predestinar.

forefathers npl antepassados mpl.

forefinger n (dedo) indicador m.

forefront n frente f, vanguarda; a primeira linha.

forego vt/vi = **forgo**.

foregoing adj antecedente; precedente; anterior.

foregone adj: **it's a ~ conclusion** é uma conclusão f antecipada, resultado m previsto.

foreground n primeiro plano.

forehand n jogada a direito, sem mudar de mão (ténis).

forehead n (ANAT) testa f.

forehold (NAUT) n porão m da proa.

forehook n (NAUT) grinalda f.

foreign n estrangeiro,-a; ♦ adj (from abroad) estrangeiro,-a; **2** (stranger, alien) estranho,-a, alheio,-a; **to lie is ~ to his nature** mentir é alheio à sua maneira de ser; **3** (trade, policy) externo,-a; **~ aid** n ajuda f internacional; **~ body** n corpo m estranho (in the eye, etc); **~ currency** n moeda f estrangeira; **~ exchange** n câmbio.

Foreign Affairs Negócios npl Estrangeiros, (BR) Relações fpl Exteriores.

foreignism n estrangeirismo m.

Foreign Office npr (UK) Ministério dos Negócios Estrangeiros.

Foreign Service n **the ~** o Serviço m Diplomático (in the UK).

forel n espécie de pergaminho para capas de livros.

foreland n cabo m; promontório m.

foreleg n (animal) perna f dianteira.

forelock n madeixa de cabelo sobre a testa; **2** (MEC) (peg in a bolt) chareta f.

foreman n capataz m; contramestre m; **2** chefe, principal; **3** (JUR) presidente de júri.

foremast (NAUT) n mastro junto à proa de navio.

foremost adj principal; eminente; melhor; ♦ **first and ~** antes de mais, em primeiro lugar.

forename *n* nome *m* de ba(p)tismo; primeiro nome.

forensic *adj* forense; ~ **medicine** medicina *f* legal; ~ **science** *n* ciência *f* forênsica.

forepeak *n* esporão, espigão na proa do de navio.

forerunner *n* (*person*) precursor-ora; **2** (*institution, theory*) antigo,-a; **3** sinal *m*, indício *m*.

foresee (*irr: like* **see**) *vt* prever.

foreseeable *adj* previsível *m,f*; **in the** ~ **future** num futuro próximo.

foreseen (*pp of* **foresee**) **it was** ~ era previsto, era de se esperar.

foreshadow *vt* pressagiar; prenunciar.

foreshore *n* parte da praia deixada a descoberto pela maré-baixa.

foreshortened *adj* condensado,-a.

foresight *n* clarividência *f*; perspicácia *f*.

foresighted *n* previdente *m,f*.

foreskin *n* prepúcio *m*.

forest *n* floresta; ◆ *vt* arborizar.

forestall *vt* prevenir; **2** açambarcar (mercadoria) (para vender com mais lucro).

forester *n* guarda florestal; **2** habitante da floresta.

forestry *n* silvicultura *f*.

foretaste *n* antegosto *m*; amostra *f*.

foretell (*irr: like* **tell**) *vt* predizer, profetizar.

foretelling *n* profecia, sinal *m* anunciador; ◆ *adj* profético,-a.

forethought *n* premeditação *f*; ◆ *adj* premeditado,-a.

foretold (*pp of* **foretell**).

forever *adv* para sempre; ~ **yours** tua para sempre.

forevermore *adv* sempre; **and** ~ e para sempre mais.

forewarn *vt* pressagiar, prevenir.

forewarning *n* aviso *m*; pressentimento *m*.

forewoman *n* (*JUR*) presidente de júri.

foreword *n* prefácio *m*, prólogo *m*.

forfeit *n* perda; **2** multa *f*; **game of** ~**s** jogo das prendas; ◆ *vt* perder (direito a).

forfeiture *n* perda de direitos por confiscação.

forgave (*pt of* **forgive**).

forge *n* forja; ferraria; oficina metalúrgica; ◆ *vt* falsificar; forjar; **to** ~ **ahead** *vi* avançar constantemente.

forged *adj* forjado; falsificado; ~ **iron** ferro forjado; ~ **scrap iron** sucata de ferro.

forger *n* ferreiro, ferrador; **2** falsificador, falsário.

forgery *n* falsificação; documento falsificado.

forget (*pt* **forgot**, *pp* **forgotten**) *vt* esquecer; ◆ *vi* esquecer-se (de); **forgive and** ~ perdoa e esquece; ◆ *exc* ~ **it!** não penses mais nisso!, (*drop the subject*) deixa lá isso!

forgetful *adj* esquecido,-a.

forgetfulness *n* esquecimento; descuido; falta de memória.

forget-me-not *n* (*flower*) miosótis *m*; (*pop*) não me esqueças.

forgettable *adj* que se esquece facilmente; para esquecer.

forgivable *adj* perdoável.

forgive (*pt* **forgave**, *pp* **forgiven**) *vt* perdoar; **to** ~ **sb for sth** perdoar algo a alguém.

forgiveness *n* perdão *m*.

forgiving *adj* clemente; **she is a** ~ **person** ela é uma pessoa que perdoa facilmente.

forgo (*irr: like* **go**) *vt* renunciar a; abster-se de.

forgoing *n* abstenção de; renúncia *f*; abandono *m*.

forgot (*pt of* **forget**).

forgotten (*pp of* **forgot**).

fork *n* (*for food*) garfo *m*; **2** (*farming tool*) forquilha; **3** (*road*) bifurcação *f*; ◆ *vi* bifurcar-se; **to** ~ **out** *vt* (*coll*) (*money*) desembolsar; ~**ed** *adj* em ziguezague; bifurcado,-a; ~**-lift truck** *n* empilhadeira *f*.

form *n* (*type, way of being/doing*) forma *f*, tipo *m*; **a** ~ **of entertainment** uma forma, um tipo de entretimento; **2** (*EDUC*) ficha *f*; (*questionnaire*) formulário *m*; **application** ~ ficha *f* de inscrição, de candidatura; **3** (*in school–year*) ano; **she is in the sixth** ~ ela está no décimo ano; **4** (*at the bank etc*) impresso *m*; **blank** ~ impresso em branco; **fill in this** ~ preencha este impresso; **5** (*health, condition*) aparência *f*; **in good** ~ em boa forma; **6** (*ART, etc*) (*kind*) género *m*; **true to** ~ como de costume, como era de esperar; ◆ *vt* formar, dar forma a; ◆ *vi* formar-se.

formal *adj* oficial; **2** (*event, dress*) de cerimónia, a rigor; (*person, speech*) cerimonioso,-a, formal; ~ **notice** um aviso oficial; ~ **education** ensino tradicional de educação.

formaldehyde *n* (*CHEM*) formaldeído.

formalin *n* (*CHEM*) formol *m*.

formalism *n* formalismo *m*.

formalist *n* formalista.

formalistic *adj* formalístico.

formality *n* (*social/legal convention*) formalidade *f*; **2** (*of occasion*) cerimónia *f*, etiqueta; **3** (*LING*) formalismo *m*; **formalities** *npl* formalidades *fpl*.

formalize *vt* (*make official*) oficializar; **2** (*in logic*) formalizar; **3** dar um aspecto rígido, convencional.

formally *adv* formalmente; cerimoniosamente.

format *n* formato *m*; ◆ (-**ted**) *vt* (*COMP*) formatar.

formation *n* (*gen*) formação *f*; estrutura *f*.

formative *adj* (*years, experience*) formativo,-a; de formação.

formatting *n* (*COMP*) formatação *f*.

former *n*: **the** ~ (*the first of two*) o primeiro; **the** ~ **is lazy and the latter is a liar** o primeiro/aquele é mandrião e o segundo/este é um mentiroso; ◆ (*in compounds*) **the sixth** ~ (*UK*) (*EDUC*) aluno de sexto ano; **2** (*previous, ex*) anterior, precedente; ex-; **your** ~ **husband** oteu ex-marindo; (*older times*) antigo,-a; **of** ~ **times** de antigamente; de tempos idos.

formerly *adv* antigamente; (*previously*) antes.

form feed *n* alimentação *f* de formulário.

formica® *n* (*placa usada em mobília*) fórmica *f*.

formicant *adj* (*MED*) formicante.

formication *n* (*itching*) formicação *f*; formigueiro *m*.

formidable *adj* (*intimidating*) terrível, temível; **2** (*inspiring*) impressionante, formidável.

forming *n* formação *f*; constituição *f*.

formless *adj* informe.

formol *n* (*CHEM*) formol *m*.

Formosa *npr* Formosa *f*; **in** ~ na Formosa.

formula *n* fórmula *f*.

formulary (*pl:* -**ies**) *n* formulário *m*; ♦ *adj* formal.
formulate *vt* formular; exprimir; elaborar.
formulation *n* formulação *f*; elaboração *f*.
fornicate *vi* fornicar.
fornication *n* fornicação *f*.
forsake (*pt* **forsook**, *pp* **forsaken**) *vt* abandonar; renunciar a.
forsaking *n* renúncia *f*; acto de pôr de parte.
forswear (*pt* **forswore**; *pp* **forsworn**) *vt* (*formal*) repudiar; renegar; **2** (*JUR*) (*perjure*) cometer perjúrio, negar.
fort *n* forte *m*, fortaleza *f*; **to hold the** ~ tomar conta de algo (para alguém).
forte *n* (*strong point*) forte *m*; **2** (*MUS*) música forte, com força.
forth *adv* para adiante; **back and** ~ de cá para lá; **and so** ~ e assim por diante; (*onwards*) **from this** ~ a partir de hose.
forthcoming *adj* (*book, event*) próximo,-a; **2** disponível; **3** (*person*) comunicativo,-a.
forthright *adj* franco,-a; dire(c)to,-a, frontal *m,f*.
forthrightness *n* franqueza *f*; frontalidade *f*.
forthwith *adv* imediatamente.
fortieth *adj* quadragésimo,-a.
fortification *n* (*act of fortifying*) fortificação *f*; **2** (*structure*) forte *m*.
fortify (*pt, pp* -**ied**) *vt* (*place*) fortificar; **2** (*fig*) (*person, decision*) fortalecer.
fortitude *n* determinação *f*; fortaleza *f* (de espírito); força *f* moral.
fortnight *n* quinzena *f*.
fortnightly *adj* quinzenal; ♦ *adv* quinzenalmente.
fortress *n* fortaleza *f*.
fortuitous *adj* (*accidental*) fortuito, casual.
fortunate *adj:* **to be** ~ ter sorte; **it is** ~ **that**... é uma sorte que...
fortunately *adv* felizmente.
fortune *n* sorte *f*, fortuna; ~-**hunter** *n* caçador *m* de dotes; ~**s** *npl* destino *fpl*; ~-**teller** *n* cartomante *m,f* vidente *m,f*.
forty *num* quarenta *m inv*.
forum (*pl:* **fora**) *n* (*HIST*) fórum, praça *f* pública; **2** debate.
forward *n* (*SPORT*) avançado *m*, atacante *m*; ♦ *adj* dianteiro,-a; **2** (*cheeky*) descarado, impudente; **3** (*advanced*) prematuro,-a, precoce; ♦ *vt* (*send on-letter, parcel*) enviar, expedir, fazer seguir; **2** (*return to sender*) remeter; **3** (*make progress*) progredir; ♦ *adv* para a frente; **from this day** ~ a partir de hoje; **to move** ~ avançar; **to put the clock** ~ adiantar o relógio; **to step** ~ dar um passo em frente; **to wind sth** ~ (*video, tape*) bobinar algo para a frente.
forward delivery *n* (*COMM*) entrega *f* numa data futura.
forwarder *n* (*of mail*) expeditor; (*of freight*) transitário.
forwarding *n* (*COMM*) expedição *f*; despacho *m;* **no** ~ **address** endereço desconhecido do destinatário; ~ **to new address** remeter para novo endereço.
forward-looking *adj* (*person*) de visão; **2** (*project*) prospe(c)tivo,-a.

forwardness *n* (*insolence*) atrevimento *m*, insolência *f*; (*from child*) impertinência *f*.
forwards *adv* = **forward.**
forward slash *n* barra *f* inclinada (para a frente).
forwent (*pt of* **forgo**).
fossil *n* fóssil *m*; **2** (*pej*) pessoa antiquada; fóssil; ~ **fuel** *n* combustível *m* fóssil.
fossilize *vt* fossilizar.
foster *adj* (*father, mother, son, daughter*) de criação *vt* criar/proteger uma criança; **2** (*idea, plan*) fomentar; encorajar; ~ **family** família de acolhimento; **in** ~ **care** sob prote(c)ção.

De notar que 'foster' em relação a crianças e pais, não significa adotivo.

fought (*pt, pp of* **fight**).
foul *n* (*SPORT*) falta *f*; ♦ *adj* (*filthy*) (*conditions, place*) repugnante *m,f*; imundo,-a; **2** (*smell, breath*) fétido,-a; **3** (*person, taste*) nojento,-a; **4** (*language*) grosseiro,-a; obsceno,-a, ordinario,-a; **5** (*criminal*) odioso,-a; **it was a** ~ **deed** foi uma infâmia; **6** (*grim*) (*weather, mood*) horrível *m,f*, péssimo,-a; **she is in a** ~ **mood** ela está de péssimo humor; ♦ *vt* (*make dirty*) sujar; poluir; **2** (*SPORT*) (*obstruct*) cometer uma falta; **3** (*rope*) enredar(-se).
foul play *n* (*SPORT*) jogada *f* suja; **2** a(c)ção *f* traiçoeira ou criminosa.
foul smelling *adj* nauseabundo,-a.
foul up *n* trapalhada *f* asneirada *f*; ♦ *vt* estragar, fazer trapalhada.
foul water *n* água estagnada.
found (*pt, pp of* **find**) *vt* fundar; **she has** ~ **my cat** ela achou o meu gato.
foundation *n* fundação *f*; base *f*; **2** (= ~ **cream**) creme *m* base; **3** ~**s** *npl* alicerces *mpl*, fundações *mpl*.
founder *n* fundador,-ora; ♦ *vi* (*sink*) afundar-se; **2** (*fig*) fracassar.
foundering *n* afundamento *m*; submersão *f*.
founder member *n* sócio-fundador *m*; sócia-fundadora *f*.
founding *n* fundação *f* (**of**, de); ~ **father** *n* pai-fundador.
foundling *n* criança enjeitada, abandonada pelos pais; ~ **hospital** hospício para as crianças abandonadas pelos pais.
foundry *n* fundição *f*.
fount *n* (*LITER*) (*source*) origem *f*, fonte; ~ **of all knowledge** fonte de sabedoria; **2** fonte *f*, nascente *f*; **3** (*spelling variant of* **font**).
fountain *n* fonte *f*; fontanário; **2** ~ **pen** *n* caneta de tinta permanente, (*BR*) caneta-tinteiro.
four *num* quatro; ♦ *adj* **on all** ~**s** de gatas; (*BR*) de quatro; ~-**figure** *adj* (*amount, sum*) com quatro algarismos; ~-**footed** *n* quadrúpede *m*; ~-**letter word** *n* palavrão *m*, asneira *f* feia; ~-**poster** *n* cama *f* de dossel; ~**some** *n* grupo de quatro pessoas; ~**score** (*dated*) oitenta; ~-**stroke** *adj* (*AUT*) (*engine*) a quatro tempos; ~-**wheel brake** travão às quatro rodas; ~-**wheel drive** (*AUT*) tracção às quatro rodas; **to the** ~ **winds** aos quatro ventos.

fourforld adj adv quádruplo; quatro vezes mais; **to increase** ~ quadruplicar.

fourteen num catorze.

fourteenth num décimo quarto.

fourth num, adj quarto; **one** ~ um quarto; ~ **rate** adj (hotel, etc) de terceira categoria; **the** ~ **of July** quatro de julho; **George IV (fourth)** Jorge IV (quarto).

> Todos os anos, os americanos, por todo o mundo, celebram o 4 de Julho, dia da independência dos E.U.A.

fourthly adv em quarto lugar.

fowl n ave f de capoeira; ~**ing** n caça a aves para subsistência ou desporto.

fox n (ZOOL) raposa f; ~ **cub** n filhote de raposa; raposinho,-a; ♦ vt (outwit) lograr, enganar; **2** (baffle) desconcertar, atordoar, deixar alguém perplexo,-a.

foxglove n (BOT) dedaleira f.

foxhole n toca f de raposa; **2** (for soldier) trincheira f.

fox-hound cão de caça à raposa.

fox-hunt caça à raposa; **to play the** ~ ser matreiro, usar de manha.

foxtrot n foxtrote m.

foxy adj (crafty) manhoso,-a, astuto,-a; **2** (sexy) sexy, atraente; **3** semelhante à raposa.

foyer n vestíbulo, (THEA) foyer.

fr. (abbr for **franc**) franco m.

Fr (abbr for **friar**) frade m.

fracas n desordem f, rixa f.

fraction n (MATH) fra(c)ção f; **2** (a little bit) um pouquinho; **a** ~ **too big** um pouco grande demais.

fractional adj fra(c)cionário,-a; **2** (difference) ínfimo,-a; pequeníssimo,-a.

fractionally adv ligeiramente.

fracture n (MED) fra(c)tura f; ♦ vt fra(c)turar.

frag (-gg-) vt (US) (slang) matar soldado-colega com explosivo deliberadamente.

fragile adj frágil.

fragility n fragilidade f; fraqueza f.

fragment n fragmento m; ♦ vi fragmentar-se.

fragmentary adj fragmentário.

fragrance n fragrância, aroma, perfume.

fragrant adj fragrante, perfumado.

frail adj frágil m,f; fraco,-a; delicado,-a.

frailty n (of person) fragilidade f; **2** (of state, structure) fraqueza, debilidade f.

frame n estrutura; talhe m; **2** (TECH) armação f; **3** (for pictures) moldura f; **4** (for window) caixilho m; ♦ vt encaixilhar; **2** (subject) contextualizar formular; **3** (fam) incriminar; tramar; IDIOM ~ **of mind** n estado de espírito.

framed adj com armação; com moldura ou caixilho; estruturado; **2** incriminado,-a; tramado,-a.

framer n armador m; moldureiro m.

frame-up n (coll) armadilha f, cilada f.

framework n armação f; **2** (of building) esqueleto m; **3** estrutura f; base f; **legal** ~ quadro m jurídico.

franc n (antiga unidade monetária francesa) franco m.

France npr França; **in** ~ na França.

franchise n (POL) direito m de voto; sufrágio; **2** (COMM) franquia f; concessão f; ~**holder/agent** n concessionário,-a; ♦ vr (COMM) (sub-contract) concessionar (services, product).

franchising n franchising.

Franciscan n adj (monk, order) franciscano,-a.

francium n (metal) frâncio m.

Francophile adj francófilo,-a.

Francophobe adj francófobo,-a.

Francophone adj francófono,-a.

frangipane n (almond-flavoured tart) pastel m de amêndoa almiscarado; frangipana f.

frangipani n (perfum, shrub with strong scent) frangipana.

frank adj (honest, open) franco,-a, aberto,-a, sincero,-a; ♦ vt (Post) franquear.

Frank npr (race) franco.

frankfurter n salsicha f defumada.

frankincense n olíbano m; incence.

franking n franquia; ~ **machine** n máquina f de selagem/de franquear.

frankly adv francamente.

frankness n franqueza.

frantic adj (activity, excitement) frenético,-a; **2** (desperate) desesperado,-a, desvairado,-a; **3** (person) fora de si; **to drive someone** ~ fazer perder a cabeça a alguém.

frantically adv freneticamente.

fraternal adj fraterno.

fraternally adv fraternalmente, fraternamente.

fraternity n fraternidade f; (US) congregação f; clube m de estudantes; (of Order) confraria f.

fraternize vi confraternizar; **to** ~ **with sb** confraternizar-se com alguém; (pej) dar-se com alguém.

fraud n (crime) fraude f; (person) impostor,-ora; **computer** ~ n fraude f informática.

Fraud Squad npr departamento m de investigação de fraudes.

fraudster n impostor; pessoa que comete fraude.

fraudulent adj fraudulento,-a; **2** (signature) falsificado,-a; **3** (statement) falso,-a.

fraught adj: ~ **with sth** cheio de, repleto de.

fray n (LITER) luta, rixa f; ♦ vi esfiapar-se; desgastar; **my nerves were** ~**ed** estava com os nervos em frangalhos/em franja (fam).

frayed adj (clothes, curtains) coçado,-a, esfiapado,-a; **2** (nerves) em franja.

frazzle vt: **to burn sth to a** ~ calcinar algo; **to be** ~**d** estar estafado,-a (fam).

freak n (deformed person) anormal m,f; **2** (strange person) (fig) excêntrico,-a; **3** (event) anomalia; aberração f; **a** ~ **of nature** um aborto da natureza; **4** (enthusiast) fanático,-a de; ♦ **to** ~ **out** vi (fam) (get angry) encolerizar-se, ir aos ares (fam).

freakish n grotesco,-a; **2** esquisito,-a; fora do vulgar, excêntrico,-a.

freakishly adv duma maneira bizarra/fora do comum.

freckle n (on skin) sarda f.

freckled, freckly (person) adj sardento,-a; **2** (animal) malhado,-a.

free *adj (unrestricted)* livre; **feel ~ to speak/to do** fale/faça à vontade; **2** *(unattached)* livre; **I am a ~ woman** sou uma mulher livre/solteira; **to break ~ from/of** libertar-se de *(obligation, person)*; **3** *(released)* solto,-a, em liberdade; **to set ~** libertar *(person, animal)*; **4** *(no charge)* gratuito,-a; **5** *(not affected by)* sem; **~ from worries** sem preocupações; **~ and easy** *adj (person)* descontraído,-a; à vontade; **~ assets** *npl* bens *mpl* de raiz livres; **~ enterprise** *n* iniciativa *f* privada; **~ fall** *n (SPORT)* queda *f* livre; **~-for-all** *n (brawl)* desordem *f* geral, *(BR)* quebra-quebra *m*; **~-handed** *adj* generoso,-a, liberal *m,f*; **~hold** *n* propriedade *f* livre e alodial; **~holder** proprietário de casa/terra alodial; **~ kick** *(football, rugby)* tiro *m* livre; pontapé *m* (na bola) livre; **~thinker** *n* pensador livre; **~ trade** *(Vd:* **~market***)*; **~way** *n (US)* autoestrada; **~wheel** *vi (AUT)* ir em ponto morto; *(cyclist)* andar sem parar; **~ will** *n* livre arbítrio *m*; vontade *f* própria; **to do sth of one's own ~** fazer algo de sua livre vontade; ♦ *adv (no payment)* grátis; *(coll)* de borla, de graça; ♦ *vt* pôr em liberdade; soltar; **2** isentar alguém *(of blame, duty)*; ♦ *vr* **to ~ o.s.** libertar-se; IDIOM **to have a ~ hand** ter carta branca.

free *suffix* sem; **salt-~** sem sal.

freebie *n (coll: free gift)* brinde *m*.

freebooter *n* pirata *m*.

freebootering *n* pirataria.

freedom *n* liberdade *f*; **~ fighter** *n* combatente *m,f* da liberdade.

freelance *n* trabalhador,-ora independente; *(profession)* *n* profissão *f* liberal; ♦ *adv (writer, etc)* por conta própria.

freely *adv* livremente; à vontade.

free market *n* comércio *m* livre.

freemason *n* mação *m*; pedreiro-livre *m*.

freemasonry *n* maçonaria.

free range *adj (chicken, eggs)* caseiro,-a.

free ride *adj (car)* boleia *f*; *(BR)* carona *f*; *(on carousel, etc)* gratuito.

freesia *n (BOT)* freesia *f*.

freestone *n* grés, arenito *m*.

freeze *(pt* froze, *pp* frozen*)* *vi* gelar-se, congelar-se; ♦ *vt* gelar; congelar, enregelar; *n* congelação *f*; *(BR)* congelamento.

freeze-dried *adj* congelado a vácuo.

freeze-dry *vt* liofilizar.

freeze-out *n* ♦ *vt* boicotar, eliminar (goods).

freeze-over *vr* gelar *(lake)*; **freeze-up** *n* congelação da água *(in car)*.

freezer *n* congelador *m*.

freezing[1] *n (METEOR)* zero-graus; ♦ *adj (room, house)* gelado,-a.

freezing[2] *adj* gelado,-a; **~ point** *n* ponto de congelação *(BR:* congelamento*)*; **6 degrees below ~** 6 graus abaixo de zero.

freight *n* carga; frete *m*; carregamento; **~ car** *n (US)* vagão de mercadorias *(BR:* carga*)*; ♦ *vt* transport goods by freight; **to be ~ed with** (**laden with**) estar sobrecarregado,-a; **each word was ~ with** meaning cada palavra estava carregada de significado.

freightage *n* acto de fretar, fretagem; transporte de mercadorias.

freighter *n* fretador; agente de transportes.

freightliner *n* comboio rápido de mercadorias.

French *npr, adj* francês, francesa; *n (língua)* francês *m*; **the F~** os franceses *mpl*; **~ bean** *n* feijão *m* verde; *(BR, Reg)* vagem *f*; **~ door** *n* porta *f* envidraçada que dá para o jardim; **~ dressing** *n* molho *m* vinagrete; *(US)* molho rosé; **~ fries** *npl* batatas *fpl* fritas; **~ horn** *n* trompa *f*; **~ kiss** *n* linguado *m (col)*; **~ letter** *n (UK: fam) (condom)* camisinha *f*; **~ polish** *n* verniz para madeira; **~ toast** *n (Portuguese dessert made of bread, eggs, milk, sugar)* fatias douradas *or* rabanadas; **~ window** *n* janela *f* de sacada envidraçada.

frenchify *vt* afrancesar, afrancesar-se.

frenzied *adj* frenético,-a; enlouquecido,-a.

frenzy *n* frenesim *m*, *(BR)* frenesi *m*, furor *m*.

frequency *(pl:* -ies*)* *n* frequência *f*.

frequence *n* frequência *f*.

frequent *adj* frequente; ♦ *vt* frequentar.

frequently *adv* frequentemente, a miúdo.

fresco *(pl:* -es*)* *n* fresco *m*.

fresh *adj (food)* fresco,-a; **2** *(coffee, bread)* acabado de fazer; **3** *(idea, evidence)* novo,-a; **4** *(beginner)* noviço,-a; **5** *(air)* puro; **6** *(drink – cool)* fresco,-a.

freshen *vt* renovar; **to ~ up** *vi* refrescar-se; lavar-se.

fresher *n (fam: 1st year university student)* caloiro,-a, calouro,-a.

freshly *adv* novamente; recentemente, recém.

freshness *n* frescura *f*.

fresh water *n* água *f* doce.

fret *n* desenho repetitivo de linhas geométricas; **2** *(MUS)* trastes *(in violin. guitar)*; **3** agitação das águas; ♦ *(-tt-)* *vi* afligir-se, arreliar-se; **what are you ~ting about?** que se passa contigo? **2** corroer, estar corroído; **3** *(road)* estar descalcetado,-a; com buracos.

fretful *adj* irritável; *(child)* rabugento,-a; mal-disposto,-a; *(night, sleep)* agitado,-a.

fretfulness *n* agitação *f* (das águas); rabugice *f*.

fretsaw *n* serra *f* tico-tico.

fretted *adj* com ornamentações em relevo (no te(c)to, etc).

fretting *n* ornamentação *f*; **2** *(worry)* arrelia *f*.

fretwork *n* obra de talha; ornamentação (de teto).

Freudian *adj* Freudiano, de Freud; **~ slip** *n* lapso *m*.

friable *adj* friável; frágil; quebradiço,-a.

friar *n* frade *m*; (título) Frei; **F~ Anton** Frei Antão; **Black ~** frade dominicano; **Grey ~** frade franciscano; **White ~** carmelita.

friary *n* convento de frades, mosteiro *m*.

fribble *n* disparate; frivolidade; ♦ *vt* entreter-se, passar o tempo com futilidades.

fricassee *n (CULIN)* fricassé.

friction *n* fricção *f*; **2** atrito; desacordo.

frictional *adj* de atrito, de fricção; **~ electricity** electricidade produzida por atrito.

frictionally *adv* por atrito, por fricção.

Friday *npr* sexta-feira *f.*

fridge *n* frigorífico, *(BR)* geladeira; ~-**freezer** *n* frigorífico-congelador *m.*

fridge *n (coll)* frigorífico *m.*

fried *(pt, pp of* **fry***).*

friend *n* amigo; **a ~ of mine** um amigo meu; **bosom ~** amigo íntimo; **2 my honourable ~** o ilustre deputado (na Câmara dos Comuns); **3 my learned ~** o meu ilustre colega (entre advogados no tribunal); **to make ~ with** tornar-se amigo de; **he is ~ with** ele é amigo de; IDIOM **a ~ in need is a ~ indeed** os amigos são para as ocasiões.

friendless *adj* desamparado,-a, sem amigos.

friendliness *n* simpatia.

friendly *adj* amigável; simpático,-a.

friendship *n* amizade *f.*

fries *npl* batatas *fpl* fritas.

Friesian (cow) *n* vaca *f* holandesa.

frieze *n (ARCH)* friso *m.*

frigate *n* fragata *f.*

fright *n* susto *m;* pavor *m;* **to get a ~** apanhar *(BR:* levar) um susto; **to give someone a ~** pregar um susto a alguém; **to take a ~ at** ter medo de; **2** *(coll)* **she is a ~** ela é um pavor.

frighten *vt* assustar, amedrontar; **to ~ away/off** *vt* espantar.

frightened *adj* assustado,-a; amedrontado,-a.

frightening *adj (experience)* assustador,-ora.

frightful *adj* assustador,-ora, horrível.

frightfully *adv* terrivelmente.

frigid *adj (MED)* frígido; **2** *(person, manner)* frio,-a, distante *m,f.*

frigidity *n* frieza *f; (MED)* frigidez *f.*

frill *n* folho *m;* ~**s** *n* floreados; **2 pleated ~** plissado,-a; **3** *(coll)* **to put on ~s** armar, proceder com afectação.

frilled *adj* aos folhos; com pregas, pregueado; **2** *(gathered)* franzido,-a.

frillies *n (coll)* folhos, *mpl.*

frill-necked lizard *n (ZOOL)* lagarto da Austrália.

frilly (-ier, -iest) *adj* franzido; com folhos.

fringe *n (hair; for shawl)* franja *f;* **2** *(border)* orla *f,* margem *f;* **on the ~ of society** à margem da sociedade; **3** *(of town)* periferia *f;* ~ **benefit** *n* benefício *m* adicional; vantagem *f* suplementar; ~ **benefits** *npl* regalias; ~ **group** *n* fa(c)ção *f;* ~ **theatre** *n* teatro de vanguarda; ♦ *vt (put trim on clothes, curtain)* ornar (de franjas); *(arrange border with trees)* orlar.

fringed *adj (clothes)* com franjas; **2** *(edged)* orlado,-a, ladeado,-a.

Frisian Islands *npr pl:* **the ~** as Ilhas *fpl* Frísias.

frisk *vt (security check)* revistar *(person);* ♦ *vi* saltar; brincar; pular.

frisky (-ier, -iest) *adj (fam)* brincalhão *m,* bricalhona *f;* duma maneira brincalhona.

frit-fly *n (harmful to cereals)* mosca *f* do trigo.

fritter *n (CULIN) (sweet)* fritura; fritos; ♦ **to ~ away** *vt* desperdiçar *(time, money).*

Fritz *npr* alcunha dada aos alemães pelos ingleses.

frivol *vt (US)* passar o tempo com bagatelas, frivolidades.

frivolity *n* frivolidade *f;* futilidade *f.*

frivolous *adj* frívolo,-a.

frizz *vt* frisar.

frizzy *adj (hair)* frisado,-a.

fro *(Vd:* **to***).*

frock *n* vestido *m;* **2** hábito *m* de monge.

frock coat *n (man's) (dated)* sobrecasaca *f.*

frog[1] *n (ZOOL)* rã *f;* ~**man** *n* homem-rã *m;* ~-**spawn** *n* ova *f,* ovos de rã; ♦ **to ~ march** *vt (of prisoner)* arrastar/levar à força (pelos braços e pernas). IDIOM **to have a ~ in one's throat** ter pigarro.

frog[2] *(feature of militry uniform)* alamar.

Frog, Froggy *n* alcunha dada aos franceses pelos ingleses.

frolic *n (fun, merryment)* brincadeira *f;* galhofa *f;* ♦ *(pt, pp* **frolicked***) vi* brincar, divertir-se.

frolicsome *adj (fond of merrymaking)* brincalhão *m,* brincalhona *f,* folgazão *m,* folgazona *f.*

from *prep (origin, source)* de; ~ **afar** de longe; ~ **end to end** de ponta a ponta; **they are ~ London** eles são de Londres; **where is he ~?** de onde/donde é ele? *(in comparatives)* de; ~ **bad to worse** de mal a pior; *(expressing time, distance)* **as ~ today** a partir de hoje; ~ **now on** d'ora avante, de agora em diante; **the shops are far ~ here** as lojas são longe daqui; *(expressing protection)* **sheltered ~ the rain** protegido da chuva; **2** *(time span) (since)* desde; ~ **the age of ten** desde os 10 anos (de idade); ~ **day one** desde o primeiro dia; **3** *(by)* por; ~ **experience** por experiência própria; ~ **her appearance, I would say** pela aparência, eu diria; **4** *(among)* entre; **to select/choose ~ among** escolher entre; *(subtraction)* menos; **thirteen ~ 22 leaves 9** 22 menos 13 são 9.

frond *n (a kind of fern, seaweed)* fronde *f,* fronda *f.*

frondose *adj* frondoso, abundante em folhas, em ramos (a árvore).

front *n (of house)* fachada *f,* frente *f;* **2** *(of fabric) (side)* direito *m;* **3** *(of book)* capa *f;* **4** *(MIL, POL)* frente; **5** *(sea front)* orla *f* marítima, beira-mar *f;* **6** *(fig) (outward appearance)* fachada *f;* ♦ *adj (window, garden, door)* da frente; **2** *(seat, tyre, animal's leg/paw)* dianteiro,-a; ~ **desk** *n* rece(p)ção; ~ **door** *n* porta principal; ~**page/row** primeira página/fila; ♦ *adv* na frente, à frente; **who is in ~?** quem está à frente, quem está primeiro?; ♦ *prep* **in ~ of** *(in presence of sb; opposite sth)* em frente de; ♦ *vt (facing) (house)* ser de frente para; dar para; **2** *(lead)* estar à frente de; **3** *(person, etc)* servir de cobertura a *(dubious group).*

frontage *n (ARCH)* frontaria *f;* fachada *f* principal.

frontal *adj* frontal *m,f.*

frontbench *n (POL: UK) (in House of Commons)* banco *f* da frente/dianteira (onde se sentam os líderes do governo ou da oposição); ~**benchers** ministros do governo ou da oposição.

frontier *n* fronteira.

frontispiece *n* frontispício *m.*

front-line *n (MIL)* linha *f* da frente.

frontman *(of group)* representante; **2** *(figurehead)* testa *f* de ferro; **3** *(TV)* apresentador.

fronton *n (ARCH)* frontão *m.*

frontroom *n (UK)* salão *m*, sala de estar.

front-runner *n* favorito,-a (**for** para); **2** *(runner in lead)* corredor à cabeça da corrida.

front-wheel drive *n* tra(c)ção *f* dianteira.

frost *n* geada *f*, gelo *m*; **~bite** *n* frieira *f*; **~bitten** *adj* gelado,-a; enregelado,-a; ♦ **to ~ over/up** *vi (windscreen)* cobrir-se de geada.

frosted *adj (person, body)* enregelado,-a; **2** *(glass)* vidro *m* fosco; *(drinking glass, mirror)* embaciado,-a; **3** *(plant)* queimado,-a; **4** *(cake)* coberto de glacé; **5** *(garden)* coberto de geada.

frostily *adv* friamente.

frosting *n (on cake)* glacé *m*.

frosty *adj* coberto,-a de geada; gélido,-a.

froth *n (gen)* espuma; **2** *(fig) (trivia)* banalidades, futilidades *fpl*; ♦ *vi (gen)* espumar; **to ~ at the mouth** *(MED, ZOOL) (fig)* espumar; *(with anger)* espumar de raiva.

frothy *adj* espumoso; **2** *(fig)*; fútil.

frown *n* olhar *m* carrancudo, franzimento da testa; ♦ *vi* franzir as sobrancelhas; franzir, carregar o sobrolho; **~ on/upon** criticar; **her behaviour was ~ed upon** o comportamento dela foi malvisto.

frowning *adj* carrancudo; de sobrancelhas carregadas.

froze *(pt of* **freeze**).

frozen *(pp of* **freeze**) *adj (lake, person)* gelado,-a; **to be ~ still/to the bones** estar transido,-a de frio, gelado,-a até aos ossos; **2** *(ECON, FIN) (assets, prices, salaries)* congelado,-a.

FRS *(abbr for* **Fellow of the Royal Society**) membro da R. S. = associação dedicada à pesquisa científica.

fructiferous *adj* frutífero,-a.

frugal *adj* frugal *m,f*.

frugality *n* frugalidade; sobriedade.

frugally *adv* sobriamente; economicamente.

fruit *npl inv* fruto, -a; **to bear ~** dar frutos; *(fig)* dar resultados; ♦ *vi* dar frutos.

fruitcake bolo inglês com passas; **2** *(coll) (mad)* maluco,-a.

fruiterer *n* fruteiro; **~'s (shop)** frutaria *f*.

fruit-farming pomicultura.

fruitful *adj (soil, tree)* fértil, fecundo,-a; **2** *(partnership)* produtivo,-a, proveitoso,-a.

fruitfully *adv* com sucesso; **2** *(spend time)* de modo útil.

fruit-grower *n* pomicultor.

fruition *n*: **to come to ~** realizar-se.

fruit juice *n* sumo *m (BR)* suco *m* de fruta.

fruitless *adj* sem fruto; improdutivo; *(soil, tree)* estéril; **2** *(fig)* em vão, sem resultado.

fruit machine *n (UK)* caça-níqueis *m inv*.

fruity *adj (aroma, sabor)* a fruta, frutado,-a; **2** *(joke)* picante; sabor a escândalo; **3** *(voice)* sonante *m,f*.

frumpish, frumpy *adj* mulher desmazelada, malvestida ou fora da moda.

frustrate *vt* frustrar.

frustrated *adj* frustrado, desapontado, desiludido.

frustration *n* frustração *f*.

fry *(pt, pp* **fried**) *vi* fritar, frigir; ♦ *n (pl: -fries)* (= **small fries**) peixe *m* miúdo, peixinho; **2** *(pej) (people)* gente *f* sem importância; ♦ **fried eggs** ovos *mpl* estrelados; **~ fish** peixe *m* frito.

fryer/frying pan *(UK)* fry-pan *(US)* *n* frigideira *f*, sertã *f*.

fry-up *n (UK)* fritada *f*; fritos *mpl*.

ft *(abbr for* **foot, feet**)

FT *(abbr for* **Financial Times**) o jornal britânico sobre economia e finanças.

FTC *(abbr for* **Federal Trade Commision**) *(US)* órgão responsável pelo cumprimento da lei sobre monopólios.

FT-SE 100 Index (abbr for: **Financial Times Stock 100 index**) FTSE *m* **the ~ index** o índice FTSE; **the ~ 100**, *índices das ações das 100 maiores empresas britânicas, publicados no FT, para refletir vários aspetos dos preços na Bolsa de Valores.*

fuchsia *n (BOT)* fúcsia *f*.

fuck *vt (vulg)* copular, foder *(vulg)*; **to ~ off** *(vulg)* foder-se; ♦ *exc* **~!** *(shit)* merda!; **~ off!** *(vulg)* vá à merda! *(less vulgar)*; vá foder-se! *(very vulgar)*.

fucking you ~ idiot! *(vulg)* seu grande merda!

fuck-up *n* asneirada, cagada.

fuddled *adj* ébrio,-a; **2** *(mind, ideas)* confuso,-a, desorientado,-a.

fuddy-duddy *(pl:* **fuddy-duddies***)* *n (old and conservative person)* bota-de-elástico *m inv* (BR) careta *m,f*.

fudge *n (soft sweet)* caramelo *m* mole; **2** *(nonsense)* disparate *m*; ♦ *vt* falsificar; **2** disfarçar *(problem)* evitar, escapar-se de *(confusion)*.

fuel *n* combustível *m*; carvão *m*, lenha; *(for car, plane)* carburante *m*; *(fig)* **to provide ~ for** dar azo a *(demand, anger, claims)*; **~ cell** *n* célula *f* a combustível; **~ oil** *n* óleo *m* combustível; **~ pump** *n* bomba *f* de combustível; **~ tank** *n* depósito de combustível; ♦ **(~led)** *vt (supply)* abastecer.

fuelling *n* abastecimento *m* de combustível.

fug *n (warm, stuffy, stale atmosphere)* ar *m* abafado, sala bafienta.

fugacious *adj* fugaz; efémero,-a; transitório,-a.

fugitive *n* fugitivo,-a.

fugue *n (MUS)* fuga *f*.

fulcrum *(pl:* -**cra**) *n* fulcro *m*; ponto *m* de apoio; sustentáculo; suporte.

fulfil *(UK)* **fulfill** *(US)* *(pt, pp* **fulfilled**) *vt* cumprir *(promise)*; **2** satisfazer *(hope, desire, ambition)*; **3 to ~ one's role** desempenhar o seu papel; **4** realizar *(dream, prophecy)*.

fulfilling *adj (mission, job, experience)* gratificante, enriquecedor,-ora.

fulfillment *n* satisfação *f*; **2 personal ~** realização *f* pessoal; **3** *(of promise)* cumprimento *m*; **4** *(of role)* desempenho *m*.

fulfilment *n* satisfação *f*; realização *f*.

full *adj* cheio,-a (**of**, **de**) **to be ~** *(gen)* estar cheio,-a; **I have my hands ~** tenho as mãos cheias; *(work)* estou cheio,-a de trabalho; **to be ~ of o.s.** ser presunçoso,-a, ser cheio,-a de si; **2** *(of praises)* repleto; **3** *(name, all-in)* completo,-a; **~ board** pensão *f* completa; **~ day** dia *m* inteiro; **~ dress** traje de cerimónia; **~ house** *(CIN, THEAT)* casa cheia; esgotado.-a; *(coll)* à cunha; *(BR)* lotado,-a; **4** *(all)* todo,-a; **do you have the ~ amount?** você tem a quantia toda?; **at** ~ **speed** a velocidade toda; **at/to the** ~ *(sound, volume)* no máximo; *(box)* abarrotado,-a; **5** *(total)* **I have** ~ **trust in you** tenho uma confiança total em você/em si; **7** *(body, lips)* cheio,-a; **8** *(flavour)* intenso, rico; **9** *(rights, clarity)* pleno,-a; **in** ~ **daylight** em pleno dia; **10** *(agenda)* preenchido,-a; **11** *(life, work)* intenso,-a; **12** *(story, report)* detalhado ♦ *adv* ~ **well** perfeitamente; **in** ~ em cheio, **you hit it in** ~ você acertou em cheio; **2** *(writing)* por extenso; **3** *(payment)* na íntegra; IDIOM **to enjoy life to the** ~ viver à grande; **to be** ~ **of beans** *(person)* estar cheio de energia; **to be in** ~ **swing** estar a todo o vapor; *(party)* estar bem animado,-a; ~**back** *n* *(FOOT)* defesa; *(BR)* zagueiro; ~**-blooded** *adj* de raça *f* pura, de sangue puro; **2** enérgico,-a; ~**-blown** *adj* bem desenvolvido,-a; bem caracterizado,-a; ~**-bodied** *adj* *(wine)* encorpado; **2** *(voice, music)* forte, poderoso,-a; ~**-face** *adj* *(photo, portrait)* de frente; ~ **fare** *n* passagem *f* completa; ~**-frontal** *adj* em nu frontal; ~**-length** *adj* *(photo)* de corpo inteiro; **2** *(dress, curtains)* comprido,-a; ao comprido; **3** ~ **film** filme de longa metragem; ~ **moon** *n* lua *f* cheia; ~**-page** *adj* *(advert)* de página inteira; ~ **powers** *adj* plenos poderes; ~**-sized** *adj* em tamanho real/natural; ~ **stop** *n* ponto *m* final; ~**-time** *adj,adv* a tempo inteiro; ~ **up** *(coll)* *(after meal)* estar cheio; **2** *(bus, train etc)* abarrotado,-a; *(coll)* à cunha; *(BR)* lotado,-a.

fullness *f* plenitude *f*; **in the** ~ **of her life** na sua plenitude; **2** abundância *f*; **3** *(sound)* amplitude *f*.

fully *adv* completamente, totalmente; *(in details)* detalhadamente; ~**-fledged** *adj* *(UK)* *(bird)* capaz de voar; emplumado,-a; **2** *(fig)* *(professional)* experiente, diplomado,-a; ~**-grown** *adj* adulto,-a; **2** desenvolvido,-a.

fulminant *adj* fulminante.

fulminate *n* *(CHEM)* fulminato *m*; ♦ *vt* encolerizar-se (**against**, contra); **2** explodir.

fulsome *adj* *(praise, complaint)* exagerado,-a; **2** *(manner)* obsequioso,-a.

fumble *n* falta de jeito; ♦ *vt*: **to** ~ **with** atrapalhar-se com.

fume *vi* fumegar, soltar fumo; ~**s** *npl* fumaça *sg*, gases *mpl*; vapor *m*.

fumigate *vt* fumigar, desinfe(c)tar.

fuming *adj* que deita fumo; fumegante; **2** *(person)* irado,-a, irritado,-a.

fun *n* divertimento; alegria; **to have** ~ divertir-se; **for** ~ a brincar, por brincadeira; **to make** ~ **of** *vt* fazer troça de, zombar de.

function *n* função *f*; **2** cargo *m*; **3** *(social event)* cerimónia; ♦ *vi* funcionar.

functional *adj* funcional; **2** *(machine)* operacional.

functionary *n* funcionário,-a público,-a; *(pej)* burocrata.

function key *n* *(COMP)* tecla *f* de função.

fund *n* *(cash reserve)* provisão *f*, fundo *m*; ~**s** *npl* fundos *mpl*; capital *m* disponível; recursos *mpl*; **no** ~**s** sem provisão.

fundable *adj* *(FIN)* consolidável.

fundamental *adj* fundamental.

fundamentalist *adj* fundamentalista.

fundamentally *adv* fundamentalmente.

funding *n* *(FIN)* *(of debt)* consolidação; recursos *mpl*.

fund-raising *n* angariação *f* de fundos.

funeral *n* funeral *m*, enterro; exéquias *fpl*; ~ **director** *m* dire(c)tor,-a funerário,-a; ~ **pile** pira crematória; ~ **urn** urna funerária, caixão; **the** ~ **procession** o cortejo fúnebre, o enterro; ~ **service** *n* cerimónia *f* de enterro.

funereal *adj* fúnebre; sepulcral; sombrio,-a.

funfair *n* parque *m* de diversões, feira popular.

fungal *adj* fungíco,-a.

fungicide *n* fungicida *m*.

fungus *(pl*: **-gi)** *n* *(MED)* fungo *m*; *(BOT)* cogumelo *m*; **2** *(mould)* bolor.

funicular *n adj* funicular.

funk *n* *(MUS)* música norte-americana, funk; **2** *(dated)* medo, pavor.

funky (-ier, -iest) *adj* *(MUS)* ritmado,-a, vibrante; **2** *(person in fashion)* à/na moda; **3** *(US)* fedorento,-a

funnel *n* funil *m*; **2** *(on ship)* chaminé *m*.

funnelled *adj* em forma de funil, afunilado,-a.

funnies *n* *(US, Canada)* *(comic strip in a newspaper)* quadradinhos.

funnily *adv* divertidamente; *(oddly)* curiosamente.

funny *adj* engraçado, divertido; **2** *(odd)* esquisito,-a, invulgar, estranho,-a; ~ **bone** *(MED)* osso *m* do cotovelo; **to feel** ~ sentir-se indisposto, esquisito.

fun run *n* *(as an exercise and pleasure)* corrida de lazer com outros; **2** *(raise money)* maratona caritativa.

fur *n* *(on animal)* (pêlo) pelo *m*; **2** *(garment)* pele *f*; ~ **coat** *n* casaco de peles; **3** *(in pipes)* sarro *m*, depósito *m*.

furbish *vt* polir; dar lustre a; renovar.

furious *adj* furioso,-a; violento,-a; **he was** ~ ele estava fora de si.

furiously *adv* furiosamente, com fúria.

furl *vt*: ~ **up** *(umbrella, flag)* enrolar, dobrar; **2** *(NAUT)* colher, amarrar (velas).

furlong *n* *(measurement)* de uma milha 1/8=201,168 m.

furnace *n* forno *m*, fornalha *f*.

furnish *vt* mobiliar; *(provide)* fornecer.

furnished *adj* mobiliado,-a.

furnishings *npl* mobília, mobiliário *m*; equipamento.

furniture *n* mobília, móveis *mpl*; **piece of** ~ móvel *m*.

furore *n* furor *m*; entusiasmo *m* excessivo.

furred *adj* forrado a peles; vestido de peles.

furrier *n* peleiro,-a.

furrow *n* *(in field)* sulco *m*, rego; **2** *(on forehead)* ruga *f*; ♦ *vt* sulcar, arar *(land)*; **2** *(forehead)* enrugar, fazer rugas.

furry *adj* *(animal)* peludo,-a.

further *adj* novo, adicional; **until** ~ **notice** até novo aviso; ♦ *adv* mais longe; ~ **on/back** mais adiante, mais atrás; ♦ ~ **to** *prep* com referência a; ♦ *vt* promover, impulsionar; adiantar.

Further Education *npr* *(UK)* educação *f* vocacional, complementar.

furthermore *adv* além disso.

furthermost *adj* mais distante.

furthest (*sup of* **far**).

furtive *adj* furtivo,-a.

furtively *adv* furtivamente; às escondidas.

fury *n* fúria *f*, ira *f*; **in a ~** num acesso de fúria; **the ~ of the waves** a fúria das ondas; **to get into a ~** enfurecer-se.

fuse *n* (*ELECT*) fusível *m*; **2** (*of bomb, fireworks*) detonador *m*; **3** (*cord for explosive*) mecha *f*; ◆ *vt* fundir; (*equip with fuse*) munir (algo) com um fusível; ◆ *vi* fundir-se; (*ELECT*) queimar; **~ box** *n* quadro (*BR*: caixa) de fusíveis.

fused *adj* (*ELECT*) com fusível.

fuselage *n* fuselagem *f*.

fusil *n* fusil, mosquete antigo.

fusilier *n* (*MIL*) fuzileiro.

fusillade *n* fuzilaria *f*; fuzilamento *m* por descarga sucessiva; **2** (*fig*) (**~ of**) avalanche (de).

fusing *n* fusão; **~ burner** maçarico que corta por fusão.

fusion *n* (*PHYS*) fusão *f*; **2** (*of styles, colours*) mistura *f*; (*fig*) união *f*.

fuss *n* (*agitation*) rebuliço *m*; **2** (*angry scene*) espalhafato *m*; **to make a ~ over trivial things** fazer ondas; **to kick up a ~** armar rebuliço; **so much ~ for nothing** tanto barulho para nada; ◆ *vi* preocupar-se com ninharias; **to ~ over sb** mimar, estragar (alguém) com mimos.

fussiness *n* reboliço *m*; **2** (*decorations*) espalhafato *m*; **3** (*being particular*) esquisitice *f*, meticulosidade.

fussing *n* exigência; **stop ~ about** deixa-te dessas coisas.

fusspot *n* (*fam*) (*over meticulous*) picuinhas; (*exhibition of affection*) exagerado,-a; (*interested in trivial things*) coca-bichinhos *m,f*.

fussy (**-ier**, **-iest**) *adj* (*choosy*) exigente *m,f*, esquisito,-a; **to be ~** (*to pick at anything*) (*pej*) ser picuinhas; **2** (*over-ornate*) exagerado,-a, espalhafatoso,-a.

fustigate *vt* fustigar.

fusty *adj* mofento,-a; bafiento,-a; malcheiroso,-a.

futile *adj* fútil, inútil.

futility *n* futilidade *f*; frivolidade *f*; inutilidade.

future *n* futuro *m*; **the foreseeable ~** o futuro próximo; (*LING*) (*tense*) futuro (tempo); ◆ *adj* futuro,-a; vindouro,-a; **in ~ years** nos anos vindouros.

futures *npl* (*COMM*) mercado *m* de futuros.

futurism *n* futurismo *m*.

futuristic *adj* futurístico,-a.

fuze *n* = **fuse**.

fuzz *n* (*hair on young man*) penugem *f*; **2** (*beard*) barbicha; **3** (*coll*) **the ~** os chuis *mpl*, (*BR*) os tiras *mpl*; ◆ *vi* (*also:* **~ over**) (*vision*) turvar-se.

fuzzy *adj* (*blurry*) indistinto,-a, desfocado,-a; **2** (*hair*) encrespado,-a; **3** (*downy*) penugento,-a; **4** (*mind, memory*) confuso,-a.

fwd. (*abbr for* **forward**).

f-word *n*: **the ~** (*euph. for the word 'fuck'*).

g

G, g *n (letter)* G, g *m*; **2 G** *n (MUS)* sol; **G clef** clave de sol; **3** *(coll) (US)* = **grand** *(Vd: grand).*

gab *vt (pt,pp:-bb-) (coll)* tagarelar; *(Vd.* **gift***).*

gabardine *n (material)* gabardine *f*; **2** *(garment)* gabardina *f.*

gabble *n* algaraviada *f*, palratório *m*, tagarelice *f*; ♦ *vi* tagarelar.

gable *n (CONSTR, ARCH) (façade)* empena *f*; **2** *(of a roof)* espigão *m*, cumeeira *f.*

Gabon *npr* Gabão; **in** ~ no Gabao.

Gabonese *n, adj* gabonês,-esa.

gad *n (MIN) (tool)* tipo de cinzel; ♦ *(-dd-) vt* quedrar o minério com este cinzel; **2** ~ **about** *vt* vadiar.

gadabout *n* pessoa que anda sempre no laré, no gandaia.

gadget *n* aparelho; **2** dispositivo; **3** *(coll)* engenhoca.

Gaelic *n (LING)* gaélico; ♦ *adj* gaélico,-a.

gaffe *n (blunder)* gafe *f.*

gag *n (joke)* piada; **2** *(for mouth)* mordaça *f*; ♦ *(-gg-) vt* amordaçar.

gaga *adj (coll)* gagá; **to go** ~ ficar gagá.

gaggle *n (flock of geese)* um bando de gansos; ♦ *vi (cackle)* grasnar.

gaiety *n* alegria, boa disposição.

gain *n (profit)* lucro, ganho *m*; **2** *(advantage)* vantagem *f*; **3** *(increase)* aumento *m*; ♦ *vt* ganhar; obter; alcançar; **to** ~ **by/from sth** tirar proveito de; lucrar com algo; **to** ~ **ground** ganhar terreno; **2** *(watch, clock)* adiantar-se; **3** *(experience)* adquirir; **4** *(support)* conquistar, obter *(apoio)*; **to** ~ **in sth** *(increase)* crescer em algo; aumentar; **she has ~ed weight** ela engordou; **to** ~ **in popularity** tornar-se mais popular; **to** ~ **on/upon sb** *(speed – close on)* aproximar-se de; **2** *(distance)* distanciar-se de; **3** alcançar; **he has gained on his rival** ele está a levar a melhor sobre o rival.

gainful *adj (job, business)* lucrativo,-a, vantajoso,-a.

gainfully *adv* vantajosamente.

gainings *npl* lucros *mpl*; vencimento(s).

gains *npl* lucros, ganhos; **ill-gotten** ~ ganhos *mpl* ilícitos.

gainsay *(pt, pp* -**said***) vt (LITER)* contradizer, negar; **to** ~ **a statement** negar uma afirmação.

gait *n* modo de andar; passo.

gaiters *npl* polainas *fpl.*

gal¹ *n (US) (coll)* rapariga *f*; moça *f.*

gal² *(also:* **gall***) (abbr for:* **gallon***).*

gala *n* festa, gala *f*; ~ **dinner** jantar de gala.

Galapagos *npr* the ~ **Islands** as Ilhas Galápagos.

galaxy *n* galáxia *f.*

gale *n* ventania *f*; vendaval *m.*

Galicia *npr (N-W Spain)* Galiza; **in** ~ na Galiza.

Galician *npr adj* galego,-a; *(LING)* galego *m.*

gall *n (inpudence)* descaramento *m*; *(coll)* lata *f*; **to have the** ~ **to** ter a lata de.

gall. *(abbr for* **gallon***).*

gallant *adj* valente; **2** galante.

gallantry *n* coragem, valentia *f*; **2** galanteio, cortesia.

gall-bladder *n (MED)* vesícula *f* biliar.

galleon *n (ship)* galeão *m.*

gallery *n (in mines, shop)* galeria *f*, corridor *m*; **art** ~ galeria de arte; **2** *(THEAT)* geral, *(coll)* galinheiro.

galley *(pl:* **galleys***) n (kitchen)* cozinha *f* (de navio); **2** *(ship)* galé *f*, galera *f*; **3** *(TYPO)* ~ **proof** prova *f* de granel.

Gallic *adj* gaulês,-esa.

gallicism *n* galicismo.

galling *adj (annoying)* irritante, humilhante *m,f.*

gallium *n (ore)* gálio *m.*

gallivant *(allivant or galavant) vi* vaguear/laurear à procura de prazer.

gallon *n* galão *m (UK* = 4.54 litros); *(US* = 3.785 litros).

gallop *n* galope *m*; **at a** ~ a galope; ♦ *vi* galopar; **2** *(fig)* **to** ~ **through sth** expedir algo a toda a velocidade.

gallows *n* forca *sg.*

gallstone *n* cálculo biliar.

galore *adv* em quantidade.

galosh *npl (pl* -**es***)* galocha *f.*

galvanize, galvanise *vt (TECH)* galvanizar; **2** *(impel)* incentivar; **to** ~ **into action** estimular (alguém) a entrar em a(c)ção.

Gambia *npr* Gâmbia; **in** ~ na Gâmbia.

Gambian *npr adj* gambiano,-a.

gambit *n (ploy)* tá(c)tica, estratagema; **2** *(in chess)* gambito *m.*

gamble *n* risco; **2** *(bet)* aposta; **3** *(luck)* jogo de azar; ♦ *vt*: **to** ~ **on** apostar em; **2** *(fig)* confiar em; ♦ *vi (at cards)* jogar; **2** apostar (**on** em); **3** *(COMM)* especular; **to** ~ **away** espatifar *(money, fortune).*

gambler *n* jogador,-ora.

gambling *n* jogo.

game *n* jogo; **2** *(of cards, darts etc)* partida; **3** *(of football)* desafio; **4** *(hunting)* caça; ~**keeper** *n* couteiro, guarda-caça *m*; ~ **park/reserve** *n* coutada; ~ **warden** guardia *m* florestal; **5** *(children's)* **let us have a** ~ **of** vamos brincar a; **6** *(fig) (trick)* manobra, esquema *f*, jogo *m*; **7** *(coll)* activity, profession, campo; ♦ *adj (plucky)* valente; *(willing to try/do)* **to be** ~ **for anything** estar pronto para qualquer coisa; IDIOM **that's the name of the** ~ é isso mesmo.

game-cock *n* galo lutador, *(BR)* galo-de-briga.

gamma rays *npl* raios *mpl* gama.

gammon *n* gamão *m*; fiambre *m*; toucinho (defumado); presunto.

gammy *adj* (-**ier**, -**iest***) (leg, knee)* estropiado,-a.

gamut *n* gama *f*; **to run the** ~ percorrer toda a gama *t.*

gander *n (male goose)* ganso; IDIOM **what is sauce for the goose is sauce for the** ~ o que é bom para um, é bom para o outro.

gang *n (thieves)* quadrilha, gangue *f*; **2** *(coll) (group)* malta; ♦ *vi*: **to ~ up on** *or* **against** aliar-se contra; ♦ **~ bang** *n (slang)* sexo em grupo; **~land** *n* submundo *m* do crime; **~ leader** *n* chefe do bando; **~ling** *adj* desengonçado.

ganglion *n* gânglio *m*.

gangplank *n* prancha de embarque.

gangrene *n (MED)* gangrene.

gangrenous *adj (MED)* gangrenoso,-a.

gangster *n* gângster *m*.

gangway *n* passagem *f*, coxia. *f*; **2** *(gangplank)* passadiço; **3** *(NAUT)* portaló *m*, ponte *f* movediça.

gannet *n (bird)* alcatraz.

gantry *(pl: -ies)* *n (for barrel)* canteiro; **2** *(for crane)* cavalete.

gaol *n* prisão *f*, cadeia; **~-bird** *n* cadastrado,-a.

gaoler *n* carcereiro.

gap *n (hole, crack)* brecha, fenda *f*, buraco *m*; **2** *(in knowledge)* lacuna *f*; **to fill in a ~** preencher uma lacuna; **3** *(in between; space)* abertura; espaço; **the ~ between two planets** a distância entre os dois planetas; **4** *(of time)* intervalo; **5** *(emptiness)* vazio; **6** diferença, divergência *f*, disparidade f; **7** *(FIN)* défice *m*; **8** *(in conversation)* silêncio *m*; **9** *(TV, performance)* interrupção *f*.

gape *vi* estar/ficar boquiaberto; **2** *(stare)* olhar para alguém embasbacado.

gaping *adj (wound)* aberto,-a; **2** *(surprised)* boquiaberto,-a, de boca aberta; **3** *(hole)* enorme.

garage *n* garagem *f*; **2** oficina *f* mecânica.

garb *n* maneira de vestir, traje *m*.

garbage *n* lixo *m*; **2** *(fig) (nonsense)* asneira *f*, disparate *m*, *(BR)* besteira; **~ can** *n (US)* lata de lixo.

garbled *adj (transmission, message)* confuso,-a; adulterado,-a.

garden *n* jardim *m*; **~ party** *n* festa/receção ao ar livre.

gardener *n* jardineiro.

gardening *n* jardinagem *f*.

gargle *n* gargarejo; *(coll)* bebida; ♦ *vi* gargarejar.

gargling *n* gargarejo.

gargoyle *n* gárgula.

garish *adj (clothing)* espalhafatoso, extravagante; **2** *(colour)* berrante.

garland *n* grinalda *f*, *(BR)* guirlanda *f*.

garlic *n* alho; **clove of ~** dente *m* de alho.

garment *n* peça de roupa; **~s** *npl* vestuário.

garnet *n (red stone)* granada *f*; ♦ *adj (colour)* grená.

garnish *n* enfeite *m*, guarnição *f*; ♦ *vt* adornar; *(CULIN)* enfeitar.

garret *n* águas-furtadas *fpl*; sótão com janela no telhado; mansarda *f*.

garrison *n* guarnição *f*; ♦ *vt* guarnecer.

garrote (UK) **garote** (US) *n* garrote *m*.

garrulous *adj* tagarela, palrador.

garter *n* liga; **~ belt** *n* cinta-liga; **Order of the G~** *n* Ordem da Jarreteira (ordem de cavalaria instituída na Inglaterra no século XIV).

gas *(pl: gases)* *n* gás *m*; **2** *(US) (for car)* gasolina *f*; **~ chamber** *n* gas câmara; **~ cooker** *n* fogão *m* a gás; **~ cylinder** *n* garrafa *f*, botija *f*, *(BR)* botijão *m* de gás; **~ mask** *n* máscara *f* antigas; **~ meter** *n* medidor *m* de gás; **~ pedal** *n (US) (AUT)* acelerador *m*; **~ ring** *n* bico *m* de gás; **~ station** *n (US)* posto *m* de gasolina; **to step on the ~** *(AUT)* acelerar; ♦ *(pt, pp -sed)* *vt* asfixiar com gás.

gaseous *adj* gasoso,-a.

gas gauge *n* medidor *m* de gás.

gash *n (cut on the leg, hand)* corte *m*, golpe *m* (comprido e fundo), cutilada; ♦ *vt* acutilar, ferir, cortar.

gashinge *n* gonzo *m* do portão.

gasket *n (MED) (BR)* gaxeta *f*; *(EP)* junta *f* da colaça.

gasoline *(US)* gasolina *f*.

gasometer *n* gasómetro, *(BR: -ô-)*.

gasp *n* suspiro, arfada *f*; **at the last ~** *(fig)* no último momento (da morte); ♦ *vi* arfar; esforçar-se por respirar; **to ~ for breath** recuperar o fôlego, respirar com dificuldade, arquejar; **to ~ out** *vt* dizer com voz entrecortada, ofegante por.

gas pump attendant *n (US)* gasolineiro; *(BR)* frentista *m,f*.

gassy *adj (pej) (water beer)* com muito gás.

gastric *adj* gástrico; **~ juice** *n* suco gástrico; **~ ulcer** *n* úlcera gástrica.

gastritis *n (MED)* gastrite *f*.

gastronomic *adj* gastronómico,-a *(BR: -ô-)*.

gastronomy *n* gastronomia *f*.

gasworks *npl* fábrica *f* de gás.

gate *n* portão *m*; **2** *(RAIL)* barreira; **3** *(COMP)* porta; **garden/farm ~** cancela; **~house** *n* portaria *f*; **~keeper** *n* porteiro,-a; **~ money** *n* receita das entradas; **~post** *n* coiceira *f*.

Desde o escândalo de Watergate em 1972, nos E.U.A. durante a presidência de Richard Nixon, o sufixo 'gate' tem vindo a ser acrescentado a outras palavras para designar casos políticos sensacionais: **Irangate** – venda ilegal de armas dos E.U.A. ao Irão; **Monicagate** – escândalo sexual em redor do Presidente Clinton e Monica Lewinski no final da década de 1990.

gateau *n* bolo *m* enfeitado, recheado.

gate-crash *vt (fam)* entrar como penetra.

gate-crasher *n* intruso,-a; *(fam) (at parties)* penetra *m,f*; *(concerts, etc.)* borlista *m,f*.

gateway *n (entrance)* portão *m*; **~ to** *n* entrada *f*; passagem *f*, caminho, acesso a.

gather *vt (fruit, flowers)* colher; **2** *(gente)* reunir; **3** *(sewing)* franzir; **4** *(understand)* compreender; ♦ *vi* reunir-se.

gathering *n* reunião *f*, assembleia.

gauche *adj (person)* desastrado,-a; **2** *(remark)* sem tato.

gaudy (-ier, -iest) *adj* berrante *m,f*, espalhafatoso,-a; **she had the gaudiest dress I ever saw** ela tinha o vestido mais berrante que eu jamais vi.

gauge *n* padrão *m*, medida, indicador *m*; medidor *m*; *(RAIL)* bitola *f*; indicador *m*; ♦ *vt* medir; calcular.

Gaulish *npr* gaulês; ♦ *adj* gaulês,-esa.

gaunt *adj (face, figure)* descarnado,-a, emaciado, esquelético,-a; **2** *(of places)* desolado,-a.

gauntlet *n (HIST)* manopla *f*; *(fig)* **to run the ~** expôr-se (à crítica); **to throw down the ~** desafiar.

gauze *n (fabric)* gaze *f.*
gauzy *adj* transparente.
gave *(pt of* **give**).
gavel *n (used by chairman, auctioneer)* martelo *m.*
gavotte *n (dança)* gavota *f.*
gawk *vt (stare)* olhar alguém de boca aberta, com um ar estúpido, pasmado.
gawky *adj (clumsy)* desajeitado,-a.
gawp *vt (UK)* olhar atónito (**at**, para); *vi* embasbacar-se; ♦ ficar embasbacado,-a.
gay *n (pej)* homosexual; ♦ *adj (dated)* alegre, jovial.
Gaza Strip *npr (GEOG)* **the** ~ a faixa de Gaza.
gaze *n* olhar fixo; **to** ~ **at sth** fitar algo,-alguém; **to** ~ **around/about** contemplar, olhar à sua volta; em redor; *(LITER)* mirar.
gazebo *n* mirante *m,* belvedere; **garden** ~ caramanchão *m.*
gazelle *n (ZOOL)* gazela *f.*
gazetteer *n* dicionário geográfico.
gazump *vt (UK) (pej)* comprometer-se a vender uma casa a alguém e depois vendê-la a outro por mais dinheiro.
GB *(abbr for* **Great Britain**).
GDP *(abbr for* **Gross Domestic Product**) PIB.
gear *n* equipamento *m; (personal effects)* pertences *mpl;* apetrechos *mpl;* **fishing** ~ apetrechos de pesca *mpl;* **2** *(TECH)* engrenagem *f;* **3** *(AUT)* mudança, velocidade, *(BR)* marcha; ~**box** *n* caixa de velocidades, mudanças; *(BR)* caixa de câmbio; **in** ~ engrenado, engatado; ~ **lever,** ~ **shift** *(US) n* alavanca das mudanças; **out of** ~ desengatado,-a; ♦ **to** ~ **up** *vi* aparelhar; preparar-se (**for**, para); engrenar; ~ **wheel** *n* roda dentada.
gee *exc (US) (surprise, admiration)* caramba! *(BR)* nossa! **2** *(to horse)* ~ **up!** eia cavalo!.
gee-gee *n (infant's talk)* cavalo *m.*
geese *(pl of* **goose**).
geisha (girl) *n* gueixa.
gelatin(e) *n* gelatina.
gelding *n* cavalo *m* castrado
gelignite *n* gelignite *f.*
gem *n* jóia, gema, pedra preciosa; **2** *(fig) (person)* jóia; **she is a** ~ ela é uma jóia.
Gemini *npr (ASTROL)* Gémeos *mpl.*
gender *n (sex)* sexo *m;* **2** *(gram)* género.
gene *n* gene *m.*
genealogist *n* genealogista *m,f.*
genealogy *n* genealogia *f.*
genera *(pl of* **genus**).
general *n (MIL)* general *m;* ♦ *adj* geral; **in** ~ em geral; ~ **elections** *n* eleições *fpl* gerais; ~ **knowledge** *n* cultura *f* geral; ~ **practitioner (GP)** *n* clínico geral *m;* médico de família; ~-**purpose** *adj* de uso geral.
generality *n* generalidade.
generalization *n* generalização *f.*
generalize *vi* generalizar.
generally *adv* geralmente.
generate *vt (ELECT)* gerar; *(fig)* produzir.
generation *n* geração *f;* ~ **gap** *n* conflito *m* de gerações.

generator *n* gerador *m.*
generic *adj* genérico,-a.
generosity *n* generosidade *f.*
generous *adj* generoso; abundante.
generously *adv* generosamente.
genesis *(pl: -eses) n (origin)* génese.
genetically-modified *adj* geneticamente modificado,-a.
genetic engineering *n* engenharia *f* genética.
genetics *n* genética.
Geneva *npr* Genebra; **the** ~ **convention** *n* a convenção de Genebra.
genial *adj* jovial, simpático,-a.
geniality *n* cordialidade *f.*
genitals *npl* órgãos *mpl* genitais.
genius *n* génio, *(BR)* gênio; **a stroke of** ~ um golpe de mestre.
Genoa *npr* Génova; **in** ~ em Génova.
genocide *n* genocídio.
genre *n (art, film)* género.
gent *(abbr for* **gentleman**).
genteel *adj (refined)* fino, elegante; amaneirado, afectado.
gentile *adj* gentio, gentílico, não-judeu.
gentle *adj (kind)* amável; **2** *(loving)* meigo, doce; *(soft)* leve, suave, brando; **the** ~ **breeze** a brisa suave, a doce brisa; **3** *(tame)* manso, dócil; **the dog is** ~ o cão é dócil; ~ **folk** *n* fidalguia, of good family.
gentleman *(pl:* **gentlemen**) *n* senhor *m;* cavalheiro; ~'**s agreement** *n* acordo de cavalheiros.
gentlemanly *adj* cavalheiresco,-a.
gentleness *n* doçura, meiguice *f;* **2** suavidade *f;* brandura.
gently *adv* devagar, suavemente.
gentry *n* gente *f* de pequena nobreza; burguesia.
gents *n* (lavabos de) cavalheiros *mpl,* de homens.
genuine *adj (work of art)* genuíne; **2** *(feeling, person, truth)* autêntico; sincero.
genuinely *adv* genuinamente; sinceramente.
genus *(pl:* **genera**) *n* género *m.*
geographic(al) *adj* geográfico.
geography *n* geografia.
geological *adj* geológico.
geologist *n* geólogo,-a.
geology *n* geologia.
geometric(al) *adj* geométrico.
geometry *n* geometria.
Geórgia *npr* Georgia; **in** ~ na Geórgia.
Georgian *adj (UK) (period)* Georgiano,-a.
geranium *n (BOT)* gerânio, sardinheira.
Gerbil *n (ZOOL)* gerbo *m.*
geriatric *adj* geriátrico,-a.
germ *n* micróbio, bacilo; *(BIO, fig)* germe *m.*
German *npr adj* alemão/mã *m,f;* alemães *mpl,* alemãs *fpl;* **2** *(LING)* alemão *m;* ~ **measles** *n* rubéola.
Germany *npr* Alemanha; **in** ~ a Alemanha.
germination *n* germinação *f.*
gesticulate *vi* gesticular.
gesticulation *n* gesticulação *f.*
gesture *n* gesto.

get *(pt, pp* **got,** *(US) pp* **gotten)** *vt* obter; receber; conseguir; encontrar; apanhar; ir buscar; compreender; ♦ *vi* fazer-se, chegar a; **to ~ old** envelhecer; **to ~ to** chegar a; **to ~ ready** preparar-se; **to ~ washed** lavar-se; **to ~ sb to do sth** convencer alguém a fazer algo; ♦ **to ~ about** *vi* sair muito, viajar muito; *(news)* divulgar-se; **to ~ along** *vi* entender-se; pôr-se a andar, ir embora; **to ~ at** *vt* atacar; chegar a; descobrir; **to ~ away** *vi* partir; escapar; **to ~ away with** *vt* safar-se, fazer impunemente; **to ~ back** *vi* regressar; ♦ *vt* voltar; **to ~ by** *vi* passar; arranjar-se; **to ~ down** *vi* baixar-se; ♦ *vt* baixar; deprimir; **to ~ down to** *vt* pôr-se a (fazer); **to ~ in** *vi* chegar; voltar para casa; ♦ *vt* subir a; **to ~ off** *vi* descer, saltar; ♦ *vt* sair de, saltar de; **to ~ in a mess/trouble** meter-se em sarilhos/dificuldades; **to ~ on** *vi (well)* ter sucesso; ♦ *vt (train etc)* subir a; **to ~ on well with** dar-se bem com; **to ~ out** *vi* sair; *(news)* saber; ♦ *vt* tirar; **to ~ out of** *vt* sair de; escapar de; **to ~ out of sight** desaparecer da vista; **to ~ over** *vt* restabelecer-se de, recuperar-se; **to ~ rid of** libertar-se de, desembaraçar-se de; **to ~ round** *vt* rodear; **to ~ through to** *vt (TEL)* comunicar-se com; **to ~ together** *vi* reunir-se; **to ~ up** *vi* levantar-se; **~ well!** as melhoras!.

getaway *n* fuga, escape *m;* **~ car** *n* carro *m* de escape.

get-together *n (fam)* encontro *m* entre amigos.

get-up-and-go *n (fam)* iniciativa *f;* energia *f.*

geyser *n* esquentador *m* (*BR:* aquecedor *m*) de água.

Ghana *npr* Gana; **in ~** na Gana.

Ghananian *npr adj* ganense *m,f.*

ghastly *adj* horrível; **2** *(pale)* pálido, lívido.

gherkin *n* pepino em conserva.

ghetto *n* gueto *m.*

ghost *n* fantasma *m;* **the ~ of a smile** a sombra *f* de um sorriso; **~ writer** *n* escritor,-ora fantasma; **~ town** *n* cidade *f* fantasma.

ghostly *adj* espiritual, spectral; **2** *(story)* fantasmagórico,-a.

ghoul *n* espírito *m* do mal.

ghoulish *adj* macabro,-a.

GI *(abbr for* **government issue)** soldado raso dos E.U.A.

giant *n* gigante *m;* ♦ *adj* gigantesco, gigante.

gibber *vt (nervous)* gaguejar, titubear; falar atabalhoadamente; **2** *(monkey)* imitar sons humanos, algaraviar.

gibberish *n (unintelligible way of speaking)* algaraviada *f,* engrimanço *m.*

gibbon *n* gibão *m.*

gibe *n* zombaria *f,* troça *f,* piada *f;* **to ~ at sb** zombar de alguém, dar uma piada a alguém.

giblets *npl* miúdos *mpl (of chicken).*

giddiness *n* vertigem *f.*

giddy (-ier, -iest) *adj* tonto,-a; atordoado,-a; **to feel ~** ter tonturas; **2** *(heights)* vertiginoso,-a; **3** estouvado,-a.

giddy-up (giddap) *exc (make horse go)* eia cavalo!, vamos!

gift *n* presente *m,* oferta *f;* **2** talento *m,* dom *m;* **to have the ~ of the gab** ter o dom da palavra; *(pej)* ter lábia.

GIFT *(abbr for* **gamete in fallopian transfer)** técnica de inseminação artificial.

gifted *adj* talentoso,-a; dotado,-a; superdotado,-a.

gift token/voucher *(UK);* **gift certificate** *(US)* vale-presente *m.*

gig *n (MUS) (fam)* concerto *m* de rock; **2** *(carriage)* cabriolet *m.*

gigantic *adj* gigantesco.

giggle *n* risadinha tola; ♦ *vi* rir-se tolamente.

giggly (-ier, -iest) *adj* com risinho tolo; **to be in a ~ mood** rir-se por tudo e por nada.

gigolo *n* gigolô *m.*

gild *vt* dourar.

gill *n (measure)* = 0.141; **2** *(of fish)* guelra, brânquia.

gills *npl (of fish)* guelras *fpl.*

gilt *(=gilding) n* douradura *f;* ♦ *adj* dourado,-a; de ouro; **~-edged** *(page)* de cercadura dourada; **2** *(FIN) (securities)* de máxima garantia.

gimlet *n (tool)* verruma *f;* **2** *(US)* bebida de gin ou vodka com lima.

gimmick *n (device to attract)* artemanha *f;* truque *m;* estratagema *m.*

gin *n* gim *m,* genebra.

ginger *n* (BOT) gengibre *m;* **~ ale** *n* cerveja de gengibre; **~-haired** *adj* ruivo.

gingerly *adv* cuidadosamente, cautelosamente.

gingham *n (cloth)* guingão.

gingivitis *n (MED)* gengivite *f.*

gipsy *n* cigano,-a.

giraffe *n* girafa.

girder *n* viga, trave *f.*

girdle *n (clothing)* cinta *f;* **2** *(fig)* cintura *f;* ♦ *vt* cintar; **2** *(fig)* cercar.

girl *n* menina, moça, jovem; rapariga; **~ Friday** *n* auxiliar de escritório.

girlfriend *n* amiga *f;* **2** *(female lover)* namorada.

girl guide *(UK),* **girl scout** *(US)* escuteira; *(BR)* bandeirante.

girlish/girly *adj* ameninado,-a; femenino,-a.

girth *n* perímetro *m;* **2** *(person)* corpolência *f;* **3** *(saddle's belt)* cilha *f; (BR)* cincha *f;* ♦ *vt* cingir *(person);* rodear; **2** cilhar.

gist *n* o essencial; ideia *f* geral.

give *(pt* **gave,** *pp* **given)** *vt* dar; entregar; oferecer; ♦ *vi (stretch: fabric)* dar de si; **to ~ the bride** levar a noiva ao altar; **to ~ away** *vt (give free)* dar de graça; **2** *(disclose)* revelar; **to ~ back** *vt* devolver; **to ~ in** *vi* ceder; ♦ *vt* entregar; **to ~ notice** despedir; **to ~ out** *vt* distribuir; **to ~ up** *vt* desistir, renunciar, dar-se por vencido; **to ~ up smoking** deixar de fumar; **to ~ way** *vi* ceder; *(AUT)* deixar passar.

given *adj* dado; **~ that** *conj* dado que; **giver** *n* dador.

glacier *n* glaciar *m;* geleira.

glad *adj* contente; alegre **(of, about,** com).

gladden *vt* alegrar, animar.

glade *n* clareira *f.*

gladiator *m* gladiador.

gladioli *npl* gladíolos *mpl.*

gladly *adv* com muito prazer, de bom grado.

glamorize/-ise *vt* embelezar; **2** *(story)* fantasiar.

glamorous *adj* atraente *m,f;* **2** *(dress, appearance)* elegante *m,f;* glamoroso,-a; **2** *(event)* brilhante.

glamour *n* encanto, glamour *m,* sedução *f.*

glance *n* olhar; **2** *(quick)* olhadela *f;* ♦ **at a** ~ de relance; ♦ *vt* **to give a** ~ **at sth** dar uma vista de olhos a algo; **to** ~ **round** olhar para trás; olhar em volta; **3** bater em algo a um ângulo oblíquo.

gland *n* glândula.

glandular fever *n (MED)* mononucleose infeciosa *f.*

glare *n* luz *f,* ofuscante; brilho *m* intenso; **2** olhar *m* penetrante; **to** ~ **at sb** *vt* lançar um olhar furioso *(a alguém);* fulminar *(alguém)* com o olhar.

glaring *adj (luz)* brilhante; **2** *(glance)* furioso; **3** *(colour)* berrante; **4** evidente.

glass *n* vidro, cristal *m;* **2** *(for drinking)* copo; cálice *m,* taça; ♦ (= **looking** ~) espelho *m;* ~ **blowing** *n* modelagem *f* de vidro a quente.

glasses *npl* óculos *mpl;* **dark** ~ óculos escuros.

glassfibre *n (UK)* fibra de vidro.

glasshouse *n (greenhouse)* estufa *f;* **2** *(conservatory)* marquise *f* envidraçada.

glassmaker *n* vidreiro,-a.

glassware *n* objectos de cristal/de vidro.

glassy (-ier, -iest) *adj* vidrado,-a; **2** *(shiny)* cristalino,-a.

glassy-eyed *adj (from fever, drink)* olhos vítreos; **2** *(look)* olhar sem expressão.

Glaswegian *adj* de Glasgow; *relativo a Glasgow, grande cidade da Escócia.*

glaucoma *n* glaucoma.

glaze *n (on pottery)* verniz; **2** *(china)* vidrado,-a; **3** *(CULIN)* cobertura *f,* glacé; ♦ *vt (pottery)* vidrar; **2** *(window, door)* envidraçar; **3** *cobrir com glacé.*

glazed *adj* vidrado; vitrificado.

glazier *n* vidraceiro.

gleam *n (glow)* brilho *m;* **2** lampejo *m;* **3** raio *m* (**of,** de); **4** *(fig)* vislumbre *m* ♦ *vi* brilhar, reluzir; **2** raiar.

gleaming *adj* brilhante.

glean *vt,vi (remnants of crops)* colher; **2** *(of information)* recolher; *(BR)* coletar.

glee *n* alegria *f,* regozijo *m.*

glen *n* vale *m.*

glib *adj (person)* com muita lábia; insincero,-a; **2** *(excuse)* de momento.

glibness *n* verbosidade *f.*

glide *n (skating, dancing)* deslizamento *m;* **2** *(in air)* voo *m* planado; ♦ *vi (move smoothly)* deslizar; **2** *(plane, birds)* planar.

glider *n (in air)* planador *m;* **2** *(SPORT)* asa-delta.

gliding *adj* deslizante; **2** ~ **joint** *n (ANAT)* artródia *f.*

glimmer *n (light)* luz *f* trêmula; **2** vislumbre *m;* ♦ *vt (light)* bruxulear.

glimpse *n* vislumbre *m;* **to catch a** ~ **of** ver de relance; ♦ **to** ~ entrever.

glint *n (look)* brilho *m;* fulgor; **2** *(metal)* cintilação *f;* ♦ *vt* brilhar; luzir; **2** *(eyes – with anger)* faiscar; ~**s** *npl (hair)* reflexos *mpl.*

glisten *vi* brilhar; reluzir; cintilar (**with,** com); ~**ing** *n* brilho *m;* cintilação *f;* ♦ *adj* brilhante; cintilante.

glitchy *adj (TECH) (equipment)* avariado,-a; com falha; com problemas técnicos.

glitter *n* brilho; **all that** ~**s is not gold** nem tudo que brilha é ouro; ♦ *vi* reluzir, brilhar.

glitterati *npl* a sociedade famosa e rica.

glitzy (-ier, -iest) *adj* faustoso,-a; ostensivo,-a.

gloat *n* exultação *f* maligna; ♦ *vi* **to** ~ **over sb's bad luck** regozijar-se com a má sorte de alguém.

global *adj* global; **2** mundial; ~ **warming** *n* aquecimento *m* global.

globalization, globalisation *n* globilização *f.*

globabalize, globalise *vt* globalizar; universalizar.

globe *n* globo *m,* esfera *f.*

globetrotter *n* viajante *m,f* incansável; *(BR)* globetrotter.

globule *n* glóbulo *m.*

gloom *n* escuridão *f,* trevas *fpl;* **2** *(sadness)* tristeza; melancolia *f.*

gloomy (-ier, -iest) *adj (dark)* escuro,-a; sombrio,-a; **2** *(sad)* triste; pessimista.

glorify *vt* glorificar.

glorious *adj* glorioso.

glory *n* glória *f.*

gloss *n* brilho *m;* lustro *m;* **2** ~ **paint** tinta *f* esmalte brilhante; **3** *(cosmetics)* de brilho; **4** *(fig)* falsa aparência; verniz; **to** ~ **over** encobrir.

glossary *n* glossário *m.*

glossy *adj* lustroso, polido.

glove *n* luva; ~ **compartment** *n (AUT)* porta-luvas *m inv.*

glow *n* brilho; ardor *m,* incandescência *f;* ♦ *vi* brilhar; *(fire)* arder.

glower *vi:* **to** ~ **at** olhar de modo ameaçador.

glucose *n* glicose *f.*

glue *n* cola; **to sniff** ~ inalar cola; ♦ *vt* colar; **2 to be glued to** *(fig) (TV, etc)* estar colado,-a a; ~ **ear** *n (MED)* otite serosa.

gluey *adj* pegajoso,-a.

glum *adj* abatido; triste; carrancudo, de mau humor.

glut *n* abundância, fartura; ♦ (-**tt**-) *vt (CHEM)* saturar; ~**ted** *adj* saciado,-a (**with,** de); **2** empanturrado,-a.

gluten *n* glúten.

glutinous *adj* pegajoso, glutinoso.

glutted *adj* saciado,-a (**with** de).

glutton *n* glutão,-tona; comilão,-lona; **a** ~ **for work** *(fig)* um trabalhador incansável; **a** ~ **for punishment** *(fig)* um,-a masoquista *m,f.*

gluttony *n* gula *f;* voracidade *f.*

glycerin(e) *n* glicerina *f.*

gm *(abbr for* **gram***)* g.

GM foods *npl* alimentos *mpl* geneticamente modificados.

GMT *(abbr for* **Greenwich Mean Time***)* horário official de Greenwich, TMG.

gnarled *adj* nodoso, cheio de nós.

gnash *vt/vi* ranger os dentes.

gnat *n* mosquito.

gnaw *(pt:* -**ed**, *pp:* **gnawn***) vt (chew)* roer *(bone);* **2 to** ~ **away at sb** *(torment)* atormentar alguém.

gnawing *n* acção de roer; ♦ *adj* roedor,-ora; **2** *(doubt)* torturante *m,f;* atormentador,-ora.

gnome *n* gnomo.

GNP (*abbr for* **Gross National Product**) Produto Nacional Bruto, PNB.

gnu *n* gnu *m*, antílope africano.

go *n* (*turn*) vez; **it's your** ~ é a sua vez; (*attempt*) tentativa; **to have a** ~ tentar; experimentar; tentar a sorte com; **to be on the** ~ estar sempre a trabalhar; a mexer-se; ♦ (*pt* **went**, *pp* **gone**) *vi* (*move, travel*) ir; **I am going to tell you a story** vou contar-te uma história; **to** ~ **by car/train/bus** ir de carro (*drive*)/de comboio (*BR:* trem)/de autocarro (*BR:* de autobus); **to** ~ **on horseback/riding** ir a cavalo; **to** ~ **to** ir a/para; **to** ~ **on foot** (*walk*) ir/andar a pé; **to** ~ **home** ir para casa; **to** ~ **and do sth** ir fazer algo; **to** ~ **in** entrar; **2 to** ~ **in for** (*competition*) concorrer; **3 to** ~ **into** (*room, conversation, business*) entrar em; (*matter*) investigar; **4 to** ~ **across** atravessar; **5 to** ~ **for a walk/stroll** ir dar um passeio; ~ **for a spin** (*by car*) (*ir*) dar um passeio de carro; **6** (*leave, depart*) ir-se; **to** ~ **away** ir-se embora; **7 to** ~ **down** descer, baixar; (*sun*) pôr-se; (*ship*) afundar-se; **the ship went down** o barco afundou-se; **8 to** ~ **by** (*person, place*) passar por; **to** ~ **by what another says** guiar-se por; **9 to** ~ **halves** partir a meias; dividir (contas, etc); **10 to** ~ **mad** enlouquecer; **11 to** ~ **with** (*match*) ir bem com, combinar com, condizer com; **12 to** ~ **about/around** *vi* (*rumour*) propagar-se; **13 how do I** ~ **about this?** como é que eu faço isso?; **14 to** ~ **against** ir contra; **15 to** ~ **ahead** ir avante, continuar, avançar; **16 to** ~ **along with** acompanhar (alguém); (*agree*) concordar, aquiescer; (*take place*) realizar-se; **17 to** ~ **around** rodar; **18** (*short of*) **not enough to** ~ **around** não há suficiente para todos; **there's a month to** ~ **before the wedding** falta um mês para o casamento; **19** (*become*) **to** ~ **red in the face** ficar vermelha, corar; **20** (*function*) **the engine won't** ~ a máquina não vai, não funciona; **21 to** ~ **well/badly** correr bem/mal; **how did your exam** ~? como te correu o exame?; **how goes business?** (*fam*) como vão os negócios?; **22 to** ~ **back** voltar, retroceder; **to** ~ **back on one's word/promise** faltar à palavra/promessa; **23 to** ~ **for** (*like*) gostar de; (*fetch*) ir buscar; (*attack*) atacar; **24** (*depart*) **to** ~ **off** ir-se; (*food*) estragar-se, (*fruta*) apodrecer, (*leite*) azedar; (*explode*) explodir; (*event*) realizar-se; **25 to** ~ **on** seguir, continuar; (*happen*) **a lot is going on** está a acontecer muita coisa; **to** ~ **out** sair; (*fire, light*) apagar-se; **to** ~ **over** repetir; (*check*) revisar, rever; **to** ~ **through** *vt* (*town etc*) atravessar; (*suitcases, drawers*) revistar; (*experience*) passar por; (*spend*) gastar; **to** ~ **up** (*stairs, hill*) subir; (*increase*) subir, aumentar; **prices have gone up** os preços subiram; ~ **up a class** (*school*) passar para a classe/turma acima; **to** ~ **without** *vt* passar sem; **to let** ~ **of sth** deixar largar; **to** ~ **let of sb** largar alguém; **my hopes are gone** as minhas esperanças foram-se.

goad *vt* aguilhoar; **2** (*fig*) (*provocar*) **to** ~ **sb into doing sth** incitar alguém a fazer algo.

go-ahead *n* luz *f* verde, permissão *f* para prosseguir; ♦ *adj* empreendedor,-ora.

goal *n* (*target, aim*) meta, alvo; **2** (SPORT) gol(o) *m*; ~**keeper** *n* guarda-redes *m*, (BR) goleiro; ~-**post** *n* poste *m* de baliza.

goat *n* cabra; **billy-**~ bode *m*; ~**'s cheese** *n* queijo de cabra.

goatee (*also:* **goat's beard**) *n* cavanhaque, pêra, barbicha.

gob *n* (*slang*) (*mouth*) bico; **2** (*spittle*) escarro; ♦ (*pt, pp* -**bed**) *vi* (*spit*) cuspir, escarrar.

gobble *vt* (~ **down/up**) engolir rapidamente, devorar; tragar, gorgorejar; **2** *vi* (*turkey's gurgling sound*) fazer gluglu.

gobbledygook *n* (*pretentious or incomprehensible jargon*) palavreado (sem nexo).

go-between *n* intermediário,-a; **2** (COMM) açambarcador.

Gobi *npr:* **the** ~ **Desert** o Deserto de Gobi.

goblet *n* cálice *m*.

goblin *n* duende *m*.

gobsmacked *adj* (*coll*) embasbacado,-a; **to be** ~ ficar de cara à banda.

go-cart *n* andadeira, andador *m*; go-kart.

god *n* deus *m*; **G~** *npr* Deus *m*; **G~ Almighty** Deus Todo Poderoso; **G~ willing** se D~ quiser; **for G~'s sake** por amor de Deus.

godchild *n* afilhado,-a.

goddam(n) (*slang*) maldito; **the** ~ **noise** maldito barulho; ♦ **goddamn!** *exc* (*slang*) que porra! (*cal*).

goddess *n* deusa.

godfather *n* padrinho.

god-forsaken *adj* miserável; abandonado, esquecido por Deus.

godmother *n* madrinha.

godparents *mpl* padrinhos.

Em inglês só se usam os termos '**godparents and god-children**' (padrinhos e afilhados) quando se trata de batizados e nunca a respeito de casamentos.

gods *npl* (THEAT) galleria *f*.

godsend *n* dádiva do céu.

godson *n* afilhado.

goer *n* (*coll*) (*energetic person*) **to be a** ~ ser dinâmico, energético; **2 theatre-**~ frequentador,-ora (de teatro/ópera); (*of cinema*) cinéfilo,-a.

go-getter *n* (*person*) lutador,-ora, ambicioso,-a.

gogglebox *n* (*coll*) televisor *m*, televisão *f*.

goggles *npl* óculos *mpl* de prote(c)ção; ♦ *vt* arregalar os olhos.

go-go *n* (MUS) go-go *m*; ♦ *adj* dinâmico,-a, enérgico,-a

going *n* (*progress*) progresso *m*, marcha andamento *m*; **that's good** ~ está a correr bem, rápido; **the** ~ **is tough** o andamento é difícil; ♦ *adj* corrente, em vigor do momento: **the** ~ **rate** tarifa corrente, em vigor; ~ **concern** (em funcionamento) empresa em laboração; ~-**over** *n* revisão, verificação.

goings-on *npl* acontecimentos *mpl*, coisas *fpl* estranhas *fpl*; (*coll*) manigâncias *fpl*; **there are some** ~ **between those two** há uns segredos entre aqueles dois.

gold *n* ouro; **to be as good as ~** *(child)* ser bem comportado; parecer ouro; ♦ *adj* de ouro; **~ leaf** ouro *m* em folha; **~-mine** *n* mina de ouro; **~plated** *adj* banhado a ouro, em banho de ouro; **~ standard** *adj* padrão-ouro *m*; **~smith** *n* ourives *m,f sg/pl; (shop)* ourivesaria *f*.

golden *adj* de ouro; dourado; **~ handshake** *n (UK)* indemnização por despedimento ou gratificação por aposentadoria; **~ jubilee** bodas *fpl* de ouro; *(other)* jubileu; **~ mean** *n (happy medium)* o justo meio termo *m*; **~ goose** *n* a galinha *f* dos ovos de ouro; **~ rule** *n* regra de ouro.

goldfish *n* peixe-dourado *m*; **~ bowl** *n* aquário *m* para peixes-dourados.

golf *n* golfe *m*; **~ club** *n* clube *m* de golfe; *(stick)* taco; **~ course** *n* campo de golfe.

golfer *n* jogador,-ora *m,f* de golfe.

gondola *n* gôndola; **gondolier** *n* gondoleiro.

gone *(pp of* go*)* **she has ~ to her mother's** ela já foi para casa da mãe; **it has just ~ twenty past two** já passa das duas e vinte; **sorry, the article you have asked for is ~** desculpe, mas o produto que deseja já foi vendido.

gong *n* gongo *m*.

gonorrhea *n* gonorreia.

goo *(fam)* substância *f* pegajosa, **2** *(sentimental talk)* *m* meleca *f*.

good *n* bem *m*, proveito *m*; **~ and evil** o bem e o mal; *(beneficial)* **it is for your own ~** é para teu bem; **2** *(use)* **to be ~ for** servir para; **it's no ~ complaining** não vale a pena queixar-se; ♦ *adj (comp* **better,** *superl* **best)** *(gen)* bom *m*, boa *f*; *(kind)* bondoso,-a, com bom coração; **in ~ spirits** *(happy)* animado,-a, bem disposto,-a; **a ~ deed** uma boa acção; **to do a ~ turn to sb** fazer um favor a alguém; **2** *(useful)* útil; **3** *(very)* bastante, muito,-a; **a ~ deal of money** muito dinheiro; **a ~ many** muitos,-as; **4** *(repair)* **to make ~** compensar, reparar; **5** *(tasty food)* **the soup tastes ~** a sopa sabe bem; **6** *(appearance)* **you look ~ in that dress** fica-lhe bem esse vestido; **7** *(skilled)* **to be ~ with one's hands** ter jeito, ser hábil; ♦ *adv* **as ~ as** *(practically)*quase; **to be as ~ as new** como se fosse novo; **for ~** *(forever)* para sempre; ♦ *exc* **that's a ~ one!** *(in approval or anger)* essa é boa!

good afternoon! *exc* boa tarde!

good bye! *exc* adeus! *(EP)*, tchau! *(BR)*; até logo!; **to say ~** despedir-se.

good evening! *exc* boa noite!

good-for-nothing *n adj* inútil; **this is ~** isto não presta *(para nada)*.

Good Friday *npr* Sexta-feira Santa.

goodies *npl (anything that is good and sweet = chocolates, puddings, etc)* guloseimas *fpl*.

good-looking *adj* bonito,-a, atraente.

good-natured *(person) n* bonacheirão,-ona, com boa disposição; **2** *(person)* de/com bom coração.

goodness *n (of person)* bondade *f*; **2** *(food)* de valor nutritivo; ♦ **for ~ sake!** *exc* por amor de Deus!

goods *npl* artigos, produtos *mpl*; mercadorias; *(electrical)* materiais; **~ services** bens *mpl* de consumo; **~ and chattels** pertences, haveres; artigos pessoais; *(JUR)* posses pessoais; **~ train** comboio de mercadorias *(BR)* trem *m* de carga.

good-tempered *adj (person)* com bom feitio.

goodwill *n* boa vontade *f*; **2** *(COMM) (customers)* clientela *f*; **with ~** de boa vontade *f*; **I come in ~** venho de boa vontade/em fé.

goody *(pl:* **goodies)** *n (gentle, good person)* um bonzinho, uma pessoa boa; ♦ *exc* **goody!** ó(p)timo!

gooey *adj (fam) (sticky)* grudento,-a.

goof *(US, fam) n (mistake)* manaca, gaffe, asneira, bobagem; **2** *(pessoa)* palerma; ♦ **~ around** *(UK)* **~ off** *(US) (fool around)* *vi* vaguear; andar na brincadeira.

goofy *n (person)* pateta; **2** *(clothes, comportamento)* simplório, patego.

goon *n (coll)* palhaço-maluco; **2** *(pej)* idiota *m,f*; **3** *(US) (thug)* rufião.

goose *(pl:* **geese)** *n* ganso; ♦ *exc (coll)* **you silly ~!** *(fam)* tontinho,-a! pateta *m,f*; *(BR)* seu bobo/sua boba!

gooseberry *n (fruit)* groselha *f*; IDIOM **to be/play ~** *(chaperon)* fazer de pau de cabeleira.

gooseflesh *(=* **goose pimples** *npl)* *n* pele *f* arrepiada.

gore *n* sangue coagulado; **2** *(in fabric)* nesga *f* de pano triangualar); ♦ *vt (bull)* espetar, trespassar, ferir com os chifres.

gorge *n* garganta *f*; **2** *(valley)* desfiladeiro; ♦ *vr:* **to ~ o.s. (on, with)** *(to eat a lot)* empanturrar-se de/com.

gorgeous *adj (place, work, weather)* magnífico,-a, maravilhoso,-a, jeitoso,-a; **she is ~** ela é encantadora; é muito querida.

gorilla *n* gorila *m*.

gormless *adj (UK) (fam)* simplório,-a; parvalhâo,-lhona.

gorse *n (BOT)* tojo *m*, urze *f*.

gory *adj* sangrento,-a.

gosh! *exc* Deus meu!, caramba!

gosling *n* ganso *m* pepueno.

go-slow *n* greve *f* de zelo, *(BR)* operação *f* tartaruga.

gospel *n* evangelho; **2** verdade absoluta; **Gospel** *npr (in Bible)* o Evangelho *m*.

gossip *n* conversa fútil, tagarelice *(BR)* bate-papo *m*; **2** *(malicious)* bisbilhotice *f*; sarilho *m*, fofoca; **malicious ~** rumores maldizentes; **~ column** *n* coluna social; ♦ *vi* falar mal das pessoas, bisbilhotar, fofocar.

gossiper *n (person)* intriguista *m,f*; bisbilhoteiro,-a, coscuvilheiro,-a; *(BR)* fofoqueiro,-a.

gossipy *(adj) (fond of gossip)* mexeriqueiro, bisbilhoteiro,-a.

got *(pt, pp* **get)**.

Gothic *adj* gótico,-a.

gotta *(coll =* **got to)**.

gotten *((US) pp of* get)*.

gouge *n* goiva *f*; ♦ *(eyes, object)* **~ out** *vt* arrancar, *(with the fingers or pointed instrument)* esburacar com uma goiva.

gourd *(BOT)* tipo de abóbora; cabaça; **2** *(container)* cabaço *m*.

gourmet *n* gastrónomo,-a; ♦ *adj* gastronómico,-a.

gout *n (MED)* gota.
govern *vt* governar; **2** controlar, dominar; **3** dirigir, administrar.
governess *n* governanta *f*; **2** *(school)* preceptora.
governing *adj* governante, dirigente; *(person)* no poder; ~ **body** *n* conselho *m* administrativo, directivo, corpo *m* directivo.
government *n (POL)* governo; **2 household** ~ o governo da casa; **3** *(department, policy, etc)* governamental.
governor *n (Bank, State, Colony)* governador *m*; dire(c)tor,-ora; ~**ship** *n* cargo *m* de governador.
Govt *(abbr for* **Government**).
gown *n* vestido; **2** *(REL)* toga; **3** *(Univ, JUR)* beca; **4** *(MED, school)* bata.
GP *n (abbr for* **general practitioner**).
grab *(pt, pp* **grabbed**) *vt/vi* agarrar, arrebatar, apoderar-se de; **2** *(snatch)* gesto rápido de agarrar; ~ **a sandwich** agarra um sanduíche; **3 to have the** ~ **on sb** ter vantagem sobre alguém; **4** *(coll)* **how does this** ~ **you?** *(does it appeal to you?*) agrada-te?, que lhe parece?; **5 it's up for** ~**s** *(available)* isto está pra quem for o primeiro.
grace *n (REL)* graça *f*; elegância, fineza; **to do sh with good** ~ fazer algo de boa vontade; ♦ *vt* honrar; agraciar, adorrnar; **8 days'** ~ *(extra time for payment)* um prazo de 8 dias; *(prayer at meal time)* **to say** ~ dar graças a Deus (às refeições); **Your Grace** *(form of address) (archibishop, cardinal)* Vossa Eminência; *(duke, duchess)* Vossa Alteza; **to be in the good** ~**s of sb** estar nas boas graça *fpl* de alguém.
graceful *adj* elegante, gracioso.
graceless *adj* desajeitado; **2** *(manner)* deselegante; **3** sem graça.
gracious *adj* gentil, afável; **2** pessoa refinada; **3** gracioso; **by** ~ **permission of H.R.H. Prince Michael** por graça de S.A.R. o Príncipe Miguel.
gradation *n (on a continuum)* gradação *f*; **2** *(colour, light)* gradação *f*; **3** *(of feeling)* grau *m*; **4** *(on scale)* graduation.
grade *n* classe *f*, categoria *f*; **2** grau *m*; **3** *(US: EDUC)* classe; ~ **crossing** *n (US)* passagem *f* de nível; ♦ *vt* classificar; 2 ter sucesso.
grader *n (of produce) (machine)* máquina de calibrar; **2** *(US):* **sixth-grader** *n* aluno,-a do sexto ano.
gradient *n (slope)* declive *m*; **2** *(degree of slope)* inclinação *f*.
grading *n* classificação; **2** *(school) (marks)* notas.
gradual *adj* gradual, suave.
gradually *adv* gradualmente.
graduate *n* graduado, licenciado; ♦ *vi* formar-se, licenciar-se.
graduation *n* graduação *f*.
graft *n (AGR, MED)* enxerto; **2** *(coll) (hard work)* labuta; **3** *(US) (corruption)* suborno; ♦ *vt* enxertar.
grain *n* grão *m*; grãos *mpl*, cereais *mpl*; **2** veio, fibra.
grainy *adj* granuloso, granulado.
gram *n* grama *m*.
grammar *n* gramática; ~-**school** *(UK)* liceu *m*; escola secundária.

grammatical *adj* gramatical.
gramme *(UK)* *n* = **gram**.
gramophone *n* gramofone *m*; giradiscos *m inv*, *(BR)* toca-discos *m inv*.
granary *n* celeiro; **Alentejo is Portugal's** ~ o Alentejo é o celeiro de Portugal; ~ **bread** *n* pão *m* de trigo.
grand *n (fam) (money)* **thousand pounds/thousand dollars** mil libras/mil dólares; ♦ *adj (impressive)* grande, magnífico; **2** ~ **project** proje(c)to ambicioso; **3** *(family, etc)* ilustre; ~**dad** *n* vovô; ~**children** *npl* netos *mpl*; ~**daughter** *n* neta; ~ **duchess** *n* grã-duquesa; ~ **duke** *n* grão-duque; ~**eur** *n* grandeza, magnificência; ~**father** *n* avô *m*; ~**father clock** *n* relógio *m* de pêndulo; ~**iose** *adj* grandioso, *(pej)* espalhafatoso,-a; ~ **jury** *n* júri *m* principal; ~**ma** *n* vovó; ~ **master** *n* grão-mestre; ~**mother** *n* avó *f*; **the G~ National** *npr* grande e famosa corrida de cavalos que se realiza anualmente em Liverpool, Inglaterra; ~**parents** *n* avós *m*; ~ **prix** *(pl:* **grands prix**) grande prémio; ~ **piano** *n* piano *m* de cauda; ~**son** *n* neto; ~**stand** *n (SPORT)* tribuna *f* principal, de honra; ~ **total** *n* some total.
granje *n (UK)* quinta *f*, solar *m*.
granite *n (MIN)* granito.
granny *n* avozinha *f*; ~ **flat** *n (UK)* apartamento, suíte para os avós, ligado à, ou dentro da casa principal.
granny smith (apple) tipo de maçã verde e dura, geralmente, para cozinhar = maçã *f* reineta.
grant *n (EDUC)* bolsa, subsídio (de estudo); **2** *(from Govt, local authority)* subsídio; **to take sth for** ~**ed** dar algo por certo; ♦ *vt* conceder, dar; **2** *(formal language)* reconhecer (que); **granted/ granting that** admitido que …
grant-aided *adj* subsidiado, subvencionado,-a.
granulated sugar *n* açúcar-cristal *m*.
granule *n* grânulo.
grape *n* uva, bago de uva; **2** *(bunch of)* cacho de uvas; **3** *(~ stone)* gráinha; **to harvest** ~**s** vindimar; ♦ ~**fruit** *n (BOT)* toranja *f*; ~ **hyacinth** *(BOT)* muscari *m*; ~**shot** *(mil)* metralha *f*; *(BOT)* ~**vine** videira *f*, parreira *f*; IDIOM *(coll) (non-official information)* **I heard it on the** ~**vine that …** ouvi dizer que …
graph *n (COMP, MATH)* gráfico; **rising/falling** ~ *(curva)* ascendente/descendente; ~ **paper** *n* papel *m* quadriculado.
graphic *adj* gráfico; **2** *(description)* vivo,-a; ~**s** *npl* grafismo *m*; ~**s card** *(COMP)* placa *f* gráfica.
graphite *n (MIN)* grafita; **2** *(objects)* em fibra de carbono.
grapnel *n (small anchor)* fateixa *f*; **2** arpão *m*.
grapple *vt (NAUT)* prender com uma fateixa; **2 to** ~ **with sth** *(fig)* esforçar-se por resolver algo, lidar com; **3 to** ~ **with sb** engalfinhar-se com alguém, lutar com alguém.
grappling *n (hand-to-hand fight)* luta *f*; ~ **hook/ iron** *n* arpão *m*.
grasp *n* a(c)to de agarrar; **2** *(reach)* alcance *m*; **3** *(understanding)* compreensão *f*; ♦ *vt* agarrar,

segurar; **2** compreender; **I** ~ **the sense** compreendo muito bem; **to** ~ **the opportunity** agarrar a oportunidade.

grasping *n* compreensão *f*; *(strong handshake)* aperto *(de mão)*; ◆ *adj (pej) (greedy person)* avaro,-a, ganancioso,-a.

grass *n (wild)* erva, *(BR)* grama; **2** *(cared for)* relva *f (for lawn)*; **3** *(coll)* (marijuana) erva; IDIOM **the ~ is greener on the other side of the fence** a galinha da minha vizinha é mais gorda do que a minha.

grasshopper *n (ZOOL)* gafanhoto *m*.

grassland *n* pradaria.

grassroots *npl* o povo; **2** raíz *f*, fundamento *m*; ◆ *adj (movement, organization)* popular; de base.

grass snake *n* cobra *f (comum)*.

grassy *adj* coberto de erva/relva, relvado.

grate *n* lareira; grelha; ◆ *vi* ranger; ◆ *vt (CULIN)* ralar.

grateful *adj* agradecido,-a, grato,-a.

grater *n* ralador *m*, raspador *m*.

gratify *vt* gratificar, satisfazer.

gratifying *adj* grato, gratificante.

grating *n (grille)* grade *f*; ◆ *adj (rough)* áspero; ◆ *adj (voice)* irritante.

gratitude *n* agradecimento *m*; gratidão *f*.

gratuitous *adj* gratuito.

gratuity *n* gratificação *f*, gorjeta.

grave *n* túmulo *m*, cova *f*; ~ **digger** *n* coveiro; ◆ *adj* sério, grave; **2** ~ **accent** *(gram) (accentuation)* acento *m* grave; IDIOM **one foot in the ~** ele está com os pés para a cova.

gravel *n (coarse)* cascalho.

gravely *adv (ill)* gravemente, *(solemnly)* seriamente.

gravestone *n* lápide *f*.

graveyard *n* cemitério.

gravitate *vi* **to ~ towards sb/sth** be attracted to sb/sth.

gravity *n* gravidade *f*; seriedade *f*.

gravy *n (CULIN)* molho; ~ **sauceboat** molheira *f*.

gray *n adj ((US)* = **grey)** *(colour)* cinzento, de cinzas; *(murky river)* pardacento; *(cat)* pardo; *(sky)* cinzento, carregado.

grayish, greyish *adj* acinzentado.

graze *n* arranhadura, esfoladela; ◆ *vt (scratch skin)* esfolar; arranhar; *(touch lightly)* roçar; ◆ *vi (sheep, cows)* pastar.

grease *n (animal's fat)* gordura; *(of oil)* lubrificante *m*; ~**proof** *adj* à prova de gordura; ~ **paper** papel *m* de cera vegetal, impermeável; *(dirty fat from skin)* sebo; ◆ *vt* engordurar; ~ **the cake tray** unta o tabuleiro dos bolos.

greasy *adj (meal)* gorduroso; gordorento; *(dirty with grease)* engordorento; engordurado.

great (-**er**, -**est**) *adj (gen)* grande; **2** ilustre *m,f*; **a ~ man** um grande homem; **2** *(vastness)* imenso,-a, vasto,-a; **3** *(coll) (good at)* **she is ~ at cooking** ela é uma fantástica cozinheira; **4** magnífico,-a, estupendo,-a; ◆ *exc (fam)* ~! ó(p)timo!,-a, porreiro!; IDIOM **everything is going ~** tudo corre ás mil maravilhas.

great-aunt *n* tia-avó.

Great Barrier Reef *npr:* **the ~** a Grande Barreira.

Great Bear *npr:* **the ~** (a) Ursa Maior.

Great Britain *npr* Grã-Bretanha; **in ~** na Grã-Bretanha.

A Grã-Bretanha, G.B., compreende a Inglaterra, a Escócia e o País de Gales. **Vd: United Kingdom**.

greatcoat *n* capote *m*.

Great Dane *n (dog)* grande danois.

great-grandchild *n* bisneto,-a.

great-grandfather *n* bisavô.

great-grandmother *n* bisavó.

greatly *adv* muito, grandemente; consideravelmente; **he shall be ~ missed** vamos sentir muito a falta dele.

greatness *n* grandeza *n*.

great-uncle *n* tio-avô.

Great Wall of China *npr:* **the ~** a Grande Muralha da China.

Grecian *adj* grego.

Greece *npr* Grécia; **in ~** na Grécia.

greed *n* (= **greediness**) avidez *f*, cobiça; gula; sofreguidão *f*.

greedily *adv* com avidez.

greedy *adj* avarento; guloso.

Greek *npr adj* grego,-a; *(LING)* grego; IDIOM **it's all ~ to me** *(I can't understand it)* para mim é tudo chinês.

green *n (colour)* verde; **2** *(grassy area)* relvado; **3** *(of golf)* green *m*; **4 The G~s** *(environmentalist)* os Verdes; **5** ~**s** *npl* hortaliças, verduras *fpl*; ◆ *adj (colour)* verde; **be ~ with envy** ter dor de cotovelo.

green bean *n* feijão *m*, vagem *f* verde.

green belt *(UK)* zona verde protegida; **2** *(BR)* cinturão *m* verde; **3** *(inexperienced)* novato,-a.

green card *n (UK) (driving insurance)* carta *f* internacional (que protege o veículo e motorista no estrangeiro); **2** *(US)* carta *f* verde (certificado de residência que permite trabalhar nos E.U.A.).

greenery *n* folhagem.

green fingers: to have ~ ter dom para jardinagem.

greenfly *n* pulgão *m* das roseiras.

greengage *n (fruto)* rainha-cláudia.

greengrocer's *n* frutaria; *(BR)* quitanda.

greenhorn *n (US) (new arrival)* recém-chegado, novato; *(Univ)* caloiro; **2** *(UK)* pessoa inexperiente.

greenhouse *n* estufa; **the ~ effect** o efeito estufa.

greenish *adj* esverdeado,-a.

Greenland *npr* Gronelândia, *(BR)* Groenlândia.

Greenlander *n, adj* gronelandês,-esa; *(BR)* groenlandês.

greenness *n (landscape)* verdura *f*, viço *f*; **2** *(inexperience)* inexperiência *m*.

Green Paper *(POL, ADMIN)* Livro Verde.

Green Party *npr:* **the ~** o Partido Verde.

greet *vt (salute)* saudar, dar as boas vindas (**to sb** alguém); **2** *(handshake, bow)* cumprimentar (alguém); **3** *(receive)* acolher; **the news were ~-ed with jubilation** a notícia foi acolhida com júbilo.

greeting *n* cumprimento, saudação; acolhimento; **seasons ~s** votos *mpl* de Boas Festas.

gregarious *adj* gregário.

grenade *n* Granada.

grenadier *n (MIL)* granadeiro *m*.

grew (*pt of* **grow**).

grey (*Vd:* **gray**) *adj* cinzento; ~**-haired** *adj* grisalho; ~**hound** *n* galgo.

grey matter *n* massa *f* cinzenta; cérebro *m*.

grid *n (grating)* grade *f*, gradeamento *m;* **2** *(ELECT)* rede *f* eléctrica nacional; **3** *(UK)* network; **4** *(pattern)* grade *f*, quadriculado *m*.

griddle *(CULIN)* n *(for pancakes, etc)* grelha, placa *f* em ferro fundido.

gridlock *n* engarrafamento *m; (fig)* deadlock, impasse.

grief *n* dor *f*, mágoa *f*, pena *f*, desgosto *m;* ~**-stricken** *adj* esmagado,-a pela dor, pelo desgosto; ♦ *exc* **good** ~! cruzes!, *(BR)* nossa!

grievance *n (feeling of injustice)* motivo de queixas (**against** contra) agravo; ressentimento.

grieve *vt* afligir-se, sofrer; ♦ *vt* dar/fazer pena a; **to** ~ **for** chorar por.

grievous *adj* penoso, doloroso; **2** *(wound, damage)* grave, profundo.

grill *n (on/in cooker, barbecue)* grelha; ♦ *vt* grelhar; **2** *(coll)* interrogar alguém cerradamente (**about** acerca de).

grille *n* grade *f*.

grim (**-mer**, **-mest**) *adj* sinistro; **2** *(local) (somber)* soturno; **3** *(fam)* horrível, assustador; **he will have the grimmest future** ele terá o futuro mais deprimente.

grimace *n* careta; **2** *(of pain)* esgar *m;* ♦ *vi* fazer caretas.

grime *n* sujidade *f; (BR)* sujeira.

grimy *adj* sujo, encardido.

grin *n* sorriso largo ou de careta; ♦ *(pt, pp* **-ned**) *vi* arreganhar os dentes num sorriso; IDIOM **to** ~ **and bear it** *(pain, loss)* aguentar estoicamente; aguentar e não bufar.

grind *n* trabalho pesado e aborrecido; **the daily** ~ a labuta, rotina diária; ♦ *(pt, pp* **ground**) *vi/vt (coffee, grains)* moer; (faca, pedra) afiar; **to** ~ **one's teeth** ranger os dentes; **to** ~ **down/out** *vt* esmagar; **to** ~ **on** prosseguir (conversa); **to** ~ **up** *vt (bottles)* triturar.

grinder *n (machine for crushing) (industrial)* britadeira; *(domestic)* trituradora *f*, moedor *m*.

grinding *adj (work)* opressivo,-a.

grindstone *n* pedra de afiar/amolar.

grinning *adj* sorridente *m,f*.

grip *n (strong)* aperto; **2 to have a** ~ **on sth/sb** ter controlo sobre algo/alguém; **a good** ~ **on** *(history, situation)* boa compreensão; **to get a** ~ **on o.s.** controlar-se; ♦ *(pt, pp* **-ped**) *vt (grasp)* agarrar; **2** *(hold o.s. to)* segurar-se bem a (algo); **3 to come to** ~**s with** debater-se com, encarar a situação; **4** *(tyres, etc)* ter aderência.

gripe *n (MED) (complaint)* queixa; ~**s** cólicas *fpl;* ~ **water** remédio para bebés para acalmar a cólica.

griping *adj (MED)* **to have** ~ **pains** ter cólicas.

gripping *adj (story, film)* cativante, absorvente *m,f*.

grisly *adj* horrendo, medonho.

grist *n* grão *m* para moer; IDIOM **it's all** ~ **to his mill** ele sabe tirar proveito de tudo.

gristle *n* cartilagem *f*.

grit *n* areia, grão *m* de areia, de poeira; **2** *(roads)* saibro; **3** *(coll)* coragem *f;* ♦ *vt* pôr, encher areia, saibro *(on road);* IDIOM **to** ~ **one's teeth** ranger os dentes.

gritter *n* veículo que espalha areia grossa nas estradas de gelo.

grits *n (UK: oats, US: corn)* farinha de aveia ou trigo, farelo servido com leite como cereal.

gritty *adj (sandy)* arenoso; ~ **particles** grãos *mpl* de poeira; IDIOM **nitty-**~ os aspe(c)tos mais básicos de qualquer assunto; **let us get down to the nitty-**~ vamos ao que interessa.

grizzle *vi (UK) (child)* choramingar; estar rabujento,-a.

grizzled *adj (hair)* grisalho; algo acinzentado, pardo.

grizzly *n (bear)* urso *m* pardo.

groan *n (of pain, sorrow)* gemido *m*, lamento *m;* ♦ *vt/vi* gemer, lamuriar; **2** *(moan)* resmungar; **3** *(creak) (floorboards)* ranger; **4** *(fig)* **the shelves groaned under the weight of the books** as prateleiras gemiam com o peso dos livros.

grocer *n* merceeiro; ~**'s** *(shop)* n mercearia.

groceries *npl* comestíveis *mpl*.

grog *n (alcoholic drink)* grogue, *m*.

groggy *adj* embriagado,-a, cambaleante *m,f*.

grogram *n* gorgorão *m*.

groin *n (ANAT)* virilha.

groom *n* moço; moço de estrebaria; lacaio; **bride**~ noivo; ♦ *vt* tratar de cavalos, cuidar de si.

groomed *adj:* **well/badly-** ~ bem-vestido, bem tratado,-a, maltratado,-a.

groove *n (on record)* ranhura *f; (on wood)* entalhe, encaixe *m; (on seashell)* estria *f;* **2** *(coll)* rotina *f;* ♦ *vt* entalhar; *(US)* curtir.

groovy *adj* fantástico,-a.

grope *vi (find one's way in the dark)* andar, procurar às apalpadelas; **2** tatear o caminho; **3** tentar às cegas.

gross *n (twelve dozen)* grosa; **by the** ~ à grosa; *adv* por junto; ♦ *adj (coarse manner)* ordinário, grosseiro; **2** ~ **indecency** *(JUR)* ultrage ao pudor; **3** ~ **injustice** injustiça *f* flagrante; **4 a** ~ **interpretation** um mal entendido; **5** *(exaggeration)* enorme; **6** *(ignorance)* crasso; **7** *(COMM)* bruto; **8** ~ **weight** peso bruto; **9** *(coll) (obeso)* gordo, balofo; **Gross Domestic Product (GDP)** Produto Interno Bruto (PIB); **Gross National Product (GDP)** Producto Nacional Bruto (PNB).

grossly *adv* grosseiramente, extremamente; ~ **overdone** escandalosamente exagerada.

grotesque *adj* grotesco.

grotto *n* gruta.

grotty (**-ier**, **-iest**) *adj (UK, fam)* asqueroso,-a; cadavérico,-a.

grouch *vi (coll)* resmungar (**about** acerca de).

grouchy *adj* resmungão,-ona; macambúzio,-a.

ground (*pp, pp of* **grind**) *n* terreno, chão *m;* **above/below** ~ acima/abaixo da terra; **to fall on the** ~ cair no chão; **to fall to the** ~ cair por terra; **to get off the** ~ *(AER)* descolar; levantar voo; **to get sth**

off the ~ (projecto) arrancar; **2** (*area of land*) terreno, campo; **3** *(AGR, CONSTR, SPORT)* (*earth*) solo *m*, terra *f*; terreno *m*, campo *m*; **we have covered a lot of** ~ andámos bastante; *(negotiations)* conseguimos discutir muito; **4** ~**s** *(motive)* causa, razão *f*; **there are ~s for divorce** há motivo para divórcio; **5** ~**s** *npl* (*of coffee*) borras, restos; (*around castle, house*) jardins *mpl*, terrenos *mpl*, parque *m*; **6** *(ELECT: US)* ligação à terra; **to go to** ~ esconder-se; **to run o.s. into the** ~ trabalhar até cair morto; **to stand one's** ~ manter-se firme nas suas opiniões; ♦ *vt* **to be grounded** *(AER)* impedido de levantar voo; **2** (*child*) ser castigado,-a; **3** (*boat*) ficar encalhado,-a; ~**breaking** *adj* inovador.

groundfloor *n* rés-do-chão *m*; *(BR)* andar *m* térreo; ~ **frost** *n* geada *f*.

grounding *n* (*preparation*) conhecimentos *mpl* básicos.

groundless *adj* infundado, sem fundamento.

ground level *n*: **at** ~ ao nível do solo.

groundnut *n* amendoim *m*.

ground rice *n* sémola.

groundsheet *n* capa impermeável, lona.

ground staff *n* *(AER)* pessoal *m* de terra.

groundswell *n* *(NAUT)* maremoto *m*; **2** (*upsurge*) **a** ~ **of support for** uma onda de solidariedade por.

groundwork *n* base *f*, preparação *f*; esboço; fundamento *m*.

group *n* grupo; conjunto, banda; ♦ (= **to** ~ **together**) *vt* agrupar; ♦ *vi* agrupar-se.

grouper *n* (*fish*) garopa *f*.

grouse *npl inv* tetraz *m*, galo-silvestre *m*; ♦ *vi* (*coll*) (*complain about*) queixar-se.

grout *n* (*to fill in between tiles*) gesso *m* fino para encher espaços entre os azulejos.

grove *n* arvoredo; **2** (*UK*) alameda *f*; (*of fruits*) pomar *m*.

grovel *vi* (*fig*) ~ **before** humilhar-se, prostrar-se (perante/diante).

grovelling (*UK*) **groveling** (*US*) *adj* servile.

grow (*pt* **grew**, *pp* **grown**) *vi* crescer; germinar; aumentar; (*spread*) espalhar-se, estender-se; (*become*) tornar-se; **to** ~ **rich/weak** enriquecer-se, enfraquecer-se; ♦ *vt* cultivar, deixar crescer; **to** ~ **up** *vi* crescer, fazer-se homem/mulher.

grower *n* cultivador,-ora, produtor,-ora.

growing *adj* crescente; **a** ~ **concern** uma crescente preocupação.

growl *vi* rosnar.

grown (*pp of* **grow**) **your son has** ~ **up** o seu filho está muito crescido.

grown-up *n* adulto, pessoa mais velha.

growth *n* crescimento, desenvolvimento; aumento; *(MED)* (*lump*) tumor *m*; ~ **rate** *n* taxa de crescimento.

grub *n* larva, lagarta; **2** (*coll*) comida.

grubby *adj* sujo, porco.

grudge *n* motivo de rancor; ♦ *vt*: **to** ~ **sb sth** dar algo a alguém de má vontade, invejar algo a alguém; **to bear sb a** ~ guardar rancor a alguém; **he ~s the money** ele dá dinheiro de má vontade.

gruelling *adj* duro, árduo.

gruesome *adj* horrível.

gruff *adj* (*voice*) rouca; (*person*) brusco,-a.

grumble *vi* resmungar, queixar-se.

grumpy (-ier, -iest) *adj* resmungão,-gona; rabugento,-a.

grunt *n* (*of pig*) grunhido; **2** (*of person*) resmungo *m*; ♦ *vi* grunhir; **2** (*person*) resmungar.

G-string *n* *(MUS)* corda G; **2** (*men's bikini*) tanga; (*BR*) tapa-sexo.

Guadeloupe *npr* Guadalupe; **in** ~ em Guadalupe.

guarantee *n* garantia; ♦ *vt* garantir.

guarantor *n* fiador,-ora.

guard *n* guarda; (*RAIL*) condutor de comboio (*BR*: trem), guarda-freio *m*; ~ **dog** cão *m* de guarda; ♦ *vt* guardar; ~ **against** prevenir-se (contra); ~**ed** *adj* (*fig*) cauteloso.

guardian *n* *(JUR)* protector,-ora, curador,-ora; guardião,-iã, tutor,-ora; ~ **angel** *n* anjo da guarda.

guardianship *n* tutela *f*.

guard rail *n* *(AUT)* barreira *f* prote(c)tora.

Guatemala *npr* Guatemala; **in** ~ na Guatemala.

Guatemalan *npr adj* guatemalteco,-a.

guava *n* *(BOT)* goiaba; ~ **tree** goiabeira *f*.

Guernsey *npr* *(GEOG)* (ilha do Canal da Mancha) Guernsey; **in** ~ em Guernsey; **2** (*sweater*) camisola *f* de lã (à moda dos pescadores).

guerrilla *n* guerrilheiro,-a; ~ **warfare** *n* guerrilha.

guess *n* suposição *f*, conjectura; **to take/have a** ~ adivinhar; ~**work** *n* conjecturas *fpl*; ♦ *vt/vi* adivinhar; ~ **what!** advinha! supor, crer; **I** ~ **it is all right** suponho que esteja bem, suponho que sim.

guest *n* convidado; ~**-house** *n* casa de hóspedes, pensão *f*; ~ **room** *n* quarto de hóspedes; **paying** ~ *n* hóspede *m,f*.

guff *n* asneiras, patetices *fpl*.

guffaw *n* gargalhada; ♦ *vi* rir-se às gargalhadas.

Guiana *npr* Guiana; **in** ~ na Guiana.

Guianese *npr adj* guianês,-esa.

guidance *n* orientação *f*; conselhos *mpl*.

guide *n* guia *m,f*; (*fig*) guia *m*; ~ **dog** *n* cão-guia *m*; ♦ *vt* guiar; orientar.

Guide (Association) *npr* (*equivalent to the Scouts*), (*US* = **Girl Scout**) as Escoteiras *fpl*.

guidebook *n* guia *m*; roteiro *m*.

guided missile *n* míssil *m* guiado.

guidelines *npl* (*fig*) princípios *mpl* gerais, dire(c)trizes *fpl*.

guiding *adj* norteador,-ora; orientador,-ora.

guild *n* grémio (*BR*: grê-); (*HIST*) guilda; associação *f*.

guildhall *n* centro de reuniões das corporações de uma cidade; (*equiv to*) Grémio Literário de Lisboa.

guile *n* astúcia.

guileless *adj* ingénuo (*BR*: -gê-), cândido.

guillotine *n* (*gen*) guilhotina.

guilt *n* *(JUR)* culpa; ~ **sense** sentido *m* de culpa.

guiltily *adv* com a consciência pesada.

guilty *n, adj* culpado,-a; **to feel** ~ ter a consciência pesada; ter remorsos.

guinea¹ *n* (*old English gold coin* =21 *shilings*) guineu *m*.

Guinea² *npr* Guiné; **in** ~ na Guiné.

Guinea-Bissau *npr* Guiné-Bissau; **in** ~ na Guiné-Bissau.

guinea fowl *n* (*ZOOL*) galinha *f* d'angola.

Guinean *npr* guinense *m,f.*

guinea pig *n* (*ZOOL*) porquinho-da-Índia *m;* (*fig*) (*experiment*) cobaia.

guise *n*: **in** *or* **under the** ~ **of** sob a aparência de, à maneira de.

guitar *n* guitarra, (*BR*) violão *m.*

guitarist *n* guitarrista *m,f* (*BR*) violonista *m,f.*

gulch *n* (*US*) ravina.

gulf *n* (*GEOG*) golfo *m;* **2** (*fig*) abismo *m*, fosso *m;* **the G~** *npr* o Golfo Pérsico; **the G~ of Aden** o Golfo de Áden; **the G~ of Mexico** o Golfo do México; **the G~ Stream** *npr* a corrente *f* do Golfo.

gull *n* (*ZOOL*) gaivota.

gullet *n* goela (esófago); **2** (*fam*) garganta.

gullibility *n* ingenuidade *f.*

gullible *adj* crédulo.

gully *n* barranco, ravina *f.*

gulp *n* gole, trago; **at one** ~ de um gole; ♦ *vi* engolir saliva; ♦ *vt* (= **to** ~ **down**) engolir.

gum *n* (*ANAT*) gengiva; **2** (*adhesive*) goma; **3** chiclete *m*, pastilha elástica; **4** borracha; ~**boil** *n* (*MED*) abcesso *m* nas gengivas; ~ **boots** *npl* botas *fpl* de borracha, galochas *fpl;* ~**shoe** *m* (*US*) crime detective; ~ **tree** *n* árvore *f* de borracha; ♦ (*pt, pp* -**med**) *vt* collar.

gumption *n* (*fam*) (*common sense*) senso comum *m*, perspicácia *f*, espírito *m* empreendedor.

gun *n* arma de fogo; pistola; (*shotgun*) espingarda; canhão *m;* **at** ~ **point** sob ameaça de uma arma; ~**boat** *n* canhoneira; ~**fire** *n* fogo, tiroteio; ~**man** *n* pistoleiro; ~**ner** *n* artilheiro; ~**powder** *n* pólvora; ~**shot** *n* tiro de arma de fogo; ~**smith** *n* armeiro.

gunge *n* (*fam*) substância pegajosa e nojenta; ♦ *vt* **to** ~ **up sth** encher, bloquear algo com substância pegajosa ou borrachenta.

gung-ho *adj* (*UK*) (*fam*) muito entusiasmado,-a, impulsivo,-a.

gunwale *n* (*often pl*) amurada *f* de um navio.

gurgle *n* (*water*) gorgolejo *m;* ♦ *vi* borbulhar; gorgolejar.

gush *n* entusiasmo; efusão *f;* ♦ *vi* jorrar; **2** brotar; (*fig*) entusiasmar-se.

gushing, gushy *adj* (*person*) arrebatado,-a, efusivo,-a.

gusset *n* (*sewing*) (*cloth for underlining*) entretela.

gust *n* rajada de vento, lufada; rabanada (de vento); **2** (*fig*) irrupção *f*, ataque *m.*

gusto *n* entusiasmo; **with** ~ com prazer.

gut *n* intestino *m;* **2** bucho; (*of animals*) vísceras; **3** (*MUS*) corda de tripa; ~ **feeling** *n* pressentimento *m.*

gutless *n* pessoa mole, (*pop*) banana.

guts *npl* tripas *fpl;* **2** (*coll*) coragem *f;* **to have** ~ (*coll*) ter coragem, ter estômago (**for** para); IDIOM **I hate his** ~ tenho-o atravessado na garganta.

gutsy *adj* (*coll*) (*spirited*) fogoso; **2** corajoso,-a, destemido,-a, com garra.

gutter *n* (*on roof*) calha, goteira; **2** (*in street*) sarjeta; ~ **press** *n* imprensa *f* sensacionalista; ~**snipe** *n* garoto *m* da rua.

guttural *adj* gutural.

guy *n* (*fellow*) (*fam*) sujeito, fulano, (*BR*) cara; **2** Guy (Fawkes) espantalho (uma efígie de G.F. que queimam nas fogueiras anualmente no dia 5 de Novembro). (*Vd:* **Guy Fawkes Night**).

Guy Fawkes Night (também conhecida por: **Bonfire Night**, ou **Fireworks Night**) *npr* festividade britânica que comemora a Conspiração da Pólvora, liderada por Guy Fawkes em 1605, cujo objectivo era destruir o Parlamento inglês.

Guyana *npr* Guiana; **in** ~ na Guiana.

Guyanese *npr adj* guianês,-esa.

guy rope *n* (*also* ~ **wire**, ~ **chain**) amarra *f.*

guzzle *vi* (*food*) devorar; (*drink*) beber com sofreguidão; emborcar.

gym *n* (= **gymnasium**) ginásio.

gymnast *n* ginasta *m,f.*

gymnastics *n* ginástica.

gym shoes *npl* sapatilhas *fpl* (*BR*: sapatos *mpl*) de ginástica.

gymslip *n* fato (*BR*: túnica) de ginástica.

gynaecologist *n* ginecologista *m,f.*

gynaecology *n* ginecologia.

gypsum *n* gesso *m;* ~ **mould** molde *m* de gesso.

gypsy (= **gipsy**) *n* cigano,-a.

gyrate *vi* girar.

gyroscope *n* giroscópio *m.*

h

H, h *n (letter)* H, h.

ha *exc* ah!

habeas corpus *n* habeas corpus.

haberdashery *n (UK – in department store) (sewing materials)* retrosaria *f,* loja de miudezas; *(US: notions); (BR)* armarinho *m.*

habit *n* hábito, uso, costume *m;* **bad ~** vício *m;* **2** *(addiction)* **drug ~** habituação à droga; dependência *f;* **3** *(REL)* hábito *m;* **to make a ~ of** habituar-se a; acostumar-se a; **to break a ~** perder o hábito.

habitable *adj* habitável.

habitat *n* habitat *m.*

habitation *n (casa)* habitação *f.*

habitual *adj (customary)* habitual, costumeiro; **2** *(drinker, offender)* inveterado.

habitually *adv* habitualmente.

hack *n (blow, kick)* golpe *m,* pontapé *m;* pancada *f;* **2** *(writer) (pej)* jornalista *m,f* medíocre; *(BR)* escrevinhador,-ora; **3** *(COMP)* pirataria *f* informática; **4** *(US)* taxi *m;* **5** *(in rugby)* pontapé *m,* canelada *f;* **6** cavalo velho e estafado; ♦ *adj* banal, medíocre; ♦ *vt* cortar; agredir; abrir; **to ~ sth to pieces** cortar algo aos pedaços; **~ to bits** *(fig) (reputation)* arruinar por completo; **3** reduzir um artigo de modo prejudicial; **4 ~ into** *(COMP)* invadir/ entrar em ilegalmente; **5** *(slang)* aguentar, tolerar; **I joined the party, but I couldn't ~ it** juntei-me ao partido mas não aguentei; **to ~ off** cortar; **2** *(arm)* decepar; **to ~ sb off** *(annoy)* arreliar alguém; **to ~ one's way** *(in woods)* abrir caminho.

hacker *(COMP)* pirata *m* informático.

hackering *n* pirataria *f* informática.

hacking cough *n* tosse *f* seca e espasmódica.

hackle *n* pena *f* no pescoço do galo; **hackles** *npl (on animal)* pelos *mpl* eriçados; **to make sb's ~ rise** enfurecer alguém.

hackneyed *adj* corriqueiro,-a, trivial *m,f.*

hacksaw *n* serra *f* para metais.

had *(pt, pp of* have*).*

haddock *n (fish)* eglefim *m.*

hadn't = had not.

haemorrhage (UK) hemorrhage (US) *n* hemorragia.

haemorrhoids (UK) hemorrhoids (US) *npl (piles)* hemorróidas *fpl.*

hag *n:* old **~** *(woman)* velha e feia; *(fig)* bruxa.

haggard *adj (appearance)* extenuado, emaciado, abatido; **2** *(expression)* perturbado.

haggis *n* tipo de salsicha escocesa, em formato de bola e com enchidos de miudos picados de carneiro = bucho *m* de carneiro recheado.

haggle *vi:* **to ~ over the price** regatear o preço; pechinchar.

haggler *n (person)* regateador,-ora.

haggling *n* regateio *m.*

Hague *npr:* **The ~** Haia.

hail *n (frozen rain)* granizo; ♦ *vt* cumprimentar, saudar; **2** chamar; **~ a taxi** chamar um táxi; **3** *(acclaim)* aclamar; **to ~ sb as sth** aclamar alguém/ algo como algo; ♦ *vi* chover granizo.

hailstone *n* pedra de granizo.

hailstorm *n* chuva *f* de granizo.

hair *n* cabelo *m;* **a head of ~** cabeleira; **2** *(on body, animal, plant)* pelo *(pêlo) m;* ♦ **to do one's ~** pentear-se; **to have one's ~ done** ir ao cabeleireiro; ir arranjar o cabelo; **to brush one's ~ back** arrepiar o cabelo; **to lose one's ~** perder o cabelo; ficar calvo,-a; **to wear the ~ piled high** usar o cabelo ao alto; ♦ **~brush** *n* escova de cabelo; **~ blow-dry** *n* brushing; **~cut** *n* corte *m* de cabelo; **~ conditioner** *n* amaciador *m;* **~-do** *n* penteado *m;* **~dresser** *n* cabeleireiro,-a; **~dresser's** *n* (salão de) cabeleireiro; **~ drier, ~ dryer** *n* secador *m* de cabelo; **~ gel** *n* fixador *m;* **~grip** *n* gancho *(BR)* grampo *m* do cabelo; **~line** *n* raíz dos cabelos; linha muito fina; **~line fracture** *n (crack in porcelain, bone)* cabelo *m;* **~ oil** *n* óleo *m*/loção *f* capilar; **~ parting** *n* risco do cabelo; **~piece** *n* cabelo postiço; peruca *f;* **~pin** *n* gancho *m* de cabelo; **~pin bend** *n* curva *f* fechada; **~-raising** *adj (story, case)* assustador,-ora; de arrepiar os cabelos; **~ remover** *n* depilador *m;* créme *m* depilatório; **2** *(electrical machine)* depiladora *f;* **~'s breath** *n* grossura de um cabelo; **2** *(fig)* **by a ~s breath** por um triz; **~ slide** *n* travessão *m* de cabelo; **~style** *n* penteado *m;* IDIOM **to let one's ~ down** *(behave without reserve)* descontrair-se; agir à vontade; **to keep one's ~ on** manter a calma; **to make sb's ~ stand on end** *(story, incident)* de pôr os cabelos em pé a alguém; deixar alguém de cabelos em pé; **to split ~s** debater ninharias/minúcias.

hair's breadth *n* grossura de um cabelo; **2** *(moment)* triz; **by a ~** por un triz.

hairy *adj* cabeludo, peludo; **2** *(fam)* arriscado.

hake *n (fish)* pescada *f.*

half *(pl:* halves*) n* metade *f,* meio,-a; **to cut sth in ~** cortar ao meio; **~ of what she said is a lie** metade do que ela disse é mentira; **by ~** pela metade; **he is too honest by ~** ele é honest de mais; **2** *(SPORT)* parte *f;* **in the first ~ of the match** na primeira parte do jogo; **3** *(fraction)* meio; **~-brother** meio-irmão *m;* **4** *(school)* semestre *m;* ♦ *adj* meio,-a: **~ a dozen** *n* meia dúzia *f;* **~ an hour** *n* meia hora *f;* **~-board** *n* meia pensão *f;* **a ~ done job** um trabalho meio feito; ♦ *adv (equal parts)* meio; pela metade; semi, quase; **~ the battle** meio caminho andado; **better ~** *(spouse)* cara-metade; **2** *(partly, almost)* quase; meio; **I ~ expected him to run away** eu quase esperava que ele fugisse; ♦ **~ and ~** *n* metade de cada; **~back** *n (SPORT)* médio *m; (BR)* meio-campo; **~-caste** *adj* mestiço,-a; **~-hearted** *adj* desanimado,-a; **~-hourly**

adj a/de cada meia hora; ~-**length** *adj* de meio corpo; ~-**life** *n* (PHYS) (radioactive decay) meia-vida *f*; ~ **note** (MUS) mínima *f*; ~-**open** *adj* (door) entreaberto,-a; ~-**mast** *n*: **at** ~ (flag) a meio pau; ~ **measures** *npl* meios termos *mpl*; meias medidas *fpl*; ~ **note** *n* (MUS), (US) mínima *f*; ~-**price** *adj* **at** ~-**price** *n* a/pela metade do preço; ~-**sister** *n* meia irmã *f*; ~-**step** *n* (MUS) (US) semitom *m*; ~-**term** *n* (UK) recesso *m* escolar; ~-**time** *n* (SPORT) intervalo; **2** (work) meio tempo; tempo parcial; **halves** *np*: **two** ~ *npl* (equal parts) duas metades *fpl*; **to go** ~**s** repartir, ir a meias; **to go** ~ **on** (meal) pagar a meias; **by halves** (com negativo) **we don't do anything by** ~**s** não fazemos nada pela metade.

halfway *adv* a meio caminho; a meio; **to meet sb** ~ chegar a um acordo com; **that doesn't go** ~ **towards my needs** isso não chega nem pensar para o que eu preciso.

half-wit *n* (pej) atrasado mental; idiota *m,f*.

half-witted *adj* pateta, *m,f*.

halfyear *n* semestral.

halibut *n* (fish) halibute *m*.

halitosis *n* (mau hálito) halitose *f*.

hall *n* (for concerts) sala; (in house, theatre) hall *m*, vestibule *m*, entrada *f*; (in hotel, airport) átrio; **town** ~ câmara *f* municipal, (BR) prefeitura; ~ **of residence** (Univ) residência *f* universitária, casa *f* do estudante.

halleluja *exc* Aleluia!

hallmark *n* marca *f*; selo *m*.

hallmarked *adj* (silver, gold) marca (na prata, no ouro) de autenticidade e de quilate.

hallo *exc* = **hello**.

hallow *vt* santificar, consagrar.

hallowed *pp adj* venerado, santificado, santo; ~ **be Thy Name** (REL) santificado seja o Vosso nome.

Halloween *npr* véspera do Dia de Todos os Santos; Dia das Bruxas.

A noite de Halloween, 31 de Outubro, é celebrada nos E.U.A. e no R.U., quando as crianças se mascaram de bruxas e diabinhos e vão de porta em porta, pedindo rebuçados ou dinheiro. Nas janelas e jardins vêem-se grandes abóboras amareladas desmioladas, com o interior iluminado por uma vela.

hallstand *n* bengaleiro *m*.

hallucinate *vi* ter alucinações, alucinar.

hallucination *n* alucinação *f*.

hallucinogenic *adj* alucinogéneo.

hallway *n* (US) entrada *f*.

halo (pl: **halos**, **haloes**) *n* (around head) auréola; **2** (ASTRON) (around moon) halo *m*.

halogen *n* (CHEM) halogénio (BR: -ê-); **2** (COMP) halógeno,-a.

halt *n* paragem *f*, (BR) alto, parada; ♦ *vi* parar; ♦ *vt* (stop person, train) deter; **2** interromper; **3** (FIN) suster (inflation); **to call a** ~ **to sth** pôr fim a algo (discussion, fight); **to grind to a** ~ (stop moving) parar lentamente; ♦ *exc* **H~!** Alto!

halter *n* cabresto *m*; (for hanging) nó *m* corredio; laço *m*.

halterneck *n adj* (dress) vestido *m* sem costas (com alças em redor do pescoço).

halting *adj* vacilante *m,f*.

halve *vt* dividir ao meio.

halves (pl of **half**).

ham *n* (CULIN) fiambre *m*; **2** pernil *m* de porco; **3** a(c)tor *m* exagerado; ♦ (pt, pp -med) *vt*: **to** ~ **it up** (THEAT) exagerar na actuação.

hamburger *n* hambúrguer *m*.

hamlet *n* aldeola *f*, lugarejo *m*, vilarejo *m*, povoação *f*.

hammer *n* martelo; ♦ *vt* (beat) martelar; **to** ~ **sth falt** achatar algo à martelada; **2** (with fist) bater; **3** (fig) (insist) **to** ~ **sth into sb's head** meter algo na cabeça de alguém; **they had history** ~**ed into them** eles tinham a história enfiada na cabeça (fam); ♦ *vi* bater insistentemente; **2** (with tool) martelar; **to** ~ **away at sth** *vi* trabalhar com afinco em algo; **to** ~ **on/at window** tamborilar; **to** ~ **out sth** *vt* (negotiate) negociar; **3** alcançar com esforço; **4** (with tool) malhar; **the** ~ **and sickle** *n* (POL) a foice e o martelo.

hammering *n* (noise) barulho *m* de marteladas; **2** (coll) **to take/get a** ~ (defeat) levar um enxerto (fam), uma porrada (slang).

hammock *n* rede *f* (de dormir).

hamper *n* (for picnics, Christmas present) cabaz *m* de comida e vinhos; (US) (laundry) cabaz, cesto *m* de roupa; ♦ *vt* dificultar; **2** (progress) impedir; (get in one's way) atrapalhar, estorvar.

hamster *n* (ZOOL) criceto; hamster.

hamstring *n* (ANAT) tendão *m* do jarrete; ♦ (pt, pp -**strung**) *vt* (fig) arruinar, dificultar impedir andamento.

hand *n* (ANAT) mão *f*; **2** (clock) ponteiro; **3** (applause); aplauso *m*, palmas *fpl*; **4** (EQUIT) measure = 16cm) palmo; **5** (AGR) trabalhador,-ora, (BR) peão; (in factory) operário,-a; (on ship) tripulante; **6** (games) (cards) jogo *m*, mão *f*; **to show one's** ~ mostrar o jogo; **to throw in one's** ~ abandonar o jogo; **7** (handwriting) letra, caligrafia *f*; **to give/lend sb a** ~ dar uma mão a alguém, ajudar alguém; **to ask for sb's** ~ (in marriage) pedir a mão de alguém (em casamento); **to give sb a free** ~ dar carta branca a alguém; **to try one's** ~ **at** experimentar; ~**s up!** mãos no ar!; ♦ *adv* **at** ~ à mão, disponível; (near) perto; **at first** ~ dire(c)tamente; **by** ~ (letter) por mão própria; **in** ~ (situation) sob controle; (COMM) (money) em caixa; **on one's** ~**s and knees** de gatas; (pleading) de joelhos; **on the one** ~ … **on the other** ~ … por um lado …, por outro (lado) …; **on the other** ~ pelo contrário; **out of** ~ (situation) fora de controlo; ♦ *vt* **to** ~ **down** (to generations) legar; **to** ~ **in** entregar; dar; transmitir; **to** ~ **on** passar adiante; **to** ~ **out** *vt* distribuir; **to** ~ **over** *vt* entregar; (power) transferir; ceder; (telephone) passar a ligação.

handbag *n* mala *f* de mão, carteira, (BR) bolsa.

handbarrow padiola *f*.

hand basin bacia *f* da cara (BR) pia.

handbill panfleto *m*.

handbook manual *m*.

handbrake *n (AUT)* travão *m*, *(BR)* freio de mão.

handclasp *(Vd:* **handshake**).

handcuff(s) *m(pl)* algema(s) *f(pl)*; ♦ algemar.

hand, foot and mouth disease *n* aftose *f*.

handful *n* punhado *m*.

handgun *n* arma *f* de mão, pistola *f*, revólver *m*.

handicap *n* desvantagem *f*; ♦ *vt* pôr obstáculos; **mentally/physically ~ped** deficiente mental/físico.

handicraft *n* artesanato, trabalho manual.

hand-in-hand *adv (walking together)* de mãos *fpl* dadas.

handkerchief *n* lenço *m*.

handle *n (of door etc)* maçaneta *f* puxador *m*; **2** *(of cup etc)* asa; **3** *(of knife, axe, etc)* cabo; **4** *(for winding)* manivela; **~ with care** cuidado, frágil; ♦ *vt* manusear, manejar; **2** *(deal with)* tratar de, lidar com; ♦ *vi* governar; **2** *(situation)* controlar; **3** *(car)* guiar; **4** *(ship)* comandar; IDIOM **to fly off the ~** perder as estribeiras, perder a cabeça.

handlebar(s) *n(pl)* guiador *m*, *(BR)* guidão *m*.

handler *m (of animals)* treinador,-ora; **2** *(of baggage)* carregador de bagagem; **3** *(of stolen goods)* receptor,-ora.

handling *n (COMM)* manutenção *f*; **2** *(dealing with)* tratamento *m*; *(JUR)* **~ of the case** tratamento do caso; **3** *(touching)* manuseamento *(fragile, precious items)*; **~ charges** *npl (COMM)* despesas/taxas *fpl* de manutenção.

hand-luggage *n* bagagem *f* de mão.

handmade *adj* feito à mão.

hand-me-downs *npl* roupas *fpl* usadas.

handout *n* distribuição *f*; **2** *(gift)* doação *f*; **3** *(leaflet)* folheto.

handover *n* transferência *f*.

handpicked *adj* escolhido,-a a dedo.

handrail *n* corrimão *m*; **~saw** *n* serrate *m*.

handset *(TEL)* combinado *m* portátil.

handshake *n* aperto de mão.

hands-off *adj* sem interferência; **2** *(of a machine, device)* funcionamento sem ser manual; ♦ *exc* **~!** tire as mãos!

hands-on *adj* experiência de equipamento; prá(c)tico,-a; **~ training in the use of computers** *npl* treinamento *m* prá(c)tico no uso de computadores.

handsome *adj* belo; atraente; bonitão *(fam)*.

handsomely *adv (amply)* **~ rewarded** generosamente recompensado.

hand-to-hand *adj (fight)* corpo a corpo.

hand-to-mouth *adj* precário; **to live ~** viver precariamente, viver do seu trabalho diário.

handwriting *n* caligrafia *m*, letra *f*.

handwritten *adj* escrito,-a à mão; manuscrito *m*.

handy *adj (near)* à mão; prático,-a; **2** *(skilful)* habilidoso,-a, hábil *m,f*; **to come in ~** vir a calhar.

handyman *n* biscateiro, topa-tudo *m*.

hang *(pt, pp* **hung***) vt* pendurar; **2** *(head)* baixar; **3** *(criminal: pt, pp* **hanged***)* enforcar; ♦ *vi* pendurar-se; **to get the ~ of sth/of doing sth** *(coll)* apanhar, pegar o jeito de algo/fazer algo; estar familiarizado com; *(coll)* **I get the ~ of your meaning** percebo o que você quer dizer; já compreendi; **to ~ about/around** *(coll) vi* rondar; **2** demorar-se; **3** *(aimlessly)* vaguear; ♦ **to ~ down** *vi* pender; ♦ **to ~ on** *(coll) vi* esperar; **2** aguentar; **3 ~ (sth)** depender de, estar suspenso de; **~ on to** agarrar-se a; *(fig) (retain)* reter, manter; ♦ **to ~ out** *vt (washing)* estender *(a roupa)*; **2** *(protrude)* sair para fora *(shirt tails)*; **3** *(flag)* arvorar; **4** *vi* frequentar; ♦ **to ~ over** pairar sobre; **2** inclinar-se; ♦ **to ~ together** *(argumento)* ser consistente; ♦ **~ up** *vi* suspender; **2** *(TEL)* desligar.

hangar *n* hangar *m*.

hanger *n* cabide *m*; **~~on** *n (person)* parasita *m,f* pendura *m,f* filão,-lona.

hanging *n (punishment)* forca, enforcamento *m*; **~s** *(curtains)* cortinados *mpl*; *(wall tapestry)* tapeçaria *(para a parede)*.

hang-glider *n* asa-delta *f*.

hang-gliding *n* voo *m* livre (com asa-delta).

hangman *n* carrasco.

hangover *n (after drinking)* ressaca *f*.

hang-up *n (PSIC)* mania *f*, complexo *m*.

hank *n (of wool)* novelo *m*; *(of wire, rope)* rolo *m*, meada *f*.

hanker *vi*: **to ~ after** sentir saudade de; *(long for)* ansiar por, desejar ardentemente.

hankie, hanky *n (abbr for* **handkerchief***)*.

hanky-panky *n* comportamento *m* duvidoso; **I sense some ~** pressinto qualquer marotice *f*; **2** *(coll) (illicit sexual relations)* arranjinho *m*.

haphazard *adj* fortuito, accidental; caótico, desordenado.

haphazardly *adv* ao acaso, desordenadamente.

hapless *adj* desgraçado, infeliz; ♦ *adv* ao acaso, à sorte.

happen *vi* ocorrer, suceder; acontecer, realizar-se; **do you ~ to have some change?** por acaso tem troco?; **if he ~ed to come** se por acaso ele viesse.

happening *n* acontecimento *m*, ocorrência *f*.

happily *adv* felizmente; alegremente.

happiness *n* felicidade *f*, alegria *f*.

happy *adj* feliz, contente; **to be ~ (with)** estar contente (com); **to be a ~ person** ser feliz; **~~go-lucky** *adj* sem cuidados; **~ medium** *n* meio-termo.

hara-kiri *n* haraquiri *m*.

harangue *n* arenga, ladainha *f*; ♦ *vt* arengar.

harass *vt* atormentar, assolar; **2** *(sexually)* molestar.

harassment *n* perseguição *f*; *(worry)* preocupação *f*; **sexual ~** assédio sexual.

harbinger *n* precursor, anunciador *m*; **2** *(LITER)*, arauto *m*; **3** prenúncio *m*.

harbour *(US:* **harbor***) n* porto; *(fig)* refúgio, porto de abrigo; ♦ *vt (hope etc)* acalentar; **2** *(hide)* esconder; **3** *(give shelter to)*, abrigar, albergar; **4 ~ a grudge against sb** guardar rancor contra alguém.

hard *adj* duro; **2** *(difficult)* difícil; **3** *(strenuous)* árduo; **4** *(person)* severo, ríspido; **5** *(winter)* rigoroso,-a; **6** *(facts, news)* concreto,-a; **~ facts** *mpl* indiscutíveis; **7** *(POL)* extremo,-a, **~ left** extrema esquerda; **~ bitten** duro, inflexível, realista; **~-boiled** *(egg)* (ovo) cozido; **~ board** *n* madeira *f* compensada, aglomerado *m*; **~ cash** dinheiro m vivo; **~ day** dia *m* difícil; **~ drugs** *npl* drogas *fpl* duras; ◆ *adv (work)* muito duro; *(study)* intensamente; **~-fought** *(competition)* renhido,-a; **no ~ feelings!** sem ressentimento!; pazes!; **to be ~ done by** ser tratado injustamente; **~ of hearing** ser surdo, ouvir mal; **to be ~ to please** ser difícil de contentar; **to be ~ pressed/ pushed** ver-se em apuros (para fazer algo); **to look ~ (at)** olhar firme/fixamente (para); **to think ~** pensar bem/seriamente; **to work ~** trabalhar muito.

hard and fast *adj (rule)* firme, absoluto, rígido.

hardback *n* livro de capa dura.

hardcore *n (of group)* núcleo duro; ◆ *adj (porn)* explícito, obsceno.

hardcurrency *n* moeda *f* forte.

harden *vt (butter, wax)* endurecer; **2** *(steel)* temperar; **3** *(fig)* tornar insensível; ◆ *vi* endurecer-se.

hardened *adj* endurecido,-a; **2** *(person)* calejado,-a; **3** *(steel)* temperado,-a; **4** *(drinker)* inveterado,-a.

hard labour *(US: labor)* *n* trabalhos *mpl* forçados.

hardline *adj (POL)* firme e duro; **~r** *n* partidário de linha dura.

hardly *adv* apenas, mal; **that can ~ be true** dificilmente pode ser verdade; **~ ever** quase nunca.

hardness *n* dureza; **2** dificuldade; *(of heart; person)* insensibilidade *f*.

hard rock *n (MUS)* rock *f* da pesada, hard rock.

hard sell *n* venda *f* agressiva.

hardship *n* sofrimento *m*; **2** privação *f*, privações *fpl*.

hard shoulder *n (AUT)* acostamento *m*.

hard-up *adj (coll) (without money)* teso, *(BR)* duro.

hardware *n* ferragens *fpl*, maquinaria, **2** *(COMP)* equipamento, hardware; **~ shop** *n* loja de ferragens.

hard-wearing *adj* resistente, duradouro.

hard-working *adj* trabalhador,-ora, diligente *m,f*.

hardy *adj (person)* forte, robusto,-a; **2** *(plant)* resistente.

hare *n (ZOOL)* lebre *f*; IDIOM **be as mad as a March ~** ser doido varrido *(fam)*.

hare-brained *adj* estouvado, cabeça-no-ar.

hare-lip *n* lábio-leporino.

harem *n* harém *m*.

harm *n* dano, mal *m*; ◆ *vt* ferir, causar dano, prejudicar, danificar; **out of ~'s way** a salvo.

harmful *adj* prejudicial; nocivo.

harmless *adj* inofensivo.

harmonica *n* gaita de boca, harmónica *(BR:* -mô-*)*.

harmonious *adj* harmonioso.

harmonize *vt/vi* harmonizar.

harmony *n* harmonia.

harness *n (for horse, oxen)* arreios *mpl*, arnês *m*; **2** *(for child)* andador *m*; **in ~** em serviço a(c)tivo; ◆ *vt (horse, ox)*, arrear, pôr arreios em; *(dog)* pôr trela; aparelhar **(a** to); **2** *(resources, energy)* aproveitar, explorar; **to ~ the solar energy** aproveitar a energia solar.

harp *n* harpa; ◆ *vi:* **to ~ on about** bater sempre na mesma tecla; repisar.

harpist *n* harpista *m,f*.

harpoon *n* arpão *m*; ◆ *vt* arpoar.

harpsichord *n (MUS)* cravo *m*.

harrow *n (farm utensil)* grade; ◆ *vt (AGR)* gradar.

harrowing *adj (ordeal)* atroz; **2** *(history; case)* doloroso, pungente.

harsh *adj* duro, cruel, severo; **2** desagradável; **3** *(note)* dissonante; *(voice)* áspera; **4** *(weather)* rigoroso; **5** *(light)* cru,-a; **6** *(landscape)* desolado; **7** *(colour)* forte; **8 ~ laugh** riso seco; **9 ~ words** *npl* palavras duras *fpl*.

harshness *n* dureza.

harum-scarum *adj adv (reckless person)* estouvado, cabeça-no-ar, inconstante; **to do sth in a ~ way** fazer algo à toa.

harvest *n* colheita *f*; **2** *(of grapes)* vindima *f*; ◆ *vt/vi (fruit)* colher, apanhar; **2** *(corn)* ceifar; **to reap a bitter ~** *(fig)* pagar as favas.

harvester *n (machine)* segadeira *f*; *(person)* ceifeiro,-a.

has *(3rd person pres ind of* **have***)*; **~-been** *(coll)* *n (pej)* pessoa acabada.

has-been *n (coll) (pej)* pessoa *f* acabada; velha glória *f*.

hash *n (CULIN)* picadinho *m*; **2** *(fig)* confusão *f (BR)*, bagunça *f*; ◆ *vt (CULIN)* picar.

hash browns *npl* batatas *fpl* salpicadas.

hashish *n* haxixe *m*.

haslet *n* fressura (de porco).

hasn't = **has not** (**to have**).

hasp *n* anel *m* de cadeado; ferrolho; gancho; ◆ *vt* fechar com ferrolho, com cadeado.

hassle *n (inconvenience)* maçada *f*; *(coll)* chatice *f*; **2** dificuldade *f*; ◆ *vt* molestar, chatear; **stop hassling me** deixa-me em paz, não me chateies *(fam)*.

hassled *pt/pp adj (person)* sob tensão, pressionado; chateado,-a.

hassock *n (cushion for kneeling in church)* almofada; **2** *(grass)* tufo *m* de relva; *(in Kent-UK)* grés calcário *m*.

haste *n* pressa.

hasten *vt* acelerar; ◆ *vi* apressar-se.

hastily *adv* depressa.

hasty *adj* apressado, precipitado.

hat *n* chapéu *m*; *(men's)* **straw ~** chapéu à panamá; **top ~** chapéu alto; bowler chapéu de coco; **~ box** chapeleira *f*; IDIOM **at the drop of a ~** *(without hesitation)* sem mais nem menos; **to keep sth under one's ~** guardar segredo; **to talk through one's ~** dizer tolices, dizer o que vem à cabeça; **to take off one's ~** tirar o chapéu; **to take one's ~ off to sb** *(greet)* cumprimentar; **2** congratular.

hatch *n (NAUT:* = **-way***)* escotilha; **2** *(aviation)* painel *m* móvel; ◆ *vi* sair do ovo, chocar; ◆ *vt* incubar, tramar, maquinar.

hatchback *n (AUT)* carro com porta traseira.

hatchet *n* machado *f*; IDIOM **to bury the ~** pôr fim às hostilidades; **~ job** *n (JOURN)* crítica *f* acerba; **to do a ~** denegrir sb.

hate *n* ódio *m*; ◆ *vt* odiar, detestar.

hateful *adj* odioso,-a.

hatred *n* ódio *m*.

hat trick *n (SPORT)* três triunfos seguidos; tripla vitória.

haughty adj soberbo, arrogante.

haul n (of fish) redada; pilhagem f, presa; ♦ vt puxar; carregar, fretar.

haulage n transporte m; custo de frete.

haulier (US: -er) n (person) contratador m de frete, transportador; 2 (business) transportadora f.

haunch n anca, quadril m; quarto traseiro.

haunt n lugar m frequentado (BR: -quen-); ♦ vt assombrar; frequentar (BR: -quen-); obcecar; ~ed house casa assombrada, com fantasmas; ~ing memory ideia (BR: idéia) fixa.

have (pt, pp had) vt ter; she does not ~ any money ela não tem (nenhum) dinheiro; (possess) ter, possuir; they ~ a great fortune eles possuem uma grande fortuna; (take, eat, drink) tomar; comer; what will you ~? que vai tomar/beber?; (aux) I ~ been thinking tenho estado a pensar; haven't you finished that yet? ainda não acabaste isso?; if we had been told se eles nos tivessem dito; to ~ to, to ~ (got) to (must, obligation); we had to leave tivemos de partir; you ~ got to work hard tens de trabalhar duro; do we ~ to reply now? é preciso responder agora?; to ~ to do ter que fazer; he had better leave é melhor que ele se vá embora; to ~ sth done mandar fazer (mandar dizer, ir, vir, etc) algo; ~ you sent for the wine? já mandou vir o vinho?; I am having my dress made mandei fazer o meu vestido; I won't ~ it não vou aguentar isso, não vou permitir isso; he has gone ele foi embora; to ~ it out with sb ajustar as contas com alguém, discutir algo; I ~ had enough! (in anger) estou farta (disto)!; what ~ you got there? o que tem você aí?; I've got it! já percebi!; ~ back (sth) (returned) ter algo de volta; to ~ on (wear) trazer vestido, chapéu; 2 (TV, etc) estar ligado; 3 (engagement, date) ter compromisso; I have sth on tonight tenho uma coisa/um compromisso esta noite; 4 (joke, tease) are you having me on? estás a brincar/zombar comigo?; to ~ out vt tirar, extrair; 2 to ~ it out with sb pedir satisfações a alguém; discutir (um assunto); to ~ (sb) over convidar alguém (para casa); to ~ up (coll) levar a tribunal; to be had up (coll) ser julgado,-a (for por).

haven n porto; 2 (fig) abrigo, refúgio.

have-nots npl: the ~ os desfavorecidos; the haves and the ~ os ricos e os pobres.

haven't = have not.

haversack n mochila f.

havoc n destruição f, ruína f, caos m.

Hawaii npr Havai.

Hawaiian n, adj havaiano,-a.

hawk n falcão m.

hawker n vendedor m ambulante.

hawk-eyed adj com olhos de lince.

hawkish adj semelhante a falcão.

hawser n (NAUT) sirga f; amarra f.

hay n feno; ~ fever n febre f do feno; ~stack n palheiro.

haywire adj (coll) (person) to go ~ ficar maluco; (plan, things) estar/ficar; descontrolado,-a, desorganizado,-a; ♦ descontrolar-se, (BR) degringolar.

hazard n risco, acaso; ♦ vt aventurar.

hazardous adj perigoso; arriscado.

haze n névoa, neblina f.

hazelnut n (fruit) avelã f.

hazy adj nublado; 2 (idea, memory) confuso.

he pron ele; ~ who ... ele que ..., aquele que ...; ~-man n macho.

head n (ANAT) cabeça; 2 (leader) chefe m,f, líder m,f; 3 (of river, bed, table) cabeceira f; 4 (of letter, newspaper) cabeçalho m; 5 (of flower) corola f; 6 (ELECT) cabeçote m; ~ache n dor f de cabeça; ~der n (top of page) cabeçalho m; 2 (SPORT) cabeçada f; ~hunt vt (recruit) procurar, contratar (novos talentos); ~ hunter n caça-talentos m,f; ~ing n título, cabeçalho; ~lamp n farol m (de veículo); ~land n promontório; ~long adv (fall) de cabeça; (rush) precipitadamente; ~master n dire(c)tor m (de escola); ~ of hair n cabeleira f; ~-on adj (collision) de frente; ~phones npl fones mpl de ouvido; ~quarters (HQ) npl sede f geral; (MIL) quartel m general; ~-rest n apoio para a cabeça; ~scarf n lenço de cabeça; ~sea (NAUT) mar de proa; ~stone n lápide f; ~strong adj voluntarioso, teimoso; ~waiter n maitre m, garçom m chefe; ~way n progresso; to make ~way avançar, fazer progresso; ~wind n vento contrário; ~word n (dictionary) entrada f, verbete m; ♦ at the ~ of (company, etc) à testa, à cabeça de; at the ~ of the queue à frente da fila; at the ~ of stairs ao cimo/topo das escadas; ~ first de cabeça; from ~ to toe da cabeça aos pés; ♦ ~ over heels de pernas para o ar; completely; 2 (in love with) loucamente apaixonado por; ~ over ears in debt cheio de dívidas; off the top of one's ~ de improviso; off one's ~ louco, desvairado, fora de si; ♦ exc on your ~ be it! que fique à sua responsabilidade!; que arque com as consequências!; ♦ to come to a ~ (crisis, conflict) culminar, chegar ao ponto crítico; 2 (MED = boil) rebentar; to have a ~ for heights não ter medo de alturas; to keep one's ~ (calm down) controlar-se, conservar o sangue-frio; to keep one's ~ above water conseguir superar um problema; to make neither ~ nor tail of não fazer sentido; não perceber patavina; to sing one's ~ off cantar a plenos pulmões; to shake one's ~ (disapproval, denial) abanar a cabeça; ♦ vt (list) encabeçar; 2 (group) liderar; to ~ the ball (SPORT) dar uma cabeçada na bola; to ~ for dirigir-se a/para (person; place); IDIOM to bang one's ~ against a brick wall malhar em ferro frio; (tossing a coin) heads you win, tails you lose preso por ter cão e preso por não o ter; ~s (or tails) (tossing coin) cara (ou coroa).

headword n (dictionary) entrada f; verbete f.

heady adj excitante; 2 (guidiness) estonteante.

heal vt curar; ♦ vi cicatrizar.

healing n curativo m.

health n saúde f; good ~! saúde!; ~ food n comida natural, saudável; H~ Service npr (UK) Serviço Nacional de Saúde (EP); to your ~ à sua saúde; ~ farm n spa m; ~ hazard n risco m à saúde; ~ visitor n enfermeiro,-a comunitário,-a.

healthy *adj (gen)* são/sã, sadio, saudável; **2** *(appetite)* bom; **3** *(crop)* abundante; **4** *(ECON)* forte; **5** *(respect)* salutar.

heap *n* pilha, montão *m*; ♦ *vt* amontoar, empilhar; encher.

hear *(pt, pp* **heard***) vt* ouvir; escutar; ♦ *vi* ouvir; **to ~ about** ouvir falar de; **to ~ from sb** ter notícias de alguém.

hearing *n (sense)* audição *f*, ouvido; **2** *(JUR)* audiência *f*; **~ aid** *n* aparelho *m* auditivo.

hearsay *n* boato *m*, zunzum *n*.

hearse *n* carro fúnebre.

heart *n* coração *m*; **2** *(fig)* centro, seio; **3** *(fig)* coragem *f*, ânimo; **at ~** no íntimo, fundo; **by ~** *(learn, know)* de cor; **to cry one's ~ out** chorar muito; **to open one's ~** desabafar, falar com franqueza; **~ ache** *n* angústia *f*; **~attack** *n* ataque *m* cardíaco, do coração; **~beat** *n* pulsação *f*; **~breaking** *adj* desolador,-ora; de partir o coração; **to be ~broken** estar desolado; **~burn** *n* azia; **~ failure** *n* colapso cardíaco, *(BR)* parada cardíaca; **~felt** *adj* cordial; sincero; **~rending** *adj* dilacerante; pungente, consternador,-ora; **~-searching** *adj* exame *m* de consciência; **~throb** *n* galã *m*; **~-warming** *adj* reconfortante; **2** *(touching)* enternecedor,-ora; **~ transplant** *n (MED)* transplante *m* de coração.

heartening *adj* animador,-ora, encorajador,-ora.

hearth *n* lar *m*; **2** *(fireplace)* lareira.

heartily *adv* sinceramente; **2** *(laugh)* a gargalhadas; *(willingly)* com vontade; **3** *(eat)* apetitosamente; **4** *(to do sth)* de boa vontade.

heartland *n (of rural centre)* coração *m*; *(of region)* centro.

heartless *adj* desumano,-a; pessoa sem coração, cruel *m,f*.

hearts *npl (cards)* copas *fpl*.

heart-to-heart *adj* sincero, franco; **to have a ~ chat** falar de coração aberto, com o coração nas mãos.

hearty *adj (manner, voice)* jovial; **2** *(smile, laugh)* franco; **3** *(meal)* abundante, farto; **4** *(energetic)* vigoroso,-a; **5** *(deeply felt)* profundo,-a.

heat *n (sun)* calor *m*; **2** *(passion)* ardor *m*; **~ of youth** ardor da juventude; **3 ~ proof** à prova de calor; **~rash** *n* brotoeja *(pelo calor)*; **~ resistant** *adj* refratário,-a; resistente *m,f* ao calor; **~ stroke** *n* insolução *f*; **~ treatment** *n* tratamento *m* térmico; **~wave** *n* onda, vaga *f* de calor; **4** *(SPORT)* **qualifying ~** prova eliminatória, rodada eliminatória; **5** *(CULIN)* temperatura; **boiling ~** *(PHIS)* temperatura de ebulição; **6 on ~** *(ZOOL)* no cio; **7** *(fig)* **in the ~ of the moment** no calor do momento; ♦ **to ~/~ up** *vt/vi*; aquecer *(EP)* esquentar *(BR) (food, room)* **2** *(give heat to)* acalorar.

heated *adj* quente, aquecido,-a; *(fig) (excited, angry)* acalorado,-a, inflamado,-a; **~ discussion** discussão exaltada; **to get ~** *(enthusiasm)* animar-se; **2** *(argument)* exaltar-se, acalorar-se.

heater *n (radiator)* aquecedor *m, (combi-boiler)* esquentador *m;* **electric ~** radiador *m* elé(c)trico.

heath *n (moor)* charneca *f*.

heathen *n adj* pagão,-ã; **2** *(uncivilized)* bárbaro,-a.

heather *n* urze *f*.

heating *n* aquecimento *m; (TECH)* calefação *f;* **~ plant** *n* central *f* de aquecimento; **~ power** *n* poder *m* calorífico.

heave *n* puxão *m;* **2** *(push)* empurrão *m;* **3** *(effort)* esforço *m; (throw)* arremesso; **4** *(chest)* arquejo *m;* **5** *(swell of sea)* ondulação, agitação *f;* ♦ *vt* puxar; **2** *(push)* empurrar; **3** *(lift)* levantar (com esforço); **4** *(throw)* arremessar, atirar; ♦ *vi (rise and fall) (of shoulders)* sacudir-se; *(of sea)* agitar-se; *(ground)* elevar-se; *(stomach)* dar voltas, *(person)* ter vómitos.

heave! *exc* upa!, força!

heaven *n* céu *m; (REL)* paraíso; **the kingdom of ~** o reino dos céus; ♦ *exc* **thank ~s** graças a Deus; **good ~s!** céus!, meu Deus!; IDIOM **to be in one's seventh ~** estar no sétimo céu, nas suas sete quintas; **to move ~ and earth** fazer todos os possíveis, mover céus e terra.

heavenly *adj* celestial; **2** *(REL)* divino; **3** *(wonderful) (fam)* maravilhoso.

heavily *adv* pesadamente; **2** *(drink, spend, etc)* excessivamente; **3** *(deeply)* profundamente; **4** *(in debt)* seriamente; **5** *(~ populated)* densamente; **6** *(noisily)* ruidosamente.

heavy *(-ier, -iest) adj* pesado; **2** duro; **3** violento; **a ~ storm** uma tempestade violenta; **4** *(deep – sleep, etc)* profundo; **5** *(quantity)* em grande número; **6** *(aroma)* forte; **~ build** *(person)* forte; **7** *(traffic)* intenso; **8** *(wine)* encorpado; **9** *(oppressive; laden)* carregado,-a; **10 ~ with fruit** *(tree)* carregado,-a de fruta; **11 ~ with child/young** grávida em estado avançado; **with a ~ heart** *(fig)* com o coração despedaçado, triste.

heavy-duty *adj (material)* muito resistente; **2** *(transport)* para grandes cargas.

heavy-handed *adj (clumsy)* desajeitado,-a, desastrado.

heavy industry *n* indústria *f* pesada.

heavy weight *n (SPORT)* peso-pesado.

Hebrew *npr adj* hebreu,-eia; *(LING)* hebraico.

heck *n (fam):* **a ~ of a lot** uma grande quantidade; **a ~ of a good guy** um tipo porreiro; *(BR)* um cara e tanto; **what the ~ are you doing?** mas que diabo estás a fazer?; ♦ *exc* **~!** diabos!

heckle *vt (comb/disentangle flex, hemp)* cardar, **2** interromper persistentemente, importunar *(public speaker)*.

heckler *n* interpelações *fpl; (person)* que está sempre a interromper discursos.

hectic *adj (activity)* intenso, agitado; febril.

hedge *n* cerca-viva, sebe *f;* **2** *(FIN)* cobertura de risco; **~ funds** *npl* fundos *mpl* de cobertura de alto risco; ♦ *vt* cercar (com uma sebe); ♦ *vi* dar evasivas; **to ~ one's bets** *(fig)* resguardar-se.

hedgehog *n (ZOOL)* ouriço, porco-espinho.

hedgerow *n* sebe, cerca-viva *f*.

hedonism *n* hedonismo *m*.

hedonist, hedonistic *adj* hedonista *m,f*.

heebie-jeebies *npl (coll)* ataque *m* de nervos/de apreensão *f;* tremeliques *mpl*.

heed vt (= take ~ of) prestar atenção a; levar em consideração; **I din't pay any ~ to what she said** não liguei nenhuma ao que ela disse (pop).

heedless adj desatento, distraído, indiferente, negligente; imprudente.

heel¹ n (ANAT and of sock/shoe) calcanhar m; **2** (of shoes) salto m; **low/flat/high ~ shoes** sapatos de salto baixo/raso/alto; ♦ vt (repair) pôr saltos em; IDIOM **to dig one's ~s in** ser obstinado, não ceder (to a query, argument); não dar a mão à palmatória (BR) fincar o pé; **to take to one's ~s** fugir; (coll) pernas para que te quero (BR) dar no pé; **to fall head over ~s in love** estar perdidamente apaixonado; **to turn on one's ~** dar meia-volta.

heel² vt adernar; (building, etc) inclinar-se; **~ over** (ship) inclinar-se para o lado; **~ over into** tombar, cair sobre algo.

hefty adj (person) corpulento, pesado (BR) troncudo; **2** (sum, bill) grande, considerável; **3** (price) alto.

Hegira (=Hejira) n Hégira.

heifer n (ZOOL) bezerra f, novilha f.

height n (person's) estatura; **2** (of room, tree, etc) altura f; **3** (of mountain) altitude f; **at the ~ of the season** (fig) (peak) em plena estação; (of dispute) no auge da disputa; **heights** npl alturas; **Wuthering Heights** (romance, film) O monte dos Vendavais.

heighten vt elevar; intensificar; ♦ vi (fear, worry) aumentar (fear); (tension) subir.

heinous adj abominável, nefando, hediondo.

heir n herdeiro; **~ apparent** n successor dire(c)to (to de); **~ presumptive** n (property law) herdeiro presuntivo.

heiress n herdeira.

heirloom n herança; relíquia de família.

heist n (coll) roubo m.

held (pt, pp of hold).

helices (pl of helix).

helicopter n helicóptero.

heliport n heliport m.

helium n hélio m.

helix (pl: -ces, -xes) n hélice f.

hell n inferno; **life in the army was ~** a vida no exército era um inferno; **a ~ of a fright** um susto m terrível; **a ~ of a noise** um barulho infernal; **what the ~ are you doing?** que diabo estás tu a fazer?; **didn't you enjoy the party? like ~ I did** não te divertiste na festa? nada mesmo; **let's get the ~ out of here** é melhor fugirmos/sairmos daqui agora; **~ broke loose** desencadeou-se um autêntico inferno; ♦ exc **~!** diabos!, que diabos!; IDIOM **there will be ~ to pay** alguém vai pagar caro; **to make sb's life a ~** fazer a vida negra a alguém.

hellbent adj: **to be ~ on doing sth** determinado,-a a fazer algo.

hellfire n fogo m do inferno; (sermon) apocalítico,-a.

hellish adj infernal; (fam) terrível.

hello exc olá!, oi!; alô!; caramba!

hellraiser n (person) bêbado,-a ou brigão,-ona.

Hell's Angels npl grupo de motoqueiros que praticam a(c)tos violentos.

helluva adj, adv (fam) formidável; **a ~ job** um emprego formidável.

helm n (NAUT) timão m, leme m; **2** (of a company) (fig) dire(c)ção f, governo m.

helmet n elmo, capacete m.

help n ajuda f; **2** empregada doméstica, (BR) faxineira; auxiliar m,f; **3** (emergency) socorro m; ♦ ajudar (with, com); auxiliar (with, com); **2** (emergency) socorrer; **3** ser útil; **may I help you?** posso ajudá-lo? **4** (pain) aliviar; **5** (avoid) evitar, deixar de; **I couldn't ~ overhearing** não pude evitar ouvir; ♦ **to ~ oneself (to sth)** vr servir-se (de algo); **to ~ sb out** dar uma mão a; ♦ exc **help!** socorro!

helper n ajudante m,f.

helpful adj útil, prestável m,f; **2** benéfico,-a.

helping n (food) porção f.

helpless adj incapaz; indefeso.

helplessness n incapacidade; vulnerabilidade.

helpline n (TEL) serviço m de assistência telefónica.

Helsinki npr Helsínquia.

helter-skelter n confusão f; **2** (in a funfair) tobogã m; ♦ adv à toa, desordenadamente, a trouxe-mouxe.

hem n (clothes) bainha; **to take up/let down the ~** subir/baixar a bainha; **to make a ~** embainhar; ♦ **to ~ in** vt encerrar; (animals) encurralar; **to ~ in/round** cercar.

hemisphere n hemisfério m.

hsemlock (BOT) cicuta f.

hemp n (fibre) cânhamo m; **2** (drug) haxixe.

hen n (chicken) galinha; (female bird, lobster) fêmea; **clucking ~** galinha no choco; **she is a cackling ~** (fig) ela é uma tagarela; IDIOM **scarce as hens' teeth** (very rare or never) quando as galinhas tiverem dentes.

hence adv daí, portanto; **one month ~** daqui a um mês.

henceforth adv de agora em diante, doravante.

henchman n braço direito, homem de confiança; **2** (pej) valentão m, guarda-costas (BR) capanga m.

hen party n a festa da despedida de solteira.

henpecked adj (husband) dominado pela esposa.

her pron (direct) a; **I saw ~** eu vi-a (BR) eu a vi; **2** (indirect) **I gave ~ (to ~) a book** eu dei-lhe um livro (BR, pop) dei a ela; **3** (stressed, after prep) ela; **I like ~** gosto dela; ♦ adj seu/sua or dela; **~ coat** o casaco dela.

herald n precursor,-ora; arauto; ♦ vt anunciar.

heraldry n heráldica.

herb n erva; (aromatic) erva aromática; (CULIN) erva seca.

herbaceous adj herbáceo; (border) canteiro m.

herbal adj à base de ervas.

herbalist n herbanário,-a.

herbivore n herbívoro,-a.

herb tea n infusão f de ervas.

herd n (gen) rebanho; (of elephants) manada (of pigs) vara; (of people) multidão f, chusma f; populaça f.

herdsman n (of sheep, goats) pastor; (of cattle) vaqueiro; (of bulls) (cowboy: in Portugal) campino.

here adv aqui, cá; **~ she is** aqui está ela; **come ~** vem cá; **~ and there** aqui e acolá; **from ~** daqui; **Carnival is ~** o Carnaval está próximo; **the weather**

is bad (over) ~ o tempo está mau por cá; ~! presente!; **it's neither** ~ **nor there** isso não tem importância; **the** ~**after** *n* a vida de além-túmulo; ♦ ~**about(s)** *adv* por aqui, aproximadamente; ~**after** *adv* daqui por diante; ~ **and now** *n* o presente; ♦ *adv* ~**by** imediatamente *(in letter, document)* por este meio, pela presente.

hereditary *adj* hereditário.
heredity *n* hereditariedade *f*, herança.
heresy *n* heresia.
heretic *n* herege *m,f*.
heretical *adj* herético.
herewith *adv (formal)* incluso.
heritage *n (cultural)* herança *f; (bens)* património *(BR:* -mô-).
hermit *n* eremita *m*.
hernia *n* hérnia *f*.
hero *(pl:* -**es**) *n* herói *m; (in book, film)* protagonista *m,f*.
heroic *adj* heróico,-a.
heroin *n (drug)* heroína.
heroine *n* heroína; *(in book, film)* protagonista.
heroism *n* heroísmo.
heron *n (ZOOL)* garça *f*.
herring *n (fish)* arenque *m*.
hers *pron* o seu/a sua, o,-a dela.
herself *pron (reflexive)* se; *(emphatic)* ela mesma; *(after prep)* si *(mesma)*.
hesitant *adj* hesitante, indeciso.
hesitate *vi* hesitar, duvidar.
hesitation *n* hesitação *f*, indecisão *f*.
hessian *n (jute or hemp material)* serapilheira *f*.
hew *vt* cortar (com machado).
hexagon *n* hexágono.
hexagonal *adj* hexagonal.
heyday *n* auge *m*, apogeu *m; (of person)* flor *f* da idade.
hi *exc* olá!, ei!; (BR) oi!
hibernate *vi* hibernar.
hiccough, hiccup *vi* estar com soluço; ~**s** *npl* soluço *sg*.
hid *(pt of* **hide**).
hidden *(pp of* **hide**).
hide *n (skin, leather)* pele *f*; ♦ *(pt* **hid**, *pp* **hidden**) *vt* esconder, ocultar; ♦ *vi:* **to** ~ **(from sb)** esconder-se, ocultar-se (de alguém).
hide-and-seek *n* jogo *m* das escondidas, *(BR)* esconde-esconde *m*.
hideaway *n* refúgio, esconderijo *m*.
hideous *adj* horrível; horroroso,-a.
hideout *n* esconderijo *m*.
hiding *n (beating)* surra; **2 to be in** ~ estar escondido; ~ **place** *n* esconderijo.
hierarchy *n* hierarquia.
hieroglyphics *npl* hieróglifos *mpl*.
high *n (highest point)* pico; ♦ *(-***er**, -**est**) *adj (gen; tall)* alto; **the building is very** ~ o prédio é muito alto; ~ **tide** maré alta; **how** ~ **do you want the skirt to be?** de que altura (até que altura) quer a saia?; **2** *(number, volume, price)* grande, elevado; **at** ~ **speed** a grande velocidade; ~ **price** preço

elevado; **3** *(wind; cooking)* forte; **to cook on** ~ **heat** cozinhar em lume forte; **4** *(mountain, plane)* altitude; **how** ~ **are we?** a que altura estamos?; **5** *(voice: high-pitched)* agudo; **6** *(influential)* importante; **7** *(on drugs) (person)* eufórico,-a, alucinado,-a *(BR)* baratinado,-a; ♦ *adv* alto, a grande altura; *(in degrees)* em alto grau; ~ **in the air** nas alturas; **it's** ~ **time** já é mais que tempo; ~ **and mighty** arrogante; ~ **altar** altar-mor; ~**ball** *n (US)* uísque com soda e gelo; ~**brow** *adj* culto, erudito; ~**born** *adj* (de nascimento) aristocrata; ~-**chair** *n* cadeira *f (alta)* de bebé; *(in College)* poltrona, *f*, cadeirão *m*; ~ **Church** *npr* Igreja Anglicana; ~-**class** *(restaurant, etc)* superior, de primeira categoria/class; *(person)* de alta roda; ~ **Court (of Justice)** *n (UK)* Supremo Tribunal *m* de Justiça; ~**lighter** *n (pen)* caneta *f* marca-texto, sublinhador; ~**lights** *npl (hair)* realces, madeixas *fpl*; ~ **mass** missa *f* solene; ~-**minded** *adj* arrogante; ~ **noon** *n* meio-dia; ~-**pitched** *adj (som)* agudo; ~-**pressure** *adj* de alta pressão; ~ **priest** *n* sacerdote *m*; ~-**ranking** *adj* de destaque; ~ **rise block** *n* edifício alto, espigão *m*; ~ **school** *n* escola secundária, liceu *m*; ~ **spirited** *adj* cheio de alegria, vivaz; audacioso, desenvolto; ~ **street** *n* rua principal; ~ **tea** *(UK)* *n* (refeição ligeira à tardinha) lanche *m* ajantarado; ~ **tech(nology)** *n* tecnologia *m* de ponta.
higher *adj* mais alto, superior; ~ **Education** *n (Univ)* Educação *f* Superior.
highest *adj* o mais alto, supremo.
high-flown *adj (speech, person)* bombástico.
high flyer *n (person)* ambicioso,-a.
high-handed *adj* despótico.
high-heeled *adj* de salto alto.
highjack *n (plane, ship)* sequestro *m*, desvio *m* de avião; ♦ *vt* sequestrar; **2** *(business)* comprometer.
highjacker *n* sequestrador,-ora; bandido *m* armado; *(plane)* pirata *m* do ar.
high jinks *npl* folia *f*, pândega *f*.
high jump *n (SPORT)* salto em altura.
Highlands *npl* the ~ *(Scotland)* as Terras Altas *fpl*.
high life *n* vida *f* de luxo.
highlight *n (fig: of event)* ponto alto; **2** *(ART)* realce; ♦ *vt* realçar.
highly *adv* altamente; ~ **strung** *adj* tenso, irritadiço.
highness *n* altura; **Her Royal H**~ Sua Alteza Real.
high seas *npl:* the ~ o alto mar.
highway *n* estrada, rodovia; ~ **and byways** *npl* caminhos e atalhos; ~ **man** *n* salteador *m* da estrada.
hijack *n (plane)* sequestro; ♦ *vt* sequestrar; **2** *(COMM)* comprometer *(business)*.
hijacker *n* sequestrador,-ora *(BR:* -qües-); bandido armado.
hike *n* caminhada *f*; ♦ *vi* viajar a pé; *(tramp)* vagar.
hiker *n* caminhante *m,f* andarilho.
hiking *n* excursões *fpl* a pé.
hilarious *adj* hilariante, alegre.
hill *n* colina, outeiro; *(high)* montanha; *(slope)* ladeira, rampa.
hillock *n* outeiro *m*.

hillside *n* vertente, encosta *f*.

hilly *adj* montanhoso; acidentado, escarpado.

hilt *n* *(of sword)* punho, guarda; **to the ~** plenamente.

him *pron* *(direct)* o; *(indirect)* lhe; *(stressed, after prep)* ele.

Himalayas (the ~) *npr* *(os)* Himalaias.

himself *pron* *(reflexive)* se; *(emphatic)* ele mesmo; *(after prep)* si (mesmo).

hind *n* corça; ♦ *adj* traseiro.

hinder *vt* *(impede)* impedir, estorvar; atrapalhar; pôr obstáculos.

hindrance *n* impedimento, estorvo.

hindsight *n*: **with the benefit of ~** olhando em retrospe(c)to, em retrospectiva.

Hindu *adj, npr* hindu *m,f*.

hinge *n* dobradiça, gonzo; ♦ *vi*: **to ~ on to sth/sb** depender de (alguém/algo); *(TECH)* articular-se sobre.

hint *n* insinuação *f*, alusão *f*; *(clue)* pista *f*, dica *f*; *(suggestion)* palpate *m* ♦ *vt*: **to ~ that** insinuar que; ♦ *vi* **to drop a ~** *(nasty hints)* dar piadas a, *(BR)* dar indire(c)tas a; **to ~ at** fazer alusão a, dar a entender.

hinterland *n* *(GEOG)* interior *m* de um país.

hip[1] *n* anca, quadril *m*; **~ bone** *n* osso *m* ilíaco; **~ flask** frasco *m* de bolso.

hip[2] *(also:* **hep, hipper, hepper**) *adj (slang)* bem informado,-a; a par de; à moda.

hip[3] *(Vd:* **rosehip**).

hippo *(abbr for* **hippopotamus**) *(pl:* **-es** *or* **-mi**) *n* *(ZOOL)* hipopótamo.

hippy *n* hippi *m,f*.

hire *n* *(EP)* aluguer *m*, *(BR)* aluguel *m* (de carro, casa); *(of person)* salário; **for ~** aluga-se (bicicleta, quarto); *(taxi)* livre; **~ purchase (HP)** *n* compra a prazo; ♦ *vt* alugar (carro, equipamento, etc); *(worker)* contratar.

his *pron* (o) seu, sua, o,-a dele; ♦ *adj* seu, sua *or* dele; **~ sister** a irmã dele.

Hispanic *adj* hispânico,-a.

hiss *(pl:* **-ses**) *n* *(from person)* assobio *m*; **2** *(of train, snake)* silvo *m*; **3** *(of kettle, gas, steam)* chiar *m*; **4** *(from audience)* vaia *f*, apupo *m*; ♦ *vi* silvar, assobiar; chiar; produzir um som sibilante; **to ~ off** *(actor, play)* vaiar, assobiar.

historian *n* historiador,-ora.

historic(al) *adj* histórico.

history *n* história; **~ tells us** a história reza; **to go down in ~ as ...** entrar na história como...; **case ~** *n* *(MED)* *(JUR)* *(record)* antecedents *mpl*; **2** passado; **he has a ~ of violence** ele tem um passado de violência.

histrionics *npl* *(pej)* melodrama *m*.

hit *n* golpe *m*, pancada; **2** *(car, person)* colisão *f*; **3** *(on target)* tiro *m* certeiro; **I scored five ~s** acertei cinco vezes ao alvo; **4** sucesso *m*, grande êxito *m* **to be a big ~** *(show, film)* ser/ter um grande sucess; **~ list** *n* lista *f* negra; **~ man** *n* *(gangster)* assassino *m* contratado; **~ parade** *n* lista *f* de êxitos; ♦ *(pt, pp* **hit**) *vt* bater em, golpear; **2** *(target)* acertar, *(by bullet)* atingir; **you ~ it** você

acertou; é isso mesmo; **3** *(car)* chocar com, embater, *(BR)* colidir com; ♦ **to ~ the roof/ceiling** ir aos arames *(fam)*; ♦ **to ~ back** *vi* ripostar; defender-se; **to be hard ~ by** ficar chocado, magoado com; **~ out** *vi* **~ at sb/sth** atacar, criticar; **to ~ upon/on** descobrir por acaso, achar; IDIOM *(occur to mind)* **suddenly the truth ~ me** de repente dei-me conta da verdade; **to ~ it off with sb** dar-se bem com alguém.

hit-and-miss *adj* aproximado, aleatório; **2** *(affair)* ao acaso.

hit-and-run *(attack, raid)* de surpresa; **2** *(car accident)* de atropelamento e fuga.

hitch *n* dificuldade *f*, empecilho *m*; **2** *(NAUT)* nó; ♦ *vt* amarrar, prender com nó; **2** *(skirt, trousers)* levantar, puxar para cima; **to ~ a lift/to ~-hike** *vi* pedir/andar à boleia, *(BR)* pedir carona (a alguém); **to ~ up** *(horse)* atrelar (cavalo).

hitch-hike *vi* viajar pedindo boleia *(BR)* carona *f*.

hither *adj* de cá, deste lado, daqui; **~ and thither** de cá para lá; aqui e acolá.

hitherto *adv* até agora, até então; **~ unknown** até agora desconhecido.

HIV *(abbr for* **human immunodeficiency virus)** HIV *m*.

hive *n* *(beehive)* colmeia; **2 ~ of activity** *(fig)* centro de a(c)tividades.

HM *(abbr for* **His/Her Majesty)** S.M.

HMG *(UK)* *(abbr for* **His/Her Majesty's Government)** governo *m* de Sua Majestade.

hoard *n* *(of treasure)* tesouro *m*; **2** *(provisions)* provisão *f*; ♦ *vt* acumular *(BR)* estocar; **2** *(animal)* armazenar.

hoarding *n* acumulação *f*; **2** *(for posters)* painel *m* publicitário; **3** *(over a shop)* tabuleta; **4** *(type of fence; around building site)* tapume *m*.

hoarse *adj* rouco,-a, roufenho,-a.

hoax *n* *(deceit)* burla *f*, logro *m*; *(practical joke)* partida *f*.

hob *n* *(modern cooker)* placa *f* do fogão (sobre a bancada da cozinha); **2** *(MEC)* tarraxa, fresa *f*.

hobble *vi* *(limp)* coxear; ♦ *vt* *(horse)* pear, estar peado.

hobby *n* hobby *m*, passatempo predileto.

hobby horse *n* cavalinho *m* de pau; **2** *(fig)* tema *m* favorito; **she is on her ~** ela volta à carga, ela está a carregar na mesma tecla.

hobnail *n* tachão; ♦ *vi* pregar com tachões: **~ed boots** *npl* botas *fpl* ferradas, cardadas; **~ liver** *n* fígado com cirrose.

hobnob *(-bed)* *vi* socializar, falar familiarmente com alguém.

hobo *n* *(vagrant)* vagabundo.

hock *n* *(of horse, etc)* jarrete *m*; **2** vinho *m* branco do Reno.

hockey *n* hóquei *m*; **ice ~** hóquei no gelo; **roller-skates ~** hóquei de patins; **~ stick** *n* bastão *m* de hóquei.

hocus-pocus *n* *(trickery)* trapaça *f*; *(BR)* tapeação *f*; **2** truques *mpl*; prestidigitação *f*.

hoe *n* enxada *f*; ♦ *vt* trabalhar com enxada, capinar.

hog *n (animal)* porco *m* castrado; ♦ *(pt, pp* **-gg-)** *vt (fig)* monopolizar; **to go the whole** ~ ir até ao fim.

Hogmanay nome dado pelos escoceses à Noite de Ano Novo = véspera do Ano Novo.

hoi-polloi *npl (pej)* populaça *f,* gentalha *f,* malta *f,* ralé *f (pej).*

hoist *n* guindaste *m;* **2** grua; ♦ *vt (load, anchor)* levantar, içar; **2** *(flag)* hastear; **to** ~ **with one's petard** ser vencido com suas próprias armas.

hoity-toity *adj (pej)* pretensioso,-a.

hokum *n (US) (nonsense)* disparates *mpl,* parvoíce *f; (sentimentality–in a play)* pieguices *fpl.*

hold *n (grasp)* apoio *m;* **2** *(fig)* influência *f m;* **3** *(NAUT)* porão *m* de navio; ♦ *(pt, pp* **held)** *vt (have)* ter; *(contain)* conter; **2** *(keep back)* reter; **3** segurar; **4** *(take weight)* aguentar *(BR:* -güen-); **5** *(meeting)* realizar; ♦ *vi (withstand pressure)* resistir; ♦ ~ **the line!** *(TEL)* não desligue!; **to** ~ **an office** exercer um cargo; **to** ~ **the floor** *vt* dominar o auditório; **to get a** ~ **on sth** *vt (obtain)* arranjar algo; **2** encontar alguém; **3 to get a** ~ **on o.s.** controlar-se; ♦ **to** ~ **sth against sb** *vt* ter algo contra alguém, estar ressentido contra alguém; ♦ **to** ~ **back** *vt (words, temper)* conter-se, reprimir-se; **2** *(laughter, tear)* conter; **3** *(information, privacy)* guardar, não divulgar; **4** *(prevent progress of)* retardar; **to** ~ **sb/sth dear** estimar, ter afeição a algo, alguém; ♦ **to** ~ **down** *vt (person)* oprimir; **2** *(item)* segurar; **3** *(job)* manter; **4** *(figures, costs)* limitar, restringir; **5** *(find sb)* encontrar alguém; ♦ **to** ~ **on** *vi (grip)* agarrar-se; **2** *(fam) (TEL)* esperar um momento; **3** *(endure)* aguentar; ♦ **to** ~ **off** *vt (enemy)* afastar, repelir; **2** manter-se à distância; **to** ~ **one's own** manter-se firme; ♦ **to** ~ **onto** segurar-se bem; **2** *(algo)* reter; **to** ~ **out** *(hand, etc) vt* estender; ~ **out for** *vt* insistir em; ♦ *vi* resistir (a alguém); ♦ **to** ~ **steady/still** segurar firme; **to** ~ **up** *vt* levantar; **2** apoiar; **3** *(delay)* atrasar; **4** *(rob)* assaltar; **to** ~ **with** *vt (approve of)* aprovar.

holdall *n* saco de viagem.

holder *n (of ticket, record)* possuidor,-ora; *(of title)* titular *m,f;* detentor,-ora de.

holding *n (farm)* propriedade *f;* **2** **~s** *npl (shares)* títulos *mpl,* a(c)ções *fpl;* participação *f* a(c)cionária; ♦ *adj (company)* controladora; holding; **3** *(Austral) (fam)* com fundos.

hold-up *n (robbery)* assalto *m* à mão armada; **2** *(delay)* empecilho; **3** *(in traffic)* engarrafamento *m.*

hole *n* buraco *m;* furo *m;* **2** falha *f;* **3** *(coll)* embaraço *m;* **4** *(fig)* lugar horrível; buraco; **5** *(of rabbit)* toca.

holiday *n* férias *fpl;* **on** ~ de férias; **bank** ~ feriado nacional; *(day off)* dia de folga *m;* ~ **camp** colónia *f* de férias; ~ **maker** *n* veraneante *m,f* excursionista *m,f;* ~ **resort** *n* local *m,* estância de férias.

holiness *n* santidade *f;* **His H**~ **the Pope** Sua Santidade o Papa.

holistic *adj* holístico,-a.

Holland *npr* Holanda; **in** ~ na Holanda.

holler *vt (fam)* gritar, berrar.

hollow *n* buraco *m;* cavidade *f;* depressão *f;* ♦ *adj (empty)* oco, vazio; **2** *(eyes)* encovados; **3** fundo,-a;

4 *(sound)* surdo; **5** *(voice)* cavernoso,-a; **6** *(ceiling)* côncavo; **7** *(riso)* forçado; ♦ *vt:* ~ **out** escavar.

holly *n* azevinho *m;* ~**hock** *n* malva-rosa *f.*

holocaust *n* holocausto *m;* **the H**~ o Holocausto.

hologram *n* holograma *m.*

hols *npl (fam)* folgas *fpl,* férias *fpl.*

holster *n* coldre *m.*

holy (**-ier, -iest**) *adj* santo, sagrado; bento; **H**~ **Ghost/Spirit** *npr* Espírito Santo; **the holiest of all men** o mais santo de todos os homens; ~ **water** *n* água benta.

homage *n* homenagem *f;* **to pay** ~ **to** prestar homenagem a.

home *n (dwelling)* casa *f; (family unit; institution)* lar *m;* **I am going** ~ vou para casa; **my** ~ **is my family** o meu lar é a minha família; **broken** ~ lar desfeito; **retirement** ~ lar *m* da terceira idade; **2** *(country)* pátria *f,* terra *f* natal; ♦ *adj (of home, homely)* caseiro, doméstico; *(ECON, POL)* nacional, interno; ~ **consumption** consumo doméstico; ~ **address** *n* endereço/dire(c)ção de casa/residencial; ~**brew** *n* cerveja *f* caseira; ~ **cooking** *n* comida *f* caseira; ~ **coming** *n (return)* regresso *m* ao lar; ~**ground** *adj* em seu território; ~**grown** *adj (vegetables etc)* plantado em casa; ~ **land** *n* terra natal; ~**less** *adj* sem casa; **the** ~**less** *n* os sem-teto, os sem-abrigo; ~**ly** *adj* caseiro; simples; ~**-made** *adj* caseiro; ~**owner** *n* proprietário,-a; ~ **rule** *n* autonomia *f* interna; ~**secretary** *(UK)* Ministro,-a do Interior; ~**sick** *adj:* **to be** ~**sick** ter saudade(s), estar saudoso; ~**sickness** *n* nostalgia *f;* ~**stead** *n (land and house)* solar *m; (farm)* herdade *f;* ~**town** *n* terra, cidade natal; ~**truth** *n* verdades *fpl* desagradáveis; a verdade nua e crua; ~**ward** *adj* para casa/para a terra natal; de retorno/regresso, em direcção a casa; ~**work** *n* dever *m* de casa; ♦ *adv (direction)* para casa; **on the way** ~ a caminho de casa; *(from abroad)* no regresso; **at** ~ em casa; **to live at** ~ viver, morar com os pais; **make yourself at** ~ esteja à vontade; *(SPORT) (own ground)* **to play at** ~ jogar em casa; ♦ *vi* **to** ~ **in on sth** dirigir-se dire(c)tamente a algo.

Home Office *npr* Ministério da Administração Interna.

homeopathic *adj* homeopático,-a.

homeopathy *n* homeopatia *f.*

homespun *adj* caseiro,-a; feito em casa.

homey *(also:* **homy)** *adj (fam) (cosy)* acolhedor.

homicidal *adj* homicida *m,f.*

homicide *n (murder)* homicídio *m.*

homily *n (lecture)* homilia *f.*

homing *n:* ~ **instinct** instinto de animais de saber voltar a casa, de longe; ♦ *adj (plane)* autodirecional, em direção ao alvo; ~ **pigeon** *n* pombo-correio.

homogeneity *n* homogeneidade *f.*

homogenise, homogenize *vt* homogenizar.

homogeous *adj* homogéneo,-a.

homonym *n* homónimo *m.*

homophobia *n* discriminação *f* dos homossexuais.

homosexual *n adj* homossexual *m;* **2** *(coll, pej)* barbosa, maricas, *(BR)* bicha.

homosexuality *n* homossexualidade *f.*

Honduran *n, adj* hondurenho,-a.

Honduras *npr* Honduras.

hone *n* pedra *f* de amolar; ♦ *vt (knife sword)* amolar, afiar; **2** *(fig) (knowledge, techique)* aprimorar, aperfeiçoar.

honest *adj* honesto; sincero, franco.

honestly *adv* honestamente, francamente.

honest-to-goodness *adj* simples; autêntico.

honesty *n* honestidade *f*, sinceridade *f*.

honey *n* mel *m*; ~**bee** *n* abelha ~**comb** *n* favo de mel; ~**combed with** *(holes) adj* cheio de alveólos, esburacado,-a; **2** *(sewing, dress)* em forma de favos; ~**ed** *adj* melífluo,-a, doce; ~**moon** *n* lua-de-mel *f*; *(trip)* viagem *f* de lua-de-mel.

honeysuckle *n (BOT)* madressilva *f*.

honk *n (of horn)* buzinada *f*; **2** *(of goose)* grasnada; ♦ *vi (AUT)* buzinar; **2** grasnar.

honky *n (US) (slang) (pej)* homem branco.

honky-tonk *n (US, Canada) (slang)* cabaré *m* reles; **2** música de cabaré (em piano).

honorary *adj* não remunerado; **2** *(duty, title)* honorário,-a; ~ **doctorate** doutoramento honorário.

honour *(UK)*, **honor** *(US) n* honra, fama; **Your H~** Vossa excelência *m,f*; **maid of** ~ dama de honor *(BR:* honra); ♦ *vt* honrar; IDIOM **to do the** ~ fazer as honras da casa.

honourable, honorable *adj (pessoa)* honrado, honesto; **2** *(action, profession)* honroso,-a, nobre; **3** *(titles)* **the** ~ **colleague** o digníssimo colega; **The H~ Gentleman** *(in debates, Parliament)* Vossa Excelência.

honourably, honorably *adv* honrosamente.

honoured, honored *adj* honrado,-a; **to feel** ~ sentir-se honrado.

honours degree *n (EDUC) (UK)* licenciatura, graduação *f* com distinção (= 1º ano do mestrado).

hood *n* capuz *m*, touca; **2** *(AUT)* capota.

hooded *adj* com capuz, encapuzado,-a; ~ **eyes** *npl* pálpebras *fpl* descaídas.

hoodlum *n* arruaceiro, gângster *m*.

hoodwink *vt* lograr.

hoof *(pl:* **hooves)** *n* casco *m*, pata *f*.

hook *n* gancho *(on dress; zip)*; **2** ~ **and eye** colchete *m*; **3** *(for fishing)* anzol *m*; **to take the telephone off the** ~ tirar o telefone do descanso *(BR)* do gancho; **4 take sb off the** ~ *(out of trouble)* livrar alguém de um problema; ♦ *vt* enganchar; fisgar; apanhar no anzol; prender com gancho; ~ **sth through** passar algo por/através; **to** ~ **up** *(garment)* apertar com colchete; **2** *(BR)* conetar.

hookah *n (pipe)* narguilé.

hooked *adj (obsessed)* obcecado,-a; **2** *(coll) (on drugs)* viciado em (algo); **3** *(married)* estar casado,-a.

hooker *n (fam)* prostituta *f*.

hook(e)y *n (US: fam):* **to play** ~ *(students)* fazer gazeta às aulas.

hooknose *n (aquiline)* nariz *m* adunco/de cavalete.

hook-up *(Radio, TV)* cadeia *f* de estações transmitindo em simultâneo; **2** *(AER)* acoplamento; ligação; **3** aliança.

hooligan *n* desordeiro, vadio; rufião *m*, *(BR)* arruaceiro, hooligan; ~**ism** *n* vandalismo, hooliganismo.

hoop *n* arco; *(of metal, wood, etc)* aro *m*; argola *f*.

hooray *exc (Vd:* **hurrah)**.

hoot *n (AUT)* buzinada *f*; toque *m* de sirena; **2** *(of owl)* pio *m*; ♦ *vi (AUT)* buzinar; **2** *(siren)* tocar a sirena; **3** *(owl)* piar; **4** *(crowd)* apupar; **to** ~ **an actor** assobiar *(BR:* vaiar) um a(c)tor; IDIOM **I don't give a** ~ quero lá saber! estou-me nas tintas.

hooter *n (of car)* buzina *f*; **2** *(siren)*; **3** *(coll) (nose)* narigueta *f*, narigão *m (fam)*.

hoover® *n* aspirador *m*; ♦ *vt* **to** ~ **the carpet** aspirar a carpete.

hooves *(pl of* **hoof)**.

hop *n* salto, pulo *m*; **2** *(BOT)* lúpulo *m*; ♦ *(pt, pt -pp-) vt/vi* saltar, pular; *(on one foot)* pular num pé só; andar ao pé coxinho; **2** *(bird)* saltitar, andar aos saltinhos; **3** *(jump over)* **he** ~**ped the hedge** ele saltou por cima da sebe; ~ **in!** *(let sb in the car)* entre!; ~ **on the bus** pular para o autocarro; **to be on the** ~ andar numa azáfama louca.

hope *n* esperança *f*; ♦ *vi* esperar, ter esperança (de), confiar (em); **I** ~ **so/not** espero que sim/que não; ~ **it won't rain** se Deus quiser não vai chover.

hopeful *adj* o(p)timista, esperançoso; promissor.

hopefully *adv* esperançosamente, o(p)timisticamente.

hopeless *adj* desesperado, irremediável; **it is** ~ não tem remédio; **a** ~ **case** um caso perdido.

hopper *n (bin)* tremonha *f*; máquina para ceifar lúpulo.

hopping *adj*: ~ **mad** furioso,-a; **she is** ~ **about with excitement** ela está a pular/pulando de contente.

hops *npl (BOT)* lúpulo *sg*.

hopscotch *n (children's games)* jogo *m* da macaca.

horde *n* horda *f*, bando *m*.

horizon *n* horizonte *m*.

horizontal *adj* horizontal *m,f*.

hormone *n* hormona *f*, *(BR)* hormônio *m*.

horn *n* chifre *m*, *(fam)* corno *m*; **2** *(MUS)* trompa; **3** *(AUT)* buzina; **4** *(of ship)* apito *m*, sereia *f*; ~**ed** *adj (animal)* cornudo, com chifres; IDIOM **on the horns of a dilemma** (estar) entre a espada e a parede.

hornet *n* vespão *m*.

horn-rimmed *adj (glasses etc)* feito com aro de chifre/tartaruga.

horny *adj* córneo; **2** *(hands)* calejado, caloso; **3** *(fam) (sexually excited)* com tesão.

horoscope *n* horóscopo *m*.

horrible *adj* horrível.

horribly *adv* horrivelmente.

horrid *adj (person)* antipático,-a; **2** *(incident)* desagradável; **3** *(place, film, idea)* horroroso,-a.

horrific *adj* horrível.

horrify *vt* horrorizar.

horrifying *adj* horripilante.

horror *n* horror *m*; ~ **film** *n* filme *m* de terror; **in** ~ horrorizado,-a.

hors d'œuvre *n* acepipes *mpl*, entrada *f*.

horse *n* cavalo; **on** ~**back** a cavalo; ~ **box/car** atrelado/reboque *m* para transportar cavalos; ~**chestnut** *n (BOT)* castanha-da-índia; ~**drawn** *adj* puxado,-a a cavalos; ~**laugh** gargalhada estrondosa; **~fly** *n (ZOOL)* mutuca *f*; **~hair** *n* crina *f*, pêlo *m* de cavalo; **~man** *n* cavaleiro; **~power (hp)** *n* potência *f*, cavalo-vapor *m*; **~-racing** *n* corrida de cavalo; **~radish** *n (BOT)* rábano *m* picante, raiz-forte *f*; **~riding** *n* equitação *f*; **~ show** *n* concurso/evento hípico, rodeio *m*; **~shoe** *n* ferradura; **~whip** *n* chicote *m*; **~woman** *n* amazona *f*.

horticulture *n* horticultura *f*.

hose *n* tubo; **~pipe** *n* mangueira; ♦ **to ~ down** *vt* lavar com mangueira.

hosiery *n* loja de meias e roupa interior (lingerie).

hospice *n* hospício, asilo *m*.

hospitable *adj* hospitaleiro,-a.

hospital *n* hospital *m*.

hospitality *n* hospitalidade *f*.

host *n* anfitrião *m*, dono da casa; **2 ~ country** país acolhedor; **3** *(compere)* apresentador,-ora; **4** *(REL)* hóstia; **5** *(army)* hoste *f*; **6 a ~ of** uma multidão de; ♦ *vt (show, etc)* apresentar; *(country hosting congresso, etc)* acolher, receber.

hostage *n* refém *m*.

hostel *n* hospedaria; **youth ~** *n* albergue *m* para jovens.

hostelry *n* estalagem *f*.

hostess *n* anfitriã *f*; dona da casa; **2** (= **air ~**) hospedeira de bordo, *(BR)* aeromoça; **3** *(TV, RADIO)* apresentadora *f*.

hostile *adj* hostil.

hostility *n* hostilidade *f*.

hot *adj (from heat)* quente; **to feel ~** *(weather)* ter calor; *(sexually)* sentir-se ardente; *(spicy)* picante; *(passionate)*, ardente; *(fig) (speech, discussion)* veemente; *(day, sand, topic)* escaldante; *(new, fresh)* recente; **to be ~ at sth** *(expert)* ser bom/boa em algo; **to have a ~ temper** encolerizar-se, exaltar-se; ♦ **~ flash** *n (menopause)* afrontamento *m (BR)* calorão *m*; **~foot** *adv* a toda a velocidade; **~headed** *adj* impetuoso; fogoso; **~house** *n* estufa; **~line** *n (between governments)* linha direta; **~ly** *adv* ardentemente, calorosamente; **~ money** *n* capital transferido de um centro financeiro para outro, para ter melhores juros; **~ pants** *npl* calções muito justos (ao corpo); **~pot** *n (CULIN)* estufado; **~potato** *n (cooked in the oven)* batata *f* quente; **~pursued** *adj* perseguido,-a de perto; **~ seat** *n (fam)* posição *f* difícil ou perigosa: **to be (always) in the ~** ser quem tem sempre que se desenrascar (de uma situação); (BR) ser quem tem sempre que descascar o abacaxi; **~shot** *n* craque *m*; **~spot** *n (POL)* ponto *m* crítico, área *f* de tensão; **2** lugar *m* da moda do entretimento; **~ springs** *npl* termas *fpl*; **~-tempered** *adj* de mau génio, arrebatado *(BR)* esquentado,-a; **~-water bottle** *n* saco *(BR:* bolsa) de água quente; IDIOM **to be in ~ water** *(in trouble)* estar/ficar em maus lençóis; **to get into ~ water** meter-se em apuros/ em sarilhos; **to blow ~ and cold** ser de humor variável/mercurial.

hot air *n (coll) (from person)* basófia; **~ balloon** *n* balão *m* de ar quente.

hot-blooded sangue quente, fogoso.

hotchpotch *(UK)* **hodgepodge** *(US) n* mixórdia *f*.

hotcross bun *n* pãozinho doce que se come pela Páscoa.

hotdog *n (sausage in a roll)* cachorro-quente *m*.

hotel *n* hotel *m*.

hotelier *n* hoteleiro,-a.

hound *n (dog)* cão *m* de caça, sabujo; **2 autograph ~** *(US; coll)* caçador,-ora de autógrafos; **3 ~ dog** *n* cão vadio; **4** *(despicable person)* miserável; ♦ *vt* perseguir, assediar.

hour *n* hora; **every ~** de hora a hora, cada hora. **after ~s** fora de horas; **at the eleventh ~** à última hora; **at an early ~** cedo; **by the ~** à/por hora; **~glass** *n* ampulheta *f*; **~hand** *n* ponteiro *m* (do relógio); **~ly** *adv* de hora; ♦ **hours** *npl* horas *fpl*; **in the small ~ of the night** a altas horas da noite; **2 business ~** horas de expediente; **3** *(timetable)* horário *m*; *(REL) (prayers)* horas *fpl*; **hourly** *adv* de hora em hora; *(pay)* à hora.

house *n* casa, moradia *f*, vivenda *f*; **2** *(COMM) (restaurant, shop)* casa; **on the ~** por conta da, oferta da casa; **3** *(THEAT) (audience)* assistência, audiência, platéia *f*; "**full ~**" *(on notice)* "lotação esgotada", "esgotado"; **empty ~** *(THEAT)* às moscas *(coll)*; **packed ~** *n (coll) (THEAT, CIN)* casa à cunha; **~-proud** *adj* meticuloso, fanático com o aspe(c)to da casa, pessoa muito asseada; **~-trained** *adj (animal)* treinado,-a *(to defecate, urinate in a particular place)*; **~-warming party** *n* festa da estreia de uma casa; ♦ *vt* alojar, *(temp.)* abrigar, albergar; IDIOM **to bring the ~ down** *(with applause)* deitar a casa abaixo (com aplausos), ser muito aplaudido,-a; **to get on like a ~ on fire** entender-se às mil maravilhas; **to put one's ~ in order** *(organize one's affaires)* pôr as coisas (assuntos) em ordem, arrumar as gavetas.

house arrest *n* prisão *f* domiciliária; **under ~** sob prisão domiciliar.

houseboat *n* casa flutuante.

housebound *adj* confinado,-a em casa.

housebreaking *n* assalto.

housebroken *(Vd:* housetrained).

housecoat *n* bata *f*.

houseguest *n* convidado *m* de passagem.

household *n* pessoas *fpl* da casa, agregado *m* familiar; **2** *(ECON, ADMIN)* governo *m* da casa; ♦ *adj (tasks, products, etc)* doméstico; **2** *(insurance)* habitação; *(appliances)* aparelho *m* ele(c)trodoméstico; **head of ~** chefe *m* de família; **~ name** pessoa muito conhecida, toda a gente o conhece; **~ name (word)** *n* nome muito conhecido.

householder *n* residente; *(owner)* dono *m* da casa; **2** *(tenant)* inquilino,-a.

house-hunting *n* procura de casa.

housekeeper *n* governanta *f*.

housekeeping governo *m* doméstico; *(managing the money)* economia *f* doméstica.

housemaid criada *f*, empregada *f* doméstica.

housemaster *n (boy's private school)* professor/tutor *m*.

House of Commons *npr* Câmara dos Comuns.

House of Lords npr Câmara dos Lordes/Pares (Peers).

House of Representatives npr (US) **the** ~ a Câmara dos Representantes mpl (dos Estados Unidos da América).

Houses of Parliament npr pl Parlamento m britânico.

house-to-house adj de casa em casa, de porta-a-porta.

housewife n dona de casa.

housework n trabalhos mpl domésticos.

housing n (houses, flats) residência, habitação; **2** (accommodation) alojamento; **3** (any box, device housing sth) encaxe, caixa; cárter; (cereals) armazenamento m; (AUT) invólucro m (do farol); ~ **association** n organização que aluga por mais barato ou ajuda a comprar casa por mais barato; ~ **benefit** n (UK) subsídio m para a habitação; ~ **development** n urbanização f.

housing estate n conjunto residencial; **2** habitação f social, fogos mpl habitacionais.

hovel n choupana f, casebre m.

hover vi pairar; ~**craft** n hidroplanador, aerodeslizador m.

how adv como; ~ **are you?** como está?; ~ **are you doing?** como vai (fam)?; como tem passado? ~ **do you do!** (introduction) muito prazer!; ~ **long have you been here?** há quanto tempo está aqui?; I **don't know** ~ **to do this** não sei como se faz isso; ~ **do you feel about it?** qual é a sua opinião disto? ~ **about it?**/~ **is that?** (asking for an opinion/comment) que tal?; ~ **far is it** a que distância fica?; ~ **lovely!** que lindo!; ~ **many/much?**; quantos/quanto?; ~ **old are you?** quantos anos tem?; ~ **come?** como? porquê?; ~ **come he gets all your attention?** como é que ele recebe sempre a tua atenção?

however adv de qualquer modo; ~ **rich** por muito rico que (+ subjunctive); ~ **much it may cost** custe o que custar, qualquer que seja o preço; ~ **did you pay?** como é que pagaste?; ◆ conj no entanto, contudo, todavia.

howitzer n obus m.

howl n uivo; ◆ vi (wolf, dog, wind) uivar; (pessoa) gritar; (child, wail) berrar.

howler n (coll) (error) bacorada f; asneira f.

howling n uivo, urro m; (child, crowd) berros mpl; **the** ~ **of wind** o bramido m/sibilar m do vento; ~ **success** adj (fig, coll) êxito m retumbante, estrondoso.

hp n (abbr for **horsepower**) h.p. m.

HP n (abbr for **hire purchase**) (UK).

HQ n (abbr for **headquarters**) QG m.

HRH npr (abbr for **His/Her Royal Highness**) Sua Alteza Real.

HRT n (abbr for **hormone replacement therapy**) (MED).

hub n (TECH) (of wheel) eixo m; (fig) (center) centro m.

hubbub n (many voices; shouting) algazarra f, vozerio m; (fig) tumulto m.

hubcap n calota f.

huckleberry n (US) mirtilo m.

huddle (cluster of people, buidings) amontoado; ◆ vi (cluster) agrupar-se; (crowd together) apertar-se uns contra os outros; **to** ~ **together** (in affection) aconchegar-se um ao outro/uns aos outros; **give me a** ~ aconchega-te a mim.

hue n (colour) matiz m; **2** (aspect) aspeto m, tendência f; ~ **and cry** n (outcry) protesto m público.

huff n: **to be in a** ~ estar amuado,-a; **to get into a** ~ ficar zangado, estar com a mosca (fam); ◆ vi soprar; **to** ~ **and puff** (with anger) bufar de cólera.

huffiness n mau humor m.

huffy (-ier, -iest) adj (fam) ressentido,-a; (touchy) sensível.

hug n (embrace) abraço; **a bear** ~ (pop) (with affection) um xi-coração; (at the end of loving letter) um Xi! Love!; ◆ (-gg-) vi abraçar.

huge adj enorme, imenso.

hugely adv extremamente.

hugeness n vastidão, imensidade f.

huggable adj que apetece abraçar; **a** ~ **child** uma criança f fofinha.

hula-hoop n bambolé m.

hulk n (wreck) navio velho abandonado, casco, carcaça; **2** (fig) (of mountain, building) massa f imensa; **3** (fig) (clumsy person) pessoa pesada e desajeitada.

hulking n (pessoa) enorme e desajeitado,-a.

hull n (of ship) casco.

hullabaloo n (fam) (shouting, fuss) celeuma f, estardalhaço m; (agitation, clamour) alarido, alvoroço m, algazarra f.

hullo exc = **hello!**

hum exc hum! ◆ n som m indistinto (de incerteza) ◆ vi (-mm-) murmurar; **2** (in hesitation) tartamudear; **3** cantarolar de lábios fechados; **4** (fam) (UK) cheirar mal.

human n adj humano; ~ **being** n o ser humano m; ~ **race** n género m humano.

humane adj (kind) humano, humanitário; ~ **decision** decisão f humanitária.

human engineering n gestão f de recursos humanos.

humanism n humanismo; **2** kindness.

humanitarian adj humanitário, humanista.

humanities npl (field of study) humanidades.

humanity n humanidade f.

humanize vt humanizar.

humankind n género m humano.

humanly adv humanamente.

humble adj humilde; **2** (unpretencious) modesto, despretensioso; ◆ vt humilhar; **to** ~ **o.s.** vr humilhar-se; IDIOM **to eat** ~ **pie** ser obrigado a aceitar seu erro e pedir desculpa.

humbly adv humildemente; ~ **born** de origem modesta.

humbug n fraude f, embuste m; **it's all** ~ é tudo intrujice f; **2** (UK) (sweet) bala/caramelo de hortelã.

humdrum n monotonia f, insipidez f; ◆ adj monótono, enfadonho; ~ **tasks** tarefas fpl rotineiras.

humid adj (h)úmido.

humidity (h)umidade f.

humiliate *vt* humilhar, rebaixar.
humiliating *adj* humilhante.
humiliation *n* humilhação *f.*
humility *n* humildade *f.*
humming *n* (*insect, plane*) zumbido; **2** (*of person*) cantarola *f,* trauteio *m;* ~ **bird** *n* (*ZOOL*) colibri *m,* beija-flor *m.*
hummock *n* (*of earth*) montículo; **2** (*of ice*) elevação.
humorist *n* humorista *m,f.*
humorous *adj* engraçado, divertido.
humour (*UK*) **humor** (*US*) *n* humorismo *m,* senso de humor *m;* ♦ *vt* condescender; fazer a vontade a (alguém).
hump *n* (*in ground*) elevação *f;* **2** (*animal's, person's back*) corcova, corcunda; ♦ *vt* (*carry*) carregar; (*back*) arquear.
humpback bridge *n* (*road*) ponte *f* arqueada.
humus *n* humo *m.*
hunch *n* (*premonition*) palpite *m,* pressentimento **to have a** ~ **that** ... ter um pressentimento que ...; ♦ *vt/vi* arquear as costas; **to** ~ **one's shoulders** encolher os ombros; ~ **over** curvar-se, inclinar-se sobre.
hunchback *n* marreco,-a (*fam*).
hundred *num* cem; ~ **euros** cem euros; **2** cento; **one** ~ um cento; **one** ~ **and twenty** cento e vinte; **be one** ~**-year old** ser centenário; **two** ~ duzentos,-as; **3** (*collective*) centena *f;* **there was one** ~ **people** havia uma centena de pessoas; **I have a** ~**-and-one things to do** (*fig*) tenho mil e uma coisas a fazer; ~**fold** cem vezes, cêntuplo; **multiply** ~ centuplicar; ~ **odd** cento e tantos; ~**s of presents** centenas de presentes; **in the eighteen** ~**s** nos anos mil e oitocentos.
hundredth *n* centésimo *m;* ♦ *adj* centésimo,-a.

NOTE: between two hundred and nine hundred, the numbers are in the masculine and in the feminine.

hundredweight *n* (*medida inglesa*) quintal *m* métrico = 50.8 kg; (*UK*) = 112 lb; (*US*) = 45.3 kg; 100 lb.
hung (*pt, pp* of **hang**) *adj* (*jury, parliament*) em suspenso; (*of a situation*) que não pode ser resolvida; ~ **on knife edge** apoiado sobre cutelo; ~ **up on** (*slang*) obcecado,-a; **he is** ~ **on jazz** ele está obcecado pelo/com o jazz.
Hungarian *npr adj* húngaro,-a.
Hungary *npr* Hungria; **in** ~ na Hungria.
hunger *n* fome *f;* ♦ *vi:* **to** ~ **for/after** ter fome de; ansiar por, desejar ardentemente; ~ **strike** *n* greve *f* de fome.
hungover *adj:* **to be** ~ estar com uma ressaca.
hungrily *adv* avidamente, com fome; **to eat** ~ comer vorazmente.
hungry *adj* faminto, esfomeado; **to be** ~ estar com, ter fome.
hung-up *adj* tenso; (*obsessed with*) **be** ~ **on sb/sth** estar obcecado,-a com alguém/algo.
hunk *n* (*large piece*) naco; **a** ~ **of bread** um naco de pão; **2** (*attractive man*) um pedaço *m* de homem.

hunker *vi* (*squat*) (*also:* ~ **down**) agachar-se, acocorar-se; ♦ **hunkers** *npl* cócoras; **on** ~ de cócoras.
hunky-dory *adj* (*fam*) satisfatório,-a para todos; ó(p)timo.
hunt *n* (*SPORT, food*) caça (*activity, game*), caçada *f;* **2** (*search*) busca; **3** (*chase*) perseguição; ♦ *vt* (*seek, chase*) procurar, perseguir; **2** (*SPORT*) caçar ♦ *vi* (*look for*) procurar; **to** ~ **for** procurar, andar à procura; ~ **down** (*pursue, chase*) perseguir; **they** ~**ed down the thief** eles perseguiram o ladrão; (*com sucesso*) perseguiram e agarraram o ladrão; ~ **about** (*of gauge, engine speed*) oscilar; ~ **up a friend** procurar um amigo.
hunter *n* caçador *m.*
hunting *n* caça.
hurdle *n* (*SPORT*) barreira; **2** (*fig*) obstáculo; **hurdles** *npl* (*SPORT*) corrida *f* de obstáculos.
hurdy-gurdy *n* (*MUS*) realejo *m.*
hurl *vt* arremessar, lançar (*projectile*) (**at** sobre); **to** ~ **stones** atirar pedras; **to** ~ **insults** insultar; **to** ~ **o.s. at** precipitar-se para; atirar-se para baixo; **to** ~ **threats** proferir ameaças.
hurling *n* arremesso *m,* lançamento *m.*
hurly-burly *n* alvoroço *m,* barafunda *f,* confusão *f.*
hurrah, hurray *n* viva!, hurra!
hurricane *n* furacão *m.*
hurried *adj* apressado.
hurriedly *adv* depressa, apressadamente, precipitadamente; ~ **made/eaten** feito/comido à pressa.
hurry *n* pressa; ♦ *vi* apressar-se; ♦ *vt* apressar; acelerar; **to be in a** ~ estar com pressa; **to** ~ **up** despachar-se, apressar-se; aviar-se; **to** ~ **up sb** pressionar, apressar a pessoa; ♦ *exc* ~ **up**! aviese!, despache-se!, apresse-se!
hurt *adj* magoado, (*BR*) machucado; ferido; ♦ (*pt, pp* **hurt**) *vt* ferir; doer; (*BR*) machucar, magoar; ♦ *vi* doer.
hurtful *adj* prejudicial, ofensivo; doloroso, que magoa; **to** ~ **sb's feelings** ofender alguém.
hurtle *vi:* **to** ~ **past** passar como um raio; **to** ~ **down** cair com violência.
husband *n* marido, esposo; **to live as** ~ **and wife** viver maritalmente.
husbandman *n* (*AGR*) agricultor.
husbandry *n* (*farming*) lavoura, agricultura; **animal** ~ criação *f* de gado.
hush *n* silêncio, quietude *f;* ♦ *vt* fazer calar; **2** ~ **up** (*person, crowd*) fazer calar; **3** (*cover up*) abafar, encobrir (*scandal*); ♦ *exc* ~! silêncio!; caluda!, nem uma palavra!; **hush up** *vt* (*scandal*) abafar.
hushed *adj* (*conversation, room*) abafado,-a, em voz baixa; (*person*) calado,-a.
hush-hush *adj* (*coll*) (*secret*) confidencial; ~ **money** *n* (*fam*) suborno *m* (para comprar o silêncio de alguém).
husk *n* (*of seed, grain*) casca *f;* **2** (*affecting cattle*) bronquite.
husky *n* cão *m* esquimó; ♦ (**-ier, -iest**) *adj* rouco; **2** (*fam*) (*strong, big*) (*male*) forte, robusto *m.*
hussar *n* hussardo.

hustings *npl (UK)* tribuna *f* para eleições; campanha *f* eleitoral.

hustle *n* agitação *f*; a(c)tividade *f* febril; ~ **and bustle** *n* azáfama *f*, grande a(c)tividade *f*, vaivém *m*; ♦ *vt* empurrar; **2** *(US) (persuade)* **to ~ sb into doing sth** pressionar alguém a/para fazer algo.

hustler *n (coll)* vigarista; **2** *(US)* prostituto,-a.

hut *n* choupana, barraca; **2** *(shed)* alpendre *m*.

hutch *n (for rabbits)* coelheira; **2** caixa, arca para guardar mantimentos; **3** *(carrying ore)* vagonete *m* (para minério).

hyacinth *n (BOT)* jacinto *m*.

hybrid *n adj* híbrido,-a.

hydrangea *n (BOT)* hortênsia *f*.

hydrant *n* (= **fire** ~) hidrante *m*; boca *f* de incêndio.

hydraulic *adj* hidráulico,-a; **~s** *n* hidráulica *f*.

hydrocarbon *n* hidrocarboneto *m*.

hydrochloric acid *n* ácido *m* clorídrico.

hydroelectric *adj* hidroelé(c)trico.

hydrogen *n* hidrogénio *(BR: -gê-)*.

hyena *n (ZOOL)* hiena *f*.

hygiene *n* higiene *f*.

hygienic *adj* higiénico *(BR: -giê-)*.

hygienist *n* higienista *m,f*.

hymen *n (ANAT)* hímen *m*.

hymn *n* cântico *m*; hino *m*; ~ **book** *n* livro *m* de cânticos; hinário *m*; **hymnal** *adj* hínico,-a.

hype *n* publicidade *f* exagerada; **2** *(coll) (drug)* injeção; ♦ *vt* promover; **2** *(news, case)* empolar; **3** *(prices)* fazer subir; ~ **up** estimular; **~ed up** *(coll)* sobreexcitado,-a., como uma pilha de nervos.

hyper- *prefix* hiper-.

hyperactive *adj* hiperativo,-a.

hyperbole *n* hypérbole *f*.

hyphen *n* hífen *m*.

hyphenate *vt* hifenizar.

hypnosis *n* hipnose *f*; **under** ~ sob hipnose.

hypnotic *adj* hipnótico.

hypnotism *n* hipnotismo.

hypnotist *n* hipnotizador,-ora.

hypnotize, hypnotise *vt* hipnotizar.

hypo *n (coll) (CHEM)* hipopossulfito de soda *m*.

hypoallergenic *adj* hipoalergénico,-a *(BR: -ê-)*.

hypochondria *n (MED)* hipocondria *f*.

hypochondriac *n adj* hipocondríaco,-a.

hypocrisy *n* hipocrisia.

hypocrite *n* hipócrita *m,f*.

hypocritical *adj* hipócrita.

hypodermic syringe *n* seringa *f* hipodérmica *(BR: -ê-)*.

hypothermia *n* hipodermia *f*.

hypothesis *(pl: -ses) n* hipótese *f*.

hypothesize, hypothesise *vi* fazer hipóteses.

hypothetic(al) *adj* hipotético.

hysterectomy *n (MED)* histerectomia *f*.

hysteria *n* histeria.

hysterical *adj* histérico.

hysterically *adv* histericamente.

hysterics *npl* histeria *f*, histerismo *m*.

i

I, i *n (letter)* I, i *m*.

I *pron* eu; **both my husband and I** eu e o meu marido; **tanto eu como o meu marido.**

Iberia *npr* Espanha e Portugal.

Iberian *adj* ibérico,-a; **the ~ Peninsula** *npr* a Península *f* Ibérica.

ibex *n* cabra *f* alpina, cabrito *m* montês.

ibis *(pl: -es) n (ZOOL)* íbis *m*.

ICA *(abbr for* **Institute of Contemporary Art***)* Instituto de Arte Contemporânea.

ice *n* gelo *m*; **2** *(UK)* gelado *m*, sorvete *m*; **on thin ~** inseguro,-a; *(fig)* em situação *f* delicada; ♦ **to break the ~** quebrar o gelo; *(fig)* entabular conversa; **to put sth on ~** pôr algo a refrescar; **2** *(fig)* pôr algo de lado à espera de melhor oportunidade; ♦ **~ age** *n* era *f* glacial; **~ axe** *n* machado *m*/ picareta *f*; **~ box** *n (freezer)* congelador *m; (BR)* geladeira *f*; **~bound** *adj (barco)* bloqueado,-a pelo gelo; **~ breaker** *n (NAUT)* navio *m* quebra-gelo; **~ cap** *n (on mountain)* calota *f* glacial; **~-cold** *adj* gelado; **~ cream** *n* gelado, sorvete *m*; **~ cube** *n* cubo *m*, pedra *f* de gelo; **~floe** *n* gelo *m* flutuante, banco *m* de gelo; **~ hockey** *n* hóquei *m* no gelo; **~ pick** *n (tool to break ice for drinks)* picador *m*; **~ cream/lolly** *n* sorvete *m*; gelado; *(BR)* picolé; **~ rink** *n* pista *f* de gelo; **~ skating** *n* patinagem *f (BR:* patinação *f)* no gelo; **~ water** *n* água *f* gelada; ♦ *vt (cake)* cobrir com glacé; **2** *(water)* gelar; **to ~ over/up** *vi* congelar-se.

iceberg *n* icebergue *m; ~* **lettuce** *n* alface *f* americana; **2** *(fig)* pessoa fria.

iced *pp adj (water)* gelado,-a; **2** *(CULIN)* coberto,-a de/com açúcar *m* cistalizado,-a/glacé *(BR:* ê).

Iceland *npr* Islândia *f*; **in ~** na Islândia.

Icelander *npr* islandês,-esa.

Icelandic *adj* islandês,-esa; *(LING)* islandês.

icicle *n* pingente *m* de gelo.

icily *adv* friamente; geladamente.

icing *n (CULIN) (sugar)* glacé *m*, cobertura *f* de açúcar; **2** congelação; crosta/formação *f* de gelo; **~ sugar** *n* açúcar *m* glacé/cristalizado; IDIOM **the ~ on the cake** a cereja em cima do bolo.

icky *(-ier, -iest) adj (fam)* pegajoso,-a; **2** *(unpleasantly sentimental)* sentimalóide, piegas *m,f*.

icon *n* ícone *m*.

iconoclast *n* iconoclasta *m,f*.

iconography *(pl: -phies) n* iconografia *f*; **2** *(fig)* imagem *f*.

ICU *(abbr for* **Intensive Care Unit***)* UCI.

icy *adj* gelado,-a; *(street)* coberto,-a de gelo; *(wind)* glacial; **2** *(fig) (glance)* glacial; indiferente; **~ hands** mãos *fpl* geladas.

I'd *(abbr for* **I would, I had***)*.

ID *(abbr for* **identification***) ~* **card** *n* bilhete *m* de identidade, *(BR)* carteira *f* de identidade.

idea *n* ideia.

ideal *n* ideal *m*; ♦ *adj* ideal.

idealist *n* idealista *m,f*.

identical *adj* idêntico,-a.

identifiable *adj* identificável.

identification *n* identificação *f*; **means of ~** documentos *mpl* pessoais.

identify *vt* identificar.

identikit picture *n* retrato-robot, *(BR)* retrato-falado.

identity *n* identidade *f*; **~ parade** *n* identificação *f* dos supeitos.

ideological *adj* ideológico.

ideology *n* ideologia *f*.

idiocy *n* idiotice *f*; estupidez *f*.

idiom *n* expressão *f* idiomática; idioma *m*, linguagem *f*.

idiosyncrasy *n* idiossincrasia *f*; *(coll)* mania *f*.

idiosyncratic *adj* idiossincrático,-a.

idiot *n* idiota *m,f*; tolo, imbecil.

idiotic *adj* idiota *m,f* parvo,-a.

idle *adj* indolente, vadio; **2** ocioso,-a preguiçoso,-a; **3** inútil, vão *m*, vã *f*; **~ talk** palavreado; ♦ *vi* funcionar com a transmissão desligada, em ponto morto, em marcha lenta; **to ~ away the time** perder/desperdiçar tempo.

idleness *n* ociosidade *f*; preguiça; inutilidade *f*.

idler *m* preguiçoso,-a, ocioso,-a.

idly *adv (lazily)* preguiçosamente; **2** casualmente; **to stand ~ by** *(person)* ficar de braços cruzados, não fazer nada.

idol *n* ídolo *m*.

idolize *vt* adorar *(family)*; idolatrar *(icon)*.

idyll *n* idílio *m*.

idyllic *adj* idílico,-a.

i.e. *(abbr for* **id est***)* isto é, ou seja.

if *conj (gen)* se; *(supposition, in the event that)* **~ you had invited me** se me tivesses convidado; **~ I were you** se eu fosse a ti/a você; **~ he likes** se ele quiser; **2** *(though)* ainda que; se bem que; quando mesmo; **she is a good person ~ a bit crazy** ela é uma boa pessoa se bem que um pouco maluca; **3** *(whether)* **I don't know ~ he is coming** não sei se ele vem; **4** *(that)* que; **do you mind ~ I don't sit down?** importa-se que eu não me sente?; **5** *(used with 'what')* **what ~ he does not pay the bill?** e se ele não pagar a conta?; **6** *(surprise)* **what ~ it isn't our Mr. Lopes!** olha se não é o nosso senhor Lopes!; **7 ~ not** se não; caso contrário; **~ only** se ao menos; quanto mais não seja; **~ only I saw him** se ao menos eu o visse; ♦ **~ only!** *(I wish)* quem me dera!; **as ~ you didn't know!** como se tu não soubesses!

iffy (-ier, -iest) *adj (fam)* inseguro,-a, duvidoso,-a; **2** *(outcome)* incerto,-a.

igloo *n* iglu *m*.

ignite *vt/vi* acender; **2** incendiar(-se); **3** inflamar(-se).

ignition *n (AUT)* ignição *f;* **to switch on/off the ~** ligar/desligar o motor; **~ key** *n (AUT)* chave *f* de ignição.

ignoble *adj* ignóbil.

ignominious *adj* ignominioso,-a; vergonhoso,-a.

ignominy *n* ignomínia, infâmia *f.*

ignoramus *(pl: -es) n (fam)* ignorante *m,f* estúpido,-a.

ignorance *n* ignorância; **~ of law is no excuse** a ignorância da lei não serve de atenuante; **~ is a bliss** a ignorância impera/é uma benção.

ignorant *adj* ignorante; **to be ~ of** desconhecer; ignorar.

ignore *vt* não fazer caso de; não levar em consideração; ignorar.

iguana *n (ZOOL)* iguana *f.*

ikebana *n (Japanese art of arranging flowers)* ikebana *f.*

I.L.E.A. *npr (abbr for* **Inner London Education Authority**) *(former)* antigo órgão responsável pela educação em Londres.

ilex *n (holm oak)* azinheira *f.*

ilk *n:* espécie *f;* **of that ~** do mesmo tipo.

I'll = **I shall, I will.**

ill *n* mal *m;* **to speak ~ of** falar mal de; **2** *(fig) (misfortune)* desgraça; ♦ *adj (sick)* doente, indisposto,-a; **to be taken ~ (with sth** com algo); **to fall ~** adoecer; **2** mau *m,* má *f,* ruim; **~ management** má/pobre administração/gerência; ♦ *adv(badly)* mal; **2** *(hardly)* **we can ~ afford to go to cinema** mal podemos pagar os bilhetes do cinema.

ill-advised *adj (misled)* mal aconselhado,-a.

ill-at-ease *adj* constrangido,-a pouco à vontade.

illbred, ill-mannered *adj* malcriado,-a, grosseiro,-a.

ill-disposed *adj* de/com má vontade.

illegal *adj* ilegal, ilegítimo,-a.

illegible *adj* ilegível.

illegitimate *adj* ilegítimo,-a.

ill-equipped *adj* mal preparado,-a.

illfated *adj* malfadado,-a, infeliz.

ill feeling *n* ressentimento *m;* animosidade *f.*

ill-gotten mal adquirido,-a; **~ gains** *npl* ganhos *mpl* ilícitos.

illhealth *n* falta *f* de saúde/má saúde.

illicit *adj* ilícito,-a.

ill-informed *adj* mal informado,-a.

illiterate *adj* analfabeto,-a.

illiteracy *n* analfabetismo *m.*

illness *n* doença *f.*

illogical *adj* ilógico,-a.

ill-suited *adj* **to be ~ for** ser inadequado,-a para; **2 an ~ couple** um casal mal ajustado, incompatível.

ill-tempered *adj (person)* mal-humorado,-a; de/com mau feitio.

ill-timed *adj* inoportuno,-a, em má hora.

ill-treat *vt* maltratar.

ill-treatment *n* maus tratos *mpl.*

illude *vt* iludir, deceive.

illuminate *vt* iluminar, clarear; **2** *(subject)* esclarecer.

illumination *n* iluminação *f;* **2** *(manuscript)* iluminura.

illuminations *npl* luminárias *fpl.*

illusion *n* ilusão *f;* engano; **to be under the ~ that ...** estar com a ilusão de que...

illusionist *adj* ilusionista.

illusory *adj* ilusório,-a.

illustrate *vt* ilustrar; esclarecer; exemplificar.

illustration *n* exemplo *m;* esclarecimento *m;* **2** *(in book)* gravura *f,* ilustração *f.*

illustrative *adj:* **~ of** elucidativo,-a de.

illustrator *n* ilustrador,-ora; desenhador,-ora.

illustrious *adj* ilustre.

ill will *n* animosidade *f,* má vontade *f.*

I'm = **I am.**

image *n* imagem *f;* **2** *(idea)* ideia **(of** de); **to be the spitting ~ of sb** *(be alike)* ser a cara chapada de alguém.

imagery *n* imagens *fpl;* imagética *f.*

imaginable *adj* imaginável.

imaginary *adj* imaginário,-a.

imagination *n* imaginação *f;* inventividade *f;* **2** *(illusion)* fantasia *f.*

imaginative *adj* imaginativo,-a.

imagine *vt* imaginar; fantasiar.

imaging *n* imagética *f.*

imagining *n* fantasia *f.*

iman *n (islamismo)* imã *m.*

imbalance *n* desequilíbrio *m;* desigualdade *f.*

imbecile *n* imbecil *m,f.*

imbecility *n* imbecilidade *f.*

imbibe *vt (ideas, knowledge)* absorver, assimilar.

imbroglio *n* embróglio.

imbue *vt:* **to ~ sth with** imbuir, impregnar algo de.

IMF *(abbr for* **International Monetary Fund**) *n* Fundo Monetário Internacional.

imitate *vt* imitar.

imitation *n* imitação *f;* cópia; *(of jewel)* falso,-a; **2** *(mimicry)* mímica.

immaculate *adj (dress, work)* impecável; perfeito,-a; *(REL)* imaculado,-a; **the I~ Conception** a Imaculada Conceição.

immaterial *adj (intangible)* imaterial; **2** irrelevante, sem importância; **it is ~ if you believe me or not** éme indiferente se me acreditas ou não.

immature *n (child-like)* criança *m,f;* **don't be ~** não sejas criança; ♦ *adj (not grown)* imaturo,-a; *(fruit)* verde; *(person) (childish)* pueril.

immediate *adj* imediato,-a; premente; **in the ~ future** no futuro próximo.

immediately *adv (at once)* imediatamente; já; **2** dire(c)tamente; **~ next to** bem junto a; mesmo ao lado.

immense *adj* imenso,-a, enorme.

immensely *adv* muito; imensamente; extremamente.

immensity *n* imensidade *f,* vastidão *f.*

immerse *vt* submergir; *(sink)* imergir, mergulhar; **to be ~d in** *(fig)* estar absorto em.

immersion *n* imersão *f;* **2** *(fig)* absorção *f;* **~ heater** *n* esquentador *m,* aquecedor *m* de imersão.

immigrant *n* imigrante *m,f.*

immigrate *vi* imigrar.

immigration *n* imigração *f.*

imminent *adj (about to)* iminente.

immobile *adj* imóvel.

immobilize *vt* imobilizar *(car, patient).*

immodest *adj* imodesto,-a; presunçoso,-a; **2** *(improper)* indecente, *(fam)* sem vergonha.

immoral *adj* imoral.
immorality *n* imoralidade *f.*
immortal *adj* imortal.
immortalize *vt* imortalizar.
immune *adj*: ~ **to/be** ~ **to** *(indifferent)* imune a *(flattery, criticism)*; **2** imunizado contra *(virus)*; **3** isento; **to be** ~ **from** *(exempt)* estar isento de *(tax)*; estar protegido,-a de algo; **4** *(reaction)* imunitário,-a; ~ **deficiency** *n* imunodeficiência *f.*
immunity *n (MED)* imunidade *f*; **2** *(COMM)* isenção *f*; **tax** ~ isenção *f* fiscal.
immunization *n* imunização *f.*
immunize *vt* imunizar.
immutable *adj* imutável.
imovable *adj* fixo,-a; **2** *(unchanged)* inabalável; *(person)* imutável; **3** ~**s** *npl (JUR)* imóveis *mpl.*
imp *n (child)* diabinho *m*, criança *f* endiabrada.
impact *n* impacto *m* (**on**, **upon** em).
impair *vt* prejudicar.
impaired *pp adj (vision, hearing)* enfraquecido,-a; *(mobility)* reduzido,-a; **his speech is** ~ tem problemas de fala; **visually-**~ *adj* invisual; **visually-**~ **people** *n* os invisuais *mpl.*
impairment *n* disfunção *f*; deficiência, insuficiência *f.*
impale *vt* perfurar; **to** ~ **sth/sb on sth** empalar algo/ alguém em algo.
impart *vt* dar, comunicar.
impartial *adj* imparcial.
impartiality *n* imparcialidade *f.*
impassable *adj* intransponível; intransitável.
impasse *n* beco sem saída; **2** *(fig)* situação *f* difícil.
impassive *adj* impassível; indiferente; **2** *(unruffled)* impertubável.
impatience *n* impaciência *f.*
impatient *adj* impaciente *m,f*, ansioso,-a (**for**, por); **to get/grow** ~ impacientar-se.
impeach *vt (JUR)* acusar (**for**, **with** de); **to** ~ **sb with a crime** acusar alguém de um crime.
impeachment *n* acusação *f*; *(Govt officials)* acusação por erros graves.
impeccable *adj (dress)* impecável; *(work)* perfeito; *(behaviour)* irrepreensível.
impecunious *adj* sem dinheiro.
impede *vt* impedir, estorvar.
impediment *n (hindrance)* obstáculo *m*; *(to marriage)* impedimento *m.*
impel (**-ll-**) *vt* impelir, empurrar; *(encourage, urge)* incitar; **to feel** ~**led to do sth** sentir-se obrigado,-a a fazer algo.
impending *adj* iminente *m,f*; ~ **disaster** um iminente desastre; **2** próximo,-a.
impenetrable *adj* impenetrável; incompreensível.
imperative *n (LING)* imperativo; ♦ *adj* imperioso,-a, obrigatório,-a; indispensável; *(urgent)* premente.
imperceptible *adj* imperceptível.
imperfect *adj (gen)* imperfeito,-a; *(faulty goods)* defeituoso,-a; *(incomplete)* incompleto,-a; **2** *(gram)* **the** ~ **tense** o imperfeito.
imperfection *n (goods, person)* defeito *m*; **2** *(state)* imperfeição *f.*
imperial *adj* imperial.

imperialism *n* imperialismo *m.*
imperialist *n adj* imperialista.
imperil *vt* pôr em perigo, arriscar.
imperious *adj* urgente, premente.
impersonal *adj* impessoal.
impersonate *vt (mimic, imitar)* imitar; fazer-se passar por; **2** personificar; **3** *(THEAT)* representar o papel de.
impertinent *adj* impertinente, insolente *m,f.*
impervious *adj* impenetrável; **2** *(fig)* ~ **to** insensível a, imune a algo.
impetuous *adj* impetuoso,-a, precipitado,-a.
impetuousity *n* impetuosidade *f.*
impetus *n* ímpeto *m*; *(fig)* impulso *m.*
impinge *vt*: **to** ~ **on/upon** *(encroach)* afe(c)tar; invadir; **to** ~ **on somebody's time** tirar o tempo a alguém; **2** violar algo.
impious *adj* irreverente; *(REL)* ímpio,-a.
impish *adj* travesso,-a.
implacable *adj* implacável.
implant *n* implante *m*; ♦ *vt (MED)* implantar (**in** em); **2** incutir.
implausibility *n* implausibilidade *f.*
implausible *adj* improvável.
implement *n (tool)* utensílio *m*, ferramenta *f*; *(in farms)* alfaia *f*; ♦ *vt* implementar, realizar, executar.
implicate *vt* comprometer; implicar, envolver.
implication *n (involvement)* implicação *f*; consequência.
implicit *adj* implícito,-a; inerente; **2** *(completo)* absoluto,-a.
implied *adj* implícito,-a.
implore *vt* implorar, suplicar.
imply *vt* implicar; **2** insinuar, dar a entender que; **it is implied** *(that)* subentende-se (que).
impolite *adj* indelicado,-a, descortês.
import *n (COMM)* importação *f*; mercadoria importada; **2** significado *m*, sentido *m*; **3** importância *f*; ♦ *vt* importar *(feeds).*
importance *n* importância *f*; **of the utmost** ~ da maior importância.
important *adj* importante; **it's not** ~ não tem importância; não faz mal.
importantly *adv* de forma relevante; essencialmente; **2** *(pompously)* com um ar *m* importante.
importer *n* importador,-ora.
importune *vt* importunar (**sb** alguém).
impose *vt* impor *(condition)*; ♦ *vi*: **to** ~ **on sb** *(take for granted)* abusar de *(kindness)*; **2** infligir *(sanction)*; **3** *(intrude)* importunar (**on sb** alguém).
imposing *adj* imponente *m,f.*
imposition *n* imposição *f.*
impossible *adj* impossível *m,f*, insuportável.
impostor *n* impostor,-ora.
impotence *n* impotência *f.*
impotent *adj* impotente.
impound *vt (JUR)* apreender bens; **2** confiscar *(document, passport, etc)*; **3** confinar, aprender num depósito de carros *(illegally parked car)*; **4** apropriar; **5** *(of waters)* represar.
impoverished *adj* empobrecido,-a.
impoverishment *n* empobrecimento *m.*

impracticable *adj* impraticável, inexequível.

impractical *adj* pouco prático *m,f*; inviável *m,f*.

imprecise *adj* impreciso,-a, vago,-a.

impregnable *adj* invulnerável; inexpugnável.

impregnate *vt (pervade)* impregnar (**with sth** de algo); **2** *(absorb)* embeber; **3** *(fertlize)* fecundar.

impresario *n* empresário,-a artístico, teatral.

impress *vt* imprimir; impressionar; ♦ *vi* causar boa impressão; **to ~ sth on sb** convencer alguém de alguma coisa; meter alguma coisa na cabeça de alguém; **it is ~ed on me** fiquei com isso gravado (na memória).

impression *n (gen)* impressão *f*; **to be under the ~ that** estar com a impressão de que; **to make a good ~** causar boa impressão; **2** *(from teeth)* marca *f*, **3** *(print)* edição *f*.

impressionable *adj* impressionável; sensível.

impressionist *n* impressionista *m,f*.

impressive *adj* impressionante; *(building)*, imponente.

imprint *n* impressão *f*; marca *f*.

imprison *vt* encarcerar.

imprisonment *n* encarceramento *m*.

improbable *adj* improvável *m,f*, duvidoso,-a.

impromptu *adj* improvisado; ♦ *adv* de improviso.

improper *adj* impróprio,-a; *(unsuitably)* indecoroso, indecente.

impropriety *n* falta *f* de decoro; indecência *f*; **2** *(unseemingly)* inconveniência *f*; impropriedade *f*; **3** irregularidade *f*.

improve *vt* melhorar; ♦ *vi* aperfeiçoar-se; progredir.

improvement *n* melhoramento *m*; melhoria *f*, progresso *m*.

improvise *vt/vi* improvisar.

imprudent *adj* imprudente.

impudent *adj* insolente *m,f* impudente.

impulse *n* impulso *m*, ímpeto *m*; **to act on ~** agir sem pensar.

impulsive *adj* impulsivo,-a.

impunity *n* impunidade; **with ~** impunemente.

impure *adj* adulterado,-a, impuro,-a.

impurity *n* impureza *f*; **2** impuro,-a.

imputation *n* imputação *f* (**of**, de).

impute *vt* atribuir (**to**, a).

in *prep* em; *(place)* **in the garden** no jardim; **~ London** em Londres; **2** *(wearing)* de: **~ a blue suit** de fato azul; *(BR)* de terno azul; **3** *(season, time, future)* em, de, a; **~ the summer** no verão; **~ the afternoon** à tarde; **it's five ~ the morning** são cinco horas da manhã (5 a.m.); **4** *(denoting future)* de, dentro de; **~ a little while** daqui a pouco; **in a week's time** dentro de uma semana; **5** *(state of being)* com; **~ fear/hunger/pain** com; com medo/fome/dores; **6** *(numbers, light, shade, weather)* a; **~ hundreds** às centenas; **~ millions** aos milhões; **~ in the dark** às escuras; **~ the shade** à sombra; **~ the rain** à chuva; **~ the sun** ao sol; **7** *(means, way)* por; **I want your reply ~ writing** quero a tua resposta por escrito; **to be ~ foal** *(pregnant mare)* estar prenhe; **to be ~ love** estar apaixonado,-a; ♦ *adv* dentro, para dentro; **all ~** *(inclusive)* tudo incluído; **to bend ~** dobrar para dentro; **day ~,**

day out dia após dia; **to be ~** estar em casa/local *m* de trabalho; *(fashion)* estar na moda/em voga; **the train is ~** o comboio/trem acaba de chegar; **the Tories are ~** os Conservadores estão no poder; **to invite sb ~** convidar alguém a entrar; **to be ~ for theft** estar na prisão por roubo; **registration must be ~ by the end of the month** o registo *(BR: registro)* deve dar entrada até ao fim deste mês; IDIOM **the ins and outs** *(of a story)* os cantos e recantos (**of**, de) os pormenores; **to be in on** *(have knowledge)* estar ao par de; saber de; **to be ~ for** estar prestes a; **you are ~ for a surprise!** prepara-te para uma surpresa! **to be ~ with sb** dar-se bem com alguém; **we are ~ the same boat** *(not good news)* estamos na mesma situação.

inability *n* incapacidade *f*.

inaccessible *adj* inacessível.

inaccuracy *n* inexa(c)tidão *f*. imprecisão *f*.

inaccurate *adj* inexa(c)to.

inactivity *n* ina(c)tividade *f*.

inadequate *adj* insuficiente; inadequado,-a; impróprio,-a.

inadvertent *adj* inadvertido,-a negligente.

inadvertently *adv* inadvertidamente, sem querer; **I trod on his foot ~** pisei o pé dele sem querer.

inadvisable *adj* não aconselhável, inoportuno,-a.

inane *adj* tolo,-a; idiota *m,f*, imbecil *m,f*.

inanimate *adj* inanimado,-a.

inapplicable *adj* inaplicável.

inapproachable *adj* inacessível.

inappropriate *adj* inadequado,-a; inconveniente; impróprio,-a.

inapt *adj* inapto,-a, inadequado,-a.

inaptitude *n* incapacidade *f*, inaptidão *f*.

inarticulate *adj* incapaz de expressar-se (bem); inarticulado,-a.

inasmuch: **~ as** *adv (insofar as)* na medida em que; ♦ *conj* visto que; desde que, já que.

inattentive *adj* desatento,-a.

inaudible *adj* inaudível.

inaugural *adj* inaugural; de posse.

inaugurate *vt* inaugurar; **2** *(induct)* empossar.

inauguration *n* inauguração *f*.

inauspicious *adj* de mau agouro; pouco propício.

in-between *adj* intermediário,-a entre dois extremos.

inboard *adj (student, etc)* interno,-a; **2** *(NAUT)* de bordo; interior; ♦ *prep/adv* a bordo de.

inborn *adj* inato,-a inerente; congénito,-a (BR: -ê-).

inbound *adj (NAUT)* que se aproxima do porto; de regresso (a casa); *(AER)* **the ~ flight fom Manchester** o voo que chega de Manchester.

inbred *adj (characteristic)* inato,-a; natural; **2** (de animal) de procriação *f*, cruzamento *m* consanguíneo,-a; *(family, tribe)* endogâmico,-a.

inbreeding *n (humans)* endogamia *f*; **2** *(animals)* cruzamento *m* consanguíneo.

inbuilt *adj (furniture)* embutido,-a; **2** *(quality, fault)* inerente.

Inc. *(abbr for **incorporated**)* S.A.

inca *n, adj, inv* inca.

incalculable *adj* incalculável.

incantation *n* feitiço *m*, encantamento *m*.

incapable *adj* incapaz.

incapacitate *vt*: **to ~ sb** incapacitar alguém.

incapacity *n* incapacidade *f*.

incarcerate *vt* encarcerar.

incarnate *adj* encarnado,-a, personificado,-a; ♦ *vt* encarnar.

incarnation *n* encarnação *f*.

incendiary *adj* incendiário,-a.

incense *n* incense *m*; ♦ *vt* exasperar, enraivecer.

incentive *n* incentivo *m*, estímulo *m*.

incessant *adj* incessante, contínuo,-a.

incessantly *adv* constantemente.

incest *n* incesto *m*.

inch *n* polegada (= 2.54 cm); **every ~** completamente; **not an ~** nada, nem um passo; **within an ~ of** muito perto,-a um passo de; ♦ *vt/vi*: **to ~ forward** avançar palmo a palmo.

Embora a Grã-Bretanha tenha ado(p)tado o sistema métrico, ainda há pessoas que usam as medidas de jarda e polegada.

incidence *n* incidência *f*.

incident *n* incidente *m*, ocorrência *f*; episódio *m*; ♦ *adj* respeitante (**to** a).

incidental *n* imprevisto *m*; **~s** *(expenses)* despesas *fpl* adicionais; ♦ *adj (minor detail)* acessório,-a, não essencial; casual.

incidental music *n (CIN, TV)* música *f* de fundo.

incidently *adv* a propósito; *(by chance)* por acaso.

incinerator *n* incinerador *m*.

incipient *adj* incipiente.

incise *vt* cortar, fazer uma incisão em; **2** *(engrave)* talhar, gravar.

incision *n* incisão *f*, golpe *m*, corte *m*.

incisive *adj (mind)* penetrante, perspicaz; **2** *(remark)* incisivo,-a, sarcástico,-a; **3** *(tooth)* dente; incisivo.

incisor *n (ANAT)* dente incisivo.

incite *vt* incitar; instigar, provocar.

incitement *n* incitamento *m* (**to** a/para); **2** estímulo *m*.

incivility *n* indelicadeza *f*, incivilidade *f*.

inclement *adj (judge, weather)* inclemente; *(climate)* rigoroso,-a.

inclination *n* tendência *f*; inclinação *f*, propência *f* (**to/towards** para); **2** *(liking)* gosto *m* (**for** por).

incline *n (slope)* declive *m*, ladeira *f*; ♦ *vt (bend)* inclinar; curvar; ♦ *vi* inclinar-se; **to be ~d to** tender a, ser propenso a; estar disposto a.

include *vt* incluir, conter; anexar.

including *prep* inclusive, inclusivo,-a.

inclusion *n* inclusão *f*.

inclusive *adj* inclusivo, incluso; ♦ *adv* inclusivo.

incognito *adv* incógnito,-a.

incoherence *n* incoerência *f*.

incoherent *adj* incoerente.

income *n* rendimentos *mpl*, *(BR)* renda *f*; receitas *fpl*; **2** ordenado, salário *m*; **~ policy** *(UK)* *n* política *f* de rendimentos; **~ support** *(UK)* *n* auxílio adicional dado a pessoas desempregadas ou com rendimento baixo; **~ tax** *n* imposto sobre o rendimento, *(BR)* imposto de renda; **~ tax inspector** *n* fiscal *m,f* (de

impostos); *(BR)* fiscal do imposto de renda; *(coll)* o fisco; **~ tax return** *n* declaração *f* de rendimentos, *(BR)* declaração do imposto de renda; **unearned ~** rendimento *m* de propriedade (= **earned**).

incoming *adj* de chegada; próximo,-a; **~ flight** voo *m* de chegada; **2** *(phone call)* recebido,-a do exterior; ♦ **~s and outgoings** *npl (COMM)* receitas e despesas *fpl*.

incommunicado *adj* incomunicável *m,f*.

incommensurate *adj* desproporcionado em relação a algo; incomensurável; insuficiente.

incomparable *adj* incomparável.

incompatible *adj* incompatível.

incompetence *n* incompetência *f*.

incompetent *adj* incompetente.

incomplete *adj* incompleto,-a; por terminar.

incomprehensible *adj* incompreensível.

inconceivable *adj* inconcebível.

inconclusive *adj* inconclusivo,-a; pouco convincente.

incongruous *adj* ridículo, absurdo,-a; incongruente, ilógico,-a.

inconsequential *adj* insignificante, sem consequência.

inconsiderate *adj (action, remark)* impensado,-a, irrefletido,-a; **how ~ of him!** que falta de consideração!

inconsistent *adj* inconsistente. *(erratic)* irregular; **~ with sth** contraditório a algo; (que) não está de acordo com.

inconspicuous *adj (person)* que passa despercebido,-a, modesto,-a, discreto,-a; **to make o.s. ~** não chamar a atenção.

inconstancy *n* inconstância.

inconstant *adj (lover)* inconstante; **2** *(conditions)* instável.

incontinent *adj* incontinente.

inconvenience *n* inconvenientes *mpl*, inconveniência *f*; incómodo *m*, transtorno *m*; ♦ *vt* incomodar.

inconvenient *adj* inconveniente, incómodo,-a *(BR: -cô-)*; inoportuno,-a.

incorporate *vt* incorporar; compreender; incluir; **~d company** *(US: abbr for* **Inc.***)* Sociedade *f* Anónima *(BR: -nô-)*.

incorrect *adj* incorre(c)to,-a.

incorrupt *adj* incorrupto,-a.

incorruptible *adj* incorruptível; insubornável.

increase *n* aumento; ♦ *vi* aumentar; crescer; subir.

increasing *adj* crescente, em aumento.

increasingly *adv* cada vez mais.

incredible *adj* incrível.

incredulous *adj* incrédulo,-a.

increment *n* aumento *m*, incremento *m*.

incriminate *vt* incriminar.

in-crowd *n* grupo *m* da moda; **to be in the ~** andar com o jet set, o grupo da moda.

incubation *n* incubação *f*.

incubator *n (for baby)* incubadora *f*; **2** *(birds, eggs)* incubador *m*, chocadeira *f*.

inculcate *vt*: **to ~ sth in (to) sb** inculcar algo em alguém.

incumbent *n* beneficiado,-a; titular; pessoa responsável por; ♦ *adj* incumbente *m,f*; **it is ~ on you**

to do sth compete-lhe/cabe-lhe fazer algo; *(JUR)* incumbe ao senhor fazer algo.

incur (-rr-) *vt (gen)* incorrer em *(expenses, risk)*; contrair *(debt)*; suscitar *(displeasure)*.

incurable *adj* incurável; **2** *(optimism)* incorrigível; **3** *(hopeless)* irremediável.

incursion *n* incursão *f*; *(fig)* invasão *f*.

indebted *adj*: **to be ~ to sb** estar em dívida para com alguém.

indecent *adj* indecente *m,f*; **2** *(JUR) (offense)* **~ assault** *n* atentado contra o pudor; **~ exposure** *n* exibição *f* obscena.

indecipherable *adj* indecifrável.

indecision *n* indecisão *f*.

indecisive *adj* indeciso,-a; *(election)* inconcludente, inconclusivo,-a.

indecorous *adj (speech, behaviour)* impróprio,-a.

indeed *adv* na verdade, sem dúvida, de fa(c)to; **yes ~!** claro que sim!; *(for emphasis)* **thank you ~** muitíssimo obrigado; **indeed?** *(surprise, doubt)* realmente?; IDIOM **a friend in need is a friend ~** os amigos conhecem-se nas ocasiões.

indefatigable *adj* incansável.

indefensible *adj (morally)* indesculpável; **2** indefensável.

indefinable *adj* indefinível.

indefinite *adj* indefinido,-a; impreciso,-a; **the ~ article** *(gram)* o artigo *m* indefinido.

indefinitely *adv* indefinidamente.

indelible *adj* indelével.

indelicacy *n (discourtesy)* indelicadeza; *(coarseness)* grosseria *f*.

indemnify *vt* inde(m)nizar, compensar.

indent *n* recorte *m* dentado; **2** mossa, marca *f*; **3** encomenda *f*; ♦ **to ~** *vt (text)* indentar; **2** talhar.

indentation *n (depression)* depressão *f*; **2** *(coastline)* reentrância *f*; *(in text)* parágrafo novo, recuo *m*.

indented *pp, adj (text word)* recuado,-a; *(edge)* recortado,-a.

indenture *n* escritura *f* de contra(c)to; acordo entre partidos; **2** contra(c)to de aprendizagem.

independence *n* independência *f*.

Independence Day *(US)* nome oficial do dia 4 de Julho, em que se comemora nos E.U.A. a sua independência (1776).

independent *adj* independente; **to become ~** tornar-se independente.

in-depth *adj (study, knowledge)* profundo, em profundidade; **2** *(text)* exaustivo,-a; **3** *(description)* pormenorizado,-a.

indescribable *adj* indescritível.

indestructible *adj* indestrutível.

index *(pl: -es, indices)* *n (of book)* índice *m* remissivo; **2** *(in library)* catálogo; **3** *(ECON) (value, system)* índice; **4** *(MATH)* expoente *m*; **~card** *n* ficha de arquivo/de indexação; **~finger** *n* dedo indicador; **~linked** *adj* vinculado ao índice (do custo de vida); indexado *(bonds, etc)*; ♦ **to ~ sth to sth** *(FIN, ECON)* indexar algo a algo; **2** fazer um índice.

indexation *n* indexação *f*.

India *npr* Índia; **in ~** na Índia; **~ ink** *(US)* tinta *f* nanquim, da China.

Indian *npr adj* indiano,-a; **2** *(from the Americas)* índio,-a; ♦ **~ file** *n (single file)* fila *f* indiana; **~ corn** *n* milho; **~ ink** *(UK)* tinta *f* nanquim, tinta da China; **the ~ Ocean** *n* o Oceano *m* Índico; **~ summer** *n* verão de São Martinho.

india rubber *n (eraser)* borracha *f*.

indicate *vt* indicar.

indication *n* indício, sinal *m*.

indicative *adj*: **~ of sth** indicativo,-a de algo.

indicator *n* indicador *m*; *(on car)* pisca-pisca *m*.

indices *(pl of index)*.

indict *vt (US) (to charge with a crime)* indiciar; **to ~ sb for sth** indiciar alguém por algo; **2** inculpar.

indictable *adj* sujeito a sanção *f* penal.

indictment *n (JUR)* acusação *f* por escrito, denúncia *f*; **to bring in an ~ against** intentar uma a(c)ção criminal contra;

indie *adj (fam)* independente.

indifference *n* indiferença *f*.

indifferent *adj* indiferente, insensível (**to** a); **2** regular, medíocre.

indigenous *adj* indígena *m,f*; nativo,-a; natural *m,f* do país.

indigestion *n* indigestão *f*.

indignant *adj* indignado,-a (**at** perante; **about, over** por).

indignation *n* indignação *f*.

indignity *n (humiliation)* indignidade *f*; **2** *(injury to one's feelings)* ultraje *m*, afronta *f*.

indigo *n* indigo *m*, anil *m*; ♦ *adj* cor de anil.

indirect *adj* indire(c)to.

indirectly *adv* indire(c)tamente.

indiscreet *adj* indiscreto,-a; imprudente.

indiscretion *n* indiscrição *f*; imprudência *f*.

indiscriminate *adj* indiscriminado.

indiscriminating *adj* sem discernimento.

indispensable *adj* indispensável, imprescindível.

indisposed *adj* indisposto,-a, mal disposto,-a.

indisputable *adj* incontestável, indisputável.

indissoluble *adj* indissolúvel; insolúvel.

indistinct *adj* indistinto,-a; confuso,-a, vago,-a.

indistinguishable *adj* indistinguível; imperceptível.

individual *n* indivíduo, pessoa; ♦ *adj* individual; pessoal; particular.

individualist *n* individualista *m,f*.

individuality *n* individualidade *f*.

individually *adv* individualmente, particularmente.

indoctrinate *vt* doutrinar.

indoctrination *n* doutrinação *f*.

indolent *adj* indolente, preguiçoso,-a.

indomitable *adj* indomável; indómito,-a.

Indonesia *npr* Indonésia; **in ~** na Indonésia.

Indonesian *npr adj* indonésio,-a; *(LING)* indonésio.

indoor *adj* interior; de casa; da porta para dentro; *(covered area)* coberto,-a; **2** *(games)* de salão; ♦ **indoors** *adv* dentro; em casa.

induce *vt* induzir, persuadir; **2** *(bring about)* causar; **3 to ~ labour** *(MED)* induzir o parto.

inducement *n* incentivo *m*, estímulo *m*; aliciante *m*.

inducer *n* instigador,-ora; *(ELECT)* indutor *m*.

induct *vt* empossar; **2** indigitar.

induction *n (MED, MATH, ELECT)* indução *f*; ~ **course** *n* curso *m* de indução; **2** *(US) (MIL)* incorporação; **3** *(inauguration)* instalação *f*; **4** *(introduction to job)* apresentação *f*.

indulge *vt (give in to)* ceder a, satisfazer; *(whim, desire)*; **2** fazer a vontade de *(person, child)*, estragar com mimos *(child)*; ♦ *vi*: **to ~ in** entregar-se a, permitir-se um luxo.

indulgence *n* satisfação *f*; indulgência *f*, tolerância *f*.

indulgent *adj* indulgente.

Indus: the (River) Indus *npr* o (Rio) Indus.

industrial *adj* industrial; *(accident etc)* do/no trabalho; ~ **action** *n* a(c)ção *f* reivindicativa; *(strike)* greve *f*; ~ **disease** doença profissional; ~ **dispute** *n* conflito *m*, disputa *f* laboral; ~ **estate** *n* zona industrial; ~ **waste** resíduos *mpl* industriais.

Industrial Tribunal *n (N. Ireland)* Justiça do Trabalho.

industrialist *n* industrial.

industrialize *vt* industrializar.

industrious *adj* diligente; aplicado,-a.

industry *n* indústria *f*; **oil** ~ indústria *f* petrolífera; **2** diligência *f*.

inebriate *n* ébrio,-a; ♦ *adj* inebriado,-a; entusiasmado,-a; ♦ *vt* embriagar, inebriar.

inebriated *adj* embriagado,-a; inebriado,-a.

inedible *adj* intragável; *(plant)* não comestível.

ineffaceable *adj* indelével.

ineffective *adj* ineficaz, ineficiente.

ineffectively *adv* inutilmente.

ineffectual *adj (person)* incapaz, inútil; **2** *(policy)* ineficaz; **3** *(attempt)* infrutífero,-a.

ineffectually *adv* em vão.

inefficiency *n* ineficácia.

inefficient *adj* ineficaz, ineficiente.

inelegant *adj* deselegante.

ineligible *adj* inelegível; **to be ~ for sth** não estar qualificado para algo.

inept *adj* inepto,-a; **2** *(clumsy) (person)* desajeitado,-a; *(work)* malfeito,-a.

ineptitude *n* inépcia *f*; inaptidão *f* incompetência *f*.

inequality *n* desigualdade *f*.

inert *adj* inerte; imóvel.

inertia *n* inércia *f*; preguiça *f (BR)* lerdeza *f*.

inescapable *adj* inevitável.

inestimable *adj* inestimável, incalculável.

inevitable *adj* inevitável; forçoso,-a; necessário,-a.

inexcusable *adj* imperdoável, indesculpável.

inexhaustible *adj* inesgotável, inexaurível.

inexorable *adj* inexorável.

inexpensive *adj* barato,-a, económico,-a *(BR:*-nô-*)*.

inexperience *n* inexperiência *f*, falta de experiência.

inexperienced *adj* inexperiente.

inexplicable *adj* inexplicável.

inextricable *adj* inextricável.

infallible *adj* infalível.

infamous *adj* infame, abominável.

infamy *n* infâmia *f*.

infancy *n* infância *f*.

infant *n* bebé *m*; *(young child)* criança; ~ **school** *(UK) n* (para crianças entre 4 e 7 anos) escola *f* infantil.

infanticide *n* infaticida *n*.

infantile *adj* infantil; *(pej)* acriançado,-a, pueril.

infantry *n* infantaria *f*; ~ **man** *n* soldado de infantaria.

infatuated *adj* enfatuado,-a; ~ **with** apaixonado, enamorado por, *(BR)* gamado por.

infatuation *n* paixão *f* passageira *(BR)* gamação *f*; fascinação *f*; **to have an ~ for sb** enamorar-se de, enfeitiçar-se por alguém.

infect *vt* infectar; contagiar; *(fig)* corromper, contaminar.

infection *n* infecção *f*; *(fig)* contágio.

infectious *adj (disease)* infeccioso,-a; **2** *(laughter)* contagioso,-a.

infer (-**red**, -**ring**) *vt* deduzir, inferir.

inference *n* dedução *f*, inferência *f*; conclusão *f*; **by** ~ por dedução.

inferior *n, ad* inferior, subordinado,-a.

inferiority *n* inferiorídade *f*; ~ **complex** *n* complexo de inferioridade.

infernal *adj* infernal; *(annoying)* diabólico,-a.

inferno *n (hell)* inferno; **2** *(fig) (fire)* inferno de chamas.

infertile *adj* infértil, estéril.

infertility *n* infertilidade *f*, esterilidade *f*.

infestation *n* praga *f*, infestação *f*.

infested *adj* infestado,-a (**with**, de); **2** assolado (por).

infidelity *n* infidelidade *f*.

infighting *n* conflitos *mpl* internos; **2** *(boxing)* luta de perto, corpo a corpo.

infiltrate *vt* infiltrar-se em; ♦ *vi* infiltrar-se.

infinite *adj* infinito,-a.

infinitely infinitamente.

infinitesimal *adj* infinitesimal.

infinitive *n* infinitivo,-a; *(gram) (mode)* infinitivo *m*.

infinity *n* infinito; **an** ~ *(time, quantity)* uma infinidade *f*; **to gaze into** ~ *(fig)* fitar o vazio.

infirm *n:* **the** ~ os enfermos *mpl*; ♦ *adj* enfermo, fraco.

infirmary *n (in prison, hospital)* enfermaria *f*.

infirmity *n* enfermidade *f*.

inflame *vt/vi (MED)* inflamar, irritar; **2** *(provoke)* atiçar; *(fig) (emotion)* exaltar-se.

inflamed *adj (MED)* inflamado,-a; **2** *(fig) (emotion)* exaltado,-a, excitado,-a.

inflammable *adj* inflamável; explosivo,-a.

inflammation *n* inflamação *f*.

inflammatory *adj (MED)* inflamatório,-a; **2** *(remark)* provocador,-ora, excitante.

inflate *vt (gen)* insuflar, encher de ar, *(BR)* inflar; **2** *(fig)* inchar *(ego)*; *(ECON)* inflacionar *(price)*.

inflated *adj (person)* empolado,-a pomposo,-a; **2** *(tyre, balloon)* insuflado,-a; **3** *(price)* excessivo,-a.

inflation *n (ECON)* inflação *f*.

inflationary *adj* inflacionário.

inflect *vt (LING)* conjugar; declinar; *(voice)* modular *(also: noun, adj)*.

inflection *n (LING) (radical)* flexão; *(of voice, vowel)* inflexão; **2** curva.

inflexibility *n* inflexibilidade *f*.

inflexible *adj* inflexível.

inflict *vt*: **to ~ on sb** infligir em, fazer sofrer alguém; **2** **to ~ o.s. on sb** *(impose)* impor a sua presença a alguém.

in-flight *adj* de bordo; durante o voo; ~ **meals** refeições servidas *fpl* durante o voo.

inflow *n (of people)* afluência *f; (into tank) (of goods)* afluxo *m.*

influence *n* influência; ♦ *vt* influir sobre, influenciar; persuadir; **under the ~ of alcohol** em estado de embriaguez.

influential *adj* influente.

influenza *n* gripe *f.*

influx *n (of people)* afluência *f* (**of**, de); **2** *(of water)* influxo *m* (**of**, de); **3** *(river mouth)* foz *f.*

inform *vt* informar; avisar; comunicar; **to ~ against/ on** denunciar, acusar; fazer queixa de.

informal *adj* sem cerimónia *(BR: -mô-)* informal *m,f; (person = clothes, manner)* simples *m,f; (language)* informal *m,f; (attire)* casual; extra-oficial; *(relaxed)* à vontade; **an ~ dinner** um jantar sem cerimónia.

informality *n* simplicidade *f;* sem cerimónia *(BR: -mô-);* informalidade *f.*

informally *adv (without ceremony)* informalmente; **2** *(unofficially)* oficiosamente.

informant *n (informer)* informador,-ora *(EP);* informante *m,f (BR);* **2** *(source of information)* fonte *f* de inspiração.

informatics *nsg* (= **computer science**), informática *f.*

information *n* informação *f,* informações *fpl* (**on**, **about** sobre, acerca de); **a piece/item of ~** uma informação *f,* um dado *m;* **2** conhecimento *m;* **for your ~** para seu conhecimento; **~ bureau/ desk** *n* balcão *m* de informações; **~ technology** *n* informática *f.*

informative *adj* informativo,-a, instrutivo,-a.

informed *adj* informado,-a; **2** *(decision, debate)* fundamentado,-a; **~ guess** conje(c)tura *f* bem fundamentada

informer *n* delator,-ora; **police ~** informador,-ora, *(BR)* informante; **to turn ~** tornar-se informador.

infrared *adj* infravermelho.

infrastructure *n* infraestrutura *f.*

infrequent *adj* infrequente; invulgar.

infringe *vt (law, agreement)* infringir; **2** transgredir, violar *(regulations);* ♦ *vi:* **to ~ on/upon sth** violar, transgredir algo.

infringement *n* transgressão *f;* violação *f* (**of** de); **2** *(SPORT)* infra(c)ção *f.*

infuriate *vt* enfurecer, enraivecer.

infuriating *adj* enfurecedor,-ora; **it is ~** é de dar raiva.

infuse *vt* instil: **to ~ into sb** incutir, infundir em alguém; **2** inspirar alguém; **3** *(CULIN) (brew)* pôr de infusão.

ingenious *adj* engenhoso,-a.

ingenuity *n* engenho *m,* habilidade *f.*

ingenuous *adj* ingénuo,-a *(BR: -gê-).*

ingest *vt* ingerir *(food);* assimilar *(facts).*

inglorious *adj (LITER)* inglório,-a.

ingot *n (metal)* lingote *m,* barra *f.*

ingrained *adj (deeply rooted)* arraigado,-a enraizado,-a; *(dirt)* entranhado,-a; **2** *(habit)* inveterado,-a; *(fig) (utter)* total; **an ~ fool** um idiota total, um perfeito idiota.

ingratiate *vt* captar as boas graças de; **to ~ o.s. with** insinuar-se, granjear as simpatias de.

ingratitude *n* ingratidão *f.*

ingredient *n* ingrediente *m.*

ingrowing *adj* que cresce para dentro; **~ toenail** uma unha do pé encravada.

inhabit *vt* habitar, viver em; ocupar.

inhabitable *adj* habitável *m,f.*

inhabitant *n* habitante *m,f.*

inhale *vt* inalar; ♦ *vi* aspirar.

inhaler *n* inalador *m.*

inherent *adj:* inerente (**in/to** a).

inherit *vt* herdar.

inheritance *n* herança *f;* **2** sucessão *f;* **genetic ~** *(MED)* herança *f* genética.

inherited *adj (BIOL)* hereditário,-a; **2** *(assets)* herdeiro,-a.

inheritor *n (gen)* herdeiro,-a.

inhibit *vt* inibir, reprimir; **to ~ sb from doing sth** impedir alguém de fazer algo.

inhibition *n* inibição *f.*

inhospitable *adj* inospitaleiro,-a; inóspito,-a.

in-house *adj, adv (within an organization)* interno,-a; **~ doctor** *(in hospital)* médico *m* interno.

inhuman *adj (cruel)* desumano,-a; **2** *(not human)* inumano,-a.

inimical *adj* inimigo,-a, adverso,-a, hostil.

inimitable *adj* inimitável.

iniquitous *adj* iníquo,-a.

iniquity *n* iniquidade *f;* injustice *f.*

initial *n* inicial *f;* ♦ *adj* inicial, primeiro,-a; ♦ *vt* marcar com iniciais; **~s** *npl* iniciais *fpl;* abreviatura, sigla.

initialize, initialise *vt (COMP)* inicializar, lançar programa.

initially *adv* inicialmente, a princípio.

initiate *vt* iniciar, começar; *(talk, chat)* encetar; **2 ~ proceedings against sb** *(JUR)* abrir, encetar um processo contra alguém.

initiation *n (start)* início *m;* começo *m;* **2** *(introduction into an organization, knowledge)* iniciação *f.*

initiative *n* iniciativa *f.*

inject *vt* inje(c)tar; *(fig)* introduzir.

injection *n* inje(c)ção *f.*

in-joke *n* piada *f* privata; **it's the ~ between us** é uma graça/piada entre nós.

injure *vt (MED)* ferir, lesar; **~ oneself** magoar-se ferir-se; **2** *(hurt)* ofender, magoar, fazer mal a; *(health)* prejudicar.

injured *adj (MED)* ferido,-a; **2** *(fig) (pride, feelings)* magoado,-a; ferido,-a; **the ~ party** *(JUR)* a parte lesada; **3** *(husband/wife)* enganado,-a; **the ~** *(people)* os feridos.

injury *n* ferida *f;* lesão *f;* **2** *(offense)* injúria *f;* golpe *m;* **3** *(JUR)* dano *m;* **~ time** *n (SPORT)* período *m* de desconto.

injustice *n* injustice *f;* **to do sb/an ~** fazer uma injustiça a alguém.

ink *n* tinta (de escrever); **in ~** a tinta; **~-jet printer** *n* impressora-jato *f* de tinta.

inkling *n* suspeita, insinuação *f;* **2** ideia *f* vaga.

inkpot, inkwell *n* tinteiro *m.*

inlaid *adj* embutido,-a marchetado,-a; *(with gems)* incrustado,-a de.

inland *adj* interior; interno; ♦ *adv* para o interior; **the I~ Revenue** *npr (UK)* departamento Britânico responsável pelos impostos; o fisco *(fam) (equiv)* a Receita do Estado *(EP);* a Receita Federal *(BR).*

in-laws *npl (the couple's parents)* sogros *mpl; (brothers/sisters)* **in-laws** cunhado(s), cunhada(s); **I have all the ~ coming tonight** esta noite, vem toda a família do meu marido, da minha mulher.

inlay *n (of gems, mother-of-pearl)* incrustação *f;* **2** *(on furniture)* obra de embutido; ♦ *(pt, pp* **laid)** *vt (wood)* marchetar, embutir; *(gems)* incrustar.

inlet *n (GEOG)* enseada, angra, braço *m* de mar; **2** *(way-in)* entrada; admissão *f;* **3** *(AUT)* **~ valve** válvula *f* de admissão.

inmate *n (of prison)* preso,-a; **2** *(of hospital)* doente *m,f;* **3** *(mental hospital)* internado,-a.

inmost *(also:* **innermost)** *adj (deepest)* no mais íntimo.

inn *n (arc)* estalagem *f,* hospedaria *f;* **2** *(superior accommodation)* pousada; *(UK) (public house)* taberna *f.*

innards *npl* entranhas *fpl,* vísceras *fpl.*

innate *adj* inato,-a.

inner *adj* interno,-a; interior; *(fig)* (=~ **self)** íntimo *m;* **~ city** *n* centro *m* da cidade; **2 ~ tube** *n* câmara *f* de ar.

innermost *adj* mais íntimo; **in my ~ thoughts** nos meus mais íntimos pensamentos.

innocence *n* inocência.

innocent *adj* inocente; **~ until proved guilty** prova *f* contrária, o réu está inocente.

innocuous *adj* inócuo,-a, inofensivo,-a.

innovate *vi* inovar.

innovation *n* inovação *f,* novidade *f.*

innuendo *(pl:* **-es)** *n* insinuação *f; (coll)* indire(c)ta.

innumerable *adj* inumerável.

inoculation *n* inoculação *f,* vacinação *f.*

inopportune *adj* inoportuno,-a.

inordinate *adj (quantity, size)* imenso,-a, excessivo,-a; *(passion)* imoderado,-a.

inordinately *adv* desmedidamente.

inorganic *adj* inorgânico,-a.

in-patient *n* doente *m,f* interno (de hospital).

input *n (ELECT, COMP-data)* entrada; **2** *(ECON) (analysis of industrial production), (often pl.)* insumo *m;* **3** contribuição *f;* ♦ *(pt, pp* **input** *or* **-ted)** *vt* entrar; *(COMP)* introduzir *(data)* **(in** em); **~-output** *n (ELECT, COMP)* entrada-saída *f.*

inquest *n* inquérito *m* policial; *(coroner's)* inquérito judicial.

inquire *vi* inquirir; indagar; ♦ *vt* perguntar; pedir informação sobre; **to ~ about** *vt* perguntar por; informar-se sobre; **to ~ into** *vt* investigar, indagar.

inquirer *n* inquiridor,-ora, investigador,-ora.

inquiring *adj (mind)* curioso,-a; *(look)* interrogador.

inquiry *n* pedido *m* de informação; '**inquiries**' 'informações'; **2** *(JUR)* investigação *f,* inquérito *m* **(into** sobre); **3** *(research, search)* pesquisa *f;* **4 ~ commission** comissão *f* de inquérito; **~ office** *n* guichê *m* de informações.

inquisition *n (investigation)* inquérito *m;* **the I~** *(REL)* a Inquisição *f.*

inquisitive *adj* inquisitivo,-a; curioso,-a, indiscreto,-a.

inroad *n (rights, time)* incursão *f; (fig)* invasão *f;* **to make ~s into** *(place, situation)* abrir caminho (gradualmente) em.

inrush *n (influx)* afluxo *m.*

insane *adj* louco, doido; *(MED)* demente *m,f;* **to go/ become ~** enlouquecer; **to drive sb ~** fazer alguém maluco,-a.

insanitary *adj* insalubre.

insanity *n* insanidade *f,* demência *f.*

insatiable *adj* insaciável.

inscribe *vt (write in book)* inscrever **(in** em); *(on tombstone)* gravar em; *(sign)* assinar, dedicar **(to sb** a alguém).

inscription *n* inscrição *f;* **2** dedicatória *f.*

inscrutable *adj* inescrutável, impenetrável.

insect *n* inse(c)to; **~'s bite** picada *f* de inse(c)to.

insecticide *n* inse(c)ticida *m.*

insecure *adj* inseguro,-a, sem confiança.

insecurity *n* insegurança *f.*

inseminate *vt* inseminar.

insemination *n* inseminação *f.*

insensible *adj* impassível, indiferente; *(unaware)* inconsciente.

insensitive *adj (unfeeling)* insensível; **~ to pain** insensível à dor; **2** *(tactless)* sem ta(c)to.

inseparable *adj* inseparável.

insert *vt* introduzir, inserir **(in** em); **2** publicar; *(advertisement)* pôr (anúncio); **3** *(clause)* intercalar *(between* entre).

insertion *n* inserção *f;* publicação *f;* **2** *(enclosed leaflet)* folha *f* solta.

in-service training *n* formação *f* contínua; *(BR)* treinamento *m* contínuo no serviço.

inset *n* coisa inserida; pequena ilustração, dentro de margens, num jornal; **2** *(sewing)* entremeio *m.*

inshore *adj* perto da costa; costeiro,-a; ♦ *adv* perto da costa; em direção à costa.

inside *n* interior *m;* **the ~** o lado de dentro; **on the ~** *(prison)* de cana *(cal);* **2** *(person)* que está por dentro; de confiança; **3** *(lining)* forro *m;* ♦ *adj* interior, interno; **2** *(knowledge)* de dentro; **the ~ story** a história *f* autêntica; **3 an ~ source** uma fonte confidencial; ♦ *adv* (por) dentro; para dentro; **2** *(fam)* na prisão; ♦ *prep* dentro de; **~ of 5 minutes** em menos de cinco minutos; **~ forward** *n (SPORT)* avançado-centro, *(BR)* centro-avante; **~ lane** *n (AUT) (in Europe, Americas)* faixa/via da direita; *(GB, Australia etc)* via/faixa da esquerda; **~ out** *adv* às avessas; **to know sb/ sth ~ out** conhecer alguém/algo a fundo; **the ~s** *npl (coll)* as entranhas *fpl.*

inside job *n* crime, roubo cometido com a conivência de um conhecido da vítima.

insider *n* pessoa bem informada dentro de uma organização; **~ dealing** *n* uso indevido de informações privilegiadas na Bolsa.

insidious *adj* insidioso,-a; clandestino,-a.

insight *n* intuição *f;* **2** *(wisdom)* discernimento *m* **(into sth** sobre algo); ideia *f* luminosa; *(glimpse)* vislumbre *m* **(into** de).

insignia *n* insígnia *f*.
insignificant *adj* insignificante.
insincere *adj* insincero,-a.
insincerity *n* insinceridade *f*.
insinuate *vt* insinuar, sugerir.
insinuation *n* insinuação *f*, indire(c)ta.
insipid *adj (dull)* insípido,-a, sem graça; **2** *(without salt)* insosso,-a.
insist *vi* insistir; **to ~ on doing** teimar em fazer; **to ~ that** insistir em que; exigir que.
insistence *n* insistência; teimosia; tenacidade *f*.
insistent *adj* insistente, pertinaz.
in situ *adv* no local.
insofar *(in so far) adv:* **~ as** na medida em que.
insole *n (within the shoe)* palmilha *f*.
insolence *n* insolência *f*, atrevimento *m*.
insolent *adj* insolente *m,f*; **2** *(cheeky)* atrevido,-a.
insoluble *adj* insolúvel.
insolvency *n* insolvência *f*.
insolvent *adj* insolvente, falido,-a.
insomnia *n* insónia *(BR: -sô-) f*.
insomuch as *conj* a tal ponto que; **insomuch that** *conj* de modo que.
inspect *vt* inspe(c)cionar, examinar; *(MIL)* passar revista em; *(premises, works)* vistoriar.
inspection *n* inspe(c)ção *f*; exame *m*.
inspector *n* inspe(c)tor,-ora; fiscal *m*.
inspiration *n* inspiração *f*.
inspire *vt* inspirar.
inst *(abbr for* **instant)** *(dated) (COMM: letter)* do corrente mês.
instability *n* instabilidade *f*.
install *(UK)* **instal** *(US) vt* instalar.
installation *n* instalação *f*.
instalment *(UK)* **instalment** *(US) n (FIN, COMM)* prestação *f*; **payment by ~** pagamento *m* a prestações; *(story)* episódio *m*; *(serial)* fascículo *m*; folhetim *m*.
instance *n* exemplo; **for ~** por exemplo; **in the first ~** em primeiro lugar; **2** pedido *m*, urgência *f*; **at the ~ of** a pedido de; **3** *(JUR)* instância; ♦ *vt* to cite as an example, ilustrar.
instant *n* instante *m*, momento; **at that very ~** nesse mesmo momento; ♦ *adj* instantâneo, imediato.
instantly *adv* imediatamente.
instead *adv* em vez disso; **~ of** em vez de, em lugar de.
instep *n* peito *m* do pé.
instigate *vt* instigar; **2** estimular; fomentar.
instigation *n* instigação *f*, incitamento *m*.
instil (-ll-) *vt* instilar, infundir, inspirar; **to ~ into** incutir em; **to ~ trust in sb** inspirar confiança em alguém.
instinct *n* instinto *m*.
instinctive *adj* instintivo,-a.
instinctively *adv* por instinto, instintivamente.
institute *n (EDUC)* instituto; *(organization)* associação *f*; ♦ *vt* começar, iniciar, fundar, instituir, estabelecer.
institution *n (ger)* instituição *f*; *(prison, hospital, college)*, estabelecimento *m* prisional/hospitalar/de ensino; **2 financial ~** organismo *m* financeiro; **3** *(established custom, etc)* costume *m*.

instruct *vt:* **to ~ sb in sth** instruir alguém em alguma coisa; **to ~ sb to do sth** dar instruções a alguém para fazer alguma coisa.
instruction *n* instrução *f*; **2** *(for use)* modo *m* de usar; manual *m*.
instructive *adj* instrutivo,-a.
instructor *n* instrutor,-ora.
instrument *n (gen)* instrumento.
instrumental *adj (MUS)* instrumental; **to be ~ in** contribuir para; **~ panel** *n* painel *m* de instrumentos.
insubordinate *adj* insubordinado,-a.
insubordination *n* insubordinação *f*; desobediência.
insubstantial *adj* inconsistente; pouco substancial; *(evidence)* insuficiente; *(flimsy)* pouco sólido,-a.
insufferable *adj* insuportável.
insufficient *adj* insuficiente.
insular *adj (GEOG)* insular; **2** *(isolated)* isolado,-a; **3** *(outlook)* tacanho,-a, de mente limitada.
insulate *vt* isolar.
insulating tape *n* fita *f* isolante.
insulation *n* isolamento, isolante *m*.
insulator *n* isolante *m*; *(ELECT)* isolador *m*.
insulin *n* insulina *f*.
insult *n* insulto *m*; ofensa *f*, afronta *f*; **and to add ~ to injury** e para cúmulo do insulto, e em cima da afronta, a injúria; ♦ *vt* insultar, ofender.
insulting *adj* insultante; ofensivo,-a.
insuperable *adj* insuperável.
insupportable *adj* insuportável.
insurance *n* seguro; **fire ~** seguro contra incêndio; **life ~** seguro de vida; **comprehensive ~** seguro contra todos os riscos; **~ agent** *n* agente *m,f* de seguros; **~ company** *n* seguradora *f*; **~ policy** *n* apólice *f* de seguro.
insure *vt* fazer um seguro, segurar; **2** *(take precautions)* prevenir-se contra; **3** *(US: ensure)* make certain.
insured *n (person, organization)* **the ~** o segurado,-a segurada; ♦ *adj (against fire, etc.)* segurado,-a *(contra fogo, etc.)*; **2** *(US) (sure)* assegurado,-a.
insurer *n (broker, company)* segurador,-ora.
insurgent *n* rebelde, revoltoso,-a; ♦ *adj* revoltado,-a.
insurmountable *adj* intransponível, insuperável.
insurrection *n* insurreição *f*.
intact *adj (complete)* intacto, íntegro,-a; **2** ileso,-a.
intake *n (TEC)* entrada, tomada; **2** *(of food)* quantidade *f* ingerida; **an ~ of 100 (students) a year** *(EDUC)* 100 matriculados por ano.
intangible *n:* **the ~** o imponderável; ♦ *adj* intangível.
integer *n (MATH)* número *m* inteiro.
integral *n (MATH)* integral; ♦ *adj (intrinsic)* essencial; integrante *m,f*.
integrate *vt* integrar; ♦ *vi* integrar-se.
integrity *n* integridade *f*; honestidade *f*; re(c)tidão *f*.
intellect *n* intelecto *m*.
intellectual *n adj* intelectual.
intelligence *n* inteligência *f*; **I~ Department** Serviços *mpl* Secretos; **~ quotient** *n* quociente *m* de inteligência.
intelligent *adj* inteligente.
intelligentsia *n:* **the I~** a Inteligência; os Intelectuais *mpl*.

intelligible *adj* inteligível, compreensível.

intemperate *adj* intemperado; *(remark, attitude)* imoderado,-a; ~ **rage** fúria incontrolada; *(excessive)* desmedido,-a; *(weather)* rigoroso,-a; **2** *(person)* dado,-a à bebida.

intend *vt* tencionar; **to ~ sth for** destinar algo a.

intended *n (dated) (fiancé/fiancée)*, o (seu/a sua) prometido,-a, noivo,-a; ♦ *adj (effect)* desejado,-a.

intense *adj* intenso,-a; muito emotivo,-a; ♦ *adv* intensamente; extremamente.

intensify *vt* intensificar; aumentar.

intensity *n* intensidade *f* (**of** de); força, veemência *f*.

intensive *adj* intensivo,-a; **an ~ course** curso *m* intensivo; ~ **care unit** *n (emergencies)* serviço m de reanimação; **2** *(for the very ill)* serviço de cuidados intensivos.

intent *n* intenção *f*; ♦ *adj* absorto,-a; atento,-a; **to all ~s and purposes** para todos os efeitos; **to be ~ on doing sth** estar resolvido a fazer alguma coisa.

intention *n* intenção *f*, propósito *m*; proje(c)to *m*.

intentional *adj* intencional, premeditado.

intentionally *adv* de propósito.

intently *adv* atentamente, decididamente.

inter (-rr-) *vt* sepultar; **he was interred yesterday** ele foi sepultado, enterrado ontem.

interact *vi* interagir.

interaction *n* intera(c)ção *f*, a(c)ção *f* recíproca.

interactive *adj* intera(c)tivo.

interbreed *(pt, pp* -**bred)** *vt* cruzar raças diferentes.

interbreeding *n* cruzamento *m* (de raças).

intercalate *vt (in between)* intercalar; interpolar, inserir.

intercede *vi:* **to ~ (with)** *(plead)* interceder (junto a); ~ **on behalf of sb** a/em favor de alguém; **2** *(mediate)* mediar, intervir.

intercept *n (MATH)* segmento *m* de linha entre dois pontos; ♦ *vt* interceptar; deter.

interception *n* intercepção *f*, interceptação.

interchange *n* intercâmbio *m*; troca *f*, permute *f*; junção *f* (de estradas), *(BR)* trevo *m*; ♦ *vt/vi* trocar; alternar.

interchangeable *adj* permutável.

inter-city *n (UK) (train)* intercidades; ♦ *adj* interurbano,-a.

intercom *n* interfone *m*, telefone *m* interno.

interconnect *vt* interligar; ♦ *vi* interligar-se.

intercourse *n* trato; **2** coito, relações *fpl* sexuais.

interest *n* interesse *m* (**in**, em); **in the ~s of my client** em nome de; em benefício de; **2** hobby *m*; **3** *(FIN)* juro *m*; **4** *(shares in a company)* participação ♦ *vt* interessar; **the subject ~s me** o assunto interessa-me; **to ~ sb in sth/to do sth** convidar alguém em algo/para fazer algo; ♦ ~-**earning** *adj* com juros.

interested *pp, adj* interessado,-a; **the ~ parties** *npl* os interessados.

interest-free *adj* sem juros.

interesting *adj* interessante *m,f* curioso,-a; **an ~ thing** uma coisa curiosa.

interest rate *n* taxa *f* de juros.

interface *n (COMP)* interface; **2** *(TECH)* junção *f*; ♦ ligar; *(BR)* conectar (**to, with** a, com).

interfere *vi:* **to ~ in** interferir/intrometer-se em; **to ~ with** impedir; prejudicar; interferir com.

interference *n* intromissão *f*; *(BR)* intrometimento *m* (**in, with** em); *(RADIO, TV, PHYS)* interferência.

interim *n:* **in the ~** neste ínterim, nesse meio-tempo; ♦ *adj* provisório,-a interino,-a; ~ **judge** juiz interino.

interior *n* interior *m*; **Minister of the ~** *(Home Office Minister)* Ministro do Interior, da Administração *f* Interna; ♦ *adj* interno,-a, interior; íntimo,-a; ~ **designer** *n* decorador,-ora de interiores.

interject *vt* inserir, interpor.

interjection *n* interjeição *f*; exclamação *f*; **2** interrupção *f*.

interlace *vt* entrelaçar; entrecruzar.

interleaf *(pl:* **interleaves)** *n (in a book)* folha *f* intercalada.

interlock *vi (fingers, textiles)* entrelaçar-se; *(tiles)* encaixar-se; *(MECH)* engatar-se, engrenar-se.

interloper *n* intruso,-a.

interlude *n (MUS)* interlúdio *m*; *(THEAT)* entrea(c)to; **2** intervalo *m*.

intermarriage *n (within a family, tribe)* endogamia *f*; **2** *(of different races, etc)* casamento misto

intermediary *(pl:* -**ies)** *n* intermediário,-a, mediador, -ora.

intermediate *n* medianeiro,-a, mediador,-ora; ♦ *adj (stage)* intermédio,-a; **the ~ level** *(school)* o segundo nível.

interment *n* enterro *m*.

interminably *adv* interminavelmente; sem fim.

intermingle *vi:* **to ~ (with people)** misturar-se (com as pessoas).

intermission *n (THEAT)* intervalo *m*.

intermittent *adj* intermitente.

intern *n (US)* médico-interno júnior; *(US: trainee teacher)* estagiário,-a.

internal *adj* interno,-a; *(security of a country)* interno,-a, nacional; *(flight)* doméstico,-a; ~ **revenue** *n (US)* receitas *fpl* do Estado, receita *f* pública; *(BR)* receita federal.

internally *adv* internamente, no interior; '**not to be taken ~**' *(medicines)* 'uso externo'.

international *n (UK; SPORT)* partida *f* internacional; **2** *(player)* jogador,-ora, atleta da seleção; ♦ *adj* internacional.

internecine *adj (conflicts)* interno,-a; **the ~ rows in the office** os conflitos *mpl* internos no escritório.

internee *n (POL, MIL)* prisioneiro,-a de guerra, de política.

internet: ~ **access** *n* acesso à internet; ~ **café** *n* cybercafé; ~ **service provider** *n* provedor *m* de serviços de internet.

internment *n* prisão *f*, reclusão *f* (por razões políticas ou de guerra).

interplay *n* intera(c)ção *f*.

interpose *vt* interpor; **2** *(interrupt)* intervir.

interpret *vt* interpretar; traduzir; **2** compreender; ♦ *vi* interpretar.

interpretation *n* interpretação *f*; tradução *f*; entendimento *m*.

interpreter *n* intérprete *m,f*; tradutor,-ora.
interrelated *adj* inter-relacionado.
interrogate *vt* interrogar.
interrogation *n* interrogatório; ~ **mark** *(US) (LING)* ponto *m* de interrogação.
interrogative *adj (LING)* interrogativo; **in the** ~ na interrogativa; **2** *(tone, look)* interrogador.
interrogator *n (person)* interrogador,-ora.
interrupt *vt/vi* interromper.
interrupter *n (ELECT)* interruptor *m*.
interruption *n* interrupção *f*.
intersect *vt* cruzar; *(MATH)* interceptar; ♦ *vi (roads, ideas)* cruzar-se.
intersection *n* intercepção *f*; *(junction)* cruzamento *m*; encruzilhada *f*.
intersperse *vt* intercalar, entremear; **to be ~d with sth** *(jokes, etc)* ser entremeado,-a de algo.
interstice *n* interstício.
intertwine *vt* entrelaçar *(vines, threads, hands)*; ♦ *vi* entrelaçar-se.
interval *n* pausa *f*; *(EDUC)* recreio *m*, intervalo *m*; **at ~s** de vez em quando, de tempos em tempos.
intervene *vi* intervir.
intervening *adj* **in the ~ period** entretanto, no período decorrente.
intervention *n* intervenção *f*.
interview *n* entrevista; ♦ *vt* entrevistar.
interviewee *n* entrevistado,-a.
interviewer *n* entrevistador,-ora.
intestate *adj (JUR)* intestado,-a, sem testamento.
intestine *n* intestino *m*; *(coll)* tripa *f*; **large/small ~** intestino grosso/delgado.
intimacy *(pl: -ies) n* intimidade *f* **(between, with** entre, com**)**; familiaridade *f*; ♦ **intimacies** *npl* relações *fpl* sexuais.
intimate *adj* íntimo,-a; profundo,-a; ♦ *vt* insinuar, sugerir.
intimidate *vt* intimidar, amedrontar.
intimidation *n* intimidação *f*.
into *prep* em; **to break ~ pieces** quebrar em pedaços; para; **to gaze ~ her eyes** olhar para os olhos dela; para dentro de; **look ~ your heart** *(fig)* olha para dentro do teu coração; em dire(c)ção a; **to go ~ town** ir à cidade.
intolerable *adj* intolerável, insuportável.
intolerance *n* intolerância.
intolerant *adj*: ~ **of** intolerante com/para com.
intonation *n* entoação *f*, *(BR)* entonação *f*, inflexão *f*.
intone *vt/vi* entoar; recitar.
intoxicate *vt* embriagar.
intoxicated *adj* embriagado.
intoxication *n* intoxicação *f*, embriaguez *f*.
intractable *adj (person)* intratável; **2** *(substance)* difícil de trabalhar; *(fig)* espinhoso,-a.
intramural *adj* intramuros.
intransigent *adj* intransigente.
intransitive *adj* intransitivo,-a.
intrauterine device (IUD) *n (MED)* dispositivo *m* intrauterino, DIU *m*.
intravenous *adj* intravenoso,-a.
in-tray *n* cabaz *m* dos assuntos pendentes.

intrepid *adj* intrépido,-a.
intricacy *n* complicação *f*, embrulhada.
intricate *adj* intricado,-a; complexo,-a, complicado,-a.
intrigue *n* intriga *f*; ♦ *vt* interessar, intrigar; ♦ *vi* fazer intriga.
intriguing *adj* intrigante *m,f*.
intrinsic *adj* intrínseco,-a.
introduce *vt* introduzir, inserir **(in** em**)** *(key, etc)*; **to ~ sb (to sb)** apresentar alguém (a outrém); **to ~ sb to** *(job)* iniciar, introduzir alguém em; *(establish)* estabelecer *(reform, law)* **(into** em**)**; **to ~ the subject** abordar, introduzir o assunto.
introduction *n* introdução *f*; apresentação *f*; ~ **agency** *n* agência *f* de encontros.
introductory *adj* introdutório,-a, preliminar; **2** *(COMM) (offer)* de lançamento.
introspection *n* introspecção *f*.
introspective *adj* introspectivo,-a.
introvert *n adj* introvertido,-a.
intrude *vi* intrometer-se; **to ~ on/into** importunar.
intruder *n* intruso,-a.
intrusion *n* invasão **(into/on** em**)** intromissão *f* **(into/upon** em**)**; interrupção *f*.
intrusive *adj* indiscreto,-a; **2** *(phone call)* inoportuno,-a.
intuition *n* intuição *f*.
intuitive *adj* intuitivo,-a.
inundate *vt* inundar **(with** de**)**.
inundation *n* inundação *f*.
inured *adj* habituado,-a **(to,** a**)**; ♦ **inure** (=**enure**) *vt* habituar-(se) **(to,** a**)**; **2** *(law)* entrar em vigor.
invade *vt* invadir; **to ~ sb's privacy** invadir a privacidade de alguém.
invader *n* invasor,-ora.
invalid *n* inválido,-a; ♦ *adj* inválido, nulo; ~ **chair** *n* cadeira *f* de rodas.
invalidate *vt* invalidar, anular.
invaluable *adj* inestimável, incalculável.
invariable *adj* invariável.
invasion *n* invasão *f*.
invective *n* invective *f*; diatribe *f*; expressão *f* injuriosa.
invent *vt* inventar.
invention *n* invenção *f*; engenho; ficção *f*, mentira.
inventive *adj* engenhoso,-a, inventivo,-a.
inventiveness *n* inventividade *f*; imaginação *f*; creatividade *f*.
inventor *n* inventor,-ora.
inventory *(pl: -ies) n (lista)* inventário *m*; *(US)* (goods) estoque *m*.
inverse *n adj* inverso.
inversely *adv* inversamente.
invert *vt* inverter, transpor; **~ed commas** *npl* aspas *fpl*; **in ~** entre aspas; **~ed snob** *n* (pessoa que finge desprezar as convenções de sua classe) snobe ao contrário.
invertebrate *n* invertebrado,-a.
inverter *n (ELECT)* inversor *m*; ~ **converter** *n (ELECT)* inversor-conversor.
invest *vt* investir; **to ~ in** *vt* comprar; **to ~ in shares** aplicar dinheiro em a(c)ções; **2 to ~ sb with** *vt* investir de; empossar (alguém); **3** *(time, effort)* empregar, consagrar.

investigate *vt* investigar; estudar, examiner.
investigation *n* investigação *f*, pesquisa.
investigator *n* investigador,-ora.
investiture *n* investidura *f*.
investment *n* investimento *m*; ~ **trust** *n* fundo *m* de investimento.
investor *n* a(c)cionista *m,f* investidor,-ora.
inveterate *adj* inveterado,-a; incorrigível.
invidious *adj* (*task*) odioso,-a; **2** (*choice*) injusto,-a.
invigilate *vt/vi* vigiar (*exams*) estar de vigilância.
invigilation *n* (*exam*) invigilância *f*.
invigorating *adj* revigorante.
invincible *adj* invencível.
inviolable *adj* inviolável.
inviolate *adj* inviolado,-a.
invisible *adj* invisível; ~ **ink** *n* tinta *f* invisível; ~ **assets** *npl* (*bens*) intangíveis.
invitation *n* convite *m*.
invite *n* (*fam*) convite; ♦ *vt* convidar (**to**, para); **2** (*opinions*) pedir; **3** (*quarrel*) provoke.
inviting *adj* tentador,-ora; convidativo,-a, sedutor,-ora; (*food*) apetitoso,-a.
in-vitro fertilization *n* fertilização *f* in vitro.
invoice *n* fa(c)tura; **as per** ~ conforme fa(c)tura; **pro = forma** ~ fa(c)tura provisória; ♦ *vt* fa(c)turar; fazer uma fa(c)tura.
invoke *vt* (*to call upon*) invocar; **2** (*JUR*) pôr a lei em uso; **the union** ~**d the dispute procedure** o sindicato invocou o regulamento das disputas; **2** (*help, pardon*) implorar.
involuntary *adj* involuntário,-a.
involve *vt* implicar; **to** ~ **sb** (**in**) envolver alguém (em).
involved *adj* envolvido; comprometido.
involvement *n* envolvimento; compromisso *m*.
invulnerable *adj* invulnerável.
inward (*US*: -s) *adj* (*inner*) (*calm*) interior; íntimo; **2** (*satisfaction*) pessoal.
inwardly(s) *adv* para si, para dentro; no íntimo; (*freight, etc*) à chegada.
I/O (*abbr for* **input/output**) E/S *f*.
iodine *n* (*CHEM*) iodo; (*antiseptic*) tintura *f* de iodo.
Ionian Sea *npr* **the** ~ o mar *m* Jónio (*BR*: -ô-).
iota *n* iota *f*; (*fig*) pouquinho, parcela mínima; **not one** ~ **of truth** nem uma ponta de verdade.
IOU *n* (*abbr for* **I owe you**) nota de dívida, (*BR*) vale.
IQ *n* (*abbr for* **intelligence quotient**) quociente *m* de inteligência (QI).
IRA (*abbr for* **Irish Republican Army**) Exército Republicano da Irlanda.
Iran *npr* Irão *m;* **in** ~ no Irão; (*BR*) Irã *m*.
Iranian *npr adj* iraniano,-a.
Iraq *npr* Iraque *m;* **in** ~ no Iraque.
Iraqi *npr adj* iraquiano,-a.
irascible *adj* irascível.
irate *adj* irado,-a; enfurecido,-a.
Ireland *npr* Irlanda; **in** ~ na Irlanda.
iridescent *adj* iridescente.
iris (*pl:* **-es**) *n* íris *f*.
Irish *n adj* irlandês,-esa; ♦ *npl:* **the** ~ os irlandeses.
Irish stew *n* (*CULIN*) prato tradicional de carne e legumes tipo de guizado.

irk *vt* (*dated*) aborrecer.
irksome *adj* enfadonho,-a.
iron *n* ferro *m*; ~ **railings** *npl* grades de ferro; **2** (*pressing fabrics*) ferro de engomar/de passar roupa; **3** (*golf*) taco *m*; ♦ *adj* (*hard, strong*) duro,-a; de ferro; ~ **constitution** saúde *f* de ferro; ~**-handed** inflexível; rígido,-a; ♦ *vt* (*fabrics*) engomar, passar a ferro; **to strike while the** ~ **is hot** agarrar a oportunidade; **to** ~ **out** passar a ferro; **2** (*problems, situation*) resolver.
Iron Age *npr* a Idade *f* de Ferro.
Iron Curtain *n* a Cortina de Ferro.
ironic(al) *adj* irónico,-a (*BR*: -rô-).
ironing *n* roupa para passar (a ferro); ~ **board** *n* tábua de passar roupa.
Iron Lady *n* (*Mrs Thatcher*) a Dama de Ferro.
iron lung *n* pulmão *m* de aço.
ironmonger *n* ferreiro; ~**'s shop** *n* loja de ferragens.
iron ore *n* minério *m*; ~ **works** *npl:* **steel and** ~ **industry** *n* indústria *f* siderúrgica.
irons *npl* (*chains*) grilhões; **2 in** ~ (*NAUT*) (*sailing*) navegar ao vento.
ironware *n* louça *f* de ferro.
irony *n* ironia; **the** ~ **of it is that** ... a piada é que ...
irradiate *vt* irradiar.
irradiation *n* irradiação *f;* radiação *f*.
irrational *adj* irracional.
irreconcilable *adj* irreconciliável, incompatível.
irredeemable *adj* (*loss*) irremediável, irredímible; **2** (*FIN*) (*shares*) não reembolsável; **3** (*loan*) não amortizável; **4** (*REL*) incorrigível.
irrefutable *adj* irrefutável.
irregular *adj* irregular; desigual; ilegal.
irregularity *n* irregularidade *f;* desigualdade *f*.
irrelevant *adj* irrelevante, insignificante *m,f*, descabido,-a.
irreligious *adj* descrente.
irreparable *adj* irreparável.
irreplaceable *adj* insubstituível.
irrepressible *adj* irreprimível, irrefreável.
irreproachable *adj* irrepreensível.
irresistible *adj* irresistível.
irresolute *adj* irresoluto,-a, indeciso,-a.
irrespective: ~ **of** *prep* independente de, sem ter em conta.
irresponsible *adj* irresponsável.
irretrievable *adj* irrecuperável.
irreverent *adj* irreverente, desrespeitoso,-a.
irreversible *adj* irreversível.
irrevocable *adj* irrevogável.
irrigate *vt* irrigar.
irrigation *n* irrigação *f*.
irritable *adj* irritável; de mau humor, nervoso,-a.
irritate *vt* irritar.
irritating *adj* (*annoying person*) irritante *m,f*; **2** (*MED*) irritação *f*.
irritation *n* irritação *f*.
IRS (*abbr for* **Internal Revenue Service**) Departamento *m* das Finanças (*EP*) Secretaria da Fazenda (*BR*).
is (*Vd:* **be**) **it is** é; **she is** ela é; **he is** ele é.
ISA (*abbr for* **individual savings account**) sistema britânico de poupanças isentas de impostos.

Islam *npr* Islã(o).
Islamic *adj* islâmico,-a.
Islamism *npr* islamismo *m*.
island *n* ilha *f*; **2 traffic** ~ *(middle of the road)* refúgio para peões; ♦ *adj* da ilha; insular.
islander *n* ilhéu,-oa.
isle/islet *n* ilhota *f*; **I**~ **of Wight** *npr* Ilha de Wight.
isn't = is not.
isobar *n (METEOR)* isóbara.
isolate *vt* isolar.
isolated *adj* isolado.
isolation *n* isolamento.
isotope *n (atoms)* isótopo *m*.
Israel *npr* (Estado de) Israel *m*; **in** ~ em Israel.
Israeli *npr adj* israelita *m,f (BR)* israelense.
issue *n* questão *f*, tema *m*; **2** resultado; **3** emissão *f*; número; **4** sucessão *f*, descendência *f*; ♦ *vt* distribuir; dar; emitir; promulgar; publicar.
Istanbul *npr* Istambul.
isthmus *n* istmo.
it *pron (subject: neuter)* ele/ela; *(direct object)* o,-a; a; *(indirect object)* lhe; *(impersonal)* isto, isso; *(after prep)* ele, ela; ~'s **snowing** está a nevar; **how is** ~ **that ...?** como é possível que ...?; **he felt better for** ~ sentiu-se melhor com isso.

it – sujeito neutro – usa-se quando se refere a coisas, animais e como pronome impessoal dos verbos. Neste caso, não se traduz em português ou é substituído por 'isto', 'isso'. *Vd:* acima.

Italian *npr adj* italiano,-a; *(LING)* italiano.
italic *adj* itálico, cursivo; ~**s** *npl* itálico *sg*.
Italy *npr* Itália; **in** ~ na Itália.
itch *n* comichão *f*; prurido *m*; *(fig)* desejo ardente; ♦ *vi* ter comichão; fazer comichão; *(BR)* coçar; **I'm** ~**ing to/for** ... estou morto/em brasas por/para ... .
itching *n* comichão *m*.
itchy *adj*: ~ **feet** *n (coll)* desejo de viajar; ~ **palm** *(coll) n* desejo de receber dinheiro.
item *n* item *m*; artigo *m*; rubrica *f*; detalhe *m*; assunto *m*; *(programme)* número *m*; (= **news** ~) notícia.
itemize *vt* pormenorizar, especificar.
itinerant *adj (worker)* itinerante; **2** *(tribe)* nómada *(EP)* nómada *(BR)*.
itinerary *n* itinerário *m*.
its *adj* seu/sua, seus suas; ♦ *pron* (o) seu/(a) sua, os seus, as suas (para animais, coisa); **it's = it is.**
itself *pron (reflexive)* a si mesmo,-a; *(emphatic)* ele mesmo/ela mesma; **in** ~ em si/por sigo.
IUD *n (abbr for* **intra-uterine device***)* dispositivo intra-uterino.
I've = I have.
IVF *n (abbr for* **in vitro fertilization***)* FIB.
ivory *n* marfim *m*; **the I**~ **Coast** *npr* a Costa *f* do Marfim; ~ **tower** *n (fig)* torre *f* de marfim.
ivy *n* hera.
Ivy League *n (US) grupo das oito mais prestigiadas universidades nos USA.*

j

J, j *n (letter)* J, j.

jab *n (in boxing)* soco, murro *m*; **2** *(sharp poke)* golpe *m*, pancada *f*; **3** *(MED: coll) (injection)* picadela; injeção *f*; ♦ *(pt, pp* -**bed**, -**bbing**) *vt (poke)* espetar (**into sb/sth** em alguém/algo); cravar (**sth into sb/sth** algo em alguém/algo).

jabber *vt/vi (speak incomprehensibly)* taramelar; *(with timidity)* tartamudear; **2** *(chatter)* algaraviar, tagarelar; *(foreign idiom)* arranhar *(fam)*.

jacaranda *n (BOT)* jacarandá.

jack *n (AUT) (crank)* macaco; **2** *(bowling)* boliche *f*; **3** *(in cards)* valete *m*; **4 Union J~** *(British flag on a ship)* bandeira britânica; ♦ **to ~ in** *vt (coll) (attempt)* desistir, deixar; **to ~ up** *vt (AUT) (lift with jack)* levantar com o macaco; **2** *(price)* aumentar; IDIOM **every man ~** (**of them**) todos sem exce(p)ção; **~ of all trades** homem dos sete ofícios/pau para toda a obra.

jackal *n (ZOOL)* chacal *m*.

jackass *n (fam)* burro *m*; **2** *(fam)* estúpido, burro.

jackboot *n* bota *f* militar de cano alto; **2** *(policy, attitude, rule)* autoritário,-a.

jackdaw *n (ZOOL)* gralha *f*.

jacket *n (garment)* jaqueta, casaco curto; **2** *(book cover)* sobrecapa *f*; *(US) (of record)* capa *f*; **3** *(of boiler, machine)* revestimento *m*, camisa *f*; **~ potato** *n* batata *f* assada com casca.

jackfish *n (fish)* carapau.

Jack Frost *n* o Senhor Inverno.

jack hammer *n (US)* britadeira *f*; *(mines)* martelo pneumático.

jack-in-the-box *n (toy)* caixinha *f* de surpresas.

jacknife *n* canivete *m*; ♦ *vt (articulated lorry)* derrapar a dianteira para o lado.

jack-o'-lantern *n* lanterna feita de abóbora para a noite das bruxas.

jackpot *n* sorte *f* grande.

Jacobean *adj (relating to James 1st of England)* jacobino.

Jacobite *npr adj* jacobita *m,f*.

jade *n* jade *m*.

jaded *adj (exhausted)* estafado,-a; **2** *(satiated)* farto,-a.

jagged *adj* dentado,-a, recortado,-a; **2** *(ragged)* escabroso,-a; **a ~ tear** um rasgão em ziguezague.

jail *n* prisão *f*, cadeia; ♦ *vt* prender; **~bird** *n* preso,-a reincidente, presidiário,-a; **~break** *n* fuga da prisão.

jailer *n* carcereiro.

Jakarta *npr* Jacarta; **in ~** em Jacarta.

jalopy *n (coll)* carripana *f*.

jam *n (CULIN)* compota *f*, geleia *f*; **carrot ~** compota de cenoura; **2** (= **traffic ~**) engarrafamento *m*;

aperto *m*; **to be in a traffic ~** estar em apuros; ♦ *(pt, pp* -**med**) *vt* obstruir, fechar; **2** *(between)* entalar; **I was ~med between the wall and the man** estava entalado entre a parede e o homem; **3** *(also: ~ up) (to cause to stick)* emperrar *(lift, etc)*; encravar *(window, door)*; **4** *(to block)* bloquear; *(block drains)* entupir, bloquear (**with sth** com algo); **5** *(RADIO)* interferir; **6 to ~ sth into sth** enfiar algo à força dentro de outra coisa; ♦ *vi (tightly packed)* comprimir; abarrotar, apinhar.

Jamaica *npr* Jamaica; **in ~** em/na Jamaica.

Jamaican *npr adj* jamaicano,-a.

jamb *n (door, window) (doorpost)* ombreira *f*, umbral *m*.

jamboree *n* festa *f* pública; grande reunião *f* de escuteiros.

jammed *adj* entalado,-a, encravado,-a; **~ communications** *npl* comunicações *fpl* bloqueadas.

jamming *n (RADIO)* interferência *f*.

jammy (-ier, -iest) *adj (face, fingers)* com geleia; **2** *(coll) (person)* felizardo,-a sortudo,-a.

jam packed *adj* abarrotado,-a, apinhado,-a; **the theatre was ~** o teatro estava à cunha.

jangle *n (noise) (of bells, saucepans)* barulho *m*; *(of alarm)* som *m* estridente; *(of keys)* tilintar; ♦ *vi* soar estridentemente; fazer soar/tocar; *(cow bells)* chocalhar; (keys) tilintar.

jangling *n* tilintar, chocalhada; ♦ *adj* tilitante.

janitor *n (caretaker)* zelador,-ora, guarda *m,f (of school)*; porteiro *(of building)*.

January *npr* Janeiro/janeiro *m*.

Japan *npr* Japão *m*; **in ~** no Japão.

Japanese *adj* japonês,-esa; ♦ *npr pl inv* japonês,-esa; *(LING)* japonês *m*.

jar *n (earthenware)* jarro *m*, pote *m*; **2** frasco; boião *m*, pote *m*; **~ of cream/marmalade** boião de creme/marmelada; ♦ *vt (jolt)* sacudir, abalar *(person structure)*; ♦ *(-rr-) vi* causar vibração; **2** *(rattle)* tremer, ranger *(windows, doors)*; **3** chiar *(cart)*; **4** *(colours)* destoar, chocar; ♦ **to ~ on** *vt* irritar; *(voices, noise)* causar nervos a alguém.

jardinière *f* floreira *f*; **2** *(CULIN)* jardineira *f*.

jargon *n* calão *m*, gíria *f*, *(BR)* jargão *m*.

jarring *adj (noise, voice)* enervante.

jasmin(e) *n* jasmim *m*.

jaundice *n* icterícia *f*.

jaundiced *adj* amargurado, despeitado; **2** *(attitude)* negativo,-a.

jaunt *n* passeio *m*, excursão *f*.

jauntily *adv* alegremente.

jaunty (-ier, -iest) *adj* alegre, jovial.

Java *npr* Java; **in ~** em/na Java.

javelin *n* dardo de arremesso.

jaw *n (lower) (person, animal)* mandíbula *f*; *(upper)* maxila *f*; **~bone** maxilar *m*; **2** *(coll) (chat)* conversa *f*, cavaqueira *f*; *(BR)* bate-papo *m*; ♦ *vt (chat idly or cheekily)* estar no paleio, na cavaqueira, *(BR)* estar no bate-papo.

jawbone *n* osso *m* maxilar; **~s** *npl* maxilares, mandíbulas.

jaw-dropping *adj (in amazement)* atónito,-a, de boca aberta.

jay *n* (ZOOL) gaio *m*.

jaywalker *n* pedestre *m,f* distraído, peão *m*, imprudente.

jazz *n* (MUS) jazz *m*; (coll) **and all that** ~ e toda essa tralha; ♦ **to ~ up** *vt* animar, avivar.

jazzy *adj* (colour, dress) vistoso,-a; (pej) berrante.

jealous *adj* (rel to: love) ciumento,-a; **2** (rel to: material things) invejoso,-a; **to be ~** estar com ciúmes (of wife, brother, etc); estar com inveja (of person's achievement, beauty, job).

jealousy *n* ciúmes *mpl*; inveja *fpl*.

jean *n* (material) cotim *m*; ganga *f*; **jeans** *npl* jeans *mpl*, calças *fpl* de ganga.

jeep *n* jipe *m*.

jeer *n*: **~s** (from crowd) apupos *mpl*; (from person) chacota; ♦ *vt* (boo) vaiar, apupar, fazer chacota; ♦ *vi* **~ at** ridicularizar, fazer pouco de, troçar de (alguém).

jeering *n* vaias *fpl*; zombaria *f*; ♦ *adj* (person, remark) trocista *m,f*

Jehovah *npr* Jeová *m*.

jellied *adj* (CULIN) em geleia; **~ eels** enguias *fpl* em geleia.

Jell-o® *n* (US) (trademark) gelatina, geleia *f*.

jelly *n* (CULIN) (sweet or salty) geleia, (BR) geléia; gelatina; **~fish** *n* alforreca, (BR) água-viva.

jelly baby *n* rebuçado em forma de bebé.

jemmy (pl: -ies) *n* (crowbar) pé-de-cabra *m*.

jeopardize *vt* arriscar, pôr em perigo; comprometer.

jeopardy *n*: **to be in ~** estar em perigo.

jerk *n* sacudidela *f*; (pull) puxão *m*; movimento *m* brusco; (jolt) solavanco; **2** (fig, fam) idiota; **with a ~** de repente, bruscamente; ♦ *vt* mover abruptamente; ♦ *vi* (vehicle) andar aos solavancos, dar solavancos; **to ~ off** (vulgar) (male) masturbar-se.

jerky *adj* (movement) brusco,-a sacudido,-a; **2** (twitch) espasmódico; **3** (in jolts) aos arrancos, aos solavancos.

jerry-built *adj* construído,-a à pressa; com materiais inferiores.

jersey *n* camisola, *f*; suéter *m,f*.

Jersey *npr* (island in the English Channel) Jersey; **in ~** em Jersey, na Ilha de Jersey.

Jerusalem *npr* Jerusalém; **in ~** em Jerusalém; **~ artichoke** *n* pera-da-terra *f*, girassol-batateiro *m*, tupinambo.

jest *n* gracejo, brincadeira; **I did it in ~** eu fiz isso de/ por brincadeira; ♦ *vi* brincar, gracejar; IDIOM **many a true word is spoken in ~** a brincar se dizem as verdades.

jester *n* (court) bobo; **2** (clown) palhaço,-a; **3** (playful person) brincalhão,-ona *m,f*.

Jesuit *npr* jesuíta *m*.

Jesus *npr* Jesus; **baby ~** o Menino Jesus; **~ Christ** Jesus Cristo.

jet *n* (of stream, water spout) repuxo *m*, esguicho *m*; jorro *m*; **2** ja(c)to; (AER) avião *m* a ja(c)to; **3** (on gas ring) queimador; **4** (stone) azeviche; **~-black** *adj* da cor do azeviche; **~ engine** *n* motor *m* a ja(c)to.

jetfoil *n* hidroflutuador *m*.

jetlag *n* cansaço *m* por desfazamento horário.

jet-powered, jet-propelled *adj* de/com propulsão a ja(c)to.

jettison *vt* (from ship) lançar a carga ao mar; (from plane) alijar; **2** (fig) renunciar a, rejeitar (ideas); abandonar (hope); desembaraçar-se de (old things); descartar (rubbish).

jetty *n* quebra-mar *m*, molhe *m*; cais *m*, desembarcadouro *m*.

Jew *n* judeu *m*, judia *f*.

jewel *n* jóia; (fig) (person) jóia; **2** (in watch) rubi.

jeweler *n* joalheiro; ourives *m*; **~'s (shop)** *n* joalharia.

jewelery *n* jóias *fpl*, joalharia.

Jewess *n* judia *f*.

Jewish *adj* judeu, judia; judaico,-a.

Jew's harp *n* (MUS) berimbau *m*.

jib *n* (NAUT) (sail) bujarrona *f*; (beam) vau *m*; **2** (of crane) guindaste de lança; ♦ **(-bb-)** *vi* (person) mostrar relutância (**at doing sth** em fazer algo); hesitar em; **2** (horse) recusar-se a avançar; **the cut of sb's ~** (fam) maneira, atitude.

jibe, gibe *n* zombaria, troça *f*; ♦ *vt* troçar de; ♦ *vi* estar de acordo com; **2** (= **gybe**) (boat) mudar de rota.

jiffy *n* (coll): **in a ~** num instante.

jiffy bag *n* envelope *m* acolchoado.

jig *n* (dance) jiga *f*; ♦ **(-gg-)** *vt/vi* dançar a jiga; **to ~ around/about** saltitar, saracotear; mover, mexer-se com rapidez.

jiggle *n* movimento curto e brusco; ♦ *vt* agitar, sacudir; **to ~ about/around** *vi* mexer-se/andar de um lado para o outro; andar aos saltinhos; **2** bambolear-se.

jigsaw *n* (= **~ puzzle**) puzzle, quebra-cabeças *m*; **2** (saw) serra *f* de vaivém.

Jihad *n* (REL) jiade *m*.

jilt *vt* abandonar, deixar, (BR) dar o fora em; **he ~ed his girlfriend** ele deixou a namorada.

jingle *n* (som) (bells, keys) tilintar *m*, tinido *m*; **2** (song verse) aliteração, rima *f*; ♦ *vi* (bells) tilintar; (coins, keys) retinir, tinir.

jingoism *n* jingoismo *m*.

jinx *n* (coll) (evil force, curse) praga *f*, maldição *f*, má-sorte *f*, mau olhado; (BR) caipora *f*.

jinxed *adj* enguiçado,-a, de, com má sorte.

jitter *n* grande agitação *f*; **~s** *npl* (coll): **to get the ~s** ficar muito nervoso,-a.

jittery *adj* nervosa,-a.

jive *n* (dance) swing *m*; **2** (US: coll) (deceptive talk) tretas, mentiras *fpl*; ♦ *vi* dançar o swing; **2** (US) enganar, dizer mentiras.

Job *npr* (Bible) Job *m*.

job *n* trabalho, emprego *f*; **~ description** *n* descrição *f* do cargo; **~ hunting** *n* procura de emprego; **2** (task) tarefa *f*; (coll) (difficult task) **quite a ~/a hell of a ~** um trabalho dos diablos (fam); **3** (duty, responsibility) dever *m*, obrigação *f*; **it's your ~** é o seu dever; **4** (cosmetic) **she had a nose ~** ela fez uma plástica, ao nariz (BR no nariz); **5** (coll) (robbery, etc) trabalho *m*; **odd ~s** *npl* serviços *mpl* miúdos, biscates *mpl*; IDIOM **to make the best of a bad ~** fazer o melhor que se pode; fazer das tripas coração; **to fall asleep on the ~** dormir em serviço; **that's just the ~** é mesmo o que faltava.

jobber n (US) intermediário,-a; 2 (UK) (=**stockjobber**) corrector de Bolsa.

jobbing n adj (person) que trabalha de, por empreitada; à tarefa.

job centre, job center n centro de emprego.

job creation scheme n projeto de geração de emprego.

jobless adj desempregado.

joblot n (auction) lote m; 2 bugiganga f variada.

job-related adj (illness, problem) de foro professional.

job-sharing n partilha f de trabalho (duas pessoas dividindo um trabalho a tempo inteiro entre elas).

Joburg, Jo'burg npr (abbr for **Johannesburg**) (fam) Joanesburgo; **in** ~ em Joanesburgo.

jockey n jóquei m; ♦ vi: **to** ~ **for position** manobrar/trapacear para conseguir uma melhor posição f.

jockstrap n suspensório (BR, Angola) sunga f.

jocular adj jocoso,-a divertido,-a; alegre.

jodhpurs n calças fpl de montar, (BR) culote m de montar.

jog n (run) corrida f a meio trote, jogging; ♦ (-**gg**-) vt sacudir levemente; 2 (nudge) dar do cotovelo em, acotovelar, (BR) cutucar; 3 ~ **sb's memory** refrescar a memória de alguém; ♦ vi fazer jogging; andar a meio-trote; **to** ~ **along/jog on** (person, business) ir andando.

jogger n praticante m,f de jogging.

jogging n jogging m; meio-trote m.

join n junção f; ♦ vt (attach, glue, link) juntar, unir; 2 ~ **alguém/algo** juntar-se a, associar-se a, afiliar-se a; I ~**ed the party** eu juntei-me à festa 3 (meet) reunir-se, encontrar-se com; 4 (unite) ~ **in** (matrimony) unir em (matrimónio); 5 (talk, mission) participate (**in** em); 6 (work for) **she** ~**ed the firm** ela entrou para a companhia; ♦ vi (rivers) confluir; ♦ **to** ~ **forces** aliar esforços; **to** ~ **battle** travar combate; **to** ~ **up** vi (link, connect) unir-se; 2 (MIL) alistar-se; IDIOM ~ **the club** junte-se a nós; não é (fam: és) o único; ~ **hands** dar as mãos.

joiner n (CONSTR) marceneiro m.

joinery n marcenaria carpintaria f.

joint n (TEC) junta, união f; encaixe m; ~ **account** conta f conjunta; ~ **consent** (JUR) comum acordo; 2 (ANAT) articulação f; 3 (CULIN) (of meat) corte m pedaço m de carne; 4 (coll: disreputable place) espelunca; 5 (slang: cannabis cigarette) charro; ♦ adj comum, conjunto; combinado; misto; **by** ~ **agreement** por comum acordo.

jointed adj articulado,-a.

jointly adv junto, em comum; cole(c)tivamente; conjuntamente.

joint-stock company n sociedade f por a(c)ções, sociedade anónima.

joint venture n (ECON) joint venture.

joist n (CONSTR) trave f, viga f (de madeira).

jojoba (BOT) jojoba m.

joke n (funny story) piada, anedota; 2 (= **practical** ~) brincadeira f, (funny remark) gracejo m; **he can't take a** ~ ele não é para brincadeiras; **this is no** ~ isto é a sério; I **am not joking** estou a falar a sério; ♦ vi brincar; **to play a** ~ **on** (prank) pregar uma partida (BR: peça) em.

joker n (person) brincalhão,-lhona 2 (playing card) curinga m, jóquer m.

jolly adj alegre; divertido; ♦ adv (coll) (UK) muito, bastante; **this pudding is** ~ **good** este pudim é muito bom; **he is a** ~ **good fellow** ele é um tipo porreiro (fam); **you are** ~ **well going to do** (in anger; emphatic) tu vais mesmo fazer isso.

jolt n (jerk) solavanco m, sacudidela f; 2 (fright) susto; ♦ vt sacudir; ♦ vi (vehicle) andar aos solavancos.

Joneses npl (fig): **to keep up with the** ~ não ficar atrás dos outros.

Jordan npr Jordânia; **in** ~ na Jordânia.

joss stick n pau m de incenso, pau aromático.

jostle vt acotovelar, dar encontrões, empurrar (other passengers, pedestrians).

jostling n empurrão m; aos encontrões.

jot n ponto; **not one** ~ nem nada; I **don't care one/a** ~ estou-me nas tintas (fam); ♦ vt: **to** ~ **down** vt anotar, tomar nota.

jotter n bloco (de apontamentos); (EDUC) caderno.

jottings n apontamentos mpl; notas fpl (BR) recadinhos mpl.

journal n revista f especializada; jornal especializado; 2 diário.

journalese n (pej) gíria f jornalística, jornalês m.

journalism n jornalismo.

journalist n jornalista m,f.

journey n (long) viagem f; (short) traje(c)to; jornada f; **pleasant** ~! boa viagem!; ♦ vi viajar.

joust n (combat with lances) justa f, torneio m.

jovial adj jovial, alegre.

jowl n maxilla f, maxilar m; ~**s** n (of person) papada f; (of animals) papo m.

joy n alegria; **to jump for** ~ saltar de alegria.

joyful adj satisfeito,-a.

joyless adj infeliz, triste; (discussion) monótono,-a.

joyous adj alegre, feliz.

joyously adv alegremente.

joyride n passeio em transporte roubado.

joyrider n pessoa que viaja num carro (ou mota) roubado,-a.

joyriding n passeio m em carro roubado.

joystick n (in airplane) alavanca f de controlo; (COMP) joystick.

JP n (abbr for **Justice of the Peace**).

Jr, Jun., Junr (abbr for **junior**) Jr (júnior).

jubilant adj jubilante, exultante.

jubilation n júbilo m, regozijo m.

jubilee n jubileu m.

Judaism npr judaísmo.

judder n (of machines) vibração m.

judge n (JUR) juiz, árbitro,-iza; ♦ vt julgar; 2 sentenciar; 3 (estimate) considerar; **to** ~ **by/from** ... a julgar por ....

judgement n opinião f, parecer m; **in my** ~ no meu parecer; 2 decisão f; sentença f.

judicial adj judicial.

judiciary n magistratura, o poder judiciário.

judicious adj judicioso, prudente.

judo n judô m.

jug *n* jarro; *(earthenware/pot-bellied)* bilha *f.*

juggernaut *n* veículo longo, camião *m* TIR; *(BR)* jamanta; **2** força *f* destruidora.

juggle *vt* fazer malabarismos.

juggler *n* malabarista *m,f.*

jugular *n adj* jugular.

juice *n* sumo, *(BR)* suco *m.*

juicy *adj* suculento,-a.

jukebox *n* máquina de tocar música automática, juke box *m.*

July *npr* Julho/julho *m.*

jumble *n* miscelânia; **2** trapalhada *f,* confusão *f, (BR)* bagunça; **3** *(useless items)* tralha *f,* quinquilharia *f;* ◆ *vt* (= ~ **up**) baralhar; misturar *(papers, letters)* confundir *(ideias).*

jumble sale *n* venda de caridade de objectos usados.

jumbo *n (child's language)* elefante; ~ **(jet)** *n* avião *m* jumbo; **~-sized** *adj* gigantesco,-a.

jump *n (leap)* pulo, salto; **2** *(in horse-jumping)* obstáculo; **3** *(sudden increase)* salto; *(ECON)* subida em flecha, disparo *m;* **4** *(fig) (progress)* avanço *m;* **5** *(sudden movement due to surprise/fright)* sobressalto *m,* susto *m;* ◆ ~ **leads** *npl* cabos para ligar a bateria; **~-start** *vt (car)* empurrar para pegar; **~-suit** *n* fato-macaco, *(BR)* macacão; ◆ *vi* saltar, pular; aumentar; sobressaltar; ◆ *vt* pular, saltar; **to ~ the queue** furar a fila; ~ **at** *vt (chance, proposal)* aproveitar imediatamente; agarrar com as duas mãos; **to ~ down sb's throat** atirar-se verbalmente a alguém; ◆ **to ~ in** *(conversation)* intrometer-se; **2** entrar de um salto; **to ~ on sb** cair em cima de (alguém); criticar; **3** *(mount)* subir para *(bus, train);* ◆ **to ~ out** *(from bed, car)* saltar; *(from window)* saltar por; **to ~ up** levantar-se de um salto.

jumped-up *adj (pej) (clerk, petty officer)* pretensioso,-a.

jumper *n (garment)* suéter *m,f,* pulóver *m,* camisola de lã; **2** *(person)* saltador,-ora.

jumper cables *npl (US) (vehicle)* cabos *mpl* de reboque.

jumpy *n* nervoso.

junction *n (roads)* cruzamento *m; (motorway)* nó *m* rodoviário; *(BR)* trevo *m; (RAIL)* entroncamento *m.*

juncture *n* conjunctura *f.*

June *npr* Junho/junho *m.*

jungle *n* selva, bush; floresta; **2** *(fig) (overgrown garden)* jungle.

junior *n* jovem; ◆ *adj* mais novo; **2** juvenil; **3** subalterno; **4** *(competition)* de juniors; **Henry Goldsmith** ~ Henry Goldsmith Filho; ~ **minister** *n* ministro-adjunto; ~ **partner** *n* sócio *m* minoritário; ~ **school** *n* escola *f* primária.

juniper *n* (BOT) zimbro *m,* junípero *m.*

junk *n (unwanted things)* ferro *m* velho *m;* **2** *(second hand)* velharias *fpl;* **2** *(rubbish)* traste *m;* lixo; **3** *(NAUT)* junco; ◆ ~ **bond** *n* obrigação de alto rendimento e risco; ~ **food** *n* comida *f* de plástico.

junkie *n (drugs)* drogado,-a; viciado,-a *m,f.*

junk shop *n (of second hand furniture etc)* loja de velharias; *(cheap quality items)* loja *f* de ferro velho.

junkyard *n (place)* sucata *f;* ferro velho *m.*

jurisdiction *n* jurisdição *f,* alçada *f.*

jurisprudence *n* jurisprudência.

jurist *n* jurista *m,f.*

juror *n* jurado,-a.

jury *n* júri *m,* jurados *mpl;* ~ **box** *n* bancada *f* do júri; ~ **service** *n (UK)* **to do** ~ fazer parte dum júri.

just *npl: (impartial, fair)* **the** ~ os justos *mpl;* **the sleep of the** ~ o sono dos justos; ◆ *adj (impartial, fair)* justo,-a; ◆ *adv* exa(c)tamente; ~ **right** exa(c)to, perfeito; **2** *(only)* apenas, somente, só; ~ **milk** só leite; **3** *(very recently)* acabar de; **I've** ~ **seen her** acabo de vê-la; **4** *(approx)* ~ **about** mais ou menos; **5** ~ **after** (um) pouco depois; *(place)* logo a seguir; *(barely)* mal; **I could** ~ **control myself** eu mal me podia controlar; **6** ~ **as** *(in comparison)* tal como, tão bem como; **7** ~ **as well that ...!** ainda bem que ...!; **8** *(that very moment)* ~ **as he was about to sit** no momento em que ele ia sentar-se; **9** ~ **now** agora mesmo; **that's** ~ **what I want** é precisamente o que eu quero; **he** ~ **missed it** ele falhou por pouco; ◆ *conj* ~ **as** assim que; **IDIOM** ~ **as well!** tanto melhor!; ~ **so** exa(c)tamente.

justice *n* justiça *m;* **to do o.s.** ~ desempenhar-se bem; **to do** ~ **to sb** fazer justiça a alguém; **to do** ~ **to sth** apreciar algo; **J~ of the Peace** (**JP**) *npr* juiz/ juiza *m,f* de Paz.

justifiable *adj* justificável; ~ **homicide** *n* homicídio *m* em legítima defesa.

justifiably *adv* justificadamente.

justification *n* justificação *f;* **2** *(COMP)* **right-hand** ~ alinhamento *m* justificado à direita.

justified *adj* justificado,-a; **to be** ~ **in doing** ter razões para fazer.

justify *vt* justificar.

justly *adv* justamente, imparcialmente; **2** *(right)* com razão.

justness *n* justiça, justeza.

jut (-tt-) *vi* (= ~ **out**) proje(c)tar-se; **2** salientar-se (**over** sobre); **3** *(brow, chin)* sobressair; fazer ressalto.

jute *n* juta *f;* ~ **yam** *n* fio *n* de juta.

juvenile *n* jovem *m,f; (JUR)* menor; ◆ *adj (person)* juvenil; **2** *(childish)* infantil; **3** *(joke)* pueril; ~ **court** *n* tribunal *m* de menores.

juxtapose *vt* justapor (**sth with sth** algo com algo).

juxtaposed *adj* justaposto.

juxtaposition *n* justaposição *f.*

K

K, k *n (letter)* K, k; **2** *(symbol for* **kilo**); **3** *(UK money)* *(abbr for* **thousand**) **the project comes to £200k** o proje(c)to custará 200 mil libras.

Kabul *npr* Cabul; **in** ~ em Cabul.

kaddish *n* oração *f* fúnebre dos judeus.

kaftan *n (garment)* cafetã *m*.

kale *(also:* **kail)** *n* couve *f* (semelhante à 'couve portuguesa', mas as folhas são encaracoladas).

kaleidoscope *n* caleidoscópio.

Kaleidoscopic *adj* caleidoscópico,-a.

Kampochean *npr adj* cambojano,-a.

Kampuchea *npr (Cambodia)* Camboja *f*; **in** ~ no Camboja.

kangaroo *n* canguru *m*; ~ **court** *n (pej)* tribunal *m* popular, improvisado *(fam) (often set up by prisoners or strikers)*.

kaolin *n (MED)* caulino *m*.

kapok *n (silky fibre from a tree used for stuffing pillows)* sumaúma *f*, capota *f*.

kaput *adj (fam) (ruined, broken)* arruinado,-a, acabado,-a; ◆ ~! pronto, é o fim!

karaoke *n* karaoke.

karat *n (US)* quilate *m*.

karate *n* karaté *(BR:* -ê).

karma *n* carma *m,f*.

Kashmir *npr* Cashemira *f*; **in** ~ na Cashemira.

kayak *n (canoe)* caiaque *m*.

Kazakhstan *npr* Cazaquistão *m*; **in** ~ no Casaquistão.

KB, Kb *(abbr for* **kilobyte(s))** *n (COMP)* KB.

KBE *(abbr for* **Knight Commander of the Order of the British Empire)** Comendador da Ordem do Império Britânico.

KC *(abbr for* **King's Counsel)** advogado da coroa na Grã Bretanha.

Kcal *(abbr for* **kilocalorie)** quilo-calorias, kcal.

kebab *n (CULIN) (Eastern dish)* espetada de carne picante.

kedgeree *n (CULIN)* prato britânico feito com arroz, peixe e ovos cozidos, vindo originariamente da India.

keel *n (NAUT)* quilha *f*; **on an even** ~ *(fig)* em equilíbrio; ~ **over** *vi* virar de pernas para o ar, emborcar; *(person)* ir-se abaixo, desmaiar; *(tree)* cair, desabar.

keelhauling *n* castigo; fazendo passar um marinheiro por debaixo da quilha.

keen *adj (eager)* entusiasmado,-a, interessado,-a, apaixonado,-a; **to be** ~ **on** ser entusiasta por *(sth* algo); **she is not that** ~ **on golf** ela não gosta muito de golfe; **2** *(intellectually acute)* vivo,-a,

perspicaz; **to have a** ~ **eye for sth** *(coll)* ter bom olho para algo; **3** *(sharp) (blade)* afiado,-a; **4** *(strong, intense)* ~ **appetite** apetite *m* devorador; ~ **competition** competição *f* renhida.

keenly *adv* entusiasmadamente.

keenness *n* entusiasmo *m*, interesse *m*; **2** *(intensity)* intensidade *f*; **3** *(sharpness)* perspicácia *f*.

keep *n* torre *f* de menagem; **2** *(provide for the upkeep)* sustento *m*; **to earn one's** ~ ganhar o seu sustento; ◆ *(pt, pp* **kept)** *vt (retain)* reter, ficar com; **2** *(put away)* guardar, ficar com; ~ **this key in a safe place** guarda esta chave num lugar seguro; **3** ter; **he** ~**s good health** ele tem boa saúde; **4** manter; **she** ~**s her house clean** ela mantém a casa limpa; **5** *(bring up, maintain)* ficar com; **she didn't want to** ~ **me** ela não quis ficar comigo; **6** cumprir; **he** ~**s his word** ele cumpre a sua palavra; **7** criar; **they** ~ **rabbits and chicken** eles criam coelhos e galinhas; **8** ficar; **this will** ~ **till later** isto fica para mais tarde; **9** atrasar; **what kept you?** porque estás atrasado?, porque me fizeste esperar?; ◆ *vi* conservar-se, continuar; **to** ~ **doing** continuar a fazer; **to** ~ **sb from sth** privar alguém de algo; **to** ~ **sth from happening** impedir que alguma coisa aconteça; **to** ~ **sb happy** fazer alguém feliz; **to** ~ **sth to o.s.** guardar algo para si mesmo; **to** ~ **sth (back) from sb** ocultar algo de alguém; **to** ~ **a secret** guardar um segredo; ◆ *vt:* **to** ~ **at it** *(work hard)* esforçar-se, empenhar-se; **to** ~ **away/off from** *vt (stay away)* afastar-se de; **to** ~ **back** *vt* conter, reprimir; **to** ~ **down** *vt (stop from increasing)* limitar; controlar; **to** ~ **in** reter; **2** conter *(emotions)*; **to** ~ **on** *vi* persistir, continuar; **to** ~ **off** *vt* afastar-se; ~ **off my land** saia da minha propriedade; **to** ~ **out** *vi* ficar/deixar de fora; ~ **out of the conversation** não te metas na conversa; '~ **out**' 'entrada proibida'; **to** ~ **up** *vt* mantêr; ◆ *vi* acompanhar; **to** ~ **up with** acompanhar; manter-se ao nível de; **2** *(progress)* **he** ~**s up with the technology** ele mantém-se informado sobre tecnologia.

keeper *n (gen)* guarda *m*; **2** *(of zoo)* zelador,-ora, guarda *m,f*; **3** *(in charge of someone)* guardião,-iã.

keep fit *n* ginástica *f*; ginástica *f* de manutenção.

keeping *n (care)* cuidado, **in sb's** ~**/in the** ~ **of sb** ao,-aos cuidado/s de alguém; **in** ~ **with sth** *prep (rules, tradition)* de acordo com, conforme; **out of** ~ **with** em desacordo com.

keepsake *n* lembrança *f*, recordação *f*, souvenir *m*.

keg *n* barrilete *m*, barril *m* pequeno; *(BR–South)* barrilote *m*; ~ **beer** *n* cerveja *f* de barril.

kelp *n* alga *f* marinha, barrilha *f*.

Ken *n* perceção; **in your** ~ na sua compreensão.

kennel *n* casota do cão/do cachorro; ~**s** canil *m*.

Kenya *npr* Quénia, *(BR)* Quênia; **in** ~ no Quénia.

Kenyan *npr adj* queniano,-a.

kept *(pt, pp of* **keep) he** ~ **me waiting** ele fez-me esperar.

kerb *(UK)* **curb** *(US)* *n* berma do passeio, *(BR)* meio-fio; ~ **crawler** *(UK)* motorista que guia vagarosamente e rente ao passeio, buscando prostitutas.

kerfuffle *n* *(UK)* *(fam)* *(commotion)* escarcéu *m*.

kernel *n* *(of melon, pumpkin etc)* pevide *f*; **2** *(fruit stone)* caroço *m*; **3** *(grain)* grão *m*; *(of bread)* miolo; **4** *(of pine)* pinhão *(pl:* pinhões); **5** *(of nut)* amêndoa *f*; **6** *(central part)* cerne, núcleo *m*; **a ~ of truth** um cerne, fundo *m* de verdade.

kerning *m* espaçamento *m*.

kerosene *n* querosene *m*.

kestrel *n* *(falcon)* francelho *m*; mioto *m*.

ketchup *n* molho *m* de tomate condimentado; ketchup *m*.

kettle *n* chaleira *f*.

kettledrum *n* *(MUS)* timbale *m*.

key *n* chave *f*; **under lock and ~** a sete chaves; **2** *(MUS)* clave *f*; **3** *(of computer, piano)* tecla; **4** *(fig)* solução; **5** *(clue to exercises/quiz)* chave; **6** *(on map)* legenda *f*; ♦ *adj* principal, chave ~ **issue** questão-chave *f*; ♦ **to ~ in** *vt* digitar.

keyboard *(COMP)* *n* teclado *m*; *n* **~boards** *npl* *(MUS)* sintetizador *m*.

keyboarder *n* digitador,-a; operador,-ora de texto.

keyed up *adj* *(person – excited)* nervoso,-a, excitado,-a, tenso,-a.

keyhole *n* buraco da fechadura; ~ **journalism** *n* jornalismo *m* sensacional.

keynote *n* *(MUS)* tónica *(BR:* tô-) dominante; ~ **speech** *n* *(POL)* discurso *m* programático.

keyring *n* chaveiro *m*, porta-chaves.

keystone *n* pedra *f* angular.

kg *(abbr for* **kilogram(s))** quilograma.

khaki *n* *(colour)* cor de cáqui; ♦ *adj* *(material)* cáqui.

kibbutz *n* kibutz *m*.

kick *n* pontapé *m*, patada *f*; **to ~ sb** dar um pontapé em alguém; *(of horse, donkey; firearm)* coice *m*; **2** *(SPORT)* chuto, chute *m*; **3** *(swimmer)* batimento *m* dos pés; **4** *(fig)* *(excitement)* **she does it for ~s** ela faz isso para se divertir; **5** *(of drink)* efeito *m* estimulante; **6** *(coll)* *(zest)* dinamismo *m*, energia *f*; ♦ *vt/vi* dar coices; dar coices; **2** *(SPORT)* chutar; **3** *(of gun)* recuar ao disparar, dar coice; **to ~ o.s.** *(fig)* **I could have ~ed myself for (say/do)** eu mordi-me de raiva por, devia bater-me por (dizer, fazer); ♦ **to ~ around/about** *(coll)* andar a vaguear; **2** *(treat badly–person, animal)* maltratar; **to ~ against** resistir a; **to ~ down** *vt* derrubar a pontapé; **a ~ in the pants** *(slang)* repreenda *f*; **to ~ in (sb's teeth/face)** *(slang)* partir as ventas a alguém *(cal)*; **to ~ off** *vi* *(SPORT)* dar o pontapé inicial, de saída; **~off** *n* *(SPORT)* pontapé *m* de saída, pontapé inicial; **to ~ sb out** *vt* despedir alguém; pôr alguém na rua; **~-start** *n* *(motorbike)* arranque; ♦ *vt* fazer arrancar com o pé; **2** *(fig)* arrancar, começar; relançar; **3** dar um impulso a algo; **to ~ up a fuss/a row** *(fam)* armar zaragata, fazer um escarcéu.

kid *n* *(coll)* criança *m,f*; garoto,-a, miúdo,-a; **my ~ sister** minha irmã mais nova; **2** *(young goat)* cabrito; **3** *(goatskin)* pelica; ♦ *(-dd-)* *vt* *(fam)* *(tease)* **to ~ sb** arreliar alguém, caçoar; *(playfully)* brincar; **I was just ~ding you** estava apenas a brincar contigo; **2** *vt* *(delude)* enganar, *(BR)*

embromar *(fam)* **to ~ o.s.** iludir-se; **to ~ sb into believing that** fazer crer a alguém que.

kid glove *n* luva *f* de pelica; **kid gloves** *npl*: **to treat/ handle sb with ~** tratar alguém com muito ta(c)to.

kidnap *vt* raptar, sequestrar.

kidnapper *n* raptor, sequestrador,-ora.

kidnapping *n* rapto, sequestro.

kidney *n* *(ANAT)* rim *m*; ~ **bean** *npl* feijão *m* vermelho *(BR)* feijão roxo; ~ **machine** *n* rim artificial; **to be on a ~ machine** fazer hemodiálise; ~ **stone** *n* cálculo *m* renal.

kif *(kaif, keef)* *n* condição eufórica produzida por marijuana ou outra droga.

kill *n* a(c)to *m* de matar; **2** *(in hunting)* matança; **3** *(prey)* presa *f*; ♦ *vt* matar; assassinar; **he was ~ed in action** ele foi morto na batalha, em combate; **2** *(fig)* *(hurt)* **my feet are ~ing me** estão a doer-me os pés; **3** *(end)* acabar com *(rumour)*; **4** *(JOURN)* suprimir; fazer malograr *(proposal)*; *(delete)* cancelar *(paragraph, etc)*; **5** *(Bill, project)* derrotar; **6** *(fig)* *(attractive effect)* **she was dressed to ~** *(fig)* ela estava vestida p'ra matar; **to ~ time** passar o tempo, esperar; **to ~ off (sth), to ~ sth off** *vt* destruir, eliminar; ♦ *vr* *(suicide)* matar-se; **2** *(fig)* *(of exhaustion)* cansar-se; IDIOM **to ~ two birds with one stone** matar dois coelhos de uma cajadada.

killer *n* assassino,-a; **2** ~ **whale** *n* *(ZOOL)* orca *f*.

killing *n* assassinato; matança; ♦ *adj* cansado,-a, fatigante; **2** **(at) a ~ pace** a um ritmo, passo fatigante; **3** *(fam)* *(very funny)* hilariante; IDIOM **to make a ~** *(COMM)* fazer um bom negócio; fazer um negócio da China.

killjoy *n* desmancha-prazeres *m,f*, *(BR)* estraga-prazeres *m,f*.

kiln *n* forno *m*, fornalha *f*.

kilo *n* quilo *m*.

kilobyte *n* *(COMP)* *(1024 bytes)* quilobyte *m*.

kilogram(me) *n* quilograma *m*.

kilohertz *n* quilohertz *m*.

kilometre *(US)* **kilometre** *n* quilómetro *(BR:* -lô-).

kiloton *n* mil toneladas.

kilowatt *n* quilovátio *m* *(EP)*, quilowatt *(BR)* quilowatt.

kilowatt-hour *n* quilovátio-hora *m*.

kilt *n* saiote *m* escocês (usado por homens e mulheres).

kimono *n* quimono.

kin *n* parente(s) *m*; **next of ~** parente(s) mais próximo(s).

kind *n* espécie *f*, classe *f*; género *(BR:* gê-); tipo; **to pay in ~** *(COMM)* pagar em géneros *(BR:* gê-); **a ~ of** uma espécie de; ~ **of** de certo modo; mais ou menos; **of a ~** da mesma espécie, do mesmo tipo; **nothing of the ~** nada disso; **they are two of a ~** os dois são muito semelhantes; ♦ *(-ier, -iest)* *adj* generoso,-a, bom,boa, bondoso,-a (**to** para, para com); **2** *(nice, helpful)* amável; **you are very ~** o senhor/a senhora é muito amável.

kindergarten *n* jardim *m* infantil, *(BR)* de infância.

kind-hearted *adj* de bom coração, bondoso.

kindle *vt* acender, pôr fogo a, atiçar; **2** *(fig) (idea)* incentivar; **3** *(passion)* inflamar, atiçar; **4** *(memories)* reavivar.

kindling *n (firewood)* gravetos *mpl*, cavacos *mpl*.

kindly (**-ier, -est**) *adj* bondoso,-a; **2** gentil; amável; **3** *(mild)* agradável *(climate)*; ♦ *adv* bondosamente, amavelmente; **would you ~ ...** fazia o favor de ...; ♦ **to look ~ on** ver com bons olhos, com tolerância, aprovar; **not to take ~ to** não gostar de.

kindness *n* bondade *f*; amabilidade *f*.

kindred *n* afinidade *f*, parentesco *m*; ♦ *adj (similar)* afim; **~ spirit** alma *f* gémea *(BR:* gê-*)*.

king *n* rei *m*; **~ cobra** *n (ZOOL)* cobra-capelo.

kingdom *n* reino; **the plant/animal ~** o reino vegetal/ animal; IDIOM **send sb till ~ come** *(fam)* mandar alguém para os anjinhos.

kingeagle *(ZOOL)* águia *f* real.

kingfisher *n* pica-peixe *m*, martim-pescador; **~ blue** *n (colour)* azul-marinho.

kingly *adj* real, digno de rei.

kingpin *n (TECH)* pino-mestre *m*; cavilha mestra; pivô; **2** *(most important person in an organization)* manda-chuva *m*.

kingsize(d) *adj* tamanho gigante; *(cigarette)* extra longo.

kinetic *adj* cinético.

kinetics *n* cinética *f*.

kink *n (rope, hose)* dobra *f*, nó *m*; **the pipe has a ~** o tubo está torcido; **2** *(hair)* jeitos; **your hair has a ~** o teu cabelo tem jeitos; **3** *(fig)* mania.

kinky (-ier, -iest) *adj (behaviour, idea)* excêntrico,-a, esquisito,-a; **2** *(pej) (sexual)* pervertido,-a; **3** *(hair)* um pouco encaracolado; com jeitos.

kinship *n (blood relationship)* parentesco *m*; **2** *(fig) (empathy)* afinidade *f* (**with** com).

kiosk *n* quiosque *m*; **2** *(TEL)* cabine *f* telefónica.

kip *n (nap)* sesta *f*, soneca *f*; **to get some ~** arranjar um lugar para dormir; ♦ (**-pp-**) *vi (also: ~ down)* dormitar.

kipper *n* arenque *m* fumado.

kiss *n* beijo; **big/little ~** *n (fam)* beijão *m*, beijoca *f*/ beijinho *m*; **2** *(in letter)* **give a ~ to your children for me** dê beijinhos de mim aos seus meninos; **~ of life** respiração *f* boca-a-boca; **~ of death** *n* golpe *m* de misericórdia; **to blow a ~** atirar um beijo; **to snatch a ~** roubar um beijo; ♦ *vt* beijar; **to ~ (each other)** beijar-se; *(fig)* **to ~ one's job goodbye** dizer adeus ao emprego; **to ~ and make up** fazer as pazes.

kit *n (gen)* apetrechos *mpl*; equipamento; **2** *(of tools)* caixa de ferramentas; **3** *(small box)* estojo; **4** kit *m* para montar; ♦ **to ~ out/up** *vt* equipar (**with/in** com).

kitchen *n* cozinha; **~ garden** *n* quintal *m*, pequena horta; **~ sink** *n* lava-louças; *(BR)* pia (de cozinha); **~ware** *n* bateria, utensílios de cozinha.

kite *n (bird)* milhafre *m*; **2** *(toy)* papagaio *m* de papel *(BR)* pipa *f*.

kith and kin *n* amigos *mpl* e parentes *mpl*.

kitten *n* gatinho,-a.

kitty *n (shared fund)* fundo comum; **2** *(for bills, drinks)* vaquinha; **3** *(cat) (affectionately)* gatinho,-a, tareco,-a *(pop)*.

kiwi *n (bird)* quivi *m*; **2** *(fruit)* quivi *m*, kiwi *m*; **3** *(fam) (neozealander)* neozelandês,-esa.

klaxon *n* buzina *f* elé(c)trica.

kleenex® *n* lenço de papel.

kleptomaniac *n* cleptomaníaco,-a.

km *(abbr for* **kilometre(s))** quilómetro *(BR:* -lô-*)*.

km/hour *(abbr for* **kilometres per hour)** km/h.

knack *n (flair)* jeito *m*, queda *f*, habilidade *f*; **the ~ of** o dom de; **to have the ~ for** ter jeito para; **get the ~** apanhar o jeito.

knacker *n* pessoa que compra cavalos para os abater.

knackered *adj (coll)* estafado.

knapsack *n* mochila.

knave *n (jack-in cards)* valete *m*; **2** *(rogue)* malandro,-a, velhaco,-a.

knavery *(pl:* **-ies)** *n* velhacaria *f*.

knead *vt (CULIN)* amassar *(dough)*; **2** *(masseur)* massajar, *(BR)* massagear.

knee *n* joelho; **~cap** *n (ANAT)* rótula *f* do Joelhos; **~-deep** *adj (mud, water)* até aos joelhos; **to be on one's ~s** estar de joelhos; **to bring sb down to their ~s** humilhar alguém.

knee-breeches *n* Bermudas.

knee-high *n (stocking, sock)* até ao joelho; ♦ *adj* da altura/à altura dos joelhos; **2** *(person)* pequeno,-a.

knee-jerk reaction reacção *f* automática, instintiva.

kneel *(pt, pp* **knelt)** *vi (also:* **~ down)** ajoelhar-se; pôr-se de joelhos.

kneepad *n (cover, protection)* joelheira *f*.

knees-up *n (fam)* festa *f* barulhenta, farra *f*.

knell *n* dobre *m* de finados; **to toll the ~** dobrar a finados; ♦ *vt/vi* dobrar os sinos.

knelt *(pt, pp of* **kneel)** **I ~ before the altar** ajoelhei-me perante o altar.

knew *(pt of* **know)** **I ~ all along he was liying** eu sabia que ele estava a mentir/mentindo.

knickerbockers *npl* calças *f* à golfe.

knickers *npl (fam) (ladies' underwear)* cuecas *fpl*, *(BR)* calcinha *fsg*; **don't get your ~ in a twist** *(coll) (get excited or angry)* não te exaltes.

knick-knack *n* bugiganga *f*, bibelô *m*.

knife *(pl:* **knives)** *n* faca; **to go under the ~** submeter-se a uma operação *f* cirúrgica; ♦ *vt* esfaquear (**sb** alguém); IDIOM **to have one's ~ in sb** *(fig)* ter rancor por alguém; **to twist the ~ in sb** agravar uma situação desagradável; mexer numa ferida; **knives are out (for sb)!** é guerra (para alguém)!

knife edge *n* gume *m* da faca, fio *m* da navalha; **2** *(fig) (situation)* tenso,-a; **to be on a ~** estar numa situação crítica; estar à beira do abismo.

knifing *n* facada *f*; ataque *m* com uma faca.

knight *n* (título honorífico) cavaleiro *m*; **2** *(CHESS)* cavalo; ♦ **to ~ sb** armar alguém cavaleiro; ♦ **~ errant** *n* cavaleiro andante; **the K~s of the Round Table** *npl (UK)* os cavaleiros da Távola Redonda.

knighthood *n (UK)* ordem de cavaleiros; título, dignitade de cavaleiro; **to get a ~** ser condecorado, receber o título de cavaleiro.

knit (**knit** or **-ted**) *vt* tricotar, fazer malha; ♦ *vi* tricotar; **2** *(broken bones)* consolidar-se; **to ~ the eyebrows** franzir o sobrolho; **to ~ together** *(fig)* unir, juntar.

knitting *n* trabalho de tricô, malha; **~ machine** *n* máquina de tricotar; **~ pattern** *n* molde *m* de tricô; **~wear** *n* artigos de malha.

knives *(pl of* **knife***)*.

knob *n (of door)* maçaneta; *(of drawer)* puxador *m* redondo; *(of cane)* castão *m* de bengala; **2** *(rounded projection) (from a tree, etc)* protuberância *f*; **3** *(control button)* botão *m*; **4** *(fig)* **a ~ of butter** uma noz, porção *f* de manteiga.

knobbly, knobby *adj (tree)* nodoso,-a; *(knees)* ossudo,-a.

knock *n (blow)* pancada *f*, batimento *m*; **a ~ on the door** uma pancada na porta; **I hear a ~ on the door** estão a bater à porta; **2** *(fam) (setback)* revés, golpe *m*; **3** *(criticism)* crítica *f* severa; ♦ *vt* bater; **2** *(fig, coll)* criticar, denegrir *(person)*; **to ~ a hole in the wall** abrir/fazer um buraco na parede; ♦ **to ~ about/around the world** *vi* vaguear, viajar pelo mundo fora; passar tempo com (amigos); **2 to ~ sb about** dar pancada em alguém; **3 to ~ about with a (gang)** *(associate)* associar-se a um bando; **to ~ at/on the door** bater à porta; **to ~ back (drink)** beber de uma só vez; *(BR)* enxugar; **2** *(ball)* devolver; **3** *(slang)* rejeitar, recusar; acontecer algo desagradável/desconcertante a alguém; ♦ **~ down** *(cause to fall)* deitar por terra; **2** *(bring down)* derrubar *(door, building, etc)*; desmontar *(machinery)*; desmantelar; **3** *(to reduce price)* abater, fazer desconto; **4** *(run over sb)* atropelar alguém; **5** *(at an auction) (hammer down)* confirmar venda; **to ~ in a nail** pregar um prego; ♦ *vi (collide)* **~ into/against** colidir, esbarrar-se contra; ♦ **to ~ off** *vi (coll)* parar, largar o trabalho; **2** fazer cair; **3** *(coll) (steal)* fanar *(cal)*; **4** *(lower price)* baixar o preço; ♦ **to ~ sb out** *(boxing)* derrotar; *(from competition)* eliminar; *(make unconscious)* deixar inconsciente; deitar ao tapete *(opponent)*; **2** *(with drugs)* aturdir; **3** *(overwhelm)* maravilhar, espantar; ♦ **to ~ up** *vt (do sth hurriedly)* improvisar, fazer apressadamente; **2** *(tennis)* fazer o aquecimento batendo bolas; **3** *(SPORT)* totalizar (points); ♦ **to ~ sb up** *(UK: awaken)* acordar; **2** *(coll) (US)* engravidar; IDIOM **my knees were knocking** os meus joelhos tremiam de medo; **~ it off!**, basta!, acabe(m) com isso!

knockabout *n* (SPORT) *(US)* barco à vela; ♦ *adj* *(UK) (slapstick comedy)* burlesco,-a, de palhaçada; **~ farse** farsa de palhaçada.

knock-back *n (col)* recusa *f*; **2** *(prison jargon)* insucesso em obter liberdade condicional.

knockdown *adj* forte; **a ~ blow** uma pancada forte; **2** *(price)* de liquidação.

knocker *n (on door)* aldraba *f*; argola de porta, batente *f*; **2 ~s** *(fam)* a woman's breasts.

knocking *n (noise)* pancada *f*; **2** crítica *f*.

knock-kneed *adj* de pernas *fpl* tortas, cambaias.

knockout *n (boxing)* knock-out, K.O., *(BR)* nocaute; **2** *(sensational)* sucesso, espanto *m*; **to be a ~** *(fig) (person, event)* ser de arromba, ser de arrasar.

knoll *n* outeiro *m*.

knot *n* nó, laço; **2** *(NAUT)* milha nautical; **dead ~** nó cego; ♦ **(-tt-)** *vt/vi* dar/fazer nós, atar, dar um nó em; **to undo a ~** desfazer/desatar um nó.

knotted *adj* atado; emaranhado; **get ~!** *(UK coll)* vá passear!, vá à fava!

knotty **(-ier, iest)** *adj (full of knots)* nodoso; **2** *(fig) (problem)* difícil, bicudo,-a.

know *n:* **to be in the ~** estar bem inormado,-a sobre; ♦ **(*pt* knew,** *pp* **known)** *vt/vi* conhecer; *(have knowledge)* saber; **to ~ about** saber de, estar ao corrente; **2** *(skill)* saber, perceber; **he ~s about machines** ele sabe/percebe de máquinas; **as far as I know ...** que eu saiba ...; **to ~ by heart** saber de cor; **to let sb ~** informar, dar a conhecer; **well, what do you ~?** então, o que sabes?; **how should I know!** sei lá!; **2** *(be acquainted with)* **~ by sight** conhecer de vista; **to ~ one's place** não abusar de; **to ~ the ropes** conhecer por fora e por dentro; **to ~ one's place** *(fig)* não abusar de; ♦ *exc* **how should I ~!** sei lá!; **well, what do you ~!** *(ironically)* mas que surpresa!

know-all *(coll) n* sabichão, chona.

know-how *n* conhecimento *m*, experiência *f*.

knowing *adj* astucioso,-a; sagaz; **a ~ look** um olhar de cumplicidade, de entendimento.

knowingly *adv* com conhecimento, com um ar de entendido; **2** *(insult, action)* deliberadamente.

knowledge *n* conhecimento, saber *m*; sabedoria *f*; inteligência; entendimento; ciência; **to the best of my ~** tanto quanto eu sei, no meu fraco entendimento; **it has come to my ~ that** fiquei a saber que; **not to my ~** que eu saiba não.

knowledgeable *adj* entendido,-a, versado,-a (**about** em).

known *(pp of* **know***) adj* conhecido,-a; **he is well ~** ele é muito conhecido; **it is ~ that** sabe-se que.

know-nothing *n* pessoa ignorante.

knuckle *n* articulação *f* dos dedos; nó *m* dos dedos; **to crack one's ~s** fazer estalar os dedos; **2** *(on animal)* junta; **3** *(as meat)* pernil *m*; ♦ **to ~ down** *vi* concentrar-se (**to** em), dedicar-se (**to** a); **to ~ under** *vi* dar-se por vencido, ceder.

knucklebone *n* articulação dos dedos.

knuckle-duster *n (luta)* manopla.

knur (**knurr, knar**) *n* nó *m*, saliência *f* numa árvore.

knurled *adj* serrilhado,-a.

KO *(pl:* **KOs***) n (slang)* (knockout, knock out) K.O. *m*; *(BR)* nocaute *m*.

koala (bear) *n* coala *m*.

kodak® *n* máquina fotográfica *f*.

kodiak (bear) *n (a variety of the brown bear from Alaska)* urso *m* ártico *(ursus arctus)*.

kooky, kookie (-ier, iest) *adj* excêntrico,-a maluco,-a; *(coll)* nutcase.

Koran *npr* (REL) Corão *m*; **the ~** Alcorão *m*.

Koranic *adj* do Alcorão; corânico,-a.

Korea *npr* Coreia, *(BR)* Coréia.

Korean *npr adj* coreano,-a.

kowtow *vi (pej)* curvar a espinha, curvar-se perante outro; fazer salamaleques; **to ~ to sb** adular alguém; *(coll)* lamber as botas.

Krakow *npr* Cracow; **in ~** em Cracow.

krona *n* unidade monetária da Suécia.

króna *n* unidade monetária da Islândia.

krone *n* (unidad monetária da Dinamarca, Noruega) Coroa *f.*

krypton *n* cripton *m.*

Kuala Lumpur *npr* Cuala Lumpur; **in ~** em Cuala Lumpur.

kudos *n* prestígio *m,* glória *f;* admiração.

NOTE: '**Kudos**' é um substantivo singular.

kumquat *n (BOT)* fruto cítrico da China, kumquat *m.*

Kurd, Kurdish *npr adj* curdo,-a; **2** *(LING)* curdo.

Kurdistan *npr* Curdistão; **in ~** no Curdistão.

Kuwait *npr* Kuwait; **in ~** no Kuwait.

Kuwaiti *npr adj* kuwaitiano,-a.

L, l *n (letter)* L, l *m*; **2** *(abbr for* **litre** *(UK)* **liter** *(US))* l.

L *(abbr for* **lake)** lago *m*; **2** *(abbr for* **large)** G; **3** *(abbr for* **left)** esq.; **4** *(abbr for* **learner)** aprendiz *m,f*; **5** *(in combination)* **an L-shaped table** mesa em feitio de L; **6** *(Roman numeral for 50)* L.

LA *(abbr for* **Legislative Assembly)** Assembleia Legislativa *f*; **2** *(abbr for* **Los Angeles)**.

lab *n (abbr for* **laboratory)** *(fam)* laboratório *m*.

label *n* etiqueta *f*, rótulo *m*; marca *f*; ♦ *vt* etiquetar, rotular.

labia *(pl of* **labium)**; **labial** *adj* labial *m,f*.

labium *n (ANAT) (of mouth; of vulva)* lábio *m*; **2** *(of some insects)* saliência *f* bocal.

laboratory *n* laboratório *m*.

laborious *adj* laborioso,-a, trabalhoso,-a.

labour *(UK)* **labor** *(US)* *n* trabalho; **2** *(workforce)* mão-de-obra *f*; trabalhadores *mpl*; ~ **dispute** *n* conflito *m* entre o patronato e os trabalhadores; ~ **costs** *npl* custos *mpl* com o pessoal; **hard** ~ *n* trabalhos *mpl* forçados; ~ **of love** *n* trabalho por amor à arte; ~ **market** *n* mercado *m* de trabalho; **the L~ Party** *n (POL)* o Partido *m* Trabalhista; ~ **shortage** *n* falta *f* de mão d'obra; ~ **union** *n* sindicato de trabalhadores; **3** *(MED) (giving birth)* parto; **to go into** ~ entrar em trabalho de parto; ♦ *vt* insistir em; ♦ *vt* insistir em; **2** *(struggle)* esforçar-se, trabalhar no duro; **to** ~ **under an illusion** ser vítima de uma ilusão, estar enganado,-a; **3** *(problem)* lutar contra.

laboured *(UK)* **labored** *(US)* *adj (discurso)* elaborado,-a; **2** *(breathing)* difícil *m,f*.

labourer *n* operário,-a; trabalhador,-ora rural.

labouriously, laboriously *adv* diligentemente.

labour saving *adj (equipment)* que economiza trabalho; **2** *(device)* *n* electrodoméstico *m*.

labrador *n (dog)* labrador *m*; **L~** *npr (GEOG)* Labrador.

laburnum *n (BOT)* laburno *m*.

labyrinth *n* labirinto *m*.

lace *n (fabric and crochet)* renda *f*; **2** *(shoe)* cordão *m*; atacador *m (EP)*, cadarço *(BR)*; ♦ *vt* atar; amarrar; **coffee ~d with brandy** café *m* com aguardente, conhaque; ♦ ~ **up** *adj* de cordões; ♦ **to** ~ **up** *vi (shoes, etc)* apertar; ~-**making** *n* fabrico *m* de renda.

laceration *n (gen and MED)* laceração *f*.

lack *n* falta; escassez *f*; ♦ *vt* carecer de, ter falta de; **to be ~ing** faltar.

lackadaisical *adj (person, attitude)* indolente *m,f*.

lackey *n* lacaio *m*; *(pej)* pau-mandado *m (pl:* paus-mandados*)*.

lack-lustre *(UK)* **lack-luster** *(US)* *adj (person, style)* sem graça, sem brilho; *(fig)* insípido,-a.

laconic *n* lacónico,-a *(BR: -cô-)*.

lacquer *n* laca *f*, verniz *m*.

lactaction *m (MED, BIOL)* latação *f*.

lactose *n (CHEM)* lactose *f*.

lacy *adj* de renda, semelhante a renda.

lad *n* menino, rapaz *m*, moço *m*.

ladder *n* escadote *m*, *(BR)* escada-de-mão *f*; **2** *(in tights, stockings, knitting)* malha *f* caída, desfiada.

laden *adj* carregado **(with** de); **basket ~ with fruit** cesto carregado de fruta.

la-di-da, lah-di-dah *adj (fam) (pretensious)* pretensioso,-a, afe(c)tado,-a; ~ **person** *n (fam)* um,-a pedante *m,f*.

ladies *n (UK)* senhoras *fpl*; damas *fpl*; ~ **room** *(US) (in a private house)* casa *f* de banho, *(BR)* banheiro *m*; **2** *(addressing the public)* ~ **and gentlemen** minhas senhoras e meus senhores.

ladle *n* concha *f* (de sopa).

lady *n* senhora *f*; **2** *(by birth, honourable position)* dama; **young ~** menina; ~ **of the house** senhora, dona de casa; **~bird** *(UK)* **~bug** *(US)* *n (insect)* joaninha *f*; ~-**in-waiting** *n* dama *f* de companhia *(pl:* damas-de-companhia*)*; ~-**killer** *n* mulherengo *m*, Don Juan *m*; ~-**like** *adj (manners, behaviour)* elegante, refinada; como uma senhora.

lady's finger *n (BOT, CULIN) (okra)* kiabo *m*.

Ladyship *n (title)* Senhoria, Excelência; **Your/Her ~** Vossa/Sua Senhoria.

lag *n (time)* atraso *m*; **2** *(with police record)* **old ~** cadastrado,-a; ♦ **(-gg-)** *vi* (= ~ **behind)** atrasar-se, ficar para atrás; ♦ *vt* revestir com isolante térmico.

lager *n* cerveja *f* branca e leve.

lagging *n (cladding of pipes)* revestimento *m*.

lagoon *n* lagoa *f*.

laid *(pt, pp of* **lay)** **she ~ the table** ela pôs a mesa.

laid-back *adj* descontraído,-a.

lain *(pp of* **to lie)** **she had ~ in the chapel of rest before ...** ela tinha reposado, jazido na câmara-ardente antes de ...

lair *n* covil *m*, toca *f*.

laird *n (Scottish landowner)* fidalgo *m* rural, proprietário escocês.

lake *n* lago *m*.

lamb *n* cordeiro *m*; **2** *(CULIN)* borrego *m*, carne *f* de carneiro; ~ **chop** *n* costeleta *f* de carneiro; ~ **down** *vi (ewe)* parir; ~ **skin** *n* pele *f* de ovelha; ~**'s wool** lã *f* de ovelha.

lambast(e) *vt* bater, chicotear; **2** repreender, censurar severamente.

lame *adj* coxo,-a, manco,-a; **2** *(fig) (excuse, argument)* pouco convincente, fraco; ~ **duck** *n (fig) (ineffectual)* pessoa incompetente, incapaz; *(company, business)* fracasso *m*; **3** *(fig) (President – US)* pessoa eleita entre mandatos como interino, ou que não vai ser re-eleito.

lament *n (grief, regret)* lamento *m*; ♦ *vt* lamentar-se de.

lamentable *adj* lamentável.

lamentably *adv* lamentavelmente.
laminated *adj* laminado,-a; **2** *(wood)* contraplacado,-a; **3** *(card, book)* plastificado,-a.
lamp *n* lâmpada; **2** *(with lampshade)* candeeiro *m*; ~**post** *n* poste *m*; ~**shade** *n* abajur *m*.
lampoon *vt* satirizar.
lance *n* lança; ♦ *vt (MED)* lancetar.
lancet *n* lanceta *f*.
land *n (country, region)* terra *f*, país *m*; **native** ~ terra *f* natal; **dry** ~ terra fime; *(NAUT)* **ahoy** ~ *(sailors)* terra à vista!; **2** *(AGR) (soil)* solo *m*, terra *f*; **3** *(farmland)* terreno *m*; **this** ~ **is not arable** este terreno não é arável; **4** *(countryside)* campo *m*; ♦ *vt/vi (NAUT)* desembarcar *(person)* **(on** em); descarregar *(cargo)*; **2** *(ship)* acostar; **3** *(aircraft)* aterrar, *(BR)* aterrissar; **4** *(fig, fam) (get)* conseguir *(position, prize)*; **5** *(coll)* **to** ~ **sb in trouble** meter, pôr alguém em apuros; **6** *(coll) (give)* dar; ~ **sb a punch** dar um murro, soco em alguém; ~ **up** *vi* acabar com; **to** ~ **up in/at** ir parar em.
landed *adj* rural; ~ **gentry** fidalguia *f* do campo; proprietários de terra.
landfill *n* aterro *m*.
landing *n* desembarque *m*; **2** aterragem *f*; *(BR)* aterrissagem *f*; **3** *(staircase)* patamar *m*; ~ **gear** *n* trem *m* de aterragem, *(BR)* aterrissagem; ~ **stage** *n* cais *m* de desembarque; ~ **strip** *n* pista de aterragem *(BR:* aterrissagem).
landlady *n* senhoria; proprietária.
land-locked *adj* cercado de terra; **Bolivia is a** ~ **country** Bolívia é um país sem litorais, cercado de terras; **2** *(lake)* *n* lago *m* interior.
landlord *n* senhorio dono, proprietário *m*.
landmark *n (important feature)* ponto *m* de referência; **2** *(fig) (in history)* marco *m* divisório; **3** *(fig)* etapa *f* importante, decisiva.
landmine *n (MIL)* mina *f* terrestre.
landowner *n* proprietário,-a rural; *(of many lands)* latifundiário,-a.
Land Rover® *n* Land-Rover *m*; *(pop)* todo-o- terreno *m*.
landscape *n* paisagem *f*; ~ **gardener** *n* jardineiro,-a paisagista *m,f*; ♦ *vt* ajardinar; arranjar o jardim.
landslide *n (GEOL)* desmoronamento *m*, desabamento *m*; **2** *(fig: POL, DESP)* vitória *f* esmagadora; derrocada *f*.
landslip *n (GEOL)* *(Vd: landslide)*.
lane *n (rural)* azinhaga *f*; *(urban)* viela *f*, rua *f* estreita; **2** *(AUT)* via *f*; faixa *f* (de rodagem); **3** *(AER)* corredor *m*; *(NAUT)* rota *f*.
langoustine *n (shellfish)* lagostim *m*.
language *n* idioma *m*, língua *f*; **2** *(style of)* linguagem; **foul** ~ linguagem *f* indecente, grosseira; **we talk the same** ~ nós entendemo-nos muito bem.
languid *adj* lânguido,-a.
languish *vi (become languid)* elanguescer; **2** *(become weak)* debilitar-se, enfraquecer; **to** ~ **for sb** ansiar por alguém, ter saudades de alguém.
lank *adj* magro,-a; descarnado,-a; **2** *(hair)* liso e fino.
lanky *adj* alto,-a e magro,-a; *(fam)* magricela *m,f*.
lanolin *n* lanolina *f*.

lantern *n (torch)* lanterna *f*; **2 roof** ~ *(ARCH)* telhado-lanterna, lucerna, lucarna *f*; ~-**jawed** *adj (person)* de queixo saliente.
Laos *npr* Laos; **in** ~ em Laos.
Laotian *adj* laosiano,-a; *(LING)* laosiano.
lap *n (SPORT) (track)* volta; **2** percurso *m*, etapa *f*; **2** *(knees)* regaço *m*, colo *m*; **to sit in sb's** ~ sentar-se no colo de alguém; **3 in the** ~ **of luxury** no seio da riqueza; **in the** ~ **of gods** *(open to chance)* nas mãos dos deuses; **4** *(ondas)* marulhar *m*; ♦ **(-pp-)** *vt (animal)* lamber; **2** *(SPORT) (car, runner)* dar volta de avanço; ♦ *vi (water, waves)* marulhar **(against, at** contra); ♦ ~ **up** *vt* beber com sofreguidão; *(the plate)* lamber o prato; **2** *(fig) (compliments)* receber com júbilo, absorver, aceitar sem questão.
lapdog *n (dog)* cão *m* de luxo; **2** *(pej)* **he is her** ~ ele é o cachorro dela; ele faz tudo o que ela quer.
lapel *n (of the coat)* lapela *f*.
lapidate *vt* lapidar.
Lapland *npr* Lapónia; **in** ~ na Lapónia.
Lapp *n adj (person)* lapão,-ona; *(LING)* lapão *m*.
lapse *n (slip)* lapso *m*, falha *f*; **2** *(error)* engano *m*, deslize *m*; **3** *(of time)* intervalo *m*; ~ **of memory** esquecimento *m*; ♦ *vi (contract, passport)* caducar, expirar; **2** *(time)* passar, transcorrer; **3** adquirir; **to** ~ **into bad habits** cair em maus hábitos; **to** ~ **into silence** calar-se.
lapsed *adj (document)* caducado,-a; ~ **catholic** *n* um católico não praticante.
laptop *n* computador *m* portátil.
larceny *n* furto *m*, roubo *m*; **petty** ~ furto *m* simples.
larch *n* larício *m*.
lard *n* banha de porco.
larder *n (for food)* despensa *f*.
large *adj (big)* grande; *(intestine)* grosso; **2** *(substantial)* importante, grande; *(number of)* numeroso,-a; ♦ **at** ~ *adj* escaped, *(prisoner, animal)* em liberdade; ♦ *adv* em geral; **by and** ~ em geral.
largely *adv* em grande parte.
larger-than-life *adj (person, description)* exagerado,-a.
large-scale *adj* em grande escala.
largesse *(UK)* **largess** *(US) (generosity of spirit)* generosity.
lark *n (ZOOL)* cotovia; **2** *(fig)* brincadeira *f*; ♦ **to** ~ **about** *vi* divertir-se, brincar.
larva *(pl:* **larvae)** *n* larva *f*.
laryngitis *n* laringite *f*.
larynx *n* laringe *f*.
lascivious *adj* lascivo,-a.
laser *n* laser *m*; ~ **beam** *n* raio *m* laser; ~ **printer** *n* impressora *f* a laser.
lash *n (of whip)* chicote *m*; chicotada *f*; **he got ten lashes** ele recebeu dez chicotadas; **2** (= **eye** ~) pestana, cílio *f*; ♦ *vt* chicotear, açoitar; **2** *(wind, waves, rain)* fustigar; ♦ **to** ~ **out** *vi (money)* esbanjar (dinheiro); **to** ~ **out at/against sb** atacar alguém verbalmente; *(physically)* com violência.
lashing *n (beating)* chicotada *f*; **2** (also: *criticism*) *(fig)* tareia, coça *f*; **3** *(scolding)* repreensão *f*; **4** *(rope)*

corda *f* ♦ ~s *npl* *(fam)* *(lots of)* montes **(of** de); ~ **of chocolate on the ice-cream** montes de chocolate no gelado.

lass, lassie *n* *(fam)* *(Scots)* moça.

lassitude *n* lassidão *f.*

lasso *n* *(cowboy)* laço; ♦ **(-es, -ed)** *vt* laçar (algo com algo).

last *n* o último,-a; **he was the ~ (person) to arrive** ele foi o último a chegar; ♦ *adj* *(gen)* último,-a; ~ **but one** penúltimo,-a; **in the ~ five years** nos últimos cinco anos; **2** *(with dates)* passado,-a; ~ **month** no mês passado; ~ **night** ontem à noite; **3** *(unlikely)* **he was the ~ person I expected to see** ele era a última pessoa que eu esperava ver; **4** *(final)* **the ~ breath** o derradeiro suspiro; ♦ *adv* *(last position)* em último lugar, por último; **at ~!, at long ~!** finalmente!; **to the ~** até ao fim; ♦ *vi* durar; continuar; **to ~ out** *vt* *(be sufficient)* durar, chegar; **2** *(endure)* aguentar; IDIOM **that is the ~ straw!** *exc* *(yet another incident)* é a última gota (que transborda o copo); era só o que faltava!

last-ditch *adj* *(attempt)* desesperado,-a; derradeiro,-a.

lasting *adj* durável, duradouro.

lastly *adv* final mente, por fim.

last-minute *adj* *(booking, cancellation)* de última hora, tardio,-a.

last rites *npl* últimos sacramentos; extrema-unção *f.*

Last Supper *n* a Última Ceia *f.*

latch *n* *(fastening)* trinco *m*, fecho *m*; ♦ *vt/vi* fechar com o trinco; **2 to ~ on** *(coll)* compreender; *(realize)* dar-se conta de; ♦ ~ **on** *vt* *(coll)* *(grasp)* entender, chegar lá; **to ~ onto sth** agarrar-se a.

latchkey *n* chave *f* do trinco, chave da porta da rua; ♦ *adj* *(child)* que fica sozinho em casa.

late **(later, latest)** *adj* *(behind time)* atrasado,-a, tarde; **I am ~** estou atrasado,-a; **it was already ~** já era tarde; **her ~ present** um presente tardio; ~ **developer** *n* *(child)* ser de desenvolvimento lento; **2** *(at the end of day, etc)* tardio *m*, avançado *m*, fim *m*, final *m*; **I went to bed ~** deitei-me tarde; ~ **in the Spring** no fim da Primavera; **at this ~ hour** a esta hora tardia; ~ **August** nos finais de Agosto; **3** *(age)* **she is in her ~ 60s** ela está nos seus sessenta avançados; deve estar perto dos sessenta anos; **3** *(dead)* falecido; **the ~ Mr Smith** o falecido, defunto Senhor Smith; **4** *(recent)* **I heard the ~/latest news** ouvi as últimas notícias; ♦ *adv* tarde; atrasado,-a; **of ~** recentemente.

latecomer *n* atrasado,-a, retardatário,-a.

lately *adv* ultimamente, recentemente.

lateness *n* atraso *m*; demora *f.*

late-night *adj* no(c)turno,-a; da noite; ~ **party** *n* festa *f* até altas horas da noite; ~ **shopping on Thursdays** as lojas estão abertas até tarde às quintas-feiras.

latent *adj* latente *m,f.*

later *(comp of* **late)** *adj* posterior; mais recente; ♦ ~ **on** *adv* mais tarde, depois; **see you ~!** até logo!

lateral *adj* lateral.

laterally *adv* lateralmente.

latest *(superl of* **late)** *adj* último,-a; **at the ~** o mais tardar.

lath *n* ripa *f*; fasquia *f.*

lathe *n* torno *m* mecânico.

lather *n* *(of soap)* espuma (de sabão); ♦ *vt* ensaboar; ♦ *vi* fazer espuma.

Latin *n* latim *m*; ♦ *adj* latino; ~ **America** *n* América Latina; **in ~ America** na América Latina; ~ **American** *n adj* latino-americano,-a.

latitude *n* *(GEOG)* latitude *f.*

latrine *n* *(MIL)* latrina *f*

latter *n*: **the ~** o último, este; ♦ *adj* *(second)* segundo,-a; **the former manager and the ~** o primeiro gerente e o segundo; ~-**day** contemporâneo,-a.

latterly *adv* recentemente.

lattice *n* *(for plants, fence)* treliça *f*; **2** *(screen for windows)* gelosia *f.*

latticework *n* entrançado,-a.

Latvia *npr* Letónia; **in ~** na Letónia.

Latvian *n adj* letão,-ona.

laudable *adj* louvável.

laugh *n* riso *m*; risada *f*; *(loud laughter)* gargalhada *f*; **to do/say sth for a ~** fazer/dizer algo por brincadeira; ♦ *vi* rir; dar gargalhadas; **she ~ed like mad** ela riu-se às gargalhadas; ♦ **to ~ at sb** *vt* *(derisively)* troçar de; rir-se de (alguém); **to ~ off** *vt* rir-se de; **to ~ one's head off** rebentar de riso; IDIOM **he who laughs last, laughs longest** ri melhor quem ri por último; ~ **all the way to the bank** *(fam)* *(pleased to make a lot of of money)* rindo a caminho do banco; **don't make me ~** *(in disbelief, irony)* não acredito por um momento; **to ~ up one's sleeve** *(secretly)* rir-se divertido, sem ninguém ver.

laughable *adj* risível *m,f*, ridículo,-a.

laughing *adj* *(person)* risonho,-a; **it is not a ~ matter** isso não é p'ra rir; ~ **gas** *n* gás *m* hilariante.

laughingly *adv* a rir, rindo.

laughing stock *n* motivo *m* de riso, de chacota *f*; **he is the ~ of the club** ele é o alvo de chacota no clube.

laughter *n* riso *m*; risada *f*; risos, *mpl*; **2** *(of mirth)* risota *f*; **3** *(of scorn)* chacota *f* de troça.

launch *n* *(NAUT)* lancha *f*; *(for pleasure)* barco *m* de recreio; **2** *(setting in motion)* lançamento *m*; *(initiation)* início *m*, inauguração *f*; ♦ *vt* *(gen)* lançar; **2** *(initiate)* iniciar; ♦ *(boat, rocket, new product)* lançar; **2** *(start)* iniciar; **to ~ into/forth** lançar-se a; *(work)* entregar-se a; **to ~ at sth/sb** *(attack)* lançar-se a algo/alguém.

launching *n* lançamento *m.*

launching pad, launch pad *n* rampa *f*/plataforma de lançamento.

launder *vt* lavar e passar (a ferro); **2** *(fam)* *(money)* branquear.

launderette *(UK)* **laundromat** *(US)* *n* lavandaria automática, *(BR)* lavanderia automatizada.

laundering *n* lavagem *f*; *(money)* branqueamento *m.*

laundry *n* lavandaria *f*, *(BR)* lavanderia *f*; roupa para lavar; **to do the ~** lavar a roupa.

laureate *adj* laureado,-a.

laurel *n* *(BOT)* *(bay)* louro *m*; ~ **tree** loureiro *m.*

laurels *npl*: **to rest on one's ~** descansar à sombra dos louros conquistados; ~ **wreath** *n* coroa *f* de louros.

lava *n* lava *f*.

lavatory (*pl:* **ies**) *n* (*in the house*) casa *f*, quarto *m* de banho; (*público*) lavabo, toalete *m*, WC *m*; (*BR*) banheiro, toalete *m*; ~ **bowl** *n* sanita *f*; (*BR*) vaso *m* sanitário; ~ **paper** (**toilet paper**) papel *m* higiénico.

lavender *n* alfazema *f*, (*BR*) lavanda *f*.

lavish *adj* sumptuoso,-a, suntuoso,-a; **2** ~ **with** generoso,-a com; **to live in** ~ **style** viver à grande; **to be** ~ **with praises** ser pródigo em; ♦ *vt* **to** ~ **on sb** encher, cobrir alguém de algo; **2** esbanjar (*dinheiro*) (**on** em); **3 to** ~ **praise on sb/sth** ser pródigo em elogios sobre alguém/algo.

law *n* lei *f*; **case** ~ (*case by case*) caso-a-caso *m*; **common** ~ lei ordinária; **constitutional/** ~ **of the Land** (*UK*) *n* lei *f* orgânica; ~ **and order** *n* ordem *f* pública; **2** (*body of rules*) regulamento *m*; **3** (*of games etc*) regras; **to study/read** ~ estudar direito; **to break the** ~ infringir, transgredir a lei; **to lay down the** ~ impor a lei; (*pej*) ditar as ordens; **pursuant the** ~ consoante/segundo a lei; **under the** ~ ao abrigo da lei; ♦ ~**-abiding** *adj* obediente à lei; ~**-breaker** *n* transgressor,-a; (*Vd:* **bylaw**); ~ **court** *n* tribunal *m* de justiça; ~**ful** *adj* legal, lícito,-a; ~**fully** *adv* legalmente.

lawless *adj* illegal *m,f*; (*streets*) sem lei; (*person*) rebelde *m,f*.

Law Lords *npl* (*UK*) (*JUR*) **the** ~ o supremo tribunal.

lawmakers *n* legislador,-a; **officer of the** ~ polícia, agente/delegado da polícia.

lawn *n* relvado, (*BR*) gramado; ~**mower** *n* máquina de cortar relva, (*BR*) cortador *m* de grama; ~ **tennis** *n* ténis *m*.

law school *n* faculdade *f* de Direito.

Law Society *n* (*UK*) Ordem *f* de advogados.

lawsuit *n* a(c)ção *f* judicial; processo *m* legal; **to bring a** ~ **against sb** processar alguém.

> A lei inglesa não inclui o sistema judicial da Escócia, da qual difere em alguns pontos.

lawyer *n* advogado,-a; ~ **of defence/prosecution** advogado de defesa, procuração.

lax *adj* frouxo,-a; negligente, descuidado,-a.

laxative *n* laxante *m*.

laxity *n* (*slackness*) frouxidão *f*; **2** negligência *f*.

lay *adj* (*REL*) leigo,-a; (*untrained*) laico; ♦ (**lays, laying**, *pt, pp* **laid**) *vt* colocar; pôr; **2** (*prepare*) preparar, armar, pôr; **to** ~ **the table** pôr a mesa; **3** (*foundations, pipes*) preparar; **4** (*bricks*) assentar; **5** (*cable*) afixar; **to** ~ **a trap** armar uma cilada; **6 to** ~ **eggs** *vi* (*chickens*) pôr ovos; **7** (*lean*) encostar; ~ **your head on/against my shoulder** encosta a cabeça ao meu ombro; **8** (*to make a bet with sb*) apostar; ♦ ~ **aside** *vt* (*abandon for temporarily*) pousar, pôr de lado (*livro, etc*); **2** (*relinquish*) abandonar (*plans, studies*); **3** (*save*) poupar; ♦ **to** ~ **bare** (*explain*) revelar, explicar; **to** ~ **before** (*put forward*) apresentar; expor; ♦ **to** ~ **by sth** (*save*) pôr de lado; **2** (*NAUT*) ser posto em doca

seca; ♦ **to** ~ **down** (*rules*) formular, estabelecer; impor; **2** (*arms*) depor; **3** (*the baby*) deitar o bebé; ♦ **to** ~ **off** *vt* (*dismiss*) demitir, suspender (*employees*); **2** (*give up*) abandonar, deixar de; **she laid off smoking** ela deixou de fumar; ♦ **to** ~ **on** *vt* (*apply*) aplicar (*paint*); **2** (*supply*) providenciar; ♦ **to** ~ **out** *vt* preparar (*defunto*) para o funeral; **2** (*spread out*) dispor; **3** projectar (*plan, design*); ♦ **to** ~ **over** *vi* (*US*) pernoitar; IDIOM **to** ~ **the ghost to rest** enterrar o passado.

layabout *n* vadio,-a.

lay-by *n* desvio *m* para estacionamento; berma *f*; (*BR*) acostamento *m*.

lay days *npl* prazo estipulado para a carga e descarga de um navio.

layer *n* camada *f*.

layette *n* enxoval *m* de bebé (*BR: -bê*).

laying *n* (*of cables, floor*) colocação *f*, construção *f*.

layman *n* pessoa não especializada; laico,-a; **2** (*REL*) leigo,-a.

layout *n* esboço *m*; composição *f*; ~ **artist** *n* maquetista *m,f*.

laze *vi* viver na ociosidade; **2** (*pej*) vadiar, malandrar.

laziness *n* preguiça *f*.

lazy *adj* preguiçoso,-a, indolente, mandrião,-ona.

lazybones *n* preguiçoso,-a, mandrião,-ona.

lb (*abbr for* **pound**) libra (peso) = 453 gramas aprox.

L/C (*abbr for* **letter of credit**) carta de crédito.

LCD (*abbr for* **Liquid-Crystal Display**) monitores eletrónicos em cristais líquidos.

lead¹ *n* (*CHEM*) chumbo; (*fig*) (*bullets*) ameixa; ~ **pellets** *npl* bagos *mpl* de chumbo (*pigeon shooting*); **2** (*graphite*) (*in pencil*) mina *f*; **3** (*coll*) (*exams*) failure; **to go down like a** ~ **balloon** *vt* não ter sucesso, não ser popular; ~**-free** *adj* (*petrol*) sem chumbo; ~ **pencil** *n* lápis *m* de grafite; ~ **poisoning** *n* saturnismo *m*; ~ **time** *n* (*COMM*) prazo *m* de entrega.

lead² *n* (*winning position*) dianteira; **to take the** ~ tomar a dianteira; **2** iniciativa *f*, exemplo *m*; **3** (*distance ahead*) vantagem *f*, estar à frente; **4** (*clue*) pista *f*; **police are following a** ~ a polícia está a seguir uma pista; **5** (*CIN, THEAT*) **the** ~ o papel *m* principal; **6** (*JOURN*) história, estória *f* principal, (*article*) artigo *m* de fundo; **7** (*cable, wire*) cabo *m*, fio *m*; **8** (*for dog*) trela *f*; ♦ (*pt, pp* **led**) *vt* (*be in front of*) dirigir; **2** (*at the head of*) liderar, comandar, chefiar; **3** (*influence*) induzir, levar a; **to** ~ **sb to do sth** induzir alguém a fazer algo; **this incident led me to think** este incidente levou-me a pensar; **4** (*existence*) reger; ♦ *vi* (*give access to*) dar, levar; **this door ~s to the study;** esta porta dá para o escritório; (*road*) ir dar (**to**); **2** (*winning – race*) passar à frente; ♦ ~ **astray** *vt* desencaminhar; **to** ~ **back** *vt* fazer voltar, levar de volta; **this road ~s back to the beach** esta rua vai dar outra vez à praia; ♦ **to** ~ **on** *vt* provocar; **to** ~ **on to** *vt* incitar a; **to** ~ **to** (*result to*) levar a, resultar em; **the discussion led to a fight** a discussão resultou/acabou numa luta/briga; **to** ~ **up to** conduzir a, (*in conversation*) levar a, conduzir a.

leaded *adj (petrol)* com chumbo; ~ **window/lights** *(CONSTR) n* janela *f,* vidraças *fpl* com tiras de chumbo, chumbadas *(UK: estilo Tudor).*

leaden *adj (made of lead)* de chumbo; *(colour) (sky)* plúmbeo,-a, cor de chumbo.

leader *n* líder, chefe; *(of party, opposition)* dirigente; **2** *(head of gang, terrorism)* cabeça *m; (of strike, mutiny)* cabecilha *m;* **3** *(in excursion, etc)* guia *m,f;* **4** *(of company)* responsável; **5** *(MUS)* maestro/trina *m,f.*

leadership *n* liderança *f,* dire(c)ção *f;* chefia *f.*

lead-free *adj* sem chumbo.

leading *adj* principal; **2** *(SPORT) (at the front)* primeiro,-a; ~ **article** *m* editorial; ~ **lady** *n (THEAT)* a(c)triz *f* principal; ~ **question** *n* questão *f* capciosa.

leaf *(pl: leaves) n* folha; ♦ *vi:* **to** ~ **through** folhear; **to turn over a new** ~ começar vida nova.

leaflet *n* folheto *m.*

league *n* associação *f; (football)* liga *f,* **to be in** ~ **with** estar de comum acordo com, *(BR)* confabulado com alguém; ~ **table** *n* tabela *f* da classificação da liga.

leak *n (gas)* fuga *f;* **2** *(hole)* buraco *m; (vessel)* rombo *m;* **3** *(of liquid into sth)* vazamento *m;* **4** *(of oil into sea)* derrame, derramamento *m;* **5** *(in the roof)* goteira; **6** *(NAUT)* veia de água; **7** *(JOURN, POL) (disclosure)* fuga *f (of information);* **8** *(ECON, COMM)* desfalque *m;* ♦ *vi* meter, fazer água; **2** *(to empty, lose water)* vazar; *(dripping)* gotejar; **3** *(escape)* sair, escapar; **the news ~ed out** a notícia veio a público; **4** *(seep)* transpirar; **5** *(coll)* **to go for a** ~ *(urinate)* mijar (cal).

leakage *n* vazamento *m;* fuga *f.*

leaking: to be ~ *vt (torneira)* estar a pingar; **2** *(rain)* estar com infiltração.

leaky (-ier, -iest) *adj (torneira)* a pingar; **2** *(pipe)* com fuga; **3** *(vessel)* a entrar água.

lean *adj (thin)* magro,-a; **2** *(insufficient: air, oil in mixture)* pobre; **3** *(harvest)* improdutivo,-a; ~ **years** anos *mpl* de vacas magras; ♦ *(pt, pp* **leaned/leant)** *vt/vi:* **to** ~ **back in the armchair** *vi* recostar-se no sofá; encostar-se para trás; **2** *(slope)* inclinar-se; ♦ **to** ~ **forward** *(person)* inclinar-se para a frente, debruçar-se (de); **to** ~ **on** *vt/vi* contar com (o apoio de); apoiar-se em; encostar-se a; **to** ~ **out (of)** *vi* debruçar-se (de); **to** ~ **over** *vt/vi* debruçar-se sobre *(book, subject);* **to** ~ **over backwards** *(fig)* fazer todos os possíveis; **to** ~ **to/towards** *vt* inclinar-se para; favorecer.

leaning *n* inclinação *f,* tendência *f* (**towards** para); **the** ~ **building** *n* edifício *m* inclinado.

leap *n* pulo *m,* salto *m;* **2 a giant** ~ um passo gigante; **3 to give a** ~ **in the dark** dar um passo *m* arriscado, um tiro *m* no escuro; **by ~s and bounds** com progresso rápido; ♦ *(pt, pp* **leaped/leapt)** *vi* saltar; **to** ~ **at** *(opportunity)* aproveitar, agarrar; **to** ~ **to one's feet** pôr-se em pé dum salto.

leapfrog *n* jogo *m* do eixo; ♦ (**-gg-)** *vt* saltar ao eixo; *(fig)* saltar por cima de obstáculos.

leapt *(pt, pp of* **leap**).

leap year *n* ano *m* bissexto.

learn *(pt, pp* **learned/learnt**) *vt* aprender; informar-se de; ~ **sb's news** ouvir dizer, saber; **I learnt that your sister is here** soube/ouvi dizer que a tua irmã está aqui; **to** ~ **how to do** aprender a fazer; ♦ *vi* aprender.

learned *adj (person)* culto,-a, erudito,-a.

learner *n* principiante *m,f,* aprendiz *m,f;* ~ **driver** *n* aprendiz de condução.

learning *n (study)* aprendizagem *f;* **2** *(knowledge)* erudição *f;* ~ **curve** *n* curva *f* de aprendizagem.

learnt *(pt, pp of* **learn**).

lease *n (JUR)* arrendamento; compra de um imóvel por um período determinado, leasing; *(shop)* trespasse *m;* ♦ *vt* arrendar, vender/comprar lease; *(business, factory)* trespassar; **to** ~ **out to sb** arrendar a alguém; IDIOM **to give sb a new** ~ **on life to sb** dar uma nova vida a alguém; **2** *(experience, holiday)* reanimar/dar forças a alguém.

leaseholder *n* proprietário,-a, dono,-a da lease; arrendatário,-a.

leasing *n* leasing *m.*

leash *n (for the dog)* trela *f.*

least *n:* o mínimo, a mínima; **the** ~ **possible effort** o menor esforço possível; ♦ *adj* menor; mínimo; ♦ *adv (with adj or noun)* menos; **the** ~ **demanding of them** o menos exigente deles; **at** ~ pelo menos; **not in the** ~ de maneira nenhuma, nada; **not bored in the** ~ nada aborrecido,-a; **last but not** ~ e por último, mas não menos importante.

leather *n* couro, pele *f; (hard leather)* cabedal; **2** *(also:* **wash ~)** camurça *f;* **a** ~ **coat** um casaco de pele; **a** ~ **belt** um cinto de cabedal.

leatherette *n* napa *f;* imitação *f* de couro.

leave *n (time off)* licença *f;* ~ **of absence** *n* licença; **2** *(permission)* autorização *f;* **on** ~ de licença; **to take one's** ~ *(say good-bye)* despedir-se, dizer adeus; **3** *(JUR)* **by** ~ **of the judge** por autorização do (único) juiz; ♦ *(pt, pp* **left**) *vt (leave behind)* deixar; abandonar; ♦ *vi (go away/out)* ir-se embora; sair; partir; **the plane has left** o avião já partiu; **to** ~ **on** *(coat, hat)* deixar ficar, não tirar; **to** ~ **off** *(stop)* parar de; ~ **off doing sth** parar/deixar de fazer algo; ~ **out** *vt (paragraphs)* omitir; excluir; *(name, subject)* esquecer; **to feel left out** sentir-se excluído/ignorado *(in a group);* **to be left over** *(food, drink)* sobrar; **so much food was left over!** sobrou tanta comida!; ♦ *exc* ~ **me alone** deixa-me em paz; ~ **it for another day!** isso fica para a outra vez!; ~ **it there!** deixa (isso) aí!

leaves *(pl of* **leaf**).

Lebanese *n adj* libanês *m,* libanesa *f.*

Lebanon *n* Líbano; **in** ~ no Líbano.

lecher *n (pej) (of man)* mulherengo; devasso,-a.

lecherous *adj* lascivo,-a.

lechery *n* lascívia *f.*

lecithin *n* lecitina *f.*

lectern *n (a support for reading-book, music)* atril *m.*

lector *n (UK) (reader)* leitor na Igreja; *(in certain universities) (lecturer)* assistente professor,-ora.

lecture *n* conferência; ~ **hall** *n* sala *f* de conferências; **2** *(talk)* palestra; **3** *(in class)* aula; ~ **theatre** *n* anfiteatro *m*; **to give a** ~ **on sth** dar uma palestra (sobre algo); **4** *(reprimand)* sermão *m*; ♦ *vi* *(Univ)* dar uma aula (sobre algo); ♦ *vt* *(scold)* dar, passar um sermão em.

lecturer *n* conferencista *m,f*; *(speaker)* palestrante; **2** *(Univ)* assistente professor,-ora.

led *(pt, pp of* **lead**).

ledge *n* *(of mountain)* saliência *f*, ressalto *m*; **2** *(of window)* peitoril *m*; *(on wall)* rebordo *m*.

ledger *n* *(COMM)* livro-caixa *m;* livro *m* contábil.

lee *n* sotavento *m*; **in/under the** ~ **of** ao abrigo de.

leech *n* *(sucking worm)* sanguessuga *f;* **2** *(fig, pej)* **to cling to sb like a** ~ colar-se a uma pessoa como uma sanguessuga.

leek *n* alho-porro *m*; *(BR)* alho-poró *m*.

leer *n* *(lustful)* olhar lascivo; ♦ *vi:* **to** ~ **at sb** olhar maliciosamene para alguém; olhar de soslaio.

leeway *n* *(AER)* deriva *f*; **2** *(coll)* espaço de segurança; **to have some** ~ *(fig)* ter certa liberdade de a(c)ção.

left *n* esquerda *f;* **the L~** *(POL)* a esquerda; ♦ *adj* esquerdo,-a; ♦ **on/to the** ~ *adv* à esquerda; **turn to your** ~ vire à esquerda; ~-**hand drive** com dire (c)ção do lado esquerdo; ~-**handed** *adj* *(person)* canhoto,-a, esquerdino,-a; **Leftist** *adj* *(POL)* esquerdista; ~ **luggage** (**office**) *n* depósito de bagagem; ~**over** *adj* restante; ~**overs** *npl* sobras *fpl;* ♦ *(pt, pp of* **leave**) **have you any sugar** ~**?** tem algum açúcar de sobra/de sobejo?

left-wing *n* *(POL)* esquerda; *adj* de esquerda, esquerdista.

leg *n* *(ANAT)* *(person, animal)* perna; **2** *(of furniture)* pé *m*, perna *f*; **3** *(CULIN)* perna, pernil *m* *(of lamb, pork)*; coxa *f* *(of chicken)*; **4** *(journey, tournament)* etapa; IDIOM **to pull sb's** ~ *(tease)* brincar com alguém; **you don't have a** ~ **to stand on** você não tem em que se basear; **to shake one** ~ *(fam)* *(hurry up)* despachar-se; **my computer is on its last** ~**s** o meu computador está nas últimas.

legacy *n* *(JUR)* legado *m*; *(of era, history)* legado; herança *f*, **2** *(of war)* sequela *f*.

legal *adj* *(relating to Law)* lícito,-a; legal; jurídico,-a; **2** *(mistake)* judiciário,-a; **3** *(owner)* legítimo,-a; ~ **action** a(c)ção *f* legal; **to bring/take** ~ **action against sb** instaurar um processo contra alguém; ~ **aid** *n* *(UK)* assistência *f* jurídica; ~ **costs** *npl* custas; ~ **tender** *n* moeda com curso legal.

legalese *n* *(lawyers; jargon)* legalês.

legality *n* legalidade.

legalize *vt* legalizar.

legally *adv* legalmente.

legend *n* lenda *f*; legenda *f*.

legendary *adj* lendário,-a.

legged *adj* *(in combination)*; **long-**~ de pernas altas, longas.

leggings *npl* collant(s) *mpl*.

leggy *adj* *(person)* de pernas altas e bonitas.

legible *adj* legível *m,f*.

legion *n* legião *f*; ~**naire's disease** *n* doença de legionário.

legislate *vi* legislar.

legislation *n* legislação *f*.

legislative *adj* legislativo.

legislature *n* legislatura.

legitimacy *n* legitimidade *f*.

legitimate *adj* legítimo.

legitimize *vt* legalizar; **2** *(justify)* justificar.

leg-room *n* espaço para as pernas.

legwork *n* *(going from one place to the other)* deslocação *f*; **2** *(work)* **you need to do much** ~ tens de andar muito.

leisure *n* *(spare time)* lazer *m*, tempo *m* livre; **at** ~ à vontade; **to be at** ~ *(relaxed)* estar descontraído,-a; **do it at your** ~ faça (isso) quando quiser; ~ **centre** *n* centro de lazer; **gentleman/lady of** ~ senhor/senhora que vive dos rendimentos.

leisurely *adj* calmo,-a vagaroso,-a; tranquilo,-a; ♦ *adv* calmamente.

lemming *n* *(ZOOL)* lemo *m*.

lemon *n* limão *m*; ~ **squash** *n* limonada; ~ **tree** *n* limoeiro *m*; ~**ade** *n* limonada gasosa.

lemur *n* *(ZOOL)* lémure *m*.

lend *(pt, pp of* **lent**) *vt* emprestar; **2** *(support)* dar apoio, ajudar; **to** ~ **a helping hand** ajudar; **3** *(abstract quality)* contribuir; **her presence lent elegance to the party** a presença dela contribuiu com a sua elegância para a festa; **to** ~ **one's ear to** prestar atenção a; **to** ~ **itself to** *(sth be right/ good for sth)* algo prestar-se para algo.

length *n* *(gen)* comprimento *m*; **the carpet is ten metres in** ~ a carpete tem dez metros de comprimento; **2** *(of river, land)* extensão; **to walk the breadth and the** ~ **of Europe** caminhar, andar por toda a Europa; **3** *(duration)* **a film four hours in** ~ um filme com quatro horas de duração; **4** *(piece of cloth, string etc)* pedaço *m*; **5** *(in compounds)* *(clothing)* altura; **knee-**~ **skirt** saia pelo joelho; **shoulder-**~ **hair** cabelo pelos ombros; ♦ **at** ~ *adv* *(eventually)* finalmente; *(in detail)* por extenso, detalhadamente; **to go to great** ~**s to do sth** fazer todos os possíveis para fazer algo.

lengthen *vt* alongar, prolongar; ♦ *vi* alongar-se.

lengthways *adv* longitudinalmente, ao comprido.

lengthy *adj* comprido,-a; **2** *(speech)* prolixo,-a; **3** *(trip, conversation)* prolongado,-a.

leniency *n* indulgência.

lenient *adj* indulgente *m,f*, clemente *m,f*.

lens *n* lente *f*; *(in camera)* obje(c)tiva *f*, lente *f*; **2** *(contact)* lente de conta(c)to; **soft/hard** ~ *(for eyes)* lentes *fpl* de contato moles, rígidas.

Lent *n* Quaresma *f*.

lent *(pt, pp of* **lend**).

lentil *n* *(BOT, CULIN)* lentilha *f*.

Leo *n* *(ASTROL, ASTRON)* Leão *m*.

leopard *n* *(ZOOL)* leopardo *m*.

leotard *n* *(gymnasts, dancers)* (BR) collant *m* de corpo *m*; (EP) malha *f* justa.

leper *n* leproso,-a.

leprosy *n* lepra.

leprous *adj* *(MED)* leproso,-a.

lesbian *n adj* lésbica; ~**ism** *n* lesbianism.

Lesotho *npr* Lesoto *m*.

less *adj (of little)* menor; menos; ~ **food** menos comida; **of ~ influence** de menor influência; ♦ *adv, pron* menos; ~ **and** ~ cada vez menos; **the** ~ **he speaks the better** quanto menos ele falar, melhor.

lessee *n* arrendatário,-a; locatário,-a.

lessen *vi* diminuir, minguar; ♦ *vt* diminuir, reduzir.

lesser *adj* menor; **to a** ~ **degree** em menor grau; **a** ~ **mortal/being** um ser inferior.

lesson *n* lição *f*; *(school)* aula; 2 *(fig)* **moral** ~ lição de moral; *(warning)* **let this be a** ~ **to you!** que isto te sirva de lição.

lessor *n* arrendador,-ora, senhorio,-a.

lest *conj: (in case that)* ~ **it happens** para que não aconteça.

let[1] *(pt, pp of* **let**) *vt* deixar, permitir; 2 alugar; ~**'s go** vamos!; ~ **me write** deixa-me escrever; ~**'s say** digamos; ~**'s not do it** é melhor não fazermos (isso); **I won't** ~ **them trick you** não permito que eles te enganem; ♦ ~ **alone** *conj (much less)*; quanto menos; para não falar em; **she couldn't speak Chinese** ~ **alone write it** ela não conseguia falar chinês, quanto menos escrevê-lo; ♦ **to** ~ **sb down** *vt (deflate)* esvaziar; 2 disappoint, desiludir; ♦ **to** ~ **go** *vt/vi* soltar; pôr em liberdade; 2 renunciar a; ~ **go of sb/sth** largar; 3 esquecer; ♦ **to** ~ **in** *vt* deixar entrar **(oneself)** com a chave; **to** ~ **o.s. in for** *(trouble, etc)* meter-se em *(apuros, etc)*; **to** ~ **in on a secret** revelar um segredo; ♦ **to** ~ **sb off** *vt* deixar sair *(student)*; 2 dispensar alguém de *(homework, duties)*; 3 *(naughty child)* deixar impune, não castigar; *(adulto)* deixar livre; ~ **sth off** *(bomb, gun)* explodir, disparar; *(fireworks)* lançar; ♦ **to** ~ **on** *vt (coll)* divulgar, contar; ♦ **to** ~ **out** *vt* deixar sair; 2 *(sewing)* alargar *(garment)*; 3 emitir *(scream, laugh)*; ♦ **to** ~ **up** *vi (rain, wind)* abrandar; parar, diminuir.

let[2] *n* aluguer *(BR)* aluguel; ♦ *(pt/pp* **let**, *cont* -**ting)** *vt* alugar *(carro, cycle, house, flat)*; arrendar *(house, flat)*; '**to let**' 'aluga-se'.

letdown *n (disappointment)* dece(p)ção *f*; **it was quite a** ~ foi bastante dece(p)cionante.

lethal *adj* letal; mortal.

lethargic *adj* letárgico,-a.

lethargy *n* letargia *f*.

let-out *n (coll) (excuse)* escapatória *f*; pretexto *m*.

let's = let us.

letter *n (alphabet)* letra *f*; 2 *(written message)* carta *f*; ~**bomb** *n* carta-bomba, carta *f* amadilhada; ~**box** *n* caixa *f* do correio; *(na porta)* portinhola *f* do correio; ~**head** *n* cabeçalho *m*; ~**ing** *n* letras *fpl*.

letter opener *n* abre-cartas *m*; *(BR)* abridor de cartas.

letting *n* aluguer *m (BR)* aluguel; **holiday** ~**s** *npl* alugueres *mpl* para férias.

lettuce *n (BOT)* alface *f*.

letup *n (interval)* pausa; *(respite)* trégua; *(weather, atmosphere)* acalmia *f*.

leukaemia *n (MED)* leucemia *f*.

level *n (gen)* plano *m*, nível *m*; 2 *(floor)* andar; **your car is on the third** ~ o seu carro está no terceiro andar; 3 **to be** ~ **with** estar/no ao mesmo nível que; 4 *(fig)* **on the same** ~ a sério, honestamente,

to speak on the ~ falar a sério; ♦ *adj (equal in height)* nivelado,-a; 2 *(voice, tone)* uniforme *m,f*; 3 *(equal in standard)* em pé de igualdade; 4 *(floor, field)* plano,-a; 5 *(CULIN)* raso,-a; **a** ~ **spoonful of sugar** uma colher rasa de açúcar; ♦ *adv* no mesmo nível; ♦ *vt* nivelar, aplanar; **to** ~ **off/out** *vi* estabilizar-se.

level crossing *n* passagem *f* de nível.

level-headed *adj* sensato,-a, equilibrado,-a.

levelling (~-**off**) *n (making smooth, flat)* nivelamento *m*; 2 *(demolition)* demolição *f*.

lever *n (AUT, TECH)* alavanca *f*; ♦ *vt:* **to** ~ **up** levantar com alavanca.

leverage *n (fig) (ECON, POL)* influência *f*, poder *m*.

levity *n* leviandade *f*, frivolidade *f*.

levy *n (TAX)* imposto, tribute *m*; cobrança; ♦ *(pt, pp* -**ied**) *vt* cobrar; aplicar *(fine)*; *(collect/demand taxes)* arrecadar, exigir.

lewd *adj* obsceno,-a; lascivo,-a.

lexical *adj* lexical.

lexicographer *n* lexicógrafo,-a.

lexicon, lexis *n* léxico *m*.

liability *n (JUR)* responsabilidade *f*; 2 *(risk)* risco *m*; **liabilities** *npl (FIN)* obrigações *fpl*; *(COMM)* dívidas *fpl*, passivo *sg*; **assets and** ~ *npl* a(c)tivos e passivos *mpl*.

liable *adj:* ~ **to** sujeito a; **to be** ~ **to do** ser capaz (de), ser provável que; **to be** ~ **for** ser responsável por; **to be** ~ **to** ter uma tendência para; **to be** ~ **to do (sth)** ser capaz de, ser provável que; **this is** ~ **to cause** … isto é provável que cause …

liaison *n* ligação *f*; relação *f* amorosa.

liar *n* mentiroso,-a.

lib (= **liberation**) *n* emancipação *f*.

libel *n* libelo, calúnia; ♦ *vt* caluniar, difamar.

libellus *(UK)* **libelus** *(US) adj* defamatório,-a.

liberal *adj* liberal *m,f*; ~ **with** generoso,-a com; **L~ Party** *n* o Partido Liberal.

liberalism *n* liberalismo.

liberality *n* liberalidade; 2 generosidade.

liberalization *n* liberalização *f*.

liberalize *vt* liberalizar.

liberal-minded *adj* de vistas largas, liberal.

liberate *vt* libertar.

liberation *n* libertação *f*, emancipação *f*.

liberator *n* libertador,-ora.

Liberia *npr* Libéria; **in** ~ na Libéria.

Liberian *adj* liberiano,-a.

libertarian *n adj (POL)* libertário,-a.

libertine *adj* libertino,-a; devasso,-a.

liberty *n* liberdade *f*; **to be at** ~ ter permissão para; 2 *(cheek)* atrevimento *m*; **to take the** ~ **of doing sth** tomar a liberdade de; fazer algo; **to take liberties with sb** *(cheeky, familiar)* ser atrevido,-a.

libidinous *adj* libidinoso,-a

libido *n (PSICH)* líbido *m*.

Libra *n (ASTROL, ASTRON)* Libra; Balança.

librarian *n* bibliotecário,-a.

library *n* biblioteca *f*.

libretto *n* libretto *m*.

Libya *n* Líbia; **in** ~ na Líbia.

Libyan *n adj* líbio,-a.

lice *(pl of* **louse***).*

licence *n (for trading)* licença *f* (**to** para); **2** autorização *f*; (= **driving** ~) carta *f* de condução, *(BR)* carteira *f* de motorista; ~ **number** *n* número da matrícula *(do automóvel) (BR)* placa; ~ **plate** *n* matrícula *(BR:* placa).

license *vt* autorizar, permitir.

licensed *adj (person, shop, taxi)* autorizado,-a; *(shop, restaurant)* ~ **to sell alcohol** autorizado,-a, que tem licença para vender bebidas alcoólicas; ~ **to do sth** autorizado a fazer algo; **2** *(dog)* com licença; *(-gun)* registado,-a *(BR)* registrado,-a; **3** *(pilot)* com brevet, brevê; **4** *(vehicle)* em ordem.

licensee *n* titular *m,f* de licença.

licensing *n* concessão *f*, autorização *f*; ~ **hours** *npl (UK)* horário de funcionamento dos bares.

licentious *adj* licencioso,-a, sem vergonha.

lichen *n (fruit)* líquem *m*.

licit *adj* lícito,-a.

lick *n* lambidela, *(BR)* lambida; **2** *(a little)* um pouco (**of** de); ♦ *vt* lamber; **to** ~ **sb's boots** *(pej)* lamber os pés a alguém; **2** derrotar; IDIOM **a** ~ **and a promise** algo feito à pressa.

licking *n* tareia.

licorice *n =* **liquorice**.

lid *n (cover)* tampa *f*; **saucepan's** ~ a tampa do tacho; **2** *(eyelid)* pálpebra *f*.

lido *n (UK)* piscina pública ao ar livre; praia *f* (com desportos náuticos).

lie[1] *n* mentira; **to tell** ~**s** contar mentiras; ♦ *(pt, pp* **lied***, pres p* **lying***) vi* mentir; **he lied to me** ele mentiu-me.

lie[2] *(pt* **lay***, pp* **lain***, pres p* **lying***) vi (horizontal position)* estar deitado *(person, animal)*; *(be lying down)* estar deitado; **2** *(be situated)* situar-se; encontrar-se; estar; **the city lies ahead** a cidade está adiante; **the book is lying on the table** o livro está na mesa; **his concentration lies somewhere else** a sua concentração encontra-se noutro lugar; **3** *(corpse)* jazer; ♦ **to** ~ **about/ around** *vi (scattered things)* estar espalhado; **2** *(person)* vadiar, andar sem fazer nada; ♦ **to** ~ **down** deitar-se; **to have a** ~**down** ir descansar, ter uma soneca; descansar; **2** *(accept without protest)* aceitar; **she won't take it lying down** ela não vai aceitar isso de braços cruzados; ♦ **to have a** ~**in** ficar na cama até tarde; ♦ **to** ~ **low** *(concealed, be quiet)* esconder-se, estar calado,-a; **if I were you, I would** ~ **low** se eu fosse a você, ficaria caladinho, escondido.

lie dete(c)tor *n* detector *m* de mentiras.

lieu *n*: **in** ~ em troca; ♦ *prep* **in** ~ **of** em vez de.

lieutenant *n* lugar-tenente *m*; *(MIL)* tenente *m*; ~**-colonel** *n* tenente-coronel *m*.

life *(pl:* **lives***) n* vida; **way of** ~ modo de viver/de vida; **for** ~ para toda a vida; **to lay down one's** ~ dar a sua vida; **run for your** ~ salve-se quem puder; **2** *(vigour)* vida; **to come to** ~ *(person)* animar-se; *(to object)* dar vida a; **to paint from** ~ pintar de acordo com o modelo; ♦ ~ **belt** *n* cinto

m de segurança; ~**boat** *n* barco salva-vidas; ~ **buoy** *n* bóia *f* de salvação; ~**guard** *n* salva-vidas; **high**~ *n* alta roda; ~ **insurance** *n* seguro de vida; ~**-jacket** *n* colete *m* salva-vidas; ~**less** *adj* sem vida; inanimado; *(fig)* sem graça; ~**like** *adj* natural; ~**line** *n* linha salva-vidas; ~**long** *adj* vitalício, perpétuo; ~ **member** *n* membro natalício; ~**-saver** *n* nadador-salvador; ~ **sentence** *n* prisão *f* perpétua; ~**-sized** *adj* de tamanho natural; ~ **span,** ~**time** *n* vida, duração *f*, longevidade *f*; **the chance of a lifetime** *n* oportunidade única; ~ **support system** *n (MED)* sistema *m* de respiração artificial; ~ **vest** *n (US)* = **life jacket**.

lift *n (UK) (for people)* elevador, ascensor; **2** *(for goods)* monta-cargas *sg/pl*; ~**-bridge** ponte *f* levadiça; **2** *(ride)* boleia *f (BR)* carona *f*; **she asked me for a** ~ ela pediu-me uma boleia; **3** *(coll) (boost)* estímulo; **to** ~ **sb's spirits** *(morale)* animar alguém, levantar o moral a alguém; ♦ *vt* levantar *(person, object)*; **2** *(ban)* revogar; **3** *(coll) (steal)* roubar, apropriar-se de; *(copy)* plagiar; ♦ *vi (fog)* dispersar-se, dissipar-se; **2** *(morale, spirits)* animar alguém, levantar o moral a alguém; **to** ~ **sth off a place** tirar algo de um lugar; **to** ~ **up one's head** levantar a cabeça; **to** ~ **a child up** pegar numa criança ao colo; IDIOM **she won't** ~ **a finger to help** ela não faz nada para ajudar.

lifting *n* levantamento *m*; ~**-off** *n (AER)* descolagem *f*; *(BR)* decolagem *f*.

ligament *n* ligamento *m*.

light *n (gen)* luz *f*, claridade *f*; **by the** ~ **of** à luz de; **to stand in sb's** ~ fazer sombra alguém, prejudicar; **to throw some** ~ **on** *(subject, mystery)* esclarecer; **to bring to** ~ revelar; **to turn on/off the** ~ acender/apagar a luz; **2** *(perspective)* **to see sb/sth in a different** ~ ver a pessoa/as coisas sob um prisma/de uma forma diferente; **3** *(AUT) (headlight)* farol *m*; **rear** ~ luz traseira; **traffic** ~**s** *npl* semáforos *mpl*; ♦ *adj (not heavy)* leve *m,f*, ligeiro,-a; **2** *(not dark)* claro,-a; ~ **blue** azul claro; **3** *(traffic)* fraco,-a; **4** *(touch)* suave; ~ **ale** *n (UK)* cerveja escura e suave; ~ **bulb** *n* lâmpada; ~ **beacon** baliza luminosa; ~**-emiting diodo** *n* diodo *m* emissor de luz; ~**er** *n (cigarette)* isqueiro *m*; ~**-fingered** *adj (gatuno)* ágil de mãos; ~**-headed** *adj* aturdido,-a, tonto,-a; estouvado,-a; ~**-hearted** *adj* alegre, despreocupado; ~**house** *n* farol *m*; ~ **industry** *n* indústria *f* leve; ~**ing** *n* iluminação *f*; ♦ *(pt, pp* **lighted/lit***) vt* acender; iluminar; **to** ~ **the fire** acender o lume; **the room was well lit** a sala estava muito bem iluminada; ♦ **to** ~ **up** *vi (lamp)* acender-se; **2** *(cigarette)* acender um cigarro; **3** *(fig) (face)* iluminar-se; *(eyes)* brilhar; IDIOM **there's always a** ~ **at the end of the tunnel** há sempre uma luz ao fundo do/no fim do túnel.

lighted *adj* iluminado,-a; **2** *(fire)* aceso,-a.

lighten *vi* clarear; ♦ *vt* iluminar; clarear; **2** *(make less heavy)* aliviar *(burden, cargo)*.

lightly *adv* ligeiramente; despreocupadamente; levemente; **2** *(remark)* levianamente; **to get off** ~ ser ligeiramente castigado.

lightmeter n (PHOT) fotómetro (BR: -tô-).

lightness n claridade f; **2** (not heavy) leveza f; **3** agilidade f.

lightning n relâmpago m, raio m; ~ **conductor** n pára-raios m inv.

light opera n opereta f.

lights npl (knowledge) conhecimento m, ideias fpl; ~**-out** n (time) hora em que se apagam as luzes.

lightweight n (boxing) peso-leve m; ♦ adj leve.

light year n ano-luz m.

like n coisa igual, semelhante; **I never saw the** ~ nunca vi coisa igual; **pots and the** ~ panelas e semelhantes; **~s and dislikes** simpatias fpl e antipatias fpl, gostos mpl e aversões fpl; **the ~s of you** (pej) gente como vocês, gente da vossa laia; ♦ adj semelhante; parecido,-a; provável; **your dress is** ~ **mine** o seu vestido é parecido com o meu; **it looks** ~ **snowing** é provável que neve; **to look** ~ parecer-se com, assemelhar-se a; **2** (suffix+adj) (same characteristics) **spring**~ como a primavera; ♦ prep como; **he is acting** ~ **a fool** ele porta-se como um idiota; **it is just** ~ **him** é típico dele; **2** (such as) tal/tais como; **there are many solutions,** ~ **the one we have given you** há muitas soluções tais como as que te demos; ♦ conj (as though) como se; ♦ vt gostar de; simpatizar com (person); **I** ~ **him** gosto dele; **2** (to want) **I would** ~ (eu) gostaria de; **would you** ~ **a beer?** quer uma cerveja?; **he would** ~ **you to give him tea** ele quer que você lhe dê um chá; **if you** ~ se quiser; **as you** ~ **it** como quiser; é típico dele.

> Quando se quer alguma coisa em inglês, diz-se "**would like**" (gostaria) em vez do verbo "want" (querer), por ser considerado mais cortês. Em português, na mesma situação usa-se o verbo "**querer**" (want) seguido de "**por favor**" ou "**se faz favor**" (please).

likeable adj simpático, agradável.

likelihood n probabilidade f.

likely adj provável; **he's** ~ **to leave** é provável que ele se vá embora.

like-minded adj da mesma opinião.

liken vt: **to** ~ **to** comparar com.

likeness n semelhança f, parecença f.

likewise adj igualmente; **have a nice holiday!** ~! boas férias! ~! igualmente!

liking n: ~ **for sb, sth** afeição por alguém, algo; **to his** ~ ao seu gosto.

lilac n lilás m; ♦ adj (colour) lilás.

lilt n (of tune) cadência f; (of voice) entoação f; ~**ing** adj cadenciado,-a.

lily (pl: -ies) n (BOT) (gen) lírio m, açucena f, jarro; ~ **of the valley** n lírio-do-vale m; lírio-do-campo; ~**-white** adj of a pure white; **2** (fam) puro,-a, sem mácula.

limb n (ANAT) membro m; (of tree) ramo m; IDIOM **to be out on a** ~ estar em apuros.

limber: **to** ~ **up** vi (fig) tornar-se flexível; (SPORT) fazer aquecimento.

limbo (pl: **limboes**) n (REL) limbo; **2** (fig) incerteza f, esquecimento m; **to be in** ~ (fig) cair no esquecimento; **3** dança das Caraíbas.

lime n (tree) tília f, limeira f; (fruit) lima f; ~ **cordial** n refresco de lima.

limelight n luz/luzes da ribalta; **to be in the** ~ (fig) ser o centro das atenções.

limerick n quintilha f humorística.

limestone n (GEOL) pedra f calcária.

limit n limite m; **within ~s** dentro de limites; até certo ponto; **she is the** ~ ela é o cúmulo; ♦ vt limitar.

limitation n limitação f.

limited adj limitado; restrito; **to be** ~ **to** limitar-se a; ~ **(liability) company (Ltd)** n companhia (de responsabilidade) limitada, Lda.

limitless adj ilimitado.

limo n (abbr for **limousine**) (car) limusine f.

limp n: **to have a** ~ mancar, ser coxo,-a; ♦ adj (slack) frouxo,-a; sem firmeza; (lettuce, etc) murcho,-a; (excuse) fraco,-a, mole; ♦ vi coxear.

limpet n lapa.

limpid adj (lakes, eyes) límpido,-a cristalino-a.

linchpin n (fig) (important person/item) peça-chave f.

linctus n (for the cough) expectorante m.

line n linha; (shorter – in drawing) traço; **washing** ~ estendal m (BR) corda de varal; **2** (TEL) linha; **the** ~ **is dead** o telfone não dá sinal; **3** (row of people, cars) fila f; (of trees, etc) fileira f; **4** (queue) fila f; (fig, fam) (EP) bicha f; **5** (alignment) alinhamento m, linha f; **in** ~ **with** de acordo com; **6** (in writing) linha f; **between ~s** nas entrelinhas; **7** (attitude, position) **to step out of** ~ estar fora da linha; **to take a firm** ~ **with sb** manter-se firme com alguém; **8** (wrinkle) ruga; **9** (speciality) ramo (de negócio); **10** (THEAT, CIN) deixa f; **11** (rail, railway – track) linha f férrea; (route) linha; **12** ~ **of vision** campo m de visão; **13** (genealogy) linha; **he comes from a long** ~ **of artists** ele vem duma (longa) geração de artistas; ♦ vt (garment, curtain) forrar; **2** alinhar; **the crowds ~d the streets** a multidão alinhava-se ao longo das ruas; **the trees ~d the avenue** as ávores ladeavam/orlavam a avenida; ♦ **to** ~ **up** vi (to be in a queue) fazer fila; fazer bicha (EP); ♦ vt alinhar, pôr em fila.

lineage n (genealogy) linhagem f, linha f; **to trace one's** ~ traçar a genealogia.

lined adj (with wrinkles – person) enrugado,-a; (paper) pautado.

linen n roupa branca, roupa de cama; ~ **basket** n cesta f de roupa suja; **2** (material) linho m; **a** ~ **dress** um vestido m de linho; IDIOM **to wash one's dirty** ~ **in public** lavar a roupa suja em público.

liner n (NAUT) paquete m, transatlântico m.

lines n texto m; **to forget one's** ~ esquecer o texto.

linesman n (UK) (SPORT) juiz m de linha.

line-up n formação f em linha, alinhamento.

linger vi (dawdle) demorar-se, retardar-se; **2** (memory, smell) persistir, continuar; **to** ~ **after sb** suspirar por alguém; **to** ~ **on** (memory) persistir; **to** ~ **over** saborear (food, drink).

lingerie n lingerie f, roupa interior (BR: de baixo) de mulher.

lingering adj persistente; **2** lento,-a; vagaroso,-a; **a ~ kiss** um beijo demorado.

lingo (pl: -es) n (pej) algaraviada f, (coll) gíria f, jargão m.

linguist n linguista m,f.

linguistic adj linguístico,-a.

linguistics n sg linguística f.

lining n (of garment, curtain, floor) forro m; **2** (TECH, AUT) revestimento m; **3** (ANAT) parede.

link n (in chain) elo m; **2** (connection) relação f (**between** entre); **3** (connection) vínculo m (**to** a); **trade ~s** vínculo commercial; **4** (fig) (bond) laço m; **5** (TRANSP, RADIO, TEL) ligação f, (BR) conexão f (**between** entre); ♦ vt vincular; unir; **2** ligar; relacionar (**to** com); **to ~ up** vt acoplar; ♦ vi associar-se (**to** a); (BR) conetar-se.

linkage n (connection) vínculo, ligação f (BR) conexão f.

linked relacionado,-a; ligado,-a, vinculado; **2** (physically) enlaçado,-a; **with arms** ~ de braço dado.

links npl (short for: ~ **course**) campo sg de golfe; **trade** ~ vínculo comercial msg, vínculos comerciais mpl.

link-up n acoplamento; **2** (TV) transmissão simultânea; ligação f.

linnet n (bird) pintarrocho m.

lino, linoleum n linóleo m, oleado m.

linseed oil n óleo m de linhaça.

lint n (MED) (dressing) gaze f.

lintel n (for door, window) lintel m.

lion n leão m; ~ **cub** n filhote m de leão.

lioness n leoa f.

lip n (of person, wound) lábio; (animal; person; slang); **2** (jug) bico; **3** (of cup, plat; crater) borda; **to give ~ to** responder malcriadamente a; **to keep a stiff upper** ~ ficar impassível; ~**read** vi ler os lábios; ~ **service** n adulação f; ~**stick** n batom m; IDIOM **to pay ~ service to** elogiar falsamente; (fig) **my ~s are sealed** a minha boca está fechada.

liposuction n (MED) lipsuccção f.

liquefy vt liquefazer; ♦ vi liquefazer-se.

liqueur n licor m.

liquid n adj (fluid) líquido; ~ **assets** npl a(c)tivo m disponível.

liquidate vt liquidar.

liquidation n liquidação f.

liquidator n liquidador,-ora.

liquidity n liquidez f.

liquidize, liquidise vt liquidificar, passar no liquidificador.

liquor n licor m, bebida alcoólica.

liquorice (UK), **licorice** (US) n (planta) alcaçuz f.

lira n (Italian currency) lira f.

Lisbon npr Lisboa f; **in** ~ em Lisboa.

Lisbonner n adj (Lisbon-born) lisboeta m,f; **2** adj (clubs, associations) lisbonense m,f.

lisp n ceceio; ♦ vi cecear, falar com a língua presa.

lissom(e) adj esbelto,-a.

list n lista, rol; **2** (NAUT) inclinação f; ♦ vt fazer uma lista/relação de; enumerar; ♦ vi (NAUT) inclinar-se, adernar.

listed adj (buildings) classificado,-a; **to be ~ under** ser classificado como; (person) figurado,-a entre; **2** (COMP) listado,-a; **to be ~ in the Stock Exchange** ser cotado na Bolsa.

listen vi escutar, ouvir; (pay attention/heed) prestar atenção; ♦ **to ~ in** vi ouvir rádio; **2** (eavesdrop) pôrse à escuta; interceptar uma conversa telefónica; ♦ **to ~ to sb** vi escutar, prestar atenção a alguém.

listener n ouvinte m,f.

listless adj apático,-a, indiferente m,f.

lit (pt, pp of **light**).

litany n ladainha f, litania f.

literacy n alfabetização f; ~ **campaign** campanha f de alfabetização.

literal adj literal.

literally adv literalmente; ao pé da letra; (translation) à letra.

literary adj literário,-a; **a ~ man** um homem de letras; literato.

literate adj alfabetizado,-a, instruído,-a; **she is not ~** ela não sabe ler nem escrever; **2** (well-read) culto,-a, letrado,-a.

literature n literatura; **2** (printed information) folhetos mpl, panfleto m; informação f; **pulp ~** literatura f de cordel.

lithe adj ágil, flexível m,f.

lithium n lítio m.

lithograph, lithography n litografia f.

Lithuania npr Lituânia; **in** ~ na Lituânia.

Lithuanian adj (person, language) lituano,-a.

litigation n litígio m; **litigious** adj (JUR) contencioso,-a.

litre (UK) **liter** (US) n litro m.

litter n (rubbish) lixo; **2** (newborn animals) ninhada; **3** (stretcher) maca; (portable chair carried on poles by men) liteira; (handbarrow) padiola; ~ **bin** n lata de lixo; ~ **ed** adj espalhado,-a (**with**, com), juncado de (papers, leaves).

little adj (comp **less** menos, menor; superl **least** o menos, mínimo) (gen) pequeno,-a; ~ **finger** n dedo mindinho, dedo mínimo (BR) dedo minguinho; **my ~ sister** miha irruã mais nova; **2** (short time, distance) curto,-a; **3** (suffix) -inho,-a, -zinho,-a; ~ **house** casinha; ~ **man** (pej or affectionate) homenzinho; ♦ pron (small amount) pouco; ♦ adv (not enough) pouco; **a** ~ um pouco (de); ~ **by** ~ pouco a pouco; (minimum) **I go shopping as** ~ **as possible** vou às compras o mínimo possível.

Little Bear n Ursa Menor f.

liturgy n liturgia f.

live adj vivo,-a; **2** (burning) aceso,-a; (coal) ardente; **3** (ELECT) vivo,-a; (wire) carregado,-a; **4** (MUS, TV) em dire(c)to; (translation) ao vivo; ♦ vi viver; **2** (reside) morar, viver, habitar; ♦ vt (conduct) levar (uma vida); **to ~ one's life again** recomeçar a vida; ♦ **to ~ down** vt fazer esquecer; **to ~ in** (student) ser interno; (empregado doméstico) viver na casa; **to ~ off** (savings, assets) viver de; (parents) viver à custa dos pais; **to ~ on sth** vt viver de, sustentar-se de algo; ♦ vi (memory) perdurar; **to ~ out** vi dormir fora; **to ~ out sth** vt (survive) aguentar, sobreviver; **to ~**

together *vi (cohabit)* viver juntos; *(with lover)* em união de facto; ♦ **to ~ up to** *vt* cumprir; **2** *(to a person/ideal)* estar à altura de; **to ~ it up** divertir-se; **to ~ with** *vt* conviver; IDIOM **to ~ on the fat of the land** viver à grande; **to ~ from hand to mouth** viver com poucos meios, viver do seu trabalho diário.

live-in *adj* household resident.

livelihood *n* meio de vida, subsistência, o ganha-pão; **to earn one's ~** ganhar a vida.

lively *adj (vivacious)* vivo,-a, cheio,-a de vida; **2** *(party, day, atmosphere)* animado,-a; **3** *(pace)* rápido,-a; alegre *m,f.*

liven: to ~ up *vt* animar; ♦ *vi* animar-se.

liver *n (ANAT, CULIN)* fígado; *(CULIN) (Port. dish with thinly-cut liver steaks)* iscas *fpl.*

liverish *adj (fig)* rabugento,-a; mal-humorado,-a.

livery *n* libré; uniforme de lacaios; **~ horse** cavalo de aluguer *(BR: aluguel).*

lives *(pl of* **life***).*

livestock *n (cattle)* gado *m*, pecuária *f;* **2** *(chickens)* criação *f.*

livid *adj* lívido,-a; furioso,-a.

living *n (people):* **the ~** os vivos; **2** *(lifestyle)* estilo *m* de vida; **healthy ~** vida *f* saudável; **3 ~ room** sala de estar; **what do you do for a ~?** em que é que trabalha?; **to make a ~** ganhar a vida; ♦ *adj* vivo,-a; **~ proof** prova *f* viva; **~ conditions** *npl* condições *fpl* de vida; **~ standards** *npl* padrão *m*, nível *m* de vida; **~ wage** *n* salário *m* de subsistência.

lizard *n* lagarto *m;* *(smaller)* lagartixa *f.*

llama *n* lhama *f.*

LLB *n (abbr for* **Batchelor of Laws***)* licenciatura em Direito.

LLD *(abbr for* **Doctor of Laws***)* doutoramento em Direito.

load *n* carga *f;* *(on van, ship)* carregamento *m;* **a ~ of work** uma carga de trabalho; **2** *(TECH)* peso *m*, carga **(on** sobre); **3** *(ELECT, COMP)* carga; **4** *(fig)* **it is a great ~ off my chest** é um grande alívio para mim; ♦ *vt* carregar; *(COMP)* **to ~ a programme** carregar um programa; **2** *(fig) (inundate)* encher **(with** de); **to ~ the Christmas tree with decorations** encher a árvore com decorações; ♦ **a ~ of/ ~s of** *(fig)* (grande) quantidade de, um montão de; **get a ~ of that girl!** olha para aquela moça!; ♦ **to ~ down** *vt* sobrecarregar **(with** com); **to ~ up** *vt* carregar.

loaded *adj* carregado,-a **(with** de); **2** *(meaning)* com duplo sentido; *(question)* tendencioso,-a; **3** *(coll) (filthy rich)* podre de rico; **4** *(coll)* bêbedo,-a, bêbado,-a *(BR)* chumbado,-a; **5 ~ with** *(fig) (inundated)* cheio de *(presents)*, coberto em *(medals).*

loading bay *n* zona *f* de carga.

loaf *(pl:* **loaves***) n* um pão *m;* **to ~ about/around** vadiar, levar uma vida ociosa; **use your ~!** use a sua massa cinzenta, os seus miolos.

loafer *n (idler)* vadio,-a; **2** *(shoe)* mocassim *m.*

loam *n* marga *f.*

loan *n* empréstimo *m;* ♦ *vt* emprestar; **to ask for a ~** pedir emprestado; **on ~** emprestado; *(person)*

destacado,-a **(to** a/para); **~ shark** *n* usurário,-a, agiota *m,f.*

loath *adj:* **to be ~ to do** estar pouco inclinado a fazer.

loathe *vt* aborrecer; odiar.

loathing *n* aversão *f;* ódio *m;* **it fills me with ~** tenho-lhe (uma) aversão.

loathsome *adj* repugnante.

loaves *(pl of* **loaf***).*

lob *n (SPORT)* bola *f* alta; ♦ **(-bb-)** *vt* lançar; *(FOOT)* jogar uma bola alta; *(tennis)* rebater com um lob/ uma bola.

lobby *(pl:* **-ies***) n* vestibule *(BR)* saguão *m;* **2** *(POL)* grupo de pressão, lobby *m;* ♦ **(-ied)** *vt* pressionar.

lobbyist *adj* lobista.

lobe *n (ANAT)* lóbulo *m.*

lobotomy *(pl:* **-ies***) n* lobotomia *f.*

lobster *n* lagosta *f;* **~ pot** *n* covo *m* para apanhar lagostas.

local *n (UK) (pub)* bar *m* local; **2** *(local)* **the ~s** *npl* os moradores *mpl* locais; ♦ *adj* local *(UK).*

locale *(US)* local.

locality *n* localidade *f.*

locally *adv* localmente, *(in the region)* nos arredores; *(neighbourhood)* na vizinhança.

locate *vt* localizar, situar; colocar.

location *n* localização *f.*

location *n* posição *f;* **on ~** *(CIN)* no local; exteriores, *(BR)* externas.

loc. cit. *(abbr for* **loco citato***)* loc. cit.

loch *n (Scot)* lago *m.*

lock *n* fechadura *f*, fecho *m;* **2** *(on canal, river)* eclusa, comporta; **3** *(steering lock)* ângulo *m* de giro; **4** *(of hair)* mecha *f*, anel *m* (do cabelo); ♦ *vt (with key)* fechar à chave; **2** *(with bolt)* trancar; **3** *(mecanismo)* bloquear; **4** *(hold)* **to be ~ed in an embrace** estar fortemente abraçado; **~ in** (o.s.) fechar-se; **to ~ sb in** prender alguém; **to ~ out sb** trancar do lado de fora; **(o.s.)** fechar-se do lado de fora; **to ~ up sb** meter alguém na prisão; **to ~ up sth** fechar algo à chave; IDIOM **to keep sth under ~ and key** fechar algo a sete chaves.

locker *n (for clothes in school)* compartimento com chave; cacifo *m;* **~ room** *n* vestiário *m.*

locket *n (charm)* medalhão *m.*

lockgate *n* porta *f* de eclusa.

lockjaw *n* tétano *m;* trismo *m.*

lockout *n* greve *f* patronal.

locksmith *n* serralheiro,-a.

lock-up *(prison)* prisão *f*, cárcere *m;* **2** *(garage)* garagem *f* com tranca.

loco, locomotive *n* locomotiva *f.*

locum *n* (médico, farmacêutico, etc) interino,-a, substituto,-a.

locust *n* gafanhoto *m;* **a plague of ~s** uma praga de gafanhotos.

lodge *n* casa do guarda/do porteiro; *(Univ) (porter's)* portaria; **2** *(freemasonry)* loja *f;* **hunting~** pavilhão *m* de caça; ♦ *vi:* **to ~ (with)** alojar-se (na casa de); ♦ *vt (register)* apresentar *(complaint, appeal).*

lodger *n (paying guest)* hóspede.

lodgings *npl* alojamento *sg;* *(house)* casa *sg* de hóspedes.

loft *n (in the roof vault)* sótão *m;* **converted** ~ águas furtadas *fpl,* mansarda *f;* **2** *(church)* galeria *f.*

lofty (-ier, -iest) *adj (tower)* alto,-a; **2** *(noble)* sublime, elevado,-a; **3** *(pej)* arrogante.

log *n (of a tree)* tronco; **2** *(firewood)* lenho, toro, cepo; ♦ *(-ged-) vt (AGR)* cortar em toros; cortar lenha; **2** *(record)* registar *(BR)* registrar; *(COMP)* registar em log; **to** ~ **in** *(COMP)* entrar no sistema; **to** ~ **out** *(COMP)* sair do sistema; IDIOM **to sleep like a** ~ dormir como uma pedra.

loganberry *(pl: -ies) n* framboesa *f* silvestre.

logarithm *n* logaritmo *m.*

logbook *n (NAUT)* diário de bordo; **2** *(AER)* caderneta de voo; **3** documentação *f* (do carro).

log cabin *n* cabana *f.*

log fire *n* fogueira *f.*

logger *n (lumberjack)* lenhador *m;* **2** *(tractor)* tractor para os cepos.

loggerhead *n* tartaruga *f* marítima; **to be at** ~**s** (**with**) em desacordo, disputa (com).

logic *n* lógica *f.*

logical *adj* lógico,-a.

logistics *n* logística *f.*

logo *n* logótipo *m.*

logojam *n* problema *m* crónico *(BR: -ô-).*

loin *n* (carne do) lombo; ~ **cloth** *n* tanga; ~**s** *npl* lombo *sg,* dorso *sg;* ♦ **loins** *npl* ancas *fpl;* **2** *(crotch)* entrepernas; **3** *(euph for womb, genitals)* **child of my** ~ fruto do meu ventre.

loiter *vi (hang about)* perder tempo, demorar-se; *(pej)* vadiar, vagabundar.

loll *vi* (= ~ **about**) refestelar-se, reclinar-se; **2** *(cabeça)* pender.

lollipop *n* chupa-chupa, *(BR)* pirulito; picolé *m.*

lolly *(pl: -ies) n (UK) (sweet)* chupa-chupa; **ice** ~ gelado *m* de gelo; **2** *(coll) (money)* bago *m,* massa *f (fam).*

London *npr* Londres; **Londoner** *n* londrino,-a.

lone *adj* solitário,-a.

loneliness *n* solidão *f,* isolamento *m.*

lonely (-ier, -iest) *adj (gen)* solitário,-a; **she is** ~ ela está só; **2** *(place)* isolado,-a.

loner *n (person)* solitário,-a.

lonesome *adj (person)* solitário,-a, pessoa só.

long *n:* **the** ~ **and the short of it is that** em poucas palavras é que; ♦ *(-er, -est) adj (in length)* longo, comprido; **the table is four metres** ~ a mesa tem quatro metros de comprimento/mede quatro metros; **2** *(time)* longo,-a; com duração; **how** ~ **does the plane take?** quanto tempo vai levar o avião?; **how** ~ **will you be?** quanto tempo vai você demorar-se?; **a friend of** ~ **standing** um amigo de longa data; **in the** ~ **run/term** a longo prazo; **3** *(fig)* no final de contas; *(distance, place)* **a** ~ **way down** no fim de *(street);* lá embaixo *(hill, stairs);* ~**-faced** *adj* desanimado,-a com cara de aborrecido; ~**-gown** *n* vestido de noite; ~**-haired** *adj* de cabelo/s *m* comprido/s; **in** ~**hand** *n* escrito,-a à mão; ~**-haul** *adj* de longa distância; *(AER)* de longo curso; ~ **in the tooth** *adj (person)* velho,-a; ~**johns** *n* ceroulas *fpl;* ~**jump** *n* salto em

comprimento *(BR:* em distância); ~**-lost** *adj* perdido há muito (tempo); ~**-playing record** (**LP**) álbum *m,* LP *m;* ~**-range** *adj* de longo alcance; ~**s** *npl (FIN)* valores retidos na esperança que os preços subam; ~**-sighted** *adj (MED)* hipermetrope *m,f* presbita *m,f; (fig)* perspicaz; ~**-standing** *adj* de muito tempo; ~**-suffering** *adj* paciente, resignado,-a; ~**-term** *adj* a longo prazo; ~ **wave** *adj* onda *f* longa; ~**-winded** *adj (speech, conversation)* prolixo,-a, cansativo,-a; ♦ *adv (for a long time)* **how** ~ **have you been here?** há quanto tempo está você aqui?; **don't be** ~ não te demores; **it won't be** ~ (**now**) isto não vai levar muito tempo; ♦ ~ **ago** há muito tempo; ~ **after** muito depois; **before** ~ *(future)* dentro de pouco tempo; ~ **before** *(= past)* muito antes; *(after noun)* **all night** ~ toda a noite; **those days are** ~ **gone** esse tempo já se foi há muito; isso foi outrora; ♦ **at** ~ **last!** por fim, finalmente; **so** ~**!** até logo!; até à vista; ♦ *conj* **as** ~ **as** *(provided that)* desde que *(+ pres subj);* **as** ~ **as you are quiet** desde que estejas calado; **2** *(while, whilst)* enquanto *(+ fut subj)* **as** ~ **as I am the boss** enquanto eu for a patroa; **3** *(time)* tanto/tão ... quanto; **as** ~ **as possible** tão cedo quanto possível; ♦ *vi* **to** ~ **for sb/sth** ansiar por, ter saudades de alguém/algo; **2** *(be impatient)* **to** ~ **to do sth** estar impaciente por fazer algo.

long arm of the law *n* poder *m* da lei.

long-distance *adj* de longa distância, de longo curso; *(TEL)* interurbano, chamada *f* de longa distância.

long-drawn-out *adj* interminável.

longer, longest *(comp and super of* **long***) adj* mais longo, comprido; **her hair is longer** o cabelo dela está mais comprido; **2** *(time)* **no ... longer** não ... mais; **I cannot stand this any longer** não aguento mais isto; **I no longer speak to him** já não falo com ele; **it was the longest day of my life** foi o dia mais longo da minha vida.

longevity *n (person)* longevidade *f.*

longing *n* desejo, anseio *m* (**for** por); **2** *(nostalgic)* saudade *f.*

longingly *adv* ansiosamente.

longitude *n (GEOG)* longitude *f.*

longshot *n (fig)* possibilidade *f* remota; **by a** ~ de modo algum.

loo *n (coll)* retrete *m,* toalete *m,* casa de banho, *(BR)* banheiro *m;* ~ **roll** *n* rolo *m* de papel higiénico.

loofah *n* esponja *f* vegetal.

look *n (expression)* olhar *m;* **2** *(glance)* olhadela *f* vista *m* de olhos; **to** ~ **over sth briefly** dar uma vista de olhos; **3** aparência *f,* aspecto *m;* **I like the** ~ **of the house** gosto da aparência da casa; ~**s** *npl* **her good** ~**s** sua beleza, seu belo físico; **I don't like the** ~**s of him** não gosto do ar dele; **by the** ~**s of it** pelo jeito; ♦ *vi (gaze, stare)* olhar; **2** *(appear)* aparentar; **he doesn't** ~ **his age** ele não aparenta a idade que tem; ♦ ~ **at** *vt* olhar para; **2** *(closely)* examinar, considerar; **3** *(TV)* ver; ♦ ~ **after** *vt* cuidar de; ~ **after o.s.** cuidar-se;

♦ ~ **back** *vi* olhar para trás; **2** *(memories)* recordar, rever o passado; ♦ ~ **down** *vt* olhar para baixo; ~ **down on** *vt (fig)* desdenhar, desprezar (alguém); **to** ~ **for** *vt* procurar; ~ **forward to** *vt* aguardar com prazer, ansiar por; ~ **into** *vt* investigar, analisar; ♦ ~ **like** *vi* parecer-se com; **she ~s like her father** ela parece-se com o pai; **2** parecer; **he ~s lost** ele parece perdido; ~ **as if/as though** parecer como se; ♦ ~ **on** *vi (watch)* observar; **2 to** ~ **onto** dar para, ter vista para; ♦ **to** ~ **out (for)**; ♦ *vi* ter cautela (com), estar atento,-a; ♦ **to** ~ **out for** *vt (search) vt* procurar; **2** esperar (alguém); ~ **round** *vi* olhar em redor; **to** ~ **through** olhar por/ através; **she ~s through the window** ela olha pela janela; **2** *(document)* examinar; ♦ ~ **to** *vt* contar com; **2** *(think about)* pensar em; ♦ ~ **sb up** visitar alguém; ~ **sth up** tentar encontrar algo; **to** ~ **up** *vi* levantar os olhos; olhar para cima; **2** melhorar; **things are ~ing up** as coisas parecem melhorar; **to** ~ **up to sb** *vt* admirar, respeitar (alguém).

lookalike *n* sósia *m,f*.

looker *adj (fam) (very attractive)* **she is not a bad** ~ ela não é nada feia; ela é bonita.

look-in *n* oportunidade de participar, ter sucesso em.

looking-glass *n* espelho *m*.

lookout *m (place)* posto *m* de observação *f*, guarita *f*, vigia *f*; **2** *(person)* vigilante; **3** *(search)* **to be on the** ~ estar à espreita de algo, estar de atalaia; **4** *(fig)* perspe(c)tiva; **look-up** *n* pesquisa.

loom *n* tear *m*; ♦ *vi* assomar-se; erguer-se; **2** *(fig)* (ameaça) estar iminente; aproximar-se; ~ **large** *(exams, events)* aproximar-se ameaçadoramente.

loony *n (coll)* lunático,-a; ~ **bin** *(coll, pej)* asilo *m* para doentes mentais, manicómio *(BR: -ô-)*; ♦ (-**ier**, -**iest**) *adj* lunático,-a.

loop *n (gen)* círculo *m*; **2** *(bow)* laço *m*; **3** *(AER; SPORT)* salto *m*, volta *f*, curva *f* (no ar); **4** *(contraceptive)* D.I.U. *m*; **5** *(ELECT)* circuito *m* fechado; **6** *(COMP)* círculo *m*; ~ **of Henle** *n (COMP) (instructions)* instruções repetidas num programa.

loophole *n* buraco; **2** *(omission)* lacuna *f*.

loopy *adj (coll)* pateta, tarado,-a, doido,-a.

loose *n adj (free)* solto,-a, livre; **on the** ~ *(criminal, animal)* à solta; **2** *(slack)* frouxo,-a; **3** *(garment: not tight)* folgado,-a amplo-a; **4** *(COMM) (unpackaged)* avulso,-a, a granel; **5** *(screw)* desaparafusado,-a; **6** *(handle, tooth)* abalado,-a; **7** *(dated) (promiscuous woman)* fácil; ~ **living** vida *f* airada; **8** *(MED) (bowels)* diarreia; *(fam)* **the runs**; ~ **change** *n* troco, trocado *m*; ~ **cover** *(sewing)* cobertura *f* solta; ~ **end** ponta *f* solta; **to be at a** ~ estar indeciso,-a; atrapalhado,-a; ~-**leaf** *adj (of a folder, album)* de páginas *fpl* soltas, removíveis; ~-**limbed** *adj (of a person)* flexível, elástico,-a; **to break** ~ escapar-se, libertar-se; **to let** ~ largar, soltar; **to** ~ **weight** emagrecer; ♦ *vt* perder; **2** *(shake off)* escapar de; ♦ *vi (fail to win)* perder-se; **2** *(time)* atrasar-se; IDIOM **to be at a** ~ **end** não saber o que fazer; **to have a screw** ~ ter um parafuso a menos, não regular bem da cabeça.

loose-fitting *adj (clothes)* folgado,-a, largo-a

loosely *adv* livremente; afrouxadamente; **2** *(translation)* livremente, de modo aproximado.

loosen *vt* soltar, livrar, desprender; **2** afrouxar; **to** ~ **one's purse strings** *(coll)* alargar a bolsa; **to** ~ **one's grip on sth** relaxar o seu domínio sobre; ♦ *vi* soltar-se, livrar-se; **to** ~ **up** *vi (fam)* descontrair-se; *(before a sport)* aquecer-se.

loose-tongued *adj (person) (irresponsible chatter)* linguareiro,-a.

loot *n* saque *m*, despojo *m*; ♦ *vt* saquear, pilhar.

looter *n* saqueador *m*; gatuno,-a.

looting *n* pilhagem *f*, saque *m*.

lop (-**pp**-) *vt* podar, cortar *(tree)*; ~**off** *(branches)* reduzir, cortar; **he ~ped off part of the tree** ele cortou parte da árvore.

lope: to ~ **along** *vi* avançar aos saltos, andar a passos largos; trotar.

lop ear *n (of animal)* orelha *f* pendente.

lopsided *adj (uneven)* assimétrico,-a; torto,-a; inclinado,-a para o lado.

loquacious *adj* locaz.

loquat *n (fruit)* nêspera *f*; *(also called:* nêspera-do-Japão).

lord *n (English title)* senhor *m* (**of** de), Lorde; **the L~** *(REL)* o Senhor, Deus; **good L~!** meu Deus!; **the (House of) L~s** a Câmara dos Lordes; **L~ Mayor** *n (UK)* Presidente *m* da Câmara Municipal.

Lord Chancellor *(UK: POL)* Presidente da Câmara dos Lordes e responsável pela Justiça na Inglaterra e País de Gales.

lordly *adj (like a lord)* senhorial; *(person)* com um porte *m* distinto; **2** *(proud)* altivo,-a.

Lordship *n*: **your** ~ Vossa Senhoria; Vossa Excelência; **his** ~ Sua Senhoria, Sua Excelência; **2** *(judge)* Meritíssimo; **3** *(bishop, etc)* Reverendíssimo.

lore *n (of a people)* sabedoria popular, tradições *fpl*.

lorry *n* camião *m*, *(BR)* caminhão *m*; ~ **driver** *n* camionista *m,f*; *(BR)* caminhoneiro,-a.

lose *(pt, pp* lost) *vt* perder; **to** ~ **sight of** perder de vista; ♦ *vi (*= **to** ~ **out)** perder, ser vencido; ♦ *vi* ~ **one's way** perder-se; **2** *(in the post)* extraviar-se; **the letter got lost (in the post)** a carta extraviou-se; ♦ **to** ~ *(clock)* atrasar-se.

loser *n* perdedor,-a; vencido,-a.

losing *adj* perdido,-a.

loss *n* perda *f*, prejuízo *m*; **I have suffered a** ~ **of £30 K** sofri uma perda de trinta mil libras; **to be at a** ~ *(fig)* estar perplexo; não saber como; **I am at a** ~ **for words** faltam-me as palavras; **to be a dead** ~ *(useless)* ser totalmente inútil; ser uma grande perda, um grande prejuízo.

loss adjuster *n* especialista *m,f* em determinar danos.

lost *(pt, pp of* lose); ♦ *adj* perdido,-a; ~ **property** *n sg (objects) mpl* achados e perdidos; ♦ *exc* **get** ~! vai ver se chove!

lot¹ *n (at auction)* lote *m*; *(US: of land)* lote *m*; **2 the lot** *(whole quantity)* tudo, o todo; **two ~s of tickets** dois lotes de bilhetes; **3** *(of people)* grupo; **one** ~ **of tourists has arrived** um grupo de turis-tas já chegou; *(pej)* **that** ~ *(people)* essa gentinha *f*; **the best of a bad** ~ o menos mau; ♦ *pron (fam)* **a** ~

of, ~s of *(a greal deal)* muito, bastante; **I go to the cinema a** ~ vou muito ao cinema.

lot² *n (fate)* destino, sorte *f*; **to draw ~s** tirar à sorte.

lotion *n* loção *f*.

lottery *n* lotaria, *(BR)* loteria; ~ **ticket** *n* bilhete *m*.

lotto® *n* lotaria *f* nacional britânica.

loud (-**er**, -**est**) *adj (voice, music)*, alto,-a; **2** *(bang, scream)* forte; **3** *(noise)* barulhento,-a; **4** *(showy, garish)* espalhafatoso,-a; **5** *(colour)* berrante; **6** *(applause)* vivo, grande; **the TV is very** ~ a TV está muito alta; **I heard a** ~ **scream** ouvi um grito *m* forte; **speak louder** fale mais alto; ♦ *adv* em voz alta; com muito barulho; ~ **and clear** alto e claro, em alto e bom som.

loud-hailer *n* megafone *m*.

loudly *adv* ruidosamente; em voz alta.

loudmouth *n* indiscreto,-a.

loudspeaker *n* alti-falante *m*.

lough *n (Irlanda)* braço de mar.

lounge *n* sala de estar *f*, salão *m*; *(in airport, station)* sala de espera; ~ **suit** *n (men's matching trousers/ coat)* fato *m*; *(BR)* terno; ♦ **to** ~ **(around)** *vi (in a chair)* recostar-se, espreguiçar-se; **to** ~ **around/about** estar sem fazer nada, sentar-se indolentemente.

lounger *n (chair)* espreguiçadeira; ♦ *adj (person)* ocioso,-a, indolente.

louse *(pl: lice)* *n* piolho *m*.

lousy *adj* piolhento,-a; *(fig)* desprezível, vil.

lout *n* rústico,-a; grosseiro,-a, labrego,-a.

lovable *adj* adorável *m,f*, *(fig)* querido,-a.

love *n* amor *m*; ~ **affair** ligação, aventura *f* amorosa, caso *m (de amor)*; **2** ~**bird** *n (ZOOL)* periquito; ~**birds** *(fig) npl* amantes, namorados; ~ **bite** chupão *m*; ~ **child** *n* filho,-a ilegítimo; ~ **life** vida *f* amorosa; ♦ *vt* amar, adorar; **to be in** ~ **with** estar apaixonado por; **to fall in** ~ **with** apaixonar-se por; **to make** ~ fazer amor; **for the** ~ **of** pelo amor de; ♦ *vt* amar, adorar.

loveless *adv* sem amor.

loveliness *n* encanto *m*, beleza *f*.

lovelorn *adj (due to unrequitted love)* doente de amor.

lovely *adj (delightful)* encantador,-ora; *(gen)* lindo,-a; **2** *(weather)* bom, boa, belo,-a maravilhoso,-a; **3** *(child)* adorável; **4** *(meal)* delicioso,-a; **it smells** ~ cheira bem.

lovemaking *n (sex)* a(c)to de fazer amor; relação *f* sexual.

lover *n* amante; namorado,-a; **2 a** ~ **of** um apreciador, amante de.

lovesick *adj* loucamente apaixonado,-a; com saudades do seu amor.

lovey *n (UK) (fam)* amorzinho *m*; ~-**dovey** *adj (coll) (sentimental display of love)* piegas; **to get all** ~ ficar todo pinga-amor.

loving *adj* carinhoso,-a, terno,-a; **a** ~ **family** uma família unida.

lovingly *adv* carinhosamente.

low *n (METEOR)* depressão, área *f* de baixas pressões; **2** *(fig) (low point)* depressão *f*, nível *m* mais baixo; ♦ (-**er**, -**est**) *adj (gen)* baixo,-a; **a** ~ **chair**

uma cadeira baixa; **we are** ~ **on petrol** estamos com pouca gasolina; **2** *(health)* debilitado,-a, fraco,-a; **3** *(opinion)* pobre; **4** *(depressed)* deprimido; ~-**fat** *adj* com baixo teor de gordura; *(cheese)*magro,-a; *(leite)* desnatado,-a; ~-**flying** *adj* de voo rasante, a baixa altitude; ~-**grade** *adj* de baixa/má qualidade; ~-**key/keyed** *adj* discreto,-a; discreto,-a; contido; ~-**life** *(pl:* -**lifes)** *n (coll) (person)* crápula; *(scene, contact, friend)* do submundo; ~-**necked** *adj (dress)* decotado,-a; ~**ness** *n (ceiling)* baixa altura; ~-**paid** *adj* mal pago; ~ **season** *(tourism)* época *f* baixa; ~ **tide** *n* maré *f* baixa; ♦ *adv* baixo, abaixo *(BR)* embaixo; **I rate her pretty** ~ não a tenho em grande conta; **I wouldn't sink/stoop so** ~ não me rebaixaria assim.

low-alcohol *adj* de baixo teor alcoólico.

low-born *adj* de origem *f* modesta.

low-brow *adj (pej)* inculto,-a.

Low Countries *npl* Países *mpl* Baixos.

low-cut *adj (dress)* decotado.

lowdown *n* information, detalhe *m*, factos *mpl*; **2** *adj (action)* baixo,-a, desonesto,-a.

lower *adj* mais baixo; inferior; ♦ *vt (bring down)* baixar *(basket, blind)*; *(CONSTR)* rebaixar *(ceiling, door)*; **2** *(reduce)* reduzir *(price)*; diminuir *(temperature)*; **3** *(drop)* **to** ~ **one's voice, arms, eyes** baixar a voz, os braços, os olhos; **4** *(NAUT)* arriar *(sail)*; ♦ *vr:* **to** ~ **o.s. to** *(demean o.s.)* rebaixar-se a; ~ **o.s. into** sentar-se cuidadosamente em *(chair, bed)*.

lower case *n (TYPO)* em letras *fpl* minúsculas, caixa *f* baixa.

Lower House *n (POL)* Câmera *f* Baixa.

lowering *n (gen)* descida *f*; *(of flag, sail)* descida; **2 the** ~ **of barriers** abolição *f*.

lower sixth *n (UK) (school)* primeira classe *f*.

lowest *adj* o/a mais baixo,-a, o menor; ínfimo,-a; **the** ~ **common denominator** *n (MATH)* o menor denominador comum.

Lowlands *npl* as regiões *fpl* baixas da Escócia; terras baixas.

loyal *adj* leal **(to** a).

loyalist *n* patriota *m,f*, leal ao governo; **Loyalists** *npr (POL) (Northern Ireland)* leais ao governo britânico lealistas.

loyalty *(pl:* -**ies)** *n* lealdade, fidelidade *f*; ~ **card** cartão *m* de fidelização.

lozenge *n* losango; *(MED)* pastilha *f*.

LP *n (abbr for* **long-playing record)** álbum *m*, LP *m*.

L-plates *npl* placa de aprendiz de motorista.

LSD *(abbr for* **lysergic acid diethylamide)** LSD.

LSE *(abbr for* **London School of Economics)** faculdade de Londres de Ciências e Económicas.

Lt *(abbr for* **lieutenant)** Ten (tenente).

LT *n (abbr for* **low tension)** *(ELECT)* baixa tensão *f*.

Ltd *(abbr for* **limited company)** Ltda (companhia limitada).

Luanda *npr* Luanda.

lubricant *n* lubrificante *m*.

lubricate *vt* lubrificar.

lucerne *n (UK) (BOT) (alfalfa)* luzerna *f*; alfafa/alfalfa.

lucid *adj* lúcido,-a; *(clearly understood)* claro,-a nítido,-a.
lucidity *n* lucidez *f.*
luck *n* sorte *f;* **bad/hard** ~ má sorte *f,* azar *m;* **good** ~! boa sorte!; **to be in good** ~ estar com sorte.
luckily *adv* felizmente; ~ **for me** felizmente para mim.
lucky *adj* feliz; ~ **fellow/dog/devil** *(fam)* felizardo, sortudo; ~ **girl** felizarda; **to strike it** ~ ganhar a sorte grande; ~ **charm** *n* amuleto *m;* ~ **dip** *n* saco *m* de surpresas.
lucrative *adj* lucrativo,-a.
ludicrous *adj* ridículo,-a.
ludo *n (game with dice)* ludo *m,* jogo *m* da glória.
lug *(-gged, -gging) vt* arrastar; puxar.
luggage *n* bagagem *f;* ~ **rack** *n* rede *f* para bagagem; porta-bagagem *m;* ~ **porter** *n* bagageiro *m.*
lug hole *n (fam) (UK) (ear)* orifício do ouvido; orelha.
lugubrious *adj* lúgubre *m,f.*
lukewarm *adj* morno,-a; tépido,-a; **2** *(pessoa)* indiferente *m,f.*
lull *n* trégua *f;* calmaria *f;* **the** ~ **before the storm** *(fig)* a bonança antes da tempestade; ♦ *vt* embalar; acalentar; acalmar.
lullaby *(pl: -ies) n* canção *f* de embalar *(BR:* de ninar).
lumbago *n* lumbago *m.*
lumber *n (US) (timber)* madeira *f* serrada, tábua; **2** *(UK) (bric-a-brac)* trastes *mpl* velhos; ♦ *vi (heavy person, animal)* andar a custo; ~ **with** *vt (fam) (to be burdened with an unwanted thing/person)* **he is** ~ **with his mother-in-law** ele está encarregado da sogra/sobrecarregado com a sogra; ~**jack** *n* madeireiro, lenhador *m;* ~**mill** *n* serraria.
luminary *(pl: -ies) adj (US) (fig) (person)* sumidade *f.*
luminous *adj* luminoso,-a.
lump *n (of sugar)* torrão *m;* **2** *(a piece of)* pedaço *m;* **3** *(med) (tumor)* caroço *m;* **4** *(fig)* **a** ~ **in the throat** *(with emotion)* nó *m;* **5** *(swollen)* inchaço *m;* **6** *(on the head from a bump)* galo *m;* ♦ *vt* (= ~ **together)** amontoar; **a** ~ **sum** soma global, montante *m.*
lumpy *adj (lumps in the soup, sauce)* granuloso,-a; grumoso,-a; ~ **mattress** colchão *m* com covas.
lunacy *n* loucura *f.*
lunar *adj* lunar.
lunatic *n adj* lunático,-a; louco,-a; ~ **asylum** *n* manicómio *(BR:* -cô-), hospício; ~ **fringe** *n* minoria *f* extremista.
lunch *n* almoço *m;* ~ **time** *n* hora do almoço; ♦ *vi* almoçar.
luncheon *n* almoço *m* formal.
lung *n* pulmão *m;* ~ **cancer** *n* cancro *m (BR:* câncer *m)* do pulmão.
lunge *vi* (= ~ **forward)** precipitar-se (para a frente), arremessar-se; dar estocada em; **to** ~ **at sb** arremeter-se contra.
lupin *(UK)* **lupine** *(US) n (BOT)* planta trepadeira; ~ **seed** *n* tremoço *m.*
lupine *adj (of wolf)* lupino, de lobo.

lupus *n (MED) (skin disease)* lúpus *m.*
lurch *n* guinada *f,* solavanco *m;* **to leave sb in the** ~ deixar alguém em dificuldades; ♦ *vi (person, vehicle)* guinar, andar de um lado para o outro; **2** ~ **forward/along** *m (sway, stagger)* cambalear, andar aos ziguezagues.
lure *n* atra(c)ção *f;* **2** *(fishing)* isca *f;* **3** *(hunting)* chamariz *m,* engodo *m;* ♦ *vt* atrair **(with** com), seduzir; **to** ~ **sb away from sth** desviar alguém de algo.
lurid *adj (colour)* berrante, gritante; **2** *(shocking detail)* sensacional; **3** *(violence)* horrível; **4** *(wan)* pale.
lurk *vi* esconder-se; estar à espreita, estar à coca.
luscious *adj (woman)* voluptuoso,-a; **2** *(food)* delicioso,-a, suculento,-a.
lush *n (US: drunkard) (slang)* bêbado,-a; ♦ *adj (vegetation)* viçoso, exuberante, luxuriante; **2** *(surroundings)* luxuoso,-a.
Lusitanean *n adj (Portuguese)* lusitano,-a; **the** ~ **horse** *n* o cavalo lusitano.
Lusitania *n (Portugal's old and poetic name)* Lusitanea *f.*
Luso- *(combining form) (indicating Portugal, Portuguese).*
lusophile *n adj* lusófilo,-a.
lusophone *adj* lusófono,-a.
lust *n* desejo *m* (sexual); **2** *(deadly sin)* luxúria *f;* **3** *(greed)* cobiça *f;* ♦ **to** ~ **after/for** *vi (person)* desejar; **2** *(money, power)* cobiçar; ambicionar por.
lustful *adj* lascivo,-a, sensual *m,f.*
lustre *n (UK)* luster *(US) (of a polished item)* lustre *m;* brilho *m.*
lustreware, lusterware *n* cerâmica *f* vidrada.
lusty *adj* robusto,-a forte *m,f.*
lute *n* alaúde *m;* ~ **player** *n* tocador de alaúde.
Lutheran *n adj* luterano,-a.
luv, luvvie *n (UK) (fam; pretentious)* (linguagem de atores) amorzinho *m,f.*
Luxembourg *n* Luxemburgo; **in** ~ em Luxem-burgo.
Luxembourger *n adj* luxemburguês,-esa.
luxuriant *adj* luxuriante *m,f,* exuberante *m,f.*
luxurious *adj* luxuoso,-a; ♦ *adj* de luxo.
luxury *n* luxo *m;* **in the lap of** ~ no luxo; ~ **articles** artigos *mpl* de luxo.
LW *n (abbr for* **long wave)** *(RADIO)* onda longa, OL.
lychee *n (fruit)* líchea *f.*
lying *n* mentira *f;* ♦ *adj* mentiroso,-a, falso,-a; **2** *(pres. pp of:* **to lie)** situado,-a; **3** deitado,-a.
lymph gland *n* glândula *f* linfática.
lynch *vt* linchar.
lynching *n* linchagem, *(BR)* linchamento.
lynx *(pl: -es) n (ZOOL)* lince *m.*
lyre *n* lira *f.*
lyric *adj* lírico,-a.
lyrical *adj* lírico,-a.
lyricism *n* lirismo *m.*
lyricist *n (in a composition)* escritor,-ora da letra.
lyrics *npl* letra de canção.

m

M, m *(letter)* M, m; **2 M** *(UK)* *(abbr for* **motorway***)* rodovia *f.*

m *(abbr for* **metre/s***)* metro/s *m*; **2** *(abbr for* **mile/s***)* milha/s *f*; **3** *(abbr for* **million***)* milhão *m*; **4** *(abbr for* **minute/s***)* minuto/s *m.*

MA *(abbr for* **Master of Arts***)* mestre,-a em Letras, Ciências Humanas; mestrado *m* em Letras; **2** *(abbr for* **Military Academy***)* Academia *f* Militar; **3** *(abbr for* **Massachusetts***, US).*

Ma'am *n* *(abbr for* **madam***)* Senhora *f*, madame *f* (modo também de endereçar membros da família real inglesa).

maar *n* *(GEOL)* vulcão *m* embrionário.

Maastricht *npr* Maastricht; ~ **Treaty** *n* *(POL)* Tratado *m* de Maastricht, Tratado *m* da União Europeia.

macabre *adj* macabro,-a.

macadam *n* *(road surface)* macadame *m.*

macadamise *vt* macadamizar.

macadamia *n* *(BOT)* *(nut)* noz *f* de macadâmia.

Macao *npr* Macau; **in** ~ em Macau.

macaroni *n* *(CULIN)* macarrão *m*; ~ **cheese** macarrão gratinado.

macaronic *adj* macarrónico,-a.

macaroon *n* maçapão *m* (bolinho feito com amêndoa pisada, clara de ovo e açúcar).

macaw *n* *(ZOOL)* arara *f.*

maccaboy *(also:* **maccabaw***)* *n* *(tobacco)* variedade de rapé *m* perfumado.

macchiato *n* café *m* pingado.

mace *n* *(old weapon)* maça *f*, clava *f*; **2** *(ceremonial staff)* bastão *m*; **3** *(spice)* macis *m.*

Mace® *n* gás *m* lacrimogéneo.

Macedonia *npr* Macedónia *f.*

Macedonian *npr adj* macedónio,-a; *(LING)* macedónio.

macerate *vt* macerar.

machete *n* faca *f* de mato, machete *f.*

Machiavelli *npr* Maquiavel.

machiavellian *adj* maquiavélico,-a, diabólico,-a.

machinations *npl* maquinações *fpl*, intrigas *fpl.*

machine *n* máquina *f*; ~ **gun** *n* *(weapon)* metralhadora *f*; ~ **intelligence** *n* inteligência *f* artificial; **printing** ~ *n* máquina *f* para impressão; **saw** ~ *n* *(tool)* serra *f* mecânica; **sewing** ~ *n* máquina *f* de costura; ~ **translation** *n* tradução *f* automática; ~ **tool** *n* ferramenta *f* mecânica; ♦ *vt* *(sewing)* coser à máquina; **2** *(TECH)* usinar.

machinery *n* maquinaria *f*; **2** *(fig)* *(system)* mecanismo *m.*

machinist *n* maquinista *m,f*, operário,-a, *(BR):* operador,-ora de máquinas.

machismo *n* machismo *m.*

Mach number *n* *(AER)* número *m* Mach.

macho *n* homem *m* viril; ♦ *adj* viril *m,f*, másculo,-a; **2** *(pej)* machista *m,f.*

mack¹ *(also:* **mac***)* *(abbr for* **mackintosh***).*

mack² *n* *(slang)* *(pimp)* chulo *m.*

mackerel *npl* *(ZOOL)* *(fish)* cavala *f*; **2** ~ **shark** *(ZOOL)* *(fish)* anequim *m*; **3** ~ **sky** *n* *(streaked)* céu *m* coberto de pequenas nuvens.

mac(k)intosh *n* *(clothing)* capa *f* impermeável.

mackle *n* *(TYPO)* impressão *f* tremida; **2** *(blot)* borrão *m*; ♦ *vt* *(mend)* consertar à pressa ou sem cuidado.

macle *n* *(crystallography)* macla *f.*

macramé *n* *(type of lace)* renda *f* macramé.

macro *n* *(COMP)* macro *m*; ♦ *prefix* macro; *(in compounds)* macro.

macrobiotic *adj* *(diet)* macrobiótico,-a.

macrocosm *n* macrocosmo *m.*

macroeconomics *n* macroeconomia *f.*

macrograph *n* macrografia *f.*

macron *n* *(LING)* *(diacritic)* mácron *m.*

macrophysics *n* *(PHYS)* macrofísica *f.*

macroscopic *adj* macroscópico,-a.

macrostructure *n* macroestrutura *f.*

macula *n* mácula *f*, mancha *f*; **2** ~ **lutea** *n* *(MED)* *(eye)* mácula *f* lútea.

maculate *vt* manchar.

mad *adj* *(MED)* louco,-a, demente *m,f*; **to go** ~ enlouquecer; **2** *(fig)* *(crazy)* louco,-a; **I am** ~ **about her** estou louco por ela; **3** *(furious)* doido,-a; *(animal)* enraivecido,-a; **4** *(pej)* *(foolish)* maluco,-a; **5** ~ **cow disease** *n* doença *f* das vacas loucas.

Madagascan *n adj* malgaxe *m,f*; *(LING)* malgaxe.

Madagascar *npr* Madagascar; **in** ~ em Madagascar.

madam *n* senhora *f*, madame *f*; **2** *(coll)* *(UK)* *(young woman – pretentious)* pretensiosa *f*; sabichona *f.*

madcap *adj* desmiolado,-a, estapafúrdio,-a.

madden *vt* *(go crazy)* enlouquecer; **2** *(anger)* irritar.

made *(pt, pp of* **make***)*; ♦ *adj* feito,-a; constituído,-a **(from, of, on/by, up** de, por, sob); **a** ~ **man** um homem de sucesso; **Chinese** ~ feito na China; ~ **to order** feito por encomenda.

Madeira *npr* *(GEOG)* Ilha *f* da Madeira; **in** ~ na Madeira; **2** ~ **wine** vinho da Madeira.

made-to-measure *adj* feito sobre medida *(BR)*; feito por medida *(EP).*

made-up *adj* *(wearing make-up)* maquilhado,-a, *(BR)* maquiado,-a; ~ **story** história *f* inventada.

madhouse *n* *(coll)* casa *f* de malucos; **2** manicómio *(dated)* hospital *m* psiquiátrico.

madly *adv* loucamente; ~ **in love** loucamente apaixonado,-a.

madman *n* louco *m*; **madwoman** *n* louca *f.*

madness *n* loucura *f*, demência *f.*

Madonna *n* *(REL)* Madona *f*, Nossa Senhora; **2** *(ART)* madona *f*, imagem *f* que representa Nossa Senhora.

madrigal *n* *(MUS)* madrigal *m.*

madwort *n* *(BOT)* alisso *m.*

Maecenas *n* mecenas *m,f.*

maelstrom *n* remoinho *m* de água, turbilhão *m*.
maestro *n* (MUS) mestre *m*, maestro *m*.
MAFF (abbr for **Ministry of Agriculture Fisheries, and Food**) Ministério *m* Britânico da Agricultura, da Pesca e dos Alimentos.
Mafia *n*: **the** ~ a Máfia.
mag¹ (abbr for **magazine**).
mag² *n* (Vd: **magpie**); ♦ *vi* (fam) (to chatter) tagarelar.
magazine *n* revista *f*; **2** (ammunition) depósito *m* de munições.
magenta *n adj* (colour) magenta *m*.
maggot *n* (ZOOL) larva *f* de inse(c)to.
maggoty *adj* podre *m,f*, com bichos.
Maghreb *npr* Magrebe; **the** ~ o Maghreb.
magic *n* magia *f*; **black** ~ magia *f* negra; **like** ~ como por magia; ~ **carpet** (in fairy tales) tapete *m* voador; ~ **eye** *n* (UK) (telecom) olho *m* mágico; ~ **mushroom** *n* (drug) cogumelo *m* mágico; ~ **wand** varinha *f* mágica; ♦ *adj* mágico,-a; **2** (dazzling) deslumbrante *m,f*.
magical *adj* mágico,-a; **a** ~ **moment** um momento mágico, maravilhoso.
magician *n* (wizard) mago *m*; **2** (conjurer) mágico *m*, prestidigitador *m*; ilusionista.
magisterial *adj* (authoritative) magistral *m,f*, autoritário,-a; **2** (JUR) (duties, office) judicial *m,f*.
magistracy *n* magistratura *f*.
magistrate *n* magistrado *m*, juiz-a; **to appear before the** ~**s** comparecer diante dos magistrados; ~**s' court** *n* (UK) tribunal *m*.
maglev *n* (abbr for **magnetic levitation train**) (high-speed train) MagLev *m*, comboio *m* de levitação magnética.
magma *n* (GEOL) magma *m*.
Magna Carta *n* base das liberdades políticas e individuais inglesas elaborada em 1215.
magnanimous *adj* magnânimo,-a.
magnate *n* (powerful person) magnata *m,f*.
magnesia *n* (CHEM) óxido *m* de magnésio.
magnesite *n* carbonato *m* de magnésio.
magnesium *n* (CHEM) magnésio *m*.
magnet *n* íman *m*, (BR) ímã *m*.
magnetic *adj* magnético,-a; ~ **axis** *n* eixo *m* magnético; ~ **compass** *n* bússola *f* magnética; ~ **constant** *n* constante *f* magnética; ~ **field** *n* campo *m* magnético; ~ **resonance** *n* (medical scanning) ressonância *f* magnética.
magnetism *n* magnetismo *m*.
magnetize *vt* magnetizar.
magnific *adj* magnificente *m,f*, imponente *m,f*.
magnification *n* aumento *m*; ampliação *f*.
magnificence *n* magnificência *f*.
magnificent *adj* magnífico,-a; suntuoso,-a.
magnify *vt* (enlarge) aumentar; ampliar; **2** (exaggerate) exagerar.
magnifying glass *n* lupa *f*, lente *f* de aumento.
magniloquent *adj* (speech) grandiloquente *m,f*.
magnitude *n* magnitude *f*, grandeza *f*; **earthquake** ~ *n* magnitude *f* sísmica.
magnolia *n* (BOT) magnólia *f*.

magpie *n* (ZOOL) (bird) pega *f*; **2** (chatterbox) fala-barato *m,f*.
mahogany *n* mogno *m*; ♦ *adj* de mogno.
Mahomet *n* (REL) Maomé *m*.
maid *n* empregada *f*, criada *f*; **old** ~ (pej) solteirona *f*; ~ **of honour** dama *f* de honor.
maiden *n* moça *f*, donzela *f*; **2** (horse) cavalo que nunca ganhou uma corrida; ♦ *adj* solteirona *f*; **2** (speech, voyage) inaugural *m,f*, **3** (century, flight) primeiro,-a; ~ **name** *n* nome *m* de solteira; ~**head** *n* (virginity) virgindade *f*, hímen *m*; ~ **speech** *n* discurso *m* inaugural.
maieutic (method) *n* (PHIL) maiêutica *f*.
maigre *n* (ZOOL) (fish) corvina *f*.
mail *n* correio *m*; correspondência *f*; ~**bag** (for transport) mala *f* postal; ~**box** *n* (US) caixa *f* de correio, (in the street) marco *m* do correio; (COMP) caixa *f* de entrada; ~ **order** *n* encomenda *f* por correspondência; ~ **shot** *n* publicidade *f* postal; **e-~** *n* email *m*, correio *m* elec(c)-trónico; ♦ *vt* (to mail) pôr no correio; (BR) postar; **2** (send) mandar pelo correio.
mailing *n* (dispatch) envio *m* (pelo correio); **2** (for advertising) mailing *m*.
maillot *n* (female swimsuit) fato-de-banho *m* feminino; (BR) maiô *m*.
mailman *n* carteiro *m*; (pop) o correio.
maim *vt* mutilar, aleijar, estropiar.
main *n* (pipe) (gas, water) cano *m*, conduta *f* principal; **2 the** ~**s** (ELECT) a rede *f* elé(c)trica; canalização *f* principal; ♦ *adj* principal *m,f*; ~ **course** (of a meal) prato *m* principal; ~ **office** sede *f*; ♦ **in the** ~ *adv* dum modo geral.
mainframe *n* (COMP) unidade *f* principal.
mainland *n* continente *m*.
mainline *n* (RAIL) linha *f* principal, ferroviária *f* principal.
mainly *adv* sobretudo, principalmente.
mainsail *n* (NAUT) vela *f* grande.
mainspring *n* mola-mestra *f*; **2** (cause) causa *f*.
mainstay *n* (NAUT) *n* estai *m* do mastro grande; **2** (fig) pilar *m*, base *f*, suporto.
mainstream *n*: corrente dominante; **the** ~ a tendência *f* geral; ♦ *adj* predominante, tradicional.
maintain *vt* manter; **2** (preserve) conservar (em bom estado); **3** (assert) afirmar.
maintenance *n* manutenção *f*; **2** sustento *m* pensão.
maître d'hôtel *n* chefe de mesa *m,f*.
maize *n* (corn) milho *m*.
Maj.-Gen. (abbr for **Major-General**).
majestic *adj* majestoso,-a, imponente *m,f*.
majesty *n* majestade *f*.
majolica *n* (pottery) majólica *f*.
major *n* (MIL) major *m*; **2** (US) (subject) disciplina *f* principal; ♦ *adj* (main) principal, importante *m,f*; **2** (MUS) maior; ♦ *vi* (US) **to** ~ **in sth** (Univ) especializar-se em algo.
Majorca *npr* Maiorca *f*; **in** ~ em Maiorca.
Majorcan *n adj* maiorquino,-a.
majorette *n* baliza *f*.
major-general *n* (MIL) general-de-divisão *m*.

majority *(pl: -ies) n (greater part of)* maioria *f*; **2** *(age)* maioridade *f*; ♦ *adj (votes, shareholder)* maioritário,-a; **2** *(decision opinion)* da maioria.

make *n (brand, type)* marca *f*; ~ **over** *n* transformação *f*; ~-**up** *n* maquil(h)agem *f*; carácterização *f*; ♦ *vi* reconciliar-se; maquil(h)ar-se; ♦ *(pt, pp* **made)** *vt* fazer; fabricar, produzir; **to** ~ **the bed** fazer a cama; **to** ~ **sb happy/sad** alegrar/entristecer alguém; **3** *(cause to do)* **to** ~ **sb do sth** fazer com que alguém faça alguma coisa; **she** ~**s me laugh** ela faz-me rir; **4** *(sums)* ser; **five plus five** ~**s ten** cinco e cinco são dez; **5** *(commit)* **I made a mistake** fiz um erro; **6** *(reach, have success)* **we'll never** ~ **it on time** nunca conseguiremos chegar lá a tempo; **7** *(become)* **she will** ~ **a good cook** ela vai tornar-se uma boa cozinheira; ♦ **to** ~ **do with** contentar-se com; **to** ~ **for** *(in haste)* *vt* dirigir-se para *(lugar, pessoa)*; **2** *(bring about)* **your money will** ~ **for the happiness of many** o seu dinheiro fará a felicidade de muitos; **to** ~ **of** *(opinion)* achar; **what do you** ~ **of this?** que acha disto?; ♦ **to** ~ **off** *vi* fugir, sair depressa; ~ **off with sb/sth** arrebatar alguém, roubar algo; ♦ **to** ~ **out** *vt (see)* decifrar; distinguir, avistar; **2** *(cheque, receipt)* passar; **3** *(form)* preencher; **4** *(pretend)* **he made out that he didn't know** ele fingiu que não sabia; **5** *(do well, manage)* **how did you** ~ **out in the interview?** como se saiu na entrevista?; **to** ~ **out with sb** *(coll) (US) (necking)* namoriscar; *(coll)* fazer marmelada com alguém; ♦ ~ **up** *vt* inventar; embrulhar; **to** ~ **up for** *vt* compensar.

make-believe *n* fantasia *f*; **the land of** ~ o país do faz-de-conta; ♦ **to make believe** *vt* fingir.

make-do *adj* substituto,-a; ♦ **to** ~ **with** *vt* arranjar-se com.

maker *n* fabricante *m,f*.

makeshift *adj* provisório,-a, improvisado,-a.

make-up *n (THEAT)* maquil(h)agem *f*; **2** *(character)* caracterização; **to be part of sb's** ~ fazer parte do cara(c)ter de alguém; **3** *(TYPO)* composição *f*.

making *n* preparação *f*, produção *f*; **2** ~**s** potencialidades *fpl*, lucros *mpl*; **3 in the** ~ em vias de formação.

malachite *n (GEOL)* malaquite *f*.

malacophily *n* malacofilia *f*, polinização *f* com a intervenção de moluscos.

maladjusted *adj* desajustado,-a; inadaptado,-a.

maladjustment *n* inadequação *f*, desajustado,-a.

maladministration *n* má gestão *f*.

maladroit *adj* desajeitado,-a.

malady *n* enfermidade *f*.

mala fide *n (JUR)* má fé *f*.

malaise *n* mal-estar *m*, indisposição *f*.

malapropism *n* emprego inapropriado da palavra.

malapropos *adj* despropositado,-a.

malar *n (ANAT) (facial bone)* malar *m*.

malaria *n (disease)* malária *f*, febre *f* palustre.

malarky, malarkey *n (coll)* baboseira *f*, parvoíce *f*.

Malawi *npr* Maláui; **in** ~ no Maláui.

Malawian *n adj* malauiano,-a.

Malay *n adj* malaio,-a; **2** *(LING)* malauio.

Malaysia *npr* Malásia *f*; **in** ~ na Malásia.

Malaysian *n adj* malaio,-a.

malcontent *adj* descontente *m,f*, insatisfeito,-a.

Maldives (the ~) *(as)* Maldivas.

male *n (animal)* macho *m*; *(man)* homem *m*; ♦ *adj* macho, masculino *m*; ~ **chauvinist** *n (pej)* porco *m* chauvinista; ~ **issue** *n* filhos varões.

malefactor *n (criminal)* malfeitor *m*.

malevolent *adj* malévolo,-a.

malformation *n* malformação *f*; imperfeição *f*.

malformed *adj (nose, ears)* disforme *m,f*; *(heart)* malformado,-a.

malfunction *n* funcionamento defeituoso; **2** avaria.

malice *n* malícia *f*; maldade *f*.

malicious *adj* malicioso,-a, maldoso,-a; ~ **intent** *n* intenção *f* criminosa.

malign *adj* maligno,-a; ♦ *vt (slander)* difamar, falar mal de (alguém).

malignant *adj (MED)* maligno,-a.

malinger *vi (pej)* fazer-se de doente.

malingerer *n* doente *m* fingido.

mall[1] *n (US) (shopping)* mercado *m*, centro *m* comercial.

Mall[2]**: the** ~ avenida am Londres que vai ter ao Palácio de Buckingham.

mallard *n (ZOOL)* pato *m* bravo.

malleable *adj* maleável *m,f*.

mallet *n (tool)* maço *m*, marreta *f*; malho *m*.

mallow *n (BOT)* malva *f*.

malm *n (soft limestone)* marga *f*.

malnutrition *n* desnutrição *f*; subnutrição *f*.

malpractice *n* negligência *f*, incompetência *f* profissional; **2** conduta contrária à ética.

malt *n* malte *m*; ~ **whisky** uísque *m* de malte.

Malta *npr* Malta.

Maltese *n adj* maltês,-esa; *(LING)* maltês.

maltose *n (CHEM)* maltose *f*.

maltreat *vt* maltratar.

maltreatment *m* maus tratos *npl*.

malware *n (COMP)* programas *mpl* malignos, programas desenhos para prejudicar o sistema.

mammal *n (ZOOL)* mamífero *m*.

mammaplasty *n (MED)* mamoplastia *f*.

mammary *adj* mamário,-a.

mammography *n (MED)* mamografia *f*.

mammon *n* avareza *f*, gula *f*.

mammoth *n* mamute *m*; ♦ *adj (huge)* gigantesco,-a, imenso *m,f*.

man *(pl: **men**) n* homem *m*; **2** *(mankind)* humanidade *f*; **an old** ~ um velho; ~ **and wife** marido e mulher; ~**eater** *n (fam)* mulher *f* promíscua; ~~**made** *adj* artificial *m,f*, ♦ *(-nn-) vt (NAUT)* tripular; **2** *(MIL)* guarnecer de homens; **3** ocupar-se de; IDIOM **no** ~'s **land** *n* terra de ninguém.

manacle *n* algema *f*; ~**s** *npl* grilhões *mpl*.

manage *vi* arranjar-se; ♦ *vt* dirigir, administrar; influenciar, saber lidar com.

manageable *adj* manejável *m,f*; executável *m,f*.

management *n* dire(c)ção *f*, gerência *f*; gestão *f*.

manager, manageress *n* gerente *m,f*; *(SPORT)* treinador,-ora.

managing director *n* dire(c)tor-geral *m*.

Mancunian *adj* de Manchester; manchesteriano,-a.

mandarin *n* mandarim *m*; (= ~ **orange**) tangerina *f*.
Mandarin *n* (*LING*) mandarim *m*.
mandate *n* mandato, mandado *m*.
mandatory *adj* obrigatório,-a.
mandible *n* mandíbula; ~**s** *npl* (*insect*) pinças *fpl*.
mandolin(e) *n* (*instrument*) bandolim *m*.
mane *n* (*of horse*) crina; (*of lion*) juba *f*; **2** (*fig*) (*of person*) cabeleira *f*.
manfully *adv* virilmente; corajosamente.
manganese *n* (*CHEM*) manganésio *m*.
mange *n* (*VET*) sarna *f*; rabugem *f*.
manger *n* manjedoura *f*.
mangle *n* calandra *f*; ♦ *vt* mutilar, estropiar.
mango (*pl*: -**es**) *n* (*BOT*) manga *f*.
mangy *adj* (*with mange*) sarnento,-a; **2** (*shabby*) esfarrapado,-a; miserável *m,f*.
manhandle *vt* maltratar, tratar com rudeza.
manhole *n* poço *m* de inspe(c)ção.
manhood *n* (*adulthood*) idade *f* adulta; **2** (*manliness*) virilidade *f*.
man-hour *n* hora-homem *f*.
manhunt *n* caça *f* ao homem.
mania *n* (*PSYCH*) mania *f*; (*obsession*) paixão *f*.
maniac *n* maníaco,-a; (*fig*) louco,-a.
manic *adj* maníaco,-a; ~-**depressive** *n, adj* (*MED*) maníaco-depressivo,-a.
manicure *n* manicura *f*; ~ **set** *n* estojo *m* de unhas, de manicura; ♦ *vt* tratar das unhas.
manifest *adj* manifesto,-a, evidente *m,f*; ♦ *vt* manifestar, mostrar; **to** ~ **itself** manifestar-se.
manifestation *n* manifestação *f*.
manifesto *n* manifesto *m*.
manifold *adj* variado,-a; múltiplo,-a.
manipulate *vt* manipular, manejar.
mankind *n* humanidade *f*, raça *f* humana.
manky *adj* (*coll*) imundo,-a.
manly *adj* másculo,-a, viril.
manna *n* (*REL*) maná *m*.
mannequin *n* (*dummy, person*) manequim *m*.
manner *n* modo *m*, maneira *f*; **in the same** ~ da mesma maneira; **2** (*behaviour*) conduta *f*, comportamento *m*; **3** (*type*) espécie *f*, género (*BR*: gê-) *m*; **4** (*style*) **in/after the** ~ **of** à maneira de; **5** ~**s** *npl* modos *mpl*, maneiras *fpl* educação *f*; **bad** ~**s** falta *f* de educação; (*fam*) falta *f* de chá; **where are your** ~**s?** isso são maneiras?
mannered *adj* (*pej*) afe(c)tado,-a; amaneirado,-a; **well/ill** ~ bem/mal educado,-a.
mannerism *n* (*habit, trait*) particularidade *f*; afetação *f*; **2** (*gesture*) trejeito *m*.
Mannerism *n* (*ART*) maneirismo *m*.
mannerless *adv* malcriado,-a, grosseiro-a.
manning (*pres participle of:* **man**): **who is manning the office?** quem está encarregado do escritório?
mannish *adj* (*woman*) maculino,-a.
manoeuvre *n* manobra *f*; ♦ *vt* manobrar.
manometer *n* manómetro *m*.
manor *n* (= ~ **house**) casa *f* senhorial, solar *m*.
manpower *n* potencial *m* humano, mão de obra *f*.
mansard *n* (*flat in the roof*) mansarda *f*; águas-furtadas *fpl*.

manse *m* presbitério *m*.
mansion *n* mansão *f*, palacete *m*; solar *m*.
manslaughter *n* homicídio *m* involuntário.
manta *n* (*ZOOL*) (*fish*) jamanta *f*.
mantelpiece *n* (*over fireplace*) prateleira *f* da lareira; console *f* da lareira; parapeito *m* de chaminé; **2** (*frame round fireplace*) guarnição *f* de lareira.
mantic *adj* profético,-a.
mantis *n* (*ZOOL*) (*insect*) louva-a-deus *m*.
mantle *n* (*of fog, night*) manto *m*; **2** (*fig*) camada *f*; **to assume the** ~ **of** (*leadership, high position*) assumir a responsabilidade de.
mantra *n* (*Buddhism and Hinduism*) mantra *m*.
manual *n* manual *m*; **2** (*MUS*) teclado *m* (de órgão); ♦ *adj* manual *m,f*.
manufacture *n* manufa(c)tura *f*, fabrico *m*; fabricação *f*; ♦ *vt* manufa(c)turar, fabricar.
manufacturer *n* fabricante *m,f*.
manure *n* estrume *m*, adubo *m*.
manuscript *n* manuscrito *m*; obra *f* original; (*before printing*) **in** ~ em manuscrito.
many *adj* (*comp* **more**, *superl* **most**) muitos,-as; ~ **of us** muitos de nós; ♦ *pron* muitos,-as; **a great** ~ muitíssimos; ~ **a time** muitas vezes.
Maoism *n* (*POL*) maoísmo *m*.
Maori *n adj* (nativo da Nova Zelândia) maori *m,f*; (*LING*) maori.
map *n* mapa *m*, planta *f*; **2** plano *m* topográfico; ♦ *vt* traçar o mapa de; **to** ~ **out** *vt* planear, (*BR*: plane (j)ar) cuidadosamente; IDIOM **to be wiped off the** ~ desaparecer do mapa.
maple *n* (*BOT*) bordo *m*; ~ **syrup** xarope *m* de bordo.
mapping *n* cartografia; **2** (*COMP*) proje(c)ção topográfica.
mar (-**red**) *vt* estragar, danificar; **2** (*reputation*) prejudicar, manchar.
marasmus *n* (*MED*) marasmo *m*, atrofia *f* infantil.
marathon *n* maratona *f*.
marauder *n* saqueador; gatuno.
marble *n* (*rock*) mármore *m*; **2** (*in children's games*) berlinde *m*, (*BR*) bola *f* de gude; ~ **cake** *n* bolo *m* mármore; IDIOM **to lose one's** ~**s** (*coll*) perder a cabeça/o juizo.
marbled *adj* marmorizado,-a; **2** (*papel, carne*) jaspeado,-a.
March *n* Março, março *m*.
march *n* marcha *f*; **2** (*fig*) (*progress*) curso *m*, avanço *m*; **3** (*public demonstration*) manifestação *f*; ♦ *vi* (*MIL*) marchar; ~-**past** *n* desfile *m*; parada *f*.
marcher *n* (*protester*) manifestante *m,f*.
marching orders *npl* **to give sb his/her** ~ mandar alguém passear; **2** ordem *f* de despedimento.
marchioness (*pl*: -**es**) *n* marquesa *f*.
Mardi Gras *n* Terça-feira de Carnaval, Terça-feira Gorda.
mare *n* égua *f*.
margarine *n* margarina *f*.
margin *n* (*ger*) margem *f*; **2** (*of field*) orla *f*; **I lost by a small** ~ perdi por pouco.
marginal *adj* marginal *m,f*; **2** secundária; **3** ~ **seat** *n* (*UK*) (*votos*) lugar ganho por uma pequena maioria.

marguerite *n* (*flower*) malmequer *m*.

Mariana Trench *npr* (*GEOG*) a Fossa *f* das Marianas.

mariculture *n* aquacultura, aquicultura *f*.

marigold *n* (*flower*) margarida *m*.

marijuana *n* (*drug*) marijuana *f*; (*BR*) maconha *f*.

marina *n* marina *f*.

marinade *n* (*CULIN*) escabeche *m*; ♦ *vt* pôr de escabeche, pôr em salmoira.

marine *n* fuzileiro *m* naval; marinha *f*; ♦ *adj* marinho,-a; ~ **insurance** seguro marítimo; **2** naval.

marionette *n* marioneta *f*.

marital *adj* marital *m,f*; conjugal *m,f*; ~ **status** estado *m* civil.

maritime *adj* marítimo,-a.

marjoram *n* (*CULIN*) (*herb*) manjerona *f*.

mark *n* (*tag*) marca *f*, sinal *m*, etiqueta; **2** impressão *f*; **3** (*stain*) mancha *f*; **4** (*EDUC*) nota *f*, valor *m*; **5** (*currency*) marco *m*; alvo *m*; **to hit the** ~ acertar no alvo; **6** (*punctuation*) *n* sinal *m* (de pontuação); **question** ~ ponto *m* de interrogação; **7** (*CULIN*) (*level of temperature*) marca *f*; **trade~** *n* marca *f* registada; **to be quick/slow off the** ~ reagir depressa/devagar; ♦ *vt* marcar; **2** (*stain*) manchar; **3** (*exam, test*) marcar, classificar; ♦ **to ~ down** *vt* anotar; **2** (*price, note*) baixar (preço, nota); ♦ ~ **off** (*name, item on a list*) riscar, assinalar; **2** distinguir (**from** de); **3 wide off the** ~ longe da verdade; ♦ **to ~ out** *vt* traçar; marcar; **2** demarcar (*area*); **3** (*select*) designar; ♦ **to ~ up** *vt* (*COMM*) (*prices*) aumentar; ~-**up** *n* margem *f* de lucro; IDIOM **he is not up to the** ~ ele não está à altura de; **to ~ time** marcar o passo; **overstep the** ~ passar das marcas.

marked *adj* (*noticeable*) notável, evidente *m,f*; **2** acentuado,-a; **3** (*for punishment*) assinalado,-a.

marker *n* (*pen*) marcador *m*, **2** (*tag*) marca *f*; **3** (*SPORT*) marcador.

market *n* (*place*) mercado *m*; praça; **2** ~ **for** (*demand*) mercado para; **3** feira; **black** ~ mercado *m* negro, mercado *m* paralelo; **Common M~** Mercado Comum; ~ **day** *n* dia *m* de mercado; **domestic/ foreign** ~ mercado interno/externo; **open** ~ mercado livre; **stock** ~ mercado de valores; **to play the** ~ especular; ~ **value** valor comercial; ♦ *vt* vender; **2** (*large scale*) lançar (no mercado).

marketing *n* compra e venda *f*, marketing *m*.

marketplace *n* mercado *m*.

marksman *n* bom atirador *m*.

marksmanship *n* boa pontaria *f*.

marmalade *n* (*CULIN*) geleia *f*, doce *m* de laranja.

marmot *n* (*mammal*) marmota *f*.

maroon *adj* de cor castanho-avermelhado; **to be ~ed** *vt* ficar abandonado (numa ilha).

marquee *n* (*for events*) tenda *f*, barraca *f*.

marquess (*also*: **marquis**) (*pl*: **-es**, **marquis**) *n* marquês *m*.

marquetry *n* marchetaria *f*.

marquis (*also*: **marquess**) (*pl*: **-es**, **marquis**) *n* marquês *m*.

marriage *n* matrimónio (*BR*: -mô-) *m*; núpcias *fpl*, boda *f*; casamento *m*; ~ **bureau** *n* agência *f* matrimonial; ~ **certificate** *n* certidão *f* de casamento.

marriageable *adj* em idade de casar; (*person*) casadouro,-a.

marriage guidance *n* aconselhamento *m* a casais; ~ **counsellor** n terapeuta *m,f* para casais.

married *adj* casado,-a; conjugal *m,f*; **to get** ~ casar-se.

marrow *n* (*vegetable*) abóbora *f*, (*BR*) abobrinha *f*; **2** (*ANAT*) (*in bones*) medula *f*; tutano *m*; **2** (*fig*) âmago *m*.

marry (*pt, pp* **-ied**) *vt* casar(se) (**to** com); **it was Father Anthony who married them** foi o Padre António que os casou; **she is married to an Englishman** ela casou-se com um inglês; ♦ *vi* (= **get married**) casar-se; **to ~ sb off** (*find husband/wife*); **she is trying to ~ me off** ela está a tentar arranjar-me marido; **to ~ up** *vt* (*join, match up*) unir, corresponder.

Mars *npr* (*ASTROL*) Marte *m*.

marsh *n* pântano *m*; marisma *f*; ~ **fever** *n* (*disease*) malária *f*.

marshal *n* (*MIL*) marechal *m*; **2** (*US*) funcionário *m* com o cargo de xerife; ♦ *vt* dispor, ordenar; formar.

marshland *n* (*EP*) (*on the banks of river*) lezíria *f*; **2** pântano *m*; (*BR*) pantanal *m*.

marshmallow *n* (*plant*) alteia *f*; **2** (*sweet*) goma *f*.

marshy *adj* pantanoso,-a.

mart *n* (*abbr for* **market**) feira *f*, mercado *m*.

marten *n* (*ZOOL*) marta *f*; pele *f* de marta.

martial *adj* marcial *m,f*; ~ **art** *n* artes *fpl* marciais; ~ **law** *n* lei *f* marcial.

Martian *adj* marciano *m*.

martin *n* (*bird*) andorinhão *m*, gaivão *m*.

martinet *n* (*bossy*) pessoa *f* autoritária que mantém disciplina.

Martinique *npr* Martinica; **in** ~ na Martinica.

martyr *n* mártir *m,f*; ♦ *vt* martirizar.

martyrdom *n* martírio *m*.

marvel *n* maravilha *f*; pródigio *m*; assombro *m*; ♦ *vi* **to ~** (**at**) maravilhar-se (**de** com).

marvellous *adj* maravilhoso,-a, incrível *m,f*.

Marxism *n* marxismo *m*.

Marxist *n adj* marxista *m,f*.

marzipan *n* (*CULIN*) maçapão *m*.

mascara *n* (*cosmetic*) rímel *m*.

mascot *n* mascote *f*.

masculine *adj* masculino *m*.

masculinity *n* masculinidade *f*.

mash *n* mistura *f*; pasta *f*, papa *f*; ♦ *vt* esmagar, reduzir a papa.

mashed *adj* (*coll*) (*drunk*) embriagado,-a; ~ **potatoes** puré *m* de batata.

mask *n* máscara *f*; ♦ *vt* mascarar; disfarçar.

masking tape *n* fita *f* adesiva.

masochist *n* masoquista *m,f*.

mason *n* (= **stone ~**) (*worker*) pedreiro *m*; **2 free ~** maçom *m*; (*BR*) maçom *m*.

masonic *adj* maçónico *m* (*BR*: -çô-).

masonry *n* maçonaria *f*; alvenaria *f*.

masquerade *n* (*party*) baile *m* de máscaras; **2** (*fig*) (*sham*) farsa *f*, disfarce *m*; ♦ *vi* **to ~ as** disfarçar-se de, fazer-se passar por.

mass *n* multidão *f*; **2** *(PHYS, GEOG)* massa *f*; **3 M~** *(REL)* Missa *f*; **4** *(quantidade)* grande número *m* (**de** of); montão *m*, montes (**de** of); ◆ **the ~es** as massas *fpl*; ◆ *vi* reunir-se; *(MIL)* concentrar-se.

massacre *n* massacre *m*, carnificina *f*; ◆ *vt* massacrar.

massage *n* massagem *f*; ◆ *vt* dar massagens, massajar, *(BR)* massagear.

masseur *n* massagista *m*.

masseuse *n* massagista *f*.

massive *adj* sólido,-a; enorme *m,f*; **2** *(campaign, task)* de grande envergadura; **3** maciço,-a.

mass media *npl* meios *mpl* de comunicação social.

massotherapy *n* massagem *f* terapêutica.

mass-production *n* produção *f* em massa, série.

mass together *vt* aglomerar-se.

mast *n* *(NAUT)* mastro *m*; **2** *(RADIO)* antena *f*.

mastectomy *n* *(MED)* mastectomia *f*.

master *n* *(person in control)* senhor *m*; **to be his own ~** ser independente; **2** *(teacher)* mestre *m*; **3** *(who excels)* **he is ~ of his craft** ele é mestre do seu ofício; *(also* **M~)** *(ART)* mestre *m*; **the masters of Impressionism** os Mestres do Impressionismo; **4** *(Univ.)* **M~'s degree** mestrado *m*; **M~ of Arts** *n* Mestre *m*, Mestra *f* em Letras, Ciências Humanas; **5** *(owner)* dono *m*; **the dog and his ~** o cão e o seu dono; **6** *(title of young man)* **M~ X** o menino *m* X; **7** *(NAUT)* capitão (de navio mercante); ◆ *vt* dominar; conhecer a fundo, **2** dirigir, planejar.

master bedroom *n* quarto *m* principal *m*.

masterful *adj* *(dominant)* autoritário,-a.

master key *n* chave *f* mestra.

masterly *adj* *(technique)* magistral *m,f*.

mastermind *n* cérebro *m* (**of, behind** de, por detrás); *(BR)* cabeça *m,f*; ◆ *vt* **to ~** organizar, dirigir.

masterpiece *n* obra-prima *f*.

masterplan *n* plano *m* piloto.

masterstroke *n* golpe *m* de mestre.

mastery *n* domínio *m*.

mastic *n* almécega *f*.

masticate *vt* mastigar; esmagar.

mastiff *n* *(dog breed)* mastim *m*.

masturbate *vi* masturbar-se.

masturbation *n* masturbação *f*.

mat *n* esteira *f*; **2** (= **door ~**) capacho *m*, tapete; **3** (= **table ~**) prote(c)tor *m* de cortiça (debaixo dos pratos quentes), suporte *m* para pratos; ◆ *adj* (-**tt**-) mate *m,f*, baço,-a, sem brilho *m*, fosco,-a.

match *n* fósforo *m*; **2** *(competition)* jogo *m*, partida *f*; desafio *m*; **3** *(fig)* *(suitable)* igual; em igualdade; **to be a good ~ for sb** *(love)*; **4** *(colours, style)* combinar bem, ir bem com, condizer; **to meet one's ~** encontrar alguém à sua altura; **3** *(fig)* *(suitable)* igual, em igualdade; **to be a good (for sb)** ~ estar à altura (de alguem); *(love)* ser uma boa união; **4** *(colour, style)* combinação *f*; ◆ *vt* *(also* ~ **up)** condizer, combinar bem, igualar (**in for** em); ser compatível; ~ **up to** estar à altura de; ◆ *vi* combinar, casar-se.

matchbox *n* caixa *f* de fósforos.

matching *adj* que combina (com).

matchless *adj* sem igual, incomparável *m,f*.

matchmaker casamenteira *f*; **2** fabricante *m,f* de fósforos.

mate *n* *(UK)* *(friend)* amigo,-a, camarada *m,f*, companheiro,-a; **hey ~!** ó pá!; **2** ajudante *m,f*; **3** *(chess)* parceiro,-a; **4** *(ZOOL)* *(male)* macho; *(female)* fêmea; *(person)* cônjuge *m,f*; companheiro,-a; **5** *(NAUT)* imediato *m*; ◆ *vi* acasalar-se; ◆ *vt* acasalar.

material *n* matéria *f*; **2** material *m*; **3** *(cloth)* pano *m*, tecido *m*; **4** dados *mpl*; **~s** *npl* materiais *mpl*.

materialistic *adj* materialista *m,f*; material *m,f*; importante *m,f*.

materialize *vi* materializar-se, concretizar-se.

maternal *adj* maternal *m,f*, materno,-a.

maternity *n* maternidade *f*; ~ **hospital** *n* maternidade *f*; ~ **benefit** *n* subsídio *m* de maternidade; ~ **leave** *n* licença *f* de maternidade.

mathematical *adj* matemático *m*; exa(c)to,-a.

mathematician *n* matemático,-a.

mathematics, maths *n* matemática *fsg*; *(COMP)* de matemática.

matinée *n* matiné *f*.

mating *n* acasalamento *m*; ~ **call** *n* chamamento *m* do macho; ~ **season** *n* época *f* de cio.

matriarchal *adj* matriarcal *m,f*.

matriarchy *n* matriarcado *m*.

matrices *(pl of* **matrix)**.

matricide *n* matricídio *m*.

matriculation *n* *(Univ)* matrícula *f*.

matrimonial *adj* matrimonial *m,f*.

matrimony *n* matrimónio *(BR:* -mô-) *m*, casamento *m*.

matrix *(pl:* **matrices)** *n* matriz *f*.

matron *n* mãe *f* de família; **2** *(in a hospital)* enfermeira-chefe *f*.

matronly *adj* matronal; *(fig)* *(plump)* corpulento,-a.

matt *(UK)* **matte** *(US)* *adj* fosco,-a, baço,-a.

matted *adj* *(hair)* emaranhado,-a; **2** *(yarn, wool)* embaraçado,-a.

matter *n* questão *f*; assunto *m*; **2** *(PHYS)* *(substance)* matéria *f*, substância *f*; ◆ *vi* importar; **it doesn't ~** não importa, não faz mal; **what's the ~?** o que é que há?; **no ~ what** aconteça o que acontecer; **no laughing ~** não é caso para rir; **~s** *npl* estado *m* das coisas; assuntos *mpl*; ◆ **as a ~ of course** o que se é de esperar; por rotina; **as a ~ of fact** por acaso, por sinal, de fa(c)to; **~-of-fact** *adj* prosaico,-a, prático,-a.

matting *n* (= **mat**) *(for the floor/beach)* esteira *f*.

mattock *n* *(tool)* enxadão *m*; **2** picareta *f*.

mattress *n* colchão *m*; **spring ~** colchão de molas.

mature *adj* maduro,-a, adulto,-a; **2** *(policy)* vencido,-a; **3** *(wine)* envelhecido *m*; ◆ *vi* amadurecer; crescer; **2** *(FIN)* vencer-se.

maturity *n* maturidade *f*; **2** *(payment, cheque)* vencimento *m*.

maudlin *adj* *(song, tale, film)* sentimental; **2** *(person)* melancólico,-a; piegas *m,f*.

maul *n* *(hammer)* malho *m*; marreta *f*; ◆ *vt* maltratar; *(lion)* lacerar; *(fig)* dizer mal, deitar (alguém) abaixo.

Maundy *n* *(REL)* lava-pés *m*.

Maundy Thursday *n* Quinta-feira Santa *f.*
Mauritania *npr* Mauritânia *f;* **in** ~ na Mauritânia.
Mauritian *n adj* mauriciano,-a.
Mauritius *npr* Ilha Maurícia *f; (BR)* Maurício *m.*
mausoleum *n* mausoléu *m.*
mauve *adj* cor de malva *m,f.*
maven *n (US)* perito,-a, especialista *m,f.*
maverick *n (calf)* animal sem marca de dono; *(person)* vagabundo,-a; ♦ *adj* inconformista *m,f.*
mawkish *adj* insípido,-a, lamecha *m,f.*
maxim *n* máxima *f.*
May *n* maio *m;* ~**Day** primeiro de maio; **2 Mayday** *n (SOS)* socorro; SOS.
may *n (BOT) (hawthorn)* espinheiro-alvar *m.*
may *(pt* **might***) aux* poder; **he** ~ **come** *(doubt)* pode ser que ele venha; **2** *(asking permission)* ~ **I smoke?** posso fumar?; **if I** ~ **say** se me é permitido dizer; **3** ~ **God bless you!** que Deus o/a abençoe; **4 come what** ~ aconteça o que acontecer.
maybe *adv* talvez, pode ser.
mayday *n* SOS *m.*
mayhem *n (chaos)* confusão *f,* caos; **2** *(quarrel) (EP)* zaragata *f; (BR)* brigalhada *f.*
mayonnaise *n* maionese *f.*
mayor(ess) *n* presidente *m,f* da câmara (municipal), *(BR)* prefeito,-a.
maypole *n* mastro *m* engalanado usado nas danças folclóricas inglesas em Maio *(Vd:* **morris dancers***).*
maze *n* labirinto *m.*
Mb *(abbr for* **megabyte***)* Mb.
MBA *(abbr for* **Master of Business Administration***)* Mestrado *m* em Gestão de Empresa.
MBE *(abbr for* **Member the Order of the British Empire***) (UK)* membro *m,* beneficiário *m* da ordem do império britânico.
MC *n (abbr for* **master of ceremonies***)* mestre *m* de cerimónias; **2** *(abbr for* **Member of Congress***) (POL) (US)* Deputado,-a do Congresso.
McCoy *n (slang):* **the real** ~ *(authentic, genuine) (person, item)* de gema *f;* o autêntico.
MD *(abbr for* **Doctor of Medicine***)* médico,-a.
MDF *(abbr for* **medium-density fibreboard***) (wood substitute)* MDF.
me *pron* me; **2** *(stressed, after prep)* mim; **with** ~ comigo; **it's** ~ sou eu; ~-**time** tempo para mim.
meadow *n* prado *m,* campina *f.*
meagre *adj* escasso,-a, pobre *m,f.*
meal *n* refeição *f;* **2** *(ground grain)* farinha *f;* **square** ~ refeição *f* substancial; ~**s-on-wheels** *n* serviço *m* de refeições grátis aos idosos e pobres; ~ **ticket** *n (coll)* ganha-pão *m;* IDIOM **to make a** ~ **of sth** engonhar, demorar muito a fazer algo.
mean *n (MATH)* média *f;* **2** meio *m,* meio-termo *m;* ♦ *adj (person) (stingy)* avarento,-a, sovina *m,f; (coll)* unhas-de-fome; **2** *(coll) (person)* cruel *m,f,* de maus fígados; ~ **trick** ação mesquinha/baixa; suja; ♦ *(pt, pp* **meant***) vt* significar, querer dizer;

to ~ **to do** pretender, tencionar fazer; **do you** ~ **it?** está a falar a sério?; **what do you** ~**?** que quer dizer você?
meander *n* meandro *m,* sinuosidade *f;* ♦ *vi (river, path)* serpentear; **2** *(walking about)* vaguear; **3** *(in speaking)* divagar.
meaning *n* sentido *m,* significado *m.*
meaningful *adj* significativo,-a.
meaningless *adj* sem sentido.
meanness *n* avareza *f;* vileza *f,* baixeza *f,* mediocridade *f;* maldade *f,* mesquinhez *f.*
means *n (method)* meio *m;* **by** ~ **of** por meio de; **2** *npl (money)* recursos *mpl,* meios *mpl;* **person of** ~**s** pessoa de posses, de meios; ♦ **by all** ~ *adv* claro que sim; **2** *(please do)* faz favor; **by no** ~ *adv* de modo algum; **by any** ~**s** a todo o custo; ♦ *exc* **by all** ~**s!** claro que sim!, com certeza!
means test *n (UK)* averiguação oficial quanto aos meios do indivíduo necessitado, para fins de recebimento de subsídios extra da assistência social.
meant *(pt, pp of* **mean***).*
meantime, meanwhile *adv* (= **in the** ~) entretanto.
measles *n (disease)* sarampo *m;* **German** ~ rubéola *f.*
measly *adj (coll)* miserável *m,f;* **2** com sarampo.
measurable *adj* medível *m,f.*
measurably *adv* consideravelmente.
measure *n* medida *f;* escala *f;* **2** régua *f;* **3** limite *m;* **made to** ~ feito por medida ♦ *vt/vi* medir; tirar as medidas de; avaliar, ponderar.
measured *adj* medido,-a; **2** ponderado,-a.
measurement *n* medida; **2** *(of land; scale)* medição *f;* ~**s** *npl* medidas *fpl.*
meat *n* carne *f;* **cold** ~ frios *mpl;* ~ **ball** *n* almôndega *f;* ~ **pie** *n* empada/bolo de carne.
meaty *adj* carnudo,-a; substancial.
Mecca *npr (holy city of Islam)* Meca *f.*
mechanic *n* mecânico *m.*
mechanical *adj* mecânico *m.*
mechanics *n* mecânica *fsg.*
mechanism *n* mecanismo *m;* **2** *(PHIL)* mecanicismo *m.*
mechanization *n* mecanização *f.*
mechanize *vt* mecanizar.
mechanotherapy *n (MED)* mecanoterapia *f.*
mechatronics *n* mecatrónica *fsg.*
meconium *n (BIOL)* mecónio *m.*
MEd *(abbr for* **Master of Education***).*
medal *n* medalha *f,* condecoração *f*
medalist *n* medalhista *m,f.*
medallion *n* medalhão *m*
meddle *vi:* **to** ~ **in** meter-se em, intrometer-se em; **2** **to** ~ **with** mexer em; IDIOM **to** ~ **with sb's affairs** intrometer-se na vida de.
meddler *n* metediço,-a, que mete o nariz em tudo.
meddlesome *adj* intrometido,-a, bisbilhoteiro,-a.
medfly *n* mosca *f* da fruta.
media *n* órgãos, meios *mpl* de comunicação social; **the** ~ *n* os media *mpl, (BR)* a mídia *f;* ~ **studies** *npl* curso *m* de comunicação; ♦ *adj (event)* mediático,-a.
mediaeval *adj* (= **medieval***)* medieval *m,f.*
medial *adj* central *m,f;* **2** *(size)* médio,-a; normal *m,f.*

median *n (statistics)* média *f;* **2** *(US) (of road)* divisória *f* central; ♦ *adj (income, value)* médio.
mediate *vi* mediar.
mediation *n* mediação *f.*
mediator *n (JUR)* mediador,-ora.
medicable *adj (condition or disease)* tratável por medicação.
medical *n* exame *m* médico; ♦ *adj* médico,-a.
medicate *vt* medicar.
medicated *adj* medicado,-a, higienizado,-a.
medication *n* medicamento *m;* tratamento *m.*
medicinal *adj* medicinal *m,f;* ~ **leech** *n (animal)* sanguessuga *f* medicinal.
medicine *n (science)* medicina *f;* **2** *(medication)* remédio *m,* medicamento *m;* ~ **chest** *n* armário *m* de remédios; IDIOM **to give sb a taste of their own** ~ pagar (alguém) na mesma moeda.
medieval *adj* medieval *m,f.*
mediocre *adj* medíocre *m,f.*
mediocrity *n* mediocridade *f.*
meditate *vi* meditar; ♦ *vt* refle(c)tir, pensar sobre.
meditation *n* meditação *f.*
Mediterranean *adj* mediterrâneo,-a; **2 the** ~ **(Sea)** *m* o (mar) Mediterrâneo; **3** ~ **fever** *n (MED) (disease)* brucelose *f.*
medium *(pl: -iums or -ia) (CIN, TV)* meio *m* de expressão, de comunicação; **2** *(spiritualist)* médium *m,f;* ♦ *adj (average, middle)* médio,-ia; **2** meio; **in the** ~ **term** no meio termo; ~-**sized** *adj* de tamanho médio.
medley *n* mistura *f;* salgalhada *f;* **2** *(MUS)* miscelânea *f,* *(BR)* pot-pourri *m.*
medulla *n (ANAT)* medula *f.*
Medusa *npr (MITOL)* Medusa *f.*
meek *adj* manso,-a, dócil *m,f;* **2** fraco,-a.
meet *(pt, pp* met*) vt (find)* encontrar, achar, dar com; **2** *(encounter)* reunir-se com, ir ao encontro de; **to** ~ **sb at the station** ir buscar alguém à estação; **3** conhecer, ser apresentado,-a a; **I met him in Paris** conheci-o em Paris, fui-lhe apresentada em Paris; **4** *(to face)* enfrentar; cumprir; **5** *(demand, request) (COMM)* satisfazer; ♦ *vi (come together)* unir-se, reunir-se; **to** ~ **up with sb** encontrar-se com alguém; **to** ~ **with** *vt* reunir-se com; **2** tropeçar em; IDIOM **there's more to him than** ~**s the eye** ele não é o que parece; **to make ends** ~ fazer face às despesas.
meeting *n* encontro *m;* reunião *f;* **2** entrevista *f;* **2** *(COMM)* junta *f,* sessão *f;* **3** *(POL)* assembleia *f;* comício *m;* **to call a** ~ convocar uma reunião.
mega *prefix (in compounds)* mega; **2** *exc (coll) (UK)* ~! porreiro,-a!, colossal!
megabyte *n (COMP)* megabyte *m.*
megahertz *n (PHYS)* megahertz *m.*
megalomaniac *n adj* megalomaníaco,-a.
megaphone *n* megafone *m.*
megapixel *n (COMP)* megapixel *m.*
melancholy *n* melancolia *f;* ♦ *adj* melancólico,-a.
melanoma *n (MED)* melanoma *m.*
mellow *adj* melodioso,-a; suave *m,f;* maduro,-a; ♦ *vi* amadurecer.

mellowing *n* maturação *f,* amadurecimento *m.*
melodious *adj* melodioso,-a.
melodrama *n* melodrama *m.*
melody *n* melodia *f.*
melon *n* melão *m.*
melt *n* degelo *m;* **2** fusão *f;* ♦ *vi* fundir-se; **2** derreter-se *(snow, butter);* **3** enternecer-se *(person, heart);* **4** *(fig)* desvanecer-se; ♦ **to** ~ **away** desaparecer; **to** ~ **down** *(metal)* findir; *(wax)* derreter; **to** ~ **into** *(crowd)* fundir-se com; misturar-se, desfazer-se em; IDIOM **to** ~ **into tears** ficar lavado em lágrimas; desfazer-se em lágrimas.
meltdown *n (PHYS)* fusão *f;* **2** *(incident)* acidente *m* nuclear; **3** *(FIN) (crash)* declínio *m,* queda *f* vertiginosa.
melting point *n* ponto *m* de fusão.
melting pot *n (of races)* cadinho *m* de culturas.
member *n (of association, club)* membro *m;* sócio *m;* *(of staff)* empregado,-a; **M~ of Parliament (MP)** *(UK)* membro do Parlamento; deputado,-a.
membership *n* associação *f;* **2** quadro *m,* número *m* de sócios; **to seek** ~ **of** candidatar-se a sócio de; ~ **card** *n* cartão *m (BR:* carteira *f)* de sócio; ~ **fee** *n* quota; ~ **entrance fee** *n* jóia/joia.
membrane *n* membrana *f.*
memento *n* lembrança *f,* recordação *f.*
memo *n* memorando *m,* nota *f.*
memoirs *npl* memórias *fpl.*
memorable *adj* memorável *m,f.*
memorandum *(pl: -da) n* memorando *m,* lembrete *m.*
memorial *n* memorial *m,* monumento *m;* ♦ *adj* comemorativo,-a.
memorize *vt (commit to memory)* memorizar, decorar.
memory *n* memória *f;* recordação *f;* **2** *(sth remembered)* lembrança *f;* **3** *(commemoration)* **in loving** ~ **of** à memória de; IDIOM **to have a** ~ **like an elephant** ter memória de elefante; **to take a walk down** ~ **lane** recordar bons velhos tempos.
men *(pl of* man*).*
menace *n* ameaça *f;* ♦ *vt* ameaçar.
menacing *adj* ameaçador,-a.
menagerie *n* cole(c)ção *f* particular de animais selvagens.
menarche *n (PHYSIOL)* menarca *f.*
mend *n* remendo *m;* ♦ *vt* consertar, reparar, remendar; ♦ *vi* restabelecer-se; IDIOM **to be on the** ~ estar a melhorar; **to** ~ **one's ways** corrigir-se.
mendacity *n* falsidade *f,* mentira *f.*
mendicant *adj* pedinte *m,f.*
mending *n* reparação *f,* conserto *m.*
menfolk *msg* homens *npl* em geral.
menial *adj* doméstico,-a; *(pej)* baixo,-a; ~ **job** trabalho *m* inferior; **2** *(attitude)* servil.
meningitis *n (MED) (disease)* meningite *f.*
menopause *n* menopausa *f.*
men's room *n (US)* casa de banho *(EP);* banheiro *(BR).*
menstruate *vi* menstruar.
menstruation *n* menstruação *f.*
mensurable *adj* medível *m,f.*
menswear *n* vestuário *m* para homem.

mental *adj* mental *m,f*; **2** *(coll) (crazy)* maluco,-a; ~ **hospital** hospício *m*.

mentality *n* mentalidade *f*.

mentally *adv* mentalmente; ~ **handicapped** *adj* deficiente *m,f* mental.

menthol *n (CHEM)* mentol *m*.

mention *n* menção *f*; ♦ *vt* mencionar; referir-se a; **2** don't ~ **it!** não tem de quê!, de nada!

mentor *n* mestre *m*, conselheiro *m*; tutor,-ora.

menu *n* ementa *f*; *(BR)* menu *m*; lista *f*, cardápio *m*.

MEP *n (abbr for* **Member of the European Parliament)** deputado,-a ao Parlamento Europeu.

mercantile *adj* comercial *m,f*, mercante *m,f*.

mercenary *n* mercenário *m*.

merchandise *n* mercadorias *fpl*.

merchant *n (COMM)* negociante *m,f*, comerciante *m,f*; ♦ *adj* mercante, mercantil, do comércio; ~ **navy** *n* marinha *f* mercante.

merchantable *adj* negociável, vendável *m,f*.

merciful *adj* piedoso,-a, misericordioso,-a; benevolente *m,f*.

merciless *adj* impiedoso,-a; desumano,-a.

mercury *n (CHEM)* mercúrio *m*.

mercy *n* piedade *f*; **2** *(REL)* misericórdia *f*; **at the ~ of** à mercê de; ~ **killing** *n* eutanásia *f*.

mere *adj* mero,-a, simples *m,f*.

merely *adv* simplesmente, somente, apenas.

merge *vt* unir; misturar; fundir; ♦ *vi* unir-se; *(COMM)* fundir-se.

merger *n (COMM)* fusão *f*.

meridian *n* meridiano *m*.

meringue *n (CULIN)* suspiro *m*, merengue *m*.

merit *n* mérito *m*; valor *m*; ♦ *vt* merecer; ter direito a.

mermaid *n* sereia *f*.

merrily *adv* alegremente; divertidamente.

merriment *n* alegria *f*, júbilo *m*, divertimento *m*.

merry *adj (happy)* alegre *m,f*, jovial *m,f*, divertido,-a; **2** *(fam) (slightly drunk)* alegre; **M~ Christmas!** Feliz Natal!; ~-**go-round** *n* carrossel *m*.

mesh *n* malha *f* (de rede, peneira, ferro); **2** *(MECH)* engrenagem *f*; ♦ *vi* engrenar.

mesmerize *vt* hipnotizar.

mesne *adj (JUR) (in propriety)* intermediário,-a.

mess *n* confusão *f*; desordem *f*; **2** *(coll) (untidy and dirty)* chiqueiro *m;*, *(BR)* bagunça *f*; **3** *(MIL)* messe *f*; rancho *m*; ♦ **to ~ about** *vt (coll)* ocupar-se com trivialidades, perder tempo, empatar; **to ~ about with** *vi (meddle)* manusear, mexer em; *(US)* cometer adultério; **to ~ up** *vt* desarrumar; estragar; sujar; IDIOM **he is in a ~** ele está em maus lençóis/em apuros.

message *n* recado *m*, mensagem *f*; ~ **board** *n* quadro *m* de mensagens, *(COMM) (internet)* fórum *m*; **I get the ~** já percebi; **to get the ~ across** explicar, fazer entender.

messenger *n* mensageiro,-a; ~ **boy** *(office boy)* moço *m* de recados.

mess hall *n (MIL)* grande sala de jantar.

Messiah *n* messias; **the M~** o Messias.

Messrs *(abbr for* **messieurs)** Senhores (em cartas comerciais).

messy *adj (dirty)* sujo,-a; **2** *(untidy)* desarrumado,-a; **3** *(lawsuit)* difícil, complicado,-a.

met *(pt, pp of* **meet)**.

metabolism *n* metabolismo *m*.

metacarpus *n (ANAT) (hand)* metacarpo *m*.

metal *n* metal *m*; ~ **detector** *n* dete(c)tor *m* de metais.

metallic *adj* metálico,-a.

metallurgy *n* metalurgia *f*.

metamorphosis *(pl:* -**ses)** *n* metamorfose *f*.

metaphor *n* metáfora *f*.

metaphysics *n* metafísica *fsg*.

metastasis *n (MED)* metástase *f*.

mete *n* limite *m*, marco *m*; ♦ **to ~ out** *vt* distribuir; dar, conceder, infligir.

meteor *n (ASTRON)* meteoro *m*.

meteorite *n (ASTRON)* meteorito *m*.

meteorological *adj* meteorológico,-a.

meteorology *n* meteorologia *f*.

meter *n* medidor *m*; contador *m*; **parking ~** *n* parquímetro *m*.

methane *n (CHEM) (gas)* metano *m*.

method *n* método *m*.

methodical *adj* metódico,-a.

Methodist *n adj* metodista *m,f*.

meths, methylated spirits *n* álcool *m* metílico, desnaturado *m*.

meticulous *adj* meticuloso,-a.

metre *(UK)* **meter** *(US) n* metro *m*.

metric *adj* métrico,-a; ~ **system** *n* sistema *m* métrico.

metronome *n* metrónomo *n (BR:* -trô-) *m*.

metropolis *n* metrópole *f*.

mettle *n* cará(c)ter *m*, temperamento *m*, índole *f*.

mew *vi (cat)* miar *(also:* miaou, miaw).

Mexican *n adj* mexicano,-a.

Mexico *npr* México; **in ~** no México.

mezzanine *n* sobreloja *f*, mezanino *m*.

MI5 *(abbr for* **Military Intelligence Section Five)** serviço *m* britânico de contra-espionagem.

miaow *n (cat's voice)* miau; ♦ *vt* miar.

miasma *n* miasma *f*.

mice *(pl of* **mouse)**.

mickey *n*: IDIOM **to take the ~ out of sb** *(coll)* gozar, fazer troça de.

micro *pref* micro.

microbe *n* micróbio *m*.

microchip *n (COMP)* microchip *m*.

microclimate *n (ecology)* microclima *m*.

microfilm *n* microfilme *m*.

microphone *n* microfone *m*.

microprocessor *n (COMP)* microprocessador *m*.

microscope *n* microscópio *m*.

microscopic *adj* microscópico,-a.

microwave *n* microondas *mpl*.

mid *adj* médio,-a; central *m,f* do meio; **in ~ May** em meados de maio; **in ~ afternoon** no meio da tarde; **in ~ air** em pleno céu; ~**day** *n* meio-dia.

middle *n (centre)* meio *m*, centro *m*; **2** *(half)* metade *f*; **3** *(waist)* cintura *f*; ~ **finger** *n* dedo médio; ~**man** *n* intermediário; ~ **name** *n* segundo nome de batismo; **M~ Ages** *npl* Idade Média *fsg*; **M~ East** *n* Médio Oriente *m*; ♦ *adj* meio,-a; mediano,-a; **~-aged** de meia idade; **~-class** de classe *f* média; IDIOM **to split sth down the ~** dividir a meias.

middle-of-the-road *adj* moderado,-a.

middleweight *n (boxing)* peso médio.

middling *adj* mediano,-a, razoável *m,f*; assim-assim.

midfield *n* (*SPORT*) meio-campo *m*; (*footballer*) médio *m*.

midge *n (insect)* melga *f*.

midget *n (small people)* anão, anã; ♦ *adj* minúsculo,-a, miniatura *f*.

midlife *n* meia-idade.

midnight *n* meia-noite *f*; **M~ Mass** *n* missa do galo.

midriff *n* diafragma *m*; (*coll*) estômago *m*.

midst *n*: **in the ~ of** no meio de, entre.

midsummer *n* solstício do Verão; **2 a ~ day** um dia em pleno Verão; **3 M~'s Day** *n* dia de São João (24 de Junho).

midway *adj adv*: no meio do caminho (**between** entre).

midweek *adv* no meio da semana.

midwife (*pl*: **-wives**) *n* parteira *f*.

midwifery *n* trabalho *m* de parteira.

midwinter *n* solstício do inverno; em pleno inverno.

mien *n* aparência *f*, semblante *m*.

might (*pt of* **may**); ♦ *n* poder *m*, força *f*.

mightn't = **might not**.

mighty *adj* poderoso,-a, forte *m,f*.

migraine *n* enxaqueca *f*.

migrant *n* migrador,-a; ave *f* de arribação; emigrante *m,f*; ♦ *adj* migratório,-a; emigrante *m,f*.

migrate *vi* emigrar.

migration *n* emigração *f*.

mike *n (abbr for:* **microphone**); **to ~ up** *vt* fornecer microfone.

mil. *adj (abbr for* **military**) milita.

Milan *npr* Milão; **Milanese** *npr,adj* milanês-esa.

mild *adj (gentle)* pacífico,-a; brando,-a; **2** *(not extreme)* temperado,-a; ameno,-a; ligeiro,-a; suave *m,f*, leve *m,f*; **3** benigno,-a.

mildew *n* mofo *m*; (*BOT*) míldio *m*.

mildness *n* suavidade *f*; doçura *f*; brandura *f*.

mile *n* milha *f* (= 1609 metros).

mileage *n* distância *f* em milhas; **2** (*AUT*) quilometragem *f*.

mileometer *n* conta-quilómetros *m*, (*BR*) marcador *m* de quilometragem.

milestone *n* marco *m* miliário; acontecimento *m* importante.

milieu *n* meio *m*, meio social.

militant *n adj* militante *m,f*.

military *adj* military *m,f*.

militate *vi*: **to ~ against** militar contra; ser contra.

militia *n* milícia *f*; guarda *f* nacional.

milk *n* leite *m*; **breast ~** *n* leite *m* materno; **~man** *n* leiteiro *m*; **~ shake** *n* batido *m*; leite *m* batido com sorvete; **~ tooth** *n* dente *m* de leite; ♦ *vt* mungir, ordenhar; **2** *(fig)* explorar, chupar.

milky *adj* leitoso, lá(c)teo; **M~ Way** *n* Via Lá(c)tea.

mill *n* moinho *m*; engenho *m*; fiação *f*; **coffee ~** moinho *m* de café; **cotton ~** fábrica *f* de fiação; **water ~**

azenha *f*; **wind ~** moinho *m* de vento; ♦ *vt* moer; triturar *(flour, pepper)*; ♦ *vi* (= **~ about/around**) aglomerar-se; mover-se em círculos; IDIOM **to be put through the ~** passar as passas do Algarve.

millennium *(pl:* **-s** *or* **-ia**) *n* milénio (*BR:* **-lê-**) *m*.

miller *n* moleiro *m*.

millet *n* milho *m* miúdo, (*BR*) milhete *m*.

milli- *pref* mili; **~gram(me)** *n* miligrama *m*.

millilitre *n* mililitro *m*.

millimetre *m* milímetro *m*.

milliner *n* chapeleiro,-a de senhoras.

millinery *n* chapelaria *f* de senhoras.

million *n* milhão *m*; **a ~ times** um milhão de vezes.

millionaire *n* milionário,-a.

millstone *n* mó *f*, pedra (de moinho) *f*.

mime *n* mimo *m*; **2** mímica *f*; **3** *(person)* comediante *m,f*, mímico,-a; ♦ *vt* imitar; ♦ *vi* fazer mímica.

mimesis *n* (*LIT*) mimese *f*.

mimic *n* mímico *m*, imitador,-ora; ♦ *adj* mímico,-a, simulado,-a; ♦ *vt* imitar, parodiar.

mimicry *n* imitação *f*.

mimsy *adj* desinteressante *m,f*, insípido,-a.

minaret *n* minarete *m*.

mince *n* (*CULIN*) carne *f* picada; picado *m* de carne; ♦ *vt* picar, moer (*meat, vegetables*); ♦ *vi* (*pej*) andar, falar com afectação; IDIOM **not to ~ one's words** falar com toda a franqueza, (*coll*) não ter papas na língua.

mincemeat *n* recheio *m* de frutos secos, especiarias e banha; IDIOM **to make ~ of** reduzir a migalhas; dar cabo de.

mince pie *n* pastel *m* recheado de frutos secos picados.

Na Inglaterra, os **mince pies** comem-se tradicionalmente pelo Natal.

---

mincer *n* picador *m* de carne, máquina *f* de picar carne, (*BR*) moedor *m* de carne.

mind *n* (*ger*) mente *f*, cabeça; **2** espírito *m*; **state of ~** estado de espírito; **2 it is on my ~** não me sai da cabeça; **3** *(thoughts, memory)* **to have sth on one's ~** estar preocupado; **to cross sb's ~** passar pela cabeça de alguém; **to bring to ~** lembrar-se de; **to cast one's ~ back,** recordar, pensar no que já foi; **4** *(concentrate)* **to keep one's ~ on sth** concentrar-se em algo; **to bear sth in ~** levar algo em consideração; **5** *(opinion)* **to my ~** a meu ver; **to change one's ~** mudar de ideias; **we are of the same ~** somos da mesma opinião; **6** *(decision)* **to make up one's ~** decidir-se; **7** *(sanity)* **to lose one's ~** perder o juízo; ♦ *vi* (*care, worry*) importar-se; **do you ~ if I smoke?** importa-se que eu fume?; **never ~!** não faz mal; não importa!; esqueça; ♦ *vt* cuidar de, tomar conta de, ter cuidado; **she minds the house** ela toma conta da casa; **~ the step!** cuidado com o degrau!; **2** *(emphasis)* (*coll*) **~ you it will not be cheap** nota bem que não vai ser barato; IDIOM **to be out of one's ~** estar fora de si/louco; **to ~ one's p's and q's** ter cuidado como se fala; medir as palavras; **your own business** *(coll)* mete-te na tua vida.

mind-boggling *adj (coll)* espantoso,-a, incrível *m,f.*
mindful *adj* atento,-a; ~ **of** consciente de.
mindless *adj* estúpido,-a, insensato,-a; negligente.
mind's eye *n*: **in my** ~ na minhar imaginação; *(poet.)* com os olhos da minh'alma.
mine[1] *pron* (o) meu *m*, (a) minha *f*, (os) meus *mpl*; (as) minhas *fpl*; ♦ *adj*: **this pen is** ~ esta caneta é minha; **2 a friend of** ~ un amigo *m* meu.
mine[2] *n* mina *f*; ♦ *vt* extrair, explorar, minar; ♦ ~**field** *n (MIL)* campo *m* minado; ~**layer** *n* lança-minas; **miner** *n* (~**worker**) mineiro,-a.
mineral *n* mineral *m*; **2** ~**s** *npl* águas *fpl* minerais, gaseificadas; ♦ *adj* mineral.
mineshaft *n* poço *m* de mina.
minesweeper *n* draga-minas *m (EP)*, caça-minas *m (BR)*.
minger *n (fam)* pessoa nojenta, fedorenta.
mingle *vi*: **to** ~ **with** misturar-se com.
mingy *adj* mesquinho,-a, avarento,-a, sovina *m,f.*
miniature *n* miniatura *f*; ♦ *adj* em miniatura.
minibus *n* autocarro *m* pequeno, *(BR)* microônibus *m.*
minicab *n* táxi (independente) *m.*
minim *n (MUS)* mínima *f.*
minimal *adj* mínimo,-a.
minimize *vt* minimizar.
minimum *(pl:* **minima**) *n adj* mínimo,-a.
minimum lending rate, MLR *n* taxa mínima de empréstimo, de juro.
mining *n* exploração *f* de minas; *(MIL) (minelaying)* colocação *f* de minas; ♦ *adj* mineiro,-a.
miniskirt *n (clothing)* mini-saia *f*, minissaia *f.*
minister *n (POL)* ministro,-a; *(REL)* pastor *m*; ♦ *vi* ministrar; prestar assistência.
ministerial *adj (POL)* ministerial *m,f.*
ministry *n* ministério *m.*
mink *n (ZOOL)* marta *f (EP)*, vison *(BR)*; ~ **coat** *n* casaco *m* de marta.
minnow *n* vairão *m*, peixinho (de água doce) *m.*
minor *n (MUS)* menor; **2** *(JUR)* menor de idade; ♦ *adj* menor *m,f*; de pouca importância; inferior *m,f*, secundário,-a.
Minorcan *n adj* minorquino,-a.
minority *n* minoria *f*; **to be in** ~ estar em minoria; **2** *(age)* menoridade *f*; ♦ *adj* minoritário,-a.
minster *n (cathedral status)* catedral *f*, basílica *f*; *(of monastery)* igreja *f* de mosteiro.
minstrel *n* menestrel *m.*
mint *n* hortelã, menta; **2** *(MED, CULIN)* hortelã-pimenta; **3** (sweet) pastilha de hortelã-pimenta; ♦ *vt* cunhar *(moedas)*; ♦ **in** ~ **condition** em perfeito estado; **the (Royal) Mint** *n (UK)* a Casa da Moeda.
minuet *n* minueto *m.*
minus *n* (= ~ **sign**) sinal *m* de subtra(c)ção; ♦ *prep* menos; sem.
minuscule *n (letter)* letra *f* minúscula; ♦ *adj* minúsculo,-a.
minute *n* minuto *m*; momento *m*, instante *m*; **it is five** ~**s past three** são 3 horas e cinco minutos; **2** *(note)* minuta *f*; **3** *(brief moment)* **the** ~ **I knew...** assim que eu soube...; ~**s** *npl (document, minutes)* a(c)tas *fpl*; ♦ *adj* miúdo,-a, diminuto,-a; minucioso,-a.

minutiae *npl* particularidades *fpl.*
miracle *n* milagre *m.*
miraculous *adj* milagroso,-a.
mirage *n* miragem *f.*
mire *n* atoleiro *m*, lodaçal *m.*
mirror *n* espelho *m*; *(in a car)* retrovisor (de automóvel) *m*; ~ **image** *n (fig)* cópia *f*; ♦ *vt* refle(c)tir; **2** assemelhar-se a.
mirrored *adj* espelhado,-a; coberto,-a de espelhos.
mirth *n (joy)* alegria *f*; **2** hilaridade *f.*
mirthless *adv* sem alegria, desconsolado.
misadventure *n* desgraça *f*, infortúnio *m.*
misanthropist *n* misantropo *m.*
misapprehension *n* equívoco *m*, má compreensão *f.*
misappropriation *n* apropriação *m* indevida; **2** desvio *m* de fundos; **3** *(JUR)* abuso *m* de confiança.
misbehave *vi* comportar-se mal.
misbehaviour *n* mau comportamento *m.*
miscalculate *vt* calcular mal.
miscalculation *n* erro *m* de cálculo.
miscarriage *n (MED)* aborto (espontâneo) *m*; **2** *(failure)* fracasso *m*, insucesso *m*; **3** *(JUR)* **a** ~ **of justice** um erro *m* judiciário.
miscarry *vi (plan, action)* fracassar, malograr-se; **2** *(MED)* abortar.
miscellaneous *adj* variado,-a, diverso,-a.
miscellany *n* miscelânea *f*; variedade *f*; **2** *(anthology)* coletânea *f.*
mischance *n* fatalidade *f*, azar *m.*
mischief *n (of children)* travessura *f*; **2** *(harm)* dano *m*, prejuízo *m*; **to make** ~ criar problemas.
mischief-maker *n* semeador,-ora de discórdia; intriguista *m,f.*
mischievous *adj* maldoso,-a; **2** *(playfully)* travesso,-a, traquinas *m,f.*
misconceived *adj* mal pensado,-a.
misconception *n* conce(p)ção *f* errada, conceito *m* errado.
misconduct *n* comportamento *m* impróprio; **professional** ~ má conduta *f* profissional.
miscount *vt/vi* contar mal.
misdeed *n* delito *m*, ofensa *f.*
misdemeanour *n* má a(c)ção *f*; **2** *(JUR)* contravenção *f*, delito *m.*
misdiagnosis *n* diagnóstico *m* errado.
misdirect *vt* orientar, informar mal; **2** *(letter)* endereçar mal.
miser *n* avaro,-a; sovina *m,f.*
miserable *adj (unhappy)* triste *m,f*, deprimido,-a; **I feel** ~ sinto-me chocho; **2** *(weather, etc.)* péssimo,-a; **3** *(wage)* de miséria *f*; **4** *(failure)* lamentável *m,f*; **a** ~ **life** *n* uma vida *f* desprezível.
miserly *adj* avarento,-a, mesquinho,-a.
misery *n* tristeza *f*, angústia *f*, sofrimento *m*, miséria *f*, penúria *f*; **she is a** ~ ela é uma choramingas.
misfire *vi* falhar (o tiro).
misfit *n* inadaptado,-a, deslocado,-a.
misfortune *n* desgraça *f*, infortúnio *m.*
misgiving(s) *n (pl)* desconfiança *f*, receio *m*; **2** *(premonition)* mau pressentimento *m.*
misguide *vt* desencaminhar.

misguided *adj* enganado,-a.

mishandle *vt* maltratar; manejar mal.

mishap *n* desgraça *f*, contratempo *m*.

misinform *vt* informar mal.

misinterpret *vt* interpretar mal.

misjudge *vt* fazer um juízo errado de, julgar mal; **2** *(distance)* fazer um erro *f* de cálculo.

mislay *(irr: like* **lay***) vt* extraviar, perder.

mislead *(irr: like* **lead***) vt* induzir em erro, enganar.

misleading *adj* enganoso, erróneo *(BR:* -rô-).

mismanage *vt* administrar mal.

mismanagement *n* má/fraca administração *f*.

mismatch *n* disparidade *f* (**between** entre); **2** *(style)* falta *f* de ligação; ♦ *vt:* **to be ~ed** *(in marriage)* ser incompatíveis, estarem desencontrados; **2** *(colours)* não combinar bem.

misnomer *n* termo *m* impróprio.

misogynist *n* misógino *m*.

misplace *vt* extraviar, perder; colocar em lugar errado.

misplaced *adj* deslocado,-a; **2** inoportuno,-a.

misprint *n* erro *m* tipográfico.

mispronounce *vt* pronunciar mal.

misrepresent *vt* desvirtuar, deturpar.

miss[1] *n* insucesso *m*, falhanço *m*; tiro *m* perdido; **2** *(accidently)* **that was a near ~** essa foi por pouco; ♦ *vt* perder *(train, bus, etc)*; **2** falhar, errar, não acertar; **she missed the target** ela não acertou no alvo; **3** *(be absent)* faltar, não comparecer; **he has missed dinner** ele faltou ao jantar; **4** *(be nostalgic about sb/sth)* sentir a falta de, ter saudade(s) de; **I ~ him** tenho saudades dele; **we ~ the sun** sentimos a falta do sol; **she misses Portugal** ela tem saudades de Portugal; **to ~ out (on sth)** *vt* omitir; ♦ *vi* falhar.

Miss[2] *n* menina *f, (BR)* senhorita *f*.

missal *n (REL)* missal *m*.

misshapen *adj* disforme *m,f*; deformado,-a.

missile *n (AER)* míssil *m*; projé(c)til *m*.

missing *adj* ausente *m,f*; perdido,-a; **2** que falta; desaparecido,-a; **to go ~** desaparecer.

mission *n* missão *f*; **on a ~** em missão; **~ accomplished** missão cumprida; **~ary** *n,adj* missionário,-a.

misspell *vt* soletrar/escrever mal; **misspelling** *n* erro *m* ortográfico.

misspent *adj (pt,pp of* **spend***)* desperdiçado,-a.

mist *n* neblina *f*; névoa *f*; bruma; ♦ *vi* (= **~ over, ~ up**) *(mirror)* embaciar-se; **2** *(eyes)* toldar-se; ficar turvo.

mistake *n* erro *m*; **by ~** acidentalmente; ♦ *(irr: like* **take***) vt* entender, interpretar mal; **to ~ X for Y** confundir X com Y.

mistaken *adj* errado,-a; **to be ~** enganar-se, equivocar-se.

mister *n* senhor *m (Vd:* **Mr***)*.

mistletoe *n (BOT)* visco *m*.

mistreat *vt* maltratar.

mistreatment *n* mau trato.

mistress *n (lover)* amante *f*; **2** *(lady of the home)* dona (da casa) *f*; **3** *(teacher)* professora *f*, mestra *f (Vd* **Mrs***)*.

mistrust *vt* desconfiança *f*; ♦ desconfiar de.

misty *adj* enevoado,-a, nebuloso,-a; nublado,-a; embaciado,-a.

misunderstand *(irr: like* **understand***) vt/vi* entender; interpretar mal; equivocar-se.

misunderstanding *n* mal-entendido *m*, equívoco *m*.

misuse *n* mau uso *m*, abuso *m*; ♦ *vt* abusar de; fazer mau uso de; desviar.

mite *n (ZOOL)* ácaro *m*.

mitigate *vt* mitigar, atenuar.

mitigation *n* mitigação *f*; atenuante *m,f*.

mitre *n* mitra *f, (BR)* mitro *m*; **2** *(carpentry)* meia-esquadria *f*.

mitt(en) *n (clothing)* mitene *f*; luva *f* de lã sem dedos.

mix *n* mistura; ♦ *vt* misturar(-se), juntar(-se); combinar(-se); **2** *(CULIN)* preparar; **3** *(socialise)* conviver (**with** com); ♦ **~ up** *n* trapalhada *f*; **2** *(mistake)* engano *m*; ♦ *vt* **to ~up** *vt (confuse)* confundir; **2** baralhar; **3** envolver-se (**with,** com).

mixed *adj* misturado,-a; sortido,-a; **2** *(food, drink)* misto,-a; **~ economy** economia mista; **~ marriage** casamento misto; **3** *(feelings)* ambivalente; **4** *(reaction, opinion)* variado,-a.

mixed-up *adj (person)* desorientado; **2** *(emotionally)* perturbado,-a; **3** misturado,-a.

mixer *n* batedeira *f* elé(c)trica; **2** *(for cement)* betoneira *f*; **3** *(MUS) (engineer)* engenheiro *m* de som; *(device)* misturador *m*; **~ tap** *n (UK)* torneira para água fria e quente; IDIOM **he is a good ~** ele é sociável, ele dá-se bem com todos.

mixing *n* mistura; **2** dosagem *f*; **~ bowl** tigela *f*.

mixture *n* mistura *f* (**of**, de); **2** *(PHARM)* preparado *m*.

ml *(abbr for* **millilitre***)* ml.

MLR *(abbr for* **minimum lending rate***)* taxa mínima de juros para empréstimos pelo Banco da Inglaterra, como referência para outros bancos.

mm *(abbr for* **millimetre***)* mm.

MMR *n (abbr for* **measles, mumps and rubella***)* MMR, SCR *f*.

MO *(abbr for* **medical officer***) (UK)* médico,-a encarregado,-a dos serviços de saúde.

moan *n* gemido *m*, lamento *m*, queixume *m*; ♦ *vi* gemer; **to ~ (about)** queixar-se (de).

moat *n* fosso *m*.

mob *n* multidão *f*; **2** *(pej)* ralé *f*, populaça *f*, povinho *m*; **3** *(of gangsters)* quadrilha *f*; **the M~** *(coll) (organized crime)* a máfia; **2** ♦ *vt* atacar; ♦ cercar, rodear.

mobile *n (decorative object)* móbil *m*; **~ home** *n* trailer; **~ phone** *n* telemóvel *m; (BR)* celular *m*; ♦ *adj* móvel *m,f*; **2** *(features)* expressivo,-a; **3** *(library)* ambulante.

mobility *n* mobilidade *f*.

mobilize *vt* mobilizar.

moccasin *n (footwear)* mocassim *m*.

mock *adj* falso,-a, fingido,-a; *(exam)* simulado *m*, prova *f*; ♦ *vt* ridicularizar; zombar de fazer troça de.

mockery *n (scorn)* escárnio *m; (in fun)* troça *f*.

mock-heroic *adj (of poetry)* herói–cómico.

mocking *adj* zombaria *f*; ♦ *adj (person)* zombeteiro,-a.

mock-up *n (print, TECH)* maqueta *f*, modelo *m*.

MOD *(abbr* for Ministry of Defense*)*.

mod con *(pl:* **mod cons***) (abbr for* **modern conveniences***) n* todo o conforto *m* moderno.

mode modo *m*, maneira *f*; **2** *(TECH)* modo de funcionamento; **3** *(MUS)* modo *m*.

model *n (in fashion)* modelo *m,f*; manequim *m*; **2** *(pattern)* padrão *m*; **3** *(example)* modelo, exemplo (**of**, de); **4** *(ARCH)* maqueta *f*; ♦ *adj* exemplar; ~ **car** carro em miniatura; ♦ *vt/vi* modelar.

modelling *(UK)*, **modeling** *(US)* *n* modelismo *m*.

modem *n (COMP)* modem *m*.

moderate *n adj* moderado,-a; ♦ *vi* moderar-se, acalmar-se; ♦ *vt* moderar.

moderation *n* moderação *f*.

modern *adj* moderno,-a; ~-**day** *adj* dos tempos *mpl* modernos.

modernism *n* modernismo *m*.

modernize/ise *vt* modernizar; a(c)tualizar.

modest *adj* modesto,-a.

modesty *n* modéstia *f*.

modicum *n*: **a** ~ **of** um mínimo de, um nadinha de.

modification *n* modificação *f*

modifier *n* modificador.

modify *vt* modificar; **2** alterar.

modulation *n* modulação *f*.

modulus *n (MATH, PHYS)* módulo *m*.

modus operandi *n* modo/método de realizar algo.

modus vivendi *n* modo *m* de viver; *(JUR)* convénio *m*.

moggy *n (UK) (fam) (cat)* gato,-a, tareco *m*.

Mogul[1] *n*: ~ **empire** império *m* mogul.

mogul[2] *n (magnate)* magnata *m*; *(fam)* manda-chuva *m,f*; **2** montículo de neve; ~ **skying** *adj* evento de ski, quando os concorrentes esquiam num declive coberto de montículos de neve.

mohair *n* pêlo *m* de cabra angorá.

Mohammed *npr (Muslim Prophet)* Maomé.

Mohican *n adj* moicano,-a *(Indian)*; **2** *(hairstyle)* crista *f*.

moist *adj* (h)úmido,-a, molhado,-a.

moisten *vt* (h)umedecer.

moistness *n* humidade *f*; **2** qualidade de estar molhado.

moisture *n* (h)umidade *f*.

moisturizer *n* creme *m* hidratante.

molar *n (tooth)* molar *m*.

molasses *n* melaço *msg*, melado *msg*.

mold *vt (US) (Vd* **mould***)*.

Moldova *npr* Moldávia; **in** ~ em Moldávia.

mole *n (ZOOL)* toupeira *f*; **2** *(MED) (on skin)* nevo *m*, sinal *m*, lunar *m*; **3** *(fig) (spy)* espião *m*, espia *f*, toupeira *m,f*; **4** *(breakwater)* molhe *m*; **5** escavadora para rochas.

molecule *n* molécula *f*.

molehill *n* montículo (feito por uma toupeira) *m*; **2** IDIOM **to make a mountain out of a** ~ fazer de um arqueiro um cavaleiro; exagerar.

molest *vt* molestar, importunar.

mollify *vt* suavizar, atenuar, aliviar.

mollusc *n (ZOOL)* molusco *m*.

mollycoddle *vt* mimar.

molten *adj (metal)* fundido,-a; em fusão.

moment *n* momento *m*.

momentary *adj* momentâneo,-a.

momentous *adj* importantíssimo,-a.

momentum *n* momento *m*; *(fig)* ímpeto *m*; **to gather** ~ ganhar ímpeto.

Monaco *npr* Mónaco; **in** ~ em Mónaco.

monarch *n* monarca *m,f*.

monarchist *n* monarquista *m,f*.

monarchy *n* monarquia *f*.

monastery *n* mosteiro *m*, convento *m*.

monastic *adj* monástico,-a.

Monday *n* segunda-feira.

monetary *adj* monetário,-a.

money *n* dinheiro *m*; **to make** ~ ganhar dinheiro; ~**lender** *n* agiota *m,f*; ~**maker** *n* mina *f* de ouro; ~**making** *adj* lucrativo,-a; ~ **order** *n* vale (postal) *m*; ~ **spinner** *n* mina *f* (de ouro).

mongol *n adj (MED)* mongolóide *m,f*.

Mongolia *npr* Mongólia; **in** ~ na Mongólia.

Mongolian *n adj* mongol *m,f*; *(LING)* mongol.

mongrel *n* cão *m* cruzado, rafeiro *m*, cão *m* vadio.

monitor *n (EDUC)* monitor,-a; **2** (= **television** ~) visor *m*; ♦ *vt* controlar.

monk *n* monge *m*, frade *m*.

monkey *n (ZOOL)* macaco *m*; ~ **business** *n (coll) (fooling)* tolices *fpl*; **2** *(cheating)* trapaça *f*; ~**nut** *n* amendoim *m*; ~**wrench** *n (tool)* chave-inglesa *f*; ♦ **to** ~ **about/around** fazer brincadeiras *fpl*, fazer macaquices *fpl*.

monkfish *n (ZOOL) (fish)* tamboril *m*.

mono *pref* mono; ~**chrome** *adj* monocromático,-a.

monocle *n* monóculo *m*.

monogamy *n* monogamia *f*.

monogram *n* monograma *m*.

monolingual *adj* monolingue *m,f*.

monologue *n* monólogo *m*.

monophobia *n* monofobia *f*.

monopolize *vt* monopolizar; açambarcar.

monopoly *n* monopólio *m*.

monorail *n* monocarril *m*, *(BR)* monotrilho *m*.

monosyllabic *adj* monossilábico,-a; *(fig) (brief)* lacónico,-a *(BR:* -cô-).

monotheism *n (REL)* monoteísmo *m*.

monotone *n* monotonia *f*; **to speak in a** ~ falar num tom monótono, monocórdico.

monotonous *adj* monótono,-a.

monotony *n* monotonia *f*.

monsoon *n (weather)* monção *f*.

monster *n* monstro *m*.

monstering *n (fam)* raspanete *m*, repreensão *f*.

monstrosity *n* monstruosidade *f*.

monstrous *adj* descomunal *m,f*; monstruoso,-a.

montage *n* montagem *f*.

month *n* mês *m*; **every** ~ todos os meses.

monthly *adj* mensal; ~ **magazine** *n* revista *f* mensal; ♦ *adv* mensalmente.

monument *n* monumento *m*.

monumental *adj* monumental *m,f*.

moo *n* mugido *m*; ♦ *vi (of cow, bull)* mugir.

mood *n* humor *m*, disposição *f*; **to be in a good/bad** ~ estar bem/mal disposto; estar de bom/mau humor.

moody *adj* caprichoso,-a, rabugento,-a; melancólico,-a, lunático,-a.

moon *n (ASTRON)* lua *f*; **full** ~ lua *f* cheia; ♦ *vi (daydream)* andar na lua, devanear; IDIOM **to**

cry for the ~ pedir impossíveis; **be over the** ~ estar nas suas sete quintas; **once in a blue** ~ quase nunca.

moonbeam *n* raio *m* de lua.

moonlanding *n* alunagem *f.*

moonlight *n* luar *m.*

moonlighting *n (coll)* atividade extra; biscate, *(BR)* bico.

moonlit *adj* iluminado,-a pelo luar.

moor[1] *n* charneca *f*, brejo *m* matagal *m*; **the York-shire ~s** as charnecas de Yorkshire; ♦ *vt (ship)* amarrar; ♦ *vi* fundear, atracar.

Moor[2] *npr (person)* mouro,-a.

moorhen *n* frango d'água *m.*

mooring *n (NAUT)* atracagem *f*, amarração *f*; **~s** *npl* amarras *fpl*; **2** *(place)* ancoradouro *sg*; ~ **tackle** *n* amarras.

Moorish *adj* mouro,-a, mourisco,-a; ~ **style** *n* estilo *m* mourisco.

moorland *n* charneca *f.*

moose *n (ZOOL)* alce *m.*

mop *n (cleaning) (for floor)* esfregona *f*; *(for saucepans)* esfregão *m*; **2** *(fig) (hair)* grenha *f*; ♦ (**-pp-**) *vt* esfregar; **2** *(wipe)* **to ~ one's face with** limpar a cara com um pano; *(from tears)* enxugar as lágrimas, a cara; ♦ **to ~ sth up** *vt (liquid etc)* limpar, absolver; **2** *(coll) (task) (after battle)* liquidar.

mope *n (gloomy person)* pessoa *f* deprimida, tristonha, sombria; ♦ *vi (be gloomy)* estar, andar deprimido,-a, esmorecer; **I spent the day moping around** passei o dia deprimido, a chorar.

moped *n* bicicleta *f* motorizada.

moral *n adj* moral *f*; ♦ **~s** *npl (morality)* valores morais, princípios *mpl.*

morale *n* estado *m* de espírito, moral *m*; **~-booster** *n*: **the book was a ~-booster (to me)** o livro levantou-me o moral, animou-me.

morality *n* moralidade *f*; *(REL)* ética *f.*

moralize *vt* moralizar (**about/on** sobre).

morally *adv* moralmente; ~ **wrong** contrário à moral, á ética.

morass *n* pântano *m*; **2** *(mess)* confusão *f.*

moratorium *(pl: -a, -s) n* moratória *f.*

morbid *adj* doentio,-a; mórbido,-a.

mordacious *adj* sarcástico,-a; mordaz *m,f.*

mordant *adj* mordaz *m,f*; incisivo,-a.

more *adj adv* mais; **once ~** outra vez; ~ **or less** mais ou menos; ~ **than ever** mais do que nunca; ~ **and ~/increasingly** ~ cada vez mais; **I could not agree ~** estou totalmente de acordo; IDIOM **the ~ the better!** quantos mais, melhor.

moreover *adv* além do mais, além disso.

morgue *n* necrotério *m*, morgue *f.*

moribund *adj* moribundo,-a.

Mormon *n (religious sect)* mórmon *m,f.*

morning *n* manhã *f*; **2** (= **early ~**) madrugada; **good ~!** bom dia!; **in the ~** de manhã; **tomorrow ~** amanhã de manhã; ~ **sickness** *n* nauseas *fpl*, enjoo *m* matinal; **~s** *adv (US)* de manhã; **the ~-after pill** *(fig)* ressaca; ~ **dress** *n (UK) (formal clothes for man)* fraque *m*, casaca *f (tail coat)*, calças cinzentas.

Moroccan *n adj* marroquino,-a.

Morocco *npr* Marrocos; **in ~** em Marrocos.

moron *n* estúpido,-a, idiota *m,f*, atrasado,-a mental.

moronic *adj* mentecapto,-a.

morose *adj* taciturno,-a, rabugento,-a.

morphine *n* morfina *f.*

morphology *n* morfologia *f.*

morris dancing *n* dança *f* folclórica inglesa.

Os **morris dancers**, homens vestidos de saiotes, ou longas camisas, e de chapéus adornados, dançam em redor de um paulito com fitas coloridas, em geral, brandindo paus. Assemelham-se, assim, aos pauliteiros de Miranda do Douro, Portugal.

Morse *n* (= ~ **code**) código *m* Morse.

morsel *n* bocado *m*, pedaço *m.*

mortal *n adj* mortal *m,f.*

mortality *n* mortalidade *f.*

mortar *n (crush seeds, herbs)* almofariz *m*; **2** *(MIL)* morteiro *m*; **3** *(cement)* argamassa *f.*

mortgage *n* hipoteca *f*; ♦ *vt* hipotecar.

mortify *vt* humilhar, mortificar.

mortuary *n* necrotério *m*, morgue *f.*

mosaic *n* mosaico *m.*

Moscow *npr* Moscovo; **in ~** em Moscovo; *(BR)* Moscou.

Moses *n (Bible)* Moisés.

Moslem *n adj (Vd* **Muslim***).*

mosque *n* mesquita *f.*

mosquito *(pl: -es) n* mosquito *m.*

moss *n* musgo *m.*

mossy *adj* com musgo.

most *adj (superl of much)* o/a mais, a maior quantidade; **2** *pron* a maioria, a maior parte *f*; ♦ *adv* muito, muitíssimo; ~ **women** a maior parte das mulheres; **at the (very)** ~ quando muito, no máximo; IDIOM **to make the ~ of** aproveitar ao máximo.

mostly *adv* principalmente, na maior parte.

MOT *n (abbr for* **Ministry of Transport Test***)* inspeção anual obrigatória em veículos com mais de três anos de fabricação = inspeção automóvel.

motel *n (US)* hotel *m* de beira de estrada.

moth *n (ZOOL)* mariposa *f*; (= **clothes ~**) traça *f*; **~ball** *n* bola *f* de naftalina; **~-eaten** *adj* roído pelas traças.

mother *n* mãe *f*; **~board** *n (COMP)* placa-mãe; ~ **country** *n* terra *f*, país *m* natal; **Mother's Day** *n* dia *f* das mães; **god~** madrinha *f*; **~hood** *n* maternidade *f*; **~-in-law** *(pl:* **mothers-in-law***)* *n* sogra *f*; **~land** *n* pátria *f*; **~ly** *adj* maternal *m,f*; **~-of-pearl** *n* madrepérola *f*; ~ **ship** *n* nave-mãe *f*; **step ~** *n* madrasta; ~ **superior** *n* madre *f* superior; **~-to-be** *n* futura mamã *(BR:* mamãe*) f*; ~ **tongue** *n* língua *f* materna; ♦ *adj* materno,-a, maternal; ♦ *vt* cuidar (como uma mãe).

motif *n* motivo *m*; tema *m*, assunto *m.*

motion *n* movimento *m*; gesto *m*, sinal *m*; **2** *(proposal)* moção *f*; **to put/set in** ~ pôr em movimento; *m,f*; ~ **picture** *n* filme (cinematográfico) *m*; ♦ *vt/vi*: **to ~ (to) sb to do sth** fazer sinal a alguém para fazer algo.

motionless *adj* imóvel *m,f.*

motivate *vt* motivar.
motivated *adj* motivado,-a.
motivation *n* motivação *f*.
motive *n* motivo *m*; ♦ *adj* motor, motriz.
motley *adj* variado,-a, heterogéneo,-a (*BR*: -gê-).
motor *n* (*engine*) motor *m*; (*coll*) (*motorcar*) carro *m*, automóvel *m*; ♦ *adj* motor, motriz; ~**bike** *n* motocicleta *f*; ~**boat** *n* barco *m* a motor; (*dated*) ~**cade** *n* (*parade*) desfile, cortejo de automóveis; ~**cycle** *n* motocicleta *f*; ~**cycle track** *n* pista *f* de motociclismo; ~**cyclist** *n* motociclista *m,f*; ~**home** *n* (US) autocaravana *f*.
motoring *n* automobilismo *m*.
motorist *n* automobilista *m,f*.
motorize, motorise *vt* motorizar.
motor racing *n* corridas de automóveis, automobilismo.
motor scooter *n* moto *f*; lambreta *f*.
motor show *n* salão automóvel.
motorway *n* auto-estrada, autoestrada *f*.
mottled *adj* mosqueado,-a, sarapintado,-a, com manchas; **2** multicolor, em furta-cores.
motto (*pl*: -**es**) *n* moto *m*, divisa *f*, lema *m*.
mould (*UK*) **mold** (*US*) *n* molde *m*; **2** (*for cakes, etc*) forma *f*; **3** mofo *m*, bolor *m*; ♦ *vi* moldar, modelar; **to ~ a person's character** moldar o carácter (duma pessoa); **2** ganhar bolor.
moulder *vt* desfazer-se, reduzir-se a pó.
mouldsing *n* (*ARCH*) (*decoration*) cornija *f*.
mouldy (-ier, -iest) *adj* bolorento,-a.
moult *n* muda *f* de pelo ou de pena (*of animals*).
mound *n* (*small hill*) morro *m*; (*small lump of soil*) montículo *m*; **2** (*of things*) pilha *f*, rima *f*.
mount *n* monte *m*, montaria *f*; **2** engaste *m*; **3** (*for pictures, paintings*) moldura *f*; ♦ *vt* montar em, subir a; ♦ *vi* (= ~ **up**) subir, aumentar.
mountain *n* montanha *f*; ♦ *adj* de montanha; ~ **chain** *n* cordilheira *f*.
mountaineer *n* alpinista *m,f*, montanhista *m,f*.
mountaineering *n* alpinismo *m*; **to go ~** praticar o alpinismo.
mountainous *adj* montanhoso,-a.
mountainside *n* lado *m* da montanha.
mourn *vt* chorar, lamentar; ♦ *vi*: **to ~ for** chorar, lamentar a morte de.
mourner *n* parente *m,f or* amigo,-a do defunto.
mournful *adj* desolado,-a, triste *m,f*.
mourning *n* luto *m*; de luto; (**to be**) **in** ~ (estar) de luto.
mouse (*pl*: **mice**) *n* rato *m*, (*BR*) camundongo *m*; **2** (*COMP*) rato *m* do computador; ~**trap** *n* ratoeira *f*.
mousseline *n* (*fabric*) musselina *f*.
moustache *n* bigode *m*.
mousy *adj* tímido,-a; **2** (*hair colour*) cor de rato.
mouth (*pl*: -**s**) *n* boca *f*; **2** (*river*) desembocadura *f*, foz *f*; IDIOM **to be all ~** ter muita garganta.
mouthful *n* bocado *m*, pedaço *m*, trago *m*.
mouth organ *n* (*musical instrument*) gaita *f*.
mouthpiece *n* (*MUS*) embocadura *f*; **2** (*phone*) bocal *m*; **3** porta-voz.
mouth-to-mouth (*resuscitation*) respiração *f* boca-a-boca.

mouthwash *n* anti-séptico/antissético *m* da boca; elixir *m* bucal.
mouth-watering *adj* que faz crescer água na boca.
movable *adj* móvel *m,f*.
move *n* movimento *m*; **2** (*SPORT*) jogada *f*; **3** turno *m*, vez *f*; **4** mudança *f*; **to get a ~ on** apressar-se; ♦ *vt* mover; **2** comover; **3** (*POL*) propor; **4** adiantar; ♦ *vi* mover-se, mexer-se; circular; **2** (= ~ **house**) mudar-se; **3** (*of emotion*) comover-se; **to ~ about** *vi* ir de um lado para o outro; viajar; **to ~ along** *vi* avançar, apressar-se; **to ~ away** *vi* afastar-se; **to ~ back** *vi* recuar; **to ~ forward** *vi* avançar; **to ~ in** *vi* instalar-se (numa casa); **to ~ on** *vi* ir andando; **to ~ out** *vi* sair duma casa, abandonar (uma casa); **to ~ up** *vi* subir; ser promovido,-a; IDIOM **to ~ heaven and earth** fazer todos os possíveis.
movement *n* movimento *m*; **2** (*TECH*) mecanismo *m*.
movie *n* filme *m*; **to go to the ~s** ir ao cinema; ~ **camera** *n* câmara *f* cinematográfica.
moving *adj* (*emotive*) comovente *m,f*; **2** (*mobile*) móvel *m,f*; **3** (*instigater*) instigador,-ora; ~ **van** *n* camião *m* (*BR*: caminhão *m*) de mudanças.
mow (*pt* -**ed**, *pp* -**ed/-n**) *vt* cortar; **2** (= **to ~ down**) ceifar; dizimar.
mower *n* ceifeira *f*; **lawn ~** máquina *f* de cortar relva, (*BR*) cortador *m* de grama.
Mozambique *npr* Moçambique *m*.
Mozambican *n adj* moçambicano,-a (língua oficial: português).
mozzarella *n* (*cheese*) mozarela *m*.
MP *n* (*abbr for* **Member of Parliament**) Membro *m* do Parlamento; deputado,-a.
mph (*abbr for* **miles per hour**) milhas *fpl* por hora.
Mr *n* (*abbr for* **Mister**) Sr. (senhor); ~ **Scott** (o) Sr. Scott.
MRI *n* (*abbr for* **Magnetic Resonance Imaging**) (*MED*) Ressonância *f* Magnética.
Mrs *n* (*abbr for* **Mistress**) (*married woman*) Sra (senhora); **Mrs (Helen) Scott** (a) Sra. Scott; *or* D. (dona) Helen.
MRSA (*abbr for* **methicillin-resistant Staphylococcus aureus**) (*MED*) (*bacterium*) Staphylococcus aureus, resistente à meticilina.
Ms *n* (*UK*) (*título moderno usadodado geralmente pora mulher profissional*) Dona
MSc (*abbr for* **Master of Science**) Mestrado *m* em Ciência.
much *n* muita coisa *f*, grande quantidade *f*; ♦ *adj adv pron* muito; **how ~ is it?** quanto custa?; **too ~** demais, demasiado; **as ~ as** tanto como; **however ~ he tries** por mais que tente; **so ~ the better** tanto melhor; ~ **to my regret** com grande pesar meu; **I very ~ doubt** duvido imenso.
muck *n* imundície *f*; (*fig*) porcaria *f*; **2** (*organic fertilizer*) estrume *m*; ♦ **to ~ about** *vi* (*coll*) perder tempo; divertir-se; **to ~ up** *vt* (*coll*) estragar.
mucky *adj* sujo,-a.
mucus *n* muco *m*.
mud *n* lama *f*, lodo *m*.
muddle *n* confusão; desordem *f*; trapalhada *f*; ♦ **to ~ through** *vi* desenrascar-se; **to ~ up** *vt* baralhar.
muddy *adj* lamacento,-a, lodoso,-a; turvo,-a.

mudguard n guarda-lamas m; pára-lamas m.

mudpack n *(cosmetic)* máscara f de argila.

mud-slinging n difamação f, maledicência f.

muezzin n almuádem, muezim.

muff n *(clothing)* regalo m; ◆ vt desperdiçar; perder; falhar.

muffin n *(CULIN)* queque m.

muffle vt abafar; agasalhar.

muffled adj abafado,-a, surdo,-a.

muffler n *(US)* tubo m de escape, *(BR)* abafador m.

mufti n: **in** ~ vestido à paisana.

mug n *(object)* caneca f; **2** *(coll)* *(silly person)* palerma m,f, pacóvio,-a, bobo,-a; **3** *(coll)* *(face)* carantonha f; ◆ vt assaltar.

mugger n gatuno,-a.

mugging n assalto m com agressão.

muggy adj (h)úmido e abafado.

mugshot n *(police)* identificação f fotográfica.

mug up *(UK)* vt *(coll)* *(exam)* marras (**for** para).

mulberry n *(fruit)* amora f; **2** *(plant)* amoreira f.

mulch n adubo m orgânico.

mule n mula f; **2** *(coll)* *(stubborn)* cabeça dura; **mules** npl *(for the feet)* pantufas.

mulish adj teimoso,-a, cabeça dura f.

mull: to ~ **over** vt cogitar, meditar sobre.

mullah n *(REL)* mulá.

mulled adj: ~ **wine** vinho m quente (aromatizado).

mullered adj *(coll)* *(drunk)* bêbedo,-a, borracho,-a.

mullet n *(fish)* salmonete m.

multi pref multi; ~**coloured** adj multicor; ~**faceted** adj multifacetado,-a; ~**media** n *(COMP)* multimédia f; ~**national** n adj multinacional m,f; ~-**purpose** adj multiusos mpl; ~**tasking** n *(COMP)* multitarefa f.

multifarious adj diverso,-a; variado,-a.

multiple n adj múltiplo,-a; ~ **personality** n *(PSYCH)* personalidade f múltipla; ~ **sclerosis** n esclerose f múltipla; ~ **store** n cadeia f de lojas.

multiplication n multiplicação f.

multiply vt multiplicar; ◆ vi multiplicar-se.

multistorey adj *(UK)* de vários andares.

multitude n multidão f, turba f; povo m.

mum n mãezinha f, mamã f, *(BR)* mamãe f; ◆ adj: **to keep** ~ ficar calado,-a.

mumble n resmungar (por entre os dentes); **2** balbuciar.

mumbling adj resmungão,-ona m,f.

mumbo-jumbo n *(coll)* *(pej)* palavreado m; treta f.

mummify vt mumificar.

mummy n mãezinha f, mamã f; *(BR)* mamãe f; **2** múmia f.

mumps n papeira fsg, *(BR)* caxumba fsg.

munch vt mastigar ruidosamente.

mundane adj mundano,-a.

Munich npr Munique.

municipal adj municipal m,f.

municipality n municipalidade f.

munitions n munições fpl; **2** provisões fpl.

muppet n fantoche; **2** *(coll)* palerma m,f, palhaço,-a.

mural n mural m.

murder n assassínio; homicídio m; ~ **in the first degree** homicídio com premeditação; ~ **in the second degree** homicídio involuntário; **attempted** ~ n tentativa f de assassinato; ◆ vt assassinar, matar; IDIOM **to shout blue** ~ fazer um escândalo.

murderer n assassino m.

murderess assassina f.

murderous adj homicida m,f, criminoso,-a.

murky adj *(river)* cinzento,-a; pardacento,-a; *(sky)* escuro, nebulado; **2** *(fig)* sombrio,-a, obscuro,-a.

murmur n murmúrio m, sussurro m; ◆ vt/vi murmurar, sussurrar.

muscle n músculo m; *(fig)* força *(muscular)* f; **2 to** ~ **in** vi abrir caminho à força.

Muscovite n adj muscovita m,f.

muscular adj muscular m,f; musculoso,-a.

muse n musa f; ◆ vi meditar.

museum n museu m.

mushroom n cogumelo m, fungo m; ◆ vi *(fig)* proliferar; crescer rapidamente, de súbito.

mushy (-ier, -iest) adj como papa mole m,f; **2** *(pej)* piegas m,f.

music n música f; ~**stand** n atril m; IDIOM **that is** ~ **to my ears!** é uma ó(p)tima notícia!

music hall n teatro m de variedades.

musical n *(film)* musical; ◆ adj musical; **2** melodious.

musician n músico,-a.

musk n *(aromatic substance)* almíscar; **2** *(ZOOL)* veado almiscareiro.

musket n mosquete m.

musketeer n mosqueteiro m.

muskrat n rato m almiscarado.

Muslim n adj muçulmano,-a.

mussel n mexilhão m; *(BR)* sururu m.

must¹ v. aux *(obligation)* dever; **I** ~ **do it** tenho que/devo fazer isso; **2** *(probability)* **she** ~ **be there by now** ela já deve estar lá; **3** *(need)* precisar; **it's a** ~ é imprescindível; **must-have** adj essencial.

must² n mosto m, bafio m, bolor m.

mustard n mostarda f.

muster n *(MIL)* revista f, inspe(c)ção f; ◆ vt reunir, juntar; ~ **up** vt *(courage, strength)* reunir, apelar a.

mustn't = must not.

musty adj mofento,-a; com cheiro a bafio/a bolor.

mutant n, adj mutante m,f.

mutation n mutação f.

mute n mudo,-a; **2** *(MUS)* abafador m.

muted adj *(som)* abafado,-a; **2** *(colour)* suave; **3** *(MUS)* em surdina.

mutilate vt mutilar; **2** *(fig)* *(misrepresent)* deturpar.

mutilation n mutilação f.

mutinous adj amotinado,-a; rebelde m,f.

mutiny n motim m, revolta f; ◆ vi amotinar-se.

mutt n *(coll)* ignorante m,f, palerma m,f; **2** *(US)* *(dog)* cão m vadio; *(BR)* vira-lata m.

mutter n resmungo m; o falar por entre os dentes; ◆ vt/vi resmungar, murmurar.

mutton n carne f de carneiro; ~ **stew** guisado de carneiro; IDIOM ~ **dressed as a lamb** velha f gaiteira.

mutual adj mútuo,-a; recíproco,-a; comum m,f.

mutually adv reciprocamente; mutuamente.

muzzle n focinho m; açaime m, *(BR)* focinheira f; **2** *(gun)* boca f; ◆ vt amordaçar; açaimar, *(BR)* pôr focinheira em; **2** *(fig)* fazer calar.

muzzy *adj* desfocado,-a, enevoado,-a; confuso,-a.

my *adj poss* meu(s) *m*, minha(s) *f*; ♦ *exc*: **Oh ~!** Meu Deus!; **2** *(of disbelief)* ~ **foot!** ora adeus! uma fava!

Myanmar *npr (Burma's modern name)* Mianmar.

mycosis *n (MED)* micose *f*.

mynah bird *n* mainá *m*.

myocardium *n (MED)* miocárdio *m*.

myopic *adj* míope *m,f*.

myriad *n (indefinite number)* míriade *f*.

myrrh *n (BOT)* mirra.

myrtle *n (BOT)* mirto *m*, murta; ~ **berry** baga *f* de mirto.

myself *pron (reflexive)* me; **2** *(emphatic)* eu mesmo; **3** *(after prep)* eu mesmo, a mim mesmo, eu próprio; **by** ~ sozinho.

mysterious *adj* misterioso,-a.

mystery *n* mistério *m*.

mystic *n adj* místico,-a.

mystical *adj* místico.

mystify *vt* mistificar, confundir; desconcertar.

mystique *n* mística *f*; **2** mistério *m*.

myth *n* mito *m*.

mythical *adj* mítico.

mythology *n* mitologia *f*.

myxoma *(pl: -mas or -mata) n (MED)* mixoma *m*.

n

N, n *(letter)* N, n *m;* **2** *(GEOG) (abbr for* **North***)* N; **3** *n (abbr for* **noun***) m.*

NA *(abbr for* **Narcotics Anonymous***)* organização de ajuda a toxicómanos *(BR:* -ô-).

NA *(abbr for* **North America***)* América do Norte.

n/a *(abbr for* **not applicable***)* não-aplicável.

nab (-bb-) *vt (coll) (catch, arrest)* apanhar (em flagrante), agarrar, prender.

nadir *n (ASTRON)* nadir *m; (fig)* ponto, grau *m* mais baixo; ~ **of despair** no fundo de desespero.

naff *adj (coll) (of bad taste)* piroso,-a; **2** *(quality)* medíocre *m,f;* ♦ **naff off!** *(slang)* pira-te!

nag *n (pej) (horse)* pileca *f (pej);* **2** *(pej) (woman)* megera *f, (pej, fam)* chata *f,* sarna *f;* ♦ (-gg-) *vt (persist) (fam)* ralar (alguém); *(fam)* chatear; **2** *(scold)* ralhar (com alguém); **3** *(niggle)* apoquentar; **4** *(moan)* resmungar; **to** ~ **(away) at sb** *(irritate)* arreliar, atormentar.

nagging *adj (complaint, pain)* persistente *m,f;* contínuo,-a; **2** *(person)* resmungão,-gona.

nail *n (ANAT)* unha *f;* ~**brush** *n* escova *f* de unhas; ~**clippers** *npl* corta-unhas *m,f, (BR)* cortador *m* de unhas; ~**file** *n* lima *f, (BR)* lixa *f* das unhas; ~**polish/varnish** *n* verniz *m, (BR)* esmalte *m* de unhas; ~**scissors** *n* tesourinha de unhas; **2** *(for hammering)* prego *m;* ♦ *vt (with hammer)* pregar; cravar; **to** ~ **(sb) down** *vt (trap thief)* agarrar; **2** expôr; **3** *(fasten)* prender, fixar *(carpet, etc);* **4** pressionar alguém para uma data precisa; **to** ~ **(sth) up** *(board up)* fechar (algo) com tábuas; IDIOM **hard as** ~**s** sem coração; **to hit the** ~ **on the head** acertar em cheio; **to bite one's** ~**s** roer as unhas.

nail-biting *n* hábito *m* de roer as unhas; ♦ *adj (film, book)* excitante, cheio de suspense; palpitante; **2** *(waiting)* angustiante.

naive *adj* ingénuo,-a *(BR:* -gê-), cândido,-a.

naivety *n* ingenuidade.

naked *adj* nu, nua; **2** *(fig)* desprotegido,-a; exposto ao ar; **with the** ~ **eye** a olho nu; **stark** ~ completamente nu; ~ **truth** verdade *f* nua e crua; ~ **to the waist** *(woman)* nua até à cintura, *(man)* de tronco nu.

nakedness *n* nudez *f.*

name *n* nome *m;* **proper (first)** ~ nome próprio; (= **surname***)* apelido *m,* sobrenome *m;* **2** reputação *f,* fama *f;* **what is your** ~**?** como se chama?; **assumed** ~ nome *m* suposto; **by** ~ de nome; **full** ~ nome completo; **in the** ~ **of** em nome de *(on behalf of);* **maiden** ~ nome em/de solteira; ~**s** *npl*

palavras *fpl* ofensivas; ~**sake** *n* homónimo; *(BR)* xará *m,f* tocaio,-a; **trade** ~ nome comercial registado *(BR)* registado; **to call sb** ~**s** chamar nomes a alguém, insultar; **to put one's** ~ **down for** inscrever-se em; ♦ *vt* chamar, dar o nome de; **2** *(boat)* ba(p)tizar; **to** ~ *(UK:* **after***) (US:* **for***)* **sb** dar a alguém o nome de; **I** ~**ed my son after his uncle** eu dei/pus o nome do tio ao meu filho; **3** *(cite names)* citar; **4** *(appoint)* nomear; **to** ~ **and shame** revelar a identidade do delitante para não voltar a fazer o mesmo; IDIOM **that's the** ~ **of the game** são as regras do jogo; **you** ~ **it!** é só dizer!

nameless *adj* desconhecido,-a, anónimo,-a *(BR:* -ô-); **2** *(horror)* indizível.

namely *adv* nomeadamente; a saber.

Namibia *npr* Namíbia.

Namibian *n,adj* namibiano,-a.

nanny *n (childminder)* ama *f, (BR)* babá *f;* **2** *(UK: coll) (grandmother)* vovó *f;* **3** ~ **goat** *n (animal)* cabra *f;* **4** ~ **state** *n (POL)* estado protetor.

nanometre *(UK)*, **nanometer** *(US)* nanómetro.

nap *n (snooze)* soneca *f; (afternoon)* sesta *f;* **2** *(textile* = **pile)** pêlo *m;* felpa *f.*

napalm *n* napalm *m.*

nape *n* nuca *f;* **the** ~ **of the neck** cachaço *m.*

napkin *n* (= **table** ~) guardanapo *m.*

Naples *npr* Nápoles; **in** ~ em Nápoles.

Napoleonic *adj* napoleónico,-a.

nappy *n (UK)* fralda *f;* ~ **liner** *n* gaze *f* descartável; ~ **rash** *n* assadura *f.*

narcissi *(pl of* **narcissus***).*

narcissism *n* narcisismo *m.*

narcissistic *adj* narcisista *m,f.*

narcissus *(pl:* -**cissuses** or -**cissi***) n (BOT)* narciso *m.*

narcotic *n adj* narcótico *m.*

nark *n (UK) (police informer)* informante *m,f, (BR) (coll)* dedo-duro *m,f;* **2** pessoa irritante; ♦ *vt* irritar, aborrecer.

narky (-ier, -iest) *adj* mal-humorado,-a; irritável *m,f,* sarcástico,-a.

narrate *vt* narrar, contar.

narrative *n* narrativa; ♦ *adj* narrativo,-a.

narrator *n* narrador,-ora.

narrow *adj (not wide)* estreito,-a; **2** *(tight, close)* apertado,-a; **3** *(eyes)* pequenos; **she is** ~ **across the hips** ela é estreita de ancas; **4** *(fig) (understanding, attitude)* intolerante, limitado,-a; ~ **minded** *adj* espírito *m* tacanho; de visão limitada; **to become** ~ estreitar-se; **to have a** ~ **escape** escapar por um triz; ♦ *vt (MED)* estreitar *(arteries);* **2** *(reduce)* diminuir, reduzir; **to** ~ **down the possibilities to** restringir as possibilidades a; ♦ *vi* estreitar-se; **2 to** ~ **the eyes** *(squint)* semi-cerrar os olhos.

narrow-gauge *adj (RAIL: track)* de bitola, via *f* estreita.

narrowish *adj* um tanto apertado,-a, estreito,-a.

narrowly *adv (barely)* por un pouco, por um triz.

narrow-minded *adj (person)* tacanho,-a; limitado,-a.

narrows *npl (of a river)* a parte mais estreita de um rio; estreitamento *m,* estrangulamento *m* de um rio; **2** *(between lands)* passagem *f* estreita.

nasal *n adj (LING)* nasal; **2** *(accent) adj* anasalado,-a.

nastily *adv (unkindly)* de modo *m* desagradável, antipático.

nastiness *n* maldade *f*; má intenção *f*.

nasturtium *(BOT)* nastúrcio *m*; capuchincha *f*.

nasty *(pl:* **nasties***) n (coll) (impurities)* impurezas *fpl*; ♦ *adj (unpleasant)* desagradável; ~ **business!** assunto, incidente *m* desagradável!; *(person)* antipático,-a; **2** *(bad)* mau *m*, má *f*; *(habit)* ruim *m,f*; **3** *(unkind) (comment, gossip)* maldoso,-a, *(bump, crack, fall)* grave *m,f*; **4** *(ugly, filthy)* muito feio,-a, repugnante, asqueroso,-a; **5** *(tricky)* difícil *m,f*; IDIOM **he is a** ~ **piece of work** ele tem maus fígados.

nation *n (country)* país *m*; *(people)* nação *f*; ~ **state** *n* estado *m* nação.

national *n adj* nacional *m,f*; *(citizen)* cidadão *m*, cidadã *f*; **N~** **Audit Office** *npr (equiv to)* Tribunal *m* de Contas; ~ **curriculum** *(UK) n* currículo *m* do ensino nacional na Inglaterra e no País de Gales; ~ **dress** roupas típicas, regionais de um país; ~ **grid** *n* rede *f* elétrica; **N~ Health Service (NHS)** *(UK)* Serviço Nacional de Saúde; **N~ Heritage Minister** *n (UK)* Ministro da Cultura, Turismo e Desporto; **N~ Insurance** *n (UK)* Segurança Social; **N~ Lottery** *n* lotaria *f* britânica; **N~ Trust (NT)** (esta instituição restora edifícios, monumentos históricos e parques e promove o seu acesso ao público) Comissão da preservação do Património Nacional.

nationalism *n* nacionalismo *m*.

nationalist *adj* nacionalista *m,f*.

nationality *n* nacionalidade *f*.

nationalization *n* nacionalização *f*.

nationalize *vt* nacionalizar.

nationalized *adj* nacionalizado,-a.

nationally *adv* de âmbito nacional; nacionalmente.

nationwide *adj* de âmbito,-a nível nacional; ♦ *adv (travel)* por todo o país; *(broadcast to)* para todo o país.

native *n* nativo,-a; **2** *(BOT, ZOOL)* originário de; ♦ *adj (people, species)* autóctone, indígena *m,f*; **2** *(country)* natal; ~ **country** país natal; **3** inato,-a, natural (**from** de); ~ **tongue** língua *f* materna.

nativity *n* natividade *f*; ~ **play** *n (THEAT)* cena, peça da Natividade; **2** *(crib)* presépio *m*.

NATO *n (abbr for* **North Atlantic Treaty Organization***)* Organização do Tratado do Atlântico Norte (OTAN).

natter *n (UK) (coll)* conversa *f* fiada, cavaqueira *f*; *(BR)* bate-papo *m*; ♦ *vt* tagarelar, cavaquear.

natty *adj* elegante, chique; *(coll)* giro,-a; catita *m,f*.

natural *adj* natural *m,f*; autêntico,-a; ~ **resources** *npl* recursos naturais *mpl*; **2** *(inborn instinct)* nato,-a, inerente; **3** *(not affected, constrained)* simples, natural; **4** normal.

naturalist *n* naturalista *m,f*.

naturalize *vt*: **to become ~d** naturalizar-se; aclimatar-se.

naturally *adv* naturalmente; claro, evidentemente; por instinto, espontaneamente.

naturalness *n* naturalidade *f*; simplicidade *f*.

natural wastage *n (war of attrition)* redução no número de empregados numa organização; (guerra de) desgaste; **2** desperdício natural.

nature *n* natureza *f*; **2** *(type)* tipo *m*, espécie *f*; **3** cará(c)ter *m*, índole *f*; **by** ~ por natureza; ~ **trail** *n* trilha *f* ecológica.

naught *(also:* **nought***) n* zero *m*; **2** *(arc) (nothingness)* nada.

naughtiness *n (of child, pet)* travessura *f*; **2** *(cunning)* marotice *f*.

naughty (-ier, -iest) *adj (person)* travesso,-a, maroto,-a; **you are a ~ girl** tu és uma marota; **2** *(adult person)* atrevido,-a, malandro,-a; **3** *(film, comment)* picante *m,f*.

nausea *n (MED)* náusea *f*; *(fig)* nojo *m*.

nauseate *vt* enjoar, causar/dar náuseas a; **2** *(fig)* repugnar.

nauseating *adj (food, smell)* nauseabundo,-a, enjoativo,-a; **2** *(fig) (filthy)* nojento,-a, repugnante.

nauseous *adj*: **to feel ~** estar enjoado,-a.

nautical *adj* náutico,-a; **2** marítimo,-a; **3** *(career)* na marinha; ~ **mile** *n* milha *f* náutica.

naval *adj* naval; ~ **dockyard** *n* arsenal *m* da marinha; ~ **officer** *n* oficial *m,f* da marinha; ~ **stores** aprovisionamento *m* naval.

nave *n (of a church)* nave *f*.

navel *n (ANAT)* umbigo *m*; ♦ ~**-gazing: to be ~** ser egocêntrico,-a.

navigable *adj* navegável *m,f*.

navigate *vt* pilotar *(plane)*; navegar *(sea);* comandar, pilotar *(ship);* *(COMP)* navegar; **2** *(fig)* dirigir; **3** ~ **by remote control** navegar à distância; ♦ *vi* navegar; **2** *(in a car)* ser/fazer de copiloto; ~ **by the stars** orientar-se pelas estrelas.

navigation *n* navegação *f*; ~ **laws** *npl* código *m* marítimo.

navigator *n* navegante *m,f*; *(in a car)* copiloto.

navvy *(pl:* **navvies***) n (CONSTR) (labourer)* trabalhador *m* braçal, cabouqueiro *m*.

navy *n* marinha *f*; armada *f*, frota *f*; **merchant ~** marinha *f* mercante; ~**-blue** *adj* azul-marinho.

nay *n (LITER)* não *m*; **2** *(POL) (negative vote)* **the ~s to the left and the ayes to the right** os nãos (contra) para a esquerda e os sins (a favor) para a direita.

Nazarene *n adj* nazareno,-a.

Nazareth *npr* Nazaré.

Nazi *n* nazista *m,f*.

Nazism *n* nazismo *m*.

NB *(abbr for* **nota bene***)* NB.

NCO *(abbr for* **non-commissioned officer***).*

NE *(abbr for* **northeast***)* nordeste, NE.

Neanderthal *adj* neandertal.

Neapolitan *n adj* Napolitano,-a.

neap tide *n* maré *f* morta, maré de quadradura.

near *(-er, -est) adv (in distance)* perto; **the station is very ~ (here)** a estação é muito perto daqui; **2** *(in time, relationship)* próximo,-a; **in the ~ future** num futuro próximo; em breve; **3** *(nearly)* quase; **a ~-perfect work** um trabalho quase, praticamente perfeito; **nowhere ~ finished** longe de estar acabado; ~ **miss** *n*: **it was a ~ miss** foi por pouco, por um triz; ♦ *prep (= ~ to) (distance)* perto de, junto de; **2** *(almost)* quase, aproximadamente; **I**

was damn ~ dismissed *(fam)* eu quase fui despedido; *(on point of)* perto de, quase, prestes a; **to be ~ to doing** estar prestes a fazer; ♦ *adj (short, close)* curto,-a, próximo,-a; **the ~er I am/ get to the sea, the happier I become** quanto mais perto estou do mar, mais feliz eu fico; **the ~est hotel** o hotel mais próximo; **the ~est and dearest** entes *npl* queridos, família *f*; ♦ ~ **at hand** *adv* à mão; ~**by** *adj adv* perto, próximo; **far and ~** *adv* em toda a parte; ♦ *vt/vi* aproximar-se de; **come ~** aproxima-te, chega-te *(fam)*.

nearly *adv* quase, por pouco.

nearness *n* proximidade *f*; intimidade *f*.

nearside *n adj* lado esquerdo, *(US)* lado direito; **2** *(AUT)* do lado oposto ao condutor.

nearsighted *adj* míope *m,f*.

near thing *n*: **it was a ~ thing** escapámos por um triz.

neat *adj* arrumado,-a, em ordem; **2** limpo,-a, asseado,-a; **3** *(theory, solution)* hábil *m,f*, engenhoso,-a; **4** *(trim) (legs, figure)* bem feito,-a; **5** *(UK) (of alcohol)* puro,-a, sem água; **6** *(summary)* conciso,-a; **7** ~**-handed** destro,-a.

neatly *adv (tidily)* impecavelmente, primorosamente; **2** *(easily)* facilmente; **3** *(adroitly)* habilmente; ~ **put/said!** bem dito!

neatness *n (tidiness)* arrumação *f*; asseio *m*; **2** *(of handwriting)* clareza *f*; **3** cuidado *m*.

nebulous *adj* nebuloso,-a; **2** *(fig)* vago,-a, confuso,-a.

necessarily *adv* necessariamente.

necessary *adj* necessário,-a, preciso,-a.

necessitate *vt* precisar; tornar necessário.

necessity *(pl:* -ies*)* *n* necessidade *f*, requisito *m*; **necessities** *npl* artigos *mpl* de primeira necessidade; **bare** ~**s** necessidades *fpl* básicas, essenciais.

neck *n (ANAT)* pescoço *m*, colo *m*; **2** *(of bottle)* gargalo *m*; **3** *(of shirt, blouse)* colarinho *m*, gola *f*; **low ~** *(of dress)* decote *m*; **with a high ~** com uma gola alta; **4** *(MED)* **the ~ of the womb** o colo do útero; **5 back of the ~** *(person, ox)* cachaço *m*; **6** *(of land)* istmo *m*; ♦ *vi (fam) (pet, kiss fondle)* andar aos beijinhos, estar na marmelada; IDIOM **to be up to one's ~ in work** estar cheio de trabalho; **a ~ and ~ race** uma corrida taco a taco; **to be ~ and ~** estar lado a lado; **to be a pain in the ~** *(fam)* ser uma carraça; **to break one's ~** *(fig)* trabalhar duro e depressa; **to stick one's ~ out** *(fam) (risk criticism)* arriscar-se; **in the ~ of the woods** *(area, locality)* sítio *m* (em, por) estas paragens; **I live in a quiet ~ of the woods** moro num sítio muito sossegado.

neckerchief *n* lenço *m* do pescoço.

necklace *n* colar *m*; *(of gold, silver)* cordão *m*.

neckline *n* decote *m*.

necktie *n* gravata *f*.

nectar *n* néctar *m*.

nectarine *n (fruit)* nectarina *f*, pêssego-careca *m*.

née *adj*: ~ **Brown** nome de solteira Brown.

need *n* falta *f*, carência *f* **(for/of** de); **2** *(necessity)* necessidade *f*; **without the ~ for/of** sem necessidade de; ♦ ~**s** *adv*: **if ~ must** se for preciso; ♦ *vt*

(require) necessitar, precisar de; **I ~ to buy a new computer** preciso de comprar um novo computador; ♦ *vb aux (to have to, must) (como auxiliar, 'need' na interrogativa e negativa, não usa 'to' e 'he', 'she' não precisa de 's'*); **he needn't tell me that** ele não tem que me dizer isso; ~ **he go?** ele tem mesmo de ir embora?; **that's all I ~!** era só o que faltava!; IDIOM **a friend in ~ is a friend indeed** o amigos conhecem-se nas ocasiões.

needle *n* agulha *f*; **pins and ~s** formigueiro *msg*, *(BR)* formigamento *m*; **the eye of the ~** o buraco da agulha; ♦ *vt (fig)* provocar, arreliar; IDIOM **it's like looking for a ~ in a haystack** é como procurar uma agulha num palheiro.

needlepoint, needlework *n* bordado *m*; trabalho *m* de agulha; costura *f*.

needless *adj* inútil, desnecessário,-a; ~ **to say** é escusado dizer que.

needy *n*: **the ~** os necessitados *mpl*; ♦ *adj* necessitado,-a, carenciado,-a.

nefarious *adj* execrável *m,f*.

negate *vt (cancel out)* anular, invalidar.

negation *n* negação *f*; anulação *f*.

negative *n (PHOT)* negativo *m*; negação *f*; **to answer in the ~** dizer que não; ♦ *adj* negativo,-a.

neglect *n (lack of care)* descuido *m*, desleixo *m* negligência *f*; **2** *(health, appearance)* falta *f* de cuidado; ♦ *vt* negligenciar, não cumprir com; não cuidar, esquecer-se de.

neglected *adj (person, child, land)* abandonado,-a; negligenciado,-a.

neglectful *adj* negligente *m,f*.

negligee *n* négligé *m*; camisa *f*, *(BR)* camisola *f* de noite; robe *m* ligeiro.

negligence *n* negligência *f*; descuido *m*; **3** *(JUR)* incumprimento do dever de cuidar de alguém

negligent *adj (JUR)* negligente; *(in appearance, manner)* desleixado,-a.

negligible *adj* insignificante *m,f*.

negotiable *adj* negociável *m,f*; transitável *m,f*.

negotiate *vi* negociar; ♦ *vt* negociar; efe(c)tuar; transpor, vencer.

negotiation *n (discussion)* negociação *f*, transa(c)ção *f*; ~**s** *npl* negociações *fpl*.

negotiator *n* negociador,-a.

Negro *n (pej)* preto,-a *(pej)*.

neigh *n* relincho *m*; ♦ *vi* relinchar.

neighbour *(UK)* **neighbor** *(US)* *n* vizinho,-a.

neighbourhood *(UK)* **neighborhood** *(US)* *n* vizinhança *f*, vizinhos *mpl*; *(area)* bairro *m*.

neighbouring *adj* vizinho,-a.

neighbourly *adj* amistoso,-a, prestável *m,f*.

neither *adj pron* nenhum-a; ~ **of us** nenhum de nós; ~ **one nor the other** nem um nem outro; ~ **good nor bad** nem bom nem mau; **that's ~ here nor there** isso não importa, é irrelevante; ♦ *adv conj* nem; tampouco, também não; nem; ~ **do I** eu também não; nem eu.

neo *prefix* neo.

Neolithic *adj* neolítico,-a.

neologism *n* neologismo *m*.

neon *n* néon (*BR*: neônio); ~ **light** *n* luz/lâmpada de néon; ~ **sign** letreiro *m* luminoso.

Nepal *npr* Nepal; **in** ~ no Nepal.

Nepalese *n adj* nepalês,-esa.

nepherites *n (MED)* nefrite *f*.

nephew *n* sobrinho *m*.

nepotism *n* nepotismo *m*.

nerd *n (pej) (stupid)* pateta *m,f*; **2** *(obsessed)* fanático,-a.

nerve *n (ANAT)* nervo *m*; ~ **centre** *n (ANAT)* centro *m* nervoso; centro nevrálgico; ~ **gas** *n* gás *m* neurotóxico; **2** *(courage)* coragem *f*; **3** *(cheek)* descaramento *m*, atrevimento *m*, arrojo *m*; **to touch a raw** ~ tocar no ponto sensível; ~**s** *npl (fig)* nervosismo *m*; **a fit of** ~ um ataque *m* de nervos; **a bundle of** ~ uma pilha *f* de nervos; **be in a state of** ~ estar com os nervos em franja; **to get on sb's** ~**s** irritar alguém.

nerve-racking *adj* exasperante *m,f*, enervante *m,f*.

nervous *adj (ANAT)* nervoso,-a; **2** *(shy)* tímido,-a, acanhado,-a; **a** ~ **breakdown** *n* um esgotamento *m* nervoso.

nervously *adv* nervosamente, timidamente.

nervousness *n* nervosismo *m*, agitação *f*; **2** *(shyness)* timidez *f*; **3** *(anxiety)* ansiedade *f*, inquietação *f*; **4** *(stage fright)* pânico *m*; **5** *(FIN)* instabilidade *f*.

nest *n* ninho *m*; **2** *(group of cats, mice, rabbits)* ninhada *f*; **3** *(of wasps)* vespeiro *m*; **4** *(of ants)* formigueiro *m*; **5** *(of tables)* conjunto *m* de mesas (de encaixar uma nas outras); ♦ *vi* aninhar-se.

nestle *vi*: **to** ~ **up to sb** aconchegar-se a alguém.

net *n (gen)* rede *f*; **2** *(fig)* armadilha *f*, teia *f*; **the** ~ **is closing in** a teia está-se a apertar, vai-se apertando; **to slip through the** ~ passar através das malhas/da rede; **the N~** *n (COMP)* a rede *f*; ~**ball** *n* bola-ao-cesto, netbol *m*; ~ **curtain** *n* cortina *f* de voile; ♦ *adj (FIN, COMM) (income, profit, price)* líquido,-a; ~ **of tax** livre de descontos; *(income)* depois dos descontos; **I earn fifty thousand euros** ~ ganho cinquenta mil euros, depois dos descontos; ~ **weight** peso *m* bruto; ♦ *(-tt-) vt* cobrir com rede; **2** *(tennis)* bater na rede; *(in football)* marcar *(goal)*; **3** *(ECON, COMM) (yield)* render; **his business** ~**ted £5 billion** o negócio dele rendeu cinco biliões *(BR*: bilhões*)* de libras; *(person)* facturar; **4** *(catch)* apanhar *(peixe)*; *(fig) (police)* apanhar *(criminal)*.

Netherlands *npr* Países Baixos; **the** ~ os Países Baixos.

netiquete *n (COMP)* netiqueta *f*.

nett *adj* (= **net**).

netting *n* rede *f*, redes *fpl*; **wire** ~ rede de arame; **2** *(of metal, plastic)* tela *f*; **3** *(of fabric)* tule grosso; *(for curtains)* voile *f*.

nettle *n* urtiga *f*; ♦ *vt (irritate)* irritar.

network *n* rede *f*, cadeia *f*; *(of people)* grupo *m*; ♦ *vt (TV, RADIO)* transmitir em rede, difundir; *(COMP)* trabalhar, ligar em rede; ♦ *vi (mutual aid, contacts)* criar uma rede de conta(c)tos.

networked *adj* interligado,-a, em cadeia.

networking *n (COMM)* estabelecimento *m*, constituição *f* de uma rede de contatos.

neuralgia *n* neuralgia *f*.

neuralgic *adj* nevrálgico,-a.

neurology *n* neurologia *f*.

neuron *n* neurónio *(BR:* -ô-*)*.

neurosis *(pl:* -ses*) n* neurose *f*.

neurotic *n adj* neurótico,-a.

neuter *adj* neutro,-a; **2** *(animal)* castrado,-a, capado,-a; ♦ *n (LING)* neutro; ♦ *vt (animal)* castrar, capar.

neutral *n (AUT)* ponto *m* morto; **to have a** ~ **effect** não ter efeito nenhum; ♦ *adj* neutro,-a; neutral; imparcial *m,f*; ~ **country** país neutro.

neutrality *n* neutralidade *f*.

neutron *n* neutrão *m*; *(BR)* nêutron *m*; ~ **bomb** *n* bomba *f* de neutrões *(BR:* nêutrons*)*.

never *adv* nunca; ~ **again** nunca mais; **2** *(expressing surprise, doubt)* **he** ~**!** impossível!; **well, I** ~**!** *(fam)* não acredito!; **3** ~ **mind!** não faz mal! não faça caso!; **4** *(poetic; emphatic)* **I shall** ~ **forget you** jamais te esquecerei; **5** *(fam) (instead of 'not')* **I** ~ **said that** eu nunca/eu não disse isso; IDIOM **it** ~ **rains but it pours** uma desgraça nunca vem só.

never-ending *adj* sem fim, interminável.

never-never *n (UK) (hire purchase system)* a prestações; **to buy on the** ~ comprar a crédito,-a prestações.

neverland *n* país *m* do nunca.

nevertheless *adv conj* todavia, contudo, não obstante.

new *n adj* novo,-a; **2** recente; **3** diferente; **4** inexperiente, principiante; **brand** ~ novo em folha; ~ **friend** *n* amigo *m* recente; ~**ish** *adj* praticamente novo,-a; ~ **look** *n* nova moda *f*, novo visual *m*; **to be** ~ **to sth** ser inexperiente em algo, estar há pouco tempo em.

New Age *n* Nova Era *f*.

newborn *adj* recém-nascido,-a.

newcomer *n* recém-chegado,-a.

New Delhi *npr* Nova Déhli; **in** ~ em Nova Déhli.

New England *npr* Nova Inglaterra; **in** ~ na Nova Inglaterra.

newfangled *adj (pej)* ultramoderno,-a.

new-found *adj* recém-descoberto,-a, recém-achado.

Newfoundland *n* Terra Nova *f*; **in** ~ na Terra Nova; **2** *(people, industry, etc)* da Terra Nova.

New Guinea *npr* Nova Guiné; **in** ~ na Nova Guiné.

New Jersey *npr* Nova Jérsei; **in** ~ em Nova Jérsei.

newly *adv* há pouco; novamente; ~**-weds** *npl* recém-casados *mpl*.

New Mexico *npr* Novo México; **in** ~ no Novo México.

newness *n* novidade *f*; **2** *(fig)* inexperiência *f*.

news *n (information)* notícia *f*, notícias *fpl*; **a piece of** ~ uma notícia; **the** ~ *(RADIO, TV)* as notícias *fpl*, o noticiário *m*; **to break the** ~ **to sb** dar uma má notícia a alguém; **2** *(new piece of information)* novidade *f*, novidades *fpl*; **what** ~ **do you bring me?** que novidades me trazes?; **I'm going to give you some** ~ *(to tell you sth new)* vou dar-te uma novidade; **that's** ~ **to me** isso é uma novidade para mim; ~ **agency** *n* agência *f* de notícias; ~**agent** *n* jornaleiro,-a; ~**caster** *n (RADIO)* locutor,-a de notícias; *(TV)* apresentador,-a de jornal; ~ **conference** *n* entrevista *f* cole(c)tiva; **daily/**

weekly ~ *n* diário *m*, semanário *m*; ~**flash** *n* notícia *f* de última hora; ~ **headlines** *npl* títulos da a(c)tualidade; ~**hound** *n* repórter *m,f*, caçador,-a de notícias; ~**letter** *n* boletim *m* informativo; ~**paper** *n* jornal *m*; ~**paper cuttings** recortes *mpl* de jornais; ~**reel** *n* documentário *m* cinematográfico; cinejornal *m*; ~**room** sala *f* de reda(c)ção; ~ **sheet** *n* folheto *m* informativo; ~**speak** *(US) n (pej)* gíria *f* administrativa e política; ~ **stand** *n* quiosque *m*, banca *f* de jornais; ~**worthy** *adj* mediático,-a.

newt *n* tritão *m*.

new wave *(new movement in art, cinema) adj* nova vaga; *(BR)* nova onda; **the New Wave** *npr (CIN) (new movement in the '60s)* nova vaga *f*; *(BR)* nova onda.

New Year *n* Ano Novo *m*; ~**'s Day** *n* dia *m* de Ano Novo; ~**'s Eve** *n* véspera *f* de Ano Novo; **Happy** ~! Feliz Ano Novo.

New York *npr* Nova Iorque, **in** ~ em Nova Iorque.

New Yorker *n adj* nova-iorquino,-a.

New Zealand *npr* Nova Zelândia; **in** ~ na Nova Zelândia.

New Zealander *n adj* neozelandês-esa.

next *adj* próximo,-a, vizinho,-a; a seguir, logo em seguida; ~ **time** na próxima vez; ~ **year** (n)o ano que vem, (n)o próximo ano; ~ **door** *adv* na casa do lado, na casa vizinha; ~ **of kin** *n* parentes *mpl* mais chegados; ~ **to** *prep* junto a, ao lado de.

nexus *(pl:* **nexuses)** *n (link)* ligação *f*; *(network)* rede *f*.

NI *(abbr for* **National Insurance)**; **2** *(GEOG) (abbr for* **North Ireland)** Irlanda do Norte.

nib *n (of pen)* aparo *m*; *(of feather)* bico *m* de pena para escrever.

nibble *n (morsel)* pedacinho *m* pequeno; petisco; **2** dentada *f*; ♦ *vt (food)* morder, dar uma dentada, comer um pouco; **to** ~ **at a cake** comer um bolo aos poucos; **2** *(person, mouse, rabbit)* roer; ♦ **to** ~ **at** *vi (playfully)* mordiscar *(neck, etc); (consider)* remoer, ruminar *(idea, subject) (fam)*.

Nicaragua *npr* Nicarágua; **in** ~ na Nicarágua.

nice *adj* simpático,-a; amável; agradável; atraente *m,f*; ~**looking** *adj (fam)* bonitão,-ona.

nicely *adv* agradavelmente, bem.

niceness *n (kindness)* gentileza *f*, ambilidade *f*, simpatia *f*.

nicety *(pl:* -**ties)** *n* delicadeza *f*, subtileza *f*; **the social** ~**ties** *npl (etiquette)* as subtilezas da etiqueta.

niche *n (gen)* nicho *m*; **a** ~ **in the market** boa posição *f*/colocação *f* no mercado.

nick *n (cut)* pequeno corte *m*, talha *f*; entalhe (**in** em); **2** *(UK: jail)* calabouço *m*; **she is in the** ~ ela está no calabouço, no xadrez *(EP fam)*; **3 in good/bad** ~ *(UK: jail) (fam)* em bom/mau estado; ♦ *vt (coll) (steal)* furtar, fanar *(cal) (BR)* passar a mão em; **2** *(UK: arrest)* prender, *(BR)* enjaular; **3** *(to chip)* talhar, entalhar *(surface, edge)*; IDIOM **in the** ~ **of time** em cima da hora, na hora H (agá).

nickel *n* níquel *m*.

nickname *n* diminutivo *m*, alcunha *f*, *(BR)* apelido *m*; ♦ *vt* pôr alcunha em, *(BR)* apelidar.

Nicosia *npr* Nicósia; **in** ~ em Nicósia.

nicotine *n* nicotina *f*.

niece *n* sobrinha *f*.

nifty (-tier, -tiest) *adj* chique, giro,-a; **2** *(on feet)* ágil, rápido,-a.

Niger *npr (country, river)* Níger; **in** ~ no Níger.

Nigeria *npr* Nigéria; **in** ~ na Nigéria.

Nigerian *n adj* nigeriano,-a.

Nigerien *adj (from Niger)* nigerino,-a.

niggardly *adj (stingy)* avarento,-a, sovina; **2** *(amount)* miserável.

niggle *n* preocupação *f* com detalhes; ♦ *vt (worry, fuss)* apoquentar, irritar; ♦ *vi (of complain)* queixar-se constantemente.

niggling *n* ninharia *f*, *(BR)* mixaria *f*; ♦ *adj (person) (petty)* mesquinho,-a; *(fussy)* miudinho,-a.

nigh *adj adv (LITER)* perto; **to draw** ~ aproximar-se; **well** ~ quáse.

night *n* noite *f*; **at/by** ~ de/à noite; ~ **after** ~ todas as noites, noite após noite; ~ **and day** (= **day and** ~) continuamente; **far into the** ~ pela noite dentro, pela noite fora; **to have an early/late** ~ ir dormir cedo/tarde; ~**cap** *n* bebida *f* tomada antes de ir dormir; ~**club** *n* clube *m* noturno; ~**dress** *(nightie) n* camisa *f* de noite, *(BR)* camisola *f*; ~**fall** *n* anoitecer; ~ **life** *n* vida *f* no(c)turna; ~**ly** *adj, adv* no(c)turno; todas as noites; ~**mare** *n* pesadelo *m*; ~ **marish** *adj* horripilante; **over** ~ de um dia para o outro; ~**shift** *n* turno *m* da noite; ~-**time** *n* noite *f*; ~-**walker** sonâmbulo; ~**wear** *n* roupa *f* de dormir; ~**watchman** *n* guarda-no(c)turno *m*.

nightingale *n (ZOOL)* rouxinol *m*.

nightowl *n (fig)* no(c)tívago,-a; **2** *(ZOOL)* mocho *m*.

nihilism *n* niilismo *m*.

nil *n* nada *m*, zero *m*.

nimble *adj* ágil *m,f*, ligeiro,-a; ~ **on one's feet** ter pés ligeiros, ser ligeiro; **2** *(with fingers)* hábil; **to be** ~ **with one's fingers** ser habilidoso,-a; **3** *(mind)* esperto,-a, vivo,-a.

nimbly *adv* agilmente.

nine *num* nove.

nineteen dezanove, *(BR)* dezenove.IDIOM **to talk** ~ **to the dozen** falar pelos cotovelos.

nineteenth *num* décimo,-a nono,-a.

ninetieth *n adj adv* nonagésimo,-a.

ninety *num* noventa.

ninny *(pl:* -**ies)** *n (fam)* simplório,-a; papalvo,-a; pateta; bobo,-a.

ninth *num* nono,-a.

nip *n (pinch)* beliscão *m*, beliscadura *f*; **2** *(bite)* mordedela *f*; *(BR)* mordiscada *f*; **3** *(of drink)* trago *m*, gole *m*; ♦ *(-ped, -ping) vt (pinch)* beliscar; **2** *(bite)* morder, *(playfully)* mordiscar; **3** *(frost)* queimar *(plants)*; ♦ *vi (bird)* dar uma bicada; **to** ~ **along** *(col)* apressar-se; **to** ~ **in/into** *(dash)* dar um salto/saltinho *m* **(to** a); **to** ~ **(sth) off** *(flower buds)* cortar; **to** ~ **out** sair rapidamente; ir de fugida; **to** ~ **upstairs** *(go)(ir)* dar um salto lá em cima; IDIOM **to** ~ **(sth) in the bud** cortar (o mal) pela raiz.

nipper *n (UK) (fam)* criancinha *f*, garoto,-a.

nipple *n (ANAT)* mamilo *m*, bico do peito *m*; **2** *(of baby's bottle)* bico *m*; **3** *(TECH)* bocal *m* (roscado).

nippy adj rápido,-a, ágil m; **2** picante m; **3** (cold) fresquinho m.

nit n lêndea f; **2** (UK) (fam) idiota m; **to pick ~s** (col) pôr defeito em tudo.

nitpick vt embirrar; pôr defeitos em tudo.

nitpicker n (fam) (person) coca-bichinhos m inv.

nitpicking adj niquento, embirrante m,f, mesquinho,-a.

nitrate n nitrato m.

nitric acid n ácido m nítrico.

nitrogen n nitrogénio (BR: -gê-) m; azoto m.

nitted adj coberto de lêndeas.

nitty-gritty n factos m reais; IDIOM **let's get down to the ~** vamos ao que interessa.

nitwit n (coll) imbecil, cretino,-a.

no n não m, negativa f; **yes or ~?** sim ou não?; **I am ~ expert** não sou perito; ♦ adj (none, not any) nenhum,-a, algum,-a; **~ woman enters the club** nenhuma mulher pode entrar no clube; **2 ~ one** ninguém; **~ one lives here** ninguém mora aqui; **3 ~ doubt** sem dúvida; **4 ~ silly tricks** nada de disparates; **5** (prohibiting) **~ smoking** proibido fumar; **~-go area** n zona f interdita; **man's land** n terra f de ninguém; **6** (for emphasis) **she is ~ actress** ela não é a(c)triz nenhuma; ♦ adv não; **~ longer** já não; **2** (distance) **~ further than** não é mais longe que; IDIOM **~ sooner said than done** dito e feito.

no. (abbr for **number**) nº.

Noah's Ark n Arca de Noé f.

nobble n (UK) (fam) (racehorse) drogar; **2** (bribe) subornar; **3** (grab) apanhar.

Nobel prize n prémio m Nobel; (winner) vencedor do N.P.

nobility n nobreza f.

noble adj nobre m,f; ♦ n (person) fidalgo,-a.

nobody pron ninguém; **I see ~** não vejo ninguém; **~ rang me up** ninguém me telefonou.

nocturnal adj no(c)turno,-a.

nod n aceno com a cabeça; ♦ vi (-dd-) cumprimentar (com a cabeça); **2** acenar (que sim) com a cabeça; **she ~ed her agreement** ela acenou que concordava **3** dormitar; ♦ vt inclinar (a cabeça); **to ~ off** dormitar, (BR) cabecear.

node n (gen) nó m; **2** (COMP) nó m, nodo m.

nodule n (COMP) nódulo m.

noise n ruído m, barulho m; **to make a ~** (cars, machines, crockery) fazer barulho; **2** (voices) algazarra f, gritaria f.

noiseless adj silencioso,-a.

noisily adv ruidosamente.

noisy adj barulhento,-a.

nomad n nómada m,f, (BR) nômade.

nomadic adj nómada m,f.

nominal adj nominal; (money, fee) mínimo,-a.

nominally adv nominalmente; teoricamente.

nominate vt propor; nomear.

nominated adj nomeado,-a.

nomination n nomeação f; proposta f.

nominee n candidato,-a, pessoa nomeada, selecionado,-a.

non pref não-, des-, in-, anti-; **~-aggression** n não-agressão; **~-alcoholic** não alcoólico,-a; **~-aligned** adj não-alinhado,-a; **~-believer** (REL) descrente m,f.

nonce[1] n (prison slang) (child molester) violador m de crianças.

nonce[2] n (for the ~) (present time) só desta vez.

nonceword n palavra inventada para a ocasião.

nonchalant adj despreocupado,-a.

nonchalantly adv com indiferença.

non-commissioned officer n oficial m,f subalterno.

non-commital adj reservado,-a; evasivo,-a.

non compliance n (with rules, standards) incumprimento m.

nonconformist adj não-conformista, dissidente.

nondescript adj indeterminado,-a; (pej) medíocre m,f.

none pron (not any) nenhum; **~ of us** nenhum de nós; **2** nada; **~ of greasy things** nada de gorduras; **3** (not one person) ninguém; **there was ~ to help** não havia ninguém para ajudar; ♦ **~ the** (+ comp) **he was ~ the richer** ele não ficou mais rico; **~ other than George Clooney himself** nenhum outro que o próprio George Clooney; ♦ adv (not, not at all) de modo algum; **~ too difficult** longe de ser difícil.

non-entity (pl: ~ties) n (pej) nulidade f; zero m à esquerda m; joão-ninguém m.

nonetheless adv no entanto, apesar disso, contudo.

non-event n acontecimento m sem importância.

non-existent adj inexistente m,f.

non-fiction adj não-ficção.

non-fulfilment n (of contract) incumprimento m.

non-infectious adj intransmissível m,f.

non-iron adj não necessita ser passado a ferro.

no-no (coll) n: **that's a ~** isso não se faz.

no-nonsense adj (person) prá(c)tico,-a.

non-partisan adj (POL) não-partidário,-a; **2** imparcial.

non-payment n incumprimento m de pagamento, não-pagamento m.

nonplussed adj perplexo,-a, pasmado,-a.

non-professional n, adj amador m.

non-profitmaking adj sem fins lucrativos.

non-returnable adj (bottle) sem retorno.

nonsense n disparate m, asneira f, ninharia f; (meaningless) sem pés nem cabeça (fam).

nonsensical adj disparatado,-a, absurdo,-a.

non-skid adj anti-derrapante.

non-stick adj não-aderente, anti-aderente m,f.

non-stop adj ininterrupto,-a; contínuo,-a; **2** (RAIL) rápido, dire(c)to; ♦ adv dire(c)tamente; (RAIL) sem paragens; (flight) voo m dire(c)to.

non-toxic adj não-tóxico,-a.

noodles npl massa fsg; macarronete msg (chinês); (BR) talharine msg.

nook n canto m, recanto m; **~s and crannies** esconderijos mpl.

noon n meio-dia m.

noose n laço m corrediço; corda da forca f.

nor (= **neither**) conj, adv nem; **neither John ~ Rita** nem o João nem a Rita.

Nordic adj nórdico,-a.

norm n norma f, regra f; **the ~** o normal.

normal adj normal m,f; comum, regular.

normally *adv* normalmente.

Norman *n adj* normando,-a.

Normandy *n* Normandia; **in** ~ na Normandia.

north *n* norte *m;* ♦ *adj* do norte, setentrional; ♦ *adv* ao/para o norte.

North Africa *npr* Norte de África; **in** ~ no Norte da África.

North America *npr* América do Norte; **in** ~ no Norte da América.

northbound *adv* com dire(c)ção norte.

northeast *n* nordeste *m.*

northeasterly *adj* a nordeste.

northern *adj* do norte, setentrional; nortista.

northerner *adj* as gentes do norte; nortenho,-a.

Northern Ireland *npr* Irlanda do Norte; **in** ~ no Norte da Irlanda.

Northern Lights *npr* aurora *f* boreal.

northernmost *adj* mais a norte.

North Korea *npr* Coreia do Norte; **in** ~ na Coreia do Norte.

North Pole *npr* o Polo *m* Norte.

North Sea *npr* o Mar *m* do Norte; ~ **gas** *n* gás *m* natural.

North Star *npr* a Estrela *f* Polar.

Northumbrian *n adj* (*from Northumberland*) nortúmbrio,-a.

northward(s) *adj, adv* para norte, virado para norte.

northwest *n adj* noroeste *m.*

northwester *n* vento *m* do noroeste.

Norway *npr* Noruega; **in** ~ na Noruega.

Norwegian *n adj* norueguês-esa.

nos (*abbr for* **numbers**) nos, n^{os}.

nose *n* (ANAT) nariz *m;* **2** (*animal, plane*) focinho *m;* **3** (*of boat*) proa *f;* **4** (*sense of smell*) (*of person*) olfa(c)to *m;* (*of dog*) faro *m;* **5** (*instinct*) instinto *m,* sexto sentido *m;* **to follow one's** ~ seguir o seu instinto; **6** (*aroma of wine*) bouquet *m;* **to** ~ **about** bisbilhotar; **to poke one's** ~ **into sth** meter o nariz em algo; **to turn up one's** ~ **at** desdenhar.

nosebag (*for animal to feed*) cevadeira *f.*

nosebleed *n* hemorragia *f* nasal.

nose-dive *n* (*plane*) voo *m* picado; **the plane** ~**d** o avião caiu a pique; **2** (*demand, prices*) cair vertiginosamente.

nosey, nozy *adj* (*pej*) bisbilhoteiro,-a; coscuvilheiro,-a.

nosh *n* (UK) (*coll*) comida *f;* (US) refeição *f;* (BR) rango *m.*

nosily *adv* indiscretamente.

nostalgia *n* nostalgia *f,* saudades *fpl.*

nostalgic *adj* nostálgico,-a, saudoso,-a.

nostril *n* (*of person*) narina *f;* (*of horse*) venta *f.*

not *adv* não; ~ **at all** não, de modo algum; ~ **always** nem sempre; ~ **that I know** não que eu saiba; ~ **even** nem mesmo; ~ **yet** ainda não; ~ **now** agora não.

notable *n* celebridade *f,* notável; ♦ *adj* notável *m,f.*

notary *n* tabelião *m,* notário *m.*

notch (*pl:* -**es**) *n* (*em madeira*) entalhe *m,* encaixe *m;* (*in fabric*) corte *m;* (*indentation*) ranhura *f;* **2** (*fam*) (*on scale*) grau *m,* ponto *m;* **a** ~ **above** um grau acima; ♦ *vt* entalhar, fazer um corte; ♦ **to** ~ **up** *vt* (*fam*) conseguir; obter (*prize, point, win*).

note *n* (*banknote*) nota *f;* **2** (*card*) bilhete *m;* **3** (*reminder*) anotação *f;* **4** (MUS) (*sound*) nota *f;* (*key of instrument*) tecla *f;* **5** (*fig*) tom *m;* **6** (*importance*) **of** ~ digno de nota, eminente; ♦ ~**s** *npl* apontamentos *mpl;* anotações *fpl;* ♦ *vt* (*observe*) observar, notar, reparar em; **2** mencionar; **3** tomar nota de; ~ **down** *vt* anotar.

notebook *n* caderno *m* (de notas), agenda *f.*

noted *adj* conhecido,-a, célebre.

notepad *n* bloco *m* (de apontamentos).

notepaper *n* papel *m* de carta.

noteworthy *adj* digno,-a de menção.

nothing *n* nada *m;* zero *m;* **for** ~ (*free*) grátis *m,f,* de graça; **2** (*in vain*) em vão; **I came here for** ~ vim aqui em vão/para nada.

nothingness *n* nada *f,* vazio *m,* vácuo *m.*

notice *n* notícia *f,* anúncio *m;* **2** atenção *f,* interesse *m;* **3** aviso *m;* **to give** ~ **to** despedir; **to give one's** ~ **in** despedir-se, pedir demissão; ~ **board** *n* quadro *m* de avisos; ~ **of appeal** *m* intimação *f;* ♦ *vt* reparar, notar; **to take** ~ **of** prestar atenção a, fazer caso de; ♦ **at short** ~ a curto prazo; **until further** ~ até nova ordem.

noticeable *adj* evidente *m,f,* óbvio,-a.

noticeably *adv* notavelmente; **2** (*increase, improve*) sensivelmente.

notification *n* aviso *m,* notificação *f.*

notify *vt* avisar, notificar.

notion *n* noção *f,* ideia *f;* opinião *f;* ~**s** *npl* (US) (*haberdashery*) retrosaria *f,* loja *f* de miudezas; (BR) aviamentos *mpl.*

notional *adj* hipotético,-a.

notoriety *n* notoriedade *f.*

notorious *adj* notório,-a (**for/as** por/como), de má fama; (*case*) famoso,-a.

notwithstanding *adv* no entanto, não obstante; ~ **this** apesar disto.

nougat *n* nogado *m,* (BR) nugá *m.*

nought *n* zero *m,* nada *m;* **one thousand has three** ~**s** um milhar *or* mil tem três zeros.

noun *n* substantivo *m.*

nourish *vt* nutrir, alimentar; (*fig*) fomentar, alentar.

nourishing *adj* nutritivo,-a, alimentício,-a.

nourishment *n* alimentação *f,* nutrimento *m.*

nouveau-riche *n* novo-rico *m,* nova-rica *f.*

novel *n* romance *m;* novela *f;* ♦ *adj* novo,-a; original.

novelist *n* romancista *m,f,* novelista *m,f.*

novelty *n* novidade *f.*

November *n* Novembro, novembro *m.*

novice *n* principiante *m,f,* novato,-a; **2** (REL) noviço,-a.

now *adv* agora; a(c)tualmente; hoje em dia; ~ **and then,** ~ **and again** de vez em quando; **any day** ~ um destes dias, qualquer dia; **from** ~ **on** d'ora avante, de agora em diante; **just** ~ agora mesmo.

nowadays *adv* a(c)tualmente, hoje em dia.

nowhere *adv* a lugar nenhum; em parte alguma, nenhures.

no-win situation *n* empate *m,* beco *m* sem saída.

noxious *adj* nocivo,-a; pernicioso,-a; tóxico,-a.

nozzle *n* (*of hose, jet, gas*) bico *m,* bocal *m.*

NP *(abbr for* **notary public***)* notário *m,* tabelião *m.*

NT *(abbr for* **New Testament***)* NT; **2** *(abbr for* **National Trust***)* organização britânica encarregada da preservação de edifícios e monumentos históricos.

nth *(maths)* representando um número ordinal não especificado; **2** *adj (coll)* **for the ~ time** pela enésima vez.

nuance *n* matiz *m, (BR)* nuança *f.*

nub *n (core)* essência *f;* fulcro *m.*

nubile *adj (girl)* núbil *f.*

nuclear *adj* nuclear *m,f;* **~ family** *n* single parent family.

nucleus *(pl:* **-lei***) n* núcleo *m.*

nude *n adj* nu,-a; **in the ~** nu, despido, em pêlo.

nudge *n* cotovelada *f; (BR)* cutucada *f;* ♦ *vt* acotovelar *(BR)* cutucar; **2** encourage.

nudist *n* nudista *m,f.*

nudity *n* nudez *f.*

nugget *n (of gold)* pepita *f;* **~s** *npl (CULIN) (of chicken)* bocadinhos *mpl* de frango.

nuisance *n* incómodo *m (BR:* -cô-*),* maçada *f, (fam)* chatice *f,* aborrecimento; **what a ~!** que maçada!, que chatice!; **2** *(person, problem)* chato,-a; macador, -ora; ♦ **~ call** *n (telephone)* chamada anónima.

nuke *n (fam)* arma *f* nuclear.

null *adj* nulo,-a, sem validade; **~ and void** nulo, sem força legal.

nullify *vt* anular, invalidar.

numb *adj* dormente *m,f;* entorpecido,-a; **2** *(fig)* paralizado,-a **(with** com**);** ♦ *vt* adormecer, entorpecer.

number *n* número; *(written)* algarismo; **a ~ of** vários, muitos; **even/odd ~** número par/ímpar; ♦ *vt* numerar; chegar a; **to be ~ed among** achar-se entre; **to be ~ed among the famous** achar-se entre os famosos; **~-crunching** *n (fam)* cálculo *f* em grande escala; **~ one** *n* o mais importante; **to look after ~ one** cuidar de si mesmo,-a; **~plate** *n (AUT)* matrícula *f, (BR)* placa *f* (de carro); ♦ *adj (main)* principal.

numberless *adj* inumerável *m,f;* sem número.

numbness *n* torpor *m,* dormência *f,* entorpecimento *m;* **2** *(fig)* insensibilidade *f.*

numbskull *n (coll)* burro,-a; cabeça *f* oca.

numeral *n* numeral *m,* algarismo *m;* **Roman ~s** numeração romana.

numerator *n (MATH)* numerador.

numerical *adj* numérico,-a.

numerous *adj* numeroso,-a.

numerously *adv* em grande número.

numismatics *n* numismática *f.*

nun *n* freira *f,* monja *f.*

nunnery *n* convento *m* (de freiras).

nuptials *n* núpcias *fpl.*

nurse *n* enfermeiro,-a; **2** ama-seca *f,* criada *f* de meninos, *(BR)* babá *f; (arc)* aia *f;* **wet ~** ama *f* de leite; ♦ *vt* cuidar de, tratar de; criar, amamentar; *(fig)* alimentar; acalentar.

nursery *n* creche *f;* infantário *m;* **2** *(bedroom)* quarto *m* das crianças; **3** *(of flowers, plants)* viveiro *m; (loja)* jardim; **~ rhyme** *n* poesia *f* infantil; **~ school** *n* infantário *m;* escola *f* infantil; **~ tale** *n* conto *m* infantil.

nursing *n (profession)* enfermagem *f;* **2** *(care)* cuidado *m,* assistência *f;* **3** que amamenta; **~ home** *n* clínica *f* de repouso, casa *f* de saúde.

nurture *n* cuidados *mpl;* ♦ *vt* alimentar *(hope, feelings);* **2** *(children, plants)* criar.

nut *n (TECH)* porca *f;* **2** *(BOT)* noz *f;* **hazel~** *n (BOT)* avelã *f;* IDIOM **a hard/tough ~ to crack** *(fam) (difficult problem/person)* osso duro de roer.

nutcase *n (fig) (foolish person)* maluco,-a.

nutcracker *n* quebra-nozes *m.*

nutmeg *n* noz-moscada *f.*

nutrient *n* nutriente *m.*

nutrition *n* nutrição *f,* alimentação *f.*

nutritious *adj* nutritivo,-a.

nuts *fpl (ger)* nuts; **2** *(fig) (mad person)* louco,-a; **he is ~ about her** ele é louco por ela; **3 the ~ and bolts** *(basics)* o essencial; **4** *(slang) (testicles)* tomates; ♦ *exc* **~ to you!** vai à fava!

nutshell *n* casca *f* de noz; **in a ~** em poucas palavras.

nutter *n (fam)* maluco,-a.

nuzzle *vt (dog, horse)* esfregar o nariz, focinho; *(pig)* fossar.

NW *n (abbr for* **northwest***)* noroeste *m.*

nylon *n (fabric)* náilon, nylon *m;* ♦ *adj* de nylon; **~s** *npl* meias *fpl* (de nylon).

NYLON *n (fam)* executivo que goza duma vida transatlântica entre Londres e Nova Iorque.

nymph *n* ninfa *f.*

nymphomania *n* ninfomania *f.*

nymphomaniac *n adj* ninfómana *f,* ninfomaníaca *f.*

NZ *(abbr for* **New Zealand***)* Nova Zelândia.

O

O, o *n (letter)* O, o; **2** *exc (calling)* ó.
oaf *n (idiot)* imbecil *m,f*; **2** *(loutish)* grosseiro,-a.
oak *n (BOT)* carvalho *m*; ~ **grove** *n* carvalhal.
oaked wine *n* vinho em barrís de carvalho.
OAP *n (abbr for* **old-age pensioner***)* pensionista *m,f*, pessoa *f* de terceira idade, reformado,-a, aposentado,-a; que recebe pensão *f* da Segurança *f* Social.
oar *n* remo *m*; ~**sman** *n* remador *m*; ~**swoman** remadora *f*.
OAS *(abbr for* **Organization of American States***).*
oasis *(pl:* -ses*) n* oásis *m*.
oatcake *n* bolinho *m* de aveia.
oath *n* juramento *m*; **on/under** ~ sob juramento; **2** *(curse)* praga *f*.
oatmeal *n* farinha *f* de aveia.
oats *n (cereal)* aveia *fsg*; IDIOM **to sow one's wild** ~ divertir-se à grande, ter muitos,-as namorados,-as.
obduracy *n (formal)* teimosia *f*, obstinação *f*.
OBE *(abbr for* **Officer of the Order of the British Empire***) (UK)* Oficial *m* da Ordem do Império Britânico.
obedience *n:* **in** ~ em obediência, em conformidade com.
obedient *adj* obediente *m,f*.
obesity *n* obesidade *f*.
obey *vt* obedecer a; cumprir.
obituary *n* obituário *m*; necrologia *f*.
object *n (item)* obje(c)to *m*; **2** *(goal)* obje(c)tivo *m*; **money is no** ~ não há problema com o dinheiro; **3** *(gram)* complemento *m*; ♦ *vi:* **to** ~ **to** desaprovar, obje(c)tar a; opor-se a; **I** ~**!** protesto!
objection *n* obje(c)ção *f*; **I have no** ~ **to** não tenho nada contra.
objectionable *adj* desagradável; censurável.
objective *n adj* obje(c)tivo.
objectivity *n* obje(c)tividade *f*.
objector *n* obje(c)tor,-ora, opositor,-ora.
obligation *n* obrigação *f*; dever *m*; **without (any)** ~ sem compromisso.
obligatory *adj* obrigatório,-a.
oblige *vt* obrigar **(to**, a); **2** obsequiar, fazer um favor (a); **I should be** ~**d if ...** ficaria muito grato, agradecido se ...; **3** agradar, ceder (a) *(request)*.
obliging *adj* amável *m,f*, obsequioso,-a.
oblique *adj* oblíquo,-a; indire(c)to,-a.
obliquely *adv* obliquamente; de esguelha; indire(c)tamente.
obliterate *vt* obliterar, apagar; destruir.
obliteration *n (memory)* apagamento *m*; **2** *(of city)* destruição *f* total.
oblivion *n* esquecimento *m*.

oblivious *adj* inconsciente *m,f* **(of to**, de); desconhecedor,-ora; alheio,-a a; **I was** ~ **to the situation** estava alheia à situação.
oblong *n* re(c)tângulo *m*; ♦ *adj* oblongo,-a, re(c)tangular *m,f*.
obnoxious *adj* odioso,-a, detestável *m,f*.
oboe *n* oboé *m*.
obscene *adj* obsceno,-a.
obscenity *n* obscenidade *f*.
obscure *adj* obscuro,-a; pouco claro, indistinto,-a; **2** *(feeling)* vago,-a; ♦ *vt* ocultar *(truth)*; **2** obscurecer.
obscurity *n* obscuridade *f*, escuridão *f*.
obsequies *(sg:* ~**quy***) (funeral rites)* exéquias *fpl*.
obsequious *adj (ingratiating)* servil *m,f*, adulador,-ora.
observance *n* observância *f*, cumprimento *m*; prática *f*, hábito *m*.
observant *adj* observador,-ora.
observation *n* observação *f*; **2** vigilância *f*; **3** *(MED)* exame *m*.
observatory *n* observatório *m*.
observe *vt* observar; cumprir.
observer *n* observador,-ora.
obsess *vt* obcecar.
obsession *n* obsessão *f*, ideia *f* fixa.
obsessive *adj* obsessivo,-a.
obsolescence *n* obsolescência *f*.
obsolete *adj* obsoleto,-a; **to become** ~ cair em desuso.
obstacle *n* obstáculo *m*; estorvo *m*, impedimento *m*; ~ **race** *n* corrida *f* de obstáculos.
obstetrician *n* obstetra *m,f*.
obstetrics *n* obstetrícia *sg*.
obstinate *adj* teimoso,-a, obstinado,-a.
obstruct *vt* obstruir; impedir; tapar; entupir; estorvar.
obstruction *n* obstrucção *f*; impedimento *m*; estorvo *m*, obstáculo *m*.
obtain *vt* obter; conseguir.
obtainable *adj (objective)* alcançável *m,f*; **2** *(in shops)* disponível *m,f*.
obtrusive *adj (colour)* gritante *m,f*; **2** *(behaviour)* chocante *m,f*; **3** *(person)* indiscreto,-a; que dá muito nas vistas; **4** *(smell)* penetrante *m,f*.
obtrusively *adv* indiscretamente.
obtuse *adj* obtuso,-a; *(coll)* bronco,-a.
obviate *vt (delay, need)* evitar, obviar.
obvious *adj* óbvio,-a evidente *m,f*; **to state the** ~ afirmar o óbvio.
obviously *adv* evidentemente.
occasion *n* ocasião *f*; *(chance)* oportunidade *f*, motivo *m*; **2** momento *m*, vez *f*; **3** acontecimento *m*; ♦ *vt* ocasionar, causar.
occasional *adj* casual, eventual; *(poem, music)* de circunstância; **an** ~ **table** *(table by the side of sofa)* uma mesinha *f*, uma mesa auxiliar.
occasionally *adv* de vez em quando.
occlude *vt* obstruir, fechar.
occult *adj* oculto,-a.
occupant *n (resident)* inquilino,-a; **2** *(of seat, building)* ocupante *m,f*; *(of car)* passageiro,-a.
occupation *n (of land)* posse *f*, ocupação *f*; **2** *(job)* trabalho *m*, ofício *m*; *(activity)* profissão *f*; **unfit for** ~ *(house)* inabitável.

occupational *adj* ocupacional; ~ **disease** *n* (MED) doença ocupacional; ~ **hazard** *n* risco *m* da profissão; ~ **therapy** *n* terapia *f* ocupacional.

occupier *n* ocupante *m,f*; **2** (of house) residente.

occupy (-ied) *vt* (time, space) ocupar; preencher, empregar; **2** (habit) morar em; **3** (country) ocupar, tomar posse de; **4** (job, position) exercer, desempenhar; **5** (entertain) entreter, divertir; **to ~ o.s. with doing sth** ocupar-se com algo,-a fazer algo; entreter-se a; **the child occupies herself with puzzles** a criança entretém-se com os quebra-cabeças.

occur *vi* ocorrer, acontecer.

occurrence *n* acontecimento; **2** incidente *m*, caso *m*.

ocean *n* oceano *m*; ~**-going** *adj* de longo curso; ~ **liner** *n* transatlântico *m*.

Oceania *npr* Oceânia.

Oceanian *adj* oceânico,-a.

ochre *adj* (colour) ocre.

o'clock *adv*: **it is 2 ~** são 2 horas; **it is one ~ p.m.** é uma hora da tarde.

Oct. (Vd: **October**).

octagon *n* octógono *m*.

octagonal *adj* octagonal.

octane *n* octano *m*; ~ **number/rating** *n* índice *m* de octana.

octave *n* oitava *f*.

octet *n* (MUS) octeto *m*.

October *n* Outubro, outubro *m*.

octogenarian *n* octagenário,-a.

octopus (pl: -**puses** or -**pi**) *n* (ZOOL) polvo *m*.

OD (abbr for **overdose**) *n* overdose *f*; **2** (abbr for **overdrawn**) *adj* (current account) saldo negativo.

odd *adj* (strange) estranho,-a, esquisito,-a, excêntrico,-a; **her attitude is very** ~ a atitude dela é muito esquisita; **2** (number) ímpar; **3** (leftover) de sobra; ~ **bits** bocadinhos de sobra; **4** (approximately) e picos, e tal, e tantos; **I have thirty ~ euros** tenho trinta euros e picos; **there were forty-~ incidents** houve quarenta e tal incidents; **5** (not matching) (gloves) desirmanado,-a; **6** (exception) **to be the ~ one out** ficar de fora; ser a exce(p)ção; **7** (occasionally) **at ~ times** às vezes, quando calha; ~**-job man** (UK), ~**-jobber** (US) *n* faz-tudo *m*, homem *m* para toda a obra; ~ **jobs** *npl* biscates *mpl*.

oddity *n* (pl: -**ies**) excentricidade *f*; particularidade *f*; estranheza *f*; **2** (person) excêntrico,-a; **she is an ~** ela é excêntrica.

oddly *adv* curiosamente, estranhamente.

oddments *npl* (fabric) retalhos *mpl*; restos *mpl*.

odds *npl* probabilidades *fpl*; **the ~ are that ...** as previsões são de que ...; **against all ~** apesar de todas as dificuldades; **he fought against all ~** ele lutou contra a adversidade; ~ **and ends** *npl* (various bits) miudezas *fpl*; **to be at ~ with sb/sth** estar em desacordo, conflito com alguém/algo; **they are at ~** eles estão zangados, de mal; **to lay the ~** *vt* apostar.

odds-on *adj* (coll) (likely) **it is ~ that she will be married this year** há fortes probabilidades que ela se case este ano.

ode *n* ode *f*.

odious *adj* odioso,-a, detestável *m,f*.

odometer *n* (in car) velocímetro *m*.

odour *n* odor *m*; fragrância *f*, perfume *m*.

odourless *adj* (CHEM) inodoro, sem cheiro; **2** (flower, etc) sem perfume.

Odyssey *n* odisseia *f*.

OECD (abbr of **Organisation for Economic Co-operation and Development**) OCDE *f*.

oedema (UK) **edema** (US) (MED) *n* edema *f*.

Oedipus complex *n* complexo *m* de Édipo.

oesophagus (UK) **esophagus** (US) *n* (ANAT) esófago *m*.

oestrogen (UK) **estrogen** (US) *n* estrogéneo *m*.

of *prep* de; **2** (relation, friend) **a cousin ~ mine** um primo meu; **3** (date) **3rd ~ September** três de Setembro/setembro; **4** (amount) **two kilos ~ potatoes** dois quilos de batatas; **5** (containing) **a glass ~ wine** um copo de vinho; **pockets full ~ money** os bolsos cheios de dinheiro; **made ~ plastic** feito de plástico; **6** (on the part of) **it was very helpful ~ you** foi muito prestável da sua parte; ♦ ~ **late** ultimamente; ~ **necessity** por necessidade; ~ **course** naturalmente, com certeza.

off *adj* (elect appliance, engine) desligado,-a; (light, fire) apagado,-a; (tap) fechado,-a; **2** azedo,-a, estragado,-a; **the milk is ~** o leite está azedo; **the meat is ~** a carne está estragada; **3** (cancelled) anulado,-a; **the meeting is ~** a reunião está cancelada, anulada; ♦ *adv* (leaving) **to be ~** estar de partida; **I am ~** vou-me embora; **to get ~** sair; (from bus, train) descer; **2** (distance in space, time) **it is a long way ~** fica a grande distância; **holidays are a month ~** as férias são dentro de um mês; **3** (removed) sem; **20% ~ the price** 20% de desconto; **4** (removal) (of clothes) despir; **take your coat ~** tire o casaco; (of shoes) descalçar; **5** (plane) **the plane took ~** o avião levantou voo; **6 ~ and on** por períodos, de vez em quando; **right/straight ~** imediatamente; ♦ *prep* (not interested) **to be ~ one's food** não ter apetite; **2 Cape Verde is ~ the coast of West Africa** Cabo Verde fica ao largo da costa ocidental da África; **3 to show ~** armar, dar nas vistas (exibir-se); (pop) **para inglês ver**; ♦ *exc* ~ **with you!** rua! põe-te a andar!; **hands ~** ! tire as mãos!; IDIOM **he is ~ his rocker** (mad) ele está maluco, ele tem um parafuso a menos; **to have an ~ day** não estar nos seus dias.

offal *n* (animal's insides) vísceras *fpl*; (CULIN) miudezas *fpl* (de frango).

off-balance *adv* sem equilíbrio; **you caught me ~** apanhou-me desprevenido.

offbeat *adj* (MUS, etc) excêntrico,-a; **off the beaten track** fora da rotina vulgar.

off-centre *adj* descentralizado,-a; fora do centro.

off colour *adj* adoentado,-a, com mau parecer.

offcut *n* (cloth) retalho *m*; (of meat) sobras *fpl*.

off-duty/work *adj* de folga; **I have two days ~** tenho dois dias de folga; ~**-duty goods** (tax-free) produtos isentos de impostos; **on the ~ chance** por acaso.

offence *(UK)* **offense** *(US)* *n* delito *m*, infra(c)ção *f*; insulto *m*, ofensa *f*; **to take ~ at** ofender-se com, melindrar-se com.

offend *vt* ofender.

offender *n* delinquente *m,f*; infra(c)tor,-ora.

offensive *n* *(MIL)* ofensiva *f*; ♦ *adj* ofensivo,-a, chocante *m,f*; repugnante *m,f*.

offer *n* oferta *f*; **'on ~'** *(COMM)* 'à venda'; **2** *(proposal)* proposta *f*; **3** *(FIN)* oferta *f*; **an ~ of millions** uma oferta de milhões; **that's my best ~** é a minha última palavra; *(COMM)* **to be on special ~** estar em promoção; **~ price** *n* preço *m* de venda; ♦ *vt* *(give, provide)* oferecer; **2** *(opinion)* dar; **3** *(sell)* vender; **4 to ~ to do sth** *(volunteer)* oferecer-se para fazer algo.

offering *n* oferta *f*; **2** *(REL)* oferenda *f*.

offertory *n* *(REL)* ofertório *m*.

off guard *adv* desprevenido,-a, sem esperar.

offhand *adj* *(unfriendly)* brusco,-a; ♦ *adv* bruscamente; *(at this moment)* de imediato, de improviso.

office[1] *n* escritório *m*; gabinete *m*; **2** *(tax, pensions,etc)* departamento *m*, repartição *f*; **3** cargo *m*, função *f*; **to be in ~** estar no poder **to take ~** tomar posse; **run for ~** *(US)* ser candidato,-a às eleições; **to stand for ~** *(UK)* tomar posse; **4** *(REL)* ofício *m*; **~ block** *n* edifício *m* de escritórios; **~ boy** *n* mensageiro *m*, contínuo *m*; **head ~** *n* sede *f*; **~ hours** *npl* horário *m* de expediente; **~ junior** *n* *(UK)* assistente *m,f* de escritório. **notary's ~** *n* cartório *m*; **public ~** *n* funções *fpl* públicas; **~ staff** pessoal *m*; **~ worker** *n* empregado,-a de escritório.

Office[2] *npr* *(ministry)* ministério *m*, gabinete *m*.

officer *n* *(MIL, NAUT)* oficial *m,f*; **2** *(police)* agente *m,f* da polícia; *(BR)* agente policial; **3** *(in an organization)* dire(c)tor,-a.

official *n* funcionário,-a; ♦ *adj* autorizado, oficial.

officialdom *n* burocracia *f*.

officiate *vt* presidir (**at** a); *(as host)* exercer as funções de anfitrião, anfitriã; *(priest)* oficiar (**at** a).

officious *adj* *(pej)* intrometido,-a, oficioso,-a.

offing *n*: **in the ~** *(fig)* em perspectiva; num futuro *m* próximo.

off-key *adj* *(MUS)* desafinado,-a.

off-licence *n* loja *f* de bebidas alcoólicas.

off limits *adj* proibido,-a.

off-load *vt* pôr de parte, livrar-se de algo (passando para outra pessoa); **2** *(COMP)* descarregar.

offpeak *adj* a horas mortas; **2** *(ELECT)* *(time)* de baixo consumo.

offputting *adj* desconcertante *m,f*.

off-road *adj* *(vehicle)* todo-o-terreno.

off-season *n* época *f* baixa; ♦ *adj* de/em estação baixa.

offset *n* (= **~ printing**) impressão *f* em off-set; ♦ *(irr: like set)* *vt* compensar, contrabalançar.

offshoot *n* *(business)* ramificação *f*; **2** *(of plant)* rebento *m*; **3** *(of idea)* consequência *f*.

offshore *adj adv* *(boat, fishing)* ao largo; perto da costa; de terra (para o mar); *(FIN)* *(funds)* extraterritorial, 'offshore'; *(oil prospecting)* em alto-mar, 'offshore'.

offside *adj* *(SPORT)* fora-de-jogo, *(BR)* impedido; ♦ *adv* do lado de dentro da pista; **2** *(UK)* *(AUT)* lado *m* direito do motorista.

offspring *n* descendência *f*, prole *f*.

offstage *adv* nos bastidores.

off-street *adj*: **~ parking** *(AUT)* carro que tem seu estacionamento.

off the cuff *adj* improvisado,-a; sem ser oficial.

off the peg *adv* pronto (a vestir).

off the record *adv* confidencialmente, extraoficial.

off the shelf *adj* *(COMM)* à venda; disponível *m,f*.

off-white *adj* *(colour)* quase branco.

OFT *npr* *(abbr for* **Office of Fair Trading***)* *(UK)* órgão que compra directamente aos produtores de países em desenvolvimento.

often *adj* muitas vezes, frequentemente.

ogle *vt/vi* comer com os olhos.

oil *n* *(vegetable)* óleo *m* vegetal; **almond ~** óleo de amêndoa; **olive ~** azeite *m*; **2** *(petroleum)* petróleo *m*; **crude ~** petróleo bruto *(also: (pop)* o crude*)*; **3 lubricating ~** óleo de lubrificação; **~ bottle** *n* azeiteira *f*; **~ can** *n* almotolia *f*; **~ cloth** *n* oleado *m*; **~ field** *n* campo *m* petrolífero; **~ fired** *adj* que usa óleo combustível; **~ industry** *n* indústria *f* petrolífera; **~ paint** *n* *(on walls)* tinta *f* a óleo; **~ painting** *n* pintura *f* a óleo; **~ pipeline** *n* oleoduto *m*; **~ refinery** *m* refinaria *f* de petróleo; **~ rig** *n* torre *f* de perfuração, plataforma de petróleo; **~ skins** *npl* capa *fsg* de oleado; **~ slick** *n* mancha *f* de óleo; **~ tanker** *n* petroleiro *m*; **~ well** *n* poço *m* petrolífero; ♦ *vt* lubrificar; olear; **2** *(baking tin)* untar azeite *m*.

oily *adj* oleoso,-a; gorduroso,-a.

ointment *n* pomada *f*, unguento *m*.

oiro *npl* *(abbr for* **offers in the region of***)* *(real estate)* ofertas à volta de, em torno de.

OK, okay *n*: **to give sb the ~** *(approve)* dar sinal verde a alguém; ♦ *adj* certo, de acordo; *(reasonable)* **the food is ~** a comida está razoável; ♦ *exc* OK!, tudo bem!, está bem; ♦ *vt* aprovar.

okra *n* *(BOT)* *(lady's fingers)* kiabo *m*.

old (**-er, -est**) *adj* velho,-a; antigo,-a, anterior; **of ~** de outrora, de há muito; **how ~ are you?** quantos anos tem?; **he's 20 years ~** ele tem 20 anos; **to grow ~** envelhecer; **to look ~** estar velho; **to be ~** servelho,-a; **~ age** *n* velhice *f*; terceira idade *f*; **~-age pensioner** (**OAP**) *n* pensionista *m,f*; reformado,-a; **the ~ ** *n* os idosos *mpl*; **~-fashioned** *adj* antiquado, fora de moda; **~ flame** *n* paixão *f* antiga; **O~ Glory** *n* bandeira *f* dos Estados Unidos da América; **~ hand** *adj* *(coll)* pessoa *f* com muita prá(c)tica; **to be an ~ hand** ter muita prá(c)tica; **~ hat** *adj* *(pej)* **to be an ~ hat** estar fora da moda; **~ maid** *n* *(spinster)* solteirona *f*; **~ master** *n* antigo quadro *m*, pintor *m* famoso; **~ people's home** *n* lar *m* de idosos; **~-timer** *n* veterano,-a, *(man/woman)* velho,-a; **~ wives' tale** *n* conto *m* da carochinha.

Old Bailey *n*: **the ~** o edifício *m* do Supremo Tribunal de Londres.

olden *adj*: **in the ~ days** antigamente, no passado, nos tempos que já lá vão.

older *(comp of* **old***) adj* mais velho,-a.

oldest *(superl of* **old***) adj* o/a mais velho,-a; **the ~ house in town** a casa mais velha da cidade.

Old Testament *n* o Velho Testamento *m*.

oligarchy *n* oligarquia *f*.

olive *n* azeitona *f*; *(tree)* oliveira *f*; ♦ *adj* (= ~-**green**) verde-oliva; ~ **grove** olival *m*; ~ **oil** *n* azeite *m*.

Olympiad *n* olimpíada.

Olympic *adj* olímpico,-a; **the ~ Games, the ~s** os Jogos Olímpicos, as Olimpíadas.

OM *(abbr of* **Order of Merit***) (UK)* Ordem do Mérito (pessoas galardoadas com esta Ordem).

Oman *npr* Omã; **in** ~ em Omã.

OMB *(abbr for* **Office of Management and Budget***) (US)* Departamento que informa, aconselha o Presidente sobre questões orçamentárias.

ombudsman *n (UK) Comissão independente que age como árbitro entre um cidadão e uma organização ou departamento governamental, investigando as queixas sobre irregularidades apresentadas pelo cidadão.*

omelet(te) *n* omelete *f*.

omen *n* presságio *m*, agouro *m*.

ominous *adj* ameaçador,-a, agoirento,-a.

omission *n* omissão *f*; descuido *m*, negligência *f*.

omit *vt* omitir; **2** esquecer.

omnibus *n (LITER)* coletânea *f*; antologia *f*, compilação *f*; **2** *(of TV programme)* retransmissão *f* dos episódios da semana; programa *m* de variedades; ~ **bill** proje(c)to de lei múltipla.

omnipotent *adj* o(m)nipotente *m,f*.

omniscient *adj* o(m)nisciente *m,f*.

on *prep* sobre, em (cima de); ~ **the contrary** pelo contrário; ~ **the sly** pela calada; **put the saddle ~ the horse** põe a sela sobre o cavalo; ♦ *adj adv* aceso,-a; ligado,-a; em funcionamento; aberto,-a; **is the meeting still** ~? ainda vai haver reunião?; ~ **Monday** na segunda-feira; **a week ~ Monday** segunda (feira) a oito olias; **and so** ~ e assim por diante, etc; ~ **pain of death** sob pena de morte; ~ **horseback** a cavalo; ~ **television** na televisão; ~ **the right** à direita; ~ **and off** de vez em quando; ~ **and** ~ continuamente; **it's not** ~! isso não se faz!; **to have/put** ~ vestir; **to go** ~ continuar; **to turn** ~ **the light** acender a luz; **to turn** ~ **the tap** abrir a torneira.

once *adv* uma vez; ~ **upon a time** era uma vez; outrora; **this house was** ~ **a palace** esta casa era outrora um palácio; ♦ *conj (since)* uma vez que; **(all) at** ~ imediatamente; ao mesmo tempo; ~ **a week** uma vez por semana; ~ **a fortnight** de 15 em 15 dias; ~ **and for all** definitivamente; duma vez para sempre; ~ **in a while** de vez em quando.

once-over *n (coll) (a quick look)* **to give sb/sth the** ~ dar uma olhadela, *(BR)* olhada rápida por alguém/ algo *(fam)*; lançar uma vista de olhos por alguém.

oncoming *adj (danger)* iminente; **2** *(vehicle)* que se aproxima em sentido inverso; que vem de frente.

one *num* um,-a; **twenty-~** vinte e um,-a, **twenty-~ reasons** vinte e umas razões; *(fraction)* ~ **third** um terço; ♦ *adj pron* um,-a; se; único; ~ **by** ~ um

a um; ~ **and all** todos; ~ **and the same** idêntico; ~ **at a time** um de cada vez; **book** ~ primeiro *m* livro; ~ **or two** alguns; **that's a good** ~! é uma boa piada!, essa é boa!; **this** ~ este,-a; **the** ~ **in the window** o/a quele que está na montra; **2** *(impersonal)* ~ **should never say** nunca se deve dizer; ~**self** se; **to comb** ~**self** pentear-se; **3 my** ~ **passion** a minha única paixão.

one another *pron* um ao outro, uma à outra; **they give presents to** ~ eles dão presentes um ao outro; **2** *(mutually, emphatically)* se; **they kiss** ~ eles beijam-se; **close to** ~ *(distance)* próximos um do outro; *(relationship)* muito amigos um do outro.

one-armed *adj* maneta *(fam) m,f*.

one-armed bandit *n (BR) (machine)* caça-níqueis *m*.

one-liner *n* piada *f* curta.

one-man *adj (for one person)* **it is a task for** ~ é uma tarefa para uma só pesssoa; **she is a** ~ **woman** ela é uma mulher de um só homem; ~ **band** *n* homem-orquestra *m*.

one model *(unique model)* modelo *m* único.

one-night stand *n (sexual relationship)* uma noite amorosa *f* de passagem, *(BR)* transa *f* passageira.

one-off *adj (opportunity)* único,-a; *(mistake, event, case)* isolado,-a.

one-parent family *n* família *f* mononuclear, monoparental.

oner *n (fam) (one continuous action)* **do it in one** ~ faça isto numa contínua a(c)ção.

onerous *adj (task, responsibility)* oneroso,-a, difícil *m,f*.

one's *adj (possessive)*: ~ **house** a nossa casa; **to be on** ~ **own** estar sozinho,-a.

oneself *pron (reflexive)* se; **to comb** ~ pentear-se; **2** *(emphatic) (after preposition)* si próprio, si mesmo; **to punish** ~ castigar-se a si próprio; **speak to** ~ falar de si para si.

one-sided *adj* unilateral; **2** *(bias)* parcial; ~ **street** *n* rua *f* com casas só dum lado.

one-time *adj (former)* antigo.

one-to-one *adj (conversation)* entre os dois; frente a frente; **2** *(tuition)* individual; **3** *(MATH)* biunívoco.

one track *adj* via *f* única; **to have a** ~ **mind** ter uma dea fixa.

one-up *adj (fam)* **to be** ~ **over sb/sth** ter uma ideia fixa.

one-upmanship *n* a arte, prá(c)tica de conseguir manter vantagem sobre alguém; **2** *(pej)* pessoa *f* sem escrúpulos.

one-way *n (one direction)* sentido único; de mão única; *(outward travel)* só ida.

one-woman man *adj (man)* de uma só mulher.

ongoing *adj* contínuo,-a, em andamento, em curso.

onion *n (BOT)* cebola *f*.

online banking *n* serviço *m* de banco on-line.

onlooker *n* espe(c)tador,-ora; **to be an** ~ assistir a *(accident, incident)*

only *adv* somente, apenas, simplesmente; **I** ~ **wanted to say** eu apenas queria dizer; ♦ *adj* único,-a; **an** ~ **child** filho,-a único,-a; **I was the** ~ **woman (who was) swimming** eu era a única mulher a nadar; ♦ *adv (exclusively)* só; *(merely, just)* apenas, somente, só, simplesmente; **a few words** ~ apenas umas palavras; *(for emphasis)* só; **I was ~ teasing** eu estava só a brincar, gozar; *(used in conditional clauses after 'if')* **if I had ~ known** se eu tivesse sabido; ♦ *conj (but)* porém, só que; ~ **just** por pouco, mesmo à justa; **not ~ but also** não só, mas também.

ono, o.n.o. *(abbr for* **or near offer***)* ou oferta mais próxima.

onomatopoeia *n (LING)* onomatopeia *f.*

onrush *n (of water)* torrente *f;* **2** *(of people)* corrida *f;* **3** arremetida *f;* **4** *(feeling)* acesso *m;* irrupção *f.*

on-screen *adj (TV, COMP)* na tela *f.*

onset *n (beginning)* começo *m;* **from the** ~ desde o princípio; **2** ataque *m;* **3** *(MED)* primeiros sintomas *mpl.*

onshore *adj* terrestre; *(towards land)* em dire(c)ção à terra, à praia.

onside *adj adv (SPORT)* em posição *f* certa.

onslaught *n* ataque *m* violento; arremetida *f* **(against** contra).

Ontario *npr* Ontário.

on the job *adj* no trabalho *m,* no local *m* de trabalho; **I caught him sleeping** ~ apanhei-o a dormir durante o trabalho.

on the spot *adj adv* no local; logo ali; **2** no a(c)to.

onto *prep (= on to)* para (cima de); **he threw the coat ~ the bed** ele atirou o casaco para cima da cama; ... **and now, ~ something else** ... e agora, vamos outra coisa, vamos a outro assunto.

onus *n* obrigação *f;* responsabilidade *f;* **the ~ is on you** a responsabilidade é sua; **the ~ is on you to do** ... incumbe a você fazer ...

onward(s) *adv* para diante, para a frente; **from this time** ~ de (ag)ora em diante.

onyx *n* ónix *m,* *(BR)* ônix *m.*

oodles *npl (fam):* ~ **of something** um montão de algo; ~ **of money** uma carrada *f* de dinheiro *(fam).*

oomph *(also:* **umph***) n* vigour, energy, garra; **2** *(sexually attractive)* sex appeal; **she has brains and** ~ ela tem miolos e sex appeal *m.*

oops *exc (fam)* opa!, upa!

ooze *n* lodo *m;* ♦ *vt* **(from/out of sth)** escorrer (de, por); ♦ *vi* transbordar; *(sweat)* transpirar *(fig)* exalar **she ~d charm from every pore** *(fig)* o encanto dela exalava por todos os poros; ela estava cheia de manteiga *(fam).*

opal *n* opala *f.*

opaque *adj* opaco,-a, fosco,-a.

OPEC *n (abbr for* **Organization of the Petroleum Exporting Countries***)* OPEC.

open *adj* aberto; livre; público; declarado; ~ **day** *n (school, univ)* dia *m* aberto aos pais e visitas; **~-ended** *adj (period)* sem prazo para acabar, aberto,-a; *(strategy)* flexível; **~-hearted** *adj* franco,-a; de coração aberto; ♦ *vt* abrir; ♦ *vi* abrir-se; começar; **to ~ on to** *vt* dar para; **to ~ up** *vt* abrir; ♦ *vi* abrir-se, começar.

open air *adj:* **in the** ~ ao ar livre; **2** *(swimming-pool)* descoberta.

open-and-shut *adj* evidente.

opener *n (gen)* abertura *f;* *(player)* aquele que abre; **can** ~ abre-latas *m.*

opening *n* abertura *f;* início *m;* oportunidade *f;* *(job)* vaga *f;* ~ **day** *n* dia *m* aberto à visitas; ~ **hours** *(shop, clinic)* horas *fpl* de expediente; ~ **night** *n* noite *f* de estreia.

openly *adv* abertamente.

open-market *n* mercado *m* livre.

open-minded *adj* aberto,-a, imparcial *m,f.*

open-mouthed *adj* boquiaberto,-a.

open-necked *adj (shirt, blouse, collar)* aberto,-a.

open-plan *adj (room, office)* aberto,-a, sem divisórias.

open season *n* temporada *f* aberta.

Open University *npr (UK):* **the** ~ cursos à distância, oferecidos pela universidade, para estudo em casa.

opera *n* ópera *f;* ~ **glasses** *npl* binóculo *msg* de teatro; ~ **house** *n* teatro *m* lírico, de ópera.

operate *vt* funcionar, fazer funcionar; trabalhar; **2** *(in business)* dirigir, manejar; **3** manobrar *(machine)* ♦ *vi* criar efeito; **2** *(MED)* operar **(on, upon...);** **to ~ on sb** operar alguém.

operatic *adj* lírico,-a, operático,-a.

operating *adj:* ~ **table** *n* mesa *f* de operações; ~ **theatre** *n* sala *f* de operações.

operation *n* operação *f;* funcionamento *m;* **to be in** ~ estar em vigor/funcionando.

operational *adj* operacional.

operative *n* trabalhador,-ora, funcionário,-a; ♦ *adj* em vigor.

operator *n* operador,-ora, manipulador,-ora; *(TEL)* telefonista *m,f.*

operetta *n* opereta *f.*

ophthalmic *adj* oftálmico,-a.

opinion *n* opinião *f;* parecer *m,* juízo *m;* **in my** ~ a meu ver; ~ **poll** *n* sondagem *f* pública.

opinionated *adj* teimoso,-a; opinioso,-a.

opium *n* ópio *m.*

Oporto *npr* Porto *m (segunda cidade de Portugal) .*

opponent *n* adversário,-a, oponente *m,f;* opositor,-ora.

opportune *adj* oportuno,-a.

opportunist *n* oportunista *m,f.*

opportunity *n* oportunidade *f.*

oppose *vt* opor-se; **to be ~d** opor-se a, estar contra.

opposing *adj* oposto,-a, contrário,-a.

opposite *n:* **the** ~ o oposto, o contrário; **the** ~ **sex** o sexo oposto; ♦ *adj* oposto; em frente; contrário; *adv* (lá) em frente; ♦ *prep* em frente de, defronte de.

opposition *n* oposição *f,* resistência *f;* **the O~** *(POL) (party)* o partido *m* da Oposição.

oppress *vt* oprimir.

oppressed *adj* oprimido,-a; **the** ~ *npl* os oprimidos *mpl.*

oppression *n* opressão *f.*

oppressive *adj* opressivo,-a; sufocante *m,f.*

oppressor *n* opressor,-ora, tirano,-a.

opt *vi:* **to ~ for** escolher; **to ~ to do** optar por fazer; **to ~ out of doing** optar por não fazer.

optic *adj* óptico,-a; **~s** *n* óptica *f.*

optical *adj* óptico,-a; ~ **fibre** *n (TECH)* fibra *f* óptica *f;* ~ **illusion** *n* ilusão *f* de óptica.

optician n oculista m,f.
optimism n o(p)timismo m.
optimist n o(p)timista m,f.
optimum adj ó(p)timo,-a.
option n opção f; **to keep one's ~s open** (fig) manter as opções em aberto.
optional adj opcional m,f, facultativo,-a.
opulent adj opulento,-a.
or conj ou; (with neg) nem; quer; **she doesn't eat ~ drink** ela não come nem bebe; **~ else** senão, ou então; **~ so** mais ou menos, ou coisa assim; **either … ~ …** ou … ou …; **whether it rains ~ shines** quer chova, quer faça sol.
oracle n oráculo m.
oral n exame m oral; ♦ adj oral m,f.
orange n laranja f; ♦ adj cor de laranja, alaranjado.
oration n oração f.
orator n orador,-ora.
orbit n órbita f; ♦ vt/vi orbitar.
orchard n pomar m.
orchestra n orquestra f.
orchestral adj orquestral.
orchid n (BOT) orquídea f.
ordain vt (REL) ordenar, decretar; decidir, mandar.
ordeal n experiência f penosa, provação f.
order n ordem f; **to give an ~** (command) dar uma ordem; **2** (condition) estado m; **in good ~** em bom estado, funcionamento; **3** (consecration; REL) Ordem/ordem; **4** (COMM) pedido m, encomenda f; ♦ vt (= put sth in ~) pôr em ordem, arrumar; **2** (COMM) encomendar, mandar (followed by her infinitive); **3** (in restaurant) pedir (drink, etc); mandar vir; **4** (give orders) mandar, ordenar; **to ~ sb about/around** mandar nas pessoas; dispor de pessoa; **5** (taxi) chamar; ♦ conj **in ~ that** para que, a fim de que; ♦ **in the ~ of** prep (amount) da ordem de cerca de; **on ~** encomendado,-a; **in ~ to (do)** a fim de (fazer); **out of ~** avariado; fora de serviço; ♦ **to ~ sb to do** mandar alguém fazer.
orderly n (MIL) (person) ordenança f; (MED) servente m,f, auxiliar m,f de enfermagem; ♦ adj arrumado,-a, ordenado,-a; metódico,-a.
Order of the Garter n (UK) Ordem f da Jarreteira.
orders npl (REL) orders fpl.
ordinance n mandado m, rito m, lei f.
ordinary adj comum, vulgar; medíocre; **out of the ~** fora do comum.
ordnance n (MIL) artilharia f; (supplies) material m militar; **~ office** n arsenal m; **O~ Survey** n (UK) serviço cartográfico e topográfico oficial.
ore n minério m.
organ n órgão m; **~ donor** n (MED) dador,-ora de órgãos; **~ grinder** n tocador m de realejo.
organic adj orgânico,-a.
organism n organismo m.
organist n organista m,f.
organization n organização f.
organize vt organizar.
organizer n organizador,-a.
orgasm n orgasmo m.
orgy (pl: **-ies**) n orgia f.

Orient n Oriente m.
oriental adj oriental m,f.
orientate vt orientar.
orifice n orifício m; abertura f; buraco m.
origin n origem f; procedência f.
original adj (genuine) original; ♦ primeiro; primitivo; **2** (not copied) original.
originality n originalidade f; **of great ~** de uma grande originalidade.
originally adv (initially) à partida, a princípio; originariamente; **2** (creativity) com originalidade.
originate vt/vi originar, causar, criar; **to ~ from/in** vi originar-se de, surgir de.
originator n originador,-ora; criador-ora; promotor,-ora.
Orkneys npr (ilhas) Órcades fpl.
Orleans n (French city) Orleães; **New ~** (US city) Nova Orleães.
ormolu n oropel m; bronze m dourado; ouro m moído para dourar.
ornament n ornamento m; (trinket) adorno m, enfeite m; ♦ vt enfeitar, ornamentar, adornar.
ornamental adj decorativo,-a, ornamental m,f.
ornate adj ornado,-a, enfeitado,-a; vistoso,-a.
ornately adv vistosamente.
ornery adj (US) (fam) genioso,-a.
ornithologist n ornitólogo m.
ornithology n ornitologia f.
orphan n órfão,-ã; ♦ vt: **to be ~ed** ficar órfão.
orphanage n orfanato m.
orthodontist n (dental) ortodontista m,f.
orthodox adj ortodoxo,-a; **the O~ Church** n a Igreja f Ortodoxa.
orthodoxy n ortodoxia f.
orthopaedic adj ortopédico,-a; **~s** n ortopedia fsg.
oryx n (pl: **-es**) n (antílope) órix m.
OS (abbr for: **Old school**, **Old Style**) a velha guarda f; **2** (for: **Ordinary Seaman**) marujo m; **3** (size) tamanho grande.
Oscar n (CIN) Óscar m.
oscillate vt oscilar (from side to side) (**between** entre); (fig) vacilar, hesitar.
oscilloscope n osciloscópio m.
osmosis n (BIOL, CHEM) osmose f.
osprey n (ZOOL) xofrango m, águia-marinha f.
ossify vi ossificar; **2** (fig) (habits) ser inflexível.
osprey n (ZOOL) xofrango m; águia-pesqueira f.
ostensible adj aparente m,f; **2** pretenso,a.
ostensibly, ostensively adv aparentemente.
ostentatious adj (house, party) pretensioso,-a; faustoso,-a.
ostentatiously adv com ostentação.
osteopath n osteopata m,f.
osteopathy n (MED) osteopatia f.
osteoporosis n (MED) osteoporose f.
ostracism n ostracismo m.
ostracize vt marginalizar, ostracizar (**sb** alguém).
ostrich n (ZOOL) avestruz m,f.
other pron (o) outro; outra coisa; **one after the ~** um após o outro; **something or ~** qualquer coisa, uma coisa ou outra; ♦ adj outro; **~ than** de outro

modo que; senão; **somehow or** ~ *adv* dum modo, jeito ou doutro.

otherwise *adv conj* de outra maneira; senão.

otter *n (ZOOL)* lontra *f.*

OU *npr (abbr for* **Open University**) *(UK)* Universidade *f* aberta; **2** Oxford University.

ouch *exc (of sudden pain)* ai!; irra!; *(child's language)* dói-dói!.

ought *aux (expressing probability, expectation)* dever, ter chance; **I** ~ **to go out** eu devia sair; **he** ~ **to get the job** ele tem uma boa chance de obter o emprego, deve conseguir; **2** *(moral obligation)* **we** ~ **to respect other people** devemos respeitar os outros; **3** *(advising, stressing a point);* **you** ~ **to know that** ... é bom que saibas que ... .

ounce[1] *n (weight)* onça *f (UK)* (= 28.35g); *(fluid) (UK)* (= 0,028m^3); *(US)* (= 0,035 m^3); **2 an** ~ **(of)** um pouco de, uma pitada de; um pingo de.

ounce[2] *n (snow leopard)* onça *f.*

our *adj* nosso,-a, nossos,-as; **Our Lady** Nossa Senhora; ~**s** *pron* (o) nosso, nossa etc; **your house and** ~ a vossa casa e a nossa; **a friend of** ~**s** um amigo nosso.

ourselves *pron pl (reflexive, after prep)* nós; *(emphatic)* nós mesmos; **we** ~ **thought that** nós mesmos pensámos isso.

oust *vt* desalojar, despojar *(person)* (**from** de); *(JUR)* desapossar; **2** expulsar.

out *adv* fora; fora (de casa); ~ **there** lá fora; **he's** ~ não está, está fora; **2** *(lights, fire)* apagado; **before the week is** ~ antes do fim da semana; **hear me** ~ ouça-me até ao fim; ~ **loud** em voz alta; ~ **of bounds** *adj, adv* fora dos limites; *(area)* interdito,-a; **2** *(SPORT)* fora de jogo; **he is** ~ **of his mind** ele está louco; ~ **of kindness** por amabilidade, por gentileza; ~ **of order** *(clock, bell, engine)* avariado,-a; ~ **of print** edição esgotada; ~ **of shape** em má condição física; ~ **of spite** por despeito, por despique; ~ **of stock** *(product)* esgotado; ~ **of the way** *adj* afastado,-a, remoto,-a; fora do caminho; **he went** ~ **of his way to be kind** ele desfez-se em amabilidades; ~ **of work** desempregado; **way** ~ saída; ♦ *exc* ~ **with it!** diga lá!, desembuche!; **get** ~**!** fora!; **get** ~ **of the way!** afasta-te, sai da minha frente *(fam)*; IDIOM ~ **of the frying-pan into the fire** de mal a pior.

out and about *adj*: **she is** ~ ela anda fora (por aí fora) a trabalhar; *(after sickness)* **he is** ~ ele já está restabelecido e a(c)tivo.

out and out *n (liar)* absoluto,-a *(before n); (success, failure)* total.

outback *n (in Australia)* o interior (da Austrália).

outbid *vt (in auction)* cobrir o lance; ultrapassar.

outboard *adj*: ~ **motor** motor *m* de popa.

outbreak *n (of war)* deflagração *f*; eclosão *f*; **2** *(of crime, violence)* explosão *f*; **3** surto *m*; **epidemic** ~ surto epidémico *(BR*: -dê-).

outbuildings *npl* dependências *fpl*; externas; anexos.

outburst *n (of emotion)* explosão, *f*, manifestação *f*; *(occurrence)* erupção *f.*

outcast *n* pária *m,f*; rejeitado,-a.

outcome *n* resultado *m.*

outcry *n* manifestação *f* de protestos, gritaria *f*, clamor *m.*

outdated *adj* antiquado,-a, fora de moda; **2** *(theory, idea)* ultrapassado,-a.

outdistance *vt (in race)* deixar para trás; **2** *(fig) (business)* ultrapassar.

outdo *(irr: like* **do***) vt* ultrapassar, exceder, eclipsar.

outdoor *adj* exterior; ~**s** *adv* ao ar livre, fora de casa.

outer *adj* exterior *m,f*, externo,-a; ~**most** *adj* mais externo,-a; *(planet)* mais afastado,-a; ~ **space** *n* o espaço (exterior/cósmico/sideral).

outfit *n* equipamento *m*; **2** *(clothes)* roupa *f*, traje *m*; **3** *(company)* firma *f*; ~**ters** *n* fornecedor *m* de roupas; especialista *m,f* em confecção; ♦ *vt* fornecer; instalar, equipar *(shop, office).*

outflank *vt (MIL)* surpreender pela retaguarda; **2** *(fig) (argument, business)* superar.

outflow *n (of money)* fluxo *m*, saída *f*; **2** *(of water)* jorro *m* de água, fluxo *m.*

outgoing *adj* extrovertido,-a; sociável *m,f*; ~**s** *npl* despesas *fpl*, gastos *mpl.*

outgrow *(irr: like* **grow***) vt* exceder; crescer demasiado.

outhouse *n* anexo *m*; dependência *f* fora da casa.

outing *n* excursão *f*; passeio *m.*

outlandish *adj* estrambólico,-a, grotesco,-a; exótico,-a.

outlast *vt* sobreviver a; durar mais tempo que.

outlaw *n* foragido,-a, proscrito,-a; ♦ *vt* banir, proscrever.

outlet *n (hole, pipe)* saída *f*, escoadouro *m*; **2** *(emotion)* desabafo *m*, escape *m*; **3** *(US: ELECT)* tomada; (= **retail** ~) posto *m* de venda.

outline *n (of object)* contorno *m*; *(of person)*, perfil *m*; **2** *(sketch)* traçado *m*, esboço *m*; *(brief description)* linhas *fpl* gerais; ♦ *vt* esboçar; delinear; **to be** ~**d against sth** *(silhouette)* delinear-se contra algo.

outlive *vt* sobreviver a.

outlook *n* perspectiva *f*; ponto *m* de vista; **to be on the** ~ estar de atalaia.

outlying *adj* afastado,-a, remoto,-a.

outmanoeuvre *vt* superar em estratégia, vencer em habilidade.

outmost *n* máximo *m*; **at the** ~ no máximo.

outnumber *vt* exceder em número.

out of date *adj (clothes, etc)* fora de moda; *(idea, theory)* ultrapassado,-a; **2** *(passport, visa)* caducado,-a.

out-of-pocket *adj* sem dinheiro; **to be** ~ *(coll)* estar teso,-a; ~ **expenses** despesas *fpl* extra.

outpatient *n* doente *m,f* externo (de um hospital).

outpost *n (bastion)* posto *m* avançado.

output *n (COMM) (volume)* produção *f*; *(yield)* rendimento *m*; **2** *(TECH)* potência *f*, rendimento *m*; **3** *(COMP-printing out)* saída *f.*

outrage *n* escândalo *m*; atrocidade *f*; ♦ *vt* ultrajar.

outrageous *adj* ultrajante *m,f*, escandaloso,-a.

outrank *vt* exceder em hierarquia.

outrider *n (motorcycle)* batedor *m* (de uma escolta).

outright *adv* completamente; **2** sem rodeios; **3** imediatamente; no a(c)to.

outsell *(like:* **sell***) vt* vender mais que, vender em excesso.

outset *n* início *m*, princípio *m*; **at the** ~ no início; **from the** ~ desde o princípio.

outshine *(like: shine) vt* eclipsar.

outside *n* exterior *m*; superfície *f*; aspecto *m* (exterior); ♦ *adj* exterior *m,f*, externo,-a; ~-**left** *n (football)* ponta-esquerda *m,f*; ~ **lane** *n (AUT) (UK, Australia)* faixa *f* da direita; *(elsewhere)* faixa da esquerda; ♦ *adv* (lá) fora; ♦ *prep* fora de; além (dos limites) de; **at the** ~ no máximo; ~ **of** *prep (US)* exce(p)to.

outsider *n (person)* estranho *m*, desconhecido *m*, forasteiro *m*.

outsize *adj* de tamanho extra-grande; enorme *m,f*.

outskirts *npl* arredores *mpl*, subúrbios *mpl*.

outsmart *vt (sb, others)* ser mais esperto que (alguém/outros); *(coll)* levar a melhor sobre (alguém); *(BR) (coll)* passar a perna em (alguém).

outsource *vt (COMM) (of a manufacturer)* subcontratar; contratar externamente; terceirizar.

outsourcing *n* contratação a terceiros.

outspoken *adj* franco,-a; **to be** ~ falar sem rodeios, ser dire(c)to.

outstanding *adj* excepcional *m,f*; **2** *(obvious)* saliente, notável *m,f*; **3** *(pending)* pendente *m,f*.

outstay *vt*: **to** ~ **one's welcome** abusar da hospitalidade (ficando mais tempo).

outstretched *adj (hand)* estendido,-a, esticado,-a.

outstrip *(-pp-) vt (person)* ultrapassar; **2** *(do better than)* superar; **3** *(demand, production)* ser superior a, exceder.

out-tray *n* cesta *f*, tabuleiro *m* de assuntos resolvidos; tabuleiro de saída.

outvote *vt*: **to** ~ **sb** vencer alguém por ter mais votos.

outwardly *adv* aparentemente.

outwards *(UK)* **outward** *(US) adv* para fora; *adj* externo,-a; **2** *(appearance)* aparente *m,f*; **3** visível *m,f*; **4** *(going away)* de ida.

outweight *vt* pesar mais que.

outwit *(-tt-) vt* ser mais esperto que (**sb** alguém).

oval *n* oval *m;* ♦ *adj* ovalado.

ovary *n* ovário *m*.

ovation *n* ovação *f*, aplauso *m*.

oven *n* forno *m*; ~**proof** *adj* refra(c)tário,-a.

over *adj adv (used with verbs) (finished)* acabado; **it's all** ~ **between us** está tudo acabado entre nós; **2** *(more than)* mais de, passar de; **women** ~ **60 …** mulheres com mais de 60 …; **she is** ~ **50** ela já passou dos 50; **3** *(remaining)* **there are two** ~ sobram dois; **4** *(repetition)* **four times** ~ quatro vezes consecutivas; **to start all** ~ **again** recomeçar de novo; *(very/too much)* **I am not** ~ **keen** não estou muito entusiasmado,-a; ♦ *prep (gen)* sobre; *(across the top of, above)* por cima de, acima de; **a bridge** ~ uma ponte por cima; **the water came** ~ **my knees** a água chegou-me acima dos joelhos; **2** *(from/on the other side)* do outro lado de; **3** *durante*; ~ **the months** durante os meses; **4** *(by means of, for the sake of)* em, por; ~ **the radio** na radio; **a fight** ~ **a trivial thing** uma luta por uma trivialidade; **5** *(recovery)* **to be** ~ **the worst** ter-se recuperado do pior; ♦ **all** ~ **the place** por todos os sítios; ~ **here** por aqui, cá; ~ **there** por ali, lá; ~ **and** ~ **(again)** repetidamente; **I have told you** ~ **and** ~ **(again)** já te disse milhares de vezes; ~ **and above** além de, para cima de; **to ask sb** ~ convidar alguém; IDIOM **to be all** ~ **sb** *(coll)* entusiasmar-se por alguém; andar sempre atrás de alguém.

overact *vt* exagerar.

overall *adj* total; global; ♦ *adv* globalmente; ~**s** *npl* fato macaco *sg*; *(BR)* macacão *msg*.

overbalance *vi* perder o equilíbrio, desequilibrar-se; avantajar-se.

overbearing *adj* autoritário,-a, dominador,-ora; arrogante *m,f*.

overboard *adv (NAUT)* ao mar; **man** ~! homem ao mar!

overburden *vt (with work, debt, guilt)* sobrecarregar (**sb** alguém).

overcast *adj (sky)* nublado.

overcharge *vt*: **to** ~ **sb** cobrar alguém em excesso.

overcoat *n (clothes)* sobretudo *m*, casaco *m*.

overcome *vt* vencer, dominar; superar; **to** ~ **one's fears** superar o medo.

overconfident *adj (previsão)* demasiado o(p)timista; com demasiada confiança.

overcooked *adj (CULIN)* cozinhado demais.

overcrowded *adj* superlotado,-a, apinhado,-a; *(coll)* à cunha.

overdid *(pt of* **overdo***)*.

overdo *(irr: like* **do***) vt* exagerar, exceder; **2** *(do too much)* fazer demais; **you have overdone the steak** cozinhou o bife demais.

overdose *n* dose *f* excessiva.

overdraft *n* saldo *m* negativo, saldo a descoberto.

overdraw *vt/vi* sacar a descoberto.

overdrawn *pp adj* a descoberto, sem fundos.

overdue *adj* em atraso, atrasado; **I am** ~ **for a consultation** já é hora de eu ter uma consulta; **2** *(COMM) (payment, etc)* vencido,-a; tardio,-a; **3** *(awaited)* **long** ~ há muito esperado.

overestimate *vt* sobrestimar.

overexcited *adj (person, atom)* superexcitado,-a, sobreexcitado,-a; *(person)* sobreexaltado,-a.

overexpose *vt (PHOT)* expor demasiado (à luz).

overflow *n* excesso *m*; inundação *f*; ~**pipe** *n* tubo *m* de descarga; ♦ *vt* transbordar.

overfund *vt* sobrefinanciar, invadir o mercado com fundos.

overgrow *vt* crescer de mais.

overgrown *adj (grass)* coberto,-a, repleto,-a (**with** de); grande de mais.

overhang *n (of cliff)* saliência *f*; **2** *(of roof)* beiral *m* ♦ *(like:* **hung***) vt* sobressair, projectar, pender.

overhanging *adj (cliff, etc)* saliente *m,f*; *(tree branch)* pendente.

overhaul *n* revisão *f*, vistoria *f*, inspeção *f*; **2** *(fig) (of system)* restruturação *f*; ♦ *vt* examinar, inspe(c)cionar; **2** *(fig)* restruturar.

overhead *adv* por cima, em cima; ♦ *adj* aéreo,-a, elevado,-a; suspenso,-a; ~ **projector** *n* retro proje(c)tor *m*; ~**s** *npl (charges)* despesas *fpl* gerais.

overhear *(irr: like* **hear***) vt* ouvir por acaso.

overindulge vt *(loved ones)* estragar com mimos; ♦ vi cometer excessos.

overindulgence n *(excess)* abuso m (**in** em); demasiada indulgência.

overjoyed adj maravilhado,-a, cheio,-a de alegria, felicíssimo,-a.

overland adj, adv por terra.

overlap vi n sobreposição f; ♦ (**-pp-**) vt sobrepor-se; **2** coincidir (**with** com).

overlapping adj que se sobrepõe; ~ **majorities** *(POL)* maiorias fpl sobrepostas.

overleaf adv no verso.

overload n sobrecarga f, carga a mais; ♦ vt sobrecarregar *(lorry, donkey)* (**with** com).

overlook vt dar para; **2** *(ignore)* deixar passar; *(fam)* *(turn a blind eye)* fazer vista grossa a; **3** *(excuse)* perdoar.

overmanning n excesso m de mão d'obra.

overnight adj: **to stay** ~ passar a noite, pernoitar; ♦ adv durante a noite; *(fig)* da noite para o dia.

overpass n passagem f elevada; ♦ vt ultrapassar, exceder.

overplay vt *(danger, etc)* exagerar (para atrair mais atenção).

overpower vt dominar; **2** *(enemy)* vencer, subjugar.

overpowering adj sufocante m,f, *(person)* dominador,-ora; *(personality)* dominante m,f; ~ **smell** cheiro m muito forte, asfixiante m,f.

overrated adj sobrestimado,-a, sobrevalorizado,-a.

override n comando m manual; ♦ *(like:* **ride***)* vt *(disregard)* não fazer caso de; ignorar; repelir arbitrariamente; **2** exceder; **3** *(person, decision)* prevalecer; desautorizar, anular.

overriding adj predominante m,f; primordial.

overrule vt dominar, predominar; **2** *(JUR)* rejeitar, indeferir.

overseas adj externo,-a; estrangeiro,-a; ♦ adv no estrangeiro, no exterior.

oversee *(like:* **see***)* superintender; supervisionar.

overseer n superintendente m,f; inspe(c)tor,-ora; **2** *(of farm)*capataz m,f.

oversell vt vender em quantidades maiores do que as que se podem fornecer.

overshadow vt eclipsar, ofuscar.

oversight n descuido m, lapso m.

oversimplification n simplificação f excessiva.

oversleep vi acordar tarde.

overspeed n excesso m de velocidade.

overspend vt *(like:* **spend***)* gastar de mais.

overspill n excedente m demográfico.

overstate vt exagerar.

overstatement n afirmação f exagerada, exagero m.

overstay vt prolongar (visit), ficar tempo de mais; **to ~ one's welcome** abusar da hospitalidade de alguém.

overstep vt exceder; ir longe demais, ultrapassar.

overstretched adj *(budget)* muito apertado,-a; **2** *(resources)* sobreexplorado,-a.

overstrung adj enervado,-a; demasiado sensível m,f, nervoso,-a; ~ **piano** piano m de cordas cruzadas.

overt adj aberto,-a, manifesto,-a, claro,-a.

overtake *(irr: like* **take***)* vt superar, exceder; *(AUT)* ultrapassar.

overtaking n *(AUT)* ultrapassagem f.

over the counter adj *(medicines)* vendido sem receita médica.

over the top, OTT adj *(coll)* exagerado,-a; **to go** ~ ir demasiado longe.

overthrow *(irr: like* **throw***)* vt derrubar *(government)* derrotar.

overtime n horas fpl extraordinárias; **to work** ~ fazer horas extraordinárias.

overtone n *(nuance)* subentendido; *(fig)* alusão f; ~**s** políticas npl conotações fpl políticas.

overture n *(MUS)* abertura f; *(fig)* proposta f.

overturn n reviravolta f; ♦ vt/vi *(boat, chair)* virar; voltar-se; **2** *(AUT)* capotar; **3** *(POL)* depor.

overuse *(of product, language)* uso m excessivo, abuso m.

overview n vista f de conjunto (**of** de); visão f geral.

overweening adj *(of a person)* presunçoso,-a, arrogante m,f; *(of opinion, appetite)* desmedido,-a.

overweight adj muito gordo,-a, com excesso de peso.

overwhelm vt esmagar; **2** *(gain control)* dominar.

overwhelmed adj *(with letters, work)* submerso,-a (**with/by** com); **2** *(joy)* **I am** ~ **by your news** estou felicíssima com as tuas notícias; **3** *(by experience)* fascinado,-a.

overwhelming adj *(victory, defeat)* esmagador,-ora; **2** *(beauty)* irresistível m,f; *(case, event)* estrondoso,-a; **3** *(response)* entusiasta m,f.

overwork n excesso m de trabalho; ♦ vt sobrecarregar de trabalho; **2** *(strength, employee)* esgotar; ♦ vi esgotar-se.

overwrought adj extenuado,-a, superexcitado,-a, muito agitado,-a; **2** *(fussy style)* estilo muito elaborado.

overzealous adj demasiado zeloso,-a; **2** *(attitude)* excessivo,-a.

ovulate vi ovular.

ovulation n ovulação f.

owe vt *(money, favours)* dever; **to ~ (to) sb** dever a alguém.

owing prep devido (**to** a), por causa de.

owl n *(barn owl)* mocho m; **screech-~** n coruja f.

own adj *(indicating possession)* próprio,-a; mesmo,-a; **he has his ~ office** ele tem o seu próprio escritório; **my ~ daughter did this to me** *(emphatic)* a minha própria filha fez-me isto; **she has her ~ style** ele tem um estilo próprio; **in his ~ way** à sua maneira; **I am my ~ master** sou senhor de mim mesmo; **the house has its ~ garden** a casa tem um jardim privativo; **of her ~ accord** de moto próprio; ♦ pron **on one's ~** sozinho,-a, sem ajuda; **2** meu, minha; **this house is my ~** esta casa é minha; **a house of my ~** a minha própria casa; **he has two cars of his ~** ele tem dois carros só para si; **to come into one's ~** receber aquilo a que tem jus, direito; **to hold one's ~** manter-se firme; **to get sb on their ~** ver alguém em privado; ♦ vt possuir, ter; **2** *(admit)* admitir, reconhecer *(fault, guilt)*; **to ~ up** vi confessar; IDIOM **to do one's ~ thing** ser independente; **to get one's ~ back** vingar-se (**on sb** de alguém); **have it your ~ way** faz como entenderes.

owner *n* dono,-a, proprietário,-a; possuidor,-ora; **sole** ~ único proprietário; ~**ship** *n* posse *f*, direito *m* de proprietário.

ox *(pl:* -**en***) n* boi *m;* **a team of** ~**en** uma parelha/ junta de bois; ~-**cart** *n* carro *m* de bois; ~-**goad** *n* aguilhão *m*.

Oxbridge *n* as universidades *fpl* de Oxford e Cambridge.

Estas universidades, assim conjuntamente designadas, foram fundadas no século XIII e são as mais antigas e as mais respeitadas da Grã-Bretanha. São rivais nas famosas regatas anuais (boat race) e em outros desportos.

Oxford *npr (city in England)* Oxónia; **in** ~ em Oxónia; ~ **University** *n* Universidade de Oxford.

oxide *n* óxido *m*.

oxidize *vt* oxidar; ♦ *vi* oxidar-se.

oxtail *n:* ~**soup** sopa *f* de rabo de boi, *(BR)* rabada *f*.

oxygen *n* oxigénio *(BR:* -gê-*) m;* ~ **mask/tent** máscara/ tenda de oxigénio.

oxygenate *vt* oxigenar.

oxyhydrogen *n* gás *m* oxídrico.

oyster *n* ostra *f;* ~ **bed** *n* viveiro *m* de ostras; **pearl** ~ *n* ostra *f* perlífera; **2** *(colour)* cinzento-pérola; IDIOM **the world is your** ~ tens o mundo à tua frente, a teus pés.

oz *(abbr for* **ounce(s)***)* onça *f*.

ozone *n (CHEM)* ozono *m*, ozónio *m* *(BR:* -ô-*);* ~ **friendly** *adj* inofensivo à camada de ozónio; amigo do ozono; *(on product)* protector do ozono; ~ **layer** *n* camada *f* de ozono.

p

P, p *n (letter)* P, p *m;* IDIOM **mind your p's and q's** vê lá se te portas bem, cuidado com o que dizes!

p *n (abbr for* **page)** *(Vd:* **page)**; **2** *(abbr for* **penny, pence)** *British currency (Vd:* **penny)**.

P *n (CHEM) (abbr for* **phosphorus)** *(Vd:* **phosphorous)**; **2** International car registration for Portugal; **3** *(abbr for* **parking)**.

p.a. *(abbr for* **per annum)** p.a.

PA *(abbr for* **personal assistant)** secretário,-a de direção; **2** *(abbr for* **Pennsylvania)**.

pa *n (US: coll)* paizinho, *(BR)* papai *m.*

paca *n (ZOOL) (rodent)* paca *f.*

pace *n (step, measure)* passo *m;* **2** *(rate, speed)* ritmo *m,* andamento ♦ *vt/vi:* **to ~ out (sth)** medir em passos; **to keep ~ with (sb/sth)** acompanhar o passo, ritmo (de alguém, de algo); **to ~ up and down** andar de um lado para o outro.

pacemaker *(also:* **pacesetter)** *n (MED)* marcapasso *m;* estimulador *m* cardíaco; **2** *(US) (in a race) (competidor que estabelece o ritmo da corrida)* lebre.

pacey (-ier, -iest) *adj (fast-moving)* veloz.

pachyderm *n* paquiderme *m.*

pacific *n:* **the P~ (Ocean)** o (Oceano) Pacífico; **P~ Islands** *n* Ilhas *fpl* do Pacífico; ♦ *adj* pacífico,-a.

pacifier *n (US) (for baby)* chupeta, chucha *f;* **2** apaziguador,-ora.

pacifist *n* pacifista *m,f.*

pacify *(pt, pp* **-ied)** *(pres p* **-ing)** *vt* apaziguar, acalmar, serenar; **2** *(landscape)* pacificar.

pack *n (bundle)* pacote *m,* embrulho *m;* **2** *(of cigarettes)* maço *m;* **3** *(group of – dogs)* matilha *f; (wolves)* alcateia; **4** *(criminals)* bando *m,* quadrilha *f;* **5** *(of cards)* baralho *m;* **6** *(of tissues etc)* caixa *f;* **7** *(SPORT) (race)* pelatão *m;* **8** *(carried by donkey, etc)* carga; **9** *(in compounds)* **a five-~ of sth** um lote *m* cinco de algo; ♦ *vi (for journey)* fazer as malas; **~ one's bags** *(fig)* ir-se embora; ♦ *vt* empacotar, embrulhar; **2** *(fill with)* encher *(hall, church);* **3** *(cram into)* apinhar; **to be ~ed** estar cheio,-a de; **4** *(push tightly)* comprimir; entulhar; ♦ **~ in (sth)** encher de (algo); **2** *(coll) (give up)* deixar; ♦ *exc* **~ it in!** deixa lá isso!, *(stop upsetting)* pára lá com isso; ♦ **to ~ sb off to** *(fam)* mandar alguém (para); **to ~ up** *vt* arrumar; ♦ *vi (suitcases)* fazer as malas; **2** encaixotar; **3** *(fam) (machines)* break down, avariar-se, *(BR) (fam)* pifar; **4** *(finish work)* sair do trabalho; IDIOM **a ~ of lies** um chorrilho *m* de mentiras.

package *n (gen)* pacote *m,* embalagem *f,* empacotamento *m,* embrulho *m;* **~ deal** *(business)* pacote *m* de acordo, de oferta; **~ holidays** férias *fpl* organizadas; **~ store** *(US)* loja *f* de venda de bebidas alcoólicas; ♦ *vt* empacotar, encaixotar, embalar.

packaging *n (materials)* embalagem *f;* **2** *(of film, artist, policy)* construção *f* da imagem pública.

packed *adj* cheio,-a; *(in a heap)* apinhado,-a; **~ with** repleto,-a (de); **2** *(coll) (crowded)* à cunha; **the theatre was ~** o teatro estava à cunha; **~ lunch** *(UK) (for school)* merenda *f;* almoço *m* piquenique.

packer *n* empacotador,-ora; **2** máquina *f* de enlatar, empacotar.

packet *n (parcel)* pacote *m,* embrulho *m; (of cigarettes)* maço *m; (of sugar rice)* pacote *m;* **2** *(coll) (lot of money)* pipa *f* de massa, um dinheirão; **this table costs a ~** esta mesa custa uma pipa de dinheiro; **~ switching** *(COMP) (data)* comutação *f* de pacotes.

packhorse *n* cavalo *m* de carga, besta *f* de carga.

packing *n* embalagem *f;* envoltório *m;* **2** enchimento *m;* **3** *(MED)* compressa *f;* **4** **~ case** *n* caixa *f* de embalagem, caixote *m;* IDIOM **to be sent ~** *(fam)* ser corrido.

pact *n (agreement)* pacto *m;* **2** *(COMM)* convénio *(BR:* -vê-).

pad *n (of paper)* bloco *m;* **2** *(material)* almofada *f,* acolchoamento *m; (shoulder)* chumaço *m;* **3** *(SPORT) (general)* proteção *f;* **4** *(to absorb liquid)* compressa *f;* **5** *(sanitary towel)* penso *m* higiénico *(EP);* pensinho *m* de proteção *(BR);* **6** *(launch)* **~ plataforma** *f;* rampa *(de lançamento);* **7** *(animal paw)* almofadinha *f;* **8** *(coll) (home)* casa *f, (fam)* cantinho *m;* **I have a ~ in Chelsea** tenho un cantinbo em Chelsea; **9** *(for small planes)* pista de aterragem; ♦ *(-dd-) adj* acolchoado,-a; ♦ *vi* caminhar sem ruído; ♦ *vt, vi* acolchoar.

padding *n (stuffing)* enchimento, acolchoado *m; (clothes, machines)* revestimento *m;* **2** *(fig) (useless information)* palavreado *m* inútil, palha *f.*

paddle *n (dinghy, canoe)* remo *m* curto; **~ boat/steamer** *n* barco/vapor *m* movido a rodas; **2** *(US)* raquete *f* de ping-pong; ♦ *vt (row)* remar; ♦ *vi (wade)* patinhar; IDIOM **to ~ one's own canoe** ser dono do seu nariz.

paddling pool *n* piscina *f* infantil, para crianças; **2** *(inflatable)* piscina *f* insuflável.

paddock *n* cercado, recinto *m (para cavalos);* **2** *(for racehorse)* padoque *m.*

paddy field *n* arrozal *m.*

padlock *n* cadeado *m;* ♦ *vt* fechar com cadeado.

padre *n* padre *m;* **2** *(in the armed forces)* capelão *m.*

padsaw *n (tool)* serrote *m* de ponta.

paediatrician *adj* pediatra *m,f.*

paediatrics *n (MED)* pediatria *fsg.*

paedology *n (development of children)* pedologia *f.*

paedophile *n* pedófilo,-a.

paedophylia *n* pedofilia *f.*

paelestra *n (HIST)* palestra *f.*

pagan *n adj* pagão,-ã.

paganism *n* paganismo *m.*

page *n (in a book, magazine, etc.)* página *f;* **over the ~** página seguinte; **a ~-turner** *n (gripping book)* obra *f* entusiasmante; **2** *(internet)* página *f*; **3** (= **~boy**) mensageiro *m*; *(in a wedding)* page *m*; paquete *m* (de hotel) *m*; ♦ *vt (paginate)* paginar; **2** *(call on loudspeaker)* mandar chamar; **3** ~ **through** *(search)* consultar, folhear.

pageant *n (parade)* cortejo *m* sumptuoso; desfile *m* alegórico.

pageantry *n* pompa *f*, fausto *f*.

pager *n (electronic device)* pager *m*.

paginate *vt* paginar.

pagination *n* paginação *f*.

pagoda *n (religious building)* pagode *m*.

paid *(pt, pp* of **pay)** *adj* remunerado; assalariado; **2 to put** ~ **to** *(end with)* acabar com, liquidar; **3** **~-up** *adj* pago, liquidado.

pail *n* balde *m*.

pain *n* dor *f*; **to be in** ~ sofrer; **on** ~ **of death** *(punishment)* sob pena de morte; **he's a** ~ **in the neck!** *(coll)* ele é um chato!; **to take** ~**s to** *(try hard)* esmerar-se, esforçar-se por; **to spare no** ~**s** não poupar esforços; ♦ *vt* magoar, irritar; **it** ~**s me to see you ill** custa-me ver-te doente; IDIOM **no** ~, **no gain** o trabalho é o pai do êxito.

pained *adj* magoado,-a; **a** ~ **expression** uma expressão *f* de dor.

painful *adj* doloroso,-a; penoso,-a.

painfully *adv* dolorosamente; *(fig)* terrivelmente.

painkiller *n* analgésico *m*.

painless *adj* sem dor, indolor *m,f*.

painstaking *adj* esmerado, meticuloso.

painstakingly *adv* meticulosamente.

paint *n* pintura *f*, tinta *f*; ~ **box** estojo *m*, caixa *f* de tintas; ~ **brush** pincel *m*; broxa *f*; **a coat of** ~ uma camada *f* de tinta; ~ **stripper** diluente, decapante *m*; ~**work** *n* obra *f* de pintura; **wet** ~ pintado,-a de fresco; ♦ *vt/vi* pintar; **to** ~ **in oils** pintar a óleo; **to** ~ **with watercolours** pintar a aguarela; **to** ~ **the nails** pintar as unhas; **2** *(smear)* cobrir, untar; **3** *(fig) (depict)* descrever, traçar um quadro, retrato; IDIOM **to** ~ **the town red** ir para a farra; pintar a manta; *(coll)* ir para a borga.

paintball (game) *n* jogo *m* de paintball.

painter *n* pintor,-ora.

painting *n (activity, study)* pintura *f*; *(work of art)* quadro *m*; *(decorating)* pinturas *fpl*.

pair *n* par *m*; casal *m*; *(of horses, oxen)* parelha *f*; **a** ~ **of scissors** uma tesoura; **the** ~ **of you** vocês dois; ♦ *vt/vi (to couple)* agrupar em pares; **to** ~ **off** formar um casal; **to** ~ **up** formar grupos de dois.

pairing *n* emparelhamento *m*; *(mating animals)* cruzamento *m*, acasalamento *m*.

pajamas *npl (US)* pijama *msg*.

Pakistan *npr* Paquistão *m*; **in** ~ no Paquistão.

Pakistani *n adj* paquistanês,-esa.

pal *n (coll)* camarada *m,f*, companheiro,-a; ♦ (-ll-) *vi* **to** ~ **up with (sb)** ser compincha de alguém; **to** ~ **about** andar na companhia de; **to** ~ **up with (sb)** ser compincha de alguém.

palace *n* palácio *m*.

palaeoanthropology *(US)* **paleoanthropology** *n* paleoantropologia *f*.

palaeolithic, paleolithic (Period) *n* Período *m* Paleolítico.

palatable *adj (tasty)* saboroso, apetitoso; **2** *(acceptable)* aceitável *m,f*.

palate *n (taste)* paladar *m*; **2** *(ANAT)* palato *m*, céu *m* da boca.

palatine *adj* palatino.

palaver *n* palavreado *m*; bla bla *m*; **2** *(bother)* maçada *f*; complicação *f*; **all the** ~ **of filling in forms** a chatice da papelada.

pale *n (stick)* estaca *f*; **2** *(fence)* vedação *m* de madeira; ♦ *adj* pálido; claro; **2** ~ **imitation** imitação *f* barata; ♦ *vt (fence off)* vedar, delimitar; ♦ *vi* (= **to grow** ~) empalidecer; *(fig)* perder a importância; IDIOM **to be beyond the** ~ passar dos limites.

paleness *n* palidez *f*.

Palestine *npr* Palestina *f*; **in** ~ na Palestina.

Palestinian *n adj* palestino,-a.

palette *n* paleta *f*; ~ **knife** espátula *f* de pintor.

Pali *n (language of India)* páli *m*.

palindrome *n* capicua *f*.

palings *npl* cerca *fsg* (de madeira).

palisade *n* paliçada *f*.

pall *n* manto *m*; pano *m* mortuário; *(fig) (of gloom, mystery)* manto *m*; ~ **bearer** *n* pessoa que ajuda a levar o caixão; ♦ *vi (become boring)* tornar-se insípido; *(fig)* perder a graça.

palladium *n (CHEM)* paládio *m*; **2** *(safeguard)* guarantia *f*, ressalva *f*, salvaguarda *f*.

pallet *n (bed)* enxerga *f*; **2** plataforma *f* de carga *f*; ~ **truck** *n* empilhadora *f*.

palliate *vt (relieve)* aliviar; **2** *(extenuate)* mitigar.

palliative care *n* cuidados *mpl* paliativos.

pallid *adj* pálido,-a, descorado,-a.

pallor *n* palidez; *(unnatural paleness)* lividez *f*.

pally *adj (coll)* muito amigo **(with** de).

palm *n (hand)* palma *f*; **2** *(measure)* palmo *m*; ~**tree** palmeira; ~ **oil** *n* óleo *m* de palma; ~ **reading** *n* quiromancia *f*; **P~ Sunday** *n* Domingo de Ramos; ~**top** *n (computer)* computador *m* de bolso, PDA; ♦ *vt* escamotear *(card, coin)*: **to** ~ **sth off on sb** *(coll)* impingir algo a alguém; IDIOM **to have sb in the** ~ **of one's hand** ter alguém na palma da mão.

palmist *n* quiromante *m,f*.

palmy *adj* próspero, bonançoso.

palomino *n* palomino.

palpable *adj* palpável *m,f*; **2** evidente *m,f*.

palpitate *vi* palpitar.

palpitation *n* palpitação *f*; **to have** ~**s** sentir palpitações.

palsy *n (MED)* paralisia *f*; **2** apatia *f*.

palter *vi* fingir, simular; **2** *(haggle)* regatear.

paltry *adj (sum)* insignificante; **2** *(excuse)* fútil.

pampas *n*: **the** ~ a pampa, *(BR)* o pampa; ~ **grass** capim *m* das pampas.

pamper *vt* mimar, dar mimos, acarinhas.

pamphlet *n* panfleto *m*.

pan *n* (= **sauce~**) *(cooking utensil)* panela *f*, tacho *m*, caçarola *f*; **frying** ~ frigideira *f*; **out of the frying** ~ **into the fire** de mal a pior; **2** *(of scales)* prato *m*; **3 lavatory** ~ sanita *f*; *(BR)* vaso sanitário; **4** *(depression in soil containing water/mud)* poça *f*;

cavidade no solo; ♦ (-nn-) vt (metais preciosos) crivar (for); 2 (coll) (criticize) arrasar, rebaixar; 3 (CIN, PHOT) fazer una panorâmica; ♦ ~ out vi (turn out) resultar em; vir a ser; ~ well ter successo.

panacea n panaceia (BR: panacéia/panaceia) f.

panache n penacho m; 2 (fig) bravata f; fanfarronada.

Panama npr Panamá m; in ~ no Panamá.

Panamanian n adj panamenho,-a.

Pan-American adj pan-americano,-a.

pancake n panqueca f; p~ Day/P~ Tuesday (also: Shrove Tuesday) n Terça-feira f de Carnaval, de Entrudo; IDIOM flat as a ~ espalmado,-a, liso,-a.

> Na Grã-Bretanha, come-se tradicionalmente a panqueca na terça-feira gorda, Terça-feira de Entrudo.

panchromatic adj (PHOT) pancromático.

pancreas n (ANAT) pâncreas m.

pancreatitis n (disease) pancreatite f.

panda n (ZOOL) panda m,f; ~ car n carro m da polícia.

pandemic n (MED) pandemia f; ♦ adj (disease) pandémico.

pandemonium n pandemónio (BR: -mô-) m, barafunda f, balbúrdia f.

pander n chulo; ♦ vi: to ~ to ceder; 2 (whims) satisfazer (to a), atender (to a).

pane n (of window) vidraça f, vidro m.

panegyric n discurso m laudatório, elogio m.

panel n (sheet of material) painel m, placa f; 2 (RADIO, TV) (team) júri m; to be on a ~ (experts) estar numa comissão, num comité; (JUR) lista f de jurados; 3 (TECH) (control board) painel m de controlo; 4 (MEC) ~ pin n tacha f de painel; ~ beater n (person) bate-chapas m; ~ saw (instrument) serra f de painel; ♦ (-ll-) vt apainelar; 2 almofadar (doors, windows).

panelling (UK) **paneling** (US) n revestimento com lambris m; apainelamento m.

panellist (UK) **panelist** (US) n (TV programme) membro do painel, convidado,-a do painel.

panful n panelada f.

pang n (physical pain) dor f; 2 (emotional pain) angústia f, aflição f; ~s of conscience peso m de consciência; ~s of hunger torturas fpl da fome.

pangram n (sentence) pantograma m.

panhandle vi (US) (fam) pedir esmola, mendigar.

panic n pânico m; ~ attack n ataque m de pânico; ~ bolt (emergency bar on doors) barra de emergência da porta; ~ disorder (PSYC) (mental disorder) transtorno m de pânico; ~-stricken adj espavorido,-a; ♦ (pt, pp -ked; p cont. -king) vi entrar em pânico, perder a cabeça,-a; ♦ exc don't ~! calma!

panicky adj nervoso,-a; em pânico.

panjandrum n (pej) pessoa pedante, em posição de autoridade.

pannier n cesta; 2 (large) gabião m.

panoply n panóplia f.

panorama n panorama m; ~ view n vista f panorâmica.

pansy n (BOT) (plant) amor-perfeito m; 2 (pej) (effeminate man) bicha m, maricas m (BR: veado m).

pant n arquejo m, arfada f; ♦ vi arquejar, arfar; to ~ out sth dizer algo em voz ofegante.

pantaloons npl (calças) pantalonas f

pantechnicon n (van) carrinha f de mudanças; 2 (warehouse) armazém m de depósito.

pantheism n (REL) panteísmo m.

pantheon n (HIST) (building) panteão m.

panther n (ZOOL) pantera f.

panties npl cuecas fpl, (BR) calcinha sg.

panting adj ofegante, palpitante; she was ~ (from running) ela estava ofegante, sem fôlego.

pantograph n (ELECT) pantógrafo m.

pantomime n pantomima f.

pantry n despensa f; copa f.

pants n (underwear) cuecas fpl (BR: also calcinha); 2 (US) (trousers) calças fpl, (BR) calça sg; IDIOM to bore the ~ off (someone) entediar, maçar; she scared the ~ off me! ela pregou-me cá um susto!; to be caught with the ~ down ser apanhado com as calças na mão.

pantsuit n (US) (clothing) fato m de calça e casaco.

panty girdle n cinta-calça f.

pantyhose n (US) meia-calça f.

pap n (food) papa f, papas fpl; puré m, (BR) mingau m; 2 (worthless information) conversa oca, disparatada; **intellectual** ~ parvoices fpl; (film; book) patetices fpl.

papa n (fam) papá m, paizinho m.

papacy n (REL) papado m.

papal adj (REL) papal m,f.

paparazzo (pl: -zzi) n (newspaper) fotógrafo,-a de pessoas famosas, paparazzi.

papaw (papaya) n (fruit) papaia f.

paper n papel m; 2 (= news~) jornal m, diário m; 3 (essay, article, etc.) artigo m, ensaio m, dissertação f; 4 (exam) ponto m; on ~ no papel, em teoria; to explain on ~ explicar por escrito; to read a ~ fazer uma palestra; (identity) ~s npl documentos mpl; ~back n livro m brochado (BR: brochura), livro de bolso; ~ bag n saco m, cartucho m de papel; ~ boy n jornaleiro m, ardina m; brown ~ papel pardo; carbon ~ papel químico; embossed ~ papel estampado; glass ~ folha f de lixa; Green P~ (policy proposals for discussion) Livro Verde; ~ knife corta-papel; ~ mill fábrica (EU) usina (BR) de papel; ~ money n papel-moeda m; ~-pulp polpa para fabrico de papel; ~s npl jornais mpl, documentos mpl; toilet ~ papel higiénico; ~weight n pisa-papéis m inv, (BR) pesa-papéis m inv; ~ work n trabalho m burocrático; (pej) papelada f; White ~ (official govt. report) Livro m Branco; ♦ adj de papel, em papel; ♦ vt (cover wall, book) forrar a/de papel, (BR) empapelar; to ~ over vt (fig) (unpleasant/controversial subject) encobrir, disfarçar.

papier-mâché n papel m machê.

papilla n (BIOL) papila f.

papilloma n (MED) (tumour) papiloma m.

papist n (often: pej) papista m,f.

paprika n (CULIN) paprica f, colorau m, pimentão-doce m.

pap test (*also:* **smear**) *n (MED)* exame *m* citológico; *(pop)* papanicolau.

Papua New Guinea *npr (GEOG)* Papua-Nova Guiné.

papyrus *n (BOT)* papiro *m;* **2** *(manuscript)* papiro *m.*

par *n* estado de igualdade; **to be on a ~ with** estar em condições iguais; **2** *(golf)* média *f;* **3** *(FIN) (market face value)* valor *m* nominal; **above/ below ~** acima/abaixo da média.

parable *n* parábola *f.*

parabola *n (MATH)* parábola *f.*

parachute *n* pára-quedas/para-quedas *m inv;* ♦ *vi* saltar de pára-quedas/de para-quedas.

paraclete *n* mediador,-ora; advogado,-a.

parade *n* desfile *m,* **2** *(MIL)* parada *f;* ♦ *vt (to march)* desfilar; **2** *(to show off)* exibir; ♦ *vi* desfilar; *(MIL)* passar revista; IDIOM **to rain on one's ~** ser desmancha-prazeres.

paradigm *n* paradigma *m.*

paradise *n* paraíso *m.*

paradox *n* paradoxo *m.*

paradoxical *adj* paradoxal *m,f.*

paradrop *n* carga *f* lançada de pára-quedas.

paraffin *n (CHEM)* parafina *f;* **~** (**oil**) querosene *m;* **~ wax** *n* cera *f* de parafina.

paragliding *n (SPORT)* parapente *m.*

paragon *n* protótipo *m,* exemplo *m;* modelo *m* de virtudes.

paragraph *n* parágrafo *m;* ♦ *vt (divide)* dividir em parágrafos; **2** *(summarize)* resumir num parágrafo.

Paraguay *npr* Paraguai; **P~an** *npr, adj* paraguaiano,-a.

parakeet *n (bird)* periquito *m.*

paralalia *n (MED) (speech disorder)* paralalia *f.*

paralanguage *n (LING)* paralinguagem *f.*

paralexia *n (MED)* paralexia *f.*

paralipsis *n (LITER)* paralipse *f.*

parallel *n (MATH)* (linha) paralela *f; (GEOG)* paralelo *m;* ♦ *adj (distance)* paralelo; **2** *(fig) (similar)* correspondente; **without ~** sem precedentes; ♦ *vt* comparar, posicionar em paralelo; IDIOM **to draw a ~** estabelecer uma comparação.

parallelism *n* paralelismo *m.*

paralyse *vt* paralisar.

paralysis *n* paralisia *f.*

paralytic *adj* paralítico; **2** *(coll) (drunk)* bêbado.

paramedic *n* paramédico,-a.

parameter *n* parâmetro *m;* indicador *m.*

paramilitary *adj* paramilitar *m,f.*

paramount *adj:* **of ~ importance** de suma importância, primordial.

paramour *n (lover)* amante *m,f,* concubina *f.*

paranoia *n* paranóia *f.*

paranoid *adj* paranóico.

paranormal *n adj* paranormal *m,f.*

parapet *n (of roof, bridge)* parapeito *m;* guarda *f* de prote(c)ção.

paraphasia *n (MED)* parafasia *f.*

paraphernalia *n* parafernalia *f;* miscelânea de acessórios *mpl,* equipamento *m;* **2** *(JUR) (of a married woman)* parafernais *mpl,* haveres pessoais *mpl.*

paraphrase *n* paráfrase *f;* ♦ *vt* parafrasear.

paraplegic *n* paraplégico,-a.

parapsychology *n* parapsicologia *f.*

parasite *n* parasita *m,f.*

parasol *n* guarda-sol/guardassol *m,* sombrinha *f.*

paratrooper *n* pára-quedista/paraquedista *m,f.*

parboil *n (CULIN)* cozer parcialmente.

parcel *n* pacote *m,* embrulho *m;* **2** *(land)* lote *m,* parcela; ♦ *vt* (= **~ up**) *(pack)* embrulhar, empacotar; **2** *(separate)* dividir; IDIOM **part and ~** parte de; **to be part and ~ of** fazer parte de.

parch *vt* secar, ressecar.

parched *adj* morto de sede.

parchment *n* pergaminho *m.*

pardon *n* perdão *m; (JUR)* indulto *m;* **I beg your ~** peço que me perdoe; **2** *(sorry)* **~!** desculpe!; *(what)* **~?** como? o quê?; ♦ *vt (forgive)* perdoar; **2** *(JUR)* indultar; absolver.

pare *vt (trim)* aparar; **2** *(peel)* descascar; **3** *(make shorter)* reduzir.

parent *n* pai *m,* mãe *f;* progenitor *m;* **~-in-law** *m* sogro,-a; **~-teacher association** *n* associação de pais e professores; **2** *(source)* origem *f;* **~ company** *n* empresa-matriz *f;* **parents** *npl* pais *mpl.*

parentage *n* ascendência *f;* parentela *f;* origem *f.*

parental *adj* paternal; maternal; dos pais.

parenthesis *(pl:* -**theses**) *n* parêntese *m.*

parenthood *n* paternidade, maternidade.

par excellence *adj* por excelência.

parget *n (plasterwork)* estuque *m.*

pariah *n* pária, marginal *m,f.*

pari passu *adv (JUR)* a par e passo.

Paris *npr* Paris *f;* **in ~** em Paris.

parish *n (REL)* paróquia *f, (ADMIN)* freguesia *f;* **~ priest** *n* pároco *m.*

parishioner *n* paroquiano,-a.

Parisian *n adj* parisiense *m,f.*

parity *n* paridade *f,* igualdade *f; (FIN)* paridade *f.*

park *n* parque *m;* jardim *m;* parque *m* natural; ♦ *vt/vi* estacionar.

parking *n* estacionamento; **no ~** estacionamento proibido; **~ fine** multa *f;* **~ lot** *n (US)* (parque de) estacionamento; **~ meter** *n* parquímetro *m.*

parkour *n (SPORT)* parkour *m.*

parkway *n (US)* avenida *f.*

parlance *n* linguagem *f;* gíria *f;* **in common/legal ~** em linguagem corrente/juridíca.

parley *n (for a truce)* convénio *m,* negociação *f.*

parleyvoo *n (coll)* franciú *m.*

parliament *n* parlamento *m,* assembleia *f;* **2** *(session)* legislature *f.*

parliamentary *adj* parlamentar.

parlour *n (room)* sala *f* de visitas, salão *m,* saleta *f;* **2** *(shop)* estabelecimento *m;* **~ game** *n* jogo de salão.

parochial *adj* paroquial *m,f;* **2** *(pej)* provinciano.

parody *n* paródia *f;* ♦ (-**ied**) *vt* parodiar.

parole *n:* **on ~** em liberdade *f* condicional, sob promessa; **to break one's ~** violar a liberdade condicional.

paronym *n (LING)* parónimo *m.*

parotid (gland) *n (ANAT)* parótida *f.*

paroxysm *n* ataque *m*; **a ~ of rage** um ataque de raiva; **2** *(MED)* paroxismo *m*.

parquet *n*: **~ floor** parqué *m*, parquete *m*, soalho *m* de tacos.

parricide *n* parricídio *m*.

parrot *n* papagaio *m*; **~ fashion** *adv* mecanicamente; ♦ *vt* imitar.

parry (**-ied**) *vt* aparar, desviar.

parsimonious *adj* parco, parcimonioso; **2** *(stingy)* avarento.

parsley *n* *(BOT)* salsa *f*.

parsnip *n* *(BOT)* cherivia *f*, pastinaga *f*.

parson *n* *(priest)* pároco *m*, padre *m*, clérigo *m*; pastor.

parsonage *n* presbitério.

part *n* *(separate piece)* parte *f*; pedaço *m*; **~ and parcel** parte integrante; **for my ~** pela minha parte; **for the most ~** na majoria dos casos; **in ~** (= **partly**) em parte; **on the ~ of** da/por parte de; **~-owner** *n* co-proprietário,-a; **2** *(component)* peça *f*; **spare ~** peça sobresselente; **3** *(THEAT)* *(role)* papel *m*; **to do one's ~** cumprir a sua obrigação; **to play a ~ in** ter influência em; **to take ~ in** participar em, tomar parte em; **4** *(portion)* episódio *m*; fascículo *m*; ♦ *vt/vi* separar(-se); partir (-se); apartar(-se); despedir-se; dispersar-se; ♦ *vt* fazer risca (no cabelo); **to ~ company (with)** *vt* separar-se (de); divergir; **to ~ with** *vt* ceder; desfazer-se de; ♦ *adv* (= **partly**) em parte, parcialmente.

partake *(like:* **take***)* *vi* participar em, partilhar; **2** *(eat)* comer.

partial *adj* parcial *m,f*; **to be ~ to** gostar de.

partiality *n* parcialidade *f*; **2** predileção *f*.

partially *adv* parcialmente, em parte; **~ sighted** *adj* com visão parcial.

partible *adj* divisível *m,f*.

participant *n* participante *m,f*.

participate *vi*: **to ~ in** participar em, tomar parte em.

participation *n* participação *f*.

participle *n* particípio *m*; **past/present ~** particípio *m* passado/presente.

particle *n* *(PHYS)* partícula *f*; grão *m*; **2** *(tiny amount)* *(fig)* bocadinho *m*, pequena parte *f*.

particular *adj* *(special)* particular *m,f*; concreto; determinado; **2** *(specific)* detalhado, minucioso; **3** *(not easily pleased)* exigente.

particularism *n* particularismo *m*.

particularly *adv* em particular, especialmente.

particulars *npl* dados *mpl*, detalhes *mpl*; pormenores *mpl*.

parting *n* *(farewell)* despedida *f*; *(separation)* separação *f*, partida *f*, adeus *m*; **2** *(UK)* *(hair style)* risca *f* (no cabelo); **~ shot** *n* comentário hóstil antes de sair; tirada *f* final.

partisan *n adj* partidário,-a.

partition *n* *(POL)* divisão *f*; partilha *f*; **2** *(dividing structure)* tabique *m*; divisória *f*; ♦ *vt* separar com tabique; *(fig)* dividir.

partitive *adj* *(LING)* partitivo.

partly *adv* em parte, até certo ponto.

partner *n* *(COMM)* sócio,-a; **2** *(SPORT; games)* parceiro,-a; *(dance)* par; **3** *(couple in a relationship)* companheiro,-a; *(married)* cônjuge *m,f*; **4** *(in crime)* cúmplice *m,f*; ♦ *vt* acompanhar.

partnership *n* *(gen)* associação *f*; *(COMM)* sociedade *f* (**between** entre, **with** com); **2** parceria *f*.

partridge *n* *(ZOOL)* perdiz *f*.

parts *npl* região *fsg*, paragens *fpl*; terra *f*; IDIOM **to be a man/a woman of ~** ser um homem uma mulher de talento; **private ~** órgãos *mpl* sexuais.

part-time *adj adv* (a) tempo parcial, *(BR)* de meio expediente, periodo.

party *n* *(POL)* partido *m*; **~ line** *(POL)* posição *f* oficial; **2** *(celebration)* festa *f*; **3** *(group)* grupo *m*; **4** *(JUR)* parte *f* interessada, litigante *m,f*; **~ animal** *n* borguista, *(BR)* farrista; **~goer** *n* frequentador,-ora de festas; **~ pooper** *n* *(coll)* desmancha-prazeres *m*; **~ wall** *n* parede *f* comum; ♦ *adj* *(POL)* do partido; ♦ *vi* festejar; IDIOM **to throw a ~** organizar uma festa.

parvenu *(f:* **-nue***)* *n* *(fam)* novo-rico-a.

pascal *n* *(COMP)* *(programming language)* pascal *m*; **2** *(PHYS)* *(unit of pressure)* pascal *m*.

paschal *n* *(relating to Easter)* pascal *m,f*.

pasquinade *n* pasquim *m*, sátira *f* pública.

pass *n* passe *m*; livre-trânsito *m*; passagem *f*; **2** *(GEOG)* garganta *f*, desfiladeiro *m*; **to get a ~ in** *(exam)* ser aprovado em; ♦ *vt* *(go past)* passar por; ultrapassar; passar por cima de; **2** *(approve)* aprovar; **3** *(change state)* passar, alterar-se; **4** *(ignore)* ignorar; ♦ *vi* *(EDUC)* ser aprovado,-a, passar *(exam)*; **to come to ~** acontecer; ♦ **to ~ away** *vi* falecer; **to ~ by** *vi* passar; **to ~ down** *(sth)* transmitir (**from** de **to** para); **to ~ for** ser tomado por; ♦ **to ~ on** transmitir *(message, wishes)*; **2** repercutir *(costs)*; ♦ **to ~ out** *vi* desmaiar; **2** distribuir *(sth* algo*)*; ♦ **to ~ over (sb)** preterir *(candidate)*; **2** ignorar *(sth* algo*)*, passar por cima; **3 ~ the hand over sb's face** acariciar; ♦ **to ~ through** estar de passagem; **2** atravessar *(sth)*; ♦ **to ~ up** ignorar, deixar passar; **to ~ water** urinar. IDIOM **to ~ the bucket** fugir a uma responsabilidade; **to make a ~ at sb** tentar seduzir alguém, atirar-se a alguém.

passable *adj* *(road)* transitável; **2** aceitável, razoável; passável.

passage *n* *(channel)* corredor *m*; **2** *(journey)* trânsito *m*; passagem *f*; travessia *f*; **3** *(quotation)* excerto *m*; **4** *(MECH, MED)* conduto *m*.

passata *n* *(CULIN)* molho *m* de tomate.

passbook *n* *(banking)* caderneta *f*.

passé *adj* ultrapassado,-a.

passenger *n* passageiro,-a, viajante *m,f*.

passer-by *n* transeunte *m,f*.

passing *adj* passageiro, fugaz *m,f*; **in ~** de passagem.

passion *n* paixão *f*; cólera *f*; **the P ~** *n* a Paixão de Cristo; **passions** *npl* paixões.

passionate *adj* apaixonado,-a; **a ~ kiss** um beijo cheio de paixão.

passionfruit *n* maracujá *m*.

passive *adj* passivo; ~ **smoker** *n* fumador,-ora passivo,-a.

passkey *n* chave-mestra *f*.

Passover *n* Páscoa *f* (dos judeus).

passport *n* passaporte *m*.

password *n* senha *f*, contra-senha/contrassenha *f*.

past *n* passado *m*; antecedentes *mpl*; ♦ *adj* passado; ex-, anterior *m,f*; ♦ *prep* para além de; depois de; **she is ~ 30** ela já fez 30 (anos); **a quarter ~ five** cinco e um quarto, (BR) cinco e quinze; **for the ~ few days** nos últimos dias; **to walk ~** passar por **sb/sth** (por alguém/algo).

pasta *n* massa *f*.

paste *n* pasta *f*; grude *m*, cola *f*; ♦ *vt* grudar; colar.

pastel *n adj* (painting/colour) (a) pastel.

pasteurized *adj* pasteurizado,-a.

pastiche *n* pastiche *m*, cópia *f*.

pastille *n* pastilha *f*.

pastime *n* passatempo *m*.

pasting *n* (coll) (thrashing) enxerto *m* de porrada; **2** (heavy defeat) derrota total.

pastor *n* pastor *m*; clérigo *m*.

pastoral *adj* pastoral *m,f*.

pastry *n* massa *f*; **2** pastéis *mpl*, folhados *mpl*; ~ **cook** *n* pasteleiro,-a.

pasture *n* pasto *m*; pastagem *f*.

pasty *n* (CULIN) empada *f*, pastel *m* de carne; ♦ *adj* pastoso; pálido.

pat *n* (stroke) palmadinha; **2** (small piece) porção *f*; **to give sb a ~ on the back** (fig) animar alguém; **off** ~ de cor; ♦ (-**ter**, -**test**) *adj* ensaiado,-a, preparado,-a; ♦ *vt* dar palmadinhas em; (dog) afagar, acariciar.

patch *n* (piece of material) retalho *m*; remendo *m*; **2** (small piece, area, land) pedaço *m*; lote *m*, terreno *m*; **3** (MED) penso *m*; **4** (COMP) corre(c)-ção *f* de programa; ♦ *vt* remendar; **to ~ up** *vt* consertar provisoriamente; **2** (small urban land) loteamento *m*; horta *f*; **3** (quarrel) resolver. IDIOM **to go through a bad ~** passar por um mau bocado.

patchwork *adj* (feito) de retalhos.

patchy (-**ier**, -**iest**) *adj* desigual *m,f*; **2** cheio,-a de remendos.

pâté *n* patê *m*, pasta *f*, (BR) patê *m*.

patella *n* (ANAT) rótula *f* (joelho).

patent *n* patente *f*; ♦ *adj* patente *m,f*, evidente *m,f*; ~ **leather** *n* verniz *m*; ♦ *vt* patentear.

patently *adv* claramente.

paterfamilias *n* patriarca *m*.

paternal *adj* (fatherly) paternal *m,f*; **2** (related to father) paterno.

paternity *n* paternidade *f*.

path *n* caminho *m*; trilha *f*, pista *f*; traje(c)tória *f*.

pathetic *adj* (pitiful) patético, digno de pena; **2** (worthless) péssimo; **3** (sad) comovente *m,f*.

pathogenic *adj* patogénico.

pathologist *n* patologista *m,f*.

pathology *n* patologia *f*.

pathos *n* elemento que exprime pena *f*/dó *m* or sofrimento *m*.

pathway *n* caminho *m*, trilha *f*, vereda *f*, atalho *m*.

patience *n* paciência *f*; **2** (card game) paciência *f*.

patient *n* (in medical care) paciente *m,f*; ♦ *adj* paciente, resignado,-a; **I am very ~** tenho muita paciência, sou muito paciente.

patina *n* (CHEM) pátina *f*, verdete *m*; **2** (fine layer) manto *m*, camada *f*.

patio *n* pátio *m*; ~ **doors** *npl* janelas *fpl* de sacada que dão para um pátio ou jardim.

patisserie *n* pastelaria *f*.

patois *n* patoá *m*.

patriarch *n* patriarca *m*.

patriarchal *adj* patri-arcal *m,f*.

patricide *n* parricídio *m*.

patrimony *n* património (BR: -ônio) *m*.

patriot *n* patriota *m,f*.

patriotic *adj* patriótico.

patrol *n* patrulha *f*; ♦ *vt* patrulhar; **to be on ~** estar de ronda; ~ **car** *n* carro *m* de patrulha, radiopatrulha *m*; ~**man** *n* guarda *m*, polícial *m*; patrulheiro.

patron *n* (customer) cliente *m,f*; **2** (supporter) prote(c)tor,-ora; benfeitor,-ora; (of hotel) cliente *m,f*; ~ **of the arts** patrono, prote(c)tor,-ora das artes, mecenas *pl*; ~ **saint** santo padroeiro.

patronage *n* patrocínio *m*; **2** mecenato *m*.

patronize, (~ise) *vt* ser cliente de; **2** (sponsor) patrocinar; **3** (pej) (superior attitude) tratar com um ar condescendente, de superioridade.

patronizing, (~ising) *adj* condescendente *m,f*, **2** paternalista *m,f*; complacente *m,f* de superioridade.

patsy *n* (US) (easily cheated) patego,-a; **2** (scapegoat) bode *m* expiatório.

patter *n* (of fingers) tamborilada *f*; (of rain) o bater da chuva *m*; **2** (steps) passos miúdos *mpl*; **3** (jargon) giria *f* professional; ♦ *vi* correr a passos miúdos; (fingers) tamborilar; (rain) bater.

pattern *n* (model) modelo *m*, padrão *m*; **2** (mould) molde *m*; **3** (design) desenho *m*; **4** (sample) amostra *f*.

patterned *adj* (cloth) estampado,-a.

patty *n* (CULIN) pastel *m*.

paucity *n* insuficiência *f*, escassez *f*.

paunch *n* pança *f*, barriga *f*; ♦ *vt* estripar.

pauper *n* pobre *m,f* indigente *m,f*; ~**'s grave** vala *f* comun.

pauperize *vt* empobrecer.

pause *n* pausa *f*; intervalo *m*; ♦ *vi* fazer uma pausa.

pave *vt* pavimentar; **to ~ the way for** preparar o terreno para.

pavement *n* (US) calçada *f*, pavimento *m*; **2** (UK) passeio *m*; ~ **artist** *n* pintor,-ora de rua.

pavilion *n* (sports building) pavilhão *m*; **2** (decorative building) coreto *m*; **3** (temporary building) barraca *f*, tenda *f*.

paving *n* pavimento *m*, pavimentação *f*; ~ **stone** *n* pedra *f* de calçada, paralelepípedo *m*.

paw *n* pata *f*; **2** (coll) (big clumsy hand) garra *f*; ♦ *vt* passar a pata; dar patadas em (to animal); **2** (pej) (touch person) apalpar; **to ~ the ground** (bull) escarvar.

pawky *n* (SCOT) chico-esperto (chicoesperto).

pawn *n (chess)* peão *m*; **2** *(fig)* títere *m*; **3** *(gage)* penhor *m*; **~broker** *n* penhorista *m,f*; **~shop** *n* loja *f* de penhores; ♦ *vt* empenhar.

pay *n* pagamento *m*; salário *m*; paga *f*; ♦ *(pt,pp: paid)* pagar; **I paid the bill** paguei a conta; **to ~ a visit to** fazer uma visita a; **to ~ attention to** prestar atenção a; **to ~ back** *vt (debt)* pagar; **2** *(retaliate)* vingar-se de (alguém); **to ~ for (sth)** pagar (algo); **to ~ in** *(money)* depositar; **to ~ off** *(debt)* saldar; **2** compensar; **to ~ out** desembolsar; **to ~ up** *(debts)* liquidar; IDIOM **to ~ through the nose (for)** dar o couro e o cabelo por.

payable *adj* pagável *m,f*.

PAYE *(abbr* **pay as you earn)** *(UK)* modalidade de pagamento do imposto sobre rendimento.

payee *n* pessoa a quem se paga; sacador *m*; portador *m*; beneficiador,-ora.

payer *n* pagador,-ora.

paying *adj* remunerador,-ora. **~ guest** *n* hóspede que paga, pensionista.

payment *n* pagamento *m*; **monthly ~** mensalidade *f*.

payoff *n* resultado *m; (UK) (redundancy payment)* inde(m)nização *f*.

payola *(US)* suborno *m*.

paypacket ordenado *m* (num envelope).

payroll *n* folha *f* de pagamento.

payslip *(UK)* **pay-stub** *(US) n* contracheque *m*.

PC *(abbr for personal computer)* computador *m*; **2** *(abbr for Police Constable)* agente da Polícia; **3** *(abbr for politically correct)* politicamente correto,-a.

p.c. *(abbr for petty cash) n* fundo de meneio.

PD *n (abbr for* **Police Department***)* Departamento *m* da Polícia.

PDA *n (abbr for* **personal digital assistant***) (COMP)* computador *m* de bolso.

PE *n (abbr for physical education)* educação *f* física.

pea *n (BOT)* ervilha *f*; **sweet ~** ervilha-de-cheiro *f*; **~brain** *n (coll)* palerma *m,f* idiota *m,f*.

peace *n (no violence)* paz *f*; **2** *(harmony)* tranquilidade *(BR*: -qüi-*) f*; **3** *(law and order)* ordem *f* pública; **~ dividend** *n* dividendo *m* da paz; **~-keeping** *n* pacificação *f*; **~maker** *n* medianeiro,-a, pacificador,-ora; **~ offering** *n* proposta *f* de paz; **~ of mind** paz *f* de espírito; IDIOM **to make ~ with** fazer as pazes com.

peaceful *adj* pacífico,-a; *(quiet)* sosse gado,-a, pacato,-a tranquilo,-a, sereno,-a; **a ~ expression** uma expressão serena.

peach *n (fruit)* pêssego *m*; **~ tree** pessegueiro *m*.

peachy *(excellent)* algo formidável, *(BR)* bacana.

peacock *n (bird)* pavão *m*; **2** *(vain person)* convencido,-a.

peahen *n* pavoa *f*.

peak *n (mountain top)* cume *m*; pico *m*; **2** *(of hat)* pala *f*, viseira *f*; **3** *(fig) (highest point)* apogeu *m*, máximo *m*; **~ hours** *npl* horas *fpl* de ponta *(BR:* do rush*)*; ♦ *vt* atingir o ponto mais elevado.

peakaboo *n* brincadeira em que esconde e mostra a cara; ♦ *exc* ~! cucu!

peaked *adj*: ~ **cap** boné *m* com viseira.

peal *n* repique *m*, toque *m* de sinos; ~ **of laughter** gargalhada *f*; ♦ *vt (bells)* repicar.

peanut *n* amendoim *m*; ~ **butter** *n* manteiga *f* de amendoim; ~ **oil** *n* óleo *m* de amendoim; **~s** *npl (fig)* ninharia *fsg*; **she paid ~s for that watch** ela pagou uma ninharia por aquele relógio.

pear *n* pera *f*; **~-shaped** *adj* em feitio de pera; **2** *(hips)* com ancas largas; ♦ **to go ~-shaped** *(go wrong)* correr mal; *(BR)* encrencar-se; ♦ ~ **tree** *n* pereira *f*.

pearl *n* pérola *f*; **2** *(fig) (person, precious thing)* jóia *f*.

peasant *n* camponês,-esa; **2** *(fig) (uncultured person)* saloio,-a, rústico,-a, campónio,-a *(BR:* -pô-*)*.

peasantry *n* campesinato *m*.

peasanty *adj* campestre *m,f*.

peat *n* turfa *f*; **~land** *n* turfeira *f*.

pebble *n* seixo *m*, calhau *m*; cascalho *m*; **2** *(MIN)* sílex *m*; **~-dash** *n (UK)* argamassa *f* com cascalho; ~ **paving** *n* calçada *f*.

pecan (nut) *n* noz *f* pecã.

peccary *n (ZOOL)* pecari *m*.

peck *vt (= ~ at) (birds)* bicar, dar bicadas em; **2** *(fig) (eat small amounts of food)* debicar; **3** *(coll) (annoy)* chatear, maçar, *(BR)* amolar; **4** *(quick kiss)* um beijinho.

pecking order *n* ordem *f* de hierarquia.

peckish *adj (UK) (coll)* com alguma fome.

pectin *n (CHEM)* pectina *f*.

pectise *vt* gelificar.

pectoral *n adj* peitoral *m,f*; ~ **muscle** *n* músculo *m* peitoral.

peculiar *adj (odd)* estranho, esquisito; **2** *(particular)* próprio, característico; **3** *(special)* especial *m,f*; ~ **to** próprio de.

peculiarity *n* peculiaridade *f*; característica *f*; excentricidade *f*, singularidade *f*.

pecuniary *adj* pecuniário,-a.

pedagogue *n* pedagogo *m*.

pedagogy *n* pedagogia *f*.

pedal *n* pedal *m*; ~ **pushers** *npl (clothing)* calças *fpl* curtas; **break ~** *n (AUT)* pedal *m* do travão; **clutch ~** *n (AUT)* pedal *m* de embraiagem; ♦ *adj* podal *m,f*; ♦ *vi* pedalar.

pedalo *n (pleasure craft)* barco a pedais.

pedant *n (pej)* pedant, formalista *m,f*.

pedantic *adj* pedante *m,f*.

peddle *vt* vender nas ruas, *(BR)* mascatear.

peddler *n (US)* vendedor,-ora ambulante; *(BR)* mascate *m,f*; passador,-ora (de drogas).

pederast *n* pederasta *m*.

pederasty *n* pederastia *f*.

pedestal *n* pedestal *m*; IDIOM **to put (someone) on a ~** enaltecer, exaltar alguém.

pedestrian *n* peão *m*, pedestre *m,f*; ♦ *adj* pedestre *m,f*, pedonal *m,f*; ~ **crossing** passadeira *f* para peões, *(BR)* faixa para pedestres.

pedicab *n* bicicleta-táxi *f*.

pedicure *n* pedicuro *m*.

pedigree *n* genealogia *f*; raça *f*; ♦ *adv* de raça.

pedlar *n* = **peddler**.

pedometer *n* pedómetro *m*.

peduncle *n (BOT, ZOOL, MED)* pedúnculo *m*.

pee *n (coll: piss)* mijo *m*; *(child's language)* chichi *m (BR:* xixi*) (fam)*; ♦ *vi (piss)* mijar; fazer chichi.

peek n espreitadela f; ♦ vi espiar, espreitar.

peekaboo n (child's language) brincadeira em que se esconde e depois se aparece; ♦ exc ~! cucu!

peel n pele f; casca f; 2 (baker's shovel) pá f do forno de lenha; ♦ vt/vi descascar; vt descolar-se; **to ~ off** tirar a pele; (outer layer) arrancar; 2 (epidermis) descamar.

peeler n descascador m.

peep n (quick look) olhadela f; (BR) olhada; 2 (of bird) pio m; (shrill sound) guincho m; ♦ vi espreitar; **to ~ out** vi surgir; 2 (sun) raiar; 3 **to make a ~** vi piar; ♦ **not a ~!** nem um pio!

peephole n vigia f; (on the door) ralo m da porta.

Peeping Tom n voyeur m; mirone.

peer n (equal in standing) par m; igual m; 2 (UK) (titled) nobre m; (House of Lords) membro da Câmara dos Lordes; **without ~** sem igual, sem rival; ♦ vi perscrutar; 2 fitar.

peerage n nobreza f.

peer group n grupo n em pé de igualdade.

peerless adj sem igual.

peeve n coisa f irritante; ♦ vt irritar.

peeved adj irritado,-a.

peevish adj rabugento, mal-humorado.

peg n (hanger) cavilha f; cabide m; 2 (= **clothes ~**) (holding pin) mola f para a roupa, (BR) pregador m; 3 (post) estaca f; **~ leg** n (coll) (wooden leg) perna f de pau; **off the ~** adv pronto (a vestir); ♦ (-**gg**-) vt prender com cavilhas, estacas; 2 (fig) fixar; **~ out** vt estender; ♦ vi (fam) (legs) esticar as canelas.

peignoir n (clothing) robe m de senhora.

pejorative adj pejorativo.

Pekinese, Pekingese n pequinês,-esa.

pelage n (animal coat) pelagem f.

pelf n (coll) (pej) (dishonestly acquired wealth) dinheiro m, lucros mpl vistos com desprezo.

pelican n (ZOOL) pelicano m; **~ crossing** n passadeira f controlada por semáforos.

pelisse n (clothing) peliça f.

pellet n (small ball) bolinha f; 2 (for gun) chumbo m; (BR) pelota f de chumbo; 3 (chicken's food) grão m.

pellicle n película f.

pell-mell n confusão f; tumulto m; ♦ adj confuso,-a; tumultuoso,-a; ♦ adv desordenadamente; de qualquer maneira.

pellucid adj translúcido; 2 (clear) límpido, claro.

pelmet n sanefa f.

pelota n (game) pelota f.

pelt n (animal hide) pele f; ♦ vt arremessar, apedrejar, atirar; ♦ **~ down** vi (rain) chover a cântaros; 2 (hurry) (coll) ir disparado; ♦ **at full ~** a toda a velocidade.

peltry n pelaria f.

pelvis n (ANAT) pélvis f; bacia f.

pelvic adj pélvico; **~ floor** n períneo m.

pen n (writing device) caneta f; 2 (enclosed space) redil m, cercado m; 3 (= **~ drive**) (COMP) pen f; 4 (US) (coll) (prison) prisão m, cana f, xilindró m (fam); **~ pal** n amigo,-a por correspondência; ~

name n pseudónimo (BR: -dô-); **fountain ~** n caneta f de tinta permanente; ♦ (-**nn**-) vt (write) escrever; 2 (enclose) fechar em cerca, cercar; IDIOM **the ~ is mightier than the sword** pode mais a pena que a espada.

penal adj penal m,f; **~ code** n (JUR) código m penal.

penalize vt penalizar; impor penalidade, punir.

penalty n pena f, penalidade f; multa f; punição f; **to pay the ~ of** sofrer as consequências de; **~ (kick)** n (football) grande penalidade f, penalty m, (BR) pênalti m.

penance n penitência f.

pence n (pl of **penny** (English money)).

penchant n inclinação f, tendência f (**for**, para).

pencil n lápis m; **propelling ~** n lapiseira f; **~ sharpener** n apara-lápis m, (BR) apontador m; ♦ (-**ll**-) vt desenhar a lápis; **~ in** vt anotar provisoriamente.

pend vi aguardar julgamento.

pendant n pingente m, pendente m.

pendent adj pendente m,f; pendurado, suspenso.

pending adj durante; até; ♦ adj pendente m,f; por dirigir; iminente; ♦ prep à espera de; **~ tray** n tabuleiro/bandeja de assuntos pendentes.

pendulous adj pendular m,f.

pendulum n pêndulo m.

peneplain n (GEOG) peneplanície f.

penetrate vt penetrar.

penetrating adj penetrante m,f.

penetration n penetração f.

penguin n (ZOOL) pinguim m.

penicillin n (MED) penicilina f.

peninsula n (GEOG) península f.

peninsular adj peninsular m,f.

penis n (ANAT) pénis (BR: pê-) m; (fam) pila f; (child's) (fam) pilinha f.

penitence n penitência f.

penitent adj arrependido; 2 (REL) penitente m,f.

penitentiary n (US) penitenciária f, presídio m; 2 (REL) penitenciário m; ♦ adj penitencial m,f.

penknife (pl: **penknives**) n canivete m.

penman n calígrafo,-a; 2 (fig) (writer) escritor,-ora.

penmanship n caligrafia f.

pennant n flâmula f, pendão m.

penne n (CULIN) massa f penne.

penniless adj sem dinheiro; (fig) sem um tostão, sem cheta (cal).

Pennsylvania npr Pensilvânia.

penny (pl: **pennies** or **pence**) n péni m; **~ pinching** n avareza f; ♦ adj (person) avarento,-as; somítico,-a; fuinhas sg, (BR) pão-duro m; ♦ **a pretty ~** um dinheirão; IDIOM **the ~ dropped** (suddenly understand) fez-se luz, já entendi; **to spend a ~** (coll) fazer chichi; **in for a ~, in for a pound** perdido por cem, perdido por mil.

penny-farthing n (early type of cycle) biciclo m.

pension n pensão f; 2 reforma f; **~ fund** n fundo m de pensões; (BR) fundo de aposentoria; ♦ **~ off** vt aposentar; **to be ~ed off** mandado para a reforma, aposentado,-a.

pensioner n pensionista m,f.

pensive adj pensativo, absorto.

penstock *n* conduta *f* para planta hidroelétrica; comporta *f.*

pentacle *n (vd:* **pentagram**).

pentadactyl *adj* pentadáctilo.

pentagon *n* pentágono *m.*

Pentagon *n (US):* **the** ~ o Pentágono.

> Pentágono em Washington, abriga o Ministerio da Defesa dos E.U.A. representando assim o poder militar do Estado.

pentagram *n* pentagrama *m.*

pentameter *n (LITER)* pentâmetro *m.*

pentane *n (CHEM)* pentano *m.*

Pentateuch *n (REL)* Pentateuco *m.*

pentathlon *n (SPORT)* pentatlo *m.*

Pentecost *n (REL)* Pentecostes *m.*

penthouse *n* apartamento *m* de luxo construído no telhado, *(BR)* apartamento *m* de cobertura.

pentode *n (ELECT) (electronic valve)* pêntodo *m.*

pent-up *adj* reprimido,-a, enervado,-a.

penultimate *adj* penúltimo,-a.

penumbra *n* penumbra *f.*

penury *n* penúria *f*, miséria *f.*

peon *n* trabalhador,-ora agrícola, *(BR)* peão *m; (in India)* mensageiro; *(foot soldier)* peão, soldado de infantaria.

people *npl* gente *f*, pessoas *fpl*; **2** *(group of persons of a country, etc.)* povo *msg*; nação *f*, raça *f*; ~ **skills** *n* competências *fpl* comunicativas; **several** ~ **came** vieram várias pessoas; ~ **say that** dizem que; ♦ *vt* povoar.

pep *n (coll)* energia *f*, dinamismo *m*; ~ **talk** *n (coll)* conversa *f* encorajadora; ♦ **to** ~ **up** *vt* animar.

pepper *n (spice)* pimenta *f*; **2** *(vegetable)* pimento *m*, *(BR)* pimentão *m*; ~**corn** *n m* de pimento; ~**mint** *n* hortelã-pimenta *f*; pastilha *f* de mentol, *(BR)* bala *f* de hortelã; ~ **spray** *n* gás *m* pimenta; ~ **pot** *n* pimenteiro *m*; ~ **spray** *n* gas *m* pimenta; ♦ *vt* apimentar.

peppery *adj* apimentado,-a; picante *m,f.*

pepsin *n (BIOL)* pepsina *f.*

peptic *adj* péptico.

per *prep* por; ~ **annum** por ano; ~ **day/person** por dia/pessoa; ~ **cent** por cento; **as** ~ **invoice** conforme fa(c)tura.

perambulate *vi* deambular; **2** *(inspect)* inspeccionar.

perceive *vt (understand)* perceber; compreender; **2** *(see)* observar.

percentage *n* percentagem *f.*

percentile *n (statistics)* centil *m.*

perception *n* percepção *f*; perspicácia *f.*

perceptive *adj* perceptivo,-a, perspicaz.

perceptual *adj* percetual *m,f*; perce(p)tivo,-a.

perch *n (fish)* perca *f*; **2** *(resting rod)* poleiro *m*; ♦ *vi* empoleirar-se, pousar.

perchance *adv* porventura.

perchloride *n (CHEM)* percloreto *m.*

percolate *vi* filtrar-se, coar-se através de; **2** *(fill)* penetrar.

percolator *n* cafeteira *f* de filtro.

percussion *n (MUS)* percussão *f*; ~ **instrument** *n* instrumento *m* de percussão; ~ **tool** *n* ferramenta *f* de percussão.

peregrine *adj* peregrino; ~ **falcon** *n* falcão *m* peregrino.

peremptory *adj* decisivo; autoritário,-a; dogmático,-a.

perennial *adj (plant)* perene *m,f.*

perfect *n* (= ~ **tense**) *(gram)* perfeito *m*; ♦ *adj (faultless)* perfeito; **2** *(precise)* exacto; ♦ *vt* aperfeiçoar;

perfection *n* perfeição *f.*

perfectionist *n* perfeccionista *m,f.*

perfidious *adj* pérfido, traiçoeiro, falso.

perforate *vt* perfurar, furar.

perforated *adj* picotado.

perforation *n* perfuração *f.*

perforce *adv* inevitavelmente.

perform *vt (execute)* realizar, fazer; executar; **2** *(entertain)* interpretar; ♦ *vi* fazer truques de amestramento; **2** *(THEAT)* representar; **3** *(TECH)* funcionar.

performance *n (execution)* cumprimento *m*, realização *f*; **2** *(manner of functioning)* desempenho *m*, a(c)tuação *f*; funcionamento *m*; performance *f.*

performer *n* artista *m,f*, a(c)tor *m*, a(c)triz *f*; *(MUS)* intérprete *m,f.*

performing *adj* amestrado; ~ **arts** artes *fpl* performáticas.

perfume *n* perfume *m.*

perfumery *n* perfumaria *f*; ♦ *vt* perfumar.

perfunctory *adj* perfun(c)tório,-a, maquinal, superficial.

perfusion *n (MED)* perfusão *f.*

pergola *n* pérgola *f.*

perhaps *adv* talvez; ~ **I shall go** talvez eu vá.

pericardium *n (ANAT)* pericárdio *m.*

peril *n* perigo *m*, risco *m.*

perilous *adj* perigoso.

perimeter *n* perímetro *m.*

perineum *n (ANAT)* períneo *m.*

period *n (time)* período *m*; época *f*, era *f*; *(US) (fig)* ponto final; **2** *(division of time)* prazo *m*; **3** *(EDUC)* tempo le(c)tivo *m*; **4** *(MED) (menstruation)* período *m*, menstruação *f*; ♦ *adj* da época; *(furniture)* de estilo.

periodic *adj* periódico.

periodical *n* periódico *m.*

periodically *adv* periodicamente, de vez em quando.

peripheral *n adj* periférico,-a.

periphery *n* periferia *f.*

periphrasis *n (LITER)* perífrase *f.*

periscope *n* periscópio *m.*

perish *vi* perecer; deteriorar-se, estragar; IDIOM ~ **the thought!** nem pensar!

perishable *adj* perecível *m,f*, deteriorável *m,f*; ♦ **perishables** *npl* géneros *mpl* perecíveis.

perishing *adj (coll) (weather)* gelado, glacial *m,f.*

peristyle *n (ARCH)* peristilo *m.*

peritoneum *n (ANAT)* peritoneu *m.*

perjure *vt:* **to** ~ **o.s.** prestar falso testemunho.

perjury *n (JUR)* perjúrio *m.*

perk *n* pagamento extra; regalia *f*; **the** ~**s** os extras, as regalias; ♦ *vt (coll) (coffee)* filtrar; **2 to** ~ **up** *vi (cheer up)* animar-se; arrebitar.

perky *adj* animado, alegre.

perm *n (hair)* permanente *f.*

permaculture *n* permacultura *f.*

permanent *adj* permanente *m,f.*
permeability *n* permeabilidade *f.*
permeable *adj* permeável *m,f.*
permeate *vt* permear, penetrar.
permissible *adj* permissível *m,f*, lícito.
permission *n* permissão *f*; autorização *f.*
permissive *adj* permissivo.
permit *n (permission)* permissão *f*; 2 *(official certificate)* licença *f*; ◆ *vt (possibility)* permitir; 2 *(consent)* autorizar; consentir em.
permutation *n* permutação *f.*
pernicious *adj* nocivo; 2 *(MED)* pernicioso,-a, maligno.
pernickety *adj (UK) (coll)* minucioso,-a; picuínhas *m,f.*
perorate *vi* perorar, discursar.
peroxide *n (CHEM)* peróxido *m.*
perp *n (US) (coll)* criminoso,-a.
perpend *n (construction)* junta *f* vertical.
perpendicular *adj* perpendicular *m,f.*
perpetrate *vt* cometer.
perpetual *adj* perpétuo,-a.
perpetuate *vt* perpetuar.
perplex *vt* deixar perplexo (**by**, com).
perplexity *n* perplexidade *f.*
perquisite *n* regalia *f*, benefício, privilégio *m* adicional.
perry *n (drink)* sidra *f* de pêra.
per se *adv (as such)* como tal; 2 *(in itself)* em si, por si mesmo.
perse *n (colour)* azul *m* petróleo.
persecute *vt* perseguir; importunar.
persecution *n* perseguição *f*; ~ **complex** *n* mania *f* da perseguição.
perseverance *n* perseverança *f.*
persevere *vi* perseverar.
Persia *npr* Pérsia.
Persian *n adj* persa *m,f*; *(LING)* farsi, persa; ~ **Gulf** *npr* Golfo *m* Pérsico.
persiflage *n* brincadeira *f*, galhofa *f*, *(BR)* zoada *f.*
persimmon *n (fruit)* dióspiro *m.*
persist *vi:* **to ~ (in doing sth)** persistir (em fazer algo).
persistence *n* persistência *f*; insistência *f.* **persistent** *adj* persistente *m,f*; teimoso; insistente *m,f.*
person *n* pessoa *f*; **average** ~ pessoa normal; **about his/her** ~ *(concealed, etc)* no seu corpo; **in** ~ *adv* pessoalmente.
persona *n* personagem *f*, figura; ~ **non grata** *f* pessoa indesejada, inaceitável.
personable *adj* atraente *m,f*, bem apessoado,-a.
personal *adj* pessoal *m,f*; particular *m,f*; em pessoa; ~ **effects** *npl* bens pessoais *mpl.*
personality *n* personalidade *f.*
personally *adv* pessoalmente.
personify *vt* personificar.
personnel *n* pessoal *m.*
perspective *n* perspectiva *f*; IDIOM **to put (sth) into** ~ analisar em perspectiva.
perspex *n* acrílico.
perspicacious *adj* perspicaz *m,f.*
perspicuous *adj* evidente *m,f*; claro.

perspiration *n* transpiração *f*, suor *m.*
perspire *vi* transpirar, suar.
persuade *vt* persuadir.
persuasion *n* persuasão *f*; poder *m* de persuasão; 2 *(belief)* convicção *f*, crença *f.*
persuasive *adj* persuasivo.
pert *adj* atrevido, descarado.
pertain *vi* pertencer, referir-se a, dizer respeito a.
pertaining: ~ **to** *prep* relativo a, próprio de.
pertinacious *adj* obstinado, inflexível *m,f.*
pertinent *adj* pertinente, a propósito.
perturb *vt* perturbar.
perturbation *n* perturbação *f.*
Peru *npr* Peru *m*; **in** ~ no Peru.
perusal *n* análise *f* minuciosa.
peruse *vt* ler com atenção, examinar.
Peruvian *n adj* peruano,-a.
perv (= **pervert**) *n (slang)* pessoa *f* perversa, depravado,-a.
pervade *vt* impregnar, penetrar em.
perverse *adj* perverso; teimoso; caprichoso.
perversion *n* perversão *f.*
perversity *n* perversidade *f.*
pervert *n* pervertido,-a; ◆ *vt* perverter, corromper.
pervious *adj* permeável *m,f*; flexível *m,f.*
pesky *adj (US)* maçador, importuno.
pessimism *n* pessimismo *m.*
pessimist *n* pessimista *m,f.*
pessimistic *adj* pessimista.
pest *n* peste *f*, praga *f*; 2 *(fig) (annoying person)* chato,-a.
pester *vt* incomodar.
pesticide *n* pesticida *m.*
pestilence *n* epidemia *f.*
pestle *n (grinding tool)* pilão *m*; ~ **and mortar** pilão e almofariz.
pesto *n (CULIN)* pesto *m*, pasta *f* de manjericão.
pet *n (house animal)* animal *m* de estimação; 2 *(favourite)* preferido,-a; mascote *f*; ~ **name** *n* nome *m* carinhoso; ◆ *vt* acariciar, afagar.
petal *n* pétala *f.*
petard *n* petardo *m*; IDIOM **hoist with one's own** ~ *(victim of one's own schemes)* sair o tiro pela culatra (a alguém).
petcock *n (MECH)* torneira *f* de descompressão.
peter: **to ~ out** *vi* acabar gradualmente; *(conversation, interest, supplies)* esmorecer, esgotar-se, acabar-se.
petite *adj* delicado, frágil *m,f.*
petition *n* petição *f*; ◆ *vt* solicitar, pedir.
petitioner *n* peticionário,-a; *(JUR)* requerente *m,f* queixoso,-a.
petrified *adj (fig)* petrificado, paralisado.
petrify *vt* paralisar; petrificar.
petrochemical *adj* petroquímico,-a.
petrodollar *n (FIN)* petrodólar *m.*
petroglyph *n* gravura *f* rupestre, petróglifo *m.*
petrol *n* gasolina *f*; ~ **bomb** *n* coquetel *m* Molotov; ~ **can** lata *f* de gasolina ~ **gauge** *n* indicador *m* do nível de gasolina; ~ **pump** *n* bomba *f* de gasolina; ~ **station** *n* bomba *f* *(BR*: posto) de gasolina; ~ **tank** depósito, tanque *m* de gasolina; ~ **tanker** *(ship)* petroleiro *m.*

petroleum *n* petróleo *m*; ♦ *adj (product, industry)* petrolífero,-a; ~ **jelly** *n* vaselina *f*.
petticoat *n (full slip)* combinação *f*; *(half slip)* saiote *m*.
pettifogger *n* picuinhas *msg*.
pettiness *n* insignificância; ninharia; **2** *(meanness)* mesquinhez.
pettish *adj* petulante *m,f*; *(peevish) (child)* rabujento,-a, com birra.
pettitoes *npl (CULIN)* pé *msg* de porco.
petty *adj* mesquinho; insignificante *m,f*; ~ **cash** *n* fundo *m* para despesas pequenas; fundo *m* de maneio; ~ **officer** *n* suboficial *m* da marinha.
petulant *adj* petulante *m,f*, impertinente *m,f*.
petunia *n (BOT)* petúnia *f*.
pew *n* banco *m* de igreja.
pewter *n* peltre *m*, estanho *m*.
PG *(abbr for* **Parental Guidance**) *(in films)* orientação *f* parental.
pg. *(abbr for* **page**).
phaeton *n* carruagem *f* aberta.
phagomania *n* fagomania *f*.
phalanx *n (ANAT, MIL)* falange *f*.
phallic *adj* fálico.
phallus *n* falo *m*.
phantom *n* fantasma *m*; ~ **pregnancy** *n* falsa gravidez *f*.
Pharaoh *n* faraó *m*.
Pharisee *n* fariseu *m*.
pharmacist *n* farmacêutico,-a.
pharmacology *n* farmacologia *f*.
pharmacy *n* farmácia *f*.
pharming *n (COMP) (computing crime)* mistificação *f* do destino.
pharyngitis *n* faringite *f*.
pharynx *n* faringe *f*.
phase *n* fase *f*; ~ **changer** *n (ELECT)* conversor *m* de fase; ~ **rule** *n (ELECT)* lei *f* das fases.
phasing *n (ELECT)* ajuste *m* de fase; ♦ *vt*: **to** ~ **in/out** introduzir/retirar gradualmente, por etapas.
phat *adj (slang)* fantástico, fabuloso.
PhD *(abbr for* **Doctor of Philosophy**) doutoramento em, *(BR)* Doutorado em.
pheasant *n* faisão *m*.
phenomenal *adj* fenomenal *m,f*.
phenomenon *(pl:* -**mena**) *n* fenómeno *(BR:* -nô-*)*.
phew *exc (relief)* uf!, ufa!, livra!
phial *n* pequeno *m* frasco, ampola *f*.
Philadelphia *npr* Filadélfia; **in** ~ em Filadélfia.
philanthropist *n* filantropo,-a.
philantropic *adj* filantrópico.
philantropy *n* filantropia *f*.
philately *n* filatelia *f*.
philharmonic *n* filarmónica *f*.
philippic *n* invectiva *f*.
Philippines (= **Philippine Islands**) *npr* as Filipinas *fpl*; **in** ~ nas Filipinas.
philology *n* filologia *f*.
philosopher *n* filósofo,-a; ~**'s stone** *n* pedra *f* filosofal.
philosophical *adj* filosófico.
philosophy *n* filosofia *f*.
phimosis *n (MED)* fimose *f*.

phishing *n (COMP) (computing crime)* mistificação *f* da interface.
phiz *n (slang)* careta *f*, tromba *f*, fuça *f (cal)*.
phlegm *n* fleuma *f*.
phlegmatic *adj* fleumático.
phobia *n* fobia *f*.
phobic *adj* fóbico.
phon *n (PHYS)* fone *m*.
phone *(abbr for* **telephone**) *n* telefone *m*; ~ **book** *n* lista *f* telefónica; ~ **box** *n* cabine *f* telefónica; ~**card** *n* cartão *m* telefónico; ~ **jack** *n* ladrão *m* de (telefone) celular; **2** *(LING)* fone *m*; ♦ *vt* telefonar; **to be on the** ~ ter telefone; estar ao telefone; **to** ~ **back** *vt/vi* ligar de volta.
phoneme *n (LING)* fonema *m*.
phonetics *n* fonética *sg*.
phoney *n (person)* impostor,-ora; **2** *(thing)* falsificação *f*; ♦ *adj* falso,-a, fingido,-a.
phonolite *n (MIN) (petrology)* fonólito *m*.
phonology *n (LING)* fonologia *f*.
phoresy *n (ZOOL)* forésia *f*.
phosgene *n (CHEM)* fosgénio *m*.
phosphate *n* fosfato *m*.
phosphatize *vt* fosfatar.
phosphite *n (CHEM)* fosfito *m*.
phosphor *n (CHEM)* fósforo *m*.
phosphorous *adj* fosforoso.
photo *n* foto *f*; ~**biology** *n* fotobiologia *f*; ~**chemistry** *n* fotoquímica *f*; ~**composition** *n* fotocomposição *f*; ~**disintegration** *n (CHEM)* fotodesintegração *f*; ~**electron** *n* fotoelectrão; ~**emission** *n* fotoemissão *f*; ~**stat** *n* cópia *f* fotostática; ~**litography** *n* fotolitografia *f*; ~**map** *n* fotoplano *m*; ~**meter** *n (CHEM)* fotómetro *m*; ~**montage** *n* fotomontagem *f*; ~**neutron** *n (PHYS)* fotoneutrão *m*; ~**receptor** *n* foto-receptor *m*; ~**shoot** *n* sessão *f* de fotografias; ~**synthesis** *n (BOT)* fotossíntese *f*; ~**therapy** *n* fototerapia *f*.
photocopier *n (machine)* fotocopiadora *f*.
photocopy *n* fotocópia *f*; ♦ *vt* fotocopiar.
Photofit® *(UK)* retrato-robot *m*.
photogenic *adj* fotogénico *(BR:* -gê-*)*.
photograph *n (picture)* fotografia *f*.
photographer *n* fotógrafo,-a.
photographic *adj* fotográfico; **to have a** ~ **memory** ter uma memória visual excelente; ~ **library** *n* fototeca *f*.
photography *n (ART)* fotografia *f*; ♦ *vt* fotografar.
photon *n (PHYS)* fotão *m*; *(BR)* fóton *m*.
photo opportunity *n (POL)* (em que um politico é fotografado em lugar de vantagem) foto-oportunidade *f*.
photosensitive *adj* fotossensível *m,f*.
photosynthesis *n* fotossíntese.
photovoltaic cell *n* célula *f* fotovoltaica.
phrasal verb *n* combinação de um verbo e de uma preposição ou de um advérbio com um sentido único.
phrase *n (syntax)* sintagma *m*; **2** *(expression)* expressão *f*; **3** *(music)* frase *f*; ♦ *vt* expressar; **2** *(music)* frasear.
phrase book *n* manual *m* de conversação.
phraseology *n* fraseologia *f*.

phycology *n (BOT)* ficologia *f.*

phyllite *n (MIN)* filito *m.*

physical *adj* físico; ~ **chemistry** *n* físico-química *f;* ~ **education** *n* educação *f* física; ~ **examination** exame *m* médico ~ **handicap** *n* deficiência *f* física; ~ **training** *n* treino/treinamento *m* físico.

physicals *npl (FIN)* mercadorias *fpl* físicas.

physician *n* médico,-a.

physicist *n* físico,-a.

physics *n* física *sg.*

physio *prefix* fisio.

physiology *n* fisiologia *f.*

physionomy *n* fisionomia *f.*

physiotherapist *adj* fisioterapeuta *m,f.*

physiotherapy *n* fisioterapia *f.*

physique *n* físico *m.*

phytochemistry *n* fitoquímica *f.*

phytogenesis *n (BOT)* fitogenia *f.*

phytography *n* fitografia *f.*

phytology *n* botânica *f.*

pianist *n* pianista *m,f.*

piano *n* piano *m;* **grand** ~ piano *m* de cauda.

pic *n (slang)* foto *f.*

pick *n* (= ~-**axe**) picareta *f,* picão *m;* ♦ *vt (choose)* escolher; **2** *(collect)* colher; **3** *(force entry)* forçar; **take your** ~ escolha o que quiser; **the** ~ **of** o melhor de; **to** ~ **one's teeth** palitar os dentes; **to** ~ **pockets** roubar carteiras; **to** ~ **on** *vt* arreliar; **to** ~ **out** *vt* escolher; distinguir; ♦ **to** ~ **up** *vi (improve)* melhorar; **2** *vt (pick)* apanhar; **3** *(telephone)* atender; **4** *(buy)* comprar; **5** *(learn easily)* aprender com facilidade; **to** ~ **up speed** acelerar; **to** ~ **o.s. up** levantar-se.

picket *n* piquete *m;* ~ **fence** *n* vedação *f;* ~ **line** *n* fila *f* de grevistas, piquete *m;* ♦ *vt* formar piquete.

pickings *npl (coll)* lucros *mpl,* espólio *msg.*

pickle *n (US)* pepino conservado em vinagre; **2** *(UK)* molho escabeche *m;* vinagre *m;* **to be in a (pretty)** ~ *(in trouble)* estar metido,-a numa alhada; ~**s** *npl* pickles, conservas em vinagre; ♦ *vt* conservar em vinagre.

pick-me-up *n (coll)* tónico *(BR: tô-).*

pickpocket *n* carteirista *m,f, (BR)* batedor,-ora de carteira, trombadinha *m,f.*

pickup *n* gira-discos *m, (BR)* toca-discos *m inv;* **2** *(truck)* pick-up *m;* camioneta *f.*

picnic *n* piquenique *m,* merenda *f;* ♦ *vi* fazer um piquenique.

picrotoxin *n (CHEM)* picrotoxina *f.*

pictograph *n* pictograma *m.*

pictorial *adj* pictórico; ilustrado.

picture *n (representation)* quadro *m;* pintura *f;* figura *f,* gravura *f,* estampa *f;* **2** *(photo)* fotografia *f;* **3** *(film)* filme *m;* ~ **book** *n* livro *m* ilustrado; ~ **messaging** *n* mensagem *f* fotográfica, MMS *m;* ~ **phone** *n* telemóvel *m* com máquina fotográfica; **the** ~**s** o cinema *m;* ♦ *vt (paint)* pintar; **2** *(view)* visualizar; IDIOM **to get the** ~ compreender.

picturesque *adj* pitoresco.

piddle *vi (fam) (urinate)* urinar; fazer chichi; **2** ~ **away** *vt* passar o tempo sem fazer nada.

piddling *(coll) adj* insignificante *m,f.*

pidgin *adj (LING)* rudimentar; misturado,-a; estropiado,-a; **2** macarrónico,-a *(BR-ô-).*

pie *n (CULIN) (small pastries)* pastel *m,* pastelão *m;* **2** *(dessert)* tarte *f;* **3** *(savoury dish)* empadão.

piebald *adj* cavalo *m* malhado, com malhas pretas e brancas, sarapintado.

piece *n (bread, cheese)* bocado *m,* pedaço *m;* **2** *(part)* peça *f;* **a** ~ **of clothing** uma peça de roupa; **a** ~ **of furniture** um móvel *m;* **4** coin; ♦ **in one** ~ *(item)* intato; *(uninjured person)* são e salvo; ♦ *vt* **to** ~ **together** unir, juntar, reunir; *(TECH)* montar; **to take to** ~**s** desmontar; IDIOM **to give sb a** ~ **of one's mind** repreender alguém; **to go to** ~**s** *(person)* ir-se abaixo; **to fall to** ~**s** desfazer-se *(em bocados);* **it's a** ~ **of cake!** *(easy)* isso é canja!

> Quando um substantivo inglês não tem singular, usa-se **'a piece of'** para indicar o singular. Ex: **a piece of advice**; ou **"some"= some advice.**

piecemeal *n* aos bocados, pouco a pouco, gradualmente; ♦ *adj (attiude)* erratic; pouco sistemático,-a.

pier *n (landing area)* embarcadouro *m;* molhe *m; (where people walk)* paredão *m; (CONSTR) (in church, etc)* pillar; ~ **glass** *n (decoration)* tremó *m.*

pierce *vt (thrust)* penetrar; **2** *(barrier)* romper; **3** *(puncture)* furar; perfurar.

piercing *n (for jewellery in ear, etc)* piercing; ♦ *adj (look)* penetrante; **2** *(sound)* agudo; **3** *(sorrow)* pungente; **4** *(wind)* cortante.

piety *n* piedade *f.*

piezoelectricity *n* piezoelectricidade *f.*

piffling *adj* fútil *m,f;* disparatado.

pig *n (ZOOL)* porco *m;* **2** *(fig) (dirty person)* porcalhão,-ona; **3** *(fig) (big eater)* alarve *m,f;* **4** *(coll) (derogatory) (policeman)* chui *m,* bófia *f;* ~ **iron** *n (metallurgy)* gusa *f;* ♦ *vt* (= **to** ~ **out**) comer demasiado; ~ **it** *(coll) (fig)* chafurdar, viver na imundície; IDIOM **to make a** ~**'s ear out of sth** estragar, deixar algo feito num oito.

pigeon *n* pombo,-a; ~~-**hearted** *adj* temeroso, tímido; ~**hole** *n* escaninho *m.*

piggery *n* pocilga *f.*

piggyback *(also:* ~ **ride)** *n* cavalitas *fpl;* ♦ *adv* às cavalitas; **to ride/go** ~ andar às cavalitas.

piggy bank *n* mealheiro *m (in the shape of a pig).*

pigheaded *adj (pej)* teimoso,-a, cabeçudo,-a, casmurro,-a.

piglet *n* leitão *m.*

pigment *n* pigmento *m.*

pigmentation *n* pigmentação *f.*

pigmy (= **pygmy**) *n* pigmeu *m.*

pigsty *n* pocilga *f; (fig)* chiqueiro *m.*

pigtail *n;* rabicho *m,* rabo-de-cavalo *m.*

pike *n* pique *m;* estaca *f;* **2** *(fish)* lúcio *m.*

pikey *n (coll)* vagabundo,-a.

pilaster *n (CONSTR)* pilastra *f.*

Pilates *n* Pilatos; **2** *(physical exercise)* Pilates *m.*

pilchard *n (fish)* tipo de sardinha inglesa.

pile n (heap) pilha f, monte m; montão m; **2** (of carpet) pêlo; (of cloth) lado felpudo; **3** (money) pipa f de massa; **4** (PHYS) pilha f, reactor m; **5** (timber column) estaca f; ♦ (= **to** ~ **up**) vt amontoar; **2** (fig) acumular; ♦ vi amontoar-se.

piles npl (MED) (pop) hemorróidas fpl.

pile-up n (AUT) acidente m em cadeia, colisão f de diversos veículos.

pilfer vt furtar, afanar.

pilfering n furto m.

pilgrim n peregrino,-a.

pilgrimage n peregrinação f.

pill n (PHARM) pílula f; (tablet) comprimido m; (sweetened) drageia f; **2** (oral contraceptive) pílula f; contraceptiva; ~ **box** n caixa f de comprimidos; IDIOM **to sweeten the** ~ dourar a pílula.

pillage n pilhagem f, saque m; ♦ vt pilhar, saquear.

pillar n pilar m; coluna f; ~ **box** n marco de correio, (BR) caixa f coletora.

pillion n assento m traseiro (da motorizada); **to ride** ~ andar na garupa.

pillock n (coll) estúpido,-a, palerma m,f.

pillory (pl: -ies) n pelourinho m; **to be pilloried** ser ridicularizado,-a; ♦ vt expor ao ridículo.

pillow n almofada f; ~**case** n fronha f; ~ **fight** n luta f de almofadas; ~ **lava** n (GEOL) balões mpl de lava.

pilot n adj piloto m; ~ **balloon** n (METEOR) balão-sonda m; ~ **circuit** n (ELECT) circuito m piloto; ~**light/burner** n (gas) chama f piloto; ~ **project/ scheme** n proje(c)to-piloto.

pilotage n pilotagem f; ♦ vt pilotar; **2 to** ~ **sb towards sth** guiar algo para; (scheme) aplicar.

pimento (pl: -s) (BOT) pimento, pimentão m.

pimp n proxeneta m, chulo m, (BR) cafetão m; ♦ vt (= **to** ~ **up**) decorar de forma extravagante.

pimpernel n (BOT) anagálide f.

pimple n borbulha f, (BR) espinha f.

pimply adj (person) cheio,-a de borbulhas.

PIN[1] n (abbr for **Personal Identification Number**) PIN m; número m de identificação pessoal.

pin[2] n alfinete m; **2** (badge) crachá m; **3** (TECH) cavilha f; **hair** ~ n gancho m de cabelo; **rolling** ~ n rolo m de cozinha, (BR) pau m de macarrão; **safety** ~ n alfinete m de dama (BR: de segurança); ~ **cushion** n pregadeira, almofada f de alfinetes, (BR) alfineteira; ~ **money** n (fig) dinheiro m para os alfinetes; ~**s and needles** n sensação f de formigueiro (BR: formigamento); ♦ vt alfinetar; **to** ~ **down** prender, segurar; **2** (fig) pôr contra a parede; **to** ~ (**sth**) **on sb** (fig) culpar alguém de (alguma coisa).

pinafore n bata f; avental m.

pinaster n (BOT) pinheiro-bravo m.

pinball n flíper m, (BR) fliperama m.

pince-nez n (glasses) luneta fsg.

pincers npl (MEC) alicate msg; turquês fsg; **2** (for eyebrows; of crab) pinça fsg; (for coal) tenazes fpl.

pinch n beliscão m; **2** (CULIN) pitada f; ♦ vt beliscar; **2** (coll) furtar; ~ **bar** n (tool) pé-de-cabra m; ♦ vi apertar; estar em apuros; **to** ~ **and scrape**

economizar; **to** ~ **the bottom** dar um beliscão no rabo; ♦ **at a** ~ (UK) **in a** ~ (US) adv em último caso; IDIOM **to feel the** ~ (financial hardship) estar num aperto; **to take what he says with a** ~ **of salt** não tomar à letra o que ele diz dar o desconto.

pinchbeck n pechisbeque m.

pinched adj (shoe) apertado; **2** (person) (look) abatido,-a, com um ar abatido; ~ **features** feições fpl macilentas, chupadas.

pinchpenny n adj avarento,-a, sovina m,f.

pine n (= ~ **tree**) (tree) pinheiro m; **2** (wood) pinho m; ~ **cone** n pinha f; ~ **grove** n pinhal m; ~ **kernel** n pinhão m; ~ **needle** n agulha f do pinheiro; ~ **tar** n (CHEM) alcatrão m vegetal; ♦ vi: **to** ~ **for** ansiar por; **to** ~ **away** consumir-se, estar definhando.

pineapple n (fruit) ananás m, (BR) abacaxi m.

pinene n (CHEM) pineno m.

ping n silvo m, sibilo m; zumbido m; **2** (COMP) pacote m rastreador da Internet; ~-**pong** n pingue-pongue m.

pinguid adj gorduroso, untuoso.

pinion n extremidade f de asa; **2** (MEC) carreto m, roda dentada f; ♦ vt (bird) aparar (as asas); **2** (person) imobilizar, agarrar.

pinite (MIN) pinita f.

pink n cor-de-rosa; **2** (BOT) cravina f; **to be in the** ~ estar em boa saúde; ♦ adj cor-de-rosa; **2** (UK) (POL) (soft left) meio-esquerdista; **3** relativo a homosexuais; ♦ vt (with sword) perfurar, tocar; **2** picotar, ♦ ~-**collar profession** n (poorly paid work) profissão cor-de-rosa; ~**eye** n conjuntivite f aguda.

pinkie n (US, Scotland, Canada) dedo m mindinho.

pinnacle n cume m; **2** (fig) auge m.

pinnule n (ZOOL, BOT) pínula f.

pinpoint vt localizar com precisão.

pinstripe n (in suits) risca f; ~ **suit** n fato às riscas.

pint n (unit of measure) pinto (0.57 litros) m, quartilho m; IDIOM **to go for a** ~ ir tomar uma cerveja.

pintail n (ZOOL) (duck) arrabio m.

pintle n (MECH) pivô m.

pin-up n pin-up f; poster m de mulher atraente e nua.

pinwheel n (foguete) girândulo m; **2** (US) (brinquedo) vira-vento.

pinworm n (ZOOL) oxiúro m.

pioneer n pioneiro,-a; ♦ vi ser pioneiro.

pious adj piedoso, devoto.

pip n pevide f, caroço m, semente f; **2** (RADIO, TV) sinal m; **3** (bad temper) mau-humor m; ♦ (-**pp-**) vt derrotar, vencer; **2** (chirp) pipilar; **3** (mood) estar chateado; **4** (defeat) derrotar.

pipe n cano m, tubo m; **2** (smoking) cachimbo m; ~**s** canalização fsg; (= **bag** ~**s**) gaita fsg de foles; ~ **dream** n sonho m impossível, castelo no ar; ~ **line** n oleoduto m; **2** (gas) gaseoduto; **to be in the** ~ **line** (fig) em preparação, em curso.

piper n gaiteiro,-a; flautista; ♦ vt canalizar; **2** (play) tocar a gaita de foles; **to** ~ **down** vi (coll) calar o bico, meter a viola no saco; **to** ~ **up** vi (voice) fazer-se ouvir, dizer o que tem a dizer; IDIOM

put that in your ~ and smoke it! toma e embrulha!

pipette *n (glass tube)* pipeta *f.*

piping *n (sound)* som *m* de gaita de foles; **2** *(conduit)* cano *m,* conduta *f;* **3** *(system)* canalização *f;* **4** *(sewing)* enfeite *m,* debrum *m;* **5** *(CULIN)* decoração *f* de açúcar; ♦ *adv:* ~ **hot** a escaldar, a ferver.

pipit *m (ZOOL)* petinha *f.*

pipsqueak *n (coll)* pessoa *f* desprezível, zé-ninguém *m.*

piquant *adj* picante *m,f,* intenso.

pique *n* ressentimento *m,* melindre *m.*

piqué *n (fabric)* piqué *m.*

piracy *n* pirataria *f;* *(of tapes, etc)* reprodução *f* pirata.

piranha *n (fish)* piranha *f.*

pirate *n* pirata *m;* ~ **ship** barco de piratas; ~ **copy** *(tape, film etc)* versão pirata.

pirouette *n* pirueta *f;* ♦ *vi* fazer piruetas.

piscary *n* pesca *f;* **common of** ~ *n* direito *m* de pesca.

piscatorial *adj* piscatório,-a.

Pisces *n (ASTROL)* Peixes *mpl.*

piss *vi (coll) (urinate)* mijar *(cal);* **2** *(rain)* chover; ♦ **to** ~ **about/around** *vi (coll)* desperdiçar tempo; ♦ **to** ~ **off** *(coll) vt* chatear *(fam);* **I am** ~**ed off** estou cheteado,-a, irritado,-a; **to take the** ~ **out of** *(coll)* gozar com; IDIOM ~ **off!** *(coll)* deixa-me em paz!; **to be on the** ~ andar na bebedeira.

pissed *adj (coll)* bêbado; **2** *(US)* chateado, zangado.

pisshead *n (coll)* bebedolas *msg.*

pistachio *n* pistácio *m.*

pistol *n* pistola *f.*

piston *n* pistão *m,* êmbolo *m;* ~ **engine** *n (MECH)* motor *m* a pistão; ~ **rod** *n* biela *f;* ~ **valve** *n* válvula *f* de êmbolo.

pit *n (hole)* cova *f,* fossa *f;* **2** *(mine)* (= **coal** ~) mina *f* de carvão; **3** *(MECH)* poço *m* de inspe(c)ção; **4** (= **orchestra** ~) fosso *m;* **5** canteira *f,* pedreira *f;* **6** *(US) (of a fruit)* pevide *f,* caroço *m;* ~ **of the stomach** boca do estômago; ~**s** *npl (AUT)* box *m;* ♦ (-**tt**-) *vt:* **to** ~ **A against B** opor A a B, enfrentar alguém.

pitch *n (throw)* arremesso *m,* lance *m;* **2** *(MUS)* tom *m;* **3** *(SPORT)* campo *m;* **4** piche *m,* breu *m;* ~-**black**/-**dark** escuro como breu; **5** barraca *f,* sítio *m* para a barraca; **6 highest** ~ cume *m,* pináculo *m;* **7** ~ **note** *(MUS)* nota *f* tónica; ♦ *vt* arremessar, lançar ♦ *vi* tombar, cair; **2** *(NAUT)* jogar, arfar; **to** ~ **a ladder against the wall** encostar o escadote à parede; **to** ~ **in** *vi* meter mãos à obra; **to** ~ **a tent** armar uma tenda; IDIOM **to queer someone's** ~ atrapalhar alguém/os planos de alguém.

pitcher *n (container)* jarro *m,* cântaro *m,* bilha *f;* **2** *(baseball)* arremessador *m.*

pitchfork *n* forcado *m.*

piteous *adj* lastimável *m,f;* comovente *m,f.*

pitfall *n* perigo (imprevisto) *m,* armadilha *f.*

pith *n (fruit)* casca *f* interna e branca; **2** *(fig) (core)* essência *f,* âmago *m;* **3** *(planta)* medula *f.*

pithead *n* boca *f* da mina.

pithy (-thier, -thiest) *adj* conciso,-a; cheio,-a de significado

pitiable *adj* deplorável *m,f;* lastimoso,-a.

pitiful *adj* comovente *m,f;* **2** *(situation)* deplorável *m,f;* **3** *(of contempt) (person)* desprezível *m,f.*

pitiless *adj* impiedoso,-a.

pitman *n* mineiro *m.*

piton *n (mountaineering)* pitão *m.*

pittance *n (money)* ninharia *f,* miséria *f.*

pituitary *adj (ANAT)* pituitário; ~ **gland** *n* glândula *f* pituitária.

pity *n (compassion)* compaixão *f,* piedade *f;* **2** *(feel sorry for)* pena *f;* ♦ *vt* ter pena de, compadecer-se de; ♦ *exc* **what a ~!** que pena!

pityriasis *n (MED)* pitiríase *f.*

pivot *n (pin)* pino *m,* eixo *m;* **2** *(fig)* pivô *m;* ♦ *vi:* **to** ~ **on** girar sobre; *(fig)* depender de.

pivotal *adj* giratório; principal.

pix *npl (fam)* photos.

pixel *n (COMP)* pixel *m.*

pixie *n* duende *m.*

pixilated *adj (US)* excêntrico; **2** *(coll) (drunk)* bêbado.

pizzazz *n (fam) (energy and style)* vitalidade, atra(c)ção, glamour *m.*

pl *(abbr for* **plural***).*

placard *n* letreiro *m,* *(BR)* placar *m;* cartaz *m.*

placate *vt* apaziguar, aplacar.

place *n (area)* lugar *m,* sítio *m;* **2** *(position)* posição *f;* **3** *(seat)* assento *m,* lugar *m;* **4** *(duty)* posto; **at/ to her** ~ em/para a casa dela; ♦ *vt* pôr, colocar; **2** *(identify)* identificar, situar; colocar; **to take** ~ realizar-se, ocorrer; **to be** ~**d** classificar-se; **to take someone's** ~ substituir, tirar o lugar a alguém; **out of** ~ fora de lugar; IDIOM **to go** ~**s** ir longe, ser bem-sucedido; **to know one's** ~ saber o seu lugar.

placebo *n (MED)* placebo *m.*

placement *n (trainee post)* colocação *f.*

place name *n* topónimo, nome *m* da localidade.

placenta *n (ANAT)* placenta *f.*

placid *adj* plácido, sereno.

placing *n (FIN)* colocação *f* de títulos.

plagiarism *n* plágio *m.*

plagiarize *vt* plagiar.

plague *n* praga *f;* flagelo *m;* **2** *(MED)* peste *f;* ♦ *vt (fig)* atormentar, importunar; **to** ~ **sb** amofinar alguém.

plaice *n (fish)* solha *f.*

plaid *n* tecido enxadrezado; xadrez *m* escocês.

plain *n* planície *f;* campina *f;* ♦ *adj (clear)* claro, evidente *m,f;* **2** *(uncomplicated)* simples *m,f,* despretensioso; **3** *(straightforward)* franco, sem rodeios; puro, natural *m,f;* ~ **flour** *n* farinha *f* sem fermento; ~-**spoken** *adj* franco; simples; **in** ~ **clothes** à paisana; ♦ *adv* claramente, com franqueza.

plainly *adv* claramente, obviamente; francamente.

plainness *n* clareza *f;* simplicidade *f;* franqueza *f.*

plaint *n* acusação *f,* queixa *f.*

plaintiff *n* queixoso,-a.

plait *n* trança *f,* dobra *f;* ♦ *vt* trançar.

plan *n* plano *m;* esquema *m;* **2** *(drawing)* proje(c)to *m,* **3** programa *m;* ♦ (-**nn**-) *vt* proje(c)tar; planear;

(BR) planejar; programar; ~ **out** traçar; ♦ *vi* fazer planos; **to** ~ **to do** tencionar fazer, propor-se fazer.

planation *n (levelling of soil)* aplanação *f.*

plane *n (AER)* avião *m;* **2** *(BOT)* plátano *m;* **3** *(tool)* plaina *f;* **4** *(MATH)* plano *m;* ♦ *adj* plano, liso.

planet *n* planeta *m.*

planetarium *n* planetário *m.*

planetary *adj* planetário,-a.

plane tree *n (BOT)* plátano *m.*

plangent *adj* ressonante *m,f;* lastimoso,-a.

planisphere *n* planisfério *m.*

plank *n* prancha *f,* *(flat piece of wood)* tábua *f;* **2** *(fig) (POL)* item *m* da plataforma política, cavalo *m* de batalha.

plankton *n (BIO)* plâncton *m.*

planner *n (drawings)* proje(c)tista *m,f;* **2** planeador,-ora.

planning *n (EP)* planeamento *m; (BR)* planejamento *m;* **family** ~ planeamento familiar; **2** *(ECON)* planificação *f.*

plant *n (vegetable)* planta *f;* **2** *(machinery)* maquinaria *f;* **3** *(factory)* fábrica *f;* ♦ *vt* plantar; semear; colocar, pôr às escondidas.

plantation *n* plantação *f, (BR)* roça *f;* fazenda *f.*

planter *n (machine)* semeador *m,* plantador *m;* **2** *(person)* proprietário,-a de plantação.

plaque *n (flat object)* placa *f,* **2** *(badge)* insígnia *f;* **3** *(MED)* placa *f.*

plashy *adj* alagado, pantanoso.

plasma *n* plasma *m;* ~ **engine** *n* motor *m* de plasma; ~ **screen** *n* ecrã *m* plasma.

plasmology *n* plasmologia *f.*

plaster *n* gesso; **2** reboco, estuque *m;* **2** (= **sticking** ~) *(dressing for a wound)* adesivo *m,* esparadrapo *m,* band-aid *m;* ~**board** *n* gesso cartonado; ~ **cast** *(MED)* gesso; ~ **of Paris** *n* gesso *m* fino; **3** *(ART)* moldagem *f;* ♦ *vt* rebocar; **to** ~ **with** encher, cobrir de.

plastered *adj* rebocado,-a, estucado,-a; **2** *(drunk)* bêbado,-a; **to get** ~ apanhar uma carraspana.

plastic *n* plástico *m;* ♦ *adj* de plástico; **2** *(fig)* superficial *m,f;* **3** *(ART)* plástica; **4** *(character)* maleável; ~ **bullet** bala *f* de borracha; ~ **money** *n* cartões *mpl* de crédito; ~ **surgery** *n* cirurgia, operação *f* plástica; ~ **wrap** *n (US)* película *f* aderente.

Plasticine® (UK) **Play-Doh**® (US) *n* plasticina *f,* massa *f* para modelar.

plate *n* prato *m;* **2** *(flat object)* folha *f,* placa *f;* **3** chapa *f;* fotográfica; **4** *(for straightening teeth)* placa *f;* **5** *(glass)* laminado; IDIOM **on a** ~ de bandeja; **to have a lot on one's** ~ estar muito ocupado, estar cheio de trabalho.

plateau *(pl: -s or -x) n (GEOG)* planalto *m;* **2** *(fig)* patamar *m;* **3** *(levelling off)* nivelamento *m; (ECON)* período de estabilidade; ~ **effect** *n (POL)* efeito *m* de planalto/de longo período de estabilidade.

plated *adj* chapeado, banhado; **gold** ~ dourado; **silver** ~ com banho de prata.

plateful *n* pratada *f.*

platelet *n (BIO)* plaqueta *f.*

platen *n (MECH)* prato *m* de prensa.

plate-rack *n* escorregador *m* de pratos.

platform *n (railways)* cais *m;* linha *f; (BR)* plataforma *f;* **2** *(raised surface)* estrado *m;* **3** *(pulpit)* tribuna *f,* **4** *(POL)* programa *m* partidário; **5** *(COMP)* plataforma *f.*

platinum *n* platina *f.*

platitude *n* banalidade *f;* lugar-comum *m.*

Plato *npr* Platão *m.*

platoon *n* pelotão *m.*

platter *n (serving dish)* travessa *f.*

plausible *adj (possible)* plausível *m,f,* aceítável *m,f;* **2** *(convincing)* convincente *m,f.*

plausive *adj* louvável *m,f.*

play *n (game)* jogo *m;* **2** (= ~ **time**) *(break)* recreio *m;* **3** *(THEAT)* obra *f,* peça *f;* ~ **on words** *n* trocadilho *m;* ~-**acting** *n* teatro *m;* ~ **wright** *n* dramaturgo,-a; ♦ *vt (game)* jogar; **2** *(instrument)* tocar; **3** *(pretend)* fingir; **4** *(THEAT)* representar; (= ~ **the role**) fazer to papel de; **5** *(fig)* desempenhar; ♦ *vi* jogar; **2** divertir-se; brincar; **to** ~ **along (with)** *vi* cooperar (com); **to** ~ **at** *vt* brincar de; **to** ~ **down** *vt* ligar, dar pouca importância a; **to** ~ **fair** fazer jogo limpo; **to** ~ **up** *vt* importunar, incomodar; **to** ~ **up to** *vt* encorajar; lisonjear; IDIOM **to** ~ **for time** ganhar tempo; **to** ~ **hard to get** fazer-se de difícil; **to** ~ **into the hands of someone** cair na esparrela (de alguém); **to** ~ **the fool** fazer figura de parvo; **to** ~ **with fire** brincar com o fogo.

playboy *n* playboy *m.*

Play-Doh® *(US) (Vd:* **Plasticine**®).

player *n* jogador,-ora; **2** *(THEAT)* a(c)tor *m,* a(c)triz *f;* **3** *(MUS)* músico,-a.

playful *adj* brincalhão,-ona.

playground *n* pátio *m* de recreio.

playgroup infantário *m.*

playing card *n* carta *f* de baralho.

playing field *n* campo *m* de jogos *(BR:* esportes).

playmate *n* companheiro *m* de brincadeira.

play-off *n (SPORT)* partida *f* de desempate.

playroom *n* quarto *m* de brinquedos.

plaything *n (person)* joguete *m.*

plaza *n* praça *f;* **2** *(US) (shopping centre)* centro *m* comercial.

plea *n (request)* apelo *m,* petição *f;* **2** *(motive)* justificativa *f,* pretexto *m;* **3** *(JUR)* defesa *f.*

plead *(-ed or pled) vt (JUR)* defender, advogar; pleitear; alegar *(insanity);* argumentar; ♦ *vi (JUR)* declarar-se; **to** ~ **guilty** confessar-se culpado,-a; **to** ~ **not guilty** negar a acusação; **2** *(beg)* rogar, implorar; **to** ~ **with sb** implorar, suplicar a alguém.

pleadings *n (JUR)* actos *mpl* processuais.

pleasant *adj* agradável *m,f;* simpático.

pleasantness *n* amabilidade *f,* simpatia *f;* encanto *f.*

pleasantries *npl* amabilidades *fpl;* cumprimentos *mpl.*

please *vt* agradar, dar prazer a; **do as you** ~ faça como quiser; ~! faça favor, por favor!; ~**d to meet you** muito prazer em conhecê-lo,-a.

pleased *adj* satisfeito, contente *m,f.*

pleasing *adj* agradável.

pleasure *n* prazer *m;* deleite *m;* ~ **trip** *n* viagem *f* de recreio; **it's a** ~ é um prazer, o prazer é todo meu!

pleat n (sewing) prega f.

plebby adj (fam) rasca m,f.

plebeian n plebeu, eia.

plebiscite n (vote) plebiscito m.

plebs npl (pej) plebe fsg; gentalha f.

pledge n (collateral) garantia m, penhor m; 2 (promise) promessa f, voto m; ♦ vt prometer (to a); comprometer-se (to do sth a fazer algo); to ~ one's own word dar a sua palavra de honra.

pledget n (MED) compressa f.

plenary n,adj plenário,-a; 2 pleno,-a.

plenitude n plenitude f.

plenteous adj abundante m,f

plentiful adj abundante, copioso; muitos,-as.

plenty n abundância f; fartura f; ~ of muito; in ~ em abundância.

pleonasm n (LITER) pleonasmo m.

plethora n superabundância f.

pleura n (ANAT) pleura f.

pleurisy n (MED) pleurisia f.

plexus n (ANAT) plexo m.

pliable adj flexível m,f; maleável m,f; 2 (fig) adaptável m,f, influenciável m,f.

pliant adj (body) flexível; 2 maleável; 3 influenciável.

plication n plicado m.

pliers n alicate m; a pair of ~ um alicate.

plight n situação f difícil; in a ~ em apuros.

plimsolls npl ténis (BR -ê-) mpl; calçado sg de lona.

plinth n (ARCH) plinto m.

plissé n (sewing) plissado m.

plod n marcha f lenta e difícil; labuta f, canseira f; ♦ (pt, pp, pres p -dd-) vi (= ~ along) caminhar a custo, vagarosamente; trabalhar laboriosamente, labutar.

plodder n (coll) marrão,-rona, labutador-ora.

plonk[1] n (coll) (wine) vinho m ordinário, zurrapa.

plonk[2] n (sound) baque; ♦ vt to ~ down (hands, body) deixar(-se); cair (pesadamente).

plonker n (coll) parvo,-a, idiota m,f.

plop n (onomat) (water) chape.

plot n (plan) trama f, conspiração f; intriga, (BR) complô m; 2 (storyline) enredo; 3 (land) lote m de terreno; (of plants) canteiro de plantas; ♦ (-tt-) vt traçar; 2 (conspiracy) tramar, plane(j)ar; ♦ (pt, pp, pres p -tt-) vi conspirar; IDIOM to lose the ~ perder o fio à meada; the ~ thickens a história adensa-se.

plotter n conspirador,-ora.

plough n arado m, charrua m; ♦ vt (AGR) arar; to ~ back vt (COMM) reinvestir; to ~ on prosseguir; ~ through vt abrir caminho por.

ploughman n lavrador,-ora; ~'s lunch n almoço ligeiro de pão, queijo, cebola e picles.

ploughshare, plowshare n relha f de arado.

plover n (ZOOL) tarambola f.

ploy n estratagema f; artimanha f.

pluck n coragem f, puxão m; ♦ vt (pick) colher; 2 (play strings) dedilhar; 3 (take feathers) depenar; to ~ up courage reunir coragem; IDIOM to ~ (sth) out of the air inventar.

plucky adj corajoso,-a, valente m,f.

plug n (stopper) tampão m; 2 (ELEC) tomada, ficha; 3 (notice) anúncio; 4 (AUT) (= spark ~) vela (de ignição); ♦ (-gg-) vt tapar; (coll) fazer propaganda de; to ~ in (ELECT) ligar; IDIOM to pull the ~ on sb/sth cancelar algo.

plughole n (in bath, basin) ralo m.

plum n (fruit) ameixa f; ~ tree n (BOT) ameixoeira f; ♦ adj (coll) vantajoso.

plumage n plumagem f.

plumb n: ~line fio m de prumo; (NAUT) chumbo m de sonda náutica; ♦ adv precisamente; (US) totalmente; ~ stupid totalmente idiota; ♦ vt sondar; ir ao fundo de; to ~ the depths of penetrar no âmago de.

plumbago n (planta) plumbagem; 2 (MIN) plumbagina f.

plumber n canalizador m, (BR) encanador m.

plumbing n canalização f, (BR) encanamento f.

plume n pluma f; penacho m.

plummet vi: to ~ (down) cair verticalmente (plano), cair a pique.

plump adj roliço, rechonchudo; ♦ vt: to ~ for (coll) optar por.

plumule n (BOT) plúmula f.

plunder n saque m, pilhagem f; despojo m; ♦ vt pilhar, espoliar; saquear.

plunge n salto m; mergulho m; imersão f, banho m; ~-board n prancha de saltos; ♦ vt mergulhar, afundar; ♦ vi cair; mergulhar; lançar-se; afundar-se; IDIOM to take the ~ atirar-se de cabeça, decidir-se, arrojar-se.

plunger n desentupidor.

plunging adj mergulhante; ~ neckline decotado.

pluperfect n (gram) mais-que-perfeito.

plural n plural m.

plurality n pluralidade f.

plus n (= ~ sign) sinal m de adição; ♦ prep mais, extra, e; ten ~ dez e tantos; 2 ~ 4 dois mais/e quatro.

plush n felpa f; ♦ adj de pelúcia; 2 luxuoso,-a.

plutocracy n plutocracia f.

plutonium n (CHEM) plutónio m.

pluvial adj pluvial m,f.

ply n camada f; expessura f; three-~ (wool) (lã) de três fios; ♦ (pt, pp plied) vt exercer; ♦ vi ir e vir; oferecer-se para alugar; to ~ sb with food insistir para que alguém coma; to ~ sb with questions bombardear alguém com perguntas.

plywood n (CONSTR) contraplacado m (de madeira); (BR) madeira f compensada.

PM n (abbr for Prime Minister) Primeiro Ministro.

pm adv (abbr for post meridiem) da tarde, da noite.

PMT (abbr for pre-menstural tension) TPM m.

pneumatic adj pneumático; ~ drill n broca f pneumática.

pneumatics nsg (PHYS) pneumática fsg.

pneumatology n (REL) pneumatologia f.

pneumonia n pneumonia f.

P.O.= Post Office estação dos correios.

poach vt (cooking) escalfar; 2 (stealing) furtar; ♦ vi caçar, pescar em propriedade alheia.

poached adj (egg) escalfado.

poacher *n* caçador *m* furtivo.
poaching *n* caça *f* furtiva.
PO Box *n* caixa *f* postal.
pochard *n* (ZOOL) zarro *m*.
pocket *n* bolso *m*, algibeira *f*; **2** *(billiards)* ventana *f*, ventanilha *f*; **3** *(GEO)* **air** ~ poço *m* de ar; **4** *(in gums)* cavidade; ♦ *adj* de bolso; portátil; ~ **book** *n* *(US)* carteira; livro de bolso; ~**knife** *n* canivete *m*; ~ **money** *n* *(per month)* mesada; ♦ *vt* embolsar, meter no bolso; apropriar-se de; IDIOM **to be/ live in each other's ~s** *(coll)* ser inseparáveis; **to be out of** ~ estar sem dinheiro; **to be in (someone's)** ~ ter (alguém) na palma da mão; dominar alguém; **to dip into one's** ~ puxar os cordões à bolsa; **to line one's ~s** encher os bolsos (de dinheiro).
pod *n* (BOT) *(pea, bean)* vagem *f*; *(empty pod)* vagem; **vanilla** ~ vagem de baunilha.
podcast *n* (TECH) podcast *m*.
poddle *vi* *(coll)* andar nas calmas.
podgy *adj* *(coll)* *(person)* atarracado,-a; rechonchudo,-a; *(substance)* mole.
podiatry *n* quiropodia *f*.
podium *n* pódio, estrado.
poem *n* poema *m*.
poet *n* poeta *m,f*.
poetess *n* poetisa *f*.
poetic, poetical *adj* poético,-a; ♦ ~ **justice** *n* justiça justa.
poet laureate *n* poeta laureado.
poetry *n* poesia *f*.
pogo-stick *n* pula-pula *m*.
pogrom *n* massacre *m* organizado.
poignancy *n* comoção *f*; pungência *f*.
poignant *adj* comovente *m,f* pungente *m,f*; **2** *(piercing)* agudo.
point *n* *(small mark)* ponto *m*; **2** *(sharp end)* ponta *f*; **3** *(objective)* finalidade *f*, obje(c)tivo *m*; **4** *(idea)* relevância *f*; **5** *(characteristic)* característica *f*; **at that** ~ naquele momento, naquele lugar; **beside the** ~ irrelevante, fora da questão; ~ **blank** *adj adv* dire-(c)to, categórico; **at** ~ **blank** à queima-roupa; **to have a** ~ ter razão; **to miss the** ~ não compreender; **sore** ~ questão *f* delicada, dolorosa; ~ **of view** ponto de vista; **to the** ~ pertinente; **up to a** ~ até certo ponto; ♦ *vt* mostrar, indicar; **to** ~ **at** apontar para; ♦ *vi* indicar com o dedo; *(CONSTR)* encher as juntas; **to** ~ **out** *vt* mostrar, realçar; **to** ~ **to** indicar com o dedo; *(fig)* indicar; **to** ~ **the way** mostrar o caminho; IDIOM **to make a** ~ **of** fazer questão de, insistir em; **to get the** ~ compreender; **to come to the** ~ ir ao que interessa, falar sem rodeios; **there's no** ~ **(in doing)** não adianta nada (fazer); **to** ~ **the finger at (somebody)** apontar o dedo a (alguém), acusar.
pointed *adj* pontiagudo,-a, bicudo,-a; aguçado,-a; *(comment)* mordaz *m,f*; penetrante, intencional *m,f*.
pointedly *adv* intencionalmente.
pointer *n* indicador *m*; *(for teaching)* ponteiro *m*; **2** *(piece of information)* indicação; *(tip)* dica *f*; **3** *(dog)* pointer, perdigueiro; *(on screen)* seta *f*.
pointing *n* (CONSTR) enchimento *m* das juntas.

pointless *adj* inútil *m,f*, sem sentido.
points *npl* *(AUT)* platinado *m*; conta(c)to *msg*; *(RAIL)* *npl* agulhas *fpl*.
poise *n* *(composure)* porte *m*, compostura *f*; **2** *(aplomb)* sangue-frio *m*.
poised *adj* *(calm)* equilibrado,-a; **2** preparado,-a; **to be** ~ **for sth** estar pronto para.
poison *n* veneno *m*; ~-**pen letter** *n* carta *f* anónima; ♦ *vt* envenenar.
poisoning *n* envenenamento.
poisonous *adj* venenoso; tóxico; *(fig)* pernicioso.
poke *n* remexida *f*; empurrão *m*; cotovelada *f*; ♦ *vt* atiçar; espetar; **to** ~ **about** *vi* escarafunchar, espiolhar; **to** ~ **fun at** zombar de; **to** ~ **in(to)** meter em; **to** ~ **one's nose into** meter o nariz em.
poker *n* atiçador *m*; **2** *(cards)* póquer *(BR:* pô-*)* *m*; ~-**faced** *adj* (com) rosto impassível, cara de pau.
poky (-**ier**, -**iest**) *adj* acanhado, apertado; **2** *(slow)* lento, frouxo.
Poland *npr* Polónia *(BR:* -lô-*)* *f*; **in** ~ na Polónia.
polar *adj* polar *m,f*; ~ **axis** *n* eixo *m* polar; ~ **bear** *(ZOOL)* urso *m* polar; ~ **front** *n* *(METEOR)* frente *f* polar.
polarity *n* *(ELECT, PHYS)* polaridade *f*; *(fig)* oposição *f*.
polarization *n* *(PHYS)* polarização *f*; **2** *(fig)* *(split)* divergência *f*.
polarize *vt* polarizar; **2** dividir *(opinion)*; desviar-se de.
pole¹ *n* vara *f*; pau *m*, viga *f*; ~ **vault** *n* *(SPORT)* salto *m* com vara, salto à vista; **2** *(GEOG)* pólo *m*; **the** ~ **star** a Estrela *f* Polar; **3** *(TEL)* poste *m*; mastro *m*; estaca *f*; IDIOM **to be up the** ~ ser maluco; **to be** ~**s apart** ser muito diferente.
Pole² *n* polaco,-a; *(BR)* polonês,-esa.
poleaxe *vt* nocautear.
polecat *n* *(ZOOL)* *(ferret)* furão *m* bravo; *(BR)* brabo *m*; *(skunk)* *(US)* gambá *(BR)*.
polemic *n* polémica *f*.
polemical *adj* polémico,-a *(BR* -ê-*)*, controverso,-a.
polenta *n* *(CULIN)* polenta *f*; creme *m* de sêmola de milho.
police *n* polícia *f*; ~ **car** *n* radiopatrulha *m*; ~**man** *n* polícia *m*, guarda *m*; ~ **officer** agente *m,f* da polícia; ~ **state** *n* estado *m* policial, totalitário; ~ **station** *n* esquadra *f*, *(BR)* delegacia *f* (de polícia); ♦ *vt* policiar.
policy *n* *(orientação)* política *f*; (= **insurance** ~) apólice *f*; ~-**holder** *n* segurado,-a.
polio *n* poliomielite *f*, pólio *f*, paralisia *f* infantil.
Polish¹ *n adj* polaco,-a, *(BR)* polonês,-esa.
polish² *n* *(wax)* graxa *f*; cera *f*; **2** *(varnish)* verniz *m*; **3** *(shine)* polimento *m*; **4** *(style)* refinamento *m*, cultura *f*; ♦ *vt* engraxar; encerar; lustrar, dar brilho a; **2** *(refine)* refinar, polir; **to** ~ **off** *vt* dar os arremates a.
polished *adj* culto; refinado.
polite *adj* gentil *m,f*, bem-educado; cortês *m,f*.
politeness *n* gentileza, cortesia.
politic *adj* prudente *m,f*.
political *adj* politico,-a; ~ **economy** *n* economia *f* política; ~ **science** *n* ciência *f* política.
politically correct politicamente correcto *m*.

politician n político m.

politicize vt politizar.

politics npl política sg.

polka n (dance) polca f; ~ **dot** n pinta f.

poll n votação f; **opinion** ~ (survey) sondagem f pública; ~ **tax** n (dated) imposto m de habitação per capita; ◆ **polls** npl urnas fpl; **to go the ~s** ir a votos; ◆ vt receber, obter.

pollard n (of animal) com hastes, chifres tirados; **2** (top of tree) árvore de copas cortadas, árvore decotada; ◆ vt cortar, talhar, decotar (árvore).

pollen n pólen m; ~ **count** n contagem de pólen.

pollination n polinização f.

polling n votação; eleição; ~ **booth** n cabine f de votar; ~ **day** n dia m de eleição; ~ **station** n centro m eleitoral.

pollster n especialista m que dirige a sondagem pública.

pollute vt poluir.

pollution n poluição f, contaminação f.

polo n (SPORT) pólo m; ~ **shirt** n (clothing) pólo m; ~**-neck** adj de gola alta (BR: rolê).

polonium n (CHEM) polónio m.

poltergeist n espírito m.

poltroon n cobarde m, poltrão m.

polyandry n poliandria f.

polyarchy n poliarquia f.

polychrome adj policromo.

polyclinic n policlínica f.

polyester n polyester m, (BR) poliéster m.

polygamy n poligamia f.

polyglot adj poliglota m,f.

polygon n (GEOM) polígono m.

polygraph n polígrafo m.

polymath n polímato m.

polyp n pólipo m.

polyphase adj (ELECT) polifásico.

polyphony n polifonia f.

polysemy n (LING) polissemia f.

polytechnic n politécnico m, escola f politécnica.

polytheism n (REL) politeísmo m.

polythene n (CHEM) politeno m, polietileno m.

polyunsaturated adj polinsaturado.

polyvalent adj polivalente m,f.

pomace n pasta f, polpa f.

pomade n pomada f; **2** (hair) brilhantina f.

pomegranate n romã f; ~ **tree** n romãzeira.

pommel n botão m do punho da espada; maçaneta f; ◆ vt esmurrar.

pomology n pomologia f.

pomp n pompa f.

pompom n pompom m.

pompous adj pomposo, ostentoso.

ponce n (coll) (pej) maricas msg; **2** (pimp) chulo.

pond n lago m pequeno; tanque m.

ponder vt ponderar, meditar (sobre).

ponderous adj (book, discourse) pesado,-a.

pong n (UK) (coll) (smell) pivete m, fedor m, cheirete m.

pongo n (ZOOL) pongo m.

poniard n punhal m.

pontiff n pontífice m; **Supreme P~** Sumo Pontífice.

pontificate vi: **to ~** (**about**) (fig) pontificar (sobre).

pontoon n pontão m; **2** (cards) vinte-e-um m.

pony n pónei (BR: pô-) m; ~**tail** n rabo m de cavalo m; ~ **trekking** n excursão f em pónei.

pooch n (coll) cão m.

poodle n caniche m, poodle m.

poof n (coll) (pej) maricas msg; (BR) veado.

poo(h) exc (an expression of disdain) ora bolas!; (smell) que cheirete!; **2** n (child's language for faeces) **to do a ~** fazer cocó.

pooh-pooh vt desdenhar, rebaixar.

pool n poça f, charco m; lago m; **2** (swimming ~) piscina f; **3** (game) pool m; **a ~ of blood** um mar de sangue; (of employees) grupo m; ◆ vt reunir; (football) ~**s** totobola m, (BR) loteria f esportiva.

poop n (NAUT) popa f; **2** (child's language for faeces) cocó m.

pooped adj esgotado,-a; exausto,-a.

poor adj pobre m,f; **2** inferior m,f; **3** (small amount) fraco; escasso; **4** (bad) mau; **the ~** npl os pobres mpl; ~ **relation** n primo,-a pobre.

poorly adj indisposto, doente.

pop n (sound) ruído m seco; estalo m; estouro m; **2** (MUS) pop m; **3** (drink) bebida f gasosa; **4** (coll) (father) pai m; ~**corn** n pipoca f; ◆ vt pôr; ◆ (-**ped**, -**ing**) vi (burst) estourar; estalar, saltar; **2** (spring, etc) saltar-se desprender-se; **3** (eyes) arregalar; **4** (balloon, bubble) repentar; ◆ **to ~ along** prestes a chegar, partir; **the doctor will be popping along** o médico já aí vem; **to ~ in** vi (brief visit) dar um salto; **to ~ in(to)** meter em; ◆ **to ~ off** (leave) partir de repente; **2** (die) morrer; ◆ **to ~ out** sair por uns minutos; **to ~ upstairs** dar um salto lá em cima; IDIOM **to ~ the question** propor casamento; **to ~ one's clogs** bater as botas (morrer).

pope n Papa m.

popinjay n (fig) fala-barato; **2** (conceited) presumido,-a.

poplar n álamo m, choupo m.

poplin n (clothing) popeline f.

poppet n (UK) (addressing baby/child affectionately) pequerrucho,-a.

poppy (pl: -**ies**) n papoula f; **P~ Day** n Dia m do Armistício.

> Poppy Day ou Remembrance Day celebra-se no segundo domingo de novembro por todo o Reino Unido e os britânicos têm uma papoula de papel nas lapelas, em memória dos soldados que pereceram nas duas guerras mundiais.

poppyhead n papoula de papel.

populace n populaça f, **2** (coll) o Zé Povinho.

popular adj popular m,f; na moda.

popularity n popularidade f.

popularize vt popularizar; vulgarizar.

populate vt povoar.

population n população f.

Populist n adj populista.

populous adj populoso.

pop-up n: ~ **toaster** n torradeira automática (sistema de ejeção); **2** (book, greeting card) com ilustrações tridimensionais.

porcelain *n* porcelana *f.*

porch *n* pórtico *m*; entrada *f*; *(US)* alpendre *m.*

porcupine *n (ZOOL)* porco-espinho *m*, ouriço-do-mar *m.*

pore *n (ANAT)* poro *m*; ♦ *vi*: **to ~ over** examinar com atenção, esquadrinhar.

porgy *n (ZOOL)* pargo *m.*

pork *n* carne *f* de porco; **~ pie** *n* empada *f*; **~ scratchings** *n* couratos *mpl*, terresmos *mpl.*

porn, pornographic *adj* pornográfico.

pornography *n* pornografia *f*; **hard/soft ~** pornografia pesada/leve.

porous *adj* poroso,-a.

porpoise *n* golfinho *m*, boto *m.*

porridge *n* papa *f* de aveia.

port *n* porto *m*; **2** *(NAUT)* bombordo *m*; **3** *(wine)* vinho do Porto.

portable *adj* portátil.

portal *n* entrada *f*; **2** *(COMP)* portal *m.*

portcullis *n* portão *m* levadiço (num castelo).

portend *vt* pressagiar.

portent *n* presságio *m*, portento *m*, prognóstico *m.*

porter *n (for luggage)* carregador *m*; **2** *(doorman)* porteiro *m.*

portfolio *n* dossier *m.* pasta *f*; **minister without ~** ministro sem pasta; *(FIN)* carteira *f.*

porthole *n* vigia *f.*

portico *n* pórtico *m.*

portion *n* porção *f*, quinhão *m*; ração *f.*

portly *adj* corpulento.

portrait *n* retrato *m.*

portraitist *n* retratista *m,f.*

portray *vt* retratar; descrever.

portrayal *n* representação *f.*

Portugal *npr* Portugal *m.*

Portuguese *n adj* português,-esa; **2** *(LING)* português *m*; **~ man-of-war** *n* caravela *f*; **2** fisália *f.*

pose *n* postura *f*; pose *f*; **2** *(pej)* afe(c)tação *f*; ♦ *vt* representar *(risk, threat)*; **2** *(question)* levantar; ♦ *vi (model)* posar; **to ~ as** fazer-se passar por.

poser *n (=poseur)* pessoa que dá nas vistas; **2** *(question)* n questão *f* complicada; quebra-cabeças msg.

posh *adj (coll)* fino, elegante *m*; chique *m,f*; queque.

posit *vt* postular.

position *n* posição *f*; **2** *(job)* cargo *m*; **3** *(point of view)* opinião *f*; ♦ *vt* colocar, situar.

positive *adj* positivo; **2** *(certain)* certo; definitivo.

positivism *n* positivismo *m.*

posology *n* posologia *m.*

posse *n (US)* destacamento *m*; pelotão *m* de civis armados, gangue *m* armado.

possess *vt* possuir.

possession *n* posse *f*, possessão *f.*

possessive *adj* possessivo.

possibility *n* possibilidade *f.*

possible *adj* possível; **as far as ~** na medida do possível; **as much as ~** tanto quanto possível; **as big as ~** o maior possível.

possibly *adv* possivelmente; talvez.

post *n (mail)* correio *m*; **~card** *n* cartão *m* postal; **~ code** *n* código *m* postal; **~ man** *n* carteiro; **2** *(job,*

place) posto *m*; **3** *(pole)* poste *m*; **4** *(in compounds)* a partir de, pós; ♦ *vt* pôr no correio; **2** *(MIL)* nomear; **3** afixar, pregar; **to ~ to** destinar a; **to ~-date** *vt* pre-datar.

postage *n* porte *m*, franquia *f.*

postal *adj* postal *m,f*; **~ order** *n* vale *m* postal.

postbox (P.O. box) *n* caixa *f* postal, apartado *m.*

posted *adj (person)* colocado **(in** em**); to keep sb ~** manter alguém ao corrente de algo.

poster *n* cartaz *m.*

posterior *n (coll)* traseiro *m*, nádegas *fpl*; ♦ *adj* posterior *m,f.*

posterity *n* posteridade *f.*

post-free (= post-paid) *adj* com porte pago, franco de porte.

postgraduate *n* pós-graduado,-a.

posthaste *adv* a grande velocidade, com pressa.

posthumous *adj* póstumo.

postiche *adj* postiço.

postil *n* apostila *f.*

posting *f (job)* colocação *f* **(in** em**);** *(mailing)* envio *m.*

postman *n* carteiro,-a.

postmark *n* carimbo *m* do correio; ♦ *vt* carimbar.

post-master *n* chefe *m,f* do correio.

post-mortem *n* autópsia *f*; ♦ *adj* após a morte.

postnatal *adj* pós-natal *m,f.*

post office *n* correios *mpl.*

post-operative *adj (MED)* pós-operatório,-a.

post-paid *adj (Vd:* **post-free).**

postpone *vt* adiar.

postponement *n* adiamento *m.*

postscript *n* pós-escrito *m*, post scriptum **(P.S.).**

postulate *vt* postular.

posture *n* postura *f*, atitude *f.*

post-war *adj* do pós-guerra.

posy *n* ramalhete *m.*

pot *n (pan)* panela *f*; **2** *(container)* vaso *m*; pote *m*; **chamber ~** *n* bacio *m*; *(coll)* penico *m*; **3** *(coll)* *(drugs)* marijuana *f*, *(BR)* maconha *f*; ♦ *vt* plantar em vaso; pôr em conserva.

potable *adj* potável *m,f*; *(water)* drinkable.

potassium *n (CHEM)* potássio *m.*

potato *(pl: -es) n* batata *f*; **sweet ~** batata doce; **mashed ~** purée de batata; **~ chips** batatinha frita; **~ crisps** *npl* batatinha *fsg* inglesa.

pot-bellied *adj* barrigudo,-a.

pot belly *n* grande barriga *f*; *(fam)* pança *f.*

potent *adj* potente *m,f*, poderoso; forte *m,f.*

potential *n* potencial *m*; ♦ *adj* potencial *m,f*, latente *m,f.*

pother *n* confusão *f*, algazarra *f.*

pothole *n* buraco *m* na estrada, cova *f.*

potholer *n* espeleólogo,-a.

potholing *n*: **to go ~** dedicar-se à espeleologia.

potion *n* poção *f.*

pot luck *n*: **to take ~** contentar-se com o que houver; tentar a sorte.

pot-roast *n* carne *f* assada, estufada em panela ao lume.

pot shot *n*: **to take a ~ (at)** atirar a esmo (em).

potted *adj* em conserva.

potter *n* oleiro *m*; ♦ *vi*: **to ~ around/about** desperdiçar tempo com ninharias; **~'s wheel** *n* roda *f* de oleiro.

pottery *n* cerâmica *f*, olaria *f*.

potty[1] *n* (*child's language for* **chamber pot**) bacio *m*; **~-trained** *adj* criança que aprendeu a ir ao bacio; **he is ~ trained** ele já não usa fraldas.

potty[2] *adj* (*coll*) (*idiotic*) maluco, doido; **~mouth** *n* (*coll*) asneirento,-a.

pouch *n* (*ZOOL*) bolsa *f*; **2** (*container*) tabaqueira *f*.

pouf(fe) *n* (*type of floor cushion*) pufe *m*.

poultice *n* cataplasma *f*.

poultry *n* aves *fpl* domésticas/de criação; **~ farm** *n* granja avícola *f*; aviário *m*.

pounce *n* salto *m*, arremetida *f*; ♦ *vi*: **to ~ on** lançar-se sobre.

pound *n* (*UK*) (*unit of currency*) libra *f*; **sterling ~** libra *f* esterlina; **2** (*for dogs*) canil *m*; **3** (*for cars*) depósito *m*; **4** (*unit of measure*) libra *f* (*4536 grs*); ♦ *vt* (*crush*) moer, triturar; reduzir a pó; **2** (*beat*) bater (*waves*); ♦ *vi* (*heart*) bater; (*throb*) latejar (*head*); **2** (*knock loudly*) bater à porta com força, dar pancadas na porta.

pounding *n* pancadas *fpl*; (*heart, head*) o latejar *msg*.

poundland *n* (*all articles at a pound*) = loja *f* dos 300 (trezentos).

pour *vt* (*pour*) despejar; **2** (*serve*) servir, deitar; **~ a bit more milk** deite um pouco mais de leite; ♦ *vi* fluir, correr; chover; **the letters ~ed from every corner** as cartas choviam de todos os cantos; **~ down** (*tears, water, rain*) escorrer por/de; **tears ~ed down her cheeks** as lágrimas escorriam pela cara abaixo; (= **to ~ down**) chover a cântaros; **to ~ out of/from** (*liquid*) esvaziar, (*fumes, smoke*) escapar (de), espalhar-se (*por*); **~ away/off** *vt* decantar; **to ~ in** *vi* entrar em torrente (*sun, light*); **to ~ out** *vi* sair aos borbotões (**from** de); **to ~ scorn** *vt* escarnecer; IDIOM **to ~ one's heart out** desabafar; **it never rains, but it ~s** uma desgraça nunca vem só; **to ~ oil on troubled waters** deitar água na fervura.

pouring *n* vazamento *m* (*of melted metal*); ♦ *adj*: **~ rain** chuva torrencial.

pout *vi* fazer beicinho, amuar; mostrar má cara.

poverty *n* pobreza *f*; (*fig*) falta *f*, escassez *f*; **~-stricken** *adj* indigente *m,f*, necessitado,-a, carente, carenciado,-a.

POW (*abbr for* **prisoner of war**) prisioneiro,-a de guerra.

powder *n* pó *m*; **2** (= **face ~**) pó-de-arroz *m*; **3** (= **gun ~**) pólvora *f*; **~ compact** *n* estojo *m* (de pó-de-arroz); **~ room** *n* toucador *m*; ♦ *vt* pulverizar; empoar; IDIOM **to take a ~** (*US*) dar de frosques.

powdery *adj* semelhante ao pó, como pó.

power *n* (*control, strength*) poder *m*; força *f*; **2** (*ELECT*) potência *f*; propulsão *f*; energia *f*, luz *f*; **~base** *n* reduto *m* (de força); **~ cut** *n* corte *m* de energia; **~ drill** *n* (*tool*) berbequim *m*; **~ house** *n* (*fig*) fonte *f* de influência; **horse-~** cavalo-vapor *m*; **~ line** *n* fio *m* de alta tensão; **~ of attorney** *n*

(*JUR*) procuração *f*; representação *f*; **~ plant** *n* central *f* elétrica; usina *f* elétrica; **~ point** *n* tomada *f*; **propelling ~** força *f* matriz, propulsora; **~ station** *n* central *f* elétrica; **~ steering** *n* direcção *f* hidráulica; ♦ *vt* (*ELECT*) alimentar.

powered *adj* com motor; **~ by** com propulsão a.

powerful *adj* (*power*) poderoso,-a; **2** (*strength*) potente, vigoroso,-a; intenso,-a.

powerhouse *n* centro de atividade/de energia; **2** (*person*) (*fig*) poço *m* de energia

powerless *adj* impotente *m,f*.

p & p (*abbr for* **postage and packing**) selo e embalagem.

powwow *n* (*fig*) discussão *f* importante; (*meeting*) assembleia; cerimonial *m* mágico entre alguns índios dos E.U.A.

pox *n* pústula; (*coll*) sífilis *f*; **chicken ~** varicela *f*, bexigas-doidas *fpl*, catapora *f*; **small ~** varíola *f*, bexigas *fpl*.

PR (*abbr for* **public relations**) relações *fpl* públicas, RP; **2** (*abbr for* **proportional representation**) representação *f* proporcional.

practicable *adj* praticável *m,f*, viável *m,f*.

practical *adj* prático,-a; **~ joke** *n* brincadeira *f*, partida *f*.

practically *adv* praticamente.

practice *n* (*regular activity*) costume *m*, hábito *m*; **2** (*exercise*) prática *f*, exercício *m*; treino *m*; **3** (*MED*) clínica *f*; **out of ~** destreinado.

practise *vt* praticar; ter por costume; exercer; fazer exercícios de; ♦ *vi* exercer (*profissão*); **2** (*exercise*) treinar, exercitar-se.

practising *adj* praticante *m,f*; que exerce.

practitioner *n* praticante *m,f*; **2** (*MED*) médico,-a.

pragmatic *adj* pragmático.

pragmatics *n* pragmática *fsg*.

pragmatism *n* pragmatismo *m*.

prairie *n* campina *f*, pradaria *f*.

praise *n* louvor *m*, elogio *m*; ♦ *vt* louvar, elogiar, exaltar; IDIOM **to sing someone's ~s** tecer elogios a alguém.

praiseworthy *adj* louvável; digno de elogio.

praline *n* (*CULIN*) pralina *f*.

pram *n* carrinho *m* de bebé (*BR*: -bê).

prance *vi* (*horse*) saracotear; saltitar; **2 ~ (about)** (*person*) gingar-se, pavonear-se.

prancing *n* (*horse*) a(ç)ão de saltitar; **2** (*of person*) maneira emproada de andar.

prandial *adj* prandial *m,f*.

prang *n* (*coll*) (*impact*) colisão *f*, batida *f*; **2** (*bombing*) bombardeio *m*; ♦ *vt* colidir, bater; **2** (*bombing*) bombardear.

prank *n* travessura *f*, partida *f*; **baby's ~s** gracinhas *fpl*.

prankster *n* brincalhão *m*; gozão *m*.

prat *n* (*coll*) palerma *m,f*, inútil *m,f*.

prate *vt* (*chat*) tagarelar; (*talk nonsense*) dizer disparates; (*boast*) gabar-se.

pratincole *n* (*ZOOL*) perdiz-do-mar *f*.

prattle *n* (*fam*) paleio *m*, tagarelice *f*; ♦ *vi* tagarelar; palrar.

prawn *n* camarão *m*.

praxis *n* prática *f*.

pray *vi* rezar, orar; pedir; **pray!** *(very formal)* por favor diga!; **2** *(beg, implore)* *(v. formal)* **I ~ I have not offended you** espero que eu não o tenha ofendido.

prayer *n* oração *f*, prece *f*; súplica *f*, rogo *m*; ~ **beads** *npl* terço *msg*; ~ **book** *n* missal *m*, livro *m* de orações; IDIOM *(slang)* **not have a ~ of** não ter hipótese de; **he hasn't a ~ of winning the game** ele não tem qualquer hipótese de ganhar o jogo.

preach *vi* pregar.

preacher *n* pregador,-ora.

preamble *n* preâmbulo *m*.

prearranged *adj* combinado de antemão.

prebend *n (REL)* prebenda *f*.

precarious *adj* precário.

precaution *n* precaução *f*.

precede *vt/vi* preceder.

precedence *n* precedência *f*; **2** *(priority)* prioridade *f*.

precedent *n* precedente *m*.

preceding *adj* precedente *m,f*.

precept *n* preceito *m*.

preceptive *adj* preceptivo.

precession *n* precessão *f*.

precinct *n* recinto *m*; distrito *m*; jurisdição *f*; ~**s** *npl* arredores *mpl*; **pedestrian** ~ área *f* de pedestres; **shopping** ~ zona *f* comercial.

precious *adj* precioso; de grande valor; ~ **metal** *n* metal *m* precioso; ~ **stone** *n* pedra *f* preciosa.

precipice *n* precipício *m*.

precipitate *adj* precipitado, apressado; ♦ *vt* precipitar, acelerar; **2** *(originate)* causar.

precipitation *n (METEOR) (rain, snow)* precipitação *f*.

precipitous *adj* íngreme *m,f* escarpado.

precise *adj* exa(c)to, preciso; escrupuloso, meticuloso. **precisely** *adv* exa(c)tamente.

precision *n* precisão *f*.

preclude *vt* excluir.

precocious *adj* precoce.

precognition *n* conhecimento *m* antecipado, precognição *f*.

preconceived *adj* preconcebido.

preconception *n* preconcepção *f*.

preconize *vt* preconizar.

precursor *n* precursor,-ora.

predator *n* predador *m*.

predatory *adj* predatório, rapace *m,f*.

predecessor *n* predecessor,-ora, antepassado,-a.

predestination *n* predestinação *f*, destino *m*.

predetermine *vt* predeterminar, predispor.

predicable *adj* predicável *m,f*.

predicament *n* predicamento *m*, apuro *m*; IDIOM **to be in some** ~ estar em apuros.

predicate *vt* afirmar; conotar; predicar.

predicative *adj* predicativo.

predict *vt* predizer, prognosticar.

prediction *n* prognóstico *m*.

predilection *n* predilecção *f*.

predispose *vt* predispor.

predisposition *n* predisposição *f*.

predominant *adj* predominante *m,f*, preponderante *m,f*.

predominate *vi* predominar.

pre-eminent *adj* preeminente.

pre-empt *vt* adquirir por preempção, de antemão.

preen *vt*: *(bird)* **to** ~ **itself** limpar e alisar as penas (com o bico); **to** ~ **o.s.** enfeitar-se, envaidecer-se.

prefab *n* casa *f* pré-fabricada.

prefabricated *adj* pré-fabricado.

preface *n* prefácio *m*.

prefect *n* monitor,-ora, tutor,-ora; chefe *m,f* de turma.

prefer *vt* preferir.

preferable *adj* preferível *m,f*.

preferably *adv* de preferência.

preference *n* preferência *f*, prioridade *f*.

preferential *adj* preferencial *m,f*; ~ **rate of interest** juros *mpl* bonificados.

prefix *n* prefixo *m*.

preggers *adj (coll)* grávida *f*.

pregnable *adj* expugnável *m,f*; capturável *m,f*.

pregnancy *n* gravidez *f*.

pregnant *adj (with child)* grávida; *(euph)* no seu estado interessante; **2** *(animal)* prenhe; **3** ~ **with meaning** cheio,-a de significado.

preheat *vt* pré-aquecer (preaquecer).

prehistoric *adj* pré-histórico.

prejudge *vt* fazer um juízo antecipado de, prejulgar.

prejudice *n (intolerance)* preconceito *m*; **2** *(JUR) (dano)* prejuízo *m*; ♦ *vt* predispor; prejudicar.

prejudiced *adj (pessoa)*, preconceituoso; **2** *(idea, opinion)* preconcebido,-a, parcial.

Notar que **prejudice** tem o mesmo significado que 'prejuízo' só no sentido jurídico.

prelate *n* prelado *m*.

preliminary *adj* preliminar *m,f*, prévio.

prelude *n* prelúdio *m*.

premarital *adj* pré-nupcial *m,f*.

premature *adj* prematuro, precoce *m,f*.

premeditated *adj* premeditado.

premier *n (POL)* Primeiro-ministro (da Austrália, N. Zelândia, Canadá); ♦ *adj* primeiro, principal *m,f*.

première *n* estreia *f*.

premise *n* premissa *f*; ~**s** *npl* local *msg*; casa *fsg*; loja *fsg*; **on the** ~**s** no local.

premium *n* prémio *m (BR: prê-)*, bónus *m (BR: bô-)*, recompensa *f*; **to be at a** ~ ser difícil de obter.

premonition *n* presságio *m*, pressentimento *m*.

prenatal *adj* pré-natal *m,f*.

prenup *n (coll) (on assets)* acordo *m* pré-nupcial.

preoccupation *n* preocupação *f*.

preoccupied *adj* absorto; preocupado, apreensivo.

prep *n*: ~ **school** (= **preparatory school**) *(EDUC)* deveres *mpl*.

prepaid *adj* com porte pago; pago antecipadamente.

preparation *n* preparação *f*; ~**s** *npl* preparativos *mpl*.

preparatory *adj* preparatório, introdutório; ~ **to** antes de; ~ **school** *n* escola *f* preparatória.

prepare *vt (plan)* preparar, organizar; **I am preparing the party** estou a preparer a festa; *(get ready)* preparar, aprontar (**for** para); ♦ *vi (get ready)* preparar-se, aprontar-se (**for** para) *(trip, outing)*; **she is preparing for an exam** ela prepara-se para o exame.

prepared *adj* preparado,-a; **I am ~ for the worst** estou preparado, pronto para o pior; **2** *(ready made)* já pronto, já feito.

prepay *vt* pagar adiantadamente.

prepense *adj (JUR)* deliberado,-a.

preponderance *n* preponderância *f*; predomínio *m*.

preposition *n* preposição *f*.

prepossess *vt (occupy)* preocupar; **2** *(influence)* influenciar.

prepossession *n* preconceito *m*, inclinação *f*.

preposterous *adj* prepóstero, absurdo, disparatado.

prepuce *n (ANAT)* prepúcio *m*.

prequel *n (CIN)* prequela *f*.

prerequisite *n* pré-requisito *m*, condição *f* prévia.

prerogative *n* prerrogativa *f*, privilégio *m*.

presage *n* presságio *m*.

presbyterian *n adj* presbiteriano,-a.

pre-school *n* pré-escola *f*; ♦ *adj* pré-escolar.

prescience *n* presciência *f*.

prescind *vt/vi* separar abruptamente, prescindir (de).

prescribe *vt* prescrever; **2** *(MED)* receitar.

prescription *n* prescrição *f*; ordem *f*; **2** *(MED)* receita *f* médica.

prescriptive *adj* prescritivo.

presence *n* presença *f*; assistência *f*; **~ of mind** *n* presença *f* de espírito.

present *n (gift)* presente *m*; prenda *f*; **2** *(time)* a(c)tualidade *f*, momento *m*; **3** *(gram)* presente *m*; **for the ~** por enquanto; **at ~** de momento, agora; ♦ *adj* presente; ♦ *vt* apresentar; expor; **2** *(offer)* presentear, oferecer; **3** *(THEAT)* representar.

presentable *adj* apresentável *m,f*.

presentation *n* apresentação *f*; exposição *f*; **2** *(THEAT)* representação *f*.

present-day *adj* a(c)tual.

presenter *n* apresentador,-ora.

presentiment *n* pressentimento *m*.

presently *adv* logo, em breve.

presentment *n* apresentação *f*.

preservation *n* conservação *f*, preservação *f*.

preservative *n* preservativo *m*.

preserve *n (area)* reserva *f* de caça, coutada *f*; **2** *(preserved goods)* compota, conserva; ♦ *vt (protect)* preservar, proteger; **2** *(keep)* conservar, manter; pôr em conserva; salgar.

preset *n (ELECT)* programar.

preside *vi* presidir.

presidency *n* presidência *f*.

president *n* presidente,-a.

presidential *adj* presidencial *m,f*.

press *n (printing)* prelo *m*; **to come off the ~** sair do prelo; *(machine)* impressora *f*; **2** *(JOURN)* imprensa *f*; **3** *(push)* apertão *m*; **4** *(TECH) (for pressing fruit, metal)* prensa; **5** *(with iron)* passagem *f* a ferro; ♦ **~ baron** *n* magnata *m* da imprensa; **~ box** *n* camarote *m* para jornalistas; **~ conference** *n* conferência *f* de imprensa; **~ cutting** *n* recorte *m* de jornal; **~ release** *n* comunicado *m* para a

imprensa; **~ stud** *n* mola *f*; ♦ *vt (push)* empurrar; **2** *(squeeze)* apertar; comprimir; **3** *(to iron)* vincar, passar a ferro; **4** *(TECH)* prensar; ♦ **to ~ down** carregar em; **2** *(bell)* premir; **to ~ charges against** *(JUR)* apresentar queixas contra; ♦ *vi* apertar; **to ~ on** *vi* continuar; **2** pressionar; **to ~ forward** *vt* prosseguir.

pressed *adj (ironed)* engomado,-a, vincado,-a; **2** *(in haste)* **to be ~ for time** estar com pressa; **3** comprimido,-a; **4** *(metal)* prensado,-a; **5 to be ~ for money** estar apertado,-a; atrapalhado,-a.

pressing *adj* urgente *m,f*, premente *m,f*.

pressure *n (force)* pressão *f*; **2** *(urgency)* premência *f*, urgência *f*; **3** (= **blood ~**) tensão *f* arterial; *(BR)* pressão *f* sanguínea; **high blood ~** hipertensão *f*; **low blood ~** hipotensão *f*; **~ cooker** *n* panela *f* de pressão; **~ gauge** *n* manómetro *m* (BR: -nô-).

prestige *n* prestígio *m*.

prestigious *adj* de prestígio.

presumably *adv* presumivelmente, provavelmente.

presume *vt* presumir, supor; **to ~ to do** ousar, atrever-se a.

presumption *n* suposição *f*; presunção *f*; **2** *(insolent behaviour)* atrevimento *m*, audácia *f*.

presuppose *vt* pressupor, implicar.

pretence *n* pretensão *f*; ostentação *f*; vaidade *f*; fingimento *m*; **on the ~ of** sob o pretexto de.

pretend *vt/vi* fingir; **to ~ to** aspirar a, pretender a.

pretender *n (to the throne)* pretendente *m,f*; **2** fingidor,-ora.

pretension *n* presunção *f*; pretensão *f*; **2** *(claim)* reclamação *f* de um direito.

pretentious *adj* pretensioso, presunçoso; exibicionista *m,f* ostentativo; afe(c)tado.

preterite *n (gram)* pretérito *m*.

pretext *n* pretexto *m*.

pretty *adj* lindo, bonito; **2** *(large amount)* considerável *m,f*; ♦ *adv* bastante.

prevail *vi (win)* triunfar, vencer; **2** *(stand out)* estar na moda; **3** *(predominate)* prevalecer, vigorar; IDIOM **to ~ (up) on sb to do** persuadir alguém a fazer.

prevailing *adj* reinante; predominante, corrente.

prevalence *n* predomínio *m*.

prevalent *adj* predominante *m,f*; corrente *m,f*; dominante *m,f* da moda; a(c)tual *m,f*.

prevaricate *vi* prevaricar.

prevent *vt* impedir.

preventable *adj* evitável *m,f*.

preventative *adj* preventivo.

prevention *n* prevenção *f*, impedimento *m*.

preventive *adj* preventivo.

preview *n (filme)* pré-estreia, ante-estreia *f*; ♦ *vt* ver antecipadamente.

previous *adj* prévio,-a, anterior *m,f*; apressado,-a.

previously *adv* previamente, antecipadamente; antes, anteriormente.

prevision *n* previsão *f*.

prewar *adj* pré-guerra, anterior à guerra.

prey *n* presa *f*; ♦ *vi*: **to ~ on** viver à custa de; alimentar-se de; saquear, pilhar; **birds of ~** aves *fpl* de rapina; IDIOM **it was ~ing on his mind** preocupava-o, atormentava-o.

price n preço m; **at a** ~ a que preço; **at any** ~ a todo o custo; **~-cut** n baixa f de preço; ~ **list** n lista f de preços; ♦ vt apreçar; fixar o preço de.

priceless adj de preço inestimável; **2** (amusing) impagável.

prick n picada f; alfinetada f; ferroada f; **2** (coll) pénis m, (BR) pênis m; ♦ vt picar, furar; IDIOM **to ~ up one's ears** apurar os ouvidos, ficar alerta.

prickle n comichão f; **2** (BOT) espinho m; **3** (ZOOL) acúleo m.

prickly adj espinhoso; **2** (fig) susce(p)tível m,f, melindroso; ~ **heat** (MED) brotoeja f.

pricy adj dispendioso.

pride n orgulho m; **2** (pej) soberba f; altivez f; (self respect) amor próprio m; **a ~ of lions** npl um bando, um bando de leões; ♦ vt: **to ~ o.s. on** orgulhar-se de, vangloriar-se de.

priest n sacerdote m, padre m.

priestess n sacerdotisa f.

priesthood n sacerdócio m; clero m.

prig n (fam) pedante m,f, conceituado.

prim adj empertigado; afe(c)tado.

primacy n primazia f.

primal adj primitivo; essencial m,f.

primarily adv fundamentalmente, antes de (mais) nada; em primeiro lugar.

primary adj primário; fundamental m,f; principal m,f; ~ **colours** npl cores primárias fpl; ~ **school** n escola f primária.

primate n (REL) primaz m; **2** (ZOOL) primata m.

prime adj (first) primeiro, principal m,f; **2** (most important) fundamental m,f, primário; **3** (superior) superior m,f; ~ **minister** n (POL) Primeiro-ministro m; ~ **number** n número m primo; ~ **time** n (TV) hora (BR: horário) nobre; **in the ~ of life** na primavera da vida; **of ~ importance** de importância primordial; ♦ vt escorvar; **2** (fig) aprontar, preparar.

primeval adj primordial m,f, primeiro.

primitive adj primitivo; rudimentar m,f; **2** (rude) grosseiro, inculto.

primogenitor n primogenitor m; antepassado m.

primordial adj primordial m,f.

primp vt/vi aperaltar-se.

primrose n (BOT) prímula f, primavera f; **2** (colour) amarelo-claro m; **evening** ~ (BOT) onagra f.

primus (stove) n fogareiro, fogão m portátil a petróleo.

prince n príncipe m.

princess n princesa f.

principal n dire(c)tor,-ora; ♦ adj principal m,f, fundamental m,f.

principality n principado m.

principle n princípio m; **in** ~ teoricamente.

principled adj detentor de bons princípios.

print n (text, finger) impressão f, marca f; **2** (ART) estampa f; gravura f; **3** (PHOT) prova f; ♦ vt (= ~ **out**) imprimir; gravar; **2** (PHOT) tirar prova; ♦ **out of** ~ esgotado,-a; **~ed matter** n impresso(s); ~ **run** n tiragem.

printer n impressor,-ora.

printing n imprensa f; impressão f; tiragem f; ~ **press** n prelo m, máquina f impressora.

prior n (REL) prior m; ♦ adj anterior m,f, prévio; ~ **to doing** antes de fazer.

priority n prioridade f.

prise vt: **to ~ open** abrir com alavanca, arrombar.

prism n prisma m.

prison n prisão f, cárcere m, cadeia f; ~ **record** n cadastro m (policial).

prisoner n preso,-a, prisioneiro,-a, detido,-a; ~ **of war** n prisioneiro,-a de guerra; IDIOM **to take no ~s** não estar com meias medidas.

prissy (**-ier, -iest**) adj (fussy and prudish) cheio de nove-horas.

prittle-prattle n (coll) conversa f de chacha.

privacy n (seclusion) isolamento m, solidão f; **2** (secrecy) intimidade f, privacidade f.

private adj (individual) particular m,f; ~ **lessons** lições fpl particulares; **2** (secret) confidencial m,f; **in** ~ em particular; em privado; **to speak with sb in** ~ falar com alguém a sós, à parte; (JUR) (hearing) a portas fechadas; **3** (talk, relationship) íntimo,-a; **4** (person, reserved) privado,-a, reservado,-a; ~ **bill** n proje(c)to m de lei (apresentado por deputado); ~ **enterprise** n iniciativa f privada; ~ **income** n rendimento m pessoal; (also: **privates**) ~ **parts** npl (external sexual organs) partes fpl íntimas; ~ **sector** n sector m privado.

privately adv em particular, em privado; **2** (secret) em segredo; confidencialmente.

privation n privação f.

privatise vt privatizar.

privatization n privatização f.

privet n (BOT) alfena f.

privilege n privilégio m. prerrogativa m.

privileged adj privilegiado.

privy n latrina f; ♦ adj: **to be ~ to** ter conhecimento de; **P~ Council** (of the monarch) n Conselho m Privado do rei/da raínha.

prize n prémio m (BR: prê-); ♦ adj premiado; de primeira classe; ♦ vt estimar, apreciar; ~ **fighter** n pugilista m,f profissional; **~-giving** n distribuição f de prémios; **~winner** n premiado,-a.

pro n (SPORT) profissional m,f; **the ~s and cons** os prós e os contras.

probability n probabilidade f.

probable adj provável m,f; verosímil m,f.

probably adv provavelmente.

probate n (JUR) aprovação, oficial de testamento.

probation n: **on** ~ em estágio m probatório; **2** (JUR) em liberdade f; condicional.

probe n (MED, TECH) (tool) sonda f; **2** (research) pesquisa f; ♦ vt sondar; investigar, esquadrinhar.

probity n integridade f.

problem n problema m.

problematic adj problemático.

procedure n (method) procedimento m; método m, processo m; **2** (protocol) protocolo m.

proceed vi proceder; **to ~ to the next** passar ao seguinte; **to ~ to (do)** continuar a (fazer); **to ~ (with)** prosseguir (com); (JUR) **to ~ against sb**

instaurar processo contra alguém; ♦ **proceeds** *npl* rendimento *m* (**from** de); **net** ~ lucro *m* líquido; **2** *(money)* receitas *fpl*; *(of sale)* resultado da venda (**from** de).

proceedings *npl* procedimento, a(c)tuação *f*; *(JUR)* a(c)ção *f*, processo *m*; reunião *f*.

process *n* processo *m*; método *m*, sistema *m*; ♦ *vt* processar, elaborar; **in** ~ em andamento.

processing *n* processamento *m*.

procession *n* procissão *f*; **funeral** ~ cortejo *m* fúnebre.

processor *n* (COMP) processador *m*; **word** ~ *n* processador *m* de texto.

proclaim *vt* proclamar; declarar; anunciar.

proclamation *n* proclamação *f*; promulgação *f*.

proclivity *n* tendência *f*, propensão *f*.

procrastinate *vi* adiar.

procrastination *n* adiamento *m*; protelação *f*.

procreate *vt* procriar.

procreation *n* procriação *f*, reprodução *f*.

procuration *n* (LAW) procuração *f*.

procurator *n* procurador,-ora.

procure *vt* obter; ♦ *vt/vi* alcovitar, servir de proxeneta.

prod *n* empurrão *m*; cotovelada *f*; espetada *f*; ♦ (*pt, pp, pres p* -**dd**-) *vt* empurrar; acotovelar; espetar.

prodigal *adj* pródigo.

prodigious *adj* prodigioso, extraordinário.

prodigy *n* prodígio *m*.

produce *n* (AGR) produtos *mpl* agrícolas; ♦ *vt* *(make)* produzir; render; **2** *(show)* apresentar; exibir; **3** *(THEAT)* pôr em cena.

producer *n* produtor,-ora; industrial *m,f*.

product *n* produto *m*; **2** *(result)* fruto *m*, resultado *m*; ~ **life cycle** *n* *(marketing)* ciclo *m* de vida dos produtos.

production *n* *(action)* produção *f*; **2** *(result)* produto *m*; **3** *(THEAT)* representação *f*, encenação *f*; ~ **line** *n* linha *f* de produção, montagem.

productive *adj* produtivo.

productivity *n* produtividade *f*.

profanation *n* sacrilégio *m*.

profane *adj* profano, irreverente *m,f*, sacrílego.

profess *vt* professar; manifestar, declarar.

profession *n* profissão *f*; carreira; ~ **of faith** *n* profissão *f* de fé; ♦ *adj* perito; de carreira.

professional *n* profissional *m,f*; especialista *m,f*.

professionalism *n* profissionalismo *m*.

professor *n* professor,-ora universitário,-a; catedrático,-a.

proffer *vt* oferecer.

proficiency *n* proficiência *f*, capacidade *f*.

proficient *adj* proficiente *m,f*, capaz *m,f*.

profile *n* perfil *m*.

profit *n* lucro *m*; *(fig)* vantagem *f*; ~ **and loss** ganhos e perdas *pl*; ~-**sharing** *n* participação *f* nos lucros; ♦ *vi*: **to** ~ **by/from** aproveitar-se de, tirar proveito de.

profitability *n* rentabilidade *f*.

profitable *adj* lucrativo, rendoso; proveitoso.

profiteering *n* *(pej)* lucros *mpl* excessivos.

profligate *adj* libertino, devasso.

profound *adj* profundo.

profuse *adj* profuso, pródigo.

profusely *adv* abundantemente.

profusion *n* profusão *f*, abundância *f*.

progenitor *n* antepassado,-a; progenitor,-ora **progeny** *n* progénie (BR: -gê-) *f*.

progesterone *n* progesterona *f*.

prognosis (*pl*: -**oses**) *n* prognóstico *m*.

programme *n* programa *m*; ♦ *vt* programar; ~ **program** *n* (COMP) programa *m* gerador.

programmer *n* (COMP) programador,-ora.

programming *n* programação *f*.

progress *n* progresso *m*; desenvolvimento *m*; ♦ *vi* progredir, avançar; **in** ~ em andamento.

progression *n* progressão *f*, avanço *m*.

progressive *n* progressista *m,f*; ♦ *adj* progressivo.

prohibit *vt* proibir; impedir.

prohibition *n* proibição *f*; **2** *(US)* lei *f* seca.

prohibitive *adj* proibitivo, excessivo.

project *n* proje(c)to *m*, plano *m*; ♦ *vt* proje(c)tar; ♦ *vi* ressaltar, sobressair.

projectile *n* projé(c)til *m*.

projection *n* proje(c)ção *f*; saliência *f*.

projector *n* proje(c)tor *m*.

prolapse *n* (MED) prolapso *m*.

prolepsis *n* (LITER) prolepse *f*.

proletarian *n adj* proletário,-a.

proletariat *n* proletariado *m*.

proliferate *vi* proliferar, multiplicar-se.

proliferation *n* proliferação *f*.

prolific *adj* prolífico.

prologue *n* prólogo *m*.

prolong *vt* prolongar, estender.

prolusion *n* preâmbulo *m*.

prom *n* (= **promenade concert**) concerto com parte da assistência em pé.

promenade *n* marginal *f*; passeio *m*, esplanada *f*; ♦ *vi* passear, dar um passeio.

prominence *n* *(fig)* eminência *f*, importância *f*.

prominent *adj* proeminente *m,f*; saliente *m,f*; eminente *m,f*.

promiscuous *adj* promíscuo, libertino.

promiscuity *n* promiscuidade *f*.

promise *n* promessa *f*; ♦ *vt/vi* prometer; IDIOM **to** ~ **the moon/earth** prometer o céu e a terra.

promising *adj* prometedor, promissor.

promontory *n* promontório *m*.

promote *vt* promover; fomentar; fazer propaganda de.

promoter *n* promotor,-ora, patrocinador,-ora.

promotion *n* promoção *f*, fomento *m*; desenvolvimento *m*.

prompt *adj* pronto, rápido; ♦ *adv* pontualmente; ♦ *vt* *(raise)* incitar, impelir; **2** *(suggest)* sugerir; **3** *(THEAT)* servir de ponto a.

prompter *n* (THEAT) ponto *m*.

promptitude *n* prontidão *f*, solicitude *f*.

promptly *adv* pontualmente; rapidamente.

promptness *n* pontualidade *f*; rapidez *f*.

promulgate *vt* promulgar; propagar.

promulgation *n* promulgação *f*.

prone *adj* inclinado, de bruços; ~ **to** propenso a, predisposto a.

prong *n* dente *m* de garfo; garra *f*; ♦ *vt* perfurar.

pronged *adj* dentado.
pronoun *n* pronome *m*.
pronounce *vt* pronunciar; declarar, afirmar; ♦ *vi*: **to ~ (up)on** pronunciar-se sobre.
pronounced *adj* acentuado, marcado, nítido.
pronouncement *n* pronunciamento *m*.
pronunciation *n* pronúncia *f*.
proof *n* prova *f*; **2** *(alcohol)* graduação *f* alcoólica; ♦ *adj*: ~ **against** à prova de; **water~** *adj* impermeável *m,f*; **~reader** *n* revisor,-ora de provas.
prop *n* suporte *m*, amparo *m*, apoio *m*; ♦ *vt* (= **up**) apoiar.
propagable *adj* propagável *m,f*.
propaganda *n* propaganda *f*.
propagate *vt* propagar; espalhar, divulgar.
propagator *n* propagador,-ora.
propel *vt* impelir; propulsionar.
propeller *n* hélice *f*.
propelling-pencil *n* lapiseira *f*.
propene *n* *(CHEM)* propeno *m*.
proper *adj* próprio; preciso; apropriado, conveniente; oportuno; decente, respeitável; genuíno; **the ~ way** como deve ser.
properly *adv* corre(c)tamente; bem.
property *n* propriedade *f*; posses *fpl*, bens *mpl*; **2** *(piece of land)* propriedade *f*, fazenda *f*; **that's your ~** isso pertence-lhe.
prophecy *n* profecia *f*.
prophesy *vt* profetizar; *(fig)* predizer.
prophet *n* profeta *m,f*.
prophetic *adj* profético.
propitious *adj* propício, favorável *m,f*.
proportion *n* proporção *f*; parte *f*, porção *f*. **proportional** *adj* proporcional.
proportionate *adj* proporcionado.
proposal *n* proposta *f*; oferta *f*; plano *m*; pedido *m*; sugestão *f*.
propose *vt* propor; oferecer; ♦ *vi* declarar-se; **to ~ to do** propor-se fazer.
proposition *n* proposta *f*, proposição *f*.
propound *vt* propor; expor.
proprietary *adj* *(rights, duties)* do proprietário; *(manner)* de proprietário; **2** *(COMM)* patenteado,-a, registado *(BR)* registrado,-a; ~ **name** *n* marca registada, *(BR)* registrada.
proprietor *n* proprietário,-a, dono,-a (**of** de).
propriety *n* propriedade *f*; corre(c)ção *f*; decência *f*.
props *npl* *(THEAT)* adereços *mpl*, acessórios *mpl*.
proptosis *n* *(MED)* proptoma *m*.
propulsion *n* propulsão *f*.
propyl *n* *(CHEM)* propilo *m*.
pro rata *adv* pro rata, proporcionalmente.
prorogue *vt* interromper os trabalhos parlamentares.
prosaic *adj* prosaico,-a.
proscribe *vt* banir, extinguir.
prose *n* prosa *f*.
prosecute *vt* *(JUR)* processar, intentar uma a(c)ção.
prosecution *n* acusação *f*, a(c)ção *f* judicial.
prosecutor *n* promotor,-ora; procurador,-ora; delegado,-a.
prosody *n* prosódia *f*.

prospect *n* vista *f*, probabilidade *f*; perspectiva *f*; esperança *f*; ♦ *vt* explorar; ♦ *vi* procurar.
prospecting *n* prospecção *f*; exploração *f*.
prospective *adj* provável *m,f* esperado; futuro; presumível *m,f*; em perspectiva.
prospector *n* explorador,-ora.
prospects *npl* probabilidades *fpl*.
prospectus *n* prospecto *m*, programa *m*.
prosper *vi* prosperar.
prosperity *n* prosperidade *f*.
prosperous *adj* próspero, bem-sucedido.
prostate *n* *(ANAT)* próstata *f*.
prostitute *n* prostituta *f*.
prostrate *adj* prostrado; **2** *(fig)* abatido, aniquilado.
prostyle *n* *(ARCH)* prostilo *m*.
protagonist *n* protagonista *m,f*.
protect *vt* proteger.
protection prote(c)cão *f*.
protectionism *n* *(POL)* prote(c)cionismo *m*.
protective *adj* prote(c)tor; preventivo.
protector *(person)* *n* prote(c)tor,-ora, patrocinador,-ora; *(machine)* dispositiro de prote(c)ção.
protégé *n* protegido,-a.
protein *n* proteína *f*.
protest *n* protesto *m*; ♦ *vi* protestar; ♦ *vt* afirmar, declarar.
Protestant *n adj* protestante *m,f*.
protester *n* manifestante *m,f*.
protocol *n* protocolo *m*.
proton *n* *(FIS)* protão *m*; *(BR)* proton *m*.
prototype *n* protótipo *m*.
protracted *adj* prolongado, demorado.
protrude *vi* proje(c)tar-se, sobressair, ressaltar.
protruding *adj* saliente *m,f*.
protrusion *n* saliência *f*, protuberância *f*.
protuberance *n* saliência, protuberance.
proud *adj* *(pleased)* orgulhoso; **2** *(pej)* *(arrogant)* vaidoso, soberbo; **3** *(distinguished)* imponente, magnífico.
prove *vt* provar, comprovar; mostrar, demonstrar; **to ~ on** mostrar o que se vale.
proven *adj* (com)provado, verificado.
provenance *n* proveniência *f*.
proverb *n* provérbio *m*.
proverbial *adj* proverbial *m,f*.
provide *vt/vi* fornecer, providenciar, munir; **to ~ against** prevenir-se contra, precaver-se contra; **to ~ for** cuidar de; prover às necessidades de; **to ~ o. s. with** munir-se de.
provided (= **providing**) *conj* desde que, contanto que.
provident *adj* previdente *m,f*, prudente *m,f*.
providential providencial *m,f*; oportuno.
province *n* província *f*; **2** *(fig)* esfera *f*.
provincial *adj* da província; provincial *m,f*; **2** *(pej)* provinciano.
proving ground *n* (= **testing ~**) zona *f* de testes, campo *m* de prova.
provision *n* *(of food, equipament)* provisão *f*; fornecimento *m*; abastecimento *m*; **2** *(of services)* prestação *f*; **3** *(for old age)* disposições *fpl*; **4** *(JUR)* cláusula *f*; condição *f*; **under the terms of** ~ nos

termos de; **provisions** *npl* víveres *mpl*, mantimentos *mpl*; **2** providências *fpl*.
provisional *adj* temporário,-a, provisório,-a.
Provisional IRA *npr* membro da facção dura do Sinn Féin (Irlanda do Norte).
proviso *n* condição *f*, disposição *f*, cláusula *f*.
provisory *adj* provisório.
provocateur *n* provocador,-ora.
provocation *n* provocação *f*, estímulo *m*.
provocative *adj* provocante *m,f*; suggestivo; irritante *m,f*.
provoke *vt* provocar; causar, motivar; irritar, exasperar.
provost *n* director,-ora; chefe *m,f*; **2** (*UK*) (*Univ*) reitor,-ora.
prow *n* proa *f*.
prowess *n* destreza *f*, proeza *f*; perícia *f*; coragem *f*.
prowl *n*: **on the** ~ (*vigiando*) de ronda; **2** à procura de presa, pilhagem; ~ **car** *n* carro *m* de patrulha; ♦ *vi* (= **to** ~ **about/around**) rondar, vaguear, em busca de *algo*) deambular.
prowler *n* estranho,-a rondando furtivamente; (*fig*) gatuno,-a.
proximal *adj* (*ANAT*) proximal *m,f*.
proximity *n* proximidade *f*.
proxy *n* procuração *f*; procurador,-ora; **by** ~ por procuração.
prude *n* puritano,-a.
prudence *n* prudência *f*, cautela *f*.
prudent *adj* prudente *m,f*.
prudish *adj* puritano,-a, pudico,-a.
prune *n* (*CULIN*) ameixa *f* seca; ♦ *vt* podar (*trees);* ~ **back** (*thin out*) desbastar, aparar.
prurient *adj* lascivo,-a.
prurigo *n* (*MED*) prurido *m*.
pry (*pt, pp* -**pried**) *vi* bisbilhotar; ♦ **to** ~ **into** (intro) meter-se em, (*coll*) meter o nariz em.
prying *adj* indiscreto, intrometido.
psalm *n* (*REL*) salmo *m*.
pseudo- *pref* pseudo-.
pseudonym *n* pseudónimo *m* (*BR*: -dô-).
psoriasis *n* (*MED*) psoríase *f*.
psst *exc* psiu!
psych (*Vd:* **psych up**).
psyche *n* psique *f*.
psychedelic *adj* psicodélico.
psychiatric *adj* psiquiátrico.
psychiatrist *n* psiquiatra *m,f*.
psychiatry *n* psiquiatria *f*.
psychic *n* médium *m,f*; ♦ *adj* psíquico; paranormal *m,f*.
psycho *n* *adj* (*coll*) psicopata *m,f*.
psychoanalyse *vt* psicanalisar.
psychoanalysis *n* psicanálise *f*.
psychoanalyst *n* psicanalista *m,f*.
psychogenesis *n* psicogénese *f*.
psychognosis *n* psicognose *f*.
psycholinguistics *n* psicolinguística *f*.
psychological *adj* psicológico.
psychologist *n* psicólogo,-a.
psychology *n* psicologia *f*.
psychometry *n* psicometria *f*.
psychopath *n* psicopata *m,f*.

psychosis (*pl:* -**choses**) *n* (*MED*) psicose *f*.
psychosomatic *adj* psicossomático.
psychotherapy *n* psicoterapia *f*.
psychotic *n* *adj* psicótico,-a.
psych up *vt* (*fam*) preparar-se psicologicamente (para).
pt (*abbr for* **pint**); **2** (*abbr for* **point**).
PT *n* (*abbr for* **physical training**) treino *m*, (*BR*) treinamento físico.
PTA (*abbr for* **parent-teacher association**) APM *f*.
pterodactyl *n* pterodáctilo *m*.
PTO (*abbr for* **please turn over**) vide verso, V.S.F.F.
ptosis *n* (*MED*) ptose *f*.
PTV (*abbr for* **pay television**) televisão *f* por assinatura.
pub *n* (*abbr for* **public house**) bar *m*, taberna *f*; ~ **crawl** *n*: **to go on a** ~ andar de pub em pub; ~ **grub** *n* refeições simples servidas em bares.

O **pub** faz parte da vida social de todos os britânicos e encontra-se praticamente em cada esquina das cidades sendo um centro indispensável nas aldeias. Além das bebidas, especialmente a cerveja, os pubs servem também 'batatinha inglesa', amendoins e, muitos deles, refeições tradicionalmente britânicas. Entrada proibida a menores de 16 anos, a não ser acompanhados.

puberty *n* puberdade *f*.
pubes *n* (*ANAT*) púbis *f*; **2** (*coll*) pêlos *mpl* púbicos.
pubescent *adj* púbere *m,f*.
pubic *adj* púbico.
pubis *n* (*ANAT*) púbis *f*.
public *n* *adj* público,-a; ~ **convenience** *n* lavabos *mpl*; ~ **debt** dívida *f* pública; ~ **domain** domínio *m* público; ~ **expenditure** despesa *f* pública; ~ **goods** bens *mpl* públicos; ~ **holiday** feriado; ~ **relations** relações *fpl* públicas; ~ **school** *n* escola *f* privada, colégio *m*; ~ **service** função *f* pública; ~-**spirited** *adj* patriótico; ~ **transports** transportes *mpl* públicos; **to go** ~ revelar algo confidencial.
publican *n* taberneiro *m*.
publication *n* publicação *f*.
publicity *n* publicidade *f*.
publicly *adv* publicamente, abertamente.
Public Prosecutor *n* procurador,-a da República, (*BR*) promotor,-ora público,-a.
publish *vt* publicar.
publisher *n* editor,-ora.
publishing house *n* (casa) editora.
puce *adj* castanho (*BR*: marrom) arroxeado, (*coll*) cor *f* de pulga.
pucker *vt* (*skin, lips*) enrugar; franzir.
pudding *n* pudim *m*, doce *m*; **black** ~ *n* morcela *f*.
puddle *n* poça *f*, charco *m*.
pudency *n* pudor *m*.
puerile *adj* pueril *m,f*.
puerperile *adj* (*MED*) puerperal *m,f*.
Puerto Rico *npr* Porto Rico; **Porto Rican** *npr, adj* porto-riquenho,-a
puff *n* (*of wind, smoke*) sopro *m*; baforada *f*; lufada *f*; **2** (*cigarette, cigar*) inalação *f*; **3** (= **powder** ~) pompom *m*; **4** (*coll*) (*pej*) (*homosexual*) paneleiro *m*; ♦ *vi* (*blow*) soprar; (*pant*) arquejar; **to** ~ **on**

his/her pipe fumar o seu cachimbo; **to ~ out** *(chest)* inflar; *(sails)* enfunar; *(bird's feathers)* eriçar; **to ~ out smoke** lançar uma baforada; **to ~ out/up** *vt/vi* inchar; ♦ **~ pastry** *n* massa *f* folhada.

puffed *adj (coll)* sem fôlego, ofegante *m,f;* inchado,-a; **~ sleeve** manga *f* tufada, bufante.

puffiness *n (of face, neck)* inchaço *m.*

puffy (-ier, -iest) inchado,-a.

pug *n (dog)* dogue.

pugilism *n* pugilismo *m.*

pugnacious *adj* combativo,-a.

pug-nosed *adj* com o nariz a chatado.

puke *n* vómito *m* (BR: vô-); ♦ *vt/vi* vomitar.

pule *vt* choramingar.

pull *n (advantage)* vantagem *f;* influência *f;* **2** *(movement)* puxão *m;* sacudidela *f;* **to give (sth) a ~** dar um puxão em; ♦ *vt* puxar; rebocar; distender; arrastar; **2** *(seduce)* engatar; ♦ *vi* puxar; arrancar; **to ~ away** *vi* afastar-se; **to ~ down** *vt* demolir; **to ~ in** *vi (RAIL)* chegar (à estação); *(AUT)* parar (na berma); **to ~ off** *vt* conseguir (com sucesso); **to ~ out** *vt* tirar, arrancar *(tooth);* retirar *(troops);* ♦ *vi (RAIL)* partir, ir-se embora; **to ~ over** *(AUT)* *vt/vi* parar (na berma); **to ~ together** trabalhar em conjunto; **to ~ through** *vt/vi (MED)* restabelecer-se; levar a melhor; **to ~ up** *vi (AUT)* parar, deter-se; IDIOM **to be on the ~** andar no engate; **to ~ a face** fazer caretas; **to ~ a fast one (on)** enganar (alguém); **to ~ a gun** sacar duma arma; **to ~ to pieces** desfazer; *(fig)* criticar; **to ~ one's weight** fazer o que se pode; **to ~ o.s. together** recompor-se, voltar a si; **to ~ sb's leg** *(coll)* entrar com (alguém), gozar com alguém; **to ~ strings** mexer os cordelinhos.

pulley *n* roldana *f;* polé *m;* polia *f.*

pullout *n (of troops)* retirada *f; (in magazine)* encarte *m.*

pullover *n* pulóver, (BR) pulôver *m.*

pullulate *vi (sprout)* brotar; **2** *(spread)* proliferar.

pulp *n* polpa *f* (de papel); pasta *f,* massa *f;* ♦ **~ literature** *n* de má qualidade, sensacionalista; literatura de cordel.

pulpit *n* púlpito *m.*

pulsar *n (star)* pulsar *m.*

pulsate *vi (heart, vein)* pulsar, palpitar.

pulsating *adj* que palpita; *(rhythm)* vibrante; *(fig)* palpitante.

pulse *n (ANAT)* pulso *m;* pulsação *f;* **to take sb's ~** sentir o pulso de alguém; **2** *(of music)* cadência *f;* **3** *(ELECT, PHYS)* impulso *m;* IDIOM **to keep one's finger on the ~** andar em cima dos acontecimentos.

pulses *npl* grãos *mpl,* leguminosas *fpl.*

pulverize *vt* pulverizar; **2** *(fig)* esmagar, aniquilar.

puma *n* puma *f,* onça *f* vermelha.

pumice stone *n* pedra-pomes *fsg.*

pummel (-led, -ling) *vt* agredir a soco, esmurrar, surrar.

pump *n* bomba *f;* **2** *(shoe)* sapatilha *f* (de dança); ♦ *vt* dar à bomba; **2** *(fig)* sondar; **to ~ up** *vt* encher.

pumpkin *n* abóbora *f.*

pun *n* trocadilho *m.*

punch[1] *n (blow)* soco *m,* murro *m;* **~ line** *n* remate *m* de anedota; **2** *(act of piercing)* punção *m;* **3** *(machine)* furador *m;* **4** *(drink)* ponche *m;* ♦ *vt (blow)* dar socos, bater; **2** *(pierce)* perfurar; picotar.

Punch[2] *npr* Polichinelo *m;* IDIOM **to be as pleased as ~** estar nas suas sete quintas.

Punch-and-Judy show *n* teatro ambulante de fantoches para crianças nos parques, nas praias.

punchbag *n* saco *m* de boxe.

punchball *n* bola para (para treino dos pugilistas).

punchbowl *n* poncheira *f.*

punch-drunk *adj (in boxing)* aturdido.

punch(ed) card *adj* cartão *m* perfurado,-a.

puncheon *n (estaca)* escora *f;* **2** *(container)* buril *m.*

punching bag *n (US)* *n* saco *m* de areia para treino dos pugilistas.

punchline *n (joke)* remate *m;* **2** conclusão *f.*

punch-up *n (coll)* briga *f,* rixa *f.*

punchy (-ier, -iest) *adj* incisivo,-a; **2** enérgico,-a.

punctilious *adj* meticuloso, miudinho.

punctual *adj* pontual *m,f.*

punctuality *n* pontualidade *f.*

punctuate *vt* pontuar; interromper.

punctuation *n* pontuação *f.*

puncture *n (skin)* picada *f, (pneu, balloon)* furo *m;* perfuração *f;* ♦ *vt* picar, furar.

pundit *n* erudito, sábio; especialista *m,f.*

pungent *adj* pungente *m,f;* mordaz *m,f;* acre *m,f.*

punish *vt* punir, castigar.

punishable *adj* punível.

punishing *adj* penoso,-a.

punishment *n* castigo *m,* punição *f.*

punitive *adj* punitivo,-a.

punk *n adj* punk.

punnet *n* cestinha feita de tiras de madeira; (de plástico) caixinha; **each ~ of raspberries costs ...** cada caixinha de framboesas custa ...

punt *n* barco *m* de fundo chato à vara, chalana (um passatempo tradicional em Oxford); **2** *(SPORT)* pontapé *m* dado na bola; **3** jogo aposta contra a banca.

punter *n* apostador,-ora, jogador,-ora; **2** *(UK) (customer)* cliente *m,f;* **3** pessoa que propela o barco *(punt)* com a vara.

puny *adj (person)* débil *m,f,* fraco, raquítico,-a; *(effort, sum)* insignificante *m,f.*

pup *n* cachorro *m;* **in ~** *(animals)* grávida.

pupil *n* aluno,-a; **2** *(ANAT)* pupila *f.*

puppet *n* fantoche *m,* marioneta *f,* marionete *f.*

puppy *n* cachorrinho *m;* **~ fat** *n* gordura *f* de bebé; **~ love** *n* amor *m* adolescente; namorico *m.*

purchase *n* compra *f,* aquisição *f;* **to take ~ on** apoiar-se sobre; ♦ *vt* comprar.

purchasing power *n* poder *m* de compra.

purdah *n* (prática muçulmana de cobrir as mulheres ou isolá-las do conta(c)to dos homens) purdá *m.*

pure *adj* puro; **~-bred** *adj* puro-sangue.

puree *n* puré *m*.

purely *adv* simplesmente.

purfle *n* (*ornamental band*) debrum *m*, orla *f* bordada; folhos *mpl*.

purgatory *n* (*suffering*) purgatório *m*; **P~** (*REL*) Purgatório *m*.

purge *n* (*MED*) purgante *m*; purga *f*; **2** (*POL*) expulsão *f*, expurgo *m*; ♦ *vt* (*cleanse*) purgar; purificar; **2** (*POL*) expurgar; **3** sanear; **to ~ o.s. of sth** livrar-se de algo.

purging *n* (*POL*) saneamento *m*, expurgo *m*; ♦ *adj* laxativo.

purification *n* purificação *f*; depuração *f*.

purifier *n* purificador *m*.

purify (-fied) *vt* purificar, depurar.

purine *n* (*CHEM*) purina *f*.

purist *n* purista *m,f*.

puritan *n* puritano,-a.

puritanical *adj* puritano.

purity *n* pureza *f*, limpeza *f*.

purl *n* (*knit*) ponto *m* reverso (de malha).

purloin *vt* surrupiar.

purple *adj* roxo, púrpura *m,f*.

purplish *adj* arroxeado.

purport *vi*: **to ~ to be/do** dar a entender que é/faz.

purpose *n* obje(c)tivo *m*, propósito *m*; **on ~** de propósito; **for the ~ of** com o fim de; **to no ~** em vão; **~-built** *adj* feito sob medida.

purposeful *adj* intencional *m,f*, resoluto.

purposely *adv* deliberadamente; expressamente.

purpura *n* (*MED*) púrpura *f*.

purpurin *n* (*CHEM*) purpurina *f*.

purr *n* (*contented sound of a cat*) ronrom *m*; (*of engine*) ronco *m*; ♦ *vi* ronronar.

purse *n* carteira *f*; bolsa *f*; porta-moedas; **~ snatcher** *n* (*thief*) carteirista *m,f*; ladrão,-a de carteiras; ♦ **to ~ one's lips** *vt* (*em desagrado*) franzir os lábios; IDIOM **to hold the ~s strings** apertar os cordões à bolsa.

purser *n* (*NAUT*) comissário *m* de bordo; bolseiro *m*.

pursuance *n* (*JUR*) seguimento *m*, cumprimento; **the ~ of** a busca de.

pursuant *adv* (*JUR*) conforme, de acordo com; **~ the law** de acordo com a lei.

pursue *vt* perseguir, seguir; **2** exercer.

pursuer *n* perseguidor,-ora.

pursuit *n* caça *f*; perseguição *f*; ocupação *f*, a(c)tividade *f*; passatempo *m*.

purulent *adj* purulento *m*.

purvey *vt* fornecer.

purveyor *n* fornecedor,-ora.

purview *n* alcance *m*.

pus *n* pus *m*.

push *n* (*shove*) empurrão *m*; **2** (*stimulus*) impulso *m*; **to give sb the ~** despedir alguém; **3** (*attack*) ataque *m*, arremetida *f*; **4** (*advance*) avanço *m*; ♦ *vt* (*thrust*) empurrar; **2** (*press*) premir (*bell*); **3** (*develop*) promover; **~ sb to do sth** incitar alguém a fazer algo; ♦ *vi* empurrar; **2** (*fig*) esforçar-se; **to ~ahead** prosseguir; **to ~ around** *vt* (*bully*) maltratar, mandar na pessoa; **to ~ aside**

vt afastar com a mão; **to ~ for** *vt* insistir; **to ~ in** *vt* furar; **to ~ off** *vi* (*coll*) partir, pôr-se ao largo; **to ~ on** *vi* seguir em frente, avançar; **to ~ over** *vt* derrubar; **to ~ through** *vt* abrir caminho; levar até ao fim; **to ~ up** *vt* fazer subir.

push-button *adj* acionado,-a; por um botão, com teclas.

pushchair *n* carrinho *m* de bebé.

pushed *adj*: **I am ~ for time** não tenho tempo.

pusher *n* (*coll*) traficante *m,f*.

pushing *adj* empreendedor,-ora; **2** ambicioso,-a.

pushover *n* (*easily deceived*) crédulo,-a; (*pej*) trouxa *m,f*; **2** tarefa *f* simples.

push-up *n* (*physical exercise*) flexão *f*, flexões *fpl*.

pushy *adj* (*pej*) agressivo,-a, insistente *m,f*.

puss/pussy(-cat) *n* bichano,-a, gatinho,-a, tareco,-a.

pussy (*vulg*) vulva *f*; rata (*vulg*).

pussyfoot *vt* andar com pezinhos de lã.

pussy willow *n* (*BOT*) salgueiro *m*.

pustule *n* (*MED*) pústula *f*.

put (*pret, pp* put) *vt* (*place*) pôr, colocar; **2** (*express*) dizer, expressar; **to ~ about** *vi* (*NAUT*) mudar de rumo; ♦ *vt* espalhar; **to ~ across** (= ~ over) *vt* expressar, comunicar; **to ~ away** *vt* guardar; **to ~ back** *vt* repor; adiar; **to ~ by** (= ~ aside) *vt* poupar; pôr de lado; **to ~ down** *vt* pôr no chão; matar; **2** (*write down*) anotar, **3** sufocar; **4** atribuir; **to ~ forward** *vt* apresentar, propor; adiantar; **to ~ in** *vt* meter; apresentar; **to ~ off** *vt* adiar; desencorajar; ♦ **to ~ on** *vt* pôr; usar; aplicar; acender; **2** (*THEAT*) encenar; **3** (*weight*) engordar; **4** (*pretend*) fingir, simular; ♦ **to ~ out** *vt* (*extinguish*) apagar; **2** estender; **3** (*publish*) publicar, mostrar; **4** (*bother*) incomodar; **to ~ right** corrigir; **to ~ up** *vt* levantar, erguer; alçar; construir, aumentar; **2** hospedar; **to ~ up with** *vt* suportar, aguentar (BR: -güen-); IDIOM **to not know where to ~ oneself** não saber onde se enfiar; **to ~ paid to** acabar com; **to stay ~** deixar-se estar.

putative *adj* putativo.

putrefy *vt/vi* apodrecer, corromper-se.

putrid *adj* pútrido, podre *m,f*.

putt *vt* dar uma tacada leve.

putter *n* (*golf*) taco *m*.

putty *n* massa de vidraceiro.

puzzle *n* charada *f*; advinha *f*; **2** (*fig*) (*EP*) quebra-cabeças *msg*; (BR: no 's') *m*; **3** enigma *m*; ♦ *vt* confundir; ♦ **to ~ one's brains** dar voltas ao miolo; **to ~ out** *vt* descobrir depois de tentativas; **to ~ over** *vt* matutar (*sobre*); **puzzled** *adj* perplexo,-a.

puzzling *adj* enigmático,-a; intrigante *m,f*.

PVC *n* PVC (policloreto de vinilo) *m*.

Pvt. (*abbr for* **Private**) soldado *m* raso.

p.w. (*abbr for* **per week**).

pygmy *n* pigmeu *m*; pigmeia *f*.

pyjamas (UK) *npl* (also: **pajama(s)** (US)) *nsg* pijama *m sg*.

pylon *n* poste *m*; torre *f*; pórtico *m* de templo egípcio.

pyramid *n* pirâmide *f*.

pyre *n* pira *f* funerária.

Pyrenean *adj* pirenaico,-a.

Pyrenees *npr:* **the P~** os Pireneus *mpl.*
pyretic *adj (MED)* pirético.
Pyrex® *npr* pírex.
pyrites *n (MIN)* pirite *f.*
pyrolysis *n (CHEM)* pirólise *f.*
pyromania *n* piromania *f.*

pyrometer *n* pirómetro *m.*
pyrotechnics *n* pirotecnia *f; (display)* fogo *m* de artifício.
pyrrhic *adj* pirríquio; **P~ victory** *n (winnings equal to losses)* vitória de Pirro.
python *n (large snake)* pitão *m.*

q

Q, q *n (letter)* Q, q.

Q *(abbr for* **queen***)*; **2** *(abbr for* **question***)*.

Qatar *npr* Catar *m*; **in** ~ no Catar.

Qatari *n adj* catarense *m,f*.

QC *(abbr for* **Queen's Counsel***)*.

Q factor *n* fa(c)tor *m* de qualidade.

Q fever *n (MED)* febre *f* Q.

q.l. *(abbr for* **quantum libet***) (MED) (prescriptions)* na quantidade que desejar.

q.m. *(abbr for* **quaque mane***) (MED) (prescriptions)* todas as manhãs.

q.n. *(abbr for* **quaque nocte***) (MED) (prescriptions)* todas as noites.

q.t. *(abbr for* **quiet***)*.

Q-tip *n* cotonete *m*.

qty *(abbr for* **quantity***)*.

quack¹ *n (cry of duck)* grasnido *m*; ♦ *vi (duck)* grasnar.

quack² *n* curandeiro,-a; charlatão,-tã/-tona.

quad *n (coll for* **quadrangle**, **quadruplet***)*; ~ **bike** *n (UK)* motoquatro *f*.

quadrangle *n (GEOM)* quadrângulo *m*; **2** *(patio)* pátio *m* quadrangular.

quadrant *n* quadrante *m*.

quadraphonic *adj (sound)* quadrafónico,-a.

quadrate *n (GEOM)* quadrado *m*, rectângulo *m*; ♦ *adj* quadrangular *m,f*.

quadratic *adj* quadrático,-a.

quadrature *n (MATH)* quadratura *f*.

quadrennial *adj* quadrienal *m,f*.

quadric *adj (GEOM)* quádrico,-a.

quadriceps *(pl: -cepses) n (ANAT)* quadricípite *m*.

quadriform *adj* quadriforme *m,f*.

quadrilateral *n* quadrilátero; ♦ *adj* quadrilateral, quadrangular *m,f*.

quadrillion *n (UK, Portugal)* quatrilião *m*, *(BR)* quatrilhão (= 24 zeros); **2** *(US and Canada)* mil biliões *mpl* (15 zeros).

quadriplegia *n (MED)* tetraplegia *f*.

quadriplegic *adj* tetraplégico,-a.

quadruped *n adj* quadrúpede *m,f*.

quadruple *n adj* quádruplo *m*; ♦ *vt/vi* quadruplicar.

quadruplets *npl* quadrigémeos *(BR: -gê-) mpl*, quádruplos *mpl*.

quadruplex *adj* quádruplo,-a.

quadruplicate *adj* quádruplo,-a; ♦ *vt* quadruplicar.

quadrupole *n (PHYS)* quádruplo *m*.

quads *npl (coll)* = **quadruplets**.

quaff *vi (arc)* beber sofregamente, emborcar.

quaggy *adj* pantanoso,-a, alagado,-a.

quagmire *n* lamaçal *m*, atoleiro *m*, pântano *m*.

quail *n (ZOOL)* codorniz *f*; ♦ *vi* desanimar, perder o ânimo; amedrontar-se (**at**, **before** diante).

quaint *adj* curioso,-a, peculiar *m,f*, esquisito,-a; pitoresco,-a.

quaintness *n* singularidade *f*.

quake *(abbr for* **earth~***) n (coll)* tremor *m* de terra; ♦ *vi (fear, instability)* tremer (**with** de).

Quaker *n (REL)* quacre *m,f*; ♦ *adj* quacriano,-a.

quaking *adj (unstable)* instável *m,f*; **2** *(shaky)* tremedor.

quaky *adj* trémulo,-a.

quale *(pl: -ia) n (philosophy)* característica *f* essencial.

qualification *n* qualificação *f*, aptidão *f*, habilitação *f*; **2** *(requirement)* requisito *m*; **3** *(restriction)* restrição *f*; **4** *(title)* título *m*.

qualified *adj* habilitado,-a, qualificado,-a; competente *m,f*; capaz *m,f*; limitado,-a; diplomado,-a.

qualifier *adj* qualificativo,-a.

qualify *(pt, pp* **-ied**; *pres p* **-ying***) vt (entitle)* qualificar; habilitar; **2** *(change)* modificar; **3** *(limit)* restringir, limitar; **to** ~ **as** classificar (como); ♦ *vi (SPORT)* classificar-se; **to** ~ **as** formar-se (em).

qualifying *adj (LING)* qualificativo,-a; **2** *(exam)* de qualificação; *(mark)* qualificador; **3** *(SPORT)* classificatório,-a; ~ **period** *(for training)* estágio *m*.

qualitative *adj* qualitativo,-a; ~ **analysis** *n* análise *f* qualitativa.

quality *n* qualidade *f*; valor *m*; ~ **control** *n* controlo *m* de qualidade; ~ **factor** *n* factor *m* de qualidade; ~ **press** *n* imprensa *f* séria.

qualm *n (usually functions as pl)* dúvida *f*, incerteza *f* (sobre comportamento moral); **to have no** ~**s about doing/saying sth** não hesitar em fazer/dizer algo; **2** ~**s** *npl (scruple)* escrúpulos *mpl*, remorsos *mpl*.

quandary *(pl: -ies) n*: **to be in a** ~ **about/over sth** estar num dilema (sobre algo).

quango *n (UK) (pej) (abbr for* **quasi-autonomous non-governmental organisation***) n* conselho *m* administrativo, com capitais mistos, cujos membros são designados pelo governo para administrar um serviço público.

quantic *adj* quântico,-a; *(MATH)* variável *m,f*.

quantifier *n* quantificador *m*.

quantify *(pt, pp* **-ied**; *pres p* **-ying***) vt* quantificar.

quantitative *adj* quantitativo,-a; ~ **analysis** *n* análise *f* quantitativa.

quantity *n (amount)* quantidade *f*; **2** *(bulk)* volume *m*; ~ **surveyor** *n (CONSTR)* encarregado *m* de medições em obra; **unknown** ~ *(MATH)* incógnita *f*.

quantometer *n (engineering)* quantómetro *m*.

quantum *(pl: -a) n* quantidade *f*; fra(c)ção *f*; ~ **cryptography** *n* criptografia *f* quântica; ~ **efficiency** *n (PHYS)* eficiência *f* quântica; ~ **electronics** *n (ELECT)* electrónica *f* quântica; ~ **leap** *(progress)* salto em frente; ~ **number** *n (PHYS)* número *m* quântico; ~ **theory** teoria *f* dos quanta, teoria *f* quântica.

quarantine *n* quarentena *f*.

quark *n (PHYS)* quark *m*.

quarrel *n* altercação *f*, discussão *f*, briga *f*.

quarrelsome *adj (person)* brigão,-ona.

quarry *(pl: -ies) n (stone extraction)* pedreira *f*; ~**man** *n* pedreiro; cabouqueiro *m*; ~ **stone** *n* pedra *f* de cautaria; ~ **tile** *n* ladrilho *m*; **2** *(source of information)* fonte *f* de informação; **3** *(hunted animal)* presa *f*, caça *f*; ♦ *(pres. p -ying; pt, pp -ied) vt* extrair, escavar.

quart *n (measure)* quarto *m* de galão (= 1.14 litros).

quartan *n adj* (~ **fever**) quartã *f*.

quarter *n* quarto *m*, quarta *f* parte; **2** *(three months)* trimestre; **3** *(neighbourhood)* bairro *m*; **4** *(moon)* quarto; **5** *(US) (coin)* vinte e cinco cêntimos; ♦ *vt* dividir em quatro.

quarterage *n* pagamento *m* trimestral.

quarterback *n (FOOT) (US)* jogador americano que lança a bola nas jogadas ofensivas.

quarterdeck *n (NAUT)* tombadilho *m* superior.

quarterfinal *n (SPORT)* quartos-de-final.

quarter-hour *adj* de quinze minutos.

quarter-light *n (in car)* janelinha *f* para ventilação.

quarterly *adj* trimestral *m,f*; ♦ *adv* trimestralmente.

quartermaster *n (MIL)* furriel; **2** *(NAUT)* contramestre.

quarternote *n (US) (MUS)* semínima *f*.

quarters *npl (MIL)* quartel *msg*; **2** alojamentos *mpl*; ♦ **at close** ~ *adv* de perto; **from all** ~ de todas as dire(c)ções.

quartet(te) *n (MUS)* quarteto *m*.

quartile *n (statistics)* quartil *m*; ♦ *adj (ASTRON)* quartil *m,f*.

quartz *n (MIN)* quartzo *m*; ~ **crystal** *n* cristal *m* de quartzo; ~ **glass** *n (ELECT)* vidro *m* de sílica.

quartzite *n (GEOL)* quartzito *m*.

quash *vt (reject)* revogar, anular; **2** *(quell)* suprimir.

quasi *pref* quase, semi.

quaternary *adj (CHEM)* quaternário,-a; **Q~** *(GEOL)* quaternário(s).

quaver *n (MUS)* colcheia *f*; **2** *(voice)* tremor *m*; ♦ *vi (voice)* tremer; **2** *(singing)* trinar, gorgear.

quavering *adj* trémulo,-a *(BR* -ê-*)*.

quay *n* cais *m*; ~**side** *n* cais *m*.

qubit *n (COMP)* qubit *m*.

queasy *(-ier, -iest) adj* indisposto,-a, enjoado,-a.

Quebec *npr* Quebeque; **in** ~ em Quebeque *m*.

queen *n* rainha *f*; *(playing card)* dama *f*; *(in chess)* rainha *f*; **2** *(coll) (gay)* homossexual *m*; ~ **bee** abelha-mestra *(BR:* -rainha*) f*; **the** ~ **mother** a rainha-mãe.

Queen's Counsel *n (UK)* advogado eminente nomeado para a Corte, com o direito de estar presente no tribunal.

Queen's evidence *n (UK)* testemunho dado pelo detido contra os seus parceiros em crime, em troca de redução da pena.

queer *adj (weird)* esquisito,-a, estranho,-a; **2** *(doubtful)* duvidoso,-a; **3** *(pej) (gay)* homossexual *m,f*; *(BR)* bicha *f*.

Embora o termo '**queer**' continue a ser pejorativo quando se refere a uma pessoa homossexual, é agora usado entre os homossexuais como um termo positivo

quell *vt (soothe)* acalmar; **2** *(repress)* reprimir, sufocar.

quench *vt* apagar; saciar, abafar; IDIOM **to** ~ **the thirst** matar a sede.

querulous *adj* queixoso,-a, rezingão,-ona.

query *(pl: -ies) n* pergunta *f*; dúvida *f*; ~ **language** *n (COMP)* linguagem *f* de interrogação; ♦ *(pt, pp -ied; pres p -ying) vt* perguntar, pôr em dúvida.

quest *n (LITER) (search)* busca *f*; **the** ~ **for glory** a busca da glória.

question *n (query)* pergunta *f*; questão *f*; ~ **mark** *n* ponto *m* de interrogação; **2** *(matter)* assunto *m*, problema *m*; **beyond** ~ sem dúvida; **it is a** ~ **of** é questão de; **out of the** ~ impossível, fora de questão; **to ask a** ~ fazer uma pergunta; ♦ *vt* perguntar; duvidar, interrogar, inquirir; IDIOM **to pop the** ~ **(to sb)** pedir (alguém) em casamento.

questionable *adj* discutível *m,f*, questionável *m,f*.

questioner *n* interrogador,-ora.

questioning *n* interrogatório *m*.

questionnaire *n* questionário *m* escrito.

question time *n (POL)* audiência televisiva, na qual os ministros respondem às perguntas vindas da audiência.

queue *n (EP) (fam)* bicha *f*, fila *f*; *(BR)* fila *f*; **to jump the** ~/~-**jump** passar à frente (na fila); ♦*(BR)* furar a fila; **to** ~ **up** *vi* fazer fila.

quibble *n* queixa *f*; objeção *f* trivial; ♦ *vi* prevaricar; usar de evasivas; **to** ~ **over/about sth** queixar-se por trivialidades sobre algo.

quibbler *n* sofista *m,f*.

quiche *n (CULIN)* quiche *f*, tarte *f* salgada.

quick *adj* rápido,-a; vivo,-a; ágil; **2** *(child)* esperto,-a; vivo,-a; **3** perspicaz; ♦ **to be** ~ *vi* apressar-se; **to have a** ~ **temper** *vt* irritar-se facilmente; **to bite one's nails to the** ~ roer as unhas até ao sabugo; ♦ *exc* **be** ~! despacha-te!; depressa!.

quicken *vt* acelerar; ♦ *vi* acelerar-se.

quickline *n* cal viva.

quickly *adv* rapidamente, depressa.

quickness *n* rapidez *f*; agilidade *f*; vivacidade *f*.

quicksand *n* areia *f* movediça.

quicksilver *n (dated)* mercúrio *m*.

quick-tempered *adj (person)* irascível *m,f*, irritadiço,-a.

quick-witted *adj (person)* perspicaz *m,f*; **2** *(reaction)* rápido,-a, vivo,-a.

quid *n, npl (UK, coll)* libra (esterlina) *f*; **lend me ten** ~ empresta-me dez libras/dez paus *(EP)*; IDIOM **to be** ~**s in** *(UK, coll)* estar numa posição vantajosa.

quiddity *n (philosophy)* quidadade *f*.

quid pro quo *n* compensação *f*, retribuição *f*, troca *f*.

quiescent *adj* quiescente *m,f*.

quiet *n* sossego *m*, quietude *f*; ♦ *adj (peaceful)* tranquilo,-a; quieto,-a; **a** ~ **village** uma aldeia sossegada; **2** *(silent)* silencioso,-a; calado,-a; **he is very** ~ ele está muito calado; **3** *(discreet)* discreto,-a; ~ **dinner** jantar *m* íntimo; ♦ *vt* fazer calar, tranquilizar; **keep** ~! cale-se!; IDIOM **to do sth on the** ~ fazer algo pela calada, em segredo.

quieten (= ~ **down**) *vi* acalmar-se; **2** calar-se.

quietly *adv* tranquilamente, silenciosamente.

quietness *n* calma *f*, tranquilidade *f*; silêncio *m*.

quiff *n (hairstyle)* poupa *f*; topete *m*.

quill *n (pen)* pena *f* (de escrever); **2** (de ave) pluma *f*; **3** *(of porcupine)* espinho *m*.

quilt *n (bed linen)* colcha *f*; edredão *m*.

quilted *adj* acolchoado,-a.

quinary *adj (MATH)* quinário,-a.

quince *n (fruit)* marmelo *m*; ~ **jam** *n* marmelada *f*.

quincentenary *(pl: -ies) n* quingentésimo aniversário *m*.

quincunx *n* quincunce *m*.

quinine *n (PHARM)* quinina *f*.

quinoa *n (BOT)* quinoa *f*.

quinoline *n (CHEM)* quinoleína *f*.

quinquennial *n* quinquénio *m*; ◆ *adj* quinquenal *m,f*.

quins *(UK)* **quints** *(US) npl (Vd: **quintuplets**).*

quinsy *n (MED)* angina *f*.

quintessence *n* quinta-essência *f*.

quintessential *adj* quintessencial *m,f*; puro,-a, típico,-a.

quintet(te) *n* quinteto *m*.

quintuplets *npl* quíntuplos *mpl*.

quip *n* gracejo *m*, dito *m* espirituoso; ◆ *(-pp-) vi* gracejar.

quire *n (24 or 25 sheets of paper)* mão *f* de papel.

quirk *n (habit)* idiossincrasia *f*, mania *f*.

quirky *(-ier, -iest) adj* peculiar *m,f*, excêntrico,-a.

quisling *n (pej) (traitor)* colaboracionista *m,f*.

quit *(pres p -tt-; pt, pp **quit** or **quitted**) vt* deixar, desistir de; abandonar; ◆ *vi (stop)* parar; **2** *(give up)* desistir; **3** *(leave)* ir(-se) embora; **4** *(resign)* demitir-se.

quitclaim *n (JUR)* renúncia *f*.

quite *adv* bastante; muito; ~ **a few** bastantes, um bom número; **2** *(enough)* **it is** ~ **sufficient!** é bastante!, chega!; **3** *(after negative)* **I don't** ~ **see how you can do it** não vejo muito bem como vais fazer isso; **4** *(emphasis)* **she is** ~ **a woman** ela é uma mulher a valer; ~ **something** algo especial; **5** *(to express agreement)* ~ **so**! isso mesmo!,

perfeitamente!; **that's** ~ **all right** não faz mal; **to be** ~ **honest, I don't think that** ... para ser sincero, eu não acho que ...; *(impatience/anger)* **have you** ~ **finished?** já acabaste?

quits *adj (fam)* quite(s) *m,f*; IDIOM **to call it** ~ estar quites.

quittance *n* quitação *f*.

quitter *n* desistente *m,f*, falhado,-a; **he is not a** ~ ele não é dos que desistem facilmente.

quiver *n (shake)* estremecimento *m*; **2** *(case for arrows)* aljava *f*; ◆ *vi* estremecer.

quixotic *adj* quixotesco,-a, idealista *m,f*.

quiz *n* concurso *m* (de cultura geral); questionário *m*, teste *m*; ~ **game** *n* jogo *m* de perguntas e respostas; ~**master** *n* apresentador de concurso de cultura geral; ◆ *(-zz-) vt* interrogar.

quizical *adj* interrogativo,-a.

quizically *adv* com perplexidade.

quod *n (UK) (slang) (jail)* xelindró *m*, choça *f (cal)*.

quoits *npl* jogo *m* da malha; **to play** ~ jogar à malha.

quorate *(UK) adj* que tem quorum.

quorum *n* quórum *m*.

quota *n (COMM)* quota *f*, contingente *m*; **2** *(proportional share)* quinhão *m*; quota-parte; ~ **sampling** *n (marketing)* sondagem *f* por quotas.

quotable *adj* citável.

quotation *n* citação *f*, orçamento *m*, cotação *f*; ~ **marks** *npl* aspas *fpl*.

quote *n* citação *f*; **2** *(COMM)* cotação *f*; ◆ *vt* citar; cotar, fixar; ◆ *vi*: **to** ~ **from** citar de, transcrever de.

quotidian *adj* quotidiano,-a.

quotient *n (MATH)* quociente *m*.

q.v. *(abbr for **quod vide**)* o que vir, tanto quanto vir; veja.

qy *(abbr for **query**)*.

r

R, r *n (letter)* R, r *m*.
Ra *n (CHEM symbol for* **radium***) (Vd:* **radium***).*
RA *(abbr for* **Royal Academy***);* **2** *(UK) (abbr for* **Royal Artillery***);* **3** *(US) (abbr for* **Regular Army***).*
Rabah *npr* Rabat.
rabbet *n (CONSTR) (groove)* rebaixo *m;* **2** *(joint)* malhete *m;* ♦ *vt (cut)* abrir uma ranhura; **2** *(join)* encaixar.
rabbi *n (REL)* rabino *m*.
rabbit *n (ZOOL, CULIN)* coelho,-a; ~ **fever** *n* febre *f* do coelho; ~ **hole** *n* toca *f*, lura *f;* ~ **hutch** *n (cage)* coelheira *f;* ~ **warren** *n (tunnels for or colony of rabbits)* coelheira; ♦ *vi* **to** ~ **on** *(also: away)* **about** estar sempre a falar de; **he is always rabbiting on about his job** ele está sempre a falar do trabalho.
rabble *n (disorderly crowd)* gentalha *f*, povinho *m;* *(pej) (riffraff)* ralé *f;* **2** *(metallurgy)* esborralhador *m;* ~ **rouser** *n* agitador *m*, demagogo *m*.
rabid *adj (MED, VET)* raivoso,-a; **2** *(fig)* fanático,-a, ferrenho,-a.
rabies *n (disease)* raiva *f;* **2** *(injection, etc)* anti-rábico (antirrábico).
RAC *(abbr for* **Royal Automobile Club***)* automóvel clube britânico.
rac(c)oon *n (ZOOL)* guaxinim *m*.
race *n (ethnicity)* raça *f;* *(BOT, ZOOL)* espécie *f;* **2** *(SPORT)* corrida *f;* **3** *(contest)* competição *f;* **a** ~ **against time** uma corrida *f* contra o tempo; ~ **meeting** *n* concurso *m* hípico; ~ **relations** relações *fpl* inter-raciais (interraciais); ~ **riot** *n* conflito *m* entre raças; ~ **track** *n* pista *f* de corridas, autódromo *m;* ♦ *vi (compete)* competir, correr (**against** contra); **2** *(hurry)* apressar-se, despachar-se; **3** *(heart, pulse)* bater rapidamente; **my mind** ~**d ahead** eu precipitei-me; ♦ *vt* fazer correr; *(AUT)* acelerar.
racecourse *n (for horses)* hipódromo *m;* *(for cars)* autodrómo *m*.
racehorse *n* cavalo *m* de corrida.
racer *n* corredor,-ora.
racial *adj* racial; ~ **discrimination** *n* discriminação *f* racial.
racialism *n* racismo *m*.
racialist *n adj* racista.
racing *n (SPORT)* corrida *f;* ~ **driver** *n* piloto,-a de corridas.
racism *n* racismo *m*.
racist *n adj* racista *m,f*.
rack *n (shelf)* prateleira *f;* *(clothes hanger)* cabide *m;* **2** *(for luggage)* porta-bagagem *m;* **3** **(on the** ~**)**

(torture) tortura *f*, suplício *m;* tormento *m;* **bicycle** ~ suporte *m* para bicicletas; **coat** ~ bengaleiro *m;* ~ **and pinion** *n (TECH)* cremalheira *f* e pinhão *m;* ♦ *vt (harass)* atormentar; **2** *(torture)* torturar, **3** *(wine)* transfundir; IDIOM **to** ~ **one's brains** dar voltas ao miolo; **to** ~ **up points** acumular pontos.
racket[1] *(racquet) (SPORT)* raqueta *f; (BR)* raquete *f*.
racket[2] *n (noise, loud party)* barulheira *f;* algazarra *f;* **2** *(illegal activity)* negócio *m* illegal, fraude *f;* ♦ *vt (noise)* fazer barulho; IDIOM **to** ~ **about** andar na folia.
racketeer *n* escroque *m*.
racketeering *n (pej)* exploração *f*, extorsão *f*.
rackety *adj (rowdy)* barulhento,-a.
raconteur *n* contador *m* de histórias.
racquet *n* = **racket**.
racquets *n, sg (US) (semelhante a)* squash *m*.
racy (-ier, -iest) *adj (spirited)* vivo, espirituoso, **2** *(risqué)* ousado,-a, picante; ~ **joke** anedota *f* picante, atrevida; ~ **style** estilo *m* vivaço,-a.
radar *n* radar *m;* ~ **antenna** antena *f* de radar; ~ **receiver** receptor *m* de radar; ~**scope** *n* indicador *m* de radar; ~ **trap: to go through a** ~ passar por um radar; ~ **vehicle** *n* carro-radar *m*.
raddle *vt (weave)* entretecer; **2** *(paint)* pintar a cara com rouge.
radial *adj* radial; ~ **engine** *n* motor *m* radial; ~ **force** força *f* radial; ~ **tyre** *n* pneu *m* radial; ♦ *adj* radial, em estrela.
radian *n (GEOM)* radiano *m*.
radiance *n* brilho *m*, esplendor *m;* **2** *(PHYS)* radiação *f*.
radiant *adj* brilhante; **2** *(happy)* radiante; ~ **smile** *n* sorriso *m* radiante; **3** *(TECH)* por radiação; ~ **heat** calor por radiação.
radiate *vt* irradiar; emitir; ♦ *vi* difundir-se, estender-se.
radiation *n (PHYS)* radiação *f;* ~ **energy** energia *f* de radiação; ~ **pattern** *n* diagrama *m* de radiação; ~ **sickness** *n* mal *m* das radiações; ~ **therapy** radioterapia *f*.
radiator *n* radiador *m;* **to turn up/down the** ~ elevar/baixar o calorífero; ~ **cap** *n* tampa *f* do radiador; ~ **grille** *n* grade *f* do radiador.
radical *adj* radical.
radicalism *n (POL)* radicalismo *m*.
radically *adv* radicalmente.
radicle *n (BOT)* radícula *f*.
radio[1] *n* rádio *m;* ~ **announcer** *n* locutor,-ora; ~ **communication** *n* radiocomunicação *f;* ~**-controlled** *adj* controlado por rádio; ~ **frequency** *n* radiofrequência *f;* ~ **station** *n* emissora *f* radiofónica, de rádio; ~ **wave** onda *f* radioeléctrica.
radio[2] *pref* radio; ~**active** *adj* radioa(c)tivo; ~**activity** *n* radioa(c)tividade *f;* ~ **beam** *n* feixe *m* de rádio; ~**element** *n* elemento *m* radioactivo; ~**graphy** *n* radiografia *f;* ~**logy** *n* radiologia *f;* ~**phone** *n* radiotelefone *m;* ~**therapy** *n* radioterapia *f*.
radish *n (BOT)* rabanete *m*.
radium *n (CHEM)* rádio *m*.
radius *(pl:* **radii***) n (gen) (GEOM)* raio *m;* alcance *m;* **within a five km** ~ num raio de dez kms;

~ **of curvature** raio *m* de curvatura; **2** *(ANAT)* rádio *m*.

radix *n (BOT, MATH)* raiz *f.*

radon *n (CHEM)* rádon *m.*

RAF *npr (abbr for* **Royal Air Force**) Força Aérea Real britânica.

raffia *n (BOT)* ráfia *f.*

raffish *adj (coll)* libertino; **2** *(flashy)* espalhafatoso,-a; pessoa que dá nas vistas.

raffle *n (lottery)* rifa *f,* sorteio *m;* ♦ *vt* rifar, sortear.

raft *n (float)* jangada *f,* balsa *f;* **2** *(CONSTR)* laje *f;* **3** *(fam) (lots of)* montes de; **life** ~ *n* barco *m* salva-vidas.

rafter *n (CONSTR)* viga *f,* caibro *m,* barrote *m.*

rafting *n (SPORT)* rafting *m.*

rag *n (cloth)* trapo *m;* farrapo *m;* ~ **doll** boneca *f* de trapos; **2** *(newspaper)* jornaleco *m;* **rags** *npl* trapos *mpl,* farrapos *mpl;* **in** ~**s** esfarrapado; ♦ *vt* arreliar, zombar de; IDIOM **from** ~**s to riches** história da Cinderela; da pobreza à riqueza; **to lose one's** ~ perder a paciência.

ragamuffin *n* maltrapilho,-a.

rag-and-bone man *n* trapeiro,-a, comerciante *m,f* de coisas usadas.

rage *n (anger)* raiva *f,* furor *m;* **2** *(fashion)* voga *f,* moda *f;* **it's all the** ~ é a grande moda, está em voga; ♦ *vi* estar furioso; bramar; **to fly into a** ~ enfurecer-se; **to be blind with** ~ estar cego de cólera.

ragged *adj (person wearing torn clothes)* maltrapilho, andrajoso; **2** *(uneven)* irregular, desigual *m,f.*

raggle-taggle *adj (unkempt)* desleixado,-a.

raging *adj* furioso,-a.

raglan *adj (sleeve)* raglã.

ragout *n (CULIN)* ragu *m.*

ragtag *n (pej)* gentalha *f;* *adj (group)* desordenado,-a.

ragtime *n (MUS)* ragtime *m.*

rag trade *n* indústria *f* de vestuário.

ragweed *n (BOT)* tasneira *f.*

raid *n (MIL)* incursão *f;* assalto *m,* ataque *m;* **police** ~ rusga *f* policial; *(BR)* batida *f* policial; ♦ *vt* invadir, atacar, assaltar.

raider *n* atacante *m,f;* assaltante *m,f.*

rail *n (handrail)* corrimão *m;* **2** *(BR)* barra *f,* varão *m;* *(on bridge, tower)* parapeito *m;* *(on ship)* amurada *f;* **3** *(track for train, tram)* carril *m,* trilho *m;* ~ **strike** *n* greve *f* de ferroviários; IDIOM **to go off the rails** descarrilar.

railing *n (around street, park)* grade; *(on balcony)* balaustrada *f.*

rail in/off *vt* cercar; vedar.

raillery *n (banter)* troça *f,* brincadeira *f.*

railroad *n (US)* caminho *m* de ferro; ♦ *vt (coll) (push)* **to** ~ **sth through** *(committee)* fazer passar algo em.

railway *n (UK)* caminho *m,* *(BR)* estrada *f* de ferro; ferrovia *f;* ~ **crossing** *n* passagem *f* de nível; ~ **engine** *n* locomotive *f;* ~ **man** *n* ferroviário; ~ **station** *n* estação *f* de caminho de ferro, *(BR)* estação *f* ferroviária.

rain *n (MET)* chuva *f;* **in the** ~ à chuva; ~**bow** *n* arco-íris *m inv;* ~**coat** *n* impermeável *m,* gabardine *f,* *(BR)* capa de chuva; ~**drop** *n* pingo,-a de chuva;

~**fall** *n* chuva *f,* pluviosidade *f;* ~**forest** *n* floresta *f* tropical, pluvial; ~ **gauge** *n* pluviómetro *m;* ~**proof** *adj* impermeável; ~**storm** *n* temporal *m* de chuva; ~**ed off** cancelado devido ao mau tempo; ♦ *vi* chover; IDIOM **to** ~ **cats and dogs** chover a potes/a cântaros; **come** ~ **or shine** aconteça o que acontecer; **when it** ~**s, it pours** uma desgraça nunca vem só; **to be as right as** ~ estar como novo.

rain check *n (US) (fam):* **to take a** ~ aceitar adiamento duma oferta.

rainy *adj* chuvoso,-a.

raise *n* aumento *m;* ♦ *vt (gen: lift up)* levantar; erguer *(statue);* **to** ~ **one's hand/voice** levantar a mão, a voz; **he** ~**d the glass to his lips** ele levou o copo aos lábios; **to** ~ **the glass to sb** *(toast)* fazer um brinde à saúde de alguém; **to** ~ **sb's spirits** levantar o moral; **2** *(improve)* elevar *(standards);* **3** *(increase pay)* aumentar; **4** *(capital)* arranjar dinheiro, angariar fundos; **5** *(AGR)* cultivar; **6** *(bring up)* criar, educar *(child);* *(breed)* criar *(chicken, pigs etc);* **7** *(rouse)* suscitar, despertar; **8** *(of questions)* fazer, expor; **9 to** ~ **from the dead** *(fig)* ressuscitar; **10 to** ~ **the alarm** dar o alarme; ♦ *vr* **to** ~ **o.s.** levantar-se, erguer-se; IDIOM **to** ~ **the roof/the devil** fazer uma grande barulheira.

raisin *n (CULIN)* passa *f,* uva *f* seca.

Raja, raja *n (India)* rajá *m.*

rake *n (AGRO – tool)* ancinho *m;* **2** *(in casino)* rodo *m (de croupier);* **3** libertino,-a devasso,-a; ♦ *vt* alisar; revolver com o ancinho; **2** varrer de ponta a ponta; **3** *(scan)* sondar; **4** vascular; ♦ **to** ~ **among/through** remexer em *(drawer);* **to** ~ **in** *(fam)* encher-se de dinheiro; **to** ~ **off** partilhar de lucros ilícitos; **to** ~ **(out)** *(grass, leaves)* limpar/ juntar com ancinho; **to** ~ **up** desenterrar; **2** reavivar, trazer à baila *(past, grievance);* IDIOM **as thin as a** ~ magro como um palito.

rake-off *n* lucros *mpl* ilícitos; soborno *m.*

rakish *adj (jaunty)* elegante; **2** *(dissolute)* libertino,-a; **at a** ~ **angle** *(cap, hat)* de banda, inclinado,-a.

rale *n (MED)* rala *f;* pieira *f.*

rally *n (POL)* reunião *f,* comício *m;* **2** *(AUT)* rally *m,* rali *m;* **3** *(recovery) (health)* melhoramento *m;* *(FIN)* recrudescimento *m;* ♦ *vt* reunir *(troops);* **2** *(liven up)* animar, encorajar; **3** *(tease)* arreliar; ♦ *vi* reorganizar-se, reunir-se; **2** *(recover) (patient)* recuperar-se; *(in sport)* recobrar forças; *(dollar, prices)* subir; ♦ **to** ~ **round** *vt (supporters)* juntar-se; **to** ~ **sb** dar apoio a.

RAM *n (abb for:* **random access memory**) RAM *f.*

ram *n (sheep)* carneiro *m,* **2** *(TECH)* êmbolo *m,* **3** *(MIL)* aríete *m;* ♦ *vt* (-mm-) introduzir à força *(in* em); cravar; **2** *(crash)* embater em; **to** ~ **a pole into the ground** enterrar um poste no terreno; **to** ~ **sth down sb's throat** impingir algo a alguém.

Ramadan *n (REL)* Ramadão *m;* *(BR)* ramadã *m.*

ramble *n (unplanned)* passeio *m (in the country-side),* excursão *f* a pé; ♦ *vi (walk)* vaguear; **to** ~ **on** *(talk)* divagar.

rambler *n* caminhante *m,f;* itinerante *m,f;* **2** *(BOT)* trepadeira *f.*

rambling adj (nomadic) errante; (talk) desconexo,-a; incoerente; **a ~ old house** uma casa cheia de recantos.

ramekin n (CULIN) prato feito de queijo, pão, ovos, que vai ao forno em pequenos recipientes.

ramification n ramificação f.

ramify vt ramificar; ♦ vi ramificar-se.

ramose adj (BOT) ramificado,-a, com ramos.

ramp n (slope) rampa f; **2** (gangway) rampa de embarque.

rampage n alvoroço m; ♦ vi barafustar, esbravejar; **to be/go on the ~** sair em debandada; estar furioso,-a, alvoroçar-se.

rampant adj (heraldic lion etc standing on hind legs) rampante m,f; **2** desenfreado,-a; descontrolado.

rampart n (CONSTR) baluarte m; muralha f.

rampion n (BOT) rapúncio m.

ramshackle adj (building) decrépito,-a, em ruínas.

ran (pt of run).

ranch n (AGR) rancho m, fazenda f, granja f. **rancher** n rancheiro,-a, fazendeiro,-a.

rancid adj rançoso,-a; **to smell ~** cheirar a ranço.

rancidity n ranço m.

rancour (UK) **rancor** (US) n rancor m, ódio m.

rancourous adj rancoroso,-a (**towards sb** para com alguém).

rand n (South Africa's monetary unit) rand m.

random n acaso m; **at ~** ao acaso, à toa; ♦ adj casual m,f, fortuito; **~ access memory** n (COMP) memória f de acesso aleatório, RAM; **~ variable** n (statistics) variável f aleatória.

randomly adv aleatoriamente, ao acaso.

randy (-ier, -iest) adj (coll: sexually aroused) excitado, pronto para sexo; lascivo,-a.

rang (pt of ring).

range n (of mountains) cadeia f, cordilheira f; **2** (choice) (of products, colours) gama; (of business, activity, subject) leque m; **3** (gen, distance) distância f, alcance m; **4** (FIN) (limit) limites mpl; **5** (MUS) (of voice, instrument) registo m; **6** (NAUT) linha f; **~ of action** n raio (de a(c)ção); **at close ~** adj à queima-roupa; **at a ~ of** adv a uma distância de; **~finder** n telémetro m; **free ~ of** n acesso livre a; **gas ~** n grande fogão m a gás, a lenha; **out of ~** adv fora do alcance; **shooting ~** n o alcance de tiro; ♦ vt alinhar, arrumar, ordenar; ♦ vi: **to ~ over** percorrer, estender-se por; **to ~ from … to …** variar de … a …, oscilar entre … e …

ranger n guarda-florestal m.

Rangoon npr Rangum.

rangy adj (ANAT) delgado,-a, esguio,-a.

rank n (row) fila f, fileira f, **2** (MIL) posto m, graduação f, **3** (status) categoria f, posição f; **4** (= taxi ~) praça f (BR: ponto m) de táxis; **~ and file** n (MIL) soldados mpl rasos; gente f comum; **to be of high/low ~** ser de alta/baixa condição; (line of people) fila; (line of objects) fileira f; **ranks** npl tropa f; ♦ adj (foul smell) fétido,-a, malcheiroso,-a; **2** (utter) absoluto,-a; **3** (vegetation) luxuriante, viçoso,-a; ♦ vi: **to ~ among** (rate) figurar entre; classificar-se; **to smell ~** cheirar mal, feder; IDIOM **to rise through the ~s** ser promovido.

ranking n classificação f; ♦ adj proeminente; de alto nível; (US) do alto escalão.

rankle vi doer, causar dor; **2** (fig) ficar magoado,-a.

ransack vt (search) revistar; **2** (plunder) saquear, pilhar.

ransacking n pilhagem f.

ransom n resgate m; (fig) **a king's ~** uma pipa de massa; ♦ vi: resgatar; **to hold sb to ~** deter alguém como refém.

rant n (declamatory) declamação f afe(c)tada; discurso bombástico; ♦ vi declamar, falar em estilo bombástico, empolado; **2** (speak with agitation) barafustar.

ranting n palavreado m zangado em voz alta.

rap n (knock, tap) pancadinha f; **2** (music) música f rap; ♦ (-pp-) vt (tap) bater em; ♦ vi (tap) dar pancadinhas secas (**with** com); IDIOM **to take the ~** (for someone else) apanhar com as culpas de; **to beat the ~** escapar de uma punição, censura.

rapacious adj voraz, ganancioso,-a;

rapacity n voracidade f, ganância f.

rape n (JUR) violação f, estupro m; **2** (BOT) colza; ♦ vt violar; violentar.

rapeseed oil n (CULIN) óleo m de colza.

rapid adj (movement) rápido,-a; **~ eye movement** (REM) n movimento rapido dos olhos durante o sono.

rapid-fire n (MIL) fogo m cerrado; **2** (fast action) feito um atrás do outro.

rapidity n rapidez f.

rapidly adj rapidamente.

rapids npl (of river) rápido m, (BR) corredeira f; **to shoot the ~** transpor os rápidos (de barco).

rapier n (sword) espadim m, florete; **~ fish** n espadarte m.

rapist n violador m, estuprador m.

rappel n (SPORT) rapel; ♦ vt praticar rapel.

rapport n relação f, harmonia f, afinidade f (**with, between** com, entre); **we are in ~** estamos em harmonia.

rapporteur n relator m.

rapscallion n patife m, canalha m.

rapt adj absorto,-a; **~ with wonder** maravilhado,-a; **a ~ smile** sorriso extasiado.

rapture n êxtase m, arrebatamento m.

rapturous adj extático,-a; entusiasta.

rapturously adv entusiasticamente.

rare adj (not common) raro,-a, fora do comum **2** (CULIN) (underdone) malpassado.

rarebit n: **Welsh ~** (CULIN) torrada f coberta de queijo derretido.

rarefaction n (PHYS) rarefa(c)ção f.

rarefied adj (PHYS) rarefeito,-a; **2** (pej) elitista m,f.

rarefy vt rarefazer(-se).

rarely adv raramente.

rareness n raridade f; infrequência f.

raring adj desejoso,-a (**to** por), mortinho,-a por.

rarity n raridade f.

rascal n (affectionate) (child, pet) maroto m; (man) (scoundrel) malandro m.

rash n (MED) (skin eruption) exantema m; vermelhidão f; **nettle ~** n urticária f; ♦ adj impetuoso, precipitado; **it was a ~ decision** foi uma decisão impetuosa/imprudente/precipitada.

rasher *n (CULIN):* ~ **of bacon** fatia fina *f* de presunto.

rashly *adv (hastily)* precipitadamente; **2** sem pensar.

rashness *n* impetuosidade *f*, imprudência *f*.

rasp *n (of saw, voice)* ruído *m* irritante; **2** *(file)* lixa *f*; ♦ *vt/vi* falar com uma voz áspera; **2** *(file, saw)* ranger.

raspatory *n (MED)* raspador *m*.

raspberry *n (BOT)* framboesa *f*; ~**bush** *n* framboeseira *f*; **2** *(rude noise with the mouth)* deboche *m*; IDIOM **to blow a ~ at sb** mandar alguém passear, mandar alguém à fava.

rasping *adj (sound, voice)* irritante, áspero,-a; ♦ **raspings** *npl* pão *m* ralado *(for frying fish)*.

rastafarian *n* rastafári *m,f*.

rat *n (ZOOL)* ratazana *f*; ~ **poison** *n* veneno para ratos; ~ **race** *n (in business and in society)* competição *f* acirrada; ~**-trap** *n* ratoeira *f*; **2** *(coll, pej) (person - false)* judas *m*, canalha *m*; **3** *(spy for the police)* espião *m*, espiã *f*; ♦ *(pres p, pt, pp* -**tt**-*) vt/vi (hunt)* caçar ratazanas; **2** *(coll) (divulge)* chibar-se, contar; IDIOM **I smell a ~** *(fig)* aqui há gato *(EP)*; aí tem dente de coelho *(BR)*; **like a drowned ~** molhado que nem um pinto.

rat-arsed *adj (UK) (drunk)* bêbado,-a/bêbedo,-a.

ratatouille *n (CULIN)* ratatui *m*.

ratbag *n (coll) (despicable)* miserável.

ratcatcher *n* exterminador *m*; **2** *(cat)* caçador de ratos.

ratchet *n (TECH) (in wheel)* roquete *m*; ~ **wheel** *n* roda *f* dentada.

rate *n (value)* razão *f*; percentagem *f*; proporção *f*; **2** *(payment)* preço *m*, taxa *f*; **3** *(hotel)* diária *f*; **4** *(speed)* velocidade *f*; ♦ *vt* avaliar; **2** *(charge)* tributar; **3 to ~ as** considerar como; ♦ *adv* **any ~** de qualquer modo; **at this ~** por este andar; ~**-capping** *n* limite imposto no aumento de impostos; ~ **of exchange** *n* taxa *f* de câmbio; ~ **of interests** *n* taxa *f* de juros; ~**payer** *n* contribuinte; ~**s** *npl* imposto *sg* municipal; ~ **value** *n* valor *m* tributável.

rateable *adj (property)* sujeita a avaliação para efeitos tributáveis.

rated *adj* avaliado,-a (**at**, em); **2** nominal; **3** *(regarded)* considerado,-a; classificado,-a (entre).

ratfink *n (US) (coll)* pessoa indesejável.

rat-gnawed *adj* roído pelos ratos.

rather *adv* muito; **2** antes, preferivelmente; **3** melhor dito; **4** certamente; **its ~ expensive** é um pouco caro; **there's ~ a lot** há bastante, muito; **I would/ had ~ go dancing** eu preferia ir dançar; ~ **than** ao invés de; **I would ~ die!** preferia morrer!

raticide *n* mata-ratos *m*.

ratification *n* ratificação *f*.

ratify *(pt, pp* -**ied**) *vt* ratificar.

rating *n (rank)* avaliação *f*; valor *m*; posição *f*; **2** *(NAUT)* marinheiro *m*; ~**s** *npl (TV, RADIO)* audiências *fpl*.

ratio *n* razão *f*, proporção *f*; ~ **scale** *n* escala *f* de razão; **in the ~ of 100 to 1** na proporção de 100 para 1.

ration *n* ração *f*; **2** *(sufficient amount)* dose *f*; ~**s** *npl* mantimentos *mpl*, víveres *mpl*; ~ **book** *n* senha *f* de racionamento *m*; ♦ *vt* racionar.

rational *adj* racional *m,f*; lógico; sensato, razoável *m,f*; ~ **number** número *m* racional.

rationale *n (without pl)* lógica *f*, fundamento *m* lógico; sem razões *fpl* (**for sth** para algo).

rationalisation *n* racionalização *f*, justificação.

rationalise, rationalize *vt* racionalizar.

rationalism *n* racionalismo *m*.

rationalist *n adj* racionalista *m,f*.

rationing *m* racionamento *m*.

ratite *adj (ZOOL)* ratite *m,f*; ~ **bird** *n* ave *f* corredora.

ratoon *n (BOT)* rebento *m*; ♦ *vt/vi* rebentar.

ratsbane *n (poison)* veneno *m* mata-ratos.

rattan *n (BOT)* rotim *m*.

ratter *n (dog)* rateiro,-a.

rattle *n (sound of) (of drum) (sound)* batida *f*, rufar *m*; *(of window, door)* bater; *(of cutlery, bottles)* chocalhar *m*, chocalhada *f*; **2** *(cat's bell, toy)* guizo *m*; *(sports, instrument)* matraca *f*; ~**-brain** *n* cabeça-de-vento *m,f*; ♦ *vi* chocalhar; *(bottles)* entrechocar-se; bater; **the hail ~d against the window panes** o granizo batia fortemente nas vidraças (da janela); matraquear; ♦ *vt* fazer ressoar; **2** *(make sb nervous)* desconcertar (**sb** alguém); **to ~ off** repetir de memória; recitar rapidamente; **to ~ on** tagarelar; **to get ~ed** meter os pés pelas mãos.

rattlesnake *n (cobra)* cascavel *f*.

rattling *adj* ruidoso,-a; **at a ~ pace** a passo vigoroso, rápido; ♦ *adv* extremamente, deveras.

ratty (-ier, -iest) *adj (coll)* irritável *m,f*; embirrento,-a, rabujento,-a.

raucous *adj* áspero, rouco.

raucously *adv* roucamente.

raucousness *n* rouquidão *f*.

raunchy (-ier, -iest) *adj (slang) (lusty) (artist, song)* sexual, sexualmente explícito,-a; **2** *(book, story)* picante *(fig)*.

ravage *vt* devastar, estragar.

ravages *npl* estragos *mpl*; **the ~ of time** a devastação *f*, os estragos *mpl* do tempo.

rave *n (party)* rave *f*; **2** *(fashion)* moda *f*; **3** delírio *m*, frenesi *m*; ♦ *adj* entusiástico; ♦ *vi (anger)* encolerizar-se; **2** *(excitement)* falar com entusiasmo; **3** *(MED)* delirar, desvairar.

ravel *n (tangle)* emaranhado *m (of threads, etc)* *m*; fiapo *m*; **2** *(fig)* confusão *f*; *(plot)* enredo *m*; ♦ *(-ll-) vt/vi* emaranhar; enredar; **to ~ out** desfiar-se, desmanchar.

raven *n (ZOOL)* corvo *m*; ♦ *adj (colour)* negro *m*; ♦ *vt/vi (seize)* perseguir; roubar; **2** *(eat)* devorar.

ravenous *adj* faminto, esfaimado, voraz *m,f*; ~ **hunger** *n* fome *f* voraz.

ravenously *adv* vorazmente.

raver *n (coll)* frequentador,-ora de raves, raver.

rave-up *n* festa de rave.

ravine *n* ravina *f*, barranco *m*.

raving *adj* louco; delirante; ~ **mad** doido,-a varrido,-a.

ravings *npl* divagações *fpl*.

ravioli *n (CULIN) (pasta)* massa *f* ravioli *m*.

ravish *vt (delight)* arrebatar; encantar; **2** *(rape)* violar.

ravishing *adj* encantador,-ora, extasiante.

raw *adj (uncooked)* cru; **2** *(steel, coal)* bruto,-a, em bruto; *(oil)* crude; *(cotton, rubber, silk)* em rama, em estado natural, puro,-a; *(spirits)* puro,-a; **3** *(inexperienced person)* inexperiente *m,f*, novato; **4** *(without skin)* em carne viva; ~ **deal** *n* injustiça *f*; ~ **material** *n* matéria-prima *f*; *(fig) (basis)* base *f*; ~ **wound** *n* ferida *f* a sangrar; **5** *(realistic)* cru,-a; ~**boned** *adj (physic)* magro,-a; **to be** ~**boned** ser pele e osso *(fig)*; IDIOM **in the** ~ nu,-a; *(life)* ao natural; **to touch a** ~ **nerve** tocar no ponto fraco (de alguém); **my nerves are** ~ **today** hoje tenho os nervos à flor da pele.

rawlplug® *n* bucha *f*.

rawness *n* crueza *f*; imaturidade *f*.

ray *n (beam)* raio *m* **(of** de); **2** *(fig) (glimmer)* laivo *m*, réstia *f*; **a** ~ **of hope** uma réstia de esperança; **3** *(fish)* raia *f*; **X-**~**s** *n* raios X *mpl*.

ray-filter *n* (photo) filtro *m* ortocromático.

rayon *n (textile)* seda *f* artificial, rayon.

raze *vt* arrasar, demolir; **2** aniquilar; **to** ~ **sth to the ground** deitar (algo) por terra, destruir.

razor *n* navalha *f*; **safety** ~ *n* máquina *f* (BR: aparelho *m*) de barbear; ~ **blade** *n* gilete *m*, lâmina *f*; ~ **edge** *n* fio *m* de navalha; IDIOM **to live on** ~**'s edge** viver com um pé no abismo.

razorbill *n* (ZOOL) torda-mergulheira *f*.

razor-sharp *adj* muito afiado,-a; *(fig) (person) (quick)* ágil; perspicaz; **a** ~ **mind** *(person)* perspicaz *m,f*.

razor-shell *n (crab)* carvalheira *f*.

razzle *(UK) (fam)* farra *f*; **to go on the** ~ ir para a farra.

razzle-dazzle *n (coll)* reboliço *m*; pândega *f*.

R&B *n (abbr for **Rhythm and Blues**) (MUS)* R&B *m*.

rc *n (abbr for **reinforced concrete**) (CONSTR)* betão *m* armado.

RC *adj (abbr for **Roman Catholic**)* católico,-a romano,-a.

RC *(abbr for **Red Cross**)* Cruz Vermelha *f*.

Rd *n (abbr for **road**)*.

RDA *(abbr for **Recommended Daily Allowance**)* DDR (Dose Diária Recomendada).

re *n (MUS)* ré *m*; ♦ *prep* referente a, com referência a.

reabsorb *vt* reabsorver.

reabsorption *n* reabsorção *f*.

reaccuse *vt* acusar novamente.

reach *n* alcance *m*; **within** ~ **of** ao alcance de; na proximidade de; **2** distância *f*; ♦ *vt, vi (height, success)* chegar a; atingir; **2** *(get to)* alcançar; **3** *(achieve)* conseguir; **4** *(extend)* chegar até; estender(-se) **5** passar *(sth to sb, algo a alguém)*; **6** contatar; **to** ~ **down** abaixar-se; **to** ~ **one's hand** *(for)* estender a mão (para); **to** ~ **out for** *(affection)* procurar; **to** ~ **out to sb** *(help)* ajudar alguém; ♦ **reach(es)** *n (of river)* parte(s) *f*; **upper/lower** ~ parte superior/inferior

reachable *adj* acessível; **2** *(contactable)* **I am** ~ **by email only** só posso ser conta(c)tado,-a por email.

react *vi* reagir; **to** ~ **against** reagir contra; **to** ~ **to** reagir a.

reactant *n (CHEM)* reagente *m*.

reaction *n* rea(c)ção *f*; **chain** ~ *n* rea(c)ção *f* em cadeia; **chemical** ~ *n* rea(c)ção *f* química; ~ **chamber** *n* câmara *f* de rea(c)ção; ~ **time** *n* tempo *m* de rea(c)ção.

reactionary *n adj* rea(c)cionário,-a.

reactivate *vt* rea(c)tivar.

reactive *adj* rea(c)tivo,-a.

reactivity *n* rea(c)tividade *f*.

reactor *n (PHYS)* rea(c)tor *m*.

read *adj* lido; **well** ~ *(book)* muito lido; *(person)* culto,-a, erudito,-a, versado,-a **(in** em); ♦ *(pt, pp*: **read**) *vt,vi (gen)* ler; **she can't** ~ ela não sabe ler; **to** ~ **sb's mind** ler os pensamentos de alguém; *(ELECT, gas)* **the man came to** ~ **the meter** o funcionário veio tirar a leitura do contador; **2** *(show)* indicar, marcar; **the barometer** ~**s** o barómetro indica; **3** *(Univ study)* estudar, preparar; **to** ~ **History** estudar História; **4** *(interpret)* interpretar *(signs, reactions)*; **to** ~ **the stars** interpretar os astros; **5** *(decipher) (code, braille)* decifrar; **he is good at** ~**ing riddles** ele é bom a decifrar advinhas; **6** *(say, tell)* dizer; **the letter** ~**s thus** a carta diz assim; **7 to** ~ **proofs** corrigir provas; **the thesis** ~**s well** a tese está bem escrita; ♦ **I** ~ **you loud and and clear** compreendo aonde tu queres chegar; **2** *(on radio)* estoua compreender; ♦ **to** ~ **between the lines** ler nas entrelinhas; **to** ~ **aloud** ler em voz alta; **to** ~ **back** *(passage)* reler, tornar a ler; **to** ~ **into sth** tirar conclusões; **you** ~ **too much into her words** você levou muito a sério o que ela disse; tirou conclusões erradas; **to** ~ **on** continuar a ler; **to** ~ **out** ler em voz alta; **to** ~ **over** tornar a ler, reler; **to** ~ **up on** *(subject matter)* estudar a fundo (assunto).

readable *adj* legível; **2** que merece ser lido, interessante de se ler.

reader *n (person who reads)* leitor,-ora; **2** *(UK) (Univ)* professor,-ora adjunto,-a, assistente *m,f*; **proof** ~ *n* revisor,-ora de provas.

readership *n* leitores; público *m* leitor; **2** *(of newspaper, magazine)* número de assinantes.

readily *adv* prontamente; de boa vontade; facilmente.

readiness *n* boa vontade *f*, prontidão *f*; preparação *f*; **in** ~ preparado, pronto.

reading *n (act of reading)* leitura *f*; **2** *(understanding)* compreensão *f*; **3** *(of meter, gauge)* marcação; **4** *(interpreting)* interpretação **(of** de); ~ **glasses** *n* óculos *mpl* de ver ao perto; ~ **group** *n* grupo *m* de leitura; ~ **room** *n* sala *f* de leitura.

readjust *vt* reajustar; **to** ~ **to** reorientar-se para.

readjustable *adj* reajustável.

readjustment *n* reajustamento *m*; reorganização *f*.

readmission *n* readmissão *f*.

readmit *vt* readmitir.

ready *n*: **at the** ~ *(MIL)* pronto para disparar, atirar; ♦ *adj (prepared)* pronto, preparado; **2** *(willing)* disposto; disponível; **3** *(quick)* rápido; ~ **cash** *n* dinheiro em mão; ~~**made** *adj* feito, ; **2** *(clothes)* pronto a vestir; ~~**mix** *adj* instantâneo; ~ **reckoner** *n* tabela *f* de cálculos feitos; ~ **to hand** à mão, conveniente; ~ **to please** obsequioso; ~~**to-wear**

pronto,-a para vestir; **4** (~ **to**) prestes a; **to get** ~ preparar-se; *(groom o.s.)* arranjar-se; **to find** ~ **acceptance** ser aceite; ♦ *vt* preparar.

reaffirm *vt* reafirmar.

reagent *n* reagente *m*.

real *n (Brazillian monetary unit)* real *m*; ♦ *adj (not imaginary)* real; ~ **estate** *n (COMM) (property)* bens *mpl* imobiliários; *(sector)* se(c)tor imobiliário *m*; ~ **life** *n* vida *f* real; **2** *(not false)* verdadeiro,-a, autêntico,-a, genuíno,-a; **the** ~ **thing, the** ~ **McCoy** *(coll)* o autêntico; **this time it is the** ~ **thing** desta vez é mesmo a valer; **2 he knows the** ~ **me** ele conhece-me muito bem, ele conhece o meu verdadeiro íntimo; **3** *(coll)* grande; **a** ~ **idiot** um grande idiota; **it's a** ~ **shame!** é uma grande pena!; **4 in** ~ **terms** em termos reais; IDIOM **is he for** ~**?** ele é genuíno?; **is this friendship for** ~**?** esta amizade é a sério?

realgar *n (CHEM)* rosalgar *m*.

realign *vt* realinhar.

realignment *n* realinhamento *m*.

realism *(ART, etc)* realismo *m*; **2** (common sense) senso *m* comum.

realist *n* realista *m,f.*

realistic *adj* realista.

reality *n* realidade *f;* **2** existência *f;* **in** ~ na verdade; ~ **principle** *n (physchology)* princípio *m* de realidade; ~ **television** *n* TV realidade *f;* IDIOM **to be out of touch with** ~ viver fora da realidade.

realizable *adj* realizável; **2** *(COMM)* convertível em dinheiro.

realization *n (achievement)* realização *f;* **2** *(understanding)* compreensão *f;* **3** *(COMM)* conversão *f* em dinheiro.

realize *vt (become aware)* perceber, aperceber-se de; dar-se conta de; **2** *(achieve)* concretizar, levar a cabo *(plan, ambition)*; **3** compreender, saber; **I** ~ **that** … eu compreendo que …; **I didn't** ~ **you were out of town** não sabia que você estava fora; **do you** ~ **what time it is?** sabes que horas já são?; **to** ~ **one's potential** desenvolver as suas capacidades; **2** *(COMM) (sale)* render, fazer *(sum)*; IDIOM **to** ~ **the error of one's ways** aperceber-se do mal que se fez.

reallocate *vt* reatribuir.

really *adv* realmente, na verdade; *(emphasis)* muito, verdadeiramente, mesmo; ~ **cheap** muito barato; **you** ~ **have to see him** tens mesmo de o ver; **I had a** ~ **good time** *(fun)* diverti-me à farta; **2** *(surprise, disbelief)* ~**?** é mesmo?, deveras?; ♦ *exc (expressing annoyance)* ~**!** francamente!

realm *n (kingdom)* reino *m*; **2** *(fig) (field)* domínio *m*.

real-time *adj (COMP)* de tempo real.

realtor *n (US)* corretor *m,f* de vendas de imóveis.

realty *n* imóvel *m*; bens *mpl* imobiliários.

ream *n (paper)* resma *f.*

reamer *n* mandril *m*; escareador *m*.

reanimate *vt* reanimar.

reanimation *n* reanimação *f.*

reannex *vt* reanexar.

reannexation *n* reanexação *f.*

reap *vt* segar, ceifar; **2** *(fig)* colher; IDIOM **to** ~ **benefit from** tirar proveito *m* de; **to** ~ **the fruits of** obter os resultados de; **to** ~ **what one sows** cada um colhe o que semeia.

reaper *n* segador,-a, ceifeiro,-a; **the grim** ~ morte *f.*

reappear *vi* reaparecer.

reappearance *n* reaparecimento *m.*

reapply *vi* voltar a aplicar **(on** em/sobre); **2** *(for a job, course)* recandidatar-se a algo.

reappoint *vt* voltar a eleger, nomear.

reappraisal *n* reavaliação *f.*

reappraise *vt* reavaliar.

rear *n (of building, etc)* traseira *f; (also:* ~ **end)** *(of car)* traseiro *m*; **2** *(euph) (buttocks)* traseiro *m*; rabo *m (fam)*; bunda *f (from Angola) (fam)*; posterior *m (formal)*; **3** *(MIL) (of convoy, march)* retaguarda *f;* **to bring up the** ~ fechar a marcha *(BR)* fechar a raia; **4** *(of procession)* cauda *f;* ♦ *adj (back of house)* das traseiras, *(BR)* dos fundos *mpl*; ~ **admiral** *n (MIL)* contra-almirante *m*; ~**light** *n (AUT)* farol *m* traseiro; ♦ *vt (raise)* criar *(child, animal)*; ♦ *vi* (= ~ **up)** *(horse, etc)* empinar-se; **2** *(fig) (building, tree)* elevar-se; **3** *(head)* erguer.

rearguard *n* retaguarda *f.*

rearm *vt/vi* rearmar.

rearmament *n* rearmamento *m.*

rearmost *adj (carriage, person, etc)* último,-a; o/a de trás.

rearrange *vt (order)* tornar a arranjar, reorganizar; **2** *(schedule)* voltar a marcar.

rearview mirror *n (AUT)* espelho *m* retrovisor.

rearward/s *adj adv (position at the back) (MIL)* retaguarda *f;* atrás, de trás.

reason *n (judgement)* razão *f;* **2** *(motive)* motivo *m*, causa *f;* **3** *(prudence)* sensatez *f;* **by** ~ **of** por causa de; **within** ~ em moderação; **to listen to** ~ ser razoável; ~**s of State** *npl* razões do Estado; ♦ *vt* raciocinar; **to** ~ **out** compreender; **to** ~ **with** argumentar; chamar à razão; IDIOM **without rhyme or** ~ sem quê nem para quê; **it stands to** ~ **that** é lógico que; **to lose one's** ~ perder o juízo.

reasonable *adj* razoável; sensato,-a.

reasonably *adv* razoavelmente.

reasoned *adj* lógico,-a, fundamentado,-a.

reasoner *n* argumentador,-ora.

reasoning *n* raciocínio *m*, argumentação *f.*

reassemble *vt* tornar a montar; ♦ *vi* reunir-se de novo.

reassembly *n* reagrupamento *m.*

reassert *vt* reafirmar.

reassess *vt* reavaliar.

reassessment *n* nova avaliação *f.*

reassign *vt* readjudicar.

reassurance *n* tranquilização *f.*

reassure *vt* tranquilizar, animar.

reassuring *adj* animador.

reawaken *vt (from sleep)* voltar a despertar.

Reb *n (US)* soldado *m* na Guerra civil americana.

rebadge *vt* relançar um produto com outro nome.

rebate *n* abatimento *m*; desconto *m;* **2** *(refund)* reembolso *m*; **3** *(CONSTR)* rabbet; ♦ *vt (deduct)* descontar; **2** *(reduce)* diminuir.

rebeck *n (MUS)* arrabil *m*.

rebel *n* rebelde *m,f*; ◆ *vi* revoltar-se (**against**, contra).

rebellion *n* rebelião *f*, revolta *f*.

rebellious *adj* rebelde; revoltado,-a.

rebelliousness *n* rebeldia *f*.

rebind *vt* reencadernar.

rebinding *n* reencadernação *f*.

rebirth *n* renascimento *m*.

rebirthing *n (psychotherapy)* renascimento *m*.

reboot *vt (COMP)* reiniciar.

reborn *adj* renascido,-a.

rebound *n (SPORT)* recuo *m*, ressalto *m*; **2 on the ~** por despeito; **to marry sb on the ~** casar com alguém por despeito; ◆ *vi* repercutir; *(bounce)* ressaltar; *(for spite)* voltar-se (**on** contra).

rebound *(pp of* **rebind***)*.

rebuff *n* recusa *f* brusca; rejeição *f*; ◆ *vt* repelir; rejeitar; desdenhar ajuda.

rebuild *(pp, pt* **rebuilt***) vt* reconstruir.

rebuilding *n* reconstrução *f*.

rebuke *n (telling off)* reprimenda *f*; ◆ *vt* repreender (**sb for sth** alguém por algo); censurar alguém.

rebut (-tt-) *vt (refute)* refutar, rebater; **2** *(JUR)* ilidir.

rebuttal *n* refutação *f*.

recalcitrance *n* recalcitrância *f*; desobediência *f*.

recalcitrant *n adj* recalcitrante, teimoso,-a.

recalculate *vt* recalcular.

recalescence *n (metallurgy)* recalescência *f*.

recalescent *adj* rescalescente.

recalibrate *vt* recalibrar.

recall *n (call back)* chamada *f* (de volta); **2** *(memory)* recordação *f*; **3** *(cancellation)* revogação *f*; ◆ *vt (remember)* recordar, lembrar; **as I ~** se bem me lembro; **2** *(call back)* mandar chamar; **3** *(parliament)* convocar; **4** *(take back)* revogar, cancelar; **to sound the ~** *(MIL)* recolher.

recant *vt/vi (former statement)* retratar; repudiar; **2** *(faith)* abjurar; renegar.

recap *n* (= **recapitulation**) *(coll)* recapitulação *f*; ◆ (-pp-) *vt/vi* (= **recapitulate**) *(coll)* recapitular.

recapture *n* recuperação *f*; ◆ *vt* recapturar, retomar; recriar.

recast *(pt, pp* **recast***) vt* reatribuir; **2** *(THEAT, CIN)* fazer novo casting.

recd *(abbr for* **received***)* confirmação de recepção.

recede *vi* retroceder, afastar-se; **to ~ into the background** passar a segundo plano; **2** *(threat)* diminuir, afastar; **3** *(slope backwards)* recuar; **4** *(tide)* descer; **5** *(hair)* ter entradas.

receding *adj (person)* metido para dentro; *(hill, street)* recuado,-a; **~ chin/forehead** retraído,-a; **~ tide** maré *f* vazante; **to have a ~ hairline** ter entradas.

receipt *n* recibo *m*, fa(c)tura *f*, ticket *m*; recebimento *m*; rece(p)ção *f*.

receipts *npl (COMM)* receitas *fpl*.

receivable *adj* a receber; **accounts ~** *(awaiting payment)* a dever, a receber; **~s** *npl (COMM) (part of assets)* contas *fpl* a receber.

receive *vt (get)* receber; **2** *(welcome)* acolher; **3** *(undergo)* sofrer; **to ~ a prison sentence of ten years** *(JUR)* ser condenado a 10 anos de prisão **4** admitir, dar entrada (em); **to be ~d to/into** ser admitido em *(order, hospital)*.

receiver *n (of telephone)* auscultador *m*; **2** *(person who receives)* rece(p)tor,-ora; recebedor,-ora; depositário,-a; **3** *(JUR, FIN) (also:* **Official R~**) administrador,-ora de falências *m*.

receivership *n (FIN) (department/receiver)* recebedoria *f*; **2** *(JUR)* curadoria *f*; **to go into ~** ser colocado,-a sob administração *f* judiciária.

receiving *n* rece(p)ção *f*; **2** *(JUR)* posse *f*; IDIOM **to be on the ~ end** ser alvo de *(criticism, etc)*; arcar com as consequências.

recense *vt* fazer uma recensão crítica.

recension *n (LITER)* recensão *f*.

recent *adj* recente *m,f*; **2** *(friend, project)* novo,-a.

recently *adv* recentemente, ultimamente; **until ~** até há pouco tempo.

receptacle *n (BOT)* rece(p)táculo *m*; **2** *(container)* recetáculo, recipiente *m*.

reception *n* rece(p)ção *f*; **2** *(welcome)* acolhimento *m*; **3** *(TECH)* captação *f*; **to give sb a warm ~** receber alguém com carinho, calorosamente; **~ desk** *n* balcão *m* de rece(p)ção; **~ centre** *n* centro *m* de acolhimento; **~ room** *n* salão *m* de festas.

receptionist *n* rece(p)cionista *m,f*.

receptive *adj* rece(p)tivo,-a; IDIOM **a ~ mind** um espírito aberto.

receptiveness *n* capacidade *f* de rece(p)ção.

receptivity *n* rece(p)tividade *f*.

receptor *n (FISIOL, TECH)* rece(p)tor *m*.

recess *n (space)* recesso *m*, vão *m*; *(in wall)* nicho *m*; esconderijo *m*; **2** *(remote place)* recanto *m*; confim *m*; **3** *(POL)* férias *fpl* parlamentares, jurídicas; **to be/go into ~** estar/entrar em recesso; **4** *(US) (school break)* recreio *m*, intervalo *m*; ◆ **in the ~es of my mind** no recôndito da minha mente; **mountain ~es** recantos *mpl* da montanha; ◆ *vt* abrir/criar um vão.

recessed *adj (cupboard, etc)* embutido,-a, encastrado.

recession *n (ECON, FIN)* recessão *f*.

recessive *adj* retrocedente; **2** *(BIOL)* recessivo; **~ character** *n* carácter *m* recessivo; **~ gene** *n* gene *m* recessivo.

recharge *vt* recarregar; IDIOM **to ~ one's batteries** *(person's)* recarregar as baterias, recuperar as forças.

rechargeable *adj* recarregável *m,f*; **~ batteries** *n* pilhas *fpl* recarregáveis.

réchauffé *n (CULIN)* comida *f* reaquecida.

recidivism *n* reincidência *f* (criminosa).

recipe *n (CULIN)* receita *f*; IDIOM **a ~ for sucess** uma receita para o sucesso.

recipient *n (person)* rece(p)tor,-ora; destinatário,-a; **2** *(of benefits)* beneficiário-a; **3** *(of prize)* premiado,-a.

reciprocal *n* recíproca *f*; ◆ *adj* recíproco,-a; **~ claim** *n* crédito *m* recíproco; **~ number** *n (MATH)* número *m* recíproco; **~ treatment** *n* reciprocidade *f* de tratamento; **~ will** *n (JUR)* testamento *m* de mão comum.

reciprocate *vt/vi* retribuir.

reciprocator *n* aparelho *m* de correspondência.

reciprocity *n* reciprocidade *f*; **law of ~** *(CHEM)* lei *f* da reciprocidade.

recision *n* *(JUR)* *(annulment)* rescisão *f* *(of contract)*, revogação.

recital *n* *(LITER, MUS)* recital *m*; **2** *(JUR)* consideração *f*, fundamentação *f*.

recitation *n* recitação *f*.

recite *vt* *(LITER, MUS)* recitar, declamar; **2** *(report)* relatar; **3** *(enumerate)* enumerar.

reckless *adj* temerário, estouvado; imprudente, descuidado; **~ driving** *n* *(JUR)* condução *f* imprudente; **to be ~ with money** gastar sem pensar, ser estouvado,-a.

recklessly *adv* temerariamente; estouvadamente.

recklessness *n* *(of person)* descuido *m*; imprudência *f*.

reckon *vt* *(estimate)* calcular; **2** *(judge, consider)* considerar; **3** achar, crer; **I ~ that** acho/creio que/ suponho que; ♦ **to ~ on** depender de, contar com; **to ~ on doing** contar fazer; **to ~ with** contar com, tomar em consideração; **to ~ without** não ter em conta; **to ~ up** calcular; IDIOM **he is a man to be ~ed with** *(of considerable influence)* ele é um homem a ser considerado.

reckoning *n* *(estimate)* estimativa *f* cálculo *m* IDIOM **the day of ~** *(REL)* o Dia do Juízo Final; **2** dia do ajuste de contas.

reclaim *vt* *(luggage etc)* recuperar; **2** converter *(wasteland into crops, etc)* desbravar, *(make use of)* aproveitar; **3** *(recycle)* reciclar; **4** reclamar, reivindicar.

reclaimable *adj* recuperável *m,f*.

reclaimer *n* reivindicador,-ora.

reclamation *n* *(JUR)* reinvindicação *f*; **2** *(recycling)* reciclagem *f*, recuperação *f*; **2** *(of land)* aproveitamento *m*, melhoramento *m*; *(of marsh)* secagem *f*; *(of forests)* desbravamento *m*.

recline *vi* reclinar-se; apoiar-se, recostar-se; **to ~ on** recostar-se em/sobre.

recliner (chair) *n* cadeira *f* reclinável.

reclining *adj* reclinável.

recluse *n* *(person)* recluso,-a; eremita *m*; ♦ *adj* solitário,-a.

reclusion *n* retiro *m*; isolamento *m*.

recognition *n* reconhecimento *m*; **to be beyond ~** estar irreconhecível; **in ~** *(in thanks)* em/como reconhecimento de.

recognizable *adj* reconhecível.

recognize *vt* reconhecer; **2** *(accept)* aceitar *(claim)*; **3** identificar.

recognized *adj* *(acknowledged)* reconhecido,-a; **2** *(accredited status)* acreditado,-a.

recoil *n* *(move)* recuo *m*; **2** *(of a gun)* coice *m*; ♦ *vi* *(move)* retroceder, recuar; **2** *(of a gun)* dar coice; **to ~ from** recusar-se a; recuar perante.

recoin *vt* *(ECON)* voltar a cunhar.

recollect *vt* lembrar, recordar; IDIOM **as far as I can ~** pelo que me lembro.

recollection *n* recordação *f*, lembrança *f*; IDIOM **to have a dim ~ of** *n* ter uma vaga ideia de; **to the best of my ~** se bem me lembro.

recommence *vt/vi* recomeçar.

recommend *vt* *(suggest)* recomendar; **2** *(advise)* aconselhar; **3** *(entrust)* encaminhar.

recommendable *adj* recomendável.

recommendation *n* recomendação *f*; **letter of ~** carta *f* de recomendação; **on the ~ of** sob recomendação de; **to make a ~** *(JUR)* formular uma recomendação.

recommended retail price *n* preço *m* sugerido ao retalho *(BR)* varejo *m*.

recompensable *adj* recompensável.

recompense *n* *(reward)* recompensa *f* **(for sth**, por algo); **2** *(JUR)* inde(m)nização *f*; ♦ *vt* recompensar; **2** inde(m)nizar **(for**, por).

recompose *vt* recompor; reorganizar; **2** acalmar(-se).

reconcilable *adj* *(differences)* conciliável; *(views)* compatível.

reconcile *vt* reconciliar; conciliar, harmonizar; **to ~ o.s. to** resignar-se a, conformar-se com.

reconciled *adj* reconciliado,-a.

reconciliation *n* reconciliação *f*.

recondite *adj* abstruso,-a; obscuro,-a.

recondition *vt* renovar, modernizar.

reconfiguration *n* *(TECH)* reconfiguração *f*.

reconfirm *vt* reconfirmar.

reconnaissance *n* verificação *f*, exploração *f*; **2** *(MIL)* (patrulha de) reconhecimento; **3** estudo *m* prévio; **~ aircraft** *n* avião *m* de reconhecimento.

reconnect *vt* religar; ligar novamente.

reconnoitre *(UK)* **reconnoiter** *(US)* *vt* reconhecer; ♦ *vi* fazer um reconhecimento *m*.

reconquer *vt* reconquistar.

reconquest *n* reconquista *f*.

reconsider *vt* reconsiderar, reexaminar.

reconsideration *n* reconsideração *f*.

reconstitute *vt* reconstituir.

reconstitution *n* reconstituição *f*.

reconstruct *vt* *(rebuild)* reconstruir; **2** *(crime)* reconstituir.

reconstruction *n* reconstrução *f*.

reconvene *vt* *(formal meeting)* reunir-se novamente.

reconvert *vt* reconverter.

record *n* *(MUS)* disco *m*; **~ industry** *n* indústria *f* discográfica; **~-player** *n* gira-disco *m* *inv*; **to ~ on video** *vt* gravar em vídeo; **2** *(official proceedings)* a(c)ta *f*, minuta *f*; regist(r)o *m*; **3** *(archives)* arquivo *m*; anais *mpl*; **Jewish ~s** *npl* as a(c)tas *fpl* judaicas; **4** *(SPORT)* recorde *m*; **5 prison ~** *n* *(police file)* cadastro (criminal); **~ of service** *n* folha *f* de serviços; **~ office** *n* arquivo *m* central; ♦ **off the ~** *adj* confidencialmente; **on ~** regist(r)ado,-a; **the worst years on ~** os piores anos regist(r)ados; ♦ *vt* *(note)* assentar, anotar; regist(r)ar *(transaction)*; **2** *(provide an account)* relatar, referir; **3** *(MUS)* *(disc, tape)* gravar **(on** sobre); **4** *(gauge, meter)* indicar; **to break the ~** *(SPORT)* bater o recorde; ♦ *adv* confidencialmente; IDIOM **for the ~** para que se conste; **to keep a ~ of** manter um registo *(BR:* registro) de; **to set the ~ straight** esclarecer a situação.

record-breaker *n*: **to be a ~** ter batido um recorde.

recorded *adj* gravado; **2** registado; **~ delivery** *n* *(post)* *(letter, parcel)* *n* carta *f*, embrulho *m* registado,-a.

recorder *n (MUS)* flauta (doce) *f*; **2** *(machine)* gravador *m*; **3** *(TECH)* indicador *m* mecânico; **4** *(JUR) (in court)* escrivão,-va.

record-holder *n (SPORT)* detentor,-ora de recorde; ~ **of** recordista *m,f* de.

recording *n (MUS)* gravação *f*; ~ **channel** *n* canal *m* de gravação; ~ **studio** *n (MUS)* estúdio *m* de gravações.

recount¹ *vt (describe)* relatar, contar.

re-count² *n (POL)* nova contagem *f* (de votos); ♦ *vt (count again)* proceder a nova contagem.

recounter *n (meeting)* encontro *m*, **2** *(confrontation)* confronto *m*.

recoup *vt (recover)* recuperar; **2** *(get compensation)* ser inde(m)nizado; **3** *(JUR)* deduzir.

recourse *n* recurso *m*; **to have** ~ **to** recorrer a; **without** ~ *(FIN)* sem a(c)ção regressiva.

recover *vt (get back)* recuperar; reaver *(possessions)*; **to** ~ **consciousness** voltar a si, recuperar os sentidos; **to** ~ **one's breath** recuperar o fôlego; ♦ *vi (get better) (person, market)* restabelecer-se, refazer-se; **to** ~ **from an illness** refazer-se de uma doença.

recoverable *adj* recuperável.

recovery *n (recuperation)* recuperação *f*, convalescença *f*, melhoras *fpl*; **2** *(restoration)* restabelecimento *m*; **3** *(collection)* cobrança *f*; **4** *(exploitation)* aproveitamento *m*; **industrial** ~ recuperação *f* industrial; ~ **vehicle** *n (UK)* guincho *m*.

recreate *vt (create again)* recriar.

recreation *n (amusement)* recreio *m*, recreação *f*; ~ **ground** *n* área recreativa; campo de jogos.

re-creation *n* recriação *f*.

recreational *adj* recreativo,-a; ~ **centre** *n* centro *m* de lazer, local *m*; ~ **drugs** *n* drogas *fpl* recreativas.

recreative *adj* recreativo.

recreatively *adv* recreativamente.

recriminate *vi* recriminar.

recrimination *n* recriminação *f*.

recriminative *adj* recriminativo,-a.

rec room *n (US) (pop)* sala *f* de lazer.

recrudescence *n* recorrência *f*.

recrudescent *adj* recorrente *m*.

recruit *n* recruta *m,f*; **raw** ~ *n (MIL)* recruta *m*, soldado *m* iniciante; ♦ *vt* recrutar; ♦ *vi (staff)* recrutar.

recruiting agent *n* agente de recrutamento *m*.

recruitment *n* recrutamento.

recta *(pl of* **rectum***)*.

rectal *adj (ANAT)* rectal *m,f*.

rectangle *n (GEOM)* re(c)tângulo.

rectangular *adj (GEOM)* re(c)tangular; ~ **coordinate** *n* coordenada *f* re(c)tangular.

rectangularity *n* re(c)tangularidade *f*.

rectangularly *adv* re(c)-tangularmente.

rectifiable *adj* re(c)-tificável.

rectification *n* re(c)tificação *f*.

rectified *adj (CHEM, ELECT)* re(c)tificado; ~ **spirit** *n (CHEM)* álcool *m* re(c)tificado; ~ **signal** *n (ELECT)* sinal *m* re(c)tificado; ~ **voltage** *n (ELECT)* voltagem *f* re(c)tificada.

rectifier *n (CHEM, ELECT)* re(c)tificador.

rectify (-ied) *vt (also: ELECT)* re(c)tificar.

rectilinear *adj (GEOM)* re(c)tilíneo; ~ **motion** *n* movimento *m* re(c)tilíneo; ~ **scale** *n* escala *f* re(c)tilínea.

rectitude *n* re(c)tidão *f*.

recto *n (TYPO)* re(c)to *m*; face *f* superior.

rector *n (REL)* pároco *m*; **2** *(EDUC)* reitor,-ora de faculdade *or* de universidade.

rectory *n (REL)* reitoria *f*, residência *f* paroquial.

rectrix *n (ZOOL)* rectriz *f*.

rectum *(pl: -a) n (ANAT)* re(c)to *m*.

recumbent *adj* recumbente *m,f*; recostado; ~ **bicycle** *n* bicicleta *f* reclinada, em posição reclinada.

recuperate *vi (get better)* restabelecer-se, recuperar-se; **to** ~ **one's health** recuperar a saúde; **2** *(get back)* reaver.

recuperation *n (health)* recuperação *f*, convalescence.

recuperative *adj* recuperativo,-a.

recuperator *n* recuperador *m*.

recur (-red) *vi (repeate)* repetir-se, **2** *(reoccur)* ocorrer outra vez; surgir de novo.

recurrence *n* repetição *f*.

recurrent *adj* repetido, periódico; ~ **education** *n* educação *f* para adultos; ~ **depressive disorder** *n* transtorno *m* depressivo, recorrente.

recurring *adj* recorrente; ~ **decimal** *n (MATH)* dízima *f* periódica; ~ **hepatitis** *n (MED)* hepatite *f* recidiva.

recursive *adj* recursivo,-a recorrente; ~ **function** *n* função *f* recursiva; ~ **subroutine** *n (COMP)* sub-rotina *f* recursiva; ~ **system** *n (MATH)* sistema *f* recursivo.

recusant *n adj (refusing to submit to authority)* dissidente; recusante; não-conformista.

recyclable *adj (ECOL)* reciclável.

recycle *vt* reciclar.

recycling *n (ECOL)* reciclagem *f*; ~ **of capital** *n (ECON)* reciclagem *f* de capitais.

red *n (colour)* encarnado, vermelho; **2 R~** *(fig) (POL)* comunista, socialista; **3** *(hair)* ruivo; **4** *(wine)* tinto; **to be in the** ~ *(bank account)* estar a descoberto; **to see** ~ enfurecer-se; ♦ *adj (person, cheeks)* vermelho,-a; **she went** ~ *(blush)* ela corou, ela ficou vermelha; ~ **alert** *n* alerta *m* máximo; **on** ~ **alert** em alerta vermelho, máximo; ~ **blood cell** *n (MED)* glóbulo *m* vermelho; ~**-blooded** *adj* ardente; ~**breast** *n (bird)* pintaroxo *m*; ~ **card** *n: (FOOT)* **to get a** ~ receber cartão *m* vermelho; ~ **carpet** *n (for VIP's)* passadeira *f* vermelha; ~ **cedar** *n (BOT)* cedro *m* vermelho; ~ **currant** *n (fruit)* groselha *f*; *(bush)* groselheira *f*; ~ **deer** veado *m*; IDIOM **to be caught** ~**-handed** *(in the act)* ser apanhado,-a com a mão na botija, apanhado em flagrante; **to paint the town** ~ andar na pândega, andar na farra.

red-brick *adj (UK) (building)* de tijolo à vista; **2** *(UK) (Univ)* universidades construídas nos séculos XIX e XX.

redcoat *n (English soldier)* casaca-vermelha.

Red Crescent *npr* Crescente Vermelho.

Red Cross *npr* Cruz *f* Vermelha.

redden *vt* avermelhar; ♦ *vi* corar, ruborizar-se.

reddish *adj* avermelhado; **2** *(hair)* arruivado.

redecorate *vt* decorar de novo, redecorar.

redecoration *n* remodelação *f*.

redeem *vt (from pawnbroker)* tirar do prego; resgatar; **2** *(save, rescue)* redimir; **to ~ a debt** amortizar uma dívida.

redeemable *adj (FIN) (bonds)* convertível; **2** *(mortgage, loan)* amortizável.

Redeemer *npr (REL)* Redentor.

redeeming *adj*: **~ feature** compensação *f*; **his ~ quality is** o que o salva, redime é.

redefine *vt* redefinir.

redemption *n (REL)* redenção *f*, salvação *f*; **2** *(JUR)* quitação, remissão *f*; **3** *(FIN) (debt, loan)* reembolso *m*; **~ fund** *n (FIN)* fundo *m* de amortização; IDIOM **to be beyond ~** não ter salvação possível.

redeploy *vt (MIL) (troops – to places)* atribuir *(tasks)*.

redesign *vt (draw again)* remodelar.

redevelop *vt* renovar.

redevelopment *n* renovação *f*.

redeye *n (US) (coll)* uísque de qualidade inferior.

red eye[1] *n (PHOT)* olho *m* vermelho.

red eye[2] *n (fam)*: **a ~ flight** *(plane)* voo noturno.

red-faced *adj (florid complexion)* corado,-a; **2** *(with anger/embarrassement)* vermelho,-a de cólera, de vergonha; corado,-a.

red fir *n (BOT) (American conifer)* abeto *m* vermelho.

red-haired *adj* ruivo,-a.

red herring *n (fig)* pista *f* falsa.

red-hot *adj (metal, coal)* incandescente, ao rubro; em brasa; **2** *(enthusiastic, lover)* ardente; **3** *(news)* recente.

redial *n (TEL)* remarcação *f* automática.

redid *(pt of redo)*.

Red Indian *n (pej) (dated)* Pele Vermelha.

redirect *vt* redire(c)cionar; **2** *(traffic, aircraft)* desviar.

rediscover *vt* redescobrir; **to be ~ed** ser redescoberto,-a.

rediscovery *n* redescoberta *f*.

redivivus *adj* ressuscitado,-a.

red lead *n (CHEM)* óxido *m* vermelho de chumbo.

red-letter day *n* dia *m* memorável.

red-light district *n* bairro *m* de prostituição, de má reputação.

red meat *n (beef, mutton)* carne *f* vermelha.

red mullet *n (fish)* salmonete *m*.

redneck *n adj* ultrarreacionário,-a; **2** *(US) (poor white farmer)* lavrador pobre e branco.

redness *n* rubor *m*; vermelhidão *f*.

redo *vt* refazer.

redolent *adj (fragrant)* aromático,-a; **2** *(suggestive)* sugestivo,-a, evocativo,-a *(of sth de algo)*.

redone *(pp of redo)*.

redouble *vt*: **to ~ one's efforts** redobrar os esforços.

redoubtable *adj* formidável *m,f*; digno,-a de respeito.

red-pencil *(pt, pp -ll-) vt* revisar, corrigir *(text, book)*.

red pepper *n (CULIN)* pimentão *m*.

redpoll *n (bird)* pintarroxo *m*.

redress *n* retificação *f*; compensação *f*; **2** *(JUR)* recurso *m*; **equitable ~** *n (JUR)* reparação *f* equitativa; **judicial ~** reparação *f* legal; ◆ *vt* compensar *(to sb for a wrong)*; **~ the balance** restabelecer o equilíbrio.

re-dress *vt (clothing)* vestir novamente; **2** *(wound)* refazer um curativo.

red rose *n (UK) (HIST)* emblema da Casa de Lencastre; *(Vd:* War on the Roses*)*.

Red Sea *npr*: **the ~** o Mar Vermelho.

red-setter *n* cão *m* perdigueiro.

redstart *n (ZOOL)* rabirruivo *m*.

red tape *n (fig) (ADMIN) (bureaucracy)* formalidades *fpl*; *(pej)* papelada *f*.

red tide *n (discolouration in the sea)* maré *f* vermelha.

reduce *vt* reduzir; diminuir; baixar; **~d mobility** *n* mobilidade *f* reduzida; **at a ~d price** a preço reduzido, remarcado; **to ~ a fracture** *(MED)* reduzir uma fractura; IDIOM **to be ~d to doing sth** sujeitar-se a fazer algo.

reduced *adj* reduzido,-a.

reducer *n (PHOT)* redutor *m*.

reductase *n (BIO)* redutase *f*.

reduction *n* redução *f*, abatimento *m*; desconto *m*.

redundancy *n (LING, COMP)*, redundância *f*; **2** *(UK)* despedimento *m* por razão patronal, *(BR)* redundância *f*; **3** *(not employed)* desemprego *m*; **~ payment** *n* indemnização *f* por despedimento.

redundant *adj* dispensado,-a, despedido,-a; *(not employed)* desempregado,-a; **to be made ~** ficar desempregado,-a; **2** *(excess)* redundante; supérfluo,-a.

reduplicate *vt* reduplicar.

redwing *n (ZOOL)* tordo-ruivo comum.

redwood *n (BOT)* pau-brasil *m*.

reed *n (BOT)* junco *m*; cana *f*; **2** *(MUS) (instrument)* palheta *f*; flauta *f* pastoral; **3** *(weaving)* pente *m* de tear; **~ grass** *n* caniço *m* malhado; **~bird** *n (ZOOL)* papa-arroz *m*; **~ warbler** *n (ZOOL)* rouxinol pequeno dos caniços *m*; IDIOM **a broken ~** *(weak, ineffectual person)* pessoa em quem não se confia.

re-edify *vt* reedificar.

re-edit *vt* reeditar.

reedling *n (ZOOL)* chapim *m*.

re-educate *vt* reabilitar, reeducar.

reedy (-ier, -iest) *adj (voice, sound)* agudo,-a.

reef *n (GEOG)* recife *m*, escolho *m*; **coral ~** *n* recife *m* de coral.

reefer *n* contentor *m* refrigerado: **2** *(also: ~ jacket)* jaquetão *m*, gabão *m*; **3** *(coll) (to smoke)* charro *m*, cigarro *m* de marijuana.

reef knot *n (NAUT)* nó *m* direito.

reek *n* fedor *m*; ◆ *vi (stink)* tresandar; **to ~ (of)** cheirar a, feder (a algo).

reel *n (holder) (gen)* carretel *m*, bobina *f*; **2** *(PHOT, CIN)* rolo *m*, filme *m*; **3** *(of sewing thread)* carrinho *m* (de linhas); **4** *(dance)* dança escocesa; ◆ *vt (TECH)* bobinar, enrolar; ◆ *vi (stagger)* cambalear; *(head, mind)* girar; **my brain ~ed** fiquei com a cabeça às voltas; **to ~ in** *vt* enrolar; **to ~ off** *vt* enumerar *(names etc)*; **2** *(thread, wire)* desenrolar; **to ~ out** *(fishing line)* soltar.

re-elect *vt* reeleger.

re-election *n* reeleição *f*.

re-employ *vt* reempregar.

re-enact *vt* reconstruir, reconstituir *(story, situation)*; **2** tornar a desempenhar *(role)*; **3** *(JUR)* tornar a pôr em vigor.

re-enactment *n* reconstituição *f.*

re-enter *vt* reentrar em; **2** *(COMP)* reinserir.

re-entrant *n* reentrância *f;* ◆ *adj* reentrante.

re-entry *n* *(AER)* reentrada *f;* **2** *(into politics, etc)* regresso a; **3** *(COMP) (data)* reinserção.

re-establish *vt* restabelecer.

re-evaluate *vt* reavaliar.

re-examination *n* novo exame *m;* **2** *(JUR)* reexame *m.*

re-examine *vt* reexaminar.

ref *n* *(SPORT) (fam)* árbitro *m.*

reface *vt* reparar.

refashion *vt* remodelar.

refectory *n* refeitório *m.*

refer *vt* *(mention)* referir(-se) **(to**, a); **2** *(direct)* remeter; reencaminhar **(to**, para); **they ~red me to a surgeon** remeteram-me para um cirurgião; **3** *(assign)* atribuir; ◆ *vi* **to ~ (to**, a) aludir; **2** recorrer a *(justice)*; *(JUR)* submeter *(case)*; **3** consultar *(books)*; **4** *(FIN)* '~ **to drawer**' consultar a entidade sacadora'.

referee *n* *(SPORT)* árbitro *m,* juiz *m;* **2** *(COMM)* pessoa que pode dar referências *f;* ◆ *vt* arbitrar.

reference *n* *(allusion)* referência *f,* menção *f,* alusão *f;* **2** *(consultation)* consulta *f;* **for future ~** para informação *f,* para consulta futura; **3** *(COMM) (in letter, order)* referências *fpl;* '**please quote this ~**' favor citar esta referência; **4** *(testimonial)* referências *fpl;* carta *f* de recomendação *f;* **5** *(GEOG)* **map ~s** *npl* coordenadas *fpl;* **with ~ to** *prep* com respeito a, quanto a; **in ~ to** relativamente a; **passing ~** *n* breve menção *f;* **point of ~** *n* ponto *m* de referência; **terms of ~** *(JUR)* atribuições *fpl;* especificações *fpl;* **~ book** *n* livro *m* de consulta; **~ level** *n* nível *m* de referência; **~ library** *n* biblioteca *f* de consulta; **~ rate** *n* taxa *f* de referência.

referendum *(pl:* -da*)* *n* referendo *m,* plebiscito *m.*

referent *n* referente *m.*

referential *adj* referencial.

referral *n* recomendação *f* **(to**, a); **2** *(MED) (patient)* reencaminhamento para um especialista.

refill *n* *(for lighter, perfume, etc)* recarga *f;* **2** *(drink)* dose *f* extra; ◆ *vt* encher de novo, reabastecer.

refinancing *n* *(COMM)* refinanciamento *m.*

refine *vt* refinar *(oil, sugar)*; **to ~ on** aperfeiçoar, aprimorar *(speech)*.

refined *adj* *(state)* refinado; **2** *(cultured)* culto,-a, distinto,-a; **~ manners** *fpl* maneiras requintadas.

refinement *n* *(elegance)* refinamento *m,* requinte *m.*

refinery *n* refinaria *f.*

refit *n* *(of shop, etc)* reequipamento *m;* **the ship needs ~ting** a loja precisa duma transformação; **2** *(of ship)* reaparelhamento *m;* ◆ *(-tt-) vt* *(of shop, etc)* reequipar, transformar; **2** *(in ship)* reaparelhar.

reflation *n* *(ECON) (increase in economic activity)* novo aumento da circulação *f* fiduciária; reflação *f.*

reflect *vt* refle(c)tir; **2** *(show)* exprimir; ◆ *vi* *(think)* meditar, refle(c)tir; **2** *(bring as consequence)* recair (sobre).

reflection *n* reflexão *f;* reflexo *m;* **anti-~** *n* antirreflexo; **on ~** pensando melhor; **~ factor** *n* *(ELECT)* coeficiente *m* de reflexão.

reflective *adj* pensativo,-a; **2** *(shiny)* brilhante.

reflectometer *n* *(PHYS)* refle(c)tómetro *m.*

reflector *n* refle(c)tor *m.*

reflex *n* *(PHYS, gen)* reflexo *m;* **~ camera** *n* câmera reflex; ◆ *adj* reflexo,-a; **a ~ action** *n* um reflexo *m;* *(MATH) (angle)* obtuso,-a.

reflexive *adj* reflexivo,-a; **2** ponderado,-a; **~ relation** *n* *(COMP)* relação *f* reflexiva.

reflexology *n* reflexologia *f.*

refluence *n* refluência *f.*

reflux *n* refluxo *m;* **~ oesophagitis** *n* *(MED)* esofagite *f* péptica; **~ valve** *n* *(TECH)* válvula *f* de retenção *f.*

reforestation *n* reflorestação *f.*

reform *n* *(JUR, POL)* reforma *f;* **agrarian/land ~** reforma agrária; ◆ *vt* *(change sth)* reformar; ◆ **(oneself)** reformar-se, redimir-se, corrigir-se.

reformat *vt* *(COM)* reformatar.

Reformation *n:* **the ~** a Reforma *f.*

reformative *adj* reformativo.

reformatory *n* centro *m* de detenção para jovens.

reformed *pp adj* *(state)* reformado,-a; **2** *(person, criminal)* arrependido,-a.

reformer *n* reformador,-ora.

reformulate *vt* reformular.

refract *vt* refra(c)tar.

refracting *adj* refra(c)tor,-ora; **~ prism** *n* prisma *m* de refra(c)ção; **~ telescope** *n* refra(c)tor *m.*

refractive *adj* refra(c)tivo; **~ index** *n* índice *m;* de refra(c)ção.

refractor *n* refra(c)tor *m.*

refractory *adj* *(obstinate)* obstinado; **2** *(PHYS, MED)* refra(c)tário; **3** **~ brick** tijolo *m* refratário.

refrain *n* *(MUS, LITER)* estribilho *m,* refrão *m;* ◆ *vi* conter-se; **to ~ from doing** abster-se de fazer.

refresh *vt* refrescar; **2** *(memory)* reavivar; **3** *(replenish)* reabastecer; **4** *(COMP)* actualizar; **~ rate** *n* *(COMP)* velocidade *f* de actualização.

refreshed *adj* revigorado,-a.

refresher course *n* curso *m* de aperfeiçoamento *or* atualização, curso de reciclagem.

refreshing *adj* reconfortante *m,f; (cooling, invigorating)* refrescante; tonificante.

refreshments *npl* *(soft drinks)* refrescos *mpl;* **2** *(with a light meal)* comes e bebes *npl;* **let us take ~** vamos aos comes e bebes *(fam)*.

refrigerant *n* refrigerante *m;* fluido *m* frigorígeno.

refrigerate *vt* refrigerar, conservar no frigorífico.

refrigerated *pp adj* *(product)* refrigerado,-a.

refrigeration *n* refrigeração *f.*

refrigerator *n* frigorífico *m,* *(BR)* geladeira *f.*

refuel *vi* reabastecer (de combustível).

refuge *n* *(place of safety)* refúgio *m;* **to take ~ in** refugiar-se em; **to take ~ from** *(danger)* pôr-se ao abrigo de; *(weather)* abrigar-se de *(wind, rain)*.

refugee *n* refugiado,-a; **~ camp** *n* campo *m* de refugiados.

refulgent *adj* resplandecente, luzente.

refund *n* reembolso *m;* ◆ *vt* devolver, reembolsar.

re-fund *vt* refinanciar.

refurbish *vt* renovar *(home decoration)*; **the flat has been completely ~ed** o apartamento foi completamente renovado; *(BR)* reformar; **2** restaurar *(building)*.

refusal *n* recusa *f*; **first ~** primeira opção *f*; **to be met with a ~** receber uma resposta negativa; *(BR)* ser rechaçado,-a.

refuse¹ *vt (deny)* **to ~ sth to sb** negar algo a alguém; *(decline)* **to ~ to do sth** recusar-se a fazer algo *vi* dizer que não, negar-se.

refuse² *n (household)* refugo *m*, lixo *m*; *(industrial)* resíduo *m*; ♦ *vt/vi* rejeitar; negar-se a, recusar; **~ bin** *n* caixote *m* *(BR*: lata*)* do lixo; **~ collector** *n* lixeiro *m*, homem do lixo; **~ collection vehicle** *n* veículo *m* de recolha do lixo *(BR)* coleta de lixo; **~ disposal** *n* tratamento *m* do lixo; **~ disposal unit** *n* triturador; **~ dump** *n* aterro *m* de entulho.

refute *vt* refutar, contradizer.

regain *vt* recuperar *(senses, health, time)*; recobrar *(forces, spirit)*; readquirir *(possession)* retomar a posse de.

regal *adj* real; régio,-a; sum(p)tuoso,-a.

regale *vt:* **to ~ sb with st** deliciar, regalar, entreter *(alguém com)*; **he ~d them with old stories** ele regalou-os com histórias *(or:* a contar-lhes histórias*)*.

regalia *n* indumentária *f*; *npl* insígnias *fpl* reais; **in full ~** em trajo *m* de gala.

regally *adv* regiamente.

regard *n (respect, esteem)* respeito *m*; estima *f*, consideração *f* (**for** para com); **2** *(aspect)* **in this ~ a** este respeito; **to have/show little ~ for** fazer pouco caso de *(rude people, money)*; **with best regards** *(in letter)* com os meus cumprimentos, cordialmente; **give him my ~s** dê-lhe os meus cumprimentos; ♦ *vt (consider)* considerar; **to ~ sb with contempt** menosprezar alguém; **2** *(observe)* olhar; **he ~d me with suspicion** ele olhou-me com suspeita; **3** *(relate)* dizer respeito a; ♦ **as regards** *prep* no que se refere a; **in regards to, with ~ to** *prep* no que diz respeito, em relação a; IDIOM **to hold sb with high ~** pensar o mundo de alguém.

regarding *prep* em relação a, com respeito a, quanto a.

regardless *prep* apesar de; sem considerar, sem contar com; ♦ *adv* independentemente; apesar de tudo; **~ the cost** custe o que custar.

regatta *n* regata *f*.

regency *n* regência *f*; período *m* regencial.

regenerate *vt* regenerar; ♦ *vi (organs)* regenerar-se; **2** *(economy)* recuperar-se.

regeneration *n (of organs, tissue)* regeneração *f*; **blood ~** *n (MED)* regeneração *f* sanguínea; **2 urban ~** *n* regeneração *f*, restauração *f* urbana.

regenerative *adj* regenerativo,-a, recuperativo,-a; **~ cooling** *n (the walls of a rocket)* refrigeração *f* por recuperação; **~ furnace** *n* forno *m* regenerativo.

regent *n* regente *m,f*.

reggae *n* reggae *m*.

regicide *n* regicídio *m*.

regime, régime *n* regime *m*; **2** dieta *f*.

regiment *n* regimento *m*; ♦ *vt* regulamentar.

regimental *adj* regimental; **~s** *npl* farda *fsg* militar.

regimentation *n* organização *f*.

regimented *adj (pej)* estritamente controlado,-a; **2** *(in rows)* ordenado,-a em fileiras.

region *n* região *f*; **in the ~ of** *(fig)* por volta de, ao redor de.

regional *adj* regional.

regionalism *n* regionalismo *m*.

regionalization *n* regionalização *f*.

register *n* regist(r)o *m*; lista *f*; ♦ *vt* regist(r)ar; **2** marcar, indicar; ♦ *vi* regist(r)ar-se, inscrever-se; **2** causar impressão; **~ book** *n* livro *m* de regist(r)o; **cash ~** *n* caixa *f* regist(r)adora; **data ~** *n (COMP)* regist (r)o *m* de dados; **electoral ~** *n* livro *m* eleitoral; **national ~** *n* regist(r)o *m* nacional.

registered *adj (voter)* inscrito,-a; **2** *(AUT)* regist(r)a-do; **3** *(charity)* reconhecido,-a; **4** *(student)* matriculado,-a *(school, college)*; **~ office** *n* sede *f* estatutária; **~ post** *n* correio *m* regist(r)ado; **~ share** *n (FIN)* título *m* nominativo; **~ trademark** *n* marca *f* regist(r)ada.

registrar *n* escrivão *m*, vã *f*; oficial *m* de regist(r)o; **2** *(univ) (administrator)* secretário,-a geral; **3** *(UK: doctor in a hospital)* médico,-a em estágio de especialização.

registration *n* regist(r)o *m*, inscrição *f*; **2** *(AUT)* (= **~ number**) número *m* de matrícula *f*; **vehicle ~ document** *n (AUT)* certificado *m* de matrícula.

registry *(pl:* **-ies***) n* regist(r)o *m*; arquivo *m*; **~ office** *n* cartório *m* do registo civil; **to get married in a ~ office** casar-se pelo registo civil.

regnant *adj* reinante; prevalente *m,f*.

regrate *vt* comprar para revenda.

regress *n* retrocesso *m*; ♦ *vi* regredir.

regression *n* regressão *f*.

regressive *adj* regressivo,-a.

regret *n (sadness)* desgosto *m*, pesar *m*; **2** *(guilt)* remorso *m*; ♦ *vt (feel sorry)* sentir, lamentar; **2** *(feel guilty)* arrepender-se de; IDIOM **to have no ~s** não se arrepender.

regretfully *adv* com pesar, lamentavelmente.

regrettable *adj* deplorável; lamentável.

regroup *vt* reagrupar; ♦ *vi* reagrupar-se.

regular *n* cliente *m,f*; **~ army** *n* exército *m* regular; ♦ *adj (normal)* normal, habitual; **2** *(orderly)* regular *m,f*; de linha; **3** *(whole)* verdadeiro, completo; IDIOM **on a ~ basis** regularmente; **as ~ as clockwork** sempre a horas.

regularity *n* regularidade *f*.

regularize *vt* regularizar.

regularly *adv* regularmente.

regulate *vt* regular; **2** *(TECH)* ajustar.

regulation *n* regra *f*, regulamento *m*; ajuste *m*.

regulator *n* regulador,-ora.

regurgitate *vt* regurgitar.

rehabilitate *vt* reabilitar.

rehabilitation *n* reabilitação *f*.

rehearsal *n* ensaio *m*.

rehearse *vt* ensaiar.

reheat *vt* reaquecer.

rehouse *vt* realojar.

reify (*pres p* -**ying**; *pt, pp* -**ied**) *vt* reificar.

reign *n* reinado *m*; **2** (*fig*) domínio *m*; ♦ *vi* reinar (**over**, sobre); **2** (*fig*) imperar.

reigning *adj* (*monarch*) reinante.

reignite *vi* reacender.

reimburse *vt* reembolsar.

reimbursement *n* reembolso *m*.

rein *n* rédea *f*; IDIOM **to give a free ~ to sb** dar rédea solta a alguém, dar carta branca a alguém; **to give ~s to the imagination** dar asas à imaginação; **to keep a tight ~ on** manter a rédea curta.

reincarnate *vt* reincarnar.

reincarnation *n* reencarnação *f*.

reindeer *n pl inv* (*ZOOL*) rena *f*.

reinforce *vt* reforçar.

reinforced *adj* reforçado; armado; **~ concrete** *n* (*CONSTR*) betão *m* armado; **~ glass** *n* vidro *m* armado; **~ plastic** *n* plástico *m* complexo.

reinforcement *n* reforço *m*; **~s** *npl* (*MIL*) reforços *mpl*.

reinstate *vt* (*in job*) readmitir, reintegrar (*employee*); **2** (*policy, pay*) restabelecer.

reintegrate *vt* (*make complete*) reintegrar; **2** (*restore*) restaurar.

reintroduce *vt* reintroduzir.

reissue *n* nova *f* edição, reedição *f*; ♦ *vt* reeditar.

reiterate *vt* reiterar, repetir.

reject *n* (*COMM*) artigo *m* defeituoso, refugo *m*; ♦ *vt* (*refuse*) rejeitar; recusar; **2** (*discard*) descartar; **3** (*MED*) (*organs*) rejeitar.

rejection *n* rejeição *f*.

rejoice *vi*: **to ~ at/over** regozijar-se de; alegrar-se de.

rejoicing *m* (*jubilation*) júbilo *m*; regozijo *m*.

rejoin *vt* reintegrar, reunir; reingressar em; (*club, etc*) voltar a ser sócio; **to ~ the ship** (*NAUT*) regressar a bordo; **2** (*reply*) replicar, ripostar.

rejoinder *n* réplica *f*; **2** (*JUR*) tréplica *f*.

rejuvenate *vt* rejuvenescer.

rekindle *vt* reacender; **2** (*fig*) despertar, reanimar.

relapse *n* recaída *f*; reincidência *f*; **2** (*MED*) recidiva *f*; ♦ *vi* recair; (*crime*) reincidir; **~ing fever** *n* (*MED*) febre *f* recorrente.

relate *vt* (*narrate*) contar, relatar; **2** (*associate*) relacionar; ♦ *vi* (*connect*) relacionar-se a algo; **2** (*concern*) referir-se a; **3 to ~ sth to sb** (*empathize*) ter algo em comum com alguém.

related *adj* (*by family*) aparentado,-a; **he and I are ~** somos aparentados; (*species*) afim, similar; **drug-~** ligado à droga.

relating to *prep* relativo a, acerca de, sobre.

relation *n* (*family*) parente *m,f*; **2** (*connection*) relação *f*, conexão *f*; ♦ **relations** *npl* relações (**between**, entre, com); (*intercourse*) (*euph*) relações *fpl* sexuais; IDIOM **to bear no ~ to** não ter qualquer relação com.

relationship *n* relacionamento *m*; ligação *f*; relações *fpl*; **2** (*family*) parentesco *m*; **~ marketing** *n* (*COMM*) marketing *m* de relação.

relative *n* parente,-a familiar; ♦ *adj* relativo,-a; **~ atomic mass** *n* (*PHYS*) massa *f* atómica relativa; **~ clause** (*gram*) oração *f* relativa.

relatively *adv* relativamente.

relativity *n* relatividade *f*; **theory of ~** *n* (*PHYS*) teoria *f* da relatividade.

relaunch *vt* relançamento.

relax *vt* afrouxar, soltar (*grip, rope*); **2** abrandar (*rule, pace*); **3** relaxar (*discipline*); ♦ *vi* (*person*) acalmar-se; descontrair-se; relaxar-se; **2** (*grip*) soltar-se.

relaxant *n* (*MED*) relaxante *m,f*, calmante *m,f*.

relaxation *n* descanso *m*, descontração *f*; (*of body*) relaxamento *m*, relax *m*; **2** (*of rule, grip*) afrouxamento *m*, abrandamento *m*.

relaxed *adj* descontraído,-a, (*laid back*) relaxado,-a.

relaxing *adj* relaxante *m,f*, repousante *m,f*.

relay *n* (*of workers*) turno *m*; (*BR*) (*revezamento*); **2** (*radio, TV*) trasmissão *f*; **3** (*ELECT*) relé *m*; **4** (*MECH*) inversor *m*; **~ race** *n* corrida *f* de estafetas; ♦ *vt* (*replace*) substituir; **2** (*alternate*) revezar; **3** (*retransmit*) retransmitir; **4** repor (*carpet, etc*).

release *n* (*freedom*) libertação *f* (**from** de); saída *f* de; **2** (*CIN*) (*coming out*) saída *f*; **on ~** em exibição; **3** (*MIL, JOURN*) lançamento *m*; **4** (*TECH*) fuga *f*, escape *m*; ♦ *vt* (*set free*) pôr em liberdade, libertar; **2** (*go loose*) soltar; escapar; **3** (*from promise, contract*) liberar; **4** (*CIN, MIL*) lançar; **5** (*JOURN*) divulgar (*story, news*); **6** (*TECH*) desengatar, desapertar; afrouxar; **press ~** *n* comunicado *m* de imprensa; **~ device** *n* (*TECH*) mecanismo *m* de disparo; **~ valve** *n* (*TECH*) válvula *f* de segurança.

relegate *vt* relegar, afastar; **to be ~d** (*SPORT*) descer de divisão; (*BR*) ser rebaixado.

relent *vi* ceder, condescender; **2** (*storm*) abrandar-se.

relentless *adj* implacável.

relevance *n* relevância *f*, pertinência *f*; relação *f*.

relevant *adj* relevante *m,f* pertinente *m,f*; apropriado.

reliable *adj* digno de confiança; seguro; fidedigno.

reliably *adv*: **to be ~ informed that** saber de fonte segura que.

reliance *n*: **~ (on sb/sth)** dependência de (alguém/ algo).

reliant *adj* dependente (**on/upon**, de)

relic *n* (*REL*) relíquia *f*; **2** (*remnant*) vestígio *m*; **3** (*object*) recordação *f*.

relief *n* (*feeling*) alívio *m*; **2** (*assistance*) ajuda *f*, auxílio *m*; socorro *m*; **3** (*ART, GEOG*) relevo *m*; **4** (*FIN*) abatimento *m*; isenção *m*; **5** (*JUR*) compensação *f*; **~ map** *n* (*GEOG*) mapa *m* em relevo; **~ road** *n* via *f* de descongestionamento; desvio *m*.

relieve *vt* (*lessen*) aliviar (*pain, distress, burden*); **2** (*give help to*) ajudar, auxiliary, socorrer; **3** atenuar, mitigar; **4** (*substitute*) substituir, revezar; **to ~ congestion** (*MED, AUT*) descongestionar; **to ~ sb of sth** tirar algo de alguém; **to ~ o.s.** (*urinate, defecate*) (*euph*) fazer as necessidades.

relieved *adj* aliviado,-a.

religion *n* religião *f*; **freedom of ~** *n* liberdade *f* religiosa; IDIOM **to practise a ~** ser seguidor,-ora de uma religião.

religious *adj* religioso.

re-line *vt* (*gen*) forrar novamente, revestir de novo; **2** (*brakes*) trocar o forro.

relinquish *vt* abandonar *(responsibility)*; **2** renunciar a, desistir de *(claim, title)* (**to** em favor de); **3** *(surrender)* ceder (power); **4** *(let go of)* largar, libertar.

reliquary *n* relicário *m.*

relish *n* *(CULIN)* condimento *m,* tempero *m;* **2** *(idea, task)* prazer *m,* entusiasmo *m;* **3** *(flavour)* sabor *m,* gosto *m;* **with** ~ com prazer; ♦ *vt* *(savour – food)* saborear; gostar de *(fazer)*; **2** *(idea)* gostar de, agradar, look forward to) **I don't much** ~ **the idea of going to her house** não me agrada a ideia de ir a casa dela.

relive *vt* reviver.

reload *vt* recarregar.

relocate *vt* realocar; transferir; ♦ *vi* transferir-se.

reluctance *n* relutância *f.*

reluctant *adj* relutante, hesitante.

reluctantly *adv* de má vontade; ♦ *adj* contrariado,-a.

reluctivity *n* *(PHYS)* relutividade *f.*

rely *vt:* **to** ~ **on** confiar em, contar com; **2** depender de (família, amigos).

REM *(abbr for* **Rapid Eye Movement***)* *(in sleep)* movimento rápido dos olhos.

remain *vi* *(stay)* ficar; permanecer; **2** *(be left over)* sobrar; **3** *(continue)* continuar, manter-se; **to** ~ **the same** continuar a ser o mesmo; **to** ~ **seated/standing** ficar sentado/de pé; **it** ~**s to be seen** veremos; **the bed** ~**ed to be made** a cama ficou por fazer.

remainder *n* *(things, money)* resto *m,* restante *m;* *(remaining people)* outros *mpl;* *(remaining time)* resto *m* (do tempo); **2** *(MATH)* sobrar; ♦ **remainders** *npl* *(COMM)* sobras *fpl;* saldo *m.*

remaining *adj* restante *m,f;* que resta; ♦ **my only** ~ **hope is...** a única esperança que resta é...; **2** *(leftovers)* sobras *fpl;* IDIOM **the fact** ~**s** a verdade é que; **it** ~**s to be seen** veremos.

remains *npl* *(corpse)* restos *mpl* mortais, **2** *(leftovers)* *(food, etc)* restos *mpl,* sobras *fpl;* **3** *(of building, civilization)* ruínas *fpl,* vestígios *mpl.*

remake *n* nova versão *f;* **2** *(CIN)* remake *m;* ♦ *vt* fazer uma nova versão, fazer de novo.

remand *n* adiamento *m;* *(JUR)* **on** ~ sob detenção *f* preventiva; ♦ *vt:* **to** ~ **in custody** recolocar em prisão preventiva, manter sob custódia; ~ **centre** *n* *(UK)* instituição *f* do juizado de menores; **2** centro *m* de detenção preventiva; IDIOM **he was** ~**ed on bail** ele foi solto/posto em liberdade sob fiança, caução *f.*

remanence *n* *(PHYS)* remanescência *f.*

remark *n* observação *f;* reparo *m,* comentário *m;* ♦ *vt* *(comment)* comentar (**about sb/sth** sobre alguém/algo); **2** *(notice)* notar, reparar.

remarkable *adj* notável *m,f;* extraordinário,-a.

remarry *vi* casar-se de novo, contrair segundas núpcias.

remedial *adj* curativo,-a; corre(c)tivo,-a; de reforço; ~ **measures** medidas *fpl* corre(c)tivas; *(MED)* terapêutico,-a.

remedy *(pl:* -ies*)* *n* *(MED)* remédio *m;* **2** *(fig)* cura, solution *f;* *(JUR)* **legal** ~ recursos *mpl* legais; ♦ *(-ied)* *vt* remediar, curar.

remember *vt* *(recall)* lembrar-se de, recordar-se de; **2** *(euph)* **he remembered me in his final letter** ele não se esqueceu de mim na sua derradeira carta; **3** *(give regards)* **please** ~ **me to your father** faz favor de dar os meus cumprimentos ao seu pai; **4** *(commemorate)* comemorar *(battle)*; ♦ *vi* lembrar-se; ♦ **to if I** (**rightly**) ~ ... se bem me lembro ...; **not as far as I** ~ que eu saiba, não; **to** ~ **by heart** saber de cor.

remembrance *n* memória *f;* lembrança *f,* recordação *f;* **R**~ **Day** *npr* Dia *m* do Armistício.

remind *vt:* **to** ~ **sb to do sth** lembrar a alguém de fazer algo; **2** ~ **of** *(similarity)* **he** ~**s me of my son** ele faz-me lembrar o meu filho.

reminder *n* aviso *m,* lembrete *m;* lembrança *f.*

reminisce *vi* relembrar velhas histórias.

reminiscence *n* reminiscência *f.*

reminiscent *adj* retrospectivo,-a; rememorativo,-a.

remise *vt* *(JUR)* renunciar *(a right, claim)*.

remiss *adj* remisso,-a desleixado,-a, negligente, descuidado,-a; **how** ~ **of me!** que descuidado,-a que eu sou! **remissible** *adj* remissível, desculpável.

remission *n* perdão *m;* absolvição *f;* responsabilidade *f;* **2** *(REL, MED)* remissão *f.*

remit *n* alçada *f;* incumbência; **that's outside my** ~ isso não é da minha alçada, da minha incumbência; responsabilidade *f;* **2** *(JUR)* transferência dum processo para outro tribunal; ♦ *(-ted)* *vt* *(JUR)* *(send back)* remeter *(case, proceeding)*; enviar *(money, payment)*; **2** *(postpone)*; cancelar, deferir.

remittance *n* *(money)* remessa *f;* *(pay)* pagamento *m;* *(by post)* envio *m.*

remittent *adj* *(MED)* remitente.

remnant *n* *(leftover)* resto *m;* **2** *(trace)* vestígio *m;* **3** *(leftover fabric)* retalho *m.*

remodel *(-ll-)* *vt* remodelar; **2** *(US)* *(renovate)* renovar, reformar.

remonstrance *n* protesto *m.*

remonstrate *vi* protestar (**with sb about th** com alguém acerca de algo).

remorse *n* remorso *m.*

remorseful *adj* arrependido,-a, cheio,-a de remorso.

remorseless *adj* *(fig)* sem piedade, desumano,-a; **2** implacável, impiedoso,-a.

remote *adj* *(place)* remoto,-a, longínquo,-a, afastado,-a; **2** *(village)* isolado,-a; **3** *(time, era)* distante; **4** *(aloof person)* reservado,-a, distante; **5** *(slight chance, idea)* vago,-a, mínimo,-a, ínfimo,-a; ~ **access** *n* *(COMP)* acesso *m* remoto; ~ **control** *n* comando *m* à distância, *(BR)* controle *m* remoto; ~-**controlled** *adj* telecomandado.

remotely *adv* remotamente; **2** *(slightly)* vagamente; **it is** ~ **possible that** é pouco provável que; **3** *(place)* afastado.

remoteness *n* afastamento *m;* isolamento *m;* alheamento *m.*

remould *(UK)* **remold** *(US)* *n* pneu recauchutado; ♦ *vt* *(AUT)* recauchutar *(tyre)*.

removable *adj* removível, desmontável.

removal *n* *(removing)* remoção *f,* retirada (**of** de); **2** *(of house)* mudança *f;* **3** *(dismissal)* demissão *f,* exoneração; **4** *(MED)* ablação *f*; **organ** ~ *n (MED)* colheita *f* de órgãos; **~s** *npl (firm)* n empresa *f* de mudanças; **~ van** *n* camião *(BR:* caminhão) *m* de mudanças.

remove *vt (take away)* tirar; **to ~ stains** tirar nódoas; **2** eliminar, remover *(doubt, player etc)*; **3** *(dismiss)* demitir **(from,** de); **4** *(move away)* afastar(-se), retirar(-se); **5** *(TECH)* retirar, separar; **6** *(take off) (hat shoes)* tirar; ♦ *vi (clothes)* despir-se.

removed *adj (family relations)* afastado,-a; **a cousin twice/three times ~** primo em segundo/terceiro, etc. grau; IDIOM **to be far ~ from the truth** estar longe de ser verdade.

remunerate *vt* remunerar.

remuneration *n* remuneração *f*.

Renaissance *n*: **the ~** o Renascimento *m*; ♦ adj *(ART, LIT)* renascentista *m,f*.

renal *adj* renal *m,f*.

rename *vt* dar novo name a.

rend *(pt, pp* of **rent)** *vt* rasgar, despedaçar.

render *vt (COMM) (submit)* entregar; **2** *(provide)* dar, prestar; **to ~ good services** prestar bons serviços; **3** *(ART, MUS, LITER)* produzir; **4** *(cause to change)* fazer, tornar; **to ~ sb speechless** deixar alguém boquiaberto,-a; **5** *(translate)* traduzir **(into** para); **6** *(CONSTR)* rebocar.

rendering *n (MUS, ART, LITER)* interpretação *f*; **2** tradução *f* **(of** de); **3** *(CONSTR)* reboco *m*.

rendez-vous *n* encontro *m*; ponto *m* de encontro.

rendition *n (of music)* execução *f*, interpretação *f*; *(of poem)* declamação *f*.

renegade *n* renegado,-a; rebelde.

renege *vi* renegar; **to ~ on sth** deixar de cumprir algo, voltar com palavra atrás.

renegociate *vi* renegociar.

renew *vt* renovar, retomar; *(start again)* recomeçar.

renewable *adj* renovável; **~ energy** *n* energia *f* renovável; **~ resources** *n* recursos *mpl* renováveis; **renewables** *npl* fontes *fpl* renováveis de energia.

renewal *n* renovação *f (of document)*; **2** reatamento **(of,** de) *(hostilities)*.

renewed *adj* renovado,-a.

renitent *adj* renitente.

renk *adj* desagradável.

rennet *n (leavening for milk)* coalho *m*.

rennin *n (BIOL) (enzyme)* quimosina *f*.

renounce *vt (give up)* renunciar a; abdicar de; **2** *(reject)* repudiar, rejeitar.

renovate *vt* renovar.

renovation *n* renovação *f*; **~ work** *n* obras *fpl*; **~s** *npl* obras de restauro.

renown *n* renome *m*; reputação *f*.

renowned *adj* célebre *m,f*, famoso,-a **(for sth** por algo).

rent *n (for accommodation)* renda *f*, aluguer; *(BR)* aluguel *m*; **2** *(tear)* rasgão *m*; ♦ *vt* alugar, arrendar *(appartment, bedroom)* **how much is the ~ per month?** quanto é a renda por mês?; **~ allowance** *n* subsídio *m* da renda de casa; **~ book** *n* livro *m* do registo da renda; **~ control** *n* regulamentação *f* de arrendamentos; **~-free** *adj* isento de renda

(EP); isento de aluguel *(BR)*; **~-roll** *n* registo *m* das rendas; ♦ *vi* arrendar, alugar *(EP) (BR)*.

rental *n (EP)* aluguer *m*, arrendamento *m*; *(BR)* aluguel *m*.

rented *adj (villa, apartment)* arrendado,-a, alugado,-a.

renunciation *n* renúncia *f*; *(of faith, family)* repúdio *m*.

reopen *vt* tornar a abrir; reabrir *(process)*.

reorganize, reorganise *vt* reorganizar; ♦ *vi* reorganizar-se.

rep[1] *n (abbr for* **representative)** *(fam)* representante *m,f*; **2** *(THEAT) (abbr for* **repertory)**.

Rep[2] *(abbr for* **Representative)** *(US)* deputado,-a; **2** *(abbr for* **Republican)** republicano,-a.

repair *n* reparação *f*, conserto *m*; remendo *m*; ♦ *vt* reparar, remediar; consertar; **in good/bad ~** em bom/mau estado; **~ kit** *n* caixa *f* de ferramentas (de bicicletas).

repaper *vt (wall)* trocar o papel da parede, forrar a parede de papel de novo.

reparation *n* reparação *f*; *(JUR)* indemnização *f*.

repartee *n* resposta pronta e engenhosa, espirituosa.

repartition *n* repartição *f*; distribuição *f*; ♦ *vt* repartir.

repast *n (meal)* repasto *m*.

repatriate *n* repatriado,-a; ♦ *vt* repatriar.

repay *(pt, pp* **repaid)** *vt (pay back-money)* reembolsar, pagar de volta; *(loan, debt)* saldar, liquidar; **2** *(favour)* retribuir, recompensar **(sb for sth** alguém por algo).

repayment *n* reembolso *m*; *(kindness, favour)* retribuição *f*; *(sum)* pagamento *m*.

repeal *n* revogação *f*; anulação *f*; ♦ *vt* revogar, anular.

repeat *n* repetição *f* reprise *f*; ♦ *vt/vi* repetir; **~ to o.s.** repetir-se.

repeatedly *adv* repetidamente.

repeater *n (TECH)* repetidor *m*.

repel (-ll-) *vt* repelir, repugnar.

repellent *n* repelente; **insect ~** repelente de inse(c)tos; ♦ repugnante.

repent[1] *adj (BOT) (creeper)* rastejante *m,f*.

repent[2] ♦ *vi*: **to ~ of** arrepender-se de.

repentance *n* arrependimento *m*.

repentant *adj* penitente, arrependido,-a; contrito,-a.

repercussion *n* repercussão *f*; **to have ~s** repercutir.

repertoire *n* repertório *m*.

repertory *n* (= ~ **theatre/company)** teatro *m* de repertório.

repetition *n* repetição *f*.

repetitive *adj* repetitivo,-a; **~ strain injury** *n (MED)* lesão *f* por esforços repetitivos.

rephrase *vt* reformular *(remark)*; **perhaps I should ~ that** talvez eu deva dizer isto de outra maneira.

replace *vt* repor, substituir, ocupar o lugar de (outro).

replacement *n* substituição *f*; reposição *f*; *(person)* substituto,-a.

replay *n* repetição *f*; **2** *(recording)* replay *m*; **3** *(game)* novo jogo, jogo de desempate; ♦ *vt (cassette, DVD)* ver novamente.

replenish *vt* reabastecer *(stock)*, prover novamente (algo com algo).

replete *adj* repleto,-a **(with,** com), cheio,-a; *(after meal)* cheio,-a; saciado,-a.

replevin *n (also:* **replevy**) *(JUR)* recuperação *f* e reivindicação de de bens roubados.

replica *n* réplica *f*, cópia *f*, reprodução *f*.

replicate *vt* copiar, fazer uma reprodução; ♦ *vi (MED)* reproduzir-se.

reply *(pl:* -**ies**) *n* resposta *f*, réplica *f*; ♦ *vi* responder, replicar.

reply-paid *adj* pré-pago,-a, com porte pago.

repopulate *vt* repovoar.

report *n (written account)* relatório *m*; **2** *(JOURN)* reportagem *f*; **3** ~ **card** *(school)* boletim *m* de avaliação, caderneta *f* escolar; **4** *(noise)* estampido *m*, *(of gun)* detonação *f*; **composite** ~ *n* relatório *m* de síntese; **weather** ~ boletim *m* meteorológico; ♦ *vt* relatar, informar sobre; fazer uma reportagem sobre; comunicar, anunciar; ♦ *vi* apresentar um relatório; **to** ~ *(to sb)* apresentar-se (a), comparecer; **to** ~ **to duty** apresentar-se ao serviço; ~ **back** informar (alguém), apresentar um relatório.

reportage *n* reportagem *f*.

reportedly *adv* alegadamente, segundo se diz.

reporter *n* jornalista *m,f*, repórter *m,f*.

repose *n (formal)* repouso *m*; ♦ *vi (rest)* repousar; **2** *(be based on)* assentar sobre; **3** *(place)* colocar, depositar.

reposition *n (MED) (surgery)* reposição, restituição de um órgão ou membro.

repository *(pl:* -**ies**) *n (items kept for safety)* repositório *m*; **2** *(for goods before they are sold)* depósito *m*, armazém.

repossess *vt* reaver a posse.

repossession *n (of house, property)* recuperação *f* imobiliária; *(of council property)* devolução *f*; ~ **order** *n* ordem *f* de despejo.

reprehend *vt* repreender.

reprehensible *adj* repreensível, censurável, condenável.

reprehension *n (reprimand)* repreensão *f*, censura *f*.

represent *vt* representar; *(fig)* falar em nome de; **2** *(COMM)* ser representante de.

representation *n* representação *f*; petição *f*; ♦ ~**s** *npl* reclamação *fsg*, protesto *msg*.

representative *n* representante *m,f*; ♦ *adj* representativo,-a.

repress *vt* reprimir, dominar.

represser *n, adj (person)* repressor *m*.

repression *n* repressão *f*.

repressive *adj* repressivo,-a.

reprieve *n (JUR)* suspensão *f* temporária (da pena), **2** *(delay)* adiamento *m*; **3** *(temporary relief)* alívio *m*, ajuda *f* temporária *(to person, company)*; ♦ *vt* suspender temporariamente, conceder um adiamento; aliviar.

reprimand *n* reprimenda *f*; **2** *(coll)* raspanete *m*; ♦ *vt* repreender, censurar; *(to tell off)* dar um raspanete a (alguém), ralhar (com alguém).

reprint *n (TYPO)* reimpressão *f*, reedição *f*; ♦ *vt* reimprimir, reeditar; **the book was** ~**ed last year** o livro foi reimpresso no ano passado.

reprisal *n* represália *f*; **fear of** ~ medo de represálias.

reprise *n* repetição *f*.

reproach *n (rebuke)* repreensão *f*, censura *f*; ♦ *vt*: **to** ~ **sb (with)** repreender alguém **(for doing sth** por fazer algo**); beyond** ~ irrepreensível, impecável *m,f*.

reproachful *adj (look, comment)* reprovador,-ora; *(look, word)* de reprovação.

reprobate *n* réprobo,-a; ♦ *adj* imoral; ♦ *vt* reprovar.

reprocessing plant *n* fábrica *(BR)* usina *f* de tratamento de (detritos)

reproduce *vt* reproduzir; ♦ *vi* reproduzir-se.

reproduction *n* reprodução *f*; **image** ~ *n* reprodução *f* de imagens; **sexual/asexual** ~ *n (BIOL)* reprodução *f* sexuada/assexuada.

reproductive *adj* reprodutivo.

reprography *n* reprografia *f*.

reprove *vt* reprovar, censurar; **to** ~ **sb (for)** repreender alguém (por).

reptile *n (ZOOL)* réptil *m*.

reptilian *adj* reptile.

republic *n* república *f*.

republican *n adj* republicano,-a.

repudiable *adj* repudiável.

repudiate *vt (reject)* rejeitar, **2** *(refuse to acknowledge)* negar; desconhecer; **3** *(disown)* repudiar.

repugnant *adj* repugnante, repulsivo,-a.

repulse *vt* rejeitar; *(MIL, gen)* repelir.

repulsion *n* repulsa *f*.

repulsive *adj* repulsivo,-a

repurchase *n* reaquisição *f*; ~ **agreement** *n (FIN)* acordo *m* de recompra; ♦ *vt* readquirir.

reputable *adj (person)* bem conceituado,-a, de confiança; **2** *(profession)* respeitável.

reputation *n* reputação *f*; **to have a good/bad** ~ ter uma boa/má reputação, ter bom/mau nome; IDIOM **to live up to one's** ~ cumprir as expe(c)tativas.

repute *n* reputação *f*, renome *m*.

reputed *adj* suposto, pretenso.

reputedly *adv* segundo se diz, supostamente, ao que consta.

request *n* pedido *m*, solicitação *f*; **on** ~ a pedido; ~ **stop** *n (for buses)* paragem *(EP)*, parada *f (BR)* não-obrigatoria; ♦ *vt* pedir, solicitar; **to** ~ **sth of/ from sb** pedir/solicitar alguma coisa a alguém; **as** ~**ed** conforme foi solicitado.

requiem *n* réquiem *m*.

require *vt (want/need)* precisar de, necessitar; **2** *(formally request)* requerer, pedir; **3** *(demand)* exigir; mandar, ordenar.

required *adj* necessário,-a; *(payment, punctuality)* exigido,-a; **visitors are** ~ **to display their badge** exige-se que os visitantes mostrem os seus crachás.

requirement *n* condição *f*, requisito *m*; necessidade *f*; IDIOM **to meet the** ~**s** cumprir os parâmetros; satisfazer as necessidades.

requisite *n* requisito *m*; ♦ *adj* necessário, indispensável *m,f*; **travelling** ~**s** artigos *mpl* de viagem.

requisition *n* requisição *f*; ~ **(for)** requerimento (para); ♦ *vt (MIL)* requisitar, confiscar.

requital *n* recompensa *f*; compensação *f*, a(c)to *m* retribuído.

reredos *n (REL) (screen, panel behind altars)* retábulo *m*.

reroute *vt* desviar.

resale *n* revenda *f*; ~ **price** *n* preço *m* de revenda; ~ **price maintenance** *n* (COMM) imposição *f* de preços de venda.

reschedule *vt* reagendar.

rescind *vt* rescindir (contract, agreement); (JUR) revogar (law), anular (decision).

rescission *n* rescisão *f*.

rescue *n* salvamento *m*, resgate *m*; ♦ *vt* salvar, livrar; resgatar; **to** ~ **from** livrar de; ~ **aid** *n* auxílio *m* de emergência; ~ **party** *n* grupo, expedição *f* de salvamento; **emergency** ~ **service** *n* serviços *mpl* de emergência; **search and** ~ *n* busca e salvamento.

rescuer *n* salvador,-ora, libertador,-ora.

research *n* pesquisa *f*, investigação *f*; ~ **and development** *n* investigação e desenvolvimento; ~ **work** *n* trabalho de pesquisa; ♦ *vt* pesquisar.

researcher *n* investigador,-ora, pesquisador,-ora.

resell *vt* revender.

resemblance *n* parecença *f*, semelhança *f*; **to bear a** ~ **to** assemelhar-se a.

resemble *vt* parecer-se com.

resent *vt* ressentir-se; ofender-se com.

resentful *adj* ressentido,-a (**of** com).

resentment *n* ressentimento *m* (**against** contra; **about** acerca de; **at** em relação a).

reservation *n* reserva *f*; **2** (booking) marcação *f*; (restaurant, hotel) **have you made a** ~**?** tem reserva?; **3** (doubt) **without** ~ sem reservas; **with some** ~**s** com certas reservas; **4** (US) (for native Americans) reserva *f*.

reserve *n* reserva *f*; **2** (SPORT) suplente *m,f*; ~**s** *npl* (MIL) (tropas da) reserva *sg*; ~ **bank** *n* (US) (ECON) banco *m* de reserva federal ~ **currency** *n* (ECON) moeda *f* de reserva; ~ **price** *n* (COMM) preço *m* limite; **emergency aid** ~ *n* reserva para as ajudas de emergência; **in** ~ de reserva; **nature** ~ *n* reserva *f* natural; ♦ *vt* reservar; **2** (retain) reservar-se.

reserved *adj* (gen) reservado,-a; ~ **list** *n* (MIL) quadro *m* de reserva; ~ **word** *n* (COMP or programmed language) palavra *f* reservada.

reservoir *n* reservatório *m*; tanque *m*; depósito *m*; **2** (water storage) represa *f*.

reset (-tt-) *vt* engastar de novo (pedras preciosas) repor; **2** fazer nova composição (de tipografia); acertar (clock); reajustar, regular (mechanism); **3** (bone) recolocar; **4** (COMP) reinicializar; ~ **time** *n* (ELECT) tempo *m* de reposição.

resettle *vt* reinstalar (person); **2** repovoar (area); ♦ *vi* instalar-se em novo lugar.

resettlement *n* restabelecimento *m*.

reshape *vt* remodelar.

reshuffle *n*: **Cabinet** ~ (POL) remodelação *f* do Gabinete do Governo, Ministério; ♦ *vt* remodelar (cabinet); **2** baralhar (cards).

reside *vi* residir, viver, morar.

residence *n* residência *f*; domicílio *m*; permanência *f*, estadia *f*; ~ **permit** *n* autorização *m* de residência.

resident *n* residente; hóspede *m,f*; ♦ *adj* permanente; interno, residente.

residential *adj* (sector, zone) residencial; **2** em regime de internato.

residents' association *n* associação *f* de moradores.

residual *adj* residual; ~ **charge** *n* (ELECT) carga *f* residual; ~ **unemployment** *n* desemprego *m* residual.

residue *n* (CHEM) resíduo *m*, resto *m*; **2** (COMM) montante *m* líquido.

resign *vt* renunciar a; ♦ *vi* demitir-se (from job, position); **to** ~ **o.s. to one's fate** resignar-se com a sua sorte; sujeitar-se a (circumstances, work).

re-sign *vt* assinar de novo.

resignation *n* renúncia *f*; resignação *f*, submissão *f*; **2** (of a job) demissão *f*.

resigned *adj* conformado, resignado (to loss, grief).

resilience *n* elasticidade *f*, resistência *f*.

resilient *adj* resiliente *m,f*; elástico.

resin *n* resina *f*; ♦ *vt* cobrir com resina.

resist *vt* resistir.

resistance *n* resistência *f*; impedimento *m*; ~ **thermometer** *n* (TECH) termómetro *m* de resistência; ~ **welding** *n* (metallurgy) soldadura *f* por resistência; **magnetic** ~ *n* (ELECT) resistência *f* magnética; IDIOM **to take the path of least** ~ seguir o caminho mais fácil.

resistant *adj* resistente.

resistor *n* (ELECT) resistência *f*.

resit (pt: **resat**, pres p -**ting**) *vt* repetir o exame; fazer o exame outra vez.

resolute *adj* resoluto,-a, firme.

resolution *n* (determination) resolução *f*; **2** (decree) resolução (**against** contra); **to pass a** ~ aprovar uma resolução *f*.

resolve *n* resolução *f*; intenção *f*; ♦ *vt* resolver; ♦ *vi* resolver-se; **to** ~ **to do** resolver-se a fazer; IDIOM **to** ~ **one's differences** (**between** entre) fazer as pazes (**with** com).

resolved *adj* decidido,-a.

resonance *n* ressonância *f*; **magnetic** ~ *n* (MED) ressonância *f* magnética.

resonant *adj* ressonante.

resonate *vi* ressoar.

resort *n* (holiday) local *m* turístico; estação *f* de veraneio; **2** (means) recurso *m*; **in the last** ~ em último caso, em última instância; **seaside** ~ *n* estância *f* balnear; ♦ *vi* **to** ~ **to** recorrer a, fazer uso de, frequentar.

resound *vi* ressoar, ecoar; **the room** ~**ed with shouts** os gritos ressoaram no quarto.

resounding *adj* retumbante; ressonante; **2** (fig) clamoroso,-a.

resource *n* recurso *m*; expediente *m*; **renewable** ~ *n* recurso *m* natural renovável; ~ **centre** *n* centro *m* de recursos; ♦ ~**s** *npl* recursos *mpl*, meios *mpl*; **human** ~ *n* recursos *mpl* humanos.

resourceful *adj* engenhoso,-a, expedito,-a, versátil.

respect *n* respeito *m* (**for** por); **out of** ~ **for him** por respeito a ele; **2** (courtesy, consideration) consideração *f* (**for** para com); **with** (**all**) **due** ~ salvo o devido respeito, com todo o respeito; ~**s** *npl* (formal) (to man) respeitos a; (to woman) homenagem *f*; **to pay one's** ~**s to** prestar homenagem a; **2** *(regards)* cumprimentos *mpl*; apresentar os seus cumprimentos; **to pay one's last ~s to sb** prestar, render a última homenagem a *(deceased)*; **2** *(aspect)* **in some ~s** em certos aspe(c)tos; ♦ *vt* respeitar, ter consideração; ♦ **in that ~** quanto a isso; **with ~ to** *prep* com respeito a.

respectability *n* respeitabilidade *f.*

respectable *adj* respeitável; considerável; aceitável.

respectful *adj* atencioso,-a, respeitador,-ora, respeitoso,-a (**of** de, **towards** para com).

respecting *prep* no que diz respeito a.

respective *adj* respe(c)tivo,-a.

respectively *adv* respe(c)tivamente.

respiration *n* respiração *f*; ~ **rate** *n* ritmo *f* de repiração.

respirator *n* (MED) *(machine)* respirador *m*; **2** *(gas mask)* máscara *f* antigás; máscara *f* respiratória.

respiratory *adj* respiratório,-a; ~ **failure** *n* (MED) paragem *f* respiratória; ~ **passage** *n* (ANAT) vias *fpl* respiratórias; ~ **quotient** *n* (MED) quociente *m* respiratório.

respite *n* *(formal)* pausa *f*, descanso *m*; **2** (JUR, COMM) *(delay)* adiamento *m*, suspensão *f.*

resplendent *adj* resplandecente, brilhante.

respond *vi* *(react)* reagir; **2** *(answer)* responder; **3** (REL) *(by singing)* cantar responsos; *(by speaking)* responsar.

respondent *n* (JUR) arguido,-a; **2** *(to questions)* interrogado,-a.

response *n* resposta *f*; **2**, rea(c)ção *f*; **3 the ~s** (REL) os responsos *mpl*; ~ **time** *n* (COMP) tempo *m* de resposta; **conditioned ~** *n* (MED) resposta *f* condicionada.

responsibility *n* responsabilidade *f* (**for doing sth** de fazer); **to accept ~ for** assumir a responsabilidade; **we take no ~ for lost suitcases** não nos responsabilizamos pela perda de malas.

responsible *adj* sério,-a respeitável; de responsabilidade; responsável (**for** por).

responsive *adj* sensível; que responde.

rest *n* *(repose)* descanso *m*, repouso *m*; **2** (MUS) pausa *f*; intervalo *m*; **3** *(support)* apoio *m*; **4** *(remaining)* resto *m*; **arm** ~ *n* apoio *m* para braços; **at ~** tranquilo; **eternal ~** *n* descanso *m* eterno; ~ **cure** *n* (MED) cura *f* pelo repouso; ~ **home** *n* lar *m*, casa *f* de repouso; ~ **room** *n* (US) lavabo *m*, casa de banho; (BR) banheiro *m*; ♦ *vi* descansar; repousar; **to ~ on** apoiar-se em; ♦ *vt*: **to ~ (sth) on/against** apoiar (alguma coisa) em/sobre, encostar a; **to ~ assured** ficar descansado; IDIOM **to ~ on your laurels** descansar à sombra da bananeira; **she was laid to ~ yesterday** ela foi a enterrar ontem; ~ **in peace!** descansa em paz!; **give it a ~!** *(fam)* vê se te calas! *(fam)*; **I ~ my case** não tenho mais nada a dizer.

restart *vt* (AUT) arrancar de novo; **2** reiniciar, recomeçar.

restate *vt* refirmar.

restaurant *n* restaurante *m*; ~**car** *n* vagão-restaurante *m*; ~ **service** *n* serviço *m* de restauração.

restful *adj* sossegado,-a, tranquilo,-a; repousante.

restitution *n* (JUR) restituição *f*, devolução *f*; **to make ~ to sb for** restituir, inde(m)nizar alguém de.

restive *adj* *(person)* inquieto,-a; *(crowd)* agitado,-a, frenético,-a; *(animal)* irrequieto,-a.

restless *n* impaciência *f*, agitação; ♦ *adj* *(night, sleep)* agitado,-a; *(child)* irrequieto,-a; impaciente.

restlessly *adv* impacientemente.

restock *vt* reabastecer.

restoration *n* restauração *f*, renovação *f.*

restorative *adj* restaurador,-ora; **2** revigorante; fortificante; ~ **justice** *n* (JUR) justiça *f* reparadora.

restore *vt* restaurar; **2** restituir (**sth to sb** algo a alguém) **3** restabelecer *(power, order)*; **my health is ~d** a minha saúde está recuperada.

restrain *vt* reprimir, restringir, coibir; **to ~ (from doing)** impedir (de fazer).

restrained *adj* moderado, comedido.

restraint *n* limitação *f*, coibição *f*, constrangimento *m*; moderação *f*, sobriedade *f.*

restrict *vt* restringir, limitar.

restriction *n* restrição *f*, limitação *f.*

restrictive *adj* restritivo, limitativo; ~ **practice** *n* (JUR) prática *f* restritiva.

restructure *vt* restruturar.

result *n* resultado *m*; **no ~s** sem resultados; ♦ *vi*: **to ~ in** resultar em; **as a ~ of** como consequência de.

resume *vt/vi* retomar, recomeçar.

résumé *n* resumo *m*; **2** (US) currículo *m.*

resumption *n* recomeço *m.*

resurface *vi* reaparecer; ♦ *vt* *(road)* repavimentar.

resurgence *n* ressurgimento *m.*

resurrect *vt* ressuscitar, renascer.

resurrection *n* ressurreição *f.*

resuscitate *vt* (MED) ressuscitar, reanimar.

resuscitation *n* ressuscitação *f.*

resuscitator *n* (MED) aparelho *m* de reanimação.

retail *n* (COMM) venda *f* a retalho, (BR) a varejo *m*; ~ **price** *n* (COMM) preço *m* de revenda; ~ **therapy** *n* *(coll)* terapia *f* das compras; ♦ *adv* a retalho, (BR) a varejo; ♦ *vt* vender a retalho (BR: varejo).

retailer *n* retalhista *m,f*, (BR) varejista *m,f.*

retain *vt* *(keep)* reter; conservar; manter; **to ~ one's composure** manter a calma *f*, (BR) compostura *f*; **2** (JUR) contratar.

retainer *n* *(arc)* *(servant)* empregado; **2** *(fee)* sinal *m*, pagamento *m* adiantado.

retaliate *vi* vingar-se; retaliar; **to ~ (against)** fazer represálias (contra).

retaliation *n* represália, vingança.

retard *n* *(offensive)* atrasado mental; ♦ *vt* atrasar.

retarded *adj* mentalmente retardado; atrasado.

retch *vi* fazer esforço para vomitar.

retention *n* *(gen)* retenção *f*; **2** *(of pride, independence)* manutenção.

retentive *adj* retentivo,-a, *(of memory)* que retém.

rethink *(pt, pp* **rethought)** *vt* repensar, reconsiderar.

reticence *n* reserva *f*; **2** discrição *f*; ♦ **reticent** *adj* reservado,-a.

reticle *n* (ELECT) retículo *m.*

retina *n* (ANAT) *(eye)* retina *f.*

retinitis *n* (MED) retinite *f.*

retinopathy n (MED) retinopatia f.

retinue n séquito m, comitiva f, escolta f.

retire vi (work) aposentar-se, reformar-se; **2** (go away) retirar-se; **3** (go to sleep) deitar-se, ir dormir.

retired adj (pensioner) aposentado,-a; reformado,-a.

retiree (US) n aposentado,-a; reformado,-a.

retirement n aposentação f, reforma f (BR) aposentadoria.

retiring adj (person) reservado,-a; retraído,-a; (from work) **to be ~** estar a ponto de se reformar, aposentar.

retort n réplica f; **2** resposta f incisiva f ou espirituosa; ◆ vi replicar, retorquir; (answer back rudely) refilar, respingar.

retrace vt retroceder; voltar atrás; **2** (memory) recordar, reconstituir; **to ~ one's steps** arrepiar caminho.

retract vt (draw in) retrair, recolher (landing gear, snail's horns); retratar, revogar (statement); ◆ vi retratar-se, desdizer-se.

retractable adj (landing gear, snail's horns) retrá(c)til; (pencil) lapiseira f; **2** revogável.

retrain vt reeducar, retreinar.

retraining n readaptação f profissional, reciclagem profissional.

retreat n (fado night club) retiro m; **mountain ~** refúgio m; (REL) retiro m; **2** (withdrawal) retraimento m; **3** (MIL) retirada f; ◆ vi retirar-se; refugiar-ser; **2** (MIL) bater em retirada; **3** (glacier, land) recuar, retroceder; **to ~ from** não cumprir, voltar atrás (word, promise).

retrench vt cortar, reduzir (expenses); ◆ vi economizar.

retrial n (JUR) revisão f (de processo).

retribution n desforra f, vingança f; IDIOM **divine ~** castigo m divino.

retrievable adj recuperável.

retrieval n recuperação f.

retrieve vt (get back) reaver; **2** (COMP) recuperar; **3** (rescue) reparar; remediar.

retriever n cão m de caça, perdigueiro.

retro n adj retro m.

retroactive adj retroa(c)tivo,-a.

retrograde adj retrogrado,-a; **~ amnesia** (MED) amnésia f retrógrada; **2** (backwards) para trás; retrocesso.

retrogress vi andar para trás; retroceder, **2** degenerar.

retrospect n: **in ~** retrospectivamente, em retrospecto.

retrospective adj retrospe(c)tivo,-a, retroa(c)tivo,-a.

retroversion n (back to the original) retroversão f.

retrovirus n (BIOL) retrovírus m.

return n (come back) retorno m; regresso m, volta f; **~ ticket** bilhete de ida e volta; **2** (give back) devolução f, restituição f; (of payment) reembolso m; **3** (reward) recompensa f; **4** (tennis) rebatida f; **5** (FIN) rendimento m, lucro m (**on** sobre); **tax ~** declaração de impostos; **joint ~** (tax) n declaração f conjunta (de impostos); **~ officer** n presidente m,f da mesa de escrutínio; **6 ~ current** n (ELECT) contracorrente f; **7 ~ pump** n (MEC) bomba f de retorno; ◆ **returns** npl (POL) (from votes)

resultados mpl; **2** (anniversary) **many happy ~!** parabéns, felicidades!; ◆ vi (come back) voltar, regressar; **2** (resume) retomar; **3** (symptom) reaparecer; ◆ vt (give back) devolver (ball, book etc); **2** (reciprocate) retribuir; **3** (JUR) proferir, anunciar (verdict); **4** (POL) eleger; **5** (MIL) ripostar a (fire) (FIN) (yield) render; ◆ adv prep **in ~** em troca (de).

returnable adj devolvível; (bottle) restituível; devolutivo,-a.

reunion n reunião f; reunião social.

reunite vt reunir; reconciliar.

reusable adj reutilizável.

reuse vt reutilizar.

rev (-ved) vt/vi (AUT) (= **~up**) acelerar o motor, a velocidade; **~ counter** n (AUT) conta-rotações m inv.

rev (abbr for **revolution**) rotação f.

Rev (abbr for **Reverend**).

revalue vt reavaliar.

revamp vt (house, image) modernizar, redecorar; **2** (text) aprimorar.

reveal vt revelar, mostrar.

revealing adj revelador,-ora, esclarecedor,-ora; **2** (fig) provocador,-ora; **~ dress** vestido m decotado.

reveille n (MIL) toque m de alvorada.

revel (UK: -led, -ling) (US: -ed, -ing) vi divertir-se; andar na pândega; **to ~ in sth** deleitar-se, divertir-se com.

revelation n revelação f.

reveller n farrista m,f, folião,-liã.

revelry (pl: **revelries**) n festança f, folia f, pândega f, patuscada f (fam); **2** (with food) patuscada.

revenge n vingança f, desforra f; **to take ~ on** vingar-se de; desforrar-se de.

revengeful adj vingativo,-a.

revenue n receita f; **~s** n (FIN) receitas fpl públicas; **inland ~ tax** (UK) n (FIN) receita f nacional, (BR) receita federal; **tax ~** n receitas fpl fiscais; **total ~** n (FIN) volume m de negócios.

reverberate vi ressoar, repercutir, reverberar.

reverberation n reverberação f, repercussão f.

revere vt venerar; respeitar.

reverence n reverência f; respeito m.

reverend adj venerável m,f; **R~** n (Roman Catholic) padre; (addressing him) Reverendo (padre), pai; (protestante, envangélico) pastor m; (addressing) **~ Smith** pastor Smith; (Anglican) reverendo; (addressing) Reverendo Smith; **~ Mother** n Madre f Superior.

reverent adj reverente.

reverie n devaneio m, sonho m, fantasia f.

reversal n inversão f; mudança f em sentido contrário; **2** (of policy) viragem f; **3** (JUR) revogação f.

reverse n: **the ~** (opposite direction) o contrário m; **2** (inside out, fabric) o avesso m; **the ~ of** o reverso m de (coin); (page) o verso m; (of book) o dorso m; **3** (AUT = **~ gear**) marcha f atrás f, (BR) marcha à ré f; ◆ adj (order) inverso,-a; **to begin in ~ order** (questions) começar pela última; oposto,-a; contrário,-a; (upside down) invertido;

~-**charge call** *n* chamada à cobrança; ~ **osmosis** *n* osmose *f* inversa; ~ **video** *n* *(COMP)* visualização *f* em negativo; ♦ *vt (turn inside out)* virar do lado do avesso; **2** *(invert)* inverter; **3** *(change)* mudar (totalmente) de; ♦ *vt (AUT)* fazer marcha atrás, *(BR)* dar marcha à ré.

reversible *adj* reversível.

reversion *n* reversão *f*, volta *f* a algo.

revert *vi* reverter; retroceder; **to** ~ **to** voltar a.

review *n* *(MIL)* revista *f*; **2** *(critic)* crítica *f*, **3** *(assessment)* análise *f* (**of** sobre); **4** *(exam)*, revisão *f*, reavaliação *f*; ♦ *vt (examine again)* rever, reconsiderar; **2** *(MIL)* passar em revista; **3** *(make a critical assessment)* fazer a crítica de.

reviewer *n* crítico,-a.

revile *vt* ultrajar, injuriar, insultar.

revise *vt* corrigir; **2** *(alter)* alterar, modificar, rever; **3** fazer a revisão de.

revision *n* corre(c)ção *f*, revisão *f*.

revitalization *n* *(of economy)* relançamento *m*; *(degraded zone)* revitatilização *f*.

revitalize *vt* revitalizar, revivificar.

revival *n* *(COMM)* reativação *f*, recuperação *f*; **2** *(of language, culture)* renascimento *m*; revitalismo **3** *(THEAT)* reposição *f* em cena; **4** *(awakening)* despertar *m*.

revivalist *n* *(person who promotes religion, customs)* revivalista *m*.

revive *vt* *(from coma etc)* reanimar, fazer recuperar os sentidos; **2** *(reactivate)* restabelecer *(custom)*; **3** *(economy)* revitalizar; **4** *(memories)* trazer à baila, reviver; restaurar; reapresentar; **5** *(awaken)* despertar, reanimar *(interest, hope)*; ♦ *vi (regain consciousness)* voltar a si; recuperar os sentidos; *(interest)* renovar-se.

revocable *adj* revogável *m,f*.

revocation *n* revogação *f*.

revoke *vt* revogar, anular, cancelar.

revolt *n* revolta *f*, rebelião *f*, insurreição *f*; ♦ *vi* revoltar-se, indignar-se; ♦ *vt* causar aversão, repugnar.

revolting *adj* revoltante *m,f*, repulsivo,-a; nojento,-a.

revolution *n* revolução *f*.

revolutionary *adj, n* revolucionário,-a.

revolutionize *vt* revolucionar.

revolve *vi* revolver, girar.

revolver *n* revólver *m*.

revolving *adj (chairs, shelves)* giratório,-a; *(cylinder)* rotativo,-a; ~ **credit** *n (FIN)* crédito *m* renovável; ~ **door** *n* porta *f* giratória; ~ **fund** *n (FIN)* fundo *m* de rotação.

revue *n (THEAT)* revista *f*.

revulsion *n* aversão *f*, repugnância *f*.

reward *n* prémio *(BR: prê-)* *m*, recompensa *f*; ~ **given to whoever finds my puppy** dão-se alvíssaras a quem encontrar o meu cachorro; ♦ *vt*: **to** ~ **(for)** recompensar, premiar (por).

rewarding *adj (fig)* gratificante *m,f*, compensador,-ora.

rewind *(pt* **rewound**) *vt* rebobinar.

rewire *vt* renovar a instalação elé(c)trica de.

reword *vt* reformular, exprimir em outras palavras.

rewound *(pt, pp of* **rewind**).

rhapsody *n (MUS)* rapsódia *f*; **2** *(fig)* elocução *f* empolada.

rheology *n (PHYS)* reologia *f*.

Rhesus factor *n (MED)* factor *m* rhesus (Rh).

rhetoric *n* retórica *f*; **empty** ~ palavras *fpl* ocas.

rhetorical *adj* retórico; ~ **question** *n* pergunta *f* retórica.

rheumatic *adj* reumático.

rheumatism *n* reumatismo *m*.

rheumatoid arthritis *n* artrite *f* reumatóide.

Rhine *npr*: **the** ~ o (rio) Reno.

Rhineland *npr* Reunânia *f*.

rhinestone *n* diamante *m* falso.

rhinitis *n (MED)* rinite *f*.

rhino *n (fam)* rino *m*.

rhinoceros *(pl:* **-es**) *n* rinoceronte *m*.

rhinology *n (MED)* rinologia *f*.

rhinoplasty *n (MED)* rinoplastia *f*.

Rhodes *npr* Rodes; **in** ~ em Rodes.

Rhodesia *npr (formerly)* Rodésia *f*.

rhododendron *n (BOT)* rododendro *m*.

rhombus *n* losango *m*.

rhonchus *(pl:* **rhonchi**) *n* ronco *m*.

Rhone *npr*: **the** ~ o (rio) Ródano.

rhubard *n (BOT)* ruibarbo *m*.

rhyme *n* rima *f*; verso(s) rimado(s), poesia *f*; **nursery** ~ *n* verso *m* infantil; IDIOM **with no** ~ **or reason** sem quê nem para quê.

rhythm *n* ritmo *m*, cadência *f*, compasso *m*; **2** ~ **method** método *m* anticonce(p)cional.

rhythmic(al) *adj* rítmico compassado, cadenciado.

rhythmic gymnastics *n* ginástica *f* rítmica.

RI *(abbr for* **Religious Instruction**) instrução *f* religiosa; **2** *(abbr for* **Rhode Island**) Rhode Island.

ria *n (long narrow inlet of sea)* ria *f*.

rib *n (ANAT)* costela *f*; costeleta *f*; ~ **cage** *n* caixa *f* toráxica; **2** *(CULIN)* entrecosto *m*; **3** *(in knitting-stitch)* ponto *m* canelado *f*; **4** *(of umbrella)* vareta *f* do guarda-chuva; **5** *(groove, line)* estria *f*, aresta *f*, nervura *f*; **6** ~ **of a pipe** *(TECH)* nervura *f* de reforço dum tubo; **7** *(of leaf)* nervura *f*; **8** *(boat, plane)* armação *f*; ♦ *(-bb-)* *vt (tease, annoy)* arreliar, chatear *(fam)*; ~ **tickle** zombar, fazer troça (**of sb** de alguém); IDIOM ~ **tickler/tickling** *n*, *adj (joke)* muito cómico; de matar a rir.

ribald *adj* vulgarmente engraçado, grosseiro; irreverente *m,f*.

ribbed *adj (garment, ceiling, vault)* com nervuras; **2** *(with grooves, lines)* estriado,-a.

ribbon *n* fita *f*; faixa *f*, tira *f*; **in** ~s em tiras; esfarrapado,-a.

rice *n* arroz *m*; ~ **field** *n* arrozal *m*; ~ **paper** *n (CULIN)* papel *m* de arroz; ~ **pudding** *n (CULIN)* arroz *m* doce; **brown** ~ *n* arroz *m* integral; **puffed** ~ *n* arroz *m* tufado.

rich *n*: **the** ~ *n* os ricos *mpl*; **the** ~**es** *npl* riquezas *fpl*; ♦ *adj (wealthy)* rico,-a; **2** *(building, décor)* sumptuoso,-a, opulento,-a; **3** *(fertile)* fértil *m,f*; **4** *(of food)* suculento,-a, pesado,-a; **5** *(of colour, sound)* forte *m,f* cativante *m,f*; **6** *(odour)* forte *m,f*.

richly *adv* ricamente; ~ **deserved** bem merecido,-a.

richness *n* riqueza *f*; 2 abundância *f*; fertilidade *f*.

Richter scale *n* escala *f* de Richter.

rick *n* (*stacks of hay*) meda *f*; (*of other cereals*) moreia *f*; 2 (*sprain*) entorse, mau jeito (*ankle*).

rickets *n* raquitismo *m*.

rickety *adj* (*infirm*) raquítico; enfezado; 2 (*shaky*) vacilante *m*.

rickshaw *n* riquexó *m*, (BR) jinriquixá *m*.

ricochet *n* ricochete *m*; ♦ *vi* ricochetear.

rid (*pt, pp* rid) *vt*: to ~ **sb of** livrar alguém de; **to get ~ of** livrar-se, desembaraçar-se de.

riddance *n* libertação *f*; ♦ *exc* good ~! ainda bem que ele se foi!, que bons ventos o levem!

ridden (*pp of* ride).

riddle *n* (*charade*) adivinha *f*, enigma *m*, charada *f*; 2 (*sieve*) crivo *m*, peneira *f*; ♦ *vt*: to be ~d **with** estar cheio,-a/crivado de (*debts, bullets*).

ride *n* passeio *m*; passeio *m* a cavalo; percurso *m*; traje(c)to *m*; **can you give me a ~?** pode dar-me uma boleia?, (BR) carona?; ♦ (*pt* rode, *pp* ridden) *vi* cavalgar, montar; passear, andar (a cavalo, de bicicleta); viajar; ♦ *vt* montar; viajar; **to ~ at anchor** (*NAUT*) estar ancorado; **to ~ on** depender de; IDIOM **to take sb for a ~** (*fig*) enganar alguém; **to ~ roughshod over someone** passar por cima de alguém, dominar.

rider *n* cavaleiro,-a; ciclista *m,f*; motociclista *m,f*.

ridge *n* (*on mountain*) cume *m*, crista *f*; 2 (*roof*) cumeeira *f*; 3 (*ploughed land, sea*) sulco *m*; 4 (*on rock*) estria *f*; 5 (*METEOR*) ~ **of high pressure** área, linha *f* de altas pressões; ♦ *vt* (*AGR*) abrir sulcos em; fazer estrias em (*rock, metal*).

ridicule *n* ridículo *m*, zombaria *f*; ♦ *vt* ridicularizar, zombar de.

ridiculous *adj* ridículo, absurdo.

riding *n* equitação *f*, passeio a cavalo; (*SPORT*) hipismo *m*; ~ **breeches** *npl* calças *fpl* de montar; ~ **crop** *n* pingalim *m*, chicote *m*; ~ **high** *adj* (*person*) autoconfiante, popular; ~ **school** *n* escola *f* de equitação; (*practice area*) picadeiro *m*; IDIOM **to be ~ for a fall** (*invite disaster*) arranjar lenha para se queimar; **to be ~ high** estar nas suas sete quintas.

rife *adj* abundante; **to be ~ with** estar repleto de; **crime is ~ in ...** o crime impera/reina em ...

riffle *vi*: to ~ **through** folhear (*book*).

riffraff *n* plebe *f*; ralé *f*, canalha *f* (*pej*).

rifle *n* (*MIL, hunting*) espingarda *f*, carabina *f*; ~ **range** *n* carreira *f* de tiro; alcance *m* do tiro ao alvo; ~ **shot** *n* tiro *m* de espingardor; ♦ *vt* roubar, esvaziar (*drawer, safe*); ♦ *vi* to ~ **through sth** vascular, esquadrinhar algo.

rift *n* (*crack*) fenda *f*, racha *f*; 2 desacordo *m* (**between** entre); 2 (*permanent*) rompimento *m*; 3 (*in rock*) fissura *f*.

Rift Valley *n* vale *f* de fissura.

rig *n* (= oil ~) torre *f* de perfuração; **floating ~** plataforma petrolífera; 2 armação *f*, aparelho *m*; ~-**out** *vt* vestimenta *f*, traje; ♦ (-**gg**-) *vt* (*POL*) falsificar os resultados; 2 (*NAUT*) armar, aparelhar;

to ~ out *vt* equipar (**with**); 3 (*coll*) (*in passive use*) vestir, trajar, ataviar; **to ~ up** *vt* equipar, instalar, montar.

rigging *n* (*NAUT*) cordame *m*; 2 (*fraudulent*) (*of election, competition*) fraude *f*; 3 (*FIN*) (*of shares*) manipulação *f*.

right *n* (*entitlement*) direito *m*; **to be in the ~** ter razão; **to have the ~ to** (**do**) ter o direito de; 2 (*direction*) direita *f*; **turn to your ~** vire/volte à sua direita; **on your ~** à sua direita; 3 (*titles*) **the R~ Honourable** (UK) Sua Excelência; (*form of address in Parliament*) **the R~ Honourable Gentleman/Lady** o nosso distinto colega, a nossa distinta colega; ♦ *adj* (*correct*) certo,-a, corre(c)to,-a; **this bill is not ~** esta conta não está corre(c)ta; 2 (*appropriate*) conveniente; apropriado, próprio; **the dress is not ~ for this occasion** o vestido não é apropriado para esta ocasião; **it is not ~ for her to do that** não é próprio que ela faça isso; 3 (*fair*) justo,-a; **to put things ~** remediar as coisas; 4 (*not left*) direito,-a; 5 ~ **wing** *n* (*POL*) a direita *f*; (*accurate - time*) exa(c)to,-a, oportuno,-a; ♦ *adv* bem, corre(c)tamente; dire(c)tamente; 2 (*emphatic*) ~ **now** agora mesmo; ~ **here** aqui mesmo; **he punched him ~ in the eye** ele deu-lhe um soco bem no olho; **he is a ~ idiot** ele é mesmo um idiota; 3 (*immediately*) **I'll be ~ back** eu já volto; ~ **away** logo, em seguida; ♦ *exc* muito bem!, certo!, bom! oh, ~ **you are!** (UK) está bem!; **by ~(s)** por direito; ♦ *vt* endireitar; **to ~ a wrong** reparar um erro; IDIOM **it serves you ~ !** bem feito! let this be a lesson to you!; **he is being accused ~, left and centre** ele está a ser acusado de todas as dire(c)ções; ~ **and wrong** o bem e o mal; ~ **or wrong** com ou sem razão.

righteous *adj* justo,-a, justificado,-a.

righteously *adv* de forma íntegra.

righteousness *n* justiça, re(c)tidão *f*.

rightful *adj* legítimo,-a.

right-handed *adj* (*person*) destro,-a.

right-hand man *n* braço *m* direito.

rightly *adv* (*gen*) corre(c)tamente; (*justifiably*) com razão; (*precisely*) exa(c)tamente; **I can ~ say** eu posso dizer com exa(c)tidão.

right-minded *adj* (*person*) re(c)to,-a, sensato,-a.

right of way *n* (*AUT*) prioridade *f*; **to give ~ to** dar passagem a.

rights *npl* direitos *mpl*; **human ~** direitos humanos; 2 (*finance*) privilégios de acionistas numa empresa.

rigid *adj* rígido,-a; inflexível, intransigente.

rigidity *n* rigidez *f*, inflexibilidade *f*.

rigmarole *n* (*process*) (*pej*) ritual *m*; 2 (*story*) ladainha *f*; 3 (*incoherent*) trapalhada *f*.

rigorous *adj* rigoroso,-a.

rigour *n* rigor *m*, severidade *f*; rigidez *f*.

rile *vt* irritar, enervar.

rill *n* riacho *m*; pequeno canal *m*.

rim *n* borda *f*, bordo *m*, rebordo *f*; **plate with a silver ~** prato com um rebordo prateado; 2 (*spectacles*) aro *m*.

rimless *adj (spectacles)* sem aros.
rimmed *pt adj*: **gold-** ~ *(plate)* com bordo dourado.
rind *n (fruit skin)* pele *f*; casca *f*; **2** *(cheese) (crust)* crosta *f*; **grated lemon** ~ raspa *f* de limão.
ring *n (hoop)* aro *m*; **2** *(jewellery)* anel *m*; **3** *(circle)* círculo *m*, **4** *(group)* grupo *m*; **5** *(SPORT)* ringue *m*; pista *f*; **6** (= **bull** ~) picadeiro *m*, arena *f*; **7** *(sound)* toque *m*, badalada *f*; **8** *(phone call)* chamada *f* (telefónica), telefonema *m*; ♦ (*pt* **rang**, *pp* **rung**) *vi* telefonar; tocar, **2** badalar; **3** (= ~ **out**) soar; zumbir; ♦ *vt* (*TEL*: = ~ **up**) telefonar; badalar; tocar; **to** ~ **back** *vt (TEL)* telefonar, ligar de volta; **to** ~ **off** *vi (TEL)* desligar; **to** ~ **out** *vi* soar claramente; **2** ligar *(telephone)*; IDIOM **to throw one's hat in the** ~ candidatar-se, concorrer; **that ~s a bell** isso faz-me lembrar uma coisa; **to** ~ **hollow** soar a falso.
ring binder *n* dossier *m* de argolas.
ring finger *n* dedo *m* anular.
ring gauge *n (TECH)* anel *m* calibrador.
ringing *n (of bell, etc)* toque *m*; *(of church bells)* repicar **2** *(in ears)* zumbido *m*.
ringleader *n* cabecilha *m*.
ringlet *n (hair)* caracol *m* (*pl*: -óis); **2** argolinha *f*.
ringmaster *n* dire(c)tor *m* de um espe(c)táculo de circo.
ringroad *n* circular *f*, cintura.
ringside *n (SPORT)*: **at the** ~ na primeira fila.
ringtone *n (for mobile phone)* toque *m* musical.
ringworm *n (MED)* tinha *f*.
rink *n* (= **ice** ~) pista *f* de patinagem (*BR*: patinação); **2** ringue *m*.
rinse *n (clothes)* enxaguadela *f*; *(BR)* enxaguadura *f*; **2** *(hair)* coloração *f*; ♦ *vt* enxaguar; **2** *(boca)* bochechar; **3** *(hair)* pintar.
riot *n* distúrbio *m*, motim *m*; desordem *f*; ~ **police** *n* polícia *f* de choque; ~ **shield** *n* escudo *m* antimotim; **2** *(of colour)* profusão *f* (de cores); ♦ *vi* provocar distúrbios, amotinar-se; **to run** ~ *vt* desenfrear-se; ♦ *vi (crowd)* amotinar-se.
rioter *n* desordeiro,-a, arruaceiro,-a.
rioting *n* desordem *f*, motins *npl*; **2** *(between persons)* zaragatas *fpl*; ♦ *adj (crowd)* insurre(c)ta.
riotous *adj* desenfreado,-a; barulhento,-a; **2** *(person)* desordeiro,-a; **3** *(living)* dissoluto,-a; **to lead a** ~ **life** levar uma vida de estroina.
rip *n* rasgão *m*; abertura *f*; ♦ *vt* rasgar, romper; **to** ~ **sth to pieces/shreds** reduzir a pedaços, a farrapos *(cloth)*; desperdaçar; **2** *(snatch, pull)* arrancar; ♦ *vi* rasgar-se; **to** ~ **off sb** roubar, explorar alguém; **to** ~ **through sth** *(bomb)* destruir *(building)*; **to** ~ **sth up** arrancar *(boards, nails)* (**from** de); **2** rasgar *(document)*.
ripcord *n* corda *f* de abertura (de pára-quedas).
ripe *adj* maduro,-a.
ripen *vt/vi* amadurecer.
ripeness *n* maturidade *f*, amadurecimento *m*.
rip-off *n* exploração *f*, roubo; IDIOM **this is a** ~ *(coll)* isto é uma roubalheira.
riposte *n* réplica *f* pronta; ♦ *vt* ripostar.
ripple *n (waves)* ondulação *f*, encrespação *f*; **2** *(sound)* murmúrio *m*; **a** ~ **of applause** uma onda

f de aplauso; ~ **control** *n (ELECT)* telecomando *m* centralizado; ~ **effect** efeito *m* secundário; ♦ *vi* encrespar(-se); **2** *(corn, reed)* ondular; ♦ *vt* fazer ondular *(hair, water)*; *(muscles)* fazer ressaltar (músculos).
rip-roaring *adj (coll: noise)* ensurdecedor,-ora; *(success)* estrondoso,-a.
rise *n* elevação *f*, ladeira *f*; rampa *f*; *(increase)* aumento *m*; subida *f*; **2** *(fig)* ascensão *f*; ♦ (*pt* **rose**, *pp* **risen**) *vi (person, wind)* levantar-se, erguer-se; **2** *(price, temperature, tone, etc)* subir, aumentar; **3** *(dough, cake)* crescer, levedar; **4** *(building, hill)* erguer-se; **5** *(ascend)* nascer *(sun, moon)*; elevar-se no ar *(balloon, plane, bird)*; **to** ~ **to fame** atingir a fama; *(rebel)* (= ~ **up**) revoltar-se (**against** contra); *(have source)* nascer *(river)*; **to give** ~ **to** dar origem a, ocasionar; **to** ~ **to the occasion** mostrar-se à altura da situação; **to** ~ **above sth** superar; ~ **and shine!** toca a acordar!
risk *n* risco *m*, perigo *m*; **at** ~ em perigo; **at one's own** ~ por sua própria conta e risco; ~ **capital** *n (FIN)* capital *m* de risco; ~ **factor** *n (MED)* factor *m* de risco; **to take/run the** ~ **of doing** correr o risco de fazer; ~ **taker** *n (person)* intrépido,-a; **to be a** ~ gostar de tomar riscos; ♦ *vt* arriscar; atrever-se a.
risky *adj* arriscado,-a, imprudente; *(share, investment)* de risco.
risqué *adj (daring, naughty)* ousado,-a, picante; indecente; **a** ~ **joke** uma anedota marota, picante.
rite *n* rito *m*; **initiation** ~ *n* rito *m* de iniciação; **funeral** ~s exéquias *fpl*, cerimónia *f (BR*: -mô-) fúnebre; **last** ~s *npl* extrema-unção *f*.
ritual *(pl*: **-ais)** *n* ritual *m*, rito *m*, cerimonial; ♦ *adj* ritual.
ritzy *adj (coll)* chique.
rival *(pl*: **-ais)** *n* rival; concorrente; ♦ *adj* rival, adversário,-a, competidor,-ora; ♦ (*pres p, pp, pt* -ll-) *vt* rivalizar, competir com.
rivalry *n* rivalidade *f*, concorrência *f*.
river *n* rio *m*; **up/down** ~ rio acima/abaixo; ~**bank** *n* margem *f* (do rio); ~**bed** *n* leito *m* (do rio); ~ **port** *n* porto *m* fluvial; ~**side** *n* margem *f* (do rio); ~ **traffic** *n* navegação *f* fluvial.
rivet *n* rebite *m*, cravo *m*; ♦ *vt* rebitar; *(fig)* cravar.
riveting *adj* fascinante.
rivulet *n* ribeiro *m*, regato *m*.
RN *(abbr for* **Royal Navy**) Marina Real Britânica.
RNA *(abbr for* **Ribo-nucleic acid**) ARN.
roach *n (ZOOL) (fish)* ruivaca *f*; **2** *(abbr for* cockroach*)* barator *f*; **3** *(drugs)* beata, *(BR)* begana *f* de baseado; **4** *(NAUT) (in sails)* aluamento *m*.
road *n* caminho *m*, via *f*; estrada *f*; rua *f*; ~ **accident** *n* acidente *m* de viação; ~**block** *n* barricada *f*, barreira *f* rodoviária; ~**hog** *n (selfish/aggressive driver)* dono,-a da estrada; ~ **map** *n* mapa *m* rodoviário; ~ **metal** *n* brita *f*; ~**side** *n* berma *f* (*BR*: beira) da estrada; ~**sign** *n* placa *f* de sinalização; ~ **show** *n (play, music)* espe(c)táculo *m* de tournée ~ **tax** *n* taxa *f* rodoviária; ~**way** *n* rodovia *f*; ~**works** *npl* obras *fpl*; **on the** ~ na estrada; **to**

be on the ~ all night viajar toda a noite; **to be on the ~ to success** estar no caminho do sucesso IDIOM **to hit the ~** fazer-se à estrada.

roadster *n* descapotável *m*.

roam *vt* **to ~ the streets** percorrer as ruas; **~ through the house** percorrer a casa; **2** vadiar por *(fam)*; ♦ *vi* deambular, vaguear, passear sem fim determinado.

roamer *n* vagabundo *m,f*, vadio *m,f*.

roar *n* *(of animal)* rugido *m*, urro *m*; **2** *(of person)* bramido *m*; **3** *(banging noise)* estrondo *m*; barulho *m*; ♦ *vi* rugir, bramar, bradar; IDIOM **to ~ with laughter** rir ruidosamente, espalhafatosamente; **to do a ~ing trade** fazer um bom negócio.

roast *n* *(CULIN)* carne *f* assada, assado *m*; ♦ *vt* assar; torrar.

roasting *n*: *(coll)* *(criticism)* **to give sb a ~** dar uma ensaboada a alguém; ♦ *adj* *(weather)* **it's ~!** está a escaldar!; **~ tin** *n* assadeira *f*.

rob *vt* roubar, furtar; **to ~ sb of** roubar de alguém; *(fig)* despojar alguém de.

robber *n* ladrão *m*, ladra *f*.

robbery *n* roubo *m*, furto *m*.

robe *n* *(of priest)* túnica *f*; *(of monarch)* manto *m*; *(of judge)* toga *f*, beca *f*; **2** *(US)* (= **bath ~**) roupão *m* (de banho).

robin *n* *(ZOOL)* pintarroxo *m*, *(BR)* pisco-de-peito-ruivo *m*.

robot *n* robô *m*, autómato *m* *(BR*: -tô-*)*.

robotic *adj* automatizado,-a; **robotics** *nsg* robótica *fsg*.

robust *adj* robusto, forte *m,f*.

robustness *n* robustez *f*.

rock *n* *(GEOL)* rocha *f*; **2** *(boulder)* rochedo *m*, penhasco *m*; **3** *(UK)* *(sweet)* barra *f* de caramelo; **4** *(MUS)* rock *m*; **5** *(fig, fam)* grande diamante; ♦ *vt* balançar, baloiçar, oscilar; **2** *(child)* embalar; **3** *(tremor, scandal)* abalar; ♦ *vi* baloiçar-se; ♦ **as firm as a ~** *(person)* tão firme como uma rocha; **on the ~s** *adv* *(whisky)* com gelo; **2** *(marriage, business)* em grande dificuldades, que vai mal; ♦ **~ bottom** nível *m* baixíssimo; **to hit ~ bottom** *(fig)* atingir o fundo do poço; **~-bottom price** *adj* preço mínimo; **~ climbing** *n* alpinismo *m*, escalada *f*; **~-face** *n* parede *f* de pedra; **~fall** *n* deslizamento *m* de pedras; **~-hard** *adj*, duro,-a como pedra; **~ pool** *n* piscina *f* formada por pedras na praia; **~ oil** *n* *(MIN)* nafta *f* mineral; **~ salmon** cação *m* galhudo; **~salt** *n* sal-gema *m*; **~ singer** *n* cantor de rock, roqueiro,-a.

rocker *n* *(US)* *(chair)* cadeira *f* de baloiço; **2** *(cradle)* berço *m* de baloiço *m*; IDIOM **to be off one's ~** ter um parafuso a menos, estar maluco.

rockery *n* *(UK)* jardim *m* de pedras e entermeado com plantas.

rocket *n* *(MIL)* foguete *m*; foguetão *m*; **~-launcher** lança-foguetes; **propelled ~** *adj* propulsionado a foguete; **to send a ~** *vi* lançar.

Rockies *npl* *(Vd*: **Rocky Mountains***)*.

rocking chair *n* *(UK)* cadeira de baloiço.

rocking horse *n* cavalo *m* de baloiço; *(BR)* cavalinho de balanço.

rocky (-ier, -iest) *adj* *(with rocks)* rochoso,-a, pedregoso,-a; **2** *(shaky)* bambo-a, sem firmeza.

Rocky Mountains *npr* Montanhas Rochosas.

rococo *n* *(ART)* rococó *m*.

rod *n* vara *f*, bastão *m*; **2** *(TECH)* haste *f*; **3** *(for curtains)* varão *m*; **4** (= **fishing ~**) cana *f* de pesca, *(BR)* vara *f* de pescar; IDIOM **to make a ~ for one's own back** arranjar lenha para se queimar.

rode *(pt* of **ride***)*.

rodent *n* roedor *m*.

rodeo *n* rodeio *m*.

roe *n* (= **~ deer**) *(ZOOL)* corça *f*, cerva *f*; **hard/soft ~** ovas/esperma *m* de peixe.

rogatory *adj* rogatório,-a.

roger *exc* *(AER, MIL, TEL)* *(message received)* entendido! OK!.

rogue *n* maroto *m*, malandro *m*; *(pej)* canalha *m*, pulha *m*.

roguery *n* patifaria *f*.

roguish *adj* *(pej)* patife, velhaco,-a; *(mischief)* brincalhão,-lhona.

roister *vi* *(party)* fazer uma farra; **2** *(brag)* vangloriar-se.

role *n* função *f*, **2** *(THEAT, CIN)* papel *m*, parte *f*; **to play a ~** desempenhar um papel; **leading ~** papel *m* principal **~ model** *n* modelo *m*, exemplo *m* a seguir; **~ reversal** *n* troca *f* de papéis.

roll *n* *(of fabric, paper)* rolo *m*; *(of banknotes)* maço *m*; **2** *(of film)* rolo de película; **3** (= **bread ~**) pãozinho *m*; **4** *(list)* rol *m*, lista *f*; **to call the ~** fazer a chamada; **5** *(of dice)* lançamento *m*; **6** *(gymnastics)* rotação; **7** *(sound)* *(of thunder)* ribombar; **8** *(of drums)* rufar; ♦ *vt* rolar; enrolar; ♦ *vi* rolar, rodar; rufar *(drums)*; **2** *(hips)* bambolear-se, gingar; balançar; **3** *(coll)* chegar, aparecer; **~ by** *vi* passar; **to ~ in** *vi* chegar em grande quantidade; **to ~ into a ball** *vt* enrolar algo, fazer um novelo; **to ~ one's eyes** *vt* *(with surprise, disapproval)* revirar os olhos; ♦ **~ out** *(undo roll)* desenrolar; **2** estender, lisar *(pastry)*; ♦ **to ~ over** *vi* *(of animal)* virar-se de pernas para o ar; **2** *(car, etc)* virar-se; **3** *(exhibit for first time)* mostrar, lançar; **to ~ up** *vi* *(coll)* *(vehicle)* chegar; ♦ *vt* enrolar; arregaçar *(sleeves, trousers)*; IDIOM **to set the ball ~ing** dar início a; **to be ~ing in it** *(money)* estar a nadar em dinheiro.

rolled gold *n* plaqué *m*, artigo plaqueado *m* a ouro.

roller *n* cilindro; **2** *(hair curler)* rolo *m*, bigudi; **3** *(painting)* rolo *m* de pintar; **4** *(wave)* onda *f* grande; **~ bearing** *n* *(MEC)* mancal *m* de roletes; **~ blind** estore *m*, persiana *f*; **~ chain** *n* *(MEC)* corrente *f* de rolos; **~ coaster** *n* montanha-russa *f*; **~ skates** *npl* patins *mpl* de roda; **~ towel** *n* toalha *f* de rolo.

rollicking *adj* alegre *m,f*; brincalhão,-ona, divertido, -a.

rolling *adj* ondulado,-a; **2** *(swaying)* bamboleante *m,f*; **~ mill** *n* laminador *m*; **~ pin** *n* rolo *m* de pasteleiro; *(BR)* pau *m* de macarrão; **~ stock** *n* *(RAIL)* material *m* rodante.

roll-neck *adj* *(sweater)* com gola rulé.

roll-out *n* lançamento *m*.

roly-poly *n* *(pudding)* rocambole; **2** *(person)* rechonchudo,-a.

Roma *n* (*gypsy*) cigano,-a.
Roman *n adj* romano,-a; ~ **Catholic** *npr adj* católico (romano); ~ **Empire** *n* Império *m* Romano; ~ **numerals** *n* numeração *f* romana.
romance *n* aventura *f* amorosa, romance *m*; **R~** *adj* românico *m*, línguas *fpl* românicas.
Romanesque *adj* românico, romanesco.
Romania *npr* Roménia (*BR*: -mê-); **in** ~ na Roménia.
Romanian *n adj* romeno,-a; (*LING*) romeno.
romantic *adj* romântico.
romanticism *n* (*ART, LITER*) romantismo *m*.
romanticize, romanticise *vt/vi* romantizar, fantasiar.
Romany (*pl*: -ies) *adj* cigano,-a (*LING*) romani.
romcom *n* (*fam*) (*CIN, TV*) comédia *f* romântica.
Rome *npr* Roma.
romp *n* (*frolic*) brincadeira *f*, travessura *f*; ♦ *vi* (= to ~ **about**) brincar, jogar.
rompers *npl* roupa *f* de bebé (*BR*: -bê) (*also*: **romper suit**) fato-macaco *m* de criança; (*BR*) macacão *m* de criança.
rondo *n* (*MUS*) rondó *m*.
roof (*pl*: -s) *n* telhado *m*; **2** te(c)to; ~ **garden** *n* terraço com flores no topo da casa; terraço *m*; **all under the same** ~ todos debaixo do mesmo te(c)to; **to have a** ~ **over one's heads** ter onde morar; **3** (*of car*) tejadilho *m*; capota *f*; ~ **rack** *n* (*AUT*) (na capota) bagageiro *m*; ♦ *vt* cobrir com telhas; **4** **the** ~ **of the mouth** o céu da boca; IDIOM **to go through the** ~ ir aos ares; **2** (*coll*) (*prices*) bater todos os recordes; subir em flecha.
roofer *n* telhador *m*, assentador de telhas.
roofing *n* material *m* para cobertura, trabalho *m* de cobertura.
rook *n* gralha *f*; **2** (*chess*) torre *f*.
rookie *n* (*coll*) (*US*) recruta *m*, novato *m*.
room *n* quarto *m*; sala *f*; (*formal*) aposento *m*; (= **bed~**) quarto *m* de dormir; **2** (*in school*) dormitório *m*; **double bed~** quarto para casal; **single bed~** quarto individual/de solteiro; **3** espaço *m*; **to make** ~ **for** arranjar espaço; acomodar (*sb, sth*); **~s** *npl* divisões *fpl*, assoalhadas; **how many ~s does the house have?** quantos quartos,-as assoalhadas tem a casa?; ♦ **~s** *npl* alojamento *sg*; **~s to let** alugam-se quartos.
roommate *n* companheiro,-a de quarto.
room service *n* serviço *m* de quarto.
room temperature *n* temperatura *f* ambiente; **to serve the wine at** ~ servir um vinho ao natural.
roomy *adj* espaçoso,-a, amplo,-a.
roost *n* poleiro *m*; ♦ *vt* empoleirar-se; **2** pernoitar.
rooster *n* galo *m*.
root *n* raiz *f*; ~ **canal treatment** *n* (*MED*) desvitalização *f*; ~ **cap** *n* (*BOT*) (*protection for roots*) coifa *f*; ~ **crop** (*AGR*) tubérculos; ~ **mean square** *n* (*MATH*) valor *m* médio quadrático; ~ **vegetable** *n* (*carrot, turnip*) raíz *f* comestível; **to pull sth by the** ~ arrancar algo pela raiz; **2** (*of evil*) origem *f* (do mal); **roots** *npl* raízes; **to pull out the ~s** arrancar as raízes; ♦ *adj* básico,-a, fundamental *m,f*; ♦ *vi* enraizar, lançar, criar raízes; ♦ **to ~ about** *vi* (*fig*) revirar; **to ~ for** *vt* (*US*) (*fam*)

torcer por; **to ~ out** *vt* desarraigar (*plants*), erradicar, extirpar (*corruption*); IDIOM **to be ~ed to the ground/spot** ficar pregado,-a ao chão.
rope *n* corda *f*; **2** (*NAUT*) cabo *m*; ~ **ladder** escada *f* de corda; ♦ *vt* atar, amarrar com uma corda; (= **to ~ together**) ligar-se (uns aos outros) com cordas; **to ~ sb in** (*fig*) persuadir alguém a tomar parte em algo; **to know the ~s** (*fig*) estar dentro (do assunto).
ropey (-ier, -iest) *adj* (*fam*) (*quality*) inferior, fraco,-a; rasca *m,f*; **2** indisposto,-a; **I am feeling a bit** ~ sinto-me um pouco chocho,-a.
rosary *n* rosário *m*.
rose (*pt of* **rise**); ♦ *n* (*BOT*) rosa *f*; **2** (*the emblem of England*) Rosa; **3** (*nozzle on a watering can*) crivo *m*; **4 ceiling** ~ (*ARCH*) rosácea; ♦ *adj* rosado, cor-de-rosa; **~bed** *n* roseiral *m*; **~bud** *n* botão *m* de rosa; **~bush** *n* roseira; IDIOM **every** ~ **has its thorn** não há rosa sem espinhos; **a bed of ~s** um mar de rosas; **under the** ~ pela calada. **~coloured/tinted** *adj* optimistic; **to see sb through** ~ **spectacles** ver alguém por um prisma o(p)timista, cor-de-rosa.
rosé *n* rosado *m*; (*wine*), rosé *m*.
roseate *adj* róseo,-a.
rosehip *n* roseira *f* brava, rosa-mosqueta *f*.
rosemary *n* (*BOT, CULIN*) alecrim *m*, rosmaninho *m*.
rose quartz *n* quartzo rosa *m*.

Wars of the Roses *npr* (HIST) Guerra das Duas Rosas, entre a Casa de Lencastre (com o símbolo da rosa vermelha) e a Casa de Iorque (simbolizada pela rosa branca), século XV.

rosette *n* rosácea *f*, roseta *f*.
rose-water *n n* água *f* das rosas.
rose window *n* (*ARCH*) janela *f* circular.
rosewood *n* pau rosa *m*.
roster *n*: **duty** ~ lista *f* de tarefas, escala *f* de serviço.
rostrum *n* tribuna *f*.
rosy *adj* rosado, rosáceo; IDIOM **a** ~ **future** um futuro promissor.
rot *n* putrefa(c)ção *f*, podridão *f*; **2** (*pej*) decadência *f*; ♦ *vt/vi* apodrecer; decompor.
rota *n* rodízio (*de pessoas*) *m*; **2** (*UK*) (*duty*) escala de serviço; **on a** ~ **basis** *n* em sistema de rotatividade.
rotary *adj* rotativo,-a; ~ **engine** *n* (*MEC*) motor *m* rotativo; ~ **press** *n* máquina *f* de impressão rotativa; ~ **pump** *n* (*CONSTR*) bomba *f* de disco.
rotate *vt* fazer girar, dar voltas em; alternar; revezar; ♦ *vi* girar, dar voltas.
rotating *adj* rotativo.
rotation *n* rotação *f*; **in** ~ por turnos.
rote *n* rotina *f*, repetição *f*; **by** ~ de cor, de memória.
rotogravure *n* (*TYPO*) rotogravura *f*.
rotor *n* rotor *m*.
rotten *adj* podre, apodrecido,-a; carcomido,-a; **2** (*fig*) corrupto,-a; **3** (*coll*) detestável, miserável; **to feel** ~ sentir-se péssimo.
rotter *n* (*coll*) canalha *m*, patife *m*.

rotund *adj* rotundo,-a; esférico,-a.

rouble *n* rublo *m*.

rouge *n (makeup)* ruge *m*.

rough *n (undetailed form)* rascunho *m*; ~ **translation** esboço de tradução, tradução feita à pressa; ♦ *adj (not smooth)* áspero,-a; *(terrain)* acidentado,-a; desigual, **2** *(harsh) (voice, taste, wine, skin, hand)* áspero,-a; **3** *(harsh behaviour, person)* grosseiro, rude; **they are a ~ lot** eles são rufiões *mpl*, é uma malta *f*, *(fam)* desordeira; **4** *(unpleasant person)* brutal, mau, má; *(weather)* mau *(tempo)*; **5** *(turbulent) (sea)* agitado; tempestuoso; *(wind)* violento,-a; **6** *(difficult)* duro,-a, difícil; **7** *(rock, surface)* rogoso,-a; *(diamond, glass)* (em) bruto; *(unpolished) (person)* falta *f* de polimento **8** *(crude)* rudimentar; tosco,-a; **9** aproximado,-a; **a ~ idea** uma ideia aproximada; ~ **justice** justiça *f* sumária; ~**-and-ready** *adj* improvisado,-a, feito,-a à pressa; ~**-and-tumble** *n* situação *f* desorganizada, sem regras; ~**cast** *n* reboco *m* grosso; ~**-hewn** *adj (unsophisticated) (work)* rude, simple; *(person)* grosseiro,-a; ~**house** *n* zaragata *f*; tumulto *m*; ~ **trade** *n* prostituição *f* homossexual, em geral, com sadismo; ♦ **to ~ out** *vt* esboçar; **to ~ up** *vt* dar uma tareia; IDIOM **to sleep ~** dormir na rua, dormir ao relento; **to go through a ~ time** passar por uma fase *f* difícil; **to take the ~ with the smooth** aceitar as coisas como são, enfrentar a realidade; **to travel over ~ and smooth** viajar por montes e vales.

roughage *n* fibras *fpl*.

roughen *vt/vi* tornar áspero; *(sea)* encrespar-se, encapelar-se.

roughly *adv* bruscamente; **2** *(crudely)* toscamente; aproximadamente, em geral.

roughneck *n (coll)* rufião *m*; **2** *(oil-rig worker)* homem que trabalha em campo de perfuração.

roughness *n* aspereza *f*, grosseria *f*, brusquidão *f*.

roughshod *adv* **to ride over ~ sb/sth** tratar alguém/algo a pontapés.

roulade *n (CULIN)* rolo *m* (de carne).

roulette *n* roleta *f*.

round *n (circle)* círculo *m*; **2** ronda *f*, série *f*; *(of drinks)* rodada *f*; *(SPORT)* partida; eliminatória *f*; **3** *(visit)* ronda *f*; traje(c)to *m*; visita *f*; **4** *(cartridge)* cartucho *m*; **5** *(boxing)* rounde *m*, assalto *m*; **6** *(cycle)* ciclo *m*; **a ~ of applause** uma salva *f* de palmas; ♦ *adj* redondo,-a; **2** *(curved, fat)* roliço,-a; ♦ *prep* ao/em redor de, em/à volta de; ~**about** *n (AUT)* cruzamento circular, balão *m*; carrossel *m*; ~ **numbers** *n* números *mpl* redondos; ~**-shouldered** *adj* encurvado,-a; ♦ *adv*: **all ~** por todos os lados; **the long way** ~ o caminho mais comprido; **all the year** ~ durante todo o ano; ♦ *vt* arredondar; **2** *(corner of the street, of cape)* virar; dobrar; **he rounded the Cape of Good Hope** ele dobrou o Cabo da Boa Esperança; ♦ **to ~ off** *vt* completar; arrematar; **2** arredondar; ♦ **to ~ up** *vt (cattle)* encurralar; **2** reunir; **3** arredondar por excesso; IDIOM **it's just ~ the corner** é logo depois da esquina.

rounded *adj* arredondado,-a, expressivo,-a.

roundly *adv (fig)* energicamente, totalmente.

rouse *vt (awaken)* despertar, acordar; **2** *(provoke)* suscitar; incitear; **3** *(suspeitas)* levantar.

rousing *adj* emocionante; vibrante *m,f*.

rout *n (MIL)* derrota *f*, **2** *(flight)* debandada *f*; ♦ *vt* derrotar, pôr em debandada; ~ **out sth** desencantar, descobrir algo.

route *n (gen)* caminho *m*, rota *f*; **air ~** rota *f* aérea; **bus ~** linha *f* do autocarro *(BR)* rota do ônibus; *(of person, procession)* traje(c)to *m*; itinerário *m*, percurso *m*; **2** *(of achievement) (fig)* caminho *m*; **escape ~** caminho *m* de fuga, ~ **map** *n* mapa *m* rodoviário.

routine *n* rotina *f*; **2** *(THEAT)* número *m*; ♦ *adj* rotineiro,-a.

routing *n (COMP)* encaminhamento *m*.

rove *vt* errar; ♦ *vi* ~ **around** deambular, vaguear.

roving *adj* itinerante; ambulante; nómada; ~ **eyes** olhar *m* errante.

row¹ *n (queue)* fila *f*; *(line)* fileira *f*, **2** *(knitting)* carreira *f*, fileira *f*; **a ~ of houses** uma fileira de casas; **in a ~** numa fileira; **3** *(in succession)* **five times in a ~** cinco vezes em seguida; ♦ *vt (boat)* remar; *(person)* conduzir de barco a remo; ♦ *vi* remar.

row² *(fight)* discussão *f*, briga **(between** entre); rixa *f*; *(with noise)* algazarra *f*; ♦ *vi* brigar; discutir **(with** com; **over** a propósito).

rowdiness *n* tumulto *m*, alarido *m*; *(noisy quarrel)* zaragata *f*.

rowdy (-ier, -iest) *adj* barulhento,-a; desordeiro,-a; *(street fighter)* arruaceiro,-a.

rower *n* remador,-ora.

rowing *n* remo *m*; ~ **boat** *n* barco *m* a remo; ~ **machine** *n* aparelho *m* de remar.

royal *adj* real *m,f*; majestoso,-a; **the ~ 'we'** (usado pelo,-a monarca quando se referindo a si próprio,-a) eu; **2** ~ **blue** *n* azul carregado; ~ **icing** *n (CULIN)* cobertura de açúcar para o bolo; ~ **jelly** *n* geleia *f* real; **R~ Marines** *npr pl* fuzileiros da marinha britânica; **R~ Mail** *npr* os Correios da Grã-Bretanha; **His R~ Highness** Sua Alteza Real *m,f*; **Your R~ Highness** vossa Alteza Real *m,f*.

royalist *adj* monárquico,-a.

royalty *(pl: -ties)* *n* realeza *f*, membro da realeza; ♦ **royalties** *npl* direitos *mpl* de autor.

rozzer *n (coll)* polícia *f*.

rpm *(abbr for* **revolutions per minute***)* rotações *fpl* por minuto.

RRP *(abbr for* **recommended retail price***) (UK)* preço *m* de retalho sugerido.

RSI *(abbr for* **repetitive strain/stress injury***)* lesão *f* por stress repetitivo.

RSPCC *(abbr for* **Royal Society for the Prevention of Cruelty to Children***)* sociedade *f* prote(c)tora das crianças.

RSVP *(abbr for* **répondez s'il vous plaît***)* R.S.F.F. (responder se faz favor)

rub *n (massage)* fricção *f*; *(fig)* esfregadela *f*; **2** *(polish)* polimento *m*; lustro *m*; ♦ **(-bb-)** *vt (scrub)* esfregar; *(touch)* esfregar *(eyes, hands)* **(with sth** com algo); **to ~ one's hands (with glee)** esfregar as mãos (de contentamento); **2** friccionar *(back, etc)*; **3** *(polish)* polir, lustrar; **4 to ~ against** roçar contra; ♦ *vi (chafe)* magoar; **to ~ away/off/out** *(remove)* fazer desaparecer *(stain)*; tirar *(ache)* friccionando; **to ~ down sth** limpar algo; **to ~ down a horse** almofaçar um cavalo; ♦ **to ~ in/into** *(absorb)* penetrar em *(skin)*; **2** repisar algo desagradável; **to ~ the butter into the flour** incorporar a manteiga na farinha; ♦ **to ~ off** *(erase)* apagar; **2** *(influence)* transferir-se; **her bad manners have ~bed off on you** a falta de educação dela influenciaram-te, deixaram a sua marca em ti; **to ~ sth through** *(a sieve)* passar algo por (um crivo); IDIOM **to ~ sb's nose in it** repisar; atirar à cara (algo desagradável); **~ shoulders with** *(mix socially)* ser íntimo,-a com *(alguém);* **to ~ sb the wrong way** irritar alguém; **there is the rub!** *(dated)* aí é que está o busílis!, aqui é que a porca torce o rabo! *(coll)*.

rubber *n (gen)* borracha *f; (eraser)* borracha *f;* **~ band** *n* elástico *m,* fita *f* elástica; **~ cement** *n* cola *f* de borracha; **~ cheque** *n* cheque *m* sem cobertura; **~ goods** *npl (euph)* camisinha *f;* **~neck** *n (person who stares)* pessoa que olha para outros de boca aberta; **~ plant** *n* árvore *f* da borracha; seringueira *f;* **~ stamp** *n* carimbo *m;* **to ~-stamp** *vt* aprovar (oficialmente).

rubberize, rubberise *vt* revestir de borracha.

rubbery *adj* elástico.

rubbish *n* lixo *m; (fam)* porcaria *f;* **2** *(refuse)* detritos *mpl;* **3** *(on site)* entulho *m;* refugo *m;* **3** *(pej) (nonsense)* disparates *mpl,* asneiras *fpl;* **~ bin** *n* caixote *m (BR: lata)* do lixo; **~ chute** *n* triturador *m* de lixo; **~ dump** *n* lixeira *f,* depósito (de lixo) *m.*

rubble *n* escombros *mpl; (on site)* entulho *m.*

rub-down *n:* **to ~ sb down** dar uma massagem a alguém; **2 to give sth a ~** polir *(woodwork, stone).*

rubella *n* rubéola *f.*

rubstone *n* pedra *f* de amolar.

ruby *n* rubi *m;* ♦ *adj (lips)* vermelho; **~ port** porto *m* rubi; **~ wedding** *n* bodas *npl* de casamento.

RUC *(abbr for **Royal Ulster Constabulary**)* força *f* policial do Norte da Irlanda; *(now:* **The Police Service of Northern Ireland**) os Serviços Policiais do Norte da Irlanda.

ruck *n (coll) (fight)* arruaça *f;* **2** *(rugby)* luta *f* pela posse da bola; **3** *(crease)* prega *f* (in clothes).

rucksack *n* mochila *m.*

ruckus *n (coll)* balbúrdia *f.*

ruction *n* distúrbio *m;* tumulto *m;* **~s** *pl (violent quarrel)* zaragata *f,* motim *m.*

rudder *n* leme *m.*

ruddy (-ier, -iest) *adj (face)* corado, rosado, avermelhado; *(sky)* rubro *m;* **2** *(dated swearword)* maldito,-a; **a ~ fool!** grande idiota!

rude *adj (impolite)* indelicado,-a grosseiro,-a, *(person)* mal-educado,-a; **2** *(abrupt)* brusco,-a, brutal **3** *(naughty joke/word)* grosseiro,-a, chocante *m,f.*

rudely *adv* rudemente, bruscamente.

rudeness *n* rudeza *f;* insolência *f.*

rudiment *n* rudimento *m;* **~s** *npl* primeiras noções *fpl.*

rudimentary *adj* rudimentar.

rue (rues, rued, ruing) *vt* arrepender-se de, sentir remorso.

rueful *adj* arrependido,-a; *(expression, smile)* pesaroso,-a.

ruff *n* rufo *m,* gola *f* de tufos engomados (usada pelos nobres do sec XVI); **2** *(in animals, birds)* gola *f* natural de penas, ou pelos, à volta do pescoço; **3** *(whist)* trunfo *m;* **4** *(of drum)* rufo, *(sound of drum)* rataplão *m.*

ruffian *n* rufião *m,* desordeiro.

ruffle *n (around neck)* folho *m,* franzido *m; (sleeve-around wrist)* punho *m; (on curtain)* folho *m;* **2** *(on water)* ondulação *f;* ♦ *vt* despentear *(hair); (crease)* enrugar, amarrotar; **2** agitar *(water, cornfield);* **3** *(birds)* eriçar *(the feathers);* **4** *(fig) (upset)* enervar, arreliar; **don't ~ your feathers!** *(coll)* não te exaltes! *(fam).*

rug *n (on the floor)* tapete *m; (in the car)* manta *f* (de viagem).

rugby *n (= ~ football)* (SPORT) râguebi *m,* (BR) rúgbi *m.*

rugged *adj (irregular)* acidentado, irregular; **2** *(coastline, cliffs)* escarpado,-a; **3** *(landscape)* agreste *m,f;* **4** *(man, features)* atraente *(de tipo viril);* **5** *(tough character)* duro,-a, severo,-a, austero,-a; **~ life** vida *f* dura; *(strong, durable)* forte, robusto,-a.

rugger *n (coll)* (SPORT) râguebi *m,* (BR) rúgbi *m.*

ruin *n* ruína *f;* ♦ *vt* arruinar; estragar; **~s** *npl* escombros *mpl,* destroços *mpl.*

ruinous *adj* desastroso,-a.

rule *n (norm)* norma *f,* regulamento *m;* regra *f;* **as a ~** via de regra; **2** *(authority)* governo *m,* domínio *m;* **3** *(measuring device)* régua *f;* **~ of thumb** *n* princípio *m* básico; *(CULIN)* a olho; ♦ *vt* governar; decidir; traçar; ♦ *vi* reger; *(JUR)* decretar; **to ~ out** excluir.

ruled *adj (paper)* pautado.

ruler *n* soberano,-a; **2** *(school ~)* régua *f.*

ruling *n (JUR)* decisão *f,* parecer *m;* ♦ *adj* dominante, dirigente.

rum *n (alcohol)* rum *m;* ♦ *(-mer, -mest) adj (coll)* esquisito,-a.

rumble *n* ruído *m* surdo, barulho *m; (of stomach, pipes)* gorgolejo *m; (of machines, train)* ronco *m; (of thunder)* estrondo *m,* ribombo *m;* ♦ *vt* aperceber-se de; **2** *(intentions)* adivinhar; **3** *(investigate)* ir até ao fundo (das coisas); ♦ *vi* ribombar, *(cannons)* troar; **2** *(train)* roncar; **3** *(stomach)* gorgolejar; **4** *(sound)* ressoar.

rumble strips *n (on road)* faixas sonoras *fpl.*

rumblings *npl* murmúrios *(of dissatisfaction);* **2** *(in stomach)* gorgolejos, sinais de fome.

rumbustious *adj* esfuziante *m,f;* **2** tempestuoso,-a.

ruminant *n* (ZOOL) ruminante *m.*

ruminate *vi* ruminar.

rummage *vi* remexer, revistar; escarafunchar; **~ sale** *n* bazar *m* beneficente (de artigos usados).

rumour *(UK)* **rumor** *(US) n* rumor *m;* boato *m;* ♦ *vt:* **it is ~ed that** corre o boato de que; IDIOM **~ has it** diz-se que; **there is a ~ that** há um zum-zum que.

rump n (person's) nádegas fpl, traseiro m; (of horse, etc) garupa f; ~ **steak** n alcatra f.

rumple vt amarrotar.

rumpus (pl: -es) n (coll: noise) chinfrim m, algazarra f.

run n (jog) corrida f; **on the** ~ em fuga; **2 to break into a** ~ pôr-se a correr; **to give sb a clear** ~ deixar o campo livre a alguém; **3** (series) série f; (in printing) tiragem f; **4** (THEAT) temporada f; **5** (ski) pista f; **6** percurso m; **7** (for chickens, rabbits) capoeira f, coelheira f; **8** (in tights) malha f caída; **the runs** npl diarreia f; ◆ (pt **ran**, pp **run**) vt (business) dirigir; organizar; **stop** ~**ning my life** deixa de mandares na minha vida; **2** (water) deixar correr; **3 to** ~ **a check on sb** (police) verificar os antecedentes de alguém; ◆ vi correr; funcionar; **2** (train, bus) circular, fazer o percurso; **3** (pass, move) **to** ~ **one's hand over sth** passar a mão por (face, hair, etc); **4** (operate) funcionar (engine); executar (programa); **5** (cause to flow) fazer correr (bath), preparar banho; **6** (fade) desbotar; ◆ vi correr; (flow) correr, fluir; **the tap is** ~**ning** a torneira está a correr; (sweat) escorrer; **2** (to operate regularly) funcionar; circular (buses); **3** (last) durar (contract, etc); **to** ~ **from ... to** (period) ir de ... a; **to** ~ **about** vi correr por todos os lados; **to** ~ **across** vi encontrar por acaso; cruzar com; **to** ~ **after** vi andar atrás de uma mulher/dum homem; ser persistente; ◆ **to** ~ **around** vi ser promíscuo,-a; **2** enganar com evasivas; ◆ **to** ~ **away** vi (flee) fugir, escapar (**from sb/sth** de alguém, de algo); **to** ~ **away with sb** vi (elope) fugir com alguém; **he lets his ambition** ~ **away with him** deixar-se levar pela ambição; ◆ **to** ~ **down** vi (watch) atrasar-se; **2** (batteries) descarregar-se; **to** ~ **sb/sth down** deitar abaixo; **to** ~ **sb down** (AUT) atropelar; **3** (criticise) falar mal de, denigrar; **4** (reduce in number/size) diminuir (staff); **5 to be** ~ **down** (in the passive) (person) estar enfraquecido,-a, exausto,-a; ◆ **to** ~ **for** vi correr; **he ran for his country** ele correu pelo seu país; **2** (POL) candidatar-se a (post); ◆ **to** ~ **in** (AUT) fazer a rodagem; **2** levar para a cadeia; ◆ **into** (collide) ir de encontro a; colidir com; ◆ **to** ~ **off** partir a correr; **2** (drain) escorrer; **3 to** ~ **off with sb** (elope) fugir com alguém; ~ **off with sth** (steal) furtar; ◆ **to** ~ **on** prolongar-se (meeting, etc); **2** (conversation) versar sobre; ◆ **to** ~ **out** sair a correr; **2** (blood) escorrer; **3** (resource, strength) esgotar-se; **4** (passport) caducar; **5** (deadline) vencer; acabar; **to** ~ **out of** ficar sem; ◆ **to** ~ **over** (AUT) atropelar; **2** recapitular; ◆ **to** ~ **through** examinar, **2** recapitular; **3** (squander) esbanjar, desperdiçar (money, etc); **4** (with weapon) trespassar (o corpo) (of person); ◆ **to** ~ **up** acumular (debt, bill); ◆ **to** ~ **up against** esbarrar contra (person, problem); IDIOM **in the long** ~ com o decorrer do tempo, mais cedo ou mais tarde; **on the** ~ em fuga; **to be** ~ **off one's feet** (in the passive) estar atulhado em trabalho.

run-around n: **to get the** ~ ser alvo de evasivas.

runaway n fugitivo,-a; ◆ adj que foge; (vehicle) descontrolado,-a; **2** (horse) com freio nos dentes.

rundown n (report) resumo m; **2** redução (in number, size); ◆ adj (person) exausto,-a, abatido,-a; **2** (dilapidated) em ruínas, decrépito,-a.

rung (pp of **ring**) n (of ladder) degrau m; **2** (hierarchy) escalão m.

run-in n (fam) discussão f, rixa f; ◆ vt levar (alguém) para a cadeira; **2** (UK) (AUT) fazer a rodagem.

runner n (person) corredor,-ora, **2** (horse) cavalo m de corrida; **3** (rollerblade) patim m, lâmina f; **4** (pulley) roldana f, roda f; ~ **bean** n (BOT) feijão m verde; (BR) feijão-trepador m; ~~**up** n (in competition) em segundo lugar.

running n corrida f; **2** (management) gestão f; (of machine) funcionamento m; ◆ adj adv contínuo,-a, constante, seguido,-a; **three days** ~ três dias seguidos; consecutivamente; ~ **board** n estribo m; ~ **comment** n comentário m ao vivo, ininterru(p)to; ~ **costs** npl despesas fpl de manutenção; ~ **head** n (TYPO) cabeçalho, título em cada página ou de duas em duas páginas; ~ **sore** n ferida f supurante.

runny adj (butter) derretido,-a; **2** (nose) escorrendo,-a; **3** (blood) gotejante; **4** (eyes) lacrimejante; **5** (eggs) malpassado, a escorrer.

run-of-the-mill adj comum m,f, corriqueiro,-a.

runt n (pej) (person) nanico,-a, anão m, anã f; meia-leca (EP); **2** (animal) filhote m mais fraco.

run-through n ensaio m, prá(c)tica; breve revisão f.

run-up: the ~ **to the election** n período m, campanha f para a eleição.

runway n (AER) pista f de de(s)colagem.

rupee n (monetary unit) rupia f.

rupture n rompimento m; ruptura f; **2** (MED) hérnia f; ◆ vt/vi fra(c)turar; rebentar; romper; abrir-se; romper-se; **to** ~ **o.s.** vt provocar-se uma hérnia.

rural adj rural, campestre.

ruse n ardil m, manha f, astúcia f.

rush n (impulse) ímpeto m, investida f; **2** (haste) pressa f; **3** (COMM) grande procura; **4** (BOT) junco m; **5** (flow) corrente f forte, torrente f; ◆ vt apressar; fazer depressa; assaltar; ◆ vi apressar-se, precipitar-se; ~ **hour** n hora f de ponta (BR: do rush).

rusk n rosca f, biscoito m (para bebés).

Russia npr Rússia f; **in** ~ na Rússia.

Russian n adj russo,-a; (LING) russo.

rust n ferrugem f; **2** (BOT) mofo m, bolor m; ◆ vi enferrujar.

rustic n camponês,-esa; ◆ adj rústico; rural, campestre; simples; inculto,-a.

rustle vi sussurrar, rumorejar; produzir ruídos como o do roçar de sedas; **to** ~ **up** preparar algo rapidamente (meal, etc).

rustler n (US) ladrão m de gado; (of horses) ladrão de cavalos.

rustling n sussurro m, **2** (of leaves) rumorejo m; **3** **the** ~ **of her silk dress** (onomat) o frufru de seu vestido de seda.

rustproof adj inoxidável m,f à prova de ferrugem.

rusty adj enferrujado; **2** (fig) com falta de prá(c)tica; **my French is** ~ o meu francês está enferrujado.

rut n (in ground) sulco m, trilho m carreiro m; **2** (dull routine) rotina f; **to get into/out of a** ~ entrar/sair da rotina; **to be in a** ~ ser escravo,-a da rotina; **3** *(ZOOL) (mating)* **the** ~ o cio *m*.

ruthless *adj* implacável *m,f*, sem piedade, cruel *m,f* (**in sth** em algo **towards sb** para com).

ruthlessness *n* crueldade *f*, desumanidade *f*, insensibilidade *f*.

rutting *n (mating)* cio *m*; ~ **season** *n* época do cio; ♦ *adj* com cio.

Rwanda *npr* Ruanda.

Rwandan *n adj* ruandês,-esa.

rye *n* centeio *m*; ~ **bread** n pão *m* de centeio; ~ **whisky** *n* uísque *m* destilado do centeio.

S

S, s *n (letter)* S, s; **2** *(abbr for* **south)** sul *m.*

SA *(abbr for* **South Africa)** África do Sul; **2** *(abbr for* **South America)** América do Sul; **3** *(abbr for* **South Australia)** região sul da Austrália.

sabbath *n (Christians)* domingo *m; (Jewish)* sábado *m.*

sabbatical *adj:* ~ **year** ano sabático, de licença.

sable *n (fur, animal)* zibeline *f.*

sabotage *n* sabotagem *f;* ♦ *vt* sabotar.

saboteur *n* sabotador,-ora.

sabre *(UK)* **saber** *(US) n* sabre *m.*

saccharin(e) *n* sacarina, adoçante *m.*

sack *n (bag)* saco, saca; **a** ~ **of onions** um saco de cebolas; **2** *(pillage)* saque *m*, pilhagem *f*; **3** *(coll) (UK) (job)* despedimento, demissão *f*; **to get the** ~ ser despedido,-a; ♦ *vt (dismiss)* despedir *(employee)*, pôr na rua *(fam);* **to** ~ **sb for sth** demitir alguém por algo; **2** *(pillage)* saquear, pôr a saque; pilhar.

sackcloth *n* sarapilheira *f.*

sackful, sackload *n* saco; grande quantidade de.

sacking *n (act of filling sacks)* ensacamento; **2** *(dismissal)* despedimento, demissão *f*; **3** *(material for sacks, freight)* aniagem *f.*

sacrament *n* sacramento *m*; **S~** *n (communion bread)* o Santíssimo Sacramento; a Eucaristia *f*; **to receive the** ~ comungar.

sacred *adj* sagrado,-a, divino,-a; **2** *(revered)* consagrado,-a; **3** *(trust)* inviolável *m,f.*

sacrifice *n* sacrifício *m*; ♦ *vt* sacrificar, renunciar; *(REL)* oferecer algo em sacrifício.

sacrilege *n* sacrilégio *m.*

sacrilegious *adj* sacrílego.

sacrosanct *adj* sacrossanto,-a.

sad (-**der**, -**dest**) *adj* triste; **2** *(situation, scene)* deplorável.

sadden *vt* entristecer.

saddle *n (for horse)* sela *f*; *(of bicycle, motorcycle)* selim *m*; assento *m*; ~**bag** *n* alforje *m*; **2** *(CULIN) (UK)* lombo *m*; ♦ *vt (to put* ~ *on horse)* selar; *(on donkey, mule)* albardar; **to be** ~**d with sth** *(coll)* estar sobrecarregado com algo.

sadism *n* sadismo *m.*

sadist *n* sádico,-a, sadista *m,f.*

sadistic *adj* sádico,-a.

sadly *adv* tristemente; lamentavelmente.

sadness *n* tristeza *f*; **2** *(feeling low)* abatimento *m.*

sadomasochism *n* sadomasoquismo *m.*

s.a.e. *n (abbr for* **stamped, self-addressed envelope)** envelope endereçado ao próprio e com selo.

safari *n* safári *m;* ~ **park** *n* reserva *f.*

safe *n (for money etc)* cofre *m*, caixa-forte *f*; ♦ *adj (unhurt)* ileso, intacto; salvo; **2** digno,-a de confiança; **3** *(risk-free)* seguro,-a; **4** *(animal)* inofensivo,-a; **5** *(policy, investment)* prudente, seguro,-a; **6** *(building)* sólido,-a; **7** *(reliable) (person)* de confiança; ~ **haven** *n* refúgio *m*; ~ **sex** *n* sexo *m* seguro; ~ **and sound** são e salvo; **to be on the** ~ **side** como precaução *f*; pelo sim, pelo não; ♦ *vt* proteger, defender; **to keep sb** ~ proteger alguém **(from** contra, de); **2 to keep sth** ~ *(store)* guardar algo em lugar seguro.

safe bet *n* aposta *f* segura; **2** *(be sure of sth)* aposta certa.

safe-breaker *n* arrombador *m* de cofres, caixas-fortes.

safe-conduct *n* salvo-conduto *m*; **to obtain a** ~ **for** obter um salvo-conduto para; **2** *(document)* salvo-conduto *m.*

safeguard *n* garantia *f*; ♦ *vt* proteger **(against, for** contra).

safekeeping *n* custódia, prote(c)ção; **for** ~ por umaquestão de segurança; **to entrust sth to sb's** ~ confiar algo à guarda de alguém.

safely *adv* com segurança, a salvo, ileso,-a, incólume; sem perigo; sem danos.

safety *n* segurança; ♦ *adj* de segurança; ~ **belt** *n* cinto de segurança; ~ **catch** *(on rifle)* fecho *m* de segurança; ~ **pin** *n* alfinete-de-ama *m*; ~ **razor** *n* gilete *f*; ~ **valve** *n (TECH)* válvula *f* de segurança; **2** *(fig) (for emotions)* válvula de escape.

saffron *n* açafrão *m.*

sag *n* inclinação *f*; descaimento *m*; **2** *(ceiling)* arqueamento *m*, curva *f*; **3** *(in price/vale)* abatimento *m*, baixa *f*; ♦ (-**gg-**) *vi (slacken)* afrouxar; **2** *(ceiling)* dar de si, ceder; **3** *(mattress, breasts, chin)* descair; **4** *(fall)* baixar *(price, export)*; **5** *(fig) (emotion) (weaken)* esmorecer.

saga *n (LITER)* saga *f*, narrativa *f* épica; **2** *pej (long tale)* lenglenga *f.*

sagacious *adj (person)* sagaz *m,f.*

sagacity *n* sagacidade *f.*

sage *n (herb)* salva; **2** *(wise, scholarly)* sábio *m*; ♦ *adj* sensato,-a.

sagging *adj* descaído,-a; **2** *(slackened)* bambo,-a; flácido,-a; **3** *(beam, ceiling)* abaulado,-a.

Sagittarian *n adj* sagitariano,-a.

Sagittarius *n (ASTROL, ASTRON)* Sagitário *m.*

sago *n* sagu *m;* ~ **palm** *n* sagueiro *m.*

Sahara *npr:* **the** ~ **Desert** o Deserto do Saara.

said *(pt, pp of* **say)** *adj (JUR)* citado, dito, mencionado; **the** ~ **Mr X** o referido senhor X; *(fam)* o tal senhor X.

sail *n* vela; **to set** ~ desfraldar as velas; fazer-se ao mar; **to go for a** ~ ir dar um passeio de barco à vela; **to hoist a** ~ içar uma vela; ♦ *vt (steer)* dirigir, manobrar; *(sea)* cruzar; ♦ *vi* passear de barco; **2** *(set off) (boat)* partir, zarpar; **3** *(sea)* singrar; **4** *(person-travel)* navegar; **5** *(SPORT)* velejar; **to** ~ **away** partir a todo o pano; **to** ~ **round the cape** contornar o cabo; **to** ~ **through** *vt/vi (fig)* fazer com facilidade.

sailboard *n* prancha *f* de windsurfe.

sailboat *n* veleiro.

sailing *n (SPORT)* navegação *f* à vela; ~ **boat/ship** *n* barco *m* à vela, veleiro *m*; **plain** ~ *(coll)* sem grade dificuldades.

sailor *n* marinheiro,-a; *(fig)* **I am a good** ~ nunca enjoo quando ando de barco, *(BR)* não fico mareado,-a.

sailplane *n (AER)* planador.

saint *n (a good person)* santo,-a; *(REL)* (= **St**) (santo,-a = Sto, Sta) ~ **Augustine** Santo (St) Agostinho; ~ **John** São João; ~ **Therese** Santa (Sta) Teresa.

saintly (**-ier, -iest**) *adj* santo,-a, santificado,-a.

Saint Patrick *(Ireland's patron saint)* São Patrício.

No dia 17 de Março comemora-se São Patrício, patrono da Irlanda, sendo esse dia feriado. Tradicionalmente, os irlandeses por todo o mundo celebram-no, vestindo-se de verde ou de 'trevo' (**shamrock**) por este ser o emblema da Irlanda.

sake *n* causa, motivo; **for the** ~ **of** por (causa de); em consideração a; **for the** ~ **of argument** só para argumentar; **for God's** ~ pelo amor de Deus; **for my** ~ por (causa de) mim; **for your** ~ por quem és.

salacious *adj* indecente, obsceno,-a.

salad *n* salada *f*; ~ **bowl** *n* saladeira *f*; ~ **dressing** *n* tempero *m*; **mixed** ~ *n* salada mista.

salamander *n (ZOOL)* salamandra *f*.

salami *n* salame *m*.

salaried *adj* assalariado,-a; *(job)* remunerado,-a.

salary *n* salário *m*; ordenado; *(higher bracket)* vencimento *m*.

sale *n* venda; *(at reduced prices)* liquidação *f*, saldo; 'for ~' 'à venda', 'vende-se'; **on** ~ à venda; **the ~s** *npl* os saldos *mpl*; ~**s drive** *n* campanha *f* de vendas; ~**sman** *n (pl: -men)* vendedor *(pl:* vendedores); ~**swoman/women** *n* vendedora *(pl:* vendedoras)*;* representante, agente de vendas; *(in shop)* caixeiro,-a, *(BR)* balconista *m,f.*

salesmanship *n* arte *f* de vender.

sales pitch *(talk)* *n* lábia *f* de vendedor.

salient *adj* saliente, evidente *m,f.*

saline *n (MED = solution)* soro *m* fisiológico; ♦ *adj (deposit)* salino *m.*

saliva *n* saliva *f.*

sallow *adj (complexion)* amarelado,-a; *(pale)* pálido,-a.

sally *(pl: -ies)* *n* ofensiva *f*; **2** dito *m* esprituoso; chiste *m*; ♦ *vt* **to** ~ **forth** sair destemido e com ímpeto.

salmon *n pl inv* salmão *m*; **smoked** ~ salmão fumado.

salmonella *n* salmonela *f.*

salmon-pink *n adj* rosa-salmão.

salon *n (hairdresser's)* salão *m* de cabeleireiro,-a.

saloon *n (on ship)* salão *m*; **2** *(US)* taberna *f*; *(in hotel)* bar *m*; **3** *(AUT)* *(UK)* *(car)* sedan *m*, berlina *f.*

salt *n* sal *m*; **a pinch of** ~ uma pitada de sal; ~ **cellar** *n* saleiro; **Epsom ~s** *npl* sulfato *m* de magnésio; ~ **mine/pan/pit** *n* salina *f*; **rock** ~ *n* sal-gema *m*;

table ~ sal refinado; ♦ *vt* salgar; pôr sal em; IDIOM **to be the** ~ **of the earth** ser uma excelente pessoa; **to take sth with a pinch of** ~ *(not believe)* dar desconto a algo; não levar a sério o que o outro diz.

salt away *vt (money)* meter ao bolso; guardar.

saltish *adj* um tanto salgado.

saltpetre *(UK)* **saltpeter** *(US)* *n* salitre *m*; nitrato de potássio *m.*

salty (-ier, -iest) *adj* salgado,-a.

salutary *adj* salutar.

salute *n* saudação *f*; **2** *(of guns)* salva; **3** *(MIL)* continência; ♦ *vt* saudar; *(guns)* dar salvas; *(MIL)* fazer continência a.

salvage[1] *n (rescue)* salvamento, recuperação *f*; *(goods saved)* salvados *mpl*, bens *mpl* recuperados; ♦ *vt* salvar; **2** *(for recycling)* recuperar.

salvage[2] *n (shops/centres)* *(selling parts of broken cars; iron scrap and old building materials)* sucata *f*; ~ **vessel** *n* barco *m* de salvamento.

salvation *n* salvação *f*; **the S~ Army** *npr (REL)* o Exército da Salvação.

salve *n* unguento, bálsamo *m*; **lip** ~ baton de cieiro; ♦ *vt* acalmar; **2** aliviar; **to** ~ **one's conscience** aliviar a consciência.

salver *n* bandeja, salva.

salvo *n (pl: -oes) (MIL) (of guns)* salva *f.*

Samaritan *n;* **the good** ~ o bom samaritano; **the ~s** organização caritativa que ouve ao telefone as mágoas de muitos infelizes, dando conselhos e conforto.

samba *n* samba.

same *adj* mesmo,-a; **at the** ~ **time** ao mesmo tempo; ♦ *adv* do mesmo modo, igualmente; ♦ *pron (identical)* **the** ~ o mesmo, a mesma; **the** ~ **as** o mesmo que; **it's not the** ~ não é a mesma coisa; **all/just the** ~ apesar de tudo, mesmo assim; *(indifferent)* **it's all the** ~ dá no mesmo, tanto faz; ♦ *exc (wishing the same, likewise)* **the** ~ **to you!** igualmente!

sameness *n* uniformidade *f.*

Samoa *npr* Samoa; **in** ~ em Samoa.

Samoan *npr adj* samoano,-a.

samosa *n* tipo de pastel de massa tenra indiano; chamuça.

sampan *n (vessel)* sampana *f.*

sample *n* amostra; ♦ *vt (food, wine)* provar, experimentar; *(products)* testar.

sanatorium *(pl: -ria)* *n* sanatório *m.*

sanctify *(pp, pt -ied)* *vt* santificar.

sanctimonious *adj (pej)* beato,-a; santimonial, sacripanta *m,f.*

sanction *n* sanção *f*, pena; ♦ *vt* sancionar, ratificar.

sanctity *n* santidade *f*, divindade *f*; inviolabilidade *f.*

sanctuary *n (holy place)* santuário; **2** *(for wildlife)* reserve *f*; *(safe place)* refúgio, asilo.

sanctum *n (private meditation place)* retiro *m*; *(REL)* lugar *m* sagrado, santuário *m.*

sand *n* areia *f*; ~**bag** *n* saco de areia; ~**bank** *n* banco de areia; ~**blast** *vt* (para limpar prédios, etc) ja(c)to de areia sob pressão; ~ **dune** *n* duna *f*;

~pit *n (for children)* caixa de areia; **~stone** *n* arenito, grés *m*; **stretches of ~** areal *m*; ♦ *vt* arear, cobrir de areia; **to ~ down** *(woodwork)* lixar, esfregar com lixa.

sandal *n* sandália.

sandalwood *n* sândalo, madeira *f* de sândalo.

sander *n* (máquina de lixar) lixadeira *f* mecânica.

sandman *n (sleep)* João Pestana.

sandpaper *n* lixa *f*.

sandpiper *n (bird)* maçarico.

sandwich *n* sanduíche; sande *f*; **cheese/ham ~** sanduíche de queijo/fiambre; **~ board** *n* cartaz *m* ambulante; **~ course** *n* curso de teoria e prática alternadas; ♦ *vt* (= **to ~ in**) intercalar; **~ed between** encaixado entre.

sandy (-ier, -iest) *adj* arenoso,-a; *(colour)* vermelho amarelado.

sane *adj (not mad)* são, sã *f* (do juízo); **2** *(sensible)* ajuizado, sensato.

sang *(pt of* **sing**).

sanitarium *n (US)* = **sanatorium**.

sanitary *adj (system, arrangements)* sanitário; **2** *(clean)* higiénico (BR: -giê-); **~ towel** *(UK)*, **~ napkin** *(US)* n penso higiénico, *(BR)* absorvente *m* higiénico.

sanitation *n (in house)* higiene *f*; salubridade; condições *f* sanitárias; **2** *(in public places)* saneamento.

sanitize, sanitise *vt* desinfectar; sanear; **2** *(film, news)* sanear, tornar inofensivo.

sanity *n* sanidade *f*, equilíbrio *m* mental; saúde *f* mental; **2** *(common sense)* juízo *m*, sensatez *f*.

sank *(pt of* **sink**).

Sanskrit *npr* sânscrito *m*.

Santa Claus *npr* Pai Natal *m*, *(BR)* Papai Noel *m*.

São Paulo *npr (largest city in Brazil)* São Paulo *m*.

sap *n (of trees)* seiva *f*; *(fig)* vigor *m*; ♦ *vt (strength)* esgotar, minar, enfraquecer.

sapling *n* árvore *f* jovem.

sapper *n (soldier, in engineering, who digs trenches)* sapador *m*.

sapphire *n* safira *f*.

Saracen *npr adj* sarraceno,-a.

sarcasm *n* sarcasmo.

sarcastic *adj* sarcástico.

sarcastically *adv* sarcasticamente.

sarcophagus *n* sarcófago *m*.

sardine *n* sardinha *f*.

Sardinia *npr* Sardenha; **in ~** na Sardenha.

Sardinian *npr adj* sardo,-a, sardenho,-a; *(language)* sardo.

sardonic *adj* sardónico,-a, mordaz.

Sargasso Sea *n (GEOG)*: **the ~** o Mar de Sargaço.

sarong *m* sarongue *m*.

sartorial *adj (formal) (REL)* vestuário de homem; **~ elegance** elegância no vestir.

SAS *(abbr for* **Special Air Service**) unidade do exército que se encarrega de operações de anti-terrorismo e sabotagem.

sash *n (around waist)* faixa, cinta; banda *f*; **2 ~ window** *n* janela *f* de guilhotina; *(frame)* caixilho *m* de janela de guilhotina.

sass *n (US) (coll)* insolência *f*; ♦ *vt* refilar com (alguém).

sassy *adj (US) (fam)* descarado,-a, atrevido,-a.

sat *(pt, pp of* **sit**); **2 Sat.** *(UK) (abbr for* **Saturday**).

SAT *n (abbr for* **Scholastic Aptitude Test**) *(US)* exame importante prestado no útimo ano da escola secundária para o ingresso na universidade.

Satan *npr* Satanás *m*, Satã *m*.

satanic *adj* satânico,-a diabólico,-a.

satchel *n (child's)* sacola escolar a tiracolo.

sate *vt* satisfazer; saciar.

sated *adj (pleasure, appetite)* saciado,-a (**with sth** com algo); **2** *(full) (food)* cheio,-a *(fam)*; satisfeito,-a.

satellite *n* satélite *m*; **~ dish** antena *f* parabólica.

satin *n (material)* cetim *m*; ♦ *adj* acetinado,-a.

satire *n* sátira.

satiric(al) *adj* satírico,-a.

satirist *n* satirista.

satirize *vt* satirizar.

satisfaction *n (pleasure)* satisfação *f*; **2** *(of debt)* liquidação *f*, pagamento *m*; **3** *(compensation)* compensação *f*; *(apology)* reparação *f*.

satisfactory *adj* satisfatório,-a.

satisfied *adj* satisfeito,-a, contente (**about sth** com algo); **2** *(convinced)* convencido (**by** por); **I am ~ that …** estou satisfeito que …

satisfy *vt/vi* satisfazer; **2** convencer; **3** *(fulfil)* atender a.

satisfying *adj* satisfatório,-a; **2** *(rewarding)* compensador; **3** *(marriage)* feliz; **4** *(life)* preenchido,-a.

SATs *n (abbr for* **Standard Assessment Tests**) *(UK)* (na Inglaterra e país de Gales) exame *m* de aptidão que as crianças prestam aos 7, 11 e 14 anos de idade (= **National Test**).

satsuma *n (fruit)* tipo de tangerina do Japão.

saturate *vt*: **to ~ (with)** saturar, encher (de).

saturated *adj (person) (fig)* saturado,-a; farto,-a *(fam)*; *(clothes, garden)* ensopado,-a, encharcado,-a; **2** *(CHEM)* saturado,-a.

saturation *n* saturação *f*; **~ point** *n* ponto *m* de saturação.

Saturday *n* sábado *m*; **today is ~** hoje é sábado; **every ~ I go to the cinema** vou ao cinema todos os sábados/vou ao cinema aos sábados; **every other ~** sábado sim, sábado não; **last ~** no sábado passado; **Easter ~** Sábado de Aleluia.

Saturn *npr (ASTRON)* Saturno *m*.

saturnine *adj (person, mood)* sombrio,-a, taciturno,-a.

sauce *n (CULIN)* molho *m*; tempero *m*; *(sweet)* creme *m*, calda *f*; IDIOM **what's ~ for the goose is ~ for the gander** todos têm os mesmos direitos.

sauceboat *n* molheira *f*.

saucepan *n* panela *f*, caçarola *f*, tacho *m*.

saucer *n* pires *msg*.

saucy *adj* atrevido,-a, descarado,-a; provocante.

Saudi *npr adj* saudita *m,f*.

Saudi Arabia *npr* Arábia *f* Saudita; **in ~** na Arábia Saudita.

Saudi (Arabian) *npr adj* árabe-saudita.

sauerkraut *n (CULIN)* chucrute *m*.

sauna *n* sauna *f*.

saunter *(stroll) vi* caminhar devagar, passear.

sausage *n* salsicha *f*, linguiça *f*; *(cold meat)* enchidos *mpl*; *(BR)* frios *mpl*; **~ roll** *n* folheado *m* de salsicha.

sauté *adj* salteado,-a, sauté, frito,-a rapidamente.

savage *n* selvagem *m,f*; ♦ *adj* cruel, feroz; **2** *(temper, attack)* violento,-a; *(criticism)* virulento,-a; **3** *(pej) (primitive)* selvagem; ♦ *vt (attack)* atacar ferozmente; **2** maltratar; **3** *(lion)* despedaçar.

savagery *n* selvajaria, *(BR)* selvageria, ferocidade *f*; barbaridade *f*.

savannah *n* savana *f*.

save *n* (SPORT) defesa *f*; (COMP) gravação *f*; ♦ *prep (except)* ~ **(for)** salvo, exce(p)to; ♦ *vt (rescue)* salvar; **he saved the little girl** ele salvou a menina; **2** *(time, energy, money)* poupar; **it saves time** poupa tempo; **3** *(postpone task)* ~ **it for another day** deixe isso para outro dia; **4** *(put by)* guardar; ~ **a few biscuits for me** guarde uns biscoitos para mim; **5** *(be thrifty)* economizar; **6** *(do without)* **to** ~ **oneself from doing sth** não precisar fazer; ~ **yourself an expense** não precisa de fazer esta despesa; **7** *(avoid)* evitar *(problem, bother, work)*; **8** *(SPORT)* defender; **9** ~ **on** *(COMP)* arquivar, gravar; ♦ *vi* (= **to** ~ **up**) economizar.

save as you earn *(UK)* sistema de poupança incentivada pelo governo, em que a contribuição regular por mês gera interesse isento de impostos.

saver *n*: **time, money** ~ algo que poupa tempo dinheiro; economizador,-ora; **2** *(FIN) (at bank, etc)* poupador.

saving *n (reduction on price etc)* economia *f* (**in** de, **on** sobre); ~ **clause** *(in an agreement) (JUR)* cláusula de exce(p)ção; *(in compounds)* **energy-**~ que economiza no consumo de energia; ~ **grace** *n*: **the** ~ **of** o único mérito de; o lado bom (da pessoa).

savings *npl* economias *fpl*, poupanças; ~ **account** *n* conta *f* de poupança; *(BR*: -nô-); caderneta *f* de poupança.

saviour *(UK)* **savior** *(US)* *n* salvador,-ora; **S~** *npr* Salvador *m*.

savour *(UK)* **savor** *(US)* *n* sabor *m*; *(fig)* gosto *m*; ♦ *adj (CULIN)* saboroso,-a, apetitoso,-a; ♦ *vt* saborear.

savoury *(pl*: **-ies**) *(before a meal)* salgados *mpl*; salgadinhos; *(after a meal) (sweet)* canapé *m*.

Savoy *npr (GEOG)* Sabóia; ~ **cabbage** *n* couve *f* lombarda.

saw *(pt of* **see**) *n* serra; serrote *m*; ~**dust** *n* serradura, *(BR)* serragem *f*; ~**mill** *n* serração *f (BR)* serraria *f*; ♦ *(pt* **-ed**, *pp* **sawed** or **sawn**) *vt (also:* **to** ~ **up**) serrar.

sawn-off shotgun *(UK)* **sawed-off shotgun** *(US)* *n* arma *f* de cano serrado.

sax *n (abbr for* **saxophone**) sax.

saxon *n adj* saxão,-ã.

Saxonia *npr* Saxónia *f*.

saxophone *n (MUS)* saxofone *m*.

say *n*: **to have one's** ~ exprimir sua opinião; **to have a/some** ~ **in sth** opinar sobre algo, ter que ver com algo; ♦ *(pt, pp* **said**) *vt* dizer; **I didn't** ~ **that** eu não disse isso; **to** ~ **yes/no** dizer (que) sim/não; **that is to** ~ ou seja; que quer dizer; **let us** ~ digamos; **let us** ~ **that** *(suppose)* suponhamos que; **whatever they** ~ digam o que disserem; **that**

goes without ~**ing** é óbvio, escusado será dizer; IDIOM **easier said than done** falar é fácil; **to** ~ **nothing of** para não falar de; **having said that** apesar disso (apesar de ter dito isso); **as they** ~ como se costuma dizer; ♦ *exc* **you can** ~ **that again!** bem podes dizê-lo!; **you don't** ~**!** não me digas!

SAYE *(abbr for* **Save As You Earn**).

saying *n* ditado *m*, dito *m*.

say-so *n (fam)* autorização *f*; aval *m*; **on sb's** ~ confiando na palavra de alguém.

s/c *(abbr for* **self-contained**) *(UK)* apartamento independente, dentro de uma casa ou prédio (com quarto, sala/cozinha, casa de banho) = tipo T-1 *(EP)*.

scab *n (of wound)* casca *f*, crosta *f* (de ferida); **2** *(on animal's skin)* sarna *f*; **3** *(strikebreaker)* fura-greves *m inv*; **4** *(despicable person) (pej)* canalha *m*.

scabby (-ier, -iest) *adj* cheio de crostas, cicatrizes.

scabies *n* sarna *f*.

scaffold *n (for execution)* cadafalso, patíbulo.

scaffolding *n (CONSTR)* andaime *m*.

scald *n* escaldadura; ♦ *vt* escaldar, queimar.

scalding *adj* escaldante; **the sand was** ~ a areia estava a escaldar, estava escaldante.

scale *n* escala; **on a large** ~ em grande escala; ~ **of charges** *n* tarifa, lista de preços; ~ **drawing** *n* desenho em escala; ~ **model** *n* maquete *f*; **2** *(of fish, snake)* escama; **3** *(of wound)* crosta de ferida; **4** *(in kettle, etc)* depósito *m* calcário *m*; **5** *(MUS)* scale; ♦ *vt (clean fish of scales)* escamar, amanhar; **2** *(mountain)* escalar; *(tree)* trepar, subir; **go up on the** ~ **in rank** subir de escalão; ~ **down** reduzir.

scales *npl (weighing)* balança *fsg*.

scallion *n (US)* cebolinha *f* verde.

scallop *n (shellfish)* vieira, venera; **2** *(sewing) (in scallop patterns)* barra, recortada; ♦ *vt (sewing)* guarnecer; recortar a orla da saia em curvas.

scalp *n* escalpo, couro cabeludo; ♦ *vt (MED)* escalpar; **2** *(US) (tout)* vender (bilhetes) no mercado negro.

scalpel *n (MED)* escalpelo *m*, bisturi *m*.

scalper *n (US) (tout)* vendedor de bilhetes no mercado negro; *(BR)* cambista *m inv*.

scam *n (slang) (swindle)* vigarice *f*; falcatrua *f*.

scamp *n (rascal, idle person)* malandro *m*; **2** *(mischievous child)* maroto,-a.

scamper *vi*: **to** ~ **away/off** sair a correr *(BR*: correndo), fugir precipitadamente.

scampi *npl* camarão *m* grande.

scan *n (MED) (ultrasound scan)* ecografia; **a CAT** ~ um TAC; *(BR)* exame *m*, escaneamento *m*; **2** leitura por alto; ♦ (**-ned**) *vt* esquadrinhar; *(BR)* escanear; pesquisar, explorar; **2** *(to glance at quickly)* passar uma vista de olhos por; **3** *(TV, radar)* explorar; **4** ter métrica corre(c)ta; **these lines don't** ~ **well** estes versos não têm métrica corre(c)ta; **5** *(COMP)* digitalizar, inspecionar; *(BR)* escanear.

scandal *n* escândalo *m*; **2** *(gossip)* mexerico *m*.

scandalize *vt* escandalizar.

scandalous *adj* escandaloso,-a; difamatório,-a, calunioso,-a; vergonhoso,-a.

Scandinavia *npr* Escandinávia; **in** ~ na Escandinávia.

Scandinavian *n adj* escandinavo,-a.

scanner *n (MED-CAT)* aparelho no hospital para detectar doenças; **2** *(COMP)* scanner, escaneador; **3** *(RADAR)* explorador, analisador *m*.

scant *adj* escasso,-a, insuficiente.

scantily *adv* insuficientemente; ~ **clad** em trajes *mpl* reduzidos, mínimos.

scapegoat *n* bode *m* expiatório.

scapula *(pl: -ae, or -as) n* omoplata.

scar *n* cicatriz *f*; **2** *(fig)* mazela; marca, *(BR)* sequela; ♦ *(pt, pp -red) vt* deixar com cicatriz; **2** marcar; traumatizar; **to be ~ed for life** ficar marcado,-a para sempre; ♦ *vi (healing but leaving scar)* cicatrizar.

scarce *adj* escasso,-a, raro,-a; **to make o.s.** ~ *(fig)* desaparecer, tornar-se 'invisível'.

scarcely *adv* mal, quase não; **I** ~ **spoke to him** eu mal falei com ele.

scarcity *n* escassez *f*; *(shortage)* falta, carência.

scare *n* susto *m*, pânico *m*; sobressalto *m*; **bomb** ~ ameaça *f* de bomba, alerta à bomba; **to give sb a** ~ fazer, meter medo alguém; ♦ *vt* assustar, amedrontar; espantar; ♦ *vi* **to** ~ **sb away/off** *(drive away)* afugentar, *(burglars, customers, animals, business)*; IDIOM **to be scared stiff** estar/ficar estarrecido (de medo); **to** ~ **sb stiff** *(BR)* deixar alguém morrendo de medo.

scarecrow *n* espantalho *m*.

scared *(pt, pp of scare) adj* assustado,-a, apavorado,-a.

scaremonger *n* alarmista.

scaremongering *n* alarmismo *m*.

scarf *(pl: scarves) n (square)* lenço (de pescoço, de cabeça); *(over the shoulders)* écharpe *f*; *(long woollen for neck)* cachecol *m*.

scarlet *adj* escarlate; ~ **fever** *n* escarlatina *f*.

scarp *n* escarpa *f*.

scarper *(coll) (UK) vi* esgueirar-se, fugir.

scarred *(pt, pp of scar) adj* cheio de cicatrizes; **2** (emocionalmente) marcado,-a, traumatizado,-a; dilacerado,-a.

scarves *(pl of scarf)*.

scary (-ier, -iest) *adj (coll) (giving fear)* assustador,-ora; *(causing fright, distress)* angustiante *m,f*; **it was a** ~ **moment** foi um momento angustiante; **2** *(easily frightened)* assustadiço,-a, tímido,-a.

scat *n (animal droppings) (in the shape of a ball)* caganita *f*.

scathing *adj (remark)* mordaz, duro,-a, severo,-a.

scatter *n (of houses, crowd)* dispersão *f*; ~ **diagram** gráfico de dispersão; ♦ *vt (papers, leaves, seeds)* espalhar; dispersar; ♦ *vi* espalhar-se; *(people, animals)* dispersar-se; ~ **brained** *adj* desmiolado,-a, estouvado,-a; cabeça-de-vento *f*.

scatterbrain *n (fam)* cabeça no ar, cabeça de vento.

scatterbrained *adj* estouvado,-a; desmiolado,-a.

scattered *adj*: ~ **around** espalhado,-a (por todo o lado); **the room was** ~ **with books** a sala estava juncada de livros; ~ **showers** aguaceiros *npl* dispersos.

scatty (-ier, -iest) *adj* despassarado,-a; estouvado,-a; de cabeça *f* oca; *(BR)* encucado,-a.

scavenge *vt* rebuscar, remexer, vasculhar nos sacos de lixo à procura de coisas; **2** *(fig)* solicitar *(funds, subsidies)*.

scavenger *n* pessoa que procura nos caixotes de lixo; **2** *(ZOOL)* animal *m* necrófago.

SCE *n (abbr for Scottish Certificate of Education)* exame de conhecimentos em três níveis, prestado na Escócia.

scenario *n (THEAT)* cenário *m*.

scene *n (in play, film)* cena *f*; **2** *(of crime, accident)* local; **3** *(sight, view)* vista, panorama *m*; **4** *(of quarrel, scandal)* cena *f*, fita *f*, escândalo *m*; **she made a terrible** ~ ela fez uma cena, fita terrível; **5** *(field, kind)* género, tipo *m*; **it is not my** ~ não é o meu género.

scenery *n (landscape)* paisagem *f*; *(fig)* ar, ares; **a change of** ~ **would do you good** uma mudança de ares seria bom para ti; **2** *(THEAT)* cenário *m*.

scene shifter *n (THEAT)* maquinista *m,f*.

scenic *adj* cénico *(BR: cê-)*; teatral.

scent *n* perfume *m*; aroma *m*; **2** *(fig: track)* pista, rasto; **3** *(sense of smell)* olfato; ♦ *vt* perfumar; *(smell)* cheirar; **2** *(sniff out)* farejar; **3** *(suspect)* suspeitar, pressentir.

scented perfumado,-a.

sceptic, skeptic *n* cé(p)tico,-a.

sceptical *adj* cé(p)-tico. **scepticism** *n* ce(p)ticismo.

sceptre *n* ce(p)tro; *(fig)* autoridade *f* real.

schedule *n (timetable)* horário; **2** *(of events)* programa *m*, agenda *f*; plano *m*; previsão *f*; **in accordance with** ~ de acordo com o plano, com as previsões; ~ na hora, a horas; **2** *(of prices, contents)* lista *f*; ♦ *vt* planear, *(BR)* planejar; fazer lista de; marcar algo para; agendar; **to be ahead of/behind** ~ estar adiantado/atrasado.

scheduled *adj* agendado,-a previsto,-a, marcado-a; **the discussion was** ~ **for next week** a discussão foi agendada para a semana que vem; **the plane is** ~ **to arrive in one hour's time** a chegada do avião está prevista para daqui a uma hora; ~ **flight** *n* voo *m* regular, voo de carreira.

scheduling *n* programação *f*; **2** inclusão na lista oficial; **3** *(of monument)* classificação.

scheme *n* plano *m*, esquema *m*; método *m*; **2** *(plot)* conspiração *f*; **3** *(trick)* ardil *m*; **4** *(arrangement)* disposição *f*; ♦ *vt* proje(c)tar; ♦ *vi (plan)* plane(j)ar, tramar; *(intrigue)* conspirar.

scheming *adj* intrigante; que faz intriga; ~ **liar!** mentiroso,-a; intriguista!

schism *n* cisma *m*.

schist *n (MIN) (rock)* xisto *m*, micaxisto *m*.

schistose *adj* xistoso,-a.

schizophrenia *n* esquizofrenia.

schizophrenic *adj* esquizofrénico *(BR: -frê-)*.

schmaltzy *adj (coll)* sentimalóide, lamecha *f*.

schlep *(pres p and pt -pp) vt, vr (drag, lug o.s.)* arrastar algo a custo; arrastar-se a custo.

scholar *n (learned person)* letrado,-a, sábio,-a, erudito,-a; intellectual; **Latin** ~ latinista *m,f*.

scholarly *adj* erudito, douto.

scholarship *n* erudição *f*; **2** *(grant)* bolsa *f* de estudo; **3** *(learning)* saber *m*, conhecimentos *mpl*.

scholastic *adj* escolástico,-a; educacional; **2** *(of school)* escolar.

Scholastic Aptitude Test (SAT) *n* (US) exame *m* de admissão à universidade.

school *n* escola, colégio; ~ **age** *n* idade *f* escolar; ~ **book** *n* livro escolar/de textos; ~ **boy** *n* aluno; ~ **girl** *n* aluna; *(in university)* faculdade *f*; **law** ~ faculdade *f* de Direito; ~ **report** *n* boletim *m* escolar; ~**room** *n* sala *f* de aula *f*; ~ **year** *n* ano le(c)tivo; **2** *(group of sardines, etc)* cardume *m*; *(of porpoises, dolphins)* banco *m*; ♦ *vt (train – animal)* adestrar, treinar; **2** *(educate)* ensinar; instruir.

schooling *n* educação *f*, ensino.

school-leaving age *n* (UK) idade de conclusão do ensino obrigatório.

schoolmaster *n* mestre, professor.

schoolmistress *n* professora, mestra.

schoolteacher *n* professor,-ora, mestre,-a.

schooner *n* *(ship)* escuna; **2** *(US) (glass)* copo *m* grande de cerveja, caneca *f*, *(BR)* canecão *m*; *(UK)* copo *m* grande de xerez.

sciatica *n* ciática *f*.

science *n* ciência; ~ **fiction** *n* ficção *f* científica.

scientific *adj* científico.

scientist *n* cientista *m,f*.

sci-fi *(abbr for* **science fiction***).*

scimitar *n* cimitarra.

scintillate *vi* cintilar; reluzir.

scintillating *adj* cintilante, brilhante.

scissors *npl* tesoura *fsg*; **a pair of** ~ uma tesoura.

sclerosis *n* esclerose *f* (*Vd:* **multiple sclerosise***)*.

scoff *n* escárnio *m*, troça *f*; **2** *(coll)* comida; ♦ *vt* engolir sofregamente; ♦ *vi* escarnecer, troçar; **to ~ at** zombar de.

scold *vt (reprimand)* ralhar, repreender; *(BR)* xingar.

scolding *n* repreensão *f*, raspanete *m*.

scone *n* bolinho inglês (tipo de pão que se come com natas e compota de morango), scone.

scoop *n* *(as a shovel, ladle)* colher *f*, pá *f*, concha *f*; **2** *(amount, spoonful)* colherada *f*, pazada *f*; *(for ice-cream)* bola; **one ~ of ice cream** uma bola de sorvete; **3** *(JOURN)* furo *m* jornalístico, cacha, exclusividade; **4** *(coll) (large, quick gain of money)* prémio *m*; lucro *m*; negócio da China *(coll)*; **in one ~** de uma só vez; ♦ *vt (also:* ~ **up***) (with shovel, spoon)* tirar (com pá, colher); *(with hands)* pegar em; **to ~ out** *(hollow out)* escavar; **to ~ up** *(money, prize)* ganhar.

scoopful *n* medida *f*; **2** *(of earth)* pazada *f*.

scoot *vt* correr com muita pressa.

scooter *n* *(motorcycle)* motoreta; **2** *(toy)* patinete *m*, trotinette *m*.

scope *n* *(opportunity)* possibilidade *f*; **2** *(range) (of plan)* envergadura *f*; **3** *(of report, study)* alcance *m*; escopo *m*.

scorch *vt (clothes, hair)* chamuscar; **2** *(grass, fields)* secar; queimar; ♦ *vi (face skin)* queimar.

scorcher *n* *(coll)* dia *m* escaldante.

scorching *adj (sand, water)* escaldante; *(sun, weather)* abrasador,-ora.

score *n* *(number of points) (cards)* pontuação *f*; *(SPORT)* resultado *m*; **2** *(MUS)* partitura *f*; **3** *(CIN)* banda *f* sonora; **4** *(reckoning)* conta; **to settle a ~ with sb** ajustar contas com alguém; **5** *(twenty)* jogo de vinte, vintena; **6** *(lots)* **I have ~s of things to do** tenho um monte de coisas a fazer; **7** *(mark, notch)* marca *f*, estria; ♦ *vt (golo)* marcar; **2** atingir a pontuação, ter como resultado; **3** *(make notches)* entalhar, cortar, gravar; ♦ *vi (in an argument)* ganhar; **2** *(football)* marcar um golo *(BR: gol)*; *(keep score)* marcar os pontos; **to ~ off sth/~ out** riscar; **to ~ over sb** levar vantagem sobre alguém; IDIOM **on that ~** a esse respeito, por esse motivo.

score *n* *(SPORT, quiz) (number of points gained)* resultado *m*; *(total points shown)* pontuação; **2** *(in test, competition)* nota *f*, resultado *m*; **3** *(MUS)* partitura *f*; **4** *(fam) (true facts, situation)* **you know the ~** já sabes como é; conheces bem a situação; **5** *(subject)* **on that ~** sobre esse assunto; **6** *(a great number)* lots; **I have ~s of things to do** tenho milhares de coisas p'ra fazer.

scoreboard *n* marcador *m*, painel *m*; *(BR)* placar *m*.

scorecard *n* *(SPORT)* cartão *m* de marcação.

scorer *n* marcador *m*.

scoring *n* *(MUS)* arranjo *m*; **2** *(cuts)* incisões *fpl*.

scorn *n* desprezo *m*; desdém *m*; ♦ *vt* desprezar, desdenhar, denegrir; **2** rejeitar.

scornful *adj* desdenhoso,-a, zombador,-ora; escarnecedor,-ora.

Scorpio *n* *(ASTROL)* Escorpião *m*.

scorpion *n* *(ZOOL)* escorpião *m*.

Scot *npr* escocês, esa; **the S~** *npl* os escoceses *mpl*.

Scotch *n*: ~ **whisky** *(drink)* uísque *m* escocês; ~ **tape** *n* (= **sellotape**) *(US)* fita *f* adesiva; ♦ *adj* (=**Scottish**) *adj (dated)* escocês,-esa; ♦ **to scotch** *vt (put an end to)* pôr fim a, estragar, contrariar; **bad weather ~ed our plans** o mau tempo estragou os nossos planos; **2** abafar *(rumour, talk)*.

scot-free *adj*: **to go/get** ~ *(unpunished)* sair impune; *(unharmed)* sair ileso,-a.

Scotland *npr* Escócia; **in** ~ na Escócia; ~ **Yard (New Scotland Yard)** *npr* Scotland Yard *f* (sede da polícia metropolitana de Londres, controlada diretamente pelo Ministério do Interior).

Scotsman/woman *n* escocês,-esa.

Scottish *adj* escocês,-esa.

scoundrel *n* canalha *m,f*, patife *m*.

scour *n* limpeza; ♦ *vt* limpar; **2** *(to scrub)* esfregar; arear; **3** *(search)* percorrer, procurar.

scourer *n* esponja *f* de aço.

scourge *n* flagelo *m*; calamidade *f*; tormento *m*.

scout *n* (= **boy** ~) escoteiro *m*; **2** *(MIL)* explorador *m*, batedor *m*; ♦ **to** ~ **around** explorar, fazer reconhecimento.

scowl *n* carranca *f*, cara *f* feia; ♦ *vi* franzir o sobrolho, a testa; **to** ~ **at sb** olhar alguém carrancudamente.

scrabble *vi (with hands or claws)* trepar com dificuldade; **to** ~ **around** *(grope around for sth)* procurar algo às apalpadelas.

Scrabble© *n* jogo de palavras.

scrag *n (CULIN)* pescoço *m* de carneiro.

scraggy *adj* esquelético,-a, descarnado,-a; ~ **person** magricela.

scram (-mm-) *vi (coll)* safar-se; pôr-se a andar, raspar-se *(pop)*.

scramble *n* escalada difícil; 2 *(struggle)* luta *f*; ♦ *vi (move, rush)* mexer-se com rapidez e sem jeito; **he ~ to his feet** ele levantou-se de um salto/num salto; 2 *(with hands or feet)* gatinhar ou trepar; 3 *(eggs)* fazer ovos mexidos; 4 *(struggle)* lutar (**for** por); *(compete)* disputar (**for**) *(prize, place, job)*; 5 *(RADIO, TEL) (code)* codificar.

scrambled *adj (message)* codificado,-a, feito,-a incompreensível; ~ **eggs** *npl* ovos mexidos.

scrap *n (bit)* pedacinho; *(fig)* pouquinho; bocado *m*; 2 *(fight)* rixa, luta; ~**s** *npl (left-over food)* sobras *fpl*, restos *mpl*; ~**book** *n* livro *(BR*: álbum *m)* de recortes; ~**-heap** *n (fig)*: **on the ~** rejeitado, jogado, deitado fora; ~ **dealer** *n* sucateiro; ~**ings** *npl* raspas *fpl*; ~ **iron/metal** *n* ferro-velho *m*, sucata *f*; ~ **paper** *n* papel *m* de rascunho; ~**yard** *n* ferro-velho *m*; ♦ *vt* reduzir a ferro velho, deitar para o ferro velho; 2 *(discard)* desfazer-se de, descartar (algo); ♦ *vi* brigar, armar uma briga.

scrape *n (money)* aperto *m*; *(coll)* enrascada *f*; 2 *(sound)* chiadela *f*; ♦ *vt* raspar; 2 *(carro)* arranhar; 3 *(skin)* esfolar; 4 ~ **against** roçar ♦ *vi*: **to ~ in/into** *(school, job)* conseguir com dificuldade; **to ~ through** viver a custo; ♦ **to bow and ~** portar-se com muita humildade

scrapper *n* raspador *m*; 2 espátula *f*.

scrappy (-ier, -iest) *adj* fragmentado,-a; 2 *(speech)* incoerente, desconexo; 3 *(US)* conflituoso,-a.

scratch *n* arranhão *m*; 2 *(from claw)* arranhadura; unhada; 3 *(scribble)* rabisco *m*; ♦ *vt (record)* marcar, riscar; rabiscar; *(with claw, nail)* arranhar; ♦ *vi (from itching)* coçar-se; IDIOM **to start from ~** começar do princípio, partir do zero; **to be up to ~** estar à altura (das circunstâncias).

scrawl *n* rabisco *m*, garatuja *f*; ♦ *vi* garatujar, rabiscar.

scrawny (-ier, -iest) *adj* esquelético,-a.

scream *n* grito *m*; ♦ *vi* gritar.

scree *n* detritos *mpl* na base dum penhasco.

screech *n* guincho *m*; grito *m* agudo e áspero; ♦ *vi (of tyres)* guinchar; 2 *(of bird)*, piar; 3 *(person)* dar gritos estridentes.

screech-owl *n (ZOOL)* coruja *f (das torres)*.

screen *n (CIN)* tela *f*; ecrã; *(COMP)* monitor *m*; 2 biombo *m*; divisória *f*; 3 *(wall)* tapume *m*; 4 (= **wind~**) guarda-vento; ♦ *vt* encobrir; 2 *(from wind, sun)* proteger; 3 *(film)* projetar; 4 *(candidate)* examinar, selecionar.

screening *n (MED)* teste *m* de despistagem; rastreio *m*; 2 *(CIN)* teste de imagem; 3 *(showing)* proje(c)ção *f*, exibição *f*; 4 *(vetting)* filtragem *f*; 5 *(of ore, seeds)* seleção *f*, triagem *f*.

screen off *vt* separar com divisória.

screenplay *n (CIN)* argumento *m*; *(BR)* roteiro *m*.

screw *n* parafuso *m*; tarraxa *f*; **thumb-~** *n* parafuso *m* de asas; 2 *(propeller)* hélice *f*; 3 *(coll) (prison guard)* carcereiro; *(coll)* salário *m*; ♦ *vt (attach screw)* aparafusar; (= **to ~ in**) apertar, atarraxar *(screw)*; enroscar *(light bulb)*; 2 *(vulgar: have sex with sb)* foder *(vulgar)*; 3 *(coll)* lixar; ~ **you!** lixa-te!; 4 *(money)* extorquir (**from sb** de alguém); **to ~ around** *vt* ir para a cama com uns e com outros; ♦ **to ~ up** *(crumple)* amarrotar; 2 pôr em desordem; 3 *(plans)* estragar, arruinar, fazer asneiras; 4 *(in the passive)* ficar nervoso,-a; **he is all screwed up about his exams** ele está cheio de nervos por causa do exame; 5 **to ~ up one's courage** encher-se de coragem; IDIOM **to have one's head screwed on (in the right place)** ser sensato, ter muito juízo; **to have a ~ loose** ter um parafuso a menos; ser maluco,-a.

screwball *n (US) (fam)* cabeça *f* oca; chanfrado,-a.

screwdriver *n* chave *f* de fenda, de parafuso.

screw piano stool *n* banco giratório de piano.

screwtop *n (lid)* tampa *f* de rosca, de atarraxar.

screwy (-ier, -iest) *adj (coll)* maluco,-a; excêntrico,-a.

scribble *n* rabisco *m*; garatuja *f*; ♦ *vt* escrevinhar, rabiscar; ~ **sth out** rasurar.

script *n (of film, play)* guião *m*, argumento *m*; *(BR)* roteiro *m*; 2 *(JUR)* texto *m* original; 3 *(writing)* escrita; *(handwriting)* caligrafia *f*.

scripture *n* escrito sagrado; **Holy S~** Sagrada Escritura.

scriptwriter *n* argumentista *(BR)* roteirista.

scroll *n* rolo *m* de pergaminho; **the Dead Sea ~s** os Manuscritos do Mar Morto; ♦ *vt (COMP)* rolar; ~ **down** mover parta baixo; ~ **up** mover para cima, subir; ~ **bar** *n (COMP)* barra *f* de deslocamento *(EP)*; barra de rodagem *(BR)*.

scrooge *n (fam)* avarento,-a; miserável.

scrotum *(pl: -ta, -tums)* *n* escroto *m*.

scrounge *vt (coll)*: **to ~ sth off/from sb** roubar/filar algo de alguém; pedinchar; ♦ *vi*: **to ~ on sb** viver à custa de alguém.

scrounger *n* pedinchão,-ona; *(fam)* parasita *m,f*.

scrub *n* limpeza *f*; esfregadela *f*; 2 *(land)* mato *m*, cerrado *m*; ♦ *vt (cleaning)* esfregar; 2 *(fam) (reject)* cancelar, eliminar.

scrubber *n* escova *f* de esfregar *(the floor)*; 2 *(UK) (fam, pej)* mulher de muitas aventuras amorosas e passageiras.

scruff *n* nuca, cachaço; **by the ~ of the neck** *(fam)* pelo cachaço; 2 *(untidy person)* *n* maltrapilho/s.

scruffy (-ier, -iest) *adj* sujo,-a, desmazelado,-a.

scrum, scrummage *n (rugby)* disputa *f* de bola.

scrumptious *adj (food)* delicioso,-a.

scrunch *n (sound with feet)* rangido *m*.

scrunchy *adj* que estala ao mastigar (bolacha, etc).

scruple *n* escrúpulo *m*.

scrupulous *adj* escrupuloso,-a.

scrutinize *vt* examinar minuciosamente; 2 *(votes)* escrutinar.

scrutiny *n* escrutínio *m*, exame *m* cuidadoso.

scuba diving *n* mergulho *m* submarino; **to go ~** mergulhar com tubo de oxigénio.

scuff *vt (wearing sth out)* desgastar; 2 esfregar os pés em, arrastar os pés; 3 *(surface)* riscar.

scuffle n luta f confusa.
scullery n (UK) copa f.
sculptor n escultor m.
sculptress n escultora.
sculpture n escultura.
scum n (on soup, liquid) espuma; **2** (pej – people) ralé f; escumalha f; **3** (of metals) escória f.
scurry vi correr com passos miúdos; **the mice were scurrying in the walls** os ratinhos corriam deutro das paredes; **to ~ off** sair a correr (BR: correndo), escapulir-se.
scurvy n escorbuto m.
scuttle n (= **coal ~**) balde m para carvão; **2** (NAUT) (porthole) escotilha f vigia f; ♦ vt afundar (ship) fazer ir a pique; ♦ vi correr depressa; **to ~ away/off** sair em disparada.
scythe n segadeira, foice f grande; gadanha; ♦ vt ceifar.
SDLP n (abbr for **Social Democratic and Labour Party**) (da Irlanda do Norte) Partido Social-Democrata e Trabalhista.
SE (abbr for **south-east**) sudeste m, SE.
sea n mar m; **to be at ~** (sailor) andar no mar; (fig) estar perdido,-a, desorientado,-a; **beyond the ~** além-mar; **to put out to ~** fazer-se ao mar; embarcar, fazer uma viagem de barco; **~ anemone** n (BOT) anémona f do mar; **~bed** n fundo m do mar; **~bird** n (ZOOL) ave f marinha; **~ cucumber** n lesma do mar; **~ bream** n (fish) pargo m; **~ breeze** n brisa marítima; **choppy ~** mar agitado; **~ dog** (with experience) velho marinheiro; **~farer** n marinheiro, homem m do mar; **~-faring** (nation) adj de marinheiros; **~food** n marisco; **~front** n (prom) avenida à beira-mar; paredão m; **~-going** adj (ship) de longo curso; **~grass** n sargasso m; **~-green** n adj verde-mar m; **~gull** n gaivota; **~horse** cavalo marinho, hipocampo m; **~ lane** n rota f marítima; **~ lion** n leão-marinho m; **~ plane** n hidroavião m; **~ port** n porto de mar; IDIOM **between the devil and the deep blue ~** entre a espada e a parede.
seal n (animal) foca f; **2** (gen) selo; **~ of approval** (rubberstamped) carimbo m de aprovação; selo m branco; **3** (TECH) vedação f; ♦ vt fechar; selar (envelope); **it ~ed his fate** decidiu seu destino; ♦ **~ in** vt conservar (flavour); **2** isolar; **~ off** (cordon off) vedar, encerrar, interditar (street, entry); **to ~ up** fechar hermeticamente; IDIOM **my lips are sealed** a minha boca é um túmulo/um poço.
sealing wax n lacre m.
seam n costura; (of metal) junta, junção f; **2** (of coal) veio, filão m.
seaman n marinheiro.
seamless adj sem costuras; **2** (fig) (faultless) pefeito,-a.
seamstress n costureira f.
seance n sessão f espírita.
sear vt (scorch) queimar; **2** cauterizar (wound); **3** (wither) secar, murchar.
search n (for person, thing) busca, procura; **2** (of drawer, pockets) revista; **3** (inspection) exame m; investigação f; **in ~ of** à procura de, em busca de; **~ party** n equipa (BR: equipe f) de salvamento, de

socorro; **~ warrant** n (JUR) mandado de captura (BR: busca); ♦ vt (look in) procurar em; **2** (examine) examinar; **3** (frisk) revistar (person, place); **4** (mind) vasculhar; ♦ vi: **to ~ for** buscar, procurar; **2** (try to remember) **to ~ for sth** tentar lembrar algo; **to ~ through** vt dar busca a.
searcher n investigador,-ora.
searching adj penetrante, perscrutador.
searchlight n holofote m.
seashore n praia, beira-mar f; (coast) litoral m.
seasick adj enjoado, mareado.
seaside n costa, litoral m; **~ resort** n lugar m de veraneio; estância f balnear.
season n (gen) época, período; **2** (of year) estação f; temporada; **~ ticket** n bilhete m para a temporada, ingresso m de assinatura; ♦ vt (food) temperar.
seasonal adj sazonal; periódico.
seasoning n (CULIN) condimento, tempero.
seat n (to sit on) assento m, cadeira f; **take a ~** (formal) queira sentar-se; **2** (in Parliament, Council) assento m; **3** (bicycle) selim m; **4** (euph) (bottom) traseiro, nádegas fpl; **~ of trousers** fundilhos mpl; **5** (of government) sede f; **to keep one's ~** (EQUIT) manter-se na sela; ♦ vt sentar (people); (have room for) ter capacidade para; **to be ~ed** estar sentado; **please be ~ed** (formal) queira sentar-se.
seat-belt n cinto m de segurança.
seater n: **a two-~ car** um carro de dois lugares; **a two-~** n sofa (para duas pessoas).
seating n (places) lugares mpl sentados; **2** **~ arrangements** npl distribuição f dos lugares sentados; **~ capacity** (of a place) capacidade de lugares.
sea urchin (ZOOL) ouriço do mar.
seawall n dique m; **2** (jetty) molhe m, paredão m.
seaweed n alga marinha.
seaworthy adj em condições de navegar, navegável.
sec (abbr for **second, seconds**).
secateurs npl tesoura f de poda; **a pair of ~** uma tesoura de poda.
secede vi separar-se (de).
secession n secessão f, separação f.
secluded adj isolado,-a; **2** (place) remoto,-a.
seclusion n reclusão f, isolamento m.
second n (time; gen) segundo; **2** (AUT: = **~ gear**) segunda, em segunda; **3** (date) **the ~ of August** dois de Agosto; **4 Charles II** (the second) Carlos II (segundo); **in a few ~s** dentro de segundos; **~s** npl artigo m defeituoso; (in dual) testemunhas, padrinhos; ♦ adj segundo,-a; **~ best** adj: **to settle for ~** contentar-se com o segundo melhor, segunda f opção; **~ cousin** n primo em segundo grau; **~-degree burn** n queimadura f de segundo grau; **~ sight** n intuição f; ♦ adv (in race, contest) em segundo lugar; **~-class post** correio em segunda classe; ♦ vt (motion) apoiar, secundar; (em nomeação) **I'll ~ Mr. Smith** eu secundo o Senhor Smith; **2** (MIL, COMM) destacar; IDIOM **he is ~ to none** ele não tem igual; ninguém lhe chega aos pés (coll); **on ~ thoughts**

pensando melhor; **to have ~ thoughts** mudar de ideias.
secondary *adj* secundário; **~ school** *n* escola secundária.
seconder *n* segundo apoiante.
second hand *n* (*on clock*) ponteiro de segundos; ♦ **secondhand** *adj* de/em segunda mão, usado,-a.
secondly *adv* em segundo lugar.
secondment *n* substituição *f*, transferência *f* temporária.
second-rate *adj* de segunda categoria; medíocre *m,f*.
secrecy *n* segredo *m*, sigilo *m*; discrição *f*.
secret *n adj* secreto,-a.
secretarial *adj* de secretário,-a, secretarial.
secretariat *n* secretaria, secretariado.
secretary *n* secretário,-a; **S~ of State** (*POL*) Ministro de Estado.
secretive *adj* sigiloso, reservado; (*BIO*) secretor.
sect *n* seita *f*.
sectarian *adj* sectário,-a.
section *n* se(c)ção *f*; parte *f*, porção *f*; **2** (*of document*) parágrafo, artigo; **3** (*of opinion*) se(c)tor *m*.
sectional *adj* (*drawing*) transversal, se(c)cional.
sector *n* se(c)tor *m*.
secular *adj* (*temporal*) secular; **2** (*layperson*) laico,-a; **3** (*ASTRON*) secular.
secure *adj* seguro,-a; firme, rígido,-a; ♦ *vt* assegurar, garantir, conseguir, obter.
security *n* segurança *f*; **~ camera** *n* câmara *f* de vigilância; **2** (*job, etc*) estabilidade *f*; **3** (*for loan*) fiança, garantia; (*object-pawn*) penhor *m*; **~s** *npl* (*FIN*) títulos *npl* de crédito, obrigações *fpl*; **~ deposit** caução *f*; (*on property*) sinal *m*; **~ officer** *n* responsável de segurança, guarda *m*.
Security Council *n* Conselho *m* de Segurança.
sedan *n* (*US*) sedã *m*, limusina *f*.
sedate *adj* (*lifestyle*) sossegado,-a, tranquilo,-a, estar sob o efeito de calmantes; ♦ *vt* sedar, tratar com calmantes.
sedation *n* (*MED*) sedação *f*.
sedative *n* calmante *m*, sedativo *m*.
sedentary *adj* sedentário,-a.
sediment *n* sedimento *m*.
seduce *vt* seduzir.
seduction *n* sedução *f*.
seductive *adj* sedutor,-ora.
see *n* sé *f*, catedral *f*; diocese *f*; sede *f* episcopal; **the Holy S~** a Santa Sé; ♦ (*pt* **saw**, *pp* **seen**) *vt* (*gen*) ver; **2** (*perceive*) compreender, entender; **yes, I ~** sim, compreendo; **3** (*look at*) olhar (para); **4 to ~ the doctor** consultar o médico; **5 to ~ sb to the door** acompanhar, levar alguém até a porta; **6** (*make sure*) assegurar que; **~ that he does it** veja lá se ele o faz; **7** (*tourism*) **to ~ the sights** fazer turismo; **8** (*encompass*) **as far as the eye could ~** a perder de vista; **9** (*manage*) **to ~ one's way to doing sth** arranjar meios de fazer algo; **10** (*find out*) ver; ♦ *vi* (*sight*) **I don't ~ very well** não vejo muito bem; **I'll go and ~** vou ver; **to ~ about sth** tratar de, encarregar-se de; **2** (*organize*) **I'll ~ about getting you an introduction** vou dar um jeito para arranjar-te uma apresentação; **3 to ~ about doing sth** pensar em fazer algo; **to ~ sb**

off despedir-se de (alguém); **to~ sth through** levar algo até ao fim; ♦ *vt* compreender muito bem; **2** (*help*) **to ~ sb through a difficulty** ajudar alguém em momento difícil; **to ~ to** *vt* providenciar, cuidar de.
seed *n* semente *f*; grão *m*; **2** (*in fruit*) caroço *m* (*cherry, etc*); pevide *f* (*melon, pear, grape*); **3** (*fig*) (*sperm*) sémen (*BR*: sê-) *m*, esperma *f*; **4** (*fig*) germe *m*; **5** (*tennis*) pré-sele(c)cionado.
seedbed, seeding *n* sementeira.
seedling *n* planta brotada da semente, broto *m*; muda *f*.
seedy (**-ier, -iest**) *adj* (*shabby*) gasto, surrado; **2** (*person*) maltrapilho,-a; **3** (*place, hotel*) duvidoso,-a, de mau aspe(c)to.
seeing *conj*: **~ as/that** já que, como, visto (que), considerando (que).
seek (*pt, pp* **sought**) *vt* procurar, buscar; (*request*) solicitar, pedir; **~ out** descobrir, localizar.
seem *vi* parecer.
seemingly *adv* aparentemente, pelo que aparenta.
seemly (**-ier, -iest**) *adj* decoroso,-a, próprio,-a, decente.
seen (*pp of* **see**).
seep *vi* escorrer; **to ~ through** (água, gás) infiltrar-se, penetrar, passar através de.
seepage *n* (*trickle*) gotejamento *m*; **2** (*leak*) fuga *f*; **3** (*drainage into soil*) infiltração *f*.
seer *n* (*person who sees the future*) vidente *m,f*.
seesaw *n* (*plank on which children sit at each end*) balancé; vaivém *m* (*EP*); gangorra *f* (*BR*); **2** (*price*) oscilação *f*.
seethe *n* ebulição, agitação *f*; ♦ *vi* ferver; fervilhar; **the crowd was seething** a chusma fervilhava; **the square was ~ with people** a praça transbordava de gente; **to ~ with anger** estar fulo de raiva; (*BR*) ficar uma arara.
see-through *adj* (*dress, etc*) transparente.
segment *n* segmento *m*; **~ of circle** segmento de círculo; **~ of sphere** calote *f* esférica; **~ wheel** roda *f* de segmentos dentados; **2** (*of an orange*) gomo *m*; **3** (*of economy*) se(c)tor; **4** (*of population*) parte *f*; ♦ *vt* segmentar.
segregate *vt* segregar.
segregation *n* segregação *f*.
seismic *adj* sísmico,-a.
seize *vt* agarrar, pegar; apoderar-se de, confiscar; tomar posse de; **2** (*opportunity*) aproveitar, agarrar; (*JUR*) apreender (*arms, goods, property*) prender (*person*); **to ~ (up) on** *vt* valer-se de; **to ~ up** *vi* (*TECH*) gripar, emperrar.
seizure *n* (*MED*) ataque *m*, acesso; **2** (*JUR*) confisco, embargo; apreensão.
seldom *adv* raramente; **I ~ go anywhere** eu raramente saio/vou a algum lado.
select *adj* sele(c)to, escolhido; **~ committee** *n* comissão *f* parlamentar; ♦ *vt* escolher, (*SPORT*) sele(c)cionar.
selection *n* sele(c)ção *f*; escolha; (*COMM*) sortimento.
selective *adj* sele(c)tivo,-a.
selector *n* (*SPORT*) sele(c)cionador,-ora, sele(c)tor,-ora.

self *(Vd: see* **myself, yourself, himself, herself, itself, oneself, ourselves, themselves).**

self¹ *(pl:* **selves)** *n:* **the** ~ o eu; *(emphatic)* eu próprio,-a; **he is his old** ~ ele volta a ser ele mesmo.

self² *pref* auto; **~-addressed stamped envelope (s.a.e.)** *n* envelope com selo endereçado a si mesmo; **~-appointed** *adj* autodesignado,-a; **~-assertive** *adj* seguro,-a de si; **~-assured** cheio,-a de confiança; **~-centred** *adj* egocêntrico; **~-confessed** *adj* assumido,-a; confesso,-a; **~-confidence** *n* auto-confiança; **~-conscious** *adj* inibido, constrangido; **~-contained** *adj (gen)* independente; completo, autónomo *(BR:* -tô-); **~-control** *n* autodomínio *m;* **~-criticism** *n* autocrítica *f;* **~-defence** *n* legítima defesa, autodefesa; **~-denial** *n* abnegação *f;* **~-drive** *adj (car, van)* de aluguer *m; (BR)* de aluguel *m;* **~-educated** *n* autodida(c)ta; **~-effacing** *adj* modesto,-a, humilde; **~-employed** (trabalhador) por conta própria; **~-evident** *adj* patente; **~-governing** *adj* autónomo *(BR:* -tô-); independente; **~-important** *adj* presunçoso; arrogante; **~-indulgent** *adj* que se permite excessos; comodista; **~-inflicted** *adj* infligido a si mesmo; **~-interest** *n* egoísmo; **~-ish** *adj* egoísta; **~-ishness** *n* egoísmo; **~-less** *n* altruísta; **~-lessly** *adv* desinteressadamente; **~-opiniated** *adj* presunçoso,-a; **~-pity** *n* pena de si mesmo, autocomiseração *f* **~-portrait** *n* auto-retrato; **~-possessed** *adj* calmo, senhor de si; **~-preservation** *n* auto-preservação *f;* **~-raising flour** *(UK)* **~-rising flour** *(US) n* farinha *f* com fermento **~-reliant** *adj* seguro de si, independente; **~-respect** *n* amor *m* próprio; **~-righteous** *adj* moralista, arrogante; **~-rule** *n* autonomia (de um governo); **~-same** *n* o/a mesmo,-a, mesmíssimo,-a; **~-sacrifice** *n* abnegação *f,* altruísmo *m;* **~-satisfied** *adj* satisfeito consigo mesmo; petulante **~-seeking** *adj (pej)* interesseiro,-a, egoísta *m,f;* **~-service** *adj* de auto-serviço; **~-starter** *n (AUT) n* arranque *m* automático; **2** *(person)* empreendedor,-ora; **~-styled** *adj (pej)* pretenso,-a, suposto,-a; **~-sufficient** *adj* auto-suficiente/autossuficiente; **~-tanning** *adj* autobronzeador,-ora; **~-taught** *adj* autodida(c)ta; **~-willed** *adj* obstinado,-a, tenaz.

sell *(pt, pp* **sold)** *vt* vender; **to** ~ **sth to sb** vender algo a alguém; **to** ~ **sth for £20** vender algo por vinte libras; **'cigarettes are sold here'** 'aqui vendem-se cigarros'; **2** *(promote) (due to name, reputation)* fazer vender; **to** ~ **o.s.** promover-se, vender-se; ~ **off** *vt* liquidar; ♦ *vi (shop, office)* **to** ~ **out of sth** estar esgotado; **we have sold out of meat** vendemos a carne toda; ♦ *vi* vender-se; trair uma causa; ♦ ~ **up** *vi* vender tudo; IDIOM **to** ~ **like hot cakes** vender como pãezinhos quentes.

sell-by-date *n* prazo *m* de validade.

seller *n* vendedor,-ora; **~'s market** *n* mercado *m* favorável ao vendedor.

selling *n* vendas; ~ **well** vendas de vento em proa.

sellotape® *n* fita *f* adesiva, (fita) durex; ♦ *vt* collar com fita adesiva.

sell-out *n (THEAT, match)* lotação *f* esgotada, sucesso *m* de bilheteria; **2** *(of principles)* traição *f.*

sell-through *n (US)* venda *f* dire(c)ta ao consumidor.

selves *(pl of* **self).**

semantic *adj* semântico,-a.

semaphore *n* semáforo *m.*

semblance *n* aparência *f.*

semen *n* sémen *(BR:* sê-) *m.*

semi *prefix* semi, meio; **~circle** *n* semicírculo; **~colon** *n* ponto e vírgula; **~-detached (house)** *n* (casa) geminada; **~-final** *n* meia final, *(BR)* semifinal *f.*

seminal *adj (important)* influente *m,f;* **2** *(of semen)* seminal.

seminar *n* seminário *m*

semiotics *n* semiótica *f.*

semi-skilled *adj (person)* semi-especializado,-a.

semi-skimmed *adj (milk, etc)* semidesnatado,-a.

Semite *n* semita *m,f.*

Semitic *adj* semita.

semolina *n* sêmola *f,* semolina *f.*

Senate *npr (POL):* **the** ~ o Senado *m.*

senator *n* senador,-ora.

send *(pt, pp* **sent)** *vt* mandar, enviar; expedir, remeter; **to** ~ **sb away** mandar alguém embora; **to** ~ **away for** *vt* encomendar; **2** mandar chamar ♦ **to** ~ **back** *vt* devolver; **to** ~ **for** *vt* mandar chamar, mandar buscar; **to** ~ **off** *vt (goods)* despachar, expedir, enviar pelo correio; **2** *(SPORT)* expulsar; ~ **off for** encomendar (pelo correio); ♦ **to** ~ **out** *vt (invitation)* distribuir; **2** *(signal)* emitir; **to** ~ **packing** *(coll)* mandar passear; **to** ~ **up** *vt (person)* fazer subir; **2** *(parody)* parodiar; imitar.

sender *n* remetente.

send-off *n* adeus *m;* **a good** ~ uma boa despedida.

send-up *n* sátira *f.*

Senegal *npr* Senegal; **in** ~ no Senegal.

Senegalese *n adj* senegalês, senegalesa.

senile *adj* senil.

senility *n* senilidade *f.*

senior *n* superior; senior *(BR:* -ê-); ♦ *adj (older)* mais velho/idoso; **2** *(staff)* mais antigo; **3** *(of higher rank)* superior; ~ **citizen** *n (ADMIN)* idoso,-a, pessoa de terceira idade; ~ **officer** *n (UK police)* agente *m,f* superior da polícia; *(ADMIN)* alto,-a funcionário,-a; ~ **partner** *n (COMM, law firm)* sócio,-a principal; ~ **school** *n* escola *f* secundária.

seniority *n* antiguidade *f;* **2** (em cargo) prioridade *f;* grau *m* de competência.

sensation *n* sensação *f.*

sensational *adj* sensacional.

sensationalism *n* sensacionalismo *m.*

sense *n* sentido *m;* **it makes no** ~ não faz sentido; **2** *(feeling)* sensação *f; (good* ~) bom senso; ♦ *vt* sentir, perceber, presintir.

senseless *adj* insensato,-a; *(unconscious)* sem sentidos, inconsciente.

sensibility *n* sensibilidade *f;* **sensibilities** *npl* susce(p)tibilidade *f,* sensibilidade *f.*

sensible *adj* sensato,-a de bom senso; **2** *(cautious)* cauteloso,-a, prudente; lógico,-a razoável; ponderado,-a.

sensibly *adv* sensatamente.
sensitive *adj (feelings, skin, eyes)* sensível *m,f; (person)*, impressionável; *(touchy)* susce(p)tível.
sensitivity *n* sensibilidade *f.*
sensor *n* dete(c)tor *m.*
sensory *adj (nerve, impression)* sensorial.
sensual *adj* sensual, voluptuoso,-a.
sensuality *n* sensualidade.
sensuous *adj* sensual.
sent *(pt, pp of* **send**).
sentence *n* frase *f;* **2** *(JUR)* sentença, decisão *f;* veredi(c)to; ♦ *vt:* **to ~ sb to death** condenar alguém à morte.
sentiment *n (feeling)* sentimento *m;* **2** *(opinion)* opinião *f.*
sentimental *adj* sentimental.
sentimentality *n* sentimentalismo *m; (pej)* pieguice *f.*
sentry *n* sentinela *f;* **~ box** *n* guarita *f.*
separate *n:* **separates** *npl (fashion)* duas peças de um fato usadas em conjunto ou separadamente; ♦ *adj* separado,-a; *(person, couple)* separado,-a; **2** *(distinct)* diferente; ♦ *vt* separar; dividir; ♦ *vi* separar-se.
separately *adv* separadamente.
separation *n* separação *f.*
separatist *n adj* separatista *m,f.*
separator *n (machine)* separador *m; (cream, milk)* desnatadeira.
sepia *n* sépia *f.*
September *n* Setembro, setembro *m.*
septic *adj* sé(p)tico,-a, infe(c)tado,-a; **to go/to turn ~** infe(c)tar-se.

septicaemia *(UK)* **septicemia** *(US) n* septicemia *f.*
sepulchre *n* sepulcro *m.*
sequel *n* consequência *f;* resultado *m;* **2** *(of story, film)* continuação *f.*
sequela *n (MED) (after-effect)* sequela *f.*
sequence *n* sequência *f,* ordem; **2** *(CIN)* cena *f;* **3** série **(of** de).
sequential *adj* sequencial.
sequestrate *(also:* **sequester**) *vt (JUR) (legal possession of assets until debt is paid)* confiscar, penhorar.
sequin *n* lantejoula *f,* lamella *f.*
seraph *(seraphim) n* serafim *m.*
Serb (= **Serbian**) *n adj* sérvio,-a; *(LING) n* sérvio *m.*
Serbia *npr* Sérvia; **in ~** na Sérvia.
Serbo-Croat, Serbo-Coatian *adj* servo-croata *m,f; (LING)* servo-croata *m.*
serenade *n* serenata *f;* ♦ *vt* fazer serenata a/para.
serendipity *n (occurrence by chance)* serendipidade *f,* descoberta *f* por acaso; feliz acaso.
serene *adj* sereno,-a, tranquilo,-a.
serenity *n* serenidade *f,* tranquilidade *f.*
sergeant *n (MIL)* sargento *m;* **2** *(police)* tenente *m;* **3 ~ at arms** *(UK) (parliament) (dated)* bedel,

maceiro do rei/da rainha; **~ major** *n (MIL)* primeiro sargento.
serial *n* série *f;* seriado, história em folhetim; **~ killer** *n* assasino,-a em série; **~ number** *n* número *m* de série.
serialize, serialise *vt* seriar; publicar em folhetim.
series *n* série *f.*
serious *adj* sério; grave.
seriously *adv* a sério, com seriedade; gravemente.
seriousness *n* seriedade *f;* gravidade *f.*
sermon *n* sermão *m.*
serpent *n* serpente *f.*
serrated *adj* serrilhado,-a; dentado,-a.
serried *adj* cerrado,-a; compacto,-a.
serum *n* soro *m.*
servant *n* servidor,-ora; (= **house ~**) criado,-a, empregado,-a; **civil ~** funcionário,-a público,-a.
serve *n (tennis)* saque *m;* ♦ *vt* servir; *(goods)* vender, servir; **2** *(customer)* atender; **3** *(train)* passar por; *(treat)* tratar; *(apprenticeship)* fazer; **4** *(JUR)* **to ~ a sentence** cumprir uma sentença; ♦ **it ~s you right!** é bem feito!; ♦ *vi* sacar; **to ~ as/for/to do** servir como/para/para fazer; **to ~ out/up** *vt (food)* servir.
service *n* serviço *m;* **2** *(REL)* cerimónia *f* religiosa, culto *m;* **3** *(AUT)* manutenção *f;* **4** *(JUR)* notificação, intimação *f;* **~ area** *n (on motorway)* posto de gasolina com bar, restaurante etc; **~ industry** *n (COMM)* se(c)tor *m* terciário; **~man** *(pl:* **~men**) *n* militar *m;* **~ station** *n* posto de gasolina, estação *f* de serviço; ♦ *vt (car, washing machine)* fazer a manutenção de; **2** *(repair)* consertar; **3** *(FIN)* assegurar o serviço de *(loan);* **4** *(VET)* cobrir *(cow, mare);* IDIOM **to be of ~** ser útil; **at your ~** ao seu dispor.
serviceable *adj* aproveitável, prático,-a, durável.
services *npl:* **the S~** *(armed forces)* as Forças *fpl* Armadas; **2** *(sector)* se(c)tor terciário.
servicing *n* revisão, manutenção *f;* **the car has gone for ~** o carro foi para inspeção.
serviette *n* guardanapo *m.*
servile *adj* servile *m,f.*
serving *(CULIN) (helping)* porção *f.*
session *n* sessão *f;* **to be in ~** estar celebrando uma sessão, fazer uma sessão.
set *n* jogo, cole(c)ção *f;* grupo, bando *m;* **a ~ of bedlinen** um jogo de cama; **a ~ of books** uma cole(c)ção de livros; *(of utensils)* bateria de cozinha; *(of knife, spoon, fork)* talher *m; (complete cutlery set)* faqueiro *m; (dinner, tea)* serviço *m;* conjunto *m;* **a ~ of boxes** um conjunto de caixas; *(kit, game)* jogo; **a chess ~** um jogo de xadrez; **a ~ of drawing instruments** um estojo *m* de desenho; **2 TV ~** televisão *f,* aparelho *m* de televisão; **3** *(tennis)* partida; **4 political ~** círculo político; **5 the smart ~** o mundo *m* elegante; **6 ~ price** preço fixo; **7** *(CIN)* set *m;* **8** *(THEAT)* cenário; **9** *(hair)* penteado; ♦ *adj (fixed)* marcado, fixo; **2** *(ready)* pronto; *(resolved)* decidido, estabelecido; **~ phrase** frase *f* feita; ♦ *(pt, pp* **set**) *vt (place)* pôr, colocar; **to ~ the table** pôr a mesa; **2** *(fix, glue)* fixar; **the**

ciment/mortar **is** ~ a argamassa está sólida/solidficou-se; **3** *(time)* marcar; **4** *(repair)* ajustar, concertar; **5** *(rules)* estabelecer, decidir; ♦ *vi (sun)* pôr-se; *(jam, jelly, concrete)* endurecer, solidificar-se; **to be ~ on doing sth** estar decidido a fazer algo; **to ~ aside** pôr de lado; **to ~ free** libertar; **to ~ on fire** incendiar, pôr fogo a; **to ~ to music** musicar, pôr música em (letra); **to ~ sth going** pôr algo em movimento *(NAUT)* **to ~ sail** alçar velas, fazer-se ao mar, zarpar; ♦ **to ~ about** *vt (task)* começar a; **to ~ aside** *vt* pôr à parte, deixar de lado; **to ~ back** *vt (in time)* atrasar; **to ~ off** *vi* partir, ir indo; ♦ *vt (bomb)* fazer explodir; **2** *(show up well)* realçar; ressaltar; ♦ **to ~ out** *vi*: **to ~ out to do sth** começar/pôr-se a fazer algo; **2** *(JUR) (contracto)* elaborar, estabelecer *(rules terms)*; ♦ *vt (arrange)* colocar em ordem, arrumar, providenciar; **2** *(state)* expor, explicar; **to ~ up** *vt (organization, record)* estabelecer; **to ~ up shop** *(fig)* estabelecer-se.

setback *n* contrariedade *f*, percalço *m*, revés *m*, contratempo *m*; **2** *(FIN)* recuo *m*, revés *m*.

settee *n* sofá *m*; canapé *m*.

setting *n (frame)* moldura; **2** *(placing)* colocação *f*; **3** *(location)* local *m*, cenário *m*; **4** montagem *f*; **5** pôr(-do-sol) *m*; **6** *(of jewel)* engaste *m*; *(location)* cenário.

settle *vt (decide)* resolver; **2** *(accounts)* ajustar, pagar, liquidar; **3** *(agree on)* estabelecer *(terms)*; **4** *(land)* colonizar, povoar; **5** *(calm down, get better)* acalmar *(stomach)*; ♦ *vi (dust)* assentar(-se), depositar(-se); **2** *(bird, eyes)* pousar **(on** em); *(take up residence)* estabelecer-se, fixar-se; **3** *(person)* acalmar-se; ~ **back** *vi (in a chair)* recostar-se, reclinar-se; **to ~ down** *vi* establilizar-se, instalar-se; dedicar-se a fazer algo; **2** acalmar(-se), sossegar; **to ~ for sth** *vt* concordar em aceitar algo, conformar-se; **to ~ in** *vi (house)* instalar-se; *(job)* adaptar-se; **to ~ on** *vt* decidir-se por; escolher; **to ~ to** *vi (doing sth)* concentrar-se em/a fazer algo *(work)*; **to ~ up (with sb)** *(old grievance)* ajustar contas (com alguém).

settled *adj* instalado,-a; confortável *(in house, job)*; **2** estabilizado, acalmado; ♦ *exc* **that's ~ then!** está tudo combinado!

settlement *n (payment)* liquidação *f*; **2** *(agreement, conciliation) (JUR)* acordo *m*, avença *f*; **financial ~** acordo *m* financeiro; **2** *(village etc)* povoado, povoação *f*.

settler *n* colono,-a, colonizador,-ora.

set-up *n* sistema *m*, organização *f*; **2** *(coll)* situação premeditada; armadilha *f*.

seven *num* sete *m*.

seventeen *num* dezassete *(BR)* dezessete *m inv.*

seventeenth *n* décimo sete *m inv*; *(of the month)* sete *m*; *(fraction)* dezassete avos *m*.

seventh *n* sétimo,-a; **2** *(of month)* sete *m*; **3** *(fraction)* sétimo,-a; **4** *(MUS)* sétima *f*; ♦ *adj adv* sétimo,-a.

seventies *npl*: **the ~** os anos setenta; **she is in her ~** ela está na casa dos setenta.

seventieth *adj* septuagésimo,-a.

seventy *num* setenta *m inv.*

seven-year itch *n* crise *f* conjugal (depois dos sete anos de casados).

sever *vt* cortar, separar; **2** *(relations)* romper.

several *adj pron* vários,-as *m,f pl*, diversos,-as *m,f pl*; ~ **of us** muitos, vários de nós.

severance *n* rompimento; ~ **pay** *n* inde(m)nização *f* pela demissão.

severe *adj* severo; **2** *(serious)* austero, grave *(countenance)*; **3** *(hard)* duro,-a; **4** *(pain)* intenso.

severity *n* severidade *f*; austeridade *f*; intensidade *f*.

sew *(pt* sewed, *pp* sewn*) vt* coser, costurar; **to ~ up (sth)** *vt* coser, cerzir (algo); **2** *(coll) (settle)* concluir *(business)*; **it's all sewn up!** está no papo! *(fam)*.

sewage *n (effluence)* detritos *mpl*; águas *fpl* residuais; esgotos *mpl*; **2** ~ **farm** *n* estação *f* de tratamento de águas residuais (ETAR).

sewer *n* (cano do) esgoto *m*.

sewerage *n* rede *f* de esgotos.

sewing *n (activity)* costura *f*; ~ **machine** *n* máquina de costura.

sewn *(pp of* sew*)*; **hand-~** *adj* cosido à mão.

sex *n* sexo *m*; **to have ~ with sb** fazer sexo com alguém; **the opposite ~** o sexo oposto; ~ **appeal** *n* atra(c)ção sexual; ~ **discrimination** discriminação *f* sexual; ~ **maniac** *n* maníaco,-a sexual; ~ **offender** *n* criminoso,-a, delinquente sexual; ~ **shop** *n* loja de artigos eróticos; ♦ **to ~ up** *vi* tornar (algo, alguém) mais excitante, mais aliciante.

sexagenarian *n adj* sexagenário,-a.

sexism *m* sexismo *m*.

sexist *adj* sexista *m,f*.

sextet *n* sexteto.

sexton *n* sacristão *m*.

sextuplet *n* sêxtuplo *m*.

sexual *adj* sexual; ~ **abuse** *n* violência *f*, abuso *m* sexual; ~ **appeal** *n* atra(c)ção *f* sexual; ~ **harassment** *n* assédio *m* sexual; ~ **intercourse** *n* relações *fpl* sexuais.

sexuality *n* sexualidade *f*.

sexually *adv* sexualmente; ~ **transmitted disease, STD** *n* doença *f* transmitida sexualmente, DTS.

sexy *(-ier, -iest) adj* sexy; atraente, sensual.

shabby *adj* esfarrapado, maltrapilho; **2** *(clothes)* usado,-a, surrado,-a; coçado,-a; **3** *(edifício, rua)* em mau estado, negligenciado,-a; **4** *(treatment)* mesquinho,-a, injusto,-a.

shack *n* choupana *f*, casebre *m*; ♦ **to ~ up** *(slang)* coabitar, amancebar-se **(with** com).

shackles *npl* algemas *fpl*; grilhões *mpl*.

shade *n* sombra *f*; **to be in the ~** estar à sombra; **2** *(for lamp)* quebra-luz *m*, abajur *m*; **3** *(for eyes)* viseira *f*; **4** *(of colour)* tom *m*, tonalidade *f*, matiz *m*; **5** *(nuance)* tom; **6** *(window) (US)* estore *m*; **beach ~** toldo; **7** *(small amount/degree)* pouco; **a ~ too insolent** um pouco insolente de mais; ♦ *vt* sombrear; dar sombra a.

shadow *n* sombra; *(under the eyes)* olheiras *fp*; **without a ~ of a doubt**; sem sombra de dúvida; **2** *(person who follows another)* sombra *f*; dete(c)tive *m,f*; **shadows** *npl (darkness)* **the ~s** trevas *fpl*; **cast**

a ~ **on** projectar uma sombra sobre; **S~ Cabinet** *npr* (*UK: POL*) gabinete *m* paralelo formado pelo partido da oposição; gabinete-sombra **S~ Education Minister** Ministro da Educação da Oposição; ◆ **to** ~ **sb** (*follow*) seguir de perto (sem ser visto); (*fig*) perseguir.

shadowy *adj* escuro; **2** (*dim*) vago,-a, indistinto,-a.

shady *adj* (*place*) sombreado,-a, sombrio,-a; **2** (*fig*) (*dubious*) suspeito,-a, duvidoso,-a.

shaft *n* (*of arrow*) haste *f*; (*of sword*) punho *m*; **2** (*of column*) fuste *m*; **3** (*rod, handle*) cabo *m*; (*on a cart*) varal *m*, raio *m*; **4** (*AUT, TECH*) eixo *m*, manivela *f*; **5** (*of mine/lift*) poço *m*; **6** (*of light*) raio *m*; **7** (*of sarcasm*) piada *f* sarcástica.

shag *n* tabaco *m* desfiado; **2** (*matted tangle*) emaranhamento de pelos, cabelos; **3** tecido *m* felpudo; **4** (*slang*) queca *f* (*cal*); ◆ (**-gg-**) *vt* ter relações sexuais com alguém; (*slang*) dar uma queca com alguém (*cal*).

shaggy *adj* (*animal*) peludo,-a; **2** (*carpet, material*) felpudo,-a, de pelo *m* comprido; **3** (*person's hair, beard*) hirsuto,-a, desgrenhado,-a.

shake *n* (*jerk*) sacudidela *f*; sacudida *f*; (*violent*) safanão *m*; ◆ (*pt* **shook**, *pp* **shaken**) *vt* sacudir (*person, dust, cloth etc*); (*building*) fazer tremer; **2** abanar (*tree, tooth*); **3** agitar (*bottle, liquid*); **4** (*emotionnally*) perturbar, inquietar; **5** (*weaken*) enfraquecer; ◆ *vi* estremecer, tremer; **to** ~ **hands** apertar a mão; **to** ~ **one's head** (*negative or in disapproval*) abanar a cabeça; **to** ~ **off** *vt* sacudir; (*fig*) livrar-se de; **to** ~ **up** *vt* (*COMM*) reorganizar radicalmente.

shaky *adj* (*writing*) trémulo (*BR*: trê-); (*chair etc*) inseguro,-a; **2** (*reply*) vacilante *m,f*; **3** (*evidence*) pouco sólida.

shall *aux* (*future*) **I** ~ **go** irei.

shallot *n* cebolinha *f*, chalota *f*.

shallow *adj* raso; baixo; **2** pouco profundo,-a; (*fig*) (*pej*) superficial *m,f*, leviano,-a.

shallows *npl* baixio *m*.

sham *n* fraude *f*; fingimento; ◆ *adj* falso, simulado, fingido; ◆ *vt* fingir, simular.

shamble *vi* caminhar tropegamente; bambolear-se.

shambles *n* (*mess*) confusão *fsg*, desordem *fsg*; **the house is in** ~ a casa está em desordem, de pernas para o ar.

shame *n* vergonha *f*; pena *f*; **it is a** ~ **you can't come** é uma pena que não possas vir; **what a** ~! que pena!; ◆ *vt* envergonhar.

shamefaced *adj* envergonhado,-a.

shameful *adj* indecente, escandaloso,-a; vergonhoso,-a.

shameless *adj* sem vergonha, descarado; desavergonhado.

shampoo *n* xampu *m*, champô *m*; ◆ *vt* lavar o cabelo.

shamrock *n* trevo *m* de três folhas; (*símbolo nacional da Irlanda*).

shandy *n* mistura *f* de cerveja com gasosa.

Shanghai *npr* Shangai; **to** ~ *vt* raptar homem para trabalhar em barcos.

shank *n* (*ANAT, ZOOL*) perna *f*, canela *f*; **2** (*of golf-club*) haste *f*, cabo *m*; **3** (*of button*) pé *m*; ~ **bone** tíbia *f*.

shan't = **shall not**.

shanty town *n* bairro *m* de lata; (*in Brazil*) favela *f*.

shape *n* forma *f*; **in the** ~ **of** (*guise*) na forma de; **in any** ~ de maneira nenhuma; **2** feitio *m*, molde *m*; **3** (*figure*) silhueta *f*; **to be in good/bad** ~ estar em boa/má forma; ◆ *vt* formar, modelar; moldar; **2** (*life*) determinar; ◆ *vi* (= **to** ~ **up**) (*events*) desenrolar-se; **2** (*person*) amadurecer, tomar jeito; **to take** ~ tomar forma.

shaped (*dress*) cintado,-a; **2** (*in combinations*): **heart-~** em forma de coração; **well-~** (*body*) bem feito,-a.

shapeless *adj* informe, sem forma definida.

shapely *adj* bem proporcionado,-a, talhado,-a, escultural.

share *n* parte *f*, porção *f*; **2** (*contribution*) quota; **3** (*COMM*) ação *f*; ~**holder** *n* acionista *m,f*; ◆ *vt* dividir; **2** (*have in common*) compartilhar; **to** ~ **out** (**among/between**) distribuir (entre).

shark *n* (*ZOOL*) tubarão *m*; **2** (*fig*) (*dishonest person*) burlão *m*; intrujão,-jona.

sharp *n* (*MUS*) sustenido *m*; ◆ *adj* cortante *m,f*; (*razor, knife*) afiado,-a; **2** (*pointed*) pontiagudo,-a; fino,-a; **3** (*features*) anguloso,-a; **4** (*sudden change, movement*) brusco,-a, brutal; **5** (*drop, increase*) acentuado,-a forte; **6** (*pain, som*) agudo,-a; **7** (*cold, wind*) cortante; **8** (*fig*) (*tongue*) afiada,-a; **9** (*tone*) áspero,-a, seco,-a; **10** (*eyesight*) penetrante; **11** (*hearing, taste*) apurado,-a; (*bitter taste*) acre; **12** (*person, mind: quick-witted*) astuto,-a, perspicaz; **13** (*contrast*) marcado,-a; (*outline*) definido,-a, nítido,-a; **14** (*clever*) esperto,-a; (*pej*) manhoso,-a; ◆ *adv*: **at 5 o'clock** ~ às 5 (horas) em ponto; **2** (*quickly, suddenly*) de repente.

sharpen *vt* afiar, amolar (*knife, etc*); **2** (*pencil*) apontar, fazer a ponta de; (*fig*) aguçar; **3** (*appetite, interest*) aumentar.

sharpener *n* (= **pencil** ~) apara-lápis *m*, (*BR*) apontador *m*; **2** (*for knife*) amolador *m*.

sharply *adv* (*abruptly*) bruscamente; (*harshly*) asperamente; severamente; (*defined*) nitidamente; (*aware*) vivamente.

sharpness *n* (*of blade etc*) fio *m*; **2** (*of road bend*) ângulo *m* apertado; **3** (*of mind, sound*) agudeza *f*; **4** (*of pain*) intensidade *f*; **5** (*of tone, criticism*) aspereza *f*; **6** (*of outline*) nitidez *f*; **7** (*of taste*) acridez *f*; **8** ~ **of tuning** (*radio, etc*) exatidão *f* de sintonização.

sharpshooter *n* atirador,-ora de primeira.

sharp-tongued *adj* de língua *f* afiada.

sharp-witted *adj* perspicaz, espirituoso,-a.

shatter *vt* despedaçar; **2** (*ruin*) destruir, acabar (*hope*); **3** arrasar (*nerves*); **4** (*glass*) quebrar; **5** (*window*) estilhaçar; **6** (*peace, silence*) romper; ◆ *vi* despedaçar-se; esmigalhar-se.

shattered *pp, adj* (*heart, objects*) despedaçado,-a, feito,-a em bocados; destruído,-a; ~ **hopes** esperanças *fpl* destruídas; **2** (*health*) abalado,-a; **3** (*nerves*) escangalhados; **I feel** ~ (*from working*) estou morto,-a de cansaço.

shattering *adj* esmagador,-ora; angustiante.

shave *n*: *vt* barbear, fazer a barba; ◆ *vi* barbear-se; ◆ **to have a** ~ barbear-se.

shaver *n* aparelho, máquina de barbear, barbeador *m*; **electric** ~ máquina de barbear elétrica, *(BR)* barbeador *m* elétrico.

shaving *n*: ~ **brush** *n* pincel *m* de barba; ~**s** *npl (of wood etc)* aparas *fpl*.

shawl *n* xaile *m*, *(BR)* xale *m*.

she *pron* ela; ~ **is lovely** ela é linda; ~ **herself admitted it** ela mesmo admitiu isso.

sheaf *(pl:* **sheaves***) n (of corn)* molho; *(of arrows)* feixe *m*; *(of paper)* maço.

shear *(pt* **sheared***, pp* **sheared** *or* **shorn***) vt (sheep)* aparar; tosquiar; **2** *(grass, hair)* cortar; **to** ~ **off** *vt* cercear.

shears *npl (for hedge)* tesoura *sg* de podar; *(sheep)* máquina *f* de tosquiar.

sheath *n (for sword)* bainha *f*; **2** (condom) camisa-de-vénus *f*, *(BR)* camisinha *f*.

sheathe *pp adj* **sheathed in** revestido,-a de, envolto,-a *(silk, etc)*; ♦ *vt (dagger, etc)* embainhar; **2** revestir *(cable, pipe)*.

sheaves *(pl of* **sheaf***)*.

shed *n* alpendre *m*; ♦ *(pt, pp* **shed***) vt* desprender-se de; **2** *(skin)* mudar; **3** *(tears, blood)* derramar; **to** ~ **a few kilos** perder alguns quilos, emagrecer; **to** ~ **light on sth** esclarecer algo, elucidar.

she'd = **she had; she would**.

sheep *n pl inv (ZOOL)* carneiro *m*, ovelha; **black** ~ ovelha *f* ronhosa, ovelha negra; ~ **dog** *n* cão *m* pastor; ~**skin** *n* pele *f* de carneiro; IDIOM **to cast** ~**s eyes at sb** lançar olhos amorosos a alguém.

sheepish *adj* tímido, acanhado.

sheer *adj* puro, completo; **2** *(steep)* íngreme, empinado,-a; **3** *(clear)* fino,-a, límpido,-a; *(stockings, dress)* transparente; **in** ~ **desesperation** totalmente desesperado,-a; **by** ~ **accident** por mero acaso; ♦ *adv (rise, fall)* a pique.

sheet *n (for bed)* lençol *m (pl:* lençóis*)*; **2** *(of paper)* folha; **3** *(of glass, metal)* lâmina *f*, chapa *f*.

sheik(h) *n* xeque *m*.

shelf *(pl:* **shelves***) n* estante *f*, prateleira; IDIOM **she's been left on the** ~ ela ficou para tia.

shell *n (on beach)* concha *f*; **2** *(of egg, nut etc)* casca *f*; **3** *(MIL)* granada; *(cartridge)* cartucho *m*; *(pyrotechnic)* invólucro *m* pirotécnico; **4** *(of building)* armação *f*, esqueleto *m*; ♦ *vt (peas)* descascar; **2** *(MIL)* bombardear.

she'll = **she will; she shall**.

shellfish *n pl inv* crustáceo *m*, molusco *m*; *(pl: as food)* marisco *m*.

Shelter *npr* organização *f* caritativa que dá abrigo e comida a desalojados = centro *m* de acolhimento.

shelter *n* abrigo *m*, refúgio *m*; ♦ *vt (give support)* amparar; proteger; abrigar; *(hide)* esconder; ♦ *vi* abrigar-se, refugiar-se.

sheltered *adj* protegido,-a; abrigado,-a.

shelve *vt (fig)* pôr de lado, engavetar.

shelves *(pl of* **shelf***)*.

shepherd *n* pastor *m*; ♦ *vt* guiar, conduzir; ~**ess** *n* pastora *f*; ~**'s pie** *n* empadão *m* de carne e batata.

sheriff *n (US)* chefe da polícia, xerife *m*; **2** *(JUR)* oficial de justiça.

sherry *n* (vinho de) Xerez *m*.

she's = **she is; she has**.

Shia *n adj (REL)* xiita *m,f*.

shield *n (armour)* escudo *m*; **2** *(herald)* brasão *m* de armas; **3** prote(c)ção *f* (**against** contra); **4** *(sports trophy – in the style of shield)* troféu *m*; **5** *(TECH)* placa *f* de prote(c)ção; **6** *(US) (policeman's badge)* insígnia *f*; ♦ *vt:* **to** ~ **from** proteger contra.

shield fern *(BOT)* aspídio *m*.

shield grid *(ELECT)* grade *f* de blindagem.

shift *n* mudança *f*; transferência *f*; **2** *(of workers)* turno; ♦ *vt* transferir; *(remove)* tirar; ♦ *vi* mudar; mudar de lugar; ~ **work** *n* trabalho por turnos.

shifty (-ier, -iest) *adj* trapaceiro,-a, matreiro,-a; velhaco,-a.

Shiite *n adj (muslim sect)* xiita *m,f*.

shilling *n (UK: pre-decimalisation coin)* xelim *m*.

shilly-shally *(pp, pt* -**ied***) vi* vacilar, titubear.

shimmer *n* reflexo *m* trémulo; **2** *(peals)* cintilação *f*; luz difusa; **3** *(silk)* brilho *m*; ♦ *vi* cintilar, tremeluzir.

shimmering *adj* que brilha; cintilante; tremeluzente.

shin *n (ANAT)* canela (da perna); ~**bone** *n* tíbia *f*.

shindig (shindy) *n* barulheira *f*; *(many loud voices)* algazarra *f*; **2** *(coll) (rowdy party)* festa *f* (ruidosa).

shine *n (gen)* brilho *m*; **2** lustro *m*; **to give a** ~ **to** *(table, floor, etc)* dar lustro a, polir; **to take a** ~ **to sb** simpatizar com alguém à primeira vista; ♦ *(pt, pp* **shone***) vi* brilhar, reluzir; **2** luzir; **3** *(fig) (radiant face)* resplandecer; ♦ *vt (shoes)* engraxar; **2 to** ~ **a torch on** apontar uma lanterna para; **3** *(to excel in sth)* brilhar em algo; IDIOM **come rain come** ~ quer chova quer faça sol.

shingle *n* pedrinhas *fpl*, seixo *m*, cascalho *m*; **2** ripas *fpl*, tabuinhas *fpl* (para o telhado, paredes); **3** ~**s** *n (MED)* zona *f* herpes-zoster *mpl*.

shining *adj* brilhante *m,f*; luminoso,-a; notável.

shiny *adj* brilhante, lustroso,-a.

ship *n* navio, barco; ♦ *vt (goods)* embarcar; **2** *(oars)* desarmar, guardar; **3** *(send)* transportar, mandar (por via marítima); ~**building** *n* construção *f* naval.

shipment *n (act)* embarque *m*; **2** *(goods)* carregamento.

ship owner *n* armador.

shipper *n* exportador,-ora.

shipping *n (act)* embarque *m*; **2** *(traffic)* transporte *m*; *(ships)* navegação *f*.

shipping forecast *n* previsão *f* das condições marítimas.

shipping lane *n* rota marítima.

shipshape *adj* em ordem.

shipwreck *n* naufrágio *m*.

shipyard *n* estaleiro *m*.

shire *n* condado (= **Gloucester**~, etc.); **the Shires** *npr pl* os condados centrais da Inglaterra.

shire horse *n (English horse)* cavalo *m* de tiro.

shirk *vt* eludir, esquivar-se; **2** *(obligations)* não cumprir, faltar a.

shirker *n* vadio,-a; mandrião,-riona.

shirt *n* camisa *f*; **in** ~ **sleeves** em mangas *fpl* de camisa; ~ **tail** *n* fralda *f* (da camisa); **2** *(coll) (US) (newspaper)* comentário *m* por baixo de um artigo.

shit *n* *(slang)* *(excrement)* merda *f (cal)*; caca *f*, bosta *f (cal)*; **2** *exc* **shit!** merda! *(BR: also)* droga!; ◆ *(pt, pp* **shit** *or* **shitted)** *vt (slang)* cagar *(cal).*

shiver *n* tremor *m*, arrepio *m*; calafrio *m*; ~**s** *npl* arrepios *mpl*; **she gives me the ~** ela causa-me arrepios; ◆ *vi (with cold, fear)* tremer; **2** *(with emotion)* estremecer; **3** *(with cold)* tiritar.

shivery *adj (feverish)* febril.

shoal *n (GEOG)* banco *m* de areia; *(shallows)* baixio *m*; **2** *(of fish)* cardume *m*.

shock *n* choque *m*; **2** *(impact, collision)* choque; **3** *(ELECT)* descarga *f*; choque *m*; **4** *(of earthquake)* abalo *m*; **5** *(of corn)* meda *f*; *(fig) (of hair)* gudelha *f*; **6** *(MED)* trauma *m*; ◆ *vt* chocar; escandalizar; horrorizar; ~ **absorber** *n* amortecedor *m*; ~**proof** *adj* à prova de choque; ~ **treatment** *n* tratamento *m* por electrochoques.

shocked *adj* chocado,-a; ofendido,-a.

shocking *adj (appalling)* chocante; **2** escandaloso,-a; ~ **red** *adj* encarnado *m* berrante; ~ **weather** *adj* tempo péssimo, horrível.

shod *pt, pp of* **shoe**; ◆ *adj (horse)* ferrado.

shoddy (-ier, -iest) *adj (material)* de qualidade *f* inferior; **2** *(product)* refugo *m*; *(work)* malfeito.

shoe *n* sapato *m*; **2** *(for horse)* ferradura *f*; **3** *(AUT)* (= **brake** ~) sapata *f*; **flat** ~**s** sapatos de salto raso, baixo; **to step into sb's** ~**s** ocupar o lugar de alguém; ~**brush** *n* escova *f* de sapato; ~**horn** *n* calçadeira *f*; ~ **industry** *n* indústria *f* de calçado; ~**lace** *n* atacador *m*; *(BR)* cadaço *m*; cordão *m* (de sapato); ~**maker** *n* sapateiro *m*; ~ **polish** *n* graxa *f*; ~ **shop** *n* sapataria *f*; ◆ *(pt, pp* **shod)** *vt* calçar; **2** *(horse)* ferrar.

shoestring budget *n* orçamento *m* de miséria; **artists on a ~ tour** *npl* artistas numa turné de pé descalço.

shone *(pt, pp of* **shine).**

shoo *exc (onomat) (to animals)* xó!; ◆ *vt (also: ~* **away)** enxotar; **to ~ the chickens away** enxotar as galinhas.

shook *(pt of* **shake).**

shoot *n (new plant)* rebento *m*; *(BR)* broto *m*; **2** *(trough)* conduta *f*; ◆ *(pt, pp* **shot)** *vt* disparar (contra alguém); *(kill)* matar (com um tiro); **2** *(execute)* fuzilar; **3** *(film)* filmar, rodar; ◆ *vi:* **to ~ (at)** atirar (em); *(football)* dar um pontapé em bola, *(BR)* chutar; **to ~ down** *vt (plane)* derrubar, abater; **to ~ in/out** *vi* entrar/sair como um raio; **to ~ up** *vi* subir vertiginosamente.

shooting *n (shots)* tiros *mpl* tiroteio *m*; *(hunting)* caçada *f* (com espingarda); ~ **star** *n* estrela *f* cadente.

shop *n (COMM)* loja *f*, estabelecimento *m*; **2** *(MEC) (workshop)* oficina; **3** **one-stop ~** *(advice, help)* Loja *f* do Cidadão; ~ **assistant** *n* vendedor,-ora, empregado,-a; ~ **floor** *n (workers and machines)* local de trabalho; ~**keeper** *n* comerciante *m,f*; ~**lifter** *n* ladrão,-ra, larápio,-a de loja; ~**lifting** *n* furto (em lojas); ~**per** *n* comprador,-a; ~**-soiled** *adj* manchado,-a, manuseado,-a; ~ **steward** *n* representante *m,f* sindical; ~ **window** *n* montra *f*; ◆ *vi* (= **to go** ~**ping)** ir fazer compras; ~ **around**

comparar preços; **to set up** ~ *(fig)* estabelecer-se; **to shut up** ~ fechar a loja; *(fig)* desistir do negócio, fechar permanentemente.

shopping *n (goods)* compras *fpl*; ~ **bag/basket** *n* saco *m*, cesta *f* das compras; ~ **trolley/cart** *n* carrinho *m* das compras; ~ **centre/mall** *(US)* **plaza** *n* centro comercial *m*.

shore *n* costa, praia *f*; margem *f*; ◆ *vt:* **to ~ (up)** reforçar, escorar.

shorn[1] *(pp of* **shear).**

shorn[2] *pp adj (fig)* despojado,-a **(of** de).

short *n* (= ~ **film)** de curta-metragem *f* **(a pair of)** ~**s** calções *mpl*, *(BR)* (um) short *m*; ◆ *adj* curto,-a; **2** *(in time)* breve, de curta duração; **3** *(height)* baixo; **4** *(curt)* seco, brusco; insuficiente, em falta; ~**-sighted** *adj* míope; *(fig)* imprevidente; ~ **story** *n* conto *m*; ~**-tempered** *adj* irritadiço, de mau génio; ~**-term** *adj (effect)* a curto prazo; ~**ton** *(US)* 907 kg; ~**wave** *n (RADIO)* onda curta; ◆ *vi (ELECT)* dar um curto-circuito; ◆ **to be ~ of sth** ter falta de algo; **in ~** em resumo; em suma; **it is ~ for** é a abreviação de; **to cut ~** encurtar, interromper; **to fall ~** ser deficiente; **to stop ~** parar de repente; **to stop ~ of** chegar à beira de.

shortage *n* escassez *f*, falta.

short-circuit *n* curto-circuito *m*; ◆ *vt* provocar um curto-circuito.

shortcoming *n* defeito *m*, imperfeição *f*, falha.

short(crust) pastry *n* massa *f* amanteigada.

shortcut *n* atalho *m*.

shorten *vt* encurtar, reduzir; **2** *(visit)* abreviar, interromper.

shorthand *n* taquigrafia; ~ **typist** *n* estenoda(c)tilógrafa.

shortlist *n* lista dos candidatos escolhidos.

shortlisted *adj* finalista.

short-lived *adj* efêmero,-a, fugaz.

shortly *adv* em breve, dentro em pouco.

shortness *n (of distance)* curteza *f*; **2** *(of time)* brevidade *f*; **3** *(manner)* maneira *f* brusca.

shot *(pt, pp of* **shoot)** *n (from gun)* tiro *m*, disparo *m*; **I heard some** ~**s** ouvi uns tiros; **he went out like a ~** ele partiu como um raio; **to take a ~ at sb/sth** dar um tiro em alguém/algo; *(marksperson)* atirador,-ora; **he is a good ~** ele é um bom atirador; **2** *(in golf, cricket, tennis)* lance *m*; **good ~!** *(SPORT)* boa jogada!; *(in football)* chuto *m*; **3** *(attempt) (fam)* tentativa *f*; **4** *(injection)* inje(c)ção *f*; **to give sb a ~** dar uma inje(c)ção a alguém; **5** *(PHOT)* fotografia *f*; *(CIN)* tomada *f*; **6** *(dose) (coll)* **a ~ of whisky** uma dose *f* de whisky; IDIOM **to give one's best ~** dar o seu melhor; **to call the ~s** ditar a lei; **he always call the ~s** ele é que manda; **it's a ~ in the dark** é uma tentativa; **it was ~ in the dark** foi um acaso, uma tentativa.

shotgun *n* espingarda *f*; ~ **wedding** *n* casamento *m* forçado.

should *pret of* **shall**; ◆ *aux:* *(ought to)* devia; **I ~ go now** devo ir embora agora; **2** *(indicating some doubt)* **he ~ be there now** ela já deve ter chegado; **3** *(in conditional clauses);* **I ~ go if I were you** se eu fosse você eu iria; **4** *(conditional form)* **I ~ like**

to rest eu gostaria de descansar; **5** *(have to)* **how ~ I say it?** como havia eu de dizer?; **that I ~ like to see!** eu sempre gostaria de ver isso!

shoulder *n (ANAT)* ombro *m,* espádua *f; (of animal)* quarto dianteiro *m;* ~ **bag** *n* saco *m* a tiracolo; ~ **blade** *n* omoplata *f;* ~ **strap** *n (of dress, bras)* alça *f; (of bag)* correia *f;* **to look over one's ~s** olhar para trás; **to straighten one's ~s** endireitar os ombros; **to rub ~s with sb** conhecer *or* conviver com alguém *(rico, famoso);* **2 hard ~** *(motorway)* acostamento *m; (road)* berma *f;* **3** *(mountain)* planalto *m, (BR)* platô *m.*

shouldered *pt pp adj:* **round-~** que tem os ombros redondos, costas curvadas; ♦ *vt* levar/carregar nos ombros; **2** *(fig) (responsibility)* arcar com.

shout *n* grito; ♦ *vt* gritar; ♦ *vi* gritar, berrar; **to ~ down** *vt* apupar.

shouting *n* gritaria *f,* berreiro *m.*

shove *n* empurrão *m;* ♦ *vt* empurrar; **to ~ sb** dar um empurrão a alguém **to ~ sth in** fazer algo entrar à força; **to ~ off** *vi (NAUT)* zarpar, partir; **2** *(fig: col)* dar o fora; cavar; ~ **off!** põe-te a andar!

shovel *n* pá *f; (mechanical)* escavadeira *f;* ♦ *vt* cavar com pá.

show *n* demonstração *f; (appearance)* aparência; exibição *f; (exhibition)* exposição *f, (THEAT)* espe(c)táculo, representação *f;* ~ **business** *n* o mundo do espe(c)táculo; ~ **jumping** *n* (exibição *f* de) hipismo; ♦ *(pt* **showed**, *pp* **shown**) *vt* mostrar, demonstrar, dar prova de; exibir, expor; *(film)* passar; ♦ *vi* mostrar-se; **he does not ~ his age** ele não aparenta a idade que tem; **to ~ sb in** mandar alguém entrar; **to ~ off** *vi (pej)* mostrar-se, exibir-se; ♦ *vt* exibir, mostrar; *(pej)* pavonear-se; **to ~ up** *vi (stand out)* destacar-se; *(col)* aparecer; ♦ *vt* descobrir; *(unmask)* desmascarar.

showdown *n* ajuste *m* de contas.

shower *n (rain)* aguaceiro *m,* chuvada, *(BR)* pancada de chuva; **2** (~ **bath**) duche *m,* banho *m* de chuveiro *(BR)* ducha *f;* **to take a ~** tomar um duche *(BR)* uma ducha; **3** (~ *apparatus)* chuveiro *m;* **4** *(of confetti, petals, etc)* chuva *f;* ♦ *vi* chover; **2** tomar um duche; ♦ *vt:* **to ~ sb with sth** cobrir alguém com *(kisses, blessings, gifts); (ash, stones)* cair.

showerproof *adj* impermeável.

showers *npl (rain)* chuviscos; **April ~** *(proverb)* Abril, águas de mil.

showery *adj* chuvoso,-a.

showing *n (of film)* projeção *f,* exibição *f.*

shown *(pp of* **show**).

show-off *n (coll: person)* exibicionista *m,f; (male) (boastful)* gabarola, *(BR)* faroleiro.

showpiece *n (of exhibition etc)* obra mais importante.

showroom *n* sala de exposição.

shrank *(pt of* **shrink**).

shrapnel *n* estilhaços *mpl* de metralhadora.

shred *n (of paper, cloth)* tira *f; (a bit)* pedaço *m,* bocado *m;* **2** *(of emotion, evidence)* parcela *f;* **there wasn't a ~ of truth** não havia um mínimo

de verdade; ♦ *vt* rasgar em tiras, retalhar; **2** *(CULIN)* desfiar *(bacalhau, etc),* picar *(cebola, etc);* ralar *(queijo, verduras).*

shredder *n (CULIN) (machine)* triturador *m; (for paper)* picadora *f* de papel.

shrew *n (ZOOL)* musaranho *m;* **2** *(woman) (pej)* megera *f.*

shrewd *adj* astuto,-a, perspicaz, su(b)til.

shrewdness *n* astúcia *f.*

shriek *n* guincho, grito *m;* ♦ *vt/vi* guinchar, gritar.

shrieking *adj* agudo,-a, penetrante.

shrill *adj* agudo,-a, estridente.

shrimp *n (shellfish)* camarão *m;* **2** *(coll) (small person)* anão *m,* anã.

shrine *n* santuário *m,* relicário *m.*

shrink *n (fam) (psychoanalist)* psicanalista *m,f;* ♦ *(pt* **shrank**, *pp* **shrunk**) *vi* encolher; reduzir-se; ♦ *vt* fazer encolher *(clothes);* **2** contrair *(wood);* **3** reduzir; **the school staff has shrunk by half** o pessoal da escola foi reduzido para metade; **4** *(recoil)* **to ~ from doing sth** não se atrever a fazer algo; ~ **away** recuar *(frente a algo).*

shrinkage *n* encolhimento *m;* redução *f;* **2** *(ECON)* recuo *m;* **3** *(timber)* contra(c)ção *f.*

shrinking *adj* em diminuição; **2** *(market)* em baixa; ~ **violet** *n* pessoa *f* tímida.

shrivel *vt* (= **to ~ up**) secar; enrugar; **a ~led man** um homem enrugado e velho; ♦ *vi (skin)* secarse, enrugar-se; **2** *(also:* ~ **up**) *(plant, etc)* murchar; **3** *(meat, forest)* ressequir-se.

shroud *n* mortalha; ♦ *vt:* ~**ed in mystery** envolto em mistério.

Shrove Tuesday *n* Terça-feira Gorda/de Entrudo.

shrub *n* arbusto.

shrubbery *n* arbustos *mpl.*

shrug *n* encolhimento dos ombros; ♦ *vt/vi:* **to ~ one's shoulders** encolher os ombros; **to ~ off** *vt* negar a importância de.

shrunk *(pp of* **shrink**).

shudder *n* estremecimento, tremor *m;* ♦ *vi* estremecer, tremer de medo; **I ~ just to think** estremeço só de pensar.

shuffle *vt (cards)* embaralhar; **to ~ one's feet** arrastar os pés.

shun *vt* evitar, afastar-se de.

shunt *vt (RAIL)* manobrar, desviar *(wagon, engine);* **2** *(usually in passive)* marginalizar, colocar na prateleira *(person);* ♦ *vi:* **to ~ to and fro** mandar daqui para lá.

shush *(onomat)* *exc* chiu!, caluda! nem um pio!; ♦ *vt* mandar calar alguém.

shut *(pt, pp* **shut**) *vt* fechar; **the office ~ at 5 p.m.** o escritório fecha às 17 horas; ~ **your mouth!** *(fam)* cala a boca!; ♦ *vi (gen)* fechar-se; **the lid ~s automatically** a tampa fecha-se automaticamente; **to ~ away** *(valuables)* guardar a sete chaves; **to ~ o.s. away** isolar-se, encerrar-se (**from** de); **to ~ down** *vt/vi (business)* fechar, encerrar; *(machinery, amenities)* parar; ~**-eye** *n:* *(coll)* **to get some ~-eye** passar pelo sono; **to ~ o.s. in** trancar-se; ♦ **to ~ off** *vt* cortar *(gas, water);* **2** *(TV, machine)* desligar; ♦ **to ~ out** excluir; **2** não deixar entrar; **to feel ~ out** sentir-se excluído,-a; **to ~ up** vi (coll) calar-se; calar a boca; ♦ vt fechar; (silence) calar; IDIOM **to ~ one's eyes to** (faults, demeanour) fazer vista grossa a.

shutter n (on window) persiana f; estore m; (over shop) estore m metálico; **2** (PHOT) obturador m; **~ speed** n velocidade f de obturação.

shuttle n (in sewing machine, loom) lançadeira; **2** (badminton) volante m; **3** (transport) vaivem m.

shuttlecock n volante m, (BR) peteca; **~ service** n (planes) ponte f aérea; (bus) serviço m regular.

shy adj tímido,-a, envergonhado,-a; reservado,-a; (not friendly) esquivo; insociável.

shyness n timidez f; acanhamento m.

Siam npr Sião; **in ~** no Sião.

Siamese n adj (person) siamês m, siamesa f; **~ cat** gato siamês; **~ twins** npl irmãos mpl siameses, irmãs fpl siamesas.

Siberia npr Sibéria; **in ~** na Sibéria.

Siberian n adj siberiano,-a.

sibilant adj sibilante.

sibling n irmão, irmã; **the ~s are playing** os irmãos estão a brincar.

Sicilian n adj siciliano,-a.

Sicily npr Sicília; **in ~** na Sicília.

sick adj (ill) doente; (nauseated) enjoado,-a, indisposto,-a; **~ benefit** n subsídio de doença; **~ leave** n licença por doença; **to be on ~ leave** estar e baixa; **~ pay** n subsídio de doença; **2** (humour) negro; **to be ~** vomitar; **to feel ~** estar enjoado; **to be ~ of** (fig) estar cheio,-a de, farto,-a de; **to make sb ~** enojar alguém.

sickbay n (em escola) enfermaria f.

sicken vt enojar; dar nauseas; fazer (alguém) doente.

sickening adj enjoativo,-a; (smell) nauseabundo,-a; **2** (fig) revoltante; **3** (offensive) de mau gosto; **to be ~ for sth** vi andar a chocar, estar a ficar doente.

sickle n foice f, segadeira f.

sickly adj doentio,-a; (unhealthy) fraco,-a; (plant) definhado,-a; **2** (causing nausea) nauseante; **3** (sentimental) (pej) piegas m,f; **4** (too sweet: person) (pej) enjoativo,-a.

sickness n doença, indisposição f; **2** (vomiting) náusea f, enjoo m (BR: -jôo).

side n (person's body) lado m; **2** (of animal) flanco m; **3** (of lake) margem f; **4** (of problem) aspecto m; **5** (of story) versão f; **6** (of hill) encosta, declive m, vertente f; **7** (SPORT) (team) equipa f; **~ by ~** lado a lado; **by the ~ of** ao lado de; **from all ~s** de todos os lados; **on my right ~** ao meu lado direito, à minha direita; **on my father's ~** por parte do meu pai; **to put sth on/to one ~** pôr/colocar algo de lado; ♦ **to do sth on the ~** fazer algum trabalho extra (para ganhar dinheiro); **2** (dishonestly) fazer por malícia, fazer por fora; **to be on the safe ~** por via das dúvidas; ♦ adj lateral; **~board** n aparador m; **~boards**, **~burns** npl suíças fpl; **~ dish** prato m de acompanhamento; **~ effect** n efeito m secundário, colateral; **2** repercussão; **~ kick** n (coll) acólito; **~ long** adj (glance)

de lado, de soslaio; **~ road** n rua lateral, transversal; **~saddle** adv de silhão; de lado; **~ table** mesa f de apoio, mesinha f; **~walk** n (US) passeio, (BR) calçada.

sideline n (SPORT) linha f lateral; **2** (fig) (extra business) linha adicional de produtos; ocupação f secundária; **to kick the ball over the ~** lançar a bola para fora.

sideshow n (at the fair) atra(c)ção f espe(c)táculo, divertimento (numa feira); **2** (fig) exibição f suplementar.

sidestep n passo m lateral; ♦ vt (fig) evitar, esquivar-se de; **2** fujir à questão.

sidetrack n desvio, via secundária; ♦ vt (fig) desviar (do assunto/propósito).

sideways adv de lado; **2** (parking) obliquamente; **3** (glance) de esguelha, de soslaio; ♦ vi: **to ~ with sb** tomar o partido de alguém.

siding n (RAIL) desvio m, ramal m; **2** (weatherproof coating) revestimento m exterior.

sidle vi: **to ~ up (to)** aproximar-se furtivamente (de).

siege n sítio m, assédio m; **2** cerco m.

siesta n (nap) sesta f.

sieve n (for flour) peneira; **2** (for stones, coal) crivo m; ♦ vt peneirar; passar por crivo; IDIOM **to have a head like a ~** ter uma memória terrível; **to leak like a ~** (secrets) ser um saco roto.

sift vt peneirar; **2** (fig: information) esquadrinhar, analisar minuciosamente.

sigh n suspiro m; ♦ vi suspirar.

sight n vista, visão f; **2** (spectacle) espe(c)táculo; **3** (scenery); **a beautiful ~!** que linda vista!; **4** (on riffle, telescope) alça, mira, visor; **to know sb by ~** conhecer alguém de vista; **to set one's ~ on doing sth** decidir-se a fazer algo; ♦ vt avistar, mirar; **in ~** à vista; **out of ~** longe dos olhos; **a ~ of money** um dinheirão.

sightseeing n turismo; **to go ~** visitar lugares turísticos.

sightseer n turista m,f; **2** (witnessing an incident) expe(c)tador,-ora.

sign n sinal m; sintoma m; **it is a good ~** é um bom sinal; (indication) indício; símbolo m; **2** (trace) rastro, vestígio; **3** (notice, any board) letreiro m, tabuleta f; **4** (zodiac) signo m; **5** (gesture) gesto m, aceno m; **~ language** n mímica, linguagem f através de sinais; lingua f gestual; **~ post** indicador m; placa f de sinalização; ♦ vt assinar, firmar; **to ~ sth over to sb** assinar a transferência de algo para alguém; **2** (employee) contratar; **3** (soldier) recruit; **to ~ in** vi dar entrada, informar de sua presença; **to ~ on** vi (enrol) inscrever-se em; ♦ **to ~ up** vi (MIL) alistar-se; **2** (for course) inscrever-se; ♦ vt (contract) firmar contrato com.

signal n sinal m, aviso m; ♦ (-ll-) vi (AUT) (indicating a turn) sinalizar; ♦ vt **to ~ sb to do sth** fazer sinal para alguém fazer algo; **2** (message) transmitir.

signalman n sinaleiro m.

signatory (pl: -ies) n signatário,-a.

signature n assinatura f; **~ tune** n tema m, indicativo m do programa.

signet ring *n* anel *m* com sinete, chancela; **2** *(seal)* selo *m*.

significance *n* significado *m*; importância *f*.

significant *adj* significativo,-a, importante *m,f*.

signify *vt* significar.

silence *n* silêncio; ◆ *vt* silenciar, impor silêncio a.

silencer *n* *(on gun)* silenciador *m*; **2** *(AUT)* silencioso,-a.

silent *adj* silencioso,-a; *(not speaking)* calado,-a; **2** *(film)* mudo; ~ **partner** *n* *(US)* *(COMM)* sócio,-a comanditário,-a.

silently *adv* silenciosamente; em silêncio.

silhouette *n* silhueta *f*; ~**d against** em silhueta contra.

silicon *n* *(CHEM)* silício *m*; ~ **copper** cobre *m* silicioso; ~ **chip** *n* *(COMP)* pastilha *f*, chip *m* de silício.

silicone *n* *(CHEM)* silicone *m*.

Silicon Valley *npr* Vale *m* do Silício.

Silk[1] *npr* *(rank of Queen's Counsel)* advogado da Coroa.

silk[2] *n* seda; ◆ *adj* de seda; ~ **screen printing** *n* serigrafia *f*; ~**worm** *n* bicho *m* de seda.

silky *adj* *(hair, material)* sedoso,-a; *(skin)* macio,-a; *(voice)* doce.

sill *n* *(of window)* peitoril *m*, parapeito *m*; **2** *(of door)* soleira *f*.

silliness *n* estupidez *f*; parvoíce *f*.

silly *adj* tonto, parvo, idiota, imbecil, *(BR)* bobo; absurdo, ridículo; ~-**billy** *(coll)* *(childish talk)* tonto,-a, tontinho,-a.

silo *n* *(AGR, MIL)* silo *m*.

silt *n* sedimento *m*, lodo *m*, aluvião *m*.

silver *n* prata; **2** *(coins)* moedas *fpl*; ◆ *adj* de prata; ~ **birch** *n* bétula; ~ **foil** *n* prata em folhas; ~-**haired** *adj* grisalho; ~-**plated** *adj* prateado, banhado a prata; ~**smith** *n* ourives *m* de prata; ~**ware** *n* *(silver tableware)* baixela *f* de prata; ~ **wedding** *n* bodas *fpl* de prata; IDIOM **every cloud has a ~ lining** não há mal que bem não tenha.

silvery *adj* prateado,-a.

similar *adj*: ~ **to** parecido com, semelhante a.

similarity *n* semelhança, similitude *f*.

similarly *adv* da mesma maneira, semelhantemente.

simmer *n* fervura *f* em lume brando; ◆ *vi* cozinhar a fogo lento, ferver lentamente.

simnel-cake *n* bolo tradicional inglês feito especialmente pela Páscoa.

simper *n* sorriso *m* pretensioso; ◆ *vi* sorrir de maneira afe(c)tada.

simpering *adj* *(pej)* *(person, smile)* afe(c)tado,-a.

simple *adj* *(easy)* fácil; **2** *(food, tastes, task)* simples **this exercise is** ~ este exercício é simples; **3** *(naïve person)* ingênuo,-a; **4** *(unsophisticated)* simples; ~ **folk** pessoas simples, humildes; ~ **house** casa *f* modesta, singela; ~-**minded** *adj* *(pej)* *(person)* *(not clever)* ingénuo,-a, simples.

simpleton *n* *(dim-witted)* simplório, pateta *m,f*.

simplicity *n* simplicidade *f*; ingenuidade *f*.

simplify *vt* simplificar.

simplistic *adj* *(pej)* simplista.

simulate *vt* simular.

simulated *adj* *(faked)* artificial *m,f*; artigo *m* de imitação; **2** *(feigned)* fingido,-a.

simulation *n* simulação *f*.

simultaneous *adj* simultâneo,-a.

simultaneously *adv* simultaneamente.

sin *n* pecado; ◆ *vi* pecar.

since *adv* desde então, depois; ◆ *prep* desde; ◆ *conj* *(time)* desde que; *(because)* porque, visto que, já que; ~ **then** desde então.

sincere *adj* sincero,-a; **yours** ~**ly** *(in a letter)* cumprimentos, atenciosamente.

Termina-se uma carta comercial ou formal com '**yours sincerely**' quando esta começa por '**Dear Mr Smith**' = Caro Senhor Smith. Quando não se sabe o nome da pessoa e a carta começa por '**Dear Sir**' = '**Exmo Senhor**', deve-se terminá-la por '**yours faithfully**'.

sincerity *n* sinceridade *f*.

sinecure *n* sinecure *f*.

sinew *n* tendão *m*.

sinful *adj* *(behaviour)* imoral; **2** *(thought, world)* pecaminoso; *(person)* pecador.

sing *(pt* **sang**, *pp* **sung**) *vt* cantar; ◆ *vi* cantar; **2** *(bird)* gorjear, cantar.

Singapore *npr* Singapura.

singe *vt* chamuscar.

singer *n* cantor,-ora.

singing *n adj* *(MUS)* canto *m*; de canto, de canção *f*; **2** *(in the ears)* zumbido.

single *n* (= ~ **ticket**) bilhete *m*, passagem *f* de ida; **3** *(MUS)* *(record)* disco, compa(c)to *m*, single; **every** ~ **day** todo o santo dia; ~**s** *npl* *(tennis)* simples *f inv*; ◆ *adj* *(only one, alone)* único, só; **one** ~ **present** um presente só/um único presente; **2** *(unmarried)* solteiro,-a; **3** *(not double)* *(in garment)* simples; ~ **bed** *n* cama *f* de solteiro; ~-**breasted** *adj* *(garment)* não trespassado, só com uma fileira de botões; ~ **cream** *n* nata *f* fresca líquida; ~ **currency** *n* moeda *f* única; **S~ European Market** *n* Mercado Comum Europeu; ~-**handed** *adv* sem ajuda, sozinho,-a; **in** ~ **file** *adv* em fila *f* Indiana; ~-**lens** *(camera)* de uma só obje(c)tiva/lente *f*; ~-**minded** *adj* determinado,-a; tenaz; ~ **parent** *n* pai solteiro, mãe solteira; ~-**parent family** *n* família *f* mononuclear; monoparental; ~-**party** *n* *(POL)* partido *m* único; ~ **room** *n* quarto individual, de solteiro; ◆ *vt* **to** ~ **out sb** escolher; alguém (para algo).

singlet *n* *(vest)* camisola *f* interior; T-shirt em managas.

singly *adj* *(one by one)* um a um; individualmente.

singsong *n* *(UK)* reunião *f* para cantar; canto *m* orfeónico; **to have a** ~ *(fam)* cantar em conjunto; **2** *(rhythm)* monótono.

singular *n* *(LING)* singular; ◆ *adj* *(unusual)* singular *m,f*, peculiar.

singularity *n* singularidade *f*.

sinister *adj* sinistro,-a.

sink *n* lava-louças *m* (-loiças); *(BR)* pia *f* de lavar loiça; **2** *(in bathroom)* lavatório *m*, bacia *f*; ~ **unit** *n* lava-loiça encastrado; ◆ *(pt* **sank**, *pp* **sunk**) *vt* *(ship)* afundar; **2** *(foundations)* escavar; **to** ~ **sth**

(embed) enterrar algo (**into** em); **3** *(FIN)* amortizar *(debt)*; **4 to ~ low** cair baixo; **5 to ~ a beer** *(coll)* beber uma cerveja; ♦ *vi (also: ~ down)* afundar-se, ir a pique; **to ~ in** *vi (building, wall)* desmoronar-se, desabar (**to the floor** por terra); **2** ceder; **to ~ under weight** ceder sob o peso; **to ~ to one's knees** cair de joelhos; **to ~ into a deep sleep** mergulhar num sono profundo; **to ~ into debts** atolar-se de dívidas; ♦ **to ~ in** *(water, cream)* penetrar; **2** ser compreendido,-a; **3** *(ground)* entranhar-se (em); IDIOM **my heart sank** *(fig)* perdi o ânimo; *(with surprise)* o meu coração caiu aos pés.

sinking *n* naufrágio *m*; afundamento *m*; **2** *(mining)* perfuração *f*; **3 a ~ feeling** *n* *(fig)* um vazio no estômago; ♦ *adj* angustiante; **~ fund** *n* *(ECON)* fundo *m* de amortização.

sinner *n* picador,-ora.

Sinn Féin *npr* Sinn Féin *m* (movimento político irlandês fundado em 1905).

sinuous *adj* sinuoso,-a.

sinus *n* *(ANAT)* seio *m*; cavidade *f* (nasal).

sinusitis *n* sinusite *f*.

sip *n* gole *m*; trago *m*; ♦ *vt* tomar um golinho de, sorver; *(little and slowly)* bebericar; *(with pleasure)* saborear.

siphon *n* sifão *m*; ♦ **to ~ off** *vt* extrair com sifão.

sir *n* senhor *m*; título de baronetes; **Dear S~** *(formal/ commercial letters)* Exmo Senhor; **yes, ~** sim, senhor.

Sire *n* (dirigindo-se ao rei) Majestade, Senhor; ♦ *vt* (cavalo, pessoa) procriar; *(formal)* ser pai de; **the king sired two sons** o rei foi pai de dois filhos.

siren *n* *(of ship)* sirene *f*; **2** *(mermaid)* sereia *f*.

sirloin *n* *(CULIN)* lombo de vaca; **~ steak** *n* bife *m* do lombo.

sissy *(pl: -ies)* *n* *(pej)* maricas *msg*.

sister *n* irmã *f*; **2** *(nurse)* enfermeira-chefe *f*; **3** *(nun)* freira; **~hood** *n* irmandade *f*, confraria; **~-in-law** *n* cunhada *f*.

sit *(pt, pp sat)* *vi* sentar-se; **to ~ on the floor** sentar-se no chão; *(be sitting)* estar sentado; **2** *(assembly)* reunir-se; ♦ *vt* *(exam)* prestar (exame); **to ~ about/around** *vi* não fazer nada; **to ~ back** *vi* recostar-se; **to ~ down** *vi* sentar-se; **to ~ in on** *vi* assistir a; **to ~ out** *vt* não participar de algo; **to ~ through** *vt* aguentar até o final; **to ~ tight** *vi* aguardar pacientemente uma melhor ocasião; ♦ **to ~ up** *vi* endireitar-se; **2** *(not go to bed)* aguardar acordado.

sitcom *(coll)* comédia *f* de situação.

sit-down strike *n* greve *f* de braços cruzados.

site *n* *(for development)* local *m*, sítio *m*, localização *f*; *(area of land)* lote *m* (de terreno); (= **building ~**) edifício em construção; ♦ *vt* situar, localizar.

sit-in *n* greve-branca *f* (ocupação *f* de um local como forma de protesto, manifestação *f* pacífica).

sitting *n* *(of assembly etc)* sessão *f*; **2** *(serving of meal)* turno *m* (para as refeições); **3 at one ~** de uma assentada *f*; **4** *(incubation period)* choco *m*; **~ duck** *n* *(coll)* alvo *m*, vítima *f* fácil; **~ room** *n* sala de estar.

situated *adj* situado,-a.

situation *m* situação *f*.

sit-up *(pl: sit-ups)* *(physical exercise)* abdominal *(pl: abdominais)*.

six *num* seis *m inv*; IDIOM **at ~s and sevens** *(person)* toda confusa.

sixteen *num* dezasseis, *(BR)* dezesseis.

sixteenth *adj* décimo,-a sexto,-a.

sixth *n* sexto,-a; *(day of the month)* seis; **one ~** *(fraction)* um sexto; **~ form** *n* *(UK)* *(school)* o ano terminal do liceu, da escola secundária; **~ sense** *n* sexto *n* sentido *m*.

sixtieth *n* sexagésimo,-a.

sixty *num* sessenta; *(decade)* **the sixties** *n* os anos *mpl* sessenta.

size *n* tamanho *m*; dimensão *f*, proporção *f*; medida; **2** *(of shoes)* número; **3** *(glue)* cola *f*, goma *f*; ♦ *vt* **to ~ up** avaliar, formar uma opinião sobre *(person)*.

sizeable *adj* considerável, bastante grande.

sizzle *n* *(frying sound)* chiadeira *f*, estalidos *mpl*; ♦ *vi* chiar.

skate *n* patim *m*; *(fish: pl inv)* arraia *f*; **~board** *n* skate *m*, patimtábua *m*; ♦ *vi* patinar.

skater *n* patinador,-ora.

skating *n* patinagem *f*, *(BR)* patinação *f*; **~ rink** *n* ringue *m* de patinagem *(BR: de patinação)*.

skeleton *n* *(ANAT)* esqueleto *m*; **2** *(TECH)* armação *f*; estrutura *f*; **3** *(outline)* esquema *m*, esboço; IDIOM **to have a ~ in the cupboard** ter um segredo *m* de família; **~ key** *n* chave *f* mestra; **~ staff** *n* pessoal *m* reduzido (ao mínimo).

sketch *n* desenho *m*; esboço *m*, croqui *m*; *(THEAT)* pequena peça teatral, esquete *m*; **~book/pad** *n* caderno, bloco *m* de desenho; ♦ *vt* desenhar, esboçar.

sketchy *adj* vago,-a; artificial; por alto.

skewer *n* espeto, *(BR)* espetinho; ♦ *vt* espetar *(carne, etc)*.

ski *n* *(on snow)* esqui *m*; *(water)* esqui *m* aquático; **cross-country ~** esqui de fundo; **downhill ~** esqui alpino; **~ boot** *n* bota de esqui; **~ jumping** *n* salto em esqui; **~ pants** *npl* calça *sg* de esquiar; ♦ *vi* esquiar; *(hobby)* fazer esqui.

skid *n* derrapagem *f*; **~ mark** *n* marca da derrapagem; ♦ *vi* derrapar, deslizar.

skier *n* esquiador,-ora.

skiing *n* *(SPORT)* esqui *m*; **~ jump** *n* pista para saltos de esqui.

skilful *adj* habilidoso,-a, jeitoso,-a; *(clever)* esperto,-a.

skill *n* habilidade *f*, jeito *m*; **2** *(know-how)* perícia *f*.

skilled *adj* hábil; **2** especializado,-a; *(trained)*, qualificado,-a; **to be ~ in** ser um perito em.

skim (-mm-) *vt* *(milk)* desnatar; **2** *(glide over)* roçar, deslizar; ♦ *vi:* **to ~ through** *(glance through)* dar uma vista de olhos por, ler superficialmente.

skimmed milk *n* leite desnatado; leite magro.

skimp *vt* *(work)* executar de maneira imperfeita, atamancar; **2** *(cloth, effort, money)* economizar.

skimpily *adv* *(eat)* frugalmente; *(work)* à pressa.

skimpy (-pier, -piest) *adj* *(meagre)* escasso,-a; mínimo,-a; **2** *(person)* sovina *m,f*; **3** *(excuse, fact)* insuficiente *m,f*; ~ **skirt** saia *f* curtíssima; **2** *(work)* atamancado,-a.

skin *n* pele *f*; *of (leather)* couro; *(complexion)* cútis *f*; ~**-deep** *adj* superficial; ~**-diving** *n* mergulho *m* submarino; ~**flint** *n* avarento,-a, sovina; ~ **graft** *n* *(MED)* *(process)* transplante *m* de pele; *(grafted area)* enxerto *m*; ~**head** *n* *(UK)* skinhead, cabeça rapada; ◆ *vt (fruit etc)* pelar, descascar; **2** *(animal)* esfolar, tirar a pele a.

skinny *adj* muito magro,-a; descarnado,-a.

skint *adj* *(coll)* *(no money)* teso,-a; liso,-a *(cal)*.

skin-tight *adj* *(dress etc)* justo (ao corpo), *(BR)* grudado (no corpo).

skip *n* salto *m*, pulo *m*; **2** *(container)* recipiente para elevação de materiais; **3** *(building)* contentor *m* para lixo; ◆ *vi* saltar, pular; *(with rope)*, saltar à corda; ◆ *vt (pass over)* omitir, saltar; pôr de lado; *(class, meal)* faltar a.

skipper *n* *(NAUT, SPORT)* capitão *m*.

skipping rope *n* corda de saltar.

skirmish *n* escaramuça *f*; *(disagreement)* desavença (**between** entre).

skirt *n* saia *f*; ◆ *vt* rodear; orlar, circundar, contornar **to ~ around sth** evitar algo; ~**ing board** *n* rodapé *m*.

skit *n* paródia, sátira; **its a ~ on the minister** é piada ao ministro.

skittish *adj* *(person)* volúvel, imprevisível; **2** *(playful)* brincalhão,-ona, frívolo,-a.

skittle *n* pau, pino *m* do jogo da laranjinha *(BR)* do boliche; **2** ~**s** *n* *(UK)* (semelhante ao bowling) jogo *m* da laranjinha; *(BR)* do boliche.

skive *n* *(coll)* evasiva *f*, desculpa, escusa *f* para faltar ao trabalho; **swine flu** ~ escusa da gripe suína; **2** *(loafing)* vadiagem *f*; ◆ *vt/vi (UK)* *(coll)* evitar trabalhar; **to ~ off** *(class, etc)* faltar a, fazer gazeta, baldar a; ◆ *vt* raspar *(leather's surface)*, polir *(precious stones)*.

skiver *n* *(leather remnant)* retalho *m* de couro, cabedal.

skivvy *(pl:* -ies) *(UK)* *(fam)* serviçal *m,f*; ◆ *(pt, pp* -ied) *vi* **to ~ for sb** servir de empregado para alguém.

skulk *vi* estar à espreita; **to ~ in/out/off** entrar/sair/afastar-se furtivamente.

skull *n* caveira; *(ANAT)* crânio.

skunk *n* doninha fedorenta; *(BR)* gambá *m*; **2** *(coll, fig, pej)* canalha *m,f*.

sky *n* céu *m*; ~**-blue** *adj* azul celeste; ~**-high** *adj* nas alturas; **2** *(price)* exorbitante; ~**lark** *n* calandra *f*; ~**line** *n* linha *f* do horizonte; ~**light** *n* claraboia *f*, escotilha *f*; ~**scraper** *n* arranha-céu(s) *m*.

slab *n* *(of wood)* prancha, tábua *f*; **2** *(of stone)* laje *f*; **3** *(of cake)* fatia *f* grossa; *(chocolate)* tablete *f*.

slack *n* *(part of the rope)* bamba *f*; *(loose)* afrouxamento; **2** *(slowing down)*, abrandamento; período *m* de ina(c)tividade; ◆ *adj* frouxo,-a, brando,-a; **business is** ~ o negócio afrouxou; **2** *(slow)* lento,-a; **3** *(careless)* descuidado,-a.

slacken (= **to ~ off**) *vi* afrouxar-se; *(rain, wind)* abrandar; ◆ *vt (pace, hold)* afrouxar; *(speed)* diminuir.

slackening *n* *(of economy, pace)* abrandamento *m*; *(of discipline)* afrouxamento *m*; *(of tension)* diminuição *f*.

slackness *n* *(businesss)* estagnação *f*; *(security, organization)* relaxamento *m*; *(by worker, student)* desleixo *m*.

slag *n* *(waste material)* escória *f*, escombros *mpl*; ~**heap** *n* monte *m* de entulho; **2** *(pej) (person)* badalhoca *f*, porca *f* *(pej)*; *vt* **to ~ sb** *(UK)* falar mal de *(alguém)*; **they ~ged each other off** insultaram-se uma à outra.

slain *(pp of slay)*.

slam *n* *(of door)* estrondo *m*; pancada *f* forte; ◆ (-**mm**-) *vt* bater, fechar (com violência); **to ~ a door in sb's face** bater com a porta na cara de alguém; **to ~ one's fist on the table** bater com o punho na mesa; **to ~ on the brakes** travar a fundo, travar repentinamente; **to ~ sth on (to) sth** atirar *(BR:* jogar*)* algo com violência para/sobre sth; **2** *(fig) (criticize)* malhar, criticar; ◆ *vi (shut)* bater.

slander *n* calúnia, difamação *f*; ◆ *vt* caluniar, difamar.

slanderous *adj* calunioso,-a, difamatório,-a.

slang *n* gíria; calão *m*, *(BR)* jargão *m*.

slant *n* *(of land)* declive *m*; *(of picture, table)*, inclinação *f*; plano inclinado; **2** *(fig)* ponto de vista.

slanted, slanting *adj* inclinado; **2** *(glance)* de esguelha.

slap *n* *(gentle)* palmada, tapa *f*; *(on face)* bofetada *f*, sopapo *m*; *(on back-friendly)* palmada *f*, palmadinha (nas costas); **a ~ in his face** *(fig) (insult, reprimand)* uma bofetada na cara dele; ◆ *vt* dar um tapa em, esbofetear alguém; **to ~ on sth on sth** dar um retoque, *(BR)* retocada em; ◆ *adv (exactly)* em cheio, exa(c)tamente; ~ **in the middle of the park** bem no meio do parque.

slapdash *adj* *(person)* descuidado,-a; *(doing things in any way)* trapalhão,-ona; *(work)* atamancado,-a.

slapstick *n* *(CIN, THEAT)* *(comedy)* palhaçada *f* comédia *f* física.

slap-up *adj* *(fam)* *(of meals)* excelente, porreiro,-a *(pop, fam)*.

slash *n* *(long cut)* golpe *m*; *(fabric, tyre, etc)* corte *m*; **2** *(in wood)* entalhe *m*; **3** *(oblique stroke)* barra *f* oblíqua; **forward** ~ barra inclinada; ◆ *vt (reduce drastically)* cortar, reduzir *(price, amount)*; **2** *(fabric, etc)* rasgar; **3** *(wood)* talhar; **4** *(with knife, blade)* golpear; **to ~ prices down** abater, reduzir os preços drasticamente; **to ~ one's wrists** golpear os pulsos.

slat *n* ripa *f*, tabuinha *f*; sarrafo *m*.

slate *n* lousa, ardósia *f*, *(on roof)* telha *f* de ardósia; ◆ *vt (fig)* criticar duramente, arrasar; **to wipe the ~ clean** *(fam)* começar vida nova; esquecer o passado e recomeçar.

slaughter *n* *(of animals)* matança; *(of people)* carnificina; ~**house** *n* matadouro *m*; ◆ *vt* matar.

Slav *n* eslavo,-a.

slave *n* escravo,-a; ~ **trade** *(HIST)* *n*: **the ~** o comércio de escravos; ◆ *vi* (= **to ~ away**) trabalhar como um escravo.

slaver *n* *(saliva)* baba *f*; **2** *(fig)* lisonja servil; ◆ *vi (drool)* babar-se; **to ~ over the idea** babar-se com a ideia.

slavery *n (practice)* escravatura *f; (condition)* escravidão *f.*

slavish *adj* servil.

Slavonic *adj* eslavo,-a.

slay *(pt slew, pp slain) vt* matar.

sleaze *n (pej) (of place)* sordidez, sujeira; **2** *(of behaviour)* comportamento *m* imoral; **3** corrupção *f;* ~**ball** *n (slang)* pessoa odiosa e vil.

sleazy *adj (place)* sórdido,-a; de reputação *f* duvidosa.

sled *n (US)* = **sledge.**

sledge *n* trenó *m;* ~ **hammer** *n* marreta, malho.

sleek *adj (hair)* liso e brilhante; *(animal)* com o pelo lustroso; **2** *(elegant person)* requintado,-a, elegante; **3** *(prosperous appearance)* cheio,-a de verniz; **4** *(car)* polido; **5** *(person's character)* pouco sincero,-a, untuoso,-a.

sleep *n* sono *m;* **2** *(euph)* morte; **sound** ~ sono profundo, sono solto; **to drop with** ~ cair de sono; ~ **walker** *n* sonâmbulo; ♦ *(pt, pp slept) vi* dormir; **I** ~ **eight hours** eu durmo oito horas; **to go to** ~ ir dormir; *(doze off)* adormecer; *(go numb)* ficar dormente *(leg, etc);* **to put a child to** ~ ir deitar, adormecer uma criança; **to put an animal to** ~ *(VET) (euph)* matar humanamente; ~ **tight!** dorme bem! **the hotel sleeps 250 people** *vt* o hotel tem capacidade/camas para 250 pessoas; **to** ~ **rough** dormir ao relento/na rua; **this bed hasn't been slept in** ninguém dormiu nesta cama; **to** ~ **around** *vi (be promiscuous)* dormir com qualquer pessoa; **to** ~ **away** *vt* passar a vida a dormir; ~ **in** *vi* dormir demais; ~ **it off** curar (bebedeira, etc) dormindo; **to** ~ **on** continuar a dormir; **to** ~ **on sth** *(problem, etc)* esperar pela manhã para se decidir; consultar o travesseiro; **to** ~ **out** dormir fora; IDIOM **to** ~ **like a log** dormir como uma pedra; **I didn't** ~ **a wink** não preguei olho; **to** ~ **round the clock** dormir 12 horas a fio.

sleeper *n (person)* dorminhoco,-a; **2** *(RAIL: on track)* travessa, dormente *m;* **3** *(berth)* carruagem-cama.

sleepily *adv* com sono, sonolentamente.

sleeping *adj* adormecido,-a; ~ **bag** *n* saco *m* de dormir; ~ **Beauty** *npr* a Bela Adormecida; ~ **car** *n (RAIL)* carruagem-cama *f, (BR)* carro-leito; ~ **partner** sócio,-a comanditário,-a; ~ **policeman** *(UK) (coll) (for spped control)* lomba; ~ **tablet** *n* soporífero *m,* comprimido *m* paradormir; IDIOM **let** ~ **dogs lie** o que lá vai, lá vai.

sleeplessness *n* insónia *f; (BR)* insônia *f.*

sleepover *n (fam)* dormida ocasional em casa de alguém.

sleepy (-ier, -iest) *adj* sonolento,-a; **2** *(place)* sossegado,-a; ~**head** *n (fam)* dorminhoco,-a; **in a** ~ **voice** numa voz ensonada.

sleet *n* granizo *m;* ♦ *vi imp* chover granizo.

sleeve *n* manga *f;* **2** *(TECH)* (revestimento) camisa de cilindro; **3** *(for record, book)* capa *f;* IDIOM **to turn the** ~**s up** arregaçar as mangas.

sleeveless *adj* sem mangas.

sleigh *n* trenó *m.*

sleight *n* destreza; ~ **of hand** prestidigitação *f;* **2** truque *m* de mãos.

slender *adj* magro,-a, esbelto,-a; **2** *(narrow, thin)* delgado; **3** *(means)* escasso,-a, insuficiente.

slept *(pt, pp of* **sleep**).

sleuth *n (US)* dete(c)tive *m,f,* polícia *m,f.*

slew *(pt of* **slay**).

slice *n* fatia *f;* **2** *(of lemon, salame)* rodela; **3** *(of fish)* posta; **4** *(utensil)* espátula, pá *f* de bolo; **5** *(proportion: of income, profit)* parte *f;* *(SPORT)* golpe *m* de bola enviesado, *(BR)* cortada *f;* ♦ *vt (also:* ~ **up)** cortar em fatias *(bread, cake);* **2** cortar em rodelas *(cucumber, onion);* *(SPORT)* cortar, desviar *(ball).*

slick *n (=* **oil** ~) mancha, poça *f* de petróleo; *(on shore)* maré *f* negra; **2** *(US) (magazine)* revista *f* luxuosa; ferramenta para polir/alisar; ♦ **(-ier, -iest)** *adj (smooth, well devised)* talentoso,-a; **a** ~ **show** um espe(c)táculo bem feito, harmonioso; **2** *(style, publication) (often pej)* superficial, lustroso,-a; **3** *(shrewd person)* astuto, com muita lábia; **a** ~ **salesman** um vendedor com muita lábia; *(insincere)* manhoso,-a e/ou bajulador,-ora; *(criminal)* engenhoso,-a; **4** *(hair)* liso, lustroso; **5** escorregadio,-a *(on oil, mud);* ♦ *adv* = **in the middle** mesmo no meio; ♦ *vt* polir, lustrar; *(hair)* alisar *(com loção);* **to** ~ **oneself up** aparaltar-se.

slicker *n (US) (shiny raincoat)* impermeável *m;* **2 city** ~ *(fam) (cunning business person)* esperto, com muita lábia.

slid *(pt, pp of* **slide**).

slide *n (in playground)* escorrega *m;* **2** *(PHOT)* slide *m;* diapositivo; *(=* **hair**~) trevessão *m;* ~ **rule** *m* régue *f* de cálculo; ♦ *(pt, pp* **slid**) *vt* deslizar, patinar; ♦ *vi (slip)* escorregar; *(glide)* deslizar.

sliding *adj (door)* corrediço.

slight *n* afronta *f,* desfeita *f;* ♦ *adj* fraco,-a, franzino,-a; leve; insignificante; pequeno,-a; ♦ *vt* desdenhar, menosprezar; **at the** ~**est hint** à mais pequena alusão; **not in the** ~**est** em absoluto, de maneira alguma.

slightly *adv* ligeiramente, um pouco.

slim *adj* magro,-a esbelto,-a; ♦ *vi* emagrecer, tornar-se esbelto.

slime *n* lodo *m,* limo *m,* lama *f.*

slimming *n* emagrecimento; ~ **diet** dieta, regime *m* para emagrecer.

slimy *adj* viscoso,-a, pegajoso,-a; **2** *(pej) (person)* falso,-a, fingido,-a.

sling *n (MED)* tipóia; **2** *(weapon)* estilingue *m,* funda; ♦ *(pt, pp* **slung**) *vt* atirar, arremessar, lançar.

slingshot *n* fisga *f.*

slink *(pt, pp* **slunk**) *vi:* ~ **away/off** entrar/sair furtivamente, escapulir-se.

slip *n* escorregadela *f; (stumble)* tropeção *m;* **2** *(mistake)* erro, lapso *m;* **3** *(underskirt)* combinação *f;* **4** *(of paper)* tira *f,* pedaço de papel; **tear-off** ~ cupão *m* destacável; **2** *(landslide)* desabamento *m;* **3** *(slender person)* **a** ~ **of a girl** uma garota magrinha; **4** *(clay)* engobo *m;* ~ **road** *n* acesso *m* à auto-estrada; ~**shod** *adj (person)* desleixado,-a; **2** *(work, appearance)* negligente; sem cuidado; desmazelado,-a; ~**stream** *n* esteira *f;* rastro *m;* ~~**up** *n*

descuido *m*; deslize *m*; *(BR)* mancada; **~way** *n*
(NAUT) (in a shipyard) plano *m* inclinado, carreira
f; ♦ *vt (slide)* deslizar; ♦ *vi* escorregar; **2** *(stumble)*
tropeçar; **3** *(decline)* decair; **to give sb the ~**
esgueirar-se, escapar de alguém; **to ~ away** *vi*
partir discretamente; **to ~ by** *(time, life)* passar;
to ~ in *vt* meter; ♦ *vi* meter-se; **to ~ off** *(remove)*
tirar *(gloves, coat, jewellery)*; **to ~ on** *(clothes, shoes)*
enfiar; **to ~ out** *vi (go out)* sair (por pouco tempo);
the words ~ped out as palavras escaparam-se da
boca; **to ~ up** cometer uma gaffe, um deslize.
slippage *n (delay in the work)* atraso *m*; **2** *(TECH)*
perda de energia; **3** discrepância *f*.
slipped disc *n (MED)* hérnia *f* discal.
slipper *n (house shoe)* chinelo *m*.
slippery *adj* escorregadio,-a; **2** *(coll) (untrustworthy)*
não ser de confiança.
slit *n* fenda; corte *m*; ♦ *(pt, pp* **slit)** *vt* rachar, cortar,
fender.
slither *n* resvalamento *m*; ♦ *vi* escorregar, resvalar;
(snake) deslizar.
sliver *n* pequeno pedaço *m*; **2** *(of meat)* bocado
fininho; **3** *(of cheese)* uma tira fina; **4** *(of wood)*
lasca *f*.
slob *n (fam)* desmazelado,-a, preguiçoso,-a; *(fig)*
(disgusting person) porcalhão,-ona.
slobber *n (saliva)* baba *f*; ♦ babar-se; **~ over (sb,**
sth) babar-se todo (em frente de alguém); dizer
baboseiras.
sloe *n* abrunho *m*; **~-eyed** *adj (person)* com olhos
escuros de feitio de amêndoa.
slog *n (hard work)* trabalho duro,-a, árduo,-a; **it was**
a ~ foi um trabalho *m* louco, foi uma estafa; **2**
(beating) tareia *f*, sova *f*, pancada *f* forte; **3**
caminhada *f* extenuante; ♦ **(-gg-)** *vi (to hit with*
heavy blows) dar pancadas fortes; mourejar; **2**
mover-se com dificuldade; **3** *(also:* **~ away)** trabalhar
duramente, esfalfar-se.
slogan *n* lema *m*, slogan *m*.
sloop *n (boat)* chalupa *f*.
slop *n (AGR)* lavagem *f (coll)* mistela *f*; **~s** *npl*
(liquid food of low quality) alimento *m* líquido, de
papas; **2** *(soft mud, snow)* neve ou lama aguada;
♦ *vi (=* **to ~ over)** transbordar; ♦ **(-pp-)** *vt* entornar;
~ around andar de modo descuidado; **she is**
slopping around in slippers ela anda pela casa
de pantufas.
slope *n (up)* ladeira, rampa; **2** *(down)* declive *m*; **3**
(mountain) encosta, vertente *f*; ♦ *vi:* **to ~ down**
estar em declive; **to be on the slippery ~** ir dire(c)to
para *(misfortune, vice)*; **to ~ up** inclinar-se.
sloping *adj* inclinado, em declive.
sloppy (-ier, -iest) *adj (work)* descuidado; trabalho
malfeito; **2** *(appearance)* desleixado,-a; **3** *(discipline)*
relaxada; *(SPORT)* fraco; *(sentimental, too sweet)*
piegas, lamechas *m inv*, untuoso,-a; sentimentalóide.
slosh *n* lama, neve *f* aguada; som de pancada na
água, chape; ♦ *vt (apply)* esparrinhar *(liquid)*; **2**
(hit) surrar; ♦ *vi (also: ~* **about)** chapinhar.
sloshed *pp adj* bêbedo,-a, embriagado,-a; **to get ~**
apanhar uma bebedeira.

slot *n (groove)* ranhura *f*; fenda *f*; **2** *(for letters)*
abertura *f*; **3** *(place in programme, timetable)* espaço
m; lugar *m* na grelha horária; ♦ *vt/vi ~* **in** *(insert, fit*
in) encaixar; inserir; **2** *(time)* arranjar tempo para.
slot machine *n (game)* caça-níqueis, **2** *(food, stamps)*
máquina automática.
sloth *n (laziness)* ociosidade *f*, preguiça; **2** *(ZOOL)*
preguiça *f*; *(BR)* bicho-preguiça *m*.
slouch *n (person)* postura desleixada, com os ombros
descaídos; **2** *(fig) (slovenly person)* incompetente
desleixado; **he is a ~ at football** ele é incompetente no futebol; **~ hat** *n* chapéu *m* mole; ♦ *vi (in*
posture) ter má postura, curvar os ombros,
curvar-se.
slough¹ (=~off) *vt (shed)* trocar, mudar de pele
(snake); **2** livrar-se de; **3** cobrir-se de crosta *(wound)*.
slough² *n* charco *m*, pântano *m*.
Slovak *n adj* eslavo,-a; *(LING)* eslavo.
Slovakian *n adj* eslovaco,-a.
Slovenia *n* Eslovénia *(BR:* ê); **in ~** na Eslovénia
(BR: -ê-).
slovenliness *n* desmazelo *m*; desleixo *m*.
slovenly *adj* desalinhado,-a, sujo,-a; desmazelado,-a.
slow *adj* lento,-a, vagaroso,-a; **2** *(watch)* atrasado; **to**
be ~ to do demorar a fazer; **3** *(business)* lento,-as,
4 *(oven, flame)* baixo,-a; **~ handclap** *n* aplauso
lento e rimado em sinal de protesto; **~ motion** *n:*
in ~ motion *(foto, film)* em câmara *f* lenta; ♦ *adv*
lentamente, devagar; ♦ *vt/vi (=* **to ~ down/up)** ir
lento, retardar *(train, economy)* abrandar *(speed,*
progress); IDIOM **to go ~** *(workers)* travar a
produção.
slowcoach *n (coll)* molengão,-gona papa-açorda *m*,
f; **you are a ~** tu és uma lesma *(fig)*.
slowdown *n (ECON)* abrandamento; *(BR: also* desace-
leração *f)*; **2 ~ in demand** diminuição, baixa *f* da
procura; **3 ~ in speed** diminuição da velocidade.
slowly *adv* lentamente.
slowness *n* lentidão *f*.
slowpoke *n =* **slowcoach**.
slow-witted *adj (person)* obtuso,-a; de raciocínio lento.
slowworm *n (ZOOL)* anguinha *f*.
SLR *(abbr for* **single-lens reflex)** máquina *f* fotográfica
reflex de uma só lente, obje(c)tiva.
sludge *n (mud)* lama *m*, *(sediment)* lodo *m*; **2** *(sewage)*
águas *npl* residuais; **~ door** *(NAUT)* porta *f* de
limpeza.
slug *n (ZOOL)* lesma *f*; **2** *(bullet)* bala.
sluggish *adj (slow)* vagaroso,-a, lerdo,-a; **2** *(business,*
work) moroso,-a.
sluice *n (channel)* canal *m*; ♦ *vt* **to ~ down** escoar-se;
to ~ down sth *vt (rinse)* lavar com muita água,
enxaguar; **to ~ out** *vt* jorrar.
sluice gate *n* comporta *f*, represa *f*.
slum *n (area) (BR)* favela; *(EP)* bairro *m* de lata;
bairro *m* degradado **2** *(house)* cortiço *m*, barraco
m, barraca *f*.
slumber *n* sono *m*, soneca *f*.
slump *n (economic)* queda *f*, baixa *f*; **2** *(recession)*
crise *f*; **3** *(popularity)* em baixa; ♦ *vi* baixar
repentinamente.

slung (*pt*, *pp of* **sling**).

slur *n* (*aspersion*) calúnia *f*, mancha *f*; **2** pronúncia, palavra ininteligível; ♦ (**-rr-**) *vt* difamar, caluniar; **2 to ~ one's words** comer as palavras; articular mal.

slurp *vt* sorver (*drink*) fazendo barulho.

slurry *n* purina *f*.

slush *n* neve *f* meio derretida; **2** (*coll*) baboseira *f*; pieguice *f*; **~ fund** *n* fundo *m* para compra de favores políticos.

slushy *adj* (*snow*) meio derretida; **2** (*street*) lamacento,-a; **3** (*fig*) (*coll*) (*novel*, *film*) sentimentalóide (*pop*); piegas *sg pl*.

slut *n* (*coll*) (*slovenly woman*) mulher *f* desmazelada, badalhoca *f*; porca (*offensive*); **2** (*slang*, *pej*) (*promiscuous*) devassa *f*, rameira *f*; (*slang*: *offensive*) puta (*vulg*).

sly *n*: **on the ~** às escondidas; atrás pela calada; ♦ (**-ier/-yer**, **-iest/-yest**) *adj* manhoso,-a, astuto,-a; **2** fingido,-a, velhaco,-a.

smack[1] *n* (*slap*) palmada *f* (*on bottom*), bofetada *f* (*on face*); **2** (*blow*) tabefe *m*; **3** heroína *f*; ♦ *adv* em cheio; **~ in the middle of** mesmo no meio de; ♦ *vt* dar uma palmada, um tabefe em; **~ one's lips** dar um estalo com os lábios.

smack[2] *vi*: **to ~ of** (*taste*, *suggestion of sth*) cheirar a; saber a; **it ~s of greed** isso cheira a ganância.

smacker *n* (*fam*) (*loud kiss*) beijoca (*fam*); **2** uma libra *f* esterlina; (*US*) um dollar.

small *adj* pequeno,-a; (*short person*) baixo,-a; **~ adds** *npl* classificados *mpl*; **~ change** *n* (*money*) troco, trocado; **~ fry** *n* peixe *m* pequeno; arraia *f* miúda; **~holder** *n* pequeno proprietário; **~holding** *n* (*UK*) minifúndio *m*; **~ hours** *npl* primeiras horas *fpl* da manhã; **~ish** *adj* de pequeno porte; **~-minded** *adj* mesquinho,-a; **~pox** *n* varíola; **~ print** *n* as letras miúdas (de um contra(c)to); **~ talk** *n* conversa *f* fiada; **~ time** *adj* insignificante; **the ~ of the back** *n* a região *f* lombar.

smart *n* dor *f* aguda; ♦ *adj* elegante; **2** (*clever*) esperto,-a, astuto,-a; **3** (*quick*) vivo,-a; ♦ *vi* arder, coçar; **~ aleck** *m* sabichâo *m*; **~ arse** (*coll*) (*pej*) espertinho,-a *m*; **~-set** gente de alta-roda; **to ~en up** *vi* melhorar o aspeto (de); **to ~en oneself up** arranjar-se; ♦ *vt* arrumar.

smash *n* (= **~-up**) colisão *f*, choque *m*; ♦ *vt* (*break*) escangalhar, despedaçar; **2** (*car etc*) chocar-se com; **3** (*record*) quebrar; ♦ *vi* colidir; **2** (*against wall etc*) espatifar-se.

smashing *adj* (*coll*) genial *m,f*, porreiro,-a (*pop*).

smattering *n*: **a ~ of** conhecimento superficial de.

SME (*abbr for* **small** or **medium-sized enterprise**) pequenas e médias empresas, PME.

smear *n* mancha *f*, nódoa *f*; **2** (*MED*) rastreio *m*, (*cervical*) papanicolau *m*; ♦ *vt* untar, lambuzar; (*fig*) caluniar, difamar.

smell *n* cheiro *m*; **2** (*sense*) olfa(c)to; ♦ (*pt*, *pp* **smelt** *or* **smelled**) *vt/vi* cheirar; **to ~ of** cheirar a; **it ~s good** cheira bem; **I ~ a rat** aqui há gato, eu desconfio.

smelly *adj* fedorento, malcheiroso.

smile *n* sorriso *m*; ♦ *vi* sorrir.

smiling *adj* sorridente, risonho,-a.

smirk *n* sorriso *m* falso,-a/fe(c)tado,-a.

smith *n* ferreiro.

smithy *n* forja, oficina de ferreiro.

smock *n* guarda-pó *m*, bata *m*, fato-macaco; (*children's*) avental *m*, bibe.

smocking *n* (*sewing*) (*honeycomb stitch*) (favos-de-mel).

smog *n* nevoeiro misturado com fumo, fumaça da cidade; **~ mask** *n* máscara *f* antipoluição.

smoke *n* fumaça, fumo; **~ screen** *n* cortina de fumaça; **~ shop** *n* (*US*) tabacaria; ♦ *vi* fumar; **2** (*chimney*) fumegar; ♦ *vt* fumar.

smoked *adj* (*bacon*) defumado; (*glass*) fumée.

smoker *n* fumador,-ora, fumante. **2** (*RAIL*) vagão *m* para fumadores (*BR*: fumantes).

smoking *n*: '**no smoking**' 'proibido fumar'.

smoky *adj* fumegante; **2** (*room*) cheio de fumaça.

smooth *adj* liso,-a, macio,-a; **2** (*sea*) tranquilo,-a, calmo,-a; **3** (*flat*) plano; **4** (*flavour*, *movement*) suave; **5** (*person*) culto, refinado; **6** (*pej*) meloso; **~-talking** *adj* de lábia *f* fácil, com lábia; ♦ *vt* alisar; (= **to ~ out**) (*difficulties*) acalmar.

smother *vt* cobrir (**with** de), sufocar; **~ with kisses** cobrir de beijos; **2** sufocar; **3** (*extinguish*) abafar; **4** (*repress*) reprimir.

smoulder *vi* arder sem chamas, estar latente.

smouldering *adj* (*fire*, *cigarette*) que se consome; (*ashes*) fumegante; **2** (*fig*) (*passion*) intenso,-a, ardente; **~ eyes** olhos ardentes.

smudge *n* mancha *f*; ♦ *vt* manchar, sujar.

smug *adj* convencido,-a, presunçoso,-a.

smuggle *vt* contrabandear.

smuggler *n* contrabandista *m,f*.

smuggling *n* contrabando.

smutty *adj* (*fig*) obsceno,-a, indecente, manchado,-a.

snack *n* merenda, lanche *m*, petisco, tira-gosto *m*; **~ bar** *n* lanchonete *f*.

snag *n* (*hitch*) dificuldade *f*, obstáculo *m*; **to run into a ~** deparar-se com uma dificuldade; **2** pequeno buraco devido a objeto cortante ou saliente; ♦ (**-gg-**) *vt* (*tear*, *catch*) rasgar; ficar preso,-a, repuxar (*clothes*, *tights*); **to ~ on sth** (*become entangled*) prender-se (em algo); **2** (*US*) (*coll*) conseguir.

snail *n* caracol *m*, (*BR*) caramujo *m*; **~-slow** lento como um caracol; (*traffic*) **at ~'s pace** a passo de caracol.

snake *n* serpente *f*; (*fam*), cobra; **~ bite** *n* mordedura de serpente/cobra; **a ~ in the grass** (*fig*) inimigo,-a na sombra, pessoa velhaca.

snap *n* estalo; estalido; clique *m*; **2** (*clothes*) colchete *m*, mola de pressão; **3** (*PHOT*) foto *f*; ♦ *adj* repentino; ♦ *vt* estalar; quebrar; (*PHOT*) tirar uma foto de; ♦ *vi* (*break*) partir-se, quebrar-se; **2** (*fig*) (*lose control*) perder as estribeiras (*fam*); **to ~ sb's head off** falar bruscamente; **to ~ shut** fechar com estrondo; ♦ **to ~ at** *vt* falar asperamente; **2** (*dog*) tentar morder; **to ~ at an offer** aceitar uma oferta imediatamente; agarrar (*chance*); **to ~ off** *vi* partir-se (*ruidosamente*); **to ~ out** (*fam*) (*recover from depression*) animar-se; **~ out of it!** vamos, acaba lá com essa depressão, esses pensamentos!; **to ~ up** *vt* arrebatar, comprar rapidamente.

snappy *adj (person)* arisco,-a; **2** *(style)* vigoroso,-a; **3** *(person)* animado,-a; **make it ~!** *(fam)* despacha-te (com isso)!, faz isso depressa!

snapshot *n* foto *f* instantânea.

snare *n* armadilha, laço; ♦ *vt* apanhar no laço/na armadilha; *(fig)* enganar.

snarl *n (growl)* rugido *m*, rosnar *m*; ♦ *vi (of animal)* rosnar; **2** *(person)* resmungar; **~ up** *(rope)* emaranhar-se; **to be ~ed up** *(in traffic)* preso,-a (no trânsito).

snatch *n (fig)* roubo; **~es of** *(conversation)* pedacinhos *mpl* de; ♦ *vt* arrebatar; agarrar; tirar à força; **~ at** *vt* tentar agarrar.

snatcher *n* ladrão *m*; ladra *f*; *(of bag, purse)* carteirista.

snazzy (-ier, -iest) *adj (coll) (person)* vistoso,-a, catita *m,f*, pessoa em voga.

sneak *n* mexeriqueiro,-a; queixinhas *sg, pl*; ♦ *adj* furtivo,-a; *(to do sth)* à socapa, às escondidas; ♦ *vt* levar escondido; **to ~ a glance at** lançar um olhar furtivo; ♦ *vi (move furtively)* **to ~ away/off** escapar-se sem ninguém notar; **to ~ in/out** entrar/sair furtivamente; **to ~ up behind sb** aproximar-se de mansinho, por detrás de alguém.

sneakers *npl (US) (shoes)* sapatilhas *fpl*; ténis *m inv*.

sneaking *adj (feeling, suspicion)* vago,-a; **I have a ~ feeling he won't come** eu tenho a impressão de que ele não vem.

sneaky (-ier, -iest) *adj* sorrateiro,-a, furtivo,-a.

sneer *n* sorriso de desprezo, de escarninho, de chacota; ♦ *vi* rir-se com desdém; *(leer)* zombar de, escarnecer de.

sneeze *n* espirro; ♦ *vi* espirrar.

snide *adj* falso,-a insidioso,-a.

sniff *n (of dogs)* farejada; *(of person)* fungadela; ♦ *vi* fungar; ♦ *vt* fungar, farejar.

sniffer *n* fungão *m*, fungona *f*; **2** *(of drugs)* viciado,-a; **~ dog** *n* cão *m* farejador; cão-polícia *m*.

snigger *n* riso *m* abafado; ♦ *vi* rir por dentro.

snip *n* tesourada *f*; **2** *(piece of cloth)* pedaço *m*, retalho *m*; **3** *(bargain)* pechincha *f*; ♦ *vt* cortar com tesoura.

sniper *n* franco-atirador,-ora.

snippet *n (of music, text)* fragmento *m* pedacinho *m*; recorte *m*; **~s** *(of conversation)* frases *fpl* soltas.

snivel (-ll-) *vi* choramingar; pingar do nariz.

sniveling *adj* ranhoso,-a; lamuriento,-a.

snob *n* snob, presumido,-a, *(BR)* esnobe *m,f*.

snobbery *n* snobismo, *(BR)* esnobismo.

snobbish *adj* snob, pedante, *(BR)* esnobe.

snooker *n* sinuca *f*.

snoop *n* bisbilhoteiro,-a; ♦ *vi*: **to ~ about** bisbilhotar.

snooper *n* bisbilhoteiro,-a.

snooty *adj* arrogante.

snooze *n* soneca *f*, sesta *f*; ♦ *vi* tirar uma soneca, dormitar.

snore *n* ronco *m*; ♦ *vi* roncar, ressonar.

snorkel *n* tubo snorkel, tubo para respirar sob a água.

snort *n (sound) (of horse, bull)* resfôlego *m*; *(of pig)* grunhido *m*; *(of person)* bufo, bufido; ♦ *vi* resfolegar, grunhir, bufat; **he ~ with anger** ele bufou

de raiva; **to ~ at** desdenhar de; ♦ *vt (drugs)* cheirar, snifar.

snout *n (of animal)* focinho *m*; *(of person) (coll)* nariz *m*.

snow *n* neve *f*; **~ball** *n* bola *f* de neve; **~bound** *adj* bloqueado,-a pela neve; **~drift** *n* monte *m* de neve (formado pelo vento); **~drop** *n (BOT)* campânula branca *f*; **~fall** *n* nevada *f*; **~flake** *n* floco *m* de neve; **~man** *n* boneco *m* de neve; **~plough** *n* máquina *f* limpa-neve; **~storm** *n* nevasca, tempestade *f* de neve; **~-white** *adj* de uma alvura/brancura; **S~ White** *npr* Branca de Neve *f*; ♦ *vi* nevar; ♦ *vi* acumular-se.

snr *(abbr for **senior**)*.

snub *n* repulsa *f*, reprimenda *f*; mau acolhimento *m*; **2 ~ nose** nariz *m* arrebitado; ♦ (-bb-) *vt* menosprezar; repreender; repelir; **to be ~bed by sb** sofrer uma recusa por parte de alguém.

snuff *n* rapé *m*.

snug *adj (sheltered)* abrigado,-a, protegido,-a; **2** *(fitted)* justo,-a, cómodo,-a *(BR: cô-)*.

snuggle *vi*: **to ~ up to sb** aconchegar-se, aninhar-se a alguém.

so *adv* tão; assim, deste modo; ♦ *conj* consequentemente *(BR: -qüen-)*, portanto; **~ that** para que, a fim de que; de modo que; **~ do I** eu também; **and ~ forth** e assim por diante; **~ what?** então por quê? e daí?; **~~** assim assim, mais ou menos; **I hope ~** espero que sim; **twenty or ~** vinte mais ou menos; **~ far** até aqui; **~ long!** tchau!; adeus!; **~ many** tantos; **~ much** *adv* tanto; **~-and-~** *n* fulano,-a; **Mr ~** o Senhor Fulano do Tal; **to do ~** fazer isto e aquilo.

soak *vt* embeber, ensopar; *(in water)* pôr de molho, estar de molho, impregnar; ♦ *vr (get wet)* encharcar-se; **to ~ in** *vi* infiltrar; **to ~ off** *(stamp, etc)* descolar-se; **to ~ up** *vt (plants, sponge)* absorver *(water)*; *(person)* impregnar-se de; encher-se de sol.

soaked *adj* encharcado,-a, molhado,-a; **2** *(fig) (drunk)* bêbado,-a; **I am ~ to the bones** estou molhado até aos ossos.

soaking *adj* encharcado,-a; *(fam)* a pingar; **I am ~ in a hot bath** estou a embeber-me, a relaxar-me num banho quente.

soap *n* sabão *m*; **toilet ~** sabonete *m*; **~ flakes** *npl* flocos *mpl* de sabão; **~ powder** *n* sabão *m* em pó; **~ opera** *n* telenovela *f*.

soapstone *n (MIN)* esteatite *f*, greda *f*.

soapy *adj* ensaboado,-a.

soar *vi* elevar-se em voo, voar alto; **2** *(building, hill)* levantar-se; **3** *(sound, smoke)* elevar-se; **4** *(prices)* aumentar, subir rapidamente; **your ambitions ~ high** tu tens grandes ambições.

soaring *adj* crescente.

sob *n (from weeping)* soluço *m*; ♦ *vi* soluçar, dizer soluçando.

s.o.b. *(abbr for **son-of-a-bitch**) (US) (coll, pej)* filho,-a da puta *(vulg)*.

sober *adj* sério,-a; sensato,-a; moderado,-a; **2** sóbrio,-a; **3** *(colour, style)* discreto,-a; ♦ **to ~ up** *vi* tornar-se sóbrio.

Soc *(abbr for* **society***)*.

so-called *adj* suposto, assim chamado.

soccer *n* futebol *m*.

sociable *adj* sociável, afável, dado,-a.

social *n* reunião *f* social; ♦ *adj* social; sociável; ~ **climber** *n* arrivista *m,f*; ~ **club** *n* clube *m*; ~ **evening** serão *m* recreativo; ~ **science** *n* ciências *fpl* sociais; ~ **security** *n* segurança (*BR*: previdência) social; ~ **work** *n* assistência, serviço social; ~ **worker** *n* assistente *m,f* social.

socialism *n* socialismo.

socialist *n adj* socialista *m,f*.

socially *adv* socialmente.

society *n* sociedade *f*; **2** associação *f*, coletividade *f*; **3** **high** ~ de alta roda.

sociologist *n* sociólogo,-a.

sociology *n* sociologia *f*.

sock *n* meia *f* (curta); peúga *f*.

socket *n* (*ELECT*) (*for plug*) tomada *f*; **2** (*ANAT*) (*joint*) cavidade *f* articular; (*of eye*) órbita *f*; (*of tooth*) alvéolo *m*.

sod[1] *n* (*of turf*) torrão *m*, relvado *m*.

sod[2] (*person*) (*slang*) pessoa desprezível; sacana *m* (*cal*); **2** (*short for*) sodomita *m*; **3** (*fam*) **the poor** ~! coitado do homem!; ♦ *exc* ~ **off!** (*coll*) ponha-se a andar!; vá à merda! (*cal*).

soda *n* (*CHEM*) soda; (= ~ **water**) água com gás.

sodden *adj* (*wet through*) encharcado,-a; **2** (*fig, coll*) ~ **with drink** embrutecido,-a pelo álcool.

sodium *n* sódio *m*.

sofa *n* sofá *m*; ~**bed** *n* sofa-cama *m*.

Sofia *npr* (*GEOG*) Sófia; **in** ~ em Sófia.

soft *adj* (*silky*) macio,-a; **2** (*not hard*) mole; **3** (*breeze, climate*) suave, leve; **4** bondoso,-a; **5** (*weak*) fraco,-a; **6** (*bed, jumper*) fofo,-a; **7** (*muscle*) flácido,-a, frouxo,-a; **8** (*ground, soil*) movediço,-a; **9** (*voice*) meiga, branda; **10** (*POL*) moderado,-a; ~ **steps** passos *mpl* abafados; ~ **option** *n* facilidade *f*; **to choose the** ~ **option** escolher a facilidade; ~ **porn** *n* (*coll*) soft (*fam*); ~ **spot** *n*: (*coll*) **to have a** ~ **spot for sb** ter um fraquinho por alguém; ~ **toy** *n* animal *m* de pelúcia; ♦ **to be** ~ **on sb** (*lenient*) ser indulgente para com alguém; **to be** ~ **in the head** (*fig*) ser mentecapto,-a.

soft-boiled *adj* (*egg*) ovo *m* quente.

soft drink *n* refrigerante *m*, bebida sem álcool, refrescos.

soft drug *n* droga *f* leve.

soften *vt* amolecer, amaciar, suavizar; ♦ *vi* abrandar-se, enternecer-se, suavizar-se.

soft focus *n* focagem *f* artística.

soft-hearted *adj* bondoso,-a, caridoso,-a.

softly *adv* suavemente; delicadamente; (*sound, voice*) baixinho.

softness *n* suavidade *f*; **2** maciez *f*; **3** maleabilidade *f*; **4** (*sweetness*) doçura; **5** (*kindness*) bondade *f*.

soft pedal *n* (*MUS*) pedal *m* abafador; ♦ (-ll-) *vi* (*MUS*) tocar em surdina (ao piano); **2** (*AUT*) (*fig*) fazer marcha atrás; ♦ *vt* (*fig*) atenuar, suavizar.

soft-spoken *adj* brando no falar, de voz suave; (*glib*) bem falante.

software *n* (*COMP*) software *m*.

softwood *n* (*timber*) madeira *f* macia; **2** (*tree*) conífera *f*.

softy (*pl:* -ies) *n* (*fig, pej*) (*weak*) maricas *m*, banana *m* (*pop*); **2** (*kind, sentimental person*) coração de manteiga.

soggy (-ier, -iest) *adj* ensopado, encharcado; (*food*) empapado,-a.

soil *n* terra *f*, solo *m*; ♦ *vt* sujar, manchar.

soiled *adj* sujo,-a.

solace *n* consolo *m*; ♦ *vt* aliviar, consolar.

solar *adj* solar; ~ **energy** *n* energia *f* solar; ~ **panel** *n* painel *m* solar.

solarium *n* solário *m*.

sold (*pt, pp of* **sell**) ~ **out** *adj* (*COMM*) esgotado,-a.

solder *n* solda *f*; ♦ *vt* soldar.

soldier *n* (*gen*) soldado; **2** (*army man*) militar *m*; **regular** ~ *n* military *m* de carreira; ♦ ~ **on** *vt* aguentar firme.

sole *n* (*of foot, of shoe*) sola; **2** (*fish: pl inv*) linguado *m*; ♦ *adj* único.

solely *adv* somente, unicamente.

solemn *adj* solene *m,f*, cerimonioso,-a.

solemnize *vt* celebrar (*marriage*); ratify (*treaty*).

sole trader *n* comerciante *m,f* individual, por conta própria.

sol-fa *n* (*MUS*) solfejo.

solicit *vt* (*request*) solicitar; **2** prostituir-se.

soliciting *n* angariação *f*.

solicitor *n* (*JUR*) solicitador,-ora; **2** (*in court*) advogado *m* em causas simples; **3** (*US*) promotor,-ora.

Solicitor-General *n* (*UK*) (*JUR*) assistente do procurador-geral.

solicitous *adj* (*caring, helpful*) solícito,-a; **2** (*anxious*) desejoso,-a de algo.

solid *n* (*CHEM*) sólido *m*; ~**s** *npl* (*food*) alimentos *mpl* sólidos; ♦ *adj* sólido,-a; **2** (*gold, etc*) maciço,-a; **3** (*reliable, firm*) sério,-a, honesto,-a; **4** (*dense*) compa(c)to *m*; **5** ~ **rock** massa *f* rochosa; **6** (*uninterrupted*) **ten** ~ **hours** (*at work*) dez horas inteiras, sem parar; (*colour*) de uma só cor, contínuo,-a.

solidarity *n* solidariedade *f*; **to be/feel** ~ **with sb** sentir-se solidário com alguém.

solidify *vi* solidificar-se.

soliloquy (*pl:* -ies) *n* solilóquio *m*.

solitaire *n* (*jewel*) solitário *m*; **2** (*card game*) solitário, jogo de paciência.

solitary *adj* (*loner*) solitário,-a, sozinho,-a, a sós; **2** (*remote place*) isolado,-a, afastado,-a; **3** (*single*) único,-a; ~ **confinement** *n* prisão *f* solitária.

solitude *n* solidão *f*, isolamento *m*.

solo *n* solo *m*; ♦ *adj* (*MUS*) solo; **2** (*single-handed*) desacompanhado,-a.

soloist *n* solista *m,f*.

solstice *n* solstício *m*.

soluble *adj* solúvel.

solution *n* solução *f*.

solve *vt* resolver, solucionar.

solvency *n* (*FIN*) solvência *f*.

solvent (*CHEM*) solvente *m*; ♦ *adj* (*CHEM*) (*cleaner*) dissolvente *m*; (*FIN*) (*person*) solvente; ~ **abuse** *n* uso/abuso de solventes, inalação *f* de solventes.

sombre *(UK)* **somber** *(US) adj* sombrio,-a, escuro,-a; **2** *(mood)* lúgubre *m,f*.

some *adj (a few)* alguns/algumas; **2** *(certain)* algum,-a; um pouco de; ♦ *pron* alguns/algumas; *(a bit)* um pouco; ♦ *adv*: ~ **thirty people** umas trinta pessoas; ~ **more cake?** mais um pouco de bolo?; ~ **day** *adv* um dia; ~ **party!** e que festa!; **there's** ~ **milk in the fridge** há leite na geladeira; **I've got** ~ *(books etc)* tenho alguns; *(milk, money etc)* tenho um pouco de; ~ **body** *pron* alguém; ~**day** algum dia, um dia *(in future)*; ~**how** *adv* de alguma maneira; *(for some reason)* por uma razão ou outra; ~ **one** *pron* alguém; ~**one else** outra pessoa.

somersault *n* salto *m* mortal; **2** *(of gymnast, vehicle)* cambalhota *f*; ♦ *vi* dar um salto mortal/uma cambalhota; *(vehicle)* capotar.

something *pron* algo; alguma coisa.

sometime *adv (in future)* algum dia, em outra oportunidade; **2** *(in past)* ~ **last month** durante o mês passado.

sometimes *adv* às vezes; de vez em quando.

somewhat *adv* um tanto.

somewhere *adv* algures; *(be)* em algum lugar; *(go)* para algum lugar; ~ **else** *(be)* em outro lugar; *(go)* para outro lugar.

son *n* filho.

song *n* canção *f*; ~ **writer** *n* autor,-ora de letra; compositor,-ora de canções; **to burst into a** ~ desatar a cantar; **2** *(of bird)* canto *m*; **3** *(REL; lyrical poem)* cântico *m*; **4** *(fig)* bagatela, ninharia; IDIOM **I bought the picture for a** ~ comprei o quadro por uma bagatela/pechincha.

sonic *adj* sónico,-a *(BR: -ô-)*, acústico,-a; ~ **boom** *n* ruído *m* sónico; ~ **interference** *n* interferências *fpl* sonoras.

son-in-law *n* genro *m*.

sonnet *n* soneto *m*.

soon *adv* logo, brevemente, em breve; **2** *(early)* cedo; ~ **afterwards** pouco depois.

sooner *adv* antes, mais cedo; *(preference)* **I would** ~ **do that** preferia fazer isso; ~ **or later** mais cedo ou mais tarde.

soot *n* fuligem *f*; ♦ *vt* enfarruscar.

soothe *vt* acalmar, sossegar; **2** *(pain)* aliviar, suavizar.

sooty (-ier, -iest) *adj (covered in soot)* enfarruscado,-a; *(atmosphere)* fuliginoso,-a; **2** *(cat, fur)* todo preto; *(such cat) n (name)* farrusco.

sop *n* pequena compensação *f*, suborno (para apaziguar); **2** *(of bread)* pão embebido em algo (azeite, etc); **3** *(weak, gullible person)* pessoa fraca, idiota; ♦ *(-pp-) vt* ensopar *(bread, biscuit)*; **to** ~ **the soup with bread** encher a sopa com pão; **to** ~ **up** absorver.

sophisticate *vt* alterar, sofisticar.

sophisticated *adj* sofisticado,-a, cosmopolita.

sophomore *n (US) (Univ)* estudante *m,f* do 2º ano da universidade.

soporific *adj* soporífico,-a.

sopping *adj*: ~ **wet** totalmente encharcado.

soppy *adj (pej) (silly sentimental)* sentimentalóide; piegas *m,f/sg/pl*; *(always kissing, hugging)* terno,-a demais; **2** ensopado,-a, encharcado,-a.

soprano *n (person)* soprano; *(voice)* soprano *f*.

sorcerer *n* feiticeiro *m*.

sorceress *n* feiticeira; bruxa *f*.

sorcery *n (witchcraft) n* feitiçaria *f*; mágica *f*.

sordid *adj* sórdido,-a.

sore *n* chaga *f*, ferida; ♦ *adj* doloroso, doído; **2** *(offended)* magoado,-a, ofendido,-a; *(topic, subject)* delicado; ~ **at** irritado,-a com; **in** ~ **need** carente, em necessidade desesperada.

sorely *adv* imensamente; ~ **tried** *(patience)* posto a rude prova.

sorrel *n (BOT)* azeda-miúda.

sorrow *n* tristeza *f*, mágoa *f*, dor *f*.

sorrowful *adj* triste, aflito,-a, magoado,-a.

sorry *adj (regretful)* arrependido,-a; **2** *(condition, action, business)* deplorável, lamentável; ♦ *exc* ~! *(failing to hear)* desculpe! como!; **2** *(apologising)* desculpe! perdão!; **3** *(feeling sad for sb)* sinto muito!; **4** *(correcting o.s.)* **on Sunday,** ~, **Saturday** domingo, quero dizer, sábado; **to feel** ~ **for sb** sentir pena de alguém; **to feel** ~ **for o.s.** lamentar-se, ter pena de si próprio lamuriar-se; **I feel** ~ **to have to say that** lamento ter de dizer que.

sort *n* espécie *f*, género *(BR:* gê-*)*, tipo *m*; ♦ *vt* (= **to** ~ **out**: *papers)* classificar; *(problems)* solucionar, resolver.

sorted *adj* escolhido,-a, sortido,-a; ~ **of** mais ou menos.

sortie *n (MIL) (of troops)* surtida.

sorting *n* escolha *f*, distribuição *f*; **2** *(post)* tiragem *f* postal.

so-so *adv* mais ou menos, regular.

soufflé *n* suflê *m*.

sought *(pt, pp* of **seek)**; ♦ *adj* ~**-after** *(person, skill)* procurado,-a, solicitado,-a; *(product)* apreciado,-a.

soul *n* alma *f*; ~**-destroying** *adj* embrutecedor,-ora; ~**ful** *adj* emocional; *(eyes, voice)* triste; ~**less** *adj* desalmado,-a; ~ **mate** *n* alma *f* gémea; ~**-searching** *n* exame *m* de consciência.

sound *n* som *m*, ruído *m*; *(noise)* barulho *m*; ~ **barrier** *n* barreira do som; ~ **effects** *npl* efeitos *mpl* sonoros; **2** *(GEOG)* estreito *m*, braço *m* *(de mar)*; *(MED)* sonda *f*; ♦ *adj (healthy)* saudável, sadio,-a; **in** ~ **health** em boa saúde; **2** *(in good condition)* sólido,-a, completo,-a; ~ **asleep** dormindo profundamente; completamente; ~ **grounds for** motivos *npl* sólidos; **3** *(safe) (investment)* seguro,-a; **4** *(person)* digno de confiança; ~ **mind: to be in** ~ **mind** *(JUR)* estar em plena posse e gozo das suas faculdades mentais; ♦ *vt (alarm)* soar; **to** ~ **like** soar como; parecer; **to** ~ **out** *(opinions, ground, rock)* sondar *(alguém, algo)*; ♦ *vi* soar, ressoar; **2** *(AUT)* buzinar; **3** *(fig) (seem)* parecer; **by the** ~ **of it** ao que parece; **4** *(MED)* **to** ~ **out one's chest** auscultar o peito de alguém.

soundbite *n (JOURN)* citação *f* curta de um discurso.

soundcard *n (COMP)* placa *f* de som.

sounding *n (NAUT) (measurement of depth)* prumada *f*; sondagem *f*; *(probing, questioning)* sondagem;

~-board n *(above stage)* difusor m acústico; **2** *(instrument)* tampa f de ressonância.

soundly adv profundamente.

soundproof adj à prova de som; ♦ vt insonorizar *(room)*.

soundtrack n *(of film)* trilha f sonora.

soundwave n onda f sonora.

soup n *(thick)* sopa; *(thin)* caldo; **green**; **~** m *(Portuguese)* caldo verde; **to be in the ~** *(fig)* estar (metido,-a) numa encrenca; **~ spoon** n colher f de sopa.

sour adj *(milk etc)* azedo,-a; ácido,-a; *(wine)* avinagrado,-a; *(fruit)* verde m,f; **~ cream** n nata f azeda; **~ grapes** n inveja f pura; pessoa com dor de cotovelo; **sweet and ~** n agro-doce m; **~ 2** *(fig)* *(person)* mal-humorado,-a; **to go ~** azedar, talhar; ♦ vt *(fig)* estragar *(atmosphere)*; ♦ vi *(attitude, mood)* azedar-se.

source n *(gen)* fonte f; *(of river)* fonte, nascente f *(fig)* origem f; **at ~** na fonte; **from reliable ~s** de fonte fidedigna, de fonte segura.

sourness n azedume m; *(acidity)* acidez f.

sourpuss n *(fam)* rabugento,-a; pessoa com cara de poucos amigos.

south n sul m; ♦ adj do sul, meridional; ♦ adv ao/ para o sul; **S~ Africa** npr África do Sul; **S~ African** npr adj sul-africano,-a; **S~ America** npr América do Sul; **S~ American** adj sul-americano,-a; **~bound** adj para o sul; **~-east** n sudeste m; **S~-East Asia** npr Sudeste m Asiático; **S~ Africa** npr África Meridional, Austral; **S~ Pole** npr Polo Sul; **~erly** adj meridional; do sul; **~ern** adj do sul, sulista; **~ward(s)** adv para o sul; **~-west** n sudoeste m; **~western** adj de sudoeste.

souvenir n lembrança f.

sovereign n adj soberano,-a.

sovereignty n soberania f.

Soviet n adj soviético,-a; **soviet** *(council)* soviete.

sow n *(female of pig)* porca f; ♦ *(pt* -**ed,** *pp* **sown)** vt semear; **2** disseminar, espalhar; IDIOM **as you ~, so shall you reap** cada um colhe aquilo que semeia.

sowing n *(AGR)* sementeira f.

soy n: **~ sauce** molho de soja.

soya bean n semente f de soja.

spa n fonte f de água mineral; estância termal *(BR:* hidromineral); **~ water** água mineral.

space n *(gen)* espaço m; **2** lugar m; **3** *(interval)* intervalo m; **4** *(gap)* espaço m; **5** *(gap between)* distância f; ♦ vt *(= to ~ out)* espaçar; **~ bar** n *(COMP)* *(keyboard)* barra f; **~ craft** n nave f espacial, espaçonave f; **~ man/woman** n astronauta m,f, cosmonauta m,f; **~ probe** n sonda f espacial; **~-saving** adj que poupa espaço; **~ shuttle** n vaivem m espacial.

spacing n *(TYPO)* espacejamento; **2** *(of payments)* escalonamento m.

spacious adj espaçoso,-a, amplo,-a.

spade n *(AGR)* *(tool)* pá f; IDIOM **I call a ~ a ~** *(speak frankly)* digo a verdade nua e crua; eu sou pão pão, queijo queijo; **~s** npl *(cards)* espadas fpl.

spaghetti n espa(r)guete m.

Spain n Espanha; **in ~** na Espanha.

Spam® n carne f de porco enlatada.

span n *(of bird, plane)* envergadura f; *(of hand)* palma; *(of arch)* vão m; *(in time)* lapso, espaço; ♦ vt estender-se sobre, atravessar; *(fig)* abarcar.

spangle n *(small shining object for decoration)* vidrinho, lantejoula f; ♦ vt brilhar, reluzir.

Spaniard n espanhol,-ola.

spaniel n *(dog)* spaniel m.

Spanish n adj espanhol,-ola; ♦ n *(LING)* espanhol m, castelhano; **S~-American** npr adj Hispano-Americano; **S~-Portuguese** adj luso-espanhol.

Spanish guitar n *(MUS)* *(six strings)* viola f.

spank n palmada f *(on bottom)*; ♦ vt bater, dar palmadas *(on bottom)*.

spanking n açoite m; tareia f, sova f.

spanner n chave f inglesa.

spar n *(NAUT)* mastro, verga; ♦ *(-rr-)* vi *(boxing)* treinar boxe; **2** *(fig)* discutir amigavelmente.

spare n *(AUTO)* *(part, extna)* sobressalente; ♦ adj *(free)* vago, desocupado; **2** *(surplus)* de sobra, a mais; **3** *(available)* disponível, de reserva; **~ time** n tempo m livre, vagar m; **~ tyre** n pneu m sobresselente; **2** *(fig)* *(fat around hips)* pneu; ♦ vt dispensar, passar sem; **2** dispor de, ter de sobra; **3** *(refrain from hurting)* perdoar, poupar; **4** *(be grudging with)* dar frugalmente.

sparing adj: **to be ~ with** ser económico com.

sparingly adv em pequena quantidade, moderadamente.

spark n *(ELECT)* faísca; *(from fire)* faúlha, fagulha; **2** *(of genius)* centelha f, rasgo m; *(of enthusiasm)* chispa f; **~(ing) plug** n vela de ignição; ♦ **to ~ sth off** vt desencadear *(row, war)*; **2** lançar faíscas.

sparkle n cintilação f, brilho m; ♦ vi cintilar; brilhar; faiscar.

sparkling adj cintilante m,f; **2** *(wine)* espumante m; **3** **~ water** *(mineral)* com gás, gaseificado,-a, gasoso,-a; **4** *(wit)* brilhante m,f espírito m vivo; ♦ **~ clean** adv limpo,-a; a brilhar.

sparrow n pardal m.

sparse adj *(population, vegetation)* escasso; disperso,-a; *(of information)* esparso,-a; *(hair)* ralo; *(use)* moderado,-a.

sparsely adv pouco, escassamente; dispersamente.

Spartan n adj espartano,-a.

spasm n *(MED)* *(muscular contraction)* espasmo m; *(of coughing)* acesso, ataque m.

spasmodic adj espasmódico,-a, intermitente.

spastic n espasmofílico,-a; ♦ adj espástico,-a.

spat *(pt, pp of* **spit**).

spatchcock n *(CULIN)* frango aberto pelas costas (espalmado) e grelhado.

spate n série f *(of incidents)*; **2** *(outpouring)* jorro m; **a ~ of words** uma torrente de palavras; **3** *(river)* cheia f repentina de um rio; **the river was in a ~** o rio estava em cheia a transbordar.

spatial adj espacial.

spatter n *(rain)* borrifos mpl; ♦ vt/vi borrifar, salpicar; **he spattered my car with mud** ele salpicou o meu carro de lama; **2** *(fig)* difamar.

spatula n espátula f.

spawn n ovas fpl; ♦ vi desovar, procriar.

spay vt esterilizar fêmea, extrair os ovários da fêmea.

speak (pt **spoke**, pp **spoken**) vt/vi dizer, falar, discursar; **to ~ to/with sb** falar a/com alguém; **to ~ of/about sb/sth** falar de/sobre algo; **to ~ well/highly of sb** falar bem de alguém; **to ~ on sth** discursar sobre algo; ♦ **speaking: ~ as** falando como; **~ of** falando de/sobre; ♦ **~ louder!** fale mais alto!; **nothing to ~ of** nada de especial; **so to ~** adv por assim dizer; ♦ **~ out** vt falar abertamente; desembuchar; **2 ~ against sb/sth** fazer declarações contra alguém/algo; ♦ **~ up!** fale claro!; **to ~ up for sb/sth** falar em defesa de alguém/algo.

speaker n (of a language) falante; **2** (in public) palestrante; orador,-ora, conferencista; **3** (= loud) alto-falante m; (system) caixa f de som; **S~** (POL) (UK) Presidente da Câmara dos Comuns.

spear n lança f; **2** (for fishing) arpão m; ♦ vt lancear, arpoar; germinar; **~-grass** (BOT) grama; **~head** n ponta-de-lança.

special adj especial; (edition etc) extra; (delivery) rápida; **~ist** n técnico, especialista.

speciality n especialidade f.

specialize vi: **to ~** (in) especializar-se (em).

specially adv sobretudo, especialmente.

species n espécie f.

specific adj específico,-a.

specifically adv especificamente.

specification n especificação f; **~s** npl detalhes mpl, características fpl.

specify vt/vi especificar, pormenorizar.

specimen n (of plants, species) espécime m; **2** (of urine, semen, handwriting) amostra f; **3** (fig) (person) exemplar m.

speck n (on skin) mancha f pequena, sinal m; **2** (on fabric) pinta f; **3** (of dust, salt) grão m; **4** (dot) ponto m; **5** (of metal) partícula f; ♦ vt manchar, salpicar, mosquear.

speck© (=salted ~) (fat from pork belly) banha f.

speckled adj manchado,-a; **2** (on bird, cat) malhado,-a, sarapintado,-a; **3** (material) (with dots) as pintas; (with flecks, sequins) salpicado,-a (with de).

specs (abbr for **spetacles**) npl (coll) óculos mpl.

spectacle n espe(c)táculo; **~s** npl óculos mpl.

spectacular adj espe(c)tacular; (success) impressionante m,f, tremendo,-a.

spectator n espectador,-ora, observador,-ora.

spectral adj espe(c)tral.

spectre n espectro m (of de), aparição f.

spectrum (pl: -tra) n espectro m.

speculate vi especular; **to ~ about** especular sobre; (FIN) **to ~ on the Stock Exchange** especular na Bolsa.

speculation n (FIN) especulação f; **2** conje(c)turas fpl.

speculative adj especulativo,-a.

speculator n especulador,-ora.

speech n (spoken form) fala f; **clear ~** fala clara; linguagem; **2** (faculty) palavra; **3** (oration) discurso m; **4** (LING) **direct/indirect ~** discurso dire(c)to/

indire(c)to; **free ~** expressão f livre; **~ impediment** n defeito m na fala; **~less** adj mudo,-a, emudecido; (fig) estupe fa(c)to,-a; **~ therapist** n fonoaudiólogo,-a.

speed n velocidade f; (rapidity) rapidez f (of answer); **at the ~ of light** à velocidade da luz; **2** (PHOT) (of film) sensibilidade f; (gear) velocidade; **at full/top ~** a toda a velocidade; **~ boat** n lancha f; **~ bump/hump** (on road) pequena elevação/lomba para impedir a velocidade; **~ily** adv depressa, rapidamente; **~ing** n (AUT) excesso m de velocidade; **~ometer** n velocímetro m; **~way** n (SPORT) pista f de corrida; ♦ (pt, pp **sped**) vt/vi apressar (process, step); **to ~ along** conduzir demasiado depressa; **to ~ up** vt/vi acelerar.

speedy adj (fast) veloz, rápido,-a; **2** (prompt) pronto, de imediato.

spell n (= magic ~) encanto m, feitiço m; **~ bound** adj encantado,-a, fascinado; **~checker** (COMP) corretor m ortográfico; **evil ~** feitiçaria f; **2** (period of time) período breve, intervalo; temporada f; **a ~ at gymnasts** uma temporada em ginástica; ♦ (pt, pp **spelt** or **spelled**) vt (= **to ~ out**) soletrar, saber escrever e ler; **2** (fig) presagiar, ser sinal de; **it ~s disaster** é um sinal de desastre; **to cast a ~ on sb** enfeitiçar alguém; **to ~ sth out** explicar algo em detalhe.

spelling n ortografia f.

spelt (pt, pp of **spell**).

spend (pt, pp **spent**) vt (money, energy) gastar; **2** (time) desperdiçar; **3** (life) passar, dedicar.

spender n gastador,-ora; **2** (who wastes money) esbanjador,-ora.

spending n gastos mpl; **~ money** n dinheiro m para despesas pessoais; **~ power** n poder m aquisitivo.

spendthrift n esbanjador,-ora, perdulário,-a.

sperm n (semen) esperma m; (coll) espermatozóide m; **~ whale** n cachalote m.

spermicidal adj espermicida.

spew vt vomitar; cuspir, expelir; ♦ vi: **to ~ out** (from sth) lançar-se (para fora) de algo.

sphere n esfera f.

spherical adj esférico,-a.

sphinx n esfinge f.

spice n especiaria f; (CULIN) tempero m, condimento m; ♦ vt condimentar; **~ up** apimentar; IDIOM **variety is the ~ of life** a variedade é o sal da vida.

spick-and-span adj (clean, neat) impecável (place).

spicy adj condimentado,-a; (fig) picante.

spider n (ZOOL) aranha f; **~'s web** n teia de aranha; **~-crab** n (ZOOL, CULIN) santola f.

spidery adj aranhoso,-a.

spiel n lábia f.

spigot n tampão m (que tapa barril); **2** (MEC) ressalto m; (US) torneira f.

spike n (point) ponta, espigão m; **2** (BOT) espiga.

spiky (-ier, -iest) adj (tree branch) com espinhos; **2** (hair) à escovinha; **3** (object) afiado,-a.

spill (pt, pp **spilt** or **spilled**) vt entornar, derramar; ♦ vi derramar-se; **to ~ over** transbordar-se.

spillage n (of oil, etc) derramamento m.

spilt (pt, pp of **spill**).

spin *n* volta, rotação *f*; *(dancer)* pirueta *f*; **2** *(AER)* parafuso *m*; **3** *(trip in car)* volta, passeio de carro; **to go for a** ~ dar uma volta, um passeio de carro; **4 to put ~ on a ball** *(SPORT)* dar efeito a uma bola; ♦ *(pt, pp* **spun***) vt* fiar, tecer *(textile)*; **2** *(wheel, top)* girar, fazer girar; **3** *(wring out)* torcer (roupa à máquina); **to ~ a coin** *(flip)* atirar uma moeda ao ar; ♦ *vi* girar, rodar; **2** (grow dizzy) **my head is ~ing** a minha cabeça está a girar, estou com a cabeça a andar à roda; **the room was ~ing around me** a sala rodopiava à minha volta; **2** *(nose dive) (plane)* descer em parafuso; **to ~ off** rodopiar; **the car spun off the road** o carro rodopiou para fora da estrada e capotou; ♦ **to ~ out** *vt* prolongar; prorrogar; **2** *(food, money)* fazer esticar/fazer durar; **to ~ round** girar, voltar-se; *(dance)* dar piruetas; **to ~ a yard** *(tell)* contar uma história em grande detalhe.

spinach *n* *(BOT)* espinafre *m*.

spinal *adj* espinhal; ~ **cord** *n* coluna vertebral, espinha dorsal.

spindle *n* *(on spinning-wheel)* fuso *m*.

spindly (-**ier**, -**iest**) *adj* alto e magro, espigado.

spin doctor *n* *(UK)* *(POL)* *(pej)* pessoa encarregada das relações com a imprensa e de manipular/adaptar as notícias.

spin-drier *n* máquina de secar; centrífuga.

spine *n* espinha dorsal; **2** *(thorn)* espinho; **3** *(book)* lombada.

spine-chilling *adj* arrepiante, de arrepiar.

spineless *adj* *(no thorns)* sem espinhos; **2** *(ZOOL)* invertebrado,-a; **3** *(fig)* fraco,-a, sem energia; **4** *(without guts)* covarde/cobarde.

spinning *n* fiação *f*; ~ **top** *n* *(child's toy)* pião *m*; ~ **wheel** *n* roca de fiar; movimento de rotação.

spin-off *n* *(by-product)* subproduto *m*; produto *m* derivado; **2** *(TV)* adaptação dum filme; **3** vantagem *f* adicional.

spinster *n* solteira *f*; *(pej)* solteirona.

spiny *adj* espinhoso,-a; com espinhas.

spiral *n* espiral *f*; ♦ *adj* em espiral: ~ **staircase** *n* escada em caracol, espiral.

spiralling *adj* *(cost, prices)* galopante *m,f* em flecha.

spire *n* *(ARCH)* flecha, agulha; **church** ~ flecha duma igreja; **2** *(of plant)* haste; **3** *(turn, coil)* volta numa estrutura espiral.

spirit *n* *(gen)* espírito *m*; **in a friendly** ~ num espírito amigável; **to enter into the** ~ **of the fun** participar na brincadeira; **2** *(courage)* coragem *f*, determinação *f*; **my** ~ **sank** perdi a coragem; **the Holy S~** o Espírito Santo; ~ **level** *n* nível *m* de bolha, de pedreiro; **methylated** ~ *(COMM, CHEM)* *m* álcool *m* metilado, desnaturado; **surgery** ~ *n* álcool *m*; **white** ~ *n* diluente *m*; *(of turpentine)* aguarrás; ♦ *vt* animor, encorajar; **to ~ sb/sth away/off** fazer desaparecer alguém/algo (em segredo).

spirited *adj* *(lively, witty)* animado,-a, espirituoso,-a.

spiritless *adj* desanimado,-a.

spirits *npl* *(mood)* **to be in good/high** ~ estar de boa disposição; **low** ~ desânimo *m*, de mau humor *m*; **to keep up one's** ~ manter o ânimo *m*; **2** *(ghost)* espíritos; **3** *(whisky, etc)* bebida *fsg* alcoólica, álcool *m* forte.

spiritual *adj* espiritual.

spiritualism *n* espiritualismo, espiritismo *m*.

spit *n* *(for roasting)* espeto *m*; **2** *(NAUT)* restinga; ♦ *(pt, pp* **spat***) vi* cuspir; *(with phlegm)* escarrar, espectorar; **to ~ blood** *(fig)* *(anger)* estar encolerizado,-a; **to ~ out** esguichar *(drink – from bottle, from tap)*; **to ~ sth out** cuspir *(algo)* para fora.

spite *n* despeito, rancor *m*, ressentimento *m*; ♦ *vt* mortificar, contrariar; **in ~ of** apesar de, a despeito de.

spiteful *adj* rancoroso,-a, malévolo,-a.

spittle *n* saliva *f*, cuspe *m*, cuspo *m*; **2** *(with phlegm)* escarro *m*; **3** *(of animal)* baba *f*.

spittoon *n* recipiente para cuspir *(especially for wine-tasting)*.

splash *n* borrifo *m*, salpico *m*; *(of colour)* mancha *f*; *(small amount)* gota *f*, respingo *m* *(in drink)*; pancada *f* na água, chape *m*; **to make a** ~ *(fig)* causar sensação, dar nas vistas; ♦ *vt/vi (mud, etc)* salpicar; *(sprinkle)* borrifar; *(with feet)* chapinhar *(in water, mud)*; **to ~ down** *vi* (pousar na agua) amarar; *(BR)* amerissar; **to ~ money about out** esbanjar, gastar um dinheirão; **to ~ water about** fazer esparrinhar a água.

splashdown *n* *(helicopter, spacecraft)* pousa *f* controlada no mar, amaragem *f*; *(BR)* amrissagem *f*.

splatter *n* *(of rain)* pingos, salpigos *mpl*; ♦ *vt/vi (with water, mud)* salpicar.

splay *n* *(ARCH)* alargamento *m*; ♦ *vt* cortar em viés *(end of pipe)*; **2** afastar; **3** *(ARCH)* alargar; **4** *(VET)* deslocar (omoplata de animal).

splayed *adj* largo e chato, virado,-a para fora, afastado,-a; ~-**feet** pés *mpl* para fora.

spleen *n* *(ANAT)* baço, *(fig)* *(anger)* cólera *f*, mau humor *m*.

splendid *adj* esplêndido,-a; soberbo,-a.

splendour *n* esplendor *m*; *(of achievement)* pompa *f*, glória *f*.

splice *n* *(in rope)* entrelaçamento *m*; **2** *(in film, tape)* junção *f*; **3** *(carpentry)* encaixe *m*; ♦ *vt (join)* unir, entrelaçar *(rope)* **2** *(film)* juntar; IDIOM **to get ~d** *(marry)* dar o nó.

splint *n* tala *f*; **to put a ~ on** *(leg, arm)* colocar, aplicar uma tala em; **2** *(ANAT)* perónio *(BR: -rô-)*.

splinter *n* *(of wood)* lasca; *(thinner)* farpa *f* **I have a ~ in my finger** tenho uma farpa no meu dedo; **2** *(of broken glass)* estilhaço *m*; ♦ *vi* lascar *(wood)*; *(fig)* dividir, separar *(grupo)*; ♦ *vi (of glass)* estilhaçar-se; *(of group)* fragmentar-se.

splinter group *n* grupo *m* dissidente.

split *n* *(fine gap)* fenda, brecha *f*; **2** *(tear, hole)* rompimento *m*, rotura *f*; **3** *(crack in a cup, etc)* racha *f*; **4** *(POL)* divisão *f*; **5** *(CHEM, PHYS)* cisão *f*, desintegração *f*; ~ **ends** *npl* *(hair)* pontas *fpl* espigadas; **to ~ hairs** *(coll)* *(comment)* fazer uma distinção desnecessária, ser miudinho,-a; ~ **infinitive** *(LING)* *n* infinitivo inglês em que se intercala o advérbio entre a partícula 'to' e o verbo (considerado incorrecto); ~ **level** *n* *(house, flat)* casa ou apartamento com dois níveis diferentes (desníveis) no mesmo piso; ~ **personality** n dupla personalidade f; ~ **second** fracção de um segundo; ~ **screen** n (CIN) tela múltipla; ~**s** npl: **to do the ~s** fazer espargata f; ♦ (pt, pp **split**) vt/vi (tear) rasgar; (share) dividir, repartir; rachar (log, rock); partir; (POL) provocar uma cisão em (party, alliance); ♦ vi dividir-se; **2** fender-se; **3** desintegrar-se; **to ~ the atom** desintegrar o átomo; **4** (slang) (leave) partir; **let's ~** vamos desaparecer; **to ~ off (from sb)** separar-se de (alguém), **to ~ off (from sth)** desprender-se de (algo); **to ~ open** (material) rasgar-se; **to ~ one's head open** partir a cabeça; **to ~ a watermelon open** rachar a melancia, abrir ao meio; ♦ **to ~ up** fracionar; **2** separar-se (**from sb** de alguém); **3** dispersar-se; **4** (path) bifurcar-se; IDIOM **to ~ one's sides with laughter** morrer de riso; **to ~ the difference** vt chegar a um meio-termo.

splitting adj a(c)to de rachar; divisão, cisão; ♦ adj **I have a ~ headache** tenho uma dor de cabeça insuportável.

splotch n borrão m, mancha f.

splotchy adj manchado,-a, sujo,-a.

splutter vt/vi (stutter) falar atabalhoadamente; **2** (spit out saliva, bits of food) deitar perdigotos/gafanhotos ao falar; **3** (from fire) lançar, saltar; **sparks ~ed from the fire** faíscas saltavam da lareira.

spoil (pt, pp **spoilt** or **spoiled**) vt danificar; estragar, arruinar; **2** (child) mimar, estragar; ~**s** npl despojo sg, saque msg; ~**sport** n desmancha-prazeres, (BR) estraga-prazeres m inv.

spoke (pt of **speak**); ♦ n (of wheel) raio m; **2** (on ladder) degrau m; IDIOM **to put ~ on sb's wheel** pôr um pauzinho na engrenagem; frustrar os planos de alguém.

spoken (pp of **speak**).

spokesman, spokeswoman n porta-voz m.

sponge n esponja; ~ **bag** n esponjeira, portaesponja; ~ **cake** n pão-de-ló m; ♦ vt (wash) lavar com esponja; ♦ vi: **to ~ on sb** viver à custa de alguém.

sponger n (person) parasita m,f.

spongy (-ier, -iest) adj esponjoso,-a, absorvente m,f.

sponsor n (as advertiser-backer; arts, events) patrocinador,-ora; **2** (as patron) mecenas m; **3** (LAW) proponente m,f; **4** (guarantor) fiador,-ora, financiador,-ora; **5** (charity, arts) benfeitor-ora, madrinha, padrinho; ♦ vt patrocinar; financiar; (idea etc) promover.

sponsorship n patrocínio.

spontaneous adj espontâneo,-a.

spoof n (parody) sátira f, paródia (**about** sobre); piada a; **a ~ on party poltics** uma paródia sobre as/uma piada às políticas do partido; (mildly deceptive) truque m, brincadeira f.

spook n (coll) fantasma m, aparição f; ♦ vt (haunt) assombrar; (frighten) amedrontar.

spooky (-ier, -iest) adj (story) fantasmagórico,-a; **2** (house) sinistro,-a.

spool n (film, tape) carretel m; rolo m; (thread) bobina f; (for wool) novelo m.

spoon n colher f; ~-**feed** vt dar de comer com colher; **2** (fig) mimar, dar de mão beijada.

spoonful n colherada.

sporadic adj esporádico,-a.

sport n desporto, (BR) esporte m; **2** (person) bom/boa camarada, bom/boa perdedor,-ora; ~**ing** adj desportivo; (BR) esportivo,-a; ~**s car** n carro desportivo (BR: esporte); ~(**s**) **jacket** n casaco desportivo (BR: esporte); ~**sman** n (d)esportista m; ~**smanship** n espírito (d)esportivo; ~**swear** n roupa desportiva (BR: esporte); ~**swoman** n (d)esportista f.

sporty adj de espírito desportista (BR: esportivo).

spot n lugar m, local m; **2** mancha; **3** ponto sinal; **black ~s** (on skin) pontos npl negros; **beauty ~** n sinal preto (**on** em) (face, etc); pinta f (on fabric); ♦ vt (notice) localizar, notar; descobrir (algo); **a ~ of** um pouquinho de; **to have a soft ~ for** ter um fraco por; **on the ~** no a(c)to, ali mesmo; ~ **check** n fiscalização f de surpresa; controle m aleatório; ~**less** adj sem mancha/mácula f; (attire) impecável; ~**light** n (THEAT, CIN) proje(c)tor; (adjustable lamp) holofote m, refle(c)tor m; **2** (fig) em foco; **to be in the ~** ser o centro das atenções; ♦ ~-**on** adj exa(c)to; **she was ~** ela acertou em cheio.

spotted adj (pattern) com pintinhas/bolinhas; ~ **dick** n (CULIN) pudim m com passas e sultanas; ~ **tie** gravata às pintas; ~ (dog) com manchas.

spotty adj: ~ **face** (adolescente) com borbulhas (BR) com espinhas; **2** (dog) às manchas.

spouse n cônjuge m,f.

spout n (of jug) bico; (pipe) cano; (of hose) bocal m; (of fountain) repuxo m; ♦ vi jorrar; (words) declamar.

sprain n distensão f, entorse f, torcedura; mau jeito; ♦ vt: **to ~ one's ankle** torcer o tornozelo.

sprang (pt of **spring**).

sprat n (fish) arenque pequeno, espadilha f.

sprawl n (of city, town) expansão f descontrolada; ♦ vi (person) estirar-se esparramar-se; (city, suburbs) expandir-se.

sprawling adj (suburb) tentacular; (person's position) esparramado,-a.

spray n (corsage of flowers) ramalhete m de flores; (single flower for lapel) botoeira f; **2** (of bullets) chuva f; **3** (can) borrifador m; **4** (of sea) borrifo m, espuma f; **5** (for perfume) vaporizador m; (for garden; throat, nose) pulverizador m; (of paint) pistola para pintar; ♦ vt pulverizar; (crops) regar; (clothes for ironning) borrifar; ♦ vi (stronger jet of water) esguichar.

spread n extensão f; (range) expansão f; **2** (of culture, news) difusão f; **3** (disease) propagação f; **4** (dimension, scope) envergadura f; **5** (CULIN) (on bread) pasta f; **bed~** colcha (para a cama); ~-**eagled** adj de braços e pernas afastados; ♦ (pt, pp **spread**) vt espalhar; **2** (wings, sails) abrir, desdobrar; **3** (apply) barrar, espalhar (on bread) com (jam etc); **4** disseminar; **5** (space out) escalonar (payments); ♦ vi espalhar-se, alastrar-se, difundir-se.

spree n: **to go on a ~** ir para o pagode, fazer uma farra; **to go on a shopping ~** fazer compras à larga.

sprig *n (of tree)* vergôntea *f*; **2** *(of lavender, parsley)* raminho; **3** *(youth)* jovem; *(boy)(fam)* fedelho, broto.

sprightly *adj* vivo,-a, esperto,-a, desembaraçado,-a.

spring *n (jump)* salto *m*, pulo *m*; **2** *(of mattress, etc)* mola; **3** *(season)* primavera *f*; **4** *(of water)* fonte *f*, nascente *f*; **hot ~s** *npl* termas *fpl*; **~ chicken** *n*: **he is no ~ chicken** ele já não é criança; **~ mattress** colchão *m* de molas; **~ onion** *n (UK)* cebolinha *f* verde; **~ tide** *n* maré *f* viva; **~time** *n* primavera *f*; ♦ *(pt* **sprang**, *pp* **sprung**) *vi* brotar, nascer; **2** pular; **to ~ into/to action/life** pôr-se em movimento; **she sprang to her feet** ela pôs-se de pé num salto; **it ~s to (my) mind** faz-me lembrar; **to ~ from sth** *(originate)* nascer de; vir de; **2** *(appear)* emergir, surgir de; **gossip ~s from jealousy** o mexerico nasce da inveja; **where did my coat ~ from?** donde surgiu o meu casaco? *(implies it was mislaid before)*; **to ~ back** *(step back) (person)* dar um salto para trás, recuar um salto; **to ~ up** *vi* aparecer de repente; *(flowers)* brotar; *(got up) (person)* pôr-se de pé. **to ~-clean** fazer a limpeza grande, limpar a fundo; **~-cleaning** *n* limpeza grande, total, *(BR)* faxina (geral).

springboard *n (trampoline)* trampolim *m*; **2** *(swimming)* prancha *f* de saltos; **3** *(launching pad)* rampa *f* de lançamento; *(fig)* ponto *m* de partida (**for sth** para algo).

springy *adj* elástico,-a, flexível.

sprinkle *vt* salpicar, borrifar; *(with sugar, flour, etc)* polvilhar; **~d with** *(fig)* salpicado, polvilhado de.

sprinkler *n (for lawn)* regador *m* automático; *(for fire)* extin(c)tor *m*.

sprint *n (SPORT)* corrida *f* de velocidade; **the final ~** a re(c)ta final; ♦ *vi* correr a toda velocidade. **sprinter** *n (person)* velocista *m*; *(horse)* sprinter *m*.

sprite *n* duende *m*, elfo.

sprout *vi* brotar, germinar; **Brussels ~s** *npl* (BOT) couve-de-Bruxelas *fsg*.

spruce *n* (BOT) abeto; ♦ *adj (tidy)* arrumado,-a, limpo,-a, elegante *m,f*.

sprung (*pp of* **spring**).

spry *adj* vivo,-a, a(c)tivo,-a, ágil.

spun (*pt, pp of* **spin**).

spur *n (of horse)* espora *f*; **2** *(fig)* estímulo; ♦ *vt* (= **to ~ on**) incitar, estimular; instigar; **on the ~ of the moment** de improviso, de repente, impulsivamente.

spurn *vt* desdenhar, desprezar, repelir.

spurt *n* esforço repentino; **2** *(of activity)* explosão de energia, de a(c)tividade; **3** *(gush of water, etc)* esguicho *m*, jorro *m*, *(of steam)* ja(c)to *m*; *(of flame)* labareda *f*; ♦ *vi* fazer um esforço supremo; **2** jorrar, esguichar; **3** *(flame, ja(c)to)* sair de; **4** *(sudden burst of speed)* arranear.

sputter *vi (oil in pan)* espirrar; *(fire)* crepitar; *(engine)* estalar.

sputum *n* expe(c)toração *f*; escarro *m*.

spy *n* espião/espiã; *(police infomer)* informador,-ora, denunciante, *(BR)* informante; **~ glass** *n* luneta *f*; **~ satellite** *n* satelite-espião *m*; ♦ (**spies**, **spied**) *vt/vi*: **to ~ on** espiar, informar sobre; **2** vigiar; espreitar descortinar *(object)*.

spying *n* espionagem *f*.

sq *(abbr for* **square**).

squabble *n* briga, rixa, *(BR)* bate-boca *m*; ♦ *vi* brigar, altercar, discutir.

squad *n (MIL, police)* pelotão *m*; esquadrão *m*; brigada *f*; *(SPORT)* sele(c)ção *f*, equipa *f*.

squadron *n (MIL)* esquadrão *m*; *(AER)* esquadrilha *f*; *(NAUT)* esquadra *f*.

squalid *adj* esquálido,-a, sórdido,-a.

squall *n* tempestade *f*; pé *m* de vento, rajada *f*.

squalor *n* sordidez *f*, imundície *f*.

squander *vt* esbanjar, dissipar; desperdiçar.

square *n* quadrado; **~ root** *n* raiz *f* quadrada; **2** *(in town)* praça; **3** *(instrument)* esquadro; ♦ *adj* quadrado,-a; **2** *(coll) (old-fashioned person)* bota-de-elástico; *(MATH, measure)* **five ~ metres** cinco metros quadrados; **a ~ meal** uma refeição *f* substancial; **back to ~ one** de volta ao ponto de partida; **we are all ~** estamos quites; **to get things ~** pôr as coisas em ordem; ♦ *vt* ajustar, acertar; *(MATH)* elevar ao quadrado; **to ~ up** *vt (bills, debts)* pagar, ajustar as contas. **to ~ accounts with** ajustar contas com; **to ~ up** *vi (settle, pay)* acertar contas com alguém; **2** *(confront)* **to ~ to sb/st** fazer frente a alguém/algo.

square brackets *npl* parênteses *mpl* re(c)tos; **between ~** entre parênteses.

squared *adj (paper, style)* quadriculado,-a.

squarely *adv* em forma quadrada; *(fully)* em cheio, dire(c)tamente; honestamente; **he looked me ~ in the eye** ele olhou-me dire(c)tamente (nos olhos).

squash *n*: *(drink)* **orange ~** laranjada; **2** *(SPORT)* squash *m*, jogo de raquetes; ♦ *vt* esmagar; **to ~ together** apinhar.

squat *n* residência ocupada ilegalmente; *(BR)* posseiros; ♦ *adj* agachado,-a; de cócoras; **2** *(dumpy person)* atarracado; ♦ *vi* agachar-se, acocorar-se; **2** *(house)* ocupar ilegalmente.

squatter *n* (duma casa, propriedade) ocupante *m* ilegal; *(BR)* posseiro,-a.

squatting *n* ocupação *f* selvagem, ilegal; ♦ *adj* agachado, de cócoras.

squawk *vi (of duck, crow)* grasnar; *(of hen)* cacarejar.

squeak *n* grito *m* estridente; **2** *(of door, wheel, bed)* rangido *m*; **3** *(of mouse)* guincho *m*, chio *m*; ♦ *vi* chiar, guinchar; ranger; **a narrow ~** *(fam)* uma escapada difícil.

squeaky *adj (voice)* esganiçada.

squeal *n (shrill noise)* guincho *m*, grito *f* agudo; ♦ *vi* guinchar, gritar agudamente; **2** *(tell on) (coll)* delatar, denunciar alguém.

squeamish *adj (easily frightened)* medricas *m,f sg/pl*; *(easily sickened)* enojado,-a.

squeeze *n* aperto, compressão *f*; **2** *(on bus etc)* aperto *m*; apinhamento *m*; **3** dificuldade, crise *f* financeira; **to give sb a ~** *(hug)* dar um abraço apertado; **~ box** *n* *(MUS)* acordeão *m*; ♦ *vt* comprimir, estreitar, apertar *(hand, arm)*; **to manage to ~ into sth/through sth** conseguir enfiar-se em algo; **to ~ out** *vt (press)* espremer *(fruit, sponge)*; *(fig)* extorquir *(money)*; **to ~ through** abrir caminho.

squeezer *n* (*of juice*) espremedor *m*.

squelch *n* som *m* de passos na lama; **the ~ of water in her boots** o plof-plof da água nas botas dela; ♦ *vi* (*water, mud*) chapinhar; **2** suprimir som, comentário.

squelchy *adj* lamacento,-a.

squib *n* (*fireworks*) bicha *f* de rabear (no fogo de artifício); **2** satira *f*; **shoot a ~ against sb** dar uma pidda a alguém; **2 damp ~** uma grande dece(p)çao.

squid *n* lula *m*.

squiggle *n* rabisco *m*, garatuja *f*; gatafunho *m*.

squint *n* (*MED*) estrabismo *m*; **to have a ~** ser vesgo,-a; ♦ *adj* estrábico,-a; vesgo,-a; ♦ *vi* **to look at sb/sth** (*with partly closed eyes*) olhar para alguém/algo semicerrando os olhos.

squire *n* fidalgo, proprietário rural.

squirm *vi* retorcer-se, contorcer-se; mostrar embaraço, mal-estar.

squirrel *n* esquilo *m*.

squirt *n* esguicho *m*, esguichadela *f*; ♦ *vi* jorrar, esguichar.

squishy *adj* mole e húmido.

Sr (*abbr for* **senior**).

Sri Lanka *npr* Sri Lanka; **in ~** na Sri Lanka.

St (*abbr for* **Saint**); **2** (*abbr for* **street**).

ST (*abbr for* **Standard Time**) hora *f* oficial.

stab *n* (*with dagger, knife*) punhalada; **2** (*of pain*) pontada; **a ~ in the back** golpe *m* traiçoeiro; ♦ (-*bb*-) *vt* apunhalar; (*with knife*) esfaquear.

stabbing *n* punhalada *f*; ♦ *adj* (*pain*) lancinante.

stability *n* estabilidade *f*.

stabilize *vt* estabiliza; ♦ *vi* estabilizar-se.

stabilizer *n* (*on bicycle, plane, ship*) estabilizador *m*.

stable *n* (*building*) estábulo *m*; (*horses*) cavalariça; ♦ *adj* estável; ♦ **~ lad/boy** *n* cavalariço *m*; **~ door** *n* (*in two halves*) porta *f* de estábulo.

staccato *n* staccato *m*.

stack *n* montão *m*, pilha *f*; **~s of time** (*coll*) imenso tempo; **chimney ~** cano *m* da chaminé; ♦ *vt* amontoar, empilhar; (*AGR*) pôr em meda; **to ~ a lorry with sth** encher o camião (*BR*) caminhão com algo; **to ~ the cards** (*prearrange*) fazer batota (*BR*) trapaça; **~ up** *vi* (*fam*) empilhar; **2** comparar-se (**with, against** com).

stadium *n* estádio *m*.

staff (*pl*: **staves**) *n* (*stick*) cajado *m*, bastão *m*; **2** pessoal *m*, corpo *m* administrativo; **~ nurse** *n* enfermeiro,-a assistente; **~ room** *n* sala *f* dos professores; sala do pessoal; **university ~** (*teaching*) corpo *m* docente; **3** (*MIL*) Estado-Maior; **the ~ comprised three women** o pessoal compreendia três mulheres; ♦ *vt* prover pessoal.

staffing *n* contratação *f* de pessoal.

stag *n* (*ZOOL*) veado, cervo; **2** (*UK*) (*FIN*) especulador,-ora da Bolsa; **3** (*US*) homem sozinho numa festa.

stage *n* (*THEAT*) palco *m*, teatro *m*; **to set the ~** preparar o cenário *m*; **2** (*actual local*) cena *f*; **3** (*JOURN, etc*) etapa, fase *f*; **by ~s** por etapas; **4** (*raised platform*) estrado *m*; **5** (*scaffolding*) plataforma; **~ coach** *n* diligência; **~ door** *n* entrada dos artistas; **~ effect** efeito cénico; **~ fright** *n*

medo *m* do palco; (*nervos antes de audição, entrevista*) borboletas no estômago **~hand** *n* assistente *m,f* de palco; **~ manager** *n* dire(c)tor,-ora de cena; **~-manage** *vt* dirigir; **~-struck** *adj* apaixonado,-a do teatro; **~ whisper** *n* (*fig*) (*THEAT*) aparte *m*; ♦ *vt* (*play*) pôr em cena, representar; (*demonstration*) montar, organizar; realizar.

stagflation *n* (*inflation combined with stagnant output*) estagnação *f*.

stagger *vi* cambalear, vacilar; ♦ *vt* (*astound*) chocar, abalar; (*arrange at different times*) escalonar; ♦ *vi* cambalear; (*drunk*) caminhar aos ziguezagues.

staggering *adj* (*news*) desconcertante; (*success*) espantoso,-a; estrondoso,-a.

staging *n* (*THEAT*) encenação *f*; **2** (*for spectators*) bancadas *fpl* provisórias.

stagnant *adj* estagnado.

stagnate *vi* estagnar(-se).

stagnation *n* (*economy*) estagnação *f*.

stag party *n* festa só para homens (na noite anterior ao casamento dum deles); despedida *f* de solteiro.

staid *adj* (*person, character*) sério,-a, sóbrio,-a, acomodado,-a (*pej*).

stain *n* mancha *f*, nódoa *f*; **2** (*colouring*) tinta, tintura; **3** (*in reputation*) desonra *f*; ♦ *vt* manchar; tingir; **~ed glass window** *n* janela com vitral.

stainless steel *n* aço *m* inoxidável.

stair *n* (*step*) degrau *m*; **~s** *npl* escada *sg*; **~case**, **~way** *n* escadaria, escada; **~well** *n* vão *m* da escada.

stake *n* (*wooden post*) estaca, poste *m*; **2** (*betting*) aposta *f*; **3** (*share*) **to have a ~ in sth** ter interesses em algo; **burnt at the ~** queimada,-a na fogueira; **to be at ~** estar em jogo; ♦ **stakes** *npl* (*prize*) prémio (*BR*: -ê-) *m*; **2** (*contest*) disputa *f*; ♦ *vt* apostar; **2** arriscar (*reputation*); **3 to ~ a claim to sth** reivindicar algo; **to sweep the ~** ganhar tudo; ♦ **to ~ out** (*field*) delimitar, marcar com balizas ou estacas; **2** (*police*) vigiar.

stakeout *n* (*police*) vigilância *f*.

stalactite *n* estalactite *f*.

stalagmite *n* estalagmite *f*.

stale *adj* (*bread, cake*) seco,-a; (*cheese*) bolorento,-a; (*biscuit*) mole; (*air*) viciado,-a; **to smell ~** cheirar a bafio; (*meat*) rançoso,-a; (*gen – food*) estragado,-a; (*joke*) sediço,-a velho,-a; (*athlete*) esgotado,-a, gasto,-a; (*idea, news*) passado,-a, velho,-a.

stalemate *n* (*chess*) empate *m*; **2** (*fig*) (*deadlock*) impasse *m*, beco sem saída.

staleness *n* (*of food*) falta *f* de frescura, rancidez *f*; (*of air*) falta de ventilação.

stalk *n* caule *m*, talo *m*, haste *f*, pé *m*; (*grapes*) engaço *m*; ♦ *vt* caçar de emboscada (*BR*: tocaia); **2 to ~ sb** perseguir alguém furtivamente; assediar; **to ~ off** sair com arrogância.

stalker *n* perseguidor,-ora.

stalking *n* perseguição *f*, assédio *m*.

stall *n* (*in market*) tenda *f*, banca *f*; **2** (*in stable*) coxia *f* manjedoura, (*BR*) baia; **~s** *npl* (*in cinema, theatre*) platéia *sg*; ♦ *vt/vi* (*cause car to stop*) parar, afogar-se; **2** (*fig*) (*play for time*) ser evasivo,-a, ganhar tempo.

stallion *n* garanhão *m*.

stalwart *n* robusto,-a, rijo,-a; valente, resoluto,-a.

stamina *n* resistência *f*, energia *f*, ânimo *m*.

stammer *n* gaguez *f*, *(BR)* gagueira; ♦ *vi* gaguejar, balbuciar; **he ~s** ele é gago.

stamp *n (postage)* selo, estampilha; **2** *(seal)* carimbo *m*, sinete *m*; **3** *(official mark)* marca, impressão *f*; *(hallmark)* marca *f*; **4** *(for making gold)* punção *f*; **5** *(type of class)* calibre *m*; **a man of his ~** um homem do seu calibre; **~ album** *n* álbum *m* de selos; **~ collection** *n* filatelia *f*; **~ collector** *n* filatelista *m,f*; **~ duty** *n* imposto *m* de selo; **embossed ~** selo branco; **the ~ of truth** *(fig)* o cunho da verdade; ♦ *vi* pisar, esmagar; ♦ *vt* bater com o pé; **to ~ on sth** pisar em algo, calcar; esmagar (com o pé); ♦ **to ~ out** *(fire)* abafar; **2** *(crime)* erradicar, eliminar; **3** *(opposition)* sufocar; *(fig) (opponent)* esmagar; ♦ **to rubber-~** *vt* aprovar, carimbar.

stampede *n* debandada, estouro (da boiada); *(of people)* fuga *f* em pânico; ♦ *vi* fugir precipitadamente.

stance *n* postura, posição *f*; **2** attitude *f*; **leftist ~** a atitude esquerdista; **3** *(SPORT) (place to stop/stand)* estância *f*.

stand *n (stance)* posição *f* **(on** em relação a); **to take a ~ on sth** tomar uma decisão em/sobre algo; **2** *(for taxis)* praça, *(BR)* ponto; **3** *(in stadium)* bancadas *fpl*; arquibancada *f*; **4 news ~** quiosque *m*, *(BR)* banca de jornais; **5** *(on market, fair)* banca, barraca *f*; **6** *(JUR) (witness box)* barra *f* das testemunhas; **7** *(for books, music)* estante *f*; **8** *(for hats, coats)* **(hall-~)** bengaleiro *m*; **9** *(for lamp)* pé *m*; **to make a ~** resistir a, be firm; ♦ *(pt, pp* **stood**) *vi* estar, encontrar-se; **2** *(remain standing)* ficar, estar em pé; **3** *(situation)* **as things ~** do modo que as coisas estão; **figures ~ at ...** os números atingem ... ♦ *vt* pôr, colocar; *(put up with)* aguentar, suportar; **2 ~ in the way** impedir; **where do I ~ in all this?** qual é o meu papel em tudo isto?; **to ~ still** ficar quieto/parado/imobilizado; **~ about/around** ficar para ali; **I stood around doing nothing** fiquei parado ali sem fazer nada; **to ~ aside** *vi* ficar de lado; **~ back** *vi* recuar, afastar-se; **to ~ by** *vi* estar pronto, estar a postos; ♦ *vt (opinion)* aferrar-se a; **to ~ by sb/sth** *(be loyal to)* ser leal a (alguém, algo); manter decisão; **2** *(as an onlooker)* **she stood by at the accident** ela estava presente no acidente; ♦ **to ~ down** *vi (resign)* demitir-se; **2** *(JUR)* deixar o banco das testemunhas; ♦ **to ~ for** *vt (defend)* apoiar; representar (alguém); **2** *(signify)* representar; *(denote)* querer dizer; **it stands for honesty** significa honestidade; **3** *(tolerate)* tolerar, permitir; **4** concorrer; ♦ **to ~ for Council** concorrer às eleições da Câmara; ♦ **to ~ in for sb** *vi* substituir alguém; ♦ **to ~ off** *vi* afastar-se; *(NAUT)* fazer-se ao largo; **2** *(reach a stalemate)* chegar a um impasse; ♦ **to ~ out** *vi (be preminent)* destacar-se; ressaltar; **it ~s out that** é evidente que; **2** *(veins)* ficar saliente; **3** distinguir-se **(from** de); ♦ **to ~ over** ser adiado; **2 ~ sb/the cooker** vigiar, supervisionar; ♦ **to ~ to** *(MIL)* estar em estado de alerta; **to ~ to attention** *(MIL)* fazer a continência;

♦ **to ~ up** *vi (rise)* levantar-se; **to ~ up for** *vt* defender; **to ~ up to** *vt* enfrentar.

standard *n* nível *m* padrão *m*, critério *m*; **~ of living** *n* nível *m* de vida; **2** *(flag)* estandarte *m*; grau *m*; ♦ *adj (general)* normal; **2** *(feature)* comun, típico,-a; **3** *(size, type)* padronizado,-a; **4** *(text, language)* padrão; **~s** *npl (morals)* valores, princípios *mpl* morais; **~-bearer** *n* porta-bandeira; **~ lamp** *n* candeeiro *m* de pé; **~ time** *n* hora *f* oficial de um país.

standardization *n* normalização *f*, standardização *f*.

standardize *vt* padronizar, uniformizar.

stand-by *n (substitute)* reserva *f*; **to be on ~** estar à espera de decisão, estar preparado, pronto.

stand-in *n* substituto,-a; *(CIN)* duplo *m,f*, *(BR)* doublé *m,f*.

standing *n* posição *f*, reputação *f*; **~ invitation** convite aberto; **~ charge** *(bank)* taxa *f* fixa; **of long ~** de longa data; **~ order** *n (at bank)* instrução de ordem permanente; **~ orders** *npl (MIL)* regulamento *sg* geral; ♦ *adj* vertical *m,f*; *(on foot)* de pé.

standoffish *adj* distante, frio,-a; reservado,-a.

standpoint *n* ponto de vista.

standstill *n*: **at a ~** paralisado, parado; **to come to a ~** ficar/estar paralisado, parado.

stand-up *adj*: *(comedian)* comediante *m,f* de plateia; artista sozinho no palco a dizer piadas; **2** *(argument)* violento.

stank (*pt of* **stink**).

Stanley knife® *npr* faca *f* muito afiada cuja lâmina está aparafusada a um cabo substituível (para carpetes).

stanza *n* estrofe *f*.

staple *n (for papers)* grampo; ♦ *adj* básico; **~ diet** dieta *f* básica; ♦ *vt* grampear.

stapler *n* grampeador *m*.

star *n* estrela; *(celebrity)* astro, estrela; **~ attraction** *n* atra(c)ção *f* principal; ♦ *vi*: **to ~ in** ser a estrela em, estrelar em.

starboard *n (NAUT)* estibordo *m*.

starch *n* amido *m*, fécula *f*, *(for ironing)* goma *f*.

starched *adj* engomado,-a; *(stiff)* teso,-a; **2** *(fig) (person)* formal, empertigado,-a.

starchy *adj* amiláceo.

stardom *n* estrelato, qualidade *f* de estrela.

stare *n* olhar *m* fixo; ♦ *vt*: **to ~ at** olhar fixamente, fitar.

starfish *n* estrela-do-mar *f*.

stark *adj* severo,-a, áspero,-a; ♦ **~ naked** *adj*/**starkers** *(coll)* completamente nu-a, em pelo; em pelote.

starlet *n (actress)* estrelinha *f*.

starlight *n*: **by ~** à luz das estrelas.

starling *n (bird)* estorninho *m*.

starry *adj* estrelado; **~-eyed** *adj* deslumbrado,-a.

star-spangled *adj (sky)* coberto de estrelas; **The ~ Banner** *n* bandeira dos EUA.

star-studded *adj (cast)* recheado de estrelas.

start *n* princípio, começo *m*; **for a ~ ...** para começar ...; **2** partida; arrancada; **3** *(jump due to fright)* sobressalto, susto; **4** ímpeto; vantagem; ♦ *vt/vi* começar, iniciar; **2** causar; **3** *(turn on)* ligar; **4** *(set up)* fundar, criar; ♦ *vi (engine)* pôr-se em funcionamento; **2** *(with fright)* sobressaltar-se, assustar-se; **3** *(annoyed)* **don't you ~ that (with**

that)! não comeces com isso!; ♦ **to ~ off** *vt* começar, principiar; **to ~ you off here is some money** para começar aqui tens algum dinheiro; **2** *(leave)* partir, pôr-se a caminho; ♦ **to ~ out (in life)** começar; **to ~ up** *vi* começar; *(car)* pegar, pôr-se em marcha; **2** *(in business)* estabelecer-se.

starter *n* *(AUT)* *(motor)* arranque *m*; **2** *(SPORT)* juiz, oficial *m,f* da partida; **3** *(runner)* corredor,-ora; *(CULIN)* entrada *f*.

starting point *n* ponto de partida.

startle *vt* assustar, aterrar.

startling *adj* surpreendente.

starvation *n* fome *f*; *(MED)* inanição *f*.

starve *vi* passar fome; *(to death)* morrer de fome; ♦ *vt* fazer passar fome; *(fig)* privar.

starving *adj* faminto, esfomeado; **I'm ~** *(fig)* estou morrendo de fome.

stash *vt* *(coll)* (= ~ **away**) esconder; *(money, valuables)* num lugar secreto.

state *n* estado *m*; **the S~** *n* o Estado *m*; *(ceremonial)* pompa *f*; aparato *m*; ~ **education** *n* ensino *m* público, do Estado; ~ **home** *n* casa senhorial aberta à visitação; ~ **of affairs** *n* situação *f* geral; ~ **of mind** *n* estado *m* de espírito; ~**-owned** *adj* estatal; ~**'s evidence** *(JUR)* *(for the prosecution)* **to turn ~'s evidence** denunciar os cúmplices; **to lie in ~** estar exposto em câmara ardente; **the S~s** os Estados Unidos; **S~ Department** *(US)* Ministério *m* dos Negócios Estrangeiros, *(BR)* M. das Relações Exteriores; **to be in a ~** estar agitado; ♦ *vt* afirmar, declarar; **2** expor, apresentar.

stateless *adj* sem pátria, apátrida.

stately (-ier, -iest) *adj* majestoso,-a, imponente.

statement *n* afirmação *f*; **2** *(JUR)* declaração *f*; **3** *(from bank)* extra(c)to *m* da conta.

state-of-the-art *adj* de vanguarda, moderno,-a.

statesman *n* estadista *m,f*.

static *n* *(RADIO)* interferência; ♦ *adj* estático; ~ **electricity** *n* eletricidade *f* estática.

station *n* estação *f*; **2** posto, lugar *m*; **3** *(RADIO)* emissora *f*; **4** *(rank)* posição *f* social; **5 police ~** esquadra *f*, posto *m* de polícia; ♦ *vt* *(position)* situar, colocar (alguém); **2** *(MIL)* designar para um posto.

stationary *adj* estacionário,-a.

stationer's (shop) *n* papelaria.

stationery *n* artigos *mpl* de papelaria; *(writing paper)* papel *m* de carta.

station-master *n* *(RAIL)* chefe *m* da estação.

station-wagon *n* carrinha *f*, *(BR)* perua.

statistic *n* estatística *f*; ~ **s** *npl* estatística *sg*.

statistical *adj* estatístico,-a.

statue *n* estátua *f*.

statuesque *adj* escultural.

stature *n* *(height)* estatura *f*; **of medium ~** de estatura média, mediana; **2** *(status)* envergadura *f*, categoria *f*.

status *(pl: -uses)* *n* posição *f*, condição *f*, estado *m*; **2** *(prestige)* ~ **symbol** *n* símbolo de prestígio.

statute *n* estatuto *m*, lei *f*; *(JUR)* *(UK)* Diploma *m* legal, parlamentar.

statutory *adj* estatutário,-a.

staunch *adj* firme, constante, fiel.

stave *n* *(MUS)* pauta *f*; ♦ *(pt, pp* **-ed**, *or* **stove)** *vt/vi* arrombar; pôr aduelas em; **to ~ off** repelir *(attack)*; evitar, afastar, protelar *(threat)*; enganar *(hunger, thirst)*; impedir *(bankruptcy)*.

stay *n* estadia *f*; **2** *(JUR)* suspensão *f*, adiamento *m*; ~ **of proceedings** suspensão do processo; ♦ *vi* ficar, permanecer; *(as guest)* hospedar-se; **to ~ the night in** pernoitar em; **2** *(spend some time)* demorar-se; ♦ **to ~ away** *vt* afastar-se (**from** de); ficar longe (**from** de); **to ~ behind** *vi* ficar atrás; **to ~ in** *vi* ficar em casa; **to ~ on** *vi* permancer **to ~ out** *vi* ficar fora de casa; **to ~ put** *vi* não arredar pé, ficar no lugar; **to ~ up** *vi* ficar acordado, ficar a pé.

staying power *n* persistência *f*, capacidade *f* de resistência.

STD *(abbr for* **sexually-transmitted disease)** DST, doença sexualmente transmissível.

stead *n* lugar *m*; **to stand in good ~** ser útil, prestar, servir.

steadfast *adj* *(friend, supporter)* fiel, firme, estável, resoluto,-a; **to be ~ in one's convictions** ser firme nas suas convicções.

steadily *adv* seguramente, firmemente; **2** *(gradually)* progressivamente; **3** sem parar; **4** *(walk)* normalmente; **5** *(drive)* a uma velocidade constante; **6** *(look gaze)* fixamente.

steady *adj* constante, regular; **2** firme; **a ~ hand** uma mão *f* firme; **3** *(sensible)* sensato, equilibrado; **4** *(job)* estável, fixo,-a; *(voice, attitude)* calmo,-a, sereno,-a; ♦ *vt* *(hold)* manter firme; ♦ *vi* controlar; **2** *(to control one's nerves)* acalmar-se; *(prices)* estabilizar-se; ♦ *exc* ~ **on!** calma!

steak *n* bife *m*; *(BR)* filé *m*; *(fish)* posta *f*; ~ **and kidney pudding** *n* empadão *m* de carne de vaca e rim.

steal *(pt* **stole**, *pp* **stolen)** *vt/vi* roubar; **to ~ a kiss** roubar; **to ~ a glance at sb/sth** lançar um olhar furtivo a alguém, algo.

stealth *n*: **by ~** furtivamente, às, escondidas.

stealthily *adv*: **to move ~** mexer-se furtivamente.

stealthy *adj* furtivo,-a secreto,-a.

steam *n* vapor *m*; **2** névoa *f*; ~**boat** *n* barco *m* a vapor; ♦ *vt* condensar (h)umidade; **2** *(CULIN)* cozer a vapor; ♦ *vi* exalar vapor; **to ~ along** *(ship)* avançar, mover-se (a vapor).

steamer *n* vapor *m*, navio (a vapor).

steaming *adj* *(bath, food)* muito quente.

steam roller *n* *(CONSTR)* *(road making)* cilindro, rolo compressor (a vapor); ♦ *vt* esmagar *(opposition)*.

steamy (-ier, -iest) *adj* cheio de vapor; **2** *(glass)* embaciado,-a, *(BR)* embaçado,-a; **3** *(heat)* húmido,-a; **4** *(erotic)* tórrido,-a.

steed *n* *(LITER)* *(horse)* corcel *m*.

steel *n* aço *m*; ♦ *adj* de aço; **nerves of ~** nervos *m* de aço; ~ **band** *n* *(MUS)* banda de metais; ~ **guitar** *n* viola *f* havaiana; ~ **industry** *n* siderurgia *f*; ~ **mill** *n* fábrica/*(BR)* usina *f* de aço; ~ **wool** *n* lã *f* de aço; ~**worker** *n* metalúrgico,-a; ~**works** *npl* siderurgia *f*.

steels *npl (FIN)* acções e títulos cotados na Bolsa provenientes de companhias siderúrgicas.

steep *adj* íngreme, escarpado,-a; **2** ~ **drop** uma queda abrupta; **3** *(price, fees)* exorbitante *f*; ♦ **to** ~ **sth in** *vt* pôr de molho algo; ♦ embeber; mergulhar em; impregnar.

steeple *n (of church)* campanário *m*, torre *f* alta; ~**chase** *n* corrida de obstáculos; ~**jack** *n* consertador *m* de torres, chaminés altas.

steer *vt* guiar, dirigir, pilotar; ♦ *vi* conduzir.

steering *n (AUT)* direção *f*; ~ **wheel** *n* volante *m*.

stellar *adj* estelar.

stem *n (of plant)* caule *m*, haste *f*; **2** *(of glass)* pé *m*; **3** *(of pipe)* tubo *m*; **4** *(LING)* raiz *f*, radical *m* do verbo; ♦ **(-mm-)** *vt* deter, reter; *(blood)* estancar; **to** ~ **from** *vt* originar-se de; ter origem em.

stench *n* fedor *m*.

stencil *n (typed)* estampilha, stencil *m*, *(BR)* estêncil *m*; **2** *(lettering)* gabarito de letra; ♦ *vt* imprimir com stencil, estêncil.

stenographer *n (US)* estenógrafa, estenoda(c)tilógrafa.

step *n (pace)* passo; **2** *(sound)* passada *f*; **3** *(stair)* degrau *m*; ~**s** *npl* escadote *m*; ~ **by** ~ *adj* progressivo,-a; ~**brother** *n* meio-irmão *m*; ~**daughter** *n* enteada; ~**father** *n* padastro; ~**ladder** *n* escadote *m*; ~**mother** *n* madrasta; ~**sister** *n* meiairmã *f*; ~**son** *n* enteado; ♦ *adv (explain)* ponto por ponto; ♦ *vt/vi* escalonar; ♦ *vi* dar um passo; **to** ~ **aside** desviar-se; ♦ **to** ~ **down** descer, appear-se *(from bus)*; **2** *(fig)* retirar-se, desistir *(from election)*; **to** ~ **forward** avançar, dar um passo em/a frente; **to** ~ **in** *(fam)* *vi* intervir; **to** ~ **on** pisar, calcar; **to** ~ **out** sair; apear-se; **to** ~ **over** *vt* passar por cima de; **to** ~ **up** *vt* aumentar.

stepping stone *n (over brook)* alpondra *f*; **2** *(fig)* *(way to success)* trampolim *m*; **3** *(step)* degrau *m*.

stereo *n* estéreo; ♦ *adj* (= ~**phonic**) estereofónico *(BR: -fô-)*.

stereotype *n* estereótipo; ♦ *vt* estereotipar.

sterile *adj* estéril.

sterility *n* esterilidade *f*.

sterilization *n* esterilização *f*.

sterilize *vt* esterilizar.

sterling *adj* esterlino,-a; *(silver)* de lei; **2** *(fig)* genuíno, puro.

stern *n (NAUT)* popa, ré *f*; ♦ *adj* severo, austero.

stethoscope *n (MED)* estetoscópio *m*.

stew *n (CULIN)* guisado *m*; *(made with rabbit)* ensopado *m*; **2** *(fig)* *(in trouble)* apuro; **in a** ~ em apuros; ♦ *vt/vi* guisar, ensopar; cozinhar; IDIOM **to** ~ **in one's own juice** deixar alguém aprender à sua própria custa.

steward *n (AER)* comissário de bordo.

stewardess *n* hospedeira de bordo, *(BR)* aeromoça.

stg *(abbr for* **sterling***)* esterlina.

stick *n (piece of wood)* pau *m*; *(for ponting)* vara *f*; **2** *(of chalk)* pedaço *m* de giz; **3** *(of celery)* talho *m* de aipo; **4 walking** ~ bengala *f*; **5** *(SPORT)* taco *m*; ♦ *(pt, pp* **stuck***)* *vt/vi (glue)* colar; **2** *(poster)* afixar; **3** *(in the mud)* atolar-se; **4 to** ~ **a pin into sth** espetar um alfinete em algo; **5 to** ~ **sth into**

cravar/enfiar algo em; **6** *(coll)* meter; **I am stuck in the house** estou metida em casa; **7** *(put up with sb)* aguentar, aturar alguém; **8** *(coll)* **he stuck me with the bill** ele fez-me pagar a conta; ♦ *vi* colar-se, aderir-se; pegar-se; **the pudding stuck to the bottom of the pan** o arroz pegou-se ao tacho; **2** *(not to move)* encravar, emperrar *(drawer, etc)*; **the lift is stuck** o elevador emperrou; **the key is stuck in the lock** a chave está encravada na fechadura; **3** *(in mind etc)* gravar-se; **4** *(pin etc)* pregar; **to** ~ **out/up** estar saliente, proje(c)tar-se; **to** ~ **up for** defender; **to** ~ **to** cinjir-se a, ser fiel, limitar-se; ~ **to what you know** limite-se a dizer o que sabe; **to** ~ **with sb** ficar com alguém; ficar em *(place, job)*.

sticker *n* etiqueta adesiva, adesivo *m*.

sticking plaster *n* adesivo *m*, esparadrapo *m*.

stick-in-the-mud *n (person)* *(coll)* retrógrado,-a; conservador,-ora; bota de elástico *m,f (fam)*.

stickleback *n (river fish)* esgana-gata *f*, peixe espinho *m*.

stickler *n*: **to be a** ~ **for** *(punctuality, etc)* ser obsessivo,-a por; ser picuínhas (por, quanto a); **2** problema *m*; **the investigation proved to be a** ~ a investigação tornou-se num problema.

stick shift *n (US)* *(gear lever)* alavanca da mudança, marcha.

stick-up *n (slang)* assalto *m* à mão armada.

sticky *adj* pegajoso,-a; **2** *(label)* adesivo,-a; **3** *(fig)* difícil.

stiff *n (coll)* *(US: corpse)* cadáver *m*; ♦ *adj (fabric)* rígido,-a, rijo,-a; **2** *(mixture)* consistente; **3** *(body)* dorido,-a; **my legs are** ~ tenho as pernas entorpecidas; **4** *(drawer-stuck)* perro,-a, emperrado,-a; **5** *(sentence)* dura, severa; **6** *(exam)* difícil; **7** *(price)* exorbitante; **I need a** ~ **drink** preciso de uma bebida forte; ♦ *adv* **to be bored** ~ *(coll)* estar a morrer de tédio; **to be frozen** ~ estar enregelado; **to scare sb** ~ *(coll)* causar um medo/susto terrível.

stiffen *vt* endurecer; *(limb)* entumecer; ♦ *vi* enrijecer-se; fortalecer-se.

stiffness *n* rigidez *f*; *(of manner)* frieza *f*.

stifle *vt* sufocar, abafar, reprimir; **she** ~**d a yawn** ela abafou um bocejo.

stifling *adj* sufocante, abafado; **the weather is** ~ o tempo está sufocante.

stigma *(pl: -ta, (fig) -s)* *n* estigma *m*.

stigmatize, stigmatise *vt* estigmatizar.

stile *n (over a fence)* degraus *m* de passagem de uma vedação; **2** couceira *f (of door)* umbral *m*.

stiletto *n* estilete *m*; (= ~ **heel**) salto (de sapato) fino.

still *adj* imóvel, quieto,-a; ♦ *adv (up to this time)* até agora; ainda; contudo.

stillborn *adj* nascido morto, nado/nato-morto, *(BR)* natimorto.

still life *n* natureza morta.

stillness *n* quietude *f*.

stilt *n (pole)* andas *fpl*; **to walk on** ~**s** andar sobre andas; **2** *(for building)* estacas *fpl*.

stilted *adj (style, speech)* forçado,-a, afe(c)tado,-a, pomposo,-a.

stimulant n estimulante m.

stimulate vt estimular.

stimulating adj estimulante.

stimulation n estímulo.

stimulus (pl: -li) n estímulo m, incentivo m.

sting n (of insect, scorpion) ferrão m, ferroada f; (of plant) picada; ♦ (pt, pp stung) vt/vi dar ferroada; (plant) picar; **2** (burning sensation) arder; (hurt) doer; (wind) fustigar; (smoke, etc) irritar; IDIOM **to have a ~ in the tail** ter um final inesperado (story, speech).

stinginess n mesquinhez f, avareza f.

stingy adj (person) sovina m,f ferreta m,f, mesquinho,-a.

stink n fedor m; ♦ (pt **stank**, pp **stunk**) vi feder, cheirar mal; **to kick up a ~** (coll) causar um escândalo; **~-bomb** n bomba f de cheirar mal.

stinker n (coll) (difficult person/thing) chatice f; seca f; **2** (smelling) de mau cheiro.

stinking adj (smell) fedorento,-a; **2 ~ rich** (pej) podre de rico.

stint n (period of work) período m, parte f; **to do one's ~** fazer a sua parte; **he did a one-year ~ in Brazil** ele trabalhou um ano no Brazil; **I have done my ~ for today** por hoje já fiz a minha parte, o suficiente.

stipend n estipêndio, remuneração f.

stipulate vt estipular, estabelecer.

stipulation n estipulação f, cláusula.

stir n (excitement) agitação f, reboliço m; **2** (fig) comoção f; **3** mexida f; **give it a ~** dá-lhe (soup, etc) uma mexida; ♦ (-rr-) vt/vi (tea, salad, etc) mexer; **2** (fire) atiçar, mover; **3** (fig) (emotionally) comover; **4** (move) mover-se, mexer-se; **5** (awaken) despertar (emotions); (breeze) agitar (leaves); ♦ **to ~ up** vt (dust) levantar; (feelings) excitar; (trouble) provocar.

stir-fry (~-fried) vt n saltear (vegetables) em óleo, azeite, fritar ligeiramente.

stirring n indício m; movimento; mexida; **the soup needs ~** precisa-se de mexer a sopa; ♦ adj (feeling, scene) comovedor,-ora; (performance) arrebatador,-ora.

stirrup n estribo m.

stitch n (sewing) ponto m; **back ~** presponto m; **cross-~** (embroidery) ponto cruzado; (knitting) malha f; **2** (sudden pain) pesponto; ♦ vt/vi costurar; cerzir, coser à mão; **2** (MED) dar pontos, suturar; IDIOM **I was in stitches** tive uma barrigada de riso.

stoat n (ZOOL) arminho m.

stock n (COMM) (in shop) provisão f, stock, (BR) estoque; **to have in ~** ter em armazém; **to be out of ~ (sth)** estar esgotado,-a algo; **2** (consignment) remessa; sortimento; **3** n (CULIN) caldo m; **~ cube** n (CULIN) cubo m de caldo; **4** raça f, estirpe f, linhagem f; **5** (FIN) fundos npl, capital m; (shares) a(c)ções fpl; **~s and shares** a(c)ções e valores; **~ exchange/market** n bolsa f, mercado m de valores; **to be listed on the ~ exchange** estar cotado na Bolsa; **~ option** n (US) opção f de aquisição de acções; ♦ adj (fig) trivial, comum; ♦

vt armazenar, (BR) estocar; **2** (supply) prover, sortir; ♦ **to take ~ of** (fig) fazer um inventário, balanço, examinar; **to be/stand ~ still** ficar absolutamente quieto,-a; **well-~ed** (shop, library) bem equipada; (house) recheada; **to ~ up with** vt abastecer-se de.

stockade n estacada f, paliçada f; (US) cadeia.

stockbroker n corrector,-a de valores, da Bolsa; **~ belt** n arredores de Londres onde moram corretores da Bolsa ricos.

stockholder n (FIN) a(c)cionista m,f.

Stockholm npr Estocolmo; **in ~** em Estocolmo.

stocking n meia f.

stockinged adj (in socks, stockings) **to be in (one's) ~ feet** estar em/de peúgas/meias.

stock-in-trade n especialidade f; arma f (fig).

stockpile n reserva; ♦ vt acumular reservas; armazenar, (BR) estocar.

stocktaking n (COMM) inventário, balanço; avaliação f.

stocky adj (person) atarracado,-a; **of ~ build** baixo,-a e forte.

stodge n (coll) comida pesada.

stodgy adj pesado,-a; (speech) enfadonho, indigesto.

stoical adj estóico,-a.

stoke vt atiçar, alimentar (fire, fornalha); **~ up** vi encher-se de comida, comer até fartar.

stole (pt of **steal**) n estola f.

stolen (pp of **steal**).

stomach n (ANAT) estômago; **2** (belly) barriga f, ventre m; **to be lying on one's ~** estar deitado de barriga para baixo; ♦ vt suportar, tolerar; **I can't ~ her behaviour** não tolero/aguento o comportamento dela.

stomachache n dor f de estômago, de barriga.

Em inglês não é cortês falar de 'belly' em público, quando nos referimos à 'barriga', salvo em tom jocoso e familiar. A palavra aceite é 'stomach' = stomachache. Assim, quando a barriga dói e precisa-se de especificar a área, deve-se então dizer 'lower abdomen'.

stomp vi: **to ~in/out** entrar/sair batendo com os pés no chão.

stone n pedra f; **2** (gem) pedra f preciosa; **3** (small lump) pedra (of salt); **4** pedrada f; **one must not throw ~s** não se deve andar a atirar pedrada; **5** (in peach, avocado, etc) caroço; **6** (weight) medida de peso (6.35 kg); **7** (standing vertical) lápide f; ♦ adj de pedra, pétreo; **S~ Age** npr a Idade f de Pedra; **~-broke** adj falido,-a, teso,-a (fam); **~ cladding** n revestimento m de pedra; **~ cold** adj gelado,-a; **~cutter** n (person) canteiro m; (machine) máquina f de lavrar pedra; (ART) (work) cantaria; **~-deaf/blind** adj totalmente surdo/cego; **kidney ~** n (MED) cálculo m renal, pedra f no rim; **~ hammer** n marreta f; **~mason** n pedreiro; **~ quarry** n pedreira f; **~'s throw: at a ~** adv a pouca distância; ♦ vt apedrejar; IDIOM **to kill two birds with one ~** matar dois coelhos de uma cajadada; **to leave no ~ unturned** fazer todos os possíveis para; **to cast a ~ at sb** criticar alguém.

stoned *adj (drunk)* bêbedo,-a por completo; **2** *(drugged)* drogado,-a, *(BR)* chapado,-a.

stonewall *n (in cricket) (batsman)* fazer jogo defensivo; **2** *(filibuster)* fazer obstrução, estar com evasivas.

stoneware *n* louça *f* de barro vidrado, faiança *f*.

stony *adj* pedregoso; **2** *(glance)* glacial; IDIOM **to fall on ~ ground** *(words, advice)* cair em saco roto.

stood *(pt, pp of* **stand**).

stooge *n* comediante que faz o papel de tolo; **2** *(coll) (dogsbody)* lacaio *m*, capacho *m*.

stool *n* tamborete *m*, pequeno banco *m*; **~s** *npl (hospital jargon)* fezes; **what are your ~s like?** como estão as suas fezes/o seu cocó?; **~ pigeon** *n (coll)* chamariz *m*.

stoop *vi* (= **to have a ~**) ser corcunda; **2** *(bend)* debruçar-se, curvar-se; **to walk with a ~** andar curvado,-a; ♦ **to ~ down** baixar-se; **2** *(debase o.s.)* rebaixar-se, descer a (esse nível); **to ~ so low as to** (**do, say**) rebaixar-se a ponto de (fazer, dizer).

stop *n* ponto; parada, interrupção *f*; *(bus etc)* paragem *f*, *(BR)* ponto, parada; **~cock** *n* torneira *f* de passagem; **~gap** *n* substituto *m* provisório; **~lights** *npl (AUT)* luz *f* do semáforo; ♦ **~over** *n* escala; ♦ *vt* parar, deter; **2** *(break off)* paralisar, cessar; **3** *(block)* tapar, obstruir; (= **to put a ~ to**) terminar, pôr firm à; ♦ *vi* parar-se, deter-se; *(end)* acabar-se; **to ~ smoking** deixar de fumar; **to ~ dead** *vi* parar de repente; **to ~ over** *vi* passar a noite (**at** em); **to ~ up** *vt* entupir.

stop-news *n* últimas *npl* notícias.

stoppage *n (strike)* greve *f*; **2** *(temporary stop)* interrupção *f*, paralisação *f*; **3** *(of pay)* suspensão *f*; **4** *(blockage)* obstrução *f*.

stopper *n (of bottle, jar)* tampa *f*; rolha *f*.

stopping *adj*: **~ train** comboio *(BR)* trem que pára em todas a s estações.

stopwatch *n* cronómetro *(BR:* -nô-*)*.

storage *n (gen)* armazenagem *f*; **2** *(furniture)* depósito *m* (**of** *de*); **3** *(COMP)* memória *f*; *(process)* gravação *fg*; **~ heater** *n (ELECT)* *n* acumulador *m* de ele(c)-tricidade (acumula durante a noite quando a luz é mais barata).

store *n (stock)* suprimento *m*; **2** *(depot, large shop)* armazém *m*; **~s** *npl* víveres *mpl*, provisões *fpl*; existências; ♦ **in ~** *adv (reserve)* em armazém, *(BR)* em estoque; **a surprise in ~** *(fig)* uma sur-presa em reserva; **who knows what fate has in ~ for us** quem sabe o que o destino nos reservou?; ♦ *vt* armazenar; guardar; **to ~ up** *vt* acumular.

store detective *n* segurança à paisana.

storeroom *(in house)* quarto *m* de arrecadação, *(for food)* despensa; **2** *(in shop)* depósito *m*.

storey *n* andar *m*, piso *m*.

stork *n* cegonha *f*.

storm *n* tempestade *f*; **2** *(wind)* borrasca; *(gale)*, vendaval *m*; **3** *(fig)* tumulto; ♦ *vi (fig)* enfurecer-se; ♦ *vt* tomar de assalto, assaltar; **~ cloud** *n* nuvem *f* de tempestade.

stormy *adj* tempestuoso.

story *n* história, estória; **2** *(LIT)* narrativa *f*; **3** *(joke)* anedota; **4** *(plot)* enredo; (= **short ~**) conto *m*; *(US)* = **storey**.

storybook *n* livro de contos.

storyteller *n* contador,-a de histórias/estórias; **2** *(pej) (liar)* mentiroso,-a.

stout *n* cerveja *f* preta; ♦ *adj (strong person)* sólido,-a, forte; **2** *(euph for fat)* corpulento,-a.

stoutly *adv (deny, affirm)* vigorosamente.

stoutness *n* corpulência *f*.

stove *n* fogão *m*; **2** *(for coal)* fogareiro; **3** *(in the room)* fogão *m* de sala.

stow *vt* guardar, meter; *(NAUT)* estivar; ♦ **to ~ away** *vi* viajar como clandestino; **~away** *n* clandestino,-a.

straddle *n* posição de quem está escarranchado; **2** *(FIN, ECON)* operação da Bolsa com opção de venda e/ou compra; ♦ *vi* escarranchar-se em; estar de pé *ou* sentado com as pernas afastadas; **2** *(across 2 sides)* atravessar; **the desert ~s the border between ...** o deserto atravessa a borda entre ...

straggle *vi (dawdle)* vaguear, deambular, perde-se; **2** *(lag behind)* ficar para trás; ir a reboque, extra-viar-se; **3** *(spread untidily)* estender-se ao acaso *(street, village)*.

straggler *n (person)* retardatário,-a.

straggly (-ier, -iest) *adj (hair)* emaranhado.

straight *n (SPORT)* **the ~** a re(c)ta final; ♦ *adj* re(c)to, corre(c)to; **2** *(honest)* honrado,-a, franco,-a, dire(c)to,-a; **3** *(upright cupboard etc)* direito; **4** *(slang)* heterossexual; **5** *(person)* que não usa drogas; **6** *(easy)* simples, fácil *m,f*; **5** *(tidy)* em ordem; **7** *(hair)* liso; **8** **~** *(JOURN) (of article, news)* dar os factos sem aformoseamentos; ♦ *adv* direito, dire (c)tamente; **2** *(whisky) (undiluted)* puro; **to put/ get sth ~** falar com franqueza; **to go ~** *(after leaving prison)* corrigir-se, ter uma vida limpa (de crime); ♦ **~ after** *adv* logo depois; **~ ahead** *adv* bem na frente; **~away** *adv* imediatamente, dire(c) tamente; ♦ **~forward** *adj (explanation, work)* simples, dire(c)to; *(person)* honesto, franco; **~ out** *adv* sem rodeios; *(CIN)* simples e dire(c)to; **~ through** (livro etc) do começo ao fim.

straighten *vt* (= **~en out**) endireitar; **2** *(tidy)* *(also:* **~ up**) pôr em ordem; ♦ *vi* endireitar-se.

straight-faced *adj* com cara séria.

strain *n (stress)* tensão *f*, pressão *f*; **2** *(pressure from weight)* pressão *f*; **to be under ~** estar sob pressão; **3** *(MED) (muscle)* distensão *f*, luxação *f*; **4** *(breed)* raça, estirpe *f*; **5** *(recurring theme)* corrente *f*; **~ in the family** tendência na família para; ♦ *vt/vi (muscle)* distender; **2** *(work hard)* forçar; **3** *(stretch)* puxar, esticar *(rope, resources)*; **4** *(filter)* filtrar; **5** esforçar-se; **~s** *npl (MUS)* sons *mpl* musicais; melodia.

strained *adj (muscle)* distendido; **2** *(laugh)* forçado; **3** *(relations)* tenso,-a.

strainer *n (kitchen utensil)* coador *m*, passador *m*.

strait *n (GEO)* estreito *m*; **~ s** *npl* dificuldades *fpl*; **in dire ~** em grandes dificuldades.

straitened *adj*: **in ~ circumstances** na penúria.

straitjacket *n* colete-de-forças *m*; **2** *(fig)* estorvo *m*.

strait-laced *adj* puritano,-a.

strand *n* *(thread, wire)* fio *m*; **a ~ of pearls** um fio de pérolas; **2** *(of hair)* fio de cabelo; *(of cable)* cordão *m*.

stranded *adj* *(helpless, lost)* abandonado, desamparado, perdido.

strange *adj* desconhecido; **2** *(odd)* estranho, esquisito.

stranger *n* desconhecido,-a, forasteiro,-a.

strangle *vt* *(kill – person)* estrangular; *(chicken)* torcer o pescoço; **2** *(fig)* *(choke)* *(collar)* asfixiar; **3** sufocar *(originality)*; *(repress)* reprimir *(cry, laugh)*; *(vine)* invadir; **~hold** *n* estrangulamento *m*; *(fig)* domínio total.

strangler *n* estrangulador,-ora.

strangulate *vt* estrangular.

strangulation *n* estrangulamento *(of person, activity)*.

strap *n* correia; **2** *(dress, BR)* alça *f*; **3** *(dated) (punishment)* chicote *m*; ♦ (-pp-) *vt* prender com correia, apertar; **2** *(bandage)* ligar, enfaixar; **he ~ped (up) my arm** ele ligou-me o braço.

strapless *adj* *(dress)* sem alças; cai-cai.

strapping *adj* corpulento,-a, robusto,-a forte; **a ~ lad** um rapaz *m* forte.

Strasbourg *npr* Estrasburgo; **in ~** em Estrasburgo.

strata *(pl of* **stratum***)*.

stratagem *n* estratagema, ardil *m*.

strategic *adj* estratégico.

strategist *n* *(MIL, POL)* estratega *m,f*.

strategy *n* estratégia *f*.

stratum *(pl*: **-ta***) n (GEOL)* estrato *m*; *(social)* camada *f*, estrato *m*.

straw *n* palha; *(for thatching)* colmo *m*; *(=* **drinking ~***)* canudo; ♦ *exc* **this is the last ~!** era só o que faltava!

strawberry *n* morango *m*; *(plant)* morangueiro *m*.

straw poll *n* *(US)* sondagem *f* de opinião.

stray *adj* *(person)* perdido,-a; *(homeless dog)* cão *m* vadio; *(sheep, gots)* extraviado,-a; ♦ *vi* extraviar-se, perder-se; afastar-se; **to ~ from the right path** afastar-se do bom caminho; desviar-se; **to ~ from the subject** desviar-se do assunto.

streak *n* lado, traço (de carácter); **2** *(of colour, water)* sinal *m*; **3** *(of light)* raio *m* de luz; **~s on hair** madeixas *fpl*; **4** estria; ♦ *vt* raiar *(sky)*; ♦ *vi*: **to ~ past** passar como um raio.

streaker *n* pessoa que anda nua em público (em eventos deportivos).

streaky *adj* listado,-a; raiado, riscado,-a; **~ bacon** *n* toucinho *m* defumado entremeado.

stream *n* *(brook)* riacho *m*; caudal *m*; **2** *(jet)* ja(c)to; **3** fluxo, corrente *f*; **4** *(of people)* fluxo *m*; ♦ *(EDUC)* classificar; ♦ *vi* correr, fluir; **to ~ in/out** *(people)* entrar/sair aos montões.

streamer *n* *(for carnival)* serpentina *f*; **2** *(pennant)* flâmula *f*.

streamlined *adj* simplificado,-a; eficiente; racionalizado,-a; **2** aerodinâmico,-a.

street *n* rua; ♦ *adj* da rua; **~car** *(US) n* carro *m*, elé(c)trico, *(BR)* bonde *m*; **~ lamp** *n* poste *m*; **~ lighting** *n* iluminação *f* pública; **~map** *n* mapa *m* da cidade, roteiro *m*; **~ market** *n* feira ao ar livre; **~ value** *n* preço *m* de revenda (drogas); **~walker** *n* prostituta, mulher da rua/da vida; **~wise** *adj* capaz de se desenvencilhar num local urbano pobre e por vezes criminoso; pessoa consciente dos perigos da rua.

strength *n* força *f*; **2** resistência *f*; **3** *(currency)* valor *m*; **to go from ~ to ~** ir de vento em popa.

strengthen *vt* fortalecer; **2** *vi* intensificar-se.

strenuous *adj* árduo,-a; extenuante *m,f*.

stress *n* *(graphic accent)* acento *m* tónico; **2** ênfase *f* importância *f*; **3** *(TECH)* tensão *f*, pressão *f* (**on sth** sobre algo); **4** *(nervous)* tensão *f*, stress *m*; **~ ball** *n* bolinha que se aperta na mão para aliviar o 'stress'; ♦ *vt* realçar, dar ênfase a.

stressed *adj* *(syllable)* tónica; *(graphic accent)* acentuado,-a; **2** *(tense)* *(also:* **~-out***)* stressado,-a; *(BR)* estressado,-a; tenso,-a.

stressful, stressing *adj* stressante; desgastante.

stretch *n* *(section of road)* troço *m*; distância *f*; *(of river)* trecho *m*; *(in gymnastics)* estiramento *m*; **~ of sand** areal *m*; ♦ *vt* *(extend)* estender (braços, pernas); esticar *(elastic)*; *(shoes)* alargar; ♦ *vi* *(extend)* estender, esticar; **to ~ one's limbs** espreguiçar-se; *(in gymnastics)* estirar-se; **to ~ in the sun** estirar-se ao sol; **3** *(extend)* estender-se (**over** por) (area); **to ~ from ... to** estender-se de ... até; **~ the truth** *vt* exagerar a verdade; **to ~ one's patience** *vt* abusar da paciência de alguém; **to ~ a point** *vt* fazer uma exce(p)ção; ♦ **to ~ out** *vi* *(have a rest)* deitar-se; **2** esticar *(hand, foot)*.

stretcher *n* maca, padiola; **~-bearer** *n* maqueiro,-a.

stretch marks *npl* estrias *fpl* *(on abdomen)*.

strew *(pt* **-ed***, pp* **strewn***)* espalhar *(clothes, papers, petals)*; **the floor was strewn with** o chão estava coberto/cheio de.

stricken *adj* ferido,-a doente; **to be ~ by/with grief** estar abalado,-a pelo desgosto; *(illness)* estar atacado por (algo).

strict *adj* *(person)* severo,-a, rigoroso,-a; **2** *(precise)* exa(c)to,-a preciso,-a; **on the ~ confidence** a título estritamente confidencial.

strictly *adv* *(exactly)* estritamente; *(totally)* terminantemente; *(severely)* rigorosamente; **'fishing is ~ forbidden'** pescar é expressamente proibido.

strictness *n* exa(c)tidão *f*; rigor *m*, severidade *f*.

stride *n* passo largo; ♦ *(pt* **strode***, pp* **stridden***) vi* andar a passos largos.

strident *adj* *(sound, voice)* estridente; **2** *(critic)* contundente.

strife *n* luta *f*, conflitos *mpl*.

strike *n* greve *f*; **2** *(of oil)* descoberta *f*; **3** *(MIL)* ataque *m*; **4** *(SPORT)* golpe *m*; ♦ *(pt, pp* **struck***) vt* *(hit)* bater, golpear; **2** *(oil etc)* descobrir; **3** *(obstacle)* chocar-se com; **4** *(to seem)* **he ~ me as an honest person** ele parece-me uma pessoa honesta; **5 I was struck by/with her beauty** fiquei impressionado com a beleza dela; **6 to ~ fear into sb** infundir medo/terror em alguém; **7 to ~ (it) lucky/rich** ter sorte/ficar rico,-a; ♦ *vi* entrar em greve; **2 to ~ against sth** bater em algo; **3** *(attack)* atacar; **4** *(clock-chime)* bater, dar horas; **5 to ~ a match** acender um fósforo; **6** *(suddenly happen)* ocorrer; **to be struck blind/deaf** ficar cego/mudo; **to ~ back** ripostar **(at sb** a alguém); **to ~ down** *vt* derrubar; **to ~ off** *vt* riscar *(name from the list)*; suspender *(licence, function)*; expulsar duma associação, Ordem; ♦ **to be struck off** perder a licença profissional; **2** ser tirado,-a (da lista); ♦ **to ~ out** *vt* cancelar, rasurar; **2** pôr-se a caminho; ♦ **to ~ up** *vt (MUS)* começar a tocar; **2** encetar, travar *(conversation, friendship)*.

strikebreaker *n* fura-greve *m,f inv.*

striker *n* grevista *m,f; (SPORT)* atacante *m,f.*

striking *n (of clock)* toque *m*, badalada *f;* **2** *(of coin)* cunhagem *f;* ♦ *adj (person, clothes, etc)* atraente, chamativo,-a; impressionante; **a ~ similarity** uma semelhança *f* impressionante; **2** *(worker, miner)* em greve; **~ distance** *n:* **to be within ~ distance (of sth)** estar muito perto de algo; **2** *(troops)* estar ao alcance de fogo.

string *n (thin rope)* cordel *m (of wire)* barbante *m; (for tennis racket, bow)* corda *f;* **2** *(row, chain)* fileira *f;* **the necklace has two ~s of pearls** o colar tem duas fileiras de pérolas; **3** *(of onions)* réstea *f;* **4** série, sucessão *(of events);* ♦ **the ~s** *npl (MUS) (musical instrument)* os instrumentos de corda; ♦ **no ~s attached** sem restrições, sem condições; **to be with no ~s attached** ser solteiro,-a, ser livre; **to pull ~s** *(fig)* puxar os cordelinhos, *(BR)* usar pistolão; ♦ *(pt, pp* **strung)** *vt/vi:* enfiar num fio; ♦ **to ~ along** *vt* ir **(with** com), acompanhar alguém; **to ~ out** *vt* estender-se so longo; **2** prolongar; ♦ **to ~ together** *vt* enfiar *(beads);* **2** *(words)* alinhavar, juntar; **3** *(ideas)* encadear; ♦ **to ~ sb up** *vt (coll)* enforcar alguém.

stringbean *n* vagem *f.*

string(ed) instrument *n (MUS)* instrumento de corda.

stringent *adj* severo,-a estrito,-a.

strip *n* tira *f;* **2** *(of land)* faixa *f;* **the Gaza ~** *n* a Faixa Gaza; **3** *(of metal)* lamina *f;* **4** *(of land)* faixa *f;* **5 cartoon ~** *n* banda *f* desenhada; **~ comic** *n* história *f* aos/em quadradinhos; **metal ~** fita *f* metálica; ♦ (**-ped)** *vt (remove)* tirar; **to ~ a wall** tirar o papel a uma parede; **2** *(clothes)* desprive; **3 to ~ the cork tree of its bark** tirar a casca/a cortiça do sobreiro, descascar o sobreiro; **4** *(deprive)* **he was ~ped of his papers** privaram-lhe os documentos; **5** despojar; **6** (= **to ~ down)** desmontar; ♦ *vi* despir-se; **to ~ naked** despir-se completamente; *(coll)* pôr-se em pelo.

stripe *n (on animal)* lista *f;* risca *f;* **2** *(on fabric, wallpaper)* risca, barra *f;* **3** *(MIL)* (de oficial) galão *m; (of sergeant)* divisa *f.*

striped *adj* listado, listrado, às riscas; com listras.

stripper *n (skin)* exfoliador *m;* **2** artista *m,f* de striptease; **paint ~** diluente *m.*

striptease *n* striptease *m.*

strive *(pt* **strove,** *pp* **striven)** *vi* **to ~ to do sth** esforçar-se por, batalhar para fazer algo.

strobe *n (light)* luz estroboscópica.

strode *(pt of* **stride).**

stroke *n (blow)* pancada *f*, golpe *m;* **2** *(SPORT) (swimming)* braçada *f;* **the breast ~** o nadar de bruços; **3** *(of golf)* tacada *f;* **4** *(in tennis)* raquetada *f;* **5** *(rowing)* remada *f;* **6** *(of brush)* pincelada *f;* **7** *(of pen)* traço *m; (punctuation – slash)* barra *f;* **8** *(of clock, church bell)* badalada *f;* **9** *(MED) (dated)* derrame *m* cerebral, trombose; *(present term)* acidente vascular cerebral, AVC; **10** *(caress)* carícia *f;* ♦ *vt* acariciar, afagar; **2** *(pet)* fazer festas a; ♦ **at a ~** de repente, de golpe; **a ~ of luck** um bambúrrio da sorte, um golpe de sorte; **a ~ of genius** um lampejo de génio; **on the ~** pontualmente; **on the ~ of midnight** pontualmente à meia-noite.

stroll *n* volta *f*, passeio *m;* ♦ *vi* passear, dar uma volta.

stroller *n* caminhante, deambulante *m,f; (US)* carrinho *m* (de bebé).

strong *adj* forte; *(sturdy)* resistente *m,f;* **~arm** *n* braço forte; pulso firme **~box** *n* cofre-forte *f;* **~hold** *n* fortaleza; *(fig)* baluarte *m*, bastião *m;* **~ language** *n* linguagem *f* pesada; **~ nerves** *npl* nervos *mpl* de aço **~ point** ponto *m* forte; **~-willed** *adj* de cará(c)ter forte, obstinado,-a.

strongish *adj* um tanto forte.

strongly *adv* fortemente, vigorosamente; *(believe)* firmemente.

strontium *n (PHYS)* estrôncio *m.*

stroppy (-ier, -iest) *adj (UK, fam)* resmungão *m*, resmungona *f.*

strove *(pt of* **strive).**

struck *(pt, pp of* **strike).**

structural *adj* estrutural.

structure *n* estrutura; construção *f.*

struggle *n* luta *f* **(against** contra; **between** entre; **for** por); *(scuffle)* briga, rixa *f; (dispute)* contenda *f; (effort, difficult task)* esforço *m;* **it was a ~ to learn Japanese** foi um esforço grande/duro para aprender japonês; ♦ *vi* lutar **(for sth** por algo), brigar; **to ~ along** avançar a custo; **to ~ to get free** esforçar-se por se livrar; **to ~ on** continuar a custo; **to ~ to one's feet** levantar-se com dificuldade; **to ~ with a problem** debater-se com um problema; **to ~ through** esforçar-se, conseguir a custo; abrir caminho *(crowd).*

strum *vt (guitar)* dedilhar.

strung *pt, pp of* **string; she is highly ~** ela é neurótica, é uma pilha de nervos.

strut *n* escora, suporte *m;* ♦ *vi (also:* **to ~ about/ around)** pavonear-se, empertigar-se.

stub *n (of cheque book, receipt, voucher)* talão *m;* **2** *(of cigarette)* beata, ponta; **3** *(of tree)* toco *m*, cepo *m;* ♦ **to ~ out** *vt* apagar; **to ~ one's toe** tropeçar, dar uma topada.

stubble *n* restolho *m;* **2** *(on chin)* barba por fazer.

stubborn *adj* teimoso,-a, renitente, obstinado,-a.

stuck *(pt, pp of* **stick)** *adj* entalado,-a preso,-a; **~-up** *adj* convencido,-a, presumido,-a, pedante.

stud *n (shirt)* botão *m;* **2** *(of boot)* cravo *m;* **3** *(for ear)* brinco *m* de mola; **4** (= **~ horse)** garanhão *m;*

he is a good ~ (*US: coll*) ele é um homem–macho, garanhão; ◆ (**-dd-**) *vt* (*sprinkle*) salpicar de (*stars*): **~ded with sequins** (*fig*) salpicado de lantejoulas; **~ with** (**studs**) guarnecido de tochas.

student *n* estudante *m,f*; ◆ *adj* estudantil; **~driver** *n* (*US*) principiante *m,f*.

studio *n* estúdio; atelier *m*, (*BR*) ateliê *m*.

studious *adj* estudioso,-a aplicado,-a; (*studied*) calculado,-a.

studiously *adv* (*carefully*) com esmero.

study *n* estudo *m*; **2** (*room*) escritório *m*, sala de estudo; ◆ *vt* estudar; examinar, investigar; ◆ *vi* estudar.

stuff *n* (*unnamed material, fabric, substance*) coisa *f*; **what kind of ~ is that?** que (tipo de) coisa é essa?; (*things*) coisas *fpl*; **2** (*stolen goods*) mercadoria *f*; **3** (*mess, clutter*) (*fig*) feira *f*; **4 the ~** (*drugs*) droga *f*; ◆ *vt* encher (**with** de); **2** (*also: ~ up*) tapar (*holes*) (**with** com); **I have my nose ~ed** (*fam*) tenho o nariz *m* entupido; **3** (*CULIN*) rechear; **~ed chicken** frango *m* recheado; **4 ~ in/into** (*pack in*) meter (em/dentro de); **5** (*taxidermist*) empalhar, embalsamar (*animals*); ◆ *vr* **to ~ o.s. with food** empanturrar-se; **to know one's ~ well** saber muito bem do seu ofício; ◆ *exc* **that's the ~!** é isso mesmo!; **get stuffed!** (*coll*) (*expressing anger*) vai pentear macacos (*fam*); (*coll*) vai à merda (*cal*).

stuffed shirt *n* (*coll, pej*) (*vain, formal*) pessoa vaidosa; ◆ *adj* pomposo,-a; **to be a ~** ter a mania (da superioridade).

stuffing *n* (*CULIN*) recheio *m*; **2** (*for upholstering*) enchimento *m*; **3** (*of animals*) empalhamento *m*; **to knock the ~ out of sb** (*coll*) destruir a autoconfiança, a força de alguém.

stuffy (-ier, iest) *adj* (*room*) abafado,-a, mal ventilado,-a; **2** (*boring person*) enfadonho,-a, muito convencional, formal.

stumble *vi* tropeçar; **to ~ across** (*fig*) encontrar por acaso, topar com.

stumbling block *n* obstáculo *m*, impedimento *m*.

stump *n* (*of tree*) cepo *m*, tronco *m*; **2** (*of candle, pencil*) toco *m*; **3** (*of cabbage*) talo *m*; **4** (*of limb*) coto *m*; **5** (*in cricket*) estaca *f*; **~s** (*wicket*) varetas *fpl* verticais; ◆ *vt* (*perplex*) deixar perplexo,-a, desconcertar (alguém); **to be ~ed for an answer** ficar atrapalhado,-a; **2** (*lop*) reduzir algo a um cepo *or* toco; **3** (*cricket*) eliminar jogador, pôr fora do jogo (*batsman*); ◆ *vi* **to ~ in/out** entrar/sair pesadamente; **to ~ up sth** desembolsar (dinheiro).

stumpy (-ier, -iest) *adj* (*person*) atarrecado,-a.

stun *vt* (*daze*) aturdir, atordoar; **2** (*surprise, amazement*) deixar estupefa(c)to; **3** assombrar.

stung (*pt, pp of* sting).

stunk (*pp of* stink).

stunned *adj* (*from blow, shock*) atordoado,-a; **2** (*astonished*) pasmado,-a, estupefa(c)to,-a.

stunning *adj* (*beautiful*) belo,-a, belíssimo,-a; assombroso,-a; **she is ~** ela é um assombro; sensacional.

stunt *n* façanha *f* sensacional; **2** (*AER*) voo (*BR*: vôo) acrobático; **3** (*publicity*) truque *m* publicitário.

stunted *adj* atrofiado, retardado.

stuntman *n* (*CIN*) duplo, (*BR*) dublê *m*.

stupefy *vt* deixar estupefa(c)to; pasmar.

stupendous *adj* assombroso,-a, estupendo,-a, prodigioso,-a.

stupid *adj* estúpido, idiota.

stupidity *n* estupidez *f*.

stupidly *adv* estupidamente.

stupor *m* estupor *m*.

sturdy *adj* robusto; **2** (*firm*) resoluto.

sturgeon *n* (*fish*) esturjão *m*.

stutter *n* gaguez *f*, gagueira; ◆ *vi* gaguejar; tartamudear, titubear; **~rer** *n* (*person*) gago,-a.

St Valentine's Day *n* Dia *m* de São Valentim, Dia dos Namorados.

sty *n* (*for pigs*) pocilga *f*, chiqueiro *m*; **2** (*MED*) (*also: ~e*) (*in the eye*) terçolho *m*.

stye *n* (*MED*) terçol *m*, terçolho.

style *n* estilo *m*; **to do things in ~** fazer tudo à grande; ◆ *vt/vi* chamar, denominar; **to ~ o.s. major** intitular-se major.

styling mousse (*for hair*) espuma *f* fixante (*BR*) musse *f* modeladora.

stylish *adj* elegante, da moda.

stylist *n* estilista *m,f*.

stylus *n* (*of record player*) agulha *f*.

stymie *vt* (*fam*): **to be ~d** (*thwarted*) estar entravado,-a; bloqueado,-a.

styrax *n* (*BOT*) estírace *f*.

Styx *npr* Estige *f*; IDIOM **to cross the ~** morrer.

suave *adj* (*sophisticated*) brando-a; cortês, polido,-a; **2** (*pleasant*), afável.

sub¹ *n* (*abbr for* **submarine**); **2** (*abbr for* **substitute**); **3** (*abbr for* **subscription**); **4** (*abbr for* **advanced payment**) adiantamento *m*.

sub² *prefix* sub; **~altern** *n* (*US*) oficial *m,f* subalterno,-a; **~aqua** *adj* relativo a desportos aquáticos; **~contract** *n* subcontra(c)to *m*; subempreitada *f*; **~divide** *vt* subdividir; **~division** *n* subdivisão *f*.

subconscious *n* subconsciente *m*; ◆ *adj* do subconsciente.

subdue *vt* subjugar; dominar.

subdued *adj* suavizado, atenuado; **2** (*voice*) sumido; **3** (*light*) coado; **4** (*person*) submisso,-a subjugado,-a.

subeditor *n* dire(c)tor adjunto (de um jornal); **2** (*checking/correcting publication*) reda(c)tor,-ora.

subheading *n* (*in text*) subtítulo *m*.

subhuman *adj* sub-humano,-a.

subject *n* (*citizen*) sú(b)dito; **2** (*EDUC*) (*at school*) disciplina *f*, matéria *f*; **3** (*topic*) assunto, tópico *m*; **4** (*GRAM*) sujeito *m*; ◆ *adj* sujeito,-a (**to** a); **to be ~ to** (*JUR*) estar sujeito a (*penalty*); submetido,-a; dominado,-a; ◆ *vt* dominar; subjugar; **2** submeter (alguém) (**to** a); **to ~ sb to sth** submeter/sujeitar alguém a algo; **to ~ sth to** (*heat, cold, light*) expor algo a.

subjection *n* submissão *f*, dependência.

subjective *adj* subje(c)tivo,-a.

subjectivity *n* subjectividade *f*.

subject matter *n* assunto; **2** (*content*) conteúdo *m*.

sub judice *adj, adv* em segredo da justiça.

subjugate vt subjugar, submeter.

subjunctive n (gram) conjuntivo m, (BR) subjuntivo m.

sublet n subaluguer m, (BR) subaluguel m, sub-arrendamento m; ♦ vt subalugar, subarrendar.

sublime adj sublime m,f; 2 (indifference, contempt) supremo,-a.

sublimely adv magnificamente; totalmente.

subliminal adj subliminar.

submachine gun n metralhadora f de mão.

submarine n submarino m.

submerge vt (plunge sth into liquid) submergir; (person) mergulhar em, imergir em; 2 (sea, flood) inundar; ♦ vi submergir-se.

submerged adj submerso,-a; imerso, mergulhado; ~ **body** corpo m submerso; ~ **submarine** submarino m em imersão.

submission n submissão f.

submissive adj submisso,-a.

submit vt submeter; ♦ vi submeter-se.

subnormal adj subnormal, abaixo do norma (temperature, etc); 2 (person) (mentalmente) atrasado,-a; 3 abaixo do normal.

subordinate adj, n subordinado,-a; ~ **clause** (GRAM) oração f subordinada.

subpoena n (JUR) intimação f judicial; ♦ vt intimar a comparecer judicialmente.

subscribe vi subscrever; **to** ~ **to** (opinion) concordar com; 2 (fund) contribuir para; 3 (newspaper) assinar.

subscriber n assinante m,f.

subscription n subscrição f; assinatura f.

subsequent adj subsequente, posterior.

subsequently adv mais tarde, depois.

subservience n subserviência f; servilismo m.

subservient adj subserviente, servil.

subside vi (fever) baixar; 2 (flood) descer; 3 (wind, emotion) acalmar; 4 (die down) diminuir, enfraquecer; 5 (land, building) aluir, desabar.

subsidence n (in property) aluimento m, desmoronamento m.

subsidiary (pl: -ies) n susidiário,-a; 2 (firm controlled by another) sucursal, filial; ♦ adj subsidiário,-a; secundário,-a.

subsiding n (GEOL, CONSTR) abaixamento m, desabamento m; (building sinking to its foundations) aluimento m.

subsidize vt subsidiar.

subsidy n subsídio m, subvenção f.

subsistence n subsistência, meio de vida; 2 (allowance) subsídio, ajuda f de custo m; ~ **level** n limiar m de subsistência.

substance n substância f; (fig) essência f.

substandard adj de qualidade m inferior.

substantial adj considerável; raro,-a; substancial; essencial; (fig) importante.

substantially adv substancialmente.

substantiate vt (JUR) comprovar, justificar.

substitute n substituto,-a; 2 (SPORT) suplente m,f reserva m,f; ~ **teacher** n suplente m,f; ♦ vt: **to** ~ **A for B** substituir B por A.

substitution n substituição f, troca f.

substratum n (basis) base f; 2 (subsoil) subsolo m; 3 (bedrock) subestra(c)to m; 4 (SOCIOL) camada f.

subtenant n sublocatário,-a.

subterfuge n subterfúgio m.

subterranean adj subterrâneo,-a.

subtitle n subtítulo; 2 ~s (film) legenda.

subtle adj su(b)til.

subtlety n su(b)tileza.

subtract vt: ~ **sth from sth** subtrair (algo de algo).

subtraction n subtração f.

suburb n subúrbios mpl; arrabalde m; **the** ~s npl os arredores mpl; (BR) periferia f.

suburban adj de subúrbio; ~ **sprawl** subúrbio m gigantesco.

suburbia n bairros mpl residenciais na periferia da cidade.

subversive adj subversivo,-a.

subvert vt subverter.

subway n (UK) (for pedestrian) passagem f subterrânea; 2 (underground) (US) metro, (BR) metrô.

sub-zero adj abaixo de zero.

succeed vi (person) ser bem-sucedido, ter êxito; 2 (achieve) **to** ~ **in doing sth** conseguir fazer algo; 3 (plan) sair bem; ♦ vt suceder a; **King Jorge was succeeded by his daughter** ao rei Jorge sucedeu-lhe a filha; **to** ~ **to the throne** subir ao trono; seguir-se a.

succeeding adj sucessivo, posterior.

success n sucesso m êxito m; triunfo m.

successful adj bem-sucedido; **to be** ~ (**in doing**) conseguir (fazer).

successfully adv com sucesso, com êxito.

succession n sucessão f, série f; (descendants) descendência.

successive adj sucessivo, consecutivo.

successor n successor,-ora.

succinct adj sucinto,-a.

succulent adj suculento,-a.

succumb vi sucumbir.

such adj tal, semelhante; ~ **a thing** uma coisa assim; **in** ~ **cases** em tais casos; ~ **courage** tanta coragem; ~ **a long trip** uma viagem tão longa; ~ **a lot of** tanto; ~ **as** tal como; **as** ~ adv como tal; ♦ pron isso, esse, essa, aquilo, os/as que; **until** ~ **time as** até que; **and** ~ (**like**) e coisas desse tipo.

suchlike adj (coll) semelhante, deste tipo, coisas assim; ♦ pron (pej) (people) gente deste tipo.

suck vt chupar; **to** ~ **one's finger** chupar no dedo; 2 (draw in) aspirar (liquid, air); **the vacuum cleaner is not sucking well** o aspirador não está a aspirar bem; 3 (extract) sorver, sugar; 4 (baby) mamar (breast); ♦ **to** ~ **in** (sea) tragar, engolir; ~ **into** (fig) (involve) **to be** ~**ed into sth** ficar/estar absorvido,-a em algo; ♦ ~ **up** aspirar (dust); ~ **up to sb** (fam) bajular, lamber as botas a alguém.

sucker n (BOT) rebento; 2 (of octopus) ventosa f; 3 chupador,-ora; 4 (coll) (gullible person) trouxa m,f, papalvo,-a, bobo,-a; 5 (attracted to a particular type) **he is a** ~ **for blondes** ele tem um fraquinho por loiras.

suckle vt amamentar (baby).

suckling adj (baby) bebé de mama; ~ **pig** n porquinho,-a; (CULIN) leitão m.

sucrose *n* sacarose *f.*

suction *n* sucção *f; ~* **pump** *n* bomba *f* de sucção.

Sudan *npr* Sudão; **in** *~* no Sudão.

Sudanese *n, adj* sudanês *m* sudanesa *f.*

sudden *adj* repentino,-a, súbito,-a; imprevisto,-a; **all of a** *~/~***ly** *adv* de repente; *(unexpectedly)* inesperadamente.

suds *npl* espuma *f* de sabão.

sue *vt (JUR)* processar, intentar uma ação.

suede *n* camurça; *~* **shoes** *npl* sapatos *mpl* de camurça.

suet *n* sebo *m.*

suffer *vt* sofrer, padecer (**from** de); **2** *(tolerate)* aguentar; **I will not** *~* **your insolence** não aguentarei mais a tua insolência; **you will** *~* **for it later** vais-te arrepender mais tarde.

sufferance *n* tolerância *f;* **to do sth on** *~* fazer algo contra vontade; como um favor.

sufferer *n* sofredor,-ora; doente *m,f,* paciente *m,f.*

suffering *n* sofrimento *m,* padecimento *m; (pain)* dor *f.*

suffice *vi* bastar, ser suficiente; *~* **it to say that** basta dizer que.

sufficient *adj* suficiente, bastante.

suffix *n* sufixo *m.*

suffocate *vi* sufocar-se, asfixiar-se.

suffocation *n* sufocação *f,* asfixia.

suffrage *n* sufrágio *m; (vote)* direito de voto.

suffragette *n* sufragista *f.*

suffragist *n* advogado,-a a/em favor do direito de voto da mulher.

suffuse *vt* espalhar-se, *(light, colour)* inundar, cobrir; **the sky was** *~***ed with red** o céu estava coberto de vermelho.

sugar *n* açúcar *m; ♦ vt* pôr açúcar em; adoçar; *~* **beet** *n* beterraba; *~* **bowl** *n* açucareiro *m; ~***cane** *n* cana-de-açúcar *f; ♦ exc ~!* exc abóbora!

sugary *adj* açucarado,-a, adocicado,-a.

suggest *vt* sugerir; aconselhar.

suggestion *n* insinuação *f;* sugestão *f.*

suggestive *adj* sugestivo; **2** *(pej)* indecente.

suicidal *adj* suicida.

suicide *n* suicídio; *(person)* suicida *m,f.*

suit *n (man's)* fato, *(BR)* terno; *(woman's)* conjunto *m,* fato *m;* **2** *(JUR)* processo *m;* **3** *(cards)* naipe *m; ♦ vt* convir a; **it doesn't** *~* **me to go out tonight** não me convém sair esta noite; **2** *(clothes)* ficar bem a (alguém); **this colour** *~***s you** esta cor fica-te bem; **to** *~* **sth to** adaptar, acomodar algo a; *♦ exc ~* **yourself!** como queiras/como quiseres.

suitable *adj* conveniente; apropriado,-a.

suitably *adv* convenientemente, apropriadamente.

suitcase *n* mala *f,* maleta *f.*

suite *n (of rooms)* apartamento, conjunto de salas; **2** *(MUS)* suíte *f.*

suitor *n* pretendente *m.*

sulcus *(linear groove)* sulco *m.*

sulk *n (usually plural)* amuo *m;* **he has got the** *~***s** ele está de mau humor; *♦ vi* amuar.

sulky (-ier, -iest) *adj* amuado,-a; ressentido,-a.

sullen *adj* taciturno,-a, carrancudo,-a.

sulphur *n* enxofre *m.*

sulphuric acid *n* ácido *m* sulfúrico.

sultan *n* sultão *m.*

sultana *n (queen)* sultana *f;* **2** *(dried fruit)* sultana.

sultanate *n* sultanato *m.*

sultriness *n (weather)* atmosfera *f* pesada e abafada; **2** *(of person)* sensualidade *f.*

sultry *adj (weather)* abafado,-a, sufocante *m,f,* mormacento *m;* **2** *(seductive)* sedutor,-ora.

sum *n* soma *f;* total *m; ~* **of money** montante *m,* soma de dinheiro; *♦* (**-med**) *vt* somar, adicionar; **to** *~* **up** *vt* sumariar, fazer um resumo; *♦ vi* resumir, recapitular; **to** *~* **up courage** encher-se de coragem.

Sumatra *npr* Sumatra; **in** *~* na Sumatra.

Sumatran *n adj* sumatriano,-a.

summarize, summarise *vt* resumir; sintetizar; **to** *~* em resumo.

summary *n* resumo *m,* sumário *m; ♦ adj (JUR)* sumário,-a; *~* **trial** (sem a presença do júri) julgamento *m* sumário.

summation *n* adição *f,* total *m;* **2** *(US) (JUR)* discurso final do advogado de defesa ou procurador num processo.

summer *n* verão *m;* estio *m;* **in the** *~* no verão; *♦ adj* estival, de verão; *~***house** *n (in garden)* pavilhão em jardim; **2** *(for holidays)* casa *f* de verão, de veraneio; *~* **resort** *n* estância *f* veranil; *~***time** *n (season)* verão *m; ~* **Time** *(by clock)* horário de verão.

summing-up *n (JUR)* resumo *m;* **2** *(gen)* recapitulação *f.*

summit *n (of mountain, top)* topo, cume *m;* píncaro *m;* **2** *(fig) (pinnacle)* auge, apogéu *(in one's career/ life);* **3** *(POL) (meeting, conference)* de cimeira *f, (BR)* de cúpula *f.*

summon *vt (person)* mandar chamar; **2** *(meeting)* convocar; **3** *(JUR)* citar, intimar; *♦ ~***s** *n (JUR)* citação *f,* intimação *f; ♦* **to** *~* **up** *vt (forces)* concentrar; **2** *(courage)* armar-se de.

sump *n (gen)* poço *m,* fossa *f;* **2** *(AUT)* cárter *m;* **3** reservatório *m.*

sumptuous *adj* sumptuoso/suntuoso,-a, magnífico,-a, esplêndido,-a.

sun *n* sol *m; ~***baked** *adj* ressequido,-a pelo sol; *~***bathe** *vi* tomar banho de sol; *~***bather** *n* banhista *m,f; ~***beam** *n* raio *m* de sol; *~***bed** *n* cama *f* solar; *~***burn** *n (painful)* queimadura; **2** *(tan)* bronzeado; *~***burned/ burnt** *adj (tanned)* bronzeado; queimado,-a; *~* **cream** *n* protetor *m* solar.

Sunday *n* domingo *m; ~* **best** *n:* **in one's** *~* **best** no seu fato, traje *m* domingueiro; **Low** *~* Domingo de Pascoela; *~* **Mass** *n* missa *f* dominical; **Palm** *~* Domingo de Ramos; *~***-school** *n* aula de instrução religiosa, catecismo (que funciona na Inglaterra ao domingo).

sundial *n* relógio *m* de sol.

sundown *n* crepúsculo *m.*

sundry *adj* vários, diversos; **all and** *~* todos; **sundries** *npl* géneros *mpl* diversos.

sunflower *n (BOT)* girassol *m.*

sung *(pp of* **sing***).*

sunglasses *npl* óculos *mpl* de sol.

sunk *(pp of* **sink***).*

sunken adj (cheeks) cavado,-a (BR) encovado; (eyes) fundos; **2** (under water) submerso,-a; **3** (boat) afundado; **4** (low-level – garden) rebaixado; (bath) embutido, encaixado.

sunlamp n lâmpada f ultra-violeta.

sunlight n luz f do sol.

sunlit adj ensolarado,-a; ~ **lounge** n saleta f envidraçada, marquise f.

sunni n adj (Muslim religion) sunita m,f.

sunny (-ier, -iest) adj cheio de sol; soalheiro; (fig) alepre; it is ~ faz sl; **2** ensolarado,-a; **a ~ house** uma casa cheia de sol; **3** (exposed to the sun) soalheiro,-a (patio, garden).

sunrise n nascer m do sol.

sunroof n terraço m.

sunset n pôr m do sol.

sunshade n (over table) parasol m; (on the beach) (hired shade/cover) toldo m.

sunshine n luz f do sol.

sunspot n mancha f solar.

sunstroke n insolação f.

suntan oil n bronzeador m.

super adj (petrol, etc) de qualidade; ~ **petrol** n gasolina f super; ♦ exc ~! ó(p)timo! porreiro!

superannuated adj (person) reformado com pensão.

superannuation n aposentação f; pensão f de reforma; (BR) aposentadoria; ~ **scheme** n regime m de reforma (BR) de aposentadoria.

superb adj soberbo,-a, magnífico,-a, excelente.

supercilious adj arrogante, desdenhoso,-a, com um ar superior.

superficial adj superficial.

superfluous adj supérfluo,-a, desnecessário,-a.

superhuman adj sobre-humano,-a.

superimpose vt sobrepor (**sth on sth** algo a algo).

superintendent n superintendente m,f; (police) chefe m,f de polícia, comandante m,f.

superior n superior m; **with a ~ air** com um ar de desdém; ♦ adj superior.

superiority n superioridade f.

superlative n (gram) superlativo m; ♦ adj superlativo,-a, excelente.

superman n super-homem m.

supermarket n supermercado m.

supernatural adj sobrenatural.

superordinate n superior; **2** hipernónimo,-a; ♦ adj superordenado,-a.

superpower n (POL) superpotência f.

supersede vt suplantar.

supersonic adj supersónico,-a (BR: -sô-).

superstition n superstição f.

superstitious adj supersticioso,-a.

superstructure n superestrutura f.

supertax (pl: -es) imposto m suplementar.

supervise vt supervisionar; fiscalizar (work, product); vigiar (child, customers); ♦ vi inspe(c)cionar.

supervision n supervisão f; fiscalização f; vigilância f.

supervisor n (person in charge) responsável; **2** (restaurant, etc) gerente; **3** (Univ) (for thesis) orientador,-ora; dire(c)tor,-ora de estudos; **4** (CONSTR) encarregado,-a.

supine n (LING) supino m; ♦ adj (person) deitado,-a de costas; **2** indolente; mole.

supper n jantar m, ceia; **to have ~** jantar. cear.

supple adj flexível.

supplement n (gen) suplemento m; ♦ vt suprir; acrescentar; completar.

supplementary adj suplementar.

supplier n abastecedor,-ora, fornecedor,-ora; **2** (COMM) distribuidor,-ora.

supply n fornecimento m, provisão f; abastecimento; ~ **teacher** n professor,-ora substituto,-a; ~ **doctor** n médico,-a suplente; ♦ **supplies** npl (food) víveres mpl; **2** provisões fpl; **3** (ECON) ~ **and demand** oferta e procura; (BR) oferta e demanda; ♦ vt (provide) abastecer, fornecer (area, ship, customer); **to ~ with** suprir de, prover a alguém (needs); responder a (demand); **to be in short ~** ser escasso.

support n apoio m; **2** (TECH) suporte m; **3** (financial) ajuda f; ♦ vt (to back) apoiar; **2** corroborar (story); **3** manter; sustentar (person, family with food etc); **4** (put up with) suportar (behaviour).

supporter n (POL etc) partidário,-a; **3** (SPORT) apoiante m,f, (BR) torcedor,-ora.

suppose vt/vi supor; imaginar; **to be ~d to do sth** dever fazer algo; **he is ~ed to be an engineer** ele é suposto ser um engenheiro; **let's ~ that** suponhamos que.

supposedly adv supostamente, pretensamente.

supposing conj se, supondo-se que; ~ **she had an accident?** e se ela teve um acidente?

supposition n suposição f.

suppository n supositório m.

suppress vt suprimir (information, activity); **2** (revolt), reprimir; **3** conter (soluço); **4** refrear (emotions).

suppression n repressão f.

suppurate vi (MED) (discharge pus) supurar.

supremacy n supremacia f.

supreme adj supremo,-a; extremo,-a; **S~ Court** n (highest court of law) Supremo Tribunal.

supremely adv extremamente; de suma importância.

surcharge n sobrecarga f; sobretaxa f.

sure adj (reliable, safe) seguro,-a; **2** (certain) certo,-a, firme; **3** (aim) certeiro; ~! claro que sim!, com certeza!; **I am ~** tenho a certeza; **4** (confident) **to be ~ of o.s.** estar seguro de si mesmo, ter confiança em si mesmo; **to make ~ that** certificar-se de (que); ♦ **for ~** adv com certeza; ~ **enough** adv efe(c)tivamente; IDIOM **as ~ as night follows day** tão certo como a noite segue o dia; tão certo como dois serem quarto.

sure-fire adj (success) garantido,-a.

sure-footed adj de andar seguro.

surely adv certamente.

surety n garantia f, fiança f; (person) fiador,-ora.

surf n (waves) rebentação (das ondas do mar);(foam) espuma f (do mar); ♦ vi fazer surf m; (COMP) surfar.

surface n superfície f; ♦ vt (road) revestir, fazer o revestimento de; ♦ vi vir à superfície/à tona, emergir.

surfboard n prancha f de surf.

surfboarder n surfista m,f.

surfeit n: **a ~ of** um excesso de.

surfing n (SPORT) surf; **to go ~** surfar, fazer surf.

surfrider n pessoa que desliza sobre a ressaca numa prancha, (BR) surfista m,f.

surge n (of sea) onda, vaga; **2** (of feelings) onda f (BR) vaga f; **3** (of demand, sales) aumento m súbito; (ELECT) sobretensão f; ♦ vi encapelar-se; **2** (crowd) crescer de repente; **3** (prices, inflation) subir em flecha; **to ~ forward** (people, vehicles) avançar em tropel/em massa.

surgeon n cirurgião m; **dental ~** dentista m,f (BR) cirurgião-dentista m.

surgery n cirurgia; (room) consultório; clínica; **to undergo ~** fazer uma/submeter-se a uma operação; (consulting period) consulta.

surgical adj cirúrgico,-a; **~ spirit** n álcool m.

surly (-ier, -iest) adj rabugento,-a; carrancudo,-a.

surmise n conje(c)tura f, suposição f; ♦ vt conje(c)turar, presumir.

surmount vt superar, vencer.

surname n sobrenome m.

surpass vt (overcome) superar (problem); **2** exceder (expectation); **3** (overtake, go beyond), ultrapassar; **4** ♦ (in size, height) ser maior que; **~ o.s.** exceder-se.

surplus n excedente m; (COMM) superávit m; ♦ adj excedente, de sobra.

surprise n surpresa f, espanto m, admiração f; ♦ vt surpreender, espantar.

surprising adj surpreendente, inesperado,-a.

surrealist, n adj surrealista m,f.

surrender n rendição f, entrega f; ♦ vt/vi entregar; render-se, entregar-se.

surreptitious adj subreptício,-a, furtivo,-a.

surrogate n substituto,-a, suplente m,f; **~ mother** n mãe-suplente f.

surround n (for fireplace) cercadura f; **2** (border) orla f; ♦ vt circundar, rodear; cercar.

surrounding adj circundante, circunvizinho; **surroundings** npl arredores mpl, cercanias fpl.

surveillance n vigilância f; **~ camera** n câmara f de vigilância.

survey n (premises; in housebuying) inspeção f, vistoria; **2** (public poll) sondagem f; pesquisa (of sobre); **3** estudo; **4** (of land), levantamento m topográfico; ♦ vt inspecionar, vistoriar; sondar, pesquisar, fazer um levantamento de.

surveyor n agrimensor,-ora; inspector,-ora.

survival n sobrevivência.

survive vi sobreviver; (custom etc) perdurar; ♦ vt sobreviver a.

survivor n (from an accident) sobrevivente m,f; (fig) (a fighter – in life) lutador,-ora.

susceptible adj susce(p)tível, sensível (**to** a).

suspect n adj suspeito,-a; ♦ vt suspeitar, desconfiar (**sth, sb** de alguém).

suspend vt suspender; (temporarily) interromper.

suspender belt n (for stockings) cinta-liga.

suspenders npl (for stockings) cintas-ligas fpl; (for trousers) suspensórios fpl.

suspense n incerteza, expectativa f; **2** (in film) suspense m; **to keep sb in ~** deixar alguém em suspense, na expe(c)tativa.

suspension n suspensão f; **~ bridge** n ponte f pênsil, ponte suspensa.

suspicion n suspeita f; **to have ~s** ter suspeitas; (mistrust) desconfiança (de alguém); **under ~** sob suspeita; **to be above ~** estar acima de suspeita; **to arouse ~s** levantar suspeitas; **to look at sb/sth with ~** olhar alguém/algo com desconfiança.

suspicious adj (story) suspeitoso,-a; **2** (causing suspicion) suspeito; **to be ~ of** (person) estar desconfiado (de).

suspiciously adv desconfiadamente; **2** (person) com um ar de (suspeito); com um ar de (algo) **this looks ~ infectious** isto tem um ar de infe(c)ção.

suss (slang) (UK) vt: **to ~ sb out** descobrir (situation, another person's character etc) I haven't **~ed him out yet** ainda não descobri o que é que ele é; **2** compreender, topar (fam); I have **~ it all** já topei tudo isso.

sustain vt (nourish sb) sustentar; (MUS) (hold) sustentar (note); **2** (gen), manter; **3** (suffer) sofrer (injury, loss, defeat); **4** (withstand) aguentar; **5** (JUR) apoiar, defender (claim) aceitar, admitir (objection).

sustainable adj (ECON) (growth) viável; (ecology) duradouro,-a; **2** (energia) renovável.

sustained adj contínuo, sustido; (JUR) **~ 'objection!'** obje(c)ção aceite!.

sustenance n sustento m; alimento m.

suture n sutura f.

SW n (abbr for **south-west**) sudoeste m, SO; **2** (RADIO) (abbr for **short wave**) onda f curta.

swab n (MED) (for cleaning) mecha de algodão; (MED) (specimen) amostra f; **2** (for cleaning floor, ship's deck) esfregão m, esfregona f.

swagger n andar m afe(c)tado; ♦ vi pavonear-se; andar com arrogância; **to ~ about** vi (boast) fazer basófia, gabar-se de.

swaggering adj (person) presunçoso,-a.

Swahili n suaíli (person, language).

swallow n (bird) andorinha; **2** (gulp) trago m; ♦ vt engolir, tragar; **2** (fig) (hold back pride/reply) engolir em seco; **to ~ up** vt consumir.

swam (pt of **swim**).

swamp n pântano, brejo; ♦ vt atolar, inundar.

swamped with/by estar inundado,-a de (letters, etc); estar invadido,-a por (guests, tourists); **to ~ sb with sth** (work, worry, etc), sobrecarregar alguém com algo.

swampy adj pantanoso,-a.

swan n (ZOOL) cisne m.

swanky (-ier, -iest) adj (posh) (car, house, hotel) aparatoso,-a, luxuoso,-a; **2** (boastful) (person) fanfarrão m, fanfarrona f.

swap n troca f; permuta f; ♦ vt: **to ~ (for)** trocar (por).

swarm n (of bees) enxame m; (of crowd) multidão f; ♦ vi formigar, aglomerar-se.

swarthy adj (person) (olive, wheat-coloured skin) moreno,-a; trigueiro,-a.

swastika *n* suástica.

swat *vt* esmagar (insectos); **to ~ flies** matar moscas.

swathe *n* faixa *f*; ♦ *vt* envolver; **~ed in veils** envolvida em véus.

swatter *n* mata-moscas *m*.

sway *n*: **to come under the ~ of sb** estar/ficar sob o domínio de alguém; ♦ *vi* balançar-se; **2** vacilar *(between options)*; **3** inclinar-se (para um lado ou vários); ♦ *vt* influenciar, ter influência sobre; **to ~ hips** bambolear-se.

Swazi *n* suazi *m,f*.

Swaziland *npr* Suazilândia; **in ~** na Suazilândia.

swear *(pt* **swore**, *pp* **sworn**) *vi* jurar; **2** *(JUR)* prestar juramento; **3 to ~ at** dizer imprecações, praguejar, *(BR)* xingar; **to ~ by** *(affirm)* apostar; jurar.

swearing dizer palavrões.

swearword *n* blasfémia *f*, *(dirty)* palavrão *m*.

sweat *n* suor *m*; ♦ *vi* suar.

sweater *n* camisola *f*; *(BR)* suéter *m,f*.

sweaty *adj* suado,-a.

swede *n* rutabaga *m*; nabo-da-suécia *m*.

Swede *npr* sueco,-a.

Sweden *npr* Suécia.

Swedish *npr* *(LING)* sueco; ♦ *adj* sueco.

sweep *n* *(of floor)* varridela *f*; **2** *(also* **chimney-~)** limpa-chaminés; **3** movimento *m* circular (majestoso); **4** *(electronic examination)* varredura; **5** *(of land, tract)* extensão *f*; **6** *(of gun, telescope)*, alcance *m*; **7 clean ~** vitória estrondosa; **8** *(steal)* **the thieves made a clean ~** os ladrões levaram tudo; **it was a clean ~** *(fig)* foi uma limpeza *f* geral; ♦ *(pt, pp* **swept**) *vt/vi* varrer; **2** *(spread through)* disseminar; *(joy, sadness, news)* espalhar-se; **3** *(for mites, things)* vasculhar; **4** *(search, go everywhere)* percorrer; **5** *(push with hand)* afastar; **to ~ sb/sth aside** afastar *(person, protest)*; ♦ **to ~ away** *vt* varrer, vasculhar; **2** *(drive)* arrastar, levar *(person, object)*; **she was swept away by his charm** ela ficou apaixonada pelo encanto dele; **he swept me up in his arms** ele enlaçou-me; **she swept me off my feet** ela arrebatou-me o coração; **to ~ in/out quickly** entrar/sair rapidamente; **~ past** roçar (por alguém/algo); **to ~ up** apanhar/recolher o lixo.

sweeper *n* *(for carpet)* máquina não-elé(c)trica de varrer (passar pela carpete); **2** *(person)* varredor,-ora; **3** *(FUT)* *(BR)* líbero *m*.

sweeping *adj* *(statement)* muito em geral, generalizado,-a; **2** *(proposals, changes)* radical, **3** *(gesture)* amplo,-a; abrangente *m,f*; **4** *(victory)* arrasador,-ora, retumbante.

sweepstake *n* *(in races)* lotaria que se baseia em apostar no cavalo suposto de ganhar; o vencedor ganha tudo.

sweet *n* doce *m*, bombom *m*; **2** sobremesa; ♦ *adj* doce; **2** açucarado; **3** *(sound)* melodioso,-a; **4** *(fig)* *(loving person)* meigo,-a, afável *m,f*; **5** *(baby)* amoroso; **~pea** *n* ervilha de cheiro *f*; **~ potato** *n* batata-doce; **~ shop** *n* confeitaria; **~-talk** *n* lábia; **to have a ~ tooth** ser guloso,-a; ♦ *adv* de bom paladar; **to smell ~** cheirar bem.

sweet-and-sour *adj* agridoce.

sweetbreads *npl* *(CULIN)* testículos *mpl* de carneiro.

sweetcorn *n* milho verde, maçaroca doce.

sweeten *vt* adoçar; pôr açúcar em; *(COMM)* tornar mais aliciante; **to ~ sb** *(persuade)* levar alguém à conversa.

sweetener *n* adoçante; **2** *(COMM)* incitação *f*; *(ilegal)* suborno *m*.

sweetheart *n* namorado,-a; *(in speech)* amor *m*.

sweetie *n* *(coll)* *(UK)* meu amor; **2** *(UK)* *(child's language)* *(lolly)* rebuçado *m*; **3** *(addressing a child)* amorzinho,-a; **~ pie** *n* *(US)* amorzinho,-a.

sweetly *adv* docemente; suavemente.

sweetness *n* doçura.

swell *n* *(of sea)* vaivém *m* do mar; elevação *f* (do mar); **2** inchaço *m*;, protuberância *f*; ♦ *adj* *(coll)* excelente, elegante; **he is a ~ guy** ele é um tipo porreiro; ♦ *(pt* **swelled**, *pp* **swollen** *or* **swelled**) *vt* inchar, inflar; ♦ *vi* inchar-se, dilatar-se; **2** *(with pride)* encher-se de; *(become louder)* intensificar-se.

swelling *n* *(MED)* inchação *f*, inchaço.

swelter *n* calor húmido e abafado; ♦ *vt* morrer de calor ♦ **~ing** *adj* *(weather)* mormacento,-a

swept *(pt,pp of* **sweep**) *adj* **~ back** *(hairstyle)* penteado, cabelo m para trás.

swerve *vi* *(AUT)* desviar-se bruscamente, dar uma guinada.

swift *n* *(bird)* gavião *m* *(BR)* andorinhão *m*; ♦ *adj* rápido, veloz.

swiftness *n* rapidez *f*, ligeireza.

swig *n* trago, golada; ♦ **(-gg-)** *vt* emborcar.

swill *n* água de lavagem; ♦ *vt* (= **to ~ out/down**) lavar, limpar com água.

swim *n*: **to go for a ~** ir nadar; ♦ *(pt* **swam**, *pp* **swum**) *vi* nadar; **can you ~?** sabe nadar?; **2** *(head, room)* girar; **to ~ across** atravessar a nado.

swimmer *n* nadador,-ora.

swimming *n* natação *f*; **~ cap** *n* touca de natação; **~ costume** *n* *(woman)* fato-de-banho *m*, *(BR)* maiô *m*; *(man)* calção *m* de banho; **~ pool** *n* piscina.

swindle *n* trapaça *f*; *(tax)* fraude *f* fiscal; ♦ *vt* defraudar.

swindler *n* vigarista *m,f* escroque *m,f*.

swine *n*, *pl inv* porcos *mpl*; **2** *(coll)* *(person)* porco, porcalhão; *(pej)* *(without principles)* canalha *msg*; **~ flu** *n* gripe *f* suína.

swing *n* *(in playground)* baloiço *m*, *(BR)* balanço *m*; **2** balanceio *m*, oscilação *f* *(of pendulum, etc)*; **3** *(change)* virada *f*; **4** *(boxing)* golpe *m*; **to take a ~ at sb** dar um soco em alguém; **5** *(of hips)* bamboleio, meneio (das ancas); **6** *(change)* variação *f*; viragem *f*; **a ~ towards** uma viragem para; ♦ *(pt, pp* **swung**) *vt* fazer girar; balançar, girar, rodar; **2 to ~ the hips** bambolear as ancas; **3** *(change)* mudar; ♦ *vi* balançar-se, mover-se; **to ~ round** voltar-se, virar-se bruscamente; **to ~ open/shut** *(door)* abrir-se, fechar-se; IDIOM **to get into the ~ of things** entrar no ritmo de algo; **in full ~** *(party)* no melhor da festa; **~ bridge** ponte *f* giratória; **~ door** *n* porta giratória, porta de vaivém.

swingeing *adj* (crítica, ataque) severo,-a; **2** *(reduction, cut)* radical.

swinging *adj (party)* divertido,-a; **the ~ '60s** a geração estimulante dos anos 60.

swipe *n* pancada violenta; ♦ *vt (hit)* **to take a ~ at sb/sth** tentar bater em alguém/algo; **2** *(coll) (steal)* afanar, roubar; **3** *(plastic card)* passar o cartão (pela máquina).

swirl *n* rodopio *m;* **2** *(eddy)* redemoinho *m;* ♦ *vi* redemoinhar, girar.

swish *n (sound: of water)* sussurro *m*, murmúrio *m;* **2** *(of silks – rustle)* frufru *m;* ♦ *vt* agitar ao vento; silvar; *(water)* murmurar; *(cause a rustling sound)* fazer frufru *m*, ruge-ruge *m;* **2** *(of whip, sword)* silvar.

Swiss *n adj* suíço,-a; **the ~** os suíços,-as; **~ army-knife** *n* canivete *m* suíço.

switch *n (for light, radio etc)* interruptor *m;* **2** *(change)* mudança *f*, viragem *f;* **3** troca *f;* ♦ *vt (change)* mudar de *(topic, channels);* **to ~ off** *vt* apagar, desligar *(lights, RADIO, TV);* **to ~ on** *vt* acender; *(engine, machine)* ligar; **to ~ over (to)** *(TV, RADIO)* mudar de canal para *(another).*

switchback *n (road, rail)* que sobe e desce, ou com curvas; **2** montanha-russa.

switchblade *n (US)* canivete *m.*

switchboard *n* mesa *f* telefónica *(BR:* -ô-) PBX; **~ operator** *n* telefonista *m,f.*

Switzerland *npr* Suíça; **in ~** na Suíça.

swivel *vi* (= **to ~ round**) girar (sobre um eixo), fazer pião; **~ chair** *n* cadeira giratória.

swollen *(pp of* **swell***).*

swoon *vi (faint)* desmaiar; desfalecer.

swoop *n (by police)* rusga *f; (BR)* batida *f;* **2** *(flight)* voo picado; ♦ *vt/vi* (= **to ~ down***) (plane, bird)* descer rapidamente/em voo picado; precipitar-se.

swop = **swap**.

sword *n* espada *f;* **~-cutter** *n* alfageme *m;* **~fish** *n* espadarte *m.*

swore *(pt of* **swear***).*

sworn *(pp of* **swear***);* **~ enemies** *npl* inimigos *mpl* ferrenhos; **~ testimony** *(JUR)* testemunho *m* sob juramento.

swot *vt/vi* trabalhar, estudar arduamente; matar-se a estudar.

swum *(pp of* **swim***).*

swung *(pt, pp of* **swing***).*

sycamore *n* sicómoro, plátano.

sycamore *n (BOT) (tree)* sicómoro *m;* falso-plátano *m.*

sycophant *n* bajulador,-ora.

syllable *n (LING)* sílaba *f.*

syllabus *n* programa *m* de estudos.

symbol *n* símbolo *m.*

symbolic(al) *adj* simbólico.

symbolism *n* simbolismo.

symbolize *vt* simbolizar.

symmetrical *adj* simétrico.

symmetry *n* simetria.

sympathetic *adj* solidário; compreensivo.

sympathetically *adv* solidariamente.

sympathize *vi* compartilhar os sentimentos; **to ~ with sb** compadecer-se, condoer-se de alguém; ter pena de alguém; **2** solidarizar-se.

sympathizer *n (POL)* simpatizante *m,f.*

sympathy *n (pity)* compaixão *f;* **2** *(liking)* simpatia; **with our deepest ~** com nossos sinceros, profundos pêsames; **~ strike** *n* greve *f* de solidariedade.

symphony *n* sinfonia *f;* **~ orchestra** *n* orquestra sinfónica *(BR:* -fô-).

symposium *(pl:* **symposia***) n* simpósio *m.*

symptom *n* sintoma *m;* **2** *(sign)* indício.

symptomatic *adj* sintomático.

synagogue *n* sinagoga *f.*

sync, synch *n (abbr for* **synchronization***) (fam)* **in ~** em sintonia, sincronia; **out of ~** *(fam)* desfasado.

synchromesh *n (AUT)* engrenagem *f* sincronizada.

synchronize *vt* sincronizar; ♦ *vi:* **to ~ with** sincronizar-se com.

syncopate *vt* sincopar.

syncope *n* síncope *m.*

syndicate *n* sindicato *m; (of newspapers)* cadeia *f;* agência *f.*

syndrome *n* síndrome *f.*

synergy *(pl:* **-ies***)* sinergia *f.*

synode *n* sínodo *m.*

synonym *n* sinónimo *(BR:* -nô-) *m.*

synonymous *adj:* **~ (with)** sinónimo (de).

synopsis *(pl:* **-ses***) n* sinopse *f.*

syntactic(al) *adj (LING)* sintático,-a; **~ errors** erros *mpl* sintáticos.

syntax *n (LING)* sintaxe *f.*

synthesis *(pl:* **-ses***) n* síntese *f.*

synthesize, synthesise *vt* sintetizar.

synthesizer *n* sintetizor *m.*

synthetic *adj* sintético, artificial; *(fig) (insincere)* artificial.

syphilis *n (MED)* sífilis *f.*

syphon *(Vd:* **siphon***).*

Syria *npr* Síria; **in ~** na Síria.

Syrian *n adj* sírio,-a.

syringe *n* seringa *f;* ♦ *vt (MED)* lavar; **to have one's ears ~ed** fazer uma lavagem aos ouvidos (com seringa).

syrup *n (MED)* xarope *m;* **cough ~** xarope *m* anti-tússico,-a; **2** *(CULIN) (sugar and water)* calda *f;* **gold ~** melado *m.*

system *n* sistema *m;* método *m;* **2** *(ANAT)* organismo; *(POL) (structure)* **the ~** o sistema; **to get sth out of one's ~** *(coll)* ver-se livre de *(worry, etc);* **~s analyst** *n* analista *m,f* de sistemas.

systematic *adj* sistemático.

systematize *vt* sistematizar.

systemic *adj* sistémico,-a; generalizado,-a.

systole *n (MED)* sístole *f.*

systolic *adj* sistólico,-a.

T

T, t *n (letter)* T, t *m*; **2 to a T** *(tee) (fam)* exactly; to perfection; IDIOM **it suits me to a T** *(tee)* isso convém-me às mil maravilhas; *(dress, suit)* assenta-me como uma luva.

t *(abbr for* **ton, tonne***)* tonelada *f*.

TA *(UK, abbr for* **Territorial Army***)*.

Ta *(CHEM) (symbol for* **tantalum***)*.

ta *exc (UK, coll for* **thank you***)* obrigadinho,-a!

tab *n (for identification)* etiqueta *f*, marca *f*; **2** *(of metal)* lingueta *f*; **3** *(US)* conta *f*; **put it on my** ~ ponha na minha conta; **to pick up the** ~ pagar a conta *f*; arcar com as despesas *fpl*; **4** *(abbr for* **tabulator***)* tecla *f*, tabulação *f*; **5** *(browser)* separador *m*; **6** *(UK) (MIL)* insígnia *f* no colarinho *m*; **7** *(slang)* comprimido *m*, pastilha ou dose *f* de LSD; ◆ **tab** *(pt,pp* **-bb-***) vt* **to** ~ **sth** *(mark)* marcar algo; IDIOM **to keep** ~**s on** vigiar, estar de olho em alguém.

tabbed *adj (cloth)* marcado,-a com uma etiqueta.

tabby *(pl:* **-ies***)* (= ~ **cat**) *n* gato *m* malhado, *(BR)* tigrado; **2** *(kitten)* gata *f*; **3** *(cloth)* tecido *m* de seda, tafetá com desenho ondeado, *or* às riscas; **4** *(fam) (old gossiping woman)* velha-mexeriqueira *f*; ◆ *vt (fabric pattern)* ondear.

tabes *n (MED)* tabes; **2 dorsalis** ~ paralisia espinal progressiva *f*.

table *n* mesa *f*; **at the** ~ à mesa; **to lay/set the** ~ pôr a mesa; **to clear the** ~ levantar a mesa; **to put an offer on the** ~ *(fig)* avançar com uma oferta/ proposta; **to wait at the** ~ servir à mesa; **2** *(of statistics, prices)* tabela *f*, lista; catálogo *m*; tábua *f*; *(chart)* quadro *m*; ~ **of contents** *(of book)* índice *m*; **3** *(GEOG)* mesa *f*, planalto *m*; **4** lápide *f*; **5** *(TYPO)* chapa de metal; **6** *(ANAT) (skull)* tábua *f*; **7** *(GEOL)* camada *f* horizontal; ◆ **under the** ~ *adv* debaixo da mesa; *(fig) (bribe)* suborno *m*; ◆ *vt* colocar/pôr na mesa; *(UK) (proposal, motion)* apresentar; **2** *(US)* adiar a discussão *(bill, proposal)*; ◆ ~**cloth** *n* toalha *f* de mesa; **head of the** ~ cabeceira *f* da mesa; ~ **d'hôte** *n* refeição *f* a preço fixo; ~ **football** *n (UK)* futebol *m* de mesa; ~ **lamp** *n* candieiro *m* de mesa; *(BR)* luminária *f*; ~**-leaf** *n* aba *f* de mesa; ~ **linen** *n* roupa *f* da mesa; conjunto *m* de toalha e guardanapos; ~ **manners** *n* comportamento *m* à mesa; ~ **mat** *n* suporte *m* de pratos quentes; **T~ Mountain** *npr (GEOG)* Montanha da Mesa; ~**spoonful** *n (measurement)* colherada *f*, colher de mesa cheia; ~ **talk** *n* conversa à mesa; ~ **tennis** *n* ténis *m* de mesa, ping-pong; **tables** *npl (six-times* ~*)* tabuada *f*; **the T~s of the Law** *(bible)* as Tábuas da Lei; IDIOM **to**

turn the ~ **s (on sb)** inverter as posições; virar o feitiço contra o feiticeiro; *(BR)* virar a mesa/ o jogo.

tablet *n (PHARM)* comprimido *m*; pastilha *f*; **2** *(of chocolate)* tablete *f*; **3** *(for writing)* bloco *m* de folhas; **4** placa *f* comemorativa.

tabloid *n (newspaper)* tablóide *m*; ~ **press** imprensa sensacionalista; ◆ *adj (pej) (JOURN)* sensacionalista *m,f*.

taboo, tabu *n* tabu *m*.

tabulate *vt* dispor em colunas/em tabelas.

tabulator *n* tecla *f* de parágrafo; tabulador *m*.

tachometer *n* taquímetro *m*; velocímetro *m*.

tacit *adj* tácito,-a, implícito,-a; ~ **consent** consentimento *m* tácito.

tacitly tacitamente.

taciturn *adj* taciturno,-a, reservado,-a, de poucas palavras *fpl*.

tack *n (for nailing)* tacha *f*; **2** *(stitch)* alinhavo *m*; **3** *(NAUT)* rumo *m*; *(NAUT)* navegação *f* em ziguezague; **to make a** ~ *(NAUT)* correr uma bordada *f*; **on the larboard/starboard** ~ amurado a bombordo/estibordo; **4** *(horse: gear)* arreios *npl*; **5** *(approach)* táctica *f*; **to change one's** ~**s** mudar de tá(c)tica; **to be on the wrong** ~ estar sob uma impressão falsa; seguir o caminho errado; **to try another** ~ procurar outra solução *f*; **6** *(fam) (shoddy)* algo sem gosto; *(coll)* porcaria *f*; ◆ *vt (nail)* prender com tacha *f*; **2** *(UK) (stitch)* alinhavar; **3** afixar; **4 to** ~ **on/onto** adicionar à pressa; anexar; ~ **this letter onto the other** anexe esta carta à outra; ◆ *vi (sailor)* virar de bordo; **2** *(course of action)* mudar de orientação *f*; **to** ~ **sth on** adicionar (a algo); IDIOM **to come/get down to brass** ~**s** tratar do que importa.

tackle *n* equipamento *m*; (= **fishing** ~) apetrechos *mpl* de pesca *f*; **2** *(SPORT) (rugby)* placagem *f*, *(soccer)* entrada *f*; **3** *(NAUT, TECH) (on ship)* talha *f*; **4** *(for lifting)* guincho *m*; **5** *(UK, slang) (drugs)* heroína *f*; **6** *(UK, slang)* genitais *mpl* masculinos; ◆ *vt (problem)* enfrentar; **2** atracar-se com; **3 to** ~ **sb about sth** confrontar alguém com determinado problema; **4** *(animal)* aparelhar; ◆ *(soccer, hockey)* obstruir; *(rugby)* placar.

tacky (-ier, -iest) *adj (sticky)* pegajoso,-a; **2** *(fresh paint)* ainda não seca; **3** *(fam)* com mau gosto; piroso,-a; *(BR)* cafona *m,f*.

tact *n* ta(c)to *m*, diplomacia *f*; **to be wanting in** ~ não ter ta(c)to; **if you use** ~, **maybe he won't say 'no'** se usares de diplomacia, pode ser que ele aceite.

tactful *adj* com ta(c)to.

tactfully *adv* discretamente, com ta(c)to.

tactic *n* tá(c)tica *f*.

tactical *adj* tá(c)tico,-a, estratégico,-a; ~ **bombing** bombardeamento *m* aéreo tá(c)tico; ~ **plan** estratégia *f*; **2** *(UK) (POL)* ~ **voting** voto *m* útil.

tactics *npl* tá(c)tica *fsg*.

tactile *adj* tá(c)til *m,f*; palpável *m,f*; **2** *(fabric, etc.)* com um toque agradável; **3** tangível; ~ **display** ecrã tá(c)til.

tactless *adj* sem diplomacia *f*; **2** sem discernimento *m*.

tactlessly *adv* sem delicadeza.

tad *n (US)* um pequeno rapaz; **2** *(US) (a little)* um pouco; **a ~ boring** um bocado chato.

tadpole *n (ZOOL)* girino *m*.

Tadznik *npr (Vd:* **Tajik**).

taffeta *n* tafetá *m*.

tag *n (label) (on luggage)* etiqueta *f*; *(goods)* rótulo *m*; *(on cat, dog)* chapa *f*; *(loop for hanging)* presilha *f*; **2** *(loose end)* rabo *m*; **3** epíteto; **4** *(children's game = tig)* pega-pega *f*; **5** *(COMP)* marca *f*; **6** *(LING) (quotation)* citação *f*; **7 ~ question** *(gram)* **isn't it?** não é? **8** *(shoelace)* pontinha de metal *or* plástico nos atacadores/cordões; **9** grafite com assinatura ou símbolo do artista; **10** *(JUR)* **electronic ~** marcador *m* ele(c)trónico **11 ~ line** ponto culminante de uma anedota *f*; **12** slogan, refrão *m*; **13** *(game)* tocar em; ♦ **(-gg-)** *vt* etiquetar; **to ~ a trunk** pôr uma etiqueta numa mala *f*; **2** *(pej) (gen)* rotular; **3** colocar o preço *m* em; **4** apelidar; **5** rimar; **to ~ lines** rimar versos; **6 to ~ sth on/to** acrescentar uma reflexão no final de uma frase; ♦ *vi* **to ~ along** andar; *(behind sb)* ir atrás de; seguir alguém; **~ sth on** acrescentar *(word, clause)*; **~ sth onto sth** juntar algo a algo; **to ~ on to** ir atrás de.

Tagus *npr (river)* Tejo *m*.

Tahiti *npr* Taiti; **in ~** no Taiti.

Tahitian *n adj* taitiano,-a.

tail *n (ZOOL)* cauda *f*, rabo *m*, rabicho *m*; *(coll) (rear)* traseiro *m*; **2 the ~ of the eye** o canto do olho *m*; **3** *(of plane, comet)* cauda *f*; **4** *(coat)* aba; **~s** *(shirt)* fralda; **5** *(of car)* parte *f* traseira; **the ~ of a procession** a retaguarda de um cortejo *m*; **6** *(TYPO)* fundo *m* da página; **~ margin** margem *f* inferior; *(trail)* rasto *m*; **to be on sb's ~** andar no encalço *m* de alguém; **to put a ~ on sb** mandar uma pessoa seguir alguém; **7 ~-end** *n* cauda, parte *f* final; **tails (~coat)** *n* fraque *m*; **8** *(of coin)* coroa; **heads or ~** cara ou coroa; ♦ *vt* seguir de perto; **2** amarrar pela extremidade *f*; ♦ *vi* **to ~ away/off** *(numbers, interest, etc.)* reduzir, diminuir; *(sound)* diminuir até se deixar de ouvir; **2 to ~ back** *(UK) (trafic)* estender-se até; IDIOM **I can't make head nor/or ~ of** não perceber patavina de; **to put one's ~ between one's legs** meter o rabinho *m* entre as pernas *fpl*; **to twist sb's ~** arreliar alguém; **with one's ~ up** confiante, contente.

tailback *n (UK)* fila *f* de trânsito.

tailed *adj (generally in compounds)* com cauda *f*; **2** de cauda; **short/long-~** de cauda curta, comprida; **a furry-~ animal** um animal *m* de cauda peluda *f*.

tailgate, tailboard *n* porta da mala *f* do carro *m*; **2** comporta *f* de descarga; ♦ *vt (cars)* ir mesmo colado (a outro).

tailor *n* alfaiate *m*; *(craft)* ofício *m* de alfaiate; **~'s dummy** manequim *m* de alfaiate; **~-made** *adj* feito,-a por/sob medida; **~-made course** curso especialmente feito para certo fim ou estudante.

tailored *adj* feito,-a por alfaiate; de corte *m* justo; ♦ *vt (suits)* talhar, fazer (à medida); **2** ajustar; adaptar algo para fim específico; ♦ *vi* trabalhar como alfaiate; IDIOM **the ~ makes the man** o hábito *m* faz o monge *m*.

tailwind *n* vento de popa/de cauda.

taint *n* nódoa *f*, mácula *f*; **2** corrupção *f*, defeito *m*; ♦ *vt* contaminar, viciar, manchar.

tainted *adj* estragado,-a, poluído,-a; **2** *(fig)* manchado,-a.

taintless *adj* imaculado,-a, inocente *m,f*.

Taiwan *npr* Taiwan.

Taiwanese *adj* taiwanês,-esa.

Tajik *n adj* tajique.

Tajikistan *npr* Tajiquistão; **in ~** no Tajiquistão.

take¹ *n (CIN) (shooting of a scene)* tomada *f*; **2** *(MUS) n* gravação *f* feita de uma só vez; **3** *(coll)* tentativa *f*; **~away** *(UK) n* restaurante *m* de comida para fora; **2** *(meal)* refeição *f* para levar.

take² *(pt* **took**, *pp* **taken)** *vt/vi* tomar, beber; **what will you ~?** que deseja beber?; **~ two pills per day** tome dois comprimidos por dia; **2** pegar (em), deitar a mão a; *(bus, train)* apanhar, *(BR)* pegar; **3** *(prize)* ganhar; **4** *(effort, courage)* requerer, exigir; **5** *(tolerate)* aguentar; **6** *(to carry; time)* levar; **I'll ~ your bag** eu levo a sua mala; **the plane ~s two hours from London to Lisbon** o avião leva duas horas de Londres a Lisboa; **7** *(lead to)* levar a, conduzir; **8** *(photo, course)* tirar, *(exam)* prestar, fazer; **9** *(JUR)* **~ an oath** prestar juramento; **10** presumir, supor; **I ~ it that ...** eu suponho que ...; **11** *(to please, have success)* ter êxito, agradar; **the book didn't ~** o livro não agradou; **12** *(BOT)* ganhar raízes; **13 to ~ sb's life** matar; **to ~ one's life** suicidar-se; ♦ **to ~ aback** surpreender *(person)*; **to ~ advantage of** tirar proveito *m*; **2** abusar; **to ~ after** parecer-se com; **to ~ apart** desmontar; **to ~ aside** *(talk in private)* puxar à parte; **to ~ around (round)** mostrar à volta *(place)*; ♦ **to ~ away** tirar; levar; **2** *(coll) (pinch)* tirar, furtar; **3** *(deduct)* subtrair, tirar; ♦ **to ~ back** devolver *(goods)*; **2** *(one's words)* retra(c)tar-se; *(what was said)* dar o dito por não dito; ♦ **to ~ a break** ter um intervalo; **~ care** ter cuidado *m*; **to ~ charge of** assumir o controlo *m* de; ♦ **to ~ down** *(building)* demolir; **2** *(letter, note)* tomar por escrito, escrever; **3** *(lower)* baixar; ♦ **to ~ sb/sth for** *(fam)* supor alguém/algo ser; **who do you ~ me for?** quem pensa você que eu sou?; ♦ **to ~ in** *(understand)* compreender; **2** *(include, cover)* abranger; **the view took in the vineyards** a vista abrangia os vinhedos; **3** *(provide accomodation)* acolher; **to ~ sb in** *(deceive)* enganar; **to ~ sb in one's arms** abraçar alguém; ♦ **to ~ off** *vi (AER)* descolar, levantar voo *(BR)* decolar; **2** *(go away suddenly)* ir-se embora; **3** *(undress)* despir (alguém); despir-se *(oneself)*; **4** *(remove)* tirar, remover *(stain, paint)*; **5** *(UK) (fam)* imitar; ♦ **to ~ on** *(work)* empreender, aceitar; **2** *(responsibility)* assumir; **3** *(employ)* empregar *(person)*; **4** desafiar *(opponent)*; **to ~ it on sb** ter pena de; **to ~ on sb's advice** seguir o conselho *m* de alguém;

♦ **to ~ out** levar para fora; **2** tirar de *(pocket, drawer)*; **3** extrair *(tooth, etc)*; **4** levantar *(from bank)*; **5** *(delete)* suprimir, tirar; **6 ~ it out on sb** *(one's mood, anger)* descarregar em; **7 to ~ it/a lot out of sb** esgotar alguém; ♦ **to ~ over** tomar posse de, assumir; **to ~ over from sb** suceder a alguém; ♦ **to ~ to sb** *(like)* simpatizar com alguém; **2** *(activity)* dedicar-se a, gostar de; **to ~ to heart** *(fig) (be offended)* levar a peito; ♦ **to ~ up sth** levantar algo; **2** *(shorten)* encurtar *(dress, etc)*; **3** *(time, space)* ocupar; **4** *(absorb)* absorver *(líquido)*; **5** *(hobby, etc.)* dedicar-se a; **6** *(activity)* começar a fazer; IDIOM **it ~ some doing** isso dá muito trabalho; **2** *(coll) (have a cheek)* é presiso ter uma lata; **to be on the ~** receber subornos; **to have what it ~s** ter as necessidades *fpl* necessárias; **it ~s the biscuit/cake!** *exc* é o cúmulo!; **it ~s the mickey/the piss out of sb** gozar com alguém; **~ it or leave it!** é pegar ou largar!

take-home pay *n* ordenado *m* líquido.

taken *pp adj* tomado,-a, levado,-a *(seat, place)*; **to be ~ sick** adoecer; **2 ~ with** *(impressed)* impressionado com.

take-off *n (plane)* descolagem, *(BR)* decolagem *f*.

takeover *n (FIN)* tomada *f* de controlo; **2** *(POL)* tomada *f* de posse; **3** *(COMM)* aquisição *f*; **~ bid** *n (FIN)* oferta pública de compra *f*.

taker *n* corretor,-ora de apostas; interessado,-a.

taking *n* toma *f*; a(c)to de tomar, pegar levar; **2** *(MIL)* captura *f*; **~s** *fpl (UK) (COMM)* receitas *fpl*; renda *f*; ♦ *adj (charming)* encantador,-ora, fascinante *m,f; (fam) (infectious)* contagioso,-a.

talc (= **~um powder**) *n* talco *m*; ♦ (**-ck-** *or* **talced**) *vt* cobrir com talco; colocar talco em; tratar com talco.

tale *n* conto *m*; narrativa *f*; **2** *(fig) (gossip)* mexerico *m*; **fairy ~** conto *m* de fadas; **folk ~** conto popular; IDIOM **a ~ of woe** um rosário *m* de desgraças; *(pej)* **to tell ~s (to sb)** dizer mentiras (a alguém); dizer fofoca (a alguém).

talent *n* talento *m*; **2** génio *m (BR: gê-)*; **~ed** *adj* talentoso,-a; de talento; **~ scout** caça-talentos *m, fpl*; **3** *(UK, coll)* **local ~** pessoas atraentes *m,fpl*.

talk *n* conversa *f*, fala *f; (fam)* fofoca *f; (BR: fam)* bate-papo *m;* conversação *f;* **2** *(lecture)* palestra *f;* **3** *(gossip)* falatório *m;* **people will ~** vai haver falatório; **small ~** conversas *fpl* triviais; ♦ *vi* falar; *(chatter)* tagarelar; dizer mal de alguém; **to ~ about** falar sobre; **get ~ed about** dar que falar; **to ~ around** *(in circles)* falar com rodeios; **to ~ down at sb** falar com condescendência; **to ~ sb into doing sth** persuadir alguém a fazer algo; **to ~ sb out of doing sth** dissuadir alguém de fazer algo; **to ~ shop** falar de assuntos *mpl* profissionais, da sua profissão *f;* **to ~ on** continuar a falar; **to ~ over** *vt (discuss)* discutir; IDIOM *(coll)* **to ~ nineteen to the dozen/to ~ one's head off** falar pelos cotovelos *mpl;* **to ~ to oneself** falar com os seus botões *mpl;* **to ~ through one's hat/~ nonsense** dizer disparates *mpl;* **to ~ big** falar com ares *mpl* de fanfarrão, *(BR)* de papo.

talkative *adj* falador,-ora, tagarela *m,f.*

talkativeness *n* verbosidade *f;* tagarelice *f.*

talking *n* conversa *f;* ♦ *(pres p.)* falando, a falar; *(fam)* **whom do you think you are ~ to?** com quem julga que está a falar?; **2** *(coll)* **now you're ~** assim já nos começamos a entender; **'no ~'** 'silêncio'; **enough ~** basta de conversas; **~-to** *n (reprimand)* reprimenda *f;* raspanete *m, (BR) (coll)* bronca *f.*

talks *npr* negociações *fpl.*

tall *adj* alto,-a; **he is 1.90m** ele tem 1.90m de altura *f;* **to grow ~** crescer; **~ story** *n* conto *m* incrível, uma patranha *f*, uma peta *f;* **~ hat** *n* cartola *f;* ♦ *adv* **talk ~** falar cheio de bazófia *f;* IDIOM **to walk ~** caminhar de cabeça *f* erguida.

tallboy *n (UK) (furniture)* cómoda *f* alta; **~ order** tarefa *f* impossível.

tallness *n (size)* tamanho *m.*

tallow *n* sebo *m.*

tally (*pl:* **tallies**) *n* conta *f;* registo *m (BR)* registro *m;* **2** rótulo *m;* **3** duplicado *m;* **4 ~ clerk** verificador *m* de mercadorias; **5 ~ sheet** folha *f* de registo; **~ing** *n* contagem *f;* **6 ~-ho** *exc* grito dos caçadores para encorajar os cães (numa caça); ♦ *(pp, pt* **tallied**) *vi* concordar (**with** com); igualar a; **her opinion tallies with mine** a opinião dela concorda com a minha; **2** *(correspond)* fechar; **3** *(SPORT)* marcar *(one point).*

talon *n* garra *f (from a bird of prey).*

tambourine *n (MUS)* pandeireta *f.*

tame *adj (animal)* manso,-a domesticado,-a; **2** *(pej)* parado,-a; **3** *(story, style)* sem graça, insípido,-a; **~r** domador,-a; ♦ *vt* domar *(wild animal);* **2** *(person)* subjugar.

Tamil *npr (language)* tamil *m.*

tam-o'shanter *n* bóina *f* escocesa.

tamper *vi* **to ~ with** intrometer-se em, *(document, etc.)* falsificar; **2** subornar; **to ~ with a lock** forçar uma fechadura *f.*

tampon *n* tampão *m*, absorvente *m* interno; ♦ *vt* aplicar tampão em.

tan *n (colour)* castanho claro; **2** bronzeado *m;* ♦ (**-nn-**) *vt/vi* bronzear(-se); ficar moreno,-a; **2** *(animal hide)* curtir.

tandem *n* tandem *m;* bicicleta *f* para duas pessoas; **2** espécie *f* de cabriolé descoberto *m;* **3 in ~ with** um atrás do outro.

tang *n* sabor *m* acidulado **2** *(smell)* cheiro *f* forte; **3** *(tool)* espigão *m;* IDIOM **there was a ~ of irony in her words** havia um tom *m* de ironia nas palavras *fpl* dela.

tangent *n (MUS)* tangente *f;* **2 ~ of an angle** *(GEOM)* tangente *f* de um ângulo *m;* **on/at a ~** *(of thought, speech)* divergente; IDIOM **to go off at a ~** *(in speech)* desviar-se do assunto *m;* escapar pela tangente.

tangerine *n (BOT)* tangerina *f; (colour)* cor *f* amarela-avermelhada.

tangibility, tangibleness *n* palpabilidade *f.*

tangible *adj* tangível *m,f*, palpável *m,f;* **2** real *m,f;* nítido,-a; **4** *(JUR)* **~ assets** valores *mpl* materiais; **the ~ world** *(phylosophy)* o mundo *m* sensível.

tangibly *adv* nitidamente.

tangle *n* *(hair, threads)* emaranhado *m*; **2** *(conflict)* escaramuça *f*; **3** *(BOT)* sargaço *m*; **to get in(to) a ~** emaranhar(-se); **to be in a ~** estar desorientado,-a; **~foot** *n* *(US, slang)* uísque *m* ordinário; ♦ *vt* emaranhar; ♦ *vi* enredar-se; atrapalhar-se; **to ~ with** *(conflict)* meter-se (com); **to ~ up** *vi* meter-se numa embrulhada *f (mess)*; IDIOM **traffic ~** engarrafamento *m*.

tangled *adj* emaranhado,-a, complicado,-a.

tango *n* *(MUS)* tango *m*; **2** *(drink)* misto *m* de cerveja *f* com groselha *f*; ♦ *pt* **tangoed** *vi* dançar o tango.

tank *n* *(AUTO)* depósito *m* de gasolina; *(water)*, cisterna *f*; **2** *(for fish)* aquário *m*; **3** *(MIL)* carro blindado *m* armado; **4** *(dive)* garrafa *f*; **5** (= **~ top**) *n* *(clothing)* camisola *f* caveada; **6** *(coll)* choça *(fam)* *f*; *(US: slang)* *(prison)* prisão *f*; **developing ~** *(PHOT)* tanque *m* de revelação; **think ~** *n* equipa,-e *f* de especialista; **~ town** *(US: fig)* *(small town)* parvónia *f* *(pej)*; ♦ *vt* colocar num reservatório *m*; **2** *(slang)* derrotar de forma esmagadora.

tankard *n* caneca *f* para cerveja; pichel *m*.

tanker *n* *(ship)* navio-cisterna *m*; **oil~** petroleiro *m*; **2** (= **~ car/wagon**) *n* *(RAIL)* vagão-cisterna *m*; **3** *(aircraft)* avião *m* de carga.

tanned *adj* bronzeado,-a; queimado,-a pelo sol; *(weather-beaten)* crestado,-a.

tantalise *(UK)* **tantalize** *(US)* *(tease)* *vt* atormentar; provocar.

tantalising *adj* torturante; **2** *(sight, possibility)* tentador,-ora; *(smile)* sedutor.

tantamount *adj*: **to ~ to** equivalente a; **this would be ~ to saying that …** isso seria o mesmo que dizer que …

tantivy *n* grito de corrida a galope *(durante a caça)*; ♦ *adv* *(at full speed)* rapidamente.

tantrum *n* *(childish outburst)* birra *f*; *(anger)* acesso *m* de fúria; **to have/throw a ~** *(of rage)* ter um ataque de fúria *f*; **to get into a ~** enfurecer-se.

Tanzanean *n adj* tanzaniano,-a.

Tanzania *npr* Tanzânia; **in ~** na Tanzânia.

Taois *n npr* taoismo *m*.

tap *n* *(UK)* *(on sink)* torneira *f*; **~ water** água *f* da torneira; **2** *(gentle blow)* palmadinha *f (on the back, etc)*; **3** *(knock)* **I heard a ~ at the door** ouvi bater à porta; **4** *(tel: bugging)* escuta *f*; **5** *(draught BR)* cerveja *f* de barril; **on ~** *(coll)* *(available)* disponível para uso imediato; ♦ *(-pp-)* *vt* *(knock)* bater à porta (**on** em, **against** contra); **2 ~ fingers on** tamborilar em; **3 ~ one's feet** *(to the music)* bater o pé no chão (ao ritmo); *(telephone)* colocar, pôr escutas em; **4** *(resources)* utilizar, explorar; **5** colocar escutas; **to ~ a tree** sangrar; extrair, recolher algo por incisão; ♦ **to ~ sb for money** *(coll)* *(BR, beg)* pedir dinheiro a alguém; **60 ~ sth in** pregar levemente *(nail)*; **6** *(COMP)* introduzir; digitar; **~-dancing/dance** *n* sapateado *m*; **~ed out** *adj* *(broke)* falido,-a, *(exhausted)* exausto,-a.

tape *n* fita; **2** (= **magnetic ~**) fita *f* magnética; **3** (= **sticky ~**) fita adesiva; **~ deck** leitor *m* de cassetes; **~ measure** *n* fita métrica, trena *f*; **~**

recorder gravador *m*; **red ~** *(coll)* *(bureaucracies)* burocracias *fpl*; **~ session** sessão *f* de gravação; *(coll)* **to have sb ~d** conhecer bem as intenções *fpl* de alguém; ♦ *vt* *(speech, music, etc.)* gravar *(em fita)*; **2** prender com fita; **3** *(stick)* colar *m* com fita-cola; **4** *(ELECT)* *(insulate)* isolar com fita; ♦ **to ~ over** *vi* gravar por cima de; **to ~ up** *vt* *(box, parcel)* fechar com fita-cola *f*; *(US)* *(MED)* *(wound)* ligar; IDIOM *(SPORT)* **to break the ~** *(win)* chegar em primeiro *m* lugar.

taper *n* *(thin candle)* círio *m*; *(narrowing)* estreitamento *m*; ♦ *adj* esguio,-a; **~ fingers** *adj* dedos *mpl* esguios; **2** *(MEC)* cónico,-a *(BR: -cô-)*; ♦ *vt* afunilar; ♦ *vi* afilar-se, estreitar-se; **to ~ off** *(gradually lessen)* diminuir gradualmente.

tapered *adj* (= **tapering** *adj*) aguçado,-a; **2** *(trousers)* afunilado,-a; **~ wing** asa *f* afunilada.

tapestry *(pl: -ies)* *n* tapeçaria *f*; **2** *(fig)* *(complexity, diversity)* mosaico *m*; **~ weaving** tecelagem *f* de tapeçarias.

tapeworm *n* *(parasite)* ténia *(BR: -tê-)* *f*, bicha-solitária *f*.

tapioca *n* *(CULIN)* tapioca *f*.

tapir *n* *(ZOOL)* auta *f*, tapir *m*.

tap out *vi* fazer sair com pequenas *fpl* pancadas; **2** *(COMP)* *(to type)* escrever; **3** *(sound)* produzir, batendo com algo (pés, dedos, etc.).

taproom *n* *(UK)* *(hotel, pub)* bar *m*.

tar *n* alcatrão *m*, piche *m*; **low ~** baixo teor de alcatrão *m*; ♦ *(-rr-)* *vt* alcatroar.

tarantula *n* *(ZOOL)* tarântula *f*.

tardiness *n* *(slowness)* lentidão *f*; **2** atraso *m*; **3** *(lateness)* demora *f*; **I regret the ~ in my reply** lamento o atraso na minha resposta.

tardy *adj* vagaroso,-a; *(late)* tardio,-a.

tare *n* *(BOT)* ervilhaca; **~ seeds** *(bird food)* sementes de ervilhaca.

target *n* *(ger)* alvo *m*, meta *f*; mira *f*; **2** *(goal)* obje(c)tivo *m*; **3** *(criticism)* ser obje(c)to de; **an easy ~** uma presa *f* fácil; **dead on ~!** em cheio!; *(project)* **to be on ~** chegar à meta; ♦ *vt* apontar; **2** *(audience, market)* visar; **to reach one's ~** atingir o seu fim; *(CIN, COMM, TV)* ter como público-alvo *m*; **to be way-off the ~** estar aquém dos obje(c)tivos; ser insuficiente.

targeting *n* *(MIL)* obje(c)tivo-alvo a atingir; **2** escolha de público-alvo *m*.

target practice *n* exercícios *m* de tiro ao alvo.

tariff *n* tarifa *f*; **2** tarifário *m*; **3** *(price list)* tabela *f* de preços; tarifário *m*; **~ing** tarifação; **~ wall** *(customs)* barreira *f* alfandegária; **~ war** guerra *f* aduaneira; ♦ *vt* aplicar tarifa a.

tarmac *n* *(on road)* macadame *m* betuminoso; **2** *(AER)* pista *f* de aterragem *(BR: aterrissagem)*.

tarn *n* pequeno lago *m* nas mountanhos.

tarnish *n* embaciamento *m*; **2** *(on mineral/metal)* mancha *f*, nódoa *f*; ♦ *vt* *(of metal)* perder o brilho *f*, embaciar; **2** *(reputation)* denegrir; ♦ *vi* *(dim)* embaciar-se.

tarpaulin *n* *(used to cover)* lona *f* oleada, alcatroada.

tarradidle *n* *(coll)* mentira *f*, *(fig)* peta *f*, patranha *(fam)*.

tarragon n *(BOT)* estragão m.

tarry[1] vi *(pp. -ying, pt -ied) (linger)* deter-se; demorar-se; **2** esperar; tardar.

tarry[2] adj alcatroado,-a.

tarrying n *(stay)* permanência f, estadia f.

tart n *(CULIN)* torta f; **2** *(slang, pej)* marafona f; **2** pega f *(cal)*; ♦ adj *(flavour)* ácido,-a; azedo,-a; **2** *(reply)* ríspido,-a; torto,-a; ♦ ~ **(sth) up** vt *(UK) (building)* melhorar; dar uma pintura, etc; **to ~ oneself up** *(coll)* arranjar-se, pintar-se.

tartademalion n maltrapilho,-a; ♦ adj andrajoso,-a.

tartan n tecido m escocês axadrezado, tartã m; ♦ adj *(pattern)* axadrezado,-a; *(coll)* escocês,-esa.

tartar n *(on teeth)* tártaro m; **2** T~ habitante m,f da Tartária; ~**(e) sauce** n molho m tártaro.

tartish adj um tanto ácido,-a.

tartly adv causticamente.

tartuf(f)e n tartufo m; **2** *(two-faced)* hipócrita m,f; *(false devotee)* falso devoto,-a, beata m,f.

task n tarefa f; dever m; **to ~ sb to ~** repreender alguém **(about, for** por); ~ **force** n força f operacional; **2** *(MIL)* destacamento m especial; ♦ vt **to ~ sb with sth** incumbir alguém de; **2** *(severe strain)* sobrecarregar alguém, pôr à prova; IDIOM **that is one endless ~** isso é um trabalho que nunca mais acaba.

taskmaster n *(person)* capataz; **2** *(pej)* tirano,-a; **a hard ~** um patrão m duro; uma patroa f dura.

Tasmania npr Tasmânia f; ~**ian** adj tasmaniano,-a.

tassle n *(tuft)* borla f; **2** *(BOT) (of a maize)* pendão m; ~**led** adj com borlas fpl; ♦ **(-ll-** UK; **-l-** US) vt *(adorn)* enfeitar com borlas; ♦ vi criar pendão.

taste n sabor m, gosto m; **2** *(sip)* prova f; golinho m; **3** *(fig)* amostra f; **4** *(aesthetics)* gosto; **in good/bad ~** de bom/mau gosto; **to have a ~ for** *(inclination)* sentir predileção por; **5** *(ANAT)* ~ **buds** papilas fpl gustativas; ♦ vt *(small amount)* provar, experimentar; ♦ vi **to ~ of/like** ter gosto de, saber a; IDIOM **everyone to his ~** gostos não se discutem.

tasteful adj de bom gosto, distinto,-a.

tastefully adv com bom gosto.

tasteless adj *(food)* insípido,-a, que não sabe a nada; ~ **food** comida f sem graça; **2** *(remark)* de mau gosto.

taster provador,-ora; **2** *(sample of food)* amostra f; **3** *(coll)* cheirinho m de.

tasting n prova f; **wine ~** prova, degustação de vinhos

tasty adj *(food)* saboroso,-a, delicioso,-a; **2** *(slang) (alcoholic drinks)* copos mpl *(col)*; **3** *(UK, coll) (atractive woman)* jeitosa f.

tat n *(shoddy)* roupas coçadas; **2** algo de mau gosto; IDIOM **to give tit for ~** pagar na mesma moeda.

ta-ta n *(child's talk)* good-bye; tchau!; **to go for a ~/to go ~s** ir dar um passeio m.

tattered adj esfarrapado,-a; **2** arruinado,-a.

tatters npl *(clothes)* **in ~** (= **tattered**) esfarrapado,-a; *(fig) (reputation, confidence)* em frangalhos, em ruína.

tattersall n *(fabric)* tecido com padrão axadrezado.

tattle *(also:* **tittle-tattle**) n tagarelice f; **2** *(gossip)* coscuvilhice f, má-língua f, fofoca ♦ vt palrar; coscuvilhar.

tattler n palrador,-ora; **2** *(bird)* pega f.

tattletale adj *(US, coll)* mexeriqueiro,-a.

tattoo n *(design)* tatuagem f; ♦ vt *(with needle)* tatuar.

tattooer, tattooist n tatuador,-ora.

tatty adj *(coll)* surrado,-a; **2** enxovalhado,-a; **3** em mau estado.

taught *(pt, pp of* teach*)*: **a ~ ship** um navio m que obedece bem ao leme m.

taunt n *(remark)* zombaria f, escárnio m; **2** *(coll)* boca *(call)*; ♦ vt *(to provoke sb)* zombar de, **2** *(annoy)* arreliar.

taunter n *(mocker)* zombeteiro,-a; arreliador,-a.

taunting n insultos; ♦ adj trocista m,f; *(remark)* insultuoso,-a.

tauromachy n tauromaquia f.

Taurus n *(ASTRON)* Touro m.

taut adj *(wire, rope)* esticado,-a, retesado,-a, teso,-a; **2** *(person, muscle)* tenso,-a; **3** *(of writing, music)* conciso,-a, sucinto,-a; **em boas** fpl **condições**; *(NAUT)* ~ **and trim** em bom m estado.

tauten vt retesar, esticar.

tautness n tensão f, retesamento m.

tautology n *(LING)* tautologia f.

tavern n *(pub)* taberna f; *(BR)* botequim m.

tawdry n arrebiques de mau gosto, adornos mpl baratos; ♦ adj de mau gosto m, espalhafatoso,-a; **2** *(topic, story)* sórdido,-a; IDIOM **a ~ existence** uma miséria f dourada.

tawny adj moreno,-a, trigueiro,-a; **2** *(wine)* aloirado,-a.

tax n *(on income, goods, etc.)* imposto m; encargo m fiscal, *(TV)* taxa; **to pay ~** ser tributável; ~ **is deducted at source** os impostos são retidos na fonte; **2** *(demand on sth/sb)* tensão f; ~ **allowance** n benefício fiscal; ~ **avoidance** n redução legal no montante sujeito a impostos; ~ **bracket** n escalão m fiscal; ~ **break/cut** n redução f tributária; ~ **collector** n cobrador,-ora de impostos; **council ~** n *(UK)* contribuição f autárquica; ~**-deductible** adj dedutível m,f nos impostos; ~ **disc** n *(AUT) (UK)* selo m *(de circulação automóvel)*; ~ **evasion** n fraude f fiscal; ~**-exempt/free** adj isento,-a de imposto(s); ~**haven** n paraíso m fiscal ~ **payer** n contribuinte m,f; ~ **relief** *(UK)* benefícios mpl fiscais; ~ **return** *(form)* impresso m de impostos; *(declaration)* declaração f de IRS = rendimentos mpl *(BR:* de renda*)*; ♦ vt tributar, lançar imposto sobre *(earnings, profits)*; **2** *(fig) (strain)* sobrecarregar; *(patience)* esgotar, pôr algo à prova.

taxable adj tributável m,f, sujeito,-a a imposto; **to be ~/liable for** ser tributável.

taxation n tributação f.

taxi *(pl:* **taxis**) n táxi m; **to flag down/hail a ~** chamar um táxi; ~**cab** *(US)* táxi; ~ **driver** motorista m,f de táxi; **2** taxista m,f; ~**meter** n taxímetro m; ~ **rank** *(UK)* praça f de táxis; ~ **stand** *(US)* praça de táxis; ♦ vt *(coll)* levar de táxi; ♦ vi andar de táxi; **2** *(AER) (before and after the flight)* deslizar ao longo da pista f.

taxidermist n taxidermista m,f; *(BR)* empalhador,-ora.

taxing adj *(task, job)* árduo,-a, exigente m,f.

TB *(abbr for* **tuberculosis**).

tbsp *n (CULIN) (abbr for* **tablespoon**).

tea *n* chá *m* (quente ou gelado); **to take ~** *(after-noon tea)* tomar chá, lanchar; **2** *(UK) (snack, meal)* lanche ajantarado *m*, merenda *f*; **3** *(leaves)* (infusão de) folhas secas *fpl* de chá; **a nice cup of ~** um chazinho; **~bag** *n* saquinho *m*, saqueta de chá; **~ break** *n (UK)* pausa *f* para o chá; **~ caddy** *n* lata *f* do chá; **~cake** *n* biscoito *m*; **2** *(UK)* bolinho *m* com frutos secos *mpl f*; **~ chest** *n* caixote *m* de madeira rude para exportação de chá e depois usada para transportar objectos numa mudança; **~ plantation** plantação *f* de chá; **~ set** *n* serviço *m* de chá; **~ room** *n* salão *m* de chá. **~ cosy/cozy** *n* abafador *m* para chá; **~ cup** *n* chávena *f; (BR, EP regional and CULIN)* xícara *f*; **~ leaf** *n (UK, slang)* gatuno; **~ leaves** *npl* borras *fpl* de chá; **~pot** *n* bule *m* de chá; **~ shop** *n* salão *m* de chá; **~time** lanche *m*, hora *f* do chá; **~ towel/cloth** *n* pano da louça; (BR) de prato; **4** *(slang) (weed)* marijuana *f*, erva *f (cal)*; IDIOM **(not) for all the ~ in China** por nada deste mundo *m*; **it's not my cup of ~** não é da minha preferência; **a storm in a ~cup** uma tempestade *f* num copo *m* de água.

teach *(pt, pp* **taught***) vt* **to ~ sb sth, ~ sth to sb** ensinar algo a alguém; ♦ *vi* ensinar, le(c)cionar; **2** educar; **3** fazer comprender algo; IDIOM **that'll ~ you!** toma lá que é para aprenderes!; **to ~ one's grandmother to suck eggs** ensinar o Pai-Nosso ao vigário *m;* **you can't ~ an old dog new tricks** burro velho não aprende línguas.

teach-in *n* curso *m* de seminários *mpl* organizado na universidade.

teacher *n* professor,-ora, mestre *m,f*; **~'s pet** *(pej)* o ai-jesus *m* do professor/da professora; **~ training** *n (EDUC)* formação *f* pedagógica; **~'s trainer** *n* formador,-ora de professores.

teaching *n (profession)* ensino *m*; ♦ *adj* docente *m,f*; que ensina; **the ~s of the Church** as doutrinas *fpl* da Igreja; **~ aids** material *m* pedagógico; **~ hospital** centro *m* hospitalar universitário; **~ practice** estágio *m* pedagógico; **~ staff** corpo *m* docente.

teak *n (BOT)* (madeira de) teca; *(colour)* castanho ou amarelo-torrado.

team *n* equipa, equipe *f*, group, *(BR: time m)*; **2** *(of horses)* parelha; *(of oxen)* junta *f*; **~ leader** *n* líder da equipa *f*; **~mate** *n* companheiro de equipa; **~ spirit** *n* espírito de equipa; **~ster** *n*; *(US)* camionista; *(BR)* caminheiro,-a, condutor duma parelha de animais; **~work** *n* trab alho em equipa; ♦ *vt (animals)* atrelar; ♦ *vi* conduzir, formar parelha; **~ up** associar-se a; **2** *(colours, clothes)* combinar (**with** com).

tear[1] *n (rip)* rasgão *m, (clothing)* pedaço *m* rasgado; **2** pressa *f*; **to go full ~** ir a toda a velocidade *f*; **3 to go off on a ~** *(US, coll) (spree)* ir para a pândega *f*; ♦ *(pt* **tore**, *pp* **torn***) vt* rasgar; **2 ~ sth from** arrancar; **3** romper *(clothes)*; **4** *(flesh)* dilacerar; ♦ **~ apart** *vt (fig)* separar; **2** despedaçar *(heart)*; ♦ *vi* rasgar-se; **to ~ at** *(by animal)* despedaçar; **2** criticize; **to ~ away** partir a toda a velocidade; **to ~**

open *(package)* abrir à pressa; **~ off** *vt* arrancar; **to ~ up** *vt (paper)* rasgar aos bocadinhos; **to ~ up/down the stairs** *(rush)* subir/descer a quatro e quatro; IDIOM **that's torn it** *(UK)* está tudo acabado!; só faltava mais essa!; **to be torn between two things** estar indeciso,-a, dividido *m* entre duas *fpl* coisas.

tear[2] *n (= teardrop)* lágrima *f*; **2** *(form, object)* gota *f*; **in ~s** chorando, em lágrimas *fpl*; **to bring ~s to sb's eyes** fazer vir as lágrimas aos olhos de alguém; **to burst into ~s** desfazer-se em lágrimas, desatar a chorar; **to shed ~s** derramar lágrimas; ♦ *vi (eyes)* encher-se de lágrimas; IDIOM **floods of ~s** num mar *m* de lágrimas; **it'll end in ~** isso vai acabar mal; **be easily moved to ~s** estar sempre com a lágrima no canto *m* do olho *m*.

tearaway *n (UK, slang)* delinquente *m,f*, arruaceiro,-a.

tearful *adj* em lágrimas; *(voice)* choroso,-a.

tearfully *adv* em lágrimas *fpl*, em pranto *m*.

teargas *n* gas *m* lacrimogéneo.

tearing *adj* tremendo,-a; **in a ~ rush** com uma pressa dos diabos.

tear-jerker *n (pej) (film, etc)* melodrama *m*; dramalhão *m*.

tearoff *adj (detachable)* destacável *m,f (coupon, receipt)*.

tear-stained *adj (face, person)* debulhado, banhado,-a em lágrimas.

tease *n (annoying joker)* arreliador,-ora; *(in fun)* brincalhão *m*, brincalhona *f*; *(coll)* gozão *m*, gozona *f*; **2** *(mocking)* trocista *m,f*; **3** provocador,-ora, arreliador,-ora; ♦ *vt (annoy)* arreliar *(person)*; atormentar *(animal); (fig) (pulling one's leg)* entrar com; **I am just teasing you** estou a entrar contigo; ♦ *vi (in negative sense)* implicar com; *(in fun)* meter-se com; **to ~ out** *(hair, threads)* desenredar; **2** *(extract information)* sacar.

teasel *n (BOT)* cardo *m*.

teaser *n (person = Vd* **tease***)*; **2** *n (puzzle)* quebra-cabeças *m*.

teaspoon *n* colher *f* de chá *m*; **(= ~ful)** (conteúdo de) colher de chá.

teat *n (breast) (coll)* mama, *(fam)* teta; **2** *(of bottle)* tetina *f* (de biberão); **3** *(animal)* teta *f*.

teated *adj (animal)* com tetas *fpl*.

tec *n (fam) (short for)* dete(c)tive *m*.

tech *n (abbr for* **technology***)* tecnologia *f*.

techie *(pl: -s) n (coll)* fanático da tecnologia.

technic *n* técnico,-a; **2** plural tecnologia *f*; ♦ **~s** *n* técnica, tecnologia *f*; ♦ *adj* raro,-a, técnico,-a.

technical *adj* técnico,-a; **~ design** *n* desenho *m* industrial;

technicality *n* detalhe *m,f*, termo *m* técnico, problema *m* de ordem *f* técnica.

technically *adv* tecnicamente.

technician *n* técnico,-a.

technique *n* técnica *f*; capacidade *f* ou habilidade *f* técnica; perfeição *f* de execução.

techno *n adj (MUS)* tecno *m*.

technocrat *n* tecnocrata *m,f*.

technocratic *adj* tecnocrático,-a.

technological tecnológico,-a.

tectonic adj (GEOL) tectónico,-a (BR: -tô-); **2** (construction) arquite(c)tónico,-a; ~**s** n tectónica (BR: -tô-).

teddy/teddies n (woman's one piece = chemise and pants) body m.

teddy bear n ursinho m de peluche/de pelúcia.

tedious adj (boring) chato,-a; **2** entediante.

tediously adv fastidiosamente.

tediousness n tédio m.

tedium n tédio m, monotonia f.

tee n (for letter **T** = tee); **2** (SPORT) (golf) (also: **teeing ground**) ponto m de partida; **2** (for ball) tee m; ◆ (**tees, teeing, teed**) vi **to** ~ **off** dar a tacada inicial.

teem vi abundar em (wildlife), pulular; **to** ~ **with** estar cheio m de; ~ **down** vi chover torrencialmente.

teeming pres p, adj cheio,-a (**with** de); IDIOM **it is** ~ (**with rain**) chove a cântaros mpl.

teen n (coll) adolescente m,f; **to be in one's** ~**s** estar na adolescência f; ◆ adj (coll) jovem m,f; ~ **years** adolescência f.

teenage adj de/para adolescentes mpl.

teenager n jovem m,f, adolescente, (BR) brotinho m, f.

teens npl: **to be in one's** ~ estar entre os 13 e 19 anos/na adolescência.

teeny-bopper n (coll) jovem m,f que anda na moda f.

teeny (weeny), teensy (weensy) adj (fam) pequenininho,-a (vd: **tiny**).

tee-shirt n T-shirt f, camiseta f.

teeter n vacilação f; cambaleio m; **2** hesitação f; ◆ vt (wobble) baloiçar, oscilar; ◆ vi balançar-se; IDIOM **to** ~ **on the brink/edge of sth** (fig) estar à beira f de algo.

teeter-totter n (US) (seesaw) balancé m (EP); gangorra (BR).

teeth (pl of **tooth**; Vd: **tooth**) n dentes mpl; (ZOOL) **dog's** ~ dentão m; ◆ vt **teethe** deitar/nascer dentes; **set of** ~ dentadura f; IDIOM **in the** ~ **of** a despeito m de; **to be armed to the** ~ estar armado m até aos dentes; **to get one's** ~ **into** familiarizar-se com; **to lie through one's** ~ mentir com todos os dentes; **to say between one's** ~ resmungar por entre dentes.

teething n dentição f; **2** nascimento m dos dentes; ~ **ring** chupeta f, mastigador m para dentição; ~ **troubles** (fig) (project, etc.) dificuldades fpl iniciais.

teetotal adj (abstinence) abstémio,-a (BR: -tê-); **2** (coll) total m, completo,-a.

teetotalism n abstenção f de bebidas fpl alcoólicas.

teetotaller (US: **teetotaler**) n abstémio,-a (BR: -tê-).

teetotally adv (US, coll) totalmente.

te-hee (= **tee-hee**) exc gagalhada f de mofa; **2** n (giggle) risadinha f, ◆ vi (snigger) rir-se à socapa.

Tehran, Teheran npl Teerão.

telaesthesia adj telestesia f; **2** telepatia f.

telecast n (TV) emissão f televisiva; ◆ vt/vi (TV) transmitir.

telecommunications n telecomunicações fpl.

telecommute vi teletrabalhar.

telecommuter n teletrabalhador,-ora.

telecommuting n teletrabalho m.

teleconference n teleconferência f.

telegram n (brief message) telegrama m; ~ **form** n impresso m para telegrama; **wireless** ~ n radiotelegrama m.

telegraph n (device) telégrafo m; **2** (NAUT) semáforo m; ◆ vt telegrafar; **2** avisar atempadamente sem intenção f; ◆ vi fazer sinais; **2** dar a entender; ~**er/~ist/~ operator** n telegrafista m,f; ~ **key** n manipulador,-ora de telégrafo; ~ **messenger** n boletineiro m; ~ **pole/post** n (UK) poste m de telégrafos.

telegraphic adj telegráfico,-a (fig) **in** ~ **style** em estilo m telegráfico.

telepath n telepata m,f; ◆ vi praticar telepatia f.

telepathic adj telepático,-a.

telepathist n telepata m,f.

telepathy n (thought transference) telepatia f.

telephone n telefone m; ~ **area code/~ dialling code** n indicativo m telefónico (BR: -fô-), (BR) catálogo m; ~ **booth** n (US), ~ **box/kiosk** n (UK) cabine f telefónica (BR: -fô-); ~ **call** n telefonema m, chamada f (telefónica); ~ **directory** n (UK) lista f telefónica; ~ **exchange** n central f telefónica; ~ **number** n número m de telefone; ~ **tapping/ bugging** n escutas flp telefónicas; ◆ vt (person) telefonar para/a; **2** chamar ao telefone; ◆ **to be on the** ~ estar ao telefone; **to put the** ~ **down (on sb)** desligar o telefone (sem avisar); **you are wanted on the** ~ você/o senhor tem uma chamada f; ◆ vi (message) transmitir por telefone; **he** ~**ed his instructions** ele transmitiu as instruções fpl por telefone.

telephonist (operator) n (UK) telefonista m,f.

telephoto n (PHOT) telefoto f, telefotografia f; ◆ adj telefotográfico,-a; ~ **lens** teleobje(c)tiva f.

telepicture n imagem de televisão f.

teleprinter n (UK) telétipo m (teleimpressor).

telesales n (= **telemarketing** n) (TV) televendas fpl.

telescope n telescópio m.

telescopic adj telescópico,-a; ~ **table** n mesa f extensível; ◆ vt (story, etc.) simplificar; ◆ vi compactar-se.

teletext n (TV) teletexto m.

televiewer n (TV) telespe(c)tador,-a.

televise vt televisionar, transmitir por televisão f; **2** (programme) pôr na televisão.

television n televisão f; **on** ~ (coll) na televisão; ~ **aerial** n antena f de televisão; ~ **broadcast** n transmissão f televisiva; ~ **licence** n (UK) licença f para ter um televisor m; ~ **set** n aparelho m de televisão f, televisor m.

teleworking n (= **telecommuting** n) teletrabalho m.

telex n telex m; ◆ vt telexar, enviar por telex.

tell (pt, pp **told**) vt (reveal) dizer; **2** (order) ordenar ou avisar (**about** de); **3** (story) contar, contar a alguém/algo a alguém; **4** discernir; **I can** ~ **what is wrong** sei ver o que está errado m; ~ **on** denunciar; **5** ressentir-se; ◆ ~ **apart** (= tell sth from) vt distinguir algo de; **she couldn't** ~ **the truth** ela não sabia qual era a verdade f; ◆ vi (coll) (secret) descair-se, falar; **2** *(have effect)* produzir efeito *m*; **3 to ~ sb to do sth** mandar alguém fazer algo; ♦ **they were twenty all told** eram vinte ao todo; **she told you so!** ela bem te disse/te avisou!, *(BR)* ela te falou!; **only time will ~** o tempo *m* o dirá; **who can ~?** sabe-se lá!; **I'll ~ you what ...** ouve, e se ...; **~ it like it is** *(US)* diz as coisas *fpl* sem rodeios *mpl*; **to ~ straight out** dizer/falar sem rodeios; IDIOM **~ that to the horsemarines** vá contar essa a outro *m*; **to ~ one's beads** rezar o terço *m*; **to ~ sb properly** dizer duas verdades *fpl* a alguém.

teller *n (in bank)* caixa *m,f*; **2** narrador,-ora; **3** *(of votes)* escrutinador,-ora.

telling *n (story, etc.)* narração *f*; ♦ *adj* impressionante *m,f*; **2** *(detail)* revelador,-ora; IDIOM **there is no ~ what may happen** ninguém sabe o que pode acontecer.

tell-off *n* reprimenda *f*, raspanete *m,f*, *(BR)* bronca *f*; **to give a telling-off** dar um raspanete *m*; *(BR)* dar bronca *f* em alguém; ♦ **tell off** *vt* repreender.

telltale *n (person)* queixinhas *fpl*; linguareiro,-a; **2** *(NAUT) (dogvane)* indicador *m* da dire(c)ção *f* do vento *m*; ♦ *adj (proof)* denunciador,-ora; **~ signs** sinais *mpl*, reveladores.

telluric *adj (GEOG, MED, CHEM)* telúrico,-a.

telly *(pl: -ies)* *n (UK, coll)* televisão *f*; **on ~** na televisão.

telpher *n (telferage)* teleférico *m*; **~ line** *n* linha *f* de teleférico; ♦ *vt (goods)* transportar por teleférico.

temerity *n (boldness)* temeridade *f*.

temp *n (abbr for* **temporary***)* *(coll)* trabalhador,-ora temporário,-a.

temper *n (mood)* humor *m*, disposição *f*; (= **bad ~**) mau *m* génio; **to be in a ~** estar de mau humor/ de má *f* maré, *(fit of anger)* cólera *f*; *(of child)* birra *f*; **to be/have a quick/hot ~** ser irascível; **to lose one's ~** encolerizar-se, perder a cabeça; ♦ *vt* moderar; **2** *(fig)* atenuar; **criticism can be ~ed with kindness** a crítica *f* pode ser contrabalançada *f* pela gentileza *f*; **3** *(MUS)* afinar; IDIOM **she has a short ~!** ela ferve em pouca água *f*, irrita-se facilmente.

tempera *n (paint, etc)* têmpera *f*.

temperament *n* temperamento *m* índole *f*, feitio *m* (da pessoa).

temperamental *adj (person)* temperamental *m,f*; **2 a ~ outburst** um acesso *m* de mau *m* génio; imprevisível *m,f*, errático,-a; **a ~ drill** um berbequim falível.

temperance *n (appetites, desires)* moderação *f*, temperança; **2** *(abstinence)* sobriedade *f*; **~ hotel** hotel *m* onde não servem bebidas *fpl* alcoólicas; **~ society** liga *f* contra o alcoolismo *m*.

temperate *adj* moderado,-a, comedido,-a; **2** *(mild climate)* temperado *m*; *(of the weather)* suavidade *f*; *(GEOG)* **T~ Zone** Zona *f* Temperada.

temperately *adv* moderadamente.

temperature *n* temperatura *f*; **to have/run a ~** ter febre *f*; **2** *(fig) (tension)* estado *m* de espírito.

tempered *adj* contido,-a, comedido,-a; **ill-~** irascível *m,f*; **quick-~** *(person)* facilmente irritável *m,f*; **2** *(steel)* temperado,-a; **~ glass** vidro *m* temperado.

tempest *n (weather)* tempestade *f*.

tempestuous *adj (stormy)* tempestuoso,-a, violento,-a; **2** *(fig) (emotional)* turbulento,-a.

tempestuously *adv* tempestuosamente.

tempestuousness *n* violência *f* de tempestade; cará(c)ter *m* tumultuoso.

template *n* modelo *m*; **2** molde *m*; **3** *(COMP)* gabarito *m*; **4** suporte *m* de viga.

temple *n (REL)* templo *m*; **2** *(ANAT)* têmpora *f*; **Knights of the T~** Cavaleiros do Templo, Templários *mpl*.

tempo *(pl: -s or* **tempi***)* *n* tempo *m*; **2** *(fig)* ritmo *m*, velocidade *f*; **3** *(MUS)* andamento *m*.

temporaizer *n* temporizador,-ora, contemporizador,-ora.

temporal *adj* temporal *m,f*; **2** secular *m,f*, temporal; **3** *(ANAT)* **~ artery** artéria *f* temporal.

temporality *n* temporalidade *f*; temporariamente; **2** (= **temporalties**) bens *mpl* temporais; **3** *(JUR)* cará(c)ter *m* provisório.

temporarily *adv* temporariamente.

temporariness *n* transitoriedade *m,f*.

temporary *adj* temporário,-a, efémero,-a *(BR: -fê-)*; transitório,-a; *(worker)* provisório,-a; **~ employment** emprego *m* temporário.

temporization *n* temporização *f*, contemporização *f*; **2** transigência *f*.

temporize *vi* temporizar, contemporizar; **2** procurar ganhar tempo *m*.

tempt *vt* tentar, **to ~ the gods** desafiar os deuses *mpl*; **2 to ~ sb into doing sth** convencer/tentar/ induzir alguém a fazer algo.

temptation *n* tentação *f*.

tempting *n* tentação *f*; ♦ *adj* tentador,-ora; atraente *m,f*; **2** *(food)* apetitoso,-a.

temptingly *adv* tentadoramente.

temptingness *n* cará(c)ter *m* tentador; **2** sedução *f*, atra(c)ção *f*.

temptress *(pl: -es)* *n* mulher *f* sedutora.

ten *n, num* dez; **he is ~ times better** ele *m* é dez vezes melhor; **~ to one he will fall for it** *(coll)* aposto que ele cai que nem um patinho *m (fam)*; **in ~s** às dezenas *fpl*; **~s of thousands** *npl* dezenas de milhar.

tenable *adj (opinion, theory)* sustentável *m,f* convincente *m,f*; **2** *(position, support)* concedido,-a, seguro,-a (**for** por).

tenableness *n* (= **tenability** *n*) defensabilidade *f*; sustentabilidade *f*.

tenably *adv* defensavelmente.

tenacious *adj* tenaz *m,f*; **2** obstinado,-a; **3** firme *m,f*; adesivo,-a; **~ memory** boa *f* memória.

tenaciously *adv* persistentemente.

tenaciousness *n* (= **tenacity** *n*) tenacidade *f*.

tenancy *(pl: -ies)* *n* aluguer *m*; arrendamento *m*; ~ **agreement** *n* contrato *m* de arrendamento; *(of house)* locação *f*.

tenant *n* inquilino,-a; *(of a pub)* locatário,-a; *(JUR)* proprietário,-a de imóvel; ♦ *vt* ocupar, habitar como arrendatário.

tenantable *adj* arrendável *m,f*.

tenantless *adj* desabitado,-a.

tenantry *n* arrendamento *m*.

tend *vt* **to** ~ **to sb** tratar de alguém; encarregar-se de; ♦ *vi (incline)* tender a; ter tendência a; **the temperature** ~**s to rise** a temperatura tende a subir; **to** ~ **towards sth** inclinar-se para algo; **I** ~ **to think** sinto-me inclinado a pensar; **2** *(look after)* cuidar, guardar; **to** ~ **the fire** vigiar o lume *m*; *(flock)* guardar; ter tendência a seguir em certa dire(c)ção; **3 she** ~**s to her needs** ela atende às suas necessidades.

tendency *(pl: -ies)* *n* tendência *f* (**towards** para); **2** *(leaning)* inclinação *f* (**towards** para); **a growing** ~ uma tendência *f* crescente.

tendentious *adj* (= **tendencious**) tendencioso,-a; **2** parcial *m,f*; ~ **speech** discurso *m* tendencioso.

tendentiously *adv* tendenciosamente.

tendentiousness *n* tendenciosidade *f*.

tender *n:* **legal** ~ moeda *f* corrente; **2** *(COMM, FIN)* oferta, proposta; **by** ~ por concurso *m* público; **to invite** ~**s for** abrir concurso para; **to sell by** ~ *(JUR)* vender por adjudicação; ♦ *adj (colour)* suave *m,f*; **2** *(loving)* meigo,-a, terno,-a; *(caring)* carinhoso,-a; **3** *(sore)* sensível *m,f*; ~ **to the touch** sensível ao toque *m*; ~ **flower** flor *f* delicada delicada; **4** *(meat)* tenro,-a; **5** *(young)* ~ **age** tenra *f* idade; ♦ *vt (proposal)* entregar; **2** *(bid)* apresentar; ♦ **to** ~ **one's services** oferecer os seus serviços *mpl*.

tenderfoot *(pl: -s or -feet)* *(US, slang)* imigrante *m,f*, acabado de chegar; **2** novato,-a, inexperiente *m,f*.

tender-hearted *adj* terno; **2** compassivo,-a.

tenderise *(US: tenderize)* *vt (CULIN)* amaciar; ~**r** *n* *(CULIN)* produto *m* para tornar a carne *f* mais tenra; amaciar; **2** *(tool)* martelo *m* da carne.

tenderly *adv* suavemente; carinhosamente.

tenderness *n* ternura *f*, meiguice *f*, carinho *m*; **2** *(of meat)* maciez *f*.

tendon *n* *(ANAT)* tendão *m*.

tendril *m* *(of plant)* gavinha *f*.

tenement *n* conjunto *m* habitacional; ~ **house** casa *f* arrendada; **2** *(JUR)* prazo *m* foreiro; **3** arrendamento *m*.

tenet *n* dogma *m*; princípio *m*.

tenfold *adj* décuplo; dez vezes maior.

tenner *n* *(coll)* nota de dez libras; **lend me a** ~ empresta-me dez libras.

tennis *n* *(SPORT)* ténis *m*, *(BR* tê-*)*; ~ **ball** *n* bola *f* de ténis; ~ **court** *n* campo *m* *(BR:* quadra *f)* de ténis; ~ **racket** *n* raqueta *f* de ténis; **table** ~ pingue-pongue *m*; ~ **shoe** *(footwear)* ténis *m*.

tenor *n* *(MUS) (male singer)* tenor *m*; **2** *(tone)* tom *m*; **3** teor (**of** de); **4** *(JUR) (exact words of a deed)* cópia *f* fiel, traslado,-a; **5** *(drift)* curso (de andamento).

tenpin bowling *(UK)*, ~**pins** *(US)* *(functioning as pl)* *n* bowling, boliche *m* com 10 paus *(BR:* pinos mpl*)* *mpl*.

tense *n* *(LING)* tempo *m*; **the future** ~ o tempo do futuro; ♦ *adj (person, situation, etc)* tenso,-a; **2** *(stretched)* estirado,-a; esticado,-a; **3** *(stiff)* rígido,-a; teso,-a; ♦ *vt* esticar; ♦ *vi* tornar tenso,-a, endurecer-se; **to** ~ **up** retesar-se; ~**ed up** *adj* tenso,-a.

tensely *adv* retesadamente; **2** sob grande tensão *f* nervosa.

tenseness *n* tensão; **2** rigidez *f*; **3** estado *m* de tensão.

tension *n* *(unease)* tensão *f*; animosidade *f*; **2** *(anxiety)* ansiedade *f*; *(ELECT)* tensão *f*; ~**s** *npl* conflitos *mpl* **tensional** *adj* relativo a tensão *f*.

tensor *n* *(ANAT)* músculo *m* tensor; *(MATH)* tensor *m*; ♦ *adj* tensor *m*.

tent *n* *(campism)* tenda *f*, barraca *f*; **a two-person** ~ uma tenda para duas pessoas; ~**peg** *n* estaca *f*; ~ **pole** *n* pau *m*; *(MED)* compressa *f*; dreno *m*; ~ **dress** *(fam)* vestido *m* sem cintura; ♦ *vt* viver, alojar em tendas *fpl*; cobrir com uma tenda *f*; *(MED) (wound)* abrir com uma compressa *f*.

tentacle *n* tentáculo *m*.

tentacled *adj* (= **tentaculate**) *adj* tentaculado,-a.

tentative *adj* provisório,-a, experimental, **2** hesitante; **3** preliminar.

tentatively *adv* tentativamente; **2** a título experimental; **3** a medo.

tenter *n* *(weaving)* tempereiro *m*; ♦ *vt* esticar (o pano).

tenterhook *n* *(weaving)* gancho *m* para firmar o pano; escápula *f*; **to be on** ~**s** *(in a rush)* estar aflito,-a; *(coll)* sobre brasas *fpl*; *(nervous)* *(coll)*, estar com os nervos *mpl* à flor *f* da pele *(fam)*.

tenth *n* décimo; **2** décima *f* parte; **three** ~ três décimos, as *mpl*, *fpl*; ~ **of June** no dia dez de junho; ♦ *adj num* décimo,-a.

tenuous *adj* ténue, fino,-a; **2** débil, frágil *m,f*; **3** subtil *m,f*; ~ **distinctions** distinções *fpl* demasiado subtis; **to have a** ~ **grasp of** ter vagas noções de.

tenuousness *n* ténue.

tenure *n* *(of property)* posse *f*; ~ **at will** posse por tolerância *f*; **2** ocupação *f*; **3** *(government)* mandato *m*; **4** *(employment)* **to get** ~ passar ao quadro *m*.

tenured *adj (post)* estável, permanente; **2** *(professor)* efetivo,-a, titular.

tepid *adj (liquid)* tépido,-a, morno,-a; **2** *(fig)* sem grande entusiasmo *m*.

tepidity (= ~**ness**) *n* tepidez *f*.

tercentenary *(pl: -ies)* *n* tricentenário; ♦ *adj* tricentenário,-a.

tercentennial *adj* tricentenário.

tergiversate *vi (shuffle)* tergiversar; **2** virar as costas *fpl*; **3** *(coll)* virar a casaca *f* *(col)*; **4** passar-se para outro partido *m*.

tergiversation *n* evasiva *f*, rodeio *m*.

term *n* *(word, expression)* designação *f*; **technical** ~**s** termos *mpl* técnicos; **2** limite *m*; **3** *(COMM)* prazo *m*; *(COMM)* cláusulas *fpl*, termos *mpl*; **4** período *m*; **in the short/long** ~ a curto/longo prazo *m*; **5** *(UK) (EDUC)* termo *m*; trimestre *m*. ♦ *vt* classificar, designar.

terminable *adj* terminável; limitável.

terminal *n* *(airport, COMP)* terminal *m*; *(ferry)* gare *f* marítima; *(bus, RAIL)* término *m*; **2** *(ELECT)* borne; ♦ *adj* terminal, fatal.

terminate *vt* terminar, acabar com, pôr fim a; **2** *(contract)* rescindir; **3** *(slang)* matar uma pessoa; ♦ *vi* *(pregnancy)* interromper; **to ~ in** *vi* acabar em.

termination *n* término *m*; **2** *(of contract)* conclusão *f*; **3** *(abortion)* interrupção *f* voluntária *f* da gravidez; **4** (LING) terminação.

terminator *n* *(ASTRON)* *(line)* terminador.

terminology *n* terminologia *f*, nomenclatura *f*. **terminological** *adj* terminológico,-a.

terminus *(pl: -uses or -mini)* *n* término *m*; **~ a quo** ponto *m* de partida; **~ ad quem** obje(c)tivo *m*, fim *m*.

termite *n* formiga-branca *f*, térmite *m* *(BR: cupim m)*.

termless *adj* ilimitado,-a.

terms *npl* termos *mpl*, condições *f*; **he dictated the ~** ele *m* impôs as condições *fpl*; **~ of reference** *(UK)* atribuições; **to come to ~ with** *(person)* chegar a um acordo *m* com; **2** enfrentar *(issue)*; **3** aceitar *(failure)*; **to be on good ~ with sb** ter uma boa *f* relação; dar-se bem com; **in ~ of** em relação a; **in no uncertain ~** sem rodeios; **in real ~** efe(c)tivamente; **on equal ~** em pé *m* de igualdade.

tern *n* andorinha-do-mar *f*; **2** *(lottery)* série *f* de três números *mpl* que dá prémio *m*.

ternary *adj* *(using three as a base)* ternário *m*.

terrace *n* *(patio)* terraço *m*; **2** *(UK)* *(row of houses)* fila *f* de casas pegadas e idênticas; **3** *(on hillside)* socalco *m* *(plantado)*; **on a ~** série *f* de edifícios em ladeira *f*; **4** *(in stadium)* bancada *f*; ♦ *vt* dispor em socalcos *mpl* *(garden, hillside)*.

terraced *adj* em terraço, escalonado,-a; **~ house** *(UK)* casa *f* pegada (a outras idênticas).

terracotta *n* *(ceramic, colour)* terracota, louça *f* de barro.

terrain *n* terreno *m*; **rocky ~** *n* terreno rochoso.

terrestrial *n* terráqueo,-a; ♦ *adj* *(animal, plant)* terrestre *m,f*; **~ magnetism** magnetismo *m* terrestre. **2** *(pleasure)* mundano,-a; **3** *(TV)* transmitido por via terrestre.

terrestrially *adv* por via *f* terrestre.

terrible *adj* terrível *m,f*, horroroso,-a; **the heat was ~** o calor *m* era insuportável; **the painting was ~** o quadro era horroroso; **I feel ~** sinto-me mal; **2** *(child)* travesso,-a; **3** *(coll)* *(intensifier)* grande *m,f*; **it would have been a ~ loss** teria sido uma grande *f* perda.

terribleness *n* aspe(c)to *m* terrível.

terribly *adv* *(very)* muito; imenso,-a, terrivelmente, extremamente; **I am ~ grateful** estou extremamente grato,-a.

terrier *n* *(dog)* terrier *m*.

terrific *adj* *(intensifier)* terrífico,-a, magnífico,-a; **a ~ artist** um artista *m* fantástico; **2** *(coll)* maravilhoso,-a; **3** enorme *m,f*.

terrifically *adv* extremamente.

terrified *adj* *(fear of sb or sth)* apavorado,-a.

terrify *vt* *(great fear or dread)* aterrorizar.

terrifying *adj* assustador,-ora, aterrorizante *m,f*; **2** espantoso,-a.

territorial *adj* territorial *m,f*; **T~ Army** *npr*: *(UK)* exército *m* voluntário; **~ waters** *n* águas *fpl* territoriais.

territory *(pl: -ies)* *n* território *m*; **2** *(area of study)* campo *m*, área *f*; **3** *(terrain)* terreno *m*.

terror *n* *(great fear)* terror *m*; **in ~** cheio *m* de medo; **to strike ~ into the hearts of people** semear o terror nos corações das pessoas; **2** *(sth feared)* horror; **3** *(coll, fig)* intimidação *f*, ameaça *f*; IDIOM **to be in ~ of one's life** temer pela vida *f*; **his son is a real ~** *(fig, fam)* o filho dele *m* é uma verdadeira *f* peste.

terrorism *n* terrorismo *m*.

terrorist *n adj* terrorista *m,f*.

terrorization *n* sujeição *f* pelo terror *m*.

terrorize, terrorise *vt* aterrorizar.

terror-stricken, terror-struck *adj* aterrado,-a.

terry *n* pano *m* atualhado,-a.

terse *adj* seco,-a; **2** *(style)* conciso,-a, sucinto,-a; **3** *(abrupt)* brusco,-a.

tersely *adv* secamente; **2** bruscamente; **3** sobriamente.

terseness *n* sobriedade *f* (de estilo).

tertiary *adj* *(age, rock)* terciário,-a; **~ sector** *(services)* sector terciário; **~ education** *n* *(EDUC)* *(further education)* educação *f* de terceiro grau, educação complementar vocacional.

TESL *(abbr for Teaching English as a Second Language)* ensino *m* de inglês como segunda língua.

tessellate *vt* *(CONSTR)* dispor em, pavimentar com pequenos mosaicos *mpl*; ♦ *vi* encaixar perfeitamente.

tessellated *adj* em xadrez *m*, com mosaicos.

test *n* *(of person, aptitude)* prova *f*; *(School, Univ)* *(in class)* teste *m*; *(= driving ~)* exame *m* de condução *(BR: motorista)*; **2** *(MED)* *(of blood)* análise *f*; *(of organ)* teste *m*; **~ ban treaty** *n* *(nuclear)* proibição *f* de testes nucleares; **~card** *n* *(UK)* *(TV)* mira *f* técnica; **~case** *n* *(JUR)* caso *m* precedente; **~-drive** *n* ensaio *m* de entrada; **~ flight** *n* voo *m* de ensaio; experimental; **~ match** *n* *(SPORT)* jogo *m* internacional; **~out** *vt* testar, experimentar; **~ pilot** piloto *m* de prova; **~ tube** *n* tubo *m* de ensaio; **~ tube baby** *n* bebé-proveta; *(BR)* nenê de proveta; ♦ *vt* *(COMM, TECH)* testar, ensaiar; pôr à prova *(patience)*; **2** *(MED)* analisar; **to ~ positive for drugs** o controlo *m* anti-doping deu positivo *m*; **to put sb/sth to the ~** pôr alguém/algo à prova.

testament *n* *(JUR)* testamento *m*; *(proof)* testemunho *m*; **2** *(REL)* **the Old/New T~** o Velho/Novo *m* Testamento.

testamentary *adj* testamentário,-a.

tester *n* *(person)* analista *m,f*; controlador,-ora; **2** *(apparatus)* aparelho *m* de controlo *m*, verificação *f*; **3** *(sample)* amostra *f*.

testicle *n* testículo *m*; **~s** *npl* ~testículos *mpl*; *(slang)* *(balls)* tomates *mpl* *(vulg)*; *(BR)* saco *m* *(vulg)*.

testify *vt* *(JUR)* *(give or be evidence)* prestar declaração *f*, testemunhar; ♦ *vi* testemunhar *(against* contra; **for** a favor de/por); **2 to ~ to sth** afirmar, asseverar algo; **3 to ~ under oath** declarar sob juramento *m*.

testimonial n carta f de recomendação; **2** *(recognition)* homenagem f.

testimony *(pl: -ies)* n *(JUR)* testemunho m, depoimento m **(of** de); **2** declaração f solene IDIOM **to give/to bear ~** dar testemunho m da sua fé f; **in ~ whereof ...** em fé do que ...

testing n examinação f; **2** realização f de experiências fpl; **nuclear ~** testes mpl nucleares; ♦ adj *(difficult)* difícil m,f; **2** *(demanding)* exigente m,f; **3 ~ time** um momento m de provação.

tetanus n *(MED)* tétano m; *(vaccine, injection)* antitetânico,-a.

tetchy adj *(person)* rabugento,-a; *(behaviour)* irritável m,f, irritante m,f.

tether vt *(animal)* amarrar, prender com corda f; IDIOM **at the end of one's ~** a ponto de perder a paciência, de não poder aguentar.

text n texto m; **2 Scripture ~** citação f tirada da Bíblia f; **3** *(TYPO)* tipo m grande de letra f manuscrita; **4** assunto m; **stick to the ~!** não te afastes do assunto m!; **~ message** n *(mobile phone)* mensagem de texto; ♦ vt *(mobile phone)* enviar mensagem de texto.

textbook n livro m didá(c)tico, compêndio m; *(BR)* livro-texto; ♦ adj clássico m; **2** modelo m.

textile n têxteis mpl, tecidos mpl; **~ weaver** tecelão m; ♦ adj têxtil m,f; **~ industry** indústria têxtil.

textual adj textual m,f, literal m,f; **~ criticism** análise f de texto.

textually adv textualmente.

texture n *(of cream, soil)* contextura f; **2** qualidade f; textura f.

Thai n adj *(person)* tailandês,-esa; **2** *(LÍNG)* tailandês.

Thailand npr Tailândia; **in ~** na Tailândia.

thalidomide n talidomida f.

Thames npr: **the ~** *(river)* o (rio) Tâmisa m; IDIOM **you'll never set the ~ on fire** nunca serás brilhante m,f.

than conj de; **more ~ once** mais de uma vez f; **2** *(do)* que; **I'd rather starve ~ eat that** antes passar fome f do que comer isso; **she is more sensible ~ you** ela f é mais sensata f do que você; **3** senão; **it is no other ~ John** não é outro senão John; **4** que não; IDIOM **no sooner said ~ done** dito m e feito.

thank n obrigado,-a; ♦ **~s** npl agradecimentos m; **my best ~s** os meus sinceros agradecimentos; **a thousand ~s!** obrigadíssimo,-a!; **~s offering** oferta f de a(c)ção de graças; **2** *(thanks to, due to)* graças a; **~ to the doctor I am better** graças ao médico, estou melhor; **~ God!** graças a Deus!; **~worthy** adj digno m de agradecimento; ♦ vt agradecer; **I ~ you for your kindness** agradeço-lhe pela sua gentileza; IDIOM **he won't ~ you for doing it** ele m não vai gostar que faças isso; **I'll ~ you (not) to do that** *(annoyed)* agradecia-lhe que (não) fizesse isso; **to ~ one's lucky stars** dar graças fpl aos céus mpl; **you have only yourself to ~** a culpa f é só tua f.

thankful adj agradecido,-a **(for** por).

thankfulness n gratidão f, reconhecimento m.

thankless adj ingrato,-a, mal agradecido,-a.

thanklessly adv ingratamente; **2** sem proveito m.

Thanksgiving (Day) n dia m de a(c)ção f de graças.

that *(pl: those)* *(det)* adj *(closer to the person you address or mention)* esse/essa; **who is ~ man you speak about** quem é esse senhor de quem falas?; **2** *(farther from both speakers)* aquele/aquela; **do you see ~ lady by the window?** vês aquela senhora ao pé da janela?; *(pointing)* **~ man is not my husband** aquele homem não é o meu marido; ♦ dem pron esse, essa; *(neuter)* isso; **that one; who is ~?** quem é esse/essa?; **what is ~?** o que é isso?; **~ is not done** isso não se faz; **~ does not concern me** isso não me diz respeito; **2** *(futher away)* aquele, aquela, *(neuter)* aquilo; **~ (one) is Manuel** aquele é o Manuel; **I don't like ~ hat, I prefer the other over there** não gosto desse chapéu, prefiro aquele ali/gosto mais daquele; *(NOTE: the combination of prep with the dem adj and pronouns: de + esse = desse; em + aquilo = naquilo, etc; a + aquela = àquela etc)*; ♦ relative pron que; **2** *(with prep)*, quem, o/a qual; **on the day ~ he said** no dia m em que ele disse; **the house ~ she lives in** a casa f na qual ela vive; **3** *(before relative pron)* **~ who** *(that one, the one who/whoever)* aquele/aquela que; **those who** aquele/a que; **the one ~, (anyone who, whoever) says the economy is good, is lying** aquele que diz que a economia está boa, mente/é porque mente; ♦ adv assim tão; **I can't drink ~ much** não posso beber tanto; **it's about ~ high** é mais ou menos dessa altura f; **was the show ~ bad?** o espe(c)táculo m foi assim tão mau?; ♦ conj que; **he said ~** ele disse que; *(expressing a wish)* **oh ~ luck would come my way!** quem me dera que a sorte me chegasse!; *(surprise, complaint)* **she should speak in ~ manner!** como é que ela pode falar-me desse modo!; IDIOM **all is well ~ ends well** tudo está bem quando acaba bem; **and that's ~** e pronto, é assim mesmo.

thatched adj *(roof)* de colmo m, de sapê m, colmado m.

Thatcherism n *(Mrs Thatcher)* thatcherismo m.

that's = that is.

thaw n degelo m; **2** *(POL)* *(fig)* diminuição f ou término m das tensões; ♦ vt *(snow)* derreter; **2** *(food)* descongelar; ♦ vi *(person)* relaxar, descontrair-se.

thawing n degelo; descongelação f.

the def art o,-a; os/as mpl/fpl; **~ Portuguese** os Portugueses mpl; **William ~ Second** Guilherme (II) Segundo m; *(era)* **~ sixties** *(in dates)* os anos 60; **~ garden's beauty** a beleza do jardim; *(NOTE: the prepositions combine with the def articles: of the = do, da, dos, das; in/on the = no/s, na/s; by/for the = pelo,-a, pelos,-as))*; ♦ adv quanto; *(with comparatives)* **~ sooner ~ better** quanto mais cedo melhor; **2** tanto; **all ~ better** tanto melhor; **so much ~ worse for you** tanto pior para si; **she is none ~ richer** nem por isso é mais rica f; **~ more I learn, ~ more I know I have to learn more** quanto mais aprendo, mais sei que tenho de aprender mais; **3** *(with superlatives)* **~ easiest way** o caminho mais fácil; **~ best** o/a melhor.

theater (US) **theatre** (UK) n (building, profession, etc) teatro; **2** (US) (building) cinema; sala de cinema; ♦ adj (MIL) ~ **of operations** teatro m de operações; zona f de combate; (MED) sala f de operações; **2** (for lectures) anfiteatro m; sala f de conferências; **3** (fig) drama m; **~-goer** n frequentador,-ora; aficionado,-a por teatro.

theatrical n a(c)tor m profissional; ♦ adj teatral m,f; **2** adaptado m ao teatro m; **3** (fig, pej) dramático,-a, teatralizar; ♦ **~s** npl teatro m amador; **2** (fig) cenas fpl; espe(c)táculo m.

theatrically adv (behaviour) teatralmente.

theft n roubo m; furto m.

their adj seu m, sua f, dele m, dela f; ~ **car** o carro deles/delas; **~s** pron (o) seu, (a) sua, dele m, dela f; **a friend of ~s** um amigo deles/delas; **these are mine, where are ~?** estes são meus, onde estão os deles/delas?

them pron (direct) os mpl, as fpl, **I see ~** vejo-as/os; **2** (indirect = to/for them) lhes; **give ~ my regards** dê-lhes os meus cumprimentos mpl; **3** (stressed after prep) a eles/a elas; **I like ~**, gosto deles; **4** (emphasis) **it was to ~** I wanted to give this era a eles que eu queria dar isto; **both of ~** ambos,-as.

thematic adj temático,-a.

thematically adv tematicamente.

theme n gen tema m; cara(c)terística f fundamental; ~ **song** tema m musical; ~ **park** parque temático.

themselves pl pron (subject) eles/elas, mesmos,-as mpl/fpl, próprios,-ias; (emphasis) **they did it ~** eles mesmos fizeram isso; **2** (reflexive) se; **they hurt ~** (they got hurt) eles magoaram-se; **3** (after prep) si (mesmos,-as); **they did that to ~** fizeram isso a si mesmos,-as; **by ~** sozinhos,-as mpl/fpl.

then n (that time) esse tempo m, essa ocasião f, essa altura f; **by ~** (at that time) por essa altura; **until ~** até essa altura; ♦ adj naquela altura **the ~ president** o então presidente m; **from ~ on** a partir de então; **now and ~** de quando em quando, uma vez por outra; ♦ conj então, portanto; **2** nesse m caso; **if she really wants to travell, well ~, let her go** se ela f quer mesmo viajar, nesse caso, é deixá-la ir; ♦ adv (at that time) então, nessa altura f; ~ **she started crying** então ela f começou a chorar; **2** (next) em seguida; **3** (later) logo, depois; **and ~ we shall see** e depois veremos; (furthermore, also) além disso.

thence adv daí; **from ~** desse lugar m; **2** por consequência f, por conseguinte, que.

thenceforth(s) adv (from that place or time) desde então.

theological adj teológico,-a.

theologist n teólogo,-a.

theology n teologia f.

theorem n teorema m.

theoretic adj teórico,-a, teorético,-a.

theoretical adj teórico.

theoretically adv teoricamente, em teoria.

theoretician n teórico,-a.

theorise (UK) **theorize** (US) vi (about sth) teorizar (sobre algo), elaborar uma teoria f.

theory (pl: **-ies**) n teoria f; **that only works in ~** isso só funciona na teoria; **2** especulação f; **3** opinião f; **4** (science) princípios mpl gerais; ~ **of chances** (MATH) teoria f das probabilidades.

therapeutic(al) adj terapêutico,-a; **2** (coll) que faz bem, salutar m,f.

therapeutically adv terapeuticamente.

therapeutics n terapêutica f.

therapist n terapeuta m,f.

therapy n terapia f; **group ~** (PSYC) terapia de grupo; **that it's good ~** (fig) faz muito bem.

there n lá, esse lugar m; ♦ pron (impersonal subject when combined with **haver** in the third person sg): ~ **is/are** há; (also: **ser, estar** in the impersonal form) ~ **is someone waiting for you** está alguém à tua espera; ♦ adv (place) ali, lá, aí (farther away) acolá; **John is ~** (pointing) **in the garden** o João está ali, no jardim; **up to ~** até ali; **2** lá (speaking of a third place); **so, you are back from America? And how was the weather ~?** vieste da América? Então como estava o tempo lá?; **in ~** lá dentro; exc ~ **she goes!** lá vai ela!; **3** (unseen, vaguely) aí; **it's right ~ by the entrance** está aí mesmo junto à entrada; **the gloves are ~** (somewhere there) as luvas estão aí; (speaking of place close to the addressee) **how is everybody ~?** como estão todos aí?; **4** (in the distance) acolá; (less used = beyond, yonder) além; **do you see that bird (over) ~?** vê aquele pássaro m acolá/além?; **here and ~** aqui e além; IDIOM ~, ~! calma!; ~ **you have it** aí está/aí o tem!; **I've been ~ before** já passei por isso; **she was not all ~** ela f não regulava bem (da cabeça); ~ **will be another day** haverá outro dia/fica para outro dia; **~'s the rub!/ the problem** aí está o busílis.

thereabouts (UK) **there about** (US) adv (around, vaguely) aí, por aí; **in Windsor or ~** em Windsor ou por ali perto; **2** cerca de; **by 1974 or ~** por volta de 1974.

thereafter adv conj depois disso; a partir daí.

thereby adv por conseguinte; desse modo; assim; ~ **losing my money** e deste modo perdi/perdendo o meu dinheiro.

therefore adv portanto.

therein adv (formal) (in that) aí, lá; ~ **lies...** é nisso que...; lá dentro, no interior; **2** (JUR) (annexed, included) incluso,-a.

thereupon adv (then) por isso; **2** logo a seguir; (as a result) em razão disso, sobre isso.

therewith adv com isso; após o que.

therewithal (formal) adv além disso.

therm n pequena caloria f.

thermal n (meteorology) corrente de ar quente ascendente; **~s** (UK, coll) roupa interior f térmica; ♦ adj (waters) termal m,f; **2** (clothing, energy) térmico,-a; ~ **baths** npl termas fpl; ~ **insulation** isolamento térmico; ~ **shock** choque térmico.

thermic adj térmico.

thermometer n termómetro (BR: -mô-) m; **Fahrenheit ~** termómetro Fahrenheit; **mercury ~** termómetro de mercúrio m.

Thermos® *npr* (= ~ **flask**) garrafatermo *f*, (*BR*) garrafa termo.

thermostat *n* termostato *m*.

thesaurus (*pl*: -**ri** *or* -**ruses**) *n* tesouro *m*; léxico *m*, dicionário *m* de sinónimos (*BR* -ô-).

these (*pl of* **this**).

thesis (*pl*: -**ses**) *n* tese *f*; **2** ensaio *m*; **3** tema *m*.

thespian *adj* (*of theatre*) tespiano,-a, dramático.

they *pron* eles *mpl*; elas *fpl*; ~ **don't want that** eles/elas não querem isso; **2** *refers to an indefinite antecedent*: **everyone did their best** todos fizeram o (seu) melhor; **there** ~ **go** lá vão eles; ~ **say that** eles dizem que … diz-se que …, dizem que …

they'd = they had, they would.

they'll = they shall, they will.

they're = they are.

they've = they have.

thick *adj* espesso,-a; com a espessura de; **how** ~ **is the wall?** qual é a espessura da parede; **2** grosso,-a; **a** ~ **coat** um casaco grosso; **3** (*quantity*) abundante; **4** (~ **with**) compato,-a; **5** (*fog*) cerrado; **6** (*coll*) (*stupid*) bronco,-a; **7** (*voice*) roufenho,-a; **8** (*atmosphere*) abafado,-a, sufocado,-a; IDIOM **in the** ~ **of it** no meio de; **through** ~ **and thin** para o que der e vier/contra a maré e os ventos; **to get a** ~ **ear** apanhar um sopapo; **to lay it on a bit** ~ *vt* exagerar (*praises, etc*); ~ **as thieves** amigos íntimos.

thicken *vt* engrossar; ♦ *vi* adensar-se; **2** complicar-se.

thickener *n* espessante *m*.

thicket *n* matagal *m*.

thick: ~**headed** *adj* bronco,-a; -**lipped** *adj* de lábios *mpl* grossos/carnudos.

thickly *adv* densamente.

thick: ~**ness** *n* grossura, espessura *f*; ~-**skinned** *adj* (*person*) insensível; **2** (*fruit*) de casca *f* grossa; ~**set** *adj* (*person*) forte; atarracado,-a.

thief (*pl*: **thieves**) *n* gatuno,-a, ladrão,-a; IDIOM **it takes a** ~ **to catch a** ~ para ladrão, ladrão e meio; **stop** ~! agarra que é ladrão!

thieve *vt/vi* roubar, furtar.

thievery (*pl*: -**ies**) *adj* roubo *m*; **2** gatunagem *f*.

thieving *n* roubo *m*, furto *m*; ♦ *adj* que rouba.

thigh *n* coxa *f*; ~**bone** *n* (ANAT) fémur *m*.

thimble *n* (*for sewing*) dedal *m*, **2** obturador,-a.

thimbleful (*coll*) tanto que cabe num dedal.

thin *adj* (*lean*) magro,-a; **to get** ~ emagrecer; **2** (*watery*) aguado,-a; **3** (*light*) tênue *m,f*, ligeiro,-a; **4** (*hair, grass*) escasso,-a, ralo *m*; **get** ~ **on top** está a ficar calvo,-a/a ficar careca (*fam*); **5** (*in width, depth*) fino,-a; **6** (*weak voice*) fina, fraca *f*; (*high-pitched*) agudo,-a; **7** pouco convincente; ~ **excuse** fraca *f* desculpa; (*air*) rarefeito; ♦ (-**nn-**) *vt* **to** ~ (**down**) diluir (*paint, etc*); **2** adelgaçar (*sauce*); ~**ning sth down/out** fazer mais fino,-a; **2** reduzir; **3** desbastar (*plants, hedge*); **4** (*crowd*) dispersar; ♦ *vi* (*fog, etc*) dispersar-se; IDIOM **as** ~ **as a rake** (*ironic*) magro como um espeto *m; **he disappeared into** ~ **air** ele *m* esfumou-se (*fam*); desapareceu sem deixar vestígio **the** ~ **end of the wedge** (*UK*) o início *m* de uma desgraça *f*; **to be** ~

on the ground (*very few*) contar-se como os dedos na mão; **you are walking on** ~ **ice** estás a arriscar muito.

thing *n* (*object, animal*) coisa *f*; **poor** ~! (*person, animal*) coitadinho,-a!; **2** (*matter*) assunto *m*, negócio *m*; **the best** ~ **would be to** … o melhor seria …; **it is just the** ~ é isso mesmo; **3** (*coll*) mania *f*; **4** (*coll*) moda *f*; **this is the latest** ~ esta é a última *f* moda; IDIOM **he was on to a good** ~ ele *m* estava numa situação *f* vantajosa; **I am doing my own** ~ faço o que me apetece; **what with one** ~ **and another** (*UK, coll*) com tanta coisa *f* que fazer.

thingamajig, thingummyjig, thingy, thingamabob (*UK*) *n* (*name not remembered of person/object*) o coiso *m* (*pop*); (*of person*) fulano,-a (*fam*).

things *npl* os acontecimentos *mpl*; **2** equipamento *m*; pertences *mpl*; **how are** ~? como vão as coisas *fpl*?; **need to pack my** ~ tenho de fazer as malas *fpl*; IDIOM **to be all** ~ **to all men/people** (tentar) agradar a gregos *mpl* e a troianos *mpl*.

think *n* pensamento *m*; **a quiet** ~ reflexão *f* ponderada; ~ **tank** *n* assessoria *f* técnica; ♦ (*pt, pp* **thought**) *vt* (*have in mind*) pensar; **she acted without** ~**ing** ela agiu sem pensar; **2** (*believe*) achar; **I** ~ **so/not** acho que sim/não; **to** ~ **about sth/sb** pensar em algo,-alguém; **3** (*imagine*) imaginar; supor; **to** ~ **of doing sth** decidir-se a fazer algo; pensar em algo; ♦ *vi* tencionar; **I thought I'd make you a surprise** pensei fazer-te uma surpresa *f*; **2** prever; contar com; **I didn't** ~ **I would see you again** eu não contava vê-la outra vez *f*; ♦ ~ **ahead** prevenir-se, antecipar-se; ~ **back** relembrar, recuar na memória; ~ **sth out/over** refle(c)tir em, bem em; ~ **sobre** (*decision*) ponderar; ~ **through** considerar todos os aspe(c)tos; ~ **up sth** (*excuse, etc*) inventar, engendrar; IDIOM **do as you** ~ **best** faz como quiseres; **I should hardly** ~ **so** parece-me pouco provável; **I wasn't** ~**ing** (*apologising*) eu não estava a pensar direito; **who would have thought it?** quem tal diria?

thinkable *adj* imaginável *m,f*; **2** admissível *m,f*.

thinker *n* pensador,-ora.

thinking *n* (*theory*) pensamento(s) *m(pl)*; **2** meditação *f*; reflexão; **to do some** ~ refle(c)tir; **3** (*opinion*) opinião *f*; ♦ *adj* pensativo,-a; **2** inteligente *m,f*; IDIOM **good** ~! (*coll*) boa ideia *f*!

thinly *adv* (*cut*) em fatias *fpl* finas, (*spread*) numa camada *f* fina, **2** (*barely*) pouco; (*forested*) escassamente.

thinner *n* dissolvente *m*; diluente *m*.

thin-skinned *adj* (*person*) susceptível.

third *n* (*fraction*) terço *m* (**of** de); **2** (*in sequence*) terceiro,-a; **3** (*date*) ~ **of July** três de julho; ♦ *adj num* terceiro,-a; ~-**class** *adj* (*UK: Univ*) nota C (*in the degree*); **2** de inferior qualidade; **3** que viaja em terceira classe; ~ **degree** interrogatório *m* exaustivo *mpl*; ~ **degree burns** queimaduras *fpl* de terceiro grau; ~ **party** (*JUR*) terceiros *mpl*; ~ **party insurance** *n* seguro *m* contra terceiros *mpl*; ~-**rate**

adj (pej) de terceira categoria, reles *m,f;* ~ **world countries** *npl* países *mpl* em desenvolvimento.

thirst *n* sede *f;* **to die of** ~ morrer à sede; **2** *(fig) (craving, yearning)* ânsia *f,* desejo *m* ardente (for de); ♦ *vi* ter sede **(for** de); *(fig)* ansiar **(for** de); IDIOM **to have a** ~ *(coll)* apetecer uma bebida *f.*

thirstily *adv* com sede; **2** cheio de sede.

thirsty *adj (person)* sedento,-a, com sede *f;* **2** *(for knowledge),* sequioso,-a.

thirteen *n* décima terceira *f* parte; ♦ *num* treze *m.*

thirteenth *num* décimo,-a terceiro,-a.

thirtieth *num* trigésimo,-a.

thirty *(pl:* **-ies)** *n num* trinta *m;* **she is in her thirties** ela anda na casa dos trinta, à volta dos trinta.

this *adj* este/esta *m,f;* ♦ *pron* este/esta *m,f; (neuter)* isto *m;* **what is** ~**?** o que é isto?; ♦ *adv (in this way)* assim; **it is like** ~ isto é assim; ~ **fat** tão gordo *m* como isto.

thistle *n* cardo *m.*

thither *adj (formal, LITER)* mais afastado,-a; **2** do outro *m* lado; **3** de lá; **hither and** ~ de lá para cá.

thong *n* correia *f,* tira *f* de couro.

thorax *n (pl:* **thoraces)** tórax *m.*

thorn *n (BOT) (prickle)* espinho *m; (tree)* espinheiro *m;* **2** *(fig)* tormento *m.*

thorniness *n* dificuldade *f;* **2** rispidez *f.*

thornless *adj* sem espinhos *mpl.*

thorny *adj* espinhoso,-a; **2** difícil *m,f;* **a** ~ **subject** um assunto *m* delicado, espinhoso.

thorough *adj* minucioso,-a; **2** profundo,-a; **3** autêntico,-a; ~**bred** *adj (horse)* de puro *m* sangue; ~**fare** *n* via *f,* pública; **'no** ~**fare'** 'passagem proibida' *f;* ~**going** *adj* completo,-a, absoluto,-a; minucioso,-a.

thoroughly *adv* minuciosamente, a fundo.

thoroughness *n* meticulosidade *f;* **2** profundidade *f;* **3** minúcia *f.*

thoroughpaced *adv (of a horse)* que mostra sua habilidade a cada passo.

those *(pl of that).*

though *conj (in spite of the fact that)* embora, se bem que; **he finished first** ~ **he began last** ele terminou em primeiro *m* lugar, embora tenha arrancado em último *m;* ♦ *adv* no entanto.

thought *(pt, pp of* **think)** *n* pensamento *m;* ~ **transference** transmissão *f* de pensamentos; **2** *(notion)* conceito *m;* **at the** ~ **of** perante a ideia de; **3** *(act of thinking)* reflexão; **want of** ~ irreflexão; **4** atenção, consideração; **5 I keep my** ~**s to myself** sou uma pessoa *f* reservada; **6** *(intention)* propósito *m;* **it's the** ~ **that counts** o que conta é a intenção *f;* IDIOM **don't give it another** ~ *(coll)* deixa lá isso; **I won't give it a second** ~ nem vou pensar mais nisso; **to have second** ~**s** ter dúvidas *fpl.*

thoughtful *adj* pensativo,-a; *(considerate)* atencioso,-a.

thoughtfully *adv* pensativamente; **2** amavelmente.

thoughtless *adj* descuidado,-a, desatento,-a.

thoughtlessly *adv* irrefle(c)tidamente.

thousand *num* mil *m;* **two** ~ dois *mpl* mil; ~**s (of)** milhares *mpl* (de).

thousandth *adj (fraction)* milésimo,-a; **T~ and One Nights** *npr* as Mil e uma Noites.

thrash *(pl:* **-es)** *n* tareia *f;* **2** *(cool) (party)* festança *f (fam);* ♦ *vt (to beat)* dar uma sova em, chicotear; **2** *(in sleep, pain)* contorcer-se; **to** ~ **(sth) out** debater, discutir a fundo *(assunto);* **2** *(swimming)* agitar (as pernas).

thrashing *n (trouncing)* sova *f,* tareia *f;* **a sound** ~ uma boa sova; **2** *(SPORT)* derrota *f.*

thread *n* fio *m,* linha *f;* **sewing** ~ linha *f* de coser; **the** ~ **of life** o fio *m* da vida; **2** *(of screw)* rosca *f,* filete *m;* **3** *(ideas, etc.) (sequence)* fio *m* da meada; **to pick up the** ~ **of** retomar; ♦ *vt (needle)* enfiar; **to** ~ **a needle** enfiar uma agulha *f;* **2** avançar com dificuldade *f;* **to** ~ **one's way through a crowd** abrir caminho *m* através da multidão *f;* **3** roscar; ♦ *vi* serpear; IDIOM **to hang by a** ~ estar suspenso *m* por um fio *m;* **to pick up the** ~**(s) of** recomeçar.

threadbare *adj* surrado,-a, puído,-a; **a** ~ **suit** um fato *m* coçado; **2** gasto,-a; **a** ~ **joke** uma piada *f* batida *(fam).*

threaded *adj* de rosca *f;* ~ **end** ponta *f* roscada.

thready *adj* semelhante a um fio *m;* **2** fibroso,-a; **3** *(voice)* esganiçada *f.*

threat *n* ameaça *f;* **to carry out a** ~ cumprir uma ameaça; **2** ameaço *m;* **3** prenúncio *m.*

threaten *vi* avisar; **2** *(endanger)* pôr em perigo *m;* **3** ameaçar; **it** ~**s to rain** ameaça chuva *f;* ♦ *vt* **to** ~ **sb with sth/to do sth** ameaçar alguém com algo/ de fazer algo.

threatened *adj* sob ameaça *f* **(with** de).

threatening *adj* ameaçador,-ora.

three *n num* três; **the** ~ **Rs** ler, escrever e contar; ♦ *adj* a três; ~**-cornered fight** luta *f* a três; ~**-dimensional** *adj* tridimensional *m,f;* **in** ~**-D** *n* em três *fpl* dimensões, dimensionalmente; ~**-fold** *adj* triplo *m;* ♦ *adv* três vezes *fpl* mais; **to increase** ~**fold** triplicar; ~**-legged** *adj* com três *fpl* pernas; ~**-phase** *adj* trifásico,-a; ~**-piece** *n* com três *fpl* peças; ~**-piece suit** *n* fato *m* de 3 peças, *(BR)* terno *m* (3 peças); ~**-piece suite** *(UK)* conjunto *m* de sofá *m* e duas poltronas *fpl;* ~**-ply** *adj (wool)* com três *mpl* fios; **2** *(wood)* contraplacado *m* triplo; *(BR)* compensado *m;* ~**-quarters** *npl* três quartos; ~**-some** *n* a(c)tividade *f* para três *fpl* pessoas; **2** *(sex)* 'ménage à trois'; ~**-way** *adj (road)* com três *fpl* vias; ~**-wheeler** *n (car)* veículo *m* de três *fpl* rodas, **2** triciclo *m.*

thresh *vt/vi (AGR) (maize)* debulhar; *(corn)* malha *f;* ~**ing floor** *n* eira *f;* ~**ing machine** *n* debulhadora.

threshold *n* limiar *m;* **2** *(of houses)* soleira *f;* **3** *(fig)* princípio *m;* ~ **of consciousness** *(PSYC)* limiar *m* da consciência; ~ **agreement** *n* indexação *f* salarial.

threw *(pt of* **throw).**

thrift *n* economia *f;* poupança *f;* **2** *(BOT)* relva-do-olimpo; ~ **shop** *(US) n* loja de beneficiência de artigos usados.

thrifty (-ier, -iest) *adj* económico,-a *(BR:* -nô-).

thrill *n (sudden feeling of joy)* emoção *f* forte de prazer; frémito *m* de alegria; excitação *f;* **2** experiência *f* estimulante; ◆ *vt* vibrar; comover, excitar *(person)*; ◆ *vi*: **to ~ to sth** emocionar-se, entusiasmar-se com algo.

thrilled *adj* (**with sth/to do sth**) encantado,-a (com algo/por fazer algo); **I am ~ to bits!** estou muito entusiasmado,-a.

thriller *n* novela *f*, filme *m* de suspense.

thrilling *adj (story, match, victory)* emocionante *m,f*; empolgante *m,f*; **2** vibrante *m,f*; **3** comovedor,-a.

thrillingly *adv* de modo *m* sensacional.

thrips *n (insect)* tripes.

thrive *(pt* **thrived** *or* **throve**, *pp* **thrived** *or* **thriven)** *vi (person, animal)* crescer, desenvolver-se; **2** *(plant)* medrar, florescer, dar-se bem em; **3** *(fig) (business, people)* prosperar.

thriving *adj (business, city etc)* florescente *m,f*, próspero,-a.

thrivingly *adv* com êxito.

throat *n* garganta *f*; **to have a sore ~** estar com dor *f* de garganta; **2** goela *f (col)*, gasganete *m (col)*; **to force sth down sb's ~** empurrar algo goela abaixo de alguém; **to seize sb by the ~** apertar o gasganete a alguém; **3** *(of bottle)* gargalo *m*; **4** *(front of neck)* pescoço *m*; **to clear one's ~** pigarrear, tossir; IDIOM **they are at each other's ~s** estar/andar engalfinhados *mpl (fam)*; **to jump down sb's ~** responder/discordar de forma agressiva.

throaty *adj (huskyvoice)* gutural *m,f*; roufenho,-a; **2** *(with sore throat)* rouco,-a.

throb *n (of heart)* palpitação *f*; **2** *(of head)* latejo *m* (BR) latejamento *m*; *(of pulse)* pulsação *f*, batimento *m*; *(of engine, machine, drums)* vibração *f*; a *f*; **heart-~** *n (famous and handsome man)* ídolo *m*, galã *m*; ◆ **(-bb-)** *vi* bater, palpitar (**with** de); **2 his head was ~bing** a cabeça *f* dele *m* estava a latejar.

throbbing *n* pulsação *f*, batimento *m*; **2** *(of pain)* dor *f* aguda, pontada *f*; *(of motor)* vibração *f*; ◆ *adj* palpitante *m,f*; **~ with activity** palpitante de a(c) tividade *f*; **2** *(pain)* latejante *m,f*; **3** *(sound, music)* lancinante *m,f*.

throes *npl* dores *fpl* agudas; **2** *(fig)* angústia *f*; **death ~** agonia *f* da morte; **in the ~ of** no meio *m* de, a braços com; **in the ~ of moving** no meio das mudanças.

thrombosis *(pl:* **-boses)** *n* trombose *f*, acidente, vascular cerebral, AVC.

throne *n* trono *m*; **to lose one's ~** perder o trono; **2** *(fig)* autoridade *f* real; **~s** *(REL)* tronos *mpl*; ◆ *vt* entronizar.

throned *adj* no trono; **2** sentado,-a no trono.

throneless *adj* destronado,-a.

throng *n* multidão *f*, aglomeração *f*; **a ~ of onlookers** uma chusma *f* de curiosos; **2** afluência *f*; ◆ *adj* de grande movimento *m*; ◆ *vt/vi* apinhar(-se); aglomerar-se; **they ~ed round me** apinharam-se à minha volta *f*.

throttle *n (AUT)* válvula *f* reguladora; **~ lever** acelerador *m*; **air ~** *(device)* obturador *m* do ar; ◆ *vt* estrangular (alguém); **2** *(fig)* abafar, reprimir; **to ~ freedom** sufocar a liberdade *f*; **3** diminuir a potência *f* de; ◆ **~ back/down** *vt (AUT)* pôr em

marcha *f* lenta; IDIOM **at (on) half, full ~** a meio *m*, a todo o gás *m*, a toda a velocidade.

throttling *n* estrangulamento *m*.

through *adj* dire(c)to,-a; **~ ticket** bilhete *m* dire(c)to; **2** *(coll) (finished with)* terminado,-a; **are you ~ with that?** já acabou isso?; **I'm ~ with you** *(coll)* já não tenho nada a ver contigo; ◆ *prep* por, através de; **to walk ~ the streets** passear pelas ruas *fpl*; **to see ~ a telescope** ver por um telescópio *m*; **2** *(time)* durante; **3** *(by means of)* por meio de, por intermédio de; **you can send it ~ my friend** pode mandar pelo meu amigo; **4** *(owing to)* devido a; **~ illness** faltar devido a doença *f*; ◆ *adv* completamente, até ao fim *m*; o outro lado; **the water went right ~** a água passou para o outro lado; **I am soaked ~** estou completamente encharcada; ◆ **~ and ~** *adv* completamente; **to know sb ~ and ~** conhecer alguém muito bem; **to put sb ~ a grill** submeter alguém a um interrogatório; IDIOM 'no ~ way' 'rua sem saída' *f*; **you are ~** *(tel)* está em linha; **to have been ~ a lot** ter passado muito na vida.

throughout *prep (place)* por todas as partes *fpl*; *(time)* durante todo,-a; através de; **~ the ages** através dos tempos; **~ my life** durante toda a minha vida; ◆ *adv (place)* por toda a parte *f*; **2** completamente.

throughput *n* produtividade *f*, rendimento *m*; *(COMP)* thoroughput.

throve *(Vd:* **thrive**).

throw *n (pitch)* arremesso *m*, tiro *m*; **2** *(SPORT)* lançamento *m*, lanço *m*; **a lucky ~ of the dice** um lanço feliz de dados; **within a stone's ~** *(distance)* muito perto; ◆ *(pt* **threw**, *pp* **thrown)** *vt* atirar; **he threw his coat onto the bed** ele atirou o casaco para cima da cama; arremessar *(stone, etc)*; **2** *(SPORT)* lançar; **3 to ~ an opponent** derrubar um adversário *m*; **4 the horse threw the rider** o cavalo derrubou o cavaleiro; **5** *(fig)* confundir, desconcertar; **the last question in the exam threw me** a última pergunta no exame confundiu-me; **6** *(doubt)* lançar; ◆ **~ about/around** *vt* afastar, rejeitar; **2** *(arms)* agitar; **to ~ her money around** esbanjar dinheiro; ◆ **~ aside** *vt* pôr de lado; **2** rejeitar; ◆ *vt* **to ~ away** deitar fora, jogar fora, descartar; ◆ *vt (revert to an earlier time)* retroceder a; **2** lançar, atirar (cabeça) para trás; **~ back on** *vt* obrigar (alguém) a recorrer a (algo); ◆ **~ in** *vt* incluir (como brinde); **2** *(SPORT)* pôr em jogo *m*; **to ~ in one's hand** desistir; **~ into** *vt* empregar em (**oneself into sth**), dedicar-se totalmente; ◆ **to ~ off** *vt* desfazer-se de; **to ~sb off balance** deixar alguém desorientado *m*; ◆ **~ out** *vt (force to leave)* expulsar; **2** despir à pressa; **3** rejeitar; ◆ **to ~ up** *vi* vomitar; IDIOM **she threw a hell of a party** ela *f* deu uma festa *f* dos diabos *mpl (col)*; **to ~ a fit** *(fig)* encolerizar-se; **to ~ a spanner in the works** sabotar as coisas *fpl*; **to ~ cold water on** *(one's enthusiasm)* atirar um balde de água fria em/sobre; **to ~ caution to the wind(s)** mandar a prudência *f* às urtigas *fpl*; **to ~**

oneself at sb *(coll) (attract attention)* atirar-se a alguém; **to ~ in one's towel** desistir, atirar a toalha ao chão.

throwaway *adj* descartável *m,f*.

throwback *n* retrocesso.

thrown *(pp of* throw*)*.

thru *(US)* = **through**.

thrush *(pl:* -es*) n (bird)* tordo *m*; **2** *(MED) (oral)* aftas *fpl*; *(fam)* sapinhos *mpl*; **3** *(MED)* infeção vaginal, candidíase *f*.

thrust *n* impulso *m*; **2** *(TECH)* empuxo *m*; **3** empurrão *m*, golpe *m*; **home ~** golpe *m* certeiro; **to give a ~ with one's foot** empurrar com o pé *m*; **4** *(with dagger)* punhalada *f*; **5** *(of argument, essay)* crítica *f*, ataque dirigido,-a (**at** contra); ◆ *(pt, pp* **thrust***) vt* empurrar; **2** *(push in)* enfiar, meter; **he ~ the money into his pocket** ele enfiou decididamente o dinheiro *m* no bolso *m*; **3** atirar; **4** abrir à força *f*; **to ~ one's way** abrir caminho *m* à força; ◆ *vi* estender-se, espalhar-se; **~ aside** *vt* empurrar para o lado *m*; **2** pôr de parte; ◆ **~ on/upon** *vt* impor a; **2** empurrar para *(coll)*.

thrusting *n (push)* empurrão *m*; **2** *(with stick)* estocada *f*; ◆ *adj* sem escrúpulos *mpl*; **2** saliente *m,f*.

thud *n* baque *m*, som *m* surdo; **to fall with a ~** cair com um baque *m*; ◆ (-**dd**-) *vi* cair, bater com um baque.

thug *n (criminal)* criminoso,-a; *(hooligan)* rufia *m,f*; facínora *m,f*.

thumb *n (ANAT)* polegar *m*; *(coll)* dedo *m*; **under sb's ~** debaixo da influência de/do poder de alguém; **the ~s down** *(coll)* desaprovação *f*; **~s up** aprovação, dar luz verde a; ◆ *vt* (= **~ through**) *vt (book)* folhear; **2 to ~ a lift** pedir boleia *f*, *(BR)* pedir carona *f*; **3** manusear com os dedos *mpl*; IDIOM **she ~s the piano** ela toca mal/matraqueia o piano; **to tweedle one's ~s** estar ocioso,-a; **to be all fingers and ~s** ser desastrado,-a.

thumb index *n* índice alfabético com reentrâncias.

thumbless *adj* sem polegar *m*.

thumbling *n (coll)* anãozinho,-a.

thumbnail *n* unha *f* do polegar *m*; **2** miniatura *f* de imagem *f*; ◆ *adj* curto,-a; **~ sketch** *n* descrição *f* muito concisa *f*.

thumbprint *n* impressão digital *f* do polegar.

thumbtack *n (US)* percevejo *m* (para fixar).

thump *n* murro *m*, pancada *f*; **2** *(sound)* baque *m*; ◆ *vt* dar um murro em *(table)*; **2 ~ on** martelar; ◆ *vi: (heart)* bater fortemente; *(head)* latejar; **to ~ upstairs** subir a escada a marchar, marchar lá para cima.

thumping *n* tareia *f*; *(of drums)* batida; ◆ *adj (big, great)* enorme *m,f*; *(loud)* alto,-a.

thunder *n* trovão *m*; **2** trovoada *f*; **there is ~ in the air** está um ar de trovoada; **3** *(fig) (noise)* estrondo *m*; **~ of applause** ovação *f* estrondosa; ◆ *vi* trovejar; *(cannon)* ribombar, atroar; ◆ *(voice)* berrar **3 to ~ past** passar como um raio *m*; IDIOM **to steal sb's ~** *(detract)* roubar as atenções *fpl* a outro; **with a face like ~** com cara *f* de poucos *mpl* amigos.

thunderbolt *n (METEOR)* raio *m*; **2** *(fig)* choque *m*.

thunderclap *n* ribombar *m* do trovão; **2** *(fig)* bomba *f*.

thundercloud *n* nuvem *f* de trovoada; **2** *(fig) (problem, threat)* nuvem *f* negra.

thundering *adj* trovejante *m,f*; **2** *(coll) (huge)* excessivo,-a, tremendo,-a; **a ~ idiot** um grandíssimo idiota *(fam)*.

thunderous *adj (applause, etc)* estrondoso,-a; **2** *(noise)* ensurdecedor,-ora, atroador,-ora; **3** *(look)* furioso,-a, fulminante *m,f*.

thunderstorm *n* temporal (com trovoada).

thunderstruck *adj* estupefa(c)to,-a.

thundery *adj* tempestuoso,-a; *(sky, atmosphere)* carregado,-a.

Thursday *n* quinta-feira *f*; **on ~s** às quintas-feiras.

thus *adv* assim, desta *f* maneira; portanto, por conseguinte; **~ far** até aqui.

thwack *n (blow)* paulada *f*; **2** pancada *f* forte; ◆ *exc (sound of beating)* zás; ◆ *vt* espancar; **2** dar pauladas *fpl* em.

thwart *vt* frustrar, contrariar; **2** *(plan, decision)* opor-se a.

thwarted *pp adj (person, plan)* contrariado,-a.

thyme *n (BOT)* tomilho *m*.

thyroid *n (ANAT) (gland)* tiróide *f*.

ti *(MUS) (note)* si *m*.

tiara *n* tiara *f*, diadema *m*.

Tibet *npr* Tibete; **in ~** no Tibete.

Tibetan *n adj* tibetano,-a.

tibia *n (ANAT) (shin bone)* tíbia *f*.

tic *n* tic *m*, tique *m*.

tick *n (of clock)* tiquetaque *m*; **2** sinal *m (de visto)*; marca *f*; **3** *(ZOOL)* carraça *f*, carrapato *m*; **4 in a ~** num instante; ◆ *vt* marcar; **to ~ away/by** *vt (watch)* marcar o tempo *m*; ◆ *vi (time)* passar; ◆ **to ~ off** *vt* assinalar, marcar; **2** *(UK)* repreender; **3** *(US)* chatear *(fam)*; ◆ **to ~ over** *vi (UK) (engine)* funcionar em marcha lenta; **2** *(fig) (business)* trabalhar no mínimo; IDIOM *(fig)* **what ticks me is ...** o que me motiva é ....

ticker *n (fig, fam)* heart; *n (coll)* relógio *m*; **~ tape** *n* fita *m* de teleimpressor; **~ parade** desfile com confeti e serpentinas.

ticket *n (gen)* bilhete *m*; **~ holder** *(passenger)* portador,-ora do bilhete *m*; **~ inspector (collector)** *n (bus, train)* revisor,-ora; **lottery ~** bilhete *m* de lotaria; **~ machine** *n* máquina *f* de vender bilhetes; **~ office** *n* bilheteira *f*, *(BR)* bilheteria *f*; **return ~** bilhete de ida e volta; *(ship, air)* passagem *f*; **2** *(AUT) (fine on parking)* multa *f*; **3** etiqueta *f (on goods)*; **4** *(for library)* cartão *m*; **5** *(cloakroom, bank, left-luggage)* ficha *f*, senha *f*, chapa *f*; ◆ *vt* vender bilhetes *mpl*; **2** etiquetar; **3** *(road)* multar.

ticketing *n* etiquetagem *f*.

ticking *n (clock)* tiquetaque *m*; **2** marcação com um sinal; **3** tecido forte para colchões.

tickle *n* cócegas *fpl*; ◆ *vt* fazer cócegas em; **2** *(fig) (amuse)* divertir; **she was ~d at the ideia** essa ideia *f* divertiu-a; **3** *(excite)* excitar *(senses)*; **4** *(blanket, etc)* picar; ◆ *vi* sentir cócegas; IDIOM

to be ~d pink estar excitado, divertido,-a; **to be ~d to death at sth** rebolar-se de riso *m* com alguma *f* coisa; **to ~ sb's vanity** lisonjear a vaidade *f* de alguém.

tickling *n* cócegas *fpl*.

ticklish *adj* coceguento,-a; ter cócegas; **2** *(fig) (tricky situation)* delicado,-a.

tick-over *n* matcha *f* em vazio.

ticktack *m (clock)* tiquetaque *m*.

tick-tack-toe *(US) n* jogo *m* do galo ou da velha.

tidal *adj* de maré *f*; **2** *(fig)* inconstante *m,f*; **~ energy power** energia *f* das marés *fpl*; **~ wave** *n* maremoto *m*, macaréu *m*.

tiddly (-ier, -iest) *adj (fam) (tipsy)* grogue, alegre *m,f*; IDIOM com um grão na asa.

tiddlywinks *n* jogo *m* da pulga.

tide *n* maré *f*; **2** *(fig) (trend)* tendência; **3** *(of events)* marcha *f*, curso *m*; **4** *(fig) (of emotion)* vaga *f*; **ebb/low ~** maré *f* vazante; **~ in/full ~** maré cheia; **rising ~** enchente *f*; ♦ *vt* transportar, levar; **2** seguir com a maré *f*; **to ~ sb over** *(difficulty)* vencer; desenrascar(-se) *(fam)*; IDIOM **to go/ swim against the ~** remar contra a maré; **the ~ has turned** a sorte mudou.

tidily *adv* cuidadosamente; *(dress)* impecavelmente.

tidiness *n (order)* arranjo *m*; *(of appearance)* asseio *m*.

tidings *npl* notícias *fpl*; **good ~!** boas notícias!

tidy *(pl: -ies) n* cestinho para arrumar coisas; **sink ~** tipo de escoador sobre o ralo do lava-louças para impedir detritos; **street ~** *n* recipiente *m* para papéis *mpl*; ♦ *adj (gen)* arrumado,-a; **2** metódico,- a; **4** *(coll)* bastante *m,f*, substancial *m,f*; **that is a ~ sum of money** essa é uma boa soma *f* de dinheiro *m*; **~ costumers** bons/boas *mpl/fpl* fregueses,-as; ♦ *vt* **(= to ~ up)** pôr em ordem, arrumar; ♦ *vi* pôr tudo em ordem; **~ o.s.** arranjar-se; **~ away** *vt* guardar; **to ~ out/up** *vi* fazer arrumações *fpl*.

tie *n (string, etc.)* fita *f*, corda *f*; **2** *(= neck~)* gravata *f*; **~ clip** travessão *m* de gravata; **~ tack/tac** *(US)*, **~pin** *(UK)* alfinete *m* de gravata; **3** *(fig) (link)* vínculo *m*, laço *m*; **family ~s** laços *mpl* de família; **4** *(SPORT)* empate *m*; **~ break** *n* desempate *m*; ♦ *vt (rope, string, etc.)* amarrar, atar, prender; **2** **to ~ in a bow** dar um laço *m*; **to ~ a knot in sth** dar um nó *m* em algo; **3** *(arrangements)* concluir; **4** *(SPORT)* empatar; **5** *(fig) (restricted)* estar limit-ado,-a a algo; ♦ **~ back** *vt (hair)* amarrar (para trás); prender; ♦ *vi (draw)* empatar (com alguém); ♦ **to ~ down** *vt* atar; **2** *(fig)* fazer (alguém) comp-rometer-se; **to ~ sb down to a contract** prender alguém a um contrato *m*; **3** **to ~ in with sth** *vt* estar de acordo com sth; ligar-se a; ♦ **to ~-in** *n (link)* relação *f*; **2** *(marketing, sales)* lote *m*; **3** *(LITER)* adaptação *f*; IDIOM **to be ~d to sb's apron strings** *(mother, woman)* andar agarrado,- às saias *fpl* de alguém; **to ~ oneself (up) in knots** *(coll)* meter os pés *mpl* pelas mãos *fpl*; **to ~ the knot** *(coll)* casar-se.

tier *n (of seats, shelves)* fileira *f*; **2** *(of cake)* camada *f*; **in ~s** em camadas *fpl*; **3** prateleira *f*; **4** *(in a amphitheatre)* fila *f*; ♦ *vt* empilhar; **2** dispor em camadas.

tie up *vt (showstring, bow)* atar; *(person, animal)* prender, amarrar; **2** *(US) (traffic)* bloquear; **3** *(FIN)* congelar, imobilizar capital; IDIOM **to ~ loose ends** acertar os últimos detalhes, esclarecer algo; **to be ~d up** *(busy)* estar ocupado,-a.

tiff *n* arrufo *m*, pequena *f* rixa, desavença *f*, zanga *f*.

tiger *n (ZOOL)* tigre *m*; **2** *(fig) (cruel person)* tigre *m*; **3** *(BOT)* **~ lily** lírio *m* tigrino; **paper ~** tigre *m* de papel.

tigerish *adj* atigrado,-a; **2** semelhante ao tigre; **3** feroz *m,f*.

tight *adj (taut)* esticado,-a; *(grip)* firme *m,f*; **2** *(money, time)* escasso,-a; *(coll) (person)* sovina *m, f*; **3** *(clothes)* justo,-a; **4** *(too small)* apertado,-a; **the shoes are ~ on me** os sapatos estão-me aper-tados; **~ knot** *(firmly)* nó *m* apertado; *(budget, programme)* apertado,-a, exigente *m,f*; **5** *(strict)* **~ security** segurança *f* apertada; **6** *(tense)* angu-stiado,-a, nervoso,-a *(person)*; **7** *(competition)* renhido,-a; ♦ **hold on ~!** segure-se bem!; **sleep ~ !** durma bem! IDIOM **to be in a ~ spot** estar numa situação *f* difícil; **to keep a ~ rein on** manter rédea *f* curta em; **to run/keep a ~ ship** controlar de forma *f* rigorosa e eficiente; **to sit ~** esperar por melhor altura; permancer firme.

tighten *vt,vi* apertar(-se); **2** esticar; **3** **to ~ up** *(security)* reforçar.

tight: ~ fitting *adj (clothes)* justo,-a; **~fisted** *adj* avar-ento-a; forreta; *(BR)* pão-duro; **~-knit** *adj (family)* unido,-a; integrado,-a; **~-lipped** *adj* silencioso,-a ; **2** *(sulky)* carrancudo,-a.

tightly *adv* apertadamente; com força.

tight: ~ness *n* aperto *m*; **2** *(strictness)* rigor *m*; **~rope** *n* corda *f* para acrobatas; **to walk on the tight-rope** dançar na corda bamba.

tights *n (UK)* collants; meia-calça *f*; **a pair of ~** uns collants.

tigress *n* fêmea *f* do tigre; *(BR)* tigresa *f*.

tile *n (on roof)* telha *f*; **2** *(on floor)* ladrilho *m*; **3** azulejo *m*; ♦ *vt* ladrilhar; **2** cobrir com telhas *fpl*; IDIOM *(UK) (coll)* **a night on the ~s** andar na farra.

tiled *adj (on roof)* coberto,-a de telhas; **2** *(on floor)* ladrilhado,-a; **3** *(on wall)* azulejado,-a.

tiler *n* ladrilhador.

tiling *n* cobertura de mosaicos/azulejos.

till *n* caixa *f* (registradora); ♦ *prep (time, limit, = until)* até; **from morning ~ night** de manhã *f* à noite; **to laugh ~ one cries** rir até às lágrimas; ♦ *conj* até que; **she won't come ~ I arrive** ela não vem até que eu chegue; ♦ *vt (land)* cultivar; IDIOM **he will be caught with his hand in the ~** *(coll)* ele vai ser apanhado com a boca *f* na botija *(fig)*.

tiller *n (NAUT)* cana *f* do leme.

tilt *n* inclinação *f*; **at a ~** a um ângulo; **2** *(fig)* ataque *m*; **3** *(in jousting, contest)* justa *f*; torneio *m*; **4** *(awning)* toldo *m*; ♦ *vi/vt* inclinar(-se); IDIOM **(at) full ~** a toda a velocidade *f*, em cheio.

timber *n (wood)* madeira *f* (para a construção); **to fell ~** cortar madeira; **~work** *n* madeiramento *m*.

time *n (spell)* tempo *m*, vagar *m*; **I don't have any ~ now** agora não tenho vagar; **to have a hard ~** ter dificuldade; **hard ~s** tempos *mpl* difíceis; *(during)* **in the course of ~** com o decorrer do tempo; **2** *(moment)* momento *m*, altura; **at that ~ I was** nessa altura eu era; **the right ~** o momento *m* certo; **3** *(by clock)* **on ~** na hora; **to arrive on ~** chegar a tempo; **have you got the ~?** tem horas?; **to be paid on ~** ser pago à hora; **to be behind ~** estar atrasado,-a; **ahead of ~** cedo; adiantado,-a; **4** *(period of days, etc)* **in a month's ~** daqui a um mês; **a long ~ ago** há muito tempo; **in no ~ at all** num instante; **in your own ~** no seu ritmo; **to take ~** levar tempo; **take ~ to do sth** tirar tempo para fazer algo; **5** *(period, era)* época *f*; **before my ~** antes de eu nascer; **6** *(occasion)* vez *f*; **once upon a ~** era uma vez; **at ~s** às vezes; **7** *(MUS)* compasso *m*; **8 ~s** *(multiplication)* vezes; **four ~ four comes to sixteen** quatro vezes quatro são dezasseis; **~ bomb** *n (fig)* bomba-relógio *f*; **~-book** *n* livro *m* de ponto; **~ consuming** *adj* moroso,-a; **~d** *(race)* cronometrado; **2** oportuno; **~keeping** *n* pontualidade *f*; **~ lag** *n* intervalo; **~less** *adj* sem fim *m*; **~ limit** *n* prazo *m* limite; **~ly** *adj* oportuno,-a; **~ off** *n* tempo *m* livre/de folga *f*; **~ out** *(pl:* **times-out)** *(US) (SPORT)* intervalo *m*; **~r** *n (in kitchen)* relógio *m* programador; **~-race** *n* corrida *f* contra-relógio; **~-saver/saving** *adj* que economiza/poupa; **~ server** *adj* oportunista *m,f*; ♦ *vt (schedule)* calcular, medir o tempo *m* de; **2** *(SPORT)* cronometrar; **3** *(watch, engine)* acertar; **4** *(MUS)* acertar no compasso *m*; IDIOM **for the ~ being** por enquanto; **from ~ to ~** de vez em quando; **it's about ~!** já era tempo!; **~ is money** o tempo é dinheiro *m*; **she is near her ~** *(pregnancy)* ela *f* está a chegar ao fim *m* do tempo; **to do ~** *(coll)* cumprir pena *f* de prisão *f*; **to have a good ~** divertir-se, distrair-se; **to keep ~** dançar a compasso *m*; **your ~ has come** chegou a tua hora *f*.

timetable *n* horário *m*.

time zone *n* fuso *m* horário.

timid *adj* tímido,-a; medroso,-a; **2** *(shy)* acanhado,-a.

timidity *n* timidez *f*; acanhamento *m*.

timing *n (of actor, musician)* timing *m*; **2** *(SPORT)* cronometragem *f*; **3** escolha *f* do momento; senso *m* de oportunidade; **good ~** bom sentido *m* de oportunidade; **4** afinação *f*; **~ of gear** afinação *f* da engrenagem; **5** sincronização *f*.

timpani *npl (MUS)* timbales *m*.

tin *n (CHEM)* estanho *m*; **2** *(can)* lata (de conserva); *(of paint)* lata *f*; *(for biscuits, etc)* caixa *f*; **~-opener** *n* abre-latas *m*, (BR) abridor *m* de latas; **3** *(for baking)* fôrma, *f*, tabuleiro *m*, assadeira *f*; **~ foil** *n* papel *m* de alumínio; (= **~plate**) folha-de-flandres *f*.

tinder *n (to light the fire in the earth)* isca *f*, mecha *f*.

ting *n* tinido *m*; ♦ *vt* tinir.

tinge *n (of colour)* matiz *m*; **2** *(touch)* toque *m*; **she feels a ~ of guilt** ela *f* sente uma ponta *f* de culpa; ♦ *vt* colorir; **~d with** tingido,-a de.

tingle, tingling *n (physical)* formigueiro *m*; *(psychological)* sensação *f* de formigueiro, arrepio *m*; *(of joy, expectation)* vibração, de alegria; *(from electricty)* choque *m*; ♦ *vt* doer; arder; *(com o frio)* entorpecer.

tinker *n* funileiro,-a; picheleiro,-a; **2** *(pej) (gipsy)* cigano,-a; **3** *(child) (rascal)* maroto,-a; diabinho,-a; ♦ *vi (fiddle)* mexer **(with** em); IDIOM **I don't care a ~'s cuss/damn** *(slang)* estou-me nas tintas *fpl*.

tinkle *n (metalic sound)* tinido *m*; **2** *(UK, coll) (phone call)* um telefonema *m*; ♦ *vt* fazer tilintar; ♦ *vi* tilintar, tinir; IDIOM **I will give you a ~** eu depois ligo-te *(BR)* eu depois bato um fio *m* para você.

tinned *adj (UK)* enlatado,-a, em conserva *f*.

tinnitus *n (MED)* tinite, zumbido *m* nos ouvidas.

tinsel *n* ouropel *m*; tiras de papel brithante.

tint *n* matiz *m*; **2** *(for hair)* tonalidade *f*, tom *m*; ♦ *vt* tingir, colorir; **2** dar tonalidade a; **3** *(hair)* pintar.

tiny *adj* pequenino, diminuto.

tip *n* ponta *f*; **2** *(horse race)* informação; **3** *(gratuity)* gorjeta *f*; **4** *(UK) (for rubbish)* depósito *m*; *(BR)* lixão *m*; **5** *(coll)* pocilga *f (fam)*; **6** *(advice)* dica *f*; ♦ **(-pp-)** *vt/vi (tilt)* inclinar; **to ~ the balance** fazer pender a balança; **2** *(to waiter)* dar uma gorjeta; *(UK) (predict)* **he is ~ped to get the job** prevêem que ele obtenha o emprego; *(spill)* derramar; (= **to ~ down**) chover a potes; **to ~ sb off** *vt* dar a alguém informação secreta, alertar; **to ~ out** esvaziar; (= **to ~ over**) virar, emborcar; *(UK) (rubbish)* despejar; IDIOM **it's on the ~ of my tongue** está na ponta *f* da língua; **that ~ped the scales** isso *m* foi decisivo *m*; **the ~ of the iceberg** a ponta do icebergue.

tip-off *n* informação *f* secreta, denúncia *f*.

tipped *adj (cigarette)* cigarro *m* com filtro; **2** *(nose) adj* nariz *m* arrebitado.

tipsy *adj* embriagado,-a, ébrio,-a; *(fig)* tocado,-a *(fam)*; *(fig)* alto,-a; **~ cake** *(CULIN)* bolo *m* borrachão.

tiptoe *n:* **on ~** na ponta *f* dos pés.

tiptop *adj:* **in ~ condition** em perfeitas *fpl* condições; óptimo (ótimo),-a).

tire *(UK)* **tyre** *(US) n (AUTO)* pneu *m*; ♦ *vt* cansar; **2** aborrecer; ♦ *vi (get tired)* cansar-se; **2 to get ~ of sth** fartar-se de; **to ~ out** *vt* esgotar (alguém).

tired *adj* cansaço *m*, fadiga *f*; **to be ~** estar exausto,-a; **2** *(sleepy)* com sono; **to be ~ of** estar farto,-a de; *(fam)* chateado,-a de/com; **3** *(hackneyed)* vulgarizado,-a; *(worn out) (machine, clothes)* usado,-a; gasto,-a.

tiredness *n* cansaço *m*, fadiga.

tireless *adj* incansável *m,f*.

tiresome *adj* enfadonho,-a, chato,-a.

tiring *adj* cansativo,-a, fatigante *m,f*.

tiro (tyro) *n* principiante *m,f*.

tissue *n (ANAT, BOT)* tecido *m*; **2** *(paper)* papel *m* de seda; **3** *(handkerchief)* lenço *m* de papel; IDIOM **a ~ of lies** *(fig)* uma teia/série de mentiras.

tit *n (ZOOL)* melharuco, chapim *m*; **2** *(slang)* mama *f*, teta *(cal)*.

titanium *n* titânio *m*.

titbit *(UK)* **tidbid** *(US) n (of food)* petisco *m*; *(of news, gossip)* boato *m*, fofoca *f*.

titchy *n (slang) (small)* muito pequeno,-a; *(person) (pej)* meia-leca *m,f (pej)*.

tit for tat *n* olho por olho; **to give** ~ pagar na mesma moeda *f*.

titillate *vt* titilar, excitar; ♦ *vi* excitar-se.

titillating *adj* titilante *m,f*; excitante *m,f*.

titivate *vt* arrumar, enfeitar.

title *n* título *m*; ~ **deed** *n* (*JUR*) título *m* de propriedade; ~**-holder** *n* detento,-a de um título; ~ **role** *n* papel *m* principal.

titled *adj* titular *m,f*, nobre *m,f*; intitulado,-a.

titter *n* riso *m* nervoso, risinho *m*; ♦ *vi* dar risadinhas.

tittle-tattle *n* tagarelice *f*; fofoca *f*, (*coll, pej*) mexericos *mpl*.

titular *adj* nominal *m,f*, titular *m,f*.

titularly *adv* como titular.

tizzy (*pl*: **-zies**) *n* (*fam*) confusão *f*; nervosismo *m*.

T-junction (*road*) cruzamento em forma de T.

to *prep* (*indicating direction*) (*for long period*) **I am going** ~ **Mozambique** vou para Moçambique; (*purpose, in order to*) ~ **work** para trabalhar; (*reaction, effect*) ~ **my surprise** para meu espanto *m*; (*towards*) para; **the road** ~ **the beach** a rua para a praia; **2** (*position*) **she had her face turned** ~ **the wall** ela estava virada para a parede; **3** (*attitude*) para com; **he was kind** ~ **her** ele foi amável para com ela; **4** (*telling time*) **a quarter** ~ **oito** um quarto *m*/quinze *m* para as oito *mpl*; **5** (*for briefer stay*) a; **I am going** ~ **Paris** vou a Paris; **we are going** ~ **the park** vamos ao parque (*NOTE the contraction of prep and def. article*); (*indicating position*) ~ **to the left/right** à esquerda/à direita; **6** **twenty** ~ **thirty people** entre vinte e trinta pessoas; **7** (*with object pron. emphatic*) **give the book** ~ **me** dá o livro a mim; **to dance** ~ **the music** dançar ao som da música; **8** (*infinitive; following another verb*) **to begin** ~ **speak** começar a falar; **9** (*up to*) até; **I am going** ~ **the bar** (*casually*) vou até ao bar; **10** (*of*) de; **the answer** ~ **that question must be** a resposta *f* a essa pergunta *f* tem de ser; (*following an infinite*) **impossible** ~ **do** impossível de fazer; ♦ *adj* de um lado *m* para outro *m*; ~**-and-fro** *n* vaivém *m*; **much** ~**-do** *n* (*pl*: **-s**) (*coll*) azáfama *f*; IDIOM **that's all** ~ **it** é simples; **what a** ~**-do!** mas que história!; **this has nothing** ~ **do with you** isto não tem nada a ver contigo.

toad *n* sapo *m*; ~**stool** *n* (*BOT*) cogumelo *m* venenoso; ~**-in-the-hole** *n* (*CULIN*) salsichas dentro de uma empada; ♦ *vt* (*pej*) adular; **2** (*coll*) dar graxa *f* (**to sb** a alguém) (*cal*).

toady *n* bajulador,-ora.

toast *n* (*CULIN*) (= **piece of** ~) torrada *f*; **2** (*drink, speech*) brinde *m*; ♦ *vt* (*CULIN*) torrar; **2** (*drink*) brindar, beber à saúde da pessoa; IDIOM **he is the** ~ **of the school** ele é o herói da escola.

toaster, toast rack *n* torradeira *f*.

tobacco *n* tabaco *m*, fumo *m*.

tobacconist *n* vendedor,-a de tabaco; ~**'s (shop)** *n* tabacaria *f*.

toboggan *n* tobogã *m*.

today *n* (*this day*) hoje *m*; **2** dos nossos *mpl* dias; ♦ *adv* hoje; **we must do this** ~ temos de fazer isto hoje; **2** (*nowadays*) a(c)tualmente, hoje em dia.

toddle *vi* (*small child*) dar os primeiros passos; andar com passos incertos; **he** ~**s to you** ele vai bamboleando para ti; ♦ *vi* andar (*walk unsteadily*); (= ~ **along/off**) ir-se embora, (*coll*) pôr-se a andar, (*BR*) cair fora; ~ **in** *vi* entrar hesitantemente.

toddler *n* bebé *f* que começa a andar.

toddy (*pl*: **-ies**) *n* (*CULIN*) grogue *m*, ponche *m* quente.

toe *n* dedo *m* do pé; **2** (*of shoe*) bico *m*, biqueira *f*; ~ **cap** *n* (of shoe) biqueira *f*; ~**nail** *n* unha *f* do pé; ♦ *vt* **to** ~ **the line** (*fig*) conformar-se, cumprir as obrigações *fpl*.

toffee *n* (*sweet*) caramelo *m*, rebuçado *m*; ~ **apple** *n* maçã *f* do amor.

tofu *n* tofu *m*.

tog *n* unidade de resistência térmica usada em edredões.

toga *n* toga *f*.

together *adj* (*coll*) atinado,-a; ♦ *adv* juntos,-as; **2** uns *mpl* aos outros *mpl*; simultaneamente; **3** de seguida; ~ **with** *prep* junto *m* com.

togetherness *n* companheirismo *m*, camaradagem *f*.

toggle *n* cavilha de madeira; (*NAUT*) trambelho *m*; ~ **switch** (*ELECT*) chave *f* articulada; (*COMP*) comutador *m*.

togs *npl* (*fam*) traje *m*, roupa *f*.

toil *n* faina *f*, labuta *f*; ♦ *vi* labutar, trabalhar arduamente.

toilet *n* (*fam*) retrete *m*, W.C. *m*; **2** (*public*) lavabos *mpl*; (*polite*) casa de banho *f*, (*BR*) banheiro *m*, W. C. *m*; ~ **bowl** *n* sanita *f*, (*BR*) vaso *m* sanitário; ~ **paper** *n* papel *m* higiénico (*BR*: -giê-); ~ **soap** *n* sabonete *m* ~**ries** *npl* artigos *mpl* de toalete; ~ **water** *n* água-de-colónia *f*.

to-ing and fro-ing *n* idas e vindas *fpl*.

token *n* (*symbol*) sinal *m*, símbolo *m*; prova *f*; (*of love*) em sinal *m* de meu amor *m*; **as a** ~ **of my friendship** como prova *f* da minha amizade *f*; **2** (*for machine*) ficha *f*; **3** (*voucher*) cupão *m*, (*BR*) vale *m*; **book/record** ~ cheque-livro *m*; ♦ *adj* (*often pej*) simbólico,-a; ~ **payment** pagamento *m* simbólico de dívida *f*; **by the same** ~ do mesmo modo *f*.

Tokyo *npr* Tóquio; **in** ~ em Tóquio.

told (*pt, pp* of **tell**).

tolerable *adj* suportável *m,f*; passável *m,f*.

tolerance *n* tolerância *f*.

tolerant (**of**) *adj* tolerante *m,f* com; **2** resistente *m,f* a algo.

tolerate *vt* (*put up with*) tolerar.

toll *n* (*of casualties*) número *m* de baixas; **the death** ~ o número de mortos; **2** (*bridge/road charge*) portagem *f*, (*BR*) pedágio *m*; **3** prejuízo *m*; **to take its** ~ ter consequências/implicações; ♦ *vt/vi* (*bell*) badalar, dobrar, tanger; **to** ~ **for the dead** dobrar pelos,-as mortos,-as.

tolling *n* (*for the dead*) toque *m* a finados *mpl*.

tomato (*pl*: **-es**) *n* (*BOT, CULIN*) tomate *m*; ~ **sauce** molho *m* de tomate.

tomb *n* tumba *f*, túmulo *m*; **2** monumento *m* funerário; **3** (*fig*) morte *f*.

tombola *n* (*UK*) tômbola *f*.

tomboy *n* maria-rapaz *f*, (*BR*) menina-moleque *f*.

tombstone *n* lápide *f*.

tomcat *n* (*male*) gato *m*.

Tom, Dick and Harry *npr* fulano, beltrano e sicrano; toda a gente; *(BR)* todo mundo.

tomfoolery *(pl: -ies) n* tolices *fpl;* **stop this** ~ deixa-te dessas tolices, brincadeiras.

tomorrow *n* amanhã *m;* **2** *(fig)* futuro *f;* ♦ *adv* amanhã; **the day after** ~ depois de amanhã; ~ **morning** amanhã de manhã.

ton, tonne *n* tonelada *f;* ~**s of** *(coll)* um monte *m* de, carradas de.

tonality *(pl: -ies) n* tonalidade *f.*

tone *n (manner of speaking)* tom *m;* *(of music)* som *m,* timbre *m;* ~~**deaf** *adj* que não tem ouvido *m* musical; ~**less** *adj* átono,-a; ♦ *vt* tonificar; ♦ *vi* dar o tom, harmonizar; **to** ~ **down** *vt* suavizar; **2** *(sound)* baixar; ~ **in** *(colours)* combinar; **to** ~ **up** *vt* fortalecer.

Tonga *npr* Tonga; **2** *n adj (African language, people)* tonga.

Tongan *n adj* tonganês,-esa.

tongs *npl (for coal)* tenazes *fpl;* **2** *(for sugar, eyebrows)* pinças *fpl;* IDIOM **to go at it with hammer and** ~ *(coll)* vou discutir com toda a fúria *f; (work)* trabalhar afincadamente.

tongue *(ANAT)* língua *f;* **to stick one's** ~ **at sb** deitar a língua de fora a alguém; **to bite one's** ~ morder a língua; *(fig)* arrepender-se de ter dito; ~~**tie** *n* língua *f* presa; ~~**tied** *adv (fig)* calado,-a, mudo,-a; ~ **twister** *n* expressão *f* difícil de pronunciar; trava-língua *m;* **2** *(language)* língua, linguagem *f;* **3** *(flap of shoe/lock)* lingueta *f;* IDIOM **a slip of the** ~ um lapso *m,* deslize *m;* ~**s will wag** vai haver falatório; **watch your** ~! cuidado com o que dizes!; **(with one's)** **in one's cheek** com descaramento/ironia, por brincadeira.

tonic *n (MED)* tónico *m (BR:* tô-) **(for** para); **a gin and** ~ um gim *m* tónico; **2** *(MUS)* tónica *f (BR:* tô-); **3** *(fig) (relief)* bálsamo *m;* ♦ *adj (LING)* acentuado,-a; **2** revigorante *m,f.*

tonicity *n* tonicidade *f.*

tonight *n adv* esta noite *f,* hoje à noite.

toning *n* tonalidade *f;* ~ **down** abrandamento *m.*

tonnage *n (NAUT)* tonelagem *f.*

tonsil *n* amí(g)dala *f,* anginas *fpl.*

tonsillitis *n* ami(g)dalite *f.*

too *adv (excessively)* demasiado *m,f,* demais; ~ **good** demasiado bom/boa *m,f;* bom/boa demais; ~ **many** demasiados,-as; ~ **much** *adv* demais; **2** *(also)* também; **he is a journalist** ~ ele *f* também é jornalista *m,f;* **3 that's** ~ **bad!** que pena! *(with negatives)* muito; **not** ~ **sure** não muito certo,-a.

toodle-oo! *(fam) (affectatious) (good-bye)* tchau!

took *(pt of* take).

tool *n* instrumento *m,* ferramenta *f;* ~ **box** *n* caixa *f* de ferramentas; **2** *(fig) (means)* ferramentas *fpl;* IDIOM **to down** ~**s** *(UK)* protestar parando de trabalhar.

toot *n (of horn)* buzinadela *f,* buzinada *f;* **2** *(of whistle)* apito *m;* ♦ *vt* buzinar; ♦ *vi (with car-horn)* buzinar.

tooth *(pl:* teeth) *n (ANAT, TECH)* dente *m;* molar *m;* **wisdom** ~ dente do siso; **brush one's** ~ *npl*

lavar os dentes; **to show one's teeth** *(in anger or smile)* arreganhar os dentes; IDIOM ~ **and nail** com unhas *fpl* e dentes *mpl;* **I am fed up to the back teeth** estar farto,-a até à ponta dos cabelos; **to lie through one's teeth** mentir com quantos dentes tem; **to set sb's teeth on edge** pôr os nervos em franja a alguém; **escape by the skin of one's** ~ escapar por um triz.

toothache *n* dor *f* de dente(s).

toothbrush *n* escova *f* de dentes.

toothless *adj* desdentado,-a.

toothpaste *n* pasta *f* de dentes.

toothpick *n* palito *m.*

tootle *vi (coll) (go for a pleasant drive)* passear.

top *n (of mountain)* cume *m* **(of** de); **2** cimo *m* **(of** de); **3** *(of head)* o alto *m,* cocuruto *m;* **4** *(of ladder)* o alto *m;* **5** *(of, table)* superfície *f,* topo *m;* **6** *(lid)* tampa *f;* **7** *(of list, etc.)* cabeça *m;* **8** *(toy)* pião *m;* **9** *(clothing)* parte de cima *f,* blusa *f;* ♦ *adj (highest)* mais alto,-a, máximo,-a; **2** *(in rank)* principal *m,f,* superior *m,f;* **3** *(best)* melhor *m,f;* ♦ **on** ~ **of** *prep (place, space)* em cima de, sobre; **2** *(in addition)* além de; ♦ **(-pp-)** *vt* liderar; *(table, party)* encabeçar; **2** *(be first in)* estar em primeiro lugar; *(better)* superar; *(exceed)* passar de; **to** ~ **off** rematar; ♦ *vi (sales, etc)* atingir um recorde; **to** ~ **out** *vi* dar os últimos retoques; *(price)* atingir o máximo; IDIOM **and to** ~ **it all** e para cúmulo *m;* **from** ~ **to toe** da cabeça *f* aos pés *mpl;* **to get on sb's** ~ deixar alguém preocupado,-a; **to go over the** ~ *(UK) (coll)* passar das marcas *fpl (col);* exagerar.

topaz *n adj* topázio *m.*

top brass *n (coll)* barões *mpl (fam).*

topclass *adj* de primeira categoria, excelente *m,f.*

topcoat *n* sobretudo *m;* **2** *(painting)* última *f* demão.

top dog *(coll)* manda-chuva *m,f.*

topdrawer, top-flight *adj* excelente; de primeira categoria *m,f.*

top hat *n* chapéu *m* alto, cartola *f.*

top-heavy *adj (object)* desequilibrado,-a; **2** *(person)* pesado,-a na parte superior do corpo; **3** *(euph)* com seios grandes.

topic *n* tópico *m.*

topical *adj* a(c)tual, da a(c)tualidade.

topless *adj* topless *f,* sem a parte superior *f* do biquíni *m.*

top level *adj (talks)* de alto nível *m,f.*

topmost *adj* supremo,-a, o mais alto,-a.

top-notch *adj (fam)* de primeira.

topographer *n* topógrafo,-a.

topped *adj:* ~ **by/with sth** com algo em cima; **steak** ~ **with an egg** *(Portuguese dish)* um bife a cavalo.

topple *vt* derrubar, cair para a frente; **to** ~ **over** *vi* vir abaixo.

top ranking *adj* de alto nível *m,f;* **2** em posição *f* elevada; **3** *(SPORT)* de alta *f* competição.

topsecret *adj* ultra-secreto,-a.

topsecurity *adj* de segurança *f* máxima.

topsoil *n* solo *m* arável; camada *f* superficial do solo.

topsy-turvy *adj (messy)* de pernas para o ar; **2** confuso,-a; às avessas.

top-up *vt* encher (**with** com) novamente; **may I ~ your glass?** mais um pouco de (vinho)?; **2** *(FIN) (fund)* aumentar; **3** *(mobile)* carregar.

topview vista *f* de cima.

torch *n* *(flaming)* tocha *f*, archote *m*; **2** *(electric)* lanterna *f*.

tore *(pt of* **tear**).

torment *n* tormento *m*; **2** suplício *m*; **3** angústia *f*; **to be in** ~ estar em sofrimento *m*; ♦ *vt* atormentar; **2** *(annoy)* chatear, aborrecer, arreliar; **3** consumir; **I am** ~ **by jealousy** isto consome-me de ciúmes *mpl*; IDIOM **his son is a positive** ~ o filho *m* dele é uma autêntica *f* peste.

torn *(pp of* **tear**).

tornado *(pl:* **-es**) *n* tornado *m*.

torpedo *(pl:* **-es**) *n* torpedo *m*.

torrent *n* torrente *f*, corrente *f*.

torrential *adj* torrencial *m,f*.

torso *n* *(ANAT)* torso *m*.

tortoise *n* cágado *m*; **~shell** *adj* de tartaruga *f*.

tortuous *adj* *(twisty)* sinuoso,-a; **2** *(complicated)* tortuoso,-a.

torture *n* tortura *f*; **instruments of** ~ instrumentos *mpl* de tortura; **2** tormento *m*; **it was sheer ~!** *(fig)* foi um verdadeiro *m* suplício! *f*; ♦ *adj* torturante; ~ **chamber** *n* câmara *f* de horrores; ♦ *vt* torturar; **2** *(fig)* atormentar *f*.

Tory *n adj* *(POL)* do partido *m* conservador.

tosh *n* *(fam)* disparate *m*.

toss *(pl:* **-es**) *n* *(turn)* **to give sth a** ~ mexer; **2** *(throw)* arremesso *m* *(de moeda ao ar)*; *(of head)* sacudida *f*; ♦ *vt* *(throw)* atirar, arremessar; derrubar; **he was ~ed by a bull** ele *m* foi atirado ao ar por um *m* touro; **the ship ~es in a storm** o navio rola na tespestade; **2** *(head)* sacudir, lançar para trás; **3** *(move about)* **to** ~ **and turn in bed** virar de um lado *m* para o outro *m* na cama *f*; **4** ~ **in** *(CULIN)* acrescentar, deitar; ♦ ~ **about/around** *vt* passar de um para outro *m*; bater *(ball)*; **2** *(fig)* remoer *(ideias)*; ♦ *vi* *(with pain)* contorcer-se; ~ **away** *(waste)* desperdiçar *(opportunity)* ~ **aside** *vt* pôr de lado *m*; ~ **back** *vt* *(ball, object)* devolver; **to** ~ **off** masturbar(-se); **to** ~/~**up a coin** tirar cara *f* ou coroa *f*; atirar a moeda ao ar, disputar no cara ou coroa; ~**-up** *n* incerteza *f*; **let's have a** ~ vamos tirar à sorte; IDIOM **I don't give a** ~ **about it** quero lá saber disso.

tosser *n* *(UK)* *(slang)* imbecil; **2** antipático,-a.

tot *n* *(drink)* copinho *m*, golinho *m*; **a** ~ **of whisky** um pouco de uísque; **2** *(child)* criancinha *f*, *(BR)* nenezinho,-a; ♦ *vt* **to** ~ **up** adicionar.

total *n* total *m*, soma *f*; **in** ~ no total; ♦ *adj* total *m,f* inteiro,-a; ♦ *(pt, pp* **-ed**) *vt* *(add up)* somar; **2** *(amount to)* totalizar; *(US)* *(wreck)* arruinar.

totalitarian *adj* totalitário,-a.

totality *n* totalidade *f*.

totally *adv* totalmente.

total recall *n* *(PSYC)* memória *f* perfeita.

totem *n* totem *m*; **2** *(symbol)* símbolo *m*; ~**-pole** *n* totem, mastro *m* totémico *(BR:* -tê-).

totter *vi* cambalear.

toucan *n* *(ZOOL)* tucano *m*.

touch *(pl:* **-es**) *n* toque *m*, conta(c)to *m*; **to keep in** ~ manter conta(c)to com alguém; **out of** ~ **with reality** afastado,-a da realidade; **2** *(of bell, button)* pressão *f*, toque *m*; **I felt a** ~ **on my shoulder** senti um toque no meu ombro; **this is rough to the** ~ isto é áspero ao toque; *(sense)* ta(c)to; **by** ~ pelo ta(c)to; **3** *(small amount)* **a** ~ **of** *(fig)* uma pitada *f* de, um pouco *m* de; **a** ~ **of sadness** uma nota de tristeza; **4** *(skill, style)* estilo *m*, habilidade *f*, a mão de; **5 with a** ~ **of elegance** com um toque de elegância; **4 finishing** ~**es** retoques *mpl* finais; **6** *(football)* **in** ~ fora do campo *m*; na lateral; ♦ *vt* *(physically)* tocar, apalpar; **2** *(food)* comer; *(drink)* beber; *(smoke)* fumar *(cigarettes)*; **3** *(matter of concern)* dizer respeito a; **4** *(emotionally)* comover, sensibilizar; **I was ~ed by his words** fiquei sensibilizada com as palavras dele; ♦ *vi* *(be in contact)* tocar-se; *(make contact)* tocar; **2** *(to dock) (ship)* acostar *(at* em); **3** *(compare – in quality)* igualar; **there is no one to** ~ **him** não há ninguém como ele, ninguém que lhe chegue aos pés *(fam)*; pedir emprestado *(money)*; IDIOM **at the first** ~ à primeira; **to be an easy/soft** ~ *(coll)* deixar-se cravar facilmente.

touch-and-go *adj* arriscado,-a, duvidoso,-a.

touchdown *n* aterragem *f*, *(BR)* aterrissagem *f*.

touched *adj* *(emotionally)* comovido,-a, sensibilizado,-a; **2** *(coll) (mad)* louco,-a, tatã *m,f*.

touching *adj* comovedor,-ora, comovente *m,f*.

touchline *n* *(SPORT)* linha *f* de fundo *(BR:* lateral).

touch off *vt* *(with match)* ser o rastilho *m* para algo, lançar *(fireworks)*; **2** *(fig)* desencadear *(riots, etc)*.

touch on/upon *vt* aludir a; abordar *(subject)*.

touchstone *n* pedra *f* de toque.

touchtyping *n* dactilografia sem olhar para as teclas.

touch up *vt* *(paint)* retocar; **to** ~ **photograph** retocar uma fotografia; **2** *(slang) (parts of a female/male)* apalpar.

touchy *adj* *(person)* susce(p)tível *m,f*, melindroso,-a; **2** *(question)* delicado,-a.

tough *n* *(person)* duro,-a; ♦ *adj* duro,-a, forte *m,f*; ~ **meat** carne *f* dura; ~ **person** pessoa *f* forte, robusta; **2** *(plant, metal)* resistente *m,f*; **3** *(life, task)* penoso,-a, difícil *m,f*; ~ **luck** má sorte, azar; **4** *(person)* inflexível *m,f* firme; **5** *(unfeeling)* insensível *m,f*; **6** *(criminal)* da pesada *f* *(fam)*; **7** *(law, measures)* severo,-a.

toughen *vt* endurecer *(character, skin)*.

tough-minded *adj* prá(c)tico,-a, de ideias *f* firmes.

toughness *n* *(hardness)* dureza *f*, firmeza *f*; **2** *(of character, material)* resistência *f*.

toupee *n* peruca *f*.

tour *n* viagem *f*, excursão *f*; **to start on a** ~ ir em viagem; **2** *(of town, museum)* visita *f*; digressão *f*; ~ **guide** guia *m* *(turístico)*; ♦ *vt* excursionar por; **2** *(MUS)* fazer digressão; ♦ *vi* *(go on trip)* fazer uma excursão, viajar.

touring *n* viagens *fpl* turísticas, turismo *m*.

tourism *n* turismo.

tourist *n* turista; ~ **office** *n* agência *f* de turismo.

tournament *n* *(competition)* torneio *m*.

tourniquet *n* torniquete *m.*

tousled *adj (hair)* despenteado,-a, desgrenhado,-a; **2** *(person)* desleixado,-a; *(house)* desarrumado,-a.

tout *n* cambista *m,f; (UK) (selling tickets)* revende-dor,-ora de bilhetes; *(BR)* de ingressos *mpl* no mercado negro; **2** *(COMM) (soliciting custom)* angariador,-ora ♦ *vt (illegally) (UK)* revender no mercado negro; ♦ *vi (publicize)* apregoar as vantagens *(of a product);* **2 to ~ for (business)** angariar clientela, aliciar; **3** informar e receber ilegalmente dados sobre os cavalos que têm a possibilidade de ganhar, para efeitos de apostas.

tow *n* veículo *m* reboque; **2** *(UK)* a reboque *m;* **in ~** sob a influência de; **he is always in her ~** ele *m* anda sempre a reboque dela *f;* **~bar** *n* engate para reboque; **~ rope** *n* cabo *m* de reboque; ♦ *vt* rebocar; **'on ~'** *(UK) (AUT)* rebocado,-a; **~ away** *(police)* levar *(car, etc)* para o depósito; **~away zone** *n* zona *f* de estacionamento proibido.

towards *(UK)* **toward** *(US) prep* para, em dire(c)ção *f* a; **2** *(of attitude)* com respeito a, para com; **I like your attitude ~ them** gosto da sua atitude *f* para com eles; **3** *(time and space)* por volta de; **~ the end** lá para o fim *m.*

towel *n* toalha *f;* **bath ~** toalhão *m* de banho; **~ rail** *(UK)* toalheiro *m;* ♦ *vt* secar-se com uma toalha; IDIOM **to throw in the ~** *(fig)* atirar a toalha para o chão *m*, dar-se por vencido,-a.

towelling *(UK)* **toweling** *(US) n (cloth)* turco *m,* atoalhado *m;* **~ rail** *n* toalheiro *m.*

tower *n* torre *f;* **2** fortaleza *f;* **~ block** *n* arranha-céus *m;* ♦ *vi* elevar-se; IDIOM **he is my ~ of strength** *(UK)* ele *m* é o meu grande apoio *m.*

tower above/over *vt* destacar-se em relação a.

towering *adj* elevado,-a, eminente *m,f.*

town *n* cidade *f;* **2** *(city centre)* centro *m;* **~ clerk** *n* funcionário,-a municipal, administrador,-ora municipal; **~ council/hall** *n* câmara *f* municipal; **~ councillor** *n* vereador,-ora municipal; **~ mayor** *n* presidente,-ta da câmara; **~ planning** *n* urbanismo *m;* **~ship** *n (US) (in S. Africa)* município *m;* IDIOM **to go to ~ on sth** fazer algo com entusiasmo *m, (BR)* botar para quebrar; **to go out on the ~ (night out)** andar na pândega/farra; **she is the talk of the ~** ela é o assunto das conversas.

towpath *n* caminho *m* de sirga.

toxic *adj* tóxico,-a.

toy *n* brinquedo *m;* **2** *(fig)* joguete *m;* **I was a ~ in her hands** eu era um joguete nas mãos *fpl* dela *f;* **~ boy** *n* gigolô *m;* amante *m* de uma coroa; **~ shop** *n* loja *f* de brinquedos; ♦ *vt* **to ~ with** jogar com; **2** *(idea)* pensar em *(doing sth),* andar com a ideia; **3** entreter-se com.

trace *n* sinal *m;* **2** *(evidence)* traço *m,* rasto *m;* **~ element** *n (CHEM)* elemento-traço; **3** *(drawing)* traçado *m;* **4** *(US)* caminho *m;* ♦ *vt (draw)* traçar, esboçar; **2** *(follow)* seguir a pista *f* de; **3** *(locate)* encontrar; **to ~ sb** localizar alguém; **4** descobrir a origem *f* de; **~ back** *vi* remontar **(to** a); **~ out** *vt* delinear, traçar.

traceable *adj* localizável; **2** que pode traçar-se.

traced *adj* traçado,-a.

traceless *adj* que não deixou vestígios *mpl.*

tracing *n* decalque *m.*

track *n (mark)* pegada *f,* marca *f,* vestígio *m;* **the bear left ~s** o urso *m* deixou pegadas *fpl;* **2** *(path)* caminho *m,* vereda *f,* trilho *m;* **3** *(of bullet, etc.)* traje(c)tória *f;* **4** *(of suspect, animal)* peugada *f,* pista *f,* rasto *m;* **to follow the ~ of** seguir a pista de; **5** *(RAIL)* via *f,* trilhos *mpl;* **6** *(on record, disc, etc.)* faixa *f;* **7** *(SPORT)* pista *f;* **~ dog** *n* cão *m* de caça *ou* de polícia; **~ event** *n* atletismo *m* na pista; **~ radar** *n* radar *m* de rastreio; **~ record: to have a ~** ter uma boa reputação/folha de serviço; **~ shoes** *npl* sapatos de bicos/de corrida; **~ suit** *n* fato de treino; ♦ **~ down** *vt (prey)* seguir a pista *f* de; **2** *(sth lost)* procurar e encontrar; ♦ *vt* seguir a pista de; IDIOM **don't get off the ~** não mudes de assunto *m;* **I lost ~ of Peter** perdi conta(c)to *m* com o Peter; **he lost ~ of time** ele perdeu a noção do tempo; **I threw him off the ~** consegui despistá-lo; **the police are on his ~** a polícia está na peugada dele; **off the beaten ~** *(place)* isolado,-a; **you are off ~!** estás fora da linha *f (fig).*

tracker *n (of animal)* batedor; *(of person)* perseguidor,-ora.

tracking *n* perseguição; rastreamento *m.*

tract *n (GEOG)* região *f;* extensão *f;* **2** *(pamphlet)* folheto *m;* **3 digestive ~** aparelho *m* digestivo.

traction *n (PHYS, MED)* tração *f.*

tractor *n* tra(c)tor *m.*

trade *n* comércio *m,* negócio *m;* **2** *(skill, job)* ofício *m,* emprego *m;* **3** clientela *f;* **4** *(US)* troca *f;* **5 by ~** por formação; **2** *(fig)* sinal *m* particular; **~ barrier** *n* barreira *f* comercial; **~ discount** *n* desconto *m* para revendedor; **~ gap** *n* défice *m* na balança comercial; **~-in** *n (exchange)* troca, retoma de um artigo usado; ♦ **~ mark** *n* marca *f* comercial, de indústria *f;* **2** *(fig)* imagem *f* de marca; **3** *(fig)* sinal *m* particular; ♦ **~-off** *n (balance)* compromisso *m* **(between** entre), equilíbrio,-a; **2** *(exchange)* troca *f;* ♦ **~ secret** *n* segredo *m* de ofício; **~ union** *n* sindicato *m;* **~ unionist** *adj* sindicalista *m,f;* **~ wind** *n* vento *m* alísio; ♦ *vi (stocks)* vender; **2** negociar; **to ~ sth for another** trocar algo por algo; **to ~ in** dar como parte do pagamento (um carro velho por um carro novo).

trader, tradesman/woman *n* comerciante *m,f;* **2** *(FIN) (Stock Exchange)* operador,-ora (na Bolsa).

trading *n (COMM)* comércio *m;* *(FIN)* transa(c)ções *fpl.*

tradition *n* tradição *f.*

traditional *adj* tradicional *m,f.*

traffic[1] *n* trânsito *m;* tráfego *m;* **heavy ~** trânsito *m* intenso; **~ accident** *n* acidente *m* de trânsito; **~ control** prevenção *f* rodoviária; **~ island** *n (in the middle of the road)* canteiro *m* central; **~ jam** *n* engarrafamento *m,* congestionamento *m;* **~ lights** *npl* semáforo(s) *mpl;* **~ offence** *(UK),* **violation** *(US) n* infra(c)ção de trânsito; **~ warden** *n (UK)* guarda *m,f* de trânsito; ♦ *(pt, pp* **-ked)** *vi* **to ~ in** *(arms, drugs)* traficar com.

traffic² *n* (*illegal trade – drugs, arms*) tráfico *m*; ♦ (-pt, pp: -ked) *vt* traficar.

trafficker *n* traficante *m,f*.

trafficking *n* (*drugs, etc*) tráfico *m*.

tragedy (*pl:* -ies) *n* (*ill fate, dramatic form*) tragédia *f*; 2 (*THEAT*) tragédia *f*.

tragic *adj* trágico,-a.

trail *n* (*tracks*) rasto *m*, pista *f*; **the lion left a long ~** o leão *m* deixou um grande rasto *m*; 2 (*path*) caminho *m*, trilha *f*; **to blaze the ~** desbravar caminho *m*; 3 (*wake*) esteira *f*; 4 (*comet, dress*) cauda *f*; ♦ *vt* (*drag*) arrastar; 2 (*follow*) seguir a pista de; 3 (*follow closely*) vigiar; 4 (*plants*) trepar; ♦ *vi* (*drag behind*) arrastar-se; 2 (*move slowly*) andar lentamente; 3 (*SPORT*) (*loose*) perder; ♦ **to ~ away/off** *vi* diminuir de intensidade *f*; 2 perder-se; **to ~ behind** *vi* atrasar-se.

trailblazer *n* pioneiro,-a.

trailer *n* (*AUT, BOAT*) reboque *m*, carro de reboque *m*; 2 (*CIN*) trailer *m*.

train *n* comboio *m*, (*BR*) trem *m*; **to go by ~** viajar de comboio, trem; 2 (*of dress*) cauda *f*; 3 ~ **of thought** *n* (linha de) raciocínio *m*; 4 (*retinue*) séquito *m*, comitiva *f*; **the Queen's ~** o séquito *f* real; ~ **crash** acidente *m* ferroviário; ~ **driver** *n* maquinista *m,f*; ~ **resistance** resistência *f* à tra(c)-ção; ~ **set** *n* comboio *n* em miniatura; ~ **spotter** *n* apaixonado,-a por comboios; ♦ *vt* ensinar; 2 instruir, (*SPORT*) treinar; 3 (*dog*) adestrar; amestrar; 4 (= **to ~ on/upon** *vt*) (*gun*) apontar para; 5 (*plant*) dirigir; ♦ *vi* (*EDUC*) formar-se (**for** para); (*SPORT*) treinar-se (**for** para).

trained *adj* (*worker*) treinado,-a; instruído,-a; especializado,-a, profissional *m,f*; 2 (*Univ*) formado,-a.

trainee *n* aprendiz *m*, estagiário,-a.

trainer *n* treinador,-ora; instrutor,-ora; ~**s** *npl* (*shoes*) ténis (*BR:* -ê-).

training *n* formação *f*; 2 instrução *f*; (*learning*) aprendizagem; 3 (*MIL, SPORT*) treino, (*BR*) treinamento *m*; ~ **college** (*UK*) escola *f*, instituto *m* profissional.

traipse *vi* arrastar os pés *mpl* (cansados), andar com passos lentos e pesados.

trait *n* (*personality*) traço *m*.

traitor *n* traidor,-ora.

trajectory *n* traje(c)tória *f*.

tram *n* (= ~**car**) elé(c)trico *m*, (*BR*) bonde *m*.

tramp *n* vagabundo,-a; (*fig*) maltrapilhos *mpl*; 2 (*hike*) caminhada *f*; ♦ *vt* (*hike*) ir a pé; caminhar com passos pesados; ♦ *vi* **to ~** (**around**) vaguear; **I have been ~ing around in search of work** tenho andado a pé por aí à procura de trabalho; 2 caminhar pesadamente.

trample *n* ruído *m* de passos; 2 (*of horses*) tropel *m*; ♦ *vt* **to ~** calcar, esmagar com os pés; ♦ *vi* (*tread*) **to ~ on sb/sth** pisar em algo; 2 (*fig*) (*act cruelly*) espezinhar alguém/algo, calcar aos pés; 3 (*fig*) magoar, ferir (*sb's feelings*); IDIOM **to ~ on sb's toes** usurpar os direitos *mpl* de alguém.

trampoline *n* trampolim *m*.

trance *n* êxtase *m*; 2 (*MED*) transe *m* hipnótico.

tranquil *adj* tranquilo,-a.

tranquility *n* tranquilidade *f*.

tranquilizer *n* (*MED*) tranquilizante *m*.

transact *vt* (*business*) negociar; levar a cabo.

transaction *n* transação *f*, negócio *m*; negociações *fpl*.

transatlantic *adj* transatlântico,-a; 2 (*on the other side of the Atlantic*) além-mar.

transcend *vt* (*go beyond*) transcender, exceder; 2 ser superior *m* a.

transcendence *n* transcendência *f*.

transcendental *n* transcendental *m,f*.

transcribe *vt* transcrever; 2 copiar.

transcript *n* cópia *f*, traslado,-a; 2 (*of speech*) transcrição *f*.

transept *n* transepto *m*.

transfer *n* (*gen*) transferência *f*; 2 (*picture, design*) decalcomania *f*; 3 (*JUR*) cedência *f*; 4 (*US*) (*ticket*) bilhete *m* que permite mudar de transporte *m*; 5 ~ **passenger** passageiro,-a em trânsito *m*; ~ **student** aluno,-a de intercâmbio; ♦ (-rr-) *vt* transferir, trasladar; **to ~ a right to sb** ceder um direito *m* a alguém; ♦ *vi* transferir-se; **to ~ the charges** (*TEL*) ligar a cobrar.

transferable *adj* transferível *m,f*; **not ~** intransferível *m,f*.

transference *n* (*gen*) transferência *f*; (*of thought*) transmissão *f*.

transfigure *vt* transfigurar.

transfix *vt* (*immobilize*) paralisar.

transform *vt* transformar; **to ~ sb/sth into sth** transformar alguém/algo *m* em algo.

transformation *n* transformação *f*.

transformer *n* (*ELECT*) transformador *m*.

transfusion *n* transfusão *f*.

transgress *vt* transgredir; ♦ *vi* cometer uma transgressão *f*.

transgression *n* transgressão *f*.

transhipment *n* trasbordo *m*.

transient *adj* (*fleeting*) transitório,-a.

transilience *n* descontinuidade *f*.

transistor *n* (*ELECT*) transistor *m*; ~ **radio** *n* rádio *m* transistor.

transit *n*: **in ~** em trânsito *m*, de passagem *f*; ~ **camp** *n* acampamento *m* provisório.

transition *n* transição *f*.

transitional *adj* transitório,-a.

transitive *adj* (*LING*) transitivo *m*.

transitory *adj* transitório,-a.

translate *vt* (*languages*) traduzir; 2 (*fig*) transformar; 3 explicar, interpretar; ♦ *vi* (*words*) traduzir-se; (*person*) traduzir.

translation *n* (*act, work*) tradução *f*; 2 versão *f*; interpretação *f*; 3 decifração *f*.

translator *n* tradutor,-a.

translucent *adj* translúcido,-a.

transmission *n* transmissão *f*.

transmit (*pp, pt* -ted) *vt* transmitir.

transmitter *n* transmissor *m*; 2 (*station*) emissora *f*.

transparency (*pl:* -ies) *n* transparência, claridade; (*PHOT*) transparência *f*, diapositivo *m*; 2 limpidez *f*, claridade *f* (de vidro, etc.).

transparent *adj* transparente *m,f*.

transplant *n* (*MED*) transplante *m*; ♦ *vt* transplantar; 2 (*population*) transferir.

transport *n* transporte *m*; (= **road/rail** ~) transporte *m* rodoviário, ferroviário; ♦ *vt* transportar; acarretar.

transportation *n* transporte *m*.

transverse *adj* transversal *m,f*.

transvestite *n* travesti *m,f*.

trap *n* *(gen)* armadilha *f*, cilada *f*; *(for humans)* emboscada *f*; **to fall into a** ~ cair numa armadilha *f*; **2** *(fig)* *(trick)* cair numa ratoeira; ♦ **to set a** ~ armar uma armadilha, cilada; **2** *(carriage)* aranha *m*, charrete *f*; **3** *(coll)* boca; **4** bloquear; ~**door** *n* alçapão *m*; **mouse**-~ *n* ratoeira *f*; ~**ped** *adj* apanhado,-a no laço *m*, na armadilha *f*; **2** *(horse, mare)* arreado,-a; ♦ (-**pp**-) *vt* armadilhar, pegar em armadilha *f*; **2** colocar armadilhas *fpl*; **3** (criminal) apanhar.

trapeze *n* trapézio *m*.

trappings *npl* *(fig)* adornos *mpl*, enfeites *mpl*.

trappy *adj* cheio,-a de armadilhas.

trash *(pl:* -**es**) *n* refugo *m*, escória *f*; **2** *(nonsense)* disparate *m*, *(BR)* besteira *m,f*; **3** *(art)* porcaria *m,f*; *(US)* lixo *m*; *(US)* *(pej)* ralé *f*; ~ **can** *n* *(US)* lata *f* de lixo; ♦ *vt* *(coll)* destruir; **2** *(US)* *(coll)* deitar fora; **3** *(US)* *(coll)* denegrir.

trashy *adj* de qualidade inferior; **2** de mau gosto.

trauma *n* *(distress)* trauma *m*.

traumatic *adj* traumático,-a.

traumatize, traumatise *vt* traumatizar.

travel *n* viagem *f*; ~ **agency** *n* agência *f* de viagens; ♦ (-**ll**-) *vt* percorrer; **his eye** ~**led over the scene** percorreu a cena *f* com o olhar *m*; **2** *(distance)* viajar; ♦ *vi* *(gen)* viajar; **2** *(news)* voar.

travelator *n* tapete, escada *m* rolante

traveller *(UK)* **traveler** *(US)* *n* viajante *m,f*; **2** *(UK)* *(euphemism for gipsy)* cigano,-a; ~**'s cheque** *n* cheque *m* de viagem.

travelling *n* as viagens *fpl*, viajar *m*; **to be** ~ andar em viagem *f*; ♦ *adj* ambulante *m,f*; **2** rolante *m,f*; **3** *(portable)* de viagem; ~ **bag** saco *m* de viagem; ~ **expenses, allowance** despesas de viagem/de deslocação; ~ **library** *n* biblioteca *f* itinerante, ambulante; ~ **salesman** *n* caixeiro *m* viajante.

travelogue *(UK)*, **travelog** *(US)* *n* livro, filme ou documentário sobre viagens.

travel-sick *adj*: **to be** ~ estar/sentir-se enjoado,-a. **travel-sickness** *n* enjoo *(sea, air, car)*.

traverse *vt* atravessar.

travesty *(pl:* -**ies**) *n* paródia *f*, farsa *f*, imitação *f*, grotesca.

trawl *n* *(net)* rede *f* de arrasto; **2** *(search)* busca *f*; ♦ *vi* pescar com rede de arrasto.

trawler *n* traineira *f*.

tray *(pl:* -**s**) *n* bandeja *f*; tabuleiro *m*; **serve the tea on the** ~ sirva o chá no tabuleiro.

treacherous *adj* *(plan)* traiçoeiro,-a; **2** *(person)* traidor,-ora; **3** perigoso,-a.

treachery *n* traição *f*.

treacle *n* melaço *m*, melado *m*.

treacly *adj* semelhante a melaço; **2** demasiado *m* doce.

tread *n* *(step)* passo *m*, pisada *f*: **2** *(sound of steps)* passadas *fpl*; **3** *(of tyre)* banda *f*, trilho *m* de rodagem; **4** *(shoe)* sola *f*; ♦ *(pt* **trod**, *pp* **trodden)** *vi* pisar; **to** ~ **on sb's corns** pisar os calos a

alguém; esmagar com os pés *fpl*; **to** ~ **grapes** pisar uvas *fpl*; ♦ *vt* *(crush)* esmagar algo em algo; ♦ *vi* *(place foot)* pisar em algo; **2** *(walk)* caminhar; ~ **down** *vt* calcar *(ground)*; *(fig)* dominar, oprimir; ~ **in** *vt* *(seeds)* enterrar com os pés *mpl*; ~ **out** tirar o sumo de algo pisando *(grapes, corn)*; ~ **water** boiar na água *f* em posição vertical. IDIOM **to** ~ **lightly** ser prudente *m,f* ser diplomático,-a; **to** ~ **on sb's toes** ofender alguém; **to** ~ **the boards** *(actor)* pisar o palco *m*.

treadle *n* pedal *m*; ♦ *vt* pedalar.

treadmill *n* roda *f* de moinho; **2** *(fig)* rotina *f*.

treason *n* traição *f*.

treasonable *adj* traidor,-ora; **2** de traição; **3** desleal *m,f*.

treasure *n* tesouro *m*; **2** *(darling person)* jóia *f*; ♦ *vt* *(value)* apreciar, estimar; ~ **hunt** *n* caça *f* ao tesouro.

treasurer *n* tesoureiro,-a.

treasury *(pl:* -**ies**) *n* tesouraria *f*; **the T~** *(UK)* Ministério *m* das Finanças, *(BR)* da Fazenda.

treat *n* *(food)* delícia *f*, guloseima *f*; **2** *(gift)* prenda *f*, presente *m*; **3** convite *m* para comer e/ou beber; ♦ *vt* *(MED)* tratar; **2 to** ~ **sb to sth** convidar alguém para algo; **3** presentear alguém with sth; **he** ~**ed to the opera** ele levou-me à ópera; **I'll** ~ **you to a drink** eu pago-te um bebida; IDIOM **this is my** ~ quem paga sou eu.

treatable *adj* *(MED)* tratável *m,f*.

treatise *n* tratado *m* (**on sth** sobre algo).

treatment *n* tratamento *m*, trato *m*; **2** *(illness)* cuidados *mpl*.

treaty *n* *(written)* tratado *m*, acordo *m*.

treble *n* *(MUS)* voz *f* de soprano; ♦ *adj* tríplice *m,f*; ♦ *vt/vi* triplicar(-se).

trebly *adv* três vezes mais; **2** triplicadamente.

tree *n* árvore *f*; **family** ~ *n* árvore *f* genealógica; ~-**felling** *n* corte *m* de ávores; ~ **house** *n* cabana numa árvore *(for children to play)*; ~-**lined** *adj* arborizado,-a; ~-**surgeon** *n* jardineiro especialista em cortar/podar árvores; ~**top** *n* copa *f* (árvore); ~ **trunk** *n* tronco *m* de árvore; **up a** ~ *(US, coll)* *(person)* numa situação *f* difícil; **to climb a** ~ trepar a uma árvore; IDIOM **at the top of the** ~ no ponto mais alto da profissão; **to be barking up the wrong** ~ acusar erradamente.

trek *n* *(long journey)* viagem *f* penosa, jornada *f*; ♦ (-**ked**-) *vi* fazer uma jornada.

trekking *n* *(SPORT)* fazer caminhadas (**through** através).

trellis *n* grade *f* de ripas, latada *f*, treliça *f*.

tremble *n* tremor; estremecimento *m*; ♦ *vi* *(with cold, fear, rage)* tremer de; **2** *(horror, aversion)* estremecer; IDIOM **he was all of a** ~ *(coll)* ele tremia como varas *fpl* verdes.

trembling *adj* trémulo,-a *(BR:* -ê-), trepidante *m,f*.

tremendous *adj* *(impressive)* tremendo,-a; enorme *m,f*; *(excellent)* formidável *m,f*.

tremor *n* tremor *m*; (= **earth** ~) tremor *m* de terra; **2** *(machine)* vibração *f*.

tremulous *adj* *(voice)* *(with emotion)* trémulo,-a; *(from weaknesss)* vacilante *m,f*.

trench n (MIL) trincheira f; (narrow channel), vala f; **Marianas T~** npr (GEOG) Fossa das Marianas.

trenchant adj mordaz m,f; **2** cortante m,f.

trend n inclinação f, tendência; **2** moda, voga f; **3** orientação f; **4** (ECON) **production ~s** npl evolução f da produção.

trendily adv à última f moda.

trendsetter n iniciador,-ora.

trendy adj (idea) de acordo com a tendência f; **2** (person) a par da moda f; de moda, criador,-a de moda; **3** (product) último grito m da moda.

trepidation n trepidação f; **2** (fear) apreensão f.

trespass vi penetrar ilegalmente; (JUR) violar (property); 'no ~ing' 'passagem f proibida'; **2 to ~ on sb's kindness** abusar da bondade de alguém; **3 to ~ against** (REL) ofender.

trespasser n intruso,-a.

tress n trança f; ♦ vt entrançar.

trestle n cavalete m; ~ **table** n mesa f de cavaletes.

trial n (JUR) julgamento m, processo m; **to stand ~** ser julgado,-a; **2** (test) prova f, teste m; ~ **of strength** prova f de força; **3** (hardship) provação f; **4** experiência f; **on** ~ à prova, em testes; **5** (attempt) tentativa; **by ~ and error** por tentativa e erro; (car, flight, engine) ensaio m; ~ **run** n ensaio m; ~ **size (d)** em tamanho de amostra; ♦ (-ll-) vt testar.

triangle n (gen) triângulo m; **2** (MUS) ferrinhos mpl; **3** (US) (set square) esquadro m.

triangular adj triangular.

triathlon (pl: -s) n (SPORT) trialto m.

tribal adj tribal.

tribalism n tribalismo m.

tribe n (social group) tribo f; **a ~ of politicians** (coll) uma cambada f de políticos; ~**sman** n membro m de uma tribo.

tribulation n tribulação f, aflição f.

tribunal n (JUR) tribunal m.

tribune n tribuna f.

tributary (pl: -ies) n (river) afluente m.

tribute n (respect, admiration) tributo m; **to be a ~ to sb/sth** ser um tributo m para alguém/algo; **to pay ~ to sb** prestar homenagem f a alguém; **2** (evidence) prova f; **as a ~ of my admiration** como prova da minha admiração.

trice n: **in a ~** num instante m, num abrir e fechar de olhos mpl.

triceps (pl: -cepses) n tríceps m inv.

trick n truque m; **you found out my card ~** descobriste o meu truque m de cartas; **2** (deceit) fraude f, trapaça f; **3** (joke) brincadeira f; (children's) travessura; **to play a ~ on sb** pregar uma partida f (BR: peça em) a alguém; **4** (cards) vaza f; **to take/win a ~** ganhar uma vaza f; **5** (knack) habilidade f hábito m, mania f; **my cat knows many ~s** o meu gato faz muitas habilidades; **you'll soon learn the ~ of it** você depressa apanha, pega o jeito; ♦ vt enganar; **she has been ~ed by a scoundrel** ela deixou-se enganar por um patife; **I have been ~ed!** fui levado!; **to ~ out/up** vt enfeitar (in/with com); IDIOM **this will do the ~** isto vai pô-lo a funcionar or resolver o assunto.

trickery (pl: -ies) n trapaça f.

trickle n (of water, etc.) fio m de água; **2** (of people or things) pingo m; ♦ vi (liquid) gotejar, pingar; ~ **away** (water) escoar-se lentamente; ~ **down** correr (num fio); ~ **in/out** entrar/sair aos poucos; **to ~ in** chegar a conta-gotas; ~ **into** infiltrar-se.

trick question n pergunta f capciosa; (fam) pergunta f rasteira; (BR) (fam) pega-ratão m; **that is a ~** essa pergunta f tem uma rasteira f, (BR: é uma pega-ratão).

trickster n (crook) vigarista; (in fun) amigo,-a de truques.

tricky adj difícil m,f, complicado,-a; **2** (person) manhoso,-a.

tricycle n triciclo m.

tried (pt, pp of try) adj à toda a prova; **2** posto,-a à prova; **3** (person) atormentado,-a.

triennial adj trienal m,f.

triennially adv de três em três anos.

trifle n (triviality) (gift) bagatela f; (trivial details) miudezas fpl, ninharias fpl; **I won't waste my time with ~s** não vou perder tempo m com miudezas fpl; **2** (CULIN) tipo de pudim com gelateia, frutos e natas; **3** (small amount) pouco m; **a ~ of** um pouco de; ♦ vt brincar com (feelings); proceder levianamente; **don't ~ with him** ele m não é pessoa f para brincadeiras fpl; ♦ adv **a ~ long** um pouquinho m longo.

trifling adj insignificante m,f; (gifts; matters) ninharias fpl.

trigger n (of gun) gatilho m; **2** (fig) estímulo m; ♦ vt (gun) disparar; **2 to ~ off sth** desencadear algo; **3** (protest) provocar.

trigger-happy adj (coll) ansioso,-a por disparar, à menor provocação; **2** (coll) que age sem pensar.

trigonometry n trigonometria f.

trilby n (hat) chapéu m de feltro de homem.

trill n trinado m, trilo m; **2** (of birds) gorgeio m; **3** (LING) rolado m; ♦ vt trinar; (LING) rolar os 'rr'.

trillion n trilião m, trilhão m; **2** (UK: arc 18 zeros) trilião; (currently represented by 12 zeros) billion; **2** (fig); ~**s of** milhares de, monte de; (many) montes de.

trim n (haircut, etc.) corte m; **2** (hedge) poda f; **3** (good condition) em boa forma f, em bom estado; **4** decoração f, enfeite m; **5** (of braid) galão m; ♦ (-mer, -miest) adj (slim) esbelto,-a; **2** (house) arrumado,-a; **3** (garden) bem cuidado,-a; ♦ (-mm-) vt (cut) aparar, cortar (hair, hedge); **to ~ one's nails** arranjar as unhas fpl; **2** (decorate dress) enfeitar; **3** arrumar; **4** ~ **down** (sail) ajustar; ~ **away/off** vt cortar.

trimmings npl decoração fsg; enfeites mpl; **2** (CULIN) guarnição f; **3** (scraps) aparas fpl.

Trinidad and Tobago npr Trindade e Tobago.

Trinity npr (REL) **the ~** a Trindade f; **the Holy ~** a Santíssima Trindade.

trinket *n* bugiganga *f*; **2** *(piece of jewellery)* berloque *m*, bijuteria *f*; **3** *(without value)* bagatela *f*.

trio *n* trio *m*, terceto *m*.

trip *n* *(journey)* viagem *f*; **2** excursão *f*; **3** *(stumble)* tropeção *m*; **4** *(with drugs)* tripe *f* *(coll)*; ♦ *vi* (= **to ~ up**) tropeçar; ♦ *vt* (= **to ~ up**) fazer tropeçar; **2** passar uma rasteira *f*.

tripe *n* *(CULIN)* bucho *m*, tripa *f*; **2** *(rubbish)* tolice *f*, *(BR)* bobagem *f*.

triple *adj* triplo,-a, tríplice *m,f*; **~ jump** *n*: **the ~ jump** o salto *m* triplo; ♦ *vt/vi* triplicar.

triplets *npl* trigêmeos,-as.

triplicate *n*: **in ~** em triplicata *f*, triplicado,-a.

tripod *n* tripé *m*.

tripper *(also:* **day ~**) *n* excursionista *m,f*.

trite *adj* *(pej)* banal *m,f*; **that is a ~ remark** isso é uma banalidade *f*; **2** gasto,-a.

tritely *adv* corriqueiramente.

triumph *n* *(success and satisfaction)* triunfo *m*; ♦ *vi* **to ~** **(over)** triunfar (sobre).

triumphant *adj* triunfante *m,f*.

triunvirate *n* *(HIST)* triunvirato *m*.

trivia *npl* trivialidades *fpl*.

trivial *adj* *(pej)* insignificante *m,f*; trivial *m,f*.

triviality *(pl:* **-ies**) *n* trivialidade *f*.

trod *(pt of* **tread**).

trodden *(pt of* **tread**) *adj* espezinhado,-a; **(down~)** *(person)* oprimido,-a.

Trojan *n adj* troiano,-a.

trolley *(pl:* **-s**) *n* *(UK)* *(gen)* carrinho *m*, *(for drinks and in the supermarket)*; **2** carro-elé(c)trico *m*; **~ bus** *n* trólei; *(BR)* bonde *m*.

trombone *n* *(MUS)* trombone *m*.

troop *n* *(animals)* bando *m*; **2 ~s** *npl* *(MIL)* tropa *fsg*; ♦ *vi* *(march)* andar em grupo; **~ along** *(UK)* *(MIL)* desfilar em grupo; **~ in/out** entrar e sair em bando.

trooper *n* *(MIL)* soldado *f* de cavalaria; **2** *(coll)* cavalo *m* do exército; *(police)* polícia *m,f* montada; **3** *(THEAT)* elemento *m* de grupo *m* de comediantes; IDIOM **to swear like a ~** praguejar como um carroceiro.

trooping *n*: **T~ the Colour** *(UK)* cerimónia tradicional militar para saudação à bandeira.

trophy *(pl:* **-ies**) *n* troféu *m*; **2** *(spoils)* despojo *m* de guerra.

tropic *n*: **the T~ of Cancer/Capricorn**; o Trópico de Câncer/de Capricónio; **the ~s** *npl* os trópicos *mpl*.

tropical *adj* tropical *m,f*.

trot *n* *(horse)* trote *m*; **2** *(person)* passo *m* apressado; **trots** *npl* *(fam)* diarrea *f*; ♦ **on the ~** *adj* atarefado,-a; ♦ *adv* *(continuously)* vezes *fpl* de enfiada; ♦ (**-tt-**) *vt* *(horse, person)* trotar; andar com pressa; **to ~ along** *vi* seguir a trote; **to ~ away/off** pôr-se a andar; **to ~ out** *(fam)* *(excuses, argument)* sair-se com; **to ~ out the same story** repetir/apresentar a mesma história.

trotter *n*: pessoa ou cavalo que anda a trote; **2 ~s** *npl* *(pig's feet)* chispe *m*; *(sheep's)* mãozinhas *fpl* de carneiro; **globe-~** *n* pessoa *f* que corre o mundo.

trouble *n* problema *m*, dificuldade *f*; **I am in ~** estou cheia de problemas; **2** *(concern)* preocupação *f*; **3** incómodo *m* *(BR:* -cô-), esforço *m*; **to go to the ~ of doing sth** dar-se ao trabalho *m* de fazer algo; **~ maker** *n* criador-de-casos *m*; **2** pessoa conflituosa; **3** encrenqueiro,-a; **~shooter** *n* *(in conflict)* conciliador,-ora; **stomach ~** problemas *mpl* gástricos; **~s** *npl* *(POL, etc.)* distúrbios *mpl*; ♦ *vt* *(disturb)* perturbar, incomodar; **I don't want to ~ you** não a quero incomodar; ♦ *vi* **to ~ to do sth** incomodar-se, preocupar-se de fazer algo; IDIOM **to be in ~** estar em apuros, em maus lençóis.

troubled *adj* *(person)* preocupado,-a; **2** *(mind, spirit)* inquieto,-a; **3** *(times, water, sleep)* agitado,-a.

troublesome *adj* incómodo *(BR:* -cô-), chato,-a *(fam)*; problemático,-a; **~ cough** tosse *f* desagradável.

trough *n* *(tub)* selha *f*; **2** *(channel)* calha *f*; **3** *(for animals)* **drinking ~** bebedouro *m*, cocho *m*; **feeding ~** gamela *f*; **4** *(between hills)* vão *m*; **5** depressão *f*; **kneeding-~** amassadeira *f*.

troupe *n* companhia *f* teatral; grupo *m*.

trousers *npl* calças *mpl*.

trouser-suit *n* *(UK)* conjunto *m* calça-casaco.

trousseau *(pl:* **-x** *or* **-s**) *n* *(of the bride)* enxoval *m*.

trout *(pl:* **inv/-s**) *n* *(fish)* truta *f*.

trowel *n* *(for cement)* pá *f* de trolha *(BR:* de pedreiro); **2** *(for gardening)* pá de jardim.

Troy *npr* Tróia.

truancy *n* absentismo *m* *(from school, work)*.

truant *n*: **to play ~** faltar à aula; fazer gazeta; *(BR)* gazear aula.

truce *n* trégua *f*, armistício *m*.

truck camioneta *f* de carga; **2** *(lorry)* camião *m*, *(BR)* caminhão *m*; *(RAIL)* vagão *m* de mercadorias; **~ farm** *n* *(US)* horta; *(BR)* chácara *f*; **~ driver** *n* camionista *m,f* *(BR)* caminhoneiro,-a; **~load** *n* *(amount)* carregamento *m* de; **by the ~** em quantidade *f* industrial; **~ stop** *n* *(US)* bar *m* de estrada.

truckle *n* roda *f* pequena; ♦ *vi* submeter-se (**to** a); **~ bed** pequena *f* cama de montar.

truculent *adj* agressivo,-a, truculento,-a.

trudge *n* estirão *m*; **2** caminhada *f* difícil; ♦ *vi* andar com dificuldade *f*; *(fig)* arrastar-se.

true *adj* *(fact)* verdadeiro,-a; *(accurate)* exa(c)to,-a; **a ~ copy** uma cópia exa(c)ta; **2** *(real)* a sério; **3** *(heartfelt)* sincero, leal; **a ~ friend** um amigo leal; **~ blue** fiel a uma causa *f* ou ideia *f*; **~ lies** autênticas mentiras; **~-life** *adj* baseado,-a na vida real; ♦ *vt* ajustar, afinar; ♦ *adv* verdadeiramente; **2** sinceramente; IDIOM **to be ~ to life** ser realista *m,f*; **a dream come ~** tornar-se realidade *(dream)*; concretizar-se.

truffle *n* trufa *f*.

truly *adv* verdadeiramente; **2** fielmente; **yours ~** *(at end of a letter)* atenciosamente; IDIOM **that won't do for yours ~** essa comigo não pega.

trump *n* *(card)* trunfo *m*, naipe *m* de trunfo; **2** *(coll)* boa *f* pessoa; **3 ~ card** vantagem *f*; *(person)* pessoa *f* influente; **~ed-up** *adj* *(pej)* forjado,-a, inventado,-a; IDIOM **to hold the ~ card** estar em posição vantajosa (sobre alguém).

trumpet *n* *(MUS)* trombeta *f*, trompete *m*.

truncheon *n* cassetete *m*.

trundle *vt/vi* exercer pressão; **to ~ along** rolar, rodar pesadamente, chiando.

trunk *n (of tree, person)* tronco *m*; **2** *(of elephant)* tromba *f*; **3** *(case)* baú *m*; *(US: in car)* porta-bagagens *m inv*; **~ call** *n (TEL)* ligação *f* inter-urbana; **~ road** *n* via *f* eixo, rodovia *f* nacional; **(swimming) ~s** calção *m* de banho.

truss *(pl: -es) n (MED)* funda *f*; **2** *(CONSTR)* arma-ção *f* para suporte; **3** *(clothes)* trouxa *f*; **4** *(fruit)* cacho *m*; ◆ **to ~ (up)** *vt* amarrar; atar *(chicken)* com cordel (para assar); enfeixar *(hay)*.

trust *n (faith)* confiança *f*; **to have ~ in sb/sth** ter confiança em alguém/algo; **2** *(COMM) (credit)* truste *m*, monopólio *m*; **3** *(FIN, JUR)* fideicomisso *m*; **~ company** *n* sociedade *f* fiduciária; ◆ *vt (confidence)* confiar em; **2** *(rely on)* **I ~ you!** conto com você!; **3** *(entrust)* **to ~ sb with sth/sb** confiar algo/alguém a alguém; **4** *(hope)* **I ~ you are not tired** espero que você não esteja cansado; **to take sth on ~** tomar algo como verdade; **to sell/give on ~** vender a crédito, à confiança.

trusted *adj* de confiança *f*.

trustee *n (JUR)* fideicomissário *m*; **2** *(of school, etc.)* administrador,-ora, curador,-ora.

trustful, trusting *adj* confiante *m,f*, crédulo,-a.

trustfund *n* fidúcia *f*, fundo *m* fiduciário.

trustworthy *adj* digno,-a de confiança; fidedigno,-a.

trusty (-ier, -iest) fiel *m,f*.

truth *(pl: -s) n (gen)* verdade *f*; veracidade *f*; **to find out the ~** apurar a verdade.

truthful *adj (person)* sincero,-a, honesto,-a; **~ drug** *n* soro *m* da verdade.

truthfully *adv* sinceramente.

try *(pl: -tries) n (attempt)* tentativa *f*; **at the second ~** à segunda tentativa; **2** experiênca *f*; **can I have a ~ at?** posso experimentar?; **3** *(rugby)* ensaio *m*; ◆ *vt* tentar; **I am going to ~ my luck** vou tentar a sorte; **2** *(JUR)* levar a juízo; **3** *(test)* provar, pôr à prova; **4** *(strain)* cansar; *(patience)* esgotar; ◆ *vi* **to ~ for sth** tratar de obter algo; **to ~ on** *vt (clothes, shoes)* experimentar; **~ out** *vt (car, machine)* testar, pôr à prova; **to ~ over** *(music, etc)* ensaiar.

trying *adj* difícil, árduo,-a; **that noise is very ~** esse barulho é muito irritante; **~ moments** momentos *mpl* críticos.

tsar *n* czar *m*.

tsetse *n (fly)* tsé-tsé *(mosca) f*.

T-shaped *(pipes etc)* em forma de T.

T-shirt (tee-shirt) *n* camiseta *f*.

tsunami *n* maremoto *(BR: -â-) m*.

Tuareg *n adj* tuaregue *m,f*.

tub *n (bath)* banheira *f*; **2** tina *f*; **3** bacia grande *(BR)* pia *f*; alguidar *m*; **4** *(of cream, paté)* boião *m*; caixa *f*.

tub-thumping *n* opiniões trocadas em voz alta e agressiva.

tuba *n (music)* tuba *f*.

tubby *adj* gorducho,-a; **2** atarracado,-a.

tube *n* tubo *m*, cano *m*; **2** *(glue, etc.)* bisnaga *f*; **3** *(ANAT)* trompa *f*, canal *m*; **4** *(underground)* metro(politano) *m*, *(BR)* metrô *m*; **~ station** *(UK)* estação *f* de metro; **5** *(US, coll)* televisão *f*; **6** *(for tyre)* câmara-de-ar *f*; **~ steak** *(US, coll)* cachorro-quente *m*; ◆ *vt* entubar.

tubeless *adj* sem câmara.

tuber *n (US)* tubérculo *m*.

tuberculosis *n* tuberculose *f*.

tubing *n* tubagem *f*; **2** canalização *f*; **3** *(BR)* encanamento *m*, tubulação *f*; **a piece of ~** um pedaço *m* de tubo.

tubular *adj* tubular *m,f*; **2** *(furniture)* tubiforme *m,f*.

TUC *npr (abbr for **Trades Union Congress**) (UK) (equir)* União Geral de Trabalhadores (UGT).

tuck *n (sewing)* prega *f*, dobra *f*; **~ shop** *n* confeitaria *(in station, near school)*; ◆ *vt* enfiar, meter; **he ~ed his hands in his pockets** ele enfiou as mãos nos bolsos; ◆ **to ~ away** *vt (store)* guardar; **2** *(hidden)* esconder; ◆ **to ~ in** *vt* enfiar, meter; **2** *(child in bed)* cobrir bem (a criança); ◆ (= **to ~ up**) aconchegar na cama *f*; **to ~ up one's sleeves** arregaçar as mangas *fpl*; **to ~ under** *vt* recolher; ◆ *vi* (= **~ into**) *(coll) (eat)* comer bem.

Tuesday *n* terça-feira *f*; **Shrove ~** Terça-Feira Gorda, de Carnaval.

tuft *n (of feathers, hair)* penacho *m*; **2** *(of grass, bush)* tufo *m*.

tug *n (boat)* rebocador *m*; **2** *(pull)* puxão *m*; **3** *(fig) (row)* disputa *f*; **~-of-war** *n* cabo-de-guerra *m*; ◆ (-gg-) *vt (tow boat)* rebocar; ◆ *vi* **to ~ at sth** darum puzão em algo.

tuition *n* ensino *m*; **2** *(private)* explicações *fpl*; **~ fees** *(UK)* propinas *fpl*; **private ~** aulas *fpl* particulares.

tulip *n (BOT)* tulipa *f*.

tumble *n* queda *f*, tombo *m*, trambolhão *m*; **I had a big ~** dei um grande trambolhão *m*; **2** *(fig)* con-fusão *f*; **the room was in a ~** o quarto *m* estava em desordem *f*; ◆ *vi* cair; **2** *(water)* jorrar; **3** *(fig) (prices)* cair; ◆ *vt* tombar, desabar.

tumbledown *adj* em ruínas *fpl*.

tumble-dryer *n* máquina *f* de secar roupa *f*.

tumbler *n (glass)* copo *m*.

tumescent *adj* intumescente *m,f*.

tumid *adj* inchado,-a, empolado,-a.

tumidity *n* saliência *f*; **2** estilo *m* empolado e pomposo.

tummy *(pl: -ies) n (coll) (lower abdomen)* barriga *f*; **2** estômago *m*; **~ button** *(coll)* umbigo *m*; **~ tuck** *(MED)* abdominoplastia *f*.

tumour *n* tumor *m*.

tumult *n* tumulto *m*; **2** alvoroço *m*; **3** desordem *f*.

tumultuous *adj* tumultuado,-a, tumultuoso,-a.

tun *n (for wine)* pipa *f*, casco *m*.

tuna *n pl inv* (= **~ fish**) atum *m*.

tune *n (song)* melodia *f*; ◆ *vt (MUS)* afinar; **2** *(RADIO, TV)* sintonizar; **3** *(AUT)* ajustar; **to be in/out of ~** *(instrument)* estar afinado, desafinado,-a; **4** *(singer)* cantar bem/mal; *(in agreement with sb)* em sinto-nia com alguém; **out of ~ with sb** fora de sintonia com alguém; **~ in** *vi (RADIO, TV)* sintonizar-se; **2** ficar à escuta (**to** de); ◆ **to ~ up** *vi (musician)* afinar (instrumento); **2** *vt (engine)* afinar; **3** *vi (orchestra)* afinar os instrumentos *mpl*.

tuned *adj* (= **in tune**) afinado,-a; **2** sintonizado,-a.

tuner *n (RADIO, TV)* sintonizador *m*; **2** *(MUS)* -afinador *m*; **piano ~** afinador *m* de pianos.

tungsten *n (wolfram)* tungsténio *m*.

tuning *n (RADIO)* sintonização *f*; ~ **in to a station** sintonização *f* de uma emissora *f*; **2** *(instrument, engine)* afinação *f*; ~ **fork** *n* diapasão *m*.

Tunisia *npr* Tunísia *f*; **in** ~ na Tunísia.

Tunisian *n adj* tunisiano,-a.

tunnel *n* túnel *m*; **they are driving a ~ through rock** eles *mpl* estão a abrir um túnel *m* na rocha *f*; **2** *(in mine)* galeria *f*.

tunnelling *n* abertura *f* de túneis ou passagens *fpl* subterrâneas.

tunny *(pl: -ies) n (fish)* atum *m*.

turban *n (headgear)* turbante *m*.

turbid *adj* turvo,-a; **2** lodoso,-a; **3** *(fig)* emaranhado *m*.

turbine *n* turbina *f*.

turbo *m* turbo *m*; **~prop** *n* turbopropulsor *m*; *(plane)* turboja(c)to.

turbulence *n* turbulência *f*; **2** violência *f*.

turbulent *adj* turbulento,-a; **2** indisciplinado,-a; **3** *(wind)* instável *m,f*.

tureen *n* terrina *f*, *(BR)* sopeira *f*.

turf *(pl: -s/-ves) n* relva *f*, grama *f*; *(= turfed adj)* relvado *m*, *(BR)* gramado *m*; **2** *(peat)* turfa *f*; **3** *(horse racing)* **the ~** *n* as corridas *fpl* de cavalo; ♦ *vt* arrelvar; *(BR)* gramar; **to ~ out** *vt (UK, coll)* chutar; dar patadas; *(throw away sth)* deitar fora; **to ~ sb out** pôr alguém no olho *m* da rua *(cal)*.

turgid *adj (speech)* pomposo,-a, empolado,-a.

turgidity *n (style)* empolamento *m* (de estilo).

Turk *n* turco,-a.

Turkestan *npr* Turquestão *m*.

Turkey[1] *npr* Turquia *f*; **in** ~ na Turquia.

turkey[2] *n (bird and meat)* peru,-ua.

Turkish *n adj* turco,-a; *(LÍNG)* turco; ~ **bath** *n* banho *m* turco.

Turkmenistan *npr* Turquemenistão *m*

turmeric *(BOT)* açafrão-da-índia *m*; *(BR)* açafrão-da-terra *m*.

turmoil *n* tumulto *m*, distúrbio *m*; **2** *(emotionally)* agitação *f*; **3** barafunda *f*, desordem *f*.

turn *n (key)* volta *f*; **give the key two ~s** dê duas voltas à chave; **2** turno *m*, vez *f*; **it's your ~** é a sua vez; **to take ~s (to do sth)** revezar-se; fazer à vez; **3** (MED) *(of events)* reviravolta *f*; **4** *(change)* curso *m*; mudança *f*, viragem *f*; **to take a ~ for the worse** mudar para pior; **5** (THEAT) *(act)* número *m*; **6** *(bend)* curva *f*; **twists and ~s** curvas e contracurvas; *(walk)* passeio *m*; ♦ **at every ~** a cada passo, momento; **by ~s** sucessivamente, por turnos; ♦ *vt/vi (rotate)* girar, dar volta a, virar; **2** *(change of position/direction)* **he turned left** ele virou à esquerda; **'no right ~'** proibido virar à direita; *(person)* (~ **around**) voltar-se; *(in bed)* virar-se; **3** *(become)* ficar, virar; *(go off)* **the milk ~ed sour** o leite ficou azedo; **4** *(convert)* **she ~ed Budhist** ela converteu-se ao Budismo *(BR)* ela virou Budista; **5 to ~ into sth** transformar-se algo; **6 to ~ pale** empalidecer, ficar branco; **he ~ed white when he saw her** ele ficou branco quando a viu; ♦ ~ **about** *vi* dar uma volta *f* completa; ~ **against** *vt* revoltar-se; ~ **around** *vt (change)* dar a volta *f* a; **2** *(business)*

ajudar a recuperar; ♦ *vi* voltar-se; **2** dar meia-volta *f*; ♦ ~ **aside** *vt* desviar; **2** *vi* afastar-se *(from* de); ♦ ~ **away** *vt (person)* mandar embora; **2** rejeitar; ♦ *vi* desviar-se *(from* de), afastar-se de; **his eyes ~ed away from** os olhos dele desviaram-se de; **2** virar *(a* cabeça *f*, as costas *fpl)*; ♦ ~ **back** *vi (return)* voltar para trás *(in book – page)* voltar atrás; **2** *(watch)* atrasar; **3** *(decision, etc.)* retroceder; ♦ ~ **down** *vt (refuse)* recusar; **2** *(reduce)* baixar; **3** *(fold)* dobrar, virar para baixo; ♦ ~ **in** *vi (coll)* ir para a cama, dormir; ~ **into** *vt* transformar-se em; **she ~ed into a princess** ela transformou-se numa princesa; ~ **a novel into a play** adaptar um romance a uma peça de teatro; ~ **off** *vt (light, RADIO, etc.)* apagar; desligar ♦ **to ~ the subject** *vi* desviar-se do assunto; *(from road)* desviar-se; ~ **on** *vt (light, RADIO, etc.)* acender; ligar; ~ **out** *n* assistência; afluência *f*; comparecimento *m*; ~ **out to be** *vt* revelar-se (ser), resultar (ser); IDIOM **to do sb a ~** fazer um jeito *m* a alguém.

turncoat *n (pej)* (POL) vira-casaca *m,f*.

turned *adj (furniture feet)* torneado,-a; **well ~ sentence** frase *f* elegante; **2** ~ **up** *(trousers, nose)* virado,-a para cima; **3** *(lathe)* trabalhado ao torno.

turning *adj (side road, turn)* volta, curva *f*; **2** mudança *f*; **a ~ for the better/for worse** uma mudança para melhor/pior; **3** torneio *m*; **~-point** *n (fig)* momento *m* decisivo, ponto *m* de viragem; ♦ *adj* que gira; rotativo,-a.

turnip *n* nabo *m*; ~ **tops** *npl* nabiças *fpl*.

turnover *n (COMM)* volume *m* de negócios, produção; fa(c)turação *f*; **2** *(personnel)* rotatividade *f* de funcionários; **3** (CULIN) pastel com recheio de frutos secos; ♦ **to turn over** *vt* derrubar; **2** *(a page)* voltar a folha *f*; **3** *(a new leaf)* regenerar-se; ♦ *vi* revirar-se.

turnpike *n* estrada *f*, rodovia com portagem *(BR)*, pedágio.

turnstile *n* roleta *f*, torniquete *m*.

turntable *n (on record player)* prato *m*.

turn-up *n (on trousers)* volta *f*, dobra *f*; ♦ **to turn up** *vi (person)* aparecer, chegar.

turpentine *n (= turps)* terebentina *f*, aguarrás *f*.

turquoise *n (colour, gem)* turquesa *f*; ♦ *adj* cor *f* turquesa.

turret *n* torre *f* pequena, torreão *m*.

turtle *(pl inv/-s) n* tartaruga *f*; ♦ *vi* ir à pesca de tartarugas *fpl*; ~ **dove** *n* rola *f*; **~neck** *n (of sweater)* gola *f* alta, *(BR)* gola *f* olímpica.

tusk *n (of elephant)* defesa *f*; *(incisive tooth) (of boar etc)* presa *f*, colmilho *m*.

tussle *n (fight)* luta *f*; **2** *(scuffle)* contenda *f*, rixa *f*; ♦ *vi* lutar; **2** disputar; **we ~d over the flowers** disputámos as flores *fpl*.

tutor *n* professor,-ora; **2** orientador,-ora; **3** tutor,-a; ♦ *vi* dar explicações *fpl* (a).

tutorial *n (EDUC)* seminário *m*.

tutoring *n* ensino *m*; **2** explicações *fpl*.

tuxedo *(men's evening attire)* smoking *m*.

twaddle *n* **2** disparates *mpl*; *(BR)* bobagens *fpl*; **she talks ~** ela *f* fala no ar *m*; ♦ *vi* dizer tolices *fpl*.

twang n (of instrument) som m agudo; (of string, rope) vibração f, ruído m de corda; (of voice) timbre m nasal, fanhoso,-a; ♦ vi vibrar; ♦ vt (guitar) tanger.

twat n (vulg) estupor; filho m da mãe; 2 (vulg) rata f.

tweak n puxão m; beliscão m; ♦ vt puxar; 2 beliscar; 3 fazer pequenas melhorias.

twee adj (UK) excessivamente sentimental ou afe(c)tado; (room, decor, etc) querido,-a, porreiro,-a.

tweed n tweed m, pano grosso m de lã.

tweedy adj de tweed, feito de tweed.

tweet n (chirp) chilreio m; (onomat) '~ ~' 'piu-piu; ♦ vi chilrear; 2 pipilar.

tweezers npl (for eyebrows) pinça fsg.

twelfth n décima f segunda parte; ♦ adj num décimo m segundo; ♦ adv em décimo m segundo lugar; T~ **Night** npr Noite f de Reis, Epifania f.

twelve n, num doze m; ~-**tone** adj (MUS) dodeca-fónico,-a (BR: -fô).

twentieth n, num, adj vigésimo,-a.

twenty (pl: -ies) n, num vinte m; ~**fold** adj, adv vinte vezes mais.

twerp n (UK) (fam, pej) imbecil m,f.

twice adv duas fpl vezes; ~ **as much** duas vezes mais; 2 dobro m; **I am ~ as old as she is** tenho o dobro da idade f dela f.

twiddle vt mexer (entre os dedos) torcer; **he is always twiddling his moustache** ele m está sempre a torcer o bigode m; ♦ vi brincar (**with** com); 2 mexer (**with** com); IDIOM **to ~ one's thumbs** (fig) estar sem fazer nada.

twig n galho m, rebento m; ♦ (-**gg**-) vt (UK, coll) perceber; **do you ~ it?** percebeste?; 2 observar.

twigged adj com ramos mpl ou galhos mpl finos.

twiggery n ramagem f; 2 raminhos mpl.

twilight n (evening) crepúsculo m, lusco-fusco m; **in the ~ of my life** no crepúsculo da minha vida; 2 (fig) decadência f, declínio m.

twin n adj gémeo,-a (BR: gê-); ~ **cities** cidades-gémeas mpl, (BR) cidades-irmãs mpl; ~-**bedded** adj com duas fpl camas; ~-**engined** (plane) bimotor; ~**ning** n geminação f; ~-**set** n (women's fashion) conjunto de camisola e casaquinho de malha; ♦ (-**nn**-) vi irmanar-se, geminar; emparelhar.

twine n barbante m, guita f.

twinge n (of pain) pontada f; 2 (of conscience) remorso m; **I have some ~s of conscience** estou cheio,-a de remorsos mpl; ♦ vt provocar dor f aguda; ♦ vi sentir pontadas fpl.

twinkle n cintilação f, piscadela f; 2 movimento m breve; 3 (fig) momento m; ♦ vi (stars) cintilar; **when she saw him, her eyes ~d** quando ela f o viu, os olhos mpl brilharam; 2 (eyes) pestanejar, (for fun) piscar (o olho); **in the ~ of an eye** num abrir e fechar de olhos.

twinkling adj cintilante m,f.

twirl n giro m, volta f; ♦ vt fazer girar; ♦ vi girar rapidamente.

twist n (action) torção f; 2 (foot, arm) entorse f; 3 (in road) curva f; 4 (in wire, flex) torcedela f; 5 (in story) mudança f imprevista, um desfecho m inesperado; ♦ vt (gen) torcer, retorcer; 2 (weave) entrelaçar; 3 enroscar, enrolar; 4 (lid) desa-tarrochar; **to ~ the key** entortar a chave; (fig) deformar (truth); distorcer (words, meaning); **he ~ed his ankle** ele torceu o pé m; **his face ~ed with pain** o rosto dele contorcia-se com as dores; ♦ vi (river) serpentear; ~ **about/around** vi (rope, etc.) enroscar-se; 2 (road, etc.) serpentear; ♦ ~ **off** vt desenroscar; 2 desaparafusar; ♦ ~ **up** vt/vi (rope, string, etc.) enrolar(-se); IDIOM **to ~ sb's arm** (persuadir) torcer o braço de alguém; **he said with a ~ of the mouth** ele disse com um esgar da boca.

twisted adj (pej) retorcido,-a; deturpado,-a; 2 entrançado,-a; 3 em espiral.

twisting adj tortuoso,-a.

twit n (UK, coll) idiota m,f, bobo, m.

twitch n puxão m; 2 (nervous) tique m nervoso; ♦ vt (ears, nose) tremer; **to ~ away** vt arrancar (**from** a); ♦ vi contrair-se, puxar bruscamente, contorcer-se.

twitching n súbita f contra(c)ção muscular; 2 tique m; 3 convulsão f; 4 puxão f.

twitchy adj inquieto,-a; 2 com tiques mpl nervosos.

twitter n (bird) chilreio m; (fig) alvoroço m; ♦ vi chilrear; 2 ~ **on** (person) tagarelar, palrar.

two n, num dois/duas m,f; ~-**faced** adj (pej) (person) de duas fpl caras; 2 falso m; **the ~ of us** nós dois/duas m,f; **to increase ~fold** duplicar; **to put ~ and ~ together** (fig) tirar conclusões fpl; **to run a train in ~ parts** desdobrar um comboio m (BR: trem); ~-**seater** n sofá m; (car) veículo m de dois mpl lugares; ~-**sided** (story) adj controverso,-a.

tycoon n (business) ~ magnata m,f, ricaço,-a.

type n (gen) tipo, espécie f; **he is my ~ of man** ele m faz o meu género m; 2 modelo m; 3 (TYPO) tipo m, letra f; **I will print the document in large ~** vou imprimir o documento m em tipo m grande; ~**cast** vt (THEAT) ser rotulado,-a, catalogado,-a (**as** como); ~**script** n texto m da(c)tilografado; ~**writer** n máquina f de escrever; ♦ vt da(c)tilo-grafar, (computer) digitar (= vi); 2 (blood type) classificar (sangue).

typhoid n febre f tifóide.

typhoon n tufão m.

typhus n tifo m.

typical adj típico,-a.

typically adv tipicamente; 2 (usually) geralmente.

typify vt tipificar, simbolizar.

typing n da(c)tilografia f; (COMP) digitação f.

typist n da(c)tilógrafo,-a, (COMP) digitador,-ora.

tyranny n tirania f.

tyrant n (person) tirano,-a.

tyre (UK) **tire** (US) n pneu m, pneumático,-a; **spare ~** pneu m sobressalente; ~ **gauge** n manómetro m (BR: -nô-).

tyro n aprendiz m,f, principiante m,f.

tzar n czar m.

tzarina n czarina f.

u

U, u *n (letter)* U, u *m*; **2** *(abbr for* **universal**) filme de censura livre.
UAE *(abbr for* **United Arab Emirates**) *npr* EUA *mpl*.
U-bend *n* curva em U; *(pipe, etc)* curvatura em U.
ubiquitous *adj* ubíquo, o(m)nipresente.
UCL *npr (abbr for* **University College London**) uma das faculdades de Londres.
udder *n* úbere; teta.
UFO *n (abbr for* **unidentified flying object**) objeto voador não identificado OVNI *m inv*.
Uganda *npr* Uganda *f*; **in** ~ na Uganda.
Ugandan *n adj* ugandês,-esa.
ugh *exc (displeasure, disgust)* ui!
ugliness *n* fealdade *f*, feiura.
ugly (-lier, -iest) *adj* feio,-a; **2** *(dangerous)* perigoso,-a; ~ **aspect** efeito *m* negativo; IDIOM **as ~ as sin** tão feio como o pecado/como o bode; **the ~ duckling** *n (fig)* patinho *m* feio.
UK *npr (abbr for* **United Kingdom**) RU = Reino Unido.

O Reino Unido compreende a Inglaterra, o país de Gales, a Escócia, a Irlanda do Norte (Ulster) e ilhas no Canal da Mancha e no Mar da Irlanda.

Ukraine *npr*: **the** ~ a Ucrânia *f*; **in** ~ na Ucrânia.
Ukrainian *n adj* ucraniano,-a; *(LING)* ucraniano *m*.
ukulele *n* ukulele *f*.
ulcer *n (MED)* úlcera; **mouth ~** *n (pop)* afta *f*.
ulcerated *adj* ulcerado,-a.
Ulster *npr (Northen Ireland)* Ulster *m*.
ulterior *adj (hidden intention)* oculto; **without any ~ motive** sem interesse pessoal; sem ideia pre-concebida; **2** *(subsequent)* ulterior.
ultimate *n*: **the** ~ o máximo *m* (**in sth** em algo); ♦ *adj (aim, wish)* último,-a, final, derradeiro,-a; **2** *(sacrifice)* supremo,-a; **3** *(question)* fundamental.
ultimately *adv* no final, no final de contas, por último; no fundo, basicamente; em última análise.
ultimatum *n* ultimato *m*.
ultra *prefix* ultra.
ultrasonic *adj* ultrasónico,-a *(BR: -ô-)*.
ultraviolet *adj* ultravioleta.
um! *exc (hesitação em discurso)* hum!
umber *n (ART)* umbra *f*; *(colour)* castanho amarelado, cor de ferrugem.
umbilical cord *n* cordão *m* umbilical.
umbrage *n*: **to take ~** *(get touchy)* melindrar-se, ofender-se (**at** com).

umbrella *n* guarda-chuva *m*; ♦ **2** *(protection)* **under the ~ of** sob a proteção de; *(entity)* sob a égide de.
umpire *n* árbitro *m*; ♦ *vt* arbitrar.
umpteen *adj* inúmeros; centenas; **for the ~th time** pela centésima/enésima vez.

un prefixo usado em substantivos, adjetivos, (contrário a) e em verbos que representam o inverso de ação. Em português os principais são: **des**; **i**; **in**, **im**; **não**, **sem**; **sub**. Ex. **desinfetar** – disinfect. Os outros prefixos ingleses são: **dis-**; **i**, **im**, **in**; **non**, **sub**, **under**, mas eles nem sempre têm as mesmas equivalências; e.g.: **unhappy** – infeliz.

UN, UNO *npr (abbr for* **United Nations Organization**) Organização *f* das Nações Unidas *fpl* (ONU *f*).
unabashed *adj (not ashamed)* descarado,-a; imperturbável; **he looked ~** ele não parecia desconcertado.
unabated *adj (fighting storm)* incessante.
unable *adj*: **to be ~ to do sth** ser incapaz de, não poder fazer algo, não conseguir (fazer algo).
unabridged *adj* integral, na íntegra.
unacceptable *adj* inaceitável.
unaccompanied *adj* só, desacompanhado,-a; **she is travelling ~** ela viaja só; **2** *(MUS)* sem acompanhamento *m*.
unaccountable *adj* incompreensível; **2** *(not responsible)* que não é responsável (**for sth** por algo); **to be ~ to anyone** não ter de dar satisfações a ninguém.
unaccountably *adv* inexplicavelmente.
unaccounted *adj*: ~ **for** desaparecido,-a; **2** *(occurrence, etc)* sem explicação.
unaccustomed *adj (person)* desacostumado,-a (**to** a); **to be ~ to** não estar acostumado a.
unacknowledged *adj (talent, contribution)* não reconhecido,-a; **2** *(without reply)* **her letter was ~** não acusaram a rece(p)ção da carta dela.
unacquainted *adj*: ~ **with sb/sth** sem conhecer alguém/algo.
unadulterated *adj (unspoiled)* não-adulterado,-a; **2** *(water)* puro,-a.
unaffected *adj (untouched)* não-afetado,-a; **2** *(unpretensious, natural)* natural, simples, descontraído,-a.
unafraid *adj* destemido,-a.
unaided *adj* sem ajuda, por si só.
unanimous *adj* unânime.
unanimously *adv* unanimemente.
unannounced *adj* não-anunciado,-a; ♦ *adv (arrive)* sem prevenir, sem anunciar.
unanswerable *adj* irrespondível, irrefutável *m,f*.
unanswered *adj* sem resposta.
unappreciated *adj (work, talent)* não reconhecido,-a; **2** *(person)* subestimado,-a.
unappreciative *adj (person, public)* ingrato,-a.
unapproachable *adj* inacessível.
unapt *adj* inapto,-a; pouco disposto,-a (**to do** a fazer).
unarmed *adj* desarmado,-a; **2** indefeso,-a; ♦ **3** *n (combat)* sem armas.
unashamed *adj* descarado,-a; sem vergonha; franco,-a, aberto,-a.
unashamedly *adv* sem vergonha, com franqueza.

unassuming *adj* modesto,-a, desprentensioso,-a.

unattached *adj (not fastened)* solto,-a, separado,-a, destacado,-a; **2** *(organization)* independente; **3** *(without partner)* descomprometido,-a, solteiro,-a, livre.

unattended *adj (child, luggage, car)* sem vigilância, abandonado,-a.

unattractive *adj (style, place)* feio,-a, sem atrativos; **2** *(person)* pouco atraente; **3** *(idea)* sem brilho.

unauthorized *adj* não autorizado,-a, proibido,-a.

unavailable *adj* indisponível, inacessível.

unavailing *adj* que não está disponível.

unavoidable *adj* inevitável.

unaware *adj* desprevenido,-a; **2** *(ignorant of)* desconhecedor,-ora; **3** *(not conscious of)* alheio,-a (**to** a); **to be ~ of** ignorar, não perceber; **~s** *adv* improvisadamente, de surpresa; **to be taken ~s** ser apanhado de surpresa, estar desprevenido,-a.

unbalanced *adj* desequilibrado,-a, instável; **2** *(biased)* parcial *(report, accounts)*.

unbearable *adj* insuportável, insustentável.

unbeatable *adj (team)* invencível; imbatível *m,f.*

unbeaten *adj (person, game, city)* invicto,-a; **2** *(ground, matter)* inexplorado,-a.

unbecoming *adj (manner, behaviour)* impróprio,-a; **2** *(clothing, colour)* pouco favorecedor.

unbeknown(st) *adv* sem o conhecimento (**of** de); **~ to me** desconhecido por mim.

unbelievable *adj* inacreditável, incrível.

unbeliever *adj* incrédulo,-a, cé(p)tico,-a; **2** *(REL)* descrente, infiel.

unbend (*irr: like* **bend**) *vi (relax)* descontrair-se; relaxar-se; ♦ *vt (wire)* desentortar.

unbending *adj* inflexível, intransigente *m,f.*

unbias(s)ed *adj* imparcial, sem preconceito.

unbind (*pt, pp* **-bound**) *vt (bow, rope)* desatar; **2** *(prisoner)* libertar.

unblemished *adj* sem defeito; **2** *(pure)* sem mácula, sem mancha.

unblock *vt* desentupir *(pipe, sink; nose).*

unblushing *adj* sem corar, imodesto,-a, desavergonhado,-a

unbolt *vt (door)* destrancar; desaferrolhar.

unborn *adj (child)* nascituro,-a, por nascer; **2** futuro.

unbounded *adj (joy)* ilimitado,-a, imenso,-a; **2** *(love)* desmesurado,-a.

unbreakable *adj* inquebrável; **2** *(view)* contínuo,-a, ininterrupto; **~ record** um record que não foi batido.

unbridled *adj (of a horse)* sem rédeas *fpl*; **2** *(fig) (without restraint)* desenfreado,-a; *(joy)* imenso,-a.

unbroken *adj* intacto; **2** ininterrupto; **3** *(horse)* não domado, indómito; **4** *(record)* mantido; **5** imbatível *m,f.*

unburden *vt* desafogar; descarregar; **to ~ o.s. with sb** *(worries)* desabafar com alguém.

unbusinesslike *adj (conduct)* contrário,-a à ética profissional.

unbutton *vt* desabotoar.

unbuttoned *adj* desabotoado.

uncalled for *adj* desnecessário, injusto,-a.

uncanny (-ier, -iest) *adj* incauto; **2** estranho, sinistro,-a; **3** *(accuracy)* espantoso,-a, incrível.

uncared for *adj (unkempt)* descuidado,-a, desleixado,-a; **2** negligenciado,-a; **3** *(left to his/her fate)* ao Deus-dará.

unceasing *adj* sem cessar, contínuo.

unceasingly *adv* incessantemente.

unceremonious *adj (departure)* brusco, abrupto; **2** *(person, manner)* sem cerimónia.

uncertain *adj* incerto; indeciso.

uncertainty *n* incerteza.

unchanged *adj* inalterado.

uncharitable *adj (person, deed)* desumano,-a, impiedoso,-a; pouco caridoso,-a.

uncharted *adj (terrain)* inexplorado,-a; desconhecido,-a; **2** *(map)* não-cartografado,-a.

unchecked *adj (unrestrained)* desenfreado,-a; **2** *(baggage, bill)* não verificado,-a.

uncivil *adj* grosseiro, rude.

uncivilized *adj* incivilizado.

uncivilly *adv* incivilmente; rudemente.

unclaimed *adj (lost property, prize)* não reclamado,-a.

uncle *n* tio *m.*

unclean *adj* sujo,-a; **2** *(REL)* impuro.

unclear *adj (purpose, meaning)* pouco claro; confuso; **2** *(handwriting)* ilegível; **3** *(future)* incerto.

unclench *vt* abrir *(fist, jaw).*

unclouded *adj (sky)* claro, desanuviado.

uncoil *vt* desenrolar; ♦ *vi (snake)* desenrolar-se.

uncomfortable *adj (furniture, clothes)* incómodo,-a (*BR:* -cô-), desconfortável; **2** *(ambience)* desconfortável; **3** *(person: ill at ease)* constrangido, pouco à vontade; **4** *(shy)* acanhado.

uncommon *adj* raro, incomum, excepcional.

uncomprehending *adj* atónito,-a (*BR:* -ô-), sem compreender.

uncompromising *adj* intransigente, inflexível.

unconcerned *adj* indiferente, despreocupado,-a, desinteressado,-a.

unconditional *adj* incondicional.

unconditionally *adv* incondicionalmente.

uncongenial *adj (person)* pouco simpático,-a; *(atmosphere, person)* desagradável; incompatível; que não é congénere.

unconnected *adj (incident)* isolado; **2** *(appliances)* desligado,-a; **3** *(wires)* sem conta(c)to, desconexo,-a; **4 ~ with** *(subject, facts)* alheio,-a a.

unconscious *n:* **the ~** o inconsciente *m*; ♦ *adj* sem sentidos; **2** *(unaware)* inconsciente; **~ of** não estar consciente de; sensibilizado quanto a.

unconsciously *adv* inconscientemente.

unconsidered *adj* irrefle(c)tido, imponderado, sem consideração.

uncontrollable *adj* incontrolável, violento,-a; indomável.

uncork *vt* tirar/sacar a rolha, desarrolhar, abrir *(wine bottle).*

uncouth *adj* rude, grosseiro.

uncover *vt* descobrir *(plot, mystery)*; destapar *(blanket)*; destampar *(saucepans).*

uncovered *adj* descoberto,-a; *(in bed)* destapado; *(undressed)* despido,-a.

uncritical *adj* acrítico.

unctuous *adj* untuoso, oleoso.

undecided *adj* indeciso; **2** *(question, case)* pendente.

undeniable *adj* inegável.

under *adj* inferior, subordinado; ♦ *prep* debaixo de; por baixo de; **the briefcase is ~ the table** a pasta está debaixo da mesa; **2** sob; **~ oath** sob juramento; **~ pain of death** sob pena de morte; **~ repair** em concerto; **3** *(less than)* menos de; abaixo de; inferior a; **~ fifty pounds** menos de cinquenta libras; **a rent ~ two thousand dollars** uma renda, *(BR*: aluguel) inferior a dois mil dólares; **4** *(JUR) (according to)* segundo, de acordo com, consoante; **~ the terms of ...** de acordo com os termos de ...; **~ the law** ao abrigo da lei; **5** *(MED) (undergoing)* **he will go ~ the knife** ele vai ser operado; **6** *(hierarchy)* **~ orders of ...** às ordens de/ segundo as ordens de; **to work ~ somebody** trabalhar como subordinado; **7** *(classification)* em; **filed ~ the letter 'P'** arquivado na letra P; **I am ~ the impression** que tenho a impressão que; ♦ *adv* por baixo, debaixo de; **the train goes ~ the bridge** o comboio passa por baixo da ponte; **~age** *adj* por menores de idade; **2~arm** *n* axila *f*; *(deodorant, etc)* para as axilas; **2** *(bowling)* com a mão por baixo do ombro; **~brush** *(in forest)* vegetação *f* rasteira *(in a forest)*; **~ carriage** *n* *(AER)* trem *m* de aterragem; **~charge** *vt* cobrar/levar menos dinheiro; ♦ *n* *(in gun)* carga *f* insuficiente; **~clothes** *npl* roupa *fsg* interior/de baixo; **~coat** *n* *(paint, varnish)* primeira demão *f*; **~cover** *adj* clandestino,-a; secreto, furtivo; **~current** *n* corrente *f* submarina; **2** *(fig) (in a situation)* corrente *f* subjacente; **~ cut** *n* filete *m* de carne de vaca; ♦ *vt* *(price)* baixar, vender mais barato; **~developed** *adj* subdesenvolvido; *(countries)* em vias de desenvolvimento; **~dog** *n* *(in society)* injustiçado, oprimido; **~done** *adj* *(food)* mal cozido; *(UK) (steak)* malpassado; **~estimate** *vt* subestimar; **~exposed** *adj (PHOT)* sub-exposição *f*; **~fed** *adj* subnutrido; **~feed** sub-alimentar; **~ floor heating** *n* aquecimento *m* por baixo do chão; **~foot** *adv* sob os/ debaixo dos pés; **~ funding** *n* fundos *mpl* insuficientes; **~go** *(pt:* **~went**, *pp:* **~gone)** *vt* sofrer; **2** *(MED) (treatment)* receber; **3** *(surgery)* submeterse a; **~graduate** *n* estudante *m,f* universitário,-a; **~ground** *n* *(RAIL)* metropolitano, (=metro) *m*; *(BR*: metrô); ♦ *adj* subterrâneo,-a; debaixo de terra; **to go ~** *vi (secret)* ser clandestino,-a; **~ economy** *(US) n* economia *f* subterrânea; **~grown** *adj* pouco crescido,-a; **~growth** *n* matagal *m*; **~hand/ed** *adj* desonesto, clandestino, às ocultas; **2** *(SPORT)* com a mão por baixo; **~lie** *vt* estar subjacente, *(fig)* justificar; **~line** *vt* subinhar; **2** salientar; **~ling** *n* *(pej)* subalterno,-a; **~lying** *adj* essencial; **2** subjacente; **~manned** *adj* com falta de mão-de-obra; **~mentioned** *adj (item)* abaixo; *(person)* abaixo nomeado,-a; *(name)* abaixo citado,-a; **~mine** *vt* *(dig)* minar, escavar; **2** *(fig) (position)* enfraquecer; **3** *(confidence)* abalar; **~neath** *n:* **the ~** a parte *f* de baixo; ♦ *adj* inferior ♦ *adv* debaixo, por baixo; ♦ *prep* debaixo de, sob; **~nourished**

adj subnutrido,-a; **~paid** *adj* mal pago; **~pants** *npl* cueca(s) *fpl* *(BR)*: calcinhas *fpl*; **~pass** *n* *(for traffic)* via *f* inferior; *(for pedestrians)* passagem *f* subterranean; **~pin** (-ned) *vt* *(CONSTR)* escorar, reforçar os alicerces; **2** *(strength)* reforçar *(belief)*; sustentar *(theory)*; **~play** *vt* minimizar a importância; **2** *(THEAT) (actor)* representar pobremente, mal; **~populated** *adj* subpovoado; **~price** *vt* vender abaixo do valor real; **~privileged** *adj* desfavorecido,-a; *(children)* desamparado,-a; **~rate** *vt* depreciar, subestimar; **~ sea** *adj* submarino,-a; **~score** *vt* sublinhar; **2** *(fig) (emphasize)* salientar; **~-secretary** *n* *(POL)* subsecretário,-a **(of State)** do Estado; **~sell** *(pt, pp* **~sold)** *vt* *(COMM)* vender mais barato que *(competitor)*; vender a baixo preço; desvalorizar-se; **~side** *n* parte *f* inferior, de baixo; **2** *(fig) (dark side)* lado *m* sombrio; **~signed: the ~** *adj* o/os abaixo assinado/s; **~sized** *adj (person)* enfezado,-a; *(animal)* raquítico,-a; pequeno,-a; **~skirt** *n* saiote *m*.

understand *(irr: like* **stand)** *vt/vi* entender, compreender; perceber; **to make o.s. understood** fazer-se entender; *(LING) (imply)* subentender.

understandable *adj* compreensível.

understanding *n* compreensão *f*, entendimento *m*; acordo *m*; ♦ *adj* compreensivo.

understate *vt* atenuar, diminuir.

understatement *n* descrição *f* atenuada; modéstia *f* excessiva; eufemismo *m*.

understood *(pt, pp of* **understand)** *adj* entendido, subentendido, implícito; ♦ *exc* **~!** está compreendido!.

understudy *n* *(THEAT)* a(c)tor *m* substituto, atriz substituta **(to** de); **2** *(gen)* suplente *m,f*.

undertake *(irr: like* **take)** *vt* empreender; **to ~ to do sth** comprometer-se a fazer algo.

undertaker *n* *(person)* agente *m* funerário; cangalheiro.

undertaking *n* empreendimento *m*; promessa *f*.

under the table *adj* **(under-the-table** *pron)* *(ilicit dealings)* ilícito; *(payment)* debaixo da mesa.

undertone *n* (meia voz) voz *f* baixa; **2** *(undercurrent)* tom; **3** *(vague feeling)* traço; **4** *(hint)* cambiante.

undertook *(pt, pp of* **undertake)**.

undertow *n* *(of wave)* refluxo; corrente submarina; ressacano mar.

undervalue *vt* depreciar; subavaliar; **2** subestimar, menosprezar *(work, person)*.

underwater *adj* subaquático, submerso; ♦ *adv* sob a água.

underway *adj:* **to be ~** estar em progresso/andamento/ marcha; *(on the road)* a caminho; *(film)* em rodagem.

underwear *n* roupa interior/de baixo.

underweight *adj* de peso inferior ao normal; **2** *(person)* magro.

underworld *n* inferno; *(of crime)* mundo de crime, submundo.

underwriter *n* *(shares)* subscritor,-ora; *(insurance)* agente *m,f* de seguros marítimos.

undesirable *adj* indesejável.

undetected *adj* despercebido,-a; *(MED)* nãodete(c)tado,-a; *(crime)* não descoberto.

undetermined *adj* indeterminado,-a; *(unresolved)* não resolvido,-a; *(outcome)* desconhecido,-a.

undeterred *adj*: **to be** ~ ser imperturbável; não se amedrontar (**by sb/sth** por alguém/algo).

undies *npl* roupa interior/de baixo.

undignified *adj* indigno,-a; indecoroso,-a.

undisclosed *adj* não revelado,-a.

undismayed *adj* impávido (**at/by sth**).

undisputed *adj* incontestável; evidente.

undo *(irr: like* **do**) *vt* desmanchar, desfazer; *(unfasten)* desapertar.

undoing *n* ruína *f*, desgraça *f*, perdição *f*.

undone *adj (button)* desabotoado; **2** *(not done)* por fazer; **the bed is** ~ a cama está por fazer.

undoubted *adj* indubitável.

undoubtedly *adv* sem dúvida, indubitavelmente.

undreamed, undreamt (of) *adj* jamais sonhado,-a, jamais imaginado,-a.

undress *vi* despir-se; ◆ *vt* despir.

undue *adj* indevido,-a, excessivo,-a.

undulating *adj* ondulante.

unduly *adv* indevidamente; excessivamente.

undying *adj (love)* eterno.

unearned *adj* imerecido; ~ **income** *(TAX)* rendimentos *mpl* diferidos, *(BR)* renda *f* diferida.

unearth *vt* desenterrar; **2** *(secret)* descobrir.

unearthly *adj* sobrenatural; estranho; **at an** ~ **hour of the night** na calada da noite, a uma hora insólita.

uneasy *adj (ill at ease)* mal à vontade; *(restless)* inquieto; desassossegado; *(worried)* preocupado.

uneconomic(al) *adj* antieconómico *(BR:* -nô-), dispendioso, *(wasteful)* esbanjador,-ora.

uneducated *adj* inculto,-a, sem instrução.

unemotional *adj (person)* imperturbável, impassivo,-a; **2** *(voice, manner)* frio,-a; **3** *(statement)* obje(c)tivo,-a.

unemployed *n*: **the** ~ os desempregados; ◆ *adj* desempregado; **2** *(FIN) (capital)* ina(c)tivo,-a.

unemployment *n* desemprego; ~ **benefit** seguro-desemprego.

unending *adj* interminável.

unenterprising *adj* sem iniciativa; *(person, policy)* tímido,-a.

unenthusiastic *adj* sem entusiasmo.

unequal *adj* desigual.

unequalled *adj* sem igual.

unequivocal *adj* inequívoco.

unerring *adj* infalível.

unethical *adj* contrário à ética, antiético,-a.

uneven *adj (teeth, pattern)* desigual, assimétrico,-a; *(performance, pulse, results, surface)* irregular; *(road)* acidentado; *(voice)* trémula.

uneventful *adj (life, day)* rotineiro,-a; *(travel, function)* sem maiores incidentes, sem sobressaltos.

unexpected *adj* inesperado.

unexplained *adj* inexplicado,-a.

unexploded *adj (bomb)* a que não detonou, explodiu.

unexposed *adj (PHOT)* virgem.

unexpurgated *adj* na íntegra, sem cortes.

unfailing *adj (support, humour, loyalty)* infalível, fiel. *(care, efforts)* constante; *(source)* inesgotável.

unfair *adj* injusto (**to, on sb** para, com alguém); **it is** ~ **that she should pay** não é justo que ela tenha de pagar; ~ **dismissal** *n (JUR)* despedimento *m*/demissão *f* sem justa causa.

unfairly *adv* injustamente.

unfairness *n* injustiça *f*.

unfaithful *adj (sexually)* infiel, desleal.

unfaithfulness *n* infidelidade *f*.

unfaltering *adj (voice)* firme; *(devotion)* a toda a prova.

unfamiliar *adj* pouco familiar, desconhecido; ~ **with sth** desconhecedor,-ora de algo.

unfashionable *adj* fora de moda.

unfasten *vt* desatar, desprender, soltar, desabotoar.

unfavourable *adj* desfavorável.

unfazed *adj (person)* impertubável; sem se desmanchar.

unfeeling *adj* insensível; *(voice, manner)* seco,-a, frio,-a.

unfettered *adj (market, liberty, right)* sem entraves irrestrito, livre.

unfinished *adj* incompleto,-a, inacabado,-a.

unfit *adj* sem preparo físico, mental; incompetente, incapaz; ~ **for work** inapto para trabalhar.

unflagging *adj* incansável.

unfledged *adj* implume, novato, inexperiente.

unflinching *adj* resoluto, firme.

unfold *vt* desdobrar *(story, newspaper)*; **2** *(fig) (disclose)* revelar; ◆ *vi* abrir-se, desdobrar-se.

unforeseeable *adj* imprevisível.

unforeseen *adj* imprevisto,-a; ~ **circumstances** circunstâncias imprevistas.

unforgettable *adj* inesquecível.

unforgivable *adj* imperdoável.

unforgiving *adj* implacável.

unfortunate *adj* infeliz *m,f*; **2** *(event, remark)* inoportuno,-a.

unfortunately *adv* infelizmente, lamentavelmente.

unfounded *adj* infundado,-a.

unfriendly *adj (person)* antipático,-a, pouco amistoso,-a; *(place, climate)* adverso,-a; *(reception)* hóstil.

unfulfilled *adj (ambition, potential)* não realizado, que não se realizou; *(need, desire)* insatisfeito,-a.

unfurl *vt (flag, sail)* desfraldar; *(umbrella)* abrir.

unfurnished *adj* sem mobília, desmobilado *(BR)* desmobiliado,-a.

ungainly *adj* desalinhado, desajeitado,-a.

ungentlemanly *adj* descortês; *(pej) (fam)* bruta-montes; **he was** ~ ele foi um bruta-montes.

ungodly *adj (irreligious)* ímpio,-a; **2** *(fam) (unreasonable)*: **at this** ~ **hour** a esta hora da noite, da madrugada.

ungovernable *(country)* ingovernável; *(temper)* incontrolável.

ungracious *adj* indelicado,-a.

ungrammatical *adj* incorre(c)to,-a.

ungrateful *adj* ingrato,-a.

ungratefulness *n* ingratidão *f*.

ungrudging *adj* dado, feito de bom grado; *(support)* incondicional.

unguarded *adj* desprotegido,-a; **2** *(careless)* desprevenido,-a descuidado,-a; ~ **moment** momento de descuido.

unhappiness *n* tristeza.

unhappy *adj (sad)* triste; *(unfortunate)* desventurado; *(childhood)* infeliz; ~ **with** *(arrangements etc)* descontente com, insatisfeito com.

unharmed *adj* ileso, incólume; são e salvo; *(object)* inta(c)to.

unhealthy *adj (climate, place)* insalubre, pouco saudável; *(fig)* prejudicial; *(person)* doentio, doente.

unheard *adj:* **we went out** ~ saímos despercebidos; ~ **of** *adj* inaudito, insólito; *(shocking)* chocante; *(unknown)* desconhecido.

unheeded *adj:* **to go** ~ *(warning, advice)* ser em vão.

unhelpful *(person)* pouco prestável; *(attitude)* com má vontade; *(useless)* inútil.

unindered *adj* livre, sem impedimentos; *(without bother)* sem ser estorvado por.

unhinge *vt* desengonçar *(door)*; *(fig, coll)*; transtornar, desestabilizar *(person, mind)*.

unhook *vt* desenganchar, desengatar; **2** *(open brackets)* desacolchetar; desapertar *(dress)*.

unhurt *adj (from accident)* ileso,-a, são e salvo *m* (sã e salva *f*); *(object)* inta(c)to,-a.

unicorn *n* unicorne, unicórneo *m*.

unidentified *adj* não-identificado.

unification *n* unificação *f*.

uniform *n* uniforme *m*; farda; ♦ *adj* uniforme.

uniformity *n* uniformidade *f*.

unify *vt* unificar, unir.

unilateral *adj* unilateral.

unintentional *adj* involuntário, não intencional.

uninterested *adj* desinteressado.

union *n* união *f*; *(trade)* sindicato (de trabalhadores); ♦ *adj* sindical.

unionism *n* unionismo *m*, sindicalismo *m*.

unionist *adj* indacalista *m,f*; **U~** *n (POL)* apoiante *m,f* da união entre a Irlanda do Norte e da G.B.; **U~ Party** *n (POL)* o principal partido protestante do Norte da Irlanda a favor da união com a G.B.

Union Jack *npr:* **the** ~ a bandeira *f* britânica a bordo (de um navio, barco).

unique *adj* único, sem igual, invulgar, exclusivo,-a (**to** a).

unisex *adj* unissexo.

unison *n:* **in** ~ em harmonia, *(simultaneous)* em uníssono.

unit *n (whole)* unidade *f*; **2** *(team, squad)* grupo; **kitchen** ~ móvel *m*, módulo de cozinha; **3** *(subdivision)* departamento; ~ **price** *n* preço m unitário; ~ **trust** *n (UK)* fundo *m* de investimento.

unitary *n (US)* unitário,-a.

unite *vt* unir, unificar; ♦ *vi* unir-se.

united *adj* unido,-a, unificado,-a; ~ **front** *n:* **to present a** ~ **front** fazer frente *f* única; IDIOM ~ **we stand, divided we fall** a união faz a força.

United Arab Emirates *npr:* **the** ~ os Estados Árabes Unidos *mpl*.

United Kingdom (UK) *npr* (o) Reino Unido (RU).

United Nations (UN) *npr* as Nações Unidas *fpl* (a ONU).

United States of America (US, USA) *npr:* Estados Unidos *mpl* da América (EUA).

unity *n* unidade *f*; união *f*.

universal *adj* universal.

universe *n (ASTRON)* universo *m*.

university *n* universidade *f*.

unjust *adj* injusto.

unjustifiable *adj* injustificável.

unkempt *adj* desleixado, descuidado; *(hair)* desgrenhado, despenteado.

unkind *adj* descortês, indelicado; *(remark)* cruel; **to be** ~ **to sb** ser desagradável para com alguém, ser mau/má para com alguém; **some shampoos are** ~ **to the hair** certos champôs são nocivos para o cabelo.

unkindness *n (of person, act)* dureza *f*; *(act, fate)* crueldade *f*.

unknowing *adj* desconhecedor,-ora, ignorante *m,f*.

unknown *adj* desconhecido; **the U~ Soldier** *npr* o Soldado *m* Desconhecido.

unlace *vt* desapertar; desatar *(shoes)*.

unladylike *adj* deselegante.

unlatch *vt* destrancar a porta.

unlawful *adj* illegal; illicito,-a, contra as regras.

Embora ʻ**unlawful**ʼ e ʻ**illegal**ʼ sejam aparentemente sinónimos, existe uma ligeira diferença no seu uso, em inglês: **illegal** é contra a lei constitucional, enquanto **unlawful** infringe os regulamentos numa situação particular como, por exemplo, os regulamentos do futebol.

unleaded *adj (petrol)* sem chumbo *m*.

unleash *vt (release)* soltar; **2** *(fig)* desencadear *(fury, war)*.

unless *conj* a menos que, a não ser que; ~ **he comes** a menos que ele venha; **2** *(except)* salvo, salvo quando; ~ **otherwise stated** salvo indicação contrária.

unlicensed *adj* sem autorização *f*, sem licença; não autorizado,-a; *(fishing, hunting)* proibido,-a.

unlike *adj* diferente; ♦ *prep* diferente de, ao contrário de.

unlikely *adj* improvável, inverossímil.

unlimited *adj* ilimitado.

unlined *adj (garment, curtain)* sem forro; *(face)* sem rugas; *(paper)* liso.

unlisted *adj* fora da lista; não-classificado,-a.

unlit *adj (street, room)* às escuras; **2** *(cigarette)* apagado.

unload *vt (goods, gun)* descarregar; *(COMM)* escoar *(surplus goods)*; *(fig) (unburden o.s.)* ~ **sth on (to) sb** desabafar algo com alguém.

unloading *n* descarregamento *m*.

unlock *vt (door)* destrancar, abrir uma porta com a chave; *(machinery)* destravar; **2** *(fig) (mysteries)* resolver; *(secrets)* revelar; *(heart)* abrir.

unloving *adj (person)* duro,-a, sem ternura.

unlucky *adj* infeliz; de mau agouro; **to be** ~ ter azar, ser azarado.

unlukily *adv* infelizmente.

unmanageable *adj* indócil, indomável; *(hair)* rebelde; difícil de resolver, de dirigir.

unmanly *adj* pusilânime.

unmanned *adj* não-tripulado,-a; *(office)* sem ninguém; *(RAIL crossing)* sem guarda.

unmarked *adj* sem etiqueta; sem identificação; *(unblemished: skin, etc)* não ter rugas, marcas; *(SPORT)* desmarcado.

unmarried *adj* solteiro,-a; ~ **mother** mãe solteira.

unmask *vt* desmascarar.

unmentionable *adj* que não se pode mencionar; ~ **subject** assunto *m* vergonhoso, indecente; **2** *(suffering)* indescritível.

unmerciful *adj* cruel, desumano,-a.

unmindful *adj* esquecido,-a, descuidado,-a.

unmistakable *adj* inconfundível; sem engano.

unmitigated *adj* não mitigado,-a, absoluto,-a.

unmoved *adj* indiferente (**by** a); insensível (**by** a).

unnatural *adj* artificial; invulgar; *(person, laughter)* afe(c)tado,-a; *(unhealthy interest)* depravado, desnaturado.

unnecessary *adj* desnecessário, inútil.

unnerve *vt* perturbar, enervar.

unnerving *adj* enervante.

unnoticed *adj*: **to go** ~ passar despercebido.

UNO *(abbr for* **United Nations Organization)** ONU *f*.

unobtainable *adj* *(ambition, goal)* inalcançável; *(goods, etc)* impossível de obter.

unobtrusive *adj* discreto,-a; *(person)* apagado,-a.

unoccupied *adj* *(seat etc)* desocupado, livre.

unofficial *adj* não-oficial, informal; **2** *(strike)* greve *f* illegal, desautorizado.

unopened *adj* fechado,-a; por abrir.

unorthodox *adj* pouco ortodoxo, heterodoxo.

unpack *vi* desfazer as malas; *(parcel)* desembrulhar.

unpaid *adj* não-remunerado,-a; **2** *(bills)* por pagar.

unpalatable *adj* *(food, wine)* não apetecível; *(fig: speech)* intragável; desagradável.

unparalleled *adj* sem paralelo; único, incomparável.

unpatriotic *adj* antipatriótico,-a.

unpick *vt* desfazer, desmanchar *(knitting, swing)*; **2** *(fig)* deslindar *(facts, truth)*.

unplaced *adj* (SPORT) desqualificado,-a.

unpleasant *adj* desagradável; *(person)* antipático,-a.

unplug (**-gg-**) *vt* (ELECT) (retirar a ficha da tomada) desligar; **2** destampar, tirar o tampão *(sink, bath)*.

unpolluted *adj* despoluído,-a; impoluto.

unpopular *adj* impopular.

unprecedented *adj* inédito, sem precedentes.

unpredictable *adj* imprevisível.

unprejudiced *adj* imparcial, sem preconceitos.

unpretensious *adj* despretencioso,-a.

unprincipled *adj* *(person)* sem princípios.

unprivileged *adj* desfavorecido,-a.

unproductive *adj* improdutivo.

unprompted *adj* não solicitado,-a.

unqualified *adj* leigo; sem qualificações, habilitações; **2** *(success)* absoluto,-a; *(support)* incondicional.

unquenchable *adj* *(fire)* inextinguível; **2** *(thirst, passion)* insaciável.

unquote *adv* fim de citação.

unravel (UK: pres. **-vels**; *pt, pp* **-ll-**); (US: **-l-**) *vt* *(plot)* desenredar; **2** *(mystery, problem)* deslindar; **3** *(threads, hair)* desembaraçar-(se), desemaranhar (-se); **4** resolver(-se).

unreadable *adj* *(illegible)* ilegível; **2** *(tedious to read)* difícil de ler.

unreal *adj* irreal, ilusório.

unrealistic *adj* pouco realista, prático; irrealista.

unreasonable *adj* *(views)* irrealista; *(insensato)* irracional; absurdo; *(unfair) (price)* exorbitante.

unrelated *adj* sem relação; *(family)* sem parentesco.

unrelenting *adj* *(weather, person)* implacável, impiedoso,-a; *(pressure)* contínuo,-a.

unreliable *adj* *(person)* indigno de confiança; inconfiável; inconstante; **2** *(machine)* incerto,-a, perigoso,-a.

unrelieved *adj* *(no change)* monótono; **2** *(person)* não suavizado,-a; **3** *(shift work)* não revezado,-a.

unremarkable *adj* comun, banal.

unremarked *adj* sem ser notado, percebido.

unremiting *adj* incessante, contínuo,-a.

unrepeatable *adj* *(offer)* irrepetível.

unrepresentative *adj* pouco representativo, característico.

unrequited *(love)* não correspondido.

unreserved *adj* *(seat)* não reservado,-a; **2** *(person)* sincero,-a, sem reserva.

unresponsive *adj* pouco rece(p)tivo,-a; indiferente.

unrest *n* inquietação *f*, agitação *f*; *(POL)* distúrbios *mpl*.

unroll *vt* desenrolar.

unruffled *adj* *(calm)* sereno,-a, despreocupado,-a; imperturbável.

unruly *adj* indisciplinado, insubordinado; *(troublesome)* turbulento; *(unmanageable)* intratável.

unsafe *adj* perigoso; inseguro,-a.

unsaid *adj*: **to leave sth** ~ deixar algo por dizer.

unsalted *adj* insosso,-a, insípido,-a.

unsatisfactory *adj* insatisfatório.

unsavoury (UK) **unsavory** (US) *adj* *(objectionable)* moralmente ofensivo; **2** *(business)* duvidoso,-a; *(smell, taste)* desagradável; vil.

unscarred *adj* sem cicatrizes.

unscathed *adj* ileso,-a.

unscheduled *adj* imprevisto,-a; *(visit)* de surpresa.

unscramble decifrar *(code)*, pôr em ordem *(ideias)*.

unscrew *vt* *(taking out screw)* desaparafusar; *(jar)* desenroscar, desatarraxar.

unscripted *adj* de improviso.

unscrupulous *adj* sem escrúpulos; imoral.

unsealed *adj* (envelope) aberto,-a.

unseasonable *adj* fora da estação; fora da sazão; **2** inoportuno,-a.

unseasoned *adj* *(fruit)* verde; *(person)* inexperiente; **2** *(food)* não temperado.

unseat *vt* derrubar *(sela)*; **2** *(fig)* *(politician)* depor.

unseeded *adj* *(of a competitor in sports)* não apurado para (posição de preferência).

unseemingly *adj* indecoroso,-a; impróprio,-a.

unseen *adj* *(unnoticed)* despercebido; *(not visible)* escondido,-a; **2** *(translation)* não preparado,-a, ao vivo; **3 the** ~ *n* o além.

unselfish *adj* desinteressado,-a; altruísta *m,f*.

unsettled *adj* incerto, duvidoso; *(weather)* variável, instável.

unsettling *adj* inquietante.

unshaven *adj* *(face)* com a barba por fazer.

unsheathe *adj* desembainhar *(sword)*.

unsightly *adj* de péssima aparência; feio,-a; desagradável à vista.

unsinkable *adj (ship, etc)* insubmergível.

unskilled *adj*: ~ **worker** operário não-especializado.

unskimmed *adj* nao desnatado,-a; *(milk)* gordo.

unsociable *adj* anti-sociável/antissociável *m,f.*

unsocial *adj*: ~ **hours** horas impróprias; ~ **work** trabalho fora d'horas.

unsophisticated *adj (gen)* simples; *(clothes, attitude, taste)* pouco refinado, sofisticado; **2** *(analysis)* simplista.

unsound *adj* doente, fraco; *(idea)* inconsistente; *(FIN)* duvidoso; **to be of** ~ **mind** estar demente; *(JUR)* não estar em posse das suas faculdades mentais.

unspeakable *adj* indizível, indescritível; **2** *(pain)* terrível, tremendo,-a; **3** *(noise)* pavoroso.

unspoiled, unspoilt *adj (person)* incólume; **2** *(place)* preservado,-a, intocado,-a; **3** *(product)* não estragado,-a.

unspoken *adj (without words)* subentendido,-a; tácito,-a.

unsteady (-ier, -iest) *adj (person, voice)* inseguro, vacilante; *(chair, ladder)* pouco seguro.

unstressed *dj (LING) (vowel)* não acentuada.

unstructured *adj* não estruturado,-a, desorganizado,-a.

unstrung *adj (instrument)* desafinado; **2** *(nerves)* descontrolado,-a.

unstuck *adj*: **to come** ~ despregar-se; *(stamp)* descolar-se; *(fig) (plan)* fracassar.

unstudied *adj (unaffected)* natural; *(manner)* espontâneo.

unsubstantiated *adj (report)* não corroborado, confirmado; **2** *(accusation)* sem provas.

unsuccessful *adj (attempt)* frustrado, gorado; *(writer, proposal)* sem êxito; **to be** ~ ser mal-sucedido.

unsuccessfully *adv* em vão; sem sucesso.

unsuitable *adj (area, subject)* inadequado, inconveniente, inapropriado,-a **(for sth** para algo).

unsuited *adj* inadequado,-a; *(not compatible)* incompatível.

unsung *adj (LITER) (poets, etc)* desconhecido,-a, não cantado,-a, não celebrado,-a.

unsupervised *adj* sem vigilância.

unsupplied *adj* não fornecido, desprovido.

unsure *adj* inseguro, incerto.

unsurpassed *adj* incomparável; **to be** ~ ser único,-a **(in sth** em algo).

unsuspected *adj* insuspeito,-a.

unsuspecting *adj* de boa-fé, sem desconfiança.

unswerving *adj* inabalável, firme, resoluto,-a.

unsympathetic *adj (person)* frio,-a, indiferente; sem compaixão; ~ **to the cause** não simpatizar com a causa.

untamed *adj* indómito,-a; em estado selvagem; *(bird, fox)* não adestrado,-a.

untangle *vt* desemaranhar, desenredar *(of thread, wool)*; ♦ *vr (extricate o.s.)* desenvencilhar-se **(from** de).

untapped *adj (resources)* inexplorado,-a.

untaxed *adj (income, goods)* não tributado,-a.

untenable *adj (position)* insustentável; *(argument)* injustificável.

unthinkable *adj* impensável, inconcebível, incalculável.

unthinking *adj (person)* irreflectido,-a; *(remark)* descuidado,-a.

unthinkingly *adv* sem pensar.

unthought-of *adj* inédito,-a, original; desconhecido,-a.

untidy *adj (room)* desarrumado,-a; *(garden)* pouco cuidado; *(person)* desleixado,-a; desmazelado,-a, desalinhado.

untie *vt* desatar, desfazer.

until *prep (up to, till)* até; ~ **one day!** até um dia!; ~ **then** até então; *(after negative)* antes de; **don't come** ~ **I ring you up** não venha antes de eu lhe telefonar; ♦ *conj* até que; ~ **she speaks** até que ela fale.

untimely *adj* inoportuno, intempestivo; **2** *(event)* prematuro.

untiring *adj* incansável, infatigável.

untold *adj* indizível; não revelado; *(endless)* ~ **stories** estórias sem fim; *(suffering)* incalculável; *(wealth)* inestimável.

untouchable *adj* intocável *m,f.*

untoward *adj* inconveniente; adverso,-a; indesejado,-a.

untraceable *adj* indetetável.

untried *adj (recruit)* sem experiência; **2** *(JUR) (prisoner)* não julgado,-a.

untrue *adj* falso, inexa(c)to,-a; **2** *(to spouse)* infiel.

untrustworthy *adj (person)* indigno,-a de confiança; *(information)* duvidoso,-a.

untruthful *adj* falso,-a.

unused *adj* sem ser usado,-a; *(unaccustomed)* ~ **to** não habituado,-a (a).

unusual *adj* incomum, raro,-a, invulgar, extraordinário,-a.

unveil *vt* desvelar, revelar, descobrir.

unvoiced *adj* omitido, não expresso,-a; *(LING) (vowel)* muda; *(consonant)* surda.

unwanted *adj* indesejado,-a; **2** supérfluo,-a.

unwarranted *adj* sem garantia; sem motivo; indevido; injustificável.

unwary *adj* incauto,-a; imprudente.

unwavering *adj* firme, inabalável.

unweaned *adj (baby)* lactante.

unwelcome *adj* inoportuno, indesejável; que não é bem-vindo,-a; **2** ~ **news** notícias desagradáveis.

unwell *adj*: **to feel/to be** ~ estar indisposto, adoentado, sentir-se mal.

unwieldy (-ier, -iest) *adj* difícil de manejar; *(weighty)* pesado,-a.

unwilling *adj*: **to be** ~ **to do sth** estar relutante em fazer algo.

unwillingly *adv* de má vontade; **to go** ~ ir contrariado,-a.

unwind *(irr: like* **wind***) vt (uncoil)* desenrolar; ♦ *vi (relax)* descontrair-se.

unwise *adj* imprudente.

unwitting *adj* inconsciente, involuntário,-a; não premeditado,-a.

unwittingly *adv* inadvertidamente.

unwonted *adj* invulgar, incomum.

unworkable *adj* impraticável.

unworldly *adj (spiritual)* espiritual *m,f*; que não liga a materialismo; **2** *(naïve)* ingénuo,-a.

unworthy (-ier, -iest) *adj* indigno,-a.

unwrap *vt* desembrulhar *(parcel)*.

unwritten *adj* verbal; *(tradition)* oral; *(JUR)* ~ **law** *n* direito consuetudinário.

up *prep*: **to go/be** ~ **sth** subir algo/estar em cima de algo; ♦ *adv* em cima, para cima; ~ **there** lá em cima; ~ **above** em cima; **to be** ~ *(out of bed)* estar levantado; **it is** ~ **to you** isso é com você, você é quem sabe; **what is he** ~ **to?** o que é que ele quer?; **he is not** ~ **to it** ele não é capaz de fazê-lo; **I'll be** ~ **(in the North)** estarei lá em cima (no Norte); ~ **to now** até agora; **what's** ~**?** o que se passa?; ~**s and downs** *npl (fig)* altos e baixos *mpl*.

up-and-coming *adj* prometedor,-ora; **2** *(economy)* emergente.

upbraid *vt*: **to** ~ **sb for sth** repreender alguém por algo.

upbringing *n* educação *f*, criação *f (of child)*.

up-country *adj (GEOG)* no/do interior;

update *vt* pôr em dia; a(c)tualizar.

upend *vt (stand upright)* pôr de pé; *(turn sth upside down)* virar algo ao contrário, de pernas para o ar.

upfront *adj* franco, frontal; **2** conspícuo, visível; ♦ *adv (pay)* (pagamento) adiantado.

upgrade *vt* elevar o nível de; promover.

upheaval *n* transtorno; perturbação *f*; convulsão *f*.

uphill *adj* ladeira acima; **2** *(fig) (task)* trabalhoso, árduo; ♦ *adv*: **to go** ~ ir morro acima, pela ladeira *f* acima.

uphold *(irr: like hold)* *vt (law, faith, principle)* suster; defender; confirmar; apoiar; **to** ~ **the law** fazer respeitar a lei.

upholster *vt* estofar; **2** *(edredão)* acolchoamento *m*.

upholstery *n (stuffing)* estofo, estofamento; acolchoamento.

upkeep *n* manutenção *f*.

upland *adj* no planalto, **the** ~**s** *npl* as terras altas *fpl*.

uplift *vt (raise moral)* elevar, erguer; **2** animar, encorajar; ~**ing** *adj* edificante.

uplifting *n* estimulante, elevação moral.

upload *n (COMP)* carregamento *m*; ♦ *vt* carregar.

up-market *adj* de alta categoria.

upon *prep* sobre, em cima; ~ **my word** minha palavra de honra; **once** ~ **a time** era uma vez; **Easter is** ~ **us** a Páscoa está quase a chegar; **chat** ~ **chat** conversa após conversa.

upper *n (of shoe)* gáspea *f*; ♦ *adj* superior; de cima; **2** *(GEOG) (inland)* alto,-a; ~ **case** *adj (letters)* letras *fpl* maiúsculas; ~ **circle** *(THEAT)* segundo balcão; ~**-class** *n* aristocracia; **the** ~**-class** a classe *f* alta; **in** ~ **circles** na alta roda *f*; ~ **crust** *adj* da alta roda; ~**cut** *n (boxing) (punch)* um (soco) debaixo para cima no queixo; ~ **floor** andar de cima; ~ **hand: to have the** ~ **hand** *n* levar a melhor; controlar a palavra final; **U~ House** *npr* Câmara dos Lordes.

uppermost *adj* o mais elevado; **what was** ~ **in my mind** o que me preocupava mais; ~ **school** *n* escola secundária (a partir dos 14 anos).

uppish, uppity *adj (fam)* arrogante *m,f*, snobe, esnobe.

upright *n (CONSTR)* pilar; **2** *(SPORT)* poste (de baliza); ♦ *adj* vertical; **to stand** ~ estar ere(c)to; muito direito; **2** *(fig)* honrado, honesto; ~ **piano** *n* piano vertical *m*.

uprising *n* sublevação *f*, revolta *f*, rebelião *f*.

uproar *n (confusion)* tumulto; *(loud voices)* algazarra, *(BR)* fuzuê *m*; **2** indignation.

uproarious *adj* hilariante; **2** barulhento.

ups-a-daisy *exc (to lift child from fall)* upa!

uproot *vt* desenraizar, arrancar *(from the ground)*.

upset *n (of car, boat)* tombo, viramento; **2** *(surprise)* *(POL, THEAT)* golpe *m* (de teatro); **3** *(MED)* **stomach** ~ indisposição *f* do estômago; **4** *(reversal of plan)* contrariedade *f*; ♦ *adj (distressed)* aflito,-a; **2** *(annoyed)* aborrecido,-a, contrariado,-a; **the news** ~ **him** a notícia afligiu-o/transtornou-o; ♦ *(pt, pp:* **upset***; pres cont:* -tt-*) vt (knock over)* virar, derrubar; **the wind** ~ **the boat** o vento virou a barco; **2** *(spill)* verter; **3** *(distress)* transtornar, afligir; **4** *(annoy)* aborrecer, irritar; **to be** ~ **with sb** *(cross)* estar aborrecido,-a com alguém; **5** *(not agree with one's stomach)* fazer mala; **the red wine** ~ **me** o vinho tinto fez-me mal; ♦ *vr* ~ **o.s.** aborrecer-se; **don't** ~ **yourself** não se aborreça; **to get** ~ **with sb** zangar-se com alguém.

upsettting *adj* desconcertante *m,f*.

upshot *n* resultado *m*, conclusão *f*.

upside-down *adj adv* invertido, às avessas; ♦ *adv* de pernas para o ar/de cabeça para baixo; **to turn sb's life** ~ transtornar a vida de alguém.

upstage *adv (THEAT) (stand)* ao fundo do palco; ♦ *vt* eclipsar (alguém).

upstairs *n (the floor/flat above)* andar *m* superior, andar de cima; ♦ *adv* em cima, lá em cima.

upstanding *adj* imponente *m,f*; **2** *(fig) (person)* honrado,-a, honesto,-a.

upstart *n* arrivista *m,f*; *(fig)* novo-rico, nova-rica.

upstream *adj, adv* rio acima; contra a corrente; ~ **from here** a montante daqui.

upsurge *n (of violence)* escalada *f*; **2** *(sudden increase)* aumento repentino **(of sth** de algo).

uptake *n*: **he is quick on the** ~ ele entende rapidamente; **he is slow on the** ~ ele é de compreensão lenta.

uptight *adj (person)* nervoso,-a.

up-to-date *adj (machinery, item)* a(c)tualizado,-a, moderno,-a; **to be** ~ *(person)* estar a par **(com** de).

upturn *n* virada; mudança para melhor, melhoria **(in sth** em algo); ♦ *adj* virado,-a; **2** *(nose)* arrebitado.

upward *adj* ascendente; para cima; ♦ ~**s** *adv* para cima; ~ **of** *prep* mais de.

upwardly mobile *adj (person, group)* em ascensão social.

uranium *n* urâneo *m*.

Uranus *n (ASTROL)* Urano *m*.

urban *adj* urbano,-a; de cidade; ~ **dweller** citadino,-a.

urbane *adj* afável, urbano.

urbanization *n* urbanização *f*.

urbanize *vt* urbanizar.

urchin *n* garoto, diabrete *m*; *(BR)* moleque *m*, criança maltrapilha.

Urdu *n (LING)* urdu (língua oficial do Paquistão).

urethra *n* uretra *f*.

urge *n* impulso; desejo; ♦ *vt (also:* ~ **on***)* incitar, urgir, pedir com instância; **I** ~**d her to accept** eu insisti com ela que aceitasse.

urgency *n* urgência *f*, insistência *f*.
urgent *adj* urgente.
urgently *adv* urgentemente.
urinal *n* *(place)* urinol *m*; *(recipiente)* mictório *m*.
urinary *adj* urinário,-a.
urinate *vi* urinar; *(coll)* *(to pee)* mijar.
urine *n* urina *f*.
urn *n* *(for ashes)* urna *f* funerária; **2** *(for votes)* urna *f*.
Uruguay *npr* Uruguai *m*; **in** ~ no Uruguai.
Uruguayan *n adj* uruguaio,-a.
us *pers pron* nos; *(after prep)* nós; **he saw** ~ ele viu-nos; **he gave it to** ~ ele deu-a nós ~ somos nós; **with** ~ conosco; **2** *(emphatic)* **he gave the money to** ~ ele deu o dinheiro a nós; **all of** ~ todlos nós; **with** ~ conosco; **3 let** ~ **see** vejamos.
US, USA *npr* *(abbr for* **United States of America***)* Estados Unidos da América *mpl* (EUA).
usable *adj* utilizável, usável.
usage *n* uso, costume *m*.
use *n* uso, emprego, utilidade *f*; ◆ *vt/vi* empregar, usar; *(utilize)* utilizar; **2** *(pej)* *(exploit)* usar; **to be of** ~ servir; **to make** ~ **of** servir-se de; **she lost** ~ **of her right hand** ela não mexe a mão direita; **it's no** ~ é inútil, não serve; **out of** ~ fora de uso, antiquado; **he** ~**d to go** ele costumava ir; **to** ~ **up** esgotar, consumir.
used *adj* usado.
useful *adj* útil; **to be** ~ ser/mostrar-se útil.
usefulness *n* utilidade *f*.
useless *adj* inútil; infrutífero; **2** *(hopeless)* incorrigível; **I am feeling** ~ sinto-me inútil.
user utente *m,f*; **2** *(of computer, machine)* utilizador; **3** *(JUR)* usufrutuário,-a; ~-**friendly** *n* de fácil utilização *m*.

usher *n* arrumador *m* (de teatro), *(BR)* lanterninha *m*; *(JUR)* oficial, porteiro de tribunal, *(BR)* oficial *m* de justiça; ◆ *vt* conduzir, escoltar; **to** ~ **sb in/out** mandar alguém entrar/sair; ~ **to the door** acompanhar alguém à porta; **to** ~ **in (sth)** abrir o caminho a algo *(era)*; introduzir *(reforms)*.
usherette *n* arrumadora (de teatro), *(BR)* lanterninha *f*.
usual *adj* usual, habitual, costumário; **as** ~ como de costume.
usually *adv* normalmente, habitualmente.
usurp *vt* usurpar.
usurper *n* usurpador,-ora.
usury *n* usura *f*.
utensil *n* utensílio; **kitchen** ~**s** *npl* utensílios, apetrechos *mpl* de cozinha.
uterine *adj* uterino,-a.
uterus *(pl:* **uteruses***)* *n* útero *m*.
utilitarian *adj* utilitário,-a; funcional.
utility *(pl:* -**ies***)* *n* *(usefulness)* utilidade *f*; **2** serviço *m* público; ~ **room** *n* lavandaria; área *f* de serviços.
utilize, utilise *vt* utilizar.
utmost *n*: **to do one's** ~ fazer todo o possível; ◆ *adj* maior, extremo, máximo.
Utopia *npr* utopia *f*.
Utopian *npr* utopista *m,f*; ◆ *adj* utópico,-a.
utter *adj* completo, total; ◆ *vt* pronunciar, proferir.
utterance *n* expressão *f*; **2** *(LING)* enunciado *m*.
utterly *adv* completamente, totalmente.
U-turn *n* inversão *f* de marcha; **2** *(fig)* volta-face *f inv*.
UV *adj* *(abbr for* **ultra-violet***)* *(radiation, ray)* ultra-violeta.
uvula *n* *(ANAT)* úvula *f*.
Uzbek *n adj* uzbeque.
Uzbekistan *npr* Usbequistão *m*; **in** ~ no Usbequistão.
uzi *npr* metralhadora *f* de desenho de Israel.

V

V, v *n (letter)* V, v *m.*

v *(abbr for* **verse**); **2** *(abbr for* **versus**); **3** *(abbr for* **volt**).

vacancy *(pl:* **-ies**) *n (job)* vaga; **2** *(room)* quarto livre.

vacant *adj* vazio,-a, desocupado,-a, livre; **2** *(expression)* destraído,-a; vago,-a.

vacate *vt (leave empty)* vagar, desocupar.

vacation *n (Univ and Court)* férias *fpl* le(c)tivas/ judiciais; *(US) (gen)* férias; ~ **resort** *n (US)* colónia *(BR:* -ô-) *f* de férias.

vacationer *n (US)* veraniante *m,f.*

vaccinate *vt:* ~ **sb against** vacinar (alguém contra).

vaccination *n* vacinação *f.*

vaccine *n* vacina *f.*

vacillate *vi:* ~ **between** vacilar (entre); hesitar *(make up one's mind).*

vacillating *adj* vacilante.

vacuous *adj* vazio,-a.

vacuum *(pl:* **vacua**) *n* vácuo *m;* ~ **cleaner** *n* aspirador *m* de pó; ~ **flask** *n* garrafa – termo *f;* ~ **packed** *adj* (algo) embalado,-a a vácuo *(EP),* em vácuo *(BR);* ~ **valve** *n* válvula *f* ele(c)trónica.

vagabond *n* vagabundo,-a.

vagary *(pl:* **-ries**) *n* capricho *m,* mania *f.*

vagina *n (ANAT)* vagina.

vagrancy *n* vagabundagem *f.*

vagrant *n* vagabundo,-a, vadio,-a.

vagrantly *adv* de modo errante.

vague *adj* vago,-a, impressivo,-a, incerto,-a; evasivo,-a; **to be** ~ **about his job** ser evasivo,-a quanto ao emprego; **2** *(person)* que divaga, divagador,-ora; **3** *(memory)* fraco,-a; **4** *(feeling)* leve; *(person)* que divaga, divagador,-ora.

vaguely *adv* vagamente; com um ar distraído, distraidamente; *(reply)* de maneira imprecisa.

vain *adj (conceited person)* vaidoso,-a; *(futile attempt)* vão *m,* vã *f;* inútil; **in** ~ *adv* em vão.

vainglorious *adj* vanglorioso,-a; orgulhoso,-a.

vainglory *n* vanglória, vaidade, jactância.

valance *n (on bed)* folho *m; (on pelmet)* sanefa *f,* dossel *m.*

vale *n (LITER)* vale *m.*

valence, valency *n (UK)* valencia *f.*

valentine *n:* **V~'s Day** Dia *m* de São Valentim, Dia *m* dos Namorados.

valet *n (manservant)* criado *m* de quarto; *(US)* camareiro *m;* ~ **service** *n (wash/iron shirts etc)* serviço *m* de lavandaria/lavadaria.

valid *adj* válido,-a; *(legitimate)* irrefutável *m,f,* legítimo,-a.

validate *vt (claim)* corroborar, confirmar; **2** *(document)* validate.

validity *n* validade *f;* legitimidade *f.*

valley *n (GEOG)* vale *m.*

valour *(UK)* **valor** *(US) n* valor *m,* valentia.

valuable *adj* de valor; valioso,-a; ~**s** *npl* obje(c)tos *mpl* de valor.

valuation *n* avaliação *f,* estimativa.

value *n (gen)* valor *m;* **2** importância *f;* **to give** ~ **to sth** dar importância a; **to set great** ~ **on** dar muito apreço a; **sentimental** ~ valor estimativo, de estimação; **ethical** ~**s** valores *mpl* morais; **to take sb/sth at face** ~ levar alguém/algo ao pé da letra; **moral/ethical** ~**s** *npl* valores *mpl* morais; ♦ *vt* avaliar, calcular; *(esteem)* estimar; apreciar.

value-added tax **(VAT)** *n* imposto de valor acrescentado (IVA) *(EP),* imposto sobre circulação de mercadorias (ICM) *(BR).*

valued *adj (friend, etc.)* apreciado,-a, estimado,-a; *(opinion)* precioso,-a.

valuer *n* avaliador,-ora.

valve *n* válvula *f.*

vamp *n (pej) (woman)* vampe, mulher fatal; **2** *(upper front of a shoe)* gáspea *f;* ♦ *vt/vi* aparaltar-se para seduzir homens; **to** ~ **up** *(fam) (improve sth)* melhorar *(algo);* renovar; **2** *(MUS)* improvisar acompanhamento.

vampire *n* vampiro,-a.

van *n (AUT)* carrinha *f,* furgoneta *f; (larger)* furgão *m;* **luggage** ~ furgão *m; (BR) (AUT)* caminhonete; *(UK) (RAIL)* vagão *m* de mercadorias *(BR:* de carga); **2** *(forefront)* vanguarda *f.*

vandal *n* vândalo.

vandalism *n* vandalismo.

vandalize *vt* destruir, vandalizar.

vane *n (on windmill)* vela *f;* **2** *(of propeller)* pá *f;* **3 weather** ~ cata-vento, catavento *m.*

vanguard *n* vanguarda *f;* **in the** ~ **of** na vanguarda de.

vanilla *n (BOT, CULIN)* baunilha *f;* ~ **pod** pau de baunilha.

vanish *vi (disappear, fade)* desaparecer; desvanecer-se; **2** *(species)* extinguir(-se); **3 to** ~ **into thin air** evaporar-se; ~**ing** *n* desaparecimento *m;* **2** fuga *f;* ♦ *adj (species)* em vias de extinção.

vanity *n (pej)* vaidade *f;* inutilidade *f;* futilidade *f;* ~ **case** *n* bolsa *f* de maquilhagem.

vanquish *vt* vencer *(enemy),* derrotar.

vantage point *n* posição *f* estratégica, de vantagem; *(for view)* ponto *m* de observação.

vapid *adj* desinteressante, inconsistente.

vaporize *vi* evaporar-se.

vapour *n* vapor *m; (steam)* exalação *f.*

variable *n adj (gen)* variável.

variance *n* divergência, discrepância; **to be at** ~ **(with sth)** estar em desacordo (com alguém/algo).

variant *n (LING)* variante *f;* **English** ~**s** as variantes do inglês; ♦ *adj (opinion)* diferente divergente.

variation *n (change)* variações *fpl;* **2** ~ **between** diferença entre; *(LING) (version)* versão, variante **(of** de); *(MUS)* variação *f;* **3** ~ **compass** *n* bússola *f* de declinação.

varicela *n (MED)* varicela *f.*

varicose *adj (MED)* varicose; ~ **veins** varizes *fpl.*

varied *adj* variado,-a; diverso,-a.
variegated *adj* (BOT, ZOOL) matizado, pintalgado.
variety *n* (range, diversity) variedade *f*, diversidade *f*; sortimento *m*; **for a ~ of reasons** por várias razões; **2** (type) tipo *m*; **~ show** *n* (THEAT) espe(c)táculo de variedades.
variola *n* varíola *f*.
various *adj* vários,-as, diversos,-as; **of ~ kinds** de várias espécies, de todos os tipos; **in ~ ways** de diversas maneiras.
varnish *n* verniz *m*; **2** esmalte *m*; ♦ *vt* envernizar; pintar; **to ~ the nails** pintar as unhas.
vary *vt* variar (**in**, em; **with**, segundo); **2** (method, route) mudar de, alterar; diversificar; divergir (**from**, de); **it varies from one to the other** varia de um para o outro.
varying *adj* (weather, degrees) variável *m,f*; (circumstances, reasons) variado,-a.
vascular *adj* (ANAT, BOT) vascular.
vase *n* jarra *f*; (BR) vaso *m*; **large/tall ~** jarrão *m*.
vasectomy (pl: -ies) *n* vasectomia *f*.
vaseline® *n* (petroleum jelly) vaselina *f*.
vast *adj* vasto,-a, enorme; imenso,-a; **the ~ majority of** a grande maioria de.
vastly *adv* amplamente, completamente, infinitamente.
vastness *n* imensidão *f*; **the ocean's ~** a imensidão do oceano.
vat *n* (of wine) tina, cuba.
VAT *n* (abbr for Value-Added Tax) (UK) IVA; (BR) ICM.
Vatican *npr*: **the ~** o Vaticano.
vaudeville *n* espe(c)táculo de variedades.
vault *n* (of roof) abóbada; **2** (tomb) sepulcro; (in bank) caixa-forte *f*; (of church) cripta *f* funerária; **3** (SPORT) (jump) salto *m*; ♦ *vt* (= **to ~ over**) saltar (por cima de).
vaulted, vaulting *adj* abobadado,-a.
VC (abbr for vice-chairman) vice-presidente; (UK, Univ) (abbr for vice-chancellor) reitor,-ora (in some British universities).
VD *n* (abbr for venereal disease) MST *f*; **~ clinic** clínica *f* de venereologia.
V-Day *n* Dia da Victória (comemoração do fim da Segunda Guerra Mundial).
veal *n* carne *f* de vitela.
vector *n* (BIOL, MATH) vetor *m*; (AER) trajetória *f*.
veer *vt* virar, mudar de dire(c)ção; desviar.
veg *n* (fam) = **vegetables**.
vegan *n adj* vegan *m,f*; (theory) vegetalista.
vegetable *n* (BOT) vegetal *m*; legume *m*; ♦ **~s** *npl* legumes *mpl*; (greens) hortaliça *f*; ♦ *adj* vegetal; **~ garden** *n* horta.
vegetarian *n adj* vegetariano,-a.
vegetate *vi* vegetar.
vegetation *n* vegetação *f*.
vehement *adj* veemente; apaixonado,-a; (dislike) violento,-a; **vehemently** *adv* impetuosamente; (deny) veementemente.
vehicle *n* veículo *m*; **closed to ~s** trânsito *m* proibido; **2** means; **the ~ of communication** o veículo de comunicação.

vehicular *adj* de veículos.
veil *n* véu *m*; **2** (fig) disfarce *m*, manto *m*; **a ~ of mystery** um manto de mistério; ♦ *vt* (mist) velar, cobrir com um véu; **to take the ~** tomar o véu, tornar-se freira, professar; **2** (fig) dissimular (emotion).
veiled *adj* velado,-a.
vein *n* (ANAT) veia *f*; **2** (on insect, plant) nervura *f*; **3** (of ore) filão *m*; **4** (in marble, wood) veio *m*; **5** estilo *m*, espírito *m*.
velar *n adj* (consonant) velar.
vellum *n* papel *m* velino.
velocity *n* velocidade *f*.

Velocity termo formal usado no contexto científico; de resto, usa-se mais 'speed' para velocidade.

velours *n* tecido *m* espesso aveludado.
velvet *n* veludo *m*; ♦ *adj* aveludado,-a.
vend *vt* (JUR) vender.
vendee *n* (JUR) comprador,-ora.
vendetta *n* vendeta *f*.
vending machine *n* máquina *f* automática.
vendor *n* (JUR) (also: estate agent) vendedor,-ora.
veneer *n* capa exterior; folheado *m*; **2** (fig) verniz *m*; (social appearance) aparência *f*; ♦ *vt* folhear; **2** (móveis) embutir.
venerable *n adj* venerável.
venerate *vt* venerar.
venereal *adj*: **~ disease** (VD) doença venérea.
Venetian *npr adj* veneziano,-a; **~ blind** *n* persiana, veneziana.
Venezuela *npr* Venezuela; **in ~** na Venezuela.
Venezuelan *n adj* venezuelano,-a.
vengeance *n* vingança *f*; desforra *f*; **with a ~** com fúria; (fig) cada vez mais, muito; **out of ~** por vingança; **to take ~ (up) on sb** vingar-se de alguém.
vengeful *adj* vingativo,-a.
venison *n* carne *f* de veado.
venom *n* veneno *m*; peçonha *f*; (fig) (spite) maldade *f*.
venomous *adj* venenoso,-a; maldoso,-a.
venous *adj* (BOT, ANAT) venoso,-a.
vent *n* (TECH) (opening) abertura, conduta; **2** (air-hole) respiradouro; (in wall) abertura para ventilação; **3** (GEOG) (outlet) passagem; (ZOOL) orifício *m* anal; **to give ~ to one's feelings** (fig) desabafar (**with sb** com alguém); ♦ *vt* fazer um furo em (barrel); escoar; (fig) descarregar, dar largas a (anger) (**on sb** sobre alguém).
ventilate *vt* ventilar.
ventilation *n* ventilação *f*.
ventilator *n* ventilador *m*.
ventriloquist *n* ventríloquo,-a.
venture *n* (undertaking) empreendimento *m*; **joint-~** negócio *m* de parceria, joint-venture; **~ capital** *n* (COMM, FIN) capital *m* de risco; **2** (experiment) ensaio *m*, experiência *f*; ♦ *vt* (to risk) arriscar (money) (**on** em); **2** (to dare) ousar, atrever-se (opinion, suggestion); **I ~ to propose** atrevo-me a sugerir, ouso fazer uma proposta; ♦ *vi*: **to ~ to**

(do sth) *(also:* **to ~ out/forth)** aventurar-se a (fazer algo); **she ~d out to sea** ela aventurou-se a nadar; **2 to ~ into** lançar-se em *(new line of business).*
venue *n* local *m* (em que se realiza um evento); *(meeting place)* ponto *m* de encontro.
veracious *adj* verídico, verdadeiro.
veracity *n* veracidade *f.*
veranda(h) *n* varanda, marquise *f*, terraço.
verb *n (gram)* verbo.
verbal *adj* verbal.
verbally *adv* verbalmente; **verbalize** *vt/vi* verbalizar.
verbatim *adj* textual; literal; ♦ *adv* palavra por palavra, literalmente; textualmente.
verbena *n (BOT)* verbena *f*, urgebão *m*, verberão *m; (BR: equivalent plant)* jurujuba *m.*
verbose *adj* prolixo,-a; verboso,-a.
verdant *adj* verdejante *m,f*, viçoso,-a.
verdict *n (JUR)* veredi(c)to, decisão *f*; **2** *(fig)* opinião *f*, parecer *m*; **to bring in a ~ of** pronunciar uma veredito de.
verdigris *n* verdete *m,f.*
verge *n* limite *m*, margem *f*; **on the ~ of** a ponto de; **to ~ on** *vt* estar à beira de; tocar as raias de.
verger *n (REL)* sacristão,-ã; **2** maceiro.
verify *vt* verificar; **2** *(JUR)* provar; comprovar.
vermillion *n adj (colour)* vermelhão *m.*
vermin *npl* bichos *mpl*; inse(c)tos *mpl* nocivos; parasitas; verme; **2** *(fig) (pej) nsg (people)* canalha, ralé *f*; ♦ *adj (rogue)* patife *m*, canalha *m*; **they are ~** eles são uns canalhas.
vermouth *n* vermute *m.*
vernacular *n* vernáculo *m.*
verruca *(pl: -cae, -cas)* *n (MED)* verruga *f.*
versatile *adj* versátil; polivalente; ágil, flexível.
verse *n* verso *m*; poesia *f*; *(stanza)* estância *f*; estrofe *f*; *(in bible)* versículo *m.*
versed *adj* conhecedor,-ora; douto,-a; **(well-)~ in** versado em, especialista em.
version *n* versão *f*; tradução *f.*
versus *prep (as opposed to)* contra, versus.
vertebra *(pl: -brae)* *n* vértebra *f.*
vertebral *adj* vertebral.
vertebrate *n adj* vertebrado,-a.
vertex *n* vértice *m.*
vertical *adj* vertical.
vertigo *n* vertigem *f.*
very *adv* muito; **it's the ~ thing (I want)** é exatamente o que quero; **at that ~ moment** naquele mesmo instante; **the ~ last** o último; **at the ~ least** no mínimo; **~ much** muito, muitíssimo.
vespers *npl (REL)* vésperas *fpl.*
vessel *n (ANAT)* vaso *m*; **2** *(NAUT)* navio, barco; **3** *(container)* vaso *m*, vasilha *f*, recipiente *m.*
vest *n* camisola *f* interior, *(BR)* camiseta *f*; ♦ *vt, vi (bestow, confer)* **to ~ in** dar poder a; conferir **power was ~ed in him** foi-lhe conferido o poder; ♦ *vi (put on vestments)* vestir.
vested *adj* empossado,-a; **~ interests** *npl (COMM)* capital *m* investido; **~ rights** *npl* direitos *mpl* adquiridos.
vestibule *n* vestíbulo *m.*

vestige *n* vestígio *m*, rasto *m.*
vestry *n* sacristia *f.*
vet *n (abbr for* **veterinary surgeon**); ♦ *(-tt-) vt* examinar; **the dog was vetted** o cão foi examinado pelo veterinário.
veteran *n* veterano,-a; antigo,-a combatente; **~ car** *n (UK)* carro antigo, *(pop)* (uma) Dona Elvira.
veterinary *adj* veterinário,-a; **~ surgeon** *n* veterinário,-a cirurgião *m*, cirurgiã *f.*
veto *(pl: -es)* *n* veto *m*; **to exercise one's ~** exercer o direito de veto **(over, on** sobre); ♦ *vt (POL)* vetar, proibir.
vetting *n* controlo *m* de sele(c)ção de alguém/algo.
vex *vt* irritar, enfadar, incomodar, apoquentar; impacientar.
vexation *n* vexame *m*, irritação *f*; contrariedade *f.*
vexed *adj (annoyed)* aborrecido,-a **(with** com); **2** *(question)* controvertido,-a, discutido,-a.
vexing *adj* vexatório,-a; irritante.
VHF *n (abbr for* **very high frequency)** VHF.
via *prep* por, por via de.
viable *adj* viável.
Via Dolorosa *n* via-sacra *f.*
viaduct *n* viaduto *m.*
vial (=phial) *n* frasco *m*, ampulheta *f.*
vibes *npl (coll)* vibrações *fpl*; **good/bad ~** *(feelings about sb/sth)* boas/más vibrações *(fam).*
vibrate *vt* vibrar.
vibration *n* vibração *f.*
vicar *n* vigário *m*; pároco *m.*
vicarage *n* vicariato *m.*
vicarious *adj (situation)* indireto,-a; **2** *(power)* delegado,-a; **~ly** *adv* indiretamente; por outra pessoa.
vice¹ *n* vício *m*; **2** *(TECH)* torno mecânico.
vice² *pref* vice-; **~-chairman** *n* vice-presidente *m,f.*
vice versa *adv* vice-versa.
vicinity *n* vizinhança *f*, proximidade *f.*
vicious *adj* cruel; pessoa má; **2** *(attack)* violento,-a; *(animal)* feroz; **~ circle** círculo *m* vicioso; **~ness** *n* maldade, crueldade *f*; **2** violência *f.*
viciousness *n* violência *f*; depravação *f*; crueldade *f*; rancor *m.*
victim *n* vítima *f.*
victimization *n* perseguição *f*; *(in strike)* represálias *fpl.*
victimize *vt* fazer represália contra.
victor *n* vencedor,-ora.
Victorian *n adj* vitoriano,-a, rigoroso,-a, puritano,-a.
victorious *adj* vitorioso,-a.
victory *n* vitória *f.*
videlicet *adj* isto é; a saber.
video *n* vídeo *m*; **~(-tape) recorder** *n* gravador *m* de videoteipe/videocassette; video *m*; ♦ *(-ed, -ing) vt (using camera)* gravar um vídeo de; **2** *(using videorecorder)* gravar em disco.
vie *vi:* **to ~ with** competir com.
Vienna *npr* Viena; **in ~** em Viena.
Viennese *n adj* vienense *m,f.*
Vietnam *npr* Vietname *m*, *(BR)* Vietnã *m.*
Vietnamese *n adj* vietnamita *m,f*; **the ~** *npl* os vietnamitas.

view *n* vista *f*, panorama *m*; **2** perspetiva *f*, mira *f*; **3** opinião *f*, parecer *m*; ♦ *vt* olhar; examinar; **on ~** em exposição; **in full ~ (of)** à plena vista (de); **in ~ of the fact that** em vista do fa(c)to de que; **~er** visor *m*; **2** *(of TV – person)* telespe(c)tador,-ora.

viewfinder *n* *(PHOT)* visor *m*.

viewing *n* *(house search)* visita; **2** *(film)* projeção; **3** *(of new range)* apresentação *f*; **~ figures** *npl* taxa *f* de audiência.

viewpoint *n* *(opinion)* ponto *m* de vista.

vigil *n* vigília *f*; **to keep ~ (over sb)** velar alguém.

vigilance *n* vigilância *f*.

vigilant *adj* vigilante.

vigorous *adj* enérgico,-a vigoroso,-a.

vigour *(UK)* **vigor** *(US)* *n* energia *f*, vigor *m*.

vile *adj (person)* vil, infame; **2** *(act)* desprezível; **3** *(smell, appearance)* repugnante, horrível; *(mood)* péssimo,-a.

vilify **(-ied)** *vt* aviltar; *(slander)* difamar, caluniar.

villa *n* casa *f* de campo/de aldeia *f* turística; moradia *f*.

village *n* aldeia *f*, povoado *m*, vilarejo *m*; **tourist ~** aldeamento *m* turístico; **2** *(in Angola)* senzala *f*.

villager *n* aldeão,-a; *(of Brazil)* povoação *f* de um vilarejo; *(of Angola)* povoação (indígena) da senzala.

villain *n* *(false person)* velhaco,-a; *(scoundrel)* patife *m*; *(perverse)* meliante *m,f*; *(CIN, TV)* vilão,-ã.

villainous *adj* ignóbil.

vindicate *vt* desagravar; defender; *(JUR)* reivindicar; justificar.

vindictive *adj* vingativo,-a; *(bearing a grudge)* rancoroso,-a.

vine *n* *(BOT)* vinha *f*, videira *f*; cepa; **2** *(climbing plant)* planta *f* trepadeira; **~ grower** *n* viticultor.

vinegar *n* vinagre *m*.

vinegary *adj* avinagrado,-a; **2** azedo,-a.

vineyard *n* vinha *f*, vinhedo *m*.

vintage *n* vindima *f*; **2** *(year)* safra, colheita; **~ wine** *n* vinho velho, de boa safra, de qualidade *f* exce(p)cional.

vinyl *n* vinil *m*.

viola *n* *(MUS)* viola *f*; **2** *(BOT)* viola *f*; violeta *f*.

violate *vt* *(infringe, disregard)* transgredir, infringir *(rile, agreement)*; **2** *(rape, peace)* violar; **3** profanar *(sacred place)*.

violation *n* violação *f*.

violence *n* violência *f*.

violent *adj* violento *m*, intenso *m*.

violet *n* *(BOT)* violeta *f*; ♦ *adj (colour)* violeta.

violin *n* violino.

violinist *n* violinista *m,f*.

VIP *n* *(abbr for* **very important person***)* personalidade; ♦ *adj (place)* reservado às personalidades; **~ guest** convidado,-a importante; **~ treatment** tratamento *m* vip, tratamento especial.

viper *n* víbora *f*; **2** *(fig) (wicked person)* malvado,-a.

virgin *n* virgem *m,f*; ♦ *adj* virgem; **the Blessed V~** a Virgem Santíssima.

Virginia creeper *n* *(BOT)* videira *f* virgem.

Virgin Islands *npr pl:* **the ~** as Ilhas Virgens *fpl*.

virginity *n* virgindade *f*.

Virgo *n* *(ASTROL)* Virgem *f*.

virile *adj* viril; vigoroso,-a.

virility *n* virilidade *f*; **2** *(fig)* machismo *m*.

virtual *adj* *(COMP, PHYS)* virtual; **virtually** *adv* virtualmente, praticamente; **~ reality** *n* realidade *f* virtual.

virtue *n* virtude *f*; **by ~ of** em virtude de.

virtuoso (*pl:* **-sos** *or* **-si**) *n adj* virtuoso,-a (**of** de).

virtuous *adj* virtuoso,-a; honesto,-a.

virulent *adj* virulento,-a.

virus *n* vírus *m*.

visa *n* *(consular)* visto *m*.

vis-à-vis *prep* em relação a; ♦ *adv* cara a cara; em frente.

viscera *n* *(ANAT)* víscera *f*.

viscose *n* *(material)* viscose *f*.

viscount *n* *(titled person)* visconde *m*.

viscountess *n* viscondessa *f*.

viscous *adj* viscoso,-a, pegajoso,-a.

vise *n* *(US)* *(MEC)* torno *m*.

visibility *n* visibilidade *f*.

visible *adj* visível.

visibly *adv* visivelmente; manifestamente; indubitavelmente.

vision *n* *(sight)* vista *f*, visão *f*; percepção *f* divinatória.

visionary *n* visionário,-a; ♦ *adj* visionário,-a; imaginário,-a.

visit *n* visita; **on a ~ (to a)** de visita; **on my third ~** na minha terceira visita; **flying ~** visita rápida, *(fam)* visita de médico; **to pay sb a ~** fazer uma visita a alguém; **2** *(stay)* estada **to be/to go on a ~ to** fazer um estada em; **3** *(inspection)* vistoria; **to make a ~ to** *(premises)* inspe(c)cionar, vistoriar; ♦ *vt* visitar; fazer uma visita a; ir a; ir conhecer.

visiting *adj* de/em visita; visitante; *(orchestra)* convidado,-a; **~ card** *n* cartão *m* de visita.

visitor *n* visitante *m,f* visita *m,f*; **~s' book** *n* livro dos visitantes; livro de honra; *(hotel)* livro de registo, *(BR:* de registro); **~ passport** *n* *(UK)* passaporte *m* temporário.

visor *(also:* **vizor***)* *n* *(on helmet)* viseira *f*; *(peak on a cap)* pala *f* de boné.

vista *n* *(view)* vista *f*, panorama *m*; **2** *(fig)* perspe(c)tiva *f*.

visual *adj* visual; **~ aids** *npl* recursos *mpl* visuais.

visualize *vt* visualizar, ter uma imagem clara; **2** *(envisage)* prever.

vital *adj* essencial, indispensável, vital; crucial; vivo,-a; **~ statistics** *npl* dados *mpl* demográficos; **2** *(gen)* informações *fpl* essenciais; **3** *(of woman's figure)* medidas *fpl* vitais.

vitality *n* energia, vitalidade *f*.

vitally *adv:* **~ important** de importância *f* vital.

vitamin *n* vitamina *f*; **~ deficiency** *n* carência *f* de vitaminas.

vitreous *adj* *(TECH)* *(enamel)* vitrificado,-a; *(china)* vidrado,-a.

vitriolic *adj* acrimonioso,-a; virulento,-a.

vivacious *adj* *(lively person)* vivaz; animado,-a; vivo,-a; *(witty)* espirituoso,-a.

vivacity *n* vivacidade *f*.

viva voce *n* *(talk, exam)* oral.

vivid *adj* vívido,-a; brilhante; intenso,-a; vivo,-a.

vividly *adv* nitidamente, claramente; *(speech, etc)* de forma nítida, expressiva; ~ **coloured** de cores *fpl* vivas.

vivisection *n* vivissecção *f.*

vixen *n (ZOOL) (fêmea)* raposa *f;* 2 *(fig, pej) (woman)* megera, mulher de mau génio.

viz *(abbr for* **videlicet)** a saber.

vizier *n* vizir; **grand** ~ grão-vizir *m.*

V-neck *n* decote *m* em bico *(BR:* em V).

VOA *(abbr for* **Voice of America)** *npr* Voz *f* da América (emissora oficial de radio norte-americana com transmissões globais).

vocab *(abbr for* **vocabulary).**

vocabulary *n* vocabulário *m.*

vocal *adj* vocal; clamoroso; ~ **chords** *npl* vocais.

vocalist *n* vocalista *m,f;* cantor,-ora.

vocals *npl* canto *m.*

vocation *n* vocação *f.*

vocational *adj* vocacional *m,f; (syllabus)* de orientação *f* professional.

vociferous *adj* vociferante *m,f.*

vodka *n (drink)* vodka *f.*

vogue *n* voga, moda; **in** ~ em voga, na moda.

voice *n* voz *f;* **in a low/loud** ~ em voz baixa/alta; **hoarse/shaky** ~ voz rouca/trémula; **to shout at the top of one's** ~ berrar; 2 opinião; 3 *(speaker, representative of a group)* porta-voz; **4 active/passive** ~ *(gram)* voz a(c)tiva/passiva; ♦ *vt* expressar, exprimir; proferir; IDIOM **I have no** ~ **in the matter** não tenho voto na matéria.

voicebox *n (ANAT)* laringe.

voiced *adj (PHON) (consonant)* sonora, sonorizado,-a; sonante.

voiceless *adj* sem voz; sem expressão; *(MED)* áfono,-a; *(PHON)* surdo,-a, mudo,-a.

voice-over *n (voice of an unseen commentator heard in a film)* comentário *m,* narração *f.*

void *n* vazio; vácuo; ~ **of imagination** falto *m* de imaginação; ♦ *adj* vazio, vago; inválido,-a; *(JUR) (contract)* **null and** ~ nulo, anulado; ♦ *vt* anular; invalidar.

voile *n (material)* voile *m.*

vol *(abbr for* **volume).**

volatile *adj* volátil *m,f;* 2 *(fig)* explosivo,-a; *(person, mood)* volúvel *m,f;* 3 *(ECON)* instável.

volcanic *adj* vulcânico,-a.

volcano *(pl:* **-es)** *n* vulcão *m.*

volition *n (formal)* vontade; **of my own** ~ de minha livre vontade.

volley *n (of gunfire)* descarga, salva; 2 *(of hail stones etc)* saraivada; 3 *(fig) (of words, questions)* torrente *f* de palavras; *(SPORT)* voleio *m,* batida da bola antes de tocar no chão; ~**ball** *n* voleibol *m.*

volt *n* volt *m,* vóltio *m;* ~**age** *n* voltagem *f;* ~ **meter** *n* voltímetro *m.*

voltaic *adj (ELECT)* voltaico,-a.

volte-face *n* mudança *f (of opinion, politics);* revira-volta *f.*

voluble *adj* volúvel; loquaz; eloquente.

volume *n (ger)* volume *m;* ~ **control** *m* regulação *f* de volume; controle *m* de volume.

voluminous *adj (clothes, parcel)* volumoso,-a; *(large space)* espaçoso,-a; *(creative work)* fecundo,-a.

voluntarily *adv* livremente, voluntariamente.

voluntary *n (MUS)* solo *m* de órgão; ♦ *adj* voluntário,-a; 2 *(unpaid for, organization)* beneficente.

volunteer *n* voluntário,-a; ♦ *vi* **to** ~ **to do sth** oferecer-se de livre vontade para fazer algo.

voluptuous *adj* voluptuoso,-a; libidinoso,-a.

vomit *n* vómito *m;* ♦ *vt/vi* vomitar.

voodoo *n* vodu *m.*

voracious *adj (for knowledge)* ávido,-a; insaciável; 2 voraz; devorador,-ora.

voracity *n* voracidade *f.*

vortex *(pl:* **-texes** *or* **-tices)** *n (TECH)* vórtice *m;* 2 *(fig) (of events)* turbilhão *m,* remoinho *m.*

vote *n* voto *m;* ~ **of confidence** voto de confiança; ~ **of no confidence** voto de censura; ~ **of thanks** *n* discurso *m* de agradecimento; **to canvass for** ~**s** solicitar votos; 2 *(voting session)* votação *f;* ♦ *vt* eleger; ♦ *vi* votar; **to** ~ **for/against** votar a favor/contra.

voter *n* votante *m,f,* eleitor,-ora.

voting *n* votação *f.*

vouch *vt:* **to** ~ **for** *vt* garantir, responsabilizar-se por; responder por; 2 *(declare belief in)* dar testemunho.

voucher *n (for meal, petrol)* vale *m;* recibo.

vow *n* juramento *m;* 2 promessa *f* solene; 3 *(REL)* voto *m;* ♦ *vi* jurar que, prometer; **to fulfil a** ~ cumprir uma promessa; **to take the** ~**s** professar.

vowel *n* vogal *f.*

vox pop, vox populi *n* opinião *f* pública; *(TV, RADIO)* entrevistas *fpl* de rua.

voyage *n (journey)* viagem *f;* ~ **outward/homeward** viagem de partida/de regresso; *(crossing)* travessia; ♦ *vi* viajar.

V-sign *n (victory sign)* V *m* de Vitória; 2 *(UK)* gesto *m* obsceno.

VSO *n (abbr for* **Voluntary Service Overseas)** (organização britânica que envia jovens voluntários para ajudar países em desenvolvimento) cooperação *f* civil.

vulgar *adj* grosseiro,-a, ordinário,-a; baixo,-a; ~ **tongue** *n* vernáculo *m.*

vulgarity *n* grosseria.

vulnerable *adj* vulnerável, susceptível.

vulture *n (ZOOL)* abutre *m; (BR: also)* urubu *m; (fig) (exploitative person)* abutre *m,f.*

vulva *(pl:* **-vae** *or* **-vas)** *n (ANAT)* vulva *f.*

W

W, w *n (letter)* W, w *m*.

W *(abbr for* **watt***)*; **2** *(abbr for* **west***)* oeste; **3** *(CHEM) symbol for* **tungsten** (= **wolfram**).

w *(abbr for* **week***)*; **2** *(abbr for* **weight***)*; **3** *(abbr for* **width***)*; **4** *(cricket) (abbr for* **wicket***)*.

wacky (-ier, -iest) *adj (fam)* excêntrico,-a, cómico,-a.

wad *n (on garment's shoulder)* chumaço *m*; **2** *(of cartridge, gun)* bucha; **3** *(of bank notes)* maço *m* (**of** de).

wadding *n (stuffing)* enchimento *m*; acolchoamento *m*.

waddle *vi (way of walking)* bambolear(se), menear; mover-se bamboleando; *(BR)* gingar.

wade *vt* andar caminhar por água ou lama; **2** ~ **in/into** intrometer-se num *(debate)*; **2** *(attack energetically) (work)* pôr mãos à obra; **to** ~ **through** *(boring book/task)* conseguir a custo; **he was ~ing through a pile of papers** ele debatia-se com um montão de papeis.

wader *n* pessoa que anda na água; **2** *(ZOOL)* ave *f* pernalta; ~**s** *npl* botas *fpl* altas impermeáveis.

wadi (=wady) *n (watercourse)* seco,-a exceto quando chove.

wafer *n* bolacha-baunilha; *(REL)* hóstia.

wafer-thin *adj* finíssimo,-a.

waffle *n (CULIN)* waffle; **2** *(fig) (long, trivial talk)* lengalenga *f*; *(pej)* verborreia *f*; ◆ *vi (also:* ~ **on***)* falar/escrever sem cessar, *(speak)* falar pelos cotovelos.

waft *n* aragem *f*; *(wind)* sopro *m*; ◆ *vt* pairar, flutuar; **2** *(scent)* levar.

wag *n* abanadela *f*; ◆ *vt (dog)* sacudir *(tail)*; ◆ (-**ged**) *vi* abanar; **to** ~ **one's finger at sb** fazer uma advertência, agitando o dedo; **to** ~ **one's tongue** *(fig)* dar à língua; **tongues will** ~ vai haver falatório.

wage *n* (= ~**s**) salário *m*, ordenado *m*; ~ **claim** *n* reivindicação *f* salarial; pedido de aumento *m* salarial; **2** *(fig) (of doing sth wrong)* resultados, efeitos; **disasters are the wages ~s of sin** os desastres são os resultados do pecado; ~ **earner** *n* assalariado,-a; ~**-freeze** *n* congelamento *m* de salários; ~ **packet** *n* envelope *m* do ordenado; ◆ *vt*: **to** ~ **war** fazer guerra; empreender *(campaign)*.

wager *n* aposta *f*; ◆ *vt* apostar.

waggish *adj (person)* engraçado,-a, patusco,-a; *(remark)* jocoso,-a.

waggle *vt,vi* sacudir(-se); agitar(-se).

wag(g)on *n (horse-drawn)* carroça *f*; *(truck)* camião *m*, *(BR)* caminhão *m*; *(RAIL)* vagão *m*; ~**-lits** *n*

carruagem-cama *f*, *(BR)* carro-leito; IDIOM **to be on the** ~ não beber nem uma gota d'água.

wagtail *n (ZOOL)* lavandisca *f*.

waif *n* criança *f* abandonada.

wail *n* lamento, gemido; ◆ *vi* lamentar-se, gemer.

wailing *n* lamentos *mpl*; choro *m*, pranto *m*; **2** *(fig) (wind)* gemido *m*; *(siren)* uivo *m*; ◆ *adj (sound, etc)* estridente; lamentoso,-a; **W~ Wall** *npr (REL)* Muro *mpl* das Lamentações.

waist *n* cintura, cinta *f*; ~ **band** *n* cós *m*; ~**coat** *n* colete *m*; ~ **deep in water** em água até a cintura; ~**ed** *adj* acintado,-a; ~**line** *n* cintura.

wait *n* espera; pausa; **to lie in** ~ **for sb** preparar uma emboscada (para alguém); ◆ *vt,vi* esperar; ~ **for** aguardar; ~ **on/upon sb** *(as attendant to sb)* servir *(alguém)*; *(at the table)* à mesa; ◆ **I can't** ~ **to** mal posso esperar por/para; **'no ~ing'** *(AUT)* 'proibido estacionar'; **to keep sb ~ing** deixar ficar alguém à espera.

waiter *n* empregado de mesa; *(BR)* garçom *m*.

waiting *adv* à espera de; *(BR)* esperando por.

waiting game *n*: **to play a** ~ esperar o momento oportuno.

waiting list *n* lista de espera.

waiting room *n* sala de espera.

waitress *n* empregada, criada de mesa, *(BR)* garçonete *f*.

waive *vt* renunciar a; pôr de parte (**sth** algo); desistir (**from** de); *(terms)* suspender.

waiver *n (JUR)* renúncia *f*; desistência *f*, abandono *f* (**of** de); suspenção *f* de.

wake *n (for the dead)* velório *m*; **2** rasto *m (de)*; **na sequência de**; **in the** ~ **of** na sequência de; **3** *(NAUT)* esteira *f*; ◆ *(pt* **woke** *or* **waked***, pp* **waken** *or* **waked***) vt/vi* (= ~ **up***)* acordar, despertar; **2** estimular; **to** ~ **up to** *vi (be aware of)* consciencializar-se; *(BR)* conscientizar-se; **2** *(understand)* aperceber-se de.

wakeful *adj* desperto,-a; sem dormir; **2** alerta *m,f*.

waken *(pp of* **wake***)* ~**-up call** *n* serviço de despertar.

waking hours *npl* dia *m*; **2** horas *fpl* de vigília.

Wales *npr* País *m* de Gales.

walk *n* passeio *m*; *(shorter)* volta *f*; excursão *f* a pé; *(hike)* caminhada *f*; **2** *(gait)* modo de andar; *(pace)* passo *m*; *(road, path)* alameda *f*, caminho *m*; **to go for a** ~ dar um passeio/uma volta; **it's a short** ~ **from here** fica a pouca distância daqui; **people from all walks** pessoas *fpl* de todos os níveis; **side~** *n (US)* passeio *m*, *(BR)* calçada *f*; ◆ *vi* andar a pé, caminhar; *(for pleasure)* passear; *(for exercise)* marchar; ◆ *vt* andar, percorrer a pé *(in search of sth/sb)*; **2** *(dog)* levar a passear; ~ **away** *vi* ir(-se) embora, distanciar-se (**from** de); ~ **away with sth** *vt (take away)* levar algo; **2** *(also:* ~ **off***) (steal)* furtar algo; ~ **across** *vt* atravessar; ~ **in on** *vt* interromper; ~ **on** *vt (continue)* continuar a andar; ~ **out** *vi (leave suddenly)* sair de repente; ~ **out on** *vt (leave sb)* deixar, abandonar *(family)*; ◆ ~ **over sb** *(humiliate)* pôr os pés em cima de (alguém); **2** *(SPORT)* derrotar; ◆ ~ **up to** *vt* aproximar-se de; ◆ *exc* ~ **up!** anda!, despacha-te!

walkabout *n* passeio *m*; **2** *(by politicians, royals)* banho *m* de multidão.

walker *n (person)* caminhante *m,f*; peão *m*, peã *f*; **he is a good** ~ ele anda bem; **sleep-**~ sonâmbulo,-a.

walkie-talkie *n* transmissor, receptor portátil *m*, walkie-talkie *m*.

walk-in *adj (cupboard)* espaçoso,-a.

walking *n* andar *m* a pé; marcha *f*; ~ **stick** *n* bengala *f*; **to give sb his/her** ~ **ticket** despedir alguém, *(fam)* pôr alguém na rua; ~ **distance** *n*: **to be within** ~ **distance** estar a curta distância (**of** de).

walk of life *(pl:* **walks of life***)* *n* profissão *f*; **2** posição *f* social.

walk-on (part) *n (THEAT)* figurante *m,f* (em papéis secundários).

walkout *n (of spectators, workers)* saída em protesto; greve *f* branca.

walkover *n (coll) (SPORT)* barbada *f*; victória *f* fácil.

walk-up *n* (US) prêdio *m* sem elevador.

walkway *n* passagem *f* pedonal.

wall *n* parede *f*; *(exterior)* muro *m*; **city** ~ muralha *f*; ~ **bars** *npl (for gymnastics)* espaldares *mpl*; ~ **cupboard** *n* armário *m* embutido; ~ **painting** *n* mural *m*, afresco *m*; ~**paper** *n* papel *m* de parede; ~**ed** *adj (city)* cercado por muralhas, fortificado,-a; *(garden)* murado, cercado; ~ **in** *vt* cercar com muro; ~ **up** *vt* tapar, entaipar *(window)*; IDIOM **to drive sb up the** ~ fazer alguém louco.

wallaby *(pl:* -**bies***)* *n* marsupial *m* australiano; canguru *m* de pequeno porte.

wallboard *n* placa *f* de madeira plástica ou de cimento.

wallet *n (for banknotes, cards)* carteira *f*.

wall-eyed *adj (squint)* ser estrábico; *(fam)* ser vesgo,-a.

wallflower *n (BOT)* goivo-amarelo *m*; **to be a** ~ *(fig)* tomar chá de cadeira, ficar sem par num baile.

wallop *n (slap)* sopapo *m*; **2** sova *f*; **3** murro duro ♦ dar uma tareia (em); ~**ping** *adj* grande; **a** ~ **lie** uma grandíssima mentira.

wallow *n* charco *m*, lodaçal *m*; ♦ *vi (in puddle, mud, scandal)* chafurdar; **2** *(in emotion)* afundar-se em, mergulhar em *(grief)*; **3** deleitar-se em, rebolar-se em *(gossip; indignation)*; **to** ~ **in money** nadar em dinheiro.

Wall Street *npr* Wall Street; **in** ~ na Wall Street.

Esta rua em Nova Iorque, onde se situa a Bolsa de valores, representa o mais importante centro financeiro dos Estados Unidos e está entre os mais importantes do mundo.

wall-to-wall carpet *adj* alcatifa; *(room)* alcatifado,-a.

wally *(pl:* -**ies***)* *n (fam)* parvo,-a, pateta *m,f*.

walnut *n* noz *f*; *(tree)* nogueira.

walrus *(pl:* **walrus** *or* -**es***)* *n* morsa *f*, vaca marinha *f*.

waltz *n* valsa *f*; ♦ *vi* valsar.

wan (-ier, -niest) *adj* pálido,-a, abatido,-a.

wand *n* (= **magic** ~) varinha *f* de condão.

wander *vt/vi (without fixed destination)* deambular, perambular; *(around the streets)* vaguear pelas ruas; *(shops)* percorrer as lojas; andar pelas lojas; **2** *(mind, attention)* devanear, divagar; **to** ~ **about**

ir à aventura; ♦ **to** ~ **off** afastar-se; *(to get lost)* desviar-se, extraviar-se; **to** ~ **off the** *(subject, route)* desviar-se de, afastar-se de; **2** *(object)* desaparecer; ~ **through the world** percorrer o mundo, errar pelo mundo.

wanderer *n* viajante *m,f*; andarilho,-a; *(fig)* vagabundo,-a.

wandering *adj* itinerante; errante; **the** ~ **jew (W-Jew)** *n (BOT, LITER)* o judeu errante; **2** *(head in the air)* distraído,-a; inconstante; **3** *(mind)* delirante; ~**s** *npl* viagens *fpl*; **2** devaneios *mpl*.

wane *n* declinio *m*; decadência *f*; ♦ *vi (gradual decrease)* decrescer; **2** *(moon)* minguar; **3** declinar, decair.

wangle *n (coll)* tramóia *(fam)*, manobra *f*, truque *m*; ♦ *vt (coll):* **to** ~ **sth** conseguir algo através de persuasão/esperteza; **2** enganar.

wangler *n* intrujão *m*, intrujona *f*.

waning *adj* em declínio, em decadência; ~ **moon** lua *f* no quarto minguante.

wanna *(US)* (= **want to**) **I** ~ **go home** quero ir para casa.

wannabe, wannabee *n* pessoa, grupo que deseja ser outra pessoa ou grupo; **to be George Clooney** ~**s** ser um sósia de George Clooney.

want *n;* **for** ~ **of** por falta de; *(need)* necessidade, carência *f*; ♦ *vt* querer, desejar; exigir; precisar (de), necessitar; carecer de; **to** ~ **to do** querer fazer; '~**ed**' *(advert)* 'precisa-se', 'procura-se'; **your father is** ~**ed** procuram o seu pai.

wanting *adj* com falta (**in**, em); **2** deficiente, insuficiente; **to be found** ~ deixar a desejar; **to be in** ~ carecer, precisar de.

wanton *adj (playful)* brincalhão,-ona; **2** *(pej) (immoral)* lascivo,-a, desvergonhado,-a; **3** *(malicious, wasteful)* gratuito,-a, deliberado,-a.

wantonly *(US) adv* sem motivo; **2** desavergonhadamente; **3** de modo brincalhão.

war *n* guerra; **to make** ~ fazer guerra; **to go to** ~ entrar em guerra; ~ **memorial** *n* monumento *m* aos mortos, memorial *m* de guerra.

warble *vi (bird)* chilrear, gorgear, trinar; *(fig)* cantarolar.

ward *n (in hospital)* ala, enfermaria; **2** *(POL)* distrito eleitoral; **3** *(JUR)* tutela *f*, custódia; **4** pupilo; ♦ *vt* **to** ~ **off** desviar, precaver-se contra; *(attack)* evitar.

warden *n (of institution)* governador,-ora dire(c)tor,-ora **2** *(of park, game reserve)* guarda *m,f* administrador,-ora; **3** (= **traffic** ~) guarda *m,f* do tráfico, de trânsito.

warder *n (prison)* guarda *m,f* prisional; **2** carcereiro.

ward of court *n* menor *m,f* sob tutela judicial.

wardrobe *n (clothes)* guarda-roupa *m*; *(of furniture)* guarda-vestidos *m*, guarda-roupa; ~ **mistress** *(UK)* figurinista *f*.

warehouse *n* armazém *m*, depósito.

wares *npl* artigos *mpl*, mercadorias *fpl*.

warfare *n* guerra, combate *m*.

warhead *n (MIL)* ogiva (de combate).

warily *adv* cautelosamente; com desconfiança; prudentemente.

warlike *adj* guerreiro, belicoso; bélico.

warm *adj* quente; *(lukewarm)* morno,-a; **2** *(weather, sound)* cálido; **3** *(person)* cordial; afe(c)tuoso; **4** *(applause, manner)* caloroso,-a; **5** *(recent)* recente, fresco,-a; **6** *(colour)* quente; **it's** ~ faz calor, *(BR)* está quente; **I'm** ~ estou com calor; **to keep o.s.** ~ *(with coat, blanket)* agasalhar-se; **to serve** ~ *(food)* servir morno, quente; **~-hearted** *adj* generoso,-a; ~ **up** *(SPORT, exercise)* aquecimento *m*; ♦ *vt (food)* aquecer; *(BR)* esquentar; **to** ~ **one's feet by the fire** aquecer os pés junto do lume, da lareira; ♦ *vr* aquecer-se *(enthusiasm)*, animar-se; **to** ~ **over** *vt (US = BR) (food)* requentar; *(ideas)* insistir em; **to** ~ **up** *(food)* aquecer; requentar, *(BR)* esquentar; *(party etc)* animar-se; *(orchestra)* preparar-se **to** ~ **up to sb** simpatizar com alguém.

warmly *adv* calorosamente, generosamente; **to dress** ~ agazalhar-se bem.

warmonger *n* belicista *m,f.*

warmth *n (weather)* calor *m*; **2** *(smile, manner)* cordialidade, afabilidade *f.*

warn *vt* prevenir, avisar; advertir; ♦ *vi* **to** ~ **of sth** alertar para a possibilidade de.

warning *n* advertência *f*, aviso *m*; ~ **light** *n* luz *f* de advertência; ~ **triangle** *n (AUT)* triângulo *m* luminoso (do carro).

warp *n (wood)* empenamento *m*; ♦ *vt* empenar; **2** *(of weaving)* urdir; **3** merecer.

warpath *n* trilho *m* de Guerra; **to be on the** ~ andar à procura de briga, de discussão; estar em pé de guerra.

warrant *n (JUR)* mandado *m* judicial; *(of arrest against)* ordem *f* de prisão; **2** *(FIN)* **dividend** ~ cupão *m*, *(BR)* cupom de dividendo; ♦ *vt, vi* garantir; **2** *(bet)* apostar.

warranted *pp adj* garantido,-a; *(JUR)* autorizado,-a; justificado,-a.

warrantee *n (person)* afiançado,-a; ~ **officer** *n (MIL)* suboficial.

warrantor *n* fiador,-ora; abonador,-ora.

warranty *(pl: -ies) n (JUR)* garantia, fiança; justificação.

warren *n (of wild rabbits)* toca; lura; **2** *(rabbit's burrow)* coelheira.

warring *adj* antagónico,-a; contrário,-a; *(factions, countries)* em conflito.

warrior *n* guerreiro.

Warsaw *npr* Varsóvia *f*; **in** ~ em Varsóvia.

warship *n* navio de guerra.

wart *n (on feet, face)* verruga *f*; cravo *m.*

wartime *n*: **in** ~ em tempo de guerra.

wary *adj* cauteloso, precavido; prudente; **2** desconfiado,-a *(of* de); de pé atrás.

was *(pt of be)* **I** ~ fui, era, estive, estava.

wash *n* lavagem *f*; *(of clothes)* lavagem da roupa; **the ~ing on the line** a roupa *f* no estendal; **to have a** ~ *(UK)* lavar-se; **go and have a** ~ vai-te lavar; **to** ~ **o.s** *(US)* lavar-se; **2** *(from ship)* esteira *f*; **the** ~ **of the waves** o marulhar *m* das ondas; ♦ *vt (clean)* lavar; **she washes her hands** ela lava as mãos; ♦ *vi* lavar-se; **to** ~ **ashore** lançar à praia; **to** ~ **away** *vt (stain, dirt)* tirar; lavar tirando *(nódoa, etc)* **2** *(river etc)* levar, arrastar; **3** *(fig)* purificar; ♦

to ~ **down** *vt (food)* regar *(with water/wine)*; *(garden)* lavar com mangueira; **to** ~ **off** *vt* lavar; limpar; **it will** ~ **off** *(dirt)* sai com água; **to** ~ **out** *(stain)* lavar, tirar *(nódoa)*; ~ **over sth** varrer; **to** ~ **up** *vi (dishes)* lavar a louça; **2** *(sea, river)* arrastar, trazer; IDIOM **your excuse won't** ~ a sua desculpa não serve; a sua desculpa não pega *(fam).*

washable *adj* lavável.

washbasin *(UK)* **washbowl** *(US) n* bacia *f*, lavatório *m*; *(BR)* pia *f*, lavatório.

washed-out *adj (faded colour)* desbotado,-a; **2** *(person – pale)* deslavado,-a; **3** exausto,-a.

washed-up *adj (no longer successful)* acabado,-a; liquidado,-a.

washer *n (TECH)* arruela, anilha.

washing *n (dirty)* roupa suja; *(clean)* roupa lavada; ~ **machine** *n* máquina de lavar; ~ **powder** *n* detergente *m*, *(BR)* sabão *m* em pó.

washing-up *n* lavagem *f* da louça.

washout *n (coll)* fracasso, fiasco.

washroom *n* casa de banho, *(BR)* banheiro.

washy *adj* aguado; **2** *(person)* débil; fraco.

wasn't = was not.

wasp *n (inseto)* vespa.

wastage *n* desgaste *m*, desperdício; perda; **natural** ~ desgaste *m* natural.

waste *n* desperdício *m*; *(squandering)* esbanjamento *m*; *(loss)* perda *f*, **2** *(rubbish)* lixo *m*; resíduo *m*; *(detritus)* detrito *m*; **nuclear** ~ detritos *mpl* nucleares; ♦ *adj (material)* de refugo, **2** *(left over)* de sobra; **3** *(wasteland)* baldio,-a; ~ **bin** *n* lata, caixote *m* de lixo; ~ **disposal** tratamento *m* de lixo; ~ **disposal unit** *n* triturador *m* de lixo; ~**ful** *adj (person)* esbanjador,-ora; *(process)* antieconómico *(BR: -nô-)*; ~ **ground** *n* terreno *m* baldio; ~ **paper basket** *n* cesto de papéis; ~ **pipe** *n* cano de esgoto; ♦ *vt (squander)* esbanjar, dissipar; desperdiçar; **2** *(time)* perder; consumir; **to** ~ **away** *vi* definhar, consumir-se.

watch *n* relógio de pulso; **2** *(surveillance)* vigia *f*; vigilância *f*; *(MIL)* sentinela *f*; **3** *(NAUT)* quarto *m*; ~**dog** *n* cão *m* de guarda; **2** *(fig) (UK)* comissão que fiscaliza e verifica se elas estão a a(c)tuar segundo a lei; ~**ful** *adj* vigilante, atento,-a; ~**maker** *n* relojoeiro; ~**man** *(pl:* ~**men)* vigia *m*, segurança *m*; (= **night** ~**man)** guarda *m* no(c)turno; *(in factory)* vigia *m* no(c)turno; ~**strap** *n* pulseira (do relógio); ~**word** *n (slogan)* lema *m*, divisa *f*; ♦ *vt (look at)* observar, olhar, ver; assistir a; vigiar; *(take care)* tomar cuidado (com) ~ **out!** cuidado! atenção!; ♦ *vi* ver, olhar; montar guarda; **to keep** ~ vigiar, guardar; **to** ~ **for** *vt* esperar; **2** **to** ~ **out for sth** *vi* ter cuidado; prestar atenção a algo; **to** ~ **over** *vt (look after sb/sth)* cuidar de alguém/algo.

water *n* água; ~ **biscuit** *n* bolacha *f* água e sal; ~ **bottle** *(for traveller)* cantil *m*; **2** *(hot)* botija *f*/saco *m* de água quente; ~**colour** *n* aguarela, *(BR)* aquarela; ~**course** *n* curso de água; canal *m*; ~**cress** *n (BOT)* agrião *m*; **drinking** ~ água potável; ♦

diviner n vedor m ~**fall** n cascata, cachoeira; ~**front** n (harbour) cais m; ~~**heater** n esquentador m; ~**hole** n bebedouro, poço ~ **lily** n nenúfar m; ~**line** n (NAUT) linha d'água; ~**logged** adj alagado; ~ **main** n canalização f de água; ~**melon** n (BOT) melancia; ~ **polo** n polo-aquático; ~**proof** adj impermeável; à prova d'água; ~s npl águas fpl; ~**shed** n (GEOG) divisor m de água; (fig) momento crítico, ponto de viragem; ~~**ski/ skiing** n (SPORT) esqui m aquático; ~**side** n beira-mar m; ♦ adj (plant, etc) costeiro, ribeirinho; ~ **softener** n (produto) amaciador m; ~ **supply** n abastecimento m de água; ~ **table** n (GEOG) nível m do lençol de água, lençol m freático; ~ **tank** n depósito d'água; cisterna f; ~**tight** adj hermético, à prova d'água; **2** (fig) infalível; **under** ~ submerso,-a, debaixo de água; **2** (flooded) inundado,-a; ~**works** npl sistema f de distribuição de água; ♦ vt/vi (plants) regar; (field) irrigar; (eyes) lacrimejar; **to give** ~ **to** (sb/animals) dar de beber a; **to** ~ **down** vt aguar, diluir, deitar água em; (fig) atenuar; ♦ **to keep one's head above** ~ manter a cabeça à tona d'água; (FIN) fazer face aos compromissos; **it makes my mouth** ~ vi estou/fico com água na boca; **pass** ~ vi (urinate) urinar; **to throw cold** ~ **on sth** vt (enthusiasm, etc) deitar um balde de água fria em algo; **to turn the** ~ **on/off** abrir/fechar a torneira; IDIOM **to go through fire and** ~ passar por grandes dificuldades; **to fish in troubled** ~s pescar em águas turvas; **it's** ~ **under the bridge** são águas passadas; o que lá vai, lá vai.

watering n rega f; irrigação f; ~ **can** n regador m; ♦ adj (eyes) lacrimejante.

watermark n (on paper) marca d'água, **2** (NAUT) nível a que chegou a maré alta.

watery adj (colour) pálido,-a; (coffee, paint) aguado; (eyes) lacrimosos, cheios mpl de lágrimas.

watt n vátio, watt m.

wattage n potência f em watts.

wattle n (fold of skin under bird's neck) monco m de peru; **2** caniçada f, vedação f de vimes entrelaçados; paliçada.

wave n (of sea) onda f; **to make** ~s (fig) fazer ondas; **2** (of hand) aceno; sinal; **3** (RADIO) onda, vaga; **4** (in hair) onda, ondulação f; **5** (fig: series) série f; ~**length** n comprimento de onda; ~ **power** n energia f das ondas; ♦ vt (with the hand) acenar com a mão; **2** (gesture) fazer sinal para; **3** (with weapon) brandir; **4** (hair) ondular; (flag) tremular, flutuar; **5** (tree branches) ondular; ♦ vi (flag) tremular, flutuar ao vento; **2** (tree branches) ondular; **3** (flame, light) tremeluzir; ♦ ~ **aside** vt (dismiss) rejeitar com um gesto; ~ **down** vt (taxi, bus) fazer sinal para parar; ~ (**sb**) **off** vt dizer adeus a alguém.

waver vi (person) vacilar; hesitar; **2** (flickering flame, light) tremular; **3** (needle: temperature) oscilar.

wavering n indecisão; **2** (of voice) tremura f; **3** (of flame) tremelejo m; ♦ pp adj (person) hesitante; indeciso,-a; (confidence) vacilante; (light) tremulante.

wavy adj ondulado, ondulante.

wax n cera; ~ **works** npl museu m de cera; ♦ vt (furniture, floor) encerar; (car) polir; ♦ vi (moon) crescer; **2** (LITER) (speak) falar de maneira eloquente, indignada sobre.

waxed pp adj encerado,-a; **2** (fabric) impermeável.

waxy adj (texture, skin) de cera.

way n (route, path) caminho; **2** (direction) dire(c)ção f, sentido; **opposite** ~ sentido contrário; **which** ~? qual é o caminho?; **go that** ~ vá por ali; **to be on one's** ~ estar a caminho; **to be in the** ~ estorvar, atrapalhar; **keep out of my** ~ saia do meu caminho; **to be under** ~ estar a caminho; (meeting, project) estar em andamento; **to go out of one's** ~ **to do sth** dar-se ao trabalho de fazer algo; **to lose one's** ~ perder-se; **the** ~ **back** o caminho de volta; '**give** ~' (AUT) 'via preferencial'; ~ **in** entrada; ~ **out** saída; **to be on the** ~ **out** (fig) passar de moda; **there is no** ~ **out** (fig) não há escapatória f possível; **3** (distance) **all the** ~ todo o caminho; **a long** ~ **off** a grande distância; **4** (means, manner, style) modo m, maneira f; forma f, jeito m; **in a** ~ de certo modo, até certo ponto; **in no** ~ de maneira alguma; **in the same** ~ da mesma forma; **in a small/big** ~ a uma pequena/ grande escala; **to have her own** ~ conseguir o que ela quer; **to have a** ~ **with people** (knack) ter jeito para lidar com a gente; **to have one's** ~ **of doing sth** (habit) ter o costume de fazer algo; **to give** ~ (under weight) ceder; **by the** ~ adv a propósito; **by** ~ **of** (prep) por via de, passando por; **ways** npl modos; hábitos, costumes; ~ **and means** npl meios mpl; **2** (FIN) (methods, resources) meios de melhorar as receitas do Estado.

waylay (irr: like **lay**) vt fazer uma espera a (alguém); aguardar e atacar; **2** fazer parar alguém.

way-out adj (unconventional) excêntrico,-a, arrojado,-a; **2** excelente, fantástico.

wayside n beira f da estrada; **at/by** ~ à beira da estrada.

wayward adj (wilful) voluntarioso,-a, teimoso,-a; caprichoso,-a; incorrigível; **2** (child) travesso,-a; **3** (wife, husband) volúvel; (horse) incontrolável.

WC (=Water Closet) WC m, toilete m; (fam) retrete f; (public) lavabos mpl; (form) casa f de banho; (BR) banheiro m.

we pron pl nós; ~ **are happy** estamos/somos felizes.

weak adj fraco, débil; **2** (tea) aguado; ~~**minded** adj fraco,-a de espírito.

weaken vt (gen) enfraquecer (person, structure); **2** debilitar, minorar (power); **3** prejudicar, abalar (power); **4** diminuir; **5** diluir (solution); **6** (ECON, FIN) enfraquecer (economy) fazer baixar os preços; ♦ vi (physically) enfraquecer-se; **2** (give way) ceder; **3** (grip) afrouxar.

weakening n (physical) fraqueza, debilitação f; (structure) degradação f.

weakling n pessoa (ou animal) fraco,-a, delicado,-a.

weakness n fraqueza; **2** (fault) ponto fraco; **to have a** ~ **for sth/sb** ter um fraco por algo/alguém; **2** (FIN) (currency) fragilidade f.

weal n vergão m.

wealth *n* (*money, resources*) riqueza; fortuna; (*of details*) abundância.

wealthy *adj* rico, abastado,-a.

wean *vt* desmamar.

weapon *n* arma; armamento.

wear *n* uso; (*damage*) desgaste *m*; **sports** ~ /**baby** ~ roupa de desporto (*BR*: esporte), roupa de infantil; ♦ (*pt* **wore**, *pp* **worn**) *vt* (*clothes*) usar, vestir, trazer; (*shoes*) usar, calçar; (*make-up*) estar maquilhada; **2** (*damage*) desgastar; consumir; gastar; ♦ *vi* (*last*) durar; (*become damaged*) gastar-se; esgotar-se; **my patience is ~ing thin** a minha paciência está a esgotar-se; **2** (*fig*) (*age*) **she is ~ing very well** ela está muito bem conservada; ~ **and tear** *n* desgaste *m* natural; **to ~ away** *vt* gastar; ♦ *vi* (*deteriorate*) desgastar-se; **to ~ down** *vt* gastar; **2** (*strength*) esgotar; **to ~ off** *vi* (*pain, effects, etc*) desa parecer, passar; **to ~ sth off** apagar, desvanecer; **to ~ out** *vt* (*clothes, machinery*) desgastar, usar até ficar estragado; **2** esgotar-se.

wearable *adj* usável.

weariness *n* fadiga *f*; **2** (*upsetting*) aborrecimento *m*.

wearing *adj* fatigante; ♦ *vi* **to ~ out** cansar- de; ♦ *vt* fatigar, aborrecer.

weary *adj* exausto,-a; deprimido,-a; farto,-a de.

weasel *n* (*ZOOL*) doninha; **2** (*sly person*) manhoso,-a; fuinha *m,f*; ♦ *vt*: **to ~ out** livrar-se de, faltar a (*commitment*).

weather *n* tempo, estado atmosférico; **to be under the ~** estar indisposto; sentir-se chocho (*fam*); ♦ *vt* (*storm, crisis*) resistir a; superar, vencer dificuldades; ~-**beaten** *adj* batido,-a (pela intempérie); (*rock*) erodido,-a; desgastado,-a; ~**cock** *n* cata-vento; ~ **forecast** *n* previsão *f*, boletim *m* meteorológico; ~**vane** *n* (= ~**cock**) (*fig*) (*fickle person*) vira-casaca *m,f*; pessoa *f* inconstante.

weave *n* tecelagem *f*; ♦ (*pt* **wove**, *pp* **woven**) *vt* (*textile*) tecer; (*spider*) tecer; (*inter~*) entrelaçar; (*fig*) (*invent*) criar, inventar (*story*); **to ~ tales** (*pej*) tecer intrigas; ~ **through traffic** abrir caminho por entre o movimento.

weaver *n* tecelão *m*, tecelã *f*.

web *n* (*of spider*) teia; **2** (*ZOOL*) (*water birds/ animal*) membrana *f* interdigital; **3** (*fig*) (*of lies, intrigue, plot*) trama *m*, enredo *m*; série *f*; **4** (*of ropes*) entrelaçamento *m*; (*network*) rede *f*; **W~** *n* (*COMP*) Rede; ~**bed** *adj* (*foot*) palmípede; ~**bing** *n* (*material*) (*on chair*) tira *f* de tecido resistente; ~ **foot** *n* (*pl*: ~ **feet**) pé *m* palmado.

wed *n*: **the newly-~s** *npl* os recém-casados *mpl*; ♦ (*pt, pp* -**ded**) *vt* casar; ♦ *vi* casar-se.

we'd = **we had; we would**.

wedded (*pt, pp* of **wed**) *adj* casado,-a; **lawful ~ wife** (*JUR*) esposa legítima.

wedding *n* casamento, boda; núpcias *fpl*; **silver/ golden** ~ bodas *fpl* de prata/de ouro; ~ **day** *n* dia do casamento; ~ **dress** *n* vestido de noiva; ~ **night** noite *f* de núpcias; ~ **present** *n* presente *m* de casamento; ~ **ring** *n* aliança, anel *m* de casamento.

wedge *n* (*insert in wood etc*) cunha; (*hold in position*) calço; (*of cake, cheese*) fatia *f*; (*on a shoe*) ~

heel cunha; (*keep door open*) calço; (*UK*) (*slang = bribe*) cunha; ~-**shaped** cuneiforme; ♦ *vt* firmar, meter com uma cunha; apertar; **to be ~ed between/against sth** estar entalado,-a entre/ contra; **to ~ into** (*narrow space*) meter à força; IDIOM **thin end of the ~** (*algo insignificante mas com consequencias futuras*) isto é apenas o começo; de algo; pano de amostra.

wedlock *n* matrimónio (*BR*: -mô-); estado de casado.

Wednesday *n* Quarta-feira, quarta-feira.

wee *adj* pequeno, pequenino; **a ~ drop** (*drink*) uma pinguinha.

weed *n* erva daninha *f*; ~-**killer** *n* herbicida *m*; ♦ *vt* capinar, mondar; **to ~ out** *vt* livrar-se de.

week *n* semana; **a ~ from today** de hoje a oito dias; ~ **after** ~ semana após semana; ~**day** *n* dia *m* da semana; ~**end** *n* fim *m* de semana.

weekly *n* (*magazine*) semanário *m*; ♦ *adv* semanalmente; ♦ *adj* seminal; ~ **wages** ordenado semanal; ~ **pocket money** *n* semanada *f*.

weeny *adj* (*UK: fam*) pouquinho,-a; **a ~ bit** (*food, drink*) um pouquinho.

weep (*pt, pp* **wept**) *vt/vi* chorar, derramar lágrimas; **2** (*blood, joint*) escorrer.

weeping *n* pranto *m*, choro *m*; ~ **willow** *n* (*BOT*) salgueiro *m* chorão *m*.

weepy *adj* (*gen*) choroso,-a; (*person*) à beira das lágrimas.

weft *n* (*yarn woven across the width of fabric*) trama *m*.

weigh *vt/vi* pesar; **2** (*risk, consequences*) avaliar, ~ **sth against sth** comparar algo com algo; **3** (*NAUT*) **to ~ anchor** levantar âncora; **to ~ down** *vt* sobrecarregar; (*fig*) oprimir, acabrunhar; **to ~ in** *vt* intervir; **to ~ up** *vt* ponderar, avaliar.

weighbridge *n* báscula *f* automática.

weigh-in *n* (*SPORT*) pesagem *f*.

weighing machine *n* (*for people*) balança *f*.

weight *n* peso; **2** valor *m*, importância; **to lose/put on** ~ emagrecer/engordar; **3** (*power, influence*) **to carry** ~ ter peso; **4 to take the ~ off one's feet** descansar, sentar-se; **to throw one's ~ about** andar a dar ordens, ser mandão,-dona; ~-**lifter** *n* halterofilista *m,f*; ♦ *vt* lastrar, chumbar (*boat, hem, dart*); IDIOM **a ~ off one's mind** um grande alívio; **by sheer ~ of numbers** pela força dos números.

weighted *adj* com contrapeso; ~ **average** média *f* ponderda.

weighting (*UK*) (pagamento variável e adicional para se viver numa cidade com alto custo de vida) peso *m* ponderação.

weightless *adj* ligeiro,-a; sem peso.

weightlessness *n* (*of person*) leveza; imponderabilidade.

weighty (-ier, -iest) *adj* (*object, person*) pesado,-a; **2** (de peso) importante.

weir *n* represa, açude *m*.

weird *adj* (*fam*) (*strange*) estranho,-a; **2** (*odd*) esquisito,-a; misterioso,-a.

weirdo (*pl*: -**s**, *or* -**dies**) *n* (*fam*) excêntrico,-a.

welcome *n* acolhimento *m*, acolhida *f* recepção *f*; ♦ *adj* bem-vindo,-a; ♦ *vt* dar as boas-vindas; (*be* *glad of)* receber com alegria; **you're** ~ *(reply to 'thanks')* não tem de quê; *(fam)* de nada.

welcoming *adj (person, home, smile)* acolhedor,-ora; *(speech)* de boas-vindas.

weld *n* solda; ♦ *vt* soldar, unir.

welder *n (person)* soldador *m*.

welding *n* soldagem *f*, solda.

welfare *n (well-being)* bem-estar *m*; **2** *(state assistance)* assistência *f* social; previdência *f* social; ~ **meal** *n* refeição *f* gratuita.

well *n (water, oil)* poço *m*.

well *(comp.* **better**; *sup.* **best)** *adj:* **to be** ~ estar bem (de saúde); **I hope you are (feeling)** ~ espero que esteja melhor; **to do** ~ **at/in** *(job, exam, interview)* sair-se bem em; ♦ *exc* bem!, bom! então!; ~ **then!** ora bem!; ~ **I never!** *(in surprise)* ora essa!, não me diga!; **2** *(in resignation)* oh ~! enfim!; **3** *(approval)* ~ **done!** apoiado!; **4** *(concern)* **get ~ soon!** melhoras!; ♦ *adv* bem; **as** ~ *(also)* também; **2** *(approval)* **just as** ~ ainda bem (que); **just as ~ you are out of it** ainda bem que você está fora disso; **3** *(slightly contentious)* ~ **then, what is the question?** ora bem, qual é a questão?; **4** *(amazed)* ~, ~, ~, **so you are the new champion** ora com que então és o novo campeão; **5** *(with auxiliaries)* **we may as ~ eat** é melhor comermos; **6** *(advisable)* **it would be just as ~ to keep quiet about this** seria melhor calar-se acerca disto; **you can't very ~ give up now** não podes realmente desistir agora; **7** *(intensifier)* **the numbers are ~ above expectations** os números estão bem acima das expe(c)tativas; **all ~ and good** tanto melhor; **if you agree,** ~ **and good** se concordares, tanto melhor; **pretty** ~ razoavelmente, bastante bem; ~ **and truly** *adv* completamente; ♦ **as ~ as** *prep* assim como; além de; **to be** ~ **up in/on** *(acquainted with – subject)* familiar com *(tema)*, com um bom conhecimento de; ♦ *vt, vi* jorrar, transbordar, derramar(-se) *(also:* ~ **up)** *(flow)* brotar, manar; **the tears welled (up) in her eyes** as lágrimas brotaram-lhe dos olhos; **to ~ out/up/forth** *vi* jorrar, transbordar; **the blood was welling out** o sangue saía aos borbotões.

we'll = we will, we shall.

well-attended *(meeting)* bem concorrido,-a.

well-behaved *adj* bem-educado,-a, bem-comportado,-a.

well-being *n* bem-estar *m*.

well-bred *adj* bem educado,-a; **2** *(animal)* de boa raça.

well-brought-up *adj* bem-criado,-a.

well-built *adj (person)* robusto,-a.

well-connected *adj* bem-relacionado,-a.

well-done *adj (steak)* bem passado,-a; *(work, etc)* bem feito,-a.

well-earned merecido,-a.

well-groomed *adj* bem arranjado,-a; **2** bem cuidado,-a.

well-heeled *adj (coll)* rico,-a, endinheirado,-a.

wellies *npl (UK) (fam)* galochas.

well-informed *adj* bem-informado,-a, versado,-a.

wellingtons *n* (= ~ **boots)** galochas *fpl*, botas *fpl* impermeáveis.

well-kept *(garden, house)* em bom estado; conservado,-a; **2** *(secret)* bem guardado,-a.

well-known *adj* conhecido,-a, famoso,-a.

well-mannered *adj* delicado,-a; de/com boas maneiras.

well-meaning *adj* bem-intencionado,-a.

well-nigh *adv (formal)* quase.

well-off *adj* próspero,-a, com posses; ♦ **the ~ people** os abastados; **to be ~ for (sth)** *(have plentyful of sth)* ter bastante (de algo).

well-preserved *(fig) (person) (aging well)* bem conservado,-a.

well-read *adj* culto,-a. versado,-a.

well-spoken *adj* que fala bem, polido,-a; ~ **of** de/com boa reputação.

well-timed oportuno,-a.

well-to-do *adj* abastado,-a.

well-trodden: a ~ path um caminho bem concorrido,-a.

well-wisher *n* simpatizante.

well-worn *adj* (roupa) gasto,-a; **2** *(expression)* batido,-a.

Welsh *n adj* galês,-esa; ♦ *npr (LING)* galês *m*; ♦ **to ~ on** *vi* não cumprir *(promise)*; faltar à palavra; ~ **rarebit** *n (CULIN)* tosta com queijo derretido; ~ **on** *vi (slang)* welsh rarebit on.

welt *n (on skin)* vergão *m*; **2** *(on shoe)* vira; **3** *(edge of a knitted suit)* debrum; ♦ *vt* vergastar.

welter *n* reboliço; confusão; ♦ *vt* ficar encharcado,-a.

welterweight *n (boxer)* peso *m* meio-médio.

wen *n (MED: cyst on scalp)* quisto *m*; **2** *(overcrowded city)* **the great ~** *n* Londres.

wench *n* moça, mulher alegre e de físico voluptuoso.

wend *vt:* **to ~ one's way** encaminhar-se vagarosamente **(towards** para).

went *(pt of* **go)**.

wept *(pt, pp of* **weep)**.

were *(pt of* **be)**.

we're = we are.

weren't = were not.

werewolf *(pl:* ~**wolves)** *n* lobisomem *m*.

west *n* oeste *m*; poente *m*; ♦ *adj* ocidental, do oeste; ♦ *adv* a ocidente; ~ **of** ao oeste; **the W~** *n* o Oeste, o Ocidente.

West Bank *npr:* **the ~** a Cisjordânia; **on the ~** na Cisjordânia.

westbound *adj* em direção ao oeste.

West Country *npr:* **the ~** o Sudoeste da Inglaterra.

West End *n* o coração de Londres (lojas e teatros, etc).

westerly *n:* ~ **wind** vento *m* do oeste; ♦ *adj (towards the west)* **in a ~ direction** em dire(c)ção a oeste **(in, on** no; **from** do oeste).

western *n (CIN)* filme *m* de cow-boys, *(BR)* faroeste; ♦ *adj* ocidental.

westerner *n (POL, GEOG)* ocidental *m,f*; **2** *(inhabitant of western country)* habitante *m,f* do oeste.

westernize/ise *vt* ocidentalizar.

West Indian *n adj* antilhano,-a.

West Indies *npr pl:* **the ~** as Antilhas *fpl*.

Westminster *npr:* **City of ~** *(area)* distrito de Westminster no centro de Londres; **2** *(British Parliament)* Parlamento *m* britânico, situado neste distrito, à beira do rio Tâmisa.

westward(s) *adv* para o oeste.

wet *adj (dampness)* humidade *f*; **2** *(POL)* políico conservador moderado; **3** *(coll) (pej)* papa-açorda *m,f;* ♦ (*-ter, -test*) *adj* (h)úmido,-a; **2** (*soaked*) molhado; **3** (*drenched*) encharcado,-a; ~ **through** completamente encharcado; ~ **to the skin** molhado,-a até aos ossos; **to get** ~ molhar-se, andar à chuva; **4** (*rainy*) chuvoso,-a; **5** '~ **paint**' 'pintado de fresco'; **6** (*UK*) (*fig, pej*) (*feeble*) fraco,-a; **7** ~ **state** (*US*) (*allowing alcohol*) anti-proibicionista *m,f;* ♦ (*-tt-, pp* **wet**) *vt* molhar; ♦ **to** ~ **o.s.** (*urinate*) molhar as calças; mijar-se (*fam*); **to** ~ **the bed** (*child*) fazer chichi (*BR:* xixi) na cama; IDIOM **to** ~ **the whistle** (*fam*) tomar uma bebida; matar o bicho (*fam*); **to be a** ~ **blanket** (*fig*) ser um desmancha-prazeres.

wetness *n* (h)umidade *f;* **2** (*UK*) (*pej*) (*feebleness*) fraqueza *f.*

wet nurse *n* ama de leite.

wet rot *n* (*wood decay*) apodrecimento *m.*

wetsuit *n* fato *m* de mergulho, (*BR*) roupa de mergulho.

we've = **we have.**

whack *n* pancada *f;* **2** (*share*) quinhão *m;* **one's** ~ **of the profits** a sua parte nos lucros; ♦ *vt* bater; dar pancada em.

whacking *n* (*beating*) sova *f;* tareia *f.*

whacked *adj* (*coll: tired*) morto,-a esgotado,-a.

whale *n* (*ZOOL*) baleia; **to have a** ~ **of a time** diverter-se a valer; ~**bone** *n* barbas de baleia.

whaler *n* (*boat*) baleeiro *m;* **2** (*person*) pescador de baleias.

whaling (*fishing*) pesca, caça da baleia; **to go** ~ ir à pesca, caça *f* às baleias.

wham (~**ming;** *pt,pp:* ~**med**) *vt* (*door*) bater com força; ♦ *exc* (*sound of this blow*) zás! trás!.

whammy (*pl:* -**mies**) *n* azar *m,* enguiço *m;* **2** (*negative impact*) **the double** ~ **of high interest and low wage increases** o impa(c)to duplo de altas taxas de juros e baixos aumentos de salários.

wharf (*pl:* **wharves**) *n* cais *m inv.*

what *excl* quê!, como; ♦ *det* que; ♦ *pron* (*interrogative*) que, o que; (*relative, indirect: object, subject*) o que, a que; ~ **are you saying?** o que está você a dizer, (*BR*) o que você está dizendo?; **I saw** ~ **you did** eu vi o que você fez; ~ **a mess!** que confusão/bagunça!; ~ **is it called?** como se chama isto?; ~ **about me?** e eu?; ~ **else?** que mais?; ~**ever you want** o que quer que desejares; ♦ *pron:* **do** ~ **is necessary** faça tudo o que for preciso; ~ **happens** aconteça o que acontecer; **no reason** ~**ever**/~**soever** nenhuma razão.

whatitsname *n* (*fam*) o (*tal*) fulano,-a, tal fulana *f.*

whatnot *n* (*fam*) (*unspecified thing*) coiso *m;* **and** ~ e coisas assim; **2** prateleira *f* para pequenos obje(c)tos.

whatsit (*what is it*) *n* (*forgot the name of the item/person*) o coiso *m.*

whatsoever *adj pron* tudo quanto; seja o que for; **2** (*at all*) nenhum,-a; absolutamente nada; **nothing** ~ nada em absoluto.

wheat *n* (*BOT*) trigo *m;* ~ **germ** *n* germe *m* de trigo; ~**meal** *n* farinha *f* de trigo integral.

wheedle *vt* lisongear; **to** ~ **sb into doing sth** obter algo à custa de lisonjas.

wheel *n* roda; (*AUT* = **steering** ~) volante *m;* (*NAUT*) roda do leme; ♦ *vt* empurrar; ♦ *vi* (= **to** ~ **round**) girar, dar voltas, virar-se; rodar; ♦ ~**barrow** *n* carrinho de mão; ~**chair** *n* cadeira de rodas; ~ **clamp** *n* (*AUT*) grampo *m* para imobilizar veículo em estacionamento proibido; **to** ~**-clamp** *vt* grampear a roda de veículos ilegalmente estacionados.

wheeled *adj* equipado com rodas; (*in combination*) **two-~ carriage** carruagem *f* de duas rodas.

wheeler-dealer *n* (*pej*) pessoa manhosa e intriguista em negócios ou em política.

wheelhouse *n* casa *f* do leme.

wheeling and dealing *n* (*pej*) (*negotiations*) negociatas *fpl;* (*with cunning*) manigância *f.*

wheeze *vt* respiração *f* ruidosa/ofegante; ♦ *vt* respirar a custo; **2** (*UK*) (*fam*) artemanha, truque *m.*

wheezy *adj* chiante, que respira com dificuldade; **2** (*out of* breath) ofegante.

when *adv* quando; ♦ *conj* quando; ao passo que; **on the day** ~ **I met him** no dia em que o conheci.

whence (**from whence**) *adv* (*formal*) (*from what place*) de onde.

whenever *adv, conj* quando; quando quer que; sempre que; ~ **you need me, you call me** sempre que precises de mim, chama-me.

where *adv* onde; **this is** ~ **we stayed** aqui é onde ficámos; **2** *pron* (*interrogative*) onde?; ~ **is your sister?** onde está (a) sua irmã?; ~'**s the harm?** onde está o mal?; **3** (*with preposition*) de, para, a; ~ **are you from?** de onde você é?; (*to where*) ~ **are you going (to)?** aonde vais? para onde vais?; **4** (*emphatic interrogative*) ~ **do you really want to go?** onde é que tu afinal queres ir?; **5** (*place*) **my home is** ~ **I like to be** (a) minha casa é onde eu gosto de estar; ♦ ~**abouts** *n* paradeiro *m;* **does anybody know her** ~? alguém sabe do paradeiro dela?; ♦ *adv* por onde; ~**as** *conj* ao passo que, enquanto que; ~**by** *adv* através do/da qual; pelo,-a qual; ~**in** *adv* no que, naquilo que.

whereupon *conj* (*formal*) depois do que, após o que, sobre o que.

wherewithal *n:* **the** ~ os meios, recursos *mpl.*

whet (**-tt-**) *vt* (*knife*) afiar, amolar; **2** (*fig*) (*appetite*) abrir; estimular; **3** (*fig*) (*desire*) despertar.

whether *conj* se, quer ... quer; **I don't know** ~ **to go or not** (*uncertainty*) não sei se vou ou não; (*obligation*) ~ **I want to or not** quer eu queira, quer não queira.

whew *exc* (*expressing relief*) uf!

whey *n* soro *m* do leite.

which *det* (*interrogative*) que, qual; ~ **one of you?** qual de vocês? ~ **picture do you want?** (*of a choice*) que quadro você quer? qual dos quadros você quer?; ♦ *pron* (*interrogative*) qual; (*relative: subject, object*) que, o que; o,-a qual/os/as quais; cujo,-a; **I don't mind** ~ não me importa qual; (*introducing a clause*) **the subject,** ~ **we talked about** o assunto sobre o qual falámos; **the book,** ~ **she wrote, is sold out** o livro, que ela escreveu, está esgotado; **we were in Italy, during** ~ **time**

estivemos na Itália e durante esse tempo; *(preceding concept/clause)* ~ **tells me (that)** o que me diz (que); **we shall be giving a party, before** ~ … vamos dar uma festa, mas antes …; **the chair on** ~ **he is sitting** a cadeira na qual ele está sentado; **in** ~ **case** em cujo caso, nesse caso.

whichever *pron (no matter which one)* qualquer coisa que, seja qual for, qualquer um; ♦ *det:* **take** ~ **book you prefer** pegue/leve o livro que preferir; *(the one that)* o,-a que; ~ **the result** seja qual for o resultado.

whiff *n (brief smell of smoke, foul breath)* baforada *f*, odor *m*; **2** *(good smell)* cheiro *m*, perfume *m*; **2** *(gust of air)*, lufada *f*; **3** *(fig) (of scandal, danger)* alusão *f*, sinal *m*, cheirinho *m*.

Whig *n (HIST – UK)* um membro do partido político do século XVII que opôs a sucessão ao trono de Jaime VII; **2** *membro do partido Conservador que se tornou no partido Liberal (séc. XVIII–XIX)*; **3** adepto da economia sem restrições; **4** (US) partidário da Guerra da Independência da América.

while *n* algum tempo *m*, momento *m*; **I waited quite a** ~ esperei uns momentos; **a long** ~ **ago** há muito tempo; há tempo que; **for a** ~ durante algum tempo, (por) um pouco *(of time)*; **to be worth**~ valer a pena; **once in a** ~ de vez em quando, tempos a tempos; **all the** ~ todo o (este) tempo; ♦ *conj (as long as, during)* durante; enquanto; **he played the guitar** ~ **I sang** ele tocava a guitarra enquanto eu cantava; *(whereas)* enquanto (que), ao passo que; ♦ *vt:* **to** ~ **away (the time)** *(leisurely)* passar/matar o tempo.

whilst *conj. adv* (= while).

whim *n* capricho *m*; mania *f*; **on a** ~ por capricho.

whimper *n* choradeira *f*; lamúria *f*; gemido *m*; ♦ *vi* choramingar; gemer; *(dog)* ganir.

whimsical *adj (person)* dado,-a a caprichos, extravagante; **2** *(look, manner)* estranho,-a, esquisito,-a; *(story, idea)* excêntrico,-a, de fantasia.

whine *n (high-pitched moan)* queixume *m*, gemido *m*; **2** *(of engine)* zunido, guincho *m*; **3** *(of dog)* ganido *m*; **4** *(of bullet)* assobio; ♦ *vi* choramingar, queixar-se **(about de)** *(continuously)*; **2** *(engine)* zunir, guinchar; **3** *(dog)* ganir; **the dog was whining in pain** o cão estava a ganir com dores.

whinge *(pres p:* **wingeing)** *vi (UK:* **to** ~ **about sb/ sth)** queixar-se (repetidamente) de alguém/algo.

whinny *n* relincho *m*; ♦ *(-nies, -nying; -nied) vi (soft neigh)* relinchar gentilmente.

whip *n* chicote *m*; ~**lash** chicotada *f*, **2** *(POL – UK)* um membro de um partido político eleito para disciplinar, organizar seus correlegionários e encorajá-los a comparecer nas votações no parlamento; instigador do grupo parlamentar; ♦ *(-ped, -ping) vt* chicotear; bater; **2** *(wind)* açoitar *(do sth suddenly or quickly)* ~ **in/out** entrar/sair precipitadamente; **they** ~**ped into the bar for a drink** foram ao bar de saltada; **to** ~ **sth out of sb's hand** *(snatch)* arrancar algo das mãos de alguém; ♦ *(CULIN)* **to** ~ **the whites of the eggs**

stiffly bater as claras em castelo; ~**ed cream** *n* natas *fpl* batidas, *(BR)* creme *m* batido, chantilly *m*; ♦ **to** ~ **up** *vt* incitar.

whippet *n* galgo *m*.

whip-round *n (fam)* cole(c)ta; *(fam)* vaquinha.

whirl *n* rotação; **2** remoinho; **3** *(confusion)* turbilhão *m*; ♦ *vt* rodopiar; *vi* girar, andar à roda; ♦ ~**pool** *n* redemoinho *m*; ~**wind** *n* turbilhão *m*; **a** ~ **romance** um romance-relâmpago.

whirr *n* zumbido *m*; ♦ *vi* zumbir.

whisk *n (CULIN)* batedeira; ♦ *vt* bater; **to** ~ **sth away from sb** arrebatar algo de alguém; **to** ~ **sb away/off** levar rapidamente alguém.

whisker *n:* ~**s** *(of animal)* bigodes *mpl*; *(of man)* suíças *fpl*.

whisk(e)y *n* uísque *m*.

whisper *n* sussurro, murmúrio *m*; **2** *(gossip, rumour)* rumor *m*; **3** *(fig)* confidência *f*; ♦ *vi* sussurrar, murmurar; *(fig)* segredar; ~**ing campaign** *n* campanha de difamação; **not a** ~! *(keep secret)* nem um pio! *(fam)*.

whist *n (card game)* whist, *(BR)* uíste *m*; ~ **drive** *n* reunião *f* onde se joga o uíste.

whistle *n (by person, birds)* assobio *m*; **2** *(object)* apito; **3** *(of train-sound)* silvo *m*; ♦ *vi (person, wind)* assobiar; **2** *(with the whistle)* apitar; **3** *(kettle)* chiar; **4** *(bird)* piar; **5** *(move fast)* **to** ~ **past/by** *(of a bullet, arrow)* passar a sibilar; IDIOM **to blow the** ~ **on sb** denunciar alguém; ~-**blower** *n* denunciador,-ora.

whit *n:* **not a** ~ nem um bocadinho.

white *n* branco,-a; **2** *(of egg)* clara; *(of eye)* branco *m*; córnea *f*; ♦ *adj* branco,-a; alvo,-a; pálido,-a; **to go/ turn** ~ *(face)* empalidecer; **2** *(hair)* ficar branco,-a; branquear; ♦ ~**bait** *n (fish)* carapauzinho *m* de gato; peixe *m* miúdo, petinga *m*; ~ **blood cell** *n* glóbulo *m* branco; ~**board** *n* quadro *m* branco; ~ **Christmas** *n* Natal *m* com neve; ~ **coffee** *n* café com leite; *(in small cup)* garoto *(col)*; ~-**collar worker** *n* empregado de escritório; ~ **elephant** *n (fig)* elefante *m* branco; ~ **goods** *npl (household appliances)* eléctrico-domésticos *mpl* ~**horses** *mpl (on sea)* crista *f* (quebrada) da onda; ~**hot** *adj* incandescente; ~ **lie** *(fib) n* mentira *f* inofensiva; peta *f*; ~ **meat** *n (poultry)* carne *f* branca; ~**n** *vt (clothes)* branquear; **2** *(wall)* caiar; ~**ness** *n* brancura, alvura *f*; **W~ Paper** *n (POL) (government's report)* Livro *m* Branco; ~ **sauce** *n* molho bechamel; molho branco; ~ **slavery** *n* tráfico de mulheres; ~ **spirit** *n (UK)* aguarrás *m inv*; diluente *m*; ~ **squall** *n* tempestade violenta no mar em locais; ~ **tie** *n* traje *m* de gala; ~ **trash** *n (pej)* gente branca e pobre que vive nos E.U.A.; ~**wash** *n (paint)* cal *f*; ♦ *vt* caiar; **2** *(fig)* encobrir, disfarçar.

Whitehall *npr* rua em Londres que vai da Praça de Trafalgar ao Parlamento, onde se encontram os principais órgãos da administração do governo britânico e seus ministérios.

White House *npr:* **the** ~ a Casa *f* Branca; *(residência oficial e local de trabalho do Presidente dos E.U.A.,* situada em Washington, capital do país e sede do governo federal).

whitener n (for clothes) alvejante m; **2** (for shoes) branqueador m; **3** (for coffee, tea) sucedâneo m de leite em pó.

whitey (US) (pej) (termo dado à gente branca pelos negros); branquela m,f (fam).

whither adv (LITER) para onde.

whiting n pl inv (fish) badejo m; badejo-branco.

whitish adj esbranquiçado,-a.

whitlow n (MED) panarício m.

Whit Monday n segunda-feira f de Pentecostes.

Whitsun n (REL) Pentecostes m.

whittle vt (wood) aparar, cortar; **to ~ away/down** reduzir gradualmente.

whizz (UK), **whiz** (US) n (very clever) ás; ♦ n,vt (sound) zunir; sibilar; **to ~ past/by** (arrow, person) passar/voar a toda velocidade; **2** (US) (coll) mijar (cal).

whizz-kid n (coll) (menino,-a) prodígio m; ás m,f; **she is a ~ in languages** ela é um ás, menina prodígio em línguas.

WHO n (Vd: **World Health Organization**) OMS.

who pron rel. que, o qual, os quais; (interrogative) quem?; **~ is that speaking?** (phone) quem fala?

whoa exc (to stop donkey, ox) xó! aí!.

whodun(n)it n filme, romance policial.

whoever (also: **whosoever**) pron quem quer que; seja quem for.

whole n total m; conjunto; **the ~ of the town** toda a cidade, a cidade inteira; **on the ~** no total, em geral; **as a ~** como um todo, no conjunto; ♦ adj todo; inteiro; inta(c)to; **~hearted** adj sincero; **~heartedly** adv de todo o coração **~sale** n venda por atacado, grosso; **~saler** n grossista m,f, (BR) atacadista m,f; ♦ adj por grosso, atacado; (destruction) em grande escala; **~some** adj saudável, sadio.

who'll = **who will**.

wholly adv totalmente, completamente.

whom pron que, o qual, quem; (interrogative) quem?; **~ are you talking about?** de quem fala você?; **~ are these flowers for (for ~ are these flowers)?** para quem são estas flores?; **2** (relative pron) **the man, to ~ I wrote (~ I wrote to) is here** o homem, a quem escrevi, está aqui; **the victims, some of ~ were children, were taken into hospital** as vítimas, das quais algumas eram crianças, foram levadas para o hospital.

whoop n grito m; **~s of joy** gritos mpl de alegria; ♦ vi gritar (**with/of sth** de algo); (MED) tossir convulsivamente.

whoopee exc iupi! eia!; **2 ~ cushion** almofada f que dá o som de peido quandos se senta nela; **3 to make ~** (have fun) divertir-se à farta; fazer uma borga; **4** (make love) fazer amor.

whooping cough n coqueluche f, tosse f convulsa.

whoops exc (child falling) pum! pumba!

whoopsie n (fam) (pet or child's faeces) coco m, caganita f; **the puppy made a ~ on the floor** a cadelinha fez cocó, caganitas (fam)no chão; **the**

little girl made a ~ in the potty a menina fez cocó no bacio.

whoosh n (fam) (rushing sound); (of water) esguicho m; **2** (rush of emotion) **a ~ of happiness** uma torrente de felicidade; ♦ (move quickly) passar a correr; voar.

whopper n (fam) (fib) grande peta f; **2** (sth huge) **it was a ~** era enorme.

whopping adj (fam) enorme, descomunal.

whore n (pej) prostituta; **2** (fig, pej) puta; pega (vulg); **~house** n bordel m.

whorl n (of mollusc) espira f; (BOT; thumb) espiral m.

whose det: **~ book is this?** de quem é este livro?; **someone ~ name he had forgotten** alguém, cujo nome ele tinha esquecido; ♦ pron: **~ is this?** de quem é isto? **I know ~ it is** eu sei de quem é.

whosoever pron: **~it is** quem quer que seja; seja quem for.

why adv porque; **2** (pron interrogative) porque?; porquê?; (surprise) **~ not ?** (also: **~ ever**) **~ ever not?** porque não?; **~ is it that** porque é que?, por que razão?; ♦ conj por isso; **that is ~ they rejected the idea** é por isso que eles rejeitaram a ideia; **the reason ~** a razão pela qual; **tell me ~** diz-me/ diga-me porquê; **so, that's ~!** ah, então, é por isso!

wick n mecha f, pavio m; IDIOM **to get on sb's ~** (coll) dar cabo da cabeça (de alguém), irritar alguém.

wicked adj mau/má, malvado,-a, perverso,-a, infame.

wicker n (= **~work**) (trabalho de) vime m, verga f.

wicket n (cricket stumps) meta f; **2** (in croquet) arco m; **3** (pitch/field) terreno entre as metas; (sluice gate) pequena comporta f de represa; (small gate) cancela m.

wide adj largo; extenso, amplo; vasto; variado; **it is 8 metres ~** tem 8 metros de largura; **a ~ range of articles** uma vasta gama de artigos; ♦ **~-angle lens** n (PHOT) lente f de grande abertura angular; **~-awake** adj bem acordado,-a; **~ boy** n (BR) (pej) pilantra m; **~-eyed** adj (surprised) de olhos arregalados; **~ open** adj (door, window) escancarado,-a; aberto,-a; de par em par; **~-ranging** adj abrangente; amplo,-a; **2** (innocent) ingénuo,-a; ♦ adv amplamente; **to open ~** abrir bem/totalmente; **to shoot ~** atirar longe do alvo, desviar-se.

widely adv amplamente, totalmente; **2 ~-known** (belief) bem conhecido,-a; **it is ~ believed that** há uma convicção generalizada;

widen vt alargar; **2** (increase scope) ampliar, aumentar; **to ~ one's eyes** (in surprise) arregalar os olhos.

wideness n largura f, extensão f.

widespread adj (epidemic) muito espalhado,-a; **2** (belief) difundido,-a; comum m,f; **3** (destruction) vasto,-a.

widow n viúva f.

widowed adj viúvo,-a, enviuvado,-a.

widower n viúvo f.

widowhood n viuvez f.

width n (breadth) largura; **it is ten metres in ~** tem dez metros de largura; **~ways** (**~wise**) adv transversalmente.

wield vt (sword) brandir, empunhar; (power) exercer.

wife (pl: **wives**) n mulher f, esposa f.

wig *n* peruca; cabeleira postiça.

wiggle *vt* menear, agitar; **to ~ one's toes** mexer os dedos (do pé); **to ~ the hips** bambolear; rebolar as ancas; ♦ *vi (snake)* serpear; **2** *(river, road)* serpentear; **3** agitar-se, mover-se.

wigwam *n (US)* tenda *f* indígena (em forma de cone).

wild *n*: **the ~ a** natureza; **in the wilds** nas regiões selvagens *fpl*; nas terras virgens *fpl*; **~ animal** *(carnivorous)* fera; ♦ *adj (animal, tribe)* selvagem; **2** *(ferocious person, animal)* feroz; **3** *(plant)* silvestre; **4** *(landscape)* agreste; **5** *(sea)* violento, bravo; **6** *(idea)* disparatado, extravagante; **7** *(unrestrained person)* bravo,-a, louco,-a; intratável *m,f*; indisciplinado,-a; **when she heard the news she went ~** quando ouviu a notícia, ela ficou uma fera; **8** *(with joy)* delirante *m,f*; **9** *(applause, noise, race)* desenfreado,-a; **10** *(plan)* insensato; **11** *(hair)* emaranhado; **~ look in sb's eyes** olhar *m* halucinante, olhos *mpl* esbugalhados.

wild boar *n (ZOOL)* javali *m*.

wild card *n (game)* curinga *m*; **2** *(COMP)* caráter *m* de substituição; **3** *(fig) (person, element)* imprevisível.

wildcat *n (ZOOL)* gato *m* selvagem, lince *m*; **~ strike** *n (a strike without union approval)* greve *f* clandestina.

wildebeest *n (ZOOL)* gnu *m*.

wilderness *n* ermo *m*; *(barren land)* sertão *m*; deserto *m*; *(overgrown land)* matagal; **político ~** ostracismo político.

wildfire *n*: **to spread like ~** espalhar-se como fogo na mata/no mato.

wild goose chase *n* busca *f* infrutífera.

wildlife *n* fauna e flora.

wildly *adv* loucamente; violentamente; desenfreadamente, freneticamente.

wiles *npl* artimanhas *fpl*.

wilful *adj (person, action)* teimoso,-a, voluntarioso,-a; obstinado,-a; caprichoso,-a; deliberado,-a, intencional.

will¹ *n (wish)* vontade *f*; **~ power** *n* força de vontade; **2** *(legal document)* testamento *m*; **of my own free ~** de minha própria vontade; IDIOM **where there is a ~, there is a way** querer é poder.

> **will**: verbo modal que precede um infinitivo sem **to** para indicar o futuro: **She will (she'll) come back** ela voltará.

will² *aux vb (expressing future tense)* **he ~ come** ele virá; **2** *(expressing intention in a vague future)* **I ~ go to China (some day)** hei-de (hei de) ir à China; **2** *(in the negative)* **no, I won't do it** não, não o farei; **3** *(courteously)* **~ you take a drink with me?** quer tomar uma bebida comigo?; **4** *(request, order)* **~ you stop that noise?** por favor acabe com esse barulho; **~ you shut the window, please?** é capaz de fechar essa janela?; **5** *(expressing habit)* **they ~ ask for (your) documents** eles normalmente pedem documentos; **these things ~ happen** estas coisas acontecem; ♦ *adj*: **strong-willed** firme; inflexível; ♦ *(pt, pp- ll-)* *vt* desejar; querer; **to will sb to live** *(urge)* querer muito que alguém viva; pedir mentalmente que viva, etc; **he**

~ed himself to go on ele reuniu grande força de vontade para continuar; **2** *(JUR)* legar, deixar em testamento.

William *npr* Guilherme.

willies *npl (slang)* nervosismo *m*; **he gives me the ~** ele causa-me nervos, faz-me nervosa,-a.

willing *adj* disposto,-a, pronto,-a; **she is ~ to help you** ela está disposta a ajudar-te. **willingly** *adv* de bom grado, de boa vontade; voluntariamente.

willingness *n* boa vontade *f*, prontidão *f*.

willow *n*: **~ tree** salgueiro *m*; **2** *(for weaving)* vime *m*; **~ pattern** *n* motivos *npl* chineses.

willowy *adj (person, figure)* esbelto,-a, gracioso,-a.

willy *n (pl: -ies) (UK) (fam) (penis)* pirilau *m*, pila *f*; *(of child)* pilinha *f*; *(BR)* piu-piu *m*.

willy-nilly *adv (at random)* ao acaso, à toa; *(desired or not)* quer queira, quer não queira.

wilt *vi (flower, plant)* murchar, definhar; **2** *(fig) (person)* perder o vigor; **3** *(daunting)* perder a coragem (**at** perante).

wily *adj* astuto,-a; manhoso,-a.

wimp *n (fam, pej)* papa-açorda *m,f*; *(BR)* bunda-mole *m,f*.

wimple *m (nun's cap)* touca *f* de freira.

win *n* vitória; ♦ *(pt, pp* won*)* *vt* ganhar, vencer; **2** *(obtain)* conseguir, obter; ♦ *vi* ganhar; **to ~ over/ round** *vt* conquistar; convencer.

wince *n* contração *f* de dor; estremecimento *m*; ♦ *vi (with pain)* estremecer (**with** de) encolher-se, contrair-se, retrair-se.

winch *n (TECH)* guincho *m*; manivela *f*; cabrestante *m*; ♦ **to ~ sth down/up** descer/içar algo com um guincho.

wind¹ *n (METEOR)* vento; aragem *f*; **2** fôlego; **3** *(MED)* gases *mpl*, flatulência; **to break ~** soltar gases; dar um peido, uma bufa *(fam)*; **4** *(MUS)* instrumento *m* de sopro; **~ed** *adj (breathless)* sem fôlego; **~bag** *n (PHYS)* saco *m* de vento; **2** *(slang) (voluble person without substance)* pessoa com uma grande garganta; que fala muito mas nada importante; **~blown** *adj (hair)* despenteado,-a pelo vento; de cabelos ao vento; **~break** *n* quebra-vento *msg*; **~breaker** *n* pára-vento, paravento **~-borne** *adj (pollen, sand)* transportado,-a pelo vento; **~fall** *n* golpe *m* de sorte; **2** fruta caída devido ao vento;**~ farm** *n (with wind generators)* planta eólica. **~ instrument** *n (MUS)* instrumento *m* de sopro; **~lass** *n (TECH)* molinete *m*, cabrestante *m*; **~mill** *n* moinho *m* de vento; IDIOM **to get the ~ up of (sth)** *(fam)* suspeitar de algo; **to put the ~ up sb** *(slang)* assustar alguém; **to sail close to the ~** aproximar-se do perigo; andar na corda bamba.

wind² *(pt, pp* wound*)* *vt (coil)* enrolar (**onto, around** à volta de); **2** *(clock, toy)* dar corda a; **3** *(turn)* rodar *(door knob)*; *(encircle)* **to ~ around sb's neck** abraçar; *(wrap)* embrulhar, cobrir *(corpse)*; **to ~ one's way through the crowd** conseguir passar por entre a multidão; ♦ *vi (road, river)* serpentear; **2** dar volta ♦ *vt/vi* deixar sem fôlego; **to ~ down** *(business, power) (fig)* reduzir gradualmente (a a(c)tividade); **2** *(window)* baixar; **3**

(relax) descontrair-se; **to ~ forward** *vt (tape)* avançar; **to ~ on** *vt (thread, rope)* rebobinar; ♦ **to ~ up** *vt (clock)* dar corda a; **2** *(debate)* rematar, concluir; **3** *(event)* acabar (**with** em); **4** *(business)* liquidar; **5** *(plan, meeting)* pôr fim a; **6** *(car window)* abrir, levantar (a janela); **7** *(annoy, irritate)* arreliar, azucrinar (alguém).

winding *adj (road)* sinuoso, tortuoso; **2** *(stairs)* em espiral; **~ sheet** *n (shroud)* lençol de mortalha.

window *n* janela *f*; vitrine *f*; montra; **~ box** *n* jardineira (no peitoril da janela); **~ ledge** *n* parapeito, peitoril *m* da janela; **~ pane** *n* vidraça, vidro; **~sill** *n* peitoril *m*, soleira.

windpipe *n* traqueia.

windscreen, windshield *(US) n (AUT)* pára-brisa (s) *m inv*, parabrisas *n inv*; **~ washer** *n* lavador *m* de pára-brisa(s), parabrisas; **~ wiper** *n* limpa pára-brisas/parabrisas *m*; *(BR)* limpador *m* de pára-brisa/parabrisa.

windsock *n* biruta *f*.

windsurfer *n (person)* windsurfista *m*; **2** *(board)* prancha *f* de windsurfe.

windsurfing *n* windsurfe *m*.

windswept *adj* varrido,-a pelo vento.

windward *n* barlavento.

windy *adj* com muito vento; ventoso; **it's ~** está ventando; faz muito vento.

wine *n* vinho; **~ cellar** *n* adega; garrafeira; **~ glass** *n* copo (de vinho); *(of port)* cálice *m*; **~ list** *n* lista de vinhos; **~ merchant** *n* vinhateiro; negociante *m,f* de vinhos; **~ press** *n* prensa, lagar *m*; **~ tasting** *n* prova de vinhos, degustação *f* de vinhos.

wing *n* asa; **2** *(of building)* ala; **3** *(AUT)* aleta, pára-lamas, paralamas *m inv*.

winger *n (SPORT)* ponta avançado, extremo; **2 ~s** *npl (THEAT) (behind stage)* bastidor *msg*.

wink *n* piscadela; ♦ *vi (one eye)* piscar o olho; **2** *(light)* brilhar; *(flash intermittently)* piscar; **~ at** *(disregard)* fechar os olhos a; **the authorities ~ed at corruption** as autoridades fecharam os olhos à corrupção; IDIOM **I didn't sleep a ~ all night** não preguei olho toda a noite.

winner *n* vencedor,-ora.

winning *adj* vencedor,-ora; decisivo,-a; atraente, cativante; **~s** *npl* lucros *mpl*, ganhos *mpl*; **~ post** *n* meta de chegada; **to have ~ ways** ter modos encantadores; ser uma grande simpatia; ser charmoso,-a.

winter *n* inverno; ♦ *vi* invernar; hibernar; **~ sports** *npl* desportos *mpl (BR:* esportes *mpl)* de inverno.

wintry *adj* glacial, invernal, invernoso,-a.

wipe *n* limpeza; *(BR)* limpada *f*; **a quick ~** limpadela *(pop)*; *(rub)* esfregadela; **to give sth a ~** (**with** com, **on** sobre, em) limpar algo com um pano, passar um pano em algo; **2** *(paper tissue)* toalhete *m*; ♦ *vt (clean)* limpar, enxugar; **~ the floor** limpa o chão; **2** *(nose)* limpar o nariz; **to ~ sth away** limpar; *(tears)* enxugar; **to ~ off** *vt* remover esfregando; tirar *(mark, dust)*; ♦ **to ~ out** *vt (debt)* liquidar; **2** *(memory)* apagar; **3** *(destroy)* exterminar; ♦ **to ~ up** *vt* enxugar, limpar.

wiper *n (cloth)* esfregão *m*; *(AUT) (windscreen/windshield)* limpa pára-brisas/parabrisas *n inv*; *(BR)* limpador *m* de parabrisa.

wire *n* arame *m*, cabo; *(ELECT)* fio *m* (elé(c)trico); *(US) (telegram)* telegrama *m*; **~ brush** *n* escova de aço; **~cutters** *n* alicate de corta-arame; **~less** *n* rádio; trasmissor; **~netting** *n* rede *f* de arame, rede metálica; *(CONSTR) (cleaning)*; **~pad** (esfregão de) palha de aço; **~tapping** *n (bug)* escuta *f* telefónica; ♦ *vt (in house etc)* instalar a rede elé(c)trica, ligar à rede elé(c)trica; (= **to ~ up**) *(BR)* conectar; **~ a lamp** conetar um candeeiro; *(in house)* fazer a instalação elé(c)trica; **2** *(TEL)* telegrafar; IDIOM **to pull ~s** *(US)* puxar os cordelinhos; **~ wool** *n* palha d'aço *f*.

wiring *n (in house)* instalação *f* elé(c)trica; *(in appliances)* circuito *m* elé(c)trico.

wiry *adj (energetic and thin)* magro,-a; musculoso,-a; **2** *(hair)* crespo, eriçado.

wisdom *n* sabedoria, sagacidade *f*; **2** bom senso; prudência, sensatez *f*; **~ tooth** *n* dente *m* do siso.

wise *adj (learned)* sábio,-a, erudito,-a; *(sensible)* sensato; *(careful)* prudente; **to be ~ to sth** estar ao corrente (avisado) de algo; **~ man/woman** *n* sábio,-a; **the Three W~ Men** *(Bible)* os Reis *mpl* Magos *mpl*; **length ~** em relaçao ao comprimento *m*; **to be none the ~r** *(not understanding)* ficar a saber o mesmo; ♦ *(suffix) (time, etc)* no que respeita a.

wisecrack *n* chiste *m*, piada *f*, dito *m* satírico, espirituoso.

wiseguy *n (fam)* sabichão,-ona *(pej)* espertalhão,-ona.

wisely *adv* sabiamente.

wish *n* desejo *m*; vontade *f*; ♦ *vt* desejar, querer; **best ~es!** *(on birthday, etc)* parabéns! *mpl*, felicidades! *fpl*; **with best ~es** *(in letter)* cumprimentos, saudações cordiais, amigas; **to give in to sb's ~es** fazer as vontades a; **to grant sb's ~** aceder ao desejo de alguém; **make a ~** fazer um voto; **I ~ you well/good luck/all the best** desejo-lhe boa sorte/tudo do melhor; ♦ *vt (expressing longing)* **I ~ it were true!** quem me dera/tomara que fosse verdade!; **he ~ed he hadn't said that** ele arrependeu-se de ter dito isso/ele desejou não ter dito isso; **I ~ things were better** eu gostaria/queria que as coisas estivessem melhor; ♦ *vi (want)* querer; **because it is my ~** porque quero; **to ~for** desejar, esperar; IDIOM **your ~ is my command** um desejo seu é uma ordem para mim.

wishbone *n (V-shaped bone)* externo (do frango); *(fig)* osso *m* da sorte.

wishful *adj* desejoso,-a; **~ thinking** *n* fantasia, ilusão *f*; **it's ~** é mais desejo do que realidade; quem me dera!

wishy-washy *adj (fam) (watery, weak)* aguado,-a, fraco,-a; **2** *(speech, manner)* sem graça, insípido,-a; *(person)* insípido,-a, desenxabido,-a; **3** *(colour)* *(coll)* deslavado,-a; desmaiado,-a.

wisp *n (tuft of hair)* mecha, tufo; **2** *(fine thread)* fio; **3** *(of cloud, cigarette smoke)* espiral *f*; **4** *(small amount of sth)* mão-cheia *f*; **a ~ of a girl** *(fam)* um pivete *m* de rapariga.

wispy (-ier, -iest) *adj (hair)* raro,-a; **2** *(person)* small.

wisteria (=wistaria) *n (BOT)* glicínia *f.*

wistful *adj* pensativo,-a; desejoso,-a; *(yearning)* nostálgico,-a.

wistfully *adv* melancolicamente; com um ar nostálgico.

wit *n (humour)* presença de espírito; *(intelligence)* astúcia *f,* engenho *m;* **to have the ~ to say that** ter a astúcia de dizer isso; **wits** *npl (mind)* **to be out of one's ~** estar espavorido,-a, desorientado,-a; **to keep (all) one's ~ about one** manter-se alerta/ vigilante *m,f;* **to collect/gather one's ~** dominar-se; **to live by one's ~** viver de expedientes; **a battle of ~** uma batalha verbal; **I am at my wits' end** já não sei o que fazer.

witch *n* bruxa; **~craft** *n* bruxaria; **~ doctor** *n* curandeiro; **~-hunt** *n* caça às bruxas.

with *prep* com; **~ me** comigo; **~ you** consigo/com você; *(fam)* contigo; **he is coming ~ us** ele vem conosco; **2** *(person)* **red ~ anger** vermelho de raiva; **to be ~ it** *(aware)* estar a par da situação; *(fashionable)* estar na moda; **yes, I am ~ you** *(I understand)* sim, compreendo; **God be ~ you!** Deus o acompanhe!.

withdraw *(pt* -drew, *pp* -drawn) *vt* tirar, retirar *(hand, etc);* **to ~ sth from sth** retirar (algo de algo); **2** *(JUR)* anular; **3** *(FIN)* sacar; *(from bank)* levantar *(dinheiro);* **4** *(MIL)* retirar; **5** renunciar a; *(BR)* arrenegar *(title, position, claim);* ♦ *vi* retirar-se **(from** de; **to** para); **he withdrew from politics** ele retirou-se da política; **2** desistir de *(plan, etc);* **3** abandonar *(position);* **4** *(go back on promise)* voltar atrás com a sua palavra, promessa; **5** retratar-se; **6** *(PSYCH)* recolher-se; **to ~ into silence** encerrar-se em silêncio.

withdrawal *n (MIL)* retirada *f;* **2** *(ambassador)* chamada *f;* **3** *(FIN)* saque *m;* *(from bank)* levantamento *m;* **4** afastamento *m* **(from sth** de algo); **5** remoção *f;* **6** *(retraction)* retratação *f;* **7** *(JUR) (of order)* revogação *f;* **8** *(PSYC)* recolhimento *m;* introversão *f;* **9 ~ of labour** suspensão *f* de trabalho; **~ symptom** *n* síndrome *f* de abstinência; sintomas *fpl* de privação.

withdrawn *adj (person)* retirado; reservado, introvertido.

wither *vi (plant)* murchar, secar; **2** *(skin)* enrugar-se; **3** *(feelings)* definhar; **to ~ away** *vi (spirit, hope)* desvanecer-se.

withered *adj (plant)* murcho,-a, seco,-a; **2** *(skin)* seco,-a; *(face)* enrugado,-a; **3** mirrado,-a.

withering *adj:* **a ~ glance** um olhar fulminante/de desprezo.

withers *npl (of horse's back)* cernelha *f.*

withhold *(pt, pp* -held) *vt* reter *(information, money);* **2** adiar *(payment);* **3** recusar.

within *prep* dentro de; ♦ *adv* dentro; **~ reach** ao alcance da mão; **~ sight of** à vista; **~ the week** antes do fim da semana.

without *prep* sem; **~ fail** sem falta; ♦ *adv* fora, no exterior; **from ~** de fora; **within and ~** por dentro e por fora.

withstand *(pt, pp* -stood) *vt* resistir a, opor-se a.

withstanding *n* resistência *f,* oposição *f.*

witness *n* testemunha; ♦ *vt (event)* testemunhar, presenciar; **to bear ~ to** prestar testemunho; **eye~** *n* testemunha ocular; **~ box/stand** *(US) n* banco das testemunhas.

witticism *n* observação *f* espirituosa, chiste *m.*

witty *adj* espirituoso,-a; *(funny)* engraçado,-a; *(astute)* engenhoso,-a.

wives *(pl of* **wife).**

wizard *n* feiticeiro, mago; **2** *(fig) (skilled person)* génio *(BR:* -ê-).

wizened *adj (person, face)* enrugado,-a, encarquilhado,-a, mirrado,-a.

wk *(abbr for* **week).**

wobble *n (in movement)* oscilação *f;* *(fig)* vacilação *f;* ♦ *vi (person)* cambalear; **2** *(in movement)* oscilar; **3** *(chair)* balançar, oscilar; **4** *(voice, hand)* tremer; *(legs)* a fraquejar.

wobbly *adj (chair, table)* bambo,-a; **2** *(voice, hand, writing)* trémulo,-a; **a bit ~** *(person)* um pouco vacilante.

woe *n* dor *f,* mágoa *f;* *(misfortune)* infortúnio *m;* *(often pl)* desgraças *fpl;* **~ betide** *(befall on you)* a desgraça cairá em ti; ♦ **~!** *exc* que desgraça!

woebegone *adj (in appearance)* abatido,-a; desolado,-a.

woke *(pt of* **wake).**

woken *(pp of* **wake).**

wolf *(pl:* **wolves)** *n* lobo; **a ~ in sheep's clothing** lobo vestido em pele de cordeiro; **~ whistle** *n (of appreciation when a woman goes by)* assobio (de apreciação); ♦ *vt:* **to ~ sth down** devorar algo.

wolfram *(=* **tungsten)** *n* volfrâmio *m.*

woman *(pl:* **women)** *n* mulher *f;* **~ president** presidenta; *(ambassador)* embaixadora; **~ prime minister** a primeira ministra; **she has become a ~** ela está uma mulher; **~hood** *n* sexo feminino; *(adult life)* maioridade *f* feminina; *(women)* mulheres; **he is going around with women** ele anda com o mulherio.

womanizer, womaniser *n* mulherego, 'Don Juan'.

womanly *adj* feminino,-a.

womb *n (ANAT, MED)* útero *m;* *(pop)* ventre *m.*

wombat *n (ZOOL)* seriqueia *f* australiana.

women *(pl of* **woman).**

won *(pt, pp of* **win).**

wonder *n* maravilha, prodígio; **2** *(amazement)* espanto; **lost in ~** maravilhado,-a; **~ of ~s** maravilha das maravilhas; ♦ *vi:* **to ~ whether** perguntar-se a si mesmo; **to ~ at** admirar-se de; **to ~ about** pensar sobre/em; **it's no ~ that** não é de admirar que; **I ~ if he has arrived?** será que ele já chegou?; **I ~ if she is lying** será que ela mente/ está mentindo?

wonderful *adj* maravilhoso,-a.

wonderfully *adv* maravilhosamente; esplendidamente.

wonderland *n (fairy land)* o país *m* das maravilhas.

wonk *n* pessoa excessivamente interessada num tema em particular.

wonky (-ier, -iest) *adj* pouco firme *(furniture)* desengonçado,-a; *(picture, etc)* torto,-a; **~ chair** cadeira *f* manca.

won't = **will not.**

woo vt: **to ~ a woman** cortejar; **2** (fig) (try to win over) persuadir.

wood n madeira; (forest) floresta, bosque m; mata; **~ carving** n escultura em madeira, entalhe m; **~cutter** n lenhador,-ora; **~ed** adj arborizado.

wooden adj de madeira; **2** (fig) (face) inexpressivo,-a; **~ spoon** n colher f de pau; (fig) prémio m de consolação.

woodpecker n (bird) pica-pau m.

woodwind n (MUS) instrumentos mpl de sopro de madeira.

woodwork n carpintaria f.

woodworm n carcoma m, caruncho m.

wool n lã f; **to pull the ~ over sb's eyes** (fig) enganar alguém, enfiar o barrete a alguém.

woollen adj de lã; **~s** npl artigos mpl, roupa f de lã.

woolly adj de lã, coberto de lã; **2** (cloud) em flocos; **3** (ideas) (fig) confuso,-a, vago,-a.

word n palavra f; notícia f; aviso m; ♦ vt (express) expressar; (document) redigir; **in other ~s** em/por outras palavras; **to break/keep one's ~** faltar à palavra, não cumprir a promessa; **~game** n jogo de palavras; trocadilho; **~ order** n (LING) ordem f das palavras; **~ processing** n (COMP) processamento m do texto; **~ processor** n (COMP) processador m de texto.

wording n reda(c)ção f.

wordless adj sem palavras; mudo.

wordy adj prolixo,-a, palavroso,-a.

wore (pt of **wear**).

work n trabalho m; (job) emprego; **2** (ART) obra; **he is a nasty piece of ~** (fam) ele é detestável; (fig) ele tem maus fígados; **to be out of ~** estar desempregado,-a; ♦ **works** npl (factory) fábrica fsg, usina fsg; **2** npl (of clock, machinery) mecanismo m; **3** (CONSTR) obras fpl; **~able** adj viável; **~aday** adj rotineiro,-a, de todos os dias; **~aholic** adj (person) obcecado pelo trabalho; **~day** n dia m de trabalho; **2** (COMM) dia útil; **~er** n trabalhador,-ora, operário,-a; (ant, bee) obreira; ♦ vt (wood etc) talhar; **2** (mine etc) explorar; **3** (machine, staff) fazer trabalhar, manejar; **4** (machine) operar; **5** (cause) fazer, produzir; ♦ vi trabalhar; fazer trabalhar (staff); **2** (machine) operar; **3 to ~ overtime** trabalhar horas extraordinárias; **to ~ shifts** trabalhar por turnos; **to ~ one's way** (physical progress) avançar; (in career) progredir; ♦ vi (do a job) trabalhar; **2** (mine) esgotar; **3** (mechanism) funcionar; **4** (medicine) ser eficaz; ter efeito; ♦ **to ~ loose** (part) soltar-se, desprender-se; **2** (knot) afrouxar-se; **to ~ at** vt trabalhar em; tentar melhorar; ♦ **to ~ in** insinuar-se; **2** fazer entrar à força; **to ~ into** penetrar em; ♦ **to ~ on/upon** vt trabalhar em, dedicar-se a; **2** (principle) basear-se em; **3** tentar persuadir; ♦ **to ~ out** vi (turn out) dar certo, surtir efeito; **2** (be successful) dar (bom) resultado; **3** (exercise) treinar; ♦ vt (solve) resolver; (calculate) calcular; (devise), elaborar, formular; **2** compreender; desvendar (mystery, puzzle); resolver (problema); ♦ **to ~ up** vt (generate) gerar; **2** (excite) exitar-se; **to get ~ed up** exaltar-se; **~in-progress** n trabalho

em andamento; **~load** n carga f de trabalho; **~ man** n operário, trabalhador m; **~manship** n acabamento; habilidade f; **~out** n treino m (BR) treinamento m; **~ permit** n licença f de licença; **~ placement** n colocação f no mercado de trabalho; **~ sheet** n (school, etc) ficha f, registo m de trabalho; **2** (training) sessão f de trabalho; **~shy** adj preguiçoso,-a; avesso,-a ao trabalho; **~shop** n oficina; **~-to-rule** n paralisação f de trabalho extra.

working n funcionamento m; **~ capital** n capital m de giro; dinheiro m em caixa; (assets) ativo m circulante; **~ class** n proletariado, classe f operária; **in ~ order** em funcionamento; em perfeito estado; **~ knowledge** n conhecimento m de causa.

world n mundo; **to think the ~ of sb** (fig) ter alguém em alto conceito/em alta estima; **the ~ over/all over the ~** no mundo inteiro; **a ~ of good** um bem infinito; **a man of the ~** um homem cheio de experiência; **out of this ~** extraordinário,-a; **to go to a better ~** morrer; ir desta para melhor; **how in the ~ did you manage to do it?** como foi que conseguiste fazer isso?; **what in the ~ is the matter with you?** que diabo tem você?; **I wouldn't do it for the ~** eu não o faria de modo algum/nenhum; **~-class** adj muito superior; **W~ Cup** n taça f, (BR) Copa f Mundial; **~s apart** diametralmente opostos,-as; **~ power** n potência f mundial; **~-weary** adj fatigado, farto,-a do mundo; **~wide** adj mundial, universal.

World Health Organization, WHO npr Organização f Mundial de Saúde, OMS f.

worldly adj mundano,-a; material; **~-wise** adj experiente.

worm n verme m; (= **earth~**) minhoca; **tape~** (MED) lombriga; solitária; (person: pej) infame.

worn pp of **wear**; ♦ adj usado; **~-out** adj (threadbare) muito usado,-a, gasto,-a; **2** (exhausted) esgotado,-a exausto,-a; **a much-~ jumper** uma camisola muito velha/esburacada.

worried adj preocupado,-a; inquieto,-a; apoquentado,-a.

worry n preocupação f; inquietação f; (concern) cuidado; ♦ vt preocupar, inquietar; ♦ vi preocupar-se; **~ about sth/sb** com algo alguém; (get into a state of worry) afligir-se; **don't worry!** não se preocupe!.

worrying n inquietação f, aflição f; ♦ adj inquietante, preocupante.

worse n o pior; **for the ~** para o pior; ♦ adj, adv pior; **to get ~** piorar; **to go from bad to ~** ir de mal a pior; **~ off** em pior situação **~n** vt/vi piorar; agravar; **~ning** adj agravante.

worship n culto m; veneração f; **2** prática f religiosa; **act of ~** devoção f; ♦ (-ped) (US) -ed) vt (REL) adorar, venerar; **Your W~** (UK) (mayor addressing, magistrates) Vossa Excelência; (EP: to judge) Senhor Juiz.

worshipper n devoto,-a, fiel; (non-religious) adorador,-ora, admirador,-ora.

worst n o pior; ♦ adj (o,-a) pior; ♦ adv pior; **at ~** na pior das hipóteses; **if the ~ comes to the ~** se o pior acontecer.

worsted *n* tecido *m* de lã penteada.

worth *n* valor *m*, mérito; **two pounds ~ of olives** *(equivalent to)* duas libras (esterlinas) de azeitonas; ♦ *adj*: **to be ~** valer; **it's ~ it** vale a pena.

worthless *adj* sem valor; inútil.

worthwhile *adj* que vale a pena; de mérito; louvável.

worthy *adj* merecedor,-ora, respeitável; *(motive)* justo,-a; **~ of** digno de.

would *aux (conditional)* **I ~ like to do it** eu gostaria de fazer isso; **he ~ come and talk to us** ele costumava vir conversar conosco; **~ that I could** se eu pudesse; ♦ **would-be** *adj (pej)* aspirante, pretenso; que pretende ser.

wouldn't = would not.

wound *pt, pp of* wind; ♦ *n* ferida *(fig)* golpe *m*; ♦ *vt* ferir.

wounded: the ~ os feridos *mpl*; ♦ *adj* ferido,-a; **2** *(hurt)* magoado,-a; **~ pride** amor-próprio magoado.

wounding *adj* prejudicial; *(remark)* ofensivo,-a.

wove *(pt of* weave*)*.

woven *(pp of* weave*)*.

wow *n (col)* sucesso *m*; ♦ *exc* olálá!, fantástico! ♦ *vt (enthuse)* entusiasmar-se, empolgar.

wrack *n* alga marinha; sargaço; **2** *(fragments of wreckage washed ashore)* bodelha *f*.

wraith *n (ghost)* espectro *m*; **2** *(fig) (thin and pale)* esquelético,-a.

wrangle *n* briga *f*; querela *f*, disputa *f*; rixa *f*; ♦ *vi* brigar, disputar, questionar;.

wrap *n (warm clothes)* agasalho *m*, abafo *m*; *(shawl)* xaile *m*, *(BR)* xale *m*; **2** *(packaging)* embalagem; ♦ *(-ped) (also: ~* **up***) vt* agasalhar, abafar; **2** *(parcel)* embrulhar; **to ~ sb in cotton wood** *(overprotective)* proteger alguém demasiado; **to ~ up** *vt* agazalhar-se; **~ up well!** agazalha-te bem!; **2** embrulhar.

wrapped *adj (in warm clothes)* abafado,-a, agazalhado,-a; **2** *(parcel)* embrulhado,-a; **3** *(mystery, corpse)* envolto,-a; **4** *(deep in thought)* absorto,-a; **she is ~ up in him** ela só tem olhos para ele *(EP)*, estar afundado em alguém *(BR)*.

wrapper *n* invólucro; *(of book)* capa; *(of sweets, chocs)* papel *m*.

wrapping *n* embalagem *f*; invólucro *m*; **~ paper** *n* papel *m* de embrulho.

wrath *n* cólera, ira.

wrathful *adj* irado; colérico.

wreak *vt* causar, infligir; **to ~ one's rage upon sb** descarregar a ira contra/em cima de alguém; **to ~ havoc/damage** causar caos/estragos.

wreath *n (pl: -s) n (=* funeral **~***)* coroa *f*; **funeral ~** coroa fúnebre; *(of flowers)* grinalda *f*; **2** *(spiral effect)* espiral *f*.

wreathe *vt/vi* enroscar; **the snake ~d around the tree** a serpente enroscou-se à volta da árvore; cingir; entrelaçar; *(encircle with flowers)* fazer coroa, grinalda; **~ up** *(smoke)* subir em espiral.

wreck *n* naufrágio *m*; **2** *(of ship, plane)* restos *mpl* do naufrágio; escombros, destroços *mpl*; **2** *(of car)* socata *f*; **3** *(pej) (person)* ruína, caco, **to be a nervous ~** ter os nervos em franja; ♦ *vi* naufragar; ♦ *vt* destruir, devastar; **2** *(fig)* arruinar, arrasar.

wreckage *n* restos *mpl*; *(of building)* escombros *mpl*; destroços *mpl*.

wrecker *n (US) (NAUT)* reboque *m*.

wren *n (ZOOL)* carriça.

wrench *n (TECH = monkey-~*) *(tool)* chave *f* inglesa; **2** *(tug)* puxão *m*; **3** *(on ankle, wrist)* distensão *f*, entorse *f*; ♦ *vt* arrancar; **2** torcer; **to ~ one's ankle** torcer o tornozelo; **to ~ sth from sb** arrancar algo de alguém; **to ~ free** libertar-se com um sacão; IDIOM *(cause sadness)* **the situation ~ed my heart**, a situação era de cortar o coração.

wrestle *n* luta *f* corpo a corpo, luta livre; ♦ *vi*: **to ~ (with sb)** lutar (com/contra alguém); **to ~ down** *vt* derrubar.

wrestler *n* lutador *m*.

wrestling *n* luta romana; **~ match** *n* partida, sessão *f* de luta greco-romana.

wretch *n (unlucky)* infeliz; **2** *(child)* diabrete *m,f*;

wretched *adj (unlucky)* infeliz *m,f*; desgraçado,-a; **2** *(vile)* miserável; **2** *(weather)* péssimo,-a; **it makes me feel ~** faz-me sentir em baixo; **3** *(coll) (damned)* malvado,-a.

wriggle *n* contorção *f*; meneio; ♦ *vt/vi* mover sinuosamente; menear-se; **2** *(one's fingers, toes, nose)* remexer, retorcer; *(snake, worm)* contorcer-se; **to ~ the tail** *(dog, cat)* agitar a cauda/o rabo; **to ~ out of sth** *(coll)* escapar-se de.

wring *(pt, pp* wrung*) vt (also: ~* **out***) (squeeze)* torcer, espremer; **to ~ the clothes out** torcer a roupa; **2 I felt like ~ing his neck** tive ganas de lhe deitar as mãos ao pescoço, torcer-lhe o pescoço; **to ~ money out of sb** extorquir dinheiro de alguém; *(fig)* **to ~ sth out of sb** arrancar à força algo de alguém; IDIOM **to ~ sb's heart** confranger o coração.

wringing wet *adj* encharcado,-a.

wrinkle *n (face)* ruga *f*; **2** *(on material)* crease; ♦ *vt* enrugar; *(nose)* fazer uma careta (**at sb** a alguém); **to ~ one's brow** franzir o sobrolho; **~ one's forehead** carregar a fronte; ♦ *vi* enrugar-se.

wrist *n* pulso; punho; **~watch** *n* relógio *m* de pulso.

writ *n* mandado *m* judicial; intimação *f* judicial; ordem; **to issue/serve a ~ against sb** demandar alguém judicialmente.

write *(pt* wrote, *pp* written*) vt/vi* escrever; **2** passar *(cheque, prescription)*; **3** elaborar *(legislation)*; **4** *(COMP)* gravar; **~back** *vt* responder (a uma carta); **to ~ down** *vt* tomar nota; assentar; anotar; **to ~ in pencil** *vt* escrever a lápis; **to ~ into** *vt* acrescentar *(clause)*; **~ off** *vt (debt)* cancelar; **to ~ out** *vt* escrever por extenso; **to ~ up** *vt* redigir; elogiar por escrito; **~-off** *n (car)* perda total; **the car is a ~-off** o carro vai para *(BR:* virou) sucata; **2** anulação *f* por escrito.

writer *n* escritor,-ora.

writhe *vi* contorcer-se; **she ~d in pain** ela contorceu-se com as dores.

writing *n* escrita; *(=* **hand-~***)* caligrafia, letra; *(of author)* obra; **in ~** por escrito; **~ paper** *n* papel *m* para escrever.

written *pp of* write; **~ evidence** *adj* evidência por escrito.

wrong *n* mal *m*; **right and ~** o bem e o mal; **2** injustiça *f*; ♦ *adj* errado; **this sum is ~** esta soma está errada; *(bad)* mau; *(unfair)* injusto; *(mistaken)* equivocado, enganado; **you are ~ about her** você está enganado acerca dela; impróprio,-a; inconveniente **you came at the ~ time** vieste a uma hora inconveniente; ♦ *adv* mal, erroneamente; **~ side out** de dentro para fora; ♦ *vt* ser injusto com; ofender; **to get out of bed on the ~ side** acordar de mau humor; **to say the ~ thing** cometer um lapso; **to be in the ~** não ter razão; **what's ~?** o que se passa?; **to go ~** *(person)* desencaminhar-se; *(plan)* não ser bem-sucedido; *(machine)* sofrer uma avaria.

wrongdoing *n* maldade *f*; **2** ação desonesta.

wrongdoer *n* malfeitor,-ora.

wrongful *adj* injusto.

wrongly *adv* injustamente; **~ informed** mal informado,-a.

wrote *(pt of* **write***)*.

wrought *adj*: **~ iron** ferro forjado; **~ up** excitado.

wrung *(pt, pp of* **wring***)*.

wry *adj (smile)* irónico *(BR:* -rô-*)*; **to make a ~ face** fazer uma careta.

wt. *(abbr for* **weight***)*.

WTO *(abbr for* **World Trade Organization***)* OMC, Organização Mundial de Comércio.

wuss *n (slang)* pessoa fraca, incompetente; *(pej)* palerminha *m,f*.

wych elm *n (BOT)* olmo-escocês.

WYSIWYG *adj (COMP)* (= **what you see is what you get**) interação entre o texto no monitor e o utlizador em que: o que se vê no ecrã é aquilo que se obtém na impressora.

wyvern *n (heraldry)* dragão alado.

X

X, x *n (letter)* X, x *m;* **2** *(unknown person)* **Mr/Mrs X** o Senhor/a Senhora X (Xis); **3** *(unknown amount, number)* X *m;* **4** *(at the end of letter)* **XXX** *(any quantity of x's)* beijinhos *mpl.*

Xanthine *n (CHEM)* xantina *f*

X-axis *n* (MATH) eixo *m* das abcissas.

X certificate *n (film): the film was given an ~* o filme foi interdito a menores de 18 anos.

xebec *n (NAUT) (small vessel with 3 sails)* xaveco *m.*

xenia *n (BOT)* xénia *f.*

xenophobia *n* xenofobia *f.*

xenophobic *adj* xenofóbico,-a.

Xerox® *npr (machine)* fotocopiadora *f;* Xerox *m;* *(process)* fotocópia *f;* ♦ *vt* fotocopiar; *(BR)* xerocopiar, xerocar.

Xmas *n (abbr for* **Christmas**).

X-rated *adj* classificação de filmes para adultos; pornográfico,-a.

X-ray *n* radiografia; *~s npl* raios *mpl* X; ♦ *vt* radiografar, tirar uma chapa, examinar aos raios X.

xylophone *n* xilofone *m.*

xystus, xystos *(pl: xisti) n* xisto, antigo pórtico grego para ginástica.

y

Y, y *n (letter)* Y, y *m*; **2** *(BIOL, MATH)* y.

yacht *n (SPORT)* iate *m*; ~ **club** *n* clube *m* náutico; ~ **race** *n* regata *f*; ~**ing** *n (SPORT)* iatismo; vela *f*; **to go** ~ praticar vela; ~**sman/woman** *n* iatista *m,f*; dono,-a de iate.

yahoo *(pl: -hoos) n (crude, brutish person)* brutamontes *m,f (fam)*.

yak *n (ZOOL)* iaque *m*; **2** *(coll)* tagarelice *f* contínua e trivial; ♦ *vt (coll) (pessoa)* tagarelar, palrar.

Yale *(= **Yale lock**®) npr* fechadura *f* de segurança, fechadura *f* cilíndrica.

yam *n* inhame *m; (US) (potato)* batata-doce.

yammy *(Vd:* **yummy***)*.

yang *n (Chinese philosophy)* yang.

Yangon *npr* Rangoon.

yank *n* puxão *m*; ♦ *vt (pull, pull out/off)* arrancar, tirar (algo de).

Yank, Yankee *n (pej) (American)* ianque *m,f*, pessoa dos Estados nortistas dos E.U.A.

> Durante a Guerra de Secessão dos E.U.A., '**Yank(ee)**' designava os soldados nortistas. Ainda hoje, os sulistas usam este termo em tom pejorativo.

yap *(-pp-) vi (dog)* latir, ganir; **2** *(person) (pej)* palrar.

yapping *n* latidos *mpl*.

yard *n* patio *m*; **back** ~ quintal *m*; **church** ~ adro *m* **2** *(unit of measurement)* jarda (914 mm).

yardstick *n (fig)* critério, padrão *m*, ponto *m* de referência (**for** para).

yarn *n (thread, wool)* fio *m*; **2** *(coll) (tale)* patranha, peta, história inverossímil; *(BR)* lorota *f*.

yashmak *n (veil covering Muslim women's face)* véu *m* islâmico.

yawn *n* bocejo; ♦ *vi* bocejar; **2** *(abyss)* abrir-se; ♦ *exc (fig) (bore)* **what a** ~**!** que chato! *(coll); (BR)* puxa, saco! *(fam)*.

yawner *n adj* bocejador,-ora.

yawning *n* bocejos *mpl;* ♦ *adj (abyss)* enorme; **2** *(fig) (in one's life)* vazio *m*.

yd *(abbr for* **yard**(s)*)*.

ye *pron pess (arc, poetic) (you)* vós; ~ **sinners!** vós pecadores!

yea *adv (old/formal use)* sim; **the** ~**s and the nayes** *(POL)* votos a favor, votos contra.

yeah *adv (fam) (yes)* sim.

year *n* ano *m*; **to be four** ~**s old** ter quatro anos; **every** ~ todos os anos; **all the** ~ **round** durante todo o ano; **for** ~**s and** ~**s** *(ages)* há séculos; ~**book** anual *m;* **financial** ~ ano fiscal.

yearling *n (horse)* potro *m*; **2** *(sheep)* filhote *m*.

yearly *adj* anual; ♦ *adv* anualmente.

yearn *vi:* **to** ~ **for sth** ansiar, suspirar por algo; ter saudade(s) de.

yearning *n* ânsia; desejo *m* ardente, aspiração *f*; saudade *f*; **I am** ~ **for your touch** tenho saudades das tuas carícias.

yeast *n* levedura *f*, levedo, fermento *m*; **2** ~ **infection** *n* candidíase *f* vaginal.

yell *n* grito, berro; ♦ *vi* gritar, berrar.

yelling *n* gritaria *f*, alarido *m*.

yellow *n (colour)* amarelo *m*; ~ **lines** *n (on the road)* faixas *fpl* amarelas; **the** ~ **Pages**® *npl (UK) (telephone directory)* as Páginas *fpl* Amarelas; **Y**~ **River** *n:* **the** ~ o Rio *m* Amarelo; **Y**~ **Sea** *n:* **the** ~ o mar *m* Amarelo; ♦ *adj (coll, pej)* cobarde; **2** *(jornais)* sensacionalista; ♦ *vi* amarelecer, amarelar.

yellowing *n* amarelecimento *m*.

yelp *n* latido; ♦ *vi* latir, ganir.

Yemen *npr:* **the** ~ o Iémen.

Yemeni, Yemenite *n adj* iemanita *m,f*.

yen *n (Japanese currency)* iene *m*.

yeoman *(pl:* **yeomen***) n (UK: HIST)* pequeno proprietário rural.

Yeoman of the Guard *n* alabardeiro *m* do monarca, da Torre de Londres, guarda real da Torre de Londres.

yep *adv (coll) (yes)* sim.

yer *(pron pers) (coll)* = **you**.

yes *n, adv,* sim *m*; **to say** ~ *(in agreement)* dizer que sim; ~-**man** *(pl:* ~-**men***) n (coll)* homem *m* servil, capacho *m*, lambe-botas *m inv (pej)*.

yesterday *n adv* ontem *m*; ~ **afternoon** ontem à tarde; ~ **morning** ontem de manhã; **the day before** ~ anteontem.

yesteryear *n adv (LITER) (bygone times)* passado *m*; **the snows of** ~ as neves de antanho.

yet *adv (with negatives)* ainda, por enquanto; **not** ~ ainda não; **I haven't seen him** ~ ainda não o vi; *(with questions)* **have you eaten** ~ **?** já comeste?; **have you got up** ~**?** já te levantaste?; *(formal)* já se levantou?; *(with comparatives)* even, still; **even more dresses** ~ ainda mais vestidos; **2** *(still) (with superlatives)* ainda, até agora; **it's the best** ~ é o melhor até agora; **the worst is** ~ **to come** o pior ainda está por vir; ♦ *conj (nevertheless)* porém, no entanto; ~**, I did advise him** no entanto, eu aconselhei-o.

yew *n (BOT)* teixo.

Y-fronts *npl (UK) (men's underpants)* cuecas abertas à frente.

YHA *(abbr for* **Youth Hostels Association***)* associação britânica de albergues da juventude.

Yiddish *n adj* (i)ídiche *m*.

yield *n* produção *f*; **2** *(AGR)* colheita; **3** *(COMM)* rendimento; ♦ *vt (cereais, fruit, clues)* produzir; **2** *(profit)* gerar, render; ♦ *vi (give up, surrender)* render-se; *(give in)* ceder; **to** ~ **to a wish** ceder a um desejo; *(US) (AUT)* ceder; ~ **up** *vt* revelar um segredo.

yielding *adj* flexível; *(person) (compliant)* submisso,-a.

Y2K *(= **year 2000***) n* ano *m* 2000.

yin *n (Chinese philosophy)* yin.

YMCA *n (abbr for* **Young Men's Christian Association**) Associação Cristã dos Moços, ACM *f.*

yo-heave-ho *exc (sailors' cry when pulling nets)* arriba! força!

yob, yobbo *n (UK) (coll)* adolescente rebelde e agressivo.

yodel (-ll-) *vi* cantar à moda dos tiroleses; **they yodelled all night** eles cantaram à tirolesa toda a noite.

yoga *n* ioga.

yog(h)ourt, yog(h)urt *n* iogurte *m.*

yogi *n (master at yoga)* iogue *m.*

yoke *n (for oxen)* jugo *m,* canga *f;* **2** *(pair of oxen)* junta; **3** *(burden, oppression)* jugo *m;* servidão *f;* submissão *f;* **under the** ~ debaixo do jugo (**of** de); **to bear the** ~ suportar o jugo; ♦ *vt (join)* unir, ligar; *(to pair off),* emparelhar.

yokel *n* campónio,-a; *(fig)* saloio,-a; *(BR)* caipira *m,f.*

yolk *n (of egg)* gema.

yonder *adv (LITER)* além, acolá.

yonks *npl (coll)* muito tempo, séculos (fam); ~ **ago** há montes de tempo.

Yorkshire pudding *n* pastel tradicional de Yorkshire que leva farinha, um ovo, água ou leite, sal e vai ao forno. Serve-se com rosbife.

you *pron (subject)* tu, você; o senhor, a senhora; *(pl)* vós, vocês; *(polite form)* os senhores, as senhoras; **2** *(direct object)* te *(fam);* **I love** ~ eu amo-te *(fam);* **I saw** ~ **yesterday** *(female; formal)* eu vi-a ontem; *(in the negative)* **I didn't see** ~ não a vi; *(pl)* vos, os, as; **I give** ~ *(pl)* **the good news** dou-vos a boa notícia; **3** *(indirect object)* te, lhe; *(pl)* vos, lhes; **I told** ~ **that** *(sg)* disse-lhe que; **4** *(after preposition)* ti, a si, a você; *(polite form)* ao senhor, à senhora; *(pl)* vós, vocês; **it is** ~ **I love** *(emphasis)* eu amo-te a ti; **5 with** ~ contigo *(fam),* consigo, com você; *(pl)* convosco, com vocês; *(formal)* com o senhor *etc;* **6** *(impersonal)* se; ~ **can never tell** nunca se pode dizer; *(coll)* a gente nunca sabe; ~ **can't do that** isso não se faz.

you'd = **you had; you would.**

you'll = **you will; you shall.**

young: the ~ *nsg* a mocidade *fsg,* a juventude *fsg;* ~**s** *npl (of animal)* filhotes *mpl,* crias *fpl;* **to be with** ~**s** *(animal)* estar prenhe; ♦ (-**er,** -**iest**) *adj* jovem, juvenil; novo,-a; júnior; **he is younger than his sister;** ele é mais jovem, mais novo do que a irmã (dele); **she was the youngest in the group** ela era a mais jovem do grupo; **2** *(experience)* novato,-a; **3** *(vegetables)* frescos, tenros *mpl.*

youngish *adj* ainda novo.

youngster *n* jovem, moço,-a, broto,-a; *(BR)* moço,-a.

your *adj* teu/tua, teus, tuas *(fam);* seu, sua, seus, suas; ~ **house** *(addressing one person)* a tua/sua casa; *(formal)* do senhor, da senhora; ~ **daughters** *(addressing one person)* as suas filhas *(fam),* *(formal)* as filhas do senhor; **2** *(addressing more than one person)* vossò,-a, vossos, vossas; ~ **horses** os vossos cavalos; *(formal)* os cavalos dos senhores, das senhoras; ~ **hats** os chapéus das senhoras.

you're = **you are.**

yours *pron poss (addressing one person)* o teu, a tua, os teus, as tuas *(fam);* o seu, a sua, os seus, as suas *(formal);* **my home is far but** ~ **is near** a minha

casa é longe, mas a tua é perto; *(formal)* do senhor/ da senhora; **my son and** ~ **are very good friends** o meu filho e o seu *or* e o da senhora são muito amigos; **2** *pl (addressing more than one person)* o vosso, a vossa, os vossos, as vossas; **my job is similar to** ~ o meu trabalho é semelhante ao seu; **our cars and** ~ **are both green** os nossos carros e os vossos são ambos verdes; **4** *(at the end of a formal letter)* ~ **sincerely,** ~ **faithfully** atenciosamente.

yourself *pron sg (emphatic) (fam)* tu mesmo, você mesmo; **you** ~ **said that** você mesmo disse isso; *pl* vocês mesmos/mesmas; *(polite form)* os senhores mesmos, as senhoras mesmas; **2** *(after prep) (emphatic)* ti mesmo,-a, *(fam)* você mesmo,-a; **I gave the money to you** ~ eu dei o dinheiro a ti mesmo *(it was to you I gave the money);* *(polite form)* o senhor mesmo, a senhora mesma; **2** *(reflexive, direct/indirect object) (fam) sg* te, se; ♦ **(all) by** ~ *adv (alone)* sozinho; **you are not quite** ~ tu não estás bem disposto,-a/ você não está bem disposto,-a; **yourselves** *pron (subject) pl* vós mesmos, vocês mesmos; **blame (it) (on)** ~ censurem-se a vós mesmos; **2** *(reflexive, direct/indirect object) pl* vocês mesmos/mesmas; se; **consider** ~ **employed** podem crer-se aceites para o emprego; **are you by** ~ vocês estão sozinhos?, *(polite form)* os senhores mesmos, as senhoras mesmas; **did you** ~ **make this cake?** foram os senhores mesmos que fizeram este bolo?

youth *n (period of being young)* mocidade *f,* juventude *f;* adolescência; **2** *(young man/woman)* moço,-a, jovem; ~**s** os jovens; **a gang of** ~**s** um bando de rapazes e de raparigas/de moços e moças; ~**ful** *adj* juvenil; ~ **hostel** *n* albergue *m* da juventude.

you've = **you have.**

yo-yo *(pl:* -**yos**) *n* ioió, ioiô.

yr *(abbr for* **year**).

yucca *n (BOT)* iúca *f.*

yucky (-**ier,** -**iest**) *adj* nojento,-a; ♦ *exc* ~! que porcaria!

Yugoslav *n adj (dated)* jugoslavo,-a.

Yugoslavia *(formerly) npr:* **a** ~ Jugoslávia.

Yule *n* Natal; ~ **log** *n* bolo *m* de feitio dum tronco d'árvore.

Yuletide *n* época natalina, do Natal.

yummy (-ier, -**iest**) *(coll) adj (food)* delicioso,-a; ♦ *exc (also:* **yum-yum**) ~! que delícia!

yuppie, yuppy *n (abbr for* **young urban professional**) yuppie; ♦ *exc* lupi!

YWCA *n (abbr for* **Young Women's Christian Association**) *(BR)* ACM *f* (Associação Cristã de Moças).

Z

Z, z *n (letter)* Z, z *m.*
Zabreb *npr* Zabrebe *m.*
Zaire *npr* Zaire; **in** ~ no Zaire.
Zairese *n adj* zairense *m,f.*
Zambezi, Zambese *n:* **the** ~ o Zambezi.
Zambezian *adj* do Zambezi, zambeniano,-a.
Zambia *npr* Zâmbia; **in** ~ na Zâmbia.
Zambian *n adj* zambiano,-a.
zany *n (buffoon)* truão *m,* bobo *m;* palhaço *m;* ◆
  (-**ier**, -**iest**) *adj (comical)* excêntrico e cómico; **2**
  (foolish) tolo,-a, bobo,-a.
zap *n (energy)* vigor *m,* tónus *m;* ◆ (-**pp-**) *vt*
  (destroy) destruir; matar; *(get rid of)* despachar,
  desembaraçar-se de; **we must** ~ **stress fast** temos
  de nos desembaraçar rapidamente do stress; **2** *(in*
  video games) destruir; **3** *(COMP) (delete)* apagar;
  ◆ *vi (rush)* correr; **to** ~ **off to** correr para; **to** ~
  into the shops dar um salto às lojas; **to** ~ **through**
  sth dar uma vista de olhos por algo; **2 to** ~ **from**
  channel to channel *(with the remote control)*
  trocar de canal para canal; ◆ *exc* ~! exclamação
  que imita o som de rapidez de acção.
zapper *n (coll) (TV)* telecomando *m.*
zeal *n* zelo, fervor *m.*
zealot *n* fanático,-a.
zealous *adj* zeloso,-a.
zebra *n (ZOOL)* zebra *f;* ~ **crossing** *n* passadeira,
  faixa de pedestre.
zenith *n (ASTRON)* zénite (BR zê-) *m; (fig) (highest*
  point) apogeu *m.*
zephyr *n* zéfiro *m.*
zero *(pl: -s or -es) n* zero *m;* **below** ~ abaixo de zero; **2**
  (nothing) nada; nulo,-a; **to** ~ **in on** *(target) vt* alvejar, visar; ◆ *vi (fam) (to bear on)* concentrar-se em
  (issue); **2** *(adjust)* ajustar um instrumento a zero; **3**
  (converge upon) convergir, centrar-se; **the police**
  ~**ed in on the site of the crime** a polícia convergiu/
  concentrou-se no lugar do crime.
zero hour *n (hour of beginning attack)* hora *f* zero.
zeroload *n* carga *f* nula.

zero-rated *adj* isento de taxa.
zest *n* vivacidade *f,* entusiasmo *m;* **to do sth with** ~
  fazer algo com gosto; **2** *(of citrus fruit) (outer*
  skin) casca *f.*
zigzag *n* ziguezague *m; (road, etc)* em ziguezagues;
  ◆ (-**ged**) *vi* ziguezaguear.
zilch *pron (coll) (nothing)* nada, peva.
zillion *n (coll)* um monte de, milhares; **I have a** ~ **of**
  letters to reply tenho milhares de cartas para
  responder.
Zimbabwe *npr* Zimbabué *m;* **in** ~ no Zimbabué.
Zimbabwean *n adj* zimbabuano,-a *(also:* zimbabuense *m,f).*
Zimmer frame® *n* andador *m.*
zinc *n (CHEM)* zinco *m.*
Zionism *n* sionismo.
Zionist *n* sionista *m,f.*
zip *n (=* ~ **fastener/zipper)** fecho ecler, zíper *m;* **2**
  (fam) energia; *(US) pron* absolutamente nada; ~
  code *(US)* código *m* postal; ◆ *vt (=* ~ **up)** fechar,
  subir o fecho ecler de.
zippy (-ier, -iest) *adj (fam) (car)* possante.
zircon *n (zirconium silicate) (gem)* zircão *m.*
zirconia *n (CHEM:* **Zr**) zircónio *m.*
zit *n (fam)* borbulha *f.*
zitty *adj* cheio,-a de borbulhas.
zither *n (MUS)* cítara *f.*
zodiac *n* zodíaco *m.*
zombie *n (fig):* **like a** ~ como um zumbi.
zone *n* zona, região *f;* ~ **of saturation** *n* saturação *f*
  da camada freática.
zonked *(also:* **zonked-out)** *adj (coll) (exhausted)*
  estafado,-a, **2** *(coll) (drunk)* **to be** ~ estar com os
  copos; **3** *(on drugs)* passado,-a, pedrado,-a.
zoning *n* divisão *f* em zonas.
zoo *n (jardim m)* zoológico *m;* ~ **keeper** *n* guarda
  m,f de jardim zoológico.
zoological *adj* zoológico,-a.
zoologist *n* zoólogo,-a.
zoology *n* zoologia *f.*
zoom *n (PHOT) (also:* ~ **lens)** zoom *m;* ◆ *vi:* **to** ~ **past**
  (thunder, arrow) passar zunindo; zunir; **2** *(coll)*
  (prices) subir em flecha; **3** *(plane)* subir a pique; **to**
  ~ **in on** ampliar fazer uma alteração na distância
  focal sobre; ~ **out** fazer um afastamento focal.
zoroastrian *n adj* zoroastriano,-a; zoroástrico,-a,
  relativo à doutrina de Zoroastres.
zucchini *n (BOT) (courgette)* curgete *f.*
zulu *n adj* zulu.
zygote *n (BIOL)* zigoto *m.*
Zürich *npr* Zurique; **in** ~ em Zurique.

List of weights and measures

Sistema Métrico	Imperial equivalents (British system)
medidas lineares	*linear measures*
1 km – 1 quilómetro/quilômetro = 1000 m	0.6214 mile
1 légua = 5 km	3 miles
″ ″	1.094 yard
″ ″	3.28 feet
1 cm – 1 centímetro	0.39 inches
1 mm – 1 milimetro	0.04 inches
medida de capacidade	*capacity measure*
1l – um litro	1.76 pints liq.
″ ″	1.06 quarts liq.
″ ″	0.265 gallons liq.
unidade de peso e superfície	*unit of weight and area*
1 kg – 1 quilograma	2.2046 pounds (*NB: no comércio é calculado a 10% mais do que duas libras-peso*)
1 g – 1 grama	0.035 ounces
1 mg – 1 miligrama	0.015 grains
1 arroba (*batatas, carvão*) (*dated*)	15 kgs approx. in current terms
1 arrátel (*dated*)	0.459 grams approx.
1 quintal – quintal métrico	100 kilograms
1 t – 1 tonelada métrica = 1000 kg	2204.6 pounds
1 alqueire (*medida de líquidos e grãos, variando entre 13 e 22 litros*)	
1 alqueire do Pará (Brasil) equiv a 30 kilos.	
1 alqueire (*de superfície em RJ, MG, Go no Brasil*)	48.400 m^2
(*de superfície*)	(*of area*)
1m^2	1.196 sq. yards
1 are = 100 m^2	119.6 sq. yards
1 ha – 1 hectare = 100 ares	2.471 acres

Medidas britânicas em relação ao sistema métrico

units of length and of area	*unidades de comprimento e de superfície*
1 mile (milha terrestre) = (1760 yards)	1609.34 metros
5 miles	8 kms aprox.
1 square mile (milha quadrada) = 640 acres	259 hectares
1 nautical/air mile (milha marítima/aéria) = (6076.12 ft)	1853.18 m
1 furlong (*dated*) = 1/8 of a mile	201.164 metros
1 yard (*dated*) (jarda) = 36 inches	0.914 m
1 foot (*dated*) (pé = 12 inches)	0.3048 m
1 inch (*dated*) (polegada)	2.539 cm
1 acre (acre) = 4840 sq. yd	0.405 ha

List of weights and measures

<table>
<tr><td>*(Avoirdupois weight)*</td><td>*(de peso)*</td></tr>
<tr><td>1 pound (libra-peso) = (16 ounces)</td><td>0.4536 kg</td></tr>
<tr><td>1 ounce (onça)</td><td>28.35 gramas</td></tr>
<tr><td>1 stone = (14 pounds-libras-peso)</td><td>6.35 kgs</td></tr>
<tr><td>1 hundredweight</td><td>50.80 kgs</td></tr>
<tr><td>1 long ton (British) = (2240 pounds = 1.016 tonnes</td><td>1016,046 kgs</td></tr>
<tr><td>1 short ton (America) (2000 pounds = 0.907 tonne)</td><td>907.184 kgs</td></tr>
</table>

<table>
<tr><td>*(of capacity)*</td><td>*(de capacidade)*</td></tr>
<tr><td>1 pint (quartilho)</td><td>0.468 l (*UK*); 0.437 (*US*)</td></tr>
<tr><td>1 quart = 2 pints</td><td>1.136 litros</td></tr>
<tr><td>1 gallon (galão) = 4 quarts</td><td>4.546 litros</td></tr>
<tr><td>1 peck = 2 gallons</td><td>9.092 litros</td></tr>
<tr><td>1 bushel (alqueire) (secos ou líquidos) =
   8 gallons (*UK*)</td><td>36.348 litros</td></tr>
<tr><td>1 bushel (*US*) = 64 US pints</td><td>35.238 litros</td></tr>
</table>